STOCK
EXCHANGE PRESS

1991
WHO'S
WHO
IN THE
CITY

STOCK
EXCHANGE PRESS

1991
WHO'S WHO IN THE CITY

M

© Macmillan Publishers Limited, 1991

Who's Who in the City 1991 is published by Macmillan
Publishers Limited under licence from The International
Stock Exchange of the United Kingdom and The Republic of
Ireland Limited.

The Stock Exchange Press is a trade mark of The International
Stock Exchange of the United Kingdom and The Republic of
Ireland Limited who own all proprietary rights to the name
'Stock Exchange Press'.

First published in the United Kingdom by
MACMILLAN PUBLISHERS LTD, 1991

Editor
Lisa Williams

Distributed by Globe Book Services Ltd
Brunel Road, Houndmills, Basingstoke
Hampshire RG21 2XS

British Library Cataloguing in Publication Data

Who's Who in the City.
    I. Williams, Lisa
    332.09421

    ISBN 0-333-54926-0

Correspondence

Letters on editorial matters should be addressed to:

Who's Who in the City
Macmillan Publishers Limited
Stockton House, 1 Melbourne Place
London WC2B 4LF

Typeset and printed in Great Britain

SC

STEPHENSON COBBOLD LIMITED

SOLVING THE PROBLEM

For further information please contact

Nicholas Cobbold or Tim Stephenson

84 Palace Court London W2 4JE Telephone 071 727 5335

EXCELLENCE IN EXECUTIVE SEARCH

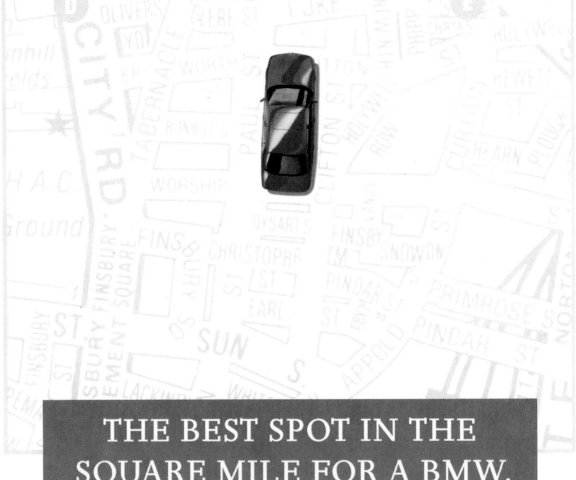

THE BEST SPOT IN THE SQUARE MILE FOR A BMW.

The best BMW cars are to be found at Cooper Bishopsgate in Paul Street, EC2.

We offer everything you'll ever need, all under one roof.

Including new and BMW approved used cars, same day service, BMW approved parts and a 24 hour reception.

So if you drive a BMW in the City, or would like to, we're streets ahead.

Cooper Bishopsgate

20 Paul Street EC2. 071-377 8811.

Contents

The City's present situation and recent successes – not least in adjusting to Big Bang – entitle it to a certain self-confidence. After all, the City of London is far and away the most important business and financial centre in Europe. It is easily the largest foreign exchange market, dominates the international bond and eurodollar markets, turns over around half of measured global equity and is the fourth largest domestic equity market by capitalisation. It is also a major centre for futures and options, international insurance, domestic and international fund management and corporate finance advice.

Yet we must ask ourselves how these comparative advantages can be maintained. The principal answer must lie with the 300,000 or so people who come flooding into the Square Mile every working day. We have to be sure that this work force is second to none in terms of knowledge of banking, insurance, accountancy, commercial law, trading and other areas. Just as important, City people have to be the best in interpretive skills, guiding clients towards the right solutions and arrangements. I foresee a continuing emphasis on quality of recruitment and training.

It is also vital that the working environment remains acceptable and indeed improves. To this end, the Corporation of London has taken a major initiative in setting up a task force on transport as it affects the City. Further, the new City Research Project will examine a whole range of issues concerning business. The Corporation will also be continuing its extensive programme of traffic management measures, schemes to govern the activities of contractors and the maintenance of the Square Mile's many gardens and open spaces.

I believe that continued development of both people and infrastructure is the key to a prosperous outlook for the 10,000 or so names and over 1400 companies and organisations who make up the pages of this third edition of Who's Who in the City. It is an invaluable guide and an essential companion to those working in the City and to others doing business here.

Alexander M Graham.

Lord Mayor

People in the City

By Christopher Fildes

The publishing house of Macmillan, where Who's Who in the City has now found its home, ought next to contemplate a companion volume. Another year like the last, and what we shall need is a Who Was Who.

Pride of place in the casualty lists must go to the First Lord of the Treasury. Dressed for a state occasion like Queen Elizabeth the First, Margaret Thatcher descended on the City to tell the Lord Mayor's fellow-guests in Guildhall how she planned to hit her enemies for six. Within days she retired hurt.

In the simplest sense this was a good result for the City; two of its old boys got the top promotions. John Major, overseas banker, keeps up his friendships in Standard Chartered, where he first made his name in the press office. Norman Lamont, merchant banker, becomes the first Rothschild man to be Chancellor – the second, if the definition were stretched wide enough to include Disraeli. Moving in the opposite direction, a Chancellor came to rest (or at least to perch) at Barclays de Zoete Wedd and on the parent bank's board: Nigel Lawson.

From the oil analysts' desk at Greenwell, the brokers now partially digested by the Midland Bank, Peter Lilley has become Secretary of State for Trade and Industry. There he has shown a belief in competition and a distrust of French nationalised industries – but, given that he sits in Whitehall's most notoriously unstable revolving chair, all this could change. More eyes are on his junior, John Redwood – another Rothschild man, with the unofficial title of minister for the City. Mr Redwood's vigorous style and flow of ideas please some and rile others, but he is agreed to have one decisive advantage over earlier ministers for the City, who gave it the Financial Services Act: he knows what he is talking about.

The political shock-wave which brought down the Prime Minister can be said to have reached Westminster from the financial markets. Her sudden conversion to the joys of the European Monetary System and its exchange rate mechanism left the markets unconvinced. That in turn put paid to talk of a 'golden scenario' – in which ERM membership would so strengthen sterling that interest rates could come rattling down, bringing cheaper mortgages and a better looking figure for inflation, and setting the scene for a fourth triumphant election. The scenario turned to lead, the pound sank with it, and her Euro conversion blew up in the Prime Minister's face.

When the smoke cleared, the Governor of the Bank of England, Robin Leigh-Pemberton, was found standing on the wreckage and saying 'I told you so.' It had been a mistake to cut interest rates when we joined the ERM – an obvious political horse-trade, as the Governor did not need to add. He had taken the trouble to call it a mistake at the time, and in writing. The moral was evident: this sort of monetary decision ought to be left to the central bankers.

How quickly times change! Mr Lawson as Chancellor had a simple rule about interest rates. 'When I say they go up, they go up', he explained, 'and when I say they go down, they go down.' No Chancellor before or since has so exerted the Treasury's supremacy over the Bank. When in his resignation speech he made known that he had planned to make the Bank independent, it seemed as unlikely as Cromwell offering independence to Connaught. Yet it was an idea whose time had recurred.

The historical rule which equates England's difficulty with Ireland's opportunity applies with equal force to the Treasury and the Bank. When things go wrong for the Treasury, the skies darken, the pound weakens, then the Bank comes into its own. Now, too, there are the examples of Europe and its dominant central bank, the Bundesbank, which in theory has the delegated power and duty to take care of the currency. Mr Leigh-Pemberton signed the demand for a European central bank on the lines of the Bundesbank but even less accountable. He had already signed Jacques Delors' proposals for European monetary union.

City opinions differ, and not everyone is happy to see the affable Governor so ready to whip out his fountain pen and sign alongside his European colleagues. It is an article of faith, though, that a strong Bank and a strong City go together, and it is beyond argument that in the Governor's second five-year term of office, which should see him through to 1993, the Bank has regained strength.

It has lost to retirement (his second) Sir George Blunden, the Deputy Governor for whom more than forty years' experience had served to mature his wisdom, refine his craft, and enrich his compendious knowledge of where the City's bodies were buried. Eddie George, home finance director and the Bank's market supremo, was a certainty to succeed him.

The Bank's busiest man can only have been Pen Kent. His title, associate director in charge of industrial finance, may be deliberately soporific. What it means is that, when companies threaten to collapse on their bankers, the bankers form up to him. They have been sidling through his door in numbers not seen for a decade, amd still they come. Who Was Who could get its index from Mr Kent's files. One of the earliest entries must make Mr Kent wince: Kentish Homes.

This was a property company with a spectacular building deep in London's docklands, a bad habit of not deducting the interest it paid from the profit it showed, and a debt of millions to that normally level-headed lender, the Halifax Building Society. In the year that followed Kentish's failure, companies like that would go down once a week or so, and lost the power to surprise. Kentish was the omen.

Among the corporate collapses that followed, two stand out, for sheer size and for close involvement with the City. British & Commonwealth came first – once the merchant shipping company whose Union Castle liners sailed to Cape Town, then transformed into a financial services empire by John Gunn. Known and liked in the City since his days as a money-broker, Mr Gunn overreached himself and bought into the notoriously trappy business of leasing computers. Down it all came.

Polly Peck came down six months later. This was the glamorous stock of the 1980s, the penny share of every punter's dream, multiplying in price by some 1200 times as its creator, Asil Nadir, seemed to be able to squeeze miraculous profits out of oranges and lemons. Every broker's private clients wanted Pollies. The institutional investors waited and bought from the private clients at the top of the market. Mr Nadir's brokers, buying after that, were left pressing their client for payment.

Property companies, builders and retailers (Sophie Mirman's Sock Shop soon ran) were casualties of a downturn which, unusually, started in the service industries and in the south-east. The Treasury, doggedly forecasting that there would be no recession, had in the end to face the fact. The City had long since recognised a savage squeeze on cash and a worldwide contraction of credit.

Barclays' experiences give one measure of events. In the results for 1989 Barclays cleared the decks on its overseas lending, making provisions of close on a billion. Sir John Quinton, the chairman, called it the end of an era – adding that, thanks to good credit management at home, his bank had steered clear of the major trouble-spots.

Within weeks, Barclays was having to provide £100 million against British & Commonwealth. Bad-debt provisions jumped in the half-yearly figures, with Sir John talking of shallow-rooted customers but denying recession. By the autumn, he and the other High Street bank chairmen were pressing for cheaper money and warning the Bank of England that something had to give. As the year ended, the High Street banks were preparing to provide billions for bad debts at home.

The bank can take it. Barclays is among the world's strongest banks, one of the few with a triple A rating. In New York and New England, famous banking names had their credit called into question. In the City, nothing much worse was questioned than the outlook for profits and dividends, but the Midland had a notably unhappy time, ending in the collapse of its long engagement to the Hongkong & Shanghai – a match which was to be the culmination of chairman Sir Kit McMahon's master plan for the Midland's recovery.

Across the world from the City but reverberating within it came the crash of Antipodean tycoons going down like ninepins, from Alan Bond to Warwick 'Wocky' Fairfax. Only the other day they seemed to have all the money in the world, to bid for everything from Lonrho to Van Gogh, picking up a merchant bank or two along the way. The money, as it turned out, was only borrowed, quite a lot of it from City banks. All the world over, there was no substitute for cash.

Cold days in the City's stock markets brought a steady drip of sackings – timed, some of them, to rule out any lingering hope of a Christmas bonus. Citicorp, which had brought itself a whole clutch of respected City names, pulled out with nothing to show but its building in Billingsgate, offered to let; it would make a good fish-market. James Capel parted with its senior partner, Peter Quinnen, and Kleinwort Benson with its enterprising deal-maker, Charles Hue Williams – also with about £30 million when one of his deals went sour. Gordon Pepper, the stockbroker who at Greenwell first taught the City that money mattered, hung up his bowler hat and donned his professorial gown at the City University.

Change came most thoroughly to the Stock Exchange itself. Chairman Andrew Hugh Smith and chief executive Peter Rawlins, still representing the shock of the new, said goodbye to one departmental head after another, and looked forward to saying goodbye to their Tower itself – a splendid site, and now a pointless building. The last inhabitants of the market floor, the traded options dealers, are leaving to throw in their lot with Liffe, the London International Financial Futures Exchange, above the tracks at Cannon Street station.

The most remarkable change, little noticed, is in the Exchange's business – where, for the first time, the volume of trade in overseas stocks overtook domestic stocks. Justifying its ambitious label 'International', the Exchange is evolving away from the home market and the retail market. Mr Rawlins has said in so many words that the private investor is commercially unattractive. Ministers still trying to create a nation of private share owners, and trusting in privatisations to introduce them to the stock market, urgently need to think of something else.

At Lloyd's of London, too, change must be on the way, with a powerful new chairman in David Coleridge, chairman of the Sturge group. He will be urged to take example from the Stock Exchange, and make his market more of a business and less of a club. (He could always have a word with Mr Rawlins, who used to work for him.) The membership elected two reformers to the ruling Council, in Peter Nutting and Rona, Lady Delves Broughton, and the days when Lloyd's members would pay up and shut up are over.

Change of another kind has made itself felt among the big institutional investors – and, often painfully, in the boardrooms of companies where they have investments. Criticised as British industry's absentee landlords, the institutions have become more active and more demanding owners. Overpaid heads of underperforming companies – Sir Ralph Halpern of Burton the most conspicuous example – have found their shareholders calling them to account.

That left one question unresolved: who should call the boards of the institutions to account? Eagle Star has an expensive commitment to underwriting the finance of property, General Accident had a specific accident in New Zealand, Guardian Royal Exchange went shopping for insurance companies in Naples, of all places. Even the Prudential, right marker of the institutions, found itself out of line, saying goodbye to a fortune as its new chief executive, Mick Newmarch, took the axe to its dearly-bought estate agents. Sir Brian Corby, the Pru's chairman, became the first City president of the Confederation of British Industry – but an old rule of investment says that a CBI presidency is a signal to sell.

The institutions' opposite numbers are the big companies' finance directors and treasurers. Their right marker has long been Alan Clements, finance director of Imperial Chemical Industries for the unusual span of a dozen years, and founding father of the Association of Corporate Treasurers. He, more than anyone else, turned a backroom job into a discipline and a profession – and it was a tribute of a sort that the institutions and banks pressed him to take a retirement job on the board of Brent Walker, one of their stickiest situations.

Most exotic arrival in the City is undoubtedly Jacques Attali. Until now best known to the City as the unauthorised biographer of Sir Sigmund Warburg (a book on the banned list at S G Warburg) he has come to set up the European Bank for Reconstruction and Development. This, the first international financial agency to be based in Britain, was rated a capture for the City, and for John Major, who as Chancellor landed it.

M Attali means to do things in style. He likes to speak of his charge as the Bank of Europe. He quickly recruited the Bank of England's economics director, John Flemming. Used to the grandeurs of François Mitterand's presidential palace, he scorned Downing Street's clumsy and ill-judged attempt to divert him down the road to the docks, preferring the idea of leasing the Midland Bank's head office, itself a palace, built by Lutyens. (Charing Cross station was a later destination.) He then set Europe's schoolchildren to design a logotype for a bank, in a competition to be judged by President Havel of Czechoslovakia.

The City remains a male-dominated society. The pattern of recruitment might well have changed this by now, but, though women have long been drawn on the inside track (representing, for instance, a third of the merchant banks' graduate entrants) few have stayed the course to the top. There are complaints of bumping and boring. Three winners, though, have at last come through.

Rosalind Gilmore takes over command at the Building Societies Commission. Alison Wright is the new director-general of British Invisibles, promoting the City's earnings abroad and seeking recognition for them at home. (At a time when Britain's invisible earnings were foolishly said to have vanished, our net exports of financial services were still covering our net imports of cars.) The new Prime Minister, looking for a head of his policy unit, turned to the Daily Telegraph and its economics editor, Sarah Hogg.

Who Was Who will acquire more draft entries – most likely from the securities houses, and from the banks. Brian Pitman, Lloyds Bank's chief executive, has warned that his industry stood where manufacturing industry stood a decade earlier: that is, on the edges of a shock and a shake-out. The City will need its strengths – adaptability, informality, toughness, speed and a sense of the practical. Its greatest strength and its central resource must always be its people.

Editor's Note

This third edition of Who's Who in the City has been completely revised and updated. As in the previous two editions, coverage is not limited to individuals working within the Square Mile; senior personnel based in regional financial centres are included; where inclusion has been requested by the company, those temporarily or permanently based overseas also appear.

The scope of the Sector Index has been expanded to include several new areas of business and the company index has been split into two new indexes: the Index of Companies contains traditional city companies, while the Index of Service Companies & Organisations lists other companies associated with city business, such as solicitors, PR companies, advertising agencies and the media. Both of these indexes give the address, telephone, telex and fax numbers of the companies and list the senior decision-making executives who appear in the Biography Section. The list of directors/partners is not in every case complete but indicates those put forward for inclusion by the company. The Sector Index lists the companies according to their area of business and indicates the company index in which they can be found.

I would like to thank Anne Williams and John Normansell at Macmillan. We are grateful to all individual and corporate contributors. The generous cooperation we have received has greatly assisted us in our aim to provide accurate and current information on a wide range of city businesses.

Lisa Williams
Editor

Abbreviations

AB	Bachelor of Arts (US)	Assoc	Association
ABA	American Bar Association	Asst	Assistant
ACA	Associate, Institute of Chartered Accountants	ATII	Associate Member, Institute of Taxation
Acct	Accountant	b	Date of birth
ACBSI	Associate, Chartertered Building Societies Institute	BA	Bachelor of Arts
		BBA	British Bankers' Association
ACIArb	Associate, Chartered Institute of Arbitrators	BBS	Bachelor of Business Studies
		BCL	Bachelor of Civil Law
ACIB	Associate, Chartered Institute of Bankers	BCom	Bachelor of Commerce
		BEcon	Bachelor of Economics
ACII	Associate, Chartered Insurance Institute	BIIBA	British Insurance and Investment Brokers' Association
ACIS	Associate, Institute of Chartered Secretaries and Adminstrators	BIICL	British Institute of International and Comparitive Law
ACMA	Associate, Institute of Cost and Management Accountants	BIM	British Institute of Management
		Biog	Biographical Details
ACT	Association of Corporate Treasurers	BL	Bachelor of Law
Admin	Administration	BS	Bachelor of Science (US)
AFA	Associate, Institute of Financial Accountants	BSBA	Bachelor of Science for Business Adminstration (US)
AFBD	Association of Futures Brokers & Dealers Ltd	BSc	Bachelor of Science
		BSocSc	Bachelor of Social Science
AIA	Associate, Institute of Actuaries	Bt	Baronet
AIB	Associate, Institute of Bankers		
AIBD	Association of International Bond Dealers	CA	Chartered Accountant (Scotland)
		CACA	Chartered Association of Chartered Accountants
AICS	Associate, Institute of Chartered Shipbrokers	CB	Companion of the Order of the Bath
AID	Associate, Institute of Directors	CBE	Commander of the Order of the British Empire
AIPM	Associate, Institute of Personnel Management	CBI	Confederation of British Industry
AIPPI	Association Internationale Pour la Protection de la Propriete Industrielle	CBIM	Companion, British Institute of Management
AITC	Association of Investment Trust Companies	CC	County Council; Cricket Club
		CCAB	Consultative Committee of Accountancy Bodies
AKC	Associate, King's College London	CDipAF	Certified Diploma in Accounting and Finance
AM	Master of Arts (US)		
AMP	Advanced Management Programme	CEng	Chartered Engineer
AMSIA	Associate Member, Society of Investment Analysts	ch	Children
		Chm	Chairman
API	American Petroleum Institute	CI	Channel Islands
ARAM	Associate, Royal Academy of Music	CIMA	Chartered Institute of Management Accountants
ARCO	Associate, Royal College of Organists		
ARCS	Associate, Royal College of Science	CIPFA	Chartered Institute of Public Finance and Accountancy
ARICS	Professional Associate, Royal Institution of Chartered Surveyors	Co	Company
ARSM	Associate, Royal School of Mines	Con	Conservative
ASA	Associate Member, Society of Actuaries	Corp	Corporation; Corporate
ACSA	Associate, Society of Company and Commercial Accountants	Ctee	Committee
		CVO	Commander of the Royal Victorian Order
ASIA	Associate, Society of Investment Analysts		

d	daughter(s)		Brokers Regulatory Association
DCB	Dame Commander of the Order of the Bath	FIMC	Fellow, Institute of Management Consultants
decd	deceased	FIMechE	Fellow, Institute of Mechanical Engineers
DEcon	Doctor of Economics		
Dep	Deputy	Fin	Finance; Financial
Dept	Department	FInstD	Fellow, Institute of Directors
DFC	Distinguished Flying Cross	FIPM	Fellow, Institute of Personnel Management
DIC	Diploma of The Imperial College		
Dir	Director	FIS	Fellow, Institute of Statisticians
Diss	Dissolved (Marriage)	FKC	Fellow, King's College London
Div	Division; Divisional	FLIA	Fellow, Life Insurance Association
div	divorced	FPMI	Fellow, Pensions Management Institution
DL	Deputy Lieutenant		
DLit	Doctor of Literature; Doctor of Letters	FRGS	Fellow, Royal Geographical Society
DMS	Diploma in Management Studies	FRICS	Fellow, Royal Institution of Chartered Surveyors
Dr	Doctor		
DSc	Doctor of Science	FRS	Fellow, Royal Society
DTI	Department of Trade and Industry	FRSA	Fellow, Royal Society of Arts
		FRSE	Fellow, Royal Society of Edinburgh
ECGD	Export Credits Guarantee Department	FRVA	Fellow, Rating and Valuation Association
Ed	Editor; Edited		
EDC	Economic Development Committee	FSIA	Fellow, Society of Investment Analysts
Educ	Education	FSS	Fellow, Royal Statistical Society
Eng	Engineer; Engineering	FX	Foreign Exchange
EEC	European Economic Community	FZS	Fellow, Zoological Society
ERD	Emergency Reserve Decoration (Army)		
Exec	Executive	GCVO	Knight or Dame Grand Cross of The Royal Victorian Order
FAIB	Fellow, Australian Institute of Bankers	GEMMA	Gilt-Edged Market Makers Association
FBCS	Fellow, British Computer Society	Gen	General
FBIM	Fellow, British Institute of Management	Gov	Governor
		Gp	Group
FCA	Fellow, Institute of Chartered Accountants		
		HAC	Honourable Artillery Company
FCBSI	Fellow, Chartered Building Societies Institute	Hon	Honourable; Honorary
FCCA	Fellow, Chartered Association of Certified Accountants	IAPIP	International Association for the Protection of Industrial Property
FCIArb	Fellow, Chartered Institute of Arbitrators	IBA	International Bar Association
		IBRC	Insurance Brokers Registration Council
FCIB	Fellow, Chartered Institute of Bankers	ICA/ICAEW	Institute of Chartered Accountants in England & Wales
FCII	Fellow, Chartered Insurance Institute		
FCIS	Fellow, Institute of Chartered Secretaries and Administrators	ICCH	International Commodities Clearing House Ltd
FCIT	Fellow, Chartered Institute of Transport	ICSA	Institute of Chartered Secretaries and Administrators
FCT	Fellow, Association of Corporate Treasurers	IES	Institute of Engineers and Shipbuilders in Scotland
FFA	Fellow, Faculty of Actuaries	ILA	International Law Association
FIA	Fellow, Institute of Actuaries	IMC	Institute of Management Consultants
FIB	Fellow, Institute of Bankers	IMF	International Monetary Fund
FIB (Scot)	Fellow, Institute of Bankers in Scotland	IMRO	Investment Management Regulatory Organisation
FICB	Fellow, Institute of Canadian Bankers		
FICS	Fellow, Institute of Chartered Shipbrokers	Intl	International
		IP	Institute of Petroleum
FIGasE	Fellow, Institute of Gas Engineers	IPE	International Petroleum Exchange
FIIB	Fellow, Indian Institute of Bankers	IPFA	Institute of Public Finance and Accounting
FIMBRA	Financial Intermediaries, Managers and		

IPR	Institute of Public Relations		MIB	Member, Institute of Bankers
IProdE	Institute of Production Engineers		MIBiol	Member, Institute of Biology
			MIBS	Member, Institute of Bankers in Scotland
JD	Doctor of Jurisprudence		MIDPM	Member, Institute of Data Processing Management
Jr	Junior			
JP	Justice of the Peace		MIMC	Member, Institute of Management Consultants
KBE	Knight Commander, Order of the British Empire		MInstM	Member, Institute of Marketing
KCB	Knight Commander, Order of Bath		MIPA	Member, Institute of Practitioners in Advertising
KCMG	Knight Commander, Order of St Michael and St George		MIPR	Member, Institute of Public Relations
KCVO	Knight Commander, Royal Victorian Order		MIProdE	Member, Institute of Production Engineers
KRRC	Kings Royal Rifles Company		MIT	Massachusetts Institute of Technology
KStJ	Knight Commander of the Most Venerable Order of the Hospital of St John of Jerusalem		Mktg	Marketing
			ML	Master of Laws
			MP	Member of Parliament
Kt	Knight		MPA	Master of Public Administration
			MPhil	Master of Philosophy
LA	Los Angeles		MSIA	Member, Society of Investment Analysts
Lab	Labour			
Lautro	Life Assurance and Unit Trust Regulatory Organisation		MSc	Master of Science
LCE	London Commodity Exchange		NAPF	National Association of Pension Funds
LIFFE	London International Financial Futures Exchange		Nat	National
			NEDC	National Economic Development Council
LLB	Bachelor of Laws			
LLD	Doctor or Laws		NEDO	National Economic Development Office
LLM	Master of Laws			
LME	London Metal Exchange		non-exec	Non-Executive
LSE	London School of Economics and Political Science		NP	Notary Public
			NUJ	National Union of Journalists
Lt	Lieutenant		NY	New York
LTC	Lawn Tennis Club		NZ	New Zealand
Ltd	Limited			
			OBE	Officer, Order of the British Empire
m	married		ODI	Overseas Development Institute
MA	Master of Arts		OstJ	Officer of the Most Venerable Order of the Hospital of St John of Jerusalem
MAAT	Member, Association of Accounting Technicians			
			PC	Privy Counsellor
MBA	Master of Business Adminstration		PCC	Parochial Church Council
MBCS	Member, British Computer Society		PGCE	Post Graduate Certificate of Education
MBE	Member, Order of the British Empire		PhD	Doctor of Philosophy
MBIM	Member, British Institute of Management		plc	Public Limited Company
			PMD	Programme for Management Development (US)
MC	Military Cross			
MCBSI	Member, Chartered Building Societies Institute		PPE	Philosophy, Politics and Economics
			PR	Public Relations
MCC	Marylebone Cricket Club		Pres	President
MCIS	Member, Institute of Chartered Secretaries and Administrators		Ptnr	Partner
			QC	Queen's Counsel
MCT	Member, Association of Corporate Treasurers		QMC	Queen Mary College
MD	Managing Director		RAC	Royal Automobile Club
MEcon	Master of Economics		RAeS	Royal Aeronautical Society
Mem	Member		RAF	Royal Air Force
Mgmnt	Management			
Mgr	Manager			

ABBREVIATIONS

Reg	Regional	sep	separated
Rep	Representative	SEP	Senior Executive Programme
RIPA	Royal Institute of Public Administration	SIB	Securities and Investment Board
		Snr	Senior
RN	Royal Navy	SVP	Senior Vice President
RNLI	Royal National Lifeboat Institution		
ROYC	Royal Ocean Racing Club	TA	Territorial Army
Rt Hon	Right Honourable	TD	Territorial Decoration
RTYC	Royal Thames Yacht Club	TSA	The Securities Association
s	son(s)	VP	Vice President
SCI	Society of Chemical Industry		
SDP	Social Democratic Party	WS	Writer to the Signet
Sec	Secretary		

BIOGRAPHIES

A

à BRASSARD, Nigel Courtenay; Director, Kleinwort Benson Ltd, since 1986; International Corporate Finance and International Equity and Equity Linked Issues. *Career:* Samuel Montagu & Co Ltd Asst Dir (London) 1977-84; Dominguez Barry Samuel Montagu Ltd (Sydney, Australia) 1984-85; Samuel Montagu & Co Ltd Asst Dir (London) 1984-86. *Biog: b.* 7 June 1955. *Nationality:* British. *Educ:* Cheltenham College; King's College, London University (BA Hons). *Other Activities:* Member, Australian Business in Europe. *Publications:* Modern Merchant Banking (Contributor) 1990; Sterling Commercial Paper (Contributor) 1988. *Clubs:* Buck's Club, Cirencester Park Polo Club. *Recreations:* Polo, Cricket, Theatre, Travel, Wine.

AARONS, Mrs Elaine (née Freedman); Partner, Jaques & Lewis, since 1989; Head of Employment Law Department. *Career:* Norton Rose 1980-89. *Biog: b.* 7 February 1958. *Nationality:* British. *m.* 1977, Stephen; 1 s; 1 d. *Educ:* Manchester High School for Girls; Kings College, University of London (LLB Hons). *Other Activities:* Member, Employment Law Sub-Committee of City of London Solicitors' Company; Member, Employment Lawyers' Group. *Professional Organisations:* Member, Law Society; Member, Industrial Law Society. *Recreations:* Ice Skating, Cricket.

ABANTO, Julio Nelson; Managing Director, Kleinwort Benson Ltd, since 1989; Joint Head of Treasury, since 1990. *Career:* Morgan Stanley, Associate 1973-75; Goldman Sachs International Corp, Partner 1982-89. *Biog: b.* 6 October 1946. *m.* 1968, Cynthia Susan (née Heitz); 4 s. *Educ:* University of Cincinnati (BBA); Harvard University (MBA). *Directorships:* Kleinwort Benson Gilts Ltd Chairman. *Other Activities:* Metropolitan Opera, New York (Dir). *Professional Organisations:* International Primary Markets Assoc.

ABBEY, B G; Partner, Grimley J R Eve.

ABBISS, A B; Managing Director, Management Services, Denis M Clayton & Co Limited.

ABBOTT, C W; Managing Director & Chief Operating Officer, Swiss Bank Corporation.

ABBOTT, D; Joint Chairman & Creative Director, Abbott & Mead Vickers.

ABBOTT, K A; Executive Director, Redland plc.

ABBOTT, Richard David; Director, Morgan Grenfell & Co Ltd, since 1988; Banking.

ABBOTT, Ronald William; CVO, CBE; Consultant Partner, Bacon & Woodrow, since 1982; Occupational Pensions. *Career:* Atlas Assurance Co Actuarial Asst 1934-38; Friends Provident Century Life Office 1938-46; Bacon & Woodrow Snr Actuary 1946-48; Bacon & Woodrow Ptnr 1948-72; Bacon & Woodrow Snr Ptnr 1972-82; Occupational Pensions Board Dep Chm 1975-82; Occupational Pensions Board Chm 1982-87. *Biog: b.* 18 January 1917. *Nationality:* British. m1 Hilda (née Clarke) decd; m2 1973, Barbara Constance (née Clough); 1 s; 2 d. *Educ:* St Olaves & St Saviours Grammar School. *Other Activities:* Life Member, Industrial Society; Master, Worshipful Company of Ironmongers, 1986-87; FRSA; Member, Deptl Ctee on Property Bonds and Equity-Linked Life Assurance 1971-73. *Professional Organisations:* FIA; ASA; FPMI. *Publications:* Contributor to Journal of Institute of Actuaries. *Clubs:* RAC. *Recreations:* Music, Reading, Drama, Walking.

ABEL, J; Director, CIN Marketable Securities.

ABELL, John Norman; Vice Chairman, Wood Gundy Inc, since 1986; Europe & Middle East. *Career:* Wood Gundy Inc (Vancouver) 1955-57; Mgr, Money Markets 1957-62; Wood Gundy International, MD 1962-66; (New York) President 1966-72; Vice Chm 1978; Dir, Corp Finance 1972-82; Orion Royal Bank, CEO & Chm 1982-85; Wood Gundy Inc (Toronto), Vice Chm 1986-88; (London) Vice Chm 1988-. *Biog: b.* 18 September 1931. *Nationality:* British. *m.* 1957, Mora Delia (née Clifton-Brown); 2 s; 1 d. *Educ:* Marlborough College; Worcester College, Oxford (MA). *Directorships:* Echo Bay Mines Ltd 1982 (non-exec); First Australian Prime Income Fund 1986 (non-exec); CIBC Wood Gundy Inc 1988 (exec); Euro-Clear Clearance System plc 1989 (non-exec); Minorco 1984-89 (non-exec); Varity Corporation (Massey Ferguson) 1984-88. *Clubs:* Boodles, Toronto, York Club, MCC, City of London. *Recreations:* Shooting, Fishing, Tennis.

ABELL, P M; Partner, Field Fisher Waterhouse.

ABELL, Timothy George; Vice President, Equitable Life Assurance Society; Non-Executive. *Career:* Baring Brothers & Co Ltd 1953-86; Director 1969; Resigned from Baring Brothers & Co Ltd Following Reorganisation 1986; Baring Investment Management Ltd,

Deputy Chairman 1986; Retired 1989. *Biog: b.* 29 April 1930. *Nationality:* British. *m.* 1961, Philippa (née Whishaw); 3 s. *Educ:* Marlborough College; Corpus Christi College, Oxford (MA). *Directorships:* Equitable Life Assurance Society (non-exec) VP; Greig Fester Group Ltd (non-exec); Stratton Investment Trust plc (non-exec); Tribune Investment Trust plc (non-exec); F & C Eurotrust plc Chairman. *Other Activities:* Past Chairman, Assoc of Investment Trust Companies, 1985-87. *Clubs:* MCC, Flyfishers.

ABIELA-CUDJOE, F S; Branch Manager, First Bank of Nigeria Limited.

ABIRU, Tatsuo; General Manager, London Branch, The Mitsui Taiyo Kobe Bank Ltd, since 1989. *Career:* The Mitsui Bank Limited, Tokyo 1964; New York Branch 1972; Foreign Banking Division, Tokyo 1977; Main Banking Division, Tokyo 1979; Senior Dep Gen Mgr International Treasury Division, Tokyo 1982; Senior Dep Gen Mgr International Finance Division, Tokyo 1985; Senior Dep Gen Mgr Europe Division Headquarters, London 1987; Managing Director Seconded to Mitsui Finance International Ltd, London 1988; General Manager London Branch 1989. *Biog: b.* 25 December 1940. *Nationality:* Japanese. *m.* Akiko. *Educ:* Hitotsubashi University. *Recreations:* Golf, Photography, Motoring.

ABRAHAM, A Richard; Executive Director, Bank of America International Limited.

ABRAHAMS, Anthony Sidney; Executive Director, Smith New Court plc.

ABRAHAMS, Michael David; Chairman, M D Abrahams & Company. *Career:* AW (Securities) Ltd, Deputy Chairman & Chief Executive 1968-73; Champion Associated Weavers Ltd, Chairman 1973-80; Weavercraft Carpets Ltd, Chairman 1980-85; John Crowther Group plc, Deputy Chairman 1985-88. *Biog: b.* 23 November 1937. *Nationality:* British. *m.* 1968, Amanda (née Mita); 1 s; 2 d. *Educ:* Shrewsbury; Worcester College, Oxford. *Directorships:* John Waddington plc 1984 (non-exec); Prudential Corporation plc 1984 (non-exec); Dalepak plc 1984 (non-exec); Drummond Group plc 1989 (non-exec); Chepstow Racecourse plc 1989 (non-exec). *Other Activities:* Assistant, Worshipful Company of Woolmen.

ABRAM, D; Partner, Nabarro Nathanson.

ABRAMS, Charles; Partner, S J Berwin & Co, since 1986; Financial Services; Securities Law. *Career:* Linklaters & Paines, Articles 1974-76; Solicitor 1976-85. *Biog: b.* 2 November 1952. *Nationality:* British. *m.* 1987, Georgia (née Rosengarten); 1 d. *Educ:* St Paul's School; Trinity College, Cambridge (BA Hons 1st). *Other Activities:* Speaker at Conferences on the Financial Services Act and Securities Regulation. *Professional Organisations:* The Law Society; Member, CBI City Regulatory Panel. *Publications:* Guide to the Financial Services Act and Securities Regulation 2nd Edition (Co-Author), 1989; Financial Services Reporter (CCH) (Contributor); Pension Fund Investment (Contributor); Articles on Securities & Compliance Topics. *Recreations:* Squash, Theatre.

ABU EL-ATA, Ahmad A; Managing Director, Citymax Integrated Information Systems Ltd, since 1984; Overall Management and Business Planning. *Career:* University of Menufia Egypt, Lecturer 1964-72; Polytechnic of Central London, Research Fellowship 1973-77; Hoskyns Group, Consultant 1978-79; Buckmaster & Moore, Data Processing & Information Systems Department Manager 1979-84; Citymax Integrated Information Systems Ltd, Managing Director 1984-. *Biog: b.* 4 August 1943. *Nationality:* British. *m.* 1970, Monira (née El-Kashef); 1 s. *Educ:* University of Cairo (BSc Electronic Engineering); Cairo Polytechnic (MPhil Electronic Engineering). *Directorships:* Credit Suisse Buckmaster & Moore (exec); Citymax Integrated Information Systems Ltd (exec); Citymax Egypt (non-exec). *Other Activities:* Member, Board of Studies in Computer Science, University of London. *Professional Organisations:* Member, International Stock Exchange; Member, Institute of Electrical & Electronic Engineers. *Publications:* Several Papers in Digital Signal Processing, 1969-78; Papers, Articles and Conference Contributions on Design and Implementation of Integrated Business Systems and Related Subjects, 1979-90. *Recreations:* Travel, Reading, Classical Music, Theatre.

ABURDENE, Dr Odeh; Executive Vice President, First City, Texas - Houston NA.

ACHEN, N C; Director, Royal Bank of Canada Europe Limited.

ACHESON, J F; Director, Metheuen (Lloyds Underwriting Agents) Limited.

ACKERMAN, Nigel Geoffrey; Trading Director, NGA Trading Ltd, since 1985; Financial Futures. *Career:* Bache & Co (London) Ltd, Operations Assistant 1968-70; E Bailey Commodities Ltd, Trader 1970-85. *Biog: b.* 2 February 1951. *Nationality:* British. *m.* 1971, Penelope; 2 s. *Educ:* Pangbourne College, Berks. *Directorships:* LIFFE 1989 (non-exec); NGA Trading Ltd 1985 Chief Executive. *Clubs:* Newmarket Golf Club, Cannons, Barbican Centre. *Recreations:* Golf, Cricket, Squash, Fishing, Shooting.

ACKLAM, Wing Commander G; Clerk, The Worshipful Company of Furniture Makers.

ACKLAND, T F; Clerk, Masons' Company.

ACKROYD, D E; Director, Williams de Broe plc, since 1987; UK Government Securities. *Biog: b.* 9 August 1955. *Nationality:* British. *m.* 1984, Sandra; 3 s. *Educ:* Chesterfield School; Durham University (BSc Mathematics). *Directorships:* Williams de Broe plc 1987 (exec). *Professional Organisations:* FIA. *Recreations:* Golf, Squash.

ACKROYD, Keith; Managing Director, Retail Division, The Boots Co plc, since 1984; Retailing. *Career:* Boots The Chemists Ltd, Area Director 1976; Boots Drug Stores (Canada), President 1977; The Boots Co plc, Director 1979; Boots The Chemists, Managing Director 1983. *Biog: b.* 6 July 1934. *Nationality:* British. *m.* 1959, E Gwenda (née Thomas); 2 s; 1 d. *Educ:* Heath School, Halifax; Bradford School of Pharmacy (PhC). *Directorships:* The Boots Co plc 1979 (exec); Halfords Ltd 1989 Chairman; Boots Opticians Ltd 1987 Chairman; Childrens World Ltd 1987 Chairman; A G Stanley Ltd 1989 Chairman; Do-It-All Ltd 1990 (non-exec). *Other Activities:* Chairman, British Retailers Association; Worshipful Society of Apothecaries. *Professional Organisations:* Fellow, Royal Pharmaceutical Society; Fellow, Institute of Directors; Companion, British Institute of Management. *Recreations:* Game Shooting.

ACLAND, David Alfred; DL; Chairman, Barclays De Zoete Wedd Asset Management, since 1986; Investment Management. *Career:* Barclays Unicorn Group Ltd Chm 1980-85; Barclays Investment Management Ltd Chm 1985-86. *Biog: b.* 21 October 1929. *m.* 1960, Elizabeth (née Kleinwort); 1 s; 1 d. *Educ:* Eton College; Oxford University (MA). *Directorships:* Kleinwort Overseas Trust 1965 (non-exec); Electric & General Investment Co 1980 Chm; Various other Barclays Directorships; Alm Ltd 1989. *Other Activities:* VP, RNLI. *Clubs:* Royal Yacht Squadron. *Recreations:* Sailing, Tennis, Country Pursuits.

ADAM, Miss Beverley Ann; Partner, Linklaters & Paines, since 1984; Commercial Litigation. *Biog: b.* 11 February 1953. *Nationality:* British. *m.* 1977, Graham Starling; 2 s. *Educ:* King George V School, Hong Kong; Warwick University (LLB). *Professional Organisations:* Member, Users Committee of the Mayor's and City of London County Court; Member, Law Society; Member, City of London Solicitors' Company.

ADAM, R W; Deputy Chairman, General Accident Fire Life Assurance Corp.

ADAMI, Dr Manfred John; Managing Director, CSFB Investment Management Ltd, since 1983; Investment Management, Merchant Banking. *Career:* SG Warburg & Co Ltd, London 1970-78; Treuhand Vermoegens Verwaltungs GmbH, Munich 1978-80; SG Warburg & Co Ltd, London 1980-83. *Biog: b.* 1940. *Nationality:* German. 1 s; 3 d. *Educ:* University of Hamburg (Dipl Kfm, PhD). *Directorships:* Credit Suisse First Boston Ltd (non-exec); CS Money Market Fund Management Co, Luxemburg; Credit Suisse (Guernsey) Ltd; First Boston Asset Management (USA); CS First Boston Global Fund Managers Ltd.

ADAMS, David Howard; Chief Executive, Henry Cooke Group plc, since 1988; Stockbroker and Banker. *Career:* Royce Peeling Green & Co, Articled Clerk 1961-66. *Biog: b.* 15 November 1943. *Nationality:* British. *m.* 1969, Zoe (née Dwek); 2 d. *Educ:* Manchester Grammar School. *Other Activities:* Worshipful Company of Chartered Accountants; Manchester Stock Exchange Assoc; Inst for Fiscal Studies, NW; Fellow, Royal Society Arts. *Professional Organisations:* Member, The International Stock Exchange; FCA; Registered Representative, The Securities Association. *Recreations:* Reading, Trying to Get Fit.

ADAMS, David Yeates; Partner, Travers Smith Braithwaite, since 1987; Corporate & Commercial. *Career:* Crossman Block & Keith, Articled Clerk/ Assistant Solicitor 1978-81; Brecher & Co, Assistant Solicitor 1981-83. *Biog: b.* 6 August 1955. *Nationality:* British. *m.* 1987, Dr Alison Mary Adams (née Chalk). *Educ:* The Leys School, Cambridge; Queen Mary College, London (LLB); Guildford College of Law (Solicitors' Part II Finals). *Professional Organisations:* The Law Society; City of London Solicitors Company. *Clubs:* Langess Golf Club, Barbican Sports Club, Old Leysian Society. *Recreations:* Skiing, Golf, Shooting.

ADAMS, Douglas William; Marketing Director, Templeton Investment Management Ltd, since 1988; Marketing, Economics. *Career:* Scottish Office, Economist 1975-78; European Commission, Economist 1978-82; Scottish Development Agency, Economist 1982-86; Scottish Provident, Economist 1986-88. *Biog: b.* 17 May 1953. *Nationality:* British. *m.* 1975, Jacqueline (née Ferguson); 1 s; 1 d. *Educ:* Perth Academy; Glasgow University (MA Political Economy & Economic Statistics); Strathclyde University (MBA). *Directorships:* Templeton Investment Management Ltd 1988 (exec); Templeton Unit Trust Managers Ltd 1988 (exec); Templeton Emerging Markets Investment Trust plc 1990 (exec). *Clubs:* Dunbar Golf Club, Luffness Golf Club, Islay Golf Club. *Recreations:* Golf, Running.

ADAMS, Mrs Elizabeth J (née Swan); Partner, Beachcroft Stanleys, since 1986; Litigation, in Particular Employment Law. *Career:* Beachcroft Hyman Isaacs, Articled Clerk 1978-80; Beechcroft Hyman Isaacs (now Beachcroft Stanleys), Assistant Solicitor 1980-86; Partner 1986-. *Biog: b.* 15 April 1955. *Nationality:* British. *m.* 1987, Roger Henry. *Educ:* Bristol Polytechnic (BA Hons). *Professional Organisations:* Law Society. *Recreations:* Tennis, Travel, Theatre.

ADAMS, Francis Peter Leslie; Director, Kleinwort Benson Investment Management, since 1986; International Private Funds Management. *Career:* Rowe Reeve & Co, Asst, Dealing Room 1961-62; Grieveson Grant 1962-86; Mgr, Private Clients 1965-76; Assoc Ptnr 1976-79; Ptnr 1979-86. *Biog: b.* 1944. *Nationality:* British. *m.* 1968, Norma (née Lockey); 1 s; 2 d. *Educ:* Tottenham Polytechnic. *Professional Organisations:* Member, International Stock Exchange. *Recreations:* Athletics, Swimming, Cycling.

ADAMS, J G; Director, Minories Holdings Ltd.

ADAMS, John Trevor; Partner, Clark Whitehill, since 1972; Personal Taxation and Financial Planning. *Career:* Temple Gothard Articled Clerk 1957-63; Shipley Blackburn Sutton & Co Audit Snr 1963-66; Arthur Andersen Tax Snr 1966-68; Josolyne Miles & Cassleton Elliot Tax Snr/Tax Ptnr 1968-71. *Biog: b.* 2 April 1936. *Nationality:* British. *m.* 1963, Elizabeth (née Lacey); 1 s; 1 d. *Educ:* University College School. *Professional Organisations:* FCA. *Recreations:* Badminton, Rugby, Cricket, Fine Art, Music, Gardening.

ADAMS, N H H; Partner, J K Shipton and Company.

ADAMS, S; Director, Charterhouse Tilney.

ADAMS, Terence; Chief Executive & Director, Skipton Building Society, since 1986. *Biog: b.* 4 June 1941. *Nationality:* British. *m.* 1962, Vera Frances (née Meachen); 2 s. *Educ:* Stratton Grammar School, Biggleswade. *Professional Organisations:* ACII. *Clubs:* Ilkley Golf Club. *Recreations:* Theatre, Chess, Most Sports.

ADAMSON, Sir Cambell; Kt; Chairman, Abbey National plc, since 1979. *Career:* Richard Thomas Baldwins Ltd, Exec Dir 1959-67; Dept of Economic Affairs, Dep Sec & Chief Industrial Adviser 1967-69; CBI, Dir Gen 1969-76; Imperial Group plc, Non-Exec Dir 1976-90; Lazard Bros & Co Ltd, Non-Exec Dir 1976-90; Doulton Ltd, Non-Exec Dir 1977-90; Revertex Ltd, Chm 1978-90; Tarmac plc, Dir 1980-90; Renold plc, Chm 1980-85. *Biog: b.* 26 June 1922. *Nationality:* British. *m.* m2 1984, Mimi (née Lloyd); 2 s; 2 d. *Educ:* Rugby School; Cambridge University (Hons). *Other Activities:* Trustee, Horticultural Therapy; Trustee, SANE; Governor, Rugby School; Chm, Independent Television Telethon Trustees. *Professional Organisations:* CBIM. *Publications:* Various Technical Articles. *Clubs:* Naval & Military. *Recreations:* Music, Exploring empty parts of the world.

ADAMSON, D H; Executive Director, UK & International, FennoScandia Bank Limited.

ADAMSON, Stephen James Lister; Partner, Ernst & Young, since 1978; Head of Insolvency & Recovery Services (London). *Career:* KMG Thomson Mclintock Mgr 1960-71; Joviel Properties Ltd Dir 1971-76. *Biog: b.* 10 July 1942. *Nationality:* British. *m.* 1972, Elizabeth (née Tunley); 3 s. *Educ:* John Lyon School, Harrow. *Directorships:* Virginia Water Preparatory School 1979 (non-exec) Chm. *Other Activities:* President, Insolvency Practitioners' Association (1988); Institute of Directors; Treasurer, Insolvency International. *Professional Organisations:* FCA; CA; FIPA. *Publications:* Contributor to Practical Financial Management, 1975. *Recreations:* Theatre, Golf, Fishing.

ADDA, Michael Elie Smouha; Director, S G Warburg & Co Ltd, since 1987; Overseas Advisory Division. *Career:* Touche Ross & Co 1964-75; S G Warburg & Co Ltd Corp Fin Dept 1975-80; Overseas Advisory Div 1980-. *Biog: b.* 11 November 1945. *Nationality:* British. *m.* 1972, Judith (née Henderson); 3 s; 1 d. *Educ:* Harrow; Magdalene College, Cambridge (MA). *Other Activities:* Council Mem, Textile Conservation Centre, Hampton Court Palace. *Professional Organisations:* FCA. *Clubs:* Royal Southampton Yacht Club.

ADDERSON, Peter; Director, Queen Anne's Gate Asset Management Limited. *Biog: b.* 16 June 1951. *Nationality:* British. *m.* 1974, Gillian (née Benson); 2 d. *Directorships:* Beta Global Emerging Markets Investment Trust plc 1990 (non-exec); Korea Liberalisation Fund Limited 1990 (non-exec).

ADDISCOTT, Graham; Director, Nicholson Chamberlain Colls Limited.

ADDISON, G R; Director, Greenwell Montagu Gilt-Edged.

ADDISON, Gerald Peter Lacey; Director, English Trust Company Limited; Corporate Finance.

ADEANE, The Hon Edward; CVO; Director, Hambros Bank Ltd, since 1986; Group Compliance Officer. *Career:* Member of the Bar (Practising) 1962-78; Private Sec/Treasurer to HRH The Prince of Wales 1979-85. *Biog: b.* 4 October 1939. *Educ:* Eton College; Magdalene College, Cambridge (MA). *Directorships:* Guardian Royal Exchange Assurance plc 1985 (non-exec); English & Scottish Investments plc 1986 (non-exec).

ADLER, P T; Director, Robert Bruce Fitzmaurice Ltd.

AGAR, N S D; Partner, Cameron Markby Hewitt.

AGAR, T; Chairman, Co-operative Bank plc.

AGATA, Masahiko; Chief Representative, The Export-Import Bank of Japan. *Career:* The Export-Import Bank of Japan Mgr, Lending for CMEA Countries 1983-86; Mgr, Intl Relations 1986-88. *Biog: b.* 4 September 1943. *Nationality:* Japanese. *m.* 1969,

Toshiko; 1 s; 1 d. *Educ:* Keio University, Tokyo (BA Econ). *Clubs:* Institute of Directors, Overseas Bankers Club.

AGER, R S; Company Secretary, Tesco plc.

AGIUS, Leslie Arthur; Executive Director, Eagle Star Insurance Co Ltd, since 1987; UK General Insurance Business. *Career:* Eagle Star Group, Branch Mgr 1965-67; Gen Mgr (Personnel) 1982-87. *Biog: b.* 9 November 1936. *m.* 1988, Sheila; 2 d. *Directorships:* Home and Overseas Insurance Co Ltd 1987 (exec); Tobacco Insurance Co Ltd 1987 (non-exec); The Loss Prevention Council 1987 (non-exec); Eagle Star Insurance Company Ltd 1987; Eagle Star Group Engineering Insurance Ltd 1987; Midland Assurance Ltd 1987; The Motor Insurance Research Centre 1987; Eagle Star Group Services Ltd 1990. *Professional Organisations:* FCII; MIPM. *Clubs:* RAC, Pall Mall.

AGIUS, Marcus Ambrose Paul; Vice Chairman, Lazard Brothers & Co Ltd, since 1990; Corporate Finance. *Career:* Vickers plc 1968-70. *Biog: b.* 22 July 1946. *Nationality:* British. *m.* 1971, Kate Juliette (née De Rothschild); 2 d. *Educ:* St George's College, Weybridge, Surrey; Trinity Hall, Cambridge (MA); Harvard Business School (MBA). *Directorships:* Exbury Gardens Ltd 1982 (non-exec). *Clubs:* Whites, London, Swinley Forest, Berkshire. *Recreations:* Gardening, Tennis, Shooting, Skiing.

AGNEW, Alexander James Blair; Director, Allied Provincial Securities Ltd, since 1988; Private Clients. *Career:* H M Forces, Capt 1954-65; S M Penney & MacGeorge, Trainee 1965-67; Partner 1967; Senior Partner 1980; Penney Easton & Co Ltd, Chairman 1983; Parsons Penney & Co, Director 1988. *Biog: b.* 6 October 1935. *Nationality:* Scottish. *m.* 1958, Gillian Margaret (née Gray Newton); 2 s; 1 d. *Educ:* Rugby School. *Directorships:* The Securities Association 1988 (non-exec); City of Glasgow Friendly Society 1989 (non-exec). *Other Activities:* Deacon Convener of the Trades of Glasgow, (1987-88); Hon Colonel, 1st Bn 52nd Lowland Volunteers, TA. *Professional Organisations:* CBIM. *Clubs:* Army & Navy, Western Club (Glasgow). *Recreations:* Gardening, Walking.

AGNEW, Jonathan Geoffrey William; Chief Executive, Kleinwort Benson plc; Chairman, Kleinwort Benson Ltd, since 1989. *Career:* World Bank, Exec 1965-67; Hill Samuel & Co Ltd, Dir 1967-73; Morgan Stanley & Co Incorporated, MD 1973-82; Self-employed Financial Consultant 1983-86; ISRO (Formation) Ltd, Chief Exec 1986; Kleinwort Benson Ltd, Head of Securities 1987; Chm of Exec Ctee 1988; Kleinwort Benson Group plc, Chief Executive 1989; Chm 1989. *Biog: b.* 30 July 1941. *Nationality:* British. m1 1966, The Hon Joanna (née Campbell) (Diss 1986); 1 s; 2 d; m2 1990, Marie-Claire (née Dreesmann). *Educ:*

Eton College; Trinity College, Cambridge (MA). *Directorships:* Thos Agnew & Sons Ltd 1967 (non-exec); International Financial Markets Trading Ltd 1984 (non-exec). *Clubs:* White's, Automobile (Paris).

AGOSTINELLI, Robert Francesco; Managing Director, Lazard Freres & Co, since 1987; International Investment Banking Group Specialization; Mergers & Acquisitions and Financial Advisory. *Career:* J Rothschild & Co Associate 1981; Goldman Sachs & Co, VP & Co-Head, Intl Mergers & Acquisitions 1982-87. *Directorships:* Lazard Freres & Co (New York) 1987 Gen Ptnr; Lazard Brothers & Co Ltd 1988 (non-exec); Burklin, Kuna & Co 1989 Member of Supervisory Board; Frontera SA 1989 Advisory Committee(non-exec); The European Institute 1990; The Council for the United States & Italy 1990.

AHLÅS, Lars Peter Richard; Managing Director - Marine Division, Gibbs Hartley Cooper Ltd, since 1986; Marine Insurance Broking. *Career:* Royal Swedish Navy Lt-Commander 1969-71; WK Webster 1971-73; Liberian Insurance Agency Gen Mgr 1973-74; Bland Payne Broker 1974-78; Jardine Glanvill Marine Dir 1978-86. *Biog: b.* 22 September 1948. *Nationality:* Swedish. *m.* 1973, Sian Fiona (née Holford-Walker); 2 d. *Educ:* Högre Allmäna Läroverket å Kungsholmen, Stockholm; London School of Foreign Trade (Dip, Shipping & Marine Insurance). *Directorships:* Gibbs Insurance Holdings Ltd; Gibbs Hartley Cooper Ltd. *Other Activities:* Royal Swedish Navy Reserve (Active). *Professional Organisations:* IBRC. *Clubs:* Lansdowne. *Recreations:* Shooting, Squash, Riding.

AHLQVIST, Per O F; Senior Vice President & Head of Banking, Skandinaviska Enskilda Banken, since 1988. *Career:* Scandinavian Bank Group plc 1981-87; Skandinaviska Enskilda Banken 1972-81; Hambros Bank 1966-72. *Biog: b.* 19 January 1937. *Nationality:* Swedish. *m.* 1964, Gunilla (née Kristensen); 1 s; 2 d. *Educ:* University of Lund (Bachelor of Law). *Recreations:* Skiing, Sailing, Golf, Literature, Art.

AHMADZADEH, Mohammed; Director, Rudolf Wolff & Co Ltd.

ÅHRELL, Dr Lars Olof; Director, Gyllenhammar & Partners International Ltd, since 1988; Investment. *Career:* GVA (UK) Ltd, Managing Director 1981-88; SIAR AB, Managing Director 1973-81; Various Academic & Consultancy Assignments 1966-72. *Biog: b.* 25 May 1943. *Nationality:* Swedish. *m.* Eva (née Holmin); 1 s; 2 d. *Educ:* Stockholm University (Dr of Business Administration, MSc,BSc). *Directorships:* Epicure Industries 1988 (non-exec); Guild Entertainment Ltd 1988 (non-exec); Saatchi & Saatchi plc 1987 (non-exec); S L P 1983 (non-exec); Quality Trading 1979 (non-exec). *Publications:* Academic Work about six titles, 1967-72; Export of Services, 1981; Can You Understand The Brits?, 1985. *Clubs:* Annabels, Arts Club, Royal Wimbledon.

AINGER, Colin; Director, GCI Sterling.

AINSCOE, Raymond; Partner, Hepworth & Chadwick.

AINSWORTH, Brian C; Director, Alexander Howden Limited.

AINSWORTH, Philip Gee; Director, Kleinwort Benson Investment Management. *Biog: b.* 24 December 1955. *Educ:* Hertford College, Oxford (MA); City University Business School (MBA).

AINSWORTH, R R; Partner, Jaques & Lewis.

AINSWORTH, S J; Partner (Guernsey), Bacon & Woodrow.

AIRS, Graham John; Partner, Slaughter and May, since 1987; Corporate Tax. *Career:* Slaughter and May, Articled Clerk 1976-78; Asst Solicitor 1978-80; Airs Dickinson Ptnr 1980-84; Slaughter and May, Asst Solicitor 1984-87. *Biog: b.* 8 August 1953. *Nationality:* British. *m.* 1981, Stephanie Annette (née Marshall). *Educ:* Newport, Essex Grammar School; Emmanuel College, Cambridge (MA, LLB). *Professional Organisations:* ATII, The Law Society. *Publications:* Chapter on Losses in Tolleys Tax Planning (Annual). *Recreations:* Theatre, Cinema, Football (as Spectator).

AISBETT, Alan; Partner, S J Berwin & Co.

AISH, Malcolm; Executive Director, N M Rothschild & Sons Limited.

AITCHISON, Jimmy; Partner, Property Finance, Cameron Markby Hewitt.

AITKEN, Ian Spencer; Partner, Clay & Partners Consulting Actuaries, since 1969; Group Pension Schemes, Small Self-Administrated Pension Schemes. *Career:* Legal & General Assurance Society, Actuarial Student 1964-65; British Rail, Operations Research, Assistant 1965-67; Meat & Livestock Commission, Junior Statistician 1967-69. *Biog: b.* 31 October 1942. *Nationality:* British. *m.* 1967, Valerie Evelyn (née Hagger); 1 s; 1 d. *Educ:* Erith Grammar School; University College, London (BSc). *Other Activities:* Livery Company of Actuaries. *Professional Organisations:* Fellow, Institute of Actuaries. *Recreations:* Tennis, Golf.

AITKEN, J B; Director, County NatWest Limited.

AITKEN, Neil Cameron; Partner, McKenna & Co, since 1986; Commercial Litigation. *Career:* Trower Still & Keeling 1977-78; Coward Chance 1978-83;

McKenna & Co, Assistant Solicitor 1983-. *Biog: b.* 16 November 1952. *Nationality:* British. *m.* 1985, Claire (née Jetten); 1 d. *Educ:* Lorretto School; College of Law (Solicitors Qualifying Exams Part I & II). *Professional Organisations:* Law Society; City of Westminster Law Society; City of London Law Society (Applied for). *Clubs:* Royal Ocean Racing Club.

AITKENHEAD, L; Director, Systems and Administration, Thornton Management Limited, since 1989. *Career:* Whinney Murray & Co 1972-76; Peat Marwick Mitchell & Co, Hong Kong 1977-78; Hong Kong & Shanghai Banking Corp, Hong Kong 1978-81; Bank of Bermuda Ltd, Bermuda 1981-86; Bank of Bermuda Ltd, Hong Kong 1986-88; Bermuda Trust (Far East) Ltd, Manager. *Biog: b.* 2 June 1951. *Nationality:* British. *m.* 1985, Shelley. *Educ:* University of Newcastle upon Tyne (BA Economic Studies). *Directorships:* Thornton Management Ltd 1989 (exec). *Professional Organisations:* FCA.

AIZAWA, Takashi; Managing Director and Chief Executive Officer, LTCB International Limited, since 1990. *Career:* LTCB International Limited, Managing Director 1987-90; Long Term Credit Bank of Japan, Associate General Manager, Marchant Banking Group 1985-87; Long Term Credit Bank of Japan 1969. *Biog: b.* 16 October 1946. *Nationality:* Japanese. *m.* 1977, Kiyomi; 2 d. *Educ:* Hitotsubashi University (Economy). *Directorships:* LTCB F & C Investment Management Co Ltd 1990 (exec); LTCB Leasing (UK) Limited 1989 (exec). *Recreations:* Golf, Skiing, Swimming.

AKAGASHI, M; Chief Representative, Iyo Bank.

AKAMATSU, Yoshitaka; Director and Head of Corporate Finance, Mitsubishi Finance International plc; Si Corporate Finance, New Issues, Swaps. *Career:* The Mitsubishi Bank Ltd, Mgr, Corp Finance 1981-87. *Biog: b.* 6 April 1950. *Nationality:* Japanese. *m.* 1986, Hisako; 1 d. *Educ:* Keio University, Tokyo (BEcon Hons); INSEAD, France (MBA). *Professional Organisations:* TSA.

AKATSUKA, T; Director, Cosmo Securities (Europe) Limited.

AKERS-DOUGLAS, Frank; Director-Private Client Services, BDO Binder Hamlyn.

AKIHAMA, W; Joint General Manager, The Dai-Ichi Kangyo Bank Ltd.

AKITA, Satoshi; Managing Director, Sanwa International Ltd.

AL SABAH, Faho M; Chairman, Kuwait Investment Office.

AL SABAH, K N; Deputy Chairman & Chief Executive, Kuwait Investment Office.

ALBERT, Alan J; Managing Director (Investment Management), Merrill Lynch Asset Management UK Limited.

ALBERT, David Edward Peter; Partner, Ashurst Morris Crisp, since 1978; Commercial Property. *Biog: b.* 8 July 1944. *Nationality:* British. *m.* 1973, Katherine (née Beer); 3 s. *Educ:* Douai School; Trinity Hall, Cambridge (MA). *Clubs:* MCC, RAC.

ALBERTI, Kerry B; Midland Securities Services Director, Midland Bank plc, since 1988; Stockbroking, Securities Processing, Global Custody, Trust Services. *Career:* US Air Force, Captain 1968-72; The Chase Manhattan Bank, VP, Corporate Banking Dept 1972-79; Avis Inc (New York), VP, Strategic Management 1979-82; Bankers Trust Co (New York), Snr VP, Global Securities Services Gp 1982-88. *Biog: b.* 26 July 1944. *Nationality:* American. *m.* 1966, Linda (Lynn); 1 s; 1 d. *Educ:* University of Iowa (BBA,MA). *Directorships:* Young Life, Colorado Springs, USA 1985 (non-exec); Midland Stockbrokers 1989 (non-exec) Chm; International Commodities Clearing House 1989 (non-exec). *Recreations:* Tennis, Running.

ALBERTINI, Peter Sinclair; RD; Partner, Hill, Taylor Dickinson, since 1981; Company/Commercial, Commercial Property, Taxation, Intellectual Property. *Career:* Tolhursts Solicitors Ptnr 1963-80. *Biog: b.* 4 May 1937. *Nationality:* British. *m.* 1967, Vanessa Ann (née McIntyre); 1 s; 2 d. *Educ:* Uppingham School; Nottingham University; Solicitor. *Directorships:* Cosmos Coach Tours Ltd 1977 (non-exec); Cosmos Intercontinental Ltd 1979 (non-exec); Richard Klinger Ltd 1988 (non-exec); Klinger Automotive Ltd 1989 (non-exec); Naturebrook Ltd 1990 (non-exec). *Other Activities:* Captain, Royal Naval Reserve (Commanding Officer HMS President). *Professional Organisations:* The Law Society. *Clubs:* Royal Naval Sailing Association, Wildernesse Golf Club. *Recreations:* Sailing, Golf, Music, Reading.

ALBRECHT, Dr Klaus L; General Manager, Deutsche Bank AG.

ALDIS, Peter; Partner, Walker Martineau Stringer Saul.

ALDOUS, Hugh Graham; Managing Partner, Robson Rhodes, since 1987; Leadership and Management of the Practice Nationally; Investigating Accountant for Inquiries & Litigation. *Career:* Robson Rhodes, Articles 1967; Partner 1976; Seconded to Department of Transport 1976-79; Head of Special Services 1979-84; Investigated Loan Guarantee Scheme for Dept of Trade & Industry 1982-84; Robson Rhodes, Head of Corporate Finance 1984-85; Deputy Managing Partner 1985-87; Managing Partner 1987-; DTI Inspector into the Affairs of House of Fraser Holdings plc 1987-88. *Biog: b.* 1 June 1944. *Nationality:* British. *m.* 1967, Christabel (née Marshall). *Educ:* Scarborough High School & Colchester Royal Grammar School; Leeds University (BCom). *Directorships:* Sealink UK Ltd 1981-84; Freightliner Ltd 1979-84; British Waterways Board 1983-86; City and Inner London North Tec 1990. *Professional Organisations:* FCA. *Publications:* Report in the Affairs of House of Fraser Holdings plc (with Sir Henry Brooke QC) 1988. *Clubs:* RAC. *Recreations:* Opera, Music, Walking, Tennis.

ALDRED, P D; Partner, Cameron Markby Hewitt.

ALDRIDGE, Simon Anthony; Director, Baring Securities Limited, since 1989; International Sales. *Career:* Savory Milln, Partner 1968-86; Managing Director 1986-88; Swiss Bank Corporation, Stockbroking, Co-Chairman 1988-89. *Biog: b.* 12 April 1942. *Nationality:* British. *m.* 1968, Jennifer Roberta Anne (née Clarke); 1 d. *Educ:* Marlborough College; Grenoble University, France (French Language & Literature). *Directorships:* Baring Securities (France) SA 1990; Northgate Pacific Fund, Jersey 1982 Chm; French Prestige Fund, Paris 1985; Croissance Immobilier, Paris 1987; Croissance Britannia, Paris 1987 Dep Chm. *Other Activities:* Chevalier dans l'Ordre National du Mérite. *Clubs:* Cercle de l'Union Interalliée (Paris), City of London Club. *Recreations:* Golf, Shooting, Tennis.

ALDWINCKLE, William Ralph; Partner, Linklaters & Paines, since 1969; Corporate and Financial Services Law. *Career:* Articled to Linklaters & Paines 1961. *Biog: b.* 13 July 1937. *Nationality:* British. *m.* 1972, Elizabeth. *Educ:* Haileybury; Clare College, Cambridge (MA, LLB). *Professional Organisations:* Solicitor.

ALEXANDER, Andrew; City Editor, Daily Mail.

ALEXANDER, Charles; Executive Director, N M Rothschild & Sons Limited.

ALEXANDER, G R; Partner, R Watson & Sons Consulting Actuaries.

ALEXANDER, John Randle; Director, Touche Remnant Investment Management Ltd UK Smaller Companies. *Career:* Drayton Montagu, Investment Mgr 1980-83; Hill Samuel Investment Management, Investment Mgr 1983-84; Touche Remnant & Co, Investment Mgr 1984. *Biog: b.* 2 November 1958. *Nationality:* British. *m.* 1986, Sophia Alexander (née Mareen). *Educ:* Oundle School; Oxford University (Modern History). *Directorships:* T R Trustees Corporation 1988 (exec). *Recreations:* Antiques, Restoring Old Houses, Horse Driving, Gardening.

ALEXANDER, Kevin John; Partner, Bracewell & Patterson, since 1988; General Corporate & Financial Law. *Career:* Lovell White & King Articled Clerk 1977-79; Boodle Hatfield Solicitor 1979-81; Bracewell & Patterson Attorney 1981-83; Boodle Hatfield Solicitor, Ptnr 1983-86; Sidley & Austin Attorney 1986-88. *Biog:* b. 26 December 1953. *Nationality:* British. *m.* 1983, Barbara Lynn (née Evans); 1 s. *Educ:* Wimbledon College; St John's College, Cambridge (BA, MA). *Professional Organisations:* New York Bar; The Law Society. *Clubs:* Oxford & Cambridge. *Recreations:* Jogging, Tennis, Golf.

ALEXANDER, Sir Lindsay; Director, Wellington Underwriting Agencies Limited.

ALEXANDER, Peter James; Partner, Penningtons, since 1990; Family Law. *Career:* Gamlens (merged with Penningtons 1990), Ptnr. *Biog:* b. 16 November 1943. *Nationality:* British. *m.* 1973, Carol; 3 s. *Educ:* Haileybury College, Herts; Manchester University Law Faculty (LLB). *Other Activities:* Member, The Solicitors' Family Law Association Sub-Committee Relating to the Welfare of Children. *Professional Organisations:* The Law Society; The Solicitors' Family Law Association. *Recreations:* Long Distance Running.

ALEXANDER, Robert Scott; The Lord Alexander of Weedon; QC; Chairman, National Westminster Bank plc, since 1989. *Career:* Called to the Bar (Middle Temple) 1961; Queen's Counsel 1973; Bencher of Middle Temple 1979; Queen's Counsel (NSW) 1983; Chairman of the Bar of England & Wales 1985-86; Trustee of the National Gallery 1986-; Chairman, Panel on Takeovers & Mergers 1987-89; Created Life Peer 1988. *Biog:* b. 5 September 1936. *Nationality:* British. *m.* Marie (née Anderson); 2 s; 1 d. *Educ:* Brighton College; King's College, Cambridge (MA). *Other Activities:* Chairman of Trustees of CRISIS; Chairman of Council of JUSTICE; Governor, Wycombe Abbey School; President, Parkinson's Disease Society; Chairman, Society of Conservative Lawyers, etc. *Clubs:* Garrick. *Recreations:* Tennis, Theatre.

ALEXANDER, Roger John Blake; Partner, Milne Ross, since 1968. *Career:* Milne Gregg & Turnbull, Articled Clerk 1959-64; Manager 1964-68; Milne Ross, Partner 1968-. *Biog:* b. 9 April 1942. *Nationality:* British. *m.* 1970, Jane Hamilton (née Jackson); 1 s; 1 d. *Educ:* Blundells. *Other Activities:* Anglo Spanish Society. *Professional Organisations:* Fellow, Institute of Chartered Accountants.

ALEXANDER, S H; Managing Director, John Siddall & Son Ltd.

ALEXANDER, S M; *Career:* Sole Practioner 1976-82; Oppenheimer & Co Ltd, Administrative Manager 1973-76; Deloitte Haskins & Sells, Audit Senior 1969-73; J & A W Sully & Co, Articled Clerk 1963-69; Candover Investments plc, Company Secretary & Treasurer 1982-90. *Biog:* b. 21 April 1946. *Nationality:* British. *m.* 1981, Vivienne Frances (née Vicary); 1 s; 1 d. *Educ:* Clifton College. *Professional Organisations:* Institute of Chartered Accountants in England & Wales.

ALEXANDER, W R; CBE; Director, Clydesdale Bank plc.

ALFORD, George Francis Onslow; Group Personnel Director, Kleinwort Benson Ltd, since 1987; Full Personnel, Training & Welfare Function for K B Group. *Career:* Kleinwort Benson Group, Asst Mgr, Asia Pacific 1973-76; (Tokyo), Banking Rep 1976-79; (Tokyo), Chief Rep 1980; Mgr, Middle East Dept 1980-83; Fendrake Ltd, MD 1983-87; Asst Dir, Intl Cap Mkts 1985-86; Asst Dir, Personnel 1986. *Biog:* b. 10 October 1948. *Nationality:* British. *m.* 1974, Adronie-Elizabeth (née Gall). *Educ:* Winchester College; University College, London (BSc). *Other Activities:* British Export Houses Assoc (Former Council Member); Worshipful Company of Basketmakers (Liveryman). *Professional Organisations:* FIPM. *Clubs:* Royal Solent Yacht, City Livery, Langbourne Ward. *Recreations:* Sailing, Skiing, Riding.

ALI, A; Partner, Nabarro Nathanson.

ALISTWICK, Malcolm P; Partner, Beachcroft Stanleys.

ALLAIN, B J A; Director, S G Warburg Akroyd Rowe & Pitman Mullens Securities Ltd.

ALLAM, R J; Finance Director & Company Secretary, J H Minet & Co Ltd.

ALLAN, Bill; Partner, Linklaters & Paines.

ALLAN, Leslie Stewart; Executive Director, Barclays Development Capital Ltd, since 1981; Management of Investments in Unlisted Companies. *Career:* Keyser Ullmann Ltd, Investment Mgr 1966-69; First National Finance Corporation Ltd, Exec, Corporate Finance 1970-72; Barclays Merchant Bank Ltd, Dir, Corporate Finance 1973-81. *Educ:* Aberdeen University (MA Hons Economics/Politics). *Directorships:* The Alumasc Group plc 1984 (non-exec); Gold Crown Group Ltd 1987 (non-exec); Eurocamp Group Ltd 1988 (non-exec); Superbreak Mini-Holidays Ltd 1990 (non-exec).

ALLAN, Nicholas Timothy; Director, Kleinwort Benson Securities Limited, since 1988; International Sales. *Career:* Grieveson Grant & Co, Building Analyst 1980-81; Grieveson Grant Intl Ltd (Boston), Sales 1981-82; Grieveson Grant and Co, Sales 1982-85; Kleinwort Benson Inc, Vice-President, Sales 1985-86; Senior Vice-President, Sales 1986-88. *Educ:* Eton College; Trinity

College, Cambridge (MA). *Directorships:* Berkeley Nurseries Ltd 1984 (non-exec). *Professional Organisations:* Member, ISE; Registered Principal, Branch Office Manager and Supervisory Analyst with NYSE/NASD. *Publications:* Various Songs. *Clubs:* Lansdowne, Manchester United FC. *Recreations:* Music.

ALLAN, Philip; Managing Director, Philip Allan Publishers Limited.

ALLAN, Walter; Publishing Director, Institute of Economic Affairs, since 1990; Micro-Economics. *Career:* Repton School, School Teacher 1981-84; Allen & Unwin, Economics Editor 1984-86; Macmillan Press, Senior Editor 1986-89; IEA, Publishing Director 1990-. *Biog:* b. 16 December 1955. *Nationality:* Scottish. *m.* 1979, Sylvia (née Wilson); 2 s. *Educ:* Hawick High School; Heriot-Watt University (BA Hons Economics). *Directorships:* B E Fencing Ltd 1989 (non-exec). *Other Activities:* Advisory Council Member, Housing Choice; Major Shareholder, Hibernian Football Club. *Publications:* Concise A-Level Economics, 1984; Economics at University, Economic Affairs, 1988; Economics of Publishing, IEA (Forthcoming). *Clubs:* Hampstead Golf Club, St Boswells Rugby Football Club, Committee Member.

ALLARD, J P; Director, M & G Investment Management Ltd.

ALLATT, Derrill Victor; Director, S G Warburg & Co Ltd, since 1990; Overseas Advisory Division. *Career:* Sotheby's 1976-80; International Energy Bank 1982-84. *Biog:* b. 3 April 1954. *Educ:* Sherborne School; Emmanuel College, Cambridge (MA); Manchester Business School (MBA).

ALLBRITTON, J L; Joint Deputy Chairman, Riggs A P Bank Ltd.

ALLCHORNE, D; Director, County NatWest Securities Limited.

ALLCOCK, John Paul Major; Partner, Bristows Cooke & Carpmael, since 1981; Patent and other Intellectual Property Litigation and Licensing. *Career:* Gill, Jennings & Every, Trainee Patent Agent 1964-68; Assistant Patent Agent 1968-69; Honeywell Limited, Patent Agent and Subsequently Manager Patent Department 1969-72; Langner Parry, Assistant Patent Agent 1972-73; Coward Chance, Patent Manager and Solicitor's Articled Clerk 1973-77; Assistant Solicitor 1977-78; Bristows Cooke & Carpmael, Assistant Solicitor 1978-81. *Biog:* b. 8 July 1941. *Nationality:* British. *m.* 1981, Caroline Anne (née Rocke); 1 s; 2 d. *Educ:* St Edwards School, Oxford; Kings College, University of London (BSc Eng); Facultée Polytechnique de Mons, Belgium (MSc). *Professional Organisations:* Law Society; Chartered Patent Agent; European Patent Attorney;

Institution of Electrical Engineers; CEng; MIEE. *Recreations:* Walking, Sailing.

ALLDAY, John Philip; Partner, Ernst & Whinney.

ALLEN, Derek James; Director, J H Rayner.

ALLEN, G K; Investment Director, ICI Investment Management Ltd, since 1989; Asset Allocation & Worldwide Equity Portfolios. *Career:* Colegrave & Co, Investment Analyst, UK Equities 1973-74; ICI Investments Department, Investment Analyst, UK Equities 1974-81; Fund Manager, US Equities 1981-82; Assistant Investment Manager, Overseas Equities & Venture Capital 1982-85; Assistant Investment Manager, Worldwide Equities & Asset Allocation 1985-86; ICI Investment Management Ltd, Investment Manager, Securities, Worldwide Equities & Asset Allocation 1986-89; Investment Director, Worldwide Equities & Asset Allocation 1989-. *Biog:* b. 12 January 1951. *Nationality:* British. div; 1 s; 2 d. *Educ:* Cambridgeshire High School for Boys; Polytechnic of Central London (BA Business Studies). *Directorships:* ICI Investment Management Ltd 1989 (exec). *Other Activities:* Member, NAPF Investment Committee; Chairman, NAPF European Affairs Sub-Committee; Member, NAPF International Committee. *Publications:* Article in Pensions World, Overseas Ordinary Shares, 1983. *Recreations:* Photography, Motor Racing, Gardening.

ALLEN, Gary James; Managing Director & Chief Executive, IMI plc, since 1986. *Career:* IMI, Management Accountant 1965; IMI Range Ltd, Managing Director 1973-77; Eley Ltd, Chairman 1981-85; IMI Components Ltd, Chairman 1981-85; IMI plc, Director 1978-; Assistant Managing Director 1985-86. *Biog:* b. 30 September 1944. *Nationality:* British. *m.* 1966, Judith Anne (née Nattrass); 3 s. *Educ:* King Edward VI Grammar School, Birmingham; Liverpool University (BCom). *Directorships:* NV Bekaert SA, Belgium 1987 (non-exec); Marley plc 1989 (non-exec); Birmingham European Airways Ltd 1989 (non-exec). *Other Activities:* Member, National Council, CBI, 1986-; Member of the Council, Birmingham Chamber of Industry and Commerce, 1983-, Vic President, 1989-; Hon Life Member of Court, Birmingham University, 1984-; Liveryman, Worshipful Company of Gunmakers; Chairman, West Midlands Regional Committee, The Lord's Taverners. *Professional Organisations:* Fellow, Institute of Cost & Management Accountants; Fellow, Royal Society of Arts; Companion, British Institute of Management. *Recreations:* Sport, Reading, Gardening.

ALLEN, Gregory; International Equity Manager, Crown Financial Management Limited.

ALLEN, Ken; Financial Reporter, Daily Mail.

ALLEN, Lindsay James; Partner, Ernst & Whinney Management Consultants.

ALLEN, M D; Director, Kleinwort Benson Limited.

ALLEN, Michael Guy Tothill; Partner, Theodore Goddard, since 1990; Commercial. *Career:* Theodore Goddard, Articled Clerk, Solicitor 1978-90. *Biog: b.* 18 October 1954. *Nationality:* British. *m.* 1987, Krzysztofa Romana (née Blaszkowska); 1 s. *Educ:* King's School, Canterbury; Bristol University (LLB); C E U, Nancy France (DESS). *Other Activities:* City of London Solicitors' Company. *Professional Organisations:* The Law Society.

ALLEN, P J; Director, USA, Denis M Clayton & Co Limited.

ALLEN, P M; Director, Hambros Bank Limited.

ALLEN, Peter John; Director, Kleinwort Benson Investment Management, since 1986; Fund Management, UK Institutional Client Relationships. *Career:* Kenneth Anderson & Co, Trainee 1967-68; Centre-File Analyst 1968-69; Rowe Swann & Co, Portfolio Mgr 1969-75; Sheppards & Chase, Discretionary Fund Mgr 1975-77; Kleinwort Benson, Investment Management 1977; Asst Mgr 1979-81; Mgr 1981-85; Asst Dir 1985-86. *Biog: b.* 3 July 1949. *Nationality:* British. *m.* 1973, Jennifer (née Groves). *Educ:* Wallington. *Professional Organisations:* International Stock Exchange; MBIM; Institute of Directors. *Clubs:* RAF. *Recreations:* Riding, Ballet, Circus.

ALLEN, Peter Rowland; Partner, Turner Kenneth Brown, since 1969; Company Commercial. *Biog: b.* 13 June 1940. *Nationality:* British. *m.* 1965, Heather (née McKenzie); 1 s; 2 d. *Educ:* Uppingham School. *Professional Organisations:* Law Society. *Clubs:* City of London, Honourable Artillery Company, Royal Solent Yacht Club.

ALLEN, Peter William; Deputy Chairman, Coopers & Lybrand Deloitte, since 1990. *Career:* Coopers & Lybrand Gen Practice & Investigations 1966-75; Ptnr/Chm, Intl Personnel Ctee 1975-79; Ptnr Venture Capital/Bus Servs 1980-83; Ptnr in charge, London Office 1984; Managing Partner 1985-90. *Biog: b.* 22 July 1938. *Nationality:* British. *m.* 1965, Patricia Mary (née Dunk); 3 d. *Educ:* Cambridge University (MA). *Directorships:* Coopers & Lybrand Subsidiary Companies. *Other Activities:* Coopers & Lybrand Deloitte Board; Liveryman, Glaziers. *Professional Organisations:* FCA. *Clubs:* Reform. *Recreations:* Golf, Bridge.

ALLEN, T E; Secretary, Securities and Investments Board.

ALLEN, Wilfred; General Manager, The Royal Bank of Scotland Group plc.

ALLEN, William Anthony; Head of Foreign Exchange Division, Bank of England, since 1990; Official Operations in the Foreign Exchange Market and Management of The Official Reserves. *Career:* Bank of England, Economic Intelligence Dept 1972-77; Gold & Foreign Exchange Office 1977-78; Bank for International Settlements (Seconded) Monetary & Economic Dept 1978-80; Bank of England, Asst Adviser, Economics Division 1980-82; Mgr, Gilt-Edged Division 1982-86; Head of Money Market Operations Division 1986-90; Head of Gilt-Edged and Money Markets Division 1990. *Biog: b.* 13 May 1949. *Nationality:* British. *m.* 1972, Rosemary Margaret (née Eminson); 1 s; 2 d. *Educ:* King's College School, Wimbledon; Balliol College, Oxford (BA); London School of Economics (MSc). *Publications:* Various Articles in Economics Journals. *Recreations:* Gardening, Jazz.

ALLEN-JONES, Charles; Partner, Linklaters & Paines.

ALLIBONE, D; Partner, Cameron Markby Hewitt.

ALLINSON, Miss C M; Partner, Lovell White Durrant.

ALLISON, John Gerard; Chairman, Allison Mitchell Partnership Ltd, since 1990. *Biog: b.* 25 October 1949. *Nationality:* British. *m.* Kathy; 3 d. *Educ:* (BA Hons Business Studies). *Directorships:* Money Marketing (Design) Ltd 1984 (exec); Moorgate Group plc 1986 (exec).

ALLISON, Shaun; Director (Sales), Hoare Govett International Securities.

ALLISTON, Nicholas; Director - Prudential Business Services, Prudential Corporation plc.

ALLSOPP, Michael; Controller (Advances), Yorkshire Bank plc, since 1986; Corporate and Personal Lending. *Biog: b.* 8 July 1942. *m.* 1966, Angela Denise (née Clegg); 1 s; 1 d. *Professional Organisations:* FCIB.

ALLSOPP, Michael Edward Ranulph; Chairman, Granville & Co Ltd, since 1987. *Career:* Allen Harvey & Ross 1952; Board 1955; London Discount Market Association Chm 1974-76; Cater Allen Holdings plc Dir 1981-85; Allied Dunbar & Co plc Chm 1979-86. *Biog: b.* 9 October 1930. *Nationality:* British. *m.* 1955, Patricia Ann (née Berners); 4 d. *Educ:* Eton College. *Directorships:* Subsidiaries of Granville & Co; BFSS Investments Ltd 1985; HSBS Investments Ltd 1977; Berners-Allsopp Estate Management Co Ltd 1975 Chm; Baronsmead Venture Capital plc 1985 Chm; Strata Investments plc 1985 (non-exec); St Davids Investment

Trust plc 1986 Chm. *Clubs:* Pratt's White's. *Recreations:* Foxhunting.

ALLSOPP, Ronald James; Partner, Penningtons, since 1974; Head of Company and Commercial Department. *Career:* College of Law Guildford, Lecturer 1971-73; Penningtons, Assistant Solicitor 1973-74. *Biog: b.* 12 May 1947. *Nationality:* British. *m.* 1977, Greta; 1 s; 1 d. *Educ:* St Andrews University (LLB). *Professional Organisations:* Solicitor. *Clubs:* Cannons. *Recreations:* Food & Wine, Walking, Reading, Shooting.

ALLUM, Geoffrey Michael; Director, County NatWest Securities Limited, since 1988; Conglomerates and other Industrial Materials Analyst. *Career:* Fielding Newson-Smith 1982-86; County NatWest Securities Limited 1986-. *Biog: b.* 12 October 1957. *Nationality:* British. *m.* 1986, Amanda Jane (née Fleming); 1 s; 1 d. *Educ:* Hampton School, Aston University (BSc Hons Managerial & Administrative Studies); Manchester Business School (Diploma Business Administration).

ALLUM, Jonathan; Vice President, Morgan Stanley Asset Management, since 1990; Management of Morgan Stanley Japanese Warrant Fund. *Career:* Laing & Cruickshank, Trainee & then UK Chemicals & Pharmaceuticals Analyst 1980-82; James Capel, Japanese Equity Analyst 1982-85; Morgan Stanley International, Head of Equity Derivative Research 1985-90; Morgan Stanley Asset Management, VP 1990-. *Biog: b.* 6 September 1956. *Nationality:* British. *m.* 1981, Moira Lacey; 2 s; 2 d. *Educ:* The Oratory School; Magdalen College, Oxford (BA, BPhil).

ALONSO, Fernando; General Manager, Banco Central, since 1986; International Finance, Corporate Finance, Trade Finance. *Career:* Banco Central (Bilbao, Spain), Official 1970-76; Banco Central (London), Chief Cashier 1977-79; Asst Mgr 1979-81; Snr Asst Mgr 1981-82; Dep Mgr 1982-86. *Directorships:* Casa de Espana Ltd 1986 (non-exec).

ALT, Anthony; Managing Director (Investment Management), N M Rothschild & Sons Limited.

ALTMANN, Rosalind; Executive Director, N M Rothschild International Asset Management Limited.

ALUN-JONES, Sir Derek; Director, Royal Insurance Holdings plc.

ALWEN, R N; Director, R H M Outhwaite (Underwriting Agencies) Limited.

AMARI, Corrado; Senior Deputy General Manager, Banco Di Roma, London Branch, since 1990. *Career:* Banca Nazionale Del Lavoro, Comprehensive Training Period at Numerous Branches in Italy 1975-79; (Barcelona Branch) Manager, Corporate Finance 1980-83; (London Branch) Manager 1983-86; (Luxembourg Subsidiary) Joint General Manager with Overall Responsibility for all the Bank's Activities 1986-88; Banco Di Roma SpA (Head Office, Rome), Deputy Chief Manager, International Finance Department 1988-90; (London Branch) Senior Deputy General Manager with Overall Responsibility for all the Bank's Activities 1990-. *Biog: b.* 6 November 1950. *Nationality:* Italian. *m.* 1974, Alda (née Parlato); 1 s; 1 d. *Educ:* Palermo University (Doctorate in Law with Honours). *Clubs:* Overseas Bankers Club. *Recreations:* Various Sports, Cinema, Literature.

AMATO, M; Director, IMI Securities Ltd.

AMBLER, H S; JP; Director, Yorkshire Building Society.

AMBROSE, J V; Secretary, Willis Corroon plc.

AMES, Christopher; Director of Regional Offices, Price Waterhouse.

AMETANI, K; Director, IBJ International Limited, since 1988; New Issue Marketing, Swaps. *Career:* IBJ (The Industrial Bank of Japan) Head Office 1973; Secondment to Ministry of Finance, Japan 1975; IBJ Head Office, Research Department, Finance Section 1976; IBJ Osaka Branch, Assistant Manager/Loan Division and Assistant Manager/Forex Division 1980; IBJ Head Office, Manager/Capital Markets Department 1985; IBJ International Ltd 1988. *Biog: b.* 23 December 1949. *Nationality:* Japanese. *m.* 1976, Sonoko; 1 s; 1 d. *Educ:* Tokyo University (Law); Harvard Business School (PMD).

AMLÔT, Robin André; Deputy Financial Editor, London Broadcasting Co Ltd, since 1987. *Career:* Tin International, Assistant Editor, Metal Markets 1982-83; Editor 1983-85; Global Analysis Systems, Company News Editor, Corporate Analysis 1985-87. *Biog: b.* 18 August 1958. *Nationality:* British. *m.* 1990, Anna (née Wolf). *Educ:* Wirral Grammar School; Lancaster University (BA Politics). *Directorships:* MIIDA Ltd 1989. *Publications:* Guide To World Markets, 1991. *Recreations:* History, Painting, Film Noir, Sleeping.

AMOS, C J; Partner, Ashurst Morris Crisp.

AMOS, Charles Anthony; Finance & Operations Director, ICI Investment Management Limited, since 1989; Accounting, Information Technology, Compliance. *Career:* Price Waterhouse (London) 1974-76; (Southampton) 1976-78; ICI Plastics Division (Welwyn), Accountant 1978-80; ICI Hillhouse Works (Fleetwood), PVC Accountant 1980-83; ICI Colours & Fine Chemicals (Manchester), Project Leader 1983-87; ICI Investment Management Ltd, Financial Controller 1987-89. *Biog: b.* 1952. *Nationality:* British. *m.* 1974, Sally Sau Lui; 2 s; 1 d. *Educ:* Cheltenham Grammar

School; Jesus College, Cambridge (MA English). *Directorships:* ICI Investment Management Ltd 1989 (exec). *Other Activities:* Business Adviser, Business in the Arts; Chairman, Quasar London Users' Group. *Professional Organisations:* FCA. *Recreations:* Poetry, Theatre, Running.

AMPHLETT, Philip Nicholas; Senior Vice President & Branch Manager, Bank Julius Baer & Co Ltd, since 1985; Banking. *Career:* W H Brandts Sons and Co Trainee Manager 1971-73; Henry Ansbacher and Co Ltd Manager/Director 1973-85; Bank Julius Baer & Co Ltd SVP 1985-; Branch Mgr 1989-. *Biog: b.* 20 October 1948. *Nationality:* Dutch. *m.* 1969, Marjolein Erantha (née De Vries); 1 s; 2 d. *Educ:* Winchester; Balliol College, Oxford (BA). *Recreations:* Sailing, Walking, Swimming, Tennis.

AMY, Ronald John; Group Compensation and Benefits Director, Grand Metropolitan plc, since 1988; Pensions and Executive Compensation on a Worldwide Basis. *Career:* Scottish Mutual Assurance Society, London Actuary 1978-80; Philips Electronics, UK Pensions Manager 1980-84; Metal Box plc, Group Pensions Manager 1984-86; Barclays de Zoete Wedd Investment Management Ltd, Director, Responsible for New Business Development 1986-87; Grand Metropolitan plc, Group Pensions Director 1987-88; Group Compensation & Benefits Director 1988-. *Biog: b.* 17 June 1950. *Nationality:* British. *m.* 1975, Evelyn (née Morrison); 2 d. *Educ:* Hermitage Academy; Dalziel High School; Glasgow University (BSc Hons Pure Mathematics). *Directorships:* National Association of Pension Funds 1988 Honorary Treasurer. *Other Activities:* Member, Occupational Pensions Board; Chairman, States of Jersey Public Employees Contributory Retirement Scheme Management Committee; Member, CBI Pensions Panel. *Professional Organisations:* Fellow, Faculty of Actuaries. *Clubs:* Wentworth Club, Caledonian Club. *Recreations:* Golf.

AMZALLAG, Robert Meyer; Managing Director, Banque Nationale de Paris plc, since 1988. *Career:* Sprecher und Schuh, Aarau (Switzerland), Computer Designer 1967-68; Rotopark SA, Geneva (Switzerland), Commercial Manager 1969-71; Banque Nationale de Paris (Mexico), Deputy Representative 1972-74; Banque Nationale de Paris (Paris), Inspector 1974-78; Banque Nationale de Paris (Hong Kong), Secrtaire Général 1978-82; Banque Nationale de Paris (London), Attachment 1982-83; Banque Nationale de Paris (Ireland), General Manager 1983-85; Banque Nationale de Paris (Australia), General Manager 1985-88; Banque Nationale de Paris (London), Managing Director 1988. *Biog: b.* 18 December 1944. *Nationality:* American. *m.* Tennille (née Dix); 1 s; 2 d. *Educ:* Ecole des Mines, Nancy, France (Engineering Degree, Solid State Physics & Applied Mathematics); European Institute of Business Administration, INSEAD (MBA). *Recreations:* Tennis, Ski, Modern Art.

ANAND, Dr Indira; Producing Manager, Merrill Lynch Pierce Fenner & Smith Ltd, since 1987; Japanese Institutional Sales, UK & Europe. *Career:* Co-operative Insurance Society, International Economist 1970-72; Economist & Fund Manager (Europe & Far East) 1972-75; Fund Manager (Europe, Japan, Australia & Canada) 1975-79; also Forex Manager & Fund Manager, US 1979-83; Head of International Investments 1983-85; Prudential Portfolio Managers, Assistant Director (Far East) 1985-87; Merrill Lynch Pierce Fenner & Smith, Associate Director, Producing Manager (Japan & Australia) 1987-89; Director 1990-. *Educ:* (BA Hons Econ, MA Econ, PhD).

ANASTASI, George; Director, Svenska International plc, since 1986; Treasury, Short-Term Instruments, Commercial Paper/CD Capital Market Products. *Career:* Banque Belge Ltd (London), Securities Officer 1960-69; Deltec Trading Co Ltd (London), Assistant Vice President 1969-73; First Boston Corporation (London), Manager 1973-74; Williams & Glyn's Bank Ltd, Manager 1974-78; Donaldson Lufkin & Jenrette (London), Director 1978-80; Arab International Securities Ltd (London), Executive Manager 1980-83. *Biog: b.* 20 October 1941. *Nationality:* British. *m.* 1964, Maureen Gilian (née Adams); 1 s. *Educ:* Quintin School, London; Goldsmith's College, London (Diploma in Economics).

ANASTASSIADES, M S; Director, Crédit Lyonnais Euro-Securities Ltd.

ANATOLE, Kaletsky; Economics Editor, The Times.

ANDERSEN, G R; Partner, Wedlake Bell.

ANDERSON, A P; Executive Director, Equities, Swiss Bank Corporation.

ANDERSON, D J L F; Director, Lazard Brothers & Co Limited.

ANDERSON, D M; Executive Director, Allied Dunbar Assurance plc.

ANDERSON, David; Director & General Manager (Corporate Development), Yorkshire Building Society, since 1990; Planning, Strategy, Diversification, Property. *Career:* Dun & Bradstreet International, Field Sales Manager 1980-83; PA Management Consultants, Senior Consultant 1983-87; Yorkshire Building Society 1987-. *Biog: b.* 23 October 1955. *Nationality:* British. *m.* Fiona; 1 s; 1 d. *Educ:* St Edmund Hall, Oxford (MA). *Directorships:* Yorkshire Building Society Estate Agents Ltd 1989 (non-exec); Yorkshire Guernsey Ltd 1990 (non-exec); Yorkshire Properties Ltd 1990 (non-exec).

ANDERSON, Dickson B; Director, Templeton Unit Trust Managers Limited.

ANDERSON, G A; Chairman, Ernst & Young.

ANDERSON, Gordon; Director, Dunedin Fund Managers Ltd.

ANDERSON, Gordon Scott; Assistant General Manager, Commerzbank AG, since 1985; International Capital Markets. *Career:* Locana Corp (London) Ltd 1964-68; Bankers Trust International Ltd 1968-72; Robert Fleming & Co Ltd, Eurobond Mgr 1972-77; Chase Manhattan Ltd, Exec Dir 1977-84; Chase Manhattan Asia Ltd, Exec Dir 1984-85. *Biog: b.* 27 May 1944. *Nationality:* British. *m.* 1970, Rosemary (née King); 2 s. *Educ:* Hampton School. *Other Activities:* Chm, UK Regional Ctee of Assoc of Intl Bond Dealers; Chm, Securities Ctee, Foreign Banks & Securities Houses Association; Member, Securities Ctee, British Bankers' Assoc. *Recreations:* Badminton, Golf, Rowing, Woodwork.

ANDERSON, Ian; Director, Rudolf Wolff & Co Ltd.

ANDERSON, J H; Executive Director, Philipp & Lion Ltd.

ANDERSON, J I W; Director, Unilever plc.

ANDERSON, James; Partner, Baillie Gifford & Co.

ANDERSON, James Douglas; Director, Dunedin Fund Managers Limited, since 1989; Venture Capital. *Career:* Nuclear Enterprises Ltd, Accountant 1967-69; Ivory & Sime, Investment Manager 1970-79; British Linen Bank Limited, Director 1980-89. *Biog: b.* 30 January 1943. *Nationality:* British. *m.* 1970, Isabel Nyria (née Lawson); 2 s. *Educ:* Dunfermline High School; University of Edinburgh (MA, BCom). *Directorships:* Belwood Nurseries Limited; Dunedin Berkeley Management Company Limited (Jersey); Dunedin Fund Mergers Limited; Dunedin Ventures Limited Chm; Dunfermline Building Society; Intermediate Capital Group Limited; Latchways Limited; Romarsh Transformers Limited; Suncan Group Limited; Suncan Wholesale Electrical Limited; Thistle Investment Co Limited; Travel & General Insurance Company plc; Veitchi (Holdings) Limited; Forth Oil Limited -1986; Smith Ladder Limpit Limited -1987; Mountjoy Finance Limited -1987; Scottish Unit Managers Limited -1987; Skytec Aviation Limited -1987; Seven Seas Inspection Limited -1987; Melville Street Leasing (Edinburgh) Limited -1988; Kineticon Limited 1989; Melville Street Assets (Edinburgh) Limited -1989; British Linen Pension Fund Managers Limited -1989; The British Linen Bank Limited -1989. *Professional Organisations:* CA.

ANDERSON, K R; Director, Bunzl Plc.

ANDERSON, Mrs Kathleen (née Harker); Director, County NatWest Limited, since 1988; Credit Risk Evaluation and Administration Group. *Career:* Continental Illinois Corporation, Vice President Commercial Banking 1966-87. *Biog: b.* 18 July 1944. *Nationality:* American. *m.* 1983, A Peter Anderson II. *Educ:* University of Chicago (MBA); University of Wisconsin (BA). *Other Activities:* City Women's Network. *Recreations:* Theatre, Reading, Walking, Gardening.

ANDERSON, Kenneth Warren; Managing Director, JP Morgan Investment Management Inc, since 1987; Head of London Office, Investment Management. *Career:* Morgan Guaranty Trust Co (New York), Analyst/Portfolio Mgr, VP 1976-84; JP Morgan Investment Management (New York), Portfolio Mgr, VP 1984-87. *Biog: b.* 18 November 1948. *Educ:* Harvard College (BA); Harvard Business School (MBA). *Clubs:* RAC.

ANDERSON, M H F; Director, Hill Samuel Bank Limited.

ANDERSON, Peter William; Partner, S J Berwin & Co, since 1986; Corporate Finance Solicitor. *Career:* Stephenson Harwood 1976-81; Stephenson Harwood & Co (Hong Kong) 1980; Lewis Lewis & Co 1981-82; Jaques & Lewis 1982-85. *Biog: b.* 29 May 1954. *Nationality:* British. *m.* 1980, Jean (née Thomas); 2 d. *Educ:* Shrewsbury School; Downing College, Cambridge (BA,MA). *Professional Organisations:* The Law Society; Holborn Law Society.

ANDERSON, Raymond; Director & General Manager, Scottish Amicable Life Assurance Society, since 1984; Actuarial. *Career:* Scottish Amicable, Various 1951-. *Biog: b.* 20 November 1934. *Nationality:* British. *m.* 1958, Maureen (née Kerr); 2 s; 2 d. *Educ:* Lenzie Academy. *Professional Organisations:* FFA.

ANDERSON, Ross Kenyon; Treasurer, The General Electric Company plc, since 1979; Treasury, Investment Management and Company Structure. *Career:* Royal Artillery, 2nd Lieutenant 1954-56; Peat Marwick Mitchell & Co, Articled Clerk/Qualified Snr 1959-63; Dufay Ltd, Group Chief Acct 1963-66; Metropole Industries Ltd, Fin Dir & Sec 1966-71; Keith Prowse Group, Fin Dir & Sec 1971-75; The General Electric Company plc, Dep Treasurer 1975-79. *Biog: b.* 9 April 1936. *Nationality:* British. *m.* 1969, Anne (née Craigie) (decd 1985); 2 d. *Educ:* The Edinburgh Academy; Corpus Christi College, Oxford (MA Law Hons). *Directorships:* GEC Group or its Associates. *Other Activities:* Auditor, Local Methodist Church. *Professional Organisations:* FCA. *Recreations:* Bridge, Golf.

ANDERSON, Stewart; Associate, James Gentles & Son.

ANDERSON, T J; Managing Director, Buchanan Communications Ltd.

ANDERTON, John Robin; Dealing Director, Parrish Stockbrokers, since 1988; All Dealing within Group. *Career:* L Messel, Specialist Inv Trust Dealer 1959-79; Sheppards & Chase, Institutional Gilt Edged Dealer 1979-85; Sternberg Thomas Clarke, Head of Dealing 1985-87. *Biog:* b. 24 April 1941. *Nationality:* British. *m.* 1969, Susan Lynda (née Swaffin); 1 s; 1 d. *Educ:* Framlingham College. *Clubs:* MCC, Thorndon Park Golf Club. *Recreations:* Sport, Gardening.

ANDO, K; General Manager, Kyowa Bank.

ANDREW, I R D; Director, Brewin Dolphin & Co Ltd.

ANDREW, Richard Arnold; Executive Chairman, The Private Capital Group (Subsidiary of Scandinavian Bank Group).

ANDREWARTHA, Miss Elizabeth Jane; Partner, Clyde & Co, since 1980; Marine Aviation and Insurance Law. *Career:* Clyde & Co, Articled Clerk 1974-76; Qualified Solicitor 1976-80. *Biog:* b. 20 December 1952. *Nationality:* English. 1 d. *Educ:* 13 Different State Schools; Exeter University (LLB Hons 2:1). *Professional Organisations:* Law Society. *Clubs:* London Motor Boat Racing Club. *Recreations:* Powerboat Racing, Skiing, Diving.

ANDREWES, E W E; Director, Granada Group.

ANDREWS, Christopher Henry; Group Secretary, Ladbroke Group plc, since 1974. *Career:* Ladbroke Group plc, Dir 1986-. *Biog:* b. 24 January 1940. *Nationality:* British. *m.* 1964, Moira Kathlyn Frances (née Dunn); 2 d. *Educ:* Chislehurst and Sidcup Grammar School. *Professional Organisations:* FCIS.

ANDREWS, Ian; Manager, National Westminster Growth Options Ltd.

ANDREWS, Ian S; Director, Kleinwort Benson Securities Limited.

ANDREWS, John M; Head of National Tax Practice, Coopers & Lybrand Deloitte, since 1986; Taxation. *Biog:* b. 11 June 1942. *Nationality:* British. *m.* 1966, Elizabeth (née Smith); 2 s. *Educ:* Bromley Grammar School. *Professional Organisations:* Member, Tax Legislation Ctee, FCA; Fellow and Member, Technical Committee, Institute of Taxation. *Publications:* Taxation of Directors and Employees, (3rd Edition), 1990; The Potential Use of Stock Option Plans and Incentives by New Technology Companies within the EEC (Report for the EEC); Butterworths Income Tax (Contributor); Taxation of Foreign Nationals in the UK. *Recreations:* Sport.

ANDREWS, M; Director, Crédit Lyonnais Capital Markets plc.

ANDREWS, Mark B; Partner, Wilde Sapte Solicitors, since 1979; Head of Litigation Department. *Career:* Clarks Solicitors (Reading), Articled Clerk 1974-76; Wilde Sapte 1976-. *Biog:* b. 12 July 1952. *Nationality:* British. *Educ:* Reading Grammar School; Hertford College, Oxford (BA Jurisprudence). *Other Activities:* Director, Pimlico Opera. *Professional Organisations:* Member, Law Society; Licensed Insolvency Practitioner. *Recreations:* French Horn Playing, Singing, Ornithology.

ANDREWS, N F; Managing Director, Greig, Middleton & Co Ltd.

ANDREWS, R D; Group Controller, Redland plc, since 1983. *Career:* Redland Roof Tiles BTR plc, Director 1979-83. *Biog:* b. 12 December 1942. *Nationality:* British. *m.* 1967, Charmian; 1 s; 1 d. *Directorships:* Redland Funding plc 1989; Redland Capital plc 1987; Redland Finance plc 1985. *Professional Organisations:* Chartered Accountant.

ANDREWS, W Denys C; Partner, Shepherd & Wedderburn WS.

ANGEL, Anthony Lionel; Partner, Linklaters & Paines, since 1984; Tax. *Career:* Linklaters & Paines, Articled Clerk 1976-78; Assistant Solicitor 1978-84. *Biog:* b. 3 December 1952. *Nationality:* British. *m.* 1975, Ruth Frances Barbara (née Hartol); 2 s. *Educ:* Haberdashers' Aske's School, Elstree; Queens' College, Cambridge (MA Cantab). *Professional Organisations:* Solicitor; Member, Law Society. *Recreations:* Tennis, Swimming.

ANGEL, Gillian; Marketing Director, Morison Stoneham Chartered Accountants.

ANGEL, Philip Charles; Senior Partner, S P Angel & Co, since 1980; Investment Management. *Biog:* b. 6 June 1937. *Nationality:* British. *m.* 1960, Elizabeth Jane (née Logan); 2 d. *Educ:* Brighton College. *Other Activities:* ISE Regional Ctee; Chm, London Regional Assoc of the ISE; Ctee of New Trade Assoc APCIMS. *Recreations:* Fishing, Gardening.

ANGELKOSKI, Jovan; Director, Stopanska Banka AD Skopje, since 1990; Trade Finance, Project Financing and SAVE. *Career:* National Bank of Macedonia, Skopje Senior Officer 1968-75; Stopanska Banka AD Skopje, Asst Director 1975-90. *Biog:* b. 11 February 1941. *Nationality:* Yugoslav. *m.* 1963, Viktorija (née Muratovska); 1 s; 1 d. *Educ:* Faculty of Economics Yugoslavia (BA Econ). *Directorships:* Anglo-Yugoslav Bank London 1990 (non-exec) alternate. *Professional Organisations:* Yugoslav Bank Association. *Clubs:* Yugoslav Club. *Recreations:* Skiing.

ANGELL, Nicholas; Managing Director, Nicholas Angell Limited; Responsible for London & Paris Offices of Executive Search Practice. *Career:* Coopers & Lybrand, Audit Snr 1965-71; British Building Trust, Chief Accountant 1972-73; Nicholas Angell (Paris), MD 1974-; (London), MD 1984-. *Biog: b.* 1947. *Nationality:* British. *m.* 1978, Jean (née Tattersall); 1 s; 1 d. *Educ:* Moseley Grammar School, Birmingham. *Professional Organisations:* FCA. *Recreations:* Sailing.

ANGLE, Martin David; Managing Director, Morgan Stanley International, since 1989; Mergers & Acquisitions. *Career:* Peat Marwick Mitchell & Co London 1972-76; UAE Currency Board 1976-78; S G Warburg & Co Ltd, Corporate Finance Department 1978-88; Director 1986; Morgan Stanley International 1988-. *Biog: b.* 8 April 1950. *Nationality:* British. *m.* 1977, Lindsey A (née Blake); 2 s; 1 d. *Educ:* St Dunstan's College; University of Warwick (BSc). *Professional Organisations:* FCA.

ANGST, K; Director, Allstate Reinsurance Co Limited.

ANGUS, John A; Director, Merrill Lynch Europe Limited.

ANGUS, Sir Michael; Chairman, Unilever plc, since 1986. *Career:* Royal Air Force 1951-54; Unilever plc 1954-; Thibaud Gibbs (Paris), Marketing Director 1962-65; Research Bureau (London), Managing Director 1965-67; Lever Brothers UK, Sales Director 1967-70; Unilever plc and Unilever NV, Director 1970-; Toilet Preparations Co-ordinator 1970-76; Chemicals Co-ordinator 1976-80; Regional Director (North America) 1979-84; Unilever United States Inc (New York), Chairman and CEO 1980-84; Lever Brothers Company (New York), Chairman and CEO 1980-84; Unilever plc, Vice Chairman 1984-86; Chairman 1986-; Unilever NV, Vice Chairman 1986-. *Biog: b.* 5 May 1930. *Nationality:* British. *m.* 1952, (Eileen) Isabel (May) (née Elliott); 2 s; 1 d. *Educ:* Marling School, Stroud, Gloucestershire; University of Bristol (BSc Hons,Honorary DSc). *Directorships:* Whitbread and Company plc 1986 (non-exec); Thorn EMI plc 1988 (non-exec); British Airways plc 1988 (non-exec); British Airways plc 1989 (non-exec) Joint Deputy Chairman. *Other Activities:* Trustee, Leverhulme Trust; Trustee, Conference Board, New York; Member, President's Committee, CBI; Member, Governing Body, ICC United Kingdom; Member, UK Advisory Board, British-American Chamber of Commerce; A Vice President, Netherlands-British Chamber of Commerce; Visiting Fellow, Nuffield College, Oxford; Governor, Ashridge Management College. *Professional Organisations:* Companion, British Institute of Management. *Clubs:* Athenaeum, University Club (New York), Knickerbocker (New York). *Recreations:* Countryside, Wine, Mathematical Puzzles.

ANGUS, Robin John; Director, County NatWest Securities Ltd Inc Wood Mackenzie, since 1988; Investment Trusts. *Career:* Baillie Gifford & Co, Investment Mgr 1977-81; Wood Mackenzie & Co, Investment Analyst 1981-85; Asst Dir 1985-88; Hill Samuel Securities Ltd, Dir 1985-88. *Biog: b.* 15 September 1952. *m.* 1977, Lorna Christine (née Campbell). *Educ:* Forres Academy; St Andrews University (MA); Peterhouse, Cambridge. *Directorships:* Personal Assets Trust plc 1984 (non-exec); Scottish Episcopal Church Clergy Widows & Orphans Fund 1987 (non-exec). *Other Activities:* Mem, General Synod, Scottish Episcopal Church; Mem, Faith & Order Brd, Scottish Episcopal Church; Auditor, Fin Adviser, Diocese of Moray, Ross & Caithness; Member of Core Group, Scottish Centre for Economic and Social Research; Mem, Working Party on Ethics & Fin, Centre for Theology and Public Issues, Edinburgh University. *Publications:* Independence, The Option for Growth, 1989; Numerous Articles on Investment Trusts. *Clubs:* New Club (Edinburgh), Scottish Arts Club (Edinburgh), Royal Scottish Automobile Club (Glasgow), McSkate's (St Andrews). *Recreations:* Church Work, Politics (Scottish Nationalist), History, Music, Reading, Writing Verse.

ANKARCRONA, Jan Gustaf Theodor Stensson; Managing Director, FennoScandia Bank Ltd, since 1983; CEO. *Career:* American Express Securities SA Paris, Sous Directeur 1969-70; Nordic Bank Ltd London Mgr, Associate Director 1971-76; Deputy Managing Director 1976-83. *Biog: b.* 18 April 1940. *Nationality:* Swedish. *m.* 1981, Sandra (née Coxe); 2 s; 2 d. *Educ:* Ostra Real, Sweden; Royal Swedish Naval Academy, Stockholm; Stockholm School of Economics (MBA); University of California, Berkeley (MBA). *Directorships:* Swedish Chamber of Commerce for the UK 1981-84 Chm (non-exec); 1984-90 (non-exec); Association of British Consortium Banks 1986 Chm. *Other Activities:* Order of St John, Sweden. *Clubs:* Brooks's, Hurlingham, Annabel's, Nya Sallskapet (Stockholm). *Recreations:* History, Music, Sailing, Tennis, Shooting.

ANSDELL, John Reginald Wardhaugh; Group Finance Director, Trafalgar House plc, since 1988. *Career:* Binder Hamlyn & Co 1967-72; Ashland Oil Inc 1972-78; Merck & Co Inc 1978-85; Hepworth plc 1985-88. *Directorships:* Trafalgar House plc 1988; ABS Computers Limited 1988; Eastern International Investment Trust plc 1988; The Cunard Steam-Ship Company plc 1988; Trafalgar Associates Ltd 1989; Trafalgar House Construction Holdings Ltd 1988; Trafalgar House Construction Ltd 1988; Trafalgar House Group Finance plc 1988 Chm; Trafalgar House Group Premises Ltd 1988; Trafalgar House Group Services Ltd 1989 MD.

ANSLOW, David Keith; Executive Director, Brown Shipley & Co Limited, since 1986; Corporate Finance. *Career:* Price Waterhouse & Co 1963-68; Forte & Co Ltd, Divisional Accountant 1968-69; Lazard Brothers &

Co Limited, Assistant Dir 1969-79; Lloyds Merchant Bank, Dir 1979-85. *Biog: b.* 3 May 1941. *Nationality:* British. *m.* 1980, Angela (née Colburn); 1 s; 1 d. *Educ:* St Paul's (Foundation Scholar); Jesus College, Cambridge (MA). *Directorships:* Council of the Corporation of Foreign Bondholders 1974-90 Member; Garfield Lewis Limited 1985-89 (non-exec). *Professional Organisations:* FCA.

ANSLOW, Maurice; Editor, Financial Weekly.

ANSON, George; Director, Prelude Technology Investments Limited.

ANSON, S; Managing Director, BMP Business.

ANSTEE, Eric Edward; Partner, Ernst & Young, since 1984; Director of Privatisation and Utilities Services & Partner, Public Sector Audit Services. *Career:* (Secondments) Dept of Trade & Industry, Accountancy Adviser 1976-77; Ministry of Agriculture, Fisheries and Food Monitoring Govt Grants 1976-77; HM Treasury, Commercial Accountancy Adviser 1983-85. *Biog: b.* 1 January 1951. *Nationality:* British. *m.* 1982, Suzanne (née Piller); 1 s; 1 d. *Educ:* St Albans School. *Other Activities:* Member of Editorial Board, Utilities Policy; Founder Member, British Privatisation Export Council. *Professional Organisations:* FCA. *Clubs:* Athenaeum. *Recreations:* Golf, Philately.

ANTHONY, Lionel Thomas; Founder Director, Causeway Capital Limited. *Other Activities:* Past Chairman, Coal Industry Society; Past Chairman, British Venture Capital Association. *Recreations:* Choral Music, Painting, Welsh Rugby.

ANTONELLI, Pietro; Count Antonelli; Director, Hambros Bank Ltd, since 1971; European Group Investment. *Career:* Banca Commerciale Italiana, Jnt Mgr 1948-62; Caboto SpA, MD & Vice Chm 1962-71. *Biog: b.* 14 March 1924. *Nationality:* Italian. *Educ:* University of Rome. *Directorships:* Energon SpA 1978 Chm (exec); Sanpaolo-Hambros Società Internazionale Gestione Fondi SpA 1987 (non-exec); Sanpaolo Invest SpA 1988 (non-exec).

AOKI, M; Deputy General Manager, Mitsubishi Bank.

AOSAKI, M; Senior Deputy General Manager, The Saitama Bank Ltd.

ap SIMON, David Charles; Partner, Freshfields, since 1982; Company Department. *Career:* Mullens & Co, Trainee 1969-71; Cazenove & Co, Research/Corporate Fin 1971-75; Knapp-Fishers, Articled Clerk 1975-77; Freshfields, Solicitor 1977-82. *Biog: b.* 28 June 1947. *Nationality:* British. *m.* 1973, Kyle Anne Bewley (née Cathie); 2 s; 1 d. *Educ:* Epsom College; Christ's College, Cambridge (MA, LLB). *Professional Organisations:*

Law Society; City of London Solicitors' Company. *Recreations:* Opera, Wine.

APPELBOAM, George G; Director, Burlington Asset Management Ltd, since 1991; Investment Management, Life Assurance & Pensions. *Career:* National Mutual Life of Australasia (Birmingham), Branch Mgr 1960-63; George Appelboam Ltd, MD 1963-72; C T Bowring & Hughes Ltd, Dep Chm 1972-73; George G Appleboam Ltd Chm, MD 1973-88; Whitehouse Moorman & Partners Ltd 1988-90; Whitehouse Moorman Financial Planning Ltd 1990. *Biog: b.* 5 March 1927. *Nationality:* British. 1979, Josephine Elizabeth (née Midwinter) (decd 1988); 2 step s 2 d. *Educ:* East Ham Grammar School. *Directorships:* FIMBRA 1986 (non-exec); Burlington Asset Management Ltd 1991 (exec). *Professional Organisations:* FLIA, FIMBRA (Dep Chm, Fin & Gen Purposes and Rules & Legislation Ctees); BIIBA (Council, Fin Services Ctee). *Recreations:* Sculls, Yoga, Singing, Tennis.

APPLETON, Anthony W J; Clerk, The Company of Constructors.

APPLETON, David; Financial Editor, The Scotsman.

APPLETON, Kevin E; Partner, Bristows Cooke & Carpmael, since 1989; Commercial and Intellectual Property Litigation. *Career:* Bristows Cooke & Carpmael, Legal Clerk; Legal Executive; Solicitor; Partner. *Biog: b.* 18 April 1956. *Nationality:* English. *m.* 1975, Lorraine; 1 s; 1 d. *Educ:* Springhead; Kingsway Princeton; College of Law. *Recreations:* Karate, Theatre, Building Design & Refurbishment, Motor Racing.

ARAI, Jiro; Director and Company Secretary, Taiheiyo Europe Ltd, since 1987; Financial Administrator. *Career:* Koyanagi Securities Co Ltd, Various 1957-83; Taiheiyo Securities Co Ltd, Snr Gen Mgr of Accounts Dept 1985-86; Snr Gen Mgr of Audit Dept 1986-. *Biog: b.* 13 January 1934. *Nationality:* Japanese. *m.* 1963, Sumiko; 1 s; 1 d. *Educ:* School of Political Science and Economic; Waseda University, Tokyo.

ARAI, Kiyoshi; Director, Kleinwort Benson Securities Limited.

ARAI, Shuzo; Chief Executive, Sanwa International plc, since 1989; Merchant Banking. *Career:* Sanwa Bank Limited, Osakaekimae Branch 1963-65; Namba Branch 1965-66; Tokyo, Head Office 1966-68; New York Branch-Assistant Manager, Foreign Exchange 1968-72; Tokyo, Head Office, Foreign Exchange & Corporate Banking 1972-75; London-Senior Manager, Chief Dealer, Head of Corporate Banking 1975-; International Corporate Banking 1979; International Treasury Dept 1983; Kichijoji Branch, General Mgr 1983-86; Brussels Branch, General Manager 1986-89; Sanwa Intl Ltd (1990 Sanwa Intl Ltd Merged with Associated Japanese

Bank and Became Sanwa Intl plc), Chief Executive 1989-. *Biog: b.* 17 May 1940. *Nationality:* Japanese. *m.* 1964, Klyoko; 2 d. *Educ:* Osaka City University (Bachelor of Commercial Science). *Clubs:* Les Ambassadeurs, Mosimanns, Overseas Bankers Club, Wentworth. *Recreations:* Golf, Opera, Ballet.

ARBER, L; Director, S G Warburg & Co Ltd.

ARBUTHNOT, Andrew Robert Coghill; Director, Sun Alliance.

ARBUTHNOT, Charles Robert Denys; Director, Hambros Bank Limited, since 1990; Capital Markets. *Career:* S G Warburg & Co Ltd, Graduate Trainee Finishing in Capital Markets Division 1978-84; Hambros Bank Ltd 1984-. *Biog: b.* 12 June 1956. *Nationality:* British. *m.* 1985, Jennifer Rosemary; 2 d. *Educ:* Eton College; Trinity College, Cambridge (BA Hons Natural Sciences). *Directorships:* None other than Hambros Bank. *Other Activities:* Provincial Church Council, St Martin's Church. *Recreations:* Running, Walking, Painting.

ARBUTHNOTT, John Campbell; The Viscount of Arbuthnott; CBE, JP; Director, Clydesdale Bank plc.

ARCHARD, P N; Director, Murray Lawrence Members' Agency Limited.

ARCHER, J R; Vice-Chairman, Grandfield Rork Collins Financial Ltd, since 1987; Jack of all trades, master of most. *Career:* 4th/7th Royal Dragoon Guards 1962-70; Various Public Relations Appointments 1970-76; Charles Barker Group 1976-87; Charles Barker City, Vice-Chairman 1986; Grandfield Rork Collins, Vice-Chairman 1987-. *Biog: b.* 14 August 1941. *Nationality:* British. *m.* 1967, Victoria (née Leigh); 1 s; 1 d. *Educ:* Cheltenham; RMA Sandhurst. *Publications:* Various. *Clubs:* Cavalry and Guards. *Recreations:* Skiing, Not Taking Life too Seriously.

ARCHER, M P; Partner, Cazenove & Co.

ARCHER, Dr Mary Doreen (née Weeden); Non-Executive Director, Anglia Television Group, since 1987. *Career:* St Hilda's College, Oxford, Junior Research Fellow 1968-71; Somerville College, Oxford, Temporary Lecturer in Chemistry 1971-72; Royal Institution of Great Britain, Research Fellow 1972-76; Trinity College, Cambridge, Lecturer in Chemistry 1976-86; Newnham College, Cambridge, Fellow and College Lecturer in Chemistry 1976-86; Bye-Fellow 1987-. *Biog: b.* 22 December 1944. *Nationality:* British. *m.* 1966, Jeffrey Howard; 2 s. *Educ:* Cheltenham Ladies College; St Anne's College, Oxford (BA, MA); Imperial College, London (PhD). *Directorships:* Anglia Television Group 1987 (non-exec); Mid Anglia Radio plc 1988 (non-exec); Cambridge and Newmarket FM Radio Ltd

1988 (non-exec). *Other Activities:* Member, Council of Lloyd's, 1989; Chairman, National Energy Foundation, 1989; Director, Fitzwilliam Museum Trust, 1984; Trustee, Science Museum, 1990. *Professional Organisations:* Fellow, Royal Society of Chemistry (FRSC). *Publications:* Rupert Brooke and the Old Vicarage, Grantchester, 1989; Contributions to Scientific Journals. *Recreations:* Singing, Theatre, Cats, Squash.

ARCHER, N J; Partner, Slaughter and May.

ARCHER, R W; Director, Unilever plc & Unilever NV, since 1989; Member of Plural Chief Executive, since 1978. *Career:* Unilever plc 1953-; Economics, Finance, Accountancy 1953-66; Financial Director and Vice-Chairman, Hindustan Lever Ltd India 1966-70; Member, Overseas Committee 1970-74; Treasurer & Deputy Financial Director 1974-78; Commercial Director 1978-83; Personnel Director 1983-89. *Biog: b.* 12 December 1929. *Nationality:* British. *m.* 1959, Catherine (née Overton); 3 s; 1 d. *Educ:* Winchester College; Magdalene College, Cambridge (BA, MA). *Directorships:* Halifax Building Society 1983 (non-exec) Deputy Chairman 1987. *Other Activities:* Executive Committee, National Institute of Economic & Social Research (NIESR).

ARCHIBALD, C S; Executive Director, James R Knowles Limited.

ARDUINO, Lawrie; Deputy Branch Manager, Swiss Volksbank.

ARFWEDSON, Anthony Carl Christopher; Director, Samuel Montagu & Co Ltd, since 1982; Northern Europe. *Career:* Deutsche Unionbank, Germany 1964-71; Hambros Bank, London 1971-77; Dillon Read Overseas Corporation 1977-82. *Directorships:* Matthiessen International Limited 1985 (non-exec); Midland Montagu AS, Norway 1985 (exec); Midland Montagu Osakepankki, Finland 1986 (exec); Midland Montagu Bank, Sweden 1989 (exec) Deputy Chairman.

ARGUS, D R; Director, Clydesdale Bank plc.

ARIMOTO, W; Company Secretary, Cosmo Securities (Europe) Limited.

ARMITAGE, David William Kenyon; Partner, Hammond Suddards, since 1988; Corporate and Commercial Work, Acquisitions, Disposals, Take overs, Joint Ventures, Contracting. *Career:* Alexander Tatham 1981-85; Ferranti plc 1985-86; AV Hammond (Now Hammond Suddards) 1986-. *Biog: b.* 7 July 1958. *Nationality:* British. *m.* 1983, Caroline (née Horsfall); 1 s; 1 d. *Educ:* Queens' College, Cambridge (MA). *Professional Organisations:* Law Society; Solicitor. *Recreations:* Golf, Sailing.

ARMSTRONG, A C; Director, Robert Fleming & Co Ltd, since 1986. *Biog: b.* 15 March 1959. *Nationality:* British. *m.* 1981, Jacqueline (née Roberts); 2 s. *Clubs:* Overseas Bankers.

ARMSTRONG, Alan Gordon; Senior Lecturer, Department of Economics, University of Bristol, since 1970; Economic Statistics and Industrial Economics. *Career:* Reed Paper Group, Economist, Forecasting & Market Intelligence 1960-62; Department of Applied Economics Cambridge University, Research Officer, Input-Output Modelling 1962-70; Selwyn College, Cambridge, Fellow and Director of Studies 1967-69. *Biog: b.* 11 February 1937. *Nationality:* British. *m.* 1963, Margaret Louise (née Harwood); 1 s; 1 d. *Educ:* Bede GS, Sunderland; Queens College, Cambridge (BA). *Other Activities:* Part-Time Member, Monopolies and Mergers Commission. *Professional Organisations:* Royal Economic Society. *Publications:* Input-Output Tables & Analysis, 1973; Structural Change in The British Economy, 1974; The Demand for New Cars, 1974; Sixteen Articles in Academic Journals. *Recreations:* Badminton, Cricket, Church Affairs, Gardening.

ARMSTRONG, Bruce Fraser; Group Finance Director, Credit Lyonnais Capital Markets plc, since 1990. *Career:* Gulf Riyad Bank EC, Bahrain, Manager, Administration 1978-82; Credit Lyonnais, Paris, Chef de Mission 1982; Kuwait French International Exchange Co, Kuwait, General Manager 1982-84; Credit Lyonnais Bank Netherland NV, Rotterdam, Deputy General Manager 1984-89; Credit Lyonnais Capital Markets, Group Controller 1989-90; Group Finance Director 1990-. *Biog: b.* 10 November 1948. *Nationality:* British. *m.* 1974, Alison Lesley (née Mackie). *Educ:* University of Nottingham (BSc). *Directorships:* Credit Lyonnais (Investments) Limited 1989; CL-Alexanders Laing & Cruickshank (Overseas) Limited 1989; Credit Lyonnais Information Services Limited 1989; CL Property Services Company Limited 1989; Credit Lyonnais Capital Markets plc 1990; Laing & Cruickshank 1990. *Professional Organisations:* Associate, Institute of Bankers; Qualified ACA, 1978.

ARMSTRONG, Robert Temple; Lord Armstrong of Ilminster; Non-Executive Director, N M Rothschild & Sons Limited.

ARMSTRONG, J S; Partner, Cameron Markby Hewitt.

ARMSTRONG, Stephen Richard; Tax Partner, Pannell Kerr Forster, since 1965; Business Taxation & Management. *Career:* Wilkins Kennedy (City), Audit Student to Audit Manager 1968-75; Ball Baker (Merged with Pannell Kerr Forster in 1989), Tax Senior to Senior Tax Manager 1975-85; Partner 1985; Head of Corporate Tax 1987; Business Tax Partner 1990. *Biog: b.* 18 February 1952. *Nationality:* British. *Professional Organisations:* CACA (FCCA).

ARNANDER, Cristopher James Folke; Director, Barclays de Zoete Wedd Ltd, since 1985; Marketing. *Career:* University of Minnesota Lecturer 1957; Hill Samuel & Co Ltd 1958-65; Glyn Mills & Co Dir & Local Dir 1965-70; Williams & Glyn's Bank Dir 1970-73; (Kuwait) Various 1973-79; Riyad Bank (Saudi Arabia) Chief Advisor 1979-85. *Biog: b.* 22 December 1932. *Nationality:* British. *m.* 1961, Pamela Primrose; 3 s; 1 d. *Educ:* Harrow School; Oriel College, Oxford (MA Hons). *Professional Organisations:* Mem of Council, Royal College of Music (1986). *Clubs:* Travellers. *Recreations:* Music, Sports, Reading, Travel.

ARNEY, M J J; Director, Providence Capitol Life Assurance Ltd.

ARNOLD, John; Group Investment Manager, Crown Financial Management Ltd. *Career:* National Provident Institution 1969-82; Crown, Investment Manager 1982-. *Directorships:* Crown Unit Trust Co. *Other Activities:* Member, Society of Investment Analysts; Member, Chartered Institute of Secretaries. *Professional Organisations:* ACIS; AMSIA.

ARNOLD, Lugman; Executive Director, Crédit Suisse First Boston Limited.

ARNOLD, M J; Partner, Ernst & Young.

ARNOLD, Michael; Partner, Hymans Robertson & Co, since 1974; Actuarial Consulting. *Career:* Prudential Assurance Co Actuarial Student 1969-71; Hymans Robertson & Co. *Biog: b.* 16 September 1947. *m.* 1972, Pauline Ann (née Pritchard); 2 s. *Educ:* Royal Wolverhampton School; Reading University (BSc). *Directorships:* Robertson Trustees 1986 (exec); City of London Computer Services 1980 (exec); Oaklife Assurance Ltd 1985 (non-exec); Transatlantic Life Assurance 1990 (non-exec). *Other Activities:* Institute of Actuaries (Council Member), Association of Consulting Actuaries, Livery Company of Actuaries. *Professional Organisations:* FIA. *Clubs:* RAC, Epsom Golf Club. *Recreations:* Golf, Squash.

ARNOLD, Michael R; Partner (Birmingham), Evershed Wells & Hind.

ARNOLD, Robert Lenox Michael; Partner, Bacon and Woodrow, since 1988; International Employee Benefits. *Career:* Callund and Company, Director International 1976-83; Willis Faber Advisory Services, Director International 1983-87. *Biog: b.* 31 May 1946. *Nationality:* British. *m.* 1973, Geraldine; 2 d. *Educ:* Methodist College, Belfast; Trinity College, Dublin (BA Hons Maths II ii); Manchester University (MSc Statistics). *Other Activities:* Joint Institute/Faculty of

Actuaries Committee on Europe. *Professional Organisations:* FIA; ASA. *Publications:* Various Articles on International Pension Issues. *Clubs:* Colony Club. *Recreations:* Tennis, Gardening, Music.

ARNOLD, Simon Rory; Chairman & Chief Executive, Bain Clarkson Limited.

ARNTZEN, Morten; Senior Vice President, Manufacturers Hanover Trust Co.

ARR, David Michael; Director, Hambros Bank Ltd, since 1990. *Career:* Barclays Bank plc 1971-86. *Biog: b.* 4 June 1950. *Nationality:* British. *m.* 1975, Susanne Edith (née Stockwell); 1 s; 1 d. *Educ:* University College of Wales, Aberystwyth (BSc Econ). *Directorships:* CNC (Washington) Estates Ltd 1990 (exec). *Professional Organisations:* AIB. *Clubs:* Royal Overseas League. *Recreations:* Music, Walking, Talking.

ARSCOTT, Alan Francis; Director, PK English Trust Company Ltd.

ARSCOTT, Simon Peter; Partner, Titmuss Sainer & Webb, since 1988; Development Division of Commercial Property Department. *Career:* Titmuss Sainer & Webb, Articles 1982-84; Assistant Solicitor 1984-88; Partner 1988-. *Biog: b.* 27 August 1958. *Nationality:* British. *m.* 1984, Clarissa (née Pilkington). *Educ:* St Pauls School, Barnes, London; Trinity College, Cambridge (BA, MA). *Other Activities:* Committee Member, London Young Solicitors Group, National Young Solicitors Group & Property & Commercial Services Sub-Committee of The Law Society; Member, City of London Solicitors' Company. *Recreations:* Tennis, Cycling, Skiing.

ARTHUR, J R; OBE; Company Secretary, CCF Holdings Ltd, since 1987; Company Secretary, CCF Foster Braithwaite Ltd, since 1989, and Credit Commercial de France (UK) Ltd, since 1986, General Administration. *Career:* Commissioned 1955; Regular Army, Scots Guards, Lieutenant Colonel 1955-84; Ministry of Defence 1979-84; Nigerian Staff College, Instructor 1976-79; Staff College 1966. *Biog: b.* 1935. *Nationality:* British. *m.* 1965, Valerie Isolde Mary (née Mahe de Chenal de la Bourdonnais (De Mahe)); 2 s; 1 d. *Educ:* Winchester College; RMA Sandhurst; Staff College, Camberley (PSC). *Clubs:* Cavalry and Guards Club, Berkshire Golf Club, Royal St Georges GC, HCEG Muirfield. *Recreations:* Golf, Gardening.

ARTHUR, Richard Andrew; Executive Director, Scimitar Development Capital Limited, since 1986. *Career:* Citibank, US Bonds Advisor 1966-68; Metric Press, Director 1968-71; Commonwealth Development Finance Co Ltd, Investment Manager 1971-76; Regional Director, SE Asia 1976-80; Chief Executive CDFC Australia 1981-82; Head of Operations 1982-86. *Biog: b.*

24 March 1944. *Nationality:* British. *m.* 1986, Akiko (née Shindo); 2 s; 1 d. *Educ:* The King's School, Canterbury; Christ's College, Cambridge (MA Economics); London Business School (MBA). *Directorships:* International Twist Drill (non-exec); Scimitar Development Capital Ltd (exec); Stalwart Assurance Group plc (non-exec); over 30 past directorships held. *Publications:* Metrication Decimalisation Price Converter, 1969. *Clubs:* Singapore Cricket Club. *Recreations:* Tennis, Gardening, Reading.

ARTHUR, Stephen Joseph; Partner, Turner Kenneth Brown, since 1980; Corporate & International Taxation. *Career:* Herbert Smith & Co, Articled Clerk/Asst Solicitor 1972-76; Berwin Leighton, Asst Solicitor (Tax Dept) 1976-78; Morgan Grenfell & Co Ltd, Exec (Tax/Corporate Finance) 1978-79; Turner Kenneth Brown 1979-. *Biog: b.* 27 October 1950. *m.* 1977, Anna Maria (née Foley); 1 s; 2 d. *Educ:* Cardinal Vaughan Memorial School; Queen Mary College, London (LLB). *Other Activities:* Revenue Law Ctee, City of London Law Society; Tax & Law Ctee, French Chamber of Commerce in GB. *Professional Organisations:* Law Society; ATII. *Publications:* Butterworths Encyclopaedia of Forms & Precedents: Gifts, 1988. *Recreations:* Opera, Gardening, DIY, Reading.

ARTHUR, Terence Gordon; Partner, Bacon & Woodrow, since 1989; Chief Exec, Investment Consultancy Dept. *Career:* Equity & Law Life Assurance, Actuarial Student 1963-66; Assistant Actuary 1966-67; Duncan C Fraser (Consulting Actuaries), Asst Actuary 1967-69; Partner 1969-76; T G Arthur Hargrave (Consulting Actuaries, Merged with Bacon & Woodrow, 1989), Sole Founder 1976-89. *Biog: b.* 5 September 1940. *Nationality:* British. m1 1 s; 2 d; m2 Mary Clare (née Austick). *Educ:* West Hartlepool GS; Manchester University (Hons Maths); Cambridge University (Post Graduate Diploma/Statistics). *Directorships:* Wesleyan Assurance Society 1988 (non-exec). *Other Activities:* Founder Member, Company of Actuaries (Livery), 1978; Council Member, Institute of Actuaries, 1976-. *Professional Organisations:* Fellow, Institute of Actuaries; Fellow, Institute of Statisticians; Fellow, Pensions Management Trust. *Publications:* 95 Per Cent is Crap: A Plain Man's Guide to British Politics, 1976; Various Other Books, Papers, Articles. *Clubs:* Cambridge Blue, 1962 and England Rugby International, 1966. *Recreations:* Sport, Bridge, Reading.

ARTUS, Ronald; Director, Prudential Corporation plc, since 1984. *Career:* Prudential Assurance Company Ltd, Head of Economic Intelligence Dept 1958-71; Joint Secretary & Chief Investment Manager 1975-82; Deputy Chairman 1985-90; Prudential Corporation plc, Group Chief Investment Manager 1982-90; Prudential Portfolio Managers Ltd, Chairman 1981-90. *Biog: b.* 8 October 1931. *Nationality:* British. m1 1956, Brenda Margaret (née Touche); m2 1987, Dr Joan (née

McCarthy); 3 s; 1 d. *Educ:* Sir Thomas Rich's School, Gloucester; Magdalen College, Oxford (MA). *Directorships:* Celltech Group plc 1980 (non-exec); The General Electric Company plc 1990 (non-exec); Electrocomponents plc 1990 (non-exec); The Securities Association Ltd 1990 (non-exec); The Solicitor's Indemnity Fund Ltd 1990 (non-exec); Imperial Cancer Research Technology Ltd 1988 (non-exec); Charterhouse Group Ltd 1980-82 (non-exec). *Other Activities:* Accounting Standards Committee 1982-86; Council of Society of Investment Analysts 1964-76, Chairman 1973-75; City Capital Markets Committee, 1982-90, Chairman 1988-90; Council, Institute for Fiscal Studies 1988-. *Publications:* Contributions to Various Journals on Economic and Investment Matters. *Clubs:* MCC. *Recreations:* Music, British Painting.

ARZYMANOW, Miss Barbara J; Director, Kleinwort Benson, since 1988; Pharmaceuticals. *Career:* Greenwell, Pharmaceuticals Analyst 1984-87. *Biog: b.* 9 December. *Nationality:* British. *Educ:* Upper Chine; University of London. *Publications:* Journal of Anatony; Journal of Physiology; Developmental Brain Research; Revista Española de Fisiologia. *Recreations:* Italian History & Culture, Various Sports.

ASAI, S; General Manager, Bank of Yokohama Ltd.

ASAKAWA, Masao; Executive Director, Yamaichi International (Europe) Limited.

ASBURY, N B; Partner, Grimley J R Eve.

ASCHWANDEN, Bruno; Non-Executive Director, Citymax Integrated Information Systems Ltd.

ASCOTT, David; Director, Gresham Trust plc.

ASHBY, Julian Frederick Kirkbride; Publishing Director, Macmillan Press, since 1985; Financial & Business Reference, General Reference Books. *Career:* Macmillan London, Publisher 1983-85; Macmillan Education, General Manager Overseas Division 1968-74; Book Club Associates, Editor Literary Guild 1966-68; Longman, Editor 1962-66; Royal Navy, Sub Lieutenant 1957-58. *Biog: b.* 25 June 1935. *Nationality:* British. *m.* 1962, Mary; 1 s; 1 d. *Educ:* Canford School; King's College, Cambridge (BA). *Other Activities:* Chairman, Public Relations, Hampshire Wildlife Trust. *Clubs:* Garrick. *Recreations:* Reading, Gardening, Golf, Walking, Theatre.

ASHCROFT, Charles Patrick; Partner, Rowe & Maw, since 1980; Corporate Finance, Mergers & Acquisitions & Financial Services. *Career:* Rowe & Maw, Solicitor 1977-80. *Biog: b.* 21 October 1951. *m.* 1986, Josanne (née Cameron). *Educ:* Uppingham School; Christ Church College, Oxford (BA Hons 1st); Cliffords Inn, John Marshall and City of London

Solicitors Co. *Professional Organisations:* The Law Society. *Recreations:* Bridge, Walking, Reading, Foreign Travel, Golf.

ASHER, Alistair Hugh; Partner, Allen & Overy, since 1987; Corporate Finance. *Biog: b.* 30 December 1955. *Nationality:* British. *m.* 1985, Patricia (née Robinson); 1 d. *Educ:* Norwich Grammar School; Southampton University (LLB); Amsterdam University. *Professional Organisations:* Law Society, City of London Law Society. *Clubs:* Cannons. *Recreations:* Cycling, Squash, Swimming.

ASHER, B H; Non-Executive Director, James Capel & Co Ltd.

ASHFORD-RUSSELL, B J D; Director, Touche Remnant Investment Management, since 1988; TR Technology Investment Trust, TR Global Technology Unit Trust, TR Ecotec Environmental Fund. *Career:* Touche Remnant & Co 1981-. *Biog: b.* 31 January 1959. *Nationality:* British. *Educ:* Winchester College; Brasenose College, Oxford (BA Hons). *Directorships:* TR Technology plc 1988 (exec); TR International 1990 (exec); TR Investment Management 1988 (exec).

ASHLEY, Martin; Chairman, Ashley Palmer Holdings Limited, since 1984. *Educ:* BSc. *Directorships:* Ashley, Palmer & Hathaway Limited 1987 (exec); Clifford Palmer Underwriting Agencies Limited 1984 (exec); Martin Ashley Underwriting Agencies Limited 1977 (exec). *Professional Organisations:* AIA.

ASHLEY MILLER, Peter; Non-Executive Director, Arbuthnot Latham Bank Ltd, since 1986. *Career:* Kenneth Anderson & Co Stockbroker 1964-66; Ionian Bank Ltd Investment Mgr 1966-69; Hoare Govett Stockbroker 1970-72; Ionian Bank Ltd Investment Dir 1972-77; Arbuthnot Investment Mgmnt Services (MD) 1978-80; Arbuthnot Securities Group Exec Chm 1981-85. *Biog: b.* 26 December 1925. *Nationality:* British. *m.* 1956, Catherine (née MacNaughton); 1 s; 2 d. *Educ:* Royal Naval College, Dartmouth; Royal Naval College, Greenwich (PSC). *Directorships:* Archimedes Investment Trust Ltd 1973 (non-exec); Norland Nursery Training College Ltd 1969 Chm. *Other Activities:* Chm, Burlingham House Home for the Mentally Handicapped. *Professional Organisations:* FCA; AMSIA. *Clubs:* The Norfolk, Special Forces. *Recreations:* Sailing, Bell Ringing.

ASHMORE, Anthony John; Chief Executive, Merchant Navy Officers Pension Fund.

ASHPLANT, Anthony John; Company Secretary, M & G Group plc, since 1990; Company Secretarial, Corporate Legal, Compliance. *Career:* Barrister Lincoln's Inn, Criminal Law 1979-80; Craigmyle & Co (Fund-Raising Consultants to Charities), Company Secretary/

Tax Law 1980-82; M & G Group plc, Unit Trust Mananagment, Unit-Linked Life & Pensions, Institutional Pension Fund Managment, Personal Equity Plans, Assistant Group Legal Adviser 1983-. *Biog: b.* 3 February 1954. *Nationality:* British. *m.* 1983, Jennifer Anne (née West). *Educ:* St Francis Xavier's College, Liverpool; King's College, London University (LLB Hons); Inns of Court School of Law (Bar Finals). *Directorships:* M & G Financial Services Limited 1989 (exec). *Professional Organisations:* Member, Middle Temple, 1977.

ASHTON, Charles E G; Partner, Theodore Goddard, since 1990; Corporate Finance & Company Law. *Career:* Speechly Bircham, Articled Clerk 1982-84; Assistant Solicitor 1984-86; Theodore Goddard, Assistant Solicitor 1986-90; Partner 1990-. *Biog: b.* 6 May 1959. *Nationality:* British. *m.* 1987, Helen (née Brakefield). *Educ:* Winchester College; Exeter University (LLB). *Recreations:* Sailing, Walking.

ASHTON, David Julian; Partner, Arthur Andersen & Co, since 1982; Head of UK Financial Consulting Services & European Head of Claims Consulting. *Career:* Arthur Andersen & Co 1970. *Biog: b.* 23 October 1948. *Nationality:* British. *m.* 1976, Marilyn (née Geller); 2 s. *Educ:* St Marylebone Grammar; London School of Economics (BSc). *Professional Organisations:* FCA; ACIArb; Member, Institute of Petroleum; BAE. *Recreations:* Skiing, Golf, Bridge.

ASHTON, P; Director, Arbuthnot Latham Bank Limited.

ASHTON-JONES, Christopher James; Director, Brunswick Public Relations Limited, since 1989. *Career:* N M Rothschild and Sons, Trainee 1966-69; Hoare Govett Ltd, Trainee/Institutional Sales Executive 1969-73; Leo Burnett, Executive, Financial Public Relations Division 1973-76; Dewe Rogerson Ltd, Executive 1976-79; Director 1979-83; The BOC Group plc, Corporate Communications Executive 1983-85; Dewe Rogerson Ltd, Director, Investor Relations 1985-88. *Biog: b.* 18 March 1948. *Nationality:* British. *m.* 1972, Carmen (née Don-Fox); 1 s; 2 d. *Educ:* Nailsea Grammar School, Somerset. *Directorships:* Brunswick Public Relations Ltd 1989 (exec). *Other Activities:* Member, Institute of Public Relations' City and Financial Group, 1980-(Chairman 1983-84); Past Member, Institute of Public Relations Council, 1984-85. *Professional Organisations:* Member, Institute of Public Relations. *Publications:* Contributor, This Public Relations Consultancy Business, 1984. *Clubs:* City of London, Chichester Yacht. *Recreations:* Motor Boating, Gardening.

ASHURST, Robert Gerald; Partner, R Watson & Sons, since 1978; Actuarial Advice to Pension Funds, Advice on Investment Management Arrangements & Manager Selection. *Career:* R Watson & Sons, Actuarial Asst 1972-78. *Biog: b.* 10 February 1951. *m.* 1979, Stella (née Collinson); 3 d. *Educ:* Reigate Grammar School; University College, London (BSc Econ). *Professional Organisations:* FIA. *Recreations:* Committed Christian, Family.

ASHWORTH, Anne; Personal Finance Editor, The Mail On Sunday.

ASHWORTH, Christopher John; Partner, Ashurst Morris Crisp.

ASHWORTH, Keith Richard; Director of Research, Henry Cooke, Lumsden plc, since 1988; Engineering/Industrial Companies Analytical Research. *Career:* British Aerospace, Systems Control Engineer 1978-79; Henry Cooke, Lumsden, Engineering Analyst 1981-83; Capel-Cure Myers, Snr Engineering Analyst 1983-84; Smiths Industries Medical Systems, Business Development Mgr 1985; Henry Cooke, Lumsden, Investment Exec 1985-88. *Biog: b.* 25 January 1956. *Nationality:* British. *m.* 1984, Carole Veronica (née Sarginson); 1 s. *Educ:* Howarth Cross & Greenhill; Queen Mary College, London University (BSc); Imperial College, London University (MSc, DIC). *Professional Organisations:* Member, The International Stock Exchange. *Publications:* Import Controls & The UK Economy, 1980.

ASKEW, Henry John; Managing Director, Gerrard & National Holdings plc. *Career:* Gerrard & National Holdings plc, Dir 1967-. *Biog: b.* 5 April 1940. *m.* 1978, Rosemary Eileen (née Taylor); 2 s. *Directorships:* Gerrard & National Discount Co Ltd 1967 (exec); International Discount Co Ltd 1970; Gerrard & Reid Nominees Ltd 1983; Reeves Whitburn Investments 1983; Gerrard & National Ltd 1986 (exec); Reeves Whitburn & Co Ltd 1982; Ladykirk Estates Ltd.

ASKEW, P R; Director, Bain Clarkson Limited.

ASLET, Graham Kenneth; Actuary & General Manager, Friends' Provident Life Office, since 1987; Life Office Management. *Career:* Friends' Provident Life Office, Various 1969. *Biog: b.* 27 May 1948. *Nationality:* British. *m.* 1981, Jean Marjorie Douglas (née Tutt); 1 s; 1 d. *Educ:* King's College School, Wimbledon; Pembroke College, Cambridge (MA). *Directorships:* Friends' Provident Life Office; Friends' Provident Linked Life Assurance Ltd; Friends' Provident Managed Pension Funds Ltd; Friends' Provident Unit Trust Managers Ltd. *Professional Organisations:* Fellow, Institute of Actuaries. *Clubs:* Effingham Golf Club. *Recreations:* Music, Gardening.

ASPERY, M; Partner, Cameron Markby Hewitt.

ASQUITH, J P; Director, Morgan Grenfell & Co Limited, since 1988; Deputy Head/Treasury. *Career:* Morgan Grenfell 1979-. *Biog: b.* 1956. *Nationality:* British. *m.* 1984, Sarah (née Negretti); 1 s. *Educ:* Eton

College; Trinity Hall, Cambridge (MA Modern Languages, Law); Inns of Court School of Law (Bar Finals). *Directorships:* International Swap Dealers Association Inc 1990 (exec); Morgan Grenfell & Co Limited 1988 (exec); Morgan Grenfell Futures & Options Limited 1990 (exec).

ASSHETON, The Hon Nicholas; Director, Coutts & Co, since 1987. *Career:* Montagu Loebl Stanley & Co, Ptnr 1960-77; Snr Ptnr 1977-86; Montagu Loebl Stanley Ltd, Chm 1986-87. *Biog: b.* 23 May 1934. *Nationality:* British. *m.* 1960, Jacqueline Jill (née Harris); 1 s; 2 d. *Educ:* Eton College; Christ Church, Oxford (MA). *Directorships:* The Harleian Society 1978; Stock Exchange Council 1969-88; NM UK Ltd 1986; The United Services Trustee 1986; The Englefield Estate Trust Corporation Ltd 1987; Coutts & Co 1987; Church House Conference Centre Limited 1990. *Other Activities:* Vintners Company; Society of Antiquaries. *Clubs:* Whites, Pratt's.

ASSHETON, Ralph John; Lord Clitheroe; Chairman, Yorkshire Bank plc, since 1990. *Career:* RTZ Corp plc, Executive Director 1968-89; RTZ Borax Ltd, Chairman 1980-89; RTZ Corp plc, Deputy Chief Executive 1988-89. *Biog: b.* 3 November 1929. *Nationality:* British. *m.* 1961, (née Hanbury); 2 s; 1 d. *Educ:* Eton College; Christ Church, Oxford (MA). *Directorships:* The Halliburton Company 1987- (non-exec); First Insterstate Bank of California 1981-89 (non-exec). *Other Activities:* House of Lords Select Committee, Science & Technology; Worshipful Company of Skinners. *Clubs:* Boodles, Pratts. *Recreations:* Field Sports.

ASTON, John; Director, J Henry Schroder Wagg & Co Limited.

ASTOR, D; Non-Executive Director, Dartington & Co Group plc.

ASTOR, The Hon Hugh Waldorf; JP; *Career:* The Times Publishing Co Ltd, Dep Chm 1959-67; The Times Book Company Chm 1959-67; Olympia Ltd, Exec Vice-Chm 1971-73. *Biog: b.* 20 November 1920. *Nationality:* British. *m.* 1950, Emily Lucy (née Kinloch); 2 s; 3 d. *Educ:* Eton College; Oxford University. *Directorships:* Phoenix Assurance Co Ltd 1962-85 (non-exec); Hambros plc 1960- (non-exec); Winterbottom Energy Trust 1961-86 (non-exec); Sotra Property Co Ltd 1968- Chm. *Other Activities:* Chm, Peabody Trust, 1981-; Chm, King Edward VII's Fund, 1983-88; JP, 1953-86; Member of Court, Fishmongers' Company (Prime Warden 1976-7); High Sheriff of Berkshire, 1953; Vice President, Aircraft Owners & Pilots Association. *Clubs:* Brooks's, Buck's, Royal Yacht Squadron. *Recreations:* Sailing, Flying, Shooting.

ATKIN, Christopher Mark; Partner, Bacon & Woodrow, since 1990; Pension Schemes. *Career:* Friends

Provident Life Office 1973-79; Hogg Robinson (Benefit Consultants) Limited 1979-81; Bain Dawes Limited 1981-84; R Watson & Sons, Partner 1984-90. *Biog: b.* 17 February 1952. *Nationality:* British. *m.* 1974, Judith Sandra (née Brookes); 2 s; 2 d. *Educ:* King Edward VII Grammar School; Loughborough University of Technology (BSc Hons 1st in Computer Studies). *Professional Organisations:* Fellow, Institute of Actuaries. *Recreations:* Running, Orienteering, Family.

ATKIN, Mrs T J; Associate Director, Grandfield Rork Collins Financial Ltd.

ATKINS, C R; Deputy General Manager, Societe Generale Merchant Bank plc, since 1987; Administration. *Career:* Ernst & Young, Audit Senior 1959-61; Societe Generale, Chief Accountant 1962-68; Societe Generale Merchant Bank plc, Company Secretary 1968-; Deputy General Manager 1987-. *Biog: b.* 27 March 1934. *Nationality:* British. *Educ:* Latymer Upper. *Directorships:* Casadas Ltd; S G Leasing Ltd. *Professional Organisations:* Fellow, Institute of Chartered Accountants in England and Wales. *Recreations:* Putney Music (Treasurer) Theatre.

ATKINS, Roger; Chairman, James Capel Pacific Ltd, since 1988; Japan. *Career:* James Capel & Co Ltd, London 1978-87; James Capel Pacific Ltd, Tokyo 1987-. *Biog: b.* 26 April 1938. *Nationality:* British. *Educ:* Allen's School, Dulwich. *Directorships:* James Capel & Co Ltd 1990 (exec); James Capel Pacific Ltd 1988 (exec). *Clubs:* Commonwealth Club. *Recreations:* Music, Theatre.

ATKINSON, Eddie; Council Member, The Office of the Banking Ombudsman.

ATKINSON, F B; Group Solicitor, Asda Group plc, since 1988; Legal.

ATKINSON, J; Director, Yorkshire Building Society.

ATKINSON, Nigel; Director, Prudential Bache Capital Funding (Equities) Ltd, since 1987; Head of Mergers & Acquisitions. *Career:* Singleton Fabian & Co Articled Clerk 1963-68; Price Waterhouse Audit/Investigation Snr 1968-72; Kleinwort Benson Ltd Asst Dir 1972-87. *Biog: b.* 10 July 1945. *Nationality:* British. *m.* 1978, Susan Norah (née Dobbs); 2 d. *Educ:* Lysses School. *Professional Organisations:* FCA. *Recreations:* Fishing, Tennis, Georgian Furniture.

ATLING, E B; Director UK Business Sector, Barclays Bank plc, since 1989; UK Banking Division, Corporate Banking. *Career:* All With Barclays. *Biog: b.* 13 September 1946. *Nationality:* British. *m.* 1968, Margaret. *Directorships:* Barclays Development Capital 1990 (non-exec); Ebbgate Holdings; Barclays Industrial Developments

Ltd 1990 (non-exec). *Professional Organisations:* Chartered Institute of Bankers. *Clubs:* Royal Overseas.

ATSMA, B F; Controller, Unilever plc, since 1989. *Career:* Financial Director Unilever Brazil 1987-89; Various other positions within Unilever since 1969. *Biog: b.* 24 April 1942. *Educ:* Erasmus University, Rotterdam (Business Admin). *Professional Organisations:* Member, Nivra (Dutch Institute of Chartered Accountants).

ATTARD, D; Director, Société Générale Strauss Turnbull Securities Ltd.

ATTENBOROUGH, Michael John; Director, J K Buckenham Ltd, since 1989; Non Marine Reinsurance. *Career:* Holmwood Back & Manson Ltd, Insurance Broker 1962-64; Morice Tozer & Beck Ltd, Insurance Broker 1964-73; Traill Attenborough Ltd (changed to Lyon Holdings Ltd), Exec Director Insurance Broker 1973-86; PWS International Ltd, Exec Director Insurance Broker 1986-89. *Biog: b.* 14 January 1944. *Nationality:* British. *m.* 1967, Penelope Diane; 1 s; 3 d. *Educ:* Summerfields School; Harrow School; Ecole Lemania, Switzerland (Certificat d'Etudes de Langue Française). *Directorships:* J K Buckenham Ltd 1989 (exec). *Other Activities:* Trustee, Harpenden Music Foundation. *Professional Organisations:* Annual Subscriber to Lloyd's; Member, Chartered Insurance Institute; Registered Insurance Broker. *Clubs:* Harpenden Tennis Club. *Recreations:* Tennis, Golf.

ATTERBURY, John Michael David; Secretary, Barclays Bank plc, since 1983; Company Law. *Career:* Barclays Bank plc (UK and Overseas) Various 1952-. *Biog: b.* 14 June 1935. *m.* 1959, Margaret Rose (née Evans); 1 s; 2 d. *Educ:* Whitgift School, Croydon; Harvard, Switzerland (SMP). *Other Activities:* ICSA Company Secretaries' Panel, Law & Professional Services Panel; ICSA City Group. *Professional Organisations:* FCIB, FCIS. *Recreations:* Travel, Music, Chess, Photography.

ATTERTON, Dr David Valentine; CBE; Member of the Court, Bank of England, since 1984. *Career:* Foundry Services Ltd, Various to MD 1952-63; Foseco Ltd, MD 1963; Foseco Minsep Ltd, Dep Chm 1969; Foseco Minsep plc, Chm 1979-87; Associated Engineering plc, Dir & Dep Chm 1972-86; Camlab Ltd, Dir 1951-86. *Biog: b.* 13 February 1927. *Nationality:* British. *m.* 1948, Sheila (née McMahon); 2 s; 1 d. *Educ:* Peterhouse; University of Cambridge (MA, PhD). *Directorships:* Barclays Bank plc 1982 (non-exec); British Coal 1986 (non-exec); Imperial Metal Industries 1976 (non-exec); Investors in Industry Group 1980 (non-exec); The Rank Organisation plc 1987 (non-exec); Marks & Spencer plc 1987 (non-exec); Notietta Enterprises Ltd 1987 Chairman; Formula Group Europe Ltd 1990 Chairman. *Other Activities:* Worshipful Company of Founders.

Professional Organisations: Fellow, The Institute of Metals. *Publications:* Various Scientific Papers.

ATTFIELD, Jeffrey Charles; Director, MIM Ltd, since 1983; Head of UK Pension Fund Investment Management. *Career:* Morgan Grenfell & Co Asst Dir 1971-83; GRE Assurance 1968-71. *Biog: b.* 16 July 1946. *Nationality:* British. *m.* 1971, Elizabeth Margaret (née Gregg); 2 s; 1 d. *Educ:* Cranbrook School; University of East Anglia (BA). *Professional Organisations:* SIA.

ATTRILL, F E G; Assistant General Manager, Scottish Widows Fund & Life Assurance Society.

ATTWOOD, Christopher R; Tax Partner, Ernst & Whinney.

ATTWOOD, Frank Albert; Partner, Robson Rhodes, since 1974; Chief Executive Officer, Dunwoody Robson McGladrey & Pullen (DRM), since 1990; International Client Services. *Career:* Robson Rhodes, Articled Clerk 1965-68; Snr Acct 1968-70; Mgr 1970-74. *Biog: b.* 19 January 1943. *Nationality:* British. *m.* 1965, Pamela (née Hunter); 1 d. *Educ:* University of Hull (BSc Econ). *Directorships:* Hon Treasurer Schoolmistresses & Governesses Benevolent Inst 1980 (non-exec). *Other Activities:* Member, Scriveners Company. *Professional Organisations:* FCA; ACIS. *Publications:* de Paula's Auditing (with others), 15th ed 1976, 16th ed 1982, 17th ed 1986; Auditing Standards: From Discussion Drafts to Practice, 1980. *Recreations:* Travel, Hill Walking, Modern Novels, Gardening, Weight Training.

ATTWOOD, Thomas Roger; Director, James Capel Corporate Finance, since 1988; Development Capital, MBOs and LBOs. *Career:* W Greenwell & Co, Head of Investment Trust 1974-81; Laing & Cruickshank Investment Trust, Sales/Analysis 1981-82; Stephen Rose & Partners, Dir, Development Capital 1982-87. *Biog: b.* 22 August 1952. *Nationality:* British. *m.* 1979, Sara Moira (née Raybone); 3 d. *Educ:* Bradfield College, Berkshire; Manchester University IST (BSc). *Directorships:* Bruton Kitchens Ltd 1984 N Chm; ACS Communications Inc 1984 (non-exec); Intermediate Capital Group Ltd 1989 Alternate; Wisley Golf Club Limited 1989 (non-exec); IMT James Capel Limited 1989 (non-exec). *Professional Organisations:* AMSIA. *Clubs:* Royal Cinque Ports Deal, Royal Dornoch, Denham and Rye Golf Clubs, Flyfishers, Whale Club. *Recreations:* Golf, Fishing, Shooting, Fine Wine.

AUBER, Thomas Frederick; Partner, Gouldens, since 1970; Commercial Conveyancing. *Biog: b.* 11 August 1939. *m.* 1965, Jennifer Jane (née Berry); 2 s. *Educ:* Bancroft's School; Magdalen College, Oxford (MA Jurisp). *Other Activities:* Past President, Old Bancroftians' Association. *Professional Organisations:* Law Society.

AUBREY, M H L X; Director, Hambros Bank Limited.

AUGAR, Dr P J; Head of Research, County NatWest Wood Mackenzie, since 1989. *Career:* Fielding Newson-Smith, Investment Analyst 1978-82; Wood Mackenzie, Investment Analyst 1982-87; St Catharine's College, Cambridge, Fellow and Bursar 1987-89. *Biog: b.* 1951. *m.* 1978, Denise (née Milross); 1 s; 1 d. *Educ:* Clane College, Cambridge (MA, PGCE, PhD). *Directorships:* County NatWest Securities 1989 (exec). *Recreations:* Running, Tennis, History.

AUGER, George Albert; Senior Insolvency Partner, Stoy Hayward; Corporate and Personal Insolvency. *Career:* Dept of Trade, Official Receivers' Dept 1956-66; Stoy Hayward 1967-. *Biog: b.* 21 February 1938. *Nationality:* British. *m.* 1962, Pauline (née Wilson); 2 d. *Educ:* Finchley County Grammar School. *Other Activities:* Chm of Governors, Channing School, Highgate. *Professional Organisations:* FCCA; Fellow, Insolvency Practitioners' Assoc (Pres 1981-2). *Publications:* Hooper's Voluntary Liquidation, 1978. *Recreations:* Cricket, Tennis, Music.

AUSTEN, Mark Edward; Partner in Charge of Financial Services Consulting in Europe, Price Waterhouse, since 1985; Consulting in Europe in Financial Institutions & Managing UK Financial. *Career:* Reed International Corp, Fin Trainee 1967-72; Henry Ansbacher, Asst Chief Acct 1972-75. *Biog: b.* 25 August 1949. *Nationality:* British. *m.* 1977, Priscilla (née Hart); 1 s; 1 d. *Educ:* City of London Freemen's School. *Professional Organisations:* Chartered Institute of Management Accountants. *Publications:* Price Waterhouse/Euromoney International Treasury Management Handbook. *Clubs:* Carlton, Thames Ditton Squash Club. *Recreations:* Squash, Piano, Good Food.

AUSTIN, Clive H; Director, Merrill Lynch International Limited.

AUSTIN, Guy Robert; Director, Barclays de Zoete Wedd Securities Limited, since 1990; Derivatives Products Development. *Career:* Wood Mackenzie & Co, Equity Salesman 1975-80; Wardley Investment Services Ltd (Hong Kong), Fund Manager 1980-83; Wardley Investment Services (UK) Ltd (London), Managing Director 1983-86; Wood Mackenzie & Co, Risk Management 1986-88; Barclays de Zoete Wedd Securities Limited 1988-. *Biog: b.* 27 July 1951. *Nationality:* British. *m.* 1981, Amanda (née Waldy); 2 s. *Educ:* Woolverstone Hall; Southampton (BSc).

AUTON, Dr (John) Paul; Managing Director, Cambridge Consultants Limited, since 1983. *Biog: b.* 1940. *Nationality:* British. *m.* 1970, Colette; 1 s; 1 d. *Educ:* Brentwood School; Imperial College, London (BSc Eng); University of Essex (PhD). *Directorships:* Cambridge Consultants Limited; Prelude Technology Investments Limited; Arthur D Little International Inc. *Professional Organisations:* Member, Institute of Physics.

AVELING, A R (Tony); General Manager, Europe, Westpac Banking Corporation, since 1990; European Division. *Career:* Westpac Banking Corporation (formerly Bank of New South Wales) 1963-; Positions in Queensland, New South Wales and United Kingdom 1963-86; Executive General Manager assisting the Managing Director 1986-87; General Manager, Retail Banking 1988-90; General Manager, Europe 1990-. *Biog: b.* 21 August 1943. *Nationality:* Australian. *m.* 1967, Mary (née Marsden); 2 s. *Educ:* St Mark's, Mbabane, Swaziland. *Directorships:* Mase Westpac Limited; Westpac Overseas BV; Westpac Banking Corporation (Jersey) Limited; Westpac (CI) Limited; Westpac Securities (Jersey) Limited; Westpac (CI) Nominees Limited. *Other Activities:* Graduate of the Advanced Management Programme of the Harvard Business School. *Professional Organisations:* FAIB; FAIM. *Clubs:* The Australian Club, Killara Golf Club, Harvard Club of Australia.

AXTEN, Peter Colin; Managing Director, Lloyds Investment Managers, Lloyds Merchant Bank Limited.

AYDON, Richard Hinchliffe; Partner, Stephenson Harwood, since 1984; Company Law. *Career:* Admitted as a Solicitor 1979. *Biog: b.* 4 March 1955. *Nationality:* British. *m.* 1983, Tanya (née Van Hasselt); 3 s. *Educ:* Marple Hall Grammar School; Trinity Hall, Cambridge (MA). *Professional Organisations:* The Law Society; The City of London Solicitors' Company. *Recreations:* Gardening.

AYLWIN, J M; Executive Partner, Richards Butler, since 1984; Management and Strategic Planning. *Career:* Richards Butler, Articled Clerk 1965-67; Assistant Solicitor 1967-72; Partner 1972-; Executive Partner 1984-. *Biog: b.* 23 July 1942. *Nationality:* British. *m.* 1970, Angela; 2 s. *Educ:* Uppingham; Emmanuel College, Cambridge (MA Law Solicitor). *Other Activities:* City of London Solicitors Company; Professional Practice Sub-Committee; The Law Society. *Professional Organisations:* Solicitor. *Clubs:* Richmond FC, Dorking RFC. *Recreations:* Tennis, Golf, Rugby.

AYLWIN, Nicholas Claude; Executive Director, Credit Commercial de France (UK) Ltd, since 1990; Mergers & Acquisitions. *Career:* PaineWebber International, Managing Director, European Mergers & Acquisitions 1986-90; Hill Samuel & Co Ltd, Director and Head of Mergers and Acquisitions 1978-86; Chemical Bank, Paris, Assistant Vice President 1977-78; Arthur Young & Company. *Biog: b.* 24 June 1944. *Nationality:* British. *m.* 1968, Nicki (née Boon); 1 s; 1 d. *Educ:* Haileybury & ISC. *Professional Organisations:* FCA. *Clubs:* Royal Wimbledon Golf Club.

AYNSLEY, P; Director, County NatWest Securities Limited.

AYRES, A; Director, Hoare Govett Corporate Finance Limited.

AYRES, Graham; Director (Sales), Hoare Govett International Securities.

B

BABCOCK, J V; Director, York Trust Group plc.

BABTIE, William John; Director, James Capel Fund Managers Ltd, since 1988; UK Clients and Marketing. *Career:* AECI Ltd, Treasurer's Asst 1971-74; UAL Ltd, Dep Head of Research 1974-78; NM Rothschild Asset Management, Asst Dir 1978-86; James Capel & Co, Snr Exec 1986-88. *Biog: b.* 20 August 1948. *Nationality:* British. *m.* 1978, Patricia Ann (née Barry); 1 s; 1 d. *Educ:* Harrow; University of Cape Town (BComm, BA Hons). *Clubs:* Hurlingham, Inanda (Johannesburg). *Recreations:* Tennis, Fishing, Jogging.

BACH, Harold; Group Financial Director & Company Secretary, The Guidehouse Group plc, since 1985. *Career:* Mackie & Clark Chartered Accountants, Partner 1963-66; Grindlays Bank (Scotland) Ltd, Assistant General Manager 1966-69; Director 1969-77; The Scottish Heritable Trust plc, Financial Controller 1977-81; Finance Director 1982-83. *Biog: b.* 27 November 1934. *Nationality:* British. *m.* 1960, Philippa (née Margolyes); 3 d. *Educ:* University of Glasgow (MA Hons, LLB). *Directorships:* Greyfriars Trust Limited 1984 (exec); Guidehouse Securities Limited 1984 (exec); Orbital Financial Services plc 1987 (exec); Guidehouse Finance Limited 1988 (exec). *Other Activities:* Chairman, Eastwood District Council, 1970-74; Member, National Savings Committee for Scotland, 1975-77. *Professional Organisations:* Member, The Institute of Chartered Accountants of Scotland; Member, The International Stock Exchange. *Recreations:* Skiing, Travel, Theatre.

BACH, John Theodore; Partner, Stephenson Harwood, since 1966; Banking, Commercial and Company Law. *Biog: b.* 18 February 1936. *Nationality:* British. *m.* 1967, Hilary Rose (née Birley); 1 s; 2 d. *Educ:* Rugby School; New College, Oxford (MA). *Other Activities:* Governor, Moorfields Eye Hospital. *Professional Organisations:* Law Society. *Clubs:* City University Club.

BACKHOUSE, David Miles; Chairman, TSB Trust Company Ltd.

BACKHOUSE, William; Director and Chief Operating Officer, Baring Asset Management Limited, since 1989. *Career:* Coopers & Lybrand, Articled Clerk/ Executive 1962-69; Baring Brothers & Co Limited, Executive/Manager/Assistant Director/Director 1970-84. *Biog: b.* 29 May 1942. *Nationality:* British. *m.* 1971, Deborah Jane (née Hely-Hutchinson); 1 s; 2 d. *Educ:* Eton College. *Directorships:* Baring Fund Managers Limited 1985-90 MD; Baring, Houston & Saunders Limited 1984- (non-exec) Chairman; Baring Investment Services Limited 1988 Chairman & MD; Guernsey International Fund Managers Limited 1987 (non-exec); International Fund Managers (Ireland) Limited 1990 (non-exec). *Other Activities:* Worshipful Company of Gunmakers. *Professional Organisations:* Institute of Chartered Accountants (1967) FCA. *Clubs:* City of London Club. *Recreations:* Photography, Contemporary Art, Travel, Shooting, Fishing.

BACON, Timothy R; Director, Brown Shipley & Co Limited; Corporate Finance. *Career:* Brown Shipley 1970-. *Biog: b.* 4 December 1947. *Nationality:* British. *m.* 1985, Marylyn (née Grant); 2 s. *Educ:* Eton College; Bristol University (BSc Economics/Politics). *Directorships:* Brown Shipley & Co Ltd 1989 (exec); The Colville Estate Limited 1975 (non-exec). *Professional Organisations:* Member of the Institute of Bankers. *Clubs:* Pratts, City University Club. *Recreations:* Opera, Theatre, Travel.

BACOT, F D; Director, S G Warburg Akroyd Rowe & Pitman Mullens Securities Ltd.

BADCOCK, C L; Managing Director, Swiss Bank Corporation; Merchant Banking.

BADEN, (Edwin) John; Managing Director & Chief Executive, Girobank plc, since 1989. *Career:* Deloitte Plender & Griffiths (Chartered Accountants), Audit Clerk 1951-54; H Parrot & Company (Wine Importers), Financial Director/Company Secretary 1954-61; C & A Modes (Departmental Stores), Director of Various Subsidiaries 1961-63; Samuel Montagu & Company (Bank is a Subsidiary of Midland Bank), Managing Director 1963-78; Italian International Bank plc (a Subsidiary of Monte dei Paschi di Siena), Managing Director & Chief Executive 1978-89. *Biog: b.* 18 August 1928. *Nationality:* British. *m.* 1952, Christine (née Grose); 2 s; 3 d. *Educ:* Winchester College; Corpus Christi College, Cambridge (MA Economics & Law). *Directorships:* Alliance & Leicester Building Society 1990 (exec) Mem Gp Exec Ctee; North American Property Unit Trust 1975 (non-exec) Chm; Paneuropean Property Unit Trust 1973 (non-exec) Mem Mgmnt Ctee. *Other Activities:* Trustee, International Centre for Research in Accounting, University of Lancaster; Companion, British Institute of Management; Fellow, Company of Information Technologists; Fellow, Royal Society of

Arts; Cavaliere Ufficiale (an Order of Merit of the Italian Republic). *Professional Organisations:* Member, Institute of Chartered Accountants of Scotland; Member, Institute of Taxation. *Clubs:* Overseas Bankers' Club, Parkstone Yacht Club, Drascombe Association (Chairman). *Recreations:* Sailing, Shooting, Reading.

BADGER, R G; Director, Lonrho plc.

BADGER, Stephen Tarrant; Director, Morgan Grenfell & Co Ltd, since 1977; Corporate Finance. *Career:* Morgan Grenfell 1962-. *Biog: b.* 5 February 1940. *m.* 1972, Katharine Mary (née Newbold); 1 s; 1 d. *Educ:* Sherborne School; Pembroke College, Oxford (MA). *Professional Organisations:* ACIB; ACIS.

BADROCK, Raymond; Director, J Henry Schroder Wagg & Co, since 1967. *Directorships:* Schroder Executor & Trustee Co Ltd 1966 (exec); Intl Services Ltd (Bermuda); Schroder Cayman Bank & Trust Co Ltd (Grand Cayman); Schroder Intl Trust Co Limited.

BAEHR, Laurence Josef; Partner, Clark Whitehill, since 1986; Head of Corporate Recovery and Insolvency Services. *Career:* Stoy Hayward, Insolvency Senior 1964-67; West Danes, Senior Management Consultant 1967-75; Thornton Baker, Insolvency Senior 1975-77; Touche Ross, Assistant Manager, Insolvency 1977-79; Cork Gully, Manager/Senior Manager, Insolvency 1980-86. *Biog: b.* 5 January 1941. *Nationality:* British. *m.* 1990, Shirley (née Natanson). *Educ:* Whitgift. *Other Activities:* Freeman, City of London. *Professional Organisations:* ACA; Insolvency Practitioners Association; British Institute of Management; Institute of Directors. *Clubs:* David Lloyd. *Recreations:* Travel, Music, Chess, Theatre.

BAGEHOT, R S; Partner, Field Fisher Waterhouse.

BAGLIN, Richard John; Managing Director, New Businesses, Abbey National plc, since 1988; Estate Agency, Insurance, Housing Development, Overseas. *Directorships:* Various Abbey National Subsidiaries.

BAGRI, Raj K; Chairman, Metdist Ltd, since 1970. *Career:* Worldwide Interests in the Metal Trade & Industry. *Biog: b.* 24 August 1930. *m.* 1954, Usha (née Maheshwary); 1 s; 1 d. *Directorships:* The London Metal Exchange Ltd 1987 (non-exec); Metal Market & Exchange Co Ltd 1983 (non-exec); Metdist Ltd 1970 (exec); Metdist Trading Ltd 1981 (exec); Metdist International Ltd 1981 (non-exec); Minmetco Ltd 1966 (exec); Metrod India Holdings Ltd 1990 (non-exec); Bagri Foundation 1990 (non-exec). *Other Activities:* Indian Chamber of Commerce in UK (Chm), Indian Institute of Culture (Vice-Chm). *Clubs:* Rotary.

BAILEY, Brian; Director of Finance, West Midlands Metropolitan Authorities Superannuation Fund. *Educ:* BSc. *Professional Organisations:* IPFA.

BAILEY, Christopher Robert; Partner, Jaques & Lewis, since 1988; Trusts & Tax. *Career:* Currey & Co, Assistant Solicitor 1972-74; Slaughter & May, Asst Solicitor 1974-79; Bird & Bird, Asst Solicitor 1979-80; Lovell, White & King, Asst Solicitor 1981-88. *Biog: b.* 17 February 1947. *Nationality:* British. *Educ:* Dover College, Dover; New College, Oxford (MA). *Directorships:* Ledger Trustee Company 1989 (exec). *Other Activities:* Treasurer, Dover College War Memorial & Endowment Fund. *Professional Organisations:* Law Society. *Recreations:* Skiing.

BAILEY, D D; Director, Hambros Bank Limited.

BAILEY, J W; Director, S G Warburg & Co Ltd. *Career:* Ernst & Young (Chartered Accountants) 1975-80. *Biog: b.* 1955. *Nationality:* British. *m.* 1986, Ruth; 1 s; 1 d. *Other Activities:* Worshipful Company of Haberdashers. *Professional Organisations:* Institute of Chartered Accountants in England and Wales. *Clubs:* City of London Club.

BAILEY, James R; Chief Executive Officer, Aetna International (UK) Ltd, since 1989. *Career:* College Life Ins, Norman, OK, Sales Rep 1949-51; US Army, 1st Lt to Captain 1951-54; College Life Ins, Norman, OK, Sales Rep 1954-55; Fidelity Union Life Ins, College Div, Dallas, Director 1955-61; Mercantile Security Life Ins, Dallas, Exec VP & Agency Director 1961-71; Republic National Life Ins, Dallas, SVP & Director of Special Mkts 1971-72; AL&C, College Marketing Sales, LVAM, PFSD, Director 1972-73; AL&C, LVAM, PFSD, National Sales Director 1973-80; AL&C, Sales & Marketing Services, LVAM, PFSD, VP 1980-81; Aetna Life & Casualty, Field Management, PFSD, VP 1981-85; Aetna Life Insurance Co Ltd, UK, CEO 1989-. *Biog: b.* 25 August 1925. *Nationality:* American. *m.* 1946, Margery; 3 s. *Educ:* University of Oklahoma (BA Business Management). *Directorships:* Aetna International (UK) Ltd 1989 (exec); Aetna Life Ins Co 1989 (exec); Aetna Unit Trusts Ltd 1989 (exec); Aetna Pensions Ltd 1989 (exec); Aetna Investment Management Ltd 1989 (exec). *Recreations:* Golf.

BAILEY, Jeffrey; Partner, Linklaters & Paines, since 1980; Commercial Property Lawyer. *Biog: b.* 28 July 1949. *Nationality:* British. *m.* 1988, Yvonne Mary (née Gallagher); 1 s. *Educ:* Neath Grammar School; University of Wales (LLB Hons). *Directorships:* Bacardi (Europe) Ltd 1987 (non-exec). *Professional Organisations:* Member, Law Society; Member, City of London Law Society. *Publications:* Land Taxation (co-author), 1986. *Clubs:* Moor Park Golf Club (Herts). *Recreations:* Reading, Piano, English Porcelain.

BAILEY, L A; Partner, Ashurst Morris Crisp.

BAILEY, M R; Director, London International Financial Futures Exchange.

BAILEY, Michael William; Partner, Morison Stoneham Chartered Accountants. *Educ:* (BA Econ). *Professional Organisations:* FCA.

BAILEY, P; Secretary, Next plc.

BAILEY, Richard; Managing Director, N M Rothschild and Sons Limited, since 1989; Northern Division/Corporate Finance. *Career:* Marks & Spencer plc, Commercial Manager 1974-76; Price Waterhouse, Audit Manager 1976-81; N M Rothschild & Sons Limited, Corporate Finance Executive 1981-. *Biog: b.* 26 December 1951. *Nationality:* British. *m.* 1977, Hilary (née Bullock); 2 s. *Educ:* The King's School, Pontefract; Manchester University (English and American Literature). *Directorships:* N M Rothschild & Sons Limited 1989 (exec). *Professional Organisations:* ACA. *Clubs:* St James Club, Manchester. *Recreations:* Theatre, Music, Gardening, Swimming, Skiing.

BAILLIE, Brian William; Group Director, Development, The Peninsular and Oriental Steam Navigation Company, since 1990; Asia Pacific. *Career:* Brisbane Stevedoring & Wool Dumping Co Pty Ltd, Supervisor 1951-54; Bulk Handling & General Stevedoring Co Pty Ltd, Manager 1954-62; Brisbane Wharves & Wool Dumping Pty Ltd, Asst Gen Mgr 1962; ConAust (Australia) Ltd, Chairman 1970; Australport Services Pty Ltd, Chairman; Robert Laurie Carpenters Pty Ltd (PNG); Lindeman Island Pty Ltd; Heron Island Pty Ltd; Burleigh Marr Distributions Pty Ltd; Mercantile Stevedores (WA) and (SA) Pty Ltd; Brisbane Wharves & Wool Dumping Pty Ltd, Chairman/MD 1970; P&O Australia Ltd, Deputy MD 1981-82; MD 1983-89; Overseas Containers Australia Pty Ltd, Director 1986. *Biog: b.* 4 December 1925. *Nationality:* Australian. *m.* 1951, Cynthia May; 4 s; 2 d. *Directorships:* Kelang Container Terminal Sdb, Bhd (Malaysia) 1984; Konnas Terminal Kelang Sd, Bhd (Malaysia) 1984; Century Group Pty Ltd 1989; P&O Australia Ltd 1990 Vice Chairman; The Peninsular and Oriental Steam Navigation Company, London 1990 Group Dir; Command Pacific Pty Limited 1988. *Professional Organisations:* FAIM; FAIT. *Clubs:* Queensland Club, Union Club (Sydney), Tattersalls.

BAILLIE, Robin Alexander MacDonald; Non-Executive Director, Standard Chartered plc, since 1983. *Career:* National Service, Royal Navy Sub-Lt 1953-55; Grindlays Bank Group 1955-66; Exporters Refinance Corp Ltd 1966-73; Chief Exec 1971-73; Grindlays Bank plc, Div Dir 1973-; Wallace Bros Bank Ltd, Exec Dir 1973-76; Wallace Bros Group, MD 1977-83. *Biog: b.* 20 August 1933. *Nationality:* British. *m.* 1959, Elizabeth (née Ordish); 1 s; 1 d. *Educ:* Larkhall Academy, Scotland. *Directorships:* London & Strathclyde Trust plc 1981 (non-exec); Burson-Marsteller Ltd 1988 (non-exec) Chm; Burson-Marsteller Financial Ltd 1988 (non-exec); PaineWebber International Bank Ltd 1987 (non-exec) Chm; TransAtlantic Holdings plc (non-exec); Capital & Counties plc (non-exec); Boustead plc (non-exec). *Other Activities:* Hon Director, The International Triangle. *Professional Organisations:* Fellow, Royal Society of Arts; Fellow, Institute of Directors; FIB (Scot). *Clubs:* City of London, Overseas Bankers'; *Clubs:* Lombard Association. *Recreations:* Opera, Ballet, Oriental Art.

BAILLIEU, Colin Clive; Executive Chairman, Gresham Underwriting Agencies Ltd, since 1990. *Career:* Council of Lloyd's 1983-88; Monopolies & Mergers Commission 1984; Bury & Mas Co Industries Ltd, Non Executive Director 1979-80; Ultrasonic Machines Ltd, Chairman 1970-79; Arthur Sanderson & Sons, Commercial Director 1967-69; Chemstrand (Monsanto), Commercial Director 1960-66; Reynold/TI Aluminium & British Aluminium; British Metal Corporation; Evening Standard. *Biog: b.* 2 July 1930. *Nationality:* British. *m.* 1968, Renata (née Ricater); 2 s; 2 d. *Educ:* Dragon School; Eton College. *Clubs:* Travellers Beefsteak, MCC, Shikar. *Recreations:* Skiing, Polo.

BAIN, N C; Finance Director and Deputy Chief, Cadbury Schweppes plc. *Career:* Inland Revenue (NZ) 1957-59; Anderson & Co, Chartered Accountants, NZ Senior Manager 1960-62; Cadbury Schweppes Group (New Zealand), Accountant, Financial Controller, Finance Director, Sales Export Director 1963-75; (South Africa), Group MD 1976-80; (United Kingdom), Strategic Planning Director 1980-83; Mem Board of CS plc 1981; Cadbury Ltd, Managing Director 1983-86; Managing Director, World Wide (Confectionery) 1986-89; Finance Director and Deputy Group Chief Executive 1989-. *Biog: b.* 14 July 1940. *Nationality:* British/New Zealander. *m.* 1987, Anne Patricia (née Kemp); 1 s; 1 d (by previous marriage); 1 stepd. *Educ:* Kings High School, NZ; Otago University, NZ (MCom Hons, BCom Acctg, BCom Econ). *Directorships:* Cadbury Schweppes plc 1981; Various Companies Within Cadbury Schweppes plc Group; London International Group 1989 (non-exec). *Professional Organisations:* FCA; CMA; FCIS; CBIM; FRSA. *Recreations:* Music, Sport.

BAIN, William Edmond Adam; Director, Warburg Securities, since 1987; Corporate Finance. *Career:* Hays Akers & Hays, Articled Clerk 1966-71; J & A Scrimgeour, Equity Salesman 1971-77; W Greenwell & Co, Partner 1977-87. *Biog: b.* 9 October 1947. *m.* 1978, Jennifer; 1 s; 1 d. *Educ:* Haileybury. *Directorships:* Rowe & Pitman Ltd 1987 (exec); Austin Desmond Fine Art Ltd 1988 (non-exec); Contemporary Books Ltd 1990 (non-exec). *Professional Organisations:* FCA. *Clubs:* Burhill, Wisley. *Recreations:* Golf.

BAINES, Paul Martin; Director, Charterhouse Bank Limited, since 1988; Corporate Finance. *Career:* Freshfields Solicitors 1978-80; Antony Gibbs & Sons Ltd 1980-86. *Biog: b.* 28 January 1956. *Nationality:* British. *m.* 1984, Rosemary Margaret; 2 s; 1 d. *Educ:* Trinity

Hall, Cambridge (MA Cantab). *Directorships:* Charterhouse Bank Ltd 1988 (exec). *Professional Organisations:* Solicitor.

BAIRD, Eric; Associate Business Editor, The Glasgow Herald.

BAIRD, John Stewart; Managing Partner, Pannell Kerr Forster, since 1987; Insolvency. *Career:* Pannell Kerr Forster (Glasgow), Apprentice 1962-67; (Liberia), Audit Snr 1967-69; (The Gambia), Ptnr 1969-72; (Sierra Leone), Ptnr 1972-85; (London), Ptnr 1985-. *Biog: b.* 8 June 1943. *m.* 1980, Lorna (née Bayne); 1 s; 3 d. *Educ:* Allan Glens School; Glasgow University. *Other Activities:* Liveryman, Worshipful Company of Loriners; Freeman, City of London; Member, West Africa Ctee. *Professional Organisations:* CA (Scot); CA (Ghana); Institute of Directors. *Clubs:* Caledonian, Walton Heath Golf Club, Kingswood Golf Club. *Recreations:* Golf, Reading.

BAIRSTOW, Peter David; Assistant Managing Director & Chief Actuary, Sun Life Assurance Society plc, since 1980; Overall Actuarial Responsibility. *Career:* Sun Life Assurance Society plc 1953-73; Executive 1973-75; Actuary & Director 1975-76; Assistant General Manager & Actuary 1976-80. *Biog: b.* 13 February 1932. *Nationality:* British. *m.* 1960, Brenda Christine (née Hanson); 2 s; 1 d. *Educ:* Eltham College; University College, London (BSc Mathematics 1st Class Honours). *Directorships:* Subsidiary Companies of Sun Life Assurance Society plc (exec); POSTEL Investment Management Ltd 1983 (non-exec); Chelsfield Park Resident's Association Ltd 1986. *Professional Organisations:* Fellow, Institute of Actuaries.

BAKER, A F; Director, Sharps Pixley Ltd.

BAKER, Alan B; Partner, Walker Morris Scott Turnbull.

BAKER, Andrew Piers; Head of Corporate Department, Wedlake Bell, since 1987; Commercial and Corporate Law. *Career:* Slaughter and May, Articled Clerk/Solicitor 1969-79. *Biog: b.* 12 October 1946. *Educ:* Reigate Grammar School; University of Birmingham (LLB Hons). *Directorships:* The Global Group plc 1985 (non-exec); The College Group Limited 1988 (non-exec). *Other Activities:* Director and Councillor, Egyptian-British Chamber of Commerce. *Professional Organisations:* Solicitor.

BAKER, Anthony Thomas; Director, County NatWest Ltd, since 1988; Corporate Advisory-Public Sector. *Career:* Department of Transport, Asst Sec 1983-87; Seconded to Coopers & Lybrand 1983; Serpell Committee on Railway Finances, Asst Sec 1982-83; Department of Transport, Asst Sec 1978-81; H M Treasury, Principal, Home Finance 1975-78; Department of Environment, Principal, Water Directorate 1973-75; Prvt Sec to Parliamentary Under-Sec 1972-73; Department of Transport, Other Posts 1965-72. *Biog: b.* 13 March 1944. *Nationality:* British. *m.* 1969, Alicia Veronica (née Roberts); 2 s; 1 d. *Educ:* Chatham House Grammar School, Ramsgate; Lincoln College, Oxford (MA Hons). *Other Activities:* Freeman, City of London. *Recreations:* Theatre, Opera, Literature, Sport.

BAKER, Cecil John; *Career:* The Insurance Institute of London, Sec 1945-49; The London Assurance, Investment Mgr 1950-64; Hambros Bank Ltd, Investment Consultant 1964-74. *Biog: b.* 2 September 1915. *Nationality:* British. *m.* 1971, Joan (née Barnes); 1 s; 1 d. *Educ:* Whitgift School; London School of Economics (LLB, BSc). *Directorships:* Alliance & Leicester Chm; Girobank plc (non-exec). *Other Activities:* Worshipful Company of Actuaries. *Professional Organisations:* FIA, ACII. *Clubs:* Savile. *Recreations:* Golf.

BAKER, D M; Director, County NatWest Securities Limited.

BAKER, Derek; Operations Director, Greenwell Montagu Stockbrokers.

BAKER, J S G; Director, Providence Capitol Fund Managers Ltd.

BAKER, J W; Senior Vice President and Branch Manager, Bank Julius Baer & Co Ltd.

BAKER, Keith R; Vice-President and Treasury Manager, Mellon Bank NA, since 1990; Control/Supervision of all FX, Money Market, Option, Derivative Sales and Trading. *Career:* Citibank NA (London), Vice-President/Chief FX Dealer 1969-84; Drexel Burnham Lambert (London), Vice President/Chief FX Dealer 1984-86; Manufacturers Hanover (London), Managing Director/European FX Manager 1986-89; Bank of America (London), Vice President/Chief Dealer Strategic Trading 1989-90. *Biog: b.* 11 June 1950. *Nationality:* British. *m.* 1972, Carol (née Martin); 2 s; 1 d. *Educ:* Beaufoy School. *Recreations:* Tennis, Swimming, Motor Sport, DIY.

BAKER, Leon Walter; Director, Touche, Remnant & Co, since 1978; Compliance Officer. *Career:* Touche, Remnant & Co, Various 1956-. *Biog: b.* 10 May 1940. *Nationality:* British. *m.* 1968, Margaret Nicola (née Philp); 2 d. *Educ:* Fawcett School, Brighton. *Professional Organisations:* FCIS.

BAKER, M F; Partner, Cameron Markby Hewitt.

BAKER, Mrs Mary; Director, Barclays Bank plc. *Educ:* MA. *Directorships:* Thames Television plc 1975 (non-exec); Prudential Corporation plc 1988 (non-exec);

Avon Cosmetics Ltd 1981; London Tourist Board 1980-83 Chairman.

BAKER, Michael G; Director, Kleinwort Benson Limited, since 1985; Corporate Finance. *Career:* Kleinwort Benson, Various 1972-. *Biog: b.* 3 July 1947. *Nationality:* British; 2 s; 1 d. *Educ:* Bedford Modern School; Leicester University (SA Coy Senior Open Scholarship) (BSc); Manchester Business School (DipBA, PhD). *Recreations:* Family, Skiing, Sailing.

BAKER, Nicholas; MP; Partner, Frere Cholmeley, since 1973. *Career:* MP for North Dorset 1979-; PPS to Sec of State for Defence 1984-86; PPS to Sec of State for Trade & Industry 1988-89; Government Whip 1989-. *Biog: b.* 23 November 1938. *Nationality:* British. *m.* 1970, Penelope Carol (née d'Abo); 1 s; 1 d. *Educ:* Clifton College; Exeter College, Oxford (MA). *Professional Organisations:* Law Society. *Publications:* Better Company, 1973; This Pleasant Land, 1987; Low-Cost Housing in Rural Areas, 1989. *Clubs:* Blandford Constitutional, Wimborne Conservative.

BAKER, Peter John; Dealing Director, Panmure Gordon Bankers.

BAKER, Ms Rhonda; Partner, S J Berwin & Co, since 1990; Media & Communications Law, Intellectual Property. *Career:* Barrister 1982-84; Denion Hall Burgin & Warrens, Barrister/Assistant Solicitor 1984-88; S J Berwin & Co, Assistant Solicitor 1988-90; Partner 1990-. *Biog: b.* 1959. *Nationality:* British. *m.* 1987, Simon Laycock. *Educ:* North London Collegiate School; Trinity Hall, Cambridge (MA Law). *Professional Organisations:* Law Society. *Publications:* Contributor, Rights Clearances. *Clubs:* Copinger Society. *Recreations:* Reading, Writing, Walking.

BAKER, Richard Clive Jonathan; Director, County NatWest Limited, since 1988; Corporate Finance. *Career:* Price Waterhouse Trainee Acct 1979-82. *Biog: b.* 14 September 1957. *Nationality:* British. *m.* 1985, Alison Evelyn (née Naumann); 2 s. *Educ:* Leys School, Cambridge; Jesus College, Cambridge (BA). *Professional Organisations:* ACA. *Clubs:* Saints Cricket Club. *Recreations:* Shooting, Skiing, Cricket, Wine.

BAKER, Richard William Shelmerdine; Senior Vice-President, Sun Life of Canada Group, since 1979; British National Organisation; Senior Advisory Council Member for International Operations. *Career:* Marks & Spencer plc, Mgmnt 1954-60; Sun Life of Canada Rep to Agency Officer 1960-72; Barbour Index plc Sales Dir to Gp MD 1972-79. *Biog: b.* 17 December 1933. *Nationality:* British. *m.* 1975, Vanda (née Macey); 1 s; 1 d. *Educ:* Buxton College. *Directorships:* Sun Life of Canada (UK) Ltd 1979 (exec); Sun Life of Canada Unit Managers Ltd 1986 (exec); Sun Life of Canada Home Loans Ltd 1987 (exec); LAUTRO 1988 (non-exec).

Other Activities: Past President, Canada-UK Chamber of Commerce; Pres, Great Britain Wheelchair Basketball Assoc. *Professional Organisations:* Honorary Life Member, Life Insurance Assoc; Mem, Institute of Directors; Member of the Council of Lord's Taverners. *Clubs:* Canada Club, East India Club, MCC. *Recreations:* Racing, Golf, Tennis, Cricket, Collecting Antiques.

BAKER-BATES, R; Managing Director - UK Banking, Midland Bank plc.

BAKER-FALKNER, David John; Director, C S Project Consultants.

BAKOVLJEV, Sreten; Director, Fixed Income, MIM Ltd, since 1988; Asset Allocation, Currencies & Fixed Income. *Career:* New Japan Securities (Europe) Ltd, Dealer/Salesman 1977-81; County Bank Investment Management, Assistant Director 1981-86; Goldman Sachs Intl, Sales Associate 1986-87. *Biog: b.* 28 September 1955. *Nationality:* British/Yugoslavian. *m.* 1987, Karen (née King); 1 s. *Educ:* University of Warwick (BA Hons Economics & Economic History). *Directorships:* Central European Asset Management 1990 (exec); MIM Luxembourg 1990 (exec).

BAKR, Hassan M; Operations Director, Citymax Integrated Information Systems Limited, since 1987; Operations, Administration, Finance, Research, Development, Communications & Systems. *Career:* Cairo University, Lecturer 1968-73; Polytechnic of Central London, Research Assistant 1974-78; CMES, Consultant 1978-79; Hoskyns Group plc, Director 1979-87; Citymax Integrated Information Systems, Director 1987-. *Biog: b.* 23 November 1946. *Nationality:* British. *m.* 1970, Soad; 2 s. *Educ:* Cairo University Faculty of Engineering (BSc, MSc); Polytechnic of Central London. *Professional Organisations:* Institute of Electrical and Electronic Engineering (USA). *Recreations:* Tennis.

BALAAM, Ms Kay; Partner, Gouldens.

BALDOCK, Anne E; Partner, Allen & Overy.

BALDOCK, Norman Frank; Chairman, Gresham Trust plc.

BALDWIN, Mrs Ann Shirley (née Clement); Executive Partner, Grant Thornton, since 1989; Finance & Personnel. *Career:* Grant Thornton, S West Group, Managing Partner, Bristol 1985-89; Tax Partner, Kettering 1978-85; Senior & Manager, Kettering 1972-78; Pinkney Keith Gibbs & Co, Articled Clerk 1967-72. *Biog: b.* 24 June 1946. *Nationality:* British. *m.* 1974, William; 2 d. *Educ:* Heriotswood Grammar School, Stanmore. *Professional Organisations:* FCA. *Recreations:* Swimming (doing), Theatre (watching).

BALDWIN, Barry Anthony; Director, Independent Business Services, Price Waterhouse Europe, since 1985; Emerging Businesses, Single European Market. *Career:* Price Waterhouse, Partner 1969; Partner in Charge, Independent Business Group, London 1975-83; Partner in Charge, Windsor Office 1983-85. *Biog: b.* 7 January 1935. *Nationality:* British. *m.* 1976, Liz (née McKeown); 3 s. *Educ:* Kings College School, Wimbledon. *Other Activities:* Special Trustee, Guy's Hospital; Honorary Director, Theatre Royal, Windsor; Council Member, Small Business Research Trust; Vice President, Small Business Bureau; Executive Member, Union of Independent Companies, Chairman, 1985-87. *Professional Organisations:* Fellow, Institute of Chartered Accountants in England & Wales. *Publications:* An Independent Enterprise Agency; A Loan Guarantee Scheme for Independent Enterprises, 1980; Year of Small & Medium Sized Enterprises – Management Training for Small Enterprises (co-author), 1983; Government Finance for SMEs: Some International Comparisons – An Overview (co-author), 1990. *Recreations:* Golf, Swimming, Theatre.

BALDWIN, K; Executive Director, Allied Dunbar Assurance plc.

BALDWIN, R K; Partner, Touche Ross & Co.

BALDWIN, T; Partner, Moores Rowland.

BALFOUR, A G; Partner, Slaughter and May.

BALFOUR, Charles George Yule; Executive Director, Banque Paribas, since 1986; Corporate & International Banking, Acquisition Finance and Export Finance. *Career:* Hoare Govett & Co, Executive, Institutional 1971-73; Hill Samuel & Co Ltd, Executive, Capital Markets 1973-76; Dillon Read, Overseas Corporate VP, Capital Markets 1976-79. *Biog: b.* 23 April 1951. *Nationality:* British. m1 1978, Audrey (née Hoare). m2 1987, Gräfin Svea (née Goëss) 1 d. *Educ:* Eton College. *Directorships:* Paribas Finance Ltd 1986 (exec); Paribas Development Services Ltd 1986 (exec); Eltonbrook Properties Ltd 1989 (exec); Intermediate Capital Group 1990 (exec) Alternate. *Other Activities:* Member of Queen's Body Guard for Scotland (Royal Company of Archers). *Clubs:* White's, City of London, Puffins (Edinburgh). *Recreations:* Fishing.

BALFOUR, Christopher Roxburgh; Director, Hambros Bank Limited, since 1984; Corporate Finance with Special Responsibility for Europe. *Career:* FCA 1967; Hambros 1968-. *Biog: b.* 24 August 1941. *Nationality:* British. *Educ:* Ampleforth College, York; Queen's College, Oxford (BA). *Professional Organisations:* FCA, 1967. *Clubs:* Pratts. *Recreations:* Shooting, Tennis, Skiing.

BALFOUR, George Patrick; Partner, Slaughter and May, since 1973; Corporate Finance/Company & Commercial Law. *Biog: b.* 17 September 1941. *m.* 1978, Lesley Ann (née Johnston); 3 s. *Educ:* Shrewsbury School; Pembroke College, Cambridge (MA). *Other Activities:* Solicitors' Benevolent Assoc (Dir). *Professional Organisations:* The Law Society; IBA. *Recreations:* Music, Golf.

BALFOUR, Michael John; Chairman, IMI Capital Markets (UK), since 1987; Chairman, IMI Securities Ltd. *Career:* Bank of England, Chief Adviser (European Affairs), Assistant Director Overseas Affairs) 1950-85. *Biog: b.* 17 October 1925. *Nationality:* British. *m.* 1951, Mary Campbell (née Penney); 2 s; 1 d. *Educ:* Eton College; Oxford University (MA Foreign Languages). *Directorships:* Balgowie Estates Ltd 1955 (non-exec) Chm; IMI Bank (International) 1987 (non-exec) Dep Chm. *Recreations:* Fishing, Boating, Music, DIY.

BALFOUR, Neil Roxburgh; Chairman, York Trust Group plc.

BALFOUR, Peter Edward Gerald; CBE; Vice Chairman, Royal Bank of Scotland.

BALFOUR, Robert Bruce; The Rt Hon Lord Balfour of Burleigh; Deputy Governor, Bank of Scotland, since 1977. *Career:* Royal Navy, Leading Radio Elec Mate 1945-48; English Electric Co Ltd, Various Mfg Mgmnt 1951-57; English Electric Co of India, Gen Mgr 1957-64; English Electric Netherton Works, Gen Mgr 1964-66; D Napier & Son Ltd, Dir & Gen Mgr 1966-68. *Biog: b.* 6 January 1927. *m.* 1971, Jennifer (née Manasseh); 2 d. *Educ:* Westminster School. *Directorships:* Bank of Scotland 1968 (non-exec); Scottish Investment Trust 1971 (non-exec); Tarmac plc 1981-90 (non-exec); Turing Institute 1983 (non-exec) Chm; Cablevision (Scotland) plc 1984 (non-exec) Chm; Wm Lawson Distillers Ltd 1984 (non-exec). *Other Activities:* Member, BR Scotland Regional Board. *Professional Organisations:* CEng; FIEE; FRSE; Hon FRIAS. *Clubs:* New (Edinburgh). *Recreations:* Music, Climbing, Woodwork.

BALL, A P J; Director, Morgan Grenfell & Co Limited.

BALL, A Scott; Director, Scottish Financial Enterprise.

BALL, C J W; Chief Executive & Director, The Private Bank and Trust Company Limited.

BALL, Christopher Charles; Director of Administration, Capel Cure Myers Capital Management Ltd, since 1986; Administration. *Career:* Grindlays Bank, Gen Mgr 1973-88; ANZ Merchant Bank Ltd Dir, Administration 1985-88. *Biog: b.* 25 December 1945. *Nationality:* British. *m.* 1971, Frances Jean (née Elliott); 1 s. *Educ:* Harold Hill Grammar School. *Directorships:* Capel Cure

Myers 1986 (exec); Capel Cure Myers Nominees Ltd 1987 (exec); Linton Nominees Ltd 1987 (exec); Richardson Glover & Case Nominees Ltd 1987 (exec); Capel Cure Myers Unit Trust Managers Ltd 1990 (exec); Key Fund Managers Limited 1990 (exec); Ridgefield Management Limited 1990 (exec). *Recreations:* Reading, Drawing.

BALL, Graham Wakely; Managing Director, Fleming Private Asset Management Ltd, since 1989. *Career:* Moore Stephens 1965-68; J M Finn & Co, Partner 1968-84; Sheppards, Consultant 1984-87; Fleming Private Asset Management, Director 1987-89; Managing Director 1989-. *Biog: b.* 25 May 1942. *Nationality:* British. *m.* 1973, Andrea Frances (née Bromage); 1 s; 3 d. *Educ:* Felsted School. *Directorships:* Oliver & Co 1987 (non-exec); Fleming Private Asset Management Ltd (formerly Fleming Montagu Stanley) 1987 (exec). *Professional Organisations:* FCA; International Stock Exchange. *Clubs:* Hankley Common Golf Club, Aston Martin Owners Club. *Recreations:* Golf, Motor Racing.

BALL, John Malvern; Director, Sharps Pixley Ltd, since 1987. *Career:* Barclays Bank Ltd 1963-64; Barclays Bank DCO 1965-71; Exporters Refinance Corporation Ltd 1971-72. *Biog: b.* 23 July 1945. *m.* 1972, Eva Catharina (née Brunnstrom); 2 d. *Educ:* Rutlish School.

BALL, Professor Sir (Robert) James; Professor of Economics, London Business School, since 1965. *Biog: b.* 15 July 1933. *Nationality:* British. *m.* 1970, Lindsay Jackson (née Wonnacott); 1 s; 1 steps; 3 d. *Educ:* St Marylebone Grammar School; Queen's College, Oxford (BA Hons 1st, MA); University of Pennsylvania (PhD). *Directorships:* IBM Holdings UK Ltd 1979; Legal & General 1979 Chm; London & Scottish Marine Oil (LASMO) 1988. *Other Activities:* Trustee, Civic Trust, The Economist Newspaper, Foulkes Foundation; Member, Marshall Aid Commemoration Commission; Freeman, City of London, 1987; Hon DSc, Aston University,1987; Hon DSoc Sci, University of Manchester, 1988. *Publications:* An Economic Model of the United Kingdom, 1961; Inflation and the Theory. *Clubs:* Royal Dart Yacht Club, RAC. *Recreations:* Chess, Gardening.

BALL, Simon Peter; Finance Director, Kleinwort Benson Securities Limited, since 1990; Finance. *Career:* Price Waterhouse 1981-85; Kleinwort Benson Limited, Corporate Finance 1985-87; Kleinwort Benson Securities Limited, Assistant Finance Director 1987-89; Finance Director 1990-. *Biog: b.* 2 May 1960. *Nationality:* British. *Educ:* Chislehurst & Sidcup Grammar School; University College, London (BSc Econ). *Professional Organisations:* Institute of Chartered Accountants in England & Wales. *Recreations:* Golf, Tennis.

BALL, Stephen Quentin; Senior Legal Counsel, Bankers Trust Company, since 1989; Europe, Middle East & Africa Operations. *Career:* Slaughter and May, London 1984-86; Linklaters & Paines, New York 1986-89. *Biog: b.* 30 January 1958. *Nationality:* British. *Educ:* Windsor Boys School; Fitzwilliam College, Cambridge. *Other Activities:* Member, City of London Solicitors' Company; Freeman of the City of London. *Professional Organisations:* Member, Law Society.

BALLANTYNE, Rob; News Editor, The Times.

BALLARD, R M; Partner, Freshfields.

BALLIN, Robert Andrew; Deputy Chairman, FCB Advertising Ltd, since 1988; Client Service. *Career:* Shell-Mex and BP Ltd, Sales and Marketing 1962-67; S H Benson Ltd, Advertising Account Executive 1967-69; Gallagher Smail Ltd/Doyle Dane Bernbach Ltd, Advertising Account Manager 1969-73; Foote, Cone and Belding Ltd, Account Director 1973-75; Impact/FCB, Belgium, Director International Business 1976-77; Foote, Cone and Belding Ltd, Director 1977-86; Vice Chairman 1986-88; Deputy Chairman 1988-. *Biog: b.* 8 July 1943. *Nationality:* British. *m.* 1975, Serena Mary Ann (née Goode); 1 s; 2 d. *Educ:* Highgate School; City of London College (HNC Business Studies). *Directorships:* FCB Advertising Ltd 1977 (exec). *Professional Organisations:* MIPA; MInstM. *Clubs:* Naval & Military, RAC, MCC. *Recreations:* Music, Sport, Theatre.

BAMFORD, Colin; Partner, Richards Butler, since 1988; Banking. *Career:* Herbert Oppenheimer Nathan & Vandyk, Articled Clerk 1972-74; Assistant 1974-77; Partner 1977-88. *Biog: b.* 28 August 1950. *Nationality:* British. *m.* 1975, Nirmala (née Rajah); 2 s; 1 d. *Educ:* Queen Elizabeth's Grammar School, Blackburn; Trinity Hall, Cambridge (MA). *Other Activities:* Chm, Old Chiswick Protection Society. *Professional Organisations:* International Bar Association; Union Internationale des Avocats. *Recreations:* Collecting Oriental Textiles, Poetry.

BAMFORD, R J E; Partner, MacIntyre Hudson.

BANCROFT, Ian Powell; Lord Bancroft; GCB; Deputy Chairman, Sun Life Corporation plc. *Career:* HM Treasury, Civil Servant 1947-69; Dept of Environment, Permanent Secretary 1970-77; Head of Home Civil Service 1977-81. *Biog: b.* 23 December 1922. *Nationality:* British. *m.* 1950, Jean (née Swaine); 2 s; 1 d. *Educ:* Coatham School, Redcar; Balliol College, Oxford (MA Scholar Hon Fellow). *Directorships:* Bass plc 1982 (non-exec); The Rugby Group plc 1982 (non-exec); Bass Leisure Ltd 1984 (non-exec); ANZ Grindlays Bank plc 1983 (non-exec); ANZ Merchant Bank Ltd 1987 (non-exec). *Other Activities:* Management Board, Royal Hospital & Home Putney; Chairman of Trustees, Mansfield College, Oxford; President, Building Centre Trust; Governor, Cranleigh School. *Professional Organi-*

sations: CBIM. *Clubs:* United Oxford & Cambridge, Civil Service.

BAND, David; Chief Executive, Barclays de Zoete Wedd, since 1988. *Career:* J P Morgan Securities Ltd, Chm and Morgan Guaranty Trust Co, Executive Vice President 1964-88; The Securities Association, Deputy Chairman 1986-88. *Biog: b.* 14 December 1942. *Nationality:* British. *m.* 1973, Olivia Rose (née Brind); 1 s; 1 d. *Educ:* Rugby School; St Edmund Hall, Oxford (MA). *Directorships:* Barclays Bank plc 1988; Barclays plc 1988. *Recreations:* Tennis.

BAND, J; Executive Director, Daiwa Europe Limited.

BANHAM, John Michael Middlecott; Director-General, Confederation of British Industry, since 1987. *Career:* HM Foreign Service, Asst Principal 1962-64; Reed International, Dir of Marketing, Wallcoverings Div 1965-69; McKinsey & Co Inc 1969-83; Associate 1969-75; Principal 1975-80; Director 1980-83; Controller, Audit Commission 1983-87. *Biog: b.* 22 August 1940. *m.* 1965, Frances Barbara Molyneux Favell; 1 s; 2 d. *Educ:* Charterhouse; Queens' College, Cambridge (Foundation Scholar, BA 1st Class Natural Sciences). *Directorships:* English China Clays 1985-87 (non-exec). *Other Activities:* Member, BOTB; Director & Board Member, Business in the Community, 1989-; Member of Council, BIM, 1985-87; PSI, 1986; Member, Council of Management, PDSA, 1982-; Finance Ctee, BRCS, 1987; Governing Body, London Business School, 1987; Managing Trustees, Nuffield Foundation, 1988; Hon Fellow, Queens College, Cambridge, 1989. *Professional Organisations:* Hon LLD, Bath; Hon DSc, Loughborough. *Publications:* Future of the British Car Industry, 1975; Realizing the Promise of a National Health Service, 1977; numerous reports for Audit Commission on Education, Housing, Social Services and Local Government Finance, 1984-87. *Clubs:* Travellers', Oriental. *Recreations:* Ground Clearing, Cliff Walking in W Cornwall, Ocean Sailing.

BANKES, U W; Senior Partner, Field Fisher Waterhouse, since 1990. *Biog: b.* 15 October 1927. *Nationality:* British. *m.* 1958, Mary (née Burder); 1 s; 1 d. *Educ:* Eltham College; New College, Oxford (MA,BCL). *Other Activities:* President, Holborn Law Society 1987-88. *Clubs:* United Oxford and Cambridge University. *Recreations:* Opera, Bridge.

BANKHEAD, Nigel R; Partner, Clay & Partners, since 1988; Pensions and Employee Benefits Consultancy. *Career:* Commercial Union, Trainee/Qualified Actuary 1978-83; Fenchurch Life & Pensions Ltd, Actuary & Director 1983-85; Tillinghast Nelson & Warren, Consultant 1985-87. *Biog: b.* 2 July 1957. *Nationality:* Irish. *m.* 1986, Josephine (née Dooney); 1 s; 1 d. *Educ:* Leeds University (BA Economics). *Professional Organisations:*

Fellow, Institute of Actuaries. *Recreations:* Climbing, Golf.

BANKIER, I P; Partner, McGrigor Donald, since 1981; Corporate Finance – Mergers & Acquisitions. *Career:* Biggart Baillie & Gifford, Law Apprenticeship 1975-77; McGrigor Donald & Co, Assistant Solicitor in the Corporate Department 1977-80; Moncrieff, Warren, Patterson (Later McGrigor Donald), Corporate Partner 1981. *Biog: b.* 14 March 1952. *Nationality:* British. *m.* 1979, Elaine (née Steven); 1 s; 1 d. *Educ:* St Aloysius College, Glasgow; Edinburgh University (LLB Hons). *Other Activities:* Incorporation of Hammermen of Glasgow. *Professional Organisations:* Law Society of Scotland; Notary Public in Scotland. *Clubs:* Caledonian Club, London. *Recreations:* Golf, Swimming, Gardening, Music.

BANKS, D D R; Director, Panmure Gordon & Co Limited.

BANKS, I F; Partner (Leeds), Bacon & Woodrow.

BANKS, Lawrence; Director, Robert Fleming Holdings Limited.

BANKS, Neil D; Director of Finance/Company Secretary, The London Metal Exchange Ltd, since 1989; Finance/Regulation/Compliance/Membership. *Career:* The Commercial Metal Company Ltd, Assistant Chief Accountant 1975-79; Sogemin (Metals) Limited, Chief Accountant 1979-81; Drexel Burnham Lambert Ltd, Operations Manager, LME Dept 1981-87; Philipp Brothers Ltd, Financial Controller, LME Dept 1987-89; ABB Futures (UK) Ltd, Financial Controller/Company Secretary 1989. *Biog: b.* 11 December 1948. *Nationality:* British. *m.* 1974, Rosemary (née Duff); 3 d. *Educ:* St Albans Grammar School; Ipswich School. *Professional Organisations:* Fellow, Chartered Association of Certified Accountants. *Clubs:* Royal Yachting Association. *Recreations:* Sailing.

BANKS, William Lawrence; Deputy Chairman, Robert Fleming & Co Ltd, since 1986; Director in Charge of Worldwide Corporate Finance. *Career:* Robert Fleming 1961-63; Save & Prosper Group Ltd, Investment Mgr 1963-66; Robert Fleming Corp, Fin Exec 1966-68; Robert Fleming Inc, Founder & Pres 1968-73; Save & Prosper Group Ltd, Investment Dir 1973-79; Robert Fleming, Dir 1979-85. *Biog: b.* 7 June 1938. *m.* 1963, Elisabeth Christina (née Saunders); 2 s. *Educ:* Rugby School; Christ Church, Oxford (MA). *Directorships:* Robert Fleming Holdings Ltd 1974. *Other Activities:* Hon Treasurer of Royal Horticultural Soc; Chelsea Physic Garden; Royal Graduate Medical School; Trustee, Chevening Estate; Vice-Chm, Intl Dendrology Soc; Chm, Nat Council for Conservation of Plants & Gardens. *Clubs:* MCC, Pratt's. *Recreations:* Gardening, Fishing, Shooting.

BANNER, John Charles; Director, Panmure Gordon & Co Ltd, since 1978; Private Clients. *Career:* Shaw & Co Partner's Asst 1960-67; Panmure Gordon & Co Various 1967-. *Biog:* 1 s; 1 d. *Educ:* Felsted School. *Directorships:* Rectory Nominees Ltd 1978 (exec); Anchor Estate Co Ltd 1987 (non-exec).

BANNISTER, Mrs Andrea; Group Pensions Manager, Harrisons & Crosfields plc.

BANNISTER, Nicholas John; Managing Editor (City), The Guardian, since 1988; Financial News Editing. *Career:* Birmingham Evening Mail; Solihull News; Birmingham Evening Mail, Reporter 1965-70; The Guardian, City Sub-Editor 1970; Financial Reporter 1970-76; Deputy Financial News Editor 1976-78; Financial News Editor 1978-88. *Educ:* Harrow.

BANNISTER, R; Chief Executive, Eurobenefits Limited, since 1989. *Career:* Legal & General Assurance Society Ltd, Assistant Controller, Statistical Services, Overseas Business 1970; Mobil Europe Inc, Compensation & Benefits Adviser, European Affiliate Companies 1977; Clay & Partners, Partner 1986. *Educ:* Exeter University (BSc). *Professional Organisations:* Fellow, Institute of Actuaries; Fellow, Society of Actuaries in Ireland.

BANNOCK, B H; *Biog: m.* Widowed 1989. *Directorships:* National Inspection Board 1980 (exec); Insurance Ombudsman Bureau 1983 (exec); Loss Prevention Certification Board 1987 (exec); Market Building Limited 1989 (exec); The Ajax Insurance Association Ltd 1989 (exec); Ajax Insurance Holdings Limited 1989 (exec); National Approval Council for Security Systems 1990 (exec).

BANSZKY, Mrs Caroline Janet; Chief Financial Officer and Director, N M Rothschild & Sons Limited, since 1988. *Career:* KMPG Peat Marwick Mitchell 1975-81; N M Rothschild 1981-. *Biog: b.* 24 July 1953. *Nationality:* British. *m.* 1984, Nicholas L Banszky von Ambroz; 2 d. *Educ:* Wycombe Abbey School, High Wycombe, Bucks; University of Exeter (BA Hons II). *Other Activities:* Liveryman, Worshipful Company of Farriers. *Professional Organisations:* Member, Institute of Chartered Accountants of England and Wales.

BANSZKY, Nicholas Laszlo; Baron Bansky Von Ambroz; Executive Director, Smith New Court plc, since 1988; Corporate Finance. *Career:* N M Rothschild & Sons Ltd, Corporate Finance 1974-84; Kitcat & Aitken, Corporate Finance 1984-86; Smith New Court plc, Corporate Finance 1986-. *Biog: b.* 18 July 1952. *Nationality:* British. *m.* 1984, Caroline (née While); 2 d. *Educ:* Westminster School, London; Oxford University (MA). *Directorships:* Smith New Court Securities Ltd 1987 (exec); Smith New Court Corporate Finance Ltd 1986 (exec). *Professional Organisations:* Member, The

International Stock Exchange. *Recreations:* Skiing, Riding, Opera, Cooking.

BANTON, Michael; Director, Baring Asset Management Ltd, since 1980; Quantative and Erisa. *Career:* Phillips & Drew 1965-68; Provincial Insurance (Prolific) 1969-78; Barings (including 4 Years in Hong Kong) 1978-. *Biog: b.* 26 June 1947. *Nationality:* British. *Directorships:* Various Baring Asset Management Subsidiaries.

BARBER, Anthony C; Senior Director, Corporate Funding, Continental Bank NA.

BARBER, Anthony Paul; Secretary to the Council of Lloyd's, Lloyd's of London, since 1986. *Biog: b.* 13 June 1946. *Nationality:* British. *m.* 1976, Katharine (née Baldwin); 1 s; 1 d. *Educ:* University College, London (LLM). *Professional Organisations:* Barrister.

BARBER, J; Director, TH March & Company Limited.

BARBER, Michelle; Committee Member, Unit Trust Association.

BARBER, Stephen Douglas; Managing Director, MIM Tokyo KK, since 1987; Japan. *Career:* Samuel Montagu & Co Ltd 1977-85; Assistant Director 1983-85; MIM Limited, Director 1985-. *Biog: b.* 18 January 1955. *Nationality:* British. *m.* 1983, Kimiko; 1 s. *Educ:* Dulwich College; St Johns College, Oxford (MA Mathematics & Philosophy). *Directorships:* MIM Limited 1985 (exec); MIM Tokyo KK Ltd 1987 (exec) MD; Nippon Warrant Fund 1986 (exec) Chm; MIM Asia Limited 1990 (exec). *Other Activities:* Guild of Rahere. *Clubs:* Vincents, Liszt Society. *Recreations:* Books, Trees, Wine, Music.

BARBIER DE LA SERRE, René; President and Chief Operating Officer, Crédit Commercial De France, since 1987; Investment Banking Department and Chairman of Nobel. *Career:* Union Européenne et Financière, Compagnie Financière de l'Union Européenne and Banque de l'Union Européenne,; Technical Adviser and then Senior Vice President 1963-73; Crédit Commercial de France (CCF), Senior Vice President, Head of Corporate Department 1973-77; Senior Vice President and Executive Vice President, Finance Department 1977-82; Group Executive Vice President, Head of Finance Department 1982-83; Senior Executive Vice President, Head of Finance Department (including International Finance since 1986) 1983-86. *Biog: b.* 3 July 1940. *Nationality:* French. *m.* 1964, Françoise (née le Pecq). *Educ:* Ecole Polytechnique; Ecole des Manufactures de l'Etat; Institut d'Etudes Politiques. *Directorships:* Nobel Chairman; CCF UK Chairman; Crédit Commercial de France; SAFR; Crédit Commercial de France Suisse SA; Continentale d'Entreprise; Européenne de

Banque; Sicovam; Union de Banque à Paris; Investimo; Facom; Framlington; Prouvost; Vitos Etablissements Vitoux; Electrobanque; Epeda Bertrand Faure; Japan Gamma. *Professional Organisations:* Member, Conseil des Bourses de Valeurs Paris. *Clubs:* Polo de Bagatelle, Paris.

BARCLAY, David Martin; Director, County NatWest Limited, since 1989; Corporate Finance. *Career:* Department of Transport 1974-83; Cabinet Office 1983-85. *Biog: b.* 23 January 1954. *Nationality:* British. *m.* 1979, Catharine (née Muir); 1 s; 1 d. *Educ:* Clifton College; Trinity College, Cambridge (MA). *Other Activities:* Member, Corporation of Trinity College of Music, London. *Clubs:* Cavalry and Guards Club.

BARCLAY, James Christopher; Chairman, Cater Allen Holdings plc, since 1985. *Career:* Sun Alliance Insurance, Clerk 1967; Sheppards & Chase, Clerk 1968-73; Member 1973-76; Cater Ryder & Co Limited, Clerk 1976-78; Director 1978-81; Chairman 1981; Cater Allen Holdings plc, Deputy Chairman 1981-85. *Biog: b.* 7 July 1945. *Nationality:* British. *m.* 1974, Rolleen (née Forbes); 1 s; 1 d. *Educ:* Harrow School; Grenoble University. *Directorships:* Cater Allen Securities Limited 1986; Cater Allen Limited 1978; Cater Allen Lloyd's Holdings Limited 1987; Cater Allen Holdings (Jersey) Ltd 1984; Sheppards Moneybrokers Limited 1989 (non-exec). *Clubs:* Pratts. *Recreations:* Fishing, Shooting, Gardening.

BARCLAY, John Alistair; Executive Director, The Royal Bank of Scotland plc, since 1989; International Division. *Career:* Entered Service 1949; National Service 1952; Inspector of Branches 1971; Audit Controller 1972; Assistant Superintendent of Branches 1974; Manager, Dunfermline Central Branch 1977; Regional Superintendent of Branches 1980; Manager, London Lombard Street 1980; Chief City Manager, London 1982; Seconded to Williams & Glyn's Bank, Assistant General Manager 1984; Executive Vice President, North America 1985; Senior General Manager UK Banking, South 1988; Executive Director, International 1989; Banco de Comercio e Industria, Lisbon, Portugal, Director 1990. *Biog: b.* 5 December 1933. *Nationality:* British. *m.* Mary Tierney Barclay; 3 d. *Other Activities:* Governor, The Royal Scottish Corporation; Member, Caledonian Society, London; Member, Institute of Directors, London; Member, The English Speaking Union; President, The Institute of Bankers, London Centre. *Professional Organisations:* Fellow, Institute of Bankers in Scotland. *Clubs:* Overseas Bankers'. *Recreations:* Travel, Golf, Reading, Gardening, Curling, Photography, Good Food & Wine.

BARCLAY, Peter; Non-Executive Partner, Killik & Co.

BARCLAY, Richard Fenton; Deputy Chairman, National Provident Institution, since 1987; Chairman Staff

Committee. *Career:* Barclays Bank plc, Various to Snr Local Dir 1948-86. *Biog: b.* 3 December 1926. *Nationality:* British. *m.* 1957, Alison Mary (née Cummings); 3 s; 1 d. *Educ:* Gresham's School; Trinity College, Cambridge (MA). *Directorships:* Portsmouth Building Society 1987 (non-exec); National Provident Institution 1967 (non-exec). *Other Activities:* Ctee of Mgmnt, RNLI; Court of the Mary Rose. *Professional Organisations:* FCIB; Fellow, Institute of Directors. *Clubs:* Army & Navy. *Recreations:* Pottering on Land & Sea, History.

BARDELL, R C W; Senior Warden, The Worshipful Company of Insurers.

BARDER, J H; Chairman, Seascope Special Risks Ltd, since 1989; Personal Stop Loss, Excess Loss & Financial Reinsurance. *Career:* Lyon de Falbe International Ltd 1977-80; Seascope Insurance Brokers Ltd 1980-85; Lochain Patrick Insurance Brokers Ltd 1985-89. *Biog: b.* 22 July 1959. *Nationality:* British. *m.* 1988, Charlotte (née Lamb); 1 d. *Educ:* Winchester House School; Marlborough College. *Directorships:* Leslie & Godwin Ltd 1990 (exec); Seascope Reinsurance Brokers Ltd 1989-90; Lochain Patrick Insurance Brokers Ltd 1987-89; Ablebrim Ltd (Holding Company to Lochain Patrick) 1985-89. *Clubs:* Richmond Hockey Club, RAC. *Recreations:* Hockey, Squash, Fishing, Skiing.

BAREAU, Peter John; General Manager, Lloyds Bank plc, since 1990; Organisation Development, UK Retail Banking. *Career:* Bank of London & South America Ltd/Various 1966-; Lloyds Bank Intl Ltd/Lloyds Bank plc. *Biog: b.* 1 June 1942. *Nationality:* British. *m.* 1976, Karen Maria (née Giesemann); 2 s; 3 d. *Educ:* Eton College; Queens' College, Cambridge (MA).

BARFIELD, P F; Partner, Hill Taylor Dickinson.

BARHAM, Bernard F; Director, J Henry Schroder Wagg & Co Limited.

BARING, (Andrew) Michael (Godfrey); Director, Baring Brothers & Co Ltd.

BARING, Hon Sir John (Francis Harcourt); CVO, Kt, KCVO; Director, Barings plc, since 1989. *Career:* Baring Brothers & Co Ltd, MD 1955-74; Chm 1974-89; Barings plc, Chm 1985-89. *Biog: b.* 2 November 1928. *Nationality:* British. m1 1955, Susan Mary Renwick (diss 1984). m2 1987, Sarah Cornelia Spencer Churchill; 2 s 2 d. *Educ:* Eton (Fellow 1982); Trinity College, Oxford (Hon. Fellow 1989, MA). *Directorships:* British Petroleum Company plc 1982; Jaguar plc 1989; Stratton Investment Trust 1986 Chm. *Other Activities:* Rhodes Trustee (1970-), Chm (1987-); Receiver-General Duchy of Cornwall (1974-).

BARING, Nicholas Hugo; Non-Executive Chairman, Commercial Union plc. *Biog: b.* 2 January 1934. *Nation-*

ality: British. *m.* 1972, Diana; 3 s. *Educ:* Eton; Cambridge (BA Classics and History). *Directorships:* Baring Brothers & Co Limited 1963-86 Managing Director; Barings plc 1986-89 Deputy Chairman; F&C Germany Investment Trust plc 1990; PosTel Investment Management Limited 1990; Swaziland Settlement Limited 1963. *Other Activities:* Member of Council, Baring Foundation; Trustee, National Gallery. *Professional Organisations:* Chairman, City Capital Markets Committee 1984-87. *Clubs:* Brooks's. *Recreations:* Gardening, Tennis, Music.

BARING, Oliver Alexander Guy; Director, S G Warburg Ackroyd Rowe & Pitman Mullins Securities.

BARING, Peter; Chairman, Barings plc, since 1989. *Directorships:* Provident Mutual Life Assurance Assoc 1969 (Deputy Chm non-exec); Inchcape plc 1978 (non-exec).

BARKER, A M; Director, County NatWest Securities Limited.

BARKER, Alan; Partner, Linklaters & Paines.

BARKER, Andrew Charles; Joint Vice Chairman, Foreign & Colonial Management Ltd, since 1987; The North American Investments of the F&C Group. *Career:* Cassel & Co, Stockbrokers 1969-70; Foreign & Colonial Management 1970-; Dir 1973-. *Biog: b.* 19 March 1945. *Nationality:* British. *m.* 1970, Janeke (née Kaas); 2 s; 1 d. *Educ:* Leighton Park School, Reading; St Edmund Hall, Oxford (MA). *Directorships:* Bankers Investment Trust 1979 (non-exec) Chm; F&C Smaller Companies plc 1977 (exec); F&C Enterprise Trust 1981 (exec); River & Mercantile American Capital & Income Trust 1988. *Professional Organisations:* ASIA. *Clubs:* City, Vincent's, Royal Wimbledon Golf Club, Richmond Rugby Football Club, Ends of the Earth. *Recreations:* Golf, Shooting.

BARKER, B; Treasurer, Ladbroke Group plc.

BARKER, Bridget Caroline; Partner, Macfarlanes, since 1988; Corporate Finance, Financial Services and Offshore Fund Work. *Biog: b.* 7 March 1958. *Educ:* Haberdashers'; Monmouth School for Girls; University of Southampton (LLB). *Other Activities:* City of London Solicitors' Company. *Professional Organisations:* The Law Society; IBA.

BARKER, Colin; Chairman, British Technology Group, since 1984. *Career:* London Co-operative Society, Dep Chief Exec 1960-63; Ford Motor Co Ltd, Dir of Fin 1963-67; Blue Circle Group, Dir of Fin 1967-70; Standard Telephone & Cables Ltd, Dir of Fin 1970-79; International Telephone & Telegraph Group Gen Mgr 1979-80; British Steel MD, Finance 1980-83. *Biog: b.* 20 October 1926. *Nationality:* British. *m.* 1951, Beryl (née

Parker); 3 s; 1 d. *Educ:* Hull Grammar School; Hull University (BCom). *Directorships:* CIN Ltd 1986 Chm; British Investment Trust 1986 Chm; British Coal 1985 (non-exec); Reed International 1983 (non-exec); Edinburgh Fund Managers 1989 (non-exec); Globe Investment trust 1990 Chm; MCD (UK) Ltd 1990 Chm. *Other Activities:* FRSA. *Professional Organisations:* CBIM. *Recreations:* Golf, Watching Rugby.

BARKER, David Breton; Partner, Simmons & Simmons.

BARKER, J P; Partner, Slater Heelis.

BARKER, K L; Managing Director, Johnson Fry plc, since 1990. *Career:* Various 1970-79; Hacker Young CA, Manager 1979-81; Deloitte Haskins & Sells, Senior Manager, Small Business Unit 1981-85; Johnson Fry 1985-; Finance Director; M & A Corporate Finance; Financial Planning & Investment CEO; Managing Director. *Biog: b.* 30 June 1954. *Nationality:* British; 2 d. *Educ:* Edmonton County Grammar. *Directorships:* Jersey General Group Holdings Ltd 1989 (non-exec); LIT Holdings plc 1989 (exec); Molynx Holdings plc 1987-89 (non-exec). *Professional Organisations:* ATII. *Publications:* Joint Editor, Check Your Tax, 1987. *Clubs:* Champneys, Arsenal FC. *Recreations:* Tennis, Swimming.

BARKER, Nicholas; Assistant Director, Markets Policy, NASDAQ International, since 1989; General Regulatory Policy and Institutional Investments. *Career:* IFF Research Ltd 1983-84; Mitsui-OSK Lines Ltd 1984-85; HM Treasury 1985-89. *Biog: b.* 28 August 1961. *Nationality:* British. *Educ:* University College School; Christ Church, Oxford (BA, MA). *Clubs:* United Oxford and Cambridge University.

BARKER, P G; Director, York Trust Group plc.

BARKER, R E J; Secretary, Frank Fehr & Co Ltd.

BARKER, R J E; Director of Administration, Allen & Overy, since 1988; Personnel/Human Resources, IT, Facilities. *Career:* MSL, Consultant 1971-77; Grindlays Bank Group, Group Appointments Manager 1977-81; Charterhouse Group, Personnel Director 1981-86; Security Pacific/Hoare Govett, Personnel Director 1986-88. *Biog: b.* 27 November 1942. *Nationality:* English. *m.* 1971, Helen; 1 s; 1 d. *Educ:* Birkenhead School, Cheshire; University of Warwick (BA Hons Econometrics). *Directorships:* Charterhouse Group 1982-86 (exec); Charterhouse Pensions 1986-86 (exec) Chm; RNVR Officers' Association 1976 (exec) Chm; LHRG 1989 (exec). *Other Activities:* Member, London Human Resource Group. *Professional Organisations:* Fellow, Institute of Personnel Management; Fellow, British Institute of Management. *Clubs:* Naval Club (Chairman).

BARKER, Timothy Gwynne; Vice Chairman, Kleinwort Benson Ltd, since 1989; Corporate Finance, Head of Division. *Career:* Kleinwort Benson Ltd 1963-; The Panel on Take-overs & Mergers (Secondment), Dir Gen 1984-85; Council for The Securities Industry (Secondment), Dir Gen 1984-85. *Biog: b.* 8 April 1940. *m.* 1964, Philippa Rachel Mary (née Thursby-Pelham); 1 s; 1 d. *Educ:* Eton College; McGill University, Montreal; Jesus College, Cambridge. *Directorships:* Kleinwort Benson Group plc 1988 (exec).

BARKER BENNETT, Charles Robert; Deputy General Manager (Overseas), General Accident Fire & Life Assurance Corp plc, since 1990. *Career:* General Accident, Mgr, India 1966-72; Asst Gen Mgr, South Africa 1975-78; Dep Mgr (UK) 1979-83; Asst Gen Mgr (Overseas) 1984-90; Dep Gen Mgr (Overseas) 1990-. *Biog: b.* 19 June 1935. *m.* 1965, Barbara Ray (née Turner); 1 s; 2 d. *Educ:* Rugby School. *Clubs:* Bombay Gymkhana, Rand (Johannesburg). *Recreations:* Golf, Bridge.

BARKLEY, R; Senior Manager, Banca Commerciale Italiana.

BARKSHIRE, Robert Renny St John; CBE, TD, JP, DL; *Career:* Cater Ryder 1955-72; Joint MD 1963-72; Mercantile House Holdings plc, Chm 1972-87; International Commodities Clearing House Ltd, Chm 1986-90. *Directorships:* LIFFE 1982-; ICCH 1986 Chm; Savills plc 1988 (non-exec); Sun Life Assurance Society plc (non-exec); Household Mortgage Corporation Group plc (non-exec); Bank Julius Baer & Co Ltd (non-exec).

BARLOW, David Ian Gunn; Technology Director, County NatWest Securities Limited, since 1990; Operational Technology into CNWS at all locations. *Career:* Wood Mackenzie & Co, Partner, Office Admin 1971-84; Wood Mackenzie & Co Ltd, Director, Technology 1984-86; Hill Samuel & Co Ltd, Director, Technology 1986-88; County NatWest Securities Ltd, Associate Director, Technology 1988-89. *Biog: b.* 10 February 1946. *Nationality:* British. *m.* 1972, Hilary Jane; 2 s. *Educ:* Inverness Royal Academy; Leith Academy. *Directorships:* Wood Mackenzie & Co Ltd 1984 (exec); County NatWest Securities Ltd 1990 (exec). *Professional Organisations:* Member, International Stock Exchange. *Clubs:* Riley Register,Lotus Cortina Register, Mercedes Owners,Dunfermline Car Club. *Recreations:* Motoring-Motor Sport & Classic Cars.

BARLOW, Frank; Managing Director & Chief Operating Officer, Pearson plc, since 1990. *Career:* Daily Times, Nigeria, Dir 1960-63; Ghana Graphic Ltd, Dir 1963-66; Barbados Advocate Ltd, MD 1966-67; Trinidad Mirror Ltd, MD 1967-69; Mirror Group Newspapers Ltd, Gen Mgr 1963-69; King & Hutchings Ltd, MD 1969-76; Westminster Press Ltd, Dir & Gen Mgr 1976-83; Chief Exec 1986-90; Financial Times Ltd, Chief Exec 1983-90. *Biog: b.* 25 March 1930. *Nationality:* British. *m.* 1950, Patricia; 1 s; 2 d. *Directorships:* Pearson plc 1986 (exec); Financial Times Ltd 1983 (exec); Financial Times Group Ltd 1984 (exec); Area Editorial SA (Spain) 1988 (exec); Financial Post Co Ltd (Canada) 1988 (exec); Hera SA (France) 1986 (exec); Les Echos SA (France) 1988 (exec); Royal Philharmonic Orchestra Ltd 1989 (exec); The Economist Newspaper Ltd 1984 (non-exec); Business People Publications Ltd 1985 (non-exec); Elsevier (Netherlands) 1990 (exec); The Press Association Ltd 1986 (non-exec). *Recreations:* Golf, Angling, Fell-Walking.

BARLOW, James; Partner, Clifford Chance, since 1980; Unit Trusts, Funds & Financial Regulation. *Biog: b.* 23 December 1943. *Nationality:* British. *Educ:* Mill Hill School; University of Nottingham (LLB). *Professional Organisations:* Solicitor; Associate Member, Institute of Taxation.

BARLOW, P F; Director, Charlton Seal Schaverien Limited.

BARLOW, Steven; Divisional Director, Royal Trust Bank.

BARLOWSKI, T; General Manager and Managing Director, Bank Handlowy w Warszawie.

BARNARD, David; Partner, Linklaters & Paines.

BARNARD, I S; Partner, Field Fisher Waterhouse.

BARNARD, S G; Partner, Herbert Smith.

BARNEBY, John Henry; Joint Managing Director, C Czarnikow Ltd, since 1984; East Asia. *Biog: b.* 29 July 1949. *Nationality:* British. *m.* 1978, Alison (née Donger); 1 s; 2 d. *Educ:* Radley College; Christ Church, Oxford (MA). *Directorships:* Czarnikow Holdings Ltd 1989 (exec).

BARNES, Adrian Francis Patrick; Remembrancer, Corporation of London.

BARNES, C A; Non-Executive Director, City Merchants Bank Ltd.

BARNES, Miss C J C; Director, Barclays de Zoete Wedd Securities Ltd.

BARNES, David; Finance Director, Cheltenham and Gloucester Building Society, since 1989; Fin & Man Accounting, Treasury, Internal Audit, Property. *Career:* Girling Bremsen GmbH, Asst to Finance Dir 1978-81; Cummins Engine Co Ltd, Mgr, International Treasury 1981-85; Abbey National Building Society, Asst Treasurer (Medium Term Funding & Investment Portfolio)

1985-88. *Biog: b.* 6 February 1949. *Nationality:* British. *m.* 1972, Lynn (née Johnston). *Educ:* Bedford School; Leeds University (BA); London School of Economics (MSc Intl Relations); Warwick University (MSc). *Professional Organisations:* ACMA. *Recreations:* Karate, Horse-Riding.

BARNES, David Michael Sedgley; Partner, Lawrence Graham, since 1990; Commercial Property. *Career:* Alsop Stevens, Articled Clerk 1975-77; Assistant Solicitor 1977-85; Partner 1985-87; Lawrence Graham, Assistant Solicitor 1987-90. *Biog: b.* 1952. *Nationality:* British. *m.* 1989, Helen. *Educ:* University College, Oxford (MA Law). *Professional Organisations:* Law Society.

BARNES, John Hampton; Partner, The Barnes Partnership, since 1987; Executive Search. *Career:* J P Morgan & Co, Incorporated VP 1962-78; Korn/Ferry International (New York), Partner 1978-82; (London) MD, European Financial Services Div 1982-87. *Biog: b.* 15 May 1938. *Nationality:* American. *m.* 1960, Laura (née Levine); 1 s; 2 d. *Educ:* Westminster School, Connecticut; Columbia University (BA). *Clubs:* Buck's, Mark's, Royal Automobile, Philadelphia.

BARNES, Judith; Partner, Jaques & Lewis.

BARNES, Oliver; Partner, Travers Smith Braithwaite, since 1980; Company Law. *Biog: b.* 13 November 1950. *Nationality:* British. *Educ:* Eton College; Trinity Hall, Cambridge (BA Hons). *Other Activities:* City of London Solicitors' Company. *Professional Organisations:* Member, International Bar Association. *Clubs:* MCC. *Recreations:* Skiing.

BARNES, Roger Anthony; Assistant Director, Bank of England, since 1986; Head of Banking Supervision Division. *Career:* Bank of England, Various 1961-. *Biog: b.* 29 May 1937. *m.* 1961, Tessa Margaret (née Soundy); 2 s; 2 d. *Educ:* Malvern College; St John's College, Oxford (BA). *Recreations:* Golf, Folk Dancing.

BARNES, S W S; Director, S G Warburg & Co Ltd.

BARNES, Simon S; Managing Director, Alexander Howden Reinsurance Brokers Limited.

BARNES, Stephen Ronald; Managing Director, Schlesinger Asset Finance Limited, since 1990; Control Growth & Profitability. *Career:* Lombard North Central, Manager 1974-88; Soc Gen Lease, Area Manager 1988-90. *Biog: b.* 29 August 1951. *Nationality:* British. *m.* 1986, Nicola (née Jones). *Educ:* Newport High School. *Clubs:* Newport Golf Club. *Recreations:* Rugby, Skiing, Golf.

BARNES, Timothy John Osmond; Assistant General Manager, Jordan International Bank plc, since 1988;

Credit. *Career:* RMA, Sandhurst 1955-57; Regular Army Officer UK, Cyprus & Germany, retiring as Temporary Captain 1957-62; J Henry Schroder Wagg & Company Limited, Trainee, Merchant Banking Depts, latterly Manager's Asst 1962-65; Gray Dawes & Company Limited, Foreign Exchange Section 1965-67; Barclays Bank International Limited 1967-74; London 1967; Relief Manager (Kenya) 1968-71; Manager, Masaka Branch, Uganda 1971-72; Asst to Planning Adviser & Group Oil Adviser, UK 1972-73; International Officer, UK Business Development 1973-74; Refson Group, London, Asst Mgr, PS Refson & Co Ltd 1974-75; City Merchants Limited, Manager, Business Development & Assessment Director 1975-77; Italian International Bank Ltd, Export Finance Sector 1978-79; Khalij Commercial Bank Ltd, Abu Dhabi, UAE, Asst Mgr, Al-Ain Branc h 1979-82; Al Saudi Banque, London, Manager for UK Business Development 1982-84; Division Manager, International Credits Division 1982-88. *Biog: b.* 13 August 1937. *Nationality:* British. *m.* 1981, Dinah (née Burges); 2 s; 1 d. *Educ:* Haileybury & Imperial Service College, Hertford; RMA, Sandhurst; Cranfield School of Managemnet (MBA Finance, International Business and French). *Other Activities:* Chairman, Trade Finance Committee of Association of British Consortium Banks. *Professional Organisations:* Associate, Chartered Institute of Bankers. *Recreations:* Theatre, Swimming, Travel.

BARNES, William D; Partner, Touche Ross & Co, since 1986; Advising Partnerships. *Career:* Spicer & Pegler (now Touche Ross) 1977; Partner 1984. *Biog: b.* 15 October 1955. *Nationality:* British. *Educ:* Woodbridge School; Bristol University (BSc). *Other Activities:* Worshipful Company of Woolmen. *Professional Organisations:* ACA.

BARNETT, Geoffrey Grant Fulton; Director, Baring Brothers & Co Limited, since 1979; Corporate Finance. *Career:* Baring Brothers Asia Ltd, MD 1979-83. *Biog: b.* 9 March 1943. *Nationality:* British. *m.* 1968, Fiona (née Milligan); 2 s; 2 d. *Educ:* Winchester College; Clare College, Cambridge. *Directorships:* Panel on Takeovers & Mergers 1989-91 Director General.

BARNETT, J F; Director, Gibbs, Hartley, Cooper Ltd.

BARNETT, M J N; Director, Kleinwort Benson Limited.

BARNETT, P C; Director, London International Financial Futures Exchange Limited.

BARNETT, Ulric David; Partner, Cazenove & Co, since 1972. *Career:* Cazenove & Co 1965-. *Other Activities:* Goldsmiths Company (Liveryman), Reeds School (Governor). *Clubs:* MCC, City University.

BARNFIELD, M A; Director, Lowndes Lambert Group Holdings Limited.

BARON, Rupert Nigel Kendall; Associate Director, Albert E Sharp & Co, since 1990; Private Client Fund Management. *Career:* Heseltine Moss & Co 1983-85; E B Savory Milln & Co 1985-87; Parrish Stockbrokers, Director 1987-90. *Biog: b.* 18 April 1961. *Nationality:* British. *Educ:* Kings School, Canterbury; School of Business Studies (BA Hons Economics). *Professional Organisations:* Member, International Stock Exchange. *Clubs:* Member of 4th Battalion Royal Green Jackets.

BARR, Brian; Director, Royal Trust Bank.

BARR, I S; Group Financial Controller, Cookson Group.

BARR, John Malcolm; CBE; Group Executive Chairman, Barr & Wallace Arnold Trust plc, since 1988. *Career:* Royal Navy Sub-Lt RNVR 1944-48; Wallace Arnold Tours (Devon) Ltd, General Mgr 1952-; Wallace Arnold Tours Ltd, Asst General Mgr; Barr & Wallace Arnold Trust Ltd, Chm & Group Managing Dir 1962-88; Hickson International plc, Non-Exec Dir 1971-; Leeds Permanent Building Society, Dir Non-Exec 1970-89; Pres 1989-. *Biog: b.* 23 December 1926. *Nationality:* British. *m.* 1955, Elaine Mary (née Rhodes); 2 d. *Educ:* Shrewsbury School; Clare College, Cambridge (MA,LLM). *Directorships:* Leeds Permanent Building Society 1970 Chm; Hickson International plc 1971 (non-exec); British Equestrian Promotions Ltd (non-exec). *Other Activities:* President, City of Leeds YMCA. *Professional Organisations:* Barrister-at-Law, Inner Temple; British Show Jumping Association. *Clubs:* Royal Ocean Racing Club, Climbers Club. *Recreations:* Drama, Literature, Music, Show Jumping.

BARRATT, Eric George; Senior Partner, MacIntyre Hudson, since 1982; General Practitioner. *Career:* Arthur Andersen & Co, Partner 1979-82; Tansley Witt & Co, Partner 1966-79; Manager 1962-66; R M Blaikie & Co, Articled Clerk 1954-62. *Biog: b.* 15 April 1938. *Nationality:* British. *Educ:* Oriel College, Oxford (MA). *Directorships:* Esthwaite Estates Limited 1975 (non-exec); S Brannan & Sons Limited 1982 (non-exec); Heathfield School Limited 1986 (non-exec); Land Estates & Property Limited 1989 (non-exec); MacIntyre Investments Limited 1987 (non-exec); Automotive Products plc 1974-85 (non-exec); Milton Keynes Development Corp 1978-86 (non-exec); Montague Boston Investment Trust plc 1980-85 (non-exec); Commission for the New Towns 1986-90 (non-exec). *Other Activities:* Treasurer, Oriel College, Oxford; Vice-Chairman, Buckinghamshire County Council 1982-86. *Professional Organisations:* FCA. *Clubs:* Atheneaum, Carlton, City of London. *Recreations:* Racing, Shooting, Farming.

BARRATT, W M; Director, Steel Burrill Jones Group plc.

BARRETT, David R; Partner, Theodore Goddard, since 1989; Commercial and Technology Law, Intellectual Property, Computer & Telecommunication Law. *Career:* IBM United Kingdom Limited, Legal Adviser 1979-85; IBM Europe SA (Paris), Senior Attorney 1985-88; IBM United Kingdom Limited, Senior Legal Adviser 1988-89; Theodore Goddard, Consultant 1989-. *Biog: b.* 30 April 1953. *Nationality:* British. *m.* 1984, Anne (née Whittle); 1 d. *Educ:* Kings School, Tynemouth; Gonville & Caius College, Cambridge (MA, LLM); University of Michigan (LLM). *Other Activities:* Computer Law Association; International Bar Association; (Telecommunication and Computer/Technology Committees). *Professional Organisations:* Law Society. *Clubs:* Royal Overseas League. *Recreations:* Sailing, Theatre, Travel.

• **BARRETT, Elizabeth Ann;** Partner, Slaughter and May, since 1989; Litigation. *Career:* Oswald Hickson Collier & Co, Articled Clerk 1979-81; Asst Solicitor 1981; Peter Carter-Ruck & Partners, Ptnr 1982-86; Slaughter and May, Asst Solicitor 1986-89. *Biog: b.* 23 November 1956. *Nationality:* British. *m.* 1980, Geoffrey; 1 s; 1 d. *Educ:* Ealing Grammar School for Girls; Kings Lynn High School; University College, London University (LLB Hons). *Professional Organisations:* The Law Society.

BARRETT, G S; Partner, Cameron Markby Hewitt.

BARRETT, Michael J; Chief Executive Officer, Alexander Stenhouse Europe Ltd, Alexander & Alexander Europe plc.

BARRINGTON, Charles P; Managing Director, Banking, Brown, Shipley & Co Limited, since 1989; Corporate and Private Banking. *Career:* Touche Ross & Co 1965-70; Galbraith Wrighton Ltd 1970-72; First National Bank of Boston, Loan Officer 1972-73; Galbraith Wrighton Ltd, Director 1973-78; Bulkships Limited, Executive Director 1978-80; Grindlays Bank, Head of Corporate Banking, Head of Shipping 1980-85; Salomon Brothers International Ltd, Vice President 1985-88; Bankers Trust, Vice President 1988-89; Brown, Shipley & Co Limited, Managing Director, Banking 1989-. *Biog: b.* 5 October 1946. *Nationality:* British. *m.* 1969, Ann (née Foster); 1 s. *Educ:* Wellington College. *Directorships:* Brown, Shipley & Co Limited 1989 (exec). *Other Activities:* TSA Capital Committee (Co-opted Member). *Professional Organisations:* FCA (qualified 1970). *Clubs:* Boodles. *Recreations:* Sailing.

BARRON, D D; Chairman, Ford Motor Credit Company.

BARRON, Sir Donald (James); Chairman, Joseph Rowntree Foundation, since 1981. *Career:* Rowntree Mackintosh Ltd 1952; Dir 1961; Vice-Chm 1965; Chm 1966-81; Dir 1972; Vice-Chm 1981-82; Chm 1982-87;

Midland Bank plc, Dep Chm, CLCB 1983-85; Cttee of London and Scottish Bankers, Chm 1985-87; Investors in Industry Gp plc, Director 1980-; Canada Life Assurance Co of GB Ltd 1980-; Canada Life Unit Trust Managers Ltd 1980-; Canada Life Assurance Co, Toronto 1980-; Clydesdale Bank 1986-87. *Biog: b.* 17 March 1921. *m.* 1956, Gillian Mary; 3 s; 2 d. *Educ:* George Heriot's School, Edinburgh; Edinburgh Univ (BCom). *Other Activities:* Mem, Inst Chartered Accountants of Scotland; Mem, Bd of Banking Supervision, 1987-; Dir, BIM Foundation, 1977-80; Mem, Council, BIM, 1978-80; Trustee, Joseph Rowntree Memorial Trust, 1966-73; 1975-; Chm 1981-; Treasurer, 1966-72; Pro-Chancellor, 1982-; York Univ; Member, Council of CBI, 1966-81; Chm, CBI Education Foundation, 1981-85; SSRC, 1971-72; UGC, 1972-81; Council, PSI, 1978-85; Council, Inst of Chartered Accountants of Scotland, 1980-81; NEDC, 1983-85; Governor, London Business Sch, 1982-88; DL N Yorks (formerly WR Yorks and City of York), 1971; Hon doctorates: Loughborough, 1982; Heriot-Watt, 1983; CNAA, 1983; Edinburgh, 1984; Nottingham, 1985; York, 1986. *Clubs:* Athenium, Yorkshire (York). *Recreations:* Golf, Tennis, Gardening, Travelling.

BARRON, Edward William; General Manager, National Westminster Bank plc, since 1989; Subsidiary & Associated Businesses; UK Financial Services. *Career:* National Westminster Bank (Birmingham), Area Director 1981-84; Dep Regional Director, North Region 1984-87; Dep Gen Mgr, Domestic Banking Div 1987-88. *Biog: b.* 19 March 1933. *Nationality:* British. *m.* 1956, Norma (née Davies); 2 s. *Educ:* Grammar School. *Directorships:* Lombard North Central plc 1989 (exec); Ulster Bank Ltd 1989 (exec); ICCH 1989 (non-exec); Isle of Man Bank Ltd 1989 (exec). *Professional Organisations:* ACIB. *Recreations:* Golf, Music, Walking.

BARRON, Michael; Partner, Dickson Minto.

BARROW, Captain M E; DSO, RN; Clerk, Haberdashers' Company.

BARROW, Martin; City Reporter, The Times.

BARROW, R; General Manager, Halifax Building Society, since 1989; IT and Money Transmission. *Career:* Halifax Building Society, IT Division. *Biog: b.* 14 December 1945. *Nationality:* British. *m.* 1971, Jill; 2 s. *Educ:* Bristol University (BSc Hons Physics). *Directorships:* Link 1989 (non-exec); BDCS 1989 (non-exec); EFTPOS UK 1987 (non-exec).

BARROWMAN, Andrew Kenneth; Administration & Finance Director, Private Asset Management Ltd, since 1988; Accounting & Finance, Computer & Administration Services. *Career:* Peat Marwick Mitchell & Co, Snr Mgr 1970-84; Hapag-Lloyd (UK) Holdings Ltd, Group Financial Dir & Co Sec 1984-88. *Biog: b.* 31

December 1947. *Nationality:* British. *m.* 1976, Jennifer (née Dorrington); 2 s. *Educ:* Seaford College, Sussex; University College, Dublin (BComm Hons 1st). *Directorships:* Monlostan Nominees Limited 1988 (exec); Fleming Private Asset Management Ltd 1988 (exec); Fleming Asset Management Services Ltd 1988 (exec); Fleming Private Nominees Ltd 1989 (exec); Fleming Personal Portfolio Management Ltd 1989 (exec); Fleming International Portfolio Management Ltd 1989 (exec); Fleming Private Fund Management Ltd., 1989 (exec). *Professional Organisations:* FCA, (Fellow, Institute of Chartered Accountants in England and Wales. *Clubs:* Epsom Golf Club. *Recreations:* Golf.

BARROWS, David Anthony; Deputy General Manager, Credit Agricole, since 1989; Administration/ Operations. *Career:* First National Bank in Dallas, Vice-President, Operations 1970-80; Kreditanstalt-Bankverein, Asst General Manager, Administration 1980-85; Caisse National de Credit Agricole, Asst General Manager, Admin 1985-89. *Biog: b.* 6 September 1944. *Nationality:* British. *m.* 1968, Lynsaye; 1 s; 1 d. *Educ:* Sir Walter St Johns (Sinjuns). *Directorships:* CAFCO 1988 (exec). *Other Activities:* Committee Member, Foreign Banks Association; Overseas Bankers Club. *Clubs:* Banstead Downs Golf Club. *Recreations:* Scouting, Social Work, Golf, Squash, Watching Cricket.

BARRY, Colin Campbell; Managing Partner, Overton Shirley & Barry, since 1976; International Search & Selection. *Career:* Dorland Recruitment Ltd, Dir, Client Services 1970-75; Foster Turner & Benson, Head, Recruitment Div 1975-76. *Biog: b.* 2 February 1936. *Nationality:* British. *m.* 1967, Caroline (née Bevan); 1 s; 1 d. *Educ:* Marlborough College. *Directorships:* Overton Shirley & Barry Ltd 1980 (exec). *Other Activities:* Liveryman of Broderers. *Clubs:* City of London, Naval & Military, Royal Lymington Yacht Club. *Recreations:* Sailing, Skiing, Sub Aqua.

BARRY, David John; Director, J H Rayner (Mincing Lane) Ltd.

BARRY, Dr David Walter; Vice President, Wellcome plc, since 1989; Research, Development & Medical. *Career:* Rockefeller Foundation Yale Arbovirus Research Unit, Part-time Research Associate 1967-69; Yale-New Haven Hospital, Medical Intern 1969-70; Medical Resident 1970-72; US Public Health Service, Commissioned Officer, Senior Surgeon 1972-77; Bureau of Biologics, FDA, Staff Associate, Viral Pathogenesis Branch, Division of Virology 1972-73; Director, General Virology Branch 1973-77; Acting Deputy Director 1973-77; Director, Influenza Vaccine Task Force 1976-77; Burroughs Wellcome Co, Medical Division, Head, Anti-Infectives Section, Dept of Clinical Investigation 1977-78; Head, Dept of Clinical Investigation 1978-85; Head, Dept of Virology, The Wellcome Research Laboratories 1983-89; Director, Division of

Clinical Investigation 1985-86; Vice President of Research, The Wellcome Research Laboratories 1986-89; Burroughs Wellcome Fund, Board of Directors 1986-; Burroughs Wellcome Co, Vice President of Research, Development and Medical, The Wellcome Research Laboratories 1989-; Board of Directors 1989-; The Wellcome Foundation, Board of Directors 1989-. *Biog:* b. 19 July 1943. *Nationality:* American. *Educ:* Yale College (BA magna cum laude); Sorbonne, Paris; Yale University School of Medicine (MD). *Other Activities:* Visiting Fellow (Infectious Diseases), University of Maryland, 1975-76; Junior Consultant (Infectious Diseases), National Naval Medical Center, 1975; Temporary Consultant (Yellow Fever), World Health Organisation, 1975; Attending Physician (Infectious Diseases), Laboratory of Clinical Investigation, NIAID, NIH, 1976; Adjunct Professor of Medicine, Duke University School of Medicine, 1977-; Advisor, Infectious Disease Branch, NIAID, NIH, 1973-77; Armed Forces Epidemiologic Board, 1977; Viral & Rickettsial Vaccine Efficacy Review Panel for the FDA, 1973-77; Committee on Public-Private Sector Relations in Vaccine Innovation, Institute of Medicine, National Academy of Sciences, 1983; National Institutes of Health AIDS Task Force, 1986; National Institutes of Health AIDS Program Advisory Committee, 1988; Workshop on Vaccine Supply and Innovation, Institute of Medicine, National Academy of Sciences, 1986; Institute of Medicine, National Academy of Sciences, Conference on Promoting Drug Development Against AIDS and HIV Infection, 1987; Institute of Medicine Roundtable on Drugs and Vaccines Against AIDS, 1989; Deans Council for the Yale School of Medicine, 1989; Wellcome Scientist Lecturer, 1981. *Professional Organisations:* Fellow, Infectious Diseases Society of America; Fellow, American College of Physicians; Member of Various Medical Societies; Honorary Member, Venezuelan Society of Internal Medicine, 1976; FDA Group Award of Merit, 1977; Public Health Service Meritorious Service Medal, 1977. *Publications:* Numerous Medical Papers, Articles, etc.

BARRY, P A; Director, Chartered Trust plc. *Biog: Nationality:* British. *Educ:* Harvard Business School (PMD). *Directorships:* Chartered Trust plc (exec); ACL Ltd (non-exec); Chartered Insurance Services Ltd (non-exec). *Other Activities:* Member of Senate, Institute of Chartered Accountants in England & Wales; Member, Commercial Affairs Committee, Finance Houses Association. *Professional Organisations:* FCA.

BARRY, Robert; Director, Samuel Montagu & Co Limited.

BARSH, A; Partner, Nabarro Nathanson.

BARSTOW, M James; Director, John Govett & Co Ltd, since 1990; UK Equities, Investment Management. *Career:* Peat Marwick Mitchell Ltd, Articled Clerk,

Senior 1973-81; John Govett & Co Ltd, Investment Manager 1981-88; Director of Pension Fund Co 1988-. *Biog:* b. 7 January 1950. *Nationality:* British. *Educ:* Winchester College; Magdalene College, Cambridge (MA Hons). *Directorships:* John Govett & Co Ltd 1990 (exec). *Professional Organisations:* FCA. *Recreations:* Tennis, Fishing, Shooting.

BARTER, Ian Stuart; Fellow & First Bursar, King's College Cambridge, since 1989. *Career:* Practised at the Bar 1958-60; Cambridge University, Taught Law 1957-63; Cow & Gate Ltd, Director; Chairman 1968-76; Unigate plc, Director 1976-89; Unigate International Division, Chairman 1976-89. *Biog:* b. 9 March 1933. *Nationality:* British. *m.* 1960, Gillian Frances (née Ide); 2 s; 1 d. *Educ:* Cranleigh; Cambridge University (MA, LLB). *Directorships:* International Council of Infant Food Industries 1975-80 (exec) President. *Other Activities:* Governor, Monkton Combe School, Bath. *Professional Organisations:* Barrister-at-Law, Gray's Inn.

BARTHELEMY, Michel; Credit Manager, Credit Lyonnais (London). *Biog:* b. 12 June 1946. *Nationality:* French; 1 s; 1 d. *Educ:* Paris University (Economics). *Directorships:* CLEF 1988 (non-exec).

BARTINGTON, J; Director, Lowndes Lambert Group Ltd, since 1982; Professional Indemnity/Errors & Omissions/ Directors & Officers Liability. *Career:* Lambert Brothers Insurance Ltd 1952; Lowndes Lamberts Hammond, Director 1974; Architects & Professional Indemnity Agencies Ltd, Director 1974; Managing Director 1975; Lowndes Lambert International Ltd, Director 1976; Lowndes Lambert Group, Director 1982; APIA, Chairman 1985; RIBA Insurance Agency Ltd, Managing Director 1986. *Biog:* b. 15 July 1936. *Nationality:* British. *m.* Natalie; 3 s; 3 d. *Directorships:* Lowndes Lambert Group Ltd; Architects & Professional Indemnity Agencies Ltd Chairman; RIBA Insurance Agency Ltd Managing Director. *Other Activities:* Underwriting Member of Lloyds. *Recreations:* Tottenham Hotspur FC.

BARTLAM, T H; Non-Executive Director, Fenchurch Insurance Group Limited.

BARTLETT, Bernard James; Partner, Berwin Leighton, since 1972; Head of Company and Commercial Department. *Biog:* b. 10 June 1941. *Nationality:* British. *m.* 1967, Jenny (née Strang); 2 d. *Educ:* Leighton Park School. *Professional Organisations:* The Law Society. *Clubs:* Wentworth. *Recreations:* Golf, Tennis, Skiing.

BARTLETT, Peter Yorke; Director, County NatWest WoodMac, since 1988; Head of UK Equity Sales into Europe and Middle East. *Career:* Strauss Turnbull & Co UK Equity Salesman 1965-83; Sheppards UK Equity Salesman 1983-85; W I Carr (UK) Ltd Dir 1985-87. *Biog:* b. 18 April 1946. *National-*

ity: British. *m.* 1973, Jennifer Elizabeth (née Horne); 1 s; 1 d. *Educ:* Wycliffe College, Glos. *Professional Organisations:* Member, Fruiterers Livery Co. *Clubs:* RAC, Wig & Pen, Stock Exchange Sailing Club, Shark Angling Club of Great Britain. *Recreations:* Sailing, Tennis.

BARTLETT, T J; Director, Billinton-Enthoven Metals Ltd.

BARTMAN, Flavio C; Director, Merrill Lynch International, since 1989; Head of Investors' Strategies Group. *Career:* Eletrobras (Rio de Janeiro), Special Assistant to the President 1975-76; Universidade Estadual de Campinas (S Paulo), Professor of Statistics 1982-85; Columbia University (N York), Adjunct Professor of Statistics 1985-86; Morgan Guaranty Trust Company of NY, Assistant Treasurer, Assistant Vice President 1986-88; Merrill Lynch International (London), Associate Director, Director 1988-. *Biog: b.* 8 July 1952. *Nationality:* Brazilian. *m.* 1985, Katherine Chan. *Educ:* ITA (BSc Mech Eng); Princeton University (MA, PhD). *Professional Organisations:* Bernoulli Society.

BARTON, Eric Anthony; Director, Investors in Industry plc, since 1986. *Career:* ICFC (West Midlands, Leeds, Nottingham) Controller 1968-74; ICFC Corporate Finance Ltd Mgr 1974-83; Investors in Industry plc Mgr subsequently Director, City Office 1983-90. *Biog: b.* 18 April 1945. *Nationality:* British. *m.* 1970, Gillian Margaret (née Strain); 1 s; 1 d. *Educ:* St Bede's College, Manchester; St Andrews University (MA Hons). *Directorships:* 3i plc 1986 (exec); Nestor BNA plc 1986-87 (non-exec); Moore Group Ltd 1987-90 (non-exec); Associated Fresh Foods Ltd 1989 (non-exec); Chartprint Ltd 1990 (non-exec); Cymric Hotel Co Ltd 1990 (non-exec); Toplis & Harding Ltd 1990 (non-exec). *Recreations:* Walking, Gardening, Literature.

BARTON, John; Group Chief Executive, Jardine Insurance Brokers Group.

BARTON, K; Partner, Pensions (St Albans), Bacon & Woodrow.

BARTON, N; Director, County NatWest Ltd, since 1989; International Merger & Acquisitions (Food & Drink Industry). *Biog: b.* 12 April 1955. *Nationality:* British. *m.* 1977, Deborah; 1 s; 1 d. *Educ:* University College, London (BSc Econ Hons). *Recreations:* Skiing, Travel.

BARTON, Roger Nigel; Managing Director, Business Development, LIFFE, since 1990; Market, Product & Strategic Development. *Career:* British Rail, Operational Research Analyst 1975-77; Tube Investments, Systems Consultant 1977-80; Chicago Bridge & Iron, Systems Manager (Europe, Africa, Middle East) 1980-82; Price Waterhouse, Management Consultant 1982-

86; LIFFE 1986-. *Biog: b.* 12 June 1954. *Nationality:* British. *m.* 1983, Dianne (née Cotton); 1 s; 1 d. *Educ:* Forest School; St John's College, Cambridge (MA Hons 1st); Brunel University (MSc). *Directorships:* LIFFE Development Ltd 1989 (exec). *Professional Organisations:* Member, Chartered Institute of Management Accountants. *Recreations:* Music, Sport.

BARTON, S J; Partner, Herbert Smith, since 1978. *Career:* Herbert Smith, Articled Clerk 1969-71; Assistant Solicitor 1971-78. *Biog: b.* 4 May 1947. *Nationality:* British. *m.* 1974, Catherine Monica Lloyd (née Buttery); 2 d. *Educ:* Birkenhead School; Jesus College, Cambridge (MA). *Other Activities:* Insolvency Law Sub-Committee of City of London Law Society. *Professional Organisations:* Licensed Insolvency Practitioner; Member of Law Society, City of London Law Society, Insolvency Lawyer's Association; International Bar Association; United Kingdom Oil Lawyers Group; Society for Computers & Law. *Publications:* Contributing Editor, Butterworths Company Law Service, 1985-. *Clubs:* Barbican Health & Fitness Centre. *Recreations:* Reading, Photography, Boating, Gardening, Walking.

BARTOS, James M; European Counsel, Shearman & Sterling, since 1987. *Educ:* Yale College (BA); Columbia Law School (JD). *Professional Organisations:* Member, International Bar Association; Member, American Bar Association; Member, Association of the Bar of the City of New York.

BASHAM, B; Managing Director, Broad Street Associates PR Ltd.

BASHER, R E; Chairman & Chief Executive Officer, Provincial Bank plc, since 1984. *Career:* First National Finance Corporation, New Business Director 1960-71; Western Trust & Savings, New Business Director 1971-72; London Scottish Finance, Assistant Managing Director 1972-76; Security Pacific Credit, CEO & Managing Director 1976-79; Security De Espana SA, Chairman & CEO 1979-83; Roxburghe Guarantee Corporation Ltd, Managing Director 1983-84. *Biog: b.* 20 March 1931. *Nationality:* British. *m.* 1958, Mary; 1 s; 1 d. *Educ:* BEC Grammar School. *Directorships:* Provincial Bank Group plc 1984 Chairman; British & Commonwealth Merchant Bank Group 1989 (exec); Provincial Credit Ltd 1988 Chairman; Norfolk & Suffolk Finance Ltd 1988 Chairman; Rimco Ltd 1988 Chairman; Chainbreaking Services Ltd 1987 Chairman; Compteam Ltd 1987 Chairman; Finance Industry Standards Association 1988 Chairman; B&C Banks Holdings Ltd 1989 (exec). *Other Activities:* Chairman, Finance Industry Standards Association, 1988-89. *Recreations:* Fishing, Shooting, Walking.

BASIROV, Dr Azhic; Associate, MSB Corporate Finance Limited, since 1988; M&A, Venture Capital. *Career:* The LEK Partnership, Strategy Consulting 1984-

86; Kleinwort Benson, Corporate Finance Division 1986-88. *Biog: b.* 2 May 1957. *Educ:* Imperial College, London University (BSc); Keble College, Oxford (DPhil). *Clubs:* Traveller's. *Recreations:* Skiing, Tennis, Squash, Reading.

BASS, P; Director, S G Warburg Akroyd Rowe & Pitman Mullens Securities Ltd.

BASS, Trevor Wyndham; Chairman, Trevor Bass Associates Limited, since 1989; Press Relations. *Career:* Evening News, Financial Journalist 1952-62; Daily Mirror, Assistant City Editor 1962-66; Daily Express, Assistant City Editor 1966-68; City Editor 1968-69; Shareholder Relation, Director 1969-76; Trevor Bass Associates, Managing Director 1976-90. *Biog: b.* 26 January 1930. *Nationality:* British. *m.* 1953, Eileen Joan; 2 s; 1 d. *Educ:* Beckenham Technical College. *Directorships:* Trevor Bass Associate 1976 (exec). *Other Activities:* President, Financial Advertising Golfing Society; Committee Member, Duffers Club. *Clubs:* The Addington, Ritz, Crockfords, Duffers. *Recreations:* Golf, Racing, Theatre.

BASSET, Ms J J N; Director, Grandfield Rork Collins Financial Ltd.

BASSET, Philip; Industrial Editor, The Times.

BASSIL, Dr F; Chairman & General Manager, Byblos Bank Sal.

BATCHELOR, P R; Clerk, The Worshipful Company of Glaziers.

BATEMAN, B R; Committee Member, Fidelity, Unit Trust Association.

BATEMAN, M R S; Executive Director, Allied Dunbar Assurance plc.

BATEMAN, Paul Terence; Chief Executive, Save and Prosper Group Ltd, since 1988. *Career:* Save and Prosper Group, Graduate in Secretarial Dept 1967-68; Assistant to Group Actuary 1968-73; Marketing Manager 1973-75; Group Marketing Manager 1975-80; Executive Director, Marketing 1981-88. *Biog: b.* 28 April 1946. *Nationality:* British. *m.* 1970, Moira (née Burdis); 2 s. *Educ:* Westcliff High School; University of Leicester (BSc Mathematics). *Directorships:* Robert Fleming Holdings Ltd 1988 (exec); Robert Fleming Asset Management Ltd 1988 (exec); Robert Fleming (France) SA 1989 (exec); Fleming Finance SA 1989 (exec); Fleming Fund Management (Luxembourg) SA 1990 (exec); Fleming Flagship Fund 1990 (exec); Fleming (FCP) Management SA 1990 (exec); Save & Prosper Group Ltd 1981 (exec); Save & Prosper Insurance Ltd 1987 (exec); Save & Prosper Insurance (Overseas) Ltd 1984 (exec); Save & Prosper (Jersey) Ltd 1988 (exec); Save & Prosper Bal-

anced Fund 1989; Save & Prosper Linked Investment Trust plc 1987; Save & Prosper Optionable Securities Investment Trust plc 1986; Save & Prosper Return of Assets Investments Trust plc 1984; Save & Prosper Securities Ltd 1987; Save & Prosper Equity Plan Managers Ltd 1986; Scotbits Investments Ltd 1989; Grove Services Ltd 1988; Robert Fleming Pension Trust Ltd 1989-90; Hexagon Services Ltd 1986; Laing & Cruickshank Unit Trust Management Ltd 1986; Lautro Limited 1989; Hexagon Administration Systems Limited 1988; Save & Prosper Financial Services Limited 1989; Save & Prosper Sales Limited 1989; James Capel Unit Trust Management Ltd 1989; Save & Prosper Investment Management Sales Ltd 1989. *Other Activities:* Chairman of the Governors, Westcliff High School for Boys. *Clubs:* Royal Burnham Yacht Club. *Recreations:* Yachting, Squash.

BATES, Malcolm R; Deputy Managing Director, The General Electric Company plc. *Career:* British Government's Industrial Reorganisation Corporation; Managing Director of Principal subsidiaries of Delta Metal. *Biog: m.* Lynda; 3 d. *Educ:* Portsmouth Grammar School; University of Warwick; Harvard Business School (MSc). *Directorships:* GEC Inc Pres; GEC Central Management Team 1976; Picker International Inc Chm. *Professional Organisations:* FCIS; CBIM.

BATES, Robert; Partner, Moore Stephens, since 1971; General Business Partner. *Career:* Articled 1959-64; Partner 1971. *Biog: b.* 20 September 1941. *Nationality:* British. *m.* 1966, Susan; 1 s; 1 d. *Educ:* Emanuel. *Other Activities:* Hon Treasurer, Royal Shakespeare Theatre Trust. *Professional Organisations:* FCA. *Recreations:* Golf, Gardening, Reading, Archaeology.

BATES, Mrs Sarah Catherine; Director, MIM Ltd, since 1989; UK Pension Funds. *Biog: b.* 30 January 1959. *Nationality:* British. *m.* 1982, Steven. *Educ:* Cambridge University (BA Hons); London Business School (MBA). *Other Activities:* Treasurer, The Maternity Alliance.

BATESON, Lynne; Personal Finance Editor, Sunday Express.

BATEY, M; Divisional Chief Executive, Cookson Group plc; Ceramics & Plastics Division.

BATTAGLIA, L; Controller & Compliance Manager. *Career:* Banca Popolare di Milano (Milano) 1962. *Biog: b.* 14 March 1943. *Nationality:* Italian. *m.* 1969, Anna; 1 s. *Educ:* Universita' Cattolica del Sacro Cuore, Milano (Accountancy & Banking).

BATTARBEE, E; Partner, Kidsons Impey.

BATTYE, J D; Director, S G Warburg Akroyd Rowe & Pitman Mullens Securities Ltd.

BATTYE, Peter G; Partner (Birmingham), Evershed Wells & Hind.

BAUGH, K F; Director, S G Warburg Akroyd Rowe & Pitman Mullens Securities Ltd.

BAUGHAN, Michael Christopher; Managing Director, Lazard Brothers & Co, Ltd.

BAULK, Michael; Director, Abbott Mead Vickers plc.

BAUM, Robin Frederic; Director, PK English Trust Company Limited.

BAX, Ms Rosalind; Partner, Clifford Chance.

BAXTER, Charles; Divisional Director, Royal Trust Bank.

BAXTER, David A; Director, Newton Investment Group.

BAXTER, Mrs Gillian Marcia (née Gelding); Partner, Titmuss Sainer & Webb, since 1989; Property & Development. *Career:* Nabarro Nathanson, Articled Clerk 1980-82; Titmuss Sainer & Webb, Assistant Solicitor 1982-89. *Biog: b.* 24 June 1958. *Nationality:* British. *m.* 1990, M A Baxter. *Educ:* Haberdashers' Aske's School for Girls; Kings College, London (LLB); College of Law, Chancery Lane (Law Society Finals). *Other Activities:* Member, London Young Solicitors Group; Member, Association of Women Solicitors.

BAXTER, Harold J; President & CEO, Pilgrim, Baxter, Greig & Associates, Inc, since 1982. *Career:* Institutional Sales, Bankers Trust Company, Vice President 1970-79; Philadelphia National Bank, Institutional Marketing 1979-82; Pilgrim, Baxter, Greig & Associates, Inc, President & CEO 1982-. *Biog: b.* 5 December 1946. *Nationality:* American. *m.* 1968, Christine; 1 s; 3 d. *Educ:* St John's University, USA (BS Marketing). *Directorships:* Framlington Group, plc; CCF & Partners Asset Management; Capstone Financial Services, Inc (USA). *Other Activities:* Chairman, Board of Trustees, Notre Dame Academy (USA). *Recreations:* Golf, Tennis.

BAYER, Mrs Elissa; Director, Parrish Stockbrokers, since 1987; Head of Private Client Department. *Career:* Joseph Sebag, Investment Clerk 1972-76; Grenfell & Colegrave, Ptnrs' Asst 1976-78; Savory Milln 1978-87; Dir, Head of Private Client Dept 1986-87. *Biog: b.* 13 August 1953. *Nationality:* British. *m.* 1974, Dr Max M Bayer; 2 d. *Educ:* Heriots Wood Grammar School; Harrow College of Technology. *Directorships:* Northgate UT 1986-87. *Professional Organisations:* Member, International Stock Exchange. *Recreations:* Entertaining, Lecturing, Theatre.

BAYFIELD, Stephen Peter; Partner, Robson Rhodes, since 1985; Corporate Finance and Tax. *Career:* Eagle Star Insurance Company Ltd, Trainee Underwriter 1974-75; Inland Revenue, Tax Office (Higher Grade) 1975-77; Frazer Whiting & Co (Chartered Accountants), Manager 1977-81; Robson Rhodes 1981-. *Biog: b.* 21 May 1954. *Nationality:* British. *m.* 1974, Margaret Ann (née Barrett); 2 s; 1 d. *Educ:* Brays Grove, Harlow; Walbrook College, London. *Professional Organisations:* ATII. *Recreations:* Athletics, Walking.

BAYLEY, Gordon Vernon; CBE; Chairman, Swiss Reinsurance Company (UK) Ltd, since 1985. *Career:* Equitable Life Assurance Society Various to Asst Actuary 1946-54; Duncan C Fraser & Co Ptnr 1954-57; National Provident Institution Dir, Gen Mgr, Actuary 1957-85. *Biog: b.* 25 July 1920. *Nationality:* British. *m.* 1945, Miriam Allenby (née Ellis); 1 s; 2 d. *Educ:* Abingdon School. *Directorships:* National Provident Institution 1970 (now non-exec); Companies House Steering Board 1988 (non-exec). *Other Activities:* Court Assistant, Worshipful Company of Insurers; Governor, Abingdon School; Occupational Pensions Board 1973-74; Ctee to Review the Functioning of Financial Institutions 1977-80. *Professional Organisations:* Fellow and Past Pres, Institute of Actuaries; Fellow, Institute of Mathematics & its Applications; Companion, British Institute of Management. *Publications:* Miscellaneous Papers to Institute of Actuaries. *Clubs:* Sea View Yacht Club, Athenaeum. *Recreations:* Sailing, Skiing.

BAYLIS, Andrew Robert Lindsay; Director, Baring Securities Limited, since 1984. *Career:* Samuel Montagu & Co Ltd, Portfolio Mgr 1970-74; Fielding Newson-Smith & Co, Portfolio Mgr 1975-82; W I Carr & Sons (Overseas) Ltd, Institutional Sales 1982-83. *Biog: Nationality:* British.

BAYLIS, C A; Partner, Field Fisher Waterhouse, since 1988; Licensing, Environmental Law. *Career:* New Scotland Yard, Solicitor 1981-84; Field Fisher Waterhouse, Solicitor 1984-88; Partner 1988-. *Biog: b.* 9 February 1957. *Nationality:* British. *m.* 1983, Sandra (née Burrows); 1 s. *Educ:* Exeter University (LLB).

BAYLISS, John; Managing Director, Abbey National Building Society.

BAYMAN, T H; Compliance Officer, Gresham Underwriting Agencies Limited.

BAYOUMI, Dr O H; Director, S G Warburg & Co Ltd, since 1990; Corporate Finance. *Career:* Price Waterhouse, Trainee Accountant 1981-84. *Biog: b.* 28 April 1955. *Nationality:* British. *Educ:* St Alban's School, London School of Economics (BSc,PhD). *Professional Organisations:* ACA. *Recreations:* Scuba Diving, Swimming.

BAZALGETTE, Vivian Paul; Managing Director, Gartmore Specialist Fund Management, since 1990; UK Pension Funds. *Career:* Department of Trade & Industry, Civil Servant 1975-79; James Capel & Co, Institutional UK Equity Salesman 1979-83; Mercury Asset Management, UK Pension Fund Manager 1983-86; Gartmore Pension Fund Managers Ltd, Director 1986-; Gartmore Investment Management Ltd, Director 1989-; Gartmore Specialist Fund Management, Managing Director 1990-. *Biog:* b. 7 May 1951. *Nationality:* British. m. 1976, Katharine Diana (née St John-Brooks); 1 s; 2 d. *Educ:* Dulwich College; St John's College, Cambridge (BA, MA). *Recreations:* Classical Music, Bridge, English Poetry, Psychology.

BAZIN, Dominique Maurice; Managing Director, Banque Paribas (London), since 1990. *Career:* Chase Manhattan Bank (Paris), Deputy General Manager 1976-78; Banque Paribas (New York), Deputy General Manager 1978-86; Banque Paribas (Paris), Directeur des Operations de Negoce International 1986-87; Banque Paribas (London), Co-Managing Director 1987-90. *Biog:* b. 4 January 1947. *Nationality:* French. m. Susan Bazin (née Ostle); 2 s; 1 d. *Educ:* ENSAE (Diploma); INSEAD (Diploma).

BEALE, M J; Director, Amalgamated Metal Trading Limited.

BEALE, Robert E; General Manager, Dresdner Bank AG, since 1989; Treasury/Securities. *Career:* Samuel Montagu Co Ltd 1962-89; Managing Director 1985-89. *Biog:* b. 27 May 1940. *Nationality:* British. m. 1964, Clodagh Drusilla (née Dobson); 1 s; 1 d. *Educ:* Shrewsbury School; Jesus College, Cambridge (BA). *Other Activities:* Chairman, London Bullion Market Association Market Development Committee. *Publications:* Trading in Gold Futures, 1985.

BEALES, D J; Partner, Slaughter and May.

BEALES, M D; Director, Holman Franklin Ltd.

BEAMISH, B; Senior Executive Director, J H Minet & Co Ltd.

BEAMISS, Richard; Director, Chartfield & Co Limited.

BEAR, C Rupert; Partner (Nottingham), Evershed Wells & Hind.

BEARD, J A; Managing Director, King & Shaxson Money Brokers Ltd, since 1985; Stock Exchange Money Broking. *Career:* NM Rothschild Nostro Accounts Clerk 1961-62; Samuel Montagu Sterling Dealer 1962-66; Bank Leumi Sterling and Foreign Currency Dealer 1966-68; Banque Paribas Sterling and Foreign Currency Dealer 1968-70; C Fulton Dir 1970-80; Hoare Bovett

Money Broking Ltd Asst Dir 1980-85. *Biog:* b. 31 May 1937. m. 1963, Jacqueline M; 1 s; 1 d. *Educ:* Christs College, Finchley; London School of Economics (BSc Hons). *Directorships:* King & Shaxon Holdings plc 1985 (non-exec). *Clubs:* Wentworth. *Recreations:* Golf, Gardening, Reading, Charity Work.

BEARD, Michael; Director, G T Management plc.

BEARD, Rob I; Partner, Touche Ross & Co, since 1963; London and International Security Industry. *Career:* Spicer and Pegler & Co, Executive Director in Charge 1965-78. *Biog:* b. 14 September 1932. *Nationality:* British. m. 1961, Diane B (née Sanders); 2 s; 1 d. *Educ:* Epsom County Grammar School; Bristol University (BA). *Other Activities:* Council Member, Institute of Management Consultants. *Professional Organisations:* FCA; FIMC; FInstD. *Recreations:* Swimming, Travel, Theatre, Gardening.

BEARD, Susanna; Director, GCI Sterling.

BEARDSLEY, Miss Alison M; Partner, Allen & Overy.

BEARE, Stuart Newton; Senior Partner, Richards Butler, since 1988; Shipping Law. *Career:* Northern Cameroons Trust Territory, Assistant Plebiscite Supervisory Officer 1960-61; Simmons & Simmons, Articled Clerk 1961-64; Assistant Solicitor 1964-66; Richards Butler & Co, Assistant Solicitor 1966-69; Richards Butler, Partner 1969-. *Biog:* b. 6 October 1936. *Nationality:* British. m. 1974, Cheryl (née Wells). *Educ:* Clifton College; Clare College, Cambridge (MA, LLB). *Other Activities:* Member, Court of Assistants, City of London Solicitors' Company; Titulary Member, Comité Maritime International. *Clubs:* Alpine Club, City of London Club, Oriental Club, MCC. *Recreations:* Mountaineering, Skiing, Travel.

BEATON, K; Member of the Council, The International Stock Exchange.

BEATSON-HIRD, J; Director, County NatWest Securities Limited, since 1986; US Equities. *Career:* 1st The Queen's Dragon Guards, Captain 1979-84; Scottish Reel, Director 1984-86; Merrill Lynch, Executive 1985-86; County NatWest 1986-. *Biog:* b. 14 April 1960. *Nationality:* British. m. 1989, Suzannah (née Starkey). *Educ:* Stonyhurst College; RMA Sandhurst. *Directorships:* County NatWest (non-exec); Scottish Reel (exec). *Professional Organisations:* Series 3, 7, 42 (Secretary). *Clubs:* Cavalry Club, Regie Club.

BEATTIE, D F; Personnel Director, STC plc.

BEATTIE, David Wilson; Chairman, Grosvenor Venture Managers Limited, since 1985; Venture Capital. *Career:* Cadbury Limited, Statistician 1960-64; Johnson

47

& Johnson, Quality Control Manager 1964-65; Cadbury Schweppes Ltd, Operational Research Manager 1966-73; Cadbury McVitie Foods Ltd, Development Director 1973-74; Mapleton Foods Ltd, Managing Director 1974-76; Cadbury Schweppes Speciality Foods Ltd, Managing Director 1974-76; National Enterprise Board, Divisional Director 1976-82; Grosvenor Development Capital plc, Managing Director 1982-85; Grosvenor Venture Managers Ltd, Chairman 1985-. *Biog: b.* 30 September 1938. *Nationality:* British. *m.* 1963, Pauline Beattie (née Holloway); 1 d. *Educ:* Carlisle Grammar School; Manchester University (BSc Hons Mathematics). *Directorships:* Grosvenor Development Capital plc 1982 (non-exec); Electron House plc 1983 (non-exec); Severn plc 1989 (non-exec) Dep Chairman; Grosvenor Technology Ltd 1985 (exec); Third Grosvenor Ltd 1988 (exec); Marcol Group plc 1983-88 (non-exec) Chairman; Twinlockk plc 1979-83 (non-exec). *Professional Organisations:* Fellow, Royal Statistical Society; Associate, Chartered Institute of Management Accountants.

BEATTY, D; Director, Allied-Lyons plc.

BEAUMAN, Christopher; Planning Director, Morgan Grenfell Group Limited, since 1989. *Career:* Hill Samuel & Co Ltd, Exec Mgr, Issues & Mergers Dept 1968-72; Guinness Mahon & Co Ltd, Dir (Corporate Finance) 1972-76; British Steel Corp, Adviser to the Chairman 1976-81; Central Policy Review Staff, Cabinet Office, Adviser 1981-83; Morgan Grenfell Group Positions in Privatisation Business; Devel and Reg of Inv Mgmnt Business; Strategic Planning 1983-. *Biog: b.* 12 October 1944. *Nationality:* British. *m.* 1976, Nicola (née Mayers); 1 s; 1 d; 3 stepch. *Educ:* Winchester College; Trinity College, Cambridge (MA); Columbia University (MA). *Directorships:* Morgan Grenfell & Co Limited 1989 (exec). *Recreations:* Family, Political Economy, Literature.

BEAUMONT, Michael Eric; Director, Kleinwort Benson Investment Management Ltd, since 1986; Investment Management. *Career:* Grieveson Grant & Co, Stockbrokers' Clerk, Ptnr 1956-86. *Biog: b.* 13 September 1933. *Nationality:* British. *m.* 1964, Hilary Gwythian (née Parsons); 2 s; 1 d. *Educ:* Charterhouse; Pembroke College, Oxford (MA Hons). *Directorships:* Kleinwort Benson Unit Trust Managers Ltd 1987 (exec); Kleinworth Overseas Investment Trust plc 1989 (non-exec). *Professional Organisations:* The International Stock Exchange. *Clubs:* Rye Golf Club. *Recreations:* Golf, Skiing, Walking, Georgian Flatware.

BEAUMONT, Rupert Roger Seymour; Partner, Slaughter and May, since 1974; Company and Commercial Law. *Career:* Appleton, Rice & Perrin (New York), Lawyer 1968-69; Beaumont & Son, Articled Clerk 1962-68. *Biog: b.* 27 February 1944. *Nationality:* British. *m.* 1968, Susie (née Wishart); 1 s; 1 d. *Educ:* Welling-ton College. *Professional Organisations:* The Law Society. *Publications:* Contribution to Euronotes; Various Contributions to Legal Journals. *Clubs:* Cavalry & Guards. *Recreations:* Tennis, Fishing.

BEAVEN, J C; Director, Greenwell Montagu Gilt-Edged.

BEAVEN, Philip Edwin; Managing Director, UK Operations, Hill Samuel Investment Management Ltd. *Biog: b.* 4 March 1946. *Nationality:* British. *m.* 1984, Anna Margaret; 1 s. *Educ:* Dulwich College; The Queen's College, Oxford (MA Mathematics). *Directorships:* Hill Samuel Unit Trust Managers Ltd 1981 (exec); Hill Samuel Sterling Fixed Interest Fund Ltd (Jersey) 1981 (exec). *Professional Organisations:* AIA.

BEAZER, Brian C; Chairman & Chief Executive, Beazer plc, since 1983. *Career:* Beazer plc, MD 1968-83. *Biog: b.* 22 February 1935. *Nationality:* British. *m.* 1958, Patricia; 1 d. *Educ:* Wells Cathedral School. *Clubs:* Reform. *Recreations:* Walking, Reading, History, Theology.

BEAZLEY, Charles J S; Director, Merrill Lynch Pierce Fenner & Smith Limited, since 1990; Institutional Equity Sales Manager, Europe and Middle East. *Career:* Merrill Lynch, Vice President, Capital Markets & Fixed Income; Orion Royal Bank, Manager International Capital Markets, Fixed Income; Lazard Brothers, Assistant Fund Manager Lazard Securities. *Biog: b.* 29 September 1959. *Nationality:* British. *m.* 1988, Ileana (née Eva). *Educ:* School of Slavonic and East European Studies, University of London (Masters, Politics & International Relations); Haileybury College (BA Hons History). *Professional Organisations:* Diploma AIBD 1984. *Recreations:* Skiing, Shooting, Travel.

BEBB, Peter John; Business Systems Director, Kleinwort Benson Investment Management, since 1989. *Career:* British Leyland, Oxford, O&M Analyst 1968-73; British United Provident Association, London, Senior System Analyst 1974-76; Edward Lumley & Sons, London, Data Processing Manager 1976-77; Management & Computer Consultancy, Kuwait 1977-79; Tom Pederson International, Kuwait, Senior Consultant 1979-80; Datamation Syems, Dubai, UAE, Senior Consultant 1981-82; World Systems Ltd, Kingston, Principal Consultant 1983-85; CACI Incorporated, Richmond, Principal Consultant 1985; James Martin Associates, Middlesex 1985-89. *Biog: b.* 2 April 1946. *Nationality:* British. *m.* 1975, Susan Elizabeth (née Bolt); 1 s; 1 d. *Educ:* Rossall School; Oxford University (PPE). *Professional Organisations:* Member, British Computer Society.

BEBB, Timothy Francis Montfort; Director, Laurence Keen Ltd, since 1966; Investment Management. *Career:* Thomas Skinner & Co Ltd Asst to MD

1956-61. *Biog: b.* 6 April 1935. *Educ:* Winchester College. *Other Activities:* Honourable Artillery Company. *Professional Organisations:* The International Stock Exchange. *Clubs:* Royal & Ancient Golf Club of St Andrews, Worplesdon Golf Club. *Recreations:* Golf, Bridge.

BECK, Charles Theodore Heathfield; Finance Partner, J M Finn & Co, since 1988; In charge of International Bond Operations, Co-Developer of Genesis Securities Computer Software. *Career:* Bank of England 1975-79; J M Finn & Co 1979-. *Biog: b.* 3 April 1954. *Nationality:* British. *Educ:* Winchester College; Jesus College, Cambridge (MA). *Directorships:* Finn Financial Futures Ltd 1982 (exec). *Other Activities:* Liveryman, Worshipful Company of Broderers. *Professional Organisations:* AMSIA. *Recreations:* Fencing, Japanese Fencing, Archaeology.

BECK, F W R; Managing Director (Investment Management), Billiton-Enthoven Metals Limited.

BECK, P Joan; Director, Crédit Suisse First Boston Ltd.

BECKET, Michael; City News Editor, The Daily Telegraph, since 1968; Accountancy, Insurance and Computers. *Publications:* Computer by the Tail; Economic Alphabet; Bluffer's Guide to Finance.

BECKETT, W C; CB; Solicitor to the Corporation, Lloyd's of London, since 1985. *Career:* Treasury, Solicitor's Dept 1956; Board of Trade 1965; DEP, Asst Solicitor 1969; DTI, Under-Secretary 1972; Deputy Secretary 1977; Law Officers' Dept, Legal Secretary 1975-80; DTI, Solicitor 1980-84. *Biog: Nationality:* British. *Educ:* Manchester University (LLM). *Other Activities:* Committee Member, Departmental Advisory Committee on Arbitration Law. *Professional Organisations:* Barrister of the Middle Temple. *Clubs:* Reform Club.

BECKITT, Jonathan Paul; Partner, McKenna & Co, since 1990; Commercial Property. *Career:* McKenna & Co, Articled Clerk 1982-84; Assistant Solicitor 1984-90. *Biog: b.* 14 August 1960. *Nationality:* British. *Educ:* Bristol University (LLB). *Professional Organisations:* City of Westminster Law Society. *Clubs:* Alfa Romeo Owners, David Lloyd Slazenger Racquets Club. *Recreations:* Skiing, Tennis, Squash.

BECKLEY, George William Roy; Managing Director, J Trevor Mortleman & Poland Ltd, since 1982. *Career:* J Trevor Mortleman & Poland Ltd 1960-; Liverpool & London & Globe Insurance Co Ltd 1956-60. *Biog: b.* 7 September 1939. *Nationality:* British. *m.* 1972, Patricia Ellen (née Rooke). *Educ:* Wembley County Grammar. *Other Activities:* Executive, Buckinghamshire Association of Cricket Umpires. *Professional*

Organisations: Associate, Chartered Insurance Institute; Chartered Insurance Practioner. *Clubs:* Chairman, Green Dragon Cricket Club. *Recreations:* Cricket Umpiring, Fishing, Travel.

BECKWITH, J L; Chairman, London & Edinburgh Trust plc, since 1971. *Career:* Beresford Lye & Co, Articled Clerk 1967-69; Arthur Andersen & Co, Articled Clerk 1969-71; London & Edinburgh Trust plc, founded in 1971. *Biog: b.* 19 March 1947. *Nationality:* British. *m.* 1975, Heather Marie (née Robbins); 2 s; 1 d. *Educ:* Harrow School. *Directorships:* Rutland Trust plc (non-exec) Chairman; Owen Owen plc (non-exec) Chairman; Oppidan Estates Ltd (non-exec) Chairman; Stratagem plc (non-exec); Riverside Racquet Centre plc (non-exec). *Other Activities:* City & Industrial Liaison Council; Chairman, RNIB Looking Glass Appeal. *Professional Organisations:* FCA; ATII. *Clubs:* Royal Mid-Surrey Golf Club, St George's Hill Golf Club, Riverside Racquet Centre. *Recreations:* Golf, Shooting, Tennis, Soccer.

BEDELL-PEARCE, Keith Leonard; Director & General Manager, The Prudential Assurance Co Ltd, since 1987; Marketing & Sales. *Career:* Plessey, Systems Analyst 1969-70; Wiggins Teape, Project Manager 1970-71; Prudential Assurance, Systems Manager 1971-74; Legal Adviser, Company & Commercial Law 1975-78; Solicitor to Company 1978-82; Prudential Portfolio Managers Ltd, Director 1982-85; Prudential Assurance, General Manager, Field Operations 1986-. *Biog: b.* 11 March 1946. *Nationality:* British. *m.* 1971, Gaynor (née Trevelyan); 1 s; 2 d. *Educ:* Trinity School of John Whitgift; University of Exeter (LLB); University of Warwick (MSc). *Directorships:* The Prudential Assurance Co Ltd 1988 (exec). *Professional Organisations:* Solicitor; Member, Law Society; Member, Association of MBAs; Member, Marketing Society. *Publications:* Checklists for Computer Contracts, 1978; Computers & Information Technology, 1979, 2nd Ed 1982. *Recreations:* Squash, Shooting, Theatre.

BEDFORD, Michael Geoffrey; Director, Kleinwort Benson Securities Ltd, since 1986; UK International Equity Marketing. *Career:* Hoare Govett & Co Joseph Sebag Ptnr 1975-79; Carr Sebag Ptnr 1979-82; Grieveson Grant Ptnr 1982-86. *Biog: b.* 24 January 1947. *Nationality:* British. *m.* 1974, Deborah (née Sitwell); 2 s; 2 d. *Educ:* Malvern College; Clare College, Cambridge (BA Hons).

BEDFORD, Nicholas C; Managing Director, Salomon Brothers International Limited.

BEDFORD, P H D; Partner, Allen & Overy.

BEDFORD, Peter Wyatt; Chairman, Fenchurch Insurance Brokers Ltd, since 1980; UK Retail Broking. *Career:* Willis Faber & Dunmas Ltd, Broker 1956-70;

Bland Payne Ltd, Director 1970-78; Fenchurch Insurance Holdings Ltd, Director 1978-. *Biog: b.* 9 March 1935. *Nationality:* British. *m.* 1959, Valerie (née Collins); 4 s. *Educ:* Marlborough College. *Directorships:* Fenchurch Insurance Group Ltd 1989 (exec); Fenchurch London Ltd 1983 Chairman; Fenchurch Midlands Ltd 1982 Chairman; Fenchurch Northern Ltd 1981 Chairman; Fenchurch North Western Ltd 1979 Chairman; Fenchurch Financial Services Ltd 1979 Chairman; Protection House Insurance Services Ltd 1979 Chairman; Credit Insurance Services Ltd 1979 Chairman; Pet Plan Group 1988 (non-exec). *Other Activities:* Haberdashers' Company; Governor, Haberdashers' Aske's Schools; Director, Hackney Business Venture; Chairman, Royal Humane Society. *Professional Organisations:* Member, Lloyd's Insurance Brokers' Committee. *Clubs:* MCC, Sunningdale Golf Club, Swinley Forest Golf Club. *Recreations:* Golf, Shooting, Horse Racing.

BEDWELL, F P L; Director, Touche Remnant & Co, since 1988; Private Clients, Pension Funds, Investment Trust Portfolio Management. *Career:* Dunkley Bedwell & Marshall (Stockbrokers), (later Dunkley Marshall & Smithers and Dunkley Marshall, taken over by Parrish plc in 1987) 1960; Partner 1967-; Parrish Stockbrokers, Director 1987-88. *Biog: b.* 22 November 1938. *Nationality:* British. *Educ:* Charterhouse. *Directorships:* Touche Remnant Investment Management Limited 1989 (exec). *Professional Organisations:* Member, International Stock Exchange, London. *Clubs:* Royal Ashdown Forest Golf Club. *Recreations:* Steam Railway Enthusiast, Music Lover, Golf.

BEEBE, Joseph P; Vice President, Midlantic Bank, since 1990; Corporate Lending and Acquisition Finance for European Companies investing in the US. *Career:* Irving Trust Company (New York), Staff Mgr 1981-83; Midlantic Bank (New Jersey) AVP and Corporate Loan Officer, Special Industries Div 1985-87. *Biog: b.* 30 December 1958. *Nationality:* American. *m.* 1983, Nancy (née Korsch). *Educ:* Pope John XXIII, New Jersey; Villanova University, Pennsylvania (BA); Graduate School, Pace University, New York (MBA). *Professional Organisations:* American/UK Chamber of Commerce; American Society in London British American Associates; Woolnoth Society. *Clubs:* Raritan Valley Golf Club (New Jersey), Villanova University Alumni Club. *Recreations:* Golf, Tennis.

BEECROFT, (Paul) Adrian (Barlow); Director, Alan Patricof Associates Limited, since 1984; Venture Capital. *Career:* ICL, Account Executive 1968-73; Ocean Transport & Trading, Project Development 1973-74; Boston Consulting Group, Vice President 1976-84. *Biog: b.* 20 May 1947. *Nationality:* British. *m.* Jacqui; 1 s; 1 d. *Educ:* Queen's College, Oxford (MA Physics); Harvard Business School (MBA). *Directorships:* Alan Patricof Associates Limited; Auto-Mek Limited; Border

Holdings Ltd; Computacenter Limited; Computacenter Maintenance Limited; Hey (UK) Limited; Minden Group; Mohawk Limited; Music Market Limited; National Telecommunications plc; REL Limited; Satellite Cafe Limited; Satellite Holdings plc; Satellite Leisure Limited; Satellite Merchandising Limited; Soundcraft Limited; BTS Group plc; British Venture Capital Association. *Other Activities:* Vice Chairman, British Venture Capital Association; Chairman, British Venture Capital Association Taxation Committee. *Clubs:* Incogniti. *Recreations:* Cricket, Travel.

BEER, Andrew M S; Partner, Wilde Sapte.

BEERY, James Ralph; Partner, Morrison & Foerster, since 1980; London Office, European Managing Partner. *Career:* United States Marine Corps Captain 1963-67; Cleary Gottlieb Steen & Hamilton Associate Attorney 1970-73; Nagashima & Ohno Foreign Law Consultant 1973-75; Erickson & Morrison Ptnr 1976-79; Morrison & Foerster Ptnr 1980-. *Biog: b.* 29 May 1941. *Nationality:* American. *m.* 1969, Caroline (née Eaker); 2 d. *Educ:* Harvard College (AB); Stanford Law School (JD). *Directorships:* Friends of Benjamin Franklin House 1987 (non-exec). *Other Activities:* Member, Assoc of Bar of the City of New York Ctee on Relationships with European Bars. *Professional Organisations:* ABA; IBA; Assoc of the Bar of the City of New York. *Clubs:* Buck's, RAC, Harvard Club of New York City. *Recreations:* Tennis, Skiing, Shooting, Reading.

BEESLEY, Professor M E; CBE; Member, Monopolies and Mergers Commission, since 1988. *Career:* University of Birmingham, Lecturer in Commerce 1951-60; University of Pennsylvania, Visiting Associate Professor 1959-60; London School of Economics, Rees Jeffreys Research Fellow 1961-64; University of London, Reader in Economics of Transport 1964-65; University of British Columbia, Visiting Professor 1968; Department of Transport, Chief Economic Advisor 1965-69; Harvard University, Visiting Professor 1974; Maquarie University, Sydney, Visiting Professor 1979-80; London Business School, Professor of Economics 1965-90; Emeritus Professor of Economics 1990. *Biog: b.* 3 July 1924. *Nationality:* British. *m.* 1947, Eleanor (née Yard); 3 s; 2 d. *Educ:* University of Birmingham (BCom Div I, PhD). *Directorships:* Rofsole Ltd (exec). *Other Activities:* Non-Executive Member, Harrow Health Authority. *Publications:* Too numerous to list! (about 130-150 at last count). *Clubs:* Reform. *Recreations:* Music.

BEESON, Andrew Nigel Wendover; Chief Executive, Beeson Gregory Ltd, since 1989. *Career:* Capel-Cure Myers, Partner 1972-85; ANZ Merchant Bank, Director 1985-87; ANZ McCaughan, Director 1987-89. *Biog: b.* 30 March 1944. *Nationality:* British. *m.* 1986, Carrie (née Martin); 1 s; 2 d. *Educ:* Eton College.

Professional Organisations: Member, Stock Exchange. *Clubs:* Whites, Pratts, Swinley, MCC.

BEETON, D F; National Director-Finance, Wellcome plc.

BEEVER, David Milton Maxwell; Director, S G Warburg & Co Ltd. *Directorships:* Pallas Leasing Group Ltd (Chm); S G Warburg & Co (Leasing) Ltd.

BEEVERS, W L; Institutional Sales Director, Charlton Seal, a Division of Wise Speke; Smaller UK Companies/Australia. *Career:* International Combustion Ltd, Investment Analyst 1969-70; Intersca Ltd, Market Research Analyst 1970-71; National Westminster Bank, Graduate Trainee 1971; Orme & Eykyn, Senior Partners Assistant 1971-72; Lyddon & Co, Senior Partners Assistant 1972-76; Charlton Seal, Senior Partners Assistant 1976-79; Charlton Seal, Partner 1979-. *Biog: b.* 29 May 1949. *Nationality:* British. *m.* 1975, Gillian Frances (née Johnson); 1 s; 3 d. *Educ:* The Gordon Boys School; Guildford Technical College; Bristol University (BSc Honours). *Directorships:* Wise Speke 1990 (exec); Duckwari plc 1988 (non-exec); Gwalia Consolidated Ltd (formerly Gwalia Minerals) 1987 (non-exec); Biotech Ltd 1989 (non-exec). *Professional Organisations:* Member, Stock Exchange. *Clubs:* Bowdon Hockey Club. *Recreations:* Tennis, Hockey, Cricket.

BEEVOR, Antony Romer; Executive Director, Hambros Bank Ltd, since 1982; Head of Corporate Finance. *Career:* Ashurst Morris Crisp & Co Solicitors 1962-72; Partner 1968-72; Takeover Panel, Director General 1987-89. *Biog: b.* 18 May 1940. *Nationality:* British. *m.* 1970, Cecilia (née Hopton); 1 s; 1 d. *Educ:* Winchester College; New College, Oxford (PPE Hons). *Directorships:* Hambros plc 1990 (non-exec). *Professional Organisations:* Solicitor, 1965. *Clubs:* Hurlingham. *Recreations:* Skiing, Sailing, Squash.

BEGG, Alastair Currie; Director, Kleinwort Benson Investment Management Ltd, since 1986; Head of International Fund Management. *Biog: b.* 6 February 1954. *Nationality:* British. *m.* 1982, Patricia (née Wigham Richardson); 1 s; 1 d. *Educ:* King's School, Canterbury; Sidney Sussex College, Cambridge (MA Hons). *Professional Organisations:* Member, The International Stock Exchange.

BEGG, Wallace; Senior Partner, James Gentles & Son.

BEHARRELL, Steven Roderic; Founder Member & Partner, Beharrell Thompson & Co, since 1990; Energy International Joint Ventures & Investment, Privatisation, Commercial and Corporate Law. *Career:* Denton Hall Burgin & Warrens 1963-90; Articled Clerk 1963-68; Partner 1973. *Biog: b.* 22 December 1944. *Nationality:* British. *m.* 1967, Julia (née Powell); 2 d. *Educ:* Uppingham School; Cours de Civilisation, British Institute and Sorbonne University, Paris; College of Law, Lancaster Gate London (Part I and Part II Solicitors Exams). *Other Activities:* Justice of the Peace, 1976-86; Member, International Bar Association Oil Committee; Various Charities; Member, Drapers Company. *Professional Organisations:* Law Society. *Publications:* Various Articles in Professional Journals and Publications of Lectures and Papers including (Recently): Contracting in an Uncertain Environment, International Energy Forum Malaysia, 1987; 'Privatisation of Energy Projects - the Legal Techniques and Consequences', Paper Presented to the Lawasia Conference, 1988; Joint Ventures Between Foreign Companies and Host Government: the Choice of Law and Related Issues, 1985-86; Common Aspirations of Host Governments and Multi-nationals Concerning Management and Control of a Joint Venture Company, IBA Munich, 1986; Special Legal Considerations for BOT and Other Non-Recourse Finance; Second International Construction Projects Conference, London, 1989. *Recreations:* Fishing, Shooting, Sailing.

BEITH, Ian Mark; Managing Director, Head of Debt Services, Charterhouse Bank Limited, since 1988; Debt Services, Corporate Banking, Property Credit. *Career:* Citibank 1972-88; Assistant Manager UK Corporate Bank, Energy Department 1972-75; Marketing Officer, Corporate Banking, Metals & Mining Department, New York 1975-80; Team Head, Oil & Mining Department, London 1980-82; Director, European Training Centre, London 1982-84; Head of North European Shipping Group 1984-86; Head of UK Corporate Banking 1986-88; Charterhouse Bank Ltd, Director, Marketing Debt Related Services 1988. *Biog: b.* 2 December 1950. *Nationality:* British. *m.* 1975, Mary Jane (née Few); 2 s. *Educ:* Cambridge University (MA History); Harvard University (Programme for Management Development). *Clubs:* Whites. *Recreations:* Shooting, Films, Theatre.

BELCHAMBER, Peter John; Director, College Hill Associates, since 1989; Corporate & Financial Public Relations. *Career:* Nottingham Evening Post, Morning Guardian Journal, Journalist; Nottingham Observer, Editor; JWT (Lexington Internationa) & Ogilvy & Mather, Account Dir/Mgr; Charles Barker PR Group 1974-88; Charles Barker Traverse-Healy, Divisonal MD 1987-89; Head of Corporate Affairs, Health & Science Division 1983-87; Head of Health & Science Division, (Ethical Pharmacheuticals, Medical Research/Hospitals, Medical Technology & Diagnostics, Biotechnology) 1980-87. *Biog: b.* 5 September 1943. *Nationality:* British. *m.* 1972, Margaret (née Bowes); 1 s; 2 d. *Educ:* Monkton Combe; Nottingham People's College; Alexander Hamilton Business School. *Other Activities:* Executive Committee, British Association of Cancer United Patients (BACUP); Honorary PR Adviser to National Association for the Welfare of Children in Hospital, Health Information Trust and Great Ormond Street

Hospital. *Publications:* East Midlands Airport, 1965. *Clubs:* Scribes. *Recreations:* Opera, Ballet, Reading, Gardening.

BELL, A C O; Director, Laurence Keen Ltd, since 1973; Investment Management. *Career:* Rowe Swann & Co 1964-68. *Biog: b.* 24 July 1945. *Nationality:* British. *m.* 1979, Julia Emily (née Grant); 1 s; 2 d. *Educ:* Charterhouse. *Directorships:* Laurence Keen Holdings Ltd 1990 (exec); Well Marine General Advisers Ltd 1987 (non exec). *Professional Organisations:* The International Stock Exchange. *Recreations:* Family & Country Pursuits.

BELL, Adrian John; Director, Hambros Bank Limited; Head of International Debt Issues Division. *Career:* Hambros Bank Ltd, Graduate Trainee 1972; Various, including Credit Analyst, Banking Division, Accounts Executive, Leasing Division & Senior Manager, Marketing Division; Director 1984. *Biog: b.* 25 May 1950; 1 s; 1 d. *Educ:* St Catherines College, Oxford (Economics & History). *Directorships:* Hambros Bank Ltd 1986 (exec); Hambros France SA 1986; International Primary Markets Association (IPMA) 1988. *Other Activities:* Member, IPMA Market Practices Committee.

BELL, Alexander Scott; Managing Director, The Standard Life Assurance Company, since 1988; General Management. *Career:* The Standard Life Assurance Company, Asst Actuary for Canada 1967-70; Asst Actuary 1970-72; Dep Actuary 1972-75; South Reg Mgr 1975-79; Asst Gen Mgr (Finance) 1979-85; Gen Mgr (Finance) 1985-88. *Biog: b.* 4 December 1941. *Nationality:* British. *m.* 1965, Veronica Jane (née Simpson); 2 s; 1 d. *Educ:* Daniel Stewart's College, Edinburgh. *Directorships:* The Bank of Scotland 1988 (non-exec); The Hammerson Group 1988 (non-exec); Scottish Financial Enterprise 1989 (non-exec). *Professional Organisations:* FFA; FPMI. *Clubs:* New Club (Edinburgh), Bruntsfield Links Golfing Society. *Recreations:* Golf, Gardening, Reading.

BELL, Andrew Richard; Director, Kleinwort Benson Securities Ltd, since 1988; Specialist Selling of Building Materials & Construction/Contracting Sectors. *Career:* E B Savory, Milln & Co, Assoc Dir 1981-86; Wood Mackenzie & Co Ltd, Asst Dir 1986-88. *Biog: b.* 23 July 1960. *Nationality:* British. *m.* 1990, Elizabeth Jane (née Grant). *Educ:* Glyn School, Epsom; Mansfield College, Oxford (BA, MA). *Professional Organisations:* Member, The International Stock Exchange; AMSIA. *Clubs:* RAC, Oxford & Cambridge University. *Recreations:* Skiing, Horseriding, Tennis, Running, Football.

BELL, B J; Director, Steel Burrill Jones Group plc.

BELL, Christopher; Partner, Travers Smith Braithwaite. *Biog: b.* 31 December 1945. *Educ:* Marlborough College; Pembroke College, Cambridge (BA).

BELL, Christopher; Partner and Head of Department, Taylor Joynson Garrett.

BELL, D W H; Director, Laurence Keen Limited, since 1990; Private Clients. *Career:* Imperial Tobacco, Marketing 1979-84; Laurence Keen Ltd, Private Client Stockbroking 1985-. *Biog: b.* 8 January 1959. *Nationality:* British. *Educ:* Eton College. *Directorships:* Laurence Keen Limited 1990; Renshaw UK Limited 1989. *Professional Organisations:* Individual Member, ISE; Securities Industry Examination Diploma. *Clubs:* The Gresham Club.

BELL, G McD; Partner, R Watson & Sons Consulting Actuaries.

BELL, Geoffrey; Managing Director, Brown Shipley & Co Ltd; Banking Division and Treasury. *Career:* Banque Belge Ltd Treasurer 1963-73; Iran Overseas Investment Bank Ltd Dep MD 1973-78; European American Banking Corporation Mgr & VP 1979-81. *Biog: b.* 18 February 1938. *Nationality:* British. *m.* 1974, Joyce (née Hunter); 1 s; 2 d. *Educ:* Royal Liberty School. *Directorships:* Brown Shipley Holdings Ltd (exec); Brown Shipley Finance (Holland) BV (exec); Lease Management Services Ltd. *Clubs:* Overseas Bankers', Royal Harwich Yacht Club, Wimbledon Park Golf Club. *Recreations:* Sailing, Golf.

BELL, Geoffrey Lakin; Chairman, Guinness Mahon Holdings plc, since 1988. *Career:* HM Treasury, Economic Assistant 1961-63; Federal Reserve System, Visiting Scholar, principally with Federal Reserve Bank of St Louis 1963-64; HM Treasury & Special Lecturer at London School of Economics 1964-66; British Embassy (Washington), Economic Adviser 1966-69; J Henry Schroder Wagg, Assistant to Chairman; Schroder Wagg, Director 1969-81; Schroder International, Executive Vice President; Schroder Bank and Trust Company, New York, Snr Adviser; The Times, Special Columnist on International Economics and Finance 1969-74; Geoffrey Bell and Company, New York, President 1982-. *Biog: b.* 8 November 1939. *Nationality:* British. *m.* 1973, Joan; 1 d. *Educ:* Grimsby Technical School; London School of Economics. *Directorships:* Guinness Mahon Group Limited 1987 (exec) Chairman; Guinness Mahon & Co Limited 1987 (exec) Chairman. *Publications:* The Euro-Dollar Market and the International Financial System, 1973; Numerous Articles on International Economics and Finance in the UK and USA.

BELL, I P; Partner, Jaques & Lewis.

BELL, Ian; Managing Director, Town & Country Building Society, since 1987. *Career:* Royal Insurance 1960-69; Leeds Permanent Building Society, Asst Gen Mgr 1969-81; National & Provincial Building Society, Gen Mgr 1981-87. *Directorships:* Town & Country Property Services Ltd 1987; Town & Country

Homebuilders Ltd 1987; Town & Country Financial Services Ltd 1987; Commercial Union Assurance Co (Ipswich Board).

BELL, John William; City Editor, The Times, since 1986; News, Features & Comment on City Financial & Business Matters. *Career:* Evening Standard, Reporter 1970-72; Sunday Times, Reporter 1972-76; City Editor 1976-81; Sunday Standard, City Editor 1981-83; Sunday Express, City Editor 1983-86. *Biog: b.* 28 November 1940. *Nationality:* British. *m.* 1969 (div); 2 s. *Educ:* St Ignatius College, Stamford Hill. *Recreations:* Hill Walking, Photography, Jazz, Cooking, Golf.

BELL, L A; Partner, Holman Fenwick & Willan.

BELL, Martin George Henry; Senior Partner, Ashurst Morris Crisp, since 1986; Corporate. *Career:* Ashurst Morris Crisp, Ptnr 1963-. *Biog: b.* 16 January 1935. *m.* 1965, Shirley (née Wrightson); 2 s. *Educ:* Charterhouse. *Other Activities:* The City of London Solicitors' Company; International Bar Association; Associate Member, American Bar Association. *Professional Organisations:* The Law Society.

BELL, Michael Jaffray de Hauteville; Partner, R Watson & Sons, since 1967; Life Assurance & Employee Benefit Consulting. *Biog: b.* 7 April 1941. *Nationality:* British. *m.* 1965, Christine (née Morgan); 1 s; 4 d. *Educ:* Charterhouse. *Directorships:* Century Group Ltd 1985 (non-exec); Century Life Assurance Company Ltd (non-exec); Group Plans Marketing Ltd (non-exec); Sentinel Life plc (non-exec); Watson Services Ltd. *Professional Organisations:* FIA, FPMI, ASA.

BELL, Steven Richard; Director and Chief Economist, Morgan Grenfell plc, since 1984; Economics. *Career:* HM Treasury, Economic Adviser 1974-84. *Biog: b.* 10 July 1953. *Nationality:* British. *m.* Arlene (née Jones); 2 s; 2 d. *Educ:* Royal Grammar School, Newcastle upon Tyne; London School of Economics (BSc Econ); Stanford University, California (AM Econ). *Professional Organisations:* Member, Royal Institute. *Publications:* Foreign Exchange Market, 1982; An Econometric Model of UK Balance of Payments, 1981. *Recreations:* Reading, Golf, Failing to Finish Crosswords, Bridge.

BELL, Stuart Henry; Partner, Hymans Robertson & Co.

BELL, Timothy Mark; Property Investment Director, Electricity Supply Pension Scheme, since 1989; Property Activities of the Pension Scheme. *Career:* Sun Life Properties Ltd, Estate Surveyor, Property Activities in South East England 1979-82; Jones Lang Wootton, Management Surveyor, Management of Pension Fund Property Asset 1975-79. *Biog: b.* 12 March 1953. *Nationality:* British. *m.* 1989, Susan Ann (née Tucker); 1 s; 1 d. *Educ:* Berkhamsted School; North East London

Polytechnic (Diploma in General Surveying, Estate Management). *Directorships:* ESNIM 1989 (exec); ESN Property Management Co Ltd 1989 (exec); Hillbank Farming Ltd 1989 (exec). *Professional Organisations:* FRICS. *Recreations:* Badminton, Fishing.

BELL, W E; CBE; Chairman, Enterprise Oil plc, since 1984. *Career:* Royal Dutch Shell Group, Tech & Managerial (Appts: Venezuela, USA, Kuwait, Indonesia) 1948; Shell International Petroleum Co, Gen Mgr 1965-73; Shell UK, Expl & Production Director 1973; Man Dir 1976-79; Shell Intl Pet Co, Middle East Regional Co-ordinator & Director 1980-84. *Biog: b.* 4 August 1926. *Nationality:* British. *m.* 1952, Angela; 2 s; 2 d. *Educ:* Birmingham University (BSc Civil Engineering); Royal School of Mines, Imperial College. *Directorships:* Costain Group (non-exec). *Other Activities:* Member of Advisory Committee, Brown & Root. *Clubs:* Nevill Golf Club, Chichester Yacht Club. *Recreations:* Golf, Sailing.

BELLEW, The Hon Christopher; Director, C Czarnikow Ltd, since 1989; Energy Futures. *Career:* C Czarnikow Ltd 1976-. *Biog: b.* 3 April 1954. *Nationality:* British. *Educ:* Eton; Durham University (BA). *Directorships:* International Petroleum Exchange of London Ltd 1986 (exec).

BELLHOUSE, D G; Partner, Cameron Markby Hewitt.

BELLINGER, Roger; Assistant General Manager, Norwich Union Life Insurance Society.

BELLINGHAM, Keith; Director, Guidehouse Securities Limited.

BELLIS, Peter Timothy; Partner, Herbert Smith, since 1987; Company Law. *Career:* Herbert Smith, Articled Clerk and Assistant Solicitor 1979-87. *Biog: b.* 17 May 1957. *Nationality:* British. *m.* 1984, Lindsey (née Fry); 2 s. *Educ:* George Watson's College, Edinburgh; St John's College, Cambridge (MA). *Clubs:* Jesters. *Recreations:* Squash, Walking.

BELLOTTI, Stephen M; Director, Merrill Lynch Pierce Fenner & Smith (Brokers & Dealers) Limited.

BELLOW, Irwin Norman; The Rt Hon Lord Bellwin; JP; Non-Executive Director, Taylor Woodrow plc.

BELLUT, J; Director, Crédit Lyonnais Euro-Securities Ltd.

BELMONT, Michael Jeremy Kindersley; *Career:* Cazenove & Co, Partner 1957-90. *Biog: b.* 26 February 1990. *Nationality:* British. *m.* 1953, Virginia (née Tate); 2 s; 1 d. *Educ:* Eton. *Directorships:* Frobisher Fund Ltd (non-exec); Ivory & Sime plc (non-exec); LASMO plc (non-exec); Monterey Trust plc 1967 (non-exec); Omnicor Inc 1990 (non-exec). *Other Activities:* Liveryman, Fishmongers Company. *Clubs:* City of London Club, Bohemian Club (San Francisco), Pratt's, Cavalry & Guards.

BELTON, John; Deputy Head of Business Services, Coopers & Lybrand Deloitte.

BENAIM, Solomon (Solly) Benjamin; General Practice Partner, Stoy Hayward, since 1985; Additional Responsibility for Technical Services and Training. *Career:* Stoy Hayward 1977-. *Biog: b.* 10 December 1955. *Nationality:* British. *m.* 1978, Annette; 2 d. *Educ:* Carmel College; London School of Economics (BSc Econ). *Professional Organisations:* FCA. *Recreations:* Reading, Travelling, Sport.

BENANAV, G G; Director, Aetna International (UK) Ltd.

BENDALL, P A; Deputy Managing Director, Benchmark Bank plc, since 1989; Property Lending, Banking. *Career:* Lloyds Bank plc, Senior Securities Clerk 1969-76; Northwest Securities, Branch Manager 1976-78; Provident Financial Group plc, Divisional Director 1978-84; Benchmark Group plc, Deputy Managing Director, Bank Developments 1984-. *Biog: b.* 7 May 1951. *Nationality:* British. *Educ:* West Hatch Grammar School, Chigwell Essex. *Directorships:* Benchmark Group (exec); All Group Companies (exec). *Professional Organisations:* ACIB; MICM. *Clubs:* Theydon Bois Golf Club, Swallow Health & Fitness Club, Mortons. *Recreations:* Golf, All Sports.

BENHAM, Keith Peter; Partner, Linklaters & Paines, since 1973; Corporate Department. *Career:* Linklaters & Paines, Articled Clerk 1963-68; Asst Solicitor 1968-73. *Biog: b.* 10 March 1943. *Nationality:* British. *m.* 1969, Merilyn Anne (née Holbrook); 3 d. *Educ:* Marlborough School. *Other Activities:* Member of the Board of Southern Region of British Rail (1989); Governor of St Mary's School, Calne (1989). *Professional Organisations:* The Law Society; City of London Law Society. *Clubs:* City Law, Sea View Yacht Club. *Recreations:* Gardening, Music, Tennis, Sailing, Skiing.

BENITZ, Bryan; Chairman, Benitz and Partners Limited.

BENJAMIN, Miss Diana Gwenllian; Partner, Walker Martineau Stringer Saul, since 1988; Commercial Property Law. *Career:* Coward Chance/Clifford Chance 1972-88. *Biog: b.* 23 September 1943. *Nationality:* British. *Educ:* Llwyn-y-Bryn Grammar School, Swansea; Lowther College, Nr Rhyl. *Other Activities:* The Law Society's Land Law and Conveyancing Committee, The City of London Solicitor's Company; Liveryman, City Womens Network. *Professional Organisations:* The Law

Society. *Recreations:* Theatre, Music, Good Food & Wine, Antiques, Gardening.

BENJAMIN, R M; Partner (Guernsey), Bacon & Woodrow.

BENJAMIN, Sidney; Partner, Bacon & Woodrow.

BENJAMIN, Victor Woolf; Partner, Berwin Leighton, since 1958; Corporate Finance. *Biog: b.* 2 March 1935. *Nationality:* British. *m.* 1981, Judith (née Powell); 3 s; 2 d. *Educ:* Malvern. *Directorships:* Lex Service plc 1971 Dep Chm (non-ex); Tesco plc 1982 Part-time Dep Chm. *Other Activities:* Dir, The Blackheath Concert Halls; Director, Guilford Mills (Europe) Ltd; Director, Grandcart Ltd; Director, Lex Pension Trustees Ltd; Director, Tesco Pension Trustees Ltd; Chairman, Central Council for Jewish Social Services. *Clubs:* Savile, City of London, Royal Thames Yacht Club. *Recreations:* Sailing, Skiing, Opera.

BENNETT, Barrie; Director, Kleinwort Benson Securities Ltd, since 1986; International Equities. *Career:* Wedd Durlacher Mordaunt & Co, Ptnr 1976-86. *Biog: b.* 20 August 1943. *Nationality:* British. *m.* 1963, Maureen Patricia (née Driscoll); 2 d. *Educ:* Stationers' Grammar School. *Directorships:* Kleinwort Benson Ltd 1986. *Professional Organisations:* Member, The International Stock Exchange.

BENNETT, David Jonathan; Treasurer, Cheltenham & Gloucester Building Society, since 1989; Treasury. *Biog: b.* 26 March 1962. *Nationality:* British. *Educ:* Queens' College, Cambridge (MA Hons Economics); King's College School, Wimbledon.

BENNETT, Mrs Elizabeth Anne (née Allen); Partner, Linklaters & Paines, since 1985. *Career:* Williams & James, Articled Clerk 1973-75. *Biog: b.* 30 September 1950. *Nationality:* British. *m.* 1971, Professor Robert J; 2 s. *Educ:* Merchant Taylors' School for Girls, Crosby; Girton College, Cambridge (MA). *Professional Organisations:* The Law Society; The City of London Solicitors' Company; The Association of Women Solicitors. *Recreations:* Music, Watching Ballet.

BENNETT, Geoffrey W; Senior Vice President & General Manager, The Bank of New York. *Career:* Bank of New York 1966; (London), General Manager 1987. *Biog: Nationality:* American. *m.* Anne; 3 s. *Educ:* Washington & Jefferson College (BA Economics & Political Science); New York University (MBA Banking & Finance); Harvard University (Graduate, Credit & Financial Management). *Directorships:* Inter Maritime Bank Geneva, Switzerland 1990 (exec). *Other Activities:* Member, Overseas Bankers Club; Member, Lombard Association.

BENNETT, Graham R; Partner, Wilde Sapte.

BENNETT, Guy Patrick de Courcy; Director, CIN Management, since 1988; UK Investment Management (Marketable Securities Division). *Career:* Equity & Law Graduate Trainee 1980-81; Investment Analyst 1981-83. *Biog: b.* 27 October 1958. *Nationality:* British. *m.* 1988, Monica Beatrice (née Brodermann); 1 d. *Educ:* Wimbledon College; Manchester University (BSc). *Recreations:* Rugby, Tennis, Squash.

BENNETT, J D S; Group Financial Director, John Menzies plc, since 1981. *Career:* Binder Hamlyn 1968-72; Anglo Continental Trust London, Financial Director 1972-75; Chloride Group, Financial Director, Various Subsidiaries & Divisions 1975-81. *Biog: b.* 1 March 1942. *Nationality:* British. *m.* 1969, Lorna (née Peat); 2 s. *Educ:* Fettes College, Edinburgh; University of Edinburgh (MA); Institute of Chartered Accountants of Scotland (CA). *Directorships:* East of Scotland Industrial Investments plc 1984 (non-exec); Edinburgh Old Town Trust 1987 (non-exec); Edinburgh Old Town Charitable Trust 1987 (non-exec); Scottish Provident Institution 1989 (non-exec); Member of Commission for Local Authority Accounts in Scotland 1983 (non-exec). *Other Activities:* Institute of Directors; University of Edinburgh Business Studies Advisory Group; Group of Scottish Finance Directors. *Professional Organisations:* FBIM; FRSA. *Clubs:* New (Edinburgh), Denham, Luffness New, Murrayfield. *Recreations:* Golf, Reading.

BENNETT, Jeffrey A; Managing Director (Investment Management), Merrill Lynch International Limited.

BENNETT, Jeffrey John; Director, Unibank plc, since 1990; Corporate & Private Banking. *Career:* Midland Bank Various Branches 1964-74; Charterhouse Bank Ltd 1974-85; Director 1985-89. *Biog: b.* 7 April 1946. *m.* 1968, Susan Mary(née Carr); 1 s; 2 d. *Educ:* Wimbledon College. *Professional Organisations:* AIB; ARCIB. *Recreations:* Golf, Gardening, Squash (Previously Rugby).

BENNETT, John Henry; Financial Director, Beazer Europe & Overseas Ltd, since 1989; Financial. *Career:* Stanley Blythen & Co, Articled Clerk to Qualified ACA 1964-72; British Enkalon Ltd, Financial Accountant 1972-76; William Coran Ltd, Company Accountant 1976-77; Second City Group, Company Accountant to Group Secretary 1977-83; Beazer Group, Financial Director of Division to Main Board Director 1983-. *Biog: b.* 11 November 1947. *Nationality:* British. *m.* 1973, Penny (née Morris); 1 s; 1 d. *Educ:* Ilkeston Grammar School. *Directorships:* Beazer plc 1989 (exec); Beazer Europe and Overseas Ltd 1989 (exec); Beazer Homes Ltd 1984 (exec); Beazer Property Ltd 1984 (exec). *Professional Organisations:* FCA. *Recreations:* Family.

BENNETT, Martin Malcolm Bertram; Partner, Nabarro Nathanson, since 1982. *Career:* Egerton Sandler Summer & Co, Articled. *Biog: b.* 31 January 1952. *Nationality:* British. *m.* 1981, Jacqueline Mary (née Gambrell); 2 d. *Educ:* Simon Langton Grammar, Canterbury; Gonville and Caius College, Cambridge (MA).

BENNETT, Neil; Banking Correspondent, The Times.

BENNETT, Nick; Consultant (Equities & Fund Management), BBM Associates.

BENNETT, P R; Managing Director Finance & Accounting, UBS Phillips & Drew Securities Limited.

BENNETT, Philip F J; Partner, Slaughter and May, since 1986; Pensions and Employment. *Career:* Slaughter and May, Solicitor 1979-86. *Biog: b.* 2 March 1954. *Educ:* Haileybury; Durham University (BA Hons). *Professional Organisations:* Legislative & Parliamentary Ctee; The Law Society; Assoc of Pensions Lawyers; The City of London Solicitors' Company. *Publications:* Pension Fund Surpluses: Takeovers, Acquisitions, Taxation, 1989.

BENNETT, Robert Frederick; General Manager, Leeds Permanent Building Society, since 1988; Finance and Estates. *Career:* National Coal Board Cost Clerk 1965-66; Spicer & Pegler (CA) Articled Clerk 1966-70; Bridge Upholstery (Leeds) Ltd Chief Acc 1970-73; National Coal Board Cash Flow Acc 1973-76; Barnsley Metropolitan Borough Council Principal Acc 1976-79; Leeds Permanent Building Society Asst Acc 1979-82; Fin Acc 1982-85; Asst Gen Mgr 1985-88. *Biog: b.* 30 May 1947. *Nationality:* British. *m.* 1987, Margaret Mary (née Ward); 3 s. *Educ:* Kings' School, Pontefract. *Directorships:* Leeds Permanent Financial Planning 1989 (exec); Leeds Permanent Financial Services 1990 (exec). *Professional Organisations:* FCA; Assoc Mem, Chartered Institute of Management Accountants; Assoc Mem; Chartered Institute of Public & Finance Accountants. *Recreations:* Rugby League, Squash, Music, Reading.

BENNETTS, Peter; Partner, Beavis Walker, since 1981; Audit Partner. *Biog: b.* 24 August 1955. *Nationality:* British. *m.* 1983, Roxane Cressy (née Palmer). *Professional Organisations:* FCA. *Recreations:* Shooting.

BENNIE, Thomas; General Manager, Bank of Scotland, since 1984; General Management. *Career:* The British Linen Bank, Various Branches and Departments 1949-69; Assistant Superintendent of Branches 1969-73; Scotland Finance Company Ltd, Assistant General Manager 1973-77; The British Linen Bank Limited, Deputy Chief Executive & Assistant Director 1977-78; Director 1978; Bank of Scotland, Divisional General Manager, International Division 1980; General Manager 1983;

General Manager, UK Banking - West 1989. *Biog: b.* 7 November 1932. *Nationality:* British. *m.* 1956, Jean (née Wallace); 2 s; 2 d. *Educ:* Falkirk High School; Harvard Business School. *Professional Organisations:* Institute of Bankers (Scot). *Clubs:* The New Club Edinburgh. *Recreations:* Golf, Fishing.

BENNINGTON, William E; Director, Bradstock Financial Services Ltd.

BENSEN, L; Director, Ultramar plc.

BENSON, Sir Christopher (John); Chairman, MEPC plc, since 1988. *Career:* Chartered Surveyor and Agricultural Auctioneer 1957-64; Arndale Developments Ltd Dir 1965-69; Dolphin Developments Ltd (Salisbury) Chm 1969-71; The Law Land Co Ltd Asst MD 1972-74; Adviser to Farmer 1975-; Civic Trust Chm 1976-88; MEPC plc Vice Chm & MD 1976-88; British Petroleum Pension Fund 1979-84; London Docklands Development Corporation Chm 1984-88; Property Advisory Group to Department of the Environment Chm 1988-90; The Boots Company plc, Chairman 1990-; The Housing Corporation, Chairman 1990-. *Biog: b.* 20 July 1933. *Nationality:* British. *m.* 1960, Margaret Josephine OBE, JP (née Bundy); 2 s. *Educ:* Worcester Cathedral King's School The Incorporated Thames Nautical Training College HMS Worcester. *Directorships:* House of Fraser plc 1982-86 (non-exec); Royal Opera House 1984-; Sun Alliance & London Insurance plc 1988- (non-exec); Reedpack 1989-90 Chm. *Other Activities:* Hon Fellow, Wolfson College; Chm, Westminster Christmas Appeal; Founder Member, Jo Benson Day Centre for the Physically Handicapped, Salisbury; Trustee, Advance in Medicine, The London Hospital; Liveryman, Guild of Air Pilots. *Professional Organisations:* Honorary Bencher of The Middle Temple. *Publications:* FRICS. *Clubs:* City Livery Club, Naval Club, RAC, MCC. *Recreations:* Aviation, Opera, Ballet, Swimming.

BENSON, David Holford; Vice Chairman, Kleinwort Benson Group plc, since 1989. *Career:* Shell Transport & Trading Exec, Shell Company of Singapore 1957-63; Kleinwort Benson Ltd Exec 1963-72; Dir 1972-87; Kleinwort Benson Group plc, Director 1988. *Biog: b.* 26 February 1938. *Nationality:* British. *m.* 1964, Lady Elizabeth Mary (née Charteris); 1 s; 2 d. *Educ:* Eton College. *Directorships:* British Gas plc; The Rouse Company 1986 (non-exec); Marshall & Cavendish 1986 (non-exec); Charities Official Investment Fund (Trustee) 1985. *Other Activities:* English Speaking Union (Hon Treasurer 1973-78). *Clubs:* White's, English Speaking Union. *Recreations:* Painting.

BENSON, David L; Executive Director, Crédit Suisse First Boston Limited.

BENSON, H C; Finance Director, Morgan Grenfell Asset Management Limited.

BENSON, Keith; Senior Manager of Treasury, Kredietbank NV.

BENSON, The Hon Michael D'Arcy; Managing Director, Scimitar Asset Management Ltd, since 1985; Global Management Operation. *Career:* L Messel & Co, Research Analyst 1963-67; Lazard Securities Ltd, Fund Manager 1967-80; Director 1980-85; Lazard Brothers Ltd, Director 1980-85; Lazard Brothers (Jersey) Ltd, Director 1982-85; Lazard Securities (HK) Ltd, Director 1984-85; Lazard Securities (Guernsey) Ltd, Director 1984-. *Biog: b.* 23 May 1943. *Nationality:* British. *m.* 1969, Rachel Candida; 1 s; 2 d. *Educ:* Eton. *Directorships:* Scimitar Asset Management Ltd 1985 MD; Parham Park Ltd 1985 (exec). *Other Activities:* Trustee, The Lambeth Fund; Trustee, Royal Hospital & Home, Putney; Trustee, King George VI & Queen Elizabeth Foundation of St Catharine's. *Clubs:* Brooks's, St James'. *Recreations:* Gardening, Tennis, Shooting, Sailing, Bee-Keeping, Carpentry.

BENSON, R N H; Partner, Lawrence Graham, since 1986; All Aspects of Commercial Property Law. *Career:* Turner Peacock, Articled Clerk 1979-81; Lawrence Graham, Assistant Solicitor 1981-86. *Biog: b.* 24 November 1956. *Nationality:* British. *m.* 1980, Cidalia Santos Beja Abraao; 1 s. *Educ:* Queen Elizabeth Grammar School, Blackburn, Lancashire; Queen Mary College, University of London (LLB Hons); City of London Polytechnic. *Other Activities:* External Tutor and Examiner, College of Estate Management. *Professional Organisations:* Law Society; Westminster Law Society; Holborn Law Society; British Council of Shopping Centres. *Clubs:* National Liberal Club. *Recreations:* Skiing, Sailing, Golf.

BENSON, Stuart H; Partner, Turner Kenneth Brown.

BENTLEY, F R; Director, Yorkshire Building Society.

BENTLEY, Jacqueline Ann; Group Treasurer, Slough Estates plc.

BENTLEY, John H; Partner, Touche Ross & Co.

BENTLEY, Michael John; Joint Deputy Chairman, Electra Investment Trust plc, since 1986. *Career:* S G Warburg & Co Ltd 1962-76; Director 1968-76; Mercury Securities Ltd, Director 1974-76; Korea Merchant Banking Corporation (Seoul), Director & Exec Vice President 1977-79; Lazard Brothers & Co Ltd, Director 1977-80; J Henry Schroder Wagg & Co Ltd, Joint Vice Chairman 1980-85; Schroders plc, Director 1980-85; Group Man Director, Corporate Finance 1983-85. *Biog: b.* 23 November 1933. *Nationality:* British. *m.* 1961,

Sally Jacqueline (née Hogan); 4 s. *Educ:* Morrisons Academy, Crieff Scotland; Institute of Chartered Accountants in England & Wales. *Directorships:* Electra Kingsway Ltd 1989 (exec) Deputy Chairman; Electra Kingsway Managers Holdings Ltd 1989 (exec) Deputy Chairman; Nimex Resources Ltd 1987 (exec). *Other Activities:* Chairman, Finance Committee, London Borough of Islington, 1968-71; Islington National Savings Committee, 1968-71. *Professional Organisations:* ACA, 1958; FCA, 1963. *Clubs:* Links Club, New York. *Recreations:* Music, Opera, Gardening, Sailing.

BENTLEY, Peter H; Director, Bradstock Blunt & Crawley Ltd.

BENTLEY, Peter John; Group Finance Director, M W Marshall & Company Ltd, since 1982; Group Finance, Technical and Administrative Services. *Career:* Prideaux Frere Brown & Co, Articles of Clerkship 1960-67; Price Waterhouse, Various to Snr Mgr 1967-77; Mercantile House Holdings plc, Group Acct 1978; M W Marshall & Company Ltd, Group Fin Dir 1982-. *Biog: b.* 10 October 1943. *Nationality:* British. *m.* 1969, Jane (née Waller); 2 d. *Educ:* Chigwell School. *Directorships:* M W Marshall & Company Limited; Marshalls Pension Trustee Company Limited; M W Marshall (Overseas) Limited; Marshalls (Bahrain) Limited; Forex Limited; Marshalls (London) Investment Limited; Interforex (Pty) Limited; M W Marshall (Capital Markets) Holdings Limited; Pan Arab Management Co, KSCS; Marshalls 106 Limited; M W Marshall (International) Limited; M W Marshall Nominees Limited; M W Marshall (Options) Holdings Limited; M W Marshall (Options) SA; Marshalls (Japan) Limited; Marshalls (Jersey) Trust Company Limited; Marshalls Finance Limited; Depthhold Limited; Marshalls Finance Trustees (Jersey) Limited. *Professional Organisations:* FCA; FCT. *Clubs:* Royal Burnham Yacht. *Recreations:* Sailing.

BENTON, Robert John; Executive Director, James Capel & Co Ltd, since 1990; UK Sales. *Career:* Cazenove, Trainee; Capel & Co, Salesman, Deputy Head of Sales, Head of Sales, Executive Director. *Biog: b.* 16 August 1957. *Nationality:* British. *m.* 1982, Belinda (née Wills); 2 s; 2 d. *Educ:* King's School, Canterbury; Exeter University (BA Politics/Economic Hist). *Other Activities:* Member, Turners Company. *Clubs:* Tandridge Golf Club. *Recreations:* Golf, Acting, Pictures.

BENTS, N A; Director, Crédit Lyonnais Rouse Limited.

BENWELL, G; Partner, Nabarro Nathanson.

BENWELL, R T; Director, Knight & Day Ltd.

BENZECRY, Cecil; Partner, Penningtons (Solicitors), since 1986; Corporate Finance/Property. *Career:* Montagu's Cox & Cardales (Solicitors), Partner 1950-70; Jessel Securities Group, Legal and Property Director 1958-74; Full Time Executive 1969-72; Cardales (Solicitors), Partner 1970-86. *Biog: b.* 22 July 1922. *Nationality:* British. *m.* 1958, Susan Jane (née Warren); 3 s; 1 d. *Educ:* Cranleigh School; Downing College, Cambridge (MA). *Directorships:* Linton Park plc 1970 (non-exec); Leeds Fireclay Company Limited 1963 (non-exec) Chairman; Johnson & Firth Brown plc; Maple & Company Limited; The London Australian and General Exploration Company Limited; Algrey Developments Limited Chairman; Constellation Investments Limited Deputy Chairman; Leeds Assets Limited. *Professional Organisations:* Member, Law Society. *Clubs:* RAC. *Recreations:* Squash, Tennis, Golf, Theatre.

BERESFORD, W; Director of Marketable Securities, CIN Management Limited.

BERESFORD JONES, David; Chairman, Steel Burrill Jones Group plc, since 1990. *Career:* Bland Welch & Co Ltd 1954; National Service in RAF, Pilot Officer 1954-56; Bland Welch & Co Ltd 1957; Bland Welch (Reinsurance Brokers Ltd), Director 1971-74; Bland Payne Reinsurance Brokers Ltd, Director 1974-76; Steel Burrill Jones Ltd, Co-Founder and Director 1977-. *Biog: b.* 19 August 1936. *Nationality:* British. *m.* 1972, Lynda (née Dolleymore); 1 s; 3 d. *Educ:* King's School, Bruton, Somerset. *Directorships:* Steel Burrill Jones Corp plc 1983 (exec) Chairman 1990; Steel Burrill Jones Ltd 1977 (exec) Chairman 1990; SBJ Marine Reinsurance Brokers Ltd 1988 (exec); SBJ Marine Ltd 1989 (exec) Chairman; Meacock Samuelson & Devitt Ltd 1989 (exec) Chairman; R Mears & Co Ltd 1983 (non-exec); R Mears & Co (Holdings) Ltd 1986 (exec); J Ryder-Smith & Co Ltd 1988 (exec). *Other Activities:* Member, National Committee Paul O'Gorman Foundation for Children with Leukaemia. *Professional Organisations:* Institute of Directors; Insurance Brokers Registration Council. *Clubs:* MCC, HAC, RTC, RBRTC. *Recreations:* Golf, Real Tennis.

BERGENDAHL, C Anders; Managing Director (Investment Management), Merrill Lynch International Limited.

BERGER, Alfred B; Non-Executive Director, Merrill Lynch International Bank Limited.

BERGER, Geoffrey David; Deputy Chief Executive, Chancery plc, since 1976; Banking. *Directorships:* Chancery plc and Subsidiaries (exec); Consolidated Finance Holding Ltd and Subsidiaries (exec); General Portfolio Group plc (non-exec); General Portfolio Life Insurance Company plc (non-exec); Grosvenor Terrace Developments plc (non-exec). *Professional Organisations:* FCA.

BERGER, S H; Partner, Milne Ross.

BERGMANN, Finn; Senior Representative, Bikuben Bank A/S, since 1987; Head of London Office. *Career:* Dew Danske Bank, Asst Manager 1966-89; Scaninavian Bank plc (London), Asst Manager 1979; Citibank (Copenhagen), Manager & Group Head in The Corporate Bank 1981-86. *Biog: b.* 25 February 1949. *Nationality:* Danish. *m.* 1987, Vibere (née Mollegaard); 1 d. *Educ:* Copenhagen Business School. *Recreations:* Tennis, Music, Literature.

BERINGER, Guy Gibson; Partner, Allen & Overy, since 1985; Company Law. *Career:* Allen & Overy, Asst Solicitor 1980-85. *Biog: b.* 12 August 1955. *m.* 1979, Margaret Catherine (née Powell); 3 d. *Educ:* Campbell College, Belfast; St Catharine's College, Cambridge (MA). *Professional Organisations:* The Law Society.

BERKE, David Maurice; Partner, Neville Russell, since 1988; Business Services. *Career:* Berke Fine (formerly Sherwood Cohen Fine) Partner 1966-88. *Biog: b.* 12 May 1935. *Nationality:* British. *m.* 1962, Esther (née Ovicher); 1 s; 1 d. *Educ:* Highbury County. *Professional Organisations:* FCA; ATII.

BERKELEY, David J; Managing Director, Brown, Shipley & Co Limited, since 1987; Offshore Banking. *Career:* E D & F Man Limited, Group Finance Director 1971-85. *Biog: b.* 7 August 1944. *Nationality:* British. *m.* 1968, Gay; 2 d. *Educ:* Rugby School. *Directorships:* Brown Shipley Offshore Holdings Limited 1989 (exec) Chm; Brown Shipley (Jersey) Limited 1985 (exec) Chm; Brown Shipley Stockbroking (CI) Limited 1988 (exec) Chm; Brown Shipley Trust Company (OI) Limited 1985 (exec) Chm; Brown Shipley Trust Company (IOM) Limited 1988 (exec) Chm; Brown Shipley (Isle of Man) Limited 1990 (exec) Chm; Brown Shipley International Currency Fund Ltd 1988 (exec) Chm; Brown Shipley International Bond Fund Ltd 1988 (exec) Chm; Brown Shipley Sterling Capital Fund Ltd 1988 (exec) Chm; Brown Shipley Sterling Bond Fund Ltd 1988 (exec) Chm. *Professional Organisations:* Member, International Stock Exchange; Fellow, Institute of Chartered Accountants in England & Wales. *Recreations:* Tennis, Hockey.

BERKOWITZ, Leonard Terry; Partner, Linklaters & Paines, since 1972; Corporate Law. *Career:* Supreme Court of South Africa, Advocate/Attorney 1959-64; Anglo African Shipping Co Ltd, Executive/Director 1965-67. *Biog: b.* 11 October 1936. *Nationality:* British. *m.* 1964, Ruth (née Greenfield); 2 s; 1 d. *Educ:* Parktown Boys High School, Johannesburg; University of Witwatersrand, Johannesburg (BCom, LLB). *Professional Organisations:* Law Society; City of London Solicitors Company. *Recreations:* Golf, Tennis.

BERLIAND, David Michael; Deputy Chairman, Bain Clarkson Ltd, since 1990; Chairman & Managing Director, International Division. *Career:* Bain Clarkson Ltd Companies 1958-. *Biog: b.* 17 December 1935. *Nationality:* British. *m.* 1961, Diana Jill (née Puckle); 1 s; 2 d. *Educ:* Charterhouse. *Directorships:* Bain Clarkson 1990 (exec) Deputy Chairman; Clarkson Puckle 1980-87 (exec) Deputy Chairman. *Other Activities:* Worshipful Company of Insurers. *Professional Organisations:* ACII. *Clubs:* Boodles, MCC, Sunningdale Golf Club. *Recreations:* Tennis, Golf.

BERNAERT, Marc; General Manager, Kredietbank NV, since 1988. *Career:* Handelsbank NV (Brussels) 1970-74; Kredietbank NV (Brussels) 1974-76; Kredietbank NV (New York) 1977-83; Kredietbank NV (London) 1983-. *Biog: b.* 28 December 1945. *Nationality:* Belgian. *m.* 1970, Tonia Bernaert Coene; 1 d. *Educ:* University Faculties, Saint Ignatius (Commercial & Consular Sciences Commercial Engineer. *Directorships:* Kredietfinance (UK) Ltd; Belgo Luxembourg Chamber of Commerce in Great Britain; Kredietlease (UK) Ltd. *Professional Organisations:* Lombard Association. *Clubs:* Anglo-Belgian Club, Overseas Bankers Club. *Recreations:* Sport, reading.

BERNAYS, Richard Oliver; Director, Mercury Asset Management Group plc, since 1986. *Career:* S G Warburg & Co Ltd 1971-78; Dir 1978-85. *Biog: b.* 22 February 1943. *m.* 1972, Karen; 3 d. *Educ:* Eton College; Trinity College, Oxford (MA). *Clubs:* Brooks's. *Recreations:* Fishing, Golf.

BERNSTEIN, Alex; Chairman, Granada Group.

BERNTSSON, John; Executive Director, Svenska International plc.

BERRIDGE, David Anderson; Chief Executive, Scottish Equitable Life Assurance Society, since 1982; Overall Responsibility. *Career:* Scottish Equitable Life Assurance Soc, Actuarial Trainee 1966-69; Systems Analyst 1969-72; Asst Actuary 1972-75; Asst New Business Mgr 1975-76; Pensions Mgr 1976-80; Asst Gen Mgr (Finance) 1980-82. *Biog: b.* 24 June 1944. *Nationality:* British. *m.* 1973, Maggie (née Lane); 1 s; 2 d. *Educ:* Edinburgh University (BSc). *Directorships:* Scottish Equitable (Managed Funds) Ltd 1978 (exec); Scottish Equitable Fund Managers Ltd 1980 (exec); Scottish Equitable Trustees Ltd 1979 (exec); Scottish Equitable Life Assurance Society 1987 (exec); CAMIFA Ltd 1987 (exec); Royal Scottish Assurance 1990 (exec). *Professional Organisations:* FFA.

BERRILL, Paul; Business Correspondent, Lloyd's List.

BERRILL, R K; Director, Henderson Administration Group plc, since 1990; MD of Henderson Unit Trust Management Limited. *Career:* Royal Green Jackets, Rank on leaving Captain 1977-82; Cadbury Schweppes 1982-83; Prescotts Limited 1983-84; Chemical Bank,

Marketing of Master Trust 1984-86; John Govett & Co Ltd, Director 1986-89; John Govett Pensions Limited, Deputy Managing Director. *Biog: b.* 8 December 1958. *Nationality:* British. *m.* 1986, Wendy (née Harrison); 2 d. *Directorships:* Henderson Administration Group plc 1990 (exec); Henderson Unit Trust Management Limited 1989 MD; Henderson Unit Funds Limited 1989 MD. *Other Activities:* Unit Trust Association Executive Committee. *Clubs:* Woburn Golf and Country Club. *Recreations:* Golf, Cricket, Showjumping (Watching).

BERRY, Brian S; Manaing Director, CSFB (Gilts) Limited.

BERRY, C M; Head of International Banking Dept, Morgan Grenfell & Co Limited, since 1990. *Career:* Mitsui & Co Ltd 1972-81. *Biog: b.* 3 March 1951. *Nationality:* British. *m.* 1975, Patricia (née Guterres); 1 s; 1 d. *Educ:* Bemrose School, Derby; Hertford College, Oxford (MA).

BERRY, Christopher; Partner, Gouldens.

BERRY, D; Director, Chartered WestLB Limited.

BERRY, D C; Director, British Land.

BERRY, Ian; Senior VP Director, Bonds, ScotiaMcLeod Incorporated.

BERRY, John Charles Howard; Managing Director, Berry Palmer & Lyle Limited, since 1983. *Career:* Hogg Group plc, Broker 1974-82. *Biog: b.* 17 May 1952. *Nationality:* British. *Educ:* Ampleforth College, York; Lincoln College, Oxford (BA); Harvard Business School (MBA). *Directorships:* BPL (Holdings) Ltd 1988 (exec); Berry Palmer & Lyle Ltd 1983 (exec); Rudd Huntley & Tate Ltd 1988 (exec). *Other Activities:* Committee, Harvard Business School Club of London. *Professional Organisations:* FCII.

BERRY, Paul; Partner, Titmuss Sainer & Webb.

BERRY, Peter Michael; Director, Hoare Govett International Securities Ltd, since 1989; International. *Career:* Jackson Smith & Knights Jessop 1968-1973; Stocken & Lazarus 1973-1977; Akroyd & Smithers 1977-85. *Biog: b.* 9 May 1951. *Nationality:* British. *m.* 1980, Susan Maureen (née Clack); 1 s; 1 d. *Educ:* Kynaston School, St John's Wood. *Clubs:* Croydon Amphibians SC, Stock Exchange SC. *Recreations:* Water Polo, Windsurfing.

BERTON, E D; Partner, Field Fisher Waterhouse.

BERTRAM, Robert David Darney; Partner, Dundas & Wilson.

BERWEIN, Paul; Member of the Board, Berwein Wertpapierhandels- und Börsenmakler AG, snce 1988. *Career:* Kreissparkasse, München, Banking Trainee 1950-52; Kreissparkasse, Tegernsee, Bank Clerk 1952-54; Kreissparkasse, München, Asst Bank Manager 1954-57; Language & Interpreter Inst, Student 1957-59; Feuchtwanger Bank, Dealer 1959-64; Independent Stock Broker 1964-77; Paul Berwein GmbH, Proprietor & MD 1978-88; Berwein Wertpapierhandels- und Börsenmakler AG, Member of the Board 988-. *Biog: b.* 1 July 1932. *m.* Gerda Annamaria (née Wicke); 1 s; 3 d. *Educ:* Sprachen-und Dolmetscher-Institut, München, Language & Interpreter Institute (English and French). *Directorships:* S G Warburg Securities Ltd 1989 (exec). *Other Activities:* Spokesman, Bundesverband der freien Börsenmakler (Federal Association of Independent Stock Brokers). *Publications:* Several Articles and Lectures on Stock Exchange Development. *Clubs:* Land- und Golfclub (St Eurach). *Recreations:* Golf.

BERWIN, N M; Director, Morgan Grenfell & Co Limited.

BESSE, Mrs Eryl; Partner, Linklaters & Paines, since 1990; International Finance. *Career:* Freshfields, Articled Clerk 1981-83; Assistant Solicitor 1983-86; Linklaters & Paines (Paris), Assistant Solicitor 1986-87; Linklaters & Paines (London), Assistant Solicitor 1987-90; Partner 1990-. *Biog: b.* 4 July 1958. *Nationality:* British. *m.* 1986, Antonin Louis Philippe Henri. *Educ:* Ardwyn Grammar School/Penglais Comprehensive School, Abersytwyth; Birmingham University/Limoges University (LLB Law with French 1st Class Hons). *Other Activities:* Member, City of London Solicitors' Company. *Professional Organisations:* Member, The Law Society. *Recreations:* Piano, Flute.

BEST, David; Partner, Clyde & Co.

BEST, J D; Managing Director, Prudential-Bache Capital Funding. *Career:* First Chicago, Vice Chairman 1985-87; First Boston ICSFB 1976-84. *Biog: b.* 23 July 1949. *Nationality:* Canadian; 2 s. *Educ:* University of Western Ontario (BA). *Directorships:* Emerging Germany Fund (non-exec). *Clubs:* Flyfisher's. *Recreations:* Fishing, Rare Books.

BEST, Roger Simon Melliship; Partner, Clifford Chance; Banking and Insolvency Litigation. *Biog: b.* 27 November 1955. *Nationality:* British; 1 s. *Educ:* The Judd School, Tonbridge; University of Durham (BA Hons Economics & Law). *Other Activities:* City of London Solicitors Company. *Professional Organisations:* Law Society. *Recreations:* Sailing, Squash, Running, Theatre.

BEST, Simon Peter Francis; Director, Baring Brothers & Co Limited, since 1989; Capital Markets New Issues. *Career:* Australian Treasury 1973-82; Baring

Brothers & Co Limited 1983-; Director 1989-. *Biog: b.* 6 December 1950. *Nationality:* Australian. *m.* 1977, Alexis Jane (née Walker); 4 s. *Educ:* Pulteney Grammar School, Adelaide; Adelaide University (BA Hons); University of Oxford (BPhil). *Directorships:* Baring Brothers & Co Limited 1989 (exec); Baring Sterling Bonds 1990 (non-exec).

BETHELL-JONES, Richard James Stephen; Partner, Wilde Sapte, since 1975; Banking, Finance, Insolvency. *Career:* Ashurst Morris Crisp & Co Articled Clerk 1968-70; Asst Solicitor 1970-73. *Biog: b.* 16 September 1945. *Nationality:* British. *m.* 1973, Sarah Landells (née Hodson); 2 d. *Educ:* St Johns School, Leatherhead; Churchill College, Cambridge (MA). *Professional Organisations:* The Law Society, City of London Law Society (Insolvency Law Sub-Ctee). *Clubs:* Queenhithe Ward Club, Hurlingham Club. *Recreations:* Tennis.

BETHENOD, Gilles; Deputy Managing Director, Yamaichi International (Europe) Ltd, since 1986; Corporate Finance. *Career:* Banque Nationale de Paris Various, Cap Mkts (Paris) 1975-86. *Biog: b.* 28 September 1948. *Nationality:* French. *m.* 1974, Sylvie (née Colin); 2 s; 1 d. *Educ:* Ecole des Roches, France; Paris University (Doctorate - Economics). *Recreations:* Tennis, Skiing.

BETTELHEIM, Eric C; Senior Resident Partner, Rogers & Wells, since 1988; Banking, Securities and Commodities Law. *Biog: b.* 27 January 1952. *Nationality:* American. *Educ:* Oxford University (BA, MA); University of Chicago (JD). *Professional Organisations:* American Bar Association; Barrister, Inner Temple; New York Bar Association; California Bar Association.

BETTENCOURT, Bruce; Vice President, Manufacturers Hanover Trust Company, since 1986; Corporate Finance, Group Head, Benelux & France MNC's,Acquisition Finance, France. *Career:* Political Consulting Enterprises Member Mgmnt Ctee 1977-79; Manufacturers Hanover Mgmnt Trainee/VP 1979-. *Biog: b.* 27 November 1955. *Nationality:* French-American. *Educ:* La Salle Academy, Providence, RI, USA; Brown University USA (BA); Institut des Etudes Politiques de Paris (Certificat); Institut des Hautes Internationales, Paris (Certificat); New York University (MBA). *Other Activities:* Council on Foreign Affairs (New York). *Recreations:* Squash, Skiing, Running.

BETTON, David John William; Partner, Clark Whitehill, since 1989; Director, VAT Group. *Career:* In Practice at the Bar 1972-76; HM Customs and Excise, Securities Office, Senior Legal Adviser 1976-86; Clark Whitehill 1986-. *Biog: b.* 30 December 1947. *Nationality:* British. *m.* 1980, Nicola Mary; 1 s; 3 d. *Educ:* Dulwich College, London; Emmanuel College, Cambridge (Classics/Law). *Other Activities:* Worshipful Company of Plumbers. *Professional Organisations:* The Bar. *Publications:* The VAT Factbook, 1989; VAT in

Printing, 1990. *Clubs:* MCC, RAC. *Recreations:* Cricket, Theatre, Dog Walking.

BETTS, D; Partner, Raphael Zorn Hemsley Ltd.

BEVAN, Judi; City Journalist, The Sunday Telegraph, since 1989. *Career:* Investors' Chronicle; Financial Weekly; Daily Mail; Sunday Telegraph; The Sunday Times, Dep City Editor 1986-89. *Educ:* (BA English History). *Publications:* The New Tycoons (with John Jay).

BEVAN, Sir Timothy (Hugh); Chairman, BET plc, since 1988. *Career:* Called to Bar 1950; Barclays Bank Dir 1966; Chm 1981-87. *Biog: b.* 24 May 1927. *Nationality:* British. *m.* 1952, Pamela Murray (née Smith); 2 s; 2 d. *Educ:* Eton College. *Directorships:* Foreign & Colonial Investment Trust plc 1988 (non-exec); Barclays Bank 1966. *Other Activities:* Chm, The Ocean Youth Club; Trustee, The Winston Churchill Memorial Trust. *Clubs:* Cavalry & Guards, Royal Yacht Squadron, Royal Ocean Racing Club. *Recreations:* Sailing, Gardening.

BEVERLY, John Stephen; Head of Wholesale Markets Supervision Division, Bank of England, since 1990. *Career:* Bank of England, Governor's Private Secretary 1978-80; Banking Supervision Division, Policy Work both Domestic and International 1981-87; Banking Supervision Division, Deputy Head, N American and European Banks 1987-90. *Biog: b.* 24 April 1947. *Nationality:* British. *m.* 1969, Farida (née Raja); 1 s; 1 d. *Educ:* Queens' College, Cambridge (MA); London Business School (MSc Business Studies). *Clubs:* Overseas Bankers Club. *Recreations:* Golf, Classical Music (particularly Opera), Theatre.

BEVITT, Robin Wilfrid; Company Solicitor, Pearl Assurance plc.

BEWES, Michael Keith; Assistant General Manager, Guardian Royal Exchange plc, since 1981; Corporate Affairs and Personnel Development. *Career:* British Rail (NE Region), Various culminating in Mgmnt Selection & Development Asst 1959-66; Royal Exchange Assurance Mgmnt Development Officer 1966-68; Guardian Royal Exchange Personnel Mgr 1968-71; Field Services Mgr 1971-75; Mgr, Corporate Affairs & Personnel Development 1975-81. *Biog: b.* 4 March 1936. *Nationality:* British. *m.* 1964, Anrõs (née Neill); 3 s; 1 d. *Educ:* Marlborough College; Emmanuel College, Cambridge (MA). *Directorships:* Stowe School Ltd (non-exec); Stowe School Educational Services (non-exec); Scripture Union (non-exec); Various GRE Subsidiaries (exec). *Other Activities:* President, The Chartered Insurance Institute 1988-89; Mem, Governing Council, Business in the Community; Chm, Insurance Industry Training Council 1982-88; Governor of Stowe; Chm, Scripture Union; Fellow, Royal Society of Arts. *Professional Organisations:*

MBIM, Institute of Training Development (Fellow). *Clubs:* Hawks, RAC. *Recreations:* Fly Fishing, Heraldic Painting, Napoleana, Sport.

BEXON, R; Director, Lazard Brothers & Co Limited.

BEYNON, D J; Executive Director, Allied Dunbar Assurance plc.

BIBBY, Ewart Brian; Compliance Director & Company Secretary, Henry Cooke, Lumsden plc. *Career:* Royal Navy 1944-63. *Biog: b.* 20 May 1930. *Nationality:* British. *m.* 1957, Ann (née Gresham); 2 s; 1 d. *Educ:* R N College, Dartmouth. *Directorships:* NMW Computers plc 1977 Chm (non-exec). *Professional Organisations:* Member, The International Stock Exchange.

BIBBY, J M; Partner, R Watson & Sons Consulting Actuaries.

BICK, David; Executive Director, Lombard Communications Limited.

BICKERS, John Leonard; Director Human Resources, Cookson Group plc, since 1985; Management Development, Succession Planning, Corporate Relations, Health & Safety. *Career:* Nestle/Crosse & Blackwell, Sales Manager Chocolat Tobler 1958-62; Product Manager, Confectionery 1963-65; Tobler Meltis, Marketing Controller 1966-67; Jeyes (Ireland) Ltd, MD 1967-70; Jeyes Group, Marketing Director 1970-71; Brobat Group, MD 1971-72; Lead Industries Group, MD, Goodlass Wall & Co Ltd 1972-85. *Biog: b.* 1 July 1930. *Nationality:* British. *m.* 1953, Dawn (née Crook); 2 s; 1 d. *Educ:* Eltham College. *Directorships:* Cookson Group plc 1980 (exec); Goodlass Nerolac - Bombay 1985-90 (non-exec); Cookson Investments Ltd 1990 (non-exec).

BICKERTON, Gary; Director of Finance, W C R S Mathews Marcantonio.

BICKERTON, Peter William; Managing Director, Manufacturers Hanover Limited, since 1987; Corporate Finance. *Career:* Kock-Light Laboratories Ltd, Various 1962-65; Miles Laboratories, New Products Development Executive 1965-68; Fisons Ltd, Various (Finance Dept) 1968-75; Sime Darby Group, Group Treasurer 1975-80; Finance Director 1980-83; Manufacturers Hanover Limited, Associate Director 1983-84; Executive Director 1984-87; Managing Director 1987-. *Biog: b.* 4 July 1940. *Nationality:* British. *m.* 1967, Anne Bickerton (née Mitchell). *Educ:* Abbotsholme School, Derbyshire; University of Durham (BSc Chemistry); University of Grenoble; INSEAD. *Professional Organisations:* Foundation Fellow, Association of Corporate Treasurers (FCT). *Recreations:* Collecting Chinese Ceramics, Classical Music, Fine Wines.

BICKNELL, Gerard; Managing Director, Walter Judd Public Relations Ltd, since 1987; Public Relations. *Career:* Infoplan Ltd, Director, Public Relations Group Head 1968-72; Thompson & Partners Ltd, Managing Director 1972-76; Citibank/Citicorp, VP & Director of Public Affairs/Europe 1976-84; St James' PR Ltd, Director 1984-87. *Biog: b.* 19 August 1937. *Nationality:* British. *m.* 1965, Caryl (née Morley); 1 s; 2 d. *Educ:* Beaumont College. *Professional Organisations:* MIPR. *Recreations:* Tennis, Skiing.

BIDWELL, Sir Hugh Charles Philip; GBE; Vice Chairman, Allied-Lyons Eastern Ltd, since 1990. *Career:* National Service, Commissioned in East Surrey Regiment and seconded to First Battalion KAR, Nyasaland 1953-55; Viota Foods Ltd 1956-70; Board Member 1962; Managing Director 1967; Robertson Foods plc, (Parent Company of Viota Foods) 1969. *Biog: b.* 1 November 1934. *m.* 1962, Jenifer Celia; 2 s; 1 d. *Educ:* Stonyhurst College. *Directorships:* Ellis, Son & Vidler Ltd 1986-88 Chm; Pearce Duff Holdings Ltd 1970-84 Chm; Gill & Duffus Foods Ltd 1984-85 Chm; Allied-Lyons Eastern Ltd 1988 Chief Exec/Dir; Glendronach Distillery Co Ltd 1989; Baskin-Robbins Eastern Ltd 1990; Riggs AP Bank Ltd 1989 (non-exec). *Other Activities:* Lord Mayor of London, 1989-90; Sheriff of City of London, 1986-87; Alderman of Billingsgate Ward, 1979-; President, Billingsgate Ward Club; President, Billingsgate Christian Mission & Dispensary; President, Fishmongers' and Poulterers' Institution; Governor, Berkhamsted Schools; Worshipful Company of Grocers, Master, 1984-85; Hon Liveryman, Marketors Company; London Chamber of Commerce and Industry, Council Member 1976-85; Food and Drink Federation, Deputy President 1985-86; Food Manufacturers Federation, Member of Executive Committee 1973-86; British Food Export Council, President 1980-87; Food from Britain Council, Member 1983-89, Export Board, Chairman 1983-86; The British-Soviet Chamber of Commerce, Executive Council Member 1989-; Sino-British Trade Council, Council Member 1989; European Trade Committee BOTB, Member 1989; China Britain Trade Group, Council Member 1990; British Invisibles, Director 1990. *Clubs:* Boodles, City of London, Denham Golf Club (Captain 1980), Royal St Georges, MCC. *Recreations:* Golf, Tennis, Cricket, Fishing.

BIGGART, Thomas Norman; CBE, WS; Partner, Biggart Barllie & Gifford WS Solicitors, Glasgow & Edinburgh, since 1959. *Career:* Served RN, Sub-Lt RNVR 1954-56. *Biog: b.* 24 January 1930. *m.* 1956, Eileen Jean Anne (née Gemmell); 1 s; 1 d. *Educ:* Morrisons Academy, Crieff (MA); Glasgow University (LLB). *Directorships:* Clydesdale Bank 1985; New Scotland Insurance Gp 1986. *Other Activities:* Member of Council, Law Society of Scotland, 1977-86; Vice President, 1981-82; Pres, 1982-83; Pres, Business Archives Council, Scotland, 1977-86; Member, Exec Ctee, Scottish Council (Development and Industry) 1984-; Scottish Tertiary Education Advisory Council, 1984-87; Scottish Records Advisory Council, 1985-; Member, Council on Tribunals (Chm, Scottish Ctee), 1990-. *Clubs:* Royal Scottish Automobile, The Western Glasgow. *Recreations:* Golf, Hill Walking.

BIGGS, Adrian Hugh; Solicitor, Jaques & Lewis, since 1978; Commercial Property. *Biog: Nationality:* British. *Educ:* Felsted School, Essex. *Professional Organisations:* Solicitor; Member, Law Society. *Clubs:* West Mersea Yacht Club, Royal Ocean Racing Club, Suffolk Aero Club, Royal Aero Club. *Recreations:* Yachting, Flying, Skiing.

BIGGS, M N; Director, Morgan Grenfell & Co Limited.

BIGGS, O A W; Director/Agency Manager, MFK Underwriting Agencies Ltd.

BIGNELL, Geoffrey; Chief Executive, PaineWebber International Bank Ltd.

BILES, Michael J; Partner, Robson Rhodes, since 1977; Client Service, Audit. *Career:* Robson Rhodes Student 1967-70; Qualified Acct 1970-72; Mgr 1972-77. *Biog: b.* 23 June 1946. *Nationality:* British. *m.* 1971, Angela (née Griffin); 1 s; 1 d. *Educ:* St Nicholas Grammar School, Northwood, Middx; Nottingham University (BA). *Other Activities:* Treasurer, Hornsey Housing Trust Ltd. *Professional Organisations:* FCA. *Recreations:* All Sports, Walking, Family.

BILL, Jamieson; Deputy City Editor, The Sunday Telegraph, since 1986; Stock Market Analysis, Insurance, Drinks & Leisure, Mining & Metals. *Career:* Broadcaster for BBC, LBC, Radio 3AW Melbourne. *Educ:* (BA Econ). *Publications:* Goldstrike! The Oppenheimer Empire in Crisis.

BILLINGTON, Guy; Partner, McKenna & Co, since 1977; Corporate Finance. *Career:* Lovell White & King, Articled Clerk 1969-72; McKenna & Co, Asst Solicitor 1972-77. *Biog: b.* 12 November 1946. *Nationality:* British. *m.* 1966, Christine (née Bonner); 2 d. *Educ:* Kings College School, Wimbledon; St John's College, Cambridge (MA). *Professional Organisations:* The Law Society; City of London Solicitors Company. *Clubs:* Gresham, Rosslyn Park Football Club, British Sub-Aqua Club. *Recreations:* Rugby, Music, Scuba Diving.

BILLSON, Hew; Partner (Private Clients), Frere Cholmeley.

BINDER, Peter L; Director, Hambros Bank Limited, since 1989; Hambro Pacific Limited, Hong Kong. *Career:* Touche Ross & Co, Articled Clerk 1973-76; County NatWest Limited, Corporate Advisory Depart-

ment 1976-84; Hambro Bank Limited, Corporate Finance Department 1984-; Director 1987. *Biog: b.* 8 October 1952. *Nationality:* British. *m.* 1975, Wendy Jane (née Thum); 1 s; 2 d. *Educ:* Mill Hill School; University of Kent, Canterbury (BA Hons). *Directorships:* Hambro Pacific Limited (Hong Kong) 1989 Managing Director; Kwang Hua Securities Investment and Trust Co (Taipei) 1989 (non-exec). *Other Activities:* Member, Hong Kong Committee on Takeovers and Mergers. *Professional Organisations:* Fellow, Institute of Chartered Accountants. *Clubs:* Royal Hong Kong Jockey Club, Sheko Country Club. *Recreations:* Tennis, Walking.

BINDING, David; Secretary, Saatchi & Saatchi Company plc.

BINGHAM, M C; Chairman, Development Capital Group Ltd.

BINGHAM, Peter William; Director, Barclays de Zoete Wedd Ltd.

BINKS, Alan C; Director, Charterhouse Tilney, since 1986; Research. *Career:* R S Dawson (Bradford), Acct 1953-62; Thornton Baker (Leeds), Acct 1962-63; Charterhouse Tilney, Asst 1963-69; Ptnr 1969-86. *Biog: b.* 1937. *Nationality:* British; 2 s. *Educ:* Pudsey Grammar School. *Professional Organisations:* FCA. *Recreations:* Keep Fit, Squash, Cricket, Fell Walking.

BINKS, Robin Paul; Director, S G Warburg & Co Ltd.

BINNEY, I R; Director, A J Archer Holdings plc.

BINT, R S; Partner, Pannell Kerr Forster.

BINYON, R F; Director, Morgan Grenfell & Co Limited.

BIRCH, Peter Gibbs; Group Chief Executive, Abbey National plc, since 1984. *Career:* The Jamaica Regiment 2nd Lt 1956-58; Nestle (Switzerland, Singapore, Malaya) Various Positions 1958-65; Gillette (UK) Mktg Dept 1965-67; (Australia) Mktg 1968-71; (NZ) MD 1971-73; (SE Asia) MD 1973-75; (Africa) Group Gen Mgr 1975-81; (UK) MD 1981-84. *Biog: b.* 4 December 1937. *Nationality:* British. *m.* 1962, Gillian (née Benge); 3 s; 1 d. *Educ:* Allhallows School, Devon. *Directorships:* Abbey National plc 1984 Group Chief Executive; Hoskyns Group plc; Argos plc 1990 (non-exec). *Professional Organisations:* FCBSI. *Recreations:* Active Holidays, Swimming.

BIRCH, Philip; Chairman, Lombard Communications Limited.

BIRCH, S H; Clerk, Lightmongers' Company.

BIRD, Alistair Francis; Partner, Simmons & Simmons, since 1986; Corporate Finance. *Career:* Slaughter and May Asst Solicitor 1980-84. *Biog: b.* 10 December 1955. *Educ:* Bloxham College; University of London (LLB).

BIRD, Anthony G; Managing Director, J P Morgan Investment Mangement Inc.

BIRD, Colin Graham; Partner, Price Waterhouse, since 1990; London Corporate Reconstruction & Insolvency Department. *Career:* Price Waterhouse 1968-. *Biog: b.* 17 December 1949. *Nationality:* British. *m.* 1971, Janet (née Beard); 1 s; 1 d. *Educ:* The Latymer School, London. *Other Activities:* Chairman, Society of Practitioners of Insolvency Technical Committee; Member of Council, SPI; Member of Council, Insolvency Practitioners Association; Member, Insolvency Court Users Committee; Member, Insolvency Practitioners Joint Liaison Committee. *Professional Organisations:* FCA; FIPA.

BIRD, G R; Director, United Dominions Trust Limited.

BIRD, K C; Assistant General Manager, The Bank of Nova Scotia.

BIRD, N M H; Partner, Allen & Overy.

BIRD, Robert; Assistant General Manager (Treasury), Banque Internationale à Luxembourg.

BIRD, Stephan; Partner, Wilde Sapte, since 1972; Banking, Asset Financing. *Biog: b.* 3 January 1934. *m.* 1983, Aw Yee (née Tan). *Educ:* King Edward VII School, Sheffield; Brasenose College, Oxford (MA). *Professional Organisations:* The Law Society. *Publications:* How to Prune those Loan Agreements 1979; The State Immunity Act, 1978. *Recreations:* Theatre, Tai Chi, Fell Walking.

BIRKIN, Sir Derek; TD; Chief Executive & Deputy Chairman, The RTZ Corporation plc, since 1985. *Career:* Tunnel Holdings Ltd, Chm & MD 1971-83; Nairn Williamson Ltd, MD 1967-70; Velmar Ltd, MD 1966-67. *Biog: b.* 30 September 1929. *Nationality:* British. *m.* 1952, Sadie (née Smith); 1 s; 1 d. *Educ:* Hemsworth Grammar School; Cranfield College; Administrative Staff College, Henley; Harvard Business School. *Directorships:* Barclays plc 1990 (non-exec); British Steel plc 1986 (non-exec); George Wimpey plc 1984 (non-exec); The Merchants Trust plc 1986 (non-exec); CRA Ltd (Australia) 1985 (non-exec); Rio Algom Ltd (Canada) 1985 (non-exec); British Gas Corporation 1982-85 (non-exec); Smiths Industries plc 1977-84 (non-exec); The RTZ Corporation 1982- (exec); The RTZ Corporation 1983-85 Deputy Chief Executive. *Other Activities:* Member, Council of The Industrial

Society; Trustee, Royal Opera House Trust. *Professional Organisations:* Companion, British Institute of Management; Fellow, Royal Society of Arts. *Clubs:* MCC, Harlequins. *Recreations:* Cricket, Rugby, Opera.

BIRLEY, D K; Head of Commercial Property Dept, Field Fisher Waterhouse.

BIRNEY, J D; Director, S G Warburg & Co Ltd.

BIRRELL, Christopher Ros Stewart; Company Secretary, Steel Burrill Jones Group plc, since 1985; Lloyd's Brokers Finance Director. *Career:* Price Waterhouse 1977-81; Matheson & Co Ltd 1981-83; Henderson Administration Ltd 1983-85; Steel Burrill Jones Group plc 1985-. *Biog: b.* 11 March 1954. *Nationality:* British. *m.* 1984, Georgina (née Breton); 2 s. *Educ:* Radley College; Mansfield College, Oxford (MA). *Directorships:* Steel Burrill Jones Ltd 1987 (exec); Meacock Samuelson & Devitt Ltd 1989 (exec). *Professional Organisations:* ACA. *Clubs:* Bucks. *Recreations:* Fishing, Shooting.

BIRRELL, David; Senior Partner (Retired), Dundas Wilson C S, since 1984; Corporate & General Business. *Career:* Mackenzie Innes & Logan, Apprentice 1941-50; D & D Carruthers, Qualified Asst 1950-51; McArthur Stuart & Orr, Qualified Asst 1951-52; Davidson & Syme, Qualified Asst 1952-54; Ptnr 1954-. *Biog: b.* 6 November 1924. *Nationality:* British. *m.* 1955, Jean Pamela (née Grant) (deceased); 2 s; 1 d. *Educ:* Knox Academy, Haddington; Edinburgh University (BL). *Directorships:* The Scottish Business Achievement Award Trust Ltd; The Scotsman Communications Ltd; Milsey Bay Investments Ltd; Nipknowes Investments Ltd; Prestonfield Catering Ltd; Prestonfield House Hotel Ltd; Slitrig Nominees Ltd; Securities Trust of Scotland Ltd; William Nimmo & Co Ltd; Irvine Robertson Wines Ltd; The Scottish Life Assurance Co; The Scottish Life Pensions Annuity Co; The Scottish Life Investment Assurance Co Ltd; The Scottish Life Investment Management Co Ltd; Martin & Son (Edinburgh) Ltd; Martin & Son (Edinburgh) Ltd; Clydesdale Bank plc; Prestonfield L'Aperitif Ltd; Brackett Agency Ltd; Saltire Insurance Investments plc; Morgan Grenfell Ltd 1990 (non-exec). *Other Activities:* Law Society of Scotland. *Clubs:* The Honourable Company of Edinburgh Golfers, Haddington Rugby Football, Club, Bruntsfield Links Golfing Society. *Recreations:* Golf, Rugby Football.

BIRRELL, James Drake; Chief Executive, Halifax Building Society, since 1988. *Career:* Boyce Welch & Co, Articled Clerk 1949-55; RAF, Pilot Officer 1955-57; Price Waterhouse, CA 1957-60; ADA Halifax Ltd, Acct 1960-61; Empire Stores, Mgmnt Acct 1961-64; John Gladstone & Co Ltd, Dir & Co Sec 1964-68; Halifax Building Society 1968-. *Biog: b.* 18 August 1933. *Nationality:* British. *m.* 1958, Margaret Anne (née Pattison); 2 d. *Educ:* Belle Vue Grammar School, Bradford. *Professional Organisations:* FCA; FCBSI. *Recreations:* Golf, Gardening, Archaeology, Keep Fit, Local History.

BIRRELL, James Gibson; WS; Partner, Dickson Minto, since 1985. *Career:* Brodies WS, Partner 1976-85. *Biog: b.* 10 June 1948. *Nationality:* British. *m.* 1970, Angela Hilary (née Soame); 2 s; 1 d. *Educ:* Loretto School; Queen Mary College, University of London (BA Hons). *Professional Organisations:* The Law Society of Scotland; The Law Society; International Bar Association. *Publications:* Contributor, Stair Memorial Encyclopaedia. *Clubs:* Caledonian. *Recreations:* Squash, Skiing, Golf.

BISCHOFF, Winfried Franz Wilhelm; Chairman, J Henry Schroder Wagg & Co Limited, since 1983; Investment Banking. *Career:* J Henry Schroder Wagg & Co Ltd 1966-; Dir 1978-; Schroders Asia Ltd (Hong Kong), MD 1971-82. *Directorships:* Schroders plc 1983 Group Chief Exec; Schroders International Ltd 1973 (exec); Schroders Asia Ltd 1971 (non-exec).

BISHOP, Christopher David; Partner, Ernst & Young, since 1985; Insurance Industry Group. *Career:* Baker Sutton & Co, Articled Clerk/Mgr 1956-71; G R Merton (Agencies) Ltd, Company Sec 1971-74; Christopher Bishop & Co, Principal 1974-85. *Biog: b.* 18 September 1938. *Nationality:* British. *m.* 1961, Judith (née Wise); 3 s; 1 d. *Educ:* Eastbourne College. *Professional Organisations:* FCA. *Clubs:* City of London. *Recreations:* Hunting, Equestrian Sports, Golf.

BISHOP, Errol Simon Owen; Director, Barclays Development Capital Ltd, since 1981. *Career:* Dihurst Holdings Ltd, Dir, Group MD 1976-80; Systems Designers International Ltd, Dir, Dep Chm 1976-81. *Biog: b.* 1 August 1938. *Nationality:* British; 1 s; 2 d. *Educ:* Charterhouse; University of Southampton (BSc Eng). *Directorships:* Barclays Development Capital Ltd & Related Companies 1981 (exec); Carpet Express Holdings Ltd 1986 (non-exec); Mecro Group Ltd 1986 (non-exec); NE Technology Ltd 1987 (non-exec). *Professional Organisations:* CEng; MIMechE; FBIM.

BISHOP, John A; Director, N M Rothschild & Sons Ltd, since 1987; Bullion Trading/Banking plus related Treasury Activities. *Career:* Babcock Int, Graduate Engineer 1974-77. *Biog: b.* 17 October 1953. *Nationality:* British. *m.* 1986, Barbara (née Smith). *Educ:* Addey & Stanhope School; University College, London (BSc). *Directorships:* Rothschild Australia 1987 (non-exec); Rothschild Gold Ltd 1990 (exec). *Professional Organisations:* MIMechE.

BISHOP, Michael John; Director, Gartmore Investment Management Limited.

BISHOP, P A; Director, Riggs AP Bank Limited, since 1990; Head of Treasury. *Career:* Sale Tilney Group

1964-70. *Biog: b.* 16 April 1947. *Nationality:* British. *m.* 1971, Valerie (née Ticehurst); 1 s; 1 d. *Educ:* Eastbrook, Dagenham, Essex. *Clubs:* Thorpe Hall Golf Club. *Recreations:* Golf, Travel.

BISHOP, R K; Master, The Worshipful Company of Insurers.

BISHOP, Ronald Kenneth; Director, Sun Alliance & London Assurance Co Ltd.

BISHOP, Steven Michael Wear; Director, Barclays de Zoete Wedd Securities Ltd, since 1988; International Equity Sales & Distribution. *Career:* de Zoete & Bevan, Partner 1977-85; de Zoete & Bevan Inc (New York), President 1985-86; BZW Securities Inc (New York), President 1987-89; Barclays de Zoete Wedd Securities Ltd, Director 1989-. *Biog: b.* 8 March 1956. *Nationality:* British. *m.* 1981, Cecilia Anne (née Scott); 2 s. *Educ:* Marlborough College; University College, Oxford (BA Hons). *Professional Organisations:* Member, ISE, NASD. *Clubs:* MCC, Vincent's. *Recreations:* Hockey, Skiing, Cricket, Tennis, Trombone Playing.

BISHOP, William Archie; Senior Partner, Holman Fenwick & Willan, since 1989; Admiralty Department. *Career:* P & O Line, Deck Officer 1954-60; Holman Fenwick & Willan, Mgr 1960; Solicitor & Ptnr 1970-89. *Biog: b.* 21 July 1937. *Nationality:* British. *m.* 1961, Joan Beatrice (née Skerman); 1 s; 1 d. *Educ:* Thames Nautical Training College HMS Worcester (1st Class Extra Nautical Studies); Sir John Cass College (2nd Mates FG Certificate, 1st Mates FG Cert); College of Law (Solicitors Qualifying Final Exam). *Directorships:* International Salvage Union 1983 Legal Adviser. *Other Activities:* Freeman, City of London; Freeman, The Company of Watermen & Lightermen; Member, The Law Society; Freeman, The Hon Company of London Solicitors. *Recreations:* Golf, Horse Riding, Hunting, Fishing, Painting.

BISS, Ms A; Non-Executive Member, British Railways Board.

BISSET, Thomas Melville; Chairman, Builders' Accident Insurance Ltd, since 1987. *Career:* F J C Lilley plc MD 1975-84; Fin Dir 1954-75; Chm 1983-84; Industrial Scotland Energy plc 1984-87. *Biog: b.* 7 September 1927. *Nationality:* British. *m.* 1954, Lorna (née Stephen); 2 s; 2 d. *Educ:* Waid Academy, Anstruther, Fife; Glasgow University. *Directorships:* Scottish Amicable Life Assurance Society 1985 (non-exec). *Professional Organisations:* CA, CBIM. *Clubs:* Royal & Ancient Golf Club of St Andrews, Golf House Club (Elie). *Recreations:* Golf, Gardening.

BISSETT, Alfred A; Managing Director, Esco Oil Management Ltd (Subsidiary of Edinburgh Fund Manager plc), since 1982; Management of Oil Exploration

Companies. *Career:* Edinburgh Fund Managers plc Investment Mgr 1972-82. *Biog: b.* 31 May 1949. *m.* 1973, Jennifer (née Dow); 2 s; 1 d. *Educ:* Boroughmuir High School; Heriot Watt University BA Economics. *Directorships:* Edinburgh Fund Mgrs plc 1978 (non-exec); Edinburgh Oil & Gas plc 1980 (exec). *Recreations:* National Coach Scottish Women's Basketball.

BISSON, R J; Fund Manager/Director, James Capel Fund Managers Ltd, since 1984; Continental Europe. *Career:* James Capel & Co 1983-; James Capel Fund Managers Ltd (Created in May 1988). *Biog: b.* 11 July 1960. *Nationality:* British. *m.* 1986, Elizabeth-Ann (née Harvey-Lloyd); 1 s; 1 d. *Educ:* Blue Coat School, Liverpool; Christ Church, Oxford (MA). *Directorships:* James Capel Unit Trust Management Ltd 1990 (non-exec). *Recreations:* Golf.

BJORKMAN, Sven I; Head of Treasury Division, Skandinaviska Enskilda Banken, since 1990; Treasury all Aspects. *Career:* Skandinaviska Enskilda Banken, London Branch, Head of Treasury 1988-90; Skandinaviska Enskilda Banken, Göteborg, Head of Treasury 1983-87; Head of Foreign Exchange 1980-83; Chief Dealer 1977-80. *Biog: b.* 23 May 1949. *Nationality:* Swedish. *m.* 1972, Lena A K (née Lundberg); 2 s. *Educ:* 'A' Levels Equivalent in Sweden Economics Line. *Recreations:* Golf, Skiing, Theatre, Art.

BLACK, A; CBE, DL; Clerk, Bowyer's Company.

BLACK, A D; Partner, Ernst & Young.

BLACK, A K; Director, P & O Steam Navigation Company.

BLACK, Alan William; Partner, Linklaters & Paines, since 1983; Corporate Finance/Project Finance. *Biog: Nationality:* British. *Educ:* King Henry VIII School; King's College, London (LLB). *Other Activities:* Freeman, Worshipful Company of Solicitors (1983). *Professional Organisations:* Law Society, UK; Law Society, HK. *Clubs:* The Second Eleven, The Inner Theatre, Pacific. *Recreations:* Tennis, Opera & Early Music, Far East, Searching for Schrodinger's Cat.

BLACK, Colin Hyndmarsh; Non-Executive Chairman, Kleinwort Benson Investment Management Ltd, since 1988. *Career:* Brander & Cruickshank (Aberdeen), Ptnr 1957-71; Globe Investment Trust 1971-90; Dir 1977-90; Deputy Chairman 1983-90. *Biog: b.* 4 February 1930. *Nationality:* British. *m.* 1955, Christine (née Browne); 1 s; 1 d. *Educ:* Ayr Academy; Fettes College; St Andrews University (MA); Edinburgh University (LLB). *Directorships:* Scottish Widows Fund & Life Assurance Co 1968 (non-exec) Chm; Kleinwort Benson Group plc 1988 (non-exec); Electra Investment Trust 1975 (non-exec); Temple Bar Investment Trust 1963 (non-exec); Clyde Petroleum plc 1976 (non-exec);

Globe Investment Trust plc 1977-90 (exec) Dep Chm 1983-90; Scottish Power plc 1990 (non-exec). *Other Activities:* Chm, Assoc of Investment Trust Companies, 1987-89; Consultant to Richard Ellis UK Partnership, 1989-. *Clubs:* New Club (Edinburgh). *Recreations:* Golf, Gardening, Reading, Walking Labradors.

BLACK, Donald Sinclair; Director, Panmure Gordon & Co Ltd.

BLACK, William Armstrong; Director, Baring Brothers & Co Limited.

BLACKBORN, Bryan; Deputy Head of Audit, Coopers & Lybrand Deloitte.

BLACKBURN, Jeffrey Michael; Director & Chief Exec, Leeds Permanent Building Society, since 1987. *Career:* Lloyds Bank plc (Business Advisory Service), Chief Mgr 1979-83; Joint Credit Card Company Ltd (Access), Dir and Chief Exec 1983-87. *Biog: b.* 16 December 1941. *Nationality:* British. *m.* 1987, Louise Clair (née Vasquez); 1 s; 1 d; (by previous marriage). *Educ:* Northgate Grammar School, Ipswich. *Directorships:* Royal Philharmonic Orchestra Ltd 1985 (non-exec); Mastercard International 1984-87 (non-exec); Eurocard International 1983-87 (non-exec); Joint Credit Card Co Ltd 1983-87 (exec). *Other Activities:* Member, Court and Council, University of Leeds; Governor, City of Leeds College of Music. *Professional Organisations:* FCIB; CBIM. *Clubs:* The Oriental. *Recreations:* Music, Theatre, Sport.

BLACKBURN, Michael John; Chairman, Touche Ross & Co, since 1990. *Career:* Touche Ross & Co, Ptnr in Charge Mgmnt Consultancy 1964-75; Ptnr in Charge London Practice 1975-84; Managing Partner 1984-90. *Biog: b.* 25 October 1930. *m.* 1955, Maureen (née Dale); 1 s; 2 d. *Educ:* Kingston Grammar School. *Directorships:* GEI International plc 1990 (non-exec) Chairman. *Professional Organisations:* FCA. *Clubs:* City of London. *Recreations:* Horse Racing, Family Tennis, Gardening.

BLACKBURN, P H; Chairman, Rowntree Limited.

BLACKBURN, Richard John; Partner, Touche Ross & Co, since 1969; Audit & Advice, Financial Institution Sector. *Career:* Touche Ross & Co 1961-. *Biog: b.* 22 February 1938. *Nationality:* British. *m.* 1966, Jennifer Ann (née Yelland); 1 s; 2 d. *Educ:* Eastbourne College; Worcester College, Oxford (MA). *Other Activities:* Member of Council, Roedean School, Brighton; Member of Council, Hazelwood School, Limpsfield. *Professional Organisations:* FCA. *Clubs:* City of London, Royal Northern & Clyde Yacht Club, United Oxford & Cambridge University Club.. *Recreations:* Sailing, Skiing, British Domestic Architecture.

BLACKER, B J; Director, Fenchurch Insurance Holdings plc.

BLACKER, G S; Joint Deputy Chairman, A J Archer Holdings plc.

BLACKER, John; Partner, Clyde & Co.

BLACKETT, David; Executive Director, N M Rothschild & Sons Limited.

BLACKHURST, Chris; City Editor, Sunday Express.

BLACKMAN, Maurice; Director, County NatWest Ltd, since 1988; Development and Implementation of Technology Strategy and Business Survival Contingency Plan for Natwest Investment Bank Group. *Career:* Vickers Armstrong (Aircraft), Apprentice Engineer 1955-59; International Computers & Tabulators Programmer, Analyst 1959-62; ISIS Computer Services, Various 1962-65; Central London Polytechnic, Lecturer 1965-66; Arthur Andersen & Co, Senior Consultant (London) 1966-68; Manager, Consulting (London and Chicago) 1968-80; Partner, Consulting (Houston) 1980-85; Asst Director, Technical Support (Chicago) 1985-87; County NatWest Ltd, Associate Director, IP Production 1987-88. *Biog: b.* 5 November 1936. *Nationality:* British. *m.* 1958, Anne (née Richardson); 1 s; 1 d. *Educ:* Tiffin Boys Grammar; Kingston College of Technology (HND); Central London Polytechnic (Dipl Mgmnt Studies). *Professional Organisations:* CEng; FBCS; MBIM; MIProdE. *Publications:* The Design of Real Time Applications, 1975. *Recreations:* History, Photography.

BLACKMORE, (Edward) Anthony; Senior Partner, Simpson Curtis, since 1988; Corporate Law & Tax. *Career:* Slaughter and May, Assistant Solicitor 1957-59; Simpson Curtis 1959-. *Biog: b.* 13 April 1933. *Nationality:* British. *m.* 1959, Caroline (née Jones); 2 s; 1 d. *Educ:* Winchester College; Emmanuel College, Cambridge (BA). *Directorships:* Liberty plc 1970 (non-exec). *Other Activities:* President, The Leeds Law Society; Visiting Professor in Commercial Practice, Leeds Polytechnic; Chairman, Information Technology Sub-Committee; Member, Training Sub-Committee; Governor, Bramcote School. *Professional Organisations:* Law Society; Freeman, City of London Solicitors' Company; British Computer Society; Society for Computers and the Law. *Clubs:* The Leeds Club. *Recreations:* Skiing, Computers, Walking, Tennis, Gardening.

BLACKSHAW, C D H; Dealing Director, Chambers & Remington Ltd.

BLACKSHIELDS, B P; Director, Lowndes Lambert Group Holdings Limited.

BLACKTOP, Graham Leonard; Managing Director, Alexanders Discount plc, since 1983. *Career:* Standard Bank of South Africa Ltd, Junior Clerk 1949-51; Royal Fusiliers/Royal W African Frontier Force, Commissioned 1951-54; Alexanders Discount Co Ltd 1954-. *Biog: b.* 21 July 1933. *Nationality:* British. *m.* 1959, Alison Margaret (née Campbell); 3 d. *Educ:* Christ's College, Finchley. *Directorships:* Alexanders Discount plc 1983 (exec). *Other Activities:* Non-Stipendiary Anglican Priest; Liveryman, Worshipful Company of Painter-Stainers, 1969; Worshipful Company of Parish Clerks, 1980. *Publications:* Thou Shalt Not Lend Upon Usury, 1987; Background to New Testament Politics, 1989; Articles in Financial & Sporting Journals. *Clubs:* MCC, Army & Navy. *Recreations:* Travel, Watching Cricket.

BLACKWELL, J; Partner, Nabarro Nathanson.

BLAIKLOCK, Anthony; Director, Samuel Montagu & Co Limited, since 1989; Corporate Finance. *Career:* Touche Ross & Co, latterly Audit Supervisor 1978-83. *Biog: b.* 26 March 1956. *Nationality:* Canadian. *m.* 1982, Jennifer; 1 s. *Educ:* St Pauls School, London; St Johns College, Cambridge (BA, MA). *Directorships:* Zurmont Finanz SA 1988 (non-exec); Square Mile Nominees Limited 1988 (non-exec). *Professional Organisations:* ACA. *Recreations:* Skiing, Golf, Tennis, Travel.

BLAIR, J W; Director, Edinburgh Fund Managers plc.

BLAIR, Michael; Group Director, Securities and Investments Board.

BLAIR, Robin Orr; Managing Partner, Dundas & Wilson CS, since 1988; Administration & Finance. *Career:* Dundas & Wilson, Partner 1966-. *Biog: b.* 1 January 1940. *Nationality:* British. *m.* 1972, Caroline (née McCallum Webster); 2 s; 1 d. *Educ:* Rugby School; St Andrew's University (MA); Edinburgh University (LLB). *Directorships:* Tullis Russell & Co Ltd 1976 (non-exec); Top Flight Leisure Ltd 1977 (non-exec) Chm; Technology & Law Ltd 1977 (exec); Ardanaiseig Hotel Ltd 1986 (non-exec). *Other Activities:* Purse Bearer to the Lord High Commissioner to the General Assembly of the Church of Scotland; Member, Royal Company of Archers. *Professional Organisations:* Member, Law Society of Scotland; Member, Society of Writers to the Signet. *Clubs:* New, (Edinburgh), Hon Company of Edinburgh Golfers.

BLAKE, Anthony Martin; Partner, Neville Russell, since 1974; Lloyd's/Finance. *Career:* Jacob, Cavenagh & Skeet Student 1964-68. *Biog: b.* 18 August 1946. *Nationality:* British. *m.* 1970, Marion (née Davey); 2 d. *Educ:* Whitgift School. *Other Activities:* Church PCC. *Professional Organisations:* ICA. *Clubs:* City of London; Surrey CCC. *Recreations:* Church Work, Cricket, Chess, Photography.

BLAKE, B G; Assistant General Manager (Customer Services), National Provident Institution.

BLAKE, B P P; Director, Chartered Trust plc.

BLAKE, Miss Charlotte Mary; Group Company Secretary, The MDA Group plc, since 1990; Legal Advice on all Matters Affecting the Company. *Career:* Asher Fishman & Co (Solicitors), Legal Articled Clerk 1975-79; Assistant Solicitor 1980-83; Wm F Prior & Co (Solicitors), Assistant Solicitor 1983-85; Blakemores (Accountants), Trainee Chartered Accountant 1985-89; Qualified as Chartered Accountant 1989; The MDA Group plc (formerly Monk Dunstone Associates Investments Ltd), Group Company Lawyer 1989-90. *Biog: b.* 5 May 1955. *Nationality:* British. *Educ:* Lycée Français de Londres (now Lycée Charles de Gaule) (Baccalauriat); London University (LLB Hons, Ext). *Professional Organisations:* Law Society of England.

BLAKE, Professor Christopher; Director, The Alliance Trust plc.

BLAKE, Jonathan Elazar; Partner, S J Berwin & Co, since 1983; Venture Capital Management Buy Outs and Buy Ins and Related Taxation Issues, Corporate Finance Law Generally. *Career:* Stephenson Harwood, Solicitor 1977-82. *Biog: b.* 7 July 1954. *Nationality:* British. *m.* 1980, Isabel (née Horovitz); 1 s; 1 d. *Educ:* Haberdashers' Aske's, Elstree; Queen's College, Cambridge (MA, LLM). *Other Activities:* Member Tax Ctee of The British Venture Capital Assoc; Euromatters Ctee of The European Venture Capital Assoc; Negotiation with the DTI and The Inland Revenue an Agreed Statement and Guidelines on the Use of Ltd Partnerships as Venture Capital Investment Funds. *Professional Organisations:* Law Society; ATII; Member, British Venture Capital Assoc. *Recreations:* Family, Theatre, Walking, Skiing.

BLAKE, Richard John Bowden; Chairman, Baker Tilly. *Career:* Baker Rooke, Snr Ptnr 1986-88. *Biog: b.* 12 March 1936. *Nationality:* British. m2 1988, Shirley (née Lee). m1 1 s 2 d. *Educ:* Aldenham School. *Directorships:* Rights & Investments Ltd 1978 (non-exec); Parkside School Trust Ltd 1976 (non-exec); Emberdove Ltd 1978 (non-exec); Keir & Cawder Ltd 1986 (non-exec); Throphyswing Ltd 1987 (non-exec); Attenborough Holdings & Subsidiaries 1988 (non-exec). *Professional Organisations:* FCA. *Clubs:* Turf, MCC, Surbiton Hockey Club, Trevose Golf Club. *Recreations:* Golf, Theatre.

BLAKELEY, A G; General Manager, The Scottish Mutual Assurance Society.

BLAKELEY, James Steven; Partner, Wilde Sapte, since 1988; Mergers & Acquisitions/Corporate Finance. *Career:* Rudd Moorfoot & Davenport (Westcliff-on-Sea, Essex), Articled Clerk 1978-80; Herbert Oppenheimer, Nathan & Vandyk, Asst Solicitor, Company & Commercial 1980-85; Ptnr, Company & Commercial Dept 1985-88. *Biog: b.* 14 March 1956. *Nationality:* British. *m.* 1980, Alison Jane (née Bannerman); 2 s. *Educ:* Sir Antony Browne's School, Brentwood; Trinity College, Oxford (MA Hons). *Professional Organisations:* Member, City of London Solicitors Company; Member, The Law Society. *Recreations:* Working, Family, Supporter of Blackburn Rovers FC, Music.

BLAKENEY, H J M; Chairman, Quill Underwriting Agency Limited.

BLAKENHAM, Michael John Hare; Viscount Blakenham; Chairman & Chief Executive, Pearson plc, since 1983. *Career:* Life Guards 1956-57; English Electric 1958; Harvard 1959-61; Lazard Brothers 1961-63; Standard Industrial Group 1963-71; Royal Doulton 1972-77; Pearson 1977-; Managing Director 1978-83. *Biog: b.* 25 January 1938. *m.* 1965, Marcia Persephone; 1 s; 2 d. *Educ:* Eton College; Harvard University (AB Econ). *Directorships:* Lazard Brothers 1975; Lazard Partners 1984 Partner; Lafarge Coppee 1979 Mem Intl Adv Bd; Sotheby's Holdings Inc 1987; Elsevier NV 1988; MEPC plc 1990; The Financial Times 1983 Chm. *Other Activities:* Member, House of Lords Select Cttee on Science and Technology, 1985-88; Nature Conservancy Council, 1986-90; President, Sussex Wildlife Trust (formerly Sussex Trust for Nature Conservation), 1983-; Chairman, Royal Society for Protection of Birds, 1981-86; Vice-President, 1986-.

BLAKESLEY, Andrew Laurence; Managing Director, Lazard Brothers & Co Ltd, since 1989; Finance. *Career:* W T Copeland & Sons Ltd, Management Accountant 1960-63; Price Waterhouse & Co Ltd (London), Managing Consultant 1963-68; UKO International Ltd, Optical Manufacturers, Finance Director 1969-77; Managing Director, Optical Group 1977-80; Manchester Exchange & Investment Bank Ltd, Managing Director 1981-87; Lazard Brothers & Co Ltd, Finance Director 1988-89. *Biog: b.* 30 September 1936. *Nationality:* British. *m.* 1960, Maureen Pamela (née Neath); 1 s; 1 d. *Educ:* Eltham College. *Directorships:* Lazard Brothers & Co Ltd 1988 (exec); Lazard Brothers & Co (Jersey) Ltd 1989 Chairman; Lazard Brothers & Co (Guernsey) Ltd 1989 Chairman. *Other Activities:* Liveryman, Spectacle Makers Company. *Professional Organisations:* FCA; MIMC; MBCS. *Clubs:* MCC. *Recreations:* Theatre, Golf.

BLAKEY, Steven A; Director, Head of European Private Placements, Merrill Lynch International Limited, since 1990; International Asset Swaps. *Career:* Chase Investment Bank Limited, Director, Structured Distribution 1984-90; Manager, Corporate Finance 1982-84. *Biog: b.* 14 August 1959. *Nationality:* British. *Educ:* Bristol University (LLB Hons). *Professional Organisations:* Barrister-at-Law, Lincolns Inn, 1981.

BLAMEY, B; Director, Edwards & Payne (Underwriting Agencies) Limited.

BLANC, J M; Director (Corporate Finance), Granville & Co Limited.

BLAND, Adrian D; Partner (Birmingham), Evershed Wells & Hind.

BLAND, David Edward; Director General, Chartered Insurance Institute, since 1990; Chief Executive. *Career:* University of Sheffield, Lecturer 1966-82; Senior Lecturer 1982-89; Warden of Sorby Hall 1980-89; Dean of Social Sciences 1982-84; Pro Vice-Chancellor 1984-88. *Biog: b.* 9 December 1940. *Nationality:* British. *m.* 1986, Christine. *Educ:* Queens Elizabeth's GS, Blackburn; University College, Durham (BA, MLitt); University of Sheffield (PhD). *Directorships:* CII Enterprises 1990 MD; Insurance Orphans 1990 (non-exec). *Other Activities:* Worshipful Company of Insurers; Guild of Firefighters. *Professional Organisations:* FSCA; President, Institute of Company Accountants. *Publications:* Can Britain Survive? (with K W Watkins), 1971; Basic Economics, 1985; Mixed Economy, 1987; Managing Higher Education, 1990. *Recreations:* Walking, Music, Travel.

BLAND, Leslie Martin; Director, Close Brothers Limited, since 1984. *Career:* Midland Bank Limited 1956-59; Royal Navy, Serving to Rank of Lieutenant on the General List 1959-69; Credit Factoring International Ltd (NatWest Group), Management Trainee 1969-71; Assistant Company Secretary and Administration Manager 1971-73; Company Secretary and Head of Personnel 1973-77; Personnel and Management Service Director 1977-78; International Director 1978-81; Operations Director 1981-84; Century Factors Limited, Managing Director 1984-; Close Brothers Limited, Director 1984-. *Biog: b.* 25 March 1939. *Nationality:* British. *m.* 1964, Janet Ray (née Stephens); 1 s. *Educ:* Beal Grammar School, Ilford; Royal Naval College, Dartmouth; Royal Naval College, Greenwich. *Directorships:* Close Brothers Limited 1984 (exec); Century Factors Limited 1984 (exec); Sales Ledger Finance Limited 1984 (exec); Watermill Theatre Limited 1987 (non-exec); Kamfarma Limited 1987 (non-exec). *Other Activities:* Chairman, Association of British Factors and Discounters, 1989-; Member, Business in the Community. *Professional Organisations:* Member, Institute of Credit Management. *Publications:* Various Articles on Factoring, Discounting, Small Business and Personnel Management. *Recreations:* Rowing, Scuba Diving, Theatre.

BLAND, R W; Executive Chief Exploration and Production Officer, Ultramar plc.

BLANK, Maurice Victor; Chairman & Chief Executive, Charterhouse Bank Limited, since 1985. *Career:* Clifford-Turner, Articled Clerk 1964-66; Solicitor 1966-69; Ptnr 1969-81; Charterhouse Bank Limited, Head of Corporate Finance 1981-85. *Biog: b.* 9 November 1942. *Nationality:* British. *m.* Sylvia Helen (née Richford); 2 s; 1 d. *Educ:* Stockport Grammar School; St Catherine's College, Oxford (MA). *Directorships:* Pentos Limited 1979 (non-exec); Charterhouse plc 1985 (exec); The Royal Bank of Scotland Group plc 1985 (exec); Business in the Community 1986; Porter Chadburn plc 1988 (non-exec); Coats Viyella plc 1989 (non-exec). *Professional Organisations:* The Law Society; IBA; Institute of Directors. *Publications:* Weinberg and Blank on Take-overs and Mergers (Jointly). *Recreations:* Family, Tennis, Cricket, Theatre.

BLANKESTIJN, A; Director, Cargill UK Ltd.

BLATCHFORD, David; Vice President & Financial Engineering and Risk Mgt, Bank of America.

BLIGHT, Mrs Catherine (née Montgomery); Part Time Member, Monopolies and Mergers Commission, since 1990; Councillor for Scotland, Gas Consumers Council. *Career:* Solicitor and Economist in Private, Commercial, Local Authority and Agricultural Practice. *Biog: Nationality:* British. *m.* David Philip; 2 d. *Educ:* Laxdale School, Isle of Lewis; George Watsons Ladies College, Edinburgh; University of Edinburgh (BL, MSc). *Directorships:* David Hume Institute (non-exec); Comunn na Gaidhlig (non-exec). *Other Activities:* Contested (Cons) Lothians Euro Constituency, 1989. *Professional Organisations:* Member, Law Society of Scotland; Agricultural Law Association; Agricultural Economics Society; European Association of Law & Economics. *Publications:* Many Articles on Law and Economics. *Clubs:* Farmers. *Recreations:* Growing Camellias, Collecting Books and Maps.

BLOGGS, C A J; Director, Wilson, Smithett & Cope Limited.

BLOODWORTH, Philip; Executive Director, Yamaichi International (Europe) Ltd.

BLOOMER, R C; Partner, Milne Ross.

BLOOMFIELD, Stephen; Managing Director, Cambridge Capital Management Ltd, since 1989; Venture Capital. *Career:* Department of Employment, Administration Trainee 1975-77; Federation of Civil Engineering Contractors, Economist 1977-78; Building Magazine, Business Editor 1978-80; Phillips & Drew, Building Industry Analyst 1980-83; Coal Industry Nominees Industrial Investments, Manager 1983-86; Director; Korda & Co, Director 1986-88; Royal Trust Bank, Director Development Capital 1988-89; Cambridge Capital 1989-. *Biog: b.* 5 January 1953. *Nationality:* British. *m.* 1982, Gillian Elizabeth (née Thomas); 1 s. *Educ:* London (BSc Econ); Manchester (MA Econ). *Directorships:* Cambridge Capital Management Ltd 1989 (exec); Cambridge Capital Ltd 1989 (exec); Kirton Healthcare Ltd 1990 (non-exec); Mackins Ltd 1990 (non-exec); Elles Ltd 1989 (non-exec). *Professional Organisations:* ICSA. *Recreations:* Flying.

BLOWER, Geoffrey; Partner, Alexander Tatham.

BLOWS, S K; Partner, Holman Fenwick & Willan; Commercial Litigation. *Biog: b.* 15 November 1955. *Nationality:* British. *m.* 1985, Juliet Anne (née Gladstone); 1 s. *Educ:* The Royal Liberty School; University College, Durham (BA).

BLOXHAM, Jeremy Nicholas; Director, Sphere Drake Underwriting Management Ltd, since 1990; Marine Underwriter. *Career:* Victory Reinsurance Company Ltd, Marine & Aviation Underwriter 1976-83; Sphere Drake Underwriting Management Ltd, Marine Underwriter 1983-90. *Biog: b.* 2 May 1954. *Nationality:* British. *m.* 1978, Andrea; 1 s; 1 d. *Educ:* University of London (BSc Hons). *Directorships:* Sphere Drake Underwriting Management Ltd 1990. *Professional Organisations:* Associate, Chartered Institute of Insurers.

BLOXHAM, P J R; Partner, Freshfields.

BLOXHAM, William Edward; Chief Executive, R H M Outhwaite (Underwriting Agencies) Limited, since 1988; General Management. *Career:* Thomas Warren & Co, Auditor 1962-67; Armour & Co Ltd, Corporate Accounting Manager 1967-71; Edward Arnold (Publishers) Ltd, Chief Accountant 1971-80; Academic Press Inc (London) Ltd, Finance Director 1980-83; Corporation of Lloyd's, Manager Members' Deposits 1983-85; R H M Outhwaite (Underwriting Agencies) Ltd, Finance Director 1985-88; Chief Executive 1988-. *Biog: b.* 23 November 1942. *Nationality:* British. *m.* 1970, Sara (née Howlett); 1 s. *Educ:* Doncaster Technical College; Kelham College. *Directorships:* R H M Outhwaite (Underwriting Agencies) Ltd 1985 (exec); Andisy Limited 1988 (exec). *Professional Organisations:* FCCA; FBIM; Member, Institute of Directors. *Recreations:* Music, Travel, Cricket.

BLOXSOME, John R; Partner, Touche Ross, since 1988; Audit Department. *Career:* Spicer & Oppenheim, Audit Department 1972-83; IASC, Assistant Secretary 1983-85; Spicer & Oppenheim International, Deputy Executive Director 1985-88. *Biog: b.* 27 October 1950. *Nationality:* British. *Educ:* Felsted School; Corpus Christi, Cambridge (MA). *Professional Organisations:* FCA. *Recreations:* Gardening, Music.

BLUM, N; Head of Sugar, J H Rayner (Mincing Lane).

BLUMSON, John David; TD; Director, Hambros Bank Limited, since 1986; Marketing. *Career:* Hambros Bank Limited 1971-; Electrolux Ltd, Commercial Manager 1959-71; Moore Stephens & Co, Articled Clerk 1953-59. *Biog: b.* 7 December 1932. *Nationality:* British. *m.* 1957, Gillian Mary (née Paul); 3 s; 2 d. *Educ:*

Merchant Taylors School; London Business School. *Directorships:* Hambros Bank Limited 1986 (exec); Hambros Scotland Limited 1985 (exec); Hemmington Scott Publishing Ltd 1986 (non-exec). *Other Activities:* Chairman, Hertfordshire Committee, Army Benevolent Fund. *Professional Organisations:* FCA. *Recreations:* Golf, Squash, Walking.

BLUNDELL, D C; Chairman and Managing Director, Sogemin Metals Ltd.

BLUNDEN, George Patrick; Director, Warburg Securities, since 1986; Money Markets. *Career:* United Biscuits, Production Mgr 1971-79; Secombe Marshall & Campion, MD 1979-86. *Biog: b.* 21 February 1952. *m.* 1978, Jane Rosemary (née Hunter); 1 s; 2 d. *Educ:* St Edward's, Oxford; University College, Oxford. *Other Activities:* Sir Abraham Dawes Almshouses (Chairman), FWA Almshouse Committee; Samuel Lewis Housing Trust (Trustee); Goldsmiths' Company, Liveryman. *Clubs:* Reform, MCC.

BLUNDEN, Robin Charles; Director, J Henry Schroder Wagg, since 1990; Capital Markets. *Career:* Citibank NA, Originally Lending Officer and Ultimately Vice President, Responsible for Lending to Trading Companies 1975-83; Citicorp Investment Bank, Capital Markets, UK Marketing 1983-86; J Henry Schroder Wagg, UK Capital Markets, Marketing Director 1986-. *Biog: b.* 17 March 1959. *Nationality:* British. *m.* 1983, Sarah Jane (née Parry); 1 s; 2 d. *Educ:* St Edwards School; University College, Oxford (BA Hons History & Economics). *Other Activities:* Goldsmiths Livery Company. *Recreations:* Tennis, Hockey, Mountain Climbing, Sailing.

BLUNT, R J; Director/Underwriter, MFK Underwriting Agencies Ltd.

BLURTON, Neil; Director of Technical Services, London International Financial Futures Exchange, since 1990; Computer & Telecommunications Systems. *Career:* Burmah Engineering (Part of Burmah Oil Ltd), Eng/Consultant 1976-80; Britoil (Formerly British Nat Oil Corp), Telecomms Eng 1980-84; Price Waterhouse, Management Consultancy 1984-85; LIFFE 1985-. *Biog: b.* 19 January 1955. *Nationality:* British. *Educ:* Openshaw Technical College, Manchester (C&GLI Final Telecommunications Engineering).

BLYTH, David; Partner (Birmingham), Eversheds Wells & Hind.

BLYTH, J; Finance Director, United Biscuits (Holdings) plc.

BLYTH, W B; Director, Special Projects, Chartered WestLB, since 1990; Mining, Africa. *Career:* Standard Chartered Merchant Bank Zimbabwe, Managing Director 1986-90; Various Corporate Finance & General Management Positions 1976-. *Biog: b.* 19 September 1945. *Nationality:* Zimbabwean. *m.* 1968, Diana (née Stone); 2 s; 1 d. *Educ:* Plumtree, Zimbabwe (BSc Chemistry & Agriculture Hons); University of Natal, Pietermaritzburg (DMS).

BLYTHE, Trevor; Partner, Beachcroft Stanleys.

BOANAS, Arthur T; Director, Newton Investment Group.

BOARDMAN, Geoffrey A; Partner, MacNair Mason.

BOARDMAN, John Kenneth; Head of Corporate Department, Alexander Tatham, since 1989; Corporate Law. *Career:* Alexander Tatham, Articled Clerk 1977-79; Assistant Solicitor 1979-84; Associate Partner 1984-86; Partner 1986; Head of Corporate Department 1989; Eversheds, Board Member 1987. *Biog: b.* 26 July 1955. *Nationality:* British. *m.* 1984, Julie; 1 s; 1 d. *Educ:* Manchester Grammar; Downing College, Cambridge (MA Cantab). *Directorships:* Eversheds Legal Services Limited 1989 (non-exec). *Professional Organisations:* Law Society.

BOARDMAN, The Hon N P; Partner, Slaughter and May.

BOAS, John Robert Sotheby; Director, S G Warburg & Co Ltd, since 1971; Corporate Finance. *Career:* National Service (2nd Lieutenant, Royal Signals) 1956-58; Price Waterhouse 1960-65; ICI, Treasurers Department 1965-66; S G Warburg & Co Ltd 1966-. *Directorships:* Chesterfield Properties plc 1979 (non-exec); English National Opera 1990 (non-exec); The Securities Association Ltd 1989 (non-exec). *Professional Organisations:* Fellow, Institute of Chartered Accountants.

BOBASCH, Steven Henry Andrew; Director, Kleinwort Benson Ltd, since 1988; Director, Account Relationship Department, Shipping. *Career:* ICI Ltd, Research Asst, Plastics Div 1968; Guest Keen & Nettlefolds Ltd, Graduate Trainee 1971; GKN Contractors Ltd, Project Engineer 1971-74; Grindlay Brandts Ltd, Mgr, Export Finance 1974-77; Amex Bank Ltd, Mgr, Project Finance 1977-78; Guinness Mahon & Co Ltd, Asst Dir, Banking and Shipping 1978-87; Guinness Mahon Export Finance Ltd, Director 1979-87. *Educ:* Manchester University (BSc Hon Physics); Vienna University (German). *Directorships:* British Financial Union Ltd 1988 (exec); Ryehart Ltd 1988 (exec); HIT Finance Ltd 1988 (exec); Kings Cross House plc 1989 (exec).

BODDINGTON, Christopher; Partner, Nabarro Nathanson, since 1977; Company. *Career:* Western, Sons & Neave Solicitors, Assistant 1966-69; McKenna & Co Solicitors, Assistant 1969-72; Ziman & Co Solicitors, Partner 1972-77. *Biog: b.* 4 May 1941. *Nationality:*

British. *m.* (div 1982); 2 d. *Educ:* Rugby; Queen's College, Oxford (MA Juris). *Professional Organisations:* Solicitor. *Clubs:* Brooks's. *Recreations:* Food, Travel.

BODEN, G; Deputy Chairman, Steel Burrill Jones Group plc.

BODEN, Roger John; Managing Director, Private Bank, Kleinwort Benson Investment Management Ltd, since 1989. *Career:* Kleinwort Benson Development of N American Banking 1973-83; Director in charge of Personal Banking responsible for development of mortgage business, formation of mortgage funding corp & KB Group information services 1983-86; Joint Managing Director, Sydney 1986-87; (London) Responsible for Banking Activities in N America 1987-89. *Biog: b.* 26 June 1947. *Nationality:* British. *m.* Jennifer Jane; 3 s. *Educ:* St Philip's Grammar School, Birmingham; Keble College & Nuffield College, Oxford (PPE); London University Institute of Education. *Directorships:* Kleinwort Benson Ltd 1973; Kleinwort Benson Investment Management Ltd 1989; Kleinwort Benson Unit Trusts Ltd 1990. *Recreations:* Sailing, Cycling.

BOECKMANN, John William; Director, M & G Investment Management Ltd.

BOESCH, Bruno W; Resident Partner, Froriep Renggli & Partners.

BOGAARD, William J; Non-Executive Director, First Interstate Capital Markets Limited.

BOGNI, Rodolfo; Chief Executive, Swiss Bank Corporation, since 1990; London Office. *Career:* Midland Bank plc, Group Treasurer 1989; Midland Montagu Ltd, Managing Director, Treasury and Capital Markets & Member, Group Executive Committee 1989-; Midland Montagu Ltd, Managing Director International 1988-89; Euromobiliare SpA, Deputy Chairman (Member, Supervisory Board, Trinkaus und Burkhardt, Midland Bank SA in Paris and Midland Bank AS in Oslo, also Board Member, Guyerzeller and Handelsfinanz) 1988-89; Midland Montagu, Chief Operating Officer 1987-88; Midland Bank plc, Special Projects Director 1986-87; Chief Financial Officer, Global Banking Sector 1985-86; Assistant General Manager, International Banking 1984; Regional Manager, Middle East, Africa & Eastern Mediterranean Region, Global Banking Sector 1983; Country Manager 1980-82; Chase Manhattan Bank NA, Greece Greek Branches, Assistant General Manager 1978; Central European Controller, Frankfurt 1976; Manager Central Operations, Italy 1975; Branch Manager Bari, Italy 1973; International Credit Department New York, Section Head 1973; Credit Analyst, Milan 1972. *Biog: b.* 2 October 1947. *Nationality:* Italian. *m.* 1972, Florence (née Ravel). *Educ:* Bocconi University, Milan (Doctorate in Economics and Business Administration). *Recreations:* History, Physics, Opera, Scuba-Diving.

BOHLING, H H; Partner, Waltons & Morse.

BOLEAT, Mark John; Director-General, The Building Societies Association, since 1987. *Career:* Dulwich College Assistant Master 1972-74; Industrial Policy Group Research Economist 1974-75; The Building Societies Association Assistant Secretary 1975-76; Under Secretary 1976-79; Deputy Secretary 1979-81; Deputy Secretary-General 1981-86; Secretary-General 1986-87. *Biog: b.* 21 January 1949. *Nationality:* British. *Educ:* Victoria College, Jersey; Lanchester Polytechnic (BA); Reading University (MA). *Other Activities:* Chairman, Circle 33 Housing Trust; Board Mem, Housing Corporation. *Professional Organisations:* FCBSI, MIH. *Publications:* The Building Society Industry, 1982; National Housing Finance Systems, 1984; Housing in Britain, 1989; The Mortgage Market, 1987. *Clubs:* Carlton. *Recreations:* Squash, Golf.

BOLIVER, Diane; Financial Reporter, Today.

BOLLAND, H W; Director, J Henry Schroder Wagg & Co Limited.

BOLMER, Diane; Financial Reporter, The Times.

BOLSOVER, John Derrick; Chief Executive & Chief Investment Officer, Baring Asset Management Ltd. *Career:* GT Management, Manager 1971; GT Management Asia (Hong Kong), Director 1971-75; Baring International Investment Management Ltd (Hong Kong), Director 1975-85. *Biog: b.* 21 June 1947. *m.* Susan Elizabeth (née Peacock); 2 s; 1 d. *Educ:* Repton School; McGill University, Canada (BA). *Directorships:* Baring International Investment Management Ltd 1975; Baring Pacific International Fund SA 1983; China & Eastern Investment Company Ltd 1985; Baring Investment Management Holdings Ltd 1986; Baring America Asset Management 1987. *Clubs:* Boodle's, City. *Recreations:* Sport.

BOLSTERLI, H W; Director, S G Warburg Akroyd Rowe & Pitman Mullens Securities Ltd.

BOLTON, A M; Partner, Pannell Kerr Forster.

BOLTON, O A; Partner, Cameron Markby Hewitt.

BOLTON, Anthony Hale; Chairman, Bowring Aviation Limited, since 1980; Worldwide. *Career:* Leslie & Godwin Aviation, Chairman 1980; C T Bowring, Aviation Division, Deputy Chief Executive, Director, Assistant Director, Senior Broker 1966-80; J H Minet/F Bolton & Co, Clerk 1960-66. *Biog: b.* 8 August 1942. *Nationality:* British. *m.* 1962, Olive Muriel (née O'Loughlin); 1 s; 1 d. *Educ:* St Albans School, Hert-

fordshire. *Directorships:* Marsh & McLennan Inc 1983 (exec) MD; C T Bowring & Co Ltd 1982 (exec); Bowring International Insurance Brokers 1988 (exec) Chm; Bowring Space Projects 1976 (exec). *Other Activities:* Aviation Executive Committee, LIBC; President, London Insurance Football Association. *Recreations:* Football, Theatre, Music, Golf.

BOLTON, David Martin; Partner, Herbert Smith, since 1973; Company Department. *Biog: b.* 2 March 1941. *Nationality:* British. *m.* 1965, Edith Helene; 1 s; 2 d. *Educ:* King Edward VI School, Southampton; Oxford University (BA Jurisprudence). *Directorships:* Swiss Re (UK) Limited 1990 (non-exec). *Professional Organisations:* Solicitor; Member, Law Society. *Clubs:* St George's Hill Golf Club, Royal Solent Yacht Club.

BOLTON, Lyndon; Managing Director, Alliance Trust plc & Second Alliance Trust plc, since 1987; Investment Management. *Career:* Alliance Trust 1964-. *Biog: b.* 24 January 1937. *Nationality:* British. *m.* 1957, Rosemary Jane Toler (née Mordaunt); 2 s. *Educ:* Wellington College. *Directorships:* Second Alliance Trust plc 1887 (exec) MD; General Accident Fire & Life Assurance Corp plc 1982 (non-exec); TSB Group plc 1986 (non-exec); Secdee Leasing Ltd; Alliance Trust (Finance) Ltd; TSB Pension Trust Ltd (non-exec) Chairman. *Other Activities:* Dundee University Court. *Professional Organisations:* ASIA. *Clubs:* New (Edinburgh). *Recreations:* Painting, Sailing, Country Life.

BONANNO, Anthony; Senior Partner, Gibson Dunn & Crutcher; US International and Corporate Taxation. *Career:* US Internal Revenue Service, Asst Branch Chief, Chief Counsel Office, US 1974-78; Georgetown Law School, Adjunct Professor of US International Tax Law 1981-82. *Biog: b.* 13 December 1946. *Nationality:* American. *m.* 1973, Mary J (née Thum); 1 s; 1 d. *Educ:* Dickinson College (BA); George Washington Law School (JD Law); Georgetown Law School (LLM). *Other Activities:* Formerly Adjunct Professor of Law, Georgetown Law School and Notre Dame Law School (London); Speeches and Lecturing; US IRS Markham Award for Outstanding Tax Lawyer. *Professional Organisations:* ABA; American Tax Institute. *Clubs:* RAC. *Recreations:* Children, Cooking, Skiing, Biking, Swimming.

BONAR, Mrs Mary P; Partner, Wilde Sapte, since 1989; Solicitor Specialising in Asset Finance. *Career:* Gamlens Solicitors, Partner 1973-89; Solicitor 1971-72. *Biog: b.* 28 July 1947. *Nationality:* British. *m.* 1969, Alastair James Bonar; 2 d. *Educ:* University College, London (LLB). *Other Activities:* Member, City of London Solicitors' Company; Member, Law Society's Remuneration & Practice Committee; Member, Women Solicitors' Association. *Professional Organisations:* Solicitor; Member, Law Society.

BOND, Christopher Michael; Partner, Field Fisher Waterhouse, since 1981; International Financial & Commercial Law. *Career:* Herbert Smith & Co, Articles 1966-69; Frere Cholmeley, London and Paris, Corporate Law 1969-72; Reuters Ltd, Principal Lawyer & Assistant Company Secretary 1972-76; Berger & Associates, London, Taxation Law 1976-78; Field Fisher Martineau, International Commercial and Work Permit Law 1978-86; Securities and Banking 1986-89; International Law Trading and Financial Law 1989-. *Biog: b.* 28 June 1943. *Nationality:* British. *m.* 1966, Lindsay; 1 s; 1 d. *Educ:* Wellington College, Berkshire; Trinity Hall, Cambridge (Hons). *Other Activities:* Member, Business Development Committee, Field Fisher Waterhouse, 1986-; Member, British Invisible Exports Committee, Missing to Taiwan and Korea, 1988 & 89; Lectured in Japan, Korea, Taiwan, UK and USA on Commercial, Securities and Trading Law. *Professional Organisations:* Solicitor; Member, Law Society of England and Wales and European Law Group. *Publications:* Investing in the United Kingdom, Japan Export Trade Organisation, 1986; Doing Business and Trading in the UK, Arab-British Chamber of Commerce, 2nd Edition 1990. *Recreations:* Reading, Tennis, Music, Sailing, Hill Walking.

BOND, Ian Douglas Barker; Deputy Chairman, Cork Sully, since 1990; Insolvency and Corporate Recovery. *Career:* Deloitte Plender Griffiths & Co, Articled Clerk to Partner 1957-68; London Insolvency Partner 1968-78; National Insolvency Partner 1978-90; Coopers & Lybrand Deloitte, Deputy Chairman of Insolvency Division, Cork Sully 1990-. *Biog: b.* 29 May 1937. *Nationality:* British. *m.* 1979, Marilyn; 1 s; 1 d. *Educ:* Marlborough College, Wiltshire. *Other Activities:* President, Insolvency Practitioners Association 1990/91; Liveryman, Worshipful Company of Shipwrights. *Professional Organisations:* FCA; FIPA. *Clubs:* MCC, City of London, Flyfishers. *Recreations:* Fishing, Shooting.

BOND, Sir Kenneth; Vice Chairman, The General Electric Company plc.

BOND, Matthew; City Reporter, The Times.

BOND, Richard Douglas; Partner, Herbert Smith, since 1977; Corporate and Energy Law. *Career:* Halsey Lightly & Hemsley, Articled Clerk 1964-69; Herbert Smith 1969-. *Biog: b.* 23 July 1946. *Nationality:* British. *m.* 1973, Anthea (née Charrington); 2 d. *Educ:* Berkhamsted (Solicitor). *Other Activities:* City of London Solicitors Company. *Professional Organisations:* Law Society; International Bar Association. *Clubs:* Lansdowne, MCC.

BONET, J; General Manager, Confederaciòn Espãnola de Cajas de Ahorros (CECA).

BONFIELD, P L; CBE; Deputy Chief Executive, and Chairman and Managing Director, ICL, STC plc.

BONNER, Frederick Ernest; CBE; Member of Commission, Monopolies & Mergers Commission, since 1987. *Career:* Fulham BC, Accountancy Positions 1940-44; Ealing BC, Accountancy Positions 1944-49; British Electricity Authority, Senior Accountant 1949-50; Assistant Finance Officer 1950-58; Central Electricity Generating Board, Assistant Chief Financial Officer 1958-61; Deputy Chief Financial Officer 1961-65; Chief Financial Officer 1965-69; Member 1969-75; Deputy Chairman 1975-86; Electricity Council, Member 1969-86; UKAEA, Part-Time Member 1977-86; British Airways Helicopters Ltd, Chairman 1983-85. *Biog: b.* 16 September 1923. *Nationality:* British. *m.* 1977, Ethel Mary (née Beardon); 3 s. *Educ:* St Clement Danes; Holborn Estate Grammar School; London University External (Diploma in Public Admin, BSc Econ). *Directorships:* Nuclear Electric plc 1990 (non-exec). *Other Activities:* Hon Treasurer, British Institute of Energy Economics; Member, Royal Society of Arts; Member, TAC (District) SE Society of Chartered Accountants. *Professional Organisations:* Fellow, Institute of Chartered Accountants in England & Wales; Member, Institute of Public Finance & Accountancy; Companion, British Institute of Management. *Recreations:* Music, Gardening, Reading.

BONNER, P A; Director, Crédit Lyonnais Rouse Limited.

BONNERMAN, D; Senior Manager, Corporate and Commercial Banking, Amsterdam-Rotterdam Bank NV (AmRo Bank).

BONNET, Michel Maurice Denis; Deputy General Manager, UK, Credit Lyonnais, since 1990; Corporate Banking, International Trade Finance, Leasing, Hire Purchase, Property Finance, Banks and Financial Institutions. *Career:* Credit Lyonnais Luxembourg, Managerial Assistant, Senior Account Officer, Sub-Manager (Corporate Banking/Euro-Credits) 1974-82; Credit Lyonnais Zurich, Sub-Director 1982-85; Director 1985-88; Credit Lyonnais New York, First Vice-President, Head of Credit Portfolio Management 1988-89; First Vice-President & Manager, Banking & Trade Finance 1989-90. *Biog: b.* 15 January 1947. *Nationality:* French. *m.* (div); 2 d. *Educ:* Lycée Hoche Landau, West Germany; Lycée Turenne Fribourg, West Germany; (Brevet Etudes du Premier Cycle (BEPC); Baccalaureat Elementary Mathematics); Université de Nancy, France, Faculty of Sciences (Mathematics, Physics, Chemistry); Centre Universitaire de Saarbrücken West Germany; University de Nancy, France, Faculty of Law and Economic Sciences, Nancy, France, (Diploma, Licence Maitrise in Economic Sciences). *Directorships:* Credit Lyonnais London Nominees 1990 Shareholding Director. *Recreations:* Tennis, Skiing, Windsurfing.

BONNETT, Ralph; Partner, Linklaters & Paines, since 1967; Property Law. *Career:* Suffolk Regiment & Royal Artillery Lieutenant 1946-49; Speechly Mumford & Craig Articles 1952-54; Long & Gardiner, Ptnr 1954-60; Linklaters & Paines, Ptnr 1960-. *Biog: b.* 6 January 1928. *Nationality:* British. *m.* 1964, Jean (née Sloss); 1 s. *Educ:* Bedford; Pembroke College, Cambridge (BA). *Other Activities:* Liveryman of the Worshipful Company of Coachmakers and Coach Harness Makers; Liveryman of the Worshipful Company of Solicitors. *Recreations:* Music, Gardening, Walking.

BONNEY, P W; Head of UK Mergers & Acquisitions, Hill Samuel Bank Limited, since 1988. *Career:* Laurence, Prust & Co, Stockbrokers 1976-81; Hill Samuel 1981-. *Biog: b.* 2 July 1949. *Nationality:* British. *m.* 1980, Jane (née Ireland-Blackburne); 3 d. *Educ:* Liverpool College; Lancaster University (BA Hons Economics). *Clubs:* MCC.

BONSALL, David Charles; Partner, Freshfields, since 1987; Company Law. *Career:* Freshfields, Articled Clerk 1979-81; Assistant Solicitor 1981-87; Partner 1987-. *Biog: b.* 26 July 1956. *Nationality:* British. *m.* 1980, Margaret Ruth (née Shaw); 1 d. *Educ:* Winchester College, Scholar; St John's College, Cambridge, Scholar (MA, LLM). *Other Activities:* Liveryman, City of London Solicitors' Company. *Publications:* Securitisation, 1990. *Clubs:* Royal St George's Golf Club, Woking GC, Rye GC, Royal Worlington & Newmarket GC. *Recreations:* Golf, Skiing, Classical Opera, Wine.

BONSALL, Mrs Margaret Ruth (née Shaw); Partner, Linklaters & Paines, since 1990; Project & Asset Finance. *Career:* Roche Products Limited, Legal Department 1979-81; BP Chemicals Limited, Legal Department 1981-85; Linklaters & Paines, Assistant Solicitor 1985-90. *Biog: b.* 24 August 1956. *Nationality:* British. *m.* 1980, David Charles; 1 d. *Educ:* St Albans High School for Girls; Girton College, Cambridge (MA). *Other Activities:* Member, City of London Solicitors' Company. *Professional Organisations:* Solicitor. *Recreations:* Skiing, Golf.

BONSOR, Sir Nicholas; Bt; Member of the Council, Lloyd's of London.

BOOK, Mrs Patricia Ruth; Director, Lazard Investors Limited, since 1989; Fixed Income. *Career:* Hoblyn & Co, Private Client Investment Management 1971-74; Northcote & Co, Private Client Investment Management 1974-75; Phillips & Drew, Head of a Sterling Bond Sales Team 1975-88; Phillips & Drew, Bond Division, Director 1986. *Biog: b.* 9 June 1948. *Nationality:* British. *m.* 1972, Robert Book; 2 s. *Educ:* South Hampstead High School (GPDST); London School of Economics, University of London (BSc Soc). *Directorships:* Lazard Investors Limited 1989 (exec). *Other Activities:* International Stock Exchange Diploma Examination Panel, Bond & Fixed Interest Markets 1984-. *Professional Organisations:* Member, Stock Exchange; Associate Member of the Society of Investment Analysts. *Clubs:* Network. *Recreations:* Swimming, Theatre, Music/Opera.

BOOME, Simon Adrian Kenneth; Partner, Cameron Markby Hewitt, since 1970; Corporate Finance. *Biog: b.* 7 November 1943. *Nationality:* British. *m.* 1968, Barstow; 2 d. *Educ:* Wellington College. *Clubs:* Royal Wimbledon Golf Club.

BOON, Gerald W (Gerry); Partner, Touche Ross & Co, since 1984 (with predecessor firm); Owner Managed Businesses. *Career:* Spicer and Pegler, Articled Clerk Rising to Manager 1974-81; Midland Bank plc, (Seconded) Corporate Finance Executive 1981-82; Spicer and Pegler, Senior Manager 1983-84. *Biog: b.* 1 April 1953. *Nationality:* British. *m.* 1976, Lesley Marion (née Wright); 3 d. *Educ:* Hulme Grammar School, Oldham; Bristol University (LLB). *Professional Organisations:* FCA. *Clubs:* The Cornhill Club. *Recreations:* Theatre, Cricket, Golf.

BOOT, George Robert; Chief Executive, The MDA Group plc, since 1990. *Career:* Norton Slade & Co, Articled Clerk 1968-71; Norton Keen & Co, Audit Senior 1971-72; Federated Land & Building Co Ltd, Assistant Finance Director 1972-75; CMG Computer Management Group Ltd, Accountant 1975-76; ABS Group of Companies, Accountant 1976-77; Director 1977-78; Managing Director 1978-85; The MDA Group plc, Finance Director 1985-90. *Biog: b.* 31 October 1949. *Nationality:* English. *m.* 1971, Christine Mary (née Roffey); 1 s; 2 d. *Educ:* Bromley Grammar; City of London College (Inter ICA). *Directorships:* ABS Litho Ltd 1977 (exec); ABS Oldacres Computers Ltd 1977 (exec); The MDA Group plc 1985 (exec); Monk Dunstone Associates Ltd 1985 (exec); Monk Dunstone Associates Management Ltd 1985 (exec); ESL Engineering Services Ltd 1985 (exec); Monk Dunstone Associates (Overseas) Ltd 1985 (exec); The MDA Group International Ltd 1985 (exec); Monk Dunstone Associates (Hong Kong) Ltd 1987 (non-exec); The MDA Group Australia Pty Ltd 1987 (non-exec). *Professional Organisations:* Fellow, Institute of Chartered Accountants in England & Wales. *Recreations:* Travel, Reading.

BOOTE, Gervase William Alexander; Director, Samuel Montagu & Co Limited, since 1984; Corporate Finance. *Career:* Peat Marwick Mitchell & Co 1962-72; Samuel Montagu & Co Limited 1972-. *Biog: b.* 2 April 1944. *Nationality:* British. *m.* 1967, Janet (née Stott) (diss 1987); 1 s; 1 d. *Educ:* Cheltenham College. *Professional Organisations:* FCA. *Clubs:* Hurlingham, Worplesdon Golf Club. *Recreations:* Golf, Tennis, Fishing.

BOOTH, A; Committee Member, Target Trust Managers, Unit Trust Association.

BOOTH, Geoffrey; Partner, Clay & Partners, since 1981; Pensions Consultancy. *Career:* Legal & General, Actuarial Trainee 1968-73; General Insurance Actuary 1973-80; Clay & Partners, Consulting Actuary 1980-81; Partner 1981-. *Biog: b.* 5 February 1947. *Nationality:* British. *m.* 1969, Katrina Jean; 1 s; 3 d. *Educ:* Prices Fareham; Manchester University (BSc Hons). *Directorships:* Masterwood Limited 1985 (exec). *Professional Organisations:* Fellow, Institute of Actuaries. *Publications:* Number of Technical Documents for Institute of Actuaries. *Recreations:* DIY, Gardening, Sailing, Horse Racing.

BOOTHMAN, Philip Comrie; Director, Kleinwort Benson Ltd, since 1989; Corporate Finance. *Biog: b.* 25 April 1953. *Nationality:* British. *Educ:* Manchester Grammar School; New College, Oxford (MA). *Professional Organisations:* Barrister (Inner Temple).

BOOTLE, R P; Director, Greenwell Montagu Gilt-Edged.

BORLAND, Mrs Margaret (née Miller); Sales & Marketing Director, Citymax Integrated Information Systems Ltd, since 1990; Sales & Marketing. *Career:* C Hoare & Co, Programmer, Development of Banking Systems 1974-75; Hoskyns Group Ltd, Programmer & Analyst, Design & Development of Turnkey Systems 1975-80; Software Sciences, Analyst, Design & Development of Turnkey Systems 1980-82; Enterprise Business Systems, Account Manager, Customer Support & Sales of Accounting Packages 1982-83; Victor Technologies, Applications Consultant, Marketing and Support of Distribution Network 1983-84; Buckmasters & Moore, Analyst Design of Back Office Systems 1984-86; Citymax, Sales Support Manager 1986-. *Biog: b.* 3 May 1953. *Nationality:* British. *m.* 1986, Andrew. *Educ:* University of Manchester (BA Honours History 2:1). *Recreations:* House Renovation.

BORRELLI, Michael Alexander; Director, Credit Commercial de France (UK) Ltd, since 1989; Corporate Finance. *Career:* Deloitte, Haskins & Sells (now Coopers & Lybrand Deloitte) 1978-82; Guinness Mahon & Co Limited, Corporate Finance Executive 1982-84; Samuel Montagu & Co Limited 1984-88, seconded to Stockbrokers; W Greenwell as a Corporate Finance Executive; Corporate Finance Manager 1986-88; Credit Commercial de France (UK) Ltd, Corporate Finance Director, initially with CCF's stockbroking subsidiary (Laurence Prust) and subsequently with CCF's UK investment banking operations 1988-. *Biog: b.* 17 February 1956. *Nationality:* British. *m.* 1987, Grace; 1 d. *Educ:* Epsom College, Surrey; Manchester University (BA Econ Hons). *Directorships:* Saxon Inns Limited 1987 (non-exec) Founder Dir. *Other Activities:* ACA, Member of Institute of Chartered Accountants in England & Wales. *Recreations:* Squash, Tennis, Sailing, Windsurfing, Third World Travelling.

BORRETT, Jack Geoffrey Kingsley; Director, The Frizzell Group Limited, since 1990; Man Dir, Frizzell Professional Indemnity Ltd. *Career:* Bevington Vaizey & Foster Ltd, then Wigham Poland Ltd, UK Director in charge of Broking 1956-79. *Biog: b.* 25 April 1938. *Nationality:* British. *m.* (div); 2 d. *Educ:* Pangbourne College. *Other Activities:* Insurers Livery Co; Liab & Acc Ctee, BIBA, 1983-89. *Professional Organisations:* ACII. *Publications:* Various Professional Indemnity Papers for Insurance Press. *Clubs:* Denham, Royal & Ancient, Clube De Golf Quinta Do Lago. *Recreations:* Golf, Reading, Racing.

BORRETT, Paul Jeffrey; Chairman, Baronsmead plc. *Career:* Barclays Bank plc, Trainee & Supervisory Positions 1944-58; Various Management Appointments 1958-78; Assistant General Manager 1978-82; Director, Corporate Division 1982-88; Non-Exec Director, Various Group of Companies 1980-88; BZW (Holdings) Ltd, Director 1986-88; International Commodities Clearing House Ltd, Non-Exec Director 1982-84; Technology Requirements Board of Department of Trade and Industry, Member 1985-88. *Biog: b.* 30 April 1928. *Nationality:* British. *m.* 1953 (widower 1974); 2 d. *Educ:* Hendon Grammar School. *Directorships:* Varity Holdings plc 1988 (non-exec); Private Bank and Trust Ltd 1989 (non-exec); Private Financial Holdings Ltd 1989 (non-exec); Celluware Ltd 1988 (non-exec); Anamartic Ltd 1988 (non-exec); Paul Borrett Associates Ltd 1988 (non-exec). *Other Activities:* Steering Board Member, Insolvency Service of Department of Trade and Industry, 1989-; Industry and Finance Committee Member of National Economic Development Corporation, 1987-. *Professional Organisations:* FCIB. *Recreations:* Music, Art, Travel, Cricket.

BORRIE, Sir Gordon; QC; Director General of Fair Trading, Office of Fair Trading.

BORROWDALE, Peter Edward Maxwell; Partner, Allen & Overy, since 1984; Company Law and Corporate Finance. *Career:* Allen & Overy, Asst Solicitor 1977-83. *Biog: b.* 4 May 1953. *Nationality:* British. *m.* 1977, Anne Arden (née Lea); 1 s; 1 d. *Educ:* Abbeydale Boys' Grammar School, Sheffield; Manchester University (LLB). *Other Activities:* Worshipful Company of Solicitors, City of London Law Society, Clerk to the Ward of Farringdon Within. *Professional Organisations:* The Law Society, IBA. *Clubs:* RAC. *Recreations:* Golf, Squash, Playing the Drums (when allowed).

BORROWS, S A; Director, Baring Brothers & Co Limited, since 1989; Corporate Finance. *Directorships:* Baring Brothers & Co Limited 1989.

BORWELL, G B; Director, Taylor Woodrow plc.

BOS, J G; Director, Panmure Gordon & Co Limited.

BOSANQUET, Christopher; Managing Director, Christopher Bosanquet Ltd.

BOSHELL, Stephen Robin; Portfolio Manager, The Scottish Mutual Assurance Society, since 1982; Far Eastern Equity Markets. *Biog: b.* 26 June 1950. *Nationality:* British. *Educ:* Shawlands Academy; Glasgow University (MA). *Directorships:* The Society of Investment Analysts Council Member 1985.

BOSKY, Dmitry; Managing Director, Security Pacific Venture Capital, since 1987. *Career:* Security Pacific Venture Capital Group, Senior Investment Analyst 1983-84; Investment Officer 1984-86; Vice President 1986-89; Managing Director, Europe 1987-; First Vice President 1989-90; Senior Vice President 1990-. *Biog: b.* 21 May 1959. *Nationality:* American. *m.* 1989, Marina. *Educ:* University of California, Berkeley (BS Hons, Phi Beta/Cappa, Beta Gamma Sigma); Harvard Graduate School of Business Administration (MBA). *Clubs:* HBS, Association of Orange County, Maserati Information Exchange. *Recreations:* Music, Chess, Maseratis.

BOSWELL, Roderick; Head of Business Services, Coopers & Lybrand Deloitte.

BOSWELL, S J J; Director, S G Warburg Securities, since 1987; UK Equities, UK Derivatives. *Career:* Rowe Rudd & Co 1968-75; Akroyd & Smithers (Merged with S G Warburg, Rowe & Pitman, Mullens & Co) 1975-86; S G Warburg Securities 1986-. *Biog: b.* 9 February 1952. *Nationality:* British. *m.* Pauline (née Holland); 2 s; 1 d. *Other Activities:* ISE Options Committee, 1988-. *Recreations:* Squash, Travel, Reading.

BOTHAM, Trevor; Director, Samuel Montagu & Co Limited.

BOTSFORD, D N; Director, Bain Clarkson Limited.

BOTT, Ms Rosemary (née Thorpe); Partner, Frere Cholmeley, since 1986; Company & Commercial: Corporate Finance, Mergers & Acquisitions. *Career:* Frere Cholmeley, Articled Clerk 1978-80; Assistant Solicitor 1980-86. *Educ:* Southampton University (LLB Hons); College of Law, Guildford.

BOTTENHEIM, Michael Charles; Executive Director, Lazard Brothers & Co Ltd.

BOTTERILL, Deryck; Partner, Kidsons Impey, since 1971. *Career:* Phillips Frith & Co Articled Clerk 1951-56; Tribe Clarke & Co Mgr 1956-59; Cooper Brothers & Co Supervisor/Snr Mgr 1959-64; Wm Brandt's Sons & Co Limited Mgr, New Issue Dept 1964-66; Inchcape & Co Limited Asst (Corp Fin) to the Fin Dir 1966-71; Gray Dawes & Company Limited Dir 1966-71. *Biog: b.* 31 May 1933. *Nationality:* British. *m.* 1958, Anne Fraser (née Treweek); 1 s; 1 d. *Educ:* St Austell Grammar

School. *Other Activities:* Inspector appointed by the DTI under section 177, Financial Services Act 1986 (1987-89); Member, Worshipful Company of Patternmakers. *Professional Organisations:* Fellow of The Institute of Chartered Accountants in England and Wales. *Publications:* Chapter on Share Valuations in The Creation and Protection of Capital, 1974. *Recreations:* Church - licensed reader, Flat Green Bowls, Walking, Cross-Country Skiing, Family History.

BOTTOMLEY, Alan Ingham; Joint Senior Partner, Hammond Suddards, since 1984; Company and Commercial. *Career:* Gaunt Fosters & Bottomley Ptnr 1960-70; A V Hammond & Co Ptnr 1970-84. *Biog: b.* 14 November 1931. *Nationality:* British. *m.* 1961, Jane Susan (née Werner); 1 s; 1 d. *Educ:* Shrewsbury School. *Professional Organisations:* Law Society; Solicitor. *Clubs:* Army and Navy, Bradford Club. *Recreations:* Sailing, Opera, Theatre, Travel.

BOTTOMLEY, M J; Home Shopping Director, Next plc.

BOTTOMLEY, Stephen John; Partner, Rowe & Maw, since 1988; Company & Commercial Law. *Career:* Bartletts De Reya, Articled Clerk 1978-80; Assistant Solicitor 1980-83; Partner 1983-88; Johnson Fry Corporate Finance Ltd, Director 1988-. *Biog: b.* 23 October 1954. *Nationality:* British. *m.* 1984, Gail Barbara (née Ryder); 2 d. *Educ:* Sutton Valence School; University of East Anglia (BA Hons). *Other Activities:* Treasurer, The Devas Club; City of London Solicitors' Company. *Clubs:* Dulwich & Sydenham Golf Club, Dulwich Hockey Club. *Recreations:* Squash, Golf, Hockey.

BOUCKAERT, A J; Director, Crédit Lyonnais Euro-Securities Ltd.

BOUCKLEY, C; Managing Director, Carnegie International Ltd.

BOUGHTON, Stephen David; Partner, Linklaters & Paines, since 1986; Corporate Finance. *Career:* Linklaters & Paines, Articled Clerk 1978-80; Assistant Solicitor 1980-82; Sullivan & Cromwell (New York), Foreign Associate 1982-83; Linklaters & Paines, Assistant Solicitor 1983-86. *Biog: b.* 29 September 1955. *Nationality:* British. *m.* 1989, Tracey (née Howcroft); 1 s. *Educ:* Trinity Hall, Cambridge (MA). *Professional Organisations:* Law Society.

BOULD, R J; Partner, Grimley J R Eve.

BOULTON, D J; Executive Director, Allied Dunbar Assurance plc.

BOURKE, J O P; Director, Hill Samuel Bank Limited.

BOURNE, Anthony; Head of Equity Syndicate, Paribas Limited.

BOURNE, Stephen Charles; Partner, Pannell Kerr Forster, since 1988; Corporate Finance. *Career:* Pannell Kerr Forster, Trainee/Accountant 1978-81; Auditor 1981-84; Corporate Finance Manager 1984-88. *Biog: b.* 4 January 1957. *Nationality:* British. *Educ:* Wolverhampton Grammar School; Reading University (BA Hons). *Professional Organisations:* ACA.

BOURNE, Teddy; Partner, Clifford Chance.

BOUTCHER, D J; Company Partner, Richards Butler.

BOVINGDON, N B; Director, Hogg Group plc.

BOVINGTON, J R; Director, Wendover Underwriting Agency Limited.

BOWDEN, Francis William; Partner, Hymans Robertson & Co, since 1985; Pension Scheme Advice and Administration. *Career:* Godwins Ltd Actuary 1969-73; Fenchurch Group Actuary 1973-84. *Biog: b.* 21 May 1944. *Nationality:* British. *m.* 1970, Bridget (née Smith); 1 s; 1 d. *Educ:* Manchester Grammar School; Christ's College, Cambridge (MA). *Professional Organisations:* FIA, FPMI. *Publications:* Joint Author, Kluwer Handbook on Pensions, 1988. *Recreations:* Gardening, Philately.

BOWDEN, Paul; Partner, Freshfields, since 1987; Litigation Department. *Career:* Freshfields (London), Articled Clerk 1978-81; Assistant Solicitor 1981-84; Freshfields (Singapore), Assistant Solicitor 1984-87. *Biog: b.* 30 July 1955. *Nationality:* British. *m.* 1976, Lynne (née Dyer); 1 s. *Educ:* Canon Slade Grammar School, Bolton; Bristol University (LLB, LLM). *Other Activities:* Law Society; City of London Solicitors' Company; International Law Association; International Bar Association. *Professional Organisations:* ACIArb.

BOWDITCH, Gillian; City Reporter, The Times.

BOWE, Colette; Group Director, Securities and Investments Board.

BOWEN, A L J; Director, Kleinwort Benson Limited, since 1990; UK Financial Institutions, Banking Division. *Career:* Kleinwort Benson Limited, Graduate Trainee 1972; Senior Manager 1978; Assistant Director 1984; Senior Vice-President 1984. *Biog: b.* 26 July 1950. *Nationality:* British. *m.* 1972, Margaret; 1 s; 2 d. *Educ:* Ruthin School, N Wales; Sheffield University (BA Hons). *Professional Organisations:* ACIB, 1975. *Recreations:* Walking, Squash, Children's Work.

BOWEN, Dr J M; OBE; Exploration Director, Enterprise Oil plc; Geology. *Career:* Exploration Billiton Intl Metals, Vice-Pres 1977-83; Royal Dutch Shell plc, Various 1954-77; Royal Dutch Shell plc, Dir of Exploration 1969-77. *Biog: b.* 23 August 1928. *Nationality:* British. *m.* 1961, Margaret (née Guthrie); 3 d. *Educ:* Edinburgh University (PhD Geology); Lincoln College, Oxford (BA Geology 1st Class). *Other Activities:* APIPG; PESGB; Geological Society. *Clubs:* Little Ship Club.

BOWEN, Martin J; Partner, S J Berwin & Co.

BOWER, Michael J E G; Executive Director, Rea Brothers Group plc.

BOWES-LYON, David James; Director in Charge of Scotland, Aitken Campbell & Co Ltd; Union Discount Co L Discount House Banker. *Career:* HM Forces (Army), Captain 1970-78; Union Discount Company of London, Various 1979-87. *Biog: b.* 21 July 1947. *Nationality:* British. *m.* 1976, Harriet (née Colville); 2 s; 2 d. *Educ:* Ampleforth College. *Directorships:* Aitken Campbell & Co Ltd 1987 (non-exec); Aitken Campbell (Gilts) Ltd 1987 (non-exec); Union Discount Company Ltd 1987 (exec); Union Discount Scotland (Underwriting) Ltd 1986 E Chm; Union Discount Asset Management Ltd 1987 (exec); The Scottish Business Achievement Award Trust Ltd 1982 (exec); Edinburgh Racecourse Ltd 1986 (exec). *Other Activities:* Ctee Mem, The Intl Bankers In Scotland; Mem, The Royal Co of Archers, The Queen's Bodyguard In Scotland. *Professional Organisations:* Mem, TSA. *Clubs:* Whites, New (Edinburgh). *Recreations:* Various Field Sports, Reading.

BOWES LYON, The Hon M Albemarle; Director, Coutts & Co.

BOWIE, Ronald Stewart; Partner, Hymans Robertson & Co.

BOWLER, Geoffrey; Non-Executive Director, N M Rothschild Asset Management (Holdings) Ltd.

BOWLER, M M; Partner, Kidsons Impey.

BOWLES, George Anthony John; Partner, McKenna & Co, since 1979; Construction. *Career:* McKenna & Co, Articled Clerk 1970-72; Assistant Solicitor 1973-79. *Biog: b.* 7 May 1946. *Nationality:* British. *m.* 1979, Miranda (née Neave); 2 s; 1 d. *Educ:* Eton College; Sussex University (BA). *Other Activities:* FRMETS; Freeman, City of London Solicitor's Company. *Professional Organisations:* Law Society; Society of Construction Law. *Recreations:* Meteorology, Flying Light Aircraft, Walking.

BOWLES, Godfrey Edward; Managing Director, Pearl Assurance plc, since 1989. *Career:* Australian Mutual Provident Society, Deputy Manager, Wellington, New Zealand 1976-80; Manager, Western Australia Branch, Perth 1980-83; Manager, Victoria Branch, Melbourne 1983-86; Chief Manager, Corporate Services, Sydney 1986-88; General Manager, Corporate Services, Sydney 1988-89. *Biog: b.* 21 December 1935. *Nationality:* British. *m.* 1958, Elizabeth Madge (née Donnel); 2 s; 2 d. *Educ:* Oxford University (1st Class Hons Modern History, MA). *Directorships:* Pearl Group plc 1989 (exec); Pearl Assurance plc 1989 (exec). *Professional Organisations:* AASA; FAII; ACIS; ASIA. *Recreations:* Running (inc Marathons), Reading, Music, Theatre, Cinema.

BOWLES, Richard; Head of Investment Office, Manulife International Investment Management Limited.

BOWLES, S A; Group Treasurer, BOC Group plc.

BOWLEY, Roger Quintin; Assistant General Manager/Secretary, The Equitable Life Assurance Society; Administration and Central Services. *Career:* The Equitable Life Various 1961-. *Directorships:* Reversionary Interest Society Ltd 1984 (non-exec); The Equitable Life Assurance Society 1989 (exec). *Other Activities:* Dep Chm, Assoc of British Insurers; Life European Cttee. *Professional Organisations:* FIA.

BOWLING, Geoffrey J; Group Director, MIM Ltd.

BOWMAN, Jeffery Haverstock; Senior Partner, Price Waterhouse, since 1982. *Career:* Price Waterhouse Articles 1958-61; New York 1963-64; Ptnr 1966; Dir Technical Services 1973-76; Dir London Office 1979-81; Snr Ptnr 1982-. *Biog: b.* 3 April 1935. *Nationality:* British. *m.* 1963, Susan Claudia (née Bostock); 1 s; 2 d. *Educ:* Winchester College; Trinity Hall, Cambridge (BA Hons 1st). *Other Activities:* Union of Independent Companies (VP 1983-); The Industrial Society (Council Member 1985-); Business in the Community (Council Member 1985-); Governor of Brentwood School (1985-). *Professional Organisations:* FCA (Council Member 1986-89). *Clubs:* Garrick. *Recreations:* Golf, Opera, Gardening, Sailing.

BOWMAN, N R; Partner, Ernst & Whinney.

BOWN, Richard David; Director, Treasury & Trading, J Henry Schroder Wagg & Co Limited.

BOWRING, Clive John; Chief Executive, Robert Fleming Insurance Brokers Limited, since 1990. *Career:* C T Bowring & Co Ltd, Various Directorships 1957-80. *Biog: b.* 1 September 1937. *Nationality:* British. *Educ:* Rugby School. *Directorships:* Robert Fleming Insurance Brokers Ltd 1980 (exec); Robert Fleming Marine Ltd 1982 (exec); Robert Fleming Insurance Brokers (UK) Ltd 1987 (exec); Robert Fleming Benefit Consultants Ltd 1988 (exec); Robert Fleming Fox Craig & Co Ltd

1990 (exec); Robert Fleming Pension Trust Ltd 1990 (exec). *Other Activities:* Worshipful Company of Insurers. *Professional Organisations:* London Business School Association. *Clubs:* Royal Ocean Racing Club, Hurlingham Club, City of London Club, Poole Yacht Club, Lloyd's Yacht Club.

BOWRING, H C; Director, Robert Fleming Insurance Brokers Limited.

BOWS, David; Partner, Clifford Chance.

BOWS, Michel; Financial Reporter, Daily Mail.

BOXALL, J H; General Manager (Estate Agents), General Accident Fire Life Assurance Corp.

BOXALL, R C; Director, County NatWest Securities Limited.

BOXFORD, Michael John; Director & Partner, Foreign & Colonial Ventures Ltd, since 1989; Venture/ Development Capital. *Career:* Advent Limited, Director 1987-89; Boosey & Hawkes plc, Group Chief Executive & Director 1980-86; Parfums Yves Saint Laurent/ Charles of The Ritz, European Operations Director (Based in Paris) 1975-80; UK Sales Director 1973-75; Squibb Corporation, Various Operational and Corporate Positions in UK & USA 1964-73. *Biog: b.* 5 April 1942. *Nationality:* British. *m.* 1984, Pilar (née Misteli); 2 s; 1 d. *Educ:* Marlborough College; Trinity College, Cambridge (MA); London Graduate School of Business Studies (MSc). *Directorships:* Foreign & Colonial Ventures Ltd 1989 (exec); Foreign & Colonial Management Ltd 1990 (non-exec); Several Investee Companies; Johnsen & Jorgensen plc 1982-86 (non-exec). *Other Activities:* Liveryman, Worshipful Comoany of Musicians. *Recreations:* Sailing, Skiing, Flying, Playing the Piano.

BOYCE, Mrs J R Z (née Galt); Company Secretary, NCL Investments Limited, since 1985. *Career:* Hays Allan Chartered Accountants, Auditor 1981-85. *Biog: b.* 21 June 1960. *Nationality:* British. *Professional Organisations:* ACA.

BOYCE, Thomas Anthony John; Director, Hambros Bank Limited, since 1981; International Banking. *Career:* Hambros Bank Ltd, Various Positions 1965-77; CIBC Limited, Managing Director 1978-80; Hambros Australia Ltd, Executive Director 1980-81. *Biog: b.* 4 December 1942. *Nationality:* British. *m.* 1973, Lucy Caroline Penelope (née Parsons); 1 s; 1 d. *Educ:* Eton College; Christ Church, Oxford. *Directorships:* Hambros Australia Ltd (non-exec); Wellesley House School Governor. *Other Activities:* Renter of the Salters Company. *Clubs:* Boodles, Pratts. *Recreations:* Hunting, Stalking, Racing.

BOYD, Ian Stewart; Partner, Shepherd & Wedderburn WS.

BOYD, James Edward; Director and Financial Adviser, Denholm Group of Companies, since 1968. *Biog: b.* 14 September 1928. *m.* 1956, Judy Ann Christey (née Scott); 2 s; 2 d. *Educ:* Kelvinside Academy; The Leys School, Cambridge (CA Scot dist). *Directorships:* Lithgows (Holdings) 1962-87; Ayrshire Metal Products plc 1965-; Invergordon Distillers (Holdings) plc 1966-88; GB Papers plc 1977-87; Jebsens Drilling plc 1978-85; Scottish Widows' Fund & Life Assurance Society 1981-; Shanks & McEwan Group Ltd 1983-; Scottish Exhibition Centre Ltd 1983-; British Linen Bank Ltd 1983-; Governor 1986; Bank of Scotland 1984-; Yarrow plc 1984-86 Chairman 1985-86; Bank of Wales 1986-88; Save and Prosper Group Ltd 1987-; James River UK Holdings Ltd 1987-; London & Gartmore Investment Trust plc 1978 Chairman; English & Caledonian Investment plc 1981-; McClelland Ker & Co CA (subseq McClelland Moores & Co) 1953-61 Partner; Lithgows Ltd 1962-69 Finance Director; Scott Lithgow Ltd 1970-78; Fairfield Shipbuilding & Engineering Co Ltd 1964-65 Chairman; Invergordon Distillers (Holdings) Ltd 1966-67 Managing Director; Nairn & Williamson (Holdings) Ltd 1968-75 Director; Carlton Industries plc 1978-84; BAA plc (formerly British Airports Authority) 1985- Deputy Chairman. *Other Activities:* Member, CAA (part-time), 1984-85; Clyde Port Authority, 1974-80; Working Party on Scope and Aims of Financial Accounts (the Corporate Report), 1974-75; Executive Committee, Accountants Joint Disciplinary Scheme, 1979-81. *Professional Organisations:* Member Council, Institute of Chartered Accountants of Scotland, 1977-83 (Vice-President, 1980-82, President, 1982-83); Member Council, Glenalmond College, 1983-. *Recreations:* Tennis, Golf, Gardening.

BOYD, Lindsay J; Assistant Director-Markets Policy, Hodgson Martin Limited.

BOYD, Michael Neil Murray; Finance Partner, Member of the Executive, Ernst & Whinney.

BOYD MAUNSELL, Nevill Francis Wray; City Editor, The Birmingham Post, since 1986. *Career:* Reuters 1955-57; The Financial Times 1957-60; Time & Tide 1960-62; Daily Sketch 1962-66; Freelance Journalist 1966-74; The Birmingham Post, Dep City Ed 1974-86. *Biog: b.* 22 December 1930. *m.* 1957, Lyghia (née Peterson); 1 s; 1 d. *Educ:* Winchester College; University College, Oxford (BA).

BOYES, R F; Finance Director, Leeds Permanent Building Society.

BOYLE, Allan Cameron Wilson; Director, County NatWest Ltd, since 1988. *Career:* De Zoete & Bevan, Salesman 1962-67; Francis Dupont, Salesman 1967-69; Wood Gundy Inc, Vice Pres 1970-81; Gardiner Watson Ltd, Vice Pres 1981-84; Wood MacKenzie Ltd, Director 1984-88. *Biog: b.* 11 November 1937. *Nationality:* British. *m.* 1975, Rowan (née Davies); 1 d. *Educ:* Merchiston Castle, Edinburgh; Pembroke College, Cambridge (MA). *Directorships:* Hill & Samuel 1985-87. *Professional Organisations:* International Stock Exchange. *Clubs:* London Scottish FC, Caledonian, Hon Company of Edinburgh Golfers. *Recreations:* Golf, Rugby Football Administration.

BOYLE, J Desmond; Group Director, Schroders plc, since 1985; Personnel. *Educ:* Galashiels Academy; University of Edinburgh (MA). *Directorships:* J Henry Schroder Wagg & Co Ltd 1985 (exec). *Professional Organisations:* FIPM.

BOYLE, Michael James; Partner, Pannell Kerr Forster, since 1977; Audits, Personnel & Training. *Biog: b.* 30 January 1943. *Nationality:* British. *m.* 1970, Pamela Gay (née Headland); 1 s. *Educ:* St Mary's Grammar School, Sidcup. *Other Activities:* Treasurer, Bassishaw Ward Club. *Professional Organisations:* FCA.

BRACKEN, Jonathan; Secretary and Compliance Officer, N T Evennett and Partners Ltd.

BRACKFIELD, Andrew; Partner, Linklaters & Paines.

BRADBURNE, Jeremy Randal; Chief Financial Officer, Salomon Brothers International Limited, since 1989. *Career:* Salomon Brothers International Limited, European Tax Director 1985-89; Clifford Chance, Solicitor 1981-85; Kenwright & Cox 1979-81. *Biog: b.* 5 December 1955. *Nationality:* British. *m.* Carolyn. *Educ:* Queen Elizabeth's School, Blackburn; University of London, Queens College, Cambridge; Law School. *Professional Organisations:* Solicitor, 1981. *Publications:* Butterworths International Taxation of Financial Instruments and Transactions, 1988. *Clubs:* Oxford & Cambridge Club. *Recreations:* Golf.

BRADFIELD, Nicholas Alan; Company Secretary, R H M Outhwaite (Underwriting Agencies) Limited, since 1989; Financial Aspects of the Business. *Career:* Ernst & Whinney, Articled Clerk to Manager 1980-88; Qualified Accountant 1983; R H M Outwaite (Underwriting Agencies) Limited, Financial Controller 1988. *Biog: b.* 8 September 1958. *Nationality:* British. *Educ:* Peter Symonds Grammar; University College, Cardiff (BSc Econ Hons). *Professional Organisations:* ACA. *Recreations:* Football, Tennis, Golf, Current Affairs.

BRADFIELD, R A R; Partner, Cazenove & Co.

BRADFORD, Michael David; Senior Partner, Hall Graham Bradford, since 1982. *Career:* Levett Betts & Co, Ptnr 1967-69. *Biog: b.* 9 September 1942. *Nationality:*

British. *m.* 1966, Carole Patricia (née Wadsworth); 2 s; 1 d. *Educ:* Brentwood School. *Professional Organisations:* Member, The Stock Exchange, 1963. *Clubs:* MCC, City of London, Thorndon Park Golf Club. *Recreations:* Golf, Watching Cricket, Reading.

BRADFORD, Robin E; Director, Bradstock Blunt & Thompson Ltd.

BRADLEY, Alan; Partner, Lane Clark & Peacock, since 1976. *Biog: b.* 15 December 1942. *Nationality:* British. *Educ:* King George V Grammar School, Southport; Trinity College, Cambridge (MA). *Directorships:* Lanbur Limited; The Fountain Society Projects Ltd 1990. *Other Activities:* Liveryman, Worshipful Company of Actuaries; Member, Westminster City Council. *Professional Organisations:* Fellow, Institute of Actuaries; Associate, Pension Management Institute. *Clubs:* Carlton. *Recreations:* Walking, Music, Theatre, Food and Wine.

BRADLEY, Edward Leonard; Partner, Clifford Chance, since 1990; Company Law. *Biog: b.* 2 November 1957. *Nationality:* British. *m.* 1988, Norah Sara; 1 d. *Educ:* Magdalene College, Cambridge (MA Law Degree). *Clubs:* Vintage Sports Car Club. *Recreations:* Vintage Motoring.

BRADLEY, I L; Treasurer, Pilkington plc.

BRADLEY, Joseph Clyde; Executive Director, Eagle Star, since 1990; Information Technology. *Career:* Prudential Property Services, Managing Director 1987-89; Town & Country Building Society, Managing Director 1981-87; Nationwide Building Society, General Manager (Marketing & Planning) 1974-81; Assistant General Manager (Marketing) 1972-74; Unilever Ltd, Succession of Commercial & Marketing Appointments 1961-72. *Biog: b.* 21 May 1940. *Nationality:* British. *m.* 1962, Ute Brunhilde; 1 s; 1 d. *Educ:* Great Yarmouth Grammar School; University College, London (BA Hons); London University (BSc Hons). *Directorships:* Eagle Star 1990 (exec); Best Solutions Ltd 1990 (non-exec); Prudential Property Services 1987-89; Town & County Building Society 1982-87. *Professional Organisations:* Fellow, Chartered Institute of Management Accountants; Fellow, Chartered Institute of Marketing; Fellow, British Institute of Management.

BRADLEY, Nigel Jonathan; Chairman, European Project Investment Trust, since 1989. *Career:* Morgan Grenfell & Co Ltd, Director of Morgan Grenfell Investment Services Limited 1976-80; Tyndall Unit Trust Managers Limited, Managing Director 1980-86; Tyndall Investment Management Limited, Managing Director 1987-90; Bristol Polytechnic, Lecturer in Political Economy 1990-. *Biog: b.* 9 July 1951. *Nationality:* British. *m.* 1975, Anne Veronica; 1 s; 1 d. *Educ:* Repton School; Bristol University (BA Hons). *Directorships:*

Tyndall Holdings plc 1987 (non-exec); Pacific Horizon Investment Trust plc 1989 (non-exec); Pacific Property Investment Trust plc 1989 (non-exec); First Philippine Investment Trust plc 1989 (non-exec). *Professional Organisations:* Institute of Directors. *Clubs:* Clifton. *Recreations:* Music, Books, Butterflies.

BRADLEY, Philip H G; Director, Robert Fleming & Co Ltd, since 1984; Corporate Finance/Investment Banking. *Career:* Jardine Fleming Ltd (HK), Mgr 1979-81; Coopers & Lybrand 1975-78. *Biog: b.* 11 November 1950. *Nationality:* Irish. *m.* 1978, Charlotte (née Wood); 3 s. *Educ:* Charterhouse; Trinity College, Dublin (BA,BAI). *Professional Organisations:* ACA. *Clubs:* Kildare St (Dublin), Lansdowne. *Recreations:* Shooting, Fishing.

BRADLEY, R; National Director Business Finance, AIB Bank Ltd; Commercial Mortgages.

BRADLEY, Roger Lindsay; Deputy Underwriter Syndicate, G P Eliot & Co Ltd. *Biog: Nationality:* British. *m.* 1970. *Educ:* Oundle; Cambridge (BA Hons). *Directorships:* G P Eliot & Co Ltd Director (exec).

BRADMAN, (Edward) Anthony; Director, Morgan Grenfell & Co Limited, since 1987; Group Financial Regulation. *Career:* Eric H Ascher & Co Articled Clerk 1953-58; Price Waterhouse & Co Audit Snr 1959-64; Philip Hill Higginson Erlangers Ltd Asst Accountant; Hill Samuel & Co Limited 1964-67; N M Rothschild & Sons Dep Chief Accountant 1967-69; Morgan Grenfell & Co Limited Grp Financial Controller 1969-85; Morgan Grenfell Securities Holdings Ltd Finance Dir 1986-87. *Biog: b.* 11 October 1936. *m.* 1967, Susan (née Magnuson); 1 d. *Educ:* Orange Hill County Grammar School. *Directorships:* Croham Hurst School for Girls, S Croydon 1975 (non-exec); Croham Hurst School for Girls, S Croydon 1986 Chm; Morgan Grenfell Securities Ltd; Morgan Grenfell Development Capital Limited 1990 (non-exec). *Other Activities:* Worshipful Company of Chartered Accountants; Member of British Bankers' Assoc & ICA Sub-Committees. *Professional Organisations:* FCA (Member of Council 1981-87).

BRADSHAW, Adrian; Director, Arbuthnot Latham Bank, since 1989; Corporate Finance. *Career:* Citicorp Scrimgeour Vickers 1978-81; Bell Lawrie McGregor 1981-82; County Bank 1982-83; Guidehouse Group plc 1983-89; Arbuthnot Latham Bank 1989-. *Biog: b.* 24 February 1957. *Nationality:* British. *m.* 1984, Valerie (née Citron); 1 s; 1 d. *Educ:* Urmston Grammar School; Birmingham University (BA Hons Law). *Directorships:* Arbuthnot Latham Bank 1989 (exec); Arbuthnot Corporate Finance 1990 (exec). *Clubs:* Riverside Racquet Club, Groucho Club. *Recreations:* Tennis, Squash, Music, Theatre.

BRADSHAW, John Michael; Partner, Simmons & Simmons; Litigation, Recruitment. *Career:* National Service, Subaltern 4RHA 1957-59; Simmons & Simmons, Articled Clerk 1962-65; Asst Solicitor 1965-71. *Biog: b.* 22 October 1938. *Nationality:* British. *m.* 1965, The Hon Alison Margaret (née Herbert); 3 d. *Educ:* Corpus Christi College, Cambridge (MA). *Clubs:* Bosham Sailing Club. *Recreations:* Sailing, Skiing, Walking.

BRADWELL, W; Managing Director, Credit Lyonnais Rouse Limited, since 1984. *Biog: b.* 23 December 1946. *Nationality:* English. *m.* Caroline Marjorie; 2 d. *Directorships:* Credit Lyonnais Capital Markets plc 1989 (exec). *Professional Organisations:* FCCA.

BRADY, Peter; Executive Director, Finance, AETNA International (UK) Ltd.

BRAFMAN, Guilherme (William); Partner, Cameron Markby Hewitt; Advertising, Communications & Businesses which exploit Intangibles & Acquisitions & Disposals thereof; responsible for International Strategy, especially in North/South America. *Career:* Slaughter & May, Articles 1977-79; Herbert Oppenheimer, Nathan & Vandyk, Assistant 1979-83; Brafmans, Principal 1983-84; Brafman Morris (Following Merger), Partner 1984-89; Cameron Markby Hewitt (Following Merger), Partner 1989-. *Biog: b.* 9 October 1953. *Nationality:* Brazilian. *m.* 1974, Jane; 2 s. *Educ:* Kingston Grammar School; Lycée Français de Londres; Downing College, Cambridge (MA Law). *Other Activities:* City of London Solicitors' Company; ICC International Marketing Committee; Lecturing on Company Law and Related Matters in England/USA. *Professional Organisations:* Law Society; Associate Member, Chartered Institute of Arbitrators; Member, Panel of Arbitrators, American Arbitration Association. *Clubs:* RAC. *Recreations:* Tennis, Cycling, Food, Literature.

BRAHAM, Michael D; Chairman (and Executive Producer, C4 Business Daily), Business Television Limited.

BRAITHWAITE, C P; Chairman, Minories Holdings Ltd.

BRAITHWAITE, J N; Director, CCF Foster Braithwaite Ltd.

BRAITHWAITE, Michael; Partner, Touche Ross, since 1976; Information Technology. *Biog: b.* 10 December 1937. *Nationality:* British. *m.* Margaret; 1 s; 1 d. *Other Activities:* Information Technologists. *Professional Organisations:* BSc; CEng; MBCS.

BRAITHWAITE, Paul John; Partner, Cyril Sweett and Partners.

BRAITHWAITE, Stephen James; Partner, Wragge & Co, since 1980; Corporate Law. *Career:* Kenneth Brown Baker Baker Articled Clerk 1971-73; Freshfields

Solicitor 1973-76; Wragge & Co Solicitor 1976-80. *Biog: b.* 3 May 1947. *m.* 1975, Alyson (née King-Reynolds); 1 s; 1 d. *Educ:* Sedbergh School; Queens' College, Cambridge (MA Law). *Professional Organisations:* The Law Society. *Clubs:* The Birmingham Club, The Edgbaston Priory Club. *Recreations:* Game Fishing, Farming, Tennis, Theatre & Music.

BRAITHWAITE-EXLEY, Bryan; Director, Skipton Building Society. *Directorships:* Tuff-Link Ltd; The Ribblesdale Trust.

BRAKEFIELD, Alan; Group Property Legal Adviser, Prudential Corporation plc.

BRAMBLE, P J; Finance Director, Credit Lyonnais Rouse Limited.

BRAMLEY, Ian; Partner, Hepworth & Chadwick, Solicitors, since 1977; Company & Commercial Law. *Career:* Slaughter & May, Assistant Solicitor 1970-76. *Biog: b.* 18 April 1944. *Nationality:* British. *m.* 1970; 2 s. *Educ:* Ecclesfield Grammar School, Sheffield; Wadham College, Oxford (BCL,MA). *Professional Organisations:* The Law Society. *Clubs:* The Leeds Club. *Recreations:* Reading, Watching Sport, Gardening, Walking.

BRAMSON, David; Senior Property Partner, Nabarro Nathanson. *Career:* Kaufman & Segal, Articled Clerk 1963-66; Mobil Oil & Co Ltd, Assistant Solicitor 1966-67. *Biog: b.* 8 February 1942. *Nationality:* British. *m.* 1966, Lilian (née de Wilde); 1 s; 1 d. *Educ:* University College, London (LLB, Law Degree). *Directorships:* Bride Hall Group plc (non-exec). *Other Activities:* Member, The Anglo American Real Property Institute; Member, The Investment Surveyors Forum. *Clubs:* RAC.

BRANCH, Nicholas M; Managing Director, The Chartfield Group Ltd, since 1984. *Career:* Binder Hamlyn Fry & Co, Articled Clerk/Consultant 1957-67; Director/Managing Director/Partner 1967-78; Larpent Newton & Co Ltd, Founder-Director 1978-84; The Chartfield Group Ltd, Founder-Managing Director 1984-. *Biog: b.* 21 December 1938. *Nationality:* British. *m.* 1963, Marietta (née Grazebrook). *Educ:* Eton College. *Directorships:* Renaissance Holdings plc 1986 (exec) Chairman; Casket plc 1989 (non-exec) Chairman; Butler Cox plc 1981 (non-exec); FTC Holdings plc 1988 (non-exec) Chairman; Larpent Newton & Co Ltd 1978 Former MD; Binder Hamlyn Fry & Co 1967 Former Partner; The Chartfield Group Ltd 1984 (exec) MD. *Professional Organisations:* FCA; FIMC; DipOR (M); FIOD.

BRANCH, Philip M; Director, Bradstock Blunt & Thompson Ltd.

BRAND, Michael; Finance Director, The Union Discount Company of London plc.

BRANDENBURGER, Rachel Clara; Partner, Freshfields, since 1988; UK and EEC Competition Law. *Career:* Freshfields 1977-. *Biog: b.* 2 April 1954. *Nationality:* British. *Educ:* North London Collegiate School, Middlesex; St Hilda's College, Oxford. *Professional Organisations:* Solicitor.

BRANDMAN, R N L; Vice President, The Bank of Nova Scotia.

BRANDON, D Rhett; Resident Partner, Simpson Thacher & Bartlett.

BRANDOW, Paul W; European Risk Management Executive, Chase Investment Bank Limited, since 1987. *Career:* Chase Manhattan Bank (Brazil), Capital Markets and FX Executive 1986-87; (Hong Kong), Treasury Executive 1983-86; (New York), Global Management Executive 1980-83; Various Positions within Treasury and Financial Controls in New York 1972-80. *Biog: b.* 23 May 1947. *Nationality:* American. *m.* Ann; 1 s. *Educ:* Hamilton College, New York (BA Hons); Harvard University (MBA). *Directorships:* Chase Manhattan Dealing Room Limited; Chase Manhattan FX Net Limited; Chase Manhattan Gilts Limited; Chase Manhattan Milbank Limited.

BRANDT, F B; Clerk, Gunmakers' Company.

BRANDT, Ralph; Executive Director, Bank of America International Ltd.

BRANN, Alan C; Vice President, Chemical Bank.

BRANNAN, Guy Christopher Hugh; Partner, Linklaters & Paines, since 1987; Corporate Tax. *Career:* Linklaters & Paines, Articled Clerk 1978-81; Assistant Solicitor 1981-87. *Biog: b.* 17 May 1955. *Nationality:* British. *m.* 1988, Jane Mary (née MacHale). *Educ:* The Becket School, Nottingham; Trinity Hall, Cambridge (MA); School of Law, University of Virginia (LLM). *Other Activities:* Member, Permanent Tax Commission of the Union Internationale Des Avocats. *Professional Organisations:* Law Society of England & Wales; Admitted as Solicitor, 1981. *Publications:* Co-Editor, Taxation of Companies and Company Reconstructions, 1988. *Recreations:* Walking, Cricket, Ships.

BRANSTON, George Michael; Chairman, Branston and Gothard Ltd.

BRAU, Pierre-Etienne; Director Base Metals, Brandeis Ltd, since 1990. *Career:* Various positions within the Pechiney Group in France and US including, Managing Director FRIGUIA 1975-79; Vice President, Petrochemicals Division PLUK 1979-81; CGEP, Man-

aging Director 1981-88; Executive Chairman 1988-89. *Biog: b.* 1941. *Nationality:* French. *Educ:* Ecole des Mines, France (Ingenieur des Mines); Paris Law School, France (DES Sciences Economiques); Yale University, USA (MJA). *Directorships:* Brandeis Limited 1990 (exec); CGEP (France) 1982 (non-exec).

BRAUNWALDER, Peter Franz; First Vice President and Branch Manager, Union Bank of Switzerland, since 1990. *Career:* Morgan Guaranty Trust Company of New York (Paris Branch), Trainee 197173; UBS Zurich, Trainee 1982-83; Lending Officer, Responsible for US Corporate Clients 1983-84; Assistant Vice President, Responsible for Syndication of Sfr Public Bond and Note Issues 1984-85; Assistant Vice President & Head of Evaluation Department of Capital Market Group Worldwide 1985-86; UBS Phillips & Drew International Limited (Tokyo Branch), Vice President & Branch Manager & Member of the Exec Committee 1986-88; President & Chief Executive Officer 1988-. *Biog: b.* 23 November 1950. *Nationality:* Swiss. *m.* 1985, Alexandra (née Rattin); 1 s. *Educ:* University of Berne (Economics, Law & Industrial Management). *Directorships:* UBS Phillips & Drew International Limited (Tokyo) 1988 President & CEO.

BRAY, Julian Charles; Managing Director, Leadenhall Associates Ltd, since 1986; Corporate & Financial Public Relations. *Career:* Granfield Rork Collins, Financial Head of Personal Fin; Extel Public Relations, Business Development Dir; Editorial Services Ltd, Dir Corporate Services; Welbeck PR Ltd, Head of Media Relations; Brian Dowling (Corporate Relations) PR Exec; BBC Radio Broadcaster; Lex Hornsby & Partners, PR Exec. *Biog: b.* 23 May 1945. *Nationality:* British. *Educ:* Ayr Academy. *Directorships:* NTN Television News Ltd 1988; CNS - City News Service 1986 (non-exec). *Professional Organisations:* National Union of Journalists (London Radio). *Publications:* Information Technology in the Corporate Environment, 1980. *Clubs:* Bloggs, Scribes. *Recreations:* Theatre, Travel, Motor Sport, Radio.

BRAY, Michael; Partner, Clifford Chance (formerly Coward Chance), since 1976; Banking and Finance Law. *Career:* Coward Chance 1970-. *Biog: b.* 27 March 1947. *Nationality:* British. *m.* 1970, Elizabeth-Ann (née Harrington); 2 d. *Educ:* Liverpool University (LLB). *Other Activities:* Freeman, City of London Solicitors Company. *Professional Organisations:* Member, Law Society; Member, Banking Law Sub-Committee, City of London Solicitors Company; Member, Joint Working Party on Banking Law of The Law Reform Committees of The Law Society and The Bar Assoc. *Recreations:* Theatre, Reading, Skiing, Photography.

BRAYNE, J L F; Partner, Allen & Overy.

BRAYSHAW, David Arthur; Managing Director, Gerrard & National Holdings plc, since 1980; Bond & Money Market Activities. *Career:* National Provincial Bank 1965-69; Mellon Bank, Snr Dealer 1969-73. *Biog:* b. 13 May 1948. *Nationality:* British. *m.* 1973, Jennifer (née Troughton); 2 s; 2 d. *Directorships:* Subsidiaries of Gerrard & National 1980-87 (exec).

BRAZEL, Peter A; Partner, Beachcroft Stanleys.

BRAZIER, David Richard; Partner, Cazenove & Co.

BREACH, Andrew; CBE; Chairman, Bristol & West Building Society.

BREACH, G E; Group Director, Export Credits Guarantee Department. *Clubs:* Overseas Bankers. *Recreations:* Rambling, Boating, Reading, Music.

BREACH, Peter John Freeman; Finance Director, Bristol & West Building Society, since 1984; Treasury & Finance. *Career:* Coopers & Lybrand, Dep Chief Training Officer 1963-67; Hoare Govett, Asst to Snr Ptnrs 1967-68; County Bank Ltd, Mgr 1969-71; Major Holdings & Developments P & Chief Exec Officer 1971-73; Bath & Portland Group plc, Div Dir 1974-77; Principality Holdings Group & Assoc Co's, Dir 1978-84. *Biog:* b. 12 January 1942. *Nationality:* British. *m.* 1966, Joan (née Livesey); 3 s. *Educ:* Clifton College; University of Bristol (BA Hons Special Economics & Accounting). *Directorships:* B & W 1976 non-exec; 1984 exec) 1988 Fin Dir; Principality Holdings Ltd 1975 (non-exec); Stockmead Ltd 1984 (non-exec); Farthingford Properties Ltd 1984 (non-exec); Hawksworth Securities plc 1989 (non-exec). *Other Activities:* Liveryman, Basketmakers. *Professional Organisations:* FCA; ATII; ACT; ASIA. *Clubs:* Royal Dart Yacht Club. *Recreations:* Sailing, Skiing, Historic Houses & Gardens.

BREALEY, Professor Richard; Professor of Finance, London Business School, since 1973. *Career:* Sun Life Assurance Co of Canada, Manager, UK Equity Portfolio 1959-66; Keystone Custodian Funds (Boston), Manager, Computer Applications 1966-68; London Business School, Research Fellow/Senior Lecturer 1968-73. *Biog:* b. 9 June 1936. *Nationality:* British. *m.* 1967, Diana (née Brown Kelly). *Educ:* Exeter College, Oxford (MA). *Directorships:* Swiss Helvetia Fund Inc 1987 (non-exec). *Professional Organisations:* Honorary Fellow, Society of Investment Analysts. *Publications:* Introduction to Risk and Return From Common Stocks, 2nd Ed, 1983; Principles of Corporate Finance (with S C Myers), 4th Ed, 1991.

BREED, C E; Managing Director, Dartington & Co Ltd, since 1987; Banking. *Career:* Midland Bank Group plc 1964-82. *Biog:* b. 4 May 1947. *Nationality:* British. *m.*

1968, Janet (née Courtiour); 1 s; 1 d. *Professional Organisations:* ACIB.

BREESE, Charles Jonathon; Managing Director, Larpent Newton & Co Ltd, since 1986; Venture Capital. *Career:* Peat Marwick McLintock, Accountant to Snr Manager 1969-82. *Biog:* b. 24 September 1946. *m.* 1988, Rebecca Alys. *Educ:* Stowe School. *Directorships:* McCann International Programme Marketing Ltd; Zepberry Ltd; Luke Hughes & Co Ltd; Bimec Industries plc; W M T Holdings Ltd; Thistleshire Ltd; Surrey Medical Imaging Systems Ltd; Biotal Ltd; Maindrive Ltd; Pi Holdings plc; Buckham Hill Meetings Ltd; Barnato Brooks Ltd. *Professional Organisations:* Fellow, Institute of Chartered Accountants in England and Wales. *Clubs:* Brooks's. *Recreations:* Skiing, Shooting, Tennis.

BRENAN, Patrick; Chairman, London Italian Bank Ltd, since 1989. *Career:* Hambros Bank Group, Director and Chief Financial Officer 1968-83; Independent Financial Management Consultant 1984-. *Biog:* b. 24 July 1927. *Nationality:* British. *m.* 1965, Rosemary Ann; 4 s. *Educ:* Hove County Grammar School; Strathcona Academy, Montreal. *Directorships:* London Italian Bank Ltd 1989 Chairman; Minories Finance Ltd(Formerly Johnson Matthey Bankers) 1984 (appointed by Bank of England); Business Expansion & Exchange Group Ltd 1984 (non-exec); Mase Westpac Ltd 1986 (non-exec); Investors Compensation Scheme Ltd 1990 Deputy Chairman (appointed bySIB). *Other Activities:* Member, Monopolies and Mergers Commission, 1990; Member, Financial Services Act Tribunal, 1988-90; Member of Court, Worshipful Company of Chartered Accountants; Hon Treasurer and Chairman of Finance Committee, Action Research; Chairman, Brighton Festival Trust. *Professional Organisations:* Institute of Chartered Accountants in England & Wales, Admitted 1950, Member of Council 1976-. *Clubs:* Athenaeum. *Recreations:* Dyke Golf Club, Captain 1974-75, Chairman 1977-87.

BREND, A L; Chief Executive, Commercial Union plc.

BRENNAN, J; Director, Bain & Company (Securities) Ltd.

BRENT, Peter Harry; Director, Philipp Bros Ltd, since 1986. *Career:* Alreco SA (Brussels), Mgr 1951-55; Alreco Metal Corp (New York), Gen Mgr 1956-62; Phibrotec SA (France), Chm/MD 1962-85; Philipp Brothers (France) SA, Chm/MD 1962-85. *Biog:* b. 2 March 1925. *Nationality:* British. *m.* 1984, Claudine (née Auger). *Educ:* London School of Economics (BComm). *Professional Organisations:* The London Metal Exchange Ltd (Dir of a Member Co). *Clubs:* Cercle de l'Union Interalliee (Paris).

BRETHERTON, P J; Partner, Simmons & Simmons, since 1979; Property and Property Development. *Career:* Slaughter and May, Trainee Solicitor 1972-74; Assistant Solicitor 1974-78; Simmons & Simmons, Assistant Solicitor 1978-79. *Biog: b.* 22 March 1950. *Nationality:* British. *m.* 1973, Caroline (née Stephen); 2 s; 1 d. *Educ:* Kings School, Gloucester; Trinity College, Oxford (MA). *Other Activities:* City of London Solicitors Company.

BRETT, Andrew; Vice President, Manufacturers Hanover Trust Company.

BRETT, R J A; Director, Sedgwick Lloyd's Underwriting Agents Limited.

BRETT, R P; Director, The Frizzell Group Limited.

BRETTON, John; Managing Director, John Bretton Financial Public Relations, since 1948. *Career:* Former Journalist in Fleet Street and Regions. *Biog: Nationality:* British. *m.* Edwina; 2 s. *Educ:* BEC School. *Professional Organisations:* PRCA; IPR; NIRI. *Recreations:* Golf, Bridge.

BREUER, Dr Rolf-Ernst; Director, Morgan Grenfell Group plc.

BREWER, G R; Executive Director, James R Knowles Limited.

BREWER, R J; Director, Greenwell Montagu Gilt-Edged.

BREWERTON, David Robert; Executive Editor, Finance & Industry, The Times, since 1988. *Career:* Financial Times Reporter 1967-69; Daily Telegraph City Reporter 1969-71; Commercial Property Corresp 1971-74; Insurance Correspondent 1974-77; Policy Holder Editor 1977-78; Daily Telegraph £Questor£ 1978-86; The Independent City Editor 1986-88. *Biog: b.* 25 February 1943. *m.* 1963, Patricia Ann (née Driscoll); 2 s; 1 d. *Educ:* Coopers' Company's. *Clubs:* Millbeach. *Recreations:* Sailing.

BREWSTER, David; Investment Management Regulatory Organisation Ltd. *Professional Organisations:* Barrister.

BRIAM, Tony; Partner, Clifford Chance.

BRIANCE, Richard Henry; Executive Director, Credit Suisse First Boston Ltd, since 1984; Institutional Sales. *Biog: b.* 23 August 1953. *Nationality:* British. *m.* 1979, Lucille Hardin (née De Zalduondo); 1 s; 2 d. *Educ:* Eton College; Jesus College, Cambridge (BA Hons). *Clubs:* Hurlingham, Hawks, Jesters, RAC.

BRIDEL, John Dickins; Director, Towry Law Holdings Ltd, since 1984; FSA Compliance. *Career:* Royal Navy, Fleet Air Arm, Lieutenant 1952-60; Legal & General, Inspector 1961-63; Malin Thorpe Insurance Brokers, Director 1964-69; Towry Law Group 1969-; Towry Law & Co Ltd, Director 1971-. *Biog: b.* 31 March 1934. *Nationality:* British. *m.* 1967, Patricia (née Fraser); 1 s. *Educ:* Brighton College (Matric). *Directorships:* Towry Law Holdings Ltd 1984 (exec); Various Subsidiary Companies 1971 (exec); Lautro Ltd 1988 (non-exec). *Other Activities:* Deputy Chairman, Financial Services Committee, BIIBA. *Clubs:* Woking Golf Club. *Recreations:* Piscatorial Society.

BRIDGE, M; Partner, Pannell Kerr Forster.

BRIDGEMAN, (John) Michael; CB; *Career:* Board of Trade 1954-56; HM Treasury 1956-81; Under Sec, Home Finance Group 1975-80; Under Sec, Gen Expenditure Policy Gp 1980-81; Registry of Friendly Societies, Chief Registrar 1982-. *Biog: b.* 26 April 1931. *Nationality:* British. *m.* 1958, June (née Forbes); 1 s; 4 d. *Educ:* Marlborough College; Trinity College, Cambridge (BA). *Clubs:* Reform. *Recreations:* Hill Walking, Reading History, Railways.

BRIDGEMAN, John Stuart; Divisional Managing Director, British Alcan Enterprises, since 1987. *Career:* Alcan (UK) Ltd, Commercial Director 1977-80; Alcan Basic Raw Materials, Vice President (Europe) 1978-82; Alcan Aluminum (UK) Ltd, Divisional Managing Director 1981-82; British Alcan Aluminum plc, Managing Director, Extrusion Division 1983-87. *Biog: b.* 5 October 1944. *Nationality:* British. *m.* 1967, Lindy Jane (née Fillmore); 3 d. *Educ:* Whitchurch School, Cardiff; University College, Swansea (BSc). *Directorships:* Aluminum Corporation Ltd Chairman; Alcan Building Products Ltd Chairman; Alcan Ekco Packaging Ltd Chairman; British Alcan Conductor Ltd Chairman; British Alcan Consumer Products Ltd Chairman; British Alcan Extrusions Ltd Chairman; British Alcan Wire Ltd Chairman; Luxfer Holdings Ltd Chairman; Pentagon Radiator Ltd Chairman. *Other Activities:* Deputy Lieutenant of Oxfordshire; Member, Aluminum Extruders Association Council; Member, British Airways Consumer Council; Chairman, Bunbury Business & Industry Group; Chairman, Enterprise Cherwell Ltd; Member, Tavra Employer Liason Committees in Oxon & Eastern Wessex; Vice Chairman, Heart of England Training & Enterprise Council; Member, Monopolies & Mergers Commission. *Professional Organisations:* Fellow, British Institute of Management; Associate Member, Institute of Personnel Management. *Recreations:* Territorial Army (Major), Gardening, Public Affairs, Education.

BRIDGER, David; Partner in Charge of Computerised Information Systems & Audit Business Services, Price Waterhouse.

BRIDGER, Derek Andrew; Chief Registrar, Bank of England, since 1990. *Career:* Bank of England, Assistant Chief Registrar 1981-85; Deputy Chief Registrar 1985-90. *Biog: b.* 11 January 1938. *Nationality:* British. *m.* 1960, Susan Elizabeth Turnbull (née White); 3 d. *Educ:* King's College School, Wimbledon. *Recreations:* Music, Antiques, Walking.

BRIDGES, Thomas Edward; Lord Bridges; GCMG; Independent Board Member, The Securities Association Limited, since 1989. *Career:* HM Foreign Service (later Diplomatic Service) 1951-87; Served in Bonn, Berlin, Rio de Janeiro, Athens and Moscow 1952-70; Private Secretary (Overseas Affairs) to the Prime Minister 1972-74; Minister (Commercial), Washington 1976-79; Deputy Secretary (for International Economic Affairs), Foreign Office 979-82; Ambassador to Italy 1983-87. *Biog: b.* 1927. *Nationality:* British. *m.* 1953, Rachel Mary (née Bunbury); 2 s; 1 d. *Educ:* Eton; New College, Oxford (MA). *Directorships:* Consolidated Gold Fields plc 1988-89 (non-exec); Abinger Hall Estate Co 1977 (non-exec); South Eastern Recovery Assured Homes plc 1989 (non-exec); Anglian Region, British Rail 1989 (non-exec) Board Member. *Other Activities:* Chairman, UK National Committee for UNICEF; Member, House of Lords Select Committee on the European Communities; Member, East Anglian Regional Committee, National Trust. *Professional Organisations:* FRSA. *Clubs:* Athenaeum.

BRIDGEWATER, Allan; Director & Group Chief Executive, Norwich Union Insurance Group, since 1989; General Management. *Career:* Norwich Union Insurance Group, Asst Gen Mgr 1979-83; Norwich Union Fire Insurance Society, Dep Gen Mgr 1983-84; Gen Mgr 1984-88; Norwich Union Insurance Group, Dep Chief Gen Mgr 1988-89. *Biog: b.* 26 August 1936. *Nationality:* British. *m.* 1960, Janet (née Needham); 3 d. *Educ:* Wyggeston Grammar School, Leicester. *Directorships:* Norwich Union Group Boards; Norwich Winterthur Group Boards; Heritage Insurance of Zimbabwe Ltd; Scottish Union de Portugal Compannia de Seguros SARL. *Other Activities:* Chairman, Endeavour Training; Council Member, Business in the Community; Past President, Chartered Insurance Institute. *Professional Organisations:* ACII; FIPM; CBIM; FRSA.

BRIDGEWATER, M; Partner, Nabarro Nathanson.

BRIDGMAN, P D M; Executive Director, Wardley Unit Trust Managers Limited.

BRIERLEY, David; Business Correspondent, Sunday Times Business News.

BRIERLEY, Michael; Senior Associate Director, Royal Trust Bank.

BRIFFETT, Richard; Tax Advisory, Continental Bank NA.

BRIGGS, B S; Director, Rutland Trust plc.

BRIGGS, H J; Secretary & Compliance Officer, Leeds Permanent Building Society.

BRIGHT, S L; Partner, Kidsons Impey.

BRIGHT, Stephen; Director/General Manager, Birmingham Midshires Building Society; Group Finance. *Career:* Hodgson Harris & Co, Audit Senior 1969-74; Peat Marwick Mitchell, Consultant 1974-77; Bone Fitzgerald & Co, Finance & Admin Director 1977-82; A J Bekhor & Co, Finance & Admin Director 1982-83; Self-employed Consultant 1984; Birmingham Midshires Building Society, General Manager, Group Finance 1985-89; Finance Director 1990. *Biog: b.* 15 October 1949. *Nationality:* British. *m.* 1973, Kathleen (née Lygo); 2 s; 2 d. *Educ:* St Columba's College, St Albans. *Directorships:* Birmingham Midshires Property Services 1989; Perkins Slade Ltd 1990; Mortgage Asset Management Limited 1989; Northern Mortgage Corporation 1989; Birmingham Midshires Building Society Land Development 1989; Birmingham Midshires Building Society Land Investment 1989. *Other Activities:* Member, Building Societies Association's Advisory Capital Markets Panel. *Professional Organisations:* FCA; ATII; Member, Association Corporate Treasurers. *Clubs:* Army & Navy. *Recreations:* Wolverhampton Rugby (non-Playing).

BRIGNALL, A F; Director, Hambros Bank Limited.

BRIGSTOCKE, Nicholas Owen; Managing Director, Barclays de Zoete Wedd Securities Ltd, since 1986; UK Equity Origination and Business Development. *Career:* Shell Mex and BP Ltd Sales Exec 1961-69; De Zoete & Bevan (Stockbrokers) 1969-86; Barclays de Zoete Wedd Securities Limited 1986-. *Biog: b.* 25 June 1942. *Nationality:* British. *m.* 1969, Carol Barbara (née Pretty); 2 s; 1 d. *Educ:* Summerfields, Oxford; Epsom College. *Clubs:* MCC, City of London Club, Escorts Squash Racquet Club, Twelve Club. *Recreations:* Cricket, Shooting, Tennis, Golf.

BRIL, Seno; Head of Equity Sales, Paribas Capital Markets Group, since 1990; Equity Sales Worldwide. *Career:* Paribas Capital Markets Group (London), Head International Equity Sales 1988-90; Bond/Equity Sales 1985-88; Banque Paribas (Miami), General Manager 1984-85; (Panama), Vice-President 1981-84; (Paris), Commercial Banking Dept 1980-81; (Amsterdam), Commercial Banking Dept 1978-80. *Biog: b.* 3 January 1952. *Nationality:* Dutch. *Educ:* Nederlands Lyceum, The Hague; University of Geneva (Sciences Politiques); Graduate, Institute of International Studies, Geneva (Lic, Sciences Politiques Etudes Internationales).

BRILL, Cyril; Chief Investment Manager, since 1976; Director, Royal London Mutual Insurance Society, since 1978; All Stock Exchange Securities and Property of Life, General Funds, Unit Trusts and Pension Funds. *Career:* Friends Provident Life Office Actuarial Student 1951-57. *Biog: b.* 5 January 1933. *Nationality:* British. *m.* 1960, Paselle; 3 d. *Educ:* Central Foundation. *Directorships:* Royal London Mutual 1978 (exec); Royal London Asset Mgmnt 1988 (exec). *Professional Organisations:* FIA. *Recreations:* Music, Gardening.

BRILL, John; Chairman, GCI Sterling, since 1976; Corporate & Financial Public Relations. *Career:* Rank Organisation, Dep PR Officer 1960-64; LPE Public Relations Account Exec 1964-65; Brian Dowling PR, MD 1965-76. *Biog: b.* 21 August 1935. *m.* 1960, Elizabeth (née Hughes-Morgan); 3 s. *Educ:* King's School, Macclesfield; Jesus College, Cambridge (MA). *Professional Organisations:* FIPR. *Clubs:* Savile. *Recreations:* Golf, Tennis.

BRIMBLECOMBE, Roy E; CBE; Executive Director & Chief Actuary, Eagle Star Insurance Company, since 1986; Chairman, Life & Investment Services Division. *Career:* Eagle Star Insurance Group Various 1956-72; Chief Executive, Life & Pensions Div 1972-89. *Biog: b.* 21 June 1937. *Nationality:* British. *m.* 1962, Diana Melanie (née Clyne); 1 s; 1 d. *Educ:* Highgate School. *Directorships:* Numerous Directorships of Eagle Star Companies; Eagle Star Mortgages Limited 1989 Chairman. *Other Activities:* Council of the Inst of Actuaries (Hon Secretary 1982-84; Vice President 1987-90); Chm, Life Insurance Council of ABI, 1988-90; VP, Insurance Inst of London; Pres, Pensions Management Inst, 1980-82. *Professional Organisations:* FIA. *Recreations:* Bridge, Watching Cricket.

BRINDLE, Ian; Director of Technical Services, Price Waterhouse.

BRINDLEY, Bernard James; Finance Director, National Provident Institution, since 1984; Finance Director and Appointed Actuary. *Career:* Commercial Union Assurance, Actuary 1969-79; Appointed Actuary 1979-84; Nationale Nederlanden Merchant Investors, Appointed Actuary. *Biog: b.* 15 February 1944. *Nationality:* British. *m.* 1968, Penelope Anne (née Burgess); 1 s; 2 d. *Educ:* High Wycombe Royal Grammar School; University College, London (BSc). *Directorships:* National Provident Institution 1986 (exec); NPI Trustees Services 1986 (exec). *Other Activities:* Member, Council of Institute of Actuaries. *Professional Organisations:* FIA; Associate, of Physics Management Institute (APMI). *Recreations:* Theatre.

BRISBY, S J M; Vice-Chairman Head of Corporate Finance, UBS Phillips & Drew Securities Limited.

BRISTER, Edward John; Assistant General Manager, Pensions, Norwich Union, since 1988; Occupational Pensions. *Career:* Norwich Union. *Biog: b.* 4 November 1934. *Nationality:* British. *m.* 1958, Jill; 1 s; 1 d. *Educ:* City of Norwich School. *Directorships:* OPIC 1984 (non-exec); Norwich Union Pensions Management 1985 (exec). *Other Activities:* ABI Pensions Ctee. *Professional Organisations:* Fellow, Institute of Actuaries. *Recreations:* Golf, Bridge.

BRISTER, Graeme Roy; Partner, Linklaters & Paines, since 1985; Litigation. *Biog: b.* 8 May 1955. *m.* 1986, Ashley (née Hines); 1 d. *Educ:* Forest School; Phillips School, New Hamp; Brasenose College, Oxford (MA). *Other Activities:* City of London Solicitors' Company; Partner, Rural Retreats. *Professional Organisations:* The Law Society, International Bar Association, American Bar Association; Administrative Law Bar Association, London Solicitors Litigation Association. *Clubs:* Oxford & Cambridge. *Recreations:* Travel, Sports.

BRITT, E R; Senior Warden, The Worshipful Company of Carmen.

BRITTAIN, Bruce; Managing Director (Investment Management), Salomon Brothers International Limited.

BRITTAIN, Frederick Humphrey; General Manager, Oesterreichische Laenderbank.

BRITTAIN, Nicholas John; Chief Accountant, Barclays plc, since 1986; Financial Control. *Career:* Unilever plc 1960-82; Legal & General plc Head of Gp Finance 1983-86. *Biog: b.* 8 September 1938. *Nationality:* British. *m.* 1964, Patricia Mary (née Hopewell); 1 s; 2 d. *Educ:* Lord Wandsworth College; Jesus College, Oxford (MA). *Directorships:* Limebank Property Co Ltd 1986 Chm; Bardco Property Investments Ltd 1986 Chm; Various Barclays Bank Subsidiary Companies 1986. *Other Activities:* Chairman, British Bankers' Association, Accounting Committee; Chairman, British Bankers' Association, SORPs Steering Committee; Governor, The Alexandra Trust; Committee Member, Providence Row Housing Association; Chairman, Finance Committee, Providence Row Housing Association. *Professional Organisations:* Council Member, The Chartered Association of Certified Accountants; Committee Member, General Purposes & Education Committees, The Chartered Association of Certified Accountants; FCCA. *Clubs:* Cannons, Brook CC, Privateers CC, '59 Club', Walbrook Ward Club. *Recreations:* Politics, Cricket, Gardening.

BRITTAN, Samuel; Principal Economic Commentator, Financial Times, since 1966; Assistant Editor, since 1978. *Career:* Financial Times, Various 1955-61; Observer, Economics Editor 1961-64; Department of Economic Affairs, Adviser 1965; Financial Times 1966-. *Biog: b.* 29 December 1933. *Nationality:* British. *Educ:*

Kilburn Grammar School; Jesus College, Cambridge (Economics 1st Class Hons). *Other Activities:* Senior Wincott Award for Financial Journalists, 1971 (1st Winner); Research Fellow, Nuffield College, 1973-74; Visiting Fellow, Nuffield College, 1974-82; Visiting Professor, Chicago Law School, 1978; Member, Peacock Committee on the Finance of the BBC, 1985-86; Winner, Ludwig Erhard Prize, 1987; Winner, George Orwell Prize (for Political Journalism), 1980. *Professional Organisations:* Honorary D Litt, Heriot-Watt University, 1985; Hon Professor of Politics, University of Warwick, 1987-; Hon Fellow, Jesus College, Cambridge, 1988-. *Publications:* Steering the Economy (third edition), 1971; Left or Right: The Bogus Dilemma, 1968; The Price of Economic Freedom: A Guide to Flexible Rates, 1970; Is There an Economic Consensus?, 1973; *Capitalism and the Permissive Society, 1973; *(New Edition), A Restatement of Economic Liberalism, 1988; The Delusion of Incomes Policy (with Peter Lilley), 1977; The Economic Consequences of Democracy, 1977; How to End the Monetarist Controversy (Hobart Paper 90), Institute of Economic Affairs, 1981; Role and Limits of Government: Essays in Political Economy, 1983.

BRITTON, David; Treasurer (Europe), Union Bank of Finland, since 1990; Treasury and Foreign Exchange Activities for London and Continental Branches outside Helsinki. *Career:* American Express Bank London, Chief Dealer, Treasury and FX Dealing 1967-74; Nordic Bank Ltd, Chief Dealer, Treasury and FX Dealing 1975-78; Banque Belge Ltd (Generale Bank), Director Treasury and FX Dealing 1978- 90. *Biog: b.* 3 August 1946. *Nationality:* British. *m.* 1967, Linda Diana; 1 s; 1 d. *Educ:* Grammar School, Weston-super-Mare. *Directorships:* Quin Cope Ltd 1985-90 (non-exec); Belgian and General Investments 1988-90 (non-exec). *Other Activities:* Member, Membership and Rules Committee of Liffe; European Advisory Committee of the Chicago Mercantile Exchange; Foreign Banks Assoc Foreign Exchange Committee. *Recreations:* Fell Walking, Oriental Antiques, Swimming, Art.

BRITTON, Richard; Director, International Securities Regulations, Securities and Investments Board Oversight of the Securities.

BRITZ, Lewis; Member, Monopolies & Mergers Commision.

BROACKES, Sir Nigel; Chairman, Trafalgar House Public Limited Company.

BROAD, Donald Andrew Robertson; Partner, Clark Whitehill, since 1987; Audit and Business Services. *Career:* Coopers & Lybrand (Bristol), Articled Clerk 1972-75; Coopers & Lybrand (Bristol/London) 1975-82; Clark Whitehill, Deputy Technical Director 1982-85; Senior Manager 1985-86. *Biog: b.* 19 May 1951.

Nationality: British. *m.* 1982, Margaret Elizabeth (née Bradley); 2 s. *Educ:* Bristol Grammar School; Manchester University (BA Econ). *Professional Organisations:* FCA.

BROADBENT, Adam Humphrey Charles; Director, J Henry Schroder Wagg & Co Limited.

BROADBENT, Miles; Chief Executive, Norman Broadbent International Ltd, since 1983; Executive Search. *Career:* IBM (UK) Ltd 1956-67; Watney Mann Ltd, MD, Intl Dept 1967-79; Russell Reynolds Associates, MD, UK 1979-83. *Directorships:* Roux Restaurants Waterside Ltd 1986 (non-exec); St Georges Hill Lawn Tennis Club 1981 (non-exec).

BROADBENT, Richard John; Director, J Henry Schroder Wagg & Co Ltd, since 1989; Corporate Finance. *Career:* HM Treasury 1975-86; J Henry Schroder Wagg 1986-. *Biog: b.* 22 April 1953. *Nationality:* British. *m.* 1974, Rosalind (née Scarland); 1 s; 1 d. *Educ:* City of Norwich Grammar; Queen Mary College, London University (BSc); Manchester University (MA); Stanford Graduate School of Business, USA (Harkness Fellow).

BROADHURST, John; Director, Barclays Financial Services Ltd, since 1986; Sales. *Career:* Barclays Bank plc, Various 1960-84; Barclays Insurance Brokers International Ltd, Jt MD 1985-86. *Biog: b.* 2 January 1943. *Nationality:* British. *m.* 1967, Josephine (née Oram); 2 d. *Educ:* St Albans School. *Directorships:* Barclays Bank Trust Co Ltd 1988 (exec); Barclays Life Assurance Co Ltd 1988 (exec); Barclays Unicorn Ltd 1988 (exec); Barclays Broker Services Ltd 1990 Chm; Barclayshare Ltd 1990 Chm; Barclays de Zoete Wedd Portfolio Management Ltd 1990 Chm; Barclays General Insurance Services Ltd 1990 (exec). *Professional Organisations:* ACIB. *Recreations:* Tennis, Industrial Archaeology.

BROADLEY, Robin David; Managing Director, Baring Brothers & Co Ltd.

BROCKBANK, Thomas Frederick; Director, Hill Samuel Bank Limited, since 1985; Corporate Finance; Joint Head of Smaller Companies Team. *Career:* Courtaulds Ltd (Coventry) Mechanical Engineer; Internal Consultant 1960-65; Arthur Andersen & Co Mgmnt Consultant 1965-68; RTZ Consultants 1968-73. *Biog: b.* 6 March 1938. *Nationality:* British. *m.* 1967, Joan Emma (née Israelski); 3 d. *Educ:* Bootham School, York; Loughborough College (DLC Hons 1st). *Other Activities:* FRSA. *Professional Organisations:* MIMC, GIMechE. *Publications:* Numerous Lectures and articles, particularly on Finance for Growing Companies, Flotation and General Strategy. *Recreations:* Music, Theatre, Photography, Travel.

BROCKLEBANK, Roger James; Director, Schroder Securities Ltd, since 1985. *Career:* Various Positions in Financial & General Management Areas, (Primarily in Technology Companies); Schroder Securities 1985-. *Biog: b.* 1 June 1938. *Nationality:* British. *m.* 1964, Alana (née Lloyd); 2 s; 1 d. *Directorships:* Schroder Securities Ltd 1988 (exec). *Professional Organisations:* FCMA; ACIS; MBIM.

BROCKMAN, M J; Partner, Life & General (Epsom), Bacon & Woodrow.

BROCKSOM, Christopher John; General Manager/ Chief Executive, Equity & Law Life Assurance Society plc, since 1986. *Career:* Joined Equity & Law from University 1960. *Biog: b.* 17 April 1936. *Nationality:* British; 2 d. *Educ:* Trinity College, Cambridge (MA). *Directorships:* Equity & Law Life Assurance Society plc & subsidiaries (exec); AXA-Midi Assurances; Equity & Law plc & subsidiaries. *Professional Organisations:* Fellow, Institute of Actuaries.

BRODIE, A T; Partner, Allen & Overy.

BRODIE, Ian Gibson; General Manager, Banco Espirito Santoe Commercial de Lisboa, since 1986; International Banking, Trade Finance. *Career:* Lloyds Bank plc, Domestic Banking 1948-69; (Portman Sq) Mgr 1964-69; (Overseas Div/International Banking Div) Correspondent Banking 1969-86; Chief Mgr-Bank Relations 1984-86. *Biog: b.* 6 November 1930. *Nationality:* British. *m.* 1956, Jill (née Page); 3 d. *Educ:* Woodbridge School; Administrative Staff College, Henley. *Other Activities:* Executive, Bromley Arts Council. *Professional Organisations:* FCIB. *Clubs:* Overseas Bankers. *Recreations:* Sport, Sugarcraft.

BRODIE, James Bruce; Chairman, Frere Cholmeley, since 1990; Commercial Litigation and Arbitration. *Career:* Frere Cholmeley, Partner 1971; Managing Partner 1987-90; Chief Executive 1990-. *Biog: b.* 19 March 1937. *Nationality:* British. *m.* 1962, Amie Louise (née James); 2 d. *Educ:* Union High School, South Africa; Natal University (BA); Fitzwilliam College, Cambridge (MA). *Clubs:* Hawks (Cambridge), MCC. *Recreations:* Cricket, Fishing, Travel.

BRODIE, William Walker; Director, County NatWest Securities Ltd (inc Wood Mackenzie).

BRODRICK, D J; Director, Leslie & Godwin Limited.

BROKE, A V B; Partner, Ernst & Young.

BROMAGE, Peter R; Partner (Birmingham), Evershed Wells & Hind.

BROMLEY, Mrs Diana H (née Irving); Partner, Touche Ross & Co, since 1990; Audit/Investigations. *Career:* Deloitte, Haskings & Sells 1976-85; Spicer & Oppenheim, Group Manager, Investigations 1985-90; Partner 1990-. *Biog: b.* 2 June 1955. *Nationality:* British. *m.* 1987, Stephen. *Educ:* St Andrews, Bahamas; Methodist Ladies College, Perth, Australia; University College of Swansea (BSc). *Professional Organisations:* Associate, Institute of Chartered Accountants in England and Wales. *Recreations:* Riding.

BROMWICH, Professor Michael; Professor of Accounting & Financial Management, London School of Economics Management Accounting and Finance. *Career:* Ford Motor Co, Trainee to Accountant 1958-62; LSE, Lecturer 1966-70; UWIST, Professor 1971-77; University of Reading, Professor 1977-85. *Biog: b.* 29 January 1941. *Nationality:* British. *m.* 1971, Dr C M E Whitehead. *Educ:* Wentworth Secondary Modern, Southend; LSE (BSc Econ). *Other Activities:* Past Pres, CIMA, 1987-88; Mem, Accounting Standards Ctee, 1981-84. *Professional Organisations:* Fellow, CIMA; Member, CIPFA. *Publications:* Economics of Capital Budgeting, 1976; Economics of Accounting Standard Setting, 1985; Management Accounting, Evolution not Revolution (with A Blimani), 1989.

BRONSTEIN, Michael Simon; Partner, Forsyte Kerman, since 1988; Litigation. *Career:* Forsyte Kerman, Articled Clerk 1981-83; Assistant Solicitor, Litigation Department 1983-88. *Biog: b.* 16 August 1956. *Nationality:* British. *Educ:* Haberdashers' Aske's School, Elstree; Christ's College, Cambridge University (MA Hons Law). *Professional Organisations:* Solicitor; Member, Law Society.

BROOK, M; Director, Chartered WestLB Limited.

BROOK, Nigel Geoffrey; Partner, Clyde & Co, since 1985; Reinsurance, Insurance. *Career:* Clyde & Co 1979-. *Biog: b.* 13 December 1956. *Nationality:* British. *m.* 1984, Ann (née Carrington); 1 d. *Educ:* Bablake School, Coventry; St Catherine's College, Oxford (David Blank Scholarship, 2nd Class Honours in Jurisprudence). *Professional Organisations:* Solicitor, The Supreme Court. *Publications:* Various Articles in Insurance & Reinsurance Magazines. *Recreations:* Music, Reading.

BROOKE, Anthony L; Director, Warburg Securities.

BROOKE, Christopher Roger Ettrick; Chairman, Candover Investments plc, since 1990; Organisation of, and Investment in, Management Buy-outs and Development Capital. *Career:* HM Diplomatic Service, Various 1955-66; Industrial Reorganisation Corp, Deputy MD 1966-69; Scienta SA, MD 1969-71; S Pearson & Son Ltd, Dir 1971-79; EMI Ltd Group MD 1979-80; Candover Investments plc, Chief Exec 1980-90. *Biog: b.* 2 February 1931. *Nationality:* British. *m.* 1958, Nancy (née Lowenthal); 3 s; 1 d. *Educ:* Tonbridge School; Trinity College, Oxford (MA). *Directorships:* Subsidiary Companies of Candover Investments plc; Slough Estates plc 1980; Agridata Resources Inc (USA) 1982; Hoare Candover Ltd 1984; Benchwood Properties Ltd 1984; Centaur Communications Ltd 1984; Friday's Court Ltd 1985; CCL Developments plc 1987; Allenwest Ltd 1987; Lowndes & Lambert Group Holdings Ltd 1988; Chawton Developments Ltd 1990; Equity Leisure Group Ltd 1990. *Other Activities:* CBI City Industry Group; NEDO Ctee of Industry and Finance; RBK&C Investment Ctee. *Publications:* Santa's Christmas Journey, 1984. *Clubs:* Brooks's, Woking Golf Club. *Recreations:* Golf, Tennis, Music, Theatre.

BROOKHOUSE, S D; Investment Development Manager, Life Association of Scotland, since 1990; Marketing and Development of Investment Product Range. *Career:* BXL Plastics (BP Chemicals), Graduate Accountant 1983-86; Wood Mackenzie (Hill Samuel) Stockbrokers, Management Accountant 1986-87; Life Association of Scotland, Administration Manager, Unit Trusts 1987-90; Investment Development Manager 1990-. *Biog: b.* 9 July 1962. *Nationality:* British. *m.* 1988, Amanda Tracy. *Educ:* King Edward VI Grammar School, Stratford on Avon; University of Wales, Cardiff (BSc Hons Economics). *Directorships:* LAS Unit Trust Managers Ltd 1990; LAS Investment Management Ltd 1990. *Professional Organisations:* ACMA.

BROOKS, E A; Secretary, Slough Estates plc.

BROOKS, E R; Partner, Slater Heelis.

BROOKS, J F; Partner, Waltons & Morse.

BROOKS, M F; Director, Phillips & Drew Fund Management Limited.

BROOKS, P A; Director, TSB Unit Trusts Limited.

BROOKS, Peter Malcolm; Partner, Clifford Chance, since 1984; Corporate Finance. *Career:* Macfarlanes, Partner 1977-84. *Biog: b.* 12 February 1947. *Nationality:* British. *m.* 1987, Patricia Margaret (née Garratt); 2 s. *Educ:* Marlborough College; Southampton University (LLB). *Professional Organisations:* The Law Society. *Recreations:* Cricket, Real Tennis, Opera, Travel.

BROOKS, R S; Director, James Capel Unit Trust Management Ltd.

BROOKS, Robert Anthony; Director, Kleinwort Benson Group plc, since 1987; Group Compliance. *Career:* Viney Price & Goodyear, Articled Clerk 1951-56; Cooper Bros, Acct 1957-60; Robert Benson Lonsdale & Kleinwort Benson 1961-; Kleinwort Benson Ltd, Dir 1967-. *Biog: b.* 12 April 1931. *Nationality:* British. *m.* 1955, Sally (née Armistead); 3 d. *Educ:* Eton

College. *Directorships:* Commercial Union 1976 (non-exec); M & G Group plc 1979 (non-exec); The Securities Association 1989. *Other Activities:* Liveryman, The Grocers Company. *Professional Organisations:* FCA. *Clubs:* City Club.

BROOMFIELD, James Douglas; National Director of Marketing, BDO Binder Hamlyn, since 1987; Marketing. *Career:* RAF, Officer 1967-77; McDermott Inc Business Development 1978-81; Hobsons Press, Executive Director 1981-85; KMG Thomson McLintock, Director of Marketing 1985-87. *Biog: b.* 26 August 1947. *Nationality:* British. *m.* 1971, Lucy (née Schupbach); 2 s; 1 d. *Educ:* Cranleigh School; Hatfield Polytechnic (DMS); Cranfield (MBA). *Other Activities:* Chairman, CoSIRA County Committee 1984-88. *Professional Organisations:* FInstM; MIPR. *Clubs:* Carlton Club. *Recreations:* Vintage Cars.

BROSSIER, Luc; Président Directeur Général, AXA International, since 1985; Reinsurance/Overseas. *Career:* La Préservatrice 1968-75; Secretaire General Adjoint 1975; AXA 1975-; Mutuelles Unies, Directeur de l'Etranger et de la Reassurance 1975; AXA International, Directeur General 1984; Ancienne Mutuelle Reassurance (now AXA RE), Directeur General 1985. *Biog: b.* 26 April 1938. *Nationality:* French. 4 children. *Educ:* Baccalauréat de Philosophie; Ecole Spéciale Militaire de Saint-Cyr; Centre des Hautes Etudes d'Assurances. *Directorships:* Equity & Law Life Assurance Society plc.

BROUGHTON, Alan William; Managing Director, Guinness Mahon & Co Ltd, since 1988; International Division. *Career:* Orion Bank Ltd, Exec Dir 1978-81; Orion Royal Bank, Managing Dir 1981-83; Royal Bank of Canada, VP 1983-85; Guinness Mahon & Co Limited, Executive Director 1985; Member of Executive Committee 1986; Managing Director 1988. *Biog: b.* 22 May 1944. *Nationality:* British. *m.* Pamela; 2 s; 1 d. *Directorships:* Guinness Mahon Guernsey Ltd. *Recreations:* Golf, Sailing.

BROWER, Stephen Jonathan; Partner, Wilde Sapte, since 1989; Commercial Property. *Career:* Rayner De Wolfe, Articled Clerk 1982-84. *Biog: b.* 6 July 1960. *Nationality:* British. *m.* 1986, Suzanne Elaine (née Simms). *Educ:* Kings School, Macclesfield; Kent University (BA Law). *Professional Organisations:* Law Society of England & Wales.

BROWN, A J; Company Secretary, Sturge Holdings plc.

BROWN, Adrian James; Senior Investment Manager, Refuge Assurance plc, since 1988; UK Equities. *Career:* Phillips & Drew Investment, Manager 1968-79; London & Manchester Assurance Investment, Manager 1979-81; Britannia Group of Unit Trusts & Pension, Manager 1982-88. *Biog: b.* 25 November 1946. *Nationality:* British. *m.* 1976, Jill (née Harmsworth); 1 s; 2 d. *Educ:* Birmingham University (BSc Hons). *Directorships:* MIM Ltd 1986-88 (exec). *Professional Organisations:* ASIA.

BROWN, Alan Edward; Director, Japan, Barclays Bank plc, since 1990; Corporate Banking & Treasury for the Large Company Sector in Japan. *Career:* Barclays Bank plc, Various Managerial Positions 1973-79; Barclays Merchant Bank Ltd, Dir for Special Transactions 1979-82; Barclays Bank plc, Corp Finance Dir, Worldwide Aerospace Banking 1982-86; Barclays Development Capital Ltd, Director 1987-90; Barclays Bank plc, Deputy Divisional Director, Large Corporate Banking 1986-90. *Biog: b.* 8 January 1946. *Nationality:* British. *m.* 1968, Diane June (née Oakley); 2 d. *Educ:* Wolverhampton Grammar; St Peter's College, Oxford (MA Hons). *Directorships:* Barclays De Zoete Wedd Securities Ltd 1990 (non-exec). *Other Activities:* Freeman of town of Bridgworth, Shropshire. *Professional Organisations:* ACIB. *Clubs:* Pinner Hill Golf Club, Rickmansworth Windsurfing Club. *Recreations:* Golf, Windsurfing.

BROWN, Alasdair Stuart; Partner, Bacon & Woodrow, since 1974; Consulting Actuary Specialising in Life Assurance. *Career:* Bacon & Woodrow Actuarial Trainee 1969-72; Actuary 1972-73. *Biog: b.* 18 April 1948. *m.* 1982, Sandra Christine (née Langmuir). *Educ:* St Paul's School; London School of Economics (BSc Econ). *Professional Organisations:* FIA; FSS. *Publications:* Valuation of Individual Investment-Linked Policies (Co-Author). *Clubs:* Phiatus.

BROWN, Anthony Philip; Director, Riggs A P Bank Limited, since 1988; Corporate Finance. *Career:* Sterling Industrial Securities Limited 1971-75; Tozer Standard & Chartered Limited 1975-77; Standard Chartered Merchant Bank Limited 1977-88. *Biog: b.* 23 July 1947. *Nationality:* British; 1 s; 1 d. *Educ:* Hutchesons', Glasgow; University of Glasgow (MA). *Directorships:* Riggs A P Bank Limited 1988 (exec). *Professional Organisations:* Member, Institute of Chartered Accountants of Scotland. *Clubs:* City of London.

BROWN, Antony Delano Gordon; Director, Kleinwort Benson Limited, since 1989; Corporate Finance, Compliance. *Career:* Allen & Overy, Solicitor 1973-75; S G Warburg & Co Ltd, Corporate Finance 1975-86; Robert Fleming & Co Limited, Corporate Finance Director 1987-89. *Educ:* Charterhouse; Birmingham University (LLB).

BROWN, Dr Brendan; Director Research Department, Mitsubishi Finance International Limited.

BROWN, Brian Michael John; Chief Executive, TSB Trust Company Limited, since 1983; Life Insurance, Pensions, General Insurance, Unit Trusts, Offshore Funds. *Career:* South Eastern Trustee Savings Bank, Assistant Branch Manager 1959-67; TSB Unit Trusts Managers Ltd, Marketing Manager 1967-71; General Manager 1971-83. *Biog: b.* 11 February 1937. *Nationality:* British. *m.* 1989, Elizabeth Charlotte (née Saywell); 1 s; 2 d. *Educ:* Sir Roger Manwoods Grammar School, Sandwich. *Directorships:* TSB Trust Company Limited 1982 (exec); TSB Life Limited 1976 (exec); TSB Pensions Limited 1982 (exec); TSB Unit Trusts Limited 1982 (exec); TSB Investment Services Limited 1986 (exec); TSB Insurance Brokers Limited 1989 (exec); TSB Properties (Andover) Limited 1984 (exec); TSB Equity Plan Limited 1987 (exec); TSB General Insurance Limited 1988 (exec); TSB General Insurance Services Limited 1989 (exec); TSB Insurance Services Limited 1982 (exec); TSB Motor Insurance Services Limited 1989 (exec); TSB Health Insurance Services Limited 1989 (exec); Wessex Life Limited 1986 (exec); TSB Gilt Fund Limited 1978 (exec); TSB Gilt Fund (Jersey) Limited 1978 (exec); TSB Offshore Investment Fund Limited 1983 (exec); TSB Fund Managers (Channel Islands) Ltd 1978 (exec); TSB Unit Trust Managers (Channel Islands) Limited 1984 (exec). *Other Activities:* Member, LAUTRO Selling Practices Committee; Governor, Cricklade College, Andover. *Professional Organisations:* FCIB; FBIM. *Clubs:* Reform. *Recreations:* Eating Out, Reading, Gardening, Steam Railways, Coin/Stamp Collecting.

BROWN, Claude Read; Chairman, Pannell Kerr Forster, since 1984. *Career:* Charles Comins & Co, Articled Clerk 1962-66; Pannell Kerr Forster 1966-; Ptnr 1968-; National Chm 1984-90; European Chm 1987-; International Vice-Chm 1990-. *Biog: b.* 12 November 1939. *Nationality:* British. *m.* 1975, Juliette Olivia (née Hubert); 1 d. *Educ:* University of Manchester (BCom). *Other Activities:* Liveryman, Worshipful Company of Carmen. *Professional Organisations:* FCA.

BROWN, Clive; Partner, Cameron Markby Hewitt; Litigation Department/Aviation Group (Non-Marine Liability Insurance, Product Liability Insurance, Reinsurance). *Career:* Bowen, Sessel & Youdvis Johannesburg, Assistant Solicitor 1969-72; Hewitt Woollacott & Chown London (now Cameron Markby Hewitt), Articled Clerk 1972-75; Solicitor 1975-77; Partner 1977-. *Biog: b.* 6 March 1944. *Educ:* Stellenbosch, S Africa (BA); Cantab (LLB). *Other Activities:* City of London Solicitors Company; BILA; British Pilot's Licence. *Professional Organisations:* Law Society; Attorney, The Supreme Court of South Africa; Solicitor, The Supreme Court of England & Wales, 1976.

BROWN, Colin Ian; Director of Finance, Europe, Price Waterhouse, since 1988; Finance, Planning, IT Systems, Legal and Secretarial. *Career:* James Worley & Sons, Training 1951-56; National Service (Army) 1956-58; Price Waterhouse 1958; Partner 1966-; National Recruitment, Partner 1966-72; Partner in Charge, London Audit/Tax Group 1972-79; Price Waterhouse

World Firm 1979-87; Vice Chairman, Human Resources 1979-82; Chairman's Office, Responsible for Human Resources, Finance, Business Development and Asia/Pacific 1979-82; UK Firm, Head of Audit and Business Advisory Services 1987-88. *Biog: b.* 3 December 1933. *Nationality:* British. *m.* 1965, Lorna (née Jarrett); 3 d. *Educ:* Raynes Park County Grammar School. *Professional Organisations:* Member, Institute of Chartered Accountants in England and Wales; Chairman, Institute of Chartered Accountants in England & Wales Banking Committee, 1977-89; Member, Institute of Chartered Accountants Practice Regulation Directorate; Chairman, Audit Registration Committee. *Publications:* Joint Author of the Institute Guide on Accounting and Auditing for Banks. *Clubs:* Royal Lymington Yacht Club, North Downs Golf Club. *Recreations:* Golf, Sailing, Skiing, Photography.

BROWN, D; Director, Allied-Lyons plc.

BROWN, D P; Director, Barclays de Zoete Wedd Securities Ltd.

BROWN, D R; Partner, Jaques & Lewis.

BROWN, David J C; Intellectual Property Partner, Bristows Cooke & Carpmael.

BROWN, Denis Osborne; JP; Partner, Independent Financial Advisory Centre.

BROWN, Professor Ewan; Director, Noble Grossart Limited, since 1971; General. *Biog: b.* 23 March 1942. *Nationality:* Scottish. *m.* 1966, Christine; 1 s; 1 d. *Educ:* Perth Academy; St Andrews University (MA, LLB). *Directorships:* Scottish Development Finance Ltd 1983 (non-exec); John Wood Group plc 1984 (non-exec); Stagecoach Holdings Ltd 1989 (non-exec); James Walker (Leith) Ltd 1971 (non-exec); Pict Petroleum plc 1973 (non-exec). *Other Activities:* Member of Council, Institute of Chartered Accountants of Scotland; Assistant, The Merchant Company of Edinburgh; Honorary Professor in Finance, Heriot Watt University. *Professional Organisations:* CA. *Clubs:* New (Edinburgh), Royal and Ancient (St Andrews). *Recreations:* Mah Jongg, Collecting Scottish Watercolours, Golf, Skiing.

BROWN, G H; Director, Schlesinger & Company Limited.

BROWN, Geoffrey Edward Martyn; Director, Plantations, Harrisons & Crosfields plc.

BROWN, Howard Roger; Partner, Chairman of Banking & Financial Services, Ernst & Young, since 1975; Services in UK & Worldwide to Clients in Banking & Financial Services Industry. *Career:* Grant Thornton Trainee Acct 1963-69; Ernst & Young Snr to Ptnr 1969-. *Biog: b.* 25 February 1945. *Nationality:*

British. *m.* 1970, Elizabeth (née Hillyar); 3 d. *Educ:* Portsmouth Grammar School. *Other Activities:* Auditing Practices Ctee; Member, Auditing of Banks Sub-Ctee. *Professional Organisations:* FCA. *Publications:* Leasing-Accounting & Tax Implications, 1978; International Bank Accounting, 1987. *Recreations:* Sport, Reading.

BROWN, Hugh McCartney; Partner, Coopers & Lybrand.

BROWN, Hugh Merrick; Partner, Holman Fenwick & Willan, since 1983; Admiralty Litigation. *Career:* E F K Tucker (Johannesburg RSA), Assistant Solicitor 1974-75; Winter Taylor Woodward & Webb (High Wycombe), Assistant Solicitor 1971-74.

BROWN, Jeremy; Partner, Linklaters & Paines, since 1982; Laws Concerning Intellectual Property, Technology and Communications. *Career:* Spoor & Fisher, Patent Attorneys, Johannesburg, Pretoria & Durban, South Africa 1971-78; Linklaters & Paines, London, Intelectual Property Lawyer 1978-82. *Biog: b.* 2 May 1948. *Nationality:* British. *Educ:* Westville Boys High, Natal, South Africa; University of Natal, Durban, South Africa (MSc Chemical Engineering); University of South Africa (BIuris). *Other Activities:* Licensing Executives Society, Britain and Ireland, Vice President 1990-91; AIPPI (British Group), Member of Council; London Chamber of Commerce and Industry, Committees on Patents and Trade Marks; City of London Solicitors' Company; Membership of Various Bodies, including Chartered Institute of Patent Agents (Associate); American Bar Association; American Intellectual Property Lawyers' Association; Patent Solicitors' Association. *Professional Organisations:* Solicitor of Supreme Court of England and Wales; Member, Law Society; Attorney, Supreme Court of South Africa; Registered Patent Agent (South Africa) & Fellow, South African Institute of Patent Attorneys. *Publications:* Various Papers on Technology Transfer; Intellectual Property Law; EEC Law and 1992; Doing Business in Europe. *Clubs:* Roehampton. *Recreations:* Tennis, Travel, The Arts.

BROWN, John Forster; Deputy Managing Director, CIN Venture Managers Ltd. *Career:* Economist Intelligence Unit, Consultant 1980-83; Greater London Enterprise Board, Investment Exec 1983-84. *Biog: b.* 11 December 1952. *Nationality:* British. *m.* 1990. *Educ:* Newcastle Royal Grammar School; Oxford University (BA). *Directorships:* Numerous Non-Executive Directorships. *Professional Organisations:* FCA.

BROWN, Johnstone Edwards; Director of Finance & Administration, Henderson Pension Fund Management Limited.

BROWN, K A; Director, Panmure Gordon & Company Limited.

BROWN, Keith; Managing Director, Morgan Stanley International, since 1988; Bank Analyst. *Career:* Greenwell Montagu & Co 1962; Partner 1977; Head of Research 1985; Managing Director 1987. *Biog: b.* 14 January 1943. *Nationality:* British. *m.* 1972, Rita Hildegard (née Rolfe); 1 s; 1 d. *Educ:* Forest School, Snaresbrook; City of London College (Diploma in Stock Exchange Law and Practice). *Directorships:* London Regional Transport 1984 Board Member; British Aerospace plc 1989 Government Director. *Other Activities:* Member, Department of Transport Panel on Disability 1985-89; Member, Lloyds' of London; Freeman, City of London; Liveryman, Coopers' Company. *Professional Organisations:* Member, Society of Investment Analysts; Member, International Stock Exchange. *Recreations:* Tennis, Cricket, Horse Racing.

BROWN, M M; Chief Manager (Corporate), Northern Bank Ltd; Corporate Banking/Treasury/International. *Career:* Northern Bank, Chief Manager (Retail) 1987-89; Asst General Manager 1984-87; Corporate Planner 1982-84. *Biog: b.* 1943. *Nationality:* British. *m.* 1970, Barbara Elizabeth (née Byers); 3 s. *Educ:* Bangor Grammar School; Queens University, Belfast; IMEDE, Lausanne. *Directorships:* Northern Bank Factors Ltd 1987 (non-exec); Northern Bank Development Corporation Ltd 1990 (non-exec). *Professional Organisations:* Fellow, The Institute of Bankers; Council Member, Institute of Bankers in Ireland. *Clubs:* Royal Belfast Golf Club.

BROWN, M T; Partner, Waltons & Morse.

BROWN, Martin Robert; Director, Kleinwort Benson Limited.

BROWN, Michael; Partner, Clifford Chance.

BROWN, Michael A; Director, Minet Holdings plc.

BROWN, Michael Jarvis; Director, Henry Cooke Corporate Finance Limited, since 1989; Corporate Finance. *Career:* Economist Intelligence Unit Economist 1958-61; Henry Cooke, Lumsden plc 1961-89. *Biog: b.* 13 July 1935. *Nationality:* British. *m.* 1964, Susan (née Thompson); 3 s. *Educ:* St Edward's School, Oxford; Oxford University (BA). *Directorships:* Henry Cooke Group plc 1988 (exec); Henry Cooke, Lumsden plc 1965 (non-exec); Oak Venture Management Ltd 1982 (exec). *Professional Organisations:* Member, International Stock Exchange. *Recreations:* Skiing, Walking, Photography.

BROWN, Neil; Partner, Hepworth & Chadwick, since 1987; Commercial Property. *Career:* Breeze & Wyles, Enfield & Hertford, Articled Clerk 1980-82; Watson Burton, Newcastle upon Tyne, Assistant Solicitor, General Commercial Work 1982-86; Hepworth & Chadwick, Assistant Solicitor, Commercial Property 1986. *Biog: b.* 17 January 1957. *Nationality:* British. *m.* 1982, Jacqueline (née Hurst); 1 s; 1 d. *Educ:* Hertford Grammar; University of Warwick (Law IIi). *Professional Organisations:* Law Society. *Clubs:* Round Table, Conjarily, Newcastle Utd FC.

BROWN, Neil Douglas; Director, Baring Brothers & Co Ltd, since 1989; Banking and Capital Markets. *Career:* Baring Brothers & Co Ltd, Various to Dir, Capital Markets 1969-87; UBS Securities/Phillips & Drew, Exec Dir to Dep MD 1987-89. *Biog: b.* 10 April 1943. *Nationality:* British. *m.* 1968, Adrienne (née Heizmann); 1 s; 1 d. *Educ:* Loretto; Peterhouse, Cambridge (BA Hons). *Professional Organisations:* FCA. *Clubs:* Worplesdon Golf Club. *Recreations:* Golf, Reading, Gardening.

BROWN, Nicholas Arthur; Partner, McKenna & Co, since 1980; Property. *Career:* McKenna & Co, Articled Clerk 1972-74; Assistant Solicitor 1974-80. *Biog: b.* 21 November 1949. *Nationality:* British. *m.* 1977, Charlotte (née Bompas-Smith); 2 s; 2 d. *Educ:* Bristol University (BA). *Other Activities:* Member, Land Law Sub-Committee, City of London Law Society. *Professional Organisations:* City of London Law Society; Law Society of England and Wales.

BROWN, Paul Gregorius; Director, Lloyds Bank plc, since 1990; Private Banking & Financial Services. *Career:* Lloyds Bank International, Principal Mgr (Germany) 1980-81; Exec VP (New York) 1982-83; Schroder, Munchmeyer, Hengst, Partner/CEO 1984; Lloyds Bank plc, Gen Mgr (Europe, Middle East & Africa) 1985-86; Lloyds Merchant Bank, Snr Gen Mgr, Investment Banking 1987-88; Snr Gen Mgr, Debt Mgmnt Group 1988-89; Snr Gen Mgr, Private Bkg & Fin Serv 1989; Director, Private Bkg & Fin Serv 1990. *Biog: b.* 10 September 1942. *Nationality:* British. *m.* 1969, Jessica (née Faunce); 1 s; 2 d. *Directorships:* Schroder, Munchmeyer, Hengst & Co 1988 Chairman; Lloyds Bank International (Guernsey) Ltd 1989 Chairman; Lloyds Bank International (Bahamas) Ltd 1989 Chairman; Lloyds Bank International (Jersey) Ltd 1990 Chairman; Lloyds International Money Market Fund Ltd. *Other Activities:* Executive Committee Member, Lloyds Bank plc.

BROWN, Peter Charles; Group Company Secretary, 3i Group plc, since 1985. *Career:* Henry E Goodrich, Articled Clerk 1956-62; Ptnr 1962-66; Midland Bank plc, Reg Legal Adviser 1966-70; Industrial & Commercial Finance Corp Ltd, Principal Legal Officer (North) 1970-75; Investors in Industry plc, Dep Chief Legal Adviser 1975-85. *Biog: b.* 11 July 1940. *Nationality:* British. *m.* 1962, Kathleen Joyce (née Newsham); 1 s; 2 d. *Educ:* King Edward VI Grammar School, Chelmsford; London University (LLB). *Directorships:* Companies within the 3i Group. *Professional Organisations:* The Law Society. *Recreations:* Music, Badminton.

BROWN, Peter John; Administration Partner, Cazenove & Co. *Career:* Cazenove & Co 1965-. *Biog: b.* 3 August 1947. *Nationality:* British. *m.* 1970, Linda (née Leek); 1 s; 1 d. *Professional Organisations:* Member, International Stock Exchange.

BROWN, Peter Stewart; Partner, Winthrop Stimson Putnam and Roberts, since 1985; London Resident Partner. *Biog: b.* 8 January 1951. *Nationality:* American. *m.* 1978, Charlotte (née Tileston); 1 s; 2 d. *Educ:* Regis High School; Drew University (BA); Harvard University (JD). *Professional Organisations:* Member, IBA; Admitted to the Bar of the State of New York and to the Federal Courts (Southern District of New York). *Recreations:* Riding, Reading, Music.

BROWN, Philip; Managing Partner, Wilde Sapte, since 1988; Management of Firm. *Career:* Wilde Sapte, Partner 1975-88; Ormerod, Morris & Dumont, Croydon 1972-74; Newark, New Jersey Law Reform Project 1969-71. *Biog: b.* 24 June 1942. *Nationality:* British/ American. *m.* 1975, Geraldine; 2 d. *Educ:* US and UK Secondary Schools; Hobart College, Geneva, New York (BA); Columbia University (LLB); College of Law, Guildford, England. *Professional Organisations:* Law Society of England and Wales; City of London Solicitors Company; International Bar Association. *Recreations:* Pottery, Art History, My Children.

BROWN, Philip Anthony Russell; CB; Director of Policy, Investment Management Regulatory Organisation Ltd, since 1986; Strategy. *Career:* Board of Trade Asst Principal 1947-55; Civil Service Selection Board Principal Observer 1955-57; Board of Trade Principal 1957-62; Overseas Information Co-ordination Office Asst Sec 1962-69; Dept of Trade & Industry Under Sec 1969-74; Deputy Sec 1974-83; Lloyds of London Head, External Relations 1983-85. *Biog: b.* 18 May 1924. *Nationality:* British. *Educ:* Malvern College; King's College, Cambridge (MA). *Directorships:* National Provident Institution 1985-90 (non-exec). *Other Activities:* Member, London Advisory Board, Salvation Army; Member, Disciplinary Committee, Inst of Chartered Accountants in England & Wales. *Publications:* Articles in Professional Journals in the UK & USA. *Clubs:* United Oxford & Cambridge University.

BROWN, Robert; Finance Director, Lucas Industries plc.

BROWN, Roderick Michael; Partner, Allen & Overy, since 1981; Commercial Property. *Career:* Allen & Overy, Articled Clerk 1973-75; Assistant Solicitor 1975-80.

BROWN, Mrs Sarah Elizabeth (née Dean); Head of Companies Division, Department of Trade & Industry, since 1986; Company Law. *Career:* Board of Trade, Asst Principal 1965-70; DTI, Principal 1970-78; Crown

Agents, Tribunal Sec 1978-82; DTI, Asst Sec, Pers Mgmnt Div 1982-85; Asst Sec, Fin Services Div 1985-86. *Biog: b.* 1943. *Nationality:* British. *m.* 1976, Philip A R. *Educ:* St Paul's Girls School; Newnham College, Cambridge (BA). *Clubs:* United Oxford & Cambridge University. *Recreations:* Gardening, Walking, Travel, Theatre.

BROWN, Timothy Colin; Director & Deputy Chief Executive, City & Commercial Communications plc, since 1987; Financial Public Relations, Investor Relations. *Career:* HM Forces 4th/7th Royal Dragoon Guards 1976-82; City & Commercial Communications 1983-. *Biog: b.* 20 September 1957. *Nationality:* British. *m.* 1987, Lady Vanessa (née Pelham). *Educ:* Eton College; RMA Sandhurst. *Clubs:* Cavalry & Guards, Lansdowne. *Recreations:* Shooting, Squash, Skiing, Backgammon.

BROWN, Timothy Frank; Head of Trading Strategy, UBS Phillips & Drew. *Career:* Larking & Larking, Articled Clerk 1963-68; Deloitte Haskin & Sells, Audit Snr 1968-69; Phillips & Drew 1969. *Biog: b.* 7 November 1944. *Nationality:* British. *m.* 1967, Kathleen (née Smith); 2 s; 2 d. *Educ:* Sir Joseph William's Mathematical School. *Professional Organisations:* FCA, ATII, ASIA.

BROWN, W; CBE; Chairman, Scottish Amicable Life Assurance Society, since 1989. *Career:* Scottish Television plc, Managing Director 1966-90; Deputy Chairman 1974-. *Biog: b.* 24 June 1929. *Nationality:* British. *m.* Nancy Jennifer (née Hunter); 1 s; 3 d. *Educ:* Ayr Academy; Edinburgh University (BCom). *Directorships:* Scottish Television plc (non-exec); Scottish Amicable Life Assurance Society (non-exec); Radio Clyde plc (non-exec); Scottish Opera Theatre Royal Ltd (non-exec). *Clubs:* Caledonian, Royal & Ancient, Prestwick Golf. *Recreations:* Golf, Cinema.

BROWN, W M; Assistant General Manager, Equity & Law Life Assurance Society plc.

BROWN-HUMES, Christopher; Business Editor, Lloyd's List.

BROWNE, Anthony George; Director of Privatisation Services, Price Waterhouse, since 1989; Privatisation. *Career:* Price Waterhouse 1971; CA 1974; Exchequer and Audit Department 1980-82; Partner 1983. *Biog: b.* 18 June 1950. *Nationality:* British. *m.* 1969, Monique Odette; 2 d. *Educ:* Downside; Brasenose College, Oxford (MA). *Publications:* Guide to Evaluating Policy Effectiveness. *Clubs:* Reform, Royal Cruising, Royal Southern YC. *Recreations:* Sailing, Opera, Art, Literature.

BROWNE, Benjamin Chapman; Partner, Clyde and Co, since 1985; Admiralty/Marine Insurance. *Career:* Lovell White and King, Articled Clerk 1976-78; Assistant Solicitor 1978-79; Morrell Peel and Gamlen, Oxford, Assistant Solicitor 1979-81; Clyde and Co, Assistant Solicitor 1981-85; Partner 1985-; Resident Partner in Dubai Office, UAE 1989-90. *Biog: b.* 18 May 1953. *Nationality:* British. *m.* 1979, Sara K (née Pangbourne); 2 s; 1 d. *Educ:* Eton College, Windsor, Berkshire; Trinity College, Cambridge University (MA). *Recreations:* Walking, Tennis, Gardening, Reading, Soccer.

BROWNE, E J P; Managing Director & Chief Executive Officer, The British Petroleum Company plc, since 1989; BP Exploration. *Career:* BP, University Apprentice 1966; Various Exploration and Production Posts (Anchorage, New York, San Francisco, London & Canada) 1969-83; BP Finance International, Group Treasurer & Chief Executive 1984; Standard Oil Company, Cleveland, Ohio, Exec Vice Pres and Chief Financial Officer 1986. *Biog: b.* 1948. *Educ:* Cambridge University (Physics); Stanford University, California (MS Bus). *Other Activities:* Board Member, Stanford Graduate School of Business. *Professional Organisations:* C Eng.; Fellow, Institute of Mining and Metallurgy.

BROWNE, Geoffrey Ernest; Director, Sun Alliance Insurance Group, since 1988; Managing Director, Sun Alliance Investment Management Ltd. *Career:* Sun Alliance Insurance Group Chief Investment Mgr 1980-88. *Biog: b.* 21 July 1930. *Nationality:* British. *m.* 1955, Edith (née Heller); 1 s; 1 d. *Educ:* Luton Grammar School; London School of Economics (BSc Econ). *Directorships:* Securitas Gilde Lebensversicherung AG 1982 (non-exec); Sun of New York Inc 1974 (non-exec); Capital International Fund SA 1978 (non-exec); Henry Venture Fund II Ltd 1987 (non-exec); Henry Venture Fund Ltd 1983 (non-exec). *Professional Organisations:* FCII.

BROWNE, Terence Michael; International Tax Partner, Touche Ross & Co, since 1976. *Career:* UK Inland Revenue Exec Officer 1959-65; Touche Ross & Co UK Tax Assistant 1966; Price Waterhouse Peat & Co (Peru) Peruvian & Intl Tax Adviser 1967-71; Touche Ross & Co UK Intl Tax Mgr 1972-75; Touche Ross International Regional Tax Dir, Europe 1976-79; Touche Ross & Co National Dir of Marketing 1979-81; Touche Ross International Intl Dir of Tax Services 1981-85; Intl Dir of Advanced Technology (Tax) 1986-. *Biog: b.* 8 October 1941. *Nationality:* British. *m.* 1968, Nelida (néeEstupinan); 1 s. *Educ:* Clare Hall School, Halifax. *Other Activities:* Joint Treasurer, European Atlantic Group; Intl Tax Representative, North American Ctee, London Chamber of Commerce. *Professional Organisations:* FCCA, FTII. *Recreations:* Tennis, Badminton.

BROWNING, J Robin; General Manager, Bank of Scotland, since 1986; Accounting and Finance, Card Services, Property. *Career:* Bank of Scotland 1956-77; The British Linen Bank, Mgr 1977-79; Asst Dir 1979-81; Dir 1981-82; Bank of Scotland Asst Gen Mgr 1982-83; Div Gen Mgr 1983-86. *Biog: b.* 29 July 1939. *m.* 1965, Christine (née Campbell); 1 s; 1 d. *Educ:* Morgan Academy, Dundee; University of Strathclyde (BA Hons); Harvard Business School. *Directorships:* NWS Bank plc 1990 (non-exec); Halifax Credit Card Ltd 1990 (non-exec). *Other Activities:* Member, APACS Council. *Professional Organisations:* FIB(Scot), (Council Member, 1987). *Recreations:* Gardening, DIY, Curling.

BROWNLOW, Jeremy Taylor; Partner, Clifford Chance, since 1973; Company Department. *Career:* Clifford-Turner Articled Clerk 1968-70; Asst Solicitor 1970-73. *Biog: b.* 4 December 1945. *m.* 1971, Lynden (née Snape); 3 s; 1 d. *Educ:* Heversham School; St Catharine's College, Cambridge (MA). *Directorships:* Cannon Street Investments plc. *Professional Organisations:* The Law Society; City of London Solicitors' Company.

BROYLES, Professor John Enloe; Professor of Treasury Management & Director of Centre for Treasury Management, Cranfield School of Management, since 1990; Association of Corporate Treasurers. *Career:* United Technologies, Nuclear Engineer 1956-60; Ludlow Corporation, Planning Manager, Forecasting, Planning and Coordinating International Manufacturing Operations 1960-65; London School of Economics, Doctoral Student, Thesis on 'A Stochastic Model of New York Stock Exchange Transactions' 1965-68; London Business School, Senior Research Officer 1968-71; Lecturer in Finance, Founding Director of the Corporate Finance Programme 1971-73; Templeton College, Oxford, Harold W Siebens Fellow in Finance Teaching & Research & Dir of Corp Fin & Strategy Programme 1973-89. *Biog: b.* 20 January 1933. *Nationality:* American. *m.* 1960, Anthea (née Bean); 2 s; 1 d. *Educ:* Principia Upper School; Massachusetts Institute of Technology (BSc); Rensselear Institute of Technology (MSc); London School of Economics (PhD). *Directorships:* Oxford Economic Forecasting Ltd 1987-89 (non-exec). *Other Activities:* Member, The Technical, Educational and Publication Committees and the Examination Review Board, Association of Corporate Treasurers; Former Editor, London Business School Journal; Formerly on Editorial Board of Journal of Business Finance and Accounting. *Professional Organisations:* Fellow, Association of Corporate Treasurers; Member, European Finance Association; Member, Western Finance Association; Member, American Finance Association. *Publications:* Modern Managerial Finance (With J R Franks), 1979; Financial Management Handbook 2nd Ed with I Cooper & S Archer, 1983; Corporate Finance with J R Franks and W T Carleton, 1985; Participation at Lloyd's as a Portfolio Investment, in Journal of Business Finance with M Aczel and B Masajoda, 1990; Debt and Equity, in Lander, Directors Guide to Corporate Finance, 1990; Risk and the Cost of Capital, The Treasurer, 1990. *Recreations:* Skiing, Mountain Hiking, Drawing.

BRUCE, Andrew Douglas Alexander Thomas; The Rt Hon The Earl of Elgin and Kincardine; Kt, JP; President, Scottish Amicable Life Assurance Society.

BRUCE, Brian Cecil; Director, Panmure Gordon & Co Limited, since 1989; Settlements. *Career:* T C Coombs & Co, Office Manager 1955-87; Panmure Gordon & Co Ltd, Office Manager 1987-89. *Biog: b.* 27 October 1939. *Nationality:* British. *m.* 1962, Veronica Muriel (née Tully); 1 s; 1 d. *Educ:* Ashburton. *Other Activities:* Committee Member, The Stock Exchange Managers Association. *Professional Organisations:* International Stock Exchange.

BRUCE, David Ian Rehbinder; Group Finance Director, Guiness Mahon Holdings plc, since 1990; Finance and Systems. *Career:* Peat Marwick Mitchell & Co, Chartered Accountants 1968-72; Cazenove & Co, Investment Analyst 1972-79; Consultant to Committee to Review the Functioning of Financial Institutions 1977-79; The Royal Dutch/Shell Group, Shell International Co Ltd, Assistant Treasury Adviser 1979-80; Shell Canada Ltd, Manager, Financial Planning 1980-83; Shell UK Ltd, Treasurer & Controller 1983-86; The International Stock Exchange, Executive Director, Finance & Administration 1986-90. *Biog: b.* 16 August 1946. *Nationality:* British. *m.* 1976, Anne (née Colbeck); 2 s. *Educ:* Eton College, Oriel College, Oxford (MA). *Directorships:* Guiness Mahon Holdings plc 1990 Group Finance Dir; Guiness Mahon Group Limited 1990 Finance Dir; Guiness Mahon & Co Limited 1990 Finance Dir; Guiness Mahon Asset Management Limited 1990 Finance Dir; Guiness Flight Global Asset Management Limited 1990 Finance Dir; Guiness Mahon Properties Limited 1990 Finance Dir. *Other Activities:* Freeman, The City of London, 1977; Liveryman, The Merchant Taylors' Company, 1980; The Hundred Group, 1982; Technical Committee of the Association of Corporate Treasurers, 1988. *Professional Organisations:* FCA; ASIA; FCT. *Clubs:* Turf, Pratt's City of London, White's. *Recreations:* Opera (Spectator), Shooting, Fishing.

BRUCE, The Hon James Henry Morys; Director, Robert Fleming & Co Limited, since 1989; Corporate Finance. *Career:* Jardine Fleming Holdings Limited (Hong Kong), Head of Corporate Finance and Banking 1987-89; Head of Corporate Finance 1983-87. *Biog: b.* 28 December 1948. *Nationality:* British. 1977 (div 1987); 1 d. *Professional Organisations:* FCA.

BRUCE, Leigh H; City Editor, International Herald Tribune.

BRUCE, Penelope; Partner, Cameron Markby Hewitt.

BRUCE, Robert; Associate Editor, Accountancy Age.

BRUCE, (Robert) Andrew; Managing Director, Morgan Guaranty Trust Company of New York, since 1988; Head of UK & Scandinavia Corporate Finance. *Career:* Morgan Guaranty, Energy & Project Finance 1973-82; Head Corporate Finance Southwestern USA 1982-86; J P Morgan Securities Ltd, Executive Director, Credit Risk Management & Funding 1986-88; European Transportation Group, Managing Director 1988-89; Managing Director, Head of UK & Scandinavia Corporate Finance 1989-. *Biog: b.* 23 June 1949. *Nationality:* British. *m.* 1975, Claire (née Leeper); 4 s. *Educ:* Pembroke College, Cambridge (BA; MA); Manchester Business School (MBA). *Recreations:* Sailing, Squash, Golf.

BRUCE, Roderick; Partner, Dickson Minto WS, since 1986; Corporate Law. *Career:* Dundas & Wilson CS 1970-86. *Biog: b.* 8 March 1948. *Nationality:* British. *m.* 1988, Jane (née Thom); 1 s; 2 d. *Educ:* Boroughmuir School, Edinburgh; Edinburgh University (LLB Honours). *Professional Organisations:* Law Society of Scotland; Writer to the Signet. *Recreations:* Golf, Theatre, Tennis.

BRUCE-JONES, Christopher; General Manager, Lloyds Bank plc, since 1989; Personnel. *Career:* Lloyds Bank plc Group, Deputy General Manager, The National Bank of New Zealand Ltd, Wellington 1977-79. *Biog: b.* 16 February 1933. *Nationality:* British. *m.* 1957, Patricia Mary; 1 s; 2 d. *Educ:* Christ's Hospital. *Other Activities:* Liveryman, Skinners Company; Governor, Christ's Hospital. *Professional Organisations:* Fellow, Chartered Institute of Bankers; Fellow, Institute of Personnel Management.

BRUCK, Steven Mark; Partner and National Director of Corporate Advisory Services, Pannell Kerr Forster; Investigations and Corporate Finance. *Career:* Chalmers Impey, Articled Clerk & Audit Snr 1969-73; Halma Ltd, Group Acct 1973-74; Overseas Containers Ltd, Special Projects Acct 1974-75; Pannell Kerr Forster, Audit Mgr 1975-77; Mercers Bryant, Ptnr 1977-83; Pannell Kerr Forster, Ptnr 1984-. *Biog: b.* 30 September 1947. *Nationality:* British. *m.* 1971, Miriam; 1 s; 1 d. *Educ:* Hendon County Grammar School; Southampton University (BSc Hons); London University (MSc). *Professional Organisations:* FCA. *Publications:* Various Articles. *Recreations:* Family, Theatre, Eating out.

BRUDER, Gottfried O; General Manager, Commerzbank AG, since 1975. *Career:* Deutsche Unionbank, Frankfurt 1954-58; Standard Bank of South Africa, Johannesburg 1958-60; Commerzbank Repr Office, Johannesburg 1960-65; Commerzvbank AG, Duesseldorf 1965-70; Frankfurt 1970-73; J Henry Schroder Wagg & Co 1973-75; Commerzbank AG, London 1975-. *Biog: b.* 7 March 1934. *Nationality:* German; 2 s. *Directorships:* International Commercial Bank plc (non-exec). *Other Activities:* Member, Committee Lombard Association; Confederation of British Industry, Council Member; Vice Chairman, London Regional

Council; Member, Economic & Financial Policy Committee; Member, EFPC/EMU Working Group; Member, Trade & Investment Committee, German Chamber of Industry & Commerce. *Recreations:* Chess, Gardening, History, Music, Reading.

BRUEGGER, Edmund Peter; Director, Singer & Friedlander Limited, since 1990; South West England, Corporate Finance. *Career:* Hill Samuel, Director, Corporate Finance Midlands & South West 1989-90; Stock Beech & Co, Director, Corporate Finance 1984-88; Amsterdam-Rotterdam Bank NV, Amsterdam, AF Delings Director, Capital Markets USA 1977-84. *Biog: b.* 8 May 1951. *Nationality:* British/German. *m.* 1979, Susan Louise; 3 s; 2 d. *Educ:* Trinity College, Cambridge (MA Law). *Directorships:* Frew Mackenzie plc 1985 (non-exec); Bath Festival Society Ltd 1988 (non-exec). *Other Activities:* Member, Council of Management, Bath Festival. *Professional Organisations:* Barrister-at-Law, Middle Temple. *Clubs:* Oxford & Cambridge. *Recreations:* Sport (Particularly Cricket), Oenology, The Arts.

BRUEHL, W F; General Manager, Berliner Bank AG.

BRUMMER, Alexander; Financial Editor, The Guardian, since 1989; Editor of Economic, Financial, Industrial, Business Coverage. *Career:* The Guardian, Foreign Editor 1989; Washington Correspondent 1979-89; Financial Correspondent 1973-79; Haymarket Publishing, Financial Reporter 1973; De La Rue, Management Systems 1972-73. *Biog: b.* 25 May 1949. *Nationality:* British. *m.* 1975, Patricia (née Magrill); 2 s; 1 d. *Educ:* University of Southampton (BSc Economics); University of Bradford Management Centre (MBA). *Professional Organisations:* NUJ. *Publications:* Part Author, Altered State, 1990; Co-Author, American Destiny, 1986. *Recreations:* Antiques, Reading, American Studies.

BRUMMER, Malcolm Howard; Chairman of the Board, Berwin Leighton, since 1990; Property Banking/ Secured Lending. *Career:* Berwin Leighton, Head of Property Department 1983-90. *Biog: b.* 21 March 1948. *Nationality:* British. *m.* 1980, Yvonne (née Labos); 1 s; 1 d. *Educ:* Haberdashers' Askes'; Downing College, Cambridge (MA Hons). *Publications:* Various Published Lectures including Blundell Memorial Lecture. *Recreations:* Family, Opera, Bridge.

BRUNDAGE, T; Director, J H Minet & Co Ltd.

BRUNET, Antoine; Secretaire General, AXA MIDI Assurances, since 1988; Insurance Overseas Operations. *Career:* Civil Service to 1983; Delegue General Adjoint of the Federation Française des Societes d'Assurances 1983; Secretaire General of Assurances du Groupe de Paris (AGPSA) in charge of overseas operations of Compagnie du Midis Insurances 1988; London & Hull Insurance Co, Deputy Chairman 1988; AGP merged with AXA Assurances to form AXA Midi Assurances 1988. *Biog: b.* 10 August 1935. *Nationality:* French.

BRUNNER, David; Head of Swaps and Fixed Income Marketing, Paribas Limited.

BRUNNING, Paul; Divisional Director, Royal Trust Bank.

BRUNOZZI, L; Director, IMI Capital Markets (UK).

BRUPBACHER, Mario C; Non-Executive Director, Merrill Lynch International Bank Limited.

BRYAN, Sir Arthur; President, Josiah Wedgwood & Sons Ltd, 1986-88; HM Lord Lieutenant for Staffordshire KstJ. *Career:* RAF RAFVR Aircrew 1941-45; Josiah Wedgwood & Sons Ltd, Mgmnt Trainee 1947-49; Mgr 1953-57; Gen Sales Mgr 1959-60; Dir & Pres 1960-62; (USA) MD, UK 1963-67; Chm 1968-86; Waterford Wedgwood Holding plc, Pres 1986-88. *Directorships:* Friends' Provident Life Office 1985 (non-exec); The Rank Organisation plc 1985 (non-exec); Wedgwood Museum Trust Ltd; JCB Excavators Inc, USA; United Kingdom Fund Inc, USA (non-exec); Consumer Market Advisory Group, DTI 1988-90 Chm.

BRYAN, Colin; Director, Nicholson Chamberlain Colls Limited.

BRYAN, Howard; Head of Litigation Department, Hepworth & Chadwick, since 1988; Employment Law, Matrimonial Law. *Career:* Hepworth & Chadwick, Solicitor 1967-71; Partner 1971-. *Biog: b.* 24 April 1944. *Nationality:* British. *m.* 1972, Jacquelyn; 1 s; 1 d. *Educ:* Silcoates School, Wakefield; Leeds University (LLB). *Other Activities:* Liveryman, Wheelwrights Company; Governor & Clerk to Board, Silcoates School, Wakefield. *Professional Organisations:* Law Society; Industrial Law Society; Anglo-German Jurists Association. *Clubs:* Leeds Club, Royal Northern & Clyde Yacht Club, Clyde Cruising Club. *Recreations:* Sailing, Squash, Skiing.

BRYAN, Simon; Director, BDO Consulting, since 1987; Information Technology. *Career:* Mann Judd & Co, Chartered Accountants 1975-80; Dearden Farrow, Chartered Accountants 1980-87; BDO Binder Hamlyn, Chartered Accountants 1987-. *Biog: b.* 30 April 1954. *Nationality:* British. *Educ:* Leeds University (BA Econ Hons). *Professional Organisations:* Associate, Institute of Chartered Accountants; Member, Institute of Management Consultants.

BRYANS, Paul Michael Alexander; Director, Charterhouse Bank Limited, since 1990; Corporate Banking. *Career:* Charterhouse Bank Ltd 1974-. *Biog: b.* 26 November 1951. *Nationality:* British. *m.* 1979, Ruth (née Stoney); 1 s; 1 d. *Educ:* Bangor Grammar School;

Warwick University (BSc). *Directorships:* Charterhouse Bank Ltd 1990 (exec). *Clubs:* Royal Ocean Racing Club.

BRYANT, Michael Keith; Group Treasurer, Sears plc, since 1988; Corporate Finance, Funding, Liquidity, Currency Management. *Career:* NatWest Bank, Operational Research Manager 1970-73; British Leyland, Manager, Cash Management 1973-77; BICC, Asst Head Group Financing 1977-81; Gotaas-Larsen, Asst Treasurer 1981-83; Hertz Europe, Treasurer 1983-88. *Biog: b.* 26 July 1947. *Nationality:* Welsh. *m.* 1972, Margaret Suzanne (née Jones). *Educ:* West Monmouthshire School; Manchester University (BSc Chemistry); Imperial College (MSc Operational Research). *Other Activities:* Programme Committee, Association of Corporate Treasurers. *Professional Organisations:* FCT. *Clubs:* Sonning GC, Sindlesham Squash Club. *Recreations:* Golf, Squash.

BRYANT, R; Banking Director, Riggs A P Bank Ltd.

BRYCE, Andrew; Partner, Cameron Markby Hewitt, since 1973; Environmental Law. *Career:* Articled with Cameron Kerby Norden (now part of CMH 1968-71; Asst Solicitor 1971-73; Partner 1971-73. *Biog: b.* 31 August 1947. *Nationality:* British. *m.* (separated); 2 s; 1 d. *Educ:* Thorpe Grammar School; Newcastle University (LLB Hons). *Other Activities:* Chairman, United Kingdom Environmental Law Association, 1988-; Vice Chairman, Planning & Environmental Sub-committee of City of London Solicitor's Company. *Professional Organisations:* Law Society. *Publications:* Several Articles on Environmental Law 1986-90; Editorial Board, Land Management & Environmental Law Report. *Clubs:* David Lloyd Racquets Club. *Recreations:* Travel, Tennis, Ornithology, Natural History.

BRYCE-SMITH, Nicholas M; Director, Bradstock Blunt & Thompson Ltd.

BRYDIE, James Wilson; Partner, Shepherd & Wedderburn WS, since 1964; Commercial Property. *Career:* Shepherd & Wedderburn, Qualified Asst 1959-64. *Biog: b.* 9 February 1932. *Nationality:* British. *m.* 1971, Judith (née Carrie); 2 s; 1 d. *Educ:* Dollar Academy; Edinburgh University (BL). *Professional Organisations:* Member, Law Society of Scotland; Member, Society of Writers to The Signet. *Clubs:* Royal Burgess Golfing Society (Edinburgh). *Recreations:* Golf, Skiing, Hill Walking.

BRYDON, Donald Hood; Managing Director, Barclays de Zoete Wedd Investment Management Ltd, since 1989; Investment Management. *Biog:* 1 s; 1 d. *Directorships:* National Association of Pension Funds.

BRYSON, Dr Norval MacKenzie; General Manager, Scottish Provident Institution.

BRYSON, R A G; Partner, Pannell Kerr Forster, since 1988; Taxation. *Career:* Binder Hamlyn, latterly Tax Manager 1974-86. *Biog: b.* 20 January 1952. *Nationality:* British. *m.* 1988, Mary Margaret (née Crowley); 1 d. *Educ:* Prior Park College, Bath; Manchester University (BSc Mechanical Engineering). *Professional Organisations:* ACA. *Recreations:* Sailing.

BUBIER, T; Vice President, First National Bank of Boston.

BUCHAN, C A M; Director, S G Warburg Akroyd Rowe & Pitman Mullens Securities Ltd.

BUCHAN, (Charles Walter) Edward (Ralph); Director, Hill Samuel Bank Limited, since 1985; Corporate Finance, Joint Head of Smaller Companies Unit. *Career:* Deloitte Haskins & Sells, Acct 1972-77. *Biog: b.* 5 August 1951. *Nationality:* British. *m.* 1982, Fiona Jane (née Carlisle); 1 s; 2 d. *Educ:* Magdalen College School, Oxford; Southampton University (BSc). *Professional Organisations:* FCA. *Clubs:* Travellers'.

BUCHAN, Hamish Noble; Director, County NatWest Wood MacKenzie.

BUCHANAN, A B; General Manager, Lloyds Bank plc, since 1987; Latin America. *Career:* Lloyds Bank 1956-. *Educ:* Ayr Academy; University of Glasgow (MA). *Directorships:* Banco Anglo Colombiano (Bogota, Colombia) 1988 (non-exec); Lloyds Bank (BLSA) Ltd 1988 (exec).

BUCHANAN, Nigel James Cubitt; Partner & Director of European Financial Services, Price Waterhouse, since 1989; Banking & Financial Services. *Career:* Slater, Dorning & Swann (Cambridge), Articled Clerk/Asst 1961-68; Price Waterhouse, London 1968-; Partner 1978-. *Biog: b.* 13 November 1943. *Nationality:* British. *m.* 1968, (Katherine) Mary (née Armitage); 1 s; 2 d. *Educ:* Denstone College, Staffs. *Professional Organisations:* FCA. *Publications:* Accounting for Pensions (Co-Author Michael Young); Pro/Euromoney Debt, Equity Swap Guide (Co-Author). *Clubs:* Carlton. *Recreations:* Tennis, Golf.

BUCHANAN-BARROW, Paul; Managing Director, Goddard Kay Rogers & Associates, since 1988. *Career:* IBM UK 1969-72; County Bank Ltd, Director 1976-86. *Biog: b.* 23 April 1945. *Nationality:* British. *m.* 1969, Eithne (née O'Shea); 2 d. *Educ:* St Andrews University (MA). *Directorships:* Royal Star & Garter Home 1989 Governor. *Clubs:* MCC, HAC, Reform Club.

BUCHANAN-DUNLOP, Robert Daubeny (Robin); CBE; Clerk, Goldsmiths' Company, since 1988. *Career:* William Thomson & Co, Managers Ben Line 1957-61. *Biog: b.* 11 August 1934. *Nationality:* British. *m.* 1972, Nicola (née Goodhart); 2 s. *Educ:*

Loretto School; Staff College, Camberley; United States Armed Forces Staff College. *Other Activities:* Member, British Hallmarking Council; Member, Governing Body, Imperial College, University of London; Member, Council Goldsmiths' College, University of London. *Clubs:* Army and Navy. *Recreations:* Destructive Gardening, Scottish 20th Century Paintings, Opera.

BUCK, R M; Head of Property Department, Berwin Leighton, since 1990; Property Investment Development and Funding. *Career:* Qualified 1967; Leighton & Co (Predecessor to Berwin Leighton) 1969-; Berwin Leighton, Partner 1971-. *Biog: b.* 14 August 1943. *Nationality:* British; 1 d. *Recreations:* Music, Literature, Golf.

BUCKENHAM, Ms Joanna Amanda; Director, J K Buckenham Ltd, since 1990; Reinsurance Broking. *Career:* Morgan Stanley International, London, Analyst in Corporate Finance Dept 1983-86; Morgan Stanley, Sydney, Capital Markets Area 1986-87; J K Buckenham Ltd 1987-. *Biog: b.* 26 July 1961. *Nationality:* British. *Educ:* St Mary's Convent, Ascot; Eton College; Université de Neuchâtel (Diplôme); Harvard University (VUS); Newnham College, Cambridge (MA Hons). *Directorships:* Bii Lda 1988 (exec); J Buckenham Holdings 1987 (exec). *Clubs:* Various. *Recreations:* Tennis, Squash, Theatre.

BUCKENHAM, John Keith; Chairman, J K Buckenham Limited. *Career:* J K Buckenham Limited, Founder 1967-. *Biog: b.* 25 September 1929. *Nationality:* British. *m.* 1957, Joan; 1 d. *Educ:* Downside School; Magdalene College, Cambridge (MA Hons). *Directorships:* J Buckenham Holdings 1984 (exec). *Other Activities:* Governor, St Mary's School, Ascot. *Clubs:* City University. *Recreations:* Fishing, Tennis, Windsurfing, Skiing.

BUCKLAND, Nicholas Simon; Partner, Bacon & Woodrow.

BUCKLAND, Sidney; Manager, Treasury, Banco Bilbao Vizcaya.

BUCKLAND, T W; Director, Phillips & Drew Fund Management Limited.

BUCKLE, J F; Partner, Kidsons.

BUCKLE, K F; Director, Hambros Bank Limited.

BUCKLEY, Professor Adrian Arthur; Professor, Cranfield School of Management, since 1986; International Finance. *Career:* Wood Albery & Co, Articled Clerk, University Business School 1959-63; Merrett Cyriax Associates, Management Consultant 1967-71; Charterhouse Group, Merchant Banker 1971-74; Redland Group, Group Treasurer 1974-80; Cranfield School of Management, Professor 1980-. *Biog: b.* 1940. *Nationality:* British. *m.* 1966, Jennifer Rosalie (decd); 2 s. *Educ:* Poole Grammar School; Sheffield University, Bradford University (BA, MSc). *Directorships:* Pearce Management Consultants Ltd 1988 (non-exec); City of London Unit Trust Managers Ltd 1989 (non-exec). *Other Activities:* Association, Corporate Treasurers Education Committee. *Professional Organisations:* Fellow, Inst of Chartered Accountants in England & Wales; Fellow, Chartered Association of Certified Accountants; Fellow, Association of Corporate Treasurers. *Publications:* Multinational Finance, 1986; The Essence of International Money, 1990; Multinational Finance, (2nd Edition) 1991; Over 100 Articles. *Recreations:* Fell Walking, Skiing, Cricket.

BUCKLEY, Brian Holden; Deputy Chairman, Singer & Freidlander Ltd.

BUCKLEY, Brian Norman; Partner, Simmons & Simmons, since 1973; Company Law & Banking. *Career:* Simmons & Simmons, Asst Solicitor 1968-72. *Biog: b.* 15 September 1943. *m.* 1974, Janis (née Edwards). *Educ:* Royal Grammar School, High Wycombe; Jesus College, Cambridge (BA). *Other Activities:* Society for Computers and Law.

BUCKLEY, Guy James McLean; Partner, Macfarlanes.

BUCKLEY, Ian Carysfort; Head of Corporate Finance, Sheppards, since 1989; Corporate Finance. *Career:* Citicorp Scrimgeour Vickers Ptnr, Corp Finance 1983-85; Dir, Institutional Sales 1985-88; Morgan Grenfell Securities Dir, Corp Finance 1988. *Biog: b.* 31 May 1955. *Nationality:* British. *m.* 1981, Susan (née Harmer); 2 d. *Educ:* Eastbourne College; Durham University. *Directorships:* Sheppards Ltd 1989 (exec). *Professional Organisations:* ACA. *Recreations:* Picture Collecting, Birdwatching.

BUCKLEY, Katherine A; Partner, Allen & Overy.

BUCKLEY, Michael Arthur; Partner and Head of Shipping Group, Waltons & Morse, since 1971; Shipping Law. *Career:* Sun Life Assurance Society, Clerk 1959-60; Waltons & Co, Conveyancing Assistant 1960-62; Articled Clerk 1962-67; Waltons Bright & Co, Assistant Solicitor 1967-71; Partner 1971; Waltons & Morse, Managing Partner 1982-87; Head of Litigation Dept 1987-. *Biog: b.* 20 November 1942. *Nationality:* British. *m.* 1965, Marie; 2 s; 2 d. *Educ:* Buckhurst Hill County High School; Law Society College of Law, Lancaster Gate. *Other Activities:* Freeman, City of London Solicitors Co; Institute of Maritime Law; Associate Member, Association of Average Adjusters; Subscribing Member, London Maritime Arbitrators Assoc. *Professional Organisations:* Member, Law Society.

BUCKLEY, S W; Chairman, Mercantile Credit Company Limited.

BUCKLEY, Thomas George McLean; Partner, Slaughter and May, since 1966; Company/Commercial. *Biog: b.* 14 January 1932. *m.* 1963, Valerie (née Shearer); 3 s. *Educ:* Eton College; Magdalen College, Oxford (MA). *Other Activities:* Member, Skinners' Company. *Professional Organisations:* The Law Society. *Clubs:* West Mersea Yacht Club. *Recreations:* Sailing.

BUCKNELL, A L; Director, Greenwell Montagu Gilt-Edged.

BUCKS, D; Deputy Chairman, Hill Samuel & Co Ltd.

BUCKS, Peter; Director, Hill Samuel Bank Ltd, since 1987; Corporate Finance. *Career:* Hill Samuel & Co Ltd Various 1969-; (New York) Rep 1973-78; (Houston, Texas) Rep 1979-81; (London) Corp Finance Dept 1981-. *Biog: b.* 30 September 1947. *Nationality:* British. *m.* 1973, Sarah Ann (née Dobson); 2 s; 1 d. *Educ:* Sevenoaks School, Kent; Southampton University (BSc Hons). *Recreations:* Bridge, Opera, Squash.

BUCKWELL, Anthony Basil; Director, Kleinwort Benson Limited, since 1985; Banking, UK & Middle East. *Career:* MIBSPA (Rome) 1966-72; Kleinwort Benson Ltd 1973-. *Biog: b.* 23 July 1946. *Nationality:* British. *m.* 1968, Henrietta J (née Watson); 2 d. *Educ:* Winchester College. *Directorships:* Centrobank (Vienna) 1985 Supervisory Board; Fendrake 1978 (exec); Absentminders 1976 (non-exec). *Clubs:* Brooks's. *Recreations:* Riding, Fishing, Music.

BUDENBERG, R F; Director, S G Warburg & Co Ltd, since 1990; Corporate Finance. *Career:* Price Waterhouse 1980-84. *Biog: b.* 8 May 1959. *Nationality:* British. *m.* 1989, Jacqueline. *Educ:* Rugby School; Exeter University (Law). *Professional Organisations:* ACA. *Recreations:* Golf, Cricket.

BUDGE, Duncan; Director, J Rothschild Capital Management Limited. *Career:* Lazard Brothers & Co Limited 1980-85.

BUDGETT, Tom; Partner, Clifford Chance.

BUFFIN, Colin John; Investment Manager, Candover Investments plc, since 1985; Management and Leveraged Buyouts. *Career:* Deloitte Haskins & Sells 1980-85. *Biog: b.* 23 October 1957. *Nationality:* British. *m.* 1989, Susan; 1 s. *Educ:* Trinity College, Oxford (MA Chemistry). *Directorships:* Motor World Group Ltd 1988 (non-exec); Bishopcross Ltd 1986 (non-exec). *Professional Organisations:* ACA. *Recreations:* Sailing, Skiing.

BUGDEN, Paul William; Partner, Clyde & Co, since 1983; Commercial/Insurance Litigation. *Biog: b.* 18 April 1953. *Nationality:* British. *m.* 1984, Nicola; 1 s; 1 d. *Educ:* Merchant Taylors School; University of Kent (BA Law). *Professional Organisations:* Law Society; International Bar Association; British Insurance Law Association. *Recreations:* Golf, Squash.

BUGGE, Peter Edward; Director, Baring Brothers & Co Ltd, since 1987; Banking & Capital Markets-Japan, Korea & South East Asia.

BUGGINS, C J; Director, Euro Brokers Holdings Limited.

BUIST, Robert C; Director, Scottish Widows' Fund and Life Assurance Society.

BULFIELD, Peter William; Managing Director & Chief Executive, Yamaichi Bank (UK) plc, since 1988. *Career:* Peat Marwick Mitchell & Co 1948-59; J Henry Schroder Wagg & Co Ltd, Mgr 1959-66; Dir, Banking 1966-86. *Biog: b.* 14 June 1930. *Nationality:* British. *m.* 1958, Pamela (née Beckett); 2 d. *Educ:* Beaumont College. *Directorships:* London Italian Bank Ltd 1988 (non-exec). *Professional Organisations:* CA. *Clubs:* Royal Thames Yacht Club. *Recreations:* Sailing, Painting, Music.

BULL, A C; Director, National Investment Group plc.

BULL, C R H; Group Finance Director, BTR plc.

BULL, Christopher; Director, Price Waterhouse, since 1990; Inward Investment Europe, Japanese Business Development. *Career:* Goodland Bull & Co 1957-68; Price Waterhouse, Trinidad 1968-72; London 1972-; Partner 1974-. *Biog: b.* 6 September 1936. *Nationality:* British. *m.* Patricia; 1 s; 2 d. *Educ:* Taunton School. *Other Activities:* London Chamber of Commerce & Industry, Japan Section; Member, Japan Association. *Professional Organisations:* ICAEW. *Clubs:* Carlton Club, Northants Golf Club. *Recreations:* Golf.

BULL, Douglas; Director, Samuel Montagu & Co Limited.

BULL, G J; Chief Executive, Drinks, Grand Metropolitan plc.

BULL, N J D; Director, Morgan Grenfell & Co Limited.

BULL, Peter Anthony; Head of Financial Statistics, Bank of England, since 1987; Collection Processing, Presentation, Development of Statistics. *Career:* Bank of England Various 1964-; Foreign Exchange Mgr 1978-80; Adviser, Staff Mgr, Econ 1980-84; Adviser, Banking/Monetary 1984-87. *Biog: b.* 17 November 1942. *m.* 1967, Caroline Susan (née Papps); 2 s; 1 d. *Educ:* Dewsbury Grammar School; Gonville & Caius

College, Cambridge (BA). *Professional Organisations:* Royal Statistical Society. *Recreations:* Cycling, Running, History, Music.

BULLARD, P H F; Secretary, RMC Group plc.

BULLEY, Philip Marshall; Partner, Theodore Goddard, since 1987; Mergers and Acquisitions. *Career:* Thompson Schwab & Co, Dealer 1958-61; News of the World Organisation, Managing Director 1961-69; Publishing Subsidiary; Willis Faber, Data Processing Adviser 1970; Sundry Small Company Rescue Consultant 1971-76; Theodore Goddard, Articled Clerk 1976-78; Solicitor 1979-87. *Biog: b.* 1 August 1934. *m.* 1963, Anne (née Leonard); 2 d. *Educ:* Radley College; Cambridge University (MA). *Professional Organisations:* The Law Society. *Recreations:* Golf.

BULLICK, Michael John; Director & Company Secretary, Edinburgh Fund Managers plc, since 1969; Administration. *Career:* Coopers & Lybrand, Auditor 1965-68. *Biog: b.* 24 November 1937. *Nationality:* British; 1 s; 2 d. *Educ:* Coleraine Academical Institution; Trinity College, Dublin (MA Hons). *Directorships:* Edinburgh Fund Managers plc 1972 (exec). *Professional Organisations:* CA. *Recreations:* Skiing.

BULLMORE, Jeremy J D; Director, W P P Group plc.

BULLOCK, John; Joint Senior Partner, Coopers & Lybrand Deloitte, since 1990; Chairman, C&L Europe. *Career:* Smallfield Fitzhugh Tillett & Co (SFT), Qualified CA 1956; Commissioned Officer in the RAF 1956-58; SFT 1958-61; Robson Morrow, Management Consultants 1961; Partner 1965; Deloitte Haskins & Sells, Partner-in-Charge, Management Consultancy Division (following merger) 1970; Deloitte Haskins & Sells UK Firm, MD 1979; Senior Partner 1985; Coopers & Lybrand Deloitte, Joint Senior Partner (following merger) 1990. *Biog: b.* 12 July 1933. *Nationality:* British. *m.* Ruth Jennifer; 3 s (1 decd). *Educ:* Latymer Upper School. *Other Activities:* Fellow, Institute of Chartered Accountants in England & Wales; Member, Institute of Chartered Accountants of Scotland; President, Institute of Management Consultants, 1978-79; Fellow, Institute of Cost and Management Accountants; Part-time Member, United Kingdom Atomic Energy Authority. *Recreations:* Ballet, Opera, Tennis, Skiing.

BULLOCK, Michael; Managing Director, Morgan Grenfell Asset Management, since 1988; Investment Management. *Career:* Morgan Grenfell Research Dept (UK) 1973-75; (Intl) 1975-79; MGIS Dir 1979-. *Biog: b.* 1 November 1951. *m.* Felicity (née Hammond); 2 s. *Educ:* London University (BSc). *Directorships:* Subsidiary Companies of Morgan Grenfell; The Target International Growth Fund 1985; NM Income & Growth Fund 1985; Morgan Grenfell International Asset Management

Co Ltd 1985; NKK Global Healthcare Fund 1986; Global System Fund 1987; System Growth Fund 1987; Morgan Grenfell Capital Management Inc 1985. *Clubs:* RAC.

BULMER, Alan Michael; Director, City & Commercial Communications; International Investor Relations. *Career:* Rowe & Pitman, Stockbroker 1963-71; Vickers de Costa, Stockbroker 1971-74; White Weld Inc US, Stockbroker 1974-78; PaineWebber US, Stockbroker 1978-80; Gartmore Investment, Investment Manager 1980-85; Kuwait Investment, Office Manager, USA 1985-86. *Biog: b.* 19 March 1950. *Nationality:* British. *m.* 1970, Rozanne (née Barwick); 2 d. *Educ:* Eton College. *Directorships:* Investor Surveys Ltd 1987; Investor Focus International 1986; Coombe Cross Management 1986; F & G Leasing Ltd 1988; Axe Houghton Ltd 1988. *Professional Organisations:* Society of Investment Analysts; Investor Relations Society. *Clubs:* Royal London Yacht Club, Royal Ocean Racing Club. *Recreations:* Sailing, Skiing, Riding, Shooting.

BULT, John; Director, PaineWebber International (UK) Ltd.

BUMSTEAD, Alan William; Director, Cater Allen Securities Ltd, since 1986. *Career:* Alexanders Discount Co Ltd, Manager 1972-84; Hill Samuel & Co Ltd, Manager 1984-85.

BUNCE, P M; Chairman, City Merchants Bank Ltd.

BUNKER, Charles Spencer; Corporate Finance Partner, Kerburn Rose, since 1990. *Career:* National Westminster Bank 1969-75; Longcrofts 1975-79; Spicer & Pegler 1979-81; Longcrofts 1981-84; Moores Rowland 1984-90. *Biog: b.* 6 June 1951. *Nationality:* British. *m.* 1975, Suzanne (née Bailey); 2 s; 1 d. *Educ:* Bedford School. *Directorships:* North Hertfordshire Health Authority 1990 (non-exec). *Professional Organisations:* ICA.

BUNN, Jeremy Robert; Deputy General Manager, Mitsubishi Bank Ltd, since 1986; Operations. *Career:* Midland Bank Ltd, City Branches 1963-73; Societe Generale, Securities Dept 1973-78; Settlement Mgr 1978-83; Operations Mgr 1983-86. *Biog: b.* 31 July 1946. *Nationality:* British. *m.* 1967, Patricia (née Coomber); 4 s. *Educ:* Beal Grammar School, Ilford. *Recreations:* Family, Squash, Badminton, Travel.

BUNN, Richard Herbert; Director, Partner, Hoare Govett Limited.

BUNTING, G C; Joint Managing Director, Prudential-Bache Capital Funding (Equities) Ltd.

BUNTING, J M; Managing Director, Daiwa Europe Limited.

BUNTING, Michael Geoffrey; Group Treasurer, The Boots Company PLC, since 1984. *Career:* Rolls Royce Ltd, Metallurgist 1968-72; Manchester Business School 1972-74; ICFC, Investment Controller 1974-77; Tootal Group plc, Asst Group Treasurer 1977-82; Group Treasurer 1982-84. *Biog: b.* 20 May 1947. *Nationality:* British. *m.* 1984, Sheila Carolyn (née Booth); 2 s; 1 d. *Educ:* King Edward VII School, Lytham; Trinity College, Cambridge (MA); Manchester Business School (MBA). *Professional Organisations:* ACT. *Recreations:* Mountaineering.

BUNTON, Christopher John; Group Treasurer, Saatchi & Saatchi Company plc, since 1986; Corporate Treasury. *Career:* Unilever 1969-71; Gulf Oil Corporation 1973-85; Dir (Financing) 1979-81; Dir (Banking) 1981-85. *Biog: b.* 22 February 1948. *Nationality:* British. *m.* 1975, Jane (née Cartmell); 2 s. *Educ:* Charterhouse; Trinity College, Cambridge (MA); London Graduate School of Business Studies (MSc). *Other Activities:* Education Committee Member, FCT. *Recreations:* Music, Wine.

BURBRIDGE, Stephen Nigel; Secretary, Monopolies & Mergers Commission, since 1986. *Career:* Board of Trade 1958-63; Foreign & Commonwealth Office (Pakistan), First Sec (Economic) 1963-67; Dept of Trade & Industry, Principal 1967-71; Asst Sec 1971-80; Under Sec 1980-86. *Biog: b.* 18 July 1934. *Nationality:* British. *Educ:* King's School, Canterbury; Christ Church, Oxford (MA). *Clubs:* Rye Golf Club, West Sussex Golf Club. *Recreations:* Sport, Collecting, Reading.

BURCH, Mark Lowrie; Director, Baring Brothers & Co Inc, since 1989; Mergers & Acquisitions. *Career:* Baring Brothers (London), Corporate Finance Department 1989; Kleinwort Benson Ltd (London), Corporate Finance Department 1983-88; American Express Bank (London and New York) 1977-82. *Biog: b.* 17 December 1955. *Nationality:* British. *m.* 1982, Victoria (née Marmion); 1 s; 1 d. *Educ:* Harrow School; New College, Oxford (BA); Columbia University, New York (MBA).

BURDITT, P W; Director, Singer & Friedlander Limited.

BURDON, Peter Vincent; Deputy Managing Director, Britannia Life Ltd, since 1990; Marketing, Investment Management. *Career:* Friends Provident Life Office Various 1968-86; FS Assurance Ltd (merged with Britannia Building Society in 1990 became Britannia Life Ltd), Dep Gen Mgr 1986-90. *Biog: b.* 15 May 1947. *Nationality:* British. *m.* 1969, Eileen (née Hooper); 4 s. *Educ:* Bexhill-on-Sea Grammar School; Churchill College, Cambridge (MA). *Directorships:* FS Investment Managers Ltd 1986 (exec); FS Investment Services Ltd 1986 (exec). *Professional Organisations:* FIA. *Recreations:* Golf, Jogging, Music.

BURGESS, Arthur William; Group Treasurer, British Gas plc, since 1987. *Career:* Standard Telephone & Cables, Accountancy Trainee 1963-65; British Cellophane, Operational Research 1965-67; Standard Telephone & Cables, Business Planning 1967-68; Shell International Petroleum, Operational Research 1968-73; Kleinwort Benson, Project Finance 1973-75; British Gas, Mgr, Financial Analysis 1975-81; Chief Acct, East Midlands 1981-84; Financing Mgr 1984-87. *Biog: b.* 26 November 1940. *Nationality:* Irish. *m.* 1965, Judith Margaret (née Burden); 1 d. *Educ:* The High School, Dublin; Trinity College, Dublin (MA). *Professional Organisations:* ACMA, Member, Operational Research Society. *Recreations:* Drawing.

BURGESS, Christopher Lawrie; Regional Managing Director & Main Board Director, Bain Clarkson Ltd.

BURGESS, John; Director, Baring Capital Investors, since 1986; UK and European MBOs and Development Capital. *Career:* Brandts Ltd, Account Executive 1972-74; Boston Consulting Group (Paris), Consultant 1975-78; Manager 1978-81; Vice-President 1981-84; F & C Ventures, Director 1984-86; Baring Capital Investors, Director 1986-. *Biog: b.* 2 June 1950. *Nationality:* British. *m.* 1979, Anne (née Bizot); 1 s; 2 d. *Educ:* Tonbridge School; St Catherines, Cambridge (BA 1st Class Engineering); INSEAD (MBA). *Directorships:* Computacenter Limited 1987 (non-exec); Video Arts Group Limited 1989 (non-exec); Kontron Instruments Holding NV 1989 (non-exec); Société Arquoise de Participations SA 1990 (non-exec). *Clubs:* New Zealand Golf Club, Foxhills. *Recreations:* Golf, Tennis, Swimming, Classical Music.

BURGESS, Mark Geoffrey William; Director, CIN Venture Managers Ltd, since 1989. *Career:* Robson Rhodes, Chartered Accountants, Audit Trainee and Senior 1980-84; Specialist Fund Raising Department 1984-85; on Secondment to CIN Industrial Investments Ltd, Asst Manager/Investment Manager 1985-86; CIN Venture Managers Ltd, Venture Capital Investment Arm of British Coal Pension Funds, Assistant Director 1987. *Biog: b.* 10 June 1959. *Nationality:* British. *Educ:* Glyn County Grammar School, Epsom; Exeter University (BA Hons Econ). *Directorships:* Furmanite plc 1986; Caltech Industries (UK) Limited 1986; CIN Venture Managers Limited 1989; CIN Venture Nominees Limited (formerly CIN Industrial Investments Ltd) 1989; CIN Investors Nominees Limited (formerly CIN Investors Nominees Ltd) 1989; Prelude Technology Investments Limited 1989; Prelude Technology Investments Holdings Limited 1989; Strand VCI plc (formerly Bealaw (236) plc) 1989; Farmdata Limited 1985-86; Duncan Vehicles Limited (In Receivership) 1986-87; Fortbrave Limited 1986-88; Stratford Colour Company Limited 1987-88; Blue Ridge Care Limited 1987-89;

Freda Holdings plc 1988-89; The Technology Partnership Limited 1988-89. *Professional Organisations:* ACA.

BURGESS, Patrick; Head of Corporate Department, Gouldens, since 1982; Stock Exchange, International Structuring Tax. *Career:* Gouldens, Partner 1974-. *Biog:* b. 31 October 1944. *Nationality:* British. *m.* 1969; 2 s; 1 d. *Educ:* Beaumont College; Gonville & Caius College, Cambridge (MA). *Directorships:* London Forefathers Company plc 1987 (non-exec). *Other Activities:* Liveryman, Worshipful Company of Feltmakers. *Clubs:* Naval & Military, Leander, Bosham Sailing Club.

BURGESS, R A; Operations Director, Charterhouse Tilney, since 1987. *Biog:* b. 24 March 1951. *Nationality:* British. *m.* 1974, Gabrielle Ruth (née Duddy). *Educ:* Stockport Grammar School; St Catherine's College, Oxford (MA). *Professional Organisations:* FCA. *Clubs:* Vincents Club (Oxford). *Recreations:* Golf, Squash.

BURGESS, Richard Trevor; Director, J H Rayner (Mincing Lane) Ltd.

BURGESS, Robert E; Vice-President and Regional Treasurer, The Toronto Dominion Bank, since 1990; Foreign Exchange, Capital Markets, Money Markets, Investment Banking. *Career:* Toronto Dominion Bank, Treasury (Calgary) 1977; Treasury (Vancouver) 1978; Treasury Manager (Hong Kong) 1980-82; Treasury Manager (Tokyo) 1982-86; General Manager, Foreign Exchange (Toronto) 1987-90. *Biog:* b. 20 January 1953. *Nationality:* Canadian. *m.* 1977, Sheila (née Marling); 1 s. *Educ:* Seneca College, Toronto (International Business). *Directorships:* Toronto Dominion (UK) Ltd 1990; Toronto Dominion (Curacao) NV 1990; Toronto Dominion Holdings BV 1990. *Professional Organisations:* Associate, Institute of Canadian Bankers.

BURGESS, Stephen H; Director, Newton Investment Group.

BURKE, John Joseph; General Manager (Business Development), Bristol & West Building Society, since 1990. *Career:* Bristol & West Building Society, Branch Mgr 1968-72; Area Mgr 1972-76; Agency Mgr 1976-85; Asst Gen Mgr (Branch Operations & Planning) 1985-88; General Manager (Retail Operations) 1988-90. *Biog:* b. 18 September 1942. *Nationality:* British. *m.* 1967, Sally; 3 s. *Educ:* Bridlington Grammar School; Sutton High School, Plymouth. *Directorships:* Bristol & West Property Services (Holdings) Ltd 1987; Westmorland Development Trust Limited; Bristol & West International Ltd 1990. *Other Activities:* Chairman of Board Governors, Chew Valley School, Bristol; Chairman of Bristol Committee, Community Action Trust.

BURKE, M J; Partner, Cameron Markby Hewitt.

BURKE, R J; General Manager (Europe), Norwich Union Insurance Group, since 1988. *Biog:* b. 6 October 1935. *Nationality:* Irish. *m.* Marie; 3 s; 2 d. *Professional Organisations:* Fellow, Chartered Insurance Institute.

BURKITT, L; Executive Director, James R Knowles Limited.

BURLEIGH, Robin; Partner, Clifford Chance, since 1971; Company Law. *Career:* Clegg & Sons, Articled Clerk 1965-67; Clifford-Turner 1968-. *Biog:* b. 16 August 1941. *Nationality:* British. *m.* 1969, Ann (née Steddy); 1 s; 1 d. *Educ:* Repton School; Trinity College, Oxford (MA). *Clubs:* Royal & Ancient, City of London. *Recreations:* Family, Golf, Fishing, Music.

BURLTON, G L W; Director, Parrish Stockbrokers.

BURN, Adrian Lachlan; Partner, Linklater & Paines, since 1982; Finance. *Career:* Linklaters Paris Office 1982-86. *Biog:* b. 4 April 1951. *Nationality:* British. *m.* 1982, Jo; 1 s; 2 d. *Educ:* Bristol University (LLB). *Professional Organisations:* Solicitor; Member, Law Society. *Recreations:* Music, Cookery, Gardening, Reading.

BURNAND, Paul William; Director, Exco International plc.

BURNELL, B S; Council Member, FIMBRA.

BURNET, Sir Alastair; Council Member, The Office of the Banking Ombudsman.

BURNETT, David; Executive Director, Samuel Montagu & Co Limited, since 1988; Capital Markets, Origination. *Career:* Orion Royal Bank Limited, Director 1976-88. *Biog:* b. 16 December 1951. *Nationality:* British. *Educ:* Tonbridge School; Churchill College, Cambridge (MA).

BURNETT, David John Stuart; Director, Warburg Securities.

BURNETT-HALL, Richard Hamilton; Partner, McKenna & Co, since 1974; Environmental Law, Intellectual Property, EEC. *Career:* Carpmaels & Ransford, Technical Asst 1961-68; The International Synthetic Rubber Co Ltd, Mgr, Patents & Licensing 1968-71; McKenna & Co 1971-. *Biog:* b. 5 August 1935. *Nationality:* British. *m.* 1964, Judith Diana (née Newton); 2 s; 1 d. *Educ:* Marlborough College; Trinity Hall, Cambridge (MA). *Other Activities:* Council Member, The United Kingdom Environmental Law Association. *Professional Organisations:* The Law Society; Fellow, The Chartered Institute of Patent Agents; The Licensing Executives Society. *Clubs:* United Oxford & Cambridge University.

BURNETT-HITCHCOCK, James; Partner, Property Litigation, Cameron Markby Hewitt.

BURNHAM, John Richard; Director, J Henry Schroder Wagg & Co Limited, since 1989; Project Finance, Privatisation. *Career:* Schroder Wagg, London 1976-85; Schroders South East Asian Regional Representative, Singapore 1985-88.

BURNS, B F; Partner, Ernst & Young.

BURNS, J N; Partner, Milne Ross.

BURNS, John Anthony; Director; Group Chief Financial Officer, National Westminster Bank plc, since 1989. *Career:* Natwest Bank plc, Fin Controller, Domestic Banking Div 1975-79; Chief Mgr, Planning & Mktg Div 1979-82; Dep Reg Dir, City Region 1982-84; Dep Gen Mgr, Business Development Div 1984-86; Gen Mgr & Chief Fin Officer, Fin Control Div 1986-88. *Biog: Nationality:* British.

BURNS, M H; Director, UBS Phillips & Drew Futures Limited.

BURNS, Michael; Senior Associate Director, Royal Trust Bank.

BURNS, Professor P J; Professor of Small Business Development, Cranfield School of Management, since 1984; Small Business & Entrepreneurship. *Career:* Arthur Andersen & Co, Accountant 1971-75; University of Warwick, Lecturer 1976-84; Harvard Business School, Visiting Scholar 1979; Open University, Visiting Professor 1987-89. *Biog: b.* 21 December 1949. *Nationality:* British. *m.* 1974, Susan. *Educ:* St Mary's School, Darlington; University of Durham (BA); University of Warwick (MSc). *Other Activities:* Board of Consultants for Modern Medicine; Director, Small Business Programme; Director, 3i European Enterprise Centre. *Professional Organisations:* FCA. *Publications:* Small Business, Finance and Control, 1983; Small Business in Europe, 1986; Small Business and Entrepreneurship, 1988; Small Business, Planning, Finance and Control, 1988; Entrepreneur, 1988; The Small Business Programme Handbook, 1990. *Recreations:* Skiing.

BURNS, R; Partner, Hammond Suddards.

BURNS, S P; Finance Director, Janson Green Limited.

BURNS, Sir Terence; Kt; Chief Economic Adviser, H M Treasury, since 1980. *Career:* London Business School 1965-79; Lecturer in Economics 1970-74; Senior Lecturer in Economics 1974-79; Professor of Economics 1979; London Business School Centre for Economic Forecasting, Director 1976-79; H M Treasury, Chief Economic Adviser & Head of Government Economic Service 1980-. *Biog: b.* 11 March 1944. *Nationality:* British. *m.* 1969, Anne; 1 s; 2 d. *Educ:* Houghton-le-Spring Grammar; University of Manchester (BA Econ Hon). *Other Activities:* Member of Council, Royal Economic Society; Vice President, Society of Business Economists; Fellow, London Business School; Visiting Fellow, Nuffield College, Oxford. *Publications:* Various articles in Economic Journals. *Clubs:* Reform, Ealing Golf. *Recreations:* Music, Golf, Soccer Spectator.

BURNSIDE, Bryan; Managing Director, Alexander Howden Reinsurance Brokers, since 1984; Non-Marine Reinsurance. *Career:* Sterling Offices Limited 1958-74; Alexander Howden Reinsurance Brokers, Director 1976-84; Managing Director 1984-.

BURR, Alan William; Director, International Commodities Clearing House Ltd, since 1987; ICCH Financial Markets Ltd; Executive Director, Market Services. *Career:* ICCH Ltd Systems Designer 1972-74; Mktg Mgr 1974-78; Member Services Mgr 1978-81; Clearing Services Mgr 1981-84; ICCH (Hong Kong) Ltd MD 1984-87. *Biog: b.* 11 December 1946. *Nationality:* British. *m.* 1971, Ann (née Edwards); 1 s; 2 d. *Educ:* Bromley Grammar School. *Clubs:* Hong Kong Club, Royal Hong Kong Jockey Club.

BURR, Stephen H; Administration Director, Baring Fund Managers Ltd, since 1985. *Career:* Bishopsgate Progressive Unit Trust Management Ltd, Director 1975-85.

BURRELL, Mark William; Executive Director, Pearson plc, since 1986; Director of Development/New Media. *Career:* Pearson plc, Non-Executive Director 1977-86; Lazard Brothers & Co Ltd, Head of Venture Capital Div 1984-86; Managing Director 1984-86. *Biog: b.* 9 April 1937. *Nationality:* British. *m.* 1966, Margot Rosemary (née Pearce); 2 s; 1 d. *Educ:* Eton College; Pembroke College, Cambridge (BA Hons 1st); Harvard Business School (SMP). *Directorships:* Lazard Brothers & Company Ltd 1974; Whitehall Petroleum Ltd 1964-88 Chm; BSB Holdings Ltd 1987; British Satellite Broadcasting Ltd 1990; The Cowdray Trust Ltd 1964; The Dickinson Trust Ltd 1985; Millbank Financial Services Ltd 1986; Pearson plc 1977; Pearson Services Ltd 1986; Spinmerit Ltd 1990; Testchange Ltd 1990; Whitehall Securities Corporation Ltd 1987; Whitehall Electric Investments 1989; The Whitehall Trust 1987; Yorkshire Television Holdings plc 1989; Yorkshire Television Ltd 1989. *Clubs:* RAC. *Recreations:* Skiing, Hunting, Sailing, Tennis.

BURRIDGE, J G; Management Board Director, GNI Ltd, since 1984; Fund Management. *Career:* Intercommodities Ltd (now called GNI) 1979. *Biog: b.* 20 March 1956. *Nationality:* British. *m.* 1983, Siobhan Mary Anne (née Watson); 1 s; 1 d. *Educ:* Sherborne School; Trinity College, Cambridge (MA Hons). *Clubs:* Annabel's, Queens.

BURROUGHS, Philip Anthony; Partner, Lawrence Graham, since 1985; Commercial Property. *Career:* Messrs Sedgwick Turner Sworder & Wilson, Trainee Solicitor 1978-80; Messrs Freshfields, Assistant Solicitor 1980-83; Messrs Lawrence Graham, Assistant Solicitor 1983-85; Partner 1985-. *Biog: b.* 2 October 1955. *Nationality:* British. *m.* 1977, Katharine (née Doughty); 1 s; 1 d. *Educ:* University of Bristol (LLB Hons Upper Second Class Honours). *Other Activities:* City of London Solicitors Company; Westminster Law Society; British Council of Shopping Centres. *Professional Organisations:* Law Society. *Clubs:* Round Table.

BURROW, J; Non-Executive Director, Dartington & Co Group plc.

BURROW, Robert Philip; Partner, S J Berwin & Co, since 1985; Corporate Finance. *Career:* Clifford Turner, Articled Clerk 1973-76; Linklaters & Paines, Solicitor 1976-78; J Rothschild & Co Ltd, Director 1978-85. *Biog: b.* 24 March 1951. *Nationality:* British/Irish. *m.* 1984, Angela Mary (née Hill); 2 s. *Educ:* St George's College, Weybridge; Fitzwilliam College, Cambridge (MA). *Directorships:* Wickes plc 1989 (non-exec); Control Components Ltd 1983 (non-exec). *Professional Organisations:* The Law Society.

BURROWS, Malcolm; Manager, Bacon & Woodrow, since 1970; Life Insurance. *Biog: b.* 10 May 1947. *Nationality:* British. *Educ:* George Stephenson County Grammar School, Newcastle upon Tyne; Worcester College, Oxford (MA). *Other Activities:* Member of Committee, Staple Inn Actuarial Society. *Recreations:* Diving, Travel, Reading.

BURT, John Gordon Morrison; Executive Director, Pensions Division, Allied Dunbar Assurance plc, since 1985; Pensions Administration Division. *Career:* Legal & General Assurance Society plc Pensions Superintendent 1952-74. *Biog: b.* 26 March 1936. *Nationality:* British. *m.* 1976, Rita (née Hey); 1 s. *Educ:* Greenford County Grammar. *Directorships:* Allied Dunbar (Pension Services) Ltd 1988 (exec). *Professional Organisations:* ACII; APMI. *Recreations:* Tennis, Gardening, Marquetry.

BURT, Peter A; Manager, Bank of Scotland.

BURTON, Anthony David; Executive Director, S G Warburg & Co Ltd, since 1979. *Career:* Bank of America NT SA, Chief Dealer 1966-72; S G Warburg & Co Ltd, Exec Dir 1972-. *Biog: b.* 2 April 1937. *Nationality:* British. *m.* 1964, Valerie (née Swire); 1 s; 2 d. *Educ:* Arnold School, Blackpool. *Directorships:* The London International Financial Futures Exchange Ltd 1988 Chm; LIFFE Options plc 1985 Chm; Warburg Futures & Options Ltd 1989 Chm; Marshall's Finance Ltd 1989 Chm. *Other Activities:* Liveryman, The Worshipful Company of Glass Sellers; City Liaison Committee; British Invisible Exports Council; BIEC, European Committee; Deputy Chairman, Joint Exchanges Committee. *Professional Organisations:* ACIB; FCT. *Clubs:* MCC. *Recreations:* Antique Glass, German Pottery, Music, Outdoor Activities.

BURTON, C M; Joint Managing Director, A J Archer Holdings plc.

BURTON, Ms Caroline Mary; General Manager, Investments, Guardian Royal Exchange plc, since 1989; Investment Management. *Career:* GRE Investment Department 1973; Investment Department, Various, International Investments, Manager 1978; GRE Asset Management, Managing Director 1987. *Biog: b.* 14 January 1950. *Nationality:* British. *m.* 1981, Nigel John Fletcher. *Educ:* Oxford High School for Girls GPDST; Oxford University (MA). *Directorships:* Scottish Metropolitan Properties 1990 (non-exec); Guardian Royal Exchange plc 1990 (exec).

BURTON, Martin John; Managing Director Trading 1988, Citicorp Scrimgeour Vickers & Co Ltd.

BURTON, Nigel Foster; Executive Director, Allied Dunbar Assurance plc, since 1983; New Developments, Particularly International. *Career:* Royal Heritage Dep Actuary 1972-83; Royal Heritage Intl Gen Mgr 1979-81. *Biog: b.* 20 September 1951. *Nationality:* British. *m.* 1973, Alwyn (née Robson); 3 s. *Educ:* Cheltenham Grammar School; Pembroke College, Oxford (MA). *Directorships:* Allied Dunbar Insurance & Investments Ltd 1987 (exec); Allied Dunbar Intl Funds Ltd 1984 (non-exec); Allied Dunbar Intl Ltd 1983 (exec); Dunbar Analisis de Mercados SA 1988 (exec). *Professional Organisations:* FIA.

BURTON, P J; Agency Director, Gravett & Tilling (Underwriting Agencies) Ltd.

BURTON, R W; Partner, Arthur Andersen & Co Chartered Accts.

BURTON, Timothy James; Partner, McKenna & Co, since 1989; Insurance & Reinsurance. *Career:* Simanowitz & Brown, Articled Clerk 1978-80; Kenwright & Cox, Assistant Solicitor 1981-83; Kingsley Napley & Co, Assistant Solicitor 1983-85; McKenna & Co, Assistant Solicitor 1985-89. *Biog: b.* 8 August 1956. *Nationality:* British. *m.* 1980, Frances; 2 d. *Educ:* Southampton University (LLB). *Other Activities:* City of London Solicitors Company; British Insurance Law Association. *Professional Organisations:* Law Society of England & Wales. *Publications:* Regular Contributor to Insurance & Reinsurance Periodicals.

BUSCH, C A M; Chairman & Managing Director, Philips Electronic & Associated Industries Ltd.

BUSH, Claude Harry; Managing Director, NWS Ltd.

103

BUSH, Trevor; Assistant General Manager (Treasury), Banco Santander, since 1989. *Biog: b.* 25 February 1953. *m.* 1988, Shirley Ann; 1 s; 1 d.

BUSH, Trevor John; Director, S G Warburg Akroyd Rowe & Pitman Mullens Ltd, since 1988; Responsible for co-ordinating International Banking Business in the Financing Division & Joint Chm of the Credit Ctee. *Career:* Midland Bank Lending Officer; Guinness Mahon Lending Officer 1974-79; S G Warburg & Co Ltd Dir 1979-88. *Biog: b.* 4 April 1946. *Nationality:* British. *m.* 1968, Susan (née Beckett); 2 s. *Educ:* Riddlesdown School, Surrey. *Professional Organisations:* ACIB.

BUSHELL, D H; Director, Lazard Brothers & Co Limited.

BUSHER, Thomas George Story; Group Secretary, Wellington Underwriting Holdings Limited, since 1985; Group Administration, Legal & Compliance. *Career:* Clifford-Turner Solicitors, Articled Clerk 1978-80; Assistant Solicitor 1980-84; Richard Beckett Underwriting Agencies Limited, Director 1984-85; Wellington Underwriting Holdings Limited, Group Secretary 1985-. *Biog: b.* 18 December 1955. *Nationality:* British. *Educ:* Winchester College; Clare College, Cambridge (BA). *Directorships:* Wellington Underwriting Agencies Limited 1988 (exec); Wellington Underwriting Services Limited 1985 (exec); Wellington Personal Insurances Limited 1990 (exec); Wellington Italia SRL 1990 (exec); Taylor Clayton Underwriting Agencies Limited 1989 (exec). *Other Activities:* Member, Management Committee Winchester District Housing Association Limited. *Professional Organisations:* Solicitor; Member, Law Society; Liveryman, City of London Solicitors Company.

BUSHNELL, P J; Director, Touche Remnant Investment Management Ltd.

BUSTARD, C D; General Manager, James Finlay Bank Limited.

BUTCHER, C; General Manager, Bayerische Landesbank Girozentrale.

BUTCHER, David; Deputy Managing Director, Syndicate, Yamaichi International (Europe) Limited.

BUTCHER, G C; Non-Executive Director, The Burmah Oil plc.

BUTCHER, J V C; Director, Robert Bruce Fitzmaurice Ltd.

BUTCHER, J W E; Director, Wendover Underwriting Agency Limited.

BUTCHER, M J; Partner, Wedlake Bell.

BUTLER, A J; Partner, Simmons & Simmons.

BUTLER, B R R; OBE; Managing Director (Investment Management), The British Petroleum Company plc.

BUTLER, Brian Stuart Theobald Somerset Caher; The Earl of Carrick; Director, Cargill plc. *Biog: b.* 17 August 1931. *Nationality:* British. *m.* 1986, Gillian Irene; 1 s; 1 d (by previous marriage). *Directorships:* Bowater plc; Bowater Incorporated; Cargill Financial Services Corporation Limited; Balfour Maclaine Corporation; Chloride Eastern Industries Ltd. *Clubs:* Whites, Brookes, Pratts. *Recreations:* Horse Racing, Bridge.

BUTLER, David; Deputy Director of Savings, Department for National Savings.

BUTLER, G R F; Partner, Jaques & Lewis.

BUTLER, Ian Geoffrey; CBE; Director (Non-executive), Cookson Group plc, since 1965. *Career:* Tansley Witt & Co, Ptnr 1951-55; Cookson Group plc, PA & Dir of Subs 1956-63; Treasurer 1963-65; Fin Dir 1965-73; MD 1973-85; Chairman 1976-90. *Biog: b.* 12 April 1925. *Nationality:* British. *m.* 1973, Anne (née Robertson); 2 d. *Educ:* Huyton Hill, Liverpool; Stowe, Buckingham; Trinity College, Oxford (MA). *Directorships:* Barclays Bank plc 1985 (non-exec); Nurdin & Peacock plc 1986 (non-exec); Cookson Group plc 1965 (non-exec). *Other Activities:* Council of CBI, Former Chairman of Companies Committee & Member of Presidents Committee; Member of Council, Former Hon Treasurer, Royal Yachting Association; Treasurer & Member of Executive Committee, International Yacht Racing Union. *Professional Organisations:* FCA; CBIM. *Clubs:* Royal Thames Yacht Club, Royal Yacht Squadron (Vice Commodore).

BUTLER, J H; Partner, Jaques & Lewis; Commercial Property - Investment and Development. *Biog: b.* 18 February 1945. *Nationality:* British. *m.* 1974, Natalie (née Kolychkine); 2 s. *Educ:* Pocklington School, near York; Leeds University (LLB 2:1). *Other Activities:* Member, Society of Construction Law. *Recreations:* Swimming, Piano.

BUTLER, Jeremy; Partner, Titmuss Sainer & Webb.

BUTLER, Sir Michael (Dacres); GCMG; Executive Director, Hambros Bank Limited, since 1986. *Career:* HM Foreign Service 1950; Served in: UK Mission to UN, New York 1952-56; Baghdad 1956-58; FO 1958-61 and 1965-68; Paris 1961-65; Counsellor UK Mission in Geneva 1968-70; Center for International Affairs, Harvard, Fellow 1970-71; Counsellor Washington 1971-72; FCO, Head of European Integration Dept 1972-74; FCO, Asst Under-Sec in Charge European Community Affairs 1974-76; FCO, Dep Under-Sec of

State 1976-79; European Community Affairs, FCO, Asst Under-Sec in Charge 1974-76; Ambassador and Perm UK Rep to EC, Brussels 1979-85. *Biog: b.* 27 February 1927. *m.* 1951, Ann; 2 s; 2 d. *Educ:* Winchester; Trinity Coll, Oxford. *Other Activities:* Chm, City European Ctee, British Invisible Exports Council, 1988-; Member, Standing Ctee on International Relations, ACOST, 1987-; Panel of Conciliators, International Centre for the Settlement of Investment Disputes 1987-; Mem, Council, Oriental Ceramic Soc 1977-80 and 1985-88; Dep Chm, Bd of Trustees, V&A Museum 1985-. *Publications:* Chinese Porcelain, The Transitional Period 1620-82; a Selection from the Michael Butler Collection, 1986; Europe: More than a Continent, 1986; 17th Century Chinese Porcelain from the Butler Family Collection, 1990; Contribs to Trans Oriental Ceramic Soc. *Clubs:* Brooks's. *Recreations:* Collecting Chinese Porcelain, Skiing, Tennis.

BUTLER, Michael Howard; Finance Director and Corporation Member, British Coal Corporation, since 1985; Finance and Estates. *Career:* National Coal Board, (NCB became British Coal Corporation in 1987), Deputy Chief Cashier 1962; Deputy Treasurer 1971; Treasurer & Dep Director-General 1978; Director-General 1981; Finance Director 1985; Corporation Member 1986. *Biog: b.* 14 Februry 1936. *Nationality:* British. *m.* 1961, Christine (née Killer); 2 s; 1 d. *Educ:* Nottingham High School. *Directorships:* NCB (Ancillaries) Ltd 1985; British Fuels Limited 1987; British Fuels Group Pension Scheme Ltd 1989; British Coal Enterprise Ltd 1988; British Coal International Ltd 1985; Citystone Assets plc 1990; Coal Industry Estates Ltd 1983; Coal Products Ltd 1985; CIBT Developments Ltd 1985; CIBT Insurance Services Ltd 1985; CIN Management Ltd 1986; Coal Developments (Queensland) Ltd 1988; Coal Developments (German Creek) Pty Ltd 1988; Compower Ltd 1981-87; SBC Properties Ltd 1987; Pan American Properties Inc 1987-89; Pan American Management Inc 1987-89; Bukingham Holdings Inc 1989; TR Industrial & General Trust plc 1988-89. *Professional Organisations:* Fellow, Institute of Chartered Accountants; Companion, British Institute of Management. *Recreations:* Tennis, Gardening, listening to music, watching Association Football.

BUTLER, Peter Leslie; Director, Nicholson Chamberlain Colls Group, since 1987; Managing Director Aviation Operating Company. *Career:* Stewart Smith London 1959-68; Aviation Ins Co of Africa (Johannesburg) 1968-69; Stewart Smith (Pty) Ltd Australia 1969-70; Stewart Smith London (later Stewart Wrighton Ltd) 1970-87; Stewart Smith Aviation, Director 1974-. *Biog: b.* 17 August 1943. *Nationality:* British. *m.* 1975, Diana. *Educ:* Hylands School, Romford. *Directorships:* Stewart Wrighton North America Ltd 1981-87 (exec); Stewart Wrighton Members Agency 1984-87 (non-exec). *Professional Organisations:* Associate, Chartered Insurance Institute; Fellow, British Insurance Brokers

Association. *Recreations:* Tennis, Gardening, Church Activities.

BUTLER, R J; Director, Scott Underwriting Agencies Limited.

BUTLER, R J; Managing Partner, London, Ernst & Young.

BUTLER, Sir Richard Clive; KB, DL; Chairman, County NatWest Investment Management Ltd, since 1989. *Career:* National Service, 2nd Lieutenant, Royal Horse Guards; The National Farmers' Union, Vice President 1970-71; Deputy President 1971-79; President 1979-86; COPA (Committee of Agricultural Organisations in the European Community), President 1985-87. *Biog: b.* 12 January 1929. *m.* 1952, Susan Anne Maud (née Walker). 2 s (twins) 1 d. *Educ:* Eton College; Pembroke College, Cambridge (MA Agric). *Directorships:* National Westminster Bank plc 1986 (non-exec); NatWest Investment Bank Ltd 1989 (non-exec); County NatWest Investment Management Ltd 1989 (non-exec); Dai-Ichi Life County NatWest Investment Management Ltd 1990 (non-exec); Agricola UK Ltd 1986 (exec) Chm; Ferruzzi Trading (UK) Ltd 1986 Chm; Barton Bendish Farms Ltd 1986 Chm; Saxlingham Farms Ltd 1990 (non-exec); The National Farmers' Union Mutual Insurance Society 1985; Avon Insurance plc 1990 (non-exec); Sir Richard and Lady Butler's Farms Ltd (formerly Butler's Peas Ltd) 1959 (exec); The Mathilda and Terence Kennedy Institute of Rheumatology 1987 (non-exec); Farmland Investors Ltd (formerly Landmatch Ltd) 1978 (non-exec); Essex Peas Limited 1968-83; Farmers' Meat Co plc 1983-85; Unifarm Services Ltd 1980-86; The NFU Development Co Ltd 1970-86; The NFU Trust Co Ltd 1970-86; NFU Holdings Ltd 1970-86. *Other Activities:* (Renter Warden 1989-90) Skinners' Company; Governor of Tonbridge School; Governor of the Skinners' School, Tunbridge Wells; Member of Court of the Farmers' Company; Life Member of the NFU Council; Chairman of The Butler Trust which administers the Prison Service Annual Award Scheme; Chairman of the Arthritis and Rheumatism Council for Research. *Professional Organisations:* CBIM. *Clubs:* Farmers. *Recreations:* Hunting, Shooting, Tennis.

BUTLER, S M; Portfolio Manager, BP Pensions Services Ltd.

BUTLER, Thomas Patrick; Partner, Holman Fenwick & Willan, Solicitors, since 1973; Shipping Law. *Career:* Holman, Fenwick & Willan, Assistant Solicitor 1969-73; Higgs & Johnson (Solicitors, Nassau), Legal Assistant 1968-69; Johnson, Stokes & Master (Solicitors, Hong Kong), Assistant Solicitor 1964-67; Barnes & Butler (London), Assistant Solicitor 1960-64; Taylor Willcocks & Co (London), Articled Clerk 1957-60. *Biog: b.* 17 February 1936. *Nationality:* British. *m.*

1961, Gillian Barclay Campbell (née Kemp); 2 s. *Educ:* Malvern College; Kings College, London (LLB). *Other Activities:* Hon Treasurer, Law Society's Art Group. *Professional Organisations:* Member, Law Society; Solicitor (Admitted Also in Hong Kong). *Recreations:* Painting, Music.

BUTLER, W D; Field Operations Director, Ford Motor Credit Company.

BUTT, M A; Chairman and Chief Executive, Eagle Star, since 1987. *Career:* Bland Welch Group 1964; Bland Payne Holdings, Director 1970; Sedgwick Group, Chairman 1983; Eagle Star Holdings, Chairman 1987; BAT Industries, Member of Board 1987. *Biog: b.* 1942. *Nationality:* British. *Educ:* Rugby School; Magdalen College, Oxford; INSEAD Business School (MBA). *Directorships:* BAT 1987 (exec). *Other Activities:* Board Member, INSEAD; Chairman, INSEAD'S International Council; Member, Association of British Insurers' General Insurance Council.

BUTT, Stephen; Managing Director, Morgan Stanley International, since 1985; Fund Management. *Career:* Phillips & Drew, Investment Adviser 1972-74; N.M. Rothschild & Sons Ltd, Investment Advisers 1974-79; Hill Samuel Group 1979-85; Hill Samuel Investment Management, Director 1980; Hill Samuel & Co, Director 1981; Travelers Hill Samuel, Chief Executive Officer 1982; Morgan Stanley Asset Management, Managing Director 1985-. *Biog: b.* 12 February 1951. *Nationality:* British. *m.* Carolyn,; 2 d. *Educ:* Magdalen College, Oxford (BA Hons). *Recreations:* Golf, Skiing, Art.

BUTTERFIELD, The Hon Jonathan W H; President, Banklink International, since 1988; Manage all Banklink Intl's Non-US Activities. *Career:* NatWest Bank plc, International Division, Team Leader, Marketing & Co-ordination Dept, Credit/Market Analysis 1974-76; Chemical Bank (London & New York), Account Executive, UK Multinational Group 1976-82; New York, Head of Transaction Services Product Management Group 1982-84; Banklink Inc, Manager, International Sales (London) 1984-86; Banklink WS (NY), MD 1986-89; Banklink International (London), President 1989-. *Biog: b.* 23 October 1948. *Nationality:* British. *m.* 1973, Sharon (née Traverse-Healy); 2 s; 1 d. *Educ:* Bryanston School; Reading University (BA Econ). *Clubs:* New Canaan Field Club. *Recreations:* Tennis, Reading.

BUTTERFIELD, William John Hughes; The Rt Hon Lord Butterfield of Stechford; KV, OBE; Deputy Regius Professor of Physic, University of Cambridge, since 1987; Medicine & Education. *Career:* Guys Hospital, First Professor of Medicine 1958-70; University of Nottingham, Vice Chancellor 1970-75; University of Cambridge, Regius Professor of Physic 1976-87; University of Cambridge, Vice Chancellor 1983-85; Educational Trusts etc in UK, Hong Kong & Tokyo, Chairman; Medical Dictionary, New York, Editor. *Biog: b.* 28 March 1920. *Nationality:* British. *m.* 1950, Isabel Ann (née Kennedy); 3 s; 1 d. *Educ:* Solihull School; Johns Hopkins (MD); Oxford University (DM). *Directorships:* Prudential Corporation 1982 (non-exec); Cemor Ltd (Cambridge) 1987 Chairman; Medical Education International 1984; Nuffield Health & Social Services Fund 1983; International Sciences 1988; Hawks (Cambridge) Company 1989. *Other Activities:* Chairman, Health Promotion Research Trust; Canada Foundation, Hong Kong; Jardine Trust, Hong Kong; Vice Chairman, GB-Sasakara Foundation, London & Tokyo; Liveryman, Company of Apothecaries. *Professional Organisations:* Fellow, Royal College of Physicians; Fellow, American College of Physicians; Fellow, New York Academy of Medicine (Hon). *Publications:* Health Behaviour in Bermondsey & Southwark, 1967; Priorities in Medicine, 1968; International Dictionary of Medicine & Biology, 1986. *Clubs:* MCC, Atheneum, Beefsteak.

BUTTERWICK, John Newton; Non-Executive Director, Duncan Lawrie Limited.

BUTTERWORTH, Hugh Barham; Chief Executive, Clark Whitehill, since 1986; General Management. *Career:* Touche Ross, Articled Clerk/Assistant Manager 1958-68; Clark Whitehill, Manager 1968-70; Partner 1970-. *Biog: b.* 16 August 1941. *Nationality:* British. *m.* 1967, Penelope (née Knowles); 1 s. *Educ:* Merchant Taylors' School. *Professional Organisations:* FCA. *Recreations:* Golf.

BUTTON, P C; Director, Charterhouse Bank Limited.

BUTTON, Peter Lowther; Director, Kleinwort Benson Ltd.

BUTTON, Roger; Partner, Messrs Jaques & Lewis, since 1983; Head of Building & Engineering Department. *Career:* London Borough of Southwark, Articled Clerk 1969-71; Sir Lindsay Parkinson & Co Limited, Assistant Solicitor, Legal Department 1971-73; Church Adams Tatham & Co, Assistant Solicitor 1973-75; Partner 1975-79; Taylor Tyrrell Lewis & Craig, Partner 1980-82; Jaques & Lewis, Assistant Solicitor 1982-83. *Biog: b.* 6 August 1946. *Nationality:* British. *m.* 1980, Elisabeth Anne (née Wiles). *Educ:* Millfield School; Oriel College, Oxford (BA Oxon). *Professional Organisations:* Member, Law Society and Society of Construction Law.

BUXTON, Andrew Robert Fowell; Vice Chairman and Managing Director, Barclays Bank plc, since 1988. *Biog: b.* 2 February 1943. *Nationality:* British. *m.* 1965, Jane Margery (née Grant); 2 d. *Educ:* Winchester College; Pembroke College, Oxford. *Clubs:* RAC Club.

BUXTON, Richard Edward; Partner, Field Fisher Waterhouse, since 1988; Licensed Property. *Career:* Woodham Smith, Articled Clerk 1975-77; Nayler Benson & Co, Assistant Solicitor 1977-78; Radcliffes & Co, Assistant Solicitor 1978-81; Douglas Goldberg & Co, Assistant Solicitor 1981-82; Richard Buxton & Co, Founder 1982-85; Ellis & Fairbairn, Assistant Solicitor 1986-87. *Biog: b.* 29 August 1953. *Nationality:* British. divorced; 1 s. *Educ:* St Paul's School, London; Hull University (LLB Hons); College of Law, Guildford. *Other Activities:* Member, Holborn Law Society Conveyancing & Law Reform Sub-Committees; Liaison Officer with City of London Law Society; Member, Holborn Law Society. *Professional Organisations:* Associate, Institute of Chartered Arbitrators; Solicitor. *Clubs:* RAC. *Recreations:* Swimming, Cricket.

BYAM SHAW, Nicholas Glencairn; Chairman and Managing Director, Macmillan Publishers Ltd, since 1990; Publisher. *Career:* William Collins Sons & Co Ltd, Glasgow, Salesman 1956-60; Sales Manager 1960-64; Macmillan & Co (later Macmillan Publishers Ltd), Sales Manager 1964-65; Sales Director 1965-67; Macmillan Publishers Ltd, Deputy Managing Director 1967-69; Managing Director 1969-. *Biog: b.* 28 March 1934. *Nationality:* British. *m.* 1987, Constance; 2 s; 1 d. *Educ:* Royal Naval College, Dartmouth. *Directorships:* St Martin's Press 1980 (exec); Pan Books Ltd 1986 (exec) Chairman; Pan Macmillan Ltd 1990 (exec) Chairman. *Other Activities:* Member, British Council Publishers Advisory Committee. *Recreations:* Gardening, Travel.

BYATT, Roger W; General Manager, National Westminster Bank, since 1990; Global Corporates and Financial Institutions. *Career:* National Westminster Bank, Various Managerial Positions Intl Div 1964-78; Head, Energy & Natural Resources 1979-83; Snr Intl Exec, Corp Finance 1983-85; Regional Gen Mgr, Corp Financial Services 1985-88; Gen Mgr, Corp Banking 1988-90. *Biog: b.* 22 May 1940. *Nationality:* British. *m.* 1964, Pam; 2 s. *Educ:* Dorking County Grammar, Surrey. *Professional Organisations:* FCIB. *Recreations:* Badminton, Tennis, Theatre, Opera, Music.

BYFORD, L G; Chairman, Walker Crips Weddle Beck plc.

BYNOE, R W; Partner, Jaques & Lewis.

BYRNE, David; Partner, Titmuss Sainer & Webb.

BYRNE, J; Partner, Nabarro Nathanson, since 1990; Company, Commercial Law. *Career:* British Coal, Legal Department Solicitor 1985-90. *Biog: b.* 28 December 1958. *Nationality:* British. *m.* 1987, Caroline. *Educ:* LSE (LLB, LLM). *Professional Organisations:* Solicitor. *Publications:* Contributor to Vaughan Law of European Communities Service, 1990.

BYRNE, J N; Partner, Freshfields.

BYRNE, Kevin; Partner, BBM Associates.

BYRNE, Michael Francis; General Manager, Nedperm Bank Ltd, since 1982; General Management. *Career:* Peat Marwick, Acct 1958-61; Consultant 1962-66; BICC, Productivity Acct 1967; UAL Merchant Bank, Corp Fin Mgr 1968-72; Dir & European Rep 1973-78; Nedbank Group, European Exec 1979-81; Nedbank Ltd, Dep Gen Mgr 1982-89; Gen Mgr 1989-. *Biog: b.* 9 February 1936. *Nationality:* British. *m.* 1964, Elizabeth (née Proctor); 1 s; 1 d. *Educ:* Stonyhurst College; Pembroke College, Oxford (MA). *Professional Organisations:* FCA; ACMA. *Clubs:* Hurlingham, Johannesbury Country Club, Royal Wimbledon Golf Club, Overseas Bankers'. *Recreations:* Golf.

BYRNE, Vincent J; Director, Bradstock Blunt & Crawley Ltd.

BYROM, Peter; Executive Director, N M Rothschild & Sons Limited.

BYRON, Robert James; Lord Byron; Partner, Holman Fenwick & Willan, since 1984; Shipping/ International Trade/Commodities. *Career:* Called to the Bar 1974; Chambers of Lord Rawlinson QC, Barrister 1974-77; Holman Fenwick & Willan 1978. *Biog: b.* 5 April 1950. *Nationality:* British. *m.* 1979, Robyn Margaret (née McLean); 1 s; 3 d. *Educ:* Wellington College; Trinity College, Cambridge (MA). *Other Activities:* Member, House of Lords; Member, Parliamentary Shipping Group. *Professional Organisations:* Solicitor, Supreme Court.

C

CABOT-ALLETZHAUSER, Mrs A; Director, MIM Limited.

CABOURN-SMITH, Anthony Thomas; Partner in Charge London Audit & Business Advisory Service, Ernst & Young, since 1986. *Career:* Ernst & Young 1969-80; Ptnr 1980-86. *Biog: b.* 24 March 1946. *Nationality:* British. *m.* 1969, Kitt (née Courtney); 3 d. *Educ:* Downside School; Wadham College, Oxford (BA). *Professional Organisations:* FCA. *Recreations:* Music, Reading, Bridge.

CACKETT, J R; Director, Wendover Underwriting Agency Limited.

CADBURY, Sir Adrian; Chairman, Pro Ned, Bank of England, since 1984. *Career:* Cadbury Ltd, Dir 1958-65; Chm 1965-69; Cadbury Schweppes, Dep Chm & MD 1969-74; Cadbury Schweppes plc, Chm 1974-89. *Biog: b.* 15 April 1929. *Nationality:* British. *m.* 1956, Gillian Mary (née Skepper); 2 s; 1 d. *Educ:* Eton College; King's College, Cambridge (MA Econ); Aston & Cranfield (Hon DSc); Bristol & Birmingham (Hon LLD). *Directorships:* Bank of England 1970 (non-exec); IBM UK Holdings Ltd 1975 (non-exec); Pro Ned 1984 Chairman; DAF NV 1988 Member, Supervisory Board; National Exhibition Centre Ltd 1989 (non-exec). *Other Activities:* Livery, Grocers' Company; Chancellor, University of Aston; Panel Member, International Centre for Settlement of Investment Disputes, Takeover Panel Member; President, Birmingham Chamber of Commerce & Industry, 1988-89. *Professional Organisations:* Companion of British Institute of Management; Fellow, Insitute of Marketing; Insitute of Personnel Mgmnt; Institute of Food Science & Technology; Institute of Linguists; Royal Society of Arts. *Publications:* Nuffield Memorial Lecture, Need for Technological Change, 1969; Institute of Personnel Management, Organisation & the Personnel Manager, 1970; The Stockton Lecture, Participation in UK Management, 1974; Directors' Handbook, Company Environment & Social Responsibility, 1975; Blackett Memorial Lecture, Work and the Future, 1983; 5th Annual Campden Lecture, The Structure of the Food Industry, 1983; Hitachi Lecture, The 1980's: A Watershed in British Industrial Relations, 1985; Foreword to Social Psychology of Industry, 1985; Harvard Business Review, Ethical Managers make their own rules, 1987; The Company Chairman, 1990. *Clubs:* Athenaeum, Boodles, Hawks' Leander.

CADBURY, N D; Chief Executive & Director, Cadbury Schweppes plc.

CADBURY, Peter Hugh George; Group Director, Morgan Grenfell & Co Limited.

CADE, David Patrick Gordon; Partner, Arthur Andersen & Co.

CAHILL, J C; Chief Executive & Director, BTR plc.

CAIN, Brian; Partner, Insolvency, Cameron Markby Hewitt.

CAINE, Sir Michael; Non-Executive Chairman, Booker plc.

CAINE, R A W; Director, Land Securities plc.

CAIRD, Richard F; Partner, Wilde Sapte.

CAIRNS, A S; Partner, Pensions (Epsom), Bacon & Woodrow.

CAIRNS, Christopher John; Director, J Henry Schroder Wagg & Co Limited.

CAIRNS, Elizabeth; Partner, Jaques & Lewis.

CAIRNS, Ian E; Partner, Beachcroft Stanleys.

CAIRNS, Peter Granville; Director, Cater Allen Ltd.

CAIRNS, Simon Dallas; The Rt Hon The Earl Cairns; Vice Chairman, S G Warburg Group plc.

CAISLEY, Christopher S; Partner, Walker Morris Scott Turnbull, since 1979; Commercial Litigation. *Biog: b.* 2 June 1951. *Nationality:* British. *m.* 1989, Rosemary (née Kitson); 1 s; 1 d. *Educ:* Grange Grammar School, Bradford. *Directorships:* Bradford Northern RLFC (1964) Ltd 1987 (exec); Dales Public Relations Ltd 1987 (exec). *Other Activities:* Chm, Bradford Northern Rugby League Football Club; Leeds Vice-Consul to the Netherlands with responsibility for North and West Yorkshire. *Professional Organisations:* Mem, Law Society.

CALCROFT, Stephen W; Deputy Managing Director, Bradstock Blunt & Thompson Ltd.

CALCUTT, D C; QC; Chairman, Panel on Takeovers & Mergers.

CALDECOTT, P Dominic; Principal, Morgan Stanley Asset Management, since 1990; Far East.

CALDECOTT, Rupert; Director and Head of Japanese Department, Schroder Securities Limited, since 1986. *Biog: Nationality:* British. *Directorships:* Schroder Securities Ltd; J Henry Schroder Wagg.

CALDER, Alistair Campbell; Director, MIM Ltd, since 1982; City Merchants Investment Management, Executive Director. *Biog: b.* 27 April 1946. *Nationality:* British. *Educ:* Brighton. *Other Activities:* Fruiterers Company. *Professional Organisations:* AIB; STA.

CALDER, W; Director, County NatWest Securities Limited.

CALDERAN, F John; Partner, Theodore Goddard.

CALEY, M J; Director, Lowndes Lambert Group Holdings Limited.

CALI, M; General Manager, Banco di Sicilia. *Career:* Banco di Sicilia 1969; Several Assignments Abroad. *Biog: b.* November 1947. *Nationality:* Italian. *Educ:* Master in Economics.

CALLAGHAN, M D; Director, MIM Ltd, since 1985; Marketing. *Career:* MPA, Consultant 1967-74; Equitable Life, Manager, Marketing 1974-85. *Biog: b.* 6 March 1947. *Nationality:* British. *m.* 1970, Vanessa (née Gates); 1 s; 1 d. *Educ:* Shoreham Grammar; Chichester College of FE (OND Business Studies). *Directorships:* MIM Ltd 1985 (exec); MIM France SA 1988 (exec); MIM Luxembourg SA 1988 (exec); MIM Britannia Finanziaia 1988 (exec). *Clubs:* Goodwood Flying. *Recreations:* Flying, Sailing, Shooting.

CALLAHAN, J D; Director, Allstate Reinsurance Co Limited.

CALLAHAN, J Loughlin; Director, SG Warburg Securities, since 1986; Joint Head of Fixed Interest Division. *Career:* Davis Polk & Wardwell Associate 1972-80; SG Warburg & Co Ltd Dir 1980-86. *Biog: b.* 18 January 1948. *Nationality:* American. *m.* 1973, Mary (née Reilly); 1 s; 1 d. *Educ:* Holy Cross College, Massachusetts (BA Hons); Harvard Law School, Massachusetts (JD Cum Laude). *Directorships:* International Primary Markets Association 1986 (non-exec); 1987 Vice Chm. *Professional Organisations:* Member, New York Bar; American Bar Association. *Recreations:* Art Collecting, Tennis.

CALLANDER, Alexander James; Partner, Baillie Gifford & Co, since 1986; Pension Fund Management.

Career: Baillie Gifford & Co, Investment Manager/ Investment Trainee Oil Sector 1982-86. *Biog: b.* 1 April 1960. *Nationality:* British. *Educ:* Trinity College, Glenalmond; St John's College, Cambridge (MA). *Directorships:* Baillie Gifford & Co Ltd 1986 (exec). *Other Activities:* Member, Education Committee of Society of Investment Analysts. *Professional Organisations:* Associate Member, Society of Investment Analysts.

CALVER, Ronald; General Manager UK Life (Operations), Norwich Union Life Insurance Society.

CALVERLEY, D M; Director, Trafalgar House Public Limited Company.

CALVERT, John Stafford; Partner, Simmons & Simmons, since 1966; Property. *Career:* Simmons & Simmons, Articled Clerk 1954-60; National Service, Subaltern 1961-62; Simmons & Simmons, Asst Solicitor 1962-65. *Biog: b.* 17 February 1936. *m.* 1969, Carolyn Joanna (née Potter); 1 s; 2 d. *Educ:* Epsom College. *Other Activities:* Glaziers' Company. *Professional Organisations:* The Law Society. *Clubs:* Cavalry and Guards. *Recreations:* Golf, Skiing, Shooting.

CALVERT, Malcolm; Partner, Cazenove & Co, since 1988; Market-Making. *Career:* Cazenove & Co, Various 1961; Dealer 1967-86. *Directorships:* Cazenove Securities Ltd 1986 (exec).

CALVOCORESSI, James Melville Ion; Divisional Director, Hoare Govett Securities Ltd. *Biog: b.* 26 March 1948. *Nationality:* British. *m.* 1971, Richenda (née Blandy); 3 s. *Educ:* Eton College; Université D'Aix-Marseille. *Professional Organisations:* International Stock Exchange. *Clubs:* Pratt's, City of London, MCC.

CAMA, J E; Partner, Cameron Markby Hewitt.

CAMANO, Alfonso; Joint General Manager, Banco Bilbao Vizcaya, since 1989; Corporate & Commercial Banking. *Career:* Banco Bilbao, Joint International Division 1979; New York Bank, Account Officer 1981; Madrid International Finance 1982; Deputy Manager International Finance 1984; London Manager Capital Markets 1986; Banco Sautauder de Negocios, Joint General Manager 1988; Banco Bilbao Vizcaya London, Joint General Manager 1989. *Educ:* Madrid Autonomous University (MSc).

CAMDEN, John; Chairman, RMC Group plc, since 1974. *Career:* Royal Tank Corps and Intelligence Corps 1943-47; Ready-Mixed Concrete (now RMC) 1952; Director, Group Operations (Europe) 1962; MD 1966-85; Chairman 1974. *Biog: b.* 18 November 1925. *Nationality:* British. m1; 1 s; 2 d; m2 Diane Mae; 1 s; 2 d. *Educ:* Worcester Royal Grammar School; Birmingham University (BSc). *Directorships:* RMC Group plc 1974 (exec) Chairman. *Other Activities:* Grand Decoration of

Honour in Silver for Distinguished Services to the Republic of Austria. *Recreations:* Golf, Gardening.

CAMERON, D R O'C; Director, Kleinwort Benson Limited.

CAMERON, Donald Alexander; General Manager, The Royal Bank of Scotland plc, since 1983; Trustee, Legal, Registrar's Department. *Career:* The Royal Bank of Scotland plc 1949-72; Planning Mgr 1972-77; Asst to MD 1977-78; Bank Sec 1978-83. *Biog: b.* 27 January 1933. *m.* 1959, Chirsty Ann (née MacDonald); 2 s; 1 d. *Educ:* Royal Academy, Inverness; Edinburgh University (BL). *Professional Organisations:* The Law Society of Scotland; The Institute of Bankers in Scotland.

CAMERON, Gerard G; Senior Vice President, Morgan Guaranty Trust Company of New York.

CAMERON, Ian Donald; Director, Panmure Gordon & Co Ltd, since 1957; Private Clients. *Biog: b.* 12 October 1932. *Nationality:* British. *m.* 1962, Mary Fleur (née Mount); 2 s; 2 d. *Educ:* Eton College. *Directorships:* John D Wood 1987 (non-exec); Cater Allen Gilt-Edge Financial Futures Fund; Colin Allen Equity Growth; Envopak Group Ltd. *Clubs:* White's.

CAMERON, Ian Sandifer; Director, Causeway Group Limited, since 1984. *Career:* Peat Marwick McLintock, Articled Clerk 1976-79; Chase Manhattan Bank, Assistant Treasurer 1979-81; 3i plc, Investment Controller 1981-84. *Biog: b.* 1 December 1953. *Nationality:* British. *m.* Annie McClure; 1 s; 1 d. *Educ:* Sherborne School, Dorset; Pembroke College, Cambridge (MA Cantab Social & Political Science). *Directorships:* Causeway Capital Limited 1985 (exec); KI Sintacel Limited 1985 (non-exec); Elderlycare Limited 1985 (non-exec); Deltest Systems Limited 1989 (non-exec); Sintacel Limited 1989 (non-exec); Causeway Group Limited 1990 (exec); Causeway Capital (Guernsey) Limited 1990 (exec); Licenced Clothing Group Limited 1990 (non-exec); Westerkirk Limited 1990 (non-exec). *Professional Organisations:* FCA. *Recreations:* Tennis, Squash, Skiing.

CAMERON, J B; Non-Executive Member, British Railways Board.

CAMERON, John Alastair Nigel; Director, Kleinwort Benson Ltd, since 1988; Corporate Finance. *Career:* Jardine Matheson & Co, Exec 1976-79; McKinsey & Co Consultant 1981-83; County NatWest 1983-88. *Biog: b.* 29 June 1954. *m.* 1982, Julia (née Wurtzburg); 1 s; 1 d. *Educ:* Harrow School; Oxford University (BA); Sloan School, MIT (MSc, BA). *Clubs:* Pratt's.

CAMERON SMAIL, Barry James; Director, British Telecommunications plc, since 1991; Financial Control; Personal Communications Division. *Career:* Commercial Union Assurance, Group Treasurer 1979-88; British Telecom, Gp Treasurer 1988-91. *Biog: b.* 8 September 1954. *Nationality:* British. *m.* 1979, Jennifer (née Wynne); 2 s. *Educ:* Edinburgh Academy; Southampton University (BSc). *Directorships:* Marshalls Finance Ltd 1989 (non-exec). *Other Activities:* Council Member, Association of Corporate Treasurers. *Professional Organisations:* CA; MCT. *Recreations:* Golf.

CAMOIN, M A L; Chairman, Crédit Lyonnais Euro-Securities Ltd.

CAMPBELL, A J W; Director, Campbell Lutyens Hudson Co Ltd.

CAMPBELL, A M; Partner, Simmons & Simmons.

CAMPBELL, C; Group Treasurer, Inchcape plc.

CAMPBELL, Christopher Robert James; WS; Partner, Dundas & Wilson CS, since 1987; Corporate Law. *Career:* Dundas & Wilson CS, Legal Assistant 1982-87. *Biog: b.* 1 December 1958. *Nationality:* British. *m.* 1983, Kay (née Macdonald); 1 s. *Educ:* Daniel Stewart's and Melville College; Edinburgh University (LLB Hons). *Professional Organisations:* Scottish Lawyers' European Group. *Clubs:* Caledonian (Edinburgh), Murrayfield Golf Club. *Recreations:* Golf, Badminton, Football, Photography.

CAMPBELL, D R; Partner, Life & General (Epsom), Bacon & Woodrow.

CAMPBELL, George; Deputy City Editor, Today.

CAMPBELL, Gordon Thomas Calthrop; The Rt Hon Lord Campbell of Croy; PC, MC, DL; Director, Alliance & Leicester Building Society, since 1983; Special Knowledge of Scottish affairs. *Career:* Commissioned in Regular Army 1939-45; Major 1942; HM Foreign Service, FO, UN (New York), Vienna Private Sec to the Sec of the Cabinet 1946-57; MP Moray and Nairn 1959-74; Member of the Cabinet, Sec of State for Scotland 1970-74; Privy Councillor 1970; Peer of the Realm 1974. *Biog: b.* 8 June 1921. *Nationality:* British. *m.* 1949, Nicola Elizabeth Gina (née Madan); 2 s; 1 d. *Educ:* Wellington College. *Directorships:* Stoic Financial Services 1979 (non-exec) Chairman; Croy Potatoes Limited 1988 (non-exec) Chairman; Stoic Insurance Services 1988 (non-exec) Chairman; Chevron Group of Companies 1975 (non-exec) Consultant; Holme Rose Farms 1976 and Holme Rose Estate 1969 (non-exec) Partner. *Other Activities:* Trustee, The Thomson Foundation; First Fellow, Nuffield Provincial Hospitals Trust Queen Elizabeth the Queen Mother Fellowship; Vice-Lieutenant of Nairnshire; Chairman, Alliance & Leicester Building Society Scottish Board; Chairman for Scotland, International Year of Disabled People, 1981.

Publications: Disablement: Problems and Prospects in the UK, 1981. *Recreations:* Music, Birds.

CAMPBELL, James Dugald; Partner, Gouldens, since 1990; Corporate Finance and Finance. *Biog: b.* 22 March 1959. *Nationality:* English. *Educ:* St Johns College, Cambridge (MA Cantab, LLM). *Directorships:* Al-Hayat Publishing Company Limited 1989 (non-exec). *Professional Organisations:* Law Society. *Clubs:* RNVRYC, Ski Club of GB. *Recreations:* Sailing, Climbing, Skiing.

CAMPBELL, John A; Partner, Wilde Sapte.

CAMPBELL, John William Duffus; Assistant General Manager, The Scottish Mutual Assurance Society.

CAMPBELL, L A; Director, Asda Group plc.

CAMPBELL, Malcolm Godfrey Wilson; Partner, Linklaters & Paines, since 1977; International Finance. *Biog: b.* 30 July 1945. *Nationality:* British. *Educ:* The King's School, Canterbury; Jesus College, Oxford (MA). *Professional Organisations:* Law Society. *Recreations:* Sport, Flying, Travel, Photography.

CAMPBELL-FRASER, Patrick Alexander; Director, Stewart Ivory & Co Ltd.

CAMPBELL-HARRIS, Alastair Neil; Chairman, Citigate Communications Group Ltd, since 1988. *Career:* Foster Turner & Benson Ltd, Head of PR 1971-74; Streets Financial Ltd, Dir 1975-86; Streets Financial Strategy Ltd, Dep Chm 1986-87. *Biog: b.* 9 February 1926. *Nationality:* British. *m.* 1962, Zara Carolyn (née Harrison); 1 s; 2 d. *Educ:* Royal Naval College, Dartmouth. *Recreations:* Shooting, Golf, Gardening.

CAMPBELL-HART, Andrew James; Chief Operating Officer, E W Payne Companies Ltd, since 1989; All non-broking areas. *Career:* Commercial Union Manager 1973-84; Royal Reinsurance Finance Director 1984-87; Royal Insurance General Manager and Director 1987-89. *Biog: b.* 21 May 1947. *m.* 1972; 2 s; 1 d. *Educ:* Balliol College, Oxford (BA). *Directorships:* E W Payne Companies Ltd 1989 (exec); E W Payne Ltd 1989 (exec); Aldgate Consultants Ltd 1989 (exec); E W Payne (Overseas)Ltd 1990 (exec). *Professional Organisations:* FCA.

CAMPBELL-JOHNSTON, G F B; Chairman, CJA (Management Recruitment Consultants) Ltd.

CAMPBELL-LAMERTON, Jeremy Robert Edward; Director, Baring Securities Limited, since 1988; Head of Corporate Finance. *Career:* Scots Guards (Army), Captain 1979-82; Lazard Brothers & Co Limited, Intl Corp Fin Negotiator 1982-86; Baring Securities Ltd, Head of European Equities 1986-89; Head of

Corporate Finance 1989-. *Biog: b.* 21 February 1957. *Nationality:* British. *m.* 1985, Mary Louise (née Thorneycroft); 1 s; 2 d. *Educ:* Downside School; Durham University (BA). *Directorships:* Baring Securities Ltd 1988 (exec). *Clubs:* British Sportsmans, Cavalry and Guards, London Scottish. *Recreations:* Field Sports, Rugby Union, Theatre.

CAMPION, Hilary P; Partner (Nottingham), Evershed Wells & Hind.

CAMPION-SMITH, Nigel; Partner, Travers Smith Braithwaite, since 1982; Corporate Finance & Financial Services. *Biog: b.* 10 July 1954. *Nationality:* British. *m.* 1976, Andrea (née Willacy); 1 s; 1 d. *Educ:* St Johns College, Cambridge (MA). *Professional Organisations:* Solicitor.

CAMPKIN, Sidney John; Director, Hill Samuel Bank Limited, since 1987; Customer Services. *Biog: b.* 17 May 1940. *m.* 1968, Pauline Frances (née Rollo); 1 s; 1 d. *Educ:* Lascells Secondary Modern School. *Clubs:* United Services, Pinner. *Recreations:* Horse Racing, Growing Vegetables.

CAMU, Alain; Director, Hill Samuel Bank Limited, since 1972. *Career:* National Bank of Belgium 1959-65; Economic Adviser to Prime Minister 1965-68; Banque de Bruxelles (BBL), Assistant Manager, Foreign Department 1969-72; Lille University (France), Part-time Lecturer in International Economics; Economische Hogeschool (Hasselt, Belgium), Part-time Lecturer in International Economics 1968-72; Hill Samuel Bank, London, Director 1972-; Petercam Securities, Joint Managing Director 1982-. *Biog: b.* 31 August 1934. *Nationality:* Belgian. *m.* 1984, Christina (née Fornari); 3 s; 2 d. *Educ:* Christ Church, Oxford (BA Philosophy, Politics and Economics); University of Louvain, Belgium (Licencié en Sciences Economiques); Yale University, USA (MA Economics). *Directorships:* Peterbroeck, Van Campenhout & Cie SCS 1982 Group Partner; Petercam Securities SA 1982 Managing Director. *Other Activities:* Member, Executive Committee of the Belgo British Union; Founder-President, Yale Club of Belgium. *Publications:* Many Articles and Conferences. *Clubs:* Brook's Club. *Recreations:* Gardening, Photography, Art Collecting.

CANBY, Michael William; Partner, Linklaters & Paines, since 1986. *Biog: b.* 11 January 1955. *Nationality:* British. *m.* 1980, Sarah; 1 s. *Educ:* Buckhurst Hill County High School; Cambridge University (MA, LLB).

CANDY, T F; Director, Hambros Bank Limited.

CANN, (John William) Anthony; Partner, Linklaters & Paines, since 1978. *Career:* Linklaters & Paines, Articled Clerk 1970-72; Solicitor 1972-78; Partner

1978-; New York Office 1975-82. *Biog: b.* 21 July 1947. *Nationality:* British. *m.* 1973, Anne (née Clausen); 2 s; 1 d. *Educ:* Shrewsbury School; Southampton University (LLB Hons); College of Law (Solicitor Hons). *Professional Organisations:* Law Society; City of London Solicitors Company. *Publications:* Mergers & Acquisitions Handbook (Part D), 1986; Mergers & Acquisitions in Europe (The United Kingdom), 1990. *Clubs:* MCC, Wimbledon, Wimbledon Squash and Badminton. *Recreations:* Sports, Photography.

CANNAN, Michael Barry; Chief Executive, Electricity Supply Pension Scheme, since 1981; Overall Responsibility. *Biog: b.* 7 December 1932. *Nationality:* British. *Directorships:* APT Committee of Management Limited; Brighton Marina Company Limited 1986 (non-exec); City Nominees Limited; Electricity Supply Nominees Limited; ESN Investment Management Limited 1987 Chm; ESN Property Management Company Limited 1984 Chm; French Property Trust plc 1990 (non-exec) Chm; Millbank Farming Company Limited 1981 Chm; Millbank Securities Limited Chm; Undercliff Holdings Limited; Undercliff Trustees Limited; Eastern Realty Investment Corporation 1981 Chm; UK American Properties 1984 Chm. *Professional Organisations:* FCA. *Clubs:* MCC, Royal Thames Yacht Club. *Recreations:* Cricket, Sailing.

CANNOCK, V L; Director, Close Brothers Limited.

CANNON, Christopher Charles; Institutional Sales Director, Charterhouse Tilney, since 1986; Institutional Sales. *Career:* Grants of St James's 1964-72; Kemp, Gee and Co, Institutional Salesman 1972-79; Tilney and Co, Institutional Salesman 1979-80; Partner, Institutional Sales 1980; Charterhouse Tilney, Director, Institutional Sales 1986. *Biog: b.* 14 November 1942. *Nationality:* British. *m.* 1975, Valerie June (née Parrish); 1 s; 1 d. *Educ:* Marlborough College; Fitzwilliam College, Cambridge (BA). *Directorships:* Charterhouse Tilney 1986 (exec). *Other Activities:* Liveryman, Vintner. *Professional Organisations:* ASIA. *Recreations:* Shooting, Fishing, Golf, Tennis, Wine.

CANNON BROOKES, M; Director, NCL Investments Limited.

CANSICK, Terence David; Director, Close Brothers Limited, since 1987; Finance, Administration. *Career:* Associated Electrical Industries Ltd, Asst Cost Accountant 1956-62; Essex County Council, Snr Fin Accounts Clerk 1962-65; Lloyds Bank plc, Bank Officer 1966-70; Revertex Ltd, Group Treasurer 1970-73; Close Brothers Ltd, Company Sec 1973-. *Biog: b.* 4 March 1935. *m.* 1960, Maureen Mary (née O'Brien); 2 s. *Educ:* Chatham House School, Kent; City University (MBA). *Directorships:* Close Nominees Ltd 1974 (exec). *Other Activities:* Lions International. *Professional Organisations:* ACIB. *Recreations:* Golf, Theatre.

CANTLAY, Charles P T; Managing Director, Alexander Howden Reinsurance Brokers Limited.

CAPAROSS, Miguel; Managing Director (Corporate Finance), Morgan Stanley International.

CAPEL, Royston Ian; Managing Director, James Capel Moneybroking Ltd, since 1986. *Career:* Pike & Bryant Asst Mgr 1967-72. *Biog: b.* 28 July 1937. *Nationality:* British. *m.* 1969, Patricia (née Hayward); 2 s; 2 d. *Educ:* Collegiate, Winchmore Hill. *Recreations:* Walking, Gardening.

CAPITMAN, Andrew William; Managing Director, International Mergers & Acquisitions, Bankers Trust Company; Cross-Border Corporate Finance. *Career:* Drexel Burnham Lambert,Account Exec 1975-78; Art Deco Hotels, Gen Ptnr 1979-84; Bankers Trust Company (New York), VP 1984-86. *Biog: b.* 17 August 1950. *Nationality:* American. *m.* 1980, Margaret Anne (née Doyle); 1 s; 1 d. *Educ:* Groton School, Radley College; Yale University, (USA) (BA); University of Miami, (USA) (MA). *Clubs:* Yale Club. *Recreations:* Collector, (English Arts & Crafts Movement), Cycling.

CAPLIN, J H; Secretary, The General Electric Company plc.

CAPPER, Richard Gerald; Managing Director, James Finlay plc.

CARBUTT, Francis (Billy); Partner, Ernst & Young, since 1967. *Career:* Rifle Brigade Lt 1954-56; Ernst & Young (or predecessoer firms 1956-. *Biog: b.* 16 July 1936. *Nationality:* British. *m.* 1958, Sally Fenella (née Harris); 1 s; 1 d. *Educ:* Eton College. *Other Activities:* Master of the Grocers' Company, Chm of Court of the Mary Rose. *Professional Organisations:* FCA. *Clubs:* Boodle's, City of London, MCC. *Recreations:* Swimming, Gardening, Photography, all kinds of Music.

CARBY, K A; Director, Allied Dunbar Assurances plc.

CARCIERI, D L; Chief Executive, Cookson America & Member of Group Executive Committee, Cookson Group.

CARDALE, D M; Executive Director, County NatWest Securities.

CARDEN, Anthony Richard Paul; Director, Corporate & Financial Sectors, Barclays Bank plc.

CARDEN, Graham Stephen Paul; CBE, TD, DL; Partner, Cazenove & Company, since 1964; Corporate Finance & Overseas. *Career:* Cazenove & Co 1956-. *Directorships:* Greenfriar Investment Co plc 1966- (non-exec).

CARDEW, Anthony John; Chairman, Grandfield Rork Collins Financial Limited, since 1985; Financial Public Relations and Advertising Company. *Career:* United Press International News Reporter 1969-70; Reuters Financial Correspondent 1971-74; Charles Barker City 1974; Charles Barker Lyons Dir 1976; Head of Fin Public Relations 1979; Grandfield Rork Collins Deputy Chm 1983-85. *Biog: b.* 8 September 1949. *Nationality:* British. *m.* 1971, Janice Frances (née Smallwood); 1 s; 1 d. *Educ:* Marlborough College, Wiltshire; Bishop Wordsworth's School, Salisbury. *Clubs:* Reform, Thunderers. *Recreations:* Book Collecting, Walking, Shooting.

CARDONA, Christopher Andrew; Partner, Wilde Sapte, since 1990; Commercial Litigation. *Career:* Theodore Goddard, Articled Clerk 1982-84; Assistant Solicitor 1984-88; Associate 1988-89. *Biog: b.* 9 December 1959. *Nationality:* British. *m.* 1983, Katherine (née Winfield); 2 d. *Educ:* St Georges College, Weybridge; Trinity College, Cambridge (MA Law). *Professional Organisations:* Member, Canning House; Member, Anglo-Spanish Society. *Clubs:* RAC. *Recreations:* Travel, Theatre, Music.

CAREFULL, Robert Charles; Finance Director/ Company Secretary, Brown Shipley Holdings plc, since 1987; Finance/Accounting. *Career:* Deloitte Haskins & Sells, Acct 1965-74; Brown Shipley & Co Ltd, Various 1974-. *Directorships:* Dumpton Gap Co 1976 (non-exec); Trace (Computer Holdings) Ltd 1978 (non-exec).

CAREY, B B; Divisional Chief Executive, Metals & Chemical Division & Member of Group Executive Committee, Cookson Group.

CAREY, Jeremy; Chief Executive, City & Commercial Communications, since 1989; Corporate Public Relations. *Career:* Sterling Public Relations, Director 1974-80; City & Commercial Communications, Managing Director 1981. *Biog: b.* 12 August. *Nationality:* British. *m.* Julie Elizabeth (née Kent); 1 d. *Educ:* Charterhouse. *Directorships:* Corporate Communications 1989 (exec). *Clubs:* Savile. *Recreations:* Skiing, Sailing.

CAREY, Sir Peter; GCB; Chairman, Dalgety plc, since 1986. *Career:* Department of Industry, Permanent Secretary 1973-83. *Biog: b.* 26 July 1923. *Nationality:* British. *m.* Thelma; 3 d. *Educ:* Portsmouth Grammar School; Oriel College, Oxford; School of Slavonic Studies, London University. *Directorships:* Dalgety plc 1983 (non-exec); Cable & Wireless plc 1984- (non-exec); BPB Industries plc 1983- (non-exec); Morgan Grenfell Group 1983-90 (exec); Chairman 1987-89; Philips NV (Supervisory Board) 1984-. *Professional Organisations:* British Institute of Management; Council of Industrial Society. *Clubs:* United Oxford & Cambridge University.

CAREY, R W; Executive Director, Slough Estates plc.

CAREY, T P A; General Manager, Corporate Development, Allied Irish Banks plc.

CAREY, W E S; Associate Director, James Capel Unit Trust Management Ltd, since 1990; Unit Trust Sales. *Career:* Army, The Blues and Royals, Short Service Commission 1980-84; Allied Dunbar Assurance plc, Trainee Broker Consultant, Broker Department 1984-86; Henderson Unit Trust Management Ltd, Marketing Executive 1986-88; John Lamb Group Ltd, Investment Manager 1988; James Capel Unit Trust Management Ltd 1988-. *Biog: b.* 22 April 1961. *Nationality:* British. *m.* 1987, Carina (née Kirch). *Educ:* Greshams School, Holt, Norfolk. *Clubs:* Boodles, The Berkshire Golf Club. *Recreations:* Golf, Skiing, Sailing.

CARL, Michael; Partner, Frere Cholmeley.

CARLON, Claes Gustav Manfred; Director, Svenska International plc, since 1989; Nordic Desk. *Career:* Svenska Handelsbanken 1968-70; Pension Guarantee Mutual Insurance Co 1970-74; Sundsvallsbanken 1974-79; Sparbankernas Bank, Stockholm 1979-80; Sundsvallsbanken, Deputy General Manager 1980-84; Fennoscandia Limited, London 1984-87; Svenska International plc 1987-. *Biog: b.* 17 January 1944. *Nationality:* Swedish. *m.* Maud; 2 s. *Educ:* Stockholm, Sweden (Master of Political Science).

CARLTON, Ian; Director, Personnel, County NatWest.

CARLTON, Vivienne Margaret; Director, Leadenhall Associates Ltd, since 1986; Corporate, City and Financial Services Public Relations. *Career:* OSCA plc, Div Dir; Opus Public Relations Ltd, Account Dir; Biss Lancaster plc, Account Dir. *Biog: b.* 28 September 1947. *Nationality:* British. *Educ:* Herts & Essex High School, Bishops Stortford; Trent Park College (University of London Teaching Certificate, Drama/English). *Professional Organisations:* MIPR; Institute of Directors. *Recreations:* Theatre, Music, Interior Design.

CARMICHAEL, Andrew; Partner, Linklaters & Paines, since 1987; International Finance. *Biog: b.* 8 August 1957. *Nationality:* British. *Educ:* (MA).

CARMICHAEL, Keith Stanley; CBE; Managing Partner, Longcrofts, since 1981; General Management. *Career:* H Foulks Lynch & Co Ltd Dir 1952-69; Wilson Bigg & Co Ptnr 1957-69; Radio Rentals Ltd Dir 1966-69; Monopolies & Merger Commission, Member 1983-. *Biog: b.* 5 October 1929. *Nationality:* British. *m.* 1958, Cynthia Mary (née Jones); 1 s. *Educ:* Bristol Grammar School. *Directorships:* Rickmansworth Masonic School Ltd 1962 Chm (non-exec). *Other Activities:* Panel Member Monopolies & Mergers Commission; Court of The

Worshipful Company of Chartered Accountants in England & Wales. *Professional Organisations:* FCA, FTII. *Publications:* Spicer & Pegler's Income Tax, 1965; Corporation Tax, 1966-78; Capital Gains Tax 1969-74; Ranking Spicer & Pegler's Executorship Law & Accounts, 1965-87; Taxation of Lloyd's Underwriters (Co-Author) 1986-88. *Clubs:* Carlton, MCC, Lords Taverners, City of London. *Recreations:* Gardening, Reading, Golf, Tennis.

CARMICHAEL, William Black; Chairman, Aitken Campbell & Co Ltd, since 1986; Managing Director. *Career:* Aitken MacKenzie & Fyfe, Ptnr 1960-72; Snr Partner 1972-75; Aitken Campbell & Co, Snr Partner 1975-86; Aitken Campbell & Co Ltd, Chairman 1986-; Aitken Campbell (Gilts) Ltd, Managing Director. *Biog:* b. 8 June 1933. *Nationality:* British. *m.* 1968, Rosemary; 1 d. *Educ:* North Kelvinside Academy. *Directorships:* The Union Discount Company of London plc 1987. *Other Activities:* Member, International Stock Exchange. *Clubs:* Royal Scottish Automobile Club, Western (Glasgow). *Recreations:* Tennis, Golf.

CARNEGIE, William Traquair; Partner, Baillie Gifford Co, since 1966; Investment Management. *Career:* McLleland Moores & Co, CA Glasgow, Apprentice Chartered Accountant 1960-63. *Biog:* b. 25 December 1936. *Nationality:* British. *m.* 1966, Mary (née Irving); 2 s; 1 d. *Educ:* Fettel College; Oxford University (BA). *Other Activities:* Association of Investment Trust Committee, Executive Committee, Deputy Chairman 1988-90. *Professional Organisations:* Chartered Accountants. *Clubs:* New Club, Edinburgh; Honourable Company of Edinburgh Golfers. *Recreations:* Golf, Shooting.

CARNWATH, Mrs Alison J (née Tresise); Director, J Henry Schroder Wagg & Co, since 1988; Corporate Finance. *Career:* Lloyds Merchant Bank 1980-84; Peat Marwick Mitchell 1975-80; Schroder Wagg 1984-87 & 1988-; Wertheim Schroder Inc 1987-88. *Biog:* b. 18 January 1953. *Nationality:* British. *m.* 1979, Peter Andrew. *Educ:* Reading University (BA Economics/German 2:i). *Directorships:* J Henry Schroder Wagg & Co Ltd 1988 (exec). *Professional Organisations:* ACA. *Recreations:* Skiing, Reading, Opera.

CARNWATH, Michael Stewart; Director, J S Gadd & Co Ltd, since 1989; Corporate Finance. *Career:* Peat Marwick McLintock 1971-84; Senior Manager 1982-84; Larpent Newton & Co Ltd, Director, Venture Capital 1984-87; J S Gadd & Co Ltd 1987. *Biog:* b. 17 July 1951. *Nationality:* British. *m.* 1974, Sara (née Pilkington); 1 d. *Educ:* Eton. *Directorships:* London American Mining plc 1988 (non-exec); Justitia International Ltd 1989 (non-exec). *Professional Organisations:* FCA. *Recreations:* Golf, Shooting.

CARPENTER, David; Associate Director, Mayer Brown & Platt.

CARPENTER, M S E; Partner, Slaughter and May.

CARR, Alan Michael; Partner, Simmons & Simmons, since 1966; Corporate Finance. *Biog:* b. 1 September 1936. *m.* 1963, Dalia Carr (née Lebhar); 2 s; 1 d. *Educ:* Gresham's School, Holt; King's College, Cambridge (MA). *Other Activities:* City of London Solicitors' Company (Company Law Sub-Committee). *Recreations:* Oriental Travel.

CARR, Michael Lewis; Deputy Chairman, Gresham Trust plc.

CARR, N B; Partner, Field Fisher Waterhouse.

CARR, Dr Stephen Paul; Director, Warburg Securities, since 1989; Investment Analysis-Head of UK Research. *Career:* Warburg Securities, Food Analyst 1979-89; Head of UK Research 1989-. *Biog:* b. 1 May 1955. *Nationality:* British. *m.* 1977, Pamela; 1 s. *Educ:* Marple Hall Grammar School; University of Warwick (BA); Oxford University (DPhil).

CARRARO, Philip A; Chief Credit Officer, Continental Bank NA.

CARRATU, N F R; Partner, Ernst & Young, since 1971; Partner in Charge of Financial Management Consultancy. *Career:* Mann Judd & Co, Student Accountant 1959-64; McLintock & Whinney Murray, Consultant/Partner 1965-76; Ernst & Young, Partner 1976-. *Biog:* b. 9 January 1937. *Nationality:* British. *m.* 1964, Judith Ann; 2 s; 1 d. *Educ:* St Lawrence College, Ramsgate. *Professional Organisations:* FCA; FIMC. *Clubs:* The Gresham Club, The Little Ship Club. *Recreations:* Sailing, Skiing, Painting.

CARRICK, B R B; Financial Director, Benchmark Bank plc.

CARRINGTON, Tim; Economics Correspondent, Wall Street Journal.

CARROLL, Christopher; Partner, Travers Smith Braithwaite, since 1986; Company Law. *Career:* Travers Smith, Articled Clerk 1978-. *Biog:* b. 21 May 1953. *Nationality:* British. *m.* 1988, Mary. *Educ:* Bedford School; Southampton University (Politics and Law Upper Second). *Clubs:* Chairman Archery Tavern Cricket Club.

CARROLL, Roger Joseph; Managing Director, Grandfield Rork Collins Consumer Finance, since 1989; Personal Finance, Public Relations & Advertising. *Career:* Thomson Regional Newspapers, Financial Journalist 1965-66; Deputy City Editor/Political Correspondent 1966-69; The Sun, Political & Diplomatic Correspondent 1969-73; Political Editor 1973-78; 10 Downing Street, Special Adviser to Prime Minister

1978-79; The Sun, Money Editor 1979-82; SDP Director of Communications 1982-83; Sunday Telegraph, Personal Finance Editor 1983-89. *Biog: b.* 9 January 1943. *Nationality:* British. *m.* 1970, Teresa (née Carey); 3 s. *Educ:* St Cuthbert's Grammar School, Newcastle upon Tyne; London School of Economics (BSc Econ). *Directorships:* Grandfield Rork Collins 1989 (exec); BESt Investment 1989 (non-exec). *Other Activities:* Life Aid (Charity Steering Committee); BESt Investment (Joint Editor). *Publications:* The Two Wage Worker - Common Ownership & Economic Democracy, 1980; The Sun Money Guide, 1981; When You Retire, 1982; Joint Editor, BESt Investment. *Recreations:* Music, Swimming, Newcastle United.

CARROLL, Stuart; Head of Litigation Department, Nabarro Nathanson, since 1982; Senior Litigation Partner. *Biog: b.* 24 July 1951. *Nationality:* British. *Educ:* University of London (LLB Hons). *Professional Organisations:* Solicitor.

CARSON, Iain; Business Correspondent, BBC TV.

CARSON, J; Partner, Baillie Gifford & Co, since 1990; Pension Fund Management. *Career:* Arthur Young 1973-87; Partner 1983; Baillie Gifford & Co 1987-; Partner 1990. *Biog: b.* 11 March 1952. *Nationality:* British. *m.* 1979, Clare (née Bruce); 1 s; 4 d. *Educ:* Eton College; Edinburgh University (Scots Law LLB). *Professional Organisations:* FCA. *Clubs:* New Club (Edinburgh). *Recreations:* Fishing, Golf, Gardening.

CARSON, R V; Partner, Slaughter and May, since 1990; Corporate Tax. *Biog: b.* 28 February 1959. *Nationality:* British. *m.* 1988, Kate (née Naylor). *Educ:* St Pauls School, London; Trinity College, Cambridge (MA). *Publications:* Chapter on Leasing in Tolley's Tax Planning (Annual).

CARSON, William Montgomery; CBE; Chairman, TSB Bank Northern Ireland plc, since 1990; Overall Responsibility. *Career:* Price Waterhouse (Northern Ireland), Snr Partner; TSB Northern Ireland, Trustee 1981; Dep Chm 1984-86; TSB Northern Ireland plc, Dep Chm 1986; TSB Bank Northern Ireland plc, Chm 1990. *Biog: b.* 1929. *Directorships:* Ulster Bus Group; Milk Marketing Board; Moy Park Ltd Chm; William Clark & Son Ltd Chm; Enterprise Equity (NI) Ltd Chm. *Other Activities:* Former Pres, Institute of Chartered Accountants in Ireland. *Professional Organisations:* FCA.

CARSWELL, Richard Ian Edward; Marketing Director, Ivory & Sime plc.

CARSWELL, Robert Dean; Partner, McGrigor Donald, since 1990; General Corporate Law/International Transactions. *Career:* McGrigor Donald & Co (Glasgow), Legal Apprentice 1962-65; Winthrop Stimson Putnam & Roberts (New York NY), Legal Associate 1966; McGrigor Donald & Co (Glasgow), Legal Assistant 1967-70; McGrigor Donald & Co (Glasgow, Edinburgh), Partner 1971-79; Gearhart Industries Inc (Fort Worth TX), Vice-President International Counsel 1980-85; Gearhart Industries Inc (Later Halliburton Logging Services Inc), Vice-President General Counsel 1985-89; International Legal Consultant (Fort Worth TX) 1989-90. *Biog: b.* 23 July 1940. *Nationality:* British. *m.* 1967, Elizabeth Ann (née Turner) (div 1988); 2 s; 1 d. *Educ:* High School of Glasgow; Loretto School; University of Glasgow (MA, LLB); Cornell University (Fulbright Fellow). *Professional Organisations:* Law Society of Scotland; American Bar Association; International Bar Association; Union Internationale Des Avocats. *Publications:* Articles in Legal Journals & Soaring Journals. *Clubs:* Western (Glasgow), Texas Soaring Association. *Recreations:* Gliding.

CARSWELL, Thomas S; Director, Carswell Ltd.

CARTE, Brian Addison; TD; Chief Executive, Lombard North Central plc, since 1989. *Career:* Westminster Bank, Branch and Head Office Duties 1960; County Bank, Sub-Manager 1971; Banking Manager 1973; Director 1975; Director and Head of Banking Division 1980; Senior Director 1983; National Westminster Insurance Services Ltd, Managing Director 1985; Lombard North Central plc, Chief Executive 1989. *Biog: b.* 7 August 1943. *Nationality:* British. *m.* 1969, Shirley Anne (née Brinkley); 2 d. *Educ:* St Lawrence College, Ramsgate. *Directorships:* North Central Finance Limited 1989 Chm; Various Lombard Subsidiaries. *Other Activities:* General Commissioner of Income Tax, 1980-85; Freedom of City of London; Freeman of Worshipful Company of Scriveners, 1975-; Past President, Association of Corporate Treasurers; Service Record 1963-87, Territorial Army (Company Commander and Staff Officer at HQ London District), now on Regular Army of Reserve of Officers. *Professional Organisations:* FCIB; FCT; FRSA. *Clubs:* New Zealand Golf Club, Bristol and Clifton Golf Club, RAC. *Recreations:* Golf, Gardening, Opera.

CARTER, Geoffrey H B; *Career:* Marsh & Parsons Chartered Surveyors, Senior Partner 1958-68; Trafalgar House Developments Ltd, Managing Director 1968-73; Trafalgar House plc, Director & Chm, Trafalgar's Commercial and Residential Property Divisions 1973-88; Kensington Housing Trust (Charitable), Chm 1967-79. *Biog: b.* April 1929. *Educ:* Stowe School; Pembroke College, Cambridge (MA). *Directorships:* Grosvenor Developments Limited (non-exec) Chm; Trafalgar House plc (non-exec); TR Property Investment Trust plc (non-exec); Grosvenor Estate Holdings (non-exec); Portman Homes (non-exec) Chm. *Other Activities:* Member of the Council of the British Property Federation (President 1987-88); Worshipful Company of Chartered Surveyors. *Professional Organisations:* FRICS; FRSA. *Clubs:*

Bucks. *Recreations:* Reading, Music, Fishing, Sailing, Gardening.

CARTER, I Christopher; Executive Director, Credit Suisse First Boston Limited.

CARTER, Isobel Jane (née Gracie); Assistant Director - Marketing, NASDAQ International Ltd, since 1988; Marketing the NASDAQ Electronic Stock Market, the Portal Market and the OTC Bulletin Board. *Career:* Marks & Spencer Ltd Fashion Buyer 1971-72; Heathfield School, Harrow Languages Teacher 1972-74; Self Employed Simultaneous Conference Interpreter 1975-84; Mintel Publications Limited Marketing Consultant 1984; Extel Advertising & PR Ltd Dir, New Business Development 1984-85; The International Stock Exchange Marketing Mgr, Settlement Services 1985-87; Business Mgr, SEQUAL 1987-88. *Biog: b.* 1 December 1948. *Nationality:* British. *m.* 1972, Nigel; 1 s; 1 d. *Educ:* The Mary Erskine School for Girls, Edinburgh; St Anne's College, Oxford (BA Hons); George Washington University, Washington DC (MBA). *Professional Organisations:* Member, AIIC (Association for International Simultaneous Conference Interpreters, Geneva). *Publications:* Retail Banking, 1984. *Recreations:* Golf, Scottish Country Dancing, Jogging, Aerobics, Theatre, Cinema.

CARTER, John Gordon Thomas; Executive Director, Commercial Union plc, since 1989. *Career:* Commercial Union Assurance Co Ltd, General Manager, UK Division 1984-89; Director 1987-. *Biog: b.* 28 December 1937. *Educ:* Jesus College, Oxford (MA). *Directorships:* The British Aviation Insurance Co Ltd (non-exec); British & European Reinsurance Co Ltd Chm; Hibernian Insurance Co Ltd (non-exec); Loss Prevention Council (non-exec); Midland Life Ltd (non-exec); Trade Indemnity plc (non-exec). *Other Activities:* Worshipful Company of Insurers. *Professional Organisations:* FIA.

CARTER, K C; Director, Providence Capitol Fund Managers Ltd.

CARTER, Peter Alan; Partner, Forsyte Kerman; Company/Commercial Departmental Manager Finance Partner. *Career:* Forsyte Kerman, Articled Clerk 1972-74; Assistant Solicitor, Company/Commercial Department 1974-77; Partner, Company/Commercial Department 1977-; Managing Partner 1985-87. *Biog: b.* 11 May 1949. *Nationality:* British. *m.* 1988, Rosemary Elizabeth; 1 s; 3 d. *Educ:* Emanuel School; University of Nottingham (BA); College of Law (Solicitor). *Directorships:* The Britten-Pears Foundation 1987 (non-exec). *Professional Organisations:* Law Society.

CARTER, Peter James Reinier; Director, Barclays de Zoete Wedd Ltd.

CARTER, Stephen McCart; Secretary General, The Baltic Futures Exchange Ltd, since 1987; Futures Market Management. *Career:* Associated Bulk Carriers Ltd, Dir 1971-83; Pres 1983; P&O Bulk Shipping Ltd, MD 1978-83; Boyle Financial Services Ltd, MD 1984-; Biffex Ltd, Chief Exec 1985-87. *Biog: b.* 3 July 1935. *m.* 1962, Diana (née Foice); 1 s; 1 d. *Educ:* Claysmore School; Cranfield Business School; Harvard Business School. *Directorships:* Boyle Financial Services Ltd 1984 (exec) MD. *Professional Organisations:* The Baltic Exchange; FICS. *Recreations:* Golf, Shooting, Fishing.

CARTWRIGHT, Christopher Egerton; Head of Equities, Paribas Ltd. *Career:* L Messel & Co, Analyst/Sales 1970-75; Wood MacKenzie & Co Ltd 1975; County NatWest Securities, Managing Director 1980-89. *Biog: b.* 19 October 1944. *Nationality:* British. *m.* 1967, Susan Lois (née Mindham); 2 s; 1 d. *Educ:* King's School, Worcester; Bristol University. *Professional Organisations:* FCA. *Clubs:* Chiselhurst Golf. *Recreations:* Angling, Microcomputing, Gardening, Guitar.

CARTY, J P; Partner, Robson Rhodes, since 1987; National Technical Partner & Investigatory and Expert Witness Work. *Career:* Price Waterhouse, Student and Manager 1965-72; University of Lancaster, Lecturer 1972-74; Accounting Standards Committee, Secretary 1974-81; James Carty & Co, Chartered Accountants 1981-87. *Biog: b.* 3 March 1937. *Nationality:* British. *Educ:* Cotton College; University of London (BSc Econ); University of Lancaster (MA). *Other Activities:* International Sub-Committee, Auditing Practices Committee. *Professional Organisations:* Institute of Chartered Accountants in England and Wales; Chartered Association of Certified Accountants. *Publications:* Practical Financial Management (Editor) 1985.

CARVALHO, Ciaran Peter; Partner, Titmuss Sainer and Webb, since 1990; Commercial Property. *Educ:* Salesian College Grammar School, Battersea; University of Kent at Canterbury (Upper Second); The College of Law, Lancaster Gate. *Professional Organisations:* Law Society. *Clubs:* Drift Golf Club (East Horsley, Surrey).

CARVER, Jeremy; Partner, Clifford Chance.

CASADY, Mark S; Head of Global Custody Operations, The Northern Trust Company, since 1990; Operations Manager. *Career:* Northern Trust, Personal Trust Assistant 1982-84; Manager Employer Benefit Operations 1984-88; Manager Global Custody Accountancy 1988-89; Head of Operations London Global Custody Operations 1990-. *Biog: b.* 21 September 1960. *Nationality:* American. *m.* 1981, Julia; 3 d. *Educ:* Indiana University (BS); De Paul University (MBA). *Directorships:* Nortrust Nominees 1990 (exec). *Professional Organisations:* Certificate of Trust Management; AIB; University of Winsconsin.

CASE, N J; Director, Pine Street Investments Limited, since 1989; Venture Capital Investments. *Professional Organisations:* ICAEW.

CASEY, Gavin Frank; Chief Operating Officer, Smith New Court plc, since 1989; Finance Operations Technology. *Career:* Harmood Banner & Co 1965-70; Coopers & Lybrand 1970-71; County NatWest 1972-89. *Biog: b.* 18 October 1946. *Nationality:* British. *Directorships:* Smith New Court plc 1989 (exec). *Other Activities:* Member, Worshipful Company of Chartered Accountants in England and Wales. *Professional Organisations:* FCA. *Clubs:* City of London. *Recreations:* Horse Racing, Shooting, Theatre.

CASEY, William; Managing Director, BDO Consulting, since 1988. *Career:* Peat Marwick 1971-80; Herman Miller UK, Financial Controller 1980-83; Coopers & Lybrand Associates, Managing Consultant 1983-86; BDO Binder Hamlyn, Partner 1986-. *Biog: b.* 1949. *Nationality:* British. *Educ:* Downside School; Brasenose College, Oxford (BA). *Professional Organisations:* FCA; MIMC. *Recreations:* Skiing, Hill Walking.

CASKIE, Donald B; Partner, W & J Burness WS, since 1986; Private Client and Banking Law. *Career:* Maclay Murray & Spens, Apprentice 1964-66; Wright Johnston & Mackenzie, Asst Solicitor 1966-71; Clydesdale Bank plc, Law Secretary 1971-85; W & J Burness, WS, Asst Solicitor 1985-86. *Biog: b.* 8 March 1941. *Nationality:* British. *m.* 1976, Katherine (née Pollard); 1 s; 1 d. *Educ:* High School of Glasgow; University of Glasgow (MA,LLB); Cornell University, NY. *Professional Organisations:* Law Society of Scotland; Associate, Institute of Bankers in Scotland; Writer to the Signet. *Publications:* Wallace & McNeil's Banking Law (9 ed) 1986. *Clubs:* Western, Glasgow Golf Club. *Recreations:* Golf, Cycling, Hillwalking, Bird Watching.

CASLING, R C; Partner, Milne Ross.

CASS, Alain; News Editor, Financial Times.

CASS, G S; Director, Baring Asset Management Ltd.

CASSAIGNE, Helene; Manager of Trade Finance Department, United Overseas Bank (Banque Unie Pour Les Pays d'Outre-Mer) Geneva.

CASSELS, Alexander; Director, Edinburgh Fund Managers plc.

CASSEY, S B; Director, Fenchurch Insurance Group Ltd.

CASSON, Jeremy; Partner, Touche Ross & Co. *Professional Organisations:* ACA.

CASTELLO, Lorenzo; UK Representative, Cassa di Risparmio di Genova e Imperia.

CASTLE, Dr Paul; Chief Executive, MTI Managers Limited, 1983; Policy, Strategy, Investment & Disinvestment Decisions. *Career:* University of Leeds, Post-Doctoral Research Fellow 1968-70; N Corah, Research Manager 1971-72; PA Consulting Services, Consultant 1972-75; Engineering Group Manager 1975-77; Deputy General Manager UK Laboratories 1977-78; Divisional Director & Unit Chief Executive of Benelux Laboratories 1978-82. *Biog: b.* 17 October 1943. *Nationality:* British. *m.* 1966, Valerie Jill (née Disbrey); 2 s. *Educ:* Royds Hall Grammar School; Leeds University, BSc, 1st Class Honours, Avery Prize PhD. *Directorships:* Highfield Industrial Holdings Ltd 1975 (non-exec); Highfield Gears Ltd 1975 (non-exec); Clayton's Lockwood Properties Ltd 1975 (non-exec); MTI Managers Ltd 1983 (exec); Prism Electronics Ltd 1984 (non-exec); Linx Printing Technologies Ltd 1986 (non-exec); Pace Communications (UK) Ltd 1987 (non-exec); Aimtest Ltd 1987 (non-exec); MTI Ventures General Partner Ltd 1988 (exec); MTI Trustees Ltd 1988 (exec); Integrated Vision Systems Ltd 1989 (non-exec); Intelligent Environments Ltd 1990 (non-exec); Intelligent Environments (UK) Ltd 1990 (non-exec); Intelligent Environments Inc 1990 (non-exec). *Professional Organisations:* CEng, MIMechE, CDipAF. *Publications:* Several Scientific & Venture Capital papers & articles. *Recreations:* Tennis, Gardening, Property Restoration, Motor Sport, Photography.

CASTLEMAN, Christopher Norman Anthony; Chief Executive, LIT Holdings plc, since 1989. *Career:* Hill Samuel & Co Limited (formerly M Samuel & Co Limited) Corporate Finance Department 1965-69; Hill Samuel Australia Limited, General Manager 1970-72; Hill Samuel & Co Limited, Corporate Finance Director 1973-75; Hill Samuel International Limited, Managing Director 1976-77; Hill Samuel Group (SA) Limited, Chief Executive 1978-80; Hill Samuel Group plc, Chief Executive 1980-87; Blue Arrow plc, Chief Executive 1987-88; Christopher Castleman & Co, Financial Adviser 1988-89; LIT Holdings plc, Chief Executive 1989. *Biog: b.* 23 June 1941. *Nationality:* British. m1 1965, Sarah Victoria (née Stockdale); m2 1980, Caroline Clare (née Westcott); m3 1990, Susan Mary (née Twycross); 1 s; 3 d. *Educ:* Harrow School; Clare College, Cambridge (BA Law 1st). *Directorships:* Asset Trust plc; Johnson Fry Asset Managers plc; Johnson Fry Development Capital Limited; Johnson Fry plc Chm; LIT Finance Limited; LIT Holdings plc; LIT Management Services Limited; LIT (Trustees) Limited; Macquarie Bank Limited (non-exec); National Investment Holdings plc Chm; National Investment Group plc. *Recreations:* Sport, Travel.

CATER, (Edward) Paul; Executive Director, Corporate Finance, Banque Paribas, since 1988; European Cross-Border Mergers & Acquisitions, Corporate Advisory. *Career:* Williams & Glyn's Bank (now The Royal Bank of Scotland), Manager, International Division Head of Credit Control 1972-77; Williams Glyn & Co, Corporate Finance; The Royal Trust Company of Canada, Head of Banking 1977-80; Banque Paribas, Head of Banking Division, London 1980-; Sous-Directeur, Paris Direction Des Engagements; Executive Director, London Corporate Finance. *Biog: b.* 15 November 1943. *Nationality:* British. *m.* 1977, Gloria Cater (née Elliott); 2 s; 2 d. *Educ:* King's College, Wimbledon; King's College, London University (BSc,AKC Postgraduate Diploma Chemical Engineering); London Business School (MSc Masters in Business Administration). *Professional Organisations:* Chartered Engineer. *Recreations:* Gardening, Reading, Tennis.

CATES, Armel; Partner, Clifford Chance, since 1976; Financial Law. *Career:* Vinters (Cambridge), Articled Clerk 1967-69; Coward Chance, Assistant Solicitor 1969-72; Clifford Turner, Assistant Solicitor 1972-76; Clifford Chance, Partner 1976-. *Biog: b.* 3 May 1943. *Nationality:* British. *m.* 1967, Susan (née Walker); 2 s; 1 d. *Educ:* Charterhouse; Southampton University (LLB Hons); College of Law. *Other Activities:* Editorial Adviser, International Financial Law Review; Trustee, Charterhouse Mission. *Professional Organisations:* Law Society; International Bar Association. *Recreations:* Golf, Photography.

CATOR, Albemarle J; Vice President, Chemical Bank.

CATOR, F; Vice-Chairman, Norwich Union Insurance Group.

CATT, A F; Managing Director, Dowa Insurance Company (UK) Limited.

CATT, Benson F; JP; Clerk, Marketors' Company.

CATTERMULL, Paul Gurney; Managing Director, Binder Hamlyn Investment Management, since 1987; Investment Management. *Career:* HM Forces (Army), Captain, The King's Regiment 1977-82; Schroders plc 1983-87; Manager, Unit Trust Portfolio Management Service 1983-85; Schroder Investment Management, Manager Smaller Companies and Private Clients 1985-87. *Biog: b.* 4 March 1955. *Nationality:* British. *Educ:* Worth School; Lancaster University (BSc Hons); Cranfield School of Management (MBA); London Business School (Pass Inv Management Programme). *Directorships:* Binder Hamlyn Investment Management 1987 (exec); BDO Binder Investment Management Limited 1988 (exec). *Recreations:* Shooting, Cricket, Tennis, Bridge, Theatre.

CATTO, The Hon Alexander Gordon; Managing Director, Lazard Brothers & Co Limited, since 1988;

Capital Markets. *Career:* Morgan Guaranty Trust Co VP 1973-85; Morgan Grenfell & Co Ltd Director 1986-88. *Biog: b.* 22 June 1952. *m.* 1981, Elizabeth (née Boyes); 2 s; 1 d. *Educ:* Westminster; Trinity College, Cambridge, BA Hons. *Directorships:* Yule Catto & Co plc 1982- (non-exec).

CATTO, Stephen Gordon; Baron Catto of Cairncatto; President, Morgan Grenfell Group plc, since 1987. *Career:* RAFVR, Fl Lt 1943-47; Morgan Grenfell & Co Limited, Director 1957-73; Chairman 1973-79; Morgan Grenfell Group plc, Chairman 1980-87. *Biog: b.* 14 January 1923. *Nationality:* British. m1 1948; 2 s; 2 d; m2 1966, Margaret (née Forrest); 1 s; 1 d. *Educ:* Eton College; Trinity College, Cambridge University. *Directorships:* Yule Catto & Co plc 1971 Chairman; Australian Mutual Provident Society (UK Branch) 1972 (non-exec) Chairman; The General Electric Company plc 1959 (non-exec); News International plc 1969 (non-exec); Pearl Group plc 1989 (non-exec) Chairman; Anglo & Overseas Investment Trust plc 1971 (non-exec); The Overseas Investment Trust plc 1960 (non-exec); Member, Advisory Council, ECGD 1959-65; Part-time Member, London Transport Board 1962-68. *Other Activities:* Chairman of Executive Committee, Westminster Abbey Trust; Chairman of Council, The Royal Air Force Benevolent Fund. *Professional Organisations:* Fellow, Chartered Institute of Bankers. *Clubs:* Oriental (London), Melbourne (Australia). *Recreations:* Music, Gardening.

CAULFEILD, J A T; Director, M & G Investment Management Ltd.

CAVE, Mrs Malvina Alice (née Cranfield); Director, Gerrard Vivian Gray; Marketing. *Career:* Roger Mortimer & Co, Clerk 1950-64; Zorn & Leigh-Hunt, Clerk 1964-74; Parrish Stockbrokers, Director 1975-90. *Biog: b.* 25 June 1944. *Nationality:* British. *m.* 1964, Brian David. *Educ:* Parsloes School, Barking. *Other Activities:* Freeman, The City of London; Chairman, Stock Exchange Christian Association. *Professional Organisations:* Member, International Stock Exchange. *Recreations:* Reading, Theatre, Walking.

CAVENDISH, Leo; Chairman, Citigate Communications Limited, since 1988. *Career:* Chalmers, Impey, Cudworth & Co, Articled Clerk 1962-64; Investors Chronicle, Financial Analyst 1964-67; Financial Press Information Services, Director 1967-74; Bryan Balls & Partners, Director 1974-76; Dewe Rogerson, Associate Director 1976-79; Good Relations City, Director 1979-85; Financial Strategy, Joint Managing Director 1985-86; Streets Financial Strategy, Chairman 1986-87; Citigate Communications Group, Joint Deputy Chairman 1988-; Citigate Communications Limited, Chairman 1988-. *Biog: b.* 19 March 1940. *Nationality:* British. *m.* 1968, Sarah (née Bucknall); 1 s; 1 d. *Educ:* Ampleforth College; Gonville & Caius College, Cambridge (BA Hons History). *Clubs:* Lansdowne. *Recreations:* Swimming, Gardening, Reading, Theatre, Arguing.

CAVILL, Brian John; Managing Director, Instinet UK Ltd, since 1990; (Electronic) Stockbrokers. *Career:* Wedd Durlacher 1962-70; Bisgood Bishop (changed to County NatWest Securities), Director, Equity Market Makers 1970-86; ANZ McCaughan Securities (UK) Ltd (formerly Capel-Cure Myers & McCaughan Dyson Capel-Cure), Managing Director, Institutional Stockbrokers 1986-90; ANZ Stock Securities (UK) Ltd (formerly ANZ Securities (UK) Ltd), Managing Director, Market Makers 1986-90; ANZ Merchant Bank Ltd, Director, Management Committee Member 1986- 90; Zealand Nominees, Managing Director (a Nominee Company) 1986-90; ANZ McCaughan Futures (UK) Ltd, Director 1988-90. *Biog: b.* 19 January 1945. *Nationality:* British. *m.* 1984, Maria Teresa (née Nunes); 2 s. *Educ:* City of London School. *Directorships:* The PINs Association (a property unitisation scheme) 1986-90 (non-exec); Instinet UK Ltd (a subsidiary of Reuters) 1990 (exec) MD; Richard Ellis FInancial Services 1987 (non-Exec). *Recreations:* Shooting, sailing.

CAWDRON, P E B; Group Strategy Development Director, Grand Metropolitan plc.

CAWDRON, Richard Arthur; Finance Director, Hill Samuel Investment Management Group Limited, since 1990. *Career:* Peat Marwick Mitchell, Articled Clerk 1963-68; Hill Samuel & Co Ltd, Investment Trust Department 1968-73; Hill Samuel Investment Management Limited, Pension Fund Department 1973-85; Company Secretary 1985-87; Finance Director 1987-. *Biog: b.* 19 January 1945. *Nationality:* British. *m.* 1973, Lesley (née Laver); 2 d. *Educ:* Merchant Taylors'. *Directorships:* Hill Samuel Investment Management Group Limited 1990 (exec); Hill Samuel Investment Management Limited 1987 (exec); Hill Samuel Property Services Limited 1990 (non-exec). *Professional Organisations:* FCA. *Clubs:* Denham Golf Club. *Recreations:* Golf, Bridge.

CAZALAA, Patrick Raymond; Executive Director, CCF (UK) Ltd, since 1989; International Mergers & Acquisitions. *Career:* Crédit du Nord (Paris), Département Financier 1979-86; CCF Paris, Corporate Finance Dept 1984-87; CCF (London), International Corporate Finance 1988-. *Biog: b.* 28 December 1954. *Nationality:* French. *m.* 1978, Chantal Precloux; 2 s; 1 d. *Educ:* Institut d'Etudes Politiques, Paris (Master in Law). *Directorships:* CCF (UK) Ltd 1989 (exec).

CAZALET, Charles Julian; Partner, Corporate Finance, Cazenove & Co, since 1989; Syndication Department. *Career:* Whinney Murray 1969-73; Cazenove & Co 1973-; Ptnr 1978-. *Biog: b.* 29 November 1947. *Nationality:* British. *m.* 1986, Jenny (née Little); 1 s;

1 d. *Educ:* Uppingham School; Magdalene College, Cambridge (MA). *Professional Organisations:* FCA. *Clubs:* City University Club.

CAZALET, Sir Peter; Non-Executive Director, P & O Steam Navigation Company.

CAZALY, E; Director, S G Warburg & Co Ltd.

CAZENOVE, B M de L; Partner, Cazenove & Co, since 1982; Pension Funds. *Career:* Commisioned Coldstream Guards 1967-73; Cazenove & Co 1973-. *Biog: b.* 14 June 1947. *Nationality:* British. *m.* 1971, Caroline (née Moore); 2 s; 1 d. *Educ:* Radley College; RMA Sandhurst.

CAZENOVE, Henry de Lerisson; Partner, Cazenove & Co, since 1972. *Career:* Lt Northamptonshire Yeomanry TA 1963-69; Cazenove & Co 1963; Member, Stock Exchange 1967. *Biog: b.* 13 January 1943. *Nationality:* British. *Educ:* Eton. *Other Activities:* Freeman, City of London, 1980; Governor & Trustee, St Andrews Hospital, Northampton. *Publications:* A Short History of the Northamptonshire Yeomanry. *Clubs:* Whites, Pratts, City of London, MCC. *Recreations:* Shooting, Travel, Gardening.

CAZENOVE, R P de L; Director, Robert Fleming Insurance Brokers Limited.

CEDRASCHI, T; Non-Executive Director, S G Warburg Group plc.

CELIN, E; Director, IMI Capital Markets (UK).

CERVENKA, Geoffrey Roy; Director, Midland Montagu Asset Management, since 1989; UK Pension Fund Management, UK Equities. *Career:* Vickers Da Costa & Co, Investment Analyst 1964-73; Hoblyn & Co Investment, Analyst 1973-74; Midland Montagu, Investment Analyst to Portfolio Mgr 1974-88. *Biog: b.* 15 January 1945. *Nationality:* British. *m.* 1971, Jill Elizabeth (née Boggis); 2 s. *Educ:* Harrow County Grammar for Boys. *Directorships:* Midland Montagu Asset Management 1989 (exec). *Professional Organisations:* AMSIA. *Recreations:* Music, Cricket, Golf.

CHADBURN, C; Partner, Moores Rowland.

CHADWICK, C N P; Commercial Director, Leeds Permanent Building Society.

CHADWICK, Peter; Partner, Hepworth & Chadwick.

CHADWICK, Peter; Production Director, Kogan Page Limited.

CHAGGAR, Rabinder Singh; Partner, Forsyte Kerman, since 1990. *Career:* Muscatt Walker & Co, Articled

Clerk 1982-85; Phillip Hodges & Co, Asst Solicitor 1985-87; Forsyte Kerman, Asst Solicitor 1987-90. *Biog:* b. 3 June 1960. *Nationality:* British. *m.* 1985, Balvinder (née Chadha). *Educ:* Elthorne High School, Ealing; The University College of Wales, Aberystwyth (LLB Hons). *Professional Organisations:* Law Society. *Recreations:* Theatre, Reading, Sport.

CHALK, Clive Andrew; Executive Director, Samuel Montagu & Co Limited, since 1982; Corporate Finance. *Career:* Coopers & Lybrand 1968-73; Williams & Glyn's Bank 1973-77; Samuel Montagu 1977-. *Biog:* b. 2 November 1946. *Nationality:* British. *m.* 1985, Iris Marita (née Hjelt); 2 s; 2 d. *Educ:* St Dunstan's College; Exeter University (LLB); Harvard Business School (AMP). *Directorships:* Samuel Montagu & Co Limited 1982 (exec). *Professional Organisations:* FCA. *Clubs:* Royal Thames Yacht Club, Little Ship Club, Harvard Business School Club of London. *Recreations:* Sailing, Skiing, Golf, Bridge, Opera.

CHALK, Gilbert J; Managing Director, Hambro European Ventures Limited, since 1987; Management Buy-Outs and Development Capital. *Career:* Brandts Limited, Executive, Corporate Finance Dept 1973-75; Hill Samuel & Co Limited, Executive, Corporate Finance Dept 1975-80; Hambros Bank Limited 1980-; Director, Corporate Finance Dept 1984; Hambro European Ventures Limited, Managing Director 1987. *Biog:* b. 21 September 1947. *Nationality:* British. *m.* 1975, Gillian (née Blois); 3 s; 2 d. *Educ:* Lancing College; Southampton University (BSc); Lancaster University (MA); Columbia University, New York (MBA). *Directorships:* Hambros Bank Limited 1984 (exec); Hambros European Ventures Ltd 1987 (exec); Hambros Group Investment Ltd 1989 (exec); Centaur Communications Limited 1982 (non-exec); Sieima Corporation Limited 1984 (non-exec); Courtwell Group plc 1986 (non-exec). *Other Activities:* Member, Goldsmiths Company. *Clubs:* Queens Club, Berkshire Golf Club.

CHALLEN, David; Head of Investment Banking Division, J Henry Schroder Wagg & Co Limited. *Biog:* b. 11 March 1943. *m.* Elizabeth; 1 s; 1 d.

CHALLIS, G H; Clerk, Chartered Secretaries' and Administrators' Company.

CHALMERS, Harvey Paxton; Partner, Simmons & Simmons, since 1986; Banking, International Finance and Capital Markets. *Career:* Shepherd & Wedderburn WS, Law Apprentice 1972-74; Linklaters & Paines, Asst Solicitor 1974-85. *Biog:* b. 18 February 1947. *Nationality:* British. *Educ:* Pollokshields School/Bellahouston Academy, Glasgow; University of Glasgow (LLB Hons); Magdalene College, Cambridge (PhD). *Professional Organisations:* The Law Society; Law Society of Scotland.

CHALMERS, Norman; Chairman, City & Commercial Communications plc.

CHAMBERLAIN, Geoffrey Howard; Chief Operating Officer, L Messel/Shearson Lehman Hutton International.

CHAMBERLAIN, Nigel; Joint Managing Director, Nicholson Chamberlain Colls Limited.

CHAMBERLAYNE, Michael Thomas; Managing Director, Baring Brothers Private Asset Management Limited, since 1989. *Biog:* b. 14 August 1943. *Nationality:* British. *Educ:* Wellington. *Directorships:* Baring Asset Management Limited 1986 (exec); Banque Baring Brothers (Suisse) SA 1986 (non-exec); Baring Brothers (Guernsey) Limited 1989 (non-exec); Baring Brothers Private Asset Management Limited 1989 (exec); Baring Brothers Trust Co Limited 1989 (exec); Baring Private Investment Management Limited 1989 (exec); Baring Unit Trust Management Service Limited 1987 (non-exec); Stratton Investment Trust plc 1989 (exec). *Professional Organisations:* FCA. *Clubs:* Royal Thames Yacht Club, The City of London Club.

CHAMBERLEN, Nicholas Hugh; Chairman, Clive Discount Company Limited, since 1977. *Career:* NCR (London) 1962-67; Clive Discount Company Limited Dir 1967. *Biog:* b. 18 April 1939. *Nationality:* British. *m.* 1962, Jane Mary (née Lindo); 3 s; 1 d. *Educ:* Sherborne School; Lincoln College, Oxford (BA Hons). *Directorships:* Clive Discount Holdings International Limited (exec) Chm; Page & Gwyther Holdings Limited (exec) Chm; Page & Gwyther Investments Limited (exec) Chm; Prudential-Bache Capital Funding (Equities) Limited (exec); Prudential-Bache International (UK) Limited (exec); London Global Funding Limited (exec); Clive Investments Limited (exec) Chm; Clive Investments (Cambridge) Limited (exec) Chm; Clivco Nominees Limited (exec) Chm; Clivwell Securities Limited (exec) Chm; Page & Gwyther Limited (exec) Chm; P-B Capital Partners (UK) Limited (exec); P-B Interfunding (UK) Limited (exec); Prudential-Bache Capital Funding (Gilts) Limited (exec) Chm; Mithras Investment Trust plc (exec). *Other Activities:* Chartered Society of Queen Square, British Ski Club for the Disabled. *Clubs:* Turf, Portland. *Recreations:* Shooting, Golf, Cricket.

CHAMBERS, Antony; Director, Robert Fleming & Co Limited, since 1984; Commercial Banking. *Career:* Military Service, Grenadier Guards, Served Cyprus, Muscat, Trucial States and Northern Ireland 1966-70; Hill Samuel, Assistant Investment Manager 1970-71; First Chicago, N Sea Project Finance 1972-74; Business Dept, UK Branch Network 1975-77; Group Head, Banking and Marketing to UK 1978-82; Head, Strategic Planning, Europe 1983-84. *Biog:* b. 8 December 1943. *Nationality:* British. *m.* 1965, Rosemary Isabel (née Constable Maxwell); 3 s; 2 d. *Educ:* Ampleforth

College; St Catherine's College, Oxford (MA); Manchester Business School (MBA). *Directorships:* Maxwell Cress Co Ltd 1974; Robert Fleming & Co Limited 1984; Brompton Developments Ltd 1988; Crosby Finance Ltd 1988; Crosby Leasing Ltd 1988; Fledgeling Finance Ltd 1988; Robert Fleming Finance Ltd 1988; Robert Fleming Leasing Ltd 1988; Robert Fleming (Stock Lending) Ltd 1990. *Other Activities:* Executive Committee and Control Board, Army Benevolent Fund, 1979 and Officers Association 1985; Trustee, Help The Aged, 1987. *Recreations:* Sailing.

CHAMBERS, J R; Clerk, Dyers' Company.

CHAMBERS, Robert; Director (Market-Making), Hoare Govett International Securities.

CHAMBERS, Victor; Deputy Chairman, Ulster Bank Ltd.

CHAMBERS, Vincent James; Partner, R Watson & Sons.

CHAMPION, J A; Director, Allied Trust Bank Limited.

CHAMPNESS, J A; Director, Lowndes Lambert Group.

CHANCELLOR, Antony Charles Beresford; Director, Thornton Management Ltd, since 1985; Managing Director, Thornton Unit Managers Ltd, since 1986. *Career:* Friends Provident, Assistant Inv Manager 1957-62; Henry Ansbacher & Co, Inv Director 1962-68; Dawnay Day Co Ltd, Inv Director 1968-80; Tring Hall, Director 1980-81; University Medical & General, Assoc 1981-83; IFICO Investment Services, Director 1983-85. *Biog: b.* 26 March 1929. *Nationality:* British. *m.* 1957, Honor Rosemary (née Boucher); 3 s. *Educ:* Stowe. *Directorships:* Thornton Pan-European Investment Trust plc 1987 (non-exec); Thornton Management Ltd 1985 (exec); Thornton Investment Management Ltd 1985 (exec); Thornton Unit Managers Ltd 1986 (exec); Thornton International Opportunities Fund 1986 (non-exec). *Other Activities:* Member of Council of Counsel & Care for the Elderly; Member, Finance Committee of RELATE, National Marriage Guidance Council. *Professional Organisations:* Associate Member, Society of Investment Analysts. *Clubs:* Institute of Directors.

CHANDLER, Edward James; Director, S G Warburg Securities, since 1986; International Financing. *Career:* Chemical Bank Intl 1975-81; Asst Dir 1980-81. *Biog: b.* 11 January 1954. *Nationality:* British. *m.* 1981, Melanie; 1 s; 1 d. *Educ:* Epsom College; Sidney Sussex, Cambridge (MA Hons). *Directorships:* Potter Warburg Ltd (Melbourne) 1987 (non-exec); Buttle Wilson Ltd (Auckland) 1988 (non-exec). *Recreations:* Tennis, Riding, Fishing.

CHANDLER, P R; Chairman, Metheuen (Lloyds Underwriting Agents) Limited.

CHANDOS, Thomas Orlando Lyttelton; 3rd Viscount of Aldershot; Director, Kleinwort Benson Ltd, since 1985; Corporate Finance. *Career:* Kleinwort Benson Ltd, Asst Mgr 1978-80; Mgr 1980-82; Asst Dir 1982-85; Dir 1985-; Kleinwort Benson Government Securities, Dir 1988-89. *Biog: b.* 12 February 1953. *Nationality:* British. *m.* 1985, Arabella (née Bailey); 2 s. *Educ:* Eton College; Worcester College, Oxford (BA). *Directorships:* Kleinwort Benson Government Securities Inc 1988-89; Kleinwort Benson Cross Financing Inc 1985-; International Swap Dealers Assoc 1988-89. *Other Activities:* SDP Spokesman in the House of Lords on Economic & Industrial Subjects; Chairman, Social Market Foundation Ltd; Past Member, IBA General Advisory Council.

CHANG, R W C; General Manager, Malayan Banking Berhad.

CHANG, Stephen; Senior Partner, Morison Stoneham Chartered Accountants.

CHANNON, Professor Derek French; Professor of Marketing & Strategic Management, The Management School, since 1990. *Career:* Shell Intl Chemical Co, Marketing Mgr 1967-68; Manchester Business School, Lecturer 1968-70; Snr Research Fellow 1971-76; Evode Holdings plc, Joint Managing Director 1976-77; Manchester Business School, Professor 1977-89. *Biog: b.* 4 March 1939. *Nationality:* British. 1 s; 1 d. *Educ:* University College, London (BSc Hons); Manchester Business School (MBA); Harvard Business School (DBA). *Directorships:* Manchester Business School; International Banking Centre 1986-87 (exec); Bray Technologies plc 1983 (non-exec); Royal Bank of Scotland plc 1988 (non-exec). *Professional Organisations:* FInstM; Strategic Management Society 1981-, President 1986-88, Executive Director 1981-; Strategic Planning Society. *Publications:* Co-Author, Franchising, 1981; Co-Author, Retail Electronic Banking and Point of Sale, 1982; Bank Strategic Management and Marketing, 1986; Global Banking Strategy, 1988. *Recreations:* Golf, Tennis.

CHANTREY, Philip Simon; Director, County NatWest Wood MacKenzie & Co Ltd, since 1986; Corporate Stockbroking. *Career:* Peat Marwick Mitchell & Co, Accountant 1965-70; J Henry Schroder Wagg & Co Ltd, Exec 1970-73; Williams Glyn & Co, Asst Dir 1973-79; National Enterprise Board (Secondment), Exec 1977-79; Barclays Merchant Bank Ltd, Asst Dir 1979-81; Venture Advisers, Dir 1981-84; Wood MacKenzie & Co Ltd, Asst Dir 1985-86. *Biog: b.* 24 August 1947. *Nationality:* British. *m.* 1971, Susanna (née Reeves); 2 s; 1 d. *Educ:* Winchester College. *Professional Organisations:* FCA; MBIM. *Clubs:* Woking Golf Club. *Recreations:* Golf, Tennis.

CHANTRY, Jeremy D; Director, Kleinwort Benson Securities Limited, since 1989; Chemicals Research. *Career:* Kleinwort Benson Securities, Chemicals Analyst 1984-; Quilter Goodison, Chemicals Analyst 1984; British Sulphur Corp, Research Executive 1980-84. *Biog: b.* 12 April 1956. *Educ:* St John's College, Oxford (MA). *Recreations:* Skiing, Squash.

CHAPLIN, Keith Arthur; Divisional Managing Director, Bain Clarkson Limited, since 1987; Energy Division. *Biog: b.* 23rd July 1936. *Nationality:* British. *m.* 1961, Patricia (née Wicks); 2 d. *Educ:* Bloxham School. *Professional Organisations:* Fellow, Institute of Petroleum. *Clubs:* RAC, Blackwater Sailing. *Recreations:* Sailing, Walking, Golf.

CHAPMAN, A L; Partner, Freshfields.

CHAPMAN, (Alfred) Michael; Chairman, Knight Chapman Limited, since 1983; Executive Search and Recruitment. *Career:* Colgate Palmolive Limited, International Marketing Manager 1954-58; Unilever plc, Several Senior UK & International Marketing Roles 1958-65; Bostik Limited/Unimark, Marketing Controller 1966-68; Talent Brokers Limited, Director & Recruitment Consultant 1969-78; Management Appointments Limited, Director 1979-82. *Biog: b.* 24 August 1930. *Nationality:* British. *m.* 1954, Joan Margaret (née Armour); 2 s. *Educ:* Leighton Park School, Reading; Emmanuel College, Cambridge (BA, MA, Economics & Law). *Directorships:* Chapman Fraser & Co Ltd (Textile Yarn Spinners & Throwsters) 1971 (non-exec); Knight Chapman Psychological Ltd (Psychological Assessment Services) 1988 (non-exec). *Other Activities:* Master Elect/Upper Warden, Worshipful Company of Framework Knitters; Court Member, City University. *Clubs:* Lansdowne Club. *Recreations:* Trout Fishing, Music.

CHAPMAN, Antony Morris; Legal Adviser and Company Secretary, Meghraj Bank Ltd, since 1988; Legal, Secretarial, Compliance. *Career:* Linklaters & Paines, Assistant Solicitor 1963-66; Bovril Ltd, Legal Adviser/Company Secretary 1966-72; Dundee Perth & London Ltd, Legal Adviser/Company Secretary 1972-74; Monotype Corporation, Group Legal Manager 1974-76; Concord Leasing Ltd, Legal Director 1977-85. *Biog: b.* 17 January 1936. *Nationality:* British. *m.* 1977, Carol (née Worsfold); 2 d. *Educ:* Repton School; Emmanuel College, Cambridge (MA,LLB). *Directorships:* Highland Marine Ltd 1986 (non-exec); Rationalist Press Association Ltd 1968 (non-exec). *Other Activities:* Member, Charity Law Reform Committee. *Professional Organisations:* Law Society. *Recreations:* Squash, Walking, Growing Vines.

CHAPMAN, Christopher Aidan; Managing Director, Seccombe Marshall & Campion plc, since 1982; Trading of Short Term Sterling Money Market Instru-

ments. *Career:* Messrs Curwen Carter & Evans (Solicitors), Articled Clerk 1964-67; Seccombe Marshall & Campion, Asst Mgr 1967-77; Dir 1977-82; Institute of Bankers, City of London Centre, Financial Studies Group Chm 1974-76; International Banking Summers School 1984; Citicorp Investment Bank VP 1985-89. *Biog: b.* 6 February 1945. *Nationality:* British. *m.* 1974, Vanessa (née Scotland); 3 d. *Educ:* Cray Valley High School. *Directorships:* Seccombe Marshall & Campion Agency Brokers Ltd 1989. *Other Activities:* Visiting Lecturer, City University Business School; Council Member, Royal Surgical Aid Society; Hon Treasurer, Westminster Ctee for the Protection of Children. *Professional Organisations:* Institute of Bankers; FCIB (1988). *Recreations:* Music, Politics, Gardening, Tennis.

CHAPMAN, Sir David Robert Macgowan; Bt; Director, Wise Speke Limited, since 1987. *Career:* Wise Speke & Co 1966-; Partner 1971-. *Biog: b.* 16 November 1941. *Nationality:* British. *m.* 1965, Maria Elizabeth (née de Gosztonyi); 1 s; 1 d. *Educ:* Marlborough College; Université de Grenoble; McGill University, Canada (BCom). *Directorships:* North of England Building Society 1974 (non-exec); Breathe North Ltd 1987 (non-exec); British Lung Foundation Ltd 1989 (non-exec); Council of the International Stock Exchange 1979-88; James Hogg & Sons (North Shields) Ltd 1974-88; John W Pratt Ltd 1970-86. *Other Activities:* Chairman, Northern Unit of the International Stock Exchange; Vice-Chairman, Regional Committee of the ISE. *Clubs:* Northern Counties Club, Lansdowne. *Recreations:* Tennis, Reading, Skiing, Theatre.

CHAPMAN, Derek James; Partner in Charge of Taxation, Touche Ross & Co, since 1984. *Career:* Touche Ross 1968-; Admitted to Partnership in 1972. *Biog: b.* 1 October 1940; 2 s. *Educ:* King Edward IV School, Southampton. *Professional Organisations:* FCA, ATII. *Recreations:* Golf.

CHAPMAN, N; Director, Byas Mosley & Co Ltd.

CHAPMAN, Norman; Partner (Litigation), Frere Cholmeley.

CHAPMAN, Peter Edward; Director, Robert Bruce Fitzmaurice Limited, since 1988; Finance. *Career:* Benfield Lovick & Rees & Co Limited, Accountant 1976-88; Benfield Lovick & Rees (Management Services) Limited, Director 1985-88. *Biog: b.* 4 December 1955. *Nationality:* British. *m.* 1979; 2 d. *Directorships:* Fitzmaurice McCall Limited 1988 (exec); Green & Place Limited 1988 (exec); HFM Limited 1988 (exec); Fitzmaurice Byward 1989 (exec); Fitzmaurice Marine 1990 (exec). *Professional Organisations:* FCCA. *Recreations:* Squash.

CHAPMAN, Richard John; Partner, Bacon & Woodrow, since 1978; Pensions Consultancy. *Biog: b.*

28 June 1950. *Nationality:* British. *m.* 1973, Robin (née Wooding); 1 s; 1 d. *Educ:* The Leys School, Cambridge; Wadham College, Oxford (MA). *Professional Organisations:* FIA.

CHAPMAN, Robert; Partner, Hepworth & Chadwick. *Biog: b.* 14 July 1949. *Nationality:* English. *m.* 1976, Sharon; 1 s. *Educ:* Sheffield University (LLB).

CHAPMAN, Roy John; Managing Partner - UK, Arthur Andersen, since 1989; Management. *Career:* Arthur Andersen 1958-; Partner 1970-; Managing Partner - London Office 1984-; Managing Partner -UK 1989-. *Biog: b.* 30 November 1936. *Nationality:* British. *m.* 1961, Janet (née Taylor); 2 s; 1 d. *Educ:* Kettering GS; St Catharine's College, Cambridge (MA). *Other Activities:* Member of the Governing Body of SOAS (University of London). *Professional Organisations:* FCA, FIMC, CBIM, FBPICS. *Clubs:* United Oxford & Cambridge University, Hawks, MCC. *Recreations:* Cricket, Walking, Opera, Literature, Idling.

CHAPPATTE, Philippe Paul; Partner, Slaughter and May, since 1989; UK & EEC Competition Law, Computer Law & General Commercial Work. *Biog: b.* 6 October 1956. *Nationality:* Swiss. *m.* 1985, Sarah Jane (née Lang); 1 s. *Educ:* Bryanston School, Dorset; Oxford University (BA); Université Libre de Bruxelles (Lic Spec en Dr Eur).

CHAPPELL, (Edwin) Philip; CBE; Adviser, Association of Investment Trust Companies, since 1986; Publicity, Marketing, Strategy. *Career:* Morgan Grenfell & Co Ltd Various 1954-64; Director 1964-85; Vice Chm 1976-85; National Ports Council Chm 1971-77; British Broadcasting Corporation Governor 1976-81; Royal Society of Arts Treasurer 1981-86; City University Treasurer 1987-. *Biog: b.* 12 June 1929. *Nationality:* British. *m.* 1962, Julia Clavering (née House); 1 s; 3 d. *Educ:* Marlborough College; Christ Church, Oxford (MA). *Directorships:* Fisons plc 1969 (non-exec); GKN plc 1974-89 (non-exec); Bank of New Zealand (London Board) 1967-89 (non-exec); British Rail Property Board 1987 (non-exec); First Australian Funds 1986 (non-exec); Interallianz (London) Ltd 1988 (non-exec); Forestry Investment Management Ltd 1987 (non-exec); Isis Innovation Ltd 1988 (non-exec); River & Mercantile Extra Income Trust plc 1989 (non-exec); Maxilink Ltd 1987 (non-exec). *Other Activities:* Treasurer, Georgian Group; Member, Barbican Centre Ctee; Council Member, ABSA; Director, City Arts Trust; Finance Ctee, International Chamber of Commerce. *Professional Organisations:* CBIM; FCIB; FCIT. *Publications:* Personal and Portable Pensions, 1983; Personal Investment Pools, 1985; Pensions and Privilege, 1988. *Clubs:* Athenaeum, Garrick. *Recreations:* Music, Sailing.

CHAPPELL, Paul; Vice President & FX Trading and Sales, Bank of America.

CHAPPLE, Alan; Group Finance Director, Beazer plc.

CHAPPLE, Brian Bedford; Deputy Chairman & Group Finance Director, Minet Holdings plc, since 1977; Corporate Finance. *Career:* Josolyne Layton Bennett & Co Ptnr 1968-77. *Biog: b.* 6 February 1939. *m.* 1961, Wendy Ann (née Cole); 1 d. *Educ:* St Clement Danes Grammar School. *Professional Organisations:* FCA, FCT.

CHARITY, D E; Partner, Holman Fenwick & Willan, since 1971; Maritime Arbitration & Litigation. *Career:* Holman Fenwick & Willan, Articled 1964-66; Assistant Solicitor 1966-71; Partner 1971-. *Biog: b.* 6 April 1941. *Nationality:* British. 3 s; 1 d. *Educ:* Kingswood School, Bath; London School of Economics (LLB). *Directorships:* Marlyn Lodge Management Co Ltd 1984 (non-exec); Gannel Shipping Ltd 1975 (non-exec). *Professional Organisations:* Qualified Solicitor and Member of The Law Society. *Clubs:* Alpine. *Recreations:* Mountaineering, Chess, Music, Opera.

CHARKHAM, Jonathan Philip; Adviser to Governors, Bank of England, since 1985; Industrial Finance. *Career:* Morris Charkham 1952-63; Rest Assured 1963-68; Civil Service Dept Principal Management Services, Pay 1969-73; Asst Sec Personnel Management 1973-75; Dir & Under Sec Public Appointments 1975-82; Bank of England, Dir, PRO NED 1982-85; Chief Adviser 1985-88; Adviser to the Governors 1988-. *Biog: b.* 17 October 1930. *Nationality:* British. *m.* 1954, Moira Elizabeth Frances (née Salmon); 2 s; 1 d. *Educ:* St Paul's School; Jesus College, Cambridge (MA). *Other Activities:* Past Master, Worshipful Company of Upholders; Knightsbridge Association; The David Hume Institute Steering Committee of the Corporate Takeovers Inquiry; The Advisory Board, Columbia University of New York Center for Law & Economic Studies, Institutional Investor Project. *Professional Organisations:* Barrister; CBIM. *Publications:* Effective Boards, 1984; Numerous Articles in Corporate Governance, 1988-90. *Clubs:* Athenaeum, City Livery, Roehampton, MCC. *Recreations:* Music, Opera, Golf, Wine, Antique Furniture.

CHARLES, Edward; Vice President, Manufacturers Hanover Trust Company.

CHARLES-JONES, I; Partner, Waltons & Morse.

CHARLTON, Louise Elizabeth; Director, Brunswick Public Relations Ltd, since 1987; Financial PR. *Career:* Broad Street Associates 1984-87. *Biog: b.* 25 May 1960. *Nationality:* British. *m.* 1985, Andrew Durant.

CHARLTON, Philip; OBE; Deputy Chairman, TSB Group plc, since 1985. *Career:* Chester Savings Bank 1947; Chester, Wrexham & North Wales TSB, Gen Mgr 1966-75; TSB Wales & Border Counties, Gen Mgr

1975-81; TSB Group Central, Executive Dep Chief Gen Mgr 1981-82; Chief Gen Mgr 1982-85; TSB Group plc, Group MD 1985-86; Group Chief Executive 1986-90. *Biog: b.* 31 July 1930. *Nationality:* British. *m.* 1953, Jessie (née Boulton); 1 s; 1 d. *Educ:* Chester City Grammar School. *Directorships:* TSB Channel Islands Ltd 1986 (non-exec). *Other Activities:* FRSA; Vice Pres, International Savings Bank Institute, Geneva (Board of Administration); European Savings Banks Group (Board of Administration); Pres, Chartered Institute of Bankers 1990. *Professional Organisations:* FCIB; CBIM. *Clubs:* Chester City, RAC. *Recreations:* Music, Swimming, Football Spectator.

CHARLTON, Richard Wingate Edward; Chief Executive, Banque Internationale á Luxembourg SA, since 1988. *Career:* Frere Cholmeley & Co, Solicitors 1968-74; Swales & Co, Solicitors 1974-76; Hambros Bank, Manager 1977-81; Banque Paribas, Executive Director 1981-88. *Biog: b.* 3 May 1948. *Nationality:* British. *m.* 1979, Claudine (née Maringe); 1 s; 2 d. *Educ:* Eton; University of Neuchatel. *Directorships:* Oppidan Films Ltd 1990 (exec); Henry Ansbacher Holdings plc 1988 (exec) Alternate Director; Belgo-Luxembourg Chamber of Commerce in Great Britain 1989 (exec); Banque Paribas Development Services Ltd (exec); Paribas Export Finance Ltd; Paribas Finance Ltd (exec). *Other Activities:* Liveryman, Merchant Taylors' Livery Company; Freeman, City of London. *Professional Organisations:* Solicitor of the Supreme Court. *Clubs:* Whites, Turf Club. *Recreations:* Theatre, Opera, Tennis, Football, Travel.

CHARLWOOD, Anthony Arthur; Director, Argosy Asset Management plc, since 1988; US Equities, Emerging Markets. *Career:* Sun Life Assurance Society, Fund Manager, US Equities 1973-85; Merchant Navy Officers Pension Fund, Portfolio Manager, US Equities 1986-87; Seconded to Argosy Asset Management 1987-. *Biog: b.* 1 December 1950. *Nationality:* British. *m.* 1976, Felicity (née Bishop); 2 s; 1 d. *Educ:* Worthing High School for Boys; Gonville & Caius College, Cambridge (MA). *Directorships:* New Frontiers Development Trust plc 1987 (non-exec); Thai-Euro Fund Ltd 1988 (non-exec); Swire Aviation Ltd 1989 (non-exec). *Professional Organisations:* Fellow, Institute of Chartered Secretaries & Administrators. *Recreations:* Long Distance Running.

CHARLWOOD, Charles Jolyon; Group Finance Director, Aitken Hume International plc, since 1989; Group Finance. *Career:* City Merchants Bank Ltd, Dir of Fin & Administration 1976-85. *Biog: b.* 15 March 1947. *Nationality:* British. *m.* 1973, Jacqueline (née Botterill); 1 s. *Educ:* Thomas Bennett. *Professional Organisations:* FCA. *Clubs:* Lambs Squash Club. *Recreations:* Hill Walking, Squash, Tennis.

CHARNLEY, William Francis; Partner, Booth & Co, since 1990; Corporate Finance. *Career:* Slater Heelis (Solicitors), Articled Clerk 1985-87; Booth & Co, Assistant Solicitor 1987-89; Associate 1989-90. *Biog: b.* 21 August 1960. *Nationality:* British. *m.* 1983, Sylvia (née Rigby). *Educ:* Rivington & Blackrod Grammar School; Bolton Institute of Higher Education (HND Business Studies Distinction); Lancaster University (LLB Hons). *Directorships:* Barleycorn Investments Limited 1990 (non-exec). *Professional Organisations:* Solicitor; Member, Law Society; ACIS. *Recreations:* Shooting, Walking, British Impressionist Paintings.

CHARTERS, D P; Non-Executive Director, Aetna International (UK) Ltd.

CHASE, C W P; Director, Ropner Insurance Services Limited.

CHASSELS, James David Simpson; Director, 3i Corporate Finance Ltd, since 1985; Corporate Finance Advisory Activities in Scotland. *Career:* French and Cowan Chartered Accountants, Glasgow, Apprentice 1965-70; Arthur Young, Edinburgh, Audit Manager 1970-74; ICFC, Glasgow, Investment Executive 1974-78; Edinburgh, Investment Executive 1978-81; ICFC Corporate Finance, Glasgow (Now 3i Corporate Finance Ltd), Director Responsible for Scotland 1981-. *Biog: b.* 2 April 1947. *Nationality:* British. *m.* 1976, Angela (née Bulloch); 2 s; 1 d. *Educ:* Rannoch School, Perthshire. *Directorships:* Rannoch School 1972 (non-exec). *Other Activities:* Past Deacon, Incorporation of Barbers, Trades House of Glasgow. *Professional Organisations:* Member, Institute of Chartered Accountants of Scotland. *Clubs:* Royal Scottish Automobile Club, Clyde Cruising Club. *Recreations:* Sailing, Skiing, Motorcycling.

CHATAWAY, Michael Denys; Chairman, C Czarnikow Ltd, since 1985. *Biog: b.* 23 July 1934. *m.* 1970, Caroline Mary (née Colville); 1 s; 1 d. *Educ:* Sherborne School; Magdalen College, Oxford (BA).

CHATER, S P; Partner, Allen & Overy, since 1989. *Career:* Allen & Overy 1979-. *Biog: b.* 2 March 1956. *Nationality:* British. *m.* 1988, Susan (née Stuart). *Educ:* Hartlepool Grammar School; Christchurch, Oxford (MA). *Other Activities:* Freeman, City of London Solicitors' Company. *Professional Organisations:* Member, The Law Society. *Recreations:* London Philharmonic Choir.

CHATTERTON, G; Managing Director, Marlar International Limited, since 1989; Consultant – Information Technology/Senior Managerial Positions. *Career:* AGB Executive Search, Managing Director 1982-89; Redland Ltd, Group Management Services Controller 1975-82; Chrysler UK/International, Systems Manager 1972-75; Rootes Ltd, Manager, Organisation Planning/Consultant 1968-72; Lucas (Sales & Service) Ltd, Computer Development Manager 1960-68; Royal Artillery, Commissioned National Service, Malta, 2nd

Lt Troop Officer 1957-59. *Biog: b.* 28 February 1936. *Nationality:* British. *m.* 1961, Irene; 2 d. *Educ:* London University (BA Hons English). *Directorships:* Marlar International Limited 1989 (exec). *Professional Organisations:* MIDPM. *Clubs:* Army & Navy. *Recreations:* Music, Theatre, Reading, Photography, Wine, Keeping Fit.

CHEADLE, (Eric) Neville; Senior Partner, Price Waterhouse, since 1988; Europe, Management Consultancy Services. *Career:* Standard Telephones & Cables Ltd, Graduate Apprentice 1959-64; Elliot Automation Ltd, Sales & Admin Mgr 1965-68; Price Waterhouse 1968; Manager 1973; Partner 1977; London Mgmnt Consultancy Services, Partner 1981-88. *Biog: b.* 10 May 1940. *Nationality:* British. *m.* 1989, Jean Patricia; 3 s. *Educ:* Mill Hill School; London Polytechnic (Dip Commercial Admin with Engineering); Stanford Graduate School of Business (NATO Research Fellow). *Professional Organisations:* FIMC. *Publications:* Articles in Journals. *Recreations:* Sailing, Cricket, Amateur Radio.

CHEATLEY, Derek; Director, Ulster Development Capital Limited.

CHECKLEY, Jonathan Richard Parnell; Partner, Clay & Partners, since 1979; Compliance, Financial Services Act 1986. *Career:* Guardian Royal Exchange, Actuarial Trainee 1973-75; Duncan C Fraser & Co, Actuarial Trainee 1975-77. *Biog: b.* 4 December 1951. *Nationality:* British. *m.* 1978, Amanda (née Rubens); 2 s; 1 d. *Educ:* Warwick School; Oxford University (Mathematics). *Directorships:* Clay Charles Barker Ltd (now Clay Communications Ltd) 1987 (non-exec). *Other Activities:* Accounting Ctee, Assoc of Consulting Actuaries. *Professional Organisations:* Fellow of the Institute of Actuaries. *Recreations:* Cycling (to work), Gardening, Reading.

CHEDGY, Paul; Partner, Allen & Overy, since 1974; Capital Markets. *Biog: b.* 18 February 1943. *m.* 1970, Patricia Anne (née Roche); 2 s; 3 d. *Educ:* Sexey's School, Bruton, Somerset; Jesus College, Oxford (BA). *Other Activities:* The City of London Solicitors' Company. *Professional Organisations:* The Law Society. *Recreations:* Tennis, West Country Pursuits, Wine (Member of the Commanderie de Bordeaux, Bristol).

CHEESLEY, R G; Partner, Touche Ross & Co.

CHEESMAN, C A; Chairman, Gravett & Tilling (Underwriting Agencies) Ltd.

CHEESMAN, David; Investment Director, 3i plc, since 1990; High-Technology Investments. *Career:* United Kingdom Atomic Energy Authority, Engineer 1958-66; Honeywell (UK) Ltd, Development Manager 1966-73; Computer Systems Engineering Ltd, Chief Engineer 1973-74; Univac UK Ltd, Director, Technical Operations 1974-79; Prime Computer (R & D) Ltd,

Vice President 1979-87; Dowty Information Systems Ltd, Managing Director 1987-88. *Biog: b.* 31 December 1942. *Nationality:* British. *m.* 1966, Ann Valerie; 2 s. *Educ:* City University (BSc Hons Electrical Engineering). *Directorships:* 3i plc 1990 (non-exec); Eden Design Group Ltd 1989 (non-exec); International Business Software Ltd 1989 (non-exec); Winprime Group Ltd 1990 (non-exec). *Professional Organisations:* Member of the Institute of Electrical Engineers (MIEE); Chartered Engineer (CEng). *Recreations:* Sailing, Wine, Jogging, Swimming.

CHEETHAM, Anthony J V; Non-Executive Director, Venture Link Investors Ltd.

CHEETHAM, Richard Froggatt; Director, Schroder Investment Management Ltd, since 1988; UK Pension Fund Management. *Career:* Peat Marwick Mitchell, Chartered Acct 1962-65; Chase Manhattan Bank Fund Management, Analyst 1965-72; Schroder Investment Management, Asst Dir, UK Fund Mgmnt 1973-82; Dir, UK Fund Mgmnt 1982-85 and 1988; Schroder Capital Management International Ltd SVP, International Fund Mgmnt 1985-88. *Biog: Nationality:* British. *m.* 1969, Jacqueline (née Allin); 2 d. *Directorships:* Schroder Investment Management Ltd 1982-85, 1988 (exec). *Professional Organisations:* FCA.

CHEFFINGS, N; Partner, Nabarro Nathanson.

CHEN, Jie Sheng; Director and General Manager, Bank of China, since 1986. *Biog: b.* 14 February 1929. *Nationality:* Chinese. *m.* 1955, Ru Ling (née Li); 2 d. *Educ:* High School in China. *Clubs:* Overseas Bankers'.

CHEONG, Parkson; Vice President, Mellon Bank NA, since 1980; Credit Approval Officer-Europe, Middle East & Africa, since 1985; Deputy Senior Credit Officer, International Banking Dept, since 1990. *Career:* Mellon Bank NA (USA), Various 1970-; First Boston (Europe) Ltd (on secondment), Asst Dir 1974-78. *Biog: b.* 30 December 1946. *m.* 1981, Karen (née Liao); 2 d. *Educ:* Diocesan Boys' School, Hong Kong; University of Wales (BSc Econ. Hons); University of Pennsylvania (MBA). *Clubs:* The Wig & Pen. *Recreations:* Travel.

CHERRY, Tony; Partner, Beachcroft Stanleys.

CHESHIRE, Timothy; Partner, Wedlake Bell, since 1986. *Career:* Slaughter and May, Assistant Solicitor 1977-82; Assistant Solicitor, Partner 1982-. *Biog: b.* 11 January 1951. *Nationality:* British. *m.* 1983, Catherine Jane (née Hepworth). *Educ:* Stowe. *Professional Organisations:* Law Society. *Clubs:* SMTC. *Recreations:* Sailing, Travel, Winter Sports.

CHESNEY, C; Vice-President, First National Bank of Boston.

CHESSELLS, A D; Partner, Ernst & Young.

CHESTER, D R; Partner, Arthur Andersen & Co, since 1989; Tax. *Biog: b.* 21 July 1956. *Nationality:* British. *m.* 1983, Hilarie (née Jackson); 1 s; 1 d. *Educ:* St Peters School, York; New College, Oxford (BA). *Professional Organisations:* ACA; ATII.

CHESTER, Martin Graham; Partner, Theodore Goddard, since 1972; Corporate Finance & Company Law. *Career:* Theodore Goddard, Solicitor 1967-72. *Biog: b.* 24 January 1943. *Nationality:* British. *m.* 1986, Gail (née Harada). *Educ:* St Albans School; Exeter University (LLB). *Other Activities:* Member, Law Society Company Law Ctee;; Chairman, City of London Law Society Company Law Sub-Ctee; Trustee & Hon Sec, Petroleum & Mineral Law Education Trust. *Professional Organisations:* Law Society. *Publications:* English-Dutch Company Law; Contributor to two Chapters of Tolley's Company Law. *Clubs:* Hurlingham, Little Ship Club. *Recreations:* Sailing, Swimming, Scuba Diving, Tennis, Eating.

CHESTERFIELD, P D; Director, Abbey Life Investment Services Limited.

CHESWORTH, Niki; Personal Finance Writer & City Reporter, Daily Express. *Career:* World Drug Market Manual, Asst Editor 1983-85; Mini Computer News, Dep Editor 1985-87; Money Week, News Editor 1987-88. *Biog: b.* 29 December 1962. *Educ:* Royal Masonic School for Girls; London College of Printing, NCTJ. *Recreations:* DIY, Local Politics, Current Affairs.

CHETWODE, Philip; Lord Chetwode; Director, NCL Investments Limited.

CHETWOOD, Sir Clifford Jack; KB; Chairman, George Wimpey plc, since 1982. *Career:* Wimpey, Building Mgr Trainee/Jnr Eng/Departmental Contracts Mgr 1951; Wimpey Birmingham, Regional Mgr 1959; Wimpey, Dir 1969; George Wimpey, Group MD, UK Construction Division 1978; Wimpey Construction, Chm; Wimpey Homes Holdings, Chm 1981; Wimpey Group, Chief Exec 1982; Chm Designate 1983; Chm 1984. *Biog: b.* 2 November 1928. *Nationality:* British. *m.* 1953, Pamela Phyllis (née Sherlock); 1 s; 3 d. *Directorships:* George Wimpey plc 1969 (exec); Chetwood Green Partnership 1988 (non-exec). *Other Activities:* Past Chm, National Contractors Group of National Federation of Building Trades Employers; Leading Figure in the Campaign Against Building Industry Nationalization (CABIN); Fundraising Ctee for Charing Cross Medical Centre (Chm 1985); Mem, Council of the Imperial Society of Knights Bachelor; Prince Philip Gold Medal for Exceptional Contribution to the Construction Industry, 1987; Architects & Surveyors Institute Man of the Year Award, 1989; Trustee, Victoria & Albert Museum; Mem of the Council of Aims of Industry; Chm, Development Trust of the Institution of Civil Engineers; Pres, Building Employers' Confederation; Chm, Construction Industry Training Board; Worshipful Company of Basketmakers; Mem, Court of Assistants of the Guild of Freemen of the City of London; Past Pres of a Senior Amateur Soccer Side and the Guildford & Godalming Rugby Football Club; Pres, Royal Tennis Court, Hampton Court Palace. *Professional Organisations:* Hon Mem, City & Guilds Institute; Hon Fellow, Institution of Civil Engineers; FRSA. *Recreations:* Real Tennis, Tennis, Music.

CHEYNE, David Watson; Partner, Linklaters & Paines, since 1980. *Biog: b.* 30 December 1948. *Nationality:* British. *m.* 1978, Gay; 3 s. *Educ:* Stowe School; Trinity College, Cambridge (BA Law). *Recreations:* Shooting, Fishing.

CHEYNE, Iain Donald; General Manager, Lloyds Bank plc, since 1986; Strategic Planning. *Career:* Drooglever & Co Articled Clerk/Solicitor 1961-68; Alfille & Co Solicitor 1968-72; Lloyds Bank plc Legal Adviser 1972-86. *Biog: b.* 29 March 1942. *m.* 1969, Amelia Martinez (née Arriola); 2 s; 1 d. *Educ:* Epsom College; Hertford College, Oxford (BA); College of Law, Solicitor; London University; Stanford University.

CHEYSSON, Jean-Christian; Managing Director, Credit Suisse Financial Products, since 1990; Marketing. *Career:* Baxter Travenol Labs, (Chicago) Various, Finance 1976-84; Bankers Trust International Ltd, Managing Dir, Head of Capital Markets & Eurobonds 1984-90. *Biog: b.* 21 March 1947. *Nationality:* French. *m.* 1971, Jacqueline (née Denis); 2 s. *Educ:* Lycee Janson de Sailly; Ecole Sainte Genevieve, Versailles; Ecole Nationale de Statistiques et d'Administration Economique (ENSAE), Paris, France. *Recreations:* Tennis, Skiing.

CHICHESTER, D S S; Director, Panmure Gordon & Co Limited.

CHIDLEY, Mark Anton; Partner, Booth & Co, since 1984; Company and Banking Law. *Career:* Slaughter and May, Articled Clerk 1977-79; Assistant Solicitor 1979-82. *Biog: b.* 24 March 1955. *Nationality:* British. *m.* 1981, Victoria Anne (née Unwin); 2 s; 1 d. *Educ:* Ardingly College, Sussex; Southampton University (LLB). *Professional Organisations:* Member, The Law Society. *Clubs:* Lansdowne.

CHILD, Denis Marsden; CBE; Director, National Westminster Bank plc, since 1982; Non-Executive. *Career:* National Westminster Bank plc, Head of Planning & Marketing 1975-77; Head of Mgmnt Information 1977-79; Gen Mgr, Financial Control 1979-82; Dep Group Chief Exec 1982-86. *Biog: b.* 1 November 1926. *Nationality:* British. *m.* 1973, m2 Patricia (née Charlton) m1 2 s; 1 d. *Educ:* Woodhouse Grove School,

Bradford. *Directorships:* Coutts & Co 1982 (non-exec); Eurotunnel plc 1984 (non-exec); IBM UK Pensions Trust 1986 (non-exec); Securities & Investments Board 1986 (non-exec); Investors Compensation Scheme Ltd 1988-; Investors Compensation Scheme Ltd Chm; International Commodities Clearing House Ltd Chm. *Other Activities:* Worshipful Company of Chartered Secretaries & Administrators. *Professional Organisations:* FCIB; FCIS; FCT. *Clubs:* Stoke Poges Golf Club. *Recreations:* Golf, Gardening.

CHILD, Graham Derek; Partner, Slaughter and May, since 1976; EEC/Competition/Intellectual Property Law. *Biog: b.* 24 June 1943. *Educ:* Bedford School; Worcester College, Oxford (MA). *Other Activities:* Bar & Law Society, Joint Working Party on Competitive Law. *Professional Organisations:* The Law Society, IBA. *Publications:* Common Market Law of Competition (with C W Bellamy QC), 1987. *Clubs:* Highgate Golf, Vanderbilt Racquet, Hurlingham.

CHILDS, David Robert; Partner, Clifford Chance, since 1981; Corporate Finance. *Career:* Coward Chance, Articled Clerk 1974-76; Assistant Solicitor 1976-81; Partner 1981. *Biog: b.* 28 June 1951. *Nationality:* British; 2 s; 1 d. *Educ:* Sheffield University (LLB); University College, London (LLM). *Other Activities:* Member, Law Society; Liveryman, City of London Solicitors Company.

CHILTON, F Paul; Deputy Chairman and Chief Operating Officer, Alexander Howden Limited.

CHILTON, Peter Henry; Director, Sphere Drake Insurance plc, since 1984. *Career:* CI de Rougemont & Co Ltd, Lloyds Deputy Marine Underwriter 1954-76; Director 1972-76; Sphere Drake Underwriting Management Limited, Director & Cargo Specie Underwriter 1977-82; Director & Overall Marine Underwriter 1982-89; Sphere Drake Insurance plc, Consultant 1990. *Biog: b.* 29 October 1927. *Nationality:* British. *m.* 1951, Pauline Marie; 2 s. *Directorships:* Sphere Drake Insurance plc 1984; Sphere Drake Insurance Group plc 1985; Dai-Tokyo Insurance Company (UK) Ltd 1982. *Other Activities:* Freeman, City of London. *Professional Organisations:* Underwriting Member of Lloyds; Nominated Representative of Institute of London Underwriters. *Clubs:* City of London Club, RAC.

CHINN, G M; Senior Partner, Berwin Leighton.

CHINNER, Howard; Senior Director, London Origination, Continental Bank NA.

CHITTY, M P; Secretary, Willis Corroon plc.

CHO, B Y; Director, Baring Securities Limited.

CHONG, Kwang-Woo; General Manager, Korea First Bank, since 1989; London Branch. *Career:* Korea First Bank, London Rep Office 1977; Senior Deputy General Manager, International Business Dept, Seoul 1983; General Manager, Shinbangbae-dong Branch, Seoul 1985; General Manager, Nonhyon-dong Branch, Seoul 1987; General Manager, London Branch 1989. *Biog: b.* 10 October 1942. *Nationality:* South Korean. *m.* Eung-Ju; 1 s; 1 d. *Educ:* Law College, Seoul National University (Batchelor of Law). *Clubs:* Wentworth, Overseas Bankers'. *Recreations:* Golf.

CHOW, Joseph; General Manager, The Bank of East Asia Ltd.

CHOWDHURY, M Y; Senior Vice President and Branch Manager, Habib Bank AG Zurich.

CHOWN, John Francis; Chairman, J F Chown & Company Ltd, since 1962; International Tax & Finance. *Biog: b.* 12 December 1929. *Nationality:* British. *m.* 1969, Vera Marie Luise (née Wohl); 2 d. *Educ:* Gordonstoun School; Selwyn College, Cambridge (MA Hons 1st). *Directorships:* Sashless Window Co Ltd (non exec); Fixed Income Research & Management Ltd. *Other Activities:* Exec Ctee Mem, Institute for Fiscal Studies; Mem, Institute of Directors Tax Ctee; Mem, UK Ctee, International Fiscal Assoc.. *Professional Organisations:* ACT Technical Ctee. *Publications:* Tax Efficient Foreign Exchange Management 1990; The Right Road to Monetary Union (with Geoffrey Wood) 1989; Taxation of Direct Investment in the United States, 1980; Numerous articles in journals. *Clubs:* Gresham. *Recreations:* Music, Monetary History.

CHRIMES, P; Director, Lazard Investors Limited.

CHRISFIELD, Lawrence John; Tax Partner, Ernst & Young, since 1975; Corporate & Personal Taxation; Head of Entertainment & Media Specialist Division. *Career:* Merrett Son & Street, Articled Clerk/Snr 1955-63; Arthur Young, Tax Mgr 1963-72; Unilever Ltd, UK Tax Mgr 1972-74. *Biog: b.* 31 March 1938. *Nationality:* British. *m.* 1961, Patricia Maureen (née Scoble); 1 s; 3 d. *Educ:* St Olaves & St Saviours Grammar. *Other Activities:* Member, Taxation Ctee of the British Property Federation; Member, Taxation Ctee of the British Film & Television Producers Association. *Professional Organisations:* ATII; FCA. *Publications:* Various. *Recreations:* Theatre, Cinema, Photography.

CHRISTENSEN, Soren Kenneth; Senior Vice President and Manager, Bank of Montreal, since 1990; Petroleum, Real Estate, Communications & Multinationals. *Career:* Bank of Montreal, San Francisco 1973-75; Bank of Montreal, Houston 1975-80; Bank of Montreal, New York 1980-85; Bank of Montreal, Chicago 1985-90. *Biog: b.* 18 August 1949. *Nationality:* American. *m.* Darlene. *Educ:* American Graduate, School of International Management, Glendale, Arizona; Utah State University , Logan, Utah (BSc Econ, Master of International Management, Finance). *Directorships:* Bank of Montreal Capital Markets Ltd 1990; Bank of Montreal Capital Markets (Holdings) Ltd 1990.

CHRISTIAN, Nigel Robin Gladwyn; Director, Leslie & Godwin Limited.

CHRISTIANSEN, Susan; Director, Bradstock Blunt & Crawley Ltd.

CHRISTIE, A H; Director, Corporate Finance, Barclays de Zoete Wedd Limited, since 1989; UK & European Corporate Finance. *Career:* Hill Samuel & Co Limited, Assistant Director, Corporate Finance 1982-87. *Biog: b.* 15 March 1956. *Nationality:* British. *Educ:* Exeter University (MSc); London Business School (MBA).

CHRISTIE, Nicholas A; Director, Kleinwort Benson Securities Ltd, since 1990; International Equity Sales. *Biog: b.* 24 April 1961. *Nationality:* British. *Educ:* Eton College; Exeter University (BA Hons Economics & Agricultural Economics). *Recreations:* Sailing, Tennis, Kite Flying.

CHRISTIE, Peter S; Director, Minet Holdings plc.

CHRISTOFIDES, G C; Chairman, Bank of Cyprus (London) Ltd.

CHRISTOPHER, Martin G; Deputy Director & Professor of Marketing & Logistics, Cranfield School of Management, since 1978. *Career:* University of Bradford Management Centre, Research Fellow 1969-70; Lecturer in Marketing and Logistics 1970-72; Cranfield Institute of Technology, School of Management, Lecturer in Marketing & Logistics 1972-75; Senior Lecturer in Marketing and Logistics 1975-78; Professor of Marketing and Logistics Systems 1978; various administrative responsibilities including: Director of MBA Programme 1977-80; Chairman, Executive MBA Programme 1980-81; Chairman, Graduate Research & Subject Development Committee 1981-87; Head of Marketing & Logistics Group 1981; Chairman, Continuing Studies 1987. *Educ:* University of Lancaster (BA Econ); University of Bradford Management Centre (MSc); Institute of Technology (PhD). *Other Activities:* Visiting Professor, Centre for Transportation Studies, University of British Columbia, Canada, 1975; Visiting Professor, Department of Marketing, University of New South Wales, Australia, 1981; Executive Editor, British Journal of Marketing, 1968-70; European Editor, International Journal of Physical Distribution, 1970-72; Editor, International Journal of Physical Distribution & Materials Management, 1972-88; Convenor and Chairman of 1983 Marketing Educators Group Conference, Back to Basics and Editor of Conference Proceedings, 1983; Advisor to Collins English Dictionary, 1983-84; Mem-

ber of the Editorial Boards of: Journal of Business Logistics (USA), 1984; Materials Flow (UK), 1985-87; L'Enterprise Logistique (France), 1986; Asia Pacific Journal of Business Logistics, 1988; External Examiner, BA in Business Studies, Middlesborough Polytechnic; External Assessor, MSc in Advanced Management, Anglian Regional Management Centre; External Examiner, MBA Programme at Manchester Business School; External Examiner, MSc in Management, City University; Chief Examiner, Institute of Marketing; Chief Examiner, Institute of Logistics and Distribution Management; External Examiner, MA in Marketing, University of Lancaster; External Examiner, BSc in Business Studies, Loughborough University; External Examiner in Agricultural and Food Marketing at the University College of Wales, Aberystwyth; External Examiner, MSc and BSc in Management Studies, University of Manchester, Institute of Science & Technology; External Examiner, MBA and BSc, University of Bradford, Management Centre; Acted as External Examiner for various PhD theses. *Professional Organisations:* FICM. *Publications:* Numerous Papers and Books on a variety of Management related topics.

CHRISTOU, Richard; Director, STC plc, since 1987; Group Commercial & Legal Affairs Worldwide. *Career:* Stephenson Harwood, Articled Clerk/Asst Solicitor 1966-69; Lanitis Bros Ltd, Legal Dir/Gen Mgr 1969-74; Standard Telephones & Cables Ltd, Legal Adviser 1975-83; STC Telecommunications Ltd, Legal Adviser & Co Sec 1983-85; Sologlas Holdings Ltd, Legal Dir & Co Sec 1985. *Biog: b.* 1 October 1944. *Nationality:* British. *m.* 1968, Anastasia (née Zeulari); 2 s. *Educ:* Eltham College, London; Trinity College, Cambridge (MA 1st Class). *Professional Organisations:* Solicitor, Law Society. *Publications:* International Agency Distribution & Licensing Agreements, 1986. *Recreations:* Literature, Music, Horse Riding.

CHUMAS, Amanda J; Partner, Cameron Markby Hewitt.

CHURCH, Christopher J; Managing Director, McLeod Young Weir International Ltd.

CHURCHFIELD, S E; OBE; Director, Enterprise Oil.

CHURCHILL, Ann; Partner, Jaques & Lewis.

CHURCHILL, Lawrence; Director, Allied Dunbar Assurance plc.

CHURCHILL, Victor George Spencer; Viscount Churchill; Managing Director, Church, Charity and Local Authority Fund Managers Limited, since 1988. *Career:* Morgan Grenfell & Co Limited 1958-74; Assistant Director 1971-74; The Central Board of Finance of the Church of England, Investment Manager 1974-;

The Charities Official Investment Fund, Investment Manager 1974-; The Local Authorities' Mutual Investment Trust, Director 1978-. *Biog: b.* 31 July 1934. *Nationality:* British. *Educ:* Eton; New College, Oxford (MA). *Clubs:* City of London Club.

CICUREL, David Elie; Chairman, International Media Communications plc, since 1990. *Career:* Duc Lamothe Ledru, Chairman 1978-83; Independent Consultant 1983-90. *Biog: b.* 23 May 1949. *Nationality:* French. *m.* 1988, Alejandra. *Educ:* Polytechnique, Paris; INSEAD, Fontainebleau. *Directorships:* Dawnay, Day & Co Ltd (non-exec); Union Group plc (non-exec); Banque Finindus SA; HRA Europe SA.

CLAGUE, Clive Taylor; Executive Director, Electra Investment Trust plc, since 1983; Industrial Advisor to Board with Supervisory Responsibilities for After Care of Investments. *Career:* Nestlé Ltd Area Sales Mgr 1951-55; RHM plc Mgr 1955-60; Imperial Group plc Mktg Dir 1960-65; Granada Group plc Mktg Dir 1965-67; Gallaher Group plc Gen Mgr 1967-70; R & S Cuthbert plc Chm, Chief Exec 1970-80; E J Arnold & Sons Ltd Gp Chief Exec 1980-82. *Biog: b.* 22 January 1929. *Nationality:* British. *m.* 1982, Frances Mary (née Robinson); 3 s; 2 d. *Educ:* Sale Grammar School. *Directorships:* Beaujersey Holdings Limited 1988 (non-exec); Bowes Darby Design Associates Limited 1986 (non-exec) Chairman; C D B Meats Limited 1985 (non-exec); Electra Investment Trust plc 1984 (exec); Electra Management Services Limited 1984 (exec); EPEP Syndications Limited 1988 (exec); Electra Kingsway Managers Limited 1988 (exec); Electra Kingsway Limited 1988 (exec); Electra Kingsway Quoted Management Limited 1988 (exec); Electra Leisure Group Limited 1989 (non-exec); Healthcall Group plc 1990 (non-exec); Jarvis Hotels Limited 1990 (non-exec); Prospect Group Limited 1988 (non-exec) Chairman; Stadium Limited 1982 (exec) Chairman; Wardle Storeys plc 1982 (non-exec) Chairman; Electra Risk Capital plc 1984 (exec) Director; Unipart Group of Companies Limited 1986 (non-exec); Unipart Group of Companies (Trustees) Limited 1987 (non-exec); R F D Group plc 1985 (non-exec). *Recreations:* Family, Fishing, Walking.

CLAISSE, Douglas Martin; Assistant General Manager, Clerical Medical & General Life Assurance Society, since 1983; Sales & Marketing. *Career:* Employers Liability Assurance, Local Mgr 1954-63; Clerical Medical & General Life Assurance, Society Inspector 1963-66; Pensions Rep 1966-68; Pensions New Business Mgr 1968-72; Pensions Development Mgr 1972-81; Joint Agency Mgr 1981-83. *Directorships:* Clerical Medical & General Life Assurance Society 1985 (exec); Clerical Medical Unit Trust Managers Ltd 1984 (exec); Clerical Medical International Holdings 1987 (exec); CMI Financial Services Ltd 1987 (exec) Chm; CMI Group Services (Gibraltar) Ltd 1987 (exec) Chm.

CLAPPERTON, Alec Mordike; Director, County NatWest Investment Management Ltd, since 1984; UK Marketing and Head of Specialised Invesmnt Vehicles Group. *Career:* County Bank Ltd Mgr 1975-78; Asst Dir 1978-80; Snr Asst Dir 1980-84. *Biog: b.* 6 March 1945. *Nationality:* British. *m.* 1969, Gilliam Mary (née Young); 2 s. *Educ:* Stretford Grammar School. *Professional Organisations:* ACIB. *Clubs:* Channels Golf. *Recreations:* Golf, Tennis, Swimming, Reading.

CLAPPERTON, Alexander Wallace Ford; Director, Barclays de Zoete Wedd Securities Ltd, since 1986; Corporate Finance. *Career:* de Zoete & Gorton, Ptnr 1963-70; de Zoete & Bevan, Ptnr 1970-86. *Biog: b.* 22 July 1934. *Nationality:* British. *m.* 1965, Catherine Anne (née Horsman); 1 s; 1 d. *Educ:* Charterhouse. *Directorships:* de Zoete & Bevan Limited 1986 (exec). *Professional Organisations:* CA, Member, Institute of Chartered Accountants of Scotland. *Clubs:* Honourable Company of Edinburgh Golfers, Denham GC, Woburn GC, City of London Club. *Recreations:* Golf, Skiing.

CLAPTON, Derek A; Vice President, Manufacturers Hanover Trust Co.

CLARK, A W; Director, Hill Samuel Bank Limited.

CLARK, Adrian Spencer; Partner, Ashurst Morris Crisp, since 1990; Company Department. *Career:* Slaughter & May 1981-86; Ashurst Morris Crisp 1986-88; Seconded as Secretary to Takeover Panel 1988-90. *Biog: b.* 20 May 1957. *Nationality:* English. *m.* 1987, Sarah (née Cornwell); 1 d. *Educ:* King Edward VI GS, Retford; Peterhouse, Cambridge (MA). *Clubs:* United Oxford and Cambridge University Club. *Recreations:* Cricket.

CLARK, Andrew Joseph Campbell; Resident Partner;, Allen & Overy, since 1989; Middle East Regional Office in Dubai. *Career:* Allen & Overy, Articled 1978-80; Solicitor 1980; Allen & Overy (London), Assistant Solicitor 1980-81; Allen & Overy (Middle East Regional Office), Assistant Solicitor 1981-84; Allen & Overy (London), Assistant Solicitor 1984-85; Partner 1985-89; Allen & Overy (Middle East Regional Office), Partner 1989-. *Biog: b.* 29 April 1955. *Nationality:* British. *m.* 1982, Teresa Diane (née Fryer); 2 s; 1 d. *Educ:* Marist College, Hull; Trinity College, Cambridge (Master of Arts 2:1). *Professional Organisations:* Law Society; City of London Solicitors Company; London Solicitors Litigation Association; London Young Solicitors Group; Associate of the Chartered Institute of Arbitrators; International Bar Association. *Clubs:* The World Trade Club (Dubai), Hilton Beach Club (Dubai). *Recreations:* Squash.

CLARK, B J; Consultant, Lane Clark & Peacock.

CLARK, Brian Stephen; Senior Company Partner, Chairman Overseas Practice Development Committee, Nabarro Nathanson, since 1987. *Career:* International Management Group, Vice President, Jointly Responsible for Administration of London Office 1969-70; Nabarro Nathanson, Partner 1970-; Chairman, Overseas Practice Development Committee, Responsible for the Development of the Firms Practice Abroad 1987-; Managing Partner, Responsible (to the Firm's Management Committee) for the Management of the Firm 1987-89; Senior Corporate Partner, Responsible for the Administration of Firm's Corporate Department (Presently 90 Lawyers) 1988-. *Biog: b.* 11 August 1936. *Nationality:* British. *m.* 1962, Rita; 2 s. *Educ:* LSE (LLB Hons). *Professional Organisations:* Law Society. *Recreations:* Golf.

CLARK, Charles; Partner, Linklaters & Paines.

CLARK, Christopher John; Head of Strategy, Laing & Cruickshank, since 1989; Strategy & Quantitative Research. *Career:* Kemp-Gee & Co (Subsequently Scrimgeour Kemp-Gee), Partner 1975-87; Citicorp Scrimgeour Vickers, Head of Research 1986-89; Laing & Cruickshank, Head of Strategy 1989-. *Biog: b.* 16 May 1942. *Nationality:* British. *m.* 1964, Angela; 3 s; 1 d. *Educ:* Southend-on-Sea High School for Boys; Southampton University (BA Hons English). *Directorships:* Laing & Cruickshank 1989 (exec). *Other Activities:* Council Member, Society of Investment Analysts; Council Member, Institute for Quantitative Investment Analysis. *Professional Organisations:* FCIS; ASIA. *Clubs:* Royal Over-Seas League. *Recreations:* Long Distance Running.

CLARK, Christopher Richard Nigel; Executive Director, Johnson Matthey plc, since 1990; Catalytic Systems Division. *Career:* Johnson Matthey USA, Marketing Manager 1979-84; Johnson Matthey UK, General Manager 1984-87; Platinum Marketing Director 1987-89; Division Director 1989-90. *Biog: b.* 29 January 1942. *Nationality:* British. *m.* 1964, Catherine Ann (née Mather); 2 s; 1 d. *Educ:* Marlborough College; Cambridge University (MIM). *Directorships:* Johnson Matthey 1990 (exec).

CLARK, David Beatson; CBE, TD, DL; *Career:* Beatson Clark plc, MD 1974-84; Chairman 1979-88. *Biog: b.* 5 May 1933. *Nationality:* British. *m.* 1959, Ann (née Mudford); 2 s; 1 d. *Educ:* Wrekin College; Keele University (BA Hons). *Directorships:* Beatson Clark plc 1963-88 (exec); The Royal Bank of Scotland plc 1988 (non-exec); Glass Manufacturers Federation 1978-88 (non-exec); Yorkshire Electricity Group plc 1990 (non-exec); Rotherham Training & Enterprise Council 1990 (non-exec); Rotherham Enterprise Agency Ltd 1989 (non-exec). *Other Activities:* Member, Rotherham Health Authority (1985-); Council Member, University of Sheffield (1984-); Liveryman, Glass Sellers (1967-). *Professional Organisations:* CBIM. *Clubs:* Army & Navy.

CLARK, David Owen; Director, Svenska International plc, since 1988; Head of Swaps & Bond Trading. *Career:* Lloyds Bank International, Economics Research Officer 1973-75; Account Executive, Middle East & Africa Division & Cairo Branch 1975-81; Manager, Export & Project Finance Division 1981-84; Lloyds Merchant Bank Assoc Dir, Head of Swaps 1985-87. *Biog: b.* 31 August 1951. *Nationality:* British/Australian. *m.* 1978, Marilyn (née Gepp); 3 s. *Educ:* Downside School; Brasenose College, Oxford (MA). *Clubs:* United Oxford & Cambridge. *Recreations:* Walking, Restoring an Italian Mill.

CLARK, Edward Michael; Director, Charles Stanley and Co Ltd. *Biog: b.* 28 February 1947. *Nationality:* British. *m.* 1976, Penelope Ann (née Medcalf); 1 s; 1 d. *Educ:* Haileybury College. *Directorships:* The Oceana Consolidated Co plc 1988 (exec).

CLARK, I G; Vice President - Foreign Exchange, The Northern Trust Company.

CLARK, Keith; Partner, Clifford Chance, since 1977; Banking & Restructuring. *Biog: b.* 25 October 1944. *Nationality:* British. *m.* 1974, Linda Sue (née Woodger); 1 s; 1 d. *Educ:* Chichester High School for Boys; St Catharine's College, Oxford (MA,BCL). *Professional Organisations:* Law Society; International Bar Association. *Publications:* Numerous Articles and Contributions to Books Including Banking & Financial Law Review, 1987. *Recreations:* Family, Ballet, Theatre, Walking.

CLARK, M A C; Secretary, Cadbury Schweppes plc.

CLARK, Michael; Stock Market Correspondent, The Times.

CLARK, Michael John; Manager Banking, Yamaichi Bank (UK) plc, since 1989; Corporate Lending/ Derivative Products. *Career:* Midland Bank plc, Various/ Corporate Finance Division 1977-78 & 1981-85; Saudi International Bank, Various/Group Manager, International Corporate Banking 1985-89. *Biog: b.* 11 December 1958. *Nationality:* British. *m.* 1985, Frances Anne (née Leask); 1 s; 1 d. *Educ:* Selhurst Grammar School, Croydon; Loughborough University of Technology (BSc Hons Banking and Finance); City University Business School. *Professional Organisations:* Associate of the Chartered Institute of Bankers (1982). *Clubs:* Old Croydonians, Loughborough Bankers. *Recreations:* Association Football, Golf, Squash.

CLARK, Sir Robert; Director, Hill Samuel Bank Limited.

CLARK, Robert Cyril (Bob); Chairman and Group Chief Executive, United Biscuits (Holdings) plc. *Career:* Royal West Kent Regiment 1947-49; Cadbury Bros Ltd, two years Training in Production and Marketing

1952; John Forrest Ltd, General Manager, a Chain of Retail Confectionery Shops in the Midlands, owned by Cadbury Bros 1954; Cadbury Confectionery, Marketing Director 1957; Cadbury Cakes Ltd, Managing Director 1962; Cadbury Cakes, Chairman 1969; Cadbury Schweppes Foods Ltd, Director 1969; McVitie & Cadbury Cakes Ltd, Managing Director 1971; United Biscuits (UK) Ltd, Board Member 1974; UB Biscuits, Managing Director 1977; United Biscuits (UK) Ltd, Chairman and Managing Director 1984; United Biscuits (Holdings) plc, Director 1984; Group Chief Executive 1986; Thames Water plc, Non-executive Member 1988; United Biscuits (Holdings) plc, Deputy Chairman 1989; Chairman and Group Chief Executive 1990. *Biog:* b. 28 March 1929. *m.* Evelyn Mary (Lynne) (née Harper); 3 s; 1 d. *Educ:* Dulwich College; Pembroke College, Oxford (MA History). *Other Activities:* Economic Development Council for the Food and Drink Industry; Member, CCIBA; Council of ISBA; Resources Committee Food and Drink Federation; Fellow, Institute of Grocery Distribution; CBIM. *Recreations:* Reading, Walking, Renovating Old Buildings, Planting Trees.

CLARK, Roger; Deputy Chairman, Baker Tilly.

CLARK, Stewart William; Partner, Baillie Gifford & Co, since 1981; Finance and Administration. *Career:* Robert G Morton & Son CA, Trainee Accountant 1966-71; Graham Smart & Annan CA, Qualified Assistant 1971-74; Deloitte & Co CA, Qualified Assistant, Manager 1974-78; Baillie Gifford & Co, Partnership Secretary 1979-81; Partner 1981-. *Biog:* b. 1 January 1947. *Nationality:* British. *m.* 1973, Jane Cairns (née Bell); 2 s. *Educ:* George Watsons College. *Directorships:* Edinburgh Sports Club Limited 1989 (non-exec). *Clubs:* Watsonian Club, Edinburgh Sports Club, Murrayfield Golf Club. *Recreations:* Squash, Golf, Tennis.

CLARK, T M; Director, Mercantile Credit Company Limited.

CLARK, (Thomas) Alastair; Head of Financial Markets & Institutions Division, Bank of England, since 1987; Structural, Regulatory and Tax Aspects of Markets: Issues related to Institutional Investors: Competitiveness of the City. *Career:* Bank of England 1971-; PA/Dep Governor 1980-81; UK Alternate Exec Dir, IMF 1983-85; UK Alternate Dir, EIB 1986-88. *Biog:* b. 27 February 1949. *Nationality:* British. *m.* 1986, Shirley Anne (née Barker); 1 s; 1 d. *Educ:* Stockport Grammar School; Cambridge University (MA); LSE (MSc). *Recreations:* Squash, Hill Walking, Joinery.

CLARK, Timothy Nicholas; Partner, Slaughter and May, since 1983; Company and Commercial Department. *Biog:* b. 9 January 1951. *m.* Caroline; 2 s. *Educ:* Sherborne School; Pembroke College, Cambridge (History). *Clubs:* Malaprops, Euston. *Recreations:* Modern History, Music, Sport.

CLARK, William James; Regional Manager, Banking and Corporate Finance, Chemical Bank, since 1988; UK, Ireland, Nordic Countries. *Career:* Chemical Bank London, Credit Analyst 1973-74; Marketing Officer 1975-79; Singapore, Head of Marketing 1979-80; General Manager 1980-83; London, Regional Energy Head 1984-87. *Biog:* b. 3 May 1950. *Nationality:* British. *m.* 1981, Karen (née Holm); 2 d. *Educ:* High School of Dundee; Edinburgh University (BSc Hons Agriculture); University of W Ontario, Canada (MBA). *Other Activities:* Council Member, Anglo-Danish Society. *Professional Organisations:* Business Graduates Association; Institute of Petroleum. *Clubs:* RAC, Annabel's. *Recreations:* Sport, Farming.

CLARK-LOWES, Jeremy William; Equity Partner and Head of Minerals, Grimley J R Eve, since 1984; Planning/Minerals. *Career:* Carter Jonas, Chartered Surveyors, Cambridge, Senior Assistant 1969-74; J M Clark & Partners, Chartered Surveyors, Northumberland, Partner 1975-80; Kent County Council, Assistant County Land Agent 1980-83; J R Eve (Before Their Merger with Grimley & Son), Now Equity Partner, Merged Practice of Grimley J R Eve, Partner 1983-. *Biog:* *Nationality:* British. *m.* Sally (née Reeve-Tucker). *Educ:* Oundle School; Cambridge University (MA Land Economy). *Other Activities:* Member, NFCI Minerals Committee. *Professional Organisations:* FRICS. *Clubs:* The English Speaking Union. *Recreations:* Rowing.

CLARKE, Bruce; Operations Manager, United Overseas Bank (Banque Unie Pour Les Pays d'Outre-Mer) Geneva.

CLARKE, Christopher; Director, Samuel Montagu & Co Limited.

CLARKE, David Hilton; Director, Gerrard & National Holdings plc, since 1974; Domestic Money Markets. *Career:* Royal Navy National Service 1956-58; Anthony Gibbs & Sons Ltd Director's Asst & Trainee 1959-67. *Biog:* b. 9 January 1938. *Nationality:* British. *m.* 1965, Leonora (née Marshall); 2 s. *Educ:* Hurstpierpoint College, Sussex. *Directorships:* Falmouth Oil Services 1986 (non-exec). *Other Activities:* Finance Ctee, University College London; Hon Sec, Coaching Club; Chm, Finance Ctee, Middlesex Hospital Medical School; Freeman, City of London, 1985. *Clubs:* Royal Ocean Racing Club, City Club. *Recreations:* Sailing, Skiing.

CLARKE, David T H; Director, S G Warburg Akroyd Rowe & Pitman Mullens.

CLARKE, Dominic Michael Bernard; Partner, Herbert Smith, since 1987; Company Commercial. *Career:* Herbert Smith, Articled Clerk 1973-75; Assistant Solicitor 1975-87. *Biog:* b. 28 February 1949. *Educ:* Austin Friars, Carlisle; Leeds University (LLB). *Other Activities:*

City of London Solicitors Company. *Professional Organisations:* Law Society. *Recreations:* Hill Walking.

CLARKE, H E; Partner, Life & General (Epsom), Bacon & Woodrow.

CLARKE, John Leonard; Partner, Clarke & Co, since 1990; Tax Planning/Corporate Planning. *Career:* Rhodes & Rhodes 1966-72; Peat Marwick Mitchell 1972-77; Longcrofts 1978-83; Moores Rowland 1983-90. *Biog: b.* 26 December 1948. *Nationality:* British; 2 s. *Educ:* The William Grimshaw School. *Directorships:* The David Linley Co Ltd 1986-89 (non-exec). *Other Activities:* Member, The Addington Society. *Professional Organisations:* Fellow, Institute of Chartered Accountants in England & Wales.

CLARKE, Martin Courtenay; Partner in Charge, Touche Ross & Co, since 1988; Corporate Finance. *Career:* Touche Ross & Co, Audit Ptnr 1973-86; Resource Development, Dir 1982-87; Reg Ptnr-in-Charge 1986-90; Dir of Mkting 1987-90. *Biog: b.* 7 January 1941. *Nationality:* British. *m.* 1974, Esmee (née Cottrell). *Educ:* Winchester College; Trinity College, Cambridge (MA). *Directorships:* Haymills Holdings Ltd 1984 (non-exec); Auditing Practices Committee 1982-88. *Other Activities:* Liveryman, Merchant Taylors' Company; Liveryman, Loriners' Company. *Professional Organisations:* FCA. *Publications:* Co-Author, Briefing Guide to Stockbrokers, 1982. *Clubs:* City of London, Lansdowne, Lighthouse. *Recreations:* Sailing, Skiing, Opera, Military History, Gardening.

CLARKE, Michael S; Non-Executive Director & Company Secretary, J Trevor, Montleman & Poland Ltd.

CLARKE, Peter Michael; Director, Kleinwort Benson Ltd.

CLARKE, Ronald William; Senior Partner, Cyril Sweett and Partners.

CLARKE, T N; Director, Bank of Cyprus (London) Ltd.

CLARKE, Timothy David Martin; Associate Director, Panmure Gordon & Company Limited, since 1989; Research. *Career:* Kitcet & Aithen, Bank Analyst 1989-90; Citicorp Scrimgeour Vickers, Director & Bank Analyst 1985-89; Grieveson Grant, Bank Analyst 1972-85. *Biog: b.* 7 April 1945. *Nationality:* British. *Educ:* Worksop College, Notts. *Professional Organisations:* Fellow, Institute of Chartered Accountants in England & Wales; Associate, The Society of Investment Analysts. *Publications:* Banking Under Pressure (with William Vincent), 1989. *Recreations:* Sailing, Chess.

CLARKE, William Malpas; CBE; Chairman, ANZ Merchant Bank Ltd, since 1987. *Career:* Manchester Guardian, Editorial Staff 1948-56; The Times, City Editor 1957-63; Financial & Industrial Editor 1963-66; The Banker, Editor 1966-67; Consultant 1967-72; Committee on Invisible Exports, Director of Official Inquiry 1966-68; Director, Chief Executive 1968-76; British Invisible Exports Council, Director General & Deputy Chairman 1976-87. *Biog: b.* 5 June 1922. *Nationality:* British. *m.* 1973, Faith Elizabeth (née Dawson); 2 d. *Educ:* Audenshaw Grammar School; Manchester University (BA Hons Econ). *Directorships:* ANZ Grindlays Bank 1966 (non-exec); Swiss Re (UK) 1977 (non-exec); ANZ Grindlays Bank (Jersey) 1976 Chairman (non-exec). *Other Activities:* Political Economy Club. *Publications:* The City's Invisible Earnings, 1958; The City in the World Economy, 1965; Private Enterprise in Developing Countries, 1966; Britain's Invisible Earnings (ed, as Director of Studies), 1967; The World's Money (with George Pulay), 1970; Inside the City, 1979 (rev edn 1983); How the City of London Works, 1986 (rev edn 1988); The Secret Life of Wilkie Collins, 1988; Planning for Europe: 1992, 1989. *Clubs:* Reform Club.

CLARKSON, Robert Smillie; General Manager, The Scottish Mutual Assurance Society.

CLASPER, Douglas Victor; Director, Kleinwort Benson Investment Management, since 1990; Trustee and Financial Planning Department. *Career:* Charity Commission, Executive Officer 1961-67; Kleinwort Benson Group 1968-. *Biog: b.* 12 September 1941. *Nationality:* British. *m.* 1985, Pauline (née Salter); 3 s; 2 d. *Educ:* Wilson's Grammar School. *Other Activities:* Hon Treasurer, The Friends of Moorfields Eye Hospital. *Professional Organisations:* Associate, Chartered Institute of Bankers. *Recreations:* Table Tennis, Tennis, Bridge.

CLASSON, Bruce D; Managing Director, Bankers Trust Company, since 1989; European Merchant Banking. *Career:* James Talcott Inc 1958-70; VP, Parent Holding Company; EVP, James Talcott Factors, responsible for New York City and environs, Factoring Division; Bankers Trust Company, Vice President, Asst Div Head of Factoring Division 1970-72; Division Head 1972; First Vice President 1973; Responsible for Accounts Receivable Lending Function 1974; also Officer-in-Charge of District III, Corporate Banking Div 1976-79; Head of New York National Division, US Department 1981-83; Head of Administration and Business Development Group, North America Department 1983-86; Managing Director and Administrative Group Head (Investment Banking) Corporate Finance Dept 1986-. *Biog: b.* 4 January 1935. *Nationality:* American. *m.* 1955, Wilma (née Fagin); 1 s; 1 d. *Educ:* Dartmouth College (BA Cum Laude); Harvard Business School (MBA). *Directorships:* Standard Motor Products Inc (NYSE) 1985-89 (non-exec); Venice Industries, Inc

(NYSE) 1966-73 (non-exec). *Other Activities:* Past Director & Member, Executive Committee of the National Commercial Finance Conference; Past President, Esquire/Toppers Credit Club; Member, of Board of Governors, Credit Men's Fraternity; Past Chairman, of Board of Trustees, New York Institute of Credit; Member, New York Credit & Financial Management Association, the Textile Distributors Association and the 475 Club. *Publications:* Commercial Credit and Collection Guide; Numerous contributions to trade journals and publications. *Clubs:* Various. *Recreations:* Sailing, Golf, Hiking.

CLAUSEN, A W; Non-Executive Director, Wellcome plc.

CLAXTON, Roger John; Partner, Pannell Kerr Forster, since 1984; Litigation Support. *Career:* P D Leake & Co (prededessor firm of Pannell Kerr Forster) Articled Clerk 1976-80; Audit Senior 1981-82; Audit Manager 1982-84; Partner 1984-. *Biog: b.* 20 March 1955. *Nationality:* British. *m.* 1980, Karen (née Brinded). *Educ:* Lowestoft Grammar School. *Professional Organisations:* ACA. *Clubs:* RAC. *Recreations:* Literature, Wine.

CLAY, Geoffrey James; Director, Treasury, British & Commonwealth Merchant Bank plc.

CLAY, John Martin; Deputy Chairman, Hambros plc, since 1986. *Career:* Hambros Bank Limited, Director 1961-84; Deputy Chairman 1972-84; Bank of England, Director 1973-83; Johnson & Firth Brown, Chairman 1973-. *Biog: b.* 20 August 1927. *Nationality:* British. *m.* 1952, Susan Jennifer (née Miller); 4 s. *Educ:* Eton College; Magdalen College, Oxford (BA Law). *Directorships:* Charter Reinsurance Co 1986 (non-exec); C E Heath plc 1986 (non-exec); Johnson & Firth Brown plc 1973 (non-exec); Norsk Hydro (UK) Ltd 1969 (non-exec); Guardian & Manchester Evening News 1967 (non-exec); Trade Indemnity plc 1987 (non-exec); Hambro Guardian Assurance 1988 (non-exec). *Professional Organisations:* FBIM; AIB. *Clubs:* Royal Thames Yacht Club. *Recreations:* Sailing.

CLAYDON, Peter; Assistant Managing Director, Yorkshire Enterprise Limited.

CLAYSON III, G P; General Manager, Fleet National Bank.

CLAYTON, Andrew Douglas; Editor, Business Television, since 1987; Channel Four Business Daily. *Career:* BBC World Service, Producer 1968-72; BBC TV Current Affairs, Producer 1972-80; BBC TV Money Programme, Deputy Editor 1980-82; BBC TV Panorama, Deputy Editor 1983-85; Channel 4 TV Business Programme, Editor 1985-87. *Biog: b.* 9 March 1947. *Nationality:* British. *m.* 1984, Ann Elizabeth (née Short); 1 s; 2 d. *Educ:* Midhurst Grammar School; The Queen's

College, Oxford (BA). *Directorships:* Business TV 1987 (exec). *Recreations:* Cricket, Music, Gardening.

CLAYTON, J; Managing Director (Investment Management), Bankers Trust Company.

CLAYTON, Simon Anthony; Executive Director, Samuel Montagu & Co Ltd, since 1989; Corporate Finance. *Career:* Arthur Andersen & Co, Chartered Accountant 1979-83. *Biog: b.* 25 October 1956. *Nationality:* British. *m.* 1981, Judy; 1 s; 1 d. *Educ:* St Edwards School, Oxford; University of Manchester (BA Econ). *Professional Organisations:* ACA.

CLEARY, Michael; Regional Managing Partner, Grant Thornton.

CLEAVELAND, Ms Helen Mary; Partner, Wilde Sapte, since 1990; Mergers and Acquisitions and General Corporate Law. *Career:* Herbert Oppenheimer Nathan & Vandyk, Assistant Solicitor 1984-88; Wilde Sapte, Assistant Solicitor 1988-90. *Biog: b.* 1 August 1958. *Nationality:* American. *m.* 1981, W J Powell. *Educ:* Millfield; Bristol University (BSc Hons Geology). *Professional Organisations:* Solicitor. *Recreations:* Sub Aqua.

CLEAVER, Anthony B; Director, General Accident Fire Life Assurance.

CLEGG, Nicholas Peter; Vice Chairman, Daiwa Europe Limited, since 1986. *Career:* Bramcast Textile Machinery, Asst to MD 1959-60; Koningkllike Hoogovens En Staalfabrieken NV, Holland, Ind Engineering & Sales 1960-62; Procter & Gamble Benelux, Marketing Exec 1962-64; Hill Samuel & Co Ltd, Snr Exec Dir 1964-86. *Biog: b.* 24 May 1936. *Nationality:* British. *m.* 1959, Hermance (née Van Den Wall Bake); 3 s; 1 d. *Educ:* Bryanston School; Trinity College, Cambridge(BA Hons). *Recreations:* Skiing, Tennis, Gardening, Listening to Music.

CLEGG, Robert Duncan; Director, Lazard Brothers & Co Ltd; Corporate Finance.

CLEGG, Simon John; Managing Director, Hoare Govett, since 1990; UK Research. *Career:* Laing & Cruickshank, Institutional Equity Sales 1979-84; Prudential Bache, Institutional Equity Sales 1984-88; Head of Equity Sales 1986-88; Hoare Govett, Institutional Equity Sales 1988-90; Joint Head of Equity Sales 1989-90. *Biog: b.* 12 May 1957. *Nationality:* British. *m.* 1985, Gillian Sarah (née Woods). *Educ:* Shrewsbury; St Catharine's College, Cambridge (MA Modern & Medieval Languages). *Professional Organisations:* Member, London Stock Exchange. *Clubs:* Leander. *Recreations:* Golf, Running, Gardening, Music.

CLEMENT, John; Chairman and Chief Executive, Unigate plc, since 1977. *Career:* Howards Dairies 1949;

United Dairies (London) Limited 1964-68; Milk Division, London Region Director 1968; Milk Division, Marketing Director 1969; Rank Leisure Services Ltd, Assistant Managing Director 1969-73; Unigate, Chairman, Foods Division 1973; Unigate Group, Chief Executive 1976. *Biog: b.* 18 May 1932. *Nationality:* British. *m.* 1956, Elisabeth (née Emery); 2 s; 1 d. *Educ:* Bishop's Stortford College. *Directorships:* N V Verenigde Bedrijven Nutricia 1981 (non-exec); The Littlewoods Organisation 1982-90 Chairman; Securities & Investments Board 1986-89 Board Member; Eagle Star Holdings plc 1981-86 (non-exec). *Other Activities:* Chairman, Children's Liver Disease Foundation; Member, Committee for Charity Macintyre. *Clubs:* Farmers, London Welsh Rugby Football, Cumberland Lawn Tennis, Royal Harwich Yacht. *Recreations:* Shooting, Music, Bridge, Farming.

CLEMENTI, David Cecil; Director, Kleinwort Benson Limited, since 1982. *Career:* Arthur Andersen 1970-73; Kleinwort Benson Ltd 1975-. *Educ:* Winchester College; Oxford University (MA); Harvard Business School (MBA). *Directorships:* Kleinwort Benson Group plc 1989; Kleinwort Benson Limited 1982; Kleinwort Benson Securities Limited 1986 Vice Chm; KBS (1984) Limited 1986. *Professional Organisations:* FCA. *Recreations:* Sailing.

CLEMENTS, Alan William; CBE; Finance Director, Imperial Chemical Industries plc, since 1979; Finance, Territorial Director for Africa, Investor Relations, Acquisitions. *Career:* Inland Revenue, Inspector of Taxes 1952-56; ICI Taxation Officer 1956-63; Taxation Officer, Senior Assistant 1963-66; Assistant Treasurer 1966-71; Deputy Treasurer 1971-76; Treasurer 1976-79. *Biog: b.* 12 December 1928. *Nationality:* British. *m.* 1953, Pearl; 2 s; 1 d. *Educ:* Culford School, Bury St Edmunds; Magdalen College, Oxford (BA 2nd Class Hons Geography). *Directorships:* Cable and Wireless plc 1985 (non-exec); Guinness Mahon Holdings plc 1988 (non-exec); Trafalgar House plc 1980 (non-exec); SEPS Trustees Ltd 1985 (non-exec). *Professional Organisations:* Fellow, Association of Corporate Treasurers, Founder President 1978-82. *Publications:* Numerous Articles for Financial Journals. *Recreations:* Golf, Music, Reading.

CLEMENTS, Victor H J; Managing Partner, Moores & Rowland.

CLEMINSON, Sir James; MC, DL; Chairman, Riggs A P Bank Ltd.

CLERIN, M; Managing Director (Investment Management), Bankers Trust Company.

CLIFF, John C; Director, Bradstock Blunt & Crawley Ltd.

CLIFFE, E E; Managing Director, Pharmaceuticals Division, The Boots Co plc.

CLIFT, John; Partner, Lawrence Graham, Solicitors, since 1988; Commercial Property/Planning and Environmental Law. *Career:* Kingsley Wood and Co (Solicitors), Junior Clerk 1959-64; Hextall Erskine and Co (Solicitors), Clerk 1964-83; Lawrence Graham (Solicitors), Assistant Solicitor 1984-88; Partner 1988-. *Biog: b.* 8 July 1943. *Nationality:* British. *m.* 1967, Carol Ann (née Griffiths); 2 d. *Educ:* The Skinners School, Tunbridge Wells; City of London Polytechnic. *Other Activities:* Member, Law Society; Affiliate Member, British Council of Shopping Centres. *Professional Organisations:* Solicitor; Fellow, Institute of Legal Executives (1980). *Clubs:* Cottesmore Golf and Country Club, Horsham Bridge Club. *Recreations:* Bridge, Golf.

CLIFT, Noel Rhys; Partner, Hill Taylor Dickinson (Solicitors); Litigate, Insurance and Reinsurance, Maritime Law. *Career:* Hill Dickinson 1981-84; Holman Fenwick & Willan (Paris) 1984-85; Hill Dickinson (Now Hill Taylor Dickinson) 1985-. *Biog: b.* 25 December 1957. *Nationality:* British. *m.* 1989, Susan Jane; 1 d. *Educ:* Aberystwyth University (LLB Hons); Université d'Aix-en-Provence, France (DESU). *Other Activities:* Member, City of London Solicitors Company.

CLIFTON, Paul; Deputy Managing Director, Alliance & Leicester Building Society, since 1989; Management Services, Lending, Premises. *Career:* Hawker Siddeley, Computer Supervisor 1957-65; Universal Grinding (Stafford), Computer Manager 1965-70; British Shoe Corporation, Computer Services Mgr 1970-77; Leicester Building Society, Assistant General Manager (Management Services) 1977-82; General Manager & Director 1982-85; Alliance & Leicester Building Society, General Manager & Director 1985-89; Deputy Managing Director 1989-. *Biog: b.* 15 July 1936. *Nationality:* British. *m.* 1965, Margaret S; 1 s; 2 d. *Educ:* Leeds University (BSc Hons Maths). *Directorships:* Electronic Funds Transfer Ltd 1984 (non-exec); Alliance and Leicester Personal Finance Ltd Chm; Alliance & Leicester Estate Ltd Chm; Alliance & Leicester Property Services Ltd (non-exec); Alliance & Leicester (IOM) Ltd (non-exec). *Professional Organisations:* CEng; FBCS. *Recreations:* Bridge, Angling, Gardening.

CLIMIE, C G; Director, Panmure Gordon & Co Limited, since 1987. *Biog: b.* 8 June 1958. *Nationality:* British. *m.* 1986, Jane (née Muir); 2 s. *Educ:* St Edmund Hall, Oxford (MA Hons Modern History). *Clubs:* Flyfishers.

CLINTON-DAVIS, Stanley; Lord Clinton-Davis; Consultant, S J Berwin & Co, Solicitors, since 1989; EC and Environmental Law and Affairs. *Career:* Hackney Borough Council, Member 1959-71; Mayor of Hackney 1968-69; Member of Parliament for Hackney Central

1970-83; Parliamentary Under-Secretary of State for Trade, with Responsibility for Companies, Aviation and Shipping; Opposition Spokesman on Trade 1979-81; Opposition Spokesman on Foreign Affairs 1981-83; Member of the Commission of the European Communities with Responsibility for Transport, Environment, Nuclear Safety 1985-89; S J Berwin & Co, Consultant 1989-; Created Life Peer 1990. *Biog: b.* 6 December 1928. *Nationality:* British. *m.* 1954, Frances Jane; 1 s; 3 d. *Educ:* Bournemouth School; Mercers School; Kings College, London University (Bachelor of Laws). *Directorships:* Jewish Chronicle. *Other Activities:* Grand Cross, Order of Leopold II, Belgium, Member, Council of Justice; Member, British Maritime League; Chair, Refugee Council; Chair, Advisory Committee on Pollution of the Sea; Trustee, Bernt Carlsson Trust (One World); Trustee, International Shakespeare Global Centre; Member of Council, Zoological Society; Vice President, Institution of Environmental Health Officers; Joint Presidency, Society of Labour Lawyers; Member, UN Sasakawa Environment Prize Selection Committee. *Publications:* Joint Author, Report of a British Parliamentary Delegation, Good Neighbours? Nicaragua, Central America and the United States, 1982; Numerous Articles; Chapter in a Forthcoming Book: New Directions in British Politics by Professor Philip Norton, University of Hull. *Recreations:* Golf, Association Football, Political Biographies.

CLODE, Michael Leslie Hailey; Partner, Freshfields, since 1974. *Career:* Equity & Law Life Assurance Society, Trainee Actuary 1962-64; Freshfields, Articled Clerk 1965-70; Assistant Solicitor 1970-74. *Biog: b.* 5 October 1943. *Nationality:* British. *m.* 1970, Isobel McLeod (née Carrick); 4 d. *Educ:* St Edwards, Oxford. *Other Activities:* City of London Solicitor's Company. *Professional Organisations:* Law Society. *Clubs:* Aberdeen Angus Cattle Society. *Recreations:* Skiing.

CLOGG, Christopher Derek Sherwel; Partner, Theodore Goddard, since 1967; Corporate, Financial Services, Insolvency. *Career:* Theodore Goddard Asst Solicitor 1965-67. *Biog: b.* 26 March 1936. *m.* 1981, Clodagh (née Maclure); 2 s; 1 d. *Educ:* Eton College; Christ Church, Oxford (MA). *Other Activities:* City of London Solicitors' Company. *Professional Organisations:* The Law Society. *Clubs:* White's, The Garrick. *Recreations:* Theatre, Classical Literature, Golf.

CLOKE, Richard Owen; Director, Barclays de Zoete Wedd Ltd, since 1985; International Capital Markets. *Career:* Barclays Bank plc 1960-76; Asst District Mgr 1976-83; Branch Mgr 1979-83; Barclays Merchant Bank Ltd, Asst Dir, Intl Securities Div 1983-85. *Biog: b.* 3 May 1944. *Nationality:* British. *m.* 1969, Carol Ann (née Wadsworth); 2 s; 1 d. *Educ:* Reading School. *Directorships:* Barclays de Zoete Wedd Capital Markets Ltd 1986 (exec); Ebbgate Holdings Ltd 1986 (non-exec).

Professional Organisations: FCIB. *Recreations:* Badminton, Tennis, Golf.

CLOUGH, Richard Robert; Director, Singer & Friedlander, since 1987; Investment Management. *Biog: b.* 18 November 1943. *m.* 1973, Gael (née Stancliffe); 1 s; 2 d. *Educ:* King's School, Bruton; Ecole de Commerce, Neuchatel, Switzerland. *Directorships:* Various Private Family Companies; Abtrust New Dawn Investment Trust plc 1989. *Other Activities:* Member of Lloyd's. *Clubs:* Bradford, RAC. *Recreations:* Shooting, Skiing, Tennis, Sailing, Golf.

CLUCAS, Sir Kenneth; Council Member, FIMBRA.

CLUTTON, Rafe Henry; Director, Legal & General Assurance Society Ltd, since 1972. *Career:* Cluttons, Chartered Surveyors, Ptnr 1955-; Snr Ptnr 1982-; City Acre Property Investments Trust Ltd; Legal and General Assurance Society Ltd 1972-80; Legal & General Investment Management (Holdings) Ltd 1980-83; National Safe Deposit and Trustee Company (UK) Ltd; Number 1 Poultry Ltd; Oxenford Properties Ltd. *Biog: b.* 13 June 1929. *Nationality:* British. *Directorships:* Haslemere Estates plc 1990; Kingsown Property Limited 1989; Legal & General Group plc 1979; Salvation Army Housing Association 1987; The National Theatre Board Limited. *Professional Organisations:* FRICS.

COATES, C F; Executive Director (Finance), Eagle Star Insurance Company Limited.

COATES, Howard Brian; Director, Barclays de Zoete Wedd.

COATES, Mrs Katherine Ann; Partner, Clifford Chance, since 1990; Insurance and Financial Services Regulation, Investment Funds, General Corporate. *Career:* Coward Chance, Articled Clerk 1981-83; Coward Chance/Clifford Chance, Assistant Solicitor 1983-90. *Biog: b.* 1 September 1959. *Nationality:* British. *m.* 1983, Andrew (née Cooke). *Educ:* King Edward VI High School for Girls, Birmingham; Somerville College, Oxford (BA Jurisprudence). *Professional Organisations:* Law Society. *Recreations:* Travel, Theatre, Walking, Cycling.

COATES, Peter; Group Treasurer, Beazer plc.

COATS, Sir William; Director, Clydesdale Bank plc.

COBBETT, D S; Upper Warden, The Worshipful Company of Glaziers.

COBBOLD, Nicholas Sydney; Chairman, Stephenson Cobbold, since 1987. *Career:* Coldstream Guards 1952-54 & 1956; Williams De Broe 1955-65; Partner 1959; Panmure Gordon & Co Partner 1965-76; JE Sanger Ltd Deputy Chairman 1976-79; Worms &

Co Ltd Director 1979-86; Energy Recovery Investment Corporation SA Chairman & Chief Executive 1982-86. *Biog: b.* 5 May 1934. *Nationality:* British. *m.* 1980, Annette Kim (née Dearden); 7 d. *Educ:* Eton College. *Directorships:* Power Investment Trust 1962-67; Heritable & General Trust 1983-87; Haussmann Holdings 1984-86; Heliunion 1984-86; Cambridge Petroleum Royalties 1983-87; Exploration Company of Louisiana 1983-87; Drayton Consolidated Trust PLC 1988. *Clubs:* White's, Pratt's, Portland.

COCHIN DE BILLY, C R; Managing Director (Investment Management), Bankers Trust Company.

COCHRANE, Brian Philip; Managing Director, Glenbow Financial Management Ltd, since 1983. *Biog: b.* 14 January 1941. *Nationality:* Scottish. *m.* 1970, Joan Margaret (née Aspinall); 1 s; 2 d. *Educ:* (BA History/Social Science). *Directorships:* Glenbow Estates & Insurance Services Ltd 1985 (exec); FIMBRA 1988 (exec); Munro & McKenzie Ltd 1990 (exec). *Professional Organisations:* Past Chairman, Scottish Independent Intermediaries Association, 1988-89.

COCHRANE, J M T; Operations Director, Wellcome plc.

COCHRANE, Sir Marc; Director, GT Management plc, since 1988; European Marketing. *Career:* Greenshields Inc Brokers, Account Executive 1971-73; Hambros Bant Ltd, Director in Charge of Middle East Business 1973-85; GT Management plc 1985-. *Biog: b.* 23 October 1946. *Nationality:* Irish. *m.* 1969, Hala; 2 s; 1 d. *Educ:* Eton College; Trinity College, Dublin (MA,BBS). *Directorships:* Hambros Bank 1979 (exec); GT Management (UK) Ltd 1985 (exec); GT Deutchland Fund SA 1986 (exec); GT Management plc 1988 (exec). *Other Activities:* Trustee, Chester Beatty Library and Gallery of Oriental Art. *Recreations:* Collecting Art & Antiques, Target Shooting.

COCKBAIN, Philip Alexander; Partner, R Watson & Sons.

COCKELL, Michael Henry; Senior Partner, MH Cockell & Partners, since 1985. *Career:* GN Rouse Syndicate 570, Underwriter 1968-; Ctee of Non-Marine Assoc, Lloyd's Elected Member; Dep Chm 1982; Chm 1983; Lloyd's Elected Council 1984-87; Dep Chm 1986. *Biog: b.* 30 August 1933. *Nationality:* British. *m.* 1961, Elizabeth Janet (née Meikle); 1 s; 3 d. *Educ:* Harrow School. *Directorships:* GN Rouse Syndicate 570 1968 Underwriter; MH Cockell & Co 1978 Chm; MH Cockell & Partners 1986 Snr Ptnr. *Clubs:* City of London, MCC, HAC. *Recreations:* Country Pursuits, Auctions.

COCKHILL, B F G; Director, Kellett (Holdings) Limited.

COCKROFT, C S; Secretary, Halifax Building Society.

COCKROFT, Richard Robert; Director, FIMBRA, since 1988; Membership and Pratice. *Career:* Towry Law (Holdings) Ltd, MD 1961-83; M & G Group plc, Dir 1984-88; M & G Assurance Group Limited, MD. *Biog: b.* 7 March 1939. *Nationality:* British. *m.* 1962, Judith Prunella (née Wearn); 1 s; 1 d. *Educ:* Exeter School; Trinity, Cambridge (MA). *Professional Organisations:* FCII. *Clubs:* MCC, East Berks Golf. *Recreations:* Golf, Real Tennis.

COCKS, George W; Director, Bradstock Blunt & Crawley Ltd.

CODD, David; Finance Director, Winterflood Securities Ltd.

CODO, F; Operations & Finance Manager, Banca Popolare di Milano.

CODRINGTON, Capt C T; CBE, RN; Clerk, Cordwainers' Company.

CODRINGTON, Edward Anthony; Partner, Slaughter and May, since 1984; Pensions and Employment Law. *Biog: b.* 12 April 1951. *Nationality:* British. *m.* 1977, Mary Philomena (née Towey); 2 s; 4 d. *Educ:* St Benedict's School; Birmingham University (LLB Hons). *Other Activities:* City of London Solicitors' Company. *Professional Organisations:* The Law Society. *Recreations:* Family.

COE, David James; Director/Group Accountant, Cater Allen Holdings plc, since 1984. *Career:* Moore Stephens & Co Audit Clerk/Acct 1955-67; Cater Allen Acct 1967. *Biog: b.* 14 March 1938. *m.* 1972, Pauline Elizabeth (née Cast); 1 s; 2 d. *Educ:* Brentwood School. *Directorships:* Proudworth Ltd 1985 (exec); Cater Allen Securities Ltd 1978 (exec); Upminster Golf Co Ltd 1977 (exec). *Professional Organisations:* FCA. *Clubs:* Upminster Golf Club. *Recreations:* Golf.

COE, R F; Clerk, Paviors' Company.

COFFELL, F H; Partner, Field Fisher Waterhouse.

COGHLAN, Timothy Boyle Lake; Chairman, BZW Equity Division, Barclays de Zoete Wedd Ltd, since 1987; UK Equities Sales, Distribution and Market Making. *Career:* de Zoete & Gordon 1960-68; de Zoete & Bevan, Partner 1968-86. *Biog: b.* 29 March 1939. *Nationality:* British. *m.* 1966, Elisabeth; 1 s; 1 d. *Educ:* Rugby School; Pembroke College, Cambridge (BA Economics & Law). *Directorships:* Tropeast Properties 1971-. *Professional Organisations:* Member, Stock Exchange. *Clubs:* MCC, Hawks Club, Richmond Rugby Club. *Recreations:* Shooting, Bridge, Tennis, Cricket.

COGSWELL, J A; Director, Merchant Navy Investment Management Ltd.

COHEN, Harvey; Chairman & Chief Executive, Chancery plc.

• **COHEN, Mrs Janet (née Neel);** Director, Charterhouse Bank Limited, since 1982; Corporate Finance, Privatisation, Marketing. *Career:* Frere Cholmeley and Nicholsons, Articled Clerk 1963-65; Management Consultant 1965-69; Department of Trade and Industry, Principal Non Assistant Secretary 1969-81. *Biog: b.* 4 July 1940. *Nationality:* British. *m.* 1971, James Lionel; 2 s; 1 d. *Educ:* South Hampstead High School; Newnham College, Cambridge (2:1 Hons Law). *Directorships:* Charterhouse Bank Ltd 1988 (exec). *Other Activities:* Associate Fellow, Newnham College Cambridge; Member, Schools Examination and Assessment Council. *Professional Organisations:* Solicitor, 1965. *Publications:* Death's Bright Angel, 1988; Death on Site, 1989; Death of a Partner, 1991. *Recreations:* Writing, Politics.

COHEN, L; Director, IMI Capital Markets (UK).

COHEN, Laurence J; Intellectual Property Partner, Bristows Cooke & Carpmael.

COHEN, Philippe Joseph; Executive Director, Banque Paribas; Head of Commodities/Trade, Finance Department. *Career:* Banque Paribas, Asst Mgr 1981-84; (Houston), Group VP 1984-87; (Paris), VP, World Commodities Group 1987-88. *Biog: b.* 20 December 1957. *Nationality:* French. *Educ:* Louis le Grand; Ecole Superieure de Commerce de Paris. *Professional Organisations:* IP; API.

COHEN, Ronald Mourad; Founder Chairman, The MMG Patricof Group plc, since 1972; Investment Management/Corporate Finance/Venture Capital. *Career:* McKinsey & Co (UK & Italy), Consultant 1969-71; Institut de Développement Industriel (France), Charge de Mission 1972. *Biog: b.* 1 August 1945. *Nationality:* British. *m.* 1987, Sharon (née Harel); 1 d. *Educ:* Orange Hill Grammar School, London; Exeter College, Oxford (BA); Harvard Business School, USA (Henry Fellow, MBA). *Directorships:* The MMG Patricof Group plc (exec) Chm; MMG Patricof & Co Ltd (exec) Chm; Alan Patricof Associates Ltd (exec) Chm; MMG Patricof Buy-Ins Ltd (exec) Chm; My Kinda Town Ltd; Sterling Publishing Group plc Chm; James Neill Holdings Ltd Chm; Capitol Films Ltd Chm; Markoffer plc Chm; Markbalance plc Chm. *Other Activities:* Member, Royal Institute of International Affairs; Member of Task Force Committee on Wider Share Ownership, CBI. *Professional Organisations:* Member of Council & Past Chairman, British Venture Capital Association; Institute of Directors. *Clubs:* RAC. *Recreations:* Music, Art, Theatre, Tennis, Travel.

COHEN, U N; Director, Euro Brokers Holdings Limited.

COLAO, Charles; Director, Hambros Bank Ltd, since 1987; International Trade Related Transactions Marketing. *Biog: b.* 6 August 1925. *Nationality:* British. *m.* 1952, Joyce Ethel. *Professional Organisations:* AIB.

COLE, A J; Executive Director, County NatWest Limited.

COLE, Ernest; Managing Director, Samuel Montagu & Co Limited, since 1990; Specialised Financing. *Career:* Midland Bank 1949-74; Samuel Montagu 1974-. *Biog: b.* 17 May 1933. *Nationality:* British. *m.* 1956, Audrey (née Acons); 2 s.

COLE, Michael David; Group Taxation Manager, Prudential Corporation plc. *Biog: b.* 24 October 1945. *Nationality:* British. *m.* 1966, Carol; 1 s; 2 d. *Directorships:* Prudential Finance (UK) plc 1989 (exec); Prudential Leasing Services Ltd 1985 (exec). *Other Activities:* Deputy Chairman, Taxation Panel, Association of British Insurers; Member, Life Taxation Committee, Association of British Insurers; Chairman, International Advisory Council, The Hartford Institute on Insurance Taxation.

COLE, Peter; Partner, Alexander Tatham.

COLE, Richard Anthony; Partner, Mayer, Brown & Platt, since 1983; International Financial and Commercial Law. *Career:* Mayer, Brown & Platt (Chicago), Assoc Lawyer 1976-81; (London), Assoc Lawyer 1981-83. *Biog: b.* 1951. *Nationality:* American. *m.* 1975, Lois (née Hallonquist). *Educ:* Brown University (AB); Cornell Law School (JD). *Other Activities:* Trustee, University of Notre Dame in England. *Professional Organisations:* Member, The Bar of State of Illinois. *Recreations:* Travel, Antiques.

COLE, Terence Arthur; Head of Property Department, Walker Martineau Stringer Saul, since 1984. *Career:* Walker Martineau, Articled Clerk 1973-75; Solicitor 1975-76; Partner 1977-. *Biog: b.* 28 February 1951. *Nationality:* British. *m.* 1978, Rosanna (née Wollcombe); 1 s; 2 d. *Educ:* Bristol Grammar School; Corpus Christi College, Cambridge (MA). *Other Activities:* Freeman, City of London Solicitors' Company. *Professional Organisations:* Law Society.

COLE, W C; Finance Director, Olliff & Partners plc, since 1987; All Financial, Administration and Compliance Matters. *Career:* Fuller Jenks Beecroft, Chartered Accountants 1970-71; Casson Beckman Rutley, Chartered Accountants 1972-73; Stocken & Lazarus, Stock Exchange Jobbers 1973-77; Akroyd & Smithers plc, Stock Exchange Jobbers (after merger) 1977-86; Warburg Securities, Finance House (after takeover)

1986-87; Olliff & Partners plc, Stockbrokers 1987-. *Biog: b.* 13 January 1946. *Nationality:* British. *m.* 1972, Sally (née Still); 2 d. *Educ:* St Joseph's College, London. *Directorships:* County Partners Ltd 1990 (exec); Classic Papers Ltd 1984 (non-exec). *Professional Organisations:* Fellow, The Institute of Chartered Accountants in England & Wales; Member, The International Stock Exchange. *Clubs:* RAC, Cherry Lodge Golf Club. *Recreations:* Golf, Tennis, Swimming.

COLE-HAMILTON, Arthur Richard; Director and Chief Executive, Clydesdale Bank plc, since 1987. *Career:* National Service, Commissioned to Argyll & Sutherland Highlanders 1960-62; Brechin Cole-Hamilton & Co, Chartered Accountants 1962-67; Clydesdale Bank, Head Office 1967; Asst Mgr, Clydesdale Bank Finance Company 1967; Mgr, Clydesdale Bank Finance Corporation & Money Market Dept 1971; Asst Mgr, Chief London Office 1971; Superintendent of Branches 1974; Head Office Mgr 1976; Asst Gen Mgr 1978; Gen Mgr 1979; Dep Chief Gen Mgr/Chief Gen Mgr 1982; Dir & Chief Gen Mgr 1984; Dir & Chief Exec 1987. *Biog: b.* 8 May 1935. *m.* 1963, Prudence Ann (née Lamb); 1 s; 2 d. *Educ:* Ardrossan Academy; Loretto School; Cambridge University (BA). *Directorships:* Glasgow Chamber of Commerce. *Other Activities:* President, Institute of Bankers in Scotland, 1988-90; Fellow, Institute of Bankers in Scotland; Deputy Chairman, Scottish Council Development & Industry; Member of Executive Committee, Erskine Hospital; Director, Glasgow Chamber of Commerce; Member of the Board of Trustees, National Galleries of Scotland, 1986; Honorary President, Ayrshire Chamber of Industry & Commerce; Member of Finance Committee, Royal & Ancient Golf Club; Member of Championship Committee, Royal & Ancient Golf Club, 1989-; Deputy Chairman, Committee of Scottish Clearing Bankers, 1989-91; Patron, Dyslexia Institute (Scotland) Bursary Fund. *Professional Organisations:* CA; FIB (Scot). *Clubs:* Prestwick Golf Club, Royal & Ancient, Western, Club Highland Brigade, The Saints & Sinners Club of Scotland. *Recreations:* Golf.

COLEBATCH, Phillip Maxwell; Executive Director, Credit Suisse First Boston Ltd, since 1984; Head of Administration & Chief Financial Officer. *Career:* Citibank NA (& Subsidiaries), Exec Dir Head of Euro-Securities 1972-84; Asia Pacific Capital Corporation Limited 1974-81; Citicorp International Bank Limited 1982-84. *Biog: b.* 25 December 1944. *Nationality:* Australian; 2 d. *Educ:* University of Adelaide, Australia (Bachelor of Science, Bachelor of Engineering); Massachusetts Institute of Technology (Master of Science); Harvard Graduate School of Business Administration (Doctor of Business Administration). *Directorships:* Credit Suisse First Boston Ltd 1984 (exec); CSFB (Fixed Assets) Ltd 1987 (exec); CSFB Services AG 1989 (exec); White Weld Investment Ltd 1990 (exec); Glenstreet Property Development Ltd 1989 (exec); Glenstreet NV

1987 (exec); Glenstreet Investment Ltd 1990 (exec); Otisco NV 1986 (exec); Credit Suisse First Boston Nederland NV 1989 (non-exec); CSFB (UK) Holdings 1989 (non-exec); CSFB UK Ltd 1988 (non-exec); CSFB Fund Management Ltd 1989 (non-exec); CSFB Nominees Limited 1989 (non-exec); CSFB UK Nominees Ltd 1989 (non-exec); Very Finance AG 1989 (non-exec). *Other Activities:* Member of Management Committee; Member of Operating Committee, Credit Suisse First Boston Limited; Chief Financial Officer for Europe for Financiere Credit Suisse First Boston. *Clubs:* Royal Southern Yacht Club, Royal Hong Kong Yacht Club, Royal Ocean Racing Club, The Hurlingham Club, Royal Hong Kong Jockey Club, The Hong Kong Club. *Recreations:* Tennis, Sailing.

COLEBY, Anthony Laurie; Executive Director, Bank of England, since 1990; Monetary Policy. *Career:* Bank of England, Various 1961; International Monetary Fund, PA to MD 1964-67; Bank of England, Asst to Chief Cashier 1967-69; Asst Chief, Overseas Dept 1969-72; Adviser, Overseas Dept 1972-73; Dep Chief Cashier 1973-80; Asst Dir - Head of Money Mkts Div 1980-86; Chief Monetary Adviser to the Governor 1986-90. *Biog: b.* 27 April 1935. *Nationality:* British. *m.* 1966, Rosemary Melian Elisabeth (née Garran); 1 s; 2 d. *Educ:* Winchester College; Corpus Christi College, Cambridge (MA). *Clubs:* Overseas Bankers'. *Recreations:* Choral Singing, Railways, Transport.

COLEMAN, B; Director, Wellington Underwriting Agencies Limited.

COLEMAN, J W J; Director, S G Warburg & Co Ltd.

COLEMAN, John; Partner, Moore Stephens.

COLEMAN, Richard; Partner, Clifford Chance.

COLEMAN-SMITH, Brian; Director, Burson-Marsteller, since 1985; Investor Relations/Financial Public Relations. *Career:* Financial Weekly, Director 1979-81; Guardian Newspaper, Financial Sales Director 1981-85; Burson-Marsteller Financial, Director 1985-; Burson-Marsteller Limited, Director 1989-. *Biog: b.* 26 October 1944. *Nationality:* British. *m.* 1984, Frances (née Gladstone); 2 s; 1 d. *Educ:* Emanuel School, London. *Recreations:* Badminton, Theatre, Classical Music, Sport.

COLERIDGE, David Ean; Chairman, Sturge Holdings plc, since 1978. *Career:* Glanvill Enthoven 1950-57; R W Sturge & Co 1957-; Dir 1966-; A L Sturge (Holdings) Ltd (now Sturge Holdings plc), Chm 1978-; Lloyd's Underwriting Agents Association, Member of Ctee 1974-82; Chm of Ctee 1981-82; Lloyd's, Junior Deputy Chm 1985; Member of the Council and Ctee of Lloyd's 1983-86 & 1988-; Lloyd's, Senior Deputy Chm 1988-89; Lloyd's, Chm 1991-. *Biog: b.* 7 June 1932. *Nationality:* British. *m.* 1955, Susan (née Senior); 3 s.

Educ: Eton. *Directorships:* Wise Speke Holdings 1986 (non-exec). *Other Activities:* Liveryman, Worshipful Company of Grocers. *Clubs:* City of London, Mark's Club. *Recreations:* Shooting, Racing, Early English Watercolours, Family.

COLERIDGE, Peter; Group Treasurer, Granada Group.

COLES, Adrian; Head of External Relations, The Building Societies Association, since 1986; Economics, Press Relations, Statistics. *Career:* Electricity Council, Economist 1976-79; Building Societies Association, Economist 1979-81; Head of Economics & Statistics 1981-86; Head of External Relations 1986-. *Biog: b.* 19 April 1954. *Nationality:* British. *m.* 1981, Marion Alma (née Hoare); 1 s; 1 d. *Educ:* Holly Lodge Grammar School; University of Nottingham (BA); University of Sheffield. *Other Activities:* Member, Committee of Management, Thames Valley Housing Association; Member, Governing Body, Grand Avenue Primary School; Member, Council, Housing Centre Trust. *Publications:* Large Number of Articles in Journals Connected with Building Societies, Housing and Personal Finance; The Mortgage Market (with Mark Boleat), 1987; Building Societies and the Savings Market, 1986. *Recreations:* Reading, Swimming, Family.

COLES, Ian R; Partner, Mayer, Brown & Platt, since 1987; Banking, Finance. *Career:* City of London Polytechnic, Lecturer in Law 1978-80; Barrister-at-Law, Inner Temple 1979-80; Mayer, Brown & Platt, New York 1981-84; London 1984-; Partner 1987-. *Biog: b.* 12 September 1956. *Nationality:* English. *m.* 1988, Bethann (née Firestone). *Educ:* University of Cambridge (BA First Class Hons); Harvard University (LLM). *Other Activities:* Barrister-at-Law: Lincoln's Inn (Walter Wigglesworth and Hardwick Scholar) 1979; New York, 1983. *Professional Organisations:* Member: New York State Bar Association, Committee on Multi-National Reorganisation and Insolvency; Bar Association for Commerce, Finance, & Industry (England); International Bar Association (Section on Business Law); Association Internationale des Jeunes Avocats. *Publications:* Remittances (author) 1979 British Tax Review 238; A Guide to the Capital Markets Activities of Banks and Bank Holding Companies (contributing author), 1990. *Clubs:* Raffles. *Recreations:* Music, Wine, Skiing.

COLES, S J H; Financial Planning Adviser, The Thomson Corporation.

COLIVA, E; Director, IMI Securities Ltd.

COLLARD, J G; Partner, Pannell Kerr Forster.

COLLAS, Philippe-Henry; Managing Director, Societe Generale Merchant Bank plc, since 1988; Market Making European Equities, M & A Capital Markets, TFX. *Career:* Societe Generale Inspector 1977-83; Dep Gen Inspector (i/c Intl Network & Capital Markets Div) 1983-87; Adviser, Capital Market Division 1987-88. *Directorships:* Tradeb (Nominees) Ltd; Capital Home Loans Ltd; S G Leasing Ltd; Casabas Ltd; Societe Generale Asset Management Ltd; Societe Generale Trust Management Ltd; Premium Life Assurance Holdings Ltd; FIMAT UK Ltd.

COLLECOTT, John Salmon; Director, C Czarnikow Ltd.

COLLETT, Sir Christopher; GBE, JP; Partner, Arthur Young, since 1981; Audit. *Career:* National Service, Royal Artillery, 2nd Lt 1950-51; Surrey Yeomanry (QMR) RA, TA Capt 1951-60; Cassleton Elliott & Co, Articled Clerk 1954; Qualified 1958; Josolyne Miles & Cassleton Elliot/Josolyne, Layton Bennett & Co; Arthur Young (now Ernst & Young), Partner 1962-. *Biog: b.* 10 June 1931. *Nationality:* British. *m.* 1959, Christine Anne (née Griffiths); 2 s; 1 d. *Educ:* Harrow School; Emmanuel College, Cambridge (MA). *Other Activities:* Member, Court of Common Council (Broad St Ward), 1973; Alderman for Broad Street, 1979; Sheriff, City of London, 1985; Lord Mayor, London, 1988-89; JP, City of London, 1979; Worshipful Company, Glovers of London (Master), 1981; Worshipful Company, Chartered Accountants in England and Wales (Liveryman 1984, Assistant 1986); City of London TAVR Committee; Council Member, Action Research for the Crippled Child, 1984-; Governor, Haberdashers' Aske's Schools, Elstree, 1982; Music Therapy Group Limited, Bridewell Royal Hospital and King Edward's School Witley; Treasurer, Lee House, Wimbledon; President, Broad Street Ward Club, 1979-; Order of Merit (Class 2), State of Qatar, 1985; Orden del Merito Civil (Class 2), Spain, 1986; Commander, Order of Merit Federal Republic of Germany, 1986; Commander, Order of the Niger (Class 1), 1989; Order of Independence (Class 2), United Arab Emirates, 1989; Hon DSc (City University), 1988; Knight, Order of St John, 1988. *Professional Organisations:* FCA. *Clubs:* City of London, City Livery. *Recreations:* Gardening, Fishing.

COLLIER, Frank Whitworth; Partner, Titmuss Sainer & Webb, since 1973; Retail Property. *Career:* Adam F Greenhalgh & Co (Bolton), Articled Clerk 1950-55; Shasha & Hamwee (Manchester), Assistant Solicitor 1956-58; Russell & Russell (Bolton), Assistant Solicitor 1959-60; Harris Chetham (London), Partner 1960-66; Town & Commercial Properties Ltd, Secretary, Director 1966-72; Titmus Sainer & Webb (London), Partner 1972-. *Biog: b.* 13 December 1932. *Nationality:* British. *m.* 1956, Brenda (née Howarth); 1 s; 2 d. *Educ:* Bolton School. *Professional Organisations:* City of London Solicitors' Company; The Law Society. *Clubs:* Fernfell Park Golf and Country Club. *Recreations:* Golf, Music, Reading, Gardening.

COLLIER, I C; Director, James Capel Gilts Ltd, since 1990; Gilt Option. *Career:* London & Manchester Assurance, Actuarial Student 1972-75; Swiss Reinsurance Company, Actuarial Superintendent 1975-79. *Biog: b.* 19 October 1950. *Nationality:* British. *m.* 1974, Carol; 1 s; 2 d. *Educ:* University of Sussex (BSc). *Directorships:* James Capel Gilts Ltd 1990 (exec). *Professional Organisations:* Fellow, Institute of Actuaries 1977.

COLLINGHAM, Ms Rosalind; Partner, Nabarro Nathanson, since 1988; Company Law. *Biog: m.* 1986, Michael Draper. *Professional Organisations:* ATII.

COLLINGS, John; Director, N T Evennett and Partners Ltd.

COLLINS, Andrew D; Partner, Wilde Sapte.

COLLINS, C I; Director, Hoare Govett Corporate Finance Ltd.

COLLINS, Crispian Hilary Vincent; Director, Phillips & Drew Fund Management (PDFM), since 1985; UK Pension Funds. *Career:* Phillips & Drew Private Clients Department, Fund Manager 1969-75; Phillips & Drew Pension Fund Department, Fund Manager 1975-81; Partner 1981-85; Phillips & Drew Fund Management, Director 1985-. *Biog: b.* 22 January 1948. *Nationality:* British. *m.* 1974, Diane (née Bromley); 1 s; 2 d. *Educ:* Ampleforth College, York; University College, Oxford (BA Hons Modern History). *Other Activities:* Member, Committee of Management, Gulliver Property Unit Trust. *Professional Organisations:* Member, International Stock Exchange; Associate, Society of Investment Analysts. *Clubs:* Crowborough, Beacon Golf Club.

COLLINS, Ivor; Partner, Forsyte Kerman.

COLLINS, J D; Director, Lowndes Lambert Group Limited.

COLLINS, Leigh Graham; Director, Institutional Sales, Charterhouse Tilney, since 1989; UK Equity. *Career:* Simon & Coates, Partner 1976-86; Chase Manhattan Securities, I/C Institutional Equity Sales & Research 1986-89. *Biog: b.* 1 July 1948. *Nationality:* British. *m.* 1971, Elizabeth (née Freeman-Archer); 1 s. *Educ:* Birkenhead School; Jesus College, Cambridge (MA). *Directorships:* Charterhouse Tilney 1989 (exec).

COLLINS, Neil; City Editor, The Daily Telegraph, since 1986. *Career:* Sunday Times, City Editor 1984-86; Evening Standard, City Editor 1979-84; Daily Mail 1974-79.

COLLINS, Nigel E N; Director, Bradstock Blunt & Crawley Ltd.

COLLS, Alan Howard Crawford; Chairman, Nicholson Chamberlain Colls Ltd; since 1988. *Career:* Stewart Wrightson Aviation Ltd, Chairman 1975-86; Stewart Wrightson Holdings plc, Director 1981-87; Stewart Wrightson International Group, Chairman 1981-85; Stewart Wrightson Ltd, Chairman 1986-87; Nicholson Chamberlain Colls Ltd, Chairman 1988-. *Biog: b.* 15 December 1941. *Nationality:* British. *m.* 1969, Janet; 1 s; 1 d. *Educ:* Harrow. *Other Activities:* Dep Chm Lloyd's Insurance Brokers Ctee, 1986-87 & 1990-. *Recreations:* Tennis, Golf, Travel.

COLLUM, Hugh Robert; Finance Director/Chief Financial Officer, Smithkline Beecham pls, since 1987; Finance, Strategic Planning, Information Systems. *Career:* Coopers & Lybrand 1959-64; Plymouth Breweries Ltd, Dir 1965-70; Courage Western, Dir 1971-72; Courage Limited, Fin Dir 1973-81; Cadbury Schweppes plc, Dep Group Fin Dir 1981-83; Group Fin Dir 1983-86; Beecham Group plc 1986-89. *Directorships:* Sedgwick Group plc 1987 (non-exec). *Other Activities:* Chairman, One Hundred Group. *Professional Organisations:* FCA.

COLMAN, Jeremy Gye; Director, County NatWest Ltd, since 1988; Corporate Finance. *Career:* Civil Service Department 1971-75; HM Treasury, Principal 1975-78; Civil Service Dept, Principal 1978-80; Private Sec to Permanent Sec & Head of Home Civil Service 1980-81; HM Treasury, Private Sec to Permanent Sec & Joint Head of Home Civil Service 1981-82; Asst Sec 1984-87. *Biog: b.* 9 April 1948. *Nationality:* British. *m.* 1978, Patricia Ann Stewart. *Educ:* John Lyon School, Harrow; Peterhouse, Cambridge (MA); Imperial College, London (MSc). *Other Activities:* Ironmonger's Company (Yeoman). *Clubs:* United Oxford and Cambridge University, Ski Club of Great Britain. *Recreations:* Cookery.

COLMER, Peter George; Director, Svenska International plc, since 1987; Scandinavian Equity Trading. *Career:* Medwin & Lowy, Partner 1970-80; Wedd Durlacher Mordaunt, Scandinavian Specialist 1980-84; Quilter Goodison, Head Foreign Trader 1984; Svenska Handelsbanken, Internat Director 1984. *Directorships:* Svenska International plc 1987.

COLQUHOUN, Andrew John; Secretary and Chief Executive, Institute of Chartered Accountants in England and Wales, since 1990; Permanent Head of Institute Secretariat. *Career:* Service with HM Diplomatic Service in London and Overseas 1974-81; Cabinet Office (on Secondment from Foreign and Commonwealth Office) 1981-83; Foreign and Commonwealth Office 1983-84; Shandwick Consultants (on Secondment to Institute of Chartered Accountants) 1984-86; ICAEW, Director of Education and Training 1987-90; Secretary and Chief Executive 1990-. *Biog: b.* 21 September 1949. *Nationality:* British. *m.* 1975, Patricia (née Beardall); 1 s; 1 d. *Educ:* Tiffin School; Nottingham

Univ (BSc Hons); Glasgow Univ (PhD); City Univ Business School (MBA). *Publications:* Various Articles in National, Educational and Accountancy Press. *Recreations:* Boating, Bird Watching, Walking, Reading.

COLVILLE, John Mark Alexander; Viscount Colville of Culross; Independent Member, The Securities Association Limited.

COLVILLE, Thomas Craufurd; TD; Director, SG Warburg & Co Ltd, since 1985; International Banking. *Career:* SG Warburg & Co Ltd 1963-. *Biog: b.* 14 July 1943. *Nationality:* British. *m.* 1978, Nicola (née Tulk-Hart); 2 d. *Educ:* Eton College. *Directorships:* SG Warburg & Co (Jersey) Ltd 1986; Rowe & Pitman Money Broking Ltd 1989; SG Warburg (Finance) Ltd 1987; British Industrial Corporation Ltd 1989. *Other Activities:* Trustee, Game Conservancy Trust, 1987-90; Member, Honourable Artillery Company, 1964-.

COLVIN, Andrew James; Comptroller & City Solicitor, Corporation of London.

COLWELL, Rodney P; Director, Merrill Lynch International Ltd, since 1988; Mergers & Acquisition. *Career:* Ranks Hovis McDoughall, Financial Accountant 1971-73; Grieveson, Grant & Co, National Enterprise Board, Investment Analys t 1974-79; Divisional Executive 1979-80; Hill Samuel & Co, Manager (Mergers & Acquisitions) 1981-84; Merrill Lynch International, Vice President 1984; Associate Director 1986. *Biog: b.* 9 September 1947. *Nationality:* British. *m.* 1972, Julia, (née Cornish). *Educ:* Queen Elizabeth School, Crediton, Devon; University College Cardiff (Post Graduate Diploma-Statistics, Honours Degree BSc Mathematics). *Directorships:* Merrill Lynch International Limited 1988 (exec). *Professional Organisations:* FCCA.

COMBE, Kenneth Christian; TD; Director, Stewart Underwriting plc, since 1987; Chairman, Stewart Members Agency Ltd. *Career:* Galbraith Pembroke & Co Ltd 1957-68; Director 1962; Eckersley Hicks & Co Ltd 1968-86; Director 1968; Stewart Underwriting plc 1986-. *Biog: b.* 14 November 1936. *Nationality:* British. *m.* 1972, Bridget Mary (née Richardson); 2 s. *Educ:* Radley College, Abingdon, Oxon. *Directorships:* Stewart Underwriting plc 1986 (exec); Stewart Members Agency Ltd (exec) Chairman; Eckersley Hicks (UA) Ltd (exec) Chairman; Martin Ashley Underwriting Agents Ltd (non-exec) Chairman; Clifford Palmer Underwriting Agencies Ltd (non-exec) Chairman; Bradstock & Barker Chairman. *Other Activities:* Worshipful Company of Shipwrights. *Clubs:* Cavalry and Guards, City of London. *Recreations:* Shooting, Golf.

COMBER, A W Peter; Finance Director, Riggs A P Bank Ltd, since 1988; Finance, Data Processing, Communications, Treasury Operations. *Career:* Peat Marwick Mitchell (London), Articles 1972-77; Equity & Law Life Assurance, Systems Development 1977-79; North Carolina National Bank (London), Accountant 1979-82; Creditanstalt Bankverein (London), Manager (Finance) 1982-84; Riggs A P Bank, Finance Director 1984-. *Biog: b.* 20 October 1952. *Nationality:* British. *m.* 1980, Caroline Jean (née Biles); 2 s. *Educ:* Stowe School. *Professional Organisations:* FCA. *Clubs:* Sunningdale Golf Club.

COMBER, Stanley James; General Manager, Marketing, The Royal Bank of Scotland plc, since 1988; Overall Director of Marketing of all Products & Services for the Bank. *Career:* Legal & General Assurance Pension Scheme Administrator 1959-61; Prudential Assurance-Various Life and Pensions 1961-67; -General Insurance Inspector 1967-73; -Various Marketing Posts 1973-85; -Snr Marketing Mgr 1973-85. *Biog: b.* 7 November 1942. *Nationality:* British. *m.* 1965, Jean (née Childs); 3 s; 1 d. *Educ:* Glyn Grammar School, Epsom. *Directorships:* Access Brand Ltd 1990 (non-exec). *Professional Organisations:* FCII. *Recreations:* Rowing, Swimming, DIY.

COMBES, Michael; Partner, Travers Smith Braithwaite.

COMBI, Cesare; UK Representative, Gruppo Arca Nordest.

COMNINOS, Michael; Director, N M Rothschild & Sons Ltd, since 1970. *Career:* N M Rothschild & Sons, Clerk/Manager 1954-65; Partner 1965-70; N M Rothschild & Sons Ltd, Director 1970-. *Biog: b.* 25 July 1931. *Nationality:* British. *m.* 1956, Ann (née Graves); 1 s; 1 d. *Educ:* Malvern College, Worcestershire. *Directorships:* Old Court International Ltd 1980 (non-exec). *Professional Organisations:* FCIB; FCIS; FCT; AMSIA. *Clubs:* Brooks's. *Recreations:* Skiing, Collecting Antiquities.

COMYN, J C Christopher; Partner, D J Freeman & Co.

COMYN, William A; Audit Group Partner, Touche Ross & Co, since 1974; Audit & Corporate Finance. *Biog: b.* 23 June 1944. *m.* 1984, Marjorie (née Tait); 3 s; 1 d. *Educ:* Kings School, Worcester. *Professional Organisations:* FCA.

CONCANON, Brian Anthony Ross; Partner, McKenna & Co, since 1981; Corporate Tax. *Career:* Deloitte Haskins & Sells, Chartered Acct 1961-71; Norton Rose Botterell & Roche, Solicitor 1971-77; Texaco UK Ltd, Tax Advisor 1977-78. *Biog: b.* 2 March 1943. *m.* 1986, Annabell (née Wright); 2 s; 3 d. *Educ:* Downside School. *Professional Organisations:* ICA; The Law Society. *Clubs:* RAC. *Recreations:* English Cartography.

CONDREN, Colin Edward; Group Compliance Director, Barclays De Zoete Wedd, since 1985; Compliance, Internal Audit & Legal. *Career:* Bank of England, various including Secondment to the Takeover Panel, latterly Adviser on Securities Markets Regulation and Developments 1956-83; Council for the Securities Industry, Deputy Director General 1983-85. *Biog: b.* 29 June 1936. *Nationality:* British. *m.* 1961, Irene Jacqueline (née Sherratt); 2 d. *Educ:* St Ignatius College, Stamford Hill. *Recreations:* Architecture, Photography.

CONEENY, Joseph A; Vice President & Group Executive, Manufacturers Hanover Trust Company, since 1988; Head of Oil & Gas Lending, Corporate Finance Group for UK & Europe. *Career:* Manufacturers Hanover Trust Co, Oilfield Services Group 1982-86; London Energy Group 1986-. *Biog: b.* 19 May 1958. *Nationality:* American. *m.* 1983, Marina J (née Carasso); 1 d. *Educ:* Austin Preparatory School; Middlebury College, USA (BA); Pushkin Language Institute, Moscow, USSR (Diploma). *Professional Organisations:* TSA. *Clubs:* Royal St George's, Royal Mid Surrey. *Recreations:* Golf, Skiing, Squash, Cooking, Music.

CONGDEN, Tim; Financial Journalist, The Spectator.

CONGREVE, Andrew Christopher; Managing Partner, Herbert Smith, since 1987. *Career:* Herbert Smith, Solicitor 1959-62; Partner 1962; Head of Property Department 1985-88; Managing Partner 1987-. *Biog: b.* 23 May 1931. *Nationality:* British. *m.* 1968, Pauline Ann (née Owen); 2 d. *Educ:* St George's School, Harpenden; London University (LLB). *Other Activities:* Member, City of London Solicitors' Company; Member, The Law Society. *Clubs:* Hurlingham Club. *Recreations:* Travel, Theatre, Music.

CONLON, Thomas Francis; Director, Henderson Administration Group plc, since 1988; Legal Counsel & Company Secretary. *Career:* Manufacturers Hanover Trust Co, London Legal Adviser 1973-78; Graham & James Associate, Law Firm 1978-81; University of Notre Dame Law School, Adjunct Professor of Law 1981-84; Tigert & Roberts (Washington DC), Partner, US Law Firm 1984-86; Philadelphia National Ltd (London), Legal Counsel 1986-88. *Biog: b.* 4 March 1943. *Nationality:* American. *Educ:* St Johnsbury Academy; London School of Economics (LLM); University of London (Diploma - Law); University of Denver Law School (JD). *Directorships:* Henderson Administration Ltd 1988 (exec); Henderson Nominees Ltd 1988 (exec); Henderson Investment Services Ltd 1988 (exec). *Other Activities:* Delegate & Alternate, Democratic National Convention; Member, National Platform Ctee, Democratic Party; British Bankers Association's Ctee on EEC Law. *Professional Organisations:* American Bar Association, Washington DC Bar Association, Colorado Bar Association. *Publications:* Articles in Legal Journals; Series on Insider Dealing in Financial Times, 1989-90.

Clubs: Broadgate, Reform. *Recreations:* Tennis, Running, Writing.

CONN, Alastair Macbeth; Managing Director, Northern Venture Managers Ltd, since 1988; Investment Management. *Career:* Price Waterhouse, Student/Manager 1976-84; Northern Investors Services Limited, Financial Director 1984-88. *Biog: b.* 22 May 1955. *Nationality:* British. *m.* 1978, Joan (née Hepplewhite); 1 s; 1 d. *Educ:* Royal Grammar School, Newcastle upon Tyne; Oriel College, Oxford (MA). *Directorships:* Northern Venture Managers Ltd 1988 (exec); Adamson Developments Ltd 1989 (non-exec). *Other Activities:* Technical Advisory Committee, Institute of Chartered Accountants. *Professional Organisations:* FCA.

CONN, William John; Chairman, Potter Warburg Limited, since 1989; Chief Executive, since 1986; Investment Banking. *Career:* Potter Partners, Melbourne, Mining Analyst 1968-70; Morgan Guaranty, New York, Mining Analyst; Potter Partners, Executive, Corporate Finance Advisory Department 1972-78; Partner 1978; Head of Corporate Finance Advisory Department 1980-86; Deputy Chief Executive 1986; Chief Executive 1987. *Biog: b.* 10 April 1946. *Nationality:* Australian. *m.* 1968, Jan Armstrong-Conn; 3 s; 1 d. *Educ:* Bacchus Marsh High School (HSC); University of Melbourne (BCom Hons); Columbia University (MBA). *Directorships:* Potter Warburg Limited; Potter Warburg Securities Limited; Potter Warburg Discount Investments Limited; Potter Warburg Discount Limited; Potter Warburg Futures Limited; Potter Warburg Asset Financing Limited; Potter Warburg Services Pty Limited; Debonaire Pty Limited; Sipiter Pty Limited; Buttle Wilson Limited; Seahorse Nominees; Wiseman Finance Pty Limited; Buttle Wilson Pty Limited. *Professional Organisations:* Member, Stock Exchange of Melbourne Ltd (now Australian Stock Exchange Ltd); Associate, Securities Institute of Australia; Associate, Australian Society of Accountants; Member Corporate Affairs Advisory Board, 1985; Board Member, National Gallery of Victoria Art Foundation; Board of Management, Royal Children's Hospital. *Clubs:* Athenaeum, Royal Melbourne Golf Club. *Recreations:* Golf, Tennis, Farming.

CONNELL, Charles Raymond; Director, The Scottish Provident Association.

CONNELL, Richard; Managing Director, MIM Development Capital Limited, since 1986; Development/Venture Capital. *Career:* Coopers & Lybrand Deloitte 1977-80; Investors in Industry plc 1980-86. *Educ:* Keeble College, Oxford (MA). *Directorships:* MIM Limited 1988 (exec); MIM Development Capital Ltd 1986 (exec); English & International Trust 1989 (exec); Britannia Development Capital 1986 (exec); Flexpack Holdings Limited 1990 (non-exec). *Professional Organisations:* FCA.

CONNER, Laurence Hunt Penninghame; Director, Security Pacific Hoare Govett (Holdings) Ltd, since 1987; Corporate Finance. *Career:* Spicer & Pegler, Articled Clerk 1959-61; Govett Sons & Co, Ptnr. *Biog: b.* 19 January 1937. m2 1986, Sandra Margot (née Berry) 1 d. m1 4 d. *Educ:* Gordonstoun School. *Directorships:* Hoare Govett Corporate Finance Deputy Chairman. *Clubs:* Boodle's, City of London. *Recreations:* Most Outdoor Activities.

CONNICK, David A; Partner, Memery Crystal; Head of Property Department. *Biog: b.* 22 August 1956. *Nationality:* British. *m.* 1983, Denise; 1 s. *Educ:* Clifton College, Bristol; College of Law, Guildford. *Professional Organisations:* Law Society. *Clubs:* MCC.

CONNICK, Harold Ivor; Senior Partner, Thornton Lynne & Lawson (Solicitors), since 1959; Commercial Law. *Career:* RAF 1946-48; Attached Army War Crimes, Singapore 1947; Admitted as Solicitor 1952; Thornton Lynne & Lawson, Partner 1953; British ORT, Chairman 1984-89; British ORT and World ORT Union, Vice President 1989-. *Biog: b.* 25 January 1927. *Nationality:* British. *m.* 1955, Claire Grace (née Benson); 2 s; 1 d. *Educ:* Ealing Grammar School; London School of Economics (Solicitor LLB). *Directorships:* Land Securities plc 1987 (non-exec); UDS Group plc 1975-83; 1983 Deputy Chairman. *Professional Organisations:* Member, Law Society. *Clubs:* Roehampton, MCC, Institute of Directors. *Recreations:* Golf, Theatre, Cricket.

CONNOLLY, Derek John; Director, Brown Shipley & Co Limited, since 1984; Corporate Finance. *Career:* Hallett Laughlin Clarke & Co, Articled Clerk/Chartered Acct 1963-67; Attwood Group, Financial Analyst 1967-68; University of Chicago, MBA Student 1968-70; Hill Samuel & Co Limited 1970-79; Dir 1979-84. *Biog: b.* 28 April 1942. *Nationality:* British. *m.* 1965, Eve Emy Yvonne (née Wahlin) (separated); 3 d. *Educ:* Eastbourne College; Durham University (BA); Chicago University (MBA). *Directorships:* Hill Samuel & Co Limited 1979-84 (exec); Brown Shipley & Co Ltd 1984- (exec); Eastbourne Water Company 1989- (non-exec). *Professional Organisations:* FCA. *Clubs:* Roehampton. *Recreations:* Tennis, Squash, Golf, Skiing.

CONNOLLY, John Patrick; Partner in Charge of London & Southern Region, Touche Ross & Co, since 1990; Corporate Finance. *Biog: b.* 29 August 1950. *Nationality:* British. *Educ:* St Bedes College, Manchester. *Professional Organisations:* FCA.

CONNOLLY, Mark; Director, N M Rothschild Asset Management Ltd, since 1990; Fixed Interest & Current Portfolio Management. *Career:* Chemical Bank, Portfolio Manager 1980-85; Bankers Trust 1977-80. *Biog: b.* 9 July 1959. *Nationality:* British. *m.* 1990, Jacqueline. *Educ:* Clapham College Grammar; City University Business School, (MBA Finance). *Directorships:* N M Rothschild Asset Management Ltd 1990 (exec); N M Rothschild International Asset Manager Ltd 1990 (exec); N M Rothschild Asset Management (IOM) Ltd (exec). *Recreations:* Squash, Climbing, Running, Walking, Reading.

CONNOR, Christopher; Partner, Robson Rhodes, since 1986; In Charge, Yorkshire, Member of National Management Team. *Career:* Robson Rhodes (Leeds), Articled Clerk 1971-74; London, Audit Snr/Mgr 1974-80; Leeds, Audit Mgr, Ptnr 1981, 1980-83; Ptnr in Charge 1983. *Biog: b.* 12 December 1949. *m.* 1974, Michèle Annette (née Fisher); 1 s; 2 d. *Educ:* St Bedes Grammar School, Bradford; University of Sheffield (BA). *Other Activities:* Ctee Member, West Yorkshire Society of Chartered Accountants. *Professional Organisations:* FCA. *Recreations:* Cricket, Golf, Music.

CONSTABLE, Professor Charles John; Independent Management Educator & Consultant, Constable & Constable.

CONSTABLE, Peter Sebastian; Chief Executive, Black Horse Agencies Ltd, since 1986; Nationwide Responsibility. *Career:* Midland Bank 1954-57; Bank of Montreal, Canada Branch Acct 1957-59; Lloyds Bank Sub-Management 1959-71; Personnel Asst to General Mgrs 1971-73; Working for Group Chief Exec, Group Headquarters & Snr Mgr, Law Courts Branch 1973-75; PA to Chief Exec 1975-80; Dep Chief Exec of Access 1980-83; General Mgr's Asst 1983-84; Regional General Mgr 1984-86. *Biog: b.* 28 July 1934. *Nationality:* British. *m.* 1958, Kathleen; 2 s; 2 d. *Educ:* St Bedes College. *Directorships:* Abbey Life Group PLC 1988 (exec); Black Horse Agencies Ltd & 36 Subsidiary Companies 1986 (exec). *Professional Organisations:* ACIB, FCBA. *Clubs:* Institute of Directors. *Recreations:* Cinema, Reading, DIY, Walking.

CONSTANTINE, The Hon R; Partner, Touche Ross & Co.

CONWAY, Keith Mark; Partner, Titmuss Sainer & Webb, since 1990; Property and Commercial Litigation. *Career:* Binks Stern & Partners, Articled Clerk 1982-84; Assistant Solicitor 1984-87; Titmuss Sainer & Webb, Assistant Solicitor 1987-90. *Biog: b.* 14 July 1960. *Nationality:* British. *m.* 1984, Janet (née Fiferman); 1 d. *Educ:* Haberdashers Aske's (LLB); City of London. *Recreations:* Theatre, Drama, Travel.

CONWAY, Leo; Director, Ulster Development Capital Limited.

CONWAY, Michael John; Company Secretary, DKB International Limited, since 1985; Finance and Administration. *Career:* Price Waterhouse, Various to Senior Manager 1975-84; DKB International Ltd, Company Secretary 1984-. *Biog: b.* 4 February 1954. *Nationality:*

British. *m.* 1979, Sally-Anne (née Kerry); 1 s; 1 d. *Educ:* Buckhurst Hill; Trinity College, Cambridge (MA Economics). *Professional Organisations:* ACA; TSA, General Registered Representative. *Recreations:* Golf, Skiing, Music.

CONYERS, N C; Director of Financial Planning, Pearson Jones & Co Ltd, since 1985. *Career:* Towry Law, Assistant Director 1980-85. *Other Activities:* Council Member, FIMBRA (1987-), Membership & Disciplinary.

COOK, B J; Director, Morgan Grenfell & Co Limited.

COOK, B R; Managing Director, Bankers Trust Company.

COOK, Charles; Executive Director, Grandfield Rork Collins Ltd, since 1989; Business Development. *Career:* The Guardian, Business Correspondent 1972-79; British Petroleum plc, Head of Media Relations 1979-82; INSEAD Business School, France 1982; BP, Commercial General Management 1983-86; Attock Oil (UK) Ltd, General Manager 1986-89; Grandfield Rork Collins Ltd, Director 1989-. *Biog: b.* 30 March 1948. *Nationality:* British. *Educ:* Abingdon School; London University (External Business Studies). *Other Activities:* Member, Investor Relations Society; Member, Education Committee.

COOK, Chris; Manager, National Westminster Growth Options Ltd.

COOK, John; General Manager, Clydesdale Bank plc, since 1987; Corporate and International Banking. *Career:* Clydesdale Bank 1955-; Branch Acct 1966-69; Asst Inspector of Branches 1969-71; Asst Branch Mgr 1972-73; Branch Mgr 1973-76; Superintendent of Branches 1976-78; Asst Chief Mgr, Intl 1979-80; Gen Mgr's Asst 1980-82; Asst Gen Mgr 1982-87; Operations Dir (Corp Banking) 1987-88; Corporate & International Banking, General Manager 1988-. *Biog: b.* 6 June 1938. *Nationality:* British. *m.* 1967, Maureen (née Muir); 2 s. *Educ:* Rutherglen Academy, Glasgow. *Directorships:* Clyde General Finance Limited 1989 (non-exec); Clydesdale Bank Equity Limited 1989 (non-exec). *Other Activities:* Member of Council, Institute of Bankers in Scotland. *Professional Organisations:* FIB (Scot); FCIS; FBIM. *Recreations:* Church Work, Reading, Walking.

COOK, John Francis; Director, Hambros Bank Limited, since 1989; Shipping. *Career:* Spain Bros & Co, Articled Clerk 1955-61; Peat Marwick Mitchell & Co 1961-67; British Aluminium Co Ltd 1969-71; P & O S N Co 1971-86. *Biog: b.* 28 July 1938. *Nationality:* British. *m.* 1966, Patricia Anne (née Emery). *Educ:* Mayfield College; London Business School (MSc Econ). *Professional Organisations:* FCA.

COOK, John Herbert; Assistant General Manager, National Provident Institution; Sales.

COOK, Ms Lindsay; Money Editor, The Times, since 1990; Edit Weekend Money Section of The Times. *Career:* Trainee journalist, Grimsby Evening Telegraph 1969-74; Consumer Writer, Morning Telegraph, Sheffield 1974-76; Freelance Writer for Sunday Times 1976-77; Asst News Editor, United Newspapers, London Office 1977-80; Features Editor, United Newspapers London Office 1980-83; Deputy London Editor & Features Editor, United Newspapers London Office 1983-86; Personal Finance Editor, The Daily Telegraph 1986-89. *Biog: b.* 24 July 1951. *Nationality:* British. *m.* 1987, Tony Wilkinson; 1 s. *Educ:* Havelock Comprehensive School, Grimsby, South Humberside; Open University (Humanities Degree). *Publications:* The Money Diet: Three Months to Financial Fitness, 1986.

COOK, M G; Clerk, Needlemakers' Company.

COOK, Michael; Director, SG Warburg Akroyd Rowe & Pitman.

COOK, Roger Walter; Joint Managing Director, International Division, Gibbs Hartley Cooper.

COOK, Tom; Non-Executive Director, Ogilvy Adams & Rinehart.

COOKE, Brian Christopher; Partner, Linklaters & Paines, since 1989; Pension Schemes. *Career:* Bischoff & Co, Articled Clerk and Solicitor 1974-78; Bristows, Cooke & Carpmael, Solicitor 1978-86. *Biog: b.* 1 February 1951. *Nationality:* British. *Educ:* Westminster School; Peterhouse, Cambridge (MA). *Professional Organisations:* Solicitor (admitted 1976); Member, Law Society.

COOKE, David Charles; Senior Partner, Pinsent & Co, since 1986; Corporate Law. *Career:* Hall Brydon & Co (Manchester), Assistant Solicitor 1961-64; King & Partridge (Madras), Assistant Solicitor 1964-67; Pinsent & Co (Birmingham), Assistant Solicitor 1967-69; Partner 1969-. *Biog: b.* 22 March 1938. *Nationality:* British. *Educ:* Bolton School; Accrington Grammar School; Manchester University (LLB). *Professional Organisations:* Birmingham Law Society. *Recreations:* Classical Music, Fell Walking, Theatre, Reading.

COOKE, David John; Partner, Pinsent & Co, since 1983; Corporate/Commercial. *Biog: b.* 6 December 1956. *Nationality:* British. *m.* 1979, Susan Margaret (née George); 1 s; 1 d. *Educ:* Lawrence Sheriff School; Trinity College, Cambridge (MA). *Professional Organisations:* Member, Insolvency Lawyers Association; Licenced, Insolvency Practitioner. *Recreations:* Sailing.

COOKE, Howard; Partner, Frere Cholmeley.

COOKE, John Arthur; Director, Deregulation Unit, Department of Trade and Industry, since 1990. *Career:* Board of Trade, Assistant Principal 1966; UK Delegation to European Communities, Second, later First Secretary 1969-73; Department of Trade and Industry 1973-76; Office of UK Permanent Representative to European Communities 1976-77; Department of Trade 1977-80; Institut International d'Administration Publique, Paris 1979; Department of Trade, Assistant Secretary 1980-84; Seconded to Morgan Grenfell & Co as Assistant Director 1984-85; Department of Trade and Industry 1985-; Under Secretary Overseas Trade Division 2 1987-89. *Biog: b.* 13 April 1943. *Nationality:* British. *m.* 1970, Tania Frances (née Crichton); 1 s; 2 d. *Educ:* Dragon School, Oxford; Magdalen College School, Oxford; University of Heidelberg; King's College, Cambridge (MA); London School of Economics. *Directorships:* RTZ Pillar 1990 (non-exec). *Other Activities:* Committee Member, St Luke's Community Trust. *Clubs:* United Oxford and Cambridge University Club, Cambridge Union. *Recreations:* Reading, Travelling, Looking at Buildings.

COOKE, Marcus Mervyn; Director, Panmure Gordon Co Ltd, since 1989; Gilt Agency Sales. *Career:* Vickers da Costa, Dealing Director 1961-79; Strauss Turnball, Dealing Director 1979-86. *Biog: b.* 28 March 1943. *m.* 1973, Phyllida (née Carnegie); 2 s. *Educ:* Harrow School.

COOKE, Peter S; Partner, Theodore Goddard, since 1986; Employment and Pensions Law. *Career:* Greater London Council, Articled Clerk 1972-74; Solicitor 1974-78; Engineering Employers' Federation, Legal Adviser 1978-83; Theodore Goddard, Assistant Solicitor 1984-86. *Biog: b.* 13 April 1948. *Nationality:* British. *m.* 1989, Elizabeth (née Thomas); 2 d. *Educ:* Royal Grammar School, Guildford; University of Southampton (BSc Electrical Engineering). *Other Activities:* Member, City of London Solicitors' Company; Member of Employment Law Sub-Committee, City of London Solicitors' Company. *Publications:* Croners Employment Law, 1980; Croners Industrial Relations Law, 1989. *Recreations:* Sailing, Cycling, Music.

COOKE, Q G Paul; Company Commercial Partner, Bristows Cooke & Carpmael.

COOKE, Roger Malcolm; Area Coordinator, Tax - Europe, Middle East, India & Africa, Arthur Andersen & Co, since 1989; Deputy UK Managing Ptnr; Head of UK Tax Practice. *Career:* Garner & Co (Chartered Accountants), Articled Clerk 1962-68. *Biog: b.* 12 March 1945. *Nationality:* British. *m.* 1968, Antoinette (née O'Donnell); 1 s; 1 d. *Educ:* Thames Valley Grammar School. *Professional Organisations:* FCA; FTII. *Publications:* Establishing a Business in the United Kingdom, 1986 (3rd Ed). *Recreations:* Squash, Tennis, Skiing, Cricket, Soccer.

COOKE, Simon H; Partner, Bristows, Cooke & Carpmael, since 1960; Intellectual Property/ Commercial Law. *Career:* Bristows Cooke Carpmael, Articled 1954-57; Assistant Solicitor 1957-60; Partner 1960-. *Biog: b.* 16 April 1932. *Nationality:* English. *m.* 1956, Anne Gillian (née Vaizey); 3 s. *Educ:* Dragon School, Oxford; Marlborough College, Wiltshire; Gonville & Caius College, Cambridge(MA Natural Sciences/Law). *Directorships:* Critchley Group Ltd 1978 (non-exec) Chairman; Trico Folberth Ltd 1975 (non-exec); Bansah & Lamb Ltd 1975 (non-exec). *Other Activities:* Chairman, Governors of Newport Free Grammar School, Essex. *Professional Organisations:* Law Society; Associate, Chartered Institute of Patent Agents. *Recreations:* Gardening, Shooting, Skiing.

COOKE, Stephen Paul; Chief Executive, Gerrard Vivian Gray Ltd, since 1987. *Career:* Montagu Lobel Stanley Head of Institution Dept 1981-84; Montagu Loebl Stanley Financial Services Ltd MD 1984-87. *Biog: b.* 8 April 1950. *Nationality:* British. *m.* 1972, Penelope Anne (née Franklin); 2 s; 1 d. *Educ:* Cranleigh School; Imperial College, London (BSc). *Directorships:* Gerrard Vivian Gray Ltd; GVG Financial Services Ltd Chm; Vivian Group Nominees Ltd; Pacific Property Investment Trust; Venturi Investment Trust. *Other Activities:* Council, Stock Exchange; Member, Trading Markets Board; Member, Security Settlement Board. *Professional Organisations:* Society of Investment Analysts; Member, The International Stock Exchange. *Clubs:* City Club. *Recreations:* Horse Racing, Tennis, Cricket.

COOKE, William Peter; Chairman, World Regulatory Advisory Practice, Price Waterhouse, since 1989. *Career:* Bank of England 1955-88; Bank for International Settlements, Basle, Switzerland 1958-59; International Monetary Fund, Washington DC, Personal Assistant to the Managing Director 1961-65; Panel on Takeovers and Mergers, Secretary 1968-69; Bank of England, First Deputy Chief Cashier 1970-73; Advisor to the Governors 1973-76; Head of Banking Supervision 1976-85; Associate Director 1982-88. *Biog: b.* 1 February 1932. *Nationality:* British. *m.* 1957, Maureen Elizabeth (née Haslam-Fox); 2 s; 2 d. *Educ:* Kingswood School, Bath; Merton College, Oxford (MA History). *Directorships:* Financial Security Assurance, New York 1989; Safra Republic Holdings SA, Luxembourg 1989. *Other Activities:* Chairman, Group of Ten Committee on Banking Regulation & Supervisory Practices, 1977-88; Chairman, City EEC Committee 1973-80; Board Member, The Housing Corporation, 1988-; Member of National Committee, Church Housing Association Ltd, 1977-; Governor, Pangbourne College, 1982-. *Clubs:* Reform, Overseas Bankers, Denham Golf. *Recreations:* Music, Golf, Travel.

COOKLIN, Laurence; Chief Executive, The Burton Group plc, since 1990. *Career:* The Burton Group plc, Joint Deputy Managing Director 1980-90. *Biog: b.* 16

October 1944. *Nationality:* British. *Directorships:* Debenhams plc Joint MD; Burton Fashion Holdings Limited 1983-86.

COOLEY, David J; Director, E S Securities Limited.

COOMBE, Christopher Brian; Partner, Linklaters & Paines, since 1983; Commercial Property. *Career:* Linklaters & Paines 1975-. *Biog: b.* 10 March 1953. *Nationality:* British. *m.* 1974, Margaret (née Mallaband); 2 d. *Educ:* Bristol Cathedral School; Keble College, Oxford. *Other Activities:* City of London Law Society, Problems in Practice Committee.

COONEY, R; Director, J H Minet & Co Ltd.

COOPER, A J; Director Financial Markets, Credit Lyonnais Rouse, since 1990; Financial Futures. *Career:* 1st Bn Queens Regiment, Officer 1975-81; King's College London, Student 1981-85; C L Rouse 1986-. *Biog: b.* 28 February 1957. *Nationality:* British. *m.* 1981, Karen. *Educ:* Worth Abbey, W Sussex; Kings College, London (BA Hons History). *Recreations:* Rugby, Hillwalking.

COOPER, Adrian R T; Executive Director, Crédit Suisse First Boston Ltd.

COOPER, Andrew R S; Partner (Nottingham), Evershed Wells & Hind.

COOPER, Anthony Geoffrey; Group Managing Director, Wellington Underwriting Holdings Ltd, since 1990. *Career:* Price Waterhouse, Singapore and Malaysia, Partner 1971-81; Malaysia, Senior Partner 1981-85; Wellington Underwriting Agencies Ltd, Managing Director 1986-90. *Biog: b.* 6 September 1939. *Nationality:* British. *m.* 1981, Nicola Jane (née Charrington). 1 (decd) 3 d. *Educ:* Wellington College. *Directorships:* Other Companies in the Wellington Group. *Other Activities:* Council of Carr-Gomm Society. *Professional Organisations:* FCA. *Clubs:* Queens Club. *Recreations:* Family, Rackets, Tennis, Theatre, Bridge.

COOPER, B S; Executive Director, Materials Technology & Research, Johnson Matthey.

COOPER, Christopher John; Partnership Manager, Cyril Sweett & Partners, since 1989; Head of Administration. *Career:* W D Scott & Co, Senior Consultant/Head of Business Development 1969-79; General Manager, Finance & Commercial Consulting 1979-82; KMG Thomson McLintock, Partnership Secretary, London 1982-86; Holman Fenwick & Willan, Head of Administration 1986-89. *Biog: b.* 22 May 1941. *Nationality:* British. *m.* 1963, Sallie Margaret (née Collison); 2 s. *Educ:* Leighton Park School; New College, Oxford (MA, Dip Ed). *Directorships:* Effective Development

1990 (non-exec). *Clubs:* Cruising Association. *Recreations:* Sailing, Reading, Cricket.

COOPER, David; Partner, Gouldens.

COOPER, David Frederick; Deputy General Manager, Guardian Royal Exchange plc.

COOPER, E L; Director, Legal & General Ventures Ltd.

COOPER, The Rt Hon Sir Frank; GCB, CMG; Director, NM Rothschild & Sons Ltd, since 1983; Consultant. *Career:* RAF Pilot 1941-46; Air Ministry Various to Asst Under Sec 1948-62; Ministry of Defence, Asst/Deputy Under Sec 1962-70; CSD Dep Sec 1970-73; Northern Ireland Office Permanent Under Sec of State 1973-76; Ministry of Defence 1976-82. *Biog: b.* 2 December 1922. *Nationality:* British. *m.* 1948, Peggy (née Claxton); 2 s; 1 d. *Educ:* Manchester Grammar School; Pembroke College, Oxford (MA). *Directorships:* Babcock International 1983-90 (non-exec)Dep Chm; United Scientific Holdings 1985-89 Chm; Morgan Crucible plc 1983 (non-exec); High Integrity Systems Ltd 1986 Chm. *Other Activities:* Chairman, Imperial College of Science, Technology and Medicine; Chairman, Institute of Contemporary British History; Freeman, City of London; Company of Information Technologists; Hon Fellow, Pembroke College, Oxon; Fellow, Imperial College; Fellow, King's College, London. *Publications:* Numerous articles in professional journals. *Clubs:* Athenaeum, RAF, Naval and Military.

COOPER, Gyles Penry; Managing Director, First Austrian International Limited, since 1988. *Career:* Samuel Montagu & Co Ltd 1968-79; Société Générale Bank Ltd Asst Dir 1979-82; Aitken Hume Ltd Dir, Corp Finance & Banking 1982-84; Chemical Bank International Ltd Dir, Corp Finance 1984-85; First Austrian Bank Gen Mgr, London Representative Office 1986-88. *Biog: b.* 8 November 1942. *Nationality:* British. *Educ:* Felsted School; St John's College, Oxford (MA). *Other Activities:* Trustee, Highgate Cemetery Charity. *Professional Organisations:* FCA.

COOPER, John; Partner, Lovell White Durrant, since 1985; Corporate Finance. *Career:* Lovell, White & King Solicitor 1979-84. *Biog: b.* 29 April 1955. *Nationality:* British. *m.* 1984, Jane; 1 s; 1 d. *Educ:* Manchester Grammar School; King's College, Cambridge (MA, ARCM). *Other Activities:* City of London Solicitors' Company. *Professional Organisations:* The Law Society. *Publications:* Articles in Law and Tax Review, 1986 & 1987. *Recreations:* Golf, Wine.

COOPER, M J; Chief Executive, Shipping; Energy Investments, The Burmah Oil plc.

COOPER, Peter; Research Director, Wise Speke Ltd, since 1981; Investment Research. *Career:* Bank of England, Economist 1964-66; Henry Cooke Lumsden & Co, Investment Analyst 1966-81. *Biog: b.* 1 May 1942. *Nationality:* British. *m.* 1967, Betty Eileen (née Pryor); 1 s; 1 d. *Educ:* Bede Grammar School, Sunderland; Gonville & Caius College, Cambridge (MA). *Professional Organisations:* Society of Business Economists; Society of Investment Analysts. *Recreations:* Athletics, Music.

COOPER, Peter J; Chief Financial Officer and Director, Continental Reinsurance London.

COOPER, R A; Partner, Lawrence Graham.

COOPER, R D B; Partner, Slaughter and May, since 1975; Company, Commercial, Financial Law. *Career:* Slaughter and May 1965-; Paris 1973-74; Hong Kong 1986-90. *Biog: b.* 10 April 1943. *Nationality:* British. *m.* 1975, Janet (née Lyle); 3 d. *Educ:* Clifton College, Bristol; The Taft School, Connecticut, USA; Trinity College, Cambridge (MA). *Other Activities:* Goldsmiths Company; Vice President, Physically Handicapped Able Bodied (PHAB). *Professional Organisations:* Law Society; Solicitor, England & Wales; Solicitor, Hong Kong. *Clubs:* MCC, Queens, Hawks, Boodle's, Hong Kong. *Recreations:* Tennis, Lawn Tennis, Shooting, Music, Travel, Languages.

COOPER, Robert Hamilton; Director, Robert Fleming Holdings Ltd, since 1988; Head of UK Corporate Finance. *Career:* Robert Fleming & Co Ltd, Dir 1972-84; Kleinwort Benson Ltd, Dir 1984-86; Next plc, Group Fin Dir 1986-87; Robert Fleming & Co Ltd, Dir 1987-. *Biog: b.* 30 July 1946. *Nationality:* British. *m.* 1972, Carol (née Pring); 1 s; 2 d. *Directorships:* BBA Group plc 1989 (non-exec). *Professional Organisations:* FCA.

COOPER, T A; Director, Hambros Bank Limited.

COOPER-SMITH, M; Executive Director, Allied Dunbar Assurance PLC.

COOPEY, Graham S; Partner, Moores Rowland.

COPESTICK, H; Group Corporate Planning Director, Wellcome plc.

COPISAROW, Sir Alcon Charles; Member of the Council, Lloyd's of London, since 1982. *Career:* Lieutenant, Royal Navy 1943-47; HM Civil Service: Ministry of Defence; British Embassy, Paris; National Economic Development Council; Ministry of Technology 1947-66; Senior Partner, McKinsey & Company Inc 1966-76. *Biog: b.* 25 June 1920. *Nationality:* British. *m.* 1953, Diana (née Castello); 2 s; 2 d. *Educ:* Owen's College, University of Manchester; Imperial College of Science & Technology, London; Sorbonne, Parris (DSc, CEng,

CPhys). *Directorships:* British Leyland 1976-77; British National Oil Corporation 1980-83; Touche Remnant Holdings and Technology plc 1977-90. *Other Activities:* Trustee, Duke of Edinburgh's Award; Chairman, Trustees of The Prince's Youth Business Trust; Council, Zoological Society of London; Freeman, City of London. *Professional Organisations:* FIEE, FInstP, Hon FTCL. *Clubs:* Athenaeum, Beefsteak.

COPP, Peter Richard; Partner, Stoy Hayward, since 1968; Corporate Recovery and Insolvency. *Career:* Horwath & Horwath (UK) Ltd Joint MD 1968-76. *Biog: b.* 17 January 1943. *m.* 1986, Janette (née Adair); 1 s; 3 d. *Educ:* Eastbourne College. *Other Activities:* Member, Honourable Artillery Company. *Professional Organisations:* FCA; FCCA; Member, Insolvency Practitioners Assoc. *Clubs:* RAC. *Recreations:* Opera, Music, Travel, Shooting.

COPPEL, Laurence Adrian; Director, Singer & Friedlander Ltd, since 1973; Corporate Finance. *Career:* Singer & Friedlander Ltd Trainee 1964; Exec 1965-68; Local Dir 1969-73. *Biog: b.* 15 May 1939. *Nationality:* British. *m.* 1964, Geraldine Ann (née Morrison); 2 s. *Educ:* Belfast Royal Academy; Queen's University, Belfast (BSc Econ). *Directorships:* Nottingham Building Society 1985 (non-exec); British Polythene Ind plc 1989 (non-exec); Singer & Friedlander Group plc 1988. *Professional Organisations:* FCA. *Recreations:* Sailing.

COPPELL, Andrew Nicholson; Director, Information Services, Kleinwort Benson Ltd, since 1986. *Career:* IBM UK Ltd, Graduate Trainee, DP Mgr 1961-72; Operations Mgmnt Consultant; Sedgwick Group, Dir of DP; Chm of Group Property Co 1972-86. *Biog: b.* 14 March 1939. *Nationality:* British. *m.* 1964, Margaret (née Cunningham); 2 d. *Educ:* Queens Park Senior Secondary; Glasgow University (BSc). *Recreations:* Tennis, Secretary of Local Church.

COPPOCK, John; Personal Finance Editor, Today.

CORAH, G N; Director, Alliance & Leicester Building Society.

CORBEN, David Edward; Chairman and Chief Executive, Jardine Thompson Graham Limited, since 1986; Reinsurance Broking. *Biog: b.* 5 March 1945. *Nationality:* British. m1 Fiona Elizabeth Macleod (née Stern) (Dissolved 1987); 1 s; 1 d; m2 1988, Miranda (née Davies) 1 steps. *Educ:* St Paul's School. *Directorships:* Jardine Insurance Brokers Group 1971- (exec); Lloyd-Roberts & Gilkes Ltd 1976 (non-exec); Matheson & Co Ltd 1984 (exec); Anslow-Wilson and Amery Ltd 1988 (non-exec); Angerstein Fund Limited 1990 (exec); LIBC Services Limited 1990 (exec). *Other Activities:* Member, Lloyd's Insurance Brokers' Committee, 1990. *Clubs:* Gresham, Roehampton. *Recreations:* Rugby, Skiing, Riding, Tennis, Golf, Motor Racing, Collecting Historic Cars, Travel.

CORBETT, G M N; Financial Director, Redland plc, since 1987; Finance. *Career:* Boston Consulting Group, Case Leader 1975-82; Dixons Group plc, Group Financial Controller 1982-86; Corporate Finance Director 1986-87. *Biog: b.* 7 September 1951. *Nationality:* British. *m.* 1976, Virginia (née Newsum); 1 s; 3 d. *Educ:* Tonbridge School; Pembroke College, Cambridge University (MA History, Foundation Scholar); London Business School (MSc Business Studies). *Directorships:* Redland plc 1987 (exec). *Other Activities:* Liveryman, Worshipful Company of Glaziers. *Recreations:* Country Pursuits.

CORBETT, Richard Panton; Executive Director, Singer & Friedlander Ltd, since 1972; Corporate Finance. *Career:* Welsh Guards Commissioned 1957-58; Singer & Friedlander Ltd 1961; C T Bowring Trading Holdings, Director 1973-79; Saxon Oil 1980-85. *Biog: b.* 17 February 1938. *Nationality:* British. *m.* 1974, Antoinette (née Sibley); 2 s; 1 d. *Educ:* Sunningdale; Eton; University of Aix en Provence. *Directorships:* Tex Holdings plc 1988; First British American Corporation 1974; Straker Brothers 1979. *Other Activities:* Freeman of Shrewsbury; Trustee, Royal Opera House Trust; Trustee, Royal Ballet Benevolent Fund; Member, Executive Committee, Royal Academy of Dancing. *Publications:* Newspaper & Magazine Articles only. *Clubs:* Boodles, Queens. *Recreations:* Skiing, Shooting, Opera.

CORBETT, Simon Mark; Head of UK Private Clients, James Capel & Co, since 1986. *Career:* Buckmaster & Moore (Stockbrokers), Private Client Exec 1972-77; James Capel & Co 1977-. *Biog: b.* 16 December 1944. *Nationality:* British. *m.* 1974, Patricia (née Cadogan); 2 d. *Educ:* Wellington College. *Directorships:* James Capel Unit Trust Management 1988 (exec); James Capel Financial Services (exec). *Clubs:* Boodles, City of London.

CORBY, Sir Brian; Chairman, Prudential Corporation plc, since 1990; President, Confederation of British Industry, since 1990. *Career:* Prudential Assurance Co, Actuary's Office 1952; Seconded to South Africa, Returned to O & M Department 1958-62; Manager, Overseas Life Department 1966-68; Assistant General Manager (Overseas) 1968-73; Deputy General Manager 1974-75; General Manager 1976-79; Chief Actuary 1980-81; Group Chief Executive 1982-90. *Biog: b.* 10 May 1929. *Nationality:* British. *m.* 1952, Beth; 1 s; 2 d. *Educ:* Kimbolton School; St John's College, Cambridge (MA). *Directorships:* Prudential Corporation plc 1983; Bank of England; The Royal National Pension Fund for Nurses; The Incorporated Bishop's Stortford College Association; South Bank Board Chairman. *Other Activities:* First Chairman, Association of British Insurers, 1985-87; Fellow, Institute of Actuaries, 1955; Vice

President, Institute of Actuaries, 1979-83. *Professional Organisations:* Qualified Fellow, Institute of Actuaries, 1955; Honorary Degree, (DSc), City University, 1989. *Recreations:* Gardening, Reading, Variety of Ball Games.

CORCORAN, J C; Director, General Manager, General Accident Fire Life Assurance.

CORCORAN, Jerome J; Managing Director (Investment Management), Merrill Lynch International Limited.

CORDEN, R P H; Associate Director, Brewin Dolphin & Co Ltd.

CORDES, O M; Managing Director, Capital Markets, Bankers Trust International Ltd, since 1990; Head of European Capital Markets Origination. *Career:* J P Morgan, Vice President 1978-86; Bankers Trust, Managing Director 1986-. *Biog: b.* 24 August 1954. *Nationality:* American. *m.* 1980, Karen (née Ringstrand); 2 s. *Educ:* Cornell University (BA Economics); Harvard University (MBA). *Directorships:* Didier Philippe SA Conseil De Surveillance. *Clubs:* Harvard. *Recreations:* Skiing, Squash.

CORDINGLEY, J; OBE; Deputy Chairman, LASMO plc.

CORDREY, Peter Graham; Director, Head of Banking, Singer & Friedlander Limited, since 1984; Domestic Banking. *Career:* Clarke Whitehill & Co, Audit Mgr 1967-71; Standard Telephones & Cables Ltd, Fin Acct 1971; Singer & Friedlander Ltd 1972-; Dir 1982-. *Biog: b.* 1 June 1947. *Nationality:* British. *m.* 1972, Carol Anne (née Ashworth); 2 d. *Educ:* Wellingborough School; City University (MSc). *Directorships:* Singer & Friedlander Leasing Ltd 1981; First British American Corporation Ltd 1981; Singer & Friedlander Ltd 1982; City & Provincial Home Loans Ltd 1986; Singer & Friedlander Holdings Ltd 1987. *Other Activities:* Lombard Association; Freeman of City of London. *Professional Organisations:* FCA; FBIM. *Clubs:* St George's Lawn Tennis Club. *Recreations:* Golf, Tennis, Swimming.

CORFIELD, Sir Kenneth; Director, Midland Bank plc.

CORIN, Anthony H; Associate Director, Coutts & Co, since 1989; Financial Control. *Career:* Peat Marwick Mitchell, to Assistant Manager 1970-80; Samuel Montagu & Co Ltd, to Assistant Director/Financial Control 1980-88; Coutts & Co, Head of Financial Control 1988-. *Biog: b.* 29 June 1945. *Nationality:* British. *m.* 1968, Jane (née Buttle); 1 d. *Educ:* Radley College (Classics); Cambridge (Classics 2:1). *Professional Organisations:* Institute of Chartered Accountants in England and Wales.

CORK, Sir Kenneth; KStJ, Hon GSM; Non-Executive Vice Chairman, Ladbroke Group plc, since 1986; Non-Executive Director, since 1982. *Career:* WH Cork Gully & Co, Senior Partner 1946-80; Cork Gully, Senior Partner 1980-83. *Biog: b.* 21 August 1913. *Nationality:* British. *m.* 1937, Nina (née Lippold); 1 s; 1 d. *Educ:* Berkhamsted. *Directorships:* Advent Eurofund Limited; Advent Capital Limited; Advent Management Limited; Aitken Hume International plc; Aitken Hume Limited; Argunex Ltd 1989; Grimms Dyke (Liberty) Estates Limited; Institute of Credit Management Ltd; Ladbroke Group plc Vice Chm; Laser Richmount Limited Chm; Richmount Enterprise Zone Managers Limited Chm; Undercliff Holdings Ltd; Testaferrata Moroni Viani (Holdings) Ltd 1988; Royal Shakespeare Theatre - 1989; Royal Shakespeare Enterprises Ltd -1989; Arts Council of Great Britain Ltd -1987; The Brent Walker Group plc -1989; Youth Enterprise Scheme Company - 1988; Celesion Holdings plc -1988; Efamol Holdings plc -1986; Griffin Productions Ltd -1986; Malta Travel Ltd -1986; Testaferrata Moroni Viani (Holdings) Limited -1986; Argunex Ltd -1986; Efamol Holdings plc - 1985. *Other Activities:* Founding Society's Centenary Award, 1981; Enlisted HAC 1938, called up, 1939, served North Africa & Italy 1939-45 (rank Lt Col); Common Councilman, City of London, 1951-70; Alderman, City of London Ward of Tower, 1970; Sheriff, City of London, 1975-76; Liveryman, Worshipful Company of Horners (Master 1980); Master, Worshipful Company of Chartered Accountants, 1984-85; Lord Mayor of London, 1978-79; Member of Court, Guild of World Traders in London; Commandeur de l'Ordre du Merite (France); Order of Rio Branco, clIII (Brazil); Grande Official da Ordem Militaire de Cristo (Portugal); Order of Diplomatic Service Merit Gwanghwa Medal (Korea); Commander of the Royal Order of the North Star. *Professional Organisations:* Chm, EEC Bankruptcy Convention Advisory Ctee to the Dept of Trade, 1973; Chm, Insolvency Law Review, 1977-82; Chm, NI Finance Corporation, 1974-76; NI Development Agency, 1976-77; Mem of Ctee to Review the Functioning of Financial Institutions, 1977; Pres, Institute of Credit Management Ltd; Pres, City Branch Inst of Directors; Pres, City Branch of British Inst of Management; Pres, Cornhill Club; FICM; CBIM; FCISA; FInstD; FRSA. *Publications:* Cork on Cork, 1988. *Clubs:* Bosham Sailing Club, Royal Thames Yacht Club, City Livery, Little Ship, Royal Southern, Athenaeum, Cornhill (Pres), Forex, Itchenor Sailing Club. *Recreations:* Sailing, Photography, Painting, Cycling, Theatre, Music.

CORLETT, Christopher John; Joint Senior Partner, Broadbridge, since 1985; Investment Management. *Career:* Westminster Bank Ltd Various 1959-68. *Biog: b.* 22 March 1942. *Nationality:* British. *Educ:* King William's College, Isle of Man. *Other Activities:* Chm, Leeds Table Tennis League. *Professional Organisations:* ACIB; The

International Stock Exchange. *Recreations:* Table Tennis, Golf, Walking.

CORLEY, Roger David; Director and General Manager, Clerical Medical Investment Group.

CORMAN, Charles Leonard; Partner, Titmuss Sainer & Webb, since 1963; Company Law. *Biog: b.* 23 October 1934. *Nationality:* British. *m.* 1986, Ruth Kohn (née Daniels); 1 s; 1 d. *Educ:* St Pauls School; University College,London (LLB Hons); University of California at Berkeley (LLM). *Other Activities:* Treasurer,Friends of Israel Cancer Association. *Professional Organisations:* The Law Society; Society of English & American Lawyers. *Recreations:* Gardening, Swimming, Skiing.

CORMIER, Ms Julia E; Vice President, The Northern Trust Company, since 1990; Commercial Banking. *Career:* The Northern Trust Company, Commercial Banking 1983-. *Biog: b.* 23 September 1961. *Nationality:* American. *Educ:* NorthWestern University, Kellogg Graduate School of Management (Master of Management); University of Illinois (Bachelor of Science).

CORNELL, Peter; Partner, Linklaters & Paines.

CORNER, Dr Desmond; Senior Reader in Economics, University of Exeter.

CORNER, Robin; Director, J Henry Schroder Wagg & Co Ltd; Loan Syndications. *Biog: b.* 19 March 1941. *Nationality:* British. *m.* 1962, Janine Rosemary (née Thackray); 1 s; 1 d. *Directorships:* Container Leasing Ltd; Schroder (Banking) Nominees Ltd; Schroder Management Services (Jersey) Ltd (non-exec); Schroder Money Funds Ltd (Jersey) (non-exec) Chairman.

CORNESS, Sir Colin (Ross); Chairman, Redland plc, since 1977. *Career:* Taylor Woodrow Construction Ltd Dir 1961-64; Redland Tiles Ltd MD 1965-70; Redland plc MD 1967-82. *Biog: b.* 9 October 1931. *Nationality:* British. *Educ:* Uppingham School; Magdalene College, Cambridge (MA). *Directorships:* Bank of England 1987 (non-exec); Courtaulds plc 1986 (non-exec); SG Warburg Group 1987 (non-exec); WH Smith & Son Holdings plc 1980-87 (non-exec); Gordon Russell plc 1985 (non-exec); Unitech plc 1987 (non-exec). *Other Activities:* Member, UK Advisory Board of the British-American Chamber of Commerce, 1987-. *Professional Organisations:* Barrister. *Clubs:* White's, Cavalry & Guards, Australian (Sydney).

CORNFORD, Michael; Managing Director, Chemical Bank.

CORNICK, Roger Courtenay; Deputy Chairman and Group Marketing Director, Perpetual plc, since 1983; Marketing and Sales. *Career:* Hambro Life Assurance, Assistant Director 1970-77; Crown Financial Management, Director 1977-80; Courtenay Manning & Partners, Partner 1980-82. *Biog: b.* 13 February 1944. *Nationality:* British. *m.* 1975, Celia Elizabeth (née Wilson); 2 d. *Educ:* Queen Elizabeth School, Devonshire. *Directorships:* Perpetual plc & Subsidiary Companies 1983 (exec). *Other Activities:* Executive Committee Member, Unit Trust Association. *Clubs:* Royal Mid Surrey Golf Club, Riverside Club. *Recreations:* Golf, Tennis, Skiing, Bridge.

CORNICK, Timothy Croad; Partner, Turner Kenneth Brown, since 1988; Company/Commercial/Financial Services Law. *Career:* Kenneth Brown Baker Baker (now Turner Kenneth Brown) Asst Solicitor 1982-88. *Biog: b.* 1 November 1957. *Nationality:* British. *m.* 1982, Amanda Jane (née Sleep); 1 d. *Educ:* Weymouth Grammar School; Worcester College, Oxford (MA). *Other Activities:* Ctee, Holborn Law Society Business Law Section; Law Society Working Party on The Soviet Union and Eastern Europe. *Professional Organisations:* The Law Society. *Clubs:* Society of Dorset Men, The Primary Club. *Recreations:* Cricket, Tennis, Runnning, Wine Tasting, Reading History.

CORNISH, Andrew P; Chief Manager, The Rural & Industries Bank of Western Australia.

CORNISH, John Essex; Partner, Touche Ross & Co.

CORNISH, William Scott; Director, S G Warburg & Co, since 1986; Market Maker (Investment Trusts). *Biog: b.* 17 May 1947. *Nationality:* British. *m.* 1976, Beverley Jane (née Boardman); 2 s. *Educ:* Whitgift School. *Recreations:* Squash, Tennis.

CORNTHWAITE, J P; Partner, Wedlake Bell.

CORNWALL-JONES, Mark Ralph; Chairman, Govett Oriental Investment Trust plc, since 1990. *Career:* Wm Brandt's Sons & Co Ltd, Trainee 1956-59; The Debenture Corporation Ltd, Asst Mgr 1959-68; John Govett & Co Ltd 1967-90. *Biog: b.* 14 February 1933. *Nationality:* British. *m.* 1959, Priscilla (née Yeo); 3 s; 1 d. *Educ:* Glenalmond; Jesus College, Cambridge (MA). *Directorships:* Halifax Building Society 1980 (non-exec); Ecclesiastical Insurance Group 1980 (non-exec) Dep Chm; Updown Investment Co 1969 (non-exec); Trades Union Unit Trust 1986 (non-exec) Dep Chm; Century Oils Group 1988- (non-exec); Hotspur Investments 1990 (non-exec) Chm; Govett Strategic Investment Trust 1990 (non-exec). *Professional Organisations:* ACIS; Society of Investment Analysts. *Clubs:* Boodle's. *Recreations:* Stalking, Sailing, Books.

CORNWELL, Nigel Rendle; Partner, Bristows Cooke & Carpmael, since 1987; Construction Law, Largely Contentious Matters for Contractors, Sub-Contractors & Employers. *Career:* Messrs Hedleys, Arti-

cles 1980-82; Admitted as Solicitor 1982; Assistant Solicitor, Shipping, Insurance and Commercial Litigation 1982-83; Bristows Cooke & Carpmael, Asst Solicitor, Commercial Litigation Dept, Commercial & Contractual Disputes 1983-87. *Biog: b.* 7 November 1954. *Nationality:* British. *m.* 1981, Alison Elizabeth (née Walker); 2 d. *Educ:* Sir Roger Manwood's School; Bristol University (BA 2:2 Modern Languages, German and French). *Other Activities:* Freeman, City of London Solicitors Company; Member, Construction Law Society. *Professional Organisations:* Law Society, Qualifying Examinations Parts I and II. *Clubs:* Lansdowne Club. *Recreations:* Squash, Tennis, Cricket, Golf, Playing Piano, Windsurfing, Sailing, Skiing, Listening to & Performing in Choral Works & Opera.

CORNYN, J; Director (Secretary), Aitken Campbell & Co Ltd.

CORROON, R F; Non-Executive Director, Willis Corroon plc.

CORSAN, (Sidney John) David; Consultant, since 1986; Finance, Investigations. *Career:* Fleet Air Arm Pilot 1944-47; Cooper Brother & Co Various 1947-54; Coopers & Lybrand Partner 1955-86. *Biog: b.* 7 October 1925. *Nationality:* British. *m.* 1950, Jean Doris (née Cumming); 3 s. *Educ:* Wellington College; Trinity College, Oxford. *Directorships:* Institute of Neurology (non-exec); IMRO 1987 (non-exec); The Technology Partnership Co 1988 Chm; The White Ensign Association 1989 (non-exec); Pergamon Holdings Anstalt (Investment)Ltd 1990 (exec); The Great Britian Sasakana Foundation (exec). *Other Activities:* Shipwrecked Fishermen and Mariners Royal Benevolent Society. *Professional Organisations:* FCA. *Clubs:* Royal Thames Yacht Club, Naval & Military, Royal Ashdown Forest Golf Club, Itchenor Sailing Club. *Recreations:* Sailing.

CORTAZZI, Sir Hugh; GCMG; Director, Hill Samuel Bank Ltd, since 1984; Japan. *Career:* HM Diplomatic Service, 1949-84 latterly British Ambassador to Japan 1980-84; Foreign & Commonwealth Office, Deputy Under Secretary 1975-80; Washington, Minister (Commercial) 1972-75; Royal College of Defence Studies 1971; Tokyo, Counsellor (Commercial) 1966-70; Foreign Office, National Counsellor 1965-66; Tokyo, 1st Secretary 1961-65; Bonn, 1st Secretary 1958-60; Foreign Office, 2nd/1st Secretary 1954-58; Tokyo, 3rd/2nd Secretary 1951-54; Singapore, 3rd Secretary 1950-51; Foreign Office, 3rd Secretary 1949. *Biog: b.* 2 May 1924. *Nationality:* British. *m.* 1956, Elizabeth (née Montagu); 1 s; 2 d. *Educ:* Sedburgh School; St Andrews University (MA); London University (BA Hons). *Directorships:* F&C Pacific Investment Trust 1984 (non-exec); GT Japan Investment Trust 1984 (non-exec); Thornton Pacific Investment Trust SA 1986 (non-exec). *Other Activities:* Chairman, Japan Society. *Professional Organisations: Royal Society of Arts. *Publications:* Isles of Gold: Antique Maps of Japan, 1983; Dr Willis in Japan, 1985; Victorians in Japan, 1987; The Japanese Achievment, 1990; Edited: A Diplomat's Wife in Japan, 1982; Mitford's Japan, 1985; Kipling's Japan (with George Webb), 1988; Various Books & Articles in Japanese. *Clubs:* Royal Air Force. *Recreations:* Japanese Studies, Gardening, The Arts.

COSH, Nicholas; Group Finance Director, MAI plc, since 1985. *Career:* Charterhouse Japhet plc, Finance Director 1972-82; Gill & Duffus Group plc, Finance Director 1982-85. *Biog: b.* 6 August 1946. *Nationality:* British. *m.* 1973, Anne Rosemary (née Nickolls); 2 s; 1 d. *Educ:* Dulwich College; Queens', Cambridge (MA). *Directorships:* MAI plc 1985 (exec); The Fleming American Investment Trust plc 1983 (non-exec); Avenir Havas Media SA 1990 (non-exec). *Professional Organisations:* FCA.

COSSEY, Geoffrey W; Director, SG Warburg Securities Ltd.

COSSLETT, John N; Director, Bradstock Financial Services Ltd.

COSTA, K J; Director, S G Warburg & Co Ltd. *Biog: Nationality:* British. *Educ:* Cambridge (LLM, Cert Theol). *Directorships:* S G Warburg & Co Ltd.

COSTELLO, M J; Director, Kleinwort Benson Securities Ltd.

COSTER, Malcolm David; Executive Partner in Charge, Coopers & Lybrand Deloitte, since 1989; Management Consultancy. *Career:* James Martin Associates, Managing Director 1984-86; British Petroleum, Group Systems Co-ordinator 1981-84; Scicon, General Manager 1973-81; Lloyds Register, Systems & Programming Manager 1970-73; Scicon, Consultant 1966-70. *Biog: b.* 29 June 1944. *Nationality:* British. *m.* 1970, Jacqueline; 2 s. *Educ:* Kings College, London (BSc Special Honours in Mathematics). *Professional Organisations:* Member, British Computer Society; Chartered Engineer. *Clubs:* RAC Club.

COSTER, P L; Managing Director (Investment Management), C & G Guardian.

COSTIN, A G; Director, Ropner Insurance Services Limited.

COTGROVE, Peter L G; Director, John Govett & Co Limited.

COTTAM, Harold; UK Managing Partner, Ernst & Whinney.

COTTAM, Robert Gwynne; Director, Kleinwort Benson Securities Ltd, since 1986; Corporate Finance. *Career:* National Service East Surrey Regt 1952-54; Watney Combe Reid, Mgmnt Trainee 1955-58; Grieveson Grant & Co 1959-64; Wicarr Sons & Co, Ptnr 1965-79; Carr Sebag, Ptnr 1979-82; Grieveson Grant & Co Ptnr 1983-86. *Biog: b.* 5 June 1934. *Nationality:* British. *m.* 1967, Morella (née Walker); 2 s; 1 d. *Educ:* Marlborough College. *Other Activities:* JT Treasurer and Trustee, Marlburian Club. *Clubs:* City of London, Gresham, MCC. *Recreations:* Tennis, Golf, Opera.

COTTERILL, I; Director, UBAF Bank Limited.

COTTERILL, Paul; Director, Minet Holdings plc; International Non-Marine and North American Marine & Non-Marine. *Career:* BICC Work Study 1964-68; J H Minet & Co Ltd, Various 1968-. *Biog: b.* 30 September 1947. *m.* 1980, Hazel (née Cole). *Educ:* Downs School. *Directorships:* Minet International (Holdings) Ltd Chairman; J H Minet & Co Ltd MD; Hydrocarbon Risk Consultants 1984; J H Minet Energy Brokers Inc (Canada) 1987. *Professional Organisations:* Fellow, Institute of Directors. *Recreations:* Golf, Music.

COTTINGHAM, Barrie; Partner in Charge, UK Regional General Practice, Coopers & Lybrand Deloitte, since 1987; Management of Offices outside London; Audit/Corporate Fin. *Career:* Carnall Slater & Co, Articled Studentship 1950-55; Royal Air Force, Flying Officer 1955-57; Coopers & Lybrand Deloitte 1957-; Admitted to Ptnrshp 1964; Various Management Positions 1974-; Member of UK Board, Management Co-Ordination Group 1990. *Biog: b.* 5 October 1933. *Nationality:* British. *m.* 1957, Kathleen (née Morton); 1 s; 1 d. *Educ:* Carfield, Sheffield. *Other Activities:* Past Pres, Sheffield & District Society of Chartered Accts; VP, Boys' Clubs of South Yorkshire & Hallamshire; Member, Liaison Ctee on Management & Economic Studies, University of Sheffield. *Professional Organisations:* FCA; ATII. *Clubs:* Naval & Military, Sheffield Club. *Recreations:* Squash, Golf, Watching Rugby & Cricket, Painting, Opera.

COTTO, Mario; Chief Manager, Istituto Bancario San Paolo di Torino, since 1988; London Branch and North Europe. *Career:* Istituto Bancario San Paolo di Torino, Branch Experience 1957-62; Foreign Exchange Office, Dealer, Intl Div 1962-76; Head of Foreign Secretariat, Foreign Assistant Office & Corp Finance Office 1977-82; SVP 1983-85; Head of Foreign Exchange and Intl Finance Dept 1983-85; Intl Div, Head of Intl Relations-Banks 1986-90; Exec VP 1988. *Biog: b.* 4 May 1938. *Nationality:* Italian. *m.* 1968, Maria (née Gallone); 1 s; 2 d. *Educ:* Turin University (BEcon). *Other Activities:* Associazione Bancaria Italiana; Technical Ctee Member, Foreign Trade and Foreign Exchange Problems, 1983; Member, Associazione Italiana Operatori Titoli Esteri,

Chm 1983-89; Member of the Executive Ctee, Ecu Banking Association.

COTTON, Frederick George; CBE; Managing Director, Friends Provident, since 1981. *Career:* Friends Provident Various 1959-. *Biog: b.* 16 November 1931. *m.* 1985, Sacha (née Dupont); 2 s; 2 d. *Educ:* Collyers Grammar School, Horsham. *Directorships:* UK Provident 1986 (exec); Atlas Properties Ltd; Box Hill Investments Ltd; Endsleigh Insurance Services Ltd; Endura Electrical Industries Ltd; Friends Provident Holdings Ltd (formerly Precis (670) Ltd); Friends Provident Life Office; Friends Provident Linked Life Assurance Ltd; Friends Provident Managed Pension Funds Ltd; Friends Provident Nominees Ltd (formerly UK Provident Unit Trust Manager Ltd); Friends Provident Unit Trust Managers Ltd; Gracechurch Securities Ltd; Ibex Commercial & Industrial Properties Ltd; Ibex Development (Vauxhall) Ltd; Ibex Properties (City) Ltd; Ibex Properties (Ealing) Ltd; Ibex Properties (St James) Ltd; Ibex (Residential Holdings) Ltd; Land & House Property Corp Ltd; London Midland Assoc Properties Ltd; Madia Investment Ltd; Maindrive Ltd; Regional Assets Ltd; Regional Properties Ltd; Regional Properties Management Ltd; UK Provident Pensions Ltd; United Kingdom Temperance & General Provident Institution. *Other Activities:* Worshipful Company of Insurers. *Professional Organisations:* FIA; FCIA; ASA; CBIM. *Recreations:* Golf.

COTTON, John Nicholas; Managing Director, Banque Belge Ltd, since 1988; Private Banking/Asset Management/Trust Services. *Career:* Samuel Montagu & Co Ltd, Trainee 1963-65; Spencer Thornton & Co (Belgium), Mgr 1965-68; Loeb Rhoades & Co (Belgium), Asst VP 1968-72; Cogefon SA (Belgium), Exec Dir 1972-77; Edwin H Bradley (Belgium), MD 1977-81. *Biog: b.* 6 August 1941. *Nationality:* British. *m.* 1979, Martine (née du Roy de Blicquy); 2 s; 1 d. *Educ:* Downside School; Oxford University (MA). *Directorships:* Banque Belge (Guernsey) Ltd 1988 (non-exec); Generale Bank and Trust Co (Bahamas) Ltd 1988 (non-exec); Banque Belge International Financial Services Ltd 1981 MD; Banque Belge Asset Management Fund (Luxembourg) 1988 (non-exec); Generale Treasury Distribution Fund (Luxembourg) 1987 (non-exec); Generale Treasury Capitalisation Fund (Luxembourg) 1987 (non-exec); Queenborough Steel 1989 Chm. *Professional Organisations:* Member, New York Stock Exchange; Member, Belgian Society of Investment Analysts. *Clubs:* Boodles, Cercle Gaulois (Brussels). *Recreations:* Shooting, Skiing, Photography, Gardening, Reading.

COTTON, John William Gordon; Regional Director, Barclays Bank plc, since 1988. *Directorships:* Barclays Development Capital Ltd 1988 (non-exec).

COTTON, Tom; Director, Finance and Support Services, IMRO Ltd, since 1986; Finance, Accounts, Personnel, Data Processing, Premises. *Career:* Rootes Motors, Various 1958-68; Lancer Boss Group, Gen Mgr 1968; Industrial Reorganisation Corp, Snr Exec 1969-71; Imperial Continental Gas, Assoc Dir, Planning & Business Development 1971-85; Strategy & Corporate, Finance Consultant 1985-86. *Biog: b.* 6 January 1936. *Nationality:* British. *m.* 1964, Amanda Mary (née Hutchinson); 3 s. *Educ:* Cheltenham College; Pembroke College, Cambridge; Cranfield College of Aeronautics (Dipl OR). *Professional Organisations:* Institute of Directors. *Recreations:* Family.

COUCHE, P G; Director, Barclays de Zoete Wedd Securities Ltd.

COUGHLIN, T C; Non-Executive Director, Riggs A P Bank Ltd.

COULSON, Nicholas John; Director, S G Warburg & Co Ltd, since 1990; Continental Europe: Investment Banking. *Career:* S G Warburg Securities, Director 1989-90; S G Warburg & Co Ltd 1984; County Bank Limited 1982-84; Baring Brothers & Co Limited 1979-82. *Biog: b.* 7 April 1955. *Nationality:* British. *m.* 1982, Katharine Claire (née Hedworth); 1 s. *Educ:* Downside School; Oriel College, Oxford (First Class Honours Modern History).

COULTON, Andrew; Manager, Financial Futures and Options, Goldman Sachs Futures Ltd, since 1989; Fixed-Income Derivatives. *Career:* Goldman Sachs Futures Ltd 1982-. *Biog: b.* 14 November 1959. *Nationality:* British. *m.* 1986, Christine (née Strianese); 1 s. *Educ:* The Royal Grammar School, Lancaster; Exeter College, Oxford (BA Modern History).

COURTMAN, David Christopher; Director, Singer & Friedlander (Holdings) plc.

COURTNEY, Rohan Richard; Managing Director, Rohan Courtney Ltd, since 1990; Banking & Corporate Consulting. *Career:* Rothschild Intercontinental Bank Credit Analyst 1968-71; Loan Syndication Officer 1971-72; Dep Credit Mgr 1973-74; Credit Mgr 1974-75; Amex Bank Mgr for Asia 1975-77; Amex Bancom Ltd (Hong Kong) Asst Director 1977-78; European Asian Finance (HK) Ltd (Hong Kong) MD 1978-80; Creditanstalt-Bankverein Snr Mgr 1980-82; State Bank of New South Wales, General Manager, London 1982-90. *Biog: b.* 28 January 1948. *Nationality:* British. *m.* 1974, Marilyn (née Goward); 1 s; 1 d. *Educ:* William Morris Grammar School, Walthamstow. *Other Activities:* Chairman, British Overseas & Commonwealth Banks Assoc 1990; President, Australian Business in Europe 1989-90; Member of Council, British Bankers Association 1990; Chairman, Associated Australian Banks in London 1988; Worshipful Company of Woolmen. *Professional Organisations:* Lombard Association. *Clubs:*

Royal Commonwealth Society, Royal Overseas League, Hong Kong Cricket. *Recreations:* Country Pursuits.

COUSE, Philip Edward; Partner, Coopers & Lybrand.

COUSINS, John Stewart; Director, Barclays de Zoete Wedd Securities Ltd, since 1986; International Equities. *Career:* Royal Navy, Sub Lieutenant 1958-62; Kleinwort Benson Limited, Manager 1966-70; Kleinwort Benson Limited (Tokyo), Far East Representative 1970-73; Kleinwort Benson (HK) Limited, Managing Director 1973-78; Porodisa Group (Indonesia), Financial Advisor to the Chairman 1979-81; De Zoete & Bevan, Partner 1981-86; Barclays de Zoete Wedd Securities Limited, Director, International Equities Division 1986-; Barclays de Zoete Wedd Equities Limited, Managing Director, Equities Division 1989-. *Biog: b.* 31 July 1940. *Nationality:* British. *m.* 1979, Geraldine Anne (née Bowers). *Educ:* Brentwood School; Britannia Royal Naval College, Dartmouth; Jesus College, Cambridge (MA). *Directorships:* BZW Nederland NV 1987 (non-exec); BZW International Equities Limited 1986 (exec); BZW Europe Ltd 1986 (non-exec); Corney & Barrow Group plc 1990 (non-exec); Stancomb & Kenington Agencies Ltd 1990 (non-exec). *Other Activities:* Member, Lloyd's; Member, Trading Markets Board, ISE. *Professional Organisations:* Associate Member, Society of Investment Analysts; Member, The Stock Exchange. *Clubs:* Brooks's, Caledonian, Royal HK Jockey. *Recreations:* Watching Cricket, Rugby, Racing.

COUTTS, Maureen S; Partner, Dundas & Wilson C S.

COUZENS, Sir K; Director, Crédit Lyonnais Capital Markets plc.

COVELL, David Hextall; Senior Partner, Keith Bayley Rogers & Co, since 1978; Investment Advice. *Career:* Keith Bayley Rogers & Co 1955-. *Biog: b.* 16 April 1937. *Nationality:* British. *m.* 1973, Christabel Margaret (née Fisher); 1 s; 1 d. *Educ:* Seaford College, Petworth, Sussex. *Clubs:* Sloane. *Recreations:* Tennis, Swimming, Walking.

COVERDALE, R M; General Manager, Bristol & West Building Society.

COWAN, J R; Director, CIN Management Ltd.

COWAN, Michael John Julian; Principal, Morgan Stanley Asset Management, since 1987; Investment Management. *Career:* NM Rothschild & Sons Limited, Investment Adviser 1973-78; Lazard Investor Ltd, Investment Dir 1979-87. *Biog: b.* 24 June 1952. *m.* 1981, Hilary Jane Cowan (née Slade); 2 d. *Educ:* Midhurst Grammar School; Churchill College, Cambridge (MA). *Recreations:* Golf, Tennis, DIY.

COWDERY, M R; Deputy General Manager Administration, Fleet National Bank.

COWE, Lieutenant Colonel R F; Clerk, Poulters' Company & Armourers' & Brasiers' Company.

COWELL, Mrs Janice Carol (née Smith); Director, Hambros Bank Ltd, since 1988; Operations. *Career:* Esso Petroleum, Programmer 1970-71; TSB, Programmer 1971-72; ICL, Programmer 1973; Hambros, Systems Analyst 1973. *Biog: b.* 7 September 1947. *Nationality:* British; 2 d. *Educ:* Grimsby, Wintringham Girls G S; St Anne's College, Oxford (BA Honours, MA). *Publications:* Thermodynamic Properties of Nickel Diamine Diodide in the Journal of Chemical Thermodynamics, 1970. *Recreations:* Tennis, Gardening.

COWELL, Peter H; Partner, Touche Ross & Co.

COWEN, Maurice Clifford; Partner, Booth & Co, since 1974; Company Law/Corporate Finance (Head of Department). *Career:* Slaughter and May, Articled Clerk 1967-69; Slaughter and May, Asst Solicitor 1970-73. *Biog: b.* 29 January 1946. *Nationality:* British. *m.* 1968, Anne Margaret; 2 s. *Educ:* Haverstock School, London; Sheffield University (LLB Hons). *Professional Organisations:* Solicitor, The Supreme Court. *Recreations:* Music, Theatre, Literature, Fell Walking, Fishing.

COWHAM, David Francis; Assistant Manager, First National Securities Ltd.

COWIE, Ian; Personal Finance Editor, The Daily Telegraph, since 1986. *Other Activities:* BES Journalist of the Year, 1989.

COWLEY, David John; Managing Director, Corporate Division, Jardine Insurance Brokers Limited; UK & Multi-National Insurance for Corporate Clients. *Career:* Bowring London Ltd Director 1969-74; SPK Bowring (Malaysia) SDN Berhad, MD 1974-77; Bowring London Ltd, Director 1977-86; Jardine Insurance Brokers Ltd, Director 1986-87. *Biog: b.* 18 May 1948. *Nationality:* British. *m.* 1974, Nicola (née Mackenzie); 1 s; 1 d. *Educ:* Wellington College. *Directorships:* Jardine Insurance Brokers Ltd 1986; Wonderworld Insurance Services Limited 1987. *Other Activities:* Committee Member of The Not Forgotten Association. *Professional Organisations:* Institute of Directors. *Clubs:* Hurlingham. *Recreations:* Golf, Skiing, Tennis, Riding.

COWLEY, Denis Leslie; Director, Lewis and Peat (Rubber) Limited, since 1980. *Biog: b.* 7 June 1933. *Nationality:* British. *m.* 1958; 1 s; 2 d. *Directorships:* Lewis and Peat Holdings Limited; Lewis and Peat Limited; London Rubber Exchange Co Limited. *Recreations:* Golf, Rugby Union.

COWLISHAW, J P; Partner, Wedlake Bell.

153

COWPER, Barry William Meadows; Executive Director, Henderson Crosthwaite Ltd, since 1987; Private Client. *Biog: b.* 13 July 1933. *Nationality:* British. *m.* 1968, Brenda Mary (née Pelham); 2 s; 1 d. *Educ:* Aldenham; Trinity Hall, Cambridge (MA). *Professional Organisations:* The International Stock Exchange. *Clubs:* City University, Hawks, Leander.

COX, Alan; Partner, Moore Stephens.

COX, C R B; Director, Hambros Bank Limited.

COX, Christopher Charles Arthur; Partner, Nabarro Nathanson, Solicitors, since 1986; Taxation Law. *Career:* Coward Chance, Articled Clerk 1968-70; Assistant Solicitor 1970-77; Financial Techniques (Planning Services) Ltd, Tax Consultant 1977-80; Spicer and Pegler, Tax Research and Consultancy Department 1981-84; Nabarro Nathanson, Assistant Solicitor 1984-86; Partner 1986-. *Biog: b.* 21 July 1944. *Nationality:* British. *m.* 1984, Kate (née Mackenzie); 2 d. *Educ:* St Edward's School, Oxford; Hertford College, Oxford (BA, MA, BCL). *Other Activities:* Member, Tax Committee of International Chamber of Commerce. *Professional Organisations:* Solicitor. *Publications:* Partnership Taxation (with Stanton Marcus), 1979; Capital Gains Tax on Businesses (with Harry Ross) 2nd Edition, 1986. *Recreations:* Mountain Walking, Music, Theatre.

COX, Edward George; Director, Charterhouse Bank Ltd.

COX, George Harrison; Senior Partner, Booth & Co, since 1978; Town & Country Planning and Corporate Business. *Career:* Leeds City Council Snr Asst Solicitor 1953-62. *Biog: b.* 17 July 1927. *Nationality:* British. *m.* 1953, Yvonne Pamela; 2 s. *Educ:* Oxford Univeristy (BA). *Directorships:* Comet Group plc 1976-90 (non-exec); Appleyard Group plc 1983-90 (non-exec).

COX, Kenneth Geoffrey; Director, Baring Brothers & Co Limited.

COX, L G; Director, S G Warburg Akroyd Rowe & Pitman Mullens Securities Ltd.

COX, S J; Director, Metheuen (Lloyds Underwriting Agents) Limited.

COX, Susan M; Director, J Henry Schroder Wagg & Co Limited.

COX, Warwick John; Property Manager, BP Pension Fund, since 1984; As Aspects of Property Portfolio. *Career:* Morgan Grenfell, Associate Director, Responsible for Property Portfolio of Pension Fund Property Unit Trust (PFPUT) 1977-84; City Corporation, Assistant Surveyor, Corporates Property Portfolio 1974-77; Savills, Head of Industrial Department 1970-74. *Biog: b.* 10 April 1942. *Nationality:* British. *m.* 1981, Lorraine; 1 s; 1 d. *Directorships:* Weston Ground Roves; St Davids Developments; St Davids Investments; Finsbury Farms; BP Trustees. *Professional Organisations:* Fellow, Royal Institution of Chartered Surveyors. *Clubs:* MCC, Chipstead Golf Club, Chipmonks CC, Beddington CC, Banstead CC.

CRABTREE, John Rawcliffe Airey; Partner, Wragge & Co.

CRACKNELL, George Duncton; Director, UK Business Sector, Barclays Bank plc, since 1990; UK Corporate & Commercial Banking, Marketing,· Electronic Products, International Services, Securities Services. *Career:* Barclays Bank, various 1950-73; Barclays Merchant Bank, Manager & Asst Director 1973-76; Barclays Bank, Branch Director, London 1976-86; Divisional Director 1986-90; Director, UK Business Sector 1990-. *Biog: b.* 1 July 1933. *Nationality:* British. *m.* 1959, Sheila (née Francis-Clare); 1 s; 2 d. *Educ:* St Clement Danes, Holborn Estate Grammar School. *Directorships:* Barclays Commercial Services (Holdings) Ltd 1990 Chairman; Merchantile Group plc 1990 (non-exec); Barclays Financial Services Ltd 1990 (non-exec); Barclays de Zoete Wedd Holdings Ltd 1990 (alternate); Bankers Books Ltd 1990. *Other Activities:* Worshipful Company of Glaziers. *Professional Organisations:* ACIB; FLIM. *Clubs:* City Livery Club. *Recreations:* Bridge, Gardening, Listed property restoration.

CRACKNELL, John; Director, J Rothschild Investment Management Ltd.

CRAFT, Alan Leslie; Director, Kleinwort Benson Ltd.

CRAIG, G P; Director, M&G Investment Management Ltd.

CRAIG, John Egwin; OBE; Non-Executive Director, N M Rothschild & Sons Limited; Banking. *Career:* N M Rothschild & Sons Limited, Director 1970-81; Managing Director 1981-88. *Biog: b.* 16 August 1932. *Nationality:* British. *m.* 1958, Patricia; 3 s. *Educ:* Charterhouse. *Directorships:* Greyfriars Investment Company plc 1989 Chairman; Jupiter European Investment Trust plc 1990 Chairman; Jupiter Tarbutt Merlin Limited 1986; Powerscreen International plc 1989 Chairman; Standard Chartered plc 1989 (non-exec); United Dutch Holdings NV 1988. *Other Activities:* Member of the Board, International Fund for Ireland; Governor, Abingdon School. *Professional Organisations:* Fellow, Institute of Chartered Accountants; Fellow, Royal Society of Arts.

CRAIG, P; Partner, Grimley J R Eve.

CRAIG HARVEY, N R; Director, Hambros Bank Limited.

CRAIG-MCFEELY, Gerald Martin; Personnel Director, Lazard Brothers & Company Limited.

CRAIGHEAD, D H; Partner, Insurance (London), Bacon & Woodrow.

CRAMMOND, James I; Director, Kleinwort Benson Securities Limited, since 1990; International Equity Trading. *Biog: b.* 17 May 1961. *Educ:* Eastbourne College.

CRAMMOND, T R; Director, Barclays de Zoete Wedd Securities Ltd.

CRAMSIE, Marcus James Lendrum; Director, Kleinwort Benson Limited, since 1986; Corporate Finance. *Career:* Price Waterhouse 1971-76. *Biog: b.* 24 April 1950. *Nationality:* British. *m.* 1983, Carol; 1 s; 2 d. *Educ:* Charterhouse; Trinity Hall, Cambridge (BA). *Professional Organisations:* FCA. *Recreations:* Golf, Tennis.

CRANE, Ian M; Director, Underwriting Assistant, G P Eliot & Co Ltd, since 1988; Reinsurance. *Career:* E W Payne & Co Ltd 1965-75; M W Marshall & Co 1975-76; G P Eliot 1976-. *Biog: b.* 29 February 1948. *Nationality:* British. *m.* 1974, Kay M (née Gibbs); 2 d. *Clubs:* Channels Golf Club, 747 Golf Society. *Recreations:* Golf, Walking, Watching Football.

CRANE, Peter; Director, Mitsubishi Finance International Ltd.

CRANE, Robert; Director, Merrill Lynch International Limited.

CRANE, S; Director, Barclays de Zoete Wedd Securities Ltd.

CRANFIELD, Alan J; Managing Director, Alexander Howden Reinsurance Brokers Limited.

CRANFIELD, Richard William Lionel; Partner, Allen & Overy, since 1985; Corporate Finance. *Career:* Allen & Overy Assistant Solicitor 1980-85. *Biog: b.* 19 January 1956. *Nationality:* British. *m.* 1981, Gillian Isabel (née Fleming); 1 s; 2 d. *Educ:* Winchester College; Fitzwilliam College, Cambridge (MA). *Professional Organisations:* The Law Society; City of London Law Society. *Clubs:* Royal West Norfolk Golf Club, HAC. *Recreations:* Field Sports, Golf.

CRANSTON, George; Partner, Clark Whitehill.

CRAVEN, John Anthony; Chief Executive, Morgan Grenfell Group plc, since 1987-89; Chairman, Morgan Grenfell Group plc, since 1989. *Career:* Wood Grundy & Co Ltd, Toronto, Corporate Finance Executive 1963-67; S G Warburg & Co Limited 1967-73; Executive Director 1969; White Weld & Co Ltd (Subsequently Credit Suisse First Boston), Group Chief Executive 1975-78; S G Warburg & Co, Vice Chairman 1979; Merrill Lynch International Inc, Chief Executive 1980; Phoenix Securities Limited, Specialists in Financial Services Mergers & Acquisitions; (Acquired by Morgan Grenfell Group plc in 1987, Sold to Management 1990) Founder and Chairman 1981-87; Morgan Grenfell Group plc, Chief Executive 1987-89; Chairman 1989. *Biog: b.* 23 October 1940. *Nationality:* British. *m.* 1970, Jane (née Stiles-Allen); 4 s; 1 d. *Educ:* Michaelhouse, Natal, South Africa; Jesus College, Cambridge (Law). *Directorships:* Deutsche Bank A G 1990 Member of Board of Managing Directors; Tootal Group plc (non-exec) Chm; Mercury Securities Limited 1979. *Other Activities:* Member, Council d'Administration, Société Générale de Surveillance SA. *Professional Organisations:* Member, Canadian and Ontario Institute of Chartered Accountants.

CRAVEN, John; Director, Securities and Investments Board.

CRAVER, Theodore F; Non-Executive Director, First Interstate Capital Markets Limited.

CRAWFORD, Andrew John; Partner, Cameron Markby Hewitt, since 1989. *Career:* Speechly Bircham, Articled Clerk/Asst Solicitor 1980-84; Morgan Grenfell & Co Limited, Corporate Finance Executive 1984-85; Cameron Markby Hewitt 1985-. *Biog: b.* 16 December 1956. *Nationality:* British. *m.* Joanna (née Alexandroff). *Educ:* St Edwards School; Exeter University (LLB). *Professional Organisations:* Law Society.

CRAWFORD, Brian; Partner, Walker Morris Scott Turnbull.

CRAWFORD, Sir Frederick; Director, Legal & General Group plc. *Biog: b.* 28 July 1931. *Nationality:* British. *Directorships:* Aston Technical Management and Planning Services 1981; Bowater Industries plc 1989; Birmingham Technology Limited 1982; Legal & General Group plc 1988; West Midlands Technology Transfer Centre 1985.

CRAWFORD, George Michael Warren Brown; Chief Operating Officer, S J Berwin & Co, since 1990; Administration. *Career:* Bank of England 1960-63; Buckmaster & Moore 1963-65; IBM (Australia) Pty Ltd 1966-70; Buckmaster & Moore 1970-86; Credit Suisse Buckmaster & Moore Ltd, Exec Director 1986-89. *Biog: b.* 11 January 1942. *Nationality:* British. *m.* 1972, Jane (née Petrie-Hay; 2 s; 1 d. *Educ:* Rugby School. *Directorships:* Citymax Intergrated Information System Ltd 1984-89 (exec). *Professional Organisations:* International Stock Exchange. *Clubs:* Little Ship. *Recreations:* Various.

CRAWFORD, Guy Mervyn Archdall; Director, Dunedin Fund Managers Ltd, since 1985; Japan and

South-East Asia, Investment Management. *Career:* Scottish United Investors, Dir 1974-83; Edinburgh Investment Management, Dir 1983-85; Dunedin Fund Managers, Dir 1985-. *Biog: b.* 12 October 1941. *Nationality:* British. *m.* 1971, Maud (née Richmond Brown); 1 s; 1 d. *Educ:* Winchester College; Selwyn College, Cambridge (BA Hons). *Directorships:* U S Ventures SA 1981 (non-exec). *Professional Organisations:* FCA. *Clubs:* Oriental, New.

CRAWFORD, J P S; Director, Morgan Grenfell & Co Ltd.

CRAWFORD, T Eric H; Director & Chief Executive, Bank of Wales plc, since 1987; Banking. *Educ:* London LSE (BSc Econ). *Professional Organisations:* FCIB.

CRAWLEY, F W; Deputy Chairman, Alliance & Leicester Building Society.

CRAWLEY, Thomas Henry Raymond; Partner, Turner Kenneth Brown, since 1967; Commercial/Corporate Organisation, Tax. *Biog: b.* 17 May 1936. *Nationality:* British. *m.* 1961, Felicity (née Bateman); 1 s; 2 d. *Educ:* Rugby School; Trinity College, Cambridge (MA). *Directorships:* Wallace O'Connor Ltd (non-exec); Measurex International Systems Ltd (non-exec). *Other Activities:* Liveryman, City of London Solicitors' Company. *Publications:* How to Use Tax Havens Successfully (English Edition), 1978. *Clubs:* Travellers' Club, Hong Kong Club. *Recreations:* Hill Walking, Gardening, Travel, Reading.

CREE, Andrew Peter; Partner, Nabarro Nathanson, since 1990; Commercial, Company, Construction. *Career:* Regional Solicitor (Yorkshire), British Coal Corporation 1986-88; Head of Commercial Group, Legal Dept, British Coal Corporation 1988-90. *Educ:* University of Keele (BA Joint Hons). *Professional Organisations:* Law Society.

CRESSWELL, Corinna; Partner, Clyde & Co.

CRESSWELL, Peter W J; Director, Bradstock Group plc.

CREWDSON, W R I; Chairman, Management Committee, Field Fisher Waterhouse.

CRICK, Charles Anthony; Partner, D J Freeman & Co, since 1982; Company, Commercial and Banking. *Career:* Allen & Overy, Articled Clerk 1972-74; Asst 1974-80; Middleton Potts & Co, Asst 1980-81. *Biog: b.* 7 May 1949. *Educ:* Oundle School; University College, London (LLB). *Other Activities:* City of London Solicitors' Company. *Professional Organisations:* The Law Society. *Recreations:* Golf, Music, Painting.

CRICK, Richard William; Director, Barclays de Zoete Wedd Ltd, since 1988; Corporate Finance. *Career:* Deloitte, Haskins & Sells, Articled/Qualified 1967-71; Glaxo, Financial Planning Dept 1971-72; Hill Samuel & Co Ltd, Exec to Asst Dir Corp Fin 1972-78; Hill Samuel Merchant Bank (SA) Ltd, Dir Corp Fin to MD 1978-85; Hill Samuel & Co Ltd, Dir Corp Fin 1985-87. *Biog: b.* 7 June 1946. *Nationality:* British; 1 s; 1 d. *Educ:* Clifton College; Brasenose College, Oxford (MA). *Directorships:* Northern Manor School (non-exec). *Professional Organisations:* FCA. *Clubs:* St Enodoc Golf Club. *Recreations:* Golf, Tennis, Skiing, Sailing, Travel.

CRIDLAN, G R; Compliance Officer, BP Pension Services Ltd.

CRIPPS, John Heaton; Head of European Mergers and Acquisitions/Director, Corporate Finance, James Capel & Co, since 1988. *Career:* Lazard Brothers & Co Ltd, Corporate Finance Executive 1979-83; Wood Mackenzie, Corporate Finance Executive 1983; Wertheim Schroder & Co, Assistant Director Investment Banking 1984-88. *Biog: b.* 15 June 1957. *Nationality:* British. *m.* 1989, Angela Mary St Jean (née Steiner). *Educ:* Cranleigh School, Surrey; St John's College, Oxford (BA Jurisprudence). *Directorships:* James Capel Corporate Finance 1988 (exec); James Capel Europe Ltd 1989 (exec); James Capel Corporate Finance SA 1990 (exec). *Recreations:* Shooting, Golf, Tennis.

CRIPPS, R J N; Partner, Slaughter and May, since 1989; International Corporate Finance and Securities Law. *Career:* Slaughter and May (London and New York) 1984-87. *Biog: b.* 1956. *Nationality:* English. *m.* 1987, Margaret J (née Mullin); 1 s. *Educ:* Eton College (King's Scholar); St Catharine's College, Cambridge (MA Economics and Law). *Other Activities:* Member, Company of Fuellers; Member, City of London Solicitors Company. *Professional Organisations:* Law Society. *Clubs:* Brooks', Lansdowne, Tandridge Golf Club. *Recreations:* Swimming, Shooting, Golf, Skiing.

CRISFORD, J R; Director, Lowndes Lambert Group Limited.

CRISPIN, Michael Julian; Chairman, Sedgwick Lloyd's Underwriting Agents Limited, since 1991. *Career:* Price Forbes & Co Ltd, Price Forbes (Germany) GmbH, Sedgwick Forbes Ltd, Sedgwick Group 1958-. *Biog: b.* 28 May 1935. *Nationality:* British. *m.* 1961, Jane (née Munday); 4 s. *Educ:* Shrewsbury School; Pembroke College, Oxford (MA). *Directorships:* The Stop Loss Mutual Insurance Association Limited 1989 (exec). *Other Activities:* Member of Court, Worshipful Company of Fan Makers. *Professional Organisations:* Member of Lloyd's. *Clubs:* City University Club. *Recreations:* Sailing, Skiing, Travel.

CROCKETT, Andrew Duncan; Executive Director, Bank of England, since 1989; International Divisions and Audit Division. *Career:* Bank of England, Economic Intelligence Dept 1969-72; Cashiers Dept 1969-72; International Monetary Fund Personal Asst to MD 1972-74; Chief, Special Studies Div 1974-77; Asst Dir, Middle Eastern Dept 1977-82; Dep Dir, Research Dept 1982-89. *Biog: b.* 23 March 1943. *Nationality:* British. *m.* 1966, Marjorie (née Hlavacek); 2 s; 1 d. *Educ:* Woking Grammar School; Queens' College, Cambridge (MA); Yale University (MA). *Publications:* Money, Theory, Policy and Institutions, 1973; International Money: Issues and Analysis, 1977; Monographs & Papers in Economic & Financial Journals.

CROCKFORD, Peter Ronald; Partner, Titmuss Sainer & Webb, since 1989; Intellectual Property, Competition Law, Commercial Agreements. *Career:* Society of Motor Manufacturers and Traders, Legal Adviser 1978-85; International Federation of Phonogram and Videogram Producers (IFPI), Legal Adviser and Anti-Piracy Co-Ordinator, responsible for all Anti-Piracy Matters for the International Record Industry in Europe and Africa 1985-8. *Biog: b.* 1 May 1953. *Nationality:* British. *m.* 1983, Carole (née Marley); 1 s; 1 d. *Educ:* Worthing High School For Boys; Kings College, London (LLB Hons); College of Law, Lancaster Gate (Solicitors Finals). *Other Activities:* Member, IBA. *Professional Organisations:* Member, The Law Society; Solicitor. *Recreations:* Singing, Travel.

CROCKFORD, Steve A; Director, Hoare Govett International Securities.

CROFT, Roy; Executive Director & Chief Operating Officer, Securities and Investments Board.

CROFT BAKER, Michael Anthony; Partner, Theodore Goddard, since 1965; Tax. *Career:* Theodore Goddard, Articled Clerk 1957-60; Admitted as Solicitor 1960; Partner 1965. *Biog: b.* 27 April 1936. *Nationality:* British. *m.* 1968, Yvonne (née Hall); 2 s. *Educ:* City of London School; King's College, London (LLB). *Other Activities:* Stock Exchange Investors Advisory Group; Member, City of London Solicitors Company. *Professional Organisations:* Law Society. *Recreations:* Gardening, Music, Travel.

CROFT-SMITH, G; Director, Crédit Lyonnais Rouse Limited.

CROFTON-MARTIN, K; Partner, Pannell Kerr Forster.

CROMIE, Stephen John Henry; Partner, Linklaters & Paines, since 1987; EEC/Competition Law. *Career:* Qualified as solicitor 1981. *Biog: b.* 13 January 1957. *Nationality:* British. *m.* 1982, Marianne Burton; 1 s. *Educ:* Abingdon School; Downing College, Cambridge

(BA Law). *Other Activities:* Committee Member, Solicitors European Group; Liveryman, City of London Solicitors Company. *Professional Organisations:* Member, Law Society. *Publications:* International Commercial Litigation, Park and Cromie, 1990. *Recreations:* Wine, Cycling, Cooking.

CRONE, D W J; Partner, Simpson Curtis.

CROOCK, James Maxwell; Partner (Tokyo Office), Linklaters & Paines, since 1987. *Career:* Linklaters & Paines, Articles 1977; New York Office 1982-83; Opened Tokyo Office 1987. *Biog: b.* 30 January 1951. *Nationality:* British. *Educ:* University of The Witwatersrand, Johannesburg (BCom, LLB); Trinity College, Cambridge (LLB). *Recreations:* Tennis, Squash, Travel, Reading, Philately.

CROOK, C; Economics Editor, The Economist.

CROOK, Paul; Partner, Allen & Overy, since 1984; Corporate Finance. *Biog: b.* 6 March 1952. *Nationality:* British. *m.* 1976, Susan Jill (née Dossetor); 1 s; 1 d. *Educ:* Peterhouse, Zimbabwe; Jesus College, Cambridge (MA, LLB). *Professional Organisations:* The Law Society, The City of London Law Society.

CROPPER, Stephen; Partner, Hill Taylor Dickinson, since 1982; Shipping/Marine Insurance. *Career:* Dawson & Co, Articled Clerk 1971-74; Kidd, Rapinet, Badge & Co, Partner 1974-78; Hill Dickinson (now Hill Taylor Dickinson) 1978-. *Biog: b.* 10 May 1947. *Nationality:* British. *m.* 1987, Kathryn Jane (née Semmens). *Educ:* Derby School; St John's College, Oxford (MA Jurisprudence). *Professional Organisations:* Law Society; Maritime Law Association of Australia and New Zealand; Asia-Pacific Lawyers Association; Association of Average Adjusters of the United States. *Clubs:* RAC, Vincents. *Recreations:* Golf, Tennis, Skiing.

CROSLAND, John David; Director, Robert Fleming Holdings Limited, since 1973; Corporate Finance. *Career:* Simpson Curtis, Articled Clerk 1961-65; Baxter Caulfield & Co, Asst Solicitor 1965-66; Linklaters & Paines, Asst Solicitor 1966-70. *Biog: b.* 17 October 1936. *Nationality:* British. *m.* 1967, Susan Jane Frances (née Meynell); 1 s; 1 d. *Educ:* Silcoates School; St Catharine's College, Cambridge (MA). *Directorships:* The Bankers Investment Trust plc 1984 (non-exec); Bryant Holdings plc 1984 (non-exec); Concentric plc 1986 (non-exec); The Fleming Japanese Inv Trust plc 1977 (non-exec); Robert Fleming & Co Ltd 1973 (exec). *Professional Organisations:* The Law Society.

CROSS, David; Marketing Director, Philip Allan Publishers Limited.

CROSS, Denis Charles; Executive Director, Hambros Bank Limited, since 1985; Project Finance. *Career:*

Hambros Bank 1961-. *Biog: b.* 13 May 1938. *Nationality:* British. *m.* 1963, Margaret (née Black); 2 s; 3 d. *Educ:* Downside School; Balliol College, Oxford (MA, DPhil). *Other Activities:* Council, Aims of Industry. *Professional Organisations:* Associate, Society of Investment Analysts. *Clubs:* Hurlingham, Royal Solent Yacht. *Recreations:* Croquet, Sailing, Poker.

CROSS, Dr Neil; Managing Director (International), 3i Group plc, since 1990; International Development & Personnel. *Career:* ICFC (renamed 3i) 1969-71; 3i, Controller 1971-76; Local Director (Cambridge) 1976-82; Divisional Director 1982-85; 3i plc, Director 1985-; Assistant General Manager 1985-88; Member of Executive Committee 1988-; 3i Group plc, Director 1988-; Managing Director (International) 1990-. *Biog: b.* 17 March 1945. *Nationality:* British. *m.* 1972, Carol (née Gillan); 1 s; 1 d. *Educ:* Drayton Manor County Grammar; Exeter University (BSc Chemistry); Edinburgh University (PhD Chemistry). *Directorships:* ANZ Grindlays 3i Investment Services Limited (Guernsey) (formerly called Grindlays Investment Services (Overseas) Ltd) 1987; Directinvest SA (France) 1990; Foundation for Science and Technology 1990; Gilde Venture Fund BV (Holland) 1983; Imperial Exploitation Limited; India Investment Fund Limited (Guernsey) 1987; Investors in Industry (Belgium) SA 1989; Neuilly Investissements SA (France) 1988; Second India Investment Fund Limited (Guernsey); The 3i Research Trust 1989; 3iBJ Limited 1990; 3i Capital Corporation (USA) 1990; 3i Corporate Finance Limited 1989; 3i Corporation (USA) 1990; 3i Group plc 1989 (exec); 3i Ibérica de Inversiones Industriales SA (Spain) (formerly Ibérica de Inversiones Industriales SA) 1989; 3i International Holdings 1988; 3i Investments plc 1986; 3i Investors in Industry SpA (Italy) (formerly called Investors in Industry Italy Srl) 1989; 3i LP Corporation (USA) 1990; 3i Participations 86 SA (France) 1988; 3i Partnership Investments Limited 1986; 3i plc 1985 (exec); 3i Portfolio Management Limited 1988; 3i Research Exploitation Limited 1987; 3i SA (France) 1988; 3i Securities Corporation (USA) 1990; 3i Ventures Corporation (USA) 1990; Thomas Green and Son Limited 1988; Waterloo Investments 1986; European Venture Capital Association (Belgium) -1987 Chairman; Anglia Commercial Properties (Investments) Limited -1989; 3i Commercial Properties Limited -1989; 3i Developments Limited -1989; Southbank Securities Limited -1989; 3i Consultants Limited -1990. *Professional Organisations:* FCIS (1981). *Recreations:* Tennis, Swimming, Walking, Theatre, Music, Reading, Gardening.

CROSS, P J; Partner, Clay & Partners Consulting Actuaries.

CROSS, Philip; Editorial Director, Philip Allan Publishers Limited.

CROSS, William Richard Jason Blount; Partner, Grant Thornton, since 1987; UK Head of Corporate Finance. *Career:* Josolyne Layton-Bennett, Ptnr 1972-77; Investors in Industry Controller 1978-80; Local Dir 1980-87. *Biog: b.* 15 November 1945. *m.* 1969, Frances (née Ramsden); 2 s; 1 d. *Educ:* Downside School. *Professional Organisations:* FCA. *Publications:* Various Articles on Leasing & Asset Finance. *Clubs:* Army & Navy, Chichester Yacht Club. *Recreations:* History, Wine, Sailing, Armchair Sport.

CROSS BROWN, Tom; Executive Director, Lazard Brothers & Co Limited, since 1985; Corporate Finance. *Career:* National & Grindlays Bank Ltd 1970-75. *Biog: b.* 22 December 1947. *m.* 1972, Susan Rosemary (née Jackson); 1 s; 3 d. *Educ:* Uppingham School; Brasenose College, Oxford (MA); Insead (MBA). *Directorships:* Whitegate Leisure plc 1987 (non-exec).

CROSSMAN, J M; RD; Secretary, The Peninsular and Oriental Steam Navigation Company, since 1989. *Career:* Barclays Bank, Clerk 1957-59; P&O SN Co, Assistant Purser 1959-62; Donald Munro & Co, Articled Clerk/Solicitor 1962-70; Overseas Containers Ltd, Assistant Secretary/Legal Adviser 1970-83; Secretary 1983-86; P&O SN Co, Group Pensions Controller 1986-88. *Biog: b.* 11 October 1940. *Nationality:* British. *m.* 1965, Margaret; 1 s; 1 d. *Educ:* Owens School, London. *Professional Organisations:* Solicitor. *Clubs:* Naval and Military Club. *Recreations:* Sailing.

CROSTHWAITE, Charles Michael; Partner, Ashurst Morris Crisp, since 1981; Company/Commercial. *Career:* Ashurst Morris Crisp Articled Clerk 1974-77; Asst Solicitor 1977-81. *Biog: b.* 21 June 1952. *Nationality:* British. *m.* 1976, Penelope Mary (née Miles); 1 s; 1 d. *Educ:* Downside School; York University (BA).

CROSTHWAITE, Christopher David; Partner, Ashurst Morris Crisp.

CROSTHWAITE, Patrick Tudor; Executive Director, Henderson Crosthwaite Ltd, since 1987; Private Client. *Career:* Military Service 11th Hussars (PAO) 1963-67; Henderson Crosthwaite Ltd Ptnr 1971-86. *Biog: b.* 1 January 1943. *Nationality:* British. *m.* 1968, Sally Margaret (née Casement); 1 s; 2 d. *Educ:* Eton College. *Other Activities:* Liveryman, The Skinners' Company. *Professional Organisations:* International Stock Exchange. *Clubs:* City of London, Cavalry & Guards. *Recreations:* Riding, Sailing, Skiing.

CROSTHWAITE, Peregrine Kenneth Oughton; Director, Henderson Crosthwaite Institutional Brokers Ltd, since 1986; Institutional Stockbroking (UK Equities). *Career:* Henderson Crosthwaite & Co Ptnr 1976-86. *Biog: b.* 24 March 1949. *m.* 1983, Valerie Janet (née Cahn); 2 s; 1 d. *Educ:* St Paul's School; Trinity College,

Oxford (MA). *Other Activities:* Merchant Taylor's Company. *Professional Organisations:* The International Stock Exchange. *Recreations:* Cricket, Skiing, Tennis, Squash, Music, Reading.

CROTTY, R G; Director, Lombard North Central plc.

CROW, Malcolm K; Director & Company Secretary, Scandinavian Bank Group plc, since 1990. *Career:* Citicorp International Bank Ltd, Manager Swaps 1979-82; Enskilda Securities, Skandinaviska Enskilda Ltd, Manager 1982-; Director, Corporate Finance & Company Secretary 1986-; Scandinavian Bank Group plc, Director & Company Secretary 1990-. *Biog: b.* 2 March 1953. *Nationality:* British. *m.* 1982, Anna; 1 s; 2 d. *Educ:* Sherborne; Fitzwilliam College, Cambridge (Geography/Law); College of Law, Grays Inn (Barrister at Law). *Directorships:* Scandinavian Bank Group 1990 (exec); Enskilda Securities 1986 (exec). *Recreations:* Family Man.

CROW, Michael Richard Stanley; European Tax Adviser, Chemical Bank.

CROWDEN, James Gee Pascoe; JP; Consultant, Grounds & Co, since 1988. *Career:* Royal Lincs Regt Commissioned 1947. *Biog: b.* 14 November 1927. *m.* 1955, Kathleen Mary (decd 1989); 1 s (decd). *Educ:* Bedford School; Pembroke College, Cambridge (MA). *Other Activities:* Vice Lord-Lieutenant of Cambridgeshire, 1985-; Rowed in Oxford & Cambridge Boat Race, 1951 & 52 (Pres 1952); Captain, Great Britain VIII, European Championships, Macon, 1951 (Gold Medallists); also rowed in 1950 European Championships and 1952 Olympics; coached 20 Cambridge crews, 1953-75; Steward and Member of Committee of Management, Henley Royal Regatta; Member of Council, Amateur Rowing Assoc, 1957-77; Member, Court Freeman, Co of Watermen and Lightermen of the River Thames (Snr Warden, 1990-); Former Pres, Agric Valuers' Assocs for Cambs; Herts, Beds, and Bucks; Lincs; Norfolk and Wisbech; Vice-Pres, British Olympic Assoc, 1988-; Chairman, Cambridgeshire Olympic Appeal, 1984 & 1988; Appeal Exec Ctee, Peterborough Cathedral, 1979-80; Member, Ely Diocesan Pastoral Ctee, 1969-89; Governor, King's School, Peterborough, 1980-, St Hugh's School, Woodhall Spa; JP Wisbech, 1969; DL Cambridgeshire, 1971; High Sheriff, Cambridgeshire and Isle of Ely, 1970; Member, Ely Cathedral Fabric Committee, 1986-90. *Professional Organisations:* Chartered Surveyor; FRICS; FCIArb. *Clubs:* East India, Devonshire, Sports and Public Schools, Sette of Old Volumes, Hawks', University Pitt, Cambridge, County (Cambridge); *Clubs:* Leander (Henley-on-Thames). *Recreations:* Rowing, Shooting.

CROWLEY, Dr Niall; *Career:* Stokes Kennah Crowley Chartered Accountants, Ireland, Ptnr 1950;

Managing Partner 1968-77; AIB Group (Allied Irish Banks plc), Director 1968; Chairman 1977-89; Irish Life Assurance plc, Director 1966; Chairman 1974-83. *Biog: b.* 18 September 1926. *Nationality:* Irish. *m.* 1953, Una (née Hegarty); 5 s; 1 d. *Educ:* Castlebrock College (DLitt Hons, DPhil Hons). *Directorships:* Alliance & Leicester Building Society 1990 (non-exec); Reliance Gear Co Ltd 1987 (non-exec); Girobank plc 1990 (non-exec); Cahill May Roberts Group (Ireland) plc 1989 (non-exec) Chm; Ventura Catalyst (Ulster) Ltd (NI) 1989 (non-exec) Chm; Cambridge Group plc (Ireland) 1990 (non-exec); Aquaport Ltd (Ireland) 1990 (non-exec). *Other Activities:* Board Member of Anglo-Irish; Member, Walker Group Committee; Patron of British Irish Association; Member of British Irish Industry Levels Board; Patron of British Association of Irish Studies; Chairman-Designate of Co-operation; Executive Committee of Financial Services Industries Association. *Professional Organisations:* FCA (Ireland); Institute of Directors; Confederation of Irish Industries Council. *Clubs:* Portmarnock Golf Club, Stephens Green Club. *Recreations:* Golf, Bridge.

CROWSON, Phillip Charles Francis; Chief Economist, The RTZ Corporation plc, since 1981; Economic Advice of all types Mineral & Metal Industry. *Career:* Distillers Chemicals & Plastics Ltd, Economist 1961-67; BP Chemicals Ltd, Economist 1967-68; Albright & Wilson, Economist 1968-71; RTZ, Senior Economist 1971-81; National Economist Development Office, Economist 1964. *Biog: b.* 28 September 1939. *Nationality:* British. *m.* 1968, Hazel; 1 s; 2 d. *Educ:* Reed's School; Fitzwilliam College, Cambridge (MA). *Directorships:* World Bureau of Metal Statistics 1981 (non-exec); RTZ Pensions Investment Ltd 1984 (non-exec); London Metal Exchange 1988 (non-exec). *Other Activities:* President, The Mining Association of the United Kingdom. *Publications:* Economics for Managers; A Professional's Guide 1985 (Third Edition); Minerals Handbook (Biennial).

CROWTHER, Charles; Chief Investment Manager, Water Authorities.

CROWTHER, G A; Partner, MacIntyre Hudson.

CROXTON, James A; Finance Director, E S Securities Limited.

CRUMP, R W; Partner, Holman Fenwick & Willan, since 1987; Shipping & Commercial Litigation. *Biog: b.* 6 September 1957. *Nationality:* English. *m.* 1990, Rosemary Scott (née Pratt). *Educ:* St Pauls School; Oriel College, Oxford (BA). *Clubs:* Wig & Pen.

CRUTTENDEN, Martin A; Managing Director, Lloyd's Bank plc; Corporate Banking Division. *Biog: b.* 26 August 1933. *Nationality:* British. *m.* 1958, Gloria Grace (née Guille); 1 s. *Educ:* Varndean Grammar

School, Brighton; Harvard Business School AMP. *Directorships:* International Commodities Clearing House Ltd; Lloyds Leasing Ltd & Subsidiaries; Lloyds Trade & Project Finance Ltd & Others. *Other Activities:* Equity Settlement Review Committee. *Professional Organisations:* FCIB.

CRUTTWELL, Christopher George; Head of Trust Department, Gouldens, since 1963; Probate and Trusts Tax Planning. *Career:* Wood Nash & Co, Articled Clerk 1956-59; Gregory Rowcliffe, Assistant Solicitor 1959-61; Gouldens, Assistant Solicitor 1961-63; Partner 1963-. *Biog: b.* 25 July 1932. *Nationality:* British. *m.* 1970, Patricia Valerie (née Long); 1 s; 1 d. *Educ:* Kings School, Bruton; St John's College Oxford (BA Jurisprudence). *Other Activities:* Honorary Solicitor, National Philatelic Society. *Professional Organisations:* Qualified as Solicitor, 1959; Member, Law Society. *Recreations:* Philately, Hockey.

CRYSTAL, Peter M; Senior Partner, Memery Crystal, since 1982; Company/Commercial. *Career:* Qualified 1973; Clifford Turner, Assistant Solicitor 1973-78; Memery Crystal, Partner 1978-. *Biog: b.* 7 January 1948. *Nationality:* British. *m.* 1978, Lena; 2 d. *Educ:* Leeds G S; St Edmund Hall, Oxford (MA Hons); McGill University, Montreal (LLM); College of Law (Solicitor). *Directorships:* IPS (Holdings) plc 1988 (non-exec); Baxhor Travel Ltd 1988 (non-exec); Chelsea Cloisters Management Ltd 1989 (non-exec). *Publications:* Legal Aspects of Control on Entry of Multi National Corporation by the EEC, 1973. *Clubs:* Athenaeum, Reform, Hurlingham. *Recreations:* Sport, Travel.

CUBITT, Sir Hugh; Chairman, Lombard North Central plc.

CUCKNEY, Sir John; Chairman, 3i Group plc, since 1987. *Career:* Mersey Docks and Harbour Board, Chairman 1970-72; Property Services Agency, DoE, Chief Executive 1972-74; Crown Agents, Chairman 1974-78; International Military Services Ltd, Chairman 1974-85; Port of London Authority, Chairman 1977-79; Brooke Bond Group plc, Chairman 1978-84; The Thomas Cook Group Ltd, Chairman 1978-87; Midland Bank plc, Director 1978-88; John Brown plc, Chairman 1981-86; Westland Group plc, Chairman 1985-89; TI Group plc, Deputy Chairman 1985-90; Lazard Brothers and Co Ltd 1988-90 (& 1964-70). *Biog: b.* 12 July 1925. *Nationality:* British. *m.* 1960, Muriel (née Boyd). *Educ:* Shrewsbury; St Andrews University (MA). *Directorships:* Royal Insurance Holdings plc 1985 (non-exec) Chairman; Brixton Estate plc 1985 (non-exec); Trinity House Marine Resources Ltd 1987 (non-exec); Glaxo Holdings plc 1990 (non-exec); St Andrews Management Institute 1990 (non-exec). *Other Activities:* Elder Brother, Trinity House; Trustee, Royal Air Force Museum. *Clubs:* Athenaeum.

CUDMORE, James; Group Treasurer, Laporte Industries (Holdings) PLC.

CUENCA-TORIBIO, Andrés; Representative, Banco Español de Credito, since 1981; Foreign Bank Relations. *Career:* Banco Español de Credito Training, London 1961; Forex Dealer 1962; Training, Paris 1963; Br Mgr, Torremolinos 1964-70; Rep, Benelux and EEC 1970-81; Rep, UK and Ireland 1981-. *Biog: b.* 29 February 1932. *m.* 1964, Lourdes (née Torres-Villaverde); 1 s; 2 d. *Educ:* Colegio Hermanos Maristas, Sevilla; Universidad de Madrid (BA); Escuela Profesional de Comercio, Sevilla. *Professional Organisations:* Spanish Chamber of Commerce. *Publications:* Essays in Spanish Chamber of Commerce Publications, London, and Newspapers in Spain & Abroad. *Clubs:* Real Betis Balompie, Overseas Bankers. *Recreations:* Swimming, Football.

CUKIERMAN, Henri; Director, Seccombe Marshall & Campion plc.

CULL, Graeme Frank; Director, Kleinwort Benson Securities Ltd, since 1989; UK Equity Sales. *Career:* Barclays Bank Trust Co Ltd (Birmingham), Investment Administrator 1969-78; Taxation Administrator 1978-80; (London), Investment Officer 1980-84; Barclays Unicorn Group, Fund Mgr 1984-85; BZW Investment Management, Asst Dir 1985-86; Kleinwort Grieveson, Asst Dir 1986-88. *Biog: b.* 17 March 1952. *Nationality:* British. *m.* 1974, Margaret Helen (née Paskins). *Educ:* King Edward's School, Birmingham. *Professional Organisations:* AIB. *Recreations:* Golf, Cinema.

CULLEN, Andrew Stephen; Director, Barclays de Zoete Wedd Limited.

CULLEN, L G; Finance Director, STC plc, since 1990. *Career:* John Menzies, Financial Controller 1973-76; Honeywell, Factory Controller 1976-78; Black & Decker, Finance Director 1978-84; Grand Metropolitan, Group Financial Controller 1984-90. *Biog: b.* 30 January 1952. *Nationality:* British. *m.* 1974, Elaine (née Ponton); 1 s; 1 d. *Educ:* George Heriot's School, Edinburgh; Southampton University (Economics Degree); Cranfield School of Management (MBA). *Directorships:* STC plc 1990 (exec); Grand Metropolitan Finance plc 1987 (non-exec); Express Foods Group Ltd 1986 (exec); Watney Mann & Truman Holdings plc 1987 (non-exec). *Other Activities:* Parent Governor. *Professional Organisations:* FCCA.

CULLEN, W I; Partner, Simmons & Simmons.

CULLUM, Charles John Stephen; Joint Deputy Chairman & Deputy Chief Executive, C T Bowring Reinsurance Ltd.

CULLUM, Mrs Sarah (née Spowart); Controller, Marketing and Information, Department for National Savings, since 1989; Paid Advertising, Below-the-line Marketing, Press & Public R. *Career:* Journalist in Scotland; Ministry of Defence Public Relations & Press (Various) 1978-85; Department for National Savings Head, Mktng & Pres 1985-86; Head, Advertising & Press 1987-88. *Biog: b.* 10 January 1940. *Nationality:* British. *m.* 1961, Garth; 1 s; 1 d. *Educ:* Buckhaven High School. *Recreations:* Family, Home, Music, Reading, Walking.

CULVERHOUSE, Timothy P; Director, Bradstock Financial Services Ltd.

CULVERWELL, Anthony James; Director, Hoare Govett, since 1987; Health & Household Sector. *Career:* Hoare Govett Research Analyst 1982-. *Biog: b.* 5 August 1956. *Nationality:* British. *Educ:* Harrow; Aberdeen University (BSc Hons). *Recreations:* Sailing, Skiing.

CUMMING, Donald Ian; Partner, Dundas & Wilson C S, since 1981; Corporate Law. *Career:* Dundas & Wilson C S, Apprentice Solicitor 1974-76; Asst Solicitor 1976-81. *Biog: b.* 3 October 1952. *Nationality:* British. *m.* 1982, Moyra Ann (née Cumberland); 1 d. *Educ:* Nairn Academy, Daniel Stewart's College, Edinburgh; Edinburgh University (LLB Hons). *Professional Organisations:* The Law Society of Scotland; Society of Writers to H M Signet. *Recreations:* Golf, Curling.

CUMMING, John Alan; CBE; Executive Vice Chairman, Woolwich Building Society, since 1986. *Career:* Woolwich Building Society 1958; Chief Executive 1969-86; Appointed to Society's Board 1978. *Biog: b.* 6 March 1932. *Nationality:* British. *m.* 1958, Isobel Beaumont (née Sked); 3 s. *Educ:* George Watson's College. *Directorships:* Woolwich Building Society and Subsidaries (exec); URC Trust Chm (non-exec); URC Insurance Co Ltd (non-exec); Value & Income Trust plc (non-exec); National Kidney Research Fund (non-exec); Cavendish Wates First Assured plc Chm (non-exec); Cavendish Wates Third Assured plc; East End Tourism Trust Chm (non-exec); Finsbury Park (Isledon Road) Community Dev Co Ltd (non-exec); Thamesmead Town Chm (non-exec). *Other Activities:* President, International Union of Housing Finance Institutions. *Professional Organisations:* Chartered Accountant. *Clubs:* Caledonian.

CUMMING, John Alexander Letham; Director, James Finlay Bank, since 1981; Investment Management. *Career:* Abbey Life Portfolio Mgr 1972-74; General Accident Portfolio Mgr 1974-76. *Biog: b.* 25 September 1947. *Nationality:* British. *m.* 1972, Patricia (née Appleton); 1 s; 2 d. *Educ:* Kelvinside Academy, Glasgow. *Directorships:* James Finlay Investment Management 1977 (exec); James Finlay Financial Services 1987 (non-exec). *Professional Organisations:* Institute of

Chartered Accountants of Scotland; Society of Investment Analysts. *Clubs:* Western (Glasgow). *Recreations:* Curling, Golf, Fishing.

CUMMING, Michael Ralston; Managing Director, Barclays Development Capital Ltd, since 1981; Venture Capital. *Career:* ICI Metals Division, Experimental Officer 1961-63; Leo Burnett, Mgr 1965-67; Cummins Engine Co, Mgr 1967-69; Midland Montagu, Industrial Finance Dir 1969-79. *Biog: b.* 6 August 1940. *Nationality:* British. *m.* (div); 2 s; 1 d. *Educ:* Fettes College; Royal School of Mines (BSc, ARSM); Stanford Graduate School of Business (MBA). *Directorships:* Barclays de Zoete Wedd Ltd 1986 (exec); BFM Holdings Ltd 1989 (non-exec). *Other Activities:* Freeman, City of London. *Professional Organisations:* ARSM.

CUMMING-BRUCE, Edward Simon; Director, Schroder Securities Limited, since 1990; Corporate Finance. *Career:* Lawrence Prust & Co (Subsequently CCF Lawrence Prust Ltd) 1980-90; Partner 1986; Director & Head of Domestic Corporate Finance 1989. *Biog: b.* 7 June 1958. *Nationality:* British. *m.* 1984, Antonia (née Gaisford-St Lawrence); 2 s; 1 d. *Educ:* Ampleforth College; Magdalen College, Oxford (MA). *Directorships:* Schroder Securities Ltd 1990 (exec); Interlink Express plc 1990 (non-exec). *Professional Organisations:* Member, Stock Exchange.

CUMMINGS, R I; Director, Branston & Gothard Ltd.

CUNLIFFE, John Malcolm; Partner, McKenna & Co, since 1987; Pensions. *Career:* Alsop Stevens, Partner 1985-87; McKenna & Co, Partner 1987-. *Biog: b.* 6 March 1935. *Nationality:* British. *m.* 1971, Bridget. *Educ:* Liverpool University (LLB); Oxford University (BCL). *Directorships:* Provident Life (Pension Trustees) Limited 1988 (non-exec). *Other Activities:* Council and Management Committee, Occupational Pensions Advisory Service; Editor, International Pension Lawyer; Member, Committee, Association of Pension Lawyers; Co-Chair European Committee, International Foundation of Employee Benefit Plans; Member, Law Society Sub-Committee on Pensions. *Professional Organisations:* Law Society of England & Wales; Association of Pension Lawyers. *Publications:* The Role of the Pension Fund Trustee, 1989; Numerous Articles in Pension Magazines.

CUNLIFFE, M D; Partner, Ashurst Morris Crisp.

CUNNANE, Michael John; Director, Panmure Gordon & Co Ltd, since 1980; Equity Sales. *Career:* Panmure Gordon & Co Ltd Investment Analyst 1972-; Assoc Dir 1978-80. *Biog: b.* 23 September 1948. *Nationality:* British. *m.* 1979, Julia (née Harvey); 1 s; 1 d. *Educ:* Finchley Grammar School; Middlesex Polytechnic (BSc Hons); City University Business School (MSc). *Profes-*

sional Organisations: Member, The International Stock Exchange.

CUNNINGHAM, Andrew Edward Tarrant; Partner, Moore Stephens, since 1972; International. *Career:* Moore Stephens 1963-. *Biog: b.* 15 March 1945. *Nationality:* British. *m.* 1973, Mary Vivien (née Swainson); 2 s. *Educ:* The King's School, Canterbury, Kent. *Other Activities:* Livery, Upholders; Freeman, Goldsmiths. *Professional Organisations:* Fellow, Institute of Chartered Accountants in England and Wales. *Clubs:* Piltdown Golf Club, Middlesex RFC, East Grinstead RFC. *Recreations:* Golf, Music, Wine, Watching Rugby.

CUNNINGHAM, Anthony Peter; Partner, Lane Clark & Peacock, since 1990; International Benefits. *Career:* Willis Consulting Ltd, Practice Director, International Benefits 1985-90; Bain Dawes & Ptnrs Ltd, Director & Regional Actuary, Southwest Region Actuarial Services 1984-85; Willis Faber Advisory Services, Assistant Director, Southwest Region Actuarial Services 1979-84; Gresham Life Assurance Society, Actuarial Assistant, Computerised Systems 1976-79. *Biog: b.* 5 August 1955. *Nationality:* British. *m.* 1979, Jill (née Collins); 1 s. *Educ:* West Park G S; St Helen's; Fitzwilliam College, Cambridge (Natural Sciences Honours Degree). *Professional Organisations:* Fellow, Institute of Actuaries; Associate, Society of Actuaries; Member, International Actuarial Association; Member, International Association of Consulting Actuaries; Member, Association of Consulting Actuaries. *Clubs:* West Berks Golf Club, Port Solent Yacht Club, Meadowview Squash Club. *Recreations:* Sailing, Skiing, Golf, Squash.

CUNNINGHAM, James Brian; Treasurer and Group Administration Manager, Williams Holdings plc, since 1987; Treasury. *Career:* Associated Engineering plc, Treasurer 1972-87; Foseco Mensep plc, Finance Director, International Division 1963-72; Proctor & Gamble Ltd 1961-63. *Biog: b.* 20 February 1938. *Nationality:* British. *m.* 1966, Geraldine Valerie (née Huband); 1 s; 2 d. *Educ:* Bell Baxter Academy. *Directorships:* Williams Management Services Ltd; Williams Holdings Pension Trustee Ltd; Shaftesbury Commercial Properties Ltd. *Professional Organisations:* Member, Institute of Chartered Accountants of Scotland; Fellow, Association of Commercial Treasurers. *Recreations:* Golf, Tennis, Bridge.

CUNNINGHAM, John Roderick; Chairman, The Nikko Bank (UK) plc, since 1987. *Career:* RAF (Aircrew) Navigator 1943-47; Coutts & Co, Various Managerial Responsibilities, including: Head of Management Services Division; Head of International Banking Division; Member of Board of Directors 1950-87. *Biog: b.* 13 May 1926. *Nationality:* British. *m.* 1964, Monica Rachel Weathrall (née George); 1 s; 2 d. *Educ:* Beckenham School, Kent; Queen's University, Belfast (BSc Econ). *Directorships:* Loriners Investment Trust Ltd 1987 (exec). *Other Activities:* Past Master, Worshipful

Company of Loriners, 1984; Governor, Cordwainers College; Member of Council, Royal Soc of St George, City of London Branch; Ctee Member, London Harness Horse Parade Soc; Vice Chm, Vauxhall Ward, Tonbridge Conservative Assoc; Ctee Member, Institute of Directors; City of London Branch, Castle Baynard Ward Club; Bishopsgate Ward Club; Aldersgate Ward Club; Portsoken Ward Club; Woolnoth Society, City Branch; Life Member, United Wards Club, Guild of Freemen of City of London. *Professional Organisations:* FCIB; FRSA; Fellow, Institute of Directors. *Clubs:* Overseas Bankers', City Livery. *Recreations:* Gardening, City of London Civic Interests.

CUNNINGHAM, Ken; Director Risk Mgmnt/ Technical Products, Mitsubishi Finance International Limited.

CUNNINGHAM, R N; Head Dealer, IMI Securities Ltd.

CUNYNGHAME, John Philip Henry Michael Selwyn; Sales Director, Griersons, since 1986; Wholesale Wine & Spirit Sales. *Career:* City Vintagers Ltd, Managing Director 1969-85. *Biog: b.* 9 September 1944. *Nationality:* British. *m.* 1981, Marjatta (née Markus); 1 s; 1 d. *Educ:* Eton. *Other Activities:* Master, Worshipful Company of Pattenmakers (March 1991-). *Recreations:* Skiing.

CURDS, Graham Rea; Executive Director, N M Rothschild & Sons Limited, since 1987; Sterling & Eurocurrency, Trading Activities including off Balance Sheet. *Career:* N M Rothschild & Sons Mgr to Director, Trading Activities 1968-87. *Biog: b.* 25 February 1950. *Nationality:* British. *m.* 1974, Linda Frances Mary; 2 s. *Educ:* Sandringham High School. *Directorships:* N M Rothschild & Sons 1987 (exec).

CURLING, David Antony Bryan; Director, Williams de Broe plc, since 1974; Head of Private Client & Fund Management Department. *Career:* Dixon Wilson Tubbs & Gillett (now Dixon Wilson) Chartered Accountants 1962-66; Articled Clerk 1962-65; Assistant Audit Manager 1966; Peat Marwick Mitchell, Johannesburg, Audit Manager (two year contract) 1967-68; Union Acceptances Pty Ltd (Merchant Banking subsidiary of Anglo American Group) Johannesburg 1969-70; Accountant to Mutual Fund subsidiary 1969; Assistant Manager Corporate Finance Department & Manager Property Mutual Fund 1970; Williams de Broe plc (formerly Williams de Broe Hill Chaplin & Co) 1971-; Research Analyst 1971; Institutional Salesman 1972-84; Director (Corporate Member of the Stock Exchange) 1974; Headed Foreign Institutional Department 1985-89; Head of Private Client and Fund Management Department 1989-. *Biog: b.* 27 January 1943. *Nationality:* British. *m.* 1970, Jennifer (née Schlesinger); 2 d. *Educ:* Eton. *Directorships:* Europafund Advisory SA 1988 (non-exec); Banque Bruxelles Lambert Trust Co (Jersey) Ltd 1990 (non-exec); Williams de Broe (Holdings) Ltd (and its good Companies including Ward plc its main Trading Subsidiary) 1974 (exec). *Professional Organisations:* FCA; ISIE. *Clubs:* Royal Yacht Squadron, Newbridge Sailing Club. *Recreations:* Sailing, Skiing, Shooting.

CURRAN, Alan H; Head of Investor Relations, British Gas plc, since 1990; UK & Overseas. *Career:* British Gas, Research 1977; Head of Planning and Liaison, Research & Technology Division. *Biog: b.* 1947; 1 s; 1 d. *Educ:* Strathclyde University (BSc Hons Chemistry); Cambridge University (PhD Chemical Physics). *Other Activities:* Harkness Fellow, USA; Ramsay Fellow, University of London. *Professional Organisations:* Chartered Engineer; Member, Institution of Gas Engineers. *Publications:* Several Research Papers. *Recreations:* Squash, Sailing.

CURRAN, S W; Chief Executive, Candover Investments plc, since 1990. *Career:* The Bowater Co Ltd 1967-71; Grumbar & See, Analyst 1971-75; Coopers & Lybrand Associates, Managing Consultant 1975-79; NCB Pension Funds, Project Finance Manager 1979-81; Candover Investments plc, Deputy Chief Executive 1981-90. *Biog: b.* 9 March 1943. *Nationality:* British. *m.* 1968, Anne Beatrice; 1 s; 1 d. *Educ:* Marlborough House; Wellington College, Certified Accountant; RMA, Sandhurst. *Directorships:* Berkertex Holdings Limited 1986; BPCC Limited 1989; Candover Investments plc 1982; Candover Realisations Limited 1983; Candover Partners Limited 1982; Candover Overseas Investments Limited 1982; Candover Overseas Investments (ET) Limited 1982; Candover Overseas Investments (UI) Limited 1983; Candover-Pac (FL) Limited 1982; Candover-Pac (BM) Limited 1982; Candover Services Limited 1982; Candover (Trustees) Limited 1983; Candover-Pac (TV) Limited 1983; Candover Nominees Limited 1983; Candover-Pac (DP) Limited 1984; Candover Investments (West Indies) Inc 1983; Greggs plc 1981; Hoare Candover Limited 1984; Jarvis Hotels Limited 1990; Caradon plc 1985; CC&P Consultants Limited; Gower Holdings plc; Hays plc 1987; Humberclyde Finance Group Limited; Metcalfe Cooper Limited; Radyne Limited; Radyne Holdings Limited; Rentco International Limited; Security Holdings Limited; Thos Storey Limited; Thos Storey (Engineers) Limited; Timpson Shoes Limited; Koala Technologies; Lombard Investments. *Professional Organisations:* FCCA. *Clubs:* Cavalry & Guards Club, Hurlingham. *Recreations:* Skiing, Swimming, Tennis, Running.

CURRAN, T A R; Partner, Lovell White Durrant.

CURRAN, W G; Council Member, FIMBRA.

CURREY, William; Executive Director, N M Rothschild International Asset Management Limited.

CURRIE, Brian Murdoch; Partner, Arthur Andersen & Co, since 1970; Manufacturing & Public Sector Work. *Career:* Royal Tank Regiment Subaltern 1957-59; Arthur Andersen & Co Mgr & Ptnr 1965-72; HMSO Fin Dir 1972-74; Arthur Andersen & Co London Dep Managing Ptnr 1975-77; Managing Ptnr 1977-82. *Biog: b.* 20 December 1934. *Nationality:* British. *m.* 1961, Trixie (née Farr); 3 s; 1 d. *Educ:* Blundell's School; Oriel College, Oxford (MA). *Other Activities:* Department of Trade Inspector 1978-81, Restrictive Practices Court (Part-time Member 1979-); Council Mem, ICA; Chm of Parliamentary & Law Ctee; ASC Public Sector Liaison Group (Chm 1984-86); Oriel College Development Trust (1980-90). *Professional Organisations:* FCA, MIMC, FBPICS (Council Mem 1970-73). *Clubs:* Reform. *Recreations:* Natural History.

CURRIE, Professor David Anthony; Professor of Economics, Dean of Research & Director of the Centre for Economic Forecasting, London Business School; Economic Forecasting and Macroeconomic Policy. *Career:* Hoare Govett, Economist 1971-72; Economic Models, Economist 1972; Queen Mary College, University of London, Lecturer in Economics 1972-74; Reader in Economics 1979-81; Professor of Economics 1981-88. *Biog: b.* 9 December 1946. (separated); 2 s. *Educ:* Battersea Grammar School; University of Manchester (BSc Mathematics); University of Birmingham (MSc Economics); University of London (PhD Economics). *Directorships:* Joseph Rowntree Social Services Trust (Investments) Ltd 1989 (non-exec). *Other Activities:* Governor, London Business School. *Professional Organisations:* Member of Council, Royal Economic Society. *Publications:* Advances in Monetary Economics, Editor, 1985; The Operation and Regulation of Financial Markets, Editor, 1986; Macroeconomic Interactions Between North and South, Editor, 1988; Macroeconomic Policies in an Interdependent World, Editor, 1989; Numerous Articles in Academic Journals. *Clubs:* Reform Club. *Recreations:* Music, Running, Literature.

CURRIE, Patrick R; Director, Merrill Lynch International Limited.

CURRIE, W; Director of Research, Head of Retail Team, Hoare Govett Investment R esearch Ltd, since 1989; Retail. *Career:* Charterhouse Tilney 1984-87. *Biog: b.* 14 February 1962. *Nationality:* British. *m.* 1986, Hilary. *Educ:* Blue Coat School, Liverpool; University of Liverpool (BA). *Clubs:* Hanbury Manor. *Recreations:* Football, Squash, Swimming, Golf.

CURRY, J F; Managing Director, ANZ Merchant Bank Limited.

CURRY, N; Partner, Lane Clark & Peacock.

CURRY, P A M; Non-Executive Director, George Wimpey plc.

CURRY, T J A; Partner, Ernst & Young.

CURTIN, A G; Director, Hambros Bank Limited.

CURTIS, J E M; Partner, Pensions, Bacon & Woodrow.

CURTIS, J R; Partnership Secretary, Milne Ross, since 1986; Partnership Administration. *Career:* Watson Hawksley Consulting Civil Engineers, Chief Accountant 1977-86; Price Waterhouse Belgium, Assistant Audit Manager 1974-77; Audit Senior 1970-74. *Biog: b.* 14 February 1946. *Nationality:* British. *Educ:* Wimbledon College. *Other Activities:* School Governor, Charity Trustee, Handicapped Children. *Professional Organisations:* Fellow, Institute of Chartered Accountants in England & Wales.

CURTIS, J S; Director, Touche Remnant Investment Management, since 1990. *Career:* Cornhill Insurance 1985-87; Grieveson, Grant 1983-85. *Biog: b.* 27 June 1961. *Nationality:* British. *Educ:* Eton College; Christ Church, Oxford (BA Hons). *Professional Organisations:* Associate Society, Investment Analysts.

CURTIS, James; Partner, Wilde Sapte, since 1979; Commercial Property.

CURTIS, Miss Penelope; Director, N M Rothschild & Sons Limited, since 1989; Compliance. *Career:* Freshfields, Articled Clerk/Assistant Solicitor 1979-87. *Biog: b.* 20 February 1957. *Nationality:* British. *m.* 1987, Christopher Crouch. *Educ:* St Michael's School, Limpsfield; Exeter University (LLB). *Other Activities:* City of London Solicitors' Company. *Professional Organisations:* Solicitor; Law Society.

CURTIS, Pierre Alfred Douglas Pascal; Treasurer, CIC-UEI et Cie, since 1990; Treasury and Foreign Exchange Department. *Career:* Lloyds Bank plc, Cable Dealer 1967-78. *Biog: b.* 16 December 1947. *Nationality:* British. *m.* 1974, Anne Caroline (née Holt-Kentwell). *Educ:* Holloway County. *Professional Organisations:* The Securities Association. *Clubs:* Middlesex Rugby Football Union Club, Overseas Bankers Club, Lombard Association.

CURTIS, T; Treasury Manager, CIC-Union Européene Internationale et Cie.

CURWEN, M J; Executive Director, Philipp & Lion Ltd.

CURZEY, Robert S; Managing Director, Alexander Howden Reinsurance Brokers Limited.

CUSTANCE BAKER, Jonathan James; Managing Director, James Capel Unit Trust Management Limited, since 1988. *Career:* GT Global Financial Services (San Francisco, USA), President 1985-87; GT Unit Managers (London), Marketing Director 1981-84; Various Shipbroking firms, Sale & Purchase Shipbroker (London, Hong Kong, Middle East) 1974-81; Queen's Royal Irish Hussars, Cornet, Troop Leader 1971-73. *Biog: b.* 18 March 1949. *Nationality:* British. m1 1975, Jane (née Richards) 3d m2 1986, Deborah (née Bordass); 1 s 1 d. *Educ:* Marlborough; Southampton University. *Directorships:* James Capel Resources Management 1990 (exec); James Capel Unit Trust Management Limited 1988 (exec); James Capel Investment Services 1990 (exec). *Other Activities:* Unit Trust Association Executive Committee. *Clubs:* Cavalry and Guards. *Recreations:* Claret, Baseball, Shooting.

CUSTARD, William L; Executive Vice President, Prudential-Bache Securities.

CUTHBERTSON, Eric Ian; Principal, Cuthbertson Riddle & Graham WS.

CUTTS, John; Executive Director, Corporate Finance, Samuel Montagu & Co Limited, since 1988; European Mergers & Acquisitions. *Career:* Rolls Royce Limited, Apprentice 1968-72; Ansafone Limited, Technical Export Manager 1973-75; H & B Real Gewerbebau GmbH & Cokg, General Manager, Property Development 1976-79; Eupic Services BV, General Manager, Property Investment 1979-81; Amsterdam Rotterdam Bank NV, Managing Director, Mergers & Acquisitions 1981-88; Samuel Montagu & Co Limited, Executive Director, Corporate Finance, Head of European Mergers & Acquisitions 1988-. *Biog: b.* 27 September 1950. *Nationality:* British. *m.* 1976, Nicola Jane (née Dancy); 3 d. *Educ:* Dean Close School; Sussex University (BSc Hons); INSEAD, Fontainebleau (MBA Distinction). *Directorships:* Samuel Montagu & Co Ltd 1988 (exec); Samuel Montagu & Co BV 1990 (exec); BPL Holdings Limited 1988 (non-exec); Project Orbis 1988 (non-exec). *Other Activities:* Chairman, INSEAD Alumni Fund. *Clubs:* Royal Thames Yacht Club. *Recreations:* Opera, Farming.

D

D'ABBANS, William Eric Charles; Chairman & Chief Executive, King & Shaxson Holdings plc.

D'ALANCON, Louis; Director, Merrill Lynch International Ltd, since 1990; Capital Market. *Career:* Merrill Lynch International, London 1988-; Banque Paribas Capital Markets, London 1986-88; Banque Paribas, Paris 1984-86. *Biog: b.* 12 February 1959. *Nationality:* French. *Educ:* Ecole Nationale des Ponts et Chaussées, Paris; Institut d'Etudes Politiques, Paris. *Directorships:* Merrill Lynch International 1990 (exec). *Clubs:* RAC.

D'ANGERVILLE, Guillaume; Head of Financing Desk, Paribas Limited.

D'ANYERS WILLIS, P A; Director, Kleinwort Benson Limited, since 1990; Japan. *Career:* Kleinwort Benson Ltd, Executive, Middle East Department 1977; Assistant Manager, Middle East Department 1981; Assistant Manager, Asia Pacific Department 1983; Manager, Asia Pacific Department & Mgr, International Corporate Finance (Japan) 1986; Assistant Director, International Corporate Finance (Japan) 1988; Director, International Corporate Finance (Japan) 1990. *Biog: b.* 12 August 1955. *Nationality:* British. *m.* 1983, Cecilia; 2 d. *Educ:* Trinity College, Cambridge (Part I: French and German, Part II: Law Economy).

D'ESTAIS, Jacques; Head of Swaps Other Currencies, Paribas Limited.

DA COSTA, Peter Jeffrey; Executive Director, Allied Dunbar Assurance plc, since 1982; Administration Management. *Career:* A L Schaffer & Co (Chartered Accountants), Articled Clerk/Qualified Accountant 1961-66; Newton, Armstrong & Co (Management Consultants), Management Consultant 1966-70; Abbey Life Assurance, Senior Systems Analyst 1970-71; Hambro Life Assurance (now Allied Dunbar Assurance), Chief Accountant/Assistant Director/Executive Director 1971-. *Biog: b.* 8 March 1943. *Nationality:* British. *m.* 1969, Moira (née Stern); 1 s; 1 d. *Educ:* University of Natal, CTA (Certificate in Theory of Accountancy). *Professional Organisations:* Chartered Accountant (South Africa), ICMA. *Recreations:* Tennis, Reading, Cinema, Theatre, Bridge.

DABLIN, Edward Paul; Director, Crédit Lyonnais Rouse.

DACOMBE, William John Armstrong; , Director, Campbell Lutyens Hudson Co Ltd, since 1988. *Career:* National Service (Midshipman RNVR Staff of Commander in Chief, Far East Station) 1954-55; Shell International Petroleum Company 1959-61; Kleinwort Benson Limited 1961-65; N M Rothschild & Sons 1965-73; Royal Bank of Scotland Group 1973-84; Director of Williams & Glyns Bank 1973-84; Head of International Banking 1975-79; Assistant Chief Executive 1979-82; The Royal Bank of Scotland Group plc, Director 1979-84; The Royal Bank of Scotland plc, Director 1982-84; Export Guarantee Advisory Council 1982-86; Deputy Chairman 1985-86; Rea Brothers Group 1984-88. *Biog: b.* 21 September 1934. *Nationality:* British. *m.* Margaretta Joanna; 2 d. *Educ:* Felsted School; Corpus Christi College, Oxford. *Recreations:* Brooks's.

DAFTER, R M; Director, Corporate Affairs, Enterprise Oil plc, since 1990; Public Relations, Communications, Investor Relations. *Career:* Evening Advertiser, Swindon, Journalist 1961-65; Evening Post, Bristol, Journalist 1965-70; Financial Times, London, Journalist 1970-83; Public and Overseas Relations, Electricity Council, Central Director 1983-88; Valin Pollen Ltd, Deputy Chief Executive Director 1988-90; Enterprise Oil, Director, Corporate Affairs 1990-. *Biog: b.* 22 April 1944. *Nationality:* British. *m.* 1965, Christine; 2 d. *Educ:* Marlborough Grammar; Harvard University (Fellow). *Directorships:* Enterprise Oil Exploration Ltd 1990 (exec); Enterprise (E & P) Ltd 1990 (exec); Montrose Management Ltd 1989 (non-exec); Paul Hammond Productions Ltd (Chm) 1990 (non-exec). *Other Activities:* Trustee, Young Peoples Trust for the Environment. *Professional Organisations:* Fellow, Institute of Petroleum. *Publications:* Running out of Fuel; Winning More Oil; Scraping the Barrel; Numerous Academic Articles, Papers, Magazine Articles. *Recreations:* Sailing, Painting, Music, Walking.

DAHLLOF-RATNER, Mrs Birgitta Christina; Director, Svenska International plc, since 1986; Fixed Income Securities. *Career:* Svenska Handelsbanken (Stockholm), Snr Mgr 1964-82; Swedish Export Credit Corporation (Stockholm), Asst Treasurer 1982-84; Svenska Handelsbanken plc, Asst Dir/Dir 1984-. *Biog: b.* 7 February 1944. *Nationality:* Swedish. *m.* 1988, John; 2 d.

DALBY, Derek; Financial Director, GCI Sterling.

DALBY, J S; Managing Director UK Trading, UBS Phillips & Drew Securities Limited.

DALBY, P C J; Partner, Cazenove & Co.

DALDORPH, Miss Jacqueline; Partner, Clay & Partners Consulting Actuaries, since 1989; Pensions Actuary. *Career:* Clay & Partners 1981-. *Biog: b.* 19 November 1959. *Nationality:* British. *Educ:* The City University (BSc). *Professional Organisations:* FIA. *Recreations:* Gardening.

DALE, David Leslie; Senior Vice President/Senior Rep, Bahrain Middle East Bank (EC), since 1988; UK, Continental & Eastern Europe. *Career:* Westminster Bank 1964-68; Manufacturers Hanover Trust Co, London 1968-72; Toronto Dominion Bank, London 1972-74; Canadian Imperial Bank of Commerce, London & Bahrain, Dep Manager 1974-81; Al Saudi Bank, Manager Syndications 1982; Bahrain Middle East Bank SUP 1983-. *Biog: b.* 13 February 1945. *Nationality:* British. *m.* 1977, Ann M; 2 s. *Educ:* Worthing High School. *Directorships:* BMB International Ltd 1988 Dir & Gen Mgr; BMBH Ltd 1988; Forex Advisory Services Ltd 1988. *Recreations:* Tennis, Golf, Sailing, Skiing.

DALE, J F; Director, Kleinwort Benson Investment Management, since 1988; Business Development/Charities. *Career:* Grieveson Grant 1965. *Biog: b.* 18 June 1947. *Nationality:* British. *m.* 1979, Frances (née Harding); 1 s; 1 d. *Educ:* Hatfield Technical School. *Recreations:* Garden.

DALE, Peter John; Executive Director, Scimitar Development Capital Limited, since 1986; Investments in the USA. *Career:* Glacier Metal Company 1962-64; P E International 1966-76; Donny Investments 1976-78; Commonwealth Development Co Ltd 1978-86; Scimitar Development Capital Limited 1986-. *Biog: b.* 12 February 1940. *Nationality:* British. *m.* 1965, Barbara; 1 s; 1 d. *Educ:* Wyggeston Boys School; Imperial College (BSc, ARCS Mathematics). *Directorships:* Various US non-executive Directorships.

DALEY, Michael John William; Vice President, Morgan Stanley International, since 1986; Head of Fixed Income, Morgan Stanley Asset Management. *Career:* J Henry Schroder Wagg Trainee, Accounting 1972-73; S G Warburg & Co Ltd Trainee, Intl Capital Mkts 1973-77; Credit Suisse First Boston Ltd Mgr 1977-86; CSFB (Asset Management) Ltd Dir 1983-86; CSFB Investment Management Ltd Investment Mgr 1983-86. *Biog: b.* 23 September 1953. *Nationality:* British. *Educ:* Hatfield School. *Directorships:* Morgan Stanley Asset Management Ltd 1988 (exec). *Professional Organisations:* FInstD, 1984; MBIM, 1986. *Clubs:* RAC. *Recreations:* Mountaineering, Skiing, Golf, Driving.

DALHUISEN, Jan Hendrik; Director, IBJ International Ltd, since 1986; Head of International Corporate Development & Planning. *Career:* NV Philips Gloeilampenfabrieken Corp, Secretariat & Law Dept 1967-70; Gulf Oil Corp (Europe, Africa, Middle East), Member/Head of Law Dept 1970-84; Intl Primary Market Assoc, Sec Gen 1984-86. *Biog: b.* 19 July 1943. *Nationality:* Dutch. *m.* 1970, Elisabeth (née Scholtens); 3 s. *Educ:* Gymnasium, Zwolle, Netherlands; University of Amsterdam (DCL, MCL); University of California at Berkeley (LLM). *Other Activities:* Corresponding Member, Royal Netherlands Academy of Sciences; Member, Chartered Institute of Arbitrators. *Professional Organisations:* New York Bar; Netherlands Lawyers' Assoc. *Publications:* Compositions in Bankruptcy, 1968; Dalhuisen on International Insolvency and Bankruptcy (2 Vols), 1979-86; The New UK Securities Legislation and the EC 1992 Program, 1989. *Clubs:* Turf, Hurlingham, Marks. *Recreations:* Reading, Writing, Gardening.

DALLARD, C F B; Partner, Clay & Partners Consulting Actuaries.

DALLY, B J M; Non-Executive Director, Rutland Trust plc.

DALRYMPLE, Robert Gordon; Director, Grandfield Rork Collins, since 1981; Financial Communications. *Career:* Financial Journalist 1967-68; City & Industrial Publicity Services, Senior Consultant 1968-72; British Leyland, Financial & Business Affairs Manager 1972-74; Secretary General Industry Committee for Packaging and Environment 1974-76; Universal McCann, Director 1976-81; Grandfield Rork Collins, Director & Founder 1981-. *Biog: b.* 1 March 1943. *Nationality:* Scottish. *m.* 1970, Diana (née Williams); 1 s; 2 d. *Educ:* Trinity College, Cambridge (MA Hons). *Directorships:* Grandfield Rork Collins 1981 (exec). *Other Activities:* Former Chairman, Ealing Arts Council; Former Council Member, WWF. *Publications:* Education in England, 1970; England is a Foreign Country, 1971; Editor, How African was Egypt?, 1973; Robert Pilgrims London, 1987; Robert Pilgrims Endangered Species, 1988; Robert Pilgrim Resuming the Egg, 1989; Writer and Programme Maker under Robert Pilgrim. *Clubs:* Naval & Military. *Recreations:* Loving Cricket, Reading, Writing, Broadcasting.

DALTON, A S; Director, Well Marine Reinsurance Brokers Limited.

DALTON, Andrew Searle; Director, Mercury Asset Management Group plc, since 1986; Chairman, Warburg Asset Management. *Biog: b.* 18 May 1949. *Nationality:* British. *m.* 1982, Jennie (née Keane); 2 s; 1 d. *Educ:* Oundle School; Magdalen College, Oxford, (Hons Degree Modern History). *Directorships:* Mercury

Asset Management Group plc. *Other Activities:* Liveryman, Grocers Co. *Clubs:* Carlton.

DALTON, R A; Chairman & Chief Executive, FCB Advertising Ltd.

DALTON, T M H; Group Treasurer, Allied-Lyons plc.

DALTRY, T M; Partner, Jaques & Lewis.

DALVIE, A E; General Manager, The New India Assurance Company Limited.

DALWOOD, K L; Director, First National Bank PLC.

DALZIEL, Ian Martin; Deputy Group Managing Director, Adam & Company. *Directorships:* Continental Assets Trust Chairman; Lepercq-Amcur Fund MV (exec).

DAMERVAL, J C; Director, Equity & Law Life Assurance Society plc.

DANCE, Jonathan; Company Secretary, Calor Group plc, since 1987. *Career:* Admitted Solicitor 1972; Hoover Limited, Company Lawyer 1972-74; Calor Gas Limited, Assistant Solicitor 1974-77; Legal Executive 1977-84; Company Secretary 1984; Calor Group plc, Company Secretary 1987; Calor Limited, Appointed Director 1988. *Biog: b.* 17 June 1947. *Nationality:* British. *m.* 1970. *Educ:* St Edwards School, Oxford. *Professional Organisations:* Solicitor.

DANIELS, J; Director, Hill Samuel Investment Management Ltd.

DANIELS, Patrick Deane; Partner, Simmons & Simmons, since 1974; Taxation and Financial Services. *Career:* Bulcraig & Davis, Articled Clerk/Solicitor 1963-67; Freshfields, Solicitor 1968-72. *Biog: b.* 20 April 1940. *Nationality:* British. *m.* 1967, Heide Marie (née Mumm); 1 s; 1 d. *Educ:* St George's College, Weybridge; Durham University (LLB). *Other Activities:* Salzburg Seminar Alumni Assoc (England & Wales); Trustee, Institute of Cultural Affairs Charitable Trust; Taxation Ctee, Federation of Commodity Associations; Liveryman, City of London Solicitors Company. *Professional Organisations:* The Law Society; Institute of International and Comparative Law. *Publications:* Contributor to Management of Interest Rate Risk, 1988; Management of Currency Risk, 1989; Tolley's Company Law. *Clubs:* Carlton.

DANIELS, S J; Partner, Cazenove & Co, since 1990; Market Maker. *Career:* Babcock & Wilcox, Trainee Accountant 1971-73; Cazenove & Co 1973-. *Biog: b.* 3 February 1952. *Nationality:* British. *m.* 1973, Janet; 2 s. *Educ:* Harold Hill Grammar School. *Directorships:* Cazenove Securities Ltd 1986 (exec). *Professional Organi-sations:* Member, London Stock Exchange, 1983. *Recreations:* Badminton, Birdwatching.

DANIELS, T A; Director, Barclays de Zoete Wedd Securities Ltd.

DANIN, Clement Paul; Managing Director, Charles Davis (Metal Brokers) Ltd, since 1986. *Career:* H J Enthoven & Sons, LME Dealer 1960-65; Chemical Plastics/Wavin Plastics Ltd, Export Sales Manager/Group Personnel Manager 1965-73; Charles Davis (Metal Brokers) Ltd, Senior Dealer/Commercial Director 1973-86. *Biog: b.* 22 April 1937. *Nationality:* British. *m.* 1962, Bridget (née Mason); 1 s; 2 d. *Educ:* Westminster. *Directorships:* Charles Davis (Metal Brokers) Ltd 1975 (exec); London Metal Exchange Ltd 1990 (non-exec). *Other Activities:* London Metal Exchange Committee; Vice Chairman, LME Committee. *Professional Organisations:* ACI Asb. *Recreations:* Music, Art, Golf.

DARBY, John Oliver Robertson; Chairman, Ultramar plc, since 1988. *Career:* Arthur Young Chartered Accountants, Partner 1959; Chairman 1974-87. *Biog: b.* 5 January 1930. *Nationality:* British. *m.* 1955, Valerie (née Leyland Cole); 3 s. *Educ:* Charterhouse. *Directorships:* National Home Loans Holdings plc 1985 Chairman; Brel Group Limited 1989 Chairman; Property Lending Bank plc 1987 Chairman. *Professional Organisations:* Chartered Accountant. *Clubs:* Garrick, Royal & Ancient Golf, Royal Thames Yacht, City.

DARBYSHIRE, David Stewart; Partner, Arthur Andersen & Co, since 1976; Accounting & Audit Partner Specialising in Financial Markets. *Career:* Arthur Andersen & Co (London) 1966-72; (Paris) 1972-79; (Leeds) 1979-85; (London) 1985-. *Biog: b.* 14 November 1940. *Nationality:* British. *m.* 1970, Elizabeth (née Watts); 1 s; 2 d. *Educ:* Radley College; Oriel College, Oxford (MA). *Other Activities:* Inner Temple (Barrister-at-Law 1965), Ordre des Experts Comptables and Compagnie de Commissaires aux Comptes (Paris Region) (admitted 1976). *Professional Organisations:* FCA, ATII. *Clubs:* Special Forces, Sea View Yacht Club. *Recreations:* Economic & Social History, Sailing.

DARE, Andrew R; Managing Director, St Ivel Group, Unigate plc, since 1989; UK Food. *Career:* Shellmex and BP Ltd; Unigate plc, Corporate Planner 1971; Marketing & General Management Positions; St Ivel Fresh Dairy Products, Managing Director 1979; Managing Director 1989. *Biog: b.* 1942. *Nationality:* British. *m.* 1989, Sally (née Evans); 1 s; 2 d (from previous marriage). *Educ:* Blundells School; University of Keele (BA Politics Economics); University of Bradford (MSC Management Studies). *Directorships:* Galloway Cheese 1990 (exec). *Other Activities:* Past Vice Chairman, National Dairy Council; President, Dairy Trade Federation. *Professional Organisations:* Fellow, British Inst of

Management; Fellow, Institute of Grocery Distribution. *Recreations:* Windsurfing, Golf, Tennis, Theatre, Watching Rugby.

DARE, John Ashton; Director, Baring Brothers & Co Limited, since 1977; International Corporate Finance. *Career:* First National City Bank (New York & London), Various 1964-70; London Multinational Bank Ltd, Exec Dir 1970-77; Baring Brothers Asia (Hong Kong), MD & Chief Exec 1975-79. *Biog: b.* 15 November 1938. *Nationality:* American. *m.* 1989, Christine Lesley; 1 d. *Educ:* Stanford University (AB,MBA). *Directorships:* Baring Securities (Hong Kong) Limited 1984 (non-exec); Baring Brothers Hambrecht & Quist Ltd 1984 (non-exec); Baring Securities Ltd 1984 Chm; The Baillie Gifford Japan Trust plc 1977 (non-exec); Baring Hambrecht Orient Trust Co Ltd 1984 (non-exec); Offshore Racing Council Ltd 1986 (non-exec); The Korea-Europe Fund Ltd (Guernsey) 1987 (non-exec); Seahorse Holdings Limited 1988 (non-exec); Baring Brothers Private Asset Management Ltd 1989 (non-exec); Banque Baring Brothers (Suisse) SA, (Switzerland) 1982 (non-exec); Seahorse Ratings Ltd 1990 (non-exec). *Other Activities:* Vice Commodore, Royal Ocean Racing Club; Treasurer, Offshore Racing Council. *Clubs:* Overseas Bankers Club, Royal Yacht Squadron, Hurlingham Club, Royal Lymington Yacht Club. *Recreations:* Sailing.

DARE, K J; Managing Director, Royal Insurance Holdings PLC.

DARE, S J St F; Managing Director (Investment Management), Clive Discount Company Ltd.

DARKAZALLY, Mamoun; Deputy General Manager, Banque Francaise de l'Orient, since 1989; Private Banking. *Career:* Banque Francaise de l'Orient, London, Deputy General Manager, Private Banking 1989-; Al Saudi Banque, London, Branch Manager, Private Banking 1983-89; London, Manager, Africa & the Middle East 1982-83; Paris, Area Manager 1979-82; The Chase Manhattan Bank, Doha, Qatar, Deputy General Manager (The Commercial Bank of Qatar) 1975-79; Beirut, Lebanon, Assistant Regional Manager 1974-75; New York, Assistant Treasurer 1973-74. *Biog: b.* 9 October 1942. *Nationality:* British. *m.* 1971, Vivian; 1 s. *Educ:* New York University (Bachelor of Science Business Administration). *Directorships:* Syrian Arab Association in the UK 1987 Chairman; Arab Bankers Association UK 1988. *Professional Organisations:* Institute of Directors; British Management Insitute.

DARLING, Humphry Nigel; Director, Hambros Bank Ltd, since 1988; Banking for Larger Companies Worldwide (excl Scandinavia). *Career:* S G Warburg & Co Ltd, Dir, UK Banking 1983-88; Kleinwort Benson Ltd, Mgr, US Banking 1977-80; Guinness Mahon & Co Ltd, Mgr, UK Banking & Shipping 1974-77. *Biog: b.* 2 February 1946. *Nationality:* British. *Educ:* Marlborough College; Jesus College, Cambridge (MA); London Business School (MSc). *Professional Organisations:* Barrister, Middle Temple. *Recreations:* Music, The Countryside.

DARLING, J S; Executive Director and Underwriter, Gresham Underwriting Agencies Limited.

DARLINGTON, Miss Diana; Director, Panmure Gordon & Co Ltd, since 1987; Corporate Finance. *Career:* Alexander Tatham Assistant, Company & Commercial 1967-73; Halliwell Landau Assistant, Company & Commercial 1973-75; Henry Cooke Lumsden & Co Executive Corporate Finance 1975-83; Montagu Loebl Stanley Executive Corporate Finance 1983-85; Panmure Gordon Corporate Finance 1985-. *Directorships:* Panmure Gordon & Co Ltd 1987 (exec).

DARLINGTON, G L B; Partner, Freshfields.

DARROCH DE HALDEVANG, Bernard Goetz Michael Imka (Bernie); Director, Berry Palmer & Lyle Limited, Lloyd's Brokers, since 1988. *Career:* De Pinna Scorers & John Venn, Articled Clerk 1982-83; Hogg Robinson Group plc, Technician, Broker & Acct Exec, Political Risks 1983-85; Berry Palmer & Lyle Limited, Lloyd's Brokers, Broker & Acct Exec 1985-; Shareholder 1988-. *Biog: b.* 15 August 1961. *Nationality:* British. *m.* 1986, Melissa Carolyn (née Darroch of Gourock); 1 d. *Educ:* Downside. *Directorships:* Rudd Huntley & Tate Limited 1989 (exec). *Clubs:* Lansdowne. *Recreations:* Riding, Sailing, Music, Whisky-Tasting.

DART, Paul; Director, AIBD (Systems & Information) Limited.

DARWALL-SMITH, R Philip R; Director (Research and Fund Management), British & Commonwealth Merchant Bank plc.

DASGUPTA, Dipankar; General Manager, Middle East Bank Ltd, since 1990; Overall responsibility UK operations. *Career:* St Stephen's College, University of Delhi, Asst Prof of Economics 1972-73; Standard Chartered Bank plc 1973-86; Various including: Branch Operations Manager; Country Administration Manager; Branch Manager; Regional Credit Controller; Deputy Chief Executive and Chief Operations Officer, Emirate of Abu Dhabi; Middle East Bank, Asst Gen Mgr UK Operations 1986-. *Biog: b.* 17 June 1951. *Nationality:* Indian. *m.. Educ:* St Xavier's School, Calcutta; Presidency College, University of Calcutta (BSc Hons Econ); Delhi School of Economics, University of Delhi (MSc Econ) and Numerous Professional Courses. *Other Activities:* Jawaharlal Nehru Memorial Gold Medal, University of Delhi; KC Nag Memorial Prize, University of Delhi; Hiralal Bhargava Memorial Prize, University of Delhi; Merit Scholarship of the Delhi School of Economics. *Recreations:* Golf, Cricket, Squash, Swimming, Rowing, Debating, Music.

DASHWOOD, Cyril Francis; Senior Partner, Moores Rowland Chartered Accountants, since 1989. *Career:* Nevill Hovey Gardner & Co, Articled Clerk 1942-49; RAF Pilot/Flight Lt 1943-47; Moores Rowland Chartered Accts, Senior Ptnr. *Biog: b.* 15 March 1925. *Nationality:* British. *m.* 1958, Prudence Elizabeth (née Williams); 2 s; 1 d. *Educ:* Cranleigh School. *Other Activities:* Hon Treasurer & VP, The Hockey Assoc; Freedom of the City of London; Chm, Amersham & Chesham Bois Choral Society; Worshipful Co of Chartered Accountants; Council Member, English Sinfonia Orchestra. *Professional Organisations:* FCA. *Clubs:* Carlton, Wig & Pen, MCC. *Recreations:* Music, Sport, Gardening.

DAUBENY, Charles Niel; Group Director - Finance, Scandinavian Bank Group plc, since 1987; Finance, Management Services & Information Technology. *Career:* Price Waterhouse & Co, Audit Snr 1965-67; Scribbans-Kemp Ltd, Group Acct 1967-68; Mercantile & General Reinsurance Co Ltd Dep Group Chief Acct 1969-73; Bank of America International Ltd, Fin Controller 1973-78; Scandinavian Bank Group plc 1978-. *Biog: b.* 4 August 1937. *Nationality:* British. *m.* 1965, Mary Rose (née McLeod); 1 s; 2 d. *Educ:* Wellington College. *Professional Organisations:* FCA. *Recreations:* Squash, Gardening.

DAVENPORT, D H; Director, CS Investments.

DAVENPORT, John; Director, Henry Cooke Lumsden plc.

DAVENPORT, Robert Simpson; Executive Director, Hill Samuel Bank Ltd, since 1988; Corporate Finance. *Career:* Singleton Fabian & Co (now part of Binder Hamlyn), Articled 1958-62; Peat Marwick McLintock & Co, Qualified Accountant 1963-67; S G Warburg & Co Ltd 1968-88; Exec Dir 1975-88. *Biog: b.* 7 January 1941. *Nationality:* British. *m.* 1970, Patricia (née Temple); 2 s. *Educ:* Canford. *Professional Organisations:* FCA. *Publications:* Contributor to Gore Browne on Company Law. *Clubs:* Hurlingham. *Recreations:* Tennis, Music, Gardening, Windsurfing.

DAVEY, A E; Director, County NatWest Securities Limited.

DAVEY, Arthur; Partner, Moore Stephens.

DAVEY, C; Partner, Nabarro Nathanson.

DAVEY, C W; Group Tax Manager, Beazer plc, since1989; Corporate Tax. *Career:* Courtaulds plc, Deputy Tax Manager 1980-89; Ernst & Whinney 1976-80. *Biog: b.* 20 May 1955. *Nationality:* British. *m.* 1980, K E (née Selfe); 1 s; 1 d. *Educ:* Newton-le-Willows Grammar; University of Newcastle-Upon-Tyne (BA Econ). *Other Activities:* Joint Taxation Committee, Building Employers Confederation. *Professional Organisations:* ICAEW.

DAVEY, Nigel Thomas; Tax Partner, Touche Ross & Co, since 1980; Taxation of Professional Partnerships, Adviser to many City Lawyers and Stock Exchange Member Firms. *Biog: b.* 8 May 1947. *Nationality:* British. *m.* 1972, Ruth Mary (née Brown); 3 s. *Educ:* Ilford County High School; Trinity College, Cambridge (MA). *Professional Organisations:* FCA. *Publications:* The Business of Partnerships (With P J Oliver), Second Edition, 1990; Partnership Taxation (With E E Ray). *Recreations:* Badminton, Tennis, Music.

DAVEY, Richard; Corporate Finance Director, N M Rothschild & Sons Limited, since 1989, Mergers & Acquisitions. *Career:* N M Rothschild, Director 1982-86; Exco International plc, Director 1983-87. *Biog: b.* 22 July 1948. *m.* Kerstin; 3 s; 1 d. *Educ:* Lincoln College, Oxford (BA). *Other Activities:* English Chamber Orchestra & Music Society. *Recreations:* Opera, Cricket.

DAVID, Colin Prichard; Partner, Touche Ross & Co.

DAVID, Gareth; Deputy City Editor, Sunday Times Business News.

DAVID, William Nigel; Director, Hoare Govett, since 1987; UK Corporate Fin, especially Small/Medium Sized Companies. *Career:* Simon & Coates, Trainee Investment Analyst 1973-74; Touche & Ross & Co, Mgr, National Audit & Accountancy 1975-80; The Stock Exchange, Mgr, Companies Supervision Quotations Dept 1980-83; Hoare Govett Dir, Corp Fin 1983-. *Biog: b.* 13 May 1951. *Nationality:* British. *m.* 1975, Karen (née Phipps); 1 s; 1 d. *Educ:* Kent College, Canterbury; St Edmund Hall, Oxford (MA). *Professional Organisations:* FCA. *Clubs:* Vincents. *Recreations:* Cricket, Rugby, Golf, Travel.

DAVID-JONES, J D; Director, Barclays de Zoete Wedd Securities Ltd.

DAVID-WEILL, Michel Alexandre; Senior Partner, Lazard Frères & Co, New York, since 1977; Chairman, Lazard Brothers & Co Limited, London, since 1990; Partner, Lazard Frères et Cie, Paris, since 1965; Lazard Partners, Chairman, since 1984. *Career:* Brown Brothers Harriman 1954-55; Lehman Brothers, New York 1955-56; Lazard Frères & Co, New York 1956-65; Partner 1961; Lazard Brothers & Co Limited, Director 1965-. *Biog: b.* 23 November 1932. *Nationality:* French. *m.* 1956, Hélène (née Lehideux); 4 d. *Educ:* Institut de Sciences Politiques of Paris; Lycée Français de New York. *Directorships:* ITT Corporation; Eurafrance; Crédit Mobilier Industrial (SOVAC); BSN - Gervais - Danone;

Pearson plc (non-exec); Instituto Finanziario Industriale Internationale SA. *Other Activities:* Member, Institut (Académie des Beaux Arts); Member, Conseil Artistique des Musées Nationaux. *Clubs:* The Knickerbocker Club New York, The Brook New York, The Creek Club Inc Locust Valley.

DAVIDSON, D H; Founder & Group Chairman, Persimmon plc, since 1972. *Career:* George Wimpey, Commercial Manager 1963-65; Ryedale Homes, Founder & Chairman 1965-72; Persimmon plc, Founder & Chairman 1972-. *Biog: b.* 29 March 1941. *Nationality:* British. *m.* 1965, Sarah Katherine (née Wilson); 4 d. *Educ:* Ampleforth College. *Directorships:* Persimmon plc 1984 (exec) Chairman; Persimmon Homes (Yorkshire) Ltd 1984 (exec); Persimmon Homes (Midlands) Ltd 1972 (exec) Chairman; Persimmon Homes (Anglia) Ltd 1976 (exec); Persimmon Homes (South West) Ltd 1979 (exec); Persimmon Homes (Wessex) Ltd 1983 (exec); Persimmon Homes (North East) Ltd 1976 (exec); Persimmon Homes (Scotland) Ltd 1986 (exec) Chairman; Persimmon Homes (South East) Ltd 1986 (exec); Persimmon Homes (North West) Ltd 1987 (exec); Persimmon Homes (Thames Valley) Ltd 1987 (exec); Persimmon Homes (East Yorkshire) Ltd 1987 (exec); Scottish Investment Trust plc 1988 (non-exec). *Clubs:* Whites, Turf Club. *Recreations:* Country Pursuits.

DAVIDSON, David Murray; Partner, Penningtons, Incorporating Gamlens, since 1990; Family Law. *Career:* Kenwright & Cox, Partner 1977-85; Gamlens 1986-90; Penningtons, Inc Gamlens, Partner 1990. *Biog: b.* 30 January 1947. *Nationality:* British. *m.* 1973, Mary Pamela (née Sebag-Montefiore); 1 s; 2 d. *Educ:* Winchester College; Edinburgh University (LLB). *Professional Organisations:* Member, Solicitors Family Law Association; Fellow, International Academy of Matrimonial Lawyers. *Publications:* Contributor, Jointly Owned and Matrimonial Property, Volume 19, Encyclopaedia of Forms and Precedents, Fifth Edition, 1990. *Clubs:* MCC. *Recreations:* Cricket, Ornithology.

DAVIDSON, Gordon Lindsay; Partner, Dickson Minto WS, since 1988; Commercial Property. *Career:* Dundas & Wilson CS Trainee Solicitor 1974-76; Edinburgh University, Faculty of Law Lecturer, Scots Law 1976-79; Steedman Ramage & Co WS Solicitor/Ptnr, Property Law 1979-86; Dickson Minto WS Solicitor/Ptnr, Commercial Property 1986-88. *Biog: b.* 10 July 1951. *Nationality:* British. *m.* 1982, Stephanie (née Sale); 1 s; 2 d. *Educ:* Hutchesons' Grammar, Glasgow; University of Glasgow (LLB Hons); Trinity College, Cambridge (LLB, LLM). *Directorships:* DM Company Services Limited 1988; 22 Nominees Limited 1988. *Other Activities:* Fellow, Society of Antiquaries of Scotland. *Professional Organisations:* The Law Society of Scotland; Member of Society of Writers to Her Majesty's Signet. *Publications:* Conveyancing Styles Book,

1977 (and subsequent editions). *Clubs:* Scottish Arts Club. *Recreations:* Foreign Travel, Hill Walking.

DAVIDSON, K M; Director, The Frizzell Group Limited.

DAVIDSON, P A T; Finance Director, Hogg Group plc.

DAVIDSON, Sir Robert; Director, The General Electric Company plc.

DAVIDSON, W L; Director, MIM Limited.

DAVIDSON KELLY, C N; Director, Corporate Development, LASMO plc, since 1986; In Charge of Group's Acquisition & Disposal Programme. *Career:* W & J Burness WS (Edinburgh), Law Apprentice/Assistant Solicitor 1968-70; Ivory & Sime (Edinburgh), Investment Analyst & Fund Manager 1970-74; Oil Exploration Holdings Ltd (Edinburgh), Legal Adviser & Company Secretary 1974-80; LASMO plc (London), General Manager Corporate Development to Director 1980-90. *Biog: b.* 2 June 1945. *Nationality:* British. *m.* 1972, Anabella Daphne (née Graham); 1 s; 1 d. *Educ:* Edinburgh Academy; Oxford University (BA); Edinburgh University (LLB). *Directorships:* LASMO plc 1986 (exec); Sidro SA Brussels 1990 (non-exec). *Other Activities:* Director, Edinburgh & Leith Petroleum Club, 1976-80; Member, Executive Committee BRINDEX, 1978-80; Member, Oklahoma Independent Petroleum Association, 1974-90. *Clubs:* Annabels. *Recreations:* Sheep Farming.

DAVIE, Jonathan Richard; Main Board Director, Barclays de Zoete Wedd, since 1986; Fixed Income. *Career:* Robson Rhodes & Co, Articled Clerk 1965-69; George M Hill & Co, Dealer 1969-70; Wedd Durlacher Mordaunt & Co Dealer 1970-75; Ptnr 1976-86; Barclays de Zoete Wedd, Main Board Director, Managing Director Fixed Income 1986-. *Biog: b.* 21 September 1946. *Nationality:* British. *m.* 1986, Belinda Mary (née Blake). *Educ:* Tonbridge School; University of Neuchâtel. *Directorships:* BZW Gilts Ltd 1986 (exec); BZW Securities Ltd 1986 (exec); BZW Holdings Ltd 1986 (exec); BZW Futures Trading Ltd 1986 (exec); Lane Fine Art Ltd 1986 (non-exec). *Professional Organisations:* Fellow, Institute of Chartered Accountants. *Clubs:* City of London, Royal and Ancient Golf Club, Royal St Georges Golf Club, Rye Golf Club, Berkshire Golf Club, Queen's. *Recreations:* Tennis, Golf, Skiing.

DAVIES, A L M; Director, County NatWest Investment Management Ltd.

DAVIES, A M; Chairman, Calor Group plc.

DAVIES, B; Finance Director, Morison Stoneham, since 1990; Management Information & Finance. *Career:*

Egerton Trust plc, Group Financial Controller 1987-88; PPP Beaumont, Finance Director 1988-89. *Biog: b.* 10 February 1953. *Nationality:* British. *m.* 1980, Hilary; 1 s. *Educ:* Manchester Grammar; University College, London (BA Hons Philosophy). *Professional Organisations:* ACA.

DAVIES, B W; General Manager, Yorkshire Building Society, since 1987; Personnel & Mortgage/Investment Administration. *Career:* E R Squibb & Sons, (Ethical Pharmaceuticals), Production Manager 1964-68; Vick International, (Ethical & Proprietary Pharmaceuticals), Production Control Manager 1968-69; PA Management Consultants, Senior Consultant 1969-87. *Biog: b.* 3 March 1941. *Nationality:* British. *m.* 1966, Helen; 1 s; 1 d. *Educ:* Leeds University (BSc Physics). *Directorships:* Phillip Schofield & Co 1990; Phillip Schofield (Property Management) 1990; Yorkshire Key Services Ltd 1987; Yorkshire Estate Agents Ltd 1987; Yorkshire Building Society Estate Agents Ltd 1987; Yorkshire Investment Services Ltd 1987; Yorkshire Insurance Services Ltd 1987. *Clubs:* Waterloo Rugby Club.

DAVIES, David John; Chairman, Johnson Matthey plc, since 1990. *Career:* Chase Manhattan Bank (Based in London and New York) 1963-67; Hill Samuel & Co Ltd (Based in New York and London) 1967-73; MEPC Ltd, Finance Director 1973-83; Vice Chairman 1977-83; The Hongkong Land Company Limited, Managing Director 1983-86; Jardine Matheson Group, Director 1983-86; The Hongkong Land Property Company Ltd, Chairman 1983-86; Hong Kong Electric Company, Director 1983-86; The Dairy Farm Company Ltd, Chairman 1983-86; Mandarin Oriental Hotel Company Ltd, Chairman 1983-86; Hill Samuel Group plc, Chief Executive and Deputy Chairman 1987-88; Hill Samuel Bank Limited, Joint Chairman 1986-88; Nobel Lowndes & Partners, Chairman 1986-88; Wescol International Marine Services, Chairman 1986-88; Hill Samuel Investment Management Group, Chairman 1986-88; Hill Samuel Investment Services Group, Chairman 1986-88; Macquarie Bank Limited (Australia), Director 1986-88; Singapore Land Limited (Singapore), Director 1986-90; Fitzwilton plc (Ireland), Director 1986-90; Imry Merchant Developers plc, Chairman 1987-89; Asia Securities Int Ltd (Hong Kong), Director 1987-89; TSB Group plc, Director 1987-89; Charter Consolidated plc, Deputy Chairman 1988-89. *Biog: b.* 1 April 1940. *Nationality:* British. *m.* 1985, Linda Wong Davies; 1 s; 1 d. *Educ:* New College, Oxford (Closed Scholarship, MA Modern Languages); Harvard Business School (AMP). *Directorships:* American Barrick Resources Corporation (Canada); First Pacific Company (Hong Kong); Sketchley plc Chm. *Other Activities:* Board of Glyndebourne Productions Limited. *Clubs:* Hong Kong Club, Turf Club, Cardiff & County Club, Oriental, Kildare Street & University. *Recreations:* Farming, Skiing, Tennis, Travel, Opera.

DAVIES, David Keith; Partner, Lawrence Graham, since 1989; European Community and Eastern Europe. *Career:* Lloyds Bank International (London), Economist 1970-73; Lovell, White & King, Solicitors (London), Articled Clerk/Assistant Solicitor 1974-79; S G Archibald (Brussels), International Lawyer 1979-81; Eurolink (Paris, Brussels, Strasbourg), Founder and Senior Partner 1982-86; Bacardi (Europe) Ltd (London), Executive Director General Counsel 1986-89. *Biog: b.* 9 January 1948. *Nationality:* British. *m.* 1976, Annick Houssin de Saint Laurent; 3 s. *Educ:* Salesian College, Oxford (BSc Econ Hons); University College, London; College of Law, London (Solicitors Professional). *Directorships:* Eurolink 1982 Senior Partner; Bacardi (Europe) Ltd 1987. *Other Activities:* City of London Solicitors Company. *Professional Organisations:* Law Society. *Clubs:* Royal Automobile Club.

DAVIES, David Wyndham; Director & Chief General Manager/Business & Customer Services, Pearl Assurance plc, since 1987; Customer Services, Life & Non Life Insurance. *Career:* Pearl Assurance plc, Industrial Relations Mgr 1979-81; Asst Actuary 1981-83; Controller (Admin) 1983-84; Asst Gen Mgr (Systems) 1984-87; Gen Mgr (Systems) 1987-88; Gen Mgr (Business & Product Development) 1988-89; Deputy Chief General Manager 1989-90; Chief General Manager 1990-. *Biog: b.* 16 September 1947. *m.* 1970, Helen Mary (née Williams); 1 s; 1 d. *Educ:* Llandysul Grammar School; London School of Economics, BSc (Econ). *Directorships:* Pearl Assurance Unit Funds 1988 (exec); Pearl Assurance Unit Linked Pensions 1988 (exec); Pearl Unit Trusts 1988 (exec); Pearl Group 1989 (exec); Hallmark 1990 (exec); Aviation & General 1990 (non-exec); St Helen's Trust 1990 (non-exec). *Professional Organisations:* FIA. *Clubs:* RAC. *Recreations:* Computers, Golf, Tennis, Rugby.

DAVIES, G A; Director, Coutts & Co.

DAVIES, G M; Director, George Wimpey plc.

DAVIES, Gareth James; Partner, Grimley J R Eve, since 1990; City of London Property, Letting Acquisition & Development. *Career:* St Quintin, Associate, City Office Agency 1983-89; Sinclair Goldsmith & Co, Director, City Office Agency 1989-90. *Biog: b.* 21 February 1961. *Nationality:* British. *m.* 1990, Katie Jane (née Hall). *Educ:* Sevenoaks School, Sevenoaks, Kent; University of Reading (BSc Hons Land Management). *Professional Organisations:* Professional Associate of The Royal Institution of Chartered Surveyors. *Clubs:* Knole Park Golf Club. *Recreations:* Golf.

DAVIES, Gavyn; OBE; Partner & Chief UK Economist, Goldman Sachs, since 1986; Economic Forecasting. *Career:* Policy Unit, Economic Policy Adviser 1974-79; Phillips and Drew, UK Economist 1979-81; Simon and Coates, Chief UK Economist 1981-86. *Biog: b.* 27

November 1950. *Nationality:* British. *m.* 1989, Ms Susan Nye; 1 d. *Educ:* Taunton's School, Southampton; St John's College, Cambridge (BA Hons 1st); Balliol College, Oxford. *Other Activities:* Council Member, Economic and Social Research Council; Economic Adviser, House of Commons Treasury & Civil Service Ctee; Visiting Professor, London School of Economics. *Recreations:* Watching Southampton win.

DAVIES, Geoffrey Ronald; Partner, Titmuss Sainer & Webb.

DAVIES, H C; Director, Hogg Robinson & Gardner Mountain plc; Chairman, Hogg Robinson Australia Group, since 1988; International Marketing. *Career:* Hogg Robinson & Capel Cure Ltd, Management Trainee/Ass Broker 1965; CIA, Home Trade Broker 1968; Sales Director, Board 1977; Managing Director 1982; Credit & Political Risks, Director 1982; Hogg Robinson (Scotland) Ltd, Member of Board 1978-84; CIA Ltd, Chairman 1984; HRGM Retail, Managing Director 1984; Hogg Robinson Ltd, Chairman 1985; HRGM, International Marketing Director 1987; HRGM plc, On the Board 1987; HRGM Insurance Marketing Services, Chairman 1987; Hogg Robinson Australia Group, Chairman 1988. *Biog: b.* 9 October 1946. *Nationality:* British; 3 d. *Educ:* Tonbridge School, Tonbridge, Kent. *Other Activities:* Institute of Management; Institute of Marketing; Institute of Credit Management; Worshipful Company of Insurers; Freeman, City of London. *Recreations:* Golf, Skiing, Rugby, Cricket, Gardening, Travel, Photography.

DAVIES, J L; Managing Director (Investment Management), United Dominions Trust Limited.

DAVIES, Jeremy; Director, Steel Burrill Jones Group plc, since 1989; Managing Director of Reinsurance Broking Subsidiary. *Career:* Glanvill Enthoven Ltd 1966-67; WE Found Ltd, Broker 1967-73; Halford Shead Ltd, Broker 1973-76; Howson F Devitt Ltd, Broker 1976-81; Director 1981-89; Devitt Group Ltd, Director 1988-89; Meacock Samuelson Devitt Ltd, 1986- Managing Director 1990; Underwriting Member of Lloyds 1981-. *Biog: b.* 14 August 1949. *Nationality:* British. *m.* 1977, Judith Anne (née Quinn); 2 d. *Directorships:* Meacock Samuelson Devitt Ltd 1990 (exec) MD. *Other Activities:* Member, Worshipful Company of Plumbers; Freeman, City of London. *Clubs:* City Livery Club, Royal Automobile Club. *Recreations:* Golf, Racing.

DAVIES, John; Managing Director, 3i Portfolio Management Ltd, since 1982; 3i's Quoted Investment Portfolio, Investment Trusts & Pension Funds. *Career:* Midland Assurance Ltd Investment Analyst 1964-67; JM Finn & Co Investment Analyst 1968-71; National Coal Board Pension Fund Investment Analyst (UK Equities) 1971-73; Confederation Life Insurance Co Fund Manager 1973-79; Deputy Investment Manager 1979-82.

Biog: b. 12 July 1946. *Nationality:* British. *m.* 1971, Jacqueline (née Wheeler); 1 s; 3 d. *Educ:* Bournville Boys Technical School. *Directorships:* Southbank Securities Ltd 1985 (exec). *Professional Organisations:* AMSIA. *Clubs:* Girt Clog Climbing Club. *Recreations:* Music, Walking.

DAVIES, John Ormond; Secretary, The Burton Group plc, since 1989. *Career:* Harvey Nichols (Holdings) Limited, Secretary 1987. *Biog: b.* 16 September 1942. *Nationality:* British. *Directorships:* B G Pension Trustee Limited 1988; The Burton Group Pension Trustee Limited 1989; Castle Trustee Limited 1989; Debenhams plc 1989; Debenhams Pension Trust Limited 1989; Portland Pension Services Limited 1988; High Street Insurance Company Limited 1988.

DAVIES, John Thomas; Director of International Banking, Lloyds Bank plc, since 1989; Far East, Latin America, Europe & New Zealand. *Career:* Lloyds Bank plc Asst Mgr/Mgr/Asst Reg Gen Mgr 1963-78; Head Office Asst Gen Mgr 1978-83; UK Retail Banking Division Gen Mgr 1983-86; Snr Gen Mgr 1986-87; Intl Banking Division Snr Gen Mgr 1987-89. *Directorships:* The National Bank of New Zealand 1989; Lloyds Bank (Blsa) Limited 1989; Lloyds Bank (France) Limited 1989; Lloyds Bank SA 1989; Lloyds International Trading Limited 1989; Schroder Munchmeyer Hengst & Co 1989.

DAVIES, Jonathan P; Partner, Memery Crystal.

DAVIES, K C; Director, The London Metal Exchange Ltd.

DAVIES, K J; Executive Director, Allied Dunbar Assurance plc, since 1988; Mortgages (Director of Allied Dunbar Mortgages Ltd). *Career:* Deloitte & Co, Chartered Accountant/Audit Senior 1970-74; Hambro Life Assurance, Financial Accountant 1974-76; Hobourn-Eaton Manufacturing Co Ltd, Financial Accountant 1976-77; Schroders Limited, Senior Accountant 1977; Allied Dunbar Assurance, Management Accountancy Director 1987-89; Executive Director, Administration 1989-; Executive Director, Mortgages & Corporate Projects 1989-. *Biog: b.* 2 February 1947. *Nationality:* British. *m.* 1980, Judith (née Walker); 2 d. *Educ:* London University (BA Hons History). *Directorships:* Allied Dunbar Mortgages Ltd 1988. *Professional Organisations:* FCA. *Recreations:* Horse Racing, Sport.

DAVIES, Kenneth Seymour; Partner, Pannell Kerr Forster, since 1974; Insurance Audit Partner. *Career:* Hatfield Dixon Roberts Wright & Co, Articled Clerk 1965-67; Rowley Pemberton Roberts & Co, Articled Clerk 1967-69; Snr Clerk 1969-72; Mgr 1972-74; Ptnr 1974-81. *Biog: b.* 11 February 1948. *Nationality:* British. *m.* 1971, Brenda Margaret (née Cannon); 4 s; 1 d. *Educ:* St Nicholas Grammar School, Northwood Hills. *Profes-*

sional Organisations: FCA. *Recreations:* Youth Club, Badminton, Gardening.

DAVIES, Kevin Laurence; Technical Director, Bradstock Blunt & Thompson Ltd, since 1989; Corporate Account Broking & Risk Management. *Career:* Sun Alliance, London, Insurance Clerk 1969-70; Norwich Union, Insurance Clerk 1970-71; First National Insurance Brokers, Account Handler 1971-72; Norman Insurance Company, Sales 1972-77; Bradstock Blunt & Thompson, Various 1977-. *Biog: b.* 11 September 1948. *Nationality:* British. *m.* 1972, Jane (née Parson); 2 d. *Educ:* Mayfield College. *Directorships:* Bradstock Blunt (Plastics) Ltd 1986 (exec); Bradstock Blunt & Thompson Ltd 1989 (exec). *Professional Organisations:* Registered Insurance Broker.

DAVIES, Leslie John; Finance Director, Gresham Trust plc.

DAVIES, M; Director, Panmure Gordon & Co Limited.

DAVIES, M C C; Director, C S Investments Limited.

DAVIES, Mark Edward Trehearne; Managing Director, GNI Ltd, since 1985; Futures Brokers & Investment Managers. *Career:* Ralli International Commodity Broker 1969; Founded Inter Commodities 1972. *Biog: b.* 20 May 1948. *Nationality:* British. *m.* 1987, Antonia (née Chittenden); 1 s; 1 d. *Educ:* Stowe School. *Directorships:* Gerrard & National Holdings plc 1986; GNI Holdings Ltd 1976; GNI Ltd (Futures and Options Brokers) 1972; GNI Inc 1989; GNI Freight Futures 1981 Chairman; GNI Wallace Ltd (Futures Brokers) 1986 Chairman; GH Asset Management 1988; Trifutures 1989; Inter Commodities Ltd (non-Trading) 1982; Inter Commodities Trading Ltd (non-Trading) 1976; ICV Ltd 1981; Tweseldown Race Course Ltd 1979; Guy Morrison Ltd (Art Dealers) 1986. *Publications:* Trading in Commodities (Co-Author), 1974. *Recreations:* Hunting, Racing.

DAVIES, N L; Associate Director, Schlesinger & Company Limited.

DAVIES, Peter; City Reporter, Today.

DAVIES, R; Member, Monopolies and Mergers Commission.

DAVIES, Richard James Guy; Director, Lazard Brothers & Co Ltd, since 1986; Corporate Finance. *Career:* Lazard Brothers Exec 1976-78; Korea Merchant Banking Corporation Exec 1978-80; Lazard Brothers Exec 1980-. *Biog: b.* 7 December 1953. *m.* 1980, Michèle (née Lipscomb); 2 s. *Educ:* Felsted School; St Catharine's College, Cambridge (BA Hons). *Clubs:* Royal Burnham Yacht Club. *Recreations:* Sailing.

DAVIES, Roger Guy; Partner, Allen & Overy, since 1976; Oil & Gas, General Company and Commercial. *Career:* Allen & Overy Asst Solicitor 1972-75; (Dubai, UAE) Mgr 1980-83. *Biog: b.* 5 November 1946. *Nationality:* British. *m.* 1970, Diana June (née Perks); 3 s; 1 d. *Educ:* Kingswood School; Fitzwilliam College, Cambridge (MA). *Other Activities:* City of London Solicitors' Company. *Professional Organisations:* The Law Society, IBA. *Publications:* Energy Financing - A Review of Legal Considerations from the Standpoint of Both Lender and Borrower, 1979. *Recreations:* Golf, Shooting, Tennis, Opera.

DAVIES, Roger Rhys; Managing Director, Leslie & Godwin (UK) Ltd, since 1987. *Career:* PA Management Consultants Ltd Reg Dir 1976-81; Jardine Insurance Brokers Ltd MD 1982-86; Chm 1986-87. *Biog: b.* 5 July 1936. *Nationality:* British. *m.* 1963, Janet Mary (née Andrews); 1 s; 2 d. *Educ:* Lancaster Royal Grammar School. *Other Activities:* Trustee, The Rowing Foundation; Member of Council, Operation Raleigh. *Professional Organisations:* FIMC. *Clubs:* City of London. *Recreations:* Tennis, Squash, Gardening.

DAVIES, S J; Partner, Pannell Kerr Forster.

DAVIES, S R C; Director, Morgan Grenfell Securities Ltd.

DAVIES, Timothy John; Partner, Field Fisher Waterhouse, since 1985; Company/Commercial Law. *Career:* Norton Rose, Solicitor, Company/Commercial Department 1979-85. *Biog: b.* 14 May 1955. *Nationality:* British. *Educ:* Wallington High School, Surrey; Southampton University (LLB). *Other Activities:* Freeman, City of London Solicitors Company. *Professional Organisations:* Member, Law Society. *Recreations:* Squash, Skiing.

DAVIES, V J; Director, Brandeis Limited.

DAVIRON, Pierre Henri; Director, Gartmore Investment Management Limited.

DAVIS, Anthony Colin Richard; Partner, Lovell White Durrant, since 1986; Business Taxation. *Career:* Frere Cholmeley Articled Clerk 1979-81; Ashurst Morris Crisp Solicitor 1981-84. *Biog: b.* 23 May 1956. *Nationality:* British. *m.* 1984, B M (née Kilby); 3 d. *Educ:* Eton College; Worcester College, Oxford (MA); Birkbeck College, London (MA). *Professional Organisations:* Member, Law Society; Fellow, Institute of Taxation. *Publications:* Tolley's Taxation of Insolvent Companies; Various Articles.

DAVIS, Arthur John; Vice Chairman, Lloyds Bank plc, since 1984. *Career:* Lloyds Bank plc Various 1941-54; Various Mgmnt Appointments 1954-78; Chief Gen Mgr 1978-84. *Biog: b.* 28 July 1924. *Nationality:* British.

m. 1950, Jean Elizabeth Edna (née Hobbs); 1 s; 1 d. *Educ:* Grammar Schools. *Directorships:* Unibank plc 1986 (exec) Dep Chm; German Smaller Cos Investment Trust plc 1985 (exec) Chm. *Other Activities:* Member, Gardeners' Company; Member, National Trust (Thames & Chilterns Regional Ctee). *Professional Organisations:* FCIB (VP). *Clubs:* Naval, Overseas Bankers'. *Recreations:* Music, Country Life.

DAVIS, Dr Brian Elliott; Resource Director, Nationwide Anglia Building Society, since 1989; Technology, Human Resources & Estates. *Career:* Esso, Research Scientist 1969-73; Marketing Budgets Adviser/Co-ordinator 1973-77; Mgr, Heating Maintenance 1977-80; Snr Adviser 1980-82; Div Mgr 1982-83; Exec Project Leader 1983-84; Computer Applications Mgr 1984-86; Nationwide Building Society, Dep Gen Mgr 1986-87; Gen Mgr 1987-89; Resource Director 1989-. *Biog: b.* 22 September 1944. *Nationality:* British. *m.* 1972, Elizabeth (née Rose); 1 s; 2 d. *Educ:* St John's College, Southsea; Sussex University (BSc); Sheffield University (PhD). *Directorships:* Link Interchange Network 1987-89 (non-exec); Alternate Director of EFTPOS UK 1989. *Other Activities:* Member of DTI, IT Security Advisory Group; Chairman, Common Purpose (Swindon). *Professional Organisations:* FRSA. *Recreations:* Squash, Amateur Dramatics.

DAVIS, C C; Member of the Council, The Society of Investment Analysts.

DAVIS, Colin G; Partner, Touche Ross & Co.

DAVIS, D M; Director, Laurence Keen Ltd, since 1990; Investment Manager. *Career:* Grenadier Guards 1973-78; Buckmaster and Moore, Stockbrokers, Partners Assistant 1978-82; Laurence Prust/Laurence Keen, Investment Manager 1982-90. *Biog: b.* 5 August 1954. *Nationality:* British. *m.* 1983, Jane (née Shipstone); 1 s. *Educ:* Haileybury; R M A Sandhurst. *Professional Organisations:* Member, International Stock Exchange, 1986. *Recreations:* The Countryside, Gardening, Skiing, Deep Sea Fishing.

DAVIS, David William; Partner, Clark Whitehill, since 1982; Audit & Corporate Advisory Services. *Career:* Fryer Sutton Morris & Co, Articled Clerk 1961-66; Partner 1967-70; Fryer Whitehill & Co, Partner 1970-82. *Biog: b.* 29 October 1942. *Nationality:* British. *m.* 1967, Jennifer; 1 s; 1 d. *Educ:* Emanuel School. *Professional Organisations:* MBIM; CA (1966). *Clubs:* Phyllis Court. *Recreations:* Bridge, Walking, Music.

DAVIS, James Patrick Lamert; Partner, Freshfields, since 1976; Corporate Finance. *Career:* Freshfields, Articled Clerk 1969-71; Assistant Solicitor 1971-76; Partner 1976-. *Biog: b.* 23 September 1946. *Nationality:* British. *m.* 1973, Sally Anne (née Kemball); 1 s; 3 d. *Educ:* Charterhouse; Balliol College, Oxford (BA). *Clubs:*

Singapore Cricket Club, MCC, Berkshire Golf Club. *Recreations:* Golf, Tennis, Fishing.

DAVIS, John; Investment Editor & Editor of Money Observer, The Observer, since 1965. *Career:* The Observer, Business Editor and City Editor; Daily Sketch, City Editor; Financial Times, Financial Reporter; Stock Exchange Gazette, Financial Reporter. *Biog: b.* 7 September 1937. *m.* 1960, Barbara; 1 s; 1 d. *Educ:* Secondary Modern School. *Other Activities:* Investments Trust - Founder Editor & Publisher, 1986-. *Recreations:* Golf, Fishing, Table Tennis.

DAVIS, Jonathan Lewis; Managing Director, Guidehouse Ltd, since 1986; Corporate Finance/Direct Investment. *Career:* Reliance Cords & Cables Ltd Production Mgr 1974-77; Dir, Volume Mouldings 1978-81; Self Employed Consultant 1981-82; The Guidehouse Group plc 1982-. *Biog: b.* 11 November 1948. *Nationality:* English. *m.* 1972, Elizabeth (née Natali); 2 s; 1 d. *Educ:* Clifton College; The City University (BSc Hons); Cranfield School of Management (MBA, CEng). *Directorships:* The Guidehouse Group plc 1984 (exec); Guidehouse Ltd Managing Director; Greyfriars Management Advisers Ltd (dormant) (non exec); Team Greyfriars Ltd; Faverwise Ltd (non exec); Guidehouse Securities Ltd. *Professional Organisations:* MIProdE, MBIM.

DAVIS, Kenneth J; Chief Executive Officer, Alexander Stenhouse Ltd, Alexander & Alexander Europe plc.

DAVIS, Mrs Lynne (née Griffiths); Partner, Clay & Partners, since 1982; Advising Clients on Pensions & Other Employee Benefits. *Career:* Slater Walker Insurance Co, Actuarial Student 1975-76; Clay & Partners 1976-. *Biog: b.* 1 December 1952. *Nationality:* British. *m.* 1978, Philip; 1 s; 1 d. *Educ:* Copthall County Grammar School; Girton College, Cambridge (MA). *Professional Organisations:* FIA.

DAVIS, P A; Finance Director, Sturge Holdings plc.

DAVIS, P J; Chairman & Chief Executive, Reed International plc, since 1990. *Career:* General Foods, Marketing and Sales Posts 1965-72; Fitch Lovell Ltd, Marketing Director of Key Markets, Managing Director of both Key Markets and David Greig 1973-76; J Sainsbury plc 1976-86; Marketing Director 1977; Assistant Managing Director 1979; Member of the Board of SavaCentre 1979-83; Director, then Deputy Chairman, Homebase 1983-86; Director, Shaw's Supermarkets Inc 1984-86; Reed International plc, Deputy Chief Executive 1986; Chief Executive 1986-90. *Biog: b.* 23 December 1941. *Nationality:* British. *m.* 1968, Susan (née Hillman); 2 s; 1 d. *Educ:* Shrewsbury School; Graduate of The Institute of Marketing (Drexler Travelling Scholarship 1961). *Directorships:* Granada Group plc 1987 (non-exec); British Satellite Broadcasting Limited

1988 (non-exec). *Other Activities:* Chairman, Adult Literacy & Basic Skills Unit; Vice Chairman, Financial Development Board, NSPCC; Member of Business in the Community National Enterprise Team; Member of RNIB National Committee for the Looking Glass Appeal; Member of The Prince's Youth Business Trust Appeal Steering Group Committee. *Clubs:* Trearddur Bay Sailing Club. *Recreations:* Sailing, Opera, Reading, Wine.

DAVIS, Peter Anthony; Partner, Price Waterhouse.

DAVIS, Peter J; Partner, S J Berwin & Co.

DAVIS, Philip; General Manager/Treasurer, Britannia Building Society, since 1988; Treasury Operations & Policy Making. *Career:* Martins Bank, General Banking 1959-69; Britannia Building Society, Clerical 1969-81; Assistant General Manager 1981-87; Treasurer/Deputy General Manager 1987-88; General Manager/Treasurer 1988-. *Biog: b.* 11 April 1940. *Nationality:* British. *m.* 1966, Susan Yvonne (née Goodfellow); 1 s; 1 d. *Educ:* Leek High School. *Professional Organisations:* MCT; ACIB; FCBSI. *Recreations:* Church Organist, Choral Singing, Music, Photography.

DAVIS, R J; Senior Vice President and Branch Manager, Bank Julius Baer & Co Ltd.

DAVIS, Richard G L; Partner, Evershed Wells and Hind, since 1989; Pensions Law, Family Law. *Career:* Overbury Steward and Eaton, Partner, Specialising in Matrimonial and Family Law 1981-88. *Biog: b.* 29 April 1952. *Nationality:* French. *m.* 1977, Monique Colette (née Molinie); 1 s; 2 d. *Educ:* Kings School, Macclesfield, Cheshire; Leeds University (LLB Hons). *Other Activities:* Member, Solicitors Family Law Association (Nottingham) Committee. *Professional Organisations:* Associate Member, Association of Pensions Lawyers. *Recreations:* Golf, Gardening, Swimming, Reading.

DAVIS, Robert Michael Pennick; Director, Smith New Court plc.

DAVIS, Rodney; Partner, Clifford Chance.

DAVIS, Stephen; Partner, Stoy Hayward.

DAVIS, Sydney; Senior Partner, Paul E Schweder Miller & Co.

DAVIS, W G; Director, Hambros Bank Limited.

DAVIS, Sir (William) Allan; GBE; Chairman, Davis Consultancy Ltd, since 1986; Management Consultant. *Career:* Barclays Bank Ltd 1939; RNVR Fleet Air Arm, Pilot 1940-44; Dunn Wylie Ltd, Apprentice 1944; Partner 1952; Senior Partner 1972-76; Armitage & Newton, London, Partner 1976; Senior Partner 1979-86; Common Councilman, Ward of Queenhithe 1971-76; Alderman, Ward of Cripplegate 1976; Sheriff, City of London 1982-83; Lord Mayor of London 1985-86; Chancellor City University; One of HM Lieutenants City of London. *Biog: b.* 19 June 1921. *Nationality:* British. *m.* 1944, Audrey Pamela (née Lough); 2 s; 1 d. *Educ:* Cardinal Vaughan School, Kensington. *Directorships:* Catholic Herald Ltd; Crawning Tea Co Ltd; Dunkelman & Son Ltd; Fiat Auto (UK) Ltd; Internatio-Muller UK Ltd and UK subsidiaries; NRS Victory Holdings Ltd and UK subsidiaries. *Other Activities:* Cmdr Order of Orange Nassau; Knight Cmdr St Gregory; Knight Cmdr Holy Sepulcher; Order of Merit German Federal Republic; Knight Cmdr Order of Isobel The Catholic; Order of Merit, State of Qatar; Member, Institute of Chartered Accountants of Scotland; Fellow, Institute of Chartered Accountants in England & Wales; Fellow, Institute of Taxation; Companion, British Institute of Management; Fellow, Royal Society of Arts; Member of Court, Worshipful Company of Painter-Stainers; Hon Liveryman: Chartered Accountants in England & Wales, Constructors, Launderers; Alderman, Cripplegate Ward; Governor, Cripplegate Foundation; Chairman of Governors, Lady Eleanor Hollis School; Trustee, Sir John Soame Museum; Trustee, Morden College; Special Trustee, St Bartholomews Hospital. *Clubs:* Oriental, Wig & Pen, City Livery. *Recreations:* Travel.

DAVIS, William Edward; Executive Director Administration, Unibank plc, since 1982; Administration, Operations, Financial Control. *Career:* Hepburn Hagley & Knight, Articled Clerk 1955-60; Elliott Bros Ltd, Management Accountant 1961-62; Ruberoid Co Ltd, Accountant 1962-67; Containerway & Road Ferry Ltd, Chief Accountant 1967-69; Thos De La Rue International, Chief Accountant 1970-72. *Biog: b.* 9 May 1939. *Nationality:* British. *m.* 1961, Jill (née Cowee); 1 s; 1 d. *Educ:* Westminster City. *Directorships:* Unibank plc (formerly PRIVATbanken Ltd) 1982; PRIVATbanken Leasing Limited 1982; Hermes Mortgage Limited 1982; Frontrunner Finance (Netherlands) BV 1983. *Other Activities:* Foreign Banks Association. *Professional Organisations:* FCA. *Recreations:* Music, Literature, Gardening, Walking.

DAVISON, Guy Bryce; Director, CIN Venture Managers, since 1988. *Career:* Peat Marwick McLintock 1979-84; Larpent Newton & Co Ltd 1984-88. *Biog: b.* 21 July 1957. *Nationality:* British. *m.* 1986, Lucy (née Barker); 2 s. *Educ:* Winchester College; Magdalene College, Cambridge. *Directorships:* Hamleys of London Ltd 1989 (non-exec); Hay Group Holding BV 1990 (non-exec); Severn plc 1989 (non-exec). *Professional Organisations:* ACA.

DAVY, Tom; Sales And Marketing Director, Kogan Page Limited.

DAWNAY, Charles James Payan; Director, Mercury Asset Management Group plc.

DAWNAY, Edward William; Director, Lazard Brothers & Co.

DAWSON, Guy N; Director, Morgan Grenfell & Co Ltd, since 1985; Head of Corporate Finance. *Career:* ICI. *Biog: b.* 25 April 1953. *Nationality:* British. *m.* 1988, Janine Roxborough(née Bunce). *Educ:* Bradfield College; Trinity College, Oxford (Law); Barrister-at-Law, Middle Temple. *Directorships:* The Lowe Group plc 1988; Janine Roxborough Bunce Associates Ltd. *Recreations:* Tennis.

DAWSON, H; Director, Charterhouse Tilney.

DAWSON, Jonathan Frank; Partner, Nabarro Nathanson, since 1986; Banking. *Career:* Nabarro Nathanson, Articled Clerk 1976-78; Asst Solicitor 1978-81; Radcliffes & Co, Asst Solicitor 1981-84; Associate Partner 1984-86; Nabarro Nathanson, Partner 1986-. *Biog: b.* 16 March 1953. *Nationality:* British. *m.* 1977, Sarah; 3 d. *Educ:* Kings College, London (LLB Hons). *Professional Organisations:* Law Society. *Recreations:* Keep Fit, Multi Gym, Swimming.

DAWSON, Oliver Nainby; Chairman, Foreign & Colonial Management Ltd, 1984. *Career:* Alexanders Discount Co, Trainee 1952-53; Buckmaster & Moore 1954-80; Snr Ptnr 1977-80; Foreign & Colonial Management 1981-. *Biog: b.* 13 December 1930. *Nationality:* British. *m.* 1966, Elizabeth (née Copeman); 1 s; 2 d. *Educ:* Eton College; King's College, Cambridge (MA). *Directorships:* London Life Association Ltd 1977-89 (non-exec); Australian Mutual Provident Society (London Board) 1988-. *Other Activities:* Chm, Finance Ctee, Arthritis & Rheumatism Council for Research; Investment Advisory Ctee, Nuffield Foundation; Investment Advisory Ctee, Associated Newspapers Pensions Funds. *Clubs:* Boodle's, City of London. *Recreations:* Reading, Bridge.

DAWSON, Paul Anthony; Managing Director, Jardine Credit Insurance Ltd, since 1987. *Career:* ECGD 1960-70; Stewart Wrightson UK Ltd, Credit Management Consultants Ltd 1970-87. *Biog: b.* 11 August 1937. *Nationality:* British. *m.* 1959, Mary (née McGowan); 3 s; 2 d. *Educ:* Gunnersbury Grammar School; St Thomas', Warwick. *Directorships:* BIIBA-UKCIBC 1988-90 Chairman UKCIBC; Jardine Credit Insurance Ltd 1987 Managing Director; Jardine Insurance Brokers Ltd 1987; Wood & Maslem Ltd 1987; Jardine Financial Risk Mgt Ltd 1987. *Professional Organisations:* Fellow, Institute of Credit Management; Fellow, Institute of Export. *Publications:* Credit Management Handbook, (3rd Edition), 1990; International Trade Finance, 1990; Handbook of International Credit Management (Forthcoming).

DAWSON, Peter S; Director, MIM Limited, since 1989; Sterling Fixed Interest Markets. *Career:* MIM Limited 1972-. *Biog: b.* 10 March 1953. *Nationality:* British. *m.* 1975, Susan J; 1 s; 1 d. *Directorships:* MIM Limited 1989 (exec). *Recreations:* Golf.

DAWSON, V A; Chairman, C & G Guardian.

DAWSON, William Mark; Director, Duncan Lawrie Limited, since 1984; Finance & Offshore Adviser. *Career:* Price Waterhouse & Co 1972-77. *Biog: b.* 26 November 1952. *Nationality:* British. *m.* 1987, Joanna (née Crill); 2 d. *Educ:* Bloxham School. *Directorships:* Duncan Lawrie Ltd 1984 (exec). *Professional Organisations:* FCA. *Clubs:* Ski Club. *Recreations:* Motor Sports.

DAWSON PAUL, Anthony; Senior Partner, Dennis Murphy Campbell & Co.

DAY, Sir Graham; *Career:* Supreme Court of Nova Scotia, called to the Bar 1956; Ontario 1967; Canadian Pacific, Legal, Commercial & Industrial Matters 1964-71; Cammell Laird Shipbuilders Ltd, Chief Exec by HM Government appointment 1971-; Organizing Committee for British Shipbuilders, Dep Chm and Chief Exec by Government Appointment 1975-76; Dalhousie University, Halifax, Canada, Professor, Graduate School of Business; Canadian Marine Transportation Centre, Director; Dome Petroleum, Vice President, Financial & Commercial issues in marine sector; Les Chantiers Davie, Lauzon, Quebec, President and CEO; British Shipbuilders, Chairman & Chief Exec 1983; BL plc, later the Rover Group plc, Chairman & Chief Exec 1986; British Aerospace plc, Director 1988. *Biog: b.* 3 May 1933. *Educ:* Queen Elizabeth High School, Halifax, Canada; Dalhousie University, Halifax, Canada (LLB). *Directorships:* British Aerospace plc 1986; Laird Group plc 1985; Rover Group Holdings plc 1986 Chm; Cadbury Schweppes plc 1988, 1989 Chm; MAI plc 1988, 1989 Dep Chm; Altnacraig Shipping plc 1989; Thorn EMI plc 1990; Microtel Communications Ltd 1990 Chm; PowerGen plc 1990; Crombie Insurance Company (UK) Ltd 1990 Chm; VGM Capital Corporation (Canada) 1989; Crownx Inc (Canada) 1989; Bank of Nova Scotia (Canada) 1989; DAF nv (Netherlands) 1987; Avenir Havas Media SA (France) 1989; Jebsens Thun Shipping (Luxembourg) SA 1990. *Other Activities:* Member, National Health Service Policy Board; Freeman, City of London; Worshipful Company of Shipwrights, and Worshipful Company of Coachmakers & Coach Harness Makers; Fellow, University College, Cardiff, University of Wales; Industrial Fellow & Visiting Professor, Kingston Business School; Member, City University Business School Council; Chairman, Association of MBAs Advisory Council; Governor, Birkenhead School and Kingston Polytechnic; Hon LLD, Dalhousie University; Hon DCL, City University; Hon Professorship, Liverpool Polytechnic; Counsel to Stewart McKelvey Stirling Scales (Canadian Law Firm).

DAY, Martin James; Partner, Linklaters & Paines, since 1976; Corporate Department. *Career:* Linklaters & Paines, Assistant Solicitor 1969-76. *Biog:* b. 12 April 1944. *Nationality:* British. *m.* 1977, Loraine Frances (née Hodkinson); 1 s; 1 d. *Educ:* City of London School; University of Durham (BA); Christ's College, Cambridge (LLM). *Directorships:* Solicitors' Benevolent Association 1988 (non-exec). *Other Activities:* Liveryman, City of London Solicitors' Company; Fellow, Royal Geographical Society; Member, the Editorial Board of Trust Law & practice; Chairman of the Trustees, Westminster Children's Charitable Foundation and the Kibogora Hospital Trust (Rwanda). *Professional Organisations:* Solicitor; Member, Law Society; International Bar Association; Associate Member, American and Canadian Bar Associations. *Publications:* Unit Trusts: the law and practice (with P I Harris), 1974; Various Articles in Legal and Professional Periodicals. *Clubs:* Carlton Club.

DAY, Phillip; Group Finance Director, Yorkshire Enterprise Limited, since 1986; Company Finance, Taxation, Systems, General Management. *Career:* Clark Whitehill & Co, Chartered Accountants 1965-71; Henlys plc 1972-76; Inchcape Berhad, (Singapore) Financial Controller, Motors 1976-79; Istel Ltd, Director of Finance 1976-86. *Biog:* b. 23 August 1946. *Nationality:* British. *m.* 1975, Annette; 1 d. *Educ:* Bishops Stortford College. *Directorships:* European Management Strategy Advisers 1988 (non-exec); Yorkshire Enterprise Limited 1986-90 (exec); SLM Contracts Ltd 1989-90 (exec); Stern & Green Ltd 1989-90 (non-exec). *Professional Organisations:* Fellow, Institute of Chartered Accountants in England & Wales (FCA); Fellow, British Institute of Management (FBIM). *Clubs:* Mundesley Golf Club. *Recreations:* Golf, Armchair Sport, Skiing, Wine.

DAY, Rosemary; Executive Director, Allied Dunbar Assurance plc.

DAY, Timon; Business Editor, The Mail On Sunday.

DAYAL, Parimal; Assistant Vice President, Habib Bank AG Zurich, since 1980; Foreign Exchange & Trade Finance. *Career:* State Bank of India, Local Head Office (Patna, India), Credit Analyst, Corporate Finance 1972-76; London Office, Manager Foreign Exchange & Documentary Credits 1976-80. *Biog:* b. 10 April 1948. *Nationality:* British. *m.* 1977, Muku (née Bhattacharya); 1 d. *Educ:* St Xaviers American Jesuit School, Datna (Senior Cambridge Indian School Certificate); Patna University (BCom Hons). *Recreations:* Antiques, Theatres, Camping.

DAYKIN, S; Partner, Nabarro Nathanson.

DAZIN, J L; Director, Chartered WestLB Limited.

DE ALBUQUERQUE, S P; Director, Charterhouse Bank Limited.

DE BERISTAIN-HUMPHREY, J Nicholas; Partner, Theodore Goddard, since 1988; International Corporate Affairs (Europe, particularly Spain, and Latin America). *Career:* Middle Temple, Barrister (Harmsworth Exhibitioner) 1972-78; Solicitor in City Firms 1977-83; Partner McKenzie Mills 1983-85; Sole Partner of de Beristain Humphrey, Solicitors Specialising in Spanish and Latin American Work 1985-88. *Biog:* b. 8 April 1949. *Nationality:* British. *m.* 1971, Maria Angeles; 2 s. *Educ:* Westminster School; Trinity College, Cambridge (MA).

DE BERRY, Noel Alexander; Managing Director and Partner, Noel Alexander, since 1972; Directing, Marketing and Consulting. *Career:* W & C French 1956-58; Val de Travers 1958-60; Bradbury Wilkinson 1960-72. *Biog:* b. 25 December 1935. *Nationality:* British. *m.* 1990, Susan (née Steer); 1 s; 1 d. *Educ:* Felsted School, Essex. *Directorships:* Noel Alexander Associates 1972 (exec); Noel Alexander & Partners 1974 Partner. *Other Activities:* Woolnoth Society; Clothworkers' Company; Edmund Burke Society. *Clubs:* Reform, Little Ship, Ward of Cordwainer, Samuel Pepys. *Recreations:* Theatre, Music, Poetry, Sanskrit.

DE BLOCQ VAN KUFFELER, John Philip; Group Chief Executive, Brown Shipley Holdings plc, since 1988. *Career:* Peat Marwick Mitchell 1970-75; Asst Mgr 1975-77; Grindlays Bank, Asst Dir 1977-82; Brown Shipley & Co Ltd, Dir & Head, Corporate Finance 1983-88. *Biog:* b. 9 January 1949. *Nationality:* Dutch/British. *m.* 1971, Lesley (née Callander); 2 s; 1 d. *Educ:* Atlantic College; Clare College, Cambridge (MA). *Directorships:* Campbell & Armstrong plc 1986 (non-exec); Petranol plc 1984-85 (non-exec). *Other Activities:* Member, Exec Ctee, Issuing Houses Assoc, 1984-88. *Professional Organisations:* FCA. *Publications:* The Venture Capital Investors View, 1983. *Recreations:* Fishing, Shooting.

DE BOTTON, Gilbert; Chairman, Global Asset Management (UK) Ltd, since 1983; Investment Management. *Career:* UFITEC Union Financière (Zurich) 1960-68; Rothschild Bank AG (Zurich) MD 1968-81. *Biog:* b. 16 February 1935. *Nationality:* Swiss; 1 s; 1 d. *Educ:* Victoria College, Alexandria/American School, Paris (BA Econ); Hebrew University (BA Econ); Columbia University (MA). *Directorships:* Global Asset Management Limited 1983; Global Asset Management (UK) Limited 1983; GAM Sterling Management Limited 1983; Leveraged Capital Holdings Investments (Curacao) 1969; Global Asset Management Corporation (Panama) 1982; Global Asset Management GAM (Schweiz) AG 1982; GAM Tyche SA (BVI) 1983; GAMerica Inc (BVI) 1983; GAM Worldwide Inc (BVI) 1983; GAM Pacific Inc (BVI) 1983; GAM Arbitrage Inc

(BVI) 1983; GAM Boston Inc (BVI) 1983; GAM Francval Inc (BVI) 1985; GAM Funds Inc (USA) (name changed from GAM International Inc, 1986) 1984; Global Asset Management (HK) Limited 1985; GAM (Bermuda) Limited 1984; Soditic Asset Management SA (Switzerland) 1985; GAM Singapore/Malaysia Inc (BVI) 1985; GAM Australia Inc (BVI) 1985; GAM Japan Inc (BVI) 1985; GAM Hong Kong Inc (BVI) 1985; GAM Bond Fund Inc (BVI) (name changed from GSAM Interest Inc, 1989) 1985; GSAM Composite Inc (BVI) 1985; GAM France Inc (BVI) 1986; GAMut Investments Inc (BVI) 1986; GAM US Inc (BVI) 1986; GAM Money Markets Fund Inc (BVI) 1986; GAM Whitehorn Fund Inc (BVI) 1987; GAM ASEAN Inc (BVI) 1987; GAM High Yield Inc (BVI) 1987; GAM Restructuring Fund Inc (BVI) 1987; GAM Anlagefonds AG (Switzerland) 1988; GAM SFr Special Bond Fund Inc (BVI) 1988; GAM Value Inc (BVI) 1988; SAM Diversified Inc (BVI) 1989; GAM European Inc (BVI) 1989; Global Asset Management Limited(Bermuda) 1989; Global Asset Management (USA) Inc 1989; GAM Universal (Spain) Inc (BVI) 1989; GAM Multi Manager Fund Inc (BVI) 1989; GAM Multi Manager Allocated Class Inc (BVI) 1989; GAM Multi Manager Advisors Limited (Bermuda) 1989; GAM Tradition Anlagefonds AG (Switzerland) 1990; GAM Fund Management Limited, (Ireland) 1990; GAM Selection Inc (BVI) 1990; Republic GAM Fund Inc (BVI) 1990. *Other Activities:* Trustee, Tate Gallery; Chm, International Council of the Tate Gallery Foundation. *Clubs:* Carlton. *Recreations:* Art, Reading.

DE BRAY, Patrick; Director, Barclays de Zoete Wedd Securities, since 1988; Sales to Continent. *Career:* Phillips & Drew, Director 1983-88. *Biog:* b. 6 March 1958. *Nationality:* Belgian. *Educ:* KA Ekeren; Antwerp University; UFSIA. *Recreations:* Golf, Tennis.

DE BUNSEN, Jocelyn Maurice; Director, Baring Brothers & Co Limited, since 1987. *Career:* Baring Brothers & Co Limited 1966-. *Biog:* b. 7 October 1944. *Educ:* Trinity College, Cambridge (MA). *Directorships:* Canning House 1987 Committee (exec). *Clubs:* Brooks's.

DE CARLE, D D; Partner, Simmons & Simmons.

DE CARVALHO, Michel Ray; Executive Director, Crédit Suisse First Boston.

DE CHAZAL, Paul Andre; Partner, Simmons & Simmons, since 1969; International Commercial, EEC, Intellectual Property, & Insurance Law. *Career:* Crossman Block & Keith, Articled Clerk 1964-67; Simmons & Simmons, Assistant Solicitor 1967-69; Brussels, Partner, Head of Branch 1969-71; London, Partner 1971-; Hong Kong, Partner 1971-; Paris, Partner 1989-. *Biog:* b. 25 September 1942. *Nationality:* British. *m.* 1978, Donatienne (née Dierkx de Casterlé); 2 d. *Educ:*

Downside School; Madrid University, Spain; Cambridge University (BA); College of Law, London. *Directorships:* British American Insurance Co Ltd (Nassau, Bahamas) 1972-88 (non-exec); Windsor Group Ltd 1987-88 (non-exec); Windsor Life Assurance Co Ltd 1978-88 (non-exec); Hamilton Life Assurance Co Ltd 1983- (non-exec); Hamilton Insurance Co Ltd 1983- (non-exec). *Professional Organisations:* Member, The Law Society; Member, The International Bar Association; Member, The International Association for the Protection of Industrial Property (British Group) Inc; Member, The City of London Solicitors Company; Member, The French Chamber of Commerce; Member, The American Chamber of Commerce; Member, The Portuguese Chamber of Commerce; Member, The Belgo-Luxembourg Chamber of Commerce (Council Member and Honorary General Secretary); Member, Japan Association; Member, Sino-British Trade Council; Member, The Competition Law Association; Member, The European Centre of Space Law; Member, Union Internationale des Avocats.

DE FERRANTI, Sebastian Z; Non-Executive Director, The General Electric Company plc, since 1982. *Career:* Ferranti plc, Chairman 1963-82; Managing Director 1958-75; Director 1954-58. *Biog:* b. 5 October 1927. *Nationality:* British. m2 1983, Naomi Angela (née Pattinson); 1 s; 2 d (from first marriage). *Educ:* Ampleforth. *Directorships:* The General Electric Company plc 1982; Royal Commission for the Exhibition of 1851 1984 Commissioner; Halle Concerts Society 1988-Chairman; High Sheriff of Cheshire 1988-89; Tate Gallery 1971-78 Trustee. *Other Activities:* Worshipful Company of Wheelwrights; Guild of Air Pilots and Air Navigators. *Publications:* Granada Guildhall Lecture, 1966; Royal Institution Lecture, 1969; Louis Bleriot Lecture, Paris, 1970; Faraday Lectures, 1970-71. *Clubs:* Cavalry & Guards, Pratt's.

DE GEER, Gerard; Chairman, Enskilda Securities.

DE GIER, J A; President, Swiss Bank Corporation, since 1990; Corporate Finance/Investment Banking. *Career:* ABN Amsterdam, New Issue Dept and Trust Co of Algemene Bank Nederland, Curacao, Neth Antilles, Legal Counsel & Jt Gen Mgr 1970-73; Amro Amsterdam, Divisional Manager, International Capital Markets 1973-78; Deputy General Manager, International Finance 1978-79; Orion Bank, London, Executive Director - Corporate Finance 1979-80; Swiss Bank Corporation International Ltd London, Executive Director 1980; Managing Director 1983; Managing Director and Chief Executive Officer 1987; Chief Executive 1988; President 1990; Swiss Bank Corporation Switzerland, Member of the Executive Board 1990. *Biog:* b. 24 December 1944. *Nationality:* Dutch. *m.* 1969, Anne-Maria; 1 s; 1 d. *Educ:* Gymnasium, Holland; Amsterdam University (Masters Degree Law). *Directorships:* SBCI Securities Inc, NY 1984; SBCI Holland NV 1987;

SBS Sociedad de Valores 1989; M&A Mergers and Acquisitions Srl 1989; The Securities Association 1989; East European Development Ltd 1990; Polish Investment Company plc 1990.

DE HALDEVANG: see DARROCH DE HALDEVANG; .

DE HAVILLAND, Andre P; Director, Svenska International plc.

DE HAVILLAND, John Anthony; Director, J Henry Schroder Wagg & Co Limited.

DE JONCAIRE NARTEN, C; Director, Morgan Grenfell & Co Limited.

DE KERANGAL, G; Director, Crédit Lyonnais Capital Markets plc.

DE LA MORINIÈRE, Herve; Director, S G Warburg, Akroyd, Rowe & Pitman, Mullens Securities Ltd, since 1990; Seconded to S G Warburg Espana, Madrid, Spain. *Career:* The Chase Manhattan Bank NA (Paris & London), Analyst 1982-84; S G Warburg & Co Ltd 1984-; Assistant Director 1986-90. *Biog: b.* 4 January 1957. *Nationality:* French. *m.* 1983, Elisabeth; 2 s; 1 d. *Educ:* College Stanislas; Université de Droit, d'Economie et de Sciences Sociales, Paris (BA Law); Institut d'Etudes Politiques de Paris (MBA Economics & Finance).

DE LÉZARDIÈRE, Alec; Managing Director, Banque Paribas Capital Markets, since 1989. *Career:* Banque Paribas (Paris) Industrial Dept 1974-77; 1977-79; (Paris) Capital Markets Dept 1979-85; Banque Paribas Capital Markets (London) Head of Swaps 1985-89. *Directorships:* Paribas Securities Inc 1985; Banque Paribas Capital Markets Ltd 1988.

DE LIEDEKERKE, P Anthony; Executive Director, Crédit Suisse First Boston Limited.

DE LISLE, Frederick; Managing Director, De Lisle Stephens Ltd, since 1989; Mergers & Acquisitions & Executive Search in Insurance. *Career:* Quenby Prints Ltd, Managing Director 1979-83; Lor-West Ltd, International Co-ordinator 1983-84; Marlar International, Consultant 1985; Haley BDC, Director & Consultant 1986-89. *Biog: b.* 14 February 1957. *Nationality:* British. *m.* 1986, Aubyn (née Cumming-Bruce); 2 s. *Educ:* Harrow School; Magdalen College, Oxford (BA Hons). *Directorships:* Quenby Prints Ltd 1979 (non-exec); Stephens Consultancies Limited 1990 (exec); De Lisle Stephens Limited 1989 (exec). *Other Activities:* Member, The Bow Group. *Publications:* The Single Market in Insurance, Bow Group, 1990. *Clubs:* Turf Club. *Recreations:* Shooting, Hunting, Philosophy.

DE LOTBINIÈRE, Nicholas Henry Joly; Partner, Grimley J R Eve, since 1988; Planning Consultancy, particularly Greater London Area. *Career:* Debenham Tewson & Chinnocks, Valuation Surveyor 1980-83; J R Eve (Merged With Grimley & Son in 1988 to become Grimley J R Eve), Planning Surveyor 1983-90. *Biog: b.* 27 August 1955. *Nationality:* British. *m.* 1980, Catherine Plummer; 1 s; 2 d. *Educ:* Eton College; Reading University (BSc Estate Management, MPhil Environmental Planning). *Professional Organisations:* ARICS. *Clubs:* Telegraph Hill Conservation Society. *Recreations:* Tennis.

DE LUSIGNAN, Hugh; Director, County NatWest Securities, since 1989; UK Equity Sales. *Career:* Wood Mackenzie & Co 1983-. *Biog: b.* 9 April 1961. *Nationality:* British. *Educ:* Abingdon School; Cambridge University (MA).

DE MANDAT-GRANCEY, Jacques; Director, Grancey & Co (UK) Ltd, since 1990. *Career:* The Chase Manhattan Bank (New York, Paris, Luxembourg, Madrid) 1968-80; Midland Bank (Spain) Regional Coordinator, Southern Europe 1980-83; (London) Regional Dir, Latin American Region 1983-84; Gen Mgr 1984-87; Intl Banking Network Director 1987; Fin & Support Dir, Global Banking 1987-88; Midland Montagu, Chief Executive, Developing Countries Division 1988-90. *Biog: b.* 20 February 1940. *Nationality:* French. *Educ:* Nancy (MS); Columbia University (MBA). *Directorships:* Corporacion Promotores Euroeos SA, Madrid 1989 (non-exec). *Clubs:* Jockey Club, Paris.

DE MAREDSOUS, V; Director, Crédit Commercial de France (UK) Limited.

DE NADAILLAC, Geraud; Count de Nadaillac; Director, Hambros Bank Ltd; New Issues/Syndications. *Career:* Credit Commercial de France Fund Mgr 1980-83; CCF (Securities) London Fund Mgr 1983-84; Hambros Bank Ltd, Head of Syndication 1986. *Biog: b.* 11 January 1955. *Nationality:* French. *m.* 1986, Anne Victoire (née de Mailly Nesle); 1 d. *Educ:* La Rochefoucaud, Paris; Ecole Supérieure de Commerce (Rouen) (ESC). *Directorships:* Hambros Bank Ltd 1987 (exec); Hambros Bank France 1990. *Clubs:* Jockey Club, Cercle de Deauville, Club des Gentlemen Rider. *Recreations:* Riding, Shooting, Tennis.

DE NAUROIS, J; Executive Director, Banque Paribas London.

DE NEMESKERI-KISS, George; Director, Touche Remnant Investment Management, since 1987; Economics and Investment Strategy. *Career:* Chase Manhattan Bank (London), Vice President 1977-87; Chase Manhattan Bank (New York), Economist 1974-77; Stanford Research Institute SRI - Europe, London, Research Analyst 1972-74. *Biog: b.* 27 April 1949.

Nationality: American. *m.* 1990, Marie Elizabeth (née de Faultrier). *Educ:* London School of Economics (MSc Econ); City University of New York (BA). *Other Activities:* Society of Business Economists. *Publications:* Currency Hedging in International Equity Portfolios, in The Currency Hedging Debate (ed L Thomas) 1990. *Recreations:* Bridge, Tennis.

DE PASS, David Vincent Guy; Partner, Head of Private Client Department, Holman Fenwick & Willan, since 1986; Private Client Work. *Biog: b.* 27 August 1949. *Nationality:* British. *Educ:* Harrow School; The College of Law; George Washington University (MCL); London University, London School of Economics (LLM). *Directorships:* E A de Pass & Co (Holdings) Ltd 1982 (non-exec). *Other Activities:* Member, Phi Delta Phi Legal Fraternity. *Professional Organisations:* Solicitor, Admitted, 1973; Member of the Bar of the District of Columbia, 1978. *Publications:* Various Contributions to Law Journals & Precedent Book, 1979-. *Clubs:* Harrow Wanderers, Harrovian Rifle Association, Hurlingham. *Recreations:* Cricket, Philately, Music.

DE PELET, Patrick Hugh Peter; Director, Kleinwort Benson Ltd, since 1984; Corporate Finance - Project Advisory Services. *Career:* Price Waterhouse 1965-69; Citibank Resident VP 1969-74; International Energy Bank Gen Mgr (Petroleum & Mining) 1974-78; Kleinwort Benson Ltd Asst Dir 1978-84. *Directorships:* Dartford River Crossing 1986 (non-exec); Lakeland Investments 1987 (non-exec); National Economic Development Office (Construction Sector Group) 1990 (non-exec).

DE PREE, A H S; Director, Ropner Insurance Services Limited.

DE RANCOURT, F; Senior Managing Director, Banque Paribas, since 1990. *Career:* Citibank, Vice President 1964-79; Seconded to Gulf International Bank, as Executive Vice President 1977-79; Paribas Group, Executive Vice President 1980-; Seconded to the Ottoman Bank, as General Manager for Turkey 1985-90. *Biog: b.* 15 May 1939. *m.* Evelyne; 2 s; 1 d. *Educ:* Eton College; Trinity College, Cambridge (MA); INSEAD (MBA).

DE ROOS, Peter J; Executive Director and Chief Executive Officer, Saudi International Bank.

DE ROTHSCHILD, David; Non-Executive Director, N M Rothschild & Sons Limited.

DE ROTHSCHILD, Edmund L; Non-Executive Director, N M Rothschild & Sons Limited. *Career:* War Service, BEF, BNAF, CMF 1939-46; N M Rothschild, Jnr Partner 1946-60; Snr Partner 1960-68; Chm 1968-75; Non-Exec Dir 1975. *Biog: Nationality:* British. *Educ:* Harrow; University of Cambridge (MA); Memorial University of Newfoundland (Hon DLitt); University of Salford (BSc). *Directorships:* RCL 1947; British Newfoundland Corporation 1963-69 Dep Chm; Churchill Falls (Labrador) Corp 1966-69 Dep Chm; Rothman's International plc; HMC Technology Ltd 1988; Solv-Ex Corporation 1986; Exbury Gardens Ltd 1962; Exbury Enterprises 1962; Exbury Trees 1962; Tokyo Pacific Holdings 1970 Chm; AUR Hydropower Ltd 1980 Chm; Straflo Ltd 1975 Chm. *Other Activities:* Order of the Sacred Treasure of Japan, 1st Class, 1976; Court of the Royal National Pension Fund for Nurses; British Government Trustee, Freedom from Hunger.

DE ROTHSCHILD, Eric; Non-Executive Director, N M Rothschild & Sons Limited.

DE ROTHSCHILD, Leopold David; CBE; Director, N M Rothschild & Sons Ltd, since 1970. *Career:* N M Rothschild & Sons Ltd Ptnr 1956-70. *Biog: Nationality:* British. *Directorships:* Sun Alliance & London Insurance plc (non-exec).

DE ROTHSCHILD, Nathaniel; Director, J Rothschild Holdings plc.

DE SAINT REMY, B L M F; Managing Director, Bankers Trust International, since 1988; Mergers and Acquisitions Continental Europe. *Career:* The Barclays Bank Group, Paris, London, New York for 10 years; Banking Trust Pour Femme, Vice-President 1982-86; Managing Director 1986-; Bankers Trust France SA, Chm 1987-; Bankers Trust Finance SA, Chm 1988. *Biog: b.* 22 May 1946. *Nationality:* French. *m.* 1970, Marie-Helene (née de Corbiac); 3 s; 1 d. *Educ:* Ecole Saint Louis de Gouzague, Paris, France; Institut D'Etudes Politiques (IEP), Paris, France. *Clubs:* Automobile Club.

DE STE CROIX, Richard; Commercial Litigation Partner, Bristows Cooke & Carpmael.

DE SALABERRY, Pascal; Count de Salaberry; Director, Ivory & Sime plc, since 1978. *Biog: b.* 15 November 1941. *Nationality:* French. *Educ:* Ste Geneviève, Versailles; Faculté des Sciences, Mathematiques Generales, Paris; Licence Sciences Economiques, Geneva. *Directorships:* Ivory and Sime plc 1978 (exec); Sumitrust Ivory and Sime Ltd 1989 (exec) Chairman; Instate plc 1990 (exec) Chairman; Facom SA 1981 (non-exec); Personal Assets Trust plc 1983 (non-exec); Continental Assets Trust plc 1990 (non-exec). *Clubs:* Dean Lawn Tennis Club. *Recreations:* Sports, Arts, Bridge, Backgammon.

DE SIBERT, Geoffrey; Director, Kleinwort Benson Securities, since 1988; Departmental Director, KB Equity Linked Group. *Career:* Bache Halsey Stuart (New York) Arbitrage Dealer 1980-83; Sellier Gadala Suchet (Paris) Ltd Ptnr/Investment Sales 1983-84; BAII

Director/Capital Mkts Gp 1984-88. *Biog: b.* 1 April 1959. *Nationality:* American. *m.* 1984, Isabella (née von Kotze); 1 s; 1 d. *Educ:* The Choate School, USA; John Hopkins University, USA (BA); Institut d'Etudes Politiques Paris (diplomé avec mention). *Directorships:* Scott Salisbury Ltd 1986 (non-exec); DYNAMEDIX Inc 1983 (non-exec). *Clubs:* Automobile Club de France, Castel (France), Annabel's.

DE STEIGER, A M; Financial Director, Greenwell Montagu Gilt-Edged.

DE TRUCHIS, A; General Manager, Caisse Nationale de Credit Agricole.

DE TUBA, J C; Director, Hambros Bank Limited.

DE VICK, Michael; Managing Partner, Grimley J R Eve, since 1990; Professional and Agency. *Career:* Gerald Eve & Co, Assistant 1966-71; Richard Ellis, Senior Assistant 1971-74; Associate 1974-85; Head of West End Rent Review Department 1978-85; J R Eve, Partner Handling Commercial Agency and Investment Work 1985-88; Grimley J R Eve, Investment Partner 1988-89; Head of London Commercial Agency 1989-; Managing Partner, City Office 1990-; Member of Board of Management 1988-; Member of Finance Committee 1988-; Member of London Executive 1988-. *Biog: b.* 15 December 1943. *Nationality:* British. *m.* 1969, Rosalind Lorna; 1 s; 1 d. *Educ:* London University (BSc Estate Management). *Directorships:* Grimley J R Eve (Financial Services) Ltd 1988 (exec). *Professional Organisations:* FRICS. *Clubs:* Marks Club. *Recreations:* Shooting, Skiing, Cycling, Gardening, Collecting.

DE VILLE, Sir Oscar; Non-Executive Member, British Railways Board.

DE ZOETE, Simon Miles; Director, Barclays de Zoete Wedd Ltd.

DE ZULUETA, Ms L; Director, The Barnes Partnership, since 1988; Banking. *Career:* The Financial Times, Research and Marketing Associate 1978-80; Korn/Ferry International, Senior Research Associate 1980-84; Houghton Sanderson, Consultant (Banking) 1985-87. *Biog: Nationality:* British. *m.* 1981, Mark Seligman; 1 s; 2 d. *Educ:* St Mary's Convent, Ascot; St Hilda's College, Oxford (MA Modern History). *Directorships:* The Barnes Partnership 1988 (exec). *Professional Organisations:* British Association of Executive Search Consultants. *Clubs:* Roehampton. *Recreations:* Swimming, Walking, Opera, Ballet.

DEACON, Mark F; Chief Financial Officer, Maruman Securities (Europe) Ltd, since 1990. *Career:* Price Waterhouse 1980-83; Coopers & Lybrand 1983-84; Commercial Union, Treasury Dept 1984-87; Merrill Lynch, Finance Dept 1987-90. *Biog: b.* 30 March 1958.

Nationality: British. *m.* 1989, Caroline (née Waller). *Educ:* Malvern College; Christ Church, Oxford (MA Mathematics); Kings College London (MSc Mathematics & Physics). *Professional Organisations:* ACA. *Recreations:* Golf, Scuba Diving.

DEAN, Barry Malcolm; Managing Director, Kleinwort Benson Development Capital Ltd, since 1988; Unquoted Investments, Venture Capital. *Career:* Articled Clerk/Chartered Accountant in Accountancy Profession 1967-77; National Research & Development Corp, Project Acct 1977-79; Kleinwort Benson Development Capital Ltd, Various 1979-. *Biog: b.* 1 November 1949. *Nationality:* British. *m.* 1975, Sarah Elizabeth (née Wiggins); 2 s; 1 d. *Educ:* Glyn Grammar School. *Directorships:* Kleinwort Benson Ltd 1988 (exec); Stewart McColl Associates plc 1984 (non-exec); Hale Hamilton Holdings Ltd 1987 (non-exec); Kleinwort Benson Development Capital Ltd 1985 (exec); Medallion Upholstery Limited 1987 (non-exec); Pelham Business Services Limited 1988 (non-exec); Kleinwort Benson Investment Management Ltd 1989 (exec); Istel Group Ltd 1988 (non-exec). *Professional Organisations:* FCA. *Recreations:* Sports, Theatre.

DEAN, Ian Hall; Chairman, Sphere Drake Underwriting Management Limited, since 1982. *Career:* S C Lloyd Haine & Co, General Clerical/Assistant Functions 1963-71; Claims Settler 1970-71; Deputy Underwriter 1971-74; Excess Insurance Group Ltd, Treaty Reinsurance Underwriter 1974; Non-Marine Manager 1974-77; Deputy Director of Underwriting 1977-78; Director of Underwriting 1979-80; Deputy Chairman & Director of Reinsurance 1980-81. *Biog: b.* 19 September 1944. *Nationality:* British. *m.* 1976, Diane; 1 s; 2 d. *Directorships:* Arpel Trimark Underwriting Agencies Ltd 1982; Churcher & Company Ltd 1982; Dai-Tokyo Insurance Company (UK) Ltd 1982; The Drake Insurance Company Ltd 1982; Groves, John & Westrup (Underwriting) Ltd 1982; The London Underwriting Centre Ltd; Market Building Ltd; The Policy Signing & Accounting Centre Ltd; Premium Management Ltd 1983; Rystwood Estate Ltd; Sphere Drake Acquisitions (UK) Ltd 1987; Sphere Drake Holding plc 1987; Sphere Drake Insurance plc 1982; Sphere Drake Insurance Group plc 1984; Sphere Drake Leasing Ltd 1985; Sphere Drake Nominees Ltd 1987; Sphere Drake (Underwriting) Ltd 1982; Sphere Drake Underwriting (Australia) Ltd 1982; Sphere Drake Underwriting Management Ltd 1982; Sphere Drake Underwriting Management (Australia) Ltd 1982; Sphere Drake Underwriting Management (Canada) Ltd 1987; The Sterling Insurance Company Ltd 1982; Alexander Agency Administration Ltd to 1987; Alexander Howden Group (Australia) Ltd to 1986; Alexander Howden Holdings plc to 1987; Asian Reinsurance Underwriters Ltd to 1987; Halford, Shead (Holdings)Ltd to 1987; PSAC Pensions Trustees Ltd to 1988; Solar Underwriting Agencies Ltd to 1987; Sphere Drake Far East Ltd to 1987.

DEAN, Peter Henry; Freelance Business Consultant, since 1985. *Career:* Freshfields, Articled Clerk 1957-62; Asst Solicitor 1962-65; Oswald Hickson, Collier & Co, Asst Solicitor 1965-66; The RTZ Corporation plc, Solicitor 1966-72; Company Sec 1972-74; Exec Dir 1974-85. *Biog:* b. 24 July 1939. *Nationality:* British. *m.* 1965, Linda Louise (née Keating); 1 d. *Educ:* Rugby School; London University (LLB). *Directorships:* Associated British Ports Holdings plc 1982 (non-exec); Liberty Life Assurance Co Ltd 1986 (non-exec). *Other Activities:* Member, Council of Management, Highgate Counselling Centre; Deputy Chairman, Monopolies and Mergers Commission. *Professional Organisations:* The Law Society. *Clubs:* Ski Club of Great Britain. *Recreations:* Choral Singing, Skiing.

DEAN, T J; Consultant Partner, Milne Ross.

DEANE, John; National Director of Finance, BDO Binder Hamlyn, since 1989. *Career:* Whinney Murray & Co, Articled Clerk/Audit Senior 1964-69; IC Gas, Assistant Accountant/Group Management Accountant 1969-87; Contibel Holdings plc, Financial Controller 1987; Meridian International Ltd, Group Budget Manager 1988. *Biog:* b. 7 December 1944. *Nationality:* British. *m.* 1970, Jenny (née Barber); 2 d. *Educ:* Cranleigh School. *Professional Organisations:* ACA, 1968; FCA, 1978.

DEANESLY, Miss Clare Helen; Partner, Gouldens, since 1980; Commercial Property; also Partner in Charge of Articled Clerk Recruitment. *Career:* Field Fisher and Martineau, Articled Clerk 1975-77; Assistant Solicitor 1977-78; Gouldens, Assistant Solicitor 1978-80. *Biog:* b. 30 May 1953. *Nationality:* British. *m.* 1979, Robert Gray; 2 s. *Educ:* Edgbaston C of E College for Girls; Southampton University (LLB Hons). *Professional Organisations:* Law Society. *Recreations:* Skiing, Travel, The Family, Tennis, Theatre.

DEAR, A A; Partner, Ashurst Morris Crisp.

DEAR, John Simon; Managing Director, Lazard Brothers & Co Ltd, since 1990; Corporate Finance. *Career:* Lazard Brothers & Co Ltd 1974-. *Directorships:* Development Capital Securities Ltd 1987 (non-exec).

DEARING, Sir Ronald; Chairman, Financial Reporting Council, since 1990. *Career:* Post Office & National Giro Bank, Chairman 1980-87; Department of Trade & Industry, Civil Servant 1946-87. *Biog:* b. 27 July 1930. *Nationality:* British. *m.* 1954, Margaret (née Riley); 2 d. *Educ:* Doncaster Grammar School; Hull University (BSc Econ); London Business School (Sloan Fellow, DSc Econ Hon). *Directorships:* Financial Reporting Council 1990 Chm; Northern Development Company 1990 Chm; Polytechnics & Colleges Funding Council 1988 Chm; Prudential Corporation 1987 (non-exec); British Coal 1988 (non-exec); IMI 1988 (non-exec); Ericsson

Ltd 1988 (non-exec); Whitbread plc 1988-90 (non-exec); County Durham Development Co 1987-90 Chm. *Other Activities:* Chairman, London Education Business Partnership, 1989-. *Professional Organisations:* CBIM. *Clubs:* Royal Overseas League. *Recreations:* Gardening.

DEEM, W; Director, Kellett (Holdings) Limited.

DEFRIEZ, Alistair Norman Campbell; Director, S G Warburg & Co Ltd, since 1987; Corporate Finance. *Career:* Coopers & Lybrand, Chartered Accountant 1973-78; S G Warburg & Co Ltd, Corporate Finance 1978-. *Biog:* b. 2 November 1951. *Nationality:* British. *m.* 1978, Linda (née Phillips); 2 s; 1 d. *Educ:* Dulwich College; University College, Oxford (MA). *Professional Organisations:* FCA. *Clubs:* Rugby – Old Alleynians, London Scottish, Golf – Moore Place.

DEGENHARDT, Jacob Roy; Managing Director, European Corporate Finance, Continental Bank NA, since 1988; General Management of Corporate Business Development & Financial Products in Europe. *Career:* Continental Bank NA, Senior Vice President, Managing Director, Assignment in US, Europe, Asia 1970-; US Army, Major, Armor 1962-69. *Biog:* b. 27 June 1940. *Nationality:* American. *Educ:* United States Military Academy (BS); George Washington University (MBA). *Directorships:* Continental Consulting Ltd 1988 (exec); Continental Finanziaria SPA 1986 (exec); BAFT, Washington DC 1989 (non-exec). *Other Activities:* ABSAL, London. *Clubs:* Queen's Lawn Tennis Club. *Recreations:* Tennis, Golf.

DEHN, Bruce; Clerk, Distillers' Company.

DEIGHTON, Peter John; Director, County NatWest Woodmac, since 1989; Engineering Metals and Motors. *Career:* Hoare Govett Analyst, Engineering 1969-80; Dir, Engineering 1980-88; Morgan Grenfell, Dir, Engineering 1988-89. *Biog:* b. 27 June 1943. *Nationality:* British. *m.* 1967. *Educ:* Ashford County; Keele University (BA). *Other Activities:* Fund Raising Ctee for Ironbridge Gorge Museum. *Professional Organisations:* AMSIA. *Clubs:* Zanzibar. *Recreations:* Walking, Climbing, Antiques, Cartography.

DELANY, Daniel; Group Accounting Controller, Harrisons & Crosfield plc, since 1984. *Biog:* b. 5 May 1941. *Nationality:* British. *m.* 1972, Catherine Jane (née Lister); 2 s; 1 d. *Other Activities:* Chartered Association of Certified Accountants; Technical Working Parties on Various Proposed Accounting Standards. *Professional Organisations:* FCCA. *Recreations:* Golf, Swimming.

DELBRIDGE, Richard; Senior Vice President & General Manager, Morgan Guaranty Trust Company of New Yo.

DELIENNE, Philippe; Director, Seccombe Marshall & Campion plc.

DELL, David Michael; CB; Chief Executive, British Overseas Trade Board; Department of Trade and Industry, Export Promotion. *Career:* Admiralty & Ministry of Defence 1955-65; Ministry of Technology 1965-70; DTI 1970-; Under Sec 1976-83; Reg Dir, Yorks & Humberside 1976-78; Dep Sec 1983-; Dir, Industrial Development Unit 1984-86. *Biog: b.* 30 April 1931. *Nationality:* British. *Educ:* Rugby School; Balliol College, Oxford (MA). *Directorships:* European Investment Bank 1984-87 (exec).

DELLER, Michael F; General Manager, United Overseas Bank (Geneva) London Branch, since 1986. *Career:* Bank of England 1955-69; Antony Gibbs & Sons Ltd 1969-75; Bank Director 1973-75; Banco Central SA (London Branch) 1975-86. *Biog: b.* 12 July 1933. *Nationality:* British. *m.* 1957; 1 s; 3 d. *Educ:* Queen Elizabeth's, Barnet; St Catherine's, Oxford (MA). *Clubs:* Royal Over-Seas League. *Recreations:* Running, Tennis, Travel, Reading.

DELVAULX, J L E G; Director, Kleinwort Benson Limited.

DELVES, H G; Director, The Barnes Partnership.

DEMEZA, R J; Director, County NatWest Ltd, since 1989; Japanese Equities/Derivatives. *Career:* Yamaichi International (Europe) Ltd, Associate Director, Japanese Equities 1971-85; Salomon Brothers, Vice President, Japanese Equities 1985-89. *Biog: b.* 9 November 1951. *Nationality:* British. *m.* 1986, Barbara-Ann (née Williamson); 2 s; 1 d. *Recreations:* Golf.

DEMPSEY, V N J; Director, Kleinwort Benson Securities Limited.

DEMPSTER, Alastair Cox; Senior Executive Director, TSB Scotland plc.

DEMWELL, Matthew Stanley; Partner, Clay & Partners, since 1989; Pensions and Employee Benefits. *Career:* Sun Life Assurance Society plc 1976-84. *Biog: b.* 9 November 1957. *Nationality:* British. *m.* 1976, Anne Therese (née Raine) (div 1990); 2 d. *Educ:* St Joseph's Academy. *Professional Organisations:* FIA. *Clubs:* MENSA. *Recreations:* Tennis, Table Tennis.

DENBY, Steve G; Director, Hoare Govett International Securities.

DENFORD, Stephen; Director, 3i plc.

DENHAM, Stephen; Divisional Director, Royal Trust Bank.

DENHOLM, James Allan; Director, William Grant & Sons Ltd, since 1966; Insurance, Legal, Pensions, Secretariat. *Career:* McFarlane Hutton & Patrick Apprentice Chartered Accountant 1954-60; A & W Smith & Co Ltd Chief Accountant 1960-66. *Biog: b.* 27 September 1936. *Nationality:* British. *m.* 1964, Elizabeth Avril (née McLachlan); 1 s; 1 d. *Educ:* Hutchesons' Boys Grammar. *Directorships:* Scottish Cremation Society Ltd 1980 (non-exec); Scottish Mutual Life Asurance Society 1987 (non-exec); East Kilbride Development Corp 1979 (non-exec); 1983 Chm. *Other Activities:* VP of The Institute of Chartered Accountants of Scotland; Chm, David Livingstone Diamond Jubilee Appeal Committee; Member, CBI Scottish Legal Panel. *Professional Organisations:* CA. *Clubs:* RSAC. *Recreations:* Shooting, Golf.

DENISON, N B; Director, BZW Ltd, since 1989; Treasury. *Career:* Barclays Merchant Bank; BZW Ltd. *Biog: b.* 31 December 1958. *Nationality:* British. *m.* 1989, Sarah Jane (née Witherspoon). *Educ:* Tonbridge School; St Catharines College, Cambridge (Modern Languages). *Directorships:* BZW Ltd 1989 (exec).

DENLEY, F; Partner, Nabarro Nathanson.

DENMAN, J D; Partner, Jaques & Lewis.

DENNES, J M; Director, Holman Macleod Limited.

DENNIS, George John James; Managing Director, TSB Investment Management Ltd.

DENNIS, N; Partner, Milne Ross.

DENNIS, Peter; Director, Barclays Financial Services Limited, since 1986; UK and Offshore Unit Trusts. *Career:* Martins Bank/Barclays, Various 1957-71; Barclays Bank Trust Co, Mgr, Cambridge 1971-73; Mgr, Money Dr Service 1973-78; Barclays Unicorn, Snr Mktg Mgr 1978-83; Barclays Investment Management, Dir 1983-84; Barclays Unicorn, Dir 1984-86. *Biog: b.* 2 September 1934. *Nationality:* British. *m.* 1959, Eileen (née Bordessa); 2 s. *Educ:* Toxteth School, Liverpool. *Directorships:* Barclays Financial Services Ltd 1987 (exec); Barclays General Insurance Ltd 1990 (exec); Barclays Life Assurance Co Ltd 1987 (exec); Barclays Unicorn Limited 1990 MD; Barclays Unicorn (Gift Plans) Ltd 1990 (exec); Barclays Unicorn (Trustees) Ltd 1990 (exec); Barclays Unit Trust Services Ltd 1990 (exec); Barclays Unicorn International (Channel Islands) Ltd 1990 Chm; Barclays Investment Funds (Channel Islands) Ltd 1990 Chm; Barclays Unicorn (Channel Islands) Investments Ltd 1990 Chm; Barclays European Investment Holdings SA 1990 Chm; Barclays Investment Funds (Luxembourg) 1990 Chm; Barclays Unicorn Multicurrency Fund Ltd Chm. *Professional Organisations:* ACIB. *Clubs:* Harpenden Golf Club, Sandway Golf Club. *Recreations:* Golf.

DENNISON, Paul; Executive Director, Merrill Lynch Europe Ltd.

DENNY, John; Partner, Overton Shirley & Barry Partnership.

DENNY, Michael; Chairman, British Venture Capital Association. *Directorships:* Northern Venture Managers Limited Chm.

DENOON DUNCAN, R E; Partner, Cameron Markby Hewitt.

DENT, Clifford; Director, Merrill Lynch International Limited.

DENT, Robin John; Chairman, Mase Westpac Limited, since 1989. *Career:* Bank of England 1948-51; M Samuel & Co Ltd 1951-63; Director 1963-65; Hill Samuel & Co Ltd Dir 1965-67; Baring Brothers & Co Ltd MD 1967-86. *Biog: b.* 25 June 1929. *Nationality:* British. *m.* 1952, The Hon Ann Camilla (née Denison-Pender); 2 d. *Educ:* Marlborough College. *Directorships:* Barfield Bank & Trust Co Ltd 1973-1987 Chm; Barings plc 1985-89 (non-exec); TR City of London Trust 1977 (non-exec); Mase Westpac Limited 1989 Chm; Westpac Banking Corporation, London Advisory Board 1989-90; Special Trustee for St Thomas Hospital 1988. *Other Activities:* Treasurer, Cancer Research Campaign, King Edward's Hospital Fund for London; Dep Chm, Export Guarantees Advisory Council, 1983-85; Chm, Public Works Loan Board. *Professional Organisations:* Exec Ctee Chm, British Bankers Assoc, 1984-85. *Clubs:* White's.

DENTON, Miss Celia; Partner, Touche Ross & Co, since 1984; Corporate Finance/Insurance Industry. *Career:* Robson Rhodes, Student Accountant 1974-78; Spicer & Pegler, Manager Financial Investigations 1979-84. *Biog: b.* 27 August 1952. *Nationality:* British. *m.* 1987, Paul Baddiley. *Educ:* University College, London (LLB). *Other Activities:* Member of Lloyd's Accounting & Auditing Standards Committee. *Professional Organisations:* FCA. *Recreations:* Gardening, Theatre.

DENTON, Jeffrey Irvine; Treasurer, Marks & Spencers plc, since 1987. *Career:* Marks & Spencers plc, Store Financial Control 1973-84; Chief Internal Auditor 1984-87. *Biog: b.* 16 August 1946. *m.* 1969, Rosalyn (née Fagelman); 1 s; 1 d. *Educ:* King Edward V11, Sheffield. *Professional Organisations:* FCA, MCT.

DENTON, Robert William; Partner, Robson Rhodes, since 1987; Client Service. *Career:* Robson Rhodes, Various 1977-. *Biog: b.* 1 December 1955. *Nationality:* British. *m.* 1984, Laurie (née King). *Educ:* St Olaves & St Saviour's Grammar School; Sheffield University (BA Hons). *Professional Organisations:* ACA. *Recreations:* Travel, Sport, Photography, Theatre.

DENTON-CLARK, Jeremy; Managing Director, City Merchants Bank Ltd, since 1986. *Career:* Kleinwort Benson Ltd 1964-66; National Westminster Bank Group 1966-73; London Interstate Bank Ltd Dir 1973-86. *Biog: b.* 7 September 1944. *Nationality:* British. *m.* 1971, Catherine (née O'Leary); 2 s. *Educ:* Cheltenham College.

DENYER, Stephen Robert Noble; Partner, Allen & Overy, since 1987; Corporate Finance. *Career:* Allen & Overy, Articled Clerk 1978-80; Assistant Solicitor 1980-86. *Biog: b.* 27 December 1955. *Nationality:* British. *m.* 1988, Monika (née Wolf). *Educ:* Fosters Grammar School, Sherborne; Durham University (BA). *Other Activities:* Member, Executive Committee of the British Polish Legal Association; Member, International Bar Association's East/West Forum. *Professional Organisations:* The Law Society; City of London Solicitors' Company. *Recreations:* Walking, Travel, Gardening.

DERBY, Richard Outram Walker; Director, Capel-Cure Myers Capital Management Ltd, since 1990. *Career:* Brown, Bliss & Co, Trainee Stockbroker 1961-64; Mem, SE 1964; 1964-67; J & A Scrimgour, Assoc Mem 1967-72; Godfray, Derby & Co, Snr Ptnr 1972-86; National Investment Group plc, Director 1986-90; Capel-Cure Myers Capital Management Ltd, Director 1990. *Biog: b.* 27 April 1940. *Nationality:* British. *m.* 1978, Anthea (née Roberts); 1 s; 2 d. *Educ:* Harrow School. *Other Activities:* Member of Council, Stock Exchange, 1982-88.

DEREHAM, Orme Giles; Director, Chartered WestLB Limited, since 1986; Project & Export Finance. *Career:* Lazard Brothers & Co Limited, Director. *Biog: b.* 20 October 1938.

DERRICOTT, Dr Christopher John; Director, Baring Securities, since 1988; Research and Sales. *Career:* Kitcat & Aitken Sales 1979-81; Buckmaster & Moore Sales 1981-82; Henderson Crosthwaite Analyst 1982-84; Baring Securities 1984-. *Biog: b.* 1 November 1954. *Nationality:* British. *m.* 1987, Jane Elizabeth; 1 s. *Educ:* King's College, University of London (BSc, PhD). *Directorships:* Baring Securities 1988 (exec); Portfolio France 1988 (exec).

DERRY-EVANS, Robert Stephen; Partner, McKenna & Co, since 1985; Banking/Asset Finance. *Career:* McKenna & Co, Assistant Solicitor 1977-85; Partner in Hong Kong 1985-89; Partner in London 1989-. *Biog: b.* 2 March 1952. *Nationality:* British. *m.* 1981, Beccy (née Tunstall-Behrens); 2 d. *Educ:* Oxford University, (MA Degree in Classics). *Other Activities:* City of London Solicitors Company; London Solicitors Golfing Society. *Professional Organisations:* Law Society England and Wales; Law Society Hong Kong; American Chamber of Commerce; IBA. *Publications:* Chapter in

Joint Ventures in the Peoples Republic of China, Licensing/Joint Ventures, Clark Boardman, 1986.

DERX, Jeffrey Leonard; Director, Cater Allen Securities, since 1986; Sales, Government Securities. *Career:* J Sebag, Dealer 1966-68; Simon & Coates, Dealer/Salesman 1968-76; Laing & Cruickshank, Head of Gilt Dept/Sales 1976-; Alexanders Laing & Co, Dir 1985-86; Laing & Cruickshank Futures, Director 1983-84. *Biog: b.* 2 June 1948. *Nationality:* British. *Directorships:* Laing & Cruickshank Futures 1983-84 (exec); Alexander Laing & Cruickshank 1985 (exec). *Professional Organisations:* Member, The International Stock Exchange.

DESAI, D N; General Manager, The New India Assurance Company Limited.

DESCAMPS, T; Director, Crédit Commercial de France (UK) Limited.

DESMOND, Denis; Director, Ulster Development Capital Limited.

DETTMER, S J; Partner, Cazenove & Co.

DEVERELL, M C; Director, Barclays Bank plc.

DEVEREUX, R C; Operations Director, Wellcome plc, since 1972; Production, Computing, Diagnostics. *Career:* The Wellcome Foundation Ltd, Chief Engineer 1959-63; Deputy Production Director 1963-69; Chairman, Calmic Australia 1969-72; Group Operations Director 1972-. *Biog: b.* 15 December 1928. *Nationality:* British. *m.* 1954, Anna-Mary; 1 s; 2 d. *Educ:* Repton School; Cambridge University (MA). *Directorships:* Wellcome Group Operations 1972- (exec); Wellcome Diagnostics 1985- (exec) Chm; Wellcome International Trading Limited 1978-90 (exec) Chm. *Professional Organisations:* MIMechE; FBIM. *Clubs:* RAC.

DEVESON, G R; Director, Metheuen (Lloyds Underwriting Agents) Limited.

DEVINE, John Buchanan; Chairman, Alexander Stenhouse & Partners Limited.

DEVLIN, Roger William; Director, Hill Samuel & Co Ltd, since 1986; Corporate Finance (Mergers & Acquisitions). *Career:* Hill Samuel & Co Ltd, Exec 1978-83; Hill Samuel Inc (New York), VP 1983-86. *Biog: b.* 22 August 1957. *Nationality:* British. *m.* 1983, Louise Alice Temlett (née Tucker); 1 d. *Educ:* Manchester Grammar School; Wadham College, Oxford (MA). *Clubs:* Royal St George's, Worplesdon. *Recreations:* Golf, Racing.

DEVON, David; Partner, Clark Whitehill, since 1978; Audit Business Services Practice Developments. *Biog: b.* 10 August 1948. *Nationality:* British. *m.* 1974, Carol

Banwell; 2 s. *Educ:* Bexley School. *Directorships:* Grenco Matal Ltd; Matal Ltd. *Professional Organisations:* FCA.

DEW, M L; Director, Sun Alliance and London Insurance plc.

DEW, Peter George Patrick; Managing Director, Thornton Management Ltd, since 1989. *Career:* Mercury Asset Management, Director 1966-82; GT Management, Director 1982-86; Thornton Management, Director 1988-. *Biog: b.* 24 October 1945. *Nationality:* British. *m.* 1978, Edwina Frances (née Mansell); 4 s; 1 d. *Educ:* Canford School, Dorset. *Professional Organisations:* Associate Member, Society of Investment Analysts.

DEWAR, A W; Director, Parrish Stockbrokers.

DEWE MATHEWS, Bernard Piers; TD; Director, Head of International Projects Department, J Henry Schroder Wagg & Co Ltd, since 1978; Project Finance and International Advice; Dept Head, since 1983. *Career:* National Service, 2nd Lt Served Malaya 1956-57; TA Major 21 SAS Regiment 1957; Edward Moore & Sons, Articled Clerk 1957-62; British Petroleum Company Limited, Finance & Admin Dept 1962-65; Coopers & Lybrand and Associates, Management Consultants, Consultant 1965-67; Sen Consultant 1967-69; Schroders 1969-; Executive, Venture Capital Dept 1969; Manager, Group Planning 1972; Manager, Export Finance Dept, Banking Division 1973; Assistant Director, Project Finance Division 1975; Director & Deputy Head of Project Finance Division 1978; Head of International Projects Department 1983. *Biog: b.* 28 March 1937. *Nationality:* British. *m.* 1977, Catherine Ellen (née Armstrong); 1 s; 3 d. *Educ:* Ampleforth; Harvard Business School. *Directorships:* Thames Power Limited 1988 (non-exec); Barking Power Limited 1990 (non-exec). *Other Activities:* Governor, St Paul's Girls' Prep School 1987-; Member, Overseas Projects Board 1989-; Member, South East Asia Trade Advisory Group 1984-90. *Professional Organisations:* ACA 1962; FCA 1972. *Clubs:* Roehampton. *Recreations:* Music, Opera, Skiing, Landscape Gardening.

DEWEN, J M; Senior Executive Director, J H Minet & Co Ltd.

DEWHIRST, Graham; Director, County Natwest Ventures Ltd, since 1988; Provision of Venture & Development Capital. *Career:* Price Waterhouse Asst Mgr 1973-79; 3i plc Local Dir 1979-86; Robson Rhodes Ptnr 1986-87. *Biog: b.* 4 June 1951. *Nationality:* British. *m.* 1972, June Margaret; 2 s. *Educ:* Batley Grammar School; London School of Economics (BSc Econ). *Directorships:* County NatWest Limited 1989 (non-exec); Maccess Group Limited 1989 (non-exec). *Professional Organisations:* FCA. *Recreations:* Music, Watching Rugby & Cricket.

DEWHURST, Philip; Director, GCI Sterling.

DHOMBRES, Dominique-André; Correspondent, Le Monde.

DI BIASE, Paul; Chairman, Partnership Board, Forsyte Kerman Solicitors, since 1988; MBO's For Management Teams/Corporate Finance, Mergers & Acquisitions. *Career:* Forsyte Kerman, Assistant Solicitor 1960-64; Salaried Partner 1964-65; Equity Partner 1965-.

DI GIORGIO, Paride; General Manager, Banca Nazionale Dell'Agricoltura, since 1983. *Career:* Banca Popolare di Novara (Milan) 1960-63; Tradevco Bank, Monrovia (Liberia), Mgr 1963-68; Banca Nazionale Dell'Agricoltura, Dep Rep 1969-78; UK Rep 1978-83; General Manager (London) 1983-. *Biog: b.* 14 September 1935. *Nationality:* Italian. *m.* 1973, Jolanta Ewa (née Siemicka); 1 s; 1 d. *Educ:* Istituto Universitario Orientale, Napoli. *Directorships:* Nagrafin Bank Ltd (Cayman Islands) 1980-84 (exec); London & Continental Bankers Ltd 1984-87 (non-exec). *Other Activities:* Cavaliere (Italy); Counsellor, Italian Chamber of Commerce, 1985-; EEC Ctee Member, Foreign Banks and Securities Houses Assoc. *Clubs:* Overseas Bankers Club (Elected and Management Ctee Member).

DI MASCIO, R A; Director, MIM Limited.

DI STEFANO, Michele; Managing Director, Global Foreign Exchange, Merrill Lynch International Bank Limited, since 1990; Foreign Exchange Trading Management. *Career:* Credito Italiano, Rome, Participated in Training Program on General Banking Services 1974-78; Foreign Exchange and Bullion Trader 1978-80; New York, Foreign Exchange Trader 1980; Milano, Banking Management Seminar 1981; Tokyo, Foreign Exchange Manager (FX/Treasury Resp) 1982-86; Merrill Lynch Int Bank Ltd (New York) Vice President/Manager Cross Currencies & Exotic Currencies Desk 1986-88; Merrill Lynch Intl Bank Limited (London), Executive Director (Foreign Exchange) 1989. *Biog: b.* 18 July 1955. *Nationality:* Italian. *m.* 1986, Elizabeth; 1 d. *Educ:* University of Economics, Rome; Accounting High School (Rome). *Directorships:* Merrill Lynch International Bank Ltd 1989 (exec); Merrill Lynch Capital Markets 1989; Merrill Lynch International Bank Ltd 1990 (exec) MD; Merrill Lynch Capital Markets 1990 MD. *Other Activities:* Merrill Lynch Europe, Executive Committee. *Clubs:* Riverside Tennis Club. *Recreations:* Tennis.

DIAMOND, Robert; Managing Director, Morgan Stanley International.

DIBBLE, Robert Kenneth; Partner, Wilde Sapte, since 1982; Shipping, Aircraft, Banking and Trade Finance Law. *Career:* Royal Navy (1958-77), including Ministry of Defence on Naval Staff 1972-75; HMS Eskimo Commander 1975-76; Linklaters & Paines Articles and Solicitor 1978-81. *Biog: b.* 28 December 1938. *Nationality:* British. *m.* 1972, Teresa; 4 s. *Educ:* Westcliff High School for Boys; Royal Naval College, Dartmouth Defence Fellow. *Other Activities:* City of London Solicitors' Company; Company of Shipwrights. *Professional Organisations:* The Law Society; International Bar Association. *Recreations:* Family, Music, Tennis.

DICK, Brian; Director, Noble Grossart Ltd.

DICK, John Antony; Director, GT Management plc, since 1970; Investment Management. *Career:* Iraq Petroleum Co Ltd, Investment Mgr 1961-67; J Henry Schroeder Wagg & Co Ltd, Investment Mgr 1967-68; Kingsdrive Investment Management Ltd, MD 1969-70. *Biog: b.* 23 March 1934. *m.* 1968, Marigold (née Verity); 1 s; 2 d. *Educ:* Trinity College, Glenalmond; Worcester College, Oxford (BA). *Directorships:* USDC Investment Trust 1987 (non-exec); F & C Eurotrust 1989 (non-exec); Thornton Pan-European Investment Trust 1988 (non-exec); GT Investment Fund SA 1980 (non-exec). *Other Activities:* Advisory Ctee to Local Authority Mutual Investment Trust. *Professional Organisations:* CA.

DICK, John Kenneth; CBE; Director, N M Rothschild & Sons Ltd, since 1978; , N M Rothschild (Leasing) Ltd, since 1978. *Career:* Mann Judd & Co, Chartered Accountants 1936; Partner 1947; Mitchell Cotts Group Ltd, Jt Man Dir 1957; Sole Man Dir 1959-78; Dep Chm 1964; Chm 1966-78; Hume Holdings Ltd, Chm 1975-80. *Biog: b.* 5 April 1913. 1942, Pamela Madge (née Salmon); 1 s (decd); 2 d. *Educ:* Sedbergh. *Other Activities:* Member, Commonwealth Development Corp, 1967-80; Gov, City of London Soc; Member, British Nat Export Ctee, 1968-71; Covent Gdn Mkt Authority, 1976-82; Chm, Ctee for Middle East Trade, 1968-71; Pres, Middle East Assoc, 1976-81 (a Vice-Pres, 1970-76). *Professional Organisations:* FCA; FRSA. *Recreations:* Golf.

DICK, Stewart John Cunningham; Director, Brown, Shipley & Co Ltd, since 1980; Risk Asset Management. *Career:* Brown, Shipley & Co Ltd 1972-. *Biog: b.* 14 January 1946. *Nationality:* British. *m.* 1974, A Aileen M (née Dickson). *Educ:* George Watson's College; Edinburgh University (MA, LLB). *Professional Organisations:* CA. *Clubs:* Caledonian, RAC. *Recreations:* Golf, Gardening.

DICKINS, Paul; Deputy City Editor, Sunday Express.

DICKINSON, Peter Frear; Vice President, Investments, Prudential-Bache Securities (UK) Inc, since 1987; Institutional Futures. *Career:* Rionda De Pass Ltd, Trader 1978-82; Prudential-Bache Securities 1982-. *Biog: b.* 8 April 1955. *Nationality:* British. *m.* 1983, Susan Caroline (née Rodway); 1 s; 2 d. *Educ:* Rugby School;

Reading University (BSc). *Clubs:* RAC. *Recreations:* Sailing, Fishing, Shooting.

DICKINSON, R E; Finance Director, Laporte plc, since 1985.

DICKISON, Lieutenant Colonel Paul J; Deputy Chief Executive, FIMBRA, since 1984; Co-ordination of Activities of Operating Departments. *Career:* Royal Engineers 1951-76; Fairey Engineering Ltd Asst to MD 1976-78; Fairey Properties Ltd MD 1978-83; Self-employed Mgmnt Consultant 1983-84. *Biog: b.* 6 July 1930. *m.* 1955, Annette Lois (née Eden); 1 s; 2 d. *Educ:* Dartford; RMA Sandhurst; St Catharine's College, Cambridge. *Publications:* Various articles. *Clubs:* Army and Navy. *Recreations:* Rugby, Cricket, Swimming, Reading, Local Government.

DICKSON, Alastair; Senior Partner, Dickson Minto.

DIERDEN, Kenneth Norman; Partner, Freshfields, since 1987. *Career:* College of Law Lecturer 1977-80. *Biog: b.* 26 February 1952. *Nationality:* British. *m.* 1976, Margaret (née Hayward); 1 d. *Educ:* Bancroft's School; Southampton University (BA Hons). *Professional Organisations:* Member, The Law Society; ATII; Association of Pension Lawyers (Member of Main Committee and Chairman of Legislative & Parliamentary Committee). *Publications:* Contributor to Tolleys Company Law. *Recreations:* Hockey, Squash.

DIERS, P; Director, Crédit Commercial de France (UK) Limited.

DIETZ, David Charles; Senior Partner, Hays Allan.

DIFFORD, J F; Director, S G Warburg & Co Ltd.

DIGBY-BELL, Christopher Harvey; Partner, Frere Cholmeley, since 1989; Property. *Career:* Articled to Taylor & Humbert 1966-71; Admitted as a Solicitor 1972; Assistant Solicitor 1972-75; Salaried Partner 1975-77; Equity Partner 1977-84; Taylor Garrett, Equity Partner (following merger) 1984-89; Managing Partner 1987-89; Frere Cholmeley, Partner 1989-. *Biog: b.* 21 June 1948. *Nationality:* British. *m.* 1974, Claire; 2 s; 1 d. *Educ:* Marlborough College, Wilts; College of Law, London (Law Society Exams). *Other Activities:* Member of Law Society Group for the Welfare of People with a Mental Handicap; Active Interest in the Legal Rights of the Mentally Handicapped particularly in relation to Education; Member of Down's Syndrome Association. *Professional Organisations:* Law Society, Qualified Solicitor 1972. *Clubs:* MCC; Berkshire Golf Club; Steward Henley-on-Thames; Leander Rowing Club. *Recreations:* Cricket (Founder of The Brief's XI), Golf, Tennis, Swimming, American Football, Rugby, Current Affairs, Reading, Pop Music, Cinema, Photography.

DIGGLE, Ms Catherine; Partner, Forsyte Kerman, since 1984; Commercial Property & Planning Partner and Training Partner. *Career:* John Laing & Son Limited, Articled Clerk 1980; Forsyte Kerman, Assistant Solicitor 1980-84. *Biog: b.* 5 July 1955. *Nationality:* British. *Educ:* Ursuline Convent, Chester; Lanchester Polytechnic, Coventry (BA Hons). *Professional Organisations:* Legal Education and Training Group. *Recreations:* Egyptology, Manchester United.

DIGGLE, Paul Francis; Director of Research, Societe Generale Strauss Turnbull Securities, since 1989; Head of Research Department & Pharmaceutical Research. *Career:* Laing & Cruickshank, Pharmaceutical & Chemicals Analyst 1972-79; Sheppards & Chase, Pharmaceutical & Chemicals Analyst 1980-82; Warburgs, Senior Analyst, Head of Global Pharmaceuticals Research 1982-89. *Biog: b.* 11 September 1950. *Nationality:* British. *Educ:* St Mary's College, Crosby; St John's College, Oxford (MA). *Other Activities:* Council Member, Society of Investment Analysts. *Professional Organisations:* ASIA. *Clubs:* Royal Wimbledon Golf Club.

DIGHE, Sanjay; Head of Equity Derivatives, Paribas Limited, since 1988; Equity Risk Management. *Career:* NatWest Bank, Officer, Energy Lending 1979-81; Bank of America, London, Manager, New Issues Department 1983-85; Paribas Limited, (London), Officer, FRN Trading and Syndicate 1985-86; Head of Fixed Income Options 1986-87. *Biog: b.* 18 March 1957. *Nationality:* British. *m.* 1986, Smita; 2 d. *Educ:* UMIST (BSc Management Sciences); Northern Illinois University (MBA).

DIKENS, Paul; Deputy City Editor, Sunday Express.

DILLON, Terence John; Portfolio Manager, British Petroleum Pension Trust, since 1986; UK & Far East Equities. *Career:* Cash Stone & Co, Articled Clerk 1955-61; Cooper Bros, Auditor 1961-63; British Petroleum, Various Fin Mgmnt Positions 1963-73; Fin Mgr 1973-77; Snr Analyst 1977-82; Head of Investment Research 1982-86. *Biog: b.* 16 July 1939. *m.* 1968, Claire (née Harvey); 2 d. *Educ:* St Joseph's College. *Professional Organisations:* FCA, ASIA. *Recreations:* Tennis, Chess, Lepidoptera, Antiquarian Books.

DIMENT, Dr Antony Richard; Director, Gresham Trust plc, since 1988; Investment Management. *Career:* Nuclear Power Group Ltd, Design Physicist 1968-70; London University, Research Associate 1970-73; Emi Audio Visual Services Ltd, Dir 1973-78; Logica Ltd Sales, Mktg Consultancy 1978-81; Pergamon Press Ltd, Business Dev Dir 1981-82; Investors in Industry plc, Investment Mgr 1982-88. *Biog: b.* 30 January 1945. *m.* 1971, Judith (née Pritchard); 2 s. *Educ:* Greenhill Grammar School; University College of Wales (BSc); Queen Mary College, London (MSc, PhD). *Directorships:* Ajax Nominees Ltd; Gresham Trust plc; Gresham Trust Fund Managers Ltd; Gresham Trust Personal Equity Plan

Managers Ltd; Gresham Nominees Ltd; Wren Investments Ltd; Wren Trust Ltd; Covrad Heat Transfer Ltd; The Moon's a Balloon Restaurants Ltd; Rega Holdings Ltd; Barrington House Nominees Ltd; British Venture Capital Association; Data Communications Group plc; Future Components Holdings Ltd; Oakland Fairfax (Holdings) Ltd; Radstone Technology plc; Skyway Group plc; Testlink Holdings Ltd; UK Holdings Ltd. *Recreations:* Golf, Squash, Water Sports, Bridge.

DIMSON, Professor Elroy; Professor of Finance, London Business School, since 1990; Corporate Finance & Investment Management. *Career:* Tube Investments, Planning Officer 1968-69; Unilever Ltd, Operations Research Mgr 1970-72; London Business School 1974-; Dean of MBA Programmes 1986-90; Bank of England (Houblon-Norman Fellow) 1991. *Biog: b.* 17 January 1947. *Nationality:* British. *m.* 1969, Helen (née Sonn); 3 s; 1 d. *Educ:* Newcastle University (BA); Birmingham University (MCom); London University (PhD); Institute of Marketing, London (Dipm). *Directorships:* Superannuation Arrangements of the University of London (SAUL) 1982 (non-exec); Mobil Trustee Co 1984 (non-exec); The German Investment Trust 1990 (non-exec). *Other Activities:* Visiting Professor, Universities of California (Berkeley), Chicago, Hawaii, Brussels (EIASM); Co-Editor, LBS Risk Measurement Service; Editorial Board Member for Journal of Banking and Finance, Investing, MBA Review; Adviser to the SIB, Stock Exchange and Private & Public Sector Organisations. *Professional Organisations:* American and European Finance Associations. *Publications:* Risk Measurement Services 1979-90; Stock Market Anomalies, 1987; Cases in Corporate Finance (Co-Author), 1988; The Hoare Govett Smaller Companies Index (Co-Author), 1987-90; Publications in Professional and Academic Journals.

DINGEMANS, Rear Admiral P G V; CB, DSO; Director, Argosy Asset Management plc, since 1990; Administration. *Career:* Royal Navy 1953-90; Commanded Maxton 1965; Berwick 1971; Lowestoft 1972; Intrepid 1980; Flag Officer, Gibraltar 1985; Chief of Staff, Cincfleet 1987. *Biog: b.* 31 July 1935. *Nationality:* British. *m.* 1961, Faith (née Bristow); 3 s. *Educ:* Brighton College. *Directorships:* Argosy Asset Management 1990 (exec). *Other Activities:* Liveryman, Worshipful Company of Coachmakers and Coach Harnessmakers. *Professional Organisations:* FBIM. *Clubs:* Naval and Military, City Livery Club. *Recreations:* Tennis, Shooting.

DINWIDDIE, Ian Maitland; Finance Director, Allen & Overy, since 1990. *Career:* Guinness Mahon Holdings plc, Finance Director 1988-90; Arbuthnot Savory Milln Holdings Limited, Group Financial Controller, Group Internal Auditor 1982-88; Arthur Young Chartered Accountants, Audit Manager 1973-82. *Biog: b.* 8 February 1952. *Nationality:* British. *m.* 1978, Sally Jane (née Croydon); 1 s; 1 d. *Educ:* Betteshanger School, Deal, Kent; Sherborne School, Dorset; Exeter University (BA

Hons Economics). *Professional Organisations:* Member of The Institute of Chartered Accountants in England and Wales. *Clubs:* Queen Mary Sailing Club. *Recreations:* Sailing.

DINWIDDY, Charles Victor; Director, S G Warburg Securities, since 1990; Fixed Interest Division. *Career:* J Henry Schroder Wagg & Co Ltd, Investment Dept 1963-69; Mullens & Co, Stockbrokers (Later Merged into S G Warburg Securities) 1969-; Partner 1979-. *Biog: b.* 18 February 1942. *Nationality:* British. *m.* 1990, Sylvia (née Bould); 1 s; 1 d. *Educ:* Winchester College; New College, Oxford (MA). *Professional Organisations:* Member, International Stock Exchange. *Clubs:* Oriental, MCC, Vincent's. *Recreations:* Golf, Historic Buildings, Wine.

DIPLOCK, A W; Chief General Manager, National Australia Bank Limited.

DiROCCO, J; Director, Lehman Brothers Gilt Money Brokers Ltd.

DISPENZA, Adriano; Head Investment Banking - Italy, Merrill Lynch International Limited, since 1988. *Career:* First Chicago Ltd, Managing Director, Head of Western Europe Investment Banking 1979-87; Amex Bank Ltd, Assistant Manager, Corporate Finance 1977-79; Morgan Grenfell & Co Ltd, Executive, Corporate Finance Dept 1973-77. *Biog: b.* 24 May 1948. *Nationality:* Italian. *m.* 1979, Rallia; 1 d. *Educ:* Queen Mary College, London (BSc Econ Honours); Faculte de Droit et de Sciences Economiques, Paris (Diploma). *Directorships:* Merrill Lynch International Ltd 1988 (exec). *Clubs:* RAC. *Recreations:* Travel, Reading, Walking.

DISS, Paul John; Partner, Stephenson Harwood, since 1982; Banking Law. *Career:* Linklaters & Paines, Articled Clerk 1974-76; Asst Solicitor 1976-77. *Biog: b.* 30 November 1951. *Nationality:* British. *m.* 1980, Janice (née Fletcher); 2 s; 1 d. *Educ:* St Joseph's College, Stoke-on-Trent; St Catharine's College, Cambridge (BA). *Professional Organisations:* The Law Society. *Recreations:* Reading, Squash, Photography.

DIX, Robert William; Finance Director, Charterhouse Bank Limited, since 1990. *Career:* Booth (International Holdings) Ltd, Financial Accountant 1972-78; Great Northern Tanning Co Ltd (Kano, Nigeria), Financial Controller 1978-80; Charterhouse Bank Limited, Accountant, Export Finance Division 1980-83; Manager, Lending Division 1983-86; Financial Controller, Banking & Treasury Divisions 1986-90; Finance Director 1990-. *Biog: b.* 14 April 1952. *Nationality:* British. *m.* 1977, Diana Barbara (née Parker); 1 s; 1 d. *Educ:* Wellingborough School (Head Prefect, Leaving Scholar). *Directorships:* Westair Holdings Ltd 1987 (non-exec). *Professional Organisations:* FCCA. *Clubs:* Island Sailing Club. *Recreations:* Offshore Racing.

DIXEY, Charles Richard; Director, Minet Holdings plc.

DIXON, David M; Partner, Withers.

DIXON, Giles; Partner, Turner Kenneth Brown.

DIXON, James Wolryche; Partner, Ernst & Young, since 1984; Value Added Tax, Tax Information Retrieval. *Biog: b.* 20 February 1948. *Educ:* Lancing College; Corpus Christi College, Oxford (MA). *Other Activities:* FRSA. *Professional Organisations:* FCA, VAT Practitioners' Group. *Publications:* Contributor to Tolley's VAT Planning (Annual Publication). *Clubs:* United Oxford & Cambridge University. *Recreations:* Cycling, Bridge, Photography.

DIXON, John; Assistant Director-Markets Policy, Scimitar Development Capital Limited.

DIXON, John Michael Fraser; Partner, The Barnes Partnership, since 1988; Executive Search. *Career:* Lowndes Lambert Group Ltd, Personnel Dir 1970-79; Brunel Recruitment Consultants Ltd, MD 1980-84; Houghton Sanderson Associates Ltd, Dir 1984-87. *Biog: b.* 12 July 1945. *Nationality:* British. *m.* 1988, Amanda Radclyffe (née Pilkington); 1 s; 2 d. *Educ:* Rugby School; McGill University. *Professional Organisations:* MIPM. *Clubs:* Royal Worlington, Winchester House, Trearddur Bay Sailing. *Recreations:* Fishing.

DIXON, Kenneth Herbert Morley; Vice Chairman, Legal & General Group, since 1986. *Career:* Rowntree & Co Ltd, Various to Dir 1956-70; Chm (UK Confectionery Div) 1973-78; Dep Chm 1978-81; Chm 1981-. *Biog: b.* 19 August 1929. *Nationality:* British. *Directorships:* Bass plc 1988; Legal & General Group plc 1984; Yorkshire Television Holdings plc 1989; Business in the Community Council 1983-88; Rowntree plc 1970-89; The Food & Drink Federation 1986-87. *Professional Organisations:* Council Member, CBI.

DIXON, P B; Associate, Grimley J R Eve.

DIXON, Roger Harry Vernon; Partner, Travers Smith Braithwaite, since 1962; Corporate Law. *Career:* Travers Smith Braithwaite, Articled Clerk 1953-56; Assistant Solicitor 1957-61; Partner 1962-. *Biog: b.* 19 June 1929. *Nationality:* British. *m.* 1955, Mary Kathleen (née Barr); 1 s; 2 d. *Educ:* Christs Hospital; St Catharines College, Cambridge (BA,MA). *Directorships:* Consolidated Insurance Group Ltd and Subsidiaries 1979 (non-exec). *Other Activities:* Senior Warden, City of London Solicitors' Company; Governor, Christs Hospital. *Professional Organisations:* Member, Law Society. *Clubs:* City of London, MCC. *Recreations:* Music, Books, Travel.

DOBBIE, I G; Non-Executive Director, The Burmah Oil plc.

DOBBIE, S J; Vice Chairman, County NatWest Securities Ltd, since 1988. *Career:* Unilever 1962; ICI 1966; Wood Mackenzie 1975; Managing Partner 1983. *Biog: b.* 26 July 1939. *Nationality:* British. *m.* 1962, Brenda (née Condie); 2 d. *Educ:* Dollar Academy; University of Edinburgh (BSc). *Directorships:* County NatWest Limited; County NatWest Securities Ltd. *Professional Organisations:* Member, International Stock Exchange.

DOBBIE, William Robertson; Associate Director/ Financial Controller, Benchmark Bank plc, since 1989; Finance and Treasury. *Career:* Deloitte Haskins & Sells, Audit Manager 1985-86; Merrill Lynch Europe Limited, Financial Accounting Manager 1986-87; Benchmark Bank plc, Financial Accountant 1987-88; Benchmark Group plc, Group Financial Accountant 1988-89. *Biog: b.* 18 July 1957. *Nationality:* British. *m.* 1985, Sally-Anne; 1 s. *Educ:* Auchterarder High School; Dundee College of Technology (SHND Accounting). *Professional Organisations:* Member, The Institute of Chartered Accountants of Scotland. *Recreations:* Golf, Music (Electric Organ), Skiing.

DOBINSON, Henry Roy; Member of the Council, Lloyd's of London.

DOBSON, A C; Partner, Lawrence Graham.

DOBSON, Michael William Romsey; Deputy Chief Executive, Morgan Grenfell Group plc.

DOBSON, Nigel Hewitt; Partner, Ernst & Young, since 1981; Corporate Advisory Services Division. *Career:* Ernst & Whinney, Various 1968-78; Midland Bank plc (Secondment), Corporate Fin Div 1978-80; Ernst & Young (& Predecessor Firm), Various 1980. *Biog: b.* 13 August 1949. *Educ:* St Dunstan's College. *Professional Organisations:* FCA. *Recreations:* Sailing, Reading.

DOBSON, Miss Sheila Eileen; Partner, Jaques & Lewis, since 1982; Trusts and Personal Taxation. *Career:* Lewis, Lewis & Co (formerly Lewis, Haymon & Lewis), Articled Clerk 1966-71; Assistant Solicitor 1971; Partner to 1982; Jaques & Lewis, Partner 1982-. *Biog: b.* 25 February 1930. *Nationality:* British. *Educ:* Central Newcastle High School for Girls; Royal Academy of Dramatic Art. *Professional Organisations:* The Law Society; Holborn Law Society. *Clubs:* St James's Club. *Recreations:* Reading.

DODD, A M M; Director, Charterhouse Tilney.

DODD, James Edmund; Director, Kleinwort Benson Securities Ltd, since 1989; Research. *Career:* Kleinwort Benson Securities, Director, Research 1989; Citicorp

Scrimgeour Vickers, Director, Research 1987-88; Fielding, Newson-Smith & Co, Investment Analyst 1983-87; Scicon Ltd, Consultant 1978-83; Cambridge University, Post-Doctoral Research 1977. *Biog: b.* 1952. *Nationality:* British. *m.* m; 1 s; 1 d. *Educ:* Kings School, Rochester; London University (BSc Physics); Oxford University (DPhil Theoretical Physics). *Professional Organisations:* Institute of Physics; Royal United Services Institute; International Stock Exchange. *Publications:* The Ideas of Particle Physics (CUP), 1984.

DODDS, Peter; Executive Director, Unibank Limited; International and Asset Finance. *Career:* Libra Bank 1977-85; Williams & Glyn's Bank 1972-77. *Biog: b.* 12 August 1950. *Nationality:* British. *m.* 1975, Sheila Margaret (née McKenzie). *Educ:* University of Edinburgh (MA); University of London (MSc). *Professional Organisations:* AIB.

DODDS Jr, W R; The Northern Trust Company, since 1990; Global Custody, Banking, Foreign Exchange. *Career:* The Northern Trust Company 1983-; Northwest Industries 1981-83; Ford Motor Company 1976-81. *Biog: b.* 17 July 1952. *Nationality:* American. *m.* 1981, Ann (née Martin); 1 s; 1 d. *Educ:* Lafayette College (AB Honors, Economics); University of Chicago (MBA, Finance and Accounting). *Other Activities:* Trustee, John G Shedd Aquarium. *Recreations:* Broadgate.

DODDS-SMITH, Ian Charles; Partner, McKenna & Co, since 1984; Head of Health Care Group, Regulatory, Research. *Career:* McKenna & Co, Articled Clerk 1974-76; Assistant Solicitor 1976-84. *Biog: b.* 31 July 1951. *Nationality:* British. *m.* 1988, Caroline (née Clarke-Jervoise); 1 s; 1 d. *Educ:* Downing College, Cambridge (MA). *Other Activities:* Consultant Editor, Personal & Medical Injuries Law Letter; Product Liability Committee of the Association of the British Pharmaceutical Industry; Legal Affairs Committee of the Association Royal College of Physicians & Medical Research Council Working Parties; Temporary Advisor to WHO; University College London and University College Hospital Ethics Committee; Frequent Lecturer on Health Care Law and Product Liability. *Professional Organisations:* Westminster Law Society; American Bar Association. *Publications:* Legal Liabilities in Clinical Trials in Early Phase Drug Evaluation in Man (By O'Grady & Linet), 1990; Product Liability for Medicinal Products in Medical Negligence by Powers (By Harris), 1990; Implications of Strict Liability Under Consumer Protection Act in Risk and Consent to Risk (By Mann), 1989. *Recreations:* Walking, Gardening, National Hunt Racing.

DODGE, L A B; Chairman, Sanyo International Ltd.

DOERR, J C; Director, Hill Samuel & Co Ltd.

DOERR, Michael Frank; General Manager, Friends Provident Life Office.

DOHERTY, J; Senior Manager, United Mizrahi Bank Limited.

DOHERTY, Peter Gerald; Managing Director, Bank of America International Limited.

DOLAN, Liz; City Reporter, Today.

DOLBEY, Alexander Charles; Director, Kleinwort Benson Limited.

DOLMAN, R A; Partner, Wedlake Bell.

DOMAN, L A; Operations Manager, Sogemin Metals Ltd.

DOMINGUEZ, James; Director, Samuel Montagu & Co Limited.

DONAGH, Francis James; Partner, Oppenheimer & Co.

DONALD, Peter James; Director, County NatWest Securities Limited, since 1987; International Corporate Finance. *Career:* Williams & Glyn's Bank Ltd, Mgr 1969-76; First Chicago Ltd, MD 1976-86; Hill Samuel & Co Ltd, Dir 1986-87. *Biog: b.* 22 May 1946. *m.* 1974, Diana (née Scott); 1 s; 1 d. *Educ:* Sedbergh School; St Andrews University (MA Hons 1st). *Clubs:* Hurlingham, Berkshire Golf Club. *Recreations:* Golf, Tennis, Music.

DONALD, Sidney Milne; Director, County NatWest Ltd, since 1987; Development Capital. *Career:* County Bank Ltd Exec 1968-75; Asst Dir 1975-82; Snr Asst Dir 1982-84; County Natwest Ventures Ltd Dir 1984-87; County Natwest Ltd Dir 1987-. *Biog: b.* 31 July 1942. *m.* 1969, Betty (née Prepouthi); 3 s. *Educ:* Merchiston Castle School, Edinburgh; St Edmund Hall, Oxford (MA). *Professional Organisations:* ACIS.

DONALDSON, Dame (Dorothy) Mary; GBE, JP; Alderman, City of London Ward of Coleman Street, since 1975. *Biog: b.* 29 August 1921. *m.* 1945, John Francis Donaldson; 1 s; 2 d. *Educ:* Portsmouth High School for Girls (GPDST); Wingfield Morris Orthopaedic Hospital; Middlesex Hospital, London, SRN, 1946. *Other Activities:* Women's National Cancer Control Campaign, Chairman 1967-69; Voluntary Licensing Authority for Human In Vitro Fertilisation and Embryology, Chairman 1985-; British Cancer Council, Vice President 1970; NE Metropolitan Regional Hospital Board, Member 1970-74; NE Thames RHA 1976-81; London Hospital, Governor 1971-74; Gt Ormond Street Hospital for Sick Children, Governor 1978-80; Cities of London and Westminster Disablement Adv Ctee, Member 1974-79; Inner London Educ Authority 1968-71;

City Parochial Foundation 1969-75; Ctee, Royal Humane Soc 1968-83; Ctee, AA 1985-; Banking Ombudsman, Chairman Council 1985-; Counsel and Care for the Elderly, Vice-Pres 1980-; British Assoc of Cancer United Patients, Pres 1985-; City of London School for Girls, Governor 1971-83; Berkhamstead Schools 1976-80; Charterhouse School, Mem, Governing Body 1980-85; Court of Common Council, Mem 1966-75; Sheriff 1981-82; HM Lieutenant 1983; Mem, Guild of Freemen, City of London 1970; (Mem Court 1983-86); Gardeners Company, Liveryman 1975; Shipwrights Company, Hon Freeman 1985; JP, Inner London 1960; Inner London Juvenile Court Panel, Mem 1960-65; CIArb, Hon Mem 1981; Girton College, Cambridge, Hon Fellow 1983; Hon DSc City 1983; DStJ 1984; Freedom, City of Winnipeg 1968; Order of Oman 1982; Order of Bahrain 1984; Grand Officier, Ordre National du Mérite 1984. *Clubs:* Reform, Royal Cruising, Royal Lymington Yacht, Bar Yacht. *Recreations:* Gardening, Sailing, Geriatric Skiing.

DONALDSON, Hamish; Chief Executive, Hill Samuel Bank Ltd, since 1987. *Career:* De La Rue 1960-66; Urwick, Orr 1966-73; Hill Samuel 1973-. *Biog:* b. 13 June 1936. *Nationality:* British. *m.* 1965, Linda (née Bousfield); 3 d. *Educ:* Oundle School; Christ's College, Cambridge (MA). *Directorships:* TSB Group plc 1990 (exec); Macquarie Bank 1989 (non-exec). *Other Activities:* Company of Information Technologists. *Professional Organisations:* FIMC. *Publications:* A Guide to the Successful Management of Computer Projects, 1978.

DONALDSON, Thomas H; Managing Director, Morgan Guaranty Trust Company of New York.

DONKIN, Robert George; Director & Company Secretary, Foreign & Colonial Management Ltd, since 1987; Company Secretarial/Compliance. *Career:* Prudential Assurance Co Gen Asst, Securities Dept 1964-73; Foreign and Colonial Management, Asst Co Sec 1973-80; Jt Co Sec 1980-87. *Biog:* b. 12 September 1945. *Nationality:* British. *m.* 1970, Dawn Margaret (née Harding); 2 s; 1 d. *Educ:* Henry Thornton Grammar School. *Directorships:* F & C Nominees Ltd 1989; G I T Management Services Ltd 1989. *Professional Organisations:* ACIS. *Clubs:* Cannons Sports Club. *Recreations:* Squash, Windsurfing, Walking.

DONLEA, Patrick Kevin Fitzgerald; Partner, Cazenove & Co.

DONOVAN, Peter William; Finance Director, Allstate Reinsurance Co Ltd, since 1990; Finance & Data Processing. *Career:* English & American Insurance Co Ltd, Deputy General Manager, Finance -1983; Allstate Reinsurance Co Ltd 1983-. *Biog:* b. 13 February 1951. *Nationality:* British. *Directorships:* Trebury Property Management Company Ltd. *Professional Organisations:* Member, Institute of Chartered Accountants.

DORAN, Nigel John Leslie; Partner, Macfarlanes, Solicitors, since 1988; Corporate. *Career:* Barclays Bank Ltd Management Graduate 1973-78; Solartron Electronic Group Ltd Asst Fin Acct 1978-79; Bankers Trust Co Internal Auditor 1979-80. *Biog:* b. 11 March 1950. *Educ:* Glenalmond College; St Edmund Hall, Oxford (MA); University of London (LLM). *Other Activities:* City of London Law Society Corporate Tax Sub-Committee. *Professional Organisations:* The Law Society; ATII; AIB; ACCA.

DORE, B John; Partner, Neville Russell.

DORMAN, John Douglas; Senior Vice President & General Manager, Bank of New England, since 1984; General Commercial Banking and Country Responsibility for the UK, Europe. *Career:* Chase Manhattan Bank, Trainee/Lending Officer 1964-69; VP & European Shipping Coordinator 1969-73; First International Bankshares Ltd, Gen Mgr, UK Banking & Shipping 1973-79; Orion Bank, Shipping Consultant 1979-80; Bank of New England, VP & UK Rep 1980-84. *Biog:* b. 30 September 1939. *m.* 1974, Pauline (née Willert); 1 s; 2 d. *Educ:* Sedbergh School; Magdalene College, Cambridge (BA Hons). *Clubs:* Hurlingham, Vanderbilt Racquet, Hayling Island Sailing. *Recreations:* Skiing, Sailing, Windsurfing, Tennis.

DORNER, Ms Irene; Senior Legal Adviser, Midland Montagu, since 1986. *Career:* Du Pont (UK) Ltd, Company Sec & UK Legal Adviser 1984-86; Samuel Montagu & Co Ltd, Sole Legal Adviser 1982-84; Citibank NA, Legal Adviser 1978-82; Barrister at Law 1976-78. *Biog:* b. 5 December 1954. *Nationality:* British. *m.* 1986, A W Ames. 1 steps; 1 stepd. *Educ:* Whitley Bay Grammar School; St Anne's College, Oxford (MA Hons Jurisprudence). *Directorships:* Samuel Montagu 1988 (exec); Midland Montagu 1988 (exec). *Other Activities:* Chairman, Steering Committee of Banks Involved in Local Authority Swaps. *Professional Organisations:* Barrister-at-Law. *Recreations:* Golf, Theatre, Reading (Reading Somewhat Better Than Golf).

DOUBTFIRE, Graham; Deputy General Manager, Bank Leumi (UK) plc, since 1985; All Credit-Driven Functions Within the Bank. *Career:* First National Bank of Chicago, Vice President, Manager of Various Offices of The Bank in USA and Far East 1978-85; Asst Vice President, Unit Head Based in London, Responsible for Business Development 1974-78; Barclays Bank Ltd, Various 1962-74. *Biog:* b. 12 February 1944. *Nationality:* British. *m.* 1965, Diane; 1 s; 1 d. *Educ:* Belmont County. *Other Activities:* Treasurer, 3 Committees. *Professional Organisations:* Associate, Chartered Institute of Bankers (ACIB). *Recreations:* Tennis, Music.

DOUGHTY, G E J A; Director, Berry Palmer & Lyle Ltd.

DOUGHTY, Nigel Edward; Chief Executive, CWB Capital Partners Ltd, since 1989; Unquoted Equity Investment/Corporate Finance. *Career:* American Express, New York 1980-83. *Biog: b.* 10 June 1957. *Nationality:* British. *m.* 1985, Carol (née Green); 1 d. *Educ:* Thomas Magnus; Cranfield School of Management (MBA). *Directorships:* BPCC Ltd 1988 (non-exec); London Clubs International Ltd 1989 (non-exec); Chartered WestLB Ltd 1990 (non-exec).

DOUGLAS, Alasdair Ferguson; Partner, Travers Smith Braithwaite, since 1985; Corporate Tax. *Career:* Shepherd & Wedderburn WS, Apprentice Solicitor 1975-77; Freshfields, Assistant Solicitor 1977-84. *Biog: b.* 16 March 1953. *Nationality:* British. *m.* 1981, K V C Kennard; 1 s; 1 d. *Educ:* Perth Academy; Edinburgh University (LL B Hons); Queen Mary College, London University (LL M). *Other Activities:* City of London Solicitors Company. *Professional Organisations:* Law Society of Scotland; Law Society of England and Wales. *Publications:* Contributor to Tolley's Company Law; Tolley's Tax Planning. *Recreations:* Reading, Gardening.

DOUGLAS, G W; Director (UK USM), Hoare Govett Investment Research Limited.

DOUGLAS, M R; Company Secretary & Financial Controller, Rutland Trust plc, since 1987; Group Financial Controls and Reporting, Company Secretarial Administration. *Career:* Deloitte Haskins & Sells, Audit Senior 1971-77; BOC Limited (BOC International), Management Accountant 1977-80; Thebarden Corporation (UK) Ltd, Financial Director & Co Sec 1980-84; MTL Microtesting Ltd (Cambridge Electronic Industries plc), Financial Director 1984-86; Rutland Trust plc, Co Sec & Financial Controller 1987-. *Biog: b.* 16 October 1949. *Nationality:* British. *m.* 1977, Susan (née Duffield); 1 s; 1 d. *Educ:* Uppingham School; Dundee University (BSc Electronics). *Directorships:* Various Subsidiaries of Rutland Trust plc. *Other Activities:* Member, Institute of Directors. *Professional Organisations:* Fellow, Institute of Chartered Accountants in England and Wales; Approved as Manager, The Securities Association. *Recreations:* Squash, Swimming, Sailing, Jogging, Family Pursuits.

DOUGLAS, P R; Group General Manager-Britain, Allied Irish Banks plc, since 1989; Chief Executive of AIB Group in Britain. *Career:* AIB Group, Dublin Ireland, Group General Manager, Treasury 1986-89; General Manager, Treasury Management & Intl Development 1983-86; Head of Foreign Exchange 1978-83; Allied Irish Investment Bank, Dublin, Manager, Moneydesk 1974-78; Central Bank of Ireland, Dublin 1964-74. *Biog: b.* 3 June 1944. *Nationality:* Irish. *m.* 1967, Anna O'Daly; 2 s; 2 d. *Educ:* University College, Dublin (Batchelor of Commerce and Master of Business Studies). *Directorships:* AIB Bank (CI) Ltd (non-exec); AIB Fund Managers (CI) Ltd (non-exec); AIB Capital Markets plc (non-exec); AIB Holdings (UK) Ltd (non-exec); Allied Irish Banks North America Inc (non-exec); Allied Irish Australia Ltd (non-exec). *Professional Organisations:* Alumnus, Harvard International Business School (1984). *Clubs:* Howth Golf Club. *Recreations:* Golf, Squash, Theatre.

DOUGLAS-HOME, The Hon David Alexander Cospatrick; Director, Morgan Grenfell & Co Limited, since 1974. *Career:* Morgan Grenfell & Co Ltd 1966; Seconded to Morgan Guaranty Trust Company of New York 1968; Morgan Grenfell International Limited, Director, Started the Export Finance Department 1972; Morgan Grenfell & Co Ltd, Director 1974; Board of Morgan Grenfell (Asia) Limited, responsible for International Geographical Divisions of the Bank 1979; The Agricultural Mortgage Corporation, Director by Government Appointment 1980; Morgan Grenfell & Co Limited, Head of International Division 1983; Morgan Grenfell (Scotland) Limited, Chairman; COMET (Committee for Middle East Trade), Chairman 1986; Morgan Grenfell International Limited, Chairman 1987; Group Director 1988; Morgan Grenfell Asia Holdings Pte Ltd & Morgan Grenfell (Hong Kong) Limited, Director; Projects Committee ECGD, Member; Offshore Industry Export Advisory Group, Member 1989; Morgan Grenfell Thai Company Limited, Director 1990. *Biog: b.* 20 November 1943. *Nationality:* British. *m.* 1972, Jane; 1 s; 2 d. *Educ:* Eton College, Windsor; Christ Church, Oxford (MA). *Directorships:* Morgan Grenfell (Scotland) Limited Chairman; Morgan Grenfell International Limited Chairman; Committee for Middle East Trade Chairman; Morgan Grenfell (Hong Kong) Limited; Morgan Grenfell Asia Holdings Pte Ltd; Morgan Grenfell Thai Company Limited; The Agricultural Mortgage Corporation plc; EFG plc; Morgan Grenfell Export Services Limited Chairman; Credit for Exports plc. *Other Activities:* Douglas and Angus Estates; Governor and Member of the Council of Management, The Ditchley Foundation; Export Guarantee Advisory Council Member and Member of Country and Finance Committee & Projects Committee, ECGD; Member of the Board of Governors, Commonwealth Institute; Member, Offshore Industry Export Advisory Group. *Clubs:* Turf Club. *Recreations:* Outdoor Sports.

DOUGLAS-HOME, Simon; Director, Kleinwort Benson Securities Ltd, since 1986; Institutional Equity Sales. *Career:* Cooper Brothers 1967-72; Joseph Sebag & Co, Ptnr 1972-79; Carr Sebag & Co, Ptnr 1979-82; Grieveson Grant & Co, Ptnr 1982-86. *Biog: b.* 20 August 1947. *Nationality:* British. *m.* 1971, Sally Ann (née Beard); 1 s; 2 d. *Educ:* Eton College. *Professional Organisations:* MICA. *Clubs:* MCC. *Recreations:* Fishing, Gardening, Photography.

DOUGLAS-MANN, Stewart Charles Hamilton; Managing Director, Primary Markets Division, London Stock Exchange, since 1987. *Career:* Herbert

Oppenheimer Nathan & Vandyk Solicitors, Partner 1969-72; Simon & Coates Stockbrokers, Head of Corporate Finance 1972-78; Charterhouse Bank (formely Charterhouse Japhet), Director, Corporate Finance 1978-84; Hoare Govett Ltd, Managing Director, Corporate Finance Division 1984-87. *Biog: b.* 6 February 1938. *Nationality:* British. *m.* 1965, Angela (née Sykes); 2 s. *Educ:* Westminster School; St Edmund Hall, Oxford (BA Jurisprudence). *Other Activities:* Chairman, Multinational Offers Working Party established by International Organisation of Securities Commissions. *Professional Organisations:* Solicitor. *Clubs:* Leander Club, City of London.

DOVE, Anthony Charles; Partner, Simmons & Simmons, since 1973; Corporate Finance. *Biog: b.* 22 July 1945. *Nationality:* British. *m.* 1974, Susan Elizabeth (née Cant); 3 d. *Educ:* Rugby; St John's, Cambridge (MA). *Recreations:* Music, Physical Fitness.

DOWDALL, M; Director, Unilever plc.

DOWDY, M J; Finance Director, George Wimpey plc.

DOWLEY, Laurence Justin; Director, Morgan Grenfell & Co Ltd, since 1988; Corporate Finance. *Career:* Price Waterhouse, Articled Clerk 1977-80. *Biog: b.* 9 June 1955. *Nationality:* British. *m.* 1986, Emma (née Lampard); 1 s; 1 d. *Educ:* Ampleforth; Balliol, Oxford (MA). *Directorships:* Filmtrax 1989 (non-exec). *Other Activities:* Governor of St Francis School, London. *Professional Organisations:* ACA. *Clubs:* Royal West Norfolk GC, MCC, Boodles. *Recreations:* Fishing, Shooting, Cricket.

DOWLING, C B; Director, Rutland Trust plc, since 1987; Head of Corporate Finance. *Career:* Deloitte Haskins & Sells 1974-79; Barclays Australia Ltd 1979-83; Barclays Merchant Bank, BZW, Director 1983-87. *Biog: b.* 15 May 1953. *Nationality:* Australian. *m.* 1982, Shelley; 2 s; 1 d. *Educ:* Marlborough College; University of Exeter (BA). *Directorships:* Rutland Trust 1987 (exec). *Professional Organisations:* ACA. *Clubs:* Royal Wimbledon GC. *Recreations:* Golf, Skiing, Fishing, Bridge.

DOWLING, Joseph J; London Correspondent, Australian Financial Review.

DOWMAN, Robert Fleming; Director, Head of Trading, Mitsubishi Finance International plc, since 1990, Fixed/Variable Rate Government Bonds & Eurobonds, Medium Term Notes & Money Market Instruments. *Career:* Morgan Guaranty Trust, London 1971-79; Chemical Bank International, London 1979-84; Mitsubishi Finance International plc, London 1984-. *Biog: b.* 7 November 1955. *Nationality:* British. *m.* 1981, Maxine Vivien. *Educ:* Suttons Secondary Modern. *Clubs:* British Dressage Supporters. *Recreations:* Horse Riding.

DOWN, Ashley Gordon; Director, M & G Group plc; Merchant Banking, Corporate Finance. *Career:* Brisbane Stock Exchange, Sec 1957-67; White Weld Inc (New York), Associate, Investment Banking 1967-69; James Capel & Co, Ptnr, Head of Corp Fin 1969-84; Prudential Bache Capital Funding, Chairman 1984-90. *Biog: b.* 17 November 1938. *Nationality:* Australian. *m.* 1984, Christine (née McRoberts); 1 s; 1 d. *Educ:* Brisbane Boys' College; University of Queensland (BEcon); Harvard Business School. *Directorships:* M&G Group plc 1979; Folkestone Australia Ltd 1980; British Real Estate Group plc 1990. *Other Activities:* Treasurer, Esmee Fairbarn Charitable Trust. *Professional Organisations:* Member, The International Stock Exchange. *Clubs:* Brooks's, City of London, Australian, Tattersals, Brisbane, MCC. *Recreations:* Country Sports.

DOWN, Michael K; Partner, Moores Rowland, since 1960; Executive Director of Moores Rowland International. *Career:* Edward Moore & Sons, Articled Clerk 1950-55; Qualified 1955-60; Ptnr 1960-74; Joint Managing Ptnr 1974-80. *Biog: b.* 4 February 1930. *m.* 1956, Barbara (née West); 1 s; 2 d. *Educ:* Sevenoaks School. *Other Activities:* Worshipful Company of Glovers of London (Charity Officer); Trustee, The Across Trust. *Professional Organisations:* FCA; MBIM; FInstD. *Recreations:* Travel, Country Life, Local Politics.

DOWN, R F; Director, Capel-Cure Myers Capital Management Ltd.

DOWNER, Nicholas James Anthony; Director, International Equity Origination & Syndication, County NatWest Securities Limited, since 1990. *Career:* Orion Royal Bank, US Marketing Manager 1981-86; Hill Samuel & Co Ltd, Assistant Director, US Marketing 1986-88. *Biog: b.* 2 March 1956. *Nationality:* British. *m.* 1983, Francoise; 2 d. *Educ:* Downing College, Cambridge (MA Modern Languages).

DOWNES, Justin; Chief Executive & Director, Financial Dynamics Limited. *Other Activities:* Member, Family Holidays Associate Committee.

DOWNEY, Sir Gordon Stanley; KCB; Chairman, Financial Intermediaries, Managers and Brokers Regulatory Association, since 1990. *Career:* H M Treasury 1952-78; Deputy Head, Central Policy Review Staff, Cabinet Office 1978-81; Comptroller and Auditor General 1981-87; Ernst and Young, Special Advisor 1988-90; The Securities Association, Complaints Commissioner 1989-90; The Independent, Readers' Representative 1990-. *Biog: b.* 26 April 1928. *Nationality:* British. *m.* 1952, Jacqueline; 2 d. *Educ:* Tiffins School; London School of Economics (BSc Econ). *Other Activities:* Chairman, Kings College School of Medicine and Dentistry; Member, Takeover Panel. *Clubs:* Army and Navy. *Recreations:* Reading, Visual Arts, Tennis.

DOWNHILL, Ronald Edward; Head of Tax & Trust Department, Berwin Leighton, since 1983; Tax & Trusts. *Career:* Inland Revenue, Latterly Lawyer in Dept's Solicitor's Office 1960-74; Berwin Leighton, Latterly Partner 1974-77; Self-Employed Taxation Consultancy 1977-82; Berwin Leighton, Partner 1982-. *Biog: b.* 11 August 1943. *Nationality:* British. *m.* 1969, Olwen Elizabeth (née Siddle); 3 d. *Educ:* Hyde County Grammar School. *Other Activities:* Member, Revenue Law Committee of Law Society; Consultant Editor of Tax Cases Analysis. *Professional Organisations:* Member, The Law Society; ATII. *Recreations:* Walking, Reading, Watching Soccer, Model Railways.

DOWNING, James B; Managing Director, Wasserstein Perella & Co, since 1989; Co-Director, Wasserstein Perella & Co International Ltd, Corporate Finance, Mergers & Acquisitions. *Career:* The First Boston Corp/Credit Suisse First Boston, Director, European Mergers and Acquisitions 1982-89; Manufacturers Hanover Trust Co, New York, Assistant Vice President, International Banking Division, South East Asia & Middle East 1976-80. *Biog: b.* 22 April 1954. *Nationality:* American. *m.* 1981, Elizabeth A; 2 s; 1 d. *Educ:* Rensselaen Polytechnic Institute (BSc Management); Yale University School of Management (MPPM). *Directorships:* Old Bond Street Corporation 1990 (non-exec). *Clubs:* Vanderbilt Tennis Club.

DOWNING, John Cottrill Ralph; DL; Senior Director, Lyddon Stockbrokers (National Investment Group plc), since 1986; Institutional & Private Client Stockbroker. *Biog: b.* 22 May 1931. *Nationality:* British. *m.* 1959, Maureen (née Webb); 2 d. *Educ:* Felsted; Pembroke, Cambridge (MA). *Directorships:* Cardiff Exchange & Office Ltd 1967 (non-exec); Glamorgan Investments Ltd 1967 (non-exec); Cathays Cottage Co Ltd 1967 (non-exec); Barry Island Cottage Co Ltd 1967 (non-exec); Letmart Properties Ltd 1967 (non-exec). *Other Activities:* Investment Committee, Representative Body of Church in Wales. *Clubs:* Brooks's, Cardiff & County, Royal Porthcawl, I Zingari. *Recreations:* Gardening, Golf.

DOWNING, Nicholas; Partner, Clifford Chance, since 1970; Corporate & Commercial Litigation. *Biog: b.* 19 March 1947. *Nationality:* British. *m.* 1971, Suzanne Mary (née Rees); 1 d. *Educ:* Berkhamsted School; University of Essex (BA Hons). *Other Activities:* Liveryman, City of London Solicitors' Company. *Professional Organisations:* Solicitor, Member, Law Society. *Publications:* The Commercial Laws of the United Arab Emirates, 1986. *Recreations:* Riding, Sailing, Scuba Diving, Skiing.

DOWNS, W N; Partner, Hammond Suddards, since 1989; Company & Commercial/Corporate Finance. *Career:* Linklaters & Paines, Articled Clerk 1980-82; Stones Porter & Co, Solicitor 1982-85; Downs Coulter & Co Ltd 1986-87; Hammond Suddards 1987-. *Biog: b.*

10 December 1956. *Nationality:* British. *m.* 1989, Catherine Alison (née Morphet). *Educ:* Bradford Grammar School; Downing College, Cambridge (MA Hons,Law). *Professional Organisations:* Law Society. *Clubs:* Craven Lawn Tennis Club. *Recreations:* Walking, The Countryside, Tennis, Reading.

DOWSE, Andrew J; Director, Merrill Lynch Pierce Fenner & Smith (Brokers & Dealers) Limited.

DOWSETT, Robert John; Director, Morgan Grenfell & Co Limited, since 1988; Corporate Finance. *Biog: b.* 2 February 1954. *Nationality:* British. *m.* 1987, Elizabeth (née Forsyth); 1 s. *Educ:* Rugby School; St Catherines College, Cambridge (MA). *Clubs:* Hadley Wood Golf Club.

DOWYER, A David; Partner, Clifford Chance, since 1968 (then Clifford-Turner); Private Client & Trust Law. *Career:* Clifford-Turner, Articled Clerk 1963. *Biog: b.* 27 August 1940. *Nationality:* British. *m.* Ann (née Beaumont); 2 s; 1 d. *Educ:* Tonbridge School; Trinity Hall, Cambridge (BA Law). *Professional Organisations:* Law Society; International Academy of Estate & Trust Law (USA). *Clubs:* Boodles. *Recreations:* Golf, Tennis, Skiing.

DOYE, P F; Director, Charterhouse Bank Limited.

DOYLE, Julian John; Partner, Gouldens (London & Brussels), since 1989; International/EC Law. *Career:* Private Practice 1965-71; BP Australia, Legal Officer 1963; Arthur Robinson & Co, Law Clerk 1958-62; MLA (Lib), Gisborne Victoria 1967-71; Trade Commissioner, London 1972-73; Couns, Australian Mission to European Communities, Brussels 1973-75; Senior Trade Commissioner Nairobi 1975-76; Ellison Hewison & Whitehead, Melbourne, Partner 1976-77; Spencer Stuart & Assts, London, Consultant 1977-79; ICOSI, Brussels, Sec Gen 1979-81; Victoria Economic Development Corp, MD 1981-83; Sirotech Ltd, MD 1984-88. *Biog: b.* 26 July 1955. *Nationality:* Australian. 1989, Sally Anne (née Dawes); 2 s; 2 d (from previous marriage). *Educ:* Xavier College, Melbourne; University of California, Berkeley; Melbourne University (LLB). *Other Activities:* Member, Commonwealth Party Association Australia and UK Institute of Directors; Law Institute of Victoria; Law Society of England; Member, Law Cl of Australia; Member, International Trade Law Committee; Member, Australian Club, Melbourne; City Councillor, Prahan. *Recreations:* Music, Surfing.

DOYLE, Ms Noreen; Managing Director, Structured Sales-Europe, Bankers Trust Company, since 1990; Structured Sales/Syndication of Senior Debt, Subordinated Debt, Equity. *Career:* Bankers Trust Company (NY), U S Banking Department 1974-80; (Houston), Energy Finance Group 1980-83; (NY) Energy Finance, Division Manager 1983-86; (NY) Structured Sales,

Senior Product Manager 1986-90. *Biog: b.* 5 May 1949. *Nationality:* American. *Educ:* College of Mount St Vincent (BA Mathemmatics); Amos Tuck School of Business Admin, Dartmouth College (MBA Finance). *Other Activities:* Member, Board of Overseas, Amos Tuck School of Business Administration, Dartmouth College, Hanover, New Hampshire, 1989. *Professional Organisations:* Member, Financial Womens Association of New York. *Recreations:* Travel, Theatre, Golf.

DOYLE, Thomas J; Managing Director (Investment Management), Merrill Lynch International Limited.

DRAGIC, John D; Senior Director, Continental Bank NA, since 1988; Property Finance and Investment. *Career:* Continental Bank NA (Chicago, Illinois), Real Estate Department, Vice President and Manager of a Commercial Real Estate Lending Group & Member of Real Estate Loan Committee; Inland Steel Company (Chicago, Illinois), Internal Consultant in Materials Management Area 1980; Schlumberger Limited (Western Components Division, Archbald, Pa), Member of Electronics Procurement Department 1978-79. *Biog: b.* 21 January 1957. *Nationality:* American. *m.* 1982, Linda; 1 s. *Educ:* Northwestern University; Kellogg Graduate School of Management (MBA); Bloomsburg University (BSc). *Directorships:* Fort Dearborn Property Company 1988 (exec). *Professional Organisations:* International Real Estate Institute. *Recreations:* Golf, Basketball, Chicago Blues Music.

DRAKE, William Eric; Director, Granville & Co Ltd, since 1985; Head of Securities. *Career:* Webster & Sheffield, Lawyer 1975-79; Kleinwort Benson Ltd, Fin Exec 1979-81. *Biog: b.* 16 December 1953. *Nationality:* British. *m.* 1982, Henrietta Sara (née Scott); 1 s; 1 d. *Educ:* Eton College; Pembroke College, Cambridge, (MA Law). *Directorships:* Granville Davies Coleman Ltd 1985 (exec); The Colville Estate 1986 (non-exec); Bray Technologies plc 1986 (non-exec); CCL Group plc. *Other Activities:* Member of the Livery, the Merchant Taylors Company. *Professional Organisations:* Barrister-at-Law, Middle Temple. *Clubs:* Queen's Club. *Recreations:* Various.

DRAPER, A J; General Manager, Bristol & West Building Society.

DRAYTON, Patrick; Director, J Henry Schroder Wagg & Co Ltd.

DRESNER, R M; Director, LPH Group plc.

DRESSEL, W; General Manager, Bank für Gemeinwirtschaft.

DREW, P R L; OBE; Chairman, Taylor Woodrow plc.

DREW, Rodney; Director, 3i plc.

DREWITT, John; Partner (Private Clients), Frere Cholmeley.

DRIFFIELD, John Bentley; Partner, McKenna & Co, since 1976; Head of Property. *Career:* Morrish & Co, Leeds, Articled Clerk 1955-60; Army Legal Services, Staff List 1960-65; Lomer & Co, Partner 1965-74; McKenna & Co, Assistant Solicitor 1974-76. *Biog: b.* 19 August 1937. *Nationality:* British. *m.* Yvonne; 3 s. *Educ:* Leeds Grammar School; Leeds University (LLB).

DRITZ, M A; Director, Smith New Court plc.

DROWN, Peter; Partner, Beavis Walker.

DRUCE, M; Board Director, Ogilvy Adams & Rinehart, since 1985. *Career:* Bastable Dailey, Creative Director 1980-85; SSCTB Lontas, Creative Director 1972-79; BBDO, Senior Writer 1969-72. *Biog: b.* 17 July 1945. *Nationality:* British. *m.* 1970, Carol(née Williams); 1 s; 1 d. *Directorships:* Ogilvy & Mather 1985. *Professional Organisations:* AMIPA, MIPA. *Publications:* Various Articles; Daily Telegraph Young Writer of the Year (1970).

DRUMM, D; Senior Vice President & UK Branch Manager, Gulf International Bank BSC.

DRUMMON, A Howard; Partner, Keith Bayley Rogers & Co; Corporate Finance. *Educ:* Aberdeen Grammar School. *Clubs:* Thunderers, The Carlton.

DRUMMOND, Mrs Caroline S; Partner, W & J Burness WS, since 1987; Commercial Property. *Career:* W & J Burness WS 1981-. *Biog: b.* 30 May 1959. *Nationality:* Scottish. *m.* 1982, William Drummond. *Educ:* Tain Royal Academy; Aberdeen University (LLB); Edinburgh University (DIP,LP). *Professional Organisations:* Law Society of Scotland; WS Society. *Clubs:* North Berwick Golf Club, Highland Club. *Recreations:* Climbing, Skiing, Golf, Fishing.

DRUMMOND, Robert Malcolm; Managing Director, Grosvenor Venture Managers Ltd, since 1990; Venture Capital. *Career:* Spicer and Oppenheim, Accountants, Senior 1966-70; 3i plc, Venture Capital, Regional Director 1972-84; Alta Berkeley Associates Ltd, Venture Capital, Director 1984-85; County NatWest Ventures Ltd, Venture Capital, Managing Director 1985-89; Electra Kingsway Ltd, Venture Capital, Vice Chairman 1989-90. *Biog: b.* 3 June 1945. *Nationality:* British. *m.* 1981, Lorraine (née Amys); 1 d. *Educ:* Rugby School, University of St Andrews (LLB); Manchester Business School (MBA). *Directorships:* Grosvenor Development Capital plc 1990 (exec); Southnews plc 1986 (non-exec). *Other Activities:* Worshipful Company of Wheelwrights. *Professional Organisations:* FCA. *Recreations:* Tennis, Sailing, Ski, Golf.

DRURY, C E H; Director, County NatWest Limited, since 1987; Shipping & Oil Services. *Career:* Greig Middleton & Co Ltd, Director, Head of Inst Sales 1985-87; Independent World Trade Consultant 1983-85; Bulk Transport Ltd (Hamilton, Bermuda), Founder Director 1983-84; Micro Marine Ltd, Marketing Director (Shipping Software) 1980-83; W N Middleton & Co, Partner 1978-80; Independent World Trade, Consultant 1975-78; Charles W Jones & Co, Partner 1969-75; Hambros Bank Ltd, Consultant 1967-69; Kilchrenan Trading Post & Sub-Post Office, Proprietor 1965-67; W Greenwell & Co, Transfer Clerk, Investment Analyst, Institutional Salesman 1961-65. *Biog: b.* 2 March 1941. *Nationality:* British. *m.* 1983, Sarah Jane (née Gofton-Salmond); 1 s; 1 d. *Educ:* Blundell's School, Tiverton, Devon. *Directorships:* Bulk Transport Ltd 1983-84 (non-exec); County NatWest Ltd 1987 (exec). *Professional Organisations:* Member, The Society of Technical Analysts. *Publications:* Ship Finance - The Credit Crisis, Co-Author, 1983. *Recreations:* Work, Hunting, Shooting, Wife, Fishing, Children, Norway, Lech & Tarr Steps Hotel.

DRURY, John Victor; Partner, Neville Russell, since 1963; Personal Taxation. *Career:* Sharp Parsons & Co 1948-50; RAF 1950-53; Sharp Parsons & Co 1953-63. *Biog: b.* 20 August 1932. *Nationality:* British. *m.* 1958, Valerie-Siddons (née Webb); 2 s; 2 d. *Educ:* Royal Grammar School, High Wycombe. *Other Activities:* Freedom of the City of London; The Worshipful Company of Plumbers. *Professional Organisations:* FCA. *Clubs:* RAC. *Recreations:* Walking, Swimming.

DRURY, Stephen Patrick; Partner, Holman Fenwick & Willan, since 1985; Company Commercial Law, Banking, Ship and Project Finance. *Biog: b.* 20 May 1954. *Nationality:* British. *m.* 1983, Deborah Ann (née Swain); 1 s; 1 d. *Educ:* Charterhouse; Oriel College, Oxford (MA). *Other Activities:* Liveryman, Merchant Taylors Company. *Professional Organisations:* Law Society of England & Wales; Law Society of Hong Kong. *Publications:* The Arrest of Ships - Hong Kong, 1987. *Clubs:* Kingston Rowing, Royal Hong Kong Yacht. *Recreations:* Rowing.

DRYER, J F; Director, Hambros Bank Limited.

DRYSDALE, A P A; Partner, Cazenove & Co.

DRYSDALE, John Duncan; Director, Robert Fleming Holdings Ltd, since 1981; Marketing, Robert Fleming Insurance Brokers, Gulf Region. *Career:* Robert Fleming, Various 1966-. *Biog: b.* 28 April 1936. *Nationality:* British. *m.* 1962, Gay (née Daldy); 2 s; 1 d. *Educ:* Rugby School; Brasenose College, Oxford (BA). *Direc-*

torships: Ifabanque 1986 Vice Chm. *Professional Organisations:* CA. *Clubs:* Boodle's. *Recreations:* Music, Travel.

DRYSDALE, Thomas H; WS; Managing Partner, Shepherd & Wedderburn WS, since 1988; Commercial Property. *Career:* Shepherd & Wedderburn WS, Ptnr 1967-. *Biog: b.* 23 November 1942. *m.* 1967, Caroline (née Shaw); 1 s; 2 d. *Educ:* Glenalmond, Edinburgh University (LLB). *Professional Organisations:* Writer to the Signet. *Clubs:* New (Edinburgh). *Recreations:* Skiing, Golf, Walking.

DU CANN, The Rt Hon Sir Edward Dillon Lott; KBE; Chairman, Lonrho plc, since 1984; Director, since 1972. *Career:* MP (Con) for Taunton 1956-87; Econ Sec to Treasury 1962-63; Minister of State, Board of Trade 1963-64; Privy Councillor 1964; Chm, Conservative Party Organisation 1965-67; Chm, Select Committee on Public Expenditure 1971-73; Chm, Select Committee on Public Accounts 1974-79; Chm, Select Committee on Treasury & Civil Service Affairs 1979-83; Chm, Liaison Committee of Select Committee Chairmen 1974-83; Chm, 1922 Committee 1972-84; Member, Committee of Privileges 1974-87; Chm, Public Accounts Commission 1984-87; Chm, All Party Maritime Affairs Party Group 1984-87; Pres, Conservative Party EC Reform Group 1985-87. *Biog: b.* 28 May 1924. *Nationality:* British. *m.* 1990, Jenifer Patricia Evely (née King); 1 s; 2 d. *Educ:* Colet Court; Woodbridge School; St John's College, Oxford (MA Law). *Directorships:* Taunton Racecourse Company; Mayflower Management Co Ltd; Unicorn Group 1957-62 & 1964-72 Chm; Keyser Ullmann 1972-75 Chm; Cannon Assurance 1972-80 Chm; James Beattie 1965-79; Martins Bank 1967-69; London Bd, Barclays Bank 1969-72. *Other Activities:* Worshipful Company of Fruiterers, Hon Assistant, 1972-74; Renter Warden, 1988; Upper Warden, 1989; Master, 1990; Governor, Hatfield College, Durham University; Patron, Human Ecology Foundation, 1987-; FRSA, 1986; Trustee, Sasakawa Great Britain Foundation. *Professional Organisations:* Hon Life Member, RCT; Freeman, Taunton Deane, 1977; Patron, Association of Insurance Brokers; BIIBA (VP 1978). *Publications:* Investing Simplified, 1959; Control of Public Expenditure, 1977; New Competition Policy, 1984; Time to Hoist Red Ensign, 1986. *Clubs:* Carlton, Pratts, Royal Thames YC, Royal Western YC of England. *Recreations:* Travel, Gardening, Sailing.

DU PARC BRAHAM, Donald Samuel; Chairman and Managing Director, London and Exmoor Estates Ltd Group of Companies, since 1984; Property Development. *Career:* National Service 1947-50; Edward Erdman and Company, Surveyors, Auctioneers, Valuers 1950-84; Partner 1960-; Early Retirement as a Senior Partner to Found Own Group of Property Development Companies 1985; London and Exmoor Estates Ltd Group of Companies 1985-. *Biog: b.* 29 June 1930. *Nationality:* British. *m1* 1955, Tanis; *m2* 1987, Susan; 2

s; 2 d. *Educ:* Hendon Grammar School. *Directorships:* Brent Hi-Tech Industrial Park Ltd (exec); London and Exmoor Estates Ltd (exec); Highline Properties Ltd (exec); Church Row Properties Ltd (non-exec); Bishopsgate Market Fish Restaurants Ltd (exec); Highambury House Ltd (exec); Priory Properties Ltd (exec); Omenport Developments plc (non-exec); Caird Group plc 1986-89 (non-exec). *Other Activities:* Nepalese Order of Gorkha Dakshina Bahu; Past Master, Guild of Freemen of City of London, 1989; Upper Warden, Worshipful Company of Horners, 1990; Member, Westminster City Council, 1971-85; Lord Mayor of Westminster, 1981; Member, National River Authority (Flood Defence Committee), 1988-; Chairman, Westminster North Conservative Association, 1983-86; President, Westminster North Conservative Association, 1990-; Chairman, London Central European Constituency Council, 1985-; Member of Council, Christians and Jews; Member of Council, Anglo-Jewish Association; Vice Chairman, Community Charge and Rating Appeal Tribunal for Central London; Vice-Chairman, Westminster Outward Bound Committee, 1985-; Member of Council, Management of Parkinsons Disease Society of UK, 1980-; Chairman, Parkinson Disease Society of UK, 1990-. *Professional Organisations:* FRGS; IRRV; FZS; ACIArb. *Clubs:* MCC, Carlton, City Livery, Farringdon Ward Club, Tower Ward Club, Union Society of Westminster, Past Overseers Society. *Recreations:* Shooting, Gilbert and Sullivan, Reading Biographies.

DUBOIS, Roger L; Managing Director, J P Morgan Investment Management Inc, since 1987; Administration, Finance, Operations and Systems. *Career:* Bankers Trust, Snr Vice President, Pension Assets and Financial Services 1981-87; Chase Manhattan, Snr Vice President, Master Trust and Global Securities Services 1968-81; Studebaker-Worthington Inc, Director, Employee Relations 1966-68; Ford Motor Co, Manager, Labour Relations 1959-66. *Biog: b.* 26 September 1931. *Nationality:* American. *m.* 1958, Ruth (née Lennox); 2 s; 2 d. *Educ:* Business School, Harvard (Advanced Management Programme); Wharton Graduate, Pennsylvania (MBA Industry); West Liberty College (BA History). *Clubs:* RAC.

DUBOSE, Frank Elsivan; Executive Director, Goldman Sachs International Limited, since 1982; Corporate Finance. *Career:* National Bank of North Carolina, VP & Gen Mgr 1969-78; First Dallas Ltd, MD 1978-82. *Biog: b.* 24 February 1943. *Nationality:* American; 1 s; 1 d. *Educ:* Stanford Business School (MBA); Davidson College (BA).

DUCHIN, J M; Director, Kleinwort Benson Gilts Limited.

DUCKETT, John; Director, Kleinwort Benson Gilts Limited, since 1987; Gilt-Edged Sales. *Career:* Grieveson

Grant & Co, Ptnr 1978-86. *Biog: b.* 23 June 1947. *m.* 1982, Dagny (née Bain); 2 s. *Educ:* Hardye's School, Dorchester. *Clubs:* Royal Wimbledon Golf Club. *Recreations:* Golf, Skiing.

DUCKWORTH, David J; Partner, Walker Morris Scott Turnbull, since 1974; Commercial Property.

DUCKWORTH, John; Partner, Turner Kenneth Brown, since 1966; Corporate and Commercial Law. *Biog: b.* 27 October 1931. *Nationality:* British. *Educ:* Sedbergh School; Downing College, Cambridge (MA). *Professional Organisations:* Law Society.

DUDERSTADT, Stefan M; General Manager, Dresdner Bank AG.

DUDLEY, Michael; Group Finance Director, Prudential Property Services Ltd, since 1988; Finance, Admin, IT, Personnel, Premises. *Career:* Esselte Business Systems Ltd, Regional Controller 1980-84; Metal Box plc, Financial Controller UK Packaging Operations 1984-87; Metal Box Engineering, Finance Director 1987-88; PPS Ltd, Finance Director 1988-. *Biog: b.* 16 December 1949. *Nationality:* British. *m.* Anne. *Educ:* Truro School, Cornwall; Exeter College, Oxford (MA, BSc). *Directorships:* Prudential Property Services Ltd 1988 (exec). *Professional Organisations:* FCA. *Recreations:* Rowing, Squash, Running, Classical & Flamenco Guitar.

DUDLEY, R E; Partner, J K Shipton and Company.

DUDMAN, Gary Robert; Director, Kleinwort Grieveson Securities.

DUERDEN, Peter Frederick; Managing Director, Royal Insurance (UK) Ltd.

DUFF, J P J; Partner, Holman Fenwick & Willan.

DUFFICY, Frank; Partner, Cameron Markby Hewitt, since 1990; Building and Engineering Construction Law. *Career:* Linklaters & Paines London, Articled Clerk 1981-83; Solicitor 1983-89; Cameron Markby Hewitt, Partner 1990-. *Biog: b.* 11 June 1953. *Nationality:* British. *m.* 1989, Alison Louise (née Childs). *Educ:* North Carolina State University, USA (BA); City University, London (Dip LL). *Other Activities:* City of London Solicitors Company; Law Society. *Professional Organisations:* Solicitor of The Supreme Court of England and Wales, 1983. *Clubs:* Acrobatic. *Recreations:* Diving, Sailing, Skiing.

DUFFIELD, D; General Manager, Group Personnel, National Westminster Bank plc.

DUFFIELD, Peter William John; Partner, Travers Smith Braithwaite, since 1966; Private Clients, Trust Law & Tax Planning. *Biog: b.* 30 April 1935. *Nationality:*

British. *m.* 1958, Diana (née Miller); 1 s; 1 d. *Educ:* Bancroft's School; St John's College, Oxford (MA). *Directorships:* C E Heath plc 1985 (non-exec). *Other Activities:* The Worshipful Company of Wheelwrights. *Professional Organisations:* The Law Society. *Clubs:* City of London, City Livery, Flyfishers. *Recreations:* Fishing.

DUFFIELD, Stephen Leslie; Partner, Evershed Wells & Hind, since 1983; Commercial Law. *Biog:* b. 17 June 1951. *Nationality:* British. *m.* 1979, Jenny (née Chapman). *Educ:* Solihull School; Queens' College, Cambridge (MA). *Professional Organisations:* The Law Society. *Clubs:* Royal Torbay Yacht Club. *Recreations:* Water Skiing.

DUFFY, David; Managing Director (Investment Management), Ogilvy Adams & Rinehart.

DUFFY, Derek J; Partner, Walker Morris Scott Turnbull.

DUFFY, Donald Eugene; Finance Director, Prudential Bache Capital Funding (Equities) Ltd.

DUFFY, John L; Director, Kleinwort Benson Securities Limited.

DUFFY, Michael John; Partner, Lawrence Graham (Solicitors), since 1979; Commercial Property. *Career:* Lawrence Graham 1964-. *Biog:* b. 19 June 1947. *Nationality:* British. *m.* 1972, Janet; 1 s; 1 d. *Educ:* Holloway School; College of Law (Solicitors Exams). *Directorships:* Institutional Property Investments Ltd 1983 (exec); Barton House Investments Ltd (non-exec). *Other Activities:* Liveryman, City of London Solicitors Company. *Professional Organisations:* Law Society; Solicitor. *Clubs:* City Livery Club.

DUFFY, P J; Director, Touche Remnant Investment Management Ltd. *Career:* Henry Ansbacher & Co (Merchant Bank), Investment Manager 1974-82; The Daily Telegraph, Financial Columnist (Founder Member of the Questor Column) 1968-74; The Economist Intelligence Unit, Economic Research Project Manager 1966-68; James Capel & Co (London Stockbroker), Investment Analyst 1963-66; London School of Economics 1960-63; Stewart & Lloyds (now part of British Steel Corporation), PA to Export Director 1958-60. *Biog:* b. 1937. *m.* Married with 3 Children. *Educ:* Mill Hill, London; London University (BSc Hons Economics). *Directorships:* TR Property Services Ltd; County Hall Development Group plc; Eborgate Holdings plc; TR Property Finance Ltd; Touche Remnant Investment Trust Management Ltd -1988; Touche Remnant & Co -1988; Skillion Holdings Ltd -1990; Skillion plc -1990; Sibec Developments Ltd -1990. *Recreations:* Literature, Music, Art.

DUFFY, William; Director, International City Holdings.

DUGDALE, David John; Deputy Chairman & Joint Chief Executive, James Capel & Co Ltd, since 1990. *Career:* James Capel & Co 1968. *Biog:* b. 12 October 1942. *Nationality:* British. *m.* 1971, Susan (née Stewart); 1 s; 1 d. *Educ:* Wellington College. *Directorships:* Subsidiary Companies of James Capel & Co. *Professional Organisations:* FCA. *Clubs:* Boodle's. *Recreations:* Farming, Hunting.

DUGDALE, Peter Robin; CBE; Director, Guardian Royal Exchange plc, since 1984. *Career:* Union Insurance Society of Canton Mgr (India) 1957-59; Marine Mgr 1959-62; Reliance Marine Insurance Co Joint Underwriter 1962-65; Guardian Royal Exchange Assurance Chief Underwriter 1965-73; Guardian Insurance Co of Canada Pres 1973-76; Guardian Royal Exchange Assurance Gen Mgr (Overseas) 1976-78; Guardian Royal Exchange Assurance Limited/plc Managing Director 1978-90; Guardian Royal Exchange plc Managing Director 1984-90; British Insurance Association Deputy Chairman 1979-; British Insurance Association Chairman 1981-82; Trade Indemnity plc Chairman 1980-; Aviation & General Insurance Chairman 1982-84; Association of British Insurers Chairman 1987-89. *Biog:* b. 12 May 1928. *Nationality:* British. *m.* 1957, Esme Cyraine (née Norwood Brown); 3 s. *Educ:* Canford School, Wimborne; Magdalen College, Oxford (MA). *Directorships:* Trade Indemnity plc 1978 Chm (non-exec); Canford School Limited 1981 (non-exec); Guardian Assurance plc 1977 (non-exec); Guardian Royal Exchange Assurance plc 1977 (non-exec); Guardian Royal Exchange plc 1984 (non-exec); The Royal Exchange Assurance 1977 (non-exec); AHJ Investments Limited 1990 (non-exec). *Other Activities:* The Worshipful Master, Company of Insurers. *Professional Organisations:* Companion of The British Institute of Managers (CBIM). *Clubs:* Oriental. *Recreations:* Flat Coated Retrievers.

DUGGAN, A J; Director, Byas Mosley & Co Ltd.

DUGUID, Andrew Alexander; Head of Market Services, Lloyd's, since 1988. *Career:* Brunel University, Research Asst 1968-69; Interscan Ltd, Marketing Exec 1969-72; Ogilvy Benson & Mather, Marketing Exec 1972-73; Department of Industry, Principal 1973-79; Principal Private Sec to Sec of State 1977-79; Prime Minister's Policy Unit, Asst Sec 1979-82; DTI Asst Sec 1982-85; Under Sec 1985-86; Lloyd's Head of Regulatory Services 1986-88. *Biog:* b. 22 June 1944. *Nationality:* British. *m.* 1967, Janet Kathleen (née Hughes); 2 s; 1 d. *Educ:* Ashbury College, Ottawa; Sidcot School, Somerset; London School of Economics (BSc); University of Lancaster (MA). *Directorships:* Kingsway Public Relations 1982-85 (non-exec). *Publications:* Case Histories in Export Organisation (with Elliot Jaques), 1971. *Clubs:* Hartswood. *Recreations:* Skiing, Tennis, Walking.

DUMAS, H R; Director, A P Leslie Underwriting Agencies Limited.

DUNBAR, I; Executive Director (Managament Services), Eagle Star Insurance Company.

DUNCAN, Alan; Chairman, Newmarket Venture Capital plc.

DUNCAN, Frederick; Actuary, Sphere Drake Underwriting Management Ltd, since 1982. *Career:* Excess Insurance Group Ltd 1974-82. *Biog: b.* 8 August 1948. *Nationality:* Scottish. *m.* 1977, Maureen; 2 s; 1 d. *Educ:* University of Glasgow (BSc Hons). *Professional Organisations:* Fellow, Institute of Actuaries.

DUNCAN, G; Non-Executive Director, Laporte plc.

DUNCAN, Gordon Barclay; Director, Kleinwort Benson Limited, since 1990; Corporate Finance. *Career:* Price Waterhouse 1978-84; Morgan Grenfell 1984-87; Kleinwort Benson 1987-. *Biog: b.* 7 December 1956. *Nationality:* British. *Educ:* George Watsons College; Bristol University (BSc Hons). *Professional Organisations:* ACA 1981.

DUNCAN, Michael Greig; Partner, Allen & Overy, since 1987; Corporate Finance. *Career:* Allen & Overy Asst Solicitor 1981-86. *Biog: b.* 9 September 1957. *m.* 1983, Fiona Helen (née Glaze); 2 s; 1 d. *Educ:* King William's College, Isle of Man; Downing College, Cambridge (BA). *Professional Organisations:* City of London Law Society.

DUNCAN, Roger; Partner, Walker Martineau Stringer Saul.

DUNCAN, S; Manager, American Express Bank.

DUNCOMBE, Kenneth J; Senior General Manager, Royal Bank of Scotland, since 1989; UK Banking (England & Wales). *Career:* Williams Deacon's Bank, Various to Area Mgr 1959-75; Jt Head of Branch Dept 1976-82; Mgr 1982-84; Asst Gen Mgr 1984-86; Gen Mgr 1986-89. *Biog: b.* 28 February 1937. *Nationality:* British. *m.* 1960, Ann (née Sutton); 1 s; 1 d. *Professional Organisations:* FCIB. *Recreations:* Golf, Football, Reading, Gardening.

DUNDAS, James Frederick Trevor; Director, Morgan Grenfell & Co Limited, since 1987; Head of Corporate Banking Department and Deputy Head of Banking Division. *Career:* Morgan Grenfell, Banking Division 1972; Morgan Grenfell & Co Limited, Director 1981; Morgan Grenfell Australia Ltd (Sydney), Managing Director 1982-85; Morgan Grenfell Securities

Holdings Ltd, London, Director & Member of Management Committee 1985; Morgan Grenfell & Co Limited, Head of Corporate & International Banking 1987; Morgan Grenfell Group plc, Member, Management Committee 1989. *Biog: b.* 4 November 1950. *Nationality:* British. *m.* m 1979, Jennifer Ann; 1 s; 2 d. *Educ:* Eton College; New College, Oxford (BA Hons Jurisprudence); Inns of Court School of Law; Stanford University (Stanford Executive Program). *Directorships:* Governor of the Court, Polytechnic of Central London 1989 (non-exec); Member of the Board of Management, Cancer Relief Macmillan Fund 1990 (non-exec). *Professional Organisations:* Barrister, Inner Temple.

DUNDAS, Robert Alexander; Executive Director, GT Management plc, since 1984; International Investment (especially Japan). *Career:* Grieveson Grant & Co, Assistant 1970-73; Far East Portfolio Manager 1974-79; Associate Member 1978-79; GT Management (Asia) Ltd, Investment Manager 1980-84; Director 1980; GT Management Ltd (became plc in 1986), Director 1984. *Biog: b.* 12 June 1947. *Nationality:* British. *m.* 1977, Sarah Rosalind (née Wilson); 1 s; 1 d. *Educ:* Harrow School; Christ Church, Oxford (Scholar). *Directorships:* GT Japan Small Companies Fund 1980 (exec); GT Global Small Companies Fund 1987 (exec); GT Berry Japan Fund 1990 (exec). *Professional Organisations:* Member, The Stock Exchange (1978-80). *Clubs:* Boodles, Pratts, Puffins, The Argyllshire Gathering Assoc. *Recreations:* Scottish History, Art Objects, Shooting.

DUNDAS, Ronald; Business Editor, The Glasgow Herald.

DUNFORD, Neil Roy; Managing Director, Morgan Grenfell Investment Management, since 1986; UK Pension Fund Management. *Career:* J Henry Schroder Wagg Asst Dir 1972-81; Scottish Widows Fund Chief Invest Mgr 1981-85. *Biog: b.* 16 January 1947. *Nationality:* British. *m.* 1976, Gillian (née Buckmaster). *Educ:* Sedbergh School; St Andrews University (MA). *Directorships:* Morgan Grenfell Asset Management. *Professional Organisations:* CA.

DUNKERLEY, Christopher; Chief Executive, Dartington & Company, since 1989; Group Management. *Career:* WM Brandt & Sons Ltd, Graduate Trainee 1973-75; Orion Bank Ltd, Manager, Credit Dept 1975-76; Saudi Intl Bank, Ass General Manager, Corporate Finance Dept 1977-87; James Capel & Co, Senior Executive, Corporate Finance Dept 1987-89. *Biog: b.* 12 December 1951. *Nationality:* British. *m.* 1983, Kathleen Jane (née Hansen); 1 s; 1 d. *Educ:* Charterhouse School, Surrey; Pembroke College, Oxford (Exhibitioner MA PPE). *Directorships:* Dartington & Co Group plc (and other Group Subsidiaries) 1989 (exec); TR High Income Trust plc 1989 (non-exec). *Clubs:* Royal Ocean Racing Club. *Recreations:* Ocean Racing.

DUNLOP, Norman Gordon Edward; CBE; Chairman, Ferrum Holdings plc, since 1989. *Career:* Peat Marwick McLintock 1945-56; De Havilland & Hawker Siddeley Aviation 1956-63; Commercial Union Assurance 1963-77; Inch Cape Singapore 1979-82; British Airways, Finance Director 1982-88. *Biog: b.* 16 April 1928. *Educ:* Glenalmond, Perthshire. *Professional Organisations:* Scottish CA. *Clubs:* Bucks, Caledonian.

DUNLOP, Robert Fergus; Member of Board of Directors, Lonrho plc, since 1972; Executive Director. *Career:* Bristol Aeroplane Co Ltd & subsequently British Aircraft Corporation 1952-66; Westland Aircraft Ltd, British Hovercraft Corporation Ltd, Commercial Director 1966-70; Lonrho plc 1970-; Director 1972-. *Biog: b.* 22 June 1929. *Nationality:* English. *m.* 1966, Jane Clare (née McManus); 1 s; 2 d. *Educ:* Marlborough; St John's College, Cambridge (MA); Massachussetts Institute of Technology (MSc, Sloan Fellow). *Directorships:* Lonrho plc 1970 Senior Executive. *Professional Organisations:* CEng; MRAeS. *Recreations:* Sailing, Skiing.

DUNN, A; Executive Director, James R Knowles Limited.

DUNN, Christopher Frank; Partner, Slater Heelis, since 1989; Corporate Finance/Commercial. *Career:* Turner Kenneth Brown, Articled Clerk 1980-83; Pinsent & Co, Assistant Solicitor 1983-86; Slater Heelis, Assistant Solicitor 1987-89. *Biog: b.* 1 February 1957. *Nationality:* British. *m.* 1984, Helen Jessica (née Burton). *Educ:* Stockport Grammar School; Gonville & Caius College, Cambridge (MA). *Professional Organisations:* Law Society. *Clubs:* St James' Club, Manchester. *Recreations:* Squash, Tennis, Walking, Reading.

DUNN, Geoffrey Richard; Group Finance Director, Exco International plc, since 1987; Finance, Systems, Administration. *Career:* ICFC Ltd, Investment Controller 1975-78; S G Warburg & Co Ltd, Corporate Finance Executive 1978-80; GKN plc, Assistant Group Treasurer 1980-84; Midland Bank plc, Head of Finance & Planning (Intl) 1984-87. *Biog: b.* 10 July 1949. *m.* 1973, Patricia Ann (née Thompson). *Educ:* Ifield Grammar School; Manchester University (BSc Hons, MSc); Manchester Business School (DpBA). *Directorships:* Exco International plc (exec). *Professional Organisations:* MCT. *Clubs:* The Alpine Club, London Mountaineering Club. *Recreations:* Mountaineering, Skiing, Opera, Cycling.

DUNN, Ian; Director, Samuel Montagu & Co Limited.

DUNN, William James; Director, Head of Sales, Société Générale Strauss Turnbull.

DUNNE, H; Partner, Nabarro Nathanson.

DUNNE, Michael John; Director, J Henry Schroder Wagg & Co Limited, since 1990; International Advisery and Project Finance. *Career:* Costain 1973-75; Renardet-Sauti-Ice 1975-77; LRDC Limited 1977-79; Taylor Woodrow 1979-80; Saudi International Bank 1982-85; J Henry Schroder Wagg & Co Limited 1985-. *Biog: b.* 12 July 1952. *Nationality:* British. *m.* 1980, Lynn Mary (née Strangeway); 1 d. *Educ:* Bedford School; Manchester University (BSc); Manchester Business School (MBA). *Professional Organisations:* MICE; CENG. *Clubs:* Naval and Military.

DUNSCOMBE, Peter William; Joint Managing Director, Imperial Investments Ltd (Investment Management Subsidiary of Hanson plc), since 1990. *Career:* Simon & Coates (Stockbrokers), Investment Analyst 1971-75; Imperial Group Pension Funds, Specialising in Equities and Property in UK and US 1975-. *Biog: b.* 27 April 1949. *Nationality:* British. *m.* 1975, Catherine Olga (née Hooper); 2 s; 1 d. *Educ:* Clifton College, Bristol; Worcester College, Oxford University (BSc Hons Engineering and Economics). *Other Activities:* Member, Worshipful Company of Spectacle-Makers; Freeman, City of London. *Recreations:* Windsurfing, Walking, Gardening.

DUNSFORD, Anthony James; Director, James Capel Fund Managers Ltd, since 1986; Head of Fixed Interest Fund Management. *Career:* Grieveson Grant & Co, Private Client Exec 1972-78; James Capel & Co, Fund Mgr 1978-86. *Biog: b.* 20 April 1949. *Nationality:* British. *m.* 1974, Mary Ann (née Bullen); 1 s; 1 d. *Educ:* The Leys School, Cambridge; Selwyn College, Cambridge (MA). *Directorships:* James Capel Fund Managers Ltd 1986 (exec). *Other Activities:* Mem, International Stock Exchange. *Recreations:* Travel, Sport, Reading, Bridge.

DUNSTAN, J V O D; Partner, Allen & Overy.

DUNT, John; Partner, Clyde & Co.

DUNTON, B; Partner, Milne Ross.

DURDEN, Leslie William; Chief Manager, Credito Italiano, since 1988. *Career:* Lloyds Bank, Asst Mgr 1946-69; Allied Bank, Dep Mgr 1969-74; Credito Italiano, Dep Mgr 1974-85. *Biog: b.* 18 December 1930. *Nationality:* British. *m.* 1957, Patricia (née Hopkins); 2 s. *Educ:* London County High School. *Directorships:* Credito Italiano International Ltd 1984 (non-exec); Credito Italiano Nominees Ltd 1975 (exec); Wimbledon Park Golf Club 1985 (exec). *Clubs:* Overseas Bankers', Lombard Association. *Recreations:* Golf.

DURELL, G A A; Partner, Simmons & Simmons.

DUREN, Resat Mehmet; General Manager, TC Ziraat Bankasi, London Branch, since 1990; International Banking. *Career:* Akbank TAS, Foreign Operations Manager 1976-78; Pamukbank TAS, Senior Vice President 1980-89; TC Ziraat Bankasi (Head Office), Senior Vice President; Foreign Operations Department 1989-90. *Biog: b.* 19 December 1950. *Nationality:* Turkish. *m.* 1979, Emel (née Pekcan); 1 s; 1 d. *Educ:* University of Istanbul, Faculty of Political Sciences and Finance (Baccalaureate in Economics, Finance and Political Science). *Professional Organisations:* Turkish/British Chamber of Commerce.

DURIE, Alistair; Director, BDO Consulting.

DURIE, Ms Robyn; Partner, Linklaters & Paines, since 1990; Intellectual Property, Telecommunications & Broadcasting. *Career:* Linklaters & Paines, Solicitor 1987-90; Freehill Hollingdale & Page (Sydney), Solicitor 1985-87; News Limited, Solicitor 1982-85; Barrister, NSW Bar 1981-82; Allen Allen & Hemsley (Sydney), Solicitor & Articled Clerk 1975-81. *Biog: b.* 11 December 1952. *Nationality:* Australian. *m.* 1984, John Meehan. *Educ:* PLC, Pymble; Sydney University (BA, LLB Hons); London University, LSE (LLM). *Other Activities:* City of London Solicitors Company; Licensing Executives Society; British Literary & Artistic Copyright Association. *Professional Organisations:* Law Society. *Publications:* Broadcasting Law & Practice, 1985.

DURLACHER, Nicholas John; Managing Director, Futures, Barclays de Zoete Wedd, since 1986. *Career:* Wedd Durlacher 1967; Stock Exchange, Member 1971; Ptnr 1972; Wedd Durlacher Mordaunt Futures (later BZW Futures), MD 1982-. *Biog: b.* 1946. *Educ:* Stowe School; Magdalene College, Cambridge (BA Hons Economics). *Directorships:* AFBD 1985 (exec); LIFFE 1984 (exec). *Other Activities:* LIFFE Membership & Rules Ctee (Dep Chm 1988-); TSA International Policy Ctee; TSA Capital Ctee; TSA Rules Ctee.

DURLACHER, Richard Frederick; Director, Barclays de Zoete Wedd, since 1986; UK Securities. *Career:* F & N Durlacher 1951; L Messel 1953-54; Bone Oldham 1954-55; Wedd Durlacher Mordaunt Member SE 1958-88; Dep Snr Ptnr 1982-85. *Biog: b.* 28 May 1933. *Nationality:* British. *m.* 1963, Wendy Sheila (née Raphael); 1 s; 2 d. *Educ:* Radley College. *Directorships:* Barclays Broker Services. *Other Activities:* Clockmakers' Livery. *Recreations:* Swimming, Skiing.

DURNIN, Bernard J; Director, Merrill Lynch Global Asset Management Limited.

DURRANCE, Philip Walter; Partner, Withers, since 1968; Head of Company Commercial. *Biog: b.* 30 June 1941. *Nationality:* British; 1 s; 1 d. *Educ:* Harrow School; Oriel College, Oxford (BA Hons). *Directorships:* Andersen Press Limited (non-exec); F Bender Limited (non-exec); Compton Manor Farms Limited (non-exec); Copydex Limited (non-exec); Design Developments Limited (non-exec); Gloy Limited (non-exec); Henkel Chemicals Limited (non-exec); Leo Laboratories Limit-

ed (non-exec); Peter Marsh & Sons Limited (non-exec); Piccadilly Press Limited (non-exec); Sidney G Jones Limited (non-exec); Unibond Copydex Limited (non-exec). *Professional Organisations:* Institute of Directors; Law Society. *Recreations:* Tennis, Squash, Cricket, Theatre, Cinema.

DURRANT, Anthony P W; Director, SG Warburg Akroyd Rowe & Pitman.

DURRANT, Dr James; Head of Fixed Income Research, Paribas Capital Markets Group, since 1989; Bonds, Swaps, Options, FX and Equity Derivative Research. *Career:* Unilever, Research Manager 1977-84; Hoare Govett, Head of Technical Research Covering Bonds, Options, Swaps 1986-88; Security Pacific, Swaps Trader with Responsibility for Interest Rate Options 1988; Paribas Capital Markets Group, Head of Risk Management Group Providing Asset/Liability Management Advice to Sovereigns Corporates & Public Bodies Worldwide 1988-89; Paribas Capital Markets Group, Head of Fixed Income Research Responsible for Economic Research 1989-. *Biog: b.* 2 July 1953. *Nationality:* British; 1 d. *Educ:* Durham University (BSc Honours 1st Class Chemistry, PhD Chemistry); London Business School (MSc Business Administration). *Directorships:* Hoare Govett 1987 Asst Dir; Security Pacific 1988 Vice President. *Professional Organisations:* Registered Representative.

DURWARD, Alan Scott; Director & Group Chief Executive, Alliance & Leicester, since 1989. *Career:* Imperial Tobacco Co Ltd 1958-65; Rowntree & Co Ltd 1965-67; Cheltenham & Gloucester Building Society 1967-75; Leicester Building Society, Deputy General Manager 1975-77; General Manager 1977-81; Director & Chief General Manager 1981-85; Alliance & Leicester Building Society (merged with Alliance Building Society), Director & Joint Chief General Manager 1985-86; Director & Chief Executive 1986-89; Director & Group Chief Executive 1989-. *Biog: b.* 30 August 1935. *Nationality:* British. *m.* 1962, Helen Young (née Gourlay); 2 s. *Educ:* Stowe School; St John's College, Cambridge (MA). *Directorships:* Girobank plc 1990 (non-exec) Chairman; B R (London Midland) Board 1990 (non-exec); Alliance & Leicester Pension Investments Ltd 1987 (non-exec); Gourlay Properties Ltd 1985 (non-exec); John Laing plc 1987-89 (non-exec). *Other Activities:* Member of Council, Building Societies Association; Member of Council, European Federation of Building Societies; Member of Council, Chairman of the Finance Committe, Loughborough University of Technology; Underwriting Member, Lloyds. *Professional Organisations:* FCBSI; CBIM.

DURWARD, Robert Allan; Chief Executive Officer, The Alexander Consulting Group Ltd; Financial Services. *Biog: Nationality:* British. *Directorships:* Alexander Stenhouse Ltd 1987 (non-exec); Newton Management

Holdings Ltd 1986 (exec); Alexander Stenhouse Fund Managers Ltd 1986 (exec); The Alexander Consulting Group Inc 1988 (exec); Alexander & Alexander Europe plc 1989 (exec). *Professional Organisations:* ACII; FPMI.

DUTHIE, Sir Robin; CBE; Chairman, Britoil plc, since 1988. *Career:* HM Forces (Army) 1946-49; Thomson Jackson Gourlay & Taylor Chartered Accountants 1949-52; Blacks (later Black & Edgington plc) 1952; Secretary 1954; Gen Mgr 1958; MD 1962; Black & Edgington, Chm 1972. *Biog: b.* 2 October 1928. *m.* 1955, Violetta Noel (née McLean); 2 s; 1 d. *Educ:* Greenock Academy; Strathclyde University (LLD). *Directorships:* Insight International Tours Ltd Chm; British Asset Trust plc 1977; Investors Capital Trust; Royal Bank of Scotland plc; Capital House plc Chm; Carclo Engineering Group 1986; Sea Catch plc 1987; Tay Residential Investments plc Chm; Scott and Robertson plc 1989. *Other Activities:* Member, Scottish Economic Council; Treasurer, Nelson St EU Congregational Church, since 1970; Commissioner, Scottish Congregational Ministers Pension Fund; Member, Court of Strathclyde University; Member, Governing Council of Scottish Business in the Community. *Professional Organisations:* CBIM; FRSA; Chartered Accountant; Fellow, Royal Institute of Architects of Scotland. *Recreations:* Cricket, Curling.

DUVERGER, P; Chairman, Société Générale Strauss Turnbull Securities Ltd.

DUXBURY, Philip T; Chairman, Bradford & Bingley Building Society. *Biog: b.* 4 February 1928. *Directorships:* Bradford & Bingley (Douglas) Ltd (non-exec); Bradford & Bingley Homeloans Ltd (non-exec); Bradford & Bingley Homeloans Management Ltd (non-exec); Bradford & Bingley (IOM) Ltd (non-exec); Bradford & Bingley Mortgage Management Ltd (non-exec); Bradford & Bingley Mortgages Ltd (non-exec); Bradford & Bingley Pensions Ltd (non-exec); Bradford & Bingley Personal Finance Ltd (non-exec); Bradford & Bingley Properties Ltd (non-exec); Emdrove Ltd (non-exec); Exclusive Fireplaces Ltd (non-exec); Philip Homes Marketing Ltd (non-exec); Phoenix Design & Development Ltd (non-exec); Portland Bathrooms Ltd (non-exec).

DWEK, M; Director, S G Warburg & Co Ltd.

DWELLY, Michael John; Director, The MDA Group plc, since 1985. *Career:* Monk & Dunstone, Partner 1968-75; The MDA Group plc, Chief Executive 1985-90. *Biog: b.* 6 April 1937. *Nationality:* British. *m.* 1961, Gillian (née Ayers); 1 s; 1 d. *Educ:* Rutlish Grammar. *Directorships:* The MDA Group plc 1985 (non-exec); ESL Engineering Services Ltd 1985 (exec). *Professional Organisations:* FRICS; FBIM. *Recreations:* Music, Reading, Gardening.

DWERRYHOUSE, William Peter; Director, Morgan Grenfell Asset Management Ltd, since 1985; Investment Management. *Career:* 10th Royal Hussars (PWO), Captain 1959-67; Spence Veitch & Co, Stockbroker 1967-70; Laurie Milbank & Co, Ptnr 1970-84; Morgan Grenfell & Co 1984-. *Directorships:* Morgan Grenfell (Asia) Ltd 1985 (non-exec); Morgan Grenfell Investment Management 1985 (exec); Morgan Grenfell International Funds Management 1985 (exec); Morgan Grenfell Unit Trust Managers Ltd 1987 (exec); Banque Morgan Grenfell En Suisse SA 1988 (non-exec).

DWYER, D; Managing Director, Bankers Trust Company, since 1990; Structured Debt & Private Equity. *Biog: Nationality:* American; 1 s; 1 d. *Educ:* University of Illinois (BS); De Paul University, Chicago (MBA).

DWYER, J A; Chief Executive, George Wimpey plc.

DWYER, Maurice John; Partner, Wragge & Co, since 1990; Corporate Law. *Career:* Freshfields, Articled Clerk 1981-83; Wragge & Co, Assistant Solicitor 1983-86; 3i plc, Solicitor 1986-87; Wragge & Co, Solicitor/ Associate 1987-90. *Biog: b.* 1977. *Nationality:* British. *m.* 1986, Sian. *Educ:* Bablake School, Coventry; University of Warwick (LLB Hons); College of Law. *Professional Organisations:* Law Society. *Recreations:* Football, Squash, Tropical Fish, Irish History.

DYAS, Anthony Rodney Joseph; Director, Singer & Friedlander Ltd, since 1974; Corporate Finance, Property Lending. *Career:* Pearl Assurance Clerk 1957-59; Associated British Foods Ltd Acct 1959-69; Singer & Friedlander Ltd Corp Fin Exec 1969-. *Biog: b.* 14 August 1940. *Nationality:* British. *m.* 1963, Vivien Ann (née Herbert); 3 d. *Educ:* Greenford County Grammar School. *Professional Organisations:* FCCA. *Recreations:* Running, Motor Cars.

DYE, Tony J; Investment Director, Phillips & Drew Fund Management Limited.

DYER, Mark; Partner, Clifford Chance.

DYER, Roger John; Partner, Freshfields, since 1990; Banking. *Career:* Anstey & Thompson, Exeter, Articled Clerk/Assistant Solicitor 1980-83; Freshfields, London, Assistant Solicitor 1983-86; Freshfields, Singapore, Assistant Solicitor 1986-88; Freshfields, London, Assistant Solicitor 1988-90. *Biog: b.* 11 November 1957. *Nationality:* British. *m.* 1987, Susan (née Lewis). *Educ:* Torquay Boys' Grammar School; St Peter's College, Oxford (BA Law). *Professional Organisations:* The Law Society.

DYKSTRA, Ronald Gerrit Malcolm; Senior Partner, Addleshaw, Sons & Latham.

DYMOCK, John Fergus; Executive Director, Hambros Bank Ltd, since 1989; Project Finance &

Shipping. *Biog: b.* 5 March 1943. *Nationality:* British. *m.* 1968, Phillipa (née Pritchard); 1 s; 2 d. *Educ:* Cranleigh School, Surrey; University College, London (BSc); Caius College, Cambridge (PhD). *Directorships:* Hambros Bank Ltd 1981 (exec). *Recreations:* Building, Tennis.

DYSON, J W; Non-Executive Director, Riggs A P Bank Ltd.

DYSON, Maurice; Partner, Clay & Partners, since 1980; Pension Arrangements. *Career:* Grieveson, Grant & Co, Investment Analyst 1973-76; Clay & Partners 1976-. *Biog: b.* 5 June 1951. *Nationality:* British. *m.* 1977, Margaret Anne (née Craig); 2 s. *Educ:* King Williams College, Castletown, Isle of Man; Fitzwilliam College, Cambridge (MA). *Professional Organisations:* AMSIA; FIA.

E

EADES, J Martin; Group Managing Director, International Commodities Clearing House Ltd, since 1989. *Career:* IBM UK 1963-68; Canadian Federal Government, Director, Computing 1968-74; Rank Xerox UK, Head, Information Services 1974-78; Jardine Matheson (Hong Kong) Group Gen Manager, Systems 1978-85; Managing Director, Jardine Logica 1983-85; Coopers & Lybrand USA, Ptnr in Tokyo, Chief Operating Officer, Japan 1985-88; ICCH Ltd, Group Managing Director 1989-. *Biog: b.* 14 January 1942. *Nationality:* British/Canadian. *m.* 1987, Sylvia Ann (née Harratt); 1 s; 1 d. *Educ:* Birmingham University (BCom); University of Guelph, Ontario (Dip, Operations Research). *Directorships:* London Clearing House 1989 Chm; ICCH Financial Markets 1989 (exec) Chm & MD. *Other Activities:* Past President, Canadian Federal Institute of Management; Past Vice-President, Canadian Trade Simplification (COSTPRO); Past Vice-Chairman, Hong Kong Trade Facilitation. *Professional Organisations:* FBCS; FBIM. *Clubs:* Royal Hong Kong Jockey Club, LRC Hong Kong; *Clubs:* Squash, Cooking, Walking, Music.

EADIE, Craig; Partner, Company/Commercial Department, Frere Cholmeley, since 1986. *Biog: b.* 22 April 1955. *Nationality:* British. *m.* 1987, Deborah Ann (née Burnett). *Educ:* Canford School; Worcester College, Oxford University (BA); Aix-Marseilles University, France (DES). *Directorships:* Institute of Contemporary British History 1987 (non-exec); Watside Charities 1988 (non-exec).

EADY, Anthony James; Secretary, Lazard Brothers & Co Ltd, since 1979. *Career:* Theodore Goddard & Co Articled Clerk 1958-59 and 1962-66; Solicitor 1966; Schroder Executor & Trustee Co Ltd Sec 1966-71; J Henry Schroder Wagg & Co Ltd Asst Sec 1971-79. *Biog: b.* 9 July 1939. *Nationality:* British. *m.* 1973, Carole June (née Langley); 2 s (1 decd) 1 d. *Educ:* Harrow School; Hertford College, Oxford (MA). *Other Activities:* Liveryman, City of London Solicitors' Company; Member of Committee, Hertford Society (Hertford College, Oxford). *Professional Organisations:* The Law Society. *Clubs:* United Oxford and Cambridge University, Thames Hare & Hounds. *Recreations:* Long Distance Running.

EAGLES, Brian; Partner, S J Berwin & Co, since 1988; Entertainment Media & Leisure. *Career:* Bulcraig & Davis, Articled Clerk 1956-60; Solicitor 1960; J Sanson & Co, Assistant Solicitor 1960-61; Partner 1961-

67; Herbert Oppenheimer Nathan & Vandyk, Partner 1967-88; Finance Partner 1974-84; Head of Entertainment, Media & Leisure 1980-88; S J Berwin & Co, Partner 1988-. *Biog: b.* 4 February 1937. *Nationality:* British. *m.* 1961, Marje; 2 s; 1 d. *Educ:* Kilburn Grammar School; London University (LLB). *Other Activities:* Arbitrator, American Film Marketing Association; Hon Solicitor to the Celebrities Guild of Great Britain; Member, The Copenhagen Club; Member, The Variety Club of Great Britain. *Professional Organisations:* The Law Society. *Publications:* Regular Contributor to Many Entertainment Industry Trade Publications. *Recreations:* Music, Film, Theatre, Walking, Skiing.

EAGLES, L M; Partner, Life & General (Epsom), Bacon & Woodrow.

EARDLEY, Jonathan Wilmot; Chief Executive, Societe Generale Settlement Holdings, since 1989; Clearing, Settlement & Technology. *Career:* GEC Traffic Automation, Head of Planning 1967-73; Systems Programming Ltd Mgr, Consultancy 1973-78; Ian Martin Ltd Dir, Technical 1978-79; Peat Marwick McLintock Dir, Consultancy 1980-87; National Investment Group, Ops Director 1987-90. *Biog: b.* 12 July 1945. *Nationality:* British. *m.* 1971, Lindsey (née Wesil); 2 d. *Educ:* Rugby School. *Directorships:* Societe Generale Clearing Services 1989 Chief Executive; Societe Generale Security Settlements 1989 Chairman/Executive; Security Settlements Options Ltd 1989 (exec). *Recreations:* Cricket, Golf, Tennis.

EARL, Peter Richard Stephen; Chairman, Tranwood & Co Ltd, since 1985; Corporate Finance.

EARL, Roger Lawrence; Group Managing Director, Fenchurch Insurance Holdings Ltd, since 1983; Insurance Broking (Internationally). *Career:* Arbon Langrish & Co Ltd (H Clarkson/Bain Clarkson) Broker 1958-65; Bland Welch & Co Ltd (Bland Payne Ltd), Asst Dir/MD North Am Div 1965-78; Fenchurch Group, Dir 1979-. *Biog:* 2 d. *Directorships:* Valonpalm Ltd 1978 (exec); Guinness Peat Group plc 1987 (exec); Various Fenchurch Group Companies 1979 (exec).

EAST, David John; Partner, Gouldens; Company & Commercial Law/Offshore Trusts. *Career:* Frere Cholmeley, Asst Solicitor 1965-67; Taylor & Humbert, Asst Solicitor 1967-70; Gouldens, Asst Solicitor 1970-71; Partner 1971-. *Biog: b.* 7 May 1939. *Nationality:* British. *m.* 1964, Carolyn; 3 s. *Educ:* Kings School,

Canterbury; Lincoln College, Oxford (MA). *Professional Organisations:* Law Society. *Recreations:* Golf, Tennis, Music.

EAST, John; Partner, Clifford Chance.

EAST, John Richard Alan; Chief Executive, The Guidehouse Group plc, since 1989; Corporate Finance. *Career:* Speechly Bircham Solicitors Articled Clerk 1967-70; Mitton Butler Priest & Co Trainee Stockbroker 1971-73; Panmure Gordon & Co Institutional Salesman 1973-77; Kent, East, Newton & Co Snr Ptnr 1977-80; Margetts & Addenbrooke, East, Newton Managing Ptnr 1980-83; Margetts & Addenbrooke Snr Ptnr 1983-86; National Investment Group plc Group Operation Dir 1986-87. *Biog: b.* 14 May 1949. *Nationality:* British. *m.* 1986, Charlotte Sylvia (née Merriman). 2 s (by previous marriage). *Educ:* Westminster School. *Directorships:* The Guidehouse Group plc 1987 (exec); 1989 Chief Exec; Guidehouse Financial Management 1987 (non-exec); Vestry Nominees Ltd 1987 (non-exec); Barwood Securities Ltd 1977 (exec) Sec; Guidehouse Securities Ltd 1987 (exec) MD; Orbital Financial Services plc 1990 (non-exec); Guidehouse Finance Ltd 1990 (non-exec); Guidehouse Insurance Brokers Ltd 1990 (non-exec); Howard Elliot Stevens & Co Ltd 1990 (non-exec); Team Greyfriars Ltd 1990 (non-exec); Greyfriars Trust Ltd 1990 (non-exec); Newgate Securities Ltd 1990 (non-exec); Guidehouse Insurance Services Ltd 1990 non-exec); Guidehouse Marketing Consultancy Ltd 1990 (non-exec); Trent Advertising Ltd 1990 (non-exec). *Professional Organisations:* Member, Stock Exchange, 1974. *Clubs:* Carlton. *Recreations:* Music, Playing and Recording of Electronic Musical Instruments.

EAST, Stephen John; Group Treasurer, Redland plc, since 1987; Treasury, Corporate Finance and Insurance. *Career:* Binder Hamlyn, Croydon, Trainee Chartered Accountant 1979-82; Audit Supervisor 1982-83; Redland plc, Assistant Treasurer 1983-84; Deputy Treasurer 1984-87. *Biog: b.* 3 March 1958. *Nationality:* British. *Educ:* Loughborough University (BSc). *Other Activities:* Vice Chairman, Association of Corporate Treasurers Programme Committee. *Professional Organisations:* ACA; MCT.

EASTGATE, Andrew Keith; Partner, Pinsent & Co, since 1985; Flotations, Acquisitions, Corporate Finance. *Career:* Stephenson Harwood, Articled Clerk 1978-80; Asst Solicitor 1980-83; Pinsent & Co, Asst Solicitor 1983-85. *Biog: b.* 14 May 1956. *Nationality:* British. *m.* 1986, Barbara Lorraine (née Howden); 1 d. *Educ:* Uppingham School; Mansfield College, Oxford (BA). *Professional Organisations:* The Law Society. *Recreations:* Hockey, Cricket, Travel.

EASTMAN, Henry Guy; Director (Development Capital), Granville & Co Limited, since 1989; Unquoted Fund Management. *Career:* Unilever plc, Management Trainee 1974-76; Arthur Andersen & Co, Chartered Accountants, Audit Senior 1977-81; Guidehouse Group plc, Syndications Manager 1981-83; Granville & Co Limited 1983-. *Biog: b.* 26 November 1955. *Nationality:* British. *m.* 1983, Briony (née Adams); 2 d. *Educ:* Port Regis School; Bryanston School; Bristol Polytechnic (BA Hons Business Studies). *Directorships:* Granville & Co Limited 1989 (exec); Maison Caurette Holdings Limited 1990 (non-exec); Ingleton Thomas plc 1990 (non-exec); Fantastic Sams (UK) Limited 1990 (non-exec). *Other Activities:* Open Air Theatre; Regents Park Friends Committee. *Professional Organisations:* Institute of Chartered Accountants in England & Wales, 1982. *Recreations:* The English Countryside.

EASTMENT, Derek Colin; Head of Investment Banking Credit & Risk, Midland Bank plc, since 1988; Management of the Credit Risk. *Career:* Midland Bank Group, Various 1957-. *Biog: b.* 13 June 1941. *Nationality:* British. *m.* 1963, Jean Maureen (née Page); 1 s; 1 d. *Educ:* Southend High School for Boys. *Directorships:* Samuel Montagu & Co Ltd 1989 (exec). *Professional Organisations:* Associate of the Chartered Institute of Bankers. *Recreations:* Walking, Gardening, Reading.

EASTWELL, Nick; Partner, Linklaters & Paines, since 1989; International Finance. *Career:* Linklaters & Paines, Articled Clerk 1980-82; Assistant Solicitor 1982-89. *Biog: b.* 15 October 1956. *Nationality:* British. *m.* 1988, Sally Jane (née Geddes). *Educ:* Westcliff High School; Trinity Hall, Cambridge (BA Hons Law 2i, MA). *Professional Organisations:* Law Society; The City of London Solicitors' Company.

EASTWOOD, Ms A Mairi; Partner, Ernst & Young.

EASTWOOD, Miss H Tamsin; Partner, Titmuss Sainer & Webb, since 1987; Corporate Finance. *Career:* Lee & Pemberton, Assistant Solicitor 1984-85; Titmuss Sainer & Webb, Assistant Solicitor 1985-87; Partner 1987-. *Biog: Nationality:* British.

EASTWOOD, Jonathan J; Partner, Withers.

EASTWOOD, R G; Deputy Managing Director, Knight & Day Ltd.

EATES, R; Committee Member, GT Unit Managers, Unit Trust Association.

EATON, Paul Gerard; Partner, Penningtons, since 1990; Taxation/Pensions. *Career:* Gamlens, Articled Clerk/Assistant Solicitor 1968-71; Gamlens, Partner 1972-90; Managing Partner 1988-90. *Biog: b.* 17 January 1945. *Nationality:* British. *m.* 1968, Pauline (née Mills); 2 s; 1 d. *Educ:* Sir John Dean's Grammar School, Northwich, Cheshire; Trinity Hall, Cambridge (MA). *Other Activities:* Holborn Law Society, Revenue Law Committee. *Professional Organisations:* Law Society. *Rec-*

reations: Opera, Piano, Walking, Skiing, Armchair Mountaineering.

EATWELL, R J L; Partner, Wedlake Bell.

EATWELL, Robert S; Partner, Walker Morris Scott Turnbull.

EBERHARDT, Urs Hans; Executive Director, Swiss Bank Corporation, since 1989; Private Banking. *Career:* Credit Suisse, Berne, Apprenticeship 1960-63; SBC, Berne & La-Chaux-de-Fonds, Documentary Credits, Forex 1963-65; SBC, NY, Trainee, Private Clients 1965-68; SBC, Los Angeles, Assistant Representative 1968-71; SBC, Berne, Assistant Vice President/VP, Private Clients/Investments 1971-81; SBC, London, Vice President, Private Banking/Investments 1981-84; First Vice President, Private Banking/Investments 1984-85; Senior Vice President, Private Banking/Investments 1985-89; Executive Director, Private Banking/Investments 1989-. *Biog: b.* 15 April 1941. *Nationality:* Swiss. *m.* 1970, Trudy (née Hinden); 2 d. *Educ:* Secondary School, Berne; College, Berne; Banking Apprenticeship; Swiss Mercantile School, Berne. *Directorships:* Swiss Centre Limited 1986 (non-exec); Swiss Bank Corporation (Jersey) Ltd 1988 (non-exec); SBC Group (UK) Pension Trust Fund Ltd 1986 (non-exec). *Clubs:* Roehampton Club. *Recreations:* Tennis, Jogging, Travel, Reading.

ECCLES, G T G; Partner, Grimley J R Eve.

ECCLES, Terence C; Managing Director, Morgan Guaranty Trust Company of New York.

ECCLES-WILLIAMS, Simon Gavin Piers; Director, Morgan Grenfell & Co Limited, since1989; Corporate Finance. *Career:* Courtaulds plc 1975-76; Ernst & Whinney 1976-80; Morgan Grenfell & Co Limited 1981. *Biog: b.* 9 February 1953. *Nationality:* British. *m.* 1982, Elizabeth (née Harding); 3 s. *Educ:* Radley College; Keble College, Oxford (MA); Cranfield, (MBA). *Professional Organisations:* ICAEW. *Recreations:* Walking, Skiing.

ECCLESHALL, David Ernest; General Manager, Clydesdale Bank plc, since 1987; Credit Bureau. *Career:* Midland Bank plc (Manchester) Asst Mgr 1974-76; (Bristol) Controller of Advances 1976-80; Midland Bank plc Corporate Banking Exec 1980-81; (Sheffield) Asst Reg Dir 1981-85; Midland Bank plc Corp Banking Dir 1985-87. *Biog: b.* 3 March 1942. *Nationality:* British. *m.* 1964, Thelma Margaret (née Nicholas); 1 s; 1 d. *Educ:* Welshpool Grammar School, Powys. *Professional Organisations:* ACIB. *Recreations:* Walking, Gardening, Sports.

ECKERSLEY, R A; Director, Crawley Warren Group plc.

EDDLESTON, R T; Director, NCL Investments Limited.

EDDY, Michael G; Director, Schroder Securities Limited.

EDELEANU, Claire Marianne; Partner, Gouldens, since 1979; Corporate Law. *Career:* Turner Peacock, Ass Solicitor 1974-77. *Biog: b.* 27 August 1949. *Educ:* Queen Victoria High School for Girls; University of Leeds (LLB). *Professional Organisations:* Holborn Law Society.

EDELL, Stephen; Ombudsman, The Office of the Building Societies Ombudsman, since 1987. *Career:* Articled to Father 1953; Qualified as Solicitor 1958; Knapp-Fishers (Westminster), Partner 1959-75; Law Commissioner 1975-83; Crossman Block & Keith (Solicitors), Partner 1983-87. *Biog: b.* 1 December 1932. *Nationality:* British. *m.* 1958, Shirley Ross Collins; 2 s; 1 d. *Educ:* St Andrews School, Eastbourne, Uppingham, London (LLB). *Other Activities:* Oxfam, Member-Retail & Property Committee (Chairman); Member, Council; Member, Executive; Makers of Playing Cards's Company, Member of Ct of Assts; Master (1981-82). *Professional Organisations:* City of Westminster Law Society; FRSA. *Publications:* Inside Information on the Family and the Law, 1969; The Family's Guide to the Law, 1974; Articles in Conveyancer; Journal of Planning and Environmental Law; Newspapers. *Clubs:* City Livery. *Recreations:* Family Life, Music, Opera, Theatre, Early Astronomical Instruments, Avoiding Gardening, Problems of Developing Countries.

EDELMAN, Keith G; Corporate Planning Director, Ladbroke Group plc, since 1986; Exec Chairman Texas Homecare. *Career:* IBM 1968-70; Rank Xerox 1970-75; Bank of America, MD, Bank of America Finance 1976-81; Grand Metropolitan, Strategy Director 1981-85. *Educ:* Haberdashers' Aske's; University of Manchester, Institute of Science & Technology. *Directorships:* Ladbroke Group plc (exec).

EDELSHAIN, M B; Director, S G Warburg & Co Ltd, since 1984; Corporate Finance, Japan. *Career:* S G Warburg & Co Ltd 1970-. *Biog: b.* 18 December 1948. *Nationality:* British. *m.* 1984, Yasuko (née Okada); 1 s; 1 d. *Educ:* Cambridge (BA Mechanical Sciences). *Clubs:* MCC. *Recreations:* Swimming.

EDEY, Russell; Managing Director, N M Rothschild & Sons Limited; Corporate Finance.

EDGAR, Thomas Leslie; Managing Director, Sharps Pixley Ltd, since 1988; Sales and Administration. *Career:* Johnson Matthey Sales Clerk/Dealer 1961-68; Sharps Pixley Ltd, Director 1974-88. *Biog: b.* 9 July 1943. *m.* 1967, Margaret (née McEnroe); 2 d. *Educ:* Reeds School, Cobham. *Directorships:* Sharps Pixley Inc (New York) 1981 (non-exec); Sharps Pixley Brokers Inc (New

York) 1988 (non-exec). *Recreations:* Horticulture, Antiques, Music.

EDGE, Christopher Culmer; Director, British & Commonwealth Merchant Bank plc, since 1988; Management of Private Client Portfolio Businesses. *Career:* Montagu, Loebl, Stanley & Co Assoc Mem 1977-82; Lazard Investors Ltd Dir 1982-88. *Biog: b.* 30 November 1952. *Nationality:* English. *m.* 1981, Lesley Anne; 4 s. *Educ:* Whitgift School; Exeter University (BA Hons Economic History). *Directorships:* British & Commonwealth Merchant Bank plc 1988 (exec); BCMB Private Clients Limited 1989 (exec). *Clubs:* The Roehampton Club, Old Whitgiftian Assoc, The Eagles. *Recreations:* Golf, Squash, Rugby, Family, Gardening, Running.

EDGE, Christopher Thomas; Managing Director, 3i Consultants Ltd, since 1989; Company Strategy, Corporate Rescues. *Career:* Philips Electronic & Associated Industries 1971-73; British Leyland Motor Corporation, Fin Analyst 1973-75; Leyland International, Commercial Mgr 1975-77; 3i Consultants, Consultant/Senior Consultant 1977-79; (Midland Region), Mgr 1979-81; (South & Midland Region), Mgr 1981-85; Dir 1985-88. *Biog: b.* 25 July 1949. *Nationality:* British. *m.* 1972, Christine (née Wilson). *Educ:* The Hulme Grammar School, Oldham; University College, Oxford (MA); King's College, London (LLM). *Directorships:* 3i plc 1989 (exec); 3i Consultants Limited 1985 (exec); S & R Business Modelling Limited 1989 (exec). *Professional Organisations:* FCMA; FCIS; FIMC. *Publications:* ICA Practical Financial Management Handbook - Section on Computers, 1983; Managing Business Cash Problems, 1985; ICA Digest - Computers for the Accountant's Office, 1983; Small Computers for Solicitors, 1983. *Recreations:* Music, Violin, Hill Walking.

EDGE, Miss J S; Partner, Slaughter and May, since 1990; Company and Commercial. *Career:* Allison & Humphreys, Articled Clerk/Assistant Solicitor 1981-86; Slaughter and May, Assistant Solicitor/Partner 1986-. *Biog: b.* 12 February 1959. *Nationality:* British. *Educ:* Benenden School, Kent; Cranleigh School, Surrey; Trinity Hall, Cambridge University (MA Philosophy/Law). *Professional Organisations:* The Law Society. *Recreations:* Scuba Diving, Riding, Sailing.

EDGE, Peter John; Director, Exco International plc; London Agency Business. *Biog: b.* 9 August 1958. *Educ:* University of Warwick (BA Economic History). *Recreations:* Golf, Squash, Football, Rugby.

EDGE, Robert James; Vice President & Director, Wood Gundy Inc, since 1988; New Issues & Syndication. *Career:* Bank of Canada, Snr Open Market Trader 1978-82; Export Development Corp, Snr Treasury Officer 1982-85. *Biog: b.* 3 October 1955. *Nationality:* Canadian. *Educ:* Carleton University (BA); University of Western Ontario (MBA).

EDGE, Stephen Martin; Partner, Slaughter and May, since 1982; Corporate Tax. *Biog: b.* 29 November 1950. *Nationality:* British. *m.* 1975, Melanie (née Lawler); 2 d. *Educ:* Canon Slade Grammar School, Bolton; Exeter University (LLB). *Publications:* Articles and Contributions to Works on Tax.

EDLMANN, Stephen Raphael Reynolds; Partner, Linklaters & Paines, since 1985; International Finance Section. *Career:* Linklaters & Paines, Articled Clerk 1977-79; Linklaters & Paines, London and New York, Assistant Solicitor 1979-85. *Biog: b.* 13 March 1954. *Nationality:* British. *m.* 1979, Deborah (née Booth); 3 s. *Educ:* Tonbridge School; Trinity Hall, Cambridge (MA Law). *Other Activities:* Liveryman, the City of London Solicitors Company. *Professional Organisations:* Member, Law Society. *Clubs:* MCC, Hawks, Harlequins FC. *Recreations:* Cricket, Tennis, Shooting, Entertaining.

EDMANS, L M; Assistant General Manager (Marketing), National Provident Institution.

EDMONDS, David; General Manager, Property Development, National Westminster Bank plc.

EDMONDS, J C P; Board Member & Managing Director, Group Services, British Railways Board, since 1989; Transport. *Career:* British Railways, Chief Freight Manager, London Midland Region 1981-82; National Business Manager, Coal 1982-84; Director, Provincial Sector 1984-87; General Manager, Anglia 1987-89. *Biog: b.* 22 April 1936. *Nationality:* British. *m.* 1962, Christine Elizabeth; 1 s; 1 d. *Educ:* Trinity College, Cambridge. *Directorships:* British Transport Police 1989 Chairman. *Recreations:* Gardening, Music.

EDMONDSON, B J; Director, Brandeis Limited.

EDWARD, Ian; Director, Charterhouse Bank Limited, since 1990; Mergers and Acquisitions. *Career:* Bankers Trust Company 1982-85; County NatWest Limited 1985-90. *Biog: b.* 13 September 1959. *Nationality:* British. *Educ:* Winchester College; St Peter's College, Oxford (BA). *Clubs:* RAC. *Recreations:* Golf, Cricket, Tennis.

EDWARDES, Warren Henry William; Director, Charterhouse Bank Limited, since 1989; Financial Engineering, Capital Markets. *Career:* Equitable Life Assurance Society, Actuarial Clerk 1970-71; Southampton University, Research Assistant 1975-76; Government Actuary's Department, Actuarial Officer 1976-78; Barclays Bank Limited, Treasury Analyst 1978-80; British Gas Corporation, Senior Dealer, Treasurer's Dept 1980-84; Midland Bank plc, Manager, Assistant Director, Product Development, Group Treasury 1984-87; Assistant Director, Group Asset & Liability Management 1987-88; Charterhouse Bank Ltd, Divisional Director, Financial Engineering 1988-89. *Biog: b.* 13 August 1953.

Nationality: British. *Educ:* Finchley Catholic Grammar School; Sheffield University (BSc); Southampton University. *Publications:* Contributed Chapters to: Pioneering Economics, 1978; Handbook of Financial Engineering, 1990. *Clubs:* Civil Service Riding Club, Moreno Wine Club. *Recreations:* Opera, Wine, Riding.

EDWARDS, A J C; Deputy Secretary, Public Services, HM Treasury, since 1990; Public Services. *Career:* Malvern College, Assistant Master 1962-63; HM Treasury, Assistant Principal 1963-67; HM Treasury (Monetary Policy), Principal 1967-71; Harvard University, Harkness Fellow 1971-73; HM Treasury (Fiscal Policy), Principal 1973-75; HMT (Balance of Payments), Assistant Secretary 1975-77; HMT (Public Expenditure Survey), Asst Secretary 1977-78; Royal College of Defence Studies 1979; HMT (European Division), Asst Secretary 1980-83; Dept of Education (Schools Examinational), Asst Secretary 1983-85; HMT (Europe), Under Secretary 1985-88; HMT (Local Government), Under Secretary 1988-89. *Biog: b.* 3 November 1940. *Nationality:* British. *m.* 1969, Charlotte Anne (née Clycot) (diss 1987); 1 s; 2 d. *Educ:* Fettes College, Edinburgh; St Johns College, Oxford (MA Lit Hum); Harvard University (Masters Degree Economics, MPA). *Other Activities:* Secretary to Board, Royal Opera House. *Publications:* Nuclear Weapons, The Balance of Terror, The Quest for Peace, 1985. *Recreations:* Music, Writing, Reading, Walking.

EDWARDS, Alan Meredith; Partner, McKenna & Co, since 1989; Property Development. *Career:* Coward Chance, Articled Clerk 1977-79; Assistant Solicitor 1979-85; McKenna & Co, Assistant Solicitor 1986-89. *Biog: b.* 5 August 1955. *Nationality:* British. *Educ:* Aberystwyth University (LLB).

EDWARDS, C; Partner, Nabarro Nathanson.

EDWARDS, C N J; Director, S G Warburg Akroyd Rowe & Pitman Mullens Securities Ltd.

EDWARDS, (Cecil Ralph) Timothy; Director, Kleinwort Grieveson Investment Management Ltd.

EDWARDS, Christopher John; Partner, Titmuss Sainer & Webb, since 1984; Commercial Property. *Career:* Stoneham Langton & Passmore, Articled Clerk, Solicitor 1977-80; City of London Corporation, Assistant Solicitor 1980-82; Titmuss Sainer & Webb, Assistant Solicitor 1982-84. *Biog: b.* 22 February 1955. *Nationality:* British. *m.* 1988, Catherine Margaret (née Hoskins); 1 d. *Educ:* Archbishop Tenison's Grammar School Croydon; Leeds University (LLB). *Professional Organisations:* The Law Society. *Clubs:* RAC. *Recreations:* Swimming, Family.

EDWARDS, Christopher Peter; Director (Trading), CL-Alexanders Laing & Cruickshank Gilts Ltd, since

1987; Risk Management. *Career:* Akroyd & Smithers Corp Bond Dealer 1977-82; Pember & Boyle Futures Mgr 1982-83; AP Bank Ltd Futures Mgr 1983-84; Saudi International Bank Sterling Portfolio Mgr 1984-86. *Biog: b.* 20 August 1956. *Nationality:* British. *m.* 1980, Beryl Claire; 2 s. *Educ:* Winchmore Hill Comprehensive School. *Professional Organisations:* Society of Technical Analysis.

EDWARDS, G H J; Director, Parrish Stockbrokers.

EDWARDS, I; Partner, Pensions (Epsom), Bacon & Woodrow.

EDWARDS, Jeremy John Cary; Joint Managing Director, Henderson Administration Group plc, since 1983; Corporate Development & Marketing. *Career:* Unilever Ltd 1955-57; Hobson Bates & Co Ltd 1957-59; Overseas Marketing & Advertising Ltd 1959-61; Courtaulds Ltd 1961-63; Vine Products Ltd 1963-66; Loewe SA 1966-68; Jessel Securities Ltd 1968-70; Vavasseur Unit Trust Mgmnt MD 1970-74; Henderson Admin Ltd 1974-. *Biog: b.* 2 January 1937. *Nationality:* British. *m.* 1974, April Philippa (née Harding); 2 s; 1 d. *Educ:* Ridley College, Ontario; Vinehall School, Sussex; Haileybury & ISC. *Directorships:* Subsidiaries of Henderson Administration Group plc. *Other Activities:* World Wildlife Fund UK (Hon Treasurer); Church of England Children's Society (Council Member & Appeals Ctee Chairman). *Clubs:* Boodle's, City of London. *Recreations:* Walking, Swimming, Fishing, Travelling, Music.

EDWARDS, John; Personal Finance Editor, Financial Times.

EDWARDS, John Graham; Partner, Clifford Chance, since 1973; Corporate/Commercial, Telecommunications. *Biog: b.* 9 July 1943. *Nationality:* British. *m.* 1983, Ann; 1 s; 2 d. *Educ:* Nottingham University (LLB). *Professional Organisations:* City of London Solicitors Company; Chartered Institute of Secretaries; Law Society. *Clubs:* Lansdowne.

EDWARDS, M D; Partner, Lawrence Graham.

EDWARDS, Martyn Richard; Secretary and Solicitor, Coventry Building Society. *Biog: b.* 25 July 1946. *Nationality:* British. *m.* 1978, Sheila (née Clarke); 1 s. *Educ:* King Edward VI School, Stourbridge; Brasenose College, Oxford (MA). *Professional Organisations:* Solicitor; Member, Law Society.

EDWARDS, Michael John; Partner, Clifford Chance; Commercial Property. *Career:* Clifford Chance, Solicitor 1987-90; Clifford Turner, Solicitor 1986-87; Prudential, Solicitor 1984-86. *Biog: b.* 4 October 1958. *Nationality:* British. *m.* 1984, Claire (née De Negri); 1 d. *Educ:* Ashton-in-Makerfield Grammar School; Hull University (LLB). *Professional Organisations:* Law Society. *Clubs:* Ragamuffins, Ulysees FC. *Recreations:* Football, Skiing, Cycling.

EDWARDS, P R; Managing Partner, Ernst & Young.

EDWARDS, Robert Gordon; Managing Director, MNC International Bank.

EDWARDS, Roger; Director, GCI Sterling.

EDWARDS, S L; Partner, Slaughter and May.

EFRIMA, D; Executive Director, Bank Leumi (UK) plc.

EGAN, Sir John; Director, Legal & General Group plc, since 1987. *Biog: b.* 7 November 1939. *Nationality:* British. *Directorships:* Berisford International plc 1990; British Motor Industry Heritage Trust 1986; Business in the Community Council 1988; Foreign & Colonial Investment Trust 1985; Various Past Directorships of Jaguar Subsidiaries 1982-90.

EGAN, Patrick Valentine Martin; Regional Director, Unilever plc, since 1987; Latin America, South Africa, Bangladesh, Pakistan, Sri Lanka and India. *Career:* Unilever Ltd 1951; United Africa Co Ltd (Nigeria) 1951; Pan Electric Ltd (Nigeria), General Manager 1956; UNAMEC Ltd (London), Product Manager 1963; Unibeam Ltd, General Manager 1964; Holpak Ltd, Chairman & Managing Director 1966; Commercial Plastics Group of Companies, Chairman 1967; Nairn International Ltd, Chairman & Managing Director 1975; Paper, Plastics and Packaging Co-ordinator 1978; Elected to the Boards of Unilever plc and Unilever NV 1978; Unilever (UK Holdings) Ltd, Chairman, Regional Director UK & Ireland 1982; Unilever plc, Chairman of Overseas Committee 1986; Latin America and Central Asia (& South Africa), Regional Director 1987. *Biog: b.* 17 July 1930. *Nationality:* British. *m.* 1953, Mary Theresa; 3 d. *Educ:* Worth School, Sussex; St Edward's College, Simla, India; Downside School, Somerset. *Directorships:* Fisons plc 1985 (non-exec); Lloyd's of London 1989 Nominated Member of Council. *Professional Organisations:* Companion, British Institute of Management; Fellow, Institute of Directors. *Recreations:* Riding, Occasional Hunting, Walking, Gardening.

EGASHIRA, K; Executive Director, Daiwa Europe Limited.

EGERTON-SMITH, David Legh; Partner, Linklaters & Paines, since 1974; Corporate. *Biog: b.* 20 June 1942. *Nationality:* British. *m.* 1967, Susan. *Educ:* Shrewsbury School; Churchill College, Cambridge (MA). *Professional Organisations:* Council Member, Section on Energy and Natural Resources of the Interna-

tional Bar Association. *Clubs:* MCC. *Recreations:* Theatre, Walking.

EGGERSTEDT, H; Director, Unilever plc.

EGGLI, Roland; Non-Executive Director, Citymax Integrated Information Systems Ltd.

EGLIN, Roger David; Editor, Times Newspapers, since 1983; Sunday Times Business. *Career:* Financial Times, Research Assistant 1962; Deputy Editor, Business Management 1963-66; The Observer, Business Correspondent 1966-72; Sunday Times Business News 1972-. *Biog: b.* 29 June 1940. *Nationality:* British. *m.* 1964, Judith (née Kay); 2 d. *Educ:* Calday Grange Grammar School; London School of Economics (BSc Econ). *Publications:* Fly Me, I'm Freddie, 1980. *Clubs:* Island Sailing Club, Cowes Corinthian. *Recreations:* Sailing.

EGLINGTON, Charles Richard John; Director, S G Warburg Securities, since 1986; Settlement. *Career:* Akroyd & Smithers plc Dir 1978-86. *Biog: b.* 12 August 1938. *Educ:* Sherborne School. *Other Activities:* Governor, Sherborne School and Twyford School. *Professional Organisations:* The Stock Exchange (Member of Council 1975-86 and Dep Chm 1981-84), Ctee on Quotations (Chm), Property & Finance Ctee (Chm). *Clubs:* MCC, Walton Heath, Rye, Royal & Ancient.

EHRMANN, P R; Director, MIM Limited.

EILLEDGE, Elwyn Owen Morris; Senior Partner, Ernst & Young UK and Joint Chairman, Ernst & Young International, since 1989. *Career:* Farrow, Bersey, Gain, Vincent & Co (now BDO Binder Hamlyn), Articles 1959-66; Whinney Murray & Co, Liberia 1966-68; Ernst & Whinney, Hamburg, Audit Mgr 1968-71; Ernst & Whinney, London, Ptnr 1972; Managing Ptnr (London Office) 1983-86; Dep Snr Ptnr 1985; Snr Ptnr 1986; Ernst & Young (UK) Snr Ptnr 1989; Ernst & Young International, Joint Chairman 1989. *Biog: b.* 20 July 1935. *Nationality:* British. *m.* 1962, Audrey Ann Faulkner Ellis; 1 s; 1 d. *Educ:* Oswestry Boys' High School, Shropshire; Merton College, Oxford (BA Hons, MA). *Directorships:* STL plc 1989 (non-exec). *Other Activities:* Member, Financial Reporting Council; Member of Council, Institute of Chartered Accountants in England & Wales; Member, Accounting Standards Board. *Professional Organisations:* FCA. *Clubs:* Brooks's. *Recreations:* Swimming, Listening to Classical Music, Gardening.

EILON, Amir; Managing Director, BZW Ltd, since 1990; Head of Corporate Financing Unit. *Career:* British Steel O R Analyst 1970-72; Exxon Financial Analyst 1975-78; Continental Illinois Ltd Capital Market Specialist 1978-81; Samuel Montagu Director, Capital Markets 1981-85; Morgan Stanley Intl, Managing Director,

Head of Equity Capital Mkts Group 1985-90. *Biog: b.* 8 October 1948. *Nationality:* British. *m.* 1972, Louise Anne (née Kay); 1 s; 1 d. *Educ:* Christ's College, Finchley; Gonville & Caius College, Cambridge (MA); Imperial College, London (PhD). *Recreations:* Skiing, Chess, Scuba.

EILON, Professor Samuel; Senior Research Fellow, Imperial College, since 1989. *Career:* Imperial College, Head of Department 1955-87; Professor of Management Science 1963-89; Former Consultancies include: Marks & Spencer, Home Office, Maxwell Communication, Hollis Industries, Pergamon Press, Selincourt, ICL, Macmillan Publishers Ltd, ICI Plastics Division, Consolidated Goldfields. *Biog: Nationality:* British. *m.* Hannah Ruth (née Samuel); 2 s; 2 d. *Educ:* BSc, PhD, Dipl Ing, DSc (Eng). *Directorships:* ARC (previously Amey Roadstone) Main Board Director; Campari International; Spencer Stuart & Associates Principal; PE Consulting Group Consultant & Dir of Subsidiary. *Other Activities:* Member, Monopolies and Mergers Commission, 1990; Chief Editor, Omega - The International Journal of Management Science, 1972; Emeritus Professor, University of London, 1989; Consultant to Business Development Division, National Westminster Bank, 1966-90; Consultant to Westland, 1980-90. *Professional Organisations:* Two Whitworth prizes of Institution of Mech Eng; Hon FCGI Silver Medal (highest award), Operational Research Society; FEng, FIProdE, FIMechE, CBIM. *Publications:* Industrial Engineering Tables, 1962, also published in German (1964) and Italian (1968); Elements of Production Planning and Control, 1962, also published in Japan (1964), Spain (1976) and India (1981, 1985, 1989); Exercises in Industrial Management (with J R King and R I Hall), 1966; Industrial Scheduling Abstracts (with J R King), 1967; Inventory Control Abstracts (with W Lampkin), 1968; Distribution Management - Mathematical Modelling and Practical Analysis (with C D T Watson-Gandy and N Christofides), 1971; Management Control, 1971, Second Edition 1979; Applications of Management Science in Banking and Finance (edited with T R Fowkes), 1972; Applied Productivity Analysis for Industry (with B Gold and J Soesan), 1979; Aspects of Management, 1977, Second Edition 1979; The Art of Reckoning - Analysis of Performance Criteria 1984; Management Assertions and Aversions, 1985; The Global Challenge of Innovation (with Sir Basil Blackwell), 1991; Management Practice and Mispractice, 1991. *Clubs:* Athenaeum.

EKERS, M J; Director, S G Warburg Akroyd Rowe & Pitman Mullens Securities Ltd.

EL-ANSARI, Dr Osama; Director, AIBD (Systems & Information) Limited.

EL DEWEINY, Ibrahim M H; Director, Middle East Services, Bacon & Woodrow, since 1984; Actuarial

Consultancy. *Career:* Kuwait Insurance Company, Assistant General Manager 1981-84; Kuwait University, Lecturer 1977-81; Royal Insurance, Gulf Agency 1976-77; Reliance Mutual, Life Manager 1970-75; Legal & General (London) 1964-70. *Biog: b.* 16 November 1938. *Nationality:* British. *m.* 1967, Margaret D; 1 s; 2 d. *Educ:* Alexandria University (BSc). *Professional Organisations:* AIA.

EL-KASHEF, Amr Hassan Ali; Director, Citymax Integrated Information Systems Ltd, since 1984; Projects & Production. *Career:* CMES, Team Leader 1978-79; Hoskyns Group, Team Leader, Project Manager 1979; Buckmaster & Moore, Deputy Head of IT Department 1979-84; Citymax Integrated Information Systems Ltd, Director, Projects & Production 1984-. *Biog: b.* 10 November 1944. *Nationality:* British. *m.* 1974, Alexandra (née Otto); 2 s; 1 d. *Educ:* University of Alexandria (BSc Electrical Engineering); University of London (MSc Systems Engineering). *Directorships:* Citymax Integrated Information Systems Ltd 1984 (exec). *Professional Organisations:* Member, International Stock Exchange; Member, IEEE; Associate Member, IEE. *Recreations:* Bridge.

ELAND, A V; Assistant General Manager, Commerzbank AG, London Branch; Corporate Banking. *Career:* Midland Bank 1962; J Henry Schroder Wagg & Co Ltd 1972; Nordic Bank 1977; Commerzbank AG 1984. *Biog: b.* 11 July 1943. *Nationality:* British. *m.* 1969, Diane (née Huckle); 2 s. *Educ:* Lancing College. *Professional Organisations:* ACIB. *Recreations:* Sailing, Golf, Gardening.

ELBORNE, M E M; Partner, Cameron Markby Hewitt.

ELBORNE, Robert Edward Monckton; Non-Executive Director, Alliance & Leicester Building Society, since 1983. *Career:* Life Guards, Lieutenant 1945-47; Inns of Court Regiment (TA), Lieutenant 1948-57; Barrister, Inner Temple and Midland Circuit 1950-57; Solicitor 1958; Waltons & Co, Solicitors to Committee of Lloyds, Partner 1958-67; Elborne Mitchell & Co, Founder & Senior Partner 1968-82; Consultant 1982-87. *Biog: b.* 10 November 1926. *Nationality:* British. *m.* 1953, Vivienne (née Wood); 2 s; 1 d. *Educ:* Eton College; Trinity College, Cambridge (Hons Degree in Law). *Directorships:* Chancellor Insurance Company Limited 1988 (non-exec); Alliance & Leicester Building Society 1986; Leicester Building Society 1982. *Other Activities:* Freeman, Company of Watermen & Lightermen; Underwriting Member, Lloyds; External Member, Council of Lloyds 1982, 1984-88. *Professional Organisations:* Barrister, 1950-57; Solicitor, 1958-82. *Clubs:* Boodles, Beefsteak, City of London.

ELBOURNE, J; Director, Lautro Ltd.

ELBOURNE, J K; Managing Director, Legal & General Group plc.

ELCOX, D J; Director, Ropner Insurance Services Limited.

ELDER, A R; Chief Executive, Northern Stockbrokers Limited.

ELDER, Ian Francis; Partner, Allen & Overy, since 1989; Corporate Finance. *Career:* Dundas & Wilson, Apprentice & Solicitor 1974-77; Imperial Chemical Industries plc, Solicitor 1978-87; Allen & Overy, Solicitor 1987-89. *Biog: b.* 11 July 1951. *Nationality:* British. *m.* Diana (née Robinson); 1 s; 1 d. *Educ:* Loretto School; St Andrews University (MA); Edinburgh University (LLB). *Professional Organisations:* The Law Society; The Law Society of Scotland; City of London Solicitors Company; International Bar Association. *Publications:* Contributor, How to Buy a Company, 1988. *Recreations:* Golf (HCEG, Muirfield) Hockey, Fishing.

ELDER, John; Managing Director, Scottish Widows' Fund and Life Assurance Society, since 1988; Investment. *Career:* Scottish Widows' Fund & Life Assurance Society Various Positions 1954-77; Asst Gen Mgr 1978; Dep Gen Mgr & Sec 1978-88. *Directorships:* Edinburgh Investment Trust plc (non-exec).

ELDRIDGE, J; Partner, S J Berwin & Co, since 1983; Commercial Property. *Career:* Brecher & Co, Partner 1982-83. *Biog: b.* 27 July 1950. *Nationality:* British. *m.* 1977, Ann Markwick; 1 d. *Educ:* Canford School; Exeter University (BA Hons). *Professional Organisations:* Solicitor, 1979. *Recreations:* Tennis, Sailing, Diving.

ELDRIDGE, Colin J; Clerk, Spectacle Makers' Company & The Worshipful Company of Framework Knitters.

ELDRIDGE, John; Partner, S J Berwin & Co.

ELEY, D C; Divisional Director, City Merchants Bank Ltd.

ELFICK, Richard Stanley; Partner, Arthur Andersen & Co, since 1970; Practice Management. *Biog: b.* 4 October 1934. *Nationality:* British. *m.* 1968, Hilary (née Jones); 1 s; 2 d. *Educ:* Hounslow College. *Professional Organisations:* FCA. *Clubs:* RSRN Yacht Club, Royal Ocean Racing Club.

ELIOT, Robin F; Chairman and Underwriter, GP Eliot & Company Ltd.

ELKIN, D A P; Director, Crédit Lyonnais Rouse Limited.

ELKINGTON, Robert John; Managing Director, Gerrard & National Holdings plc, since 1978; Gilt Edged Market Making, Stockbroking, Finance & Banking. *Biog: b.* 7 October 1949. *Nationality:* British. *m.* 1984, Mary Patricia (née Ashley Cooper); 1 s; 2 d. *Educ:* Eton College; Exeter University (BA). *Directorships:* Gerrard & National Securities Ltd 1986 (exec); Gerrard Vivian Gray Ltd 1987 (non-exec); Gerrard & National Ltd 1990 (exec). *Clubs:* Boodle's, Pratt's, City of London.

ELKS, L; Partner, Nabarro Nathanson.

ELLACOTT, P; Director, Dowa Insurance Company (UK) Limited.

ELLARD, John; Partner, Linklaters & Paines, since 1983; Corporate Finance, Investment Funds. *Career:* Linklaters & Paines, Articled Clerk 1975-77; Assistant Solicitor 1977-83; Partner 1983-; Resident Partner in New York Office 1986-89. *Biog: b.* 1953. *Nationality:* British. *m.* 1987, Nicola M (née Pugh); 2 s. *Educ:* St Ambrose College, Hale Barns, Cheshire; John Fisher School, Purley, Surrey; King's School, Chester; Trinity Hall, Cambridge (BA). *Professional Organisations:* Solicitor. *Clubs:* Oxford & Cambridge. *Recreations:* Reading, Music, Travel, Photography.

ELLEN, S T; Director, S G Warburg Akroyd Rowe & Pitman Mullens Securities Ltd.

ELLERTON, C C; Director, S G Warburg Akroyd Rowe & Pitman Mullens Securities Ltd, since 1990; Equity Research. *Career:* Samuel Montagu, Assistant Director 1984-85; Barlays Bank International 1978-84. *Biog: b.* 16 September 1952. *Nationality:* British. *m.* 1982, Elizabeth Ellerton. *Educ:* St Edwards, Oxford; Leicester University (BA); Oxford University (MPhil). *Clubs:* Travellers.

ELLICK, P F; Director, S G Warburg Securities, since 1985. *Career:* Rowe & Pitman, Ptnr 1985-. *Biog: b.* 4 November 1950. *Nationality:* British. *Educ:* Cheshunt Grammar. *Directorships:* S G Warburg Securities 1986 (exec). *Other Activities:* Freeman, City of London. *Recreations:* Fox Hunting.

ELLICOCK, J H; Chief Executive Speciality Chemicals, The Burmah Oil plc.

ELLINGHAM, O B; Director, Robert Fleming & Co Limited, since 1989; Corporate Finance. *Career:* Ernst & Young, Accountant 1981-84; Robert Fleming 1984-. *Biog: b.* 11 March 1957. *Nationality:* British. *m.* 1981, Nicola (née Gammidge); 2 s; 1 d. *Educ:* Trinity College, Glenalmond; Middlesex Polytechnic (BA 1st Class Business Studies). *Professional Organisations:* ACA. *Recreations:* Squash, Gardening, Ballet.

ELLINGTON, Paul Robert; Partner, McKenna & Co, since 1971; Mergers & Acquisitions/Insolvency/other Corporate Work. *Career:* T Weldon Thomson & Co, Articled Clerk 1958-60; Marcan & Dean, Articled Clerk 1960-63; Clifford-Turner & Co, Asst Solicitor (incl 2 years in Paris) 1963-66; Allen & Overy, Asst Solicitor 1966-69; McKenna & Co, Asst Solicitor 1969-71. *Biog: b.* 2 August 1937. *Nationality:* British. *m.* 1960, Mireille (née Mathie); 2 s; 1 d. *Educ:* Dauntsey's; Bristol University and College of Law (Solicitors Qualifying Exam-Intermediate-Distinction Final-Distinction & 2nd Class Honours). *Directorships:* Toys R Us Ltd 1985 (non-exec); Western Union Communications Consultants Ltd 1985 (non-exec). *Other Activities:* Freeman, City of London Solicitors Company; IBA Committee J, Insolvency and Creditors' Rights; CBI Companies Act Working Group & Others; Law Society Insolvency Panel. *Professional Organisations:* Licensed Insolvency Practitioner. *Publications:* Various, London Correspondent, Revue Des Droits Des Affaires Internationales. *Recreations:* Music, Theatre, Walking, Reading.

ELLINTHORPE, B; Director, CIN Properties.

ELLIOT, Gordon Henry; Partner, Clyde & Co, since 1975; Recruitment Partner, Specialist in Commercial Litigation. *Career:* Clyde & Co, Articled Clerk 1970-72; Assistant Solicitor 1972-75. *Biog: b.* 28 June 1948. (div); 3 s. *Educ:* Nottingham High School; Bristol University (LLB). *Professional Organisations:* Member, Law Society. *Recreations:* Music, Reading.

ELLIOT, Graeme Arthur; Executive Vice-Chairman, Slough Estates plc, since 1985. *Career:* Arthur Anderson & Co 1964-67; The Rio Tinto-Zinc Corporation plc 1968-85. *Biog: b.* 28 June 1942. *Nationality:* British. *m.* 1983, Nicola Nella Simpson (née Taylor); 2 d (prev marriage). *Educ:* Rugby School; Magdalene College, Cambridge (MA Law). *Directorships:* Bredero Properties plc 1986 (non-exec); Candover Investments plc 1988 (non-exec); Thames Valley Enterprise Limited 1989 (non-exec). *Other Activities:* Member, CBI Southern Region; Member, Council of British Property Federation. *Professional Organisations:* FCA. *Clubs:* Whites, Portland, Berkshire Golf. *Recreations:* Golf, Tennis, Music, Bridge.

ELLIOT, Jo C; Executive Director, Quayle Munro Ltd, since 1988; Corporate Finance. *Career:* Scottish & Newcastle Breweries plc, Finance Division 1976-79; United Wire Group plc, Corporate Planner 1980-83; Quayle Munro Ltd, Manager/Assistant Director 1983-. *Biog: b.* 13 June 1952. *Nationality:* British. *m.* 1979, Alison Janet (née Macrae); 1 s; 1 d. *Educ:* Marlborough College; New College, Oxford (MA Physics); Cranfield School of Management (MBA). *Clubs:* New Club (Edinburgh). *Recreations:* Violin Playing, Windsurfing.

ELLIOTT, Andrew; Managing Director (Investment Management), Broad Street Group plc.

ELLIOTT, Anthony Charles Rayner; Director, S G Warburg & Co Ltd.

ELLIOTT, Anthony William; Partner, Lawrence Graham, since 1990; Commercial Property. *Career:* Herbert Oppenheimers, Articled Clerk 1974-76; Freshfields, Assistant Solicitor 1976-87; Lawrence Graham, Assistant Solicitor 1988-90. *Biog: b.* 7 July 1953. *Nationality:* British. *Educ:* Havant Grammar School; London School of Economics and Political Science (London University) (LLB Honss). *Professional Organisations:* Member, Law Society. *Recreations:* Music, Chess, Hockey, Running, Fell-Walking.

ELLIOTT, G K; Director, The Private Bank and Trust Company Limited.

ELLIOTT, Giles Roderick McGregor; Director, J Henry Schroder Wagg & Co Limited, since 1989; Corporate Finance. *Career:* Price Waterhouse, Assistant Manager 1975-80; J Henry Schroder Wagg & Co Limited, Manager 1980-83; Schroders Asia Limited, Director 1983-89; J Henry Schroder Wagg & Co Limited, Director 1989-. *Biog: b.* 6 February 1953. *Nationality:* British. *m.* 1978, Charlotte (née Davidson); 1 s; 3 d. *Educ:* Gresham's School, Holt; Magdalene, Cambridge (Engineering Sciences). *Directorships:* J Henry Schroder Wagg & Co Limited 1989 (exec). *Professional Organisations:* CA. *Clubs:* Hong Kong Club. *Recreations:* Golf, Bird Watching.

ELLIOTT, J; Director, Byas Mosley & Co Ltd.

ELLIOTT, John George; Assistant General Manager, Scottish Equitable Trustees Ltd.

ELLIOTT, Keith David; Director, S G Warburg & Co Ltd, since 1987; , S G Warburg France SA, since 1990. *Career:* Barclays Bank, Mgr; Generale Bank, Gen Mgr. *Biog: b.* 30 November 1947. *Nationality:* British. *m.* 1985, Jane Nichola (née Lee); 2 s; 1 d. *Educ:* The Stationers Company School. *Directorships:* S G Warburg & Co Ltd 1986 (exec); S G Warburg France SA 1990 (exec). *Other Activities:* Stationers Company. *Professional Organisations:* AIB. *Recreations:* Squash, Sailing.

ELLIOTT, Martin John Henry; Partner, Linklaters & Paines (Solicitors), since 1985; Commercial Property. *Career:* Linklaters & Paines, Articled Clerk to Partner 1977-. *Biog: b.* 26 August 1955. *Nationality:* British. *m.* 1984, Rosanna; 2 s. *Educ:* St Benedict's School, Ealing; Christ Church, Oxford (BA). *Other Activities:* City of London Solicitors Company. *Professional Organisations:* Member, Law Society. *Clubs:* MCC, Ealing Squash Rackets Club, Pitshanger Allotments & Garden Society.

ELLIOTT, Peter John; Partner, Clifford Chance.

ELLIOTT, R J; Executive Chairman, Willis Corroon plc.

ELLIOTT, Timothy R; Vice President, Chemical Bank.

ELLIOTT, Walter S; Director, Merrill Lynch Pierce Fenner & Smith Limited.

ELLIS, C T; Director, W H Ireland Stephens & Co Ltd.

ELLIS, David; Chief Executive, Lane Clark & Peacock, since 1989; Business Development, Marketing, Finance & Administration. *Career:* Crusader, Various to 1986; Crusader Insurance plc, Managing Director 1986-89. *Biog: b.* 13 February 1934. *Nationality:* British. (div) 2 d. *Directorships:* Co-Cam Computer Services (UK) Ltd 1989 (non-exec). *Other Activities:* Worshipful Company of Insurers. *Professional Organisations:* FCIS; FCII; FInstD. *Clubs:* Insurance Golfing Society of London, Betchworth Park Golf Club, English Speaking Union. *Recreations:* Writing.

ELLIS, H W H; Clerk, Farriers' Company.

ELLIS, M A; Partner, Simmons & Simmons.

ELLIS, M F; Executive Director and Deputy Underwriter, Gresham Underwriting Agencies Limited.

ELLIS, M T; Director, J H Minet & Co Ltd.

ELLIS, N G; Finance Director, BAA plc, since 1988; Finance and Property. *Career:* Longcrofts, Articled Clerk 1957-63; Touche Ross, Audit Clerk 1963-65; Heycock Press Ltd, Accountant 1965-67; City of London Real Property Company Ltd, Chief Accountant & Company Secretary 1967-73; Holland America UK Ltd, Finance Director 1973-79; Hammerson Property Investment and Development Corporation Ltd, Finance Director 1979-88; BAA plc, Finance Director 1988-. *Biog: b.* 19 April 1939. *Nationality:* British. *m.* 1965, Yvonne Melina Elizabeth (née Tracy); 1 s; 1 d. *Educ:* Farnborough Grammar School. *Directorships:* BAA plc 1988 (exec); Lynton plc 1988 (exec). *Other Activities:* Member, The Hundred Group; Member, The Worshipful Company of Fan Makers. *Professional Organisations:* FCA; FCCA. *Recreations:* Chess, Philately.

ELLIS, Peter Johnson; Deputy Chairman (formerly Joint Chief Executive), Kleinwort Benson Investment Management Ltd.

ELLIS, Stephen; Deputy City Editor, Daily Mirror.

ELLISON, A J; Director, Byas Mosley & Co Ltd.

ELLISON, Ian Keith Casey; CBE; Director, Robert Fleming & Co Ltd, since 1986; Corporate Finance/Telecommunications. *Career:* H M Diplomatic Service, 3rd/2nd Sec 1965-73; Govt of Gibraltar Secretariat 1969-71; Dept of Trade & Industry Principal, later Asst Sec 1973-84; Office of Fair Trading Monopolies & Mergers Division 1975-78; Principal Private Sec to Successive Secretaries of State for Industry 19 79-82; Telecommunications Div - Privatisation and Introduction of Competition 1982-84; Seconded to Robert Fleming & Co Limited 1985-86. *Biog: b.* 12 May 1942. *Nationality:* British. *m.* 1970, Mary (née East). *Educ:* Hurstpierpoint College; Keele University (BA Hons 1st); Reed College, Portland, Oregon. *Directorships:* Cable London plc 1988 (non-exec). *Publications:* The Telecommunications Monopoly Policy Review: Proposals for Policy Changes, 1990. *Recreations:* Gardens, Bridge, Mozart.

ELLISON, J J; Partner, Ashurst Morris Crisp, since 1990; European Law, In charge of Brussels Office. *Biog: b.* 6 September 1954. *Educ:* Westminster; Trinity College, Cambridge (Law). *Publications:* Longmans Practical Commercial Precedents: Computer Contracts. *Recreations:* Riding, Squash, Tennis, Skiing, Gardening.

ELLISTON, Richard Paul; Group Company Secretary, Morgan Grenfell Group plc, since 1990. *Career:* Dominion International Group plc, Director of Legal Services, Company Secretary 1987-90; The Juffaly Group, Legal Adviser 1979-89; The Rio Tinto Zinc Corporation plc, Assistant Legal Adviser 1973-78. *Biog: b.* 13 May 1947. *Nationality:* British. *m.* 1976, Monica; 1 s; 1 d. *Educ:* Uppingham School, Rutland; St Catharine's College, Cambridge (MA Hons). *Directorships:* Morgan Grenfell International Ltd 1990 (exec). *Professional Organisations:* Solicitor.

ELLWOOD, P B; Executive Director, TSB Group plc.

ELMER, Alec Francis; Director, Minster Trust Ltd, since 1968; Investment Management. *Career:* J T Lee & Co Unauthorised Clerk 1961-63; Authorised Clerk 1963-64; Assoc Member 1964-65; Akroyd & Smithers Assoc Member 1965-66; Minster Trust Ltd 1966-. *Biog: b.* 6 May 1939. *Nationality:* British. *m.* 1961, Brenda (née Lewis); 1 s; 1 d. *Educ:* Manchester Grammar School; Manchester University (BA Com).

ELMER, Patrick; Chairman, Baltic Futures Exchange Ltd, since 1987. *Career:* Pauls Agriculture Ltd, Company Director 1977-90; London Meat Futures Ltd, Chairman 1984-90. *Biog: b.* 17 March 1930. *Nationality:* British. *m.* 1955, Sybil Irene (née Turner). *Directorships:* Baltic Futures Exchanges Ltd 1987 (non-exec); London Meat Futures Ltd 1984 (non-exec). *Other Activities:* MLC Committees; NFU Industry Group Committee; NPBA. *Professional Organisations:* Fellow, British Inst Management. *Clubs:* RAC Pall Mall, Farmers Club.

ELMS, R A; Group General Manager - Britain, Royal Insurance Holdings plc.

ELSON, E E; Director, W H Smith Group plc.

ELSTOB, Eric Carl; Vice-Chairman, Foreign and Colonial Management, since 1987; International Investment Director. *Biog: b.* 5 April 1943. *Nationality:* British. *Educ:* Marlborough College; Queen's College, Oxford (MA). *Directorships:* F&C Reserve Asset Fund Chm; TR Trustees 1973 (non-exec); GT Japan 1972 (non-exec); Thornton Pan European 1980 (non-exec); F&C Pacific IT 1984 (exec); F&C Euro Trust IT 1972 (exec); Foreign & Colonial IT 1973 (exec). *Other Activities:* Treasurer, Friends of Christ Church, Spitalfields; Finance Ctee, DGAA. *Publications:* Sweden, Traveller's History of, 1979. *Clubs:* Cercle Interalliee, Paris. *Recreations:* Canoeing, Fell-Walking, Architecture.

ELTON, David Oatley; Executive Director, Ultramar plc, since 1981; Corporate Affairs. *Career:* Limebeers, Management Consultant 1969-70; Ultramar Golden Eagle, Managing Director 1970-74; Ultramar Ontario, President 1974-76; Ultramar plc, Group Marketing Coordinator 1977-87; American Ultramar, Vice President of Marketing 1978-79. *Biog: b.* 20 November 1943. *Nationality:* British. *m.* 1984, Jane (née Jenkins); 1 s; 1 d. *Educ:* Highgate School; Trinity College, Oxford (MA); London Business School (MSc). *Directorships:* Ultramar plc 1981 (exec); Agricultural Genetics Company 1983 (non-exec). *Clubs:* Carlton, MCC.

ELTON, Michael Anthony; Director General, National Association of Pension Funds, since 1987. *Career:* Cumberland CC, Solicitor 1958-61; Surrey CC, Solicitor 1961-65; Bucks CC, Assistant Clerk 1965-70; Deputy Clerk of the Peace 1967-70; Association of British Travel Agents, Chief Executive 1970-86. *Biog: b.* 20 May 1932. *Nationality:* British. *m.* 1955, Isabel Clare; 2 s; 2 d. *Educ:* Peter Symonds School; Brasenose College, Oxford (BCL, MA). *Professional Organisations:* CBIM. *Clubs:* United Oxford and Cambridge. *Recreations:* Tennis, Music, Bridge, Gardening.

ELVIDGE, Stephen René; Partner, Simmons & Simmons, since 1978; Commercial Property. *Career:* Simmons & Simmons, Articled Clerk 1972-74; Asst Solicitor 1974-77. *Biog: b.* 11 September 1949. *Nationality:* British. *m.* 1975, Gail Rosalind (née Church); 1 s; 2 d. *Educ:* Rydal School, Colwyn Bay, North Wales; Fitzwilliam College, Cambridge (MA). *Professional Organisations:* Member, Law Society; Member, City of London Solicitors' Company. *Recreations:* Squash, Walking, Gardening, Bell-Ringing.

ELVISS, M A; Compliance Partner, Broadbridge.

ELWES, Nigel Robert; Finance Director, S G Warburg Securities, since 1986; Finance. *Career:* Rowe & Pitman, Partner 1970-86; Finance Partner 1983-86. *Biog: b.* 8 August 1941. *Nationality:* British. *m.* 1965, Carolyn Peta (née McAlpine); 1 s; 2 d. *Educ:* Eton. *Directorships:* S G Warburg Akroyd Rowe & Pitman Mullens Securities Ltd 1986 (exec); The International Stock Exchange 1988 (exec). *Other Activities:* Member, Stock Exchange Council, 1983-86 and 1988-; Chairman, Special Committee on Market Developments, 1988-90 (The Elwes Committee). *Professional Organisations:* FCA. *Clubs:* White's. *Recreations:* Hunting, Shooting.

EMBLETON, Michael John; Partner, Pinsent & Co, since 1969; Corporate & Financial Law. *Biog: b.* 20 June 1941. *Nationality:* British. *m.* 1966, Carol (née Scribbans); 1 s; 1 d. *Educ:* Kingswood School. *Professional Organisations:* The Law Society; The Birmingham Law Society. *Clubs:* The Birmingham Club, Birmingham Chamber of Commerce Club. *Recreations:* Shooting, Skiing, Sailing.

EMERSON, E A; Director, Hill Samuel & Co Ltd.

EMERSON, Ronald Victor; General Manager, Banking, Nomura Bank International plc, since 1989. *Career:* British Steel Corporation 1969-70; De La Rue Group, Formica International Commercial Development Controller 1971-75; Bank of America, Various Positions Leading to Head of London Corporate Office and UK Country Manager 1975-89. *Biog: b.* 22 February 1947. *Nationality:* British. 2 s. *Educ:* Manchester University (BSc); Durham University (MSc). *Professional Organisations:* FRSA. *Recreations:* Flying, Sport, Reading.

EMLEY, M L B; Managing Director UK Corporate Finance, UBS Phillips & Drew Securities Limited.

EMLY, John Richard Keith; Main Board Director, Robert Fleming Holdings Limited, since 1985; UK Investment. *Career:* The Law Debenture Corporation Ltd 1960-75; Accountant 1968-70; Joint Investment Manager 1970-75. *Biog: b.* 1941. *Nationality:* British. *m.* 1969, Maria Joan (née Gumosz); 2 s; 2 d. *Educ:* St Dunstans College. *Directorships:* Robert Fleming Holdings Ltd 1985 (exec); Robert Fleming Asset Management Ltd 1988 (exec); Fleming Investment Management Ltd 1988 (exec); Robert Fleming Investment Trust Ltd 1981 (exec); Robert Fleming Investment Management Ltd 1978-88 (exec). *Professional Organisations:* FCIS; ASIA.

EMMERSON, John Corti; Partner, McKenna & Co, since 1983; Personal Tax Planning/Private Clients. *Career:* 4th Royal Tank Regiment (2/LT) 1956-58; Oxford University 1958-61; Air Ministry, Assistant Principal 1961-63; Warmingtons & Hasties, Partner 1967-83. *Biog: b.* 10 September 1937. *Nationality:* British. *m.* 1970, Anne; 1 s; 1 d. *Educ:* Magdalen College, Oxford (MA). *Directorships:* Woodard Schools (Southern

Division) Ltd 1984 (non-exec); Euroconsults Ltd 1985 (exec); Jasmine Trustees Ltd 1988 (exec). *Other Activities:* London Chamber of Commerce (Hong Kong Committee); Governor, Ardingly College, West Sussex. *Professional Organisations:* Law Society; International Fiscal Association; International Tax Planning Association; Law Society of Hong Kong. *Publications:* Various Articles in Legal Journals. *Clubs:* Brooks's. *Recreations:* Fly Fishing, Reading, Walking.

EMMOTT, William John; Business Affairs Editor, The Economist, since 1989; Editor for all Coverage of Business, Finance & Science. *Career:* The Economist, Brussels Correspondent 1980-82; Economics Writer 1982-83; Tokyo Correspondent 1983-86; Financial Editor 1986-89. *Biog: b.* 6 August 1956. *Nationality:* British. *Educ:* Latymer Upper School, Hammersmith; Magdalen College, Oxford (BA Hons Politics Philosophy & Economics). *Publications:* The Pocket Economist (with R Pennant-Rea), 1983, Second Edition, 1986; The Sun Also Sets: The Limits To Japan's Economic Power, 1989. *Clubs:* Reform.

EMMS, John Frederick George; Deputy Chairman, Commercial Union Assurance Co Ltd.

EMMS, Peter Anthony; Executive Director, Marketing, Allied Dunbar Assurance plc.

EMMS, V E; Prime Warden, Worshipful Company of Glass Sellers.

EMUS, Alan H; Clerk, The Worshipful Company of Butchers.

ENDACOTT, Richard John; Group Financial Controller & Treasurer, Ranks Hovis McDougall plc, since 1985; Treasury, Accounting, Taxation. *Career:* Ranks Hovis McDougall, Various 1966-. *Biog: b.* 19 May 1942. *m.* 1971, Susan (née Taylor); 2 s. *Educ:* The Leys School, Cambridge. *Professional Organisations:* ICA; MCT. *Recreations:* Golf, Cricket.

ENGINEER, Ratan; Finance Director, MIM Ltd.

ENGLAND, A M; Director, Wellington Underwriting Agencies Limited.

ENGLAND, Norman Clifford; Non Executive Director, Singer & Friedlander Ltd.

ENGLEBRIGHT, William Joseph; Director, Baltic Futures Exchange Ltd.

ENGLISH, A B; Partner, Life & General (Epsom), Bacon & Woodrow.

ENGLISH, P C; Director, Charterhouse Tilney, since 1989; Information Systems. *Career:* Charterhouse Tilney

1984-; Teaching (Mathematics & Electronics) 1978-84. *Biog: b.* 1 December 1953. *Nationality:* British. *Educ:* Hazelwick School; Gonville & Caius College, Cambridge (BA Engineering, MA); University of Technology, Loughborough (PGCE). *Clubs:* Hawks'. *Recreations:* Skiing, Rowing, Motorcycling, Theatre, Music.

ENGLISH, Peter; Partner, Venture Capital Funding, Technology Investment Management, Fleming Ventures Ltd, since 1985; Managing £20m Venture Fund Specialising in Electronics Sector.

ENGLISH, Peter John; Joint Managing Director, PWS Holdings plc, since 1989; Insurance Operations. *Career:* Tudor & Co, now P/O Fenchurch Group, Insurance Clerk 1966-68; Bevington Vaizey Foster, now P/O Sedgwick Group, Insurance Clerk 1968-70; Bland Payne, now P/O Sedgwick Group, Insurance Broker 1970-75; Pearson Webb Springbett, now PWS Holdings, from Insurance Broker, Mgr to Jt MD 1975-89. *Biog: Nationality:* British. 1 s; 1 d. *Directorships:* PWS Holdings plc 1986 (exec); PWS International Ltd 1986 (exec); PGS Ltd 1989 (non-exec).

ENGSTRÖM, Peter; Managing Director, J S Gadd & Co Ltd, since 1988. *Career:* Various Companies Journalist 1964-68; Confederation of Swedish Construction Industry Secretary of Information 1968-70; International Monetary Fund, Asst Div Chief 1970-78; Swedish National Debt Office, Director 1978-86; Union Bank of Switzerland (Securities) Ltd, MD 1986-88. *Biog: b.* 2 August 1944. *Nationality:* Swedish. *m.* 1986, Béatrice (née Bondy); 2 d. *Educ:* Whitlockska Samskolan, Stockholm; Stockholm School of Economics (Civilekonom); University of Stockholm (Fil Kand). *Directorships:* Anglo Scandinavian Investment Trust plc 1989 (non-exec); IMI Bank (International) 1989 (non-exec). *Clubs:* RAC, Sällskapet.

ENOCK, David S; Director, Commercial Union Asset Management Ltd. *Directorships:* Investment Management Regulatory Organisation Ltd (non-exec). *Professional Organisations:* FCIS.

ENTWHISTLE, R M; Executive Director, James R Knowles Limited.

ENTWISTLE, Malcolm Graham; Partner, Hill Dickinson & Company, since 1985; Company, Commercial & Corporate Law. *Career:* Norton Rose Botterell & Roche Articled Clerk 1977-79. *Biog: b.* 6 September 1954. *m.* 1987, Elizabeth Ruth (née Williams). *Educ:* Oundle School; Liverpool University (LLB Hons). *Other Activities:* Third Market Legal Sub Ctee. *Professional Organisations:* The Law Society. *Clubs:* Walton Heath Golf Club. *Recreations:* Golf, Squash, Sailing.

ENTWISTLE, R M; Executive Director, Adam & Company Group plc.

EPSTEIN, Norman; Partner, Moore Stephens.

ERITH, Robert Felix; TD; Chairman, Equities Group, Swiss Bank Corporation, since 1983. *Career:* 10th Royal Hussars (PWO), Lt 1956-58; Builders' Merchants Sales and Mgmnt Trainee 1960-65; Milln & Robinson/Savory Milln Building Industry Specialist 1966-. *Biog:* b. 8 August 1938. *Nationality:* British. *m.* 1966, Sara (née Muller); 3 s. *Educ:* Ipswich School; Writtle Agricultural College. *Directorships:* Erith plc 1977 (non-exec) Dep Chm; Cawberry Ltd 1983 (non-exec); Royal London Mutual Insurance Society Ltd 1987 (non-exec); Secure Trust Group plc 1989 (non-exec). *Other Activities:* National Economic Development Council, Housing Sub-Committee; Worshipful Company of Builders' Merchants. *Professional Organisations:* AMSIA. *Publications:* Savory Milln's Building Book, 1968-86, (annual). *Clubs:* Cavalry & Guards, City of London, MCC.

ESCOTT, John Robert Sydney; Director, Touche Remnant & Co, since 1988; Dealing & Contracts. *Career:* Hill Samuel Investment Management, Deputy Dealing Manager 1974-83; Butler Till Moneybrokers, Sterling Deposits Dealer 1983-84; Bank Julius Baer Securities, Trader 1984-85; Touche Remnant & Co 1985-. *Biog:* b. 28 December 1954. *Nationality:* British. *m.* 1988, Sharon Deborah (née Knevett). *Educ:* King Edward VI Grammar School, Chelmsford, Essex. *Recreations:* Football, Amateur Dramatics.

ESPE, R D; Deputy Chairman, E W Payne Companies Limited.

ESPENHAHN, Peter Ian; Director, Morgan Grenfell & Co Ltd, since 1983. *Biog:* b. 14 March 1944. *Educ:* Westminster; Sidney Sussex, Cambridge (MA). *Professional Organisations:* FCA.

ESPHAVN JENSEN, Carsten; Chief Executive, Unibank plc, since 1988. *Career:* Privatbanken A/S (Denmark), Assistant Manager 1979-81; Deputy Manager 1981-84; Manager 1984-86; Assistant General Manager 1986-88; Executive Vice President 1988-; Trainee, International Division 1977; Foreign Offices Department 1980; Privatbanken A/S, New York, Account Manager Business Development/Head of Business Development & Corporate Finance 1981; Privatbanken A/S Head Office (Denmark), Head of Corporate Banking Dept 1986; Chief Executive Privatbanken Limited, London (now Unibank plc) 1988-. *Biog:* b. 21 April 1951. *Nationality:* Danish. *m.* 1982, Audrey (née Schuttler). *Educ:* Business School of Economics and Business Administration, Aarhus, Denmark (Master of Economics). *Directorships:* Unibank plc 1988 (exec). *Other Activities:* Founding Chairman, Danish-UK Chamber of Commerce, now Member of Board. *Professional Organisations:* Member, Institute of Bankers; Member, Institute of Directors. *Clubs:* RAC, Overseas Bankers' Club, Lombard Association. *Recreations:* Tennis, Football, Films.

ESSEX, David Anthony Dampier; Partner, Ernst & Whinney.

ESSLEMONT, P D; Clerk, Actuaries' Company.

ESTEVA, P; Director (France), County NatWest Limited.

ETZEL, P-J K; Member of the Council, The International Stock Exchange.

EUGSTER, Christopher Anthony Alwyn Patrick; Director, Kleinwort Benson Ltd, since 1976; Corporate Finance. *Career:* Whinney Murray, Trainee Acct 1965-70; Kleinwort Benson Ltd 1970-. *Biog:* b. 17 March 1941. *Nationality:* British. *m.* 1965, Carole (née Bouwens); 2 s. *Educ:* Downside School. *Directorships:* Boddington Breweries 1976 (non-exec); Dares Estates 1988. *Clubs:* White's, Pratt's. *Recreations:* Shooting, Fishing.

EULATE, J; Deputy General Manager, Banco Santander, since 1990. *Career:* Banco Intercontinental Español, FX, Intal Division, Credit Dept, Foreign Department Manager 1981-83; Banco Arabe Español, Area Manager, Intal Division 1983-88; Banco Santander Spain, Deputy Manager, International Financial Institutions 1988-90; London 1990-. *Biog:* b. 31 March 1955. *Nationality:* Spanish. *m.* 1984, Veronica Gomez-Acebo; 1 d. *Educ:* Universidad Complutense Falcutad Ciencias Economicas (Completed 5 Years Licenciado). *Clubs:* Real Club, Puerta de Hierro, Madrid. *Recreations:* Golf, Shooting, Squash, Reading, Sailing.

EVANDER, Lars Peter; Executive Vice President, Group Chief Executive, UK Region & Managing Director, Svenska Handelsbanken Group, since 1982; All International Investment Banking & UK Commercial Banking. *Career:* City Courts (Stockholm) Law Clerk & Asst Judge 1971-73; Svenska Handelsbanken (Stockholm) Legal Advisor 1973-74; Asst VP 1975-78; European Banking Co (secondment) 1978-79; Nordic Bank (secondment) 1980-82. *Biog:* b. 12 January 1947. *Nationality:* Swedish. *m.* 1972, Maria (née Dahlgren-Tiberg); 1 s; 1 d. *Educ:* Sigtuna Hum; University of Stockholm, Law School(LLM). *Directorships:* Svenska Financial Services Ltd Chm; Svenska & Company Ltd Chm; Svenska Development Capital plc Chm; Svenska Selection Fund; Svenska Handelsbanken SA (Luxembourg); SIL (Nominees) Ltd; Svenska Handelsbanken Bond Fund; Svenska Handelsbanken OHG; Svenska Handelsbanken Asia Ltd; Svenska Capital (Japan) Ltd; Svenska Iberica SA; Nordic Capital Ltd. *Other Activities:* Trustee, Swedish Benevolent Trust.

EVANGELIDES, John; Director, Samuel Montagu & Co Limited.

EVANGELOU, S H; Financial Controller, Bank of Cyprus (London) Ltd.

EVANS, Anthony David; Partner, Macfarlanes, since 1981; Banking & Corporate Law. *Career:* Collins Woods & Vaughan Jones (Swansea), Ptnr 1971-73; Coward Chance, Asst Solicitor 1973-78; Macfarlanes, Asst Solicitor 1978-81. *Biog: b.* 14 December 1946. *m.* 1987, Diane Janet (née Pauls). *Educ:* Grove Park School, Wrexham; University College Wales, Aberystwyth (LLB). *Other Activities:* Liveryman, Coopers Company; Chm, Lion Boys Club Hoxton. *Professional Organisations:* City of London Solicitors' Company; The Law Society; IBA. *Recreations:* Sailing, Climbing.

EVANS, Christopher David; Director, Operations & Planning, Abbey Life Assurance Company Ltd, since 1989; General Management. *Career:* Equity & Law Life Assurance Society, Various to Snr Asst Sec, Group Pensions 1969-83; Abbey Life, Various to Executive Director, Marketing 1983-. *Biog: b.* 5 June 1948. *m.* 1970, Isobel; 2 d. *Educ:* King Henry VIII, Coventry; Churchill College, Cambridge (MA). *Professional Organisations:* Fellow, Institute of Actuaries.

EVANS, Christopher John; Assistant Group General Manager (Personnel), Royal Insurance Holdings plc, since 1988; Group Organisation & Succession Planning, Career Development & Training, Coordination of Employment Policy & Employee Relations. *Career:* Imperial Metal Industries (Birmingham) Personnel Officer 1964-66; ICI Europa Limited (Brussels) Snr Personnel Officer 1967-76; Sperry Remington Consumer Products European Personnel Mgr 1977-78; Sperry Information Systems (now Unisys Ltd) Regional Personnel Dir, N Europe 1978-84; Personnel Director (UK) 1984-86; Unisys Ltd Management Services Dir 1987-88. *Biog: b.* 10 August 1942. *Nationality:* British. *m.* 1977, Belinda (née Knapp); 2 s. *Educ:* Clifton College, Bristol; Kings College, Cambridge (MA). *Other Activities:* Chm, Insurance Industry Training Council. *Professional Organisations:* Member, Institute of Personnel Management. *Recreations:* Travel, National Trust, Philately, Sailing.

EVANS, D; Managing Director (Investment Management), Bankers Trust Company.

EVANS, D W; Company Secretary/Compliance Officer, Wardley Investment Services International Limited/Wardley Unit Trust Managers Limited, since 1989; UK Compliance and Offshore Regulation. *Career:* Wardley Fund Managers (Jersey) Limited, Finance Director/Company Secretary 1988-89; MIM Britannia International Limited (Jersey), Financial Controller 1985-88; Cranfield MBA Progranne 1983-84; Lorilleux & Bolton Limited, Financial Controller 1980-83; Management

Accountant 1978-80. *Biog: b.* 18 September 1953. *Nationality:* British. *m.* 1982, Louise Emily (née Wood); 2 s. *Educ:* Burnham Grammar School; Exeter University (BA Hons Law/Economics); Cranfield School of Management (MBA). *Directorships:* Wardley Fund Managers (Jersey) Limited 1988 (non-exec). *Professional Organisations:* Chartered Institute of Management Accountants - passed Finalist (CIMA). *Recreations:* Family.

EVANS, David F C; Partner, Wilde Sapte.

EVANS, David I; Managing Director, Alexander Howden Reinsurance Brokers Limited.

EVANS, Douglas F; Partner, Theodore Goddard.

EVANS, Edward; City Reporter, Today.

EVANS, Edward Thomas Huw; Partner, Freshfields, since 1986; Company Department. *Career:* Freshfields 1978-. *Biog: b.* 12 December 1954. *Nationality:* British. *m.* 1980, Alison (née Hird); 1 s; 2 d. *Educ:* RGS High Wycombe; Trinity College, Cambridge. *Professional Organisations:* Law Society. *Clubs:* UOCUC.

EVANS, Gareth Ian; Director, N M Rothschild Asset Management, since 1989; Currency Straegy. *Career:* Bank of England, Economist 1980-85; Foreign Exchange Division, Senior Investment Manager 1986-89. *Biog: b.* 6 June 1957. *Nationality:* British. *Educ:* Worcester Royal Grammar School; Hertford College, Oxford (BA Hons Mathematics); London School of Economics (MSc). *Directorships:* N M Rothschild International Asset Management 1989 (exec).

EVANS, H P; Deputy Secretary, HM Treasury.

EVANS, J C; Partner, Hill Taylor Dickinson.

EVANS, Janet; Partner, Jaques & Lewis, since 1989; Commercial Property. *Career:* Davies Arnold & Copper, Assistant Solicitor 1982-86; Jaques & Lewis, Assistant Solicitor/Partner 1986-. *Biog: b.* 10 February 1956. *Nationality:* British. *Educ:* University College, University of London (LLB Hons). *Other Activities:* Member of RHS. *Professional Organisations:* Association of Womens Solicitors. *Recreations:* Cookery, Gardening.

EVANS, John M R; Company Secretary, Guardian Royal Exchange plc, since 1985. *Career:* Deloittes, Snr Audit 1954-57; Guardian Assurance, Asst Accountant 1957-68; GRE, Chief Accountant 1968-76; Snr Mgr 1976-82; Asst Gen Mgr 1982-85; Company Secretary 1985-. *Biog: b.* 29 November 1931. *m.* 1955, Mary C (née Cooper); 1 s; 2 d. *Educ:* King George V School, Southport. *Directorships:* GRE (Various Subsidiaries) (exec). *Other Activities:* Chm, Insurance Regulations Ctee of Assoc of British Insurers. *Professional Organisa-*

tions: FCA. *Clubs:* RAC, Players Theatre. *Recreations:* Golf, Local Societies.

EVANS, John Stafford; Director, Gibbs Hartley Cooper Ltd, since 1986; Specialist Insurance Broking. *Career:* Halford Shead & Co Ltd, Dir 1970-76; Alexander Howden Insurance Brokers Div Chief Exec Officer 1976-85; Halford Shead & Co Ltd, Chm 1985-86. *Biog: b.* 19 March 1939. *Nationality:* British. *m.* 1972, Judith Mary (née Beesly); 1 s; 2 d. *Educ:* Harrow School. *Directorships:* Hartley Cooper Associates Ltd Joint Chm; Gibbs Hartley Cooper Limited. *Clubs:* RAC Club, New York Athletic Club.

EVANS, L Adrian W; Group Managing Director, Benchmark Group plc, since 1986. *Career:* Citibank, NYC, Vice-President 1963-71; First National Finance Corporation, Director 1971-76; Grindlays Bank plc, MD 1976-85; Benchmark Group plc, Group MD 1986-. *Biog: b.* 29 June 1941. *Nationality:* British. *m.* 1983, Ingela. 1 s (decd) 2 d. *Educ:* Stowe School; Cambridge University (BA History). *Directorships:* Benchmark Group Related Companies 1986 (exec); F L Smidth & Co (Holdings) Ltd 1988 (non-exec); Grovecastle Ltd 1984 (non-exec); Cliveden Group Ltd 1984 (non-exec). *Other Activities:* Chairman, Council of Management of Gap Activity Projects Ltd; Governor, Stowe School. *Clubs:* Brooks's.

EVANS, Lloyd Hanwick; Equity Partner, Berwin Leighton, since 1982; Commercial, Communications, Europe & Eastern Bloc/Entertainment. *Career:* Camrose Kemsley and Thompson Owned Papers, Journalist 1954-63; D W Harris & Co, Pontypridd, S Wales, Solicitor 1963-68; Associated Television Corporation Ltd, Group Solicitor 1968-80; Berwin Leighton, Partner 1980-. *Biog: b.* 3 February 1941. *Nationality:* British. *m.* 1984, Jane; 2 d. *Educ:* Hillstone Preparatory School; Uppingham Public School (Solicitor). *Other Activities:* Law Society; International Bar Association. *Professional Organisations:* Diploma in Journalism. *Publications:* Times and Financial Times Articles on Copyright and Eastern Bloc in Recent Years; UK Competition Law, 1989; EEC Competition Law, 1990; Soviet Joint Ventures, 1990. *Recreations:* Shooting, Motor Racing, Scuba Diving.

EVANS, M A; General Manager, Investments, Commercial Union Assurance.

EVANS, M A; Partner, Investment, Bacon & Woodrow.

EVANS, Mark Singleton; Head of Corporate Finance, Laing & Cruickshank, since 1983. *Career:* Fahnestock & Co, Ptnr's Asst 1957-59; Robert Wigram & Co, Ptnr's Asst 1959-61; Laing & Cruickshank, Research Analyst 1961-64; Ptnr 1964-86; Dir 1980-. *Biog: b.* 27 October 1933. *Nationality:* British. *m.* 1962, Belinda Jane (née Cayley); 2 s; 1 d. *Educ:* Winchester College; New College, Oxford (MA Hons). *Directorships:* Mediterranean Fund 1989 (non-exec). *Other Activities:* President, Kensington Conservative Association; Chairman of Governors, Brompton Hall Special School and Welburn Hall Special School; Committee, Kensington Day Centre; President, Scarborough & Whitby Conservative Association; Governor, Brompton-by-Sawdon Priory School; Governor, Sion-Marriet School for Girls. *Clubs:* Whites, Swinley Forest Golf Club, Ganton Golf Club, MCC. *Recreations:* Gardening, Tennis, Golf, Shooting, Fishing.

EVANS, Michael John; AE; Director, DAL Group plc, since 1988; Industrial/International Marketing. *Career:* ICI UK, Manager 1956-67; ICI Europa, Brussels, Marketing Director, Chemicals Group 1967-72; Deutsche ICI, Director 1972-75; Unilever Oleochemicals, Director 1976; Siegfried AG Switzerland, Deputy Chairman Management Board 1977-83; DTF Ltd, Chief Executive 1983-88. *Biog: b.* 20 June 1932. *Nationality:* British. *m.* 1960, Kathleen (née Roberts); 1 s; 1 d. *Educ:* B Com; Dip INSEAD. *Directorships:* Siegfried AG Switzerland 1977-83 Deputy Chairman Management Board; Ganes Chemicals Inc New York 1978-82 President; Laporte plc; DAL Group plc; Oost International Ltd; Assilec SA Paris 1984-87 Deputy Chairman; EPI Ltd 1987-89 Chairman. *Other Activities:* Local Political. *Clubs:* Royal Air Force. *Recreations:* Skiing, Sailing, Tennis, Serious Music, Languages.

EVANS, Philip W; Head of Corporate Finance, Paribas Limited, since 1988; International M&A. *Career:* Morgan Grenfell, Director, Corporate Finance 1974-88.

EVANS, Richard C; Partner, Beachcroft Stanleys.

EVANS, Robert; CBE; Partner, Nabarro Nathanson.

EVANS, Stuart John; Partner, Simmons & Simmons, since 1981; Company Law. *Career:* Stanley Brent & Co, Articled Clerk 1970-72; Slaughter and May, Asst Solicitor 1972-79; Simmons & Simmons, Asst Solicitor 1979-80. *Biog: b.* 31 December 1947. *m.* 1971, Margaret Elizabeth (née Evans); 2 s; 1 d. *Educ:* Royal Grammar School, Newcastle-upon-Tyne; Leeds University (LLB). *Other Activities:* City of London Law Society. *Publications:* A Practitioner's Guide to The Stock Exchange Yellow Book, 1989 and 1990; Chapter on Acquisitions and Realisations in Take-Overs and Mergers. *Recreations:* Pictures, Squash.

EVANS LOMBE, Peter Michael; Director, Hambros Bank Ltd, since 1983; Investment Management. *Career:* Army Regular 1951; Commissioned 3rd Carabiniers PWDG 1953; Transferred 15th/19th Hussars 1954; Retired from the Army as a Captain 1960; Kitcat & Aitken Stockbrokers 1960-83; Member of the Stock Exchange 1966-83; Kitcat & Aitken, Partner 1967;

Global Asset Management, Director 1983; Hambros Bank, Director 1983. *Biog: b.* 5 June 1933. *Nationality:* British. *m.* 1964; 2 s. *Educ:* Wellington College; RMA, Sandhurst (MB 1st). *Directorships:* Kitcat & Aitken 1967-83; Global Asset Management (UK) Ltd 1983; Hambros Bank Ltd 1983-. *Other Activities:* Liveryman, Skinners Company; Freeman, City of London; Member, The NASD 1980-83 (Registered Rep, NASD). *Clubs:* Swinley Forest Golf Club, Royal West Norfolk Golf Club.

EVE, Michael Winston; Chairman & Managing Director, Non Marine Group, Leslie & Godwin Ltd, since 1989; International Insurance Broking. *Career:* Ansbacher Insurance Holdings, Executive Deputy Chairman 1987-89; Bank America Insurance Services, Managing Director 1984-87; Jardine Insurance Brokers, Initially Chief Executive of Jardine Glanvill (UK) and then Chief Exec, Worldwide Retail 1980-84; Bland Payne/Sedgwick plc, Director Responsible for Loss Control Services and Product Development 1976-80; PA Management Consultants, Marketing and Strategic Development Consultant 1969-76; Rank Xerox, Market Analyst and then Manager Major Account Sales and Planning 1966-69; Michelin Tyre Co, Graduate Trainee and then Market Analysis Manager 1962-66. *Biog: b.* 17 September 1941. *Nationality:* British. *m.* 1969, Madeleine (née Norman); 1 s; 1 d. *Educ:* Manchester University (BSc Hons). *Directorships:* Leslie & Godwin Group Ltd (exec); Leslie & Godwin Ltd (exec); Leslie & Godwin Non Marine Holdings Ltd (exec); Leslie & Godwin Financial Risks (exec); Leslie & Godwin Energy Resources (exec); Leslie & Godwin Non Marine (exec); Leslie & Godwin North America (exec); Artscope International (exec); Property Owners Data Base (exec). *Professional Organisations:* Chartered Insurance Institute; Insurance Brokers Registration Council; Graduate, Institute of Marketing. *Publications:* Strategic Options Facing the Travel Industry, 1986. *Recreations:* Travel, Running, International Business Studies.

EVENNETT, David; Managing Director, N T Evennett and Partners Ltd.

EVENNETT, Norman T; Chairman, N T Evennett and Partners Ltd.

EVERARD, F G; Clerk, Scientific Instrument Makers' Company.

EVERARD, Marcus A L; Executive Director, Crédit Suisse First Boston Limited.

EVERARD, S; TD, DL; President, Ellis & Everard plc, since 1990. *Career:* Ellis & Everard Ltd 1952; Deputy Chairman 1975; Chairman 1980. *Biog: b.* 1928. *m.* 1955, Joceline Margaret (née Holt); 3 s; 1 d. *Educ:* Uppingham School; Clare College, Cambridge (BA Hons History). *Directorships:* Alliance & Leicester Building Society 1984 (non-exec); Uppingham School Shops Ltd 1988 (non-exec); Ellis & Everard plc 1952 (non-exec). *Other Activities:* Governing Body, Leicester Polytechnic; Trustee, Uppingham School. *Clubs:* Cavalry & Guards. *Recreations:* Golf, Shooting, Bridge.

EVEREST, Richard Anthony; Director and Group Chief Accountant, Bell Nicholson Henderson Ltd, since 1987; Finance. *Career:* Pridie Brewster & Gold, Articled Clerk 1962-66; Black Geoghegan & Till, Audit Senior 1966-70; Layton-Bennett Billingham & Co, Assistant Manager 1970-74; Josolyne Layton-Bennett & Co, Audit Manager 1974-79; Arthur Young McLelland Moores & Co, Principal Manager 1979-82; Bell Nicholson Henderson Ltd, Director 1982-. *Biog: b.* 26 April 1938. *Nationality:* British. *m.* 1969, Brenda Anne (née Ralph); 2 s. *Educ:* Highgate School; Christ Church, Oxford (MA). *Directorships:* Henry G Nicholson (Underwriting) Ltd 1986 (exec); Bell Nicholson Henderson Ltd 1987 (exec). *Other Activities:* Master, Worshipful Company of Cutlers, 1990-91. *Professional Organisations:* Institute of Chartered Accountants in England & Wales, Associate 1966, Fellow 1976. *Recreations:* Swimming.

EVERETT, M J L; Deputy Chairman, Tullett & Tokyo Forex International Ltd.

EVERINGHAM, N G A; Director, Barclays de Zoete Wedd Securities Ltd.

EVERS, Ralph Owen; Partner, Clyde & Co, since 1975; Shipping and Insurance. *Career:* Clyde & Co, Articled Clerk 1969-71; Assistant Solicitor 1971-75. *Biog: b.* 7 August 1946. *Nationality:* British. *m.* 1974, Mary Jean (née McNeil); 3 s. *Educ:* Rugby School; Oriel College, Oxford (MA). *Professional Organisations:* Law Society. *Clubs:* Roehampton.

EWART-JAMES, D O; Director, Hambros Bank Limited.

EWBANK, Jonathan J; Partner, Dennis Murphy, Campbell & Co.

EWEN, Arthur John Stanley; Executive Director, County NatWest Securities Limited; Corporate Stockbroking. *Career:* ER Syfret & Co, Articled Clerk 1948-51; Industrial Development Corp of South Africa Exec 1952-54; Johannesburg Consolidated Investment Co Ltd Exec 1954-61; Barnato Bros Ltd Dir 1961-69; Colegrave & Co Ptnr 1969-75; Private Consultant 1975-81; Wood, Mackenzie & Co 1981-87. *Biog: b.* 7 August 1927. *m.* 1966, Avis (née Blackwood-Murray); 2 s; 1 d. *Educ:* Winchester College. *Directorships:* Northamber plc 1988 (non-exec). *Recreations:* Tennis, Bridge.

EWER, D L; Director, Ropner Insurance Services Limited.

EWERS, Fred J; Head of Institutional Sales Division, Crédit Suisse Buckmaster & Moore Ltd.

EWINS, Peter; Personnel Director, 3i plc, since 1989. *Career:* Joselyne Layton-Bennett 1976-80; 3i plc 1980-. *Biog: b.* 26 June 1955. *m.* 1979; 2 d. *Educ:* Cardiff University (BSc Econ). *Directorships:* 3i plc 1989 (exec). *Professional Organisations:* ACA. *Recreations:* Travel, Active Christian Church Member.

EYNON, Richard Mark; Director, Warburg Securities, since 1986; Futures, Options. *Career:* Harris Bank, London 1977-80; Bank of America, London 1980-86. *Biog: b.* 9 November 1953. *Nationality:* British. *m.* 1980, Susan (née Allen); 1 d. *Educ:* Manchester University (BSc); Manchester Business School (MBA). *Directorships:* Liffe Ltd 1987 (non-exec); S G Warburg Futures, Options 1982 (exec). *Other Activities:* FIA, London.

EYRES, W R; Executive Director, Schroder Investment Management Ltd.

F

FACER, J R; Partner, Field Fisher Waterhouse.

FADEL, Gaby G; Manager, Byblos Bank Sal, since 1981; Manager, Head of Marketing Dept. *Career:* Banque Trad Credit Lyonnais, Beirut, Forex Dept 1975-77; Byblos Bank Belgium SA, Brussels, Training for one year; Byblos Bank, Beirut 1980-81; Byblos Bank Sal, London Branch 1981-; Account Officer, Assistant Manager, Manager. *Biog:* b. 6 February 1956. *Nationality:* Lebanese. *m.* 1985, Marcelle (née Bou Dagher); 2 s. *Educ:* College de l'Annonciation; St Joseph University, Beirut (BSc Econ); St Joseph University, Beirut (DESS Econ). *Other Activities:* Member of the ABA, London; Member of the BBA, London.

FAHERTY, Colman James Bernard; Administration Director, Foreign and Colonial Management Ltd, since 1985. *Career:* Simon and Coats, Accounts Clerk 1967-70; RA Blackwell Ltd, Arbitrage Settlements 1970-72; Buckmaster and Moore, Fin Mgr/Dep Office Mgr 1972-81; Foreign and Colonial Management Ltd, Office Mgr 1981-85. *Biog:* b. 1 September 1949. *Nationality:* Irish. *m.* 1969, Jacqueline Frances (née Ford); 2 s; 1 d. *Educ:* St Joseph's College, Nun's Island, Galway. *Directorships:* Foreign & Colonial Unit Management Ltd 1983 (exec); F & C Nominees Ltd 1986 (exec); Foreign and Colonial Pensions Management Ltd 1986 (exec); Circa Leisure plc 1988-89 (non-exec); Foreign & Colonial Management (Jersey) Ltd 1988 (exec). *Other Activities:* Member, Rochford District Council 1986-90; Member, Institute of Directors. *Recreations:* Golf, Snooker.

FAIERS, Ms Sally D; Director, Merrill Lynch Pierce Fenner & Smith Ltd, since 1988; Money Market Department. *Career:* Credit Suisse First Boston, Money Market Sales 1981-84; Merrill Lynch, Money Market Sales 1984-. *Biog:* b. 22 November 1958. *Nationality:* British. *m.* 1989, Roy Copperwaite; 1 s. *Educ:* Haberdashers' Aske's Girls School; Jesus College, Oxford (PPE MA Hons). *Recreations:* Swimming, Reading.

FAIRBAIRN, John Sydney; Chairman, Unit Trust Association, since 1989. *Career:* Monkhouse Stoneham & Co, Articled Clerk 1957-60; M & G Group 1961-89; M & G Securities, Dir 1968-89; M & G Trust Assurance Co Ltd (Now M & G Life Assurance Co Ltd), Dir 1974-89; M & G Group plc, Dir 1974-; M & G Group plc & most subsidiary Companies, Dep Chm 1980-89. *Biog:* b. 15 January 1934. *Nationality:* British. *m.* 1968, Camilla (née Grinling). 1 s; 2 d; 2 steps; 2 stepd. *Educ:* Eton; Trinity College, Cambridge (BA Economics/Law).

Directorships: M & G Group plc 1974 (non-exec); Lautro Ltd 1986-89 Dep Chm. *Other Activities:* Esmee Fairbairn Charitable Trust (Trustee 1966-, Chairman 1988-); University of Buckingham (Council Member 1986-); King's College, London University (Council Member and Treasurer 1972-86). *Professional Organisations:* FCA. *Clubs:* Brooks's, MCC.

FAIRBROTHER, Jeremy Richard Frederick; Director, Baring Brothers & Co Ltd, since 1982; Banking & Capital Markets. *Career:* Barings, Exec to Asst Dir 1971-79; Saudi Arabian Monetary Agency, Riyadh Snr Advisor 1979-86. *Biog:* b. 4 June 1939. *Nationality:* British. *m.* 1979, Linda Alison (née Reilly); 1 s; 2 d. *Educ:* Cheadle Hulme School; Balliol College Oxford (MA, DPhil); Manchester Business School (MBA). *Professional Organisations:* AIB, FCT. *Recreations:* Tennis, Skiing, Sailing.

FAIRCLOTH, R F; Director, BTR plc.

FAIRFIELD, David Peter James; Partner, Titmuss Sainer & Webb, since 1990; Corporate Finance. *Career:* Wedlake Bell, Articled Clerk, Assistant Solicitor 1982-86; Herbert Smith, Assistant Solicitor 1986-89. *Biog:* b. 29 December 1957. *Nationality:* British. *Educ:* Salesian College, King's College London (LLB, AKC). *Professional Organisations:* The Law Society; The City of London Solicitors' Company; British Italian Law Association; Italian Chamber of Commerce; Italian Institute. *Recreations:* Music, Cricket, Skiing, Golf, Tennis, Astronomy.

FAIRHURST, Charles Sebastian; Director, Syndication and Distribution, Brown, Shipley & Co Ltd, since 1990. *Career:* 13th/18th Royal Hussars, (QMO) 1968-73; Baring Brothers 1973-77; Chemical Bank 1977-84; Bankers Trust 1984-90. *Biog:* b. 14 February 1949. *Nationality:* British. *m.* 1973, Virginia (née Kewley); 2 d. *Educ:* Ampleforth College. *Clubs:* Boodle's, MCC. *Recreations:* Skiing, Gardening.

FAIRLEY, Clifford J M; Vice President, Manufacturers Hanover Trust Company, since 1979; OIC all UK Premises. *Career:* Allied Irish Banks, Clerk 1955-62; Manufacturers Hanover Trust Company, FX Clerk 1962-65; Foreign Loans Supervisor 1965-68; Deputy Manager, FX 1968-70; Assistant Vice President, FX 1970-73; Chief Accountant 1973-79; Vice President, Operations 1979-87; Vice President, Premises 1987-. *Biog:* b. 6 August 1937. *Nationality:* Irish. *m.* 1965,

Judith Roberta; 1 s; 1 d. *Educ:* Mountjoy School, Dublin; Rosse College, Dublin. *Directorships:* The Adelphi Management Co Ltd 1988-90 (non-exec). *Other Activities:* FRSA; Chairman, Petersfield Rugby Club. *Clubs:* The Rugby Club, Petersfield RFC, Steep CC, Petersfield Golf Club. *Recreations:* Golf, Rugby, Cricket.

FAIRLEY, John David; Tax Partner, Ernst & Young, since 1987; International Tax. *Career:* Inland Revenue, HM Inspector of Taxes - Trainee 1970-75; Horsham District, Mgmnt Inspector 1975-77; Somerset House, Intl Tax Division 1977-84; Regent District, District Inspector 1984; Ernst & Whinney, Snr Mgr 1984-87. *Biog: b.* 9 January 1949. *Nationality:* British. *m.* (div); 1 d. *Educ:* Chethams Hospital, Manchester; University of Kent at Canterbury (BA Hons). *Other Activities:* Member Tax Committee, International Chamber of Commerce; Treasurer & Member of Committee, UK Branch International Pistes Association. *Recreations:* Sport, especially Windsurfing, Theatre.

FAIRMAN, Bernard William; Partner, Venture Capital Funding Partners, since 1984; Venture Capital Investment Management. *Career:* Investors in Industry, Investment Manager 1981-84. *Biog: b.* 20 August 1949. *Nationality:* British. *m.* 1982, Julia. *Educ:* University of Nottingham (BA Hons Industrial Economics). *Directorships:* Ferranti Creditphone Ltd 1986 (non-exec).

FAIRSERVICE, G D; Deputy Chief Executive, Candover Investments plc, since 1990. *Career:* British Technology Group, Deputy Divisional Director & Divisional Director 1982-84; 3i plc, Various Positions 1974-82. *Biog: b.* 4 April 1947. *Nationality:* British. *m.* 1977, Judith (née Steinberg). *Educ:* Hamilton Academy; Glasgow University (BSc); London Business School (MBA). *Directorships:* Candover Investments plc & Group Subsidiaries 1986; Rechem Environmental Services plc 1985; LCE Holdings Ltd 1987; LCE Computer Maintenance Ltd 1987; Stoves Ltd 1989; Kenwood Appliances Ltd 1989; Keller Group Ltd 1990; Powerpike Ltd 1990; Office Workstations Ltd; Fairey Group plc; Crabtree of Gateshead Ltd; United Wine Producers Ltd. *Recreations:* Squash, Golf, Skiing.

FAIRWEATHER, James MacGregor Ayton; Director, Martin Currie Investment Management Ltd, since 1987; America. *Career:* Montague Loebl Stanley & Co Institutional Sales & Economics Asst 1979-82; Kleinwort Benson Ltd Eurobond Sales & Dealer 1982-84; Martin Currie Ltd Asst to Dirs on Far East Team 1984-; MC Investment Management Ltd Dir 1987. *Biog: b.* 1 May 1961. *Nationality:* British. *m.* 1988, Mary (née Tait); 1 s. *Educ:* Hitchin Boys' Grammar School; North Herts College of Further Education. *Recreations:* Squash, Golf.

FAKAHANY, Ahmass; Controller, Europe & Middle East, Merrill Lynch Europe, since 1989; Financial Management and Controls of the Firm. *Career:* Exxon Corporation, Finance Manager, International Exploration & Production 1985-87; Various Financial Mgmnt Assignments 1981-85. *Biog: b.* 18 June 1958. *Nationality:* American. *m.* Penny. *Educ:* Columbia University, Graduate School of Business (MBA Finance & Accounting); Boston University, School of Management (BSc Business Administration/Corporate Finance). *Directorships:* Merrill Lynch International Ltd 1989; Merrill Lynch Limited 1989; Merrill Lynch Pierce Fenner & Smith Ltd 1989; CLO Funding 1990; Merrill Lynch Europe Limited 1989.

FALCON, Michael Gascoigne; CBE, JP, DL; Chairman, Norwich Union Insurance Group, since 1981. *Career:* George Younger & Co (Alloa) 1948-50; Morgans Brewery (Norwich) 1951-; E Lacon & Co (Great Yarmouth), Joint MD 1951-68; Edgar Watts Willow Merchants, Exec Dir 1968-73. *Biog: b.* 28 January 1928. *Nationality:* British. *m.* 1954, April Daphne Claire (née Lambert); 2 s; 1 d. *Educ:* Stowe School; Heriot-Watt College, Edinburgh. *Directorships:* Subsidiary Companies of Norwich Union Life Insurance Society 1981 Chm; Norwich Winterthur Holdings Ltd 1984 Chm; Norwich Winterthur Overseas Ltd 1984 Chm; Norwich Winterthur Reinsurance Corporation Ltd 1986 Chm; Stronghold Insurance Co Ltd 1986 Chm; Bronpole Ltd; The Colville Estate Ltd; Matthew Brown plc 1981-87; Lloyds Bank plc, Eastern Counties Regional Board 1979 Chm; Greene King & Sons plc 1988; British Railways (Anglia) Board 1988. *Other Activities:* Chm, Norwich Health Authority; High Steward of Great Yarmouth since 1984; High Sheriff of Norfolk 1979-80; County of Norfolk (DL); Order of St John (Commander Brother). *Clubs:* Norfolk (Norwich), Royal Norfolk & Suffolk Yacht Club (Lowestoft). *Recreations:* Country Pursuits.

FALCONER, I; Director, Alexander Stenhouse UK Ltd.

FALCONER, I M; Partner, Freshfields.

FALCONER, J K R; Director, Head of UK Equity Department, Martin Currie Investment Management Ltd, since 1982; UK Equities. *Career:* Martin Currie Investment Management Ltd, Head of Far East Department 1982-87. *Biog: b.* 7 February 1955. *Nationality:* British. *m.* 1982, Stella (née Mok); 1 s; 1 d. *Educ:* Clifton Hall School; Stowe; Stirling University (BA). *Directorships:* Clifton Hall School 1989 (non-exec). *Professional Organisations:* CA. *Clubs:* New Club. *Recreations:* Stalking, Fishing.

FALK, Fergus Antony; TD; Partner, Touche Ross & Co, since 1975; Partner in Charge, Forensic Services, Charities, Various Audits. *Career:* John Lewis & Co Ltd 1959-64; C Ulysses Williams 1964-65; Touche Ross & Co 1965-. *Biog: b.* 30 August 1941. *m.* 1973, Vivian (née

Irvine); 1 s; 2 d. *Educ:* Uppingham School; London University (BSc Econ). *Other Activities:* Member, Court of Common Council, CA Livery Company; Member, Court of Assistants, HAC. *Professional Organisations:* FCA. *Publications:* Charity Accounting, Numerous Articles. *Clubs:* City Livery, Guildhall, MCC, Honourable Artillery Company. *Recreations:* Small Children, Gardening, Sport.

FALLER, Ms Carrie; Partner, Gouldens.

FALLON, Padraic Matthew; Chief Executive, Euromoney Publications plc, since 1989. *Career:* Thomson City Office (London) Financial Reporter 1969-70; Daily Mirror Financial Reporter 1970-72; Daily Mail City Pages 1972-74; Seconded to Middle East Money (Beirut) Managing Editor 1974; Euromoney Magazine Editor 1974-86; Euromoney Publications Ltd Dir 1975; Euromoney Dep MD 1982; Associated Newspapers Holdings plc, Main Board Director 1985. *Biog: b.* 21 September 1946. *m.* Gillian (née Hellyer); 1 s; 3 d. *Educ:* Blackrock College, Co Dublin; Trinity College, Dublin (BBS). *Directorships:* Euromoney Publications plc; Associated Newspapers Holdings Ltd (non-exec); Allied Irish Banks plc 1988 (non-exec); Harmsworth Media Ltd (non-exec); Latin American Financial Publications Inc Pres. *Other Activities:* Commended in Wincott Awards to Outstanding Journalists, 1982. *Clubs:* Kildare Street and University Club (Overseas Member).

FALLOWFIELD, Richard Gordon; Deputy Chairman, Grandfield Rork Collins, since 1986; Advertising. *Career:* McCann Erickson (Australia), MD 1972-73; Young & Rubicam (Australia), MD 1974-77; (Hong Kong), MD 1977-79; McCann Erickson, MD 1980-84; Grandfield Rork Collins, MD, GRC Intl 1985-86. *Biog: b.* 25 January 1935. *m.* 1963, Elfrida Charlotte (née Eden); 2 s; 1 d. *Educ:* Marlborough College. *Professional Organisations:* MIPA. *Recreations:* Walking, Squash, Tennis, Reading.

FALTON, Chris; Assistant City Editor, Daily Mail.

FANE, H; Director, Hill Samuel Investment Management Ltd.

FANSHAWE ROYLE, Anthony Henry; The Lord Fanshawe of Richmond; KCMG; Non-Executive Director, Sedgwick Group plc, since 1984. *Career:* Captain, The Life Guards (Germany, Egypt, Palestine and Tansjordan) 1945-48; 21st Special Air Service Regt (TA) 1948-51; Conservative Member of Parliament for Richmond 1959-83; Parliamentary Private Secretary to Under Secretary of State for the Colonies 1960; to Secretary of State for Air 1960-62; to Minister of Aviation 1962-64; Member Assembly of Council of Europe and WEU 1965; Vice-Chairman, Conservative Parliamentary Foreign Affairs Committee 1965-67;

Tory Opposition Whip 1967-70; Parliamentary Under Secretary of State for Foreign and Commonwealth Affairs 1970-74; Vice Chairman, Conservative Party Organisation 1979-84; Chairman, Conservative Party International Office 1979-84. *Biog: b.* 27 March 1927. *Nationality:* British. *m.* 1957, Shirley Worthington; 2 d. *Educ:* Harrow; Sandhurst. *Directorships:* Westland Group plc 1985 (non-exec); Rank Xerox (UK) Limited 1988 (non-exec); Lyell Holdings Ltd 1989 (non-exec); T I Group plc 1990 (non-exec); United Technologies Corp Atlantic Advisory Council 1988 Member. *Clubs:* Pratt's, White's, Brooks's.

FARIMANI, Mehrdad; Director, Merrill Lynch International Limited.

FARLEY, Deryk Mark William; Active Underwriter & Chairman, Pegasus Motor Policies at Lloyds, since 1972; Motor Insurance: Underwriting & General Management & Liaison with Provincial Insurance Brokers & Lloyds Brokers. *Career:* RAF Clerk 1952-54; Howson F Devitt & Sons, Clerk 1954-59; L Hammond & Co, Clerk 1959-60; EW Payne & Co, Motor Broker 1960-64; Highway Motor Policies at Lloyd's, Deputy Underwriter 1964-68. *Biog: b.* 2 April 1934. *m.* 1956, Maureen (née Goodwin); 2 d. *Educ:* North Hammersmith Central. *Directorships:* Pegasus Motor Policies (Management) Ltd 1987 Chm; Edwards & Payne (Underwriting Agencies) Ltd 1972; R A Edwards & Co (Holdings) Ltd 1985; E W Payne (Underwriting Agencies) Ltd 1969-77; Sturge Lloyd's Agencies Ltd 1987. *Professional Organisations:* Committee of Lloyd's Motor Underwriters Association, Member 1977-79, 1981-83, 1988-90; Chairman, 1983; Lloyd's Disciplinary Committee's Panel, 1986-; LMNA, Direct Motor Liaison Committee. *Clubs:* Theydon Bois Golf Club, Lloyd's Golf Club. *Recreations:* Golf, Photography, Cricket, Travel.

FARLEY, Henry Edward; Deputy Group Chief Executive, Royal Bank of Scotland Group.

FARMAR, Hugh Alexander Peregrine; Director, Chartered WestLB Limited, since 1985; Project Finance. *Career:* Lazard Brothers & Co Limited, Assistant Director Project Finance 1968-84. *Biog: b.* 28 September 1945. *Nationality:* British. *m.* Carole; 1 s; 3 d. *Educ:* Eton College; Keble College, Oxford (MA Jurisprudence). *Other Activities:* Livery of The Drapers Company. *Clubs:* Pratt's. *Recreations:* Country Pursuits.

FARMER, D; Executive Director, Banque Paribas London; Technical Banking Support Services and Systems. *Career:* UBAF Bank Ltd, Assistant General Manager 1986-88; Royal Trust Bank, Associate Director 1982-86; Toronto Dominion Bank 1970-82. *Biog: b.* 9 April 1945. *Nationality:* British. 1 s; 2 d. *Directorships:* Paribas Futures Ltd 1989 (exec). *Professional Organisations:* AIB Scot.

FARMER, David William Horace; Director, Chartered WestLB Limited, since 1984; Administration Standard Chartered Group Overseas Merchant Banks. *Career:* Slaughter and May Solicitor (1962) 1959-66; Amax International Ltd Dir 1967-76; Lonrho Ltd Group Sec 1976-79; Standard Chartered Merchant Bank (now Chartered WestLB Ltd) 1979-. *Biog: b.* 19 October 1935. *Nationality:* British. *m.* 1988, Johanna Joy (née Seligman). 2 steps; 1 stepd. *Educ:* Tonbridge School; St John's College, Cambridge (MA).

FARMER, J J S; Deputy Chairman, PWS Holdings Ltd.

FARMER, John R; Managing Director, Fixed Income, Goldman Sachs International Limited.

FARMER, Miss Rosemary A; Vice President & Representative, First National Bank of Maryland, since 1989; Head of UK Office, Working with UK & European Co's with US Operations. *Career:* Morgan Grenfell & Co Limited 1972-78; Hill Samuel & Co Limited, Manager Export Finance 1978-81; International Energy Bank, Manager Corporate Finance 1981-84; American Express Bank, Assistant Vice President 1984-86; First National Bank of Maryland, Senior International Banking Executive 1986-88; Vice President 1988-; Vice President & Representative 1989-. *Biog: b.* 3 December 1949. *Nationality:* British. *Educ:* Pipers Corner School; University of Leeds (BA). *Clubs:* Oriental. *Recreations:* Music, Reading, Fine Art.

FARQUHARSON, Robert Douglas; Vice President, Property Group, First Interstate Bank of California, since 1989; UK Commercial Property Finance. *Career:* Continental Illinois National Bank, Assistant Manager, Property Group 1981-84. *Biog: b.* 1 May 1951. *Nationality:* British. *m.* 1984, Jane (née Birtwistle); 2 s. *Educ:* Wellington College, Berkshire; Pembroke College, Oxford (MA Hons); American Graduate School of International Management (MIM Hons). *Other Activities:* Freeman; Skinners. *Clubs:* Vincents Club (Oxford), Ski Club of Great Britian, Aldeburgh Golf Club, Hurlingham Club. *Recreations:* Tennis, Golf, Skiing, Sailing.

FARRAND, Dr Julian Thomas; Insurance Ombudsman, The Insurance Ombudsman Bureau, since 1989. *Career:* Admitted Solicitor 1960; KCL, Assistant Lecturer, then Lecturer 1960-63; Sheffield University, Lecturer 1963-65; Queen Mary's College, Reader in Law 1965-68; Manchester University, Professor of Law 1968-88; Dean of Faculty of Law 1970-72; 1976-78; Law Commissioner 1984-88. *Biog: b.* 13 August 1935. *m.* 1957, Winifred Joan (née Charles); 1 s; 2 d. *Educ:* Haberdashers' Aske's School; University College, London (LLB, LLD). *Other Activities:* Rent Assessment Panel, Greater Manchester and Lancashire Area, Chm, 1973-1990; Vice-President, 1977-1984; London Area,

1984-; Supplementary Benefit Appeals Tribunal, 1977-1980; National Insurance Local Tribunal, 1980-83; Social Security Appeal Tribunal, 1983-88; Government Conveyancing Committee, 1984-85. *Publications:* (Ed with Dr J Gilchrist Smith) Emmet on Title, 15th Edn 1967 to 19th Edn (as sole editor) 1986; Contract and Conveyance 1963-64, 4th Edn 1983; (Ed) Wolstenholme and Cherry, Conveyancing Statutes, 13th Edn (vols 16) 1972; The Rent Acts and Regulations, 1978 2nd Edn (with A Arden) 1981. *Recreations:* Chess, Bridge, Wine.

FARRANT, Norman; Partner, Moore Stephens.

FARRAR, John W; Renter Warden, Worshipful Company of Joiners and Ceilers.

FARREN, G R; Partner, Pensions (St Albans), Bacon & Woodrow.

FARREN, Peter Stefan; Partner, Linklaters & Paines, since 1979. *Career:* Wm Brandt Son & Co Ltd 1973-76. *Biog: b.* 16 October 1944. *Nationality:* British. *m.* Victoria (née Small); 1 s; 2 d. *Educ:* Mill Hill School; Grenoble University; Kings College, London (LLB Hons). *Recreations:* Flying, Skiing, Squash.

FARRER, Arthur Mark; Partner, Farrer & Co, since 1968. *Career:* Lee & Pembertons/Farrer & Co, Articles to Asst Solicitor 1965-68. *Biog: b.* 25 March 1941. *Nationality:* British. *m.* 1969, Zara Jane (née Thesiger); 1 d. *Educ:* Stone House, Broadstairs, Kent; Eton College. *Directorships:* Association of Lloyd's Members 1985 (non-exec); Essex Water Co 1986 (non-exec) Dep Chm; Council of Lloyd's 1988 (non-exec); Lyonnaise (UK) plc 1988 (non-exec); East Anglian Water Co 1990 (non-exec) Dep Chm. *Other Activities:* Liveryman, Fishmongers Company. *Professional Organisations:* The Law Society. *Clubs:* Brooks's, Essex.

FARRIER, Denis J; Clerk, Basketmakers' Company.

FARROW, Christopher John; Director, Kleinwort Benson Ltd, since 1987; Corporate Finance. *Career:* Department of Trade & Industry Under Sec 1961-83; Bank of England Asst Dir 1983-87. *Biog: b.* 29 July 1937. *Nationality:* British. *m.* 1961, Alison (née Brown); 1 s; 1 d. *Educ:* King's College, Cambridge (BA). *Directorships:* London Metal Exchange Ltd 1987 (non-exec).

FARSTAD, Jan-Arne; Managing Director & Chief Executive Officer, Royal Trust Bank, since 1988. *Career:* Wells Fargo Bank, VP 1975-83; Bank of Montreal, Snr VP 1983-87. *Directorships:* Royal Trust Asset Management 1988 (non-exec); Royal Trust Bank (Isle of Man) 1988 (non-exec).

FARTHING, Peter John; Partner, Clyde & Co, since 1977; Commercial Litigation. *Biog: b.* 1949. *Nationality:*

British. *Educ:* Crypt School, Gloucester; Pembroke College, Oxford (MA). *Professional Organisations:* Solicitor.

FATTORINI, H T; Director, Skipton Building Society. *Directorships:* Thomas Fattorini Ltd and Subsidiary Companies.

FAULKNER, Laurence John; Director, Kleinwort Benson Securities Ltd, since 1990; Head of Equity Sales to Europe. *Career:* Phillips & Drew, Manager 1970-81; Grieveson Grant & Co, Associated Member 1981-86; Phillips & Drew 1986; SBCI Savory Milln, Director, Head of Equity Sales to Europe 1986-90. *Biog: b.* 23 July 1951. *Nationality:* British. *m.* 1981, Sandra (née Killelay); 1 d. *Educ:* Gillingham Grammar School. *Professional Organisations:* Member, International Stock Exchange. *Recreations:* Gardening, Walking, Reading.

FAURE, Hubert Rene Joseph; Non-Executive Director, NM Rothschild & Sons Ltd, since 1988. *Career:* French Embassy, Bogota, Attache 1947; Ateliers Metallurgiques St Urbain, Manager 1949; Ascinter Otis, Pres 1961-72; Otis Europe, Pres 1969; Otis Elevator Co, Pres, COO 1975-77; Otis Elevator Co, Pres, CEO 1977-79; Otis Elevator Co, Chm Bd, Pres, CEO 1979-81; United Technologies, Chm Bd, CEO 1981-86; United Technologies, Snr Exec VP 1981-86; Societe Imetal, Dir 1986. *Biog: b.* 5 September 1919. *Nationality:* French. *m.* (separated); 1 s. *Educ:* Ecole Libre Sciences Politiques; Sorbonne, Paris. *Directorships:* Rothschild et Associes Banque 1987 (non-exec); Rothschild Espana 1988 (non-exec); Rothschild Italia 1988 (non-exec); Gervais Danone 1988 (non-exec); Swiss Re USA 1984 (non-exec); Interclissa Carrier SA 1986 (non-exec); Sotheby's 1988 (non-exec). *Other Activities:* Chevalier, French Legion of Honour. *Professional Organisations:* American Chamber of Commerce; Association of Elevator Lift Manufacturers. *Clubs:* Nouveau Cercle, Brook.

FAURE WALKER, Rupert Roderick; Director, Samuel Montagu & Co Limited, since 1982; Corporate Finance. *Career:* Peat, Marwick Mitchell & Co 1969-77; Samuel Montagu & Co Limited 1977-. *Biog: b.* 9 September 1947. *Nationality:* British. *m.* 1975, Sally (née Sidebotham); 1 s; 2 d. *Educ:* Eton College; Bristol University (BSc). *Directorships:* Hanover Property Unit Trust 1988 (non-exec); Aubrey Investments Limited 1985 (non-exec). *Professional Organisations:* FCA.

FAVA, Peter Luke; Director, Alexanders Discount plc, since 1987; Sterling Money Markets/Funding. *Career:* Lloyds Bank Ltd, General Clerk 1968-71; Johnson Matthey Bankers, Trainee Bullion Dealer 1971-72; Merrill Lynch Inc, Bullion Dealer 1972-74; N M Rothschild & Sons, Bullion Dealer/Mgr 1974-; Mgr, Sterling Treasury 1979-; Mgr, Eurodollars 1984-85; CNCA London Branch Chief Dealer, Money Markets 1985-86; Alexanders Discount Mgr, Non-Sterling 1986-87; Executive Director 1987. *Biog: b.* 27 December

1948. *Nationality:* British. *Educ:* St Peter's School, Bournemouth. *Other Activities:* Ex-TAVR (5RRF). *Clubs:* RHS. *Recreations:* Golf, Photography, Antiques.

FAVRE-GILLY, Olivier M; Director, Credit Lyonnais Securities, since 1990; Corporate Finance. *Career:* Paribas (Paris), Corporate Finance Dept 1983-85; Paribas Ltd (London), Capital Markets Dept 1985-87; Merrill Lynch (London), Capital Markets Dept 1987-90. *Biog: b.* 12 August 1959. *Nationality:* French. *m.* 1990, Marie-Laure (née Chevrier de Varennes de Bueil). *Educ:* Lycee du Parc; Ecole des Mines (MSc); Sorbonne (MA Hons). *Directorships:* Merrill Lynch International Ltd 1989 (exec). *Clubs:* Annabels, RAC. *Recreations:* Opera, Golf.

FAWCETT, B; Director, Dalgety plc, since 1990; Agribusiness. *Career:* National Service, Royal Artillery 1953-55; United Africa Co, Nigeria (Unilever) 1956-60; United Africa Co, London (Unilever) 1960-62; BOCM Ltd (Unilever) 1962-71; Dalgety Crosfields, Regional Manager 1971-77; Dalgety Agriculture, Feed Director 1977-84; Managing Director 1984-87; Dalgety plc, Chief Executive Agribusiness Group 1987-. *Biog: b.* 11 June 1932. *Nationality:* British. *m.* 1961, Lilian Eveline (née Watson); 1 s; 2 d. *Educ:* Reading University (BA Hons Geography).

FAZAL, Zahir; Partner, Clark Whitehill.

FAZAN, Brian John; *Career:* HM Forces, Local Defence Volunteers & later Royal Sussex Regt, to Captain (served in UK, India, Burma & Assam) 1940-46; TA, Inns of Court Regt, Royal Corps of Military Police, Westminster Dragoons 1947-63; Maidstone and District Motor Services Ltd, Engineering Trainee 1948-51; Ford Motor Co Ltd, Production Buying Depts, to Snr Buyer, Engines & Special Bodies 1952-69; Dennis Brothers Ltd (Specialist Vehicle Builders), Group Purchasing Dir 1970-72; Strachans (Coachbuilders) Ltd, Purchasing Mgr 1972-75; C F Taylor (Metalworkers) Ltd (Aircraft Engineers), Purchase Mgr 1975-87. *Biog: b.* 20 December 1922. *Nationality:* British. *m.* 1948, Vera (née Wilson; 1 s; 1 d. *Educ:* Lancing College, Sussex; College of Automobile and Aeronautical Engineering, Chelsea; LCC Technical College, Wandsworth. *Other Activities:* Worshipful Company of Pewterers (Master 1990-). *Recreations:* Motor Cycling, Walking the Countryside, Pewter & the Pewter Industry.

FEAR, Raymond; Managing Partner, Milne Ross, Chartered Accountants, since 1988; General Audit Partner and Management of Firm. *Career:* Milne Ross, Partner 1979. *Biog: b.* 4 May 1946. *Nationality:* British. *m.* 1971, Gillian; 2 s. *Professional Organisations:* Fellow, Institute of Chartered Accountants in England and Wales; Associate, Institute of Taxation.

FEARFIELD, M A; Operations Director, Laporte plc, since 1988; Applied Products Sector. *Career:* Plessey Co, Management Trainee 1964-65; Albright & Wilson Ltd, Finance Department 1965-70; Marcha Spain, Managing Director 1970-73; Australia, Managing Director 1974-75; Managing Director, Agricultural Division 1976-80; Managing Director, Detergents Division 1980-84; Laporte plc, European Regional Manager 1984-86; USA, President 1986-88; Operations Director 1988-. *Biog: b.* 29 July 1938. *Nationality:* British. *m.* 1986, Wynne (née Turner); 2 d. *Educ:* Kings School, Macclesfield; Derby College of Technology (ACMA). *Directorships:* Laporte plc 1988 (exec); Various Laporte Subsidiaries 1984 (exec). *Professional Organisations:* ACMA. *Recreations:* General Reading, Theatre, Travel, Food & Wine, Golf, Cricket and Rugby Union (Spectating).

FEARNSIDES, M; General Manager, Halifax Financial Services (Holdings) Ltd, Halifax Building Society.

FEASEY, A S; Director, Wendover Underwriting Agency Limited.

FEATHER, C A; Senior Partner, J M Finn & Co, since 1988; Corporate Finance. *Biog: b.* 19 July 1935. *Nationality:* British. *m.* 1968, J M (née Gavin); 1 s; 1 d. *Educ:* Perse School, Cambridge; King Edward VII School, Lytham; New College, Oxford (MA Hons). *Professional Organisations:* MSIA.

FEATHERBY, J M; Partner, Slaughter and May, since 1990; Company/Commercial Law. *Biog: b.* 9 November 1958. *Nationality:* British. *m.* 1980, Charlotte; 3 s; 2 d. *Educ:* Haileybury College; Selwyn College, Cambridge (MA). *Other Activities:* Law Society; City of London Solicitors Company.

FEATHERMAN, Peter Maxwell; Managing Director, DCC Corporate Finance Limited, since 1986; M & A. *Career:* Price Waterhouse 1971-77; S G Warburg & Co Ltd 1977-81; Equity Finance Ltd 1981-85. *Biog: b.* 4 September 1949. *Nationality:* British. *m.* 1975, Stephanie; 1 s; 2 d. *Educ:* Roundhay School; Trinity College, Cambridge (MA). *Directorships:* Development Capital Corporation (exec); Wardell Roberts plc (non-exec); London & Provincial Factors Ltd (non-exec). *Professional Organisations:* FCA.

FEDERMAN, David; Main Board Director & MD, Coffee Division, E D & F Man Ltd.

FEENY, Kevin M; Director, S G Warburg Akroyd Rowe & Pitman.

FEENY, Maeve; Partner, Linklaters & Paines.

FEHR, Basil Henry Frank; CBE; Chairman & Managing Director, Frank Fehr & Co Ltd.

FELD, D; Managing Director, MNC International Bank.

FELDMAN, N L; Assistant General Manager, Guardian Royal Exchange Assurance.

FELL, A E; Director, Nicholson Chamberlain Colls Limited.

FELL, Colin R; Director, Kleinwort Benson Securities, since 1988; Head of Engineering & Related Industries Research. *Career:* Phillips & Drew Engineering Analyst 1968-71; Citicorp Scrimgeour Vickers Dir, Head of Engineering Research 1971-88. *Directorships:* Kleinwort Benson Securities 1988 (exec).

FELL, H G; Chairman, Skipton Building Society. *Directorships:* Robert Fell & Sons Ltd; Associated Heating Equipment Distribution Ltd.

FELL, John Arnold; Partner, Wilde Sapte, since 1964; Property, Trusts and Charities. *Career:* Messrs Kimbers 1952-56; Messrs Conquest Clare & Binns, Assistant Solicitor 1956-58; Messrs Hatchet Jones & Co, Assistant Solicitor 1958-63; Messrs Wilde Sapte 1963; Partner 1964. *Biog: b.* 31 August 1928. *Nationality:* British. *m.* 1963, Janet Eva; 2 d. *Educ:* Merchant Taylor's School; Pembroke College, Oxford (MA Jurisprudence). *Directorships:* Portman Family Settled Estates Ltd 1985 (non-exec); Portman Burtley Estate Co 1985 (non-exec); Seymour Street Nominees Ltd 1985 (non-exec); Moor Park (1958) Ltd 1984 (non-exec). *Other Activities:* Liveryman, Worshipful Company of Gardeners; Past Chairman, Queenhithe Ward Club; Past Chairman, Broad Street Ward Club; Common Councilman, Queenhithe Ward on the Corporation of London; Governor of the City of London School; Donation Governor of Christ's Hospital; Chairman of the Trustees of the Truro Fund; Trustee, Royal Academy; Trusts, Housing Associations Charitable Trust and the Lord Mayor's 800th Anniversary Trust. *Clubs:* Old Merchant Taylor's Society, Guildhall, City Livery. *Recreations:* Walking, Gardening, Youth Work.

FELL, Tony; Director, Nicholson Chamberlain Colls Limited.

FELLINGHAM, M B; Partner, Penningtons.

FELLOWES, Thomas William; Deputy Chairman, Gerrard & National Holdings plc; Director of Subsidiary Companies. *Career:* Bank of New South Wales 1964; J B Were & Son (Melbourne) 1965; Gerrard & Reid Limited 1965; Dir 1973. *Biog: b.* 3 November 1945. *m.* 1975, Rosamund Isobelle (née Van Cutsem); 2 d. *Educ:* Eton College. *Directorships:* Astley & Pearce Group 1975-79 (non-exec). *Other Activities:* A Governor, Queen Elizabeth's Foundation for the Disabled. *Clubs:* White's, Pratt's, Overseas Bankers.

FELLOWS, Derek; Executive Director, Securities and Investments Board.

FELSTEAD, Eric William; Director, J Capel Gilts Ltd, since 1989; Head of Sales, UK Bonds. *Career:* Stock Exchange 1957-; Member 1968. *Biog: b.* 7 September 1942. *Nationality:* British. 1 s; 2 d. *Educ:* The Robert Dewhurst School, Cheshunt, Herts. *Directorships:* J C Gilts Ltd. *Professional Organisations:* Stock Exchange. *Recreations:* Golf.

FENDER, John Lawrence; Director, County NatWest, since 1986; Property Advice and Finance. *Career:* Greater London Council, Various 1961-71; Taylor Woodrow Property Co, Estates Manager 1971-72; Jones Lane Wootton, Associate 1973-80; County Bank, County NatWest Director 1980-. *Educ:* London (BSc Estate Management). *Directorships:* County NatWest Property Ltd 1986 MD; Pensman Nominees Ltd (exec); Provident Fund Securities Ltd (exec); Cameron Hall Development Ltd 1986 (non-exec); Stanhope County Ltd 1990 (exec). *Professional Organisations:* ARICS.

FENHALLS, Richard Dorian; Executive Chairman, Henry Ansbacher & Co Ltd, since 1985. *Career:* Guinness Manon & Co Ltd, Dep Chm & Chief Exec Officer 1981-85; American Express Bank, Snr VP 1977-81; Marine Midland Bank, Snr VP 1972-79. *Directorships:* Henry Ansbacher Holdings plc 1985 Chief Exec; Henry Ansbacher Holdings Inc Chm.

FENN-SMITH, Clive Antony Kemp; Director, Barclays Financial Services Ltd, since 1986; Unit Trust Management, Life Assurance & Insurance Broking, Portfolio Management. *Career:* Messrs Letcher & Son (Solicitors, Ringwood) 1958-64; The Law Society Asst Sec 1965-68; M & G Group Ltd 1968-77; MD 1977-80; Barclays Unicorn Group Ltd Dir, Gen Mgr & MD 1980-85; Barclays Unit Trusts & Insurance Ltd Vice-Chm 1985-86; Barclays Bank Trust Co Ltd Dir 1984-87 and 1989-; MD 1987; Chm 1988-89. *Biog: b.* 13 March 1933. *Nationality:* British. *m.* 1961, Jane Hester (née Henderson); 2 s; 1 d. *Educ:* Charterhouse; Cambridge University (MA Hons). *Directorships:* IMRO 1986; Subsidiary Companies of Barclays; Investors Compensation Scheme Ltd 1988; Pearl Group plc 1989; Technology Services International Ltd 1989 Chm; Premier Portfolio Group plc 1989. *Other Activities:* Unit Trust Assoc (Past Chm). *Professional Organisations:* Law Society. *Clubs:* Cavalry and Guards. *Recreations:* Sailing, Messing about in the Garden.

FENNER, John Ronald; Senior Partner, Berwin Leighton; Commercial Property. *Career:* Leighton & Co Ptnr 1962-71; Berwin Leighton Ptnr 1971-; Managing Ptnr 1980-84; Chm 1984-90. *Biog: b.* 7 December 1935. *Nationality:* British. *m.* 1963, Gillian Adelaide; 2 s. *Educ:* Tonbridge School; University College, London (LLB

Hons); City of London Solicitors Company Grotius Prize. *Directorships:* Pincs Association 1989; Pincs Ltd 1989. *Other Activities:* Member, Worshipful Company of Fletchers. *Professional Organisations:* Law Society. *Clubs:* City Club, Carlton, RAC (Full Member). *Recreations:* Tennis, Skiing, Theatre, Opera, Charity Work, Politics.

FENTON, Ciaran J; Managing Director & Associate Producer, Business Television Limited, since 1989; C4 Business Daily. *Career:* Company & Film & TV Accountant, Eire & UK. *Biog: b.* 12 August 1960. *Nationality:* Irish. *Educ:* National University of Ireland (BComm Hons). *Directorships:* Broadcast Communications (Productions) Ltd 1989 (exec). *Professional Organisations:* IPPA. *Clubs:* 10D.

FENTON, Ernest John; Chief Executive, Greenwell Montagu Stockbrokers & Smith Keen Cutler Ltd, since 1988; International Equities. *Career:* W Greenwell & Co Ptnr 1968-86; Greenwell Montagu Securities Dir 1986-88. *Biog: b.* 14 October 1938. *Nationality:* British. *m.* 1965, Ann (née Ramsay); 1 s; 2 d. *Educ:* Harris Academy; St Andrews. *Directorships:* Dunham Hotels plc 1985 (non-exec); Valetrue Ltd 1984 (non-exec). *Professional Organisations:* CA. *Recreations:* Farming, Curling.

FENWICK, (Anthony) Benedict (Xavier); Director, David Sheppard & Partners Ltd, since 1984. *Career:* Investment Intelligence Ltd, Founder & Chm 1959-79; Morgan Grenfell Fund Mgmnt, Dir 1969-72; Rowe & Pitman Mgmnt Ltd, Dir 1970-71; Wrightson Wood Ltd, Dir 1980-84. *Biog: b.* 1934. *Nationality:* British. *m.* 1958, Deirdre Heber (née Percy); 1 s; 1 d. *Educ:* Ampleforth. *Directorships:* By-Pass Nurseries Ltd 1978 (non-exec) Chm; Dawes & Henderson (Agencies) Ltd 1979 (non-exec). *Clubs:* Beefsteak, Boodle's, City of London, Northern Counties, Pratt's, White's.

FENWICK, John Andrew; Finance Director, Brunswick Public Relations Limited, since 1987. *Career:* Deloitte Haskins & Sells, Articled Clerk/Accountant 1982-86; Broad Street Associates, Account Director 1986-87. *Biog: b.* 8 October 1959. *Nationality:* British. *Educ:* Eton College; Exeter University. *Directorships:* Brunswick Public Relations Ltd 1987 (exec); Merchant Corporate Design Ltd 1988 (exec). *Professional Organisations:* ACA.

FERGUSON, David William Ramsay; Finance Director, Stewart Ivory & Company Ltd.

FERGUSON, Duncan George Robin; Partner, Bacon & Woodrow, since 1988. *Career:* Bacon & Woodrow Actuarial Student 1965-69; Metropolitan Life, Cape Town Actuary & AGM 1969-72; Nation Life Actuary 1972-75; Eagle Star International Div Dir 1975-88. *Biog: b.* 12 May 1942. *Nationality:* British. *m.* 1966, Alison Margaret (née Simpson); 2 s; 1 d. *Educ:* Fettes College; Trinity College, Cambridge (MA). *Pro-*

fessional Organisations: FIA. *Publications:* Various Articles in Professional Journals.

FERGUSON, I C; Chief Executive, County NatWest Securities Limited, since 1989.

FERGUSON, J M; Director, Scott Underwriting Agencies Limited.

FERGUSON, James Gordon Dickson; Chairman, Stewart Ivory and Co Ltd, 1989; Investment Management. *Career:* Stewart Ivory (previously Stewart Fund Managers) Various 1970-74; Dir 1974-. *Biog: b.* 12 November 1947. *Nationality:* British. *m.* 1970, Nicola Hilland (née Stewart); 2 s; 1 d. *Educ:* Winchester College; Trinity College, Dublin (BA). *Directorships:* Value & Income Trust plc 1986 (non-exec); OLIM Convertible Trust plc 1989 (non-exec). *Other Activities:* Assoc of Investment Trust Companies (Former Dep Chm, Member of Gen Ctee). *Clubs:* New (Edinburgh).

FERGUSON, Nicholas; Director, J Henry Schroder Wagg & Co Limited.

FERGUSSON, A G; Director, Brandeis (Brokers) Limited.

FERGUSSON, (Frederick) James; Deputy Chairman & Joint Chief Executive, James Capel & Company, since 1986; International Operations. *Career:* S H Benson Ltd 1965-68; Unilever Ltd 1968-69; James Capel & Co, Various, Head of Research 1976-81; Head of International Division 1983-90. *Biog: b.* 28 March 1943. *Nationality:* British. *m.* 1966, Diane Frances (née Darley); 2 s; 2 d. *Educ:* Haileybury & ISC; Oxford (BA Mathematics). *Directorships:* James Capel & Co 1984 Joint Chief Executive; James Capel International Ltd 1987 Chm; James Capel (Far East) Ltd 1985 Chm; Various Other James Capel Subsidiaries.

FERGUSSON, J N; Senior Partner, Dundas & Wilson CS.

FERGUSSON, William; Executive Director, Walter Judd Limited.

FERRARO, Michael John; Director, T H March & Co Ltd, since 1979. *Biog: b.* 7 June 1947. *Nationality:* British. *m.* 1972, Antoinette (née Condon); 2 s; 1 d. *Educ:* Downside School; Peterhouse, Cambridge (MA); McMaster University, Ontario (MSc). *Professional Organisations:* Associate, Chartered Insurance Institute. *Recreations:* Mountaineering, Music, Windsurfing.

FERRARO, R F; Chairman (Non-Executive), TH March & Company Limited.

FERRY, Alexander; MBE; General Secretary, Confederation of Shipbuilding and Engineering Unions.

FETZER, Rodney Wilberforce; Director Treasury, Private Bank & Trust Company Ltd, since 1989; Member of Banks Executive Committee, Daily Responsibilities for Investment Management of Funds and Treasury Services for Private Clients. *Career:* L George Fetzer & Co, Partner 1967-69; Josiah Wedgwood & Sons, Financial Accountant 1969-71; Bank of America, Head of International Treasury Management 1972-85; Orion Royal Bank, Executive Director 1985-87; D C Gardner City and D C Gardner Group, Chief Executive 1987-89; Private Bank & Trust Co Ltd, Director Treasury 1989-90. *Biog: b.* 25 May 1944. *Nationality:* British. *m.* 1971, Sharie (née Bradley); 2 d. *Educ:* Wrekin College Public School. *Directorships:* J Whitley Investments 1988 (non-exec); Executive Director, Orion Royal Bank 1985 (exec). *Other Activities:* Education Committee, Association of Corporate Treasurers. *Professional Organisations:* Fellow, Association of Corporate Treasurers; Fellow, Institute of Chartered Accountants. *Clubs:* Lansdowne Club, Kings College Sports Club.

FEZZANI, Mohamed Ali Hussein; Deputy Chief Executive and General Manager, UBAF Bank Limited, since 1985. *Career:* Barclays Bank DCO (Benghazi) 1956-60; British Bank of the Middle East (Benghazi) Head of Dept 1960-67; Bank of North Africa (Benghazi) Asst Mgr 1968-70; Wahda Bank (Benghazi) Asst Mgr 1970-71; Mgr 1971-73; Asst Gen Mgr 1973-75; UBAF Bank Ltd Asst Gen Mgr 1975-80; Dep Gen Mgr 1980-82; Gen Mgr 1982-85. *Biog: b.* 15 January 1938. *Nationality:* Libyan. *m.* 1966, K O (née Sherif); 3 s; 1 d. *Educ:* Benghazi Secondary School. *Directorships:* Arab International Bank 1982 (non-exec). *Professional Organisations:* Arab Bankers Assoc.

FFOLKES DAVIS, Paul; Executive Director, N M Rothschild & Sons Ltd.

FFORDE, J S; Director, Alexanders (CL-) Laing & Cruickshank.

FICKLING, Paul M; Deputy General Manager, Yamaichi Bank (UK) plc, since 1987; Credit. *Career:* Arthur Andersen & Co, Articled Clerk 1968-71; Kleinwort Benson & Co Ltd, Corporate Finance Executive 1973-74; Bank of Cyprus (London) Ltd, PA to MD 1974-75; The Rossminster Group, Divisional Director 1975-79; Orion Bank Ltd, Manager 1979-83; The National Bank of Kuwait, Credit Manager 1983-87. *Biog: b.* 23 June 1946. *Nationality:* British. *m.* 1973, Gudrun (née Laidlaw); 2 s. *Educ:* Radley College; St Edmund Hall, Oxford University (BA,MA); University of Chicago (MBA). *Professional Organisations:* Institute of Chartered Accountants, FCA. *Clubs:* Moor Park Golf Club. *Recreations:* Tennis, Gardening, Walking, Travel.

FIDLER, M E; Exec Dir, The International Stock Exchange.

FIDLER, Peter John Michael; Partner, Stephenson Harwood, since 1984; Banking, Insolvency. *Career:* Peacock, Fisher & Finch Articled Clerk 1964-67; Coward Chance Asst Solicitor 1967-72; D J Freeman & Co Asst Solicitor 1972-73; Ptnr 1973-84. *Biog: b.* 16 March 1942. *Nationality:* British. *m.* 1984, Barbara Julia (née Pinto); 2 s; 2 d. *Educ:* Bradford Grammar School; St John's College, Oxford (MA Hons 1st). *Other Activities:* City of London Solicitors' Company. *Professional Organisations:* Law Society. *Publications:* Sheldon & Fidler's Practice & Law of Banking, 1982. *Recreations:* Sports, Music.

FIELD, A E; Finance Director, Arbuthnot Latham Bank Limited, since 1989; Accounting, Computer. *Career:* Arbuthnot Latham Bank Ltd 1958-.

FIELD, D W; Clerk, Master Mariners' Company.

FIELD, Geoff; Partner, Robson Rhodes.

FIELD, M D; Managing Director (Investment Management), W H Smith Group plc.

FIELD, Marshall Hayward; CBE; Consultant Partner, Bacon & Woodrow, since 1986; Insurance Division. *Career:* Phoenix Assurance plc, Actuary 1964-85; Gen Mgr 1972-85; Dir 1980-85; Life Offices' Association, Chm 1983-85; Securities & Investments Board, Consultant 1985-86; Institute of Actuaries, President 1986-88. *Biog: b.* 19 April 1930. *Nationality:* British. *m.* 1960, Barbara (née Harris); 2 d. *Educ:* Dulwich College. *Directorships:* TSB Trust Co Ltd 1985-89 (non-exec); TSB Group plc 1990 (non-exec); Phoenix Assurance plc 1980-85 (exec). *Other Activities:* Liveryman, Worshipful Company of Actuaries (Court Assistant 1989-); Chairman, Estates' Governor at Dulwich, 1988-; Governor, Dulwich College, 1987-; Governor, James Akers' Girls' School, 1981-; Committee Member, Dulwich Picture Gallery, 1985-. *Professional Organisations:* FIA. *Publications:* Presidential Address, Institute of Actuaries, 1986. *Clubs:* Bembridge Sailing Club. *Recreations:* Theatre, Bridge.

FIELD, Peter John; Director-Banking (& Compliance Officer), Duncan Lawrie Limited.

FIELD, R; Compliance Director, Walker Crips Weddle Beck plc.

FIELD, Robert David; Department Administrator, Tax Dept, Lawrence Graham, since 1989; Corporate Tax. *Career:* May May and Merrimans, Articled Clerk/Solicitor 1979-82; Hempsons, Solicitor/Partner 1982-87; Lawrence Graham, Solicitor/Partner 1987-. *Biog: b.* 31 October 1954. *Nationality:* British. *m.* 1985, Ceza (née Margossian); 2 d. *Educ:* Truro Cathedral School; Exeter College, Oxford (MA); College of Law, Guildford. *Professional Organisations:* Law Society. *Publications:*

Various Articles on Tax Matters. *Recreations:* Woodwork, Gardening, Cycling.

FIELD, Robin Shaun; Divisional Partner, Touche Ross Management Consultants, since 1980; Health Care, Defence & Engineering Industries. *Career:* Shell Intl Petroleum Co Development, Eng/Operational Research 1960-66; John Waddington Ltd, Mgmnt Services Mgr 1967-69; Plastona (John Waddington) Ltd, Commercial Dir, then Gen Mgr 1969-76; Touche Ross Management Consultants, Consultant 1976-80; Ptnr 1980-. *Biog: b.* 10 May 1938. *Nationality:* British. *m.* 1960, Wendy (Joan); 2 s; 1 d. *Educ:* Cheltenham College; Corpus Christi College, Cambridge (MA). *Professional Organisations:* MIProdE; FCMA; FSS; CEng; Member, The Operational Research Society; Licenciate of the Institute of Health Service Mgmnt. *Recreations:* Squash, Skiing, Sailing, Opera.

FIELD, Miss Sally A; Partner, Bristows Cooke & Carpmael, since 1987; Intellectual Property. *Career:* Clifford Turner, Articled Clerk 1979-81; Solicitor, Intellectual Property Department 1981-83; Bristows Cooke & Carpmael, Solicitor 1983-87; Partner 1987-. *Biog: b.* 16 May 1957. *Nationality:* British. *Educ:* Durham University (BA Hons Law); Chester College of Law (Solicitors Finals 2nd Class Hons). *Professional Organisations:* Law Society. *Recreations:* Skiing, Tennis.

FIELD, William; Partner, Clark Whitehill, since 1990; International Tax. *Career:* Tobacco Kiosks Ltd, Area Accountant 1973-75; Hill Vellacott, Trainee/Audit Manager/Tax Manager 1975-83; Clark Whitehill, Tax Manager Business Tax/Partner Spanish Matters 1983-. *Biog: b.* 14 May 1952. *m.* 1989, Jennifer Anne (née Havard); 1 d. *Educ:* Kingsbury County Grammar School; City of London Polytechnic (Diploma in Accountancy). *Professional Organisations:* Associate, Institute of Chartered Accountants in England and Wales. *Recreations:* Music, Walking.

FIELD-JOHNSON, Nicholas; Executive Director, N M Rothschild & Sons Ltd, since 1990; Corporate Finance, Europe. *Career:* Dresdner Bank AG, London, Head of M & A Corp Finance 1986-90; World Trade Bank, Los Angeles, CA, USA, Sup & Gen Manager, Merchant Banking 1983-85; Atlantic Richfield Co, Los Angeles, CA, International Investment Planning & Strategy 1979-82; Harvard Business School, MBA 1976-79; Citibank NA, London, Account Officer, Corporate Banking 1974-76. *Biog: b.* 28 March 1951. *Nationality:* British. *m.* 1977, Sarah Katherine (née Von Everitt); 3 s. *Educ:* Harrow School; St Edmund Hall, Oxford University (MA,BA); Harvard Business School (MBA). *Other Activities:* International Experience in Europe & 9 Years in USA. *Clubs:* Carlton Annabel's. *Recreations:* Fishing, Shooting, Sailing, Tennis, Bridge.

FIELDEN, David Shaw; Managing Director, Pallas Leasing Group Ltd, since 1984. *Career:* American Express Co VP Finance 1962-74; Hamilton Leasing Ltd MD 1975-82; Lloyds Bowmaker Ltd Dir 1982-83; Pallas Leasing Group Ltd 1984-. *Biog: b.* 3 November 1938. *Nationality:* British. *m.* 1965, Carola (née van der Meer); 2 s; 1 d. *Educ:* West Bridgroad Grammar School. *Directorships:* S G Warburg & Co Ltd 1986 (exec). *Professional Organisations:* FCA. *Clubs:* MCC. *Recreations:* Tennis, Golf, Watching Rugby, Cricket.

FIELDING, Richard Walter; Chairman & Chief Executive, C E Heath plc, since 1987; Insurance Broking. *Career:* Bland Welch & Co Ltd, Broker - Dir 1954-68; C E Heath & Co Ltd, Board Dir-Jt Man Dir 1968-75; Fielding Group, Chm 1986-; C E Heath plc, Chief Exec. *Biog: b.* 9 July 1933. *m.* 1983, Jacqueline Winifred (née Hussey); 1 s; 3 d; 2 stepd. *Educ:* Clifton College. *Directorships:* Subsidiaries of C E Heath plc; The Charter Reinsurance Co Ltd 1985 Chm. *Other Activities:* Member, Lloyd's. *Recreations:* Hunting, Country Sports.

FIFE, Eugene Vawter; Chairman & Managing Director, Goldman Sachs International Limited, since 1988; Head of the London Office. *Career:* Blyth & Company Associate 1968-70; Goldman Sachs & Company (New York) 1970-72; (San Francisco), Gen Mgr 1972-86; (London) Head of Investment Banking Division 1986-. *Biog: b.* 23 September 1940. m2 1984, Anne (née Leisy); 2 s; 1 d. *Educ:* Virginia Tech; University of Southern California, Los Angeles (MBA). *Other Activities:* (Chm of Board of Trustees) Lewis & Clark College; (Head) Royce School; Lafayette Orinda Presbyterian Church; Trustee, the Royal Opera House. *Clubs:* Union (New York).

FIFE, J K; Partner, Field Fisher Waterhouse, since 1978. *Career:* Admitted as Solicitor 1973; Partner 1978. *Biog: b.* 18 September 1948. *Nationality:* British. *m.* 1974, Jean (née Northedge); 1 s; 2 d. *Educ:* Leeds Modern School; Lincoln College, Oxford (MA). *Professional Organisations:* Solicitor. *Recreations:* Football, Opera.

FIFIELD, Guy; Partner, Wilde Sapte; Employment Law. *Biog: b.* 7 March 1957. *Nationality:* British. *Educ:* Cheltenham College (LLB). *Other Activities:* Whittington Committee of City of London Solicitors Company; Freeman, City of London.

FILDES, (David) Christopher; Financial Columnist, Author and Broadcaster, (The Daily Telegraph, Euromoney, The Spectator, Business Daily); Wincott Award, 1978 and 1986; The Spectator (1828) Ltd, Director.

FILLERY, Wendy; Partner, Forsyte Kerman.

FINBOW, Roger John; Partner, Ashurst Morris Crisp, since 1985; Competition Law (OFT, MMC and EEC), Corporate Finance, Commercial. *Career:* Ashurst Morris Crisp, Articled Clerk 1975-77; Asst Solicitor 1977-83; Associate 1983-85. *Biog: b.* 13 May 1952. *Nationality:* British. *m.* 1984, Janina Fiona (née Doull); 2 d. *Educ:* Woodbridge School, Suffolk; Mansfield College, Oxford (MA). *Other Activities:* Mansfield Assoc (Pres); Mansfield College Council (Member); Mansfield 2000 Appeal Ctee (Member); Mansfield Business Sub-Group (Chm). *Recreations:* Cars, Collecting Model Cars, Ipswich Town FC, Badminton.

FINCH, Julia; Money Editor, Daily Express. *Career:* Cargo Systems Research Consultants 1981-83; Insurance Age 1983-87. *Other Activities:* BIIBA Insurance Journalist of the Year, 1988.

FINCH, Robert; Partner, Linklaters and Paines, since 1974; Property. *Biog: b.* 20 August 1944. *Nationality:* British. *m.* 1971, Patricia (née Ross); 2 d. *Educ:* Felsted. *Other Activities:* Freeman, City of London; Livery of Solicitors. *Clubs:* Alpine Ski, Ski Club of Gt Britain, West Mersea Yacht Club.

FINCHAM, Anthony Leonard Rupert; Partner, Cameron Markby Hewitt, since 1984; Employment Commercial Litigation. *Career:* Markby, Articled Clerk 1978-80; Cameron Markby, Assistant Solicitor 1980-83. *Biog: b.* 19 March 1955. *Educ:* Tonbridge School; Oriel College, Oxford (Degree in Modern History).

FINDLATER, Richard Napier; Partner, Ernst & Young, since 1976; Major Client Handling, Partner in Charge of Food & Drink Industry Group. *Career:* Harry Price & Co Articled Clerk/CA 1964-70; Arthur Young Qualified Snr-Mgr 1970-76; Ptnr 1976-; (New York) 1976-77. *Biog: b.* 27 May 1947. *Nationality:* British. *m.* 1972, Susan (née Charlton); 2 s; 1 d. *Educ:* Pangbourne College. *Professional Organisations:* FCA, ATII. *Recreations:* Sports.

FINDLAY, Alastair Ian; Director, Robert Fleming & Co Ltd, since 1986; Corporate Finance. *Career:* Peat Marwick Mitchell & Co 1974-78. *Biog: b.* 1 April 1952. *Nationality:* British. *m.* 1983, Henrietta (née Burton); 1 s; 1 d. *Educ:* Fettes College; University of Lancaster (BA). *Professional Organisations:* FCA.

FINDLAY, James Anthony; Director, Foreign & Colonial, since 1990; USA. *Career:* Hoare Govett 1979-82; John Govett, USA 1982. *Biog: b.* 14 October 1957. *Nationality:* British. *m.* 1987, Venetia (née Laing). *Educ:* Harrow. *Clubs:* Brooks, Lansdowne, Prestwich Golf Club. *Recreations:* All Sports, Tennis, Golf, Shooting.

FINDLAY, James William; Partner, Cazenove & Co.

FINE, Antony Edward Martin; Partner, Bacon & Woodrow, since 1971; Insurance Consulting. *Biog: b.* 14 September 1942. *Educ:* Queen's College, Oxford (MA). *Professional Organisations:* FIA; ASA.

FINE, Jonathan Mark; Partner, Holman Fenwick & Willan, since 1983; Commercial Litigation - Maritime/Commodities/Professional Negligence; Finance Partner, since 1988. *Career:* Barrister 1984-86; Holman Fenwick & Willan, Assistant Solicitor 1983-86. *Biog: b.* 7 February 1951. *Nationality:* British. *m.* 1973, Doreen (née Charlton); 3 d. *Educ:* Bede School, Sunderland; St John's College, Cambridge (BA, LLB, MA, LLM); Middle Temple (Barrister). *Professional Organisations:* Solicitor. *Recreations:* Family, Communal Activities, School Governor.

FINEBERG, Jonathan Erich; Director, County NatWest Secs, since 1989; Customer Liquidity. *Career:* Morgan Stanley Secs, Head of Market Making 1987-89; Smith New Court plc, Market Maker 1972-87. *Biog: b.* 18 July 1956. *Nationality:* British. *m.* 1980, Dawn Elizabeth; 1 s; 3 d. *Directorships:* Perfect Produce Ltd 1990 (exec).

FINK, S; Director, E D & F Man Ltd.

FINLAY, A; Director, Stewart Ivory & Company Limited.

FINN, Geoffrey Peter John; Partner, Slaughter and May, since 1977; Mergers and Acquisitions, Leveraged Buyouts, General Commercial. *Biog: b.* 14 December 1945; 2 s; 1 d. *Educ:* Downside School; Christ's College, Cambridge (MA). *Other Activities:* Member, City of London Solicitors' Company. *Professional Organisations:* The Law Society.

FINN, Geoffrey Stuart; Financial Consultant, Godsell, Astley & Pearce Ltd, since 1989; Corporate Finance, Capital Markets & Money Markets. *Career:* Joseph Sebag & Co, Investment Analyst 1954-59; W I Carr, Sons & Co, Partner 1959-69; Rowe & Pitman, Partner 1969-86; S G Warburg Securities Ltd, Director, Fixed Interest Division 1986-89. *Biog: b.* 23 August 1930. *Nationality:* British. *m.* 1955, Miriam; 1 d. *Educ:* Bemrose School, Derby; University of London (BCom Hons). *Other Activities:* Liveryman, Tallow Chandlers Company; Liveryman & Court Assistant, Chartered Secretaries and Administrators Company; Past Master, Cripplegate Ward Club; Life Governor, Imperial Cancer Research Fund; Member of Committee, City of London Branch Leukaemia Research Fund. *Professional Organisations:* Fellow, Chartered Institute of Secretaries & Administrators; Fellow, Royal Statistical Society; Fellow, Royal Economic Society; Fellow, Royal Society of Arts; Associate Member, Society of Investment Analysts. *Publications:* Numerous Articles for Newspapers & Magazines Including Daily Telegraph, Times, Sunday Times, Investors Chronicle, Financial Weekly, The Treasurer. *Clubs:* Carlton, City of London, City Livery, MCC, Middlesex RFU, Leander, Royal Mid-Surrey Golf Club, Carmarthen Golf Club, Ashburnham Golf Club. *Recreations:* Bridge, Music, Travel, Golf, Rugby, Cricket.

FINN, Leo Peter; Deputy Managing Director, Northern Rock Building Society, since 1990. *Career:* Northern Rock 1959; Secretary 1979; Assistant General Manager & Secretary 1982-86; General Manager & Secretary 1986-89; Director & Secretary 1989; Deputy Managing Director 1990. *Biog: b.* 13 July 1938. *Nationality:* British. *m.* 1963, Alice Patricia (née Harold); 2 s; 2 d. *Educ:* Newcastle Polytechnic (BA Hons). *Directorships:* Northern Coalfields Property Co 1987 (non-exec); Northern Rock Housing Trust 1984 (exec) Dep Chm; Rock Asset Management 1987 (exec) Dep Chm; Homes Intown plc 1988 (non-exec); Community Housing Initiatives Ltd 1990 (non-exec); Northern Rock Property Services Ltd 1990 (non-exec). *Professional Organisations:* FCBSI; FRSA. *Recreations:* Photography, Victorian History, Fell-walking.

FINN, R G M; Director, Edwards & Payne (Underwriting Agencies) Limited.

FINNERTY, C W; Director, Lombard North Central plc.

FINNIGAN, John Howard; Head of Company and Commercial Department, Hepworth & Chadwick, since 1990; Banking/Insolvency. *Career:* Hepworth & Chadwick, Articled Clerk 1969-71; Assistant Solicitor 1971-74; Partner 1974-. *Biog: b.* 5 March 1947. *Nationality:* British. *m.* 1974, Hilary Jill; 2 s. *Educ:* Woodhouse Grove School; Gonville & Caius College, Cambridge (BA, MA). *Professional Organisations:* The Law Society; The Incorporated Leeds Law Society; Licensed Insolvency Practitioner. *Clubs:* The Leeds Club.

FISH, J C; Director Corporate Communications, Sedgwick Group plc.

FISHBURN, Simon Ephraim; Director of Finance, Brandeis Group, since 1989; Accounting, Administration, Foreign Exchange Commodity Finance. *Career:* Triland Metals Ltd (Mitsubishi), Financial Controller 1984-89; Primary Industries (UK) Ltd/Lonconex Ltd/M Golodetz Ltd, Group Internal Auditor 1980-84; Philips Electronics, Audit Manager 1973-80; Ernst & Whinney, Accountants Auditor 1967-. *Biog: b.* 1943. *Nationality:* British. *m.* 1972, Margaret Sally. *Educ:* Hasmonfan; University College London (BA Hons); School of Oriental and African Studies, London University (SOAJ Certificate). *Directorships:* Brandeis Limited (exec) Fin; Brandeis (Brokers) Limited 1989 (exec) Fin; Pechiney World Trade (Holdings) Limited 1989 (exec) Fin. *Other Activities:* London Metal Exchange Technical

231

Committee; Commodity Traders Group. *Professional Organisations:* FCA. *Recreations:* Hill Walking, Tennis, Bridge.

FISHER, A M; Partner, Field Fisher Waterhouse.

FISHER, Alfred Robin; Partner, Chapel Studio, since 1972; Designer and Conservator of Stained Glass. *Career:* Whitefriars Glass Ltd, Draughtsman/Designer/Manager 1951-72; Chapel Studio, Designer & Partner 1972-. *Biog: b.* 10 December 1933. *Nationality:* British. *m.* 1990, Pamela Fleur; 1 s; 1 d. *Educ:* The Liverpool Institute; Liverpool College of Art. *Directorships:* British Society of Master Glass Painters 1982-89 Chairman; Leighton Buzzard Railway 1981-87 Chairman. *Other Activities:* Art Workers Guild; National Trust; Consultant/Conservator of Glass. *Professional Organisations:* Fellow, British Society of Master Glass Painters; Associate Fellow, Guild of Glass Engravers. *Publications:* Papers on Glass Conservation. *Recreations:* Nature, Steam Locomotive Driving and Maintenance.

FISHER, Anthony Bruce; Director, C S Investments Ltd, since 1988; Fund Management. *Career:* Colonial Mutual Life, Investment Officer 1969-77; Allstate Insurance Co, Investment Mgr 1977-80; Asst Gen Mgr 1980-83; Dep Gen Mgr (Finance) 1983-85; R Nivison & Co Head, Fund Mgmnt 1985-86; Nivison Cantrade Ltd, Dir 1986-88. *Biog: b.* 8 June 1948. *Nationality:* British. *m.* 1985, Philippa (née Comer); 2 s; 1 d. *Educ:* Burton-on-Trent Grammar School; St Edmund Hall, Oxford (MA). *Professional Organisations:* FIA; ASIA. *Clubs:* Argonauts, Annabel's, Wilmslow Golf Club, King's Head Chess Club. *Recreations:* Golf, Cricket, Chess.

FISHER, C J H; Director, Orion Royal Bank Ltd.

FISHER, C M; General Manager, Lloyds Bank plc.

FISHER, Christopher Charles; Director, Lazard Brothers & Co Limited, since 1987; Corporate Finance. *Career:* Confederation of British Industry Economist 1978-80; Lazard Brothers 1980-. *Biog: m.* 2 d. *Educ:* Reading University (BA); Harvard University (Master in Public Policy). *Directorships:* Development Capital (Securities) Limited. *Other Activities:* Member of Council, University of Reading.

FISHER, Ian; Director, MMG Patricof Buy-Ins Limited, since 1988. *Career:* Army, Captain 1968-71; Winfields Enterprises 1964 Ltd, Export Manager 1974-77; Winco Ltd, Joint General Manager 1977-79; Bain & Company, London, Partner 1980-88. *Biog: b.* 22 August 1950. *m.* 1975, Daphna Fisher (née Ur); 1 s; 1 d. *Educ:* Tel Aviv University, Israel (BA English and Economics); IMEDE, Lausanne, Switzerland (MBA Distinction). *Directorships:* MMG Patricof Buy-Ins Limited 1988 (exec);

Markoffer plc 1989 (exec); James Neill Holdings Ltd 1989 (exec).

FISHER, Ian Maxwell; TD; Partner, Freshfields, since 1981; Commercial Property. *Career:* Macfarlanes, Articled Clerk 1969-71; Solicitor 1971-72; Lovell White & King, Solicitor 1972-74; Freshfields, Solicitor 1974-81. *Biog: b.* 6 April 1947. *Nationality:* British. *m.* 1975, Suzanne Gwendolyn (née Dengate); 1 d. *Educ:* Watford Grammar School; Liverpool University (LLB). *Other Activities:* Member, Territorial Army (Promoted Major 1983). *Professional Organisations:* Member, The Law Society; Member, City of London Law Society. *Recreations:* Territorial Army, Photography, Sailing.

FISHER, J D; Partner, Clay & Partners, Consulting Actuaries, since 1984. *Career:* Clay & Partners 1977-. *Biog: b.* 24 April 1956. *Nationality:* British. *m.* 1981, Michelle (née Lebetkin); 2 d. *Educ:* Latymer Upper School, London; The City University, London (BSc Hon Actuarial Science First Class). *Other Activities:* Member, Institute of Actuaries Careers Committee. *Professional Organisations:* FIA.

FISHER, Keith; Partner, Overton Shirley & Barry, since 1984; City Search Assignments. *Career:* Mercedes Benz (GB) Ltd Sales Promotion 1960-67; Baileys Farms Proprietor 1967-71; James Capel & Co Bullion/Private Clients 1971-75; Heritage Marketing Ltd MD 1975-81. *Biog: b.* 28 October 1935. *Nationality:* British. *m.* 1976, Julia (née Pattinson); 3 s (1 decd). *Educ:* Harrow. *Directorships:* Overton Shirley & Barry 1984 Ptnr (exec). *Other Activities:* Freeman, Grocers' Company; Mem, Vintry & Dowgate Ward Club. *Clubs:* Inst of Directors, Lansdowne. *Recreations:* Fishing, Shooting, Bridge.

FISHER, Max Henry; Director, S G Warburg & Co Ltd, since 1981. *Career:* Foreign Office Research Dept and Library 1949-56; Financial Times Various 1957-80; Editor 1973-80. *Biog: b.* 30 May 1922. *m.* 1952, Rosemary Margaret (née Maxwell); 2 s; 1 d. *Educ:* Fichte-Gymnasium (Berlin), Rendcomb Coll; Lincoln College, Oxford (MA). *Directorships:* Commercial Union plc 1981 (non-exec); Booker plc 1981 (non-exec). *Other Activities:* LSE (Governor). *Publications:* The Holstein Papers (Co-Editor). *Clubs:* RAC.

FISHER, Norman; Partner, Forsyte Kerman.

FISHER, P J; Partner, Lovell White Durrant.

FISHER, Ronald Ashley; Director, BDO Consulting, since 1988; Resource Management, Covering Manufacturing, Logistics, Costing. *Career:* Leyland Vehicles Snr Analyst 1974-77; Leyland Trucks Corp Planning & Inv Mgr 1978-82; Landrover-Leyland International Fin Mgr 1983-84; Peat Marwick Mging Cons 1984-87. *Biog: b.* 1951. *Nationality:* British. *m.* 1979, Noelle (née Saundry). *Educ:* Workington County Grammar; St Andrews University (BSc Hons). *Directorships:* Binder Hamlyn Management Consultants 1988 (exec). *Professional Organisations:* FCMA. *Recreations:* Music, Badminton, Cycling, Bridge, Travel.

FISHMAN, Alan Seymour; Senior Partner, Clay & Partners. *Biog: b.* 9 December 1942. *Nationality:* British. *m.* 1966, Marian (née Frankel); 1 s; 2 d. *Professional Organisations:* FIA.

FISHMAN, M A; Partner, Arthur Andersen & Co Chartered Accts.

FITCH, Colin Digby Thomas; Director, Kleinwort Benson Securities Ltd, since 1986; Corporate Finance. *Career:* The Stock Exchange, Asst Sec 1961-66; Rowe & Pitman, Ptnr 1966-76; Hong Kong Bank Group MD, Wardley Middle East 1976-80; Grieveson Grant and Co, Ptnr 1981-86. *Biog: b.* 2 January 1934. *Nationality:* British. *m.* 1956, Wendy Ann (née Davis); 4 s; 1 d. *Educ:* St Paul's School; St Catharine's College, Cambridge (MA, LLM). *Professional Organisations:* Member of the Inner Temple; Member of the Stock Exchange; FCIS. *Clubs:* Brooks's.

FITCHEN, Michael John; Director, Lowndes Lambert Group Limited, since 1983; Cargo Insurance Broking. *Career:* Wackerbarth Hardman & Co Ltd, Insurance Broker 1958-66. *Biog: b.* 28 November 1938. *Nationality:* British. *m.* Norma Ann (née Little); 1 s; 1 d. *Educ:* Aylesbury Grammar School. *Directorships:* Lowndes Lambert Cargo Ltd 1985 Chm & MD. *Professional Organisations:* ACII. *Recreations:* Golf, Gardening, Carpentry.

FITTON, D; Financial Director, Church, Charity and Local Authority Fund Managers Limited.

FITTON, Geoffrey; Deputy General Manager, Postipankki Ltd, London Branch, since 1990; Finance. *Career:* Price Waterhouse & Co, Snr 1957-60; Wm Brandts Sons & Co Ltd, Asst Mgr, Corp Finance 1960-63; Standard Industrial Group, Mgmnt Accountant 1963-66; Antony Gibbs & Sons Ltd, Chief Accountant 1966-72; Antony Gibbs Holdings Ltd, Gp Finance Dir 1972-83; Postipankki (UK) Ltd, Gen Mgr 1983-86; Executive Director 1986-90. *Biog: b.* 4 January 1933. *Nationality:* British. *m.* 1956, Mary Helena (née Howard); 2 s; 2 d. *Educ:* Newent Grammar School. *Other Activities:* The Worshipful Company of Chartered Accountants in England & Wales. *Professional Organisations:* FCA. *Recreations:* Golf, Cricket, Opera.

FITZALAN HOWARD, Mark; Lord Fitzalan Howard; Director, Robert Fleming Holdings Limited, since 1974. *Biog: b.* 28 March 1934. *Nationality:* British. *m.* 1961, Jacynth; 2 d. *Educ:* Ampleforth College. *Directorships:* Robert Fleming Holdings Limited 1974; Robert Fleming Asset Management Limited 1988; Fleming Investment Trust Management Limited 1988; Robert Fleming Investment Trust Limited 1975; The Fleming Claverhouse Investment Trust 1979; The Fleming Far Eastern Investment Trust 1965; The Fleming International High Income Investment Trust plc 1981; The Fleming Overseas Investment Trust 1979; The Fleming Universal Investment Trust 1982; BET plc 1983; National Mutual Life Assurance Society 1972; National Mutual Pensions Limited 1981; Ladybridge Developments Limited 1965; Moorgate Properties Inc 1982; The United States Debenture Corporation plc 1977; USDC Investment Trust plc 1987; Lochside Land Limited 1987; Sawpass Limited 1989; Birmingham & District Investment Trust Limited -1983; Namulas Pension Trustees Limited -1984; St George Assurance - 1980; Tempest Estates Limited -1983; Robert Fleming Investment Management Limited -1988; Rediffusion plc -1985; London Prudential Investment Trust plc -1985; Robert Fleming Properties Limited -1987; TR North America Investment Trust plc -1988; Continental Union Finance Limited -1988; Continental Union Agricultural Holdings Limited -1988; Robert Fleming Pension Trust Limited -1989; Robert Fleming France (SA) –1989.

FITZGERALD, Adrian Bruce; Director, County NatWest Securities.

FITZGERALD, Christopher Francis; Partner, Slaughter and May, since 1976; Banking/Commercial Law; Finance Partner, 1986-. *Biog: b.* 17 November 1945. *Nationality:* British. *m.* 1986, Jill (née Freshwater). m1; 1 s; 2 d, m2; 2 stepd. *Educ:* Downside School; Lincoln College, Oxford (MA). *Other Activities:* City of London Solicitors' Company. *Professional Organisations:* Law Society. *Clubs:* MCC, RAC.

FITZGERALD, E B; Non-Executive Director, STC plc.

FITZGERALD, Dr Michael Desmond; Director, Mitsubishi Finance International plc, since 1988; Head of Arbitrage & Investment Management. *Career:* CL-Alexanders, Laing & Cruickshank Ltd, Chief Economist & Head of Planning 1986-88; Ernst & Whinney, Professor of Finance, University of Strathclyde 1985-86; City University Business School, Senior Lecturer in Finance & Head of Finance Dept 1980-85; New York University Associate Professor of Finance 1977-80; Chemical Bank, London, Chief Economist 1975-77. *Biog: b.* 19 January 1947. *Nationality:* British. *m.* 1977, Krystyna Weinstein. *Educ:* De La Salle College, Salford; University of York (BA Economics); University of Manchester (PhD). *Directorships:* Unique Consultants Ltd 1985 (non-exec); London Maritime Investment Company 1984 (exec); Alexanders, Laing & Cruickshank Options Ltd 1985 (exec). *Publications:* Financial Options, Euromoney, 1987; Financial Futures, Euromoney, 1983; Numerous Academic and Professional Articles. *Clubs:* Reform. *Recreations:* Collecting Antiquities, Horse Racing.

FITZGERALD, N W A; Director, Unilever plc.

FITZGERALD, Neil; Glasgow Business Correspondent, The Scotsman.

FITZGERALD, P G; General Manager, Sales & Marketing, The Scottish Provident Institution.

FITZGIBBONS, H E; Non-Executive Director, Johnson Matthey.

FITZHERBERT, David Henry; Director, Hambros Bank Ltd, since 1988; Venture Capital/Development Capital. *Career:* Hambros Bank London, Fund Manager 1978-81; Hambros Hong Kong, Fund Manager (Japan) 1981-84; Hambros Tokyo, Chief Representative 1984-88; Hambros London, Director, Hambro Group Investment 1988-. *Biog:* b. 4 March 1957. *Nationality:* Irish. *Educ:* Trinity College, Oxford (MA). *Recreations:* Skiing.

FITZMAURICE, P; Partner, Nabarro Nathanson.

FITZPATRICK, Barry John; Company Secretary, Crawley Warren Group plc, since 1987; Finance. *Career:* Wigham Poland Group, Group Accountant 1972-77; Deloittes, Chartered Accountants, Accountant 1970-72; Reads & Co, Chartered Accountants, Articled Clerk 1965-70. *Biog:* b. 27 April 1948. *Nationality:* British. *m.* Margaret Isobel (née Collins); 1 s; 1 d. *Educ:* St Benedicts, Ealing. *Other Activities:* Lloyds of London. *Professional Organisations:* FCA; ATII. *Clubs:* City, RAC. *Recreations:* Golf, Skiing, Cricket.

FITZPATRICK, G; Director, Hoare Govett & Co, since 1989; Market Making, Specifically Recruitment & Training of Trainee Dealers. *Career:* Wedd Durlacher Mordant & Co, Stock Jobber 1985-86; Hoare Govett (Formerly C T Pulley) 1986-; Director 1989. *Biog:* b. 26 November 1961. *Nationality:* British. *m.* 1989, Bronwen Fitzpatrick (née Jones). *Educ:* Christ's Hospital; Southampton University (BA Hons Eng/Phil). *Clubs:* Cannons Sports Club, Queens LTC, Stock Exchange LTC (Captain). *Recreations:* Squash, Tennis, Golf, Travel.

FITZPATRICK, Nicholas David; Partner, Bacon & Woodrow, since 1987; Investment Adviser. *Career:* Abbey Life Investment Analyst 1972-74; Portfolio Mgr 1974-76; British Rail Pension Fund UK Equity Mgr 1976-84; Investment Mgr 1984-86. *Biog:* b. 23 January 1947. *m.* 1969, Patricia Jill (née Brotherton); 1 s; 1 d. *Educ:* Bristol Grammar School; Nottingham University (Industrial Economics Degree). *Directorships:* Charterhouse Dev Capital Fund Ltd 1984 (non-exec); CAPS Ltd 1987 (non-exec); Quantec Computers Ltd 1987 (non-exec). *Other Activities:* Member, NAPF Investment Committee. *Professional Organisations:* FIA; MSIA. *Rec-*

reations: Teenage Rugby Training (Sutton & Epsom Rugby Football Club).

FITZPATRICK, R F; Director, S G Warburg Akroyd Rowe & Pitman Mullens Securities Ltd.

FITZROY, James Oliver Charles; The Earl of Euston; Finance Director, Capel-Cure Myers Capital Management Ltd.

FITZSIMMONS, H; Director, W H Ireland Stephens & Co Ltd.

FITZSIMONS, Patrick Anthony; Managing Director & Chief Executive, Bristol & West Building Society, since 1989. *Career:* Rank Xerox, (Australia) Finance Planning & Accounting Mgr 1972-75; Regional Controller 1975-76; Finance Controller, Region 3 1976-79; Finance Director, Region 1 1979-81; Grand Metropolitan Finance Systems & Strategy Director 1981-83; Managing Director of the Host Group 1983-85; Citibank Managing Dir of Personal Banking 1985-89. *Biog:* b. 16 March 1946. *Nationality:* British; 2 s. *Educ:* St Philip's Grammar; London School of Economics (BSc Econ). *Directorships:* Leisure Retail Services 1988; Ruton Management Ltd 1985; The Bristol Initiative 1989; Avon Training & Enterprise Council 1989 Chairman. *Other Activities:* Member of Lords Taverners. *Recreations:* Squash, Riding, Antiques.

FITZWILLIAM-LAY, David Hugh; Chairman, G T Management plc, since 1989; Investment Management. *Career:* Courtaulds Ltd Synthetic Fibres Division Marketing Dir 1960-67; Baker Weeks Inc (New York) VP 1968-75; Dean Witter Reynolds Inc (New York) VP 1975-78; G T Managment plc Dir 1978-. *Biog:* b. 12 October 1931. *Nationality:* British. *m.* 1961, Ann Delmar (née Gormley); 2 s; 3 d. *Educ:* Lancing College; St Edmund Hall Oxford (BA). *Directorships:* G T Management (Tokyo) 1986 (exec) Chm; G T Capital Holdings Inc (San Fransisco) 1987 (exec) Chm; G T Management (Asia) Ltd (Hong Kong) 1985-86 (exec) Chm; G T Management plc, Chief Executive Officer 1988-89. *Other Activities:* Hong Kong Securities Commission (Member of Unit Trust Ctee 1984-85, Member of Ctee on Takeovers & Mergers 1986). *Professional Organisations:* Governor at Large, Nat Assoc of Security Dealers, Washington DC 1987-90. *Clubs:* City, Hong Kong, Hurlingham. *Recreations:* Shooting, Tennis, Skiing, Landscaping.

FLAHERTY, J; General Manager & Executive Vice President, American Express Bank.

FLAHERTY, St John Andrew; Partner, Slaughter and May, since 1985. *Biog:* b. 10 November 1946. *Nationality:* British. *m.* 1980, Lesley McGregor (née Nisbet); 1 s; 1 d. *Educ:* Ampleforth College; Cambridge

University (BA). *Professional Organisations:* Fellow, Chartered Association of Certified Accountants.

FLANAGAN, Martin L; Director, Templeton Unit Trust Managers Limited.

FLANNERY, P A; Director, Morgan Grenfell & Co Limited.

FLAVIN, Jim; Chief Executive/Deputy Chairman, Development Capital Corporation Limited, since 1976. *Career:* Allied Irish Investment Bank 1971-76; Kennedy Crowley Chartered Accountants (now KPMG Stokes Kennedy Crowley) 1969-71. *Biog: b.* 30 October 1942. *Nationality:* Irish. *m.* 1970, Mary; 1 s; 3 d. *Educ:* Blackrock College; University College, Dublin. *Directorships:* Development Capital Corporation Limited 1976 Chief Executive/Deputy Chairman; DCC Corporate Finance Limited 1985 Chairman/Chief Executive; DCC Ventures Limited 1983 Chairman/Chief Executive; DCC Business Expansion Fund Limited 1989 (exec) Chairman; Flogas plc 1978 Chairman; Fyffes plc 1981 (non-exec); Duke House Properties Limited 1982 Chairman; Zeus Management Limited 1985 (non-exec); Fannin Limited 1986 (non-exec); Printech International plc 1987 Chairman; Reflex Investments plc 1987 Chairman. *Professional Organisations:* BComm; Dip Pub Adm; FCA. *Clubs:* Royal Automobile Club, Stephen's Green Club, Royal Irish Yacht Club.

FLEISCHER, Spencer Charles; Managing Director, Morgan Stanley, since 1979; Corporate Finance. *Career:* Morgan Stanley, New York 1979-84; San Francisco 1984-87; Los Angeles 1987-89. *Biog: b.* 2 October 1953. *Nationality:* American. *m.* 1986, Caroline Mary (née Lorentz); 2 d. *Educ:* Lincoln College, Oxon (M PHIL); Michaelhouse Witwatersrand (BA Hons). *Clubs:* Vincents, University Club New York, University Club San Francisco. *Recreations:* Reading, Architecture, Wine.

FLEMING, Adam Richard; Director, Robert Fleming Holdings Limited, since 1985. *Biog: b.* 15 May 1948. *Nationality:* British. *m.* Caroline; 2 s; 1 d. *Directorships:* The Fleming Mercantile Investment Trust plc 1985; The Fleming Universal Investment Trust plc 1985; Glidrose Publications Limited; Fleming Investment Trust Management Limited 1988; Robert Fleming Investment Trust Ltd 1985; Robert Fleming Trustee Co Ltd 1981; Robert Fleming Investment Management (Jersey) Limited 1987; Fleming High Income Investment Trust Limited 1989; Fleming Private Asset Management Limited 1989; Fleming Unquoted Management Limited 1989; Crozier Securities Limited 1990; The Fairbridge Drake Society of Scotland 1990; Robert Fleming Investment Management Limited - 1988; Jardine Fleming International Inc -1984; Resource Holdings Ltd; Robert Fleming Securities Ltd - 1985; Fleming Montagu Stanley Limited -1989; Fleming Personal Portfolio Management Limited 1989;

Fleming International Portfolio Management Limited - 1989; Britannic Syndicate Limited -1990; Jardine Fleming International Limited -1990; JF Pacific Warrant Co SA -1990.

FLEMING, Andrew Somerville; Partner, Maclay Murray & Spens, since 1990; Responsible for Pensions Law Department within Firm. *Career:* Bannatyne Kirkwood France & Co, Glasgow, Apprentice Solicitor 1975-77; Solicitor 1977-78; Bishop & Co, Glasgow, Solicitor 1978-79; The Law Society of Scotland, Deputy Secretary 1979-84; John Menzies plc, Assistant Company Secretary 1984-86; Linklaters & Paines, Solicitor Pensions Law Department 1986-89; Maclay Murray & Spens, Solicitor Pensions Law 1989. *Biog: b.* 26 November 1954. *Nationality:* British. *Educ:* Kelvinside Academy; University of Glasgow (LLB). *Other Activities:* Member, Pension Committee; Law Society of Scotland. *Professional Organisations:* Law Society of Scotland, 1977; Association of Pension Lawyers, 1975. *Publications:* Accountants Magazine, 1990; Pensions and the Finance Act, 1989; What the Finance Director Needs to Know; Occupational Pensions, 1987; Financial Services Act 1986 as it Affects Pension Schemes. *Recreations:* Walking, Railways.

FLEMING, E B; Clerk, Girdlers' Company.

FLEMING, John Grierson; Partner, Stephenson Harwood, since 1960; Administration. *Career:* Reynolds Parry-Jones & Crawford, Asst Solicitor 1954-55; Evill & Coleman, Asst Solicitor 1955-56; Ptnr 1956-59; Stephenson Harwood, Asst Solicitor 1959-60. *Biog: b.* 2 February 1926. *Nationality:* British. *m.* 1953, Margaret; 1 s; 2 d. *Educ:* Lincoln School; Trinity College, Cambridge (MA, LLM); Scott Scholar; Clement's Inn; City of London Solicitors' Company's Grotius; Maurice Nordon and John Mackrell Prizes. *Directorships:* Boustead plc 1986 (non-exec). *Other Activities:* Freeman, Worshipful Company of Gardeners; Freeman, City of London Solicitors' Company; Chairman, Gresham Club; Law Society. *Clubs:* Beaconsfield Golf Club, MCC, Western Club Glasgow, Royal Overseas League, Chairman, Beaconsfield Cricket Club, Craftsman, Incorporation of Gardeners of Glasgow. *Recreations:* Golf, Cricket, Gardening, Music, Reading, Collecting Early English Watercolours.

FLEMING, Robin; Chairman, Robert Fleming Holdings Limited, since 1990. *Career:* Robert Fleming 1958-; Robert Fleming Trustee Co Limited, Director 1961; Chairman 1985; Robert Fleming Investment Trust Limited, Director 1968; Robert Fleming Holdings Limited, Director 1974; Deputy Chairman 1986. *Biog: b.* 18 September 1932. *Nationality:* British. *m.* 1962, Victoria Margaret (née Aykroyd); 2 s; 1 d. *Educ:* Eton College; Royal Military Academy, Sandhurst. *Directorships:* Robert Fleming Investment Trust Limited 1968; Robert Fleming Trustee Co Limited 1961 Chairman; Bar

Trustee Company Limited 1958; White Corries Limited Chairman; University Life Assurance Society 1966-90. *Recreations:* Country Pursuits.

FLEMING, Valentine Patrick; Director, Robert Fleming Holdings Ltd, since 1968; Investment Trusts. *Career:* Robert Fleming Group 1957-. *Biog: b.* 1 August 1935. *Nationality:* British. *m.* 1963, Elizabeth Helen (née Gibbs); 4 s. *Educ:* Eton College. *Directorships:* Robert Fleming Holdings Ltd 1968 (exec); Robert Fleming & Co Ltd 1988 (non-exec); Fleming International High Income Inv Trust plc 1975 (exec) Chairman; The Fleming Enterprise Inv Trust plc 1975 (exec); The Fleming Fledgeling Inv Trust plc 1984 (exec) Chairman; Jardine Fleming Australia Limited 1990 (non-exec); Provident Mutual Life Ass Association 1973 (non-exec); Whitburgh Investments Limited 1976 (non-exec); Dunedin Income Growth Inv Trust plc 1979 (non-exec); Dunedin Worldwide Investment Trust plc 1979 (non-exec); RCO Holdings plc 1986 (non-exec). *Recreations:* Outdoor Pursuits.

FLEMINGTON, Roger; Director & Deputy Group Chief Executive, National Westminster Bank plc, since 1990; Group Management. *Career:* National Westminster Bank Chief Intl Exec, Asia, Australasia, Africa 1979; Asst Gen Mgr, Intl Banking Div 1981; Gen Mgr, Premises Div 1984; Gen Mgr, Domestic Banking Div 1986-88; Dir & Chief Exec, UK Financial Services 19892B7 May 1932 British 1955, Doreen (née Smyter) (decd 1990). *Educ:* Nantwich & Acton Grammar School. *Directorships:* Coutts & Co 1986 (non-exec); Lombard North Central plc 1989 (non-exec); Westments Ltd 1984 (exec); Ulster Bank Ltd 1986-89. *Other Activities:* Freeman of City of London; Member, General Purposes Ctee of CIOB; Liveryman, Worshipful Co of Woolmen; Member, The Pilgrims of Great Britain & USA; Member, City Advisory Group; Trustee, Independent Broadcasting Telethon Trust; Dep Chm, Chartered Institute of Bankers; Member, British Bankers Association Executive Committee. *Professional Organisations:* FRSA; FCIB. *Clubs:* MCC, Overseas Bankers. *Recreations:* Music, Flyfishing, Country Pursuits.

FLEMMING, John Stanton; European Bank for Reconstruction & Development, since 1990; Economics. *Career:* Oriel College, Oxford Fellow in Economics 1963-65; Nuffield College, Oxford Official Fellow in Economic & Investment Bursar 1965-80; Bank of England, Chief Adviser 1980-83; Economic Adviser to the Governor 1983-88; Economics Director 1988-90. *Biog: b.* 6 February 1941. *Nationality:* British. *m.* 1963, Jean Elizabeth (née Briggs); 3 s; 1 d. *Educ:* Rugby School; Trinity College, Oxford (MA); Nuffield College, Oxford. *Other Activities:* Member, Advisory Board on Research Councils; Council, Institute of Fiscal Studies. *Professional Organisations:* Member of Council & Exec Ctee, Royal Economic Society. *Publications:* Inflation,

1976; numerous academic articles in journals & books. *Clubs:* Reform.

FLETCHER, Adrian; General Manager and Chief Operating Officer, Republic National Bank of New York, since 1988; General Operating, Financial and Personnel Management. *Career:* IBM UK Ltd, Large Systems Marketing 1966-70; Citibank UK Ltd, Vice President - UK Operations 1970-78; UK Region Financial Controller 1979-80; Trade Development Bank, Senior Manager (London) 1980-83; Samuel Montagu and Co Ltd, Executive Director 1983-84; Republic National Bank of New York, Senior Vice President 1984-86; Executive Vice President 1986-88. *Biog: b.* 21 July 1943. *Nationality:* British. *m.* 1964, Elizabeth; 2 d. *Educ:* Mill Hill School; School of Oriental and African Studies, London Univ (BA Arabic). *Directorships:* Samuel Montagu and Co Ltd 1983-84 (exec); Republic New York (UK) Ltd 1984 (exec); Republic Nominees 1984 (exec). *Clubs:* The Arts Club.

FLETCHER, G; Executive Director, Allied Dunbar Assurance plc.

FLETCHER, Ian Macmillan; WS; Partner, Richards Butler, since 1987; Finance & Banking Department experienced in Insolvency. *Career:* Richard Butler Asst Solicitor 1977-79; MacRoberts Ptnr 1980-87. *Biog: b.* 16 February 1948. *Nationality:* British. *m.* 1977, Jennifer Margaret (née Daly); 1 s; 2 d. *Educ:* Greenock Academy; University of Glasgow (LLB). *Directorships:* Chilton Bros Ltd Co Sec 1985. *Other Activities:* LTCL, LRAM, ARCO, MIPA. *Professional Organisations:* Law Society; Law Society of Scotland; Society of Writers to the Signet; Inst of Directors; IBA Section on Business Law (Member of Ctee J-Creditors' Rights, Insolvency, Liquidation and Reorganisations); Council Member, Insolvency Lawyers Association Ltd; Insolvency Practitioners Association; President, Society of Scottish Lawyers in London. *Publications:* The Law and Practice of Receivership in Scotland (Co-Author), 1987. *Clubs:* Western (Glasgow), Caledonian (London). *Recreations:* Music, Golf, Swimming.

FLETCHER, John; Associate, James Gentles & Son.

FLETCHER, John Richard; Senior Manager General Banking, The Hongkong and Shanghai Banking Corporation, since 1989; Trade Finance, Branches and Operations, including Systems and Finance. *Career:* Coopers & Lybrand, Articled Clerk 1969-72; Cripps Warburg, Manager Corporate Finance 1972-74; Consolidated Goldfields Group, Various Financial Positions in the Trade and Finance Side 1974-82; Royal Bank of Canada Trade Finance Ltd, Business Development Director 1982-83; HSBC, Various Positions 1983-. *Biog: b.* 25 September 1946. *Nationality:* British. *Educ:* Sandford Paul School; Trinity, Dublin (BBS Hons). *Directorships:* HongkongBank International Trade Finance Ltd 1984 (exec) Chm; HongkongBank Limited 1989 (non-exec); Hongkong International Trade Finance (Japan) Ltd 1985 (non-exec). *Professional Organisations:* FCA. *Recreations:* Golf, Squash, Power Boat Racing.

FLETCHER, John Wilfred Sword; Managing Director, Trafalgar House Corporate Development Limited, since 1985. *Career:* CBECL, Sandwich Course Student 1959; Site Agent, Blyth Power Station 1963; Site Agent at West Burton Power Station & Project Engineer Fiddlers Perry Power Station 1964; Project Engineer (Power Station Contracts) 1965; Contracts Manager 1968; Contracts Director UK 1971; Cleveland Bridge & Engineering Company Limited, Managing Director 1975; Trafalgar House plc, Divisional MD (Structural) 1982; Business Development & Marketing Director 1985; Trafalgar House Corporate Development, Managing Director 1989. *Biog: b.* 24 October 1940. *Nationality:* British. *m.* 1964, Jacqueline (née Aston); 2 s; 1 d. *Educ:* Uppingham School; Teeside Polytechnic (Higher Diploma in Civil & Structural Engineering). *Directorships:* City of London Heliport Limited 1989 (exec); Cleveland Bridge & Engineering Middle East (Private) Limited, Dubai 1979 (exec); Cunard Steam Ship Co plc 1989 (exec); Dartford River Crossing Limited 1989 (exec); Eurorail Limited 1988 (exec); Euroroute Construction Limited 1985 (exec); John Brown plc 1985 (exec); Poole Power Company Limited 1988 (exec); Scott Lithgow Limited 1984 (exec); Trafalgar House Construction Holdings Ltd 1990 (exec); Trafalgar House Construction Limited 1988 (exec); Trafalgar House Corporate Development Ltd 1989 (exec); Trafalgar House Environmental Services Ltd 1989 (exec); Trafalgar House Property Limited 1984 (exec); Anglo Japanese Construction Limited 1990 (exec). *Professional Organisations:* Associate Member, Institute of Civil Engineers.

FLETCHER, M G; Director, Johnson Fry plc.

FLETCHER, M J G; Clerk, Musicians' Company.

FLETCHER, Michael; Partner, Clark Whitehall.

FLETCHER, Nick; City Reporter, Daily Express. *Career:* Birmingham Post; London Daily News; Electronics Weekly; Electrical Review.

FLETCHER, Piers Michael William; Director, GNI Ltd, since 1985. *Career:* Tradax England, Trader 1978-79; GNI Ltd, Dealer 1979-. *Biog: b.* 10 August 1956. *Nationality:* British. *m.* 1986, Paula (née Levey). *Educ:* Wellington College; Christ Church, Oxford (MA). *Directorships:* GNI Freight Futures 1985 (exec); GNI Wallace 1987 (exec); London Potato Futures Assoc 1984 (exec); Baltic Futures Exchange 1987 (exec).

FLETCHER, Richard Alexander; Managing Director, Fletcher Jones Ltd, since 1984. *Biog: b.* 9 March 1956. *Educ:* Ainslie Park High School, Edinburgh;

Napier Polytechnic, Edinburgh (HND). *Directorships:* Carol Jones (Recruitment) Ltd 1979. *Clubs:* New (Edinburgh), RAC, Royal Burgess (Edinburgh). *Recreations:* Golf, Reading.

FLETCHER, Simon; Partner, Clyde & Co.

FLETCHER, T H; Director, Vale & Weetman Ltd.

FLIGHT, Howard Emerson; Joint Managing Director, Guinness Flight Global Asset Management Ltd, since 1987; International Investment Management. *Career:* N M Rothschild, Investment Adviser 1970-73; Cayzer Ltd, Mgr 1973-77; Wardley Ltd, Mgr 1977-79; Guiness Mahon & Co Ltd, Joint Head of Investment Dept 1979-87. *Biog: b.* 16 June 1948. *m.* 1973, Christabel Diana Beatrice (née Norbury); 1 s; 3 d. *Educ:* Brentwood School; Magdalene College, Cambridge (MA); Michigan University Business School (MBA). *Directorships:* Guinness Flight Global Strategy Fund 1983; Guinness Flight Intl Fund 1983; Guinness Mahon (Zurich) AG 1983. *Other Activities:* Conservative Parliamentary Candidate, Bermondsey/Southwark 1973-77, 1980; Trustee, Elgar Foundation; Governor, Brentwood School. *Publications:* All You Need to Know About Exchange Rates, 1988. *Clubs:* Carlton. *Recreations:* Conservative Politics, Worcestershire, Classical Music, Skiing.

FLOWER, J H; Director, Beeson Gregory Limited.

FLUKER, J R; Partner, Wedlake Bell.

FLUX, N; Vice President, First National Bank of Boston.

FLYNN, Daniel Patrick James; Main Board Director, The MDA Group plc, since 1985; Managing Director of The MDA Group International Ltd. *Career:* Mahon & Scears, Associate 1968-72; Monk Dunstone Associates, Associate 1972-74; Partner 1974-85. *Biog: b.* 5 August 1937. *Nationality:* British. *m.* 1959, Teresa Pauline (née Hancock); 2 s; 2 d. *Educ:* Cardinal Vaughan Grammar School; College of Estate Management. *Professional Organisations:* Fellow, Royal Institution of Chartered Surveyors. *Recreations:* Travel, Gardening, Reading.

FOGEL, Steven Anthony; Partner, Titmuss Sainer & Webb, since 1980; Head of Property Dept, Specialising in Property Development and Trainee Solicitor Recruitment. *Career:* Cohen & Meyohas, Paris 1974; Titmuss Sainer & Webb, Articles 1974-76; Assistant Solicitor 1976-80; Partner 1980; Trainee Solicitor Recruitment Partner 1982; Head of Development Division 1986-90; Head of Property Department 1990. *Biog: b.* 16 October 1951. *Nationality:* British. *m.* 1977, Joan Selma; 2 s; 1 d. *Educ:* Carmel College; King's College London (LLB); Hickling Prize Winner; Post Graduate London University (LLM). *Other Activities:* Member, City of London

Solicitors Company; Member, Law Commission Working Party on Landlord and Tenant (Privity of Contract) LCWP 95 HMSO, 1985-86; Member, Joint Working Party of Law Society and RICS on Commercial Leases (1987). *Professional Organisations:* Member, British Council of Shopping Centres, 1989; Member, British Council for Offices, 1990; Member, Anglo American Property Institute, 1990. *Publications:* Co-author, Rent Reviews, 1987; Consulting Editor, Vol 22, Butterworth Encyclopaedia of Forms and Precedents; Member, Board of Journal of Property Finance, 1989; Writes and Lectures Frequently for Law Society, RICS and Commercial Publishers. *Clubs:* Old Carmeli Association. *Recreations:* Cycling, Jazz, Photography, Gardening, Creative Writing, Family.

FOLEY, Martin John; Partner, Corporate Finance, Price Waterhouse, since 1984; Mergers & Acquisitions. *Career:* Watney Mann 1969-72; Price Waterhouse 1972-. *Biog: b.* 7 March 1947. *Nationality:* British. *m.* 1972, Joyce (née Dixon); 2 s. *Educ:* Westcliff High School; University of Manchester (BA Econ). *Professional Organisations:* Fellow, Institute of Chartered Accountants in England & Wales. *Recreations:* Tennis, Music, Bridge.

FOLWELL, Grenville John; Group Finance Director, Halifax Building Society, since 1989. *Career:* London Borough of Bexley, Director of Finance 1977-82; Sheffield MDC, City Treasurer 1982-86; Halifax Building Society, Treasurer 1986; General Manager Finance 1986-89. *Biog: b.* 6 July 1943. *m.* 1977, Linda. *Educ:* Ellis School, Leicester. *Other Activities:* Elected Council Member, IPFA; Chairman, Public Finance Ctee, IPFA. *Professional Organisations:* IPFA; FCT; IRRV. *Clubs:* RAC. *Recreations:* North Yorkshire, Chess, Rugby Union.

FOOT, Michael David Kenneth Willoughby; Head of European Division, Bank of England, since 1990; European & Community Affairs. *Career:* Bank of England Economist Balance of Payments 1969-71; Economist Economic Research 1971-75; Economist Chief Cashiers Office 1976-78; Asst Principal Monetary Policy 1978-80; Asst Principal Gilt Edged Policy 1980-82; Mgr Money Markets Div 1982-85; International Monetary Fund UK Alternate Exec 1985-87; Head Foreign Exchange Division 1988-90; Head, European Division 1990-. *Biog: b.* 16 December 1946. *Nationality:* British. *m.* 1972, Michele (née Macdonald); 1 s; 2 d. *Educ:* Latymer Upper; Pembroke College, Cambridge (MA); Yale University (MA). *Other Activities:* External Examiner, City University Business School (1983-85). *Professional Organisations:* AIB. *Publications:* Articles in Bank of England Bulletin 1972-79; Three Banks Review, 1977; City University Conference Volume, 1980-81. *Recreations:* Chess, Choral Singing, Soccer Refereeing.

FOOTERMAN, Simon; Partner, Moores Rowland.

FOOTMAN, J R E; Head of Information Division, Bank of England.

FORBES, Anthony David Arnold William; Joint Senior Partner, Cazenove & Co, since 1980. *Career:* Coldstream Guards 1956-59. *Biog: b.* 15 January 1938. *m.* m2 1973, Belinda Mary (née Earle); 1 s; 1 d. *Educ:* Eton College. *Other Activities:* Hospital & Homes of St Giles (Chm); Wellesley House Educational Trust (Chm); Cobham Hall (Governor); Royal Choral Society (Governor). *Professional Organisations:* Member, The International Stock Exchange; AMSIA. *Recreations:* Music, Shooting, Gardening.

FORBES, Trevor M; Director, Abbey Life Investment Services Ltd; UK Equities. *Career:* West Dreifontein Gold Mining Co, Geologist 1971; L Messel & Co, Investment Analyst 1972-77; Bankers Trust Co Fund Mgr, UK Equities 1977-82; Hill Samuel Pensions Investment Management Dir, UK Equity Investment Mgmnt 1982-87. *Biog: b.* 2 June 1950. *Nationality:* British. *m.* 1972, Gillian (née Richmond); 2 s. *Educ:* Sherrardswood School; Leicester University (BSc Hons). *Professional Organisations:* ASIA; IOD. *Recreations:* Music, Reading, Travel, Tennis.

FORBES-WILSON, Malcolm; Director, Crawley Warren & Co Ltd, since 1984; Non-Marine Insurance. *Biog: b.* 30 December 1946. *Nationality:* British. *m.* 1969, Susan K (née Gater); 1 s; 1 d. *Educ:* Epsom College. *Other Activities:* Non-Marine Executive, Lloyd's Insurance Brokers Committee. *Professional Organisations:* Member, Chartered Insurance Institute. *Clubs:* Lime Street Ward Club, RAC. *Recreations:* Golf, Snooker.

FORCEY, David John; Director, Steel Burrill Jones Group plc, since 1989; Deputy Chairman, Meacock Samuelson and Devitt Reinsurance subsidiary. *Career:* Shell Mex and BP Ltd, Management Training, latterly Retail Marketing Superintendent 1963-68; Glanvill Enthoven and Company Ltd (now Jardine Thompson Graham Ltd) 1968-80; Glanvill Reinsurances Ltd, Director 1976; Glanvill Enthoven Marine Ltd, Director 1979; Jardine Thompson Graham Ltd, Director, Jardine Thompson Graham (Non-Marine) Ltd 1980-81; Devitt Group Ltd now Steel Burrill Jones Ltd, Director 1985; Meacock Samuelson & Devitt Ltd, Managing Director; Steel Burrill Jones Group plc, Director 1989-; Meacock Samuelson & Devitt Ltd, Deputy Chairman 1989-. *Biog: b.* 8 December 1943. *Nationality:* British. *m.* 1974, Bernadette J N R (née Reeves); 1 s; 2 d. *Educ:* Marlborough College, Wiltshire; City of London College (HND Business Studies). *Other Activities:* Freeman, City of London; Plumbers Company; Underwriting Member, Lloyds. *Professional Organisations:* Associate, Chartered Insurance Institute. *Clubs:* RAC, MCC, I Zingari, Old Marlburian. *Recreations:* Cricket, Squash, Music, Photography, Current Affairs.

FORD, B P; Director, Bunzl Plc.

FORD, Dennis; General Manager, National Commercial Bank, since 1988. *Career:* Barclays Bank International, to Executive Director of Barclays Merchant Bank 1984. *Biog: b.* 25 November 1932. *Nationality:* British. *Directorships:* Langden P Cook Government Securities (New York) 1987 (non-exec); SNCB - Securities Ltd 1988 MD; SNCB - Investments Ltd 1988 MD; Saudi NCB Nominees Ltd 1988 MD.

FORD, M D; OBE; Group European Manager, Commercial Union Assurance Company plc, since 1987; Europe - Insurance. *Career:* Commercial Union, Management Trainee 1958; Posted to India 1961; Manager, Hong Kong 1969; The Ocean, CU Subsidiary, in the Netherlands, Manager 1970; CU Head Office, London 1974; Les Provinces Reunies, SA, CU Subsidiary in Belgium, General Manager 1976; Commercial Union London, Group European Manager 1987. *Biog: b.* 28 May 1935. *m.* 2 s; 1 d. *Educ:* Sidney Sussex College, University of Cambridge (BA). *Directorships:* Numerous Directorships and Chairmanships in Commercial Union Group of Companies. *Other Activities:* Awarded the Order of the British Empire for services to British Commercial Interests and to the British Community in Belgium, 1988. *Recreations:* Golf, Cricket, Reading.

FORD, P J; Director, P & O Steam Navigation Company.

FORD, Richard; Deputy Chief Executive, MTI Managers Limited.

FORD, Simon William Frederick; Financial Director, Charles Davis (Metal Brokers) Ltd, since 1988. *Career:* Boustead Days (Metal Brokers), Financial Controller 1985-88. *Biog: b.* 10 August 1954. *Nationality:* British. *m.* 1979, Valerie; 1 s; 1 d. *Educ:* St Peter's School, York. *Professional Organisations:* Associate, Institute of Chartered Accountants in England and Wales. *Clubs:* Cambridge Rugby Club. *Recreations:* Rugby and Other Sports.

FORDER, J D; Director, Lowndes Lambert Group Limited.

FORDHAM, John Anthony; Director, Hill Samuel Bank Limited, since 1985; Corporate Finance. *Career:* Akroyd & Smithers Ltd, Trainee 1967-69; Hoblyn & Co, Dealer/Analyst 1969-71; Commercial Union Assurance, Portfolio Manager 1971-73; Cayzer Bowater Ltd, Investment Manager/Business Development 1973-78; The Bowater Corporation Ltd, Strategic Planning Manager 1978-81; Hill Samuel Bank Ltd 1981-; Manager 1982; Assistant Director 1984; Director 1985; Head of Mergers & Acquisitions 1986. *Biog: b.* 11 June 1948. *Nationality:* British. *m.* 1974, Lynda (née Green); 2 s. *Educ:* Gresham's School, Holt. *Directorships:* Hill Samuel

Bank Limited 1985 (exec); Moorgate Nominees Limited 1986 (exec); Central European Asset Management Ltd 1990 (non-exec). *Clubs:* The Jesters, Royal Wimbledon Golf Club, Rye Golf Club. *Recreations:* Golf, Running, Theatre.

FOREMAN, Tony; Partner, Pannell Kerr Forster, since 1988; Tax. *Career:* Inland Revenue 1970-73; Peat Marwick Mitchell 1973-74; Clark Whitehill 1974-83. *Biog: b.* 12 December 1947. *Nationality:* British. *m.* 1970, Dorothy; 2 s; 1 d. *Educ:* Beckenham & Penge Grammar School; York University (BA). *Professional Organisations:* FTII. *Publications:* Allied Dunbar Retirement Planning Guide, 1985; Purchase and Sale of Private Companies, 1986; Anti-Avoidance Legislation, 1987; Leaving Your Money Wisely, 1988; Business Tax Service, 1990.

FORMAN, Craig; City Reporter, Wall Street Journal.

FORMBY, Roger Myles; Managing Partner, Macfarlanes, since 1987; Chief Executive. *Career:* Macfarlanes, Partner 1967-70; Head of Property 1970-86. *Biog: b.* 15 March 1938. *Nationality:* British. *m.* 1962, Jane (née Woof); 2 d. *Educ:* Winchester College; Magdalen College, Oxford (BA). *Other Activities:* City of London Solicitors' Company. *Professional Organisations:* The Law Society; City of London Law Society. *Clubs:* City of London. *Recreations:* Golf, Swimming, Skiing.

FORREST, Michael Alexander; Chief Investment Manager, The Life Association of Scotland Ltd.

FORRESTER, Harry O; Partner (Birmingham), Evershed Wells & Hind.

FORSTER, A W; Director, Midland Bank plc.

FORSTER, Clifford Rowland; Director, Hill Samuel Bank Ltd, since 1987; UK Corporate Lending. *Career:* National Westminster Bank, Various 1964-72; Hill Samuel Bank Ltd, Various 1972-; (New York) VP 1977-81; (Singapore) MD 1984-87. *Biog: b.* 18 June 1948. *Nationality:* British. *m.* 1984, Amara (née Chamraskul); 1 s; 1 d. *Educ:* Chailey School. *Professional Organisations:* ACIB; Financial & Operations Principal National Association Securities Dealers USA. *Clubs:* Roehampton, Tanglin, Singapore Cricket Club. *Recreations:* Cricket, Squash, Tennis, Golf.

FORSTER, Malcolm Harry; Director, Barclays de Zoete Wedd Ltd.

FORSYTH, Alastair Elliott; Director, J Henry Schroder Wagg & Co Limited.

FORSYTH, Ian; Director, City of London PR Group plc.

FORSYTH, John Howard; Group Director, Morgan Grenfell & Co Ltd, since 1988. *Career:* Morgan Grenfell 1968-; Morgan Grenfell & Co Limited, Director 1979. *Biog: b.* 23 August 1945. *Nationality:* British. *m.* 1968, Barbara (née Cook); 2 s; 1 d. *Educ:* St John's College, Cambridge (MA). *Directorships:* Luthy Baillie Dowsett & Pethick & Co Limited (non-exec). *Other Activities:* Member of Council, Royal Institute of International Affairs. *Publications:* A Policy for Sterling, 1979. *Clubs:* City of London Club.

FORTESCUE, The Hon Seymour Henry; Director, UK Personal Sector, Barclays Bank plc, since 1987; Branch Banking, Plastic Cards. *Career:* Barclays Bank, Various 1964-72; (Luton), Local Dir 1972-77; Barclays Bank, Head of Mktg 1977-80; Barclaycard, Dep Chief Exec 1980-83; Chief Exec 1983-85; Barclays Bank, Gen Mgr 1985-87. *Biog: b.* 28 May 1942. *Nationality:* British. *m.* 1990, Jennifer; 1 s; 1 d. *Educ:* Eton College; Cambridge University (MA); London Business School (MSc). *Directorships:* Visa, Europe, Middle East & Africa 1981 (non-exec); Eftpos UK Ltd 1987 (non-exec). *Other Activities:* Warden, Grocers' Company; Treasurer, British Leprosy Relief Association. *Professional Organisations:* FCIB. *Recreations:* Travel, Gardening, Opera.

FORTIN, Richard Chalmers Gordon; Managing Director, Lloyds Merchant Bank Ltd, since 1985; Head of Corporate Finance. *Career:* Lever Brothers Ltd 1964-72; Sloan Fellowship Programme, London Business School 1972-73; Morgan Grenfell & Co Ltd, Asst Dir 1973-79. *Biog: b.* 12 April 1941. *Nationality:* British. *m.* 1969, Jane (née Copeland); 3 d. *Educ:* Wellington College, Crowthorne; Corpus Christi College, Oxford (MA). *Professional Organisations:* Business Graduates Association. *Clubs:* MCC, Vincent's. *Recreations:* Sailing, Walking, Beekeeping.

FORTUNE, Donald Mackenzie; Director, Dunedin Fund Managers.

FORWOOD, Philip; Partner, Clark Whitehill.

FOSS, Mrs K M (née Arden); Chairman of Council, Insurance Ombudsman Bureau, since 1985, and Chairman of Board, Direct Mail Services Standards Board, since 1989. *Career:* National Consumer Council, Member; Consumers in European Community Group, Chairman; National Federation Womens Institutes, National Treasurer; Tidy Britain Group, Vice President; Teacher and Deputy Head 1945-60. *Biog: b.* 1925. *Nationality:* British. *m.* 1951, Robert; 1 s. *Educ:* Northampton High School; Whitelands College (University of London Teachers Certificate). *Other Activities:* Member, Data Protection Tribunal; Sales Promotion Sub-Committee of CAR; Tidy Britain; Consumers in European Community Group. *Recreations:* Golf, Bridge.

FOSSETT, B R; Director, CIN Properties.

FOSTER, Bryan Hayward; Deputy Chairman, Allied Provincial plc, since 1988. *Career:* Royal Navy 1946-68; Westlake & Co, Ptnr 1973-80; Snr Ptnr 1980-86; Chm 1986-88. *Biog: b.* 24 December 1928. *Nationality:* British. *m.* 1981, Susan Rosemary (née Colborne Mackrell). *Educ:* Clifton College. *Directorships:* Sutton Harbour Co 1986 (non-exec). *Clubs:* Army & Navy.

FOSTER, D R J; Director, Panmure Gordon & Co Limited.

FOSTER, Geoff; Market Reporter, Daily Mail.

FOSTER, J C T; Partner, Freshfields.

FOSTER, John; Partner, Hepworth & Chadwick.

FOSTER, N E; Director, City Merchants Bank Ltd.

FOSTER, Patrick; Executive Director, N M Rothschild International Asset Management Limited.

FOSTER, Peter Henry; Director, J H Minet & Co Ltd, since 1982; North America. *Biog: b.* 23 July 1934. *m.* 1957, Sonia (née Dixon); 2 s; 1 d. *Educ:* Whitgift Middle School. *Recreations:* Golf.

FOUCAR, Antony Emile; Chairman (non-exec), River & Mercantile Investment Management Ltd, 1983. *Career:* Noble Lowndes Group Dir 1951-74; Lowndes Lambert Group Ltd Dep Chm 1974-79; John Plumer & Ptnrs Ltd Chm 1979-86. *Biog: b.* 3 August 1926. *m.* 1959, Anne; 2 s; 1 d. *Directorships:* F & C Pacific Investment Trust plc 1971 Chm 1985; River & Mercantile Trust plc 1985 Chm; River & Mercantile Geared Capital & Income Trust 1999 plc 1986 Chm; River & Mercantile American Capital & Income Trust plc 1988 Chm; River & Mercantile Extra Income Trust plc 1989 Chm; Perrings Finance Ltd 1986 (non-exec); Avenue Trading Ltd 1986 (non-exec); Poutney Hill Holdings Ltd 1989 (non-exec). *Professional Organisations:* Middle Temple (Barrister-at-Law). *Clubs:* Royal Wimbledon Golf Club, Oriental.

FOULDS, (Hugh) Jon; Chairman, Halifax Building Society, since 1990. *Career:* Investors in Industry Group plc, Chief Exec 1977-88; 3i Group plc, Deputy Chairman 1988-90. *Biog: b.* 2 May 1932. *Nationality:* British. *m.* Hélène; 2 s. *Directorships:* Brammer plc 1980 (non-exec); London Atlantic Investment Trust plc 1983; Halifax Building Society 1986; 3i Group plc 1988 Dep Chm; The Channel Tunnel Group Ltd 1988; Eurotunnel Group plc 1988; Mercury Asset Management Group plc 1989. *Professional Organisations:* FIB, CBIM. *Clubs:* Garrick, Hurlingham, Cercle de l'Union Interalliée (Paris). *Recreations:* Tennis, Skiing, Looking at Pictures.

FOULIS, Michael B; Assistant Director, Scottish Financial Enterprise, since 1989. *Career:* Scottish Office 1978-89. *Biog: b.* 23 August 1956. *Nationality:* British. *m.* 1981, Gill (née Tyson); 1 s; 1 d. *Educ:* Kilmarnock Academy; Edinburgh University (BSc Hons Geography).

FOUND, Nigel Wyndham; Director, Well Marine Reinsurance Brokers Ltd, since 1980; Excess of Loss Reinsurance, Marine and Energy. *Career:* Gray Dawes & Co Ltd 1957-65; Leslie & Godwin Ltd 1966-68; Sedgwick Colins & Co Ltd 1968-73. *Biog: b.* 1 January 1936. *Nationality:* British. *m.* 1971, Jemma Mary (née Hanley); 2 s; 2 d. *Educ:* Beaumont College. *Directorships:* Well Marine Reinsurance Brokers Ltd 1986 (exec); EFGO Limited 1985 Chairman & MD; Wm Brandts Sons & Co (Insurance) Ltd 1974 (exec). *Other Activities:* Member of Lloyd's 1972-80. *Professional Organisations:* Fellowship of Chartered Insurance Institute, London; Member, International Christian Chamber of Commerce, Brussels. *Clubs:* City of London Club, Honourable Artillery Company. *Recreations:* Piano, Organ, Skiing, Gardening.

FOUNTAINE, M A; Director, Ropner Insurance Services Limited.

FOWELL, D I; Partner, Litigation Department, Jaques & Lewis, since 1976; Commercial Property Disputes. *Career:* Jaques & Co, Articled Clerk 1967; Solicitor 1969; Jaques & Co (Jersey), Partner 1972-76; Jaques & Co (London), Partner 1976; Head of Litigation Department 1980-90; Member of Finance Committee 1980-82; Management Committee 1982-90 (following merger with Lewis Lewis & Co 1982); Director of Marketing 1987-90. *Biog: b.* 7 October 1944. *Nationality:* British. 1973, Jane; 1 steps; 1 stepd. *Educ:* Mill Hill School (Scholar); Pembroke College, Oxford (BA Jurisprudence). *Professional Organisations:* Law Society; Holborn Law Society; Justice; London Solicitors Litigation Association. *Clubs:* OM's. *Recreations:* Tennis, Theatre, Cinema, Furniture Restoration.

FOWLER, Andrew; Director, Charterhouse Tilney.

FOWLER, Charles Andrew; Director, John Govett & Co Ltd.

FOWLER, Derek; CBE; Chairman, British Rail Pension Trustee Co Ltd, since 1986. *Career:* Financial Management Appointments with Grantham Borough Council 1944-50; Spalding Urban District Council 1950-52; Nairobi City Council 1952-62; Southend-on-Sea County Borough Council 1962-64; British Rail Western Region, Management Accountant 1967-69; Internal Audit Manager 1964-67; British Rail Headquarters, Senior Finance Manager 1969-71; Corporates Budget Manager 1971-72; Controller of Corporate Finance 1972-75; British Railways Board, Board Member, Finance 1975-78; Board Member, Finance & Planning 1978-81; Vice Chairman 1981-90; Deputy Chairman 1990. *Biog: b.* 26 February 1929. *Nationality:* British. *m.* 1953, Ruth (née Fox); 1 d. *Educ:* Grantham, Lincolnshire. *Directorships:* Capita Group plc 1989 (non-exec). *Other Activities:* Freeman, City of London; Liveryman, Worshipful Company of Loriners; Freeman, Company of Information Technologists. *Professional Organisations:* FCCA; CIPFA (Member Chartered Institute of Public Finance and Accountancy); J Dip MA (Joint Diploma in Management Accounting). *Recreations:* Cartophily.

FOWLER, Ian; Director and Secretary, Trafalgar House Public Limited Company.

FOX, Anthony Frederick Clifton; Managing Director, Fox Craig & Company Limited, since 1989; North American Reinsurance Broker, Production & Management. *Career:* Leslie & Godwin Ltd, Junior Technical/Broker 1972-86; Carter Wilkes & Fane Ltd, Senior Technician/Broker 1981-86; Sten RE (UK) Ltd, Director in Charge North American Department 1981-82; E W Blanch (UK) Ltd, Managing Director 1982-89; E W Blanch Co (USA) Limited, Partner 1986-89. *Biog: b.* 27 August 1954. *Nationality:* British. *m.* 1986, Alison Heather (née Jones); 1 s; 1 d. *Educ:* Tower College, Rainhill, Liverpool; Grenvill College, Bideford, Devon (OND Business Studies). *Directorships:* Fox Craig Group Limited 1989 (exec); Robert Fleming Fox Craig Ltd 1990 (exec); Robert Fleming Insurance Brokers Ltd 1990 (exec); E W Blanch (Group) Ltd 1986-89 (exec); E W Blanch (UK) Ltd 1982-89 (exec); Sten RE (UK) Ltd 1981-82 (exec). *Other Activities:* Underwriting Member of Lloyd's. *Clubs:* Marine Club. *Recreations:* Golf, Swimming.

FOX, James Seddon; Controller (Operations), Yorkshire Bank plc, since 1990; Support Services. *Career:* Yorkshire Bank plc 1951; Head Office 1960; Gen Mgr's Asst 1972; Asst Regional Controller 1972; Controller (Personnel) 1981. *Biog: b.* 5 March 1934. *Nationality:* British. *m.* 1958, Cynthia Mary (née Stanney); 1 s; 1 d. *Educ:* Huddersfield College. *Directorships:* Craft Centre & Design Gallery Ltd 1983 (exec). *Professional Organisations:* ACIB; ACIS. *Recreations:* The Fine Arts, Gardening.

FOX, L L; Executive Vice President, Bank of Nova Scotia.

FOX, Michael Pease; Director, Friends Provident.

FOX, Robert Trench (Robin); Vice Chairman, Kleinwort Benson Group plc, since 1985; Business Development. *Career:* Kleinwort Benson Ltd 1962. *Biog: b.* 1 January 1937. *Nationality:* British. *m.* 1962, Lindsay (née Anderson); 2 s; 2 d. *Educ:* Winchester College; Oxford University (BA PPE). *Directorships:* Association of Lloyd's Members 1987. *Other Activities:* Deputy Chairman, Executive Ctee, British Bankers Association; Honorary Treasurer, Royal Free Hospital School of Medicine; Member, the Overseas Project Board; Member, the Offshore Industry Advisory Board; Member, the City Advisory Panel, City University Business School. *Professional Organisations:* Fellow, the Chartered Institute of Bankers, Cost & Management Accountant. *Recreations:* Sailing, Theatre, Shooting.

FOX, Ruth Margaret; Partner, Slaughter and May, since 1986; Company and Commercial Law. *Biog: b.* 3 October 1954. *Educ:* St Helena School, Chesterfield; University College, London (LLB Hons).

FOX, S A; Partner, Pensions (Epsom), Bacon & Woodrow.

FOX BASSETT, Nigel; Senior Partner, Clifford Chance, since 1990; Financial/Corporate. *Career:* Clifford Chance, Partner 1960-90. *Biog: b.* 1 November 1929. *Nationality:* British. *m.* 1961, Anne (née Lambourne); 1 s; 1 d. *Educ:* Taunton School; Trinity College, Cambridge (MA). *Directorships:* UK Government Know-How Fund Banking & Finance - Mission To Poland 1989- Member. *Other Activities:* Liveryman, City of London Solicitors' Company; President, Justinians, 1987-88; The Pilgrims of Great Britain; Council Member, Taunton School; Old Tauntonians Sports Club, Chm until 1989. *Professional Organisations:* Council Member, Chairman Executive Committee, BIICL; British Council Member, AIPPI; ILA; Chairman, British Committee on International Securities Regulation; Committee Member, ABA; Founder Member, Law Society European Group; Assoc Europeene d'Etudes. *Publications:* English Sections of: Branches & Subsidiaries in the European Common Market, 1973; Business Law in Europe, 1982 and 1990 (Second Edition). *Clubs:* Garrick, City of London, MCC, Seaview YC. *Recreations:* Art, Opera, Shooting, Beagling, Cricket.

FOXALL, Colin; Director, Insurance Services, Export Credits Guarantee Department, since 1986; Short Term Credit Insurance Scheme. *Career:* ECGD 1966-74; Dept of Trade, Private Sec 1974-75; Principal Foreign Currency Programme 1976; Asst Sec, Middle East Project. *Biog: b.* 6 February 1947. *m.* 1980, Diana Gail (née Bewick); 2 s. *Educ:* Gillingham Grammar School. *Professional Organisations:* MICM; MIE. *Recreations:* Family, Home, Trying to Lose Weight, Shooting Clay Pigeons.

FOYLE, John Lewis; Managing Director, The London International Financial Futures Exchange Ltd, since 1987; Membership, Compliance and Trading Operations. *Career:* Price Waterhouse, Snr Mgr 1969-81; Inflation Accounting Steering, Group Sec 1976-78; LIFFE 1981-. *Biog: b.* 7 June 1948. *m.* 1971, Mary (née Ketteringham); 2 s. *Educ:* Portsmouth Northern Grammar School; St John's College, Cambridge (MA). *Direc-*

torships: AFBD 1986 (non-exec). *Professional Organisations:* FCA. *Recreations:* Sport, Music.

FRADKIN, S L; Second Vice President - Master Trust, The Northern Trust Company.

FRAHER, Gilbert Anthony Edmund; Managing Director, Morgan Grenfell Unit Trust Managers Limited, since 1987; Retail Financial Services Unit Trust. *Career:* Allied Irish Bank plc, Analyst/Portfolio Manager, Charities Specialist 1983; Grofund Label, Managing Director 1984. *Biog: b.* 4 June 1950. *Nationality:* Irish. *m.* 1974, Miriam (née McMahon); 1 s; 1 d. *Educ:* Beneavan College, Dublin (Leaving Certificate). *Directorships:* Morgan Grenfell Asset Management Limited; Morgan Grenfell Unit Trust Managers Limited; Morgan Grenfell Trust Managers Limited; Morgan Grenfell Financial Management Limited. *Other Activities:* Executive Committee, Unit Trust Association. *Professional Organisations:* Associate, Society of Investment Analysts.

FRAKER, Ford McKinstry; Assistant General Manager, Saudi International Bank, since 1982; Marketing. *Career:* Chemical Bank (New York), Corporate Credit/ Mktg Officer 1972-74; (Beirut, Lebanon), Asst Rep 1974; (Dubai, UAE), Reg Rep 1975-77; (Bahrain), VP & Gen Mgr 1978-79; Saudi International Bank, Mgr Gen Banking 1980-81; Snr Mgr, Gen Banking 1981-82; Asst Gen Mgr, Gen Banking 1982-85; Asst Gen Mgr, Credit 1985-89; Asst Gen Mgr, Marketing 1989-. *Biog: b.* 15 July 1948. *Nationality:* American. *m.* 1984, Linda Margaret Hanson; 2 s; 1 d. *Educ:* Harvard University (BA Hons). *Directorships:* Saudi International Bank (Nassau) 1987 (exec). *Clubs:* Owl Club, Nantucket Yacht Club, Vanderbilt Racquet Club. *Recreations:* Tennis, Travel.

FRAME, Sir Alistair; Chairman, Wellcome plc.

FRAMHEIN, D C G; Director, S G Warburg Akroyd Rowe & Pitman Mullens Securities Ltd.

FRANCE, B C; Director, Barclays de Zoete Wedd Securities Ltd.

FRANCE, Henry James; Chairman & Chief Executive, Crédit Suisse Buckmaster & Moore Ltd.

FRANCESCOTTI, Mario; Managing Director, Morgan Stanley International, since 1981; International Fixed Income Securities Trading. *Biog: b.* 1 December 1959. *Nationality:* British. *m.* 1982, Davina (née Napier); 2 d. *Educ:* Finchley Grammar School; LSE (BSc Econ Hons). *Directorships:* Morgan Stanley & Co (New York) 1989 (exec); Morgan Stanley Intl (London) 1989 (exec); Morgan Stanley SpA (Milan) 1990 (exec). *Other Activities:* Product Development Committee, London International Financial Futures Exchange (LIFFE). *Clubs:* RAC Club (Pall Mall & Woodcote).

FRANCIS, Barry H; Partner, Beachcroft Stanleys.

FRANCIS, George P; Partner, Beachcroft Stanleys.

FRANCIS, Julian Earnshaw; Partner, Freshfields, since 1987. *Career:* Freshfields 1980-. *Biog: b.* 1 December 1954. *Nationality:* British. *m.* 1983, Philippa Stuart (née Bate); 1 s; 1 d. *Educ:* Sir Roger Manwood's Grammar School; Trinity College, Cambridge (MA). *Professional Organisations:* Solicitor. *Recreations:* Ornithology, Modern British Prints.

FRANCIS, M C; Executive Director, Lazard Brothers & Co Limited, since 1990; Corporate Finance. *Career:* Coopers & Lybrand 1977-82; Qualified as Chartered Accountant 1981. *Biog: b.* 26 April 1956. *Nationality:* British. *m.* 1982, Lesley Ann (née Duff). *Educ:* Abbeydale School, Sheffield; Aston University (BSc). *Directorships:* Lazard Brothers 1990 (exec). *Professional Organisations:* ACA. *Recreations:* Racing, Tennis, Music, Antiques.

FRANCIS, M R; Clerk, Wheelwrights' Company.

FRANGOULIS, Jason Constantine; Director & General Manager, General Accident plc, since 1980; International Risks Division of London HQ. *Career:* General Accident, Various Areas of Corporations Worldwide Activity, Specialization Included Marine, Aviation, Reinsurance, International, EEC, Decd, UNCTAD Matters and Several Market Committees (Invisibles, CBI Etc) 1954-; Gen Mgr 1980; Member of the Board 1984. *Biog: b.* 16 July 1922. *Nationality:* British. *m.* 1947, Helen; 1 d. *Directorships:* General Accident plc 1984 (exec); Trade Indemnity plc 1990 (non-exec); Brit Aviation Ins Co Ltd 1989 (non-exec); Brit Aviation Ins Group 1990 (non-exec). *Other Activities:* Worshipful Company of Insurers; Freeman, City of London. *Professional Organisations:* Associate, Institute of Secretaries; Fellow, Australian Institute of Insurance; Institute of Directors. *Publications:* Several Technical Papers on Insurance. *Recreations:* Studies.

FRANK, David Thomas; Partner, Slaughter and May, since 1986; Commercial Law. *Biog: b.* 1954. *Nationality:* British. *m.* 1982, Diane Lillian (née Abbott); 1 s; 1 d. *Educ:* Shrewsbury School; Bristol University (LLB). *Professional Organisations:* The Law Society; City of London Solicitors' Co. *Recreations:* Lawn Tennis.

FRANK, J Michael B; Director, County NatWest Ltd, since 1988; Corporate Finance Division. *Career:* Prudential-Bache Capital Funding (Equities) Ltd Director 1987-88. *Biog: b.* 7 August 1943. *Educ:* St Peter's, York.

FRANKE, Colin; Partner, Clyde & Co.

FRANKEL, Glenn; Bureau Chief, Washington Post, since 1989.

FRANKLAND, Christopher John; Partner, Ernst & Young; Audit Partner with Specific Responsibility for Japanese Owned Companies. *Career:* Ernst & Young 1966-89. *Biog: b.* 7 November 1942. *Nationality:* British. *m.* 1966, Eve (née Chown); 1 s; 2 d. *Educ:* Forest School. *Other Activities:* Liveryman, Company of Needlemakers. *Professional Organisations:* FCA. *Recreations:* Beach and Hill Walking.

FRANKLAND, Timothy Cecil; Senior Executive Director, Hill Samuel & Co Ltd, since 1967; Bank Wide Responsibilty, Corporate Finance, Japan & Far East. *Career:* 15/19 Hussars & Inns of Court Yeomanry Lt 1950-52; Binder Hamlyn Ptnr 1952-66. *Biog: b.* 1931. *Nationality:* British. 3 s. *Educ:* Charterhouse. *Directorships:* Newman Tents Group plc 1976 (non-exec)Chm; James Neill Holdings 1981 (non-exec); Jarvis Porter Group plc 1986 (non-exec). *Other Activities:* Steering Committee, The Oxford University Business Summer School. *Professional Organisations:* FCA. *Clubs:* MCC, Berkshire & Royal Mid Surrey Golf Clubs. *Recreations:* Sailing, Gardening, Opera, Walking, Golf.

FRANKLIN, Clifford Edward; Associate Director, Coutts & Co.

FRANKLIN, D C; Director, Barclays De Zoete Wedd Limited.

FRANKLIN, J L; Director, Holman Franklin Ltd.

FRANKLIN, John Andrew; Director, Morgan Grenfell & Co Ltd, since 1979; Corporate Finance. *Career:* Slaughter and May Solicitor 1968-72; Morgan Grenfell Various 1972-; (New York) Dep Chm 1980-84. *Biog: b.* 21 November 1943. *Nationality:* British. *m.* 1976, Elizabeth Anthea (née Bartley); 2 s. *Educ:* Rugby School; Cambridge University (MA). *Directorships:* First Mortgage Securities 1987 (non-exec) Chm. *Other Activities:* Governor, United World College of the Atlantic. *Professional Organisations:* Solicitor. *Clubs:* Boodle's, HAC, Royal Harwich Yacht, The Leash (NY). *Recreations:* Skiing, Sailing, Shooting.

FRANKLIN, Sir Michael; Non-Executive Director, Barclays plc, since 1988. *Career:* Ministry of Agriculture 1950-52; Economic Section, Treasury 1952-55; UK Delegation to OECD 1959-61; Principal Private Secretary, Minister of Agriculture, Fisheries & Food 1961-64; Under-Secretary, MAFF 1968-73; Deputy Director General, EC Commission, Brussels 1973-77; Head of European, Secretariat, Cabinet Office 1977-81; Permanent Secretary, Dept of Trade 1981-82; Permanent Secretary, Ministry of Agriculture Fisheries & Food 1983-87. *Biog: b.* 24 August 1927. *Nationality:* British. *m.* 1951, Dorothy; 2 s; 1 d. *Educ:* Taunton School;

Peterhouse, Cambridge (Economics First Class). *Directorships:* Barclay Bank plc 1988 (non-exec); Agricultural Mortgage Corporation 1987 (non-exec); Whessoe plc 1988 (non-exec). *Other Activities:* Council, Royal Institute for International Affairs; Court, Henley, The Management College; International Policy Council for Agriculture & Trade; Chairman, Consultative Committee, Potato Marketing Scheme; Deputy Chairman, BIEC Europe Committee; CBI, Europe Committee. *Publications:* Richman's Farming, The Crisis in Agriculture, 1988; Review of British Invisible Export Council, 1990 (Unpublished). *Clubs:* United Oxford & Cambridge Universities Club.

FRANKLIN, Michael Charles; Director, Kim Eng Securities (London) Limited, since 1988; South East Asian Securities Sales. *Career:* WI Carr (London), Far East Analyst 1970-74; Vickers da Costa (London), SE Asian Research/Sales 1974-79; (Hong Kong), Director SE Asian Research 1979-80; Citibank NA (Hong Kong), Fund Manager SE Asian Securities 1980-82; Wardley Investment Services (Hong Kong), Director International Fund Management 1982-85; BBR International (London), Director Personal Financial Planning (HNWI) 1985-88. *Biog: b.* 24 August 1948. *Nationality:* British. *m.* 1976, Mandy (née Mellard); 1 s; 1 d. *Educ:* Churcher's College, Petersfield; Queen Mary College, London University (BSc). *Professional Organisations:* AMSIA; Institute of Directors. *Recreations:* Tennis, Travel, Music.

FRANKLIN, Peter; Director, REA Brothers Ltd, since 1989; Finance & Administration & Financial Aspects for Bank & Various Subsidiaries. *Career:* Thomson McLintock & Co Auditor, Senior 1973-78; BFI Line Ltd Financial Controller 1978-79; FMI International Treasury Manager 1979-81; Salomon Brothers International Mgr, Intl Control 1981-84; Bache Securities (UK) Ltd Asst VP 1984-86; County Natwest Ltd Director Operations 1986-88. *Biog: b.* 11 May 1952. *Nationality:* British. *m.* 1976, Susan Ann (née Edwards); 3 s. *Educ:* Peter Symonds', Winchester; University College, London (LLB Hons). *Directorships:* REA Brothers Ltd 1989 (exec); REA Brothers (Investment Management)Ltd 1989 (exec); NatWest Capital Markets Ltd 1988-89 (exec); County NatWest Ltd 1987-89 (exec). *Other Activities:* Stock Exchange, Senior Management Association. *Professional Organisations:* FCA, FRSA.

FRANKLIN, W J; Deputy Chairman, Chartered Trust plc.

FRANKS, Professor Julian; Professor, London Business School.

FRASER, The Hon Alexander Andrew MacDonell; Director, Baring Securities, since 1984; South East Asian Stockbroking. *Career:* Kleinwort Benson, Trainee 1968-70; Vickers da Costa, Analyst 1970-76; Sun Hungkai Securities, Mgr 1977-83; Henderson Crosthwaite, Salesman 1983-84. *Biog: b.* 2 December 1946. *m.* 1982, Sarah Joanna (née Jones (div)); 1 s. *Educ:* Eton College; St John's College, Oxford (MA). *Clubs:* Brooks's. *Recreations:* Shooting, Skiing, Stalking.

FRASER, Sir Charles Annand; KCVO, WS, DL; Senior Partner, W & J Burness, WS, since 1990; Corporate Law. *Career:* Cameronians & 2nd Lieutenant, Royal Artillery 1947-49; W & J Burness, WS, Partner 1956-. *Biog: b.* 16 October 1928. *Nationality:* British. *m.* 1957, Ann (née Scott-Kerr); 4 s. *Educ:* Hamilton Academy; University of Edinburgh (MA, LLB). *Directorships:* Adam and Company Group plc 1983; Adam and Company plc 1990; Anglo Continental Venture Investors SA 1981; Anglo Scottish Investment Trust plc 1984; British Assets Trust plc 1972; W & J Burness (PEP Nominess) Limited 1987; W & J Burness Trustees Ltd 1971; Edinburgh Old Town Trust; Edinburgh Old Town Charitable Trust 1987; Edinburgh Venture Enterprise Trust 1984; Ettrick Nominees Ltd 1968; Euroven SA 1983; Grosvenor Developments Limited 1981; Investors Capital Trust 1985; The John Muir Trust Ltd 1984; NSM plc 1988; The Old Course Hotel Limited 1988; The Patrons of the National Galleries of Scotland 1984; Scottish Television plc 1979; Scottish Business in the Community 1982; Scotven SA 1978; Scotven (BVI) Ltd; Selective Assets Trust 1988; Seiden & de Ceuvas International SA; Signetics (UK) Ltd 1969; Stakis plc 1987; Triptych SA 1984; United Biscuits (Holdings) plc 1977 Vice Chairman; Venture Associates SA 1969; Savem 1986; Arthur Bell & Sons plc -1986; The Murrayfield plc -1986; Morgan Grenfell (Scotland) Ltd 1986; Bison Holdings Limited (taken over by NSM plc) -1988; Solsgirth Investment Trust -1988; Walter Alexander plc -1990; Hambrecht & Quist Ivory and Sime Ltd -1990; Various Directorships in Fidelity Group of Companies; and in Scottish Widows's Group of Companies. *Other Activities:* Purse Bearer to the Queen, 1970-88; Chairman, Institute of Directors Scottish Division, 1978-81; Governor, Fettes College, 1976-86; Trustee, Scottish Civic Trust; Trustee, National Trust for Scotland Investment Committee, 1978-; Chairman, Committee of Managers of New Club, 1986-88, for their Bicentenary Celebrations; Member, Council of Law Society of Scotland, 1966-72; Served on the Court of Heriot Watt University, 1972-78; Trustee, University of Edinburgh Foundation Fund, 1989-. *Clubs:* New Club, Royal and Ancient Golf Club, Hon Co of Edinburgh Golfers, Caledonian Club. *Recreations:* Golf, Tennis, Squash, Skiing, Playing Bagpipes, Hill Walking.

FRASER, Colin Gall; TD; Partner, Taylor Joynson Garrett, since 1964; General Commercial & Copyright. *Career:* National Service in the Army, Rifle Brigade 1952-53; Commissioned into Queen's Own Royal West Kent Regiment 1953; Served with the 1st Bn as a

Platoon Commander in Malaya 1953-54; Baor 1954; Territorial Army 1954-68; Joynson-Hicks, Articled Clerk 1957-60; Admitted Solicitor 1960; Assistant Solicitor 1960-64; Partner 1964; Taylor Joynson Garrett, Partner 1989; Joint Head of Commercial Dept 1989. *Biog: b.* 18 February 1934. *Nationality:* British. *m.* 1963, Gay (née Holt-Wilson); 1 s; 1 d. *Educ:* Aldenham School; Trinity Hall, Cambridge (MA). *Other Activities:* Member, British Literary and Artistic Copyright Association; Associate, Centre for Commercial Law Studies, Queen Mary College; A Legal Adviser to the Music Copyright Reform Group. *Publications:* Articles on Copyright. *Clubs:* United Oxford and Cambridge University Club.

FRASER, Sir Ian; Director, Lazard Brothers & Co Limited.

FRASER, The Hon K I M; Director, Societe Generale Strauss Turnbull Securities Ltd; Eurobond Sales. *Career:* Scots Guards, Junior Officer 1964-67; Jardine Matheson & Co Ltd, Executive 1968-74; SGST Secs Ltd 1974-. *Biog: b.* 4 January 1946. *Nationality:* British. *m.* 1975, Joanna Katharine (née North); 3 s. *Educ:* Ampleforth College; Aix-en-Provence. *Directorships:* Fracistown Mining & Exploration Ltd 1988 (non-exec); Futures Management Ltd 1986 (non-exec). *Clubs:* City of London, Turf, White's, Royal Scottish Pipers Society, Piobreachid Society.

FRASER, Nicholas Andrew; Director, James Capel & Co, since 1987; Head of Investment Management Division. *Career:* Helbert, Wagg & Co Ltd 1957-63; Wm Heinemann Ltd, Publicity Exec 1964-65; Bank of London & South America Exec, Intl Banking Div 1965-67. *Biog: b.* 2 March 1935. *Nationality:* British. *m.* m2 1981, Charlotte (née Warren-Davis); 1 s; 2 d. *Educ:* Eton College; King's College, Cambridge (BA Hons). *Directorships:* Allied Provincial Securities 1987. *Other Activities:* Liveryman of Fishmongers' Company.

FRASER, R D A; Partner, Herbert Smith.

FRAWLEY Jr, John J; Director, Merrill Lynch Global Asset Management Limited.

FRAZER, Frank; Associate Editor (Business), The Scotsman.

FREEDMAN, Lionel; Senior Partner, Alexander Tatham.

FREDJOHN, Dennis; MBE; Chairman, Capital Ventures Ltd, since 1980; Investment Management & Corporate Finance. *Career:* Pillar Ltd MD 1961-70; RTZ plc Exec Dir 1970-73; Arbuthnot Latham Holdings Exec Dir 1973-76; Alusuisse UK Ltd Chief Exec 1976-80. *Biog: b.* 22 February 1925. *Nationality:* British. *m.* 1947, Pamela Jill (née Elliott Samms); 1 s; 2 d. *Educ:* West-

minster City; St John's College, Cambridge (MA). *Directorships:* BPB Industries plc 1980 (non-exec); London Wall Hldgs 1986 (non-exec); Chester International Hotel plc Chm; Ashford International Hotel plc Chm. *Other Activities:* Lloyd's of London (Ruling Council 1982-84, Finance Ctee 1983-88); Member, Doctors & Dentist Review Body 1989-. *Recreations:* Squash, Bridge.

FREEBORN, Tim; Financial Reporter, Daily Mail.

FREEDMAN, G D; Director, Smith New Court plc.

FREEMAN, Anthony James; Managing Director, Head of European Mergers & Acquisitions, Merrill Lynch International Ltd, since 1989. *Career:* Merrill Lynch Pierce Fenner & Smith, Vice President, Investment Banking Division 1971-77; The First Boston Corporation, Managing Director, Co-Head of European Mergers & Acquisitions 1977-89. *Biog: b.* 29 January 1948. *Nationality:* British. *m.* 1982, Jeanne M (née Schwab); 2 s. *Educ:* Pembroke College, Cambridge (BA, MA); University of Chicago (MBA). *Clubs:* The Piscatorial Society. *Recreations:* Fly Fishing.

FREEMAN, David John; Founder & Senior Partner, D J Freeman & Company, since 1952; Corporate Matters. *Biog: b.* 25 February 1928. *m.* 1950, Iris Margaret (née Alberge); 2 s; 1 d. *Educ:* Christ's College, Finchley. *Other Activities:* Governor, Royal Shakespeare Theatre; Dept of Trade Inspector into Affairs of AEG Telefunken (UK) Ltd and Credit Collections Ltd. *Clubs:* Reform, Huntercombe Golf. *Recreations:* Reading, Theatre, Gardening, Golf.

FREEMAN, John Anthony; Managing Director UK Individual Division, Prudential Corporation.

FREEMAN, M J J; Partner, Cameron Markby Hewitt.

FREEMAN, P J; Alternate Director, Wellington Underwriting Agencies Limited.

FREEMAN, Peter John; Partner, Simmons & Simmons, since 1977; EEC Law/Competition Law. *Biog: b.* 2 October 1948. *Nationality:* British. *m.* 1972, Elizabeth(née Rogers); 2 s; 2 d. *Educ:* Kingswood School; Trinity College, Cambridge, BA, MA; Institut d'Etudes Européennes, Licence Spéciale en Droit Européen. *Other Activities:* Member, Law Society/Bar Joint Working on Competition Law. *Professional Organisations:* Member, Law Society. *Recreations:* Naval History, Music.

FREEMAN, Roger John; Director, Morgan Grenfell & Co Limited, since 1990; Debt Arbitrage & Asset Trading. *Career:* Bank of London & South America, Peru & Uruguay 1968-72; Harris Trust, Chicago & London, International Banking Officer 1974-79; Libra Bank plc,

Officer Responsible for Business in Argentina 1979-81; Representative in Mexico 1981-85; General Manager & Chief Lending Officer 1985-87; General Manager, Corporate Finance, Business Development Responsibility in Latin America 1987-90; Morgan Grenfell & Co Limited, Director 1990-. *Biog: b.* 21 June 1944. *Nationality:* British. *m.* 1971, Maria Cristina; 2 s. *Educ:* Exeter University (BA Hons History); University of Pennsylvania (MBA). *Directorships:* Morgan Grenfell & Co Limited 1990 (exec). *Clubs:* MCC. *Recreations:* Sport.

FREEMAN, Ronald M; Managing Director (Investment Management), Salomon Brothers International Limited.

FREER, Miss Gillian Margaret; Partner, Nabarro Nathanson, since 1972; Commercial Property. *Career:* Nabarro Nathanson, Assistant Solicitor 1968-72. *Biog: b.* 15 June 1944. *Nationality:* British. *m.* 1968, Michael Bailey. *Educ:* Bromley High School GPDST; University College London (LLB Hons). *Professional Organisations:* Member, Law Society; Solicitor. *Clubs:* Dulwich & Sydenham Hill Golf Club, West Cornwall Golf Club. *Recreations:* Golf, Riding, Music.

FREER, Miss Penelope; Partner, Freshfields, since 1979; Property. *Career:* Lee & Pembertons, Articled Clerk 1971-73; Nabarro Nathanson, Solicitor 1973-75; Freshfields, Solicitor 1975-79. *Biog: b.* 1950. *Nationality:* British. *m.* 1975, Terence Fuller; 1 s; 1 d. *Educ:* Bromley High School for Girls; Lady Margaret Hall, Oxford (BA). *Professional Organisations:* Member, Law Society; City of London Solicitors' Company. *Clubs:* Reform Club.

FREESTONE, G A; Director, UBAF Ltd (UK).

FREETHY, Norman Derek; Senior Partner, Hymans Robertson & Co, Consulting Actuaries, since 1979; Total Management of the Practice, Responsible for Client Relations, Public Relations. *Career:* Friends Provident & Century Life Office Actuarial Supervisor 1949-61; Imperial Life Assoc Co of Canada Asst Actuary for UK 1961-67; Duncan Fraser & Co Ptnr 1967-69. *Biog: b.* 23 February 1933. *Nationality:* English. *m.* 1985, Alison; 2 s; 2 d. *Educ:* Pinner Grammar School. *Directorships:* Coulter Pension Trustees 1976 (non-exec); City of London Computer Services 1981 Chm; Robertson Trustees Ltd 1987 (exec). *Other Activities:* Worshipful Company of Actuaries; Former Committee Member of Association of Consulting Actuaries and Association of Pensioneer Trustees (Founder Member). *Professional Organisations:* FIA; FPMI. *Publications:* Control Your Own Pension; Many Articles on Pensions & Life Assurance too numerous to mention; Co-editor, Handbook on Pensions. *Clubs:* City Livery, Wig and Pen, The Addington Golf Club, Various Actuarial. *Recreations:* Golf, Music, Gardening.

FRENCH, Christopher Dennis; Head of Financial Policy, The Building Societies Association, since 1986. *Career:* Barron Rowles Bass (Chartered Accountants) 1970-82; The Building Societies Association 1982-. *Biog: b.* 25 December 1951. *m.* 1981, Cheng-Sam (née Chan); 2 d. *Educ:* Southgate County School. *Directorships:* Council of Mortgage Lenders 1989 Secretary. *Professional Organisations:* FCA; ATII.

FRENCH, Gary; Director, Continental Reinsurance London.

FRENCH, Robert Henry; Partner, Pannell Kerr Forster, since 1988; General Practice. *Career:* Leach Bright & Co, Ptnr 1970-76; Total Fire Protection Ltd, Financial Dir 1976-77; Norris Gilbert Stern, Mgr 1977-79; Ptnr 1980-88. *Biog: b.* 1 March 1946. *Nationality:* British. *m.* 1985, Christie (née Dickason); 1 s. *Educ:* Hampton. *Directorships:* Cox Associates Ltd 1986 (non-exec); Windotel Ltd 1984 (non-exec). *Professional Organisations:* FCA. *Clubs:* Richmond 41, Green Diamond Assoc. *Recreations:* London Symphony Chorus, Opera Concerts, Off Piste Ski Touring.

FRESHWATER, Timothy George; Partner, Slaughter and May, since 1975; Company/Commercial Department. *Biog: b.* 21 October 1944. *m.* 1984, Judy (née Lam). *Educ:* Eastbourne College; Emmanuel College, Cambridge (MA, LLB). *Professional Organisations:* The Law Society; Hong Kong Law Society.

FREUD, David Anthony; Director, S G Warburg Securities, since 1988; Equities. *Career:* Western Mail Journalist 1972-75; Financial Times Journalist, Industrial & Economic Coverage 1975-79; LEX Writer 1979-83; Rowe & Pitman Corp Finance Analyst 1984-87; Director 1987-88; S G Warburg Securities, Director 1988-. *Biog: b.* 24 June 1950. *Nationality:* British. *m.* 1978, Cilla (née Dickinson); 1 s; 2 d. *Educ:* Whitgift School, Croydon; Merton College, Oxford (BA Hons). *Clubs:* Ski Club of Great Britain. *Recreations:* Skiing.

FRIEDENBERG, Filippo; Head of Swaps European Currencies, Paribas Limited.

FRIEND, Adrian V S; Executive Director, Merrill Lynch International Bank Limited, since 1988; Manager for Eastern Europe. *Career:* Citibank NA, Executive Trainee 1977; London Treasury, FX Dealer 1979-80; Senior Account Manager, Commodities Dept 1981-82; Merrill Lynch Int Bank, Associate Director, Manager Trade Finance Europe, Middle East & Africa 1983-85; Marketing Director, Global Marketing 1986; Merrill Lynch Capital Markets, Director & Manager, European Emerging Markets 1987-88; Special Responsibility Central & Eastern Europe 1988-. *Biog: b.* 3 January 1954. *Nationality:* British. *m.* 1988, Jane Katherine (née Arnold); 2 d. *Educ:* St Pauls School; London School of Economics (BSc Hons). *Directorships:* Merrill Lynch

Capital Markets 1988 (exec). *Other Activities:* Great Britain, Rowing 8, 1975; Member, GB Match Racing Team, 1987-90. *Clubs:* Leander Club, Royal Thames Yacht Club. *Recreations:* Rowing, Sailing.

FRIEND, Mark W; Partner, Allen & Overy, since 1990; Competition Law. *Biog: b.* 23 November 1957. *Nationality:* British. *m.* 1990, Margaret (née Dejong). *Educ:* Hymers College, Hull; Gonville & Caius College, Cambridge (BA); Institut d'Études Européennes, Brussels (Lic Sp en Dr Eur). *Professional Organisations:* The Law Society. *Publications:* Various Contributions to Legal Periodicals. *Recreations:* Music, Painting, Golf.

FRIEND, Tony Peter; Director, Corporate Stockbroking, County NatWest Wood Mackenzie & Co Limited, since 1989; Corporate Finance. *Career:* Pannell Fitzpatrick & Co 1974-79; Grindlay Brandts/Grindlays Bank 1979-86; ounty NatWest 1986-. *Biog: b.* 30 October 1954. *Nationality:* British. *m.* 1982, Antoinette Julie; 1 s. *Educ:* Highgate School. *Professional Organisations:* Fellow, Institute of Chartered Accountants; Institute of Taxation. *Clubs:* MCC, East India, Totteridge Cricket Club.

FRITZ, Joseph Kelley; Director, Rickett & Co Limited, since 1989; Corporate Finance. *Career:* Wood Gundy Limited 1963-69; Nesbitt Thomson & Co, Director Money Markets 1969-78; Midland Doherty Limited, Director Capital Markets 1978-88; Financial Consultant 1988-89; Rickett & Co, Director Corporate Finance 1989-. *Biog: b.* 15 December 1942. *Nationality:* Canadian. *m.* 1984, Valerie (née Perkins); 1 s; 2 d. *Educ:* St Francis Xavier University (B Commerce). *Clubs:* National Club (Toronto), Halifax Club (Halifax N S Can).

FRIZZELL, Colin Frazer; Chairman, The Frizzell Group Ltd, since 1981. *Career:* Royal Fusiliers 1958-60; Norman Frizzell & Partners Ltd (now The Frizzell Group) 1957-. *Biog: b.* 8 April 1939. *Nationality:* British. *m.* 1962, Anna Georgina (née Stewart-Johnstone); 2 d. *Educ:* Oundle School. *Directorships:* All Within Frizzell Group. *Other Activities:* Member, Worshipful Co of Insurers and Worshipful Co of Coachmakers & Coach Harness Makers; Freeman, City of London; Council Member, CBI; Member, BIBA Council; Underwriting Member of Lloyd's. *Professional Organisations:* ACII; FBIBA. *Clubs:* Royal & Ancient Golf Club, Lloyd's Golf Club, Temple Golf Club. *Recreations:* Golf, Fishing, Tennis, Music.

FROGATT, H W; Partner, Insurance (London), Bacon & Woodrow.

FROGER, Patrick; Deputy General Manager Administration, Société Générale.

FROGGATT, Howard William; Partner, Bacon & Woodrow, since 1990; Life Insurance. *Career:* National Provident Institution 1965-88. *Biog: b.* 10 May 1943. *Nationality:* British. *m.* 1968, Rosemary (née Chittey); 3 s. *Educ:* Bristol University (BSc). *Professional Organisations:* FIA.

FROST, Alan John; Managing Director, Abbey Life Assurance Company Ltd, since 1989; Life Assurance. *Career:* London & Manchester Assurance Group, Assistant General Manager, Investments 1974; Sun Life Assurance Society, Assistant General Manager, Investments 1984; Abbey Life Assurance Company Ltd, Director, Investments 1986. *Biog: b.* 6 October 1944. *Nationality:* British. *m.* 1978, Valerie; 2 s. *Educ:* Stratford County Grammar School; Manchester University (BSc Honours Maths). *Directorships:* Lloyds Abbey Life plc 1986 (exec). *Other Activities:* Worshipful Company of Actuaries; President, Wessex Region BIM. *Professional Organisations:* FIA. *Publications:* A General Introduction to Institutional Investment (Joint Author), 1986; Debt Securities (Joint Author), 1990. *Clubs:* East India. *Recreations:* Reading, Opera, Family.

FROST, Cecil John William; Managing Director, Cater Allen Ltd, since 1977; Money Market. *Biog: b.* 27 May 1942. *Nationality:* British. *m.* 1962, Janice Rhoda (née Cook); 2 s. *Educ:* Royal Liberty Grammar School, Gidea Park. *Professional Organisations:* AIB. *Recreations:* Sailing, Music, Opera, Walking.

FROST, Thomas Pearson; Director & Group Chief Executive, National Westminster Bank plc, since 1984 & 1987. *Career:* National Westminster Bank 1950-; NBNA, Chief Exec Officer & Vice Chm 1980-82; National Westminster Bank plc, Gen Mgr, Business Dev Div 1982-84; Dir 1984; Dep Gp Chief Exec 1985-87. *Biog: b.* 1 July 1933. *Nationality:* British. *m.* 1958, Elizabeth (Betty); 1 s; 2 d. *Educ:* Ormskirk Grammar School; Harvard Business School (AMP). *Directorships:* British Overseas Trade Board 1986 (non-exec); Office of the Banking Ombudsman 1987 (non-exec). *Other Activities:* Freeman, City of London, 1978; Fellow, World Scout Foundation, 1984; British-American Chamber of Commerce (UK Advisory Board), 1987-; Companion, The British Institute of Management, 1987; Policy Advisory Committee, Tidy Britain Group, 1988-; Companion, Operational Research, 1987; Council Member, British-North America Research Association, 1990-. *Professional Organisations:* FCIB (Council Member). *Clubs:* MCC, Harpenden Golf Club. *Recreations:* Golf, Greenhouse, Theatre.

FROUD, Bruce Douglas Hayden; Director UK Market Making, Kleinwort Benson Securities Ltd, since 1989; Derivatives/Traded Options/UK Market Making; Head of Derivatives since 1990. *Career:* Akroyd & Smithers plc, Dealer, Traded Options & UK Equities 1981-84; Harold Rattle & Co (now Credit Suisse, Buckmaster & Moore) Mem, Stock Exchange, Traded Options 1984-86; Director 1986; Kleinwort Benson

Securities Ltd Dir, Traded Options/Market Making 1986-. *Biog: b.* 9 May 1963. *Nationality:* British. *m.* 1988, Karen Ann (née Holdgate); 1 d. *Educ:* Forest School, Snaresbrook. *Other Activities:* Member, Traded Options Floor Ctee; Member, Traded Options Rules and Supervision Ctee; Member, FTSE Eurotrack Index Sterling Ctee; Member, FTSE Eurotrack Index Working Ctee. *Professional Organisations:* Stock Exchange Practice Examination. *Clubs:* East India, Devonshire Sports & Public Schools Club.

FROW, Air Commodore B G; DSO, DFC; Clerk, Clockmakers' Company.

FROY, Robert Anthony Douglas; Managing Director, Lloyds Bank Stockbrokers Ltd, since 1987; Corporate Finance. *Career:* Montagu Loebl Stanley Ltd, MD 1969-87. *Biog: b.* 23 August 1936. *Nationality:* British. *m.* 1960, Diany Wendy (née Likeman); 2 s. *Educ:* Clarks College. *Directorships:* Otford Group Ltd 1987 (non-exec); Bertrams Investment Trust 1986 (exec); Hanover Property Unit Trust 1986 (exec); Sennocke Services Ltd 1986 (non-exec) Chairman; Bertrams Securities Ltd 1986 (exec); Lloyds Bank Stockbrokers (Nominees) Ltd 1987 (exec); Chambers Remington Ltd 1988 Deputy Chairman; Lloyds Merchant Bank Ltd 1988 (exec). *Other Activities:* Liveryman, Worshipful Company of Pattenmakers. *Professional Organisations:* Society of Investment Analysts. *Clubs:* City of London. *Recreations:* Walking, Gardening.

FRUELING, D L; Director, Maxwell Pergamon Publishing Corporation plc.

FRY, Anthony; Executive Director, N M Rothschild & Sons Limited, since 1988; Corporate Finance. *Career:* N M Rothschild & Sons Limited, Executive, Corporate Finance 1977-80; Rothschild Australia Limited, Manager, Melbourne Office 1980-85; N M Rothschild & Sons Limited, Assistant Director/Director 1985-. *Biog: b.* 20 June 1955. *Nationality:* British. *m.* 1985, Anne Elizabeth (née Birrell). *Educ:* Stonyhurst College, Lancashire; Magdalen College, Oxford (1st Class Hons Modern History). *Other Activities:* Bonnetmakers (Glasgow); Executive and Council, British Lung Foundation. *Clubs:* Carlton Club, Australian Club (Melbourne), Armadillos C C, Incogniti C C, The Blake.

FRY, C A; Chairman, Johnson Fry plc.

FRY, Jonathan Michael; Managing Director, Burmah Castrol plc, since 1990. *Career:* Pritchard Wood Ltd, Account Executive 1961-65; Norman Craig & Kummel Inc, Account Supervisor 1965-66; McKinsey & Co, Consultant 1966-73; Unigate Foods Division, Development/Marketing Director 1973; Managing Director 1973; Chairman 1976-78; Burmah Oil Trading Ltd, Group Planning Director 1978-81; Burmah Speciality Chemicals Ltd, Chief Executive 1981-87; Castrol

Limited, Chief Executive & Managing Director 1987. *Biog: b.* 9 August 1937. *Nationality:* British. *m.* 1970, Caroline Mary (née Dunkerly); 4 d. *Educ:* Repton School; Trinity College, Oxford (MA). *Directorships:* Burmah Castrol Trading Ltd (formerly Burmah Oil Trading Ltd) 1990 Managing Director; Castrol Limited 1990 Chairman & Chief Executive; Burmah Castrol plc (formerly The Burmah Oil plc) 1990 Group Managing Director. *Other Activities:* Chairman, St Francis School, Pewsey, Wilts; Chairman, Beechingstoke Parish Council. *Clubs:* MCC, Vincents (Oxford). *Recreations:* Cricket, Skiing, Archaeology.

FRY, Nicholas Rodney Lowther; Director, S G Warburg & Co Ltd, since 1982; Corporate Finance, Mergers & Acquisitions. *Career:* Peat Marwick Mitchell & Co, Supervising Senior 1968-73; Williams Glyn & Co, Exec, Corporate Finance Dept 1974-76. *Biog: b.* 28 April 1947. *Nationality:* British. *m.* 1972, Christine Sarah (née Rogers); 1 s; 2 d. *Educ:* Malvern College; Cambridge University (MA). *Professional Organisations:* FCA. *Recreations:* Music, Gardening, Recreational Sports.

FRY, R M; Director, Panmure Gordon & Co Limited.

FRYER, John; Industrial Correspondent, BBC TV.

FRYZER, William Allan; Partner, Titmuss Sainer & Webb, since 1989; Commercial Property Development. *Career:* Titmuss Sainer & Webb, Solicitor 1984-. *Biog: b.* 26 February 1957. *Nationality:* British. *m.* 1987, Gillian Sara Fryzer. *Educ:* Brighton College; Exeter University (LLB Hons). *Recreations:* Golf, Cricket, Squash.

FUJIHIRA, Naoshi; Director, Head of Trading, Mitsubishi Finance International Limited.

FUJII, Motohiko; Managing Director & Chief Executive, Mitsubishi Trust International Ltd, since 1986. *Career:* Mitsubishi Trust & Banking Corp (New York) Chief Mgr of Business Promotion 1975-81; (Panama) Dep Gen Mgr 1981-83; (Tokyo) Dep Gen Mgr Intl Planning Div 1984-86. *Biog: b.* 30 January 1942. *Nationality:* Japanese. *m.* 1972, Sumiko; 2 d. *Educ:* Keio University.

FUJIMOTO, G; Director, Nikko Bank (UK) plc.

FUJIMOTO, Masaaki; Executive Director, Yamaichi International (Europe) Ltd, since 1988; Corporate Finance. *Career:* Yamaichi Securities Co Ltd, Asst Mgr, Corp Fin 1979-85. *Biog: b.* 31 October 1954. *Nationality:* Japanese. *m.* 1981, Midori (née Kyoda); 2 s; 1 d. *Educ:* Carleton College, Northfield, Minnesota (BA); University of Chicago, Graduate School of Business (MBA). *Recreations:* Reading, Travel.

FUJTT, Y; Director & General Manager, Long Term Credit Bank of Japan.

FUKUDA, Miss Haruko; Director, Member of the Board, The Nikko Securities Co (Europe) Ltd, since 1988; Equity Brokerage. *Career:* Trade Policy Research Centre, Research Officer 1968-70; Overseas Development Institute, Research Officer 1970-71; World Bank (Washington), Economics Dept 1971-72; Vickers da Costa & Co Ltd, Economist 1972-74; James Capel & Co, Head of Japanese Dept 1974-80; Partner 1980-88. *Biog: b.* 21 July 1946. *Nationality:* Japanese. *Educ:* Channing School, London; New Hall, Cambridge (BA Hons, MA). *Directorships:* Foreign and Colonial Investment Trust plc 1988 (non-exec). *Other Activities:* Member, Council of The Japan Society, London; Member of Development Board, National Art Collections Fund. *Professional Organisations:* Member, The International Stock Exchange. *Publications:* Britain in Europe: Impact on the Third World, 1973; Japan & World Trade, 1974. *Recreations:* Art, Gardening, Foreign Travel.

FUKUNAGA, Kiyoshi; Managing Director - Fixed Income, The Nikko Securities Company (Europe) Ltd.

FULBROOK, Guy Anthony; Managing Director, Discount Corporation of New York (London) Ltd, since 1990; Primary Dealer US Government Securities. *Career:* Bankers Trust Company London, Manager, US Government Securities Sales Department 1979-83. *Biog: b.* 18 March 1960. *Nationality:* British. *Educ:* Worth Abbey.

FULLER, Graham Maitland; Investment Manager, Credit Suisse Buckmaster & Moore, since 1989; International Strategy. *Career:* Central Board, Finance of Church of England, Asst Investment Mgr 1974-0; De Zoete & Bevan, Fund Mgr 1980-86; BZW Investment Management Ltd 1986-89. *Biog: b.* 22 July 1942. *Nationality:* British. *m.* 1976, Pamela Anne (née Elgie); 2 s. *Professional Organisations:* FCA; AMSIA; Council, Society of Investment Analysts, 1986. *Clubs:* Gresham. *Recreations:* Music, Bridge, Travel.

FULLER, Robert Douglas; Director, Charterhouse Bank, since 1988; Capital Markets Systems Design. *Career:* British Bank of The Middle East Bank of England, Returns & Internal Reporting etc 1974-75; Foreign Exchange Back-Up 1975-76; Philippine National Bank, Trainee FX & L&D Dealer 1976-77; Chemical Bank/Chemical Bank International Internal Audit, Group Audit 1977-78; Chemical Bank International, Deputy Financial Controller 1980-81; Head of Systems Development Team, Eurobonds 1982-86; Head of Team Defining User Requirements for Swaps Processing 1986-87; Prudential-Bache Securities (UK) Inc, Vice President & Group Project Manager, ISD 1987-88. *Biog: b.* 30 March 1955. *Nationality:* British. *m.* 1990, Angela (née Westwood). *Educ:* Beal Grammar School for Boys, Ilford.

FUNKE, Georg; General Manager Property Finance, Bayerische Hypotheken-und-Wechsel Bank.

FURBER, Richard Mark; Managing Director, Dean Witter Reynolds.

FURLEY, Barbara A; Partner, Neville Russell.

FURLONG, James; Senior Vice President and US Equity Sales Manager, Europe, Drexel Burnham Lambert.

FURLONG, Tony; Executive Director, Yamaichi Capital Management (Europe) Ltd, since 1988; Discretionary Accounts Marketing. *Career:* Legal & General Investment Management 1978-88; Yamaichi Capital Management (Europe) Ltd 1988-. *Biog: b.* 28 April 1937. *Nationality:* British. *m.* 1959, Una (née McMahon); 3 d. *Educ:* London University (BSc Econ); Sussex University (MA). *Directorships:* Yamaichi International Europe 1988 (exec); Korea Asian Fund 1990 (exec).

FURNEAUX, Vivienne; Partner, Forsyte Kerman, since 1985; Litigation. *Biog: b.* 28 June 1956. *Nationality:* British. *m.* 1980, Peter Duffy; 2 d. *Educ:* Newnham College, Cambridge (MA, LLB). *Professional Organisations:* Member, Law Society; Solicitor.

FURNESS, David Clemens; Director, Chief General Manager, Pearl Assurance plc, since 1989; Sales & Marketing. *Career:* AMP Society, Various 1953-; Sales Manager (Auckland) 1971-72; Sales Manager (NSW) 1973-77; State Manager (Tasmania) 1977-81; Chief Sales Manager, Head Office (Sydney) 1981-88; Chief Manager, International Development 1989. *Biog: b.* 5 August 1936. *Nationality:* Australian. *m.* 1962, Lynne; 2 s; 1 d. *Educ:* Sydney University (BEc). *Directorships:* Pearl Group Board (exec); Hallmark Insurance Company Ltd (exec); Pearl Assurance plc (exec); Pearl Assurance (Unit Funds) Ltd (exec); Pearl Assurance (Unit Linked Pensions) Ltd (exec); Pearl Unit Trusts Limited (exec). *Professional Organisations:* AASA; ACIS; FAII. *Clubs:* Royal Automobile Club (Sydney). *Recreations:* First Division Rugby.

FURSE, Ms C; Executive Director & Head of Sales, UBS Phillips & Drew Futures Limited.

FURSE, Mrs C H F; Director, London International Financial Futures Exchange.

FURST, David; Partner, Clark Whitehill.

FUSSELL, N; Director, Metallgesellschaft Ltd.

FYFE, Sheila; Partner, Frere Cholmeley.

FYNN, L C; Partner, Penningtons.

FYSHE, R A D; Director, Leslie & Godwin Limited, since 1989; New Business Production. *Career:* Artscope International Insurance Services, Managing Director 1979; Seascope Insurance Services, Director 1983; Seascope Insurance Holdings, Director 1984; A P S International Insurance Services, Director 1988; Leslie & Godwin Ltd, Director 1989. *Biog: b.* 15 November 1938. *Nationality:* British. *m.* 1965, A Margaret Fyshe (née Babington); 1 s. *Educ:* Sherborne. *Directorships:* Leslie & Godwin Limited 1989 (exec); Artscope International Insurance Services Ltd 1979 (exec). *Other Activities:* Underwriting Member, Lloyd's, 1964-. *Clubs:* Boodles, City of London. *Recreations:* Shooting, Classic Italian Cars.

G

GABITASS, W M; Managing Director, Swiss Bank Corporation; Banking.

GACHOUD, Y A; Director, Williams de Broë plc.

GADD, J D; Director, The General Electric Company plc.

GADD, J S; Chairman, J S Gadd & Co Ltd, since 1988. *Career:* Confederation of Swedish Industries Secretary 1958-61; Skandinaviska Banken 1961-69, London Representative 1964-67; Scandinavian Bank in London, Deputy Managing Director 1969-71; Chief Executive & Managing Director 1971-80; Samuel Montagu & Co Ltd, Chief Executive 1980-81; Chairman & Chief Executive 1982-84; Saga Securities Ltd, Chairman 1985-; J S Gadd & Co Ltd, Chairman 1988-. *Biog: b.* 30 September 1934. *Nationality:* Swedish. *m.* 1990, Kay. *Educ:* Stockholm School of Economics (MBA). *Directorships:* Citigate Communications Ltd (non-exec); S G Investments SA (non-exec). *Recreations:* Skiing, Shooting, The Arts, Travel.

GADOW, B F; Deputy Managing Director, LTCB International Limited, since 1985; Capital Markets. *Career:* London & Continental Bankers 1981-82; Bank of America International Limited 1973-81; Weeden & Co 1966-73. *Biog: b.* 19 September 1936; 2 s. *Educ:* Wharton Graduate School (MBA); LaFaxette College (BA). *Professional Organisations:* TSA.

GADSDEN, Sir Peter Drury Haggerston; GBE; Chairman, Private Patients Plan, since 1984. *Biog: b.* 28 June 1929. *Nationality:* British. *m.* 1955, Belinda Ann (née de Marie Haggerston; 4 d. *Educ:* Rockport, Northern Ireland; The Elms, Colwall; Wrekin College, Wellington; Jesus College, Cambridge (MA, Hon Fellow 1988). *Directorships:* Ellingham Estate 1974 (non-exec); Ginsbury Electronics 1981 (non-exec); Wm Jacks plc 1984 (non-exec); World Trade Centre in London Ltd 1985 (non-exec); Aitken Hume International plc 1986 (non-exec); Penny & Giles International plc 1987 (non-exec); Gourlay Wolff Futures 1988 (non-exec); W Canning plc 1989 (non-exec); Clothworkers' Foundation 1978 (non-exec); Young Group plc 1986 (non-exec). *Other Activities:* Founder Master, The Engineers' Company; Immediate Past Master, The Clothworkers' Company; Chairman, the Britain-Australia Society; Chairman, the Britain-Australia Bicentennial Trust; Alderman of the City of London (Ward of Farringdon Without). *Professional Organisations:* Hon FCIM; FIMM

1979; CEng 1979; FEng 1980; Hon Member, Inst of Royal Engineers, 1986. *Publications:* Fellowship of Engineering Distinction Lectures, 1980; Wm Menelaus Memorial Lecture, 1983; SW Inst of Engineers, 1983; Paper to MANTECH Symposium, 1983. *Clubs:* City Livery, City of London, Farringdon Ward. *Recreations:* Skiing, Sailing, Walking, Photography, Farming, Fishing.

GAFFNEY, Thomas F; Managing Director, WestLB UK Ltd, since 1987; Investment Banking. *Career:* Chase Manhattan Bank 1955; Worked with Corporate Clients in the US 1955-62; Seconded to Executive Positions with 5 Independent Indigenous Latin American Commercial Banks including Banco Continental, Lima, CEO 1962-72; Seconded to Libra Bank plc, London, CEO 1972-84; Chase Investment Bank Limited, London, Pres, 1985; WestLB UK Limited, Chief Exec & MD 1988-. *Biog: b.* 2 April 1932. *Nationality:* American. *m.* 1955, Carmen (née Vega); 2 s; 1 d. *Educ:* St John's University (Economics); St John's Law School (Law). *Directorships:* Libra Bank 1972-89 (non-exec); WestLB Finance Curacao NV 1988 (non-exec); Bellgree Estates, Dublin 1989 (non-exec). *Other Activities:* Lombard Association; Overseas Bankers Club. *Professional Organisations:* Registered Representative, Securities Association. *Clubs:* Mark's Club, Oriental Club, End of the Earth Club. *Recreations:* Tennis, Jogging, Golf, Theatre, Latin American Studies.

GAGER, Stewart Douglas; Managing Director, Developing Countries Group & USA, Midland Montagu Ltd, since 1990; Developing Countries Group & USA, Midland Bank Group. *Career:* Chase Manhattan Bank, Various Positions 1965-73; Orion Bank Ltd, Secondment 1973-75; Chase Manhattan Bank, Various Positions 1975-83; Snr VP 1983-86; Midland America Corp Chief Lending Officer, N America 1986-87; Midland Bank plc, Group Risk Management Director 1987-88; Midland Montagu Ltd, Managing Director Risk Management 1988-90. *Biog: b.* 15 November 1940. *Nationality:* American. *m.* 1962, Virginia (Dolly) (née Vance); 1 s; 1 d. *Educ:* Westminster Schools, Atlanta, Georgia; Duke University, N Carolina (BA). *Clubs:* India House. *Recreations:* Shooting, Skiing, Music, Antiques.

GAIRDNER, Martin; National Director-Professional Services, BDO Binder Hamlyn.

GAISFORD-ST LAWRENCE, Julian Tristram; Fund Manager, Framlington Investment Management

Ltd, since 1986; UK Equities, Financial Stocks. *Career:* Carr, Sebag & Co 1980-82; Grieveson, Grant & Co 1982-83; Laurence Prust & Co 1983-86. *Biog: b.* 17 November 1957. *Nationality:* Irish. *m.* 1989, Christine (née Delalande). *Educ:* Ampleforth College; Christ Church, Oxford (MA). *Directorships:* Framlington Investment Management Ltd 1989 (exec); Framlington Unit Management Ltd 1990 (exec). *Clubs:* Brooks. *Recreations:* Fishing, Shooting, Painting.

GAIT, Robert Charles Campbell; Partner, McKenna & Co, since 1985; Commercial Property Development and Investment. *Career:* McKenna & Co, Articled Clerk 1978-80; Assistant Solicitor 1980-85. *Biog: b.* 16 July 1955. *Nationality:* British. *m.* 1978, Anne (née Nicolson); 3 s. *Educ:* Jesus College, Cambridge (MA). *Professional Organisations:* Solicitor of Supreme Court; Law Society. *Clubs:* Old Epsomians RFC, London Welsh RFC. *Recreations:* Rugby, Skiing, Eating Well.

GAITLEY, B V; Director, Ropner Insurance Services Limited.

GAITSKELL, A A; Director, Hill Samuel Investment Management Ltd.

GALAUD, M R; Partner, Cameron Matkby Hewitt.

GALBRAITH, R; Treasurer, British Airways plc.

GALE, Miss C E; Director, Barclays de Zoete Wedd Securities Ltd.

GALITZINE, G L A; Director, Fund Management, The Private Bank and Trust Company Limited.

GALLEGOS, Jorge; Director, British & Commonwealth Merchant Bank, since 1987; Media Finance. *Biog: b.* 3 March 1944. *Nationality:* Costa Rican; 2 s. *Professional Organisations:* FCA.

GALLEY, Carol; Joint Vice Chairman, Mercury Asset Management plc, since 1986; Investment. *Biog: b.* 30 September 1948. *Directorships:* Mercury Asset Management Group plc 1987; Mercury Asset Management plc 1986 Joint Vice Chairman.

GALLEYMORE, Christopher John; Director, Wardley Investment Services International Ltd, since 1989; North America. *Career:* Hill Samuel & Co 1969-74; Britannia Fund Managers 1974-79; Director 1978; Phillips & Drew, Head of North American Desk 1979-84; Geoffrey Morley & Partners, Director in Charge of North American Portfolios 1984-89. *Biog: b.* 5 July 1948. *Nationality:* British. *m.* 1986, Rosemary (née George). *Educ:* Clifton College; St Catharine's College, Cambridge (Economics). *Directorships:* Wardley Investment Services International Ltd 1989 (exec). *Professional*

Organisations: Member, New York Society of Security Analysts. *Recreations:* Music, Wine.

GALLOWAY, Andrew Marcus; Director, Samuel Montagu & Co Limited, since 1989; Corporate Finance. *Biog: b.* 23 June 1957. *Nationality:* British. *Educ:* Downside School; Oxford University, (Hons Literae Humaniores). *Clubs:* RAC. *Recreations:* Art, Golf.

GALLOWAY, David Richard; Editorial Consultant, GT Management plc, since 1975; The GT Guide to World Equity Markets, Annual Report, All Fund Reports, Investment Circulars etc. *Career:* Investors Guide, Trainee/Deputy Editor 1960-62; Daily Mail, Financial Staff 1962-64; Sunday Telegraph, Deputy City Editor 1964-67; Spencer Thornton, Partner (Research) 1967-74; GT Management, Editorial Consultant 1975-. *Biog: b.* 5 November 1931. *Nationality:* British/Irish. *m.* 1963, Ann Penelope (née Gaskell); 1 s; 2 d. *Educ:* Blackrock College, Dublin; University of Vienna; Lincoln College, Oxford (MA). *Professional Organisations:* Society of Investment Analysts. *Clubs:* Garrick. *Recreations:* Theatre, Opera, Reading, Gardening, Swimming, Skiing.

GALVANONI, John; Director, Robert Fleming Holdings Limited.

GALWEY, S H de B; Director, Robert Fleming Insurance Brokers Limited.

GAMBLE, A; Partner, Lovell White Durrant.

GAMBLE, David John; Deputy Chief Executive, County NatWest Investment Management Ltd.

GAMBLE, Philip John; Finance Director, Credit Lyonnais Rouse Ltd, since 1985; Finance and Operations. *Career:* Sime Darby Berhad, Divisional Finance Director 1975-84; Maxwell Property Holdings Ltd, Financial Controller 1972-75; Peat Marwick Mitchell, Deputy Audit Manager 1969-72. *Directorships:* Credit Lyonnais Rouse Ltd 1985 (exec); Credit Lyonnais Rouse Metals Inc 1990 (exec). *Other Activities:* Member, Capital Committee of the Association of Futures Brokers & Dealers; Member, Rules Advisory Panel of the Association of Futures Brokers & Dealers. *Professional Organisations:* FCA; ATII.

GAMMELL, Iain William; Director, Laurence Keen Ltd, since 1971. *Career:* Brown Fleming & Murray/ Whinney Murray 1959-68. *Biog: b.* 30 November 1940. *Nationality:* British. *m.* 1965, Elizabeth Ann (née King); 2 s. *Educ:* Winchester College. *Professional Organisations:* CA.

GAMMIE, Malcolm; Partner, Linklaters & Paines.

GANGULY, Dr A S; Director, Unilever plc, since 1990; Research & Engineering. *Career:* Hindustan Lever

Ltd, Management Trainee 1962; Scientist, Research Division, India, UK, Netherlands & USA; Production Management 1971; Chairman, India 1980. *Biog: m.* 2 d. *Educ:* Bombay University (BSc Hons); University of Illinois (MS, PhD). *Directorships:* Technology Development and Investment Company of India Limited; Andhra Pradesh Industrial Development Corporation Venture Capital Ltd. *Other Activities:* Business Leadership Award, Madras Management Association, 1985; Businessman of the Year, 1986; Awarded the Padma Bhusnan by President of India for Contribution to Public Service; Member, Science Advisory Council to the Prime Minister of India 1986-89; Member, Managing Committee of the Associated Chambers of Commerce and Industry of India; Chairman, Board of Governors of the Indian Institute of Technology, Kanpur; Member, Science Advisory Committee of the Department of Biotechnology, Government of India; Member, Board of Trade in the Ministry of Commerce, Government of India; Member, Society of Council of Scientific and Industrial Research; Member, Advisory Board of India Fund (Unit Trust of India and Merrill Lynch); Member, Indian & US Councils for the Program for the Advancement of Commercial Technology (PACT); Member, Governing Council of the Council of Scientific and Industrial Research (CSIR); Member, Advisory Board on Energy, Government of India. *Recreations:* Golf, Travel.

GANNON, M G J; Partner, Pensions (Epsom), Bacon & Woodrow.

GANT, Ms Elizabeth; Partner, Jaques & Lewis, since 1987; Commercial Property. *Career:* Mills & Reeve, Norwich, Articled Clerk 1978-80; Assistant Solicitor 1980-81; Allen & Overy, London, Assistant Solicitor 1981-84; Jaques & Lewis, Assistant Solicitor 1985-87; Jaques & Lewis, Partner 1987-. *Biog: b.* 1956. *Nationality:* British. *m.* 1983, John Gallop; 1 s. *Educ:* Adwick School, Doncaster; King's College, London (LLB). *Professional Organisations:* Member, Law Society; Member, Holborn Law Society. *Recreations:* The Arts, Walking.

GARBUTT, John; Director, Kleinwort Benson Investment Management Ltd, since 1987; UK Institutional Funds. *Career:* Rowe & Pitman Hurst-Brown Investment Analyst 1975-77; ICI Investment Analyst 1977-79; Touche Remnant Fund Mgr 1979-84; Schroder Investment Management Fund Mgr 1984-87. *Biog: b.* 14 June 1954. *Nationality:* British. *m.* 1986, Pat (née Sabramaniam); 1 s. *Educ:* Kettering Boys' Wellingborough Grammar; LSE (BSc Econ Hons). *Other Activities:* Life Member, University of London Convocation; Life Member, International Students Trust. *Professional Organisations:* Member, The International Stock Exchange; AMSIA. *Recreations:* Travel, Chess, The Arts.

GARBUTT, N T; Director, Wise Speke Ltd.

GARDENER, Professor E P M; Professor, Head, School of Accounting, Banking & Economics, University College of North Wales, since 1990; Banking & Finance Specialisations. *Career:* Shell-Mex & BP Ltd, Senior Financial Assistant, NW Finance & Administration 1966-71; University of Wales Bangor, Lecturer in Finance, Finance Teaching & Research 1975-80; Lecturer in Banking, Banking Teaching & Research 1980-83; Senior Lecturer in Banking 1983-86; Professor (Personal Chair) 1986-; Head of School of Accounting, Banking and Economics, Running the School 1990-; Institute of European Finance, Research and Consultancy Institute, Deputy Director 1981-85; Director 1985-. *Biog: b.* 29 March 1947. *m.* 1973, Anne-Christine; 3 s; 1 d. *Educ:* Prior Park College, Bath; University of Wales, Bangor (PhD, MSc Econ). *Directorships:* DC Gardner Group plc 1984 (non-exec). *Other Activities:* Member, SUERF and UK Money Study Group; Member, 'Wolpertinger Club' (European Club of Banking Professors); Member, Chartered Institute of Bankers Working Party on Eastern Europe; Collaborateur Scientifique at University of Namur, Belgium. *Professional Organisations:* FCIS; MBIM. *Publications:* Capital Adequacy and Banking Supervision, 1981; UK Banking Supervision: Evolution, Practice and Issues, 1986; Interest Rate Risk and Banks, 1987; Securitisation: History, Forms and Risks, 1987; The Future of Financial Systems and Services, 1990; Changes in Western European Banking, 1990. *Clubs:* Ramblers Association. *Recreations:* Mountain Walking, Cycling, Swimming.

GARDENER, W K; Director of Mergers and Acquisitions, STC plc.

GARDINER, Donald; Chief Executive, Gardiner Morgan International, since 1978; Executive Search. *Career:* RAF Flight Lt 1955-58; Ford Motor Co Employee Relations Mgr 1958-62; Powell Duffryn Personnel Mgr 1962-64; Rank Xerox UK Personnel Mgr 1964-66; ICL Personnel Controller 1966-70; The Plessey Co Dir of Manpower Resources 1970-76; Sime Darby Personnel Dir 1976-78. *Biog: b.* 1 February 1934. *Nationality:* British. *m.* 1958, Georgina (née Wharton); 2 s; 1 d. *Educ:* Bournemouth School for Boys; LSE (BSc). *Professional Organisations:* Vice Pres of Membership & Past Companion, Institute of Personnel Management; Chm, Central London Group, Northern Home Counties Region and South Herts Branch. *Clubs:* East India. *Recreations:* Cricket, Golf, Walking.

GARDINER, J A; Director, Enterprise Oil.

GARDINER, John; Director, Securities and Investments Board.

GARDINER, Michael Ian Macleod; Partner, Ernst & Young, since 1984; Management Consultancy. *Career:* James Edwards, Dangerfield & Co Articled Clerk 1965-66; Whinney Murray & Co/Ernst & Whinney Acct

1969-. *Biog: b.* 10 January 1947. *Nationality:* British. *m.* 1968, Carol A (née Johnson); 1 s; 1 d. *Educ:* St Paul's School; Selwyn College, Cambridge (MA). *Professional Organisations:* ICA; MIMC. *Clubs:* Leander. *Recreations:* Rowing, Gardening.

GARDINER, P A J; Director, Dalgety plc.

GARDINER, R; Non-Executive Director, Sheppards.

GARDINER, T; Director, Rowntree Limited.

GARDINER, William Griffiths; Finance Director, Glasgow Investment Managers Ltd, since 1987. *Career:* The Clyde Structural Steel Co Ltd, Co Sec 1960-63; South of Scotland Electricity Board, Snr Asst, Fin Dept 1963-66; Stenhouse Holdings plc, Group Acct 1966-70; Co Sec 1970-84; Scottish Development Agency, Head of Finance & Investment, Small Business 1984-87. *Directorships:* GIM Financial Planning Services Ltd 1987 (exec); Drummond Fund Management Ltd 1987 (exec). *Professional Organisations:* CA.

GARDNER, Bruce; Partner, S J Berwin & Co; Securities Law. *Educ:* Liverpool College (LLM); London University, LSE.

GARDNER, Nigel Royston; Finance Director, Clerical Medical Unit Trust Managers Ltd, since 1988. *Career:* Avon AHA Various Accountancy Positions 1971-78; Clerical Medical Various Management Positions 1978-88. *Biog: b.* 1 January 1953. *Nationality:* British. *Educ:* Lockleaze Comprehensive, Bristol. *Directorships:* CMUTM 1988 (exec). *Professional Organisations:* FCCA.

GARDNER, R A; Managing Director, Communications Systems, STC plc.

GARDNER, R C G; Director, Hill Samuel Bank Limited; Personnel. *Biog: b.* 18 December 1939. *Nationality:* British. *Other Activities:* Member, Saddlers Company.

GARFORD, Francis Stephen; Partner, McKenna & Co, since 1988; Commercial Property. *Career:* Vehicle & General Group, Legal Dept 1966-70; Confederation Life Association, Legal Dept 1970-73; Coward Chance, Asst Solicitor 1973-75; Evershed & Tomkinson, Asst Solicitor 1976-79; Hunting Gate Group, Legal Dept 1979-84; D J Freeman & Co, Asst Solicitor Later Partner 1984-87. *Biog: b.* 11 June 1944. *Nationality:* British/Canadian (Dual). *m.* 1984, Frances; 2 s. *Educ:* Reeds School, Cobham, Surrey. *Professional Organisations:* Law Society. *Recreations:* Skiing, Water Sports, Gardening, Travel.

GARIOCH, H G; Vice President, Bache Securities (UK).

GARLAND, George Michael; Head of Securities & General Division of Property Dept, Titmuss Sainer & Webb; Commercial Property. *Career:* Alfred Neale & Co, Articled Clerk 1956-60; Titmuss Sainer & Webb, Asst Solicitor 1961-65; Partner 1966-90. *Biog: b.* 16 November 1937. *Nationality:* British. *m.* 1974, Thelma Garland (née Tryon); 2 s; 1 d. *Educ:* Queen Elizabeth's Grammar School, Barnet; Law Society's College of Law. *Professional Organisations:* Member, Law Society. *Recreations:* Classical Music, Food & Wine, Spanophile with Second Home in Andalucia.

GARLAND, Mike; Partner, Clark Whitehill.

GARLAND, The Hon Sir Victor; KBE; Director, Prudential Corp plc, since 1984. *Career:* The Australian Government Minister for Supply 1971-72; Chief Opposition Whip 1974-75; Chm, Expenditure Ctee 1976-77; Minister for Special Trade Negs 1977-79; Min for Business & Consumer Affairs 1979-81; High Commissioner to the UK 1981-84. *Biog: b.* 5 May 1934. *Nationality:* Australian. *m.* 1960, Lynette May (née Jamieson); 2 s; 1 d. *Educ:* University of Western Australia (BA Economics). *Directorships:* Throgmorton Trust plc 1985; Dunedin Berkeley Development Capital Ltd 1985; South Bank Board 1985 Dep Chm; The New Throgmorton Trust 1985; Throgmorton Final Trust 1985; TR Far East Income Trust 1984. *Other Activities:* Royal Society for the Blind; Commonwealth Institute; Freeman of the City of London. *Professional Organisations:* FCA. *Clubs:* White's. *Recreations:* Music, Reading, Sports.

GARLICK, Sir John; KCB; Non-Executive Director, Abbey National plc.

GARNER, C A; Partner, Simmons & Simmons.

GARNER, John Christopher; Board Director, E W Payne Companies Limited.

GARNETT, J R; Clerk, Fletchers' Company.

GARNETT, W A; Clerk, Upholders' Company.

GARONZIK, Frederick B; Managing Director, Goldman Sachs International Limited.

GARRATT, R O; Underwriting Director, Gravett & Tilling (Underwriting Agencies) Ltd.

GARRAWAY, Brian Pattison; Deputy Chairman, BAT Industries, since 1953; Member of Chairman's Policy Committee & Financial Services. *Career:* British-American Tobacco, Travelling Auditor 1955-62; Financial Adviser 1962-70; Souza Cruz in Brazil, Finance Manager 1970-71; Finance Director 1971-74; Vice President 1974-75; British-American Tobacco UK, Tobacco Division Finance Director 1975-79; BAT Industries, Main Board Finance Director 1979-90; Number of Main Board positions including Director on Board of Batus, Director resposible for liason with Imasco, Director, Eagle Star, Director, Allied Dunbar 1979-88; Board of Farmers Group, Inc 1989; Allied Dunbar, Executive Chairman 1990-. *Biog: b.* 23 October 1931. *Nationality:* British. *m.* 1961, Jean; 1 s; 3 d. *Educ:* King Edward School, Birmingham (Institute of Chartered Accountancy). *Directorships:* BAT International Finance 1976 Chairman; BAT Industries 1983 Deputy Chairman; BAT Financial Services 1985 Chairman; Farmers Group 1989; Allied Dunbar 1990 (exec) Chairman. *Other Activities:* Member, Economic and Financial Policy Committee of Confederation of British Industries; First British Industrialist to join Board of Association for the Monetary Union of Europe 1988. *Professional Organisations:* Fellow, Institute of Chartered Accountants in England & Wales.

GARRAWAY, Mark; Director, College Hill Associates Ltd, since 1990; Financial Corporate Communications. *Career:* College Hill 1987-. *Biog: b.* 12 December 1960. *Nationality:* British. *m.* 1988, Sandra (née Jones). *Educ:* Malvern College; Durham University (BA Economic History). *Recreations:* Swimming, Squash, Going on Holiday!

GARRETT, A D; Chief Executive, Royal Mint, since 1988. *Career:* Procter & Gamble Limited, Managing Director 1968-82; Procter & Gamble Company, Vice-President (International) 1968-82; Post Office Corporation, Board Member 1983-87; The Royal Mint, Chief Executive 1988-. *Biog: b.* 26 August 1928. *Nationality:* British. *m.* 1952, Monica; 3 s; 1 d. *Educ:* Clare College, Cambridge (MA). *Directorships:* National Provident Institution 1988 (non-exec); Pitney Bowes plc 1989 (non-exec).

GARRETT, Colin Noël; Group Solicitor, 3i Group plc, since 1984; Legal. *Career:* Few & Kester, Cambridge, Solicitors 1968-69; Amoco (UK) Ltd, Wembley, Company Secretary & Solicitor 1969-73; Shell International Petroleum Company Limited, Senior Legal Adviser 1973-81; 3i Group plc, Group Solicitor 1981-. *Biog: b.* 3 June 1942. *Nationality:* British. *m.* 1967, Sarah; 2 d. *Educ:* King's College, Cambridge (BA, MA); Université de Nancy, France (DÈS). *Directorships:* 3i plc 1986 (exec). *Other Activities:* Member, International Committee of Council, The Law Society; The Law Society Commerce & Industry Group (Past Chm 1989-90); City of London Solicitors' Company; Law Society. *Professional Organisations:* The Law Society, Solicitor (1967); FBIM; Attorney-at-Law (New York 1978). *Recreations:* Violin Maker and Restorer.

GARRETT, M; Group Treasurer, National Coal Board.

GARRETT, William; Director, Robert Fleming Holdings Limited.

GARROD, Kenneth J; Senior Vice President, Morgan Guaranty Trust Company of New York.

GARROW, John Nicholas; Managing Director, Salomon Brothers International Ltd, since 1987; Managing Director in Charge of International Mergers and Acquisitions. *Career:* Morgan Grenfell, Director 1986-87; Salomon Bros International Ltd, Director 1987-88. *Biog: b.* 5 February 1943. *Nationality:* British. *m.* 1967, Diana (née Leather); 2 d. *Educ:* Charterhouse. *Directorships:* Salomon Brothers International Limited 1987 (exec). *Professional Organisations:* FCA. *Clubs:* RAC. *Recreations:* Golf, Swimming.

GARRY, J J; Director, C Czarnikow Ltd.

GARSTEN, Geoffrey; VP Director, Equities, ScotiaMcLeod Incorporated.

GARVEY, Kevin; Associate Director, Coutts & Co.

GARVEY, R J; Director, Kleinwort Benson Limited.

GARVIN, Mark S; Managing Director, Chemical Bank.

GARVIN, T M; Director, United Biscuits (Holdings) plc.

GARWOOD, John Raymond; Group Company Secretary, Smith New Court plc, since 1990. *Career:* Thomson Snell & Passmore, Articled Clerk/Assistant Solicitor 1980-85; APV plc, Assistant to the Company Secretary 1985-87; Cadbury Schweppes plc, Assistant Group Secretary 1987-90. *Biog: b.* 12 August 1958. *Nationality:* British. *m.* 1976, Sarah Anne (née Chapman); 2 s. *Educ:* Trinity School of John Whitgift; Hull University (LLB). *Professional Organisations:* Law Society. *Recreations:* Water Polo, Squash, Cricket, Golf.

GASCOIGNE, D C; Director, CCF Foster Braithwaite Ltd.

GASCOIGNE, Ian; Partner (Litigation), Frere Cholmeley.

GASKELL, R N; Investment Manager, Shell International Petroleum Company Limited, since 1990; Pension Fund Investments.

GASKIN, James Joseph; Director, FIMBRA, since 1985; Compliance. *Career:* Trust House Forte, Fin Acct 1972-74; Cory Distribution, Mgmnt Acct 1974-76; Ocean Cory Trading, Fin Controller 1976-80; Ocean Cory Energy, Fin Dir 1980-82; Repcon (UK) Ltd, MD 1982-84. *Biog: b.* 23 April 1945. *Nationality:* British. *m.*

1968, Linda (née Arundel); 1 s; 1 d. *Educ:* Wembley County Grammar School. *Professional Organisations:* FCA. *Recreations:* Riding, Classical Music, Tennis.

GASSER, Dr Erik B; Director, J Henry Schroder Wagg & Co Limited.

GATENBY, Ian Cheyne; Partner, McKenna & Co, since 1977; Head of Planning Group, Specialist in Planning & Rating. *Career:* Lovell White & King, Articled Clerk 1966-68; Assistant Solicitor/Associate Partner 1968-75; McKenna & Co, Assistant Solicitor 1975-77. *Biog: b.* 30 June 1942. *Nationality:* British; 1 s; 1 d. *Educ:* Exeter College, Oxford (MA). *Other Activities:* Land Use Society; Planning Sub-Committee, City of London Solicitors Company. *Professional Organisations:* Law Society England & Wales. *Publications:* Numerous Articles on Planning & Rating; McKenna Rating Guide, 1988 (2nd Edition 1990); Editor of Property Section, Croner's Business Law Handbook. *Clubs:* Ski Club of Great Britain, Ranelagh Sailing Club, Little Ship Club. *Recreations:* Skiing, Sailing, Gardening, English National Opera.

GATENBY, M R B; Director, Charterhouse plc.

GATENS, J; Financial Director, Texaco Ltd.

GATES, D J; Compliance Director, Brewin Dolphin & Co Ltd.

GATES, David; Managing Director, Capital Markets, Continental Bank NA.

GATLAND, G P; Associate, Grimley J R Eve.

GATTINARA, S; Managing Director, Banca Novara (UK) Limited, since 1990; Banking. *Career:* Banco Di Roma (Biella, Prato, Bangasi, Torino, Roma, Bueno Aires, Mexico, Roma, New York, Roma) 1961-86; Retail Banking, International Division Treasurer, Management Information System (MIS) Supervisor, Planning; Bayerische Vereinsbank (Munich, Milano), Head, Italian Project, General Manager, Italian Branches 1986-88; Consulentia Srl (Roma), Vice President & Managing Director, Consulentia Firm (Strategy & Financing) 1989; Banca Novara (UK) Limited (London), Managing Director 1990. *Biog: b.* 18 October 1939. *Nationality:* Italian. *m.* Rita Mattiuzzi; 1 s; 2 d. *Educ:* Istituto Camillo Cavour, Vercelli (Accountant). *Directorships:* Banca Novara (UK) Limited 1990 (exec). *Other Activities:* Cabe (Uniapac); Wine Producer. *Professional Organisations:* TSA; FOREX. *Recreations:* Walking, Jogging, Swimming, Reading, Socializing.

GAUGE, T Michael R; Director, Alexander Howden Limited.

GAULIN, J; Group Chief Executive Officer, Ultramar plc.

GAULTER, A M; Company Secretary, J Henry Schroder Wagg & Co Limited, since 1990. *Career:* J Henry Schroder Wagg & Co Limited 1976-. *Biog: b.* 4 April 1951. *Nationality:* British. *m.* 1978, Susan; 2 d. *Educ:* Merchant Taylors, Northwood; Peterhouse, Cambridge (MA Cantab). *Professional Organisations:* Solicitor; Member, Law Society. *Recreations:* Golf, Gardening.

GAUNT, Keith H; Managing Director, Amalgamated Metal Trading Limited, since 1987. *Career:* Amalgamated Metal Corporation plc, Director of Corporate Finance 1986-; Group Treasurer 1980-86; Sheerness Steel Company plc, Treasurer 1976-80; Finacor Corporate Services Ltd, Director 1975; Italian International Bank Ltd, Divisional General Manager 1972-75; National Westminster Bank Ltd, Various 1960-72. *Biog: b.* 29 April 1944. *Nationality:* British. *m.* 1972, Rosemarie (née Stokes); 1 s; 3 d. *Educ:* Pudsey Grammar, Yorkshire. *Directorships:* Amalgamated Metal Trading Ltd 1987 (exec) MD; Amalgamated Metal Investment Holdings Ltd 1986 (exec); AMT (Futures) Ltd 1989 (non-exec) Chm; Association of Futures Brokers & Dealers Ltd 1989 (non-exec); Finacor Corporate Services Ltd 1975 (non-exec). *Other Activities:* Member, Finance & General Purposes Committee, Assoc of Futures Brokers & Dealers; Chairman, Locals Advisory Panel, Assoc of Futures Brokers & Dealers; Member, Currency Committee, London Metal Exchange; Member, Committee on Banking Technique & Practice, International Chamber of Commerce UK. *Professional Organisations:* FCIB; FICM; FCT; CDipAF. *Recreations:* Skiing, Koi Keeping.

GAUTIER-SAUVAGNAC, Denis M F A; Director, Paris, Kleinwort Benson Limited, since 1990; Head of French Operations. *Career:* Ministry of Finance, Inspecteur des Finances 1967-70; Attache to the Treasury 1970-71; Finance Attache to the French Embassy to the EEC 1972-73; Financial Adviser, Dep Dir, then Dir of Cabinet of Mr Ortoli, Chairman of the EEC Commission 1973-78; Deputy Gen Sec for European Affairs in the Prime Minister's Office 1978-79; Union Laitiere Normande, Managing Director then Chief Executive 1979-85; Director of the Cabinet of M Guillaume, Minister of Agriculture 1986-88; Inspecteur des Finances, Ministry of Finance 1989. *Biog: b.* 28 May 1943. *Nationality:* French. *m.* 1965, Solange (née Fauchon de Villeplee); 2 s; 1 d. *Educ:* Lycee Janson de Sailly; Institute d'Etudes politiques (Diploma); Faculte de Paris (Licencie es Sciences Economiques). *Other Activities:* Chevalier de l'Ordre National du Merite; Commandeur du Mérite Agricole.

GAVETLY, David; Deputy City Editor, Sunday Times Business News.

GAYE, Ms M; Director, British Invisible Exports Council.

GAYMER, Mrs Janet (née Craddock); Partner, Head of Employment and Immigration Law Department, Simmons & Simmons , since 1976; Employment Law. *Career:* Simmons & Simmons, Articled Clerk 1971-73; Assistant Solicitor 1973-76. *Biog: b.* 11 July 1947. *Nationality:* British. *m.* 1971, John Michael; 2 d. *Educ:* Nuneaton High School for Girls; St Hilda's College, Oxford (MA); London School of Economics (LLM). *Other Activities:* Member, Employment Law Committee, Law Society; Chairman, Employment Law Sub-Committee, City of London Law Society; Member, Editorial Advisory Board, Sweet & Maxwell's Encyclopaedia of Labour Relations; Freeman, City of London Solicitors Company; Member, Justice Committee on Industrial Tribunals (Report Published in 1987). *Professional Organisations:* Affiliate Member, Institute of Personnel Management; Solicitor; Member, Law Society.

GAYMER, Mrs Vivien M (née Gall); Head of Legal Affairs, Enterprise Oil plc, since 1984. *Career:* Barrister, Middle Temple 1971; Mobil Oil, Counsel 1975-84. *Biog: Nationality:* British. *m.* 1978, Keith Edward; 1 d. *Educ:* University of Sheffield (LLB Hons); Middle Temple. *Directorships:* Petroleum and Mineral Law Education Trust Trustee. *Other Activities:* Editorial Advisory Board of the International Company and Commercial Law Review & the Oil and Gas Law Taxation Review. *Professional Organisations:* IBA; SERL; BACFI. *Recreations:* Village Life.

GAYNOR, John Harold Francis; Head of Finance, Lloyd's of London, since 1986. *Biog: b.* 21 November 1935. *Nationality:* British. *m.* 1972, Patricia Alice (née Taylor); 2 s; 2 d. *Educ:* Beaumont College. *Professional Organisations:* FCA; ATII. *Recreations:* Sailing.

GAYNOR, P S; Partner, Freshfields.

GAZMARARIAN, Dickran; Managing Director, Mase Westpac Limited.

GEBHARDT, Rainer G; Director of European Sales & Marketing, Manufacturers Hanover Trust Co, since 1989; Head of GEOSERVE Europe (Manufacturers Hanover' Global Services Group). *Career:* MHT, Gen Mgr (Bucharest/Roumania Branch) 1977-80; Manufacturers Hanover Bank Luxembourg SA, MD 1981-82; MHT (Zurich Branch), Gen Mgr 1983-85; MHT (New York), Dep Regional Mgr 1986-87; MHT (Frankfurt), Snr Rep for Europe 1988; MHT (London), Dir European Sales & Mktg, GEOSERVE 1989-. *Biog: b.* 21 September 1941. *Nationality:* German. *m.* 1972, Cynthia (née Ferrer); 2 d. *Educ:* State University of New York (BS Economics); University of Pittsburgh (MBA). *Recreations:* Tennis, Hiking, Music.

GEDDES, Alexander J C; Senior Vice President and General Manager, Philadelphia National Bank, since 1990; Overall Management of PNB's London Branch & Chief Executive of Merchant Bank Subsidiary. *Career:* Philadelphia National Ltd, Managing Director 1985-90; Samuel Montagu & Co Ltd, Executive Director 1982-85; Orion Bank Ltd, The Royal Bank of Canada and Orion Royal Bank Ltd 1971-82. *Biog: b.* 3 December 1948. *Nationality:* British. *m.* 1971, Vivien (née Salter); 1 s; 1 d. *Educ:* Harrow School; Oxford University (BA Hons). *Directorships:* Philadelphia National Ltd 1985 (exec); Frixa Investments Ltd 1975 (exec).

GEDDES, John Anthony; Partner, R Watson & Sons, since 1981; Actuarial Advice to Financial Institutions. *Career:* Phoenix Assurance Group; Hill Samuel Life Assurance Ltd Actuary & MD 1975-81. *Biog: b.* 17 April 1932. *Nationality:* British. *m.* 1961, Elizabeth Brodie (née Helder); 2 s; 1 d. *Educ:* Cranleigh School. *Directorships:* Computations UK 1984 (non-exec); Regency Life Assurance Ltd 1985 (non-exec); Regency Financial Group plc; Computations (Europe) Ltd. *Other Activities:* Worshipful Company of Glass Sellers. *Professional Organisations:* FIA. *Clubs:* East India Club.

GEE, Christopher John; Partner, Macintyre Hudson.

GEE, Ronald Ernest; Chairman & Managing Director, R E Gee & Co Ltd, since 1972; Financial Planning. *Directorships:* Midland Financial Consultants Ltd 1980 (exec).

GEERING, Michael William; Director, James Capel & Co.

GEIER, H G; Director, Kleinwort Benson Limited.

GEIGER, Dr Hans; Deputy Chairman, Citymax Integrated Information Systems Ltd.

GEMMELL, Gavin John Norman; Senior Partner, Baillie Gifford & Co, since 1989; Pension Fund Clients, since 1973. *Career:* Baillie Gifford, Investment Analyst 1964-67; Ptnr 1967-. *Biog: b.* 7 September 1941. *Nationality:* British. *m.* 1967, Kate (née Drysdale); 1 s; 2 d. *Educ:* George Watson's College. *Directorships:* Scottish Widows' Fund 1984 (non-exec); Baillie Gifford Overseas 1983 Chairman; Toyo Trust Baillie Gifford 1990 Chairman. *Other Activities:* Association of Investment Trust Companies (Tax Committee). *Professional Organisations:* CA. *Publications:* Newspaper and Magazine Articles on Investment Management. *Recreations:* Golf, Squash, Holiday Travel.

GEMMELL, James Henry Fife; Partner, Clark Whitehill, since 1975; Audit Investigation's Business Advice. *Career:* A C Philip & Co, Apprentice Chartered Accountant 1960-65; Graham Smart & Annan, Chartered Accountant 1965-70; Deloitte Haskins & Sells,

Manager 1970-73; FPE Group Ltd, Finance Controller 1973-74; Clark Whitehill, Manager/Partner 1974-. *Biog: b.* 17 May 1943. *m.* 1972, Morna (née Gammie); 2 d. *Educ:* Dunfermline High School; Edinburgh University (ICAS). *Directorships:* Clark Whitehill Associates Ltd 1976 (exec) Chairman; Bridford Career Management 1990 (non-exec) Chairman. *Other Activities:* Member of Disciplinary Committee, Insurance Brokers Registration Council; Elder, St Andrews United Reformed Church, Woking. *Professional Organisations:* Member of Council, Institute of Chartered Accountants of Scotland; England & Wales Area Committee Chairman, Finance and General Purposes Convenor. *Publications:* How to Value Stock, 1983; RICS Accounts Regulations, 1978; Insurance Brokers Accounts and Business Requirements Rules, 1977. *Recreations:* Gardening.

GEMMILL, Alexander David; Deputy Chief Executive, Chartered West LB Limited, since 1986. *Career:* Lazard Brothers and Co Ltd, MD 1967-86. *Biog: b.* 11 April 1941. *Nationality:* British. *m.* 1967, Jacquelyn Gaye (née Conoley); 1 s; 1 d. *Educ:* University College Oxford (MA Jurisprudence); Barrister at Law; Jurisrudence Middle Temple, Chartered Accountant. *Directorships:* The Mexico Fund 1985. *Clubs:* Brooks's, Annabel's. *Recreations:* Gardening, Tennis, Beekeeping.

GENDERS, I; Senior Executive Director, J H Minet & Co Ltd.

GENT, Brian S P; Director, The Union Discount Company of London plc.

GENT, Richard Peter; Group Treasurer, Glaxo Holdings plc, since 1981; Corporate Finance. *Career:* Touche Ross & Co 1960-62; Corn Products Co Asst to European Fin Controller 1962-66; Glaxo Various 1966-81. *Biog: b.* 25 August 1934. *Nationality:* British. *Educ:* Wycliffe College; Bristol University (BA). *Professional Organisations:* FCA; London Treasurers Club. *Clubs:* Lansdowne.

GENTRY, Bradford Stokes; Partner, Morrison & Foerster, since 1990; Environmental Law. *Career:* McKenna & Co, US Lawyer, Environmental Law Group 1988-90; Goodwin, Procter and Hoar, Boston Massachusetts USA, Partner, Environmental Law Department 1982-90; United States District Court, Boston Massachusetts USA, Law Clerk, Judge Walter J Skinner 1981-82. *Biog: b.* 21 June 1955. *Nationality:* American. *m.* 1980, Eugenie I; 1 s; 1 d. *Educ:* Harvard University, Cambridge, MA (JD Law); Swarthmore College, Philadelphia, PA (BA Biology). *Professional Organisations:* International Bar Association; American Bar Association. *Publications:* Global Environmental Issues and International Business, Bureau of National Affairs Special Report, 1990; Environmental Law of the European Communities: Emission Controls, Conference Proceedings, 1990; Environmental Regulation in Europe: Haz-

ardous Waste and Contaminated Sites, 10 Northwestern University Journal of International Law & Business 3, 1990; RCRA - Type Requirements in Europe, 15 Environmental Management Review 84, 1990; Regulation of Hazardous Waste in the United States and Britain, 19 (43) Environment Reporter 2321, 1989, 12 (2) International Environment Reporter 82 1989; Dirty Land Can Foul Up Deals, The Times, 1989; Environmental Aspects of Multinational Acquisitions, 11 (9) International Environment Reporter 505, 1988; The Impact of Environmental Liabilities on Acquisitions: What you Don't Know Can Kill the Deal, Acquisitions Monthly, 1988; Co-author and Editor, The Law of Hazardous Waste, 1987; Co-author, Superfund and Contamination of Workers' Homes, 48 American Industrial Hygiene Association Journal A-718, 1987; Actions By Private Parties Under CERCLA, 8 Chemical & Radiation Waste Litigation Reporter 532, 1984; Class Action in Toxic Tort Cases, 8th Annual Fall Meeting of the American Bar Association Litigation Section, 1983; Encouraging Electric Utility Participation in Decentralized Power Production, 5 Harvard Environmental Law Review 292, 1981.

GEORGE, Edward Alan John; Deputy Governor, Bank of England, since 1990. *Career:* Bank of England, initially East European Affairs; Seconded to the Bank for International Settlements, Basle, as Economist 1966-69; Seconded to the International Monetary Fund as Personal Assistant to Sir Jeremy Morse, Chairman of the Deputies of the IMF's Committee on International Monetary Reform (Committee of Twenty) 1972-74; Adviser, Overseas Department, External and International Monetary Questions 1974-77; Deputy Cashier, concerned particulary with the Management of the Gilt-Edged Market and Implementation of Monetary Control and with Management of Public Sector External Borrowing 1977; Assistant Director, in charge of Gilt-Edged Division 1980; Court of Directors as Executive Director with responsibility for Monetary Policy, Market Operations and Market Supervision 1982. *Biog: b.* 11 September 1938. *Nationality:* British. *m.* 1962, Vanessa (née Williams); 1 s; 2 d. *Educ:* Dulwich College; Emmanuel College, Cambridge (MA). *Recreations:* Family, Bridge, Sailing.

GEORGE, James Gemmell; Group Treasurer, LASMO plc, since 1989. *Career:* Beecham Group plc Management Accountant 1968-73; Roussel - UCLAFSA (Paris) Financial Analyst 1975-77; Roussel Laboratories Ltd (London) UK Treasurer 1977-79; Beecham Group plc Dep Treasurer 1979-89. *Biog: b.* 28 July 1947. *Nationality:* British. *m.* 1968, Mary; 2 s. *Educ:* University College, London (BSc Hons). *Professional Organisations:* ACMA; FCT.

GEORGE, Nicholas; Director, Barclays de Zoete Wedd Securities, since 1988; International Equities, South East Asia. *Career:* Edward Moore & Sons, Articled

Clerk 1973-78; Joseph Sebag, Investment Analyst 1978-79; Rowe & Pitman, Investment Analyst 1979-80; WI Carr, Overseas Dir 1981-86. *Biog: b.* 1 February 1954. *Nationality:* British. *Educ:* Radley College. *Directorships:* Barclays de Zoete Wedd International Equities 1986 (exec); BZW Securities 1988; Drayton Asia Investment Trust plc (non-exec). *Professional Organisations:* FCA; ASIA.

GEORGE, Peter M; Executive Chairman, UK and International Racing, Ladbroke Group plc.

GEORGE, R E; Director, Wellington Underwriting Agencies Limited.

GERMAN, Clifford; City Editor, The Scotsman.

GERMAN, Gary; Director, Rudolf Wolff & Co Ltd.

GERRARD, Peter Noel; Senior Partner, Lovell White Durrant, since 1980; Corporate Law. *Biog: b.* 19 May 1930. *Nationality:* British. *m.* 1957, Prudence (née Lipson-Ward); 1 s; 2 d. *Educ:* Rugby School; Christ Church, Oxford (MA). *Other Activities:* Board of Banking Supervision; City Capital Mkts Ctee; Ctee of Mgmnt, Inst of Advanced Legal Studies; Council of Mgmnt, British Inst of International & Comparative Law; Chairman, Constraints Ctee of British Invisibles. *Clubs:* Athenaeum. *Recreations:* Family Life, Music, Weekend Gardening.

GERSHUNY, Philip D; Partner, Lovell White Durrant, since 1990; Business Taxation. *Biog: b.* 6 August 1958. *Nationality:* British. *m.* 1984, Rebekah (née Marks); 1 d. *Educ:* Sussex University (BA). *Other Activities:* City of London Solicitors Company. *Professional Organisations:* Law Society.

GERSHUNY, R; Partner, Nabarro Nathanson.

GERVASIO, James; Company Secretary & Solicitor, Yorkshire Enterprise Limited.

GESUA, Danny; Director of Finance and Administration, Frere Cholmeley, since 1988; All Support Areas, including Financial Management, Planning, IT. *Career:* Price Waterhouse (London) 1972-74; Lloyds Bank plc (London) 1974-77; Canadian Imperial Bank of Commerce (London) 1977-88. *Biog: b.* 11 October 1945. *Nationality:* British. *m.* 1968, Anthea (née Rees); 1 s; 1 d. *Educ:* Quintin Grammar School; Fitzwilliam College, Cambridge (MA). *Professional Organisations:* FCA. *Recreations:* Tennis, Golf, Bridge, Skiing.

GHALI, Riad; Executive Vice President & Relationship Management, Bank of America.

GIACOMOTTO, C; Non-Executive Director, Rutland Trust plc.

GIANNOTTI, John Bernard; Managing Director, Bankers Trust International Ltd.

GIBB, J R; RD; Director, Speirs & Jeffrey Ltd, since 1970. *Career:* Scottish Amicable Life Assurance Society, Asst Investment Manager 1956-67. *Biog: b.* 1934. *m.* 1973, Elizabeth (née Henderson); 1 s; 1 d. *Educ:* University of Glasgow (MA). *Other Activities:* Chairman, RNVR (Scotland) War Memorial Fund. *Professional Organisations:* FFA.

GIBB, Samuel Boyd; Director, County NatWest Ltd, since 1988; Technology. *Career:* Citicorp, Systems Analyst 1971-75; Scandinavian Bank, Various to Asst Mgr, Data Processing 1975-85. *Directorships:* County NatWest Ltd 1988.

GIBBONS, A R; Director, County NatWest Ventures Limited.

GIBBONS, Christopher Adney Walter; Partner, Stephenson Harwood, since 1966; Company/Commercial Law. *Career:* Practised at Bar 1954-60; Admitted as a Solicitor 1961; Linklaters & Paines, Asst Solicitor 1961-66. *Biog: b.* 14 May 1930. *Nationality:* British. *m.* 1964, Charlotte Sophia (née Bull); 3 d. *Educ:* Charterhouse; Trinity College, Cambridge; 2nd Lt Grenadier Guards (National Service). *Directorships:* The Throgmorton Trust plc 1984 (non-exec); The New Throgmorton Trust (1983) plc 1984 (non-exec); The Throgmorton Dual Trust plc 1984 (non-exec); TT Finance plc 1985 (non-exec); The Fifth Throgmorton Company plc 1988 (non-exec). *Other Activities:* Member, City of London Solicitors' Company, Professional Business Committee, 1976-84 (Deputy Chairman, 1982-84); Chairman, City of London Solicitors' Company Banking Law Sub-Committee, 1980-84; Member, City of London Solicitors' Company, Company Law Sub-Committee 1968-86; Member, The Law Society Standing Committee on Company Law 1978- (Leader, Accounting Matters Group, 1987-). *Professional Organisations:* The Law Society; City of London Solicitors Company. *Clubs:* City of London Club.

GIBBONS, Michael David; Partner, Cyril Sweett and Partners.

GIBBS, Andrew Goldsworthy; Investment Director, Church Charity and Local Authority Fund Managers Ltd, since 1988; Fund Management. *Career:* Articles in Accountancy 1968-71; Save the Children Fund, Deputy Director, Refugee Relief, Bangladesh 1971-72; Peat, Marwick, Mitchell 1972-75; Methodist Church, Ivory Coast, Financial Secretary 1975-78; Church Charity and Local Authority Fund Managers Ltd (and its Forerunner, The Central Board of Finance of the Church of England) 1978-. *Biog: b.* 22 January 1947. *Nationality:* British. *m.* 1971, Juliet (née Miller); 2 s; 2 d. *Educ:* Kingswood School; St John's College, Cambridge (MA

Economics). *Directorships:* Leegate Housing Society 1986 (non-exec); CCLA 1988 (exec). *Other Activities:* Hyde Housing Association, 1979. *Professional Organisations:* FCA. *Recreations:* Theatre, Fishing, Walking.

GIBBS, D P; Director, Hambros Bank Limited.

GIBBS, Michael John; Executive Vice Chairman, Woolwich Building Society, since 1988. *Career:* Leicester Permanent Building Society, Internal Auditor 1955-61; Assistant Secretary 1961-68; Secretary 1968-71; Temperance Building Society, Assistant General Manager (Administration) 1971-75; Gateway Building Society, Deputy Chief Executive 1975-81; Managing Director 1981-88. *Biog:* b. 8 April 1931. *Nationality:* British. *m.* 1957, Pamela Jessie (née Pane); 1 s. *Educ:* Solihull School; University of Bristol (BA). *Directorships:* Woolwich (Guernsey) Ltd 1990; Woolwich Financial Advisory Services Ltd 1989 Chairman; Woolwich Pension Fund Trust Co Ltd 1989; Woolwich Life Assurance Co Ltd 1990. *Other Activities:* Nationally Elected Member of the Council of the Building Societies Association, 1982-88; Chairman of The Metropolitan Association of Building Societies, 1984-85. *Clubs:* MCC, British Sportsmens Club, Ham Manor Golf Club.

GIBBS, Roger Geoffrey; Chairman, Gerrard & National Holdings plc.

GIBBS, Ron; Partner, Linklaters & Paines.

GIBBS, S G; Partner, Field Fisher Waterhouse.

GIBBS, William; Partner (Property), Frere Cholmeley.

GIBSON, Archibald Turner; General Manager, Bank of Scotland, since 1988; Banking Administration. *Biog:* b. 6 June 1932. *Nationality:* British. *m.* 1955, Ellen Campbell (née McNiven); 1 s; 2 d. *Educ:* Paisley Grammar School. *Directorships:* Edinburgh's Capital Limited; Uberior Investments Limited 1987; Kellock Limited 1983 Chm; Kelscot Limited 1983 (exec); Kellock Leasing Limited 1983 (exec); Bank of Wales plc 1986 (exec); First Mortgage Securities Limited 1986 (exec); Bank of Scotland (Isle of Man) Ltd (exec). *Professional Organisations:* FIB (Scot). *Clubs:* Caledonian Club, New Club (Edinburgh). *Recreations:* Tennis, Gardening, Theatre.

GIBSON, Commodore B D; Clerk, Engineers' Company.

GIBSON, The Hon Clive; Director, St James's Place Capital plc (formerly J Rothschild Holdings plc). *Directorships:* RIT Capital Partners plc 1987 (exec).

GIBSON, David B; Partner, W & J Burness WS, since 1990; Commercial Property/Company Work. *Career:* W & J Burness WS, Trainee/Assistant 1984-90. *Biog:* b.

10 February 1961. *Nationality:* British. *Educ:* Bishopbriggs High School; Edinburgh University (LLB Hons, Dip LP). *Professional Organisations:* Law Society of Scotland; Scottish Law Agents' Society. *Clubs:* Royal Scottish Automobile Club, Glasgow. *Recreations:* Travel, Photography, Eating, Karate, Car Maintenance, Music.

GIBSON, David Horsburgh; Group Financial Director, Henderson Administration Group plc, since 1983; Financial Management & Corporate Secretariat, Facilities, Compliance/Internal Audit, Personnel. *Career:* Royal Navy 1956-58; Howden & Molleson, Acct Trainee 1958-63; Thomson McLintock & Co, Qualified Audit Asst 1963-65; British Technology Group, Fin Exec 1965-66; Molins Machine Co Ltd, Commercial Mgr 1966-71; King Taudevin & Gregson, Dir 1971-81; Hargreaves Reiss & Quinn, Dir 1981-83. *Biog:* b. 25 June 1937. *Nationality:* British. *m.* 1962, Elizabeth Christine (née Woodward); 2 s; 1 d. *Educ:* Gordonstoun School. *Directorships:* Subsidiaries of Henderson Administration Group plc. *Other Activities:* Worshipful Company of Distillers. *Professional Organisations:* CA; FBIM. *Clubs:* City. *Recreations:* Music, Walking, Gardening, Skiing, Golf.

GIBSON, Derek George; Associate Director, Maruman Securities (Europe) Limited, since 1987; Head of Corporate Finance and New Issue Syndication. *Career:* HM Armed Forces, The Queen's Regt 2nd Lt, Platoon Commander 1976; European Banking Company Limited Associate, Capital Markets Dept 1982-85; EBC Amro Bank Limited Manager, Capital Markets Dept 1985-87. *Biog:* b. 23 April 1957. *Nationality:* British. *m.* 1988, Katherine Maria (née Bracken); 1 s. *Educ:* Maidstone Grammar School; Heriot Watt University (BA Hons). *Recreations:* Walking, British History, Piano.

GIBSON, G; Head of Euro-Securities, Crédit Lyonnais Capital Markets plc.

GIBSON, Ian Robert; Partner, Frere Cholmeley, since 1978; Company Law & Corporate Taxation. *Career:* Frere Cholmeley, Articled Clerk 1970-72; Solicitor, Company & Commercial Department 1972-78. *Biog:* b. 19 August 1948. *Nationality:* British. *m.* 1972, Valerie Ann (née Armitage); 1 s; 2 d. *Educ:* St Peter's School, York; The Queen's College, Oxford (BA Hons Jurisprudence). *Directorships:* G Maunsell & Partners International Limited 1990 (non-exec). *Professional Organisations:* Law Society; International Fiscal Association. *Recreations:* Music, Walking.

GIBSON, M; Director, Barclays de Zoete Wedd Securities Ltd.

GIBSON, M R; Head of Construction, Berwin Leighton.

GIBSON, Michael John; Director, Martin Currie Investment Management Ltd.

GIBSON, Robert E G; Managing Director and Chief Executive, Bradstock Group plc.

GIBSON, Robert James McIntosh; Securities Investment Director, ESN Investment Management Ltd, since 1981; Responsible, for the Management of the Securities Portfolio of the Electricity Supply Pension Scheme. *Biog: Nationality:* British. *Professional Organisations:* AMSIA.

GIBSON, Ms Vanessa J; Director, Baring Securities Limited, since 1990; Japanese Equity Derivatives. *Career:* Dean Witter Reynolds, Senior Salesman 1983-85; J M Finn & Co, Eurobond Salesman & Dealer 1980-83. *Biog: b.* 26 December 1960. *Nationality:* British. *Educ:* Woodford County High School. *Directorships:* Baring Securities Ltd 1990.

GIDMAN, A C; Director, Hill Samuel Bank Limited.

GIEDROYC, Michal Graham Dowmont (Miko); Director, S G Warburg Securities, since 1990; Head of European Equities Research. *Career:* J Henry Schroder Wagg & Co, Investment Analyst 1980-84; Schroder Capital Management International, Vice President 1984-85; S G Warburg Securities, Head of European Equities Research 1985-. *Biog: b.* 5 May 1959. *Nationality:* West German. *m.* 1986, Dorothee (née Jung). *Educ:* Ampleforth College, Yorkshire; New College, Oxford (BA Mathematics); Birkbeck College, London (MSc Unfinished). *Recreations:* Jazz Piano.

GIFFEN, J A; Director, Allied-Lyons plc.

GIFFORD, David A; WS; Partner, W & J Burness WS.

GIFFORD, Michael Roger; Head of Capital Markets, Skandinaviska Enskilda Banken, since 1990. *Career:* S G Warburg & Co Ltd 1978-82; Enskilda Securities 1982-90; Manager 1982; Director 1985; Head of International Corporate Finance 1989. *Biog: b.* 3 August 1955. *Nationality:* Scottish. *m.* 1983, Jane (née Lunzer); 2 s; 2 d. *Educ:* Sedbergh School, Yorks; Trinity College, Oxford (MA). *Recreations:* Music, Gardening.

GIFFORD, Patrick; Director, Robert Fleming Holdings Limited.

GILBARD, Marc E C; Director, County NatWest Securities Ltd (incorporating Wood Mackenzie & Co Ltd), since 1990; Property. *Career:* Gerald Eve & Co, Chartered Surveyor 1982-83; Edward Erdman, Associate Director, Investment & Financial Services 1984-87; UBS Phillips & Drew, Property Specialist, Property Equities Analysis & Sales 1987-89; County NatWest Securities Ltd, Director, Head of Property Equities Sales

& Analysis 1989-. *Biog: b.* 19 May 1962. *Nationality:* British. *Educ:* St Johns School, Leatherhead, Surrey; Polytechnic of the South Bank (BSc Estate Management). *Directorships:* County NatWest Securities Ltd 1990 (exec); County NatWest Property Ltd 1990 (exec). *Other Activities:* Investment Surveyors Forum and Investment & Financial Services Committee, Royal Institute of Chartered Surveyors; Property Futures Committee (London Fox). *Professional Organisations:* ARICS. *Clubs:* Various Sports & Social Clubs. *Recreations:* Martial Art, Squash, Swimming, Travel, Classic Cars.

GILBERT, B D; Director, Maxwell Pergamon Publishing Corporation plc.

GILBERT, Daniel; *Career:* Bristol and Keynsham, Private Footwear Fitting Specialist 1938-81. *Biog: b.* 18 September 1915. *m.* 1938, Nancy Sybil; 2 s; 2 d. *Educ:* Greenhill Grammar School, Tenby. *Other Activities:* President, Nat Fed Boot Trades Assoc, 1962-63; Master, Guild of Cordwainers, 1973-75; Deacon, Incorporation of Cordiners in Glasgow, 1984-85; Master, Worshipful Company of Pattenmakers, 1990; Founder Member, Society of Shoefitters; Founder Member, Keynsham Chamber of Commerce and Trade; Member, Incorporation of Tailors in Glasgow; Life Member, City Livery Club; 30 Years Working with Scout Movement in Bristol. *Recreations:* Foreign Travel.

GILBERT, Ian Michael; Partner, Walker Morris Scott Turnbull, since 1986; Company & Corporate Law. *Career:* 3i plc, Legal Adviser 1979-85. *Biog: b.* 22 July 1957. *Nationality:* British. *m.* 1981, Susan Margaret (née Eyre); 2 s. *Educ:* Calday Grange Grammar School, Wirral; Sheffield University (LLB Hons). *Professional Organisations:* Member, The Law Society. *Recreations:* Squash, Tennis, Walking.

GILBERT, John; General Manager, Westdeutsche Landesbank Girozentrale.

GILBERT, Jonathan Sinclair; Director, Sedgwick Group plc, since 1981; Oil and Gas Insurance Broker. *Career:* Bland Payne Ltd, Board Dir 1968; Oil & Cargo Div, Chm 1977; Bland Payne Holdings Ltd, Dir 1978; Sedgwick Ltd, Dir 1980-. *Directorships:* Sedgwick Offshore Resources Ltd 1980 Chm; Sedgwick Special Risks Group 1985 Chm.

GILBERT, Mark; Partner, Theodore Goddard.

GILBERT, Martin James; Managing Director, Aberdeen Trust Holdings, since 1983. *Career:* Brander & Cruickshank, Investment Mgr 1981-83. *Biog: b.* 13 July 1955. *Nationality:* British. *m.* 1981, Dr Fiona (née Davidson); 1 s; 1 d. *Educ:* Robert Gordon's College; Aberdeen University (MA, LLB). *Directorships:* Aberdeen Trust Holdings plc and Subsidiary Companies; Bell Lawrie (Aberdeen) Ltd; Aberdeen Cable Services Ltd;

Abtrust New Thai Investment Trust plc; Abtrust Scotland Investment Company plc; Radiotrust plc; Country Gentlemens Association plc. *Professional Organisations:* CA. *Clubs:* Royal Aberdeen Golf Club, Royal Selangor Golf Club, Royal Northern & University Club. *Recreations:* Golf, Hockey, Skiing, Sailing.

GILBERT, N; Partner, Pannell Kerr Forster.

GILBERT, Robert Michael; Partner, Wragge & Co, since 1974; Company and Corporate Finance. *Biog: b.* 2 June 1948. *m.* 1973, Margaret (née Pimm); 2 s. *Educ:* University College School, London; Solihull School; London University (LLB). *Directorships:* Plumb Holdings plc 1983-1989 Chm (non-exec); Everest Foods plc 1988 Chm (non-exec); York Trailer Holdings plc 1988 (non-exec); Corello Lighting plc 1987-89 (non-exec); Insolvency Lawyers Association Ltd 1989; Birmingham City 2000 Ltd 1990. *Professional Organisations:* The Law Society, Institute of Directors, Licensed Insolvency Practitioner. *Clubs:* VSCC, VCC. *Recreations:* Motor Sport, Gardening.

GILBERT, Mrs S R; Personnel Controller, Sphere Drake Insurance plc.

GILBERTSON, David; Editor/Chief Executive, Lloyd's List.

GILCHRIST, Clive Mace; Director, Argosy Asset Management plc, since 1987. *Career:* J & A Scrimgeour Ltd, Stockbroker 1972-75; Joseph Sebag & Co, Stockbroker 1975-78; Postel Investment Management Ltd, Deputy Director of Investments 1978-87. *Biog: b.* 27 September 1950. *Nationality:* British. *m.* 1979, Angela (née Watson-Hagger); 2 d. *Educ:* Holte Grammar School, Birmingham; LSE (BSc Econ Hons). *Directorships:* Allied Provincial plc (non-exec); British Empire Securities & General Trust plc (non-exec); The Turkey Trust plc (non-exec). *Other Activities:* National Association of Pension Funds (Chm, Investment Ctee; Vice Chm, Counsel). *Professional Organisations:* AMSIA.

GILCHRIST, David; General Manager Corporate Development, Halifax Building Society, since 1989; Strategic Planning, Research, Corporate Communications. *Career:* Rowntrees of York, Accounts Asst/ Programmer 1961-64; Halifax Building Society, Snr Programmer 1964-70; DP Mgr 1970-73; Controller Comp Services 1973-75; Economist 1975-76; Sec & Member of Society's Exec 1976-80; Asst Gen Mgr 1980-83; General Manager, Strategic Planning 1983-89. *Biog: b.* 2 July 1939. *Nationality:* British. *Educ:* Archbishop Holgate's Grammar School, York; Hull University (BSc Econ); Harvard Business School. *Directorships:* Halifax Financial Services (Holdings) Ltd 1989 (exec); Halifax Financial Services Ltd 1989 (exec). *Professional Organisations:* Member, British Computer Society. *Recreations:* Theatre.

GILCHRIST, Graeme; Chairman, Winterflood Securities Ltd.

GILCHRIST, Graeme Elder; TD; Managing Director, Union Discount Company of London plc.

GILDERSLEEVES, Paul Simon; Director, Johnson Fry plc, since 1990; Finance/Administration. *Career:* Coopers & Lybrand, Trainee/Supervisor 1983-87; Chase Property Holdings plc (Trafalgar House Property Ltd, takeover), Financial Controller 1987-88; LIT Holdings plc & Subs, Head Office Acct, Group Tax Mgr, Financial Controller, Company Secretary 1988-. *Biog: b.* 18 August 1960. *Nationality:* British. *m.* 1984, Edith Lucy Pitcairn (née Colam). *Educ:* Colchester RGS; University College, Oxford (BA, MA). *Directorships:* Johnson Fry plc (& other LIT Subs) 1990 (exec). *Professional Organisations:* ACA. *Publications:* Two Notes on Sophocles' Trachiniae, Jornal of Hellenic Studies, 1985. *Recreations:* Cricket, Golf, Historic Sites.

GILES, Gordon Scott; Director, Baring Asset Management Ltd, since 1986; Management. *Career:* Bank of England 1966-71; Baring Brothers & Co Limited 1971-86; Director 1985. *Biog: b.* 3 December 1942. *Nationality:* British. *m.* 1981, Tanya Elizabeth (née Bruce-Lockhart); 1 s. *Educ:* Marlborough College; University of St Andrews (MA). *Directorships:* Baring Asset Management 1986 (exec). *Recreations:* Golf, Fishing.

GILES, J C; Partner, Pannell Kerr Forster.

GILES, J Michael; Chairman, Merrill Lynch International Banks, Merrill Lynch Europe Limited.

GILKES, R M H; Non-Executive Director, R H M Outhwaite (Underwriting Agencies) Limited.

GILL, Christopher; Secretary, Harrisons & Crosfields plc.

GILL, George Malcolm; Chief Cashier and Chief of Banking Dept, Bank of England, since 1988. *Career:* Bank of England, Various 1957-; Seconded to UK Treasury Delegation, Washington DC 1966-68; Private Sec to Governor 1970-72; Asst Chief Cashier 1975-77; Seconded to HM Treasury 1977-80; Chief Mgr, Banking & Credit Mkts 1980-82; Head of For Exchange Div 1982-88; Appointed Asst Dir 1987. *Biog: b.* 23 May 1934. *Nationality:* British. *m.* 1966, Monica Kennedy (née Brooks); 1 s; 1 d. *Educ:* Cambridgeshire High School; Sidney Sussex College, Cambridge (MA). *Professional Organisations:* FCIB. *Clubs:* Overseas Bankers'.

GILL, Ian; Director, British Bank of the Middle East.

GILL, Mark S; Partner, Wilde Sapte.

GILL, Peter; Group Development Director/Company Secretary, Abbott Mead Vickers plc, since 1987. *Career:* Arthur Andersen & Co 1977-87. *Biog: b.* 24 October 1955. *Nationality:* British. *m.* 1981, Nicola; 1 s; 1 d. *Educ:* Henley Grammar School; Sheffield University (BA Econ/Accountancy). *Professional Organisations:* ACA. *Clubs:* RAC Club. *Recreations:* Squash, Family.

GILLAM, P J; Managing Director (Investment Management), The British Petroleum Company plc.

GILLAN, David Campbell; Director, MIM Ltd, since 1986; Investment Management. *Biog: b.* 17 March 1951. *m.* 1974, Janet (née Hutcheson); 2 s. *Educ:* King's Park School, Glasgow. *Directorships:* MIM International Ltd 1985 MD; MIM Britannia Okasan Intl Investment Mgmnt Ltd 1985; Invesco MIM International Ltd 1987. *Professional Organisations:* AIB (Scot), ASIA.

GILLESPIE, B J; TD, DL; Director in Charge of Discretionary Clients, Wise Speke Limited, since 1980. *Biog: b.* 26 February 1931. *Nationality:* British. *m.* 1958, Susan Joyce (née Hilton); 2 d. *Educ:* Uppingham; St Johns College, Cambridge (MA). *Other Activities:* Chairman, North of England Cancer Research Campaign; Chairman, Youth Clubs Northumbria. *Professional Organisations:* FCA. *Clubs:* Northern. *Recreations:* Rugby Football.

GILLESPIE, D J; Director, Barclays de Zoete Wedd Securities Ltd.

GILLESPIE, H R; Director, Hill Samuel Bank Limited.

GILLESPIE, Marc; Director, 3i plc, since 1989. *Biog: b.* 7 October 1956. *Nationality:* British; 2 s. *Educ:* King Edwards School, Edgbaston; Merchant Taylors, Crosby; Leeds University (BA); Manchester Business School (MBA). *Other Activities:* Member, CBI Small Firms Committee.

GILLESPIE, Robert Andrew Joseph; Director, S G Warburg & Co Ltd, since 1987; Corporate Finance. *Career:* Price Waterhouse Accountant 1977-81; S G Warburg various 1981-. *Biog: b.* 14 April 1955. *Nationality:* British. *m.* 1987, Carolyn Sarah (née Powell); 1 d. *Educ:* Nottingham High School; Grey College, University of Durham (BA). *Professional Organisations:* ACA. *Clubs:* Leander. *Recreations:* Reading, Sailing, Gardening.

GILLET, Sir Robin Danvers Penrose; Bt, GBE, RD; *Career:* Cadet, Mediterranean & North Atlantic 1943-45; Canadian Pacific Steamships Ltd 1945-60; Master Mariner 1951; Staff Commander 1957; Wigham Poland Group, Director 1965-86; Sedgwick Insurance Brokers, Consultant 1986-87; Underwriting Member of Lloyds 1966-; St Katherine Haven Limited, Director 1979; Chairman 1990. *Biog: b.* 9 November 1925. *m.* 1950,

Elizabeth Marion Grace (née Findlay). *Educ:* Mill Crest School, Frinton-on-Sea; The Nautical College, Pangbourne. *Other Activities:* Common Councilman for Ward of Bassishaw, 1965-69; Elected Alderman for Ward of Bassishaw, 1969; Sheriff of City of London, 1973-74; Lord Mayor, 1976-77 (Queen's Silver Jubilee); Honorary Commander, Royal Naval Reserve (London Division); Elder Brother of Trinity House (Younger Brother 1973-78); Fellow & Founder Member, Nautical Institute; Vice-Chairman, Port of London Authority 1979-84; Trustee, National Maritime Museum; A Patron, National Maritime League; President, National Waterways Transport Association 1978-83; RLSS, UK President 1979-82, Deputy Commonwealth President 1982-; Vice President, City Centre St John's Ambulance; Vice President, City of London Red Cross; Chairman, Lord Mayor's Flood Relief Fund and Princess Victoria's Distress Fund; Vice President, City of London Outward Bound Association; Member of the Council and Trustee, Drake Fellowship (now Fairbridge Drake); Vice President, Lloyd's Volunteer Forces Fund; President, The Society of Young Freemen 1981-84; President, Bassishaw Ward Club; Chairman and Governor, Pangbourne College; Member of the Council, Royal College of Music; Churchwarden, St Lawrence Jewry by Guildhall; Trustee, St Paul's Cathedral Trust; Lay Vice Patron, The Missions to Seamen; Fellow, Institute of Administrative Management; (Institute Medal awarded 1982) President 1980-84; Fellow, Institute of Directors; Honourable Company of Master Mariners 1962, Master 1979-80, Warden 1971-; GBE 1976; Gentleman Usher of the Purple Rod 1985-; Reserve Decoration 1965; HM Lieutenant for City of London 1975-; City of London University, Hon Doctor of Science 1976; Chancellor, 1976-77; Hon Member, Guildhall School of Music and Drama; K St J 1976; Officer of Order of Leopold of Zaire 1974; Commander of the Order of Dannebrog 1974; Order of Johan Sedia Mahkota (Malaysia) 1974; Grand Cross of Municipal Order of Merit (Lima) 1977; Gold Medal of Administrative Management Soc (USA) 1983; Member, Guild of World Traders 1989. *Professional Organisations:* FNI, FInstAM. *Clubs:* City Livery, Guildhall, City Livery Yacht (Admiral), Royal Yacht Squadron, Royal London Yacht Club (Commodore 1984-85), Guild of World Traders Yacht Club (Admiral), Cruising Association, Hon Life Member Deauville Yacht Club. *Recreations:* Sailing, Photography.

GILLETT, A J; Clerk, Founders' Company.

GILLETT, Peter Lewis; Partner, Ernst & Young, since 1975; National Services to Leisure and Tourism Businesses. *Biog: b.* 26 May 1942. *Nationality:* British. *m.* 1969, Susan; 1 s; 1 d. *Educ:* Bancrofts School, Essex. *Professional Organisations:* FCA.

GILLIGAN, Brian Francis; National Tax Partner, Moores Rowland, since 1985. *Career:* Fuller Jenks Beecroft & Co, Tax Snr 1968-70; Neville Russell, Tax

Mgr 1970-71; Moores Rowland, Tax Mgr 1971-79; Ptnr 1980-. *Biog: b.* 22 November 1944. *Nationality:* British. *m.* 1969, Valerie (née Mathison); 1 s; 1 d. *Educ:* St Patricks, Dumbarton; Glasgow University. *Directorships:* Moores Rowland (Services) 1980 (exec); Moores Rowland (Financial Services) Ltd 1987 (exec). *Professional Organisations:* FCA; ATII. *Publications:* Tax and Financial Planning for Professional Partnerships, 1981 & 86. *Recreations:* Reading, Outdoor Pursuits.

GILLINGHAM, Adam R; Partner, W & J Burness WS, since 1989; Conveyancing/Private Client. *Career:* Brodies WS, Trainee & Assistant 1982-85; W & J Burness WS, Assistant 1985-89. *Biog: Nationality:* British. *m.* 1987, Susan; 1 s. *Educ:* Trinity College, Glenalmond; University of Aberdeen (LLB, DipLP). *Professional Organisations:* Writer to the Signet. *Clubs:* Arts Club (Edinburgh), Club Nautico.

GILLINGHAM, Richard; Director, Samuel Montagu & Co Limited.

GILLINGHAM, T M; Financial Controller, Globe Investment Trust plc.

GILLINGWATER, Richard Dunnell; Director, Barclays de Zoete Wedd Limited, since 1990; Corporate Finance. *Career:* Lovell White & King, Articles 1978-80; Kleinwort Benson Executive 1981-83; Asst Mgr 1984-85; Mgr 1985-86; Asst Dir 1986-88; Dir 1989-90. *Biog: b.* 21 July 1956. *Nationality:* British. *m.* 1981, Helen Margaret (née Davies); 3 d. *Educ:* Chesterfield Grammar School; St Edmund Hall, Oxford (MA); IMD, Lausanne, Switzerland (MBA). *Professional Organisations:* Solicitor. *Recreations:* Music, Film, Walking.

GILLITT, B; Chairman, Coventry Building Society, since 1989.

GILLON, George Marr Flemington; Partner, Drivers Jonas, since 1988; Partner in Charge of City Office. *Career:* Graham and Sibbald 1963-65; Richard Ellis 1965-86; Drivers Jonas 1986-. *Biog: b.* 14 November 1942. *Nationality:* British. *m.* 1973, Lesley (née Turner); 2 d. *Educ:* Arbroath High School; College of Estate Management. *Other Activities:* RICS (Honorary Secretary City of London 1987-); Liveryman, Chartered Surveyors Company (1987); Member, Incorporation of Masons of Glasgow (1972); Fellow, Institute of Directors. *Professional Organisations:* FRICS. *Clubs:* City of London, Caledonian, Flyfishers'. *Recreations:* Fishing, Hill Walking, Travel.

GILLON, Hamish William; General Manager (Finance) and Actuary, The Scottish Provident Institution, since 1988; Actuarial Finance. *Career:* Scottish Provident, Various Posts 1965-. *Biog: b.* 22 January 1940. *Nationality:* Scottish. *m.* 1968, Sandra (née Sibbald); 1 s; 1 d. *Educ:* Royal High School, Edinburgh. *Directorships:*

Scottish Provident Managed Pension Funds Ltd 1980 (exec); Other Companies in Scottish Provident Group. *Other Activities:* Honorary Treasurer, Faculty of Actuaries. *Professional Organisations:* FFA; FPMI.

GILMAN, David William; Finance Director, Forward Trust Group, since 1987; Financial Control, Planning, Analysis, Taxation, MIS, Balance Sheet Management. *Career:* Deloitte Haskins & Sells, Accountant 1974-78; GKN, Financial Accountant 1978-79; Midland Montagu Leasing Systems, Accountant 1979-80; Forward Trust Group, Project Accountant, Consumer Fin Mgr Planning Mgr; Chief Financial Officer Chief Accountant, Fin Controller 1980-89. *Educ:* High Arcal Grammar; Middlesex Polytechnic (BA Hons). *Directorships:* Forward Trust Group 1987 (exec); Fiat Finance Ltd 1986 (exec); Midland Montagu Leasing Ltd 1988 (exec); Midland Bank Finance Corporation Ltd 1988 (exec); Forward Trust Ltd 1988 (exec). *Professional Organisations:* FCA.

GILMORE, John W A; Director, Tranwood Earl & Company Limited.

GILMORE, Rosalind Edith Jean (née Fraser); Chairman, Building Societies Commission, since 1990. *Career:* HM Treasury Asst Principal 1960-65; International Bank for Reconstruction & Development Exec Asst to Economics Director 1966-67; HM Treasury, Principal Posts connected with International Fin Markets & Dom Financial Policy 1968-73; Principal Private Secretary to the Paymaster General (Rt Hon Maurice MacMillan) 1973-74; Cabinet Office, Principal Private Secretary to the Chancellor of the Duchy of Lancaster 1974-75; HM Treasury, Asst Secretary in Charge of Financing Various Nationalised Industries 1975-77; Head of Financial Institutions Division 1977-80; Press Sec to the Chancellor of the Exchequer (Rt Hon Geoffrey Howe) & Head of Information 1980-82; Dunlop Ltd General Manager, Corporate Planning 1982-83; National Girobank Director of Marketing 1983-86; St George's House, Windsor Castle Directing Fellow 1986-89; Building Societies Commission, Deputy Chairman 1989-90. *Biog: b.* 23 March 1937. *Nationality:* British. *m.* 1962, Brian Terrence. *Educ:* King Alfred School, N London; University College, London (BA Hons); Newnham College, Cambridge (BA, MA). *Directorships:* Mercantile Group plc; Mercantile Credit Company Ltd; London and Manchester Group plc; F I Group plc (Software) Mktg Consultant. *Professional Organisations:* FRSA; Associate Fellow, Newnham College, Cambridge; Fellow, University College, London. *Recreations:* Music, House in Greece, Languages.

GILMOUR, Ewen Hamilton; Director, Charterhouse Bank Ltd, since 1987; Corporate Finance. *Career:* Peat Marwick McLintock, Articled Clerk 1974-77; Assistant Manager 1980-; Charterhouse Bank Ltd, Corporate Finance Executive 1980-; Corporate Finance

Director 1987-. *Biog: b.* 16 August 1953. *Nationality:* British. *m.* 1978, Nicola (née van Mesdag); 3 s; 1 d. *Educ:* Rugby School; Downing College, Cambridge (MA). *Professional Organisations:* FCA. *Clubs:* Invalids, MCC. *Recreations:* Cricket, Golf, Gardening.

GILMOUR, J R; Director, PK English Trust Company Limited.

GINSBERG, Jeffrey; Director, Global Asset Management; Group Information Systems. *Career:* Easyrider (Pty) Ltd, Director 1980-81; Merchant Shippers SA (Pty) Ltd, Director 1981-86; Global Asset Management (UK) Ltd, Director 1986-. *Biog: b.* 1 November 1954. *Nationality:* South African. *m.* 1981, Nicole; 1 s. *Educ:* University of the Witwatersrand (BCom, MCom, MBA). *Directorships:* Global Asset Management UK Ltd 1988 (exec). *Recreations:* Tennis, Art.

GINSBERG, R K; Partner, Waltons & Morse.

GINSBURY, J; Non-Executive Director, Sheppards.

GIORDANO, R V; Non-Exec Director, Grand Metropolitan plc.

GITELSON, Bruce L; , Gibson Dunn & Crutcher.

GITTINGS, Harold John; Senior Managing Director, Touche Remnant Holdings Ltd, Touche Remnant & Co, Touche Remnant Unit Trust Management Ltd, since 1987; Unit Trusts & Offshore Funds. *Career:* N M Rothschild & Sons, Mgr, Investment Div 1974-81; Continental Illinois Bank Intl, Marketing Mgr 1981-82; Target Group plc, Investment Marketing Dir 1982-85; Touche Remnant Unit Trust Management, MD 1985-. *Biog: b.* 3 September 1947. *Nationality:* British. *m.* 1988, Andrea (née Fisher); 1 s; 1 d. *Educ:* Duke of York's School, Dover. *Directorships:* Various in Touche Remnant Group. *Other Activities:* Executive Committee, Unit Trust Association. *Professional Organisations:* ACIS.

GITTINGS, J; Committee Member, Touche, Remnant, Unit Trust Association.

GITTINS, Barry; Staff Director, Securities and Investments Board.

GIZZI, Julian Anthony; Partner, Beachcroft Stanleys, since 1986; Company/Commercial Law. *Career:* Beachcroft Stanleys, Articled Clerk/Assistant Solicitor 1979-86. *Biog: b.* 13 February 1957. *Nationality:* British. *Educ:* Downside School; Cambridge University (MA). *Professional Organisations:* Law Society. *Publications:* Solicitors and VAT, 1986. *Recreations:* Antique Furniture, Reading, Music.

GLADDIS, Robert A; Managing Director, Leslie & Godwin North America Ltd.

GLADWYN, M G; Chairman, Ropner Insurance Services Limited.

GLANCY, James Roland; Executive Director, County NatWest Wood Mackenzie & Co Ltd; Sales. *Biog: b.* 14 September 1947. *Nationality:* British. *m.* 1976, Rosemary (née Hume); 1 s; 1 d. *Educ:* Marlborough College; Dundee University. *Professional Organisations:* ASIA. *Clubs:* New Club (Edinburgh).

GLASGOW, David George; Deputy Chairman, Kleinwort Benson Unit Trusts Ltd, since 1989; Unit Trust & Offshore Development. *Career:* Royal Navy Officer 1961-73; Burge & Co Clerk 1973-74; Schlesinger Inv Mgmnt Services Technical Dir 1974-79; Abbey Unit Trust Managers MD 1979-87. *Biog: b.* 18 October 1942. *Nationality:* British. *m.* 1985, Bridget (née Watson). *Educ:* King's College School, Wimbledon; Britannia Royal Naval College, Dartmouth. *Directorships:* Kleinwort Benson Unit Trusts 1987; Kleinwort Benson Investment Management Ltd 1987; Kleinwort Benson International Fund Managers Ltd 1987; Kleinwort Benson Select Fund SA 1989; Insurance Ombudsman Bureau 1989. *Other Activities:* Unit Trust Association, Chairman of Customer Standards Ctee; Hon Secretary Castaways Club. *Professional Organisations:* Member, International Stock Exchange. *Clubs:* Royal Ocean Racing Club, Royal London Yacht Club. *Recreations:* Sailing, Skiing, Music, Opera.

GLASSMAN, David; Partner, Milne Ross, since 1989. *Career:* Norden & Company, Partner (Later Milne Ross) 1977-89. *Professional Organisations:* FCA; ATII.

GLASSON, J; Partner, Jaques & Lewis.

GLAZEBROOK, P G; Head of Licensing Dept, Field Fisher Waterhouse.

GLAZZARD, S V; Director, Smith Keen Cutler.

GLEADELL, Giles C; Director, Bradstock Blunt & Crawley Ltd.

GLEN, James Robert; Managing Director, The Scottish Investment Trust, since 1981; Management of Investment Trust. *Career:* The Scottish Investment Trust 1962. *Biog: b.* 27 May 1930. *Nationality:* British. *m.* 1956, Alison (née Brown); 3 s. *Educ:* Merchiston Castle School, Edinburgh. *Directorships:* The Scottish Life Assurance Company 1971 (non-exec) Chm. *Professional Organisations:* CA. *Clubs:* New Club, Hon Co, Edinburgh Golfers. *Recreations:* Golf, Fishing, Theatre.

GLENCROSS, Richard; Partner, Clyde & Co.

GLENN, Terry K; Managing Director (Investment Management), Merrill Lynch Asset Management UK Limited.

GLENNIE, Robert McDougall; Partner, McGrigor Donald, since 1980; Commercial, Banking and Insolvency Matters, Managing Partner (London). *Biog: Nationality:* British. *Educ:* Jordanhill College School, Glasgow; University of Strathclyde (LLB). *Other Activities:* Member of the Incorporation of Tailors in Glasgow; Freeman of the City of Glasgow; Member of the English Speaking Union. *Professional Organisations:* ACIS. *Recreations:* Travel, Gastronomy, Tropical Fruit Farming.

GLICHER, Julian Harvey; Partner, Director of Corporate Finance, Clark Whitehill, since 1987; National Corporate Finance. *Career:* Price Waterhouse (Paris), Snr 1968-72; Hambros Bank, Mgr 1972-77; Lloyds Merchant Bank, Asst Dir 1977-85. *Biog: b.* 15 June 1948. *m.* 1976, Adrienne Diane (née Rose); 2 s. *Educ:* Haberdashers' Aske's School, Elstree; Ashridge School of Management, Management Courses; Henley. *Professional Organisations:* FCA. *Recreations:* Badminton, Cycling, Sailing, Family.

GLOAK, Malcolm; Director, 3i plc, since 1987; London Regional Office. *Biog: b.* 8 May 1951. *Nationality:* British. *m.* 1977, Lynda (née Burgess); 2 s. *Educ:* Brentwood School; Trinity College, Oxford (BA). *Recreations:* Cricket, Golf.

GLOCK, F; Executive Director, Daiwa Europe Limited.

GLOSSOP, Peter; Director, Tyndall Holdings plc.

GLOVER, Edward Douglas; Director, Charterhouse Bank Ltd; Property. *Biog: b.* 19 July 1953. *Nationality:* British. *Educ:* Eton College. *Professional Organisations:* Member, Chartered Institute of Bankers.

GLOVER, Eric; Secretary-General, The Chartered Institute of Bankers, since 1982. *Career:* Brunei Shell Ltd, Personnel Officer 1958-60; Uganda Shell, Personnel Supervisor 1960-63; The Chartered Inst of Bankers 1963-90; Director of Studies 1968-82; Sec Gen 1982-90. *Biog: b.* 28 June 1935. *Nationality:* British. *m.* 1960, Adele Diane; 3 s. *Educ:* Liverpool Institute High School; Oriel College, Oxford (MA Classics). *Directorships:* British Accreditation Council for Independent Further & Higher Education 1985 (non-exec); Council for Accreditations of Correspondence Colleges 1982 (non-exec); Governor, South West London College 1989 (non-exec). *Professional Organisations:* Fellow, Royal Society of Arts. *Publications:* Articles in Press/Banking Magazines. *Clubs:* Overseas Bankers. *Recreations:* Golf, Squash, Tennis.

GLOVER, M H; Cerk, Skinners' Company.

GLOVER, Malcolm; Deputy Senior Partner, Wilde Sapte, since 1988; Commercial Litigation Partner. *Career:* Bridge Sanderson & Co, Solicitor 1966-69; Breeze

Benton & Co, Solicitor 1969-70; Wilde Sapte, Solicitor 1970; Partner 1971-. *Biog: b.* 3 November 1943. *Nationality:* British. *m.* 1973, Diane (née Callaway); 1 s; 2 d. *Educ:* Doncaster Grammar School; Bristol University (LLB). *Other Activities:* City of London Solicitors Company; Member, The Law Society. *Recreations:* Tennis, Theatre.

GLOYENS, Patrick; Partner, Titmuss Sainer & Webb.

GLUCKLICH, T C; Director, Lazard Brothers & Co Ltd, since 1989; Venture Capital. *Career:* BICC Cables, Group Director 1979-85; Wilkinson Match, Marketing Director 1976-79; McKinsey, Consultant 1969-76; James A Jobling, Marketing Director 1965-69. *Biog: b.* 17 June 1936. *Nationality:* British. *m.* 1 s; 2 d. *Educ:* Oxford University (BA Hons); London School of Economics (Diploma in Business Administration). *Directorships:* BPAS Limited 1984; Baker Street Investment Co Ltd 1989; Chantergrill (UK) Limited 1988; Development Capital Group Ltd 1986; Development Capital Management Ltd 1985; Henley Distance Learning Ltd 1986; Lazard Defence Fund (Management) Ltd 1989; Lazard Food & Drink Fund (Management) Ltd 1989; Lazard Unquoted Companies Fund (Management) Ltd 1989; Lazard Venture Funds (Management) Ltd 1989; Metro Office Supplies Ltd 1987; Strategic People Ltd 1987; Welsh Development Capital (Management) Ltd 1989; Welsh Development Capital (Nominees) Ltd 1988; Wessex Retirement Homes Ltd 1987-90; Wessex Secured Contracting Ltd 1987-90; Wilds Farm (Cheese Exports) Ltd 1989; Annabel Jones Ltd 1989; Silver at Annabel Jones Ltd 1989; Bawmac Ltd (now in Receivership) 1986; Griprod Ltd (formerly Griffin Productions Ltd) 1980; Melkron International Ltd 1986-88; Portapax Holdings Ltd 1986. *Clubs:* Arts Club. *Recreations:* Current Affairs, Theatre, Opera.

GLYN DAVIES, Miss Charmian Alexandra; Partner, Frere Cholmeley, since 1978; Property.

GLYN DAVIES, H M; Director, S G Warburg & Co Ltd.

GLYNN, Michael Richard; Managing Director (Formerly Finance Director), Hill & Knowlton (UK) Ltd, since 1989; All Non-Client Operations. *Career:* Deloitte Haskins & Sells (Chartered Accountants/Management Consultants), Staff Accountant 1982-84; Godfrey Davis plc, (Motor Ind/Property), Management Accountant 1984; Michael Peters Group plc (Marketing Services), Financial Controller 1985-87; Andrew Derrick Group Ltd (Design/PR Group), Financial Director 1987-89; Hill & Knowlton (UK) Ltd, (Public Relations Counsel, Sub of WPP Group plc), Financial Director 1989-90; Managing Director 1990-. *Biog: b.* 15 February 1954. *Nationality:* British. *m.* 1985, Barbara (née Burke). *Educ:* Haberdashers Aske's School; Manchester University (BA

Econ Hons). *Directorships:* Hill & Knowlton (UK) Ltd 1989 (exec). *Professional Organisations:* ACMA. *Clubs:* Scribes. *Recreations:* Skiing, Tennis, Soccer.

GOBLE, J F; Deputy Chairman, Panel on Takeovers & Mergers.

GODBOLD, Philip; Group Treasurer, Bunzl Plc.

GODBY, J A; Partner, Jaques & Lewis.

GODDARD, J P A; Partner, Freshfields.

GODDEN, Richard Westacott; Partner, Linklaters & Paines, since 1990; Corporate Finance. *Career:* Linklaters & Paines (London), Articled Clerk 1980-82; Assistant Solicitor (Commercial/Corporate Finance) 1982-85; (Hong Kong) Assistant Solicitor (Commercial/ Corporate Finance) 1985-87; (London) Assistant Solicitor (Corporate Finance) 1987-88; Takeover Panel, Joint Secretary 1988-90. *Biog:* b. 20 April 1957. *Nationality:* British. *m.* 1982, Joanna (née Perry); 1 s; 1 d. *Educ:* Sevenoaks School; Trinity Hall, Cambridge (MA Hons, First Class); College of Law, Guildford (Law Society Final Examination, Second Class). *Other Activities:* Church (St Johns, Blackheath), Various Responsibilities. *Professional Organisations:* Law Society; City of London Solicitors Company. *Recreations:* Studying History (almost any period), Watching Sport (especially Cricket), Travel, Entertaining Friends.

GODFREY, C; Secretary, C Czarnikow Ltd.

GODFREY, David; CBE; Director, Wellcome plc, since 1979; Operations Director. *Career:* Wellcome Foundation Ltd, Product Manager 1956-61; Sterling Winthrop, Director of Commercial Development 1961-66; Calmic Group, Managing Director 1966-71; Wellcome Foundation Ltd, Director 1971-; Wellcome plc, Director 1986-. *Biog:* b. 8 February 1929. *Nationality:* British. *m.* 1951, Margaret (née Wolfenden); 4 s; 1 d. *Educ:* London (BPharm, FRPSGB). *Directorships:* Wellcome plc 1986 (exec); Wellcome Foundation Ltd 1971 (exec); Calmic Ltd 1966 (exec); Coopers (Holdings) Ltd 1984-89. *Other Activities:* President, Assoc British Pharmaceutical Industry (ABPI) 1986-88; Member, Worshipful Society of Apothecaries; Member, Chemicals EDC (Neddy) 1978-88. *Professional Organisations:* Fellow, Royal Pharmaceutical Society of GB. *Clubs:* MCC, Farmers.

GODFREY, David Warren; Managing Director, European Merchant Bank, Bankers Trust Company, since 1988; Head of UK & European Credit Risk Management. *Career:* NatWest Group 1972-74; FOSECO Minsep plc 1974-76; First Pennsylvania Bank 1976-77; Bankers Trust Company, Relationship Mgr 1977-81; (New York) VP, Corp Relationship Mgr 1981-82; (Los Angeles) VP & Team Leader 1982-85;

VP/MD, UK & European Real Estate Finance and Advisory Business 1985-90. *Biog:* b. 22 September 1950. *Nationality:* British. *m.* 1981, Patricia Lynn (née Watts); 1 s; 2 d. *Educ:* The Heath School, Halifax, W Yorks; Nottingham University (BA Hons). *Directorships:* BT Pension Fund Trustees Ltd 1988 (exec).

GODFREY, K G; Partner, Allen & Overy, since 1981; Corporate Finance. *Career:* Allen & Overy, Asst Solicitor 1976-80. *Biog:* b. 21 January 1951. *m.* 1971, Margaret (née Stonier); 1 s; 1 d. *Educ:* St George's College, Zimbabwe; University of London (LLB). *Other Activities:* Member, Law Society's Company Law Committee. *Professional Organisations:* The Law Society; City of London Law Society; International Bar Assoc.

GODFREY, P M; Managing Director, River & Mercantile Investment Management.

GODFREY, Robert Antony; Company Secretary, Wendover Underwriting Agency Ltd, since 1986. *Career:* Served in Royal Navy 1949-76; Hine & Butcher Limited, Lloyd's Underwriting Agent (Later Merged into Wendover) 1976. *Professional Organisations:* Associate, Chartered Institute of Secretaries.

GODFREY, Stephen Jack Owen; Group Marketing Director, The MDA Group plc, since 1990. *Career:* Monk and Dunstone, Articled Pupil 1961-66; MDA (Cyprus), Partner 1972-79; (Middle East), Partner 1975-79; (Gulf), Partner 1978-79; Monk Dunstone Associates, Associate 1979-85. *Biog:* b. 16 February 1943. *Nationality:* British. *m.* 1970, Ann (née Weaving); 1 s; 1 d. *Educ:* Maidenhead Grammar; College of Estate Management. *Directorships:* MDA Management 1985 (exec); Monk Dunstone Associates 1990 (exec); MDA Overseas 1990 (exec); ESL Engineering Services 1990 (exec); ABS Litho 1990 (exec); Oldacres Computers 1990 (exec). *Professional Organisations:* FRICS; ACIArb; MAPM. *Clubs:* Kingswood Golf Club. *Recreations:* Golf, Fishing, Racquet Sports.

GODFREY, William Edwin Martindale; Partner, Simmons & Simmons, since 1977; International Commercial Law. *Career:* Norton, Rose, Botterell & Roche, Articled Clerk/Asst Solicitor 1968-72; Simmons & Simmons, Asst Solicitor 1972-76. *Biog:* b. 20 October 1947. *Nationality:* British. *m.* 1977, Helen Ann (née James); 2 s; 1 d. *Educ:* Repton School; Queens' College, Cambridge (Scholar) (MA). *Other Activities:* City of London Solicitors Company. *Professional Organisations:* The Law Society; IBA (Vice-Chm, Committee on Anti-Trust Law, 1981-86); Chm, Sub-Committee on Structure & Ethics of Business Law 1990-; City of London Law Society (Member, Commercial Law Sub-Committee). *Publications:* Editor of title Joint Ventures in Butterworths Encyclopedia of Forms & Precedents (5th Edn), 1990. *Recreations:* Fell-Walking, Books, Numismatics.

GODSON, Antony Graham; Director, Sedgwick Lloyd's Underwriting Agents Ltd, since 1988; Responsible for Team Handling Underwriting Affairs of Agency's Members of Lloyd's. *Career:* Bevington Vaizey & Foster Ltd, Clerk and Broker 1965-67; Sedgwick Collins & Co Ltd, Broker 1967-71; Sedgwick Forbes & Co Ltd, Broker and Administrator 1971-79; Sedgwick UK Ltd, Assistant Director 1979-84; Sedgwick Lloyd's Underwriting Agents Ltd 1984-. *Biog: b.* 9 March 1946. *Nationality:* British. *m.* 1971, Catriona (née Liddell); 3 s. *Educ:* Bradfield College. *Recreations:* Tennis, Golf.

GODWIN, David Christopher; Partner, Cazenove & Company.

GODWIN, Peter Raymond; Managing Director, Chartered WestLB Limited, since 1986; Export & Project Finance. *Career:* Lazard Brothers & Co Ltd, Exec Dir 1979-85; Korea Merchant Bank Corp, Dir & Exec VP 1976-77; Non-Exec Dir 1977-85. *Biog: b.* 16 May 1942. *Nationality:* British. *m.* 1967, Wendy Dorothy (née Slater); 1 s; 1 d. *Educ:* Harrow County Boys Grammar School. *Directorships:* CWB Export Finance Limited Chairman. *Other Activities:* President, Anglo-Taiwan Trade Committee; Member, Korea Trade Advisory Group (BOTB); Member, Tropical Africa Advisory Group (BOTB); Member, CLSB Export & Shipbuilding Policy Committee. *Professional Organisations:* ACIB. *Recreations:* Organist.

GOEKJIAN, Christopher A; Managing Director, Credit Suisse Financial Products, since 1990; Head of Trading. *Career:* Bankers Trust International Limited, Managing Director 1984-90. *Directorships:* Credit Suisse First Boston 1990 (exec).

GOHEL, Sir Jay; Director, Meghraj Bank Ltd.

GOLD, David Jeremy; Director, Phillips & Drew Fund Management, since 1988; USA Equities. *Career:* Guardian Royal Exchange, Senior Analyst, USA Equities 1979-84. *Biog: b.* 10 December 1956. *Nationality:* British. *m.* 1983, Yvonna (née Demczynska); 2 s. *Educ:* Downer Grammar; Loughborough University (BSc). *Recreations:* Cycling, Skiing.

GOLD, E H; Director, Hill Samuel Investment Management Ltd.

GOLD, Mrs Josyane Rose; Partner, S J Berwin & Co Solicitor, since 1988; Corporate Finance/Venture Capital. *Career:* Bartletts De Reya, Articled Clerk 1979-81; Assistant Solicitor 1981-83; Partner 1983-88. *Biog: b.* 16 November 1956. *Nationality:* British. *m.* 1978, Laurence; 2 s. *Educ:* North London Collegiate School; Bristol University (LLB). *Professional Organisations:* Law Society.

GOLD, Nicholas Anthony; Partner, Cazenove & Co.

GOLD, Nicholas Roger; Director, Baring Brothers & Co Ltd, since 1987; Corporate Finance. *Career:* Multitude Pty, South Africa, Ball Point Pen Salesman 1970; Touche Ross & Co, Articled Clerk 1973-76; Freshfields, Articled Clerk & Solicitor 1977-86. *Biog: b.* 11 December 1951. *Nationality:* British. *m.* 1983, Siena Laura Joy (née Arnold-Brown); 1 s; 1 d. *Educ:* Felsted School; Kent University (BA). *Directorships:* Baring Brothers & Co Ltd 1987 (Executive). *Professional Organisations:* FCA, Law Society. *Recreations:* Sailing, Travel, Stalking, The Arts.

GOLD, Paul Vincent; Deputy Managing Director, Mitsubishi Finance International Ltd, since 1990. *Career:* N M Rothschild & Sons Dealer 1964-72; WI Carr & Sons Ptnr 1972-77; Credit Suisse First Boston Mgr 1977-81; Morgan Grenfell & Co Ltd Snr Asst Dir 1981-85; Bank of America International Ltd Dep MD 1985-88; Mitsubishi Finance International Ltd, Dir Eurobond Distribution 1988-. *Biog: b.* 13 January 1944. *Nationality:* British. *m.* 1968, Anne (née Clayton); 1 s; 1 d. *Educ:* Christ College, Finchley.

GOLD, Peter Aldo Braham; Partner, Titmuss Sainer & Webb, since 1964; Company Law. *Biog: b.* 17 May 1934. *Nationality:* British. *m.* 1969, Susanna (née Schoenewald); 2 s. *Educ:* Bradfield College, London University (LLB Hons). *Other Activities:* Member, City of London Solicitors' Company; Member, The Law Society.

GOLDBERG, Ruben; Representative, N M Rothschild & Sons Limited in Mexico, since 1984; Non-Executive Dir, N M Rothschild & Sons Ltd, London; Corporate Finance. *Career:* Bank of America NT and SA, Corporate Banking, San Francisco, Canada and Mexico, Vice Pres and Corporate Group Head, Planning Supervision, Business Development, Maintenance and Control of Corporate Banking activities with the Mexican Private Sector 1974-81; Wells Fargo Bank NA International, Government & Corporate Banking Representative, Management of all areas of Administration, Credit, Risk, Control, Marketing and Public Relations 1981-84. *Biog: b.* 12 November 1948. *Nationality:* Mexican. *m.* 1971, Bertha (née Alerhand); 1 s; 1 d. *Educ:* Wharton School of Finance and Commerce, University of Pennsylvania (MBA); Facultad de Comercio y Administracion, Mexico, D F (Public Accounting). *Directorships:* N M Rothschild & Sons Limited 1989- (exec); Caribbean Management Company NV 1988-; Banco BICE, SA (Chile) 1987-; British Chamber of Commerce 1985-. *Professional Organisations:* Wharton Graduate Alumni Association, Mexico and San Francisco, California; Mexican Institute of Chartered Public Accountants; Mexican Institute of Finance Directors. *Clubs:* Bellavista Golf Club. *Recreations:* Golf, Tennis.

GOLDENBERG, Philip; Partner, S J Berwin & Co, since 1983; UK Corporate Finance, Employee Share

Schemes. *Career:* Linklaters & Paines, Asst Solicitor 1972-82; S J Berwin & Co, Asst Solicitor 1982-83. *Biog: b.* 26 April 1946. *Nationality:* British. m1 1985, Dinah Mary (née Pye). m2 Lynda Anne (née Benjamin); 2 s 1 d. *Educ:* St Paul's School; Pembroke College, Oxford (MA Hons). *Other Activities:* Immediate past Liberal/ SDP Parliamentary Candidate (Woking); Woking Borough Councillor (Liberal Democrat); Chm, Highways Ctee, 1988-90; Legal Adviser to the Liberal Party in Relation to its Merger with the SDP, and Jt Author of the Constitution of The Liberal Democrats; Member, London Regional Council of the CBI; Occasional Writer & Lecturer. *Professional Organisations:* The Law Society. *Publications:* New Outlook (Joint Ed), 1974-77; Fair Welfare, 1968; The S J Berwin & Co Businessman's Guide to Directors' Responsibilities 1988; Sharing Profits (With Sir David Steel), 1986; Part-Author, Gore-Brown on Companies, 1986; Editor, Guide to Company Law (Third Edition), 1990. *Clubs:* National Liberal.

GOLDIE, I W; Partner, Slaughter and May, since 1983. *Biog: b.* 6 February 1951. *Nationality:* British. *m.* 1976, Susan (née Moore); 2 s; 1 d. *Educ:* Trinity College, Glenalmond; Jesus College, Cambridge (BA Hons, MA). *Professional Organisations:* Member, Law Society and International Bar Association. *Clubs:* Woking, Royal St George's, Royal Blackheath.

GOLDING, Dr Anthony Michael; Director, Robert Fleming & Co Limited, since 1990; Corporate Finance. *Career:* Mullard Ltd, Trainee Executive 1970-73; Scott Goff Hancock & Co, Investment Analyst 1973-77; Flemings, Investment Analyst/Director of Research in Investment & Securities Subsidiaries, Director in Corporate Finance 1978-. *Biog: b.* 28 September 1944. *Nationality:* British. *m.* 1969, Gillian (née Harris); 1 d. *Educ:* St Clement Danes Grammar, London; Queens' College, Cambridge (MA); University of Sussex (DPhil). *Directorships:* Robert Fleming & Co Limited 1990 (exec). *Professional Organisations:* Member of the International Stock Exchange.

GOLDING, D M; Alternate Director, Wellington Underwriting Agencies Limited.

GOLDING, Dr Richard James Arthur; Director, Kleinwort Benson Ltd, since 1990; Member of Management Committee, Treasury Division, Head of Structured Finance. *Career:* Simon & Coates, Analyst/ Salesman 1976-81; Grieveson Grant & Co Gilts, Analyst 1981-84; Ptnr 1984-86; Kleinwort Grieveson & Co, Dir 1986; Kleinwort Benson Gilts, Dir 1986-. *Directorships:* Kleinwort Benson Gilts 1986-.

GOLDING, Rob; Director, S G Warburg Securities, since 1990; Motor Industry/Engineering Research. *Career:* Birmingham Post, Motoring Correspondent 1972-76; Business Editor 1976-81; The Engineer Magazine,

Editor 1981-84; Quilter Goodison, Engineering Analyst 1984-85; Warburg Securities, Motor Industry/ Engineering Analysis, 1985-. *Biog: b.* 1950. *Nationality:* British. *m.* 1976, Shirley; 3 d.

GOLDINGHAM, Hew Lyston; Partner, Richards Butler, since 1967; Corporate Finance. *Career:* Richards Butler, Asst Solicitor 1962-67. *Biog: b.* 5 September 1935. *Nationality:* British. *m.* 1968, Romey Anne (née Craig); 3 s. *Educ:* King's College, Taunton. *Other Activities:* Freeman, City of London Solicitors' Company. *Professional Organisations:* The Law Society; Institute of Directors. *Recreations:* Tennis, Travel, Fencing.

GOLDMUNTZ, David T; Managing Director (Investment Management), Salomon Brothers International Limited.

GOLDSMITH, Carl Stanley; Partner, Hill Dickinson & Company.

GOLDSMITH, J S; Chairman, Denis M Clayton & Co Limited.

GOLDSTEIN, Jerome; Managing Director, Sanwa International plc, since 1984. *Career:* Citicorp International Bank Limited, Executive Director 1964-80; Kidder Peabody International Limited, Managing Director 1980-83; European Banking Company Limited, Executive Director 1983-84. *Biog: b.* 25 December 1936. *Nationality:* British/American. *m.* 1970, Rita (née Frangakis). *Educ:* Swarthmore College, New York University (BA Hons, MA History). *Other Activities:* Member of the Board, Association of International Bond Dealers; Chairman, Council of Reporting Dealers (AIBD); Member, Market Practices Committee (AIBD). *Professional Organisations:* Fellow, Institute of Directors. *Recreations:* Photography, Fishing, Swimming.

GOLDSTEIN, John Arthur; Partner, Titmuss Sainer & Webb, since 1960; General Commercial Litigation. *Career:* Sidney L Samson & Nyman, Articles 1954-59; Admitted 1959; Assistant Solicitor 1959-60; Titmuss Sainer & Webb, Assistant Solicitor 1960; Partner 1960; Head of Litigation. *Biog: b.* 14 July 1937. *Nationality:* British. *m.* Daniele (née Ury); 1 d. *Educ:* Kilburn Grammar; College of Law (Hons). *Other Activities:* Commissioner for Oaths; Member, City of London Solicitors' Company; Children's Leukaemia Research; Wig and Pen Club. *Recreations:* Keen Sportsman, Law Society Cricket, Francophile with Affection for Tuscany, Opera, Gardening, Cooking.

GOLDTHORPE, Brian Lees; Director & Deputy Group Chief Executive, Midland Bank plc, 1989; Banking. *Career:* Midland Bank plc Various 1949-77; Gen Mgr (Operations) 1977-80; Gen Mgr Northern Div 1980-81; Snr Gen Mgr and Chief Exec 1981-83; Chief Exec (Group Risk Mgmnt) 1983-86; Chief Exec Corp

Banking 1986-87; Director and Chief Executive UK Banking Sector 1987-1989. *Biog: b.* 11 June 1933. *Nationality:* British. *m.* 1957, Mary (Molly) (née Commins); 1 s; 1 d. *Educ:* Wath-on-Dearne Grammar School. *Directorships:* Motability Finance Ltd 1985 (non-exec) Chm; Motability Ltd 1987 Governor (non-exec); International Commodities Clearing House Holdings 1989; Midland Bank Public Limited Company 1983; Midland Bank Executive Trust Limited 1989; Midland Bank (Head Office) Nominees Limited 1989; Midland Bank No 2 Pension Trust Limited 1989; Midland Bank Pension Trust Limited 1989; Midland California Holdings Limited 1984. *Other Activities:* Member of CBI Council. *Professional Organisations:* Fellow and Council Member,Chartered Institute of Bankers; Fellow, Royal Society of Arts; Companion, British Institute of Management; Member, British-American Chamber of Commerce UK Advisory Council. *Clubs:* Overseas Bankers Club, Ward of Cheap Club. *Recreations:* Music, Golf.

GOLINELLI, Walter; Chief Manager, Banca Nazionale del Lavoro.

GOLLINGS, Raymond Dennis; Director, Hill Samuel Bank Ltd, since 1985; Treasury. *Career:* Bank of Montreal, Trainee to Clerk 1962-69. *Biog: b.* 5 June 1943. *m.* 1969, Anne Elizabeth (née Nugent). *Educ:* Bexleyheath School for Boys. *Directorships:* Hill Samuel International Banking Corp, New York 1987 (non-exec); Wood Street Finance (No 3) Ltd 1987 (non-exec); Wood Street Finance (No 4) Ltd 1987 (non-exec). *Other Activities:* Freeman, The City of London. *Recreations:* Golf, Photography, Music.

GOMAR, Norbert George; General Manager, CIC-Union Européenne International et Cie, since 1988. *Career:* Crédit Industriel et Commercial (Paris) VP for Africa & the Middle East 1976-78; Banque Atlantique (Côte d'Ivoire) General Mgr 1978-83; CIC-Union Européenne Intl (Singapore) General Mgr 1983-88. *Biog: b.* 20 September 1941. *Nationality:* French. *m.* 1964, Moune (née Duez); 2 d. *Educ:* Ecole Polytechnique, Paris; University of California (Berkeley) (MSc). *Recreations:* Golf, Tennis.

GÓMEZ-BAEZA, Pedro A; Director, S G Warburg & Co, since 1989; Corporate Finance. *Career:* Morgan Guaranty (New York), Corp Fin 1980-82; The First Boston Corp New York (CS First Boston), MD Mergers and Acquisitions Corp Fin 1982-89. *Biog: b.* 21 April 1952. *Nationality:* Spanish. *m.* 1985, Maria (née Escarbaga); 2 d. *Educ:* Madrid University (Doc of Engineering); The Wharton School (MBA). *Recreations:* Tennis, Golf, Music, Reading.

GONSZOR, Charles Patterson; Partner, Phildrew Ventures, since 1988. *Career:* Citicorp Venture Capital, Head of Management Buy-outs 1982-88; Coopers &

Lybrand Associates, Consultant 1981-82. *Biog: b.* 13 February 1952. *Educ:* RGS Newcastle; Peterhouse, Cambridge (BA Hons). *Directorships:* TIP Europe plc 1986 (non-exec); SGI Ltd 1989 (non-exec); Mercado Holdings Ltd 1989 (non-exec).

GONSZOR, George Patterson; Director, Hill Samuel Bank Ltd, since 1982; Project Finance, International Banking, Shipping, Aerospace. *Career:* Hill Samuel & Co Ltd 1974-. *Biog: b.* 20 January 1949. *Nationality:* British. *m.* 1985, Margaritha Maria (née Post); 1 s. *Educ:* Royal Grammar School, Newcastle upon Tyne; Peterhouse, Cambridge (MA); St Johns College, Oxford. *Other Activities:* British Invisibles (Member of Banking Ctee). *Clubs:* Carlton. *Recreations:* Travel, Opera.

GOOCH, Stephen Leeds; Partner, Clay & Partners Consulting Actuaries, since 1974; Advising Occupational Pension Schemes, Head of Investment. *Career:* Sun Life Assurance Co 1970-71; Clay & Partners 1971-. *Biog: b.* 28 July 1948. *Nationality:* British. *Educ:* Stamford School, Lincs; Sheffield University (1st Class Honours Degree in Mathematics). *Other Activities:* Member, Association of Consulting Actuaries' Investment Committee. *Professional Organisations:* Member, Association of Consulting Actuaries; Member, International Association of Consulting Actuaries; Fellow, Institute of Actuaries.

GOOD, Charles Anthony; Managing Director, J S Gadd & Co Limited, since 1987; Corporate Finance, Property Development, Energy Finance, Flotations, Private Placing;. *Career:* Robson Rhodes Accountant 1969-72; S G Warburg & Co Ltd, Investment Banker, Corporate Finance Department 1973-75; C A Good & Co, Controlling Shareholder 1976-87. *Biog: b.* 18 May 1946. *Nationality:* British. *m.* 1967, Averil; 3 d. *Educ:* Charterhouse; University of Kent (BSc). *Directorships:* Embassy Property Group plc 1986 (non-exec); Citigate Communications Group Ltd 1988 (non-exec); Neilson Milnes Ltd 1988 (non-exec); Shoprite Group Ltd 1989 (non-exec). *Professional Organisations:* Fellow, Institute of Chartered Accountants.

GOOD, Diana; Partner, Linklaters & Paines.

GOODALL, Miss Caroline Mary Helen; Partner, Herbert Smith, since 1987; Company & Commercial, Corporate Finance. *Career:* Slaughter and May 1978-84; Herbert Smith 1984-. *Biog: b.* 22 May 1955. *Nationality:* British. *Educ:* Queen Ethelburga's School, Harrogate; Newnham College, Cambridge (MA Hons). *Other Activities:* City of London Solicitors' Company. *Professional Organisations:* Law Society. *Clubs:* Roehampton. *Recreations:* Tennis, Walking, Theatre.

GOODALL, Charles Peter; Partner, Simmons & Simmons, since 1984; Banking and International Finance. *Career:* Slaughter and May Asst Solicitor 1976-82. *Biog: b.* 14 July 1950. *Nationality:* British. *Educ:*

Sherborne School; St Catharine's College, Cambridge (MA, LLM). *Professional Organisations:* The Law Society. *Clubs:* Hawks Club (Cambridge), Royal Wimbledon Golf Club. *Recreations:* Golf, Squash.

GOODALL, E J M; Partner, Moores Rowland. *Professional Organisations:* Institute of Chartered Accountants of Scotland; Institute of Chartered Accountants in England and Wales.

GOODBODY, P R; Director, Charlton Seal Schaverien Limited.

GOODCHILD, John; Senior Analyst, Keith Bayley Rogers & Co.

GOODCHILD, Martin Roy; Partner, Pannell Kerr Forster, since 1985; Acquisition Investigation & Related Stock Exchange Matters. *Career:* Pannell Kerr Forster, Student/Senior Manager 1975-85. *Professional Organisations:* FCA; ATII.

GOODE, Professor Roy; OBE, QC; Norton Rose Professor of Law, University of Oxford and Fellow St John's College, Oxford, since 1990; Commercial Law. *Career:* Assistant Solicitor 1955-63; Victor Mishcon & Co, Partner 1963-71; Consultant 1971-88; Queen Mary College, University of London, Professor of Law 1971-73; Queen Mary College, Crowther Professor of Credit and Commercial Law 1973-89; Dean of the Faculty of Law and Head of Department of Law 1976-80; Founder and Director of the Centre for Commercial Law Studies 1979-89; Transfered to the Bar 1988; Appointed QC 1990. *Biog: b.* 6 April 1933. *Nationality:* British. *m.* 1964, Catherine Anne; 1 d. *Educ:* Highgate School (LLB); London University (Gladstone Scholar LLD). *Other Activities:* Member, Department of Trade and Industry Advisory Committee on Arbitration; Member, Civil and Family Committee of Judicial Studies Board; Member, Council of the Banking Ombudsman; Former Member, Crowther Committee on Consumer Credit; Monopolies and Mergers Commission. *Professional Organisations:* Barrister, Inner Temple; Vice President, Society of Public Teachers of Law; President-Elect, International Academy of Commercial and Consumer Law; FBA; FRSA. *Publications:* Hire-Purchase Law and Practice 1st Edn, 1962, 2nd Edn, 1970, Supplement, 1975; Hire-Purchase and Conditional Sale: A Corporation Survey of Commonwealth and American Law, Jointly With Jacob S Ziegel, 1965; Commercial Law, 1982; Consumer Credit Legislation, Original Author and Editor; Legal Problem of Credit and Security 1st Edn, 1982, 2nd Edn, 1988; Payment Obligations in Commercial and Financial Transactions, 1983; Proprietary Rights and Insolvency in Sales Transactions, 1st Edn, 1985, 2nd Edn, 1989; Principal of Corporate Insolvency Law, 1989. *Clubs:* Wig and Pen. *Recreations:* Reading, Walking, Chess, Browsing in Bookshops.

GOODEVE-DOCKER, N E; Partner, Wedlake Bell.

GOODEY, P J; Director, Hambros Bank Limited.

GOODFELLOW, J G; General Manager, Skipton Building Society.

GOODGAME, R A; Chief Dealer, Allied Trust Bank Limited.

GOODGER, J H; Managing Director, Gresham Underwriting Agencies Limited.

GOODHART, Professor C A E; Professor of Banking & Finance, London School of Economics, since 1985; Study Monetary Policy, Financial Markets, Banking, Structures & Regulations; Joint Director of Financial Markets Research Group. *Career:* Cambridge University, Assistant Lecturer 1963-64; Department of Economic Affairs, Adviser 1965-67; London School of Economics, Lecturer 1967-69; Bank of England, Chief Adviser on Monetary Policy 1969-85. *Biog: b.* 1936. *Nationality:* British. *m.* 1960, M (née Smith); 1 s; 3 d. *Educ:* Cambridge (MA); Harvard (PhD). *Other Activities:* Director, Lombard Street Research; Member, Council of Management of National Institute of Economic and Social Research. *Professional Organisations:* FBA, 1990.

GOODHILL, Alan; Managing Director (Investment Management), Morgan Stanley International.

GOODIER, W F; Director, Janson Green Limited.

GOODING, Christopher; Partner, Clyde & Co, since 1984; Insurance Law. *Career:* Clifford Turner, Articles; Clyde & Co 1980-. *Biog: b.* 27 May 1957. *Nationality:* British. *m.* 1984, Sharon (née Khajeh). *Educ:* St Lawrence College; Brunel University (LLB Hons). *Professional Organisations:* Law Society. *Publications:* Articles in Lloyds List, The Review, Single Market Monitor. *Recreations:* Motor Racing.

GOODING, P J; Director, Hill Samuel Bank Limited.

GOODISON, Sir Nicholas (Proctor); Kt; Chairman, TSB Group plc, since 1989. *Career:* H E Goodison & Co (later Quilter Goodison & Co, now Quilter Goodison Co Ltd), Members of Stock Exchange 1976-86. *Biog: b.* 16 May 1934. *m.* 1960, Judith Abel (née Smith); 1 s; 2 d. *Educ:* Marlborough College; King's College, Cambridge (Scholar, BA Classics, MA, PhD Architecture and History of Art). *Directorships:* British Steel plc 1989; General Accident Fire & Life Assurance Corporation plc 1987; Ottoman Bank 1988; TSB Bank plc 1989. *Other Activities:* Chm, International Stock Exchange; President, International Federation of Stock Exchanges (FIBV); Dep Chm, Committee of London and Scottish Clearing Bankers, 1989-; Fellow, and Vice Chm, Chartered Institute of Bankers, 1989-; Fellow, Institute of

Directors, 1989-; Member of the Council of the Industrial Society; Companion of British Institute of Management; Member, Executive Committee National Art-Collections Fund, 1976- (Chm 1986-); Chm, Courtauld Inst of Art 1982-; Dir, English National Opera 1977- (Vice Chm 1980-); Hon Treas, Furniture History Society; Hon Keeper of Furniture, Fitzwilliam Museum, Cambridge; Dir, City Arts Trust; Pres, Antiquarian Horological Society; Dir, Burlington Magazine Ltd; Governor, Marlborough College. *Professional Organisations:* Hon Fellow, RA; FSA; FRSA; Hon DLitt, City University; Hon LLD, Exeter University. *Publications:* English Barometers 1680-1860, 1968, 2nd edition 1977; Ormolu: The Work of Matthew Boulton, 1974; many papers & articles on history of furniture, clocks and barometers. *Clubs:* Arts, Athenaeum, Beefsteak. *Recreations:* History of Furniture and Decorative Arts, Opera, Walking, Fishing.

GOODMAN, David H; Group Treasurer, BICC plc, since 1990; Bank Relations, Debt, Cash Management, FX. *Career:* National Westminster Bank, Graduate Trainee 1979-82; Chase Manhattan Bank NA, Senior Auditor-Europe, Africa, Middle East Area 1982-85; BICC plc, Financing Manager 1986-87; Balfour Beatty Ltd, Group Treasurer 1988-89. *Biog: b.* 25 June 1957. *Nationality:* British. *m.* 1987, Dominique (née Goggin); 1 s; 1 d. *Educ:* Harrow School; Leeds University (BSc Hons Mgmnt St/Operations Research); Cranfield School of Management (MBA). *Professional Organisations:* Member, Association of Corporate Treasurers; Associate, Chartered Institute of Bankers. *Clubs:* MCC, Lansdowne. *Recreations:* Theatre, Cricket, Golf.

GOODMAN, L D; Director, Barclays de Zoete Wedd Limited.

GOODMAN, Michael Paul; Deputy Chairman, Bell Lawrie White & Co Ltd, since 1990. *Career:* Earnshaw, Haes & Sons, Ptnr 1987-88; Earnshaw, Haes & Sons Ltd, MD 1988-90. *Biog: b.* 3 June 1958. *Nationality:* British. *Directorships:* Comet Investments Limited; Regent Capital Holdings Ltd; Evergood Investments Ltd; Allied Freehold Property Trust Ltd; The Imperial Hotel, Hull, plc; Triumph Securities Ltd; Robert White & Co Ltd; Earnshaw, Haes & Sons Ltd; Tops Shop Centres Ltd; Tops Shop Estates Ltd. *Professional Organisations:* Member, International Stock Exchange.

GOODMAN, R A; Partner, Cameron Markby Hewitt.

GOODSON, John Francis; Partner, Client Services, Pannell Kerr Forster, since 1990; Corporate Finance, Venture & Start-Up Capital, Business Plan. *Career:* Ball Baker Deed & Co, Audit Manager 1968-72; Hambros Bank Ltd, Assistant 1972-73; Ball Baker Leake, Audit Partner 1974-89; Pannell Kerr Forster, Audit Partner 1989. *Biog: b.* 16 October 1943. *Nationality:* British. *m.* 1972, Marion (née Statham); 1 s; 1 d. *Educ:* St Be-

nedicts School, Ealing; Hull University (BSc Econ). *Professional Organisations:* FCA. *Clubs:* Royal Automobile Club, Pall Mall. *Recreations:* Gardening, Photography, Stamps, Walking.

GOODWAY, Nick; Deputy Editor, Observer Business, since 1985. *Career:* Investors Chronicle 1980-83; Evening Standard, City News Editor 1983-85. *Biog: b.* 19 August 1959. *Nationality:* British. *Educ:* Newcastle-under-Lyme High School; Sheffield University (BA Hons). *Clubs:* City Golf Club.

GOODWIN, J D; Director, S G Warburg Akroyd Rowe & Pitman Mullens Securities Ltd.

GOODWIN, J M; Partner, Allen & Overy.

GOODWIN, Ms Pauline; Publishing Director, Kogan Page Limited.

GOODWIN, Richard Anthony; Director, Commercial Banking, Hambros Bank Ltd, since 1988; Property Funding. *Career:* National Provincial Bank Ltd/National Westminster Bank plc, Various General Banking 1955-69; County NatWest, Property Funding, Snr Asst Director 1969-85; Hambros Bank Ltd, Director, Property Funding, Commercial Banking Division 1985-90. *Biog: b.* 1 June 1938. *Nationality:* British. *m.* 1961, Brenda Mary (née Richards); 1 s; 1 d. *Educ:* Beckenham Technical School. *Directorships:* Hambros Bank Ltd 1988 (exec); Appleby Westward plc 1988 (non-exec); CNC (Washington) Ltd 1990 (exec). *Professional Organisations:* AIB. *Recreations:* Squash, Tennis, Bridge.

GOODWORTH, Simon Nicholas; Partner, Theodore Goddard, since 1986; Corporate Finance & Flotations, Mergers & Acquisitions, Venture Capital & Joint Ventures. *Career:* Theodore Goddard, Asst Solicitor 1979-84; Associate 1984-86. *Biog: b.* 9 August 1955. *Nationality:* Canadian/British. *Educ:* Solihull School; Manchester University (LLB Hons). *Professional Organisations:* The Law Society. *Recreations:* Squash, Tennis, Music.

GOODYEAR, William M; Executive Vice President & Managing Director, Continental Bank NA, since 1986; Chairman, Continental Capital Markets Ltd, since 1986. *Career:* Continental Bank, Various Mgmt Positions 1972-. *Biog: b.* 3 May 1948. *Nationality:* American. *m.* 1971, Karen; 1 s; 1 d. *Educ:* University of Notre Dame (BBA); Tuck School, Dartmouth (MBA). *Directorships:* Continental Capital Markets Ltd; Continental Illinois Equity Corporation. *Professional Organisations:* Overseas Bankers Club; Chicago Council on Foreign Relations; American Institute of Certified Public Accountants in the USA. *Clubs:* Union League (Chicago), Jonathan Club (Los Angeles). *Recreations:* Tennis, Golf, Travel, Jogging.

GOOM, R J; Director, Royal Bank of Canada Europe Limited.

GORDON, Alasdair Shepherd; Partner, Lovell White Durrant; Unit Trusts, Offshore Funds, Investment Management, Financial Services. *Career:* Slaughter and May 1974-81; Lovell White & King 1981-. *Educ:* Trinity College, Glenalmond; Sheffield University (BA).

GORDON, Alastair J; WS, NP; Partner, W & J Burness WS, since 1970; Company/Commercial Law.

GORDON, David Michael; Director and Actuary, Pearl Assurance plc, since 1987; Appointed Actuary of Pearl Assurance plc, Pearl Assurance (Unit Fund) Ltd, Pearl Assurance (Unit Linked Pensions) Ltd, Pearl Trust Managers, Pearl Group plc. *Career:* Sun Life Assurance Society Actuarial Student 1959-64; Northern Assurance Actuarial Student 1964-67; Pearl Assurance plc Section Leader 1967-70; Principal 1970-72; Dept Mgr 1972-75; Asst Actuary 1975-83; Dep Actuary 1983-84; Actuary 1984. *Biog: b.* 12 December 1940. *m.* 1968, Patricia Anne (née Melamed); 1 s; 1 d. *Educ:* Davenant Foundation Grammar School. *Directorships:* Pearl Assurance plc 1987; Pearl Assurance (Unit Funds) Ltd 1987; Pearl Assurance (Unit Linked Pensions) Ltd 1987; Pearl Trust Managers Ltd 1987; Pearl Group plc 1988; Insurance Ombudsman Bureau 1988 (non-exec). *Other Activities:* Assoc of British Insurers (Member of Legislation Ctee, Home Service Actuarial and Publicity Ctees); Trustee, Overweight and Heart Disease Trust; Member, LAUTRO Selling Practices Committee. *Professional Organisations:* FIA, FSS. *Clubs:* 59, Denarius. *Recreations:* Theatre, Swimming, Gardening.

GORDON, Donald; Chairman, TransAtlantic Holdings plc.

GORDON, I R L; Director, J Henry Schroder Wagg & Co Limited, since 1987; UK and European Underwriting. *Biog: b.* 21 August 1954. *Nationality:* British. *m.* 1981, Claire (née Winterschladen); 1 s. *Educ:* Harrow School; Pembroke College, Cambridge (BA Hons History).

GORDON, Ian; Partner, McGrigor Donald, since 1983; Corporate Law, Tax Law, Pension Schemes, Employee Benefits. *Career:* McGrigor Donald Asst 1981-83. *Biog: b.* 15 August 1957. *Nationality:* British. *m.* 1988, Angela (née MacDonald). *Educ:* Biggar High School; Edinburgh University (LLB Hons). *Professional Organisations:* The Law Society of Scotland; Notary Public; Assoc of Pension Lawyers. *Recreations:* Walking, Exploring, Photography.

GORDON, J M; Director, Metheuen (Lloyds Underwriting Agents) Limited.

GORDON, J S; JP; Director, Brewin Dolphin & Co Ltd, since 1965; Maximising People's Assets within the Context of their Investment Aims. *Biog: b.* 27 March 1935. *Nationality:* British. *m.* 1960, Anne Cecilia (née Hyde); 3 d. *Educ:* Charterhouse, Godalming, Surrey. *Other Activities:* Needlemakers Company; Saffron Walden Bench. *Clubs:* Garrick, Lansdowne, City Livery. *Recreations:* Croquet, Village History.

GORDON, James Ian; Deputy Underwriter for Lloyd's Syndicate, Martin Ashley Underwriting Agencies Ltd, since 1983. *Career:* Robt Bradford Hobbs Savill Ltd (Lloyd's Broker), Dir & Gen Mgr of Non Marine Div, Responsibility for Latin America 1978-83; Martin Ashley Underwriting Agencies Ltd, Deputy Underwriter for Lloyd's Syndicate 1983-. *Biog: b.* 2 June 1942. *Nationality:* British. *m.* 1968, Maureen. *Educ:* Wimbledon College; Trinity College, Cambridge (MA Hons). *Directorships:* Martin Ashley Underwriting Agencies Ltd 1984 (exec); Clifford Palmer Underwriting Agencies Ltd 1986 (exec); Ashley Palmer and Hathaway Ltd 1987 (exec). *Professional Organisations:* Fellow, Chartered Insurance Institute. *Clubs:* United Oxford and Cambridge University Club.

GORDON, Jeffrey I; Associate Director, Mayer Brown & Platt.

GORDON, John Edwin; Head of Corporate Finance, Beeson Gregory Limited, since 1989. *Career:* Hill Samuel & Co Ltd 1968-72; Robert Fleming & Co Ltd, Director 1972-77; Laing & Cruickshank, Director 1977-82; Jackson Exploration Inc, Director 1982-85; Capel-Cure Myers, Head of Corporate Finance 1985-89. *Biog: b.* 14 December 1939. *Nationality:* British. *m.* 1968, Monica Anne (née Law); 1 s; 2 d. *Educ:* Tonbridge School; Queens' College, Cambridge (MA). *Directorships:* Beeson Gregory Ltd 1989 (exec); British Waterways Board 1987 (non-exec). *Professional Organisations:* FCA. *Clubs:* Boodles, Hawks, Leander. *Recreations:* Fishing.

GORDON, John Wallace; Snr Partner, Hays Allan, since 1967. *Career:* Deloitte Haskins & Sells, Trainee 1960-64; Touche Ross, Snr 1965-66. *Biog: b.* 6 July 1936. *m.* 1964, Gillian Margaret (née Ramage); 2 s. *Educ:* The Edinburgh Academy; St John's College, Oxford (MA). *Clubs:* Hon Co of Edinburgh Golfers, Rye Golf Club, Denham Golf Club, Caledonian. *Recreations:* Fishing, Golf, Shooting, Bridge.

GORDON, M J; Director, Royal Trust Asset Management.

GORDON, Martin Laing; Director, S G Warburg Securities, since 1972; International Finance. *Biog: b.* 19 July 1938. *Nationality:* British. *Educ:* Harrow School; Oriel College, Oxford (MA). *Other Activities:* Chairman, Japan Committee, British Invisibles.

GORDON, Robert; Senior Partner, Chiene & Tait, CA, since 1987. *Career:* Chiene & Tait, Partner 1957-. *Biog: b.* 1930. *Nationality:* British. *m.* 1955, Avril (née Wotherspoon); 3 s; 2 d. *Educ:* Loretto School. *Directorships:* Scottish Equitable Life Assurance Society 1975 (non-exec). *Other Activities:* Member, Commission for Local Authority Accounts in Scotland, 1976-85; Governor, Moray House College of Education, 1979-87; Member, Committee of Investigation for Scotland, 1980-; Governor, Loretto School (Chairman), 1981-; Member, Scottish Council of Independent Schools, 1987-89; Member, Society of High Constables and Guard of Honour of Holyroodhouse, 1965-. *Professional Organisations:* CA. *Clubs:* New (Edinburgh), Clyde Cruising. *Recreations:* Yachting.

GORDON, Stuart S; Director, Merrill Lynch Pierce Fenner & Smith (Brokers & Dealers) Limited.

GORDON, T John R; Investment Director, Providence Capitol Life Assurance Company, since 1984; Investments and Unit Trusts. *Career:* Cooperative Insurance, Actuarial Trainee 1958-61; Various Companies, Stockbroking 1961-63; Prudential Assurance, Portfolio Mgr 1963-68; Abbey Life, Investment Dir 1968-84. *Educ:* Cambridge University (BA). *Directorships:* Providence Capitol Fund Managers 1984 (non-exec); Providence Capitol Portfolio Managers 1987 (exec). *Other Activities:* Livery, Farmers' Company. *Professional Organisations:* FIA.

GORDON, William John; Director, Personnel, Barclays Bank plc, since 1990; Middle Market. *Career:* Barclays Bank plc Various 1955-80; Asst Gen Mgr Barclaycard 1980-83; Reg Gen Mgr Central UK 1983-87; Director, UK Corporate Services 1987-90. *Biog: b.* 24 April 1939. *Nationality:* British. *m.* 1963, Patricia (née Rollason); 2 s. *Educ:* King Edward VI School, Fiveways, Birmingham. *Professional Organisations:* Fellow, Chartered Institute of Bankers. *Recreations:* Bridge, Chess, Golf, Classical Music.

GORDON-LENNOX, Lord Nicholas Charles; Non-Executive Director, Sturge Holdings plc.

GORE, J S; Director, The New India Assurance Company Limited.

GORE, John Temple; Chairman & Managing Director, J H Minet & Co Ltd, since 1989; Oil and Gas Insurance. *Career:* Robert Bradford Hobbs Savill & Co Ltd, Dir 1954-74; Coldstream Guards; Robert Bradford and Co Ltd, Insurance Brokers at Lloyd's 1954; J H Minet & Co Ltd, Managing Director, Oil & Gas Division 1974; Deputy Chairman 1983-89. *Biog: b.* 30 March 1931. *Nationality:* British. *m.* 1984, Kathleen Ann (née Griffin); 1 s; 2 d. *Educ:* Eton College. *Directorships:* Minet Holdings plc 1982 (exec); J H Minet & Co Ltd 1976 (exec). *Other Activities:* Worshipful Company of Insurers; Institute of Directors. *Professional Organisations:* Lloyd's Insurance Brokers Committee. *Clubs:* City of London. *Recreations:* Sailing.

GORE, Mark; Legal Adviser, FIMBRA, since 1987; Legal Adviser. *Career:* Common Law Bar 1947-56; S Gore & Sons Ltd, Dir 1956-85; Legal Consultant 1986-. *Biog: b.* 16 March 1922. *m.* 1953, Daphne Eleanor (née Elkin); 1 s; 1 d. *Educ:* University College School, Hampstead; Balliol College, Oxford (MA). *Professional Organisations:* Barrister (1947), Inner Temple. *Recreations:* Tennis, Gardening.

GORE, Michael B G; Group Finance Director, S G Warburg Group plc. *Career:* Kemp Chatteris & Co, Audit Senior 1959-64; S G Warburg & Co Ltd 1964-. *Biog: b.* 25 October 1937. *Nationality:* British. *m.* 1972, Mozella (née Ransom); 2 s; 1 d. *Educ:* Felsted School; Peterhouse, Cambridge (BA). *Directorships:* S G Warburg & Co Ltd 1969 (exec); S G Warburg Group Management Ltd 1986 (exec) Joint Chairman; Rowe & Pitman Money Broking Ltd 1986 (exec) Chairman; Potter Warburg Ltd 1989 (exec) Deputy Chairman. *Professional Organisations:* FCA; FRSA. *Recreations:* Opera, Theatre, Reading.

GORE LANGTON, Miss C M; Director, Laurence Keen Ltd, since 1990; Private Client I M. *Career:* Lazard Securities Ltd 1978-83. *Biog: b.* 18 June 1954. *Nationality:* British. *m.* 1984, Peter E Jordan; 2 s. *Educ:* Weston Birt; Exeter University (Latin BA Hons 2:i). *Directorships:* Laurence Keen Ltd 1990 (exec). *Other Activities:* Membership Committee, Stock Exchange - Special Brief for Individual Membership. *Professional Organisations:* Stock Exchange. *Recreations:* Reading, Horse Racing, Needlework, Cinema, Theatre.

GORE-RANDALL, Philip Allan; Partner, Arthur Andersen & Co, since 1986; Audits and Business Advisory (Oil & Gas, Multinationals, Stock Exchange). *Career:* Arthur Andersen & Co 1975-. *Biog: b.* 16 December 1952. *m.* 1984, Alison (née While); 2 s. *Educ:* Merchant Taylors'; University College, Oxford (MA). *Professional Organisations:* FCA, Institute of Petroleum. *Recreations:* Classical Music, Good Food, Travel, Family, Cotswold Life.

GORMAN, Christopher; Partner, Linklaters & Paines.

GORMLY, Allan G; Director, Trafalgar House Public Limited Company.

GORRINGE, Robin; Partner, Clark Whitehill.

GORST, Blake Nicholas; Director, Singer & Friedlander Ltd.

GORTY, Peter; Partner, Nabarro Nathanson, since 1972; Company and Commercial. *Career:* Gilbert Samuel & Co 1967-69; Withers 1969-70; Nabarro Nathanson 1970-. *Biog: b.* 3 November 1944. *Nationality:* British. *m.* 1972, Mariana; 1 s; 1 d. *Educ:* Oweus School; LSE (LLB). *Directorships:* Stat Plus plc; New Balance Athletic Shoes (UK) Ltd. *Recreations:* Sport, TV, Reading Newspapers.

GORVIN, R J; Executive Director, Co-operative Bank plc, since 1982; Customer Service Division. *Career:* Midland Bank, Training Branch Tutor, District Staff Superintendent's Assistant, Accountant (Hinckley Branch), Manager (Personnel Relations) 1954-73; Federation of London Clearing Bank Employers, Assistant to Director 1971-73; Co-operative Bank plc, Personnel Manager 1974; Joint General Manager (Personnel Services) 1979; F C Finance Ltd, Managing Director 1980-81; Executive Director of Main Board & General Manager (Domestic Banking) 1982; Executive Director, Personal Banking 1987; EFT & Consumer Credit, Executive Director 1988; Executive Director, Customer Service 1990. *Biog: b.* 16 June 1983. *Nationality:* British. *m.* 1961, Josephine (née Cooper); 3 d. *Educ:* Chippenham; Cheltenham; Witney. *Directorships:* Scottish Co-operative Society Nominees Ltd 1982; Cleveland Finance Ltd 1987; First Co-operative Finance Ltd 1987; Fastline Credit Finance Ltd 1987; Co-operative Bank Financial Advisers Ltd 1987; Co-operative Handycard Service Ltd 1987; Co-operative Bank (Insurance Services) Ltd 1987; F C Finance Ltd 1988; EftPos UK Limited 1988; North West Business & Industry Awards (Charity) 1990 Chairman; North West Business & Industry Awards (Services) Ltd 1990 Trustee; Visa International EMEA Region 1990; Co-operative Bank plc 1982 (exec). *Professional Organisations:* FCIB. *Recreations:* Cricket, Gardening, Hi-Fi, Photography.

GOSCHALK, S L; Director, J S Gadd & Co Ltd, since 1987; Corporate Finance/Compliance. *Career:* Touche Ross & Co (London), Articles 1974-77; Insolvency Asst Manager 1977-80; Touche Ross & Co (Toronto), Insolvency Manager 1980-82; London Trust plc, Fund Manager 1982-85; Chartfield & Co Ltd, Venture Capital Manager 1985-87. *Biog: b.* 29 September 1952. *Nationality:* British. *m.* 1976, Julia (née Michaels); 1 s; 2 d. *Educ:* London School of Economics (BSc Econ). *Professional Organisations:* FCA.

GOSLING, J C; Partner, Holman Fenwick & Willan, since 1988; Admiralty, Spain & S America. *Biog: b.* 28 June 1955. *Nationality:* British. *m.* 1980, Brenda L; 1 s; 1 d. *Educ:* Ampleforth College; St Catharine's College, Cambridge (MA Cantab). *Professional Organisations:* Solicitor.

GOSNAY, Andrew William; Partner, Simpson Curtis, since 1990; Banking & Capital Markets. *Career:* Cameron Markby, Articled Clerk 1983-85; Banking Department Assistant Solicitor 1985-86; Simpson Curtis, Corporate Department Assistant Solicitor 1986-88; Associate Partner 1988-90; Partner (Banking Unit) 1990. *Biog: b.* 21 February 1961. *Nationality:* British. *Educ:* Uppingham School; University of Newcastle upon Tyne (LLB). *Professional Organisations:* The Law Society.

GOSTYN, Antony; Partner, D J Freeman & Co.

GOTBAUM, Joshua; Managing Director, Lazard Frères & Co Ltd, since 1989, and General Partner, Lazard Frères & Co Ltd, since 1990; Corporate Finance, principally Mergers and Acquisitions, Corporate Restructuring & General Financial Advisory Matters. *Career:* Lazard Frères & Co, Vice President/Associate 1981-89; Legislative Assistant for Economics and Budget 1981; U S Senator Gary Hart/Senate Budget Committee, Assoc Dir for Economics, White House Domestic Policy Staff, White House Coordination of Economics, Industry & Trade Matters 1980; Executive Assistant to Alfred Kahn, Advisor to the President on Inflation 1978-80; White House Office of Energy Policy and Planning/US Dept of Energy 1977-78. *Biog: b.* 1951. *Nationality:* American. *m.* 1989, Joyce H (née Thornhill). *Educ:* John F Kennedy School of Government, Harvard (MPP); Harvard Law School (JD); Stanford University (AB Sociology). *Other Activities:* Admitted to the Bar of the District of Columbia, 1978-81; Registered Representative (Series 7) NASD.

GOUBET, Jean-Claude; General Manager UK, Credit Lyonnais, since 1987. *Career:* Credit Lyonnais (France) 1966-77; (New York), Head of Corp Relations 1977-81; (Luxembourg), Gen Mgr 1981-84; (UK), Dep Gen Mgr UK 1984-87. *Biog: b.* 31 December 1943. *Nationality:* French. *m.* 1964, Françoise (née Paris); 2 s. *Educ:* Lycee Carnot, Paris; Institut National des Sciences Appliquées de Lyon (Ingenieur Diploma). *Directorships:* Credit Lyonnais Equipment Finance Ltd; The Credit Lyonnais London Nominees; Credit Lyonnais Securities; Credit Lyonnais Rouse; Woodchester Investments plc; Woodchester Bank; Moorgate Mercantile Holdings plc. *Professional Organisations:* French Chamber of Commerce in Great Britain (Vice Pres). *Clubs:* Overseas Bankers Club, Foxhills Country Club. *Recreations:* Skiing, Sailing, Theatre.

GOUGH, Ben; Partner, Frere Choleley.

GOUGH, Charles Brandon; Senior Partner & Chairman, Coopers & Lybrand, since 1983. *Career:* Evans Smith Boothroyd & Co, Articled Clerk 1961-64; Coopers & Lybrand, Audit Snr/Mgr 1964-68; Gen Practice Ptnr 1968-83. *Biog: b.* 8 October 1937. *Nationality:* British. *m.* 1961, Sarah (née Smith); 1 s; 2 d. *Educ:* Douai School; Jesus College, Cambridge (MA). *Directorships:* Coopers & Lybrand (Intl) 1982 Exec Ctee; 1985 Chm; Council of Lloyd's 1983-86; British Aerospace plc 1987-88; Coopers & Lybrand Europe 1989 Chm; British

Invisibles 1990. *Other Activities:* Mem, CCAB Audit Practices Ctee, 1976-84 (Chm 1981-84); Worshipful Co of Chartered Accountants; Governing Council, Business in the Community, 1984-88; Council, Business in the Community, 1988-; Council for Industry & Higher Education, 1985-; Management Council, GB-Sasakawa Foundation, 1985-; Council, City University Business School, 1986-; Chm, City Advisory Panel, City Univ Business School, 1987-; Mem, Accounting Standards Review (Dearing) Ctee, 1987-88; Mem, CBI Task Force, Vocational Education & Training, 1989; Chm of the Finance Committee, City University Business School, 1988-; Trustee, Common Purpose within our Cities, 1989-; Member, Japan-European Community Association's UK National Committee, 1989-; Member, Financial Reporting Council, 1990-; Member of Council, Foundation for Education Business Partnerships, 1990-; Member, CBI Education & Training Affairs Committee, 1990-; Trustee, Guildhall School, Music & Drama Foundation, 1990-. *Professional Organisations:* FCA (Council Member 1981-84). *Recreations:* Music, Gardening.

GOULD, J; Partner, Allen & Overy.

GOULD, Ms V; Executive Director, River & Mercantile Investment Management.

GOULDER, N E M; Deputy Underwriter Syndicate 1095 at Lloyd's, Wellington Underwriting Agencies Limited, since 1987; Treaty Manager. *Career:* Harman Hedley Agencies, Underwriting Assistant, Underwriting and Administration 1978-81; Munich Re UK Non-Life Branch, Underwriter, Casualty Treaty Underwriting 1981-84; Underwriting Manager, Management of Casualty Treaty Account 1984-87. *Biog: b.* 24 July 1957. *Nationality:* British. *m.* 1987, Caroline Jane (née Rennie); 2 s. *Educ:* Dragon School, Oxford; Eton College (Scholar); Merton College, Oxford (Scholar, BA Hons II Mathematics). *Directorships:* Wellington Underwriting Agencies Ltd 1987 (exec). *Recreations:* Music, Walking, Wines, Property.

GOULDER, Terence Renshaw; Director, Bain Clarkson Ltd, since 1987; Marketing. *Career:* Glanvill, Enthoven Dir, Various Subsidiary Cos 1952-70; A W Bain & Sons Ltd Dir 1970; Bain Dawes plc Div MD 1980; Dir 1984. *Directorships:* RHAIS 1985 (non-exec); TTFIS 1987 (non-exec); RICSIS 1987 (non-exec).

GOURLAY, R; Chief Executive, BP Nutrition, The British Petroleum Company plc.

GOVETT, Clement John; LVO; Deputy Chief Executive, Schroder Investment Management Ltd, since 1987. *Career:* Price Waterhouse & Co 1966-69; J Henry Schroder Wagg & Co Ltd, Various 1969-80; Director 1980-90. *Biog: b.* 26 December 1943. *m.* 1975, Rosalind (née Fawn); 3 d. *Educ:* St Paul's School; Pembroke College, Oxford (MA). *Directorships:* City & Commercial Investment Trust plc 1981 (non-exec); Schroder Ventures Ltd 1985; Schroder Properties Ltd 1987 Chairman. *Professional Organisations:* FCA. *Recreations:* Tennis, Bridge, Gardening.

GOVETT, William John Romaine; Deputy Chairman, John Govett & Company Ltd. *Biog: b.* 11 August 1937. *Nationality:* British. *Directorships:* CIN Management Ltd 1985; Corney & Barow Ltd 1979; General Overseas Investments Ltd 1975; Govett American Endeavour Fund Ltd 1988; Govett Equity Trust Ltd 1975; Govett Atlantic Investment Trust plc 1979; Govett Strategic Investment Trust plc 1975; Investors in Industry Group plc - 3i 1984; Legal & General Group plc 1979; Lep Group plc 1983; Ranger Oil (UK) Ltd 1988; Scottish Eastern Investment Trust plc 1977; Union Jack Oil Co Ltd 1983; Govett Oriental Investment Trust plc 1972; Berkeley Atlantic Income Ltd 1986; Energy Resources International Ltd; Home & Overseas Limited 1967; Basinghall Securities Limited 1975-90; Berkeley Govett & Company Limited 1987-90; Energy Resources & Services Incorporated 1981-90; Estate Duties Investment Trust plc -1984; Govett Enterprise Investment Trust plc; John Govett Portfolio Management Limited 1987-90; JGPM (Nominees) Limited - 1990; John Govett & Co Limited 1964-90; John Govett Investment Management Limited 1986-90; John Govett Services Limited 1978-90; London & Aberdeen Oil & Gas Limited 1984-88; Stockholders Far East Investments Incorporated 1981-87.

GOVIER, Peter John Hugh; Director, Sharps Pixley Ltd, since 1971; Finance. *Career:* Binder Hamlyn, Auditing & Consultancy 1961-69. *Biog: b.* 7 October 1933. *Nationality:* British. *m.* 1960, Gillian M (née Murray); 2 d. *Educ:* Haileybury & ISC. *Other Activities:* The Institute of Directors (Member). *Professional Organisations:* FCA. *Recreations:* Music, Bridges, Walking (Sometimes with Golf Clubs).

GOWAR, Martyn Christopher; Partner, Lawrence Graham, since 1973; Tax Department. *Career:* Lawrence Graham, Articled Clerk & Solicitor 1967-. *Biog: b.* 11 July 1946. *Nationality:* British. *m.* 1971, Susan Mary (née Scotchmer); 3 s. *Educ:* King's College School, Wimbledon; Magdalen College, Oxford (MA). *Other Activities:* Taxation Editor, The Law Society's Gazette; Member, The Law Society Revenue Law Ctee; Liveryman, The Worshipful Company of Glaziers. *Professional Organisations:* Law Society; FTII; MInstD. *Publications:* Chapter II of Organisation & Management of a Solicitors Practice, 1976. *Clubs:* MCC, Gresham. *Recreations:* Cricket, Gardening, Golf.

GOWARS, A J; Director, Edinburgh Fund Managers, since 1989; UK Investment. *Career:* EFM 1975-. *Biog: b.* 5 June 1955. *Nationality:* British. *m.* 1977, Lorna (née Cunningham); 1 s; 1 d. *Educ:* WAD Academy,

Anstruther. *Professional Organisations:* Society of Company and Commercial Accountants. *Recreations:* Golf, Football (Watching).

GOWER, G T; Partner, MacIntyre Hudson.

GOYDER, Daniel George; Legal Consultant, Birkett Westhorp & Long, since 1989; Competition Law. *Career:* Allen & Overy, Asst Solicitor 1964-67; Birketts, Ptnr 1968-83; Consultant 1983-89; Birkett Westhorp & Long, Consultant 1989-. *Biog: b.* 26 August 1938. *Nationality:* British. *m.* 1962, Jean Mary (née Dohoo); 2 s; 2 d. *Educ:* Rugby School; Trinity College, Cambridge (MA,LLB); Harvard Law School (LLM). *Directorships:* St Edmundsbury & Ipswich Diocesan Board of Finance 1977-85 (non-exec) Chm. *Other Activities:* University of Essex (Part-time Lecturer in Law); Commercial Law Ctee Assoc of British Chambers of Commerce (Former Member, 1976-80); Member, Monopolies & Mergers Commission 1980-. *Professional Organisations:* The Law Society. *Publications:* The Antitrust Laws of the USA, 1981; EEC Competition Law, 1988. *Clubs:* Ipswich & Suffolk. *Recreations:* Tennis, Choral Singing, Walking.

GRACE, Paul Henry; Executive Director & Actuary, Scottish Equitable Life Assurance Society, since 1987; Appointed Actuary. *Career:* Scottish Equitable, Actuarial Clerk 1960-65; Zurich Life Assurance Co, Actuary & Life Mgr 1965-80; Scottish Equitable, Actuary 1980-82; Asst Gen Mgr & Actuary 1983-84; Dep Chief Exec & Actuary 1985-. *Biog: b.* 25 September 1938. *Nationality:* British. *m.* 1963, Aileen (née Anderson); 1 d. *Educ:* Bedford Modern; St Andrews University (BSc). *Directorships:* Scottish Equitable Managed Fund Ltd 1983 (exec); SE Trustees Ltd 1983 (exec); SE Fund Managers Ltd 1983 (exec). *Other Activities:* Hon Publicity Officer, Faculty of Actuaries. *Professional Organisations:* FFA. *Publications:* Introduction to Life Assurance, 1987; Effect of Legislation on the investment Strategy of a UK Mutual Life Office (With D J Kirkpatrick), 1988. *Clubs:* East India. *Recreations:* Golf, Gardening.

GRACEY, Howard; Partner, R Watson & Sons, since 1970; Pension Fund Actuary. *Career:* Royal Insurance, Various 1953-69. *Biog: b.* 21 February 1935. *Nationality:* British. *m.* 1960, Pamela Jean (née Bradshaw); 1 s; 2 d. *Educ:* Birkenhead School. *Other Activities:* Church Commissioner (1978-); Member, General Synod of C of E (1970-); C of E Pensions Board (Chairman 1980-); Treasurer, South American Missionary Society. *Professional Organisations:* FIA; FIAA; FPMI; ASA; Past President, Pensions Management Institute (1983-85). *Clubs:* Army & Navy. *Recreations:* Fell-Walking, Photography, Sports.

GRADEL, D; Deputy Chairman, Schlesinger & Company Limited.

GRAFFTEY-SMITH, Jinx; European Representative/Manager Correspondent Banking, National Commercial Bank, since 1982; Correspondent Banking/Relations, Private Banking. *Career:* Samuel Montagu & Co 1958-65; Far East Rep 1963-65; Wallace Brothers, MD 1966-76; Allied Medical Group (Saudi Arabia), Resident Dir 1977-81; National Commercial Bank, European & UK Rep 1982-. *Biog: b.* 13 October 1934. *Nationality:* British. *m.* 1964, Lucy (née Fletcher); 2 s; 1 d. *Educ:* Winchester College; Magdalen College, Oxford (BA,MA). *Directorships:* Brendoncare Foundation 1987 Governor; SNCB Investments Ltd 1988 (exec); SNCB Nominees Ltd 1988 (exec); Saudi NCB Securities Ltd 1988 (exec). *Other Activities:* Exec Ctee Member, Saudi British Society; Intermiting Member, Lloyds of London. *Clubs:* City of London, Cavalry & Guards, Ashridge Golf Club. *Recreations:* Golf, Tennis, Shooting, Skiing, Cycling.

GRAFTON-GREEN, Paddy; Partner, Theodore Goddard; Media Law. *Career:* Theodore Goddard, Articled Clerk 1967-69; Admitted as Solicitor 1969; Partner, Advice on Media Law, in particular Copyright and the Taxation of Income and Gains Derived from the Worldwide Exploitation of Copyright 1973; Management Committee 1990. *Biog: b.* 30 March 1943. *Nationality:* British. *m.* 1982, Deborah Susan; 2 s; 2 d. *Educ:* Ampleforth College; Wadham College, Oxford (MA Jurisprudence). *Other Activities:* Law Society; City of London Solicitors. *Clubs:* MCC. *Recreations:* Cricket, Opera, Theatre.

GRAHAM, A M; Deputy Chairman, The Frizzell Group Limited.

GRAHAM, Alan Philip; Executive Director, N M Rothschild & Sons Limited, since 1988; Treasury Division. *Biog: b.* 4 December 1947. *Nationality:* British. *m.* 1974, Jennifer (née Phillips); 2 d. *Educ:* Orange Hill Grammar School. *Directorships:* N M Rothschild & Sons (CI) Ltd 1983 (non-exec); NMR Metals Inc, New York 1977-81 Chief Executive; N M Rothschild & Sons (CI) Ltd, Guernsey 1984-88 (exec) Banking Division. *Other Activities:* Freeman, City of London. *Professional Organisations:* Chartered Institute of Bankers. *Recreations:* Association Football, Theatre, Tennis, Music.

GRAHAM, Sir Alexander Michael; GBE; Lord Mayor, Corporation of London.

GRAHAM, B W C; Director, Holman Franklin Ltd.

GRAHAM, Bryan M; Partner, Moores Rowland.

GRAHAM, D R; Director, Lazard Investors Limited, since 1989; Responsible for Asia Pacific Business Activities. *Career:* Deloitte Haskins & Sells, Chartered Accountant; London 1977-82; Sydney, Audit Manager 1982-84; Lazard Investors, London, Investment Manager (Far East) 1984-87; Lazard Asia Asset Management Limited, Hong Kong, Director 1987-89; Lazard Japan Asset Management KK, Tokyo, President 1989-90. *Biog:* b. 13 December 1955. *Nationality:* British. *m.* 1981, Susan Camilla (née Peirse); 1 s; 2 d. *Educ:* Hurstpierpoint College, Sussex. *Directorships:* Lazard Investors 1989 (exec); Lazard Japan Asset Management KK, Tokyo 1989 (exec). *Professional Organisations:* Associate, Institute of Chartered Accountants.

GRAHAM, Dan W; Partner, Bristows Cooke & Carpmael, since 1971; Commercial Law, Competition Law (UK & EEC), Electrical & Mechanical Engineering Contracts. *Career:* Bristows Cooke & Carpmael, Articles 1965-67; Assistant Solicitor 1967-71; Partner 1971. *Biog:* b. 6 May 1942. *Nationality:* British. *m.* 1966, Jennifer Margaret (née Radley); 2 s; 1 d. *Educ:* Shrewsbury School; Gonville & Caius College, Cambridge (MA). *Other Activities:* Chairman, IMechE/IEE Model Forms Drafting Panel 1975-; Chairman, Holborn Law Society Business Law Section 1989-. *Professional Organisations:* Law Society; International Bar Association, Business Law Section (Committee Co-Anti Trust); Holborn Law Society. *Clubs:* Porters Park Golf Club, Radlett Cricket Club. *Recreations:* Golf, Gardening, Reading.

GRAHAM, George Ronald Gibson; CBE; Director, Scottish Widows' Fund & Life Assurance Society, since 1984.

GRAHAM, M J; Partner, Lawrence Graham.

GRAHAM, Robert T; Group Finance Director, Chancery plc, since 1990; Finance and Corporate Development. *Career:* Arthur Andersen & Co Chartered Accountants, Senior Manager 1978-87. *Biog:* b. 4 November 1956. *Nationality:* British. *m.* 1982, Sharon; 2 s. *Educ:* Haberdashers' Aske's School; Sheffield University (BA Hons Economics, Accounting and Financial Management). *Professional Organisations:* ACA. *Recreations:* Sport, Theatre, Family.

GRAHAM, Ronald; Partner, Alexander Tatham.

GRALL, Jean; Managing Director, Corporate Finance, Salomon Brothers Intl Ltd.

GRANDISON, R N S; Partner, Slaughter and May.

GRANGIÉ, François; Bureau Chief, Agence France-Presse (AFP), since 1987. *Career:* AFP (Singapore/Malaysia), Bureau Chief 1977-80; (Athens), Bureau Chief 1982-85; (Paris), Foreign Editor 1985-87. *Biog:* b. 17 May 1944. *m.* 1969, Elisabeth (née de Bascher); 1 s; 1 d. *Educ:* Lycee Gambetta, Cahors 46, France; Faculte de Droit, Paris; Institut d'Etudes Politiques, Paris (Dip). *Directorships:* AFP-Extel News Ltd 1990 (non-exec). *Professional Organisations:* Foreign Press Assoc (London).

GRANT, Charles Gamble; Solicitor, Cannons. *Career:* Clerk to the Worshipful Company of Pewterers 1967-78; Master, Cripplegate Ward Club 1977-78. *Biog:* b. 27 October 1932. *Nationality:* British. *m.* 1975, Diana (née Weston); 4 d. *Educ:* Harrow School; Oxford University (MA). *Directorships:* Association of British Pewter Craftsmen 1970 (non-exec); British Pewter Designs Ltd 1970 (non-exec). *Other Activities:* Member, Council of the City & Guilds of London Institute.

GRANT, Ian D; CBE; Partner, Ian Grant & Co; Chairman, Scottish Tourist Board, since 1990. *Career:* National Farmers Union of Scotland, Vice President 1981-84; International Federation of Agricultural Producers, Grains Committee, Chairman 1984-90; National Farmers Union of Scotland, President 1984-90. *Biog:* b. 28 July 1943. *Nationality:* British. *m.* 1968, Eileen M L (née Yule); 3 d. *Educ:* Strathallan School; East of Scotland College of Agriculture. *Directorships:* Scottish Tourist Board 1988 (non-exec) Board Member; 1990 (non-exec) Chairman; Clydesdale Bank plc 1989 (non-exec); NFU Mutual Insurance Society Ltd 1990 (non-exec); East of Scotland Farmers Ltd 1978 (non-exec); 1985 (non-exec) Vice Chairman. *Other Activities:* Council Member, Royal Smithfield Club. *Professional Organisations:* Fellow, The Royal Agricultural Societies (FRAgS). *Recreations:* Swimming, Shooting, Travel, Reading, Music.

GRANT, Ian F H; Director, The Royal Bank of Scotland plc.

GRANT, K N; Secretary, Commercial Union plc.

GRANT, Newton Keene; OBE, JP; Senior Partner, Pridie Brewster, Chartered Accountants, since 1983. *Career:* Scurr & Gilroy, Chartered Accountants, Alton, Hants 1948-55; Royal Army Pay Corps 1955-57; Tansley Witt & Co, Chartered Accountants, London 1957-60. *Biog:* b. 25 June 1931. *Nationality:* French. *m.* 1958, Mary Elizabeth (née Romagny); 3 d. *Educ:* Eggar's Grammar School, Alton, Hants. *Directorships:* Cornish Candy (Export) Limited 1989 (non-exec); Max Recoveries Limited 1989 (non-exec). *Other Activities:* Chairman, Hearing Aid Council 1984-; Council Member, Chartered Association of Certified Accountants (President 1983-84); Master, The Worshipful of Company of Horners 1990-91. *Professional Organisations:* FCA; FCCA; FCIArB. *Clubs:* City Livery Club, Savage Club. *Recreations:* Music, Cooking, Collecting Silver.

GRANT, Nicholas Airth; Chairman & Managing Director, Duncan Lawrie Limited.

GRANT, Peter James; Chairman, Sun Life Assurance Society plc, since 1983. *Career:* Edward de Stein & Co, Assistant to the Partners in Charge of Investment Management 1952-60; Edward de Stein & Co, merged with Lazard Brothers 1961; Anglo-Australian Corporation, Melbourne Seconded 1962; Lazard Brothers (London), Corporate Finance and Merger Department 1963; Executive Director 1968; Sun Life Assurance Society Limited, Director 1973; Vice-Chairman 1976; Deputy Chairman 1982. *Biog: b.* 5 December 1929. *Nationality:* British. *m.* 1964, Paula (née Eugster); 2 s; 3 d. *Educ:* Winchester College; Magdalen College, Oxford. *Directorships:* Sun Life Corporation plc 1986 (exec) Chairman; Sun Life Assurance Society plc (exec) Chairman; London Merchant Securities plc 1984 (nonexec); LEP Group plc 1988 (non-exec) Deputy Chairman; Scottish-Hydro Electric plc 1990 (non-exec); UAP International SA 1988 (non-exec); Lazard Brothers & Co Limited 1983-88 (exec) Deputy Chairman. *Other Activities:* Member, Council of Institute of Directors; Member, Industrial Development Advisory Board (DTI). *Clubs:* Boodles, Caledonian. *Recreations:* Fishing, Shooting, Golf.

GRANT, Robin William; Director, Charterhouse Bank Limited, since 1984; Corporate Finance. *Career:* Baring Brothers & Co, Corporate Finance Executive 1966-71; Williams Glyn & Co, Corporate Finance Director 1971-75; De Zoete & Bevan, Equity Salesman 1975-77; Charterhouse Bank, Corporate Finance 1977-. *Biog: b.* 14 May 1938. *Nationality:* British. *m.* 1968, Hilary (née Hamley); 1 s; 1 d. *Educ:* Rugby; Oxford (MA Hons). *Directorships:* Charterhouse Bank 1984 (exec). *Professional Organisations:* Chartered Accountant. *Clubs:* Denham Golf Club. *Recreations:* Golf, Music, Skiing, Travel.

GRANT, William; Partner, Linklaters & Paines, since 1970; Commercial Property. *Biog: b.* 27 March 1938. *Nationality:* British. *m.* 1961, Jane M (née Moon); 3 d. *Educ:* Wellington College; Selwyn College, Cambridge (MA). *Other Activities:* Court Member, The Worshipful Company of Pewterers; The Worshipful Company of Solicitors. *Professional Organisations:* Member, The Law Society.

GRANT HALL, C; Managing Director (Investment Management), N T Butterfield & Son (Bermuda) Ltd.

GRANT-PETERKIN, Mrs T J (née Baynes); Partner, Withers, since 1986; Commercial Property. *Career:* William Charles Crocker, Articled Clerk 1971-76; Linklaters & Paines, Assistant Solicitor Commercial Property 1976-83; Watson Farley & Williams, Set Up Property Department 1983-86; Withers, Commercial Property Partner 1986-. *Biog: b.* 11 October 1949. *Nationality:* British. *m.* 1977, Keith; 2 s. *Educ:* St Leonards-Mayfield School; The College of Law. *Directorships:* Norland Nursery Training College 1981 (nonexec); Association of Women Solicitors 1985-87 Chairman; St Leonards-Mayfield School 1990 Governor. *Other Activities:* Member, Women Careers Working Party, The Law Society; Member, Association of Women Solicitors; Member, Middle East Association. *Profes-*

sional Organisations: Member, The Law Society; Member, Society of Construction Law. *Clubs:* Lansdowne. *Recreations:* Tennis, Walking, Bicycling.

GRANTHAM, R J; Director, County NatWest Woodmac, since 1986; Convertibles & Warrants. *Career:* Spillers, Management Trainee 1968-71; Sternberg Thomas Clarke & Co, Analyst 1972-77; Phillips & Drew, Manager, Fixed Interest & Money Market Services Dept 1977-86; County NatWest (also County NatWest Woodmac), Director 1986-. *Biog: b.* 20 September 1947. *Nationality:* British. 1985, Cecilia; 1 d; 1 steps; 2 stepd. *Educ:* Stowe School; Wolverhampton Poly (BA Business Studies). *Directorships:* County NatWest (previously County Group) 1986 (exec); County NatWest Woodmac (previously County Securities) 1986 (exec). *Professional Organisations:* Member, International Stock Exchange (1986).

GRANVIK, Carl-Johan; General Manager, Union Bank of Finland, London Branch, since 1989. *Career:* Union Bank of Finland International SA, Luxembourg, Managing Director 1987-89; Union Bank of Finland Ltd, Helsinki, Assistant General Manager, Capital Markets 1985-87; UBF Group, Various Positions 1974-85.

GRANVILLE, B C F; Director, Robert Fleming Insurance Brokers Limited.

GRASSICK, W P C; Non Executive Director, George Wimpey plc.

GRAVES, Dr D J T; Non Executive Director, George Wimpey plc.

GRAVES, Rodney Michael; National Director, Corporate Financial Services, BDO Binder Hamlyn, since 1985; Mergers & Acquisitions, MBO's, General Financial Advice. *Career:* Cooper Brothers & Co, Chartered Accountants 1963-69; BDO Binder Hamlyn, Chartered Accountants 1969-. *Biog: b.* 13 January 1941. *Nationality:* English. *Educ:* Downside School; Pembroke College (MA). *Other Activities:* Management Committee, The Downside Settlement. *Professional Organisations:* Institute of Chartered Accountants. *Clubs:* The Hawks' Club (Cambridge), The Lansdowne Club.

GRAVETT, M A; Underwriting Director, Gravett & Tilling (Underwriting Agencies) Ltd.

GRAY, B S; Head of Operational Audit Group, County NatWest, since 1988. *Career:* National Westminster Bank plc, Assistant Administration Manager (SE Region) 1969-73; Branch Managements 1973-80; Senior Inspector 1980-86; Senior Manager, International Audit 1980-88. *Biog: b.* 14 September 1933. *Nationality:* British. *m.* 1956, Grace (née Smart); 1 s; 2 d. *Educ:* Haberdasher Askes, Hatcham. *Directorships:* County

NatWest 1988 (exec). *Professional Organisations:* ACIB. *Recreations:* Bridge, Photography, Church Organist.

GRAY, David; Partner, Hepworth & Chadwick.

GRAY, David Francis; Partner, Lovell White Durrant, since 1966; Corporate Finance. *Career:* Clifford Chance, Articled Clerk 1957-60; Solicitor 1960-62; Bischoff & Co, Solicitor 1962-63; Lovell White & King, Solicitor 1963-65; Partner 1965-88; Lovell White Durrant, Partner 1988-. *Biog: b.* 18 May 1936. *Nationality:* British. *m.* 1970, Rosemary Alison Elizabeth (née Parker); 2 s; 1 d. *Educ:* Rugby School; Trinity College, Oxford (MA). *Directorships:* SHV (United Kingdom) Holding Company Ltd 1970-90 (non-exec); Bilton Grange Trust Limited 1973 (non-exec). *Other Activities:* City of London Solicitors' Company (Master 1984-85, Almoner 1988-); Liveryman, Glaziers' Company; Joint Honorary Secretary, Trinity College, Oxford Society 1979-88, Trustee 1988-. *Professional Organisations:* City of London Law Society (VP, Chm of Ctee 1985-88); Law Society, Honorary Auditor 1988-90; International Bar Association, Assistant Treasurer 1988-; Trustee, Educational Trust 1987-. *Clubs:* Ski Club of Great Britain, Liphook Golf Club. *Recreations:* Skiing, Golf, Tennis, Swimming.

GRAY, Geoffrey George; Managing Director, TSB Trust Company, since 1989; Unit Trusts & Offshore Funds. *Career:* International Life/Cannon Assurance, Snr Underwriter 1970-78; TSB Trust Co, Mgr, Life Administration 1978-81; Unit Trust Administration, Mgr 1981-82; Head of Unit Trust Mktg 1982-85; Div Mgr; Mktg Planning 1985-86; Offshore Business, Div Mgr 1986-88. *Biog: b.* 24 November 1950. *Nationality:* British. *m.* 1987, Rosalind (née Evitts); 2 s. *Educ:* Wellingborough Grammar School. *Directorships:* TSB Offshore Investment Fund Ltd 1987 (exec); TSB Gilt Fund Ltd 1987 (exec); TSB Gilt Fund (Jersey) Ltd 1987 (exec); TSB Unit Trust Managers (CI) Ltd 1987 (exec); TSB Fund Managers (CI) Ltd 1987 (exec); TSB Unit Trusts Ltd 1989 (exec). *Other Activities:* UTA External Relations Committee. *Clubs:* Abbotts Ann CC.

GRAY, J M; Non-Executive Director, James Capel & Co Ltd.

GRAY, John; Fixed Interest Manager, Crown Financial Management Limited.

GRAY, Leslie James; General Manager, The Scottish Mutual Assurance Society, since 1990; Corporate Services. *Career:* The Scottish Mutual Assurance Society 1966-; Assistant Pensions Secretary 1973; Data Processing Controller 1977; Joint Pensions Secretary 1980; Product Development Manager 1983; Actuarial Manager 1987.; The Scottish Mutual Assurance Society, General Manager, Corporate Services 1990. *Biog: b.* 20 August 1949. *Nationality:* Scottish. *m.* 1973, Grace; 1 d. *Educ:*

Eastbank Academy. *Other Activities:* Fellow, Society of Antiquaries (Scotland); Secretary, Glasgow Archaeological Society. *Professional Organisations:* FIA. *Publications:* Co-Author, Product Pricing in Life Assurance. *Recreations:* Archaeology, Hill Walking, Jazz.

GRAY, M C; Director, Finance Department, Hill Samuel Bank Limited, since 1990. *Career:* Hill Samuel & Co Limited, Assistant Director 1970-87; Daiwa Europe Bank plc, Associate Director 1987-89; Hill Samuel Bank Limited, Assistant Director 1989-90. *Biog: b.* 5 October 1951. *Nationality:* British. *m.* 1973, Marilyn; 2 d. *Directorships:* Hill Samuel Bank Limited 1990 (exec).

GRAY, P; Partner, Linklaters & Paines, since 1989. *Career:* Clayton & Co, Articled Clerk/Assistant Solicitor 1975-78; Resident Magistrate, Kenya 1978-80; Senior State Counsel, Attorney-General's Chambers, Kenya 1980-84; Linklaters & Paines, Assistant Solicitor 1984-89. *Biog: b.* 20 May 1952. *Nationality:* British. *m.* 1982, Wendy Jane (née Seale); 2 s. *Educ:* St Albans School, Victoria; University of Manchester (LLB). *Other Activities:* Freeman, City of London Solicitors Company; Member, Institute of Petroleum. *Professional Organisations:* Law Society. *Clubs:* Royal Commonwealth Society. *Recreations:* Windsurfing, Sailing, Squash.

GRAY, Richard William; Director & Financial Controller, Sphere Drake Underwriting Management Limited, since 1984; Financial & Technical Accounts. *Career:* Peat Marwick Mitchell, Articled Clerk 1965-68; Sterling Winthrop Group Ltd, Management Accountant 1968-70; Abbey Life Assurance Co Ltd, Assistant Controller 1970-75; Hartford Europe Ltd, Management Accountant 1975-76; Excess Insurance Group Ltd, Deputy Controller 1976-84; Sphere Drake Underwriting Management Ltd, Director & Technical Controller Financial Accounts 1984-. *Biog: b.* 14 September 1943. *Nationality:* British. *m.* 1966, Wendy; 2 d. *Educ:* Sheffield University (BA Economics). *Directorships:* Arpel Trimark Underwriting Agencies Limited 1984; Churcher & Company Limited 1985; Sphere Drake Nominees Limited 1987; Groves, John & Westrup (Underwriting) Limited 1984; Sphere Drake Insurance plc 1984; The Drake Insurance Company Limited 1984; The Sterling Insurance Company Limited 1984; Sphere Drake Insurance Group plc 1984; Sphere Drake Leasing Limited 1985; Sphere Drake Underwriting (Australia) Limited. *Professional Organisations:* Fellow, Institute of Chartered Accountants.

GRAY, Tony; Deputy Editor/News Editor, Lloyd's List.

GRAYBURN, Jeremy Ward; Sales Development Director, Allied Dunbar Assurance plc, since 1989; Product Development, Promotion, Support, Sales Training and Development. *Career:* Allied Dunbar Assurance, Quotes Clerk to Exec Dir 1971-. *Biog: b.* 24 August

1952. *Nationality:* British. *m.* 1975, Pamela Anne (née Ross); 2 d. *Educ:* Lancaster Royal Grammar School. *Recreations:* Travel, Music, Bridge.

GRAYSON, R C; Company Secretary, The British Petroleum Company plc.

GREAVES, Adam; Partner, Gouldens.

GREAYER, Anthony B; Chief Executive, CCF Holdings Ltd, since 1990. *Career:* Grindlays Bank Group 1967-82; Wm Brandts, US Representative; Grindlay Brandts, Director & Head of Eurocurrency Lending; Regional Director, Pacific Basin, Grindlays Group & Director, Dao Heng Bank; Head of Merchant Banking; Goare Govett 1983-88; Head of International; Head of Strategic Planning; Deputy Chief Executive; Chief Excutive; MHHG Ltd, Director 1986-88. *Biog: b.* 27 September 1943. *Nationality:* British. *m.* 1972, Maureen Jennifer (née Bohn); 1 s; 2 d. *Educ:* Edinburgh University (MA Hons Political Economy). *Directorships:* Hoenig & Company Limited 1988 (non-exec) Chm; Credit Commercial de France (UK) Ltd 1990 Chm; CCF Foster Braithwaite Ltd 1990 Chm; Framlington Group plc 1990 (non-exec); CCF Holdings Ltd 1990 Chief Exec. *Publications:* A Guide to the Eurocurrency Market, 1974. *Recreations:* Horse Racing.

GREEN, B C; Director, E D & F Man Ltd.

GREEN, C R; Director, Knight & Day Ltd.

GREEN, C R; Director, USA, Denis M Clayton & Co Limited.

GREEN, Christopher John Britnell; Chairman & Chief Executive, Cerro Metals (UK) Ltd.

GREEN, Darryl; Head of Fixed Income Trading and Sales, Paribas Limited.

GREEN, David Anthony; Financial Director, Taylor Woodrow plc, since 1988. *Career:* Arthur Andersen, Auditor 1964-69; Dan-Air (Spain), Fin Controller 1970-72; Morton International Inc, Intl Fin Dir 1972-77; Navistar, Fin Mgr, Europe, Africa, Mid East 1978-82; Dir of Fin 1982-85. *Biog: b.* 15 August 1943. *Nationality:* British. *m.* 1972, Alice D (née Zawilenski); 2 d. *Educ:* Collyers Grammar School; LSE (BSc). *Directorships:* Taylor Woodrow plc 1985; Taylor Woodrow Services Ltd 1985-86; 1986-89 Chm; TW Investments Inc 1986; TW International BV 1986; Taylor Woodrow plc 1988 Fin Dir. *Professional Organisations:* FCA. *Recreations:* Gardening, Languages, Travel.

GREEN, David W; Head of North American & Japanese Division, Bank of England, since 1990; Advice on the North American & Japanese Economies and Financial Systems. *Career:* Bank of England, Overseas Department 1968-74; IMF, Washington, Personal Assistant to the Managing Director 1974-77; Bank of England, Economic Intelligence Department, Assistant Adviser, Balance of Payments 1977-78; Assistant Adviser, Domestic Financial Forecasting 1978-80; International Division, Assistant Adviser, Intl Financial Mkts 1980-83; Adviser, North American Affairs 1983-85; Adviser, North American & Japanese Affairs 1985-90. *Biog: b.* 8 June 1946. *Nationality:* British. *Educ:* Watford Grammar School; Corpus Christi College, Cambridge (Classical Tripos, MA 1st Class); University College of North Wales, Bangor (Financial Economics, MSc). *Professional Organisations:* Licentiate, Royal Academy of Music. *Publications:* Canadian Financial System 1965; Competition and Structural Change, 1974. *Recreations:* Chamber Music Performance (Piano & Harpsichord), Travel, Architecture, Opera, Walking.

GREEN, G H; Chief Dealer, Banca Popolare di Milano.

GREEN, Geoffrey Stephen; Partner, Ashurst Morris Crisp, since 1979; Corporate Finance. *Career:* Ashurst Morris Crisp, Articled Clerk/Asst Solicitor/Ptnr 1973-. *Biog: b.* 3 September 1949. *Nationality:* British. *m.* 1982, Sarah Charlton (née Chesshire); 3 s. *Educ:* Forest; St Catharine's College, Cambridge (MA). *Publications:* Various Articles. *Clubs:* Hurlingham. *Recreations:* Tennis, Cricket.

GREEN, Lieutenant Colonel Ian Rowland Paul; Clerk, Worshipful Company of Fan Makers, since 1986; Administration. *Career:* National Service, Commissioned in East Surrey Regt, served in West Africa 1951-53; Subsequently TA & Cadets 1956-85; Schoolmaster 1956-85; Headmaster, Warminster School 1971-78; Headmaster, Read School, Drax, N Yorks 1979-85; Universities Settlement in East London, Deputy Warden 1985-89; Care Trust, General Manager 1989-. *Biog: b.* 20 February 1933. *Nationality:* British. m1 1959, Joyce (née Russell) (Diss); m2 1979, Elizabeth (née Stovold); 2 s; 3 d. *Educ:* Westminster City School; Magdalene College, Cambridge (MA). *Other Activities:* Tower Hamlets District Scout Committee. *Publications:* Practical Literary Criticism, 1966. *Clubs:* Oxford & Cambridge, Bishopsgate Ward Club.

GREEN, Kenneth Charles; General Manager, Financial Services, Clydesdale bank plc.

GREEN, Kenneth David; Director, Barclays de Zoete Wedd Holdings Ltd, since 1986; Fixed Income/Capital Markets. *Career:* Bank of America, Senior Vice President, Corporate Banking - Midwest USA 1968-77; Bank of America International Ltd, MD/CEO, Investment Banking Activities for Bank America Gp in Europe & Middle East 1978-86. *Biog: b.* 11 April 1944. *Nationality:* American. *m.* 1969, Anne; 1 s; 1 d. *Educ:* UCLA (AB, MBA). *Directorships:* BZW Holdings Ltd 1986 (exec);

BZW Ltd 1986 MD; BZW Securities Ltd 1988 (exec); BZW Securities Inc 1987 (non-exec); Bank of America International Ltd 1978-86 MD. *Professional Organisations:* International Stock Exchange; The Securities Association. *Clubs:* Annabels, St George's Lawn Tennis Club.

GREEN, L Barrie; Director, Newton Investment Management Ltd, since 1986; Director in Charge of Investment Dealing. *Career:* Wise Speke and Company (Newcastle), Dealer 1961-72; Britannia Group of Unit Trusts, Dealer 1972-78; Newton Investment Management, Dealing Director 1978-. *Biog: b.* 16 July 1943. *Nationality:* British. *m.* 1970, Norma; 1 s; 3 d. *Educ:* Middle Street Commercial School, Newcastle upon Tyne. *Directorships:* Newton Investment Management Ltd 1986 (exec).

GREEN, Michael James Bay; Director, Hill Samuel Bank Ltd, since 1988; Head of Corporate Finance. *Career:* Peat Marwick Mitchell & Co, Articled Clerk 1960-65; G W Green & Sons, Mgr 1965-71; Kleinwort Benson Ltd 1971-88; Kleinwort Benson (Australia) Ltd, Chm & MD 1981-84. *Biog: b.* 4 June 1943. *Nationality:* British. *m.* 1971, Ann Eila (née Elliott); 1 s; 1 d. *Educ:* Harrow School. *Professional Organisations:* FCA.

GREEN, Sir Owen; Chairman, BTR plc.

GREEN, P D; Director, Charterhouse Bank Limited.

GREEN, Peter J; Head of Treasury, Leeds Permanent Building Society.

GREEN, Peter Robert; Finance Director, Charterhouse Tilney, since 1986. *Career:* Touche Ross & Co, Trainee Acct 1975-79; S A Morris, Chartered Acct 1979-81; Fred S James (New York), Account Exec 1981-84; Tilney & Co, Fin Controller 1984-. *Biog: b.* 15 March 1954. *m.* 1977, Susan (née Fullelove); 2 s. *Educ:* Baines Grammar School, Poulton-le-Fylde; Bedford College, London (BSc Hons). *Professional Organisations:* ICA.

GREEN, R W F; Director, James Capel Corporate Finance Ltd.

GREEN, Richard; Partner, Morison Stoneham, since 1969; Private Clients. *Biog: b.* 1938. *Nationality:* British. *m.* 1973, Margaret; 3 s. *Educ:* Bancrofts School; Bristol University (FCA). *Professional Organisations:* Chartered Accountant. *Recreations:* Bridge.

GREEN, Robert Frank; Director, Phillips & Drew Fund Management Ltd; Pensions & Other Funds Management. *Career:* IBM (UK) Ltd Data Processing Salesman 1965-66; Centre File Ltd Liaison Analyst Computer Bureau 1966-67; Phillips & Drew (subsequently PDFM) Fund Manager 1968-. *Biog: b.* 6 May 1944. *Nationality:* British. *m.* 1969, Audrey. *Educ:* St

Clement Danes Grammar School; City of London College (BSc Hons). *Professional Organisations:* AMSIA. *Recreations:* Swimming, Eating Out, Old Cars.

GREEN, T G; Chairman and Underwriter, Gresham Underwriting Agencies Limited.

GREEN-ARMYTAGE, John; Joint Chairman, Kelt Energy plc, since 1990. *Career:* The Guthrie Corporation plc, Managing Director 1982-88; N M Rothschild & Sons Limited, Executive Director 1977-82; Executive 1970-77. *Biog: b.* 6 June 1945. *Nationality:* Canadian. *m.* Susan (née Le Messurier); 1 s; 3 d. *Educ:* McGill University, Montreal (BA); Columbia University, New York (MBA). *Directorships:* N M Rothschild & Sons Ltd 1988 (non-exec); English & Scottish Investors plc 1988 (non-exec); International Investment Trust of Jersey Ltd 1988 (non-exec); Rowe Evans Investments plc 1988 (non-exec); Mezzanine Capital & Income Trust 2001 plc 1986 Chairman; REA Holdings plc 1984 (non-exec); Norweb plc 1990 (non-exec).

GREEN LAURIDSEN, P; Executive Director, Unibank plc.

GREENBOROUGH, Sir John; Director, Hogg Group plc.

GREENBURY, Toby Jonathan; Partner, D J Freeman & Co, since 1980; Company and Commercial, International. *Career:* Stephenson Harwood, Articled Clerk 1974-76; Asst Solicitor 1976-79; Lord, Day & Lord Associate 1976-77; D J Freeman & Co, Asst Solicitor 1979-80. *Biog: b.* 18 September 1951. *Educ:* Clifton College, Bristol; University College, London (LLB). *Other Activities:* City of London Solicitors' Company (Editor of Newsletter). *Professional Organisations:* New York Bar (1978); The Law Society of England & Wales, City of London; Law Society (Chm of Whittington Ctee). *Clubs:* RAC. *Recreations:* Gardening, Sport, Singing, Opera, Polo.

GREENE, Christopher; Partner, Clark Whitehill.

GREENE, Oliver Raymond; UK Corporate Finance Head, Chase Investment Bank Limited, since 1988; Corporate Finance. *Career:* Citibank NA, Various Appointments in Citibank, Citi Corp International Bank Ltd and Citi Corp Leasing International, Latterly Vice President World Corporate Group 1966-80; Bankers Trust Company, Managing Director, Corporate Finance 1980-88. *Biog: b.* 19 July 1943. *Nationality:* British/American. *m.* 1975, Elizabeth (née Yates); 2 s; 1 d. *Educ:* Westminster School; Oxford University (MA, PPE). *Directorships:* Graham Greene Productions Ltd; Chase Investment Bank Ltd. *Professional Organisations:* American Bankers Asociation. *Recreations:* Opera, Shooting, Tennis, 20th Century First Editions.

GREENE, Stephen; Managing Partner, Stoy Hayward.

GREENFIELD, George Nigel Ian; Partner, Hammond Suddards, since 1986; Company and Commercial Law. *Career:* Coward Chance, Articled Clerk/ Solicitor 1976-80; Brooke North & Goodwin, Solicitor 1980-84; A V Hammond & Co, Solicitor 1984-86. *Biog: b.* 5 November 1953. *m.* 1979, Pauline Linda (née Adams); 1 s; 1 d. *Educ:* Hymers College, Hull; Emmanuel College, Cambridge (MA). *Professional Organisations:* The Law Society. *Clubs:* Bradford, Northcliff Golf Club. *Recreations:* Rugby Union, Golf.

GREENHALGH, David Anthony; Head of Tax Dept, Linklaters & Paines, since1989; Corporate Tax. *Career:* March Pearson & Skelton, Manchester, Articles qualified 1968; Linklaters & Paines, Articles qualified 1969; Linklaters & Paines, Partner 1974. *Biog: b.* 4 December 1943. *Nationality:* British. *m.* 1980, Jill Marian. *Educ:* Sedbergh School. *Other Activities:* Member of Revenue Law Sub Committee, City of London Law Society. *Clubs:* St George's Hill & West Sussex Golf Clubs.

GREENHORN, A S; Director, Hill Samuel Investment Management Ltd.

GREENLEES, Loudon Ian; Finance Director, Baring Asset Management Ltd, since 1989. *Career:* Whinney Murray & Co 1971-75; Jardine Matheson & Co Ltd, Hong Kong 1975-86; Various to Director JM (South East Asia) 1984-85; Baring International Investment Management Ltd, Finance Director 1986-89. *Biog: b.* 14 October 1951. *Nationality:* British. *m.* 1990, Sally Helen (née Villar). *Educ:* Harrow School. *Professional Organisations:* FCA. *Recreations:* Cricket, Golf.

GREENSLADE, P J; Director, International Equities, Fuji Bank, since 1987; Fund Management, Covering UK, Europe, USA, etc, in International Equities & Derivatives. *Career:* British Aerospace, Training as Aerospace Engineer/Engineer 1957-64; Turner Charles Consultants (UK & USA), Senior Project Engineer, Aerospace 1964-70; Western American Bank, Lending Officer, Credit Analyst (Risk Management) 1971-73; Merrill Lynch (UK & Switzerland), Manager European/ UK Equities (Research/Marketing Fund Management) 1973-78; Grieveson Grant/Vickers Da Costa, Account Exec, Research, Fund Mgmt 1978-81; Lloyds Group, Manager Technologies Funds (USA, Europe) Incl Offshore Oil Project Management 1981-84; Quilter Goodison/Paribas, Manager European Equities (Research Marketing) 1984-87. *Biog: b.* 16 April 1941. *Nationality:* British. *m.* 1964, Karen F; 1 s; 1 d. *Educ:* Brooklands College; Kingston Polytechnic (Degree in Mechanical/Aero Engineering, Masters in Business, Management Administration); Washington University, Engineering Courses; London Business School, Courses in Finance. *Other Activities:* Local Institution of Management Chapter. *Professional Organisations:* Stock Exchange; Society of Investment Analysts, Director, 1988-89; Member, 1975-; British Institute of Management; Institution of Mechanical Engineers/ Chartered Engineers. *Publications:* Thesis, Investment Analysis and Management Efficiency; Various Papers in Response to Society of Investment Analysts Affairs. *Recreations:* Most Sports, Including Skiing, Music (Piano-Organ), House, Garden, Travel, Architecture, Conservatory & Plants.

GREENSMITH, Nicholas Ian; Partner, Clyde & Co, since 1984; Shipping Law. *Career:* Titmuss, Sainer & Webb, Articled Clerk 1978-80; Clyde & Co, Assistant Solicitor 1980-84. *Biog: b.* 3 March 1955. *Nationality:* British. *m.* 1984, Sally Jane (née Mills); 2 s; 1 d. *Educ:* William Hulme's Grammar School, Manchester; St Catharine's College, Cambridge University (MA). *Professional Organisations:* Law Society. *Clubs:* Hawks Club, Milford & Godalming Squash Club, London Marine Claims Golf Society. *Recreations:* Sailing, Squash, Golf.

GREENTREE, William Wayne Chris; Chief Executive, LASMO plc, since 1982; Managing the Group. *Career:* Shell Canada, Technical & Managerial Appointments Onshore & Offshire 1957-72; Ranger Oil (UK) Ltd, Managerial 1972-79; Managing Director 1976; Mapco Inc USA, Senior Vice President, Exploration & Production 1979-82. *Biog: b.* 6 April 1935. *Nationality:* Canadian. *m.* (div); 5 d (1 decd). *Educ:* University of Alberta (BSc Electrical Engineering). *Directorships:* LASMO plc Subsidiaries. *Other Activities:* Ordre National du Mérite, Gabon 1987. *Professional Organisations:* Fellow, Institute of Petroleum, London; Association of Professional Engineers of Alberta. *Clubs:* Petroleum (USA). *Recreations:* Golf, Skiing, Fishing.

GREENWOOD, Jeffrey Michael; Senior Partner, Nabarro Nathanson, since 1987; Property Law. *Career:* Nabarro Nathanson Head, Property Law Dept 1975-87. *Biog: b.* 21 April 1935. *Nationality:* British. *m.* 1964, Naomi (née Grahame); 3 s; 1 d. *Educ:* Raine's Foundation; Downing College, Cambridge (MA); LSE (LLB). *Directorships:* Bank Leumi (UK) plc 1988 (non-exec). *Other Activities:* Chm, Jewish Welfare Board, 1985-89; Chm, Jewish Care, 1990; Member, Hampstead Garden Suburb Trust Council, 1983-86; Worshipful Company of Glovers. *Professional Organisations:* Member, The Law Society. *Publications:* Numerous Articles on Legal Matters. *Clubs:* RAC. *Recreations:* Running, Skiing, Swimming, Literature, Theatre, Music.

GREENWOOD, Martin David; Trade Finance Manager, Banco Santander, since 1989; All Aspects International Trade. *Career:* Creditanstalt Bankverein, Manager, Trade Finance 1984-89; Deutsche Bank, London, Assistant Credit Manager 1978-84; Lloyds Bank 1967-78. *Biog: b.* 1950. *Nationality:* British. *m.* 1973, Enid; 1 s;

1 d. *Educ:* City of Oxford High School. *Professional Organisations:* Chartered Institute of Bankers, ACIB. *Recreations:* Sailing, Gardening, Walking.

GREENWOOD, Peter; Director (Market-Making), Hoare Govett International Securities.

GREENWOOD, Robin Erskine; Director, James Capel Corporate Finance Ltd; Corporate Finance. *Career:* Peat Marwick Mitchell & Co 1975-79; James Capel & Co 1979-. *Biog: b.* 27 May 1953. *Nationality:* British. *Educ:* Eton College; Selwyn College, Cambridge (MA). *Other Activities:* Trustee of Trinity Foot Beagles. *Professional Organisations:* FCA; Member, The International Stock Exchange. *Clubs:* Travellers'. *Recreations:* Fishing and Other Field Sports.

GREGG, W S; Partner, Milne Ross.

GREGORY, A A; Executive Director, Willis Corroon plc.

GREGORY, A R; Joint Managing Director, Kleinwort Benson Unit Trusts Limited.

GREGORY, A T; Non-Executive Director, Willis Corroon plc.

GREGORY, Brian Frederick; Director, Barclays de Zoete Wedd Securities Ltd, since 1986; Head of Sales Trading UK Equities. *Career:* de Zoete & Garton Trainee, Dealer 1956-70; de Zoete & Bevan Dealer 1970-76; Ptnr 1976-86; Dealing Ptnr 1981-86. *Biog: b.* 1 June 1938. *Nationality:* British. *m.* 1963, Maureen (née Rawlinson); 5 s. *Educ:* Hertford Grammar School. *Clubs:* Gresham, MCC.

GREGORY, J F; Director, Beeson Gregory Ltd, since 1989; Corporate Finance. *Career:* ANZ McCaughan Securities (Formerly Capel-Cure Myers) 1950-89; Beeson Gregory Ltd 1989-. *Biog: b.* 7 April 1935. *Nationality:* British. *m.* 1956, Ethel Currie (née Burns); 1 s; 2 d. *Educ:* Ashburton High. *Directorships:* Cussins Property Group plc 1984 (non-exec). *Clubs:* Gresham, Mosimanns. *Recreations:* Music, Fell Walking, Painting, All Sport.

GREGORY, Keith; Partner, Cameron Markby Hewitt, since 1989; Corporate Taxation. *Career:* Coward Chance, Articled Clerk 1977-80; Assistant Solicitor 1980-87; Clifford Chance, Assistant Solicitor 1987-89. *Biog: b.* 28 August 1953. *Nationality:* English. *m.* 1988, Lynn (née Clarke); 1 d. *Educ:* Hitchin Grammar School; Oriel College, Oxford (BA Hons, MA). *Other Activities:* City of London Solicitors' Company. *Professional Organisations:* Law Society. *Recreations:* History, Golf.

GREGORY, Mrs Lesley A; Partner, Memery Crystal, since 1987; Company/Commercial Law. *Career:*

Memery Crystal, Solicitor 1983; Partner 1987-. *Biog: b.* 7 January 1960. *Nationality:* British. *m.* 1990, Lyndon Morris (née Gregory). *Educ:* Charlton Park School, Cheltenham; Somerville College, Oxford (BA Hons IIi); Chester College of Law (Solicitors' Professional Qualification). *Professional Organisations:* Member, Law Society. *Clubs:* Hampstead Cricket Club, Vanderbilt Raquet Club. *Recreations:* Swimming, Tennis, Golf, Opera, Ballet.

GREGORY, Dr Paul Duncan; Director, County Natwest Securities Limited, since 1989; Business Consultancy (Oil). *Career:* Wood Mackenzie & Co Ltd, Oil Analyst 1981-87; County Natwest Securities Limited, Oil Analyst 1988-89. *Biog: b.* 1 December 1954. *Nationality:* British. *m.* 1978, Catherine; 1 s; 1 d. *Educ:* Edinburgh University, (BCom Hons); Edinburgh University, (PhD). *Professional Organisations:* Member, Institute of Petroleum. *Publications:* Factors Influencing The Export Performance of the Scottish Manufacturing Sector of the Offshore Supplies Industry; World Offshore Markets: Can Britain Compete?; Oils - A Volatile Sector. *Recreations:* Sports, Principally Golf and Squash.

GREGORY-JONES, Anne; Partner, Clark Whitehill.

GREGSON, Charles; Deputy Managing Director, MAI plc.

GREGSON, Miss Helen Margaret; Salaried Partner, Bacon & Woodrow, Actuaries and Consultants, since 1990; Pensions Consultancy. *Career:* Bacon & Woodrow 1984-. *Biog: b.* 6 March 1963. *Nationality:* British. *Educ:* Keble College, Oxford (BA, MA). *Professional Organisations:* FIA. *Recreations:* Reading, Walking, Ballroom Dancing.

GREGSON, Jonathan; City Journalist, The Sunday Telegraph, since 1988. *Career:* Which?, Fin Journalist; Financial Weekly, Fin Journalist. *Other Activities:* Research Fellow of the Centre National de la Recherche Scientifique, Paris.

GREGSON, Marcus; Chief Executive, Samuel Montagu & Co Ltd, since 1989; Private Banking. *Career:* Royal Trust UK Ltd, MD, Private Banking 1988-89; Hagen & Company, Partner, Strategic Management of and Investment in Shipping Companies 1987-88; Manufacturers Hanover Trust, Various London & New York 1976-87; Vickers Da Costa & Co, Private Client Fund Management 1970-75; Biddle & Co, Solicitors Articles 1968-70. *Biog: b.* 20 June 1946. *Nationality:* British. *m.* 1969, Grania (née Derouet); 2 s; 1 d. *Educ:* Rugby School; Magdalene College, Cambridge (MA Economics & Law). *Professional Organisations:* Solicitor.

GREGSON, P M; Partner, Touche Ross & Co.

GREGSON, Sir Peter; KCB; Permanent Secretary, Department of Trade & Industry, since 1989. *Career:* Board of Trade 1961-68; Private Secretary to the Prime Minister 1968-72; Assistant Secretary, Dept of Trade & Industry & Secretary, Industrial Development Advisory Board 1972-74; Under Secretary, Department of Industry & Secretary National Enterprise Board 1975-77; Department of Trade, Under Secretary 1977-80; Deputy Secretary 1980-81; Cabinet Office, Deputy Secretary 1981-85; Dept of Energy, Permanent Under-Secretary of State 1985-89. *Biog: b.* 28 June 1936. *Nationality:* British. *Educ:* Nottingham High School; Balliol College, Oxford University (MA); London Business School. *Professional Organisations:* CBIM. *Recreations:* Gardening, Listening to Music.

GREIG, Henry Louis Carron; CVO, CBE; Chairman, Horace Clarkson plc, since 1976. *Career:* Scots Guards Captain 1943-47; H Clarkson & Co Ltd Dir 1953-85; Chm 1973-85; Baltic Exchange Dir 1979-85; Chm 1983-85. *Biog: b.* 21 February 1925. *m.* 1955, Monica (née Stourton); 3 s; 1 d. *Educ:* Eton College. *Directorships:* Royal Bank of Scotland 1985 (non-exec); James Purdey & Sons 1972 (non-exec); United World College of Atlantic 1986 (non-exec). *Other Activities:* Not Forgotten Association (Vice-Chm); School Mistresses & Governors Institution (Vice-Chm); Gentleman Usher to HM Queen since 1961. *Clubs:* White's.

GREIG, J A M; Senior Manager, Corporate Finance, FennoScandia Bank Limited.

GREIG, John Scott; Chairman, Greig Fester Group Ltd, since 1974. *Career:* W T Greig Ltd, Office Boy 1948; Dir 1949; National Service - Royal Artillery 2nd Lt 1949-50; W T Greig Ltd, Dir 1951-72; MD 1972-73; Chm 1973-. *Biog: b.* 27 July 1931. *m.* 1965, Prudence Carolyn Meriol (née Trevor); 1 s; 4 d. *Educ:* Marlborough College. *Directorships:* S Berkeley Owen Ltd; Fester Fothergill & Hartung Ltd; Lloyd's of London Press Ltd; Wishart Wallace (Agencies) Ltd; Craven Farmer Underwriting Agents Ltd; Subsidairy Companies of Greig Fester Group Ltd. *Other Activities:* Mem, Council of Lloyd's, 1986-87, Re-elected 1989; Trustee, Lloyd's Tercentenary Foundation; Junior Warden & Mem, Court of Assts, Worshipful Co of Insurers; Mem, Board of Governors, CII College of Insurance. *Professional Organisations:* ACII; Insurance Institute of London (VP); Fellow, BIM. *Clubs:* City of London, Quinta do Lago Golf Club. *Recreations:* Opera, Ballet, Tennis, Golf, Bee Keeping.

GREIG, Kenneth John; Legal Director & Company Secretary, Templeton Unit Trust Managers Limited, Templeton Investment Management Limited, since 1989; Legal/Secretarial/Compliance. *Career:* Norton Rose, Solicitors 1981-85; First Interstate Capital Markets Limited, Manager, Corporate Finance 1986-88; Lautro Ltd, Enforcement Officer 1988. *Biog: b.* 17 September 1959. *Nationality:* British. *m.* 1986, Susan (née Froggatt); 1 s; 1 d. *Educ:* John Neilson School, Paisley; Davenant Foundation School, Loughton; Balliol College, Oxford (BA Hons Jurisprudence). *Professional Organisations:* Solicitor; Member, Law Society. *Clubs:* Leven Golfing Society, Islay Golf Club. *Recreations:* Golf, Rugby, Literature.

GRENDALE, Thomas Vazey; Director, Midland Montagu Asset Management, since 1987; Investment Management, European Equities. *Career:* Commonwealth Economic Committee, Economist 1957-61; Provident Mutual Life Assurance Association, Asst Investment Mgr 1961-64; General Electric Co Pension Fund, Asst Investment Mgr 1964-68; Courtaulds Pension Fund, Asst Investment Mgr 1968-72; Midland Bank Pension Fund, Investment Mgr 1972-87; Midland Montagu Asset Management, Dir 1987-. *Biog: b.* 20 February 1933. *Nationality:* British. *m.* 1956, Alma (née Gowland); 1 s; 2 d. *Educ:* Bede Grammar School, Sunderland; Trinity College, Cambridge (BA Hons). *Professional Organisations:* AMSIA; IMRO.

GRENSIDE, Sir John Peter; CBE; Non-Exec Director, Allied Lyons plc, since 1986. *Career:* Peat Marwick Mitchell & Co, Staff Mem/Snr Ptnr 1948-86; Peat Marwick International, Chm 1980-83. *Biog: b.* 23 January 1921. *Nationality:* British. *m.* 1946, Yvonne Therese (née Grau); 1 s; 1 d. *Educ:* Rugby. *Directorships:* Nomurch Bank Intl plc 1987 (non-exec). *Other Activities:* Trustee, Portman Family Estates; Director, Molecule Theatre of Sciences for Children; Chm, Exec Ctee Chartered Accountancy Bodies Joint Disciplinary Scheme; Past Master, Chartered Accts Livery Company; Chm, Review Board for Government Contracts 1983-86. *Professional Organisations:* FCA; PCA. *Clubs:* All England Lawn Tennis, Hurlingham, Pilgrims. *Recreations:* Tennis, Bridge.

GREVTSEV, E M; Deputy Chairman and General Manager, Moscow Narodny Bank Limited.

GREY, Andrew James Alexander; Finance Director, Chartered WestLB Limited, since 1987; Finance & Operations. *Career:* Schlesingers, Fin Dir 1974-78; Morgan Stanley International Controller 1978-87. *Biog: b.* 31 January 1943. *m.* Elizabeth (née Allon); 1 s; 1 d. *Educ:* Malvern College. *Directorships:* Subsidiary Companies of Chartered WestLB Limited. *Professional Organisations:* FCA. *Clubs:* RAC. *Recreations:* Golf, Tennis.

GREY, C J; Director, EW Payne Companies Ltd.

GREY, Major General J St J; CB; Clerk, Pewterers' Company.

GREY, Shelley; Group Legal Adviser, Prudential Corporation plc.

GRIBBEN, Roland; Business Editor, The Daily Telegraph, since 1963; Editor of Monday's Business Monitor.

GRIBBIN, Michael C; Group Director, Jardine Insurance Brokers Group.

GRICE, Julian Richard; Director, Henry Cooke Lumsden plc, since 1976; In Charge of Institution/Research Department. *Career:* Co-operative Insurance Society, Investment Dept 1963-69. *Biog: b.* 22 January 1942. *Nationality:* British. *m.* 1984, June Elizabeth Anne (née Scarr); 1 d. *Educ:* Llanelli Boys' Grammar School; University of Wales, Aberystwyth (BA). *Professional Organisations:* The International Stock Exchange. *Clubs:* Bolton Golf Club. *Recreations:* Golf.

GRICE, Mark J; Partner, Neville Russell.

GRIDLEY, W W; Executive Director, Lazard Brothers & Co Limited.

GRIER, James; General Manager, The Royal Bank of Scotland plc.

GRIERSON, Sir Ronald; Vice Chairman, The General Electric Company plc.

GRIEVE, James Crawford; Director, Hill Samuel Investment Management Ltd, since 1989; UK Operations. *Career:* Royal Bank of Scotland Ltd, Retail Banking 1962-69; Trainee Investment Analyst 1969-72; Fund Manager 1972-78; Hill Samuel Investment Management Ltd, Investment Manager (Private Clients) 1978-83; Senior Investment Manager (Pension Funds) 1983-88; Associate Director 1988-89. *Biog: b.* 9 December 1944. *Nationality:* British. *m.* 1984, Carolyn (née George). *Educ:* Knightswood School. *Other Activities:* Hon Sec, Caledonian Society of London. *Professional Organisations:* AIB (Scot); AMSIA. *Clubs:* Caledonian Club, Royal Mid-Surrey Golf Club. *Recreations:* Fishing, Golf.

GRIEVES, John Kerr; Senior Partner, Freshfields, since 1990. *Career:* Freshfields, Solicitor 1963-64; Partner 1964; Managing Partner 1979-85. *Biog: b.* 7 November 1935. *m.* 1961, Ann Gorell (née Harris); 1 s; 1 d. *Educ:* King's School, Worcester; Oxford University (MA); Harvard Business School. *Clubs:* The Athenaeum, Roehampton. *Recreations:* The Arts, Running.

GRIFFIN, Alan F; Managing Director, Alexander Howden Reinsurance Brokers Limited.

GRIFFIN, D T; Director, Pechiney World Trade (Holdings) Ltd.

GRIFFIN, John Anthony; Business Administration Director, G T Management plc, since 1988; Group's Global Business Administration & Management Information Services. *Career:* Safferys & Co Unit Trust Administrator 1970-80; G T Unit Managers Ltd Unit Trust Admin Dir 1980-87. *Biog: b.* 10 April 1946. *Nationality:* British. *m.* 1973, Martina Mary (née Casserly); 2 d. *Educ:* Clapham College. *Directorships:* G T Management (UK) Ltd 1986 (exec); G T Unit Managers 1980 (exec). *Clubs:* Chigwell MC. *Recreations:* Music, Reading (History), Snooker, Tennis.

GRIFFIN, Shane Gerard; Partner, Linklaters & Paines, since 1990; Corporate Finance. *Career:* Solicitor, Queensland 1981-84; Linklaters & Paines, Asst Solicitor 1985-90. *Biog: b.* 17 November 1957. *Nationality:* Australian. *Educ:* St Laurences CBC, Brisbane, Queensland; University of Queensland (BA, LLB); Emmanuel College, Cambridge (LLM). *Other Activities:* City of London Solicitors' Company. *Professional Organisations:* The Law Society. *Recreations:* Rugby, Skiing, Squash, Opera.

GRIFFIN, W T; Non-Executive Director, Church, Charity and Local Authority Fund Managers Limited.

GRIFFIN, (William) Thomas (Jackson); Chairman, G T Management plc.

GRIFFITH, David Vaughan; Executive Director, Banque Paribas, since 1986; Specialised Lending. *Career:* S G Warburg & Co Ltd 1970-73; Edward Bates & Sons Ltd 1973-75; Orion Bank Ltd 1975-76; Saudi International Bank 1976-86. *Biog: b.* 14 April 1947. *Nationality:* British. *m.* 1977, Tina (née Frost); 1 s; 5 d. *Educ:* Cardiff High School; Balliol College, Oxford (MA). *Directorships:* Paribas Home Loans Ltd (exec). *Other Activities:* Institute of Welsh Affairs. *Clubs:* Reform. *Recreations:* Hill-Walking, Theatre, Railways.

GRIFFITH, Miss O L; Executive Director, J O Hambro Magan & Co, since 1988; Corporate Finance. *Career:* Touche Ross & Co Chartered Accountants, latterly as Partner 1976-87; County NatWest, Corporate Finance 1987-88. *Biog: b.* 15 September 1954. *Nationality:* British. *Educ:* University of Leeds (BSc Hons Mathematics). *Directorships:* J O Hambro Magan & Co. *Professional Organisations:* ACA. *Recreations:* Opera, Food & Wine, Horse Racing.

GRIFFITHS, Anthony John; General Manager, Friends Provident, since 1987; Marketing and Sales. *Career:* SPL International Systems Consultant 1967-74; Friends Provident, Systems Mgr 1974-83; Lloyd's of London, Gen Mgr 1984-85; Friends Provident, Agency Mgr 1986-87. *Biog: b.* 28 January 1944. *m.* 1970, Jane V (née Young); 2 d. *Educ:* Holyhead; Liverpool University (BSc). *Recreations:* Running (London Marathon 1987).

GRIFFITHS, The Hon David; Partner, Clifford Chance, since 1990. *Career:* Clifford-Turner, Articled Clerk 1980-83; Assistant Solicitor 1983-87; Clifford

Chance, Assistant Solicitor 1987-90. *Biog: b.* 13 February 1958. *Nationality:* British. *m.* 1983, Henrietta (née Hall); 1 s; 2 d. *Educ:* Eton College; Magdalene College, Cambridge (BA, MA). *Publications:* Restraint of Trade and Business Secrets: Law and Practice, 1986. *Recreations:* Golf, Tennis, Skiing.

GRIFFITHS, David Howard; Director/Company Secretary, Fenchurch Insurance Group Ltd, since 1989. *Career:* Peat Marwick Mitchell & Co 1976-80; Guinness Peat Group plc 1980-82; Fenchurch Insurance Group Ltd 1982-. *Biog: b.* 22 June 1955. *Nationality:* British. *Educ:* Beckenham Grammar School; Kent University (BA). *Directorships:* Various Fenchurch Group Companies. *Professional Organisations:* ACA.

GRIFFITHS, John Henry Morgan; Deputy General Manager, Nomura Bank International, since 1990; Banking. *Career:* Samuel Montagu & Co Limited, Director, Specialised Finance 1979-90; Lloyds Bank International, Various International Management Positions 1975-79. *Biog: b.* 3 December 1953. *Nationality:* British/American. *Educ:* Rugby School; Emmanuel College, Cambridge (Economics/History). *Directorships:* Various. *Recreations:* Tennis, Squash, Shooting, Travel.

GRIFFITHS, M R; Director, Land Securities plc, since 1990; Property Development/Project Management. *Career:* Chartered Quantity Surveyor in Private Practice 1961-73; Land Securities plc, Junior to Senior Management 1973-80; Land Securities Properties Ltd, Assistant Director 1980-86; Director 1986-90. *Biog: b.* 12 May 1945. *Nationality:* British. *m.* 1970, Pauline (née Pearce); 1 s; 2 d. *Directorships:* Land Securities plc; Land Securities Properties Ltd; The City of London Real Property Co Ltd; Ravenseft Properties Ltd; Ravenseft & Murray Field (second Dundee) Ltd; Eron Investments Ltd; Sevington Properties Ltd. *Professional Organisations:* FRICS. *Recreations:* Travel, Squash.

GRIFFITHS, Michael John; Director, Allied-Lyons plc, since 1988; Retailing. *Career:* Royal Air Force, General Duties (Pilot) 1955; Ind Coope, Trainee 1962; J J Murtagh (Ireland), General Manager 1962; Ind Coope West Midlands, Director 1963; Friary Meux, Director 1966; Halls Oxford Brewery Co, Managing Director 1967; Benskins Brewery Co, Managing Director 1970; Ansells Brewery Co, Deputy Chief Executive 1974; Taylor Walker, Managing Director 1979; Ind Coope, Director 1979-89; Allied Breweries, Director 1979; Ind Coope, Managing Director 1985-89. *Biog: b.* 15 December 1934. *m.* Jennifer Elizabeth (née Stafford); 2 s; 3 d. *Educ:* Peter Symonds School, Winchester; Royal Air Force College, Cranwell; London Business School (Senior Executive Course). *Directorships:* Victoria Wine Co 1988 Chm; Taylor Walker 1985 Chm; Friary Meux 1985 Chm; Benskins 1985 Chm; Halls Oxford Brewery Co Chm; Nicholsons 1985 Chm; Ind Coope Sale 1985-89 Chm; Parasol Corporation Ltd 1985 Chm; 1989

(exec); Embassy Hotels 1989 (exec) Chm; J Lyons 1989-90 (exec) Chm; Porterhouse Restaurants 1989-90 (exec) Chm. *Other Activities:* Brewers Company; London Brewers Council; Member of Council, Design Museum. *Clubs:* RAF Club, Piccadilly. *Recreations:* Skiing, Shooting, Sailing, Gardening, Family, Home.

GRIFFITHS, Paul; Executive Director, Baring Capital Investors Limited.

GRIFFITHS, Timothy John; Finance Director, Credit Lyonnais Euro-Securities Ltd, since 1989; Finance and Operations. *Career:* Northcote & Co Dealer 1971-76; Grieveson Grant & Co Member Dealer 1976-85; Laing & Cruickshank Gilt Salesman 1985-87; Credit Lyonnais Gilts Ltd, Director 1987-89. *Biog: b.* 14 April 1953. *Nationality:* British. *m.* 1977, Patricia Stanton (née Dunne); 3 s. *Educ:* Campion Grammar School. *Professional Organisations:* International Stock Exchange.

GRIGGS, R; Partner, Cameron Markby Hewitt.

GRIMES, T; Director, Barclays de Zoete Wedd Securities Ltd, since 1988; Fixed Income Division. *Career:* Hill Samuel & Co, Director, Gilts 1986-88; Wood Mackenzie & Co, Partner 1980-86; Senior Executive, Gilts 1978-80; Post Office Staff Superannuation Fund, Assistant Investment Manager, Fixed Income 1972-78; Cooperative Insurance Society, Assistant Investment Manager 1967-72. *Biog: b.* 2 March 1942. *Nationality:* British. *m.* 1964, M Ann; 2 s. *Educ:* Imperial College (BSc, DIC). *Directorships:* B2W Securities (exec). *Other Activities:* Liveryman, Worshipful Company of Actuaries; Chairman, Stock Exchange Examination Panel, Bonds & Fixed Interest. *Professional Organisations:* FIA; AMSIA.

GRIMSHAW, Mrs Andrea; Partner, Clark Whitehill, since 1983; Audit Partner, Head of Employers Advisory Unit. *Biog: b.* 29 November 1952. *Nationality:* British. *m.* 1973, Trevor. *Professional Organisations:* Fellow, Institute of Chartered Accountants. *Clubs:* British Sub-Aqua Club. *Recreations:* Skiing, Scuba Diving.

GRIMSTONE, Gerald; Director, Investment Banking Division, J Henry Schroder Wagg & Co Ltd, since 1986; Corporate Finance. *Career:* UK Civil Service, Latterly Assistant Secretary, HM Treasury 1972-86. *Biog: b.* 27 August 1949. *Nationality:* British. *m.* 1972, The Hon Janet Elizabeth (née Svenson-Taylor); 1 s; 2 d. *Educ:* Whitgift School; Merton College, Oxford (MA, MSc). *Publications:* Various Works on Privatisation and Environmental Sciences. *Clubs:* Athenaeum.

GRINDROD, Peter Anthony Schofield; Partner, Slaughter and May, since 1979; Company and Commercial Law. *Career:* Slaughter and May, Articled Clerk 1970-72; Asst Solicitor 1972-79. *Biog: b.* 3 June 1947. *m.* 1985, Ann (née Cartwright). *Educ:* Ipswich School;

Emmanuel College, Cambridge (MA, LLB). *Other Activities:* Lord's Taverner. *Professional Organisations:* The Law Society.

GRINDY, Roger Sydney; Director, Hill Samuel & Co Ltd.

GRINYER, Brian John; Deputy Chief Executive, Town & Country Building Society, since 1981; General Management including Computing, Administration, Peronnel & Training Services. *Biog: b.* 21 June 1933. *m.* 1974, Linda (née Holland); 1 s; 2 d. *Educ:* Eastham Grammar. *Directorships:* Funds Transfer Sharing Ltd 1985 (non-exec); Town & Country Property Services Ltd 1987; Town & Country Financial Services Ltd 1987; LINK Interchange Network Ltd 1989. *Professional Organisations:* Chartered Institute of Secretaries; Institute of Bankers; Chartered Building Societies Institute.

GRIPTON, Bruce Graham James; Partner, Frere Cholmeley, since 1990; Company & Commercial Law. *Career:* Frere Cholmeley, Articled Clerk 1982-84; Assistant Solicitor 1984-90. *Biog: b.* 12 December 1959. *Nationality:* British. *m.* 1987, Jacqueline Catherine (née Hodder); 1 d. *Educ:* King Edward School, Birmingham; Exeter College, Oxford (MA). *Professional Organisations:* The Law Society. *Recreations:* Golf, Bridge.

GROBLER, O D; General Manager, Trust Bank of Africa.

GRØNDAHL, Tom; Chairman, Den Norske Bank plc.

GROOM, R J; General Manager, Gateway Building Society.

GROOM, Stephen Henry; Executive Director, Merrill Lynch Limited.

GROOME, L; OBE; Clerk, Chartered Architects' Company.

GROSE, Jeremy; Partner, Titmuss Sainer & Webb.

GROSSART, Angus McFarlane McLeod; CBE; Chairman & Managing Director, Noble Grossart Limited, since 1969. *Career:* Thomson McLintock Glasgow, CA Apprentice 1958-62; Scottish Bar, Advocate 1963-69; Noble Grossart Limited, Managing Director 1969-. *Biog: b.* 6 April 1937. *Nationality:* British. *m.* 1978, Marion Gay (née Dodd); 1 d. *Educ:* Glasgow University (MA, LLB); LLD (Hon). *Directorships:* Alexander & Alexander Inc (New York) 1985; American Trust plc 1973; British Petroleum Scottish Advisory Board 1990; Edinburgh Fund Managers plc 1983 Chairman; Hewden Stuart plc 1988; Murray International Holdings Ltd 1987; Noble Grossart Limited 1969; Phoenician Holdings Limited (Canada) 1979; The Royal Bank of Scot-

land plc 1982; The Royal Bank of Scotland Group plc 1985; Scottish Financial Enterprise 1986; The Scottish Investment Trust plc 1974 Chairman; Scottish Television plc 1986; Trustees of The National Galleries of Scotland 1989 Chairman of the Board; Scottish Cot Death Trust 1986 Trustee. *Professional Organisations:* CA. *Publications:* Climate for Leadership, 1982; The Financial Catalyst, 1984. *Clubs:* The New Club, Royal & Ancient Golf Club St Andrews, Honourable Company of Edinburgh Golfers. *Recreations:* Restoration of 16th-Century Castle, Decorative Arts.

GROSSFELD, M; Group Treasurer, Trusthouse Forte plc.

GROSSMANN, L B; Head of Metals, J H Rayner (Mincing Lane).

GROUND, Alan Geoffrey; Partner, Linklaters & Paines, since 1969; Competition and Trade Law. *Career:* Pollard & Co, Solicitors, Westminster Articles 1958-62; Linklaters & Paines, Solicitor 1962-69. *Biog: b.* 5 April 1935. *Nationality:* British. *m.* 1967, Sarah Helen (née Powell); 3 s; 1 d. *Educ:* Beckenham Grammar School; Jesus College, Cambridge (Exhibitioner) (MA, LLB Modern Languages and Law). *Other Activities:* Member, Law Society International Committee and Law Society Human Rights Working Party; Liveryman, City of London Solicitors Company. *Professional Organisations:* Member, Law Society; Qualified as Solicitor, 1962. *Publications:* EEC Merger Control Section of 'Mergers & Aquisitions in Europe', 1990. *Clubs:* RAC, Pall Mall, Royal Overseas League. *Recreations:* Music, Tennis, Theatre, Reading, Family Life.

GROUT, J; Director of Treasury, Cadbury Schweppes plc, since 1987; Tax, Treasury, Corporate Finance. *Career:* BL plc, latterly Assistant Treasurer 1970-82; BICC plc, Group Treasurer 1982-87. *Biog: b.* 26 September 1945. *Nationality:* British. *m.* 1984, Elisabeth Anne (née Berkeley); 1 s. *Directorships:* Cadbury Schweppes Finance Ltd 1987; Cadbury Schweppes Money Management plc 1988; Cadbury Schweppes Overseas Ltd 1988. *Other Activities:* Member of Council, Association of Corporate Treasurers, 1984; Vice Chairman, Association of Corporate Treasurers; Chairman, City Regulatory Panel of the CBI.

GROVE, Josceline Philip; Managing Director, Grandfield Rork Collins Ltd, since 1986. *Career:* RMA Sandhurst & 22nd Cheshire Regiment Lt 1957-62; J & P Coats Patons & Baldwins, Mgmnt Trainee 1963; CT Bowring & Co 1964-65; The Economist 1966; The Sunday Times 1967-70; J Walter Thompson Co, Account Exec 1970-73; Charles Barker 1974; Assoc Dir 1977; Dir 1978-83; Grandfield Rork Collins, Financial Dir 1983-. *Biog: b.* 8 November 1938. *Nationality:* British. *m.* 1970, Jennifer Clifton (née Calvert); 1 s (decd); 2 d. *Educ:* Hurstpierpoint College. *Other Activi-*

ties: Mem, Court of Assistants; The Worshipful Company of Bowyers; Territorial Army, Queens Royal Rifles (1963-66); 4th Volunteer Battalion, The Royal Green Jackets (1966-72); Exec Sec, Wider Share Ownership Council (1976-78). *Clubs:* Brook's, Army & Navy, The Northern Meeting Club (Invernesshire). *Recreations:* Ocean Racing, Deerstalking, Grand Opera.

GRUBB, R de C; Partner, Cazenove & Co.

GRUBMAN, W K; Director, Unilever PLC, since 1986; Specialty Chemicals. *Career:* National Starch and Chemical Corporation, 1950-85; Chemical Engineer; Technical Service Engineer; Plant Manager; Acquisitons and Mergers Manager; Vice President, General Manager, Adhesives Division 1972-75; Group Vice President, Adhesives & Resins Divs 1975-78; President, Chief Operating Officer 1978-82; Chairman & CEO 1982-85; Unilever PLC and NV, Director and Chemicals Coordinator 1986-. *Biog: b.* 12 September 1928. *Nationality:* American. *m.* 1950, Ruth W (née Winer); 2 s. *Educ:* Columbia University (BS Chem Eng); New York University (MS Chem Eng). *Directorships:* Unilever PLC and Unilever NV 1986 (exec); National Starch and Chem Corp 1978-85 (exec); 1986- (non-exec); Unilever United States 1980-85 (exec); United National Bancorp New Jersey, US 1978-86 (non-exec); 1987- Consultant to Board. *Other Activities:* Engineering Advisory Committee Columbia University, New York; Industry Advisor, Chemical Engineering London University, 1989. *Professional Organisations:* Fellow, Inst. of Directors (London); American Institute of Chemical Engineers (US); Society of the Chemical Industries (US and London); Chemical Industry Association (London); Chemical Mfg's Assoc. (US). *Clubs:* Princeton Club, NY City, Sky Club NY City, Wentworth Golf UK, Mid-Ocean Club Bermuda.

GRUEBEL, Oswald J; Deputy Chairman, Crédit Suisse First Boston Limited.

GRUMBALL, Clive Roger; General Manager Treasury, Yamaichi Bank (UK) plc, since 1989; Treasury. *Career:* HM Forces, Army Officer 1965-68; Gillett Brothers Discount Co Ltd, Assistant to the Managing Directors 1969-77; Amex Bank Ltd/American Express International Banking Corp, Assistant Treasurer 1977-80; Nordic Bank plc, Director 1980-85; County Bank Ltd/County NatWest Capital Markets Ltd, Managing Director, Treasury 1985-87; British & Commonwealth Merchant Bank plc, Director 1987-89; Yamaichi Bank (UK) plc, General Manager, Treasury 1989-. *Biog: b.* 17 December 1946. *Nationality:* British. *m.* 1971, Jennifer (div 1986); 1 s; 1 d. *Educ:* Sir Roger Manwood's School, Sandwich Kent; Priory G S, Shrewsbury Salop; Welbeck College, Worksop Notts; Royal Military Academy, Sandhurst. *Publications:* Managing Interest Rate Risk, 1986; Management, 1989. *Recreations:* Horse Riding.

GRUME, J M; General Manager, Banco de Sabadell.

GRUNBERG, Michael; Partner, Stoy Hayward, since 1985; Management Consultancy Services. *Career:* Hacker Young, Audit Supervisor 1977-81; Stoy Hayward, Consultancy Mgr 1981-85. *Biog: b.* 23 September 1956. *Educ:* City of London School; London School of Economics (BSc Hons). *Directorships:* Stoy Hayward Consulting 1985 (exec); Stoy Hayward Franchising Services 1986 (exec). *Professional Organisations:* ICAEW; Institute of Mgmt Consultants; Institute of Data Processing Mgmt. *Recreations:* Squash, Skiing, Running.

GRUNDY, Tony; Partner, Linklaters & Paines.

GRUNFELD, H; President, S G Warburg Group plc, since 1987. *Career:* S G Warburg & Co Ltd, Chairman 1969-74; President 1974-87. *Biog: b.* 1 June 1904. *m.* 1931, Berta Lotte (née Oliven); 1 s.

GUASCHI, Francis; Partner, Bacon & Woodrow, since 1985; General Insurance. *Career:* Gresham Life Actuarial Assistant 1948-59; Mercantile & General Reinsurance Co Asst Gen Mgr 1959-85. *Biog: b.* 5 April 1931. *m.* 1960, Sylvia (née Jones); 1 s; 1 d. *Educ:* St Marylebone Grammar School. *Professional Organisations:* FIA. *Publications:* Various Papers. *Clubs:* Actuaries. *Recreations:* Piano, Mathematics, English Literature.

GUBBINS, Anthony Paul; Partner, Wedlake Bell, since 1987; Company/Commercial Law. *Career:* Slaughter and May, Articled Clerk 1980-82; Assistant Solicitor 1982-84; Wedlake Bell, Assistant Solicitor 1984-87. *Biog: b.* 17 April 1958. *Nationality:* British. *m.* 1982, Jennifer (née Marr); 1 s. *Educ:* Brighton Hove and Sussex Grammar School; Durham University (BA Hons). *Professional Organisations:* The Law Society. *Recreations:* Theatre, Music, Swimming, Food.

GUBBINS, R S; Partner, Ashurst Morris Crisp, since 1989; Company/Commercial Law. *Career:* Ashurst Morris Crisp 1980; Qualified 1982. *Biog: b.* 24 May 1957. *Nationality:* British. *m.* 1984, Carolyn Mary (née Monro); 1 s; 1 d. *Educ:* Cheltenham College; University of Wales, UWIST (LLB Hons). *Professional Organisations:* Law Society. *Clubs:* MCC, I Zingari, Frogs, Sunningdale Golf Club, Roehampton Club. *Recreations:* Cricket, Golf, Tennis, Squash, Sailing.

GUBBINS, S R; Associate, Grimley J R Eve.

GUBERT, Walter A; Managing Director & Chairman of Management Committee, J P Morgan, since 1989; Advisory, Mergers & Acquisitions. *Career:* J P Morgan 1973-. *Biog: b.* 15 June 1947. *Nationality:* Italian. *m.* 1974, Caroline; 2 d. *Educ:* University of Florence; INSEAD. *Directorships:* J P Morgan Securities Ltd 1986; J P Morgan (Switzerland) Ltd 1986; J P Morgan España SA 1989. *Clubs:* Royal Automobile Club, Larchmont

Yacht Club, Wentworth. *Recreations:* Golf, Sailing, Tennis.

GUERIN, Benoît-Marie Pierre Robert; Director International Corporate Finance, Kleinwort Benson Limited, since 1987; France, Belgium. *Career:* French Chamber of Commerce in GB, Financial Attaché 1980-81; Grindlays Bank, Corporate Banking 1981-84. *Biog: b.* 30 October 1956. *Nationality:* French. *m.* 1986, Caroline (née Stapylton-Thorley); 1 s. *Educ:* Institution Saint Joseph; University of Paris X; European School for Management Studies (MBA). *Directorships:* Kleinwort Benson Europe SA (Brussels) 1990 (exec). *Clubs:* Brooks's. *Recreations:* Culture & Country.

GUEST, Jonathan; Partner, Hepworth & Chadwick, since 1986. *Biog: b.* 28 February 1958. *Nationality:* British. *m.* 1983, Sally Elizabeth (née Fox); 1 s; 1 d. *Educ:* Bristol (LLB Hons).

GUEST, R H; Assistant General Manager, The Toronto-Dominion Bank, since 1988; Foreign Exchange, Money Markets, Trading, Sales. *Career:* Midland Bank plc, Corporate Sales Manager 1985-87. *Biog: b.* 9 February 1956. *Nationality:* British. *Educ:* Wallasey Grammar School.

GUILD, Ivor Reginald; CBE; Senior Partner, Shepherd & Wedderburn WS, since 1984; Tax & Company Law. *Career:* Shepherd & Wedderburn WS Ptnr 1951-. *Educ:* Cargilfield; Rugby School; New College, Oxford (MA); Edinburgh University (LLB). *Directorships:* Edinburgh Investment Trust (non-exec); 1974 Chm; Dunedin Income Growth Investment Trust (non-exec); Dunedin Worldwide Investment Trust (non-exec); Fulcrum Investment Trust 1986 (non-exec); Fleming Universal Investment Trust 1977 (non-exec). *Other Activities:* Procurator Fiscal of the Lyon Court, 1960-; Bailie of Holyrood House, 1980-; Registrar, Episcopal Synod of Episcopal Church in Scotland, 1967-; Chancellor of the Dioceses of Edinburgh & St Andrews, 1985; Chm, National Museum of Antiquities of Scotland, 1981-85; Editor, Scottish Genealogist, 1959-. *Professional Organisations:* WS, 1930. *Clubs:* New Club (Edinburgh). *Recreations:* Golf, Genealogy.

GUILDING, Miss Rosemary; Partner, Theodore Goddard, since 1989; Commercial Property. *Career:* Cameron Markby, Articled Clerk/Assistant Solicitor 1979-81; John Welch & Stammers, Assistant Solicitor 1981-82; Farrer & Co, Assistant Solicitor 1982-83; Theodore Goddard, Assistant Solicitor 1983-89. *Biog: b.* 29 December 1953. *Nationality:* British. *m.* 1988, Timothy Walter Roche Coe; 1 s. *Educ:* The Lady Eleanor Holles School; The University of York (BA). *Professional Organisations:* The Law Society. *Recreations:* Piano, Reading, Sailing.

GUINNESS, Geoffrey Neil; Director, Barclays de Zoete Wedd Securities Ltd, since 1989; Risk Control. *Career:* Guinness Mahon & Co Ltd, Manager 1964-74; Barclays Bank International Limited, Assistant General Manager 1974-89. *Biog: b.* 27 December 1938. *Nationality:* British. *m.* 1962, Jillian Ruth (née Powell); 1 s; 2 d. *Educ:* Rugby; Trinity College, Oxford (MA). *Directorships:* BZW Securities Ltd 1989 (exec); European Schoolbooks Ltd 1970 (non-exec). *Other Activities:* Trustee, The Richmond Charities. *Professional Organisations:* Fellow, Institute of Chartered Accountants in England and Wales.

GUINNESS, T W N; Joint Managing Director, Guinness Flight Global Asset Management Ltd.

GUINNESS, William L S; Non Executive Director, Henry Ansbacher Holdings plc, since 1985. *Biog: b.* 28 Decmber 1939. *m.* 1971, Lynn (née Day); 2 s; 1 d. *Educ:* Eton College. *Directorships:* Overman Son Co Ltd 1966 (exec); GIG Engineering Ltd 1989 Chm; Euroquip Ltd 1989 Chm; Dredging & Pumping System Ltd 1989 Chm; Banque Lausanoise de Portefeuilles 1989 (non-exec). *Clubs:* White's, Pratt's. *Recreations:* Golf, Skiing.

GULLEY, Ernest Paul; Partner, Cyril Sweett and Partners.

GULLIVER, James Gerald; Executive Chairman, James Gulliver Associates Ltd, since 1977. *Career:* Urwick Orr & Partners Ltd Mgmnt Consultant 1961-65; Fine Fare (Holdings) Ltd MD 1965-72; Chm 1967-72; Associated British Foods Ltd Dir 1967-72; Oriel Foods Ltd Chm 1973-77; The Argyll Group plc Chm 1979-88; Lowndes Queensway plc, Executive Chm 1988-90. *Biog: b.* 17 August 1930. *Nationality:* British. *m.* 1985, Marjorie Hazel (née Moncrieff); 3 s; 2 d. *Educ:* Campbeltown Grammar School; Glasgow University (BSc Hons, MSc); Georgia Institute of Technology, USA; Fulbright Scholar to USA, 1954. *Directorships:* Manchester United Football Club 1982 (exec) VP; Scottish Investment Trust 1986 (exec); Waverley Cameron plc 1987 (non-exec) Chm; Ancasta Marine Holdings Ltd 1988 (non-exec) Chm. *Other Activities:* The Guardian Young Businessman of The Year; Chm, The Scottish Business Group; Member, the Governing Council of Scottish Business in the Community; The Scottish Economic Council; Trustee, Duke of Edinburgh's Award; Fulbright Scholarship to the USA, 1954; Council Member, Institute of Directors; Visiting Professor of Business Strategy & Marketing, Glasgow University; Trustee, Glasgow University Trust; Council Member, Buckingham University; Vice President, Manchester United Football Club. *Professional Organisations:* D Univ (Glasgow-1989); Fellow, Royal Society of Edinburgh, 1990; FICE; FRSA; CBIM. *Clubs:* Carlton, Royal Thames Yacht Club. *Recreations:* Skiing, Sailing, Music, Art.

GULLIVER, Ronald; Partner, Nabarro Nathanson, since 1974; Finance and Tax. *Career:* Fryer Sutton Morris Ltd, Partner 1962-66; ICAEW, Technical Officer 1966-67; P A Thomas & Co, Partner 1967-71. *Biog:* b. 12 August 1940. *Nationality:* British. m. 1967, Penelope Daphne; 1 s; 1 d. *Educ:* King Alfreds School, Wantage; London University (LLB, FCA). *Directorships:* Eagle Place Services Ltd 1974 (non-exec); Orr & Boss Ltd 1987 (non-exec); Forminster plc 1988 (non-exec) Chairman. *Other Activities:* Honourable Artillery Company. *Professional Organisations:* Solicitor; FCA. *Publications:* Various Articles in Professional Magazines and Radio Programmes on Taxation Matters. *Clubs:* Naval & Military Club, East Berks GC. *Recreations:* Farming, Golf.

GULVANESSIAN, Miss Aleen; Partner, Jaques & Lewis, since 1989; Company/Commercial. *Career:* Jaques & Lewis, Articled Clerk 1981-83; Assistant Solicitor 1983-88. *Biog:* b. 21 May 1958. *Nationality:* British. m. 1987, Neil Alisdair. *Educ:* Haberdashers' Aske's School for Girls, Elstree, Herts; University College, London (LLB Hons). *Professional Organisations:* Member, The Law Society; Member, The Holborn Law Society. *Recreations:* Opera, Theatre, Tennis, Skiing.

GUMIENNY, M S; Investment Executive, Candover Investments plc, since 1986; General. *Career:* Price Waterhouse (London) 1981-85; (Bahrain) 1985-86. *Biog:* b. 23 March 1959. *Nationality:* British. m. 1989, Iona Young. *Educ:* St Johns College, Southsea; Warwick University (BSc Maths). *Directorships:* Knickerbox Holdings Ltd 1990 (non-exec); Baillie Longstaff Holdings Ltd 1990 (non-exec); Dwek Group Ltd 1988 (non-exec); Golden Key Homes Ltd 1987 (non-exec); Don Reynolds Holdings Ltd 1987-89 (non-exec). *Professional Organisations:* ACA. *Clubs:* Canons.

GUNN, Ms Cathy; City Editor, Today Newspaper, since 1987; Financial Section. *Career:* Touche, Remnant & Co, Investment Analyst 1976-78; Investors Chronicle, Financial Journalist 1978-80; The Times, Financial Journalist 1980-81; Freelance Financial Journalist 1981-83; Financial Weekly, Features Editor/News Editor/Deputy Editor 1983-86; Today, Financial Journalist 1986; Deputy City Editor 1986-87; City Editor 1987-. *Biog:* b. 28 May 1954. *Nationality:* British. *Educ:* St Swithins School, Winchester; University of Durham (BA Joint Hons II:ii English & Philosophy); University of Edinburgh (Diploma, Business Administration). *Publications:* Fraud: The Growth Industry of the Eighties (with Mihir Bose). *Recreations:* Eating, Drinking, Entertaining, Travel, Reading.

GUNN, John Humphrey; Chairman, British & Commonwealth Holdings plc.

GUNN, R C L; Associate, Grimley J R Eve.

GUNN, William P; Non-Executive Chairman, Clerical Medical & General Life Assurance.

GUNN FORBES, A; Director, Kim Eng Securities (London) Limited.

GUNNELL, John; Chairman, Yorkshire Enterprise Limited.

GUNSON, Adrian; Senior Investment Manager, Norwich Union Fund Managers Ltd.

GUNSON, George M; London General Manager, Banca Serfin SNC.

GUNTER, Ralph Sebastian Timothy; Director, David Holman & Co Ltd, since 1989; Lloyd's Members' Agency Director. *Career:* Bland Welch Underwriting Ltd 1982-86. *Biog:* b. 3 January 1964. *Nationality:* British. *Educ:* St John's School, Leatherhead. *Directorships:* David Holman & Co Ltd 1989 (exec); Holman MacLeod Ltd 1989 (exec). *Recreations:* Secretary Old Johnian Rugby Football Club.

GURDON, Hugo; City News Editor, The Daily Telegraph. *Career:* Daily Telegraph, New York City Correspondent. *Publications:* Iran: the Continuing Struggle for Power.

GURNEY, Dr John Peter; Investment Director, Allied Dunbar Asset Management plc, since 1981; US Equities. *Career:* Hambros Bank, Investment Mgr 1968-81. *Biog:* b. 1 June 1936. *Nationality:* British. m. 1969, Irmgard; 2 s; 1 d. *Educ:* St Aloysius College, London; Gonville & Caius College, Cambridge (MA); Birmingham University (PhD). *Professional Organisations:* ASIA.

GURTIN, Mustafa Hamdi; Deputy Representative, Central Bank of the Republic of Turkey, since 1988; Representation. *Career:* Central Bank of Turkey, Researcher, Research Dept 1975-79; Land Forces Military Academy, Instructor of Economics 1979-80; Central Bank of Turkey, Economist, Research Dept 1980-85; Mgr, Forex Operations 1985-88. *Biog:* b. 23 August 1951. *Nationality:* Turkish. m. 1975, Deniz (née Zorkun); 1 s; 1 d. *Educ:* Middle East Technical University (BSc); Vanderbilt University (MA). *Professional Organisations:* Middle East Technical University Alumni Association.

GUTERRES, Miguel Mark; Director, International Department, Panmure Gordon & Co; UK Equities to Europe - Switzerland, Denmark. *Career:* Dunkley Marshall (Member of Stock Exchange), Associate 1980-84; Panmure Gordon 1984-. *Biog:* b. 18 December 1957. *Nationality:* British. m. 1986, Veronica (née Middleton); 2 s. *Educ:* Stonyhurst College; Exeter University (General Hons Degree). *Professional Organisations:* Member, Stock Exchange. *Recreations:* Squash, Tennis.

GUY, Mrs Diana (née Eade); Partner, Theodore Goddard, since 1973; EEC/Competition Law. *Career:* Theodore Goddard, Articled Clerk 1966-68; Staff Solicitor 1968-73. *Biog: b.* 27 March 1943. *Nationality:* British. *m.* 1968, John Robert Clare Guy; 2 *s. Educ:* Queen Anne's School, Caversham; Lady Margaret Hall, Oxford (MA). *Other Activities:* Chairman, Law Society's 1992 Working Party. *Professional Organisations:* Law Society. *Publications:* The EEC and Intellectual Property (with G I F Leigh), 1981.

GUY, J A; Director (Group Settlements), Baring Securities Ltd, since 1990; Settlement Responsibility for all Members. *Career:* Standard Life Assurance Co, New Business Clerk 1965-68; Grieveson Grant & Co, Accounts Clerk 1968-70; Clients Ledger Clerk 1970-71; Contracts Clerk 1971-75; Foreign Settlements Clerk 1975-82; Manager-Foreign Settlements 1982-85; Kleinwort Grieveson Securities, Manager-Foreign Settlements 1985-87; Baring Securities, Operations Manager 1987-89; Assistant Director (Operations) 1989-90; Director (Group Settlements) 1990. *Biog: b.* 28 February 1948. *Nationality:* British. *m.* 1971, Patricia Ann; 2 *d. Educ:* Secondary Modern. *Professional Organisations:* International Stock Exchange.

GUY, John Robert Clare; Director, NM Rothschild & Sons Ltd, since 1975; Treasury & Bullion. *Career:* Conservative Party Research Dept 1966-67. *Biog: b.* 30 December 1943. *m.* 1968, Diana (née Eade); 2 *s. Educ:* Kingswood School, Bath; Balliol College, Oxford (MA). *Directorships:* London Gold Market 1980; London Bullion Market Association 1988 Chm.

GUY, Philip; Director, Hill Samuel Bank Ltd, since 1989; Head of Treasury. *Career:* Sharps Pixley Limited, Chairman 1989; Kleinwort Benson Group plc, Director 1988-89; Kleinwort Benson Limited, Director 1984-88; Kleinwort Benson (Hong Kong) Ltd, Director 1982-84. *Biog: b.* 15 March 1946. *Nationality:* British. *m.* 1971, Janice Anne (née Cocksedge); 1 s; 1 d. *Educ:* Southend High School for Boys. *Directorships:* Hill Samuel Bank Ltd 1989 (exec).

GWILT, George D; Director, Hodgson Martin Limited.

GYLLENHAMMAR, Pehr G; Executive Chairman, A B Volvo, since 1990. *Career:* Mannheimer & Zetterlof, Solicitors, Gothenburg 1959; Haight Gardner, Poor & Havens, Admiralty Lawyers New York 1960; Amphion Insurance Co, Gothenburg 1961-64; Skandia Insurance Co, Stockholm, Asst Administrative Manager 1965-66; Vice President, Corporate Planning 1966-68; Executive Vice President 1968; President & Chief Executive Officer 1970; A B Volvo, Gothenburg 1970; MD 1971-83; CEO, Volvo Group 1971-90; Chairman of Board 1983. *Biog: b.* 1935. *m.* 1959, (Eva) Christina (née Engellau); 1 s; 3 d. *Educ:* University of Lund, Sweden (LLB); Studies in International Law, England & Maritime Law, USA; Centre d'Etudes Industrielles, Geneva (Management Program). *Directorships:* A B Volvo 1971; 1983 Chairman; 1990 (exec); Swedish Ships' Mortgage Bank 1976 Chairman; Procodia AB 1990 Chairman; Svensk Interkontinental Lufttrafik AB (SILA) 1982 Vice Chairman; Skandinaviska Enskilda Banken 1979; United Technologies Corporation, Hartford, Conn 1981; Kissinger Associates, Inc, New York 1982; Pearson plc, London 1983; Reuters Holdings PLC, London 1984; Svenska Cellulosa AB SCA 1989; Vin- & Sprit AB 1989; NV Phillips' Gloeilampenfabrieken, Eindhoven 1990; Renault SA, Paris 1990; Member, International Advisory Committee, The Chase Manhattan Bank, NA, New York 1972; Member, Board, Committee of Common Market Automobile Constructors (CCMC) 1977; Member, Board, Federation of Swedish Industries 1979; Founder and Member, The Roundtable of European Industrialists 1982; 1982-88 Chairman. *Other Activities:* Officer of the first class of the Royal Order of Vasa, 1973; Member of the (Royal Swedish) Academy of Engineering Sciences, 1974; Lethaby Professor of 1977 at the Royal College of Art, London; Commander of the Order of the Lion of Finland, 1977; Commander of Ordre National du Merite, France, 1980; Conferred the Golden Award of the City of Gothenburg, 1981; Conferred The King's Medal, 12th size, with ribbon of the Order of the Seraphim, 1981; Doctor of Medicine h.c., Gothenburg University, 1981; Commander of St Olavs Orden, Norway, 1984; Commander first class of the Order of the Lion of Finland, 1986; Commander of the Legion of Honour, France, 1987; Doctor of Technology h.c. Brunel University, London, 1987; Knight Grand Officer of the Republic of Italy's Order of Merit, 1987; Doctor of Engineering h.c., Technical University of Nova Scotia, Halifax, 1988; Commander of the Order of Leopold, Belgium, 1989; Doctor of Social Sciences h.c. University of Helsinki, 1990. *Publications:* Author of Mot sekelskiftet pa mafa (Toward the Turn of the Century, at Random), 1970; Jag tror pa Sverige (I Believe in Sweden), 1973; People at Work, 1977; En industripolitik for manniskan (Industrial policy for human beings), 1979; Numerous articles for domestic and international press, including contributions to several books. *Recreations:* Tennis, Sailing, Skiing, Riding.

H

HAAN, Christopher F; Senior Partner, S J Berwin & Co.

HAAN, Michael R; Partner, Stoy Hayward.

HAAS, J C; General Partner, Lazard Frères & Cie, since 1974. *Career:* Banque de Neuflize Schlumberger Mallet, Membre du Directoire 1960-71; Lazard Frères & Cie, General Partner 1974-. *Biog: b.* 21 February 1926. *Nationality:* French; 1 s; 1 d. *Educ:* Political Sciences School; Faculty of Law, Faculty of Literature. *Directorships:* Lazard Brothers & Co; Pearson plc; Sicomibail; Chargeurs SA; Eurafrance. *Other Activities:* Officer of the Légion d'Honneur. *Clubs:* Automobile Club de France. *Recreations:* Golf de Morfontaine.

HAAS, R D W; Company Secretary, James Capel Fund Managers Limited, since 1990; Accounting/Secretarial. *Career:* Deloitte Haskins & Sells 1980-87; Trainee Accountant/Auditor 1980-84; Insolvency Specialist 1984-87; James Capel & Co, Assistant to Company Secretary 1987-88; James Capel Fund Managers Limited, Financial Controller 1988-90. *Biog: b.* 27 February 1958. *Nationality:* British. *Educ:* Marlborough College, Wiltshire; University of Manchester Institute of Science and Technology, UMIST (BSc Hons). *Directorships:* Benenden School Kent Limited 1989 (non-exec). *Professional Organisations:* CA. *Recreations:* Sailing, Skiing, Travel.

HABER, Martin D; Director, Continental Reinsurance London.

HABERER, J-Y; Director, Crédit Lyonnais Capital Markets plc.

HADDON-CAVE, Sir Philip; Director, Kleinwort Benson-Lonsdale plc.

HADEN, Harold John; Legal Director, M & G Group plc, since 1984; Legal, Compliance and Regulation. *Career:* Pupillage 1964-65; Practice, English Bar 1966-69; Loss Adjuster 1970-72. *Biog: b.* 14 February 1941. *Nationality:* British. *m.* 1964, (Elizabeth) Jane (née de St Croix); 1 s; 2 d. *Educ:* Wrekin College; Hackley School, New York; Birmingham University (Law). *Directorships:* M & G Group plc 1984 (exec); M & G Limited 1982 (exec); The First British Fixed Trust Company Limited 1974 (exec); M & G Financial Services Limited 1980 (exec); More's Garden Management Limited 1982 (non-exec); M & G Life Assurance Company Limited -1984; M & G Pensions & Annuity Company Limited -1984; M & G Leasing Limited -1984; M & G Securities Limited -1988; M & G Assurance Group Limited -1988; Transatlantic and General Securities Company Limited -1989. *Professional Organisations:* Member, Gray's Inn.

HADLEY, Michael James; Director, Chemicals & Industrial, Harrisons & Crosfield plc.

HADLEY, Nicholas Martin; Partner, McKenna & Co, since 1989; Property Development and Institutional Conveyancing. *Career:* Evershed & Tomkinson, Articled Clerk 1977-79; Assistant Solicitor 1979-82; Associate Partner 1982-84; Wragge & Co, Assistant Solicitor 1985-86; Associate Partner 1986-87; McKenna & Co, Assistant Solicitor 1987-89. *Biog: b.* 30 April 1953. *Nationality:* British. *m.* 1982, Marsha; 1 s; 1 d. *Educ:* Birmingham University (LLB 2i, PhD Law). *Other Activities:* City of London Solicitors Company. *Professional Organisations:* Law Society.

HADOW, N P H; Director, Barclays de Zoete Wedd Securities Ltd.

HADOW, Paul; Partner, Penningtons, since 1979; Commercial Litigation Construction Law and Employment Law. *Career:* Penningtons, Articled Clerk 1973-75; Assistant Solicitor 1975-79. *Biog: b.* 20 November 1950. *Nationality:* British. *m.* 1983, Patricia Mary (née Cattanach). *Educ:* Ampleforth College; University of Kent (BA). *Professional Organisations:* Member, Law Society. *Recreations:* Walking, Gardening.

HAGER, David Paul; Partner, Bacon & Woodrow, since 1987; Investment Consulting Partner. *Career:* N M Rothschild & Sons Ltd Investment Adviser 1972-74; Bacon & Woodrow Ptnr 1975-85; County Group Ltd/County Investment Management Ltd Dir 1985-87. *Biog: b.* 7 January 1951. *Nationality:* British. *m.* 1972, Jeanette Carolyn (née Hares); 1 s. *Educ:* Bournemouth School; Hertford College, Oxford (BA Hons Eng Science & Econ 1st, MA). *Directorships:* Combined Actuarial Performance Services Ltd 1984-85 Chm. *Professional Organisations:* Fellow, Institute of Actuaries; Fellow, Institute of Pensions Management. *Publications:* A General Introduction to Institutional Investment (with A J Frost), 1986; Debt Securities (with A J Frost), 1990; Pension Fund Investment (with C D Lever), 1989. *Clubs:* Oxford & Cambridge Club. *Recreations:* Flying Light Aircraft, Swimming.

HAGERTY, M T; Executive Director, J H Minet & Co Ltd.

HAGGAS, John Brian; Director, Skipton Building Society. *Nationality:* British. *Directorships:* John Haggas plc Chairman.

HAGGETT, David Stephen; Senior Partner, Evershed Wells & Hind; Corporate Finance. *Career:* Evershed & Tomkinson (Birmingham) 1967; Partner 1969. *Biog: b.* 28 March 1938. *Nationality:* British. *m.* Janet Irene; 2 s; 2 d. *Educ:* Bromsgrove School; Trinity Hall, Cambridge (MA,LLM). *Directorships:* The Air Group Limited; Animal Biotechnology Cambridge Limited; Astbury Construction Group Limited; B Birks & Co Limited; Colorgraphic plc; DMC Creative World Limited; Headlam Group plc; HHT plc; High Level Hardware Limited; How Group plc; METSEC plc; Morris Ashby plc; Pearce & Cutler Group Limited; Pedigree Group Limited; Polywarm Products Limited; The Second Roman Property Trust plc; Seward Agricultural Machinery Limited; TGI plc; The Third Roman Property Trust plc; The Wensum Company plc.

HAHN, Edward William; Chief Operating Officer, Citicorp Insurance Brokers Ltd.

HAILEY, Stephen Russell; Head of Audit & Business Advisory Practice, Arthur Andersen, since 1989; Advisory Audit and Investigative Work. *Career:* Jackson Taylor Abernethy & Co 1965-69; Arthur Andersen & Co 1969-; DTI Industrial Development Unit (Secondment), Principal/Case Officer 1976-77; Arthur Andersen, Client Partner 1980-. *Biog: b.* 7 September 1945. *Nationality:* British. *m.* 1972, Susan (née Smart); 3 s. *Educ:* Atlantic College. *Other Activities:* Lloyds Committee of Enquiry (Member 1983-84); United World College of the Atlantic (Governor & Member of Council). *Professional Organisations:* FCA.

HAK, S; Director, Barclays de Zoete Wedd Securities Ltd.

HAKUTA, S; Executive Director, Daiwa Europe Limited.

HALCROW, Richard John; Director, Morgan Grenfell & Co Ltd, since 1989; Head of Debt Equity Conversions & Asset Trading Depts, Member of International Division Operating Committee. *Career:* Lloyds Bank (Overseas), Graduate Trainee 1973; European Brazilian Bank Mgr 1974-76; Libra Bank plc, Snr Regional Mgr 1976-78. *Biog: b.* 2 June 1952. *Nationality:* British. *m.* 1975, Gillian Mary (née Van Mallrik); 1 s; 1 d. *Educ:* Bradfield College; Bournemouth College (Business Administration). *Directorships:* Morgan Grenfell & Co Ltd 1989 (exec); Morgan Grenfell Trade Finance Ltd 1989 (exec) Chairman; Equitypar Cia De Investimentos Ltd, (Brazil) 1988 (non-exec); Morgan Grenfell International Ltd 1986-88 (exec); Credit for Exports plc 1989 (exec); MG Bv Assecioria Financeira Ltd, (Venezuela) 1990 (non-exec). *Professional Organisations:* Member,The Securities Assoc; Member, Inst of Bankers. *Clubs:* Special Forces Club, Wildernesse Golf Club, East India Club. *Recreations:* Shooting, Golf.

HALCROW, Robert; Head of Syndications/Senior Manager, Business Development, Banque Internationale à Luxembourg SA, since 1989; Loan Syndications/Business Development. *Career:* Manufacturers Hanover Trust Co, London Branch, Asst Regional Officer, Account Officer for Latin America/Iberian Peninsula Region 1977-79; Libra Bank Limited (London), Regional Manager, Marketing and Syndication of Eurocurrency Loans and Responsible for Placement of Existing Portfolio in Secondary Market 1979-82; Saudi International Bank (London), Head of Eurocurrency Lending and Syndications, Responsible for Marketing and Syndication Activity of all Loan Activities (excluding Middle East Related Relationship Loans and Property Finance) 1982-87. *Biog: b.* 30 June 1956. *Nationality:* British. *Educ:* Sompting Abbots School, Sussex; Bradfield College, Berkshire; Southampton University (BSc Economics and Commerce). *Clubs:* East India Club, Richmond Golf Club. *Recreations:* Golf, Tennis, Swimming, Skiing, Windsurfing, Squash.

HALE, A; Partner, Pensions (St Albans), Bacon & Woodrow.

HALE, Charles Martin; Managing Director, Donaldson Lufkin & Jenrette International Securities, since 1984; Head of International Division, Institutional Equity Sales and Trading. *Career:* Hirsch & Co Gen Ptnr 1968-70; A G Becker Inc MD 1970-83; Lehman Bros Kuhn Loeb Inc Gen Ptnr 1983-84. *Biog: b.* 19 January 1936. *Nationality:* American. *m.* 1967, Kaaren; 2 d. *Educ:* St Bernards School, NY; Culver Military; Stanford University (BSc); Harvard Business School (MBA). *Other Activities:* Chairman, U.K. Association of New York Stock Exchange Members. *Clubs:* Annabel's, Harvard Club (New York), Hurlingham, Vanderbilt Racquet. *Recreations:* Tennis, Cinema, Travel, Naval History.

HALE, Christopher George; Partner, Travers Smith Braithwaite, since 1987; Corporate Finance. *Career:* Kingsley Napley, Articled Clerk; Asst Solicitor 1979-82; Travers Smith Braithwaite, Asst Solicitor 1983-87. *Biog: b.* 27 September 1955. *Nationality:* British. *Educ:* King's College School, Wimbledon; Emmanuel College,Cambridge (MA); Wolfson College, Cambridge (LLM). *Other Activities:* Mem, & Liberal Democratic Lawyers' Association; National Council for Civil Liberties. *Professional Organisations:* The Law Society. *Recreations:* Cinema, Reading, Gardening, Walking, Legal History.

HALE, John Hampton; Director, Pearson plc, since 1983. *Career:* RAF and Fleet Air Arm Pilot 1943-46; Alcan Aluminium Ltd, Montreal, Canada 1949-60; New York 1960-63; London; Alcan Booth Industries Ltd, Managing Director 1964-70; Montreal, Executive Vice President, Finance 1970-82; Alcan Aluminium Ltd; Aluminium Company of Canada Ltd (Montreal); Nippon Light Metal Co (Japan); Indian Aluminium Co Ltd; Alcan Australia Ltd, Director 1970-85; Aluminium Company of Canada Ltd, Chairman 1979-83; Scovill Inc (USA), Director 1978-85; Ritz-Carlton Hotel, Montreal, Director 1981-83; Pearson plc, Managing Director 1983-86; Fairey Holdings Ltd, Chairman 1983-86; Pearson Inc (USA), Chairman 1983-86; SSMC Inc (USA), Director 1986-89. *Biog: b.* 8 July 1924. *Nationality:* British/Canadian. *m.* 1980, Nancy (née Birks); 1 s; 2 d (former marriage). *Educ:* Eton College (Kings Scholar); Magdoline College, Cambridge (BA Hons, MA); Harvard Business School (Henny Fellow). *Directorships:* Bank of Montreal 1985 (non-exec); Economist Newspapers Ltd 1984 (non-exec); International Stock Exchange (London) 1987 (non-exec); Pearson plc 1983 (non-exec); Pearson Inc 1983 (non-exec); Spean Insurance Company Limited 1983 (non-exec); Foundation for Canadian Studies 1988. *Other Activities:* Chairman, Chambly County Protestant Central School Board, Canada, 1957-60; Chairman, Business Graduates Association, London, 1967-70; Member, Accounting Research Advisory Board, Canadian Institute of Chartered Accountants, 1975-81; Chairman, 1978-81; Director, Canadian Advisory Board, Allendale Mutual Insurance Company, 1977-83; Director, Mont St Hilaire Nature Conservation Association, Canada, 1977-83; President, 1980-83 80-83; Director, Concordia University Business School, Montreal, 1981-83; Governor, Stratford Festival, Ontario, 1981-83; Senator, 1983-89; Governor, Montreal General Hospital, 1981-; Master, Worshipful Company of Armourers & Brasiers; Member, North American Advisory Group, British Overseas Trade Board, 1988. *Clubs:* RTYC, Mount Royal Club, Toronto Club, Aldeburgh Golf Club. *Recreations:* Fishing, Shooting, Sailing, Skiing.

HALE, Robert; Partner, Robson Rhodes, since 1974; Audit, Accountancy, Flotations and Corporate Financial Services. *Career:* Robson Rhodes, Snr Mgr 1960-. *Biog: b.* 29 August 1943. *m.* 1968, Diane Elizabeth (née Morris); 1 s; 1 d. *Educ:* Sir Gilbert Claughton Grammar School, Dudley. *Professional Organisations:* FCA. *Clubs:* Belfrey Sporting. *Recreations:* Golf, Travel.

HALES, Antony; Chief Executive, J Lyons & Company Limited, since 1989. *Career:* Ansells Limited, Managing Director 1987-89; Ind Coope Taylor Walker, Managing Director 1985-87; Halls Oxford & West Brewery, Managing Director 1983-85; Joshua Tetley, Marketing Director 1979-83; Cadbury Schweppes, Marketing Manager 1969-79. *Biog: b.* 23 May 1948. *Nationality:* British. *Educ:* Repton School; Bristol University

(BSc). *Directorships:* Allied-Lyons plc 1989 (exec); Baskin-Robbins Eastern Ltd 1990 (exec); DCA Food Industries Inc 1989 (exec); J Lyons & Company Limited 1989 Chief Executive; Dunkin Donuts Inc 1990 (exec). *Other Activities:* Brewers Company. *Professional Organisations:* MCIM.

HALES, C A; Partner, Holman, Fenwick & Willan, since 1968; Shipping Law, Chairman of Management Committee, Staff Partner. *Career:* Served at Sea in Merchant Navy, Alfred Holt & Co (Blue Funnel Line), Apprentice to 2nd Mate 1949-58; Master Mariner 1957; Barrister, Gray's Inn 1960; Alsop Stevens & Co, Articled Clerk 1961-64; Admitted Solicitor 1964; Holman Fenwick & Willan, Asst Solicitor 1965-67; Partner 1968-. *Biog: b.* 26 August 1931. *Nationality:* British. *m.* 1956, Barbara Mary (née Ryan); 2 s; 4 d. *Educ:* Wellingborough School; HMS Worcester. *Other Activities:* Deputy District Registrar, High Court; Deputy Registrar, County Courts; Liveryman, Hon Company of Master Mariners; Freeman, City of London Solicitors Company; Freeman of the City of London. *Professional Organisations:* Member, Law Society. *Recreations:* Concert & Theatre Going, Following Cricket, History.

HALEY, Geoff N; Partner, Theodore Goddard, since 1989; Construction, Energy, Urban Renewal and Transportation. *Career:* Admitted as Solicitor 1971; Walton & Weybridge UDC, Solicitor 1971-72; Peterborough Dev Corp, Deputy Legal Adviser 1972-74; Costain Group plc, Senior Solicitor 1974-76; Deputy Group Legal Adviser 1976-86; Costain UK, Director 1980-86; Legal Adviser 1978-86; Costain Ventures Division, General Manager 1986-89; Thames Barrier Consortium, Legal Adviser 1979-86; Channel Tunnel Contractors (Transmanche Link), Led Contract Negotiations for Proposal 1985-86; GKN Kwikform Ltd, Director 1986-89; British Urban Development Ltd, Alternate Director 1988-89. *Biog: b.* 12 October 1944. *Nationality:* British. *m.* Doreen (née Veitch); 1 s; 1 d. *Educ:* Accrington Grammar School; London University (LLB); Henley Management College/Brunel University (MBA). *Directorships:* Costain UK 1980-86 (exec); GKN Kwikform Ltd 1986-89 (exec); British Urban Development Ltd 1988-89 (exec) Alternate; Costain Concrete Co 1986-88 (exec); Loughside Power Co 1986-88 (exec); Invermoray Hydrocarbons Utilities Co 1987-88 (exec); CPI Securities Ltd (exec); Forward Computing Ltd (exec); GKN Kwikform Holdings Ltd (exec); JLS Plant Ltd (exec); Kwikform Investments Ltd (exec); Kent European Enterprises Ltd (exec) Alternate. *Other Activities:* Member, Ascot 41 Club; Member, Law Society; Society of Construction Law; Member of Committee on Design & Construction of Deep Basements of Institute of Structural Engineers; Strategic Planning Society; Institute of Marketing; Greenlands Association (Henley); Member, Institute of Petroleum Inaugural Committee Member of British Urban Regeneration Association. *Professional Organisations:* Solicitor; Diploma in Marketing, Chartered Institute of Marketing. *Publications:* Numerous Articles in the Fields of Construction Law, Private Financing for Infrastructure Projects, Transportation, Energy and Urban Renewal. *Clubs:* Ascot 41 Club (Round Table). *Recreations:* Swimming, Cycling, Walking.

HALFORD, W Timothy; Group Public Affairs Director, Grand Metropolitan plc, since 1984; Public/Media Relations. *Career:* Occidental Intl Oil Inc, Vice-President, European Public Affairs 1975-84. *Biog: b.* 19 February 1947. *Nationality:* British. *m.* 1969, Andrea Rosemary (née Lee); 3 d. *Professional Organisations:* FRSA; Fellow, Institute of Public Relations (FIPR); FBIM. *Clubs:* Honourable Artillery Company. *Recreations:* Theatre, Reading, Walking.

HALL, A M; Partner, Grimley J R Eve.

HALL, Adrian Charles; Partner, Turner Kenneth Brown, since 1986; Banking. *Career:* Norton Rose Botterell & Roche, Solicitor 1971-75; Borden & Elliot (Toronto), Barrister/Solicitor 1975-78; Allen & Overy, Solicitor 1978-82; Standard Chartered Bank, Snr Legal Mgr 1982-86. *Biog: b.* 8 June 1945. *Nationality:* British. *m.* 1981, Magdalena Mary (née Fiteni); 2 s; 1 d. *Educ:* Eton College; Mansfield College, Oxford (MA). *Other Activities:* City of London Solicitors' Company. *Professional Organisations:* IBA; The Law Society; Canadian Bar Association. *Clubs:* MCC, Eton Ramblers, Alfa Romeo Owners' Club, Historic Sports Car Club. *Recreations:* Historic Motor Racing, Music, Field Game, Wall Game.

HALL, Alan Richard Finden; Partner, Slaughter and May, since 1984; Corporate Finance and Commercial Law. *Biog: b.* 30 October 1952. *Nationality:* British. *m.* 1975, Helen Ann (née Duckworth); 2 s; 1 d. *Educ:* Bradfield College; Clare College, Cambridge (MA). *Professional Organisations:* The Law Society; Law Society of Hong Kong. *Clubs:* Oriental, Hurlingham, Addington Golf Club, Royal Hong Kong Jockey Club, Sheko Country Club (Hong Kong), Royal Ashdown Golf Club, The Wiseley Golf Club. *Recreations:* Sport and the Arts.

HALL, Anthony Arthur; Joint Managing Director, Rea Brothers Group plc; with responsibility for the two Offshore Companies of the Group, Rea Brothers (Guernsey) Ltd and Rea Brothers (Isle of Man) Ltd. *Career:* Barclays Bank Ltd, Jnr Securities Clerk 1955-65; Barclays Bank DCO Group Trust Officer 1965-70; N M Rothschild (CI) Ltd, (GSY) Trust Officer 1970-72; Bank of London & Montreal (Nassau), Trustee Mgr 1972-73; Italian International Bank (CI) Ltd, Trustee Mgr 1973-76; Rea Brothers (Guernsey) Ltd, MD 1976-. *Biog: b.* 25 May 1939. *Nationality:* British. *m.* 1960, Valerie Christine (née Stewart); 1 s; 2 d. *Educ:* Sir George Monoux Grammar School, Walthamstow. *Di-*

rectorships: Rea Bros (Guernsey) Ltd 1977 (exec); Rea Bros Group plc 1988 (exec). *Professional Organisations:* ACIB (Trustee Diploma). *Recreations:* Flying (Holder of Multi-Engine Instrument Rating), Target Pistol Shooting, Sea Fishing, Chess, Swimming.

HALL, B A; Executive Director, Laporte plc; Personnel. *Career:* Courtaulds, Chemical Engineering 1960-65; British Gypsum, Operational 1965-70. *Biog: b.* 20 October 1939. *Nationality:* British. *m.* 1961, Edna Anne (née Proffit); 1 s; 2 d. *Educ:* Manchester University (BSc Hons Chemical Engineering). *Directorships:* Laporte plc (exec); Laporte Pension Fund Trustees Ltd (exec); Laporte Industries Ltd (exec); Interox Chimica Spa (exec); Laporte Industries Australia Pty Ltd (exec). *Other Activities:* Member of CIA: Business & Trade Board Committee, Competition Policy Committee; Member, Institute of Environmental Assessment. *Professional Organisations:* AMCT; AMIChemE. *Recreations:* Sailing, Golf.

HALL, C Nicholas; Partner, Beachcroft Stanleys.

HALL, Colin; Partner, Slaughter and May, since 1978; Company and Commercial Law. *Career:* Foreign and Commonwealth Office 1966-68. *Biog: b.* 23 April 1945. *Nationality:* British. *m.* 1973, Philippa (née Collinson); 4 s. *Educ:* The Stationers' Company School; Bristol University (LLB Hons). *Professional Organisations:* Law Society. *Recreations:* Sailing, Ornithology, Gardening.

HALL, D J; Partner, Broadbridge.

HALL, David; Partner, Linklaters & Paines.

HALL, Dr Derek Gordon; Senior Vice President, J P Morgan, since 1987; Systems and Data Processin. *Career:* Arthur Andersen, Mgr 1970-76. *Biog: b.* 17 April 1944. *Nationality:* British. *m.* 1979, Susan (née Eaton); 2 s; 1 d. *Educ:* Penarth County Grammar School; University College, London (BSc, PhD). *Publications:* Various Scientific, 1968-70. *Recreations:* Sport, Dinner Parties, Music, Theatre.

HALL, Professor E T; CBE; Non-Executive Director, The General Electric Company plc.

HALL, Geoffrey Alan; Director, Midland Montagu Asset Management, since 1988; Smaller Companies. *Career:* Philips Industries Pension Fund, Trainee 1966-68; New South Wales Bus Company, Driver 1968-70; IPC Pension Trustee, Analyst 1970-71; Philips Pension Fund, Analyst 1972-76; British Railways Pension Fund, Investment Manager 1976-86; County Investment Management, Investment Manager 1986-87; Midland Montagu Asset Management, Investment Director 1987-. *Biog: b.* 22 October 1948. *Nationality:* British. *m.* 1971, Ethne (née McKeon); 2 s. *Educ:* City of London School. *Professional Organisations:* Associate Member,

Society of Investment Analysts. *Clubs:* Fell & Rock. *Recreations:* Climbing, Football.

HALL, Graham N; Partner, MacNair Mason.

HALL, Harold Michael; Director, Gibbs Hartley Cooper Ltd.

HALL, J E; Partner, Cameron Markby Hewitt.

HALL, J P; Managing Director (Investment Management), Brewin Dolphin & Co Ltd.

HALL, J R; Director, S G Warburg Akroyd Rowe & Pitman Mullens Securities Ltd, since 1989; European Equities. *Career:* Savory Milln, Director European Equities 1981-86; Warburg Securities 1986-; Seconded to Paris at Warburg Subsidiary, Bacot-Allain 1988-. *Biog: b.* 21 September 1958. *Nationality:* British. *m.* 1984, Marion (née Wall); 1 s; 1 d. *Educ:* Eton College; Oriel College, Oxford (BA). *Clubs:* Royal Birkdale Golf Club.

HALL, Sir John Bernard; BT; Managing Director, The Nikko Bank (UK) plc, since 1990; Banking. *Career:* J Henry Schröder & Co/J Henry Schröder Wagg & Co Ltd 1955-73; Director 1967-73; Bank of America Ltd/Bank of America International Ltd/Bank of America International SA, Director 1974-82; Bank of America NT & SA, Vice-President 1982-90; Seconded to European Brazilian Bank plc, Managing Director & Chief Executive 1983-89. *Biog: b.* 20 March 1932. *Nationality:* British. *m.* 1957, Lady Delia Mary (née Innes); 1 s; 2 d. *Educ:* Eton College, Windsor; Trinity College, Oxford (MA). *Other Activities:* Member, Court of Assistants, The Clothworkers' Company (and Governor, The Clothworkers' Foundation); FRGS; FRSA. *Professional Organisations:* FCIB. *Clubs:* Boodles, Lansdowne, Overseas Bankers'. *Recreations:* Fishing, Travel, Motoring.

HALL, John Henry; Partner, Wragge & Co, since 1966. *Biog: b.* 10 October 1931. *m.* 1966, Diane Jane (née Hanks); 1 s; 1 d. *Directorships:* Mucklow Bros Ltd 1977 (non-exec).

HALL, John James; Executive Director, Treasury, Fennoscandia Bank Ltd, since 1989; Treasury. *Career:* Bank of London & South America Ltd (London)/Lloyds Bank Intl (London), Trainee to Manager, F/E Dealing Room 1957-73; Banco Di Roma (London), Vice Directtore, Dealing Room 1973-76; Dresdner Bank AG (London), Senior Manager, F/E & Money Market 1976-87; Fennoscandia Bank Ltd (London), Senior Manager to EDT 1987-. *Biog: b.* 2 September 1936. *Nationality:* British. *m.* 1984, Diane (née Wright); 1 s; 2 d. *Educ:* Ashby De La Zouche Boys Grammar School. *Recreations:* Badminton, Stamp Collecting.

HALL, M S; Executive Director, James R Knowles Limited.

HALL, Marcus; Director (Sales), Hoare Govett International Securities.

HALL, R J L; Director, Panmure Gordon & Co Limited.

HALL, R P; Director, Charterhouse Tilney.

HALL, Richard John Jeaffreson; Head of Corporate Services Division, BDO Binder Hamlyn, since 1989; Services to Public Companies and Banks. *Career:* BDO Binder Hamlyn 1971-; Partner 1978-. *Biog: b.* 31 July 1945. *Nationality:* British. *m.* 1970, Wendy (née Thomas); 1 s; 1 d. *Educ:* Westminster School; Christ Church, Oxford (MA). *Professional Organisations:* FCA. *Clubs:* Hurlingham. *Recreations:* Squash, Tennis, Watching & Listening to Italian Opera.

HALL, Robin Alexander; Managing Director, CIN Venture Managers Ltd, since 1988; Venture Capital. *Career:* Arthur Young Audit Mgr 1967-74; National Enterprise Board Investment Exec 1975-79; Insac Products Ltd Fin Dir 1980-81; CIN Venture Managers Ltd Dir 1982-90. *Biog: b.* 19 May 1948. *Nationality:* British. *m.* 1977, Hazel (née Maidman); 2 s; 1 d. *Educ:* Highbury County Grammar School. *Directorships:* CIN Venture Managers Ltd 1982 (exec); CIN Venture Nominees 1982 (non-exec); CIN Post Houses Fund Ltd 1986 (non-exec); Spectrum Group plc 1983 (non-exec); Citylink Group Ltd 1983 (non-exec); Gabicci plc 1984 (non-exec); SEMA Group plc 1985 (non-exec); Globe Investment Trust plc 1990 (non-exec). *Professional Organisations:* FCA.

HALL, Roger Leonard; Managing Director, Smith Barney & Co, since 1990. *Career:* ICI Plastics Division 1964-70; Merrill Lynch 1975-80; Smith Barney 1980. *Biog: b.* 30 May 1942. *Nationality:* British. *m.* 1962, Patricia (née Sutcliffe); 2 s; 2 d. *Educ:* Westminster School; Sidney Sussex College, Cambridge (MA); London Business School (MSc). *Other Activities:* Needlemakers' Company. *Recreations:* Opera, Swimming.

HALL, Simon Andrew Dalton; Partner, Freshfields, since 1985; Head of Finance Group. *Career:* Freshfields, Articled 1977-79; Seconded to Cravath Swaine & Moore, New York, 1983-84; Freshfields (New York Office) 1984-85. *Biog: b.* 6 February 1955. *Nationality:* British. *m.* 1979, Teresa Ann (née Bartleet); 2 s; 2 d. *Educ:* Ampleforth College, York; St Catharine's College, Cambridge (MA Law); Lancaster Gate, College of Law (Law Society Qualifying). *Professional Organisations:* Law Society; International Bar Association. *Publications:* Co-Author, Leasing Finance (Euromoney, 1985); Editor, Aircraft Financing (Euromoney, 1989). *Recreations:* Shooting, Fishing.

HALL, Stephen Hargreaves; Partner, Ernst & Young, since 1962; Corporate Advisory Services. *Career:* Kings Own Yorkshire Light Infantry 1952-53; Territorial Army Major 1953-69; Ernst & Young 1962-. *Biog: b.* 30 April 1933. *Nationality:* British. *m.* 1960, Nuala (née Stanley); 2 s; 1 d. *Educ:* Rugby School; Christ's College, Cambridge (MA). *Directorships:* Yorkshire Television Holdings plc (non-exec). *Other Activities:* High Sheriff of Humberside 1982-82; University of Hull (Member of Council 1972-84). *Professional Organisations:* FCA. *Clubs:* City of London, Army & Navy. *Recreations:* Fishing.

HALL, Timothy Julian Dalton; Director, Martin Currie Investment Management Ltd, since 1989; UK Based Pension Funds & Charities. *Career:* Martin Currie Ltd, Assistant Fund Manager 1984-89. *Biog: b.* 18 December 1961. *Nationality:* British. *m.* 1988, Elizabeth Charlotte (née MacLeod). *Educ:* Ampleforth College, York; Edinburgh University (MA Hons History). *Directorships:* Martin Currie Investment Management Ltd 1989 (non-exec); Martin Currie Unit Trusts Ltd 1989 (non-exec). *Recreations:* Squash, Running, Fishing, Art.

HALL, Tony; Vice President, Drexel Burnham Lambert.

HALLAHANE, Dennis; Executive Director, Scimitar Development Capital Limited.

HALLAM, Cedric George; Assistant General Manager, Banque Nationale de Paris, since 1990; Treasury. *Career:* Samuel Montagu & Co Ltd 1964-68; Banque Nationale de Paris, Foreign Exchange Dealer 1968-79; Dealing Manager 1979-90. *Biog: b.* 13 March 1947. *Nationality:* British. *Educ:* Harrow County School. *Recreations:* The Countryside, Church Architecture.

HALLAM, Frank Maurice; General Manager, Bradford & Bingley.

HALLAM, S H; Partner, Cameron Markby Hewitt.

HALLE, Victor Gordon David; Director, Kleinwort Benson Securities, since 1986; Equity Salesman. *Career:* Grieveson Grant 1969-86; Ptnr 1983-86. *Biog: b.* 27 October 1950. *m.* 1972, Maria (née Templeman); 1 s; 1 d. *Educ:* Higher Grade School, Edmonton. *Professional Organisations:* The International Stock Exchange. *Recreations:* Football, Reading, Gardening.

HALLER, Frederic Zachary; Director, Morgan Grenfell & Co Limited, since 1990; Debt Arbitrage and Trading in Impaired Assets. *Career:* Chase Manhattan Bank; Credit and Marketing Officer (responsible for calling on and soliciting business from private and public sectors of Latin American countries) 1970; Second Vice President 1974; Vice President 1976; Seconded to Libra Bank 1973; Responsible for Brazil 1973-74; Responsible

for Onlending in Mexico 1975-83; Directly employed by Libra 1979-90; Chief Financial Officer 1983-87; Executive Director 1985; Executive Director, Investment Banking 1987-90; Moved to Morgan Grenfell on liquidation of Libra Bank 1990. *Biog: b.* 19 May 1946. *Nationality:* American. *m.* 1972, Josephine (née Ysaguirre); 3 s; 1 d. *Educ:* New York University Graduate Business School (BA).

HALLETT, R C; General Manager, Customer Services, Friends' Provident Life Office.

HALLIDAY, David Ralph; Partner, Bacon & Woodrow, since 1987; Pension Fund Actuary. *Career:* Bacon & Woodrow 1974-. *Biog: b.* 28 September 1952. *Nationality:* British. *Educ:* Devonport High School; Selwyn College, Cambridge (MA). *Professional Organisations:* FIA. *Recreations:* Music, Bridge, Reading, Gardening.

HALLMANN, J Clark; Director, County NatWest Investment Management Ltd.

HALLOWELL, Michael Geoffrey; Partner, Titmuss Sainer & Webb; Commercial Property and Property Development. *Biog: b.* 23 July 1954. *Nationality:* British. *m.* 1982, Karen (née Werth); 2 d. *Educ:* Highgate School; Queens' College, Cambridge (MA).

HALLY, Paul William; Partner, Shepherd & Wedderburn WS, since 1987; Corporation and Commercial Law, Insolvency & Bankruptcy Law. *Career:* Fyfe Ireland & Co, Trainee/Solicitor 1982-84; Shepherd & Wedderburn, Solicitor 1984-87. *Biog: b.* 23 June 1959. *Nationality:* British. *m.* 1989, Anne (née Weatherup). *Educ:* Perth High School; University of Edinburgh (LLB Hons). *Professional Organisations:* Law Society of Scotland. *Recreations:* Hockey, Squash, Golf.

HALSEY, Michael J; Company Secretary, Brown, Shipley & Co Limited, since 1990. *Career:* Brown, Shipley & Co Limited, Group Controller & Assistant Secretary 1985-90; E D & F Man Limited, Group Secretary 1982-85; Group Chief Accountant 1974-82. *Biog: b.* 5 May 1947. *Nationality:* British. *m.* 1976, Kristina (née Tetzeli De Rosador); 2 d. *Educ:* Haileybury; ISC. *Professional Organisations:* FCA. *Clubs:* Henden G C.

HALTON, T M; Director, CCF Foster Braithwaite Ltd.

HAM, Richard Gibson; Partner, Walker Martineau Stringer Saul, since 1987; Banking and Finance. *Career:* Midland Bank plc, Management Trainee 1978-80; Jaques & Co, Articled Clerk 1981-83; Edward Lewis & Co, Assistant Commercial Solicitor 1983-84; Walker Martineau, Assistant Commercial Solicitor 1984-87; Partner 1987-90; Walker Martineau Stringer Saul, Partner 1990. *Biog: b.* 10 November 1956. *Nationality:* British. *Educ:* Llanishen High School, Cardiff; Wadham College, Oxford (BA). *Other Activities:* Holborn Law Society. *Clubs:* The Little Ship Club, Lee on the Solent Sailing Club.

HAMA, M; Director, IBJ International Limited.

HAMBRO, Charles Eric Alexander; Chairman, Hambros plc, since 1983. *Career:* Coldstream Guards, Lt 1948-51; Hambros Bank Ltd 1952-; Dir 1957-; Chm 1972-83; Chm 1988. *Biog: b.* 24 July 1930. m1 Rose Evelyn (née Cotterell); m2 1976, Cherry Felicity (née Twiss); 2 s ; 1 d. *Educ:* Eton College. *Directorships:* Royal National Pension Fund for Nurses 1957 Chm; Taylor Woodrow plc 1962 (non-exec); Guardian Royal Exchange Assurance plc 1968-; Chm 1988; Hambros Advanced Technology Trust plc 1984 Chm; The Peninsular & Oriental Steam Navigation Co 1987 (non-exec); General Oriental Investments Ltd 1984; Istituto Bancario San Paolo di Torino 1989. *Other Activities:* Member of the Fishmongers' Company; Member of the Guild of World Traders; Hon Member of the Parlour; Trustee, The British Museum. *Clubs:* White's, MCC. *Recreations:* Shooting, Cricket, Golf.

HAMBRO, James; Joint Managing Director, J O Hambro Magan & Co Ltd.

HAMBRO, Rupert Nicholas; Chairman, J O Hambro Magan, since 1988. *Career:* Hambros Bank 1974-86; Chairman 1983-86. *Biog: b.* 27 June 1943. *Nationality:* British. *m.* 1970, Mary Robinson (née Boyer); 1 s; 1 d. *Educ:* Eton. *Directorships:* Sedgwick Group plc (non-exec). *Other Activities:* Worshipful Company of Fishmongers.

HAMBURGER, R L; Managing Director, Smith Barney, Harris Upham Europe Ltd, since 1988; Corporate Finance. *Career:* Goldman Sachs, Vice President 1979-88; Chase Manhattan Bank (New York, Milan, Rome & London), Vice President 1971-79. *Biog: b.* 18 October 1943. *Nationality:* American. *m.* 1967, Caroline (née Dull); 2 s. *Educ:* University of Notre Dame (AB, MA, PhD). *Publications:* Anti Colonialism and Anti Communism with Respect to the Algerian Question, 1970. *Recreations:* Golf.

HAMBY, Sir Derek; Non-Executive Member, British Railways Board.

HAMER, C J; Bureau Manager, Insurance Ombudsman Bureau, since 1988; Oversight of General Operation, Finance, Personnel & Procedural Matters. *Career:* HM Customs & Excise, Various Management Positions in Southampton/Southend/Westend 1974-84; Personal Assistant to the Parliamentary Ombudsman, Sir Cecil Clothier KCB, QC 1984-85; Cabinet Office/HM Treasury, Management & Efficiency; Division, General

Consultancy Work on Efficiency in The Civil Service 1985-87; Bureau Manager, Insurance Ombudsman Bureau 1988-. *Biog: b.* 26 December 1952. *Nationality:* British. *m.* 1975, Sarah Anne (née Preston); 3 s. *Educ:* Thornbury Grammar School, Gloucestershire; Dorset Institute of Higher Education (HNC Business Studies). *Recreations:* Motoring, Golf, DIY.

HAMER, Keith William; Managing Director, Credit Commercial de France (UK) Limited, since 1990; Corporate Finance. *Career:* Rothschild Intercontinental Bank, Executive 1973-75; Amex Bank Limited, Manager 1975-77; Middle East Associates, Director 1977-87; Chase Investment Bank Ltd, Director Mergers & Acquisitions Dept 1987-88; Laurence Prust & Co Ltd (now renamed Credit Commercial de France (UK) Ltd), Director, Managing Director 1988-. *Biog: b.* 5 September 1950. *Nationality:* Canadian/British. *m.* 1981, Jennifer (née Cassar); 1 s; 2 d. *Educ:* Sedbergh School; Keble College, Oxford (MA, Philosophy & Psychology); INSEAD (MBA). *Directorships:* CCF Holdings 1990 (exec); MEA Investment Co (non-exec); CPA Holdings (non-exec). *Clubs:* Boodles, Hurlingham, Roehampton, Royal Wimbledon GC. *Recreations:* Skiing, Tennis, Golf, Jazz.

HAMES, Captain P; RN; Clerk, Stationers' & Newspaper Makers' Company.

HAMILTON, A J; Non-Executive Chairman, Byas Mosley & Co Ltd.

HAMILTON, Alexander Macdonald; CBE, JP; Consultant, McGrigor Donald, since 1990; Banking, Civil Engineering and Building Contract Disputes. *Career:* McGrigor Donald Ptnr 1957-90; Senior Ptnr 1977-90; Consultant 1990-. *Biog: b.* 11 May 1925. *m.* 1953, Catherine (née Gray); 2 s; 1 d. *Educ:* Hamilton Academy; Glasgow University (MA, LLB). *Directorships:* Royal Bank of Scotland plc 1978 (non-exec); Royal Bank of Scotland Group plc 1985 (non-exec); Royal Bank of Scotland plc 1990 Vice Chm. *Other Activities:* Session Clerk, Cambuslang Old Parish Church; Vice Chm, Cambuslang Community Council; Chm, Scottish Ctee of the Scout Assoc; Member, Merchants House and Incorporation of Wrights of Glasgow. *Clubs:* Royal Scottish Automobile, Royal Northern & Clyde Yacht Club. *Recreations:* Golf, Sailing.

HAMILTON, Hugh Robert Bowsfield; Partner, Lawrence Graham, since 1983; Trusts & Estates. *Career:* Crane & Hawkins, Partner 1968-83. *Biog: b.* 4 June 1937. *Nationality:* British. *m.* 1968, Susan Elizabeth (née Knight); 2 s. *Educ:* Cheltenham College; Nottingham University (LLB). *Professional Organisations:* Solicitor; Member, Law Society; Committee, Westminster Law Society.

HAMILTON, J I M; Head of Corporate Finance, Kleinwort Benson Securities Ltd, since 1982. *Career:* Beaumont & Son, Solicitors, Articled Clerk 1966-69; Solicitor 1969-70; Tioxide Ltd, Assistant Company Secretary 1970-73; Grieveson, Grant & Co, Stockbrokers, Corporate Finance 1973-79; Partner 1979; Head of Corporate Finance 1982-. *Biog: b.* 6 January 1944. *Nationality:* British. *m.* 1977, Janet (née Man); 2 s; 1 d. *Educ:* Canford School; Bristol University (LLB). *Directorships:* Kleinwort Benson Ltd 1986 (exec); Kleinwort Benson Securities Ltd. *Professional Organisations:* Solicitor; Member, Law Society. *Recreations:* Fishing, Wine, Opera.

HAMILTON, J K; Director, S G Warburg Akroyd Rowe & Pitman Mullens Securities Ltd.

HAMILTON, Sir James; Non-Executive Director, Smiths Industries plc.

HAMILTON, M W; Assistant Director, Macey Williams Insurance Services Ltd.

HAMILTON, Nicholas I; Director, Schroder Securities Limited.

HAMILTON, Nigel James; Partner, Ernst & Young, since 1975; National Head of Insolvency Department. *Career:* Graham Proom & Smith 1959-67; Ridley and Ridley 1967-69; Whinney Murray & Co (Newcastle) Set Up Insolvency Dept 1969-74; Ernst & Young Ptnr 1975-. *Biog: b.* 27 March 1941. *Nationality:* British. *m.* 1966, Valerie Joan (née Moorwood); 1 s; 1 d. *Educ:* Loretto School. *Professional Organisations:* FCA; Chm, Insolvency Practitioners Committee; Member, Post Qualification Education Committee; Member, Insolvency Practitioners Association. *Clubs:* RAC. *Recreations:* Rugby Football, Golf, Sailing, Opera.

HAMILTON, Paul R; Director, S G Warburg Akroyd Rowe & Pitman Mullens Securities; Corporate Finance.

HAMILTON, Peter Bernard; Company Secretary, Allied Dunbar Assurance plc, since 1977; Head of Legal Department. *Career:* Barrister in Private Practice 1968-77. *Biog: b.* 20 April 1941. *Nationality:* British. *m.* 1966, Patricia Jean (née Freeman); 1 s; 2 d. *Educ:* St John's College, Johannesburg; Rhodes University (BA); Cambridge University (MA). *Other Activities:* Member of following Committees of Association of British Insurers: Chm, Data Protection Panel; Chm, Companies Regulations (Linked Life Assurance) Panel; Law Review Panel; Legalisation Co-ordinating Committee. *Professional Organisations:* Member of Inner Temple; Bar Assoc for Commerce, Finance and Industry (Member, Law Reform Committee). *Recreations:* Riding, Birdwatching, Carpentry, Theatre.

HAMILTON, Ms Sophie Charlotte; Partner (Property) & Training Partner, Frere Cholmeley, since 1985; Commecial Property. *Career:* Frere Cholmeley, Articled Clerk 1977-79; Assistant Solicitor 1979-85; Recruitment Partner 1985-90. *Biog: b.* 14 October 1955. *Nationality:* British. *m.* 1990, Peter Goldie. *Educ:* St Mary's School, Calne; Marlborough College; Clare College, Cambridge (BA). *Other Activities:* Honorary Legal Adviser, Citizens Advice Bureau.

HAMILTON, W I; Group Finance Director, Alliance & Leicester Building Society, since 1989. *Professional Organisations:* FCA.

HAMLETT, David William; Corporate Partner, Wragge & Co, since 1988; Company Law. *Career:* Linklaters & Paines, Articled Clerk 1978-80; Solicitor 1980-83; Wragge & Co, Solicitor 1983-87. *Biog: b.* 5 May 1955. *Nationality:* British. *m.* 1978, Eleanor M (née Ferns); 1 s; 2 d. *Educ:* Downing College, Cambridge (MA Law). *Professional Organisations:* Law Society.

HAMLYN, J M; Director, W H Ireland Stephens & Co Ltd.

HAMMERTON, Simon; Partner, Beavis Walker.

HAMMOND, Mark Watkin; Director, Touche Remnant, since 1990; Head of Japanese Investment. *Career:* Save & Prosper Gp 1982-88; Robert Fleming, Japanese Investment Mgr 1988-90. *Biog: b.* 27 October 1959. *Nationality:* British. *Educ:* Christ's Hospital, Horsham; Magdalen College, Oxford (MA). *Directorships:* Touche Remnant Investment Management 1990. *Recreations:* Singing.

HAMMOND-CHAMBERS, Robert Alexander; Chairman, Ivory & Sime plc, since 1985; Investment Management. *Career:* Ivory & Sire plc, Chairman 1985-; Deputy Chairman 1982-85; Director 1975-; Ivory & Sire Limited 1964-; Partner 1969-1975. *Biog: b.* 20 October 1942. *Nationality:* British. *m.* 1968, Sarah Louisa Madeline (née Fanshawe); 2 s; 1 d. *Educ:* Wellington College; Magdalene College, Cambridge (MA Hons). *Directorships:* GBC Capital Ltd (Canadian) 1971 (non-exec); I & S Optimum Income Trust plc 1990 (non-exec). *Other Activities:* Governor Fettes College, Edinburgh; Edinburgh Old Town Trust, Trustee; Governor, National Association of Securities Dealers Inc (1984-87). *Professional Organisations:* ASIA. *Clubs:* New Club (Edinburgh). *Recreations:* Photography, Sailing, Tennis, Golf, Skiing.

HAMON, Captain K G; RN; Clerk, Carpenters' Company.

HAMPEL, R C; Director, Commercial Union plc.

HAMPEL, Ronald Claus; Executive Director, Imperial Chemical Industries plc, since 1985; Territorial Director-Americas Business Director Paints Speciality Chemicals. *Career:* ICI Gen Mgr Commercial 1977-80; Chm, ICI Paints 1980-83; Chm, ICI Agrochemicals 1983-85. *Biog: b.* 31 May 1932. *m.* 1957, Jane (née Hewson); 3 s; 1 d. *Educ:* Canford School; Corpus Christi College, Cambridge (MA). *Directorships:* Commercial Union 1987 (non-exec); Powell Duffryn 1984 (non-exec); British Aerospace 1989. *Other Activities:* British North America Ctee (Executive Ctee); American Chamber Commerce (Member). *Professional Organisations:* FBIM. *Clubs:* Hawks, AELTC, MCC. *Recreations:* Skiing, Tennis, Golf.

HAMPTON, Clifford S H; Chief Executive, CSH International, since 1990; Consultant to Financial Services Industry. *Career:* Spicer & Oppenheim, Partner 1977-90; Spicer & Oppenheim International, Executive Director 1983-86. *Biog: b.* 28 October 1944. *Nationality:* British. *m.* 1973, Marjorie Jean; 2 d. *Educ:* City of London School; University of Durham (BA). *Directorships:* The Ecu Trust plc 1990 (non-exec). *Professional Organisations:* FCA. *Clubs:* Jesters, MCC, Roehampton, City of London Club, University Club New York.

HAMPTON, John; Director, Rudolf Wolff & Co Ltd.

HAMWAY, N J; Director, Charterhouse Bank Limited.

HANBURY, Antony; Director, Singer & Friedlander Holdings Ltd, since 1972; Investment Management. *Biog: b.* 31 July 1922. *Nationality:* British; 1 s; 2 d. *Educ:* Winchester College. *Directorships:* Singer & Friedlander (Isle of Man) Ltd 1979 (exec); Singer & Friedlander Investment Management Ltd 1987; Singer & Friedlander (IOM) Trust Ltd 1979. *Clubs:* Sunningdale Golf Club.

HANBURY-BROWN, Stephanie Selina (née Newby); Vice President & Manager, J P Morgan Futures Inc, since 1986; Financial Futures & Options. *Career:* Lane & Lane (Sydney) Law Clerk 1979-80; Rouse Woodstock Pty Ltd (Sydney) Client Adviser 1980-82; Rouse Woodstock Ltd (London) Snr Trader 1982-86. *Biog: b.* 26 December 1956. *m.* 1978, Robert; 1 s. *Educ:* Frensham, Mittagong NSW; University of Sydney (BA). *Directorships:* LIFFE Ltd 1987; AFBD Council 1990. *Clubs:* Ealing Ladies Hockey Club, Templars Lawn Tennis Club. *Recreations:* Hockey, Tennis, Piano, Cycling, Running.

HANBURY-WILLIAMS, Charles Lister; Executive Director, Samuel Montagu & Co Limited, since 1990; Capital Markets. *Biog: b.* 18 November 1958. *Nationality:* British. *m.* 1982, Camilla (née Krefting); 1 s; 1 d. *Educ:* Eton College; Exeter University.

HANBURY-WILLIAMS, John Michael Anthony; Chief Executive, Allied Provincial Ltd, since 1986. *Career:* Courtaulds Ltd Various 1954-64; Eurofinance Sarl Mgr 1964-66; David Q Henriques Analyst 1966-68; Ptnr 1968-86; Illingworth & Henriques (Stockbrokers) Ltd Dir 1986-. *Biog: b.* 7 July 1933. *m.* 1956, Diane (née Hartley); 3 s; 1 d. *Educ:* Eton College. *Directorships:* Allied Provincial Securities plc 1987 Marketing Dir; APS (CI) Ltd 1989 Chm.

HANBURY-WILLIAMS, N J; Director, S G Warburg Akroyd Rowe & Pitman Mullens Securities Ltd.

HANCOCK, Sir David; KCB; Executive Director, Hambros Bank Limited, since 1989. *Career:* HM Treasury, Various 1959-82; Cabinet Office, Deputy Secretary 1982-83; Dept of Education & Science, Permanent Secretary 1983-89. *Biog: b.* 27 March 1934. *Nationality:* British. *m.* 1966, Sheila Gillian (née Finlay); 1 s; 1 d. *Educ:* Whitgift School; Balliol College, Oxford (MA). *Directorships:* Hambros plc 1989 (exec). *Professional Organisations:* CBIM; FRSA. *Clubs:* Athenaeum. *Recreations:* Theatre, Opera, Walking, Gardening, Reading, Music.

HANCOCK, P D; Partner, Bacon & Woodrow.

HANCOCK, Peter Douglas; Managing Director, J P Morgan, since 1990; Head of Global Swaps. *Career:* J P Morgan 1980-. *Biog: b.* 19 June 1958. *Nationality:* British. *Educ:* Wellington College, Berkshire; Christ Church, Oxford (BA).

HANCOCK, Stephen Clarence; Partner, Herbert Smith, since 1986; Company Law. *Career:* Herbert Smith, Articled Clerk 1978-80; Assistant Solicitor 1980-86; Partner 1986-. *Biog: b.* 1 November 1955. *Nationality:* British. *m.* 1990, Jane Mary (née Hughes); 1 s. *Educ:* King Edward VI, Lichfield; City of S-O-T 6th Form College; Sheffield University (LLB First Class Hons). *Other Activities:* City of London Solicitors Company; Law Society; International Bar Association. *Professional Organisations:* Solicitor. *Recreations:* Golf.

HANCOCK, Timothy; Executive Director, N M Rothschild & Sons Limited.

HANCOX, John Philip Dale; Managing Director, Charterhouse Tilney, since 1986; Institutional Division. *Career:* Chalmers Impey & Co Articled Clerk 1963-67; Tilney & Co/Charterhouse Tilney 1967-86; Partner 1968-86. *Biog: b.* 18 January 1941. *Nationality:* British. *m.* 1967, Deborah Margaret (née Crowther); 3 d. *Educ:* Stowe School; Corpus Christi College, Cambridge (MA Hons Econ). *Directorships:* Richard Burbidge Ltd 1986 (non-exec); H Burbidge & Son Ltd 1970 (non-exec); Miles Macadam (Holdings) Ltd 1970 (non-exec); Charterhouse Securities 1986. *Other Activities:* Former Chairman, The Stock Exchange, Liverpool Committee.

Professional Organisations: FCA; ASIA. *Clubs:* Liverpool Racquet Club, Royal Dee Yacht Club, South Caernarvonshire Yacht Club, Dee Sailing Club; Offham Cricket Club, Offham Tennis Club. *Recreations:* Tennis, Sailing, Golf, Fishing, Shooting.

HANDLEY, John; Partner, Beavis Walker.

HANDLEY-JONES, Nicholas; Partner, Touche Ross & Co.

HANDRAS, Nicholas G; Vice President, Manufacturers Hanover Trust Company.

HANDS, D J; Director, Gerald Limited.

HANDS, Peter; Partner (Nottingham), Evershed Wells & Hind.

HANKEY, Martin; Director, Svenska International plc, since 1986; Legal Advisor, With Special Reference to Japan, Corporate Finance, Structured Loans. *Career:* Stephenson Harwood, Articled Clerk 1965-68; Herbert Smith, Solicitor 1968-71; Hill Samuel & Co Ltd, Manager 1971-78; Nordic Bank plc, Snr Mgr 1978-82. *Biog: b.* 12 March 1944. *Nationality:* British. *m.* 1966, Gillian (née Davies); 2 d. *Educ:* St Pauls; Trinity College, Cambridge (MA). *Other Activities:* Freeman, City of London; Freeman, City of London Solicitors' Company. *Professional Organisations:* The Law Society. *Clubs:* Ex Tabler. *Recreations:* Canoeing, Walking, Cycling, Golf, Rowing, Tennis, Bridge.

HANLON, N M; Partner, MacIntyre Hudson, since 1986; Education Sector. *Professional Organisations:* FCA; ICAEW. *Publications:* Independent Schools Cost Survey, Annual.

HANNA, John W; Director, Alexander Howden Limited.

HANNA, W F; Director, Banking, The Private Bank & Trust Company Limited, since 1989; Business Development (Corporate & Personal); Banking Division Operations & Customer Services; Credit Control & Administration. *Career:* The Bank of Nova Scotia, Manager, Cairo 1975-79; Manager, Dubai 1979-80; Supervisor, Credit 1980-83; Manager, West End, London 1983-89. *Biog: b.* 8 December 1947. *Nationality:* British. *m.* 1987, Brenda; 1 s; 1 d. *Educ:* American University of Beirut (BA Economics); University of Western Ontario (International Management). *Directorships:* The Private Bank & Trust Company 1989 (exec). *Other Activities:* Member, Executive Committee.

HANNAM, J V; Director, Crédit Lyonnais Rouse Limited.

HANOVER, Clive; Director, Mitsubishi Finance International Ltd.

HANSBERGER, Thomas L; President & Chief Executive Officer, Templeton, Galbraith & Hansberger Ltd, since 1986; Investment Counsel. *Career:* Templeton Investment Counsel Ltd, Director, President and Chief Executive Officer 1986-89; Stein Roe & Farnham, General Partner/Portfolio Manager 1974-79; First Equity Financial Corp, President and Director of Research 1969-74. *Biog: b.* 4 April 1933. *Nationality:* American. *Directorships:* Structured Asset Management Inc 1990; The DAIS Group Inc 1990; Templeton Global Bond Managers Inc 1990 Chairman; Templeton Asia Fund 1989; Templeton Management Limited 1987; Templeton Management (Lux) SA 1988; Templeton Investment Counsel Inc 1979 Chairman; Templeton Global Investors Ltd 1988; Templeton Unit Trust Managers Ltd 1988; Templeton Investment Management Ltd (UK) 1988 Managing Director; Templeton Investment Management Ltd (Australia) 1989; Templeton Investment Management (Hong Kong) Ltd 1987 Chairman of the Board; Templeton Emerging Markets Fund Inc 1987; Templeton Emerging Growth Stock Portfolio NV 1989 Supervisory Board; Templeton Global Opportunities Trust 1990 President and Trustee; Templeton, Galbraith & Hansberger Ltd 1986 President and Chief Executive Officer; John Templeton Counsellors Inc 1986 President and Chief Executive Officer; Templeton Global Investors Inc 1987 President; Templeton Financial Advisory Services SA 1988 General Manager; Templeton Growth Fund Ltd 1985 President; Templeton Funds Inc 1981 President; Templeton Global Fund Inc 1981 President; Templeton Income Trust 1986 Trustee and President; Templeton Growth Fund Inc 1986 President; Templeton Variable Annuity Fund 1988 President; Asian Development Equity Fund 1988; Templeton Global Income Fund, Inc 1988 Pres; Templeton Variable Products Series Fund 1988 Pres; Templeton Treasury Bill Fund 1988; Templeton Global Income Portfolio Ltd 1988 Pres; Templeton Global Income Fund 1988; Templeton Value Fund, Inc 1988 Pres; Templeton Global Governments Income Trust 1988 Pres; Templeton Heritage Fund 1989; Developing Growth Stock Fund 1989; Templeton Heritage Retirement Fund 1989; Templeton Emerging Markets Investment Trust plc 1989; Templeton Real Estate Trust 1989 Pres; Templeton Tax Free Trust 1989 Pres; Templeton Worldwide Investments 1989; The Bangkok Fund 1988; The India Fund 1988 Advisory Bd Mem; Templeton World Superannuation Trust 1988. *Professional Organisations:* Financial Analysts Federation; Chartered Financial Analyst; Bahamas Chapter of Institute of Financial Analysts; Association for Investment Management and Research.

HANSON, J D; Treasurer, British Aerospace plc.

HANSON-SMITH, Julian; Director/Secretary, Financial Dynamics Limited.

HARA, Akira; Deputy Managing Director General Affairs, Mitsui Taiyo Kobe International Limited.

HARADA, Robert G; Executive Director, Merrill Lynch International Bank Limited.

HARBORD-HAMOND, The Hon John Edward Richard; Partner, Cazenove & Co, since 1991; Fund Management. *Career:* Hedderwick Stirling Grumbar & Co 1979-91; Cazenove & Co 1991-. *Biog: b.* 10 July 1956. *Educ:* Eton College. *Professional Organisations:* Barrister.

HARBOUR, Karel Frederick; Director, GNI Ltd, since 1987; Operations. *Career:* Touche Ross & Co, Chartered Accountant 1972-76; International Commodities Clearing House Ltd, Dep Group Accountant 1977-78; Leopold Lazarus Ltd, Assistant Chief Accountant 1979-80; ACLI Commodity Services Ltd, Company Secretary 1980-83. *Biog: b.* 21 November 1950. *Nationality:* British. *m.* 1975, Carol Anne (née Harbury); 2 s. *Educ:* Erith Grammar; Southampton University (BSc Econ). *Directorships:* GNI Ltd 1987 (exec); GNI Wallace Ltd 1989 (exec); GNI Incorporated 1989 (exec). *Professional Organisations:* Fellow, Institute of Chartered Accountants in England & Wales.

HARDCASTLE, Alan John; Chief Accounting Adviser & Head of Government Accountancy, H M Treasury, since 1989. *Career:* KPMG Peat Marwick McLintock, Partner 1967-88. *Biog: b.* 10 August 1933. *Nationality:* British. m2 1983, Ione (née Cooney); 2 s; 2 d (from First Marriage). *Educ:* Haileybury. *Directorships:* Board of Banking Supervision 1986 Member; Lloyd's 1987-88 Nominated Member of Council; The White Ensign Association Ltd 1984 (non-exec). *Other Activities:* Worshipful Company of Chartered Accountants (Master 1978-79). *Professional Organisations:* Fellow, Institute of Chartered Accountants in England & Wales (President 1983-85). *Publications:* Joint Editor, Financial Reporting Under the Companies Act 1981, 1985; Joint Editor, Companies Act 1981 Handbook, 1982. *Clubs:* City Livery, Naval.

HARDCASTLE, Peter Robert; Partner, Bacon & Woodrow, since 1989; Pension Funds. *Career:* Bacon & Woodrow 1980-; Actuary, Pension Sections 1986-89; Partner 1989-. *Biog: b.* 20 December 1958. *Nationality:* British. *Educ:* The King's School, Chester; Mansfield College, Oxford (MA). *Professional Organisations:* FIA. *Recreations:* Walking, Watching any Sport, Reading Crime Novels.

HARDIE, (Charles) Jeremy (Mawdesley); CBE; Chairman, National Provident Institution.

HARDIE, David; NP, WS; Partner, Dundas & Wilson CS, since 1983; Corporate Law. *Career:* Dundas & Wilson CS 1976-. *Biog: b.* 17 September 1954. *Nationality:* British. *m.* 1981, Fiona Mairi (née Willox); 3 s. *Educ:* Glasgow Academy; Greenock High School; University of Dundee (LLB Hons). *Professional Organisations:* The Law Society of Scotland; International Bar Association. *Clubs:* Royal Forth Yacht Club. *Recreations:* Sailing, Golf, Swimming.

HARDIE, Richard William John; Director of Administration, S G Warburg Group Management, since 1986. *Career:* Dixon Wilson & Co, Manager, General Practice 1974-77; S G Warburg & Co Ltd, Corporate Finance Executive 1977-82; Management Executive Director 1982-86. *Biog: b.* 14 August 1948. *Nationality:* British. *m.* 1975, Elizabeth (née Newte) (Diss 1986); 2 d. *Educ:* Sherborne School, Dorset; Lincoln College, Oxford (MA). *Directorships:* S G Warburg & Co Ltd 1985 (exec). *Professional Organisations:* FCA. *Clubs:* Vincents, Free Foresters. *Recreations:* Golf, Opera, Theatre, Cinema, Travel.

HARDIE, Thomas Innes; Deputy Managing Director, Girobank plc, since 1990; Sales & Marketing. *Career:* Alliance & Leicester Building Society, Asst Gen Mgr (Retail Fin Services) 1988-89; Asst Gen Mgr (Branches) 1985-89; Mgr for Scotland 1982-85. *Biog: b.* 19 July 1935. *Nationality:* British. *m.* 1963, Irene (née Halliday); 3 s. *Directorships:* Alliance & Leicester Property Services Ltd 1988 (non-exec) Deputy Chairman; Alliance & Leicester Insurance Services Ltd 1989 (non-exec) Deputy Chairman; Alliance & Leicester (Isle of Man) Ltd 1990 (non-exec) Chairman; Alliance & Leicester Building Society 1989 General Manager (Development). *Clubs:* Royal Burgess Golfing Society of Edinburgh. *Recreations:* Golf.

HARDING, Francis John; Executive Director, Barclays Development Capital Ltd, since 1982. *Career:* Barclays Bank Ltd, Mgr 1970-72; Barclays Merchant Bank, Mgr 1972-80; Asst Dir 1980-82. *Biog: b.* 31 December 1935. *Nationality:* British. *m.* 1958, Sheila (née Rickett); 2 s. *Educ:* Colchester Royal Grammar School. *Directorships:* Barclays Industrial Development Ltd 1982 (exec); Barclays Industrial Investments Ltd 1982 (exec); John Lelliott Group plc 1984 (non-exec); Magnum Group Ltd 1987 (non-exec); Autonumis Ltd 1987 (non-exec); Thompson & Capper Ltd 1987 (non-exec); Blydut (101) Ltd 1987 (non-exec); Ebbgate Holdings Ltd 1987 (non-exec); William Shipstone & Co Ltd 1987 (non-exec); Davies Group Holdings Ltd 1988 (non-exec); Triman Investments Ltd 1989 (non-exec); Errut International Ltd 1989 (non-exec); Finesample Ltd 1990 (non-exec); Clermont Investments Ltd 1990 (non-exec); Intercraft Products Ltd 1990 (non-exec); Magnum Trustees Ltd 1990 (non-exec). *Professional Organisations:* ACIB.

HARDING, Dr Geoffrey Wright; Partner, Wilde Sapte, since 1967; Banking, Competition, European Community Law. *Career:* Federation of Civil Engineering Contractors Asst Sec (Legal) 1958-60; British Insurance (Atomic Energy Ctee) Legal Adviser 1960-63; Isham, Lincoln And Beale (Chicago Attorneys) 1964-65; Exchange Lawyer through Harvard Law School Programme 1964-65; Joynson Hicks Solicitor 1965-67. *Nationality:* British. *m.* 1972, Margaret (né Danger); 1 s; 1 d; *Educ:* King's College, London (LLB); Queen Mary's College, London (PhD); Northwestern University School of Law, Chicago (LLM) General Electric Foundation Fellowship; Gray's Inn (Barrister). *Other Activities:* Bar and Law Society Joint Working Party on Banking Law; Guild of Freemen of the City of London; Mem, National Autistic Soc & Kent Autistic Community Trust; The Prince's Youth Business Trust (Business Adviser). *Professional Organisations:* The Law Society. *Publications:* Encyclopaedia of Competition Law, 1987 (Jt Consulting Ed); Current Law Statutes Annotated, 1987 (Banking Act 1987). *Recreations:* Learning the Piano, Mountain-Biking, Avoiding Domestic DIY.

HARDING, Sir (George) William; KCMG,CVO; Director and Adviser on International Affairs, Lloyds Bank plc, since 1988. *Career:* Royal Marines 1945-48; Her Majesty's Diplomatic Service, Singapore, Burma, France, Dominican Republic, Mexico 1950-77; Ambassador (Peru) 1977-79; Ambassador (Brazil) 1981-84; The Foreign & Commonwealth Office, Dep Under Sec of State for the Americas & Asia 1984-87. *Biog: b.* 18 January 1927. *Nationality:* British. *m.* 1955, Sheila Margaret Ormond (née Riddel); 4 s. *Educ:* Aldenham School, Hertfordshire; St John's College, Cambridge (MA Hons). *Directorships:* First Spanish Investment Trust 1987 Chm; Centre for International Briefing 1987 Governor; Shelley Court Management Ltd 1986; Lloyds Merchant Bank Holdings Ltd 1988; Thai-Euro Fund 1988 Chm. *Other Activities:* Chm, The Brazilian Chamber of Commerce in GB; Member, Council Royal Geographic Society; Mem, Council Royal Institute of International Affairs; European Mem, Trilateral Commission. *Clubs:* Garrick, Beefsteak, Leander. *Recreations:* Shooting (Rifle, Pistol & Game), Fishing, Sailing, Golf.

HARDING, I M; Secretary, The Scottish Investment Trust plc, since 1979. *Biog: b.* 13 October 1948. *Nationality:* British. *m.* 1973, Barbara (née Ogden); 3 s; 1 d. *Educ:* Nottingham High School. *Professional Organisations:* FCMA; FCIS. *Recreations:* Reading, Music.

HARDING, J C; JP; Executive Director, Slough Estates plc.

HARDING, N R; Director, Charlton Seal Schaverien Limited.

HARDING, Paul Anthony; Partner, Titmuss Sainer & Webb, since 1986; Corporate Finance. *Career:* British

Coal, Articled Clerk 1979-81; Solicitor 1981-82; Forsyte Kerman, Solicitor 1982-84; Titmuss Sainer & Webb, Solicitor 1984-. *Biog: b.* 6 October 1955. *Nationality:* British. *m.* 1979, Deborah Anne (née Harvey); 1 s; 1 d. *Educ:* Hardye's Grammar, Dorchester, Dorset; London School of Economics (LLB Hons). *Recreations:* Train Spotting.

HARDING, Peter; Partner (Property), Frere Cholmeley.

HARDING, R L; Director, Barclays de Zoete Wedd Securities Ltd.

HARDING, Timothy John Randolph; Director, Peninsular and Oriental Steam Navigation Company, since 1989; Property. *Career:* Scottish Special Housing Association, Architect 1966-72. *Biog: b.* 7 April 1940. *Nationality:* British. *Educ:* Bryanston School; Bristol University (B Arch); Harvard Business School (MBA). *Directorships:* Town & City Properties (Overseas) Ltd 1974-88; P & O Properties International Ltd 1988-Managing Director; P & O Properties Holdings Ltd 1990 Deputy Chairman & Managing Director; Laing Properties plc 1990 Chairman. *Clubs:* RAC, Hurlingham. *Recreations:* Swimming, Walking, Skiing.

HARDISTY, D G; Managing Director, Close Asset Finance Limited, since 1987. *Career:* North West Securities, Divisional Director, London and South East Division, Southern Division, Sales & Marketing 1967-82; British Credit Trust, Operations Director, Sales & Marketing Countrywide 1982-87. *Biog: b.* 13 October 1942. *Nationality:* British. *m.* 1969, Elizabeth; 1 s; 1 d. *Educ:* Yew Lane School, Sheffield. *Directorships:* Close Asset Finance Ltd 1987 (exec); Close Brothers Limited 1988 (exec); Air & General Finance Ltd 1988 (exec).

HARDMAN, Alasdair F; WS; Managing Partner, W & J Burness, WS, since 1990.

HARDMAN, J N; Chairman & Chief Executive, Asda Group plc.

HARDWICK, Michael Robert; Director, S G Warburg & Co Ltd.

HARDWICKE, Roy James; Associate Director, Brewin Dolphin & Co Ltd, since 1988; Private Client Investment Adviser. *Career:* Brewin Dolphin, Office Boy to Associate Director 1972-; Orme Teykyn, General Duties 1966-72. *Biog: b.* 31 January 1947. *Nationality:* British. *m.* 1966, Linda; 2 s. *Educ:* Brook House Comprehensive. *Clubs:* Chairman, Broxbourne Saines FC (Youth Football Club).

HARDY, B A; Director, Metheuen (Lloyds Underwriting Agents) Limited.

HARDY, Brian; Director-Finance, Burmah Castrol plc, since 1990; Corporate Finance, Treasury, Insurance, Reporting. *Career:* Arthur Andersen & Co, London & Athens, Audit Assistant then Audit Senior, then Manager 1963-70; Stanford Business School 1970-72; Arthur Andersen & Co, London, Manager 1972-77; BICC plc, Group Audit Manager, then Group Controller 1977-82; Unigate plc, Group Financial Controller 1982-84; Castrol Ltd, Finance Director 1984-90. *Biog:* b. 1942. *Nationality:* British. *m.* 1970, Eirene (née Verganelakis); 1 s. *Educ:* London School of Economics (BSc Econ); Stanford Business School, California (MBA). *Directorships:* Burmah Castrol plc 1990 (exec). *Professional Organisations:* FCA. *Clubs:* RAC Club.

HARDY, David Malcolm; Managing Director, International Commodities Clearing House Ltd, since 1987; Clearing & Guarantee of London Based Futures & Options Markets. *Career:* Barclays Bank plc 1973-81; Barclays Merchant Bank Ltd 1981-85; Seconded to ICCH Ltd 1985-87. *Biog:* b. 16 July 1955. *Nationality:* British. *m.* 1981, Maureen Ann (née Petherick); 1 s; 1 d. *Educ:* Westcliff High School. *Professional Organisations:* ACIB. *Clubs:* Rochford Hundred Golf Club. *Recreations:* Golf, Gardening, Bird Watching, Photography.

HARDY, David William; Chairman & Acting Chief Executive, London Docklands Development Corporation, since 1988; Largest Development Project in the World. *Career:* Imperial Group (USA) VP Fin Admin 1964-70; HM Government Co-ordinator of Industrial Advisers 1970-72; Tate & Lyle Fin Dir 1972-77; Ocean Transport & Trading Exec Dir 1977-83; Globe Investment Trust plc Dir 1976-90. *Biog:* b. 14 July 1930. *Nationality:* British. *m.* 1957, Rosemary (née Collins); 1 s; 1 d. *Educ:* Wellington College; Harvard Business School (AMP). *Directorships:* MGM Assurance 1985 (non-exec) Chm; Swan Hunter 1986-88 (non-exec) Chm; AMC 1976 (non-exec) Vice-Chm; Waterford Glass 1984-90 (non-exec); Paragon Group 1985-89 (non-exec); Aberfoyle Holdings 1986 (non-exec); Electra Candover Fund 1986 (non-exec); London Regional Transport 1984-87 (non-exec) Dep Chm; Docklands Light Railway 1985-87 (non-exec) Chm; Sturge Holdings 1984 (non-exec); London Docklands Development Corporation 1988 (non-exec) Chm; Buckingham International 1988 (non-exec) Chm; Department of Trade and Industry-Engineering Mkts Advisory Ctee 1988-90 (non-exec) Chm; ECGD 1970-72. *Other Activities:* Hundred Group of Chartered Accountants (Chm) 1987-88; National Art Collections Development Fund (Board Member) 1988; Worshipful Company of Chartered Accountants; Worshipful Company of Shipwrights. *Professional Organisations:* FCA; CBIM; FCIT. *Clubs:* Brook's, MCC, HAC, Flyfishers. *Recreations:* Fishing, Shooting.

HARDY, M; Associate, Grimley J R Eve.

HARDY, Malcolm Keith; National Audit Partner, Robson Rhodes; Audit & Client Service, Special Emphasis on City Institutions & Investment Management. *Career:* Robson Rhodes 1963-. *Biog:* b. 27 January 1940. *Nationality:* British. *m.* 1964, Elizabeth (née Warrick); 1 s; 1 d. *Educ:* Forest School. *Directorships:* Garnier & Co Ltd 1977 (non-exec). *Professional Organisations:* FCA. *Publications:* Digest on Investment Trusts, 1976. *Recreations:* Theatre, Films, Reading.

HARDY, Peter Bernard; Director, S G Warburg Group plc, since 1987; Joint Chairman Equity Division (Worldwide). *Career:* Read Hurst-Brown Ptnr 1967-74; Rowe & Pitman Ptnr 1974-86. *Biog:* b. 1938. *Nationality:* British. *m.* 1961, Cynthia Mary (née Crouch); 2 s. *Educ:* Gordon School, Gravesend. *Recreations:* Tennis.

HARDY, S Charles; Partner, Touche Ross & Co, since 1988; Financial Services Industry Division. *Career:* Spicer and Pegler 1977-82; MacGillivray & Co (Vancouver) 1982-85; Spicer and Pegler (now Touche Ross & Co) 1985-. *Biog:* b. 4 April 1955. *m.* 1980, Julie (née Baker); 2 s. *Educ:* Royal Masonic School; Imperial College, London. *Professional Organisations:* ACA; CA (Canada).

HARDY, Timothy Paul Frank; Partner, McKenna & Co, since 1988; Commercial Litigation. *Career:* Simmons & Simmons, Asst Solicitor 1977-80; Slaughter & May, Asst Solicitor 1980-86; McKenna & Co, Asst Solicitor 1986-88. *Biog:* b. 25 July 1952. *Nationality:* British. *m.* Sarah; 1 s; 1 d. *Educ:* Cotton College. *Other Activities:* Freeman, City of London Solicitors Company. *Professional Organisations:* Law Society; American Bar Association. *Clubs:* Law Society Fishing Club.

HARFIELD, Colonel A B; CBE; Clerk, Barbers' Company.

HARGRAVE, D P; Managing Director, Brandeis Limited.

HARGRAVE, David Grant; Partner, Bacon & Woodrow, since 1979; Pensions. *Career:* Duncan C Fraser & Co (Later William M Mercer Fraser Ltd), Actuary 1973-79; T G Arthur Hargrave (Merged with Bacon & Woodrow 1989), Partner 1979-. *Biog:* b. 11 April 1951. *Nationality:* British. *m.* 1969, Celia (née Hawksworth); 1 s; 1 d. *Educ:* Howardian HS, Cardiff; University of Birmingham (BCom, MSc). *Directorships:* Homeowners Friendly Society 1982 (non-exec); T G Arthur Trustees Ltd 1979 (exec). *Other Activities:* Secretary & Treasurer, Birmingham Actuarial Society, 1979-81; Treasurer 1982-85, Secretary 1985-87, & Chairman 1987-89, National Association of Pension Funds (West Midlands); Governor, Yew Tree School, 1988-. *Professional Organisations:* Fellow, Institute of Actuaries. *Recreations:* Long Distance Running, Swimming, Windsurfing, Rugby.

HARGRAVE, R; Financial Director, Crawley Warren Group plc.

HARGREAVE, C O; Senior Partner, Marsden W Hargreave Hale & Co.

HARGREAVES, Ian Richard; Deputy Editor, Financial Times, since 1990. *Career:* Kaleidoscope Project, Community Worker 1972-73; Southway Comprehensive, Plymouth, Schoolteacher 1973; Keighley News, Reporter 1973-74; Bradford Telegraph & Argus, Reporter, Feature Writer, Sub Editor 1974-76; Financial Times, Industrial Reporter; Transport Correspondent; New York Correspondent; Social Affairs Editor; Resources Editor; Assistant Editor (Features) 1976-87; BBC, Managing Editor, News & Current Affairs 1987-88; Controller, News & Current Affairs 1988-89; Director, News & Current Affairs 1989-90. *Biog: b.* 18 June 1951; 1 s; 1 d. *Educ:* Burnley Grammar School; Altrincham Grammar School; Queens' College, Cambridge (BA English).

HARGREAVES, Dr Richard Bozza; Managing Director, Baronsmead plc, since 1982. *Career:* 3i plc 1973-82. *Educ:* Manchester Grammar School; Queen's College, Cambridge (BA); Imperial College (PhD, MSc). *Directorships:* Several Investee Companies - Baronsmead is a Venture Capital Manager. *Other Activities:* Past Chairman & Current Member of the Council of the British Venture Capital Association. *Publications:* Managing Your Company's Finances, 1980; Starting a Business, 1982.

HARGREAVES-ALLEN, Peter M; Director, J Henry Schroder Wagg & Co Limited.

HARING, Peter Alan; Director, Cayzer Ltd.

HARINGTON, Guy Charles; Director, J Henry Schroder Wagg & Co Ltd, since 1985; Central and Eastern Europe. *Career:* The British Petroleum Co Ltd, Marketing Asst 1969-71; J Henry Schroder Wagg & Co Ltd, Various 1971-. *Biog: b.* 12 December 1946. *Nationality:* British. *m.* 1984, Kay Elizabeth (née Humphreys); 1 s; 1 d. *Educ:* Malvern College, Worcestershire; University College, Oxford (MA); Loughborough University of Technology (MSc). *Directorships:* Solvay UK Holding Co Ltd 1985 (non-exec). *Other Activities:* Executive Committee Member, Cystic Fibrosis Research Trust. *Clubs:* Hurlingham. *Recreations:* Music, Sailing, Skiing.

HARKER, S J; Director, Barclays de Zoete Wedd Securities Ltd.

HARKETT, William J; Director, Schroder Securities Limited.

HARKNESS, E J G; Director, Barclays de Zoete Wedd Securities Ltd.

HARLAND, Neil; Director, Barclays Bank plc, since 1989; Global Syndications. *Career:* Barclays Bank Group, Various 1966-; Firestone Tyre & Rubber Company Ltd 1963-66. *Biog: b.* 29 November 1944. *Nationality:* British. *m.* 1963, Audrey (née Kenley); 1 s; 1 d. *Educ:* Wallsend-on-Tyne Grammar School. *Directorships:* Barclays de Zoete Wedd Ltd 1984 (exec); Barclays de Zoete Wedd (Capital Markets) Ltd 1987 (exec). *Professional Organisations:* FCIB, Mem, TSA. *Recreations:* Besotted by Cricket, Spectating & Playing (though Father Time is catching up with me on the playing side!).

HARLEY, Robert Dryburgh Nisbet; Director, Kleinwort Benson Ltd, since 1989; Head of Operations. *Career:* JH Tod & Co Securities, Clerk 1965-67; Wood Mackenzie & Co Ltd, Asst Dir, Security Operations 1967-87. *Directorships:* Kleinwort Benson Securities Ltd 1987 (exec); Kleinwort Benson Ltd 1989 (exec). *Professional Organisations:* ISE; TSA.

HARMAN, H J W; Clerk, Scriveners' Company.

HARMAN, James H K; Partner, Theodore Goddard, since 1984; Entertainment & Media Law. *Career:* Theodore Goddard, Assistant Solicitor 1979-82; Associate 1982-84; Partner 1984-. *Biog: b.* 13 November 1954. *Nationality:* British. *Educ:* Radley College; Fitzwilliam College, Cambridge (BA, MA). *Professional Organisations:* Law Society. *Recreations:* Music, Sailing, Skiing.

HARMON, B D; Partner US Firm, Ernst & Young; Expatriate Services Division. *Biog: b.* 6 July 1942. *Nationality:* American. *Educ:* Ohio State University (BA).

HARPER, David G; Director, Kleinwort Benson Securities Ltd, since 1989; European Equiity Sales. *Career:* 4th Royal Tank Regiment, Lieutenant 1974-78; Grieveson Grant, UK Private Clients 1978; UK Institutional Gilt Edged Sales 'Shorts' 1979-84; Kleinwort Benson, UK & European Institutional Sales out of Boston 1984-88; New York 1988-89. *Biog: b.* 8 May 1952. *Nationality:* British. *m.* 1980, Jackie (née Mocatta); 1 s; 1 d. *Educ:* Bedford School. *Recreations:* Skiing, Tennis, Running, Cycling, Windsurfing, Shooting, Walking.

HARPER, Ian; Financial Writer, The Scotsman.

HARPER, Jack; Partner, Titmuss Sainer & Webb.

HARPER, Professor M H; Professor of Enterprise Development, Cranfield School of Management, Cranfield, since 1978; Finance for Enterprise in Third World. *Career:* Harvard University, Teaching Fellow, Faculty of Arts & Sciences 1960-61; John Harper & Co Ltd, Marketing Director 1961-70; University of Nairobi, Kenya, Senior Lecturer 1970-74; Cranfield School of Management, Director, Enterprise Development Centre 1974-. *Biog: b.* 25 August 1935. *Nationality:* British. *m.* 1989, Ursula; 1 s; 3 d. *Educ:* Oxford (MA); Harvard (MBA); Nairobi (PhD). *Directorships:* DPM Parry Ltd 1988 (non-exec); Facet NV 1990 (non-exec); Oxfam Trading 1982 (non-exec). *Other Activities:* Various. *Publications:* Small Business in the 3rd World, 1986; Entrepreneurship for the Poor, 1987; Consultant for Small Business, 1976; Self Employment for the Disabled, 1988.

HARPER, V E G; Director, Hoare Govett Corporate Finance Ltd.

HARPUR, Ms O M; Principal Executive, Berwin Leighton, Solicitors, since 1988; Responsibilities Equivalent to Chief Executive Officer. *Career:* British Coal, Operational Research Executive 1976-80 & 1981-82; Central Secretariat 1980-81 & 1982-85; Spicer & Oppenheim, Management Consultant 1985-87; Strategic Planning Associates (Washington DC), Associate, Responsible for Strategy Advice to Companies in Telecommunications and Banking Industries 1987-88. *Biog: b.* 26 September 1953. *Nationality:* British. *m.* 1974, Peter E Clamp(div 1991); 1 d. *Educ:* Keele University (BA 1st Class Honours Mathematics and Economics). *Clubs:* Network. *Recreations:* Clarinet Playing, Opera, Kayaking.

HARRAGAN, Stephen William; Director, GNI Limited, since 1986; Futures Trading. *Directorships:* GNI Limited 1986 (exec); GNI Wallace Limited 1989 (exec); GNI Inc 1989 (exec).

HARRAP, Simon Richard; Director, Gibbs Hartley Cooper Ltd, since 1988; North America. *Career:* Stewart Wrightson plc, Director 1985-87; Willis Faber plc, Director 1987-88. *Biog: b.* 25 March 1941. *Nationality:* British. *m.* 1969, Diana (née Akers-Douglas); 1 s; 2 d. *Educ:* Harrow School.

HARREL, David T D; Partner, S J Berwin & Co, since 1982; Head of Commercial Litigation Department. *Career:* Messrs William Charles Crocker, Articled Clerk 1971-73; Admitted as a Solicitor 1974; William Charles Crocker, Assistant Solicitor then Partner 1974-79; Messrs Burton & Ramsden, Partner 1979-81; S J Berwin & Co, Partner 1982-. *Biog: b.* 23 June 1948. *Nationality:* British. *Educ:* Marlborough College; Bristol University (LLB).

HARRINGTON, Patrick Bernard; Partner, Morison Stoneham, since 1990; Insolvency/Corporate Recovery. *Career:* Peat, Marwick, McLintock, Student/Manager 1979-85; Griffins, Senior Manager 1985-89; Morison Stoneham, Associate/Partner 1989-. *Biog: b.* 22 October 1957. *Nationality:* British. *Educ:* St Brendan's College, Bristol; Birmingham University (BCom Acc). *Profession-*

al Organisations: ACA. *Recreations:* Music, Golf, Swimming.

HARRIS, Miss Brenda; Partner, Jaques & Lewis, since 1989; Commercial Litigation/Banking & Insolvency. *Career:* Jaques & Lewis, Articled Clerk & Assistant Solicitor 1981-89. *Biog: b.* 5 March 1959. *Nationality:* British. *Educ:* King's College, London (LLB First). *Professional Organisations:* The Law Society; Association of Women Solicitors; Insolvency Lawyers Association. *Recreations:* Sailing, Squash, Theatre.

HARRIS, C P; Deputy President, The Chartered Insurance Institute.

HARRIS, Colin C; Managing Director (Investment Management), Legal & General Group plc.

HARRIS, Colin R; Executive Director & Group Company Secretary, Newton Investment Management Ltd, since 1987; General Management, Legal, Compliance. *Career:* A C White Silver Young & Cosh, Apprentice/Solicitor 1975-78; Nithsdale District Council, Legal Adviser 1978-79; Reed Stenhouse Group (taken over by Alexander & Alexander Inc), Group Legal Adviser 1979-84; Newton Investment Management Ltd, Group Legal Adviser 1984-. *Biog: b.* 9 October 1953. *Nationality:* British. *m.* 1985, Elizabeth Catherine (née Vose); 3 s. *Educ:* Firth Park Grammar School; University of Strathclyde (LLB). *Directorships:* Newton Investment Management Ltd 1987 (exec); Newton Fund Managers Ltd 1987 (exec); Wellington BES Ltd 1987 (exec); Wellington Fund Managers (Guernsey) Ltd 1987 (exec); Wellington Fund Managers (Bermuda) Ltd 1987 (exec). *Professional Organisations:* Member, Law Society of Scotland. *Recreations:* Golf, Travel, Walking.

HARRIS, David Anthony; Partner, Lovell White Durrant, since 1986; Corporate Finance. *Career:* Field Fisher & Martineau, Articled Clerk 1977-79; Solicitor 1979-82; Lovell White & King, Solicitor 1982-; Partner 1986-. *Biog: b.* 31 March 1954. *Nationality:* British. *m.* 1987, Penelope Anne (née Dalton); 1 d. *Educ:* King Edward's School, Birmingham; London University, (LLB Hons). *Other Activities:* Freeman, City of London Solicitors Company. *Professional Organisations:* Law Society. *Recreations:* Tennis, Skiing, Travel.

HARRIS, David Kenneth; Partner, Stoy Hayward, since 1966; General Audit. *Biog: b.* 11 June 1939. *Nationality:* British. *m.* 1988, Jennifer (née Rick); 1 s; 3 d; (by first Marriage). *Educ:* Stationers Company School. *Directorships:* Sanderson Vere Crane (Film Editors) Ltd 1986; Racehorse Owners Assoc 1986 Pres. *Other Activities:* Owner, The Brook Stud, Cheveley, Newmarket. *Professional Organisations:* FCA. *Publications:* HAC Guide to Taxation of the Bloodstock Industry, 1987. *Recreations:* Racing & Breeding of Thoroughbred Horses.

HARRIS, Derek; Small Business Editor, The Times.

HARRIS, Edward John; Director, International Operations, Enterprise Oil plc, since 1989. *Career:* Shell International Petroleum, Maatschapij, Career in Exploration & Production Division, Starting as Wellsite Engr 1966-81; Saxon Oil plc, Exploration Manager 1981-83; Director and Gen Manager 1983-85; Enterprise Oil plc, Production Director 1985-88; Director, Projects 1988-89; International Operations Director 1989-. *Biog: b.* 12 July 1944. *Nationality:* British. *m.* 1975, Maureen; 1 s; 3 d. *Educ:* Teignmouth Grammar School; Imperial College, Royal School of Mines (BSc Hons Oil Technology). *Publications:* Production Geology of the North Rankin Gasfield, Published in Energy Resources of the Pacific Region, 1981. *Recreations:* Sailing, Gardening, Cycling.

HARRIS, G; Director, E D & F Man Ltd.

HARRIS, Hugh Christopher Emlyn; Associate Director, Bank of England, since 1988; Responsible for Corporate Services. *Career:* Bank of England 1959-. *Biog: b.* 25 March 1936. *Nationality:* British. *m.* 1968, Pamela Susan (née Woollard); 1 s; 1 d. *Educ:* The Leys School, Cambridge; Trinity College, Cambridge (MA). *Directorships:* The Securities Management Trust 1987; Houblon Nominees 1987; BE Services Ltd 1984; BE Property Holdings Ltd 1989; BE Museum Ltd 1989. *Other Activities:* Governing Council, Business in the Community; Windsor Fellowship Advisory Council; Fullemploy 500 Executive Committee; Churchwarden, St Margaret's Church, Lothbury. *Professional Organisations:* Associate, Chartered Institute of Bankers; Fellow, Royal Society of Arts; Fellow, Institute of Personnel Management. *Recreations:* Rugby, Tennis.

HARRIS, John D; Senior Vice President & General Manager, First Interstate Bank, since 1989; Commercial Banking Europe. *Career:* First Interstate Bank, Hong Kong, Senior Vice President Asia, Pacific, Middle East 1986-89. *Biog: b.* 24 July 1945. *Nationality:* British. *m.* 1978, Judi (née Lerwill); 3 s; 1 d. *Educ:* Worcester College, Oxford (MA); Institute of Chartered Accountants (FCA). *Directorships:* First Interstate Asia Limited 1986 (non-exec) Chairman; China Non-Ferrous Leasing Co Ltd 1987 (non-exec) Deputy Chairman; First Interstate Capital Markets Limited 1986 (exec). *Professional Organisations:* FCA. *Clubs:* Gresham Club, Royal Winchester Golf Club, Hong Kong Club. *Recreations:* Golf, Sailing.

HARRIS, Dr Jon Philip; Director, Company Secretary and Compliance Officer, Bank of Tokyo Capital Markets Ltd, since 1989; Finance/ Operations. *Career:* Merrill Lynch Europe & Middle East, Vice President, Operations, Systems & Telecommunications 1986-88; British Petroleum International, Co-ordinator, Oil Strategy and Marketing 1985-86; British Petroleum Oil

Limited, Manager, Special Products UK 1979-85. *Biog: b.* 28 May 1953. *Nationality:* British. *m.* 1981, Patricia Anne (née Davis). *Educ:* City University (MBA Finance/ International Business); University of Salford (BSc Hons Pure & Applied Physics, PhD). *Directorships:* Tokyo and Detroit Eurodeal (Continental) AG 1990 (exec); Euroclear Clearance Systems plc 1989 (exec); Euroclear Clearance Systems Societe Cooperative 1989 (exec). *Professional Organisations:* Member, British Institute of Management; TSA. *Recreations:* Squash, Reading, Walking, Photography, Travel.

HARRIS, Dr Keith Reginald; Managing Director, MMG Patricof & Co Limited, since 1990; Corporate Finance/Investment Banking. *Career:* Orion Bank Limited, Associate Director, Corporate Finance 1977-80; Morgan Grenfell & Co Limited, Director, Capital Markets 1980-87; Morgan Grenfell Inc, President, Investment Banking 1985-87; Drexel Burnham Lambert, Managing Director, Investment Banking 1987-90. *Biog: b.* 1953. *Nationality:* British. *m.* 1985, Judy (née Morgan); 1 d. *Educ:* University of Bradford, Management Centre (1st Class Hons Business Studies); University of Surrey (PhD Financial Economics). *Directorships:* MMG Patricof & Co Limited 1990 (exec); First Britannia Mezzanine NV 1988 (non-exec); First Britannia Mezzanine BV 1988 (non-exec); Morgan Grenfell & Co Limited 1985 (exec); Cyrus J Lawrence Inc 1988 (non-exec). *Publications:* The Merger Activity of Financial Intermediaries - the Banking Institutions, in Economic Notes, Monte dei Paschi di Siena Bank Review, 1976; A Critique of Merger Policy from an Interpretation of its Economic Foundations, 1976; The Role of Financial Intermediaries in Merger Activity, 1977; Perspective Article in Corporate Money, 1989. *Recreations:* Soccer, Tennis, Cricket, Music, Cross-words.

HARRIS, Kim; Director, City & Commercial Communications plc, since 1988; Corporate, Financial & Investor Relations. *Career:* Multicom Holdings Ltd, Dep to Chairman 1986-88; Norman Craig & Kommel, Director 1976-86; Brian Dowling Ltd, Director 1971-76. *Biog: b.* 1 June 1944. *Nationality:* Australian. *m.* (div); 1 s; 1 d. *Educ:* Wellingborough; Adelaide University, SA (BSc). *Professional Organisations:* Member, Institute of Public Relations, Australia. *Clubs:* BMYC. *Recreations:* Yachting.

HARRIS, M J; Director, A J Archer Holdings plc.

HARRIS, M John; Partner, Theodore Goddard.

HARRIS, Mark Derwent; Partner, Bacon & Woodrow, since 1989; Pensions. *Biog: b.* 14 July 1960. *Nationality:* British. *m.* 1985, Penelope Anne (née Shindler); 1 d. *Educ:* Manchester Grammar School; Haberdashers Aske's School, Elstree; St John's College, Cambridge (BA Hons Cantab, Diploma in Mathematical Statistics). *Professional Organisations:* FIA. *Clubs:* West

Middlesex Lawn Tennis Club, Ealing Squash Club. *Recreations:* Tennis, Squash, Travel.

HARRIS, Martin Richard; Non-Executive Director, National Westminster Bank plc, since 1977; Audit Committee, Remuneration Committee. *Career:* Price Waterhouse & Co 1946-74; Ptnr 1956-74; The Panel on Takeovers & Mergers Dir-Gen 1974-77; Reckitt & Colman plc Dep Chm 1977-81; Inmos Intl plc Dir 1980-84; Westland plc Dir 1981-85; Equity & Law Life Assurance Society plc Dep Chm 1983-87; TR Industrial & General Trust plc 1983-88 (non-exec). *Biog:* b. 30 August 1922. *Nationality:* British. *m.* 1952, Diana Moira (née Gandar Dower); 4 s. *Educ:* Wellington College; Trinity Hall, Cambridge. *Directorships:* The De La Rue Co plc 1981 (non-exec); NatWest Investment Bank Ltd 1977 (non-exec). *Other Activities:* The Drapers' Co (Master 1987-88); The Chartered Accts Co (Master 1984-85); Queen Mary College, University of London (Dep Chm 1978-89); Queen Mary & Westfield College University of London (Chm 1989-); Royal College of Music (Council Member 1984-); Queen Mary & Westfield College (1978-89). *Professional Organisations:* FCA; FRCM; FRSA. *Clubs:* Carlton, MCC, Pilgrims. *Recreations:* Keeping Busy.

HARRIS, Michael Charles; Director, National Provident Institution.

HARRIS, P M; Controller, Metallgesellschaft Ltd.

HARRIS, Paul Ian; Partner, Linklaters & Paines, since 1976. *Biog:* b. 13 December 1943. *Nationality:* British. *m.* 1967, Margaret (née Roer); 1 s; 1 d. *Educ:* Chatham House Grammar School, Ramsgate; Birmingham University (LLM). *Other Activities:* Trustee, World Student Drama Trust; Member, City of London Solicitor Company. *Professional Organisations:* Law Society. *Publications:* Co-Authur, Unit Trust, 1974; Co-Authur, Unit Trusts - the Law and Practice, 1979. *Clubs:* Hendon. *Recreations:* Theatre, Cinema, Cricket, Sitting on Commitees, Bridge.

HARRIS, R; Senior Partner, Seligmann Harris & Co.

HARRIS, Richard Travis; Director, The Burton Group plc, since 1984. *Biog:* b. 15 April 1919. *Nationality:* British. *Directorships:* B G Pension Trustee Limited 1985; The Burton Group Pension Trustee Limited 1985; Dollond & Aitchison Limited; Gallaher Limited; Lucy's Mill Limited; Mill Management (Stratford) Limited.

HARRIS, Richard Wilson; Partner, Freshfields, since 1970; Company Department. *Biog:* b. 14 October 1941. *Nationality:* British. *Educ:* Stamford School; Peterhouse, Cambridge (BA). *Clubs:* City of London.

HARRIS, Robert Nicholas; Commercial Director, Dalgety plc, since 1988. *Career:* BP 1958-65; Dalgety 1965-. *Biog:* b. 1939. *Nationality:* British. *m.* 1965, Caroline (née Carpenter); 1 s; 1 d. *Directorships:* Dalgety plc 1988 (exec). *Professional Organisations:* Associate, Chartered Institute of Secretaries.

HARRIS, S C; Portfolio Manager, BP Pensions Services Ltd.

HARRIS, Sue; Associate Director, GCI Sterling.

HARRIS, Sydney Michael Frank; Director, Guardian Royal Exchange Assurance plc.

HARRIS, Timothy Charles; Director, The Peninsular & Oriental Steam Navigation Company, since 1986. *Biog:* b. 11 July 1947. *Nationality:* British. *m.* Angelika (née Harris); 1 s; 1 d. *Directorships:* P&O Containers Limited 1989 (exec) Chm; P&O Cruises Limited 1986 (exec) Chm; P&O European Transport Services Limited 1990.

HARRIS-ST JOHN, Jeremy Michael; Director, Parrish Stockbrokers, since 1990; Private Clients. *Career:* Capel Cure Myers, Account Manager 1975-86; Montagu Loebl Stanley, Associate Director 1986-87; Alexanders Laing & Cruickshank, Associate Director 1987-88; Parrish Stockbrokers, Director 1988-. *Biog:* b. 1 February 1957. *Nationality:* British. *m.* 1987, Karen Elizabeth. *Educ:* Charterhouse. *Directorships:* Parrish Stockbrokers 1990 (exec). *Professional Organisations:* Stock Exchange Exams. *Clubs:* Stock Exchange Athletic Club, Basingstoke Athletic Club. *Recreations:* Race Walking.

HARRISON, A G; Chief Executive & Director, Clerical Medical Unit Trust Managers.

HARRISON, B M; Compliance Officer, Sogemin Metals Ltd.

HARRISON, Brian William; Partner, Allen & Overy, since 1987; Banking. *Biog:* b. 30 October 1953. *Nationality:* British. *Educ:* Lynfield College, Auckland, New Zealand; Auckland University (LLB). *Professional Organisations:* The Law Society; City of London Law Society. *Clubs:* Royal Ocean Racing Club, New York Yacht Club.

HARRISON, C H; Partner, Herbert Smith.

HARRISON, D H A; General Manager, Lloyds Bank plc.

HARRISON, Garnet; Managing Director, Tyndall Holdings plc.

HARRISON, John; Partner, Touche Ross, since 1981; Management Consultancy. *Career:* Coopers & Lybrand, Articled Clerk 1966-70; Tillotson, Corporate Planner 1970-72; Touche Ross, Management Consultant 1972-. *Biog: b.* 12 November 1944. *Nationality:* British. *m.* 1969, Patricia (née Alban); 1 s; 2 d. *Educ:* Sheffield University (BA Econ). *Directorships:* Granta Radio Limited 1988 (non-exec). *Other Activities:* CBI Europe Committee. *Professional Organisations:* FCA; FIMC. *Clubs:* Royal Harwich Yacht Club. *Recreations:* Sailing, Shooting, Skiing.

HARRISON, Linda; Partner, Jaques & Lewis.

HARRISON, M C; Group Personnel Director, Sedgwick Group plc, since 1989. *Career:* Royal Insurance 1968-78; Willis Faber/Stewart Wrightson, Group Personnel Director 1978-88. *Biog: b.* 19 April 1946. *Nationality:* British. *Educ:* Wallingford Grammar School; University College, London (BSc). *Professional Organisations:* FCII.

HARRISON, M S K; Director, Information Systems, The Private Bank and Trust Company Limited, since 1989; Planning, Implementation and Operation of Computer Systems. *Career:* Arthur Andersen & Co 1977-85; Cazenove & Co 1985-87; Coopers & Lybrand 1987-89. *Biog: b.* 5 September 1953. *Nationality:* British. *Educ:* Corpus Christi College, Cambridge (MA Hons Natural Sciences).

HARRISON, Martin Edward; Managing Director, Morgan Guaranty Trust Co of New York, since 1988; Investment Management and Private Banking. *Career:* Samuel Montagu & Co, Asst Dir 1961-75. *Biog: b.* 4 April 1937. *m.* 1965; 1 s; 1 d. *Educ:* Harrow School; Oriel College, Oxford (MA). *Directorships:* J P Morgan Investment Management Inc 1986 (non-exec); J P Morgan (Suisse) SA 1987 (non-exec); J P Morgan Investment Management Australia Ltd 1988 (non-exec) Chairman. *Other Activities:* Finance and General Purposes Committee, London School of Hygiene & Tropical Medicine. *Clubs:* Brooks's, United Oxford & Cambridge University.

HARRISON, Michael; Partner, Clyde & Co.

HARRISON, Sir Michael; Bt; Chairman, LPH Pitman Limited, since 1987. *Career:* Lloyds, Broker 1959-; Member of Lloyds 1964-. *Biog: b.* 28 March 1930. *Nationality:* British. *m.* 1967, Lady Olive; 2 s; 2 d. *Educ:* Rugby School. *Directorships:* Chalwyn Ltd 1980 (non-exec); Berrite Ltd 1979 (exec); Rivercourt Insurance Services Ltd 1981 (exec). *Other Activities:* Member Council & Schooner Committee, Sail Training Association; Vice President & Chairman, Association of Combined Youth Clubs; Freeman, City of London; Liveryman, Mercers Company; Master, Mercers Company, 1986-87. *Clubs:* Boodles, MCC, Royal Harwich Yacht Club, Ski Club of Great Britain. *Recreations:* Sailing, Skiing, Crosswords.

HARRISON, Nigel Alexander; Director of Research, Smith Keen Cutler, since 1986; Smaller Companies. *Career:* Smith Keen Cutler Ltd Various 1961-. *Biog: b.* 5 February 1945. *Nationality:* British. *m.* 1969, Margaret (née Cole); 1 s; 2 d. *Educ:* King Edwards FiveWays School. *Professional Organisations:* Chartered Secretary. *Recreations:* Family Interests, Gardening.

HARRISON, Richard James; Director, James Capel Corporate Finance Ltd, since 1989; UK Corporate Finance. *Career:* Angus Campbell & Co (Merged with Josolyne Layton-Bennett & Co), Articled Clerk 1970-75; James Capel & Co, Deputy Chief Accountant 1975-80; Corporate Finance 1980-. *Biog: b.* 1 August 1951. *Nationality:* British. *m.* 1979, Valerie (née Leiper); 2 s. *Educ:* Bancroft's School, Essex. *Professional Organisations:* Fellow, Institute of Chartered Accountants. *Recreations:* Golf, Cricket, Hockey, Tennis, Squash, Skiing.

HARRISON-DEES, Geoffrey; General Manager (Marketing & Sales), Sun Life Assurance Society plc, since 1989; Marketing & Sales within the UK. *Career:* Phillips & Drew 1956-65; Target Group Unit Trust Services, Gen Mgr 1966-69; Key Fund Mgrs, MD 1970-73; Keyser Ullmann Ltd, Dir 1971-73; European Financial Services, MD 1974-76; Mercantile House Group, Dir of Various Oppenheimer Subsidiaries 1977-84; Sun Life Trust Management Ltd 1984-89. *Biog: b.* 9 June 1938. *Nationality:* British. *m.* 1982, Alison Marian (née Starte); 1 s; 3 d (2 d and 1 s by previous marriage). *Educ:* Dulwich College, London. *Directorships:* Sun Life Technical Services Limited Chm; Sun Life Broker Services Limited Chm; Sun Life Direct Marketing Limited Chm; Sun Life Unit Services Limited Chm; Sun Life Financial Associates Limited Chm; Northern Education Foundation Chm. *Clubs:* Gog Magog Golf Club. *Recreations:* Music, Reading, Golf.

HARRISON-TOPHAM, Thomas R N; Director, S G Warburg Akroyd Rowe & Pitman Mullens.

HART, Alan; Partner, Theodore Goddard.

HART, Garry Richard Rushby; Head of Property Department, Herbert Smith, since 1988. *Career:* Herbert Smith, Articled Clerk 1962-65; Solicitor 1966-68; Associate Partner 1968-70; Partner 1970-. *Biog: b.* 29 June 1940. *m1* 1966, Paula (née Shepherd) (Diss 1986); m2 1988, Valerie (née Davies); 2 s; 3 d. *Educ:* Northgate GS, Ipswich; University College London (LLB Solicitor). *Other Activities:* Liveryman, City of London Solicitors Company; Member, Joint Planning Law Conference Committee of the Law Society/The Royal Institution of Chartered Surveyors/The Bar Council. *Professional Organisations:* Member, Anglo-American Real Property Institute; Member, Law Society. *Publications:* Co-

Author, Blundell & Dobrys Planning Appeals & Inquiries, 4th Edition. *Clubs:* Carlton. *Recreations:* Farming.

HART, Hugh Robert; Director, N T Evennett and Partners Ltd.

HART, M C; Director, Chartered Trust plc.

HART, Michael John; Deputy Chairman, Foreign & Colonial Management Ltd; Joint Manager Foreign and Colonial Investment Trust, since 1969. *Career:* Foreign & Colonial Management Ltd, Dir 1969-. *Biog: b.* 26 December 1932. *Nationality:* British. *m.* Sheila; 1 s; 1 d. *Educ:* London School of Economics (BSc Econ). *Directorships:* Amphion Securities Limited; Anglo-Nippon Trust Limited; BP Pension Fund Investment Committee; C & L Securities Limited; F & C Smaller Companies plc; F & C Nominees Limited; F & C Securities Limited; Foreign & Colonial Unit Management Limited; GIT Management Services Limited; Hypo Foreign & Colonial Management (Holdings) Ltd; Latin American Securities Limited; Martindale Investment Trust Limited; Martindale Securities Limited; Teesdale Investments Limited; Teesdale Securities Limited; Union Jack Oil Company Limited. *Other Activities:* Chairman, Association of Investment Trust Companies. *Professional Organisations:* ACIS.

HART, N; Director, Henry G Nicholson (Underwriting) Ltd.

HART, P J F; Director, Panmure Gordon & Co Limited.

HART, Timothy Guy Collins; Partner, Phildrew Ventures, since 1985; Management Buy-outs. *Career:* Arthur Young & Co 1974-83; Prudential Portfolio Managers 1983-85; Phildrew Ventures 1985-. *Biog: b.* 31 August 1953. *Nationality:* British. *m.* 1980, Judith Charlotte (née Elgood); 2 s; 1 d. *Educ:* The Kings School, Canterbury; Oxford Polytechnic. *Directorships:* Richard Grant 1986 (non-exec); Norcor Holdings 1989 (non-exec); Kosset Carpets 1990 (non-exec). *Professional Organisations:* ACA.

HART, Trevor John Powell; Company Secretary, Barclays de Zoete Wedd Holdings Ltd.

HARTE, Brian Arthur; Director, Chase Investment Bank Limited, since 1989; UK Compliance Officer/Company Secretary. *Career:* Deloitte Haskins & Sells, Chartered Accountants, Articled Clerk/Audit Senior 1974-80; The Chase Manhattan Bank, NA; Chief Examiner/2nd Vice President, within Europe, Middle East, Africa area of general auditing 1980-83; Vice President, Asst Area Audit Mgr, Europe, Middle East, Africa 1983-85; (Hong Kong) Regional Audit Mgr, Vice Pres, Asia/Pacific 1985-88; Vice President 1988-. *Biog:*

b. 8 February 1953. *Nationality:* British. *m.* 1980, Sandra (née Davies); 1 s; 1 d. *Educ:* Wirral Grammar School; University of Birmingham (BCom). *Directorships:* Chase Investment Bank Holdings Ltd 1989 (exec); Chase Manhattan Financial Services Ltd 1989 (exec). *Other Activities:* American Chamber of Commerce Financial Services Sub Committee; American Banking & Securities Association of London Committee, 1992. *Professional Organisations:* Member, Institute of Chartered Accountants in England & Wales. *Recreations:* Clay Pigeon Shooting, Reading, Theatre.

HARTILL, Andrea Beatrice; Senior Financial Editor, Macmillan Press Reference Books, since 1990; Publishing Books on the Capital Markets. *Career:* Dun & Bradstreet, Editor, Who Owns Whom 1982-84; Longman Books, Publisher, Capital Markets 1984-87; IFR Publishing, Publishing Manager, Capital Markets 1987-90. *Biog: b.* 18 January 1960. *Nationality:* British. *m.* 1990, Neil Harding; 1 d. *Educ:* High Arcal School, Woodsetton, Worcs; University of Nottingham (BA Hons German Studies).

HARTLEY, P S; Director, Baring Asset Management Ltd.

HARTLEY, Paul; Non-Executive Partner, Killik & Co.

HARTSTONGE, Earl W; Chief Manager, Bank of New Zealand.

HARTY, Bernard Peter; Chamberlain, Corporation of London.

HARTY, M J; Group Legal & Compliance Director, Credit Lyonnais Capital Markets plc, since 1987; Legal & Compliance. *Career:* Called to Bar Middle Temple (Harmsworth Major Law Scholar) 1976; In Practice 1976-86; Phillips & Drew 1986-87; Credit Lyonnais Capital Markets plc, Group Legal & Compliance Director 1987-. *Biog: b.* 22 April 1952. *Nationality:* British. *m.* 1982, Eily (née Goodall); 2 s; 1 d. *Educ:* Ullathorne Grammar School, Coventry; Brasenose College, Oxford (BA,MA). *Directorships:* Various Group Companies (exec). *Other Activities:* Chairman, Securities Houses Compliance Officers' Group; Chairman, TSA Client Money Working Party; TSA Arbitrator. *Clubs:* Garrick. *Recreations:* Opera, Travel, Skiing, Cricket.

HARVEY, B J; Chairman, Henry G Nicholson (Underwriting) Ltd.

HARVEY, Edward J; Director, Continental Reinsurance London.

HARVEY, Ian; Partner, Stoy Hayward Consulting, since 1985; Management Consultancy. *Career:* Thomson McLintock & Co, Computer Audit Mgr 1969-77;

Henlys plc, Group Chief Internal Auditor 1977-79; Stoy Hayward, Snr Mgr 1979-85. *Biog: b.* 31 May 1951. *Nationality:* British. *m.* 1973, Avril (née Somers); 2 d. *Educ:* City of London School. *Professional Organisations:* FCA; MIMC; MBCS; Council Member, Management Consultancies Association. *Recreations:* Family, Keep Fit, Sports, Cinema.

HARVEY, Ian Alexander; Chief Executive, British Technology Group, since 1985; Technology Development. *Career:* Vickers Ltd, Mechanical Engineer 1963-69; Laporte Industries, Project Engineer 1969-73; World Bank, Snr Loan Officer 1975-82; Sabbatical 1982-84; Logan Associates Inc, Ptnr 1984-85. *Biog: b.* 2 February 1945. *Nationality:* British. *m.* 1976, DeAnne Julius; 1 s; 1 d. *Educ:* Cardiff High School; Cambridge University (MA); Harvard Business School (MBA). *Directorships:* Logan Associates Inc 1984 (non-exec); PACS Ltd 1986 (non-exec). *Other Activities:* Advisory Panel, SPRU; British Assoc, Science & Industry Committee; CBI R&M Committee. *Professional Organisations:* CBIM. *Publications:* Transferts de Technologie en Grande-Bretagne, 1987; Technology Transfer - An International Two-Way Street, 1987; Trade Through Technology, 1987; The Cephalosporin Story, 1987; Intellectual Property - The Undervalued Resource for Competitive Advantage, 1989 & 1990. *Recreations:* Piano, Skiing, Sailing, Windsurfing.

HARVEY, J R; Director, Sedgwick Group plc, since 1985. *Career:* Chevron Corp, Engineer 1956-61; Touche Ross, Consultant 1963-64; Transamerica Corporation, Various 1965-1981; Chairman and Chief Executive Officer 1981-. *Biog: b.* 20 August 1934. *Nationality:* American. *m.* 1971, Charlene; 2 d. *Educ:* Princeton University (BSE); University of California, Berkeley (MBA). *Directorships:* Pacific Telesis Group 1983; McKesson Corporation 1987; Charles Schwab Corporation 1989; SRI International 1988; Safeway Corporation 1982-86. *Other Activities:* National Park Foundation Board; Montana Land Reliance; California Parks Foundation Advisory; Nature Conservancy Business Advisory; San Francisco Chamber of Commerce; Bay Area Council; California Economic Development Corp; California Business Roundtable; Saint Mary's College Trustee, Regent; Walter A Haas School of Business, Advisory Bd; Foundation for Teaching Economics; Fine Arts Museum of San Francisco; Meyer Friedman Institute. *Clubs:* Pacific Union (San Francisco), Bohemian (San Francisco), Union League Club (New York). *Recreations:* Fly Fishing, Nature Conservation, Ranching, Early California Art, Tennis.

HARVEY, Michael; Group Treasurer, The Royal Dutch Shell Group, since 1986. *Career:* Royal Dutch Shell Group (Indonesia, Argentina, Switzerland, France, Nigeria & The Netherlands). *Biog: b.* 12 April 1934. *Nationality:* British. *m.* 1970, Susan (née Schaffner) (decd); 1 d. *Educ:* Winchester College; Oriel College, Oxford (MA). *Professional Organisations:* ACIS; FCT.

HARVEY, Nicholas Charles; Director, Granville & Co Ltd, since 1987; Corporate Finance/Head of Mergers and Acquisitions Dept. *Career:* Oswald Hickson Collier & Co Articled Clerk 1977-80; Asst Solicitor; Chesham Amalgamations and Investments Ltd Asst to MD 1980-81; S G Warburg & Co Ltd Dep Mgr 1981-83. *Biog: b.* 5 November 1953. *m.* 1981, Diane Catherine (née Redgrave); 1 s; 1 d. *Educ:* Alleyn's School; Reading University (BA Econ). *Professional Organisations:* The Law Society. *Recreations:* Squash, Skiing, Theatre, Food, Wine.

HARVEY, Philip Martin; Director, Morgan Grenfell & Co Ltd, since 1990; LDC Debt. *Career:* Libra Bank plc, Deputy General Manager, Responsible for LDC Debt Trading 1977-90; Banque Belge Ltd, Financial Analyst 1970-77. *Biog: b.* 23 January 1954. *Nationality:* British. *m.* 1984, Cibeli (née Cunha Cardoso).

HARVEY, Richard; Partner, Morison Stoneham, since 1989; Taxation. *Career:* MacIntyre Hudson, Articled Clerk 1974-78; Arthur Andersen & Co, Tax Senior 1978-81; Tax Manager 1981-88. *Biog: b.* 26 May 1955. *Nationality:* British. *m.* 1975, Elaine Carmel (née Goodman); 3 d. *Educ:* Gilberd, Colchester; City of London Polytechnic. *Professional Organisations:* Fellow, Institute of Chartered Accountants in England and Wales. *Publications:* Tax and Financial Planning for Sportsmen and Entertainers, 1987.

HARVEY, Richard Charles; Partner, Slaughter and May, since 1969; Company/Commercial Management. *Biog: b.* 5 September 1935. *Nationality:* British. *m.* 1962, Susan (née Keeling); 1 s; 1 d. *Educ:* Caterham School; Merton College, Oxford (MA). *Professional Organisations:* The Law Society (Council); City of London Law Society. *Clubs:* Leander, Hurlingham, Royal Wimbledon Golf. *Recreations:* Fishing, Golf, Skiing, Theatre.

HARVEY, Robert William; Director, Treasury Division, Kleinwort Benson Ltd.

HARVEY, Roger Martin; Director, Kleinwort Benson Securities Ltd, since 1988; Insurance Research and Sales/Deputy Head of Research. *Career:* Royal Insurance Actuarial Trainee 1964-68; Laing & Cruickshank Investment Analyst 1968-73; W Greenwell & Co Insurance Analyst 1974-79; Ptnr, Insurance Research 1979-86; Greenwell Montagu Dir, Insurance Research 1986-87. *Biog: b.* 18 October 1946. *Nationality:* British. *m.* 1969, Diana Elizabeth (née Record); 2 s; 1 d. *Educ:* Latymer Upper School. *Professional Organisations:* FIA; Chartered Insurance Institute (Member); ASIA. *Clubs:* Fellowship, Argonauts. *Recreations:* Roadrunning, Skiing, Book-collecting, Theatre.

HARVEY, Roy William George; Executive Director, Hambros Bank Ltd, since 1975; Head of Commercial Banking Division. *Career:* Martins Bank Limited 1948-52; Hambros 1953-; Dir 1975; Exec Dir 1985. *Biog: b.* 2 November 1931. *Nationality:* British. *m.* 1953, Audrey (née Murch); 1 s; 1 d. *Educ:* Isleworth Grammar School. *Directorships:* Hambros Bank (Nominees) Ltd 1969; Hambros Bank (Jersey) Ltd 1977 Chm 1990; Hambros Bank (Guernsey) Ltd 1977 Chm 1990. *Other Activities:* Member, Lombard Assoc. *Professional Organisations:* AIB. *Recreations:* Golf, Tennis.

HARVEY-JONES, Sir John; KB, MBE; Deputy Chairman, Grand Metropolitan plc, since 1987. *Career:* Royal Navy, specialising in Submarines 1937-56; Qualified as Russian Interpreter 1946; Later German Interpreter, various in Naval Intelligence, latterly Lieutenant Commander; ICI Work Study Officer 1956; Commercial Appointments, Wilton, then Heavy Organic Chemical Div, Techno-Commercial Dir 1967; Dep Chm, HOC Div 1968; Chm, ICI Petrochemicals Div 1970-73; ICI, Main Board Dir 1973; Dep Chm 1978-82; Chm 1982-87. *Biog: b.* 16 April 1924. *m.* 1947, Mary Evelyn (née Bignell); 1 d. *Educ:* Tormore School, Deal, Kent; Royal Naval College, Dartmouth. *Directorships:* Grand Metropolitan plc 1983; 1987 Dep Chm; The Economist 1987; 1989 Chm; GPA Ltd 1987; 1989 Dep Chm; Parallax Enterprises Ltd 1987 Chm; Business International Board Committee 1988 (non-exec) Chm; Didacticus Video Productions Ltd 1989 Chm; Trendroute Ltd 1988; Burns Anderson 1987 (non-exec); 1987-89 Chm; Phillips-Imperial Petroleum 1973-75 Chm; ICI Americas Inc 1975-76; Fiber Industries Inc 1975-78; Reed Intl plc (non-exec); Carrington Viyella Ltd 1981-82; Chemical Industries Association Ltd 1980-82 Council Member. *Other Activities:* Commander's Cross of the Order of Merit of the Federal Republic of Germany; Chancellor, Bradford University; Chm of Council, St James's & The Abbey School, Malvern 1987; Chm of Council, Wildfowl Trust 1987-; President: Wider Share Ownership Council, 1988; Book Trust Appeal Fund, 1987; Vice Pres: Hearing & Speech Trust, 1985-; Heaton Woods Trust 1986-; Member: Society of Chemical Industry 1978; Royal Society of Arts 1979-, Vice-Pres, 1988-; Member, Advisory Council of the Prince's Youth Business Trust 1986; Trustee, Police Foundation 1983-; Chm of Trustees, 1984-88; Board Member, Welsh Development International 1989; Hon Consultant, Royal United Services Institute for Defence Studies,1987-; Governor, English Speaking Union 1987; Member of Advisory Editorial Board, New European 1987-; Hon Member, Economic Research Council 1984-; City of Guilds of London Institute 1988-; Patron: Cambridge University Young Entrepreneurs Society 1987-; Manpower Services Commission National Training Awards 1987-; Steer Organisation; Vice Patron, British Polio Fellowship 1988-; Fellow, Smallpiece Trust 1988-; Hon Fellow: Royal Society of Chemistry 1985; Institute of Chemical Engineers 1985;

Member of Court of Governors, Kidney Research Unit for Wales Foundation 1989; Hon Dir, RACAC (Radio Ramair, Bradford); Hon Pres, University of Bradford MBA Alumni Association 1989; Member BIM 1978-; Vice Chm, 1980-85; Vice Pres, Industrial Participation Association 1983; Hon Pres, Friends of Brecon Jazz 1989; Patron, National Canine Defence League 1990-; Hon LLD (Manchester) 1985, (Liverpool) 1986, (London) 1987, (Cambridge 1987; D Univ (Surrey) 1985; Hon DSc (Bradford 1986, (Leicester) 1986,; Hon DCL (Newcastle) 1988; Hon DSc (Keele) 1989, (Exeter) 1989; Hon DBA (International Management Centres) 1990; British Institute of Management Gold Medal 1985; Society of Chemical Industry Centenary Medal 1986; JO Hambro, British Businessman of the Year 1986; International Association of Business Communicators Award of Excellence in Communication 1987; Radar Man of the Year 1987; City & Guilds Insignia Award in Technology (Honoris Causa) 1987; Senior Ind Fellowship, Leicester Polytechnic, 1990; Member, Tees and Hartlepool Port Authority 1970-73; Vice-Pres, Conseil Europeen des Federations de l'Industrie Chimique (CEFIC) 1982-84; Member President's Committee, Confederation of British Industry 1982-87, Pres, 1984-86; Vice Chair, Policy Studies Institute 1980-85; Vice Chairman 1980-85; Hon Vice-Pres Inst of Marketing 1982-89; Member, National Economic Development Office Committee for the Chemical Industry 1980-82; Member, Northeast Development Bd 1971-73; Member of Court of British Shippers' Council 1982-87; Member of Council, British-Malaysian Society 1983-87; Member of Foundation Bd Intl Mgmnt Inst, Geneva 1984-87; Member of Council, Youth Enterprise Scheme 1984-86; Trustee, Conference Board 1984-86; Intl Council Member, European Inst of Business Admin 1984-87; Trustee, Science Museum 1983-87; Vice Chm Great Ormond Street Redevelopment Appeal; Patron, Halton Chemical Industry Museum Appeal 1986; Non-Exec Dir, Nimbus Records; Vice Pres, Newham College Appeal 1987; Television Series, Troubleshooter, 1990. *Publications:* Making it Happen, Reflections on Leadership, 1987. *Clubs:* Athenaeum, Groucho's. *Recreations:* Ocean Sailing, Swimming, The Countryside, Driving one of my donkeys, Cooking, Contemporary Literature.

HARWOOD, Ian; Head of Global Research, S G Warburg Securities, since 1990; International Economics. *Career:* Rowe & Pitman, Economist 1978-86; S G Warburg Securities, Chief Economist 1986-90. *Biog: b.* 7 March 1953. *Nationality:* British. *Educ:* Reigate Grammar; Bristol University; LSE (BSc); Cambridge University. *Professional Organisations:* Royal Economic Society; European Economic Association; Economic History Association; American Economic Association. *Recreations:* Sport (particularly Swimming, Cycling, Running), Political History.

HARWOOD, John Thomas; Director of Finance, Philips Electronic & Associated Industries Ltd, since

1980; Company Financing & Pension Fund. *Career:* Prudential Assurance Co, Investment Analyst 1958-64; Mullard Ltd Corporate Planning 1964-69; Philips Electronics, Grp Fin Mgr & Asst Mgr 1969-80. *Biog: b.* 20 July 1933. *m.* 1969, (decd); 1 s; 1 d. *Educ:* St Clement Danes Grammar; London School of Economics (BSc). *Directorships:* Philips Finance 1969 (exec); Philips Financial Services 1980 (exec); Philips Asset Finance 1987 (exec); Philips Pension Fund Trust Ltd 1980 (exec); UK Estates Ltd 1988 (exec). *Professional Organisations:* ACT; Society of Business Economists. *Publications:* Statistics of Electronics Industry, 1968. *Recreations:* Music, Skiing, Gardening.

HARWOOD, Paul; Director, Newton Investment Group.

HARWOOD, Richard Cecil; Director, Schroder Securities Limited, since 1989; Head of UK Research. *Career:* Morgan Grenfell Securities, Director, Capital Goods Research 1986-89; Smith New Court Agency, Research Director (Office Equipment, Electronics Leisure) 1985-86; Scott, Goff, Leyton, Research Partner 1973-85; Scott, Goff, Hancock, Research Analyst 1969-73; Smiths Industries, Corporate Planning, Graduate Training Programme 1962-69. *Biog: b.* 21 September 1943. *Nationality:* British. *m.* 1967, Kirsten; 1 s; 2 d. *Educ:* Sutton High School for Boys; Tiffin Boys School, Kingston-on-Thames; City University, (BSc Hons Production Engineering Class 1); City University Business School (MSc Business Studies). *Directorships:* Schroder Securities Ltd 1989 (exec). *Other Activities:* Member, Society of Investment Analysts; Member, Chartered Engineering Institute (C Eng); Member, Lloyds. *Publications:* Numerous Company and Industry Reviews Published over the Last 20 Years. *Clubs:* AMOC. *Recreations:* Classic Cars, Leisure Travel.

HASEGAWA, Taiji; Managing Director, Mitsui Trust International Ltd.

HASHIMOTO, Y; Executive Director, Daiwa Europe Limited.

HASKI, Michel; Deputy Chairman, CCF Foster Braithwaite Ltd, since 1988; Deputy Chairman, Framlington Group plc, since 1990; International Development. *Career:* Crédit Commercial de France, Senior Vice President, International Fund Management Activity 1985-90; Dorset Development, Paris, Chairman of the Board and CEO 1975-84; Caisse National du Credit Agricole Paris 1970-74. *Biog: b.* 1946. *Nationality:* French. *m.* 1981, Sylvie Nicollet; 2 s; 1 d. *Educ:* Faculte des Sciences de Paris (MBA Mathematics, PhD Statistics); Ecole Nationale de la Statistique et de l'Administration Economique. *Directorships:* Fida Holding (Italy) 1988 (non-exec); Framlington Group plc 1990 (exec); CCF Foster Braithwaite Ltd 1988 (exec); Banque Chaix 1988 (non-exec); Elysees Fonds 1989

(non-exec). *Publications:* Several Papers, Conferences and Articles on Marketing in European and French Newspapers; Statistics, 1969 (French).

HASLAM, Robert; Lord Haslam; Chairman, British Coal, since 1986. *Career:* ICI 1947-83; Main Board Dir 1974; Dep Chm 1980-83; British Steel Corp, Chm 1983-86; Tate & Lyle plc, Chm 1983-86. *Biog: b.* 4 February 1923. *Nationality:* British. *m.* 1947, Joyce (née Quinn); 2 s. *Educ:* Bolton School; Birmingham University (BSc). *Directorships:* Bank of England 1985; Unilever 1986. *Other Activities:* Manchester Business School (Chm 1985); Member of Council, CBI; Member of NIGC; Governor of NIESR; Governor of Henley Management College; Freeman of the City of London; Chairman of Governors, Bolton School. *Clubs:* Wentworth, Brooks's, Athenaeum. *Recreations:* Golf, Travel.

HASLAM, Simon M; Partner, Touche Ross & Co, since 1986; Securities Industry Audit/Consulting. *Career:* Spicer and Pegler (later Spicer & Oppenheim and Touche Ross), Articled Clerk 1978-81; Qualified Senior/Manager 1981-86; Partner 1986-. *Biog: b.* 29 May 1957. *Nationality:* British. *m.* 1982, Kate (née Alcock); 1 s; 1 d. *Educ:* Ecclesbourne School, Duffield; Magdalen College, Oxford (MA). *Other Activities:* District Councillor, Welwyn Hatfield District Council. *Professional Organisations:* ACA. *Publications:* Joint Author, The London Securities Market, 1990. *Recreations:* Music, Reading.

HASPINEALL, David W; Director, Bradstock Blunt & Crawley Ltd.

HASS, Anthony; Director, Samuel Montagu & Co Limited.

HASTINGS, Stephen; Joint Senior Partner, Broadbridge.

HASTINGS-BASS, John Peter; Managing Director, Personal Insurance Division, Jardine Insurance Brokers Limited, since 1986. *Career:* Jardine Matheson Group, Various Positions in Far East 1976-85. *Biog: b.* 5 June 1954. *Nationality:* British. *m.* 1982, Sophie (née Scarisbrick); 2 d. *Educ:* Cambridge (MA Law).

HATA, Isami; Executive Director, Yamaichi International (Europe) Limited.

HATCH, Henry Clifford; Finance Director, Allied-Lyons plc, since 1987; Finance. *Career:* Toronto Dominion Bank, Toronto, Investment Division 1963-64; Inspiration Ltd, Montreal, Executive Assistant and Treasurer 1966-68; Corby Distilleries Limited, Manager, Corporate Development 1968-70; Hiram Walker-Gooderham & Worts Limited, Windsor Ontario, Marketing Manager 1970-76; Corby Distilleries Limited, Montreal Quebec, President and Chief Executive Officer 1977-79;

Hiram Walker-Gooderham & Worts Limited, Vice President 1979-84; President & Chief Executive Officer 1984-87; Allied-Lyons plc, Finance Director 1987-. *Biog: b.* 30 April 1942. *Nationality:* Canadian. *m.* 1967, Sylvie Helene; 1 s; 2 d. *Educ:* Assumption College High School, Windsor Ontario; Neuchatel Junior College, Neuchatel Switzerland; McGill University, Montreal Quebec (BA Honours); Harvard Graduate School of Business Administration, Cambridge Massachusetts (MBA). *Directorships:* Allied-Lyons Netherlands BV 1987 Supervisory Board; Allied-Lyons plc 1986; Allied Industrial Technology BV 1987 Supervisory Board; Allied Investments Limited 1988; Allied-Lyons Australia Pty Limited; Allied-Lyons Investments Limited 1987; Allied-Lyons Overseas (Canada) Limited 1988 Chairman; Allied-Lyons Overseas (Europe) Limited 1988; Allied-Lyons Overseas Limited 1987 Chairman; Betset Limited 1988; Financiering Maatschappij D'Oranjeboom BV Supervisory Board; Gomiddle Limited 1989; Hiram Walkers-Allied Vintners Limited 1987; Recordpull Limited 1988 Chairman; Trendhigh Limited 1988 Chairman; Allied-Lyons Eastern Limited 1987; Broad Street Securities Limited 1988 Director; Business in The Community 1990; Corby Distilleries Limited; Elco Leasing Limited 1987. *Clubs:* Young Presidents' Organisation, Royal Ocean Racing Club. *Recreations:* Sailing, Hiking, Skiing, Jogging, Reading.

HATCH, John Vaughan; Chairman, Venture Link Investors Ltd, since 1987; Venture Capital Investment. *Career:* Deloitte Haskins & Sells Mgmnt Consultant 1973-82; Water Authorities Superannuation Fund Dep Dir of Investment 1982-84; Venture Link (Holdings) Ltd MD 1984-87. *Biog: b.* 25 May 1949. *Nationality:* British. *m.* 1973, Sally Margaret (née Brownscombe); 2 d. *Educ:* Worksop College; Mansfield College, Oxford (MA); St Anthony's College, Oxford (MPhil). *Directorships:* Oxfordshire County Council 1973-77 Councillor; National Consumer Council 1980-86 Member; General Optical Council 1984-88 Member; Electricity Consumers Council 1984-90 Chm; National Grid Company plc 1989- (non-exec); Century Hutchinson Ltd 1985-89 (non-exec). *Other Activities:* Member, The Company of Information Technologists, 1989; Freedom of the City of London, 1985. *Professional Organisations:* ACMA. *Publications:* Value for Money Audits 1981; Controlling Public Industries 1982. *Clubs:* City of London, Landsdowne. *Recreations:* Cricket, Bridge.

HATCHARD, Michael Edward; Partner, Theodore Goddard, since 1985; Corporate Finance and Technical Company Law. *Career:* Admitted Solicitor 1980. *Biog: b.* 21 November 1955. *Nationality:* British. *m.* 1983, Erica (née Bourdon Smith). *Educ:* Sherborne School; Reading University (LLB Hons); College of Law (2nd Class Hons). *Other Activities:* City of London Solicitors' Company. *Professional Organisations:* The Law Society; The City of London Law Society. *Publications:* Selected

Contributions. *Clubs:* RAC, Big Picture. *Recreations:* Painting, Shooting, Boating, Swimming.

HATCHER, M C; Director, Baring Securities Limited.

HATCHETT, A G; CBE; Director, P & O Steam Navigation Company.

HATHAWAY, Rodney Francis; Managing Director, Ashley Palmer Holdings Limited, since 1986.

HATTRICK, R I; Consultant, Waltons & Morse, since 1989; Shipping and Insurance. *Career:* Skelton & Co (Manchester), Articles 1955-58; Army, Infantry Officer 1958-60; Waltons & Co, Assistant Solicitor 1960-64; Waltons & Morse and Predecessor Firms, Partner 1964-89; Senior Partner 1987-89; Partner 1964-89; Consultant 1989-. *Biog: b.* 20 January 1933. *Nationality:* British. *m.* 1959, Joan Moira (née Chatterton); 3 d. *Educ:* William Hulme Grammar School, Manchester; Victoria University (LLB). *Other Activities:* Chairman, City of London Admiralty Solicitors Group; Admiralty Court Committee; Lloyd's Form Working Party; British Maritime Law Association; City of London Solicitors Company; Law Society. *Professional Organisations:* Solicitor of the Supreme Court. *Clubs:* Naval & Military, City Club, City Law Club, Little Ship Club, Colne Yacht Club, Law Society Yacht Club. *Recreations:* Sailing, Walking, Music.

HAUPTMANN, Dr Karl H; Director, Merrill Lynch, Pierce, Fenner & Smith Ltd, since 1990; Equity Derivatives (Europe). *Career:* Bankers Trust International Ltd, Equity Derivatives, Vice President 1986-90. *Biog: b.* 11 August 1960. *Nationality:* German. *Educ:* Free University of Berlin (PhD Economics, Diplom Kaufmann). *Professional Organisations:* Studienstiftung Des Deutschen Volkes. *Clubs:* Askania-Burgundia Berlin. *Recreations:* Running, Jazz, Music, Travel, Skat.

HAUSER, G; Director, Pechiney World Trade (Holdings) Ltd.

HAUTEFORT, Bernard; Director, Credit Lyonnais Securities, since 1987; International Corporate Finance Management. *Career:* Nippon Europartners (Tokyo), Chief Executive 1973-78; Europartners Securities (New York), President 1978-83; Credit Lyonnais Capital Markets (Paris) 1983-87; Credit Lyonnais Securities (London) 1987-. *Biog: b.* 3 July 1943. *Nationality:* French; 1 s. *Educ:* Faculty of Law (Paris); Institut d'Etudes Politiques (Paris). *Recreations:* Riding, Farming, Gardening, History, Music.

HAVERS, Robert Michael Oldfield; The Rt Hon The Lord Havers; Non-Executive Chairman, R H M Outhwaite (Underwriting Agencies) Limited.

HAVILAND, Christopher Philip; Director, Barclays de Zoete Wedd Ltd.

HAVILL, Brian Bond; Managing Director, Investment Banking, PaineWebber International (UK) Ltd, since 1989; Corporate Finance. *Career:* PaineWebber, Director 1987; Head of Corporate Finance 1989; Citicorp Investment Bank, Director & VP 1984-87; Thomas Tilling Inc/Thomas Tilling Ltd, Group Executive & VP 1977-83; Haden Carrier Ltd, Group Marketing Director 1974-75; Alcan Industries Ltd 1961-74. *Biog: b.* 31 August 1939. *Nationality:* British. *m.* 1969, Jenny; 2 s. *Educ:* University of Sheffield (BSc Hons); Harvard Business School (Graduate PMD). *Directorships:* PaineWebber International (UK) Ltd 1987 (exec). *Other Activities:* Committee Member, British American Chamber of Commerce. *Professional Organisations:* Harvard Business Club. *Clubs:* Royal Wimbledon Golf Club.

HAW, Jonathan Stopford; Partner, Slaughter and May, since 1977; Company and Commercial Law. *Biog: b.* 1945. *Nationality:* British. *m.* 1969, Hélène (née Lacuve); 1 s; 1 d. *Educ:* Radley College; Keble College, Oxford (MA). *Other Activities:* Armourers & Brasiers' Company; City of London Solicitors' Company; Ctee of Bassishaw Ward Club; Juvenile Diabetes Foundation (UK). *Professional Organisations:* The Law Society; IBA. *Clubs:* Leander.

HAWES, Anthony John David; Director, Baring Brothers & Co Ltd, since 1987; Treasury & Trading. *Career:* Baring Brothers & Co Ltd Various 1961-; Seconded to Saudi Arabian Monetary Agency (Jeddah) 1975-77; Intl Asset Mgmnt 1977-83; Treasury & Trading 1983-. *Biog: b.* 6 March 1943. *m.* 1966, Hilary Margaret (née Wright); 1 s; 3 d. *Educ:* Merchant Taylors' School, Northwood. *Directorships:* Baring Sterling Bonds 1986 (exec). *Professional Organisations:* FCIB.

HAWKE, Nigel Peter James; Director, Banking Division, Barclays de Zoete Wedd Limited, since 1989; Commercial Property Finance. *Career:* Barclays Bank plc 1976-83; Barclays de Zoete Wedd Limited 1983-. *Biog: b.* 3 July 1955. *Nationality:* British. *m.* 1976, Felicity Jane (née Millward); 2 s. *Educ:* Trinity School, Croydon; Keble College, Oxford (BA Hons PPE, MA). *Directorships:* Barclays de Zoete Wedd Limited 1989 (exec). *Professional Organisations:* ACIB; DipFS CIOB; The Securities Association, Registered General Representative Director. *Clubs:* Institute of Directors, United Oxford & Cambridge University Club. *Recreations:* Family, Church.

HAWKEN, James Stanley; OBE; Assistant General Manager, Equity & Law Life Assurance Society plc, since 1988; Sales, Marketing. *Career:* Equity & Law (West Germany), Gen Mgr 1976-88. *Directorships:* Equity & Law Fund Management Gesellschaft für Kapitalanlagen 1987 (exec); Equity & Law International Fund Managers Ltd 1989 (exec); Equity & Law International Life Assurance Co Ltd 1989 (exec); Equity and Law Unit Trust Managers Ltd 1988 (exec); Equity & Law Life Assurance Society plc 1988 (exec); Equity & Law Commercial Loans Ltd 1990; Equity & Law Home Loans plc 1989.

HAWKES, Ben; Partner, Clifford Chance.

HAWKES, C R C; Partner, Lane Clark & Peacock, since 1970; Pension Fund Advice/Chairman of International Committee. *Career:* National Provident Institution, Actuarial Clerk 1961-65; Hosking, Burton & Co, Actuarial Assistant 1965-67; Actuary 1967-70. *Biog: b.* 29 January 1940. *Nationality:* British. *m.* 1984, Juliet Alison (née Hicks); 1 s. *Educ:* Charterhouse; Merton College, Oxford (MA Pure Maths). *Other Activities:* Member, Committee of International Association of Consulting Actuaries; Liveryman, Worshipful Company of Actuaries; Member, Association of Consulting Actuaries. *Professional Organisations:* Fellow, Institute of Actuaries. *Clubs:* Royal Ocean Racing Club, Lansdowne Club, JOG. *Recreations:* Sailing, Gardening, Bridge, Family, Opera.

HAWKINS, D; Partner, Nabarro Nathanson.

HAWKINS, D M; Director, Panmure Gordon & Co Limited.

HAWKINS, Ian; Director, Phillips & Drew Development Capital.

HAWKINS, J; Director, Hoare Govett International Securities; Director of International Research & Marketing.

HAWKINS, M A; Director, Well Marine Reinsurance Brokers Limited.

HAWLEY, Peter; Managing Partner, Walker Martineau Stringer Saul, since 1983; Senior Commercial/Banking Partner. *Career:* 99 Gurkha Infantry Brigade Attached 1957-59; Walker Martineau, Articled Clerk 1963-66; Assistant Solicitor 1967-69; Partner 1970-. *Biog: b.* 20 July 1938. *m.* 1964, Tanya (née Ounsted); 1 d. *Educ:* Wyggeston School; Magdalene College, Cambridge (MA, LLB). *Directorships:* Pentewan Sands Ltd 1989 (non-exec). *Other Activities:* Member, Institute of Directors; Freeman, City of London. *Professional Organisations:* The Law Society. *Clubs:* Gresham. *Recreations:* Foreign Travel.

HAWTIN, Ian Alexander; Company Secretary, The Boots Company plc, since 1989. *Career:* Distillers Chemicals & Plastics Ltd, Company Secretary's Dept 1965-67; British Petroleum Ltd, Legal Dept 1967-70; Guest Keen & Nettlefolds Ltd, Legal Dept 1970-72; The Boots Company plc, Legal Adviser/Deputy Secretary 1972-88. *Biog: b.* 25 September 1942. *Nationality:* British. *m.* 1967, Patricia; 1 s; 1 d. *Educ:* Wadham College, Oxford (MA Jurisprudence). *Directorships:* None outside the Boots Group. *Other Activities:* Member, Code of Practice Committee of the Association of the British Pharmaceutical Industry. *Professional Organisations:* Member, Gray's Inn (Barrister). *Recreations:* Tennis, Bridge, Theatre, Music, Reading.

HAWTIN, Michael Victor; Director, Export Credits Guarantee Dept, since 1988; Finance & Personnel, Principal Establishment & Finance Officer, Resource Management Group. *Career:* HM Treasury, Asst Principal 1964-69; Seconded to Barclays Bank 1969-71; HM Treasury, Principal 1971-76; Asst Sec 1976-83; Property Services Agency, Under Sec (Principal Fin Officer) 1983-86; HM Treasury, Under Sec (Head of Local Gvnmt Gp) 1986-88. *Biog: b.* 7 September 1942. *Nationality:* British. *m.* 1966, Judith (née Eeeley); 1 s; 1 d. *Educ:* Bournemouth School; St John's College, Cambridge (MA); University of California, Berkeley (MA). *Clubs:* Overseas Bankers. *Recreations:* Music, Travel.

HAY, Marianne Laing; Director, Martin Currie Investment Management Ltd.

HAY, Morven Charles; Senior Vice President & General Manager, Arab Banking Corporation, since 1988; General Manager of London Branch, Head of Commercial Banking for the ABC Group. *Career:* RTZ Services Ltd Financial Analyst 1968-71; Western American Bank Mgr, Banking Div 1972-75; Crocker National Bank VP & Dep Branch Mgr 1975-78; National Commercial Bank (Jeddah) Head of Corporate Finance 1978-80; Arab Banking Corporation 1980-. *Biog: b.* 24 April 1947. *Nationality:* British. *Educ:* Latymer Upper School; Liverpool University (BSc Hons 1st); Cape Town University (MBA 1st). *Professional Organisations:* Fellow, Royal Statistical Society. *Clubs:* Carlton, Overseas Bankers', Annabel's, Crockfords. *Recreations:* Politics, Theatre.

HAY, Peter Rossant; Finance Partner, Penningtons, since 1986; Company/Commercial Affairs. *Career:* James Morgan & Co (Cardiff), Articled Clerk 1967-70; Ward Bowie (London), Articled Clerk 1971-72; Assistant Solicitor 1973; Partner 1973-86. *Biog: b.* 11 October 1948. *Nationality:* British. *m.* 1973, Christine Maria (née Battle); 2 s; 1 d. *Educ:* Clifton College. *Directorships:* Richmond Athletic Association Limited 1976 (non-exec); 1986 Chairman; Meat Trade Supplies plc 1988-89 (non-exec). *Other Activities:* Hon Solicitor, The Royal Scottish Corporation. *Professional Organisations:* The Law Society. *Clubs:* The Caledonian Club, London Scottish FC, Sunningdale. *Recreations:* Golf, Skiing, Swimming, Ex Rugby, Rowing.

HAY DAVISON, Ian F; Chairman, Laing & Cruickshank, since 1988. *Career:* Arthur Andersen & Co

1958; Partner 1966; Managing Partner 1966-82; Senior Partner 1982-83; Adviser 1986-88; Lloyd's, Dep Chm & Chief Executive 1983-86. *Biog: b.* 30 June 1931. *Nationality:* British. *m.* 1955, Maureen Patricia (née Blacker); 1 s; 2 d. *Educ:* Dulwich College; London School of Economics (BSc Econ); University of Michigan. *Directorships:* Credit Lyonnais Securities Chm; Alexanders Discount Chm; Credit Lyonnais Rouse Chm; Shorehouse plc Chm; Newspaper Publishing plc (The Independent); Chloride Group plc. *Other Activities:* Hon DSc, Aston University, 1985; Chm of the Accounting Standards Ctee of the Consultative Ctee of Accountancy Bodies, 1982-84; Member of Council, Institute of Chartered Accountants in England & Wales, 1975- (Former Member of the Inflation Accounting Steering Group, Auditing Practices Ctee, Technical Advisory Ctee and Chm of Technical and Research Ctee); Member of the Price Commission, 1977-79; Member (Chm 1975), National Economic Development Ctee for the Building Industry, 1970-77; Chm, NEDC for the Food and Drink Manufacturing Industry, 1981-83; Dept of Trade Inspector into the affairs of London Capital Group Limited, 1975-77; Inspector into the affairs of the Gray's Building Society, 1978-79; Chm, Hong Kong Securities Review Ctee, 1987-88; Chm, Lloyd's Working Party on Accounting and Disclosure, 1982-83; Parliamentary Candidate (Conservative) Stepney, 1964; Councillor and Alderman of the London Borough of Greenwich, 1961-74; Chm of the Housing Ctee, 1968-70; Chm, 1968-71 and Vice-Chm, 1971-74, of the London Boroughs Joint Computer Ctee; Governor (Chm until 1971) of the Greenwich Theatre, 1968-81; Trustee of the Monteverdi Choir & Orchestra, Victorian and Albert Museum, Royal Opera House Convent Garden and Conran Foundation; Member, Commerce and Industry Ctee, Save the Children Fund; Director, European Arts Foundation; Member of Council, Association for Business Sponsorship of the Arts; Governor, London School of Economics; Member of Standing Ctee, LSE; Chm, LSE Finance Panel; Member, Oxford University Appointments Board; Governor, National Institute of Economics and Social Research. *Professional Organisations:* FCA. *Publications:* A View of the Room, 1987. *Clubs:* Athenaeum, Arts, MCC. *Recreations:* Opera, Theatre, Music, Skiing, Gardening Under Supervision.

HAYASHI, T; Chief Representative, Bank of Kyoto Ltd.

HAYCOCK, P J; Finance Director, Riggs A P Bank Ltd.

HAYCOCKS, M; Associate, Grimley J R Eve.

HAYDEN, B G; Director, Leslie & Godwin Limited; Multinational Risks, City Broking & Risk Management Divisions.

HAYDEN, Mrs Hazel Rosemary; Director & Company Secretary, Murray Lawrence Members Agency Limited, since 1988; Co Secretary/Names Liaison. *Career:* Bowring Group Synd 360, Secretary 1965-70; Harvey Bowring Synd 362, PA to Underwriter 1971-83; Murray Lawrence & Partners, Members Agency Names Liaison & Administration 1985-1988. *Biog: b.* 2 July 1948. *Nationality:* British. *m.* 1969, Michael. *Educ:* Sutton Common Road School for Girls. *Directorships:* Murray Lawrence Members Agency Ltd 1988 (exec) Director & Co Secretary. *Professional Organisations:* Member of Lloyd's, 1985. *Recreations:* Horse Riding, Travel, French Language Studies, Arts & Crafts.

HAYDEN, Michael A J; Director, Continental Reinsurance London.

HAYES, Derek; Partner, Macfarlanes.

HAYES, J C; Director, Phillips & Drew Fund Management Limited.

HAYES, Jane; Consultant (Corporate Finance), BBM Associates.

HAYES, P B; Partner, Field Fisher Waterhouse.

HAYES, W D; Executive Director, Chartered WestLB Limited.

HAYGARTH, Nigel Charles; Director and General Manager Finance, Pearl Assurance plc, since 1987; Financial Management and Group Accounting. *Career:* Baker Sutton Co Audit Ptnr 1975-79; Ernst & Whinney Audit Ptnr 1979-81; Community Reinsurance Corporation Ltd/Norden Insurance Co (UK) Ltd 1981-83; Chief Exec 1983-85; Pearl Assurance plc Chief Acct 1986-87. *Biog: b.* 10 February 1943. *Nationality:* British. *Educ:* Leeds Grammar School; University College, Oxford (MA Hons). *Directorships:* Community Reinsurance Corporation Ltd 1983-85 (exec); Norden Insurance Co (UK) Ltd 1983-85 (exec); Pearl Assurance (Unit Funds) Limited 1988; Pearl Assurance (Unit Linked Pensions) Limited 1988; Pearl Trust Managers Limited 1988; Pearl Assurance plc 1988; Pearl Developments Limited 1988. *Professional Organisations:* FCA. *Clubs:* Royal Philharmonic Society. *Recreations:* Music, Theatre, Reading.

HAYMAN, G J; Deputy Chairman, The British Insurance and Investment Brokers' Association.

HAYNES, Derek Leslie; Technical Partner, Clark Whitehill, since 1982; Auditing and Accounting Technical. *Biog: b.* 13 June 1950. *Nationality:* British. *m.* 1973, Averil. *Directorships:* Clark Whitehill Associates Ltd 1983 (exec); Clark Whitehill Portfolio Management Limited 1988 (exec). *Other Activities:* Liveryman, The Worshipful Company of Glass Sellers of London. *Professional Organisations:* FCA. *Clubs:* City Livery Club.

Recreations: Music, Photography, Classic Cars, Victorian Engineering.

HAYNES, J A; Non-Executive Director, Booker plc.

HAYNES, N F; Director, Kleinwort Benson Investment Management.

HAYNES, P E; Partner, Kidsons Impey.

HAYNES, R; Committee Member, Abbey Unit Trust Managers, Unit Trust Association.

HAYSEY, David John; Director, S G Warburg Securities, since 1990; Head of European Equity Sales. *Career:* E B Savory Milln & Co 1979-86; S G Warburg Securities 1986-. *Biog: b.* 12 March 1957. *Nationality:* British. *m.* 1987, Linda (née Tremaine); 1 d. *Educ:* Adams' Grammar School, Newport; Trinity College, Oxford (MA Hons). *Clubs:* Arts. *Recreations:* Sailing.

HAYTER, George Anthony; Managing Director, Trading Markets Division, The Internaional Stock Exchange, since 1990; The Operation, Supervision & Development of the ISE's Equity & Fixed Interest Markets, including the Systems & Services which support them. *Career:* Elliott Automation Development Engineer 1962-64; Leo Computers/ICL Systems Support Mgr 1964-68; BOAC/British Airways Development Controller 1968-76; The International Stock Exchange Dir Information Services 1976-87; Executive Dir of Services 1987-90. *Biog: b.* 4 October 1938. *Nationality:* British. *m.* 1968, Annabel (née Strong); 2 s; 2 d. *Educ:* Malvern College; Queens' College, Cambridge (MA Physics). *Directorships:* Critchley Limited 1984 (non-exec); The ISE (London) Inc 1984; Bankinter (Spain) 1988 (non-exec). *Clubs:* Leander. *Recreations:* My Family, DIY, Sailing.

HAYTHE, David; Managing Director (Investment Management), Morgan Stanley International.

HAYWARD, David Philip; Partner, Lawrence Graham, since 1990; Commercial Property. *Career:* Wilkinson & Durham, Assistant Solicitor 1976-82; Wilde Sapte, Asst Solicitor 1982-87. *Biog: b.* 1 October 1951. *Nationality:* British. *m.* 1981, Carol (née Hilton); 3 d. *Educ:* Ellesmere College, Salop; Selwyn College, Cambridge (History IIi). *Professional Organisations:* Law Society.

HAZELL, A G; Director, Lowndes Lambert Group Limited.

HAZELL, Sharon; Partner, Titmuss Sainer & Webb.

HAZZARD, C; Partner, Life & General (Epsom), Bacon & Woodrow.

HEAD, B C; Partner, Pannell Kerr Forster.

HEAD, David Raymond John; Director, County NatWest, since 1988; European Trading. *Career:* L Messel & Co Director, Intl Trading 1985-86; Shearson Lehman International Director, Intl Trading 1986-88. *Biog:* b. 5 March 1954. *Nationality:* British. *m.* 1984, Julia Margaret; 4 d. *Directorships:* County NatWest Securities 1989 (exec); County NatWest Ltd 1989.

HEAD, John C; Partner, John Head & Partners LP, Investment Bankers, since 1987. *Career:* Morgan Stanley & Co Inc, Investment Bankers, Associate 1972-77; Vice President 1977-80; Principal 1980-82; Managing Director 1982-86; Odyssey Investors Inc, Chairman 1986-87; Seneca Insurance Group, President 1986-87. *Biog:* b. 28 April 1948. *Nationality:* American. *Educ:* Massachusetts Institute of Technology. *Directorships:* Seneca Insurance Group plc, Inc and subsidiary, Seneca Insurance Company Inc; Sphere Drake Insurance plc 1988; Sphere Drake Insurance Group plc 1988; Sphere Drake Acquisitions (UK) Ltd; Sphere Drake Holding plc; Banner Life Insurance Company (US subsidiary of Legal & General Group plc); Morgan Stanley Group, Inc and subsidiary Morgan Stanley & Co Inc; Odyssey Investors, Inc a subsidiary of Odyssey Partners, a US partnership.

HEAD, T W R; Partner, Freshfields.

HEADLAM, R D; Director, Rutland Trust plc.

HEALD, Antony; Partner, Theodore Goddard.

HEALD, G; Chief Treasury Manager Europe, HongKong and Shanghai Banking Corporation.

HEALD, N F B; Partner, Simmons & Simmons, since 1977; Property. *Career:* Simmons & Simmons, Articled Clerk 1968-72; Assistant Solicitor 1972-77; Partner 1977-. *Biog:* b. 12 November 1947. *Nationality:* British. *m.* 1971, Mary Elizabeth (née Goodhall); 2 d. *Educ:* Harrow County School for Boys. *Other Activities:* City of London Solicitors Company. *Professional Organisations:* The Law Society. *Recreations:* Travel.

HEALING, J R P; Director, Kleinwort Benson Limited.

HEANLEY, Robert Bowman; Partner, Clyde & Co, since 1980; Shipping and Transport Law, Insurance Law, Construction Law. *Career:* Clyde & Co, Assistant Solicitor 1975-80; Metson Cross and Co, Articles 1971-75. *Biog:* b. 7 February 1950. *Nationality:* British. *m.* (div); 1 s; 1 d. *Educ:* Cranleigh School; Guildford County Technical College (HND Business Studies); College of Law (Law Society Examinations). *Other Activities:* Member, International Bar Association. *Professional Organisations:* Member, Law Society; Solicitor,

Supreme Court. *Recreations:* Skiing, Windsurfing, Sailing, Tennis.

HEAP, M A; Non-Executive Director, Abbey National plc.

HEAPE, R G; Committee Member, Midland, Unit Trust Association.

HEAPS, Christopher Seymour; Partner, Jaques and Lewis, since 1971. *Biog:* b. 15 November 1942. *Nationality:* British. *m.* 1970, Ann Mary; 2 d. *Educ:* Dorking G S; University of Exeter (LLB). *Other Activities:* Council Member, Law Society, 1984-; Chairman, Law Society Planning Committee, 1988-; Deputy Chairman, London Regional Passengers Committee, 1985-; Member, Railway Heritage Trust Advisory Panel; Liveryman, Worshipful Company of Curriers, 1976; Liveryman, Worshipful Company of Coachmakers and Coach Harness Makers, 1985; President, Holborn Law Society, 1983-84. *Professional Organisations:* Solicitor, 1967; Member, Chartered Institute of Transport, 1988. *Publications:* London Transport Railway Album, 1978; Western Region in the 1960s, 1981; This is Southern Region Central Division, 1982; B R Diary, 1968-77, 1988. *Recreations:* Transport History, Transport.

HEAPS, John; Partner, Hepworth & Chadwick.

HEARD, Julian John Lennox; Partner, Cyril Sweett & Partners, since 1990. *Career:* W H Saunders & Associates 1978-81; Cyril Sweett & Partners 1981-. *Biog:* b. 19 October 1955. *Nationality:* British. *m.* 1985, Mary (née Reed); 1 s; 1 d. *Educ:* Taunton School; Portsmouth Polytechnic (BSc). *Professional Organisations:* Associate, Royal Institute of Chartered Surveyors. *Clubs:* East London Runners. *Recreations:* Running, Sailing.

HEARD, Roger Russell; Partner, Lane Clark & Peacock, since 1979. *Biog:* b. 17 September 1945. *Nationality:* British. *m.* 1972, Shelley; 1 s; 1 d. *Educ:* University of Hull (BSc Econ); London School of Economics (MSc). *Other Activities:* Company of Actuaries. *Professional Organisations:* Fellow, Institute of Actuaries. *Recreations:* Opera.

HEARN, Andrew E T; Litigation Partner, Titmuss Sainer & Webb, since 1986; Intellectual Property Litigation. *Career:* Titmuss Sainer & Webb, Articled Clerk 1980-82; Assistant Solicitor 1982-86; Partner 1986-. *Biog:* b. 23 July 1957. *Nationality:* British. *m.* 1985, Sarah P; 2 s. *Educ:* University College School, London; St Johns College, Oxford (BA, Juris). *Professional Organisations:* Member, City of London Solicitors Company; Member, Law Society. *Publications:* Misleading Advertising - The New Law, 1988. *Recreations:* Theatre, Cinema, Skiing, Tennis.

HEARNE, Graham; Non-Executive Director, N M Rothschild & Sons Limited.

HEARNE, Graham James; CBE; Chief Executive & Executive Director, Enterprise Oil plc, since 1984;; Non-Executive Director, N M Rothschild & Sons Ltd. *Career:* Pinsent & Co, Solicitor 1959-63; Fried Frank Harris Shriver & Jacobson (NY), Solicitor 1963-66; Herbert Smith & Co, Solicitor 1966-67; Seconded to Industrial Reorganisation Corp 1967-70; Courtaulds Ltd, Fin Dir 1977-81; Tricentrol plc, Chief Exec 1981-83; Carless, Capel & Leonard plc, MD 1983-84; Enterprise Oil plc, Chief Exec 1984-. *Biog: b.* 23 November 1937. *Nationality:* British. *m.* 1961, Carol Jean (née Brown); 1 s; 3 d. *Educ:* George Dixon Grammar School, Birmingham. *Directorships:* BPB Industries plc 1982 (non-exec); Enterprise Oil plc 1984 (exec); Reckitt & Colman plc 1990 (non-exec).

HEASMAN, Lawrence Frank; Director, Arbuthnot Latham Bank, since 1989. *Career:* Ionian Bank (now Arbuthnot Latham Bank), Asst Investment Mgr 1970-77; Portfolio Mgr 1977-86; Royal Trust Asset Management, MD 1986; Arbuthnot Latham Fund Managers Ltd MD , Investment Mgmnt Arm 1987-. *Biog: b.* 11 February 1946. *Nationality:* British. *m.* 1973, Elizabeth (née Barker); 3 s; 1 d. *Educ:* West Kent College. *Directorships:* Arbuthnot Fund Managers Ltd 1987; Arbuthnot Latham Nominees Ltd 1988; Arbuthnot Computer Services Ltd 1988; DSB Nominees Ltd 1988; Society of Investment Analysts 1988; NZI Investment Services Ltd 1988; Nelson Nominees Ltd 1988; Arbuthnot Unit Trust Management Ltd. *Other Activities:* AMSIA. *Recreations:* Computer Science.

HEATH, A M; Executive Director, Marketing, Eagle Star Insurance Company Ltd.

HEATH, Christopher John; Managing Director, Baring Securities Ltd, since 1984. *Career:* ICI 1964-69; George Henderson & Co, Sales Executive 1969-75; Henderson Crosthwaite & Co, Ptnr 1976-84. *Biog: b.* 26 September 1946. *Nationality:* British. *m.* 1979, Margaret Joan (née Wiggin); 1 s. *Educ:* Ampleforth College. *Directorships:* Baring Brothers & Co Ltd (exec); Subsidiaries of Baring Securities Limited 1987 (exec). *Other Activities:* National Appeals Committee, Cancer Research Campaign; Joy to the World (Save the Children, NSPCC). *Professional Organisations:* Member, Stock Exchange. *Clubs:* Turf, Flyfishers. *Recreations:* Horse Racing, Fishing.

HEATH, D C; Chairman, Billiton-Enthoven Metals Limited, since 1987. *Educ:* (MSc). *Directorships:* Billiton UK Ltd 1987 (exec) MD.

HEATH, J C; Director, Parrish Stockbrokers.

HEATH, Michael Robert; Director, Smith New Court plc.

HEATH, Ray; Editor, Equity International.

HEATH, Robin D J; Partner, Banking & Financial Services Group, Ernst & Whinney.

HEATHCOTE, Aidan; Partner, Clyde & Co.

HEATHCOTE, D J; Group Legal Advisor and Company Secretary, Beazer plc.

HEATON, Mrs Frances Anne (née Whidborne); Director, Lazard Brothers & Co Limited, since 1987; Corporate Finance. *Career:* Dept of Economic Affairs 1967-70; H M Treasury 1970-80. *Biog: b.* 11 August 1944. *Nationality:* British. *m.* 1969, Martin; 2 s. *Educ:* Queen Anne's, Caversham; Trinity College, Dublin (BA, LLB). *Directorships:* Defence Technology Enterprises Ltd 1985 (non-exec); W S Atkins plc 1990 (non-exec). *Professional Organisations:* Barrister. *Recreations:* Riding, Gardening, Bridge.

HEATON-WARD, Patrick Francis; Director, Ogilvy Adams & Rinehart, since 1988; Account Handling, Business Development. *Career:* Ogilvy & Mather Ltd, Account Director 1964-75; Ogilvy & Mather SpA (Milan), Director of Client Services 1976-77; Ogilvy & Mather Ltd, Account Director 1978-82; Livraghi Ogilvy & Mather (Milan), Director 1982-88; Ogilvy & Mather Focus (now Ogilvy Adams & Rinehart), Director 1988-. *Biog: b.* 3 October 1939. *Nationality:* British. *m.* 1976, Danielle (née Mussot); 2 d. *Educ:* Bristol Grammar School; Brasenose College, Oxford (MA). *Directorships:* Ogilvy Adams & Rinehart 1989 (exec); Livraghi Ogilvy & Mather 1982 (exec). *Other Activities:* Institute of Practitioners in Advertising (IPA) Recruitment Advertising Committee. *Professional Organisations:* MIPA. *Recreations:* Music, Skiing.

HEBBLETHWAITE, J D; Clerk, Parish Clerks' Company.

HEBERT, L I; Non-Executive Director, Riggs A P Bank Ltd.

HEDBERG, Leif I; Deputy Managing Director, Svenska International plc.

HEDGES, P; Deputy Chairman & Joint Managing Director, Taylor Woodrow plc.

HEDIEN, W E; Director, Allstate Reinsurance Co Limited.

HEDLEY, A M; Director, National Investment Group plc.

HEDLEY, S W G; Director, Robert Bruce Fitzmaurice Ltd.

HEDLEY GREENBOROUGH, Sir John; KBE; Deputy Chairman, Lloyds Bank plc.

HEDLEY-MILLER, Rosalind; Director, Kleinwort Benson Ltd, since 1987; Corporate Finance. *Career:* J Henry Schroder Wagg & Co Ltd, Exec, Investment Dept 1977-79; Kleinwort Benson Ltd 1979-. *Directorships:* Bejam Group plc 1987-89 (non-exec).

HEFFERNAN, John; City Editor, Yorkshire Post, since 1987; Stock Market Quoted Companies. *Career:* City Press Newspaper, Chm 1965-75; United Newspapers, City Editor 1965-87. *Biog: b.* 1 September 1927. *Nationality:* British. *m.* 1954, Veronica (née Laing); 2 d. *Educ:* Gunnersbury Grammar School; London University (BCom). *Other Activities:* Hon Sec of London Ctee, Yorkshire & Humberside Development Association; Hon Sec, Association of Regional City Editors; City Livery Council; Court Member, Basket Makers Co. *Professional Organisations:* Barrister (Inner Temple). *Clubs:* City Livery. *Recreations:* Tennis, Skiing.

HEFFERNAN, Patrick; Partner, Clyde & Co, since 1988; Mergers & Acquisitions, Joint Ventures, Corporate Matters. *Career:* Slaughter and May, Articled Clerk 1972-74; Solicitor 1974-75; Vinters, Solicitor 1976-80; Forsyte Kerman, Solicitor 1980-82; Lovell, White & King, Solicitor 1982-87. *Biog: b.* 17 March 1948. *m.* 1973, Elizabeth (née Essery); 1 s; 1 d. *Educ:* Wimbledon College; Jesus College, Cambridge (MA). *Professional Organisations:* The Law Society.

HEFFERNAN, Peter F J; Senior Vice-President, Investment Banking, Europe, The Bank of Nova Scotia; Capital Markets/Treasury. *Career:* Bank of Montreal Various Mgmnt 1966-77; Banque Nationale de Paris Various to VP 1977-83; The Bank of Nova Scotia Various to SVP 1983. *Biog: b.* 7 January 1947. *Nationality:* Canadian. *m.* 1974, Christine (née Hosegood); 1 s. *Directorships:* The Bank of Nova Scotia Channel Islands Limited 1988 (non-exec); The Bank of Novia Scotia Trust Company Channel Islands Limited 1988 (non-exec). *Other Activities:* Canada-UK Chamber of Commerce. *Professional Organisations:* Fellow, Institute of Canadian Bankers. *Clubs:* Annabel's. *Recreations:* Windsurfing, Skiing, Bridge.

HEGAZY, Dr A M; Chairman, Allied Trust Bank Limited.

HEIGHAM, David John; Company Secretary, Williams De Broe plc, since 1990. *Career:* Thomson McLintock 1963-71; Jardine Matheson 1971-72; The Council of the Stock Exchange 1972-73; Williams De Broe 1973-. *Biog: b.* 4 December 1944. *Nationality:* British. *m.* 1970, Pauline Elizabeth (née Payne); 1 s;

1 d. *Educ:* Haileybury College. *Professional Organisations:* Institute of Chartered Accountants of Scotland; The International Stock Exchange. *Recreations:* Golf.

HEILBRON, David James Michael; Director, County NatWest Securities Ltd, since 1989; UK Equity Sales. *Career:* Spicer & Pegler Chartered Accountants, Articled Clerk 1980-83; Grieveson Grant & Co, Stockbroker in Various Departments 1983-85; Wood Mackenzie & Co Ltd (now County NatWest Securities Limited) 1985; New York 1986-88. *Biog: b.* 15 September 1958. *Nationality:* British. *m.* 1990, Louise. *Educ:* Sevenoaks School; University of Exeter (BA Hons Economics & Economic History 2:2). *Directorships:* County NatWest Securities 1989 (exec). *Professional Organisations:* All Stock Exchange Exams. *Clubs:* Gurus, Saints. *Recreations:* Cricket, Tennis, Golf.

HEIMANN, J G; Executive Committee, British Merchant Banking and Securities Houses Association.

HEININGER, Patrick; Director, Baring Brothers & Co Ltd, since 1984; International Finance, Property. *Career:* Debevoise & Plimpton Lawyer 1969-71; University of Nairobi/Government of Kenya Lecturer/Adviser 1971-73; World Bank Legal Adviser, Finance 1973-82. *Biog: b.* 22 June 1942. *m.* 1987, Caroline (née Atack). *Educ:* Georgetown University, Washington DC (LLM, JD); American University, Washington DC (BA). *Other Activities:* Council Member, The Barkshire Committee Ltd; Director & Treasurer, Food & Agricultural Research Management Limited. *Professional Organisations:* New York Bar, D.C. Bar. *Publications:* Liability of US Banks for Deposits Placed in their Foreign Branches, 1979. *Recreations:* Tennis, Squash, Chamber Music.

HELENIUS, Joakim J; Executive Director, Merrill Lynch International Bank Limited, since 1989; Institutional FX/Currency Options. *Career:* Goldman Sachs Intl Ltd, Vice President 1987-89; Kansallis-Osake-Pankki (London Branch), Senior Manager 1984-86; Goldman Sachs Intl Ltd, Associate 1981-84. *Biog: b.* 24 November 1957. *Nationality:* Finnish. *m.* Arja; 1 s; 1 d. *Educ:* Cambridge University (MA Honours). *Directorships:* Merrill Lynch International Bank Ltd 1989 (exec); Merrill Lynch Capital Markets 1989. *Professional Organisations:* Registered Representative with the NYSE.

HELEY, Richard William; Executive Director, Hill Samuel Bank Ltd, since 1990; Corporate Finance. *Career:* Citibank NA, Managing Director, UK Corporate Finance, Head of UK Mergers and Acquisitions and General Corporate Finance Unit 1989-90; Barclays de Zoete Wedd Ltd, Managing Director, Head of UK Corporate Finance 1986-89; Hill Samuel & Co Ltd, Director, Corporate Finance Dept 1974-86; Phillips & Drew, Associate, European Economics and Investment Research 1970-74. *Biog: b.* 9 October 1948. *Nationality:* British. *m.* 1974, Barbara Alessandra (née Kidd); 1 s;

1 d. *Educ:* Forest School; University of Wales UCNW (BA Econ); University of Sussex. *Directorships:* Henlys plc 1980-85 (non-exec). *Other Activities:* Member, Corporate Finance Committee, British Merchant Bankers and Securities Houses Association 1987-89. *Professional Organisations:* AMSIA. *Publications:* Profit Forecasting (Ed C Westwick), 1981. *Recreations:* Riding, Swimming.

HELLER, John; Managing Partner, Nabarro Nathanson, since 1989; Practice Management. *Career:* Nabarro Nathanson, Trainee 1976; Qualified as Solicitor 1978; Partner Corporate Finance 1982. *Biog: b.* 29 December 1952. *Nationality:* British. *m.* 1983, Amanda (née Baker); 1 s; 2 d. *Educ:* St Edward's School, Oxford; Clare College, Cambridge (BA Hons Modern Languages and Law). *Other Activities:* General Committee of Management, Oriental Club, 1987-90. *Professional Organisations:* The Law Society. *Clubs:* Oriental, Wine Society. *Recreations:* Skiing, Tennis, Wine, Bridge.

HELLER, Lawrance; Senior Partner, Berwin Leighton, since 1986; Property Work. *Career:* Titmuss Sainer & Webb, Partner 1961-63; Leighton & Co, Partner 1963-70; Berwin Leighton, Partner 1970-. *Biog: b.* 14 April 1934. *Nationality:* British. *m.* 1961, Lilian Patricia (née Kessel); 1 d. *Educ:* Battersea Grammar School; Cambridge University (MA). *Other Activities:* Trustee of the Westminster Association for Youth. *Publications:* Commercial Property Development Section of Longmans Practical Commercial Precedents, 1987. *Recreations:* Gardening, Skiing.

HELLER, M; Director, Maxwell Pergamon Publishing Corporation plc.

HELLER, M A; Chairman, London & Associated Investment Trust plc, since 1977. *Biog: b.* 19 July 1936. *Nationality:* British. *m.* 1965, Morven (née Livingstone); 2 s; 1 d. *Educ:* Harrogate Grammar School; St Catharine's College, Cambridge (MA). *Directorships:* United Biscuits (Holdings) plc 1968 (non-exec); London & Associated Investment Trust plc 1971 (exec); Bisichi Mining plc 1973 (exec); Electronic Data Processing plc 1965 (non-exec). *Professional Organisations:* FCA. *Clubs:* RAC. *Recreations:* Collecting Modern British Paintings.

HELLINGS, David Whicher; Head of Insurance Branch 3, Department of Trade & Industry.

HELLYER, Compton Graham; Director, Serpula Ltd.

HELMORE, Charles Patrick; Director, Foreign & Colonial Management Ltd, since 1983; Marketing. *Career:* Middle Temple, Barrister-at-Law 1973-85; Jardine Matheson & Co Ltd, Merchant 1973-78; Paine Webber Mitchell Hutchins, Stockbroker 1979-82; Foreign & Colonial, Management Dir 1982-. *Biog: b.* 26 May 1951. *Nationality:* British. *m.* 1981, Rachel; 2 s.

Educ: Eton College; Magdalene College, Cambridge (MA); INSEAD (MBA). *Directorships:* F & C Unit Mgmnt Ltd 1985; F & C Overseas Ltd 1987; LTCB and F & C Investment Management Co Ltd 1988; National and Foreign Capital Management Co Ltd 1988. *Recreations:* Reading, Shooting, Fishing.

HELYAR, R; Director, Kleinwort Grieveson Charlesworth Ltd.

HEMINGWAY, J; Director, Phillips & Drew Fund Management Limited.

HEMINGWAY, John G; Chairman, Morgan Hemingway & Co Ltd, since 1974. *Career:* Messrs Freshfields, Solicitors, Partner 1960-74. *Biog: b.* 28 April 1931. *Nationality:* British. *m.* 1 s; 2 d. *Educ:* Mill Hill School; University of London (LLB). *Directorships:* Daily Mail and General Trust plc (non-exec); Associated Newspapers Ltd (non-exec); The Brent Walker Group plc (non-exec); Dartington & Co Group plc (non-exec); Howmac plc (non-exec); The Morgan Trust Co Ltd (non-exec); The Berthon Boat Co Ltd (non-exec); Pyramid Records Ltd (non-exec); William Hill Group Ltd (non-exec); New World Trust Corporation Ltd (non-exec). *Professional Organisations:* Law Society. *Clubs:* Royal Ocean Racing, Royal Thames Yacht.

HEMSLEY, Andrew Robert; Partner, Cyril Sweett & Partners, since 1989. *Career:* Wheeler Rumble & Perrin, Quantity Surveyor 1973-80; Cyril Sweett & Partners, Quantity Surveyor 1980-86; Associate 1986-89. *Biog: b.* 15 November 1954. *Nationality:* British. *m.* 1979, Eileen (née Oswin); 1 s; 1 d. *Educ:* The Old Grammar School, Lewes; Lewes Priory. *Professional Organisations:* Associate, Royal Institute of Chartered Surveyors. *Recreations:* Lethargy.

HEMSLEY, Oliver Alexander; Managing Director, Raphael Zorn Hemsley Limited, since 1989. *Biog: b.* 27 September 1962. *Nationality:* British. *Directorships:* Raphael Zorn Hemsley Ltd 1989 (exec). *Other Activities:* Member, Lloyds.

HENBREY, Eric J; Director, Schroder (J Henry) Wagg & Co Ltd.

HENDERSON, Alan Brodie; Executive Director, Newmarket Venture Capital plc.

HENDERSON, Charles Michael; The Lord Faringdon; Bt; Partner, Cazenove & Co.

HENDERSON, D A; Assistant General Manager, Scottish Equitable Life Assurance Society.

HENDERSON, Sir Denys (Hartley); KB; Chairman, Imperial Chemical Industries plc, since 1987. *Career:* Messrs Esslemont & Cameron, Advocates, Legal

Apprentice 1952-55; Army, RASC and Directorate of Army Legal Services, latterly Staff Captain 1955-57; ICI Head Office, Commerical Assistant, Secretary's Dept, London 1957; Paints Division 1958-59; Billingham Division 1959-61; Assistant Secretary, Agricultural Division 1961-64; Secretary, Nobel Division 1965-66; New Ventures Manager, Nobel Division 1966-68; General Manager, Catalysts and Licensing, Agricultural Division 1968-72; Catalysts, Licensing and Purlboard Director, Agricultural Division 1972; Fertilizer Business Area Director, Agricultural Division 1973-74; General manager, Commercial 1974-77; Chairman, Paints Division 1977-80; ICI Main Board, Variously responsible for Planning, Commercial Affairs, Polyurethanes, Speciality Chemicals and Explosives, the international businesses of Pharmaceuticals, Agrochemicals and Colours, Paints and Continental Western Europe and Eastern Europe 1980; Deputy Chairman 1986; Understudy to the Chairman only 1986; Chairman 1987. *Biog: b.* 11 October 1932. *Nationality:* British. *m.* 1957, Doreen (née Glashan); 2 d. *Educ:* Aberdeen Grammar School; University of Aberdeen (MA, LLB). *Directorships:* Barclays Bank plc 1983 (non-exec); Barclays plc 1985 (non-exec); The RTZ Corporation plc 1990 (non-exec); and various subsidiary/associated companies. *Other Activities:* Knight Bachelor; Solicitor; D Univ, Brunel, 1987; LLD, University of Aberdeen, 1987; Hon DSc, Cranfield Institute of Technology, 1989; Hon LLD, University of Nottingham, 1990; International Award, The Wall Street Transcript Annual Diversified Chemicals Awards, 1987; Member of Council, Chemical Industries Association, 1980-82; Member of the London Executive Committee, The Scottish Council Development & Industry, 1983-86; Member, BBC's Consultative Group on Industrial and Business Affairs 1984-86; Member, CEFIC (European Council of Chemical Manufacturers' Federations) Presidential Advisory Group, 1987; Member, New York Stock Exchange Listed Company Advisory Committee, 1988-90; Member of the London Advisory Group, The Scottish Council Development and Industry, 1986-; Member of the Court of Governors of Henley - The Management College 1986; Chairman of the Court of Governors, 1989; Member of Advisory Council, Prince's Youth Business Trust, 1986; Chairman, Stock Exchange Listed Companies Advisory Committee, 1987; Member of President's Committee, Confederation of British Industry 1987; Member of Council, British Malaysian Society, 1987; Vice President, Cleveland International Eisteddfod, 1987; Member, The Opportunity Japan Campaign Committee, 1988; Member, Appeal Council, Winston Churchill Memorial Trust, 1988; Member of President's Committee, The Advertising Association, 1988; Member, Industry & Commerce Group, Save The Children Fund, 1988; Trustee, The Natural History Museum, 1989; Member of Council, The Japan Festival 1991, 1989; Patron, AIESEC, 1989; President, Society of Business Economists, 1990. *Professional Organisations:* Member, The Law Society of Scotland; Companion, British Institute of Management; Fellow, Royal Society

of Arts; Fellow, Institute of Marketing; Honorary Vice-President, The Chartered Institute of Marketing, 1989. *Clubs:* Royal Automobile. *Recreations:* Family Life, Swimming, Reading, Travel, Minimal Gardening, Unskilled but Enjoyable Golf.

HENDERSON, Dr Douglas Lindsay; First Vice-President, Swiss Bank Corporation.

HENDERSON, George; Partner, James Gentles & Son.

HENDERSON, Giles Ian; Partner, Slaughter and May, since 1975; Company and Commercial Law. *Educ:* Michaelhouse, S Africa; University of Witwatersrand, S Africa (BA); Magdalen College, Oxford (MA, BCL).

HENDERSON, Guy; Partner, Allen & Overy, since 1990; Commercial Litigation. *Career:* Allen & Overy 1980-84; Porter Bartlett & Mayo, Sturminster Newton 1984-86; Allen & Overy 1986-. *Biog: b.* 9 January 1958. *Nationality:* British. *m.* 1988, Sophie (née Wingfield Digby); 1 s. *Educ:* Radley College; Downing College, Cambridge (MA). *Professional Organisations:* The Law Society.

HENDERSON, Henry Merton; Partner, Cazenove & Co, since 1982; Fund Management Cazenove Unit Trust Management Ltd. *Biog: b.* 25 April 1952. *Nationality:* British. *m.* 1976, Sarah (née Lowther); 1 s; 1 d. *Educ:* Eton College. *Directorships:* Blagoslay Ltd; Evershot Farms Ltd; Farmington Trust Ltd; Holland House Estates; Nunthorpe Investments Ltd; Strangways Estates Ltd; Cazenove Service Co 1982; Cazenove Nominees Ltd 1984; Updown Investment Company plc 1984; Stata Investments plc 1985; Greenwood Nominees Ltd 1986; Witan Investment Co plc 1988; Cazenove Unit Trust Management Ltd 1988; Hotspur Investments plc 1990. *Clubs:* White's, Pratt's.

HENDERSON, I J; Director, Land Securities plc.

HENDERSON, Ian Ramsay; Investment Director, Wardley Investment Services International Limited, since 1982; International/Senior Investment Officer. *Career:* Peat Marwick Mitchell, Accountant 1971-76; Morgan Grenfell, Investment Manager 1977-82. *Biog: b.* 6 January 1949. *Nationality:* British. *m.* 1978, Virginia (née Freeman); 3 s. *Educ:* Eton College; Edinburgh University (MA, LLB). *Directorships:* Wardley Marine Investment Management Limited 1982-85 (exec); Wardley Investment Services International Limited 1985 (exec); Wardley Unit Trust Managers Limited 1989 (exec). *Professional Organisations:* Institute of Chartered Accountants of England & Wales, FCA. *Clubs:* Brooks's, St James, West Sussex Golf Club. *Recreations:* Golf, Tennis.

HENDERSON, John Crombie; Chief Executive, Capel-Cure Myers Capital Management Limited, since 1988. *Career:* Army Lt 1959-63; Sir R W Carden & Co/ Capel-Cure Myers 1964; Ptnr 1970; Dir 1985. *Biog: b.* 8 April 1939. *Nationality:* British. *m.* 1968, Marylou (née de Guingand); 2 d. *Educ:* Uppingham School. *Directorships:* Capel-Cure Myers Capital Management Ltd (exec); Capability Trust Managers Ltd 1983 (exec); CCM Financial Services Ltd 1986 (exec). *Professional Organisations:* Member of The International Stock Exchange. *Clubs:* Turf, Berkshire Golf Club. *Recreations:* Hunting, Golf, Shooting.

HENDERSON, M A; Director, Panmure Gordon & Company Limited.

HENDERSON, M J G; Chairman & Chief Executive, Cookson Group plc, since 1990. *Career:* William Dyson Jones & Co, Articled Clerk 1956-61; Accountant 1961-63; Whinney Smith/Whinney & Co 1963-65; Goodlass Wall & Lead Industries (now Cookson Group plc) 1965-75; Cookson Group plc, Dir 1975-79; MD 1979-84; Group MD 1984-87; Chief Executive 1987-; Chm 1990-. *Biog: b.* 19 August 1938. *Nationality:* British. *m.* 1965, Stephanie; 4 s. *Educ:* St Benedict's School, Ealing. *Directorships:* LIG Canada Limited; Mainsail Insurance Company Limited (Bermuda); Spinnaker Insurance Company Limited (Gibraltar); Tioxide Group plc; Vesuvius Group Limited; Guiness Mahon Holdings plc; Zimco Holdings Pty Limited (South Africa); Various Directorships within Cookson Group. *Other Activities:* Member, Innovation Advisory Board of DTI; Catenian Association. *Professional Organisations:* FCA.

HENDERSON, Mark Ian; Director, Touche Remnant & Co, since 1989; Pension Investment Management. *Career:* RCB International Ltd, Managing Director 1987-89; Hill Samuel Pensions Investment Management Ltd, Managing Director 1978-87. *Biog: b.* 10 April 1947. *Nationality:* British. *Educ:* City of London School of Business Studies (BA Hons). *Other Activities:* Currier. *Professional Organisations:* AMSIA, London Oil Analysts Group. *Publications:* Numerous Articles on Pension Investment Management. *Clubs:* Carlton. *Recreations:* Running, Music, Scuba Diving.

HENDERSON, Philip William Alexander; Director, Argosy Asset Management plc, since 1986; Manager, Ensign Trust plc, Financial Services Development Capital. *Career:* Vickers da Costa, Analyst 1961-67; Lawrence Keen & Gardner, Analyst 1967; James Capel & Co, Analyst, Partner 1967-73; Canadian Ltd, MD 1973-76; Henderson Crosthwaite, Partner 1976-80; Dalgety plc, Group Executive (Strategy) 1980-81; Merchant Navy Officers Pension Fund, Deputy Investment Manager 1982-85. *Biog: b.* 3 April 1939. *Nationality:* British. *Educ:* Aldenham School, Elstree Herts. *Directorships:* Aberdeen Trust Holdings plc 1986 (non-exec); Advisory Board of India Fund 1986 (non-exec); Argosy Asset Management plc 1985; Banque Bruxelles Lambert SA 1987 (non-exec); Carmichael Participations Ltd 1976; CFW Securities Ltd 1989 (non-exec); Classix Investments Limited 1990 (non-exec); East Holdings Ltd 1990 (non-exec); Ensign Oil & Gas Inc 1990 (non-exec); Ensign Trust plc 1986; Etoile Investment Management Ltd 1989 (non-exec); ERI Ltd 1989 (non-exec); Figurehead Finance plc 1988 Chairman; Filmtrax plc 1987 Chairman; Meghraj Group Ltd 1986 (non-exec); Opalbrown Ltd 1990 (non-exec); Seguin Moreau SA 1989 (non-exec); Solong Ltd 1986 (non-exec); United East India Co Ltd 1987 (non-exec); Worth Investment Trust plc 1989. *Other Activities:* Organiser, Vamps Ball 1985; Organiser, Golddiggers Ball 1987; Organiser, Sweethearts Ball 1989; Ensign Prize RCA 1988, 1989 & 1990. *Clubs:* City of London. *Recreations:* Popular Music (1900-69), Charity Events.

HENDERSON, William McClaxen; Assistant General Manager, The Scottish Mutual Assurance Co.

HENDRICKS, Maureen A; Managing Director, Morgan Guaranty Trust Company of New York.

HENDRY, Bev; Managing Director, Abtrust Management, since 1987; Overall Management of Unit Trust Company. *Career:* Deloitte Haskins & Sells, CA 1974-81; Norton Christensen, Financial Director 1982-86; Abtrust Management Ltd, MD 1987-. *Biog: b.* 17 December 1953. *Nationality:* British. *m.* 1979, Lesley Elizabeth (née Napier); 2 d. *Educ:* Robert Gordons College; Aberdeen University (MA). *Directorships:* Abtrust Management Services Ltd 1987 (exec); Abtrust Realisations Ltd 1987 (exec). *Other Activities:* Vice Pres, Gordonians Hockey Club. *Professional Organisations:* CA. *Clubs:* Gordonians Hockey Club, Blackthorn Football Club. *Recreations:* Association Football, Hockey, National Hunt Racing, Golf.

HENDRY, James Alan; Managing Director, James Neville & Co, since 1984; Commercial Funding Specialising in Commercial Mortgages, Large Ticket Leasing & HP. *Career:* British Army Intelligence Corps 1965-74; Kalamazoo Business Studies Sales 1974-76; Lloyds & Scottish Finance Co Branch Mgr 1976-82; General Guarantee Finance Corporation Branch Mgr 1982-84. *Biog: b.* 20 July 1947. *Nationality:* British. *m.* 1971, Helen (née Allott); 2 s; 1 d. *Educ:* St Andrews High School, Kirkcaldy. *Directorships:* FIMBRA 1988 (non-exec); Esaren Ltd (Private Health Sector) 1988 (exec); Hepburn plc 1990 (exec); Hepburn Finance Corporation 1989 Managing Director; F P & A Humberstone 1990 (exec); James Neville & Co (Financial Services) Ltd 1984 Managing Director. *Recreations:* Photography (Cine & Still).

HENLEY, Raymond A; Director, Newton Investment Group.

HENNEFELD, Mrs Ruth (née Schiller); Director, Merrill Lynch Pierce Fenner & Smith, since 1988; European Research. *Career:* Merrill Lynch (New York), Manager/Vice President US Research 1978-88; Lehman Brothers, Analyst 1975-78. *Biog: b.* 23 May 1941. *Nationality:* American. *m.* 1960, Larry; 2 s; 1 grandd. *Educ:* Rutgers University (MA Economics); City University of New York (BA Political Science). *Professional Organisations:* NYSSA (New York Society Security Analysts).

HENNESSY, David James George; Lord Windlesham; Director, W H Smith Group plc.

HENRY, Christopher; Manager, Baring Brothers & Co Ltd, since 1987; Financial Futures. *Biog: Nationality:* Canadian. *Educ:* University of BC. *Directorships:* LIFFE Ltd 1984; LIFFE plc 1985.

HENRY, Geoffrey Ronald; Managing Director, MNPA Ltd; Vice Director of Finance, Merchant Navy Officers Pension Fund, since 1985; Overall Financial Control of the MNOPF Gp. Special Interest - International Administration, Regulation & Taxation of Investments. *Career:* British Shipbuilders Pension Fund Chief Financial Officer 1980-84; Kimber, Henry & Co (Accountants) Ptnr 1984-85. *Biog: b.* 8 June 1944. *Nationality:* British. *m.* 1966, Pamela (née Mount); 1 s; 1 d. *Educ:* Kingston College. *Directorships:* Argosy Asset Management plc 1988 (exec); Pensions Ltd 1988 (exec); Ashcombe Property Developments Ltd 1986 (exec); Merchant Navy Ratings Pensions Fund 1985 Dir of Finance. *Other Activities:* Chairman, PRAG (Pensions Research Accountants Group); Member, National Association of Pension Funds Investment Sub- Ctee on Taxation. *Publications:* Contributor to Various Works on Pension Fund Accounting & Investment Taxation. *Clubs:* Past Round Table Chm and Area Executive. *Recreations:* Family, Collecting British Motorcycles, Photography.

HENSMAN, Stuart; VP Director, International Equities, ScotiaMcLeod Inc.

HENSON, D W; Partner, Grimley J R Eve.

HEPBURN, D; Director, Providence Capitol Life Assurance Ltd.

HEPBURN, John; Managing Director (Investment Management), Morgan Stanley International.

HEPHER, Michael Leslie; Chairman & Managing Director, Lloyds Abbey Life plc (Formerly Abbey Life Group plc), since 1980. *Career:* Provident Life Assurance, Mgr, Actuarial Dept 1961-66; Commercial Life Assurance Co (Toronto), Chief Actuary 1967-70; Maritime Life Assurance Co (Canada), Pres & Chief Exec 1970-79. *Biog: b.* 17 January 1944. *Nationality:* British/

Canadian. *m.* Janice; 1 s; 2 d. *Educ:* Kingston Grammar School. *Directorships:* Abbey Life Group plc; Abbey Life Assurance Co Ltd; Abbey Unit Trust Managers; Ambassador Life Assurance Co Ltd; Abbey Life Investment Services Ltd; Abbey Life Home Loans Ltd; Abbey Life Assurance (Ireland) Ltd; Transatlantische Lebensversicherung, AG (W Germany); Life Assurance & Unit Trust; Regulatory Organisation (Lautro); Abbey Global Investment Fund; Lloyds Abbey Life plc 1980; Black Horse Agencies Ltd 1989; Lloyds Bank plc 1989; Lloyds Bank Insurance Services Ltd 1989; Lloyds Bowmaker Finance Ltd 1989. *Professional Organisations:* FIA; FCIA; ASA; FLIA; CBIM. *Recreations:* Tennis, Reading.

HEPHER, Roger Antony; Partner, Grimley J R Eve, since 1986; Managing Partner of London Town Planning Department. *Career:* Greater Manchester County Council, Planning Assistant 1978-81; G L Hearn & Partners, Planner/Surveyor 1981-85. *Biog: b.* 12 January 1956. *Nationality:* British. *m.* 1978, Ann (née Attewell); 2 s. *Educ:* Lady Manners School, Bakewell, Derbyshire; University of Manchester (BA Hons Town & Country Planning, MTP). *Professional Organisations:* FRICS; Member, Royal Town Planning Institute (MRTPI). *Clubs:* Lansdowne. *Recreations:* Boating, Hill Walking, Music, Travel.

HEPPEL, Meg E M; Partner (Birmingham), Evershed Wells & Hind.

HEPWORTH, I R; General Manager, Skipton Building Society, since 1987; Finance, Marketing. *Career:* Peat Marwick Mitchell, Articled Clerk 1969-72; Senior Audit Clerk 1972-79; Audit Manager 1979-84; Skipton Building Society, Chief Accountant & Head of Finance 1984-85; Assistant General Manager & Head of Finance 1985-87. *Biog: b.* 3 April 1949. *Nationality:* British. *m.* 1978, Wendy (née Newstead); 1 d. *Educ:* Sedbergh School; Manchester University (BA Econ). *Directorships:* Homeloan Management Ltd 1988 (exec); Mortgage Services Ltd 1990 (exec); Skipton Financial Services Ltd 1987 (exec); North Yorkshire Training & Enterprise Council 1989 (non-exec). *Other Activities:* Vice Chairman, BIM Leeds & Central Yorkshire; Governor, Harrogate College of Arts & Technology. *Professional Organisations:* FCA; FBIM. *Clubs:* Ilkley Golf Club. *Recreations:* Skiing.

HERAULT, Philippe Charles; Group Director, Framlington Group plc, since 1990; Fund Management. *Career:* Union Des Assurances De Paris, Fund Manager 1971-73; Societe Privee D'Etudes, Paris, Fund Manager 1973-74; Credit Lyonnais, Johannesburg, Assistant to the Director 1974-75; Banque Industrielle et Mobilière Privee, Paris, Fund Manager 1975-78; Credit Commercial De France, Paris, Fund Manager 1978; Seconded to Framlington 1990-. *Biog: b.* 12 May 1946. *Nationality:* French. *m.* 1980, Bocquillon Liger-Belair; 2 d. *Educ:*

Institut D'Etudes Politiques, Paris; Diplôme D'Etudes Superieures De Droit, Paris; DEA Paris, Dauphine. *Directorships:* Framlington Group plc 1990 (exec).

HERBERT, Anthony James; Partner, Allen & Overy, since 1970; Managing Partner & Head of International Capital Market Group. *Career:* Allen & Overy Asst Solicitor 1965-70. *Biog: b.* 28 March 1940. *Nationality:* British. *m.* 1968, Lowell (née Pelton); 2 s; 1 d. *Educ:* Eton College; King's College, Cambridge (MA). *Professional Organisations:* The Law Society,; City of London Law Society; IBA. *Clubs:* Roehampton. *Recreations:* Tennis, Skiing, Painting.

HERBERT, Arthur Simon; Director, James Capel Gilts Ltd, since 1988; Gilts. *Career:* Alexanders Discount Co, Mgr 1970-84; Hill Samuel, Mgr 1984-85; James Capel & Co 1985-. *Biog: b.* 12 June 1952. *Nationality:* British. *m.* 1974, Jane Lesley (née Micklefield); 1 s; 2 d. *Educ:* Winchester College. *Other Activities:* Liveryman, Clockmakers Company. *Recreations:* Tennis, Hockey, Fishing, Shooting.

HERBERT, Martin Geoffrey Greenham; Partner, Clifford Chance, since 1977; Corporate Finance. *Career:* Coward Chance, Articled Clerk 1969-71; Solicitor 1971-77. *Biog: b.* 9 December 1946. *m.* 1981, Alicia Malka (née Jolles); 1 s; 2 d. *Educ:* Rugby School; Balliol College, Oxford (BA). *Clubs:* Royal Fowey Yacht, Royal Harwich Yacht. *Recreations:* Tree Planting, Sailing.

HERBERT, Robin Arthur Elidyr; Chairman, Leopold Joseph Holdings plc. *Biog: b.* 5 March 1934. *Nationality:* British. *m.* 1988, Philippa (née King). *Educ:* Eton College; Christ Church, Oxford (MA); Harvard Business School (MBA). *Directorships:* The Union Discount Co of London plc 1990 (non-exec) Chm; National Westminster Bank plc 1972 (non-exec); Marks and Spencer plc 1986 (non-exec); Agricultural Mortgage Corp plc 1986 (non-exec); F & C Smaller Companies plc (non-exec); Financial Advisor, NRA Pension Fund. *Other Activities:* Pres & Chm, Council of The Royal Horticultural Society. *Professional Organisations:* ARICS. *Clubs:* Brook's, Pratt's. *Recreations:* Dendrology, Walking.

HERBERT-SMITH, T; Partner, Nabarro Nathanson.

HEROD, David John; Joint UK General Manager, Credit Lyonnais Bank Nederland, since 1980. *Career:* District Bank Ltd, Various/International 1961-67; NCT/ABN, International & Lending 1967-77; Schlesinger Ltd, Director 1977-80; C L Bank, Nederland, Jt UK General Manager 1980-. *Biog: b.* 17 May 1945. *Nationality:* British. *m.* 1971, Barbara Helen (née North); 1 s. *Professional Organisations:* ACIB. *Recreations:* Bridge, Hockey.

HERON, David Leslie Norton; Director, James Capel & Co, since 1987; Derivative Products, and Risk Manager- Equity Trading. *Career:* James Capel & Co Private Client Exec 1965-71; Head, Far East Department 1971-74; Institutional Sales 1974-84; Head, Options & Futures 1982-86; Head, Programme Training 1986-89. *Biog: b.* 5 October 1941. *m.* 1965, Peggy (née Berry); 3 s; 1 d. *Educ:* Christ's College, Finchley. *Other Activities:* London Traded Options Market Divisional Board Member. *Recreations:* Tennis.

HERON, G M D; General Manager Personnel, Clydesdale Bank plc.

HERON, M G; Personnel Director, Unilever plc, since 1989; International Personnel. *Career:* Unilever plc, Management Trainee 1958-; BOCM Ltd, Various Appointments 1958-71; BOCM Silcock Ltd, Director, Variously Responsible for Sales, Marketing, Feeds 1972-76; Batchelors Foods Ltd, Chairman 1976-82; Unilever plc, Deputy Coordinator for Food & Drinks 1982-86; Unilever plc & Unilever NV, Director 1986-; Director for UK & Ireland & PPP 1986-; Additionally for Continental Europe 1987-89; Director for Personnel & UK & Ireland 1989-. *Biog: b.* 22 October 1934. *Nationality:* British. *m.* 1958, Celia (née Hunter); 2 s; 2 d. *Educ:* St Joseph's Academy, Blackheath; New College, Oxford (MA History). *Directorships:* Member, Armed Forces Pay Review Board 1981-82. *Other Activities:* CBI, 1986, Member, Council, 1987, Member, Europe Committee, 1988, Member, Task Force, 1990, Member, Education Foundation Council; Food & Drink Federation, 1986 Member, Council & Exec, 1986; Chairman, Food Policy & Resources Ctee; Business in the Community, Chairman, Marketing Private Sector Initiatives, 1987; Centre of Agricultural Strategy, Member Advisory Ctee, University of Reading, 1989. *Professional Organisations:* CBIM. *Recreations:* Former Keen Sportsman, now a Spectator.

HERON, T; Director/Secretary, Aetna International (UK) Limited, since 1987; Operations, Strategy, Compliance, Marketing, Regulatory and Investments. *Career:* John Lyle & Co, Various Positions 1968-74; South Eastern Electricity Board, Various Positions 1974-76; Kurvers International plc (won Queen's Award for Export 1983), Assistant Company Secretary, Company Secretary, Director, Chief Executive 1976-87; Aetna International (UK) Ltd, Company Secretary, Group Director 1987-. *Biog: b.* 15 August 1951. *Nationality:* British. *m.* 1978, Clare (née Finn); 3 s. *Educ:* Strathclyde University, (Masters Degree in Business Administration). *Directorships:* Aetna Unit Trusts Limited 1987 (exec); Aetna Life Insurance Co Ltd 1987 (exec); Aetna Investment Management Ltd 1987 (exec); Aetna Pensions Limited 1987 (exec); Aetna Limited 1987 (exec); Kurvers International plc 1984 (exec); Cantrade & Co 1982 (exec). *Other Activities:* Member of Innovation Research Unit, City University, London. *Professional*

Organisations: Fellow, Institute of Chartered Secretaries & Administrators. *Publications:* 1992 Strategy Formulation for Unit Trust Companies, 1990. *Recreations:* Golf, Reading, Tennis.

HERRIES, Sir Michael (Alexander Robert Young); OBE, MC; Chairman, Royal Bank of Scotland Group plc, since 1976. *Career:* Jardine Matheson & Co (Far East), Chm & MD 1963-70; Matheson & Co Ltd, Chm 1970-75; Royal Bank of Scotland, Dir 1972-74; Vice-Chm 1974-75; Dep Chm 1975-76. *Biog: b.* 23 February 1923. *Nationality:* British. *Educ:* Eton College; Trinity College, Cambridge (MA). *Directorships:* Williams & Glyn's Bank (Now part of The Royal Bank of Scotland plc) 1975; National & Commercial Banking Group (Now The Royal Bank of Scotland Group plc) 1976; The Scottish Mortgage & Inv Trust plc 1975 Chm; Scottish Widows Fund & Life Assurance Society 1974. *Other Activities:* Council Member, Missions to Seamen; Scottish Disability Foundation, 1982-; Member, Royal Company of Archers; Lord Lieutenant, Stewartry of Kirkcudbright; Hon LLD, Univ of Hong Kong, 1974, Chinese Univ of Hong Kong, 1973; Hon DLitt, Heriot-Watt Univ, 1984; Hon DBA, Napier Polytechnic 1990. *Recreations:* Shooting, Walking.

HERRING, Brian John; Partner, Arthur Young.

HERRINGER, F C; Director, Sedgwick Group plc.

HERRIOTT, William Gerard; Partner, Kidsons Impey, since 1988; Audit. *Career:* Coopers & Lybrand, Trainee 1962-68; Mgr 1968-72; Kidsons, Snr Mgr 1972-79; Hope Agar Anr Mgr 1979-80; Partner 1980-88. *Biog: b.* 19 February 1941. *Nationality:* British. *m.* 1970, Eileen Jean (née MacLean); 2 d. *Educ:* Downside; Magdelen College, Oxford (MA). *Professional Organisations:* FCA. *Recreations:* Travel.

HERRON, Anthony Gavin; TD; Partner, Touche Ross & Co, since 1966; Corporate Finance Group. *Career:* Post Office Corporation (Secondment), Dir Postal Finance, Corp Planning 1973-75; Expamet International plc, Non-Exec Dir 1973-. *Directorships:* Expamet International plc 1973 (non-exec).

HERVEY-BATHURST, Frederick John Charles Gordon; Managing Director, Lazard Brothers & Company Ltd, since 1986; Banking. *Career:* Lazard Brothers 1957-; Director 1974. *Biog: b.* 1934. *Nationality:* British. *m.* 1957, Caroline (née Starkey); 1 s; 2 d. *Educ:* Eton College; Grenadier Guards; Trinity College, Cambridge (MA). *Other Activities:* Skinners' Company.

HESKETH, Blair; Director, Hill Samuel Bank Ltd, since 1982; Private Banking. *Biog: b.* 15 January 1939. *m.* 1974, Margaret (née Watkins); 1 s; 1 d. *Educ:* Stowe School. *Directorships:* C G Hacking & Sons Ltd 1989 (non-exec) Chairman. *Other Activities:* Cheam School

Board of Governors. *Professional Organisations:* FCA. *Clubs:* Turf. *Recreations:* Racing, Golf, Shooting, Jazz.

HESKETH, Michael John; Director, Warburg Securities, since 1986; Investment Research & Marketing - Insurance. *Career:* Simon & Coates, Analyst 1971-78; Ptnr 1978-81; Rowe & Pitman, Analyst 1981-82; Ptnr 1982-86. *Biog: b.* 19 May 1949. *Nationality:* British. *m.* 1973, Jennifer (née Hartnell); 2 d. *Educ:* Marlborough School; New College, Oxford (BA). *Clubs:* United Oxford & Cambridge University. *Recreations:* Swimming, Cycling, Music.

HESKETT, J E; Director, Baring Asset Management Ltd.

HESSELGREN, Claes; Head of Bond Trading and Sales, Paribas Limited.

HESTER, Stephen Alan Michael; Executive Director, Credit Suisse First Boston, since 1988; Corporate Finance. *Career:* CSFB Various 1982; Director 1987; Exec Director 1988. *Biog: b.* 14 December 1960. *Nationality:* British/American. *Educ:* Easingwood School; Lady Margaret Hall, Oxford (MA). *Clubs:* RAC, Annabel's.

HETHERINGTON, John Reid; Partner, Kidsons Impey, since 1990; Corporate Finance/Company Acquisitions and Mergers. *Career:* Cole Dickin & Hills 1960-; Ptnr 1967-72; Kidsons, Ptnr 1972-90. *Biog: b.* 12 January 1942. *m.* 1975, Diane (née Yates); 2 s. *Educ:* Highgate School. *Directorships:* Columbia House (Nominees) Ltd 1985 (non-exec); Russell Square House (Nominees) Ltd 1988 (non-exec). *Professional Organisations:* FCA; Institute of Directors.

HETTICH, Joachim Franz Xaver; Director, Dunedin Fund Managers Limited, since 1988; Finance, Administration, Information Technology. *Career:* Citicorp Scrimgeour Vickers International Ltd (Previously Vickers Da Costa Ltd), Principal & Group Financial Controller 1981-88; Acatos & Hutcheson Limited, Group Financial Controller 1979-81; AGB Publications Limited, Group Financial Controller 1978-79; Turquands Barton Mayhew and Company 1972-78. *Biog: b.* 18 November 1951. *Nationality:* German. *m.* 1976, Ann (née Donovan); 1 s; 1 d. *Educ:* The Oratory School; Queen Mary College, London University. *Directorships:* Dunedin Ventures Limited 1989 (non-exec). *Professional Organisations:* FCA; Member, International Stock Exchange London.

HEWAT, Angus Davidson; Partner, Allen & Overy.

HEWES, P L; Partner, Cameron Markby Hewitt.

HEWES, Robin Anthony Charles; Head of Regulatory Services Group, Lloyd's of London, since 1988. *Career:* Inland Revenue, Inspector of Taxes 1966-74;

Department of Industry 1974-85; Cabinet Office, Management & Personnel Office 1985-87; Department of Trade & Industry, Director, Enterprise & Deregulation Unit 1987-88. *Biog: b.* 15 April 1945. *Nationality:* British. *m.* 1967, Christine Diane (née Stonebridge); 1 s; 2 d. *Educ:* Colchester Royal Grammar School; Bristol University (LLB Hons). *Directorships:* Comforto-Vickers (formerly Vickers Business Equipment Division) 1984-88 (non-exec). *Recreations:* Swimming.

HEWETT, Keith Edwin; Administration Director, MIM Britannia Unit Trust Managers Ltd, since 1985; Trust & Client Accounting. *Career:* Stoy Hayward & Co, Audit Senior 1971-73; Aspen Securities Ltd, Acct 1973-75; Samuel Montagu & Co Ltd, Acct, Investment Div 1975-85. *Biog: b.* 13 October 1950. *Nationality:* British. *m.* 1983, Sharon (née Bloor); 2 s; 2 d. *Educ:* Hastings Grammar School. *Directorships:* MIM Limited; MIM Britannia Unit Trust Managers Ltd; Cape and General Finance Ltd; MIM Investments Ltd; MIM Group Ltd; 117 Ventures Ltd; Investment Analysis Ltd. *Clubs:* Sports Clubs. *Recreations:* Badminton, Squash.

HEWITT, Anthony Richard; Partner, Bacon & Woodrow, since 1976; Employee Benefits, Social Insurance. *Career:* Government Actuary's Department 1970-73; Bacon & Woodrow 1973-. *Biog: b.* 25 October 1949. *Nationality:* British. *m.* 1973, Sheila (née Khan); 2 s. *Educ:* Rossall School; Pembroke College, Cambridge. *Professional Organisations:* FIA.

HEWITT, Frank; Deputy Chief Executive, Industrial Development Board for Northern Ireland, since 1988; Inward Investment. *Career:* Industrial Development Board for Northern Ireland, Executive Director 1984-88; H M Consul - Inward Investment, H M Consulate - General, Los Angeles, Ca 1982-84; Dept of Commerce for Northern Ireland 1972-82. *Biog: b.* 1 July 1943. *Nationality:* British. *m.* 1968, Carol (née Burch); 2 d. *Educ:* Queens University, Belfast (BSc Econ). *Other Activities:* Member, Chartered Institute of Marketing.

HEWITT, Ian Leslie; Partner, Freshfields, since 1976; Head of Commercial Group. *Biog: b.* 9 May 1947. *Nationality:* British. *m.* 1990, Jenifer S (née Marston). *Educ:* King Edward VI School, Southampton; St Edmund Hill, Oxford (BA); London University (LLM). *Professional Organisations:* Law Society. *Clubs:* International Tennis Club of Great Britain. *Recreations:* Tennis.

HEWITT, Michael Earling; Director of Central Banking Studies, Bank of England, since 1988; Training Central Bankers. *Career:* Bank of England 1961-70; Government of Bermuda, Economic Adviser 1971-74; Bank of England, Asst Adviser, Oil 1974-76; Financial Forecaster 1976-78; Adviser, Financial Institutions 1979-83; Head of Financial Supervision, Gen Div 1984-87; Head of Finance and Industry Area 1987-88; Senior Adviser, Finance and Industry 1988-90. *Biog: b.* 28 March 1936. *Nationality:* British. *m.* 1961, Elizabeth (née Batchelor); 1 s; 1 d. *Educ:* Christ's Hospital; Merton College, Oxford (MA); London University (BSc Econ). *Other Activities:* Member, City Advisory Panel, City University Business School; Chm, City EEC Ctee; Member, British Invisible Exports Council; Member, BIEC European Ctee; Member, OECD. *Professional Organisations:* ASIA. *Recreations:* Chess, Wine, Travel, Reading, Cycling.

HEWITT, R J; Partner, Wedlake Bell, since 1987; Commercial Litigation. *Career:* Knapp-Fishers, Partner 1978-87. *Biog: b.* 1950. *Nationality:* British. *Educ:* London (LLM).

HEYES, Thomas; Managing Director, ICI Investment Management Ltd, since 1987. *Career:* ICI plc, Various, Investment Management 1959-. *Biog: b.* 2 July 1936. *Nationality:* British. *m.* 1960, Jean (née Wallace); 2 s; 1 d. *Educ:* London School of Economics (BSc Hons Econ). *Directorships:* The Lands Improvement Group Ltd 1985; Intex Yarns Pension Scheme Securities Ltd 1976; Green Property Co plc 1976; Orbisa (UK) Ltd 1980; Pension Funds Securities Ltd 1983; Pension Fund Property Unit Trust 1982; Instate plc 1990. *Other Activities:* Executive Committee, IFMA. *Recreations:* Squash, Rugby Football, Fishing, Shooting.

HEYLIN, Ms Angela; Chairman, Charles Barker City Ltd.

HEYMAN, Richard William; Director, Morgan Grenfell & Co Ltd, since 1989; Corporate Finance. *Career:* Peat Marwick Mitchell, Acct 1972-77; J Henry Schroder Wagg & Co Ltd, Exec in Corporate Finance 1977-81; Morgan Grenfell & Co Ltd 1981-. *Biog: b.* 10 September 1950. *Nationality:* British. *m.* 1977, Victoria Edith Charlotte (née Thompson); 1 s. *Educ:* Stowe School; Lancaster University (BA). *Professional Organisations:* FCA. *Clubs:* Lansdowne. *Recreations:* Racing, Hunting, Tennis.

HEYWOOD, John Nigel; Vice Chairman, Hambros Bank Ltd, since 1987; Treasury & Capital Markets. *Career:* English Electric Aviation Engineer 1957-63; Mobel Pfister (Switzerland) Acct Trainee 1964; Esso Petroleum Co Economist 1964-66; PA Management Consultants Mgmnt Consultant 1966-69; Hambros Bank Ltd 1969-. *Biog: b.* 19 October 1940. *Nationality:* British. *m.* 1965, Diane (née Clarke); 1 s; 1 d. *Educ:* Shebbear College; London University (BSc Hons 1st); Manchester Business School. *Directorships:* Hambros Australia Ltd 1984; Hambros Corporate Treasury Consultants Ltd 1987 Chm; Hambros plc 1988. *Professional Organisations:* ACT (Founding Fellow). *Publications:* Foreign Exchange & the Corporate Treasurer, 1981; Using the Futures, Forwards and Options Markets, 1984. *Recreations:* Gardening, Music, Fishing.

HIBBERT, A J; Director, County NatWest Securities Ltd, since 1990; Quantitative Research. *Career:* Prudential, Assistant Director 1987-90; Hill Samuel Investment Advisers, Senior Fund Mgr 1986-87; Prudential, Senior Analyst 1985; Wood, Mackenzie & Co, Analyst 1981-85; Scicon Consultancy, Analyst 1980-81. *Biog: b.* 20 January 1958. *Nationality:* British. *m.* 1986, Chrystine May Lynch; 2 s. *Educ:* London School of Economics (MSc Operational Research); Bristol University (BSc Economics & Accounting); Dulwich College. *Directorships:* County NatWest Securities 1990. *Professional Organisations:* Associate, Society of Investment Analysts. *Recreations:* Squash, Mountaineering, Golf.

HIBBERT, Brian Richard Ewart; Director, C T Bowring & Co Ltd.

HIBBITT, T S; Chief Executive, Sheppards Moneybrokers Ltd.

HICHENS, Antony P; RD; Chairman, MB-Caradon, Y J Lovell (Holdings) plc and Swedish Match NV. *Career:* Rio Tinto Zinc Corporation 1960-72; Redland plc, Deputy Managing Director and Financial Director 1972-81; Consolidated Gold Fields plc, Managing Director and Chief Financial Officer 1981-89; Caradon plc, Non-Executive Chairman (from Formation in 1985 to Recommended Acquisition by MB Group in 1989) 1985-89. *Biog: b.* 10 September 1936. *Nationality:* British. *m.* Sczerina Neomi; 1 d. *Educ:* Stowe; Magdalen College, Oxford (MA Law); Inner Temple (Barrister-at-Law); Wharton School, University of Pennsylvania (MBA). *Directorships:* Candover Investments plc 1989 Dep Chm; Candover Partners Limited 1989; Courtaulds Textiles plc 1989; Greenfriar Investment Company plc 1984; Y J Lovell (Holdings) plc 1989 Chm; MB Group plc 1989 Chm; South Western Electricity plc 1989; Swedish Match NV (Holland) 1990 Chm. *Professional Organisations:* Member of the European Advisory Board, Wharton School, University of Pennsylvania, 1988. *Clubs:* Naval & Military, City Club.

HICKEY, David Martin; Director, James Capel & Co, since 1989; Corporate Finance, General. *Career:* Peat Marwick Mitchell (Dublin) 1978-82; HongkongBank Group 1982-86; James Capel Group 1986-. *Biog: b.* 25 July 1955. *Nationality:* Irish/British. *m.* 1982, Jane Elisabeth; 1 s. *Educ:* Terenure College, Dublin; Trinity College, Dublin (BA Bus Stud, MA). *Directorships:* James Capel Corporate Finance 1989 (exec). *Professional Organisations:* Institute of Chartered Accountants. *Clubs:* Leander. *Recreations:* Rowing, Skiing, Music.

HICKINBOTHAM, Anthony George; Partner, Linklaters & Paines, since 1984; Corporate Law. *Career:* Linklaters & Paines, Articled Clerk/Assistant Solicitor 1966-70; The Prestige Group, Legal Adviser 1970-73; Linklaters & Paines (London and Paris), Assistant Solicitor 1974-84. *Biog: b.* 29 October 1943. *Nationality:*

British. *m.* 1969, Susan (née Curtis); 2 s; 1 d. *Educ:* Bournemouth School; Durham University (LLB). *Professional Organisations:* Solicitor; Member, Law Society. *Recreations:* Walking.

HICKINBOTTOM, Gary Robert; Partner, McKenna & Co, since 1986; Commercial Litigation, Product Liability, Pharmaceutical Law. *Career:* McKenna & Co, Articled Clerk 1979-81; Assistant Solicitor 1981-86; Partner 1986-. *Biog: b.* 22 December 1955. *Nationality:* British. *m.* 1982, Paula Jayne (née Hughes); 1 s; 1 d. *Educ:* Queen Mary's Grammar School, Walsall; University College, Oxford (MA); College of Law, Guildford and Chester. *Other Activities:* British Academy of Experts, Education and Training Committee; Part-Time Lecturer, Polytechnic of Central London, 1979-80; Part-Time Lecturer, University College, Oxford, 1987-89. *Professional Organisations:* Law Society; Westminster Law Society; Association of Commonwealth Lawyers; British Academy of Experts; Administrative Law Bar Association; International Litigators Forum. *Clubs:* London Welsh Club. *Recreations:* London Welsh Male Voice Choir.

HICKS, C A; Partner, Wedlake Bell.

HICKS, Jeremy David; Director, Hambros Bank Ltd, since 1988; Corporate Finance. *Career:* Touche Ross & Co Articled Clerk 1975-78; County Bank Ltd Corp Finance Exec, Asst Dir 1979-84; Hambros Bank Ltd 1984-. *Biog: b.* 14 May 1953. *Nationality:* British. *m.* 1976, Eve Elizabeth (née Newson); 2 s. *Educ:* Plymouth College; Pembroke College, Oxford (BA Hons). *Directorships:* Hemmington Scott Publishing Ltd 1987 (non-exec). *Professional Organisations:* ACA.

HICKSON, C J; Partner, Slaughter and May, since 1984. *Biog: b.* 10 December 1951. *Educ:* St Joseph's College, Beulah Hill, London; University of Birmingham (LLB). *Professional Organisations:* Solicitor. *Recreations:* Music, Mountaineering, Gardening, Model Railways.

HIDA, Takeo; Deputy General Manager, The Sumitomo Bank Ltd; Mortgage Dept.

HIDE, E; Partner, Nabarro Nathanson.

HIGGINS, M J; Director, Charterhouse Bank Limited.

HIGGS, Derek Alan; Director, S G Warburg & Co Ltd, since 1979; Head of Corporate Finance. *Biog: b.* 3 April 1944. *Nationality:* British. *m.* 1970, Julia (née Arguile); 2 s; 1 d. *Educ:* Bristol University (BA). *Directorships:* S G Warburg Group plc. *Professional Organisations:* FCA.

HIGH, J H; Director, Charterhouse Bank Limited.

HIGHAM, N A C; Partner, S J Berwin & Co, since 1985; Information Technology and Intellectual Property. *Career:* Osborne Clarke, Bristol, Articled Clerk 1967-72; Richards Butler, Assistant Solicitor 1972-76; Linklaters & Paines, Assistant Solicitor 1976-82. *Biog: b.* 2 March 1947. *Nationality:* British. *m.* 1985, Ursula (née De Nemeskeri-Kiss); 2 s. *Educ:* Sherborne School, Dorset. *Other Activities:* Associate Member, Chartered Institute of Patent Agents; Member, CBI Intellectual Property Forum; Member, International Chambers of Commerce Committee for Intellectual and Industrial Property. *Professional Organisations:* Member, Law Society. *Publications:* Businessman's Guide to Intellectual Property, 1987; New Opportunities in Telecommunications, 1990. *Recreations:* Bridge, Rare Animal Breeds.

HIGLETT, M N B; Director, MIM Limited.

HIKOKUBO, C; General Manager, The Tokyo Trust & Banking Company Ltd.

HILDESLEY, Michael Edmund; Director, Morgan Grenfell & Co Ltd, since 1983; Corporate Finance, Energy, Privatisation. *Biog: b.* 16 October 1948. *m.* 1972, Judith Carol (née Pistor); 3 s. *Educ:* Sherborne School; Trinity College, Oxford (MA).

HILDRETH, (Henry) Jan (Hamilton Crossley); Independent Consultant and Executive Director, Minster Trust Limited, since 1979; Development Capital & Corporate Finance. *Career:* Baltic Exchange 1956; Royal Dutch Shell Group 1957; Kleinwort Benson 1963; NEDO 1965; Member, London Transport Board 1968-72; John Laing & Sons Ltd, Asst Chief Exec 1972-74; Institute of Directors, Director General 1975-78. *Biog: b.* 1 December 1932. *Nationality:* British. *m.* 1958, Wendy Moira Marjorie (née Clough); 2 s; 1 d. *Educ:* Wellington College; The Queen's College, Oxford (MA). *Directorships:* Carroll Securities Ltd Chm; Scallop Kings plc Chm; Sea Catch plc Chm; Dexta Estates plc (non-exec); Diveships plc (non-exec); Grampian Assured plc (non-exec); Finotel plc (non-exec); and others. *Other Activities:* Governor, Wellington College; Governor, Eagle House School; Council Member, The Spastics Society; Member, Pay Review Body for Nursing & Midwifery Staff & Profession Allied to Medicine (NAPRB); President, Wimbledon Conservative Association. *Professional Organisations:* Fellow, Chartered Institute of Transport (FCIT); Fellow, Royal Society of Arts. *Clubs:* Athenaeum, Political Economy Club, Thames Hare & Hounds, Vincent's (Oxford). *Recreations:* Water Mills, Cross Country, Road & Fell Running.

HILDREY, Mark Richard William; Director, County NatWest Securities Ltd.

HILL, Sir Brian; Director, National Westminster Bank plc.

HILL, David W; Director, Bradstock Blunt & Thompson Ltd.

HILL, Henry Peter; Deputy Managing Director, CIN Management Ltd.

HILL, Sir James F; Bt; Director, Yorkshire Building Society.

HILL, Jeremy Adrian; Director, J Henry Schroder Wagg & Co Ltd, since 1977; Investment Management - Far East. *Career:* Cons Gold Fields 1965-69; Montagu Loebl Stanley 1969; J Henry Schroder Wagg 1970-. *Biog: b.* 16 January 1940. *m.* 1965, Virginia Ann (née Wilmot); 3 s. *Educ:* Eton College; Christ Church, Oxford (MA). *Directorships:* The Korea Europe Fund Ltd 1987 (non-exec); Schroder Japanese Warrant Fund LH 1990 Chm. *Other Activities:* Freeman, Worshipped Company of Goldsmiths. *Clubs:* MCC. *Recreations:* Tennis, Shooting, Gardening.

HILL, John Michael; Partner, R Watson & Sons.

HILL, Josselyn; Partner, Walker Martineau Stringer Saul.

HILL, Leslie F; Executive Director, Merrill Lynch International Bank Limited.

HILL, M D; Director, Chancery plc.

HILL, Michael Edward; Group Personnel Director, G T Management plc, since 1984; Personnel Generalist. *Career:* Ministry of Defence (Army) 1955-74; Regimental Commands 1955-65; Staff Officer and ADC to Army Commander, Singapore 1965-67; Staff College, Camberley 1967-68; Staff Officer, Directorate of Army Training 1968-70; Company Commander, Staffordshire Regiment 1970-72; Staff Officer, Directorate of Personnel Services 1972-74; Alexander Howden Group 1974-84; Personnel Manager 1974-76; Assistant Director Personnel 1976-79; Group Personnel Director 1979-84; G T Management plc, Group Personnel Director 1984. *Biog: b.* 8 June 1935. *Nationality:* British. *m.* 1959, Veda (née Ure-Whyte); 1 s; 2 d. *Educ:* Brighton College; Royal Military Academy, Sandhurst; Army Staff College, Camberley. *Directorships:* G T Management plc 1988 (exec); G T Management (UK) Ltd 1985 (exec). *Clubs:* Lansdowne. *Recreations:* Education, Drama, Sport.

HILL, P H; Director, Sanyo International Ltd.

HILL, Peter; Partner, Morison Stoneham Chartered Accountants.

HILL-SAMUEL, B C; Group Administrator, James R Knowles Limited.

HILL-WOOD, Peter Denis; Vice Chairman, Hambros Bank Limited, since 1987; Investment Management. *Career:* De Zoete & Bevan 1956-60; Hambros Bank 1960-. *Biog: b.* 25 February 1936. *Nationality:* British. *m.* 1971, Sarah (née Andrews); 2 s; 1 d. *Educ:* Eton College. *Directorships:* Arsenal Football Club 1962 (exec) Chairman; Hambros Advanced Technology Trust plc 1973 (exec); River Plate & General Investment Trust plc 1969 (non-exec); Top Technology Limited 1986 (exec). *Clubs:* White's, Pratts. *Recreations:* Association Football, Golf, Country Pursuits.

HILLIAR, Peter Bryant; Leisure Analyst, Barclays De Zoete Wedd, since 1987; Research. *Career:* Edward Moore & Sons, Clerk 1958-62; Royal Trust Company of Canada, Investment Adviser 1962-66; Kitcat & Aitken, Investment Adviser 1966-67; Mobil Pension Trust Analyst 1967-68; Moy Davies Smith Vandervell & Co, Analyst 1968-70; Hedderwick Stirling Grumbar & Co, Leisure Analyst/Ptnr 1970-81; Quilter Goodison & Co, Leisure Analyst 1981-82; Fielding Newson-Smith/ County Securities, Leisure Analyst/Ptnr/Dir 1983-87; Barclays de Zoete Wedd, Leisure Analyst/Dir 1987-. *Biog: b.* 20 December 1940. *Nationality:* British. *m.* 1970, Margaret Jean (née Williams); 1 s; 1 d. *Educ:* Kings College, Taunton. *Directorships:* County Securities 1985 (exec); Barclays de Zoete Wedd Research 1987 (exec); Barclays de Zoete Wedd Securities 1989 (exec). *Clubs:* Gresham. *Recreations:* Tennis, Music, Photography.

HILLS, D J; Director, Barclays de Zoete Wedd Securities Ltd.

HILLS, J J F; Company Secretary, Aitken Hume International plc.

HILLS, Jonathan William Macleod; Tax Partner, Pannell Kerr Forster, since 1981; International & Property Taxation. *Career:* Harmood Banner & Co (Deloitte & Co from 1974), Articled Clerk to Tax Manager 1970-76; Pannell Kerr Forster, Tax Manager 1976-; Partner 1981. *Biog: b.* 27 September 1948. *Nationality:* British; 1 d. *Educ:* Whitgift School; University College, Oxford (MA Hons Modern Languages). *Other Activities:* Member, London Society of Chartered Accountants Tax Committee; Member, Joint Tax Committee of British Hotels Restaurants and Caterers Association/British Association of Hotel Accountants. *Professional Organisations:* FCA; ATII. *Publications:* General Editor, Butterworths Business Tax Service. *Recreations:* Golf, Music.

HILLS, Roger Ernest; Director, Schroder Investment Management Ltd, since 1984; Investment Management. *Career:* Grieveson Grant (now Kleinwort Benson Secs) 1960-70. *Biog: b.* 18 September 1940. *Directorships:* Schroder Unit Trust Managers Ltd 1988 (exec); Schroder Nominees Ltd 1985 (exec); Schroder Cayman Bank & Trust Co Ltd 1989 (exec). *Other Activities:*

Causeway Business Expansion Scheme Fund 1984-85 & 1985-86. *Recreations:* Golf, Squash, Tennis, Skiing.

HILLYER, John Selby; OBE; *Career:* Hill Vellacott Ptnr 1954-88; DTI Inspector (Scotia Investments) with LJ Bromley QC 1976-80; Chantrey Vellacott Senior Partner 1988-89. *Biog: b.* 14 February 1925. *Nationality:* British. *m.* 1951, Elizabeth Ann (née Thyne); 1 s; 2 d. *Educ:* Stowe School; Trinity College, Oxford (MA). *Directorships:* Capel-Cure Myers Unit Trust Management 1983 (non-exec); T H White Ltd 1954 (non-exec). *Other Activities:* Mem, Council, Barnardo's; Past Master, Worshipful Company of Fanmakers. *Professional Organisations:* FCA; Barrister at Law, Inner Temple. *Clubs:* RAC, City Livery. *Recreations:* Gardening, Keeping Ornamental Ducks.

HILSDON, Paul J; Partner (Derby), Evershed Wells & Hind.

HILTON, Nicholas David; National Executive Partner (UK), Moore Stephens, since 1990; Management/ Development of the Moore Stephens UK National Partnership. *Career:* Spicer & Pegler 1970-76; Articled Clerk 1970-74; Training Department 1975-76; Moore Stephens 1976-; Training Manager 1976-79; Training Partner 1979-81; PA to Senior Partner 1982; General Practice 1983-84; Marketing Partner 1984-90; National Executive Partner, UK Firm 1990-. *Biog: b.* 27 June 1952. *Nationality:* British. *m.* 1984, Vanessa Jane (née Reed); 1 d. *Educ:* Marlborough College. *Directorships:* Cornhill Trustees Ltd 1989 (exec). *Professional Organisations:* Fellow, Institute of Chartered Accountants in England & Wales. *Clubs:* Richmond Golf Club, Cignets Hockey Club. *Recreations:* Golf, Hockey, Skiing, Entertaining.

HINAMAN, Robert; Managing Director & Mergers and Acquisitions Executive, Chase Investment Bank Limited.

HINCHCLIFFE, Brian J; Director, J Trevor, Montleman & Poland Ltd.

HIND, Donald Bryan; General Manager, Town & Country Building Society, since 1981; Finance and Accounts. *Career:* Practising Accountant Ptnr/Student 1947-68; Planet Building Society, Sec 1969-75; Magnet & Planet Building Soc/Town & Country B Soc, Chief Accountant 1975-81. *Biog: b.* 20 November 1931. *Nationality:* British. *m.* 1956, Audrey; 1 s; 1 d. *Educ:* Continuing. *Directorships:* Town & Country Homebuilders Ltd 1987 (exec); Town & Country Financial Services Ltd 1987 (exec); Cycleways Ltd 1989 (non-exec); Town & Country Property Services Ltd 1989 (exec). *Professional Organisations:* Fellow, Institute of Chartered Accountants in England & Wales. *Recreations:* Golf, Wandering.

HINDE, David Richard; Executive Director, Samuel Montagu & Co Limited, since 1982; International Corporate Finance. *Career:* Slaughter & May, Assistant Solicitor 1961-69; Wallace Bros Group, Executive Director 1969-77; Wardley Limited, Executive Director, Corporate Finance, Based in Hong ong 1977-81. *Biog: b.* 16 August 1938. *Nationality:* British. *m.* 1963, Jill (née Young); 3 d. *Educ:* Marlborough College, Wiltshire; Cambridge University (BA Law 2:1); London Law Society's Final Exam. *Directorships:* Samuel Montagu & Co Limited 1982 (exec); Samuel Montagu Inc 1982 (exec); American Barrick Resources Corp 1984 (non-exec); Dah Sing Financial Holdings Ltd 1986 (non-exec); Diamond Trust of Kenya Ltd 1983 (non-exec); International Pursuit Corp 1984 (non-exec). *Other Activities:* Worshipful Company of Woolmen. *Professional Organisations:* The Law Society, Solicitor. *Recreations:* Skiing, Tennis, Gardening.

HINDE, K S G; TD; Clerk, Cutlers' Company.

HINDS, S; Assistant General Manager, Arab Banking Corporation.

HINE, John; Partner, Slaughter and May, since 1983; Litigation. *Biog: m.* Margaret; 1 s; 2 d. *Educ:* Taunton School, Taunton; Bristol University (LLB). *Recreations:* Looking at Buildings, Music.

HINES, Anthony Gordon; Member, Council of Lloyds Crowe Underwriting Agency, since 1989; Aviation Underwriter. *Career:* Chandler Hargreaves Whittall (Lloyds) Broker 1955-56; R A Norman (Lloyds) Clerk, Non Marine Underwriting 1957-58; Harvey Bowring (Lloyds) Dep Underwriter 1958-74; A G Hines and Others (Lloyds) Underwriter 1974-89; Lloyds Aviation Claims Centre Dep Chm 1985-89; Lloyds Aviation Underwriters Assoc Dep Chm 1987-88. *Biog: b.* 26 May 1935. *Nationality:* British. *m.* 1975, Anthea (née Smith-Walker); 2 s; 1 d. *Educ:* Charterhouse School. *Directorships:* Crowe Underwriting Agency 1981 (exec); Lloyds Aviation Claims Centre 1991 (exec). *Clubs:* Army and Navy Club. *Recreations:* Tennis, Golf, Skiing, Equitation.

HINES, Bryan Charles; General Manager, Insurance & Investments, ICI plc, since 1982; Pension Fund Investment & Insurance Companies. *Career:* ICI plc, Various 1952-. *Educ:* Berkhamsted School. *Directorships:* I C Insurance Ltd 1966 Chairman; Prime Property Inc 1987 (non-exec); Queenswood School Ltd 1987 Governor; Kleinwort Benson Farmland Trust (Managers) Ltd 1982 (non-exec); Woolwich Equitable Building Society 1989 (non-exec); ICI Investment Management Ltd 1989 Chairman; Govett Strategic Investment Trust plc 1990 (non-exec).

HINSHAW, David; Chief Executive (Channel Islands), Kleinwort Benson Limited. *Career:* Kleinwort Benson Group 1966-. *Directorships:* Kleinwort Benson Investment Management Ltd 1988 (exec); M & G (Guernsey) Ltd 1989 (non-exec); Willis Wrightson (Guernsey) Ltd 1980 (non-exec); BHS (Jersey) Ltd 1983 (non-exec). *Professional Organisations:* Fellow, Chartered Institute of Bankers.

HINTON, Alan; Manager, National Westminster Growth Options Ltd.

HINTON, Patrick Raymond; Chairman of Professional Standards, Arthur Anderson & Co.

HIORNS, Dr Brennan Martin; Deputy Managing Director, Head of UK Equity Research, Kleinwort Benson Securities Ltd, since 1984. *Career:* ICI Plastics Division, Research Engineer 1970-74. *Biog: b.* 21 September 1943. *Nationality:* British. *m.* 1969, Mary Diana (née Long); 1 s; 1 d. *Educ:* The Lewis School, Pengam, Glamorgan; Birmingham University (BSc,PhD). *Professional Organisations:* ASIA; Member, The Stock Exchange. *Recreations:* Archaeology, Reading, Military & Naval History.

HIPPS, Paul; Senior Partner, Stoy Hayward.

HIRAGUCHI, Atsushi; Deputy Managing Director Fund Management, Mitsui Taiyo Kobe International Limited.

HIRAI, Y; Executive Director, Daiwa Europe Limited.

HIRSCH, L J; Director, Hill Samuel Bank Ltd.

HIRST, Michael B; Executive Chairman, UK and International Hotels, Ladbroke Group plc.

HISASUE, Junichiro; General Manager, The Mitsui Trust & Banking Co Ltd, since 1989. *Career:* The Mitsui Trust & Banking Co Ltd 1962; Manager, General Affairs Section, Foreign Div 1975; Manager, Business Promotion Section, London Branch 1976; Mitsui Trust Bank (Europe) SA, Director Manager 1980; Managing Director 1982; Senior Deputy General Manager, International Finance Div 1985; General Manager, International Finance Div 1986; General Manager, International Treasury Div 1988; General Manager, International Headquarters 1989; General Manager, London Branch 1989. *Biog: b.* 15 October 1938. *Nationality:* Japanese. *m.* 1966, Kikuko (née Imai); 1 s; 1 d. *Educ:* Keio University, Faculty of Business and Commerce. *Directorships:* Mitsui Trust International 1989 (non-exec); Mitsui Trust Asset Management 1990 (non-exec); Mitsui Trust Finance (Switzerland) Ltd 1989 (non-exec). *Clubs:* Coombe Hill Golf Club.

HISCOCK, Keith John; Director, Hoare Govett Securities Ltd, since 1987; UK Equity Sales. *Career:* Hoare Govett, Asst Director, UK Equity Sales 1986-87; Wood Mackenzie, UK Equity Sales 1983-86; James Capel,

Various Responsibilities 1979-83. *Biog: b.* 19 January 1958. *Nationality:* British. *m.* 1982, Annelies Rosalinda Gillian (née Doelly); 2 d. *Educ:* Christ Church, Oxford (MA Philosophy Politics & Economics); Esher College. *Recreations:* Plumbing.

HITCHINGS, Christopher David; Insurance Analyst, Hoare Govett Investment Research Ltd, since 1980; Investment Research Analyst Insurance (Composite) and Insurance Brokers. *Career:* Chase Manhattan Bank,Clerk, Investment Dept 1971-72; First National City Bank, Pension Fund Exec 1973-74; Messrs de Zoete & Bevan, Performance Analyst, Pension Funds 1974-75; Analyst, Investment Research 1976-80. *Biog: b.* 16 December 1951. *Nationality:* British. *m.* 1987, Lucinda (née Ballisat); 2 s. *Educ:* Clifton College, Bristol; Worcester College, Oxford (not completed). *Clubs:* Ronnie Scotts. *Recreations:* Listening to Jazz, Walking.

HITCHMAN, Frank Hendrick; Deputy Group Finance Director/Company Secretary, Greig Fester Group Limited, since 1989; Finance/IS. *Career:* Sedgwick Group plc 1973-89; Group Secretary/ Head of Corporate Finance 1980-85; Finance Director, E W Payne Companies Ltd 1985-89; Samuel Montagu & Co Ltd 1970-73; Coopers & Lybrand Deloitte 1964-69. *Directorships:* Greig Fester Limited 1989 (exec). *Other Activities:* Insurance Sub-Committee, Institute of Chartered Accountants. *Professional Organisations:* Fellow, Institute of Chartered Accountants.

HOAGLAND, L; Managing Director (Investment Management), Bankers Trust Company.

HOARE, Alexander S; Managing Partner, C Hoare & Co.

HOARE, Anthony Malcolm Vincent; Partner, C Hoare & Company, since 1986. *Career:* C Hoare & Company Agent/Chief Acct. *Biog: b.* 14 February 1946. *m.* 1969, Gay (née Burge); 2 d. *Educ:* St Paul's School. *Professional Organisations:* FCA. *Recreations:* Photography & Conservation of Butterflies.

HOARE, David John; Partner, C Hoare & Co.

HOARE, Henry Cadogan; Chairman, C Hoare & Company, since 1989. *Career:* C Hoare & Company, Managing Ptnr 1959-. *Directorships:* National Mutual Life 1986-89.

HOARE, Jonathan Michael Duoro; Chief Executive, BMP Business. *Biog:* 2 s; 1 d.

HOARE, Michael Rollo; Managing Partner, C Hoare & Company, since 1982. *Biog: b.* 8 March 1944. *m.* 1981, Caroline (née Abèle); 1 s; 3 d. *Educ:* Eton College; New College, Oxford. *Other Activities:* Gover-

nor, Royal Academy of Music. *Recreations:* Singing, Hunting, Gardening, Skiing.

HOARE, Q V; OBE; Managing Partner, C Hoare & Co.

HOARE, Richard Quintin; Partner, C Hoare & Co.

HOBART-HAMPDEN, George Miles; The Rt Hon The Earl of Buckinghamshire; Managing Director, Wardley Investment Services International Ltd, since 1988; Inv. *Career:* Wardley Investment Services International Ltd, Marketing Director 1986-88; Antony Gibbs Pension Services Ltd 1981-86; Noble Lowndes Ltd 1970-81; Hudson Bay Company 1968-70; Hong Kong and Shanghai Bank 1963-64. *Biog: b.* 15 December 1944. *Nationality:* British. *m.* 1975, Alison (née Wightman). 2 steps. *Educ:* Clifton College Bristol; Exeter University (BA Hons Hist); London University (MA Area Studies). *Directorships:* Wardley Investment Services International Ltd 1988 (exec); Wardley Unit Trust Managers Ltd 1988 (exec); Wardley Investment Services Bahamas 1988 (non-exec); Wardley Investment Services (UK) Ltd 1986 (exec); WISLI Nominees Ltd 1986 (exec); WISUK Nominees Ltd 1986 (exec); Wardley Investment Services (Luxemb) SA 1988 (exec); Gota Global Selection 1988 (exec); Wardley Global Selection 1989 (exec); Wardley Asia Investment Services (Lux) SA 1989 (exec); Wardley Funds Ltd 1988 (exec); Wardley Fund Managers (Jersey) Ltd 1988 (exec); The Korea Asia Fund Ltd 1990 (exec). *Other Activities:* Member, House of Lords Committee on European Affairs; Patron, Hobart Town (Tasmania) First Settlers Association. *Professional Organisations:* Institute of Directors. *Publications:* Income Taxation and Equal Treatment for Men and Women. *Clubs:* Western, West of Scotland Football Club. *Recreations:* Music, Squash, Fishing, Rugby, Football.

HOBBS, Andrew William; Chairman & Managing Director, Kim Eng Securities (London) Ltd, since 1989; South East Asia. *Career:* Vanderfelt & Co Ptnr, Mining Shares 1961-78; Laurence Prust & Co Ptnr, South East Asia 1978-83; Hoare Govett Ltd Dir, Intl Division, South East Asia 1983-88; Kim Eng Securities (Private) Ltd, London Resident Director, South East Asia 1988-89. *Biog: b.* 28 September 1941. *Nationality:* British. *m.* 1976, Diana (née Horne); 1 d. *Educ:* Fettes College. *Directorships:* Harder Investments 1964 (non-exec); Kim Eng Securities (Private) Ltd 1988 (exec); Kim Eng Properties (PTE) Ltd 1988 (non-exec); Kim Eng Holdings Ltd 1989 (exec). *Other Activities:* Worshipful Company of Poulters. *Professional Organisations:* International Stock Exchange. *Clubs:* Royal Thames Yacht Club. *Recreations:* Skiing, Tennis, Golf, Wine, Horse Racing.

HOBBS, David Henry Stuart; Director, Phillips & Drew Fund Management Ltd; Quantitative Analysis. *Career:* Guardian Assurance Actuarial Trainee 1964-68;

Phillips & Drew Research Analyst 1968-73; Pension Fund Mgr 1973-86; Phillips & Drew Fund Management Asst Dir 1986-87. *Biog: b.* 17 December 1946. *Nationality:* British. *Educ:* Westcliff High School. *Directorships:* Phillips & Drew Unit Managers 1988 (exec). *Professional Organisations:* ASIA. *Recreations:* Hockey, Opera, Welfare of the Elderly.

HOBBS, Peter Thomas Goddard; Group Personnel Director, Wellcome plc, since 1979; Personnel, Training, Public Relations, Pensions. *Career:* Imperial Chemical Industries plc 1962-79; Wellcome Foundation Ltd (now Wellcome plc), Group Personnel Director 1979-. *Biog: b.* 19 March 1938. *Nationality:* British. *m.* Victoria; 1 d. *Educ:* Crypt School, Gloucester; Exeter College, Oxford (MA Oxon). *Directorships:* Employment Conditions Abroad Ltd 1984 (non-exec); Roffey Park Institute 1989 (non-exec); London Business School Centre for Enterprise 1989 (non-exec). *Other Activities:* Vice President (International), Institute of Personnel Management, 1987-89; Trustee, Learning From Experience Trust; Chairman, Employers Forum for Disability; Chairman, Chemical Industries Association Employment Affairs Board. *Professional Organisations:* CIPM; FInstD. *Clubs:* Oxford and Cambridge. *Recreations:* Books, Opera, Film.

HOBBS, Ron; Partner, Phillips & Drew Development Capital.

HOBKINSON, A J; Partner, Cameron Markby Hewitt.

HOBLEY, D C D; Director, S G Warburg Securities.

HOBSON, Anthony; Group Director (Finance), Legal & General Group plc, since 1987; Corporate Finance and Strategic Planning. *Career:* Sperry Corporation, Finance Director (Europe); S G Warburg, Corporate Finance; Arthur Andersen and Co. *Biog: Nationality:* Dutch. *m.* Ingrid. *Educ:* University of Virginia (MBA); University of Liverpool (BA); Bootham School, York. *Other Activities:* Council Member, Association of Corporate Treasurers. *Professional Organisations:* FCT, FCA.

HOBSON, David Constable; Chartered Accountant, The Building Societies Commission, since 1950. *Career:* Army (REME), Captain 1942-47; Coopers & Lybrand, Staff Member to Mgr 1947-53; Ptnr 1953-84; Snr Ptnr 1975-83; Prime Minister's Policy Unit, Part-Time Adviser 1983-86. *Biog: b.* 1 November 1922. *Nationality:* British. *m.* 1961, Elizabeth Anne Drury; 1 s; 1 d. *Educ:* Marlborough College; Christ's College, Cambridge (MA). *Directorships:* Building Societies Commission 1986- Commissioner (Part Time); Cambrian & General Securities plc 1986-89 Chm; The Laird Group plc 1985- (non-exec); The Fleming High Income Investment Trust plc 1989- (non-exec). *Other Activities:* Chairman of Council, Marlborough College, 1987-; Hon Treasurer, The Lister Institute of Preventive Medicine, 1986-.

Professional Organisations: FCA. *Clubs:* Reform. *Recreations:* Reading, Travel, Gardening.

HOBSON, Neil Christopher; Vice President & Director, Wood Gundy Inc.

HOCK, Peter George; Director, Lazard Brothers & Co Ltd.

HOCKLESS, Peter Bruce; Partner, Allen & Overy, since 1988; Banking, Capital Markets & Corporate Finance. *Career:* Allen & Overy Articled Clerk 1979-. *Biog: b.* 9 December 1955. *Nationality:* British. *m.* 1984, Fiona (née Stackhouse); 1 d. *Educ:* Dulwich College; St John's College, Cambridge. *Professional Organisations:* Mem, The Law Society. *Clubs:* Sundridge Park Golf Club, Cooden Beach Golf Club. *Recreations:* Golf.

HODDELL, J; CBE; Chairman, Chartered Trust plc, since 1990. *Career:* Deputy Chairman 1988-90; Chartered Trust, Managing Director 1975-88. *Biog: b.* 17 June 1929. *Nationality:* British. *m.* 1952, Vera (née Jones); 1 s; 1 d. *Educ:* University College Cardiff (BA). *Directorships:* ACL Limited 1983 (non-exec); Chartered Finance Limited 1963 (non-exec); Garden Festival Wales Limited 1989 (non-exec); Finance Houses Association 1988-90 Chairman. *Professional Organisations:* Fellow, Institute of Chartered Secretaries and Administrators. *Clubs:* Cardiff and County.

HODGES, Christopher John Stratford; Partner, McKenna & Co, since 1990; Pharmaceutical and Healthcare Law, Product Liability. *Career:* Slaughter and May, Articled Clerk 1977-79; Asst Solicitor 1979-86; Clifford Chance, Asst Solicitor 1986-89; McKenna & Co, Ptnr 1990. *Biog: b.* 19 March 1954. *Nationality:* British. *m.* 1977, Fiona (née Ewart); 3 d. *Educ:* New College, Oxford (BA,MA Jurisprudence). *Directorships:* The Sixteen 1990 (non-exec). *Other Activities:* Freeman, City of London; Church Warden, St John The Divine, Richmond; British Actors Equity Association. *Professional Organisations:* Freeman, City of London Solicitors Company; IBA. *Publications:* Appeals to the Medicines Commission and Beyond in the British Institute of Regulatory Affairs Journal, 1984; Evidence Collection or Evidence Suppression? in the New Law Journal, 1990.

HODGES, Stephen Richard; Managing Director, Close Brothers Ltd, since 1990; Banking/Treasury Operations. *Career:* Hambros Bank Ltd, Snr Mgr 1977-85; Close Brothers Ltd, Director 1985-90. *Biog: b.* 23 May 1954. *Nationality:* British. *m.* 1980, Felice; 1 s; 1 d. *Educ:* Latymer Upper School; Trinity Hall, Cambridge (MA Hons). *Professional Organisations:* Barrister-at-Law. *Recreations:* Fishing.

HODGSON, Allan F; Managing Director, Hodgson Martin Ltd, since 1980; Investment Management. *Ca-*

reer: Edinburgh Investment Trust, Economist 1967-70; Ivory & Sime, Economist 1970-76; Scottish Widows Fund & Life Assurance Society, Joint Investment Secretary 1976-80. *Biog: b.* 19 May 1945. *Nationality:* British. *m.* 1969, Irene (née Rennie); 2 d. *Educ:* George Heriots; Edinburgh University (MA Hons Econ). *Directorships:* Saltire Insurance Investments plc 1987 (exec). *Other Activities:* Member, Scottish Economic Council; Member, Single Market Committee; Governor, Edinburgh College of Art.

HODGSON, David George; Vice President, Manufacturers Hanover Trust Co, since 1984; Corporate Banking. *Career:* Williams & Glyns Mgr 1961-78; Manufacturers Hanover Trust co Asst VP 1978-84. *Biog: b.* 14 June 1944. *Nationality:* British. *m.* 1968, Jane Radcliffe (née Chadwick); 2 s. *Educ:* Brighton College. *Professional Organisations:* ACIB, ACIS. *Recreations:* Waterskiing, Skiing.

HODGSON, Derek Peter Talbot; Partner, Clyde & Co, since 1981. *Biog: b.* 5 July 1952. *Nationality:* British. *m.* 2 d. *Educ:* UCL (LLB). *Clubs:* MCC.

HODGSON, H; Director, Panmure Gordon Bankers Limited.

HODGSON, K; Senior Manager, London, National Australia Bank Ltd, since 1989; Wholesale Banking. *Career:* National Australia Bank; Manager Branch Banking, Branch Manager 1982-86; Corporate Finance Manager, Corporate Manager 1986-88; Manager Credit London, Credit Control 1988-89. *Biog: b.* 16 March 1958. *Nationality:* Australian. *m.* 1980, Krysia (née Misiurski); 2 d. *Educ:* Brighton Grammar School; Monash University, Melbourne (BSc Econ). *Recreations:* Fishing, Cycling, Gardening.

HODGSON, Sir Maurice; Member of the Council, Lloyd's of London.

HODGSON, Peter J; Executive Director, Bank of America International Limited, since 1989; Head Project and Export Finance. *Career:* Arthur Andersen 1977-80; Bank of America 1980-. *Biog: b.* 6 January 1955. *Nationality:* Australian. *m.* 1981, Jan (née Dyke); 2 s. *Educ:* Tiffin Boys School; St Catharine's College, Cambridge (MA Law). *Directorships:* Severn River Crossing Limited 1990 (non-exec).

HODGSON, Robin Granville; Managing Director, Granville & Co Ltd, since 1979. *Career:* Investment Banking (New York & Montreal) 1964-67; Industry in Birmingham 1969-72; MP for Walsall North 1976-79; Granville & Co Asst/Dir/MD 1972-. *Biog: b.* 1942. *Nationality:* British. *m.* 1982, Fiona Ferelith (née Allom). 3 s (1 decd); 1 d. *Educ:* Shrewsbury School; Oxford University (BA); Wharton School of Finance, Pennsylvania University (MBA). *Directorships:* Johnson Bros &

Co Ltd 1969 (exec); Mem, West Midlands Industrial Development Board; Spotlaunch plc (non-exec) Chm; Dominick Hunter Ltd; Walker Alexander Ltd. *Other Activities:* MP Walsall North, 1976-79; Conservative Party (Area Treasurer West Midlands 1986-); Member, National Executive of Conservative Party; Trustee, Friends of Shrewsbury School; Liveryman, Goldsmith Company; Member, Wharton School International Advisory Panel. *Professional Organisations:* Council for The Securities Industry, 1980-85; Securities & Investment Board, 1985-89. *Publications:* Britain's Home Defence Gamble, 1978. *Recreations:* Squash, Book Collecting, Theatre.

HODSON, Daniel Houghton; Deputy Chief Executive and Group Finance Director, Nationwide Anglia BS, since 1989. *Career:* Chase Manhattan Bank NA, Trainee 1965-68; Various Management Positions 1968-73; Edward Bates & Sons, UK Banking Mgr 1973-74; Banking Dir 1974-76; Unigate plc, Group Treasurer 1976-81; Group Finance Dir 1981-87; Unigate Inc, Pres 1986-87; Davidson Pearce Group plc, Chief Exec 1987-88; Chm 1988; Girobank plc, Dir 1987-89; Part Time Board Member, The Post Office 1984-; GT Symen (Holdings) Ltd 1990-. *Biog: b.* 11 March 1944. *Nationality:* British. *m.* 1979, Diana Mary (née Ryde); 2 d. *Educ:* Eton College; Merton College, Oxford (MA Hons). *Other Activities:* Association of Corporate Treasurers, Council Member 1979-88, Chm 1985-86, Vice President 1989-; Governor, Yehudi Menuhin School (1985-); Member, CBI City Industry Task Force (1987-88); Member, Mercers Company (1965-). *Professional Organisations:* Fellow, ACT. *Publications:* Corporate Finance and Treasury Management, 1984 (Exec Ed & Contributor). *Clubs:* Brooks's. *Recreations:* Music, Travel, Gardening.

HODSON, David Michael; Partner, Theodore Goddard; Family Law and Family Law Tax. *Career:* Hepherd Winstanley & Pugh (Southampton) 1976-80; Anthony Collins & Co (Birmingham) 1980-81; Cooke Matheson & Co (London) 1981-84; Theodore Goddard (London) 1985-. *Biog: b.* 17 October 1953. *Nationality:* British. *m.* 1981, Gillian (née Cockburn). *Educ:* King Edward VI Grammar School, Southampton; Leicester University (LLB). *Other Activities:* Chairman, Solicitors Family Law Association Training Committee; Member of Main Committee and of European Committee of Solicitors Family Law Association; Member, City of London Solicitors Co; The Law Society; Lawyers' Christian Fellowship; Solicitors European Group; International Bar Association. *Professional Organisations:* Qualified as Solicitor, 1978. *Recreations:* Wildlife, Photography, Folk Music, Running.

HODSON, Geoffrey Allan; Managing Director, Merrill Lynch International Ltd; Mergers & Acquisitions. *Career:* ICI Ltd 1970-72; McKinsey & Co Inc 1974-76; Triad Holding Corporation 1976-78; Bankers

Trust International Ltd 1978-82; Merrill Lynch Europe Ltd, Managing Director 1982-. *Biog: b.* 26 November 1947. *Nationality:* British. *m.* 1972, Bridget Elizabeth (née Deans); 1 s; 1 d. *Educ:* Emmanuel College, Cambridge (MA); Harvard Business School (MBA). *Professional Organisations:* Member, of Business Graduates' Association. *Clubs:* Harvard Business School (London). *Recreations:* Photography, Ornithology, Railways, Rowing.

HODSON, John; Director, Singer & Friedlander Holdings Ltd.

HODSON, Simon J; Partner, Beachcroft Stanleys.

HOFFMAN, Mark; Chairman, Cambridge Capital Limited.

HOFFMAN, Michael Richard; Chief Executive, Thames Water plc, since 1989. *Career:* Rolls Royce Ltd 1961-73; AE Ltd 1973-77; Perkins Engines Ltd, Chm 1977-80; Massey Ferguson Ltd, Pres, Farm Machinery Division 1980-83; Babcock Intl plc, Chief Exec and MD 1983-87; Airship Industries Ltd, Chief Exec 1987-88; Dep Chm 1988-89. *Biog: b.* 31 October 1939. *Nationality:* British. m1 1963, Margaret Edith Tregaskes (Diss 1978); 1 d; m2 1982, Helen Judith (née Peter). *Educ:* Hitchin Grammar School; University of Bristol (BSc Hons Eng). *Directorships:* Cosworth Engineering Ltd 1988 Dep Chm; Cray Electronics Holdings plc 1990. *Other Activities:* Member, DTI Monopolies & Mergers Commission, Technological Requirements Board, 1985-88; Council Member, University of Brunel; Chm, UK South African Trade Association; Freeman, City of London, 1984; Liveryman, Worshipful Company of Engineers, 1984. *Professional Organisations:* Fellow, Institution of Production Engineers (Pres 1987-88); Fellow, Institution of Mechanical Engineers. *Clubs:* Reform, RAC, MCC. *Recreations:* Real Tennis, Shooting, Sailing.

HOFFMANN, R; Executive Director, Chartered WestLB Limited.

HOGAN, Alison; Director, Brunswick PR Ltd.

HOGAN, D C; Finance Director, Sogemin Metals Ltd.

HOGARTH, Peter Laurence; Chief Executive, Societe Generale Strauss Turnbull Securities Ltd, since 1989. *Career:* Peat Marwick McLintock Ptnr 1981-88; Societe Generale Strauss Turnbull Securities Ltd, Operations Dir 1988-9. *Biog: b.* 10 July 1949. *Nationality:* British. *m.* Margaret Rosemary (née Alison); 1 s; 2 d. *Educ:* Haileybury College; Dundee University. *Directorships:* SGST 1988 (exec). *Other Activities:* Member, The Worshipful Company of Joiners and Ceilers. *Professional Organisations:* Institute of Chartered Accountants of Scotland. *Recreations:* Golf, Bridge, Cooking.

HOGBEN, B J; Finance Director, BPB Industries.

HOGBIN, W; Joint Managing Director, Taylor Woodrow plc.

HOGG, Sir Christopher; Non-Executive Chairman, Reuters Holdings plc, since 1985. *Career:* IMEDE (Business School) 1962; Hill Samuel 1963-66; Industrial Reorganisation Corporation 1966-68. *Biog: b.* 2 August 1936. *Nationality:* British. *m.* 1961, Anne (née Cathie); 2 d. *Educ:* Marlborough College; Trinity College, Oxford (MA 1st Class Honours); Harvard University School of Business Administration (MBA High Distinction). *Directorships:* Courtaulds plc 1968 (exec); Courtaulds plc 1980 (exec) Chairman; Courtaulds Textiles plc 1990 (non-exec) Chairman. *Other Activities:* Board of Trustees, Ford Foundation; Member, International Council of J P Morgan. *Publications:* Masers and Lasers, 1963. *Recreations:* Theatre, Reading, Walking, Skiing.

HOGG, Graham Edwyn Trevor; Partner, Holman Fenwick & Willan, since 1973; Marine & Non-Marine Litigation. *Career:* Ince & Co, Articled Clerk 1960-64; Roney & Co, Solicitor 1964-66; Richards Butler & Co, Solicitor 1966-69; Waltons Bright & Co, Solicitor 1969-71; Holman Fenwick & Willan, Solicitor 1971-73; Partner 1973-. *Biog: b.* 22 December 1936. *Nationality:* British. *m.* 1972, Margaret (née Davies); 2 s. *Educ:* Greshams School, Holt; Fitzwilliam College, Cambridge (MA Law). *Other Activities:* Ex Practice Development Partner & Member of Management Committee, H F & W, 1989-90. *Professional Organisations:* Law Society. *Clubs:* RAC. *Recreations:* Squash, Swimming, Fell Walking, Music, Photography, Food & Wine, Cars.

HOGG, Sarah; Economics Editor, The Telegraph, since 1989. *Career:* The Economist, Economics Editor; The Times, Economics Editor; The Independent, City Editor. *Educ:* (BA Hons PPE). *Other Activities:* Wincott Financial Journalist of the Year Award, 1985; Broadcaster.

HOGG, Stephen; Partner, Moore Stephens.

HOGWOOD, P A; Company Secretary, Morgan Grenfell Asset Management Limited, since 1989. *Career:* Anglo & Overseas Investment Trust plc 1989-; Overseas Investment Trust plc, Company Secretary 1989-; Morgan Grenfell Securities Holdings Ltd, Company Secretary 1986-88; Morgan Grenfell & Co Ltd, Project Finance Executive 1983-86; Morgan Grenfell & Co Ltd, Chief Internal Auditor 1978-86; Coopers & Lybrand, Manager 1970-78. *Biog: b.* 18 July 1949. *Nationality:* British. *m.* 1971, Sylvia Ann (née McCulloch); 2 s. *Educ:* Haberdashers Askes Boys School; University of Hull (BSc Econ). *Professional Organisations:* Fellow, Institute of Chartered Accountants in England & Wales.

HOLBECHE, Philip; Director, Royal Trust Bank, since 1989; Private Banking/Corporate Finance. *Career:* Ford Europe Treasury 1969-71; Delta Group plc, Finance Director, Electrical Engineering Group 1973-78; General Atlantic Group, Chief Financial Officer, International Operations 1979-83; Ardmore Petroleum plc, Founder & Finance Director 1984-88; Royal Trust Bank, Director 1989-. *Biog: b.* 3 September 1944. *Nationality:* British. *m.* Andrea. *Educ:* Hull University (BSc Econ); London Business School (MBA). *Directorships:* Concurrent Technologies Limited 1990 (non-exec); Danbury Group plc 1990 (non-exec); Maccorp Holdings Limited 1990 (non-exec); RT Property Investments Limited 1989 (exec); Royal Trust Bank 1990 (exec); RTC Holdings Company 1989 (exec); Royal Trust International Limited 1989 (exec); Royal Trust Private Client Limited 1990 (non-exec); Skilladvance Ltd 1988 (non-exec); Ardmore Petroleum plc 1984-87 (exec); Ericsson Exploration Consultants 1984-87 (exec). *Professional Organisations:* Associate Member, Institute of Management Consultants. *Clubs:* Royal Automobile Club, Hampstead Cricket Club. *Recreations:* Theatre, Tennis, Music.

HOLDEN, Neil Jonathan; Director, Hambros Bank Limited, since 1990; Treasury, Financial Control & Consultancy. *Career:* Thomson McLintock & Co 1980-84; Morgan Guaranty Trust Co of New York 1984-86; Hambros Bank Ltd 1986. *Biog: b.* 7 December 1959. *Nationality:* English. *m.* 1979, Janet (née Iffland); 1 s; 2 d. *Educ:* University College, London (BSc Mathematics); Brentwood School, Essex. *Directorships:* Hambros Bank Ltd 1990 (exec); Hambros Corporate Treasury Consultants Ltd 1987 (exec). *Professional Organisations:* ACA. *Recreations:* Sailing, Mountaineering, Traditional Music.

HOLDEN, Richard Charles Thomas; Partner, Linklaters & Paines, since 1989; Corporate Department. *Career:* Linklaters & Paines, Articled Clerk 1980-82; Assistant Solicitor 1982-89; Partner 1989-. *Biog: b.* 15 March 1958. *Nationality:* British. *m.* 1986, Patricia (née Mordaunt-Crook); 1 s. *Educ:* Winchester College; St John's College, Cambridge (BA). *Professional Organisations:* Law Society.

HOLDEN-BROWN, Sir Derrick; Chairman, Allied-Lyons plc.

HOLDER, B; Director General Accident, Arbuthnot Latham Bank Limited.

HOLDSWORTH, Sir Trevor; Deputy Chairman, Prudential Corporation plc.

HOLDSWORTH HUNT, Christopher; Managing Director, Peel Hunt & Company Ltd, since 1989. *Career:* Pinchin Denny & Co Ptnr 1971-86; Morgan Grenfell Securities 1986-89. *Biog: b.* 2 August 1942. *Nationality:*

British. *m.* 1976, Joanne Lesley Starr (née Reynolds); 2 s. *Educ:* Eton College; Tours University. *Other Activities:* Liveryman, Grocers Company. *Professional Organisations:* Member, International Stock Exchange. *Clubs:* City of London, White's. *Recreations:* Golf, Tennis, Theatre/Opera.

HOLFORD, Francis; Chairman, Rudolf Wolff & Co Ltd, since 1984; Managing Director, since 1976. *Biog: b.* 1 April 1937. *Nationality:* British. *m.* 1963, Jennifer Jane (née Wolff); 2 s; 3 d. *Educ:* Collyers School, Horsham, Sussex. *Other Activities:* Council Member, The Association of Futures Brokers and Dealers Ltd. *Professional Organisations:* Fellow, Institute of Chartered Accountants in England & Wales; Member, Institute of Directors. *Clubs:* Gresham. *Recreations:* Walking.

HOLFORD, John Brian; Managing Director, Throgmorton Investment Management Ltd. *Directorships:* CFI (Assets) Ltd; Capital For Industry (1984) Ltd; Community Hospital Services plc (non-exec); R Green Properties plc; Throgmorton Finsbury Trust plc.

HOLLAND, Michael; Partner, Touche Ross & Co, since 1967; Senior Tax Partner. *Career:* National Service - RAF Flying Officer 1949-51; Teacher 1951-52; Inspector of Taxes 1953-63; Articled Clerk - CA 1963-66. *Biog: b.* 14 December 1927. *Nationality:* British. *m.* 1956, Pixie (née Morgan); 1 s; 2 d. *Educ:* Royal Liberty School; Southampton University (BA). *Other Activities:* Worshipful Co of Chartered Accountants. *Professional Organisations:* FCA; FTII. *Publications:* Many Taxation Articles for Accountancy Press. *Clubs:* City of London, Addington Society. *Recreations:* Aerobics, Theatre, Golf.

HOLLAND, Peter Rodney James; Partner, Allen & Overy, since 1972; Corporate Finance. *Career:* Allen & Overy, Asst Solicitor 1968-71. *Biog: b.* 31 July 1944. *Nationality:* British. *m.* 1975, Susan Elizabeth (née Okeby); 1 s; 1 d. *Educ:* St Edmund's School, Canterbury; Oxford University (MA). *Professional Organisations:* The Law Society (Past Chm, Co Law Ctee); City of London Law Society. *Publications:* Mergers and Acquisitions, 1986 (Contributor); Practitioners Guide to the City Code on Take-Overs and Mergers, 1989 (Contributor). *Recreations:* Skiing, Outdoor Activities.

HOLLAND-BOSWORTH, Timothy Hugh; Director, Kleinwort Benson Ltd, since 1988; Corporate Finance. *Career:* Kleinwort Benson Ltd, Dir 1969-87; Prudential Bache Capital Funding, MD 1987-88.

HOLLAND-MARTIN, Robert (Robin) George; Executive Director, Henderson Administration Group plc, since 1988. *Career:* Cazenove & Co Various 1960-68; Ptnr 1968-74; Paterson Products Ltd Fin Dir 1976-86; Newmarket Venture Capital plc, Consultant 1982-. *Biog: b.* 6 July 1939. *Nationality:* British. *m.* 1976, Dominique (née Fromaget); 2 d. *Educ:* Eton College.

Directorships: Baronsmead plc 1982-87 (non-exec); Gloucestershire Sand & Gravel Co Ltd 1983 (non-exec); Space-Time Systems (Holdings) Ltd 1983- (non-exec); New Cambridge Research Co Ltd 1986- (non-exec); Aspex Ltd 1987- (non-exec). *Other Activities:* Cons & Unionist Party Hon Dep Treasurer, 1979-82; Metropolitan Hospital-Sunday Fund, Council Member 1963- (Chm 1977-); Homeopathic Trust, 1970- (Vice-Chm 1975-); Blackie Foundation Trust, Trustee 1971- (Chm 1987-); V & A Museum (Mem of Advisory Council 1972-73 & Dep Chm, Trustees 1983-85); Ctee of Assocs of V & A 1976-85 (Chm 1981-85); Mem, Visiting Ctee for Royal College of Art, 1982- (Chm 1984-). *Clubs:* White's, RAC.

HOLLICK, C R; Director, Hambros Bank Limited.

HOLLICK, Clive; Managing Director (Investment Management), MAI plc.

HOLLIDAY, N B; Marketing Director, Touche Remnant Investment Management Ltd, since 1989; UK Institutions. *Career:* HM Forces 1973-85; Robert Fleming Asset Management, Marketing Manager 1986-89. *Biog: b.* 15 January 1955. *Nationality:* British. *Educ:* Oxford (MA Hons). *Directorships:* Touche Remnant Investment Management 1989 (exec).

HOLLIDAY, Robin Clarke; Head of Banking, British & Commonwealth Merchant Bank plc, since 1990. *Career:* County NatWest, Director of Structured Financing 1974-88. *Biog: b.* 4 March 1948. *Nationality:* British. *m.* 1971, Margaret (née Chappell); 1 s; 2 d. *Educ:* Cranbrook School; Southampton University (BSc Eng Hons). *Other Activities:* Governor, Cranbrook School. *Professional Organisations:* Associated Institute of Bankers. *Recreations:* Cricket, Hockey, Golf.

HOLLIDGE, Ron; Managing Director, Lloyds Development Capital Limited, since 1985; Investment Banking, Venture Capital. *Career:* Lloyds Bank plc, Various to Senior Mgr, Mincing Lane 1963-85. *Directorships:* Lloyds Merchant Bank Limited 1985 (exec); BWBC Holdings Limited 1986 (non-exec); Schroder Munchmeyer Hengst Beteiligungs GmbH 1988 (non-exec); Lloyds Merchant Bank Holdings Ltd 1989 (exec); Pentagon Nominees Ltd 1990; British Venture Capital Association 1990.

HOLLINGSWORTH, B; Partner, Jaques & Lewis, since 1963; Head of Property Dept. *Career:* Jaques & Co, Articled Clerk 1957-60; Assistant Solicitor 1960-63. *Biog: b.* 8 June 1936. *Nationality:* British. *m.* 1967, Barbara Mary (née Whereat); 2 d. *Educ:* Watson's College, Edinburgh; Whitgift School, South Croydon; King's College, London (LLM, AKC). *Professional Organisations:* Solicitor; Member, Law Society. *Recreations:* Gardening.

HOLLINGWORTH, Laurence David Edgar; Partner, Cazenove & Co, since 1990; North America. *Career:* Cazenove & Co 1980-. *Biog: b.* 28 May 1958. *Nationality:* British. *m.* 1987, Anne Rosalind (née Pigot). *Other Activities:* Freeman, Worshipful Company of Painter-Stainers. *Professional Organisations:* Member, International Stock Exchange.

HOLLINRAKE, J; Director, J H Minet & Co Ltd.

HOLLIS, A John; Vice President, Manufacturers Hanover Trust Company.

HOLLMEYER, Robert C; Senior Vice-President & General Manager, NCNB National Bank of North Carolina, since 1985; Commercial Banking, Treasury, Securities, Investment Banking. *Career:* NCNB (Charlotte NC) Treasury Mgr 1974-1985. *Biog: b.* 24 October 1946. *Nationality:* American. *m.* 1969, Jere (née Reddick); 3 s; 1 d. *Educ:* University of Florida (BA); University of North Carolina (MBA). *Directorships:* Panmure Gordon Bankers Ltd 1985 (exec); Panmure Gordon & Co Ltd 1985 (exec). *Professional Organisations:* American Bankers & Securities Assoc (London); London FOREX. *Clubs:* Overseas Bankers, Hampstead Golf Club. *Recreations:* Golf.

HOLLOWAY, Anthony Douglas; Assistant General Manager and Treasurer, UBAF Bank Ltd, since 1982; Treasury and Finance. *Career:* Bank of England, Clerk 1956-60; Provincial Building Society Snr Clerk; Leeds Permanent Building Society Snr Clerk and Cashier 1961-66; American Express Intl Bank Corporation Loans Dept Head 1967-74; United Dominion Trust Controller, Eurocurrency Banking 1974-75; UBAF Bank Ltd Snr Mgr, Medium Term Lending; Asst Gen Mgr. *Biog: m.* 1 s; 1 d. *Directorships:* UBAF Finance Company Ltd 1984 (exec).

HOLLOWAY, Hugh L; Marketing Director, CCF Foster Braithwaite Ltd, since 1988; Marketing. *Career:* Ladbroke Group, Admin Manager, Casinos 1975-78; Lunn Poly, Marketing Manager, Travel Marketing 1978-84; Abbey Unit Trust Managers, Marketing Manager, Unit Trusts Marketing 1984-87; Fidelity Investment Services, Senior Marketing Manager, Unit Trusts Marketing 1987-88. *Biog: b.* 2 August 1952. *Nationality:* British. *m.* 1978, Molly (née Wade); 1 s; 3 d. *Educ:* Tonbridge; University of Warwick (BA Hons Philosophy & Politics). *Directorships:* CCF Foster Braithwaite Ltd 1989 (exec); CCF Foster Braithwaite Unit Trust Management Ltd 1989 (exec). *Professional Organisations:* Member, Chartered Institute of Marketing. *Recreations:* Jazz Drums, Golf, Cricket, Tennis, Fishing, Croquet.

HOLLOWAY, Julian Pendrill Warner; Partner, McKenna & Co, since 1988; Construction and Dispute Resolution. *Career:* Denton Hall Burgin & Warrens, Articled Clerk 1979-81; Brecher & Co, Asst Solicitor

1981-83; McKenna & Co, Asst Solicitor 1984-88. *Biog: b.* 6 May 1954. *Nationality:* British. *m.* Emma; 2 s; 1 d. *Educ:* Durham University (BA). *Professional Organisations:* Law Society.

HOLLOWAY, Peter; Assistant General Manager - FX, Union Bank of Finland Ltd.

HOLLWAY, Miss Janet; Partner, Simmons & Simmons.

HOLMAN, C B; Director, David Holman & Co Ltd.

HOLMAN, David McArthur; Chairman/ Managing Director, John Holman & Sons Ltd, since 1954. *Career:* David Holman & Co Ltd, Chairman 1971; Managing Director 1971. *Biog: b.* 11 December 1928. *Nationality:* British. *m.* 1966, Valerie Brythonig (née Pryor); 3 s. *Educ:* Rugby. *Directorships:* John Holman & Sons Ltd 1954 Chm & MD; David Holman & Co Ltd 1971 Chm & MD; Their Subsidiary & Associated Companies. *Other Activities:* Chm, Phyllis Holman-Richards Adoption Society. *Clubs:* Cavalry and Guards Club, City of London Club. *Recreations:* Field Sports.

HOLMAN, R J G; Marketing Partner, Milne Ross (Chartered Accountants), since 1988; General Practice. *Career:* Edward Boyles & Co, Trainee 1961; Edward Boyles & Co, Partner 1966; Milne Gregg & Turnbull (following merger of practices), Partner 1970; Milne Ross, (following merger of Milne Gregg & Turnbull and Jones Ross Howell), Partner 1980; Milne Ross, Managing Partner 1985-88; Marketing Partner 1988-. *Biog: b.* 11 June 1943. *Nationality:* British. *m.* 1983, Angela; 1 s; 1 d. *Educ:* St Pauls School. *Directorships:* UK 2000 Ltd 1986 (non-exec); Virgin Atlantic Airways Limited 1984-86 (semi-exec). *Other Activities:* Member, Lloyds; Church Warden and Lay Reader, St Mary's, Putney. *Professional Organisations:* Fellow, Institute of Chartered Accountants, 1966; Associate, Institute of Taxation. *Clubs:* Roehampton Club. *Recreations:* Church Warden and Lay Reader, Family, Keeping Fit.

HOLMAN, R W; Partner, Ernst & Young.

HOLMES, Mrs Carol Miriam (née Simon); Partner, Titmuss, Sainer & Webb, since 1987; Property Law. *Career:* Titmuss Sainer & Webb, Articled Clerk 1969-71; Assistant Solicitor 1971-73; Partner 1973-75; Wansbroughs Bristol, Assistant Solicitor 1975-76; Titmuss Sainer & Webb, Assistant Solicitor (Part-Time) 1977-87; Partner 1987-. *Biog: b.* 18 September 1947. *Nationality:* British. *m.* 1970, Ronald David; 1 s; 1 d. *Educ:* Croydon High School GPDST; University of Nottingham (LLB). *Professional Organisations:* Law Society. *Recreations:* Music.

HOLMES, Christopher John; Assistant General Manager, National Provident Institution, since 1987; Head

of Assets Division. *Career:* George Henderson (Stockbrokers), Analyst 1968-71. *Biog: b.* 15 May 1947. *Nationality:* British. *Directorships:* NPIM 1987 (exec); NPIPM 1987 (exec); Basil Investments 1987 (exec). *Professional Organisations:* ASIA.

HOLMES, John; Managing Director (Investment Management), Morgan Stanley International.

HOLMES, John Hanby; Partner, Clifford Chance.

HOLMES, R E; Director, Charlton Seal Schaverien Limited.

HOLMES, R W; Director, Robert Fleming Insurance Brokers Limited.

HOLMES, S A; Underwriter, Quill Underwriting Agency Limited.

HOLT, Andrew Richard; Director, National InvestmentGroup plc.

HOLT, Miss Elizabeth Jane; Director Corporate Finance, Robert Fleming & Co Limited, since 1990; UK Corporate Finance. *Biog: b.* 23 January 1959. *Nationality:* British. *m.* 1987, C M Turner. *Educ:* Somerville College, Oxford (BA Literae Humaniores). *Recreations:* Gardening, Wine, Literature.

HOLT, Nicholas John; Legal & Compliance Director, Smith New Court plc, since 1989; Legal and Regulatory Matters. *Career:* Coward Chance, Solicitor 1980-83; Jardine Matheson & Co, Manager, Legal Dept 1984-87. *Biog: b.* 2 April 1958. *Nationality:* British. *m.* 1984, Georgina (née Mann); 1 s; 1 d. *Educ:* The Manchester Grammar School; Fitzwilliam College, Cambridge (BA Hons). *Directorships:* Smith New Court plc 1989 (exec). *Professional Organisations:* The Law Society. *Clubs:* The Reform. *Recreations:* Sport, Travel, Wine.

HOLT, Richard; Director, Nicholson Chamberlain Colls Limited.

HOLT, S J; Clerk, Environmental Cleaners' Company.

HOLY, Daniel L; European Controller, Cargill Europe Ltd.

HOMAN, (Andrew) Mark; National Director of Corporate Reconstruction & Insolvency, Price Waterhouse, since 1981. *Career:* Price Waterhouse 1963-. *Biog: b.* 27 June 1942. *Nationality:* British. *m.* 1970, Pamela (née Robertson); 1 s; 1 d. *Educ:* Maidstone Grammar School; Nottingham University (BA). *Other Activities:* Chairman, Joint Insolvency Examination Board. *Professional Organisations:* Fellow, Institute of Chartered Accountants in England & Wales; Fellow,

Insolvency Practitioners Association. *Clubs:* MCC. *Recreations:* Cricket, Gardening, Opera, Chess.

HOMAN, Lawrence Hugh Adair; Partner, Berwin Leighton, since 1975; Asset Finance, Staff Partner. *Career:* Allen & Overy, Articled Clerk & Assistant Solicitor 1968-73; Berwin Leighton, Assistant Solicitor 1973-75. *Biog: b.* 26 June 1945. *Nationality:* British. *m.* 1971, Lyn; 1 s; 1 d. *Educ:* Sherborne School, Dorset; Worcester College, Oxford (MA Jurisprudence). *Professional Organisations:* Law Society. *Recreations:* Sailing, Golf, Indian Affairs.

HOMER, Peter Norman; Director, James Finlay Bank Ltd, since 1986; Corporate Finance. *Career:* James A Jobling Ltd Group Development Mgr 1966-73; Simpson Lawrence Ltd Dir 1973-74; Grampian Holdings plc Dir of Subsidiaries 1974-79; Scottish Development Agency Asst Dir 1979-84; IMD Holdings Ltd Chief Exec 1984-86. *Biog: b.* 7 June 1939. *Nationality:* British. *m.* 1961, Valerie Anne (née Knight); 3 s. *Educ:* Moseley Grammar School, Birmingham; Manchester University (BSc, MSc). *Directorships:* BHR Group Ltd 1990 (non-exec); West of Scotland Assured Homes plc 1989 (non-exec); Scottish Allied Investors Ltd 1990 (exec); Scottish Offshore Investors plc 1990 (exec). *Professional Organisations:* MBIM Institute of Directors. *Clubs:* Western Club, Royal Northern & Clyde Yacht Club (Commodore). *Recreations:* Sailing, Wine.

HONEYMAN, S H; Director, W H Smith Group plc.

HONIGMANN, A P P; Partner, Field Fisher Waterhouse.

HONNOR, Christopher John; Director, Kleinwort Benson Securities Ltd, since 1986; Head of European Sales and Research. *Career:* J & P Coats Ltd, Various Mgmnt Posts 1958-67; PE Consulting Group, Mgmnt Consultant 1968-70; Grieveson Grant & Co (aquired by Kleinwort Benson in 1986); Engineering Analyst 1970-75; Head of UK Research 1975-79; Jt Head of European Sales & Research 1979-86. *Biog: b.* 29 June 1935. *Nationality:* British. *m.* 1964, June (née Günther). *Educ:* Whitgift; Christ's College, Cambridge (MA). *Professional Organisations:* ASIA. *Clubs:* Royal Wimbledon Golf Club, Roehampton Club. *Recreations:* Golf, Gardening, Food & Drink.

HOOD, Gordon; Associate, James Gentles & Son.

HOOD, Michael; Lending Manager, Bank of East Asia Limited, since 1989; All Aspects of Lending and Trade Finance. *Career:* Midland Bank plc 1976-85; Banque Bruxelles Lambert SA 1985-89; The Bank of East Asia Ltd 1989-. *Biog: b.* 21 November 1957. *Nationality:* British. *m.* 1986, Josephine Clare (née Warren); 1 s. *Educ:* House County Grammar School; Open University; The Management College, Henley. *Professional Organisations:* Associate, Chartered Institute of Bankers (ACIB); Institute of Bankers Financial Studies Diploma (Dip FS). *Recreations:* Investment Matters, DIY, Cricket.

HOOD, Stephen John; Partner, Clifford Chance, since 1978. *Biog: b.* 12 February 1947. *m.* 1971, Maya (née Togonal); 4 s; 1 d. *Educ:* Brisbane Boys' College; University of Queensland; University of London (LLM). *Other Activities:* Council Mem of Britain-Australia Society; Council Mem of Royal Commonwealth Society; Trustee of Sir Robert Menzies Memorial Fund (Chm, Exec Ctee). *Professional Organisations:* Law Society; City of London Law Society. *Publications:* Equity Joint Ventures in the People's Republic of China; Technology Transfer in the People's Republic of China. *Recreations:* Golf, Skiing.

HOOK, Christian Robert MacNachtan; Partner, Dundas & Wilson CS, since 1990; Acquisitions & Mergers. *Career:* McKenna & Co, Articled Clerk 1976; Trowers & Hamlins, Articled Clerk 1976-78; Government of the State of Bahrain (On Secondment from Trowers & Hamlins), Asst Legal Adviser, Ministry of Finance & National Economy 1978-79; Trowers & Hamlins, Articled Clerk 1979-80; Assistant Solicitor 1980-84; Government of the State of Bahrain, Legal Adviser, Ministry of Housing 1982-84; Ministry of Finance & National Economy 1984-86; Trowers & Hamlins, Partner 1984-87; Dundas & Wilson, Assistant Solicitor 1987-89; Associate 1990. *Biog: b.* 16 August 1952. *Nationality:* British. *m.* 1981, Stephanie Ann (née Taylor); 1 s; 1 d. *Educ:* The Edinburgh Academy; St Catharines College, Cambridge (BA Law). *Professional Organisations:* Law Society; Law Society of Scotland. *Clubs:* New Club, Edinburgh Academicals. *Recreations:* Sailing, Shooting.

HOOK, Mrs J; Director and Agency Manager, Henry G Nicholson (Underwriting) Ltd.

HOOK, Dr Robert Charles; Managing Director, Prelude Technology Investments Ltd, since 1985. *Career:* PYE TVT Ltd Engineer 1957-65; Cambridge Consultants Ltd Mgr 1966-75; Dir 1975-85. *Biog: b.* 18 August 1943. *Nationality:* British. *m.* 1964, Janet (née Jackson); 2 s; 2 d. *Educ:* Cambridge Grammar; Trinity College, Cambridge (PhD). *Directorships:* Cambridge Consultants Limited; Elmjet Ltd 1986 (non-exec); Creative Logic Ltd 1987 (non-exec); Prelude Technology Investments Limited; Prelude Technology Investments Holdings Limited; Xaar Limited 1990 (non-exec). *Other Activities:* British Venture Capital Association; European Venture Capital Association. *Professional Organisations:* MIEE. *Recreations:* Gardening, Music.

HOPE, Catherine D; Partner, D J Freeman & Co.

HOPE, R J d'O; Director, Henry G Nicholson (Underwriting) Ltd.

HOPE-FALKNER, Patrick M; Director, Lazard Investors, since 1985; Private Client Legal. *Career:* Freshfields, Mgr 1973-84. *Biog: b.* 1 December 1949. *Nationality:* British. *m.* 1972, Wendy (née Mallinson); 2 s. *Educ:* Wellington College. *Professional Organisations:* The Law Society. *Clubs:* Brooks's.

HOPE JOHNSTONE, Patrick Andrew Wentworth; The Earl of Annandale and Hartfell; DL; Director, Murray Lawrence Members' Agency Limited.

HOPKINS, Anthony Strother; Chief Executive, Industrial Development Board for Northern Ireland, since 1988; Overall Direction of Organisation. *Career:* Thomson McLintock & Co, Chartered Acct-Audit Mgr 1962-70; Dept of Commerce (Northern Ireland), Principal Officer 1971-75; Northern Ireland Development Agency, Dep Chief Exec 1975-79; Chief Exec 1979-83; Industrial Development Board, Dep Chief Exec 1983-88. *Biog: b.* 17 July 1940. *Nationality:* British. *m.* 1965, Moira (née McDonough); 1 s; 2 d. *Educ:* Campbell College, Belfast; The Queen's University of Belfast (BSc Econ). *Professional Organisations:* FCA; CBIM. *Clubs:* Oriental, Royal Belfast Golf. *Recreations:* Golf, Tennis, Windsurfing.

HOPKINS, Carl William Vernon; Partner, Nabarro Nathanson, since 1987; Public Law/Compulsory Purchase/Planning. *Career:* Kent County Council, Assistant Solicitor 1971-72; Senior Assistant Solicitor 1972-75; Assistant County Secretary 1975-81; Dept of Environment, Principal (Secondment), New Towns Directorate 1979-80; London Docklands Dev Corp, Corporation Solicitor & Secretary 1981-87. *Biog: b.* 18 August 1945. *Nationality:* British. *m.* 1969, Jennifer (née Sprangemeyer); 1 s. *Educ:* Haverford West & Milford Haven Grammar Schools. *Other Activities:* CBI London Regional Council. *Professional Organisations:* Law Society, Solicitor. *Clubs:* Reform Club. *Recreations:* Fishing, Sailing.

HOPKINS, Ian William; Director, Baring Brothers & Co Limited, since 1986; Finance. *Biog: b.* 23 April 1947. *Nationality:* British. *m.* 1971, Valerie (née Hughes); 1 s; 1 d. *Directorships:* The English Concert 1989 (non-exec). *Other Activities:* Hon Treasurer, The British Dyslexia Association. *Professional Organisations:* Institute of Chartered Accountants of Scotland. *Clubs:* Riverside Racquets.

HOPKINS, Martin W; Partner (Birmingham), Evershed Wells & Hind.

HOPKINS, Sidney Arthur; Director, Guardian Royal Exchange Assurance plc.

HOPKINS, William John; Chairman, March Consulting Group.

HOPKINSON, Adrian Trayton; Director, County NatWest Securities, since 1987; German Research Analyst. *Career:* Conservative Research Dept Research Officer 1975-78; JP Morgan Investment Asst Dir 1979-85. *Biog: b.* 5 August 1953. *m.* 1984, Clare Diana (née Birch Reynardson); 3 s. *Educ:* New College, Oxford (BA Hons); INSEAD (MBA). *Other Activities:* Director, English Chamber Orchestra and Music Society. *Professional Organisations:* Chartered Financial Analyst (USA). *Recreations:* Music.

HOPKINSON, David Hugh Laing; CBE, RD, DL; Chairman, Harrisons & Crosfield plc, since 1988. *Career:* RNR & RNVR 1944-68; A Clerk of the House of Commons 1948-59; Robert Fleming & Co 1960-62; M & G Group, Chief Executive 1963-87; British Rail Southern Board, Chairman 1981-87; Lloyds Bank Southern Board, Director 1979-87; Housing Corporation, Director 1987-88; Housing Finance Corporation, Chairman 1987-88. *Biog: b.* 14 August 1926. *Nationality:* British. *m.* 1951, Prudence (née Holmes); 2 s; 2 d. *Educ:* Wellington College; Merton College, Oxford (BA). *Directorships:* Harrisons & Crosfield plc 1987 (exec); English China Clays 1975 (non-exec); Wolverhampton & Dudley Breweries 1987 (non-exec); Charities Investment Managers Ltd 1970 (non-exec); Merchants Trust 1972 (non-exec). *Clubs:* Brooks's. *Recreations:* Travelling, Walking, Opera.

HOPPER, Alan Keith Thompson; Managing Director, Pannell Kerr Forster Associates.

HOPPER, Henry G; Associate Director, Coutts & Co.

HOPWOOD, Professor Anthony George; Ernst & Young; Professor of International & Financial Management, London School of Economics. *Career:* Manchester Business School, Lecturer Management Accounting 1970-73; European Institute for Advanced Studies in Management (Brussels), Visiting Professor of Management 1972-; Henley-on-Thames Administrative Staff College Mem, Snr Staff 197 3-75; Oxford Centre for Management Studies, Professorial Fellow 1976-78; London Business School, ICA Prof of Accounting & Financial Reporting 1978-85; Pennsylvania State University, Distinguished Visiting Prof, Accounting 1983-88. *Biog: b.* 18 May 1944. *Nationality:* British. *m.* 1967, Caryl (née Davies); 2 s. *Educ:* Hanley High School, Stoke on Trent; London School of Economics (BSc); Chicago University (MBA, PhD); Turku School of Economics, Finland (Hon DEcon). *Directorships:* Tavistock Institute of Human Relations 1981 Mem of Council. *Other Activities:* American Accounting Association's Distinguished International Visiting Lecturer, 1981; Mem, ICAEW Research Board; Editor-in-Chief, Accounting, Organisations and Society, 1976-; Accounting Adviser,

European Commission, 1989-90; Accounting Adviser, OECD, 1990-. *Professional Organisations:* Pres, European Accounting Assoc (1977-79 & 1987-88). *Publications:* An Accounting System and Managerial Behaviour, 1973; Accounting and Human Behaviour, 1974; Co-Author, Essays in British Accounting Research, 1981; Co-Author, Auditing Research: Issues and Opportunities, 1982; Co-Author, Accounting Standard Setting: An International Prospective, 1983; Co-Author, European Contributions to Accounting Research, 1984; Co-Author, Issues in Public Sector Accounting, 1984; Co-Author, Research and Current Issues in Management Accounting, 1986; Accounting from the Outside, 1989; International Pressures for Accounting Change, 1989; Numerous Articles in Professional and Academic Journals.

HORAN, C A; Director, Charterhouse Bank Limited.

HORE-RUTHVEN, Alexander Patrick Greysteil; The Rt Hon The Earl of Gowrie; Non-Executive Director, Ladbroke Group plc.

HORBACZEWSKA, Ms M J; London Representative, Kredietbank SA Luxembourgeoise.

HORLICK, Richard M A; Director, Newton Investment Management, since 1984; Segregated Pension Funds. *Career:* Newton Investment Management 1984-; Samuel Montagu & Co 1981-84. *Biog: b.* 4 March 1959. *Nationality:* British. *m.* 1986,Penelope Jane (née Barlow). *Educ:* Harrow School; Pembroke College, Cambridge (MA). *Professional Organisations:* Society of Investment Analysts. *Recreations:* Cricket, Rugby.

HORLOCK, K W; Director, First National Bank PLC.

HORN, Bernard Philip; General Manager, Group Strategy & Communications, National Westminster Bank plc, since 1990. *Career:* National Westminster Bank plc, early Retail Bank Experience; Various assignments in International Banking; Senior Executive responsibility for Special Financial Services; Director of Planning and Control, Corporate and Institutional Banking 1989; General Manager, Group Chief Executives Office 1989-90. *Biog: b.* 22 April 1946. *Nationality:* British. *m.* 1988, Clare (née Gilbert). *Educ:* Catholic College, Preston; Harvard Business School (Scholar, Diploma in Management Studies). *Professional Organisations:* ACIB. *Recreations:* Keeping Fit, Theatre, Ballet, Opera, Playing the Piano (for own enjoyment).

HORN, F Roger; Chief Executive and Managing Director, Smiths Industries plc.

HORNBY, Sir Simon; Director, Lloyds Bank plc.

HORNE, Christopher Malcolm; Senior Associate Director, Coutts & Co, since 1988; Secretary of the Bank. *Biog: b.* 14 June 1941. *Nationality:* British. *m.* 1964, Christine Ann (née Fradley); 2 s. *Professional Organisations:* Institute of Directors. *Clubs:* Rochester & Cobham Golf Club.

HORNE, David Oliver; Chairman and Chief Executive, Lloyds Merchant Bank Ltd, since 1988. *Career:* S G Warburg & Co Ltd, Director 1966-70; Williams & Glyn's Bank Ltd, Director 1970-78; Lloyds Bank International Ltd, Director 1978-85. *Biog: b.* 7 March 1932. *Nationality:* British. *m.* 1959, Joyce (née Kynoch); 2 s; 2 d. *Educ:* Fettes College, Edinburgh. *Directorships:* Lloyds Development Capital Ltd 1981 (non-exec) Chairman; Lloyds Merchant Bank Ltd 1985 (exec); Lloyds Merchant Bank Holdings Ltd 1985 (exec); Lloyds Corporate Advisory Services Pty Ltd 1987 (non-exec); Schroeder Muenchmeyer Hengst & Co 1987 (non-exec); Lloyds Bank Stockbrokers Ltd 1988. *Professional Organisations:* Fellow, Institute of Chartered Accountants in England and Wales. *Recreations:* Golf.

HORNER, P J; Director, J K Buckenham Limited.

HORROCKS, Julian; Partner, Hepworth & Chadwick.

HORSFALL, J; Executive Director, BMP Business.

HORSFALL, Jonathan; Partner, Allen & Overy, since 1973; Banking and Capital Markets. *Biog: b.* 27 November 1945. *Nationality:* British. *m.* 1973, Yvonne (née Thomson); 1 d. *Educ:* The Kings School, Canterbury; Gonville & Caius, Cambridge (MA). *Other Activities:* Member, City of London Solicitors Company. *Professional Organisations:* The Law Society. *Clubs:* Garrick. *Recreations:* Architecture, Antiques, Opera and Singing.

HORSFALL TURNER, R; Partner, Allen & Overy.

HORSMAN, Peter R; Director, Bradstock Blunt & Thompson Ltd.

HORTON, C M; Partner, Slaughter and May.

HORTON, D M; Director, Smith Keen Cutler Ltd.

HORTON, G J; Director & Head of Lending, Benchmark Bank plc, since 1989; Property Lending. *Career:* National Westminster Bank plc, Tutor, Personal Assistant, Area Advances Officer 1974-85; Benchmark Bank plc, Senior Lending Executive, Associate Director Lending, Director & Head of Lending 1985-. *Biog: b.* 2 May 1956. *Nationality:* British. *m.* 1982, Lisa (née Mireille); 2 s. *Educ:* Bishop Ullathorne RC School. *Directorships:* Benchmark Bank plc 1989 (exec). *Professional Organisations:* ACIB. *Recreations:* Golf.

HORTON, Michael Thomas James; Director, First National Bank plc, since 1976; Sales & Marketing. *Biog:*

b. 1 July 1935. *Nationality:* British. *m.* 1964, Pamela Ann (née Martin); 1 s; 1 d. *Educ:* Aston Commercial School, Birmingham; Birmingham College of Commerce. *Directorships:* First National Credit Ltd 1971 (exec); First National Leasing Ltd and other Group Companies 1971 (exec). *Recreations:* Politics, Theatre, Racing.

HORTON, R B; Chairman and Chief Executive Officer, The British Petroleum Company plc, since 1990. *Career:* British Petroleum 1957-; General Manager, BP Tankers 1975-76; General Manager, Corporate Planning 1976-79; Chairman, Standard Oil 1986-88; Vice Chairman & Chief Executive Officer, BP America 1987-88; Chairman, BP America 1988-89; Chairman, BP Chemicals 1989-90; Deputy Chairman, Chairman designate BP 1989. *Biog: b.* 18 August 1939. *Nationality:* British. *m.* 1962, Sally Doreen (née Wells); 1 s; 1 d. *Educ:* King's School, Canterbury; University of St. Andrews (BSc); Massachusetts Institute of Technology (SM, Sloan Fellow). *Directorships:* Emerson Electric Company 1987 (non-exec). *Other Activities:* Vice Chairman and Companion, British Institute of Management; Member, Universities Funding Council; Chairman, Tate Gallery Foundation and Business in Arts; President, Third Age Network; Governor, Kings School Canterbury; Chancellor, University of Kent at Canterbury; Member of the Boards of MIT, and Western Reserve University and the Cleveland Orchestra; Member of the Advisory Board, British-American Chamber of Commerce. *Professional Organisations:* Member, Chemical Industries Association. *Recreations:* Music, Shooting.

HORTON, Richard; Group Finance Director, Tyndall Holdings plc, since 1988. *Career:* Price Waterhouse 1973-84; First National Bank of Chicago 1984-87; Brown Shipley 1987-88. *Biog: b.* 24 April 1952. *Nationality:* British. *m.* 1977, Linda (née Garton); 1 s; 1 d. *Educ:* Merton College, Oxford (MA). *Professional Organisations:* Institute of Chartered Accountants in England and Wales. *Recreations:* Amateur Radio.

HORTON, Toby; Director, Minster Trust Ltd, since 1984; Head of Corporate Finance Department. *Career:* Kleinwort Benson Ltd, Corp Fin Exec 1970-76; Shearson Lehman Inc, Assoc Dir Intl 1976-79; Sound Broadcasting (Teeside) Ltd, MD 1979-83. *Biog: b.* 18 February 1947. *Nationality:* British. *m.* 1977, Fiona Catherine (née Peake); 2 s; 2 d. *Educ:* Westminster School; Christ Church, Oxford (MA). *Directorships:* Allied Partnership Group plc 1986 (non-exec); Molinare Visions plc 1986 (non-exec). *Other Activities:* The Foundation for Defence Studies (Chm); Prospective Conservative Euro-Parlimentary Candidate, Yorkshire South-West. *Professional Organisations:* FBIM. *Publications:* Programme for Reform, A New Agenda for Broadcasting, 1987; Going to Market: New Policy for the Farming Industry, 1985. *Clubs:* Buck's, Northern Counties (Newcastle). *Recreations:* History, Country Pursuits.

HORWELL, John Malcolm; Deputy Chairman, Steel Burrill Jones plc, since 1989; Reinsurance. *Career:* Leslie & Godwin Ltd, Non-Marine Reinsurance Broker 1952-54; Edward S Saville, Non-Marine Insurance Broker 1954-56; WE Found & Co Ltd, Director 1956-73; Halford Shead & Co Ltd, Director 1973-76; Crockford Devitt Underwriting Agencies Ltd, Director. *Biog: b.* 20 November 1932. *Nationality:* British. *m.* 1956, Gloria Lorraine; 3 s. *Educ:* Hampton School; City of London College. *Directorships:* Steel Burrill Jones Group plc 1989 Deputy Chairman; Meacock Samuelson & Devitt Ltd 1983 Chairman (previously Director); SBJ Devitt Limited (Formerly Howson F Devitt & Sons Ltd 1976 Chairman (previously Dir/MD); Devitt Insurance Services Ltd (formerly Devitt (DA Insurance) Ltd) 1989; Roger Major & Co Ltd 1987 Chairman; Devitt Group Ltd (now SBJ Group plc) 1977 Former Chief Executive. *Other Activities:* Worshipful Company of Plumbers; Worshipful Company of Insurers; City Livery Club. *Clubs:* City of London Club, Wig & Pen Club, Royal Automobile Club.

HORWOOD, W J; Director, Phillips & Drew Fund Management Limited.

HOSFORD, S R H; Director, Brewin Dolphin & Co Ltd.

HOSHINO, K; Deputy Managing Director, Nippon Credit International Limited.

HOSKER, Gerald Albery; CB; Solicitor, Department of Trade & Industry, since 1987; Legal Advice on all matters for the Department. *Career:* Treasury Solicitors Dept Legal Asst 1960-66; Snr Legal Asst 1966-73; Asst Treasury Solicitor 1973-82; Principal Asst Treasury Solicitor 1982-84; Dep Treasury Solicitor 1984-87; DTI Solicitor 1987-. *Biog: b.* 28 July 1933. *Nationality:* British. *m.* 1956, Rachel Victoria Beatrice (née Middleton); 1 s; 1 d. *Educ:* Berkhamsted School. *Other Activities:* FRSA. *Professional Organisations:* The Law Society; AFCS. *Clubs:* Royal Commonwealth Society.

HOSKIN, Peter; Partner, Beavis Walker.

HOSKINS, L; Executive Director, Booker plc.

HOSKYNS, Sir John Austin Hungerford Leigh; Chairman, The Burton Group plc, since 1990. *Biog: b.* 23 August 1927. *Nationality:* British. *Directorships:* The Burton Group plc 1990 (non-exec), 1990 Chm; Clerical Medical & General Life Assurance Society; Ferranti International plc; McKechnie plc.

HOSSACK, James David Ian; Partner, Cyril Sweett & Partners, since 1985; Cost Management of Building Process of Commercial Property. *Career:* Jon D Gibson & Simpson, Edinburgh 1962-70; Dawson & Ward, Kenya 1970; Bernard James & Partners, Capetown

1971; Jon D Gibson & Simpson, Edinburgh 1972-75; H A Brechin & Co, Kelso, Associate 1975-80; Cyril Sweett & Partners, Brighton, Manager 1980-85; London, Partner 1985-. *Biog: b.* 6 November 1943. *Nationality:* British. *m.* 1972, Hilary (née Wallen); 1 s; 1 d. *Educ:* Glenalmond College, Perthshire; Heriot Watt, Edinburgh (ARICS). *Directorships:* Norden Technical & Consultancy Services Ltd 1985 (exec); CS Project Consultants 1986-89 (exec). *Professional Organisations:* FRICS; Dipl Proj Man. *Clubs:* Ebury Court. *Recreations:* Music.

HOSSENLOPP, John J A; Partner, Gibson, Dunn & Crutcher, since 1989; International Corporate, Commercial & Financial Transactions. *Career:* Citibank, NA 1961-62; Shearman & Sterling Associate 1967-73; Gottesman & Partners Ptnr 1973-75; Coudert Brothers Ptnr 1975-89. *Biog: b.* 31 October 1939. *Nationality:* American. *m.* 1963, Patricia (née La Mar); 1 s; 2 d. *Educ:* Lafayette College (BA); Vanderbilt University (JD). *Directorships:* Threshold Investments Limited 1989 (non-exec). *Other Activities:* Trustee, Elliott E Cheatham Fund. *Professional Organisations:* Mem, NY Bar since 1968.

HOTCHIN, Michael Geoffrey; Group Company Secretary, Charterhouse plc, since 1985; Legal Administration. *Career:* Various Departments Charterhouse Bank Limited 1966-76; Secretary Charterhouse Bank Limited 1976-; Group Secretary Charterhouse plc 1985-. *Biog: b.* 25 February 1944. *Nationality:* British. *m.* 1980, Patricia Ann (née Shand) (div 1986). *Educ:* Stamford School. *Directorships:* Charterhouse International Finance BV (Holland) 1981; Charterhouse International Holdings Limited (Jersey) 1981; Charterhouse (Midlands) Limited 1984; Charterhouse (Northern) Limited 1984; Charterhouse Pensions Limited 1989; One Paternoster Row Limited 1985; Paternoster Directors Limited 1984; Paternoster Nominees Limited 1982; Paternoster Secretaries Limited 1984; Paternoster Securities Limited 1982; St Paul's Stores plc 1985; Swift 1981 Limited 1986; Swift 1987 Limited 1986; Charterhouse Management Services Limited 1988. *Professional Organisations:* Fellow, Institute of Chartered Secretaries and Administrators (FCIS). *Recreations:* Shooting, Reading, Power Boat Racing.

HOTOPF, Mark; Financial Reporter, Daily Mail.

HOTTINGER, Richard; Director, International City Holdings.

HOUGH, B D; Director, Gibbs, Hartley, Cooper Ltd.

HOUGHTON, Paul Benjamin Reynolds; Director, Wise Speke Ltd, since 1987; Administration. *Career:* H M Forces, The Green Howards. *Biog: b.* 2 February 1952. *m.* 1970, Victoria Karen (née Bryant); 2 s. *Educ:* Woodhouse Grove School; Hull University (BA); RMA Sandhurst.

HOULIHAN, William John; Director, Hoare Govett Investment Research Ltd.

HOULT, Tim; National Director of Audit & Business Advisory Services, Price Waterhouse.

HOURSTON, G M; Managing Director, Boots The Chemists, The Boots Co plc.

HOUSTON, G A; Director, UK Equities, Hoare Govett Securities Ltd, since 1985.

HOUSTON, George; Partner, James Gentles & Son.

HOUSTON, I A; Director, Charterhouse Bank Limited.

HOW, Mrs L C; Director, Phillips & Drew Fund Management Limited.

HOWARD, Adrian; Director, Hambros Bank Limited, since 1990; European Trading Operations. *Career:* Hambros Bank Ltd 1969-. *Biog: b.* 25 September 1950. *Nationality:* British. *m.* 1971, Sally-Ann (née Harvey); 2 d. *Educ:* Enfield Grammar School. *Directorships:* Hambros Bank Ltd 1990 (non-exec). *Recreations:* Golf, Travel, Reading.

HOWARD, Christopher L; Partner, Moores Rowland.

HOWARD, D F; Director, Crawley Warren Group plc.

HOWARD, David Alan; Joint Managing Director, LPH Group plc, since 1986; Lloyd's Broking/Motor Industry. *Career:* Wigham Poland (Reinsurance Brokers) Ltd Lloyd's Brokers, Graduate Trainee Southern European Reinsurance 1974-78; Oakeley Vaughan & Co Ltd Lloyd's Broker, Divisional Director/Head of Overseas Department 1978-81; Leggeter & Howard Ltd (later LPH Group plc), Founder Director 19 81-. *Biog: b.* 7 July 1953. *Nationality:* British. *m.* 1982, Charlotte Henrietta Gaylyn (née Whitelocke-Winter); 2 d. *Educ:* St Georges School, Rome, Italy; Loughborough University (Bachelor of Science Hons). *Directorships:* LPH Group plc & Subsidiaries (exec); Griffin Insurance Mutual (non-exec). *Other Activities:* Member, Bow Group. *Professional Organisations:* Associate of Chartered Insurance Institute; Member of Lloyd's. *Publications:* Internal Market Works. *Clubs:* City University Club, Royal Automobile Club. *Recreations:* Shooting, Hunting.

HOWARD, David Howarth Seymour; Managing Director, Charles Stanley & Co Ltd, since 1971. *Career:* Charles Stanley 1967-. *Biog: b.* 29 December 1945.

Nationality: British. *m.* 1968, Valerie (née Crosse); 2 s; 2 d. *Educ:* Radley College; Worcester College, Oxford (MA Hons). *Directorships:* The Oceana Consolidated Co plc (exec). *Other Activities:* Alderman, City of London (Cornhill Ward), 1986-; Common Councilman (Cornhill Ward), 1972-86; Master, Worshipful Co of Gardeners, 1990-; Vice-President, Lime Street Ward Club. *Professional Organisations:* Member of the Stock Exchange. *Clubs:* City Livery Club, United Wards Club. *Recreations:* Gardening.

HOWARD, Sir Edward; Bt, GBE; Chairman, Charles Stanley & Co Ltd. *Career:* Sheriff 1966-67; Lord Mayor 1971-72. *Biog: b.* 29 October 1915. *Nationality:* British. *m.* 1943, Elizabeth; 2 s. *Educ:* Radley College (Diploma); Worcester College, Oxford. *Other Activities:* Gardeners Company (Master 1961); Light Mongers. *Professional Organisations:* Member, International Stock Exchange. *Recreations:* City Livery, United Wards.

HOWARD, F G; Director, Scott Underwriting Agencies Limited.

HOWARD, Lionel M; Partner (Nottingham), Evershed Wells & Hind.

HOWARD, Michael Cecil; Director, E W Payne Companies Ltd, since 1985; International Broking. *Career:* Insurance Broking in South America Various 1966-74; E W Payne Various 1974-. *Biog: b.* 27 April 1945. *m.* 1969, Ingrid (née Jaeger); 1 s; 1 d. *Educ:* Charterhouse. *Directorships:* E W Payne Companies Limited 1985 (exec); E W Payne Limited 1989 (exec); Lombard Agency Limited 1989 (exec); E W Payne (Overseas) Limited 1989 (exec). *Other Activities:* Worshipful Company of Insurers. *Professional Organisations:* ACII. *Recreations:* Sailing.

HOWARD, Ross Charles; Managing Director, North American Division, D M Clayton & Co Ltd, since 1986; North American Treaty Reinsurance. *Career:* Bland Payne, Broker, North Am Division 1974-75. *Biog: b.* 14 August 1953. *Nationality:* British. *m.* Valerie; 2 s. *Educ:* Epsom College. *Directorships:* D M Clayton 1981 (exec).

HOWARD Jr, Thomas B; Chairman & Chief Executive, Beazer USA, Inc, Beazer plc.

HOWE, Elspeth Rosamund Morton; Lady Howe; JP; Director, United Biscuits (Holdings) plc.

HOWE, Geoffrey Michael Thomas; Managing Partner, Clifford Chance, since 1989; Corporate Finance and Insolvency. *Career:* Clifford-Turner, Partner 1980-87. *Biog: b.* 3 September 1949. *Nationality:* British. *m.* 1976, Alison Laura (née Sims). *Educ:* The Manchester Grammar School; St John's College, Cambridge (MA). *Professional Organisations:* The Law Society. *Recreations:* Collecting Antiques, Wine, Opera, History of Art, Tennis, Flying.

HOWE, Gordon James; Partner, Ernst & Young, since 1961; Member of the UK Executive. *Career:* Ernst & Young (or predecessor firms), Articled Clerk 1949-54; Royal Artillery 1954-56; Senior/Manager 1956-61; Partner 1961-; Arthur Young Europe, Chairman (Current Member of Executive) 1985-89. *Biog: b.* 6 January 1932. *Nationality:* British. *m.* 1957, Dawn; 1 d. *Educ:* Royal Liberty Grammar School, Romford. *Other Activities:* Chairman of the Blood Transfusion Service for the South East of England; Member of the South West Thames Regional Health Authority. *Professional Organisations:* FCA. *Clubs:* RAC. *Recreations:* Stamp Collecting, Swimming.

HOWE, I; Partner, Nabarro Nathanson.

HOWE, Dr Martin; Director, Competition Policy Division, Office of Fair Trading, since 1984; Competition Legislation, including Financial Services Act. *Career:* Sheffield University, Lecturer/Snr Lecturer 1960-73; Monopolies & Mergers Commission, Snr Econ Adviser 1973-77; Office of Fair Trading, Snr Econ Adviser 1977-80; Office of Fair Trading & DTI, Asst Sec 1980-84. *Biog: b.* 9 December 1936. *Nationality:* British. *m.* 1959, Anne Cicely (née Lawrenson); 3 s. *Educ:* High Storrs Grammar School, Sheffield; Leeds University (Bcom); Sheffield University (PhD). *Publications:* Equity Issues and the London Capital Market (Co-Author), 1967; Various Articles in Professional Journals. *Recreations:* Cricket, Amateur Dramatics, Theatre, Gardening.

HOWE, P C; Divisional Director, Legal Department, Allied Dunbar, since 1977; Financial Services Law. *Career:* Department of Environment, Legal Adviser 1976-77; Private Practice at Bar 1974-76. *Biog: b.* 16 October 1946. *Nationality:* British. *m.* 1973, Hilary; 1 s. *Educ:* UWIST (LLB Hons). *Professional Organisations:* Barrister-at-Law. *Publications:* Allied Dunbar Investment Guide (Chapter on Financial Services). *Recreations:* Keep Fit, Swimming, Languages.

HOWE, Timothy Roger; Director, Singer & Friedlander Investment Management Ltd. *Biog: b.* 1951. *Nationality:* British. *Directorships:* Singer & Friedlander Holdings 1989 (exec).

HOWEL, C R; Director, Wellington Underwriting Agencies Limited.

HOWELL, The Rt Hon David; MP, PC; International Adviser, Swiss Bank Corporation, since 1987; International Finance, European Economics, Eastern Europe, Oil, Middle East, Japan. *Career:* Journalist Economist; MP for Guildford 1966-; Secretary of State for Energy 1979-81; Secretary of State for Transport 1981-83;

House of Commons Foreign Affairs Committee, Chairman 1987-; UK-Japan 2000 Group, Chairman 1990-. *Biog: b.* 18 January 1936. *Nationality:* British. *m.* 1967, Davina (née Wallace); 1 s; 2 d. *Educ:* Eton College; King's College, Cambridge (1st Class Honours, Economics). *Directorships:* Queens Moat Houses plc (non-exec). *Other Activities:* Member, Clothworkers' Company. *Publications:* Freedom & Capture, 1980; Blind Victory, 1986; Japan & Europe, (Translated into Japanese), 1987; Numerous Articles & Pamphlets. *Clubs:* Bucks Club. *Recreations:* Countryside, Travel, Golf.

HOWELL, Michael John; Partner, Clifford Chance, since 1987; Commercial Law. *Career:* Clifford-Turner Partner 1969-87. *Biog: b.* 9 June 1939. *Nationality:* British. *m.* 1966, Caroline Sarah Eifiona (née Gray); 2 d. *Educ:* Strode's School, Egham; King's College, London (LLB); University of Chicago (JD); University of Capetown. *Other Activities:* Freeman of City of London Solicitors' Company; Liveryman of Coopers' Company (Warden). *Professional Organisations:* The Law Society; Associate Member of Chartered Institute of Patent Agents. *Clubs:* City Livery.

HOWELL, Robert; Treasurer, Tesco plc, since 1986; Treasury Management. *Career:* Blue Circle Industries plc, Asst Treasurer 1977-85. *Biog: b.* 18 April 1950. *Nationality:* British. *m.* 1984, Kathleen (née Rabey); 1 s; 1 d. *Educ:* The Brunts Grammar School, Mansfield; Manchester University (BA Hons). *Professional Organisations:* ACMA; MCT. *Recreations:* Squash, Tennis, Skiing.

HOWELL, Simon; Director, Merrill Lynch International Limited.

HOWELLS, J R; Partner, Ernst & Young.

HOWELLS, Marion J; Director, Panmure Gordon Bankers Ltd.

HOWELLS, P T; Director, Wise Speke Ltd, since 1990; Corporate Services. *Career:* Messrs Smith & Williamson, Articled Clerk 1966-69; Royal Engineers, Short Service Commission 1969-73; Grant Simmons/Mercer Fraser, Consultant 1973-83; Branch Manager 1983-86; Wise Speke Financial Services, Director 1986-89. *Biog: b.* 9 October 1946. *Nationality:* British. *m.* 1972, Anne Marie (née Puleo); 1 s; 1 d. *Educ:* Greshams School, Holt. *Directorships:* Wise Speke 1990 (exec); Wise Speke Financial Services 1988 (exec). *Other Activities:* Freeman, City of London; Governor, Royal National Lifeboat Institution. *Professional Organisations:* TSA. *Clubs:* Royal Channel Islands Yacht Club. *Recreations:* Offshore Sailing.

HOWES, J H; Deputy Chairman, Crawley Warren Group plc.

HOWES, T E; General Manager & Secretary, C & G Guardian, since 1989; Deputy to Managing Director. *Career:* Nationwide Anglia Building Society, Various Accounting and O & M Responsibilities 1954-65; Guardian Building Society, Assistant Secretary, General Admin & Responsibilty for Investment Matters 1965-72; Asst General Manager, Responsibility for Accounting and Treasury 1972-84; Asst General Manager and Secretary, Responsibilty for Secretarial Matters and Accounting and Treasury 1984-89; General Manager and Secretary, Deputy to Chief Executive with Responsibilty for Secretarial Accounting and Treasury matters 1989-90; C&G Guardian (Central Lending Division of Cheltenham & Gloucester Building Society), General Manager and Secretary, Deputy to Managing Director 1990-. *Biog: b.* 11 June 1938. *Nationality:* British. *m.* 1962, Barbara Eileen (née Cloughton); 2 s. *Educ:* Selhurst Grammar School for Boys. *Professional Organisations:* Fellow, Chartered Institute of Secretaries and Administrators; Fellow, British Institute of Management; Member Chartered Building Societies' Institute. *Recreations:* Golf, Keep Fit, Crosswords.

HOWIE, Paul; Executive Director, Broad Street Group plc.

HOWISON, James Robert Charles; Partner, Stephenson Harwood, since 1977; Company Law with emphasis on Corporate Finance. *Career:* Herbert Smith Articled Clerk 1964-68; Linklaters & Paines Asst Solicitor 1968-74; Stephenson Harwood Asst Solicitor 1974-77. *Biog: b.* 11 March 1943. *m.* 1969, Sarah Melanie (née Fraser); 2 d. *Educ:* Loretto School; Corpus Christi College, Oxford (BA). *Other Activities:* City of London Solicitors' Company. *Professional Organisations:* Law Society. *Recreations:* Tennis, Golf, Gardening.

HOWLAND JACKSON, Anthony Geoffrey Clive; Managing Director, Hogg Group plc, since 1987. *Career:* J H Minet, Broker 1959-64; H Clarkson Insurance Ltd, Business Developer 1964-74; Clarkson Puckle Ltd, Chief Exec 1974-87; Bain Clarkson Ltd, Managing Director 1987. *Biog: b.* 25 May 1941. *Nationality:* British. *m.* 1963, Susan (née Hickson); 1 s; 2 d. *Educ:* Sherborne School. *Directorships:* Gill & Duffus plc 1983 (exec). *Other Activities:* Worshipful Company of Insurers; Member, Lloyd's Insurance Brokers Committee. *Clubs:* Turf Club, City of London Club.

HOWLAND JACKSON, John David; Deputy President, Nomura International plc; European Corporate Finance and Strategic Planning. *Directorships:* Wentworth Group Holdings since 1990 (non-exec).

HOWLEY, John C; Controller, Yorkshire Bank plc.

HOWSDEN, G C; Group Secretary & Director, Philipp Bros Ltd.

HOWSON, J E; Director, Olliff & Partners plc.

HOYER MILLAR, G C; Non-Executive Director, Bunzl Plc.

HOYER MILLAR, Robert; Lord Inchyra; Secretary General, British Bankers Association, since 1988. *Career:* Barclays Bank, Latterly Director UK Financial Services 1964-88.

HOYLE, S L; Partner, Freshfields.

HOYSTED, (Desmond) Christopher (Fitzgerald); Group Personnel Director, Morgan Grenfell & Co Limited, since 1988. *Career:* Swiss Bank Corporation International Limited (SBCI), Executive Director 1982-88; Morgan Guaranty Trust Co of New York (London Office), Vice President, Head of Personnel & Services Div 1975-82; Samuel Montagu & Co Ltd, Assistant Director, Personnel 1970-75; HM Forces, Regular Army, to Captain 1961-70. *Biog:* b. 25 March 1941. *Nationality:* British. *m.* 1968, Anna Jennifer (née Duncan); 2 d. *Educ:* Rugby School; RMA Sandhurst. *Directorships:* Morgan Grenfell & Co Limited 1988 (exec). *Other Activities:* Member, Finance Committee, London Federation of Boys' Clubs. *Clubs:* IEC Wine Society, Butterfields Cricket Club. *Recreations:* Tennis, Golf, Skiing, Game Shooting.

HUA, Hsieh Fu; Director, Morgan Grenfell & Co Limited.

HUBBALL, David J; Partner (Birmingham), Evershed Wells & Hind.

HUBBARD, Andrew J; Partner, Neville Russell, since 1990; Advice to Lloyd's Syndicates. *Career:* Hemsley Miller & Co, Articled Clerk 1968-77; West Wake Price & Co, Audit Senior/Supervisor 1977-78; Neville Russell, Audit Supervisor, Manager, Senior Manager, Partner 1978-. *Biog:* b. 17 July 1950. *Nationality:* British. *m.* 1977, Jeannette Frances (née Ware); 1 s; 1 d. *Educ:* Shooters Hill Grammar School. *Directorships:* International Needs 1976 Trustee/Treasurer; The Pocket Testament League 1987 Treasurer; Brent Christian Mission 1980 Trustee/Treasurer. *Professional Organisations:* FCA. *Recreations:* Photography, Marine Models, Walking, Running, Church Activities, Travel.

HUBBARD, J C; Partner, Cazenove & Co.

HUBBARD, Robert Arthur (Bob); Head of Correspondent Banking, Midland Bank plc, since 1985; Banking Relations and Electronic Banking. *Career:* Midland Bank plc Domestic Banking 1960-72; PA to Exec Dir 1972-75; Investment Mgr (Intl) 1975-77; Corp Planner (Intl) 1977-79; Snr Exec/RegionalMgr 1979-85. *Biog:* b. 22 March 1943. *m.* 1966, Jackie (née Garrett); 2 s. *Educ:* Market Harborough Grammar

School. *Professional Organisations:* Institute of Bankers. *Clubs:* Overseas Bankers'. *Recreations:* All Sports.

HUBBLE, Terence; Executive Director, Svenska Handelsbanken plc.

HUBER, Alfred Ernst; Senior Vice President & CEO, Swiss Volksbank, since 1990; Branch Manager. *Career:* Swiss Volksbank, Bern, Project Management 1962-76; Swiss Bank Corp. (Canada), Vice President Operations 1977-86; Zurich, First Vice President 1986-1989. *Biog:* b. 12 February 1943. *Nationality:* Swiss/Canadian. *m.* 1987, Anny (née Knudsen); 1 s; 1 d. *Educ:* Swiss Mercantile School; University of Wisconsin, Madison (Bank Operation Manager). *Professional Organisations:* Swiss Society for Organisation (MbO); American Bankers Association (OM). *Recreations:* Squash, Swimming, Skiing.

HUDD, David Glyn Trefor; Head of Structured Finance, Paribas Limited, since 1990. *Career:* Linklaters & Paines, Articled Clerk/Assistant Solicitor 1981-85; Paribas Limited 1985-. *Biog:* b. 21 June 1958. *Nationality:* British. *Educ:* Gravesend Grammar School; Christ Church, Oxford (MA Hons). *Recreations:* Reading, Cinema, Travel.

HUDSON, (Anthony) Maxwell; Partner, Frere Cholmeley, since 1987; Corporate Finance, Financial Services. *Career:* Qualified as Solicitor 1980. *Biog:* b. 12 April 1955. *Nationality:* British. *Educ:* St Pauls School; New College, Oxford (Modern History). *Clubs:* United Oxford & Cambridge University Club. *Recreations:* Squash, Wine & Food.

HUDSON, Brian; Managing Director (Investment Management), Den Norske Bank plc.

HUDSON, D E C; Director, Lazard Brothers & Co Limited, since 1988; Managing Director, Venture Capital. *Career:* P & O Energy, Project Manager 1974-80; Bank of America NT & SA, Strategic Planning Europe, Middle East & Africa 1980-83. *Biog:* b. 5 June 1944. *Nationality:* British. *m.* 1970, Rosemary Juliet (née Chobb); 6 s. *Educ:* Westcliff, Essex; Birmingham University (BSc). *Directorships:* Development Capital Group Ltd 1986 (exec); Lazard Development Capital Ltd 1987 (exec); Lazard Venture Funds (Managers) Ltd 1990 (exec); Various Non-Executive Directorships of Investee Companies. *Professional Organisations:* ACMA. *Recreations:* Tennis, Shooting.

HUDSON, David Norman; Director and Principal Shareholder, Campbell Lutyens Hudson & Co Ltd, since 1990; Corporate Finance. *Career:* Kleinwort Benson Ltd, Corporate Finance Executive 1967-71; Drayton Corporation, Manager, Corporate Finance 1971-72; Director 1972-74; Samuel Montagu, Deputy Head, Corporate Finance 1974-77; Director, Head of International Banking 1978-81; Arlabank, Head of Merchant Banking 1981-84; James Capel & Co, Head of Corporate Finance 1984-87; Henry Ansbacher & Co Limited, Deputy Chairman & Chief Executive 1987-89. *Biog: b.* 29 May 1945. *Nationality:* British. *m.* 1967, Rosemary Mcmahon (née Turner); 1 s; 2 d. *Educ:* Marlborough College; Balliol College, Oxford (1st Class Hons Classical Mods & Greats). *Directorships:* Campbell Lutyens Hudson & Co Ltd 1990 (exec); Resources Capital Investments Limited 1989 (non-exec); Yellowhammer plc 1989 (non-exec); The Brooking School of Ballet 1978 (non-exec). *Recreations:* Natural History, Bridge, Opera.

HUDSON, G D; Partner, Allen & Overy, since 1974; Commercial Property, Recruitment Partner. *Career:* Allen & Overy, Articled Clerk 1967-69; Assistant Solicitor 1969-74. *Biog: b.* 8 November 1944. *Nationality:* British. m1 1969, Elizabeth Janet (née Wells) (diss 1974); m2 1976, Jane Bernice (née Hann) (diss 1986) 2 s; 1 steps. *Educ:* St Edwards School, Oxford; Exeter College, Oxford (MA Jurisprudence). *Other Activities:* General Commissioner of Taxes for City of London. *Professional Organisations:* Law Society. *Clubs:* MCC, Freeforesters CC, Beaconsfield Golf Club, BRSCC, PCGB. *Recreations:* Motor Racing, Cricket, Golf.

HUDSON, James; Client Services Director, BMP Business, since 1990; Provision of Resources to Enhance Clients Marketing & Advertising.

HUDSON, James J S; Commercial Litigation Partner, Bristows Cooke & Carpmael.

HUDSON, Jonathan Philip; Director, Barclays de Zoete Wedd Securities Ltd.

HUDSON, N J; Company Secretary, Sampo Insurance Company (UK) Limited.

HUDSON, Nigel R L; Senior Vice President, BSI - Banca della Svizzera Italiana.

HUDSON, Ms Patricia; Director, Samuel Montagu & Co Limited.

HUE WILLIAMS, Charles James; Managing Director, Kleinwort Benson Securities Ltd, since 1989; Marketmaking Worldwide, Kleinwort Benson Securities Worldwide. *Career:* Durlacher Oldham Mordaunt Godson & Co, Jobber 1961-70; Wedd Durlacher, Ptnr 1970-75; Managing Ptnr 1975-85. *Biog: b.* 28 September 1942. *Nationality:* British. *m.* 1964, Jocy; 1 s; 1 d. *Directorships:* Kleinwort Benson Ltd 1986 (exec); Kleinwort Benson Inc (New York) 1986 (exec); Kleinwort Benson Group plc 1989; Kleinwort Benson International Inc. *Clubs:* Royal St George's Golf (Sandwich), Berkshire Golf, New York Racquet & Tennis. *Recreations:* Golf, Cricket, Racquets, Lawn Tennis, Real Tennis.

HUET, Jean; UK General Manager, Société Générale.

HUFF, R C; Director, S G Warburg Akroyd Rowe & Pitman Mullens Securities Ltd.

HUGH-REES, J E; Non-Executive Director, Abbey National plc.

HUGH SMITH, Andrew Colin; Chairman, The International Stock Exchange, since 1988. *Career:* In Practice at the Bar 1956-60; Courtaulds Ltd, Exec 1960-68; Capel-Cure Carden/Capel-Cure Myers 1968-; Ptnr 1970-. *Biog: b.* 6 September 1931. *Nationality:* British. *m.* 1964, Venetia (née Flower); 2 s. *Educ:* Ampleforth College; Trinity College, Cambridge (BA). *Directorships:* ANZ Merchant Bank Ltd 1986 Dep Chm; Holland & Holland plc 1987 Chm; Billingsgate Securities plc 1986 (non-exec). *Other Activities:* Vice Chm, Council of Guide Dogs for the Blind Assoc. *Professional Organisations:* Member of Council, The International Stock Exchange. *Clubs:* Brooks's, Pratt's. *Recreations:* Shooting, Fishing, Gardening, Reading.

HUGH-SMITH, N G; Director, European Research, Hoare Govett Investment Research Ltd, since 1988; European Research, Market Strategy. *Career:* Hoare Govett, European Economist & Strategist 1987-88; Investors in Industry plc, Investment Controller 1985-87; Bank of England, Head of European Group; Head of African Group 1975-85. *Biog: b.* 29 January 1953. *Nationality:* British. *Directorships:* Hoare Govett Investment Research 1988 (exec).

HUGHES, A M; Deputy Chairman, York Trust Group plc.

HUGHES, Chris; Head of Cork Gully (Insolvency), Coopers & Lybrand Deloitte.

HUGHES, Christopher Wyndham; Partner, Wragge & Co, since 1970; Corporate and Commercial Law Soc Liaison and Chairman of Executive Committee. *Career:* Wragge & Co Articled Clerk 1964-66; Solicitor 1966-69. *Biog: b.* 22 November 1941. *Nationality:* British. *m.* 1966, Gail (née Ward); 3 s. *Educ:* Manchester Grammar School/King Edward's School, Birmingham; University College, London (LLB Hons). *Directorships:* Severn-Trent Water Authority 1982-84 (non-exec). *Other Activities:* Governor of the Schools of King Edward VI in Birmingham. *Professional Organisations:* The Law Society (Mem, Standards & Guidance and Council Membership Committees); Notary Public, The Provincial Notaries' Society (Member); Birmingham Law Society Council, President, 1989-90. *Recreations:* Travel, Theatre, The Arts, Old Buildings, Sport.

HUGHES, David Clewin; Partner, Arthur Andersen & Co, since 1987; Corporate Audit & Advice. *Biog: b.* 14 October 1953. *Nationality:* British. *m.* 1977, Rosanne

Margaret (née Graham); 3 d. *Educ:* Whitgift School; Hertford College, Oxford (MA). *Directorships:* Croydon & District Society of Chartered Accountants 1988-89 President; Young Vic Theatre, Board of Management 1988 (non-exec). *Professional Organisations:* FCA (Institute of Chartered Accountants). *Clubs:* OWA. *Recreations:* Gardening, Golf, Squash.

HUGHES, David John; Partner, Pinsent & Co, since 1987; Corporate, Corporate Finance, Banking. *Career:* Nabarro Nathanson, Asst Solicitor 1980-82; Slaughter and May, Asst Solicitor 1982-85; Pinsent & Co, Asst Solicitor 1985-87. *Biog:* b. 19 March 1955. *Nationality:* British. *m.* 1987, Linda Anne (née Hunt); 1 s; 1 d. *Educ:* Wolverhampton Grammar School; Jesus College, Oxford (MA). *Recreations:* Music, Theatre.

HUGHES, Derek John; Managing Director, The Nikko Bank (UK) plc, since 1988. *Career:* American Express Bank, London & New York 1963-71; European Co-ordinator for European Multinationals; Assistant Vice President (London); Scandinavian Bank Limited 1971-81; Deputy Managing Director; Managing Director & Dep Chief Executive, Business Development, Credit & Administration 1973; Samuel Montagu & Co Limited, Managing Director, Banking & Finance 1981-88; General Practice Corporation (Statutory Body) 1984-89; Deputy Chairman; Chairman 1987 until privatisation via primary legislation Health & Medicines Bill. *Biog:* b. 1 August 1932. *Nationality:* British. *m.* 1957, Angela Mary; 2 s. *Directorships:* The Nikko Bank (UK) plc 1988 (exec); The Nikko Securities Co (Europe) Limited 1988 Special Advisor to Board; Derek J Hughes Consultants Limited 1988 Chm; Midland Montagu Securities Limited Chm; Greenwell Montagu (Hong Kong) Chm. *Professional Organisations:* CAIB. *Clubs:* Overseas Bankers Club, Royal Automobile Club. *Recreations:* Sailing, Water Sports, Snow Skiing, Cycling.

HUGHES, Howard; Managing Partner, Price Waterhouse, since 1985. *Career:* Price Waterhouse 1960; Partner 1970; Member of Policy Committee 1979-; Director, London Office 1982-85; Managing Partner 1985-88; Joint Managing Partner Europe/Managing Partner UK 1988-; Member of World Board and World Management Committee 1989. *Biog:* b. 4 March 1938. *Nationality:* British. *m.* 1988, Christine (née Miles); 3 s; 1 d. *Educ:* Rydal School. *Directorships:* Auditor to Duchy of Cornwall 1983; Agricultural Wages Board 1990 Member. *Other Activities:* Council Member, Royal London Society for the Blind; The Worshipful Company of Chartered Accountants in England and Wales. *Clubs:* Carlton, Wildernesse Golf (Sevenoaks).

HUGHES, Hugh Llewellyn; Managing Director, Swiss Bank Corporation, since 1986. *Career:* Wedd Durlacher, Ptnr. *Biog:* b. 13 February 1952. *Nationality:* British. *m.* Brigitte (née Erb); 2 s. *Other Activities:*

Member, International Stock Exchange; Member, City Swiss Club; Freeman, City of London.

HUGHES, John; Group Financial Controller, Prudential Corporation plc.

HUGHES, Jonathan; Director, Crédit Suisse Buckmaster Securities.

HUGHES, M J; Director, J K Buckenham Limited.

HUGHES, M L; Director, Knight & Day Ltd.

HUGHES, Martin Charles Andrew; Partner, Clifford Chance, since 1980; Banking, Sovereign Debt Rescheduling.. *Biog:* b. 3 June 1948. *Nationality:* British. *m.* 1983, Eda (née Brown); 1 s; 2 d. *Educ:* Shrewsbury School; Sussex University (BA Hons). *Professional Organisations:* The Law Society; IBA. *Publications:* Robert Palache 'Loan Participation - some English Law Considerations', with IFL Rev, 1984; 'Transferability of Loans and Loans Participations', 1987; 1 JIBL, p5, 'Approches to Restructuring of Sovereign Debt' (Co-Author), 1984.

HUGHES, N; Partner, Nabarro Nathanson.

HUGHES, N B; Managing Director, (Market-Making), Hoare Govett International Securities.

HUGHES, Paul John; Director, C E Heath plc, since 1986; Group Finance Director. *Career:* Peat Marwick Mitchell, Articled Clerk-Snr 1970-74; C E Heath plc, Group Acct 1975-76; C E Heath & Co (Insurance Broking) Ltd, Chief Acct 1976-78; Finance Director 1978-. *Biog:* b. 25 September 1946. *Nationality:* British. *m.* 1974, Diana Mary (née Ballard); 1 s; 3 d. *Educ:* Swayne School, Rayleigh. *Directorships:* C E Heath plc; C E Heath & Co (Insurance Broking) Ltd; C E Heath (Broking Services) Ltd; The Heath Group; Hughes Aubrey & Partners Limited; C E Heath (IOM) Limited; Heath Nominees Limited; Heath Oil & Gas Limited; C E Heath Overseas Broking. *Professional Organisations:* FCCA; FCIS. *Clubs:* Essex Yacht Club. *Recreations:* Sailing, Gardening, Reading.

HUGHES, Richard S; Director, M & G Investment Management Ltd.

HUGHES, Robert Charles; Partner, Ernst & Young, since 1978; Corporate Advisory Services. *Career:* Ernst & Whinney (London) Student-Mgr 1970-78; Ptnr 1978-81; (Dubai, UAE) Ptnr 1981-86; (London) Ptnr 1986-. *Biog:* b. 20 January 1949. *Nationality:* British. *m.* 1973, Cindy (née Kirby-Turner); 3 d. *Educ:* Westminster School; Emmanuel College, Cambridge (MA Econ). *Professional Organisations:* FCA. *Clubs:* Sutton Tennis & Squash Club. *Recreations:* Golf, Cricket, Squash, Computing.

HUGHES, Terry Peter; Head of European Structured Finance, Continental Bank NA, since 1990; Debt Finance for Corporate Restructuring. *Biog: b.* 15 May 1964. *Educ:* St Mary's, Crosby; Hertford College, Oxford (MA Physics). *Recreations:* Art, Travel.

HUGHES, Timothy William; Director, Manning Beard Ltd, since 1989; Placing of Insurance or Reinsurance Business in Lloyd's. *Career:* Jewellery Wholesale Business to 1976; Self Employed, Jewellery Manufacturer & Sales 1976-78; W E Ginder (Diamond Ring Manufacturer), Area Sales Manager 1978-80; Manning Board, Various 1980-.

HUGHESDON, John Stephen; Partner, Neville Russell, since 1977; Audit Technical and General Practice, Speciality Areas - Lloyd's Syndicates, Insurance Broking, Solicitors, Schools, Charities. *Career:* Peat Marwick Mitchell To Asst Mgr 1962-73; Neville Russell Mgr 1973-76. *Biog: b.* 9 January 1944. *Nationality:* British. *m.* 1970, Mavis June (née Eburne); 1 s; 1 d. *Educ:* Eltham College. *Directorships:* The Girls' Brigade National Council for England & Wales 1979 Hon Treasurer (non-exec). *Other Activities:* Member, Guild of Freemen of the City of London. *Professional Organisations:* FCA; FRSA. *Clubs:* Bishopsgate Ward Club, City Livery Club. *Recreations:* Church, Family, Squash, Golf.

HUGHESDON, Michael C; Director, Leslie & Godwin, since 1990; Director, UK Retail Company. *Career:* C E Heath & Co Ltd 1958-60; Stewart Smith & Co Ltd (Stewart Wrightson & Co Ltd since 1973) 1960-80; Stewart Wrightson International Ltd, MD 1978-80; Leslie & Godwin Ltd 1980-. *Biog: b.* 11 August 1939. *Nationality:* British. *m.* 1967, Carole (née Murray Brown); 1 d. *Educ:* Charterhouse; Grenoble University (Foreign Students Diploma). *Directorships:* Leslie & Godwin Development Ltd; Leslie & Godwin International Ltd; Leslie & Godwin (UK) Ltd; Leslie & Godwin Personal Insurance Services Ltd Chm; W Fred Garner & Co Chm. *Other Activities:* Golf Commentator with BBC. *Clubs:* Sunningdale GC, MCC, Royal & Ancient Golf Club. *Recreations:* Golf, Fishing.

HUGI, Rob F; Associate Director, Mayer Brown & Platt.

HUI, K M; Director, Barclays de Zoete Wedd Securities Ltd.

HULBERT, Evelyn Gervase Carson; Chairman, Moore Stephens International, since 1989; Partner, Moore Stephens (London), since 1970. *Career:* Moore Stephens, Articled Clerk 1962-67; Moore Stephens, Butterfield (Bermuda) 1968-69; Moore Stephens (London), Partner 1970; Moore Stephens International, Chairman 1989. *Biog: b.* 1 April 1942. *Nationality:* British. *m.* 1968, Susannah (née Oliphant); 2 s. *Educ:* Winchester College; Institut Britannique Université de Paris. *Professional Organisations:* FCA. *Recreations:* Collecting Antiques, Pictures, Classic Cars.

HULETT, R M; Director, County NatWest Securities Limited.

HULL, Charles Joseph Malcolm; Purchasing Consultant & Pewter Manufacturer; Self-Employed. *Career:* Mars Ltd, Slough, Purchasing Manager, Engineering Equipment 1957-85; British Racing Motors, Bourne, Lincs, Purchasing Manager 1951-57; Parachute Regt 1946-48. *Biog: b.* 14 February 1928. *Nationality:* English. *m.* 1960, Oana Audrey (née Hodosh); 2 s; 1 d. *Educ:* Bloxham School (HNC). *Other Activities:* Worshipful Company of Pewterers, Court. *Professional Organisations:* RSA; City & Guilds, Insignia Award in Technology, Honoris Causa. *Publications:* The Techniques of Pewtersmithing, 1984. *Clubs:* Vintage Sports Car Club, The Pewter Society.

HULL, Edward Graham; Company Secretary, Ropner Insurance Services Ltd, since 1989. *Career:* Arbon Langrish & Co Ltd, Accountant 1953-66; Hinton Hill & Coles Ltd, Accountant 1966-82; Anthony Endersby Ltd, Director/Secretary 1982-88. *Biog: b.* 31 October 1936. *Nationality:* English. *m.* 1965, Shirley Kathleen (née Degge); 1 s; 1 d. *Educ:* Bec Grammar.

HULL, John Folliott Charles; Director, Legal & General Group plc, since 1979. *Biog: b.* 21 October 1925. *Nationality:* British. *Directorships:* Land Securities plc 1976 (non-exec) Chm; Goodwood Racecourse 1987 (non-exec); Lucas Industries plc 1975 (non-exec); Legal & General Group plc 1979; J Henry Schroder Wagg & Company Ltd -1985; Leadenhall Securities Corporation 1985; Legal & General Assurance Society Ltd 1976-80; Legal & General Investment Management (Holdings) Ltd 1980-83; Schroder International Ltd -1985; Schroders plc -1985; Schroder International Holdings Ltd -1985; Schroder Investment Company Ltd -1985.

HULL, John K; Partner, Wilde Sapte.

HULTON, Frederick William; Chief Executive and Managing Director, Hoare Govett Corporate Finance Ltd, since 1990; CF Advisory Services, Consolidation of M & A Activities. *Career:* Prudential-Bache Capital Funding, Chairman, European Corporate Finance 1985-90; Prudential-Bache Securities International, President 1983-85; Lehman Brothers Kuhn Loeb, New York, Managing Director, M & A Dept 1981-83; Lehman Brothers Kuhn Loeb Incorporated, London, Managing Director 1977-81. *Biog: b.* 3 August 1938. *Nationality:* British. *m.* 1973, Ruth; 2 s (twins). *Educ:* Mount St Mary's College, Sheffield; St John's College, Cambridge (BA Law and Economics, MA). *Other Activities:* Chairman, Appeal Committee, GAP Activity Projects (GAP) Ltd. *Professional Organisations:* Fellow, Institute of Chartered Accountants in England and Wales. *Clubs:*

Brooks's. *Recreations:* Sailing, Shooting, Skiing, Gardening.

HULTQUIST, Timothy Allen; Managing Director, Morgan Stanley International, since 1985; Head, London Office, since 1988. *Career:* The First National Bank of Chicago, Domestic Commercial Lending 1972-73; Admin Asst to Vice Chairman 1973-74; (London), Intl Asst 1974-75; (New York), Chief Forex Dealer 1976-79; (Chicago), VP & Forex Mgr 1979-82; Morgan Stanley & Co Inc, Principal, Head, Forex Worldwide 1982; MD, Forex 1985; Morgan Stanley International, MD, Head, London Office 1988-; Member, Mgmnt Ctee. *Biog: b.* 1 April 1950. *Nationality:* American. *m.* 1972, Cynthia (Cindy); 2 s; 1 d. *Educ:* Anoka Senior High School; Macalester College, USA (BA); University of Chicago (MBA). *Other Activities:* Trustee, Macalester College (Minnesota, USA); Mem, Securities Ctee, BMBA. *Clubs:* Westchester Hills Golf Club (USA), Winged Foot Golf Club (USA), Wentworth Golf Club. *Recreations:* Golf, Reading.

HUMAN, Henry Robin John; Partner, Linklaters & Paines, since 1969; Trusts Department. *Career:* Articled clerk (L & P) 1962-65; Assistant Solicitor (L & P) 1965-69. *Biog: b.* 5 October 1937. *Nationality:* British. *m.* 1961, Alison Phyllida (née Thompson); 1 s; 1 d. *Educ:* Repton School; Clare College, Cambridge (BA). *Directorships:* Member of the Board of Crown Agents for Overseas Governments and Administrations 1985 (non-exec). *Other Activities:* Liveryman, City of London Solicitors' Company. *Professional Organisations:* The Law Society. *Clubs:* MCC, Aldeburgh Golf Club. *Recreations:* Golf, Shooting.

HUMBLE, D R L; RD; Clerk, Woolmens' Company.

HUME, David John; Director, Stewart Ivory & Co Ltd.

HUME, Jeffrey; Group Treasurer, Hawker Siddeley Group plc, since 1988. *Career:* Clark Pixley & Co, Various 1972-78; Hawker Siddeley Group plc, Fin Exec 1978-83; Hawker Siddeley Rail Projects Ltd, Sec & Fin Controller 1980-85; Hawker Siddeley Intl Ltd, Commercial Mgr 1983-85; Brush Switchgear Ltd, Fin Dir 1985-88. *Biog: b.* 26 March 1953. *Nationality:* British. *m.* 1978, Jennifer May (née Good). *Educ:* Alleyns College, Dulwich. *Directorships:* Hawker Siddeley Finance Ltd; Hawker Siddeley Capital Corporation BV; Hawker Siddeley Finance (USA) Inc; Hawker Siddeley Power (USA) Inc; Hawker Siddeley Power I Inc; Hawker Siddeley Power II Inc; Peterborough Power Ltd; Corby Power Ltd. *Professional Organisations:* FCA.

HUME, John Edward; Partner, Titmuss Sainer & Webb, since 1973; Head of Litigation Department. *Career:* Titmuss Sainer & Webb 1970-. *Biog: b.* 22 September 1945. *Nationality:* British. *m.* 1973, Susan;

2 s. *Educ:* Cranleigh School. *Other Activities:* City of London Solicitors Company. *Professional Organisations:* Law Society. *Clubs:* RAC, Rosslyn Park Football Club, Jaguar Drivers Club, Roehampton Club. *Recreations:* Shooting, Motor Racing.

HUMM, R F; Staff Operations Director, Ford Motor Credit Company.

HUMPHREY, Anthony Robert; Partner, Allen & Overy, since 1981; Corporate Finance, Banking. *Biog: b.* 1951. *Nationality:* British. *m.* 1977, Ann Louise (née Wood). *Educ:* Douai School, Woolhampton; Durham University (BA Hons). *Other Activities:* City of London Solicitors' Company. *Professional Organisations:* The Law Society; International Bar Association. *Clubs:* RAC. *Recreations:* Numerous.

HUMPHREY, K B; Partner, Milne Ross, since 1986; Partner in Charge of Kingston Office. *Career:* Milne Ross 1976-. *Biog: b.* 26 August 1955. *Nationality:* British. *m.* 1979, Ingrid; 1 d. *Educ:* Buckinghamshire College of Further Education (HND Business Studies). *Directorships:* Milne Ross Associates Ltd 1989 (exec). *Professional Organisations:* ACA; Member, IOD (Founder Member of Kingston Area). *Clubs:* Surbiton Club. *Recreations:* Bird Watching.

HUMPHREYS, E C; Director, Dalgety plc.

HUMPHREYS, Sir Myles; Non-Executive Director, Abbey National plc.

HUMPHREYS, R G; General Manager, Field Operations, Leeds Permanent Building Society, since 1988; Branch & Area Operations, Optimising Profit Contribution, including Major Branch Refurbishment & Manpower Retraining Exercise. *Career:* N West Electricity, Project Mgr (Systems) 1968-74; Leeds Permanent, System & Programme Mgr 1974-78; Systems Procedures Mgr 1978-82; Asst Gen Mgr 1982-88; Gen Mgr, Field Operations 1988-. *Biog: b.* 13 February 1945. *Nationality:* British. *m.* 1968, Sheila; 1 s; 1 d. *Educ:* University of Manchester (BSc Electrical Engineering IIi Hons). *Clubs:* Scarcroft Golf Club. *Recreations:* Golf, Tennis, Jogging.

HUMPHREYS, T E; Director, Hambros Bank Limited.

HUMPHRIES, John Anthony Charles; OBE; Senior Partner, Travers Hill Braithwaite, since 1981; Property. *Career:* Served War RNVR 1943-46; Inland Waterways Association, Chm 1970-73; VP 1973-; Water Space Amenity Commission, Chm 1973-83; National Water Council Member 1973-83; Inland Waterways Amenity, Advisory Council Member 1971-; Environment Council, Vice Chm 1985-; Sports Council Member 1987-88; Southern Council for Sport & Recreation, Chm 1987-. *Biog: b.* 15 June 1925. *Nationality:* British. *m.* 1951, Olga

June (née Duckworth); 4 d. *Educ:* Fettes; Peterhouse, Cambridge (MA 1st). *Directorships:* Evans of Leeds 1982 Chm; Halifax Building Society (London Branch) 1985 (non-exec) Member. *Professional Organisations:* Member, The Law Society. *Clubs:* Naval & City. *Recreations:* Inland Waters, Gardening.

HUMPHRIES, S; London Branch Manager, Allstate Reinsurance Co Limited.

HUNKING, Arthur; Tax Partner, Arthur Andersen & Co, since 1980; Taxation & Business Aspects of Growing Companies including International Aspects. *Career:* Pilkington Brothers plc Trainee Acct 1963-64; Coopers & Lybrand, Articled Clerk 1967-70; Arthur Andersen 1970-. *Biog: b.* 25 February 1945. *Nationality:* British. *m.* 1979, Penny (née Wright); 1 s; 1 d. *Educ:* Hillfoot Hey High School; Hull University (BSc). *Professional Organisations:* FCA; FTII. *Recreations:* Photography.

HUNT, The Right Hon David J F; PC, MBE, MP; Secretary of State for Wales, since 1990. *Career:* Partner, Beachcroft Stanleys (& predecessor firms) 1968-; Minister for Local Government and Inner Cities 1989-90; Treasurer, HM Household 1987-89; Parliamentary Under-Secretary, Department of Energy 1984-87; Lord Commissioner of the Treasury 1983-84; Assistant Government Whip 1981-83; Parliamentary Private Secretary, Trade & Defence 1979-81; Opposition Spokesman on Shipping & Shipbuilding 1977-79; MP for Wirral 1976-83; MP for Wirral West 1983-. *Biog: b.* 21 May 1942. *Nationality:* British. *m.* 1973, Paddy (née Orchard); 2 s; 2 d. *Educ:* Liverpool College; Montpellier University; Bristol University (LLB); Guildford College of Law. *Professional Organisations:* Member, The Law Society. *Clubs:* Hurlingham.

HUNT, Dr Eric Millman; Clerk & Liveryman, Worshipful Company of Horners, since 1982. *Biog: m.* 1974, Phyllis Mary Charteris (née Burleigh); 2 s; 2 d. *Educ:* Marling School, Stroud; University of Leeds (BSc, PhD); University College, London (Postgraduate Diploma in Chemical Engineering). *Directorships:* Thomas Swan & Co Ltd, Durham 1982 (non-exec) Chm; Merton and Sutton District Health Authority 1990 (non-exec); Akzo Chemicals Ltd 1967-81 Chief Exec. *Other Activities:* Hon Treasurer and Past Chairman, The Plastics and Rubber Institute; Member of Court, University of Surrey. *Professional Organisations:* Fellow, Royal Society of Chemistry; Fellow, The Institution of Chemical Engineers; Fellow, The Plastics and Rubber Institute; Fellow, The Institute of Directors; Chartered Engineer.

HUNT, Franklin G; Resident Partner, London Office, Lord Day & Lord, Barrett Smith, since 1989; Shipping, Banking & Corporate Matters. *Career:* Lord Day & Lord and Lord Day & Lord, Barrett Smith, Partner 1965-; Lord, Day & Lord, Associate 1959-65. *Biog: b.* 21

December 1930. *Nationality:* American. *m.* 1958, Marilyn (née Maxfield); 2 d. *Educ:* Harvard University (AB, LLB). *Professional Organisations:* The New York Bar (admitted 1960); Maritime Law Association of the US; Association of the Bar of the City of New York; American Bar Association. *Publications:* Admiralty and Shipping Law in Survey of American Law, 1977, 1979, 1981, 1983; Ship Sale Contracts in Tulane Law Review, 1973. *Clubs:* India House. *Recreations:* Ballet, Skiing, Physics and Mathematics.

HUNT, Henry Holman; CBE; Deputy Chairman, Monopolies and Mergers Commission, since 1985. *Career:* Cadbury Bros, Mgmnt Trainee 1950-51; PA Management Consultants, Mgmnt Consultant 1952-57; Mgr, Office Organisation 1958-63; Dir, Computer Div 1964-69; Board Dir 1970-83; PA Computers & Telecommunications MD 1976-83; Monopolies & Mergers Commission Member 1980-. *Biog: b.* 13 May 1924. *Nationality:* British. *m.* 1954, Sonja (née Blom); 1 s; 2 d. *Educ:* Queen's Park School, Glasgow; Glasgow University (MA Hons Econ). *Professional Organisations:* FCMA, FIMC (Pres 1974-75), FBCS, FInstAM; Institute of Directors, FRSA. *Clubs:* Caledonian. *Recreations:* Music, Reading, Walking, Travel, Photography.

HUNT, John Joseph Benedict; The Lord Hunt of Tanworth; GCB; Chairman, Banque Nationale de Paris plc, since 1980. *Career:* RNVR 1940-46; Civil Service 1946-79; Secretary of the Cabinet 1973-79. *Biog: b.* 23 October 1919. *Nationality:* British. m1 1941, Hon Magdalen (née Robinson) decd. m2 1973, Lady Madeleine (née Charles); 2 s 1 d. *Educ:* Downside School; Magdalene College, Cambridge (BA Hons, Honorary Fellow). *Directorships:* Prudential Corporation plc 1980- (non-exec); Prudential Corporation plc 1985-90 Chairman; Tasler Publishing Co Ltd 1984- Chairman; Dirchley Foundation 1983- Chairman; IBM (UK) Ltd 1980-90; Unilever 1980-90 Advisory Director. *Recreations:* Gardening.

HUNT, John William Thomas; Vice President and General Manager, The Riggs National Bank of Washington DC, since 1990. *Career:* Horserace Totalisator Board 1960-70; Charles Fulton & Co, Broker 1970-77; Banco De Vizcaya, Dealer 1977-80; Hill Samuel, Dealer 1980-81; First National Bank of Maryland, Chief Dealer 1981-85; Swiss Volksbank, Treasurer 1985-86; First City National Bank of Houston, Senior Dealer 1986-87; Riggs Bank, Head of Treasury 1987-. *Biog: b.* 2 December 1942. *Nationality:* British. *m.* 1973, Margaret (née Watts); 1 s. *Educ:* Tiffins Boys School, Kingston. *Publications:* Foreign Exchange and Money Market Rates, 1983. *Clubs:* Overseas Bankers. *Recreations:* Bridge, Music.

HUNT, Maurice; Deputy Director-General, Confederation of British Industry. *Career:* ANZ Bank 1953-66; Joint Iron Council 1967; Board of Trade/DTI 1967-84;

CBI 1984-. *Biog: b.* 30 August 1936. *Nationality:* British. *m.* 1960, Jean (née Ellis); 1 s; 1 d. *Educ:* Selhurst Grammar School, Croydon; London School of Economics (BSc Econ). *Professional Organisations:* AIB.

HUNT, Michael John; Managing Director, Anthony Gibbs Financial Management Ltd, since 1984; Independent Financial Planning Consultants; Member, HongkongBank Group. *Career:* Scottish Widows Pensions Consultancy 1960-69; Anderson Finch Villiers (L & P) Ltd, MD 1970-76; Hartley Cooper/Gibbs Group 1977-. *Biog: b.* 21 September 1942. *Nationality:* British. *m.* 1967, Irene (née Saunders); 1 s; 1 d. *Educ:* Forest School, Snaresbrook. *Directorships:* Gibbs Hartley Cooper Ltd 1984; Antony Gibbs Benefit Consultants Ltd 1984. *Professional Organisations:* APMI. *Recreations:* Squash, Tennis.

HUNT, Timothy James; Company Secretary & Legal Coordinator, Ultramar plc. *Career:* Lawrence Messer & Co, Law Clerk 1964-66; City of London College, Part-Time Lecturer 1965-72; Freshfields, Corporate Lawyer 1966-69; Ultramar Company Limited, Solicitor & Legal Adviser 1970; Legal Coordinator 1973; Ultramar plc, Company Secretary 1982. *Biog: b.* 24 June 1941. *Nationality:* British. *m.* 1983, Sylvia (née Ball); 2 s. *Educ:* Catteral Hall & Giggleswick School; University of Bristol (Honours LLB); Guildford College of Law (Law Society Part II Qualifying Examination); Oxford University Business Summer School. *Directorships:* Ultramar Exploration Ltd 1986 (exec). *Professional Organisations:* The Law Society. *Clubs:* City of London Club, Royal Lymington Yacht Club, Ganton Golf Club. *Recreations:* Sailing, Golf.

HUNT, Verity Susan Stowell; Director, Kleinwort Benson Securities Limited.

HUNTER, A T F; Director/Compnay Secretary, Mase Westpac Ltd, since 1989.

HUNTER, Alex B de M; Finance Director, The Chartfield Group Ltd, since 1990. *Career:* Williams & Glyns Bank plc Chief Acct 1983-85; Royal Bank of Canada EMEA Fin Controller 1985-87; TSB England & Wales plc Fin Controller 1987-89. *Biog: b.* 28 July 1949. *Nationality:* British. *m.* 1976, Ruth (née Stocks); 1 d. *Professional Organisations:* FCA.

HUNTER, Colin; Group Treasurer, Blue Circle Industries plc.

HUNTER, D R; Partner, Cazenove & Co.

HUNTER, David; Director, 3i plc, since 1989. *Career:* Deloitte Haskin & Sells, Chartered Accountant 1976-82. *Biog: b.* 22 February 1955. *Nationality:* British. *m.* 1979, Wendy (née Tansey); 1 s. *Educ:* Brighton College; University College, London (BSc Hons Eco-

nomics). *Directorships:* 3i plc 1989. *Professional Organisations:* ACA (1980); FCA (1990). *Clubs:* RAC, Bosham Sailing Club. *Recreations:* Sailing, Skiing, Theatre.

HUNTER, David Ian; MBE; Chairman, Henry Cooke Lumsden plc, since 1972; Stockbroking. *Biog: b.* 13 November 1929. *Nationality:* British. *m.* 1954, Sybil (decd); 1 s; 3 d. *Educ:* Rugby School. *Directorships:* English National Investment Co plc 1953 (exec). *Professional Organisations:* The Stock Exchange. *Clubs:* St James's (Manchester), Sloane (London). *Recreations:* Gardening.

HUNTER, Ian William; Executive Director, Midland Montagu Asset Management, since 1987; Far Eastern Equities Investment Management. *Career:* Bank of England Economist 1974-78; Swiss Bank Corporation Investment Mgr 1979-80; Lazard Brothers Snr Investment Mgr, Unit Trust Comp 1981-87. *Biog: b.* 17 March 1955. *m.* 1986, Susan (née Morris). *Educ:* Alleyns School, Dulwich. *Professional Organisations:* ICSA; IMRO; ACCA. *Clubs:* AMOC.

HUNTER, James Martin Hugh; Partner, Freshfields, since 1967. *Career:* Freshfields Articled Clerk 1961-64; Asst Solicitor1964-67. *Biog: b.* 23 March 1937. *Nationality:* British. *m.* 1972, Linda Mary (née Gamble). *Educ:* Shrewsbury School; Pembroke College, Cambridge (MA). *Professional Organisations:* FCIArb; IBA; The Law Society. *Publications:* Law & Practice of Intl Commercial Arbitration (Co-Author), 1986; Arbitration Title, Butterworth's Encylopaedia of Firms & Precedents, (Editor). *Clubs:* Royal Cruising, Sunningdale Golf. *Recreations:* Cruising Under Sail, Golf.

HUNTER, John Stewart; Director, The British Linen Bank Ltd, since 1985; Corporate Finance. *Career:* Noble Grossart Ltd, Co Sec 1973-80; Advent Ltd, Co Sec 1981-84; The British Linen Bank Ltd Dir 1984-. *Biog: b.* 29 March 1948. *Nationality:* British. *m.* 1983, Fiona (née Henderson); 1 s; 1 d. *Educ:* Strathallan School; Edinburgh University (BCom). *Professional Organisations:* ICA (Scot).

HUNTER-JONES, S L; Director, Touche Remnant Investment Management Ltd.

HUNTINGTON, David C; Managing Director, Bradstock Blunt & Crawley Ltd.

HURCIK, Igor; Managing Director, Continental Bank NA, since 1990; Global Foreign Exchange/Global Options/Currency Asset Management. *Career:* Citibank Zurich, Asst Manager-FX 1975-79; Credit Swiss, Zurich, Asst Treasurers-FX 1979-82; Merrill Lynch Int Bank London, VP-FX 1982-85; New York, Director & Treasurer 1985-89; Merrill Lynch Capital Markets New York, Director 1987-90; Merrill Lynch Pierce Fenner Smith Ltd, London, Executive Director Global Swaps

1989-90. *Biog: b.* 20 November 1951. *Nationality:* Swiss. *m.* 1982, Susan Katherine (née Doscher); 1 s; 1 d. *Educ:* Gymnasium, Winterthur, Switzerland (MATURA); University of Zurich (Law & Economics).

HURDLEY, John R; Partner, Beachcroft Stanleys.

HURLEY, Terence Xavier; Managing Director, Merrill Lynch Europe Ltd, since 1989; Managing Director - Equity Trading - Europe. *Career:* Weeden & Co, Mgr 1962-74; Chicago Board of Trade, Trader 1974-79. *Biog: b.* 3 August 1934. *m.* 1956, Marjorie (née Edmondson); 2 s; 1 d. *Educ:* St George High School, Evanston, Illinois; University of Montana, USA (BSc). *Other Activities:* Co-Chair, Nat Sec Traders Intl Committee; Co-Chair, Nat Sec Traders' Exch Committee. *Professional Organisations:* International Stock Exchange; Chairman, Dealers Assoc; Chairman, National Security Traders Assoc (Board of Governors). *Clubs:* Hadley Wood Golf Club.

HURN, F R; Non-Executive Director, S G Warburg Group plc.

HURN, Stanley Noel; Director, Samuel Montagu & Co Limited; Head of Banking Syndicate - Loan Syndication. *Career:* Orion Royal Bank, Assoc Director Loan Syndication & Eurocurrency Lending 1978-83; Standard Chartered Bank 1968-78. *Biog: b.* 24 December 1943. *Nationality:* British. *Educ:* Royal Grammar School, Colchester; University of Hull (BSc Econ). *Directorships:* Samuel Montagu & Co Limited 1984 (exec). *Professional Organisations:* Associate of The Chartered Institute of Bankers. *Publications:* Syndicated Loans, 1990; Numerous Articles in Various Publications. *Clubs:* Overseas Bankers Club.

HURN CONSTABLE, Group Captain John; Secondary & Undersheriff & High Bailiff of Southwark, Corporation of London.

HURST, Alexander Allan; Vice Chairman & Joint Managing Director, Ogilvy Adams & Rinehart Ltd, since 1990; Corporate & Financial Communications. *Career:* British European Airways, Trainee/Marketing Projects 1966-69; Horniblow Cox-Freeman & de Uphaugh, Account Supervisor 1970-72; Wasey Campbell-Ewald, Account Director 1973-76; Foster Turner & Benson, Director/MD 1976-86; Ogilvy & Mather Focus, Vice Chm & Chief Exec 1986-90. *Biog: b.* 13 March 1945. *m.* 1990, Carmel (née McCarthy). *Educ:* Haberdashers' Aske's, Elstree; Gonville & Caius College, Cambridge (MA). *Professional Organisations:* MIPA; DMS; GInst Mktg. *Clubs:* RAC. *Recreations:* Travel, Opera, Badminton, Chess.

HURST, Andrew L T; Partner, Walker Morris Scott Turnbull.

HURST, P A; Director, Charles Stanley Corporate Finance Ltd.

HURST-BROWN, Christopher Nigel; Director, Mercury Asset Management Group plc, since 1990; Europe and Middle East; Joint Chairman, Warburg Asset Management. *Career:* Hill Samuel Investment Management Ltd, Director 1983-86; Lloyds Merchant Bank Ltd, Managing Director 1986-90; Lloyds Investment Managers Ltd, Chairman. *Biog: b.* 11 July 1951. *Nationality:* British. *m.* 1976, Candida Madelaine (née Drabble); 2 d. *Educ:* Wellington College; Bristol University (BSc Economics & Accountancy). *Professional Organisations:* FCA. *Clubs:* Berkshire Golf Club. *Recreations:* Golf, Tennis, Fishing, Shooting.

HUSBAND, John; City Editor, Daily Mirror.

HUSSEY, M W; Deputy Chairman, R H M Outhwaite (Underwriting Agencies) Limited.

HUTCHESON, K; Partner, Nabarro Nathanson.

HUTCHINSON, A; Partner, Titmuss Sainer & Webb, since 1990; Property Development. *Biog: b.* 8 March 1961. *Nationality:* British. *m.* 1985, Helen Natalie; 2 d. *Professional Organisations:* Law Society.

HUTCHINSON, John; Retail Operation Director, Nationwide Anglia Building Society. *Career:* Lloyds Bank plc, Various Posts 1960-75; Branch Manager 1975-78; Project Manager, O & M 1978-80; Project Manager, Planning & Marketing 1980-82; Deputy to General Manager, Black Horse Agencies 1982-84; Divisional Manager, UK Retail Banking 1984-87; Head, Personal Banking 1987-89; General Manager, Support and Development 1989-90. *Biog: b.* 8 August 1944. *Nationality:* British. *m.* 1967, Elspeth; 1 d. *Educ:* King Charles I Grammar School, Kidderminster; Harvard Business School (Training Courses); Cabinet Office (Top Management Programme). *Directorships:* Nationwide Anglia Trust 1990 (exec); Nationwide Anglia Independent Financial Services 1990 (exec). *Professional Organisations:* Fellow, Chartered Institute of Bankers; Fellow, British Institute of Management. *Recreations:* Skiing, Walking, Swimming.

HUTCHINSON, Michael; Managing Director, Yamaichi International (Europe) Limited, since 1990; Investment Banking Dept. *Career:* First Chicago 1980-82; Citicorp 1982-84; Samuel Montagu & Co 1984-86. *Biog: b.* 16 October 1950. *Nationality:* British. *m.* 1986, Lucinda (née Hamilton); 1 s; 1 d. *Educ:* Monkton Combe School; Queens' College, Cambridge (MA); INSEAD (MBA). *Recreations:* Active Sports.

HUTCHINSON, Michael John; Managing Director, Metallgesellschaft Ltd.

HUTCHISON, Thomas Oliver; Director, ICI plc.

HUTTON, Anthony Charles; Under Secretary, Department of Trade & Industry, since 1990; Head of Personnel Management Division. *Career:* Dept of Trade, Prin Private Sec to Sec of State 1974-77; Asst Sec CRE 5 1977-79; DTI, Asst Sec MSM 1979-80; Dept of Trade, Asst Sec Marine Div 1980-82; DTI, Asst Sec PEP 1982-84; Under Sec OT2 1984-87; Under Sec EEP 1987-90. *Biog: b.* 4 April 1941. *Nationality:* British. *m.* 1963, Sara (née Flemming); 2 s; 1 d. *Educ:* Brentwood School; Trinity College, Oxford (MA). *Clubs:* Athenaeum.

HUTTON, C N; Partner, Hammond Sutton.

HUTTON, G S; Director, Morgan Grenfell & Co Ltd, since 1989; Corporate Banking Department. *Career:* Bank of America NT & SA 1981-83; Morgan Grenfell 1983-. *Biog: b.* 27 March 1958. *Nationality:* British. *m.* 1982, Amanda Jane (née Giles); 2 s. *Educ:* Emmanuel College, Cambridge (MA 1st Class Hons History); St Stephen's House, Oxford (MA 1st Class Hons Theology). *Recreations:* Opera, Theatre, Reading, Art & Architecture, Wine.

HUTTON, H Robin; Director General, British Merchant Banking & Securities Houses Association, since 1988; Merchant Banking & Securities Industry. *Career:* Finance Corp for Industry, Asst Gen Mgr 1956-62; Hambros Bank Ltd, Dir 1962-70; HM Government, Special Adviser 1970-73; Commission of European Communities, Dir of Fin Institutions 1973-78; S G Warburg & Co Ltd, Exec Dir 1978-82; Accepting Houses Committee, Dir Gen 1982-87; Issuing Houses Association, Dir Gen 1984-88. *Directorships:* Northern Rock Building Society 1986 (non-exec); Investment Management Regulatory Organisation 1986 (non-exec).

HUTTON, William Nicholas; Economics Editor, The Guardian, since 1990; Economics. *Career:* The European Business Channel, Editor 1988-90; BBC Newsnight, Economics Correspondant 1983-88; Director BBC, 'The Money Programme', Producer 1981-83; Financial World Tonight, BBC Radio 4, Senior Producer 1978-81; INSEAD, MBA 1977-78; Phillips & Drew (Stockbrokers), Investment Analyst & Institutional Account Executive 1971-77. *Biog: b.* 21 May 1950. *Nationality:* British. *m.* 1978, Jane Anne Elizabeth (née Atkinson); 2 d. *Educ:* Chislehurst & Sidcup GS; Bristol University (Upper Second Economics & Sociology); INSEAD (MBA). *Professional Organisations:* NUJ. *Publications:* The Revolution That Never Was, 1986; Various Articles and Pamphlets. *Recreations:* Family, Cycling, Tennis, Skiing, Reading, Writing.

HYATT, Peter Robin; Group Partner, Neville Russell, since 1986; Audit & Financial Advice. *Career:* Coopers & Lybrand (London, Northampton, Tehran) 1964-80; Group Mgr in London 1977-80; Neville Russell Technical Mgr 1980-81; Snr Mgr 1981-82; Audit Ptnr 1983-. *Biog: b.* 12 May 1947. *Nationality:* British; m2 1988 Jennifer (née Taylor); 1 s; 1 d (by previous marriage). *Educ:* Cheltenham College. *Professional Organisations:* FCA. *Recreations:* Squash, Golf.

HYLAND Jr, Thomas F; Senior Vice President, Manufacturers Hanover Trust Company.

HYMAN, H; Head of Corporate Finance, Europe, Price Waterhouse, since 1990; Corporate Finance (including Privatisation) for all European Countries. *Career:* Director of Privatisation Services, HM Treasury (on Secondment) Specialist 1987-90; Advisor, Privatisations 1984-87. *Biog: b.* 23 October 1949. *Nationality:* British. *m.* 1972, Anne Moira; 2 s; 1 d. *Educ:* Bedales School, Hampshire; Manchester University (BA Hons). *Professional Organisations:* FCA. *Publications:* The Implications of Privatisation for Nationalised Industries, 1987; Articles in Journals. *Clubs:* Reform, MCC. *Recreations:* Walking, Classical Music, Cricket, Gardening.

HYMAN, Norman; Director in Charge of Dealing, Henry Cooke Lumsden plc, since 1984. *Biog: b.* 24 January 1947. *Nationality:* British. *m.* 1969, Jill (née Simons); 2 s. *Professional Organisations:* Member, International Stock Exchange.

HYPHER, David Charles; Executive Director, MIM Ltd, since 1982; Head of Fixed Interest & Currency Section. *Career:* Various Stockbroking Companies Convertible & Gilt Specialist 1958-82; Britannia Arrow Group Fixed Interest Specialist 1982. *Biog: b.* 24 July 1941. *Nationality:* British. *m.* 1978, Pamela (née Craddock); 2 d. *Educ:* Brooklands College, Weybridge. *Directorships:* MIM Britannia Unit Trust Management Ltd 1983 (non-exec). *Professional Organisations:* AMSIA.

I

IBBETT, W G; Director, Wellington Underwriting Agencies Limited.

IBBS, Sir Robin; KBE; Deputy Chairman, Lloyds Bank plc, since 1988. *Career:* ICI plc 1952-88; ICI plc, Executive Director 1976-80 & 1982-1988; Seconded to Cabinet Office as Head of Central Policy Review Staff 1980-82; Adviser (part-time) to the Prime Minister on Efficiency & Effectiveness in Government 1983-88; Lloyds Bank plc, Non-Executive Director 1985-. *Biog: b.* 21 April 1926. *Nationality:* British. *m.* 1952, Iris Barbara (née Hall); 1 d. *Educ:* Trinity College, Cambridge University (MA Mechanical Sciences). *Other Activities:* Chairman of Council, University College, London. *Professional Organisations:* Barrister-at-Law; Graduate, Institution of Mechanical Engineers. *Clubs:* United Oxford & Cambridge Universities Club.

IBETT, W G; Director, A P Leslie Underwriting Agencies Limited.

IDILBY, Z H; Chairman & Chief Executive, Aitken Hume International plc, since 1990.

IIJIMA, Mikio; President & Managing Director, Nomura Asset Management (International) Ltd.

IKEDA, Nobuhiko; Deputy General Manager, The Mitsui Trust and Banking Co Ltd, since 1988; Treasury & General Affairs. *Career:* Mitsui Trust and Banking Co Ltd 1968-. *Biog: b.* 8 April 1945. *Nationality:* Japanese. *m.* 1972, Setsuko (née Hayashi); 1 s; 2 d. *Educ:* Hibaya High School Tokyo; Hitotsubashi University, Tokyo (BCom). *Recreations:* Reading, Golf, Tennis.

IKIN, R J; Director, Wendover Underwriting Agency Limited.

ILES, Ronald Alfred; Chairman, Alexander Howden Group Limited, since 1981; General Management, Re-insurance Broking. *Career:* Alexander Howden Group Limited 1957-. *Biog: b.* 16 December 1935. *m.* 1960, Pat (née Hayes); 2 d. *Educ:* Raines Foundation Grammar School. *Directorships:* Alexander & Alexander Services Inc 1985 Snr VP; Various Overseas Subsidiaries of Alexander Howden. *Other Activities:* Member, Lloyd's. *Professional Organisations:* FCII; Corporation of Insurance Brokers (Associate).

ILEY, Dr R; Group Managing Director, Cookson Group.

ILIC, Milomir; Manager, UK Rep Office, Jugobanka United Bank.

ILKSON, Atilla S; Manager, Law & Compliance Department, Merrill Lynch Europe Limited, since 1987. *Career:* US Securities and Exchange Commission, Special Counsel, Division of Market Regulation 1974-77; Real Estate Syndication Institute, Legislative Counsel 1977-79; New York Stock Exchange, Attorney, Market Surveillance Division 1979-80; Merrill Lynch International Inc, Attorney 1981-86. *Biog: b.* 13 October 1949. *Nationality:* American. *m.* 1980, Ann; 1 d. *Educ:* New York University (BA); University of Florida (Juris Doctor). *Professional Organisations:* Mem, Florida Bar; Mem, District of Columbia Bar; Mem, US Supreme Court Bar.

ILLION, Peter J L; Partner, Beachcroft Stanleys, since 1981; IT. *Career:* Eucs & Co, Solicitors (Zambia), Articled Clerk 1956-59; Asst Solicitor 1959-63; Partner 1963-69; International Life Insurance Society, (London), Asst Solicitor 1970-73; Linklaters & Paines (London), Asst Solicitor 1974-79; Beachcroft Stanleys (London), Associate 1980; Partner 1981-. *Biog: b.* 27 October 1935. *Nationality:* British. *Educ:* Michaelhouse, Natal, RSA (Matriculator); University of Witwatersrand (1st Year BA); University of Cambridge (MA). *Professional Organisations:* Solicitor; Member, Law Society. *Recreations:* Computing, Reading, Socialising.

ILLSLEY, John Edward; Managing Director, Cater Allen Securities Ltd.

IMAIZUMI, Yokichi; Managing Director, The Nikko Bank (UK) plc.

IMAMURA, M; Deputy Managing Director, LTCB International Limited.

IMESON, Stuart; Investment Manager, West Yorkshire Superannuation Fund, since 1985. *Career:* West Yorkshire Metropolitan County Council, Group Accountant 1979-83; Principal Accountant 1983-85. *Biog: b.* 11 May 1947. *Nationality:* British. *m.* 1968, June (née Beaumont); 2 d. *Educ:* Ossett Grammar School; Open University (BA). *Professional Organisations:* CIPFA. *Recreations:* Family Interests, Swimming.

IMISON, C; Assistant General Manager (Finance), C & G Guardian.

INAGAKI, Masao; Chairman, The Nikko Securities Co (Europe) Ltd, since 1990; Overall responsibility for Europe Group. *Career:* The Nikko Securities Co Ltd 1962-; The Nikko Securities Co (Europe) Ltd, Director of Underwriting 1978-80; The Nikko Securities Deutschland GmbH, Managing Director 1980-85; The Nikko Securities Co Ltd (Tokyo), General Manager, International Finance Division 1985-86; The Nikko Securities Co (Europe) Ltd, Managing Director & Chief Executive Officer 1986-90; The Nikko Securities Co Ltd, Chairman & Chief Operating Officer Europe Group. *Biog: b.* 27 November 1938. *Nationality:* Japanese. *m.* 1967, Keiko; 1 s; 2 d. *Educ:* Kobe University of Commerce (BA Economics). *Directorships:* The Nikko Securities Co Ltd 1990; The Nikko Bank (UK) Ltd 1990. *Other Activities:* Member of Council, International Stock Exchange of the UK & The Republic of Ireland, 1990-. *Clubs:* RAC. *Recreations:* Golf, Music.

INCE, C E; Partner, Lawrence Graham.

INDACO, Thomas; Director, Dean Witter Capital Markets International Ltd.

INFANTE, Dr Neri Roberto; Representative, Unibanco-Uniao de Bancos Brasileiros SA, since 1982; Overseas Commercial Bank. *Career:* Banca Nazionale del Lavoro, Various 1957-80; (London) Dep Mgr 1980-82. *Biog: b.* 18 June 1938. *Nationality:* Italian. *m.* 1967, Diane Thérèse (née Granfield); 1 s. *Educ:* Lycee Chateaubriand, Rome; Rome University; Perugia University (Economics). *Other Activities:* CAV (Italian Decoration); Rotary Club of Kew Gardens (Past Pres). *Professional Organisations:* Foreign Bankers' Assoc; Anglo-Brazilian Society; Brazilian Chamber of Commerce Councillor; Italian Chamber of Commerce. *Clubs:* Overseas Bankers', Rotary (Kew Gardens), Effingham Golf Club, Acqua Santa Golf Club (Rome). *Recreations:* Golf, Gardening, Theatre, Music.

ING, Brian; Partner, Clark Whitehill.

INGHAM, Graham; Economics Correspondent, BBC TV.

INGHAM, M L; Director, United Dominions Trust Ltd, since 1985; Business Planning & Development. *Career:* Shell UK Oil, Account Manager, Sales of Industrial Products 1975-78; Lucas Ingredients Ltd, Marketing Manager Flavours Division, Development of New Division 1978-82; Fardem Ltd, Marketing Manager, Marketing & Business Planning 1982-85.

INGHAM CLARK, Robert James (Jamie); O St J; Finance Director, Quill Underwriting Agency Ltd, since 1988; Responsible for all Area's of Finance Function. *Career:* Ernst & Whinney, Contracted Student 1980-86; Chandler Hargreaves Ltd, Financial Accountant, Group Consolidation and Monthly Reporting, also Group

Company Secretary 1987-88. *Biog: b.* 1 December 1959. *Nationality:* British. *m.* 1986, Celia Louise (née Parsons). *Educ:* Harrow School. *Directorships:* Quill Services Ltd 1989 (exec). *Other Activities:* Liveryman, Clothworkers Company. *Professional Organisations:* ACA. *Clubs:* Buck's, MCC, HAC. *Recreations:* Music, Shooting.

INGLEBY, John Mungo; Managing Director, James Finlay Bank Ltd.

INGLIS, Andrew G D; Partner (Birmingham), Evershed Wells & Hind.

INGLIS, George Bruton; Senior Partner, Slaughter and May, since 1986; Company and Commercial Law. *Career:* Slaughter and May Ptnr 1966-. *Biog: b.* 19 April 1933. *m.* 1968, Patricia Mary (née Forbes); 3 s. *Educ:* Winchester College; Pembroke College, Oxford (MA). *Professional Organisations:* The Law Society. *Recreations:* Gardening.

INGLIS, Hamish Macfarlane; Non-Executive Director, Scottish Equitable Life Assurance Society, since 1973. *Career:* Lorimers Brewery Ltd (Subsidiary of Vaux Breweries Ltd), Managing Director 1963-79. *Biog: b.* 1931. *Nationality:* British. *m.* 1958, Lyndsay (née Laidlaw). *Educ:* The Edinburgh Academy. *Directorships:* Watson & Philip plc 1981 (exec). *Professional Organisations:* Member, Institute of Chartered Accountants of Scotland. *Clubs:* The Honourable Company of Edinburgh Golfers. *Recreations:* Golf, Shooting.

INGLIS, Ian Brownlie; Partner, Shepherd & Wedderburn WS, since 1968; Corporate Law & Insolvency Law. *Career:* The Royal Bank of Scotland, Apprentice/Clerk/Apprentice Solicitor 1957-66; Shepherd & Wedderburn WS, Apprentice Solicitor 1966-67; Asst Solicitor 1967-68. *Biog: b.* 6 February 1941. *Nationality:* British. *m.* 1965, Eleanor (née Taylor); 2 d. *Educ:* Lanark Grammar School; University of Edinburgh (LLB). *Professional Organisations:* AIB (Scot); The Law Society of Scotland; The Society of Writers to HM Signet. *Clubs:* New Club (Edinburgh). *Recreations:* Golf.

INGLIS, James Craufuird Roger; *Career:* Dundas & Wilson CS, Ptnr 1953-73; Ivory & Sime, Ptnr 1973-75; Shepherd & Wedderburn WS, Ptnr 1976-89. *Biog: b.* 21 June 1925. *Nationality:* British. *m.* 1952, Phoebe Aeonie (née Murray-Buchanan); 2 s; 4 d. *Educ:* Winchester College; Magdalene College, Cambridge (BA); Edinburgh University (LLB). *Directorships:* British Assets Trust plc 1957 (non-exec); European Assets Trust NV (Netherlands) 1972 (non-exec); Investors Capital Trust plc 1985 (non-exec); The Royal Bank of Scotland plc 1967-89 (non-exec); The Royal Bank of Scotland Group plc 1985-90 (non-exec); Scottish Provident Institution 1962 (non-exec); Selective Assets Trusts plc 1988 (non-exec); Ivory & Sime Optimon Income Trust plc 1989 (non-exec). *Professional Organisations:* Writer to the Signet. *Clubs:* Army & Navy, New (Edinburgh), Hon Company of Edinburgh Golfers, Royal & Ancient Golf Club. *Recreations:* Golf.

INGLIS, Kenneth W B; Chief Executive, Allied Dunbar Asset Management plc, since 1990. *Career:* Scottish Provident Institution, Investment Manager - 1983; UBS Phillips & Drew, Head of Research 1983-90.

INGLIS, William R H; Partner, Touche Ross & Co, since 1987; Forensic Accounting. *Career:* Student Accountant (Spicer & Pegler) 1977-80; Audit Senior (Spicer & Pegler) 1980-82; Manager (Spicer & Pegler) 1982-87; Seconded to HM Treasury 1987-89; Partner, Forensic Accounting 1989-. *Biog: b.* 11 January 1956. *Nationality:* British. *m.* 1983, Alison (née Hepburn); 2 d. *Educ:* Fettes College; Magdalene College, Cambridge (MA Law). *Professional Organisations:* ACA. *Clubs:* MCC. *Recreations:* Skiing, Real Tennis, Squash, Golf.

INGMIRE, David Richard Bonner; Partner, Neville Russell, since 1975; Corporate Taxation - Insurance and General. *Career:* Robson Rhodes, Trainee Acct 1962-65. *Biog: b.* 29 September 1940; 2 s. *Educ:* Chatham House; King's College, London (BA History). *Other Activities:* Worshipful Company of Glaziers & Painters of Glass; King's College, London (Associate). *Professional Organisations:* FCA; ATII. *Publications:* Tax Planning for Companies; Numerous Magazine Articles. *Recreations:* Golf.

INGRAM, Martin Alexander; Managing Director, Brown Shipley Stockbroking, since 1988. *Career:* Hambros Bank, Fund Manager 1968-72; Montagu Loebl Stanley & Co, Partner, Institutional Broking 1972-75; Heseltine Moss & Co Partner, Research & Corp Finance 1976-88. *Biog: b.* 1 July 1945. *Nationality:* British. *m.* 1970, Amanda (née Lockhart); 1 s; 1 d. *Educ:* Charterhouse; Kings College, London University (LLB Hons). *Professional Organisations:* Member, International Stock Excahnge; AMSIA. *Clubs:* Brook's. *Recreations:* Painting.

INGRAMS, Leonard Victor; OBE; Director, Robert Fleming Holdings Ltd, since 1985. *Career:* Baring Bros, Manager 1967-70; London Multinational Bank, Manager 1970-73; Baring Bros, Manager 1973-74; Managing Director 1975-81; Saudi Arabian Monetary Agency, Senior Adviser 1974-79; Chief Adviser 1981-84. *Biog: b.* 1 February 1941. *Nationality:* British. *m.* 1964, Rosalind (née Moore); 1 s; 3 d. *Educ:* Corpus Christi College, Oxford (MA, BLitt). *Directorships:* Robert Fleming & Co Ltd 1986; Robert Fleming International; Investment Management Ltd 1988; Pacific Growth Fund 1985; Transworld Bond Trust 1986; Equimark Ltd 1989; Equitalia Ltd 1990; Fleming European Warrant Fund 1990 Chm.

INKESTER, Andrew Peter; Partner, Turner Kenneth Brown, since 1985; Company/Commercial Partner. *Career:* Turner Kenneth Brown Articled Clerk 1978-80; Asst Solicitor 1980-85. *Biog: b.* 23 June 1957. *m.* 1986, Kathryn Lilian (née Drucker); 1 d. *Educ:* St Margaret's High School, Liverpool; King's College, London (LLB). *Other Activities:* City of London Solicitors' Company; American Chamber of Commerce. *Professional Organisations:* The Law Society; ATII; IBA. *Publications:* Comparative Study in Force Majeure (Co-Author of Section on English Law). *Recreations:* Photography, Aircraft, Travel.

INMAN, Simon Randall; Partner, Hammond Suddards, since 1985; Corporate Law. *Career:* A V Hammond & Co, Articled Clerk 1979-81; Asst Solicitor 1981-85. *Biog: b.* 2 August 1956. *Nationality:* British. *m.* 1984, Kathleen Marie (née McGowan); 1 d. *Educ:* Haileybury College; Leicester University (LLB Hons). *Professional Organisations:* The Law Society.

INNES, Duncan John Faraday; Partner, Richards Butler, since 1989; Corporate Finance. *Career:* Admitted as Solicitor (England 1980, Hong Kong 1982); Richards Butler 1988-. *Biog: Nationality:* British. *Educ:* Merchant Taylors' School; Magdalene College, Cambridge (MA Law Cantab 2:1). *Other Activities:* Member, City of London Solicitors Company. *Professional Organisations:* Member, Law Society. *Clubs:* Lansdowne, Highgate. *Recreations:* Golf, Shooting, Fishing, Tennis, Photography.

INNES, M; Executive Director, BMP Business.

INNES, M E A; Director, S G Warburg & Co Ltd, since 1990; Financing/Leasing. *Career:* British Railways Board (London Midland Region), Accountancy 1968-71; Corporate Finance/Treasury Management 1971-79; The Royal Bank of Scotland, Asset Financing 1979-86; S G Warburg & Co Ltd, Financing/Leasing 1986-90. *Biog: b.* 25 February 1946. *Nationality:* British. *m.* 1970, Marion (née Pearson); 2 s. *Educ:* City of London College (ACCA); Open University (BA). *Directorships:* British Railways Board 1972 (exec); Royal Bank Leasing Ltd 1982 (exec); S G Warburg & Co (Leasing) Ltd 1986 (exec); S G Warburg & Co Ltd 1990 (exec). *Professional Organisations:* Fellow, Chartered Association of Certified Accountants. *Recreations:* Sailing.

INNES, Richard H R; Partner, Walker Morris Scott Turnbull.

INNES, W; Partner, Ashurst Morris Crisp.

INNESS, A Paul A; Partner, Dennis Murphy, Campbell & Co.

INNS, David George; Financial Director, Bass plc, since 1986; Group Finance, Treasury, Insurance &

Computer Services. *Career:* Charrington, Dep CA 1963-66; Bass (Ireland), Fin Dir 1967-70; Bass (North), Fin Dir 1971-76; Co Dir 1976-79; Bass Mitchells & Butler, Fin Dir 1979-83; Bass plc, Fin Controller/Dir of Fin 1983-86.

INOSAKI, Takeshi; Executive Director, Bond Trading, Yamaichi International (Europe) Limited.

INSLEY, Ian A E; Partner, S J Berwin & Co.

INWARDS, Michael Anthony; Director, Philips Electronics & Associated Industries Ltd, since 1989; Finance & Administration. *Career:* Philips Electronic & Associated Industries, Director of Admin 1975-77; Philips (Spain), Director of Fin & Admin 1977-80; Gispert SA (Spain), Chief Executive Officer 1980-82; Philips (Pakistan), Chief Executive Officer 1982-84; Philips Components International (Netherlands), Managing Director, Fin and Admin 1984-89. *Biog: b.* 24 May 1939. *Nationality:* British. *m.* 1960, Dorothy Ann (née Robertson); 2 s; 1 d. *Educ:* Chigwell School. *Directorships:* Philips Elec & Assoc Ind 1989 (exec); Philips UK Ltd 1989 (exec); Philips Pension Trustees Ltd 1989 (exec); SPIN UK Ltd 1989 (exec); BYPS Communications Ltd 1990 (exec); DZB Systems Co Ltd 1990 (exec); Band Three Holdings Ltd 1989 (exec). *Other Activities:* Member, Sandilands Committee, 1973-74. *Professional Organisations:* FCA. *Clubs:* Foxhills Country Club.

IOANNIDES, C C; Director & General Manager, Bank of Cyprus (London) Ltd.

IRBY, Alton; Managing Director, J O Hambro Magan, since 1988. *Career:* US Marine Corps, Captain 1962-65; A F Irby & Company, President 1965-72; F S James & Co, Director & Executive Vice President 1972-; W'Oham Poland Holdings, Chairman 1982-85; Sedgwick Group, Director 1985-88; Sedgwick Ltd, Deputy Chairman 1985-88. *Biog: b.* 3 August 1940. *Nationality:* American. *m.* 1982, Pamela; 1 s; 2 d. *Educ:* Georgia Institute of Technology (BS Industrial Management). *Directorships:* Centaur Communications 1989 (non-exec); Input Ltd 1985 (non-exec); City Capital 1986 (non-exec); HBO & Company 1990 (non-exec). *Clubs:* Bucks, River Club NY, Prachtere Golf Club, Sunningdale, Piedmont Driving Club, Capital City Club.

IRBY, Charles Leonard Anthony; Director, Baring Brothers & Co Ltd, since 1985; Corporate Finance. *Career:* Binder Hamlyn & Co 1965-69; Joseph Sebag & Co 1971-74; Baring Exec 1974-75; Baring Brothers (Asia) Dir/Asst Dir/Mgr 1976-79; Baring Brothers Mgr 1980-81; Asst Dir 1982-84. *Biog: b.* 5 June 1945. *m.* 1971, Sarah Jane (née Sutherland); 1 s; 1 d. *Educ:* Eton College. *Professional Organisations:* FCA. *Clubs:* City of London. *Recreations:* Travel.

IRELAND, Adrian William Velleman; Director, Warburg Securities, since 1986. *Biog: b.* 1 March 1945. *m.* 1975, Victoria Jane (née Cooper); 2 s. *Educ:* Stowe School. *Clubs:* Boodle's, MCC, City of London. *Recreations:* Reading, Travel.

IRELAND, N C; Director, BTR plc.

IRELAND, P A; General Manager (Legal/Secretarial), Yorkshire Building Society.

IRVINE, Norman M; General Manager, Management Service Division, The Royal Bank of Scotland plc.

IRVING, Mrs A M; Clerk, Tin Plate Workers Alias Wireworkers' Company.

IRWIN, G H F; Director, Kleinwort Benson Limited.

ISAACS, Anthony Hyman; Senior Partner, Stephenson Harwood, since 1987. *Career:* Stephenson Harwood 1957-64; Ptnr 1964-. *Biog: b.* 9 August 1934. *Nationality:* British. *m.* 1964, Jennifer (née Cameron); 3 s; 2 d. *Educ:* Cheltenham College; Pembroke College, Cambridge (BA Hons). *Directorships:* Thornton & Co Ltd 1985 (non-exec); The Peper Harow Foundation (Charity) 1983 Council. *Other Activities:* Coopted Member, Company Law Committee of The Law Society; Member, Solicitors Disciplinary Tribunal. *Professional Organisations:* Law Society. *Clubs:* Garrick.

ISAACS, J E; Partner, Hill Taylor Dickinson.

ISHERWOOD, Patrick; Partner (Litigation), Frere Cholmeley.

ISHIDA, Masakazu; Executive Director, Japanese Equity Sales, Yamaichi International (Europe) Limited.

ISHIKAWA, Hirokazu; Managing Director and Chief Executive, Mitsui Taiyo Kobe International Limited.

ISHIKAWA, Motoji; Executive Director, Japanese Corporate Investment Services, Yamaichi International (Europe) Limited.

ISSAIAS, T J; Director, James Capel Gilts Ltd.

ITO, K; General Manager, The Saitama Bank Ltd, since 1989. *Career:* Saitama Bank, Clerk 1966-72; Asst Manager, Foreign Dept 1972-75; Manager, London Branch 1975-79; Senior Manager, International Dept 1979-82; Deputy General Manager, Osaka Branch 1982-83; General Manager, Katsushika Branch 1984-86; Chief Manager, Secretariat Division 1986-88; Senior Deputy General Manager, Int Planning Dept 1988-89; General Manager, London Branch 1989-.

ITO, Shigeichi; Managing Director, Yamaichi International (Europe) Ltd; Japanese Corporate Investment Services. *Career:* Yamaichi Securities Co Ltd, Kumamoto Branch, Branch Manager 1981-84; Yamaichi Securities Co Ltd, Head Office, Financial Institution Division, General Manager 1984-89; Yamaichi International (Europe) Ltd, Managing Director 1989-. *Biog: b.* 10 May 1936. *Nationality:* Japanese. *m.* 1964, Hiroko; 1 s; 1 d. *Educ:* Kyushu University (Economics). *Recreations:* Golf, Travel.

IVES, D; Director, Hill Samuel Investment Management Ltd.

IVES, Francis Robert; Partner, Cyril Sweett and Partners.

IVES, S; Partner, Touche Ross & Co, since 1985; Audit & Consultancy on Computer Hardware & Software Companies and Construction Property Development Companies. *Career:* Coopers & Lybrand, Computer Audit Specialist 1972-76; Binder Hamlyn, Partner 1976-85. *Biog: b.* 8 September 1949. *Nationality:* British. *m.* 1974, Sharon (née Lawton); 2 s. *Educ:* The Headlands School, Wiltshire. *Professional Organisations:* Chartered Accountant. *Clubs:* RAC Club. *Recreations:* Shooting, Vintage Cars, Gardening, Photography.

IVEY, R; Head of Direct Marketing, Leeds Permanent Building Society.

IVISON, Andrew Selwyn; Partner, McKenna & Co, since 1987; Banking and Finance. *Career:* McKenna & Co, Articled Clerk 1978-80; Asst Solicitor 1980-83; Asst Solicitor, Bahrain 1983-85; Overseas Ptnr, Bahrain 1985; Asst Solicitor 1986. *Biog: b.* 11 July 1956. *Nationality:* British. *m.* 1980, Anne Janet (née Lambert); 2 d. *Educ:* Bolton School; Pembroke College, Cambridge (MA). *Professional Organisations:* The Law Society. *Recreations:* Squash, Swimming.

IVORY, Ian Eric; Director, Stewart Ivory & Company Ltd, since 1985; Investment Management. *Career:* Ivory & Sime, Ptnr/Dir 1969-81; Ivory & Co, Ptnr 1981-85; Stewart Ivory & Co, Dir 1985-. *Biog: b.* 8 April 1944. *m.* 1971, Joanna Mary (née Marshall); 2 s. *Educ:* Eton College. *Professional Organisations:* CA. *Recreations:* Farming, The Arts.

IVORY, James; Director, Stewart Ivory & Co Ltd.

IVORY, Leon; Chief Executive, Arbuthnot Latham Bank Ltd. *Career:* Broadlands Ltd MD 1976-86; NZI Securities Western Ltd Chief Exec 1986-88. *Biog: b.* 30 May 1948. *Nationality:* New Zealander. *m.* 1987, Gwenny (née Haanappel); 2 s. *Directorships:* Western Capital Ltd 1985; Auspharm International Ltd 1986; Cortecs Ltd 1989; ALI Finance Ltd 1989. *Professional*

Organisations: Fellow, Australian Institute of Management. *Recreations:* Reading, Sailing.

IWAMOTO, M; Joint General Manager, The Dai-Ichi Kangyo Bank Ltd.

IWASAKI, M; Managing Director, Fuji International Finance Limited, since 1988; Investment Banking. *Career:* The Fuji Bank, Japan 1965-74; Fuji Bank & Trust Co, New York 1974-82; Fuji Bank, Head Office, Tokyo, Japan 1982-87. *Biog: b.* 16 November 1941. *Nationality:* Japanese. *m.* Yoshiko; 1 s; 2 d. *Educ:* Kansei Gakuin University, Japan.

IWASE, Masao; Deputy General Manager Administration, The Sumitomo Bank Limited.

J

JACK, Professor Robert Barr; CBE; Senior Partner, McGrigor Donald, since 1990; Company, Banking & Insolvency Law. *Career:* Brownlee plc, Timber Merchants, Glasgow, Director 1974-86; Chm 1984-86; Scottish Law Commission 1974-77; Scottish Observer on DoT's Insolvency, Law Review Ctee 1977-82; Council of the Securities Industry, Lay Member 1983-85; The International Stock Exchange, Lay Member of Council 1984-86; McGrigor Donald, Partner 1957-; Joint Senior Partner 1987-90. *Biog: b.* 18 March 1928. *Nationality:* British. *m.* 1958, Anna Thorburn (née Thomson); 2 s. *Educ:* Kilsyth Academy and Glasgow High School; Glasgow University (MA, LLB). *Directorships:* The Securities Association 1987 Independent Member of Board; Scottish Metropolitan Property plc 1980 (non-exec); Joseph Dunn (Bottlers) Ltd 1983 (non-exec) Chm; Bank of Scotland 1985 (non-exec); The Scottish Mutual Assurance Society 1987 (non-exec). *Other Activities:* Professor of Mercantile Law, Glasgow University; Chm of Review Ctee on Banking Services Law (1987-88); UK Member, Panel of Arbitrators - International Centre for Settlement of Investment Disputes (ICSID) 1990-; Chairman, The Turnberry Trust 1983-; President, Scottish National Union of YMCAs 1983-; Member, Board of Governors, Beatson Institute for Cancer Research, 1989-. *Professional Organisations:* The Law Society of Scotland. *Publications:* Articles on Company Law, Statutory Regulation & Self Regulation of the City and Insolvency and Floating Charges and Receivership under the Law of Scotland. *Clubs:* Caledonian, Western (Glasgow), Pollok Golf Club. *Recreations:* Golf, Football (Director of Clyde Football Club).

JACK, W H; Assistant General Manager (UK), General Accident Fire Life Assurance.

JACKMAN, D; Trading Director, Sogemin Metals Ltd.

JACKMAN, M C J; Chairman, Hiram Walker-Allied Vintners. *Biog: b.* 7 November 1935. *Nationality:* British. *m.* 1965, Valerie; 1 s; 1 d. *Directorships:* Allied-Lyons plc Vice Chm.

JACKSON, A B S; Director, S G Warburg & Co Ltd.

JACKSON, Mrs A L; Clerk, Chartered Surveyors' Company.

JACKSON, A R; Director, BTR plc.

JACKSON, Alan Francis; Marine Underwriter and Deputy Chairman, Wren Underwriting Agencies Ltd. *Career:* JH Minet & Co Ltd 1955-58; Working in Insurance in Canada 1958-62; Robert Bradford (Underwriting) Ltd 1962-78; Alan Jackson (underwriting Agencies) Ltd(merged with Wren Underwriting Agencies Ltd, 1986) 1979-. *Biog: b.* 25 April 1935. *Nationality:* British. *m.* Jean Elizabeth; 1 d. *Educ:* Westminster School. *Directorships:* Wren Holdings Ltd; Alan Jackson (Underwriting Agencies) Ltd; Joseph W Hobbs & Co Ltd; Robt Badford (Underwriting) Ltd; E R H Hill (Agencies) Ltd; Anjak Ltd. *Other Activities:* Member of The Council, Lloyd's 1987-; Deputy Chairman, Lloyds 1990; Freeman, Goldsmiths Company. *Professional Organisations:* FIIC; ACII. *Recreations:* Golf.

JACKSON, Christopher Leslie Willan; Director, Charterhouse Tilney, since 1986; Research in Retail Sector. *Career:* Charles W Jones & Co, Partner 1966-75; Tilney & Co, Partner 1975-86. *Biog: b.* 24 June 1939. *Nationality:* British. *m.* 1966, Jane Leslie (née Dee); 3 s; 1 d. *Educ:* Marlborough College; Caius College, Cambridge (MA). *Clubs:* Boodles, Fly Fishermans. *Recreations:* Bridge, Shooting, Fishing.

JACKSON, Clive; Director, Merrill Lynch International Limited.

JACKSON, Geoffrey Keith; General Manager (Field Operations), Halifax Building Society, since 1987; Retail Financial Operations. *Career:* Halifax Building Society, Assistant Regional Manager (London) 1980-82; London City Manager 1982-85; Regional General Manager (London) 1985-89. *Biog: b.* 12 January 1943. *Nationality:* British. *m.* 1966, Shirley; 2 d. *Directorships:* Halifax Estate Agency Ltd 1987 (non-exec); Halifax North Estate Agencies 1987 (non-exec); Cartwright Holt Ltd 1989 (non-exec); Building Societies Ombudsman Co Ltd 1989 (non-exec). *Other Activities:* Member of Building Societies Ombudsman Council. *Professional Organisations:* FCIS; FCBSI; DMS. *Clubs:* RAC, Oriental. *Recreations:* Cricket, Squash.

JACKSON, Gordon A; Head of Company/Commercial Department, Taylor Joynson Garrett, since 1989; Corporate Finance, International Business Law. *Career:* Bartletts de Reya, Partner 1980-88; Taylor Garrett, Partner 1988-. *Biog: b.* 25 March 1952. *Nationality:* British. *m.* 1975, Susan; 2 s; 1 d. *Educ:* Newcastle University (LLB). *Professional Organisations:* Law Society;

American Bar Association. *Recreations:* Steam Boating, Fell Walking, Photography.

JACKSON, Ian; Partner, Clifford Chance, since 1987. *Career:* Clifford Turner Partner 1959-87.

JACKSON, J P; Clerk, Farmers' Company.

JACKSON, John B H; Director, Ladbroke Group plc. *Biog:* b. 26 May 1929. *Nationality:* British. *m.* 1984, Rowena; 1 s; 2 d. *Educ:* Kings School, Canterbury; Queens' College, Cambridge (BA, LLB); Barrister at Law, Inner Temple. *Directorships:* Cambridge Electronic Industries plc Chairman; Cambridge Animation Systems Ltd 1990; Celltech Group plc Chairman; Cicada Productions Ltd; Direct Broadcasting Ltd (dormant) Chairman; Duphar Limited Deputy Chairman; History Today Ltd Chairman; History Today Productions Ltd; The Hulton Deutsch Collection Ltd 1988; John Jackson Consultants Ltd 1989; Ladbroke Group plc; National Enterprise Board; National Research & Development Corporation; National Interactive Video Centre 1989 Chairman; Peboc Ltd Chairman; Philips Electronic & Associated Industries Ltd; S W Wood Group plc 1990 Chairman; Television for the Environment Ltd Chairman; Terence Piper Co Ltd; Xenova Limited 1990 Chairman; Argent Television Ltd to 1986; Cabletel Communications Ltd to 1989; Central Independent Television plc to 1987; Context Television Ltd to 1984; Daytime Television Ltd to 1983; Molinare Visions plc to 1989; Quorum Computers Ltd to 1985; Sky Television plc to 1989; Zenith Productions Ltd to 1987.

JACKSON, L St J T; Partner, Slaughter and May.

JACKSON, Leslie Irwin; Partner, Theodore Goddard, since 1983; Corporate Finance. *Career:* Arthur Young Audit, Mgmnt Consultant 1971-72; Frere Cholmeley, Articled Clerk 1975-77. *Biog:* b. 7 July 1946. *m.* 1969, Dawn; 1 s; 2 d. *Educ:* King Edward VII School, Johannesburg; University of Witwatersrand, Johannesburg (BComm); Keble College, Oxford (MA); Columbia University (MBA). *Recreations:* Tennis, Squash, Cricket.

JACKSON, Michael Edward Wilson; Group Main Board Director, The Guidehouse Group plc, since 1983; Corporate Finance, Acquisitions and Subsidiary Company Management. *Career:* Coopers & Lybrand, Auditor 1976-79; AM International Ltd European Controller 1976-79; Itek International Inc Marketing Director 1979-83. *Biog:* b. 16 March 1950. *Nationality:* British. *Educ:* The Leys School, Cambridge; Cambridge University (MA). *Directorships:* Sage Group plc 1983 (nonexec); TSL plc 1985 (non-exec). *Professional Organisations:* FCA. *Clubs:* Vanderbilt Tennis, Richmond Hockey Club. *Recreations:* Tennis, Hockey.

JACKSON, Peter G; Partner (Resident in Jersey), Theodore Goddard.

JACKSON, R B; General Manager(Information Systems), Yorkshire Building Society, since 1987; IT. *Career:* Yorkshire Building Society, Deputy General Manager (IS) 1986-87; Assistant General Manager (IS) 1985-86; Information Systems Manager 1984-85; Midshires Building Society, Data Processing Manager 1974-83. *Biog:* b. 5 June 1951. *Nationality:* British. *m.* 1973, Lesley (née Denholm); 1 s; 1 d. *Educ:* Royal Grammar School, Newcastle-upon-Tyne; University of Essex (BA Hons Economics); University of Bradford (MBA). *Professional Organisations:* Fellow, Chartered Building Societies Institute.

JACKSON, R W; Director, Charterhouse Tilney.

JACKSON, Raymond; Partner, Linklaters & Paines.

JACKSON, T J; Associate, Grimley J R Eve.

JACOB, Andrew B; Partner, Neville Russell.

JACOBS, Howard Robert; Partner, Slaughter and May.

JACOBS, Paul Granville; Partner, Clifford Chance, since 1987; Property Law. *Career:* Clifford-Turner, Partner 1974-87. *Biog:* b. 15 February 1946. *Nationality:* British. *Educ:* The Leys School, Cambridge; Exeter University (LLB Hons). *Other Activities:* City of London Solicitors Company. *Clubs:* RAC. *Recreations:* Horse Racing, The Arts.

JACOBS, Stephen; Director, Financial Dynamics Limited.

JACOBSON, Phillip R; Partner, Stoy Hayward.

JACOMB, Anthony Keith Richard; Director, Charterhouse Tilney.

JACOMB, Sir Martin Wakefield; Kt; Chairman, Barclays de Zoete Wedd, since 1985. *Biog:* b. 11 November 1929. *Nationality:* British. *m.* Evelyn Helen; 2 s; 1 d. *Educ:* Eton; Worcester College, Oxford. *Directorships:* Bank of England 1986; Barclays Bank plc 1985 Dep Chm; Barclays de Zoete Wedd Holdings Ltd 1986 Chm; Barclays de Zoete Wedd International Holdings Ltd 1986 Chm; Barclays de Zoete Wedd Limited 1986 Chm; Barclays de Zoete Wedd Securities Limited 1986 Chm; Barclays de Zoete Wedd Government Securities Inc (USA) 1987; Barclays plc 1985 Dep Chm; Commercial Union Assurance Company plc 1984 Dep Chm; Commercial Union plc 1990; Daily Telegraph plc 1986; Ebbgate Holdings Limited 1987; Royal Opera House, Convent Garden Ltd 1987; The RTZ Corporation plc 1988; Kleinwort Benson Limited 1968-

85; Kleinwort Benson (Trustees) Limited 1971-85; Kleinwort Benson Lonsdale plc 1974-85; Kleinwort Benson Investment Trust Ltd 1974-84; Kleinwort Benson Investment Management Ltd 1977-84; Kleinwort Benson Inc 1977-85 President; Kleinwort Benson (North America) Corp 1981-85; Hudson's Bay Company 1971-86; Hudson's Bay Trustees Ltd 1971-86; Hudson's Bay Company Ltd 1971-86; Beavor House Ltd 1971-86; The Merchants Trust plc 1974-85; The Bankers' Clearing House Ltd 1987 Alternate; Mercantile Credit Company Ltd 1973-84; John Mowlem & Company 1969-79; Montagu Boston Investment Trust plc 1975-84; Harley Mullion & Co Ltd 1977-85; Christian Salvesen Ltd 1974-88; Transatlantic Fund Ind 1978-85 Chairman; British Gas Corporation 1981-88; Securities & Investments Board 1985-87; Barint Jersey Limited 1985-87; Member, European Advisory Board to Touche Remnant & Co 1982-87; City Capital Markets Committee 1980-83 Chairman; CSI Dep Chairman. *Other Activities:* External Member of the Finance Committee, Delegacy of the Oxford University Press, 1971; Trustee, National Heritage Memorial Fund, 1982; Honorary Bencher, Inner Temple, 1987; Member of the Steering Committee, Intl Capital Markets Advisory Committee, Federal Reserve Bank, 1987; Member of Committee, British Merchant Banking & Securities Houses Association, 1988, Chairman, 1989; Member of Advisory Board, CEDEL SA Luxembourg Centrale de Livraison de Valeures Mobilieres SA, 1988; Vice President, British Bankers Association, 1989. *Recreations:* Tennis, Family, Bridge, Theatre.

JAGD, Bo; General Manager, Den Danske Bank, since 1990; London Branch. *Career:* Copenhagen Handelsbank 1959-77; Nordic Bank plc London, Associate Director 1977-80; Nordic Bank plc Singapore Branch, General Manager 1980-83; Copenhagen Handelsbank, Assistant General Manager 1983-87; Managing Director 1987-90. *Biog:* b. 11 March 1943. *Nationality:* Danish. *m.* Kate; 2 d. *Educ:* Copenhagen Business School (HD).

JAGELMAN, Rodney James; Partner, Bacon & Woodrow, since 1980; Pensions. *Career:* Bacon & Woodrow 1972-. *Biog:* b. 15 August 1951. *Nationality:* British. *m.* Susan (née Bateman); 2 s; 1 d. *Educ:* Tiffin School; Emmanuel College, Cambridge (MA). *Other Activities:* Institute of Actuaries Board of Examiners (1986-1990); North Herts Conservative Association (Vice-Chairman 1989-); National Association of Pension Funds, Eastern Region (Treasurer 1990-). *Professional Organisations:* FIA.

JAGO, Hugh B G G; Director, Continental Reinsurance London.

JAHN, Juergen; Senior Manager, Commerzbank AG.

JALVING, David L; Director, Merrill Lynch Europe Limited.

JAMBON, Jacques; Assistant General Manager, Administration, Crédit Lyonnais.

JAMES, A M; General Manager, Allied Trust Bank Ltd, since 1989; Commercial & Corporate Banking, Marketing & Sales Strategies; Credit Sanctioning & Control; Business & Profit-Planning. *Career:* Chase Manhattan, Internal Audit 1972-73; Manufacturers Hanover, Internal Audit 1973-74; Bank of Montreal, Various Sales & Credit Functions Culminating in Manager, Credit 1974-85; Bank of British Columbia, Senior Manager, Credit 1985-86; Allied Trust Bank, Senior Manager to General Manager, Commercial Banking 1986-. *Biog:* b. 23 September 1949. *Nationality:* British. *m.* 1978, Veronica (née Neve); 2 d. *Educ:* Tottenham Grammar School; Colfe's Grammar School, London; Liverpool Polytechnic (BA General Arts Course). *Directorships:* Allied Trust Bank 1990 (exec). *Clubs:* Bexley Tennis Club.

JAMES, Dr Anthony Trafford; CBE; Director, Wellcome Foundation plc, since 1985; R and D. *Career:* Unilever Research Laboratory, Head of Division of Biosciences 1970-85. *Biog:* b. 6 March 1922. *Nationality:* British. m1 1945, Olga (decd). m2 1983, Linda; 3 s 1 d. *Educ:* University College School; University College, London (BSc); Harvard (PhD); University of Dijon, France (Honorary DSc); Cranfield Institute of Technology (Honorary DSc). *Directorships:* Rothampstead Research Laboratory 1990 (non-exec) Member of Board of Management. *Other Activities:* Member, Council of Royal Society. *Professional Organisations:* Honorary Member, Biochemical Society; Fellow, Royal Society; Fellow, Institute of Biology. *Publications:* Methods of Biochemical Analysis (with L J Morris), 1966; Liquid Biochemistry (with M Garr), 1971. *Recreations:* Fishing, Gardening.

JAMES, C G; Director, Hoare Govett Corporate Finance Limited, since 1978. *Career:* IBM, Sales Trainee 1968-69; Hoare Govett, Inv Analyst 1969-72; Hoare Govett (Far East) Ltd, Head of Research 1972-78. *Educ:* Epsom College; Southampton University (BSc Econ & Stats). *Recreations:* Skiing, Tennis, Golf, Sailing, Eating.

JAMES, Christopher; Partner, Linklaters & Paines.

JAMES, Christopher John; Senior Partner, Martineau Johnson, since 1989; Corporate Law. *Career:* Johnson & Co, Partner 1965-85; Senior Partner 1985-87; Martineau Johnson, Deputy Senior Partner 1987-89. *Biog:* b. 20 March 1932. *Nationality:* British. *m.* 1958, Elizabeth (née Thomson); 1 s; 1 d. *Educ:* Clifton College; Magdalene College, Cambridge (MA). *Directorships:* Birmingham Midshires Building Society (then Birmingham B S) 1980 (non-exec); 1988 Dep Chm.

Professional Organisations: Law Society. *Clubs:* The Birmingham Club, Little Aston Golf Club.

JAMES, Glen William; Partner, Slaughter and May, since 1983; Company & Commercial Law. *Biog: b.* 22 August 1952. *Nationality:* British. *m.* 1987, Amanda (née Dorrell). *Educ:* King's College School, Wimbledon; New College, Oxford (MA). *Other Activities:* City of London Solicitors' Company. *Professional Organisations:* The Law Society. *Publications:* Contributor to: A Practitioner's Guide to the Stock Exchange Yellow Book; Mergers & Acquisitions: The Complete Guide to Principles & Practice. *Clubs:* RAC. *Recreations:* Reading, Golf, Squash, Swimming, Tennis, Piano, Music.

JAMES, Mrs Helen (née Shaw); Partner, Clay & Partners, since 1977; Company Pension Schemes. *Career:* Equity & Law Actuarial Student 1972-74; Clay & Partners 1975-. *Biog: b.* 29 March 1951. *Nationality:* British. *m.* 1976, Allan; 1 s; 2 d. *Educ:* Harrytown High School; Cheadle Hulme School; Girton College, Cambridge (MA 1st Mathematics). *Other Activities:* Assoc of Consulting Actuaries (Ctee). *Professional Organisations:* FIA. *Recreations:* Walking, Activities with the Children.

JAMES, Ian; Managing Director, Fleet Communications Ltd, since 1971. *Career:* British Aircraft Corporation, Aerodynamist 1951-60; Financial Times, Editorial Asst 1960-61; Henry Greenwood, Dep Ed 1961-62; Fountain Press, Exec Ed 1962-65; Brook-Hart Ruder & Finn International, PR Exec 1965; 3M, Chief PR 1965-67; Diamond Publishing, Editorial Dir 1967-70. *Biog: b.* 3 April 1936. *m.* 1954, Marion (née Best); 1 s; 3 d. *Educ:* Brooklands College. *Publications:* Photography Year Books, 1963, 1964, 1965. *Clubs:* Vintage Sports Car Club, Bentley Drivers' Club. *Recreations:* Fine Wine Consumption.

JAMES, John Nigel Courtenay; Executive Trustee, The Grosvenor Estate.

JAMES, N R; Partner, Cameron Markby Hewitt.

JAMES, Paul; Consultancy Partner, BDO Binder Hamlyn, since 1989; Director of Financial Management Consulting. *Career:* Deloitte Haskins & Sells 1975-81; Tarmac plc 1981-83; European Ferries plc 1983-84; Coopers & Lybrand 1984-87; BDO Binder Hamlyn 1987-. *Biog: b.* 30 January 1954. *Nationality:* British. *Educ:* University of Wales, Cardiff (BSc). *Directorships:* BDO Consulting 1988 (exec). *Professional Organisations:* ACA. *Recreations:* Squash, Church, Gardening, Skiing.

JAMES, Dr Peter Charles; Chief Executive, Panmure Gordon Bankers Ltd, since 1987. *Career:* OECD (Paris), Economist 1968-73; North Carolina National Bank, General Manager 1973-78; Panmure Gordon Bankers Ltd, Managing Director 1978-85. *Biog: b.* 15 January 1943. *Nationality:* British. *m.* 1971, Vivien (née Ball);

1 s; 2 d. *Educ:* St Joseph's Academy; Magdalen College, Oxford (MA); University College, London (PhD); University of London (BSc Econ). *Clubs:* Hurlingham.

JAMES, Richard Baker; Partner, Ashurst Morris Crisp.

JAMES, Rodney Derek; Chairman, Roy James & Co.

JAMES, S E V; Director, Foreign & Colonial Management Ltd.

JAMES, Stephen Lawrence; Senior Partner, Simmons & Simmons, since 1980; Company/Commercial. *Career:* Simmons & Simmons Articled Clerk 1957-59; Solicitor 1959-61; Partner 1961-80. *Biog: b.* 19 October 1930. *Nationality:* British. *m.* (div); 2 s; 2 d. *Educ:* Clifton College, Bristol; St Catharine's College, Cambridge (BA History & Law). *Directorships:* Horace Clarkson plc 1975 (non-exec). *Other Activities:* Member of The Worshipful Company of Glaziers (1964). *Clubs:* Royal Yacht Squadron, Royal Thames Yacht, Royal Ocean Racing, Royal Lymington Yacht Club. *Recreations:* Yachting, Gardening.

JAMES, Stuart Cambell; Partner, Rowe & Maw, since 1977; Financial Services, Pensions. *Biog: b.* 3 March 1944; 1 s. *Directorships:* Pulford Winstone & Tennant Ltd (non-exec); Reliance Mutual Insurance Society Ltd; Reliance Unit Managers Ltd. *Professional Organisations:* FPMI.

JAMES, William Stirling; Director, Hill Samuel Bank Ltd, since 1980; Swaps/Syndications. *Career:* Morgan Grenfell & Co, Graduate Trainee 1964-65; Touche Ross & Co (London) 1965-68; (New York) 1968-69; Hill Samuel & Co Ltd 1969-. *Biog: b.* 20 November 1941. *Nationality:* British. *Educ:* Stonyhurst College; Magdalene College, Cambridge (MA). *Other Activities:* External Member, Lloyd's; Farmer. *Professional Organisations:* FCA. *Clubs:* Boodle's, Pratt's, Annabel's. *Recreations:* Shooting, Bridge.

JAMESON-TILL, Michael Anthony; Director, Clive Discount Company Ltd, since 1979; Marketing. *Career:* Hogg Bullimor & Co 1963-67; Butler Till Ltd 1967-70; Clive Discount 1970-74; International Discount Co Ltd, Gen Mgr 1974-78. *Biog: b.* 30 May 1944. *Nationality:* British. *m.* 1971, Rachel Clare (née Stevenson); 1 s; 1 d. *Educ:* Eton College. *Directorships:* Clive Discount Holdings Intl Ltd 1983 (non-exec). *Recreations:* Tennis, Sailing.

JAMIESON, Andrew T; Finance & Compliance Director, Panmure Gordon & Co Limited, since 1986. *Biog: m.* 1 s; 1 d. *Educ:* Edinburgh University (BSc Hons). *Directorships:* Panmure Gordon Bankers Ltd 1987 (exec). *Other Activities:* Company of Actuaries. *Professional Organisations:* Faculty of Actuaries.

JAMIESON, Bill; Deputy City Editor, The Sunday Telegraph.

JAMIESON, Ian; Director (Market-Making), Hoare Govett International Securities.

JAMIESON, Peter; Director, Robert Fleming Holdings Limited.

JANNER, The Hon Greville; QC, MP; Non-Executive Director, Ladbroke Group plc.

JANNEY, David E M; Partner, Theodore Goddard, since 1990.

JANNOTT, Dr Horst K; Non-Executive Director, S G Warburg plc.

JANSEN, Peter J; Chief Executive, MB Group plc, since 1989. *Career:* Caradon plc, Deputy Chairman & Chief Executive 1985-89; Redland plc, Main Board Director 1980-85; Divisional Chief Executive 1977-80; Management Consultant 1969-76; Pharmaceutical Industry, Manager 1959-69. *Biog: b.* 13 February 1940. *Nationality:* Dutch. *m.* 1963, Francoise Marie-Paul (née Dubois); 3 s. *Directorships:* MB Group plc 1989; Caradon plc 1985; CMB Packaging SA 1989 (non-exec) Vice Chairman. *Other Activities:* Governor, St George's College, Weybridge, Surrey.

JANSSEN, Baron Daniel; Director, Schroders plc.

JAP, Mrs C; Manager, First Vice President, American Express Bank.

JARRATT, Sir Alex; Deputy Chairman, Midland Bank plc.

JARRATT, David; Head of Human Resource Management, Leeds Permanent Building Society, since 1988.

JARRETT, D C; Director, National Investment Group plc.

JARRETT, David Robert; Director & Company Secretary, King & Shaxson Holdings plc.

JARVIS, Alan L; Partner-in-Charge, Private Clients & Institutional Services Department, Wilde Sapte, since 1988; Pensions/Charities/Immigration/Personal Tax/ Trusts & Estates. *Biog: b.* 4 April 1951. *Nationality:* British. *m.* 1978, Susan Jane; 2 s; 1 d. *Educ:* London School of Economics (LLB). *Professional Organisations:* Member, Law Society.

JARVIS, Alexander William; General Manager Printing Works, Bank of England, since 1987; General Management, Personnel & Administration. *Career:* Printing Works Personnel Manager 1982-85; Dep Gen Mgr 1985-87. *Biog: b.* 17 February 1941. *m.* 1965, Lesley Catherine (née Taylor); 2 s; 1 d. *Educ:* Bancroft's School. *Directorships:* Debden Security Printing Ltd 1987 MD; Bank of England Services Ltd 1987 (non-exec); Bassett Business Units 1990 Chairman. *Other Activities:* Vice-Chairman, Forest Enterprise Agency Trust; Council Member, Printing Industries Research Programme; Dir, Prince's Youth Business Trust in Essex; Non-Executive Director, Barking & Havering Regional Health Authority. *Professional Organisations:* Institute of Directors, BIM. *Recreations:* Tennis, Squash, Gardening.

JARVIS, David; Chairman of the Mortgage Corporation and Head of Financial Institutions, Saloman Brothers International Ltd, since 1986. *Career:* Anderson Clayton & Co SA (Mexico) VP & Gen Mgr (Consumer Foods) 1968-78; The Pillsbury Company VP, Intl Business Dev 1978-81; Northwest Corporation, Vice Chm 1981-86. *Biog: b.* 9 March 1941. *m.* 1963, Ina (née Colby); 1 s; 2 d. *Educ:* Gillingham Grammar School. *Professional Organisations:* ACMA. *Clubs:* Riverside. *Recreations:* Tennis, Golf.

JARVIS, Hugh John; Group Chief Actuary, Prudential Corporation plc, since 1988; All actuarial matters within the Corporation. *Career:* Mercantile and General Reinsurance Company, Various Positions, latterly Deputy Gen Mgr, Responsible for all Long Term Business 1947-88. *Biog: b.* 4 July 1930. *Nationality:* British. *m.* 1959, Margita; 2 s; 1 d. *Educ:* Southend High School. *Directorships:* The Mercantile and General Reinsurance Company plc (exec); The Prudential Assurance Company Ltd (exec). *Professional Organisations:* FIA. *Recreations:* Hockey.

JASCHOB, Wolfgang E; Senior Vice President and General Manager, First City, Texas - Houston NA.

JAWANMARDI, Jehangir; Director, Hill Samuel Bank Limited; Internal Auditing. *Professional Organisations:* FCA.

JAWHARY, S; Director, Allied Trust Bank Limited.

JAY, John; City Editor, The Sunday Telegraph, since 1989. *Career:* Thomson Regional Newspapers, City Reporter; The Sunday Telegraph 1984; The Sunday Times, City Editor 1986-89. *Educ:* (BA Hons History). *Publications:* The New Tycoons (with Judi Bevan).

JEAL, Christopher Rowland; Managing Director, Bell Lawrie White & Co Ltd, since 1990; Private Clients. *Career:* Govett Sons & Co (Stockbrokers), Assistant to Private Client Partner 1964-67; Myers & Co (Stockbrokers), Partner (Responsible for Private Client Dept) 1967-74; Coutt & Co (Bankers), Manager Investment Management Dept 1974-84; Hill Samuel Private Client Management Ltd, Deputy Manager Director (Reponsible for Discretionary Private Client Management Team) 1985-90; Bell Lawrie White & Co Ltd, Managing Director 1990-. *Biog: b.* 29 September 1942. *Nationality:* British. *m.* 1967, Linda Margaret (née Deamer); 2 s. *Educ:* St Joseph's Academy, Blackheath. *Directorships:* Hill Samuel Private Client Management 1985 (exec); Bell Lawrie White & Co Ltd 1987 (exec); Stable (Nominees) Ltd 1988 (non-exec). *Other Activities:* Liveryman, Worshipful Company of Blacksmiths. *Recreations:* Bridge, Literature, Theatre.

JEANES, J A; General Manager & Secretary, Skipton Building Society.

JEBENS, C F; Chief Executive, Lautro Ltd.

JEENS, Robert Charles Hubert; Finance Director, Kleinwort Benson Limited, since 1989; Merchant Banking & Securities. *Career:* Touche Ross & Co, Trainee to Audit Partner 1975-87; Partner 1984; Kleinwort Benson Securities Limited, Finance Director 1987-89. *Biog: b.* 16 December 1953. *Nationality:* British. *m.* 1978, Gillian Frances (née Thomas); 3 s. *Educ:* Marlborough College; Pembroke College, Cambridge (MA). *Directorships:* Kleinwort Benson Gilts Ltd 1987 (exec); Kleinwort Benson Securities Ltd 1987 (exec). *Professional Organisations:* FCA. *Recreations:* Music, Bridge, Wine.

JEFCOAT, N; Senior General Manager, Corporate Finance Division (Tokyo Branch), Kleinwort Benson International Inc, since 1990; M&A. *Career:* Lloyds Bank International Limited, HO, Paris, Tokyo & Osaka Branches, Various Positions 1977-84; Kleinwort Benson Limited, London & Tokyo 1984-. *Biog: b.* 22 June 1955. *Nationality:* British. *Educ:* Repton School; Worcester College, Oxford (BA Modern Languages); Queen's College, Oxford (Japanese Studies). *Directorships:* Kleinwort Benson Ltd 1989 (exec).

JEFFCOTE, P J; Partner, Freshfields.

JEFFERIES, David George; CBE; Chairman, National Grid Company, since 1990. *Career:* Southern Electricity, District Manager 1967; Chief Engineer 1972-74; North West Region, CEGB, Director 1974-77; CEGB, Personnel Manager 1977-81; LEB, Chairman 1981-86; Electricity Council, Deputy Chairman 1986-90. *Biog: b.* 26 December 1930. *Nationality:* British. *m.* 1961, Jeanette (née Hanson). *Directorships:* Electricity Supply Pensions Ltd Chairman. *Other Activities:* Wax Chandlers Livery Company. *Professional Organisations:* Fellow, Fellowship of Engineering; Fellow, Institution of Electrical Engineers. *Clubs:* Foxhills. *Recreations:* Golf, Music, Theatre.

JEFFERS, Raymond; Partner, Linklaters & Paines, since 1986; Employment and Employee Benefits. *Career:* Linklaters & Paines, Articled Clerk 1978-80; Assistant Solicitor 1980-86. *Biog: b.* 5 August 1954. *Nationality:* British. *m.* 1982, Carol (née Awty). *Educ:* University College of Wales, Aberystwyth (LLB); Wadham College, Oxford (BCL). *Other Activities:* Founder Member, City of London Solicitors' Company, Employment Law SoS Committee; Member, City of London Solicitors' Company, Commercial Law SoS Committee. *Professional Organisations:* The Law Society; City of London Solicitors' Company. *Recreations:* Tennis, Badminton, Ornithology.

JEFFREY, Richard Stephen; Managing Director, Economics, Hoare Govett Investment Research, since 1988; Head of Economic Research. *Career:* Thompson McLintock Chartered Accounting Trainee 1978-80; Hoare Govett UK Economist 1981-85; Asst Dir, Economics 1985-86; Dir of Economics 1986-88. *Biog: b.* 20 August 1957. *Nationality:* British. *m.* 1984, Marion Bernadette (née Roach); 1 s. *Educ:* Haileybury; Bristol University (MSc). *Recreations:* Music, Reading, Gardening, Hill Walking.

JEFFREYS, Simon Baden; Partner, McKenna & Co, since 1988; Partner in Charge of Employment Law Practice. *Career:* McKenna & Co, Articled Clerk 1980-82; Asst Solicitor 1982-88. *Biog: b.* 3 May 1957. *Nationality:* British. *m.* 1980, Lynn (née Coward); 2 s. *Educ:* Trinity Hall, Cambridge (MA). *Other Activities:* Member, City of London Solicitors Company. *Professional Organisations:* Law Society of England & Wales; City of Westminster Law Society; Immigration Law Practitioners Association. *Recreations:* Clay Pigeon Shooting, Fly Fishing.

JEFFRYES, Dennis Alfred Peter; Director, First National Bank plc, since 1970; Underwriting, Securities. *Career:* First National Securities Ltd (now First National Bank Ltd) 1961-. *Biog: b.* 4 October 1931. *Nationality:* British. *Educ:* Ilford County High Grammar School. *Directorships:* First National Assurance Ltd (exec); First National Management Ltd (exec); First National Leasing (exec); First National Credit (exec); Barnet Devanney Group Ltd (non-exec).

JELBART, Martin Wallis; Director, CIN Venture Managers Limited; Venture Capital, Management Buyouts. *Career:* Royal Navy 1973-78; Balfour Beatty Engineering Limited 1978-79; British Technology Group 1979-84; Robson Rhodes 1984-86. *Biog: b.* 7 May 1952. *Nationality:* British. *m.* 1980, Sandra (née Jessup). *Educ:* Tiffin School, Kingston; Downing College, Cambridge (MA). *Directorships:* Lindsey Holdings Limited 1987 (non-exec); Bartend Limited 1988 (non-exec); IAD (UK) Limited 1989 (non-exec). *Professional Organisations:* CEng; MIMechE. *Recreations:* Sailing, Gardening, Tennis.

JELLEY, Colin B; Senior Vice President, Morgan Guaranty Trust Company of New York.

JEMMETT, C M; Director, Unilever plc.

JENKIN, (Charles) Patrick (Fleeming); The Rt Hon The Lord Jenkin of Roding; PC; Chairman, Friends' Provident Life Office, since 1988. *Career:* British Government, MP for Wanstead & Woodford 1964-87; Junior Front Bench Spokesman on Treasury, Trade, Economic Affairs 1965-70; All-Party Group on Chemical Industry, Chm 1967-70; Fin Sec to the Treasury 1970-72; Chief Sec to the Treasury 1972-74; Minister for Energy 1974; Member of Shadow Cabinet & Opposition, Spokesman on Energy 1974-76; Opposition Spokesman on Social Services 1976-79; Sec of State for Social Services 1979-81; Sec of State for Industry 1981-83; Sec of State for Environment 1983-85; Back Bencher 1985-87. *Biog: b.* 7 September 1926. *Nationality:* British. *m.* 1952, Monica; 2 s; 2 d. *Educ:* Clifton College; Jesus College, Cambridge (MA Hons 1st). *Directorships:* NERA Inc 1986 (non-exec); Crystalate Holdings plc 1986 (non-exec) Chm 1988-; Lamco Paper Sales Ltd 1987 (non-exec) Chm; Arthur Andersen, Management Consultants 1985- Consultant. *Other Activities:* Chm, UK-Japan 2000 Group, 1985-90; Chm, Taverner Concerts Trust; Council Member, Centre for Economic & Environmental Development; Council Member, Guide Dogs for the Blind Association; Chm, Westfield College Trust; President, Clifton College 'Towards 2000' Appeal; Adviser, Sumitomo Trust and Banking Co Ltd; President, British Urban Regeneration Association; Chairman, Target Finland. *Professional Organisations:* FRSA; Barrister-at-Law (Middle Temple). *Clubs:* West Essex Conservative. *Recreations:* Gardening, Brick-laying, Sailing, Music.

JENKIN, M W F; Assistant General Manager and Chief Compliance Officer, Guardian Royal Exchange Assurance, since 1988; FSA Compliance. *Career:* Union Insurance Society of Canton, Various Positions in Far East from Junior to Acting Mgr Singapore 1955-67; Guardian Insurance of Canada, latterly SVP (Finance & Admin) 1967-83; GRE of America, latterly Group SVP (Admin) 1983-88. *Biog: b.* 13 November 1931. *Nationality:* British/American. *m.* 1959, Ann (née Stopford); 2 s. *Educ:* Dragon School, Oxford; Loretto School, Musselburgh; Brasenose College, Oxford (MA). *Professional Organisations:* FCII. *Clubs:* Royal Mid Surrey Golf Club. *Recreations:* Golf, Bridge.

JENKINS, Alan; Partner, Frere Cholmeley; Litigation.

JENKINS, Brian Garton; Partner, Coopers & Lybrand Deloitte, since 1969; Head of Audit, since 1986. *Biog: b.* 3 December 1935. *Nationality:* British. *m.* 1967, Elizabeth Ann (née Prentice); 1 s; 1 d. *Educ:* Tonbridge School; Trinity College, Oxford (MA). *Directorships:* Commission for New Towns 1990; Architectural Heritage Fund 1987 (non-exec); Blackheath Preservation Trust 1981 (non-exec); Royal Ordnance Factories 1976-83 (non-exec). *Other Activities:* City of London (Sheriff 1987-88); Ward of Cordwainer (Alderman 1980); Chartered Accts Co (Master); Merchant Taylors Co (Mem of Court); Info Technologists Co (Mem of Court); Royal Shakespeare Co (Gov); Corp of Sons of the Clergy; SPCK; Royal School of Church Music; St Felix School, Southwold (Gov). *Professional Organisations:* FCA (Council Member 1976-, Pres 1985-86). *Publications:* An Audit Approach to Computers (Co-Author), 3rd Ed 1986. *Clubs:* Brooks's, City of London, City Livery. *Recreations:* Garden Construction, Old Books, Large Jigsaw Puzzles, Ephemera.

JENKINS, Christopher; Secretary, Causeway Capital Limited.

JENKINS, David Stannard; Partner, Touche Ross & Co, since 1968; Group Partner/London Audit, Chm Construction Property Group. *Biog: b.* 13 April 1944. *Nationality:* British. *m.* 1978, Fiona; 1 s; 2 d. *Educ:* Tonbridge School. *Directorships:* The America-European Community Association Ltd (non-exec). *Clubs:* Hurlingham Club.

JENKINS, Derek William; Finance Director, RMC Group plc, since 1981; All Finance & Accounting Matters. *Career:* RMC Group plc, Group Financial Controller 1977-80; Group Taxation Manager 1968-77; Texaco (UK) Ltd, Assistant Tax Administrator 1966-68; Binder Hamlyn & Co, Audit/Tax Manager 1958-66; Proctor & Proctor, Articled Clerk 1950-58. *Biog: b.* 12 September 1934. *Nationality:* British. *m.* 1961, Hazel (née Watson); 2 d. *Educ:* Burnley Grammar School. *Other Activities:* Member, Worshipful Company of Chartered Accountants in England and Wales; Member, 100 Group. *Clubs:* RAC. *Recreations:* Swimming, Squash, Cartophily, Golf, Burnley FC (past & present).

JENKINS, Graham Nicholas Vellacott; Partner, Moores Rowland, since 1974; Audit. *Career:* Whinney, Smith & Whinney, London (now Ernst & Young) 1964-70; Seconded to Cardiff 1968-69; Rowland & Co, London (now Moores Rowland) 1970-. *Biog: b.* 15 December 1945. *Nationality:* British. *m.* 1977, Margaret Alice; 4 s. *Educ:* Radley College. *Other Activities:* Honourable Artillery Company; Liveryman, Worshipful Company of Barbers. *Professional Organisations:* Fellow, Institute of Chartered Accountants in England & Wales. *Clubs:* Flyfishers' Club, Ashridge Golf Club, Royal Porthcawl Golf Club. *Recreations:* Golf, Fishing.

JENKINS, Hugh; Executive Director, Prudential Corporation & CE Prudential Portfolio Managers Ltd, since 1989; Investment Management. *Career:* Allied Dunbar Assurance plc, Group Investment Director & Chairman Dunbar Bank plc, Investment Management 1986-89; Heron International NV, Director and Chief Executive, Heron Financial Corporation Inc 1985-86; National Coalboard Pension Funds, Director General of Investments, Investment Management 1972-85; CIN Properties Ltd, Managing Director, Property Investment & Management 1968-72; CIN Properties Ltd, Assistant

Controller 1962-68; London County Council, Valuer 1956-62. *Biog: b.* 9 November 1933. *Nationality:* British. *m.* Beryl Joan (née Kirk). *Educ:* Llanelli Grammar School; College of Estate Management. *Directorships:* National Assoc of Pension Funds 1979-81 Vice Chairman; Heron Financial Corp 1985-86 Chief Exec; Lay Member Stock Exchange 1984-85; Unilever Pensions Ltd 1985-89; Prudential Corp plc 1989-; Prudential Portfolio Managers Ltd 1989- Chief Exec. *Other Activities:* Chairman, Property Advisory Group, Department of the Environment; Liveryman, Leathersellers Company. *Professional Organisations:* Fellow, Royal Institute of Chartered Surveyors. *Clubs:* Garrick Club. *Recreations:* Golf.

JENKINS, Iain; European Correspondent, Sunday Times Business News.

JENKINS, Dame Jennifer (née Morris); DBE; Non-Executive Director, Abbey National plc, since 1984. *Career:* Hoover Ltd 1942-43; Min of Labour 1943-46; Political and Economic Planning (PEP) 1946-48; Part-time Extra-mural Lecturer 1949-61; Kingsway Day College, Part-time Teacher 1961-67; Consumers' Association, Chairman 1965-76; Historic Buildings Council for England 1975-84; British Standards Institute, Member, Executive Board 1970-73; Design Council 1971-74; Courtauld Institute, Committee of Management 1981-84; Ancient Monuments Board 1982-84; Historic Buildings & Monuments Commission 1984-85; Historic Buildings Adv Ctee, Chairman 1984-85; Ancient Monuments Society, Secretary 1972-75; President 1985-; N Kensington Amenity Trust, Chairman 1974-77; Wallace Collection, Trustee 1977-83; London Juvenile Courts, JP 1964-74; National Trust, Chairman 1986-. *Biog: b.* 18 January 1921. *Nationality:* British. *m.* 1945, Lord Jenkins of Hillhead; 2 s; 1 d. *Educ:* St Mary's School, Calne; Girton College, Cambridge (BA Hons). *Directorships:* Abbey National plc 1984 (non-exec); J Sainsbury 1981-86 (non-exec). *Other Activities:* President, Ancient Monuments Society. *Professional Organisations:* FRIBA (Hon); RICS (Hon); RTPI (Hon); LLD London (Hon); LLD Bristol (Hon); D Univ York (Hon).

JENKINS, John Anthony; Partner, Insurance Division, Clay & Partners Consulting Actuaries, since 1989; Life Assurance, General Insurance, Healthcare Matters. *Career:* Legal & General, Marketing Actuary 1986-88. *Biog: b.* 24 June 1962. *Nationality:* British. *Educ:* University of Exeter (BSc Mathematics 1st Class Honours). *Professional Organisations:* FIA. *Recreations:* Music.

JENKINS, Michael Nicholas Howard; Chief Executive, LIFFE, since 1981. *Career:* Shell Petroleum, Various 1956-62; IBM (UK) Ltd, Various 1962-67; Deloitte Robson Morrow, Ptnr 1967-71; The International Stock Exchange, Tech Dir 1971-77; European Options Exchange, MD 1977-80. *Biog: b.* 13 October 1932. *m.*

1957, Jacqueline Frances (née Jones); 3 s. *Educ:* Tonbridge School; Merton College, Oxford (MA). *Directorships:* LIFFE (Holdings) plc 1982. *Professional Organisations:* FBIM. *Clubs:* Wildernesse Club. *Recreations:* Golf, Tennis, Furniture Making, Music.

JENKINS, Peter Sefton; National VAT Partner, Ernst & Young, since 1986; Indirect Taxation. *Career:* HM Customs & Excise Various 1969-83; Cabinet Office (Secondment) Economic Secretariat 1975-77; HM Treasury (Secondment) Pvt Sec to Chancellor of Exchequer 1980-82; HM Customs & Excise Asst Sec, VAT Liability 1983-86; Ernst & Whinney, VAT Partner 1986-89. *Biog: b.* 9 February 1948. *Nationality:* British; 3 s. *Educ:* King's School, Canterbury; St Edmund Hall, Oxford (MA Hons). *Professional Organisations:* Customs Duty Practitioners Group; VAT Practitioners Group. *Clubs:* Reform. *Recreations:* Music, Squash, Walking.

JENKINS, R A; Director, Kleinwort Benson Limited.

JENKINS, Robert; Partner, Phildrew Ventures.

JENKINSON, Barry; Divisional Director, Regional Offices, Royal Trust Bank, since 1990; Corporate Lending with Emphasis on Property via 5 Regional Offices in the UK. *Career:* Midland Bank plc, Varied Duties 1974-79; Algemene Bank, Nederland NV, Corporate Analysis and Marketing 1979-84; Nederlandsche Middenstandsbank NV, Corporate Marketing, Assistant Manager 1984-88; Royal Trust Bank, Corporate Marketing Senior Manager to present role 1988-. *Biog: b.* 7 December 1953. *Nationality:* British. *m.* 1983, Anne (née Tunks). *Educ:* Rotherham Grammar School; Thomas Rotherham College; Matlock Teacher Training College, Part 1 Teaching Cert. *Professional Organisations:* ACIB. *Clubs:* Ardleigh Squash Club.

JENKS, Paul; Director, N T Evennett and Partners Ltd.

JENNINGS, Charles James; Partner, Wilde Sapte, since 1986; Corporate and Banking Work. *Career:* Freshfields Asst Solicitor 1980-82. *Biog: b.* 27 October 1951. *Nationality:* British. *m.* 1976, Julia Frances(née Whiffen); 1 s; 1 d. *Educ:* Harrow School; Durham University (BA). *Other Activities:* City of London Solicitors' Company. *Professional Organisations:* The Law Society. *Clubs:* City of London.

JENNINGS, John; Secretary, Nicholson Chamberlain Colls Limited.

JENNINGS, John M; Partner (Birmingham), Evershed Wells & Hind.

JENNINGS, Ms Marie Patricia; Director, Cadogan Management Limited, since 1984; Cadogan Services Ltd, since 1989; Management of Information/Finance &

Consumer Affairs. *Career:* Roy Bernard & Co, Managing Director 1957-62; Lexington International, Director 1970-76; Public Relations Consultants Association, Director 1979-85. *Biog: b.* 25 December 1930. *Nationality:* British. *m.* 1976, Brian Locke; 1 s. *Educ:* Presentation Convent College, Srinagar, Kashmir, India. *Directorships:* FIMBRA 1986 (non-exec); Money Management Ltd (The Money Management Council) 1985 (non-exec) Deputy Chairman; Cadogan Management Ltd (exec); Cadogan Services Ltd 1989 (exec); Cadogan Consultants 1976 Partner. *Other Activities:* Woman of the Year Award, 1969; Hon Treasurer & Council Member, Society of Consumer Affairs Professionals in Business; Committee Member, National Association of Womens Clubs; Committee Member Customer Standards, Unit Trust Association; Deputy Chairman, Money Management Council; Council Member, Insurance Ombudsman Bureau; Executive Committee Member, Wider Share Ownership Council. *Professional Organisations:* Fellow, Institute of Directors; Fellow, Royal Society of Arts; Member, British Academy of Experts; Member, Institute of Public Relations. *Publications:* Getting the Message Across, 1988; The Guide to Good Corporate Citizenship, 1990; Women & Money, 1988; The Money Guide, 1983; amongst others. *Recreations:* Writing Books, Admiring the Countryside, Sleeping.

JENNINGS, P T; Partner, Slaughter and May.

JENNINGS, Peter Morrison Nevill; Chief Executive, Interallianz London Ltd.

JENSEN, P; Deputy Managing Director, James R Knowles Limited.

JENSEN, Thomas George; Director, IBJ International Ltd, since 1986; Treasury, Eurobond Settlements, Banking. *Career:* First National Bank (Seattle) VP 1973-83; Saudi Investment Bank Asst Gen Mgr 1983-85; IBJ International Ltd Dir 1986-. *Biog: b.* 20 January 1948. *m.* 1971, Miki (née Hotta); 1 d. *Educ:* Netherlands School of International Business; University of Puget Sound, Seattle (BA, MBA). *Directorships:* Euroclear plc 1986 (non-exec). *Recreations:* Tennis, Shooting.

JEPSON, Jonathan Fraser; Treasury Manager, Northern Foods plc, since 1990. *Career:* Forrester Boyd, Audit Manager 1983-88; Northern Foods, Internal Audit Manager 1988-90. *Biog: b.* 18 April 1964. *Nationality:* English. *m.* 1988, Diane Maria (née Clafton); 1 s. *Educ:* Silverdale Comprehensive; Richmond College (BEc); Humberside College (Accountancy Foundation). *Professional Organisations:* ACA.

JERVIS, Brian Roy; Director, John Govett & Co Limited, since 1981; Director of Secretarial and Legal Services, Personnel Director. *Career:* John Govett & Co Ltd 1960-66; English Electric Co Ltd 1967-69; John Govett & Co Ltd 1969-. *Biog: b.* 19 August 1935. *m.*

1960, Joan; 1 s. *Educ:* Plymouth College. *Directorships:* Energy & Resources International Limited 1988 (non-exec). *Professional Organisations:* FCIS. *Clubs:* MCC. *Recreations:* Golf, National Hunt Racing, Cartography, Hill Walking.

JERVIS, David A; Director, Kleinwort Benson Securities Limited.

JESSETT, Robert Paul; Partner, R Watson & Sons, since 1976; Independent Consulting Actuary. *Career:* Australian Mutual Provident Society 1969-73. *Biog: b.* 18 March 1948. *m.* 1972, Sandra Anne (née Christie). *Educ:* Abingdon School; Exeter University (BSc). *Professional Organisations:* FIA; FPMI.

JESSUA, C A; Director, Barclays de Zoete Wedd Securities Ltd.

JEUNE, Senator Reginald Robert; OBE; Director, TSB Group plc, since 1976. *Career:* Mourant du Feu & Jeune Ptnr 1947-85; Consultant 1985-. *Biog: b.* 22 October 1920. *m.* 1946, Monica Lillian (née Valpy); 2 s; 1 d. *Educ:* De La Salle College, Jersey. *Directorships:* TSB Bank Channel Islands Ltd 1986 Chm; Hill Samuel & Co (Jersey) Ltd 1988 Chm; Jersey Electricity Company Ltd 1982 Chm; International Investment Trust Company of Jersey Ltd 1962; Royal Trust Co. of Canada (CI) Ltd 1962; Mercury Money Market Trust Ltd 1978; Metals Trust Ltd 1975; Mercury Offshore Sterling Trust 1986. *Other Activities:* Senator of The States of Jersey; The States of Jersey Finance & Economics Ctee (Pres); The States of Jersey Policy & Resources Ctee (Pres); Commonwealth Parliamentary Assoc. *Professional Organisations:* Solicitor of the Royal Court of Jersey (1945-). *Clubs:* Carlton, RAC, MCC, Victoria (Jersey), United (Jersey), Royal Jersey Golf Club, La Moye Golf Club. *Recreations:* Golf, Reading.

JEWSON, Edward Richard Rivers; Director, Cater Allen Limited, since 1988; Sterling Commercial Paper and Non Bank Business. *Career:* Pinchin Denney, Statistics Clerk 1971-72; Brown Shipley & Co, Bank Trainee 1972-73; Smith St Aubyn & Co (New York), Mgr 1973-80; Mergate Nurseries Ltd, Chm & MD 1982-86; BA Nurseries Ltd, Chm & MD 1984-86; Cater Allen Limited, Dir 1988-; Cater Allen Dublin Limited, MD 1990-. *Biog: b.* 13 June 1953. *Nationality:* British. *m.* 1980, Elizabeth Georgina (née Villiers); 2 d. *Educ:* Radley College. *Directorships:* Mergate Nurseries Ltd 1982 (exec); B A Nurseries Ltd 1984 (exec); Cater Allen Ltd 1988 (exec); Cater Allen Dublin Ltd 1990 (exec). *Clubs:* Whites. *Recreations:* Shooting, Fishing, Tennis.

JEYAKUMAR, J K; Executive Director, Wardley Unit Trust Managers Limited.

JINJUGI, Toshio; Executive Director, Bond Sales, Yamaichi International (Europe) Limited.

JISKOOT, Allard; Chairman, Securities Board of the Netherlands. *Career:* Pierson, Heldring & Pierson NV Amsterdam, Chairman Managing Board 1975-81; Amsterdam-Rotterdam Bank NV Amsterdam, Managing Director 1975-81; Philips Glocilampen Fabr NV 1980-; Canadian Pacific Ltd, Montreal, Director 1964-89. *Biog: b.* 22 November 1918. *Nationality:* Dutch. *m.* 1960; 2 s; 3 d. *Directorships:* St James's Place Capital plc. *Other Activities:* Ridder Nederlandse Leeuw.

JOB, Peter; Executive Director, Reuters Holdings plc.

JOBLING, Clive; Director, Panmure Gordon & Company Limited.

JOBSON, Clive; Director, J Henry Schroder Wagg & Co Ltd, since 1989; Treasury & Trading.

JOFFE, Joel Goodman; Deputy Chairman, Allied Dunbar Assurance plc.

JOHN, Dr Herbert Hugh; Medical Officer for the Port & City of London, Corporation of London.

JOHNS, Michael Charles; Partner, Ashurst Morris Crisp, since 1987; Corporate Law. *Career:* Withers, Ptnr 1974-87. *Biog: b.* 20 December 1947. *Nationality:* British. *m.* 1970, Lucy (née Ronald); 2 d. *Educ:* Tiffin School, Kingston; St Edmund Hall, Oxford (BA). *Directorships:* Exco International plc 1985 (non-exec); London Forfaiting Co plc 1984 (non-exec). *Professional Organisations:* The Law Society. *Publications:* Legal Considerations in the A Forfait Market (Co-Author), 1984.

JOHNS, Peter Andrew; Director, N M Rothschild & Sons Ltd, since 1987; Lending. *Biog: b.* 31 December 1947. *Nationality:* British. *m.* 1985, Rosanne (née Slayter); 2 s. *Educ:* Bridgend Grammar School; University College, London (BSc). *Directorships:* Merchant Bank of Central Africa 1985 (non-exec). *Professional Organisations:* ACIB. *Clubs:* RAC. *Recreations:* Golf, Tennis.

JOHNSON, A L; Director, Nicholson Chamberlain Colls Limited.

JOHNSON, A R B; Director, Legal & General Ventures Ltd, since 1989. *Career:* 3i plc 1983-86; Price Waterhouse (New York) 1980-83; Coopers & Lybrand Deloitte 1975-79. *Professional Organisations:* Institute of Chartered Accountants in England & Wales.

JOHNSON, Andrew; Partner, Hill Taylor Dickinson Solicitors, since 1987; Maritime & Insurance Law. *Career:* Hill Dickinson & Co, Articled Clerk 1980-84; Assistant Solicitor 1984-85; Associate Partner 1985-87. *Biog: b.* 5 February 1955. *Nationality:* British. *Educ:* (BA Hons). *Professional Organisations:* Member, Law Society. *Recreations:* Riding, Travel, Walking.

JOHNSON, Christopher Louis McIntosh; Chief Economic Adviser, Lloyds Bank plc, since 1977; UK & International Economics & Finance. *Career:* The Times, Journalist 1954-60; Financial Times, Paris Correspondent 1960-63; Diplomatic Correspondent 1963-65; Foreign Editor 1965-67; Managing Editor 1967-70; Managing Director of Business Enterprise Div 1970-76; Director 1973-76; Lloyds Bank, Chief Economic Adviser 1977-. *Biog: b.* 12 June 1931. *m.* 1958, Anne (née Robbins); 1 s; 3 d. *Educ:* Winchester College; Magdalen College, Oxford (1st Class Hons Philosophy, Politics & Economics). *Directorships:* Sadler's Wells Theatre 1987-90. *Other Activities:* Chairman, Executive Committee of the Institute for Fiscal Studies; Chairman, Executive Committee of the Employment Institute; Member of the Economic Situation & Europe Committees, Confederation of British Industry; Council Member, Royal Economic Society; Council Member, Royal Institute of International Affairs; Specialist Adviser to the Treasury and Civil Service Committee, House of Commons; Specialist Adviser, House of Lords Sub-Committee on Economic, Monetary and Political Union. *Publications:* Anatomy of UK Finance, 1977; North Sea Energy Wealth, 1979; Measuring the Economy, 1988; Privatization & Ownership (Ed), 1988; The Market on Trial (Ed), 1989; Changing Exchange Rate Systems (Ed), 1990; Monetarism and the Keynesians (Ed), 1991. *Clubs:* Overseas Bankers Club. *Recreations:* Choral Singing, Photography, Windsurfing.

JOHNSON, Christopher Michael; Finance Director, Dunbar Vida y Pensiones, since 1988; Actuarial, Legal, Accounting, Audit and Personnel Areas. *Career:* Allied Dunbar Assurance plc, Executive Director (Expatriated to Spain) 1988-; Various to Executive Director, Financial Control 1978-88; Victory Insurance Co Ltd, to Assistant Manager, Life Client Services 1974-78; Welfare Insurance Co Ltd 1971-74. *Biog: b.* 14 March 1951. *Nationality:* British. *m.* (div); 1 d. *Educ:* Queen Elizabeth Grammar School, Wakefield; Owens University, Manchester (BSc Honours Mathematics 2:1). *Directorships:* Dunbar Vida y Pensiones, SA 1988 (exec); Dunbar Analisis de Mercados, SA 1988 (exec). *Professional Organisations:* Fellow, Institute of Actuaries. *Publications:* Author and Co-Author of Three Papers to the Institute of Actuaries. *Recreations:* Chess, Reading, Travel.

JOHNSON, D P; Member of the Council, The Society of Investment Analysts.

JOHNSON, Professor G; Professor of Strategic Management & Director of Research, Cranfield School of Management, since 1988. *Career:* Manchester Business School, Senior Fellow in Strategic Management 1985-88; Aston University Management School, Lecturer in Business Policy 1979-85; Hull College of Higher Education, Senior Lecturer in Marketing 1976-79; Gower Furniture, Marketing Director 1975-76; Urwick Orr and Partners, Management Consultant 1973-75; Wall

Paper Manufacturers Retail Division, Marketing Director 1972-73; Birds Eye Foods Ltd, Marketing Executive 1968-72. *Biog: b.* 15 August 1945. *Nationality:* British. *m.* 1968, Enid; 3 d. *Educ:* University College, London (BA); University of Aston (PhD). *Directorships:* Geo Ellison Ltd 1984 (non-exec). *Publications:* Exploring Corporate Strategy, 2nd Edition 1988; Exploring Corporate Strategy (Text & Cases), 1989; Strategic Change & the Management Process, 1987; Business Strategy and Retailing, 1987; and Numerous Papers. *Recreations:* Squash, Cricket.

JOHNSON, Geoffrey Edwin; Director of UK Operations, Price Waterhouse, since 1990; UK Operations-Central Services. *Career:* Price Waterhouse 1969-. *Biog: b.* 12 October 1947. *m.* 1979, Maria; 1 s. *Educ:* Sheffield University (BA Economics). *Directorships:* Price Waterhouse 1990 (exec). *Professional Organisations:* FCA. *Recreations:* Sailing, Motoring, Swimming.

JOHNSON, Ian; Partner, Withers, since 1989; Energy/Commercial Law. *Career:* Linklaters & Paines, Articled Clerk 1975-77; Solicitor 1977-79; Cadbury Schweppes plc, Legal Adviser 1979-81; UNOCAL Corporation, Legal Counsel, Europe, Africa & Middle East 1981-89. *Biog: b.* 13 December 1951. *Nationality:* British. *m.* 1976, Gillian Helenia (née Rosewell); 1 s; 1 d. *Educ:* Morecambe Grammar School; Downing College, Cambridge (MA, LLM). *Directorships:* UNOCAL UK Limited 1985-90; Muanda Oil Company Inc 1985-90. *Other Activities:* Committee Member, UK Oil Lawyers Group, 1987-. *Professional Organisations:* Law Society; Westminster Law Society; International Bar Association; Institute of Petroleum. *Clubs:* RAC. *Recreations:* Travel, Literature.

JOHNSON, J P; Director, Wendover Underwriting Agency Limited.

JOHNSON, Kimberley; Marketing Manager, Top Technology Limited.

JOHNSON, L; Director, Hill Samuel Investment Management Ltd.

JOHNSON, Michael; Editor in Chief, International Management, since 1982. *Career:* Associated Press Moscow Correspondent 1967-71; McGraw-Hill World News Paris Correspondent 1971-76; Dir 1976-82. *Biog: b.* 23 November 1938. *Nationality:* American. *m.* 1967, Jacqueline (née Zimbardo); 3 d. *Educ:* Columbia University; San Jose State College (BA). *Professional Organisations:* American Society of Magazine Editors; Overseas Press Club. *Publications:* The Third Type Company (Translator), 1987; Business Buzzwords 1990. *Recreations:* Juggling Flaming Torches.

JOHNSON, Nicholas Anthony Donatus; Chief Executive, MIM Britannia Limited, since 1988; Investment Management. *Career:* MIM Limited Research Analyst 1976-77; Asst Mgr 1977-78; Mgr 1978-80; Dir 1980-87; MIM Ltd/MIM Britannia Unit Trust Managers, Group Director 1987-88; MD 1987-. *Biog: b.* 6 January 1953. *m.* 1981, Jennifer (née Malherbe Jensen); 1 s. *Educ:* Stonyhurst College; Magdalen College, Oxford (BA); Courtauld Institute, London University (MA). *Directorships:* Invesco MIM plc 1990 Deputy Chairman.

JOHNSON, Nigel; Partner, Commercial Litigation, Cameron Markby Hewitt.

JOHNSON, Nigel David; Partner, Allen & Overy.

JOHNSON, P J P; Director, Parrish Stockbrokers.

JOHNSON, P M; Executive Director, Redland plc.

JOHNSON, Peter Douglas; Deputy Chief General Manager & Secretary, Co-operative Insurance Society, since 1987. *Biog: b.* 15 April 1929. *m.* 1953, Frances Doreen (née Hill); 1 s; 1 d. *Educ:* Buxton College; Selwyn College, Cambridge (MA). *Professional Organisations:* FIA; FSS. *Publications:* Sundry Acturial Papers. *Recreations:* Fell Walking, Bridge, Ignoring Questionnaires.

JOHNSON, R S; Director and Company Secretary, Hammerson Property Investment and Development Corporation plc.

JOHNSON, Richard F; Managing Director, Morgan Guaranty Trust Company of New York.

JOHNSON, Roy Douglas Trevor; Director, Baring Securities Limited, since 1989; Company Secretary. *Career:* George Henderson & Co, Mgr 1960-75; Henderson Crosthwaite & Co, Mgr 1975-84. *Biog: b.* 6 November 1939. *Nationality:* British. *m.* 1969, Elenora Enid (née Hanson). *Educ:* Queen Elizabeth's, Barnet. *Recreations:* Music, Reading, Gardening, Travel.

JOHNSON-BIGGS, David; Executive Director, Yamaichi International (Europe) Limited.

JOHNSON-GILBERT, Christopher Ian; Partner, Linklaters & Paines, since 1986; (Corporate Law, Investment Funds). *Career:* Linklaters & Paines, Articled Clerk 1978-80; Assistant Solicitor 1980-86; Partner 1986-; (Hong Kong Office) 1988-. *Biog: b.* 28 January 1955. *Nationality:* British. *m.* 1981, Emma Davina Mary (née Woodhouse); 3 d. *Educ:* Rugby School; Worcester College, Oxford (BA). *Other Activities:* City of London Solicitors Company. *Professional Organisations:* Law Society; Hong Kong Law Society. *Clubs:* MCC, RAC, Vincents, Aberdeen Marina Club. *Recreations:* Cricket, Golf, Wine.

JOHNSON-HILL, Nigel; Managing Director, Hoenig & Co Ltd, since 1988; International Soft Commission Stockbroking. *Career:* Hong Kong & Shanghai Bank, Foreign Staff Officer 1965-73; W I Carr (Overseas), Stockbroker, Intl Sales 1973-78; Hoare Govett Stockbroker, MD Intl Sales 1978-88. *Biog: b.* 8 December 1946. *Nationality:* British. *m.* 1971, Catherine (née Sainsbury); 1 s; 2 d. *Educ:* Rugby. *Professional Organisations:* Member, The International Stock Exchange; Member, National Association of Securities Dealers (USA). *Clubs:* Oriental Club, Hong Kong Club. *Recreations:* Wine, Skiing, Tennis.

JOHNSTON, Alexander David; Executive Director, Lazard Brothers & Co Ltd, since 1985; Corporate Finance. *Career:* Lazard Brothers 1973-. *Biog: b.* 3 September 1951. *Nationality:* British. *m.* 1980, Jackie (née Stephenson); 2 s. *Educ:* Westminster School; Corpus Christi College, Cambridge (MA). *Recreations:* Classical Music, Reading, Skiing, Travel, Walking.

JOHNSTON, Anthony Graeme Douglas; Director, Martin Currie Investment Management Ltd.

JOHNSTON, Edmund W; Chief Executive, Ulster Development Capital Limited, since 1985. *Career:* AVX Limited, Vice President Finance 1979-85; Smedley-HP Foods Limited, Financial Accounting Manager 1976-79; Zambia Industrial and Mining Corporation, Consultant 1975-76; International Engineering Limited, Management Accountant 1970-75. *Biog: b.* 17 October 1951. *Nationality:* British. *m.* 1975, Maureen; 1 s; 1 d. *Educ:* Annadale Grammar School, Belfast. *Directorships:* Ulster Development Capital Ltd 1985 (exec); Nectar Beauty Shops Ltd 1986 (non-exec); Harmann Systems Ltd 1988 (non-exec); The Ideal Design 1988 (non-exec). *Other Activities:* Member, Council of CBI N Ireland. *Professional Organisations:* Fellow, Chartered Inst of Management Accountants. *Clubs:* Ulster Reform Club. *Recreations:* Travelling, Photography.

JOHNSTON, I; Director, County NatWest Securities Limited.

JOHNSTON, John; Director, J Rothschild Capital Management Limited.

JOHNSTON, Simon John; Partner, Nabarro Nathanson, since 1990; General Commercial/Corporate Law/Property Finance. *Career:* Articles, Messrs Robinson Cox Solicitors, Perth, Western Australia 1983-84; Solicitor, Company & Commercial Department, Messrs Robinson Cox 1984-86; Solicitor, Company & Commercial Department, Messrs Nabarro Nathanson 1986-90; Partner, Messrs Nabarro Nathanson 1990-. *Biog: b.* 13 December 1960. *Nationality:* Australian. *m.* 1990, Caroline (née Hatter). *Educ:* University of Western Australia (Bachelor of Jurisprudence, Bachelor of Laws). *Professional Organisations:* Law Society of Western Australia; Law Society, England and Wales. *Clubs:* Queens Club. *Recreations:* Tennis, Skiing, Swimming, Squash, Travelling.

JOHNSTON, Thomas; OBE; Director, Scottish Amicable Life Assurance Society. *Career:* Barr & Stroud Ltd, Managing Director 1979-88; Chairman 1989-90; Pilkington Medical Systems Ltd, Chairman 1985-89; Scottish Industrial Development Advisory Board 1980-89. *Biog: b.* 27 June 1927. *Educ:* University of Glasgow (BSc). *Directorships:* Bank of Scotland (West Board); Barr & Stroud; Science Projects (Scotland) Ltd 1982 (non-exec) Chairman. *Other Activities:* Director, Glasgow Development Agency 1990; Treasurer, University of Strathclyde. *Professional Organisations:* Chartered Engineer (CEng).

JOHNSTON, Dr Thomas L; DL; Self-Employed; Manpower Industrial Relations; Arbitration. *Career:* Lecturer, University of Edinburgh 1953-65; Professor of Economics, Heriot-Watt University 1966-76; Chairman, Manpower Services Committee for Scotland 1977-80; Principal and Vice-Chancellor, Heriot-Watt University 1981-88. *Biog: b.* 9 March 1927. *Nationality:* British. *m.* 1956, Joan (née Fahmy); 2 s; 3 d. *Educ:* Hawick High School; University of Edinburgh (MA, PhD); University of Stockholm. *Directorships:* First Charlotte Assets Trust 1981 (non-exec); Scottish Life Assurance Co & Subsidiaries 1989 (non-exec); Hodgson Martin Ltd 1989 (non-exec); Academic Residences in Scotland plc 1990 (non-exec) Chairman; Edinburgh Science Festival 1988 (non-exec). *Professional Organisations:* FRSE, FRSA, CBIM, FIPM. *Publications:* Collective Bargaining in Sweden, 1962; The Structure & Growth of the Scottish Economy (co-author), 1970; Introduction to Industrial Relations, 1981. *Recreations:* Gardening, Walking.

JOHNSTONE, David William Robert; Chairman of Principal Subsidiaries, Dartington & Co Group plc, since 1979; General Management/Corporate Finance. *Career:* Whinney Smith & Whinney Articled Clerk/Audit Snr 1960-65; Grace Darbyshire & Todd/Grace Ryland/Thomson Mclintock & Co (Bristol) Staff 1965-67; Ptnr 1967-79. *Biog: b.* 20 November 1936. *Nationality:* British. *m.* 1962, Penelope Susan (née Sloan); 3 d. *Educ:* St Bees School; Clare College, Cambridge (MA). *Directorships:* TSW Television South West plc 1980 (non-exec); JT Group Ltd 1979 (non-exec); Praxis plc 1989 (non-exec). *Professional Organisations:* FCA. *Recreations:* Gardening, Walking, Theatre, Music.

JOHNSTONE, Ian Temple; WS; *Career:* Baillie & Gifford WS, Partner 1950-74; Biggart Baillie & Gifford WS, Partner 1974-85; Senior Partner 1985-88. *Biog: b.* 25 February 1923. *Nationality:* British. *m.* 1958, Frances (née Ferenbach); 3 d. *Educ:* Edinburgh Academy; Corpus Christi, Cambridge (MA); Edinburgh University (LLB). *Directorships:* Friends Provident Life Office 1964 (non-exec); Inch Kenneth Kajang Rubber plc 1970 (non-exec); Baillie Gifford Shin Nippon plc 1985 (non-exec). *Other Activities:* Member of Council, Edinburgh Festival Society; Chairman of Governors, St Margaret's School Edinburgh. *Professional Organisations:* Society of Writers of the Majesty's Signet (former Treasurer). *Clubs:* New Club Edinburgh.

JOHNSTONE, John Raymond; CBE; Chairman, Forestry Commission, since 1989. *Career:* Chiene & Tait Apprenticed CA 1951-54; Robert Fleming & Co Ltd Research Analyst 1955-59; Brown Fleming & Murray/ Whinney Murray Ptnr in Charge, Invest Mgmnt 1959-68; Murray Johnstone Ltd MD 1968-89. *Biog: b.* 27 October 1929. *Nationality:* British. *m.* 1979, Susan Sara (née Gore); 5 s; 2 d. *Educ:* Eton College; Trinity College, Cambridge (BA). *Directorships:* Scottish Financial Enterprise 1986 Chairman; Scottish Amicable 1971; Dominion Insurance Co Ltd 1973; 1978- Chm; Glasgow Cultural Enterprises 1988 (non-exec); Summit Group plc 1989 Chm; Murray Income Trust plc 1989 (non-exec); Murray International Trust plc 1989 (non-exec); Murray Smaller Markets Trust plc 1989 (non-exec); Murray Ventures plc 1983 (non-exec); Murray Enterprise plc 1989 (non-exec); Murray Johnstone Ltd 1968 Chm & MD. *Other Activities:* Scottish Opera (Hon Pres 1986-, Chm 1983-85, Dir 1978-86); Scottish Economic Council (1988-). *Professional Organisations:* Chartered Accountant. *Clubs:* Western (Glasgow). *Recreations:* Fishing, Farming, Shooting, Opera, Art.

JOHNSTONE, William Stirling; Marketing Director, Edinburgh Fund Managers plc, since 1985. *Career:* Lloyds Bank Intl, Account Mgr 1982-84. *Biog: b.* 8 March 1948. *Nationality:* British. *m.* 1981, Jane (née McNeill); 1 s; 1 d. *Educ:* Stowe School; Heriot Watt University. *Directorships:* EFM Unit Trust Managers Ltd 1989 (exec); Private Fund Managers Ltd 1989 (exec). *Other Activities:* Member, Royal Company of Archers (Queens Body Guards for Scotland). *Clubs:* The New Club, Prestwick & Luffners Golf Club. *Recreations:* Farming.

JOLL, Christopher Andrew; Chief Executive, Charles Barker City Ltd, since 1989; Financial Public Relations. *Career:* United Scientific Holdings, Director of Corporate Affairs 1977-86; Michael Peters & Partners, Director 1975-77; Lazard Brothers & Co, Research Analyst 1975; British Army, Captain, The Life Guards 1966-75. *Biog: b.* 16 October 1948. *Nationality:* British. *Educ:* Oundle School; Oxford University (MA Hons); RMA Sandhurst. *Directorships:* Charles Barker Holdings plc 1989 (exec). *Professional Organisations:* Member, Institute of Public Relations (MIPR). *Clubs:* Garrick Club, Cavalry & Guards Club. *Recreations:* Theatre, Fine Art, Bridge, Field Sports.

JOLL, James Anthony Boyd; Finance Director, Pearson plc, since 1985. *Career:* Financial Times Journalist 1961-68; Lex Column 1963-68; N M Rothschild & Sons Ltd Merchant Banker 1968-80; Dir 1970-80; S Pearson & Son Ltd (now Pearson plc) Dir 1980-; Fin Dir 1985-. *Biog: b.* 6 December 1936. *Nationality:* British. *m.* 1977, Lucilla (née Kingsbury); 3 s; 2 d. *Educ:* Eton College; Magdalen College, Oxford (BA Hons 1st). *Directorships:* Lazard Bros & Co Ltd 1981 (non-exec); Westpool Investment Trust plc 1980 (non-exec); Janus Hotels Ltd 1990 (non-exec)Deputy Chairman. *Other Activities:* Chairman, Council for the Protection of Rural England Trust; Trustee, The Wallace Collection; Sir John Soane's Museum Society Ltd 1987. *Clubs:* Boodle's.

JOLLIE, W Ian; Partner (Birmingham), Evershed Wells & Hind.

JOLLIFFE, John Anthony; Partner, R Watson & Sons, since 1967; All Aspects of Pension Arrangements. *Career:* Royal Air Force 1955-57. *Biog: b.* 1 August 1937. *Nationality:* British. *m.* 1990, Dorothy (née Saul); 2 s; 1 d (from previous marriage). *Educ:* Dover College. *Directorships:* London Aerial Tours Ltd 1982; National Association of Pension Funds Ltd 1983. *Other Activities:* Chairman, European Federation for Retirement Provision; Chairman, Association of Consulting Actuaries, Local Government Superannuation Committee; Member, UK Steering Committee for Local Government Superannuation; Member, Council of the National Association of Pension Funds; Member, Worshipful Company of Actuaries; Freeman, City of London. *Professional Organisations:* FIA; FPMI; ASA. *Clubs:* Reform Club, Birmingham Club. *Recreations:* Flying, Travel, Tennis.

JOLLIFFE, P; Partner, Slaughter and May.

JONAS, Christopher William; Senior Partner, Drivers Jonas, since 1987; Chartered Surveyors & Urban Real Estate Consultants. *Career:* Jones Lang Wootton 1959-67; Drivers Jonas, Ptnr 1967-82; Mging Ptnr 1982-87; Snr Ptnr 1987-. *Biog: b.* 19 August 1941. *Nationality:* British. *m.* 1968, Penny (née Barker); 3 s; 1 d. *Educ:* Charterhouse; College of Estate Management; London Business School (Sloan Fellow). *Directorships:* Staffordshire County Council 1982 Property Adviser; Port of London Authority 1985 Board Member; Port of London Properties Ltd 1986 Chm; Economics Research Associates USA 1987 Chm; The Securities Association 1988 Board Member; The City University Property Centre 1988 Trustee. *Other Activities:* Mem, Governing Council Business in the Community; Chm, BIC Professional Firms Group; RICS, Vice-President; Mem, Gen Council, 1980-; Liveryman, Clothworkers' Company 1962; Liveryman, Chartered Surveyors Company 1978; Fellow, Inst of Directors; Mem, Urban Land Inst (USA); Mem, American Soc of Real Estate Counselors; Fellow, Royal Society of Arts. *Professional Organisations:* FRICS. *Clubs:* Naval &

Military, Toronto Club (Toronto). *Recreations:* Wagner, Other Music, Tennis, Skiing.

JONES, A B; National Tax Partner, Ernst & Young, since 1990; Responsible for Development of UK Tax Practice. *Career:* Dickson Middleton & Co (Stirling), Apprentice CA 1965-70; Arthur Andersen (Glasgow), Tax Senior 1970-71; Edward Moore & Sons (London), Tax Manager 1971-74; Whinney Murray (London), Tax Supervisor to Manager 1974-79; Ernst & Whinney (London), Partner 1979-; Partner in Charge of London Tax Dept 1984-88; Ernst & Whinney, National Tax Partner 1988-89; Member of Executive; Ernst & Young, National Tax Partner 1990-. *Biog:* b. 31 March 1948. *Nationality:* British. *m.* 1974, Rosemary; 2 s. *Educ:* High School of Stirling. *Professional Organisations:* Institute of Chartered Accountants of Scotland. *Recreations:* Reading, Travel, Golf, Watching Sons Perform Music/Sport.

JONES, Andrew; Group Personnel Policy Manager, Prudential Corporation plc.

JONES, Andrew Stewart Ross; Managing Director, Gerrard & National Holdings plc, since 1986; Dealing. *Biog:* b. 2 March 1959. *Nationality:* British. *m.* 1987, Annabel (née Eley). *Educ:* Ampleforth College. *Directorships:* Gerrard & National Ltd 1986 (exec); Reeves Whitburn Investments 1987 (exec); GNI Holdings Ltd 1988 (non-exec); Music Marketing Services Ltd 1988 (non-exec). *Clubs:* Hurlingham, Annabels, Overseas Bankers.

JONES, Arfon; Partner, Cameron Markby Hewitt; Corporate Finance.

JONES, B; Controller, Yorkshire Bank plc.

JONES, B M; Partner, MacIntyre Hudson.

JONES, Brian Robert; Director, The Royal London Mutual Insurance Society Ltd, since 1985; General Manager & Actuary. *Career:* The Royal London Mutual Insurance Society Ltd Asst Actuary 1970-74; Dep Actuary 1974-82; Actuary 1983-87; Dir 1985; Gen Mgr & Actuary 1987. *Biog:* b. 7 January 1946. *Nationality:* British. *m.* 1968, Sandra Thirwall (née Davies); 1 d. *Educ:* Wallington Grammar. *Directorships:* R L Unit Trust Managers Ltd 1981 (exec) Chm; R L Mutual Insurance Society 1985 (exec); R L General Insurance 1985 (exec); Triton Fund Managers 1986 (exec); R L Homebury Ltd 1987 (exec) Chm; Neptune Fund Managers Ltd 1988 (exec) Chm. *Other Activities:* Mem, Various Ctees; Assoc of British Insurers; Chm, The Advisory Ctee on Education for the Life Insurance Industry; SIB Ctee. *Professional Organisations:* FIA. *Recreations:* Gardening, Reading, Enjoyment of Countryside, Opera; Theatre.

JONES, C; Managing Director, J Walter Thompson Co Ltd.

JONES, C S; Director, Henry Cooke Lumsden plc.

JONES, D C; Chief Executive, Next plc.

JONES, D L; Member of the Council, The International Stock Exchange.

JONES, David; Divisional Director, Royal Trust Bank.

JONES, Frank E; Senior General Manager, Lloyds Bank plc, since 1986; International Banking.

JONES, Frederick Ralph; Assistant General Manager, C & G Guardian; Mortgages. *Professional Organisations:* MBIM; FCBSI.

JONES, Gareth D; Partner, Touche Ross & Co.

JONES, Graham; Managing Director, Quin Cope Ltd.

JONES, Ian Quayle; Chief Executive, Quayle Munro, since 1983; Corporate Finance. *Career:* Cowan and Stewart WS Partner 1968-72; Ivory and Sime Fund Manager 1972-73; The British Linen Bank Ltd Various/ Dir 1973-83. *Biog:* b. 14 July 1941. *Nationality:* British. *m.* 1968, Christine Ann (née Macrae); 2 s; 1 d. *Educ:* Strathallan School; Edinburgh University (MA, LLB). *Directorships:* PCT Group plc 1983 (non-exec); Nevis Range Development Co plc Chm (non-exec); International Twist Drill (Holdings) Ltd 1986 (non-exec); Gleneagles Hotels plc 1981-84 (non-exec); Granfel plc 1989 Chm (non-exec). *Other Activities:* Governor, Strathallan School. *Professional Organisations:* WS. *Clubs:* Hon Company of Edinburgh Golfers. *Recreations:* Golf, Skiing, Fishing.

JONES, J B; Secretary, The Burmah Oil plc.

JONES, John Clifford; Administration Director, Prudential-Bache Capital Funding (Moneybrokers) Ltd, since 1989; Operations/Stock Exchange Moneybroking. *Career:* S G Warburg Securities, Senior Manager, UK Equities 1973-86. *Biog:* b. 4 September 1954. *Nationality:* British. *m.* 1987, Clare Marion (née Hirst); 1 d. *Educ:* SWH County Technical School. *Other Activities:* Committee Member, SEMA (Stock Exchange Managers Assoc); Committee Member, IEDA (International Equity Dealers Assoc). *Professional Organisations:* Stock Exchange Registered Representative. *Clubs:* Broxbourne Cruising Club, Hanover Golf Club, Potters Bar Fishing Club. *Recreations:* Cruising Inland Waterways, Golf, Fishing.

JONES, John Lynton; Managing Director, Europe, NASDAQ International, since 1987; All UK & Continental European Affairs. *Career:* HM Diplomatic Service, Career Diplomat 1968-83; British Embassy (Paris), 1st Sec, Commercial/Fin 1979-83; London Stock Exchange, Intl Affairs Adviser 1983-85; Dir of Public Affairs 1985-87. *Biog: b.* 12 November 1944. *Nationality:* British. *m.* 1968, Judith Mary (née Coop); 1 s; 2 d. *Educ:* Rhyl Grammar School; University College of Wales, Aberystwyth (BSc Econ). *Other Activities:* British Invisible Exports Council, Overseas Promotions Ctee, 1983-87; BIEC European Ctee, 1983-87; Ctee Investor Relations Soc, 1985-87; Ctee, City Group of Inst of Public Relations, 1985-87. *Professional Organisations:* IOD. *Publications:* Various Articles on Intl Securities Trading in Company Lawyer, Accountancy Age and Other Journals. *Recreations:* Photography, Theatre, Music, Skiing, Squash.

JONES, Keith; Director and Head of Fixed Income Department, Lazard Investors, since 1989; Bonds and Currencies. *Career:* HM Government Economic Adviser 1974-76; Henley Centre for Forecasting, Economic Consultant on Interest Rates, Currencies and International Economies 1976-78; James Capel & Co 1978-89; Chief Economist and Head of Bond and Economic Research 1978-85; Gilt Sales Executive 1981-85; Partner 1983; Head of Fixed Income Sales & Director, James Capel Gilts Limited 1985-88. *Biog: b.* 12 November 1952. *Nationality:* British. *Educ:* Birkenhead School; Oxford University (MA Oxon Hons, Politics, Philosophy and Economics); London University (MSc Econ, Economics and Econometrics). *Directorships:* Lazard Investors 1989 (exec); Lazard International Asset Management 1989 (exec); James Capel Gilts Limited 1988-89; James Capel (Europe) 1988-89; James Capel Financial Futures 1988-89; James Capel CM & M Limited 1988-89. *Professional Organisations:* Member, Stock Exchange, 1982. *Recreations:* Skiing, Squash, Tennis, Windsurfing, Opera, Theatre.

JONES, M; Group Treasurer, The Thomson Corporation.

JONES, M Gary; Group Marketing Director, Lloyd's Abbey Life plc, since 1988. *Career:* Thomson Organisation, Marketing Mgr 1966-71; Seagram Distillers, Sales & Marketing Dir 1972-75; LBS 1976-78; United Biscuits plc, Commercial Dir 1978-82; Grand Metropolitan plc, Subsidiary MD 1983-86; Abbey Life plc, General Manager & Director 1986-88. *Biog: b.* 27 May 1945. *Educ:* University of Wales (BA Hons); London Business School (MBA). *Directorships:* Abbey Global Investment Fund 1987 (exec); Abbey Unit Trust Managers 1986 (exec); Abbey Life Assurance Co Ltd 1986 (exec). *Recreations:* Sailing.

JONES, Mark Adam; Partner, Bacon & Woodrow, since 1989; Pensions. *Career:* Bacon & Woodrow, Actuarial Staff 1978-89. *Biog: b.* 21 November 1957. *Nationality:* British. *Educ:* Forest Grammar School, Reading;

Selwyn College, Cambridge (BA Hons, MA Hons). *Professional Organisations:* FIA. *Clubs:* Kentish Sail Association. *Recreations:* Sailing, Skiing, Tennis, Squash.

JONES, Medwyn; Partner, Walker Martineau Stringer Saul, since 1983; Commercial and International Law, Corporate Finance. *Career:* Theodore Goddard, Articled Clerk 1978-80; Solicitor 1980-81; Walker Martineau, Solicitor 1981-83. *Biog: b.* 13 September 1955. *Nationality:* British. *Educ:* Chester Grammar School; Sheffield University (LLB). *Directorships:* Agnalap Ltd 1984 (non-exec); Blademead Ltd 1984 (exec); EC Productions Ltd 1984 (non-exec); Figurant Ltd 1984 (non-exec); Great Records Ltd 1984 (non-exec). *Other Activities:* The City of London Solicitors' Company; Member, Australian Business in Europe. *Professional Organisations:* The Law Society; International Bar Association. *Recreations:* Skiing, Squash, Weight Training, Sailing.

JONES, Melfyn Lloyd; *Career:* Lloyds Bank plc, Group Compliance Director 1987-90; Chief Investment Manager 1980-85; Lloyds Investment Managers (Subsidiary Lloyds Bank plc), Managing Director 1985-90. *Biog: b.* 30 July 1930. *Nationality:* British. *m.* 1956, Mair; 1 d. *Directorships:* Investment Management Regulatory Organisation (IMRO) 1985 (non-exec); Chartered Institute of Bankers, Exec Rep Appointments (non-exec). *Professional Organisations:* ACIB. *Recreations:* Theatre, Travel.

JONES, Mervyn N; Finance Director, Crédit Suisse Buckmaster & Moore Ltd.

JONES, Michael Abbott; Chief Executive, Association of British Insurers.

JONES, Nicholas Michael Houssemayne; Managing Director, Lazard Brothers & Co Ltd, since 1987; Corporate Finance. *Career:* Peat Marwick Mitchell & Co 1965-73; J Henry Schroder Wagg & Co Ltd 1975-87; Dir 1983. *Biog: b.* 27 October 1946. *Nationality:* British. *m.* 1971, Veronica Anne (née Hamilton-Russell); 1 s; 1 d. *Educ:* Winchester College; London Business School (MSc). *Directorships:* County Hall Development Group plc 1990. *Professional Organisations:* FCA. *Clubs:* Hurlingham. *Recreations:* Racing, Tennis, Bridge, Stalking, Painting.

JONES, Nick; Partner, Morison Stoneham, since 1987; Head of Corporate Services Dept. *Career:* Morison Stoneham 1983. *Biog: b.* 12 April 1956. *Nationality:* British. *Educ:* Chislehurst & Sidcup Grammar School; Sheffield University, (Accountancy). *Professional Organisations:* ACA.

JONES, Norman William; CBE TD; Deputy Chairman, Lloyds Bank plc.

JONES, Peter Nicholas; TD; Executive Director, Samuel Montagu & Co Limited, since 1989; Corporate Finance. *Career:* National Coal Board, Various 1974-78; Staff Officer to Sir Derek Ezra 1978-80; Principal Private Sec to Sir Derek Ezra 1980-81; Departmental Sec, HQ Finance Dept 1981-84; Samuel Montagu & Co Ltd, Mgr, Corp Finance 1984-85; Asst Dir, Corp Finance 1986-88. *Biog: b.* 13 June 1953. *Nationality:* British. *m.* 1985, Gillian Elizabeth (née Milbank). *Educ:* Clifton College; Clare College, Cambridge (MA). *Other Activities:* Financial and Sponsorship Adviser; Nordic/ Biathlon Executive, British Ski Federation. *Professional Organisations:* FCCA (Gold Medal, Final Exams, 1983). *Clubs:* Royal Scottish Automobile Club, Leander, Eagle Ski Club. *Recreations:* Walking, Ski-Touring, Trout and Salmon Fishing.

JONES, Philip Michael Thyer; Director, Capel-Cure Myers Capital Management Ltd, since 1970; Technical Services, Settlement. *Career:* The International Stock Exchange, Trainee/Various 1959-63; Capel-Cure Myers, Various 1963-67; Head of Investment Department 1967-70; Fin & Admin Partner/Director 1970-85. *Biog: b.* 9 October 1942. *Nationality:* British. *Educ:* Roan Blackheath. *Other Activities:* Chairman, Trustees, Stock Exchange Rifle Club; Securities Industry Steering Committee on Taurus (Siscot). *Recreations:* Flying, Climbing, Skiing, Deep Sea Fishing, Shooting.

JONES, Rhidian Huw Brynmor; Partner, Turner Kenneth Brown, since 1981; Company/Commercial. *Career:* Selection Trust Ltd, Trainee Assistant Secretary 1966-68; Total Oil Great Britain Ltd, Legal Assistant 1968-69; J E Lesser (Holdings) Ltd, Company Secretary 1969; Granada Group Ltd, Assistant Secretary 1970-76; Herbert Smith & Co, Articled Clerk, Assistant Solicitor 1976-80; Kenneth Brown Baker Baker/Turner Kenneth Brown, Senior Assistant Solicitor/Partner 1980-. *Biog: b.* 13 July 1943. *Nationality:* British. *m.* 1970, Monica Marianne (née Sjöholm); 1 s; 1 d. *Educ:* Queen Mary's Grammar School, Walsall; Keble College, Oxford (MA Hons). *Directorships:* Mornington Building Society 1986 (non-exec); Serco Group plc 1987 (non-exec); The Mortgage Agency plc 1988 (non-exec). *Other Activities:* Freeman, City of London Solicitors' Company. *Professional Organisations:* Law Society; FCIS; FBIM; Institute of Directors. *Clubs:* Wig & Pen. *Recreations:* Rugby, Scandinavian Studies.

JONES, Richard; Director, Prelude Technology Investments Limited.

JONES, Rupert James Livingston; Partner, Allen & Overy, since 1985; Property Law. *Career:* Allen & Overy, Articled Clerk 1976-78; Assistant Solicitor 1978-85. *Biog: b.* 2 September 1953. *Nationality:* British. *m.* 1978, Sheila Carol (née Kertesz); 2 s; 1 d. *Educ:* Kings College School; University of Birmingham (LLB). *Directorships:* London Young Solicitors Group

1987-88 Chairman. *Other Activities:* Freeman, City of London Solicitors' Company; Member, Whittington Committee. *Professional Organisations:* The Law Society. *Recreations:* Gardening, Cinema, Motoring.

JONES, S M; Partner (Guernsey), Bacon & Woodrow.

JONES, Stephen; Executive Director & Company Secretary, Prelude Technology Investment Limited, since 1985; Venture Capital Investment Manager. *Career:* Cambridge Consultants Ltd, Contract Research & Development Company, Licensing Manager 1983-85; London Business School, Post Graduate Student 1981-83; Lucas Cav Ltd, Automobile Components Manufacturer, Production Engineer/Production Supervisor 1978-81. *Biog: b.* 10 April 1956. *Nationality:* British. *m.* 1986, Dianne (née Griffiths); 2 d. *Educ:* Hampton School; University of Bath (BSc 1st Class Hons Engineering); London Business School (MSc with Distinction). *Directorships:* Prelude Technology Investments Limited 1987 (exec); Procal Analytics Limited 1986 (non-exec); Arun Technology Limited 1988 (non-exec); Coercive Limited 1989 (non-exec); Design Computing Limited 1990 (non-exec). *Recreations:* Swimming, Running, Motorsport.

JONES, T W; Partner, Freshfields.

JONES, Trevor Alexander; Managing Director, Gresham Trust plc, since 1990; Management Buy-Outs and Venture Capital. *Career:* Touche Ross & Co, Mgmnt Consultant 1971-80. *Biog: b.* 13 April 1950. *Nationality:* British. *m.* 1 s. *Educ:* Liverpool University (BCom Hons). *Professional Organisations:* FCA.

JONES, Dr Trevor Mervyn; Director, Wellcome plc, since 1987; Research and Development. *Career:* Nottingham University, University Lecturer 1965-71; The Boots Co Ltd, Director of Pharmaceutical Development 1971-76; The Wellcome Foundation, Director of Development 1976-87. *Biog: b.* 19 August 1942. *Nationality:* British. *m.* 1966, Verity (née Bates); 1 s; 1 d. *Educ:* Wolverhampton School; King College, London (Formerly Chelsea College) (BPharm, PhD). *Other Activities:* Member, Medicines Commission, Dept of Health; Member of Council, Kings College, London; Yeoman Member, Worshipful Society of Apothecaries; Visiting Professor, University of Strathclyde and Kings College, London. *Professional Organisations:* FPS; CChem; FRSC; MCPP. *Publications:* Drug Delivery to the Respiratory Tract (with D Ganderton); Numerous Scientific Papers. *Clubs:* The Athenaeum.

JONES, William Nigel Henry; Group Company Secretary, Prudential-Bache Capital Funding (Equities) Ltd, since 1986; Company Secretarial/Taxation. *Career:* Clive Discount Company, Financial Controller/ Secretary 1978-86; Stangard Metalworkers Ltd, Financial Accountant 1977-78; W J Calder Son & Co

Chartered Accountants, Trainee/Audit Senior 1972-77. *Biog: b.* 20 December 1951. *Nationality:* British. *m.* 1984, Helen Mary (née Seddon). *Educ:* Purley Grammar School. *Directorships:* Prudential-Bache Capital Funding (Gilts) Ltd 1988 (exec); P-B Interfunding (UK) Ltd 1989 (exec); Page & Gwyther Investments Ltd 1983 (exec); Page & Gwyther Holdings Ltd 1982 (exec); Page & Gwyther Ltd 1983 (exec); P-B Capital Partners (UK) Ltd 1989 (exec); Clivco Nominees Ltd 1987 (exec); Clive Investments Ltd 1987 (exec); Clivnell Securities Ltd 1983 (exec). *Professional Organisations:* Institute of Chartered Accountants of England & Wales; Institute of Taxation.

JOPP, Laurence; Chief Financial Officer, UK, The Chase Manhattan Bank, NA, since 1986; Accounting & Finance. *Career:* Hillier Hills Frary & Co, Articled Clerk 1966-71; H W Fisher & Co, Audit Senior 1971-72; Coopers & Lybrand, Audit Manager 1972-74; Continental Minios Nat Bank, Senior Auditor 1975-78; The Chase Manhattan Bank NA, Regional Audit Manager 1978-83; Research Management & Operations Planning 1983-86; CFO 1986-. *Biog: b.* 8 October 1949. *Nationality:* British. *m.* 1986, Amanda (née Robinson). *Educ:* Dunstable Grammar School. *Professional Organisations:* Fellow, Institute of Chartered Accountants; Member, Strategic Planning Society. *Recreations:* Gardening, Reading, Music, Jogging, Squash.

JORDAN, Andrew Robert; Partner, Hammond Suddards, since 1983; Company Law. *Career:* Last Suddards Articled Clerk 1979-81; Assistant Solicitor 1981-83; Partner 1983-88. *Biog: b.* 26 February 1957. *Nationality:* British. *m.* 1989, Victoria Mary. *Educ:* The Leys School, Cambridge; Christ's College, Cambridge (MA). *Recreations:* Fly Fishing, Hill Walking, Hockey, Tennis, Rowing.

JORDAN, Arthur; Divisional Director, Royal Trust Bank.

JORDAN, Michael Anthony; Chairman, Senior Partner, Cork Gully, since 1983; Insolvency. *Career:* R H March & Son & Co 1958-68; Partner 1959-; Saker & Langdon Davis, Partner 1963; W H Cork Gully & Co, Partner 1968-80; Coopers & Lybrand, Partner 1980-90; Coopers & Lybrand Deloitte, Partner 1990. *Biog: b.* 20 August 1931. *Nationality:* British. *m.* 1990, Dorothea (née Coureau); 1 s; 1 d. *Educ:* Haileybury. *Other Activities:* Governor, Royal Shakespeare Co, 1979-; Bakers Livery Co; Chartered Accountants Livery Co; High Court of Isle of Man (Joint Inspector into Affairs of the Savings & Investment Bank Ltd, 1983). *Professional Organisations:* FCA. *Publications:* Insolvency, 1986. *Recreations:* DIY, Opera.

JORDAN, P E; Director, Framlington Unit Management Limited.

JORDEN, R C; Clerk, Blacksmith's Company.

JORGE, C; Executive Director, Daiwa Europe Limited.

JOSCELYNE, M; Partner, Nabarro Nathanson, since 1990; Tax (Corporate and Property). *Career:* Brecher & Co, Articled Clerk 1979-81; Brecher & Co, Assistant Solicitor 1981-82; Oppenheimers, Assistant Solicitor 1982-85; Oppenheimers, Partner 1985-86; Herbert Smith, Assistant Solicitor 1986-88; Nabarro Nathanson, Assistant Solicitor 1988-90; Nabarro Nathanson, Partner 1990-. *Biog: b.* 19 September 1957. *Nationality:* British. *Educ:* St Paul's School, London; University College London (LLB 2:i). *Professional Organisations:* Law Society. *Publications:* Various Articles, Lectures on Tax. *Recreations:* Squash, Tennis.

JOSEPH, Colin Stuart; Head of Litigation Department, D J Freeman & Co, since 1990; Licensed Insolvency Practitioner. *Career:* D J Freeman & Co, Ptnr 1973-; Jt Head, Litigation Dept 1978-87; Chief Executive 1987-90. *Biog: b.* 23 December 1946. *Nationality:* British. *m.* 1979, Anne Janette (née Milloy); 1 s; 1 d. *Educ:* Bancroft's; Exeter College, Oxford (BA). *Other Activities:* City of London Solicitors' Company and Member, Insolvency Law Sub-Com mittee. *Professional Organisations:* The Law Society; IBA. *Clubs:* MCC. *Recreations:* Reading, Cricket, Theatre.

JOSEPH, Polly; Partner, Forsyte Kerman.

JOULES, Howard Alan; Head Trader Gilts, Barclays de Zoete Wedd Securities.

JOWETT, E W; Partner, Allen & Overy.

JOWETT, P R C; Partner, Pensions (Epsom), Bacon & Woodrow.

JOWETT, R A; Partner, Herbert Smith.

JOY, Andrew Neville; Director, Causeway Capital Limited, since 1984. *Career:* Hill Samuel & Co Limited 1978-84. *Biog: b.* 10 April 1957. *Nationality:* British. *m.* 1983, Caroline (née Okell); 2 s. *Educ:* New College, Oxford (PPE). *Directorships:* Causeway Group Ltd 1990 (exec); Village Green plc 1985 (non-exec); Garage Equipment Maintenance Co Ltd 1986 (non-exec); The Aristocrat Group Ltd 1988 (non-exec). *Recreations:* Tennis, Squash, Skiing, Travel.

JOYCE, Thomas; Managing Partner, London Office, Shearman & Sterling, since 1989. *Career:* Shearman & Sterling, Associate, New York Office 1963-72; Shearman & Sterling, Partner, New York Office 1972-78; Shearman & Sterling, Partner, London Office 1978-81; Shearman & Sterling, Partner, New York Office 1981-84; Shearman & Sterling, Managing Partner,

Hong Kong Office 1985; Shearman & Sterling, Partner, New York Office 1986-89. *Biog: b.* 5 October 1939. *Nationality:* American. *m.* 1962, Patricia (née Nepper); 2 d. *Educ:* St John's University (BA); Notre Dame Law School (LLB). *Professional Organisations:* International Bar Association; American Bar Association; Association of the Bar of the City of New York. *Recreations:* Reading, Walking, The Arts.

JOYNER, D P; Director, Kleinwort Benson Securities Limited, since 1988; UK Equity Sales. *Career:* Grieveson Grant & Co, Associate Partner 1969-86; Kleinwort Benson Secs 1986-. *Biog: b.* 5 March 1951. *Nationality:* British. *m.* 1973, Janet; 2 d. *Educ:* Archbishop Temple's School. *Professional Organisations:* Member of the International Stock Exchange. *Recreations:* Cricket, Football, Gardening.

JOZZO, Alfonso; General Manager International Division, Member of the Executive Board, Istituto Bancario San Paolo Di Torino, since 1986. *Career:* Employee, Foreign Department 1961-68; Manager, Research and Planning Department 1968-77; Head of Research and Planning Department 1977-86. *Biog: b.* 31 August 1942. *Nationality:* Italian. *m.* 1 s; 1 d. *Educ:* University of Turin (Degree Economics). *Directorships:* Hambros Bank Ltd, London 1987; Melita Bank, La Valletta (Malta) 1987; Sanpaolo Finance SpA, Turin 1987; Sanpaolo Lariano Bank SA, Luxemburg 1987; Banque Indosuez, Paris 1988; Abel Matutes Torres SA - Banco de Ibiza, Ibiza 1990; Ruegg Bank AG, Zurich 1990. *Other Activities:* Member, Federal Committee of the Union of European Federalists (Bruxelles).

JUBB, David Alfred Lancaster; Director and Chief Executive, London and Manchester Group plc.

JUDAH, Nigel Leopold; IMR; Company Secretary, Reuters Holdings plc, since 1990. *Career:* Reuters, Secretary & Chief Accountant 1960-67; Assistant General Manager 1967-81; Finance Director & Company Secretary 1981-90; Company Secretary 1990-. *Biog: b.* 6 December 1930. *Nationality:* British. *m.* 1970, Phoebe Anne (née Grant) div; 1 s; 2 d. *Educ:* Charterhouse; Lausanne University. *Directorships:* Visnews Ltd 1975 (non-exec). *Other Activities:* 100 Group; Governor, Charterhouse School; Member, Senate of Chartered Accountants; Member, Development Council of the Royal National Theatre. *Professional Organisations:* FCA. *Clubs:* Brook's, Garrick. *Recreations:* Opera, Wine, Collecting Pictures.

JUDD, James Hubert; Chairman & Managing Director, Walter Judd Limited, since 1971. *Biog: b.* 27 March 1933. *Nationality:* British. *m.* 1982, Lady Zinnia (née Denison). *Educ:* Eton College. *Directorships:* Walter Judd Public Relations Limited 1973 Chairman. *Professional Organisations:* IPA. *Clubs:* City of London, Whites. *Recreations:* Hunting, Shooting, Skiing, Farming.

JUDDERY, Robin Keith; Managing Director, CIN Properties Ltd, since 1976; Property Investment, Development, Funding and Management. *Career:* Prall & Prall Articled Clerk 1954-57; LCC, then GLC Valuers Dept Surveyor 1957-68; CIN Various 1969-. *Biog: b.* 3 April 1938. *Nationality:* British. *m.* 1966, Joan Margaret (née Fairbotham); 2 s. *Educ:* Dartford Grammar. *Professional Organisations:* FRICS. *Recreations:* Walking, Bowls.

JUDGE, Ian M; Intellectual Property Partner, Bristows Cooke & Carpmael.

JUDKOWSKI, Mark; Investment Analyst, March Investment Fund, since 1989; Investment Appraisal, Negotiation and Monitoring/Specialisation in High Technology Areas. *Career:* Independent Broadcasting Authority, Development Engineer 1982-85; Image Reconstruction Systems, Senior Engineer (Served on Management Team Advising on Company Strategy) 1985-89. *Biog: b.* 6 September 1959. *Nationality:* British. *Educ:* Hulme Grammar School, Oldham; Trinity College, Cambridge (BA Hons in Electrical Sciences). *Professional Organisations:* Chartered Engineer; Member, the Institution of Electrical Engineers (CEng MIEE); Certified Diploma in Accounting and Finance (CDipl AF). *Recreations:* Squash, Tennis, Skiing.

JUKES, A W; Director, Hill Samuel Bank Limited.

JULY, C L A; Partner, Freshfields.

JUSTHAM, Gordon; Actuarial Consultant, Sedgwick Financial Services Limited, since 1991; Corporate Pensions. *Career:* Standard Life Assurance Company, Trainee Actuary 1973-78; Alexander Consulting Group, Regional Actuary & Associate Dir Responsible for the Pensions Operation in Leeds Region 1978-87; Bacon & Woodrow, Partner, Pensions 1987-90. *Biog: b.* 22 September 1951. *Nationality:* British. *m.* 1977, Jacklyn Anne (née Carder); 3 s. *Educ:* Rochdale Grammar School; Hull University (BSc Hons); Durham University (PGCE). *Other Activities:* Elder within the United Reformed Church. *Professional Organisations:* FFA. *Recreations:* Bridge, Squash, Opera.

K

KABRAJI, Philip; Partner, Grant Thornton.

KADWANI, I M; Executive Vice President, Habib Bank AG Zurich.

KAHN, Gregory R; Partner, Wilde Sapte.

KAHN, Stephen; Deputy City Editor, Daily Express. *Career:* Daily Mail; Campaign; Industry Week.

KAHNAMOUYIPOUR, H; Director, S G Warburg & Co Ltd.

KAKABADSE, Professor A; Professor of Management Development, Cranfield School of Management, since 1978; Top Executive Development, Management of Change Organisation Structures & Restructuring. *Career:* Derbyshire County Council, Mental Welfare Officer 1970-71; Liverpool City Council, Psychiatric Social Welfare Worker and Child Guidance Officer 1971-72; Manchester Polytechnic, Department of Management, Research Fellow in Management Development 1973-75; Lecturer in Organisation Behaviour and Director of Organisation Research in Development Unit 1975-77; WS Atkins Group of International Consultants, Personnel Consultant 1977-78; Cranfield School of Management, Professor of Management Development 1978-. *Biog: b.* 30 March 1948. *Nationality:* British. *m.* 1979, Patricia; 1 d. *Educ:* Salford University (BSc); Brunel University (MA); Manchester University (PhD); Manchester University Medical School (AAPSW). *Directorships:* Consultant to numerous companies, including: FI Group; KPMG Peat Marwick; Bull International SA; Bank of Ireland; Royal Institute of British Architects; Rolls Royce; National Health Service; Ministry of Radio USSR; National Nuclear Corporation. *Other Activities:* Member, Academy of Management, USA; Director, Board of Organisation Development Institute, USA. *Professional Organisations:* Fellow, British Psychological Society (FBPsS); Member, Civil Service College Advisory Council; Fellow, International Academy of Management. *Publications:* Over 60 articles, 7 monographs & 11 books, including: Leadership & Organisation Development, 1980; People in Organisations: The Practitioners View, 1982; Cases in Human Resource Management, 1987; Working in Organisations, 1988; Top People Top Teams, 1991; Getting Even, 1991. *Recreations:* Swimming, Training in Gym, Travel.

KAKKAD, Sunil Shantilal; Partner, Hill Taylor Dickinson, since 1989; Company Law. *Career:* Brecher & Co, Articled Clerk 1982-84; Hill Dickinson & Co, Solicitor 1984-89. *Biog: b.* 19 May 1959. *m.* 1984, Darshna (née Hindocha); 1 s. *Educ:* Alder School & Barnet College; University of Hull (LLB Hons). *Professional Organisations:* The Law Society. *Recreations:* Reading, Music.

KAKUMOTO, Takashi; Deputy General Manager & Treasurer, Mitsubishi Bank, since 1990; Treasury. *Career:* Mitsubishi Bank International Treasury & Foreign Exchange Division, Assistant General Manager 1988-89; Treasury Department (Los Angeles Agency), Manager & Chief Dealer 1986-88; Corporate Banking Division II, Manager 1983-86; International Treasury & Foreign Exchange Division, Manager 1981-83; Head Office, Corporate Officer 1977-81; Ginza Branch, Various 1974-77. *Biog: b.* 20 December 1949. *Nationality:* Japanese. *m.* Kiyomi; 1 s; 2 d. *Educ:* Tokyo University.

KALARIS, Thomas L; Managing Director, Morgan Guaranty Trust Company of New York.

KALMAN, S L; Director, British Land.

KAMBARA, Yoichi; Deputy Managing Director, Mitsubishi Finance International plc, since 1989; Strategic Planning & Administration. *Career:* The Mitsubishi Bank Ltd, Head Office, Tokyo, Manager 1980-84; The Bank of California Corporate Banking Group, San Francisco, USA, Vice President & Manager 1984-89. *Biog: b.* 20 August 1948. *Nationality:* Japanese. *m.* 1972, Wakae; 2 d. *Educ:* Keio University, Tokyo (BA Economics); L'Institut d'Etudes Politiques de Paris (CEP); INSEAD (MBA). *Directorships:* Mitsubishi Finance International plc 1989 (exec); The Bank of California Capital Services & Consulting Inc 1985-89. *Clubs:* Richmond Golf Club.

KAMEDA, Tsutomu; Deputy Managing Director, Yasuda Trust Europe Limited, since 1990. *Career:* The Yasuda Trust & Banking Co Ltd (London), Deputy General Manager/Corporate Finance 1987-90. *Biog: b.* 28 October 1947. *Nationality:* Japanese. *m.* 1972, Kumiko; 2 d. *Educ:* Tokyo University (BA). *Directorships:* Yasuda Trust Europe Limited, London 1990 (exec).

KAMIEL, Josef Ingo; Director, First National Finance Corporation plc, since 1985; Director in Charge of Commercial Lending Division. *Career:* First National Finance Corp plc 1955-. *Biog: b.* 8 November 1931.

Nationality: British. *m.* 1964, Helen Sylvia (née Nyman); 2 s; 1 d. *Educ:* Kings, Ottery St Mary. *Directorships:* First National Finance Corp Subsidiaries 1958- (exec); First National Bank plc (exec); First National Commercial Bank plc (exec).

KAMIENICKI, Jan Anthony; Partner, Bacon & Woodrow, since 1989; Insurance Consulting. *Career:* Bacon & Woodrow, Actuarial Assistant 1988-89. *Biog: b.* 29 July 1961. *Nationality:* British. *Educ:* St Pauls School, London; Magdalene College, Cambridge (MA, Certificate of Advanced Studies). *Other Activities:* Committee, Staple Inn Actuarial Society 1988-. *Professional Organisations:* Fellow, Institute of Actuaries; Fellow, Royal Statistical Society. *Publications:* Miscellaneous Contributions to Trade and Professional Journals. *Recreations:* Reading, Skiing.

KAMINA, Y; Director, S G Warburg Akroyd Rowe & Pitman Mullens Securities Ltd.

KAMIYA, K; Deputy General Manager Administration, The Mitsubishi Bank Ltd.

KAN, Praba; Finance Director and Company Secretary, Kogan Page Limited.

KANAAN, George Elias; General Manager, Saudi American Bank, since 1987; Overall Responsibility for Branch in London and SAMBA Capital Management International Ltd. *Career:* Eno Foundation of Transport Staff Engineer/Asst Tech Dir 1969-73; Citibank/Saudi American Bank VP 1975-84; First Chicago Ltd Exec Dir/VP 1984-87. *Biog: b.* 12 November 1946. *Nationality:* American. *m.* 1971, Catherine (née Sloane); 2 s; 1 d. *Educ:* American University of Beirut (BEng); Carnegie-Mellon University (MSE); University of Bridgeport; Harvard Graduate School (MBA). *Other Activities:* Conference Ctee, Arab Bankers Assoc. *Publications:* Parking & Access at General Hospitals, 1973; Zoning, Parking & Traffic, 1972; Conjunctive Use Systems Analysis, 1970; Various Articles on Engineering and Banking. *Clubs:* Annabel's, Royal Assembly, Overseas Bankers'. *Recreations:* Opera, Theatre.

KANAZOME, Naoaki; Director & Secretary, Nichiboshin (UK) Ltd.

KANE, Frank; The Sunday Telegraph, since 1990. *Career:* Taught Economics, Government and English in London; Financial Times, Company News 1983-86; The Independent, Chief City Reporter 1986-90.

KANGLEY, Geoffrey Bruce; Chairman, Kangley Financial Planning Ltd, since 1981; Life Assurance, Investment, Pensions & Financial Planning Compliance Officer, Technical Knowledge and Discipline. *Career:* Walter Bell & Co, Articled Clerk 1959-61; Sheffield & Rotherham Constabulary, Constable 1961; Officer Re-

sponsible for Chief Constable's Administration 1969-; Nation Life Insurance Co Ltd, Various, Salesman to Regional Mgr 1969-7; Noble Lowndes Personal Financial Services Ltd, Snr Consultant, Financial Planning 1971-81; Personal Financial Services Ltd, MD 1981-; Clayton Kangley & Co, Partner 1988-90. *Biog: b.* 23 September 1941. *Nationality:* British. *m.* 1963 (div); 2 s; 1 d. *Educ:* Sheffield University, Special 2yr Course for Police Officers (Law, Psychology & Sociology); Sheffield Education Committee (Qualified Youth Leader). *Directorships:* FIMBRA 1988 (non-exec); NFIFA Services Ltd 1990 (non-exec); Sectorvogue Ltd 1990 (exec); Kangley Financial Planning Ltd 1990 (exec); Personal Financial Services Ltd 1990 (exec). *Other Activities:* Founding Chairman, National Federation of Independent Financial Advisers (NFIFA); Founder Member, Institute of Financial Planning (IFP); Member of FIMBRA, Training and Competence Committee with Responsibility to Other SROs: Industry Wide Competence Training and Testing. *Publications:* In Search of Best Advice in Money Management, 1988; Letting Rip with Roy in Pensions Management, 1990. *Clubs:* Exchange Club, Sheffield, Queen's Tower Squash Club, Hallamshire Squash Club. *Recreations:* Squash, Study of Psychodynamics, Reading, Music.

KANNAN, S; Director, The New India Assurance Company Limited.

KANTOR, Miss K T; Director of Finance & Business Planning, Grand Metropolitan plc, since 1990; Retailing & Property. *Directorships:* British Railways Board 1987 (non-exec). *Professional Organisations:* FCA.

KANTOROWICZ-TORO, D; Managing Director, Consolidado UK Ltd.

KANZAKI, Y; Director, Nikko Bank (UK) plc.

KARANJIA, D N; Director, Meghraj Bank Ltd.

KARAT, David Spencer; Managing Director, Salomon Brothers International Limited, since 1990; Corporate Finance. *Career:* Slaughter and May, Solicitor 1976-80; Orion Royal Bank/Royal Bank of Canada, Associate Director 1980-84; Merrill Lynch International Limited 1984-90. *Biog: b.* 1 August 1951. *Nationality:* British. *m.* 1976, Shirley Lessels (née Williams); 2 d. *Educ:* Merchant Taylors' School; Leicester University (LLB Hons). *Other Activities:* Finance Committee, Save the Children Fund. *Professional Organisations:* Law Society. *Clubs:* RAC. *Recreations:* Squash, Tennis, Running, Motor Cars.

KARMEL, Martin Newman; Senior Deputy Secretary, British Bankers Association, since 1975; Legal and Public Policy Issues. *Career:* Barrister, Middle Temple 1956; Solicitor 1961; Committee of London & Scottish Bankers and British Bankers Association, Assistant Secretary 1967; Deputy Secretary 1971. *Biog: b.* 9 November 1933. *Nationality:* British. *m.* 1987, Priscilla. *Educ:* Malvern College; Brasenose College, Oxford (MA, BCL). *Publications:* Articles in Professional Journals. *Recreations:* Beagling, Tennis.

KASHIWA, S; Managing Director, Daiwa Europe Limited.

KASHIWAGI, S; Director, IBJ International Limited.

KASHIZAWA, Toshihiro; Deputy General Manager, The Bank of Tokyo Limited.

KASSEM, Tarek Jamal; Chairman & Managing Director, Quanta Group (Holdings) Limited.

KATO, J S; Associate Director, Lonrho plc.

KATO, Shigeru; Joint General Manager, The Fuji Bank Ltd.

KATO, Takashi; Managing Director & Chief Executive, The Nikko Bank (UK) plc, since 1990. *Career:* The Nikko Securities Co Ltd 1959-; Dep Gen Mgr 1978-82; Gen Mgr, Intl Fin Div 1982-83; Gen Mgr, Intl Planning Div 1983-85; London Gen Mgr 1986-88; Nikko Bank (UK) plc, Deputy Managing Director 1988-90. *Biog: b.* 1 February 1935. *Nationality:* Japanese. *m.* 1965, Sonoko (née Miki); 1 s; 1 d. *Educ:* Takamatsu High School; Hitotsu Bashi University, Japan (BA).

KATSUOKA, K; Director, Sanyo International Ltd.

KATZ, Richard; Non-Executive Director, N M Rothschild & Sons Limited.

KAUFMAN, Alan; Managing Partner, since 1988; Litigation Partner Specialising in Commercial and Matrimonial Litigation. *Biog: b.* 15 April 1947. *Nationality:* British. *m.* 1973, Vivienne; 5 d. *Educ:* King's College, Cambridge (MA IIi). *Directorships:* Knightsbridge Speakers Club 1985-86 President. *Professional Organisations:* International Bar Association; Industrial Society Quality Club. *Clubs:* Highgate Tennis Club. *Recreations:* Tennis, Cricket, Theatre, Cinema.

KAUFMANN, R M S U; Director, County NatWest Securities Limited.

KAVANAGH, Peter Richard Michael; Partner, Theodore Goddard, since 1989; Corporate Law. *Career:* Theodore Goddard, Solicitor 1984-. *Biog: b.* 20 February 1959. *Nationality:* British. *m.* 1985, Vivien (née Hart); 1 d. *Educ:* Wimbledon College; Gonville & Caius College, Cambridge (MA). *Professional Organisations:* Member, The Law Society.

KAVANAUGH, John Lawrence; Main Board Director, Bain Clarkson Ltd.

KAWAMOTO, Takashi; General Manager, The Bank of Tokyo Ltd.

KAWAMURA, S; Executive Director, Daiwa Europe Limited.

KAY, David; Chairman, Goddard Kay Rogers & Associates Ltd. *Career:* ICI, Plastics Division, Various Posts in Personnel 1957-65; Rank Xerox, Personnel Manager, Industrial Relations 1965-67; Bechtel International, Personnel Manager, Organisation & Planning 1967-69; Goddard Kay Rogers & Associates, Founder & Chairman 1970-. *Biog: b.* 31 January 1935. *Nationality:* British. *m.* Margaret. *Educ:* Leighton Park School, Reading; Trinity College, Oxford (Hons Geography). *Directorships:* GKR Group and its Subsidiary Companies; British American Drama Academy; English Shakespeare Company; International Foundation for Training in the Arts.

KAY, Professor John Anderson; Director, Centre for Business Strategy, London Business School, since 1986. *Career:* St John's College, Oxford, Fellow 1970-; University of Oxford, Lecturer in Economics 1971-79; The Institute for Fiscal Studies, Research Director 1979-82; Director 1982-86. *Biog: b.* 3 August 1948. *Nationality:* British. *m.* 1986, Deborah (née Freeman). *Educ:* Royal High School, Edinburgh; Edinburgh University (MA); Nuffield College, Oxford (MA). *Directorships:* Govett Strategic Investment Trust 1982 (non-exec); Acorn Investment Trust 1987 (non-exec); Investors Compensation Scheme 1988 (non-exec). *Publications:* The British Tax System (5th Edition), 1990; Many Other Books and Articles.

KAY, P B; Director, Smith New Court plc, since 1990; Pacific Broking.

KAYE, Colin Michael Sutton; OBE; Executive Director, County NatWest Limited, since 1988; Corporate Services, Technology, Public Relations, Central Management. *Career:* HM Armed Forces 1961-87; Chief of Staff HQ, N Ireland 1986-87. *Biog: b.* 20 July 1943. *Nationality:* British. *m.* 1970, Gay (née Vernon); 1 s; 1 d. *Educ:* Harrow School; RMA Sandhurst (PSC, JSSC). *Clubs:* Army & Navy, Overseas Bankers', MCC, IZ, Free Foresters. *Recreations:* Golf, Cricket, Sailing, Reading, Photography.

KAYE, Jeremy Robin; Director & Company Secretary, Arbuthnot Latham Bank Ltd.

KEAL, Anthony Charles; Partner, Allen & Overy, since 1982; Domestic & International Banking. *Career:* Allen & Overy Articled Clerk & Asst Solicitor 1974-76; Libra Bank plc Legal Adviser 1976-78; Allen & Overy

Asst Solicitor 1978-81. *Biog: b.* 12 July 1951. *Nationality:* British. *m.* 1979, Janet Michele (née King); 4 s. *Educ:* Stowe; New College, Oxford (BA Juris). *Professional Organisations:* The Law Society; City of London Solicitors' Company. *Recreations:* Family, Sailing, Travel.

KEANE, Miss Mary Georgina; Head of Employment Unit, Titmuss Sainer & Webb, since 1988; Employment Law. *Career:* Barrister in General Practice 1975-84; Confederation of British Industry, Legal Adviser, Employment Affairs Directorate 1984-86; Titmuss Sainer & Webb, Consulting Barrister 1986-88. *Biog: b.* 3 February 1954. *Nationality:* British. *m.* 1978, Dr Saad Al-Damliyi; 2 s. *Educ:* Sacred Heart Convent, Woldingham, Surrey; Inns of Court Law School. *Other Activities:* Executive Committee Member, Industrial Law Society; Employment Committee Member, Fawcett Society; Law Society,; City of London Solicitors Company. *Professional Organisations:* Law Society Admitted as Solicitor 1988; Former Member of the Bar, Middle Temple 1975-88.

KEAT, Alan Michael; Partner, Travers Smith Braithwaite, since 1970; Company Law. *Biog: b.* 12 May 1942. *Nationality:* British. *m.* 1966, Lorna Marion (née Wilson); 3 d. *Educ:* Charterhouse; Merton College, Oxford. *Directorships:* Beazer plc 1986 (non-exec). *Other Activities:* Member, Standing Committee on Company Law, The Law Society.

KEATING, William J; Partner (London), Evershed Wells & Hind.

KEATINGE, Richard Arthur Davis; Chief Executive, Bank of Ireland, since 1986. *Career:* Reuters Ltd, Fin Jourinalist 1969-71; The Irish Times Fin Jourinalist 1971-78; The Investment Bank of Ireland, Corporate Finance Executive/Director 1978-83; Bank of Ireland, Head of Group Strategy 1983-86; Chief Executive, Britain 1986-. *Biog: b.* 30 August 1947. *m.* 1970, Athene; 2 s; 1 d. *Educ:* Portora Royal School; Trinity College, Dublin (BA Econ); University College, Dublin (MBA). *Directorships:* Bank of Ireland; Lifetime Assurance Company Limited; Bank of Ireland Britain Holdings Limited; British Credit Trust Ltd; Bank of Ireland Home Mortgages Limited; Bank of Ireland Investment Services Limited; College Green Limited; Openmulti Limited; BIF (Northern Ireland) Ltd. *Clubs:* Overseas Bankers', Royal Mid Surrey. *Recreations:* Golf, Fishing, Cricket.

KEATLEY, W H; Chairman, Laurence Keen Limited.

KEATS, Peter Gordon Stevenson; Director, Greig Fester Group Ltd, since 1986; Latin America, Spain, South Africa, Israel. *Career:* C E Golding & Co 1954-63. *Biog: b.* 9 November 1934. *Nationality:* British. *m.* 1956, Myra (née Gray); 1 s; 2 d. *Directorships:* Greig Fester Ltd 1970 (exec); Greig Fester (South Africa) (Pty) Ltd 1977 (non-exec); Greig Fester (North America) Inc 1981 (non-exec); Greig Fester (Agencies) Ltd 1984 (non-exec); Greig Fester Iberica SA 1988 (non-exec); Greig Fester Group Ltd 1986 (exec). *Professional Organisations:* ACII. *Clubs:* City of London. *Recreations:* Sailing.

KEEGAN, Dennis J; Managing Director (Investment Management), Salomon Brothers International Limited.

KEEGAN, Nicholas Francis; Director, Barclays de Zoete Wedd Ltd, since 1990; Corporate Finance. *Career:* Price Waterhouse 1978-82; Hill Samuel & Co Ltd 1982-87; Barclays de Zoete Wedd Ltd 1987-. *Biog: b.* 16 September 1955. *Nationality:* British. *Educ:* Douai School; Corpus Christi College, Oxford (MA). *Professional Organisations:* ACA. *Clubs:* Oxford & Cambridge. *Recreations:* Music, Opera, Swimming.

KEEGAN, William; Economics Editor, The Observer, since 1977. *Career:* Financial Times, Feature Writer 1963-64; Daily Mail, City Staff 1964-67; Financial Times, Economics Correspondent 1967-76; Bank of England, Economics Division 1967-77; The Observer, Economics Editor 1977-; Associate Editor 1982-. *Biog: b.* 3 July 1938. *Nationality:* British. (div); 2 s 2 d. *Educ:* Wimbledon College; Trinity College, Cambridge (BA Economics). *Other Activities:* BBC Committee on Industrial and Business Affairs (1981-88); Board of Dept of Applied Economics, Cambridge (1988-); Professor of Journalism, Sheffield University (1990-). *Professional Organisations:* Society of Business Economists. *Publications:* Who Runs the Economy?, 1979; Mrs Thatcher's Economic Experiment, 1984; Britain Without Oil, 1985; Mr Lawson's Gamble, 1989; Consulting Father Wintergreen (fiction), 1974; A Real Killing (fiction), 1976. *Clubs:* Garrick.

KEEL Jr, A G; Non-Executive Director, Riggs A P Bank Ltd.

KEELING, Christopher Anthony Gedge; Chairman, Fenchurch Underwriting Agencies Ltd, since 1987; Lloyd's Underwriting Members' Agency. *Career:* Grenadier Guards Captain 1948-54; Antony Gibbs Group Dir 1954-66; Fenchurch 1966-; MD 1972-87. *Biog: b.* 15 June 1930. *Nationality:* British. *m.* 1974, Rachel; 2 s; 1 d. *Educ:* Eton College; Royal Military Academy, Sandhurst. *Directorships:* Fenchurch Insurance Holdings Ltd 1966 (exec); KGM Underwriting Agencies Ltd 1985 Consultant; Venton Underwriting Agencies Ltd Consultant; Castle Underwriting Agencies Ltd 1986 Consultant; Stutter & Tallack (Underwriting Agencies) Ltd 1987 (exec); Jeamring Ltd 1989 (exec). *Other Activities:* Liveryman of the Fishmongers' Company; Deputy Chairman, Lloyd's Underwriting Agents' Association, -1988. *Professional Organisations:* Associate, Chartered Insurance Institute (ACII). *Clubs:* White's, Beefsteak, MCC. *Recreations:* Shooting, Watching Cricket, Reading.

KEELING, Damian John; Partner, Clark Whitehill, since 1989; Investigations. *Career:* Clark Pixley 1979-82; Clark Whitehill 1982-. *Biog: b.* 1 August 1957. *Nationality:* British. *m.* 1987, Pauline Anne (née Briggs); 2 d. *Educ:* William Hulme's Grammar School, Manchester; University of Kent at Canterbury (BA Hons). *Professional Organisations:* Institute of Chartered Accountants in England & Wales.

KEELING, Frank; Chairman and Managing Director, Fyshe Horton Finney Ltd, since 1988. *Career:* F H Finney & Co Ptnr 1962-72; Fyshe Horton Finney & Co Ptnr & Snr Ptnr 1972-88; FHF Market Makers Ltd Dir 1986-89. *Biog: b.* 10 April 1929. *Nationality:* British; 1 s; 1 d. *Educ:* Queen Mary's, Walsall; Selwyn College, Cambridge (MA). *Directorships:* Second City Securities Ltd 1987 (exec); Midbras Group Holdings Ltd 1982 (non-exec); Upfields Ltd 1986 (non-exec).

KEELING, H C V; Alternate Director, Wellington Underwriting Agencies Limited.

KEEN, N G; Partner, Milne Ross.

KEENAN, Michael John; Vice President & Director, Wood Gundy Inc, since 1977; Head of European Business, Canadian Imperial Bank of Commerce, since 1990; Financial Control, Security/Banking Operations, Human Resources, Systems Development, Facilities Management, Special Projects. *Career:* Ernst Whinney, ACA 1968-77. *Biog: b.* 13 April 1949. *Nationality:* British. *m.* 1975, Mary Elizabeth (née Clarke); 1 s; 2 d. *Educ:* Harrow School. *Directorships:* Wood Gundy (London) Ltd 1980 (exec); Wood Gundy SA 1986 (exec); Wood Gundy International Ltd 1986 (exec). *Professional Organisations:* FCA.

KEENAN, William; Financial Journalist, Daily Mirror.

KEENE, Bryan Richard; Company Secretary, Director, MIM Ltd, since 1985; Taxation, Personnel. *Career:* Drayton Corporation Ltd, Various 1963-74; Samuel Montagu & Co Ltd, Asst Dir 1974-84. *Biog: b.* 14 September 1937. *Nationality:* British. *Educ:* St James' School for Boys, Weybridge. *Directorships:* 117 Ventures Ltd 1985 (non-exec); Elliot Associates Ltd 1986 (non-exec). *Professional Organisations:* FCIS; ATII.

KEENS, David Wilson; Group Treasurer, Next plc, since 1986; Banking, Corporate Funding, Foreign Exchange, Risk Managemnt. *Career:* Gale Brown & Co Mgr, Private Client Portfolio 1970-77; Standard Brands Tunisie Chief Financial Officer 1977-80; Romix Foods Limited Financial Controller 1980-83; Nabisco Group Ltd Dep Dir, Fin Planning and Analysis 1983-84; Treasury Mgr 1984-86. *Biog: b.* 16 August 1953. *Nationality:* British. *m.* 1977, Shirley (née Cardnell); 1 s; 1 d. *Educ:* Rayleigh Sweyne Grammar. *Professional Organisa-*

tions: FCCA; MCT (Member of the Association of Corporate Treasurers). *Recreations:* Outdoor Pursuits.

KEER, C; Managing Director, Bankers Trust Co, since 1986; Head of Mergers & Acquisitions. *Career:* Price Waterhouse & Co, Assistant Manager 1972-76; Samuel Montagu & Co Ltd, Director 1976-86. *Biog: b.* 19 April 1950. *Nationality:* British. *Educ:* Radley College; Magdalene College, Cambridge (MA). *Directorships:* Bankers Trust International Ltd 1987 (exec); Samuel Montagu & Co Ltd 1984 (exec). *Other Activities:* Fellow, Royal Society of Arts. *Professional Organisations:* Fellow, Institute of Chartered Accountants. *Recreations:* Tennis, Garden Design, Trade History.

KEEVIL, Philip Clement; Head of Corporate Finance USA, S G Warburg & Co Ltd, since 1987; Merger s and Acquisitions. *Career:* Unilever plc, Manager 1968-73; Morgan Stanley & Co Inc, New York, Corporate Finance Associate 1975-78; Lazard Freres & Co (New York), Mergers & Acquisitions, Associate 1979-80; Mergers & Acquisitions, Vice-President 1981-82; General Partner 1983-87; International Department, Co-head 1986-87; S G Warburg & Co Ltd Corporate Finance Director 1987-; S G Warburg & Co Inc (New York), Managing Director and Head of Mergers & Acquisitions 1987-. *Biog: b.* 19 October 1946. *Nationality:* British. *m.* 1972, Augusta (née McGrail); 2 s; 1 d. *Educ:* Tonbridge School; Trinity College, Oxford (BA, MA); Harvard Business School (MBA). *Directorships:* Wiener Enterprises Inc (US) 1984 (non-exec). *Other Activities:* Liveryman, Poulters' Company; Governor, Piping Rock Club; Finance Comm, St John's Church, Lattington, Long Island; Director, Music at St John's. *Clubs:* Leander, Brook (NY), Knickerbocker (NY), Racquet & Tennis (NY). *Recreations:* Choral Music, Racquet Sports and Skeet Shooting.

KEEY, Christopher Wynne; Group Deputy Chairman, Minet Holdings plc, since 1985; Chairman of Minet Insurance Brokers and Minet International. *Career:* Minet Holdings (SA) (PTY) Ltd, Chief Exec 1972-85. *Biog: b.* 7 July 1938. *Nationality:* South African. *m.* 1962, Andrea (née Leyton); 1 s; 2 d. *Educ:* St Andrews, Grahamstown, South Africa. *Directorships:* Several In House Directorships. *Professional Organisations:* ACII; Fellow, Corporation of Insurance Brokers. *Clubs:* Addington Golf Club. *Recreations:* Golf.

KEEYS, Geoffrey Foster; General Manager, Prudential Corporation, since 1984; Personnel and Business Services. *Career:* Mobil Oil Co, Personnel Officer 1966-68; Massey Ferguson, Various Personnel Positions, Personnel and Industrial Relations Director 1968-2; Chubb & Son plc, Group Personnel Director 1982-84. *Biog: b.* 29 October 1944. *Nationality:* British. *m.* 1970, Donna (née Lavers); 1 s; 1 d. *Educ:* Abingdon School; Manchester University (LLB). *Other Activities:* Member, Advisory Boards for Centre for Corporate Strategy &

Change, Warwick University. *Professional Organisations:* MIPM. *Clubs:* RAC. *Recreations:* Golf, Cricket.

KEIGHER, Richard P; Executive Director, Samba Capital Management International Ltd.

KEIR, James Dewar; QC; *Career:* The United Africa Co Ltd, Legal Adviser 1954-66; Sec & Legal Adviser 1966-73; Unilever Ltd, Head of Legal Services 1973-76; UAC International Ltd, Dir 1974-77; Unilever plc & NV, Jt Sec 1976-84. *Biog:* b. 30 November 1921. *Nationality:* British. *m.* 1948, (Jean) Mary (née Orr); 2 s; 2 d. *Educ:* Edinburgh Academy; Christ Church, Oxford (MA Hons). *Directorships:* Open University Educational Enterprises Ltd 1983-88 (non-exec). *Other Activities:* Chm, Pharmacists' Review Panel; Member, Monopolies & Mergers Commission, 1987; Chm, East Grinstead Decorative & Fine Arts Society; Formerly Pres and Chm, East Grinstead Rugby Football Club. *Professional Organisations:* Bar Assoc for Commerce Finance & Industry (VP, Formerly Pres and Chm). *Clubs:* Caledonian. *Recreations:* Opera, Watching Rugby, Reading.

KEIRSTEAD, Roy; VP Compliance, ScotiaMcLeod Incorporated.

KEKHIA, Bassel; Treasury Manager, Jordan International Bank plc, since 1988; Dealing Room/Treasury. *Career:* P Murray-Jones Ltd, Spot and Forwards 1973-74; Sarabex Ltd (London), Spot, Forwards, Gold and Silver 1974-77; Allied Trust Bank (Previously Allied Arab Bank), Assistant Chief Dealer 1977-82; Chief Dealer/ Treasury Manager 1982-88. *Biog:* b. 18 November 1944. *Nationality:* British. *m.* (div); 2 s. *Educ:* Kingston Polytechnic, (Hons Aeronautical Engineering). *Professional Organisations:* Member, Arab Bankers Association, London. *Recreations:* Tennis, Swimming.

KELIHER, J A; Company Partner, Richards Butler.

KELLAWAY, Rosalind; Partner, Jaques & Lewis.

KELLEHER, Mrs Elizabeth Kate; Partner, McKenna & Co, since 1988; Corporate Taxation. *Career:* Coward Chance, Articled Clerk 1978-80; Asst Solicitor 1980-88. *Biog:* b. 5 March 1956. *Nationality:* British. *m.* 1983, John; 1 s; 1 d. *Educ:* St Hugh's College, Oxford (MA Jurisprudence); French Chamber of Commerce (Diplomé Supérieur De Français Des Affaires. *Professional Organisations:* Law Society; City of London Solicitors Company; Solicitors International Tax Group. *Recreations:* Bridge, Gardening, Cooking, Sailing.

KELLEHER, John R; Partner, Theodore Goddard.

KELLEHER, Terry; Editor, The City Programme, Thames Television, since 1987. *Career:* Hibernia Fortnightly Review (Ireland), Deputy Editor & Columnist 1970-75; Sunday Press, Ireland Senior Journalist 1975;

RTE (Irish TV & Radio), London Correspondent 1975-77; Thames TV Deputy Editor, Thames News 1977-82; Reporting London, Editor 1984-86. *Biog:* b. 2 July 1948. *Nationality:* Irish; 1 d. *Educ:* Clongowes Wood College, Kildare; University College Dublin (BCL). *Publications:* The Essential Dublin, 1971 and 1979. *Clubs:* ICA. *Recreations:* Theatre, Tennis.

KELLER, C E; Director, Hogg Group plc.

KELLER-HOBSON, D S Douglas; Director, Royal Trust Bank, since 1990; Legal Affairs. *Biog:* b. 10 June 1955. *Nationality:* Canadian. *m.* 1980, Kathleen.

KELLER Jr, Paul C; Senior Vice President and Deputy General Manager, NCNB National Bank of North Carolina, since 1990. *Career:* Republic National Bank of Dallas, Various Positions 1979-86; NCNB Texas National Bank, Senior Vice President & General Manager (London Branch) 1986-90. *Biog:* b. 29 January 1955. *Nationality:* American. *m.* 1974, Kay (née McGowan); 1 s; 1 d. *Educ:* University of Texas (BBA); Southern Methodist University (MBA); Stonier Graduate School of Banking, Rutgers University. *Other Activities:* Ambassador of the City of Dallas to London (appointed 1990). *Clubs:* Overseas Bankers Club. *Recreations:* Music, Opera.

KELLETT, Sir Brian; Director, Lombard North Central plc.

KELLETT, Bryan Philip David; Chairman, Kellett (Holdings) Ltd, since 1973. *Career:* Sedgwick Collins & Co Ltd 1954-60; National Service (Royal Artillery) 1956-58; KF Alder Syndicate Lloyd's, Asst Underwriter 1960-65; Rose Thomson Young (Reins) Ltd, Reinsurance Broker 1965-68; Edwards & Payne (U/A) Ltd, Property Underwriter 1968-73. *Biog:* b. 8 December 1937. *Nationality:* British. *m.* 1968, Brenda (née English). *Educ:* Latymer Upper School, Hammersmith. *Other Activities:* Lloyd's Underwriters Non-Marine Assoc (Former Chm); Council of Lloyds (Mem). *Professional Organisations:* FCII; Insurance Institute of London (Pres, 1989-90).

KELLETT, Sarah Jane; Director, County NatWest Limited, since 1988; Corporate Advisory. *Career:* Bank of England 1975-77; J Henry Schroder Wagg & Co Limited 1977-81. *Biog:* b. 28 May 1954. *Nationality:* British. *m.* 1989, David Howard Juster. *Educ:* Roedean School, Brighton; St Hugh's College, Oxford (BA); London Business School (MSc). *Other Activities:* Governor, Taunton School.

KELLEY, Edward William; Managing Partner, Financial Institutions, Korn/Ferry International, since 1984; Investment/Merchant Banking, International Banking, Stockbroking, Fund Management, Insurance. *Career:* State of California Asst Dir, Finance 1961-67;

Peat Marwick Mitchell Principal 1967-69; Griffen Hagen Kroeger MD 1969-74; Booz Allen & Hamilton Inc Ptnr & VP 1974-84. *Biog: b.* 18 December 1937. *Nationality:* American. *m.* 1975, Françoise (née Marion); 3 s; 1 d. *Educ:* O'Dowo High School; University of Southern California (BA, MBA). *Recreations:* Tennis, Skiing, Squash, Bike Riding, Golf.

KELLNER, P M; General Manager, Crédit Lyonnais Bank Nederland NV.

KELLNER, Peter L; Deputy Head Mergers & Acquisitions, Morgan Stanley International, since 1990. *Career:* Bank of America 1967-73; Morgan Stanley & Co Incorporated (NY) Corp Fin Analyst 1973-82; Managing Director (Mergers & Acquisitions) 1983-87; Chairman, Management Board, Morgan Stanley GmbH Frankfurt, Germany 1988-90; Morgan Stanley Intl London, England, Managing Director & Deputy Head (Mergers & Acquisitions Dept) 1990-.

KELLS, Ronald David; Director, Ulster Bank Limited, since 1984. *Career:* Wm F Coates & Co, Stockbroker; Wm Patterson & Co, Stockbroker; Ulster Bank Ltd, Investment Mgr 1969-76; Dep Head, Related Banking 1976-79; Head of Planning & Marketing 1979-82; Seconded to National Westminster Bank 1982-84. *Biog: b.* 14 May 1938. *Nationality:* British. *m.* 1964, Elizabeth (née Hanna); 1 s; 1 d. *Educ:* Sullivan Upper School, Holywood; Queen's University, Belfast (BSc). *Directorships:* Ulster Bank Trust Co (exec); Ulster Natural Resources (exec); Office of the Banking Ombudsman (exec); Ulster Bank Limited; Ulster Bank Unit Trust Managers Limited; Ulster Bank Commercial Services (NI) Limited; Lombard & Ulster Limited; Lombard & Ulster Ireland Limited; Institute of Software Engineering. *Professional Organisations:* Fellow, Institute of Chartered Secretaries in Ireland. *Clubs:* Royal Belfast Golf Club, Royal County Down Golf Club. *Recreations:* Golf, Squash, Winter Sports, Gardening.

KELLY, Bernard; , Bernard Kelly & Associates. *Career:* 8th Queen's Royal Irish Hussars, Capt 1958-62; Qualified Solicitor 1955; Simmons & Simmons, Partner. *Biog: b.* 23 April 1930. *Nationality:* Irish/British. *m.* 1952, Lady Mirabel (née Fitzalan Howard); 7 s; 1 d. *Educ:* Downside School. *Directorships:* Barnes Group Inc (USA) 1975; Investment AB Ostermalm (Sweden) 1976; Lazard Income Growth & Property Unit Trust 1984 Chm; First Equity Holdings Ltd 1987 Chm; Highcross plc 1988; Phoenix Re Corporation (USA) 1988; International Select Fund Ltd 1989 Chm; Campbell Lutyens Hudson & Co Ltd 1990 Chm; Societe Generale d'Investissements SA 1990; Phoenix Investment Counsel Ltd 1990; Stockholm & Edinburgh Investments plc 1990; S G Warburg & Co Ltd 1963-76; British and French Bank Ltd 1966-73; United Bank for Africa Ltd 1966-73; Metropolitan Pensions Association (Holdings) Ltd 1966-76; AB Motorvarden (Sweden) 1967-82; AB

Autokredit (Sweden) 1967-84; Societe d'Investissement et de Gestion SA (France) 1969-76; S G Warburg & Co, International Holdings Ltd 1970-76; British Channel Tunnel Co Ltd 1971-75; Imminvest SA (France) 1972-76; Banque de Paris et des Pays-Bas (Belgique) SA 1973-76; Warburg Pension Trustee Co Ltd 1974-76; Mercury Securities Ltd 1974-76; Stanley Gibbons International Ltd 1975-80; Compagnie Monegasque de Banque SAM 1976-85; Stanley Gibbons Monaco SAM 1978-80; Societe Europeenne de Banque (Luxembourg) 1978-80; Insilco Corporation (USA) 1978-88; Rentco International Ltd 1988 Dep Chm; Lazard Brothers & Co Ltd 1980-90 Vice Chm & MD; Lazard Brothers & Co (Jersey) Ltd 1987-90 Chm. *Clubs:* Athenaeum, Brooks's, Kildare Street, University Club.

KELLY, Mrs Caroline Margaret (née Crawford); Partner, Clyde & Co, since 1984; Marine and Commercial Litigation. *Career:* Lovell, White & King, Articled Clerk 1978-80; Clyde & Co, Assistant Solicitor 1980-84. *Biog: b.* 3 October 1956. *Nationality:* British. *m.* 1980, Donald Cornelius Kelly; 1 d. *Educ:* Cambridge House School, Ballymena; Ashford School, Kent; Newnham College, Cambridge.

KELLY, Donald Cornelius; Partner, Lovell White Durrant, since 1986; Corporate Taxation. *Biog: b.* 29 January 1956. *Nationality:* British. *m.* 1978, C M (née Crawford); 1 d. *Educ:* St Edmund's College, Ware; Jesus College, Cambridge (MA). *Other Activities:* City of London Solicitors' Company. *Professional Organisations:* The Law Society.

KELLY, Ian; Partner, Clark Whitehill.

KELLY, John Anthony Brian; Director, Brown, Shipley & Co Ltd, since 1982; Corporate Finance. *Career:* ATE Ltd Management Trainee 1963; Price Waterhouse & Co, Articled Clerk 1963-67; Audit Clerk 1967-68; Old Broad Street Securities Ltd, Exec 1968-70; Wheatsheaf Distribution & Trading Ltd, Asst Group Chief Acct 1970-71; Laurie, Milbank & Co Corp, Fin Exec 1971-75; Associate Member 1975-78; Brown, Shipley & Co Ltd, Mgr 1978-82. *Biog: b.* 21 August 1941. *Nationality:* British. *m.* 1971, Denise Anne (née Circuit); 2 s; 2 d. *Educ:* Fort Augustus Abbey School, Scotland; Queen's University, Belfast (LLB Hons). *Directorships:* Cosalt plc 1986 (non-exec); Tag Holdings Ltd 1988 (non-exec). *Other Activities:* Member of Founders Company. *Professional Organisations:* FCA. *Clubs:* The Naval Club, Royal Ulster Yacht Club. *Recreations:* Walking, Theatre-Going, Tennis, Poetry.

KELLY, Owen; QPM; Commissioner of the City Police, Corporation of London.

KELLY, P A; Partner, R Watson & Sons Consulting Actuaries.

KELLY, R W; Deputy Managing Director, Sogemin Metals Ltd.

KELLY, Reay Diarmaid Anthony; Director, Baring Securities Ltd.

KELLY, Thomas Anthony; Assistant General Manager, Norwich Union Life Insurance Society, since 1987; Sales & Marketing. *Career:* Norwich Union Life, Inspector 1966-74; Chief Inspector 1974-78; Asst Production Mgr 1978-83; Marketing Mgr 1983-87. *Biog: b.* 31 August 1942. *Nationality:* British. *m.* 1974, Janice (née Allen); 1 s; 1 d. *Educ:* St Mary's College, Merseyside. *Directorships:* Camifa Limited to 1989; Westlegate Financial Services Limited 1990 (exec); Norwich Union Healthcare Limited 1990 (non-exec); Norwich Union Pension Trustees Limited 1989 (non-exec); IFA Promotion Limited 1990 (non-exec). *Recreations:* Walking, Football.

KELSALL, John Robert; Partner, Walker Morris Scott Turnbull, since 1984; Commercial Property. *Career:* Davis Campbell & Co, Articled Clerk 1977-79; Maxwell Entwistle & Byrne, Assistant Solicitor 1979-80; Simpson Curtis & Co, Assistant Solicitor 1980-83; Walker Morris & Coles, Assistant Solicitor 1983-84. *Biog: b.* 22 August 1954. *Nationality:* British. *Educ:* Wrekin College; Hull University (LLB). *Professional Organisations:* Law Society.

KELSON, Christopher John Kerry; Chairman, M W Marshall & Co Ltd, since 1990. *Career:* M W Marshall 1970; Foreign Exchange Division, London 1970-74; Marshalls (Singapore) Pte Limited, Head of Foreign Exchange 1974-76; Marshalls (Hongkong) Limited, Director & General Manager 1976-79; Marshalls (Singapore) Pte Limited, Director & General Manager 1979-81; Marshall Woellwarth & Co Ltd, London Director, Chief Executive London Foreign Exchange 1981-87; Joint Managing Director and Asia-Pacific Regional Chairman, Hongkong 1988-89; Chief Executive, London 1989. *Biog: b.* 25 December 1946. *m.* 1972, Elizabeth Helen (née Curnow); 1 s; 1 d. *Educ:* Tudor Grange Grammar School, Warwickshire. *Directorships:* Marshalls Finance Ltd 1988 (exec). *Clubs:* Woking Golf Club.

KELTON, Robin Charles; Chairman & Managing Director, Fox-Pitt Kelton Group SA, since 1970. *Career:* York & Co Inc, Broker 1959-64; Tucker Anthony & RL Day Manager, Europe 1964-70. *Biog: b.* 24 October 1934. *Nationality:* British. *m.* 1975, Zena Lavinia (née McVittie); 3 s; 1 d. *Educ:* Stowe School; Queens' College, Cambridge (MA Law). *Directorships:* Fox-Pitt Kelton Ltd 1983 (exec) Chm; Fox-Pitt Kelton Inc 1983 (exec); Insurance Solvency International 1982 (exec); IBCA Banking Analysis Ltd 1977 (non-exec). *Recreations:* Horses, Fishing, Farming.

KEMBER, H J; Director, General Accident Fire Life Assurance Corp.

KEMNER, A; Director, Unilever plc.

KEMP, Alan Scott; Deputy Chief Executive, Dunedin Fund Managers Ltd, since 1990. *Career:* Scottish Widows Fund Investment Analyst 1970-72; Edinburgh Investment Trust Dep Mgr 1972-84; Dunedin Fund Managers North American Dir 1985-87; Investment Director 1988-90. *Biog: b.* 2 April 1944. *Nationality:* British. *m.* 1967, June (née Christie); 2 s. *Educ:* George Heriot's School, Edinburgh. *Directorships:* Dunedin Unit Trust Managers Ltd 1985 (exec); Dunedin Berkeley Management Ltd 1986 (exec); Edinburgh Sports Club Ltd 1986 (non-exec); Dunedin Fund Managers Ltd 1985 (exec); DFM Holdings Ltd 1990 (exec); Dunedin Ventures Ltd 1989 (exec). *Other Activities:* Murrayfield Cramond Rotary Club (Member). *Professional Organisations:* CA; ASIA. *Recreations:* Golf, Squash, Rotary.

KEMP, Charles Richard Foster; Director, Brown Shipley & Co Ltd, since 1988; Development & Venture Capital. *Career:* Chemical Bank (London & New York), Lending & Leasing Divisions 1978-84; Charterhouse Development Capital Ltd, Investment Exec & Director 1984-87. *Biog: b.* 5 January 1957. *Nationality:* British. *Educ:* Bedford School; Queens' College, Cambridge (BA Hons). *Directorships:* Lincat Group plc 1985-87 (non-exec); Charterhouse Development Capital Ltd 1986-87 (non-exec); Brown Shipley Development Capital Ltd 1988 (exec); Dalehead Foods Holdings Ltd 1988 (non-exec); Bridata Group Ltd 1989 (non-exec). *Recreations:* Golf, Squash, Skiing.

KEMP, D H; OBE; Partner, Penningtons.

KEMP, M; Partner, Nabarro Nathanson.

KEMP, M H D; Partner, Bacon & Woodrow.

KEMP, Timothy; Joint Managing Director, UK Division, Gibbs Hartley Cooper Ltd, since 1985; UK General Insurances. *Career:* Royal Exchange Assurance, Trainee Inspector 1966-68; E W Jessup & Co Ltd, Account Handler 1968-69; Bluett Smith & Co Ltd, Account Exec 1969-71; Gibbs Hartley Cooper, Various 1971-. *Directorships:* Gerrard Insurance Services Ltd 1985 (exec); Gibbs Hartley Cooper Ltd.

KEMP-GEE, Mark Norman; Chairman, Greig, Middleton & Co Ltd, since 1978. *Career:* Kemp-Gee & Co, Institutional Salesman/Research Analyst 1967-75. *Biog: b.* 19 December 1945. *Nationality:* British. *m.* 1980, The Hon Lucy (née Lyttelton); 3 s. *Educ:* Marlborough College; Pembroke College, Oxford (MA). *Directorships:* Maybox Group plc; Moncrieffe & Co plc. *Other Activities:* Councillor, London Borough of Lambeth, 1982-86.

Professional Organisations: AMSIA. *Clubs:* Oxford Union. *Recreations:* Steeplechasing.

KEMP-WELCH, John; Joint Senior Partner, Cazenove & Co, since 1980. *Career:* Hoare & Co 1954-58; Cazenove & Co 1959-; Partner 1961-. *Biog: b.* 31 March 1936. *m.* 1964, Diana Elisabeth (née Leishman); 1 s; 3 d. *Educ:* Winchester College. *Directorships:* Savoy Hotel plc 1985 (non-exec); Lowland Investment Co plc 1963 (non-exec); Updown Investment Co plc 1978 (non-exec). *Other Activities:* Governor, Ditchley Foundation; Governor, North Foreland Lodge School; Trustee, King's Medical Research Trust; Companion, British Institute of Management; Fellow, Royal Society of Arts; Trustee, Game Conservancy Trust. *Professional Organisations:* CBIM. *Clubs:* White's, City of London, MCC. *Recreations:* Shooting, Farming, the Hills of Perthshire, Cricket.

KEMPEN, Reginald William; Associate Director/ Company Secretary, Unibank plc, since 1990; Compliance, Facilities Management. *Career:* Richard Costain Limited, Secretarial Assistant 1961-67; Turner & Coates Limited, Assistant Company Secretary 1967-69; The Osborne Group, Management Accountant 1969-72; London Interstate Bank Limited (later SDS Bank Limited), Company Secretary 1972-90. *Biog: b.* 6 July 1945. *Nationality:* British. *m.* 1970 (div 1982); 1 s; 1 d. *Educ:* Dagenham County High School. *Directorships:* London Interstate Nominees Ltd 1990 (exec); London Interstate Finance Ltd 1990 (exec); London Interstate Export Finance Ltd 1990 (exec); London Interstate Fund Managers Ltd 1988 (exec); London Ship Venture Capital Ltd 1986 (non-exec); SDS Bank Limited 1989-90 Alternate. *Professional Organisations:* FCIS. *Recreations:* Music, Sports, Photography, Reading.

KEMPLEY, Michael; Partner, Walker Morris Scott Turnbull.

KEMPSTER, P; Partner, Nabarro Nathanson.

KENDALL, D W; Deputy Chairman, British Coal Corporation, since 1989. *Career:* Elles Reeve & Co, Chartered Accountants 1955-62; Shell-Mex & BP Ltd 1963-68; Irish Shell & BP Ltd, Finance Director 1969-70; British Petroleum Co Ltd, Crude Oil Sales Manager 1971-72; Manager, Bulk Trading Division 1973-74; Organisation Planning Committee 1975; BP (New Zealand) Ltd, General Manager 1976-79. *Biog: b.* 8 May 1935. *Nationality:* British. *m.* 1973, Elisabeth (née Rollison); 2 s; 2 d. *Educ:* Enfield Grammar School; Southend High School. *Directorships:* Bunzl plc 1988 (non-exec); STC plc 1988 (non-exec); BP (New Zealand) Ltd 1979-82 (exec) MD & CEO; BP (South West Pacific) 1979-82 (exec) Chm; BP Oil Ltd 1982-85 (exec); BP Oil Ltd 1985-88 (exec) MD & CEO; BP Chemicals International 1985-88 (exec); BP Oil International 1985-88 (exec); Associated Octel Co Ltd 1985-

88 (exec); UK Petroleum Industries Association 1987-88 (exec) Pres; Oil Industries Club 1988 (exec) Pres. *Other Activities:* Confederation of British Industry; Companion, British Institute of Management. *Professional Organisations:* Fellow, Institute of Chartered Accountants in England & Wales. *Recreations:* Golf, Music, Family.

KENDALL, Gilbert John; Partner, Allen & Overy, since 1985; Litigation, Arbitration & Constructio Law. *Career:* Articled Clerk, Stephenson Harwood 1973-76; Assistant Solicitor, Litigation Dept, Allen & Overy 1977-85. *Biog: b.* 31 May 1950. *Nationality:* British. *m.* 1986, Jennifer Lynne (née Watton). *Educ:* Rugby School; New College, Oxford (BA, MA). *Professional Organisations:* City of London Law Society; Associate Member, Chartered Institute of Arbitrators. *Recreations:* Music, Walking.

KENDALL, P; Partner, Nabarro Nathanson.

KENDALL, Thomas J; Partner, Touche Ross & Co.

KENNEDY, Andrew David; Senior Partner, Beachcroft Stanleys, since 1987. *Biog: b.* 20 May 1943. *Nationality:* British. *m.* 1970, Mary (née Turnbull); 2 s. *Educ:* Worth Preparatory School; Downside School; Gonville & Caius College, Cambridge (MA). *Directorships:* The Sutton District Water plc 1980 (non-exec); East Surrey Water plc 1980 (non-exec); Ludgate Insurance Co Ltd 1989 (non-exec); Solicitors Indemnity Fund Ltd 1987 (non-exec). *Other Activities:* Member, Council of the Law Society; Vice Chairman, Standards and Guidance Committee of the Council of the Law Society; Member, City of London Solicitors' Company. *Clubs:* MCC, City Law Club, Royal Wimbledon Golf Club, Dulwich Hockey Club.

KENNEDY, Miss Ann D M; Partner, Touche Ross & Co, since 1987; Corporate Finance. *Career:* Spicer & Oppenheim (now Touche Ross) 1979-; Kleinwort Benson 1985-87. *Biog: b.* 16 November 1957. *Nationality:* British. *Educ:* Bar Convent, York; Imperial College, University of London (BSc). *Professional Organisations:* ACA. *Recreations:* Walking, Travel.

KENNEDY, Sir Francis; KCMG, CBE; Special Adviser & Non-Executive Director, British Airways.

KENNEDY, George M; Chairman, Smiths Industries Medical Systems Group, Smiths Industries plc.

KENNEDY, George Ronald; Partner, Simmons & Simmons.

KENNEDY, Graham Norbert; Director, Group Compliance, James Capel and Co Ltd, since 1990; Moneybroking/Compliance. *Career:* Union Acceptances Ltd, Asst Mgr 1965-70; James Capel Moneybroking Ltd, Chief Executive 1971-90. *Directorships:* The International Stock Exchange Ltd 1986 (non-exec); Duncan H McLaren Ltd 1986 (non-exec); RPL Ltd 1988 (non-exec); Charities Investment Managers Ltd 1989 (non-exec); James Capel & Co 1990 (exec); Anglo Pacific Resources plc 1990 (non-exec) Chm.

KENNEDY, Ian David; General Manager, Bristol & West Building Society, since 1990; Marketing. *Career:* PRS plc, Marketing Consultant, Acquisition & Market Development Consultant 1981-83; Lloyds Bowmaker, Group Marketing Manager, Finance House 1983-85; Nevi Baltic plc, Group Marketing Manager 1985-86; MPSI, Consultant (short-term project assessing the viability of a new market) 1986; Bristol & West, General Manager, Marketing 1986-. *Biog: b.* 23 December 1954. *Nationality:* British. *m.* 1984, Dr Nichola (née Rumsey); 2 s. *Educ:* Skinners School, Tunbridge Wells; Exeter University (BSc); Cranfield School of Management (MBA). *Directorships:* Bristol & West Property Services (Holdings) Ltd. *Recreations:* Tennis, Sailing, Skiing.

KENNEDY, James A; Chief Executive & Director, Beachcroft Stanleys.

KENNEDY, John Maxwell; Senior Partner, Allen & Overy, since 1986; Corporate Finance. *Biog: b.* 9 July 1934. *m.* 1958, Margaret (née Davies); 4 s. *Educ:* University College; London University (LLB). *Professional Organisations:* The Law Society; City of London Solicitors' Company. *Clubs:* City of London, City Law, Hurlingham. *Recreations:* Sport, Music.

KENNEDY, Peter Norman Bingham; TD, DL; Managing Director, Gartmore Scotland Limited, since 1987; Investment Management. *Career:* McClelland Moores & Co, CA Apprenticeship 1960-68; R C Greig & Co, Analyst 1968-71; Alex Lawrie Factors Ltd, Regional Manager 1971-75; Chester Street Trading Ltd, Director 1976-77. *Biog: b.* 11 October 1942. *m.* 1968, Priscilla (née Graham); 4 d. *Educ:* Rugby School; Edinburgh University (CA). *Directorships:* Gartmore Investment Trust Management Limited 1987 (exec). *Other Activities:* Chairman, River Doon Fishery Board; Deputy Lieutenant, Ayrshire & Arran. *Professional Organisations:* Institute of Chartered Accountants of Scotland. *Clubs:* Western (Glascow). *Recreations:* Shooting, Fishing, Tennis.

KENNEDY, William Michael Clifford; Director, Martin Currie Limited.

KENNERLEY, Peter Dilworth; Partner, Simmons & Simmons, since 1986; Company & Commercial Law. *Biog: b.* 9 June 1956. *Nationality:* British. *m.* 1989, Anne Marie Ghislane du Roy (née Galbraith). *Educ:* Collyer's School; Sidney Sussex College, Cambridge (MA). *Other Activities:* Panel on Take-overs and Mergers (Secretary 1986-88); Major, The Royal Yeomanry (1986). *Profes-*

sional Organisations: The Law Society. *Clubs:* Cavalry & Guards.

KENNERLEY BANKES, J L; Upper Warden, The Worshipful Company of Spectacle Makers.

KENNETT, Richard; Partner, Morison Stoneham Chartered Accountants.

KENNY, Kevin A; Managing Director, Tyndall Holdings plc, since 1990. *Career:* Charterhouse Japhet & Thomason Ltd, Fund Manager 1968-70; Allied Irish Investment Bank Ltd, Investment Manager 1970-72; Harcourt International Holdings Ltd, Chief Executive 1972-81; Weybridge Management Ltd, Managing Director 1981-83; Simon & Coates, Stockbroker 1983-85; Tyndall Holdings plc 1986-; Tyndall Business Finance, Managing Director 1986-87; Tyndall Holdings plc, Banking Director 1987-90; Investment Director 1989; Managing Director 1990. *Biog: b.* 18 September 1946. *Nationality:* British. *m.* 1969, Simone; 3 s. *Educ:* Trinity College, Dublin University (BA Economics, English and Philosophy). *Directorships:* Pacific Horizon Investment Trust 1990 (exec); European Project Investment Trust 1990 (exec); Pacific Property Investment Trust 1990 (exec); Tyndall & Co Limited 1987 (exec); Tyndall Business Finance Limited 1986 (exec); Tyndall Bank International Limited 1988 (exec); Tyndall Financial Management Limited 1988 (exec).

KENNY, P W; Director, Aetna International (UK) Ltd.

KENT, Geoffrey Charles; Director, Lloyds Bank plc, since 1981; Chairman, Audit Committee. *Career:* RAF Flt Lt (Coastal Command) 1939-46; Various Advertising & Marketing Appointments 1947-58; John Player & Sons Advertising Mgr 1958-64; Marketing Dir 1964-69; Asst MD 1969-75; Chm & MD 1975-78; Courage Ltd Chm & Chief Exec 1978-81; Imperial Group plc Chm & Chief Exec 1981-86. *Biog: b.* 2 February 1922. *Nationality:* British. *m.* 1955. *Educ:* Blackpool Grammar School. *Directorships:* Lloyds Merchant Bank Holdings Ltd 1985-88; Corah plc 1986-89 Dep Chm; John Howitt Group Ltd 1986; Mansfield Brewery plc 1988; Chm 1989. *Other Activities:* Member and Master, Brewer's Society. *Professional Organisations:* Member, Lloyd's of London. *Recreations:* Flying, Skiing.

KENT, Pendarell Hugh; Associate Director, Bank of England, since 1988; Finance & Industry, Printing Works. *Career:* National Service 2nd Lt Intelligence Corps 1959-61; Bank of England 1961-; Bank of International Settlements Secondment 1965-66; Bank of England, Governors' Private Sec 1969-70; IMF UK Alternate Exec Dir 1976-79; Bank of England, Head of Information Div 1984-85; Head of International Div 1985-88. *Biog: b.* 18 August 1937. *Nationality:* British. *m.* 1960, Jill (née George); 1 s; 1 d. *Educ:* University College School; Jesus College, Oxford (MA Hons).

Directorships: British Rail (Southern Region) 1986 (non-exec) Chm 1989. *Other Activities:* Exec Committee Magistere Universite Paris Dauphine. *Publications:* Nursery Schools For All (with Wife), 1970. *Recreations:* Art, Jazz, Skiing.

KENT, Roderick David; Managing Director, Close Brothers Group plc, since 1975. *Career:* J Henry Schroder Wagg Investment Analyst/Mgr 1969-71; Banque Blyth & Che Paris 1971-72; INSEAD Business School MBA Course 1972-; Triumph Investment Trust PA to Director 1972-74; Close Brothers Ltd Corp Fin Dir 1974-75. *Biog: b.* 14 August 1947. *Nationality:* British. *m.* 1972, Belinda Jane (née Mitchell); 3 d. *Educ:* The King's School, Canterbury; Corpus Christi College, Oxford (MA); INSEAD (MBA). *Directorships:* Close Brothers Ltd 1975 (exec) Chairman; Subsidiaries Of Close Brothers Group plc 1975-87 (exec); Wessex Water plc 1989 (non-exec); English & Scottish Investors plc 1988 (non-exec). *Other Activities:* Liveryman, Worshipful Company of Pewterers. *Recreations:* Sport.

KENWORTHY, John Neil; Director, The MDA Group plc, since 1985; Project Management. *Career:* Monk Dunstone Associates, Partner 1973-85. *Directorships:* Monk Dunstone Associates Management Limited 1985 (exec) MD. *Professional Organisations:* FRICS; ACIArb; Association of Project Managers (MAPM).

KENWORTHY, Robert; Partner, Moore Stephens, since 1976; Audit & General Consultancy. *Career:* Hodgson Harris & Co Articled Clerk 1967-70; Hill Vellacot Audit Snr 1970-73; Moore Stephens Snr Mgr 1973-76. *Biog: b.* 8 March 1946. *Nationality:* British. *m.* 1976, Jane Nicola (née Dalton); 2 s. *Educ:* East Grinstead County Grammar School. *Other Activities:* Worshipful Company of Bowyers. *Professional Organisations:* FCA. *Clubs:* East Grinstead RFC, Lingfield Park Golf Club, Farringdon Ward Club. *Recreations:* Rugby (now as Spectator only), Golf, Reading, History, Family.

KEOGH, Colin Denis; Chief Executive, Close Brothers Ltd, since 1986; Corporate Finance. *Career:* Arthur Andersen & Co 1979-82; Saudi International Bank 1983-85. *Biog: b.* 27 July 1953. *Nationality:* British. *m.* 1978, Joanna Mary (née Leapman); 2 s; 2 d. *Educ:* St John's College SA, Eton College; Oxford University (MA Law); INSEAD (MBA). *Directorships:* Amman UK 1990 (non-exec); Steniford Close Registrars 1989 (non-exec). *Professional Organisations:* ATII. *Recreations:* Tennis, Skiing, Watersports, Theatre.

KER, Philip R; Executive Director, Merrill Lynch International Bank Limited.

KERFOOT, Alan; Partner, Titmuss Sainer & Webb.

KERMAN, Anthony; Partner, Forsyte Kerman.

KERMAN, Isidore; Partner, Forsyte Kerman.

KERN, David; Chief Economist & Head of Market Intelligence, National Westminster Bank plc.

KERNER, J M; Director, Panmure Gordon & Co Limited.

KERR, Duncan Alexander; Director, Equity & Law Life Assurance Society plc, since 1986; Chief Actuary. *Career:* Equity & Law Life Assurance Society plc 1958-; Pensions Manager 1973; Assistant General Manager 1978; Chief Actuary 1985. *Biog: b.* 29 December 1935. *Nationality:* British. *m.* 1961; 3 d. *Educ:* RGS Newcastle upon Tyne; Christ Church, Oxford (MA). *Directorships:* Law Reversionary Interest Society Ltd 1985 (exec); Equity & Law (Managed Funds) Ltd 1985 (exec); Equity & Law Home Loans Ltd 1988 (exec); Equity & Law Commercial Loans Ltd 1990 (exec); Equity & Law Life Assurance Society plc 1986 (exec).

KERR, John Errington; Executive Director, Samuel Montague & Co Ltd, since 1990; Capital Markets. *Career:* Orion Royal Bank, Director 1985-88; Kitkat & Aitken, Director 1987-88. *Biog: b.* 4 March 1951. *Nationality:* British. *m.* 1986, Andrea; 2 s. *Educ:* Radley College; Exeter Univerisity (BA Hons). *Directorships:* Samuel Montagu & Co Ltd 1990 (exec); Burlington Estates plc 1988 (non-exec); Burlington Two plc 1989 (non-exec). *Professional Organisations:* Solicitor. *Clubs:* Naval & Military. *Recreations:* Golf, Bridge.

KERR, Ms Mary A; Director, Kleinwort Benson Investment Management.

KERR-DINEEN, M N C; Chief Executive, Laing & Cruickshank Investment Management Ltd, since 1989; Investment Management. *Career:* Bank of England, Banking Staff 1976-79; British National Oil Corporation, Executive 1979-81; Guinness Peat Group plc, (latterly as Managing Director) 1981-88; Laing & Cruickshank Investment Management Ltd, Chief Exec 1989-. *Biog: b.* 14 July 1952. *Nationality:* British. *m.* 1988, Sally; 2 s. *Educ:* Marlborough College; Edinburgh University (MA Hons Politics). *Directorships:* Credit Lyonnais Capital Markets Ltd (exec); Laing & Cruickshank Investment Management Ltd (exec); Guinness Peat Group plc (exec). *Clubs:* MCC, St Mellion. *Recreations:* Golf, Horse Racing, Opera.

KERR-MUIR, J; Director, London Fox.

KERRIDGE, J S; Director, Legal & General Group plc.

KERRIDGE, Peter Robert; Director & Treasurer, Barclays de Zoete Wedd.

KERRIGAN, Paul S J; Director, Merrill Lynch Europe Limited.

KERRIGAN, Thomas; Director, Henry Cooke Lumsden plc, since 1986; Overseas Department, Private Client Portfolios. *Career:* Henry Cooke Lumsden 1959-63; F I Dupont (New York) 1963-64; Henry Cooke Lumsden 1964-. *Biog: b.* 17 August 1942. *Nationality:* British. 1967, Jean Margaret (née Bradley) (Diss 1976) 2 d. *Educ:* St Francis Xavier, Liverpool. *Directorships:* Henry Cooke Lumsden plc 1986 (exec); Arkwright Nominees Ltd 1989 (exec). *Recreations:* Music, Reading, Walking, Travel.

KERRY, Sir Michael James; KCB, QC; Deputy Chairman, Lautro Ltd, since 1986; Public Interest Director. *Career:* Board of Trade (later DTI), Solicitors' Dept 1951-73; DTI, Solicitor 1973-80; Treasury Solicitor 1980-84. *Biog: b.* 5 August 1923. *Nationality:* British. *m.* 1951, Sidney Rosetta Elizabeth (née Foster); 1 s; 2 d. *Educ:* Rugby School; St Johns College, Oxford (MA, Hon Fellow). *Other Activities:* Chairman, Committee of Investigation for England & Wales under Agricultural Marketing Act 1958. *Professional Organisations:* Barrister-at-Law, Lincolns Inn 1949, Bencher 1984. *Clubs:* Piltdown Golf Club. *Recreations:* Golf.

KERSEY, P; Director, County NatWest Securities Limited.

KERSHAW, David Robert; Partner, Ashurst Morris Crisp, since 1986; Corp Finance, Mergers & Acquisitions, Public Issues, Banking, Insolvency. *Career:* Ashurst Morris Crisp Asst Solicitor 1982-84; Associate 1984-86. *Biog: b.* 1953. *Nationality:* British. *m.* 1978, Christine Anne (née Sexton); 3 s. *Educ:* Urmston Grammar School; Trinity College, Cambridge (MA). *Publications:* Gore-Browne Practice Bulletin (bi-monthly), Editor; Company Law Contributor to PLC Magazine (monthly). *Recreations:* Windsurfing, Travel, Literature, Classical Guitar.

KERSHAW, F M B; Director, Mase Westpac Limited.

KESTENBAUM, Dan E; Director, Alexander Howden Limited.

KESTENBAUM, Ralph; Joint Managing Director, Gerald Metals Ltd.

KESWICK, Henry Neville Lindley; Chairman, Matheson & Co Ltd.

KESWICK, (John) Chippendale Lindley (Chips); Chairman, Hambros Bank Limited, since 1986. *Career:* Glyn Mills & Company 1961-65; Hambros Bank Limited 1965-; Chief Executive 1985; Chairman 1986; Hambros plc, Joint Vice Chairman 1986. *Biog: b.* 2 February 1940. *Nationality:* British. *m.* 1966, Lady Sarah (née Ramsay); 3 s. *Educ:* Eton College; University of Aix/Marseilles. *Directorships:* Persimmon plc 1984 (non-exec); Charter Consolidated plc 1988 (non-exec); Hunters & Frankau Group Ltd 1986 (non-exec). *Other Activities:* Hon Treasurer, Children's Country Holidays Fund; Member of Council, Cancer Research Campaign. *Clubs:* Royal Bodyguard of Archers, Portland, Whites. *Recreations:* Country Pursuits.

KETT, Peter John Louis; Partner, Slaughter and May, since 1980; Company & Commercial Law. *Biog: b.* 2 July 1946. *Nationality:* British. *m.* 1974, Julia (née Hodge); 1 d. *Educ:* Norwich School; University College of Wales (LLB).

KEVILLE, R B; Executive Director, Willis Corroon plc.

KEYS, A J; Finance Director, Steel Burrill Jones Group plc.

KHALIL, Ahmed; Assistant General Manager, UBAF Bank Limited.

KHANACHET, S; Managing Director, Sharjah Investment Co (UK) Ltd.

KHARTABIL, Khaldoun Shafiq Khalil; Main Board Director, J H Minet & Co Ltd, since 1990; Responsible for the Arab Countries Promotion and Marketing. *Career:* Bland Payne Reinsurance Brokers Ltd, Student Employee 1978-79; Arab Insurance and Re-insurance Brokers (AIRB) (Athens), Leslie & Godwin/Frank B Hall, Assistant Vice President 1979-82; AIRB (London Contact Office) Leslie & Godwin (London), Assistant Vice-President, London Office Manager 1982-87; J H Minet & Co Ltd, Divisional Executive Director, Main Board Director 1987-. *Biog: b.* 23 March 1954. *Nationality:* Jordanian. *m.* 1984, Leila; 2 s. *Educ:* High School (School Degree); American University, Washington, DC (BSBA). *Directorships:* J H Minet & Co Ltd 1990 (exec). *Professional Organisations:* Lloyds of London. *Recreations:* Tennis, Swimming.

KHODADAD, Nabil L; Associate Director, Mayer Brown & Platt.

KHURAMI, Abdul Wakil; Managing Director, Afghan National Credit and Finance Limited, since 1989. *Career:* Daafghanistan Bank, Kabul, Director General 1974-87; Mortgage and Construction Bank, Kabul, President 1988. *Biog: b.* 6 June 1930. *Nationality:* Afghan. *Directorships:* The Trading Company of Afghanistan Limited London 1990 (exec).

KIDD, Andrew Michael; Assistant General Manager (Finance), Cheltenham & Gloucester Building Society, since 1984; Accounts, Taxation, Financial Information, Budgeting. *Career:* Simpson Wood & Co, Articled Clerk

1967-70; Bass Charrington (North West) Ltd, Management Accountant 1970-72; Halifax Building Society, Assistant Accountant 1972-74; Financial Accountant 1974-80; Cheltenham & Gloucester Building Society, Assistant Secretary (Finance) 1980-84. *Biog: b.* 24 August 1946. *Nationality:* British. *m.* 1975, Christine (née Lloyd); 1 s; 1 d. *Educ:* Huddersfield New College; Bristol University (BSc). *Directorships:* C & G Homes Ltd 1989 (non-exec).

KIDD, D J; Partner, Cameron Markby Hewitt.

KIDEL, Andrey; Director, S G Warburg & Co Ltd, since 1983; Overseas Advisory Division. *Career:* Department of Economic Affairs (London), Economist 1966-68; International Monetary Fund (Washington DC, USA), Economist 1968-73; Commission of European Community (Brussels), Principal Administrator 1974; Forex Research Ltd (London), MD 1975-81; S G Warburg & Co 1981-. *Biog: b.* 20 November 1943. *Nationality:* British. *m.* 1969, Sara Jacinta (née Nadal); 4 s. *Educ:* Lycee Janson de Sailly, Paris; Oxford University (BA); London School of Economics (MSc).

KIDO, Kazue; Executive Director, Japanese Stock Trading, Yamaichi International (Europe) Limited.

KIER, Michael Hector; Group Managing Director, C E Heath plc, since 1989; Broking. *Career:* C E Heath plc, Insurance Broker 1968-77; Fielding Juggins Money and Stewart Ltd, Managing Director 1977-86; C E Heath plc, Director 1986-. *Biog: b.* 22 October 1946. *Nationality:* Danish. *m.* 1971, Jane Kier (née Childs). *Educ:* Repton School; King's College, London.

KIERNAN, Pat; Partner in Charge of London Management Consultancy Services, Price Waterhouse.

KIKANO, Khalil Naoum; Vice President, Lending & Corporate Banking in Europe, The Royal Bank of Canada; Credit Management for Europe, Middle East & Africa; Management of Dubai Branch. *Career:* Banque Sabbag SAL (Beirut) 1956-63; Whinney Murray & Co, Audit Mgr 1964-68; Royal Bank of Canada (Middle East) SAL (Beirut), Mgr 1969-77; (Montreal) Regional Officer, Middle East & Africa HQ 1977-78; (Middle East) SAL (Beirut), Gen Mgr 1978-82; Royal Bank of Canada (London) 1982; Middle East & Africa HQ, Reg Mgr 1982-83; VP 1983-84; VP, International Banking 1984-88; VP, Lending 1988-. *Biog: b.* 20 August 1938. *Nationality:* Lebanese. *m.* 1959, Hanne; 1 s; 2 d. *Directorships:* Orion Royal Bank Ltd; The Royal Bank of Canada (France) SA; The Royal Bank of Canada Trade Finance Ltd; The Royal Bank of Canada (Belgium) SA; Royal Bank of Canada Europe Ltd. *Other Activities:* Member, Centre of Arbitration and Conciliation of the Union of Arab Banks. *Clubs:* RAC.

KILLEEN, (John Gerard) Conor; Director, Schroder Securities Limited, since 1990; Syndication, Equity New Issues. *Career:* The First Boston Corporation, New York, Analyst, Commercial Paper Department 1982-84. *Biog: b.* 21 March 1960. *Nationality:* Irish. *m.* 1985, Mary (née Stacey); 2 d. *Educ:* St Michaels College, Dublin; Trinity College, Dublin (BA Mod Economics). *Directorships:* Schroder Securities Limited 1990 (exec). *Clubs:* Connemara Golf Club. *Recreations:* Fishing, Football, Golf.

KILLIK, Paul; Senior Partner, Killik & Co.

KIDD, D J; Partner, Cameron Markby Hewitt.

KILNER, Ms (Helen) Sian; Associate Partner, Grimley J R Eve, since 1989; Planning. *Career:* West Oxfordshire District Council, Planning Assistant 1982-85; Cherwell District Council, Senior Planning Assistant 1985-87; Grimley J R Eve 1987-. *Biog: b.* 20 February 1959. *Nationality:* British. *m.* 1985, Peter Robbins. *Educ:* Bolton School; Somerville College, Oxford (MA); University College, London (MPhil). *Professional Organisations:* MRTPI.

KILNER, John Stephen; Partner, Linklaters & Paines, since 1985. *Biog: b.* 1952. *Nationality:* British. *m.* 1979, Mary; 1 s; 3 d. *Educ:* Rugby School; Gonville & Caius College, Cambridge (MA). *Other Activities:* Member, Law Society.

KILPATRICK, T G E; Managing Director, Hoare Govett International Securities; Pacific Basin Equities. *Career:* Argyll and Sutherland Highlanders, Commission 1964-67; Govett Sons & Co 1967; Hoare Govett Ltd in Melbourne, Representative 1969-71; HG Asia in Hong Kong, MD 1976-79; Director, Responsible for Japanese Equities 1980-84; Security Pacific Hoare Govett, Group Development Director 1985-87; MD, International Equities 1987-. *Biog: b.* 22 February 1945. *Nationality:* British. *m.* 1967, Eileen (née Staples); 2 d. *Educ:* Stowe. *Directorships:* Security Pacific Hoare Govett Group Ltd 1987 (exec); Security Pacific Ltd (Australia) 1988 (exec); McIntosh Securities Ltd 1987 (exec). *Other Activities:* International Markets Committee of the IS, 1986-89. *Professional Organisations:* Member, London Stock Exchange, 1969; Member, ISE. *Clubs:* Hong Kong Club, Royal Victoria Yacht Club, Royal Hong Kong Yacht Club.

KILSBY, Richard Philip; Vice Chairman, Charterhouse Bank Limited, since 1990; Banking, Treasury and Capital Markets. *Career:* Price Waterhouse, London, Partner 1984-88; Charterhouse Bank Limited, Managing Director 1988-90; Vice-Chairman 1990-. *Biog: b.* 26 December 1951. *Nationality:* British. *m.* 1973, Janet; 1 s; 1 d. *Educ:* Kings School, Chester; University College, London (LLB Hons). *Directorships:* Charterhouse Bank Ltd 1988; Charterhouse plc 1990. *Professional Organisations:* FCA; ACT.

KILSHAW, David W; Partner, Theodore Goddard.

KIM, D S; Chief Representative, The Korea Development Bank, since 1990; London Representative Office. *Career:* The Korea Development Bank, Dep Gen Mgr Intl Fin Dept 1986-88; Dep Rep London Representative Office 1988-90; Chief Rep London Representative Office 1990-; KDB International (London) Ltd, MD 1990-. *Biog:* b. 29 November 1944. *Nationality:* Korean. m. 1972, S K; 1 s; 2 d. *Educ:* Seoul National University (BA); Business School, Seoul National University (MBA). *Directorships:* KDB International (London) Ltd 1990 (exec) MD. *Professional Organisations:* Registered Representative, The Securities Association. *Clubs:* Wentworth Golf Club. *Recreations:* Golf.

KIM, Young Tae; Director, Schroder Securities Limited, since 1990; Korean & Taiwanese Equities. *Career:* Korea Investment Trust Co Ltd, Fund Manager 1978-87; Schroder Securities Limited, General Manager Korean & Taiwanese Equities 1987. *Biog:* b. 23 April 1954. *Nationality:* Korean. m. 1981, Soo Hyun Kim; 1 d. *Educ:* Seoul National University (BA Law). *Directorships:* Schroder Securities Limited 1990 (exec). *Professional Organisations:* Korean Association of Investment Analysts. *Clubs:* Gatton Manor Golf Club.

KIMBALL, Marcus Richard; The Rt Hon Lord Kimball; Member of the Council, Lloyd's of London.

KIMBELL, D H S; Managing Director, Spencer Stuart & Associates Ltd.

KIMBERLEY, D O; Finance Director, English Trust Company Ltd, since 1990; Finance. *Career:* Dixon Wilson Chartered Accountants 1978-84.

KIMMINS, I J; Clerk, Tobacco Pipe Makers' & Tobacco Blenders' Company.

KIMOTO, Yasuyuki; Joint General Manager, The Sumitomo Bank Ltd.

KIMPTON, T P; Partner (Bristol), Bacon & Woodrow.

KIMURA, T; Joint General Manager, Sumitomo Trust & Banking Corp.

KINDER, John M; Director, E D & F Man Ltd, since 1987; Sugar Trading. *Biog:* b. 15 July 1956. *Nationality:* British. m. 1986, Susan (née Kirkup); 1 d. *Educ:* Sherborne; Trinity Hall, Cambridge (BA).

KINDERSLEY, C P; Partner, Cazenove & Co.

KINDERSLEY, Robert Hugh Molesworth; The Rt Hon Lord Kindersley; Non-Executive Director, Lazard Brothers & Co Limited. *Career:* London Assurance,

Director 1957-; Witan Investment Co Ltd, Director 1958-85; Steel Co of Wales, Director 1959-67; Lazard Brothers & Co Ltd, Director 1960; Vice-Chairman (Executive) 1981-85; Marconi Co Ltd, Director 1963-68; Sun Alliance London Insurance, Director 1965-; English Electric Co Ltd, Director 1966-68; General Electric Company, Director 1968-70; British Match Corporation, Director 1969-73; Swedish Match Co, Director 1973-85; Commonwealth Development Corporation, Chairman (executive) 1980-89; Mansk Co Ltd, Director 1986-; Slaim Selective Growth Trust, Chairman 1990-. *Biog:* b. 18 August 1929. *Nationality:* British. m. 1989, Tita (née Norman) (first marriage dissolved); 3 s; 1 d. *Educ:* Eton College; Trinity College, Oxford (MA); Harvard Business School (MBA). *Other Activities:* Financial Adviser to the Export Group for the Construction Industries, 1986-86; Member of Advisory Panel, Overseas Projects Group, 1975-77; Dep Chm, ECGD Advisory Panel, 1975-80; Chm of Ex Ctee, British Bankers Association, 1976-78; Pres, Anglo-Taiwan Trade Committee, 1976-86; Member, Institut International d'Etudes Bancaires, 1971-85; Member, Court of Fishmongers Co, 1973-; Prince Warden, 1989-90. *Clubs:* Pratt's, All-England Lawn Tennis, Queen's, MCC. *Recreations:* Gardening, Deer, Tennis, Skiing.

KING, B R; Assistant General Manager, Guardian Royal Exchange Assurance plc.

KING, D C; Director, Granville Davies Limited.

KING, D E; Chief Executive & Director, The London Metal Exchange Ltd.

KING, D R; Executive Director, Willis Corroon plc.

KING, John William; Assistant General Manager, Guardian Royal Exchange plc, since 1989; Strategic Planning. *Career:* Bank of England 1965-68; Guardian Royal Exchange Investment Dept, Various Positions 1968-74; Investment Mgr 1975-87; Guardian Royal Exchange plc, Asst Gen Mgr Corp Fin 1987-89. *Biog:* b. 18 October 1943. *Nationality:* British. m. 1966, Muriel (née Claridge); 1 s; 1 d. *Educ:* Birmingham University (BCom). *Directorships:* GRE Linked Life Assurance Ltd 1988 (exec); GRE Pensions Management Ltd 1988 (exec); Hambro Guardian Assurance Ltd 1988 (non-exec); Assembly & Automation (Electronics) Ltd 1983 (non-exec); British Equitable Assurance Company Ltd 1988 (exec); Bruton Estates Ltd 1988 (exec); The City of Aberdeen Property & General Investment Ltd 1985 (exec); GRE Ireland (Holdings) Limited 1990 (exec); GRE Life Ireland Limited 1989 (exec); Guardian National Insurance Company Limited 1990 (exec). *Professional Organisations:* AMSIA.

KING, Kenneth; Executive Director, N M Rothschild International Asset Management.

KING, Professor Mervyn Allister; Professor of Economics, London School of Economics, since 1984; Director, LSE Financial Markets Group. *Career:* Dept of Applied Economics (Cambridge Growth Project) Jnr Research Officer 1969-73; St John's College, Cambridge, Fellow & Dir of Studies 1972-77; Dept of Applied Economics, Cambridge Research Officer 1972-76; Faculty of Economics Lecturer 1976-77; Harvard University Visiting Prof of Economics 1982; Univ of Birmingham Esmee Fairbairn Prof of Inv 1977-84; Massachusetts Inst of Technology Visiting Prof of Economics 1983-84; Harvard University, Visiting Prof of Economics 1990-. *Biog: b.* 30 March 1948. *Nationality:* British. *Educ:* King's College, Cambridge (BA Hons 1st). *Directorships:* Bank of England 1990 (non-exec). *Other Activities:* City Capital Markets Ctee, 1989-; Fellow, The Econometric Society (Council Mem, 1986-); Journal of Public Economics; Governor, National Institute of Econ & Social Research; Assoc Mem, Inst of Fiscal & Monetary Policy. *Publications:* Public Policy & The Corporation, 1977; The British Tax System (Co-author), 1978; Indexing for Inflation, 1975; The Taxation of Income from Capital; A Comparitive Study of the US, UK, Sweden and West Germany (Co-author), 1974; Papers and Articles in Journals.

KING, Michael; General Manager, Bayerische Landesbank Girozentrale.

KING, P K; Director, Bain Clarkson Limited.

KING, P T C; Partner, Herbert Smith.

KING, Peter David Spencer; Partner, Linklaters & Paines, since 1990; Company Law and Financial Services. *Career:* Linklaters & Paines, Articled Clerk 1981-83; Assistant Solicitor 1983-90. *Biog: b.* 13 January 1960. *Nationality:* British. *m.* 1987, Sarah (née Hopkins); 1 d. *Educ:* Dulwich College; St John's College, Cambridge (MA). *Professional Organisations:* Law Society. *Recreations:* Music, Cookery.

KING, R A P; Director, Candover Investments plc.

KING, R C; Director, National Westminster Growth Options Ltd, since 1985; Venture Capital Needs of Small Businesses. *Career:* National Westminster Bank plc, Various Positions in Corporate Finance 1963-. *Biog: b.* 18 July 1939. *Nationality:* British. *m.* 1963, Elspeth; 2 d. *Educ:* Manchester University (BA Com). *Directorships:* GLE Technology Investments Ltd 1990 (non-exec); GLE Technology Ltd 1990 (non-exec); GLE Technology Fund Managers Ltd 1990 (non-exec); UCL Ventures Ltd 1990 (non-exec). *Other Activities:* Secretary, The Harry Payne Trust. *Professional Organisations:* Associate, The Chartered Institute of Bankers. *Recreations:* Motor Sports, Reading, Travel.

KING, Raymond A; Deputy General Manager Business Operations, Moscow Narodny Bank Ltd, since 1988; Bank Operations and Control. *Career:* National Westminster Bank plc, Management 1958-86; Christiania Bank of Kredithasse, General Management 1986-88. *Biog: b.* 28 July 1942. *Nationality:* British. *m.* 1963, Sandra (née Pattison); 1 s; 2 d. *Educ:* Westminster City Grammar. *Professional Organisations:* Fellow, Institute of Financial Accountants; FCIB; FCIS; MBCS. *Recreations:* Squash, Tennis, Golf.

KING, Richard; Chairman, Cambridge Capital Management Limited.

KING, Stephen H M; Director, W P P Group plc.

KING, T G; Production Director & General Manager (Asian Pacific Division), LASMO plc, since 1987; Oil & Exploration & Production. *Career:* Shell Group of Companies 1960-66; Gulf Oil Corp Group of Companies 1966-82; Burmah Group 1982-86; CEO, Trafalgar House Oil & Gas Inc 1986-87; LASMO plc 1987-. *Biog: b.* 21 May 1938. *Nationality:* British. *m.* 1960, Judie (née Clarke); 2 s; 1 d. *Educ:* Perse School, Cambridge; Imperial College (Royal School of Mines), London (BSc). *Directorships:* Burmah Oil Exploration Ltd 1982-86 (exec). *Professional Organisations:* Fellow, Institute of Directors; Fellow, Institute of Petroleum; Fellow, Geological Society.

KING, William Lawrence; Partner, Macfarlanes, since 1980; Intellectual Property and Commercial Law. *Career:* Macfarlanes 1970-. *Biog: b.* 29 December 1947. *m.* 1975, Jane (née Wrixon); 2 s. *Educ:* Oundle School; Trinity Hall, Cambridge (MA). *Other Activities:* The City of London Solicitors' Company (Member of Court). *Professional Organisations:* The Law Society; IBA; The City of London Law Society; The Society of English & American Lawyers. *Clubs:* United Oxford & Cambridge University. *Recreations:* Beagling.

KINGSHOTT, Albert Leonard; Executive Director, Banking of The Private Bank & Trust Company Limited, since 1989; Crown Agent; Member of Monopolies & Mergers Commission. *Career:* British Petroleum Company, Financial Analyst 1955-59; British Nylon Spinners, Economist 1960-62; Iraq Petroleum Company, Fin Mgr 1963-65; Ford Europe, Treasurer 1965-70; Whitbread Group, Fin Dir 1970-72; British Steel Corporation, MD Fin 1972-77; Lloyds Bank Intl, Dir & Dep Chief Exec 1977-85; Dir Intl Banking Div 1985-89. *Biog: b.* 16 Sept 1930. *Nationality:* British. *m.* 1957, Valerie (née Simpson); 2 s; 1 d. *Educ:* London School of Economics (BSc). *Directorships:* Lloyds Bank (BLSA) Ltd; Lloyds International Trading (Bahamas) Ltd; Lloyds Bank (France) Ltd; Lloyds International Trading Ltd; The National Bank of New Zealand Ltd; Lloyds First Western Corp. *Other Activities:* Governor, Ashridge Management College and Associate Member of Faculty.

Professional Organisations: FCIS. *Publications:* Investment Appraisal (Ford Motor Company), 1967. *Recreations:* Reading, Chess, Golf.

KINGSHOTT, L; Member, Monopolies and Mergers Commission.

KINGSLAND, W E; Clerk, Launderers' Company.

KINGSLEY, R C; Director, Scott Underwriting Agencies Limited.

KINGSLEY, Stephen Michael; Partner, Arthur Andersen & Co, since 1986; Capital Markets Audit Group. *Career:* Arthur Andersen & Co, Manager 1979-86. *Biog:* b. 1 June 1952. *Nationality:* British. *m.* 1982, Michelle (née Solovici); 1 d. *Educ:* Cheadle Hulme School; Bristol University (BSc). *Other Activities:* Member, Formation Ctee, The Options & Futures Society; Advisory Panel to the Securities & Investments Board 1985-87(Member, Advisory Board). *Professional Organisations:* FCA. *Recreations:* Travel, Classical Music.

KINGSMILL, D; Managing Director, Credit Agricole Personal Finance plc, since 1989. *Career:* Turquand & Young, Articled Clerk 1968-71; Price Waterhouse (Paris) Senior Accountant 1971-73; Chase Manhattan, Manager, Corporate Finance 1973-80; Chase Manhattan (London Branch) Assistant General Manager Finance 1918-84; Caisse Nationale de Credit Agricole, Assistant General Manager, Corporate Finance 1984-89. *Biog:* b. 27 July 1947. *Nationality:* British. *m.* 1970, Denise Patricia (née Byrne); 1 s; 1 d. *Educ:* Dean Close, Cheltenham; Bristol University (BSc Economics). *Other Activities:* Treasurer, Richmond Environment Trust; Treasurer, Attingham Society; Member, Livery Company of Chartered Accountants. *Professional Organisations:* FCA. *Clubs:* Gentian, Furniture History Society.

KINGSMILL, G H; Clerk, Chartered Accountants' Company.

KINGSNORTH, G Arnold; Director, Hodgson Martin Limited.

KINGSTON, Michael Ian; Partner, Herbert Smith, since 1987; Corporate Finance - Mergers and Acquisitions, New Issues; Management Buy-Outs, Joint Ventures, Oil & Natural Resources. *Career:* Freshfields, Articled Clerk 1976-78; Assistant Solicitor 1978-84; Herbert Smith, Assistant Solicitor 1984-87. *Biog:* b. 23 October 1953. *Nationality:* British. *Educ:* St Brendon's College, Bristol; Manchester University (LLB Hons). *Other Activities:* Freeman, City of London Solicitors' Company; Chairman, Whittington Committee of the City of London Solicitor's Company. *Professional Organisations:* Law Society; Law Society of Hong Kong; United Kingdom Oil & Gas Lawyers Group; British Venture Capital Association. *Publications:* Contributor to Tolley's

Company Law. *Recreations:* Literature, Music, Photography, Amateur Dramatics.

KINGSTON, P E; Managing Director, Technical, Enterprise Oil.

KINGZETT, Jan Anthony; Director, Schroder Investment Management Ltd, since 1987; Asia. *Biog:* b. 25 October 1955. *Nationality:* British. *Educ:* Eton College; Trinity College, Cambridge (MA). *Directorships:* Thos Agnew & Sons Ltd 1985 (non-exec); Schroder Investment Management (Japan) Ltd 1987 (non-exec); European 21st Century Fund Management Co 1990 Chairman. *Clubs:* Queens, MCC. *Recreations:* Ballroom Dancing, The Study of the Works of Pliny.

KINI, U M; Deputy General Manager, Syndicate Bank.

KININMONTH, Peter Wyatt; Director, Lowndes Lambert Group (Holdings) Ltd, since 1985; Overseas Operations and Reinsurance. *Career:* 3rd QAO Gurkha Rifles Capt 1942-46; F Bertram Galer 1949-50; Bahr Behrend & Co 1951-53; Thos Stephens & Son Ltd Dir 1953-67; Keith Shipton & Co Dir 1967-72; P W Kininmonth (Holdings) Ltd Chm 1972-85. *Biog:* b. 23 June 1924. *Nationality:* British. *m.* 1951, Priscilla (née Sturge); 3 s; 1 d. *Educ:* Sedbergh School; Brasenose College, Oxford (MA Hons). *Directorships:* P W Kininmonth Ltd 1987 (exec). *Other Activities:* High Sheriff, Greater London 1980-81. *Professional Organisations:* Member of Lloyd's. *Clubs:* Vincent's, City of London, The Brook (NY), Australian Club (Sydney), Royal & Ancient, Rye Golf Club, Royal St George's Golf Club, Swinley, Forest. *Recreations:* Golf, Music, Gardening.

KINKOZAN, Kazuo; Deputy Managing Director, Wako International (Europe) Ltd.

KINLOCH, Francis; Finance Director, Stirling Hendry & Co.

KINMONTH, George Frederick; Partner, Herbert Smith, since 1980; General Company/Commercial Law. *Career:* Herbert Smith, Company and Commercial Dept, Partner 1980; Hong Kong Office, Managing Partner 1986-90. *Biog:* b. 2 February 1949. *Nationality:* British. *m.* 1976, Susan; 1 s; 2 d. *Educ:* Birmingham University (LLB). *Professional Organisations:* Member of Council, Hong Kong Law Society 1987-90. *Clubs:* Hong Kong Club, Royal Hong Kong Yacht Club, Royal Automobile Club, Grafham Motor Sailing Club. *Recreations:* Sailing, Shooting.

KINNERSLEY, Thomas Anthony; Partner, Slaughter and May.

KINNIS, Shaun Munro; Assistant General Manager, Equitable Life Assurance Society; Marketing. *Biog:*

Nationality: British. *Directorships:* Equitable Investments Managers Ltd; Equitable Unit Trust Managers Ltd; Equitable Life 1989 Board Member.

KINNISON, Alexander Peter John; Director & General Manager, Banque Nationale de Paris plc, since 1988; General Banking. *Career:* Bank of Nova Scotia Mgmnt Positions 1957-70; BNP plc Mgmnt Positions 1970-77; BNP Daiwa (Hong Kong) MD 1977-81; BNP plc Dep Gen Mgr 1981-86; Gen Mgr 1986-88. *Biog: b.* 29 September 1934. *Nationality:* British. *m.* 1957, Shirley Anne (née Edwards); 1 d. *Educ:* Buckhurst Hill County High School. *Directorships:* BNP plc & Various BNP Group Subsidiaries. *Other Activities:* Freeman of The City of London. *Clubs:* Overseas Bankers'. *Recreations:* Gardening, Walking the Dogs.

KINSELLA, Paul; Head of Commercial Property, Lawrence Graham, since 1985; Property Development & Finance. *Career:* Lawrence Graham, Articles; Admitted as Solicitor 1974; Partner 1978; Head of Commercial Property Management 1978-85. *Biog: b.* 11 August 1947. *Nationality:* British. *m.* 1974, Karin; 1 d. *Educ:* Beaumont College; Cambridge University (Exhibitioner in Classics,BA Law); College of Law (Solicitor). *Directorships:* British Council of Shopping Centres 1989 Hon Treasurer. *Professional Organisations:* Member, Law Society. *Recreations:* Travel.

KINSEY, O J R; Partner, Simmons & Simmons.

KIRBY, Barry Anthony; Main Board Director, Jardine Insurance Brokers Limited.

KIRK, D F; Partner, Arthur Andersen & Co Chartered Accts.

KIRK, Ian Malcolm; Director, Head of Corporate Finance, Charterhouse Tilney, since 1989; Corporate Finance. *Career:* Fielding, Newson-Smith & Co, Corporate Finance Executive 1975-80; Corporate Finance Partner 1980-86; County NatWest Limited, Director Corporate Finance 1986-89; County NatWest Securities Limited, Director Corporate Finance 1986-89; County NatWest Wood Mackenzie & Co Ltd, Director Corporate Finance 1986-89. *Directorships:* Charterhouse Tilney 1989 (exec).

KIRK, Nicholas J; Finance Director, Newton Investment Management Limited, since 1988; Finance & Administration. *Career:* Coopers & Lybrand Chartered Accountants (London & Madrid) Latterly as Senior Manager 1976-86; Coopers & Lybrand Managing Consultants (London) Latterly as Managing Consultant 1986-87. *Biog: b.* 16 December 1953. *Nationality:* British. *m.* 1981, Ann; 1 s; 2 d. *Educ:* Exeter College, Oxford (MA Mathematics). *Professional Organisations:* Fellow, Institute of Chartered Accountants in England

& Wales; Associate Member, Association of Corporate Treasurers. *Recreations:* Sport.

KIRKHAM, Donald Herbert; Chief Executive, Woolwich Equitable Building Society, since 1986. *Career:* Woolwich Equitable Building Society (Worcester), Branch Mgr 1963; Woolwich Equitable Building Society, Gen Mgr's Asst 1967-70; Business Prod Mgr 1970-72; Asst Gen Mgr 1972-76; Gen Mgr 1976-81; Deputy Chief Gen Mgr 1981; Scotland & N Ireland Local Board Member 1979-84; Main Board Member 1982. *Biog: b.* 1 January 1936. *Nationality:* British. *m.* 1960, Kathleen (née Lond); 1 s; 1 d. *Educ:* Grimsby Technical College. *Other Activities:* Freeman of the City of London; Chartered Secretaries' Livery Company. *Professional Organisations:* FCIS (Council Member); FCBSI (Pres 1981-82, Vice Pres 1986-87); CBIM, Institute of Directors; ICSA (President Designate 1991). *Recreations:* Boating.

KIRKHAM, Peter; Deputy General Manager, Co-operative Insurance Society Limited, since 1987; Administration Personnel and Data Processing. *Career:* Co-operative Insurance Society, Mgr O&M Dept 1960-77; Mgr, Personnel & Mgmnt Services 1977-87. *Biog: b.* 29 December 1931. *m.* 1960, May (née Williamson); 1 s; 1 d. *Educ:* Ducie Avenue School, Manchester. *Professional Organisations:* FCCA. *Clubs:* Blackley Golf Club (Manchester). *Recreations:* Golf, Gardening.

KIRKMAN, Charles R; Director, Merrill Lynch Europe Limited.

KIRKPATRICK, David Jeffery; General Manager, Director, Scottish Equitable Life Assurance Soc, since 1984; Investment Management. *Career:* Standard Life Asst Investment Mgr 1963-82. *Biog: b.* 26 August 1941. *Nationality:* British. *m.* 1966, Sheila (née Bulloch); 1 s; 1 d. *Educ:* Queen Elizabeth Grammar School, Penrith; Manchester University (BSc Hons). *Other Activities:* Carnegie Trust; Church of Scotland Trust. *Professional Organisations:* FFA. *Recreations:* Music, Golf, Squash.

KIRKPATRICK, John Finlay Alexander; Chief Industrial Adviser & Director, 3i plc, since 1989; In Charge of 3i Group's Industry Dept. *Career:* Westinghouse Corp (Canada) & ASEA (Sweden), Engineer 1963-65; Electricity Board (NI), Engineer 1965-66; Sir William Halcrow & Partners, Consulting Engineer 1966-67; Unilever, Factory Management 1967-74; Shell, Tech/Production Executive 1975-77; Normand Electrical Company, Managing Director 1977-79; 3i plc, Industrial Adviser 1980-83; Senior Industrial Adviser 1983-89; Director & Chief Industrial Adviser 1989-. *Biog: b.* 27 April 1942. *Nationality:* British. *m.* 1973, Philippa (née Stokes). *Educ:* Royal Belfast Academical Institution; Queen's University (BSc Electrical Eng); Cranfield School of Management (MBA). *Directorships:* 3i plc 1989 (exec). *Professional Organisations:* AMIEE.

KIRKWOOD, C G; Secretary, The Scottish Mutual Assurance Society.

KIRMAN, Christopher John; Director, Touche Remnant & Co; Pension Funds. *Career:* William Brandt Sons & Co 1957-66; Touche Ross 1966-70; Touche Remnant & Co, Dir 1970-. *Biog: b.* 21 March 1933. *Nationality:* British. m1 1963, Urusula Elisabeth (née Franke). m2 1988, Eva Maria (née Franke). *Educ:* Bedales School; Cambridge University (BA). *Directorships:* Church of England Nominees Ltd 1976; TR Berkeley Development Capital Management Ltd 1984; Touche Remnant Group Trustees Ltd 1981; Atlas Electric & General Trust Ltd 1970-80 MD; TR Industrial and General Trust plc 1980-86 MD. *Other Activities:* Member, Advisory Panel of Charities Official Investment Funds; Member, Advisory Panel of the Local Authorities Mutual Investment Trust; Investment Mgmnt Ctee, the Central Board of Finance of the Church of England. *Professional Organisations:* Society of Investment Analysts.

KIRWAN-TAYLOR, Charles Patrick; Director, Kleinwort Benson Limited, since 1990; Equity Syndication. *Career:* Morgan Guaranty Trust Company of New York 1979-82; Kleinwort Benson Limited 1982-. *Biog: b.* 8 April 1958. *Nationality:* British. *m.* 1988, Helen (née Semler). *Educ:* Winchester College; St Johns College, Oxford.

KISSIN, Harry; The Rt Hon The Lord Kissin of Camden; Life President of, Lewis & Peat Holdings Ltd, since 1987. *Career:* Fenchurch Insurance Holdings, Chm 1962-82; Esperanza Ltd, Chm 1970-82; Guinness Peat Group, Chm 1973-79; Linfood Holdings Ltd, Chm 1974-81; Royal Opera House, Convent Garden 1973-84; Transcontinental Services Group NV, Chm 1982-86; Lewis & Peat Ltd, Chm 1982-87; Guinness Mahon Holdings plc, President 1988-89. *Biog: b.* 23 August 1912. *Nationality:* British. *m.* 1935, Ruth Deborah (née Samuel); 1 s; 1 d. *Educ:* Danzig; University of Basle, Switzerland (LLD). *Directorships:* GPG plc (formerly Guinness Peat Group plc) 1979 (non-exec) Life President; Tycon Spa Venice 1975 (non-exec). *Other Activities:* Freeman, City of London (1975); Governor, Hebrew University of Jerusalem; Chevalier, Legion D'Honneur; Commdr, Ordem Nacional Do Cruzeiro Do Sol, Brazil; 1300 Bulgaria Medal; Chm, Royal Opera House Trust (1974-80), Mem (1974-87); Chm, Council of Institute of Contemporary Arts (1968-75). *Professional Organisations:* Institute of Directors. *Clubs:* Reform, East India Devonshire Sports, Public Schools. *Recreations:* Arts, Opera, Theatre.

KITAMOTO, Yasufumi; Joint General Manager, Intl Credit Dept, The Sumitomo Bank Limited.

KITCHEN, Jonathan Aistrope; Director, Lazard Brothers & Co Ltd, since 1981; Corporate Finance. *Career:* Samuel Montagu & Co Ltd 1966-77; Panel on Take-Overs & Mergers 1978-79. *Biog: b.* 30 July 1939. *m.* 1967, Elizabeth (née Lacon); 2 s; 1 d. *Educ:* Harrow School. *Directorships:* Lazard Money Broking Ltd 1986. *Other Activities:* Worshipful Company of Gunmakers. *Professional Organisations:* AIB. *Clubs:* RAC. *Recreations:* Shooting, Skiing.

KITCHIN, Alan William Norman; Partner, Ashurst Morris Crisp, since 1986; International Finance, General Corporate. *Biog: b.* 31 January 1954. *Nationality:* British. *Educ:* Oundle School; Gonville and Caius College, Cambridge (BA, MA). *Professional Organisations:* The Law Society. *Clubs:* Walton Heath Golf Club. *Recreations:* Golf, Tennis.

KITCHING, Henry Alan; Director, Allied Provincial Securities Ltd, since 1986; Training. *Career:* R S Stancliffe & Co, Partner 1961-66; J A Scrimgeaur, Partner 1966-70; Stancliffe Todd & Hodgson, Partner 1970-86. *Biog: b.* 9 February 1936. *Nationality:* British. *m.* 1988, Ann Margaret (née Britton). *Educ:* Leighton Park, Reading; Peddie Institute USA. *Directorships:* Middlesbrough Warehousing Ltd 1965 Chairman. *Professional Organisations:* Member, Stock Exchange. *Clubs:* Cleveland.

KITCHING, John Richard Howard; Partner, Lovell White Durrant, since 1976; Corporate Finance, Venture Capital. *Career:* Lovell White & King 1971-. *Biog: b.* 30 July 1946. *Nationality:* British. *m.* 1972, Toril (née Ness); 1 s; 1 d. *Educ:* Rugby School; Caius College, Cambridge (MA). *Other Activities:* City of London Solicitors' Company. *Professional Organisations:* Law Society. *Recreations:* Golf, Choral Singing.

KITSON, Antony Bernard; Partner, McKenna & Co, since 1990; Planning, Rating, Local Government, Law and Finance. *Career:* London Borough of Newham, Articled Clerk/Solicitor 1973-77; London Borough of Islington, Principal Solicitor 1977-85; Dartford Borough Council, Legal Services Officer 1985-87; McKenna & Co, Assistant Solicitor 1987-90. *Biog: b.* 14 February 1952. *Nationality:* British. *m.* 1977, Rosaleen (née Phillips). *Educ:* Warwick University (LLB Hons). *Professional Organisations:* City of London Law Society.

KIYOYANAGI, Y; Director & General Manager, The Daiwa Bank Limited.

KLAHR, Anthony Leonard; Director, Capel-Cure Myers Capital Management.

KLEEMAN, H; Warden, Horners' Company.

KLEIN, Jonathan David; Director, Hambros Bank Limited, since 1989; Corporate Finance. *Career:* Hambros Bank Limited 1983-. *Biog: b.* 13 May 1960. *Nationality:* South African. *m.* 1988, Deborah Ann (née Hunter); 1 s. *Educ:* Bedales School; Trinity Hall College, Cambridge (MA Hons Law). *Directorships:* Hambros Bank Limited 1989 (exec). *Other Activities:* Trustee, Centre for International Environmental Law. *Recreations:* Tennis, Cricket, Theatre, Music.

KLEINWORT, Sir Kenneth; Bt; Director, Kleinwort Benson Group plc.

KLESCH, A Gary; Chairman, Quadrex Securities.

KLIEFOTH, David A; Managing Director, International Leasing, Continental Bank NA.

KLIMA, D A; Director, J H Minet & Co Ltd.

KLINGSICK, Martin G; Vice President, Royal Bank of Canada, since 1986; Treasury. *Career:* Orion Royal Bank, Head of Treasury 1978-86. *Biog: b.* 5 June 1949. *Nationality:* British. *m.* 1970, Maree (née Nelson); 1 s; 1 d. *Educ:* Sweyne School, Rayleigh. *Professional Organisations:* Member, International Forex Association. *Recreations:* Sailing.

KLUGE, P; Vice President, The Bank of Nova Scotia.

KNAPEN, Paul; Senior Manager Operations, Kredietbank NV.

KNAPMAN, David; London Managing Partner, Baker Tilly.

KNAPP, Ms Vanessa Jane; Partner, Freshfields, since 1988. *Biog: b.* 1956. *Nationality:* British. *Educ:* Northampton High School; Exeter University (LLB). *Recreations:* London Symphony Chorus.

KNEISEL, William; Managing Director (Investment Management), Morgan Stanley International.

KNIGHT, Andrew; Non-Executive Director, Reuters Holdings plc.

KNIGHT, Christopher John; Director, Morgan Grenfell & Co Limited, since 1985; Corporate Finance. *Career:* Barton, Mayhew & Co, (Chartered Accountants) 1968-73; Robert Fleming & Co Limited 1973-77; Morgan Grenfell & Co Limited, Corporate Finance Division 1978-; Morgan Grenfell (Hong Kong) Limited, Managing Director 1985-89. *Biog: b.* 18 June 1946. *Nationality:* British. *m.* 1981, Sarah (née Bolton); 2 d. *Educ:* Hymers College; Keble College, Oxford (MA). *Professional Organisations:* FCA. *Clubs:* City of London, Hong Kong.

KNIGHT, David; Assistant General Manager, Yorkshire Bank plc, since 1990; Strategic Planning and General Management. *Career:* Yorkshire Bank plc, Various in Branches & Head Office 1959-69; Personal Asst to Gen Mgr 1969-70; Mgr, Personnel Administration 1970-72; Mgr, Personnel Development & Training 1972-78; Controller Marketing 1978-83; Regional Controller 1983-86; Controller Advances 1986-90. *Biog: b.* 1 December 1939. *Nationality:* British. *m.* 1963, Eileen (née Shaw); 2 s. *Educ:* Southwell Minster Grammar School. *Directorships:* Yorkshire Bank Retail Services Ltd 1988 (non-exec); Yorkshire Bank Development Capital Ltd 1988 (non-exec); Yorkshire Bank Investments Ltd 1988 (non-exec); Brightwall Properties Ltd 1989 (non-exec). *Other Activities:* Member of House Ctee, Wheatfields Hospice Leeds. *Professional Organisations:* FCIB. *Clubs:* Scarcroft Golf Club. *Recreations:* Golf, Gardening, DIY, Boating (Own Narrow Boat).

KNIGHT, David Leonard; Director in Fixed Income Division, Barclays de Zoete Wedd Limited, since 1989; Head of UK Marketing (Capital Markets) and UK Commercial Paper Operations. *Career:* Barclays Bank plc, Various Positions 1966-81; Barclays Merchant Bank Ltd, Assistant Manager Banking; Directors Assistant; Manager, Banking 1981-86; Barclays de Zoete Wedd Ltd, Manager; Assistant Director; Director; Capital Markets 1986-. *Biog: b.* 14 November 1948. *Nationality:* British. *m.* 1970, Marion Vanessa (née Stevens); 3 d. *Educ:* Priory Vale School, Hornsey. *Directorships:* Barclays de Zoete Wedd Capital Markets Ltd 1988 (exec); Ebbgate Holdings Ltd 1988 (non-exec); Barclays de Zoete Wedd Ltd 1990 (exec). *Professional Organisations:* Institute of Bankers. *Recreations:* Squash, Keeping Family in the Lifestyle they have become accustomed to!

KNIGHT, F W; Deputy Group Chief Executive, United Biscuits (Holdings) plc, since 1988. *Career:* Colgate-Palmolive Ltd, Sales & Product Management (UK) 1960-63; Marketing Director (Denmark) 1964-65; Managing Director (East Africa) 1966-68; Booz Allen & Hamilton Inc, Management Consultant 1969-70; Lines Bros Ltd, Group Marketing Director 1971-72; Bristol-Myers Company Ltd, Managing Director, B-M Products & Clairol 1972; Asst Group MD/MD, Bristol Laboratories 1973; Group Managing Director 1974-77; Campbell's Soups Ltd, Chairman & Chief Executive 1978-81; United Biscuits (Holdings) plc, Deputy MD, UB Biscuits 1981-83; MD, UB Biscuits 1984-85; Chief Exec UB Foods (Europe) 1980-87; Deputy Group Chief Executive 1988-. *Biog: b.* 10 September 1936. *Nationality:* British. *m.* 1959, Beverley; 1 s; 2 d. *Educ:* The Roan School, Blackheath; St John's College, Cambridge (MA). *Directorships:* United Biscuits (Holdings) plc 1986 (exec); Ocean Group plc 1988 (non-exec). *Other Activities:* Member, Nedo Food Sector; Member, Council for Industry & Higher Education; President's Committee, Age Concern England; Fund Raising Committee, National Grocers' Benevolent Fund. *Recreations:* Cricket, Golf, Dickensiana, Chess.

KNIGHT, G P; Director, Hambros Bank Limited.

KNIGHT, Geoffrey Egerton; CBE; Chairman, Fenchurch Insurance Group Ltd, since 1980. *Career:* Royal Marines 1939-46; Bristol Aeroplane Co Ltd 1953; Bristol Aircraft Ltd, Dir 1956; BAC Ltd, Dir 1964-77; Vice Chm 1972-76. *Biog: b.* 25 January 1921. *Nationality:* British. *m.* 1947, Evelyn (née Bugle); 2 d. *Educ:* Brighton College. *Directorships:* GPA Gp plc 1977 (nonexec); Fenchurch Ins Holdings Ltd 1980 Chm; Trafalgar House plc 1980; Guinness Peat Group plc 1976. *Publications:* Concorde: The Inside Story, 1976. *Clubs:* Boodle's, White's, Turf.

KNIGHT, Jeremy Plowman; Director, Brown, Shipley & Co Limited, since 1989; Corporate Finance/ Mergers & Aquisitions. *Career:* Brown, Shipley & Co Limited 1981-; Executive 1981-84; Manager 1984-88; Assistant Director 1988-89; Director 1989-. *Biog: b.* 15 July 1960. *Nationality:* British. *Educ:* St Paul's School, London; Bristol University (BSc Economics/Econ Hist). *Other Activities:* Founders Company. *Clubs:* City University. *Recreations:* Wine Tasting, Cooking, Travel.

KNIGHT, M D; Company Secretary, The Thomson Corporation.

KNIGHT, P A; Group Managing Director, Knight & Day Ltd.

KNIGHT, Robin; Senior European Editor, US News & World Report, since 1985; Covering Events in UK, Ireland, NATO, Scandinavia & E Europe. *Career:* US News & World Report London Bureau Reporter 1968-74; London Bureau Chief 1974-76; Moscow Bureau Chief 1976-79; (Johannesburg) Africa Editor 1979-81; (Rome) Mediterranean Editor 1981-83; (Washington DC) General Editor 1983-84. *Biog: b.* 10 June 1943. *Nationality:* British. *m.* 1972, Jean (née Sykes). *Educ:* Nautical College, Pangbourne; Dublin University (BA Hons); Stanford University, California (MA). *Directorships:* Chiswick Wharf Residents Association 1988 Chm.

KNIGHT, Ronald David Paul; Chief Executive, Knight & Day Ltd, since 1989. *Career:* JS Knight & Son Ltd (Family Business) 1957-60; National Service 2nd Lieutenant 1960-62; JS Knight & Son Ltd, Employee 1962-69; Director 1969-71; Managing Director 1971-83; Edward Day & Baker Ltd, Managing Director 1971-83; Vale & Weetman Ltd (subsidiary of Edward Day & Baker Ltd) Chm 1983-89; Knight & Day Ltd (amalgamation of JS Knight & Son Ltd, Edward & Baker Ltd and Vale & Weetman Ltd) Chief Executive 1989-. *Biog: b.* 5 September 1939. *Nationality:* British. *m.* 1987, Lynne; 3 d. *Educ:* St Edmunds College, Herts. *Directorships:* Knight & Day Ltd 1989 Chief Executive. *Professional Organisations:* Freeman, Worshipful Company of Goldsmiths; Freeman, City of London. *Clubs:* Ombersley Tennis Club, St Pauls Club, Birmingham. *Recreations:* Tennis, Shooting.

KNIGHT, S F D; Director, Byas Mosley & Co Ltd.

KNIGHT, William John Langford; Partner, Simmons & Simmons, since 1973. *Biog: b.* 11 September 1945. *Nationality:* British. *m.* 1973, Stephanie (née Williams); 1 s; 1 d. *Educ:* Sir Roger Manwood's School, Sandwich; Bristol University (LLB). *Other Activities:* Trustee, Haydn-Mozart Society; Trustee, SCAR (Sickle Cell Anaemia Relief); FRSA. *Professional Organisations:* The Law Society (Chm, Standing Ctee on Company Law), City of London. *Publications:* The Acquisition of Private Companies, 1975 (5th Ed 1989). *Clubs:* Hong Kong Club. *Recreations:* Music, Riding, Skiing.

KNIGHTON, W M; CB; Deputy Secretary, Department of Trade & Industry.

KNIGHTS, John Brian; Managing Director, Operations, Royal London Mutual Insurance Society Ltd; Marketing, Field Personnel & Non Life Operations. *Biog: b.* 16 September 1935. *Nationality:* British. *m.* 1965, Patricia Ann (née Henshall); 1 s; 1 d. *Educ:* Rochdale Municipal High School. *Directorships:* Royal London Mutual 1980 (exec); Royal London General 1980 (exec); Lion Insurance 1989 (exec). *Professional Organisations:* FBIM. *Recreations:* Reading, Sport, Current Affairs.

KNIGHTS, Julian Paul; Director, Corporate Finance, Hill Samuel Bank, since 1988; Mainstream Corporate Finance. *Career:* Bowman Gilfillan (South Africa), Solicitor 1978-80; Hill Samuel South Africa, Mgr, Corporate Finance 1980-82; Grey Holdings, Dir, Acquisitions 1983-84; Hill Samuel South Africa, Asst Gen Mgr, Corp Finance 1984-86; Hill Samuel Bank, Corp Finance 1986-88. *Biog: b.* 15 December 1957. *Nationality:* British. *m.* 1987, Lizanne (née Killerby). *Educ:* St Stithians School; Witwatersrand University (BCom,LLB,H Dip Co Law). *Clubs:* Ascot. *Recreations:* Horse Racing, Running, Skiing.

KNOPE, Victor Ian; Director, Bradstock Blunt & Thompson Ltd, since 1988; Professional Indemnity Insurance. *Biog: b.* 23 March 1948. *Nationality:* British. *m.* 1968, Margaret; 1 s; 1 d. *Educ:* Raines Foundation School, London. *Professional Organisations:* ACII. *Recreations:* Bridge, Badminton, Music.

KNOTT, Simon Harold John Arthur; Deputy Chairman, Greig Middleton & Co Ltd, since 1988; Corporate Finance. *Career:* Greene & Co, Ptnr 1961-88; Snr Ptnr 1986-88. *Biog: b.* 26 June 1931. *Nationality:* British. *m.* 1956, Josephine (née Whowell); 1 s; 2 d. *Educ:* Trinity College, Cambridge (BA Hons 1st). *Directorships:* Automated Security (Holdings) plc (non-exec); Discretionary Unit Fund Managers; Hill & Smith plc; LPA Industries; Phosyn Ltd; Rights & Issues Investment Trust Chm; Safe Computing Ltd; Sandells plc; Shorco Group Holdings plc; United Scientific Holdings (non-exec); Platigrum Jt Chm; Alvis Pension Fund Chm. *Other Activities:* Councillor, London Borough of Hammersmith 1974-89; Chm, Social Services 1978-86; Chm, Finance 1984-86. *Professional Organisations:* Member, The International Stock Exchange. *Publications:* The Electoral Crucible (The Politics of London 1900-14). *Clubs:* National Liberal.

KNOWLAND, R R; Managing Director (Investment Management), The British Petroleum Company plc.

KNOWLES, James R; Chairman and Managing Director, James R Knowles Limited.

KNOWLES, Janet; Partner, Alexander Tatham.

KNOWLES, W A; Executive Director, James R Knowles Limited.

KNOX, Anthony; Chairman, Financial Dynamics Ltd, since 1987; Development of Business, Major Takeover Bids, Major Flotations. *Career:* Streets Financial Ltd, Chairman 1986; Addison Communications plc, Director 1985; Financial Strategy Ltd, Chairman 1978-84; Shandwick PR Ltd, Director 1976-78; John Addey Associates, Director 1974-76; ICFC Communications, Director 1972-74; Keith Prowse Ltd, Marketing Manager 1970-72; Burson-Marsteller, Account Executive 1968-70; Braban Public Relations, Account Executive 1967-68. *Biog: b.* 23 March 1945. *Nationality:* British. *m.* 1990, Adele; 1 d. *Educ:* St Dunstan's College; Christ Church, Oxford (MA Jurisprudence). *Directorships:* European Investor Communication 1987 (exec). *Clubs:* Oxford & Cambridge, City Club, Hurlingham. *Recreations:* Tennis, Skiing, Running.

KNOX, (David) Brian; Director, Kleinwort Benson Securities Ltd, since 1986; Research and Sales, Nordic Equity Markets. *Career:* Grieveson, Grant & Co Clerk 1954-61; Partner 1961-86. *Biog: b.* 22 February 1932. *Nationality:* British. *m.* 1975 (Div 1986). *Educ:* Winchester College; Balliol College, Oxford (MA 1st). *Directorships:* Kleinwort Benson Securities Ltd 1986. *Other Activities:* Trustee, Appeal Funds, Balliol College, Oxford; Fishmonger. *Professional Organisations:* ASIA. *Publications:* Architecture of Prague and Bohemia, 1963; Architecture of Poland, 1970. *Recreations:* Painting.

KNOX, J D; Director, Rea Brothers Limited, since 1989; Corporate Finance/Shipping. *Career:* Touche Ross & Co, Articled Clerk 1969-72; Wm Brandts Sons & Co Ltd, Corporate Finance, Executive 1972-75; Grindlays Bank, Banking Senior Manager 1975-79; Shipping Finance, Assistant Director 1979-88. *Biog: b.* 30 November 1947. *Nationality:* British. *m.* 1978, Shirley Anne (née Dixon); 2 s. *Educ:* Marlborough College; Bristol University (BSc). *Professional Organisations:* FCA. *Clubs:* Berkshire Golf Club. *Recreations:* Skiing, Golf.

KNOX, John; Director (Sales), Hoare Govett International Securities.

KNOX, Robert William; Partner, Kidsons Impey, since 1972; Corporate Services. *Career:* Kidsons Taylor & Co, Articled Clerk/Qualified 1961-68; Campbell Lawless & Punchard (Canada), CA 1968-70; Kidsons Impey, Mgr/Ptnr 1970-. *Biog: b.* 15 December 1943. *Nationality:* British. *m.* 1968, Susan Mary (née O'Bryen); 2 d. *Educ:* Cranleigh School. *Other Activities:* ICAEW; London West End Training Board. *Professional Organisations:* FCA. *Publications:* Statements of Source and Application of Funds (ICAEW), 1977. *Recreations:* Golf, Watching Rugby, Cricket, Tennis, Philately, Bridge.

KNOX, William Graeme; Managing Director, Scottish Amicable Investment Managers Ltd, since 1983; Investment MD, Scottish Amicable Investment Managers Ltd & Scottish Amicable Unit Trust Managers Ltd. *Career:* Scottish Amicable Actuarial Student 1966-69; Investment Analyst 1969-76; Responsible for Inv Dept 1976. *Biog: b.* 18 February 1945. *Nationality:* British. *m.* 1969, Jennifer (née Russell); 1 s; 1 d. *Educ:* Glasgow Academy; Cambridge University. *Directorships:* Scottish Amicable Investment Managers Ltd; Scottish Amicable Life Assurance Society. *Other Activities:* Institutional Fund Managers Ltd. *Professional Organisations:* FFA, ASIA.

KNUST, J F D; Partner, Ernst & Young.

KOBUSE, Shinichi; Deputy Managing Director, Bond Trading, Yamaichi International (Europe) Limited.

KODAMA, A; Chairman, Norinchukin International Ltd.

KOEHNE, Stephen D; Partner, D J Freeman & Co; Commercial Property/Banking. *Career:* Brecher & Co, Articled Clerk & Assistant Solicitor 1968-72; Zelin & Zelin, Assistant Solicitor 1972-75; D J Freeman & Co, Assistant Solicitor & Partner 1975-. *Biog: b.* 10 April 1947. *Nationality:* British. *m.* 1972, Susan J Koehne (née Mellows); 3 s; 1 d. *Educ:* Christs College, Finchley; Bristol University (LLB Hons). *Other Activities:* Member, City of London Law Society. *Professional Organisations:* Member, Law Society. *Publications:* Articles in Estates Times, 1987 & 1989. *Recreations:* Scouting, Walking, Swimming.

KOGAN, Ben; Director, Kogan Page Limited.

KOGAN, Philip; Managing Director, Kogan Page Limited.

KOMATSU, I; Managing Director, Nomura Capital Management (UK) Limited.

KON, Stephen D; Partner, S J Berwin & Co.

KONDO, Tsuneo; Deputy General Manager, The Taiyo Kobe Bank Ltd.

KONIG, Martyn; Executive Director, N M Rothschild & Sons Limited.

KONISHI, Yasuo; Deputy Managing Director, Syndicate, Yamaichi International (Europe) Limited.

KOO, Ja Sam; Chief Representative, Daewoo Securities Co Ltd; Research, Syndication & Sales in Korean & Other International Paper. *Career:* Daewoo Securities 1975-. *Biog: b.* 25 January 1949. *Nationality:* Korean. *m.* B J; 1 s. *Educ:* Graduate School of Business (MBA); Seoul National School of Business.

KOPKE, R; General Manager, French Bank of Southern Africa Limited.

KOPPER, H; Joint Deputy Chairman, Morgan Grenfell Group plc.

KOPRIVEC, Gojko; Director, Ljubljanska Banka, since 1988; Director of Representative Office. *Career:* Ljubljanska Banka Gospodarska Banka, Gen Mgr, Planning & Analysis 1974-80; Gen Mgr, Intl Div 1980-82; LB Associated Bank, Dep Gen Mgr, Intl Div 1982-84; Gen Mgr, Foreign Exchange Div & Treasury 1984-88. *Biog: b.* 6 March 1951. *Nationality:* Yugoslavian. *m.* 1976, Sonja (née Jurca); 1 s. *Educ:* University of Economics, Maribor, Yugoslavia (MSc). *Recreations:* Tennis.

KORANTENG, P S M; Deputy Chief Manager, Ghana Commercial Bank.

KORN, Julian S; Partner, Beachcroft Stanleys.

KORWIN, M; Manager, Bayerische Vereinsbank, since 1989; Corporate Banking. *Biog: b.* 26 January 1952. *Nationality:* British. *Educ:* Cambridge (MA).

KOSUGE, J; Senior Deputy General Manager, The Saitama Bank Ltd.

KOVACS, Leslie; Partner, Nabarro Nathanson.

KRAIJENHOFF, Baron; Non-Executive Director, S G Warburg Group plc.

KRAMER, Douglas; President, Draper and Kramer Incorporated, since 1972; Real Estate. *Biog: b.* 6 November 1936. *Nationality:* American. *m.* 1978, Mary Lynn Kramer (née McClatchey); 4 d. *Educ:* Westminster School, Simbsbury Conn; Claremont Men's College, Claremont CA. *Directorships:* Draper and Kramer Incorporated 1962 (exec); Slough Estates Limited (non-exec); Slough Parks Inc; Kirke Van-Orsdel, Des Moines, Iowa;

Board of River Oaks Bank and Trust Company Former Chairman; The Hull House Association Former Member Board of Directors; The Institute for Hearing and Speech Former Member Board of Directors; United Charities Former Member Board of Directors. *Clubs:* Chicago Club (Chicago, Illinois), Bohemian Club (Des Moines, Iowa), Jupiter Golf Club (Jupiter, Florida), Lake Shore Country Club (Chicago, Illinois), Standard Club (Chicago), Tavern Club (Chicago). *Recreations:* Golf, Golf, More Golf !

KRAMER, Martin C; Partner, Theodore Goddard.

KRATKE, Jan; Director, LPH Group plc.

KRAUS, Frank Charles; Group Secretary, Nationwide Anglia Building Society, since 1976; Secretariat/ Legal Services. *Career:* London Borough of Hammersmith, Solicitor 1965-71; Guildford Borough, Assistant Town Clerk 1971-73; Horsham DC, District Solicitor 1973-76. *Biog: b.* 12 December 1943. *Nationality:* British. *m.* 1965, Maya; 2 s; 1 d. *Educ:* Marylebone Grammar School; Holborn College of Law (LLB Lond). *Directorships:* Nationwide Housing Trust Ltd 1983 (non-exec); Building Societies Ombudsman Company Limited 1989 (non-exec). *Other Activities:* Chairman, Law Society Commerce & Industry Group, 1990-91; Chairman, International Bar Association Committee on Savings & Building Societies (Section on Business, Law, Committee 'U'), 1988-; Member, Holborn Law Society Committee. *Professional Organisations:* Law Society (Solicitor). *Recreations:* Skiing, Running, Music, Theatre.

KRAUS, Peter A; Partner, Beachcroft Stanleys.

KREMER, Ivan M H; Partner, Beachcroft Stanleys.

KRIEGER, Ian Stephen; Corporate Finance Partner, Arthur Andersen & Co, since 1975; Head of Buy-Outs in UK. *Biog: b.* 2 February 1952. *Nationality:* British. *m.* 1986, Caron (née Gluckstein); 1 s. *Educ:* Christ's College, Finchley; Kent University (BA Hons). *Professional Organisations:* FCA. *Publications:* Management Buy Outs, 1990.

KRIJGSMAN, Peter; Executive Director, International Financing Review, since 1988; Editorial Director/ Editor-in-Chief. *Career:* Financial Decisions, Launch Editor 1984; Corporate Money, Launch Editor 1987; International Financing Review, Editor 1988. *Biog: b.* 23 March 1955. *Nationality:* Dutch. *m.* 1987, Jocelyn Elisabeth. *Educ:* University of Sussex (MA International Relations). *Clubs:* RAC.

KRUGER, N; Director, Lonrho plc.

KUBO, Shinji; Managing Director, IBJ International Ltd, since 1990; Overall. *Career:* The Industrial Bank of Japan 1966-87. *Biog: b.* 29 April 1943. *Nationality:*

Japanese. *m.* 1970, Michiko; 1 s. *Educ:* Tokyo University.

KUCZYNSKI, Pedro-Pablo; Chairman, First Boston International, First Boston Corp, since 1982. *Career:* World Bank 1961-67; 1971-73; 1975-77; Loan Officer and Economist, Western Hemisphere Dept 1961-67; Chief Economist, Mexico, Central America & Carribean 1971-72; Chief of the Policy Planning Division 1972-73; Chief Economist, International Finance Corp 1973-75; Central Reserve Bank of Peru 1967-69; Economic Adviser; then Deputy Governor, also, Economic Adviser to the President of the Republic; Pontifical Catholic University of Peru, Lecturer in Economics; Peruvian Steamship Company, Director; Peruvian Houwing Bank, Adviser; International Monetary Fund, Senior Economist, Western Hemisphere Department 1969-71; Kuhn, Loeb & Company, Vice President, and then Partner, Kuhn Loeb International 1973-75; Halco (Mining)Inc. (a major bauxite mining consortium) President and Chief Executive Officer 1977-80; Government of Peru, Minister of Energy and Mines in the Administration of President Fernando Belaunde Terry 1980-82; First Boston Corporation, Managing Director, The First Boston Corp. and President now Chairman, First Boston International, Executive Director Credit Suisse First Boston, London 1982-. *Biog: b.* 3 October 1938. *Nationality:* Peruvian. *m.* Jane (née Casey); 1 s; 2 d. *Educ:* Schooling in Peru and England; Exeter College & Oxford University (BA MA Philosophy, Politics & Economics); Woodrow Wilson School for Public and International Affairs, Princeton University (MPA). *Directorships:* ROC Taiwan Fund International Investment Trust Co. *Other Activities:* Lecturer, Economics Department, University of Pittsburgh 1977-; Member of the Board of Visitors, Graduate School of Business, University of Pittsbugh 1979-; Member of the Board, Council of the Americas 1984-; Member of the Board, Panamerican Development Foundation 1984-; Member of the Board, International Human Rights Law Group 1985-; Member of the Board, Salzburg Seminar 1988-; Member of the Advisory Council, Rockefeller University 1984-; Member of the Advisory Council, Overseas Development Council 1987-; Member of the Advisory Council, International Center for Economic Growth 1987-; Member of the Advisory Council, Governor Guomo's Panel on the Financial Development of New York. *Publications:* The Impact of the Higher Oil Prices on the LDC's; The Case of Latin America; The Search for a New International Role, edited by Hellman & Rosenbum for the Center for Inter-American Relations, 1975; Peruvian Democracy under Economic Stress; An Account of the Belaunde Administration 1983 - 1968, 1977; The Economic Development of Venezuela in Perspective in a Council on Foreign Relations Book on Contemporary Venezuela, editor, Robert Bond, 1977; Toward Renewed Economic Growth in Latin America, with Bela Belassa, Gerardo Bueno and Mario Henrique Simonsen, 1986; Latin American Debt, a Twentieth

Century Fund Book; Japanese edition, 1990; International Emergency Lending Facilities; Are they Adequate? In The International Monetary System; Forty Years After Bretton Woods, 1984; Action Steps After Cancun, 1982; Latin American Debt I, 1982-83; Latin American Debt II, 1983; The Outlook for Latin American Debt, 1987.

KUDO, Y; Director, IBJ International Limited.

KUEHNE, Karl J; Executive Director, Crédit Suisse First Boston Limited.

KUNITAKE, Tanekiyo; Joint General Manager, The Sumitomo Bank Limited (London Branch), since 1985; Management, Head of Audit, General Affairs and Loans Administration Departments.

KURIHARA, O; Deputy Managing Director, IBJ International Ltd, since 1990; Capital Markets, Personnel. *Career:* The Industrial Bank of Japan Ltd 1968-86. *Biog: b.* 25 October 1945. *Nationality:* Japanese. *m.* 1974, Kaoru (née Miura); 3 d. *Educ:* Tokyo University (BA Law).

KUROKAWA, Kiyotaka; Joint General Manager, The Sumitomo Bank Ltd, since 1990; Japanese Corporate Personnel. *Career:* The Sumitomo Bank Ltd 1969-. *Biog: b.* 17 February 1947. *Nationality:* Japanese. *m.* 1976, Toshiko; 1 s; 1 d. *Educ:* Kyushu University.

KUSANO, Motohiko; Managing Director, Nippon Credit International Ltd, since 1986. *Career:* The Nippon Credit Bank Ltd 1971-. *Biog: b.* 15 October 1947. *Nationality:* Japanese. *m.* 1977, Mamiko (née Takeda); 1 s; 1 d. *Educ:* Keio University, Japan (BA). *Directorships:* Nippon Credit International Ltd 1986 (exec). *Recreations:* Golf.

KWEK, L H; Director, Benchmark Group plc.

KYLE, James; Director & Company Secretary, Yamaichi International (Europe) Limited.

KYLE, James Terence; Partner, Linklaters & Paines, since 1979; Head of International Finance Section. *Career:* Linklaters & Paines, Articled Clerk 1970-72; Assistant Solicitor 1972-79. *Biog: b.* 9 May 1946. *Nationality:* British. *m.* 1975, Diana (née Jackson); 1 s; 2 d. *Educ:* The Royal Belfast Academical Institution; Christ's College, Cambridge (MA). *Other Activities:* Freeman, City of London Solicitors' Company. *Professional Organisations:* Member, Law Society. *Recreations:* Cricket, Squash.

KYLE, R J; Director, Barclays de Zoete Wedd Securities Ltd.

KYTE, David Mark; Managing Director, Kyte Futures Ltd, since 1984; Financial Futures, Trading. *Career:* Tullett & Tokyo, Financial Futures Trade 1982-84; Gilbert Eliott, Fixed Interest Broker 1979-82. *Biog: b.* 29 June 1960. *Nationality:* British. *m.* 1984, Tracey (née Leigh); 1 s; 1 d. *Educ:* Christ's College, Finchley. *Directorships:* London International Financial Futures Exchange 1990 (non-exec). *Recreations:* MAL.

KYTE, Thomas Peter; Director, Brunswick, since 1988; Press Relations. *Career:* Inland Revenue 1963-66; Financial Times, Company Comments 1966-77; Daily Telegraph, Questor Column 1977-86; The Independent, Deputy City Editor 1986-87; City Editor 1987-88. *Biog: b.* 4 June 1947. *Nationality:* British. *m.* 1970, Lynn Dora (née Harding); 1 s; 2 d.

L

LA NIECE, David; Partner, Moore Stephens, since 1967; Chairman International Technical Committee, Head of Corporate Business Services. *Career:* Royal Artillery 1949-54; P D Leake & Co 1951-57; Moore Stephens 1957-67. *Biog: b.* 21 June 1931. *Nationality:* British. *m.* 1958, Beryl Jean (née Cork); 1 s; 1 d. *Educ:* Tonbridge School. *Other Activities:* Liveryman of Wax Chandlers' Company; Freeman of City of London. *Professional Organisations:* FCA. *Clubs:* Oriental, Army & Navy, Farringdon Ward, Walbrook Ward. *Recreations:* Music, Theatre, Travelling.

LA ROCHE, A P; Director, London International Financial Futures Exchange.

LABAND, Paul Alexander Kenneth; Deputy Managing Director, Abbey Life Investment Services Ltd, since 1989; Investment Management. *Career:* Simon & Coates, Analyst 1970-73; Abbey Life, Analyst 1973-75; Portfolio Mgr 1975-84; Asst Exec Dir 1984-86; Abbey Life Investment Services, Director 1986-88. *Biog: b.* 15 August 1948. *Nationality:* British. *m.* 1970, Sheila (née Russell); 2 d. *Educ:* Strathallan School; Downing College, Cambridge (BA Hons). *Professional Organisations:* ASIA. *Recreations:* Athletics, Tennis, Sailing.

LABES, Claus G; Executive Director, Crédit Suisse First Boston Ltd.

LABRAM, Nigel Anthony; Head of Cocoa, J H Rayner (Mincing Lane) Ltd, since 1989; Cocoa Dealer & Commission House. *Career:* Mars (Confectionery) Ltd, Project Engineer, Supplies Buyer, Commodity Buyer 1975-84; V Berg & Sons Ltd, Head of Cocoa, Deputy Managing Director 1984-89; J H Rayner (Mincing Lane) Ltd, Head of Cocoa 1989-. *Biog: b.* 12 September 1953. *Nationality:* British. *m.* 1974, Lesley Patricia; 2 d. *Educ:* Queen Mary's Grammar, Basingstoke; Southampton University (BSc Hons & Eustace Memorial Prize). *Directorships:* V Berg & Sons Ltd 1985-89 (exec); J H Rayner (Cocoa) 1990 (exec); Lonray Malaysia 1989 (exec); Berisford Commodities Inc 1989 (exec). *Recreations:* Fitness Training, Sailing, Driving.

LACE, John David; Partner, Bristows Cooke & Carpmael, since 1978; Corporate & Commercial Law Including Corporate Finance. *Career:* Meade King & Co, Articled Clerk 1968-73; Assistant Solicitor 1973-74; Bristows Cooke & Carpmael, Assistant Solicitor 1974-78. *Biog: b.* 11 September 1947. *Nationality:* British. *m.* 1981, Stephanie Rachel (née Ward); 3 s; 1 d. *Educ:*

Dragon School, Oxford; Malvern College. *Professional Organisations:* Law Society. *Clubs:* MCC. *Recreations:* Gardening, Sailing, Photography.

LACEY, Michael Patrick; Partner, Titmuss Sainer & Webb, since 1988; Commercial Property. *Career:* Wilde Sapte, Articled Clerk 1980-82; Assistant Solicitor 1982-85; Titmuss Sainer & Webb, Assistant Solicitor 1985-88. *Biog: b.* 14 July 1956. *Nationality:* British. *m.* 1986, Alison (née Winspear); 2 s. *Educ:* St Georges College, Weybridge; University of Wales (LLB); University of Exeter (LLM). *Professional Organisations:* Law Society. *Recreations:* Football, Hockey, Cricket, Chess.

LACY, Richard Clifford; Chairman, Exco International plc, since 1986; Money Foreign Exchange and Government Securities Broking. *Career:* Exco International Various 1966-. *Biog: b.* 17 November 1947. *Nationality:* British. *m.* 1969, Christine Mary (née Waller); 2 s; 1 d. *Educ:* Eastbourne College. *Directorships:* RMJ Securities Corp 1987. *Clubs:* Turf, Army & Navy, Royal Ashdown Forest Golf Club. *Recreations:* Golf, Skiing.

LADD, Mark; Partner, Clark Whitehill.

LADENBURG, Michael John Carlisle; Director, Robert Fleming & Co Ltd, since 1988; International Corporate Finance. *Career:* J Henry Schroder Wagg & Co Ltd Various 1966; Director 1979-88; Schroder Securities (Japan) Ltd (Tokyo) Gen Mgr & Snr Schroder Gp Exec, Japan 1985-87. *Biog: b.* 2 February 1945. *Nationality:* British. *m.* 1971, Susan Elizabeth (née Laing); 1 s; 2 d. *Educ:* Charterhouse, Godalming, Surrey; Christ Church, Oxford (MA). *Clubs:* Hurlingham, Tandridge Golf Club. *Recreations:* Golf, Skiing, Music, Tennis.

LAFFERTY, J; Director, County NatWest Securities Limited.

LAFFERTY, Michael J; Chief Executive Director, Lafferty Publications Ltd.

LAING, Andrew A; Director, Aberdeen Trust Holdings plc; Managing Director, Aberdeen Fund Managers Ltd. *Career:* Biggart Baillie & Gifford, Commercial Lawyer 1977-83; Hodgson Martin Ltd, Dir, Venture Capital 1984-87. *Biog: b.* 8 November 1952. *Nationality:* British. *Educ:* Robert Gordons College; Aberdeen University (MA, LLB). *Directorships:* Aberdeen Trust Holdings (& Subsidiaries) 1987 (exec); Scotcare Ltd 1988 (non-exec); Seaforth Maritime Group plc 1989 (non-exec); Hodgson Martin Ventures Ltd 1985-86 (exec). *Professional Organisations:* Notary Public. *Clubs:* Royal Northern & University. *Recreations:* Rowing, Flying, Outdoor Sports.

LAING, Graham Alexander A Turner; Chairman, Raphael Zorn Hemsley Limited, since 1989.

LAING, Robert John; Partner, Maclay Murray & Spens, since 1985; Corporate Finance and Commercial. *Career:* Slaughter and May, Asst Solicitor 1977-83. *Biog: b.* 12 March 1953. *Educ:* Eton College; Selwyn College, Cambridge (MA). *Professional Organisations:* The Law Society of Scotland; The Law Society. *Clubs:* New Club, Edinburgh Sports Club, Luffness Golf Club. *Recreations:* Golf, Tennis, Fishing, Shooting.

LAIRD, Gavin Harry; General Secretary, Amalgamated Engineering Union, since 1982; All Financial and Administrative Matters Relating to the AEU. *Biog: b.* 14 March 1933. *Nationality:* British. *m.* 1956, Catherine (née Campbell); 1 d. *Directorships:* Bank of England 1986 (non-exec); Scottish TV 1986 (non-exec); Scottish Development Agency 1987 (non-exec); Brittannia Life Ltd 1988 (non-exec). *Other Activities:* Governor, London Business School; Member, Strathclyde Business School Council, University of Strathclyde. *Clubs:* Clydebank AEU Social Club. *Recreations:* Looking wistfully at hills I would like to climb.

LAIRD, R H; Director, Hoare Govett Corporate Finance.

LAKE, J B; Managing Director, Greenwell Montagu Gilt-Edged.

LAMB, Richard; Executive Director, N M Rothschild International Asset Management Limited.

LAMBERSON, J R; Executive Director, Willis Corroon plc.

LAMBERT, Henry Uvedale Antrobus; Chairman, Sun Alliance Group plc, since 1985. *Career:* Royal Navy, Lt RNVR 1943-46; Barclays Bank plc 1948-85; Local Dir 1957-59; (Southampton), Local Dir 1959-69; (Birmingham), Local Dir 1969-72; Vice Chm 1973-79; Dep Chm 1979-85. *Biog: b.* 9 October 1925. *Nationality:* British. *m.* 1951, Diana (née Dumbell); 2 s; 1 d. *Educ:* Winchester College (Scholar); New College, Oxford (Exhibitioner, MA). *Directorships:* Barclays Bank plc 1966; Agricultural Mortgage Corp 1966; 1985 Chm. *Other Activities:* Council Member, Royal Agricultural Society of England; Council Member, White Ensign Association; Trustee, Imperial War Graves Endowment Fund; Trustee, National Maritime Museum. *Professional*

Organisations: FCIB. *Clubs:* Brooks's, MCC. *Recreations:* Fishing, Gardening, Naval History.

LAMBERT, J R; Executive Director, Schroder Investment Management Ltd.

LAMBERT, M; Finance Director, Philipp Bros Ltd.

LAMBERT, Patricia; OBE; Public Interest Director, Lautro.

LAMBERT, Philip S; Director, Kleinwort Benson Securities Limited.

LAMBERT, R M U; Partner, Cazenove & Co.

LAMBERT, Richard; Editor, Financial Times.

LAMBERT, Royston; Managing Director, AIBD (Systems & Information) Limited, since 1984.

LAMBIE, Bruce D; Deputy Managing Director, Den Norske Bank plc; Shipping & Offshore.

LAMBOURNE, R D; Partner, Cameron Markby Hewitt.

LAMBRECHT, T P; Director (Non-Executive), Williams de Broë plc.

LAMBRICK, Charles Trevor; Partner, Jaques & Lewis, since 1981; Commercial Litigation, Insurance Litgation. *Career:* McKenna & Co, Articled Clerk 1972-75; Bower Cotton & Bower, Assistant Solicitor 1975-77; Jaques & Co, Assistant Solicitor 1977-81. *Biog: b.* 27 September 1949. *Nationality:* British. *m.* 1981, Fiona (née Thom-Postlethwaite); 1 d. *Educ:* The King's School, Canterbury; Lincoln College, Oxford (MA Hons). *Professional Organisations:* Law Society. *Clubs:* Royal Southern Yacht Club. *Recreations:* Sailing, Architectural History, Music.

LAMOND, William Kerr Edward; Director, Barclays de Zoete Wedd Securities Limited, since 1989; South East Asia Equities. *Career:* W I Carr Sons & Co Ltd, Analyst of UK Equities 1970-75; W I Carr Sons & Co (Overseas) Limited, Research Director Far Eastern Markets 1975-83; W I Carr (America) Inc, President 1983-86; Swiss Bank Corporation International Securities Limited, Director Far East Equities 1986-87; SBCI Savory Milln Limited, Director European Research 1988-89; Barclays de Zoete Wedd Securities Limited, Director South East Asian Sales 1989-. *Biog: b.* 24 November 1947. *Nationality:* British. *m.* 1971, Darna Petronelle (née Pallot); 2 s; 1 d. *Educ:* Repton College. *Directorships:* Barclays de Zoete Wedd Securities Limited 1989 (exec). *Clubs:* Hurlingham, Hong Kong Jockey Club, LRC.

LAMPARD, M R; Director, Hambros plc.

LAMPARD, Martin Robert; Consultant, Ashurst Morris Crisp.

LAMBRECHT, T P; Non-Executive Director, Williams de Broë plc.

LAMPL, Sir Frank; Director, P & O Steam Navigation Company.

LAMPSON, The Hon Victor Miles George A; Partner, Cazenove & Co.

LANCH, C; Director, FIMBRA.

LANCHON, Mme C; Director, Crédit Lyonnais Capital Markets plc.

LAND, Brook; Partner, Nabarro Nathanson, since 1974; Corporate Finance. *Career:* Nabarro Nathanson, Articled Clerk 1967-72; Asst Solicitor 1972-74. *Biog: b.* 12 March 1949. *m.* 1975, Anita (née Grade); 1 s; 1 d. *Educ:* St Paul's School. *Directorships:* Theatre Royal Brighton Ltd 1985 (non-exec); JLI Group plc 1988 (non-exec). *Professional Organisations:* The Law Society. *Clubs:* Annabel's. *Recreations:* Work, Poker.

LAND, J W; Finance Director, Amalgamated Metal Trading Limited.

LAND, Nicholas Charles Edward; Partner, Ernst & Whinney.

LANDAIS, J P; Information Systems Director, Methuen (Lloyd's Underwriting Agents) Limited, since 1987; Computing & Communications.

LANDER, Geoffrey Ian; Partner, Nabarro Nathanson, since 1980; Real Estate. *Career:* Nabarro Nathanson Man & Boy 1973-. *Biog: b.* 11 January 1951. *Nationality:* British. *m.* 1984, Lynn. *Educ:* Moseley Hall Grammar School; Lanchester Polytechnic (BA). *Other Activities:* Executive Council Member, British Council for Offices. *Professional Organisations:* Solicitor. *Recreations:* Bridge, Watching Sport, Swimming, Walking.

LANE, James N; Managing Director - Investment Banking, Goldman Sachs International Limited.

LANE, Sir Peter (Stewart); The Lord Lane of Horsell; Kt, JP; Senior Partner, BDO Binder Hamlyn Chartered Accountants, since 1979. *Career:* RNVR, Sub-Lt 1943-46; Qualified as Chartered Accountant 1948; Binder Hamlyn or Predecessors Firms, Partner 1950-. *Biog: b.* 29 January 1925. *m.* Doris Florence (née Botsford) (decd 1969); 2 d. *Educ:* Sherborne School, Dorset. *Directorships:* Brent Chemicals International 1985 Chm; More O'Ferrall 1985 Dep Chm. *Other*

Activities: National Union of Conservative Associations, Vice Chairman 1981-83; Chairman, 1983-84; Chairman Executive Committee, 1986-; Vice-President, 1984-; Nuffield Nursing Homes Trust, Governor, 1985-; Deputy Chairman, 1990-; JP (Surrey), 1976-; Freeman, City of London. *Clubs:* Boodle's, MCC.

LANE, Robert Charles; Partner, McKenna & Co, since 1990; Corporate/Utilities Lawyer with Interest in Electricity. *Career:* Slaughter & May, Articled Clerk 1980-82; Asst Solicitor 1982-88; McKenna & Co, Asst Solicitor 1988-90. *Biog: b.* 29 August 1958. *Nationality:* British. *m.* 1986, Margaret; 2 s. *Educ:* Buckhurst Hill County High School; University College, London (LLB). *Other Activities:* Freeman, The City of London; Liveryman, Worshipful Company of City of London Solicitors. *Professional Organisations:* Law Society; International Bar Association (Section on Energy & Natural Resources). *Clubs:* Royal Automobile Club, Bentham Club. *Recreations:* Opera.

LANE, V F; Head of Branch, Department of Trade and Industry.

LANG, David Percival; Analyst, Henderson Crosthwaite.

LANG, Jonathan Andrew; Manager Fixed Interest and Treasury Functions, British Airways Pensions, since 1985; Gilts/Overseas Bonds/Foreign Exchange/Money Markets. *Career:* BOAC Manager, Dubai 1968-72; British Airways Manager, Barbados 1972-76; Chief Executive Aviation, Seychelles 1976-79; British Airways Foreign Exchange Manager 1979-85. *Biog: b.* 20 January 1937. *Nationality:* British. *m.* 1965, Catherine Mary (née Chubb); 2 s. *Educ:* Clifton College, Bristol; New College, Oxford (MA Law). *Recreations:* Golf, Walking, Opera, Wine.

LANG, M P; Director of Finance, Ford Motor Credit Company Ltd, since 1989. *Career:* Ford Motor Company Ltd 1973-89; Various Finance Positions in Truck Operations, Product Development and Finance Staff, Ford of Europe 1973-87; Controller, Parts Operations, Ford of Britain 1987-89. *Biog: b.* 1 May 1951. *Nationality:* British. *m.* 1989, Elizabeth. 1 s; 2 d (including previous marriage). *Educ:* University of Exeter (BA Hons Economics). *Directorships:* Ford Motor Credit Company Ltd 1990 (exec); Ford Automotive Leasing Ltd 1990 (exec); Ford Credit Funding plc 1990 (exec); Automotive Finance Ltd 1990 (exec); Ford Lease Finance Ltd 1990 (exec); Ford Fleet Financing Ltd 1990 (exec); Ford Financial Trust Ltd 1990 (exec). *Recreations:* Golf, Skiing, Good Food.

LANGDON, Michael Charles; Partner, McKenna & Co, since 1987; Property Litigation. *Career:* McKenna & Co, Articled Clerk 1979-81; Asst Solicitor 1981-87. *Biog: b.* 27 February 1956. *Nationality:* British. *Educ:*

Queens College, Oxford (MA Philosophy and Modern Languages). *Professional Organisations:* Law Society England & Wales; British Italian Law Association.

LANGDON, Michael R F; Deputy Chairman and Chief Executive, Rutland Trust plc, since 1987. *Career:* Price Waterhouse, Partner 1981-86. *Biog: b.* 8 February 1948. *Nationality:* Swiss. *m.* 1976, Claudia (née Luscher); 3 d. *Educ:* The Leys, Cambridge; Cambridge University (MA Economics). *Directorships:* London & Edinburgh Trust plc 1987 (non-exec); Michael Langdon Associates Ltd 1986 (exec). *Professional Organisations:* Fellow, Institute of Chartered Accountants. *Clubs:* City of London Club.

LANGDON, R N D; Chairman, First National Finance Corporation plc, since 1985. *Career:* Spicer & Pegler (now Touche Ross & Co); Partner 1953; Managing Partner 1971-82; Senior Partner 1978-84. *Biog: b.* 19 June 1919. *Nationality:* British. *m.* 1944, June Phyllis (née Dixon); 2 s. *Educ:* Shewsbury School. *Directorships:* First National Finance Corporation plc 1985 (exec); Finlay Packaging plc 1984 (non-exec); Time Products plc 1984 (non-exec); Chemring Group plc 1985 (non-exec); Rockware Group plc 1985 (non-exec); BISFISA Compania Iberica de Inversiones SA 1990 (non-exec); Beeson Gregory Ltd 1989 (non-exec). *Other Activities:* Member of Council, University of Surrey. *Professional Organisations:* FCA; MIOD. *Clubs:* City of London, Old Salopian. *Recreations:* Sailing, Gardening, Bricklaying.

LANGLEY, P J; Partner, Slaughter and May, since 1975; Commercial Property. *Career:* C F Snow & Co, Littlehampton, Assistant Solicitor 1965-66; Partner 1966-70; Slaughter and May, Assistant Solicitor 1970-74; Partner 1975-.

LANGMAN, J C; Director, Murray Lawrence Members' Agency Limited.

LANGMEAD, D F; Associate Director, Beeson Gregory Limited.

LANGTON, John Leslie; Chief Executive & Secretary General, Association of International Bond Dealers, since 1990; Self-Regulatory Body for the International Capital Markets. *Career:* Strauss Turnbull & Co (London), Eurobond Settlements Mgr 1965-69; Scandinavian Bank Ltd (London), Snr Eurobond Trader 1969-73; Williams & Glyns Bank (London), Head of Bond Trading 1973-74; Bondtrade in Brussels, General Mgr 1974-77; Morgan Stanley Intl (London), Mgr/Head Bond Trader 1977-78; Amex Bank Ltd (London), Exec Dir 1979-80; Orion Royal Bank Ltd (London), Snr Exec Dir 1980-85; SPHG Ltd (London), Exec Dir 1985-87; Gintel & Co Ltd (London), MD 1987-90; AIBD (Zurich), Chief Exec & Sec Gen 1990-; AIBD Systems & Information Ltd (London), Chm 1990-. *Biog: b.* 23 November 1948. *Nationality:* British. *m.* 1979, Raymonde. 1 steps 1 d. *Educ:* Roan Grammar School for Boys, Greenwich. *Directorships:* AIBD Systems & Information Limited 1987 (exec) Chm; AIBD (Zurich) 1981 (Chief exec & Sec Gen); ARNTON Investment Management Limited CIMRO Member (London) 1990 (non-exec) Chm. *Recreations:* Backgammon, Reading, Travel, Food & Wine.

LANZA, F; Deputy Manager, Banca Nazionale del Lavoro.

LAPPING, Ian Emmott; Director, Chartered WestLB Ltd, since 1989; United Kingdom Corporate Finance. *Career:* Hill Samuel South Africa, Gen Mgr, Corporate Finance 1975-87; Hill Samuel & Co, Dir, Corporate Finance 1988. *Biog: b.* 12 January 1947. *Nationality:* British. *m.* (div); 1 s; 1 d. *Educ:* Michaelhouse Rhodes University (BCom); University of Cape Town GSB (MBA). *Recreations:* Fishing, Reading.

LARA, F; Treasurer, Vauxhall Motors Ltd, since 1989; Pension Admin & Investment, Tax, Insurance, Corporate Finance, Banking, Foreign Exchange. *Career:* Arthur Andersen (Madrid Office), Audit & Tax 1976-80; General Motors (Espana), Tax Administrator, Manager Tax & Insurance, Assistant Treasurer, Treasurer 1980-89. *Biog: b.* 4 October 1952. *Nationality:* Spanish. *m.* 1977, Paz; 2 s; 2 d. *Educ:* Icade, Madrid, Spain (Law & Business Administration); Deusto University, Spain (Law); Icade, Madrid, Spain (Graduate Tax Advice).

LARCOMBE, Brian; Director, 3i plc.

LARCOMBE, Derek Roy; Executive Director & Fund Manager, CCF Foster Braithwaite Limited, since 1989. *Biog: b.* 28 September 1946. *m.* 1972, Lynda Sally; 1 s; 3 d. *Educ:* Hawes Down. *Directorships:* CCF Foster Braithwaite Ltd 1989 (exec); CCF Foster Braithwaite Unit Trust Management Ltd 1989 (exec). *Other Activities:* Treasurer, Broad Street Ward Club; Freeman, City of London. *Professional Organisations:* Member, Stock Exchange 1983-; TSA; Lautro; Imro. *Clubs:* Blackheath Harriers, Reedham Park Tennis Club. *Recreations:* Running, Cycling, Tennis, City History.

LARKIN, Peter; Deputy Managing Director, Mitsui Taiyo Kobe International, since 1990; Sales and Research. *Career:* Price Waterhouse (London), Articled Clerk/Auditor 1967-71; Barclays Bank (London & International), Mergers and Acquisitions, Corporate Structuring 1972-74; Credit Lyonnais (London), Representative of C L Paris for Mergers and Acquisitions 1974-77; Credit Lyonnais (Antwerp), Manager, Marketing to Domestic and Multinational Companies 1977-80; Credit Lyonnais (London), Manager, Capital Markets and Financial Institutions 1980-85; CCF Securities (London), Managing Director 1985-87; Taiyo Kobe International (London)(Merged with Mitsui Finance 1990), Deputy Managing Director, Sales and Trading

1987-90. *Biog: b.* 22 March 1945. *Nationality:* British. *m.* 1971, Jane Lee (née Kendall); 1 s; 1 d. *Educ:* St Dunstans College; Trinity College, Cambridge (MA Law); INSEAD (Diplôme). *Professional Organisations:* Fellow, Institute of Chartered Accountants in England and Wales. *Clubs:* United Oxford and Cambridge University Club, Liphook Golf Club. *Recreations:* Golf, Sailing, History.

LARKIN, Reginald W; Managing Director, Alexander Howden Reinsurance Brokers Limited.

LARLHAM, C; Partner, Cameron Markby Hewitt.

LARNER, Richard John; Managing Director, Waters Lunniss & Co Ltd, since 1990; Managing a Private Client Stockbroking Firm. *Career:* Grieveson Grant, Private Client Stockbroker 1983-85; Margetts & Addenbrooke, Associated Member 1985-88; Waters Lunniss & Co, Associated Member 1989; Private Client Director 1989-90; Managing Director 1990-. *Educ:* The Paston School, North Walsham, Norfolk; University of Exeter. *Clubs:* The Norfolk Club, The Strangers Club.

LASKEY, Peter S; Partner, Theodore Goddard.

LAST, Simon; VP Director, Bond Trading, ScotiaMcLeod Incorporated.

LASZLO, Peter John; Director, Legal & General Ventures Ltd, since 1987; Venture Capital. *Career:* Marconi Instruments Ltd, Divisional Accountant 1966-71; Small Business Capital Fund Ltd, Cost Accountant 1971-72; Blundell-Permoglaze Holdings plc, Chief Accountant then Director of Finance & Planning 1972-85. *Biog: b.* 13 March 1944. *Nationality:* British. *m.* 1970, Susanne; 1 s; 1 d. *Educ:* Clifton College, University of Manchester (BA). *Other Activities:* Member of Council, Chartered Institute of Management Accountants. *Professional Organisations:* FCMA. *Recreations:* Bach Choir.

LATCHAM, K D; Director, Amalgamated Metal Trading Limited.

LATCHMORE, Andrew Windsor; Partner, Hepworth & Chadwick, since 1978; Commercial Property. *Career:* Booth & Co, Articled Clerk 1972-75; Hepworth & Chadwick, Assistant Solicitor 1975-78; Partner 1978; Eversheds Commercial Property Group, Chairman 1990. *Biog: b.* 9 February 1950. *Nationality:* British. *m.* 1989, Clarissa Mary (née Orde); 1 s; 1 d (by previous marriage). *Educ:* Oundle School; Leeds University (LLB). *Directorships:* The Leeds Law Society 1986 (non-exec). *Other Activities:* Honorary Secretary, The Leeds Law Society, 1986-90; Honorary Secretary, Gateways School. *Professional Organisations:* The Law Society; The Leeds Law Society. *Recreations:* Golf, Tennis, Squash, Riding, Walking, Music.

LATHAM, G A; Director, Manning Beard Ltd.

LATHAM, John Martin; Head of Secretariat, James Capel & Co, since 1986; Group Finance and Secretarial. *Career:* Peat Marwick Mitchell, Articled Clerk to Asst Mgr 1965-74; James Capel & Co, Corp Finance Exec 1974-76; Co Sec 1976-86. *Biog: b.* 28 July 1942. *Nationality:* British. *Educ:* Bradfield College, Berkshire; Fitzwilliam College, Cambridge (MA). *Directorships:* James Capel Moneybroking Ltd 1986 (exec); Allied Provincial Securities plc 1988 (non-exec) Alternate. *Professional Organisations:* Fellow, ICAEW. *Clubs:* MCC, Roehampton. *Recreations:* Tennis, Squash, Music, Sailing.

LATIF, Mrs Rona; Director, Afghan National Credit and Finance Limited, since 1981; Audit. *Career:* Ministry of Finance, Kabul, Director/General Director 1970-79; Banke Millie Afghan, Kabul, Vice President 1980-81. *Biog: b.* 14 April 1945. *Nationality:* Afghan.

LATIMER, D C; Group Finance Director, Bunzl plc, since 1990. *Career:* Bunzl, Director 1980-; United Biscuits 1967-69; PRR & Co 1960-67. *Biog: b.* 24 July 1942. *Nationality:* British. *m.* 1965, Rosemary Ann (née Maxwell); 2 s; 1 d. *Educ:* Rugby School. *Professional Organisations:* FCA.

LATNER, Stephen; Director, S G Warburg & Co Ltd, since 1983; Corporate Finance, Mergers & Acquisitions. *Career:* ICL, Graduate Entrant 1968-71; S G Warburg, Exec 1973-. *Biog: b.* 23 July 1946. *Nationality:* British. *m.* 1971, Jennifer Sylvia (née Keidan); 3 s. *Educ:* Grocers'; Queen Mary College, London (BSc Hons); Manchester Business School (MBA). *Directorships:* S G Warburg & Co Ltd 1983 (exec). *Professional Organisations:* Manchester Business School Assoc. *Recreations:* Sport, Cinema, Theatre, Music, Reading.

LATSIS, Dr S J; Director, The Private Bank and Trust Company Limited.

LATTER, A R; Head of International Division, Bank of England.

LAUGHLAN, D C; General Manager, Halifax Building Society.

LAUGHLAND, H W; Director, BTR plc.

LAURANCE, Benjamin James; Deputy Financial Editor, The Guardian, since 1989. *Career:* Eastern Counties Newspapers, Reporter 1977-82; Lloyd's List, Business Correspondent, Energy Correspondent 1982-86; Freelance 1986; Daily Express, Deputy City Editor 1986-88; The Guardian, Financial Writer 1988-89. *Biog: b.* 27 May 1956. *Nationality:* British. *Educ:* Oakham School; Trinity College, Cambridge (BA Hons Economics). *Recreations:* Offshore Sailing, Chopping Wood.

LAURENSON, James Tait; Deputy Chairman & Managing Director, Adam & Company Group plc, since 1984. *Career:* Ivory & Sime, Investment Mgr 1968-70; Ptnr 1970-75; Ivory & Sime Ltd, Dir 1975-83; Tayburn Design Group Ltd, MD 1983-84; Chm 1984-89. *Biog: b.* 15 March 1941. *Nationality:* British. *m.* 1969, Hilary (née Thompson); 1 s; 3 d. *Educ:* Eton College; Magdalene College, Cambridge (MA). *Directorships:* United Scientific Holdings plc 1972 (non-exec); First Charlotte Assets Trust plc 1983 (non-exec); Nippon Assets Investments SA 1984 (non-exec) Chm. *Other Activities:* Court of Company of Merchants of the City of Edinburgh. *Professional Organisations:* FCA. *Clubs:* New Club (Edinburgh). *Recreations:* Tennis, Skiing, Shooting, Gardening.

LAURENT, M-O; Director, Crédit Commercial de France (UK) Limited.

LAURENT-BELLUE, J; Director, Crédit Commercial de France (UK) Limited.

LAURIE, Sir Bayley; Bt; Director, Murray Lawrence Members' Agency Limited.

LAURIE, John; Group Treasurer, Scottish & Newcastle Breweries plc.

LAVAL, Derek C; Executive Director, Venture Link Investors Ltd.

LAVER, John G; Director, Bradstock Blunt & Crawley Ltd.

LAVERS, Michael John; Group Treasurer, George Wimpey plc, since 1982; Treasury and Project Finance. *Career:* Esso Petroleum Ltd 1964-72; International Finance Corporation 1972-73; Kleinwort Benson Ltd 1974-76; Norcros Limited 1976-82. *Biog: b.* 3 June 1943. *Nationality:* British. *m.* 1975, Sally (née Wheeler); 2 s. *Educ:* Cranleigh School; Trinity College, Cambridge (BA Hons). *Directorships:* George Wimpey Group. *Other Activities:* Member, Examination Review Board of the Association of Corporate Treasurers. *Professional Organisations:* Fellow, Association of Corporate Treasurers. *Recreations:* Golf, Theatre.

LAW, Charles E; Managing Director, Continental Bank NA, since 1981; Corporate Finance in the UK. *Career:* British Steel Corporation, Metallurgist 1968-71; United International Bank, Manager 1973-79; Merrill Lynch, Vice President 1979-81; Continental Bank NA, Managing Director 1981-. *Biog: b.* 12 August 1946. *Nationality:* British. *m.* 1970, Clodagh (née Steele-Baume); 2 s; 1 d. *Educ:* Nottingham University (Metallurgy 2i); Manchester Business School (MBA).

LAW, Donald; Managing Director, Yorkshire Enterprise Limited.

LAW, George Llewellyn; Senior Adviser, Morgan Grenfell Group plc, since 1989. *Career:* Slaughter and May, Asst Solicitor 1955-61; Ptnr 1961-67; Morgan Grenfell & Co Ltd, Dir 1968-; Morgan Grenfell Group plc, Dir 1971-89; Vice Chairman 1987-89. *Biog: b.* 8 July 1929. *Nationality:* British. *m.* 1960, Anne Stewart (née Wilkinson); 1 d. *Educ:* Westminster School; Clare College, Cambridge (BA). *Directorships:* APV plc 1987-90 (non-exec); Blackwood Hodge plc 1968-90 (non-exec); Baker Perkins plc 1981-87 (non-exec). *Other Activities:* City of London Solicitors' Company; The Securities Association Conduct of Business Rules Committee. *Professional Organisations:* The Law Society (Standing Ctee on Company Law); Solicitor. *Clubs:* Brooks's, MCC, Surrey County Cricket. *Recreations:* History of Furniture & Decorative Arts, Music, Reading, Walking.

LAW, Gordon Malcolm; General Manager, Woolwich Building Society, since 1976; Personnel & Training. *Career:* Jessop Saville Ltd (Sheffield) Graduate Trainee/Staff Officer 1957-62; Shepherd Building Group Ltd Personnel Officer 1962-65; (York) Group Establishment Officer 1965-70; Woolwich Equitable Building Soc Personnel Mgr 1970-72; AGM (Personnel) 1972-76. *Biog: b.* 7 November 1932. *Nationality:* British. *m.* 1957, Elaine (née Whittingham); 3 d. *Educ:* King Edward VII Grammar School, Sheffield; Sheffield University (BA). *Directorships:* Thames Polytechnic Court Governor 1976, Past Chm 1985-88; National Interactive Video Centre 1986 (non-exec); National Council for Educational Technology (Council Member) 1985. *Other Activities:* Liveryman, Worshipful Company of Distillers; Freeman, City of London; CBSI Council Member, Education Ctee Member, Corporate Planning Ctee Member. *Professional Organisations:* FIPM, FCBSI, FBIM. *Publications:* Personnel Policy & Line Management 1974, revised 1983; Various CBSI/BSA. *Clubs:* City Livery, West Kent Golf Club. *Recreations:* Golf, Philately.

LAW, Michael B H; Director, Schroder Securities Limited.

LAWDEN, James Anthony Henry; Partner, Freshfields, since 1988; Capital Markets, Banking and Corporate Finance. *Career:* Freshfields, Articled Clerk 1979-81; Assistant Solicitor 1981-84 & 1986-88; Aoki Christensen & Nomoto, Tokyo 1985; Freshfields, Partner 1988-. *Biog: b.* 10 August 1955. *Nationality:* British. *Educ:* Winchester College; New College, Oxford (MA). *Other Activities:* Trustee, Wykehamist Society. *Professional Organisations:* Solicitor. *Clubs:* Naval and Military Club, Roehampton Club. *Recreations:* Tennis, Squash, Travelling.

LAWES, J T P; Director, Hambros Bank Limited.

LAWES, William E; Vice President and Chief Credit Officer, London Branch, Manufacturers Hanover Trust Company; Business Units, Risk/Credit Functions. *Career:* ANZ/Grindlays Banking Group; Head of Global Shipping 1981; General Manager, North America 1984; Various administration positions, Europe; Manufacturers Hanover Trust Company 1988-. *Biog:* married 2 children. *Educ:* Edinburgh University. *Directorships:* Manufacturers Hanover Finance Limited; Manufacturers Hanover Export Finance Limited; Manufacturers Hanover Industrial Finance Limited; Manufacturers Hanover Leasing (UK) Limited; Manufacturers Hanover Property Services Limited; Manufacturers Hanover UK Holdings Limited; G H Curzon Ltd; Engelmann & Buckham (Holdings) Ltd. *Professional Organisations:* Chartered Accountant (Scotland).

LAWRENCE, D A C; Director, Kleinwort Benson Unit Trusts Limited.

LAWRENCE, Jeffrey; Managing Director, Merrill Lynch Global Asset Management.

LAWRENCE, Sir John Patrick Grosvenor; CBE; Senior Partner, Wragge & Co, since 1982. *Career:* Wragge & Co, Articled Clerk 1949-54; Solicitor 1954-59; Partner 1959-82; Senior Partner 1982-. *Biog:* b. 29 March 1928. *Nationality:* British. *m.* 1954, Anne Patricia (née Auld); 1 s; 1 d. *Educ:* Denstone College. *Directorships:* Newey Group Pension Fund Ltd Chm (non-exec); Ingleby Holdings Ltd (non-exec); Ingleby Services (non-exec); Birmingham Chamber of Industry & Commerce (non-exec); Shooting Sports Trust (non-exec). *Other Activities:* President, West Midlands Conservative Council; Member of Council, Aston University; Member of Council, Denstone College; Conservative National Union Executive Committee; Vice Chairman, British Shooting Sports Council. *Professional Organisations:* Solicitor. *Clubs:* Carlton, Birmingham, Law Society's Yacht.

LAWRENCE, Linda J; Partner, Jaques & Lewis.

LAWRENCE, Michael John; Group Finance Director, Prudential Corporation plc.

LAWRENCE, N R; Director, Charlton Seal Schaverien Limited.

LAWRENCE, Sir Patrick; Senior Partner, Wragge & Co.

LAWRENCE, Philip Alastair; Partner, Beachcroft Stanleys, since 1988; Litigation. *Career:* Stanleys & Simpson, North, Articled Clerk 1980-82; Stanleys & Simpson, North, Assistant Solicitor 1982-88; Beachcroft Stanleys, Partner 1988-. *Biog:* b. 31 October 1955. *Nationality:* British. *Educ:* Bristol Cathedral School; Exeter University (LLB Hons). *Professional Organisations:* Solicitor; Law Society.

LAWRENCE, R L; Director, UBS Phillips & Drew Gilts Limited.

LAWRENCE, Timothy Gordon Roland; Partner, Coopers & Lybrand Deloitte, since 1967; Head of Litigation Support. *Career:* Wilson De Zouche & Mackenzie, Articled Clerk 1953-58; Army (Commissioned into Royal Irish Fusiliers) 1958-60; Coopers & Lybrand Deloitte (Formerly Cooper Brother & Co then Coopers & Lybrand) 1960-. *Biog:* b. 22 August 1936. *Nationality:* British. *m.* 1964, Ann (née Petherbridge); 1 s; 2 d. *Educ:* Wimbledon College; St George's College, Weybridge. *Other Activities:* Treasurer, St Francis' Leprosy Guild. *Professional Organisations:* Fellow, Institute of Chartered Accountants in England & Wales; Member, Institute of Experts. *Clubs:* MCC, Stoke Poges Golf Club. *Recreations:* Golf, Bridge.

LAWRENCE, (Walter Nicholas) Murray; Senior Partner, Murray Lawrence & Partners, since 1985. *Career:* C T Bowring & Co Various to Mgr, Treaty Dept 1957-62; Harvey Bowring & Others Asst Underwriter, Contract Dept 1962-68; Dep Underwriter 1968-70; Underwriter 1970-1984; Lloyd's of London Chairman 1988-90. *Biog:* b. 8 February 1935. *Nationality:* British. *m.* 1961, Sally; 2 d. *Educ:* Winchester College; Trinity College, Oxford (BA). *Directorships:* C T Bowring & Co Ltd 1976-84 (non-exec); Bowring Agencies Ltd -1984 (non-exec); Bowring Members Agency Ltd -1984 (non-exec); C T Bowring (Underwriting Agencies) 1983-84 Chm; Lloyd's 1982-83 & 84-87 Dep Chm; Murray Lawrence Members Agency Ltd 1988 Chm; Murray Lawrence Holdings Ltd 19 Chm. *Other Activities:* Ctee Member, Lloyd's Underwriters' Non-Marine Association, 1970 (Dep Chm, 1977 & Chm, 1978). *Professional Organisations:* Underwriting Member of Lloyd's 1973-. *Recreations:* Sport, particularly Golf, Music, Opera, Travelling.

LAWRIE, D A R; Chairman, R A McLean & Co Ltd, since 1987. *Career:* R A McLean & Co Ltd 1952-; Snr Ptnr 1978-87. *Biog:* b. 18 October 1922. *m.* 1951, Elizabeth Henderson (née Thom); 1 d. *Educ:* Kelvinside Academy. *Other Activities:* Glasgow & Scottish Stock Exchange (Past Ctee Member). *Professional Organisations:* The International Stock Exchange. *Clubs:* RSAC. *Recreations:* Golf, Horse Racing, Swimming.

LAWRIE, Thomas Macpherson; Partner, Maclay Murray & Spens, since 1965; Company and Commercial Law. *Career:* Dundas & Wilson, Apprentice 1956-59; Asst Solicitor 1959-60; Allen & Overy, Asst Solicitor 1960-64. *Biog:* b. 17 June 1934. *m.* 1963, Mary Elizabeth Jean (née Burnett); 2 d. *Educ:* Marlborough College; King's College, Cambridge (BA); Edinburgh University (LLB). *Directorships:* Midwynd International Investment

Trust plc 1984 (non-exec). *Professional Organisations:* Member, Company Law & Investor Protection Ctees, The Law Society of Scotland; IBA. *Clubs:* Western (Glasgow). *Recreations:* Gardening, Sailing, Skiing.

LAWS, Charles Richard Thurlou; Director, Allied Provincial Securities Ltd, since 1986; Private Client Investment Advisor. *Career:* Land Agent 1957-62; Stockbroker in Bristol 1962-. *Biog: b.* 12 April 1935. *m.* 1988, Patricia; 1 s; 2 d. *Educ:* Shrewsbury School. *Directorships:* Cheltenham & Gloucester Building Society 1984. *Other Activities:* Member, Local Committees. *Professional Organisations:* ARICS. *Clubs:* Burnham & Berrow GC, Houghton Club, Royal Overseas Bristol Commercial Rooms. *Recreations:* Golf, Fishing, Riding.

LAWS, Keith; Partner, Forsyte Kerman.

LAWSON, Alastair J; Director, Brown, Shipley & Co Limited.

LAWSON, The Rt Hon Nigel; MP; Director, Barclays Bank plc.

LAWSON, Peter Halford; Partner, McKenna & Co, since 1964; Tax. *Career:* Freshfields, Articled Clerk 1954-57; Asst Solicitor 1957-59; McKenna & Co, Asst Solicitor 1959-64. *Biog: b.* 7 January 1933. *Nationality:* British. *m.* 1966, Susan (née Ibbotson); 2 s; 2 d. *Educ:* Lancing College; Trinity College, Cambridge (MA). *Directorships:* City of Westminster Law Society 1984-85 Pres. *Other Activities:* Liveryman, Fishmongers Company; City of London Solicitors Company. *Professional Organisations:* International Tax Planning Association. *Clubs:* United Oxford & Cambridge University, City Livery. *Recreations:* Music, Theatre, Mountain Walking.

LAWSON, Philip Berthold; Chief Legal Adviser, Lloyds Bank plc, since 1990. *Career:* Linklater & Paines 1956-60; Lloyds Bank 1960. *Biog: b.* 15 December 1934. *Nationality:* British. *m.* 1966, Rosemary Hoult (decd); 2 s; 1 d. *Educ:* Lancing College; Trinity College, Cambridge (BA History/Law). *Other Activities:* City of London Solicitors Company. *Clubs:* RAC. *Recreations:* Tennis, Squash, Running, Golf.

LAWSON, Richard Henry; Chairman, Greenwell Montagu Stockbrokers, since 1987. *Career:* ICI, Trainee 1952-54; W Greenwell, Partner 1960; Partner Responsible for Private Clients 1960-73; Senior (Joint) Partner 1980-86; Stock Exchange, Deputy Chairman 1985-86; The Securities Association, Dep Chm 1987-. *Biog: b.* 16 February 1932. *Nationality:* British. *m.* 1958, Janet Elizabeth (née Govier); 3 s; 1 d (decd). *Educ:* Lancing College. *Directorships:* The Securities Association Deputy Chairman; Investors Compensation Fund. *Clubs:* Naval & Military.

LAWSON, Roger; Director, 3i plc. *Other Activities:* Member, Council of ICAEW. *Professional Organisations:* FCA.

LAX, Michael; Partner, Lawrence Graham.

LAYARD-LIESCHING, Ronald George; Executive Director, County NatWest Investment Management, since 1990; Director of Quantitative Research. *Career:* Chase Investment Bank, New York, Managing Director Swaps Department 1984-86; Chase Bank, New York, Vice President Treasury Department 1976-84; Hoare Govett Stockbrokers, Econometrician 1972-76. *Biog: b.* 11 March 1950. *Nationality:* British. *m.* 1977, Janet Rona (née Murphy); 3 d. *Educ:* Lancaster University (BA Hons).

LAZARUS, Richard; Director, J Henry Schroder Wagg & Co Limited, since 1990; Flotations and Corporate Disposals. *Career:* N M Rothschild & Sons Limited 1973-83; J Henry Schroder Wagg & Co Limited 1983-. *Biog: b.* 3 October 1951. *Nationality:* British. *m.* 1975, Deborah; 2 s. *Educ:* Westminster School; Kings College, Cambridge (Economics Degree). *Professional Organisations:* FCCA. *Clubs:* Cannons. *Recreations:* Opera, Ballet, Classical Music, Art Galleries, Fellwalking.

LE BLAN, Julia; Partner, Touche Ross & Co.

LE FEVRE, Simon Henry; Director, County NatWest Investment Management Ltd, since 1990; Business Development & International Fund Management. *Career:* Church Commissioners for England, Executive, UK Equities Research 1980-84; County NatWest Investment Management, Fund Manager, European Equities 1984-90. *Biog: b.* 17 October 1957. *Nationality:* British. *Educ:* St Paul's Cathedral Choir School, London; Sir Roger Manwood's School, Sandwich, Kent; Gonville & Caius College, Cambridge (BA Hons Modern Languages); City University Business School, London (MBA International Business & Finance). *Directorships:* CNIM 1990 (exec). *Other Activities:* Hon Secretary, The Templar Pilgrimage Trust (OTJ), regd charity. *Recreations:* Reading, Music, Travel, Swimming, Church & Charity Work.

LE NEVE FOSTER, N; Partner, Ernst & Young.

LE PARD, Geoffrey; Partner, Freshfields, since 1987; Real Property. *Biog: b.* 30 November 1956. *Nationality:* British. *m.* 1984, Linda Ellen (née Jones); 1 s. *Educ:* Purley Grammar School; Brockenhurst Grammar School and Sixth Form College; Bristol University (LLB Hons First Class). *Other Activities:* Law Society; Law Society Rugby Football Club; City of London Solicitors' Company. *Recreations:* Rugby, Cricket, Cycling, Walking, National Trust and RHS Gardens.

LEA, W H; General Manager, London and Manchester Group plc.

LEACH, Bobby; Director, City & Commercial Communications plc, since 1989; Financial Public Relations. *Biog: b.* 1957. *Nationality:* British. *Educ:* Charterhouse School; Exeter University (BA Hons). *Clubs:* Cavalry & Guards.

LEACH, Ms C; Council Member, FIMBRA.

LEACH, E J B; Group Personnel Executive, C T Bowring & Co Limited.

LEACH, Rodney; Group Chairman, Jardine Insurance Brokers Group.

LEADER, T J; Partner, Raphael Zorn Hemsley Ltd.

LEADER, Vincent W; Director, Kleinwort Benson Securities Limited.

LEADILL, S K; Treasurer, W H Smith Group plc.

LEAF, D; Director, County NatWest Securities Limited.

LEANEY, Michael; Human Resources Director, Morison Stoneham Chartered Accountants.

LEAROYD, A; Director, Corporate Finance, Panmure Gordon & Co Limited, since 1988. *Biog: b.* 23 April 1961. *Nationality:* British. *m.* 1987, Sarah (née Walker); 1 d. *Educ:* Uppingham; Downing College, Cambridge (MA). *Professional Organisations:* Member, Stock Exchange.

LEASOR, S N; Associate Director, Grandfield Rork Collins Financial Ltd.

LEATHERDALE, Peter James; Director, Capel-Cure Myers Capital Management, since 1986; Group Development for 9 Offices in South England. *Career:* Mullens & Co, Clerk 1967-69; Philip Taunton Godfrey & Dane, Asst to Ptnr 1969-72; Richardson Chubb & Co, Asst to Ptnr 1972-76; Ptnr 1976-86; National Investment Group, Director 1986-90; Capel-Cure Myers Capital Management, Director 1990-. *Biog: b.* 2 October 1947. *Nationality:* British; 3 s; 2 d. *Educ:* St Edmunds, Canterbury. *Directorships:* Rich Nominees 1984 (exec); RCLR Financial Services 1985 (exec). *Other Activities:* Chm, Dorchester Fishing Club. *Professional Organisations:* Member, International Stock Exchange. *Clubs:* Dorchester Fishing Club. *Recreations:* Dry-Fly Trout Fishing.

LEATHES, S W; Director, S G Warburg & Co Ltd.

LEAVER, Sir Christopher; GBE, JP; Chairman, Russell & McIver Ltd, since 1987; Wine Merchants. *Career:* Commissioned Army 1956-58; Express Dairy Co Ltd, Sales Manager 1959-64; Russell & McIver Ltd, MD - Chairman 1964-; Bath & Portlang Group plc, Non-Exec Dir 1982-84; Thermal Scientific plc, Non-Exec Dir 1986-88; London Tourist Board Ltd, Chairman 1983-89. *Biog: b.* 3 November 1937. *Nationality:* British. *m.* 1975, Helen; 1 s; 2 d. *Educ:* Eastbourne College. *Directorships:* Thames Water plc 1983 (non-exec) Dep Chairman. *Other Activities:* Past Master, Worshipful Company of Carmen; Honorary Liveryman, Worshipful Company of Farmers; Freeman, Company of Watermen & Lightermen; Chairman, Eastbourne College; Church Commissioner; Sheriff, City of London, 1979-80; Lord Mayor 1981-82; Alderman Dowgate Ward 1974; City Bench 1974; Order of Oman II; Retail Food Trade Wages Council, 1963-64; JP Inner London, 1970-83; Councillor, Royal Borough of Kensington and Chelsea, 1971-74; Court of Common Council, Dowgate Ward, 1973-74; Board of Brixton Prison, 1975-78; Master, Tower Ward Club, 1975-76; Governor, Christ's Hospital, 1975; Churchwarden, St Olave's Hart Street, 1975-89; Governor, City of London Girls' School, 1975-78; Court of City University (Chancellor 1981-82), 1978; Chairman, Young Musicians Symphony Orchestra Trust, 1979-81; Governor, Music Therapy Charity Ltd, 1981-89; HM Lieutenancy City of London, 1982; Trustee, Chichester Festival Theatre, 1982; Vice President, Bridgewell Royal Hospital (King Edward's School) 1982-89; Trustee, London Symphony Orchestra, 1982-90; Council of Missions to Seamen, 1983; Finance Committee, London Diocesan Fund, 1983-86; Vice President, National Playing Fields Association, 1983; Hon Colonel, 151 Transport Regiment RCT (V) 1983-88; Hon Freeman, The Worshipful Company of Environmental Cleaners; Honorary Colonel Commandant, Royal Corps of Transport, 1988. *Recreations:* Music, Gardening.

LEAVER, Colin Edward; Partner, Simmons & Simmons, since 1986; General Corporate Law, particularly Mergers and Acquisitions. *Career:* Simmons & Simmons, Articled Clerk 1980-82; Asst Solicitor 1982-86. *Biog: b.* 25 May 1958. *m.* 1986, Maria Victoria (née Simpkins); 1 s; 1 d. *Educ:* Haywards Heath Grammar School; Lincoln College, Oxford (MA). *Professional Organisations:* London Young Solicitors' Group (Member). *Recreations:* Hockey, Aviation, Philately.

LEBREDO, Jose; Managing Director, Havana International Bank Ltd, since 1990; Resident Director. *Career:* Banco Nacional De Cuba (Havana), Accountant, Domestic Division (Branches) 1958-68; Vice Director, International Division (Operational Units) 1968-73; Director, International Division (Banking Relations) 1973-75; Banco Nacional De Cuba (Zurich), Director, Representative 1975-82; Banco Nacional De Cuba (Havana), Director, International Division (Banking Relations) 1982-90. *Biog: b.* 10 June 1941. *Nationality:* Cuban. *m.* 1974, Pilar (née Gomez); 1 s; 1 d. *Educ:* Champagnat College, Havana; University of Havana (Accountant). *Recreations:* Reading, Music, Cinema.

LEBUS, Timothy Andrew; Director, Charterhouse Bank Limited, since 1989; Corporate Finance. *Career:* Barrister 1973-77; Fried, Frank, Harris, Shriver & Jacobson 1977-79; European Banking Company Limited 1979-83; Charterhouse Japhet Limited, Assistant Director 1983-86; Salomon Brothers International Limited, Vice President 1986-89; Charterhouse Bank Limited, Director 1989-. *Biog: b.* 17 April 1951. *Nationality:* British. *m.* 1974, Christina (née Fraser); 1 s. *Educ:* Eton College; Magdalene College, Cambridge (MA). *Professional Organisations:* Barrister-at-Law, England & Wales; Member, The Bar of New York State.

LECLÉZIO, M J J R; Director, Lonrho plc.

LEDAMUN, A A; Director, Lowndes Lambert Group Limited.

LEDEBOER, Nigel; Director, G T Management plc.

LEDERMAN, R A M; Director, Beeson Gregory Limited.

LEDINGHAM, Alexander; TD; Senior Partner, Edmonds & Ledingham, since 1981. *Career:* National Service, Royal Artillery, 2/Lt 1951-53; Edmonds & Ledingham Solicitors, Partner 1958-. *Biog: b.* 9 May 1931. *Nationality:* Scottish. *m.* 1963, Shelagh Rosemary (née Mackintosh); 1 s; 1 d. *Educ:* Loretto School; Aberdeen University (MA); Edinburgh University (LLB). *Directorships:* Clydesdale Bank plc 1985 (non-exec); Cala plc 1964 (non-exec). *Professional Organisations:* Law Society of Scotland; Scottish Law Agents Society. *Clubs:* Royal Aberdeen Golf Club, Royal Northern & University Club. *Recreations:* Golf, Walking, Reading.

LEDOCHOWSKI, J W; Executive Director, S G Warburg & Co Ltd, since 1990; Corporate Finance. *Biog: b.* 9 July 1953. *Nationality:* British. *m.* 1984, Joanna Maria (née Zakrzewska); 1 s; 1 d. *Educ:* Waterford School, Swaziland; Downing College, Cambridge (MA Economics). *Directorships:* S G Warburg & Co Ltd 1990 (exec). *Clubs:* Cruising Association. *Recreations:* Sailing, Swimming, Reading.

LEDSAM, Charles Edmund Royden; Company Secretary/Personnel Manager, Gibbs Hartley Cooper Ltd, since 1985; Company Secretarial/Personnel/Training. *Career:* Hartley Cooper & Co Ltd Asst Sec 1969-85. *Biog: b.* 7 April 1949. *Nationality:* British. *m.* 1973, Deborah (née Neil); 2 s; 1 d. *Educ:* Tonbridge School, Kent. *Professional Organisations:* ICSA, BIM, FCIS.

LEDWIDGE, Frank; Director, Ulster Development Capital Limited.

LEE, J D; Head of Systems & Communications, Lloyd's of London.

LEE, John Desmond (Des); Director, BCQ plc (Kingfisher Group), since 1990. *Career:* National Coal Board Computer Operations 1960-65; Centre-File Computer Services Mgr 1965-67; Rowntree Mackintosh Snr Mgr GMS 1967-80; Brooke Bond Mgmnt Services Controller 1980-86; Lloyds of London Group, Head Systems & Communications 1986-90. *Biog: b.* 18 January 1942. *Nationality:* British. *m.* 1964, Susan (née Bott); 1 s; 1 d. *Educ:* Belmont Abbey School, Hereford. *Other Activities:* IBM Computer Users' Assoc (Life Pres & Past Chm); The Bank of Kuwait IT Investment Board (Advisor); Company of Information Technologists (Member); Freedom of the City of London. *Professional Organisations:* FBCS, MIDPM; Numerous Publications on Technical & Management Issues. *Recreations:* Sport, Motor Racing, Music.

LEE, Michael David; Director, Cater Allen Ltd, since 1984; Gilts. *Career:* W Greenwell & Co Various 1970-80; Allen Harvey & Ross Asst to Dirs 1980-81; Cater Allen Ltd 1981-. *Biog: b.* 11 June 1951. *m.* 1973, Julie Elizabeth Anne (née Gillam); 3 d. *Directorships:* Cater Allen Securities Ltd 1986 (exec). *Clubs:* MCC.

LEE, Michael Patrick; Director, Dean Witter Capital Markets International Ltd.

LEE, Nicholas John; Finance Director, Jardine Insurance Brokers Ltd, since 1976; Lloyds Insurance Broking. *Career:* Arthur Goddard & Co, Articled Clerk/Audit Mgr 1959-68; Pickford Dawson & Holland Ltd (now Jardine Insurance Brokers Ltd), Chief Accountant 1968-72; Company Sec 1972-76. *Biog: b.* 14 August 1942. *Nationality:* British. *m.* 1966, Wendy Elizabeth (née White); 1 s; 1 d. *Educ:* Colchester Royal Grammar School. *Directorships:* Jardine Insurance Brokers Ltd 1978 (exec); Jardine Pensions Management Ltd 1983 (exec); Jardine Financial Consultants Ltd 1987 (exec). *Professional Organisations:* FCA. *Clubs:* Royal Overseas League. *Recreations:* Golf, Tennis, Skiing.

LEE, Simon; Manager, National Westminster Growth Options Ltd.

LEE, Yung-Woo; Regional Senior Vice President, Korea Exchange Bank.

LEECH, Peter John; General Manager, UK Retail Banking, Lloyds Bank plc.

LEECH, Stirling; Partner, Clyde & Co.

LEEMING, Charles Gerard James; Senior Partner, Wilde Sapte, since 1987. *Career:* Wilde Sapte, Ptnr 1963-87. *Biog:* b. 4 May 1936. *Educ:* Ampleforth College. *Other Activities:* City of London Solicitors' Company; Company of Watermen & Lightermen; Member of Lloyd's. *Professional Organisations:* The Law Society. *Clubs:* The Little Ship, Cruising Association. *Recreations:* Sailing, Music, Art, Books, Bee-Keeping, Collecting Electronic Gadgets.

LEES, Gordon Carrington; Director, Panmure Gordon & Co Ltd, since 1987; Equity Distribution, Insurance Research, Portfolio Advice. *Career:* Royal Insurance Group, Investment Official 1955-67; De Zoete & Bevan, Ptnr 1967-78; Panmure Gordon & Co, Ptnr 1978-87. *Biog:* b. 6 July 1934. *Nationality:* British. *m.* 1962, Jean Veronica (née Wiseman); 2 s. *Educ:* King George V School, Southport. *Directorships:* Rectory Nominees Ltd 1984 (exec). *Other Activities:* Liveryman, Worshipful Company of Carmen; Freeman, City of London; Member, Glyndebourne Festival/Operatic Society; Member, Conservative Party; Vice President, The Story of Christmas. *Professional Organisations:* FCII, ASIA; The International Stock Exchange. *Publications:* Various Insurance Research Articles. *Clubs:* Croham Hurst Golf Club, Surrey County Cricket Club, Lancashire County Cricket Club. *Recreations:* Cricket, Golf, Opera, Classical Music, Bridge, Travel, Reading, Racing.

LEESON, Ian Arthur; Partner, Ernst & Young, since 1970; Corporate Advisory & Finance. *Career:* Whinney Smith & Whinney, Articled Clerk 1960-64; Whinney Murray, Qualified Acct/Mgr 1964-68; Ernst & Ernst (Chicago), Mgr 1968-69; Whinney Murray/Ernst & Whinney/Ernst & Young, Ptnr 1970-. *Biog:* b. 13 March 1937. *m.* 1965, Margaret (née Tennent); 2 d. *Educ:* Rugby School; University College, Oxford (MA). *Professional Organisations:* FCA (Former Member of Technical Advisory Ctee, Technical & Research Ctee, Company Law Sub-Ctee). *Clubs:* Woking Golf Club, St Georges Hill Lawn Tennis Club. *Recreations:* Golf, Tennis.

LEGG, Andrew Richard; Partner, Linklaters & Paines, since 1990; Litigation. *Career:* Booth & Co, Articled Clerk 1980-82; Linklaters & Paines, Assistant Solicitor 1982-90. *Biog:* b. 30 June 1957. *Nationality:* British. *m.* 1984, Beatrix (née Ives); 2 d. *Educ:* Magnus Grammar School, Newark-upon-Trent; Leeds University (LLB); College of Law, Chester (Part II). *Professional Organisations:* Law Society. *Recreations:* Music, Theatre.

LEGG, D N; Director, Girobank plc.

LEGGE, C D; Director, Brewin Dolphin & Co Ltd.

LEGGE, M H; Director, Charterhouse Bank Limited.

LEGGE, Nigel Richard; Sales Director, James Capel & Co (Unit Trust Management), since 1988; Head of Unit Trust Sales. *Career:* Willis Faber & Dumas Aviation Broker 1976-81; Henderson Administration Ltd Unit Trust Dir; Dir of Offshore Mktg 1983-88. *Biog:* b. 29 October 1957. *Nationality:* English. *m.* 1988, Claudia Mary Louise (née Kearon). *Educ:* Charterhouse School, Godalming; Westminster College. *Directorships:* Henderson Administration International Ltd 1987 (exec); Henderson OffProperty Fund 1987 (exec); Henderson Admin Guernsey 1987 (exec); Henderson International Luxembourg 1987 (exec); Henderson Investment Services 1988 (exec); James Capel Unit Trust Mgmnt Ltd 1988 (exec). *Clubs:* Quintessence Club. *Recreations:* Art, Sailing, Flying, Golf, Chess.

LEGGE-BOURKE, William Nigel Henry; Director, Kleinwort Benson Securities Ltd, since 1986; Compliance; Member of Council of the International Stock Exchange since 1988. *Career:* Grieveson Grant & Co, Ptnr 1973-86. *Biog:* b. 12 July 1939. *Nationality:* British. *m.* 1964, The Hon Shân (née Bailey, LVO); 1 s; 2 d. *Educ:* Eton College; Magdalene College, Cambridge (MA). *Other Activities:* The Scout Association (Chm of Finance Ctee); Member of Representative Body of the Church in Wales. *Professional Organisations:* The International Stock Exchange. *Clubs:* White's. *Recreations:* Country Sports.

LEGGET, Robert W L; Executive Director, Quayle Munro Ltd. *Biog:* b. 13 July 1950. *Nationality:* British. *m.* 1985, Shelagh, (née Robson); 2 s.

LEGGETT, Jeremy James Robin; Joint Managing Director, LPH Group plc, since 1987. *Career:* Oakeley Vaughan Ltd, Broker 1972-79; Anthony Gibbs Sage Ltd, Broker 1979-80; Oakeley Vaughan Ltd, Asst Dir 1980-81; Leggett Porter Howard Ltd, Dir 1981-85; H Pitman Ltd, Dir 1985-87; L P H Pitman Ltd, Joint MD 1987-90. *Biog:* b. 16 April 1954. *Nationality:* British. *m.* 1979, Sarah Diana (née Hammond); 1 s; 3 d. *Educ:* St Johns School. *Directorships:* Finance Risk Managers 1986 (exec); MBIC 1990 (exec); L P H Pitman 1985 (exec). *Other Activities:* Member of Lloyd's. *Recreations:* Shooting, Golf, Skiing.

LEGON, James Albert; Director, Bank of Cyprus (London) Ltd, since 1983; Chairman, Audit & Remuneration Committee. *Career:* Westminster Bank, P A to General Manager 1957-62; Manager, Various Branches 1962-69; Area Advances Manager, West End 1969-72; Deputy Manager, Lombard Street Office 1972-74; Chief Manager, Lombard Street Office 1974-80; Deputy Regional Director, City 1980-82; AIM Group plc, Deputy Chairman 1982-85; Chairman 1985-87; Henshalls Ltd, Deputy Chairman 1982-85; Chairman 1985-87; Jecco Aviation Ltd; Flightform Ltd; AIM Aviation Ltd Deputy Chairman/Chairman 1982-87. *Biog:* b. 25 August 1922. *Nationality:* British. *m.* 1944, Carol (née Franklin); 1 s;

413

3 d. *Educ:* Haberdashers' Aske's School. *Directorships:* Bank of Cyprus (London) Ltd 1983 (non-exec); Total Finance Holdings Ltd 1988 (non-exec). *Clubs:* MCC. *Recreations:* Painting, Gardening, Cricket.

LEGRAIN, Gerard Marie Francois; Managing Director, International Mexican Banks, since 1974. *Career:* Citibank NA; VP 1966-74. *Biog: b.* 1937. *Nationality:* French. *m.* 1969, Katrin (née Tombach); 2 s; 1 d. *Educ:* Ecole St Louis de Gonzaque, Paris; Ecole Nationale d'Administration, Paris. *Clubs:* Hurlingham. *Recreations:* Skiing.

LEGROS, F; Adviser, Société Générale Merchant Bank plc.

LEIFER, Norman Anthony; Partner, D J Freeman & Co, since 1974; Corporate Finance & Entertainments Law. *Career:* D J Freeman & Co, Articled Clerk and Associate Solicitor 1970-74. *Biog: b.* 17 September 1945. *Nationality:* British. *m.* 1979, Susan E A (née Spieler); 2 s. *Educ:* Hackney Downs Grammar School; London School of Economics (LLB); University of California, Berkeley (LLM). *Professional Organisations:* The Law Society; The City of London Law Society. *Publications:* The Profits of Crime and their Recovery, 1984 (Joint Author of the Report of a Ctee Chaired by Sir Derek Hodgson). *Recreations:* Tennis, Cooking.

LEIGH, Guy I F; Partner, Theodore Goddard, since 1978; Head of Competition Group, Head of German Business Group. *Career:* Clifford Turner & Co, Articles 1972-74; Theodore Goddard 1974-. *Biog: b.* 22 November 1944. *Nationality:* British. *m.* 1968, Mary M; 1 s; 1 d. *Educ:* The German School in Rome; Westminster School, Simsbury, Connecticut; UCLA, California; University of Pennsylvania (BA); Law School, University of Pennsylvania (JD); Trinity Hall, Cambridge (Diploma in International Law). *Other Activities:* Member, the Law Society; Member, Bar Joint Working Party on Competition Law; Committee Member, London Chamber of Commerce West European Committee; Deputy General Reporter, International League of Competition Law (LIDC); Member, City of London Solicitors Company. *Publications:* Co-Author, The EEC and Intellectual Property (with Diana Guy), 1981; Various Articles on Anti-Trust Law and other Legal Subjects; Frequent Speaker at Conferences on UK and EC Anti-Trust Law. *Recreations:* Travel, Languages (German, Italian, Spanish and French), Photography, Swimming, Theatre.

LEIGH-PEMBERTON, J H; Director, S G Warburg Akroyd Rowe & Pitman Mullens Securities Ltd.

LEIGH-PEMBERTON, The Rt Hon Robert (Robin); Governor, Bank of England, since 1983; Central Bank. *Career:* Grenadier Guards 1945-48; Called to the Bar, Inner Temple (Hon Bencher 1983) 1954; Practised as Lawyer, London and South East Circuit

1954-60; Birmid Qualcast, Director 1966-83; Deputy Chairman 1970; Chairman 1975-77; University Life Assurance Society, Director 1967-78; Redland Ltd, Director 1972-83; Equitable Life Assurance Society, Director 1979-83; Vice-President 1982-83; National Westminster Bank, Director 1972-83; Deputy Chairman 1974; Chairman 1977-83; Committee of London Clearing Bankers, Chairman 1982-83. *Biog: b.* 5 January 1927. *Nationality:* British. *m.* 1953, Rosemary Davina (née Forbes); 5 s. *Educ:* Eton; Trinity College, Oxford (MA). *Directorships:* Bank of England 1983 Governor (exec). *Other Activities:* County Councillor, Kent County Council, 1961-77 (Chairman 1972-75); Member, National Economic Development Council, 1982-; Liveryman, Mercers Company; Lord Lieutenant of Kent, 1982- (Vice Lord-Lieutenant 1972-82); Honorary Colonel, Kent & Sharpshooters Yeomanry Squadron, 265 (KCLY) Signal Squadron, 5th (Volunteer) Battalion, The Queen's Regiment. *Professional Organisations:* Fellow, Royal Society of Arts; JP, 1961-75. *Clubs:* Brooks's, Cavalry & Guards. *Recreations:* Country Life.

LEIGHTON, Robert Smith; Vice Chairman, Credit Lyonnais Rouse Limited, since 1982; International Operations. *Career:* Gibbs Nathaniel Limited, Joint Managing Director to 1982. *Biog: b.* 1 September 1941. *Nationality:* British. *m.* 1968, Caroline Jane (née McDonnell); 2 s; 1 d. *Educ:* Kilmarnock Academy; Glasgow University. *Directorships:* Credit Lyonnais Capital Markets plc 1990 (exec); Various Credit Lyonnais Group Companies Throughout World 1987- (exec); System Trend Limited, Bermuda 1984 (non-exec); System Trend Guaranteed Limited, Bermuda 1987 (non-exec); Statrend Limited 1984 (non-exec). *Other Activities:* British Invisibles, Overseas Promotion Ctee. *Professional Organisations:* Institute of Chartered Accountants of Scotland. *Clubs:* Little Ship. *Recreations:* Sailing, Classical Music.

LEIMAN, Russell Michael; Chief Executive, Credit Lyonnais Securities and Laing & Cruickshank Institutional Equities Division, since 1989; International & UK Equities to Instititial Customer Base. *Career:* Chief Exec, Citicorp Scrimgeour Vickers International, London 1988-89; President, Vickers Da Costa Secs Inc (New York) 1985-88; Associate General Manager, Vickers Da Costa (Tokyo Branch) 1977-85; Arbitrage Trader, Vickers Da Costa (Hong Kong) 1974-77; Arbitrage Trader, Vickers Da Costa, (London) 1971-74; Stockbroker, I Jacobs, Johannesburg Stock Exchange 1968-71. *Biog: b.* 26 October 1947. *Nationality:* British. *m.* 1973, Ashley Elizabeth (née Beer); 2 d. *Directorships:* Credit Lyonnais Capital Markets 1989 (exec); Credit Lyonnais Securities 1989 (exec); Laing & Cruickshank 1989 (exec); Credit Lyonnais Secs Asia 1990 (exec).

LEITCH, A P; Joint Managing Director, Allied Dunbar Assurance plc.

LEITH, David Gordon; Vice President and Director, Wood Gundy Inc.

LEITNER, Dr Franz G; General Manager, DG Bank Deutsche Genossenschaftbank, since 1989. *Career:* DG Bank, Frankfurt, Head of Loan Syndications 1978-81; DG Bank, New York, NY, SVP and General Manager 1981-87; DG Investment Bank Ltd, Managing Director 1987-89. *Biog: b.* 18 February 1948. *Nationality:* Austrian. *m.* 1977, Marita (née Kraft); 1 s; 1 d. *Educ:* Theresianische Accademie, Vienna; University of Vienna (Doctor of Law); INSEAD, Fontainebleau (MBA); NASD (Series 7/Principal). *Directorships:* DG Investment Bank Ltd 1989 (non-exec); LCB Consultants 1987 (non-exec); Product Finance Limited 1989 (non-exec). *Recreations:* Tennis, Golf, Skiing.

LEITNER, J; Managing Director, Bankers Trust Company.

LELLIOTT, K D; Partner, Pensions (Epsom), Bacon & Woodrow.

LEMAY, M J; Director, Barclays de Zoete Wedd Limited, since 1990; Corporate Finance. *Career:* Morgan Grenfell & Co Limited 1983-86; Morgan Grenfell Inc 1986-87; Driscel Burnham Lambert Securities Limited 1987-90. *Biog: b.* 24 January 1958. *Nationality:* British. *m.* 1983, Sarah Le May (née McCormack); 1 s. *Educ:* St Olaves & St Saviours Grammar School for Boys; University College of North Wales (BA Hons). *Professional Organisations:* CA. *Recreations:* Shooting.

LEMKIN, J A; CBE; Partner, Field Fisher Waterhouse.

LEMMER, Juergen; General Manager, Commerzbank AG, London Branch; Treasury, Investment Banking,Corporate Banking. *Career:* Commerzbank AG (Frankfurt) Dep Head, Central Treasury Dept before 1983; Commerzbank International SA (Luxembourg) MD 1983-88. *Biog: b.* 13 September 1941. *Nationality:* German. *m.* 1967, Elke (née Mueller); 1 s; 1 d. *Educ:* Universities of Bonn and Mainz (MEcon). *Recreations:* Sports, Hiking, Music.

LENNARD, G L; Chairman, Gerald Limited.

LEON, Anthony; Director, BDO Consulting.

LEONARD, Carol; , City Diary, The Times.

LEONARD, P M; Partner, Freshfields.

LEONARD, Peter Alan; Director, Schroder Investment Management Ltd, since 1985; Investment Management. *Biog: b.* 2 August 1938. *m.* 1962, Jill (née Stedman); 1 s; 1 d. *Educ:* Rutlish School, Wimbledon. *Professional Organisations:* AMSIA. *Recreations:* Golf, Squash, Walking.

LEONARD, Simon; Partner, Titmuss Sainer & Webb.

LERRY, Christine; Partner, Theodore Goddard.

LERWILL, Robert E; Group Finance Director, WPP Group plc, since 1986. *Career:* Arthur Andersen & Co 1973-86. *Biog: b.* 21 January 1952. *Nationality:* British. *m.* 1980, Carol (née Ruddock); 1 s. *Educ:* Gosport Grammar School; Nottingham University (BA). *Directorships:* WPP Group plc and subsidiary Companies 1986 (exec). *Professional Organisations:* FCA.

LESLIE, Captain Alastair Pinkard; TD; Director, A P Leslie Underwriting Agency Ltd and Other Lloyds Underwriting Agencies. *Career:* Royal Scots Fusiliers (TA), Capt; Willis Faber & Dumas (Agencies) Ltd 1976-85; Utd Goldfields NL, Dir 1988. *Biog: b.* 29 December 1934. *Nationality:* British. *m.* 1963, Rosemary (née Barry); 1 s (decd); 2 d. *Educ:* Eton. *Other Activities:* Member, Queen's Body Guard for Scotland, The Royal Co of Archers; Liveryman, Worshipful Co of Clothworkers. *Clubs:* Boodle's, Pratt's. *Recreations:* Fishing, Stalking, Shooting.

LESLIE, N R; Executive Director, Allied Dunbar Assurance plc, since 1985; Management Services - Life, Unit Trusts, International. *Biog: b.* 21 August 1944. *Nationality:* British. *m.* 1971, Jean; 1 s; 1 d. *Educ:* University of Newcastle (BSc). *Professional Organisations:* Member, British Computer Society; Chartered Engineer.

LESLIE, Peter Evelyn; Deputy Chairman, Barclays Bank plc, since 1987. *Career:* Barclays Bank Limited, Gen Mgr 1973-76; Dir & Snr Gen Mgr (Intl) 1980-84; Barclays Bank plc, Chief Gen Mgr/MD 1985-88. *Biog: b.* 24 March 1931. *Nationality:* British. *m.* 1975, Charlotte (née Chapman-Andrews). *Educ:* Stowe School; New College, Oxford (MA). *Other Activities:* Chm, Export Guarantees Advisory Council; Council for Industry & Higher Education; Governor, Stowe School; Chm, Overseas Development Institute 1988-; Chm, Queen's College Council 1989-; Chairman, Commonwealth Development Corporation. *Professional Organisations:* FCIB, CBIM, MInstM. *Recreations:* Natural History, Genealogy.

LESLIE MELVILLE, I H; Chairman, Capel-Cure Myers Capital Management Ltd.

LESSELS, Norman; Partner, Chiene & Tait CA, since 1980; Non-Executive Directorships and Corporate Advice. *Career:* Graham Smart & Annan, Edinburgh, Apprenticeship; Thomson McLintock & Co Qualified Asst 1960-61; Wallace & Somerville CA, Whinney Murray & Co/Ernst & Whinney, Ptnr 1962-80. *Biog: b.* 2 September 1938. *Nationality:* British. *m.* 1981, Christine Stevenson (née Hitchman); 1 s. *Educ:* Melville College, Edinburgh Academy. *Directorships:* The Standard Life Assurance Company 1978 (Chm 1988) (non-exec); The Scottish Eastern Investment Trust plc 1980 (non-exec); Scottish Homes 1988 (non-exec); General Surety & Guarantee Co Ltd 1988 (non-exec); Bank of Scotland 1988 (non-exec); NWS Bank plc 1989 (non-exec); Cairn Energy plc 1988 (non-exec)Deputy Chm; Havelock Europa plc 1989 (non-exec); Securities & Investments Board Ltd 1989 (non-exec). *Other Activities:* Member, Companies House Steering Board, 1988. *Professional Organisations:* CA; Pres, Institute of Chartered Accountants of Scotland 1987-88; ATII. *Clubs:* New (Edinburgh), Honourable Company of Edinburgh Golfers, Royal & Ancient, Bruntsfield Links Golfing Society (Edinburgh). *Recreations:* Golf, Music, Bridge.

LESTER, Michael; Director, The General Electric Company plc, since 1983; Legal Affairs. *Career:* Teaching Fellow, University of Chicago Law School 1962-64; Articled Clerk & Solicitor in Private Practice 1964-80; Director of Legal Affairs & Associate Director, The General Electric Company plc 1980-83; Director The General Electric Company plc 1983-. *Biog: b.* 10 March 1940. *Nationality:* British. *m.* 1967, Pamela Frances (née Gillis); 1 s; 1 d. *Educ:* Coopers' Company's School; New College, Oxford (MA Hons). *Directorships:* The General Electric Company plc 1983 (exec). *Professional Organisations:* The Law Society.

LESTER, Nigel Martin; Chief Executive, County NatWest Investment Management, since 1990. *Career:* Legal and General, latterly Head of International Equity Management 1974-81; Schroders Asia (HK), Assistant Director 1981-84; Aetna Investment Management (Asia Pacific) (Hong Kong), Managing Director 1984-89; Aetna International (USA), Chief Investment Officer 1989-90; Senior Vice President 1989-90. *Biog: b.* 26 March 1953. *Nationality:* British. *m.* 1982, Rosemarie Ann (née Skoll); 1 s; 1 d. *Educ:* Banbury School; Sussex University (BSc Mathematics). *Directorships:* County NatWest Investment Management 1990 (exec). *Professional Organisations:* Fellow, Institute of Actuaries. *Clubs:* MCC. *Recreations:* Real Tennis, Golf, Squash.

LETHBRIDGE, M G; Director, Kleinwort Benson Limited.

LETHEREN, Mark; Director, LPH Group plc.

LETLEY, Peter Anthony; Finance Director, James Capel & Co, since 1988. *Career:* Hong Kong Bank Group 1974; Wardley Ltd, Head of Lending 1974-78; Director, Overseas Operations 1978-82; Wardley Australia Ltd, Joint Chief Executive 1982-83; Hong Kong International Trade Finance Ltd, Chief Executive 1983-86; James Capel Bankers, Finance Director 1986-87; Managing Director 1987-88. *Biog: b.* 11 November 1945. *Nationality:* British. *m.* 1970, Alice Emma Campbell (née Finlay); 1 s. *Educ:* Woodbridge School, Suffolk; St John's College, Oxford (BA Modern Histo-

ry). *Clubs:* Hong Kong Jockey Club. *Recreations:* Opera, Theatre.

LEUKERS, Hans; Managing Director, WestLB UK Ltd, Westdeutsche Landesbank Girozentrale.

LEUNG, Philip; Head of International & UK Equity Trading, Paribas Ltd, since 1987. *Career:* Morgan Stanley International (London) 1985-87; First Boston Corp (New York) 1983-85. *Biog: b.* 13 July 1958. *Nationality:* American. *Educ:* Columbia University (MBA); University of San Francisco (BS).

LEUTHOLD, Rudolph; Managing Director, J P Morgan Investment Management Inc, since 1985; Global Equity Management, Head of Equity & Balanced Strategy Group. *Career:* Morgan Guaranty Trust (New York), Research Officer 1975-77; (London) aVP 1977-79; VP 1979-. *Biog: b.* 10 May 1949. *Nationality:* Swiss. *Educ:* Gymnasium Zurich; Geneva University (MA); McGill University, Montreal (MBA). *Professional Organisations:* Society of Investment Analysts. *Clubs:* RAC. *Recreations:* Film, Theatre, Music, Skiing.

LEUZZI, L N; Director, S G Warburg Akroyd Rowe & Pitman Mullens Securities Ltd.

LEVACK, I; Vice President, First National Bank of Boston.

LEVER, Colin David; Senior Partner, Bacon & Woodrow, since 1982; Investment Consultancy. *Career:* Bacon & Woodrow, Actuarial Trainee 1960-66; Ptnr 1966-82. *Biog: b.* 4 September 1938. *Nationality:* British. *m.* 1962, Ruth (née Bornstein); 1 s; 3 d. *Educ:* Hendon County School; Balliol College, Oxford (MA). *Other Activities:* NAPF (Chm 1985-87, VP 1987-89). *Professional Organisations:* FIA. *Publications:* Pension Fund Investment (with D P Hager), 1989. *Recreations:* Gardening, Narrowboating.

LEVER, Jeremy Frederick; QC; , Queen's Counsel, since 1972; European Community and other Economic Law. *Career:* Dunlop Holdings Limited, Non-Executive Director 1973-80. *Biog: b.* 23 June 1933. *Nationality:* British. *Educ:* Bradfield College, Berks; University College, Oxford (1st Class Hons Jurisprudence); Nuffield College, Oxford; All Souls College, Oxford (Fellow). *Directorships:* The Wellcome Foundation Ltd; Wellcome plc 1983 (non-exec). *Other Activities:* Senior Dean, All Souls College, Oxford; Bencher, Gray's Inn; Member of the Council of the British Institute of International and Comparative Law. *Professional Organisations:* Barrister-at-Law. *Publications:* The Law of Restrictive Trading Agreements, 1964; One of the Editors of Chitty on Contracts, 21st-25th eds, 1955-83; Numerous Legal Essays, Articles, etc. *Clubs:* Garrick. *Recreations:* Music.

LEVER, Lawrence; Financial Editor, The Mail On Sunday.

LEVETT, M J; Chairman, Providence Capitol Life Assurance Ltd.

LEVETT, Tim; Investment Director, Northern Venture Managers Limited.

LEVINE, Marshall Francis; Partner, Linklaters & Paines, since 1989; Construction & Engineering Law and Head of Construction and Engineering Law Unit. *Career:* Royds Barfield 1980-82; Linklaters & Paines, Assistant Solicitor 1982-89. *Biog: b.* 20 November 1957. *Nationality:* British. *m.* 1989, Susan Claire (née Silver). *Educ:* University College School, Hampstead; University College, London (LLB); Reading University (BSc). *Other Activities:* City of London Solicitors Company. *Professional Organisations:* Associate, Chartered Institute of Arbitrators. *Recreations:* Rugby Fives, Fishing, Sailing.

LEVINSON, Steve; Economics Correspondent, BBC TV.

LEVITT, Professor Theodore; Non-Executive Director, Saatchi & Saatchi Company plc.

LEVY, Graeme David; Partner, S J Berwin & Co, since 1990; Corporate Finance. *Career:* Herbert Oppenheimer, Nathan & Vandyk 1982-88;, Articled Clerk 1982-84; Assistant Solicitor 1985-88; Associate 1988; Richards Butler, Assistant Solicitor 1988-89; S J Berwin & Co, Assistant Solicitor then Partner 1989-. *Biog: b.* 15 April 1959. *Nationality:* British. *Educ:* St Dunstans College; Trinity Hall, Cambridge (BA, MA). *Recreations:* Cinema, Music, Tennis.

LEVY, K G S; Director, Capel-Cure Myers Capital Management Ltd.

LEVY, L; Director, Mercury Asset Management Group plc.

LEVY, Victor Raphael; Tax Partner, Arthur Andersen & Co, since 1985; European Co-ordinator of Tax Services on Issues Relating to Capital Markets & Financial Products. *Career:* Arthur Andersen & Co 1976-. *Biog: b.* 14 April 1951. *Educ:* University College School, Hampstead; UMIST (BSc Hons). *Professional Organisations:* FCA; FTII.

LEW, Chung; Director, Kleinwort Benson Securities Limited.

LEW, Dr Julian David Mathew; Partner, S J Berwin & Co, since 1986; International Law - Commercial Contracts/International Commercial Arbitration & Head of School of International Arbitration, Centre for Commercial Law Studies, Queen Mary & Westfield College, University of London, since 1985. *Career:* City of London Polytechnic, Research Fellow 1973-76; Barrister-at-Law, England 1973-74; University of Namur, Belgium, Associate Professor of Law 1976-79; Dilley & Custer, Brussels, Associate Lawyer 1977-79; Briger & Associates, New York Attorneys, UK Counsel 1979-86; SJ Berwin & Co, Solicitors, London, Partner 1986-. *Biog: b.* 3 February 1948. *Nationality:* British. *m.* 1978, Margot Gillian (née Perk); 2 d. *Educ:* Carmel College; University of London (LLB Hons); Council of Legal Education Barrister, 1970 (Resigned 1981); Catholic University of Louvain (Doctorate in Intl Law). *Directorships:* London Court of International Arbitration 1985 (non-exec); Interlaw 1987 (non-exec). *Other Activities:* Member, Company of Arbitrators; Chairman, Joint Committee of Management of London Chamber of Commerce & Industry; Vice-Chairman, British Committee on Intl Commercial Arbitration of the Intl Law Association; Corresponding Member, Institute of Intl Business Law and Practice of the Intl Chamber of Commerce; American Arbitration Association; Australian Centre of Intl Commercial Arbitration (Melbourne); British Columbia Intl Commercial Arbitration Centre (Vancouver); Cairo Regional Centre for Intl Commercial Arbitration; Chartered Institute of Arbitrators. *Professional Organisations:* Solicitor (England); Attorney-at-Law (New York); Fellow, Chartered Institute of Arbitrators; Member, British Institute of Intl and Comparative Law; Member, American Society of Intl Law; Member, International Bar Association; Member, American Bar Association. *Publications:* Selected Bibliography on East-West Trade (Jt Ed), 1976; Applicable Law in International Commercial Arbitration, 1978; Selected Bibliography on International Commercial Arbitration (Jt Ed), 1979; International Trade: Law & Practice (Jt Ed), 1984; Contemporary Problems in International Commercial Arbitration (Ed), 1986; International Trade: Law & Practice 2nd Edition (Jt Ed), 1990; Immunity of Arbitrators (Ed), 1990.

LEWIS, Aneurin George; General Manager, Volkskas Bank Ltd, since 1984; Commercial Banking. *Career:* Nedbank Ltd, Mgr 1958-84. *Biog: b.* 15 September 1932. *m.* 1955, Daphne Nina (née Cutter); 3 s. *Educ:* Mitcham County Grammar. *Directorships:* Boohat Ltd 1984 (exec); Coptic Ltd 1984 (exec); Volkskas International Ltd 1984 (exec). *Other Activities:* Die Oulap Club (Secretary). *Professional Organisations:* ACIB.

LEWIS, Anthony; Partner, Venture Capital Funding, Cameron Markby Hewitt.

LEWIS, Anthony; Senior Partner, Taylor Joynson Garrett.

LEWIS, B I; Partner, Penningtons, since 1988; Insurance Litigation, International Litigation. *Career:* R I Lewis & Co Solicitors, Partner 1965-73; Barry Lewis Solicitors, Sole Principal (London and Guildford) 1973-

88. *Biog: b.* 14 August 1940. *Nationality:* British. *m.* 1972, Gill Elizabeth; 2 s; 2 d. *Educ:* Rugby School; Trinity Hall, Cambridge (MA, LLM). *Directorships:* Gilbar Investments Ltd 1973 (exec). *Other Activities:* Penningtons, European Committee. *Professional Organisations:* Law Society. *Clubs:* Hankley Common Golf Club. *Recreations:* Golf, Photography, Languages, Skiing, Tennis, Gardening.

LEWIS, C J; Vice-Chairman Head of Debt, UBS Phillips & Drew Securities Limited.

LEWIS, Clive Robert; Managing Director, Consolidated Credits Bank Ltd, since 1985; Property Finance and Investment. *Career:* Siwel International Shipping Ltd, Panocean Anco Ltd, Director 1979-83; Consolidated Credits Bank Ltd 1983-. *Biog: b.* 4 December 1956. *Nationality:* British. *m.* 1983, Sarah Louise (née Banham); 1 s; 1 d. *Educ:* Millfield School; Warwick University (LLB Hons); Inns of Court School of Law. *Directorships:* Shop and Warehouse Mutual Insurance Association Ltd; London & Overseas Property Investment Corporation Ltd. *Other Activities:* Trustee, Noonan Syndrome Foundation; Trustee, Birth Defects Foundation. *Professional Organisations:* Barrister, Middle Temple.

LEWIS, D E; Corporate Tax Partner, Allen & Overy, since 1982; Corporate Tax. *Biog: b.* 26 March 1952. *Nationality:* British. *m.* 1975, Susan (née Eccleston); 2 s; 1 d. *Educ:* Exeter University (LLB); College of Law (2nd class Honours). *Professional Organisations:* Law Society. *Clubs:* RAC. *Recreations:* Squash, Tennis, Skiing.

LEWIS, David Gwynder; Director, Hambros Bank Ltd, since 1979. *Career:* Hambros Bank Ltd 1961-; Hambros Bank (Tokyo), Rep 1972-74; Hambro Pacific (Hong Kong), MD 1975-82; Hambro America (New York), Pres 1982-85. *Biog: b.* 31 August 1942. *m.* 1966, Susan J (née Agnew); 1 s; 1 d. *Educ:* Rugby School; West London College of Commerce. *Directorships:* Hambro Countywide 1986; Other Hambro Group Companies. *Professional Organisations:* ACIB. *Clubs:* Turf, RAC. *Recreations:* Fishing, Shooting, Opera.

LEWIS, Derek C; Chief Executive Officer, Granada Group plc, since 1990. *Career:* Granada Group plc, MD 1987-; Granada Group plc, Financial Director 1984-87; Imperial Group plc, Various 1982-84; Ford Motor Company, Various 1969-82. *Biog: b.* 9 July 1946. *Nationality:* British. *m.* 1969, Louise (née Wharton); 2 d. *Educ:* Wrekin College; Queens' College, Cambridge (MA); London Business School (MSc). *Directorships:* Courtaulds Textiles 1990 (non-exec); Granada Group plc 1984 (exec).

LEWIS, Derek Trevor; Joint Senior Partner, Hammond Suddards, since 1984. *Career:* A V Hammond & Co (now Hammond Suddards), Partner 1964-. *Biog: b.* 21 October 1936. *Nationality:* British. *m.* 1961, Pamela Lewis (née Ratcliffe); 1 s; 1 d. *Educ:* Bradford Grammar School; Leeds University (LLB). *Directorships:* Herbert Roberts Ltd 1981 (non-exec); West Yorkshire Independent Hospital plc 1979-88 (non-exec) Chm; Bradford & Bingley Building Society 1990 (non-exec). *Professional Organisations:* Member, The Law Society.

LEWIS, Derek William; Partner, Theodore Goddard, since 1977; Executive Partner, Corporate Department. *Career:* Pinsent & Co, Asst Solicitor 1968-69; Evershed & Tompkinson, Asst Solicitor 1969-70; Theodore Goddard Solicitor, Partner 1970-. *Biog: b.* 23 October 1944. *Nationality:* British. *m.* 1972, Bridget Jennifer (née Stoney); 2 s; 1 d. *Educ:* Dean Close School, Cheltenham. *Professional Organisations:* Law Society; Society of Conservative Lawyers; IBA. *Clubs:* Royal Wimbledon Golf Club, Roehampton. *Recreations:* Golf, Tennis, Horse Racing.

LEWIS, G A; Director, Smith New Court PLC.

LEWIS, H; Partner, Jaques & Lewis.

LEWIS, J; Managing Director, Seymour Pierce Butterfield Ltd.

LEWIS, Jonathan Malcolm; Partner; Company/ Commercial Department, D J Freeman & Co, since 1973; Corporate Finance, Company/Commercial, Insolvency. *Career:* D J Freeman & Co Asst 1969-73. *Biog: b.* 27 March 1946. *Nationality:* British. *m.* 1971, Rosemary Anne (née Mays); 2 s. *Educ:* Harrow County School for Boys; Downing College, Cambridge (MA). *Other Activities:* City of London Solicitors' Company. *Professional Organisations:* The Law Society; International Bar Association; Authorised Insolvency Practitioner under the Insolvency Act 1986. *Publications:* City Comment in Law Society's Gazette, since 1983. *Recreations:* Walking, Theatre, Family.

LEWIS, Julian Anthony; Partner, Titmuss Sainer & Webb, since 1990; Mergers and Acquisitions and Corporate Finance. *Career:* Titmuss Sainer & Webb, Articled Clerk 1984-86; Assistant Solicitor (Corporate Department) 1986-90. *Biog: b.* 13 February 1961. *Nationality:* British. *m.* 1983, Judy (née Rich); 1 s; 1 d. *Educ:* King Edward's School, Birmingham; St Johns College, Cambridge (MA). *Professional Organisations:* The Law Society.

LEWIS, Michael; Partner, Forsyte Kerman.

LEWIS, Nigel Wickham; Director, 3i plc, since 1984; Independent Directors Programme. *Career:* Vickers Armstrongs (Aircraft) Ltd, Apprentice & Design Eng 1958-62; Glacier Metal Co Ltd, Snr Research Eng/Mgr 1962-69; McKinsey & Co Inc, Management Consultant 1969-72; Security Control Engineering Ltd, Managing Director 1972-76; Industrial & Commercial Finance Corporation (renamed 3i in 1983), Chief Industrial

Advisor 1977-89; Director, Independent Directors Programme 1989-. *Biog: b.* 3 January 1936. *Nationality:* British. *m.* 1961 Chloe Elizabeth H (née Skinner); 1 s; 2 d. *Educ:* Greshams School; Clare College, Cambridge (MA). *Directorships:* 3i plc 1984 (exec); 3i Enterprise Support Ltd 1988 (exec) Chairman. *Other Activities:* Member, Cordwainers' Company. *Professional Organisations:* CEng, MIMechE, MBCS. *Clubs:* United Oxford & Cambridge Universities Club. *Recreations:* Lawn Tennis, Real Tennis, Garden Suppression, Music.

LEWIS, Paul; Director, Merrill Lynch Pierce Fenner & Smith (Brokers & Dealers) Limited.

LEWIS, Perry Rufus; Partner, Corporate Services Dept, Morison Stoneham, since 1989; Head of Litigation Support, General Business Consultancy - Corporate. *Career:* Harris Kafton Chartered Accountants, Articled Clerk 1971-75; Manager, Audit Dept 1975-79; Partner, Audit Dept, Investigations Dept 1979-89. *Biog: b.* 30 August 1953. *Nationality:* British. *Professional Organisations:* Fellow, Institute of Chartered Accountants in England and Wales.

LEWIS, R K; Partner, Jaques & Lewis.

LEWIS, Richard Daniel Price; Partner, Waltons & Morse, since 1985; Private Clients and Pensions. *Biog: b.* 29 May 1956. *Nationality:* Welsh. *m.* 1989, Alison. *Educ:* Greenhill School, Tenby; QMC, University of London (LLB). *Other Activities:* City of London Solicitors Company. *Professional Organisations:* Law Society. *Clubs:* Woodford RFC, Marconi Sailing Club. *Recreations:* Rugby, Sailing, Gardening.

LEWIS, Richard Peter Gwynne; Partner, Kidsons Impey, since 1971; Audit, Accounting and Investigation Assignments in the Field of Shipping, the Lloyd's Environment and Farming. *Career:* Shell Tankers (UK) Ltd Deck Apprentice/Deck Officer 1960-65. *Biog: b.* 29 January 1942. *Nationality:* British. *m.* 1971, Mary Elizabeth (née Davenport); 2 s; 1 d. *Educ:* Malvern College. *Directorships:* Lewis Chartering Ltd 1980 (non-exec). *Other Activities:* The Worshipful Company of Makers of Playing Cards (Member). *Professional Organisations:* FCA. *Clubs:* Chipstead Sailing Club. *Recreations:* Sailing, Travelling, Walking, Gardening, Music.

LEWIS, Susan; Partner (Birmingham), Evershed Wells & Hind.

LEWISOHN, Oscar Max; Deputy Chairman, S G Warburg & Co Ltd, since 1987; Treasury and Internationl Investment Banking. *Career:* S G Warburg & Co Ltd 1962 -; Exec Dir 1969; S G Warburg Group plc, Dir 1985. *Biog: b.* 6 May 1938. *Nationality:* Danish. m1 Louisa (née Grunfeld) (div 1985). m2 1987, Margaret (née Paterson); 3 s 2 d. *Educ:* Sortedam Gymnasium, Copenhagen. *Directorships:* Bank S G

Warburg Soditic AG, Zurich (non-exec); S G Warburg Soditic SA, Geneva (non-exec); S G Warburg & Co Inc, New York (non-exec). *Other Activities:* Knight of The Order of Dannebrog; Life Governor, Imperial Cancer Research Fund. *Clubs:* Overseas Bankers. *Recreations:* Music.

LIBERMAN, Gerald; Director, Panmure Gordon & Company Limited, since 1984; Dealing. *Biog: b.* 23 March 1947. *Nationality:* British. *m.* 1970, Roberta Michele (née Swerner); 1 s; 1 d. *Educ:* Gearies College. *Recreations:* Family, Golf, Theatre, Music, Films.

LICHT, Leonard Samuel; , Mercury Asset Management Group plc; Investment Management. *Biog: b.* 15 March 1945. *m.* 1973, Judith (née Grossman); 1 s; 1 d. *Educ:* Christs' College, Finchley. *Directorships:* Mercury Asset Management plc 1986 Deputy Chairman; Mercury Asset Management Employee Trust Co Ltd 1987 (exec); Channel Islands & International Investment Trust Ltd 1982 Chm; Mercury Asset Management Group plc 1987 Vice Chairman; Keysec Ltd 1988 (exec); Keystone Investment Company plc 1988 (exec); Beneficial Arts UK, Limited 1990 (non-exec); Triangle PD Limited 1990 (non-exec). *Clubs:* Brooks's. *Recreations:* 18th Century British Pottery, Tennis.

LICHTENBERG, U; Director, S G Warburg Akroyd Rowe & Pitman Mullens Securities Ltd.

LICKIERMAN, Professor John Andrew; Deputy Principal, since 1990 and Professor of Accounting and Financial Control, London Business School, since 1987; Financial Control, Financial Reporting. *Career:* English Sewing Ltd (now Tootal Ltd) Mgmnt Trainee, Div Mgmnt Accountant 1965-68; Leeds University Asst Lecturer 1968-69; Qualitex Ltd Geshaeftsfuerer Div MD 1969-72; Leeds University Lecturer 1972-74; London Business School Lecturer 1974-76; Cabinet Office (CPRS) Asst Sec 1976-79; London Business School Lecturer, Snr Lecturer, Professor 1979-. *Biog: b.* 30 December 1943. *Nationality:* British. *m.* 1987, Meira (née Gruenspan); 1 steps; 1 stepd. *Educ:* Stowe; Balliol College, Oxford (BA, MA). *Directorships:* Economists' Bookshop Ltd 1981 (non-exec); 1987 Chm. *Other Activities:* Council Mem, CIMA; Advisor,House of Commons Treasury,Transport & Employment Select Ctees; Mem,Audit Commission; Mem,Financial Reporting Council; Governor, London Business Board Chm Public Money & Management. *Professional Organisations:* Fellow, CIMA; Fellow, CACA. *Publications:* Public Sector Accounting & Financial Control (jointly) 1983, 1986-89; Public Expenditure, 1988. *Clubs:* Reform. *Recreations:* Singing, Skiing, Cycling, Wine, Music.

LICKISS, Michael Gillam; President, The Institute of Chartered Accountants in England & Wales, since 1990. *Career:* Miles Watson (Bournemouth) Trainee 1955-58; Army Captain 1959-62; Sole Practitioner (Bournemouth) Ptnr 1962-65; Partner Firm (Bournemouth) Ptnr 1965-68; Thornton Baker (Bournemouth) Ptnr 1968-73; (London) Ptnr 1973; Thornton Baker National Managing Ptnr 1985-89; Grant Thornton National Senior Ptnr 1989-. *Biog: b.* 18 February 1934. 1987, Anne (née Avant). m1 2 s; 2 d m2 1 s. *Educ:* Bournemouth Grammar School; LSE (BSc Econ). *Directorships:* Grant Thornton Nominees 1977 (non-exec); The Lake Hunts Ltd 1981 (non-exec); Family Planning Sales Ltd 1982 (non-exec); Business & Technician Education Council 1985 (non-exec). *Other Activities:* Worshipful Company of CAs. *Professional Organisations:* FCA Council Member, Chm Professional Conduct Directorate, Gen Purposes & Fin Ctee; Vice-President, 1988-89; Deputy-President, 1989-90; BTEC (Chm, Fin Ctee). *Clubs:* RAC. *Recreations:* Walking, Gardening.

LICKLEY, Gavin Alexander Fraser; Banking Director, Morgan Grenfell & Co Ltd, since 1981; Corporate & Special Banking, Leasing, Public Sector Finance. *Career:* GKN plc Corp Fin Exec 1971-72; Morgan Grenfell & Co Ltd Corp Fin Exec 1972-76; Head of Leasing 1976-81. *Biog: b.* 14 August 1946. *Nationality:* British. *m.* 1973, Anne (née Forrester); 2 d. *Educ:* High School, Dundee; Edinburgh University (LLB). *Professional Organisations:* CA. *Clubs:* Royal Wimbledon Golf Club, Roehampton Club. *Recreations:* Golf, Skiing.

LICKORISH, Adrian Derick; Partner, Lovell White Durrant, since 1981; Corporate and Banking. *Biog: b.* 29 October 1948. *Nationality:* British. *m.* 1987, Vivien Gould. *Educ:* Highgate School; London University (LLB, LLM). *Clubs:* Royal Overseas League. *Recreations:* Farming, Fishing, Shooting, Military History.

LIDDIARD, Michael Richard; Vice-Chairman, C Czarnikow Ltd.

LIDDLE, D G; Executive Director, County NatWest Limited.

LIDDLE, John Stewart; Group Compliance Director, Charterhouse Bank Limited, since 1990; Compliance and Regulatory Affairs. *Career:* Morgan Grenfell & Co Limited, Corporate Finance Executive, Syndicated Loans Officer, Director in Charge of Scottish Subsidiary, Energy & Project Loans International, Director, Senior Group Compliance Officer 1974-89; Shearson Lehman Hutton, Director of Compliance for UK and Europe 1989-90; Charterhouse Group, Group Compliance Director 1990-. *Biog: b.* 25 December 1944. *Nationality:* British. *m.* 1970, Denise Moira; 2 s. *Educ:* George Heriot's School, Edinburgh; Edinburgh University (LLB Hons). *Directorships:* Charterhouse Bank Limited 1990 (exec). *Professional Organisations:* Solicitor (Writer to HM Signet); CA. *Recreations:* Golf, Gardening.

LIDSTONE, John Ross; Partner, Baillie Gifford & Co, since 1990. *Career:* Metal Box Ltd 1977-79; Texaco

Ltd 1979-84; The International Stock Exchange 1984-87; Baillie Gifford & Co 1987. *Biog: b.* 17 January 1956. *Nationality:* British. *m.* 1989, Shona (née Dickson); 1 d. *Educ:* Sherborne School; Leicester Univeristy (BA Economics). *Directorships:* Baillie Gifford Overseas Ltd 1987 (exec); Toyo Trust Baillie Gifford Ltd 1989 (exec). *Clubs:* Lansdowne, Dalmahoy. *Recreations:* Tennis, Travel.

LIECHTI, Raymond John; Managing Director, Monk Dunstone Associates, since 1989; Quantity Surveying and Cost Consultancy United Kingdom. *Career:* Robert Stevens, Assistant 1955-59; National Service (Flying Officer RAF) Air Ministry Works Department 1959-60; Armstrong & Duncan, Kenya, Senior Assistant 1961; House & Shrimpton, Senior Assistant 1962-63; Cameron & Middleton, Sydney, Australia, Senior Assistant 1963-66; Monk Dunstone Associates, Senior Assistant 1966-69; Associate 1969-74; Partner 1974-85; Director 1985-89. *Biog: b.* 5 August 1934. *Nationality:* British. *m.* 1963, Jean Pamela; 2 s. *Educ:* East Barnet Grammar School; College of Estate Management, London University (ARICS). *Directorships:* Monk Dunstone Associates 1985 (exec); Monk Dunstone Associates 1989 (exec) MD; MDA Group plc 1989 (exec). *Professional Organisations:* FRICS; ACIArb. *Clubs:* Cricketers Club, Hazelwood LTC.

LIESNER, H H; CB; Deputy Chairman, Monopolies and Mergers Commission, since 1989. *Career:* London School of Economics, Teaching Appointments 1955-59; Cambridge University, Teaching Appointments 1959-70; Emmanuel College Cambridge, Teaching Appointments 1959-70; Assistant Bursar; H M Treasury, Under Secretary 1970-76; Department of Trade and Industry (formerly Industry, Trade and Prices and Consumer Protection) Deputy Secretary & Chief Economic Adviser 1976-89. *Biog: b.* 30 March 1929. *Nationality:* British. *m.* 1968, Thelma (née Seward); 1 s; 1 d. *Educ:* German Schools; Bristol University (BA Economics); Nuffield College, Oxford (MA Cantab). *Other Activities:* Member, Executive Committee, National Institute of Economic & Social Research; Member, Economic & Social Research Council; Member of Council, Royal Economic Society. *Publications:* Academic Books & Articles in Learned Journals. *Clubs:* Reform. *Recreations:* Skiing, Gardening, Walking.

LIGHTE, Peter R; Vice President, Manufacturers Hanover Trust Company.

LILLEY, C A; Director, David Holman & Co Ltd.

LILLEY, Francis Anthony; Director, James Capel Corporate Finance Ltd, since 1989; European Corporate Finance. *Career:* Coopers & Lybrand, Senior Manager, General Practice 1975-82; Societe Fiduciaire Suisse (Geneva), Assistant Director, Financial Advisory Work 1982-86; Savory Milln Ltd, Assistant Director, European

Corporate Finance 1986-88; James Capel & Co, Assistant Director, European Corporate Finance 1988-. *Biog:* b. 12 June 1953. *Nationality:* British. *m.* 1985, Judy (née Leftwich); 1 s; 1 d. *Educ:* Downside School; Pembroke College, Oxford (History & Modern Languages 2nd Class Honours). *Professional Organisations:* ICAEW. *Recreations:* Tennis, Badminton, Skiing, Sailing, Chess, Opera, Singing.

LILLIE, Kenneth Edward; Associate Director, Schlesinger & Co Ltd/Manchester Exchange & Investment Bank Ltd, since 1989; Corporate Treasury Management. *Career:* Joseph Sebag & Co, Stockbrokers, Section Leader 1967-72; Quilter Hilton Goodison & Co, Stockbrokers, O&M Officer 1972-75; Abbott Laboratories Ltd, Deputy Treasurer 1975-77; Ellerman Lines Ltd, Deputy Group Treasurer 1977-84. *Biog:* b. 30 June 1948. *Nationality:* British. *m.* 1971, Valerie Maria (née Marshall); 2 d. *Educ:* Walpole Grammar School, Ealing; Harrow School of Art. *Directorships:* Corporate Treasury Management Ltd 1985. *Professional Organisations:* MCT. *Recreations:* Reading, Gardening, Beekeeping, Art.

LILLIS, Charles E; Director, Merrill Lynch International Limited, since 1989; Equity Syndicate Desk. *Career:* S G Warburg & Co Ltd, Fund Management 1975-79; Country Advisory Division 1979-83; Credit Suisse First Boston, Manager of Emerging Country Group 1983-86; Merrill Lynch International, Equity Syndicate Department; Specialist in Country Funds 1986-. *Biog:* b. 21 September 1952. *Nationality:* Irish. *m.* 1987, Veronica Mary; 1 d. *Educ:* Ampleforth College, York; Christ Church, Oxford (MA). *Directorships:* Merrill Lynch International Limited; Euro Spain Fund Limited. *Clubs:* Brooks's, The Turf. *Recreations:* Tennis, Shooting.

LILWALL, M R I; Director, Brewin Dolphin & Co Ltd, since 1989; Corporate Finance. *Career:* Brewin Dolphin & Co Ltd 1979-. *Biog:* b. 29 April 1958. *Nationality:* British. *m.* 1989, Julie (née Caulcott); 1 d. *Educ:* Radley College; Essex University (BSc Hons). *Directorships:* Brewin Dolphin & Co 1989 (exec). *Recreations:* Sailing, Golf, Shooting, Squash.

LILWALL, R W; Sales Director, Leasing Division, Benchmark Bank plc.

LIM, Thiam J; Managing Director, Merrill Lynch International Limited, since 1990; Head of Derivative Products. *Career:* Morgan Guaranty, VP Swaps 1983-88. *Biog:* b. 8 February 1957. *Nationality:* Malaysiam. *m.* 1981, Laura V; 1 s; 2 d. *Educ:* University of Glasgow (BSc Hons); University of Waterloo (Master in Applied Science Management Service); New York University Graduate School of Business (MBA Distinction).

LIMBERT, Roger S G; Partner, Walker Morris Scott Turnbull.

LINAKER, Lawrence Edward; *Career:* Esso Petroleum 1957-63. *Biog:* b. 22 July 1934. *Nationality:* British. *m.* Elizabeth Susan; 1 d. *Educ:* Malvern College. *Directorships:* M & G Investment Management Ltd Chairman; M & G Assurance Group Ltd Chairman; M & G Securities Ltd Chairman & MD; M & G Ltd Deputy Chairman & MD; M & G Group plc 1987-90 Deputy Chairman & MD; BIT Futures Ltd (non-exec); Brunner Investment Trust Ltd (non exec). *Other Activities:* Council, Royal Postgraduate Medical School, 1977; Governing Body, Society for the Promotion of Christian Knowledge (SPCK) 1976; Council, Malvern School. *Professional Organisations:* FCA. *Clubs:* Athenaeum. *Recreations:* Music, Wine, Gardening.

LIND, Bernard J; Director Group Treasury & Capital Markets, CIB, National Westminster Bank plc, since 1990; Treasuries/NW Futures. *Career:* Merrill Lynch, Asst VP 1965-74; Credit Industriel et Commercial, Snr VP & Dep Gen Mgr 1974-83; Midland Bank plc (New York), Exec VP & Treasurer/Branch Mgr 1984-86; Midland Montagu, Director of Fixed Income 1987-89; Director of Group Market Risk 1989-90. *Biog:* b. 8 January 1942. *Nationality:* American. *m.* 1987, Sonja; 2 s. *Educ:* Brandeis University, Mass (BA); Columbia University, NY (MBA). *Directorships:* Samuel Montagu & Co Ltd 1987-90; Greenwell Montagu Gilt-Edged 1987-90; Midland Investment Delaware Inc 1987-90; Midland Montagu Securities Inc 1987-90. *Other Activities:* Chairman, LIFFO Product Strategy Committee; CME International Advisory Committee. *Professional Organisations:* Chicago Board of Trade; Chicago Mercantile Exchange; Economics Club of New York; Money Marketeers; Forex Assoc Dealer, Bank Assoc. *Clubs:* Anglo-Belgium, University Club (NY), RAC Club.

LINDEMANN, Jurgen H; Senior Vice President, First Interstate Bank of California, since 1984; Foreign Exchange - Bond and Money Market Dealing. *Career:* Bankers Trust Company, VP and For Exchange Mgr 1974-82; Bankers Trust GmbH (Germany), Gen Mgr to VP and Treasury Mgr 1982-84. *Biog:* b. 9 January 1945. *Nationality:* German. *m.* 1974, Ute-Liz (née Auch); 1 s. *Educ:* High School, Bremen; Banking College, Bremen, W Germany. *Directorships:* First Interstate 1985 (non-exec); Capital Markets Ltd 1987 (exec); Bankers Trust GmbH (Frankfurt) 1982 MD. *Recreations:* Swimming, Skiing.

LINDEN, Brian Andrew; Director, CIN Venture Managers Ltd, since 1989; Unquoted Investments. *Career:* Whittaker London & Co 1980-83; Touche Ross & Co 1983-85; CIN Venture Managers Ltd 1985-. *Biog:* b. 12 December 1956. *Nationality:* British. *m.* 1988, Clare (née Grover); 1 s. *Educ:* St Marylebone Grammar School; Newcastle University (BA Hons Business

Finance); Thames Polytechnic. *Directorships:* Various Non-Executive Directorships. *Professional Organisations:* Chartered Accountant. *Recreations:* Various Sports.

LINDSAY, James Snodgrass; Secretary, The Royal Bank of Scotland plc, since 1988; Company Secretarial. *Career:* The Royal Bank of Scotland plc Various 1973-83; Asst Mgr, Corp Finance 1983-85; Dep Sec 1985-88. *Biog: b.* 20 July 1952. *Nationality:* British. *m.* 1973, Susan (née Brown); 2 s. *Educ:* Madras College, St Andrews; Edinburgh University (BSc); Strathclyde University (MBA). *Professional Organisations:* AIB Scot. *Clubs:* New Golf Club, St Andrews, St Andrews Golf Club, Linlithgow Golf Club. *Recreations:* Golf, Family.

LINDSAY, Robert Alexander; The Earl of Crawford and Balcarres; Vice Chairman, Sun Alliance and London Insurance plc.

LINDSELL, Charles Nicholas; Deputy Managing Director, Midland Montagu Asset Management, since 1988. *Career:* Philips & Drew Fund Mgr 1972-82; Henderson Administration plc 1982-88. *Biog: b.* 31 December 1953. *m.* 1980, Jill Penelope (née Gransbury); 1 s; 1 d. *Educ:* Monckton Combe School, Bath.

LINDSELL, D C; Senior Technical Partner, Ernst & Young, since 1988. *Career:* Ernst & Whinney, Audit Partner 1973-85; Ernst & Whinney International, Director of Planning and Marketing 1985-88. *Biog: b.* 9 May 1947. *Nationality:* British. *m.* 1969, Gaynor (née Scrimshaw); 2 d. *Educ:* Christ's College, Cambridge (MA). *Other Activities:* Member, Business Law Committee, Institute of Chartered Accountants; Chairman, Company Law Sub-Committee, Institute of Chartered Accountants. *Professional Organisations:* Fellow, Institute of Chartered Accountants in England and Wales. *Publications:* A Changing Company Framework and Accounting Standards in Planning for Europe, 1989. *Clubs:* United Oxford and Cambridge. *Recreations:* Theatre, Music.

LINDSEY, Ian Walter; OBE; Executive Director, Save & Prosper Group Ltd, since 1986; Banking Services. *Career:* Westminster Bank Branch Banker 1964-68; Williams & Glyn's Bank Marketing Exec 1971-75; Harrow College Snr Lecturer 1975-77; Price Commission Consultant 1977-78; TSB Trustcard Ltd Asst Gen Mgr 1978-83; Save & Prosper Group Ltd 1983-. *Biog: b.* 7 May 1946. *Nationality:* British. *m.* 1970, Janet (née Hewitt); 2 s; 1 d. *Educ:* Hayes County School; University of Nottingham (BA Hons, MPhil). *Directorships:* Robert Fleming & Co Ltd 1988 (exec). *Other Activities:* Wing Commander, RAFVR(T); Vice Chancellor's Advisory Committee Member, University of Nottingham. *Professional Organisations:* Council Member, FCIB. *Publications:* Nature & Extent of Competition Between the London Clearing Banks, 1979. *Recreations:* Reading, Classical Music, Flying.

LINEEN, P J; Executive Director, James R Knowles Limited.

LING, T A; Partner, Freshfields.

LING, W J N; Director, Manning Beard Ltd.

LINGER, Robert George; Partner, Arthur Andersen & Co, since 1970; Audit/Development Capital/Service Industries. *Biog: b.* 24 January 1941. *Nationality:* British. *m.* 1966, Angela (née Dunne-Neill); 1 s; 1 d. *Educ:* Mercers' School, London.

LININGTON, Miles Julian Gordon; Director, Billiton-Enthoven Metals Ltd. *Biog: b.* 15 April 1947. *Nationality:* British. *m.* 1971, Elizabeth; 1 s; 1 d. *Clubs:* Royal Naval Club, Auriol Rowing Club, Southsea Rowing Club. *Recreations:* Sailing, Rowing.

LINNETT, Simon; Director, N M Rothschild & Sons Limited, since 1987; Corporate Finance. *Educ:* Leys School, Cambridge; Balliol College, Oxford University (MA Hons Maths).

LINSELL, Richard Duncan; Partner, Rowe & Maw, since 1976; Company and Commercial Law. *Career:* Rowe & Maw, Articled Clerk 1969-71; Asst Solicitor 1972-76. *Biog: b.* 21 June 1947. *m.* 1986, Briony Margaret (née Crabtree); 1 d. *Educ:* Mill Hill School; Jesus College, Cambridge (MA). *Directorships:* DHL International (UK) Ltd 1977 (non-exec). *Other Activities:* City of London Solicitors' Company. *Professional Organisations:* IBA. *Recreations:* Classical Music, Golf, Walking.

LINTOTT, Mrs Lesley Joan; Partner, Penningtons, since 1978; Private Client Work (Tax Planning). *Career:* Penningtons, Articled Clerk 1972-75; Assistant Solicitor 1975-78; Partner 1978-. *Biog: b.* 28 June 1950. *Nationality:* British. *m.* 1972, Christopher. *Educ:* St Hilda's College, Oxford (MA Hons Oxon). *Professional Organisations:* Member, Law Society; City of Westminster Law Society.

LINWOOD, N A; Finance Director, Hoare Govett International Securities.

LION, A K M; Partner, Pension Fund Administration (Epsom), Bacon & Woodrow.

LION, D N; Director, Philipp & Lion Ltd.

LION, Jacques Kenneth; OBE; President, The London Metal Exchange Ltd.

LION, Michael Charles Elphinsto; Chairman & Chief Executive Officer, Philipp & Lion Ltd.

LIPPIATT, Stuart R; Partner, D J Freeman & Co.

LIPWORTH, Maurice Sydney; Chairman, Monopolies & Mergers Commission, since 1988. *Career:* Liberty Life Association of Africa Ltd, Dir (non-exec) 1956-64; Johannesburg Bar, Barrister 1956-64; IMEX UK Ltd, Dir 1965-67; Walker Bros (London) Ltd, Dir 1964-67; Abbey Life Assurance plc, Legal Dir 1968-70; Abbey International Corp, Dir 1968-70; Allied Dunbar Ass plc, Dir 1970-88; BAT Industries plc 1985-88. *Biog: b.* 13 May 1931. *m.* 1957, Rosa (née Liwarek); 2 s. *Educ:* King Edward VII School, Johannesburg; University of the Witwatersrand, Johannesburg (BCom,LLB). *Directorships:* Allied Dunbar Charitable Trust 1971 Trustee; Philharmonic Orchestra Trust 1982 (non-exec) Dep Chm; Royal Academy of Arts 1988 Trustee. *Professional Organisations:* Honorary Bencher, Inner Temple. *Publications:* Annual Chapters in Allied Dunbar Tax Guide and Investment Guide. *Clubs:* Queens, Reform. *Recreations:* Music, Theatre, Tennis.

LIS, Roman; Director, J Henry Schroder Wagg & Co Limited.

LISS, Ian Trevor; JP; Director, Cater Allen Ltd.

LISTER, C; Partner, Nabarro Nathanson.

LISTER, Geoffrey Richard; Chief Executive, Bradford & Bingley Building Society, since 1985; Overall Control and Management of the Society. *Career:* Bradford & Bingley Building Society Asst/Chief Accountant 1965-75; Asst Gen Mgr 1975-76; Dep Gen Mgr 1976-80; Gen Mgr 1980-84; Dep Chief Exec 1984-85; Chief Exec 1985-. *Biog: b.* 14 May 1937. *Nationality:* British. *m.* 1962, Myrtle Margaret (née Cooper); 1 s; 2 d. *Educ:* St Bede's Grammar School, Bradford. *Directorships:* Electronic Funds Transfer (Clearings) Ltd 1988 (non-exec); Electronic Funds Transfer (Point of Sale) Ltd 1988 (non-exec). *Other Activities:* The National House-Building Council and Exec Ctee (Member); Director of Bradford & District TEC. *Professional Organisations:* FCA, FCBSI, CBIM.

LISTER, M; Executive Director, Unibank plc.

LISTER, N G; Assistant General Manager (UK), General Accident Fire Life Assurance.

LITHIBY, John Grant; Chairman, Panmure Gordon & Co Limited, since 1986; Corporate Finance. *Career:* Panmure Gordon & Company Limited, Ptnr 1958-77; Snr Ptnr (Joint) 1977-86. *Biog: b.* 1 December 1930. *m.* 1961, Sarah (née Branch); 2 s; 1 d. *Educ:* Eton College. *Directorships:* Fortnum & Mason plc (non-exec); Transport Development Group plc (non-exec). *Professional Organisations:* The International Stock Exchange. *Clubs:* White's, Portland, Hurlingham.

LITTLE, Alan; Partner, European Human Resources Consultancy, Price Waterhouse.

LITTLE, Nigel Stuart; Director, Panmure Gordon & Co, since 1989; UK Equity Sales. *Career:* Kitcat & Aitken Institutional Salesman UK Equities 1977-78; James Capel & Co Senior Executive (Partner) Equities (Head of Scottish & Irish Sales) 1978-88; Morgan Stanley International Director & Head of UK Equities 1988-89. *Biog: b.* 11 March 1954. *Nationality:* British. *m.* 1986, Fiona Mary (née Lee); 2 s. *Educ:* Queen Elizabeth the First School; Queen Mary College, London University(BSc Hons). *Other Activities:* Freeman of the City of London. *Professional Organisations:* FBIM; The International Stock Exchange. *Recreations:* Driving, Golf, Watching Rugby, Shooting.

LITTLE, P S; Director, Robert Fleming Insurance Brokers Limited.

LITTLEJOHN, Anthony David Findon; Finance Director, GT Management plc, since 1983. *Career:* The Guthrie Corporation 1974-78; Kumpulan Guthrie SB, Malaysia, Finance Director 1978-81; Guthrie International, Finance Director 1981-83; GT Management plc, Finance Director 1983-. *Professional Organisations:* FCA; FCT.

LITTLEJOHNS, A; Partner, Freshfields.

LITTLEWOOD, G; Partner, Pannell Kerr Forster.

LITTLEWOOD, John Nigel; Group Director, S G Warburg Group plc, since 1985. *Career:* Read, Hurst-Brown & Co, Ptnr 1964-75; Rowe & Pitman, Ptnr 1975-86. *Biog: b.* 18 April 1935. *Nationality:* British. *m.* 1962, Rosemary (née Underwood); 2 s. *Educ:* Farnborough Grammar School; New College, Oxford (MA). *Other Activities:* Independent Governor, City of London Polytechnic. *Professional Organisations:* FSIA. *Recreations:* Cinema, Golf, Gardening, Music, Reading, Writing.

LITTMAN, Mark; QC; Director, The Burton Group plc, since 1983. *Biog: b.* 4 September 1920. *Nationality:* British. *Directorships:* Granada Group plc 1977; Rio Tinto-Zinc Corporation plc 1968; RTZ Metals plc 1983; RTZ Chemicals Limited 1987.

LIU, S L; Secretary, Berry Palmer & Lyle Ltd.

LIVENS, Leslie John Phillip; Partner, Moores Rowland, since 1983; International Taxation & Share Valuation. *Career:* Butterworths Managing Ed, Tax Books 1977-81; Freelance Author & Publisher; Tax Planning International, One Time Editor; Financial Times World Tax Report, OneTime Editor; Review of Parliament, One Time Editor; Institute of Taxation, Taxation Practitioner, One Time Editor. *Biog: b.* 13 December 1946. *Nationality:* British. *m.* 1968, Carole Ann (née Todd); 1 s; 1 d. *Educ:* Wimbledon County Secondary School. *Professional Organisations:* ATII; Institute of Taxation in Ireland (Assoc); MBAE (Associate

Member of the British Academy of Experts). *Publications:* The Daily Telegraph Personal Tax Guide, 1987; The Daily Telegraph Personal Tax, 1988; Share Valuation Handbook, 1986; Moores Rowland's Tax Guide, 1982-88; Numerous Articles. *Recreations:* Writing, Walking, Music, Family.

LIVING, Graeme A; Director, Parrish Stockbrokers, since 1988; East Anglia Region Pro-Trade Facility. *Biog: b.* 14 August 1945. *Nationality:* British. *m.* 1975, Diane C (née Sevant); 2 s; 1 d. *Educ:* Forest School. *Other Activities:* Tallow Chandlers; Makers of Playing Cards; City Livery Club. *Professional Organisations:* Member, International Stock Exchange, 1969. *Clubs:* City Livery. *Recreations:* Bridge, Skiing, Family, Genealogy, Watching Sport.

LIVINGSTON, Dorothy Kirby; Partner, Herbert Smith, since 1980; European and Competition Law/Banking Law. *Career:* Herbert Smith, Articled Clerk 1970-72; Qualified Solicitor 1972; Assistant Solicitor 1972-80. *Biog: b.* 6 January 1948. *Nationality:* British. *m.* 1971, Dr Julian Millar; 2 d. *Educ:* Central Newcastle High School, GPDST; St Hugh's College, Oxford (MA). *Directorships:* Friends of The Girls' Public Day School Trust 1981 (non-exec). *Other Activities:* Member, Banking Law Sub-Committee, City of London Law Society; Member, City of London Solicitors' Company and Law Society; Member, Law Society. *Professional Organisations:* Solicitor, Admitted 1982. *Recreations:* Family Life, Gardening, Photography.

LIVINGSTONE, Hugh Jonathan; Partner, Holman Fenwick & Willan; since 1986, Maritime Law. *Biog: b.* 14 July 1950. *Nationality:* British. *m.* 1978, Helen; 1 s; 1 d. *Educ:* Kingswood College, South Africa; University of Cape Town (BA, LLB); University College, London (LLM). *Professional Organisations:* Law Society, England and Wales, Solicitor; Law Society, Hong Kong, Solicitor; Attorney (South Africa). *Clubs:* RAC, Hong Kong CC, Highgate CC, Chung Shan GC (China).

LIVINGSTONE, Michael G; Chairman, J Trevor, Montleman & Poland Ltd.

LLAMBIAS, John Richard; Director, Sphere Drake Underwriting Management Ltd, since 1988; Personal Lines. *Career:* Excess Insurance Group Ltd, Underwriting Director, Personal and Creditor Lines 1964-88. *Biog: b.* 18 January 1942. *Nationality:* British. divorced; 2 s. *Directorships:* Sphere Drake Underwriting Management Ltd 1988; Sphere Drake Insurance plc 1988; Sphere Drake Insurance Group plc 1988; Churcher & Company Ltd 1988.

LLEWELLYN, Anthony David; Group Partner, Personal Financial Services Group, Touche Ross & Co, since 1982; Personal Tax & Trust Planning, Share Valuation of Unquoted Companies, Executorship Plan-

ning and Administration. *Career:* Midland Bank Executor & Trustee Co Ltd, Head Office Asst to the Joint Chief Accountants 1959-65. *Biog: b.* 23 March 1940. *Nationality:* British. *m.* 1967, Jacqueline (née Curtis); 2 d. *Educ:* Watford Grammar School. *Directorships:* Island Trustees Ltd 1972 (exec); Walbrook Trustees Ltd 1972 (exec); Walbrook Nominees Ltd 1972 (exec); Norstrand Trustees Ltd 1987 (exec); Touche Ross Financial Services Ltd 1990 (exec)Chairman. *Other Activities:* Member of Board of Management, London School of Hygiene & Tropical Medicine. *Professional Organisations:* FCA, ACIB, FTII. *Recreations:* Tennis, Skiing, Golf.

LLEWELYN, Gordon Ionwy David; Partner, McKenna & Co, since 1987; Commercial and Intellectual Property Law. *Career:* Reading University, Law Lecturer 1977-78; North Atlantic Treaty Organisation, Nato Fellow 1979; Max-Planck Institute for Intellectual Property Law (Munich), Research Fell 1980-81; Morris Fletcher & Cross (Brisbane), Consultant 1982; Linklaters & Paines Solicitors 1982-87; Pepperdine University (USA), Adjunct Professor of EEC Law 1984-87. *Biog: b.* 15 July 1956. *Nationality:* British. *Educ:* Wallingford Grammar School; Worcester College, Oxford (BCL); Southampton University (LLB). *Directorships:* Visiting Lecturer, Intellectual Property Law, London School of Economics 1984-. *Professional Organisations:* Member, The Law Society. *Publications:* Numerous Publications on Intellectual Property, Computer and Intl Law.

LLOWARCH, M E; Non-Executive Director, Abbey National plc.

LLOYD, Christopher E; Partner, Theodore Goddard London and Jersey, since 1973; Trust and Tax Work. *Career:* Admitted to practise in the British Virgin Islands 1967; Harvey Westwood and Lloyd, Partner 1969-73. *Biog: b.* 6 September 1944. *Nationality:* British. *m.* 1974, Christine; 1 s; 2 d. *Educ:* Eastbourne College. *Directorships:* Le Riches Stores Limited 1985 (non-exec) Chairman; Cater Allen Bank (Jersey) Ltd 1987 (non-exec); Joseph Harkom and Son (Gunmaker) Ltd 1989 (non-exec) Chairman. *Other Activities:* President, Association of English Solicitors Practising in Jersey 1989-. *Professional Organisations:* Solicitor (Admitted 1965). *Clubs:* Cruising Association, Royal Channel Islands Yacht Club. *Recreations:* Sailing, Fly Fishing.

LLOYD, David; Partner, Linklaters & Paines.

LLOYD, G G; Director, Pru-Bache Capital Funding (Equities).

LLOYD, Humphrey Alexander; Director, Close Brothers Limited, since 1988; Corporate Finance. *Career:* Coopers & Lybrand, Articled Clerk to Audit Supervisor 1977-81; (Sydney), Audit Supervisor to Audit Mgr

1981-83; (London), Audit Mgr 1983-84; N M Rothschild & Sons Ltd, Corporate Finance Mgr 1984-87. *Biog: b.* 1956. *Nationality:* British. *m.* 1984, Cassie (née Paines); 2 s. *Educ:* Winchester College; Magdalene College, Cambridge (MA Hons). *Professional Organisations:* ACA. *Recreations:* Photography, Travel.

LLOYD, J D; Director, Metheuen (Lloyds Underwriting Agents) Limited.

LLOYD, Mrs Jane Mary (née Faulkner); Company Secretary/Compliance Officer, Billiton-Enthoven Metals Ltd, since 1989; Compliance. *Biog: b.* 28 November 1962. *Nationality:* British. *m.* 1983, Mark Stephen. *Recreations:* Squash, Skiing.

LLOYD, M P W; Director, Charlton Seal Schaverien Limited.

LLOYD, Sir Richard (Ernest Butler); Bt; Chairman, Hill Samuel Bank Limited, since 1987. *Career:* Military Service in The Black Watch; Glyn Mills & Co, Cadet Trainee 1952; Board Member 1964; Williams & Glyn's Bank, the 1st Chief Executive (on its formation) 1970-78; Hill Samuel Bank Limited, successively a Deputy Chairman, Chief Executive 1978- Chairman 1987-. *Biog: b.* 6 December 1928. *Nationality:* British. *m.* 1955, Jennifer Susan Margaret (née Cardiff); 3 s. *Educ:* Wellington College; Hertford College, Oxford (PPE Exhibitioner). *Directorships:* British Heart Foundation 1977; The Ditchley Foundation 1984; Equity Consort Investment Trust plc 1988; ECIT Finance Limited 1988; Harrisons & Crosfield plc 1988; Hill Samuel & Co Ltd 1978; Hill Samuel Bank Limited (formerly Hill Samuel & Co Ltd) 1987 Chairman; Hill Samuel Securities Limited 1987; Legal & General Group plc 1979; SIEBE plc 1988; Simon Engineering plc 1988; Vickers plc 1978; 1989- Deputy Chairman; TSB Group plc 1990; TSB Bank plc -1990; TSB Hill Samuel Bank Holding Company plc -1989; Hill Samuel Investments Limited -1989; Corporate Bank Group Limited (formerly Hill Samuel Group (SA) Ltd -1988; Corporate Merchant Bank Limited (formerly Hill Samuel Merchant Bank (SA) Ltd) -1988; Hill Samuel Holdings (SA) Limited -1988; Wood Mackenzie & Co Limited -1988; Spitfire Scheme Nominees Limited -1986; Hill Samuel International Limited -1985; Hill Samuel New York Inc -1985; Hill Samuel Australia Limited -1985; Hill Samuel Pacific Limited -1984; Hill Samuel New Zealand Limited -1984; Hill Samuel & Co (Jersey) Limited -1983; Williams & Glyn's Bank Limited -1983; Legal and General International Limited -1983; Universal Credit Limited -1982; Legal & General Assurance Society Limited -1980; London Bridge Finance Limited -1979. *Other Activities:* Freeman of London; Liveryman, Mercers' Company; Member, CBI Council, 1978-; Finance and General Purposes Committee, Chairman, Investment Sub-Committee; Member, CBI City Advisory Group; Government's Industrial Development Advisory Board, 1972-77; Overseas Projects Board, 1981-85; National Economic Development Council, 1973-77; Member, Wilson Committee (Reviewing Functioning of Financial Institutions), 1977-80; Advisory Board, Royal College of Defence Studies; Hon Treasurer, British Heart Foundation; Governor of Ditchley, Chairman of Finance and General Purposes Committee. *Professional Organisations:* Companion, BIM, 1976; Fellow, Chartered Institute of Bankers, 1970. *Clubs:* Boodles. *Recreations:* Walking, Fishing, Gardening.

LLOYD, Roger Hall; Partner, Haythe & Curley, since 1979; Corporate, Administrative and Tax Lw Specialisation. *Career:* Practising Lawyer since 1958. *Biog: b.* 18 September 1934. *Nationality:* American. *m.* 1959, Svetlana (née Kassessinoff); 1 s; 1 d. *Educ:* Stowe School, Buckingham; Princeton University, USA (BA); Harvard University, USA (LLB). *Directorships:* Western Oceanic (UK) Ltd 1975 (non-exec); Western Oceanic (Overseas) Ltd 1975 (non-exec); Colony Drilling Company Ltd 1975 (non-exec); Embassy Greenly Ltd 1988 (non-exec). *Other Activities:* Dir, American Chamber of Commerce (UK); Chm, British American Arts Association. *Professional Organisations:* Member, New York State and US Federal Bars. *Clubs:* Brooks's, Knickerbocker (New York). *Recreations:* Riding, Opera, Theatre, Philosophy.

LLOYD, Thomas; Editor-in-Chief, Financial Weekly Ltd, since 1990; Editorial. *Career:* Thomson Regional Newspapers, City Reporter 1970-73; United Newspapers, Dep City Editor 1973-74; London Evening News, City Reporter 1974-79; Financial Weekly 1979-; Editor 1983-90. *Biog: b.* 26 April 1946. *Nationality:* British; 1 s; 1 d. *Educ:* Wellington College; Liverpool University (BA). *Directorships:* Financial Weekly Ltd; PRPR Ltd. *Publications:* Dinosaur & Co Studies in Corporate Evolution, 1984; Co-Author, Managing Knowhow, 1987; The 'Nice' Company, 1990. *Recreations:* Walking.

LOACH, P J; Director, Framlington Unit Management Limited.

LOADES, (Geoffrey) Geoff; Assistant General Manager, Norwich Union Fire Insurance Society Limited, since 1989; Finance, Corporate Development and Staff Development of UK General Business. *Career:* Norwich Union Pensions Schemes, Documentation 1960; Accountants (Life), Schemes Department 1962; Statistics Schemes 1966; Accountants (Life) Department 1967; Accounting Assistant, Head of Department Status 1967; Head, Central Collections 1968; Accounting Assistant (Life), Head of Department Status 1969; Accounting Assistant (Life), Superintendent Level 2 Status 1969; Staff Superintendent (Research) 1973; Staff Superintendent (Manpower) 1974; Chief Accountant, Anglo-Portuguese Bank 1975; Assistant Accountant, Accountants General 1978; Accountant (Fire) 1979;

Corporate Development Manager 1988; Assistant General Manager, Corporate Finance & Development 1989. *Biog: b.* 3 September 1942. *Nationality:* British. *m.* 1969, Elizabeth; 1 s; 2 d. *Educ:* Sir John Leman Grammar School, Beccles, Suffolk. *Directorships:* Eastlease Limited 1986; Haven Insurance Policies Limited 1989; Norwich Union Equipment Finance Limited 1986; Norwich Union Healthcare Limited 1990; Norwich Union Insurance Group (Equipment Leasing) Limited 1986; Norwich Union Leasing Finance Limited 1989; Norwich Union Leasing Holdings Limited 1990; Norwich Union Leasing Limited 1990; Norwich Union Leasing Assets Limited 1990; Norwich Union Leasing Industrial Limited 1990; Norwich Union Leasing Services Limited 1990; Norwich Union Leasing (January-December) Limited 1990; Norwich Union Finance (No 3) Limited 1990; St Stephen's Policies Limited 1990; The Ajax Insurance Association Limited 1989; Ajax Insurance Holdings Limited 1989; Aviation & General Insurance Company Limited 1989; Norwich Winterthur Holdings Limited 1989; Norwich Winterthur Leasing Limited 1989; Norwich Winterthur Overseas Limited 1989; Norwich Winterthur Reinsurance Corporation Limited 1989; Norwich Winterthur Services Limited 1989; Stronghold Insurance Company Limited 1989; Norwich Union Holdings (NZ) Finance Limited 1990; Norwich Union Holdings NZ Limited 1990. *Other Activities:* Chm, Norwich Union Athletic Association; Chm, Swardeston Edith Cavell Day Care Ctee. *Professional Organisations:* FCCA. *Recreations:* Tennis, Badminton, Following Most Sports, Gardening.

LOAT, Martin Edward; Managing Director, Merrill Lynch International Limited, since 1990; Head of Special Equity Derivatives. *Career:* Thomson McLintock (PMM) London, Account Trainee 1975-79; BICC Ltd, London, Treasury Manager 1979-82; Banker's Trust, London/New York, Associate, Project Finance 1981-83; Vice President, Various Positions in Capital Markets Area Including Marketing, Swaps and Non-Dollar Swaps 1983-88; Equity Derivatives, Managing Director 1988-90; Merrill Lynch, London, Managing Director 1990-. *Biog: Nationality:* British. *m.* Isabel; 1 s; 2 d. *Educ:* Oundle School; Manchester University (BA Economics). *Directorships:* Banker's Trust 1987 MD; Merrill Lynch 1990 MD.

LOBBENBERG, Peter; Partner, Clark Whitehill.

LOBLE, Steven Frederick; Partner, Nabarro Nathanson, since 1988; International Litigation. *Career:* Pritchard Englefield & Tobin, Articled Clerk; Herbert Oppenheimer Nathan & Vandyk, Assistant Solicitor 1984-87; Associate 1987-88; Nabarro Nathanson, Partner 1988-. *Biog: b.* 4 January 1958. *Nationality:* British. *Educ:* Royal Grammar School, Newcastle-upon-Tyne; Pembroke College, Cambridge. *Other Activities:* American Bar Association; Young American Bar Association; Association Internationale des Jeunes Avocats; British-

German Jurists Association; City of London Solicitors Company; City of Westminster Law Society; Royal Institute of International Affairs; Society of English and American Lawyers; Royal Institute of International Affairs; Society of English and American Lawyers; Westminster Law Society. *Publications:* The Procedure for Obtaining Evidence in England and Wales for Use in United States Proceedings, 1988; Various Articicles and Publications Produced by the Firm. *Recreations:* Travel, Languages, Literature, Theatre, Cinema, Skiing.

LOCK, Barry David Stuart; Partner, Clifford Chance, since 1964; Wills, Settlements, Private International Law and Pension Schemes. *Career:* Coward Chance, Assistant Solicitor 1961-64; Partner 1964-87; Clifford Chance, Partner 1987-. *Biog: b.* 28 July 1934. *Nationality:* British. *Educ:* King's School, Canterbury; Magdalen College, Oxford (BCL,MA). *Clubs:* The Athenaeum. *Recreations:* Opera, Theatre, Regency Culture.

LOCK, D A; Director, Parrish Stockbrokers.

LOCK, John; Managing Director, Mercantile & General Reinsurance Co plc.

LOCK, T G; Chairman, Amalgamated Metal Trading Limited.

LOCKE, D A; Partner, Milne Ross Chartered Accountants, since 1989; General Audit Partner, Building and Landfill Industries. *Biog: b.* 21 May 1957. *Nationality:* British. *m.* 1985, Mary Elizabeth (née Bookham). *Educ:* Merchant Taylors School, Middx; Polytechnic of The South Bank, London (BA Hons Business Studies). *Professional Organisations:* Member, Institute of Chartered Accountants in England and Wales.

LOCKE, Duncan Francis Gibbs; Associate, Grimley J R Eve, since 1988; Rent Review and Lease Renewal Negotiations. *Career:* Mann & Co, Senior Surveyor 1983-85; Conrad Ritblat & Co 1981-82. *Biog: b.* 4 August 1961. *Nationality:* British. *Educ:* Holy Trinity School, Crawley, West Sussex; Trent Polytechnic (BSc Hons Urban Estate Surveying). *Professional Organisations:* Associate, The Royal Institution of Chartered Surveyors. *Recreations:* Sailing, Skiing, Singing.

LOCKETT, Thomas Ralph Ashley; Foreign Exchange Director, Midland Montagu, since 1987. *Biog: b.* 16 May 1940. *Nationality:* British. *m.* 1962, Margaret Rose (née Dawson); 1 s; 1 d. *Educ:* Reigate Grammar School. *Directorships:* Midland Montagu Treasury Management Ltd 1987; Midland Montagu Osakipankki (Finland). *Other Activities:* Vice Chm, BBA Foreign Exchange Ctee. *Professional Organisations:* ACIB; Forex Assoc. *Clubs:* Overseas Bankers', Greenlands Association. *Recreations:* United Reformed Church, Family, Walking, Gardening.

LOCKHART, Harry Eugene; Chief Executive, Midland Bank plc, since 1988; Group Operations & UK Banking. *Career:* Arthur Andersen & Co, Snr Cons 1974-77; Nolan Norton & Co, Mgng Principal (Europe) 1977-82; C T Bowring & Co, Group Dir, Mgmnt Svcs 1982-85; First Manhattan Consulting Group, Vice Pres 1985-87; Midland Bank plc, Chief Exec, Information Technology 1987; Chief Exec, Group Operations 1988. *Biog: b.* 4 November 1949. *Nationality:* American. *m.* 1974, Terry; 1 s; 3 d. *Educ:* University of Virginia/Darden Graduate Business (Mech Eng, MBA, Cert Public Acct). *Directorships:* Midland Bank plc 1988 (exec); Midland Stockbrokers 1987-90; CHAPS & Town Clearing Co Ltd 1988 (non-exec) Chm; Thomas Cook Group Ltd 1988 Dep Chm wef May 1989; Forward Trust Group 1990 Chm; Mastercard International 1990. *Other Activities:* Member, Royal Academy Advisory Board. *Clubs:* Annabel's, RAC, Vanderbilt, St George's Hill, Liphook. *Recreations:* Tennis, Skiing, All Forms of Sport, Classical Music, Ballet.

LOCKWOOD, David; Divisional Director, Royal Trust Bank.

LOCKWOOD, Graham Henry; Executive Director, Eagle Star Insurance Co Ltd.

LOCKWOOD, Roger P; Vice President, Manufactuures Hanover Trust Co.

LOCKYER, P R; Partner, Clay & Partners, since 1987; Investment. *Career:* Clay & Partners, Actuary 1982-87. *Biog: b.* 29 February 1960. *Nationality:* British. *Educ:* Monmouth School, Gwent; Bristol University (BSc). *Professional Organisations:* Fellow, Institute of Actuaries. *Publications:* Further Applications of Stochastic Investment Models, 1990; The Implementation of Liability Driven Asset Allocations, 1990.

LODER, The Hon Robert; Director, Target Group plc.

LODGE, John Gordon; General Manager, Bradford & Bingley Building Society, since 1987; Development of Branch and Agency Network. *Career:* Bradford & Bingley Building Society 1961-76; Development Mgr 1976-79; Regional Mgr 1979-82; Asst Gen Mgr 1982-87. *Biog: b.* 9 May 1944. *Nationality:* British. *m.* 1967, Diana (née Harrison); 2 s. *Educ:* Bradford Grammar School. *Professional Organisations:* FBIM; Building Societies Institute. *Clubs:* Shipley Golf Club (Treasurer). *Recreations:* Golf, Bridge.

LOEHNIS, Anthony David; CMG; Vice Chairman, SG Warburg & Co, since 1989. *Career:* HM Diplomatic Service 1960-66; J Henry Schroder Wagg & Co Ltd 1967-80; Director 1974-80; Bank of England 1980-89; Seconded as Chief Adviser 1977-79; Associate Director for Overseas Affairs 1980-81; Executive Director for Overseas Affairs 1981-89; S G Warburg Group plc, Director 1989-. *Biog: b.* 12 March 1936. *Nationality:* British. *m.* 1965, Jennifer Forsyth (née Anderson); 3 s. *Educ:* Eton College; New College, Oxford (BA); Harvard School of Public Administration (Frank Knox Fellow). *Other Activities:* Member, Group of Thirty; Director, UK-Japan 2000 Group. *Clubs:* Garrick.

LOFFSTADT, David; Dealing Director, Kleinwort Benson Investment Management Ltd, since 1988; Chief Dealer. *Biog: b.* 23 June 1945. *Nationality:* British. *m.* 1973, Patricia Rose (née Williams); 2 s.

LOFTHOUSE, Peter; Partner, R Watson & Sons.

LOFTHOUSE, Stephen; Chairman, James Capel Fund Managers Ltd; Investment Management. *Career:* Manchester University, Research Associate 1968; Manchester Polytechnic, Snr Lecturer 1969-72; Manchester Business School, Lecturer 1972-75; Industries Assistance Commission, Dir Grade 10 1975; Price Commission, Consultant 1976-77; Capel Cure Myers, Assoc 1977-83; James Capel Group, Director 1983-. *Biog: b.* 23 March 1945. *Nationality:* British. *Educ:* Taunton's Grammar School; University of Manchester (BA Hons Econ, MA Econ). *Directorships:* James Capel & Co 1990 (exec); James Capel Unit Trust Managers Ltd 1988 (non-exec); Wardley Investment Services Ltd 1988 (non-exec). *Publications:* Approximately 50 Articles in Academic and Professional Journals.

LOGAN, Gordon Niall; Partner, Nabarro Nathanson, since 1990; Commercial Property. *Career:* Stanford and Lambert Solicitors (Newcastle Upon Tyne), Articled Clerk 1979-81; Assistant Solicitor 1981-82; British Coal, (Gateshead, Tyne & Wear), Solicitor, Property Section Legal Department 1982-83; Head of Property Section 1983-88; British Coal (Doncaster), Senior Solicitor, Property Group, Legal Department 1988-90. *Biog: b.* 15 May 1957. *Nationality:* British. *m.* 1987, Astrid Rosalind (née Molloy); 1 s. *Educ:* Kings' School, Tynemouth, Tyne and Wear; Leicester University (LLB Hons). *Professional Organisations:* Law Society. *Recreations:* Golf, Cricket.

LOGAN, W Bruce; WS; Partner, W & J Burness WS.

LOIZAGA, J M; Director, Campbell Lutyens Hudson Co Ltd.

LOMAS, John H; Partner, Theodore Goddard.

LOMAS, P F; Group Finance Director, Next plc, since 1986. *Career:* Next plc 1986-; Grattan plc, Fin Dir 1982-87; John Collier Menswear, Fin Dir 1978-82; Timson Shoes Ltd, Fin Dir 1973-78. *Biog: b.* 27 May 1939. *Nationality:* British. *m.* 1963, Ann; 2 s; 2 d. *Directorships:* British Satellite Broadcasting (exec). *Other Activities:* Mount Carmel School (Chm of Governors).

LOMAX, Dr David Frederick; Group Economic Adviser, National Westminster Bank plc, since 1974. *Career:* Federal Reserve Bank of New York 1961; H M Foreign Office 1961-65; H M Department of Economic Affairs 1965-69; National Westminster Bank plc 1969-. *Biog: b.* 25 November 1935. *Nationality:* British. *m.* 1969, Morag (née Pollock); 2 d. *Educ:* Cambridge University (MA Cantab in Maths and Economics); Stanford University, California (MA, PhD in Economics). *Other Activities:* British Invisible Exports Council - LOTIS Committee. *Professional Organisations:* Fellow, Chartered Institute of Bankers. *Publications:* The Euromarkets and International Financial Policies (Jointly with P T Gutmann), 1981; The Developing Country Debt Crisis, 1986; London Markets After the Financial Services Act, 1987. *Clubs:* RAC. *Recreations:* Golf, Bridge.

LONG, David Christopher; Director, Sphere Drake Underwriting Management Limited, since 1990; Non Marine Underwriter. *Career:* Greig Fester Limited, Reinsurance Broker 1975-81; Sphere Drake Underwriting Masnagement Limited, Deputy Pro Rata Treaty Underwriter 1981-82; Deputy X/L Underwriter 1982-87; Senior Treaty Underwriter 1987-89; Director 1990. *Biog: b.* 27 May 1957. *Nationality:* British. *m.* 1987, Sarah.

LONG, Denis Colin; Assistant General Manager, Credit Lyonnais, since 1989; General Banking UK. *Career:* Midland Bank plc, Various Positions 1960-88; General Manager 1986-88; Standard Chartered Bank plc, General Manager 1988-89. *Biog: b.* 15 September 1941. *Nationality:* British. *m.* 1969, Janet Patricia (née O'Brien); 2 s. *Educ:* Cothan Grammar School, Bristol; Administrative Staff College, Henley (GMP); Harvard Business School (AMP). *Professional Organisations:* ACIB. *Clubs:* Overseas Bankers Club.

LONG, J M; Treasury, Burmah Oil Trading Ltd.

LONG, Peter James; Partner, McKenna & Co, since 1984; Construction Law. *Career:* Mckenna & Co, Articled Clerk 1975-77; McKenna & Co (London), Asst Solicitor 1978-81; McKenna & Co (Hong Kong), Asst Solicitor 1981-83; McKenna & Co (Hong Kong), Ptnr 1984-85; McKenna & Co (London), Ptnr 1985-. *Biog: b.* 18 October 1950. *Nationality:* British. *m.* 1976, Trishya (née Tredwell); 3 s. *Educ:* Balliol College, Oxford (BA Literae Humaniores Classics First Class). *Other Activities:* Member, Executive Committee the Markfield Project. *Professional Organisations:* Law Society; Associate, Chartered Institute of Arbitrators. *Recreations:* Music, Hockey.

LONG, William John; Director, National Investment Group plc, since 1986; Group Marketing and Business Development. *Career:* Laing & Cruickshank, Ptnr, Private Clients 1972-79; Milton Mortimer & Co (now part of National Investment Group), Ptnr 1981-86. *Biog: b.*

11 November 1943. *Nationality:* British. *m.* 1969, Sarah (née Lockwood); 2 s; 1 d. *Educ:* Woodbridge School. *Directorships:* Lockwood Foods Ltd 1979-81. *Other Activities:* Served on Earl Marshall's Staff for State Funeral of Sir Winston Churchill, 1966. *Professional Organisations:* Member, The International Stock Exchange; Underwriting Member of Lloyd's. *Recreations:* Fishing, Shooting, Sailing.

LONGDON, John Charles; Partner, Travers Smith Braithwaite; Company Law.

LONGHURST, Andrew Henry; Managing Director, Cheltenham & Gloucester Building Society, since 1982. *Career:* Data Processing Industry, Various 1961-67; Cheltenham & Gloucester Building Society, Various 1967-. *Biog: b.* 23 August 1939. *Nationality:* British. *m.* Margaret. *Educ:* Glyn Grammar School, Epsom; Nottingham University (BSc Hons Mathematics & Statistics). *Directorships:* C & G Financial Services Ltd 1989 (exec) Chairman; C & G Estate Agents Ltd 1988 (exec) Chairman; C & G Channel Islands Ltd 1990 (exec); National Waterways Museum Trust 1989 (non-exec). *Other Activities:* Council Member, Building Societies Association; Executive Committee Member, National House Building Council; Executive Committee Member, Council of Mortgage Lenders; Executive Committee Member, Metropolitan Association of Building Societies. *Professional Organisations:* CBIM; FCBSI; FCS.

LONGRIDGE, David John Ernle; Director, Central Executive, Hill Samuel Bank Limited, since 1985. *Career:* Arthur Young and Co, Paris Office 1963-65; Avis Rent A Car System Inc 1965-81; Chief Executive of International Operations 1975-81; Hill Samuel Bank Limited 1981-; Head of Asset Finance, part of Corporate Finance Division 1981-85; Wood Mackenzie & Co, Finance Director 1985-86; Hill Samuel Bank Limited, Director Central Executive 1986-; Member, Executive Ctee 1986-. *Biog: b.* 15 June 1939. *Nationality:* British. *m.* 1970, Anna (née Watkinson); 2 s. *Educ:* Downside School. *Directorships:* Hill Samuel Bank Limited; The Securities Association. *Other Activities:* Member of the Board, The Securities Association Capital Ctee; Advisory Board, Centre for Strategic Change, Warwick University. *Professional Organisations:* FCA. *Recreations:* Riding.

LONGWORTH, Ian Robert; Director, County NatWest Ltd, since 1987; Responsible for Facilities (Premises, Printing, Messenger, Security). *Biog: b.* 9 June 1948. *Nationality:* British. *m.* 1978, Judy (née Wright); 2 s. *Educ:* Wrekin College; Bath University (BSc Hons). *Recreations:* Tennis, Food, TV, Amdram.

LOOSMORE, Guy; Deputy General Manager Administration, Jyske Bank.

LORD, Alan; CB; Deputy Chairman and Chief Executive, Lloyd's of London, since 1986; Provision of Services (including Regulation) to the Market. *Career:* Inland Revenue 1950-59; HM Treasury 1959-62; Office of First Sec of State, Principal Private Sec 1962-63; Inland Revenue 1963-69; Board of Inland Revenue, Mem 1969; Dep Chm 1971-73; DTI, Principal Fin Officer 1973-75; HM Treasury, Second Permanent Sec 1975-77; Dunlop Holdings, Dir of Corp Planning 1977; Main Board Dir 1978-84; Dunlop International, MD 1978-80; Dunlop Holdings Group, MD & Chief Exec 1980-84. *Biog: b.* 12 April 1929. *Nationality:* British. *m.* 1953, Joan (née Ogden); 2 d. *Educ:* Rochdale Grammar School; St John's College, Cambridge (BA Hons 1st, MA). *Directorships:* Dunlop Ltd 1984 Chm; Dunlop Tyre & Rubber Corp Inc 1984 Chm; Allied Lyons 1979-86 (non-exec); Bank of England 1983-86 (non-exec); Johnson Mathey Bankers 1985-86 (non-exec). *Other Activities:* Past Pres, Johnian Society; Governor, NIESR. *Publications:* A Strategy for Industry, 1977; Earning An Industrial Living, 1985. *Clubs:* Reform. *Recreations:* Reading, Gardening, Rough-Shooting.

LORD, David Gerald; Managing Director, First Interstate Capital Markets Limited, since 1987; Eurocurrency Corporate Finance, Capital Markets & Securities Trading. *Career:* Continental Illinois Ltd 1973-78; Continental Bank VP 1978-81; Continental Illinois Ltd, Assoc Dir 1981-84; First Interstate Capital Markets Ltd, Exec Dir 1986. *Biog: b.* 14 December 1947. *m.* 1978, (Diana) Jennifer (née Benjamin); 1 s; 2 d. *Educ:* Repton; Trinity College, Dublin (BA Hons Econ). *Clubs:* Boodle's, Oriental. *Recreations:* Sailing, Skiing, Golf.

LORD, Ms Hilary Margaret; Partner, Linklaters & Paines, since 1990; Trust Law. *Career:* Pothelary & Barratt, Articled Clerk and Assistant Solicitor 1980-83; Wilde Sapte, Assistant Solicitor 1984-85; Linklaters & Paines, Assistant Solicitor 1985-90. *Biog: b.* 30 March 1958. *Nationality:* British. *Educ:* Walthamstow Hall School; University of Bristol (LLB). *Professional Organisations:* The Law Society. *Publications:* Joint Author, Tolley's Estate Planning (first edition), 1988. *Recreations:* Reading, Travel.

LORD, Peter William; Director, Hoare Govett Corporate Finance Ltd, since 1988; North America, Corporate Finance & Mergers & Acquisitions. *Career:* The Chase Manhattan Bank NA, VP 1970-79; Chase Manhattan Ltd, Exec Dir 1979-81; Chase Manhattan Asia Ltd, Exec Dir 1981-84; Hoare Govett Asia Ltd, MD 1984-88. *Biog: b.* 11 July 1949. *Nationality:* British. *m.* 1979, Caroline (née Evans); 2 s; 1 d. *Educ:* Repton School; Bristol University (Combined Hons). *Clubs:* Boodle's, Oriental, The Hong Kong Club. *Recreations:* Skiing, Golf.

LOREAU, Alain; General Manager, Credit Du Nord, since 1990. *Career:* CIC Paris, Financial Division 1974-79; International Division 1980-83; International Division, Vice President/Head of Far East Dept 1984-88; Credit Du Nord (Paris), International Development Division, First Vice President 1989-90; Credit Du Nord (London), General Manager 1990-. *Biog: b.* 28 December 1947. *Nationality:* French. *Educ:* University of Paris X (BA History); Institut D'Etudes Politiques De Paris (Graduate); University of Paris, Assas (MA Law).

LORENZ, Andrew; Business Editor, Sunday Times Business News.

LORENZINI, P G; Director, Bunzl Plc.

LORIMER, Sir Desmond; Chairman, Northern Bank Ltd, since 1986. *Career:* Harmood, Banner, Smylie & Co, Chartered Accountants, Snr Partner 1960-74. *Biog: b.* 20 October 1925. *Nationality:* British. *m.* 1957, Patricia; 2 d. *Directorships:* Lamont Holdings plc 1973 Chairman; Old Bushmills Distillery Co Ltd 1986 Chairman. *Professional Organisations:* FCA; Companion, British Inst of Management; Fellow, Irish Inst of Management. *Clubs:* Carlton Club (London), Royal County Down Golf Club.

LORING, Anthony Francis; Partner, McKenna & Co, since 1988; Mergers & Acquisitions, Corporate Insolvency. *Career:* Coward Chance, Articled Clerk 1977-79; Asst Solicitor 1979-83; Mills & Reeve, Asst Solicitor 1984; McKenna & Co, Asst Solicitor 1985-88; Ptnr in Bahrain 1988-90; Ptnr in London 1990. *Biog: b.* 10 October 1954. *Nationality:* British. *Educ:* Ampleforth College; Bedford College (BA). *Professional Organisations:* Law Society England & Wales.

LOSSE, Dieter Ronald; Chief Executive, Greig Fester Ltd, since 1988; Reinsurance Broking. *Career:* Swiss Reinsurance Company (Zurich) Translator/Correspondent 1959-67. *Biog: b.* 23 June 1937. *m.* 1963, Lesley Jean (née Cunningham); 3 d. *Educ:* Enfield Grammar School; Queens' College, Cambridge (MA). *Directorships:* Greig Fester Group Limited (exec); Greig Fester (Agencies) Ltd (exec); JFS Greig Fester Ltd (exec); Eton End School Trust (Datchet) Ltd Chm. *Other Activities:* LIBC (Member); Brokers' Reinsurance Ctee (Chm 1988 and 1990). *Professional Organisations:* Chartered Insurance Institute. *Recreations:* The Arts, Fishing, Racing.

LOUDON, George Ernest; Director, Midland Bank plc, since 1988; Chief Executive, Midland Montagu. *Career:* Lazard Freres & Cie, Paris 1967-68; Ford Foundation, New York/Jakarta 1968-71; McKinsey & Co, Amsterdam 1971-76; Amsterdam-Rotterdam Bank NV, Amsterdam 1976-88. *Biog: b.* 19 November 1942. *Nationality:* Dutch. *m.* 1968, Angela Mary (née Goldsbrough); 1 s; 1 d. *Educ:* Christlijk Lyceum, Zeist,

The Netherlands; Balliol College, Oxford (BA); John Hopkins University, Washington DC (MA). *Directorships:* Midland Bank plc; Midland Montagu Ltd; Samuel Montagu & Co Ltd; Midland Bank SA (France); Trinkaus und Burkhardt (Germany); Euromobiliare (Italy); Geveke NV (The Netherlands); Oriental Art Magazine Ltd.

LOUDON, J; Director, Capability Trust Managers Limited.

LOUDON, John David; Director, Greenwell Montagu Stockbrokers, since 1986; Marketing & Compliance. *Career:* Peat Marwick Mitchell, Auditor 1974-80; W Greenwell & Co, Assistant to Financial & Administration Partner 1980-82; Smith Keen Cutler, Partner then Director 1982-89. *Biog: b.* 19 August 1956. *Nationality:* British. *m.* 1988, Catherine Sarah (née Ward). *Educ:* Kenilworth Grammar School; Lanchester Polytechnic. *Directorships:* Greenwell Montagu Stockbrokers and other Group Companies. *Other Activities:* Vice President, Meriden Conservative Association; Chairman, Arthritis & Rheumatism Council (West Midlands); Finance Officer, Midlands Central Euro Constituency; Member, Birmingham Stock Exchange Committee. *Professional Organisations:* The International Stock Exchange. *Clubs:* Ardencote. *Recreations:* Country Sports, Politics, Gardening.

LOUGH, R C; Director, Kleinwort Benson Limited, since 1990; Banking. *Biog: b.* 19 November 1957. *Nationality:* British. *m.* 1978, Janice; 2 d. *Educ:* University of London (BA). *Clubs:* Canning Club.

LOUGHBOROUGH, Derek Ralph; *Career:* Sun Life Assurance Society Mgr 1943-77; Post Office Insurance Society Sec/Chief Exec 1977-88. *Biog: b.* 5 March 1927. *Nationality:* British. *m.* 1951, Hazel (née Benn); 2 s. *Directorships:* Lautro Ltd 1987 (non-exec); POIS Trustees Ltd 1978-88 Sec (exec); POIS Staff Superannuation Scheme Trustees Ltd 1978-88 Sec (exec). *Other Activities:* Councillor, London Borough. *Professional Organisations:* ACII; APMI; MBIM.

LOUGHNEY, G A; Director, Rutland Trust plc.

LOUTREL, C; Non-Executive Director, Laporte plc.

LOVE, Charles Marshall; Regional Director, Northern Region & Chief Executive, TSB Bank Scotland plc, since 1990. *Career:* TSB Group, Dep Gen Mgr (Marketing) 1980-83; TSB England and Wales plc, Reg Gen Mgr 1983-86; Gen Mgr, Financial Services 1986-87; TSB England & Wales plc, Exec Director 1988-89; Managing Director, Property & Mortgage Services 1988-89; TSB Bank plc, Managing Director, Banking Services 1989-90; Regional Director, Northern Region; TSB Bank Scotland plc, Chief Executive 1990-. *Biog: b.* 27 October 1945. *Nationality:* British. *m.* 1968, June

Alexandra (née Dyball); 1 s; 1 d. *Educ:* Musselburgh Grammar School. *Directorships:* TSB Bank Scotland plc 1990 (exec); TSB Scotland Asset Finance Limited Chairman; Scottish Business In The Community (non-exec). *Other Activities:* Member, The City Ctee of National Children's Homes; Member, Rotary International; Member, CBI Scottish Council. *Professional Organisations:* Fellow, Chartered Institute of Bankers; Associate of the Institute of Bankers (Scotland); Member, Chartered Institute of Marketing. *Clubs:* RAC. *Recreations:* Reading, Music, Theatre.

LOVEDAY, Mark Antony; Partner, Cazenove & Co.

LOVELAND, Mark Jeremy Stephen; Head of UK/European Electronics, Telephone Networks Team, S G Warburg Securities, since 1981. *Biog: b.* 6 April 1954. *Educ:* Eltham College; Oxford University (BA). *Recreations:* Electronics Sector.

LOVELAND, R A; Partner, Penningtons.

LOVELESS, J A; Finance Director, Wendover Underwriting Agency Limited.

LOVELL, Christopher H; Partner (Resident in Jersey), Theodore Goddard.

LOVERD, Robert D; Executive Director, Crédit Suisse First Boston Limited.

LOVERING, John David; Finance Director, Sears plc, since 1988. *Career:* Metal Box, Commercial Executive Export Sales 1971-73; Spillers, Corporate Development Executive Planning Manager, International Division 1975-78; Lex Service, Financial Planning Manager, Corporate Strategy Manager 1978-82; Grand Metropolitan, Finance Director Retail Division, Commercial Director Express Foods 1982-85; Imperial Group, Group Financial Planning Manager 1985-86; Sears plc, Finance Director 1986-90. *Biog: b.* 11 October 1949. *Nationality:* British. *m.* 1971, Brenda; 2 s; 1 d. *Educ:* Dulwich College; Exeter University (BA Hons Economics); Manchester Business School (MBA). *Directorships:* Sears plc 1988 (exec). *Publications:* Various Articles on Planning & Financial Management. *Recreations:* Sport, Family, Model Trains.

LOVETT, I; Managing Director, Dunbar Bank plc, since 1984. *Career:* Barclays Bank plc, Sloane Square Business Advisory Service, Manager Small Business Unit 1968-84. *Biog: b.* 7 September 1944. *Nationality:* British. *m.* 1969, Patricia; 2 d. *Educ:* Selhurst Grammar School; University of Wales (BA Hons). *Directorships:* Allied Dunbar Bank International 1984 (exec); Allied Dunbar Leasing Limited 1984 (exec); Allied Dunbar Provident plc 1986 (exec); Dunbar Financial Services Limited 1984 (exec); Dunbar Group plc 1984 (exec); Dunbar Nominees Limited 1984 (exec); Dunbar Pensions Limited

1984 (exec). *Professional Organisations:* Fellow, Chartered Institute of Bankers. *Clubs:* MCC. *Recreations:* Cricket, Comedy.

LOVICK, Sara; Partner, Cameron Markby Hewitt.

LOW, Alistair James; Executive Director, William M Mercer Fraser Ltd, since 1986; Employee Benefits Consultancy. *Career:* Duncan C Fraser & Co Ptnr 1967-86. *Biog: b.* 2 August 1942. *m.* 1966, Shona Petricia (née Wallace); 2 s; 1 d. *Educ:* Dundee High School; St Andrews University (BSc). *Directorships:* Scottish Widows Fund & Life Assurance Society 1983 (non-exec). *Other Activities:* Royal & Ancient Golf Club (Chm, Championship Ctee). *Professional Organisations:* FFA, AIA, FPMI. *Clubs:* New Club (Edinburgh). *Recreations:* Golf, Skiing.

LOW, The Hon Charles; General Manager, Deutsche Bank AG, since 1988; Full Executive Responsibilty for the Branch. *Career:* Citibank NA (New York, Hong Kong & Duesseldorf), Account Officer Multintional Clients 1971-77; Grindlay's Bank plc, Ship Finance Officer, Joint Head Ship Finance Department 1978-82; Director, Corporate Banking 1982-83; Director, Continental Europe 1983-86; Deutsche Bank AG (Duisburg) Director 1986-87. *Biog: b.* 22 June 1948. *Nationality:* British. *m.* 1989, Dr Regine Low (née von Schopf). *Educ:* Winchester College; New College, Oxford (BA Hons); INSEAD (MBA). *Directorships:* Orbwise Ltd. *Other Activities:* Trustee, English International; Trustee, Friends of the Orchestra of St John's; Liveryman, Grocers' Company.

LOWE, C R; Partner, Holman Fenwick & Willan.

LOWE, D L; Managing Director, Tullett & Tokyo Forex International Ltd.

LOWE, D M; Head of Commercial Litigation Department/Partner, Field Fisher Waterhouse, since 1980; Commercial Litigation. *Career:* Kidd Rapinet Badge, Assistant Solicitor 1974-75; Kingsley Napley & Co, Solicitor 1976-78; Partner 1978-80. *Biog: b.* 17 June 1948. *Nationality:* British. *m.* 1975, Christine Anne Elizabeth; 2 d. *Educ:* Monkton Combe School; University of Kent (BA Hons). *Other Activities:* Member, Association Internationale des Jeunes Avocats; Member, Commonwealth Lawyers Association; Member, British Polish Legal Association; Member, British-Czechoslovak Law Assoc; Associate, Chartered Institute of Arbitrators; Founder Member, European Users Council, London Court of International Arbitration; Member, Society of Construction Law; Supporting Member, London Maritime Arbitrators Assoc. *Recreations:* Flying, Music, Squash, Tennis.

LOWE, Stanley Charles; Technical Director, Memaco Services Ltd, since 1984; Metallurgical Techni-

cal Services, Technical Sales, ZCCM Mine Liason, Representation Internationally. *Career:* Imperial Chemical Industries (Metals Div) Technical Plant Supervision 1947-; Mgr, All Aspects of Non-Ferrous Metals Technology -1961; Rio Tinto Corporation Development Engineer 1961-64; RTZ Ltd Development Engineer 1964-67; Anglo American Corporation Charter Consolidated Anmer Co SA Sales Tech Dir 1967-74; Memaco Services Ltd Tech Dir 1974-. *Biog: b.* 26 July 1926. *Nationality:* British. *m.* 1951, Phyllis (née Reardon); 2 s; 2 d. *Educ:* Bridge Trust School, Birmingham; University of London (CEng, BSc, AIM). *Directorships:* Memaco Trading Inc 1988 (non-exec); London Metal Exchange 1987 (exec). *Other Activities:* Vice Chm, Copper Development Association. *Professional Organisations:* Member, Institute of Metals; Member, Institute of Mining & Metallurgy. *Recreations:* Choral Music, Sail Cruising, Lawn Bowls, Cabinet Making.

LOWES, David John; Director, Robert Fleming & Co Ltd, since 1987; Corporate Finance. *Career:* Sydenham & Co, Trainee Chartered Acct 1971-77; Robert Fleming & Co Ltd, Corp Fin Exec 1978-84; Eberstadt Fleming Inc, Corp Fin VP 1984-87. *Biog: b.* 25 June 1952. *m.* 1983, Caroline (née Baily); 1 s; 1 d. *Educ:* Eton College. *Other Activities:* Ironmongers' Company. *Professional Organisations:* FCA. *Recreations:* Shooting, Photography, Classical Music.

LOWES, M J; Partner, Pensions (Epsom), Bacon & Woodrow.

LOWRIE, Anthony Carmel; Chairman International Securities, Hoare Govett, since 1986; Equities and Trading Asia & Europe. *Career:* British Army (Gurkhas) Major 1962-73. *Biog: b.* 24 March 1942. *Nationality:* British. *m.* 1969, Liv Torill Lowrie (née Ronningen); 1 s; 1 d. *Educ:* Llewellyn School, Rhodesia; RMA Sandhurst. *Directorships:* Hoare Govett International Securities Limited 1986; HGIS Nominees Limited 1989; Security Pacific Hoare Govett (Holdings) Limited 1987; J D Wetherspoon Ltd 1985 (non-exec); Hoare Govett Asia (exec); Superchalet Ltd (non-exec) Chm; Thai-Euro Fund Ltd; City Wine Bars Ltd; The Singapore SESDAQ Fund Ltd; The Malaysian Emerging Companies Fund; The Scottish Asian Investment Co. Ltd. *Clubs:* The Addington Golf Club, Walton Heath Golf Club. *Recreations:* Golf, Swimming.

LOYD, D W A; Director, Kleinwort Benson Ltd.

LOYNES, John H; Director, Continental Reinsurance London.

LUBOFF, M E; Director, Kleinwort Benson Investment Management Limited, since 1990; Treasury Services Dept. *Career:* Arthur Anderson & Co, Audit Senior 1979-84; Chloride Group plc, Assistant Group Treasurer 1984-86; Kleinwort Benson Group 1986-; Director

1990-. *Biog: b.* 26 May 1957. *Nationality:* British. *m.* 1984, Susan; 1 s; 1 d. *Educ:* Dulwich College; Reading University (Economics & Politics IIi). *Directorships:* Kleinwort Benson Investment Management Limited 1990 (exec); Mortgage Funding Corporation plc 1990 (exec). *Professional Organisations:* ACA (ICAEW), 1983. *Recreations:* Second Property in Normandy, France, Wine Tasting.

LUCAS, Jeremy Charles Belgrave; Director, Morgan Grenfell & Co Ltd, since 1986; Corporate Finance. *Career:* Denton, Hall, Burgin & Warrens, Articled Clerk 1974-76; Asst Solicitor 1976-78. *Biog: b.* 10 August 1952. *m.* 1976, Monica (née Ball); 2 s. *Educ:* Stowe School; Pembroke College, Cambridge (MA). *Clubs:* Royal West Norfolk Golf Club. *Recreations:* Golf, Tennis.

LUCAS-TOOTH, Sir John; Director, Chartfield & Co Limited.

LUCK, Christopher Alan; Partner, Nabarro Nathanson, since 1985; Corporate Finance & Commercial Matters. *Career:* Boodle Hatfield & Co, Articles, Assistant Solicitor 1981-85; Nabarro Nathanson, Solicitor & Partner 1985-. *Biog: b.* 23 April 1959. *Nationality:* British. *m.* 1987, Susan Jane (née Hatt). *Educ:* Northampton Grammar School; Kings College, London (LLB Hons). *Professional Organisations:* The Law Society. *Recreations:* Tennis, Squash, Cricket.

LUCK, G Anton; Partner, MacNair Mason.

LUCKHOO, K R L; Marketing Manager, The Life Association of Scotland Ltd, since 1990; Mortgages and Investment. *Career:* Barrister at Law, Private Practice 1973-75; Towry Law & Co, Legal Assistant 1976-77; Neville Russell (Chartered Accountants), Financial Planning Manager 1977-81; Life Association of Scotland, Technical Services Manager, Unit-Linked Development Manager, Corporate Development Manager, Marketing Manager 1982-. *Biog: b.* 13 May 1951. *Nationality:* British. *m.* 1974, Jane (née Savige); 3 s. *Educ:* Bloxham School, Nr Banbury, Oxon; King's College, London (LLB Honours London). *Directorships:* LAS Unit Trust Managers Ltd 1987 (exec); LAS Investment Management Ltd 1988 (exec); LAS Nominees Ltd 1990 (exec). *Other Activities:* PCC, St Annes, Kew, Surrey. *Professional Organisations:* Barrister at Law; Member, the Middle Temple. *Recreations:* Golf.

LUCKHURST, Raymond C; Operations Manager, Mellon Bank NA.

LUDER, I D; Tax Partner, Arthur Andersen, since 1989; Personal Tax & Financial Planning. *Career:* Arthur Andersen & Co, Tax Articled Clerk-Tax Manager 1971-78; Macintyre Hudson, Tax Partner 1978-88; Arthur Andersen & Co, Tax Associate-Tax Partner 1988-. *Biog:*

b. 13 April 1951. *Nationality:* British. *m.* 1984, Elizabeth Jane (née Gledhill); 1 s; 1 d. *Educ:* The Haberdashers' Aske's School, Elstree; University College, London (BSc Econ). *Other Activities:* Council Member & Hon Treasurer, Institute of Taxation. *Professional Organisations:* FCA, FTII. *Clubs:* MCC. *Recreations:* Music, Politics.

LUDERS, Richard Charles; Deputy Chairman, Abtrust Management Ltd, Aberdeen Fund Managers Ltd, Country Gentlemens Association, Aberdeen Trust Holdings plc, since 1989; Management of 3 Subsidiaries of Holding Company in London Office. *Career:* Local Authorities Mutual Investment Fund, Investment Accountant 1962-69; Pan Australian Unit Trust, Investment Director 1969-74; Picadilly Unit Trust Management, Investment Admin Director 1975-78; Aitken Hume, Managing Director of Unit Trust Co 1978-88; Aberdeen Trust Holdings, Managing Director of Unit Trust Co (Sentinel Funds) 1988. *Biog: b.* 21 March 1935. *Nationality:* British. *m.* 1958, Elizabeth Marion (née Pendrill); 2 s; 1 d. *Educ:* Pitmans College (Business Diploma). *Directorships:* Abtrust Management Ltd 1988 (non-exec) Deputy Chairman; Aberdeen Fund Managers Ltd 1990 (exec) Deputy Chairman; Country Gentlemen's Association 1988 (exec) Deputy Chairman; CGA Insurance Brokers Ltd 1989 (exec) Deputy Chairman; CGA Accountancy Ltd 1989 (exec) Deputy Chairman; CGA Financial & Investment Services Ltd 1989 (exec) Deputy Chairman. *Publications:* Article in Unit Trust Industry Review & Directory. *Recreations:* Investment, Gardening, Wild Life, Tennis.

LUETZOW, Hagen Helmuth; Senior Vice President, Smith Barney, Harris Upham & Co Inc, since 1990. *Career:* Hallgarten & Co (New York, Brussels, London), Partner 1965-74; Kuhn Loeb & Co (London), Vice President 1975-78. *Biog: b.* 20 May 1941. *Nationality:* German. *m.* 1971, Gunilla (née Paulsson); 1 s; 2 d. *Recreations:* Tennis, Golf, Fishing, Shooting, Travel.

LUKES, N T; Executive Director, Lazard Brothers & Co Limited.

LUMB, P G; Information Systems Director, Leeds Permanent Building Society.

LUMLEY, Henry Robert Lane; Chairman, Edward Lumley Holdings Ltd, since 1985. *Career:* Edward Lumley & Sons Limited, Director 1956-88; Chairman 1985-88; Edward Lumley Holdings Limited, Director 1974-; Chairman 1986-. *Biog: b.* 29 December 1930. *Nationality:* British. *m.* 1959, Sheena Ann (née Shearer); 2 s; 1 d. *Educ:* Eton College; Magdalene College, Cambridge (MA). *Directorships:* British Insurance and Investment Brokers Association 1990 Chairman. *Other Activities:* Nationally Elected Member, Insurance Brokers Registration Council. *Professional Organisations:* Insurance Broker. *Clubs:* East India. *Recreations:* Walking, Farming.

LUMSDEN, David Malcolm; Director, Henry Cooke Lumsden plc, since 1973; Managing Director, London Office. *Career:* Scots Guards Capt 1949-55; Lumsden & Co Ptnr 1955-73. *Biog: b.* 10 November 1930. *m.* 1959, Joanna Mary (née Cooke); 2 s; 2 d. *Educ:* Eton College. *Professional Organisations:* Member, The International Stock Exchange (Domestic Equity Rules and Compliance Committee). *Clubs:* Turf, City of London, Pratt's, HDYC, RYS. *Recreations:* Sailing, Skiing, Shooting.

LUMSDEN, Ian George; Partner, Maclay Murray & Spens, since 1980; Company/Commercial Law. *Career:* Maclay Murray & Spens, Trainee & Asst 1974-78; Slaughter and May, Asst 1978-80. *Biog: b.* 19 March 1951. *Nationality:* British. *m.* 1978, Dr Mary Ann (née Welbon); 1 s; 2 d. *Educ:* Rugby School; Corpus Christi College, Cambridge (BA Hons); Edinburgh University (LLB). *Professional Organisations:* Law Society of Scotland; Royal Faculty of Procurators, Glasgow. *Clubs:* New Club (Edinburgh), Prestwick Golf Club. *Recreations:* Golf, Shooting.

LUND, A; Senior Adviser, Norinchukin International Ltd, since 1989; General. *Career:* Articled Clerk, Price Waterhouse 1949-51; Associate, Kuhn Loeb & Co 1952-57; Investment Officer, International Finance Corp 1958-61; VP, Kuhn Loeb & Co 1961-66; Partner, Kuhn Loeb & Co 1966-77; Managing Director, Lehman Brothers, Kuhn Loeb 1977-84; Managing Director, Shearson, Lehman Brothers 1984-86; Chief Executive, EBC Amro Bank Ltd 1986-89; Senior Adviser, Norinchukin International 1989-. *Biog: b.* 24 September 1929. *Nationality:* British. *m.* 1967, Sophie (née Soumarokoff-Elston); 2 d. *Educ:* Eton College. *Other Activities:* Membership Committee, TSA. *Clubs:* White's. *Recreations:* Shooting, Tennis, Various.

LUNGOCI, F; Managing Director/General Manager, Anglo-Romanian Bank.

LUPSON, Ian; Partner, Gouldens.

LUPTON, James Roger Crompton; Director, Baring Brothers & Co Ltd, since 1986; Corporate Finance. *Career:* Lovell White & King 1977-79; S G Warburg & Co Ltd Exec 1979-80. *Biog: b.* 15 June 1955. *Nationality:* British. *m.* 1983, Beatrice Marie (née Delaunay); 2 d. *Educ:* Sedbergh School; Lincoln College, Oxford (Law). *Other Activities:* Member, CBI Under-35s \$Vision 2010\$ Group. *Professional Organisations:* The Law Society. *Recreations:* Music, Windsurfing.

LUPTON, Martin Neil; Director in Charge of Market Making, Kleinwort Benson Securities Limited, since 1987; In Charge of Electricals, Kleinwort's Best Automated Dealing. *Career:* Wedd Durlacher Mordaunt, Ptnr 1984-86. *Biog: b.* 5 August 1953. *Nationality:* British; 1 s. *Educ:* Belfairs High School. *Directorships:* Kleinwort

Benson Securities 1987. *Clubs:* Cannon's Sports Club. *Recreations:* Swimming.

LUST, G; Partner, Nabarro Nathanson.

LUSTY, C E; Director, Williams De Broe plc; Eurobond Broking. *Career:* Mitsubishi Finance International Ltd, General Manager 1983-84; Citibank Canada, Vice President 1982-83; Citicorp International, Vice President 1978-82. *Biog: b.* 10 May 1940. *Nationality:* Canadian. *m.* 1966, Diane; 2 d. *Educ:* Sir William Romneys School, Tetbury. *Directorships:* Williams De Broe plc 1990 (exec). *Clubs:* Crowborough Beacon Golf Club. *Recreations:* Golf, Tennis.

LUTER, B R F; Senior Vice President, Bank of Novia Scotia.

LUTLEY, Andrew John; Partner, Lovell White Durrant, since 1980; Company/Commercial. *Career:* Durrant Piesse, Solicitor 1976. *Biog: b.* 17 March 1951. *Nationality:* British. *m.* 1980, Hilary Margaret (née Wilson); 2 d. *Educ:* KCS, Wimbledon; Emmanuel College, Cambridge (MA). *Professional Organisations:* Law Society; IBA. *Clubs:* RAC. *Recreations:* Flying, Genealogy.

LUTOLF, Dr F J; Director, Sedgwick Group plc.

LUTYENS, D L P; Director, Fleming Private Asset Management Limited.

LUTYENS, Richard David; Director, Campbell Lutyens & Co.

LUTZ, Alfred; Director, Central Europe Region, Merrill Lynch Europe Limited.

LYBURN, Andrew Usherwood; General Manager (Administration), The Standard Life Assurance Company.

LYDALL, I R; Administration Director, Stirling Hendry & Co.

LYES, Jeffrey; Chairman & Managing Director, Good Relations Limited, since 1989. *Career:* Journalist 1963-69; Hertford PR Ltd, Executive 1969-70; Heart of England Newspapers, News Editor 1970-73; Thames Valley Police, Public Relations Officer 1973-78; J Walter Thompson, PR Director 1978-81; Granard Communications, Deputy MD 1981-85; Good Relations Technology, MD 1985-86; Good Relations Consumer, MD 1986-87; Good Relations Corporate Communications, MD 1986-87; Good Relations Ltd, MD 1988-89. *Biog: b.* 19 April 1946. *Nationality:* British. *m.* 1968, Jan (née Armstrong); 2 d. *Educ:* The Grammar School, Daventry; Technical College, Harlow (NCTJ). *Directorships:* Lowe Bell Communications Ltd 1989 (exec); Good Relations Ltd 1987 (exec); Community Media Ltd 1989 (non-exec); AMRA 1986-89 (non-exec). *Professional Organisations:* MIPR; FBIM; FIOD. *Recreations:* River/Sea Cruising.

LYGO, Admiral Sir Raymond; KGB; Director, James Capel Corporate Finance Ltd, since 1990; Aerospace. *Career:* The Times 1940; RN, Naval Airman 1942; HMS Ark Royal, CO 1969-71; Vice Chief Naval Staff 1975-78; British Aerospace, MD, Hatfield/Lostock Div 1978-79; Group Dep Chm 1980; Dynamics Gp, Chm and Chief Exec 1980-82; BAe Inc, Chairman 1983-88; Member of Supervisory Airbus Industries 1987-89; British Aerospace plc, MD 1983-86; Chief Executive 1986-89; Board Member 1980-89; BAe Enterprise Ltd, Chairman; BAe (Space Systems) Ltd; BAe Holdings Inc 1988-89. *Biog:* m. 1950, Pepper Van Osten; 2 s; 1 d. *Directorships:* London & Edinburgh Trust 1990 (non-exec); ESTA 1990 (non-exec) Chairman. *Other Activities:* Coachmaker, Shipwrights, City Livery; CBI Education Foundation; President of Appeal Ctee, SENSE; Council Member, Industrial Soc. *Professional Organisations:* Hon FRAES; Hon Fellow, PCL; FBIM; FRSA. *Clubs:* Royal Naval and Royal Albert, Les Ambassadeurs, RAC. *Recreations:* Building, Gardening, Flying, Joinery.

LYLE, David Angus; Director/Company Secretary, Scottish Enterprise, since 1990; Secretariat, Legal and Corporate Services. *Career:* Lloyds and Scottish Finance Ltd Edinburgh, Solicitor 1969-70; East Lothian County Council, Deputy County Clerk 1971-74; Dumfries and Galloway Regional Council, Director of Administration and Law 1975-79; Scottish Development Agency, Agency Secretary 1980-90. *Biog:* b. 7 September 1940. *Nationality:* Scottish. m. 1969, Dorothy Ann (née Clark); 1 s; 3 d. *Educ:* George Watson's College, Edinburgh; Edinburgh University (MA, LLB). *Directorships:* Scottish Development Finance Ltd 1982 (non-exec). *Professional Organisations:* Member, Law Society of Scotland; Fellow, The Institute of Directors; Fellow, British Institute of Management; Solicitor to the Supreme Courts of Scotland; Fellow, Chartered Institute of Secretaries; Fellow, Institute of Administrative Management. *Clubs:* RSAC Glasgow. *Recreations:* Country Sports, Golf, Bridge.

LYLE, James Robert Bryan; Vice President, Morgan Stanley Asset Managment, since 1989; European Equity Fund Management. *Career:* Research Officer, Center For Business Strategy, London Business School 1983-85; Fund Manager (European Equities), Morgan Stanley Asset Management 1985-. *Biog:* b. 31 July 1961. *Nationality:* British. *Educ:* Charterhouse; St. Edmund Hall, Oxford.

LYLE, Nicholas Roger; Partner, Touche Ross & Co, since 1990; Corporate Recovery and Insolvency. *Career:* Grant Thornton, Trainee Acct 1960-65; Peat Marwick McLintock, Supervising Snr 1965-68; Grant Thornton, Mgr 1968-69; Ptnr 1969-88; Spicer & Oppenheim, Ptnr 1988-90; Touche Ross & Co, Ptnr 1990-. *Biog:* b. 30 October 1942. *Nationality:* British. *Educ:* Bedford School. *Professional Organisations:* FCA; Insolvency Practitioners' Assoc; Institute of Credit Management. *Clubs:* Woburn Golf & Country Club. *Recreations:* Shooting, Golf, Breeding Ornamental Waterfowl.

LYLE, R A W; Director, Berry Palmer & Lyle Ltd.

LYLE, Timothy John Abram; Director of Corporate Finance, Livingstone Fisher plc, since 1990; Advice on Acquisitions, Disposals & Management Buyouts. *Career:* Ernst & Whinney, Auditor 1981-85; Lombard North Central plc, Special Projects Manager Involved in Acquisitions and Joint Ventures 1985-87; The Union International plc, Corporate Development Executive Responsible for Completing Several Acquisitions and Disposals 1987-89; Livingstone Fisher plc 1989-. *Biog:* b. 25 April 1961. *Nationality:* British. *Professional Organisations:* Member, Institute of Chartered Accountants in England and Wales. *Clubs:* RAC, MCC. *Recreations:* Both Playing & Watching Wide Range of Sports, Listening to Music, Reading.

LYMBRY, Judge Robert; Common Serjeant, Corporation of London.

LYNCH, C F; Director, Macey Williams Ltd.

LYNCH, R Vincent; Managing Director, J P Morgan & Co (or Morgan Guaranty), since 1988; Corporate Finance. *Career:* J P Morgan (London) 1985-; J P Morgan (Milan, Italy), Head of Italian Banking Division 1982-85; J P Morgan (New York), Various Corporate Finance/Banking Positions 197-82. *Biog:* b. 18 July 1950. *Nationality:* American. m. 1975, Rebecca H (née Hathaway); 1 s; 2 d. *Educ:* Princeton University (Bachelor of Arts).

LYNCH-BELL, Michael David; Audit Partner, Ernst & Young, since 1985; Group Audit Partner (Personnel Aspects), Business Development Partner (Natural Resources), Contact Partner, Ernst & Young Energy Business Centre. *Career:* UK, Intl and Overseas Oil & Gas Industry Clients 1974-. *Biog:* b. 12 May 1953. *Nationality:* British. m. 1976, Jane Elizabeth (née Rushbrook); 2 s; 1 d. *Educ:* Quarry Bank School, Liverpool; University of Sheffield (BA Economics/Accountancy). *Other Activities:* Member, Institute of Petroleum. *Professional Organisations:* Fellow, Institute of Chartered Accountants of England and Wales.

LYNESS, John F; Managing Director, Merrill Lynch International Limited.

LYNN, George; Group Finance Director, The Union Discount Company of London plc, since 1990; Group

Accounting and Finance. *Career:* Deloitte Haskins & Sells, Accountant 1976-83; Highland Leasing Ltd, Group Chief Accountant 1981-83; Baltic plc, Finance Executive 1983; Union Discount Finance & Leasing, Chief Accountant 1983-86; The Union Discount Company of London plc, Group Accountant 1986. *Biog: b.* 3 July 1955. *Nationality:* British. *m.* 1976, Elizabeth (née Muspratt); 2 s; 1 d. *Educ:* Bromley Grammar School; Hull University (BSc). *Directorships:* Union Discount Company Ltd 1987 (exec); Union Discount Finance & Leasing 1986 (exec); Herald Financial Services 1988 (exec); Sabre Leasing Ltd 1988 (exec). *Other Activities:* Equipment Leasing Assoc (Member, Tax Ctee). *Professional Organisations:* FCA.

LYNN, R J F; Associate Director, Brewin Dolphin & Co Ltd.

LYNN, Timothy; Director, Samuel Montagu & Co Ltd, since 1989; LDC Asset Trading & Arbitrage. *Career:* Libra Bank plc, Assistant General Manager (Brazil) 1979-87. *Biog: b.* 8 May 1951. *Nationality:* British.

LYON, (Colin) Stewart (Sinclair); Non-Executive Director, Aetna International (UK) Ltd.

LYON, Jeremy Malcolm; Director, County NatWest Securities; Market Making, Liaison. *Career:* Partner, Pinghin Denny & Co (Jobbers) 1971-86; Director, Morgan Grenfell Sec 1986-89. *Biog: b.* 16 February 1942. *Nationality:* British. *m.* 1963, Hannah (née Vaizey); 1 s; 3 d. *Educ:* King's School, Worcester. *Directorships:* County NatWest Securities 1989. *Other Activities:* Liveryman, Dyers Company. *Professional Organisations:* Member of London Stock Exchange since 1966. *Recreations:* Tennis, Sailing.

LYON, Richard W; Director, Merrill Lynch Europe Limited.

LYONS, Derek Jack; Executive Director, Union Discount Co of London plc, since 1982; Domestic & International Money Markets. *Career:* A C Goode Group of Companies (Melbourne), Mgr 1970-71. *Biog: b.* 5 December 1943. *Nationality:* British. 1982, Philippa Kate (née Rundle); 1 s; 1 steps; 1 stepd. *Educ:* Cranleigh School. *Directorships:* Union Discount Futures Co Ltd 1985 (non-exec). *Other Activities:* London Business School Alumni. *Professional Organisations:* Institute of Bankers. *Clubs:* Roehampton. *Recreations:* Sport, Walking.

LYONS, Michael; Director, Wise Speke Ltd.

LYONS, Robert W; Senior Manager, Amsterdam Rotterdam Bank NV, since 1990; Operations and Administration. *Career:* International Bank of Asia (Hong Kong) General Mgr, Retail Banking Division/Division Head, Operations 1985-90; First National Bank of

Chicago, Vice President Area Operations-Asia Pacific 1973-85. *Biog: b.* 21 September 1948. *Nationality:* American. *m.* 1989, Razzia. *Educ:* Northern Illinois University (BS Finance). *Recreations:* Tennis, Clay Target Shooting.

LYONS, Thomas Colvill Holmes (Toby); Deputy Chairman & Managing Director, Minster Trust Ltd, since 1973; Corporate Finance & Investment Management. *Career:* Royal Welch Fusiliers, Lt 1956-58; Linklaters & Paines, Solicitor 1964-66; Allen & Overy, Solicitor 1966-69; Minster Trust Ltd, Exec Corp Fin 1969-72. *Biog: b.* 8 March 1937. m1 1966, Heather Mary Menzies (née Forbes) (div 1971); m2 1972, Gwendolin Frances (née Gosling); 1 s 3 d. *Educ:* Harrow School; Oriel College, Oxford (MA). *Directorships:* Monument Oil and Gas plc 1984 (non-exec); R & J Hadlee plc 1985 (non-exec) Chm; Minster Assets plc (exec). *Other Activities:* Assistant, Tinplate Workers' Company. *Professional Organisations:* The Law Society. *Recreations:* Shooting, Skiing, Countryside Conservation.

LYSTER, Rae Lionel Haggard; Partner, Cazenove & Co, since 1961. *Biog: b.* 24 August 1931. *Nationality:* British. *m.* 1958, Julia Elizabeth (née Scott-Plummer); 1 s; 2 d. *Educ:* Bradfield College; Trinity College, Cambridge (BA). *Other Activities:* Reed's School (Governor & Hon Treasurer); Perry Watlington Trust (Chm). *Clubs:* Boodle's, City of London. *Recreations:* Shooting, Fishing, Golf.

LYTTELTON, The Hon Christopher Charles; Chief Executive, NCL Investments Ltd.

M

MABERLY, M A; Director, Lombard North Central plc, since 1989; Business Finance; Managing Director, Lombard Business Finance Limited, since 1990. *Career:* Shell International Petroleum Co, Managing Director 1957-63; International Factors Limited, New Business Manager 1963-67; Sales Director 1967-68; Portland Group Factors (Credit Factoring International), Sales Director 1968-85; Credit Factoring International, Managing Director 1985-90. *Biog: b.* 7 September 1936. *Nationality:* British. *m.* 1966, Diana Jane Maberly (née Glover); 1 s. *Educ:* Sutton Valence School, Kent; Diploma in Commerce. *Directorships:* Equipment Leasing Association Ltd 1990 Management Committee Member; Lombard Business Equipment Leasing Ltd 1990 (exec); Lombard Business Finance Ltd 1990 (exec) Managing Director; Lombard NatWest Commercial Services Ltd 1977 (exec); Lombard Orix Leasing Ltd 1990 (exec); Telecom Rentals Ltd 1990 (exec). *Other Activities:* Vice Chairman, Dyslexia Foundation; Governor, Sutton Valence School, Kent. *Professional Organisations:* Member, Institute of Directors. *Clubs:* St Enodoc Golf Club. *Recreations:* Gardening, Golf, Music, Travel.

MacADIE, A; Partner, Nabarro Nathanson.

McALLESTER, J S; Director, Charterhouse Tilney.

McALPINE, Stewart; Director, City of London PR Group plc.

McANDREW, Ian Christopher; Director, British & Commonwealth Merchant Bank plc, since 1988; Group Compliance Director & Company Secretary. *Career:* Coopers & Lybrand, Snr Mgr Financial Services Div 1975-88. *Biog: b.* 20 February 1953. *Nationality:* British. *m.* 1978, Geraldine (née Baker); 2 d. *Educ:* Trinity Hall, Cambridge (MA). *Directorships:* BCMB Group Ltd 1988 (exec); BCMB Private Client Ltd 1989 (exec); British & Commonwealth Banks Holdings Limited 1989 (exec). *Professional Organisations:* FCA.

MacANDREW, The Hon N R; Director, J Henry Schroder Wagg & Co Limited, since 1982; Corporate Finance. *Career:* Coopers & Deloitte 1966-71; Schroder Group 1971-. *Biog: b.* 12 February 1947. *Nationality:* British. *m.* 1975, Vicky (née Renton); 1 s; 2 d. *Educ:* Eton College. *Professional Organisations:* FCA. *Recreations:* Golf.

McARTHUR, Colin; Partner, Field Fisher Waterhouse, since 1974; Company & Commercial

Dept. *Career:* Waterhouse & Co, Partner 1974; Field Fisher Waterhouse (Following Merger), Partner 1989. *Biog: b.* 5 November 1944. *Nationality:* British. *m.* 1979, Mary Elizabeth (née Haswell); 1 d. *Educ:* Edinburgh Academy; Fettes College; Sidney Sussex College, Cambridge (BA Cantab). *Professional Organisations:* Law Society, Solicitor. *Publications:* Co-Author, A Director's Guide - Duties, Liabilities and Company Law, 1990. *Clubs:* Royal Mid-Surrey Golf Club. *Recreations:* Golf.

MACASKILL, John Harry; Partner, Slaughter and May, since 1979; Corporate Finance, Company Law. *Career:* Slaughter and May, Articled Clerk 1970-72; Asst Solicitor 1972-79. *Biog: b.* 13 February 1947. *Nationality:* British. *m.* 1974, Gwyneth June (née Evers); 3 s. *Educ:* Oundle School; Nottingham University (BA). *Professional Organisations:* The Law Society. *Recreations:* Walking, Gardening, Sheep Dog Trials.

MACAULAY, Anthony Dennis; Partner, Herbert Smith, since 1983; Company Law/Corporate Finance. *Career:* Biddle & Co, Articled Clerk/Assistant Solicitor 1972-75; Wilkinson Kimbers & Staddon, Assistant Solicitor 1975-77; Herbert Smith, Assistant Solicitor 1977-83; City Panel on Takeovers and Mergers, Secretary 1983-85. *Biog: b.* 15 November 1948. *Nationality:* British. *m.* 1978, Dominica (née Compernolle); 1 s; 2 d. *Educ:* Queen Elizabeth Grammar School, Wakefield; Keble College, Oxford (BA Litterae Humaniores). *Other Activities:* City of London Solicitors' Company. *Professional Organisations:* Solicitor; Member, The Law Society. *Recreations:* Family, Tennis, Skiing, Cinema, Reading.

MACAULAY, Glyn F; Partner, Neville Russell.

MACAULAY, J B; Director New Zealand, Arbuthnot Latham Bank Limited.

McAUSLAN, Eric David; Director, Martin Currie Investment Management Limited.

McAUSLAN, John; Chief Surveyor, Church Charity and Local Authority Fund Managers Limited, since 1988; Fund Management of Three Property Investment Portfolios with a Total Value of £183 m. *Career:* Matthews and Son, Chartered Surveyors, Assistant Valuer 1956-59; Inland Revenue, District Valuers Office, Valuer 1959-60; Legal and General Assurance Society Limited Estates Department Assistant Estates Surveyor 1960-70; Central Board of Finance of the Church of

England, Local Authorities' Mutual Investment Trust, Charities Official Investment Fund, Chief Surveyor 1970-88. *Biog: b.* 14 November 1930. *Nationality:* British. *m.* 1957, Daphne-Jill (née Butterfield); 1 s; 1 d. *Educ:* Alleyn's School, Dulwich; Regent Street Polytechnic. *Directorships:* Church Charity and Local Authority Fund Managers Limited 1988. *Other Activities:* National Economic Development Office (NEDO), Non-Housing Forecasting Sub-Committee. *Professional Organisations:* Fellow, Royal Institution of Chartered Surveyors. *Publications:* Estates Gazette, Annual Reports on Residential Building Land Values, 1968-74; Chartered Surveyor, Property Market Reports and Land Commission Survey, 1970. *Clubs:* Tonbridge Philharmonic Society, Tonbridge AC. *Recreations:* Music, Road Running.

McBRIDE, I J; Director, Arbuthnot Latham Bank Limited.

McBRIDE, J L K; Director, County NatWest Ltd, since 1988; Corporate Finance. *Career:* Lazard Brothers, Asst Director 1984-87; Charterhouse Japhet, Manager 1981-84; Peat Marwick Mitchell, Audit Senior 1978-81. *Biog: b.* 14 May 1954. *Nationality:* British. *m.* 1978, Daniela (née Maccio); 2 d. *Educ:* Kings, Cambridge (MA Mathematics); Southampton University (MSc Oceanography). *Professional Organisations:* ACA. *Recreations:* Tennis, Golf, Sports in General, Skiing.

McBRIEN, Kevin Harry; Director & General Manager, National Provident Institution, since 1985. *Career:* Phoenix Group (Australia) 1965-68; London and Manchester Assurance 1968-82. *Directorships:* Basil Investments Ltd; National Provident Investment Managers Ltd; N P I Pensions Management Ltd; N P I Trustee Services Ltd. *Other Activities:* Member, Management Committee, Life Insurance Council. *Professional Organisations:* Fellow, Institute of Actuaries. *Recreations:* Golf, Jogging.

MacCABE, Michael Murray; Partner, Freshfields. *Career:* Charles Russell & Co 1965-70; Freshfields 1970-; Freshfields (Paris), Managing Partner 1981-84; Freshfields, Managing Partner 1985-90. *Biog: b.* 20 November 1944. *Nationality:* British. *m.* 1969, Olga Marie (decd); 1 s; 1 d. *Educ:* Downside School, Bath; Lincoln College, Oxford. *Directorships:* Solicitors' Indemnity Mutual Insurance Assoc Ltd 1986. *Professional Organisations:* City of London Law Society (Committee Member); International Bar Association. *Recreations:* Fishing, Painting.

McCALL, Hilary Maurice Fitzmaurice; Chairman, Robert Bruce Fitzmaurice Ltd, since 1977; Reinsurance Brokerage. *Biog: b.* 31 May 1939. *Nationality:* British. *m.* 1974, Josephine (née Russell); 1 s; 2 d.

McCALL, John Kingdon; CBE; Partner, Freshfields, since 1969. *Career:* The British National Oil Corp

(Seconded) Head of Legal Dept 1976-79; Freshfields (New York) Snr Resident Ptnr 1983-87. *Biog: b.* 28 July 1938. *m.* 1963, Anne (née Meller); 2 s; 1 d. *Educ:* Winchester College. *Other Activities:* City of London Solicitors' Company. *Professional Organisations:* The Law Society, IBA, (Council Member); Chm, Section on Energy and Natural Resources Law, Intl Bar Assoc. *Clubs:* Racquet & Tennis Club (New York). *Recreations:* Real Tennis, Road Running and Seabirds.

McCANN, Christopher Conor; Executive Director, County NatWest Ltd, since 1987; Development Capital/Mezzanine Finance Management Buy-Outs. *Career:* Price Waterhouse 1969-73; Barclays Merchant Bank, Asst Dir 1973-80; Barclays Bank plc, Snr VP 1981-87. *Biog: b.* 26 June 1947. *Nationality:* British. *m.* 1974, Clare (née Lewis); 1 s; 2 d. *Educ:* Downside School; Clare College, Cambridge (MA). *Directorships:* Aynsley Group Ltd (non-exec); County NatWest Ventures Ltd (exec); Redifon Holdings Ltd (non-exec); Maritime Transport Services Ltd (non-exec); Mostjet Ltd (non-exec). *Professional Organisations:* Institute of Bankers; Fellow, Institute of Chartered Accountants. *Recreations:* Sailing, Skiing, Theatre.

McCANN, D M D; Partner, Stephenson Harwood.

McCANN, Michael Denis; Group Treasurer/Director, Grand Metropolitan plc, since 1988; All Group Treasury Management and Financing. *Career:* Ford of Europe Inc, Various Fin Mgmnt Areas 1970-83; Ford Motor Co Ltd, Group Treasurer 1983-86; Trafalgar House plc, Group Treasurer/Dir 1986-88. *Biog: b.* 31 March 1948. *Nationality:* British. *m.* 1975, A J (née Bannister); 1 d. *Educ:* Greatfields, Yorkshire; Hull University, (BSc Hons). *Directorships:* Grand Metropolitan Investments Ltd 1988 (exec) Treasurer; Grand Metropolitan Finance plc 1988 (exec) Treasurer; Grand Metropolitan International Finance plc 1988 (exec) Treasurer; Cappoquin Securities Ltd 1988 (exec) Treasurer; Rachel Securities Ltd 1988 (exec) Treasurer; GrandMet Hotels and Catering Ltd 1988 (exec) Treasurer; City Corporate Treasury Consultants Ltd; Stag Insurance Company Ltd (exec); Grand Metropolitan Second Investments Ltd 1988; Grand Metropolitan Third Investments Ltd 1988; Leisure International Ltd 1988; Trafalgar House Group Finance Ltd 1988; Trafalgar House Group Services Ltd 1988. *Professional Organisations:* FCT. *Clubs:* RAC. *Recreations:* Shooting, Fishing, Rugby, Reading.

McCANNAH, I J; Vice President, Bank of Nova Scotia.

McCARTHY, David; Partner, Clifford Chance, since 1978; International Capital Markets, Corporate Finance. *Biog: b.* 27 January 1942. *Nationality:* British; 2 s. *Educ:* Ratcliffe College, Leicester; Birmingham University (LLB Hons). *Directorships:* Mithras Limited 1978 (exec); Mithras Nominees Limited 1978 (exec); St George's

Hill Residents' Association Ltd 1988 (exec). *Other Activities:* Member of Company Law Sub-Committee, City of London Solicitors' Company. *Professional Organisations:* Law Society; Institute of Taxation. *Clubs:* Richmond Cricket Club, St George's Hill Tennis Club, Loch Achonachie Angling Club. *Recreations:* Cricket, Fishing, Tennis, Two Sons.

McCARTHY, Dominic E D; Director, Brown, Shipley & Co Limited.

McCARTHY, Dr Malcolm Christopher; Deputy Head of Corporate Finance, Barclays de Zoete Wedd Limited, since 1989. *Career:* Kleinwort Benson Limited, Director 1985-89; Department of Trade and Industry, Various to Under Secretary 1972-85; DTI, Responsible on behalf of Government for Policy, Legislation and Implementation of the Privatization of British Aerospace 1979-80; Principal Private Secretary to Secretary of State 1984-85; ICI, Economist, Corporate Planning of Research & Development 1965-72. *Biog:* b. 29 February 1944. *Nationality:* British. *m.* Penny; 2 s; 1 d. *Educ:* Oxford University (MA); Stirling University (PhD); Graduate School of Business, Stanford University, California (Masters Degree). *Publications:* Introduction to Technological Economics, 1968.

McCARTHY, Nicholas Christian; Director, James Capel & Co, since 1988; Corporate Finance. *Career:* EMI Ltd, Engineer 1973-74; Western American Bank (Europe) Ltd, Asst Mgr 1974-75; Guiness Mahon & Co Ltd, Dir 1975-88. *Biog:* b. 10 December 1951. *m.* 1979, Gail (née Ter Haar); 1 s; 2 d. *Educ:* Portsmouth Grammar School; Oxford University (MA Hons). *Professional Organisations:* Institute of Directors.

McCAUGHAN, Jim P; Managing Director (Investment Management), UBS Phillips & Drew Intl Investment Ltd.

McCAW, Ms L; Partner, Nabarro Nathanson, since 1990; Company & Commercial. *Career:* Day Wilson Campbell (Toronto, Canada), Articled Clerk/Barrister & Solicitor 1975-79; Barristers Chambers (Toronto, Canada), Barrister & Solicitor 1979-82; Moir & Associates (Vancouver, Canada), Barrister & Solicitor 1982-85; British Coal Corporation, Solicitor 1985-87; McKenna & Co, Assistant Solicitor 1987-89; British Coal Corporation, Solicitor 1989-90. *Biog:* b. 1 December 1945. *Nationality:* Canadian. (div); 1 s. *Educ:* Queen's University, Canada (BA Hons); York University, Canada (MA); Osgood Hall Law School (LLB). *Other Activities:* Membership Committee, Canada-UK Chamber of Commerce. *Professional Organisations:* Law Society of England & Wales; Law Society of Upper Canada. *Clubs:* Canada Club. *Recreations:* Travel.

McCAW, Robert Steel; Partner, Wilde Sapte, since 1971; Company, Commercial, Banking. *Career:*

Linklaters & Paines, Asst Solicitor 1965-69; The Brocks Group of Companies Ltd, Sec/Legal Adviser 1969-71. *Biog:* b. 21 December 1941. *m.* 1968, Madeleine (née Scammell); 2 s. *Educ:* Collyers School, Horsham; University of Exeter (LLB). *Professional Organisations:* The Law Society.

McCLEAN, Simon; Investment Director, London and Manchester Group plc, since 1987. *Career:* Panmure Gordon Graduate Trainee 1968-69; Canada Life Assurance Investment Mgr 1969-84; Manufacturers Hanover Investment Management Ltd Dir 1984; London and Manchester Group plc Investment Mgr 1984-87. *Biog:* b. 10 October 1946. *Nationality:* British. *m.* 1974, Philippa Jane (née Brice); 1 s; 1 d. *Educ:* Ratcliffe College, Leicester; St Catherine's College, Oxford (BA Hons). *Directorships:* Subsidiary Companies of London & Manchester Group; Collegia Ltd; Speciality Shops plc; APA Venture Capital Fund. *Recreations:* Golf, Theatre, Tennis, Rugby, Reading.

McCLUMPHA, Alex Donald; General Manager Overseas Trading Division, The Nestle Company Ltd, since 1988. *Career:* The Nestle Co Ltd Purchasing Mgr; Nestle (Switzerland, USA, Argentina) Various Overseas Appointments; Corporate Affairs Manager. *Biog:* b. 1932. *m.* 1960, Patricia (née Moran); 2 s. *Educ:* Mill Hill School; University of London (BSc Hons); Imede Lausanne (MBA). *Directorships:* London Futures and Options Exchange (London Fox) 1986 (non-exec); Confederation des Industries Agro-Alimentaires 1985 Leader of UK Delegation. *Other Activities:* Food & Drink Federation Council; Biscuit Cake Chocolate and Confectionery Alliance; British Soluble Coffee Manufacturers' Assoc; CAOBISCO; Association of Preserved Milk Manufacturers of the EEC. *Professional Organisations:* Association of MBAs. *Publications:* Contributor to Arbitrage, 1988; Coffee, 1988; Contributor, The Human Food Chain, 1989. *Clubs:* RAC.

McCLURE FISHER, David Anthony; Director, Hogg Group plc, since 1990; Insurance Marketing. *Career:* Hogg Group plc 1958-. *Biog:* b. 4 March 1939. *Nationality:* British. *m.* 1961, Lesley (née Chester Jones); 1 s; 1 d. *Educ:* Tonbridge School. *Directorships:* Hogg Group plc 1990 (exec); Grupo Internacional de Marketing de Seguros SA, Spain 1990 (exec); Meadows Mouldings Limited 1990 (non-exec); Insurance Marketing Services, Australia 1989 (exec); Hogg Automotive Insurance Services 1988 (exec) Hogg Insurance Brokers Limited 1987 (exec); Hogg Insurance Marketing Services 1984 (exec); Greyfriars Administrative Services 1984 (exec). *Professional Organisations:* FCII; FCIS; FBIIBA; MIMI; F Inst D. *Clubs:* Moor Park Golf Club. *Recreations:* Golf, Bridge.

McCLUSKY, Dominic; Partner, Theodore Goddard.

McCOLVILLE, Allan; Executive Director, Allied Dunbar.

McCONNELL, Brian W; Executive Director, Ulster Bank Limited.

McCONVILLE, J; Finance Director, TSB Bank Scotland plc, since 1990; Finance. *Career:* Wylie & Hutton CA 1977-79; Coopers & Lybrand, Senior Manager 1979-88. *Biog: b.* 20 July 1956. *Nationality:* British. *m.* 1984, Fiona Elizabeth; 3 s; 1 d. *Educ:* Perth Academy; Edinburgh University (Bachelor of Commerce). *Directorships:* TSB Bank Scotland plc 1990 (exec). *Professional Organisations:* Institute of Chartered Accountants of Scotland. *Clubs:* Lufness New. *Recreations:* Golf, Reading.

McCORD, M P P; Director/Underwriter, MFK Underwriting Agencies Ltd.

McCORKELL, B; Director, Stewart Ivory & Company Limited.

McCORMACK, Barry; Company Secretary, AIBD (Systems & Information) Ltd, since 1988; Finance and Legal. *Career:* Micrognosis, Accountant 1985-88; Bunzl plc, Accountant 1983-85. *Biog: b.* 13 April 1959. *Nationality:* British. *Educ:* Carnoustie High; Dundee University (MA Econ/Law). *Directorships:* AIBD (Systems & Information) Ltd 1988 (exec); TRAX Limited 1988 (non-exec); Music Business Network 1989 (exec).

McCORMICK, K S; Director, Kleinwort Benson Limited

McCORQUODALE, Alastair; Director, Guardian Royal Exchange Assurance plc.

McCRANE, Angus; Financial Writer, The Scotsman.

McCRICKARD, Donald Cecil; Group Chief Executive, TSB Group plc, since 1990. *Career:* Management Consultancy, Consultant 1966-75; Smith Doubleday Inc Gen Mgr, Europe 1971-75; American Express Co Chief Executive, UK 1975-78; Regional VP, Europe 1978-79; VP Corporate 1979-80; Chief Exec, Asia, Pacific & Australia 1980-83; Chief Exec, United Dominions Trust Ltd 1983-88; Dep Group MD & Chief Exec, Banking, TSB Group plc 1988-89; Chief Executive, TSB Bank plc 1989-90. *Biog: b.* 25 December 1936. *Nationality:* British. *m.* 1960, Stella May (née Buttle); 2 d. *Educ:* Hove Grammar School; London School of Economics; University of Malaya. *Directorships:* TSB Group plc 1987 (exec); TSB Bank plc 1988 (exec); TSB Hill Samuel Bank Holding Company plc 1990 (non-exec). *Professional Organisations:* FCIB; CBIM; Institute of Directors. *Recreations:* Golf, Theatre.

McCULLOCH, J R; Director, Speirs & Jeffrey Ltd, since 1985; Private Clients/Corporate Finance. *Career:* Coopers & Lybrand (Glasgow) 1976-79; Coopers & Lybrand (Houston, Texas) 1979-82. *Biog: b.* 19 November 1954. *Nationality:* British. *m.* 1980, Sally Lindsay (née Butters); 3 d. *Educ:* Glasgow Academy; Stirling University (BA). *Professional Organisations:* CA. *Clubs:* Glasgow Academical Club, RSAC, Pollok Golf Club. *Recreations:* Golf, Squash, Skiing.

McCURRIE, Miss Janet Grierson; Group Legal Adviser, Morgan Grenfell Group plc, since 1985; Group Legal Affairs, Domestic and International. *Career:* Butterworths Editor in Charge, Legal Textbooks 1959-65; Beaumont & Son Articled Clerk 1966-70; Linklaters & Paines Asst Solicitor 1970-76; Bankers Trust Company VP and Chief Legal Adviser 1976-82; Yorkshire Television Secretary & Group Solicitor 1982-84. *Biog: b.* 20 May 1935. *Nationality:* British. *Educ:* Dumfries Academy; Aberdeen University (MA, LLB). *Directorships:* Morgan Grenfell & Co Ltd 1988 (exec); Grierson Productions Ltd 1984 (non-exec). *Other Activities:* Mem, The Law Society; Mem, City Solicitors' Company; Mem, International Bar Association. *Recreations:* Eating Out.

McDANELL, James; Group Finance Director, Abbott Mead Vickers plc, since 1985; Finance, Investor Relations. *Career:* Ernst & Young, Asst Audit Manager 1966-73; Kimpher Group, Director of Supply Services Division 1973-76; Conway Group Holdings, Group Finance Director 1976-78; Ernst & Young (Hong Kong), Manager, Consultancy Division 1978-79. *Biog: b.* 29 March 1947. *Nationality:* British. *Educ:* Bedford School. *Directorships:* Abbott Mead Vickers plc (exec); Abbott Mead Vickers & Sons Ltd (exec); McBain Noel-Johnson Co Ltd non-exec); The Leagas Delaney Partnership Ltd (non-exec); Park Hill School Ltd (non-exec). *Clubs:* RAC.

McDERMOTT, Dermot St J; Director, Trafalgar House Public Limited Company.

McDERMOTT, Michael R; Director, Alexander Howden Limited.

McDONAGH, Robin James; Director, Kleinwort Benson Securities Limited.

MacDONALD, A J; Partner, Hays Allan.

MACDONALD, Alastair William; Managing Director, Alexander Howden Reinsurance Brokers Ltd; Marine Reinsurance (France, Holland, Belgium, USA, Bermuda, S Africa). *Professional Organisations:* ACII.

McDONALD, D A; Chief Executive & Director, Birmingham Midshires Building Society.

MACDONALD, D C W; Director, S G Warburg Akroyd Rowe & Pitman Mullens Securities Ltd.

McDONALD, Sir Duncan; CBE; Director, General Accident.

MACDONALD, Euan Ross; Director, S G Warburg & Co Ltd, since 1982; Overseas Advisory Division. *Career:* Lazard Brothers & Co Ltd, Corp Fin Dept 1964-74; IFA (Kuwait), Gen Mgr 1974-79; Ifabanque SA (Paris) 1979-82. *Biog: b.* 8 April 1940. *Nationality:* British. *m.* 1965, Anne (née Evelyn-Wright); 4 s. *Educ:* Marlborough College; Cambridge University (BA); Columbia University, New York (MBA). *Directorships:* S G Warburg & Co Ltd 1982.

MacDONALD, I H; UK Trading, Barclays de Zoete Wedd Holdings.

McDONALD, Jinny; Associate Director, GCI Sterling, since 1989; Public Relations. *Career:* Rediffusion Simulation Ltd, PR Manager 1983-86. *Biog: b.* 5 August 1959. *Nationality:* British. *Educ:* Aberdeen University (LLB). *Professional Organisations:* MIPR.

MACDONALD, J H; Chairman & Chief Executive, County NatWest Limited, since 1989. *Career:* Thomson McLintock & Co, Served Articles 1949-55; Walter Mitchell & Sons 1955-58; Aircraft Marine Products 1958; Keir & Cawder Arrow Drilling, Finance Manager 1958-60; Royal Dutch/Shell Group, Group Treasurer 1960-83; Dome Petroleum Ltd, Chairman & Chief Executive 1983-88. *Biog: b.* 5 June 1928. *Nationality:* Scottish. *m.* 1961, Anne (née Hunter); 3 d. *Educ:* Hermitage, Helensburgh. *Directorships:* NatWest Investment Bank Limited 1989 Chairman & Chief Exec; National Westminster Bank plc 1989 (exec); County NatWest Ventures Ltd 1989 Chairman; McDermott Inc 1985 (exec). *Other Activities:* Member, Advisory Committee, Energy International NV; Founder Member, Association of Corporate Treasurers. *Professional Organisations:* Member, Institute of Chartered Accountants; CA; FCT. *Clubs:* Caledonian. *Recreations:* Golf, Theatre.

MacDONALD, James G S; The Lord MacDonald of Aird & Vallay; Deputy General Manager, Nomura Bank International plc, since 1989; Marketing Bank's Services. *Career:* Kleinwort Benson Limited, Graduate Trainee to Assistant Director, Corporate Finance 1973-89. *Biog: b.* 4 February 1950. *Nationality:* British. *m.* 1981, Elisabeth (née Wolff); 1 s; 1 d. *Educ:* Eton College; Queens College, Oxford (MA Hons). *Directorships:* Scottish Heritage USA Inc 1985 (non-exec); Clan Donald Lands Trust 1989 (non-exec); Glencoe Foundation Inc 1989 (non-exec). *Other Activities:* Member of Council, National Trust for Scotland. *Recreations:* Scotland.

MacDONALD, Joseph Mackay; General Manager, UK Banking, The Royal Bank of Scotland plc, since 1985; Domestic Banking. *Career:* Royal Bank of Scotland plc Various appointments 1950-77; Superintendent of Branches 1977-80; Asst Gen Mgr, N Region 1980-82; Gen Mgr, N Region 1982-85. *Biog: b.* 16 September 1934. *Nationality:* British. *m.* 1959, Marlene Groat (née MacKay); 1 s; 1 d. *Educ:* Miller Academy, Thurso. *Professional Organisations:* FIB (Scot). *Clubs:* Royal Northern and University (Aberdeen), Aberdeen Petroleum. *Recreations:* Angling.

McDONALD, Kevan; Partner, Dickson Minto WS, since 1987; Company & Commercial Law, Oil & Gas Law. *Career:* Dundas & Wilson CS Asst, Commercial Work 1982-85; Dickson Minto WS Asst, Company & Commercial Law 1985-87. *Biog: b.* 7 July 1958. *Nationality:* British. *m.* 1988, Anne Louise (née Henderson); 1 d. *Educ:* The Edinburgh Academy; Aberdeen University (LLB); Dundee University (Diploma, Petroleum Law). *Directorships:* Nominee Companies. *Professional Organisations:* Member, IBA; Member, IBA Section on Energy & Natural Resources Law. *Publications:* Onshore Oil and Gas Pipelines: The Problems, 1980. *Recreations:* Fishing, Squash.

McDONALD, Professor M H B; Professor of Marketing Planning, Cranfield School of Management.

MacDONALD, Nigel Colin Lock; Senior Technical Partner, Ernst & Whinney.

McDONALD, P S; Non-Executive Director, Rutland Trust plc.

MACDONALD, Stuart; Partner, Clyde & Co.

McDONALD, W M; Finance Director, Framlington Group plc. *Biog: b.* 30 August 1951. *Educ:* LLB. *Professional Organisations:* CA; ACMA.

MACDONALD-BROWN, Charters; Partner, Head of Litigation, Gouldens, since 1977; Litigation/Intellectual Property. *Career:* Called to the Bar of England & Wales 1969; Gouldens, Articled 1972; Admitted as Solicitor 1974; Assistant Solicitor 1974-77; Partner 1977-. *Biog: b.* 20 August 1946. *Nationality:* British. *m.* 1969, Patricia Mary; 3 s; 1 d. *Educ:* Loretto School, Musselburgh, Scotland; Geneva University; Inns of Court Bar School. *Other Activities:* Honorary Solicitor to the Law and Parliamentary Committee, Royal Society of Chemistry; Clerk to the General Commissioner of Income & Taxes (2nd East Brixton Division). *Professional Organisations:* Associate Member, Chartered Institute of Patent Agents; Member, International Bar Association; Foreign Affiliate, American Bar Association; Member, UIA (Union Internationale des Avocats); Member, AIPPA; Foreign Affiliate, AIPLA (American Intellectual

Property Law Association). *Clubs:* RAC, Annabelles. *Recreations:* Golf, Sailing, Watersports.

McDONNELL, David; National Managing Partner, Grant Thornton, since 1989. *Biog: b.* 9 July 1943. *m.* 1967, Marieke; 3 d.

McDONOUGH, J T; General Manager, Guardian Royal Exchange Assurance plc, since 1990; Operations. *Career:* Royal Exchange, West Africa, AGM Nigeria 1955-74; Guardian Royal Exchange Assurance, Singapore, Group Manager 1974-76; Guardian Royal Exchange (Malaysia), Managing Director 1976-83; Guardian Royal Exchange (Asia), Hong Kong, Managing Director 1983-87; Union Insurance Society of Canton, Deputy Chairman 1983-87; Grea plc, Assistant General Manager 1987-90. *Biog: b.* 13 May 1933. *Nationality:* British. *m.* 1968, Fiona (née Benington); 2 d. *Educ:* The High School, Dublin. *Directorships:* Guardian Holdings, France 1988 (non-exec); Grea (Malaysia) SDN BHD 1976 (non-exec); Guardian Assurance Co (Thailand) Ltd 1982 (non-exec); PT Maskapai Asuransi Union-Far East 1982 (non-exec); Amsterdam Londen Verzekering Maatschappij NV 1989 (non-exec); Le Foyer Compagnie Luxembourgeoise D'Assurances SA 1988 (non-exec); Assicurazioni Cidas/Sipea 1989 Chm; Assicurzaioni Polaris Vita 1989 Chm. *Clubs:* Oriental, RAC, Hong Kong, Royal St George Yacht Club. *Recreations:* Golf, Music, Sailing.

McDOUGALL, Douglas Christopher Patrick; Senior Partner, Baillie Gifford & Co, since 1989; Investment Management. *Career:* Baillie Gifford & Co 1965-. *Biog: b.* 18 March 1944. *Nationality:* British. *m.* 1986, The Hon Carolyn (née Griffiths); 1 d. *Educ:* Edinburgh Academy; Christ Church, Oxford (MA). *Directorships:* IMRO 1987 (non-exec); Provincial Group plc 1989 (non-exec); Baillie Gifford Japan Trust plc 1989 (non-exec); Baillie Gifford Technology plc 1989 (non-exec). *Other Activities:* Investment Committee, 1986; Executive Committee, Institutional Fund Managers Association. *Clubs:* New (Edinburgh), City of London, Brooks's.

MACDOUGALL, Patrick Lorn; Chief Executive, Chartered WestLB Limited, since 1985. *Career:* N M Rothschild & Sons Ltd, Mgr 1967-70; Rothschild Intercontinental Bank Ltd (Amex Bank Ltd), Exec Dir 1970-77; Chief Exec 1977-78; Jardine Matheson Holdings Ltd, Exec Dir 1978-85. *Biog: b.* 21 June 1939. *Nationality:* British. m1 1967, Alison Noel (née Offer); 2 s; 2 d. *Educ:* Millfield School; University College, Oxford (MA). *Directorships:* Standard Chartered plc 1988 (exec). *Professional Organisations:* FCA. *Clubs:* RAC. *Recreations:* Golf, Opera, Bridge.

MacDOUGALL, William F; Director, International Fixed Interest, Hill Samuel Investment Management Ltd; Bond and Currency Management Economic Forecasting. *Biog: b.* 19 February 1955. *Nationality:* British.

Educ: St John's College, Oxford (MPhil Economics); Stanford University (BA Economics & History).

McDOWELL, J H; Director, S G Warburg Akroyd Rowe & Pitman Mullens Securities Ltd.

MACE, Daniel Charles; Partner, Lovell White Durrant, since 1977; Corporate & Securities Law. *Biog: b.* 16 October 1946. *m.* 1969, Marlie (née Johnston); 2 s; 1 d. *Educ:* Queen's College, Taunton; Bristol University (LLB Hons). *Professional Organisations:* Standing Ctee on Company Law, Law Society; Company Law Sub-Ctee, City of London Law Society. *Recreations:* Family, Theatre.

MacEACHAM, Captain Neil; Clerk, Leathersellers' Company.

McENERY, G M; Director, Hill Samuel Bank Limited.

McENTYRE, D J; Director, Charterhouse Tilney.

MacEWAN, N S; Director, Kleinwort Benson Group plc.

McEWEN, P G; Director, Merchant Navy Investment Management.

MACEY, Roger David Michael; Managing Director, Macey Williams Limited, since 1976. *Career:* Macey Williams Limited, Managing Director 1983-; Macdonagh Boland Group, Director 1989-; P S Mosse & Partners Ltd, Director 1977-83; George Miller Underwriting Agencies Ltd, Director 1977-86; Brandts Insurance Brokers, Director 1972-76. *Biog: b.* 15 November 1942. *Nationality:* British. *m.* 1970, Julie (née Mellors) (separated); 2 s. *Educ:* St Mary's College, Ireland. *Clubs:* Turf, Carlton, City of London. *Recreations:* Shooting, Golf, Tennis.

McFADZEAN, Christopher William; Partner, Linklaters & Paines, since 1989; International Finance. *Biog: b.* 15 March 1958. *Nationality:* British. *m.* 1987, Jane (née Alexander). *Educ:* Milnes High School, Morayshire; Trinity Hall, Cambridge (MA Hons).

MACFARLANE, Andrew Elliott; Partner, Ernst & Young, since 1987; Corporate Advisory Services. *Biog: b.* 16 October 1956. *Nationality:* British. *Educ:* King's School, Canterbury; Cambridge University (MA). *Professional Organisations:* ACA.

MACFARLANE, C K; Marketing Manager, Fleming Private Asset Management Limited.

MACFARLANE, D B; Director, J O Hambro Magan & Co Ltd. *Biog: b.* 5 June 1962. *Nationality:* American. *m.* 1988, Annesley R. *Educ:* University of Virginia (BSc);

Harvard Business School (MBA). *Professional Organisations:* Chartered Financial Analyst; Association for Investment Management and Research.

MaCFARLANE, David John; Partner, Ashurst Morris Crisp, since 1986; Corporate Finance. *Career:* Stephenson Harwood 1965-75; Ptnr 1975-85. *Biog: b.* 10 April 1946. *m.* 1969, Nicola (née Lines); 2 d. *Educ:* Radley College. *Other Activities:* City of London Solicitors' Company. *Professional Organisations:* Law Society. *Clubs:* City of London, Leander. *Recreations:* Shooting, Fishing, Tennis.

MACFARLANE, I; Partner, Kidsons Impey.

McFARLANE, John; Managing Director, Citicorp Scrimgeour Vickers Ltd.

MACFARLANE, Jonathan Stephen; Partner, Macfarlanes, since 1985; Corporate Finance and Related Areas. *Career:* Macfarlanes, Articled Clerk 1978-80; Assistant Solicitor 1980-85. *Biog: b.* 28 March 1956. *Nationality:* British. *m.* 1983, Johanna Susanne (née Foster); 1 s; 1 d. *Educ:* Charterhouse; Oriel College, Oxford (MA). *Professional Organisations:* Law Society; City of London Solicitors Company. *Clubs:* Leander. *Recreations:* Family, Sports.

MACFARLANE, Sir Norman; Chairman, Guinness plc.

MACFARLANE, Peter F; Director Finance, Rolls-Royce plc, since 1989; Finance, Treasury, Mergers, Acquisitions, Systems & Computing. *Career:* Coopers & Lybrand (Nigeria), Senior Auditor 1961-65; International Computers (UK), Asst Group Accountant 1965-66; Kimberley Clark (UK, USA, Holland & Germany), Financial Manager, later Director 1966-69; British Leyland (UK & Nigeria), International Controller, Managing Director Nigeria & Treasurer London 1969-79; Rolls-Royce plc, Treasurer, Director Industrial & Marine, Director of Corporate Development 1979-. *Biog: b.* 3 July 1938. *Nationality:* British. *m.* 1960, Dianne Jennifer (née Hotton); 2 d. *Educ:* Woodhouse Grammar School. *Other Activities:* Member of the Senate, Board for Chartered Accountants in Business; The One Hundred Group of Finance Directors. *Professional Organisations:* Institute of Chartered Accountants; Fellow, Corporate Treasurers. *Clubs:* Royal Southern Yacht Club. *Recreations:* Sailing, Tennis.

McFETRICH, Charles Alan; UK Managing Partner, Deloitte Haskins & Sells, since 1985; Coopers & Lybrand Deloitte, since 1990. *Career:* Graham Proom & Smith (Chartered Accountants), Articled Clerk 1959-61, 1964-66; Deloitte Haskins & Sells, Qualified Accountant 1966-68; Consultant 1968-73; Consultancy Partner 1973-80; Consultant Partner on Secondment at the Department of Industry as Under Secretary 1981-82; UK Operations Partner 1982-84; UK Managing Partner 1985-89; Coopers & Lybrand Deloitte, UK Managing Partner 1990-. *Biog: b.* 15 December 1940. *Nationality:* British. *m.* 1990, Janet Elizabeth (née Munro); 2 s; 1 d. *Educ:* Oundle School; Magdalene College, Cambridge (MA Economics & Law). *Other Activities:* Shipwrights' Company. *Professional Organisations:* Fellow, The Institute of Chartered Accountants in England and Wales; Fellow, The Royal Society for the Encouragement of Arts, Manufacture and Commerce. *Clubs:* Gresham. *Recreations:* Gardening, Theatre.

McGAREL-GROVES, Hugh Macmillan Julian; Group Financial Controller, Sedgwick Group plc, since 1989. *Career:* Guinness plc, Group Chief Accountant 1987-88; British Petroleum Co plc, Finance & Accounting Manager 1978-87; Peat Marwick Mitchell & Co, Auditor 1974-78. *Biog: b.* 26 June 1952. *Nationality:* British. *m.* 1978, Jane (née Perkins); 2 s; 1 d. *Educ:* Eton College; Trinity College, Cambridge (MA). *Professional Organisations:* FCA. *Clubs:* Leander. *Recreations:* Sailing, Skiing, Vintage Cars.

McGARRIGLE, C; Director, Robert Fleming Insurance Brokers Limited.

McGEACHY, A L; WS; Clerk, Gardeners' Company.

McGEORGE, R G H; Director, Dunedin Fund Managers Ltd, since 1986; Pension Funds. *Career:* British Investment Trust, Overseas Portfolio Manager 1969-82; LAS Group (Life Association of Scotland), Investment Secretary 1982-86. *Biog: b.* 5 May 1947. *Directorships:* Dunedin Fund Managers Canada Ltd 1987 (exec); Dunedin Pension Fund Managers Ltd 1986 (exec); Dunedin Unit Trust Managers Ltd 1986 (exec); Dunedin Financial Services Ltd 1987 (exec). *Professional Organisations:* ACIS.

McGIBBON, A R G; Director, Minster Trust Limited.

McGILL, Lewis Sinclair; Executive Director, UK Banking, The Royal Bank of Scotland plc, since 1989; UK Banking. *Career:* Royal Bank of Scotland 1956-; Asst Gen Mgr (Southern Region) 1980-81; Gen Man, (Southern Region) 1981-86; Exec Dir, International 1986-89. *Biog: b.* 8 April 1939. *Nationality:* British. *m.* 1965, Ann Mackintosh (née Mitchell); 2 s. *Educ:* Forfar Academy; Strathclyde University (MBA). *Professional Organisations:* FIB (Scotland). *Clubs:* Luffness Golf Club, Denham Golf Club, Gerrards Cross Lawn Tennis Club. *Recreations:* Music, Sport.

McGILLIVRAY, B; Non-Executive Director, Bunzl Plc.

MacGILLIVRAY, P A; Executive Director, James R Knowles Limited.

McGIRR, D W J; Director, S G Warburg, since 1986; Canada/International Corporate Finance. *Career:* S G Warburg & Co Ltd 1978-86; Exec Dir, Canadian Corporate Finance 1985-. *Biog: b.* 19 May 1954. *Nationality:* British. *m.* 1981, Margaret Joslin (née Richardson); 1 s; 3 d. *Educ:* University of Glasgow (BSc Civil Engineering 1st Class Hons); The Wharton School, (Thouron Scholar, MBA). *Directorships:* Bunting Warburg Limited 1989 (exec); Bunting Warburg Inc 1989 (exec); S G Warburg Canada Ltd 1989 (exec). *Clubs:* The National Club (Toronto, Ontario), Historic Sports Car Club, Vintage Auto Racing Association Canada. *Recreations:* Family, Car Racing.

McGIVERN, K; Director, Barclays de Zoete Wedd Securities Ltd.

McGONIGAL, Christopher; Partner, Clifford Chance.

McGONIGLE, R; Executive Director, Allied Dunbar Assurance plc.

McGOWAN, G; Partner, Nabarro Nathanson.

McGOWAN, John; Chief Administrative Officer, Merrill Lynch Europe Limited.

MacGOWAN, John; Director (Sales), Hoare Govett International Securities.

McGOWAN, Harry Duncan Cory; The Lord McGowan; Director, Panmure Gordon & Co Limited, since 1986; Head of Corporate Finance. *Biog: b.* 20 July 1938. *m.* 1962, Gillian (née Pepys); 1 s; 2 d. *Educ:* Eton College. *Professional Organisations:* The International Stock Exchange. *Clubs:* Boodle's, City of London.

McGOWN, Donald M; Partner, Allen & Overy, since 1989; Company, Commercial. *Career:* Allen & Overy, Articled Clerk 1981-83; Asst 1983-85; (New York), Asst 1985-88. *Biog: b.* 20 May 1957. *Nationality:* British. *m.* 1987, Lisa (née Collier). *Educ:* Marlborough College; Southampton University (LLB). *Professional Organisations:* Mem, The Law Society.

McGRANE, Joe; Director, 3i plc.

McGRATH, Anthony Charles Ormond; Director, Baring Brothers & Co Ltd, since 1985; Corporate Fin Dept, Dir Heading Research & Marketing Unit. *Biog: b.* 10 November 1949. *Nationality:* British. *m.* 1974, Margaret (née Usher); 1 s; 1 d. *Directorships:* W & F C Bonham & Sons Ltd 1987 (non-exec). *Other Activities:* Member, British Standards Institute Quality Assurance Board. *Professional Organisations:* FCA.

McGRATH, Edmund B; Director, Bradstock Group plc.

McGRATH, H A; Director, E D & F Man Ltd.

McGREGOR, Bruce William Corbet; Partner, Theodore Goddard.

MacGREGOR, Gervase; Partner, Stoy Hayward.

McGREGOR, R; Executive Director, TSB Bank Scotland plc.

McGUINNESS, Dennis; Chairman & Managing Director, Carswell Limited, since 1988; Development of the Company. *Career:* Stockbroker 1960-73; The Stock Exchange, Member 1973-79; Partner 1979-87; Carswell Ltd, Chm & MD 1987. *Biog: b.* 20 November 1943. *Nationality:* British. *m.* 1964, Maureen (decd); 1 s; 2 d. *Educ:* Holyrood Senior Secondary. *Directorships:* Bremner plc 1988-90 (exec); Carswell Ltd 1987 (exec). *Other Activities:* Chm, The Child & Family Trust. *Professional Organisations:* Member, International Stock Exchange. *Clubs:* Bonnyton Golf Club. *Recreations:* Golf, Football, Swimming, Horse Racing.

McGUIRE, Dane Steven; Assistant Geberal Manager & Treasurer, Credit Lyonnais, since 1987; Head of Market Group. *Career:* United States Peace Corps, Guatemala, Central America, US Government Peace Corps Volunteer assigned to the Ministry of Finance, Republic of Guatemala, as Credit Co-operative Promoter and Technical Adviser 1971-73; Action Peace Corps, Washington DC, USA, Placement Officer for all Individual Placements for both United Nations (of US Nationality) and United States Peace Corps Volunteer Programs worldwide 1973-74; Chemical Bank, New York, Junior Member of Foreign Exchange Advisory Service, Foreign Exchange Division, New York 1975-76; Citibank NA, New York 1977-86; Citibank NA, Quito, Ecuador, Resident Vice-President and Country Financial Controller & Treasurer for Ecuador 1977-79; Caracas, Venezuela, Vice-President and Country Treasurer for Venezuela and The Netherlands, Antilles 1979-82; London, Vice-President and Unit Head, Foreign Exchange Division, Treasury Group 1982-84; Copenhagen, Vice-President and Country Treasurer for Denmark 1984-86; Gulf International Bank BSC, London, Vice-President, London Branch Treasurer 1986-87. *Biog: b.* 6 April 1948. *Nationality:* American. *m.* Delia Margarita (née Briones); 1 s. *Educ:* The Citadel, Charleston, S Carolina, USA (BA Politcal Science); The John Hopkins School of Advance International Studies, Washington DC, USA (MA International Economics). *Recreations:* Tennis, Skiing, Canoeing, Scuba Diving.

McGURRAN, John T; Executive Director, First Interstate Capital Markets Limited.

McHALE, J F; Partner, Pannell Kerr Forster.

443

MACHARG, John Maitland; General Manager and Actuary, Scottish Provident Institution.

MACHIN, S J; Tax Partner, Ashurst Morris Crisp, since 1987; Corporate Tax. *Career:* Freshfields, Solicitor 1980-85; Ashurst Morris Crisp 1985-. *Biog: b.* 9 November 1954. *Nationality:* British. *m.* 1978, Michaela (née Tomasch); 1 s; 1 d. *Educ:* King Edward VII School, Sheffield; Pembroke College, Cambridge (MA, LLB). *Professional Organisations:* ATII. *Clubs:* Tilford Cricket Club. *Recreations:* Sport, Music.

McHUGH, Daniel Anthony; Executive Director, European Controller, Lehman Brothers Ltd, since 1986; Accountancy. *Career:* Peat Marwick Mitchell & Co, Senior Manager Investment Services Audit and Consultancy 1977-86. *Biog: b.* 14 February 1956. *Nationality:* American. *Educ:* Regis High School; Fordham University (BSc). *Directorships:* Lehman Brothers Securities 1987; Shearson UK Holdings Limited 1988; Lehman Brothers Limited 1990; Shearson Lehman Brothers Holdings plc 1988; SLB Mortgage Backed Securities (No 1) Limited 1989; SLB Mortgage Backed Securities (No 2) Limited 1989; Lehman Brothers Gilts Money Brokers Limited 1988; Lehman Brothers Equity Money Brokers Limited 1988; Lehman Brothers Nominees Limited 1988.

McHUGH, Peter James; Partner, Evershed Wells & Hind, since 1989; Corporate Services and Finance. *Career:* Evershed & Tomkinson, Articled Clerk 1980-82; Assistant Solicitor 1982-86; Associate 1986-89. *Biog: b.* 23 July 1958. *Nationality:* British. *m.* 1982, Barbara Ann (née Spence); 2 s. *Educ:* Finchley Catholic High School; University of Birmingham (LLB). *Other Activities:* Friend, The Royal Birmingham Society of Artists. *Professional Organisations:* Member, The Law Society; Member, The Birmingham Law Society. *Recreations:* Golf, Skiing, Collecting Works of Art.

McILVENNY, Robin Hugh; Assistant General Manager, Saudi International Bank, since 1990; Head of Corporate Finance Division. *Career:* Lloyds Bank plc, Management Trainee 1975-78; County NatWest, Finance Executive 1978-79; Deutsche Bank, Senior Credit Officer 1979-82; Creditanstalt-Bankverein, Deputy Group Head, Investment Banking 1982-84; Vice President, Head of US Merchant Banking Group, New York 1984-88; Senior Manager, Corporate Finance 1988; Security Pacific Merchant Bank, Vice President, Head of Acquisition Finance 1988-89. *Biog: b.* 2 February 1953. *Nationality:* British. *m.* 1982, Barbara (née Willoughby); 2 s. *Educ:* Cheltenham Grammar School; Southampton University (BSc). *Other Activities:* FRSA. *Recreations:* Golf, Tennis, Ancient History.

MacILWAINE, Bruce Rodney; Chief Executive, Schlesinger & Company Limited, since 1989. *Career:* Bank of London & South America Limited, London, Peru, Paraguay, Spain, New York, Argentina 1962-70; Lloyds Bank International Limited, New York, Chicago, various including President Corporate Foreign Exchange 1970-79; Pittsburgh, Vice President & Manager 1979-83; Principal Manager, Japan 1983-86; Lloyds Bank plc, Chief Manager, Office of Director of International Banking 1986-89; Schlesinger & Company Limited (previously Manchester Exchange Trust Company) and Manchester Exchange & Investment Bank Ltd, Chief Executive 1989-. *Biog: b.* 6 April 1945. *Nationality:* British; 1 d. *Educ:* Sutton Valence School. *Directorships:* Schlesinger & Company Limited (exec); Schlesinger Corporate Finance Limited (exec); Schlesinger Asset Finance Limited (exec); Manchester Exchange & Investment Bank Limited (exec); and various other subsidiaries of Schlesinger & Company Limited. *Recreations:* Scuba Diving, Skiing, Riding, Exercise.

McILWEE, Richard; Partner, Clifford Chance, since 1990; Taxation of Collective Investment Schemes. *Career:* Pupillage at One Gray's Inn Chambers 1982; Peat Marwick Mitchell, Tax Consultant 1982-84. *Biog: m.* 1988, Fabienne Lydie. *Educ:* Merchant Taylors School; Kings College, London (LLB Hons). *Professional Organisations:* Associate, Institute of Taxation.

McINERNEY, Peter; Partner, S J Berwin & Co.

McINNES, Robert M; General Manager, Financial Control, The Royal Bank of Scotland plc, since 1989; Financial, Management and Cost Accounting Departments and Resource Management. *Career:* The Royal Bank of Scotland, Assistant Law Secretary -1980; Law Secretary 1980-83; Secretary of the Bank 1983-85; Assistant General Manager, UK Banking 1985-88; Assistant General Manager, Special Duties 1988-89; Head of Financial Control 1989; General Manager, Financial Control 1989-. *Biog: b.* 22 January. *Nationality:* British. *m.* 1963, Kathleen (née Beattie); 2 s. *Educ:* Montrose Academy; Edinburgh University (Notary Public and Solicitor). *Other Activities:* Council Member, Institute of Bankers in Scotland. *Professional Organisations:* Fellow, Institute of Bankers in Scotland; Fellow, Chartered Institute of Secretaries; Law Society of Scotland.

McINTOSH, A Bruce; Director, John Govett & Co Limited.

McINTOSH, Derek John Hunter; Managing Director, Bell Lawrie White & Co Ltd, since 1989. *Career:* Bell Lawrie MacGregor & Co, Partner 1970-86; Bell Lawrie Ltd, Managing Director 1986-89. *Biog: b.* 28 February 1943. *Nationality:* British. *m.* 1970, Barbara (née Dixon); 3 d. *Educ:* Trinity College, Glenalmond. *Clubs:* Hon Co of Edinburgh Golfers, Gullane Golf Club. *Recreations:* Golf, Shooting, Fishing, Tennis.

McINTOSH, Ian Alexander Neville; Deputy Chief Executive, Samuel Montagu & Co Ltd, since 1989; Corporate Finance. *Career:* Coopers & Lybrand 1964-69; Samuel Montagu & Co Limited 1969-. *Biog: b.* 1938. *Nationality:* British. *m.* Gillian (née Cropp); 1 s; 1 d. *Educ:* Bradford Grammar; Edinburgh University. *Directorships:* IMI plc 1989 (non-exec). *Other Activities:* Member, Chairman's Committee & Chairman, Corporate Finance Committee of the British Merchant Banking and Securities Houses Association (BMBA); Member, Takeover Panel. *Professional Organisations:* FCA. *Clubs:* MCC, Mid Herts Golf Club, RAC.

McINTOSH, Ian William; Partner, Booth & Co, since 1989; Company Law. *Career:* Turner Kenneth Brown, Articled Clerk, then Solicitor 1981-84; Travers Smith Braithwaite, Solicitor 1984-88; Booth & Co, Associate 1988-89. *Biog: b.* 28 May 1959. *Nationality:* British. *m.* 1984, Susan Harriet (née Rosborough); 1 s. *Educ:* Alleynes School, Stone; Bristol University (LLB Hons). *Professional Organisations:* Solicitor. *Recreations:* Golf, Cinema, Walking.

McINTOSH, Robert Gilbert; Director, 3i plc, since 1986; Administration, UK Investment Activities. *Career:* Coopers & Lybrand, Audit Snr 1960-67; 3i plc, Investment Controller 1967-72; Royal Bank of Scotland plc, Mgr/Dir, Leasing 1972-79; 3i plc, Mgr, Leasing 1979-82; Head of Personnel 1982-88; Regional Director for Scotland and N Ireland 1988-90. *Biog: b.* 30 April 1943. *Nationality:* British. *m.* 1967, Pamela Lloyd (née Murray); 2 s. *Educ:* Airdrie Academy, Scotland. *Directorships:* OIC (UK) Ltd 1986 (non-exec). *Professional Organisations:* CA. *Clubs:* Caledonian, Woking Golf Club, Mortonhall Golf Club. *Recreations:* Golf, Bridge.

MacINTYRE, Robert Hamilton; Partner, MacIntyre Hudson, since 1961; General Audit Partner. *Career:* MacIntyre Hudson Trained as Chartered Accountant. *Biog: b.* 2 March 1932. *Nationality:* British. *m.* 1956, Jean-Anne (née Pizzey); 2 s; 2 d. *Educ:* St Paul's School. *Directorships:* Surrey Building Society 1988 (non-exec). *Professional Organisations:* FCA. *Clubs:* Leander RC, Thames RC. *Recreations:* Motoring, Swimming.

MACK, H G; Director, Minories Holdings Ltd.

MACKAY, Alex J R; Partner (Birmingham), Evershed Wells & Hind.

MacKAY, Angela; Finance Reporter, The Times.

MACKAY, Barry G; Managing Director, Alexander Howden Reinsurance Brokers Limited.

MACKAY, Heather; VP Bond Sales, ScotiaMcLeod Incorporated.

MacKAY, I H N; Group Chief Executive, The Frizzell Group Limited.

MacKAY, Iain; Director, Allied Provincial plc.

MACKAY, Neil Douglas Malcolm; Managing Director, Lazard Brothers & Co Ltd, since 1987; Corporate Finance. *Career:* Industrial Reorganisation Corporation 1967-68; Lazard Brothers, Asst Dir 1974-78; Exec Dir 1979-87. *Biog: b.* 28 August 1939. *Nationality:* British. *m.* 1969, Frances (née Van Namen); 2 s; 2 d. *Educ:* Loretto School. *Directorships:* Tridant Group Printers Ltd 1974-79 (non-exec); R & A G Crossland Ltd 1975-78 (non-exec); Hadson Petroleum International plc 1981-86 (non-exec); Aaronite Group plc 1983-86 (non-exec). *Other Activities:* British Merchant Banking and Securities Houses Association Corporate Finance Committee 1988-. *Clubs:* Hurlingham. *Recreations:* Bridge, Tennis.

MACKAY, P; Partner, Dundas & Wilson CS.

MACKAY, R J; Director, Hill Samuel Bank Limited, since 1989; Corporate Lending. *Career:* Hill Samuel Bank Limited 1978-. *Biog: b.* 31 May 1956. *Nationality:* British. *m.* 1979, Geraldine Mary (née Keating); 3 s; 1 d. *Educ:* Shrewsbury School; University of Edinburgh (MA Hons).

McKEAN, John Michael; Partner, Wedlake Bell (London); Resident Partner, Wedlake Bell & Partners (Geneva) and Wedlake Bell McKean (Guernsey). *Career:* National Service, Commission in RA; OC North Norfolk Transport; Qualified as Solicitor 1958; Shacklocks, Partner, Senior Partner & Managing Partner 1960-78; N M Rothschild & Sons (CI) Limited, Director, Trust Work 1978-80; British Waterways, Solicitor to the Board 1980-86. *Biog: b.* 10 November 1931. *Educ:* Worksop (Scholar); New College, Oxford. *Other Activities:* Part-time Tutor & Lecturer, Nottingham University, 1973-78; Law Society Final Examination Board, 1977-; Law Society Continuing Education Programme, Lecturer/Chm, Conduct & Ethics, 1986-. *Professional Organisations:* Nottinghamshire Law Society Prize. *Publications:* Author, Practical Precedents; Contributor, Modern Wills and Modern Conveyancing Precedents. *Clubs:* RAC, Kings, Vincents, Achilles. *Recreations:* Theatre, Sport (especially Athletics and Squash: Athletics & Cross-country for Oxford and Nottinghamshire and Pres & Sec, Nottinghamshire AAA; Squash for Nottinghamshire and Guernsey Veterans).

McKEAN, Roderick Hugh Ross; Partner, Lovell White Durrant, since 1988; Corporate Finance. *Career:* W & J Burness WS, Articled Clerk 1978-80; Maclay Murray & Spens, Asst Solicitor 1980-84; Lovell White & King, Asst Solicitor 1984-88. *Biog: b.* 13 March 1956. *Nationality:* British. *Educ:* The High School of Dundee; Edinburgh University (LLB Hons). *Professional Organisa-*

tions: The Law Society; The Law Society of Scotland. *Recreations:* Skiing, Tennis, Riding, Sailing.

McKEAND, J L; Partner, Freshfields.

MACKEITH, D H; Financial Director, Land Securities.

McKENNA, Charles; Partner, Allen & Overy.

McKENNA, Martin N; Partner (Birmingham), Evershed Wells & Hind.

McKENNA, S; Partner, Nabarro Nathanson.

MACKENZIE, Christopher Alasthair Antony Ewan; Director, J Henry Schroder Wagg & Co Ltd, since 1988; Japanese Corporate Finance. *Career:* John Swire & Sons, Hong Kong 1975-81; McKinsey & Co, Tokyo 1982-85; J P Morgan & Co, Tokyo 1985-88. *Biog: b.* 28 June 1954. *Nationality:* British. *m.* 1982, Pearl; 2 s. *Educ:* Eton College; Christ Church, Oxford (MA, BA); INSEAD (MBA). *Directorships:* J Henry Schroder Wagg & Co 1988 (exec); Schroders Japan Limited 1990 (exec); PCFM Inc 1990 (exec). *Clubs:* Brooks, Travellers. *Recreations:* Squash, Riding, Chess.

McKENZIE, Miss Dinah; Director, Midland Montagu Asset Management, since 1990.

McKENZIE, G M; Director, C & G Guardian.

MACKENZIE, J; Director, Chartered Trust plc.

MACKENZIE, M C; Partner, Field Fisher Waterhouse.

McKENZIE, R A; Executive Director, Booker plc.

McKENZIE, Ross Lindsay; Regional Chairman & Director, Alexander Howden Limited, since 1990. *Career:* Stenhouse Group, Queensland, Australia, Various, principally Broking and Marketing 1962; General Manager for Victoria 1979; General Manager for New South Wales Division 1983; Australian Board of Alexander Stenhouse 1985; Alexander Stenhouse, Australia, Managing Director and Chief Executive Officer 1987; Alexander Howden Asia Pacific, Chairman and Alexander Howden Non-Marine, London, Chief Executive 1990. *Biog: b.* 22 June 1946. *Nationality:* Australian. *m.* 1967, Therese (née Maclennan); 3 s; 1 d. *Educ:* Harvard (Advanced Management Programme). *Directorships:* Alexander Howden Limited 1990 (exec); John C Lloyd Reinsurance Brokers Pty Limited (Australia) 1985 (exec); Southern Cross Underwriting Pty Limited (Australia) 1985 (exec); Alexander Stenhouse Limited (Australia) 1985-90 (exec). *Professional Organisations:* Annual Subscriber, Lloyd's of London; Member, Australian Institute of Company Directors; Associate, Australian Insurance Institute.

MACKENZIE, W J; OBE; Non-Executive Director, Slough Estates plc.

MACKENZIE-GREEN, John Garvie; Chairman, Heath Fielding Insurance Brokers, since 1987; Broking. *Career:* Fielding Insurance Holdings Snr Dir 1978-86. *Biog: b.* 28 April 1953. *Nationality:* British. *m.* 1976, Tessa Mary (née Batten); 2 s; 1 d. *Educ:* Malvern College; Guildford Law College. *Directorships:* C E Heath plc 1986 (exec); Subsidiary Boards of C E Heath plc. *Other Activities:* Member of Lloyds. *Professional Organisations:* IBA. *Recreations:* Yachting, Golf, Shooting, Skiing.

MACKIE, David Lindsay; Senior Litigation Partner in the London Office, Allen & Overy. *Career:* Articled Clerk 1969-71; Assistant Solicitor 1971-74; Partner 1975-. *Biog: b.* 15 February 1946. *Nationality:* British. *m.* 1989, Phyllis (née Gershon); 2 s; 1 d. *Educ:* RAF School, Changi; Ardingly College; St Edmund Hall, Oxford (BA, MA). *Other Activities:* Assistant Recorder, Crown & County Courts; Chairman, International Bar Association Committee on Product Liability, Advertising, Consumer Affairs and Unfair Competition. *Professional Organisations:* Solicitor. *Publications:* Products Liability - An International Manual of Practice (jointly with others), 1988; & Various Articles. *Recreations:* Climbing.

MACKIE, Francis; Partner, Clyde & Co.

MACKIE, Miss Sheila C D; Assistant Director, Hodgson Martin Ltd, since 1989; Venture Capital. *Career:* The Alliance Trust Dundee 1985-86. *Biog: b.* 9 June 1944. *Nationality:* Scottish. *Educ:* Wellington School, Ayr; Loretto School, Musselburgh; University of Aberdeen (LLB).

McKINNON, Andrew Stephen; Partner, Bacon & Woodrow, since 1990; Actuarial Consultancy to Pension Schemes. *Career:* Norwich Union, Actuary 1981-86; T G Arthur Hargrave, Actuary 1987-89. *Biog: b.* 16 March 1960. *Nationality:* British. *m.* 1982, Sheridan (née Weaver); 1 s; 1 d. *Educ:* Netherstowe Comprehensive School, Lichfield, Staffs; Exeter University (BA). *Professional Organisations:* Fellow, Institute of Actuaries.

MACKINNON, Colin Ian Charles; Divisional Director, E D & F Man International Ltd, since 1980; Futures. *Career:* Maclaine Watson & Co Ltd 1969-73; Commodity Analysis Ltd 1973-80; E D & F Man International Ltd, Commodity Broker 1980-. *Biog: b.* 21 August 1947. *Nationality:* British. *Educ:* Harrow School. *Directorships:* London Metal Exchange Ltd 1989. *Clubs:* Royal Yacht Squadron, Seawanhaka Corinthian Yacht Club, Bembridge Sailing Club. *Recreations:* Yachting.

MACKINNON, Neil John; Chief Economist, Yamaichi International (Europe) Ltd, since 1989; Global Economic Strategy in the Fixed Income, Equities & Foreign Exchange Matters. *Career:* HM Treasury, Economist 1982-85; Fielding Newson-Smith & Co, Economist 1985-86; Nomura Research Institute, Economist 1986-88; Chase Investment Bank, Senior Economist & Director 1988-89. *Biog: b.* 17 May 1955. *Nationality:* British. *m.* 2d. *Educ:* Waterloo Grammar School, Liverpool; University of Liverpool (BA Hons Economics); University of Southampton (MSc Economics & Econometrics). *Directorships:* Yamaichi International (Europe)Ltd 1989 (exec). *Publications:* Inflation & Relative Price Variabilty: The UK Experience over the last 30 years (with A Smith), Scottish Journal of Political Economy, May 1987; The Yen Bond Market in Global Government Bonds, 1988; The Sterling Money Market (with M Dowding and foreword by Sir Douglas Wass), 1989; Gilts - Facing the Challenge (with D Corrigan & S Hartnell), 1989.

MACKINTOSH, Anthony Robert Kilgour; Head of Marketing and Research, Laing & Cruickshank, since 1990; Institutional Equities. *Career:* British Petroleum, Executive Supply & Planning 1965-71; Wood Mackenzie & Co, Oil Analyst 1972-81; Head of Research 1981-86; Hill Samuel Bank Ltd, Director Corporate Finance 1986-89. *Biog: b.* 15 June 1943. *Nationality:* British. *m.* 1967, Barbara Dorothy (née Fox); 3 s. *Educ:* Brighton Hove & Sussex Grammar School; Hertford College, Oxford (MA Modern History). *Directorships:* Laing & Cruickshank 1990 (exec). *Professional Organisations:* Associate Member, Society of Investment Analysts. *Clubs:* United Oxford & Cambridge University, Highgate GC. *Recreations:* Golf, Bridge, Chess, Reading.

MACKINTOSH, James Donald Malcolm; Partner, Lawrence Graham, since 1979. *Career:* Lawrence Graham 1973-. *Biog: b.* 16 June 1950. *Nationality:* British. *m.* 1977, Catherine (née Lea); 2 d. *Educ:* Fettes College; St Andrews University (MA). *Other Activities:* Council Member, Society for Computers & Law; Member of its Executive Committee; Chairman of its London Branch. *Professional Organisations:* The Law Society. *Clubs:* Collegium Musicum of London, Riverside. *Recreations:* Singing, Sport.

MACKINTOSH, Simon A; WS; Partner, Convenor, Private Client Department, W & J Burness WS Solicitors, since 1985; Private Client. *Career:* W & J Burness, Apprentice 1980-82; W & J Burness, Solicitor 1982-84; Boodle Hatfield, Seconded 1983-84. *Biog: b.* 2 February 1957. *Nationality:* British. *m.* 1984, Catriona (née Mann); 1 s; 1 d. *Educ:* Glenalmond; Magdalene College, Cambridge (MA); Edinburgh (LLB). *Professional Organisations:* Law Society of Scotland; WS Society. *Publications:* Revenue Law in Scotland (with M H Jones), 1987. *Clubs:* Edinburgh Academical. *Recreations:* Golf, Gardening, Rugby.

McKIRDY, J L; Deputy Chairman, Noble Lowndes & Partners Ltd, since 1990; Personal Financial Services in UK, Ireland and Australia. *Career:* Noble Lowndes & Partners Ltd, Appointed to the Board 1972; Noble Lowndes Personal Financial Services, Assistant New Business Director 1973-76; New Business Director 1976-78; Deputy Managing Director 1978-79; Managing Director 1979-87; Noble Lowndes & Partners Ltd, Deputy Chief Executive 1987-90; Deputy Chairman 1990-. *Biog: b.* 13 September 1931. *Nationality:* British. *m.* 1955, Isobel (née Brownlee); 4 d. *Educ:* Queen's Park School, Glasgow. *Directorships:* Noble Lowndes International Holdings Pty Ltd (Australia) 1985; Noble Lowndes Personal Financial Services Ltd (Australia) 1985; Noble Lowndes (New Zealand) Ltd 1985. *Clubs:* RAC, Tandridge Golf Club. *Recreations:* Golf, Bridge.

MACKLIN, Jeffrey Randall; Senior Director, Continental Bank NA, since 1987; Chairman, Product Risk Committee. *Career:* Deloitte Haskins & Sells, New York City Client Services 1974-84; Multinational Client Service Initiative (London, New York, Continental Europe) US Liaison (London) 1984-87. *Biog: b.* 29 April 1950. *Nationality:* American. *m.* 1981, Diane M Kotelnikoff; 1 d. *Educ:* Ohio State University (BSc Accounting & Computer Science); Drexel University, Philadephia (MBA Finance & Accounting). *Other Activities:* Chairman, The American Society in London, 1988-90; Executive Committee Member, 1984-; Pan Asian Repertory Theatre, Board of Directors (Vice-President, Finance and Administration/Treasurer), 1981-84; Church of The Epiphany, Member of the Vestry/Treasurer, 1981-84; Young Adult Community, President/Treasurer, 1978-80; Executive Program of the J L Kellogg Graduate School of Management, Northwestern University, 1981; Boy Scouts of America, Eagle Scout, 1964. *Professional Organisations:* CPA (Ohio, New York & California); Member, American Institute of CPAs; Member, Ohio, New York & California Societies of CPAs; The Securities Association, Registered Manager. *Recreations:* Cinema & Theatre, Photography & Travel, Running, Tennis, Skiing.

MACKLIN, Peter Richard; Departmental Managing Partner, Real Property Dept, Freshfields, since 1980; Real Property. *Career:* Clifford Turner, Assistant Solicitor 1971-77. *Biog: b.* 1 April 1946. *Nationality:* British. *m.* 1971, Pamela Adele (née Plant); 3 s. *Educ:* Wellington College; St Cuthbert's Society, Durham (BA). *Directorships:* British Property Federation 1990 (non-exec). *Professional Organisations:* City of London Solicitors' Company, The Law Society; IBA. *Recreations:* Family, Opera, Exploration.

MACKNEY, V D; Director, S G Warburg Akroyd Rowe & Pitman Mullens Securities Ltd.

MacKNIGHT, A; Partner, Cameron Markby Hewitt.

McLACHLAN, Ian Malcolm; Partner, Holman Fenwick & Willan, since 1961; Shipping & Insurance.

McLACHLAN, John James; Investment Manager & Director, United Friendly Insurance plc, since 1990; Investment Management. *Career:* Norwest Construction, Mgmnt Accountant 1966-67; Martins Bank Trust Co, Investment Analyst 1967-69; Barclays Bank Trust Co, Invest Research Mgr 1969-71; Dep Invest Mgr 1971-74; British Railways Pension Fund, Invest Mgr 1974-83; Dir, Pension Invests 1983-84; Reed International plc, Investment Mgr 1984-88; United Friendly Insurance plc, Invest Mgr 1988. *Biog: b.* 28 August 1942. *Nationality:* British. *m.* 1966, Heather Joan (née Smith); 1 s; 1 d. *Educ:* Rock Ferry High Grammar. *Directorships:* Iceland Frozen Foods plc 1984 (non-exec); Iceland Frozen Foods Pension Fund 1985 (non-exec) Chm; Hewitt High Total Return US Equity Fund Ltd 1988 Chm; National Assoc of Pension Funds Ltd 1984-90 Chm Investment Committee; Investment Management Regulatory Organisation Ltd 1985. *Other Activities:* Panel on Takeovers & Mergers (1986-88); Institutional Shareholders Ctee (1986-88). *Professional Organisations:* FCA, AMSIA, RSA. *Publications:* Number of specialised investment articles. *Recreations:* Squash.

MacLACHLAN, Neil Thacker; Deputy Managing Director, Svenska International plc, since 1990; Merchant Banking. *Career:* James Capel & Co Ltd 1986-90; Head of Corporate Finance 1987; Wardley Australia Ltd, MD 1979-86; Wardley Ltd, Various 1974-79. *Biog: b.* 3 August 1942. *m.* 1974, Elizabeth (née Rice); 2 d. *Educ:* Sevenoaks School; Manchester University (BSc Hons). *Directorships:* Wardley Holdings Ltd 1983-87; James Capel & Co Ltd 1988-90; Svenska International plc 1990. *Clubs:* Hurlingham, Queen's, Wisley, Hongkong Club, Australian Club. *Recreations:* Skiing, Tennis, Golf.

MACLACHLAN, Simon; MBE; Partner, Clifford Chance, since 1964; Chairman/Company Department. *Career:* Queen's Own Royal West Kent Rgt, Lieutenant 1953-55. *Biog: b.* 17 December 1934. *Nationality:* British. *m.* 1963, Julie (née Mannering); 2 s; 2 d. *Educ:* Downside School; Law Society's School of Law. *Other Activities:* Circle 33 Housing Trust (Trustee). *Professional Organisations:* The Law Society; IBA. *Publications:* Euromoney International Securities 1984 (UK Section), Take Overs & Mergers in Europe, 1989. *Clubs:* RAC. *Recreations:* Gardening, Swimming, Tennis.

MacLAREN, Andrew Murray; Partner, Wilde Sapte, since 1990; Banking and International Finance. *Career:* Allen & Overy Articled Clerk and Qualified Solicitor 1967-70; Linklaters & Paines, Assistant Solicitor 1972-74; Marine Midland Bank Group, Lawyer 1974-80; International Counsel (New York) 1977-80; Security Pacific Bank, Counsel for Europe, Africa & Middle East 1981-85; Deacons, Partner Hong Kong 1985-90; Legal

Adviser to the Hong Kong Association of Banks. *Biog: b.* 18 October 1944. *Nationality:* British. *m.* 1969, Elizabeth, (née Smith); 2 s; 1 d. *Educ:* Tonbridge School; Pembroke College, Cambridge (MA). *Other Activities:* International Bar Association; Member, New York Clearing House Committee on International Banking Facilities, 1978-80. *Professional Organisations:* Solicitor (England & Wales) 1968; Solicitor (Hong Kong) 1985; Notary Public (Hong Kong) 1988. *Publications:* Chapter on Syndicated Bank Lending in International Banking by E Roussakis, 1982. *Clubs:* Hong Kong Club, Clearwater Bay Golf, Naval Club, Edenbridge Golf Club; *Clubs:* Music, Golf, Pre-18th Century Cartography.

McLAREN, J A; Director, Morgan Grenfell & Co Limited.

McLAUCHLAN, R; Managing Director (Investment Management), Bankers Trust Company.

McLAUGHLIN, S; Executive Director, Wardley Unit Trust Managers Limited.

MacLAURIN, Sir Ian; Chairman, Tesco plc, since 1985. *Career:* Vatric Control Equipment 1959-60; Tesco Stores Holdings Ltd (now Tesco plc) 1960-; Director 1970; Managing Director 1973; Deputy Chairman 1983-85; Chairman 1985. *Biog: b.* 30 March 1937. *Nationality:* British. *m.* 1960, Ann; 1 s; 2 d. *Educ:* Malvern College. *Directorships:* Tesco plc 1985 Chairman; Guinness plc 1986 (non-exec); Institute of Grocery Distribution 1989 President; National Westminster Bank 1990 (non-exec). *Other Activities:* Awarded the Freedom of the City of London in 1981; Liveryman, Carmen Company. *Clubs:* MCC, Band of Brothers, RAC, Forty Club. *Recreations:* Golf.

McLEAN, Ms Deborah; Managing Director, Morgan Stanley International; Firm's Property Activities in UK and on Continent. *Biog: b.* 30 December 1954. *Nationality:* American. *m.* 1985, Keith L Kearney; 1 s. *Educ:* Harvard College (BA); Harvard Business School (MBA).

MACLEAN, George Angus; Director, Baring Brothers & Co Limited.

McLEAN, James A; WS; Partner, W & J Burness WS.

McLEAN, K; Director, LAS Unit Trust Managers.

MacLEAN, Lachlan Roderick; Director, Touche Remnant & Co, since 1985; In Charge of Private Clients. *Career:* C Tennant Sons & Co Ltd Metal Trader 1964-69; Capel-Cure Myers Acct Mgr Private Clients 1969-78; Société Générale Merchant Bank (London) Assoc Dir Investment Div 1978-83; (Singapore) Head of Investment Div 1983-85. *Biog: b.* 2 April 1944. *Nationality:* British. *m.* 1968; 2 d. *Educ:* Winchester College.

Directorships: TR High Income Trust plc 1989 (non-exec). *Clubs:* MCC.

MacLEAN, Murdo; Partner, McGrigor Donald, since 1987; Banking Law. *Career:* McGrigor Donald, Asst Solicitor 1979-84; Stephenson Harwood (London), Asst Solicitor; Stephenson Harwood & Co (Hong Kong) 1984-86. *Biog: b.* 12 June 1956. *Nationality:* Scottish. *m.* 1980, Fiona Mary (née Fern); 2 s. *Educ:* Nicolson Institute, Stornoway; University of Aberdeen (LLB Hons); University of British Columbia (LLM). *Professional Organisations:* Law Society of Scotland. *Clubs:* Clyde Canoe Club. *Recreations:* Fishing, Reading.

McLEAN, Neil M; Partner, Walker Morris Scott Turnbull, since 1980; Commercial Property, Building Society Law. *Biog: b.* 16 June 1953. *Nationality:* British. *m.* 1986, Jill Frances (née Riley); 2 s; 2 d. *Educ:* Leeds University (LLB 2i). *Directorships:* Coppergate Properties Limited 1986 (non-exec); The Park Square Trust Limited 1986 (non-exec). *Professional Organisations:* Law Society.

McLEAN, R A; Director, R A McLean & Co Ltd.

MACLEAN, Simon P; Head of Information Services, Kleinwort Benson Limited, since 1989. *Career:* Kleinwort Benson 1986 -; Director 1989-; Asst Director 1988-89; Manager 1986-87; Grieveson Grant & Co (Subsequently Bought by KB in 1986) Systems Manager/Manager, Settlements/Internal Audit, Asst Manager/Department Head, Settlements/Trainee Stockbroker 1972-86. *Biog: b.* 14 December 1950. *Nationality:* British. *m.* 1969, Pauline Lilian; 2 s. *Educ:* Tunbridge Wells Grammar School; Hastings College of Further Education. *Directorships:* Kleinwort Benson Securities Ltd. *Professional Organisations:* Stock Exchange Examination. *Recreations:* Tennis, Travel, Food & Drink.

McLEISH, Ian Clelland; Joint Manager, The Scottish Investment Trust, since 1986; Investment Management. *Career:* Kleinwort Benson, Asst Mgr 1968-73; Scottish Investment Trust, Investment Sec, Asst Mgr, Mgr 1973-. *Biog: b.* 16 July 1945. *Nationality:* British. *m.* 1969, Margaret (née Kilpatrick); 4 s. *Educ:* Royal High School of Edinburgh. *Other Activities:* General Ctee of Assoc of Investment Trust Companies; Treasurer, Alzheimer's Scotland. *Professional Organisations:* CA. *Recreations:* Golf, Tennis, Curling.

McLEISH, Stuart K; Partner, Wilde Sapte.

McLELAND, Warren; Managing Director & Global Risk Management Executive, Chase Investment Bank Limited.

MacLENNAN, Angus G; Deputy General Manager, Den Danske Bank, since 1988; Corporate Banking, Asset Financing, M & A Credit. *Career:* BFCE, Senior Manager Corporate Banking 1981-87; First Interstate Bank, International Banking Officer 1979-87. *Biog: b.* 12 December 1955. *Nationality:* British. *m.* 1976, Fiona; 2 s; 2 d. *Educ:* Napier College, Edinburgh (Dip Comm); Glasgow College of Technology (ICSA). *Directorships:* David Garrick Ltd 1990 (non-exec). *Recreations:* Golf, Squash, Rugby.

MACLEOD, A M; Director, Holman Macleod Limited.

McLEOD, Alex; Managing Director, LDC Asset Trading, Continental Bank NA.

MacLEOD, Donald Ian Kerr; RD, WS; Senior Litigation Partner, Shepherd & Wedderburn WS, since 1970. *Career:* MacPherson & Mackay WS, Apprentice 1957-59; Shepherd & Wedderburn WS, Qualified Asst 1960-64; Partner 1964-. *Biog: b.* 19 April 1937. *Nationality:* British. *m.* 1966, Mary St Clair (née Bridge); 1 s; 2 d. *Educ:* Aberdeen Grammar School; Edinburgh University (MA, LLB). *Other Activities:* Solicitor in Scotland to HM Customs and Excise (1970-), to Department of Employment (1970-) and to Health and Safety Executive and Commission (1974-); Member, Court of Session Rules Council & Rules Review Gp; Lt, Cdr, RNR (Rtd). *Professional Organisations:* Member, Law Society of Scotland; Scottish Law Agents Society; Society of Writers to HM Signet. *Clubs:* Bruntsfield Links Golfing Society. *Recreations:* Golf, Hockey (Class 1 International Umpire).

MacLEOD, Duncan James; *Career:* Ernst & Whinney, Partner 1960-89; Managing Partner, Glasgow Office 1985-. *Biog: b.* 1 November 1934. *Nationality:* British. *m.* 1958, Joanna (née Bibby); 2 s; 1 d. *Educ:* Eton College. *Directorships:* Bank of Scotland 1973 (non-exec); Scottish Provident Institution 1976 (non-exec); The Weir Group plc 1976 (non-exec); Scottish Industrial Development Advisory Board 1980 (non-exec); 1989 Chairman; Harry Ramsden's plc 1989; Motherwell Bridge Holdings Ltd 1990. *Clubs:* Western (Glasgow), Prestwick Golf Club, MCC, Royal Ancient Golf Club. *Recreations:* Shooting, Golf.

McLINTOCK, (Charles) Alan; Chairman, Woolwich Building Society, since 1983. *Career:* Army 1943-47; Thomson McLintock & Co, Ptnr 1954-82; KMG Thomson McLintock, Snr Ptnr 1982-87; Trust Houses, Dir 1967-71; Grange Trust, Dir and Chm 1954-81; National Westminster Bank, Dir 1979-90; Govett Oriental Investment Trust, Chm 1971-90. *Biog: b.* 28 May 1925. *Nationality:* British. *m.* 1955, Sylvia Mary (née Foster Taylor); 1 s; 3 d. *Educ:* Rugby School. *Directorships:* National Westminster Bank UK Advisory Board 1990 (non-exec); Ecclesiastical Insurance Office 1972 (non-exec) Chm; M & G Group 1982 (non-exec); Govett Strategic Investment Trust 1971 (non-exec) Chm; Govett Atlantic Investment Trust 1978 (non-exec) Chm; AJ's Family Restaurants Ltd 1987 (non-exec) Chm; Church Urban Fund 1990 (non-exec). *Other Activities:* Chm, Governing Body of Rugby School; VP, Clergy Orphan Corp; Member of Court, London University. *Professional Organisations:* CA. *Clubs:* Army and Navy.

McLINTOCK, Dr Clive Holt; Deputy Managing Director, Barclays Development Capital Ltd, since 1988. *Career:* Metals Research Limited, Marketing Mgr 1963-69; Scientific & Electronic Industries Trust Ltd, Dir 1970-74; Sangers Group Limited, Group Corporate Planner 1975-79; Barclays Development Capital Ltd, Dir 1979-88. *Biog: b.* 14 June 1938. *Nationality:* British. *m.* 1967, Carol (née Musker); 3 d. *Educ:* Merchant Taylors' School; University of Liverpool (BSc Hons, PhD). *Directorships:* Foster & Plumpton Group Ltd 1985 (non-exec); FEM Ltd 1985 (non-exec).

McLUSKIE, W G; Group Treasurer, GKN plc.

MacMAHON, Brian Sean; Group Benefits Executive, BET plc, since 1982; Corporate Retirement & Benefit Plans. *Career:* Irish Pensions Trust (Dublin) General Duties 1955-66; Client Services Mgr 1966-72; Allied Lyons Pension Trust Scheme Controller 1973-76; Pension Fund Manager 1976-81. *Biog: b.* 3 April 1938. *Nationality:* Irish. *m.* 1983, Colleen (née Harbottle); 2 s; 2 d. *Educ:* Terenure College, Dublin. *Directorships:* BET Pension Trust Ltd 1982 (exec); United Transport Group Pension Trustee Ltd 1982 (non-exec); Sparrow Group Pension Trustee Ltd 1987 (non-exec); BET Copenhagen Pension Trustee Ltd 1988 (non-exec); BET EPS Trustee Ltd 1988 (non-exec); National Association of Pension Funds Ltd 1983 (non-exec). *Other Activities:* Council; Occupational Pensions Advisory Service (OPAS). *Professional Organisations:* FPMI; Vice Chm, National Association Pension Funds. *Publications:* Pension Scheme Trusteeship-Discretionary Powers, 1982. *Clubs:* Bristol and Clifton Golf Club. *Recreations:* Golf, Theatre.

McMAHON, Sir Kit (Christopher William); Kt; Chairman & Chief Executive, Midland Bank plc, since 1987. *Career:* University of Melbourne, Tutor (Eng Lit) 1950; HM Treasurer, Econ Asst 1953-57; British Embassy (Washington), Econ Adviser 1957-60; Magdalen College, Oxford, Fellow & Tutor (Econ) 1960-64; Bank of England, Adviser 1964; Adviser to the Governors 1966-70; Exec Dir 1970-80; Dep Governor 1980-85. *Biog: b.* 10 July 1927. *Nationality:* British. m1 Marion (née Kelso); 2s; m2 1982, Alison Barbara (née Baimbridge). *Educ:* Melbourne Grammar School; University of Melbourne (BA); Magdalen College, Oxford (MA Hons 1st). *Directorships:* Midland Montagu Holdings 1986 Chm; Hong Kong Shanghai Banking Corp; Eurotunnel 1987. *Other Activities:* British Invisible Export Council (Chm, Overseas Promotions Ctee); Hon Fellow, University College of North Wales, 1988; Hon Fellow, Chartered Society of Designers, 1990; Awarded

rank of Chevalier dans l'Ordre National de la Legion d'Honneur, 1990. *Professional Organisations:* FInstM. *Publications:* Sterling in the Sixties, 1964; Techniques of Economic Forecasting (Editor), 1965. *Clubs:* Garrick. *Recreations:* Gardening, Books, Looking at Pictures.

McMEEHAN, Anne; Marketing Director, Framlington Group, since 1988. *Career:* British Commercial Transport Ltd, Mgmnt Trainee 1975-77; Hambro Life Assurance, Sales Assoc 1977-82; Arbuthnot Securities Ltd, Broker Consultant 1982-84; Marketing Mgr 1984-85; Framlington Overseas Fund Management Ltd, Marketing Mgr 1985-86; Dir 1986; Framlington Unit Management Ltd, Marketing Dir 1987. *Biog: b.* 25 April 1954. *Nationality:* British. *Educ:* Portsmouth High School for Girls (GPDST); Loughborough University of Technology (BA Hons). *Directorships:* Framlington Overseas Fund Management Ltd 1986 (exec); Framlington Unit Man Ltd 1987 (exec). *Recreations:* Entertaining, Squash, Tennis, Waterskiing, Reading, Theatre.

McMENAMIN, Derek; Partner, Linklaters & Paines.

MACMILLAN, Alexander Daniel Alan; The Earl of Stockton; President, Macmillan Ltd, since 1990. *Career:* Glasgow Herald, Sub-Editor 1963; Daily Telegraph, Reporter & Crime Correspondent 1965; Foreign Correspondent 1968-70; Sunday Telegraph, European Correspondent 1968-70; Macmillan Publishers Ltd 1970; Macmillan, Deputy Chairman 1984; Chairman 1985; President 1990. *Biog: b.* 10 October 1943. *Nationality:* British. *m.* 1970, Helene Birgitte (née Hamilton) (sep 1989); 1 s; 2 d. *Educ:* Highfield School, Liphook, Hampshire; Eton College, Windsor; Université de Paris, Ecole Science Politique (Diplômé Supérieur); University of Strathclyde. *Directorships:* Chemical Dependency Centre Ltd 1985; The English-Speaking Union of the Commonwealth 1986 Board Member; Book Trade Benevolent Society 1976-87 (non-exec). *Other Activities:* Joint National Chairman, National Playing Fields Association Appeal; Liveryman, The Worshipful Company of Merchant Taylors & The Worshipful Company of Stationers and Newspaper Makers; President, The Westminster Chamber of Commerce; Chairman, Central London Training and Enterprise Council (CENTEC); Member, RNIB's National Committee for the Looking Glass Appeal. *Professional Organisations:* FRSA; FInstD; CBIM. *Clubs:* Carlton, Buck's, Garrick, White's, Beefsteak. *Recreations:* Shooting, Opera, Ballet, Theatre.

McMILLAN, John; Partner, James Gentles & Son.

McMULLAN, David Malcom; Director, County NatWest Securities Ltd.

McNALLY, John J; Executive Director, Ulster Bank Limited.

McNAMARA, B G; Director, Hill Samuel & Co Ltd.

McNAMARA, K Paul; Partner, Ernst & Young, since 1979; Partner in Charge, Insurance Industry Group. *Career:* Whinney Murray 1970; Ernst & Whinney 1979-89. *Biog:* b. 9 April 1948. *Nationality:* British. *Educ:* Beaumont College; Magdalene College, Cambridge (MA). *Professional Organisations:* FCA. *Clubs:* City of London. *Recreations:* Horse Racing, Opera, Tennis, Bridge.

MACNAMARA, Rory Patrick; Director, Morgan Grenfell & Co Ltd, since 1988; Corporate Finance. *Biog:* b. 2 January 1955. *Nationality:* British. *m.* 1986, Clare (née Asquith); 1 s; 1 d. *Educ:* Stowe; Christ Church, Oxford (MA). *Professional Organisations:* ACA. *Clubs:* City.

MacNAUGHT, D K; Chairman Elect, Yorkshire Building Society.

McNAUGHT, Lewis John; Director, Gartmore Investment Management Limited.

MacNAUGHTON, Niall; Consultant (Banking), BBM Associates, since 1990; Commercial Lending, Credit, Syndications, Property Finance, Capital Markets & Transaction Management. *Career:* Michael Page plc, Consultant (Banking), Recruitment of Banking Officers for City Based Banks and Securities Houses 1987-89; Commissioned Officer H M Forces (Army) 1980-87; Operations Officer 6th (Qeo) Gurkha Rifles, Captain 1986-87; Commissioned Officer with 4th Royal Tank Regiment (stationed in West Germany, Northern Ireland & the UK), Operations Officer, Regimental Signals Officer & Tank Troop Leader 1980-87. *Biog:* b. 6 November 1961. *Nationality:* British. *m.* 1988, Caroline. *Educ:* Morrisons Academy, Crieff, Scotland; Royal Military Academy, Sandhurst (Commissioned August 1980). *Recreations:* Skiing, Sailing, Golf, Running, Theatre, Cinema, Music.

MacNEARY, A J; Director, County NatWest Securities Limited.

McNEE, Sir David; QPM; *Career:* Police Officer in Glasgow 1946-68; Deputy Chief Constable, Dunbartonshire 1968-71; Chief Constable, City of Glasgow Police 1971-75; Chief Constable, Strathclyde Police 1975-77; Commissioner of Police of the Metropolis 1977-82; Non-Exec Director of a Number of Quoted and Unquoted Companies 1982-. *Biog:* b. 23 March 1925. *Nationality:* British. *m.* 1952, Isabella Clayton (née Hopkins); 1 d. *Educ:* Woodside Senior Secondary, Glasgow. *Directorships:* Clydesdale Bank plc 1982 (non-exec); Scottish Express Newspapers Ltd 1983 (non-exec); Trusthouse Forte plc 1983 (non-exec); Integrated Security Services Ltd 1985 (non-exec); Plextel Security Systems Ltd 1986 (non-exec); Clyde Helicopters Ltd

1988 (non-exec); Memex Information Systems Ltd 1988 (non-exec); Wrightson Wood Ltd 1988 (non-exec); Scottish Business Communications Ltd 1990 (non-exec). *Other Activities:* President, The Royal Life Saving Society 1982-89; President, The National Bible Society of Scotland 1983-; President, Glasgow City Committee of Cancer Relief 1987-; Patron, The Scottish Motor Neurone Disease Association 1982-; Chairman, St John Association of Scotland (Glasgow Branch) 1987-; Honorary Colonel 32 (Scottish) Signal Regiment (Volunteers) 1988-. *Professional Organisations:* FBIM; CBIM; FRSA. *Publications:* Crime and The Young in The 1978 Basil Henriques Memorial Lecture; Policing Modern Britain in London Lectures in Contemporary Christianity, 1979; McNee's Law, 1983. *Clubs:* Caledonian, Naval (Hon Member). *Recreations:* Fishing, Golfing, Music.

McNEIL, I G; Director, County NatWest Securities Limited.

McNEIL, Ian R; JP; Partner, Moores Rowland, since 1958; Deputy President, Institute of Chartered Accountants in England & Wales, since 1990. *Biog:* b. 14 December 1932. *Nationality:* British. *m.* 1964, Ann; 2 d. *Educ:* Brighton College. *Other Activities:* Liveryman, Curriers Company; Liveryman, Chartered Accountants Company; Justice of the Peace. *Professional Organisations:* Fellow, Institute of Chartered Accountants in England & Wales.

McNEIL, (James) John; Director, County NatWest Wood Mackenzie & Co Ltd.

McNEILL, James; Director & Company Secretary, Chartered WestLB Ltd, since 1989; Personnel, Secretariat & Administration. *Career:* British Linen Bank/ Bank of Scotland 1961-72; Midland & International Banks plc, Company Secretary 1972-83; Standard Chartered Merchant Bank Ltd, Director & Secretary 1983-90. *Biog:* b. 25 December 1944. *Nationality:* British. *m.* 1971, Patricia (née Grimes); 2 s; 1 d. *Directorships:* Chartered WestLB Limited (and Subsidiaries) 1989 (exec). *Professional Organisations:* FCIS; AIB (Scot). *Recreations:* Golf.

McNEILLAGE, J K; General Manager, Finance, Clydesdale Bank plc.

McNIVEN, John; Managing Director, Merrill Lynch International Limited, since 1990; Capital Markets. *Career:* J P Morgan (Australia), M&A Department 1981-83; (New York) Commercial Banking 1983-84; (London) Capital Markets, responsible for Australia & New Zealand, responsible for executing the first Swaps in New Zealand & Australia dollars 1984-85; (New York) Swap Group, specialising in Foreign Currencies 1986-88; Merrill Lynch International Limited (London), Head of Capital Markets (Origination) 1988-. *Biog:* b. 18

December 1956. *Nationality:* Australian. *Educ:* St Stanislav's College, Bathurst; Australian National University (BEc Hons, LLB). *Professional Organisations:* Senior Associate of the Australian Society of Accountants. *Clubs:* Sydney Cricket Ground.

MACPHAIL, B D; Managing Director, Peninsular & Oriental Steam Navigation Company, since 1986. *Career:* Price Waterhouse, Accountant 1961-65; Hill Samuel & Co Ltd, Executive Corporate Finance 1967-69; Sterling Guarantee Trust, Finance Director 1969-74; Town & City Properties Ltd 1974-76; Sterling Guarantee Trust 1976-85; Peninsular & Oriental Steam Navigation Company, Managing Director 1985-. *Biog: b.* 1 May 1939. *Nationality:* British. 1983, Caroline Ruth (née Hubbard); 3 s; 1 steps; 1 stepd. *Educ:* Haileybury College; Balliol College, Oxford (BA Mathematics); Harvard University Graduate School of Business Admin (MBA). *Directorships:* The Peninsular & Oriental Steam Navigation Company; P&O Travel Limited; P&O Overseas Holdings Limited; P&O Property Holdings Limited; P&O Properties International Limited; P&O Pension Fund Investment Limited; Chelsea Harbour Limited; EF International Inc; Inmogolf SA; Earls Court & Olympia Limited; Sutcliffe Catering Group Limited; Pall Mall Properties. *Other Activities:* Governor, Royal Ballet School; Member, Council of Management of Templeton College. *Professional Organisations:* Associate, Institute of Chartered Accountants.

McPHAIL, M Douglas; Director, The British Linen Bank Limited.

MACPHERSON, Donald Charles; Executive Director, County NatWest Ltd, since 1986; Corporate Finance. *Career:* Fielding, Newson-Smith & Co, Snr Ptnr 1957-86. *Biog: b.* 3 January 1932. *Nationality:* British. *m.* 1962, Hilary Claire (née Standish). *Educ:* Winchester College. *Directorships:* Judy Farquharson Ltd 1974 (non-exec); Fuller Smith & Turner plc 1990 (non-exec). *Professional Organisations:* Member, The International Stock Exchange.

MACPHERSON, Ewen Cameron Stewart; Managing Director/Finance, 3i Group plc, since 1990; Finance/Planning. *Career:* Massey-Ferguson (UK) Ltd, Rep (Export) 1964-68; ICFC, PA to General Manager 1970-71; Planning Manager 1972-74; FCI, Controller & Manager 1975-81; FFI, Manager, Head Office 1982-85; 3i City Office, Managing Director 1985-90; 3i plc, Director, Member of Executive Committee 1985-90; 3i Group plc, Director 1989-90. *Biog: b.* 19 January 1942. *Nationality:* British. *m.* 1982, Laura Anne (née Baring); 2 s. *Educ:* Fettes College; Queens' College, Cambridge (MA); London Business School (MBA); Harvard (AMP). *Directorships:* Ship Mortgage Finance plc 1985 (non-exec); 3i International Holdings; 3i plc; 3i Portfolio Management Ltd. *Professional Organisations:* Business Graduates Assoc; Harvard Business School Assoc. *Clubs:*

Caledonian, City of London. *Recreations:* Gardening, Sailing.

MACPHERSON, Ian; Partner, Nabarro Nathanson, since 1990; Mines, Minerals Law, Environmental Litigation. *Career:* British Coal Corporation, Assistant Solicitor 1978-81; Western Area, Assistant Solicitor/Head of Litigation 1981-83; Legal Dept, Deputy Area Solicitor 1983-88; Head of Mining Group III 1988-90. *Biog: b.* 21 August 1948. *Nationality:* British. *m.* 1966, Annette Margaret (née Salter); 1 d. *Educ:* Wombourne School, Wolverhampton; Birmingham College of Commerce; Chester College of Law. *Professional Organisations:* Law Society.

MACPHERSON, (John Hannah) Forbes; CBE, OStJ; Chairman, TSB Bank Scotland plc, since 1984; Corporate Finance & Investment. *Career:* RNVR, Sub-Lieutenant 1943-47; Touche Ross & Co, Partner 1956-86; Glasgow Junior Chamber of Commerce, Chairman 1964-65; Scottish Industrial Estates Corporation, Chairman 1972-76; Irvine Development Corporation, Chairman 1976-79; Glasgow Chamber of Commerce, President 1980-81. *Biog: b.* 23 May 1926. *Nationality:* British. *m.* 1959, Margaret Graham (née Roxburgh); 1 s. *Educ:* Merchiston Castle School; Glasgow Academy. *Directorships:* The Scottish Mutual Assurance Society 1971 Chairman; TSB Group plc 1985 (non-exec); Scottish Metropolitan Property plc 1986 (non-exec); Glasgow Development Agency 1990 Deputy Chairman. *Other Activities:* Member of Court, University of Glasgow; Governor, Merchiston Castle School; Trustee, Prince & Princess of Wales Hospice; Trustee, Scottish Civic Trust. *Professional Organisations:* Member, Institute of Chartered Accountants of Scotland; Fellow, Institute of Petroleum; Fellow, Royal Society of Arts, Manufactures & Commerce. *Clubs:* East India, Western, RSAC, RNVR (Scotland). *Recreations:* Travel, Gardening, Reading.

MACPHERSON, Michael Alastair Fox; Partner, Ashurst Morris Crisp, since 1974; Company/Commercial. *Biog: b.* 17 December 1944. *Nationality:* British. *m.* 1972, Penelope Margaret (née Harper); 2 s; 1 d. *Educ:* Haileybury; Magdalene College, Cambridge (MA Hons). *Directorships:* Smith & Nephew plc 1986 (non-exec); Johnson Fry plc 1987 (non-exec); Thomas Jourdan plc 1988 (non-exec). *Other Activities:* Member, City of London Solicitors' Company. *Clubs:* Hurlingham, United Oxford & Cambridge University, I Zingari. *Recreations:* Golf, Fishing, Shooting.

MACPHERSON, Philip Strone Stewart; Director, Investment Banking, Robert Fleming & Co Ltd.

MacPHERSON, R T S; Chairman, Allstate Reinsurance Co Limited.

McPHERSON, William John Hill; General Manager (Management Services), Northern Bank Ltd, since 1987; Computerisation, Premises, General Administration. *Career:* Northern Bank Ltd, Various Mgmnt Positions 1970-80; Controller, Computerisation 1980-84; Asst Gen Mgr 1984-87. *Biog: b.* 9 May 1936. *Nationality:* British. *m.* 1971, Elizabeth Ann (née Loan); 1 s; 2 d. *Educ:* Ballycastle Grammar School; Queens University, Belfast (1-yr course). *Directorships:* Northern Computing Ltd 1984-87 (non-exec). *Other Activities:* Hon Treasurer, Northern Ireland Chest Heart & Stroke Association. *Professional Organisations:* Member, Institute of Bankers in Ireland; Member, Northern Ireland Chamber of Commerce & Industry. *Recreations:* Golf, Swimming.

McQUATER, G J; Partner, Lovell White Durrant.

McQUEEN, C J J; Executive Director, County NatWest Securities Ltd.

McQUEEN, J H J; Director, Charterhouse Tilney.

McRAE, Hamish Malcolm Donald; Business & City Editor, The Independent, since 1989. *Career:* The Banker, Editorial Asst 1967-69; Asst Editor 1969-70; Dep Editor 1970-71; Euromoney Editor 1971-74; Financial Editor, The Guardian 1975-89. *Biog: b.* 20 October 1943. *Nationality:* British. *m.* 1971, Frances Anne (nee Cairncross); 2 d. *Educ:* Fettes College, Edinburgh; Trinity College, Dublin (BA Hons). *Publications:* Capital City-London As a Financial Centre 1971-85 (with Frances Cairncross). *Recreations:* Walking, Skiing.

MacRAE, L F; Director, IMI Capital Markets (UK).

MacREDMOND, E A; Chairman, Macey Williams Ltd.

McSLOY, Peter; Managing Director, Salomon Brothers International Limited, since 1989; Finance, Technology, Operations, Administration. *Career:* Continental Bank, Senior Vice President 1969-85; Standard Chartered Bank, Exec Director 1985-89. *Biog: b.* 19 January 1946. *Nationality:* British. *m.* 1976, Deirdre (née Yuill); 1 s; 2 d. *Educ:* Salesian College, Oxford; London School of Economics (BSc Econ Hons); Fletcher School of Law & Diplomacy (MA); Harvard University; Massachussetts Institute of Technology.

McSPORRAN, Archibald Campbell; Executive Director, Aitken Campbell & Co Ltd, since 1989; Accounts and Settlement. *Career:* Campbell Neill and Co, Settlements and Accounts Mgr 1968-75. *Biog: b.* 23 April 1952. *Nationality:* British. *m.* 1979, Jacqueline (née Semple); 2 d. *Educ:* Bellahouston Academy. *Other Activities:* Stock Exchange Management Assoc. *Professional Organisations:* Member, The International Stock Exchange. *Clubs:* Douglas Park Golf Club. *Recreations:* Golf.

McSWEENEY, D K; Audit Partner, Milne Ross Chartered Accountants, since 1987; Corporate Finance. *Biog: b.* 25 October 1958. *Nationality:* English. *m.* 1982, Shiralee; 1 s; 1 d. *Educ:* Coopers' Company Grammar School; Polytechnic, South Bank (Accountancy Diploma). *Professional Organisations:* ACA (ICAEW). *Recreations:* Squash, Golf.

McVEIGH III, Charles S; Chairman, Salomon Brothers International Ltd.

McWHIRTER, A S; Partner, Freshfields.

McWILLIAMS, Professor Douglas; Chief Economic Adviser, Confederation of British Industry, since 1988; Economics. *Career:* CBI, Various Economic Posts 1974-86; IBM UK, Chief Economist 1986-88; MES, Chief Executive 1988-; CBI, Chief Economic Adviser 1988-. *Biog: b.* 24 November 1951. *Nationality:* British. *m.* 1979, Ianthe Priscilla (née Wright). *Educ:* Stonyhurst College; Lincoln College, Oxford (PPE MA, Economics MPhil). *Directorships:* MES (Economic Consultancy) 1988 (exec) Chief Executive; Quantum Management Skills Ltd 1989 (exec). *Other Activities:* Council Member, Institute for Fiscal Studies; Company of Information Technologists. *Professional Organisations:* Visiting Professor, Kingston Business School. *Clubs:* Reform. *Recreations:* Skiing, Cricket.

MADDEN, Francis John Phillip; TD; Managing Director (Founder), Cambridge Capital Limited, since 1985. *Career:* Philipe Electronic Industries (Mullard) 1962-69; Arbulthnot Latham & Co Limited (Merchant Bankers) 1969-75; City Panel on Takeover's & Mergers 1975-77; NM Rothschild & Co Limited, Director 1977-81; East Anglian Securities Trust Limited 1981-85; Cambridge Capital Limited 1985-. *Biog: b.* 23 April 1938. *Nationality:* British. *m.* 1982, Eileen (née Rawson); 2 s; 3 d. *Educ:* Stowe School; Cambridge University (MA LLB). *Directorships:* Cambridge Capital Limited 1985 (exec) MD; Cambridge Research & Innovation Limited 1987 (exec) Chm; Cambridge Capital Management Ltd 1987 (exec); International Business Communications (Holdings) plc 1985 (non-exec); Ashfield Holdings plc 1985 (non-exec). *Professional Organisations:* Barrister-at Law, (Grays Inn). *Clubs:* Special Forces. *Recreations:* Sailing.

MADDOX, Miss Bromwen M; Director, Kleinwort Benson Securities; Media Research.

MADER, William; Bureau Chief, Time Magazine, since 1989. *Career:* Time Magazine, Jnr State Dept Correspondent 1965-68; Eastern Europe Bureau Chief 1968-71; Snr State Dept Correspondent 1971-73; Chief Canada Correspondent 1973-76; Bonn Bureau Chief 1976-81; Dep Chief of Correspondents 1981-88; Diplomatic Correspondent 1988-89; London Bureau Chief 1989-. *Biog: b.* 3 July 1934. *Nationality:* American. *m.*

1958, Martha (née Jester); 2 d. *Educ:* Guildford College (BA); Columbia University. *Professional Organisations:* International Institute for Strategic Studies; Royal Institute of International Affairs. *Clubs:* Bucks, Travellers. *Recreations:* Reading, Music.

MADINAVEITIA, Juan; Corporate Banking Manager, Banco Bilbao Vizcaya SA.

MADOFF, Bernard Lawrence; Chairman, Madoff Securities International Ltd, since 1986; Broker/Dealer in US Equities. *Career:* Bernard L Madoff Investment Securities Snr Ptnr 1960-; Madoff Securities International Ltd, Director 1983-; US Infantry, 2nd Lieutenant 1960-62. *Biog: b.* 29 April 1938. *Nationality:* American. *m.* 1960, Ruth (née Alpern); 2 s. *Educ:* Hofstra University (BSc). *Directorships:* National Securities Clearing Corp 1984; International Securities Clearing Corp 1985; NASDAQ Inc 1989 Chairman. *Other Activities:* National Assoc of Securities Dealers (Chm of Intl Ctee, Member of Capital & Margin, Long Range Planning, Board Surveillance and District 12 Nominating Ctees). *Professional Organisations:* National Securities Traders' Assoc; Security Traders Association of New York; Securities Industry Association; Member, International Stock Exchange, London; Member, London International Financial Futures Exchange; Member, Cincinnati Stock Exchange. *Clubs:* City Athletic Club, New York Stock Exchange Luncheon, Fresh Meadow Country Club, Cat Cay Club, Atlantic Golf Club. *Recreations:* Boating, Skiing, Big Game Fishing, Tennis, Golf.

MADSEN, Thomas P; Head of International Equities, J P Morgan Investment Management Inc, since 1989. *Career:* JPMIM for 11 Years. *Biog: b.* 2 May 1956. *Nationality:* American. *m.* Nikki; 3 s; 1 d. *Educ:* University of Wisconsin (MBA Finance). *Recreations:* AC, Denham Golf Club, St George's Hill Tennis Club.

MAEDA, Fumiaki; Deputy Managing Director, Mitsubishi Finance International plc, since 1988; Management. *Career:* Mitsubishi Bank (Europe) SA, Mgr, Eurobond Dept 1975-81; The Mitsubishi Bank Ltd, Dep Gen Mgr, Capital Market Div 1981-88. *Biog: b.* 10 January 1946. *Nationality:* Japanese. *m.* 1976, Kazuko; 3 d. *Educ:* Keio University, Japan (MA); Insitut Superieur des Affaires, France.

MAGAN, George Morgan; Managing Director, J O Hambro Magan & Co Ltd, since 1988; Mergers, Acquistions, Corporate Finance. *Career:* Peat Marwick Mitchell 1964-71; Kleinwort Benson Ltd 1971-74; Morgan Grenfell & Co Ltd 1974-88. *Biog: b.* 14 November 1945. *Nationality:* British. *m.* 1972, Wendy Anne (née Chilton); 2 s; 1 d. *Educ:* Winchester College. *Directorships:* Asprey plc 1980 (non-exec); WCRS Group plc 1983-90 (non-exec); CCA Publications plc 1986-89 (non-exec); Bluett Holdings Limited 1988 (non-exec). *Other Activities:* Governor, Hawtreys School.

Professional Organisations: FCA. *Clubs:* Royal Yacht Squadron, Turf, Boodles.

MAGEE, N P; Director, LAS Unit Trust Managers.

MAGILL, John Walter; National Director, National Accounting and Auditing, Touche Ross & Co, since 1987. *Biog: b.* 11 March 1944. *Nationality:* British. *m.* 1971, Gil (née Hanna); 2 s. *Educ:* Merchant Taylors Crosby. *Directorships:* Touche Ross & Co Board of Partners 1984 (exec). *Professional Organisations:* Institute of Chartered Accountants in England & Wales.

MAGNUS, Alan Melvyn; Partner, D J Freeman & Company, since 1987; Company & Commercial Law, Joint Ventures, Corporate Reorganisation, Floatations on USM and Stock Exchange. *Career:* National Coal Board and CIN Investments Limited, Head of Company & Commercial Law 1973-87. *Biog: b.* 31 August 1938. *Nationality:* British. *m.* 1962, Judith (née Sack); 2 s; 1 d. *Educ:* Sir George Monoux Grammar School; Worcester College, Oxford (MA Oxon); College of Law (Solicitor Hons). *Other Activities:* City of London Solicitors Company; Joint Hon Treasurer, RSGB (1988-). *Professional Organisations:* The Law Society. *Recreations:* Scuba Diving, Opera, Ballet.

MAGNUS, Miss Caroline; Senior Consultant, Overton Shirley & Barry, since 1985; International Search & Selection. *Biog: b.* 1936. *Nationality:* British. *Educ:* Benenden School; Queens College, London; Goethe Institute (Kleines Deutsches Sprachdiplom). *Recreations:* Tennis, Literature, The Arts.

MAGNUS, George Anthony; Director, S G Warburg Securities, since 1990; Head of International Fixed Income Research. *Career:* Bank of America (London) Head of Economics, Vice President 1977-85; Laurie Milbank & Co/Chase Investment Bank, (London) Chief International Economist 1985-87; S G Warburg Securities 1987-. *Biog: b.* 17 April 1949. *Nationality:* British. *m.* 1989, Lesley; 2 s. *Educ:* London University (BSc Econ, MSc Econ). *Publications:* The International Debt Game, 1985.

MAGNUS, Sir Laurence Henry; Bt; Executive Director, Samuel Montagu & Co Limited, since 1988; Corporate Finance. *Career:* Samuel Montagu & Co Limited, Manager, Corporate Finance 1977-84; (Singapore Branch) General Manager 1984-87; Midland Bank (Singapore) Limited, Managing Director 1987-88; Samuel Montagu & Co Limited, Executive Director 1988-. *Biog: b.* 24 September 1955. *Nationality:* British. *m.* 1983, Jocelyn Mary; 1 s; 1 d. *Educ:* Eton College; Christ Church, Oxford (MA Politics, Philosophy & Economics). *Directorships:* Samuel Montagu & Co Limited 1988 (exec); Midland Bank (Singapore) Limited 1987-88 (exec); Richard Innes Limited 1989 (non-exec). *Other*

Activities: Merchant Taylors' Company. *Clubs:* Millenium Club. *Recreations:* Fishing, Walking.

MAGRIN, Edward P; Partner, Moores Rowland.

MAGUIRE, H J; Director, Hill Samuel Investment Management Ltd.

MAGUIRE, P; Partner, Cameron Markby Hewitt.

MAHE, J F X; Director, Barclays de Zoete Wedd Securities Ltd.

MAHE, Y J F; Director, Barclays de Zoete Wedd Securities Ltd.

MAHESHWARI, K R; General Manager (UK), State Bank of India.

MAHON, Vincent; Manager of Private Banking Department, United Overseas Bank (Banque Unie Pour Les Pays d'Outre-Mer) Geneva.

MAHONEY, Dennis L; Chairman, Alexander Howden Ltd, since 1984. *Career:* Sedgwick Forbes (North America) Dir 1978-79; MD 1979-82; Dep Chm 1982-84. *Biog: b.* 1951. *Directorships:* Alexander Howden Group 1985 Co Chm; Alexander Howden Holdings 1985. *Other Activities:* Member, Lloyd's Insurance Broking Ctee. *Professional Organisations:* Member of Lloyd's; Member, American Mgmnt Assoc.

MAIDEN, Robert Mitchell; Managing Director, The Royal Bank of Scotland plc, since 1986. *Career:* The Royal Bank of Scotland, Various 1950-86. *Biog: b.* 15 September 1933. *Nationality:* British. *m.* 1958, Margaret (née Nicolson). *Educ:* Montrose Academy. *Directorships:* The Royal Bank of Scotland Group plc 1985 (exec); Lothian and Edinburgh Enterprise Limited 1990. *Other Activities:* VP, Institute of Bankers (Scot); Governor, Napier Polytechnic of Edinburgh. *Professional Organisations:* FIB (Scot); FBIM. *Clubs:* New Club (Edinburgh). *Recreations:* Music, Golf, Reading, Hill Walking.

MAIDMENT, Alan Tom; Managing Director, Martin Currie Unit Trusts Ltd, since 1988. *Career:* Britannia Arrow Holdings plc, Dir & MD of Principal Invest Subs 1968-82; Oppenheimer Fund Management Ltd, Dir & MD 1982-85; Wardley Investment Services International Ltd 1985-88. *Biog: b.* 22 November 1936. *Nationality:* British. *m.* 1965, Kirsteen (née Shaw); 1 s; 1 d. *Educ:* Dauntsey's School, West Lavington, Wilts. *Directorships:* Lautro 1986-89 (non-exec). *Other Activities:* Regimental Member, Honourable Artillery Company; Company of Pikemen & Musketeers HAC. *Professional Organisations:* FCA. *Clubs:* City of London. *Recreations:* HAC, Sports, Gardening.

MAIN, G D H; Director, Leasing Division, Benchmark Bank plc.

MAIN, J J W R; Director, Charlton Seal Schaverien Limited.

MAIN, W H; Director, Brewin Dolphin & Co Ltd.

MAINELLI, Michael Raymond; Director, BDO Consulting, since 1987; Strategy and Information Technology. *Career:* Petroconsultants SA, General Manger 1979-84; ISF Inc, President 1984-86; Arthur Andersen & Co, Manager 1986-87. *Biog: b.* 1958. *Nationality:* American/Irish. *Educ:* Harvard University; Trinity College, Dublin; London School of Economics and Political Science (continuing). *Directorships:* BDO Consulting 1987 (exec). *Professional Organisations:* Member, Strategic Planning Society; Member, Institute of Management Consultants; Member, British Computer Society; Member, Institute of Directors; Member, Institute of Petroleum. *Publications:* Various Scientific Papers.

MAIR, Antony Stefan Romley; Partner, Stephenson Harwood, since 1988; Company & Commercial Law. *Career:* Holman Fenwick & Willan, Asst Solicitor 1976-79; Ptnr 1979-88. *Biog: b.* 27 December 1946. *Nationality:* British. *Educ:* Reading School; Magdalen College, Oxford (BA). *Other Activities:* Law Society Solicitors' European Group Committee. *Professional Organisations:* Law Society; IBA. *Publications:* Englische Nacherzaehlungen, 1968. *Recreations:* Dressage, Gardening.

MAIR, Keith; Director, 3i plc.

MAITLAND, Sir Donald; GCMG OBE; Non-Executive Director, Slough Estates plc. *Career:* Served with British & Indian Armies, Middle East, India & Burma; Foreign (later Diplomatic) Service 1947; Various in Foreign Office & Middle East; Ambassador to Libya 1969-70; Chief Press Secretary to Prime Minister 1970-73; UK Permanent Representative to United Nations, New York 1973-74; UK Permanent Representative to European Community, Brussels 1975-79; Permanent Under Secretary, Dept of Energy 1980-82; Independent Commission for World Wide Telecommunications Development, Chm 1983-85; Independent Broadcasting Authority, Chm 1986-89. *Biog: b.* 1922. *Educ:* George Watson's College; Edinburgh University (MA). *Directorships:* Britoil plc 1983-85 Govt Dir; Northern Engineering Industries plc 1986-89. *Other Activities:* Chairman, Health Education Authority, 1989-; Member, Commonwealth War Graves Commission, 1983-87; Chairman, Christians for Europe, 1984-; President, Bath Institute for Rheumatic Diseases, 1986-; President, Federal Trust for Education & Research, 1987-. *Clubs:* Travellers'. *Recreations:* Music, Hill-walking.

MAITLAND, W W; Deputy Chairman, Janson Green Limited.

MAITLAND HUDSON, Alexis Philip; Partner, Withers, since 1985; Head of Litigation. *Career:* Messrs Toplis & Harding, Loss Adjuster 1971-72; Withers, Articled 1972-75; Assistant Solicitor 1975-76; Bird & Bird, Assistant Solicitor 1976-78; Partner 1978-80; Holman Fenwick & Willan, Assistant Solicitor 1980-82; Partner 1982-85. *Biog: b.* 7 September 1948. *Nationality:* British. *m.* 1971, Jane Catherine; 2 s; 1 d. *Educ:* Eastbourne College, Sussex; St Johns College, Oxford (MA). *Other Activities:* Freeman, The Merchant Taylor's Company; Governor, Cumnor House School, Sussex; Member, Franco-British Chamber of Commerce; Member, The Association of Franco-British Lawyers. *Professional Organisations:* Solicitor, The Supreme Court of England & Wales; Avocat a La Cour de Paris. *Publications:* A Coarser French Course, 1970. *Clubs:* Cercle de L'Union Interalliee. *Recreations:* Tennis, Village Cricket.

MAITLAND SMITH, Geoffrey; Chairman, Sears plc, since 1985. *Career:* Thornton Baker & Co, Ptnr 1960-70; Sears plc, Exec Dir 1971-77; Dep Chm & Chief Exec 1977-85. *Directorships:* Asprey plc 1980 (non-exec); Midland Bank plc 1986 (non-exec); The Hammerson Property Investment & Development Corporation plc 1990 (non-exec). *Professional Organisations:* CBIM; FCA; FRSA.

MAJOR, Christopher Ian; Partner, Lovell White Durrant, since 1979; Taxation. *Biog: b.* 14 June 1948. *Nationality:* British. *m.* 1972, Susan Fenella (née Kirton). *Educ:* Kingston Grammar School; Wadham College, Oxford (MA). *Other Activities:* City of London Solicitors' Company; New York Bar Assoc (Intl & Comparative Law Committee); American Bar Assoc; American Arbitration Assoc Panel of Arbitrators; International Bar Association, Committee, British American Chamber of Commerce. *Professional Organisations:* Law Society. *Recreations:* Tennis.

MAJOR, R M; Director, Citymax Integrated Information Systems Ltd.

MAJOR, William; European Representative, Commercial Bank of Kuwait.

MAKER, Daljit Singh; Director, Parrish Stockbrokers.

MALCOLM, Brian Richard; Partner, Baillie Gifford & Co, since 1988; Pension Fund Management. *Career:* L Messel & Co, Research Analyst (Insurance) 1970-73; Rowe & Pitman, Research Analyst (Consumer Stocks) 1973-75; Bankers Trust, Assistant Vice-President Fund Manager 1976-81; Hill Samuel, Director, Hill Samuel Pensions Investment Management 1981-86; ABD International, Director London Operations 1986-87; Baillie

Gifford & Co 1987-. *Biog: b.* 14 August 1948. *Nationality:* British. *m.* 1975, Geraldine Sarah; 2 s; 1 d. *Educ:* Kingston School; St Andrews University (BSc Statistics). *Professional Organisations:* Associate, Society of Investment Analysts (ASIA).

MALCOLM, Clive; Partner, Clark Whitehill, since 1985; Audit. *Career:* Hancock Gilbert & Morris, Accountant 1972-75; Coopers & Lybrand, Accountant 1975-81. *Biog: b.* 30 August 1951. *Nationality:* British. *m.* 1972, Gill (née Standley); 2 d. *Educ:* St Olaves School; Hull University (BA German/Italian). *Other Activities:* Editorial Board, Audit Magazine. *Professional Organisations:* FCA.

MALCOLM, David; Deputy Group General Manager, Royal Insurance plc, since 1987; Investment, Corporate Finance & Treasury, Strategic Planng. *Career:* Royal Insurance 1956-. *Biog: b.* 7 June 1932. *Nationality:* British. *m.* 1965, Janet (née Fisher); 1 s; 1 d. *Educ:* Caius College, Cambridge (MA). *Directorships:* Scottish Metropolitan Property plc (non-exec); Charinco Chm of Trustees; Charishare Chm of Trustees. *Other Activities:* President, Insurance Chess Club. *Professional Organisations:* FCII.

MALCOLMSON, P Michael; Director, PaineWebber International (UK) Ltd.

MALJERS, F A; Vice Chairman, Unilever plc.

MALLETT, Christopher John; Director, Barclays de Zoete Wedd Limited; Corporate Finance. *Career:* Slaughter and May Solicitor.

MALLIN, Anthony; Director, Hambro European Ventures Limited.

MALLIN, M F; Partner, Hill Taylor Dickinson.

MALLINCKRODT, George W; Executive Chairman, Schroders plc, since 1984. *Career:* Agfa AG 1948-51; Muenchmeyer & Co 1951-53; Kleinwort Sons & Co 1953-54; J Henry Schroder Bank & Trust Co (NY) 1954-55; Union Bank of Switzerland 1956; J Henry Schroder Bank & Trust Co (NY) 1957-60; J Henry Schroder Wagg & Co Ltd, Dir (from 1967) 1960-83; J Henry Schroder Bank & Trust Co (NY), Chm & Chief Exec 1984-86. *Biog: b.* 19 August 1930. *Nationality:* German. *m.* 1958, Charmaine (née Schroder); 2 s; 2 d. *Educ:* Schule Schloss Salem, Germany; New York University. *Directorships:* Pfeifer & Langen (Cologne) Ltd Ptnr; Schroder International Ltd - Holding Company 1973 Chairman; European Arts Foundation Ltd; J Henry Schroder Wagg & Co Ltd; Schroders Inc (New York) Chm & Chief Exec; Wertheim Schroder & Co Inc (NY); J Henry Schroder Bank AG (Zurich) Chairman; Schroders Australia Holdings Ltd; Schroder Asseily & Co Ltd; Euris SA (Paris); Schroder International Holdings - Holding Company 1977 Chairman; Schroder International Merchant Bankers Ltd, Merchant Bank, Singapore 1988; Siemans plc - Industrial Holding Company 1989. *Other Activities:* Vice President, German Chamber of Industry & Commerce in UK; President, German YMCA in London; Verdienstkreuz Bande des Verdienstordens der Bundesrepublik Deutschland. *Professional Organisations:* FRSA; CBIM. *Clubs:* River Club (New York). *Recreations:* Shooting, Skiing.

MALLINSON, Anthony William; Non-Executive Director, Morgan Grenfell Asset Management Limited, since 1986. *Career:* Served RA to Major 1943-47; Admitted Solicitor England & Wales 1952; Hong Kong 1978; Slaughter and May, Partner 1957-86; Senior Partner 1984-86. *Biog: b.* 1 December 1923. *Nationality:* British. *m.* 1955, Heather Mary (née Gardiner). *Educ:* Cheam School; Marlborough College; Gonville and Caius College, Cambridge (Exibitioner, Tapp Post Graduate Scholar, BA LLM). *Directorships:* Bank of Scotland 1985 Member of London Board; Stratton Investment Trust 1986. *Other Activities:* Solicitor to Fishmongers' Co, Member of London Board; Member, BoT Ctee examining British Patent System (Banks Ctee) 1967-70; Chm, Cinematograph Films Council, 1973-76; Hon Legal Adviser to Accounting Standards Ctee, 1982-86; Member of Council, Section on Business Law, International Bar Assoc 1984; Financial Services Tribunal, 1988-; Exec Ctee, Essex County Cricket Club. *Professional Organisations:* Member, Law Society of England & Wales. *Clubs:* MCC. *Recreations:* Sport Watching paarticularly Cricket, Reading.

MALLINSON, Terence S; Chairman, Town & Country Building Society, since 1990. *Career:* Town & Country Building Society, Director 1958; William Mallinson, Sales Director 1965-71; Group Market Research Director 1971-75; William Mallinson & Denny Mott Ltd, Group Market Research & Sales Coordinator 1976-81; Mallinson Denny, Group Marketing Director 1981-85; Mallinson Denny Group, Group Hardwood & Marketing Director 1985-86; Mallinson Turner Hunter, Managing Director 1986-87; Mallinson-Denny, Group Director 1987-88; Mallinson-Denny Ltd, Non-Executive Director 1989-90. *Biog: b.* 9 September 1929. *Nationality:* British. *Educ:* Marlborough; Jesus College, Cambridge (MA). *Directorships:* Lydney Products Ltd 1988 (non-exec) Chm; Forestry Commission 1989 Part Time Member. *Other Activities:* Governor, The Building Centre Group; Liveryman, Worshipful Co of Carpenters; President, Timber Trade Federation; Member of Council, National Council of Building Material Producers. *Professional Organisations:* Fellow, Institute of Wood Science; Fellow, Royal Geographical Society. *Clubs:* English Speaking Union, Hurlingham.

MALLMANN, Dr Alfred Wilhelm; Director, Hambros Bank Ltd, since 1986; International Corporate Finance, Capital Markets & General European Business.

Career: Swiss Bank Corporation (Zurich), Trainee 1977-78; Creditanstalt (Vienna), Corp Finance Asst 1980-83; Seconded to European Banking Co Ltd, Asst Mgr 1981-83; Hambros Bank Ltd 1984. *Biog: b.* 17 January 1951. *Nationality:* Austrian. *m.* 1984, Tina Maria (née Thost); 1 s; 2 d. *Educ:* Salzburg, Austria; University of Salzburg, Austria (Dr of Law). *Directorships:* Hambros Bank Ltd. *Clubs:* Aigner Herrenrunde.

MALLOWS, R C R; Director, S G Warburg Akroyd Rowe & Pitman Mullens Securities Ltd.

MALONEY, P D; Partner, Stephenson Harwood.

MALONEY, T J; Partner, Jaques & Lewis.

MALPAS, R; CBE; Director, Barings plc.

MALTBY, Colin Charles; Chief Executive, Kleinwort Benson Investment Management Ltd, since 1988; Investment Management/Private Banking. *Career:* N M Rothschild & Sons Ltd, Manager, Asst Mgmnt 1975-80; Kleinwort Benson Investment Management Ltd, Director, Intl Dept 1980-85; Banque Kleinwort Benson SA (Geneva), Directeur 1985-88. *Biog: b.* 8 February 1951. *Nationality:* British. *m.* 1983, Victoria (née Elton); 1 s; 2 d. *Educ:* King Edward's School, Birmingham; Christ Church, Oxford (MA Hons Double 1st, MSc by research). *Directorships:* Kleinwort Benson Group 1989 (exec); Kleinwort Benson Unit Trusts Ltd 1988 Dep Chm; Oxford Union Society 1973 Pres. *Other Activities:* National Union Exec Ctee, Conservative Party, 1974-76. *Professional Organisations:* Member, The International Stock Exchange; Chartered Association of Certified Accountants, CDipAF. *Clubs:* Coningsby. *Recreations:* Skiing, Reading, Curiosity.

MALTBY, John Newcombe; CBE; Chairman, UK Atomic Energy Authority, since 1990. *Career:* Shell Group 1951-69; Panocean Shipping & Terminals, Managing Director 1969-80; The Burmah Oil plc, Director 1980-83; Chairman 1983-90; Dover Harbour Board, Chairman 1988-; Harrisons & Crosfield plc, Director 1988-. *Biog: b.* 10 July 1928. *Nationality:* British. *m.* 1956, Lady Sylvia Harris; 1 s; 2 d. *Educ:* Wellington College; Clare College, Cambridge (Mech Sc 1st). *Directorships:* J Bisby & Co 1986-88; Premier Consolidated Oilfields 1986; DRG plc 1986-89. *Other Activities:* President, Thirty Club of London, 1989-90; Dep Chm British Port Federation, 1990. *Clubs:* Brooks, Naval & Military.

MALTHOUSE, Richard Harold; Senior Partner, McKenna & Co, since 1987; Corporate. *Career:* McKenna & Co, Articled Clerk 1954-57; Asst Solicitor 1957-61; Partner 1961. *Biog: b.* 21 September 1931. *Nationality:* British. *m.* 1957, Jean (née Agassiz); 2 s; 2 d. *Educ:* Uppingham School; Pembroke College, Cambridge (MA). *Professional Organisations:* The Law

Society; City of London Solicitors' Company. *Clubs:* Brook's, City of London, Rosslyn Park RFC, Effingham Golf Club. *Recreations:* Rugby Football, Golf, Gardening, Wine, Travel.

MANASIAN, D; World Business Editor, The Economist.

MANDELLI, Gianfranco; Deputy Chief Manager, Banca Commerciale Italiana, since 1988; Senior Management. *Career:* Banca Commerciale Italiana 1972-; (New York) VP Intl Dept 1979-83; (Chicago) SVP & Branch Mgr 1983-88. *Biog: b.* 4 October 1946. *Nationality:* Italian. *m.* 1972, Marialuisa (née Frosio); 1 s. *Educ:* Bocconi University, Milan (Business Admin). *Professional Organisations:* Colgate Darden School of Business Administration (University of Virginia), Executive Seminar on International Lending. *Clubs:* Lyons, Overseas Bankers'. *Recreations:* Tennis, Skiing, Music, Theatre, Cinema.

MANDER, Michael Stuart; Non-Divisional Director, Hill Samuel & Co Ltd, since 1987; Corporate Finance. *Career:* Associated Newspapers 1958-71; Times Newspapers, Dep Chief Exec 1971-80; Thomson Magazines, MD 1980-83; Thomson Information Services, Chm & Chief Exec 1984-86; International Thomson plc, Director 1984-86. *Biog: b.* 5 October 1935. *Nationality:* British. *Educ:* Tonbridge School; Hackley School, New York. *Directorships:* Thomson Directories 1983 (non-exec); MAID Systems 1985 Chm; Southnews plc 1989 (non-exec). *Other Activities:* Worshipful Company of Marketors (Member); Solus Club (Pres 1979). *Professional Organisations:* Periodical Publishers' Assoc (VP); Institute of Marketing (Fellow); Institute of Directors (Council Member, Policy & Exec Ctee); Advertising Assoc 1976-86; Vice-Chm National Advertising Benevolent Society 1985-86. *Clubs:* Royal Southern Yacht Club, Royal Wimbledon Golf Club. *Recreations:* Sailing, Skiing, Golf.

MANDUCA, Paul Victor Sant; Chairman & Chief Executive, Touche Remnant & Co, since 1989. *Career:* Colegrave & Co, Graduate Trainee 1973-75; Rowe & Pitman, Portfolio Mgr 1976-79; Hill Samuel, Snr Investment Mgr 1979-83; Touche Remnant 1983-. *Biog: b.* 15 November 1951. *m.* 1982, Ursula; 2 s. *Educ:* Harrow School; Oxford University (BA Hons Modern Languages). *Directorships:* Touche Remnant Industrial & General 1987-89 (exec); TR Trustees Corp 1987 (exec); Clydesdale IT plc 1987-89 (non-exec); TR High Income plc 1989 Chairman. *Other Activities:* Bakers Livery Co. *Clubs:* Wentworth, Lansdowne. *Recreations:* Golf, Squash.

MANFORD, Bruce Robert James; Partner, Lawrence Graham, since 1988; Corporate Finance. *Career:* Heald Nickinson, Asst Solicitor 1981-85; Lawrence Graham, Asst Solicitor 1985-88. *Biog: b.* 21 March 1957.

Nationality: British. *Educ:* Haberdashers' Aske's School; Keele University (BA Hons). *Professional Organisations:* Member, The Law Society; RIPA.

MANFORD, Peter; Partner (London), Evershed Wells & Hind.

MANHEIM, Grant; Non-Executive Director, N M Rothschild & Sons Limited.

MANN, G; General Manager and Chief Executive, Bayerische Landesbank Girozentrale.

MANN, Miss Patricia K R; Member, Monopolies and Mergers Commission.

MANNERS, D N; Director, Sogemin Metals Ltd.

MANNERS, The Hon Thomas Jasper; Deputy Chairman, Lazard Brothers & Co Ltd, since 1985; Corporate Finance. *Career:* Elliot Casleton Chartered Acct 1954-; Lazard Brothers & Co Ltd 1955-65; Dir 1965-. *Biog: b.* 12 December 1929. *Nationality:* British. *m.* 1955, Sarah (née Peake); 3 s. *Educ:* Eton College. *Directorships:* Davy Corporation plc 1984 (non-exec); Legal & General Group plc 1979 (non-exec); Mercantile Group plc 1988 (non-exec); Scapa Group plc 1972 (non-exec); Govett Oriental Investment Trust plc 1978 (non-exec); British Bond & Mortgage Corporation Limited 1980-89; Grindlays Equipment Finance Limited 1981-83; Grindlays Industrial Leasing Limited 1983-84; Lazard Equipment Leasing Limited 1981-86; Lazard Investments Limited 1980-89; Lazard Investors Limited 1986-89; Lazard Leasing Limited 1984-86; Lazard Overseas Holdings Limited 1980-89; Lazard Second Leasing Limited 1983-86; Legal and General Assurance Society Limited 1972-82; Lazard Residential Property Fund (Management) Limited 1988-89; Mercantile Credit Company Limited 1987; Minden Securities Limited 1971-88; Scapa Group North America Limited 1978-89. *Professional Organisations:* ICA. *Clubs:* Pratt's, White's. *Recreations:* Fishing, Shooting.

MANNES, Roger Keith; Director, Credit Lyonnais Euro-Securities, since 1987; Head of Sales. *Career:* Popham Lyon & Smith Authorized Dealer 1962-72; Powell Popham Dawes Member Dealer 1972-74; Laing & Cruickshank Gilt Edge Dealer/Sales 1974-86; Alexanders Laing & Cruickshank Gilts Sales 1986-89; Credit Lyonnais Euro-Securities Sales 1989-. *Biog: b.* 25 May 1944. *m.* 1970, Patricia Ann (née Botten); 1 s; 1 d. *Educ:* Dover College. *Directorships:* CL Alexanders Laing Cruickshank Gilts Ltd 1987 (exec). *Other Activities:* Freeman of the City of London; Worshipful Company of the Loriners. *Professional Organisations:* Member, The International Stock Exchange.

MANNING, B W J; Director, Kleinwort Benson Ltd.

MANNING, D S; Director, Hill Samuel Investment Management Ltd.

MANNING, M J; Chairman, Manning Beard Ltd.

MANNING, Richard B; Partner, Walker Morris Scott Turnbull.

MANNOOCH, David; Partner, Morison Stoneham Chartered Accountants.

MANSELL JONES, R M; Director, Robert Bruce Fitzmaurice Ltd.

MANSER, John; Director, Securities and Investments Board.

MANSER, Paul Robert; Partner, Clyde & Co, since 1989; Company, Corporate Finance. *Career:* Berwin Leighton Ptnr 1982-86; Hammond Suddards, Partner 1988-89. *Biog: b.* 27 March 1950. *Nationality:* British. *m.* 1972, Lindy (née Myers); 2 s. *Educ:* Eltham College; Warwick University (BA Hons). *Professional Organisations:* The Law Society. *Recreations:* Tennis, Photography, Music.

MANSER, Peter John; Chief Executive, Robert Fleming Asset Management Ltd.

MANSFIELD, Brian Donald Frederick; Director, Singer & Friedlander Ltd, since 1984; Administration. *Career:* Coopers & Lybrand, Snr Mgr 1950-71; Singer & Friedlander Ltd, Grp Accountant 1971-83; Dir 1984-. *Biog: b.* 25 February 1934. *Nationality:* British. *m.* 1959, Gillian Stella (née Picken); 1 d. *Educ:* Bishop's Stortford College. *Directorships:* Singer & Friedlander Holdings Ltd 1987. *Professional Organisations:* FCA. *Recreations:* Golf.

MANSFIELD, M T N; Director, Hambros Bank Limited.

MANUEL, N; Deputy European Representative, Nacional Financiera.

MAPES, Glynn; London Bureau Chief, Wall Street Journal.

MAPLES, Charles James Julian; Partner, Theodore Goddard, since 1979; Banking. *Career:* Theodore Goddard, Articled Clerk 1972-74; Solicitor 1974-79. *Biog: b.* 26 January 1949. *m.* 1972, Anne-Francoise (née Bromley); 2 s. *Educ:* Harrow School; Liverpool (LLB Hons). *Other Activities:* Fletchers' Company; Weavers' Company; City of London Solicitor's Company. *Professional Organisations:* Law Society. *Clubs:* City University, Borgia. *Recreations:* Shooting.

MARAN, Stephen; Group Finance Director, Lloyds Abbey Life plc, since 1989; Finance. *Career:* Lloyds Bowmaker Finance Ltd, Managing Director 1984-88; Group Finance Director 1979-84; Credit Director 1977-79; Chief Manager, New Business 1974-77; Leasing Manager 1972-74; Internal Auditor 1969-72; SMT Sales & Service Co Ltd, Financial Accountant 1967-69; Scottish Gas Board, Accounting Assistant 1965-67; Walker and Walker, Apprentice Chartered Accountant 1960-65. *Biog: b.* 16 May 1940. *Nationality:* British. *m.* Sally; 1 d. *Educ:* George Watson's Boys' College, Edinburgh. *Directorships:* Lloyds Abbey Life plc 1989 (exec); Black Horse Financial Services Group 1989 (exec); Black Horse Financial Services Ltd 1989 Chairman; Black Horse Life Assurance Co Ltd 1989 Chairman; Carvan Credit Ltd 1987 (non-exec); Lloyds Bank Insurance Services Ltd 1989 (exec); Lloyds Bank Unit Trust Managers Ltd 1989 Chairman; Lloyds Bank (Channel Islands) Unit Trust Managers Ltd 1989 Chairman; Lloyds & Scottish Ireland 1987 (non-exec); Lloyds Bowmaker Finance Limited 1981 Deputy Chairman; Lloyds Bowmaker Limited 1977 Chairman. *Professional Organisations:* Member, Institute of Chartered Accountants of Scotland.

MARCELL, Philip Michael; Chairman, Continental Reinsurance, since 1986. *Career:* Royal Navy, Commander -1978; Jardine Matheson Insurance Broking Group, Company Secretary; Jardine Insurance Brokers Ltd, Director 1980-83; American Re-Insurance Company (UK) Ltd, Director & Chief Executive 1983-86. *Biog: b.* 21 August 1936. *Nationality:* British. *m.* 1962, Lucina Mary; 1 s; 3 d. *Educ:* Wimbledon College; Britannia Royal Naval College, Dartmouth; London University (LLB); Wolfson College, Cambridge. *Directorships:* Continental Reinsurance Corporation (UK) Ltd Chairman; Continental Reinsurance Management Co Ltd; Union America Insurance Company Ltd; Union America Management Company Ltd; Continental Reinsurance Management Holding Co Ltd; Market Building Ltd 1990. *Other Activities:* Executive Committee, Reinsurance Offices Association; Chairman, Technical Standing Committee, Reinsurance Offices Association; Liveryman, Worshipful Company of Chartered Secretaries & Administrators. *Professional Organisations:* FCIS; FFA; MBIM. *Clubs:* Oxford and Cambridge, Pall Mall. *Recreations:* Squash, Sailing, Golf.

MARCHANT, Andrew William; Director, CIN Venture Managers Ltd, since 1988; Unquoted Investments. *Career:* Thompson Mclintock & Co, qualified as Accountant 1977-83; Prudential Venture Managers, Executive Development Capital 1983-85; Schroder Ventures, Partner 1985-88; CIN Venture Managers Ltd, Director 1988-. *Biog: b.* 31 May 1955. *Nationality:* British. *m.* 1981, Barbara (née Bevan); 2 s. *Educ:* Malvern College, Exeter University (Econ Hons). *Directorships:* CIN Venture Managers Ltd 1988 (exec); Anagen 1989 (non-exec); Enterprise Systems Group 1989 (non-exec); Paribas Electronique SA 1990 (non-exec). *Professional Organisations:* Institute of Directors; Institute of Chartered Accountants in England & Wales. *Recreations:* Sailing, Skiing, Country Pursuits, Tennis.

MARCHANT, T F E; Director, County NatWest Securities Limited.

MARCHESE, David Lawrence; Partner, Richards Butler, since 1985; Solicitor. *Career:* Herbert Smith Articled Clerk 1973-76; Richards Butler Asst Solicitor 1976-85. *Biog: b.* 3 December 1949. *Nationality:* British. *Educ:* Tiffin School; New College, Oxford (MA). *Professional Organisations:* Law Society; Licensing Executives Society. *Publications:* Contributor to Practical Commercial Precedents, 1987.

MARCKUS, Melvyn; Editor, The Observer, since 1984; Observer Business & City Editor. *Career:* The Scotsman, Reporter 1962-66; Daily Mail, Reporter 1966-67; The Guardian, Reporter 1967; Daily Mail, Reporter 1967-70; Daily Express, Reporter 1970-72; Sunday Telegraph, Deputy City Editor 1972-82. *Biog: b.* 1 January 1944. *Nationality:* British. m2 Rachel (née King); 1 s; 1 d (from first marrriage). *Educ:* Worthing Grammar School. *Directorships:* The Observer 1987 (exec). *Clubs:* The Travellers'. *Recreations:* Several.

MARCOTTI, F; Chief Manager, Banca Commerciale Italiana, since 1989; London Branch. *Career:* Banca Commerciale Italiana Head Office (Milan) 1961-; BCI Chicago Branch, Assistant Vice President 1976-78; BCI Warsaw Representative Office, Chief Representative 1978-80; BCI Frankfurt/Main Representative Office, Chief Representative 1980-83; Sudameris Group Paris, Chief Representative 1980-83; Bancode Credito del Peru' Lima, Chief Representative 1980-83; BCI New York Branch, First Vice President & Deputy Manager 1983-85; BCI Tokyo Branch, Chief Manager 1985-89; BCI London Branch, Chief Manager 1989-. *Biog: b.* 14 February 1942. *Nationality:* Italian. *m.* 1968, Pierangela (née Tanzi); 1 s. *Educ:* (High School Degree, Accountant). *Directorships:* BCI Limited London 1989 (exec). *Other Activities:* Deputy Chairman, Institute of Foreign Bankers (Tokyo) 1986-89; Deputy Chairman, Rotary International (Tokyo) 1988-89. *Professional Organisations:* Italian Chamber of Commerce for Great Britain, London. *Clubs:* Club Di Londra, Riverside Tennis Club.

MARDON TAYLOR, Nicholas John; Finance Director, J S Gadd & Co Ltd, since 1988. *Career:* Carless plc, Finance Director 1985-88; Saxon Oil plc, Finance Director 1982-85; Total Oil Marine plc, Treasurer 1974-82. *Biog: b.* 24 October 1944. *Nationality:* British. *m.* 1973, Cynthia (née Evans); 2 d. *Educ:* Shrewsbury School. *Directorships:* Petresearch International plc 1990 (non-exec); Belle Secretarial Ltd 1988 (non-exec); Albemarle & Bond Holdings plc 1989 (non-exec); Whitehall Energy plc 1988 (exec). *Other Activities:* Governor,

Cobham Hall School. *Professional Organisations:* FCA. *Recreations:* Sailing, Skiing.

MAREMONT, Mark; London Correspondent, Business Week International, since 1986. *Career:* Business Week, New York City, Telecommunications Editor 1983-86. *Biog: b.* 3 June 1958. *Nationality:* American. *m.* 1984, Emily (née Dreifus); 1 d. *Educ:* Brown University, USA (BA History); Columbia University, USA (MSJ Journalism).

MARENBACH, Berno E; Director, J Henry Schroder Wagg & Co Limited.

MARGARSON, J D R; Group Financial Controller & Company Secretary, Allied Trust Bank, since 1989; Financial Control of the Bank & Group Companies. *Career:* Bahrain Monetary Agency, Accountant; Cook Islands Motor Centre, Deputy General Manager; Deeside Boat Building Co, Proprietor; McDermott, Corporate Auditor; Mobil Oil, Corporate Auditor; Coopers & Lybrand, Senior Auditor. *Biog: b.* 3 July 1949. *Nationality:* British. *m.* 1984, Isabel. *Educ:* Liverpool College of Commerce, Liverpool University; Warwick University. *Directorships:* Allied Trust (non-exec); Rowans PVR (non-exec). *Professional Organisations:* Fellow, Institute of Chartered Accountants in England & Wales. *Publications:* Warm Water Sailing, 1985; Pros & Cons of Catamarans for Circumnavigation, 1985. *Clubs:* Ocean Youth Club. *Recreations:* Sailing (Particularly Long Distance), Hash Hoose Harriers.

MARGERISON, Peter; Partner, Hepworth & Chadwick.

MARGREE, Roderick James; Managing Director, Settlement Services Division, The International Stock Exchange, since 1990. *Career:* Barclays Bank plc, Various Training & Junior Management Roles 1961-73; Assistant Manager, Hatton Garden 1974-76; Business Advisory Service Manager 1976-79; Manager, Camden Town 1979-81; Head of Organisations & Methods 1981-82; Assistant General Manager, Information Technology 1982-85; Corporate Finance Director, Securities Industry 1985-89; Corporate Director, Financial Institutions 1990; Seconded to ISE 1990. *Biog: b.* 17 June 1945. *Nationality:* British. *m.* 1967, Pauline; 1 s; 1 d. *Educ:* Tottenham Grammar School. *Professional Organisations:* Fellow, Chartered Institute of Bankers. *Recreations:* Motor Racing, Cricket, Rugby, Photography, Music.

MARGRETT, David Basil; Managing Director, Lowndes Lambert UK Ltd, Lowndes Lambert Group Ltd.

MARINI, Luigi; UK Representative, Banca d'Italia, since 1987; Central Banking. *Career:* University of Rome Asst Prof of Economics 1959-60; IMF-IBRD Technical Asst to Exec Dir 1961-64; Banca d'Italia Dep

UK Rep 1964-75; Ufficio Italiano dei Cambi USA Rep 1976-87. *Biog: b.* 23 February 1936. *Nationality:* Italian. *m.* 1962, Gabriella (née Ortona); 2 s; 1 d. *Educ:* University of Rome (Doctorate in Law); Cambridge University. *Other Activities:* Italian Embassy (Financial Attache), Grand'Ufficiale al Merito Della Republica Italiano. *Professional Organisations:* Institute of Directors. *Publications:* Articles on Banking & Finance Published in Italy, UK, USA & Japan. *Clubs:* Club di Londra.

MARINKOVIC, Milan; Director/Representative, Beogradska Banka DD, Representative Office, since 1987. *Career:* Beogradska Banka, Loan Officer 1964-72; Manager, Cooperations & Investments with Foreign Partners 1972-73; Manager, Foreign Financial & Commercial Credits 1973-78; Area Manager, Capital Construction Abroad 1978-82; Assistant Gen Manager, International Division 1982-87; Rep Office, London, Director/Representative 1987-. *Biog: b.* 1939. *Nationality:* Serbian. *m.* 1964, Danica; 1 s; 1 d. *Educ:* University of Novisad (BA Econ). *Directorships:* Anglo Yugoslav Bank Limited, London 1990 Alternate Dir. *Recreations:* Tennis, Walking.

MARJORIBANKS, Francis N; Chief Financial Officer, Alexander Howden Reinsurance Brokers Limited.

MARK, John Richard Anthony; Director, Panmure Gordon Bankers Limited, since 1978; Corporate Banking; Senior VP, NCNB National Bank of North Carolina. *Career:* Peat Marwick Mitchell & Co Various 1967-73; The British Linen Bank Ltd Various 1973-77. *Biog: b.* 20 January 1946. *Nationality:* British. *m.* Diane Virginia (née Roberts); 1 s; 2 d. *Educ:* Clifton College; Magdalene College, Cambridge (MA Hons). *Directorships:* Demand and Supply Co Ltd; Carolina Leasing Ltd; NCNB (Export Finance) Limited; Carolina Investments Limited; Friary Leasing Limited; Panmure Gordon Investments; Panmure Gordon & Co Ltd; Friary Nominees Limited; Collmain Customer Services Limited. *Professional Organisations:* FCA. *Recreations:* All Sports, English Literature.

MARK, Miss Mary Meiklem; Partner, Grimley J R Eve, since 1989; Chairman London Marketing. *Career:* Gerald Eve, Assistant Surveyor 1980-83; Grimley J R Eve, Associate Partner 1987; Partner 1989. *Biog: b.* 1 February 1959. *Nationality:* British. *m.* 1990, Colin B Davidson. *Educ:* Penrhos College, Colwyn Bay (MA); Girton College, Cambridge (Economics Part I/Land Economy Part II). *Other Activities:* Member, Cambridge Land Society; Member, RICS P&D Division, Marketing & Promotions Committee. *Professional Organisations:* Associate Member, Royal Institution of Chartered Surveyors. *Recreations:* Travel, Walking, Antiques.

MARK, Reuben; Non-Executive Director, Pearson plc.

MARKARIAN, M E; Financial Director, Moutafian Commodities Ltd.

MARKER, B S; Non-Executive Director, Next plc.

MARKHAM, Lawrence P; Partner, Beachcroft Stanleys.

MARKLEY, Stuart J; Partner, MacNair Mason.

MARKS, Ms Alexandra Louise; Partner, Linklaters & Paines, since 1990; Commercial Property. *Career:* Rowe & Maw (Solicitors) Articled clerk 1981-83; Assistant Solicitor 1983-84; Linklaters & Paines, Assistant Solicitor 1984-90. *Biog: b.* 9 September 1959. *Nationality:* British. *Educ:* Guildford County School for Girls; Brasenose College, Oxford (BA). *Other Activities:* Chair of Trustees of Amnesty International British Section Charitable Trust; Council Member of Amnesty International; Chair of Law Society's International Human Rights Consultative Group; Committee Member of Charity (a movement to simplify legal English). *Professional Organisations:* The Law Society. *Clubs:* President of the 63 Club. *Recreations:* Human Rights Campaigning.

MARKS, Andrew E; Director, Continental Reinsurance London.

MARKS, Anthony Louis; Partner, McKenna & Co, since 1983; Head of Commercial Litigation Group. *Career:* Clifford Turner, Articled Clerk 1973-75; Asst Solicitor 1975-79; McKenna & Co, Asst Solicitor 1979-83. *Biog: b.* 18 December 1949. *Nationality:* British. *m.* 1980, Rikki; 1 s; 2 d. *Educ:* Bristol University (LLB Honours 2:1). *Other Activities:* Former Chairman, Fulham Legal Advice Centre, 1978-79. *Professional Organisations:* City of London Solicitors Company; Committee Member, OA Society. *Publications:* Article in Acquisitions Monthly on DTI Inquiries; Articles on DTI Inquiries & FSA in the Company Lawyer and New Law Journal.

MARKS, David Michael; Director, Smith New Court plc, since 1983; Equity Trading. *Biog: b.* 27 January 1942. *m.* 1969, Ginette Gabrielle (née Crasnier). *Educ:* Southgate Grammar School.

MARKS, E S; Director, Smith New Court plc.

MARKS, Michael John Paul; Chief Executive, Smith New Court plc, since 1987. *Career:* Smith Bros 1960-71; Ptnr 1971-84; Smith New Court International Ltd MD 1984-. *Biog: b.* 28 December 1941. *Nationality:* British. *m.* 1967, Rosemary Ann (née Brody); 1 s; 2 d. *Educ:* St Paul's School. *Directorships:* Rothschilds Continuation Ltd 1990 (non-exec). *Professional Organisations:* Member, Securities Association. *Recreations:* Water Skiing, Tennis, Swimming.

MARKS, Peter Michael; Director, Brantson & Gothard Ltd, since 1987; Stockbroker, Dealing Director. *Career:* Grieveson Grant, Clerk 1967; W H Hart, Blue Button 1967-68; P E Schweider Miller, Blue Button & Dealer & Member of the S/E 1968-73; Harris Allday Lea & Brooks, Member of The Stock Exchange 1973-80; Strauss Turnbull, Member of The Stock Exchange 1980-81; Branston & Gothard, Partner 1982-87; Branston & Gothard Ltd, Director 1987-. *Biog:* b. 6 March 1950. *Nationality:* British. *m.* 1973, Mimi (née Benzaken). *Educ:* Kilburn Grammar School. *Professional Organisations:* Member, The International Stock Exchange, 1971-. *Recreations:* Work, Tennis, Golf.

MARKS, R C; Non-Marine Underwriter, Sphere Drake Insurance plc.

MARKSON, I; Director, Brandeis Limited.

MARLATTE, George Ellis; Vice President, The Bank of Nova Scotia, since 1987; Corporate Banking in the UK. *Career:* Nova Scotia Various 1968-. *Biog:* b. 9 October 1949. *Nationality:* Canadian. *m.* 1970, Donna Marie (née Read); 1 s; 1 d. *Educ:* University of Saskatchewan (BComm); Banff School of Advanced Management. *Professional Organisations:* Fellow, The Institute of Canadian Bankers. *Clubs:* Overseas Bankers'.

MARLE, William James; Director, Guidehouse Securities Limited, since 1989; Corporate Finance Division. *Career:* Bank of Nova Scotia 1982-83; London & Continental Bankers 1983-85; Allied Irish Investment Bank 1985-87; Guidehouse Group 1987-. *Biog:* b. 10 March 1958. *Nationality:* British. *m.* 1982, Audrey (née Power); 1 s; 1 d. *Educ:* Tonbridge School; Hull University (Law, LLB); Manchester Business School (MBA). *Other Activities:* Worshipful Company of Launderers; Worshipful Company of Bakers. *Recreations:* Golf, Collecting Golf Memorabilia, Bridge.

MARLOW, Alastair Rupert; Director, Kleinwort Benson Investment Management, since 1988; UK Pension Funds. *Career:* Peat Marwick Mitchell 1974-79; J Henry Schroder Wagg 1979-85; Scimitar Asset Management 1985-87. *Biog:* b. 20 November 1952. *Nationality:* British. *m.* 1979, Teresa; 1 s; 2 d. *Educ:* Uppingham School; Cambridge (MA Hons). *Professional Organisations:* Chartered Accountant.

MARLOW, David; Chief Executive & Director, 3i Group plc.

MARPER, William John; Group Finance Director, Co-operative Bank plc, since 1989; Financial Services Sectors. *Career:* ANZ Investment Banking Group, Director of Finance 1985-89; Citicorp/Citibank Investment Banking Group USA, Vice President Operations 1984-85; Individual Banking Group USA, Vice President Finance 1982-84; Individual Banking Group UK, Fi-

nance Director 1977-82; Charles Barker Group, Management Accountant 1972-77; Lyon Group, Financial Accountant 1970-72; Peat Marwick McLintock, Auditor 1965-70. *Biog:* b. 9 December 1946. *Nationality:* British. *m.* 1974, Maureen. *Educ:* Sir William Turners. *Directorships:* Co-operative Bank plc and Subsidiaries 1989 (exec); CIM Limited 1990 (exec); Unity Trust Bank plc 1989 (non-exec). *Professional Organisations:* Fellow, Institute of Chartered Accountants; Member, International Stock Exchange. *Recreations:* Tennis, Motor Sport.

MARQUARD, B A; Director, Providence Capitol Fund Managers Ltd.

MARQUARDT, Stephen C; Director, Merrill Lynch International Limited, since 1986; Equity Origination. *Career:* Warburg Paribas Becker Incorporated 1978-84; Merrill Lynch Capital Markets 1984-89. *Biog:* b. 8 August 1954. *Nationality:* American. *m.* Deborah (née Shaw); 1 d. *Educ:* Northwestern University (BA); Harvard Business School (MBA); Loyola University (JD). *Professional Organisations:* American Bar Association. *Clubs:* The Chicago Club, The Racquet Club of Chicago, The Saddle & Cycle Club, The Attic Club.

MARR, John; Director, Charterhouse Tilney, since 1986; Research, Specialising in Insurance. *Career:* Mather and Platt (Engineers), Trainee Accountant 1964-68; Co-op Insurance Society (Life Co), Investment Mgr 1968-72; Tilney/Charterhouse, Tilney Analyst 1973-77; Ptnr 1977-86. *Biog:* b. 7 March 1946. *Nationality:* British. *m.* 1972, Caroline (née Cowan); 1 s; 2 d. *Educ:* Doncaster Grammar School. *Professional Organisations:* FCCA; ACIS; ASIA. *Recreations:* Cricket, Chess, Photography.

MARR, Lindsay Grigor David; Partner, Freshfields, since 1987. *Career:* Freshfields, Articled Clerk 1979-81; Assistant Solicitor 1981-87. *Biog:* b. 14 September 1955. *Nationality:* British. *Educ:* The Perse School, Cambridge; Gonville and Caius College, Cambridge (MA). *Professional Organisations:* Law Society; City of London Solicitors' Company. *Recreations:* Reading, Music, Squash, Golf.

MARR, William Donald; Chairman & Chief Executive, Dunedin Fund Managers Limited, since 1989. *Career:* Dunedin Fund Managers Ltd, Deputy Chairman & Joint Chief Exec 1985-89. *Biog:* b. 10 September 1930. *Nationality:* British. *m.* 1957, Valerie (née Stevenson); 1 s; 3 d. *Educ:* Loretto. *Directorships:* DFM Holdings Ltd 1985 (exec); The British Linen Bank Ltd 1989 (non-exec); Dunedin Worldwide Investment Trust plc 1980 (non-exec); Dunedin Income Growth Investment Trust plc 1970 (non-exec); The Fleming Fledgeling Investment Trust plc 1984 (non-exec); Loretto School Ltd 1976 (non-exec). *Professional Organisations:* CA. *Clubs:* New, Caledonian, Royal & Ancient GC. *Recreations:* Golf, Fly Fishing.

MARRE, Richard; Partner, Clifford Chance, since 1973; Ship Finance, International Banking. *Career:* Coward Chance, Solicitor 1971-73; Partner 1973-87; Clifford Chance, Partner 1987-. *Biog: b.* 26 June 1940. *Nationality:* British. *m.* 1976, Vanna; 1 d. *Educ:* Lycee Francais de Londres; University College, London (LLB). *Professional Organisations:* Member, Law Society. *Clubs:* Yacht Club of Greece.

MARRIAGE, Jeremy Peter; Partner, Linklaters & Paines, since 1978; Paris Office. *Career:* Linklaters & Paines, Articled Clerk; Assistant Solicitor 1972-78; Seconded to Linklaters & Paines Hong Kong 1977-80; Linklaters & Paines, Partner 1978-; Linklaters & Paines Paris, Partner in Charge 1988-. *Biog: b.* 3 May 1947. *Nationality:* British. *m.* 1983, Caroline (née Williams); 1 s; 2 d. *Educ:* Rugby. *Other Activities:* Governor, The Old Malthouse School. *Professional Organisations:* Member, The Law Society; Member, The Franco-British Lawyers' Society. *Recreations:* Skiing, Sailing.

MARRIOTT, John Miles; Non-Executive Director, Phillips & Drew Fund Management Ltd, since 1986. *Career:* East Midlands Electricity Board (Nottingham), Trainee Acct/Acct Asst 1952-60; Morley Borough Council, Snr Acct Asst/Snr Audit Asst 1960-62; Wolverhampton County Borough Council, Acct/Snr Systems Analyst, Programme 1962-67; Torbay CBC, Asst Borough Treasurer 1967-70; Ipswich CBC, Dep Borough Treasurer/Borough Treasurer 1970-73; Bolton Metropolitan BC, Dir of Fin 1973-78; Greater Manchester County Council, County Treasurer 1978-86; Grant Thornton, Ptnr 1986-90. *Biog: b.* 11 October 1935. *m.* 1967, Josephine Anne (née Shepherd). *Educ:* High Pavement Grammar School, Nottingham. *Directorships:* Greater Manchester Passenger Transport Executive 1978-86 (non-exec); Manchester International Airport 1978-86 Treasurer. *Professional Organisations:* CIPFA; BCS. *Recreations:* Bird Watching, Golf, Motoring, Rotary.

MARRIOTT, O; Non-Executive Director, P & O Steam Navigation Company.

MARRIS, Ian Colquhoun; Director, Morgan Grenfell Asset Management Limited.

MARRS, A; Manager, First Vice President, American Express Bank.

MARS, P J; Director, S G Warburg Akroyd Rowe & Pitman Mullens Securities Ltd.

MARSDEN, (Austin) Philip; Executive Director, County NatWest Ltd, since 1989; Head of Intl Mergers & Acquisitions, Corporate Finance Director. *Career:* Citibank NA, Account Officer, Energy 1980-84; County NatWest, Head of Energy 1984-87; Director 1987-89. *Biog: b.* 18 April 1956. *Nationality:* British. *m.* 1985, Valerie Judith Sloan (née Hodgart); 2 s. *Educ:* Ampleforth College; St Andrews University (MA in History). *Directorships:* Galilée Investillements. *Other Activities:* Member, The Trades House of Glasgow, Incorporation of Skinners. *Clubs:* RAC, Oil Clubs, Wimbledon Park, Saints, The Kate Kennedy Club. *Recreations:* Sport, Food, Drink, Family.

MARSDEN, Philip; Director, 3i Corporate Finance Limited, since 1988. *Career:* Arthur Andersen & Co, Consultancy Division 1974-79; 3i plc, Investment Controller 1979-82; Local Director 1982-86; 3i Corporate Finance 1986-. *Biog: b.* 23 March 1952. *Nationality:* British. *m.* 1977, Angela (née Crawford); 2 s. *Educ:* St Peter's School, York; Management Centre, University of Bradford (MSc). *Directorships:* 3i Corporate Finance 1988 (exec). *Other Activities:* Institute of Chartered Accountants, Various Committees. *Professional Organisations:* FCA. *Recreations:* Shooting, Fishing.

MARSH, Brian John; Company Secretary, United Dominions Trust Limited, since 1988; Compliance. *Career:* United Dominions Trust Limited, Various Accounting Positions 1969-88. *Biog: b.* 17 March 1935. *Nationality:* British. *Professional Organisations:* Chartered Secretary.

MARSH, B R; Deputy Chairman, The British Insurance and Investment Brokers' Association.

MARSH, Bryan; Partner, Touche Ross & Co, since 1968; Taxation. *Biog: b.* 3 February 1941. *Nationality:* British. *m.* 1965, Sandra Beverley (née Webb); 1 s; 1 d. *Educ:* Barry Grammar School; Birmingham University (BCom). *Other Activities:* Assistant to the Court of the Worshipful Company of Tin Plate Workers alias Wire Workers. *Professional Organisations:* FCA. *Clubs:* City Livery Club. *Recreations:* Golf, Skiing.

MARSH, David John; Partner, Wragge & Co, since 1963; Corporate Finance. *Biog: b.* 2 November 1936. *Nationality:* British. *m.* 1963, Hilary Joy (née Pitt); 1 s; 2 d. *Educ:* Leeds Grammar School; Merton College, Oxford (MA). *Directorships:* Fownes Hotels plc 1987 (non-exec); Marla Tube Fittings Ltd 1970 (non-exec). *Professional Organisations:* Law Society.

MARSH, G A; Director, LMX, Denis M Clayton & Co Limited.

MARSH, Ian; Partner, Titmuss Sainer & Webb.

MARSH, John Bernard; Managing Director, Phillips & Drew Fund Management Ltd, since 1988. *Career:* Price Waterhouse, Audit Snr 1969-73; Phillips & Drew, Investment Analyst 1973-78; Phillips & Drew Fund Management, Fund Mgr 1979-82; Ptnr/Dir 1982-88. *Biog: b.* 29 May 1947. *Nationality:* British. *Educ:* The Leys School, Cambridge. *Professional Organisations:* FCA.

MARSH, Professor Paul Rodney; Professor of Management & Finance, London Business School, since 1985; Corporate Finance & Investment Management. *Career:* Esso Petroleum, Systems Analyst 1968-69; Scicon, Systems Analyst 1970-71; London Business School, Bank of England Research Fellow 1974-85; Director, Sloan Fellowship Programme 1980-83; Senior Lecturer in Finance 1983-85; Professor of Managment & Finance 1985-; Faculty Dean 1987-90; Deputy Principal 1989-90. *Biog: b.* 19 August 1947. *Nationality:* British. *m.* 1971 Stephanie (née Simonow. *Educ:* Poole Grammar School; London School of Economics (BSc Econ 1st Class Honours); London Business School (PhD). *Directorships:* M&G Investment Management 1989 (non-exec); Centre for Management Development 1984 (non-exec); London Business School 1987 (Governor). *Other Activities:* CBI Task Force on City-Industry Relations (1986-88); Risk Measurement Service (Joint Editor); Evidence to Wilson Committee (1980); Consultant to the SIB, The Stock Exchange & Many Leading Companies & Financial Institutions. *Professional Organisations:* European Finance Association; American Finance Association; Western Finance Association (USA); British Academy of Management. *Publications:* Cases in Corporate Finance (with E Dimson) 1988; The Hoare Govett Smaller Companies Index (with E Dimson), 1990; Accounting for Brands (with P Darwise,C Higson & A Likierman), 1989; Managing Strategic Investment Decisions (with P Barwise,R Wensley,K Thomas),1988; Plus Numerous Articles in Books & Journals. *Recreations:* Gardening, Investment.

MARSH, Richard; Partner and Head of Department, Taylor Joynson Garrett.

MARSHALL, A J; Director, The Private Bank and Trust Company, since 1989; Financial Control, Compliance. *Career:* Orion Bank Ltd, Executive Director Group Financial Control 1971-80; Swiss Bank Corporation Investment Banking, Executive Director Financial Administration and Control 1980-89. *Biog: b.* 18 June 1943. *Nationality:* British. *m.* 1971, Susan (née Sakin); 2 s. *Educ:* Radley College. *Professional Organisations:* Fellow, Institute of Chartered Accountants in England and Wales.

MARSHALL, Alexander Badenoch; Chairman, Commercial Union Assurance Company plc.

MARSHALL, Sir Colin; Non-Executive Director, Grand Metropolitan plc.

MARSHALL, D R A; Chairman, Eurobrokers Holdings Limited, since 1986. *Career:* Nesbitt Thomson & Co Ltd, Toronto, Canada, Money Market Specialist 1968-70; Euro Brokers Inc, NY 1970-; President & CEO 1986-. *Biog: b.* 24 December 1944. *Nationality:* Canadian. *Educ:* University of Toronto (BA Hons Philosophy & English); Stanford University, Graduate School of Business (MBA). *Directorships:* Euro Brokers Group Companies 1986 (exec); Yagi Euro Corp, Tokyo 1987 (exec); Caridon Company, Hong Kong 1990 (exec).

MARSHALL, David; Director (Market-Making), Hoare Govett International Securities.

MARSHALL, Sir Denis; Consultant (formerly Senior Partner), Barlow Lyde & Gilbert, since 1984. *Career:* Admitted as Solicitor 1937; Barlow Lyde & Gilbert, Admitted as Partner 1949; Senior Partner 1968-84. *Biog: b.* 1 June 1916. *Nationality:* British. *m.* 1975, Jane; 1 s. *Educ:* Dulwich College. *Directorships:* R J Kiln & Co Ltd 1987- (non-exec); Anglo American Insurance Company Limited 1988- (non-exec); Housing Standards Company Limited 1989- (non-exec); H J Weavers (Underwriting) Agencies Ltd 1990- (non-exec); Solicitor's Indemnity Fund Limited 1988- (non-exec). *Other Activities:* Associate Member, Lloyd's, 1951-; Council Member, Law Society, 1966-86, (President 1981-82); Council Member, Insurance Brokers Registration Council, 1979-90; Council Member, FIMBRA, 1986-90; Member, Royal Commission on Civil Liability (The Pearson Commission), 1972-77; Member, Lord Chancellors County Court Rules Committee, 1970-80; Member, Criminal Injuries Compensation Board, 1982-90. *Professional Organisations:* Solicitor. *Clubs:* Naval & Military.

MARSHALL, I; Director, Bain Clarkson Limited, since 1989. *Career:* Peat Marwick Mitchell & Co, Accountant 1970-74; Thomas Tilliny, Group Accountant 1974-76; TSB Group, Head of Finance 1976-81; Head of Planning 1981-86; Ogilvy & Mather Ltd, Finance Director 1986-89. *Biog: b.* 27 May 1947. *Nationality:* British. *m.* Carla. *Educ:* Edinburgh University (MA Hons English). *Professional Organisations:* Fellow, Institute of Chartered Accountants.

MARSHALL, Kenneth Richard Paul; Director, S G Warburg & Co Ltd, since 1977; Group Finance. *Career:* Morison Rutherford & Co, Partner 1963-68; Ford Motor Company, Financial Accountant 1968-70. *Biog: b.* 20 July 1935. *Nationality:* British. *m.* 1958, Dee (née Arney); 1 s; 2 d. *Educ:* Oundle School. *Directorships:* S G Warburg Group Management Ltd 1986 (exec). *Professional Organisations:* FCA. *Clubs:* Gresham. *Recreations:* Walking, Squash.

MARSHALL, Richard Sydney; Director, March Investment Fund Ltd, since 1988; General Management of March Cheshire Development Capital. *Career:* The Plessey Company Ltd, Development Engineer 1965-69; Multitone Electric Co Ltd, Group Leader 1969-73; Pye Dynamics Ltd, Project Manager 1973-78; Lexor Electronics Ltd, Chief Engineer 1978-80; B & L Microcomputers, Chief Engineer 1980-81; Prutec Ltd, Technical Business Mgr 1981-85; Fairey Engineering Ltd, Business Development Executive 1985-86; Wharton Winches

Ltd, Dir & Gen Mgr 1985-86; March Investment Fund 1986-. *Biog: b.* 28 March 1944. *Nationality:* British. *m.* 1965, Gillian Ann (née Lee); 2 d. *Educ:* Aylesbury Grammar School; Imperial College/LSE (ACGI,BSc). *Directorships:* Wharton Winches Ltd 1985-86 (exec); Bulldog Tools Ltd 1988 (non-exec); Hastypitch Ltd (Central Emplyment Agency) 1988-90 (non-exec); March Cheshire Nominees Ltd 1990 (exec). *Other Activities:* Member, Regional Funds Working Party; British Venture Capital Association. *Professional Organisations:* CEng; Member, Institute of Electrical Engineers. *Publications:* Venture Capital in the North West, 1988; Co-Author, Sources of Venture Capital, 1990. *Recreations:* Theatre, Music, DIY, Railway Modelling.

MARSHALL, Stuart Walter; Director, Coutts & Co, since 1989; Commercial Banking. *Career:* Coutts & Co, Various Management Positions 1969-81; Dep Head of Branch Banking 1981-86; Head of Mgmnt Services Div 1986-90; Head of Commercial Banking Group 1990. *Biog: b.* 9 September 1935. *Nationality:* British. *m.* 1961, Patricia (née Bentley); 1 s; 1 d. *Educ:* Beckenham & Penge Grammar School. *Other Activities:* Council Member & Hon Treasurer, Invalid Children's Aid Nationwide; Governor, Colfe's School. *Professional Organisations:* FCIB. *Recreations:* Fishing, Shooting, Gardening, Skiing.

MARSHALL, T R; Partner, Holman, Fenwick & Willan, since 1988; Commercial Litigation/Marine Law. *Biog: b.* 24 January 1952. *Nationality:* British. *Educ:* Campbell College, Belfast; Trinity College, Oxford (MA); Middle Temple (Called to the Bar 1975). *Clubs:* Oxford & Cambridge, Royal Belfast Golf Club. *Recreations:* Squash, Golf, Tennis.

MARSHALL SMITH, Mrs Rosamond Joy (née Durden); Partner, Hammond Suddards, since 1989; Corporate Tax. *Career:* Boodle Hatfield, Articled Clerk 1981-83; Boodle Hatfield, Assistant Solicitor 1983-84; Clifford-Turner, Assistant Solicitor 1984-87; Hammond Suddards, Assistant Solicitor 1987-89. *Biog: b.* 11 April 1959. *Nationality:* British. *m.* 1985, William Marshall Smith. *Educ:* Newstead Wood, Orpington; Durham University (BA). *Professional Organisations:* Law Society; Association of Women Solicitors. *Clubs:* Bradford Club. *Recreations:* Gardening, Swimming.

MARTELL, A; Director, Wise Speke Ltd.

MARTELL, B M; Director, Maxwell Pergamon Publishing Corporation plc.

MARTHALER, Kurt; Managing Director, Quadrex Securities Limited.

MARTI, D; Non Executive Director, Citymax Integrated Information Systems Ltd.

MARTIN, Adrian H; Partner, Stoy Hayward.

MARTIN, Alan Graham; Partner, Dickson Minto WS, since 1987; Corporate Law. *Career:* Dundas & Wilson CS (Edinburgh), Asst 1978-81; Vinson & Elkins, Assoc Lawyer 1981-82; Dundas & Wilson CS (Edinburgh), Ptnr 1983-84; Vinson & Elkins, Assoc Lawyer 1984-87. *Biog: b.* 28 March 1954. *Nationality:* British. *m.* 1984, Lindsey Jane (née Evans); 2 d. *Educ:* Dollar Academy; Edinburgh University (LLB Hons). *Professional Organisations:* Writer to the Signet; Member, The Law Society of Scotland. *Clubs:* Lansdowne. *Recreations:* Windsurfing, Tennis.

MARTIN, Benjamin John; Director, Barclays de Zoete Wedd Limited, since 1986; Corporate Finance. *Career:* Morgan Grenfell 1967-72; Banque De Suez 1972-74; Barclays Merchant Bank, Various 1974-81; Dir 1981-86. *Biog: b.* 21 January 1944. *m.* 1974, Mary Julia (née Laird); 1 s; 1 d. *Educ:* Allhallows School; St Andrews University (BSc).

MARTIN, C D Z; Partner, Macfarlanes, since 1990; Corporate Law. *Career:* Macfarlanes 1983-. *Biog: b.* 2 February 1961. *Nationality:* British. *m.* 1988, Sarah (née Wilson). *Educ:* Merchant Taylors', Northwood; Bristol University (LLB). *Professional Organisations:* Solicitor; Member, International Bar Association.

MARTIN, Carolyn; Associate Director, GCI Sterling.

MARTIN, David; Partner, Herbert Smith, since 1986; Tax.

MARTIN, David John; Director, Leslie & Godwin Ltd, since 1990; Financial Risks. *Career:* Corporation of Lloyd's 1976-79; Insurance Co of North America (UK), Underwriter 1979-85; Bankamerica Insurance Brokers Ltd, Managing Director 1985-89; Leslie & Godwin Financial Risks Ltd, Managing Director 1989-. *Biog: b.* 4 January 1958. *Nationality:* British. *m.* 1987, Terri (née Fleming). *Educ:* Sir Joseph Williamson's, Rochester. *Professional Organisations:* Fellow, Chartered Insurance Institute (1982-).

MARTIN, George K; Managing Director, Merrill Lynch Pierce Fenner & Smith Limited.

MARTIN, I A; Director, Grand Metropolitan plc, since 1985; Chairman & Chief Executive Officer, Grand Metropolitan Food Sector. *Career:* Timex Corporation, Dundee 1962; PA Management Consultants, Edinburgh & Glasgow; Timex, France 1967; Mine Safety Appliances Ltd, Director of Finance and Personnel 1969-72; ITT Europe, Managing Director ITT Distributors Ltd, Director, Europe Electrical Distributor Division; Chairman, ITT Distributors Ltd, UK; Grand Metropolitan plc, Watney Mann & Truman Brewers subsidiary 1979; Chm & CEO 1982; Chm & Chief Exec, Brewing and

Retailing Div; Chm, US Consumer Products Div. *Biog:* b. 1935. *m.* Phyllis. *Educ:* Harris Academy, Dundee; St Andrew's University, Scotland (MA, Economics, Prize Winner, Psychology Class Medallist). *Directorships:* The Pillsbury Company Chm, CEO & President; Burger King Corporation Chm; Inter-Continental Hotels Former Chm. *Other Activities:* Freeman, City of London; Board Member: Grocery Manufacturers of America; The Conference Board; Minnesota Business Partnership; United Way; 1991 Special Olympics; Children 2000 Commission; University of Minnesota School of Management Board of Overseers; Metropolitan Economic Development Association. *Professional Organisations:* Companion, British Institute of Management. *Recreations:* Salmon and Deep Sea Fishing.

MARTIN, Ian James; Finance Director, Baring Securities Limited.

MARTIN, J W; General Manager, BP Pensions Services Ltd.

MARTIN, Jim; Director, 3i plc, since 1988; Regional Director (East Anglia). *Career:* Touche Ross & Co, Glasgow & London, Trainee & Qualified CA 1974-78; Uniroyal Inc, Liege, Investigations Manager 1978-79; Lucas CAV, Buckingham, Financial Controller 1979-80; 3i plc (London), Investment Controller 1980-; (Sheffield), Investment Controller 1980-; (Edinburgh), Director 1980-; (Cambridge), Director 1980-. *Biog: b.* 11 November 1954. *Nationality:* British. *m.* 1982, Maureen (née Martin); 1 s; 1 d. *Directorships:* 3i plc 1988 (exec); Cambridge Quantum Fund Ltd 1990 (non-exec); Edinburgh Quantum Fund Ltd 1985 (non-exec); Scotbic Ltd 1986 (non-exec). *Other Activities:* Scottish Council Trade & Industry; Member, Public Policy Committee 1986-88. *Professional Organisations:* Member, Institute of Chartered Accountants of Scotland. *Publications:* Various. *Recreations:* Squash.

MARTIN, John; Associate, James Gentles & Son.

MARTIN, Leonard John; Senior Partner, R Watson & Sons, since 1983; Actuarial Advice to Pension Funds and Life Assurance Companies. *Career:* National Mutual 1947-52. *Biog: b.* 20 April 1929. *Nationality:* British. *m.* 1956, Elisabeth Veronica (née Hall-Jones); 1 s; 1 d. *Educ:* Ardingly College. *Other Activities:* Deputy Chairman, Occupational Pensions Board; Chairman, Groupe Consultatif des Associations d'Actuaires in EEC; Past Chairman, Assoc of Consulting Actuaries; Council Member, Institute of Actuaries, Committee of Actuaries United Nations Pensions Fund. *Professional Organisations:* FIA; FPMI; FSS. *Clubs:* Naval Club. *Recreations:* Music, Flying, Sailing.

MARTIN, Michael; Director, Kleinwort Benson Ltd, since 1987; Corporate Finance, Mergers & Acquisitions. *Career:* Price Waterhouse (Paris), Asst Mgr 1974-78;

Allied Irish Investment Bank (Dublin), Corporate Fin Exec 1978-81. *Biog: b.* 4 April 1952. *Nationality:* Irish. *m.* 1978, Marylyn (née Coombes); 2 s; 1 d. *Recreations:* Golf.

MARTIN, Paul John George Charles; Administration Director, Panmure Gordon & Co Ltd, since 1987; Day to Day Administration of General Office, Deputy Compliance Officer, Telecommunications, Data Processing, Personnel & Training. *Career:* Touche Ross & Co Articles to Audit Snr 1971-78; The Stock Exchange Quotations Dept Asst Mgr Companies Supervision 1978-80; James Capel & Co Corp Finance Exec 1980-82; Panmure Gordon & Co Ltd Corp Fin Exec 1982-86. *Biog: b.* 1 September 1949. *Nationality:* British. *m.* 1989, June Ellen Anne (nee Smith). *Educ:* Kings College, Wimbledon; Leeds University (BSc). *Directorships:* Panmure Gordon Bankers Ltd 1987 (exec). *Professional Organisations:* FCA. *Recreations:* Motorsport, Marine Fishkeeping.

MARTIN, Peter; Partner (Head of Aviation Department), Frere Cholmeley Solicitors, since 1981; Air Law. *Career:* Beaumont & Sons, Ptnr 1961-81. *Biog: b.* 9 May 1934. *Nationality:* British. *m.* 1971, Elizabeth (née de Villardi de Montlaur); 3 d. *Educ:* University College, London (LLB Hons). *Directorships:* Equitable Life Assurance Society 1983 (non-exec); Dollar Air Services Limited 1978 (non-exec). *Other Activities:* Clerk to Her Majesty's Commission for Lieutenancy for the City of London, 1964-; Visiting Professor of Aerospace Law, University College, London. *Professional Organisations:* The Law Society; FRAeS. *Publications:* Air Law, 1977 & Supplements. *Recreations:* Gardening, Shooting, Foreign Travel.

MARTIN, Peter John; Director, Kleinwort Benson Limited, since 1990; Mergers & Acquisitions. *Career:* Kleinwort Benson Limited 1981-. *Biog: b.* 9 October 1957. *Nationality:* British. *m.* 1984, Susan Jane (née Chugg). *Educ:* Gordonstoun; Birmingham University (BSc, BComm).

MARTIN, Philip Edward; Group Treasurer, Unilever plc & NV, since 1989. *Career:* Unilever 1962-; Various Accounting, Economics and Financial Appointments 1962-71; Unilever Argentina, Controller/Treasurer 1971-74; Senior Commercial Manager Overseas 1974-78; Unilever Indonesia, Financial Director 1978-82; Lever Brothers Ltd, Financial Director 1982-89. *Biog: b.* 13 September 1943. *Nationality:* British. *m.* 1987, Alison. *Directorships:* Various Unilever Subsidiary & Finance Companies. *Professional Organisations:* FCCA, FCT.

MARTIN, R J; Special Projects Co-ordinator, Ultramar plc.

MARTIN, R G; Partner, Cameron Markby Hewitt.

MARTIN, Richard Graham; Vice Chairman & Chief Executive, Allied-Lyons plc, since 1989. *Career:* Friary Holroyd & Healy's Brewery Ltd, Personal Assistant to Managing Director 1955-59; Director 1959-63; Friary Meux Ltd, Director 1963-66; Ind Coope (East Anglia) Ltd, Managing Director 1966-69; Joshua Tetley & Son Ltd, Director 1969-72; Allied Breweries Ltd, Director 1972-; Joshua Tetley & Son Ltd, Chief Executive 1972-78; Joshua Tetley & Son Tetley Walker Ltd, Vice Chairman 1978-79; Ind Coope Ltd, Chairman 1979-85; Allied-Lyons plc, Director 1981-; Allied Breweries Ltd, Managing Director 1985-86; Chairman & Chief Executive 1986-88; Allied-Lyons plc, Vice Chairman 1988-; Hiram Walker-Allied Vintners Ltd, Director 1988-; Allied-Lyons plc, Chief Executive 1989-; J Lyons & Company Ltd, Chairman 1989-. *Biog: b.* 4 October 1932. *Nationality:* British. *m.* 1958, Elizabeth (née Savage); 2 s; 1 d. *Directorships:* Allied Breweries Ltd 1972 (exec); Allied Lyons plc 1981 (exec); Hiram Walker-Allied Vintners 1988 (exec); J Lyons & Co Ltd 1989 (exec). *Other Activities:* Chairman, Brewers Society, 1991; President, Shire Horse Society, 1981-82; Brewers Company.

MARTIN, Rosemary; Partner, Turner Kenneth Brown, since 1970; Company & Commercial Law (Computer Software). *Biog: b.* 26 January 1943. *Educ:* Durham High School; London School of Economics (LLB). *Other Activities:* Member, City Women's Network; City of London Solicitors' Company Commercial Law Sub-Committee. *Professional Organisations:* Law Society. *Recreations:* Tennis, Sailing, Theatre.

MARTIN, Timothy Charles; Director, Barclays de Zoete Wedd Limited, since 1988; Corporate Finance. *Career:* Allen & Overy Articled Clerk/Solicitor 1975-79; Hill Samuel & Co Ltd 1979-87; Dir 1986-87. *Biog: b.* 17 May 1951. *Nationality:* British. *m.* 1984, Sarah (née Moffett); 2 s. *Educ:* Worthing High School; King's College, Cambridge (BA, MA). *Professional Organisations:* The Law Society; Solicitor. *Clubs:* Hurlingham, Lansdowne. *Recreations:* Tennis, Opera, Gardening.

MARTIN, William Thomas; Partner, Nabarro Nathanson.

MARTIN SMITH, Andrew Everard; Director, Hambros Bank Limited, since 1986. *Biog: b.* 13 June 1952. *Nationality:* British. *m.* 1982, Jennifer Ann (née Dent); 1 s; 2 d. *Educ:* Eton; Exeter College, Oxford (MA). *Other Activities:* Liveryman, Fishmongers Company.

MARTINEAU, Mrs Elizabeth Jane (née Hammond); Partner, Clyde & Co, since 1978; Shipping and Insurance Litigation. *Biog: b.* 27 March 1951. *Nationality:* British. *m.* 1982, John Denis (decd); 2 s. *Educ:* Cheltenham Ladies' College.

MARTINEAU, Jeremy John; Partner, Martineau Johnson.

MARTYN, C Philip; Legal Adviser/Joint General Manager, The Sumitomo Bank Ltd, since 1979. *Career:* Coward Chance, Asst Solicitor 1970-77; Clifford Turner, Asst Solicitor 1977-79. *Biog: b.* 17 July 1948. *Nationality:* British. *Educ:* St Dunstan's College; Exeter University (LLB). *Other Activities:* Trustee, Various Charities including Galahad Publishing Assoc; N & S London Rudolf Steiner Schools; Practitioner of Complementary Medicine; Teacher of Esoterics. *Professional Organisations:* Law Society. *Recreations:* Studying the Works of Rudolf Steiner, Gardening, Green Politics, Esotericism, Bach.

MARTYN, J R; Group Finance Director, Dalgety plc, since 1987. *Career:* Ford Motor Company Ltd, Various 1965-79; BICC plc, Group Finance Director 1980-84; The Littlewoods Organisation plc, Group Finance Director 1984-87. *Biog: b.* 16 June 1944. *Nationality:* British. *m.* 1967, Frances (née Williams); 1 s; 1 d. *Educ:* Exeter University (BA Hons). *Directorships:* Pilkington Glass Ltd 1989 (non-exec). *Professional Organisations:* FCMA, MCT. *Clubs:* Caledonian Club.

MARZULLI Jr, John A; Partner, Shearman & Sterling, since 1987; Mergers & Acquisitions. *Career:* US District Judges, US District Court, Trenton, New Jersey, USA 1978-80; Law Clerk, Honorable George H Barlow, The Hon Clarkson S Fisher, The Honorable Anne E Thompson. *Biog: b.* 3 January 1953. *Nationality:* American. *m.* 1986, Penelope (née Bennett); 1 s; 1 d. *Educ:* College High School (Diploma); Middlebury College (BA Magna Cum Laude Phi Beta Kappa); New York University School of Law (JD Order of the COIF). *Professional Organisations:* New Jersey, New York and American Bar Associations.

MAS MONTANES, Sir E; Director, Hambros plc.

MASDING, Robert David; Partner, R Watson & Sons, since 1972; Advice on Pension Schemes. *Career:* Prudential Assurance, Actuarial Asst 1966-69. *Biog: b.* 4 January 1944. *Nationality:* British. *m.* 1969, Jennifer Elizabeth (née Henry); 2 s. *Educ:* Wyggeston School, Leicester; Cambridge University (MA). *Other Activities:* Member of the Worshipful Company of Actuaries. *Professional Organisations:* FIA; FPMI; ASA; The Intl Assoc of Consulting Actuaries; Assoc of Consulting Actuaries. *Recreations:* Sailing, Golf.

MASKALL, Michael Edwin; Senior International Tax Partner, Price Waterhouse Europe, since 1986. *Career:* Price Waterhouse 1973-. *Biog: b.* 26 October 1938. *Nationality:* British. *m.* (div); 2 s; 2 d. *Educ:* Brentwood School, Essex. *Professional Organisations:* Fellow, Institute of Chartered Accountants. *Publications:* International Tax Management and Strategy, 1986.

MASKARA, Hare Narain; Chief Executive & Deputy General Manager, UCO Bank; Controlling UK Branches. *Career:* UCO Bank (India & Malaysia) Various Offices 1958-88. *Biog: b.* 3 January 1940. *Nationality:* Indian. *m.* 1963, Annapurna; 2 s; 1 d. *Educ:* Calcutta University (MCom). *Professional Organisations:* ACIB; Associate, Indian Institute of Bankers (Bombay).

MASKELL, P J; Director, CIN Venture Managers Ltd, since 1988; Venture Capital. *Career:* Peat Marwick Mitchell, Assistant Manager 1980-84; CIN Venture Managers Ltd 1984-. *Biog: b.* 25 May 1959. *Nationality:* British. *Educ:* Southampton University (BSc Business Economics and Accountancy. *Directorships:* Barnes Thomson Management Ltd 1986 (non-exec); The Cable Corporation Ltd 1987 (non-exec); Topdeq Ltd 1989 (non-exec). *Professional Organisations:* ACA.

MASLECK, R A; Senior Vice President, The Royal Bank of Canada.

MASLOV, Alexandre Stepanovich; Chairman & Managing Director, Moscow Narodny Bank Limited.

MASON, Anthony Denzil; Partner, Lane Clark & Peacock, since 1985; Pensions and General Insurance. *Career:* Guardian Royal Exchange, Actuarial Trainee 1975-80. *Biog: b.* 17 June 1954. *Nationality:* British. *m.* 1979, Vivien (née Long); 2 d. *Educ:* Chislehurst & Sidcup Grammar School; Birmingham University (BSocSc Mathematics, Economics & Statistics). *Other Activities:* Worshipful Company of Actuaries. *Professional Organisations:* FIA. *Clubs:* Lansdowne. *Recreations:* Squash, Walking, Bridge, Darts.

MASON, D E; Company Secretary, King & Shaxson Ltd, since 1986; Accounts/Pensions/Computers. *Career:* King & Shaxson Ltd, Assistant Secretary 1970-86; 65 Offset Ltd, Co Secretary 1969-70; Mayhew-Sanders & Co, Partner 1965-69; Articled 1959-65. *Professional Organisations:* FCA.

MASON, Ian Roger Humphrey; Vice President, Manufacturers Hanover Trust Company.

MASON, K B; Director, Euro Brokers Holdings Limited.

MASON, Keith Edward; Manager, Administration, C Hoare & Co.

MASON, Michael Hugh; Chairman, Charterhouse Tilney, since 1986; Now Mainly Administrative Formerly Institutional Sales and Technical Analyst. *Career:* Charles W Jones & Co, Ptnr 1960-75; Tilney & Co, Ptnr 1975-84; Snr Ptnr 1984-86. *Biog: b.* 1 April 1934. *Nationality:* British. *m.* 1959, Barbara Ann (née Birtles); 1 s; 2 d. *Educ:* Wrekin College. *Directorships:* Charterhouse plc 1986 (exec); Charterhouse Securities 1986

(exec). *Other Activities:* The International Stock Exchange Council (Former Member 1982-86); The International Stock Exchange (Member of the Northern Unit Ctee 1978-); The Securities Association Membership Ctee. *Clubs:* Liverpool Artists' Formby Golf Club, Waterloo Rugby Club. *Recreations:* Sailing, Golf, Watching Most Sports.

MASON, Nicholas Erskine Home; Director, C Czarnikow Ltd, since 1985; Finance. *Biog: b.* 25 January 1948. *Nationality:* British. *m.* 1969, Lois Eugenie (née Foster); 1 s; 2 d. *Educ:* Marlborough College. *Other Activities:* The Vintners' Company. *Professional Organisations:* FCA.

MASON, P; Director, CIN Properties.

MASON, Richard Graham; Executive Director, British Invisibles, since 1984; Export Promotion. *Career:* Bank of England 1962-84; Exchange Control Dept 1965-79; City EEC Committee, Sec 1980-84; City Capital Markets Committee, Sec 1980-84; City Taxation Committee, Sec 1980-82; British Invisible Exports Council, Sec & Treasurer 1982-84. *Biog: b.* 21 June 1944. *Nationality:* British. *m.* 1967, Lynda (née Tothill); 1 s; 1 d. *Educ:* Wilson's Grammar School, Camberwell. *Other Activities:* Mem, Intl Trade Ctee, London Chamber of Commerce; Mem, Development Ctee, British Tourist Authority; Mem, Guildford Diocesan Board of Finance; Treasurer, Runnymede Deanery Synod. *Professional Organisations:* ACIB; MIEX. *Publications:* Various Articles on Invisible Exports. *Clubs:* Overseas Bankers'. *Recreations:* Walking, Church Finance.

MASON, Richard J S; Partner, MacNair Mason.

MASON, William Ernest; CB; Director, Allied-Lyons plc, since 1989; Non-Executive. *Career:* Ministry of Food 1949-54; Ministry of Agriculture, Fisheries and Food 1954-89; Principal 1963-70; Assistant Secretary 1970-75; Under Secretary 1975-80; Fisheries Secretary 1980-82; Deputy Secretary (Fisheries and Food) 1982-89. *Biog: b.* 12 January 1929. *Nationality:* British. *m.* 1959, Jean (née Bossley); 1 s; 1 d. *Educ:* Brockley Grammar School; London School of Economics (BSc Econ). *Directorships:* Allied-Lyons plc 1989 (non-exec); Various Food and Drink Companies 1989 Consultant. *Other Activities:* FRSA. *Professional Organisations:* Fellow, Institute of Grocery Distribution (FIGD); Hon Fellow, Institute of Food Science & Technology (FIFST). *Clubs:* Reform. *Recreations:* Music, Reading, British Painting.

MASSEY, S; Executive Vice President, Prudential-Bache Securities (UK) Inc, since 1989; Branch Manager. *Career:* Prudential-Bache Securities (UK) Inc, Senior Vice President-Investments/Equity Sales 1982-89. *Biog: b.* 7 September 1957. *Nationality:* British. *m.* 1984, Fiorella (née Coen); 1 d. *Educ:* Lycee Francais de Londres; Hertford College, Oxford (MA Politics, Economics & Philosophy). *Directorships:* Harvington Properties 1988 (non-exec). *Other Activities:* Vice Chairman, Hampstead & Highgate Conservative Association.

MASSEY, John M; Partner, Touche Ross & Co.

MASSEY, James L; Chief Executive, Salomon Brothers International Limited, since 1988. *Career:* Salomon Brothers Inc 1967-. *Biog: b.* 9 February 1943. *Nationality:* American. *m.* Sue (née Jameson); 2 d. *Educ:* Florida State University (BS); Emory University (MBA). *Directorships:* Salomon Inc 1987 Executive Vice-President; Salomon Brothers Inc 1988 Vice Chairman. *Other Activities:* Member, Securities Trading Committee, British Merchant Banking & Securities Houses Association (BMBA). *Recreations:* Shooting, Golf.

MASTERS, C D; Consultant Partner, Milne Ross.

MASTERS, J E; Treasurer, State Bank of New South Wales Limited, since 1988. *Career:* Nikko Bank (UK) plc, Assistant General Manager, Treasury 1987-88; Caisse National De Credit Agricole, Treasurer & Head of Division, Money Markets & Foreign Exchange 1984-87; Johnson Matthey Bankers, Senior Dealer 1975-84. *Biog: b.* 19 May 1965. *Nationality:* British. *Educ:* Romford Technical High School, Romford, Essex. *Other Activities:* BBA Foreign Exchange Committee. *Professional Organisations:* TSA.

MASTERTON, Gavin George; General Manager, Bank of Scotland, since 1986; UK Banking East. *Career:* British Linen Bank Ltd, various Branch Banking followed by Departmental roles 1957-77; Executive Assistant to Gen Mgr with responsibility for creation of Corporate Lending Section 1977-78; Gen Mgr's Asst/ Secretary of East of Scotland Board 1978-83; Asst Gen Mgr, Specific Corporate relationships, including creation of niche expertise in Management Buy-Outs & Corporate Financing generally 1983-86; General Manager, East of Scotland, responsible for in excess of 50% of the retail outlets 1986-; Member of Management Board, East of Scotland and Aberdeen Board, responsible for the creation of a number of joint ventures. *Professional Organisations:* Fellow, Institute of Bankers in Scotland; Harvard University Advance Management Programme.

MATATKO, John Michael; Director, MA in Finance & Investment, University of Exeter, since 1988; Research & Teaching in Portfolio & Risk Management. *Biog: b.* 26 July 1946. *Nationality:* British. *Educ:* (BSc, MA). *Publications:* Numerous Papers, Books Include Key Developments in Personal Finance; 'Directors of Unit Trust Management'.

MATHÉ, J R E M; Partner, Penningtons.

MATHER, G; Financial Controller, Enterprise Oil.

MATHER, Howard S G; Partner, Simmons & Simmons, since 1986; Corporate Finance & Company Law. *Career:* Simmons & Simmons, Solicitor 1982-86. *Biog: b.* 10 July 1957. *Nationality:* British. *Educ:* Hutton Grammar School; New College, Oxford. *Publications:* Contributor, European Corporate Finance Law, 1990. *Recreations:* Antiquarian Book Collecting, Chess, Oriental Travel, FRGS.

MATHER, John MacGregor; Treasurer & General Manager, The Royal Bank of Scotland plc, since 1986; Treasury Divisions - UK and Overseas. *Career:* The Royal Bank of Scotland plc 1949-; Asst Gen Mgr, Intl 1976; Gen Mgr, Intl 1977; Gen Mgr, Treasury Operations 1985. *Biog: b.* 12 January 1932. *Nationality:* British. *m.* 1957, Eileen Jamieson (née Boyd); 1 s; 2 d. *Educ:* Hutchesons' Boys' Grammar School, Glasgow. *Directorships:* International Commodities Clearing House 1986 (non-exec); RBS Development Holdings (CI) Ltd 1986 (non-exec); Travellers Cheque Associates Ltd 1989 (non-exec). *Other Activities:* Forex Assoc; Anglo-Indonesian Students' Trust; American Chamber of Commerce (UK); English Speaking Union. *Professional Organisations:* FIB (Scot). *Clubs:* Caledonian, Overseas Bankers', Lombard Assoc. *Recreations:* Curling, Golf.

MATHER, Roderic Cameron; Chairman, Central Division, Allied Provincial Securities plc, since 1989; Chairman, Corporate Finance. *Biog: b.* 10 October 1942. *Educ:* Uppingham School. *Directorships:* Eadie Holdings plc 1983 (exec) Chairman. *Other Activities:* Freeman, Cutlers Company.

MATHER, William G; Joint Managing Director, Imperial Investments Limited, since 1990; General. *Educ:* Cambridge University (MA Cantab). *Professional Organisations:* Fellow, Institute of Actuaries.

MATHEWS, Michael; Partner, Clifford Chance.

MATHEWS, Roger; Managing Director, W C R S Mathews Marcantonio.

MATHEWS, Terence Francis; Commissioner, Building Societies Commission, since 1988; Balance Sheet Risk Management. *Career:* HM Treasury Various 1952-86; RAF (National Service) 1953-55; Building Societies Commission Asst Commissioner 1986-88. *Biog: b.* 1 May 1935. *Nationality:* British. *m.* 1977, Barbara Eleanor (née Scott); 1 s; 1 d. *Educ:* Balham Central School. *Other Activities:* Member, Society for Nautical Research. *Recreations:* Walking, Amateur Theatre.

MATHEWSON, David Carr; Director, Noble Grossart Limited, since 1989; Corporate Finance. *Career:* Deloittes (Edinburgh) 1968-72; Williams Glyn & Co (London), Executive 1972-75; Nedbank Group (South Africa), Assistant General Manager 1976-86; Noble Grossart Limited 1986-87; Assistant Director 1987-89;

Director 1989-. *Biog: b.* 26 July 1947. *Nationality:* British. *m.* 1972, Jan (née McIntyre); 1 s; 1 d. *Educ:* Daniel Stewarts College, Edinburgh; University of St Andrews (BSc). *Directorships:* Noble Grossart Limited 1989 (exec); Poldrait Textiles Limited 1986 (non-exec); Majors Place Industries Limited 1987 (non-exec); Isocom Components Limited 1989 (non-exec); Laidlaw Group plc 1987 (non-exec). *Professional Organisations:* The Institute of Chartered Accountants of Scotland CA. *Clubs:* The Bruntsfield Links Golfing Society, The New Golf Club, St Andrews, Johannesburg Country Club. *Recreations:* Family Interests, Golf, Bridge, Athletics.

MATHEWSON, Dr George Ross; CBE; Deputy Group Chief Executive, The Royal Bank of Scotland Group plc, since 1990; Strategic & Capital Resource Planning, Marketing & Product Development. *Career:* St Andrews University, Asst Lecturer 1964-67; Bell Aerospace, USA, Various-Avionics Engineering 1967-72; 3i, Various-Asst General Manager & Director 1972-81; Scottish Development Agency, Chief Executive 1981-87; The Royal Bank of Scotland Group plc, Director 1987-90; The Royal Bank of Scotland Group plc, Deputy Group Chief Executive 1990-. *Biog: b.* 14 May 1940. *Nationality:* British. *m.* 1966, Sheila Alexandra Graham (née Bennett); 2 s. *Educ:* Perth Academy; St Andrews University (BSc Mathematics & Physics, PhD Electrical Engineering); Canisius College, Buffalo (MBA); Dundee University (LLD Honorary). *Directorships:* The Royal Bank of Scotland Group plc 1987 (exec); The Royal Bank of Scotland plc 1987 (non-exec); Royal Bank Group Services Ltd 1987 (exec); Scottish Investment Trust plc 1981 (non-exec); EftPos UK Ltd 1988 (non-exec); Scottish Financial Enterprise 1988 (non-exec); RBSG (Europe) Ltd 1988 (exec); Citizens Financial Group Inc 1989 (non-exec); Royal Scottish Assurance plc 1989 Chairman; Royal Santander Financial Services SA 1989 President; Direct Line Insurance plc 1990 Chairman; Scottish Development Agency 1981-87 Chief Executive. *Other Activities:* Fellow, Royal Society of Edinburgh (Council Member). *Professional Organisations:* CEng; MIEE; CBIM. *Clubs:* New Club, Edinburgh. *Recreations:* Rugby (Still Active), Tennis, Skiing, Business.

MATHIAS, Dermot Colin Anthony; Partner, Stoy Hayward, since 1980; Corporate Finance. *Biog: b.* 19 October 1949. *Nationality:* British. *m.* 1973, Helen (née Lloyd Davies); 2 d. *Educ:* Ampleforth College; Surrey University (BSc). *Directorships:* Horwath Consulting Ltd 1978 (non-exec). *Professional Organisations:* ICA.

MATHIAS, Julian Robert; Director, Foreign and Colonial Management Ltd, since 1981; Investment Management. *Career:* Hill Samuel & Co Ltd, Mgr 1964-71; Buckmaster & Moore, Ptnr 1971-81. *Biog: b.* 7 September 1943. *Educ:* Downside School; University College, Oxford (MA Hons). *Clubs:* Boodle's, City of London. *Recreations:* Bridge, Shooting, Golf, Wine Tasting.

MATHIESON, Stuart D; Finance Director, Sun Life Trust Management Limited, since 1987; Finance/Administration. *Career:* Baker Sutton & Co, Articled Clerk 1966-70; Ford Motor Company, Financial Analyst 1970-72; Save & Prosper Group Limited, Group Accountant 1972-85; Sun Life Trust Management Limited, Finance Director 1985-. *Biog: b.* 5 February 1945. *Nationality:* English. *m.* 2 s. *Educ:* Brentwood School. *Directorships:* Sun Life Portfolio Counselling Services Limited 1987 (exec). *Other Activities:* Liveryman, Needlemakers Company. *Professional Organisations:* Institute of Chartered Accountants in England & Wales, FCA. *Recreations:* Music, Reading, Swimming, Gardening.

MATHIESON, William (Bill); Director, Land Securities plc, since 1987; Development & Technical Services. *Career:* Cumbernauld Development Corporation, Senior Surveyor 1958-62; Ravenseft Properties Ltd (Part of Land Securities), Manager for Scotland, Director, Managing Director 1962-. *Biog: b.* 31 May 1930. *Nationality:* British. *m.* 1956, Margaret (née Patterson); 1 s; 1 d. *Educ:* Kilsyth Academy; Royal Technical College, Glasgow. *Directorships:* Land Securites plc 1987 (exec); Ravenseft Properties Ltd 1970 (exec); City of London Real Property Co Ltd 1977 (exec); Ravenside Investments Ltd 1986 (exec). *Professional Organisations:* Fellow, Royal Institution of Chartered Surveyors. *Recreations:* Golf, Travel, Gardening.

MATHIEU, Arturo C-F; Executive Director, Crédit Suisse First Boston Limited.

MATHRANI, Ranjit; Managing Director, Chartered WestLB Limited, since 1990; Project Advisory. *Career:* DTI (& other Government Economic Ministries) Dir, Projects/Asst Sec 1967-82; Lazard Brothers Exec Dir 1982-87. *Biog: b.* 11 May 1943. *m.* 1986, Namita (née Pawjabi). *Educ:* Cathedral School, Bombay; Delhi University (BSc Hons); London University (MSc). *Clubs:* RAC. *Recreations:* Opera, Climbing, Travel, Good Food, Theatre.

MATSUDA, Keiji; Chief Representative in Europe, The Bank of Japan, since 1990. *Career:* Chief Manager, Coordination Division, Foreign Dept 1986-88; General Manager, Kumamoto Branch 1988-90. *Biog: b.* 26 April 1943. *Nationality:* Japanese. *m.* 1972, Miryo; 1 s; 1 d. *Educ:* College of Arts and Science, Tokyo University (BA).

MATSUDAIRA, Hirohisa; Managing Director, The Dai-Ichi Kangyo Bank Ltd, since 1989; General Manager, since 1988. *Career:* The Dai-Ichi Kangyo Bank Ltd 1958-; London Branch 1988-; Managing Director 1989. *Biog: b.* 29 April 1934. *Nationality:* Japanese. *m.* 1959,

Sachiko; 1 d. *Educ:* Keio University, Japan (BA Law). *Directorships:* DKB Schweiz 1988 (non-exec); DKB Nederland 1988 (non-exec); DKB Luxembourg 1988 (non-exec); DKBI 1988 (non-exec). *Other Activities:* Ward of Cordwainers. *Recreations:* Golf, Travelling, Driving, Gardening.

MATSUI, Tadashi; Managing Director, Mito Europe Ltd.

MATSUNAGA, Seiji; Deputy Managing Director, LTCB International Ltd, since 1989. *Career:* The Long Term Credit Bank of Japan Ltd 1970-; Seconded DDI Telphon, General Manager 1984-85; LTCB Kyoto Branch, Deputy General Manager 1986-88. *Biog: b.* 18 December 1946. *Nationality:* Japanese. *m.* 1971, Makiko (née Hirota); 1 d. *Educ:* Tokyo University (Bachelor of Economics). *Directorships:* LTCB International Ltd 1989 (exec). *Publications:* Industry of Medical Electronics, 1983. *Recreations:* Gardening, Tennis, Reading.

MATSUOKA, Tempei; Deputy Managing Director, DKB International Ltd, since 1989; Trading, Sales, Syndication. *Career:* DKB HO, Corporate Research Div. *Biog: b.* 23 March 1947. *Nationality:* Japanese. *m.* 1972, Yoshiko; 1 s; 1 d. *Educ:* Tokyo University (Economics). *Directorships:* DKB International Limited 1989. *Recreations:* Classic Music, Golf.

MATTEI, G F O; Director, IMI Capital Markets (UK).

MATTERSON, Miss Jean Grace Kemmis; Director, Stewart Ivory & Co Ltd, since 1988; UK Investment Manager. *Biog: b.* 26 March 1956. *Nationality:* British. *Educ:* Wycombe Abbey School.

MATTHEWS, C; Group Chief Accountant, Lonrho plc.

MATTHEWS, John Waylett; Deputy Chairman, Deputy Chief Executive, Beazer plc, since 1989. *Career:* Dixon Wilson & Co, Articled Clerk 1962-66; Qualified Exec 1966-67; Mgr 1968-69; N M Rothschild & Sons, Exec 1969-71; County NatWest Ltd, Mgr 1971-74; Asst Dir 1974-79; Dir 1979-84; Exec Dir 1984-88. *Biog: b.* 22 September 1944. *Nationality:* British. *m.* 1972, Lesley Marjorie (née Halliday); 2 s; 1 d. *Educ:* Forest School. *Directorships:* Perry Group plc 1980 (non-exec); County NatWest Ltd 1979 (non-exec); Ulster Investment Bank Ltd 1988 (non-exec). *Professional Organisations:* FCA. *Recreations:* Golf, Tennis, Squash, Hockey, Bridge.

MATTHEWS, Philip; Partner, Wedlake Bell, since 1986; Commercial Conveying/Secured Property Lending. *Career:* Penningtons, Articled Clerk 1976-78; Assistant Solicitor 1978-80; Associate 1980-82. *Biog: b.* 26 May 1954. *m.* 2 s. *Educ:* Dulwich College; University of Hull (LLB). *Professional Organisations:* The Law Society. *Recreations:* Music, Golf.

MATTHEWS, Robert Anthony; Partner, Arthur Andersen & Co, since 1989; Retailing & Media. *Career:* Arthur Andersen & Co 1976-. *Biog: b.* 29 December 1954. *Nationality:* British. *Educ:* Shrewsbury School; Southampton University (BSc Joint Hons Law & Accountancy). *Other Activities:* Treasurer of SANE (Schizophrenia Appeal) Charity; External Examiner in Accounting & Finance at Middlesex Polytechnic. *Professional Organisations:* FCA. *Clubs:* RAC. *Recreations:* Football, Golf, Music, Theatre.

MATTHEWS, Robert David; Assistant Director, Sun Alliance Investment Management Ltd, since 1989; Fund Mgmnt, Gilts, UK Fixed Interest, International Bonds. *Biog: b.* 12 December 1953. *Nationality:* British. *m.* 1980, Helen Frances (née Beames); 2 s. *Educ:* Wirral Grammar; University College Cardiff (BSc Econ). *Other Activities:* Council Mem, SIA. *Professional Organisations:* AMSIA. *Recreations:* Swimming, Reading, Theatre, Music.

MATTHEWS, William Brian; Finance Director, Electricity Supply Pension Scheme, since 1980; Financial and Legal Administration. *Career:* CEGB (N W Region), Asst Fin Controller, Mgmnt Accts 1974-78; (Headquarters), Asst Fin Controller, Salaries, Pensions, Creditors, Banking 1978-79; Secondment to set up Mgmnt College 1979-80. *Biog: b.* 1 April 1941. *Nationality:* British. *m.* 1963, Rita (née Kavanagh); 3 s; 1 d. *Educ:* Woolverstone Hall. *Directorships:* Millbank Securities Ltd 1983 (exec); Electricity Supply Nominees Ltd 1985 (exec); ESN Investment Management Ltd 1988 (exec); Fellowship of Independent Evangelical Churches Ltd 1978 (exec); ESN Property Management Company Ltd 1982 (exec). *Professional Organisations:* FCA. *Recreations:* Church.

MATTIN, G M; Director, Providence Capitol Life Assurance Ltd.

MATTINGLEY, C G; CBE; Clerk, Grocers' Company.

MATTISON, John; Chief Executive, Burson-Marsteller Financial Limited.

MAUERSBERG, U; General Manager, Bank für Gemeinwirtschaft.

MAUGHAN, M B H; Director, Sturge Holdings plc.

MAULE, T; Deputy General Manager - Forex, Nomura Bank International plc.

MAUNDER, David; Partner, Clifford Chance.

MAUNES, G; Chairman, Metallgesellschaft Ltd.

MAUNSELL, Michael Brooke; Partner, Lovell White Durrant, since 1971; Corporate & Commercial Law. *Nationality:* British. *Educ:* Monkton Combe School; Gonville & Caius College, Cambridge (MA, LLB). *Other Activities:* Liveryman, City of London Solicitors' Company; Trustee, Highgate Cemetery Charity. *Professional Organisations:* The Law Society; IBA; City of London Law Society. *Recreations:* Bird Watching, Opera, Theatre, Swimming.

MAUNSELL-THOMAS, John Richard; Director, Brewin Dolphin & Co Ltd, since 1987. *Biog:* b. 11 August 1937. *Nationality:* British. *Professional Organisations:* Society of Investment Analysts.

MAURICE, Mrs Clare Mary (née Rankin); Partner, Allen & Overy, since 1985; Private Client. *Career:* Allen & Overy, Articled Clerk 1976-78; Assistant Solicitor 1978-85. *Biog:* b. 25 February 1954. *Nationality:* British. *m.* 1980, Ian Maurice; 2 d. *Educ:* Sherborne School for Girls; University of Birmingham (LLB). *Professional Organisations:* Law Society. *Clubs:* Reform. *Recreations:* Theatre, Travel.

MAVROLEON, I G; Director, Charlton Seal Schaverien Limited.

MAW, N N Graham; Senior Partner, Rowe & Maw.

MAX, Michael; Partner, Titmuss Sainer & Webb.

MAXWELL, Barry Owen Somerset; The Rt Hon Lord Farnham; Chairman, Brown Shipley & Co Limited.

MAXWELL, (Ian) Robert; MC; Chairman and Publisher, Pergamon Holdings Ltd.

MAXWELL, J A W; Director, International Commodities Clearing House.

MAXWELL, K F H; Joint Managing Director, Maxwell Communication Corporation plc, since 1988. *Biog:* b. 20 February 1959. *Nationality:* British. *m.* 1984, Pandora Deborah Karen (née Warnford-Davis); 1 s; 3 d. *Educ:* Marlborough College; Balliol College, Oxford (BA Hons). *Directorships:* Maxwell Communication Corporation plc 1986 (exec); Central & Sheerwood plc 1987 (exec); Guinness Mahon plc (non-exec); Mirror Group plc 1987 (exec); Oxford United Football Club plc 1985 (exec); Pergamon AGB plc 1985 (exec); Scitex Corporation Limited 1989 (non-exec); GPG plc 1990 (non-exec). *Recreations:* Water Colour Painting, Football.

MAXWELL, T J W; Director, S G Warburg Akroyd Rowe & Pitman Mullens Securities Ltd.

MAXWELL-ARNOT, Miss Patricia Jeanne; Director, Lazard Investors, since 1987; Management of European Equities. *Career:* ASG Holdings 1969-70; Barclays Trust Co, Investment Research 1970-72; NM Rothschild & Sons 1972-84. *Biog:* b. 21 September 1947. *Nationality:* British. *Educ:* Moore House School; Bristol University (BA Hons). *Recreations:* Riding, Music, Travel.

MAXWELL SCOTT, Ian; Managing Director, Sheppards, since 1988; All Aspects of an Integrated Agency Stockbroker. *Career:* Scrimgeour Vickers (Kemp-Gee & Co), Ptnr 1976-80; Scrimgeour Kemp-Gee, Ptnr 1980-85; Dir 1985-87. *Biog:* b. 13 December 1945. *Nationality:* British. *m.* 1987, Caroline Jane Fiona (née Collins); 3 s; 1 d. *Educ:* Bexley Grammar, Kent. *Clubs:* Caledonian. *Recreations:* Tennis, Squash, Horology.

MAY, David Oliver; Chairman, Berthon Boat Co Ltd, since 1960. *Biog:* b. 1 March 1935. *Nationality:* British. *m.* 1960, Catherine (née Baroness Van Den Branden de Reeth) (div); 2 s; 1 d. *Educ:* Wellington College; Southampton University (Degree in Naval Architecture). *Directorships:* Lymington Marina Ltd 1968 (exec) Chairman; Lymington Marine Garage Ltd 1966 (exec); Imatronic Ltd 1987 (non-exec); Vit-Tal Hospital Products Ltd 1988 (non-exec); Transatlantic Capital General Partner A & B Ltd 1989 (non-exec); Marina Mutual Insurance Association Ltd 1990 (non-exec); Dartington & Co Group plc 1990 (non-exec); National Boat Shows Ltd 1986-88 (non-exec) Chairman; Lucas Marine Ltd (non-exec); Antigua Slipway Ltd. *Other Activities:* Liveryman, Worshipful Company of Shipwrights; Rear Commodore, Royal Thames Yacht Club; Previous Chairman of Committees, RTYC. *Professional Organisations:* Fellow, Royal Institute of Naval Architects; CEng. *Clubs:* Royal Thames Yacht Club, Royal Ocean Racing Club, Royal London YC, Royal Lymington. *Recreations:* Yacht Racing, Sailing, Shooting.

MAY, J M; Director, Hambros Bank Limited.

MAY, John Nicholas; Partner, Ashurst Morris Crisp, since 1974; Corporate Finance/Banking. *Biog:* b. 11 January 1947.

MAY, Mark Douglas; Partner, R Watson & Sons Consulting Actuaries, since 1985; Pensions Advice. *Career:* Government Actuary's Department 1970-84; R Watson & Sons 1984-. *Biog:* b. 19 July 1948. *Nationality:* British. *m.* 1971, Janet; 1 s; 1 d. *Educ:* St Dunstan's College; Downing College, Cambridge (MA). *Professional Organisations:* Fellow, Institute of Actuaries. *Publications:* Papers for International Congress of Actuaries, 1980, and International Association of Consulting Actuaries, 1990.

MAY, Peter Norman James; Director, Charterhouse Bank Ltd, since 1988; Corporate Finance. *Career:* Binder Hamlyn Audit Snr 1976-80; Britoil plc Finance Exec 1980-82. *Biog: b.* 19 November 1954. *Nationality:* British. *m.* 1981, Penny (née Clay); 1 d. *Educ:* Glasgow Academy; Glasgow University (MA). *Professional Organisations:* ACA. *Recreations:* Walking, Gardening, Bridge.

MAY, Peter Richard; Branch Manager, Swiss American Securities Inc, since 1986. *Biog: b.* 12 August 1955. *Nationality:* British. *m.* 1981, Nina (née Makhijaney); 2 s. *Educ:* Queen Elizabeth Grammar School, Darlington; Middlesex Polytechnic (BA Hons); Centre D'Etudes Supérieures Européennes de Management, Reims, France.

MAY, Dr T; Executive Director, Sheppards.

MAY, William Herbert Stuart; Senior Partner, Theodore Goddard, since 1989. *Career:* Theodore Goddard, Articled Clerk/Solicitor 1961-68; Partner (Corporate Finance, Mergers & Acquisitions) 1968-. *Biog: b.* 5 April 1937. *Nationality:* British. *m.* 1966, Sarah (née Maples); 4 s. *Educ:* Taunton School; Wadham College, Oxford (MA). *Other Activities:* City of London Solicitors' Company. *Professional Organisations:* The Law Society. *Recreations:* Gardening, Walking, Sport.

MAYDON, Gary; Company Secretary, Town & Country Building Society, since 1988; Secretary/Compliance Officer. *Career:* Town & Country Building Society, Admin Accounts 1976-78; Halifax Building Society, Asst Mgr 1978-88; Norwich & Peterborough Building Society, Manager 1988. *Biog: b.* 15 February 1957. *Nationality:* British. *m.* 1979, Gillian Katrina (née Pengelly); 2 d. *Educ:* Colbayns High School, Clacton; Colchester Institute (HNC Bus Studies). *Professional Organisations:* FCIS; FCBSI; FFA. *Recreations:* Canoeing, Swimming, Playing Guitar, Chess.

MAYES, Raymond; Partner, Shipping, Cameron Markby Hewitt.

MAYHEW, David Lionel; Partner, Cazenove & Co.

MAYLAM, R J; Chairman, A J Archer Holdings plc.

MAYNARD, Henry Charles Edward; Partner, Moores & Rowland, since 1967; Specialising in Auditing, General Financial Advice and Dealing with Overseas Companies Investing in the UK; Vice-Chairman, Moores Rowland International. *Career:* Moores Rowland, Ptnr in charge of London Office 1981-87. *Biog: b.* 10 February 1941. *m.* 1984, Susan (née Barford); 1 d. *Educ:* Bryanston School; Imperial College, London (BSc Eng). *Other Activities:* Member of the Worshipful Company of Chartered Accountants in England & Wales. *Professional Organisations:* FCA. *Clubs:* Hurlingham, Royal West Norfolk, Golf Club,

Annabels. *Recreations:* Tennis, Golf, Sailing, Skiing, Collecting Watercolours.

MAYNARD, Julia; Partner, Linklaters & Paines.

MAYNARD, P M; Director, Gibbs Hartley Cooper Ltd.

MAYO, J C; Director, S G Warburg & Co Ltd, since 1990; Corporate Finance. *Career:* Arthur Andersen & Co, Audit and Tax Manager 1978-84. *Biog: b.* 2 April 1956. *Nationality:* British. *m.* 1979, Julia (née Lumley); 2 s. *Educ:* Farnborough Grammar School; Loughborough University (BSc Hons Economics and Economic Policy). *Directorships:* S G Warburg & Co Ltd 1990 (exec). *Professional Organisations:* Institute of Chartered Accountants in England and Wales.

MAYO, John William; Director, S G Warburg Group plc, since 1985; Compliance. *Career:* Mayo & Perkins Articled Clerk 1937-39; HM Forces to Capt RA 1939-46; Seaton Taylor & Co Articled Clerk 1946-47; Linklaters & Paines Solicitor 1947-52; Ptnr 1952-85. *Biog: b.* 8 October 1920. *Nationality:* British. *m.* 1959, Susan Margaret (née Singer); 3 s; 1 d. *Educ:* St Paul's School. *Directorships:* Rothmans International plc 1960 (non-exec); St Aubyns School Trust Ltd 1972 (non-exec); S G Warburg & Co Ltd 1985 (exec); S G Warburg Group plc 1985 (non-exec); Wellington Underwriting Holdings Ltd 1986 (non-exec); Wellington Underwriting Agencies Ltd 1986 (non-exec). *Other Activities:* Mem, Regulation & Compliance Exam Panel (Securities Industry); Mem, Consumer Arbitration Panel (The Securities Assoc); Mem, Compliance Committee (BMBA). *Professional Organisations:* Mem, The Law Society. *Publications:* Companies Limited by Guarantee, 1960; Stock Exchange Chapter of Halsbury's Laws of England, 1965. *Clubs:* Royal Wimbledon Golf Club. *Recreations:* Bridge, Genealogy.

MAZZOLA, Bruno; Deputy Chief Manager, Istituto Bancario San Paolo di Torino, since 1988; London Branch. *Career:* Istituto Bancario San Paolo di Torino (Turin), Branch Employee 1973; Economic & Financial Research Dept 1973-86; (London) Capital Mkts, Gp Mgr 1986-88. *Biog: b.* 9 July 1947. *Nationality:* Italian. *m.* 1972, Ornella (née Bertero); 1 d. *Educ:* Turin University (BEcon). *Directorships:* Options & Financiere Matif 1988 (non-exec).

MEAD, A F J; Group Audit Partner, Pannell Kerr Forster, since 1986; Insurance Industry Audits and Investigations. *Career:* Lewis Bloom & Co, Articled Clerk 1963-67; Coopers & Lybrand Deloitte, Senior & Manager 1967-78; AFIA, Audit Manager 1978-79; Pannell Kerr Forster, Manager & Partner 1979-. *Biog: b.* 4 May 1941. *Nationality:* British. *m.* 1972, Alison (née Ward); 2 s; 1 d. *Educ:* Trinity School, Croydon; Hull University (BSc Econ). *Professional Organisations:* Fellow,

Institute of Chartered Accountants in England & Wales. *Recreations:* School Governor.

MEAD, P; Chairman, Abbott Mead Vickers.

MEAD, Richard Barwick; Partner/National Director of Corporate Finance, Ernst & Young Corporate Finance, since 1985; Corporate Finance. *Career:* Arthur Young, Audit Supervisor 1969-73; Wm Brandts Sons & Co Ltd, Exec 1973-75; Antony Gibbs & Sons Ltd, Dir 1975-83; Credit Suisse First Boston Ltd, Dir 1983-85. *Biog: b.* 18 August 1947. *Nationality:* British. *m.* 1971, Sheelagh (née Thom); 2 s. *Educ:* Marlborough College; Pembroke College, Cambridge (MA). *Professional Organisations:* FCA.

MEADE, Daniel J; Executive Director, Credit Suisse First Boston Ltd, since 1989; Director, Global Research. *Career:* First Boston, Associate Director of Equity Research Managing Director 1980-89. *Biog: b.* 8 November 1942. *Nationality:* American. *m.* 1969, Karen; 1 s; 1 d. *Educ:* Purdue (MBA); Youngstown University (BE). *Professional Organisations:* Chartered Financial Analysis; NYSSA. *Clubs:* Mantaloking Yacht Club. *Recreations:* Hunting, Fishing.

MEADOWS, D H; Director, Sampo Insurance Company (UK) Limited.

MEADOWS, Tony; Partner, Clark Whitehall.

MEAKIN, John; Director, Panmure Gordon Bankers Limited.

MEANEY, Sir Patrick; Chairman, The Rank Organisation plc, since 1983. *Career:* Thomas Tilling Ltd 1951-83; Chief Executive 1973-83. *Biog: b.* 6 May 1925. *Nationality:* British. *m.* Mary June (née Kearney); 1 s. *Educ:* Wimbledon College; Northern Polytechnic. *Directorships:* The Rank Organisation plc 1983 Chm; Midland Bank plc 1984 Dep Chm; ICI plc 1981 (non-exec); MEPC plc 1986 (non-exec); Horserace Betting Levy Board 1985 Dep Chm; Tarmac plc 1990 (non-exec); Thomas Tilling Ltd 1973-83 Chief Exec; Cable & Wireless plc 1974-84 (non-exec). *Other Activities:* British-North American Committee; Stock Exchange Listed Companies Advisory Committee; Advertising Association (President's Committee). *Professional Organisations:* Chartered Institute of Marketing (President & Fellow); CBI (Council); Royal Society of Arts (Council); World Economic Forum (Council); British Executive Service Overseas (Council); British Institute of Management (Companion). *Clubs:* Harlequins, British Sportsman's. *Recreations:* Sport, Music, Education.

MEARS, P M; Partner, Allen & Overy, since 1988; Corporate Tax. *Career:* Allen & Overy 1980-; Qualified as Solicitor 1982; Specialist in Corporate Tax Field 1982-. *Biog: b.* 19 January 1958. *Nationality:* British. *m.*

1983, Carol Lucia (née Anders) (decd); 1 d. *Educ:* Henley Grammar School; London School of Economics (LLB). *Other Activities:* Worshipful Company of Solicitors. *Clubs:* Dulwich Sports Club. *Recreations:* Theatre, Squash, Tennis.

MECZ, Ms Jane; Vice President, Chemical Bank.

MEDDINGS, Richard Henry; Director, Hill Samuel Bank Limited, since 1990; Corporate Finance. *Career:* Price Waterhouse 1980-84; Hill Samuel 1984-. *Biog: b.* 12 March 1958. *Nationality:* British. *Educ:* Wolverhampton Grammar School; Exeter College, Oxford (BA Hons History). *Professional Organisations:* Associate, Institute of Chartered Accountants in England & Wales.

MEDHURST, Brian; Managing Director, Prudential Corporation plc, since 1982; International Division & Prudential Property Services (from 1990). *Career:* Prudential Assurance Co, Actuarial 1958-66; Prudential Assurance Co (Investment Dept), Various Managerial 1966-80; Joint Chief Investment Mgr 1980-82. *Biog: b.* 18 March 1935. *Nationality:* British. *m.* 1960, Patricia Anne (née Beer); 2 s; 1 d. *Educ:* Godalming Grammar School; Trinity College, Cambridge (MA). *Directorships:* Subsidiaries & Prudential Corp plc. *Professional Organisations:* FIA. *Clubs:* Royal Aldershot Officers' Club, North Hants Golf Club. *Recreations:* Squash, Golf, Piano Duets, Tree Felling.

MEDLAND, David Arthur; Partner, Robson Rhodes, since 1979; Client Service/Corporate Finance. *Career:* Robson Rhodes 1965-; Assistant Manager 1973; Manager 1974; Senior Manager 1976; Partner 1979. *Biog: b.* 23 September 1946. *Nationality:* British. *m.* 1973, Patricia Ann (née Wood) (div 1979); 1 s. *Educ:* St Paul's School, Darjeeling, India. *Professional Organisations:* FCA. *Publications:* The Unlisted Securities Market - A Review, 1984. *Recreations:* Pianist, Theatre, Sport.

MEEK, Edwin Graham; Director, County NatWest Wood Mackenzie & Co Ltd.

MEHROTRA, P S; Chief Manager (Branches), State Bank of India.

MEHTA, Nikhil Vasant; Partner, Linklaters & Paines, since 1989; Corporate Taxation. *Career:* London Bar, Pupil 1976-77; Bombay Bar, Tax Advocate 1977-80; Butterworths, Tax Publishing 1980; Inland Revenue, (Solicitor's Office) 1981-83; Linklaters & Paines, Legal Assistant/Assistant Solicitor 1983-89. *Biog: b.* 12 October 1953. *Nationality:* British. *m.* 1978, Snehal; 2 s. *Educ:* Rugby School; Bristol University (LLB Hons). *Other Activities:* Member, MENSA; City of London Solicitors' Company; Friend, Royal Academy. *Professional Organisations:* The Law Society; Institute for Fiscal Studies. *Clubs:* RAC, Cricket Club of India. *Recreations:* Squash, Windsurfing, Music, Art.

MEHTA, P C S; Director, GNI Limited.

MEIER, Ian; Director, Tyndall Holdings plc.

MEIKLEJOHN, Iain Maury Campbell; Partner, Shepherd & Wedderburn WS, since 1982; Company and Commercial Law. *Career:* Allan, Dawson, Simpson and Hampton WS Law Apprentice 1976-78; Shepherd & Wedderburn WS Legal Asst 1978-82. *Biog: b.* 3 November 1954. *Nationality:* British. *m.* 1990, Margaret Jane (née MacKenzie). *Educ:* The Edinburgh Academy; University of Edinburgh (LLB Hons). *Directorships:* Scottish Trust for Underwriter Archaeology 1988 (non-exec). *Professional Organisations:* Law Society of Scotland; Society of Writers to Her Majesty's Signet; Scottish Law Agents' Society. *Clubs:* The New Club, Edinburgh.

MEINE, T; Director, IMI Securities Ltd.

MEINERTZHAGAN, Peter Richard; Chairman, Hoare Govett Corporate Finance.

MEISENKOTHEN, Walter A; Partner, Arthur Andersen & Co, since 1982; Director-International Executive Tax Services. *Career:* Arthur Andersen & Co, Partner 1982-; (London), Manager 1978-82; IMS International Inc (London), Tax Director 1975-78; Arthur Andersen & Co (Miami, Florida), Senior 1968-71; (New York City), Manager 1971-75. *Biog: b.* 20 September 1946. *Nationality:* American. *m.* 1976, Judith (née Hopkins). *Educ:* Farleigh Dickinson University, New Jersey, USA (Bachelor of Science). *Directorships:* American Chamber of Commerce (UK) 1989 (non-exec). *Other Activities:* Chairman, Tax Committee, American Chamber of Commerce (UK). *Professional Organisations:* American Institute of Certified Public Accountants; Florida Institute of Certified Public Accountants. *Clubs:* Burford Golf Club. *Recreations:* Golf.

MEISTER Jr, Gilbert Charles; Managing Director, Merrill Lynch International Limited, since 1990; Senior Investment Banker (Corporate Finance). *Career:* Harris Trust & Saving Bank (Chicago), Corporate Finance Consultant 1977-78; Merrill Lynch Capital Markets, Associate 1978-83; Merrill Lynch, Pierce, Fenner & Smith, Vice President 1983-86; Managing Director 1986-90. *Biog: b.* 30 January 1952. *Nationality:* American. *m.* 1980, Doris (née Powers). *Educ:* Kenyon College, Ohio (AB Highest Honors Economics); The University of Chicago (MBA Finance, International Economics). *Directorships:* Merrill Lynch International Limited 1990 (exec); Grace Sierra Horticultural Products Company (California) 1989 (non-exec). *Recreations:* Tennis, Golf.

MEKIE, Duncan John Cameron; Director, Leslie & Godwin Limited.

MELCHER, A Stephen; Finance Director, Eagle Star Insurance Co.

MELCHER, Richard; Bureau Chief, Business Week, since 1985; Financial, Political, Corporate Coverage of the UK. *Career:* Akron (Ohio) Beacon Journal Labour Writer 1976-78; Business Week Correspondent (Chicago) 1978-83; Correspondent (London) 1983-85. *Biog: b.* 1 August 1952. *Nationality:* American. *m.* 1980, Barbara (née Bookey); 1 s; 2 d. *Educ:* Pembroke Country Day School; Duke University (BA History). *Clubs:* Queen's, RAC. *Recreations:* Tennis, Reading, Family.

MELLEN, William Henry; Director, Kleinwort GrievesonSecurities Ltd.

MELLER, Andrew Temple; Partner, Ernst & Young, since 1971; Audit & Accountancy, Pension Schemes. *Career:* Whinney Smith & Whinney, Accountant 1958-65; Whinney Murray & Co, Snr Accountant 1965-67; Mgr, Partner 1967-71; Ernst & Whinney, Partner. *Biog: b.* 2 April 1939. *Nationality:* British. *m.* 1963, Katharine (née Barry); 1 s; 2 d. *Educ:* Lancing College. *Directorships:* E & Y Trustees Ltd 1975 (exec). *Other Activities:* Member, Worshipful Company of Chartered Accountants in England & Wales. *Professional Organisations:* FCA; Member, Pensions Research Accountants Group. *Clubs:* City of London.

MELLON, James; Co-Chief Executive, Roxy Holdings, since 1990; Fund Management in Specialist Vehicles. *Career:* GT Management (San Francisco), US Fund Manager 1978-84; Thornton Management (Hong Kong), Managing Director 1984-87; Tyndall Holdings (London), Marketing Director 1988-90; Roxy Holdings (Bahamas), Chief Executive 1990-. *Directorships:* Tyndall Holdings plc 1988; Venturi Investment Trust plc 1990; Korea Liberalisation Trust plc 1990; First Philippine Investment Trust plc 1990; CST Emerging Asia Trust plc 1989; Pacific Horizon Trust plc 1989; European Project Investment Trust plc 1989; Pacific Property Investment Trust plc 1989.

MELLOR, Christopher David; Company Secretary, Northern Venture Managers Limited, since 1988. *Career:* Spicer & Pegler, Trainee Accountant to Senior Manager 1979-86; Northern Investors Company Limited, Corporate Finance Executive 1987-88. *Educ:* (BSc). *Professional Organisations:* ACA (1982).

MELLOR, H S; Non-Executive Director, The Burmah Oil plc.

MELLOR, Simon; Director, Saatchi & Saatchi Company plc, since 1985; Management of UK Affiliate Group. *Career:* Saatchi & Saatchi Company 1976-; Corporate Development Manager, Acquisitons; Corporate Development Director, Investors Relations; Associate Director, Press Relations 1984-85; Main Board

Director 1985-86; General Management of Communications Businesses 1986-88; Management of UK Affiliate Group 1988-. *Biog: b.* 10 September 1954. *Nationality:* British. *m.* 1990, Mary (née Langford). 2 steps. *Educ:* Haberdashers' Aske's School, Elstree, Herts; Bristol University (BSc Social Sciences - Economics & Economic History). *Other Activities:* Freeman, City of London; Member, Clockmakers Company. *Clubs:* RAC. *Recreations:* Cricket, Soccer, Theatre, Cinema.

MELLORS, Keith Michael; Finance Director, York Trust Group plc.

MELLOWS, John Stanley; Partner, Neville Russell, since 1979; Member, London & National Executive, National Personnel and Training Partner, Partner in Charge of Corporate Services Department. *Career:* Griffin Stone Moscrop, Articled Clerk/CA 1965-71; Price Waterhouse (Holland & Canada), Snr Mgr 1972-76. *Biog: b.* 2 December 1947. *Nationality:* British. *m.* 1972, Gillian Margaret (née Park); 2 s; 1 d. *Educ:* Wallington Independent Grammar School. *Professional Organisations:* FCA. *Recreations:* Skiing, Tennis, Cycling.

MELLUISH, Christopher Brunton; Director, Lazard Brothers & Co Ltd; Investment Management for Private Clients. *Biog: b.* 2 June 1936. *Nationality:* British. *m.* 1973, Susan Elizabeth (née Bickerton); 1 s; 2 d. *Educ:* Rossall School; Caius College, Cambridge (MA Hons). *Directorships:* Lazard Investors Ltd 1973 (exec); MGM Assurance 1980 (non-exec). *Clubs:* Naval & Military. *Recreations:* Gardening, Singing.

MELLUISH, Michael Edward Lovelace; Director, Singer & Friedlander Holdings Ltd, since 1974; Deputy Chairman, Singer & Friedlander Investment Management Ltd. *Career:* ABCO Petroleum Co Ltd Dir. *Biog: b.* 13 June 1932. *Nationality:* British. *m.* 1957, Anna Romaine Gervis (née Green); 1 s; 2 d. *Educ:* Rossall School; Gonville & Caius College, Cambridge (MA Hons). *Directorships:* Friends Provident Life Office 1980 (non-exec); Singer & Friedlander Smaller Companies Trust Ltd Chm; Singer & Friedlander Investment Advisers Ltd. *Other Activities:* Member, Various MCC Sub-Ctees; Vice-Chm, Radley College Council; Vice-Chm, Rossall School Council; Pres, Quidnuncs CC. *Clubs:* MCC, Royal Ashdown Forest Golf Club, Trevose Golf Club, CURUFC. *Recreations:* Golf, Walking, Gardening, Listening to Music.

MELLY, Charles William; Managing Director, Smith Keen Cutler, since 1987; Institutional Sales of Smaller Companies. *Biog: b.* 19 February 1947. *Nationality:* British. *m.* 1980, Gail Elizabeth (née Watkins); 3 s. *Educ:* Warwick School. *Clubs:* RAC. *Recreations:* Motor Racing, Snooker, Horse Racing.

MELMOTH, Graham John; Secretary, Co-operative Bank plc & Co-operative Wholesale Society Ltd, since 1976; Legal, Pensions, Administration, Secretariat, Insurance Membership Services and Security. *Career:* Cryoplants Ltd, Sec 1966-69; Fisons plc, Dep Sec 1969-72; Letraset plc, Sec 1972-75. *Biog: b.* 18 March 1938. *Nationality:* British. *m.* 1967, Jenny (née Banning); 2 s. *Educ:* City of London School. *Directorships:* Subsidiaries and Associates of the CWS Group; Ringway Developments plc; New Lanark Trading Ltd 1990 (non-exec); New Lanark Enterprise Training Ltd 1990 (non-exec). *Other Activities:* Trustee, New Lanark Conservation Trust. *Professional Organisations:* FCIS. *Recreations:* Opera, Theatre.

MELSOM, Andrew John; Executive Creative Director, BMPB, since 1985. *Career:* Tractor Driver 1970; Foote Cone & Belding, Trainee 1971; J Walter Thompson, Junior Account Executive 1972; Mirror Group Newspapers, Space Salesman 1974; J Walter Thompson, Account Director then Copywriter 1976; J Walter Thompson, Director 1980; BMPB Advertising, Founding Partner 1985. *Biog: b.* 1 February 1953. *Nationality:* British. *m.* 1980, Melanie Clare; 1 s; 1 d. *Educ:* Uppingham. *Other Activities:* Fund Raiser, Foundation for the Study of Infant Deaths. *Professional Organisations:* Institute of Marketing - Certificate. *Publications:* Are You There Moriarty 1984; Play It Again Moriarty 1985. *Recreations:* Tennis, Shooting, Cricket.

MELSOM, Stuart Campbell; Director, Panmure Gordon & Co Ltd, since 1987; Financial Controller. *Career:* Pawley & Malyon, Articled Clerk 1958-63; Touche Ross & Co, Audit Snr 1964-67; Guinness Mahon, Accounts Dept 1967-69; Locana Corporation (London) Ltd, Director 1969-71; Roger Mortimer & Co, Financial Controller 1971-73; Phillips & Drew, Financial Controller 1973-82; Farrer & Co, Partnership Secretary 1982-85. *Biog: b.* 4 September 1939. *Nationality:* British. *m.* 1963, Brenda (née Gillatt); 1 s; 1 d. *Educ:* Kilburn Grammar. *Professional Organisations:* Member, The International Stock Exchange; FCA. *Clubs:* MCC. *Recreations:* Cricket, Hockey, Horse Racing, Reading.

MELTON, B; Director, County NatWest Investment Management Ltd.

MELVILL, Neil Douglas; Director, Chartered WestLB Limited, since 1987; Corporate Finance. *Career:* Standard Chartered Bank, Various 1974-78; Standard Chartered Merchant Bank, Various 1978-87. *Biog: b.* 21 April 1952. *m.* 1980, Gillian (née Lindsay); 2 s. *Educ:* Aldenham School; Middlesex Polytechnic (BA Hons). *Professional Organisations:* AIB. *Recreations:* Golf, Squash.

MELVILL, T V; Director, Knight & Day Ltd.

MELVILLE, Nigel Edward; Director & Member of Management Committee, Baring Brothers & Co Ltd, since 1983; International Corporate Finance. *Career:*

Fuller Jenks Beecroft & Co, Articled Clerk 1967-70; Samuel Montagu & Co Ltd, Corporate Fin Exec 1972-74; Baring Brothers & Co, Corporate Fin Exec 1974; Seconded to Icon Ltd (Nigeria) 1975-77; Seconded to Baring Brothers Asia Ltd (Singapore), Gen Mgr 1977-82; Baring Brothers & Co Ltd, Asst Dir, Corp Fin 1982-83; Dir 1983-; Seconded to Baring Brothers Asia Ltd (Hong Kong), MD 1983-87; Member, Mgmnt Ctee 1987-. *Biog: b.* 5 June 1945. *Nationality:* British. *m.* 1970, Maria (née Van Oosten); 1 s; 1 d. *Educ:* Sedbergh School; Trinity College, Oxford (MA); London Business School (MSc). *Directorships:* Baring Brothers (France) SA 1988; Baring Brothers (Italia) Srl 1990; Baring Brothers (Deutschland) GmbH 1990; Baring Brothers (Espana) SA 1988; Commerce International Merchant Bankers, Berhad (Malaysia) 1988. *Professional Organisations:* FCA. *Clubs:* Hurlingham, Vanderbilt. *Recreations:* Tennis, Golf.

MELVILLE-ROSS, Timothy David; Chief Executive, Nationwide Anglia Building Society, since 1985. *Career:* British Petroleum, Various 1963-73; Rowe, Swann & Co Stockbrokers 1973-74; Nationwide Building Society, Various 1974-. *Biog: b.* 3 October 1944. *Nationality:* British. *m.* 1967, Camilla (née Probert); 2 s; 1 d. *Educ:* Uppingham School; Portsmouth College of Technology (Diploma). *Directorships:* Industrial Society 1986 (non-exec) Council Mem; Policy Studies Institute 1986 (non-exec) Council Mem; Phoenix Initiative 1986 (non-exec) Chm; INSEAD (UK Advisory Board) 1985 (non-exec). *Other Activities:* Liveryman of Ironmongers' Company. *Professional Organisations:* FCIS, CBIM, FCBSI, FRSA. *Recreations:* Music, Bridge, Sport, The Countryside.

MEMERY, W V John; Consultant Partner, Memery Crystal.

MENAGE, Ian R; Assistant General Manager, Credit Lyonnais UK; Head of Corporate Banking Syndications & Structured Finance.

MÉNARD, C P M J; Managing Director, Crédit Lyonnais Capital Markets plc, since 1989. *Career:* Crédit Lyonnais Paris 1967-68; Crédit Franco-Portugais, Vice-President, Director of North Portugal Agencies 1968-73; Banco Frances & Brasileiro 1973-86; San Paulo City, Director 1973-75; San Paulo State, Director 1975-86; Commercial Managing Director 1976-78; General Manager 1978-81; Crédit Lyonnais Paris, Director of International Affairs - Regional Director of Western Europe 1981-84; Crédit Lyonnais UK, General Manager 1984-87; Director, Head Office; International Division - Risk Assessment, Computer Systems, Management Information, General Secretariat 1987-1989; Alexanders Laing & Cruickshank (now Crédit Lyonnais Capital Markets), General Manager 1989. *Biog: b.* 20 August 1941. *Nationality:* French. *m.* 1966, Anne-Marie (née Du Pré); 2 s; 1 d. *Educ:* Ecole Ste Geneviève, Versailles (HEC).

Directorships: Credit Lyonnais Property (Broadwalk) Ltd 1989; Laing & Cruickshank 1989; CL Alexanders Laing & Cruickshank (Overseas) Ltd 1989; Crédit Lyonnais Information Services Ltd 1989; AL&C Nominees Ltd 1989; Cloak Lane Securities Ltd 1989; Heritage Personal Finance Ltd 1989; Alexanders Discount plc 1989; Crédit Lyonnais Securities Ltd 1989; Crédit Lyonnais Gilts Ltd 1989; Crédit Lyonnais Euro-Securities plc 1989; Crédit Lyonnais Rouse Ltd 1989; Crédit Lyonnais (Investments) Ltd 1987; CLAH Ltd 1987; Crédit Lyonnais Canada 1987; Crédit Lyonnais Hong Kong (Finance) Ltd 1988; Crédit Lyonnais Capital Markets plc 1989; Crédit Lyonnais Properties Ltd 1989; Waiting Nominees Ltd 1989; Core Nominees Ltd 1989; Crédit Lyonnais Construction Company Ltd 1989; Rouse Woodstock Metals Ltd 1989; CL Property Services Company Ltd 1989; Marshall Rouse Woodstock Ltd 1989; Martenborow Private Ltd; Cloak Lane Commodities BV; Rouse Woodstock (Hong Kong) Ltd. *Clubs:* RAC Club. *Recreations:* Golf, Swimming, Skiing, Tennis.

MENDELBLAT, Michael; Partner, Nabarro Nathanson, since 1990; Construction Law. *Career:* GLC Legal Dept, Assistant Solicitor 1979-85; British Telecommunications plc, Legal Dept, Assistant Solicitor 1985-86; Nabarro Nathanson, Assistant Solicitor 1986-90. *Biog: b.* 13 April 1954. *Nationality:* British. *m.* 1985, Thamar Edith (née MacIver); 1 s. *Educ:* Harrow County Grammar School; Magdalen College, Oxford (BA Law); Wolfson College, Cambridge (LLB). *Professional Organisations:* Law Society; Society of Construction Law. *Recreations:* Travel, Cinema, Reading.

MENDELSSOHN, Martin Charles; Partner, McKenna & Co, since 1990; Mergers & Acquisitions, Joint Ventures, Corporate Law. *Career:* McKenna & Co, Articled Clerk 1980-82; Asst Solicitor 1982-90. *Biog: b.* 23 June 1958. *Nationality:* British. *m.* 1987, Emma; 1 s. *Educ:* Bristol University (LLB Hons). *Professional Organisations:* Law Society; City of London Solicitors Society. *Recreations:* Cricket, Golf.

MENDELSSOHN, R G; Partner, Pannell Kerr Forster.

MENENDEZ, Jose Manuel Antonio; Director, Baring Brothers & Co Ltd, since 1988. *Career:* Baring Brothers & Co Ltd, Spanish Correspondent 1969-73; Export Finance Executive 1973-79; Deputy Mgr, Export Finance & Desk Officer Mexico and Spain 1979-83; Mgr, Export Finance & Desk Officer Mexico and Spain 1983-84; Ass Dir, Project Finance and Advisory Services 1984-88. *Biog: b.* 30 May 1943. *Nationality:* Spanish. *m.* 1968, Jennifer (née Butler); 1 s; 1 d. *Educ:* Escuela de Comercio de Oviedo. *Directorships:* Baring Brothers (Espana) SA 1988 MD; BBVG Inversiones Bancobao (Spain) 1987 (non-exec); BBG Mediterraneo (Spain) 1988 (non-exec); Cie Management Limited (Guernsey)

1989 (non-exec); CIE II Management Limited (Guernsey) 1989 (non-exec). *Professional Organisations:* ACIB. *Clubs:* Canning Club. *Recreations:* Tennis, Swimming, Windsurfing.

MENHENNET, David William Mark; Partner, Wilde Sapte, since 1988; Property Department. *Biog: b.* 8 February 1956. *Nationality:* British. *Educ:* Dulwich College; Wadham College, Oxford (BA). *Professional Organisations:* Member, Law Society.

MENZIES, D M; Director, Manning Beard Ltd.

MENZIES, George M; WS; Partner, W & J Burness WS.

MENZIES, Iain Alasdair Graham; Director, Schroder Securities Limited, since 1988; UK Equity Division. *Career:* Merrill Lynch, Pierce, Fenner & Smith 1971-80; Director 1982-88. *Biog: b.* 7 January 1952. *Nationality:* British. *m.* 1974, Sandra Francoise (née Mills); 3 s. *Educ:* Eton College, Windsor; Sorbonne University (Diploma). *Directorships:* Schroder Securities Limited 1988 (exec). *Clubs:* White's.

MENZIES, Ian Caithness; General Manager/Director, General Accident Fire & Life Assurance Corp plc, since 1985; Finance & Investment. *Career:* Arthur Young, Mgr 1961-68; J Henry Schroder Wagg & Co Ltd, Dir 1969-85. *Biog: b.* 11 February 1940. *Nationality:* British. *m.* 1966, Elizabeth (née Murray); 2 s; 1 d. *Educ:* Uppingham School; Edinburgh University (MA). *Directorships:* Head Wrightson 1974-76 (non-exec); Davy Corporation 1976-79 (non-exec); LCP (Holdings) 1980-87 (non-exec). *Other Activities:* CBI Industrial Policy Ctee (1980-85). *Professional Organisations:* CA. *Clubs:* Caledonian. *Recreations:* Squash, Bridge, Shooting.

MENZIES, Ian Michael; Partner, Drivers Jonas, since 1989; Building Surveying, Partner City Office. *Career:* Greater London Council, Building Surveyor 1977-79; Hunter to Partners, Building Surveyor 1979-81; Drivers Jonas, Building Surveyor to Partner 1981-. *Biog: b.* 22 February 1956. *Nationality:* British. *m.* 1982, Beryl (née Harrow). *Educ:* Picardy School; Polytechnic of the Southbank (BSc). *Professional Organisations:* ARICS; Affiliate Member, Association of Facilities Managers. *Recreations:* Sailing, Travel, Shooting.

MENZIES, John Maxwell; Chairman, John Menzies plc.

MENZIES, M O B; Director, Macey Williams Insurance Services Ltd.

MENZIES, Rowan Robin; Partner, Baillie Gifford & Co. *Biog: b.* 30 October 1952. *Educ:* Stowe School; Trinity College, Cambridge (BA). *Directorships:* Baillie Gifford Technology plc 1984 (exec).

MERCER, H; Partner, Milne Ross.

MERCEY, Charles; Executive Director, N M Rothschild & Sons Limited.

MEREDITH, J P; Partner, Grimley J R Eve.

MEREDITH, Noel; Director, Svenska International plc, since 1989; UK Corporate Banking. *Career:* Midland Bank, Management Trainee 1977-81; County Bank, Various to Manager, County NatWest Ventures 1981-86. *Biog: b.* 25 December 1955. *Nationality:* British. *m.* 1988, Veronica; 1 s. *Educ:* St Johns College, Cambridge (MA). *Professional Organisations:* AIB (1981). *Clubs:* Sundridge Park Golf Club. *Recreations:* Golf, Theatre, Reading.

MEREDITH, Paul Michael Charles; Chairman, Phillips & Drew Fund Management Limited, since 1990. *Career:* Fund Manager 1979-82; Phillips & Drew Fund Management, Director 1982-90. *Biog: b.* 7 June 1945. *Nationality:* British. *m.* 1984, Margaret; 1 s; 2 d. *Educ:* Clifton College; Britannia Royal Naval College. *Professional Organisations:* FIA.

MEREDITH, Philip; Director, Kleinwort Benson Securities, since 1987; Smaller Company Research. *Career:* Joseph Sebag & Co, Ptnr 1968-80; Carr Sebag, Ptnr 1980-82; Grieveson Grant, Ptnr 1982-86; Kleinwort Grieveson, Dir 1986-. *Biog: b.* 17 December 1938. *m.* 1966, Marilyn (née Hunt); 3 s. *Educ:* Tonbridge School. *Professional Organisations:* FCA. *Recreations:* Golf.

MEREDITH HARDY, Simon Patrick; Executive Director, County NatWest Securities Ltd, since 1988; Continental Europe. *Career:* Commissioned, The Life Guards 1964-69; Wood Mackenzie & Co Ltd 1981-88; County NatWest Securities Ltd 1988-. *Biog: b.* 31 October 1943. *Nationality:* British. *m.* 1969, Joanna Mary (née Porritt); 2 s. *Educ:* Eton College. *Directorships:* Sellier SA 1989 (non-exec). *Professional Organisations:* Member, The International Stock Exchange. *Clubs:* City of London. *Recreations:* Yachting, Skiing.

MERNAGH, J E; Director, Barclays de Zoete Wedd, since 1986; Head of Gilt Sales, since 1990. *Career:* Cazenove & Co 1970-82; de Zoete & Bevan (Merger with Barclays & Wedd in 1986) 1982-86; BZW 1986-. *Biog: b.* 24 May 1952. *Nationality:* British. *m.* 1972, Lynn Margaret; 2 s. *Educ:* St Aloysius College. *Directorships:* de Zoete & Bevan 1985 Partner; BZW 1986. *Professional Organisations:* Member, London Stock Exchange (1984).

MERRIAM, Andrew William Kennedy; Director, Granville & Co Limited, since 1987; Head of Investment Management Department. *Career:* Singleton Fabian & Co, Articled Clerk 1967-71; Vickers da Costa, Investment Mgr, Private Clients 1972-82; Granville &

Co Limited 1982. *Biog: b.* 18 May 1948. *Nationality:* British. *m.* 1979, (Elizabeth) Jean; 1 s; 1 d. *Educ:* Eton. *Directorships:* Granville & Co Ltd and Group Companies 1984-87 (exec); Granville Trust Limited 1987 (non-exec); Various Minor Private Companies (non-exec). *Professional Organisations:* FCA. *Clubs:* MCC, St Moritz Toboganning Club. *Recreations:* Shooting, Horse Racing, Gardening.

MERRIFIELD, K J; Operations Director, Wellcome plc.

MERRIMAN, P E; Partner, Bacon & Woodrow.

MERRITT, Paul; Clerk, Worshipful Company of Pattenmakers, since 1987; Responsible for the Administration of the Livery Company. *Career:* Contract Catering with Gardner Merchants and Taylorplan Catering 1965-74; Secretary of The City of London Club 1974-86; Hotelier in North Yorkshire 1983-87; Clerk to The Worshipful Company of Pattenmakers 1987-. *Biog: b.* 30 May 1937. *Nationality:* British. *m.* 1976, Gilian Mary (née Eggleton); 3 s; 1 d. *Educ:* Canford School; Battersea College of Technology (ACT, MHCI). *Directorships:* Forest & Vale Hotel Limited 1983 (exec). *Other Activities:* Interest in Development and Management of Various Residential Properties 1966-. *Professional Organisations:* Fellow, Hotel Catering and Institutional Management Association; Member, Hotel & Catering Institute; Member, British Property Federation; Institute of Directors. *Recreations:* Squash, Study of Wines.

MESSERVY, Sir Godfrey; Non Executive Director, Asda Group plc.

MESTWERDT, Reinhold; General Manager, Westdeutsche Landesbank, since 1990. *Biog: Nationality:* German. *Directorships:* WestLB Europe (UK) Holdings Ltd 1990 (non-exec).

METCALF, John; Group Secretary, IMI plc, since 1973; Legal, Corporate Public and Investor Relations. *Career:* ICI, Personnel & Plant Management 1957-61; Company Secretarial 1961-73; Assistant Company Secretary 1966-73. *Biog: b.* 25 February 1934. *Nationality:* British. *m.* 1963, Dorinda Jane (née English); 2 s. *Educ:* Chesterfield School; Pembroke College, Oxford (MA Jurisprudence). *Directorships:* IMI Kynoch Limited; IMI Overseas Investments Limited; IMI International Limited; IMI Nederland BV; IMI Americas Inc. *Clubs:* Vincent's. *Recreations:* Sport, Hunting, Music.

METCALF, Michael Edward; Group Finance Director, Thorn EMI plc, since 1989. *Career:* UB (Biscuits), Finance Director, Branded Biscuits Division 1983-85; Thorn EMI Home Electronics (International), Finance Director 1985-88; Thorn EMI plc, Deputy Finance Director 1988-89; Group Finance Director 1989-. *Biog: b.* 10 January 1952. *Nationality:* British. *Educ:* Bristol University (BSc Econ). *Directorships:* Thorn EMI plc 1989 (exec); Thames Television plc 1989 (non-exec). *Professional Organisations:* FCA.

METCALF, Simon Railton; Executive Director, County NatWest, since 1988. *Biog: b.* 19 January 1943. *m.* 2 s.

METCALFE, M W; Managing Director, E D & F Man Cocoa Limited, since 1987; Management of Cocoa Division. *Career:* Mars UK, Slough, Various Management including Personnel, Production, Operational Research, Marketing, Supplies 1966-78. *Biog: b.* 8 April 1944. *Nationality:* British. *m.* Lenore; 1 s; 1 d. *Educ:* University of Liverpool (BSc, MSc); Slough College of Technology (Diploma of Management Studies). *Directorships:* Holco Trading Co Inc 1981 Vice President; E D & F Man Ltd 1985; Holco Trading Co Inc 1987; W G Spice & Co Ltd 1987 Chairman; E D & F Man (Bermuda) Ltd 1987; Tropival (Ivory Coast) 1989; E D & F Man Cocoa Ltd 1990 MD; Gill & Duffus Ltd 1990 MD; Holco Man Ltd 1990 MD. *Recreations:* Squash, Shooting.

METLISS, C; Director, British Land.

METLISS, Jonathan A; Partner, S J Berwin & Co.

METTERS, B; Executive Director, Allied Dunbar Assurance plc.

METZGER, Barry; Managing Partner, Coudert Brothers International Attorneys, since 1989; International Banking & Finance. *Career:* Ceylon Law College, Asst to Principal 1969-71; International Legal Center, Dir of Asian Programs 1971-74; Coudert Brothers, Assoc Attorney, NY & Hong Kong 1974-78; Managing Partner, Hong Kong 1974-78; Managing Partner, Sydney, Australia 1984-89. *Biog: b.* 11 June 1945. *Nationality:* American. *m.* 1969, Jacqueline Sue (née Ivers); 1 s; 1 d. *Educ:* Columbia High School; Princeton University (BA); Harvard University (JD). *Directorships:* Equatorial Pacific International Co 1985-89 (non-exec); Nikko Securities Australia Ltd 1986-89 (non-exec); Michael EJ Perry & Associates Pty Ltd 1985-89 (non-exec). *Other Activities:* Member, Editorial Advisory Board, International Financial Law Review; Member, Board of Trustees, Priceton in Asia. *Professional Organisations:* ABA; IBA; Assoc of the Bar of the City of New York; District of Columbia Bar Assoc; Law Assoc of Asia & the Western Pacific. *Publications:* Legal Aid and World Poverty, 1974; Journal Articles on International Banking and Finance. *Clubs:* Princeton Club of New York, American National, Sydney. *Recreations:* Reading, Collection of Contemporary Art.

MEW, M A; Director, First National Bank PLC.

MEWS, R E B; Director, Barclays de Zoete Wedd Securities Ltd.

MEYER, Peter Anthony Roger; Finance Director, Schroder Investment Management Ltd, since 1990; Finance. *Career:* Price Waterhouse 1973-78; Bankers Trust Co NA, Chief Financial Auditor, Europe ME & A 1978-84; Chase Manhattan Bank NA, Div Head, Financial Controls 1984-86; Hongkong & Shanghai Banking Corporation, UK Area Financial Controller 1986-90. *Biog: b.* 23 July 1951. *Nationality:* British/Swiss. *m.* 1981, Frances Helen (née Wheat); 1 s; 2 d. *Educ:* Dulwich College; University of Bristol (BA Hons). *Professional Organisations:* FCA. *Recreations:* Cycling, Walking, Squash, Cinema, Theatre.

MEYERMAN, Harold J; Non-Executive Director, First Interstate Capital Markets Limited.

MEYERS, Hans W; General Manager, Norddeutsche Landesbank, since 1990. *Career:* Bayerische Vereinsbank, General Manager, Hamburg 1989-90; General Manager, New York 1986-89; Managing Director, Luxembourg 1977-86; Bankers Trust Company, Vice President, London 1975-77; Asst Vice Pres, Frankfurt 1971-75; Asst Vice Pres, New York 1969-71; Commerzbank, Various Assignments, Hamburg 1958-69. *Biog: b.* 26 June 1938. *Nationality:* German. *m.* 1971, Anya; 1 s; 1 d. *Directorships:* Bremer Landesbank Capital Markets plc 1990 (exec); NORD/LB Norddeutsche Securities plc 1990 (exec).

MEYRICK, Michael James; Director, Morgan Grenfell Asset Management Ltd, since 1985; Investment Management. *Career:* Fielding Newson Smith 1960-61; Moir & Shand 1961-67; Morgan Grenfell & Co Ltd Junior Dealer 1967; Dir 1981-85. *Biog: b.* 30 June 1942. *Nationality:* British. *m.* 1972, Juliet (née Andrew); 1 s; 1 d. *Educ:* Sutton Valence School, Kent; City of London College - Stock Exchange Law & Practice. *Directorships:* Morgan Grenfell Asset Management 1985 (exec); Morgan Grenfell Investment Management 1985. *Clubs:* Royal Motor Yacht Club. *Recreations:* Sailing, Golf.

MEZGER, Theo; Assistant General Manager - Commercial Banking, Union Bank of Finland Ltd.

MGADZAH, Raymond; City Journalist, The Sunday Telegraph, since 1989; Electronics Companies, The Marketing Services Sector and Small Companies. *Career:* Marketing Week; Freelancing for the Sunday Times.

MIALL, P J; Company Secretary, Sogemin Metals Ltd.

MICHAELIDES, Costas P; Managing Director, Merrill Lynch Europe Ltd, since 1988; Finance. *Career:* Exxon Corporation, Senior Financial Analyst 1977-79; Esso Europe Inc, Senior Financial Advisor 1979-83; Esso Italiana SPA, Treasurer 1983-85; Esso Europe Inc,

Assistant Treasurer 1985-86; Salomon Brothers International, Treasurer 1986-88. *Biog: b.* 5 February 1949. *Nationality:* US Citizen. *Educ:* Ripon College (BA, Economics & Political Science); Columbia University Graduate School of Business (MBA, Finance & International Business); University of Denver Graduate School of International Studies (PhD, Economics & International Relations). *Directorships:* Merrill Lynch Europe Ltd 1988 (exec); Merrill Lynch International Ltd 1989 (exec); Merrill Lynch Ltd 1990 (exec); Merrill Lynch Pierce Fenner & Smith Ltd 1990 (exec); Merrill Lynch International Bank Ltd 1989 (non-exec). *Other Activities:* The Securities Association Capital Committee. *Recreations:* Skiing, Sailing, History.

MICHAELSON, Joe Martin; Partner in Charge, Moores & Rowland, since 1986; General Audit. *Career:* Wilson Bigg & Co, Articled Clerk 1963-67; PA to Snr Ptnr 1967-71; Edward Moore & Sons, Mgr 1971-73; Ptnr 1973-84; Moores & Rowland, Ptnr 1985-. *Biog: b.* 23 August 1940. *m.* 1968, Wendy (née Haigh); 1 s; 1 d. *Educ:* Minchenden Grammar School, Enfield. *Professional Organisations:* FCA. *Recreations:* Theatre, Opera, Football (Spectator).

MICHAELSON, Robert Paul Brandon; Director, Mercury Asset Management Group plc.

MICHEL, K; Partner, Holman Fenwick & Willan, since 1978; Maritime and Commercial Law and International Trade. *Career:* Coward (Now Clifford) Chance, Articled Clerk 1971-73; Clyde & Co, Assistant Solicitor 1973-75; Holman Fenwick & Willan, Assistant Solicitor then Partner 1975-. *Biog: b.* 19 May 1948. *Nationality:* British. *m.* 1972, Rosemary Suzannah (née Simons); 1 s. *Educ:* Bradfield College; Cambridge University (MA). *Other Activities:* Member, City of London Solicitors Company; Clerk to the Council of Governors, Bradfield College; Trustee, Cambridge University Football Club and its Representative on Council of Amateur Football Alliance. *Professional Organisations:* Solicitor. *Publications:* Various Articles in Legal Journals including Law Society's Gazette, Lloyds Maritime Commercial Law Quarterly, and Lloyds List; Contraband (First Novel), 1988. *Clubs:* Hawks, Old Bradfieldian Football Club, Grasshoppers Cricket Club, Free Foresters CC. *Recreations:* Most Sports (Cambridge Soccer Blue 1968-69 Combined Oxbridge Soccer Tour to Japan 1969), History, Archaeology, Wildlife Conservation.

MICHELMORE, Peter Guy; Partner, Richards Butler, since 1983; Corporate Finance, Company & Commercial Law. *Biog: b.* 18 May 1951. *Nationality:* British. *m.* 1985, Susan Elizabeth (née Gardener). *Educ:* Sherborne School; University of Bristol (LLB). *Professional Organisations:* The Law Society; International Bar Association; Union Internationale Des Avocats. *Publications:* UAE - Company and Commercial Law and Practice, 1981; Establishing a Commercial Presence in the Emirate of AbuDhabi, 1980. *Recreations:* Squash, Tennis, Running.

MICHELSON, A Rawle; Director, Merrill Lynch International Limited; Mergers & Acquisitions. *Career:* Merrill Lynch International Limited 1989-; Morgan Stanley (London) 1984-89; Morgan Stanley (New York) 1981-84 and 1977-79; Harvard Business School 1979-81. *Biog: b.* 1955. *Nationality:* American. *m.* 1986, Giovanna (née Vitelli); 1 s.

MICHIE, Alastair John; Company Secretary, Lloyds Bank plc, since 1985. *Career:* Lloyds Bank International Ltd, Asst Sec 1978-80; Co Sec 1981-85. *Biog: b.* 21 March 1948. *m.* 1971, Dawn Elizabeth (née Wittet); 1 s; 1 d. *Educ:* Blairgowrie High School, Perthshire. *Professional Organisations:* FCIS; AIB (Scot). *Recreations:* Squash, Golf.

MICHIE, William Guthrie McGregor; Director, Morgan Grenfell & Co Ltd, since 1988; Banking Division, Project Finance/Advisory Services. *Biog: b.* 20 December 1947. *Nationality:* British. *m.* 1976, Susan Jane (née Griffin); 3 d. *Educ:* Fettes College, Edinburgh; Aberdeen University (LLB). *Professional Organisations:* CA. *Recreations:* Golf.

MIDDLEDITCH, Matthew; Partner, Linklaters & Paines, since 1990; Corporate Finance. *Career:* Linklaters & Paines, Articled Clerk & Assistant Solicitor 1980-86; Mills & Reeve (Norwich), Assistant Solicitor 1986-88; Linklaters & Paines, Assistant Solicitor 1988-90. *Biog: b.* 12 August 1958. *Nationality:* British. *m.* 1984, Penelope; 2 d. *Educ:* Winchester College; Trinity College, Cambridge (MA). *Other Activities:* Freeman, Skinners Company; City of London Solicitors Company. *Professional Organisations:* Member, Law Society.

MIDDLEMASS, Nigel; Partner, Forsyte Kerman, since 1984; Property & Commercial Litigation. *Career:* J M Smith & Co, Articled Clerk 1978-80; Assistant Solicitor 1980-81; Forsyte Kerman, Assistant Solicitor 1981-84; Partner 1984-; Marketing Partner 1988-. *Biog: b.* 31 July 1956. *Nationality:* British. *m.* 1986, Kate (née Middlemass). *Educ:* Slough Grammar School; Nottingham University (LLB Hons). *Professional Organisations:* Law Society. *Clubs:* RAC. *Recreations:* Sport, Theatre, Films, Walking.

MIDDLETON, Alan Bruce; Director, Minet Holdings plc.

MIDDLETON, Edward Bernard; Partner, Pannell Kerr Forster, since 1979; Corporate Advisory. *Career:* Pannell Kerr Forster Mgr 1973-79; Ptnr 1979-; DTI (seconded) Dir, Industrial Dev Unit 1984-86. *Biog: b.* 5 July 1948. *Nationality:* British. *m.* 1971, Rosemary (née Brown); 3 s. *Educ:* Aldenham School. *Directorships:* Pannell Kerr Forster Associates 1987 (non-exec). *Profes-sional Organisations:* FCA. *Clubs:* Salcombe Yacht Club. *Recreations:* Sailing, Photography.

MIDDLETON, Sir Peter (Edward); GCB; Permanent Secretary, HM Treasury, since 1983. *Career:* RAPC 1958-60; HM Treaury Snr Information Officer 1962; Principal 1964; Centre for Admin Studies Asst Dir 1967-69; HM Treasury, Private Sec to Chancellor of the Exchequer 1969-72; Treasury Pres Sec 1972-75; Head of Monetary Policy Div 1975-76; Under Sec, Fin Economics 1976-80; Dep Sec, Fiscal & Monetary Policy 1980-83. *Biog: b.* 2 April 1934. *Nationality:* British. m1 1964, Valerie Ann (née Lindup (decd); 1 s; 1 d; m2 1990, Constance Owen (née Close). *Educ:* Sheffield City Grammar School; Sheffield University (BA, MA, DLitt); Bristol University. *Other Activities:* Visiting Fellow, Nuffield College, Oxford (1981-89); Governor, London Business School (1984-90); Council Member, Manchester Business School (1985); Member & Governor, Ditchley Foundation (1985); School of Mgmnt & Econ Studies, University of Sheffield (1986); Commodore, Civil Service Sailing Association. *Clubs:* Reform.

MII, K; General Manager Administration and Company Secretary, Nomura Bank International plc.

MIKOSHIBA, Yoshio; Managing Director, Yasuda Trust Europe Limited, since 1990. *Career:* The Yasuda Trust & Banking Co Ltd Tokyo, Fund Manager 1978-87; Yasuda Trust Europe London, Dep Managing Director 1987-90; Managing Director 1990-. *Biog: b.* 9 February 1945. *Nationality:* Japanese. *m.* Tomoko; 1 d. *Educ:* Waseda University (Law). *Directorships:* Yasuda Trust Europe Ltd, London 1990 (exec).

MILBOURN, Michael Peter; Managing Director, Chartered WestLB Limited, since 1990; Developing Country Finance Group. *Career:* Western American Bank (Europe) Ltd, Asst General Mgr, Banking Division 1970-77; Libra Bank plc, General Mgr, Merchant Banking Group 1977-87. *Biog: b.* 4 November 1948. *Nationality:* British. *m.* 1971, Felicity (née O'Donohoe); 2 s; 2 d. *Educ:* St Alban's School; Nottingham University (BA Hons Industrial Economics). *Directorships:* Chartered WestLB Limited 1987 (exec).

MILBURN, Robert Christopher; Director, Corporate Communications, Cadbury Schweppes plc, since 1990; Investor Relations, Public Relations, Public Affairs, Internal Communications. *Career:* Cadbury Schweppes since 1969; Various in Production Management, Industrial Engineering, Production Control, Materials Management, Finance and Information Systems Management; Group Headquarters, London, Redeveloping Financial Reporting Systems 1984; Responsibilty for Investor Relations 1988; Corporate Communications, Director 1990. *Educ:* University of Manchester Institute of Science & Technology (BSc Chem Eng).

MILDWATERS, Dr Kenneth Charles (Ken); Partner, Theodore Goddard, since 1989. *Career:* Kott Gunning (Western Australia), Articled Law Clerk 1976-77; Solicitor 1977-79; Associate 1979; Glynn and Glynn (Western Australia), Partner 1979-81; Kott Gunning (Western Australia), Associate 1981-82; Partner 1982-85; Theodore Goddard, Senior Manager 1987-88; Associate 1988-89. *Biog: b.* 8 March 1954. *Nationality:* Australian. *m.* 1974, Gretchen Jean Mildwaters (née Jones); 1 s; 1 d. *Educ:* Wesley College (Western Australia); University of Western Australia (B Juris Hons, LLB); University of Dundee (PhD). *Professional Organisations:* Law Society. *Recreations:* Reading.

MILES, Adrian Spencer; Partner, Wilde Sapte, since 1976; Head of Special Finance Group, Specialising in Aviation, Marine and Project Finance. *Career:* Boodle Hatfield, Solicitor 1972-74; Norton Rose, Solicitor 1974-76. *Biog: b.* 16 November 1947. *Nationality:* British. *m.* 1975, Hilary; 1 s; 2 d. *Educ:* Rutlish; Queen Mary College, London (LLB Hons). *Professional Organisations:* Member, The Law Society. *Recreations:* Sport, Chess, Politics, Music.

MILES, H M P; OBE; Executive Director, John Swire & Sons Ltd, since 1988; Hong Kong and Taiwan. *Career:* Swire Pacific Ltd, Chairman 1984-88; Cathay Pacific Airways Ltd (Hong Kong), Chairman 1984-88; Cathay Pacific Airways Ltd, Managing Director 1978-84; John Swire & Sons (Japan) Ltd, Managing Director 1973-76; Swire Group (Hong Kong) 1958-88. *Biog: b.* 19 April 1936. *Nationality:* British. *m.* 1967, Carol Jane (née Berg); 2 s; 1 d. *Educ:* Wellington College, Berkshire. *Directorships:* Barings plc 1989 (non-exec); Christie's Swire (Holdings) Ltd 1989; Fleming Far Eastern Investment Trust plc 1989; Johnson Matthey plc 1990; NAAFI 1989; P&O Containers (Pacific) Ltd 1988; Portals Holdings plc 1990; Sedgwick Lloyd's Underwriting Agents Ltd 1989; The Thomas Cook Group Ltd 1988. *Other Activities:* Member, Anglo-Taiwan Trade Committee; Member, Sino-British Trade Council; Board of Governors, Wellington College. *Clubs:* Berkshire Golf Club.

MILES, Nick; Director, Lowe Bell Financial Ltd, since 1986; Mergers & Acquisition, Investor Relations. *Career:* Trafalgar House 1979-83; Good Relations, Account Director 1983-85; BMP, Business Director 1984-86. *Nationality:* British. *m.* 1990, Suzanne (née Chauveau). *Educ:* Tonbridge School; Corpus Christi College, Cambridge (MA). *Publications:* The Disappearance of the God Concept in 20th Century Literature, 1972. *Clubs:* Annabels Hurlingham, Bachelors. *Recreations:* Jazz, Golf, Cricket.

MILES, Sir P T; Director, British & Commonwealth Merchant Bank plc.

MILFORD, Antony Brian; Director, Framlington Group plc, International Fund Management. *Career:* Laurence Keen & Gardner 1967; Laurence Prust & Co 1971; Ptnr 1974; Framlington Unit Management 1974. *Nationality:* British. *Educ:* Lincoln College, Oxford (BA). *Directorships:* Group Development Capital plc 1986 (non-exec); Medical Investments Ltd 1989.

MILICIC, Mrs Marija (née Mojsovska); Managing Director of a Representative Office, Vojvodjanska Banka, since 1987; Foreign Payments, Current Accounts and other Banking and Commercial Transactions. *Career:* Vojvodjanska Banka, Yugoslavia Dir, Foreign Payments Dept 1975-87. *Biog: b.* 28 September 1945. *Nationality:* Yugoslavian. *m.* 1969, Marinko; 1 s; 1 d. *Educ:* Skopje University, Yugoslavia (Dipl Ecc). *Other Activities:* Chm, The Yugoslav Commission on Banking Technique and Practice of the Association of Yugoslav Banks (1980-87).

MILLAR, Graham; Managing Director, Rowntree Mackintosh Limited, since 1988. *Career:* Larking & Larking (now Larking, Gowen & Co), Chartered Accountant 1962; Lotus plc, Accountant 1969; John Mackintosh & Son Ltd, Financial Controller 1973; Rowntree Mackintosh Ltd, Group Accountant 1975; Finance Director, European Division 1979; Wilson Rowntree (Pty) Ltd, East London, South Africa, MD 1984; Rowntree Mackintosh Ltd, MD 1988. *Biog: b.* 29 September 1944. *Nationality:* British. *m.* Pat; 2 s. *Directorships:* North Yorkshire Training & Enterprise Council Deputy Chairman; York Enterprise Ltd; Member, National Enterprise Team. *Other Activities:* Member, Biscuit, Cake, Chocolate & Confectionery Alliance Council & Operating Committee; Treasurer, York Civic Trust; Chairman, York Urological Cancer Research Fund. *Professional Organisations:* FCA.

MILLAR, J; Director, Taylor Woodrow plc.

MILLAR, John Paterson; Director, Williams De Broe, since 1985; UK Equities. *Career:* Williams De Broe 1973-90. *Biog: b.* 19 July 1950. *Nationality:* British. *m.* 1985, Richenda (née Eaton); 2 s; 2 d. *Educ:* St Edwards School, Oxford; Queen Mary College, London University (1st Class Honours).

MILLAR, Keith Malcolm Hedley; Chairman, Henderson Crosthwaite Ltd, since 1986. *Biog: b.* 3 August 1933. *Nationality:* British. *Educ:* Loretto School; Clare College, Cambridge. *Professional Organisations:* FCA.

MILLER, A J; Director, Berry Palmer & Lyle Ltd.

MILLER, David; Executive Director, Premises & Office Services, Allied Dunbar, since 1985; Property Strategy/Purchasing/Facilities Management. *Career:* IBM UK, Computer Prog 1968-71; Hambro Life, Prog

Manager 1971-80; Hambro Life (Allied Dunbar), DP Director 1980-85; Allied Dunbar, Exec Director, PSD 1985-. *Biog: b.* 9 August 1947. *Nationality:* British. *m.* (div); 1 s; 2 d. *Educ:* High School of Glasgow; Glasgow University (MA Maths/Economics). *Recreations:* Golf, Dining & Wining.

MILLER, David J; Finance Director, Global Asset Management (UK) Ltd, since 1988; Compliance, Financial, Administrative. *Career:* Deloitte Haskins & Sells, Consultant, then Manager in Charge of Assignments in a Variety of Industries, including Financial Services 1984-87; Ranks Hovis McDougall, Development & Planning Accountant, Various Planning & Line Financial Positions 1975-83. *Biog: m.* 1976; 1 d. *Educ:* Edinburgh University (BCom Hons). *Directorships:* Global Asset Management (UK) 1989 (exec). *Professional Organisations:* CA (Scottish Institute of Chartered Accountants) 1971-74; ATII (Member, Institute of Taxation) 1985. *Recreations:* Golf, Swimming.

MILLER, Geoffrey Ruscoe; Director UK Banking, Barclays Bank plc, since 1987; Whole Branch Network of UK Bank Branches. *Career:* Barclays Bank plc 1955-. *Biog: b.* 3 November 1938. *m.* 1964, Maureen (née Dobson); 2 s. *Educ:* Liverpool Institute High School for Boys. *Professional Organisations:* FCIB. *Recreations:* Sport, Gardening.

MILLER, Ian; Financial Journalist, Daily Mirror.

MILLER, J R T; Director, Hill Samuel Investment Management Ltd.

MILLER, Jem; Deputy Chairman, Lowe Bell Financial Ltd, since 1988; Administration, Major Account Responsibility. *Career:* Journalism, Various 1953-63; Anglo American Corp, Editor PRO 1963-71; Streets Financial Ltd, Head of PR, Snr Dir 1972-82; Miller & Co, Chm 1982-84; Burson-Marsteller, Financial MD 1984-87. *Biog: b.* 27 December 1934. *Nationality:* British. *m.* 1986, Margaret (née Jones); 1 s; 1 d. *Educ:* Brighton College. *Professional Organisations:* Institute of Directors. *Recreations:* Photography, Cooking.

MILLER, John Ashley Laing; WS; Group Company Secretary, Asda Group plc, since 1987; Corporate Law. *Career:* Simpson, Kinmont & Maxwell, Apprentice/ Solicitor 1970-73; Brodies WS, Solicitor 1973-75; Partner (Corporate Law) 1975-87. *Biog: b.* 4 August 1948. *Nationality:* British. *m.* 1973, Sheila Elizabeth (née Knowles); 2 s; 1 d. *Educ:* Repton School; Aberdeen University (LLB). *Professional Organisations:* Law Society of Scotland. *Clubs:* Caledonian Club (London). *Recreations:* Stalking, Tennis, Mountain Biking.

MILLER, Jonathan Alexander; Director, Garside, Miller Associates Limited, since 1990. *Career:* Grolier Inc, Asst Editor 1959-61; Sun Life Assurance Co of

Canada, Asst Resident Treasurer 1961-67; Fielding Newson-Smith & Co, Ptnr 1967-86; County Natwest, Consultant 1986-88; Consultant to Republic of Guyana on behalf of the Stock Exchange 1988; Consultant to Central Bank of Malta on behalf of The Stock Exchange 1989; Consultant to the International Stock Exchange of Gibralter Ltd 1989-90. *Biog: b.* 13 January 1936. *Nationality:* British. *m.* 1967, Brigid (née Ashby); 3 s; 1 d. *Educ:* St Paul's School; New College, Oxford (BA). *Directorships:* Garside, Miller Associates Limited 1990 (exec). *Other Activities:* Council of Society of Investment Analysts (Chm 1982-84); Stock Exchange Council (1984-86); Authorisation Ctee of The Securities Assoc (1987-89); CCAB Accounting Standards Review Committee (1988). *Publications:* Dictionary of Financial Regulation, 1988. *Clubs:* United Oxford and Cambridge University.

MILLER, K H; Partner, Cameron Markby Hewitt.

MILLER, Nicholas; Director, Svenska International plc.

MILLER, Nicholas H J; Director, Guidehouse Securities Limited, since 1989; Corporate Finance. *Career:* Price Waterhouse Chartered Accountants London, Qualifying as ACA 1979-83; GIBA International Limited London (Private Investment Bank) Executive working on Corporate Finance Projects 1983-8. *Biog: b.* 2 July 1958. *Nationality:* British. *m.* 1982, Carolyn; 1 s. *Educ:* King's College School, Wimbledon; University of Leeds (BSc Hons Civil Engineering). *Directorships:* Mercer & Miller (Office Services) Limited 1977 (exec); White Light (Electrics) Limited 1989 (non-exec). *Professional Organisations:* Associate, Institute of Chartered Accountants in England and Wales.

MILLER, P R; Partner, Milne Ross.

MILLER, Peter G G; Partner, Moores Rowland, since 1968. *Biog: b.* 14 January 1940. *Nationality:* British. *m.* 1968, Carole (née Cowl); 3 s; 1 d. *Educ:* University of Sheffield (BA Econ). *Professional Organisations:* FCA.

MILLER, R M; Chief Executive, Willis Corroon plc.

MILLER, Robert D; Vice President, Mellon Bank NA.

MILLER, Ronald Andrew Baird; CBE; Chairman, Dawson International plc, since 1982. *Biog: b.* 13 May 1937. *Nationality:* British. *Directorships:* Scottish Amicable Life Assurance Society (non-exec); Securities Trust plc (non-exec); Christian Salveson plc (non-exec). *Professional Organisations:* CA.

MILLER, Timothy Peter Francis (Tim); Director, M & G Group plc, since 1988. *Career:* Advertising Executive 1962-79; Framlington Unit Management Director 1979-83; Framlington Group plc MD 1983-88. *Biog: b.* 9 November 1940. *Nationality:* British. *m.* 1965, Lisa (née Davies); 2 s; 2 d. *Educ:* Douai School; Magdalen College, Oxford. *Other Activities:* Chm, Board Charter 88; Trustee, Child Psychotherapy Trust; Chm, EFIFC Marketing Committee; Chm, Financial Services Committee, Advertising Association. *Professional Organisations:* Board Member of Lautro (Chm, Advertising & Product Disclosure Ctees). *Clubs:* Beefsteak, City of London, MCC. *Recreations:* Opera, Rallying, Books, Pictures.

MILLER, V M; Partner, Pensions Research, Bacon & Woodrow.

MILLER, William S; Director, Merrill Lynch International Limited.

MILLER-BAKEWELL, Robert Lewis; Director, County NatWest Securities Limited. *Biog: b.* 6 February 1953. *Recreations:* Golf, Bridge, Racing.

MILLER SMITH, Charles; Financial Director, Unilever, since 1989. *Career:* Walls Meat Company, Commercial Director 1976-79; Hindustan Lever, Vice-Chairman 1979-80; Unilever, Member, Chemicals Co-Ordination 1981-83; PDR International, Chairman 1983-86; Quest International, President 1987-89. *Biog: b.* 7 November 1939. *Nationality:* British. *m.* 1964, Dorothy; 1 s; 2 d. *Educ:* Glasgow Academy; St Andrews University (MA). *Directorships:* Unilever Pension Investment Ltd (UPIL) 1989 Chm. *Other Activities:* Treasurer, St Michael's Church. *Clubs:* National Club. *Recreations:* Tennis, Walking, Shooting.

MILLGATE, V A; Associate Director/Recoveries, Benchmark Bank plc.

MILLHAM, D; Deputy Chairman & Managing Director, Shandwick Consultants, since 1979; Financial Public Relations. *Career:* Financial Times, Journalist 1959-69; Times, Journalist 1969-71; ICFC, Financial Public Relations Consultant 1971-74; Shandwick Public Relations, Founder Director 1974-; Shandwick Consultants, Deputy Chairman 1979-; Managing Director 1980-. *Biog: b.* 20 June 1938. *Nationality:* British. *m.* 1965, Frances (née Dubarry); 1 s; 1 d. *Directorships:* Shandwick Consultants 1979 (exec). *Other Activities:* Freeman, City of London. *Recreations:* Reading, Gardening, Watching West Ham FC, Drinking Red Wine.

MILLIGAN, Charles; Director, PaineWebber International (UK) Ltd.

MILLMAN, Stewart Ian; Managing Director, de Zoete & Bevan Ltd, since 1988; Corporate Finance. *Career:* Lazard Securities Ltd, Mgr 1971-78; Dir 1979-81; de Zoete & Bevan, Assoc Member 1981-84; Ptnr 1984-86; Director 1986-88. *Biog: b.* 21 November 1948.

Educ: City of London School; New College, Oxford (BA Hons, MA). *Directorships:* Wall Street Clearing Co 1987 (non-exec). *Professional Organisations:* RIC; Council Member, Society of Investment Analysts. *Publications:* Articles in Journals. *Recreations:* Playing Cricket, Watching Football.

MILLS, Colin Roger; Executive Director, County NatWest Wood Mac, since 1988; Head of Market Making, Head of Global Trading (Equities). *Biog: b.* 24 October 1945. *Nationality:* British. *m.* 1975, Helen (née Wilkinson); 1 s; 1 d. *Educ:* Hinchley Wood County Secondary School. *Directorships:* Wood Mackenzie & Co Ltd 1985 (non-exec); Hill Samuel & Co Ltd 1986 (non-exec). *Other Activities:* ISE, Domestic Equity Rules & Compliance Committee (DERCC).

MILLS, George Peter; Managing Director, Girozentrale Gilbert Eliott, since 1988. *Career:* The London Assurance, Investment Department 1956-61; MacNicoll & Co (subsequently Capel-Cure Myers) 1961-71; Member of the Stock Exchange & Ptnr 1964; Gilbert Eliott & Co, Founder of Equity Department 1971; Deputy Chief Executive 1985. *Biog: b.* 6 February 1933. *Nationality:* British. *m.* 1957, Anne Margareta; 1 s; 1 d. *Educ:* St Albans School; Queen's College, Cambridge (MA Law). *Directorships:* Girozentrale Capital Markets (exec); Hoare Govett Gilbert Eliott Ltd (exec); The Golf Fund plc (non-exec); Colin Snape Golf Consultancy plc (non-exec). *Professional Organisations:* International Stock Exchange; ACII; ACIS.

MILLS, John Wilfrid; Secretary, Association of British Consortium Banks, since 1986; Secretariat & Legal. *Career:* Royal Navy Secretariat Branch 1945-47; Mory & Co Ltd, Asst Acct 1947-56; British and French Bank Ltd (now BNP plc), Chief Acct 1956-71; Scandinavian Bank Group plc, Mgr/Comptroller 1971-86. *Biog: b.* 9 May 1927. *Nationality:* British. *m.* 1949, Catherine (née Caldwell); 1 s; 1 d. *Educ:* Clark's College; City of London College. *Directorships:* Society of Company and Commercial Accountants 1984 Council Mem (non-exec); renamed Institute of Company Accountants 1990 Vice-President. *Other Activities:* Appointed to the Order of St John, 1988. *Professional Organisations:* FSCA; MInstAM. *Recreations:* Motoring, Foreign Travel, Naval History, Music Appreciation, Photography.

MILLS, Leif Anthony; General Secretary, Banking Insurance and Finance Union, since 1972. *Career:* Banking Insurance & Finance Union, Research Officer, Assistant General Secretary, General Secretary 1960-. *Biog: b.* 25 March 1936. *Nationality:* British. *m.* 1958, Gillian Margaret (née Smith); 2 s; 2 d. *Educ:* Balliol College, Oxford (Philosophy, Politics and Economics). *Other Activities:* Member, TUC Non-Manual Committee, 1967-72; Member, Committee to Review Financial Institutions (Wilson Committee), 1977-80; Member, Civil Service Pay Research Unit Board, 1978-81; Member, BBC Consultative Group on Social Effects of Television, 1978-8; Member, Armed Forces Pay Review Body, 1980-87; Member, Monopolies and Mergers Commission, 1982-; Member, TUC General Council, 1983-; Chairman, TUC Financial Services Committee, 1983-; Chairman, TUC Education and Training Committee, 1989-; Member, TUC Finance and General Purposes Committee, Economic Committee, International Committee, Trade Union Education Committee and Committee on European Strategy; Trustee, Civic Trust; Member, Governing Body of London Business School; Member, Financial Reporting Council; Member, National Training Task Force Steering Group. *Clubs:* United Oxford & Cambridge University, Oxford University Boat, Weybridge Rowing. *Recreations:* Rowing, Chess.

MILLS, Mark T; Director, Merrill Lynch Pierce Fenner & Smith (Brokers & Dealers) Limited.

MILLS, Nigel Gordon; Corporate Finance Director, Hoare Govett.

MILLS, R H Y; Director, Metallgesellschaft Ltd.

MILLS, R J; Director, Allied Provincial plc.

MILLS, Terry Robert; Senior Vice President, J P Morgan; Heads 60 Victoria Embankment Project (New Office Development). *Career:* United Builders Merchants, Manager 1967-69; J P Morgan, various management positions, including Banking Manager, Lagos, General Manager, Seoul, General Manager, Saudi International Bank, London, Managing Director, Morgan Property Development Company Ltd 1969-. *Biog: b.* 19 October 1945. *Nationality:* British. *m.* Married with 2 Children. *Educ:* Christ Church, Oxford (MA Literae Humaniores); Manchester Business School (Diploma, Business Administration). *Directorships:* Morgan Property Development Company Ltd 1988 (exec) Chm & MD. *Other Activities:* Freeman, City of London; Member, Company of Information Technologists. *Publications:* Various Articles and Broadcasts on Ornithology. *Recreations:* Shooting, Fishing, Ornithology.

MILLWARD, H N; Director, S G Warburg Akroyd Rowe & Pitman Mullens Securities Ltd.

MILLWARD, Neil; Senior Associate Director, Royal Trust Bank, since 1988; Operations. *Career:* Gartmore Fund Managers International Ltd, MD 1983-86; County (Bank) Unit Trust Managers, Dir 1986-87; Royal Trust Asset Management, Dir 1987-88. *Professional Organisations:* ACIB.

MILLWATER, Dennis Curtis; Group Director, Bain Clarkson Limited, since 1987; Chairman/Managing Director Bain Clarkson Financial Serv Ltd. *Career:* Northern Assurance Co Ltd, Reg Supt 1957-68; Com-

mercial Union Assurance Co Ltd, Reg Pensions Controller 1968-69; De Falbe Halbey Ltd, Dir 1969-71; H Clarkson (Insurance Holdings) Ltd, Group Dir 1971-81; Clarkson Puckle Group Ltd, Group Dir 1981-87. *Biog: b.* 31 March 1934. *Nationality:* British. *m.* 1957, Marlene Beatrice (née Collins); 3 s; 1 d. *Educ:* Bassaleg Grammar School, Newport, Gwent; Bristol University. *Other Activities:* General Commissioner of Taxes. *Professional Organisations:* ACII; FPMI. *Clubs:* Royal St George's Golf Club. *Recreations:* Music, Golf, Cycling.

MILNE, B J; General Manager, Lloyds Bank plc.

MILNE, David Alistair; Director Head of Capital Markets, British & Commonwealth Merchant Bank plc, since 1987; Capital Markets and Syndications. *Career:* Nippon Credit Bank, Loan Officer 1974-77; Guinness Mahon & Co Ltd, Dir 1977-87. *Biog: b.* 29 August 1952. *Nationality:* British. *m.* 1975, Clare E A (née Crassweller); 1 s; 1 d. *Educ:* Malvern College; Pembroke College, Oxford (MA). *Professional Organisations:* MIB. *Clubs:* Riverside, Overseas Bankers Club. *Recreations:* Tennis, Theatre, Ballet.

MILNE, David L; Group Finance Director, Glynwed International plc, since 1979. *Career:* Wilmot Breeden Holdings Ltd, Group Finance Director 1975-79. *Biog: b.* 10 September 1936. *Nationality:* British. *m.* Pamela (née Harvey); 1 s; 1 d. *Educ:* Bedford School. *Directorships:* Glynwed International plc (exec); Glynwed Overseas Holdings Ltd (exec); Glynwed Properties Ltd (exec); Glynwed Property Developments Ltd (exec); Raglan Property Trust plc (non-exec). *Other Activities:* Member, Midland Industry Group of Finance Directors; CBI, Accounting Standards Working Group; City of Birmingham Orchestral Endowment Fund.

MILNE, Garth P D; Director, S G Warburg Akroyd Rowe & Pitman Mullens Ltd.

MILNE, Gordon; Business Reporter, The Scotsman.

MILNE, Sir John; Director, Royal Insurance Holdings plc.

MILNE, Malcolm Keith; Managing Director, Corporate Resource Control Limited, since 1988. *Career:* James R Knowles, Executive Director 1987-; R M Douglas Construction (Scotland), Director 1976-85; R M Douglas Construction Limited, Supervisory Quantity Surveyor 1975-76; British Lift Slab Limited, Senior Quantity Surveyor 1971-75. *Biog: b.* 12 February 1945. *Nationality:* British; 2 d. *Educ:* Bishop Vesey Grammar School, Sutton Coldfield; South Birmingham Polytechnic. *Directorships:* James R Knowles Limited 1987 (exec); Corporate Resource Control Ltd 1988 (exec) MD. *Other Activities:* Past Member, Various QS Divisional Committees RICS (Scotland); Past Chairman, Round Table; Past Member, Various Committees, Institute of Quantity

Surveyors (London); Past Member & Chairman, Institute of Quantity Surveyors (Scottish Branch). *Professional Organisations:* Fellow, Royal Institution of Chartered Surveyors; Associate, Chartered Institute of Arbitrators. *Publications:* Various Articles in Technical Publications. *Recreations:* Golf, Walking, Horology, Music.

MILNER, Elaine; Executive Director, Hoare Govett Gilbert Eliott Ltd, since 1990; Corporate Finance. *Career:* Titmuss Sainer & Webb, Asst Solicitor 1979-80; Rowe Rudd & Co, Corporate Fin Exec 1980-81; W Greenwell & Co, Corporate Fin Exec 1981-83. *Biog: b. 9* July 1955. *Educ:* Greenhead High School for Girls; Kings College, University of London (LLB). *Professional Organisations:* Member, International Stock Exchange; Member, The Law Society. *Recreations:* Shopping.

MILNER, Richard; Deputy City Editor, The Mail On Sunday.

MILTON, Paul; Director, Nicholson Chamberlain Colls Limited.

MILTON, R E; Director, Abbey Life Investment Services Ltd. *Professional Organisations:* FRICS.

MIMPRISS, Peter Hugh Trevor; Partner, Allen & Overy, since 1972; Private Clients. *Career:* Admitted Solicitor 1967; Allen & Overy 1968-. *Biog: b.* 22 August 1943. *Nationality:* British. *m.* 1971, Hilary Ann (née Reed); 2 d. *Educ:* Sherborne School. *Directorships:* Leeds Castle Foundation 1980 (non-exec); Chatham Historic Dockyard Trust 1988 (non-exec); Weston Park Foundation 1986 (non-exec). *Professional Organisations:* Law Society. *Clubs:* The Athenaeum, The Garrick. *Recreations:* Maritime History, Collecting Books & Pictures.

MINCHIN, Peter David; Deputy Chairman, Lloyds Bank Stockbrokers Ltd, since 1986. *Career:* Pidgeon de Smitt (and Predecessor Firms), Ptnr 1963-; Ptnr, Finance & Admin 1969-74; Deputy Snr Ptnr 1975-82; Securities Group SAK, Gen Mgr 1982-85; Scrimgeour Vickers Ltd, Ptnr/Dir 1985-86. *Biog: b.* 5 March 1932. *Nationality:* British. *m.* 1960, Angela (née Petley); 2 s; 1 d. *Educ:* All Hallows. *Directorships:* Chambers and Remington Ltd 1988 (exec) Chm; Lloyds Investment Managers Ltd 1990 Chm. *Other Activities:* Member, Council of the Stock Exchange, 1976-82, 1988-; Member, Board of the Securities Association, 1988-. *Professional Organisations:* Member, International Stock Exchange, 1963-. *Clubs:* Overseas Bankers Club.

MINCHINSON, N J; General Manager, Lloyds Bank plc.

MINEMATSU, T; Director, Norinchukin International Ltd.

MINERAUD, C; Director, Lowndes Lambert Group Holdings Limited.

MINERS, J M; Group Finance Controller, Beazer plc.

MINFORD, Professor (Anthony) Patrick (Leslie); Professor of Applied Economics, University of Liverpool, since 1976; Department of Economics and Accounting. *Career:* Ministry of Overseas Development, London, Economic Asst 1966; Ministry of Finance, Malawi, Economist 1967-69; Courtaulds Ltd, Economic Adviser, Director's Staff 1970-71; HM Treasury, Economic Adviser 1971-73; HM Treasury Delegation in Washington DC 1973-74; Visiting Hallsworth Fellow, Manchester University 1974-75; NIESR Review Editor 1975-76; Liverpool Quarterly Economic Bulletin, Editor 1980-. *Biog: b.* 17 May 1943. *m.* 1970, Rosemary Irene (née Allcorn); 2 s; 1 d. *Educ:* Morris Hill; Winchester College (Scholar); Balliol College, Oxford (Scholar BA); London School of Economics (MSc Econ, PhD). *Directorships:* Merseyside Development Corp 1988-89. *Publications:* Substitution, Effects, Speculation and Exchange Rate Stability, 1978; Unemployment - Cause And Cure (Jtly), 1983; 2nd Edition, 1985; Rational Expectations and The New Macroeconomics (Jtly), 1983; The Housing Morass, 1987; Articles in learned journals on monetary and international economics.

MINNS, Richard; Joint Chief Executive, Greater London Enterprise.

MINOGUE, Elizabeth Ann; Partner, McKenna & Co, since 1985; Property & Construction. *Career:* McKenna & Co, Articled Clerk 1978-80; Asst Solicitor 1980-85. *Biog: b.* 17 October 1955. *Nationality:* British. *Educ:* Clare College, Cambridge; College of Law. *Other Activities:* Forum for Construction Management, University of Reading; Anglo American Property Trust. *Professional Organisations:* Society of Construction Law. *Publications:* Regular Articles in Building.

MINOPRIO, Stephen James Calder; Main Board Director, Hogg Group plc, since 1987; Overseas Subsidiaries & Associates, Corporate Finance. *Career:* Arbuthnot Latham, MD, Factoring & Export Fin 1959-70; Development Capital 1970-76. *Biog: b.* 4 November 1940. *m.* 1977, Elizabeth (née Copinger-Hill); 2 s; 2 d. *Educ:* Harrow School. *Directorships:* Hogg Group plc 1987; Hogg Insurance Brokers Ltd 1985; Hogg Group Overseas Ltd 1985 Chm; Eastaf Holdings Ltd 1987; Commercial Credit Corporation Ltd 1978; Staple Hall Trading & Finance Company Ltd 1981; Haulfryn Estate Co Ltd 1977; Hogg Robinson Australia (Holdings) Ltd 1985; Hogg Robinson Australia (Investments) Pty Ltd 1985; Vonera Ltd (Australia) 1985; J S Johnson & Co Ltd (Bahamas) 1989; International Insurance Brokers Ltd (Jamaica) 1987; Hogg Robinson Kenya Ltd 1989; Insurance Holdings Africa Ltd (Kenya) 1987; Hogg

Robinson Malawi Ltd 1986; MIB Holding Co Ltd (Malta) 1987; Hogg Reinsurance Group Intermediarios de Reaseguro SA (Mexico) 1990; Hogg Group Netherlands BV 1985; Hogg Robinson Nigeria 1987; Nigerian Life & Pensions Consultants 1987; Sime Hogg Robinson Holdings Ltd (Singapore) 1985; Swaziland Insurance Brokers (Pty) Ltd 1987; Hogg Insurance Group SA (Switzerland) 1985; Hogg Robinson Uganda Ltd 1987; International Insurance Services Gulf (Pvt) Ltd (UAE) 1985; Hogg Venezolana CA (Venezuela) 1990; Associated Brokers International (Pvt) Ltd (Zimbabwe) 1985; Willis Faber Syfrets Holdings (Private) Ltd (Zimbabwe) 1990. *Professional Organisations:* ACT. *Clubs:* Royal Cruising Club. *Recreations:* Sailing, Tennis, Shooting.

MINOWA, T; Partner, Arthur Andersen & Co Chartered Accts.

MINSHULL-FOGG, J; TD; Clerk, Arbitrators' Company.

MINSKY, R; Director, Market-Making, Hoare Govett International Securities.

MINTER, J C; Senior Vice President and Deputy Branch Manager, Bank Julius Baer & Co Ltd, since 1989; Fund Management. *Career:* Baring Brothers & Co Ltd 1972-76; Saudi Arabian Monetary Agency, Advisor 1976-80; Baring Brothers & Co Ltd, Manager 1980-83; Saudi Arabian Monetary Agency, Advisor 1983-85; Baring International Investment Ltd, Director 1985-89; Bank Julius Baer & Co Ltd, SVP 1989-. *Biog: b.* 22 July 1949. *Nationality:* British. *m.* 1983,Diana; 1 s; 1 d. *Educ:* Repton School; University of Birmingham (BA Hons). *Directorships:* Baring International Investment Ltd 1985 (exec); Baring Intl Investment Management Ltd 1988 (exec); Julius Baer Investment Management Ltd 1989 (exec) Managing Director; Julius Baer International 1989 (exec); Julius Baer Investments Ltd 1990 (exec) Managing Director. *Other Activities:* Liveryman, Skinners Company; Member, Lawrence Atwell Committee. *Clubs:* Royal Ocean Racing Club. *Recreations:* Shooting, Sailing, Farming.

MINTER, P A; Director, Holman Franklin Ltd.

MINTO, Bruce; Executive Partner, Dickson Minto WS, since 1985; Corporate Lawyer. *Career:* Dundas & Wilson CS, Solicitors 1979-85. *Biog: b.* 30 October 1957. *Nationality:* British. *m.* 1983, Christine (née Gunn); 2 s. *Educ:* Biggar High School; Edinburgh University (LLB First Class Honours). *Recreations:* Most Sports, Music, Shooting.

MINTON, K J; Chief Executive and Managing Director, Laporte plc, since 1986. *Career:* National Coal Board, Mining Engineer; Unilever, Prod & Devl Exec in UK & France 1960-68; Laporte, Head of Res/Divisional MD/Operations Director/Group MD/Chief Exec

1968-. *Biog: b.* 17 January 1937. *Nationality:* British. *m.* 1961, Mary (née Wilson); 1 s. *Educ:* Leeds University; University College, London (1st Class Hons). *Directorships:* Jeyes plc 1989 (non-exec). *Recreations:* Antique Furniture, Clocks & Porcelain, Walking, Gardening.

MIRAT, Olivier; Deputy General Manager, CPR-Compagnie Parisienne de Réescompte; International Department. *Career:* Banque Indosuez, FX Dealer 1970-80; FX Manager & Treasury 1980-86; Manager Capital Markets 1986-88. *Biog: b.* 30 April 1944. *Nationality:* French. *m.* 1980, Marchal. *Educ:* Université de Paris (Diplômé d'Études Supérieures de Droit); l'Institut d'Etudes Politiques de Paris (Diplômé). *Directorships:* Seccombe Marshall & Campion plc (London) (non-exec); Paresco Inc (New York) (non-exec); IMI-CPR Finance France (non-exec). *Professional Organisations:* Member, French FX Association. *Recreations:* Golf, Skiing.

MIRZA, Aijaz; Group Finance Director & Company Secretary, Byas Mosley & Co Ltd, since 1988; Finance/Legal. *Career:* Clarkson Puckle Group Ltd, Group Financial Controller 1963-87. *Biog: b.* 2 September 1940. *Nationality:* British. *m.* 1969, Qamar; 2 s. *Educ:* St Joseph Convent School, Pakistan; Woolwich Polytechnic, London (BSc Eco). *Directorships:* Byas Mosley & Co Ltd 1988 (exec); Byas Mosley Group Ltd 1989 (exec). *Professional Organisations:* FCCA; MBIM.

MISHCON, The Hon Russell Orde; Partner, S J Berwin & Co, since 1987; Commercial Property. *Career:* Blatchfords, Partner 1972-80; Senior Partner 1974-80; Consultant 1980-83; Russell Mishcon, Senior Partner 1980-87. *Biog: b.* 9 July 1948. *Nationality:* British. *m.* 1975, Marcia (née Leigh); 1 s; 1 d. *Educ:* City of London School; College of Law (Solicitor). *Clubs:* Guards Polo Club (Playing Member).

MISSENDEN, Bryan; Director, N T Evennett and Partners Ltd.

MITAKE, Keiichi; Head of Corporate Finance, Capital Markets, Yamaichi International (Europe) Ltd.

MITCHARD, Ms Shirley (née Chappell); Corporate Tax Partner, Clark Whitehill, since 1987; Business Expansion Scheme Work, Reorganisations, Acquisitions, Disposals & Mergers. *Career:* KPMG Peat Marwick McLintock 1975-81; Qualified as an ACA, Specialising in Tax Post Qualification 1978; Arthur Andersen & Co 1981-85; Corporate Tax Manager 1983-85; Clark Whitehill 1985-. *Biog: b.* 15 February 1953. *Nationality:* British. *m.* (div). *Educ:* Weir Field School, Taunton (now part of Taunton School); Portsmouth Polytechnic (BA Hons Social Administration). *Professional Organisations:* Member, Institute of Chartered Accountants in England and Wales. *Recreations:* Tennis, Gardening, Drawing & Painting.

MITCHELL, A C; Managing Director, Murray Lawrence Members' Agency Limited.

MITCHELL, Alastair John; Group Financial Controller, The MDA Group plc, since 1990; All Financial Functions including International and Domestic Acquisitions/ Expansions. *Career:* Blakemores Chartered Accountants, Audit Manager 1988-89; Westcott Wilson Chartered Accountants, Trainee Chartered Acct/Audit Senior 1983-88. *Biog: b.* 21 December 1962. *Nationality:* British. *m.* 1987, Jane. *Educ:* Sandbach Grammar; Richard Hale, Hertford; City of London Poly. *Directorships:* The MDA Group International Ltd 1990 (exec). *Professional Organisations:* Chartered Accountant (1988). *Recreations:* Golf, Music.

MITCHELL, Bruce W; Senior Vice President & Global Payments Services, Bank of America.

MITCHELL, D J; Chief Executive & Director, Calor Group plc.

MITCHELL, David Oliver Carlyle; Partner, Dickson Minto WS, since 1980; Company Law. *Career:* Dundas & Wilson CS, Solicitor 1982-85; Dickson Minto WS 1985-. *Biog: b.* 1957. *Nationality:* British. *Educ:* Trinity College, Glenalmond; Worcester College, Oxford (BA); Edinburgh University (LLB, DipLP).

MITCHELL, David Smith; TD; Group Secretary, Allied-Lyons plc, since 1987. *Career:* Royal Air Force 1956-58; Secretary of Various Trading Companies within J Lyons & Company Limited 1961-72; J Lyons & Company Limited, Assistant Secretary 1972-83; Secretary 1983-87. *Biog: b.* 5 August 1937. *m.* 1963, Karin (née Hall); 1 s; 1 d. *Educ:* Chesterfield School; Pembroke College, Oxford (MA). *Directorships:* Allied-Lyons Pension Fund Companies 1990 (exec); Maidstone Insurance Company Limited 1990 (exec). *Other Activities:* Territorial Army. *Professional Organisations:* FCIS. *Clubs:* RAF. *Recreations:* Territorial Army.

MITCHELL, Desmond Gerrard; Finance Director, Tranwood plc, since 1990. *Career:* Midland Montagu, Hong Kong, Group Financial Controller 1985-87; Samuel Montagu & Co Ltd, Assistant Director 1987-89. *Biog: Nationality:* British. *m.* 1989, Eleanor; 2 s. *Educ:* Loughborough University (BSc Hons, Banking & Finance). *Professional Organisations:* ACA; ACIB.

MITCHELL, F M; Partner, Slaughter and May.

MITCHELL, G; Partner, Clay & Partners Consulting Actuaries.

MITCHELL, H; Secretary, Wellcome plc.

MITCHELL, J P; Partner, Hammond Suddards, since 1989; Corporate Finance, particulary Mergers and Acquisitions and Venture Capital. *Career:* Cameron Markby Hewitt, Solicitors, Trainee Solicitor subsequently Assistant Solicitor Corporate Finance 1979-85; The Bell Group International Limited, MRH Holmes, a Court International Holding Company, Group Legal Counsel 1986-87; Stevens Drake & Pope, Solicitors, Head of Commercial Department 1987-88; Hammond Suddards, Solicitors, Assistant Solicitor, subsequently Partner, Corporate Finance (especially Mergers and Acquisitions and Venture Capital) 1988-. *Biog: b.* 24 February 1957. *Nationality:* British. *m.* 1985, Janette (née Plumb). *Educ:* Ardingly College, Haywards Heath; Magdalen College, Oxford University (BA Jurisprudence). *Directorships:* LGW plc (Third Market) 1990 (non-exec); Pavilion Computing/Resco Limited 1989 (non-exec). *Professional Organisations:* Solicitor. *Recreations:* Marathon Running, Football, Sports Generally, Walking, Horse Racing.

MITCHELL, John David; Managing Director, Charterhouse Tilney, since 1986; Private Clients. *Career:* Thames Board Mills Mgmnt Trainee 1959-60; Henry Cooke & Son 1960-61. *Biog: b.* 7 March 1942. *Nationality:* British. *m.* 1969, Susan; 1 s; 1 d. *Educ:* Sedbergh.

MITCHELL, Philip Lindsay Rewse; Company Commercial Partner, Lawrence Graham, since 1989; Corporate Finance, Financial Services, Insurance. *Career:* Linklaters & Paines, Assistant Solicitor 1978-85; Clifford Chance, Assistant Solicitor 1985-89. *Biog: b.* 26 June 1946. *Nationality:* British. *m.* 1975, Jackie. *Educ:* Brighton College; University College, London (LLB). *Other Activities:* Former Chairman, Policy & Finance Committee, Tandridge District Council; Former Vice Chairman, Surrey District Councils Association. *Professional Organisations:* Law Society. *Publications:* Insider Dealing and Directors Duties, 2nd Ed, 1989; General Editor, Butterworths Company Law Service; Consulting Editor, Financial Services Law and Practice. *Clubs:* RAC. *Recreations:* Music.

MITCHELL, R C; Director of Investor Relations, Grand Metropolitan plc.

MITCHELL, Roger Paul; Managing Director, Allison Mitchell Partnership Ltd, since 1990. *Biog: b.* 3 February 1951. *Nationality:* British. *m.* 1975, Mary; 1 s; 1 d. *Educ:* (BA Hons Business Studies, DipM). *Directorships:* Money Marketing (Design) Ltd 1984 (exec); Moorgate Marketing Consultants Ltd 1986 (exec); Moorgate Group plc 1986 Co Sec. *Professional Organisations:* MCIM.

MITCHELL, S M; Director Non-Executive, R H M Outhwaite (Underwriting Agencies) Limited.

MITCHELL, Miss S R; Director, Hambros Bank Limited.

MITCHELL, Steven M E; Partner, Beachcroft Stanleys.

MITCHELL-HARRIS, A J; Director, Edwards & Payne (Underwriting Agencies) Limited.

MITCHELL-INNES, Alistair Campbell; Deputy Chairman, H P Bulmer (Holdings) plc, since 1990. *Career:* MacFisheries Ltd, Supermarket Director 1973-75; Walls Meat Co Ltd, Vice Chairman 1975-77; Brooke Bond plc, Chief Executive, Meat Division 1977-79; Brooke Bond Group plc, Director 1979-85; Mabisco Group Ltd, Chief Executive 1985-88. *Biog: b.* 1 March 1934. *Nationality:* British. *m.* 1957, Penelope Ann (née Hill); 1 s; 2 d. *Educ:* Charterhouse; Stanford Business School (Executive Program). *Directorships:* Next plc 1989 (non-exec); Evans Halshaw (Holdings) plc 1989 (non-exec); H P Bulmer (Holdings) plc 1984 (non-exec). *Professional Organisations:* Fellow & Master Member, Institute of Grocery Distribution; Member, Institute of Directors. *Clubs:* MCC, The Berkshire Golf Club, Caledonian Club. *Recreations:* Golf, Cricket.

MITCHENER, A A; Director, Lombard North Central plc.

MITCHINSON, Christopher MacMillan; Managing Director, Salomon Brothers International Limited.

MITFORD-SLADE, Patrick Buxton; Partner, Cazenove & Co, since 1972; Managing Director, Cazenove Money Brokers. *Career:* Royal Green Jackets, Capt 1956-67; RMA Sandhurst, Instructor 1965-67; Cazenove & Co 1968-70; Panel on Takeovers & Mergers, Asst Sec 1970-72. *Biog: b.* 7 September 1936. *Nationality:* British. *m.* 1964, Anne (née Stanton); 1 s; 2 d. *Educ:* Eton College. *Directorships:* The International Stock Exchange 1986; ISE Mutual Reference Ltd 1987 Chm; The International Stock Exchange (London) Inc 1986 Chm; Securities Industry Steering Committee on TAURUS 1988-90 Chm. *Other Activities:* Member of Joint Management Ctee, Central Gilts Office; Chm, City Telecommunications Ctee, 1983; Hon Trustee, The Stock Exchange Clerks' Fund; Chm, The Officers' Assoc. *Professional Organisations:* Member, International Stock Exchange (Council, 1976) Dep Chm 1982-85. *Clubs:* City of London. *Recreations:* Shooting, Fishing, Gardening.

MITTAL, K C; General Manager, The New India Assurance Company Limited.

MIURA, Tatewaki; Chief Representative, The Zenshinren Bank, since 1990; London. *Career:* Ministry of Finance 1957-82; Banking Bureau 1969-71; Minister's Secretariat 1971-73; Representative of Interchange Association, Taipei Office 1973-76; Ministry of Finance, International Finance Bureau 1976-77; Overseas Economic Co-Operation Fund of Japan 1977-88; Director,

Philippine and Korean Division 1977-79; Chief Representative, Jakarta Office 1979-82; Managing Director, African and Latin America Countries 1983-86; Managing Director, Asian Countries 1986-88; Nippon Koei Co Ltd, Director, Co-ordination Department 1988-90. *Biog: b.* 20 December 1933. *Nationality:* Japanese. *m.* 1964; 1 s; 1 d. *Educ:* Waseda University (Batchelor of Political Economics).

MIYAGI, Kakuei; Deputy General Manager, The Taiyo Kobe Bank Ltd.

MIYAKO, Fumio; Deputy Managing Director, DKB International Limited, since 1990; Administration & Compliance. *Career:* The Dai-ichi Kangyo Bank Ltd, Various to Deputy General Manager 1970-90; DKB International Limited, Deputy Managing Director 1990-. *Biog: b.* 24 January 1948. *Nationality:* Japanese. *m.* 1974, Noriko (née Enomoto); 1 s; 1 d. *Educ:* Hitotsubashi University (BA Economics). *Directorships:* DKB International Ltd 1990 (exec). *Professional Organisations:* TSA General Registered Representative, 1990; Japanese Securities Dealers Association, 1987. *Publications:* Co-Author, ABC of M & A 1988 in Japan. *Recreations:* Golf, Tennis.

MIYATA, Nagayoshi; Managing Director of Capital Markets, Daiwa Europe Ltd, since 1990; European & Middle East Operations. *Career:* Joined Daiwa Securities Co Ltd, International Investment Services Dept 1977-78; Director 1983-85; Managing Director 1985-88; Daiwa Securities Co Ltd Tokyo, Deputy General Manager, General Manager, International Finance Department 1988; General Manager, Capital Markets Dept/International Investment Banking Dept 1990. *Biog: b.* 4 December 1945. *m.* Sachiko; 2 s. *Educ:* Jochi University, Japan (Economics); Kölner University, Germany (Economics). *Directorships:* Chairman of Daiwa Europe (Deutschland) GmbH Frankfurt.

MIZEN, Piers M; Director, Kleinwort Benson Securities Limited, since 1990; European Dept. *Biog: b.* 13 April 1959. *Nationality:* British. *m.* 1990, Julia (née Deadman). *Educ:* Westminster School; Exeter University.

MOAR, J M; Director, Land Securities plc.

MOBBS, Sir Nigel; DL; Chairman & Chief Executive, Slough Estates plc, since 1976. *Career:* Hillier Parker 1959-60; Slough Estates plc 1960; Director (Executive) 1963-71; Managing Director 1971-76; Chairman & Chief Executive 1976-; Director of Subsidiary Companies in UK, Belguim, France, Germany, Australia, Canada, USA. *Biog: b.* 22 September 1937. *Nationality:* British. *m.* 1961, Pamela Jane (née Berry); 1 s; 2 d. *Educ:* Marlborough College; Christ Church, Oxford. *Directorships:* Barclays Bank plc 1979 (non-exec); Kingfisher plc 1982 (non-exec) Dep Chairman;

Cookson Group plc 1985 (non-exec); Howard De Walden Estates Ltd 1989 (non-exec); BZW Holdings Ltd 1986 (non-exec); Groundwork Foundation 1990 Chairman; Charterhouse Group plc 1974-83 Chairman; PSA Advisory Board CDOE 1980-86 Chairman. *Other Activities:* Chairman, Aims of Industry; Chairman of Council, University of Buckingham; President, British Council for Offices; Master, Company of Spectacle Makers; Chairman, DTI Advisory Panel on Deregulation; Commonwealth War Graves Commission; Hon DSc (City University). *Professional Organisations:* CBIM; Hon Member, Royal Institution of Chartered Surveyors; Hon Fellow, College of Estate Management. *Clubs:* Brooks, Toronto Club (Canada), York Club (Canada).

MOBERLY, William James Dorward; Partner, Pannell Kerr Forster, since 1966; Corporate Advisory Department Litigation Support. *Career:* Ball Baker Deed, Articled Clerk 1960-63; Thomson McLintock, Qualified Assistant Audit Department 1963-66; Ball Baker Deed (subsequently Ball Baker Leake, merged with Pannell Kerr Forster in 1989) Partner 1966-89. *Biog: b.* 4 September 1938. *Nationality:* British. *m.* 1970, Angela (née Mason); 2 s. *Educ:* Blundells School (Scholar); Sidney Sussex College, Cambridge (Scholar)(MA). *Directorships:* Thousand & One Lamps Ltd 1975 (non-exec). *Other Activities:* Liveryman, Curriers Company; Chairman, Conciliation Committee of London Chartered Accountants. *Professional Organisations:* Fellow, Institute of Chartered Accountants in England and Wales. *Publications:* Partnership Management, 1982. *Clubs:* Rye Golf Club, St Georges Hill Golf Club. *Recreations:* Golf, Gardening, Bridge.

MOBSBY, Peter; Assistant General Manager - Finance & Operations, Union Bank of Finland Ltd.

MOCKRIDGE, Michael John; Partner, Clifford Chance, since 1967; Company Law. *Career:* Coward Chance, Articled Clerk 1959-62; Solicitor 1962-67. *Biog: b.* 26 May 1936. *m.* (div); 1 s; 2 d. *Educ:* Shene Grammar School; Balliol College, Oxford (BA Hons History). *Directorships:* Working Mens College Corporation 1987; Mental Health Foundation 1989; Philip Morris Limited 1976-87. *Professional Organisations:* Law Society. *Clubs:* Garrick, Reform.

MOFFITT, Douglas; Financial Editor, LBC Radio and Independent Radio News, since 1975; Financial News Programming. *Career:* Investors Review, City Editor 1971-74; Financial World, Executive Editor 1970-74; LBC Radio and Independent Radio News, Financial Correspondent 1974-75. *Biog: b.* 13 February 1946. *Nationality:* British. *Educ:* St Catherine's College, Oxford (BA Modern History). *Directorships:* Ellastone plc 1989 (non-exec); Inflight Productions Ltd 1979 (non-exec); WMRS Studios Ltd 1982 (non-exec); In-Flight Video Ltd 1984 (non-exec). *Other Activities:* Trustee,

Assoc of Independent Radio Contractors' Industry Pension Scheme. *Publications:* The Family Money Book.

MOGI, Y; Deputy General Manager Administration, The Mitsubishi Bank Ltd.

MOHAMED, I; Director, Sharjah Investment Co (UK) Ltd.

MOHARRAM, C; Director, Allied Trust Bank Limited.

MOIR, Alastair Clive; Director, Panmure Gordon Bankers Limited.

MOIR, Ms Christine; Financial Editor, The Observer.

MOIR, Lance Stuart; Head of Corporate Finance & Planning, Storehouse plc.

MÖLLER, George Andre; Managing Director, International Clearing Services Ltd, since 1987. *Career:* Amsterdam-Rotterdam Bank NV, Corporate Finance/Syndicated Loans 1974-84; International Treasury; Deli Universal Inc, Corporate Treasurer & Divisional Controller 1984-87. *Biog: b.* 29 December 1947. *Nationality:* Dutch. *m.* 1974, Saskia (née Van Brederode); 2 d. *Educ:* University of Groningen, Netherlands (Econ & Bus Admin); University of Pennsylvania, USA (Management for Bankers). *Directorships:* Anglo Options Ltd 1988 (non-exec); Pierson Heldring & Pierson Holdings Limited; Pierson Heldring & Pierson Securities (UK) Limited; Pierson Heldring & Pierson (UK) Limited; Pierson Management & Licensing (UK) Limited; Pierson Heldring & Pierson Nominees (UK) Limited; International Clearing Services Limited; ICS Nominees Limited; Anglo Pierson Options Limited. *Publications:* Multicurrency Investments, 1983. *Recreations:* Hockey, Skiing, Walking.

MOLSON, R Ian; Executive Director, Credit Suisse First Boston Ltd; Head of Investment Banking. *Career:* Credit Suisse First Boston Limited, Executive Director, Member of the Operating Ctee, in Charge of Investment Banking Product Groups (excluding M&A) 1977-. *Biog: b.* 17 February 1919. *Nationality:* Canadian. *m.* Verena Brigid (née Cayzer); 1 s; 1 d. *Educ:* Harvard University (BA Honours). *Directorships:* Credit Suisse First Boston Limited (exec). *Clubs:* Harry's Bar, Annabel's.

MOLYNEUX, John Frederick; Mergers & Acquisitions Director, English Trust Co Ltd, since 1981; Corporate Finance. *Career:* Stock Exchange, Sub-Editor, Year Book 1967-68; Feuchtwanger (London) Ltd (now Greyhound Guaranty Ltd), Investment Mgr 1969-74; Spence Veitch Attache 1974; Montagu Loebl Stanley Attache 1974-78; English Trust, Investment Mgr 1978-. *Biog: b.* 18 December 1946. *Nationality:* British. *m.* 1971,

Margaret (née Fenn); 2 s; 1 d. *Educ:* Kimbolton, Hele's, Exeter. *Directorships:* PK English Trust (Investment Management) Ltd 1987 (exec); Australia Investment Trust plc 1987 (non-exec). *Clubs:* Annabels. *Recreations:* Sport.

MONAGHAN, R L; Group Finance Director, Philipp and Lion Ltd, since 1989. *Career:* John M Winter & Sons, Articles 1976-80; Moore Stephens & Co, Audit Senior 1980-84; Coopers & Lybrand, Management Consultancy 1981-84; Mundogas UK Ltd (Oil/Gas/Petrochemical Trader & Shipping Company), Group Finance Director 1984-87; County NatWest Investment Bank, Group Management Accountant 1987-88; Monaghan & Co Chartered Accountants, Partner 1988-89. *Biog: b.* 11 October 1952. *Nationality:* British. *m.* 1985; 1 s; 1 d. *Educ:* CNAA Degree, Sunderland (BSc Joint Hons Class 2-1 Economics/Geology). *Directorships:* Philipp and Lion Limited 1989 (exec). *Professional Organisations:* Institute, Chartered Accountants in England & Wales; Association, Middle East Accountants.

MONAHAN, David; Senior Manager Corporate Banking & Finance, Kredietbank NV, since 1988; Head of Banking & Finance Division. *Career:* Allied Irish Investment Bank, Banking Executive 1978-80; Irish Intercontinental Bank/Kredietbank International Group, Banking Manager 1980-85; Kredietbank NV London, Senior Manager 1985-. *Biog: b.* 4 October 1951. *Nationality:* Irish. *m.* 1982, Yvonne (née Lane); 3 d. *Educ:* University College Dublin (BA, MA Economics); Harvard Business School (MBA). *Directorships:* Krediet Finance (UK) Ltd 1986 (exec). *Clubs:* Milltown Golf Club, Fitzwilliam Lawn Tennis Club, Overseas Bankers Club.

MONCK, Nicholas; 2nd Permanent Secretary (Public Expenditure), HM Treasury, since 1990. *Career:* HM Treasury, Principal Private Sec to Chancellor 1976-77; Under Sec, Nationalised Industries 1977-80; Under Sec, Home Finance 1980-84; Deputy Secretary (Industry) 1984-90. *Biog: b.* 9 March 1935. *Nationality:* British. *m.* 1960, Elizabeth (née Kirwan); 3 s. *Educ:* Eton College; King's College, Cambridge (BA Hons, BSc); University of Pennsylvania; London School of Economics (Econ). *Directorships:* BSC Board 1978-80. *Clubs:* Battersea Amateur Football Club.

MONEY, Anthony John; Director, C E Heath plc, since 1986; Managing Director, C E Heath (Insurance Broking) Limited. *Career:* C E Heath plc, Subsidiary Company Director 1960-75; Fielding Juggins Money & Stewart Ltd, Director 1975-86. *Biog: b.* 22 March 1943. *Nationality:* British. *m.* 1982, Sally Jane (née Fielden); 3 d. *Clubs:* Old Parkonians Association.

MONEY-COUTTS, David Burdett; Chairman, Coutts & Co.

MONK, D W; Assistant Director, J K Buckenham Limited.

MONK, James Stuart Richard; Director, Leslie & Godwin.

MONK, Paul Nicholas; Partner, Allen & Overy.

MONK, Terence Charles; Managing Director, Bradstock Financial Services Ltd, since 1986; Financial Services. *Career:* Commercial Union, Clerk/Inspector/Life Superintendent 1960-77; UK Provident, Branch Manager (Maidstone, Reading & City), London Area Manager 1977-86. *Biog: b.* 10 August 1943. *Nationality:* English. *m.* 1966, Christine (née Roberts); 1 d. *Educ:* Ealing Commercial College. *Directorships:* Bradstock Financial Services Ltd 1986 (exec). *Other Activities:* Chairman (1990) of Independent Financial Advisors Forum (a Small City-Based Group of IFAs). *Recreations:* Golf, Theatre.

MONNAS, A; Executive Director, Daiwa Europe Limited.

MONNERY, Jonathan Christopher; Director, Security Pacific Hoare Govett, since 1988; Market Making. *Career:* Montagu Loebl Stanley (Stockbrokers), Stock Exchange Dealer 1983-84; Statham Duff Stoop (Stockbrokers), Stock Exchange Dealer 1984-85; C T Pulley (Stockjobbers), Stock Exchange Dealer, Dealing in Oil Shares & Large Industrial Companies 1985-. *Biog: b.* 27 November 1963. *Nationality:* British. *m.* 1985, Sally (née Holden); 2 d. *Educ:* Portslade School and Community College. *Directorships:* Hoare Govett Securities 1988 (exec). *Professional Organisations:* Member, Stock Exchange. *Recreations:* Football, Squash, Most Other Sports.

MONNICKENDAM, Peter F J; Director, Bradstock Blunt & Thompson Ltd.

MONRO, Fiona; Director of Communications, FIMBRA, since 1986; Press, Public & Membership Relations. *Career:* Stewart Wrightson, PR Officer 1974-78; British Insurance Brokers Assoc, PR Officer 1978-86; Money Marketing, Snr Reporter 1986-87. *Biog: b.* 8 February 1946. *m.* 1976, Ian Smith.

MONTAGUE, Adrian; Partner, Linklaters & Paines.

MONTAGUE, J A V; Group Treasurer, Sedgwick Group plc.

MONTAGUE-JOHNSTONE, Roland Richard; Partner, Slaughter and May, since 1973; Company and Commercial Law. *Career:* The Kings Royal Rifle Corps 1958-62. *Biog: b.* 22 January 1941. *Nationality:* British. *m.* 1968, Sara (née Whitehead); 2 s. *Educ:* Eton College. *Professional Organisations:* The Law Society. *Clubs:* Celer et Audax, Royal Green Jackets, The English Speaking Union. *Recreations:* Reading, Walking, Gardening.

MONTGOMERIE, Archibald George; The Earl of Eglington & Winton; Deputy Chairman, Gerard & National Holdings plc, since 1980. *Career:* Grieveson Grant & Co, Ptnr 1957-72; Gerrard & National, MD 1972-. *Biog: b.* 27 August 1939. *Nationality:* British. *m.* 1964, Marion Carolina (née Dunn-Yarker); 4 s. *Educ:* Eton College. *Directorships:* The Mercantile & General Reinsurance Co plc 1977 (non-exec); Charities Investment Managers Ltd 1984 (non-exec); The First Scottish American Trust plc (now called Dunedin Income Growth Investment Trust) 1985 (non-exec); The Northern American Trust plc (now called Dunedin Worldwide Investment Trust) 1985 (non-exec); DFM Holdings Ltd 1988 (non-exec).

MONTGOMERY, George H; Director, Carswell Ltd.

MONTGOMERY, J M; Clerk, Salters' Company.

MONTGOMERY, John Duncan; Member, Monopolies and Mergers Commission, since 1989. *Career:* Beecham Products, Legal Adviser 1974-75; Shell UK Limited, Head of Legal Division 1975-88; Company Secretary 1979-88. *Biog: b.* 12 November 1928. *Nationality:* British. *m.* 1956, Pauline Mary (née Sutherland); 2 d. *Educ:* Kings College School, Wimbledon; LSE (LLB, LLM London). *Other Activities:* Liveryman, Worshipful Company of Loriners. *Professional Organisations:* Solicitor; Member, Law Society; Member, International Bar Association. *Clubs:* MCC, City Livery Club.

MONTLEMAN, Brian G; Director, J Trevor, Montleman & Poland Ltd.

MONY, S V; Chairman/Managing Director, The New India Assurance Company Limited.

MOODEY, K G; Deputy General Manager, Operations, Nomura Bank International plc.

MOODY, Peter Edward; CBE; Director, Prudential Corporation.

MOODY, Tony; Managing Director, Corporate Finance, Continental Bank NA.

MOON, Alfred W; General Manager, Consumer Banking, The Royal Bank of Scotland plc, since 1990. *Professional Organisations:* FIB (Scot); Member, Institute of Management Services.

MOON, James Philip; Director, Baring Brothers & Co Limited, since 1990; Corporate Finance. *Career:* Lazard Brothers & Co Ltd, Assistant Director, Corporate Finance 1985-90. *Biog: b.* 14 May 1954. *Nationality:*

British. *Educ:* Cheltenham College; Pembroke College, Oxford (MA Hons).

MOON, P; Partner, Nabarro Nathanson.

MOONEY, Kevin Michael; Partner, Simmons & Simmons, since 1975; Senior Partner in Intellectual Property Group. *Biog: b.* 14 November 1945. *Nationality:* British. *m.* Maureen (née O'Hara); 2 s; 1 d. *Educ:* Cardinal Vaughan School; Bristol University (LLB). *Other Activities:* Member of City of London Subcommittee on Intellectual Property; Member, AIPLA; Member, AIPPI; Member, Patent Trade Mark & Copyright Section of ABA; Member, USTA. *Professional Organisations:* Member, Law Society; Solicitor of Supreme Court. *Recreations:* Gardening, Watching QPR.

MOORE, (Alan) David; Director, Midland Montagu Asset Management, since 1987; International Fixed Income, Investment Management. *Career:* Morgan Grenfell & Co Ltd, Manager 1978-86; Manufacturers Hanover Ltd, Associate Dir 1986-87. *Biog: b.* 8 May 1958. *Nationality:* British. *m.* 1982, Gabriel (née Anderson); 1 s; 3 d. *Educ:* Shrewsbury School. *Directorships:* Midland Montagu Asset Management 1987 (exec). *Recreations:* Music, Sailing.

MOORE, Alan Edward; CBE; Director of Corporate Banking and Treasury, Lloyds Bank plc, since 1988. *Career:* Glyn Mills & Co, FX Dealing Room 1953-61; RAF National Service 1954-56; Glyn Mills & Co, Various 1961-71; Williams & Glyns, Dep Dir 1971-74; Bahrain Monetary Agency, Dir Gen 1974-79; Lloyds Bank, International Dir, Middle East 1980-81; Treasurer 1981-84; Lloyds Bank plc, Dir of Treasury 1985-88; Director 1989-. *Biog: b.* 5 June 1936. *Nationality:* British. *m.* 1961, Margaret (née Beckley); 1 s; 1 d. *Educ:* Berkhamsted School. *Directorships:* Subsidiary Companies of Lloyds Bank plc. *Professional Organisations:* AIB; ACIS; FCT. *Recreations:* Photography, Steam Railway Preservation.

MOORE, C H; Partner, Raphael Zorn Hemsley Ltd.

MOORE, Christopher M; Director, Robert Fleming Holdings Ltd, since 1986; Corporate Finance, Capital Markets. *Career:* Price Waterhouse Articled Clerk/ACA 1966-70; Robert Fleming Inc Exec 1970-72; Lazard Brothers Exec 1972-73; Jardine Fleming & Co Ltd Dir 1973-76; Robert Fleming & Co Ltd Dir 1976-. *Biog: b.* 1 December 1944. *Nationality:* British. *m.* 1972, Charlotte (née Glessing); 3 s. *Educ:* Winchester College; Pembroke College, Cambridge (MA). *Professional Organisations:* FCA. *Clubs:* Leander, Pratt's, White's. *Recreations:* Riding, Flying, Tennis, Music, Books.

MOORE, G K; Director, Steel Burrill Jones Group plc.

MOORE, G S; Partner, Holman Fenwick & Willan, since 1990; Marine/Aviation Litigation. *Career:* Kennedys, Solicitor 1978-82; Ince & Co, Solicitor 1982-85. *Biog: b.* 22 February 1955. *Nationality:* British. *Educ:* RGS Worcester; University of Surrey (BSc Linguistics & International Studies); City of London Polytechnic (MA Business Law). *Professional Organisations:* Member, Law Society; Member, International Bar Association. *Recreations:* Cricket, Tennis, Flying, Photography, Creative Writing.

MOORE, George Henry; TD; General Manager (Banking), Northern Bank Ltd, since 1986. *Career:* Northern Bank Ltd, General Manager (Republic of Ireland) 1985-86; Northern Bank Ltd, General Manager (Banking) 1986-. *Biog: b.* 29 August 1935. *Nationality:* British. *m.* 1964, Helen; 2 d. *Educ:* Masonic School. *Directorships:* Belfast Banking Comp Ltd 1986 (non-exec); Belfast Bank Executor & Trustee Co Ltd 1986 (non-exec); Northern Bank Development Corp Ltd 1986 (non-exec); Northern Bank Leasing Ltd 1986 Chairman; Northern Bank Nominees Ltd 1986 (non-exec); Northern Bank Financial Services Ltd 1986 (non-exec); Northern Bank Executor & Trustee Co Ltd 1986 Chairman; Northern Bank Factors Ltd 1987 (non-exec); Northern Bank Equipment Leasing Ltd 1988 Chairman; Northern Bank Commercial Leasing Ltd 1988 Chairman; Northern Bank Industrial Leasing Ltd 1988 Chairman; Northern Bank Insurance Services Ltd 1988 (non-exec); Causeway Credit Ltd 1988 Chairman. *Other Activities:* Northern Ireland Chamber of Commerce and Industry. *Clubs:* Ulster Reform Club, Royal Ulster Yacht Club. *Recreations:* Gardening.

MOORE, M D; Managing Director (Investment Management), Bankers Trust Company.

MOORE, Neil McGowan; Director, Hambros Bank Ltd, since 1987; Investment Management. *Career:* Charterhouse Japhet Ltd, Senior Investment Manager 1969-80; Charterhouse Japhet Investment Management Ltd, Director 1980-83; Caviapen Investments Ltd, Managing Director 1983-86. *Biog: b.* 3 February 1935. *Nationality:* British. *m.* 1967, Fleur (née Hackett); 2 s; 1 d. *Educ:* The Leys School; St John's College, Oxford (BA). *Directorships:* Hambros Bank Ltd 1987 (exec); Hambros Unit Trust Managers Ltd 1986 (exec). *Other Activities:* Chairman, The Rainer Foundation. *Professional Organisations:* Associate Member, Society of Investment Analysts. *Clubs:* Oxford Union. *Recreations:* Beachcombing.

MOORE, Nicholas; Partner, Hill Taylor Dickinson, since 1976; Head of Employment Unit. *Biog: b.* 22 December 1947. *Nationality:* British. *m.* 1979, Sally; 2 s; 2 d. *Educ:* Oundle School; Trinity College, Cambridge (MA Hons). *Other Activities:* Freeman, City of London; Liveryman, Worshipful Company of Pattenmakers. *Professional Organisations:* Solicitor of the Supreme Court. *Recreations:* Riding, Gardening, Family.

MOORE, Nigel Sandford Johnson; Regional Managing Partner Eastern Europe, Ernst & Young, since 1988. *Career:* Buckley Hall Devin & Co, Articled Clerk & Snr 1962-68; Ernst & Young, Snr to Ptnr 1968-. *Biog: b.* 12 April 1944. *Nationality:* British. *m.* 1969, Elizabeth Ann (née Bowker); 1 s; 2 d. *Educ:* Radley College. *Professional Organisations:* FCA; Institute of Directors. *Clubs:* City of London, The Pilgrims. *Recreations:* Opera, Ballet, Golf, Tennis.

MOORE, Professor Peter Gerald; TD; Professor, London Business School, since 1965. *Career:* University College, London Lecturer 1951-56; National Coal Board, Asst Economic Adviser 1956-58; Reed International, Chief Statistician 1958-65; London Business School, Principal 1984-89. *Biog: b.* 5 April 1928. *Nationality:* British. *m.* 1958, Sonja (née Thomas); 2 s; 1 d. *Educ:* King's College School, Wimbledon; University College, London (BSc, PhD); Heriot-Watt University (DSc Hon). *Directorships:* Martin Paterson Associates 1984-89 (non-exec); Copeman Paterson 1978-87 (non-exec); Shell UK 1969-72 (non-exec); EIF Aquitane Holdings (UK) 1989 (non-exec). *Other Activities:* Council for Mgmnt Educ & Dev Working Party on Codes of Practice; Council for Hong Kong University of Science & Tech 1986-; Tech Adviser to Wilson Ctee on City Institutions 1977-80; Council of University College London 1988; Member, Review Body of Doctors and Dentists Renumeration 1971-89; Member, Court of Assistants, Tallow Chandlers Company 1986-; Companion of the British Institute of Management 1986. *Professional Organisations:* FIA (Pres 1984-86); Fellow, Royal Statistical Society (Hon Sec 1968-74, Pres 1989-). *Publications:* Principles of Statistical Techniques, 1958; Basic Operational Research, 1968; Anatomy of Decisions, 1976; The Business of Risk, 1983. *Clubs:* Athenaeum. *Recreations:* Golf, Walking, Travel (particularly by Train).

MOORE, Philip Brian Cecil; The Rt Hon Lord Moore of Wolvercote; Director, General Accident Fire and Life Assurance Corp.

MOORE, R R C; Director, Hill Samuel Bank Limited.

MOORE, Richard Dalzell; Partner & Member of Management Group, Bacon & Woodrow, since 1975; Employee Benefits & Communications. *Career:* Bacon & Woodrow, Actuarial Trainee 1968-70; Bacon, Woodrow & De Souza (Trinidad, West Indies), Actuarial Trainee 1971-73; Actuary 1973-74; Bacon & Woodrow, Actuary 1974-75. *Biog: b.* 25 April 1946. *Nationality:* British. *m.* 1969, Christine (née Peverley); 1 s; 1 d. *Educ:* The Royal School, Armagh, N Ireland; Emmanuel College, Cambridge (MA). *Directorships:* Triskel Communications Ltd 1985 (non-exec) Chm; Combined Actuarial Performance Services Ltd 1985-88 (non-exec). *Other Activities:* Secretary/Treasurer, International Association of Consulting Actuaries (1986-). *Professional Organisations:* FIA; FPMI. *Recreations:* Bridge, Classical Music, Theatre.

MOORE, Richard Hobart John de Courcy; Senior Partner, Moore Stephens, since 1989. *Career:* Moore Stephens, Senior Partner 1989-; London Managing Partner 1987-89; Partner 1975-87. *Biog: b.* 31 August 1949. *Nationality:* British. *m.* 1977, Lucy (née Sefton-Smith); 1 s. *Educ:* Stowe. *Directorships:* Crossburn Trustees Limited 1980 (exec); Snow Hill Trustees Limited 1987 (exec). *Other Activities:* Liveryman, The Vintners' Company; Liveryman, The Worshipful Company of Shipwrights. *Professional Organisations:* FCA. *Clubs:* Boodles, MCC. *Recreations:* Real Tennis, Squash, Cricket.

MOORE, Ronald Clive; Executive Director, Banque Arabe et Internationale D'Investissement, since 1987; Head of Property Division. *Career:* Barclays Bank plc, Various, Branch Management 1962-77; IMC Ltd (Export Consultancy), Director 1977-82; National Girobank, Senior Management 1982-83; BAII 1983-. *Biog: b.* 28 December 1944. *Nationality:* British. *m.* 1980, Diane Heather (née Taylor); 1 s; 1 d. *Educ:* Queen Elizabeth Grammar School, Penrith, Cumbria. *Directorships:* BAII Property Ltd 1988 MD; Hillgate Securities Ltd 1988 (exec); Geldercliff Construction Ltd 1990 (exec). *Professional Organisations:* ACIB. *Recreations:* Sailing, Clay Pigeon Shooting.

MOORE, S R; Executive Director, Finance Division, County NatWest Ltd, since 1988; Corporate Banking. *Career:* County NatWest, Regional Director, Manchester 1985-88; Local Director, Manchester 1982-85; Executive, Manchester 1978-82; Executive, London 1971-78. *Biog: b.* 17 December 1947. *Nationality:* British. *m.* 1972, Katharine (née Rankin). *Educ:* St Joseph's College, Blackpool. *Professional Organisations:* ACIB. *Clubs:* Hertford-Ware Athletic Club.

MOORE, Trevor Anthony; Partner, Freshfields, since 1987. *Career:* Dawson & Co Articled Clerk & Asst Solicitor 1979-81; Freshfields Mgr 1981-87. *Biog: b.* 3 February 1957. *Educ:* Christ's Hospital; St Catharines's College, Cambridge (MA). *Professional Organisations:* City of London Law Society; The Law Society. *Recreations:* Long Distance Running, Squash, French/France.

MOORES, Peter; Director, Singer & Friedlander.

MOORSOM, Patrick William Pierre; Vice Chairman, Guinness Mahon & Co Ltd, since 1988; Chairman of the Management Committee of the Bank. *Career:* Cayzer Limited, Managing Director 1981-87; Barclays Merchant Bank, Director and Head of Corporate Finance 1978-81; Rothschild Intercontinental Bank, Director 1972-78; Galbraith Wrightson Ltd, Director 1968-72; Arthur Andersen & Co, Chartered Accountant 1964-68. *Biog: b.* 30 October 1942. *Nationality:* French.

m. 1965, Dominique (née Leroy); 1 s; 3 d. *Educ:* Downside School; Jesus College, Cambridge (MA). *Directorships:* Guinness Mahon (Guernsey) Ltd 1987 Chairman; Guinness and Mahon Ltd, Dublin 1987 Vice Chairman; Regent Inns plc 1988 Chairman; Lockton Superstores plc 1989 Director. *Professional Organisations:* Fellow, Institute of Chartered Accountants. *Recreations:* Golf, Tennis.

MOOTHAM, Dolf C; Finance Director, TSB Group plc, since 1988. *Career:* Hill Samuel Bank Ltd, Dir 1967-; Hill Samuel Group plc, Dir 1978-. *Biog: b.* 2 August 1933. *Nationality:* British. *Educ:* Bryanston School; Trinity College, Cambridge (BA). *Directorships:* UIC Insurance Co 1982 (non-exec). *Clubs:* Brooks's.

MORAN, John; Director, County NatWest Ventures Limited, since 1989; North West of England. *Career:* County NatWest 1978-89; County NatWest Ltd, Regional Director 1989-. *Biog: b.* 26 June 1952. *Nationality:* British. *m.* 1973, Anne; 3 s; 1 d. *Other Activities:* Associate, Chartered Institute of Bankers. *Clubs:* St James Club (Manchester).

MORANT, Stephen Peter; Partner, Cazenove & Co, since 1983; Japan/Korea. *Professional Organisations:* FCA

MORBIN, R J; Director, Arbuthnot Latham Bank Limited.

MORDAUNT, Gerald Charles; Chairman, CL-Alexanders Laing & Cruickshank.

MORGAN, Charles Pearce; Partner, Allen & Overy.

MORGAN, D; Secretary, Royal Insurance Holdings plc.

MORGAN, D L; Director, M & G Investment Management Limited.

MORGAN, David L; Partner, Touche Ross & Co.

MORGAN, David R P; Partner, Beachcroft Stanleys.

MORGAN, Geoff; Managing Director, Lloyds Merchant Bank Ltd, since 1989; Personnel and Support Services. *Career:* Ford Motor Company Ltd, Mgr, Organisation & Personnel Planning 1968-78; Morgan Guaranty Trust Co of New York, VP, Personnel 1978-86. *Biog: b.* 16 February 1945. *Nationality:* British. *m.* 1968, Elizabeth (née Mably); 1 s; 1 d. *Educ:* Hathershaw Technical Grammar School; Sheffield University (BA Hons). *Directorships:* Lloyds Merchant Bank Ltd 1986 (exec); London Human Resource Group Ltd 1989 (exec). *Other Activities:* Member, Personnel Committee, British Merchant Banking & Investment Houses Association. *Recreations:* Most Sports.

MORGAN, Gwilym R; Partner, MacNair Mason.

MORGAN, J M; Director, Lombard North Central plc.

MORGAN, Dr J P; Director, W H Smith Group plc.

MORGAN, J R; Partner, Ernst & Young.

MORGAN, John Alfred; Chief Executive, IMRO Ltd.

MORGAN, John B; Partner, Booth & Co.

MORGAN, P W L; Director, National Provident Institution.

MORGAN, Peter; Business Correspondent, BBC TV.

MORGAN, Peter Gerard; Business Partner, Clyde & Co, since 1973. *Biog: b.* 3 December 1945. *Nationality:* British. *m.* 1971, Hilary (née Dow); 3 d. *Educ:* St Edmunds College, Ware; Exeter University (LLB). *Other Activities:* Chairman, Hertford Citizens Advice Bureau; Member, Committee of Hertfordshire County Cricket Association and Manager Hertfordshire U25 side; Vice-President, Hertford Rugby Football Club; Vice-President, Hertford Cricket Club; Member, the Hertfordshire Society of Rugby Union Football Referees. *Professional Organisations:* Solicitor (England & Hong Kong); Member, Institute of Petroleum. *Recreations:* Cricket, Golf, Fly Fishing, Lepidoptery, Cartophily, Rugby Refereeing.

MORGAN, Peter J; Partner, Touche Ross & Co.

MORGAN, Peter Jerome; Partner, Bacon & Woodrow, since 1980; International Benefit Consulting. *Biog: b.* 9 July 1950. *Nationality:* British. *m.* 1981, Elizabeth (née Rowley). *Educ:* St John's College, Cambridge (MA). *Professional Organisations:* FIA; MAAA.

MORGAN, R S; Partner, Grimley J R Eve.

MORI, Minoru; Chairman & Chief Executive, Daiwa Europe Limited, since 1989. *Career:* Daiwa Securities (Tokyo) 1961; (America), Exec Vice-Pres 1972-78; (Tokyo), Mgr to Gen Mgr 1978-86. *Biog: b.* 1 March 1938. *Nationality:* Japanese. *Educ:* Waseda University, Tokyo, Japan (BA). *Directorships:* Daiwa Securities (Tokyo) 1990 MD. *Professional Organisations:* Mem, International Stock Exchange; Principal, National Association of Securities Dealers; Registered Representative on Tokyo Stock Exchange. *Recreations:* Golf, Playing Go, Shogi.

MORIARTY, Brian; Executive Director, Fixed Interest, Yamaichi International (Europe) Ltd, since 1983. *Career:* James Capel & Co, Chief Eurobond Dealer 1967-76; Burns Fry Ltd, Govt Bond Dealer 1977-80; Deutshe Bank AG, Manager, Bond Sales 1980-83; Yamaichi International (Europe), Exec Director, Bonds 1983-. *Biog: b.* 24 March 1943. *Nationality:* British. *m.* 1982, Karen; 2 s; 1 d. *Educ:* Ridgeways School, Wimbledon.

MORIGUCHI, Takahiro; Managing Director, Bank of Tokyo Capital Markets Limited, since 1988. *Career:* Bank of Tokyo, Various Business Experiences, Corp Fin Foreign Exchange, Marketing 1967-80; The Bank of Tokyo Trust Co, Securities Dept VP, Mgr 1980-83; Bank of Tokyo Ltd (Personnel Division) Dep General Mgr 1983-86; (Capital Market Division) Snr Managing Officer 1986-87; (Head of Trading & Sales) Dep Managing Dir 1987-88; Bank of Tokyo Capital Markets Ltd Managing Director, Pres 1988. *Biog: b.* 22 May 1944. *Nationality:* Japanese. *m.* 1968, Midori (née Kitano); 2 d. *Educ:* Kobe University, Tokyo (BA). *Directorships:* Bank of Tokyo International 1988 (non-exec); Bank of Tokyo Capital Markets 1987 (exec); Euro-Clear Clearance System plc 1988 (exec); Tokyo & Detroit Eurodeal (Continental) AG, Switzerland 1988 (exec). *Other Activities:* TSA Capital Market Ctee; LIFFE Membership & Rules Ctee; EBA Capital Market Ctee. *Clubs:* Richmond Golf Club. *Recreations:* Golf.

MORISHIGE, Tetsuo; Managing Director, Daiwa Bank (Capital Management) Ltd.

MORITA, O; Deputy General Manager - Asset Management, Nomura Bank International plc.

MORIYAMA, J T; Compliance Officer, Wako International (Europe) Ltd.

MORLAND, Michael H; Director, Bradstock Blunt & Crawley Ltd.

MORLEY, David Howard; Partner, Allen & Overy, since 1988; Banking & Capital Markets, Asset Financing, Securitisation. *Career:* Allen & Overy, Asst Solicitor 1982-87. *Biog: b.* 21 September 1956. *Nationality:* British. *m.* 1982, Susan Diana (née Radcliffe); 2 s; 1 d. *Educ:* Queen's Park High School, Chester; St John's College, Cambridge (MA). *Other Activities:* City of London Law Society. *Recreations:* Sailing, Literature, Mountain Walking.

MORLEY, J; Finance Director & General Manager, Guardian Royal Exchange plc, since 1990; Finance. *Career:* Avis Europe plc, Finance Director & Deputy Chief Executive 1976-89; Arthur Andersen & Co 1970-76. *Biog: b.* 19 February 1949. *Nationality:* English. *Educ:* Winchester College; Imperial College of Science & Technology (Botany 2:i). *Directorships:* Various Subsidiary & Associated Companies. *Other Activities:* ABI, Tax Supervision & Financial Reporting Committee. *Professional Organisations:* FCA. *Clubs:* Carlton.

MORLEY, John Robert; Senior Manager, The Hongkong and Shanghai Banking Corporation, since 1988; Head of UK Corporate Banking Division. *Career:* McKinsey & Co, Consultant 1969-71; Stern Holding, Group Dir, Subsidiaries 1971-73; Dares Estate Ltd, Director 1973-78; Marine Midland Bank NA, VP 1978-82; Anthony Gibbs & Sons Ltd, Dir 1982-88. *Biog: b.* 9 November 1945. *Nationality:* British. *m.* 1973, Brenda M (née Heasman); 2 d. *Educ:* Bushey Grammar School, Herts; Gonville & Caius College, Cambridge (MA); Havard Business School (MBA). *Directorships:* HongkongBank London Ltd. *Recreations:* Gardening, Reading, Children.

MORLEY, Peter; Director, British & Commonwealth Merchant Bank plc, since 1988; Banking. *Career:* London Borough of Lewisham, Gp Accountant 1964-70; London Borough of Greenwich, Dep Chief Accountant 1970-73; London Borough of Sutton, Chief Accountant 1973-76; London Borough of Ealing, Dep Dir Finance 1976-80; Phillips & Drew, Dir Money Mkts 1980-86; UBS Phillips & Drew, Dir Corp Finance 1986-88. *Biog: b.* 17 May 1946. *Nationality:* British. *m.* 1977, Susan Frances (née Pike); 1 s. *Educ:* Colfe's Grammar School, London. *Professional Organisations:* Member, CIPFA; Member, International Stock Exchange. *Recreations:* Golf, Tennis, Theatre, Sailing.

MORLEY, Stuart; Head of Research, Grimley J R Eve, since 1989; Property Research. *Career:* John D Wood & Co, Investment Assistant 1964-67; Drivers Jonas, Land Economist 1969-72; Hillier Parker, Local Authority Consultancy 1972-73; Polytechnic of Central London, Senior, Then Principal Lecturer 1974-86; Acting Head of School of Estate Management 1986-89; Grimley J R Eve, Principal Associate Head of Research 1989-. *Biog: b.* 24 April 1947. *Nationality:* British. *m.* 1975, Karen (née Godson). *Educ:* Cranleigh School (BSc); College of Estate Management, London University (MA); Sussex University (Dip TP); Polytechnic of Central London (FRICS). *Other Activities:* Member, RICS Central London Branch (P&D Division); Member, RICS Research Working Party (GP & P&D Divisions); Examiner, Oxford Polytechnic. *Professional Organisations:* FRICS. *Publications:* Valuation & Development Appraisal (ed C Darlow), 1982 & 1988; Valuation & Investment Appraisal (ed C Darlow), 1983; Office Development (ed P & P Marber), 1984; London 2000 (ed C Darlow), 1985; Property Investment Theory (ed Macleary & Nanthakumeran), 1988; Industrial & Business Space Development, 1989. *Recreations:* Squash, Photography.

MORLEY COOPER, J B; Director, Bain Clarkson Limited.

MOROSANI, J W; Director, S G Warburg Akroyd Rowe & Pitman Mullens Securities Ltd.

MORRELL, J A; Director, Baring Asset Management Ltd.

MORRELL, J E; Director, James Capel Gilts Ltd.

MORRIS, Albert (Bert); Chief Executive, Support Services, National Westminster Bank plc, since 1989; Information Technology, Property, Clearing, etc. *Career:* National Westminster Bank plc, Various 1967-79; Head, Money Transmission Services 1979-83; Dep Gen Mgr, Management Services Division 1983-85; Gen Mgr, Management Services Division 1985-88. *Biog: b.* 21 October 1934. *Nationality:* British. *m.* 1987, Patricia (née Lane); 1 s; 1 d. *Educ:* Skerrys College, Liverpool; Massachusetts Institute of Technology (SEP); City of Liverpool College of Commerce (Associate, Chartered Institute of Bankers). *Directorships:* BACS Ltd 1986 (non-exec) Chm; Centre-File Ltd 1986 (exec) Chm; Westments Ltd 1985 (non-exec); APACS (Administration) Ltd 1987 (non-exec); National Westminster Bank plc 1989 (exec). *Other Activities:* Fellow, Royal Society of Arts; Council Member, Chartered Institute of Bankers. *Professional Organisations:* FCIB; FRSA. *Publications:* Various Articles on Banking Subjects. *Clubs:* Harpenden Golf Club. *Recreations:* Work, Politics, Golf, Sport.

MORRIS, Anne P; Partner, Cameron Markby Hewitt.

MORRIS, Anthony David; Partner, Cameron Markby Hewitt, since 1989; Media & Entertainment Law including Film, Record, Music, Video, Television, etc. *Career:* Michael Sears & Co, Articled Clerk 1975-77; Charles Boundy & Co, Partner 1977-82; Anthony Morris & Co, Sole Principal 1982-84; Brafman Morris, Partner 1984-89; Cameron Markby Hewitt, Partner 1989-. *Biog: b.* 21 July 1952. *Nationality:* British. *m.* 1976, Rosalind (née Gould); 1 s; 1 d. *Educ:* Portsmouth Grammar School; Orange Hill Grammar School, Edgware, Middx; Schools Major Open Scholarship to Manchester University; Manchester University (LLB Upper Second). *Directorships:* Wimpole Services Ltd 1985 (exec). *Professional Organisations:* Law Society. *Publications:* Numerous Articles in a Variety of Magazines including Billboard and the Treasurer. *Clubs:* Ronnie Scotts, Mortons. *Recreations:* Films, Music, Photography, Writing Fiction.

MORRIS, Anthony Richard; Group Compliance Director, Midland Bank plc (Head Office), since 1987; Group Compliance (Financial Services Act 1986). *Career:* Minestone (Zambia) Ltd, Fin Acct 1974-76; Deloitte Haskins & Sells, Audit Mgr 1976-79; The International Stock Exchange, Dep SE Inspector 1979-85; Samuel Montagu & Co Ltd, Compliance Officer 1985-86. *Other Activities:* Chairman, Investment Regulation Committee, CLSB; Committee Member, Financial Services Society, ACCA; Member, IFMA Practitioner Group. *Professional Organisations:* Member, CIPFA; FCCA. *Recreations:* Gardening, Fishing.

MORRIS, B R; Director, Ropner Insurance Services Limited.

MORRIS, Christopher; National Director Insolvency Services, Touche Ross & Co, since 1980; Insolvency & Corporate Rescue. *Biog: b.* 28 April 1942. *m.* 1971, Isabel Claire (née Ramsden-Knowles); 2 s. *Other Activities:* Worshipful Company of Wheelwrights. *Professional Organisations:* FCA. *Clubs:* Turf. *Recreations:* Fishing, Racing.

MORRIS, David J H; Financial Controller, Schroders plc. *Biog: b.* 28 February 1939. *m.* Margaret; 2 s; 1 d. *Educ:* Canford School; Bristol University; Stanford University. *Professional Organisations:* Fellow, Institute of Chartered Accountants in England & Wales.

MORRIS, E D; Director, Barclays De Zoete Wedd Limited.

MORRIS, Ernest; TD; Group General Manager, Management Services, Prudential Corporation plc, since 1989; Information Systems. *Career:* Prudential, General Manager, Management Services 1981-89; Coopers & Lybrand Associates, Director 1967-81; C T Bowring & Co, EDP & O & M Manager 1958-66; British Tabulating Machine Co, Systems Engineer 1954-58. *Biog: b.* 7 May 1932. *Nationality:* British. *m.* 1956, Barbara; 1 s. *Educ:* University of Wales (BA); Hon Fellow, University College of Swansea. *Other Activities:* Chairman, Advisory Board for Computing & Information Systems, BTEC; Member, Company of Information Technologists; Past Pres, British Computer Soc; Past Pres, Computer Services Assoc. *Professional Organisations:* FBCS; FBIM. *Recreations:* Francophigia.

MORRIS, Leslie; Senior Partner, Walker Morris Scott Turnbull, since 1988; Taxation & Corporate Finance. *Career:* Inland Revenue Estate Duty Office, Examiner 1956-61; Inland Revenue Inspector of Taxes, Inspector 1961-63; Walker Morris & Coles, Articled Clerk 1964-66; Partner 1966-87; Walker Morris Scott Turnbull, Senior Partner 1988. *Biog: b.* 28 February 1933. *Nationality:* British. *m.* 1956, Patricia Mary (née Hall); 1 s; 2 d. *Educ:* High Storrs Grammar School, Sheffield; Sheffield University (BA Hons); King's College, University of London (LLB Hons). *Directorships:* Bradford Securities Ltd 1980 (non-exec); Wood Canton Holdings Ltd 1980 (non-exec). *Professional Organisations:* FTII. *Recreations:* Family, Countryside, Sport (mainly watching), Reading.

MORRIS, N D; Partner, Jaques & Lewis.

MORRIS, Nicholas G U; Group Secretary, Unigate plc, since 1982. *Career:* Beecham Group 1966-69; H P Bulmer Holdings, Group Secretary 1969-78; British Shipbuilders, Corporation Secretary 1978-82. *Biog: b.* 15 April 1940. *Nationality:* British. *m.* 1963, Susan (née

Wilkinson); 1 s; 2 d. *Educ:* Charterhouse; Christ Church, Oxford (MA Jurisprudence). *Professional Organisations:* Barrister.

MORRIS, Paul William; Senior Corporate Tax Partner, BDO Binder Hamlyn, since 1972; Corporate Tax Planning particularly Mergers & Acquisitions, Reconstructions, Sales Flotations including International Aspects; Property Taxation. *Career:* Midgley Snelling, Senior UK Tax Department 1967-69; Harmood Banner, Manager 1969-72; BDO Binder Hamlyn 1972-. *Biog: b.* 20 May 1942. *Nationality:* British. *m.* 1965, Carole; 2 s; 2 d. *Educ:* Downsmeade School, Eastbourne (FCA). *Other Activities:* Liveryman, Painter-Stainers Co; Member, Tax Committee of the ICAEW; Chairman, Business & Corporate Tax Sub-Committee. *Professional Organisations:* FCA. *Clubs:* Marylebone Cricket Club, Eridge Cricket Club, Queenhythe Ward Club.

MORRIS, R Glyn; Executive Director, Electra Investment Trust plc.

MORRIS, Roger Philip; Director, Morgan Grenfell Asset Management, since 1986; Investment Management. *Career:* Pember & Boyle, Ptnr 1974-86; Fund Mgr/Analyst 1968-74. *Biog: b.* 15 July 1944. *Nationality:* British. *m.* 1974, Jacqueline (née Fallon); 1 s; 2 d. *Educ:* Tonbridge School. *Professional Organisations:* FCA. *Recreations:* Sailing, Skiing, Tennis.

MORRIS, Simon J; Managing Director, Foreign Exchange, Continental Bank NA.

MORRIS, Simon James; Partner, Cameron Markby Hewitt, since 1988; Commercial Dept/Financial Services. *Career:* Cameron Markby Hewitt, Solicitor 1982-. *Biog: b.* 1958. *Nationality:* British. *Educ:* Whitgift School; Gonville & Caius College, Cambridge (MA). *Publications:* Financial Services: Regulating Investment Business, 1990. *Clubs:* Member of Council, London Topographical Society. *Recreations:* Victorian Maps.

MORRIS, W H; Managing Director, Sampo Insurance Company (UK) Limited.

MORRIS-JONES, Tom; Dealing Director, Albert E Sharp Co, since 1987; Institutional Sales. *Career:* Royal Insurance Investment Asst 1968-70. *Biog: b.* 17 March 1946. *m.* 1968, Carol Eileen (née Kennard); 2 d. *Educ:* Oswestry Boys High School; Merton College, Oxford (MA). *Professional Organisations:* Society of Investment Analysts. *Recreations:* Golf.

MORRISON, David; Managing Director - Economics, Goldman Sachs International Limited.

MORRISON, David Du Bois; Director, County NatWest Wood Mackenzie & Co Ltd; Corporate Finance, Oil. *Biog: b.* 3 April 1952. *Nationality:* British. *m.*

1977, Julia (née Godden); 3 s. *Educ:* George Watson's College, Edinburgh; St Andrews University (BSc Hons). *Professional Organisations:* MInstPet; ASIA; The International Stock Exchange. *Clubs:* New (Edinburgh). *Recreations:* Music, Running, Painting, Squash, Photography.

MORRISON, Miss Fiona Jane; Partner, Lane Clark & Peacock, since 1984; Pensions. *Career:* Lane Clark & Peacock, Actuarial Trainee 1979-82; Assistant Actuary 1982-84. *Biog: b.* 2 May 1957. *Nationality:* British. *m.* 1984, Eivind James Dullforce. *Educ:* Dauntseys School, West Lavington; Selwyn College, Cambridge (MA). *Other Activities:* Staple Inn Actuarial Society (Ctee 1985-); Selwyn College Permanent Henley Fund (Ctee). *Professional Organisations:* FIA (1984). *Recreations:* Skiing, Gardening, Knitting.

MORRISON, Hilary Thomas; Senior Partner, Wm F Coates & Co, since 1984; Investment Management. *Career:* Wm F Coates & Co 1951-; Ptnr 1963-. *Biog: b.* 17 May 1936. *Nationality:* British. *m.* 1960, Mary Jane (née Haire); 2 s; 2 d. *Other Activities:* Member, General Synod & Representative Church Body, Church of Ireland, Girl Guides Assoc; Hon Treasurer, Province of Ulster; Advisory Panel, N Ireland Central Investment Fund for Charities. *Clubs:* Ulster Reform (Belfast). *Recreations:* Gardening, Reading.

MORRISON, M C; Director, Euro Brokers Holdings Limited.

MORRISON, Michael John; Senior Partner, Taylor Joynson Garrett, Solicitors, since 1988; Commercial Lawyer. *Career:* Allen & Overy, Articled Clerk 1964-66; Assistant Solicitor 1966-68; Parker Garrett (later Taylor Joynson Garrett), Partner 1969. *Biog: b.* 31 March 1939. *Nationality:* British. *m.* 1965, June (née Winskill); 1 s; 1 d. *Educ:* Fettes College, Edinburgh; St Catharines College, Cambridge (MA, LLB). *Directorships:* Ambia Marine (UK) Limited; Bessemer Group (UK) Limited; Futuremill Limited; Gainhalf Limited; Huntsmoor Nominees Limited; Leif Hoegh (UK) Limited; Philpot Trading Co Limited; Yuills Limited; Uxbridge Springwaters Developments Limited; Bride Developments Limited; Torquay Leisure Investments Limited; Churchward Limited; Beaumont House Properties Limited. *Other Activities:* City of London Solicitors Company. *Professional Organisations:* Law Society. *Clubs:* Royal Automobile Club, The Norwegian Club, Moor Park Golf Club.

MORRISON, Neil Campbell; Partner, S J Berwin & Co.

MORRISON, Nigel Douglas; Director, M & G Investment Management Ltd, since 1983; Investment Manager in UK Gilt Edged Stocks and UK Equities. *Career:* Samuel Montagu & Co Ltd, Investment Mgr 1969-81. *Biog: b.* 22 April 1944. *Nationality:* British. *m.*

1978, Mary-Anne (née Allpass); 2 s. *Educ:* Aldenham School.

MORRISON, Ralph F; Director, Continental Reinsurance London.

MORRISON, The Hon Mrs Sara Antoinette Sibell Frances; Non-Executive Director, Abbey National plc, since 1987 & 1979-86. *Career:* General Electric Co 1975-; Director 1980-. *Biog: b.* 9 August 1934. *m.* 1954, Hon Charles Andrew Morrison (diss 1984); 1 s; 1 d. *Directorships:* Imperial Group Ltd 1981-86 Chm. *Other Activities:* National Council for Voluntary Organisations, 1977-81; National Advisory Council on Employment of Disabled People, 1981-84; County Councillor, then Alderman, Wilts, 1961-71; Chairman, Wilts Assoc of Youth Clubs, 1958-63; Wilts Community Council, 1965-70; Vice-Chairman, National Assoc of Youth Clubs, 1969-71; Conservative Party Organisation, 1971-75; Member: Governing Board, Volunteer Centre, 1972-77; Annan Ctee of Enquiry into Broadcasting 1974-77; National Consumer Council 1975-77; Board, Fourth Channel TV Co, 1980-85.

MORRISON, William M; President, Faculty of Actuaries.

MORROW, Sir Ian Thomas; Kt; Chairman, MAI plc, since 1974. *Career:* Brocklehurst-Whiston Amalgamated Ltd, Chartered Accountant 1935; Robson Morrow & Co, Assistant Accountant 1937-40; Partner 1942-51; Fin Dir 1951-52; Dep Managing Director 1952-56; Joint Managing Director 1956-57; Managing Director 1957-58; H Clarkson & Co Ltd, Joint Managing Director 1961-72; Associated Fire Alarms Ltd, Chairman 1965-70; Rowe Bros & Co (Holdings) Ltd, Chairman 1960-70; Kenwood Manufacturing Co Ltd, Chairman 1961-68; Crane Fruehauf Trailers Ltd, Chairman 1969-71; Rolls Royce Ltd, Deputy Chairman 1970-71; Rolls Royce (1971) Ltd, Deputy Chairman 1971-73; Managing Director 1971-72; Collett, Dickenson Pearce International Ltd, Chairman 1979-83; Scotia DAF Trucks Ltd, Chairman 1979-83; Agricultural Holdings Co Ltd, Chairman 1981-84; UKO International plc (formerly UK Optical & Industrial Holdings Ltd), Chairman (former Managing Director & Chairman of Subsidiary Companies) 1979-86; W M Still & Sons Ltd, Chairman 1964-86; Martin-Black plc, Chairman 1977-86; Pearl & Dean Ltd (Hong Kong), Chairman 1978-86; Hugh Paul Holdings Ltd, Chairman 1979-85; Barlow Meyer Savage (subsequently Harlow Ueda Savage) (Eurodollars), Chairman 1980-88. *Biog: b.* 8 June 1912. *Nationality:* British. m1 Elizabeth Mary (née Thackray) (diss 1967); 1 s; 1 d; m2 1967, Sylvia Jane (née Taylor); 1 d. *Educ:* Dollar Academy, Dollar; Stirling University; Heriot-Watt (Hon DLitt). *Directorships:* Additional Underwriting Agencies (No 3) Ltd 1985 Chairman; Beale Dobie & Co Ltd 1989 Chairman; C E Heath Public Limited Company 1988; Efamol

Holdings plc 1986 Chairman; Gisburne Park plc 1987 Chairman; Hambros Industrial Management Ltd 1965; Insport Consultants Ltd 1988 Chairman; MAI plc 1974 Chairman; PSion plc 1987; Scotia Pharmaceuticals Ltd 1986 Chairman; Strong & Fisher (Holdings) plc 1981 Chairman; The Laird Group plc 1973; Walbrook Insurance Co Ltd 1990 Chairman; Zeus Management Ltd 1985. *Other Activities:* Freeman, City of London; Liveryman, Worshipful Company of Spectaclemakers; Lay Member, Press Council, 1974-80; Member, Grand Council FBI, 1953-58; Member, Institute of Management Accountants, 1952-70 (President 1956-57, Gold Medallist 1961); Performing Rights Tribunal, 1968-74; Council Member, Inst of Chartered Accountants of Scotland, 1968-72, 1979-82 (Vice-President 1972-79, 1979-80, 1980-81, President 1961-82). *Professional Organisations:* CA; FCMA; JDipMA; FBIM; CompIEE. *Publications:* Papers and Addresses on Professional and Management Subjects. *Clubs:* National Liberal, Royal Automobile, Royal & Ancient (St Andrews). *Recreations:* Reading, Music, Golf, Skiing.

MORROW, William B; Deputy Managing Director, Bank of America International Limited, since 1989; Corporate Finance (Europe), Covering Leveraged Finance, Eurofacilities, Syndications, Project Finance, Mergers & Acquisitions and Specialised Trade Services. *Nationality:* American. *Educ:* Wharton Graduate School, University of Pennsylvania (MBA); Bucknell University (BA); The George Washington University (MA).

MORSE, Sir Christopher Jeremy; KCMG 1975; Chairman, Lloyds Bank, since 1977; Deputy Chairman, Lloyds Bank, 1975-77. *Career:* Glynn Mills & Co, Dir 1964; Bank of England, Exec Dir 1965-72; IMF, Alternate Governor for UK 1966-72; Chm of Deputies of Ctee of Twenty 1972-74; Lloyds Bank, Dep Chm 1975-77. *Biog:* b. 10 December 1928. *m.* 1955, Belinda Marianne; 3 s; 2 d (1 decd). *Educ:* Winchester; New College Oxford (1st Class Lit Hum). *Directorships:* ICI plc; Business in the Community Dep Chm; Lloyds Bank International 1979-80 Chm; Lloyds Merchant Bank Holdings 1985-88 Chm; Alexanders Discount Co Ltd 1975-84; Legal & General Assurance Society 1964 & 1975-87. *Other Activities:* President, British Bankers' Assoc, 1984; Banking Federation of the European Community, 1988; Warden, Winchester College, 1987 (Fellow 1966-82); Chancellor, Bristol University 1989; London Clearing Bankers (Deputy Chairman 1978-80, Chairman 1980-82); Per Jacobsson Foundation,1987-; Member, Council of Lloyd's, 1987-; President, Institut International d'Etudes Bancaires, 1982-83; British Overseas Bankers' Club, 1983-84; International Monetary Conf, 1985-86; London Forex Assoc, 1978-; Member, NEDC, 1977-81; Chairman, City Communications Centre, 1985-87; Hon Member, Lombard Association, 1989; Governor, Henley Management College, 1966-85; Chairman, Trustees, Beit Memorial Fellowships for Medical Research, 1976-; Member, British Selection

Ctee, Harkness Fellowships, 1986-; Freeman, City of London, 1978; Chairman, City Arts Trust, 1976-79; Fellow, All Souls College, Oxford, 1953-68, 1983-; Hon Fellow, New College, Oxford, 1979-; Hon DLitt City, 1977; Hon DSc Aston, 1984; FIDE International Judge for Chess Compositions, 1975; President, British Chess Problem Society, 1977-79; Hon Life Member, British Chess Federation, 1988. *Clubs:* Athenaeum. *Recreations:* Poetry, Problems and Puzzles, Coarse Gardening, Golf.

MORSE, Rodney John; Director, Wellington Underwriting Agencies Ltd, since 1986; Underwriter Syndicate 97, Aviation Syndicate at Lloyd's. *Career:* Price Forbes 1960-64; Willis Faber & Dumas Ltd 1964-85. *Biog:* b. 26 January 1944. *Nationality:* British. *m.* 1968, Ann (née Woodward); 1 d. *Directorships:* Wellington Underwriting Agencies Limited 1986 (exec). *Other Activities:* Committee Member, Lloyd's Aviation Claims Centre; Committee Member, Lloyd's Aviation Underwriters Assoc. *Professional Organisations:* ACII. *Recreations:* Gardening, DIY.

MORSMAN, Peter Douglas; Director, Wellington Underwriting Agencies Ltd, since 1986; Administration and Managing Agency. *Career:* Willis Faber Dumas Agencies Ltd, Asst Director -1985.

MORTIMER, David; Controller, Yorkshire Bank plc, since 1987; Marketing. *Career:* Yorkshire Bank Group, Various 1959-85; Yorkshire Bank Finance Ltd, Dep Chief Exec 1985-87. *Biog:* b. 1942. *Educ:* Bellevue Grammar School, Bradford. *Professional Organisations:* ACIB; FCIS; MBIM.

MORTON, Guy Wallis; Partner, Freshfields, since 1986. *Career:* Hodgkinson & Tallents (Newark-on-Trent), Articled Clerk 1976-79; Freshfields, Assistant Solicitor 1980-86. *Biog:* b. 1 October 1952. *Nationality:* British. *m.* 1983, Anne Melissa (née Phillips); 1 s; 2 d. *Educ:* Winchester College; Corpus Christi College, Oxford (BA, MA). *Other Activities:* Liveryman, Worshipful Company of Musicians; Liveryman, City of London Solicitors Company. *Professional Organisations:* The Law Society.

MORTON, John Andrew; Partner, Allen & Overy, since 1973; Corporate Finance, Commercial, Intellectual Property. *Career:* Allen & Overy, Asst Solicitor 1968-73. *Biog:* b. 5 July 1943. *Nationality:* British. *m.* 1975, Angela Fern Gage (née Wheeler); 2 d. *Educ:* Charterhouse; Merton College, Oxford (BA). *Directorships:* Canadian Pacific Newsprint Ltd 1976 (non-exec); International Paper Company (UK) Ltd 1977 (non-exec); Canadian Pacific Forest Services Ltd 1982 (non-exec). *Other Activities:* Dir, The Solicitors' Benevolent Assoc. *Professional Organisations:* The Law Society; The City of London Law Society. *Clubs:* Royal Harwich

Yacht Club, Royal Wimbledon Golf Club. *Recreations:* Sailing, Golf, Skiing.

MORTON, Kenneth John; Group Financial Director, Kleinwort Benson Group plc, since 1988. *Career:* Hill Samuel & Co Ltd, Mgr, Dir 1967-73; Sime Darby Holdings Group, Finance Dir 1976; Reed International plc, Group Treasurer 1976-81; Group Finance Dir 1981-86; Hill Samuel Group, Exec Dir 1986-88. *Biog: b.* 11 February 1940. *Nationality:* British. *m.* 1974, Marguerite (née Wright); 1 s. *Educ:* Rugby; University College, Oxford (BA Hons,PPE). *Directorships:* Steel Brothers Holdings 1982-87 (non-exec); Asda Group plc 1986 (non-exec); North British Newsprint Holdings 1987 (non-exec); South West Water plc 1989 (non-exec); Her Majesty's Stationery Office 1990 (non-exec). *Other Activities:* Ctee, 100 Group. *Professional Organisations:* FCA; FCT.

MORTON, Lee Robert; Director, Hoare Govett Securities Ltd, since 1989; UK Equity Sales. *Career:* Giles & Overbury, Administration 1975-77; Fielding Newson-Smith, Analyst (Special Situations) 1977-80; Hoare Govett, Engineering Analyst 1980-85; Hoare Govett (New York), Head of US Research 1985-87; Corporate Finance 1988-89. *Biog: b.* 13 May 1956. *Nationality:* British. *m.* 1986, Tina Marguerite (née Ashington). *Recreations:* Running, Cycling.

MORTON, Reginald John; Partner, Titmuss Sainer & Webb, since 1987; Company Law. *Career:* George Davies & Co (Manchester), Articled Clerk 1973-75; Clifford Chance, Asst Solicitor 1975-85. *Biog: b.* 17 September 1951. *Nationality:* British. *m.* 1979, Jennifer (née Carr); 2 s. *Educ:* Manchester Grammar School; Birmingham University (LLB). *Professional Organisations:* The Law Society. *Clubs:* Paddocks Snooker Club. *Recreations:* Snooker, Golf.

MOSCROP, Gerald Ian; Tax Partner, Neville Russell, since 1976; Personal Taxation. *Career:* Griffin Stone; Moscrop & Co Articled Clerk 1964-69; Greenhaven Securities Ltd/Capital & Counties Property Co Ltd Asst Co Sec/Asst Group Fin Controller 1969-71; Robson Rhodes Tax Snr/Management 1971-74; Neville Russell Ptnr 1974-. *Biog: b.* 15 January 1944. *Nationality:* British. *m.* 1971, Jennifer; 1 d. *Educ:* Chace County. *Directorships:* Christian Action (Enfield) Housing Association 1981 (non-exec) Chm; Haggai Institute for Advanced Leadership Training 1987. *Other Activities:* Christ Church; Churchwarden, Cockfosters. *Professional Organisations:* FCA. *Publications:* Papers Arising from Lectures, Institute of Chartered Accountants in England, Scotland and Wales. *Clubs:* St James's. *Recreations:* Sailing, Squash, Badminton, Golf.

MOSER, Robin Allan Shedden; Managing Director, Chief Executive, Alexanders Discount plc, since 1984; Discount House. *Career:* Deloitte Plender & Griffiths, Articled Clerk 1965-71; Hahn & Co Ltd, Chief Acct 1973-75; Gillett Bros Discount Co, MD 1976-83; Jessel Toynbee & Gillett plc, MD 1983-84. *Biog: b.* 3 June 1947. *Nationality:* British. *m.* 1973, Sally (née Knowles); 3 s. *Educ:* Radley College. *Directorships:* Credit Lyonnais Capital Markets plc 1986 (exec); Alexanders Discount Futures Ltd 1982 (exec). *Professional Organisations:* FCA. *Clubs:* Saffron Walden Golf Club, Southwold Golf Club. *Recreations:* Golf, Sailing.

MOSS, B T; Director, Maxwell Pergamon Publishing Corporation plc.

MOSS, Malcolm Kennedy Hunt; Senior Executive, Guinness Mahon Development Capital Ltd, since 1989; Venture Capital Investment. *Career:* Baxter Healthcare Inc, Business Analyst, London 1981-83; Snr Business Analyst, Brussels 1983-85; Uniroyal Inc, European Budget and Planning Manager, Capital Investment 1985-87; TSB Group, Snr Business Analyst, Central Executive 1987-89. *Biog: b.* 29 July 1959. *Nationality:* British. *Educ:* Kings School, Canterbury; Thames Polytechnic Business School (BA); Kingston Polytechnic Business School (MBA). *Directorships:* Mobilia Ltd 1989 (non-exec); Scorpio Marine Electronics Ltd 1989 (non-exec); All Childrens Co Ltd 1990 (non-exec). *Professional Organisations:* Chartered Institute of Marketing, Diploma in Marketing. *Clubs:* Metropolitan Club. *Recreations:* Tennis.

MOSS, Philip; Director, Svenska International plc.

MOSS, R; Chairman & Chief Executive, Allied Breweries Ltd. *Biog: b.* 2 December 1929. *Nationality:* British. *Professional Organisations:* MIMechE.

MOSS, Sally-Anne; Director, Financial Dynamics Limited.

MOSSELMANS, Carel Maurits; TD; Chairman, N M Rothschild Asset Management Limited, since 1989. *Career:* Sedgwick Collins & Co 1952; Director 1963; Sedgwick Collins (Underwriting) Ltd, Director 1971; Managing Director 1972; Sedgwick Forbes Underwriting Agencies Ltd, Chairman 1974-89; Sedgwick Forbes Marine Ltd, Chairman 1974-78; Sedgwick Forbes Holdings Ltd, Director 1978; Sedgwick Forbes Services Ltd, Chairman 1978-81; Sedgwick Ltd, Chairman 1981-84; Sedgwick Group plc, Deputy Chairman 1982-84; Chairman 1984-89; The Sumitomo Marine & Fire Insurance Co (Europe) Ltd, Director 1975-81; Chairman 1981-90. *Biog: b.* 9 March 1929. *Nationality:* British. *m.* 1962, The Hon Prudence Fiona McCorquodale; 2 s. *Educ:* Stowe; Trinity College, Cambridge (MA Modern Languages and History). *Directorships:* Coutts & Co 1981 (non-exec); N M Rothschild Asset Management Limited 1989 Chairman; N M Rothschild International Asset Management Limited 1989 Chairman; N M Rothschild Asset Management

(Isle of Man) Limited 1989 Chairman; N M Rothschild Fund Management Limited 1990 Chairman; Rothschild Asset Management (Japan) Ltd 1990 Chairman; Rothschilds Continuation Limited 1990. *Clubs:* White's, Cavalry and Guards. *Recreations:* Shooting, Fishing, Golf, Tennis, Music.

MOSSON, Dr Michael; General Manager, The Royal Bank of Scotland plc.

MOTT, Henry; Clerk, Plaisterers' Company.

MOUCHTY-WEISS, Harriet; Director, GCI Sterling.

MOUGHTON, Barry John; Partner, Turner Kenneth Brown, since 1963; Commercial Use of Trusts. *Biog:* b. 28 May 1932. *Nationality:* British. *m.* 1958, Elizabeth Anne (née Parr); 1 s; 2 d. *Educ:* Merchant Taylors School; Oxford University (MA); McGill University (MCL). *Other Activities:* Past President, Rotary Club of London. *Professional Organisations:* The Law Society. *Clubs:* Rotary. *Recreations:* Choral Singing.

MOULE, M B; Director, Touche Remnant & Co.

MOULT, Barry Vincent; Director, Major Projects, Girobank plc.

MOULTON, Jonathan Paul (Jon); Managing Partner, Schroder Ventures, since 1985; Venture Capital, Buy-Outs. *Career:* Coopers & Lybrand, Mgr 1973-81; Citicorp Venture Capital, Dir 1981-83; Gen Mgr 1983-85. *Biog:* b. 15 October 1950. *Nationality:* British. *m.* 1972, Pauline (née Dunn); 1 s; 1 d. *Educ:* Hanley High School; Lancaster University (BA). *Directorships:* Parker Pen Ltd 1986 (non-exec); Haden MacLellan Holdings plc 1987 (non-exec); Halls Homes & Gardens plc 1982 (non-exec); Hornby Hobbies plc 1981 (non-exec); Interconnection Systems Ltd 1987 (non-exec); Technology plc 1989 (non-exec); Appledore Holdings Ltd 1990 (non-exec). *Professional Organisations:* FCA; FBIM. *Recreations:* Chess.

MOUNTFIELD, Robin; CB; Deputy Secretary, Department of Trade and Industry, since 1984; Financial Services, Insurance, Company Law (inc Companies House), Insolvency Service, Competition Policy & Consumer Affairs. *Career:* Ministry of Power 1961-69; Ministry of Technology 1969-70; DTI 1970-; Private Sec to Minister 1973-74; Asst Sec 1974-80; Seconded to The Stock Exchange 1977-78; Under Sec 1980-84; Dep Sec, Manufacturing Industry 1984-87. *Biog:* b. 16 October 1939. *Nationality:* British. *m.* 1963, Anne (née Newsham); 2 s; 1 d. *Educ:* Merchant Taylors' School, Crosby; Magdalen College, Oxford (BA).

MOUNTFORD, Ms Margaret; Partner, Herbert Smith.

MOUNTFORD, R P; Director, Hambros Bank Limited.

MOURGUE D'ALGUE, Pierre-Andre; Co-Head, European Equities & Director, Schroder Securities Ltd, since 1990; Continental European Equities. *Career:* Hoare Govett Inc (New York), Vice-President European Equities 1986-88; Citicorp Intl Private Banking (New York), Account Manager 1984-86. *Biog:* b. 25 August 1960. *Nationality:* French/Swiss. *Educ:* Columbia Graduate School of Business Admin, NY (MBA); Long Island University (BS Cum Laude).

MOURSY, M F K; Director, Lehman Brothers Equity Money Brokers Ltd.

MOUSSA, Pierre Louis; Chairman, Pallas Limited, since 1984. *Career:* Inspection des Finances; French Administration, Technical Advisor to the Sec for Fin & Economic Affairs 1949-51; Director of Cabinet to the Minister for French Overseas 1954; Under-Sec for Economic Affairs & Planification for French Overseas 1954-59; Director of Civil Aviation 1959-62; World Bank for Reconstruction & Development Dir, Dept of Operations, Africa 1962-64; Federation of French Insurance Companies, Chm 1965-69; Paribas Group, in succession, Snr exec VP, Pres, Dep Chm, Chm & Chief Exec 1969-81; Created Finance & Development Inc, Holding Co Chairman 1982-87; Created, Pallas Holdings (Luxembourg) (formerly Pallas Group), Chairman 1983. *Biog:* b. 5 March 1922. *Nationality:* French. *m.* 1957, Anne-Marie Denise (née Trousseau). *Educ:* Lycee Ampere; Lycée du Parc; Ecole Normale Supérieure (Agregé des Lettres). *Directorships:* Pallas Invest 1988 (exec); Frandev 1986 (exec) Chm; Cresvale Partners 1987 (exec) Chm; Pallas Finance 1986 (exec); Pallas Monaco 1988 (exec) Chm; Banque Pallas France 1987 (exec); Pallas Gestion 1986 (exec); Parindev, France 1987 (exec); Banque Pallas (Suisse) 1988 (exec); Broad Inc, USA 1983 (non-exec); Kaufman & Broad Home Corp, USA 1986 (non-exec); CERUS, Compagnies Européennes 1986 (non-exec); Reunies, France 1987 (non-exec); Marceau Investissements, France 1987 (non-exec); Sedgwick Group plc, UK. *Other Activities:* Foreign Orders and Decorations; Officier de la Légion d'Honneur (France, 1976); Officier de l'Ordre National du Mérite (France 1966). *Professional Organisations:* Inspection Generale des Finances, France. *Publications:* Les Chances Economiques de la Communauté Franco-Africaine, 1957; Les Nations Prolétaires, 1959; L'economie de la Zone Franc, 1960; Les Etats-Unis et les Nations Prolétaires, 1965; La Roue de la Fortune, Souvenirs d'un Financier, 1989; Prix Européen des Affaires du Livre, 1989. *Clubs:* Automobile Club de France (Paris).

MOUTAFIAN, Artine Nicholas; Chairman, Moutafian Commodities Ltd, since 1958; Commodities Dealer (Cocoa, Coffee, Sugar). *Career:* Foreign Trading

Agency, Principal & Founder; Foreign Trading Agency Ltd, Chairman, Specialising in Nuts and Nut Kernels 1962-. *Biog: b.* 21 March 1912. *m.* 1955, Helena MBE. *Educ:* Saint Benoit College, Istanbul. *Directorships:* London Armenian Community Trust 1962-87 Chairman; Armenian General Benevolent Union 1974-87 Chairman; Armenian General Benevolent Union London Trust 1980-87 Chairman.

MOUTAFIAN, H; MBE; Director, Moutafian Commodities Ltd.

MOWAT, Magnus Charles; Director, Barclays de Zoete Wedd Ltd, since 1984; Corporate Finance & Banking. *Career:* Peat, Marwick McLintock 1959-68; Hill Samuel & Co Ltd 1968-70; Illingworth & Henriques, Ptnr 1970-84. *Biog: b.* 5 April 1940. *Nationality:* British. *m.* 1968, Mary Lynette St Lo (née Stoddart); 3 s. *Educ:* Haileybury. *Directorships:* Barclays de Zoete Wedd Ltd. *Other Activities:* Trustee, Booths Charities; Chm, Manchester YMCA; Governor, Packwood Haugh. *Professional Organisations:* FCA. *Clubs:* St James's (Manchester). *Recreations:* Music, Gardening, Shooting.

MOWLL, Christopher M; Clerk, Clothworkers' Company.

MOXON, J W J; Director, Beeson Gregory, since 1989; Institutional.

MOY, C H N; Deputy Managing Director, Granville & Co Limited.

MOZZINO, Jorge; General Manager, Banco de La Nacion Argentina, since 1988.

MUDD, Philip John; Partner, Walker Morris Scott Turnbull.

MUELLER, Dame Anne; DCB; Non-executive Director, STC plc, since 1990. *Career:* Various appointments in different Government Departments 1953-72; Under Secretary, Department of Industry & Head of Industrial & Comercial Policy Division 1972-77; Deputy Secretary, Department of Trade & Industry, responsible for Regional Industrial Policy 1977-84; Second Permanent Secretary, Cabinet Office & Head of Management & Personnel Office 1984-87; Second Permanent Secretary, HM Treasury, responsible for Civil Service Management & Pay 1987-90. *Biog: b.* 15 October 1930. *Educ:* Wakefield Girls High School; Somerville College, Oxford (MA). *Directorships:* Cere Britain 1989 (non-exec); Phonepoint Limited 1990 (non-exec); European Investment Bank 1978-84 (non-exec); Business in the Community 1984-88 (non-exec). *Other Activities:* Member of Council, Institute of Manpower Studies; Manchester Business School; London Education Business Partnership; Governor Templeton

College, Queen Mary & Westfield College and Leicester Polytechnic; Trustee Whitechapel Art Gallery; Royal Armouries Development Trust. *Professional Organisations:* CBIM; FIPM. *Clubs:* United Oxford & Cambridge University.

MUELLER, O O H; Director, Unilever plc.

MUELLER, Rudolf G; Chairman and Chief Executive, Union Bank of Switzerland Phillips & Drew Ltd.

MUENTER, J H B; Director, Benchmark Group plc.

MUIR, A H J; Partner, Cazenove & Company.

MUIR, Graeme Murray; Company Secretary, Rea Brothers Limited, since 1989; Legal Director, Compliance Officer, Marketing Director. *Career:* Hill Samuel Investment Services Ltd, Marketing Manager 1981-86; Company Sec & Legal Director 1986-89. *Biog: b.* 19 February 1954. *Nationality:* British. *Educ:* Glasgow University (LLB). *Directorships:* Rea Brothers Limited 1989 (exec); Rea Brothers Group plc 1989 Co Secretary. *Professional Organisations:* Law Society.

MUIR, R J K; Executive Chairman, James Finlay plc, since 1990. *Career:* National Service Commission; James Finlay 1960-; South India 1960-63; Calcutta 1964-67; Nairobi 1967-80; General Manager 1974-80; James Finlay Board in Glasgow 1980; Chairman 1990. *Biog: b.* 25 May 1939. *Nationality:* British. *m.* 1975, Lady Linda Cole; 4 d. *Educ:* Glenalmond. *Clubs:* Oriental. *Recreations:* Fishing, Tennis, Trying to Make a Scottish Estate Pay.

MUIR, R Keith; Partner (Nottingham), Evershed Wells & Hind.

MUIR, Robert Wallace; Partner, McKenna & Co, since 1987; Commercial Property. *Career:* Titmuss Sainer & Webb, Articled Clerk 1977-79; Asst Solicitor 1979-82; Herbert Oppenheimer Nathan & Vandyk, Asst Solicitor 1982-83; Knapp-Fishers, Salaried Ptnr 1983-86; McKenna & Co, Ptnr 1986. *Biog: b.* 7 September 1954. *Nationality:* British. *m.* 1987, Carole. *Educ:* University College, London (LLB). *Other Activities:* Member, City of London Solicitors Company. *Professional Organisations:* Law Society of England & Wales. *Clubs:* Royal Automobile Club.

MUIRHEAD, Alastair William; Managing Director, Charterhouse Bank Limited, since 1989; Corporate Finance. *Career:* Price Waterhouse 1976-80; Saudi International Bank (Banking Division) 1980-84. *Biog: b.* 12 September 1953. *Nationality:* British. *m.* 1980, Linda Anne (née Johnson); 3 d. *Educ:* Tonbridge School; St Johns College, Oxford (Scholar, First Class Natural Sciences Chemistry). *Professional Organisations:* ACA. *Publications:* The Optical Study of the Magnetic Phase

Diagram of Metamagnetic Ferrous Bromide in the Journal of Physical Chemistry, 1978. *Recreations:* Fly Fishing, Walking, Gardening.

MULCAHY, R K; Partner, Pensions Research (Epsom), Bacon & Woodrow.

MULCAHY, T P; Group General Manager, AIB Venture Capital.

MULLARKEY, David; Partner, Tax Department, Linklaters & Paines, since 1988; Corporate Taxation, International Tax, Investment Funds, Corporate Finance. *Career:* Theodore Goddard & Co, Articles 1980-82; Linklaters & Paines (London), Asst Solicitor 1982-84; Linklaters (Hong Kong), Asst Solicitor 1984-86; Linklaters (London), Asst Solicitor 1986-88; Linklaters & Paines, Partner 1988-. *Biog: b.* 4 February 1956. *Nationality:* British. *m.* 1984, Beverley Ann (née Carter); 1 s; 1 d. *Educ:* Finchley Catholic High School; Nottingham University (LLB 2:i). *Other Activities:* Member, Unit Trust Association Taxation Committee. *Professional Organisations:* Law Society. *Publications:* Tax Editor, Linklaters & Paines' Unit Trusts: The Law and Practice.

MULLEN, A I; Director, Midland Bank plc; UK Corporate Banking.

MULLER, Sidney; Chairman, Marshall Hoellwarth & Co Ltd.

MULLEY, Michael J; Vice President, Chemical Bank.

MULLIGAN, Aynia M; Partner, Wilde Sapte.

MULLINGS, R; Senior Vice President and Treasury Manager, NCNB National Bank of North Carolina.

MULLINS, T; Assistant General Manager (Personnel), National Provident Institution.

MULLION, R D P; Director, C Czarnikow Ltd.

MULLY, R S; Director, County NatWest Ltd, since 1989; Property Finance, Advice & Investment. *Career:* Deloitte Haskins & Sells (Management Consultants), Consultant 1984-86; County NatWest 1986-90. *Biog: b.* 29 July 1961. *Nationality:* British. *Educ:* University College, London (BSc Economics 1st Class Hons); City University Business School (MBA with Distinction). *Directorships:* County NatWest Property Limited 1988 (exec); Stanhope County Limited 1990 (exec); Stanhope County (St George's) Limited 1990 (exec). *Recreations:* Soccer, Cricket.

MUMFORD, David John; Director, Schroder Investment Management Ltd, since 1985. *Career:* Grieveson Grant & Co 1957-67; J Henry Schroder Wagg, Dir 1977-89. *Biog: b.* 2 January 1937. *m.* 1961, Sally (née

Costello); 2 d. *Educ:* Sherborne School. *Directorships:* Schroder Property Fund for Pension Funds & Charities 1981 (exec). *Clubs:* RNSA, RMSC. *Recreations:* Sailing.

MUMFORD, Hugh A L H; Executive Director, Electra Investment Trust plc.

MUMFORD, R C H; Managing Director & Chief Executive, TH March & Company Limited.

MUMMÉ, Susan Anna Louise; Finance Director/City Search Executive, BBM Associates, since 1986. *Career:* Arthur Andersen & Co Grad Audit Trainee 1980-85; Rochester Group Fin Consultant 1985-86. *Biog: b.* 11 March 1959. *Nationality:* British. *m.* 1984, Paul John Ackford. *Educ:* Taunton School; Kent University (BA Hons). *Professional Organisations:* ICA. *Recreations:* Skiing, Theatre, Bridge, Rugby, Golf.

MUNCHAU, Wolfgang; European Biz Correspondent, The Times.

MUNDAY, C H; Director, Corporate Finance, Security Pacific Hoare Govett, since 1986; Property. *Career:* Legal & General Assurance Society, Investment Analyst 1959-62; GEC Pension Fund, Assistant Investment Manager 1963-64; Borthwick, Investment Analyst 1965; Govett Sons & Co, Construction Analyst 1965-70; Hoare Govett, Property Analyst 1970-86; Corporate Finance Director, Property 1986-. *Biog: b.* 12 September 1943. *Nationality:* British. *m.* 1965, Suzanne Caroline (née Tadhunter); 1 s; 2 d. *Educ:* Bishopshalt School, Hillingdon; Nottingham University (BA Industrial Economics 2:i). *Clubs:* Wadhurst Cricket Club (Chairman). *Recreations:* Cricket.

MUNN, Dr C W; Secretary, The Institute of Bankers in Scotland, since 1988; Chief Executive. *Career:* The British Linen Bank, Clerk 1964-67; Dept of Finance & Accounting, Glasgow College of Technology, Lecturer 1975-78; Dept of Economic History, University of Glasgow, Lecturer/Senior Lecturer 1978-88. *Biog: b.* 26 May 1948. *Nationality:* British. *m.* 1973, Andrea; 1 s; 1 d. *Educ:* University of Strathclyde (BA Hons); University of Glasgow (PLD); Jordanhill College of Education (Lecturer's Certificate). *Directorships:* The Adam Smith Bicentenary Ltd 1989 (non-exec). *Other Activities:* Church and Nation Committee, Church of Scotland; Ethics and Finance Group, Centre for Theology and Public Issues, University of Edinburgh; Council Member, Scottish History Society. *Professional Organisations:* Associate, The Institute of Bankers in Scotland. *Publications:* The Scottish Provincial Banking Companies, 1747-1864, 1981; Banking in Scotland, 1982; Clydesdale Bank, The First 150 Years, 1988; Numerous Articles in Academic and Banking Journals; Editor in Chief, The Scottish Banker, 1988. *Clubs:* College Club (Glasgow), Burntisland Golf House Club. *Recreations:* Reading, Rookie Golf.

MUNN, Geoffrey Thomas; Director, Morgan Grenfell & Co Ltd, since 1976; Treasury. *Career:* Midland Bank Ltd, Snr Foreign Exchange Dealer 1950-67. *Biog: b.* 1 November 1933. *Nationality:* British. *m.* 1959, Ann Rebecca (née Wood); 1 s; 1 d. *Educ:* Wallington County Grammar School. *Directorships:* Morgan Grenfell (Jersey) Ltd 1985 (non-exec); Morgan Grenfell (Guernsey) Ltd 1985 (non-exec); Morgan Grenfell Government Securities Ltd 1987 (non-exec); Morgan Grenfell Financial Futures Ltd 1987 (non-exec). *Other Activities:* Foreign Exchange Ctee. *Professional Organisations:* Association Cambiste Internationale; London Forex Assoc. *Recreations:* Golf, Gardening.

MUNRO, A W W; Director, Hambros Bank Limited.

MUNRO, Allan; Director, Ivory & Sime plc, since 1984; Chairman of the Management Committee, Investment Management. *Career:* Ivory & Sime 1964; Head of Dealing Room 1972-87; Responsible for Management of Fixed Interest Portfolios 1976-; Director 1984. *Biog: b.* 20 September 1947. *Nationality:* British. *m.* 1969, Elizabeth (née Brand); 2 s. *Educ:* Broughton School. *Directorships:* Bankside (Underwriting Agencies) Ltd 1985 (non-exec); Edinburgh Hibernian plc 1989 (non-exec); Edinburgh Sports Club Ltd 1989 (non-exec). *Clubs:* Edinburgh Sports Club, Bruntsfield Links Golf Club. *Recreations:* Squash, Golf, Football, Rugby.

MUNRO, Miss C; Director (UK Consumers), Hoare Govett Investment Research Limited.

MUNRO, C I C; Director, Robert Fleming Holdings Limited.

MUNRO, Charles John; Partner, Ernst & Young, since 1978; Securities industry and overseas privatisations. *Career:* W I Carr, Stockbrokers Client Exec 1971-75. *Biog: b.* 25 July 1943. *Nationality:* British. *m.* 1973, Alison (née Close); 2 s. *Educ:* Trinity College, Glenalmond; Pembroke College, Oxford (BA). *Professional Organisations:* FCA. *Recreations:* Fishing, Shooting.

MUNRO, David Michael; Joint Managing Director, Quayle Munro Ltd, since 1983; Corporate Finance. *Career:* Kleinwort Benson, Analyst 1968-70; Chiene & Tait, Ptnr, Investment Mgr 1970-83. *Biog: b.* 3 November 1944. *m.* 1973, (née Lindsay-Stewart); 3 d. *Educ:* Glenalmond College. *Directorships:* Shanks & McEwan Group plc 1982 (non-exec); The Life Association of Scotland Ltd 1981 (non-exec). *Professional Organisations:* CA. *Clubs:* New (Edinburgh). *Recreations:* Shooting, Fishing.

MUNRO, F F C; Director, Finance & Planning, Cookson Group.

MUNRO, Robert Malcolm; Executive Director, The Union Discount Company of London plc, since 1984; Leasing, Marketing, General Management. *Career:* Lloyds & Scottish, Finance Branch Mgr 1960-68; Hambros Leasing, Asst Gen Mgr 1968-72; Williams & Glyns Leasing Co Ltd, MD 1972-80; Nordic Finance International, BV MD 1980-83. *Biog: b.* 16 May 1937. *Nationality:* British. *m.* 1961, Irene M (née Percy); 2 s. *Educ:* Trinity School, Mid-Essex Technical College; Manchester Business School. *Directorships:* Union Discount Leasing 1983 MD; Union Discount Futures 1985 (non-exec); Union Discount Company 1986 (exec); Union Discount Asset Management 1987 (non-exec); Union Discount Invoice Financing 1987 Dep Chm; Herald Financial Services; Sabre Leasing Ltd. *Other Activities:* Mgmnt Ctee, Equipment Leasing Assoc. *Professional Organisations:* Fellow, Institute of Directors. *Recreations:* Tennis, Golf, Music, Theatre.

MURAKAMI, A; Managing Director, Tokai International Ltd.

MURAKAMI, Takeshi; Director, Schroder Securities Limited.

MURAKAMI, Tetsuya; Managing Director - Investment Division, The Nikko Securities Co (Europe) Ltd.

MURAKAWA, G; Director, Sanyo International Ltd.

MURBY, D J; Partner, Arthur Andersen & Co Chartered Accountants.

MURDOCH, J S; Deputy Chairman, Shaw & Co.

MURDOCH, Ms M Gaye; Director, British Invisibles.

MURDOCH, Rupert; AC; Non-Executive Director, Reuters Holdings plc.

MURLEY, Richard Andrew; Director, Kleinwort Benson Ltd.

MURMANN, Johann Horst; Managing Director, Metallgesellschaft Ltd, since 1982. *Career:* Metallgesellschaft AG (Frankfurt/Main) Various/Metal Dealer 1958-70; Metallgesellschaft Ltd Dir 1970-. *Biog: b.* 6 February 1938. *m.* 1966, Ursula B (née Koch); 1 s; 1 d. *Educ:* Leibniz Realgymnasium, Frankfurt-Hoechst. *Other Activities:* Councillor, German Chamber of Industry and Commerce in the UK; Awarded Bundesverdienstkreuz am Bande. *Professional Organisations:* Institute of Directors. *Recreations:* Tennis, Travel, Historic Studies.

MURPHY, Christopher Hugh; Director & Company Secretary, Sedgwick Lloyd's Underwriting Agents Limited, since 1985. *Career:* Bevington, Vaizey & Foster Limited, Assistant Company Secretary 1968-70; Wigham-Richardson and Bevingtons Limited, Assistant

Company Secretary 1970-74; Wigham Poland Holdings Limited, Assistant Company Secretary 1974-82; Wigham-Richardson and Bevingtons (Underwriting Agencies) Limited 1983-85; Director 1984; Sedgwick Lloyd's Underwriting Agents Limited, Director & Company Secretary 1985-. *Biog: b.* 13 May 1940. *Nationality:* English. *Directorships:* Sedgwick Lloyd's Underwriting Agents Limited 1985 (exec); Bland Welch Underwriting Limited 1985 (exec); Wigham-Richardson and Bevingtons (Underwriting Agencies) Limited 1984 (exec).

MURPHY, Miss Frances Mary; Partner, Slaughter and May, since 1990; Company/Commercial. *Career:* Slaughter and May (London), Articled Clerk 1981-83; Assistant Solicitor 1983-86; (Hong Kong) 1986-87; (London) 1987-90. *Biog: b.* 24 September 1957. *Nationality:* British. *Educ:* St Dominic's Independent Grammar School, Harrow-on-the-Hill; University of Sheffield (LLB Hons). *Professional Organisations:* The Law Society.

MURPHY, Miss Jane Frances; Partner, Linklaters & Paines, since 1982. *Biog: b.* 20 December 1951. *Nationality:* British. *Educ:* Lady Margaret Hall, Oxford (MA Law). *Professional Organisations:* Member, Law Society; Member, City of London Solicitors Company; Licensed Insolvency Practitioner. *Recreations:* Yachting.

MURPHY, John T; Partner, Theodore Goddard.

MURPHY, M E; Financial Controller, Candover Investments plc.

MURPHY, Philip Thomas; Partner, Beachcroft Stanleys Solicitors, since 1982; Commercial Property Law. *Career:* Herbert Smith & Co, Articled Clerk 1968-70; Assistant Solicitor 1970-77; Associate 1977-81. *Biog: b.* 10 March 1946. *Nationality:* British. *m.* 1980, Sara Gillian (separated). *Educ:* Lewes County Grammar School; London School of Economics (LLB Hons). *Other Activities:* Freeman, City of London Solicitors Company. *Professional Organisations:* Solicitor; Member, The Law Society. *Recreations:* Reading, Walking, Swimming, Cycling, Badminton, American History, Travel.

MURRAY, Alan Adams; Director, The British Linen Bank Ltd, since 1987; Head of Banking, The British Linen Bank Ltd, since 1989. *Career:* Bank of Scotland 1965-75; British Linen Bank, Asst Loans Controller 1975-77; Loans Controller 1977-79; Exec Asst 1979; Asst Mgr 1980-82; Mgr 1982-83; Asst Dir 1983-84; Divisional Dir 1984-87. *Biog: b.* 16 December 1948. *Nationality:* British. *m.* 1970, Margaret (née McBeth); 1 s; 1 d. *Educ:* Perth Academy; Heriot-Watt University (Diploma in Banking & Financial Studies). *Directorships:* Gillies Melville Associates Limited 1988 (non-exec); McLaren Cross Developments Limited 1988 (non-exec); GA Holdings Limited 1988 (non-exec); Elitho Limited 1988 (non-exec); Melville Street Assets (Edinburgh)

Limited 1989 (non-exec); The Northampton Business Park Limited 1990 (non-exec); Cala Homes (Headley Down) Limited 1990 (non-exec). *Professional Organisations:* Associate, Institute of Bankers in Scotland. *Recreations:* Badminton, Tennis.

MURRAY, Alexander Barclay; Managing Director, Ford Motor Credit Co Ltd, since 1986; UK Operations. *Career:* Decca Group, Management Accountant 1960-62; Ford Motor Company, Junior Management Roles 1962-72; Ford Motor Credit Co Ltd, Director, Regional Sales Manager 1977-86; Director, Asia Pacific and Latin America 1977-86. *Biog: b.* 27 May 1938. *Nationality:* British. *m.* 1964, Helen; 1 s; 1 d. *Educ:* Forfar Academy. *Directorships:* Ford Credit Funding plc 1987 (exec); Ford Automotive Leasing Ltd 1987 (exec); Ford Lease Financing Ltd 1987 (exec); Ford Financial Trust Ltd 1987 (exec); Automotive Finance Ltd 1987 (exec); Ford Motor Co Ltd 1987 (non-exec). *Professional Organisations:* CA; ACMA. *Recreations:* Bridge, Reading.

MURRAY, Alexander Thomas; Executive Director (Geneva), Baring Securities Ltd, since 1989; Japanese Equity Sales. *Career:* Nippon Kangyo Kakumaru (Ldn), Equity Dept 1982-83; Henderson Crothswaite (Tokyo), Equity Dept 1983-84; Baring Securities (Tokyo), Equity Dept 1984-87; (London), Asst Dir 1987-88; Exec Dir 1988-90. *Biog: b.* 20 September 1960. *Nationality:* British. *m.* 1989, Kathelyna Marie Louise (née van Lierde); 1 s. *Educ:* Charterhouse; University College, Oxford (MA Hons). *Clubs:* City University.

MURRAY, Angus M M; Barrister, Theodore Goddard; European Community Law & Competition Law. *Career:* Called to Bar 1978; Butterworths (Legal Publishers) Ltd, Senior Sub-Editor 1981; Government Legal Service, European Court Litigation, Advising on European Community Law 1983; Theodore Goddard, European Community Law & Competition Law 1988. *Biog: b.* 22 August 1950. *Nationality:* British. *m.* 1973, Caroline (née Thorpe); 2 s; 1 d. *Educ:* Manchester Grammar School; Christ's College, Cambridge (MA). *Professional Organisations:* Barrister, Middle Temple; Member, Union Internationale Des Avocats; Member, Ligue Internationale Du Droit De La Concurrence.

MURRAY, Colin Keith; Chairman, R J Kiln & Company Ltd, since 1985. *Career:* C T Bowring & Co (Ins) Ltd, Clerk & Broker 1953-63; R J Kiln & Co Ltd, Dep Underwriter 1963-74; Active Underwriter 1974-84. *Biog: b.* 18 June 1932. *Nationality:* British. *m.* 1964, Precelly (née Davies-Scourfield); 1 s; 2 d. *Educ:* Wellington College. *Directorships:* Dann, Kiln & Co 1977 (exec); Spurr, Kiln & Co 1981 (exec); Street Underwriting Agency 1984 (exec); R J Kiln & Co 1963 (exec). *Other Activities:* Lloyd's (Dep Chm, 1989-91, Council 1983-86, Training Ctee, 1983-86 & 1988); Governor, College of Insurance. *Clubs:* City. *Recreations:* Music, Tennis, Fishing, Gardening, Shooting.

MURRAY, G M; Honorary Secretary, The Faculty of Actuaries.

MURRAY, Gordon L K; WS; Partner, W & J Burness, since 1982; Property. *Biog: b.* 23 May 1953. *Nationality:* British. *m.* 1978, Susan Patricia; 1 s; 3 d. *Educ:* Lenzie Academy; Edinburgh University (BA History & Law, LLB). *Directorships:* Scottish National Orchestra Society Limited 1990 (non-exec); Scottish National Orchestra Society Limited 1985 (non-exec) Past Secretary 1985-90. *Other Activities:* Rotary Club of West Linton. *Professional Organisations:* Law Society of Scotland. *Clubs:* Scottish Arts Club, Edinburgh Wanderers FC, Edinburgh Borderers RFC. *Recreations:* Music, Rugby, Golf.

MURRAY, James Anthony Stoddard; Managing Partner, Maclay Murray & Spens, since 1987. *Career:* Maclay Murray & Spens Apprentice/Solicitor 1970-73; Slaughter and May Asst Solicitor 1973-75; Richards Butler Asst Solicitor 1975-76; Maclay Murray & Spens Ptnr (Corporate Law) 1976-87. *Biog: b.* 26 October 1946. *m.* 1977, Albinia Jane (née Townshend); 2 d. *Educ:* Rugby School; Cambridge University (BA); Edinburgh University (LLB). *Professional Organisations:* Law Society of Scotland. *Clubs:* Western, Glasgow, Prestwick Golf Club. *Recreations:* Shooting, Golf, Sailing.

MURRAY, James Iain; Partner, Linklaters & Paines, since 1967. *Career:* Freshfields Articled Clerk 1956-59; Robert Fleming & Co Ltd Trainee Investment Dept 1960-62; GH Walker (Investment Bankers) Wall Street Seconded 1962; Linklaters & Paines Asst Solicitor 1963-67. *Biog: b.* 12 November 1932. *m.* 1969, Ursula Jane (née Sayle); 1 s; 2 d. *Educ:* Rugby School; Corpus Christi College, Cambridge (BA, MA). *Other Activities:* Liveryman, City of London Solicitors' Company; Member, Companies Ctee of CBI. *Professional Organisations:* The Law Society. *Clubs:* New (Edinburgh), City of London, Travellers'. *Recreations:* Walking, Fishing.

MURRAY, John H; Executive Director, Swiss Bank Corporation, since 1987; Corporate Finance. *Career:* Morgan Stanley Group Inc (New York) 1975-77; (London) 1977-83; (Australia) 1983-86; Chilmark Partners, Chicago, Illinois, USA, General Partner 1986-87; Swiss Bank Corporation 1987-. *Biog: b.* 21 May 1946. *Nationality:* American. *m.* 1981, Jennifer (née Hadow); 1 s. *Educ:* Williams College (BA Hons Economics); Harvard University Business School (MBA).

MURRAY, John Joseph; Partner, Nabarro Nathanson, since 1986; Pensions. *Career:* Smallpiece & Merriman, Articled Clerk 1977-79; Nabarro Nathanson, Assistant Solicitor 1979-83; Biddle & Co, Assistant Solicitor 1983-84; Brecher & Co, Assistant Solicitor 1984-85; Nabarro Nathanson, Assistant Solicitor/Partner 1985-. *Biog: b.* 10 May 1953. *Nationality:* British. *Educ:* Fort Augustus Abbey School; Leeds University (LLB). *Professional Organisations:* Law Society. *Recreations:* Reading, Travel, Music.

MURRAY, Professor Leo Gerard; Director, Cranfield School of Management, since 1986. *Career:* Rothmans International plc, General Manager 1979-82; Director, Overseas Manufacturing & Licensing 1982-85; Middle East Regional Director 1985-86; A T Kearney Limited, Consultant 1975-76; Consulting Manager 1977-79; Courtaulds Group, PA to Divisional MD 1968; Assistant to Group Supplies Director 1968-71; Divisional Supplies and Planning Manager 1971-73; European Sales Manager 1973-75; British Petroleum Company Limited, Graduate Management Trainee 1965-66; Supplies Programmer 1967. *Biog: b.* 21 May 1943. *Nationality:* British. *m.* 1970, Pauline (née Murray); 1 s; 1 d. *Educ:* Glasgow University (MA Honours); University of Rennes, France (Diploma French Language and Literature). *Directorships:* ICI/Cranfield Business Games Ltd 1987 Chairman & Director (exec); Council of University Management Schools 1988 Treasurer & Executive Ctee Member (exec); Comité d'Orientation d'Ecole Internationale des Affaires, Marseille 1988 Member (non-exec). *Professional Organisations:* Member, Institute of Directors; Member, Institute of Marketing; Member, Institute of Management Consultants.

MURRAY, Malcolm Alexander; Director, Phillips & Drew Fund Management Ltd.

MURRAY, Marsali C; Partner, W & J Burness WS.

MURRAY, Norman Loch; Deputy Chief Executive, Morgan Grenfell Development Capital Limited, since 1989; Development Capital. *Career:* Scottish & Newcastle Breweries plc, Project Manager 1971-73; Arthur Young, Trainee Chartered Accountant 1973-76; Peat Marwick Mitchell & Co, Hong Kong Office, Deputy Manager Auditing 1977-80; The Royal Bank of Scotland plc, Manager in the Corporate Finance Department 1980-85; Charterhouse Development Capital Limited, Director Equity Investments in Unquoted Companies 1985-89; Morgan Grenfell Development Capital Limited, Deputy Chief Executive Equity Investments in Unquoted Companies 1989-. *Biog: b.* 17 March 1948. *Nationality:* British. *m.* 1972, Pamela Ann (née Low); 2 s. *Educ:* George Watson's College, Edinburgh; Heriot-Watt University, Edinburgh (BA Economics & Commerce); Harvard University, Boston, USA (Program for Management Development). *Directorships:* Morgan Grenfell & Co Limited 1989 (exec); Morgan Grenfell Development Capital Holdings Limited 1989 (exec); Morgan Grenfell Development Capital Limited 1989 (exec); Morgan Grenfell Capital (GP) Limited 1989 (exec); Morgan Grenfell Capital Trustee Limited 1989 (exec); Morgan Grenfell (Scotland) Limited 1989 (exec); Burn Stewart Group Limited 1988 (non-exec); BSM Group Limited 1990 Alternate (non-exec);

Maccess Group Limited (non-exec); Dalmore Distillers Limited Alternate (non-exec); Charterhouse Development Capital Limited (exec); Charterhouse Development Limited (exec); Charterhouse Development Capital Holdings Ltd (exec); National Commercial & Glyns Limited (exec); Royal Bank Development Limited (exec); GSM plc (non-exec). *Other Activities:* Member, Research Committee of The Institute of Chartered Accountants of Scotland. *Professional Organisations:* Chartered Accountant, The Institute of Chartered Accountants of Scotland; Fellow, Royal Society of Arts. *Publications:* Co-Author, Making Corporate Reports Valuable, 1988. *Clubs:* Royal Scottish Automobile Club, Watsonian Club, Royal Hong Kong Yacht Club, Harvard Business School Club of London. *Recreations:* Squash, Golf, Hill-Walking.

MURRAY, Roger; Chairman, Cargill UK Ltd.

MURRAY, W R; Group Financial Controller, Thorn EMI plc.

MURRAY, William David Mungo James; The Rt Hon The Earl of Mansfield; Director, General Accident Fire & Life Assurance Corp.

MURRAY, W T; Executive Director, Baring Securities Limited, since 1990; SE Asian Equity Sales. *Career:* Baring Securities (Hong Kong) Ltd, Exec Director 1985-89; Sun Hun Kai Securities (HK) Ltd 1977-85. *Biog: b.* 4 January 1956. *Nationality:* British. *m.* 1981, Helen (née Sohn). *Educ:* Barstable Grammar. *Clubs:* HK Football Club; *Clubs:* Discovery Bay Golf Club.

MURRAY-JONES, Allan Gordon; Partner, Lovell White Durrant.

MURRELL, Barry L; Market Making Director, Hoare Govett International Securities, since 1985; Far East Securities. *Career:* Akroyd & Smithers Ltd, Market Maker Far East Securities 1968-85. *Biog: b.* 22 January 1953. *Nationality:* British. *Professional Organisations:* Member, London Stock Exchange.

MUSGRAVE, Christopher Francis; National Director of Finance, Touche Ross & Co, since 1978; Finance/Administration/Legal/IT. *Career:* Clark Brownscombe & Co 1958-65. *Biog: b.* 17 January 1940. *Nationality:* British. *m.* 1968, Jennefer Susan; 3 s; 4 d. *Educ:* St Edmund's, Canterbury, Kent. *Professional Organisations:* FCA.

MUSGRAVE, Michael Henry Baxter; Chairman & Managing Director, Edenhall Securities Ltd, since 1980; Investment Management. *Career:* Royal Marines Officer 1949-72; Anthony Gibbs & Sons Ltd, Reg Mgr 1972-77; Westavon Investment Consultants Ltd, MD 1977-80. *Biog: b.* 5 April 1931. *Nationality:* British. *m.* 1963, Yvonne Margaret (née Meade); 2 s; 2 d. *Educ:* Malvern

College. *Directorships:* Edenhall (Life & Pensions) Ltd 1980 MD; Edenhall Properties Ltd 1988 MD. *Other Activities:* Commandeur of Commanderie de Bordeaux. *Professional Organisations:* FIMBRA (Council Member). *Clubs:* Clifton (Bristol). *Recreations:* Golf, Tennis, Travel.

MUSKIE Jr, Edmund Sixtus; Vice President & Deputy General Manager, The Riggs National Bank of Washington, DC - London Branch, since 1988; Corporate Banking. *Career:* United States Senate, Office of Senator George J Mitchell, Legislative Assistant, Washington, DC 1982-84; Herbert Smith & Co (Solicitors), Articled Clerk, London 1984-85; The Riggs National Bank of Washington, DC 1985-. *Biog: b.* 4 July 1961. *Nationality:* American. *m.* 1989, Dr Julia Jane (née Biggart). *Educ:* Duke University (BA). *Directorships:* Riggs Keep Limited 1990 (non-exec). *Clubs:* Royal Mid-Surrey Golf Club, Overseas Bankers'. *Recreations:* Golf.

MUSSON, Geoffrey Charles; Director of Investments, Merchant Navy Officers Pension Fund, since 1977. *Career:* James Capel & Co, Partner and Head of Research 1966-77. *Biog: b.* 2 July 1942. *Nationality:* British. *m.* 1966, Caroline Margaret (née Ivinson); 3 d. *Educ:* King's School, Canterbury; London School of Economics & Political Science (BA Hons Philosophy & Economics). *Directorships:* New Plan Realty Trust (New York) 1983 Trustee; TR Property Investment Trust plc 1982; Trust Union Finance Limited 1982; Ensign Holdings Inc 1989 Chairman; Ensign Oil & Gas Inc 1989 Chairman; Ensign Trust plc (formerly Murray Growth Trust plc) 1985; Argosy Asset Management plc (formerly Merchant Navy Investment Management Ltd) 1985 Managing Director; Ivory & Sime plc 1987; New Frontiers Development Trust plc (formerly CDFC Trust plc) 1987; The Clydesdale Investment Trust plc (formerly Unitycorp Trust) 1987 Chairman; CDFC Berkeley Ltd 1987; CDFC International Ltd 1988; Argosy Asset Management Inc 1988; First Hungary Fund Limited 1990; Merchant Navy Officers Pension Investments Ltd; Merchant Navy Investment Management Australia Limited -1988; The Plantation Trust Company plc; Ashcombe Property Developments Ltd; ERI Ltd -1989; Argosy Investment Management Limited (formerly Merchant Navy Unit Trust Management Ltd); National Association of Pension Funds Ltd; Aberdeen Trust Holdings Ltd (formerly Aberdeen Fund Managers Ltd) 1988-90; Solong Ltd (formerly Commonwealth Development Finance Company Ltd) 1986 Chairman. *Recreations:* Gardening, Collecting Russian Stamps, Opera.

MUULS, P; Director, Campbell Lutyens Hudson Co Ltd.

MYDDELTON, Professor David Roderic; Professor of Finance & Accounting, Cranfield School of Management, since 1972. *Career:* Cranfield School of Management Lecturer, Fin & Accounting 1965-69; London Business School, Lecturer in Accounting 1969-72. *Biog: b.* 11 April 1940. *Nationality:* British. *m.* 1986, Hatherley d'Abo; 1 s; 1 d. *Educ:* Eton College; Harvard Business School (MBA). *Professional Organisations:* FCA; ACIS. *Publications:* The Power to Destroy: a Study of the British Tax System, 1969; The Meaning of Company Accounts (4th ed), 1988; The Economy and Business Decisions, 1984; On a Cloth Venture: Inflation Accounting, Net Way Forward, 1984; Essential Management Accounting, 1988; Accounting and Financial Decisions (2nd ed), 1991.

MYDDELTON, R H; Group Legal Director/Company Secretary, Grand Metropolitan plc, since 1988; Company Secretarial/Risk Management/Legal. *Career:* Rank Xerox plc, Commercial Lawyer 1968-73; Manager Legal Services 1973-78; Courtaulds plc, Group Legal Advisor 1978-86; Group Public Affairs 1986-88; Grand Metropolitan plc, Group Legal Director & Company Secretary 1988-. *Biog: b.* 31 August 1942. *Nationality:* British. *m.* Brigitte; 1 d. *Educ:* Cambridge (MA, LLB, Cantab, Solicitor). *Recreations:* Golf, Music, Bridge.

MYERS, Bernard Ian; Managing Director, N M Rothschild & Sons Limited, since 1988; Group Finance and International. *Career:* Arthur Andersen & Co, Audit Manager 1965-72; N M Rothschild & Sons Ltd 1972-. *Biog: b.* 2 April 1944. *Nationality:* British. *m.* 1967, Sandra (née Barc); 1 s; 2 d. *Educ:* London School of Economics (BSc Econ); Hendon County Grammar School. *Directorships:* Smith New Court plc 1985 (non-exec); Rothschilds Construction Holdings AG 1983 (non-exec); Rothschild Bank Zurich 1988 (non-exec). *Professional Organisations:* FCA. *Recreations:* Golf, Tennis, Opera, Theatre.

MYERS, Ian David; Director of European Sales, PaineWebber International (UK) Ltd, since 1990; US Equities and Derivatives throughout Europe. *Career:* White Weld & Co Inc (taken over by Merrill Lynch), Institutional Portfolio Adviser 1976-78; PaineWebber Mitchell Hutchins (later just Paine Webber) 1978-. *Biog: b.* 3 August 1954. *Nationality:* British. *m.* 1976, Helen Rosemary; 2 s; 1 d. *Educ:* Latymer Upper; Pembroke College, Oxford (MA Oxon). *Directorships:* PaineWebber Inc 1990.

MYERS, Simon; Finance Director, Swiss Bank Corporation, since 1990; Finance. *Career:* Coopers & Lybrand Associates Ltd, Partner Financial Services 1982-90; Motolease Ltd, Financial Controller 1980-82; Coopers & Lybrand, Audit 1975-80. *Biog: b.* 30 May 1952. *Nationality:* British. *m.* 1975, Milly (née Caplan); 2 s; 1 d. *Educ:* Hasmonean Grammar School; University of Hull (BSc); University of London (MSc). *Professional Organisations:* Associate, Institute of Chartered Accountants. *Publications:* Various Articles for Pensions World, 1985-90; Internal Publications within Coopers Deloitte.

Recreations: Sport (watching now more than participating).

MYERS, Stephen Francis; Vice President, Chemical Bank.

MYERSON, Brian Alan; Managing Director, Euro Suisse Securities Limited. *Career:* UAL Merchant Bank, Corporate Banking Executive 1984-86; Jesup & Lamont, Corporate Finance Director 1986-87; Oceana Development Investment Trust plc, Director 1988-89; Yamato Equity Warrant Fund, Chairman 1988-89. *Biog: b.* 22 October 1958. *Nationality:* Irish. *m.* 1982, Ingrid Dianne (née Lawrie); 2 s. *Educ:* King David School; University of the Witwatersrand, South Africa. *Directorships:* E S Securities Limited. *Clubs:* Houghton Golf Club, Guards Polo Club. *Recreations:* Yachting, Polo, Flying, Golf.

MYNERS, Paul; Chairman & Chief Executive, Gartmore Investment Management Ltd, since 1985; Investment Management. *Career:* N M Rothschild & Sons, Dir 1974-85. *Biog: b.* 1 April 1948. *Nationality:* British. *m.* 3 d. *Directorships:* English & Scottish Investors plc 1985 (non-exec); Scottish National Trust plc 1987 (non-exec); Celltech Group plc 1988 (non-exec); PowerGen plc 1988 (non-exec); Gartmore Value Investments plc 1989 Chm; Capital Strategy Fund Limited 1986 Chm.

N

NAAMANI, Anis Abdel-Kader; Manager, Jordan International Bank plc, since 1990; Business Development and Correspondent Banking. *Career:* Bank of Lebanon & Kuwait SAL, Beirut 1977-85; Manager, Hamra Branch 1980; Tetrad Group of Saudi Arabia, London Financial Adviser 1985-87; Thomson McKinnon Futures Ltd, London Manager, Foreign Exchange Dept 1987-89. *Biog: b.* 5 January 1955. *Nationality:* Lebanese. *Educ:* International College, Beirut; American University of Beirut (BBA, Management/ Marketing Courses, MBA) & various business seminars. *Other Activities:* Member of Voluntary Committee, IC Alumni Association UK, 1989-; Member of Board of Directors, AUB Alumni Association UK, 1988-; Participated in 3 'Career Panels' for Graduate Students Graduate School of Business & Management AUB, 1983-84; President, American University of Beirut Chess Club, 1973-75; President, International College in Beirut Chess Club, 1970-72.

NABOULSI, F H; Chief Executive UK Operations, Bank of Oman Ltd, since 1990; UK Branches. *Career:* Fidelity Bank, Vice President & Head of Middle East Division 1978-88. *Biog: b.* 28 July 1950. *Nationality:* British. *m.* 1987, Soraya Al-Sa'di; 1 s. *Educ:* Buckingham College of Higher Education (HND Business Studies, Post Graduate Export Marketing Diploma). *Professional Organisations:* Arab Bankers Association.

NACHAMKIN, Boris A; Managing Director, Bankers Trust Co.

NAGAMATSU, Hiroshi; Managing Director, DKB International Ltd. *Career:* The Dai-Ichi Kangyo Bank Ltd, Tokyo 1963-89. *Biog: b.* 2 October 1939. *Nationality:* Japanese. *m.* 1966, Mitsuko (née Yamamoto); 1 s; 2 d. *Educ:* Tokyo University (BA Law). *Directorships:* DKB International Limited 1989 (exec); DKB Investment Management International Ltd 1989; DKI Nominee Company Limited 1989. *Professional Organisations:* General Registered Representative, The Securities Association.

NAGANO, E; Director, Dowa Insurance Company (UK) Limited.

NAGASAKI, Komaki; Managing Director, Sumitomo Finance International, since 1990. *Educ:* University of Tokyo (Bachelor of Law).

NAGATA, S; Director, Dowa Insurance Company (UK) Limited.

NAGAYA, Yoshihiko; General Manager, The Bank of Tokyo Ltd, since 1990; Overall Responsibility for Bank of Tokyo Specialising in Foreign Exchange. *Biog: b.* 29 April 1941. *Nationality:* Japanese. *Educ:* Hitotsubashi University, Tokyo (BA).

NAGAYAMA, Y; Chief Representative, Seventy-Seven Bank.

NAGGAR, Guy Anthony; Chairman, Dawnay, Day & Co Ltd, since 1981. *Career:* Banque Financiere de la Cite Geneva, Director 1970-88; The Charterhouse Group Ltd, Director 1980-81. *Biog: b.* 14 October 1940. *Nationality:* Italian. *m.* 1964, The Hon Marion (née Samuel); 2 s; 1 d. *Educ:* Ecole Centrale des Arts et Manufactures, Paris.

NAISH, John Alexander; Director, Hill Samuel Bank Ltd, since 1985; Chief Representative in Japan. *Biog: b.* 12 April 1948. *m.* 1982, Bonnie (née Fan); 2 s. *Educ:* Queen Elizabeth's Hospital, Bristol; Dr Challoner's Grammar School, Amersham; City of London Polytechnic (BA Hons). *Professional Organisations:* FCIB. *Clubs:* Oriental. *Recreations:* Golf, Astronomy.

NAITO, Takeshi; Deputy Managing Director, Mitsui Taiyo Kobe International Limited, since 1990; Europe & Middle East. *Career:* Taiyo Kobe Bank, London Branch, Manager 1976-80; International Dept, Manager 1980-82; New York Branch, Assistant General Manager 1982-85; International Business Dept, Asst Gen Mgr 1985-88; International Planning Dept, Asst Gen Mgr 1988-90. *Biog: b.* 8 April 1946. *Nationality:* Japanese. *m.* 1975, Yumiko. *Educ:* Keio University (Economic). *Recreations:* Golf, Skiing.

NAKAGAWA, Moto; Deputy Managing Director, IBJ International Limited, since 1989; Investment Management. *Career:* IBJ Trust Company (New York), Senior Vice President 1984-89.

NAKAJO, Noriyasu; Executive Director, Yamaichi International (Europe) Limited, since 1988; Japanese Equities Development. *Career:* Yamaichi Securities, Securities Salesman 1973-82; Stock Trader, Trading Dep 1982-83; Senior Stock Market Analyst, Stock Information Dept 1983-87; Yamaichi International (Europe) Ltd, London, Associate Director of Japanese Equity Sales

1987-88; Executive Director, Japanese Equities Development 1988. *Biog: b.* 22 October 1948. *Nationality:* Japanese. *m.* 1974, Machiko; 1 s; 1 d. *Educ:* Tokyo University of Foreign Studies. *Recreations:* History of Art.

NAKAMITSU, Tomohiko; President & Managing Director, Sumitomo Finance International, since 1987. *Career:* The Sumitomo Bank Ltd Graduate Trainee to Gen Mgr 1965-85; Sumigin Bankers Investment Mgmnt Co Ltd President 1985-87. *Biog: b.* 10 December 1941. *Nationality:* Japanese. *m.* 1972, Yasuko (née Okamachi); 1 s; 1 d. *Educ:* Tokyo University (Economics); University of Pennsylvania (MBA). *Recreations:* Bird Watching, Golf.

NAKAMURA, Shuzo; Managing Director, Wako International (Europe) Ltd, since 1988. *Career:* Wako Securities Co Ltd (Tokyo) 1969-77; Wako International (Hong Kong) Ltd 1977-82; Wako Securities Co Ltd (Tokyo) 1982-84; Wako International (Europe) Ltd 1984-88. *Biog: b.* 16 March 1944. *Nationality:* Japanese. *m.* 1976, Atsuko; 2 d. *Educ:* Doshisha University (MA). *Clubs:* Richmond Golf Club. *Recreations:* Tennis, Golf.

NAKAZATO, Kenichi; Deputy Managing Director, Bank of Tokyo Capital Markets Ltd.

NALLY, M F; Director, Granville Davies Limited.

NAPIER, J A; Finance Director, W H Smith Group plc.

NAPIER, R S; Managing Director, Redland plc, since 1988. *Career:* Fisons Limited, Fin Dir 1975-81; Redland plc, Fin Dir 1981-87; MD 1988-. *Biog: b.* 21 July 1947. *Nationality:* British. *m.* Patricia Gray (née Stewart); 1 d. *Educ:* Sedbergh School; Sidney Sussex College, Cambridge (Natural Sciences, Economics); Harvard Business School (AMP).

NARBROUGH, Colin; Economics Correspondent, The Times.

NARULA, Krishan Kumar; Development Manager, State Bank of India.

NARUSE, Tomonori; Resident Managing Director For Europe, The Bank of Tokyo Ltd, since 1989; Europe. *Career:* The Bank of Tokyo Ltd, General Manager, Head Office, Tokyo (International Project Finance Div) 1981; General Manager, Jakarta Office 1983; General Manager, New York Office 1984; President, Bank of Tokyo Trust Company, New York 1986; Director (Member of the Board of Directors in Europe); Director (Member of the Board of Directors in Tokyo) 1988; Resident Managing Director for Europe, London and Chief Executive Officer for the Bank of Tokyo Group in London 1989-. *Biog: b.* 26 July 1933. *National-*

ity: Japanese. *Educ:* Tokyo University (BA Diploma Liberal Arts in International Relations). *Directorships:* Bank of Tokyo Ltd, Tokyo MD; Bank of Tokyo International Ltd (exec) Chairman; Bank of Tokyo Capital Markets (exec) Chairman. *Recreations:* Golf.

NASH, Alan; Assistant General Manager, The Equitable Life Assurance Society, since 1985; Pensions Administration. *Career:* The Equitable Life 1971-. *Biog: b.* 28 June 1948. *Nationality:* British. *m.* 1986, Eileen (née Baker). *Educ:* St Olave's Grammar School; King's College, London (MSc). *Professional Organisations:* FIA.

NASH, David Harwood; Partner, Pannell Kerr Forster. *Career:* Binder Hamlyn 1966-76; Robertson Nash 1977-87; Pannell Kerr Forster 1987-. *Biog: b.* 4 November 1937. *Nationality:* British. *m.* 1963, Susan Margaret; 1 s; 2 d. *Educ:* St Albans School. *Directorships:* Midstates plc 1986 (non-exec); Chesterfield Properties plc 1973-80 (non-exec); John Townsend Underwriting Agencies Ltd 1982-84 (non-exec); ORME Developments Ltd 1977-80 (non-exec). *Professional Organisations:* FCA. *Clubs:* MCC. *Recreations:* Tennis, Skiing, Shooting, Golf, Sailing.

NASH, David Percy; Company Director, Grand Metropolitan plc, since 1990. *Career:* Peat, Marwick, Cassleton Elliot & Co (Nigeria), Senior Auditor 1963-65; Imperial Chemical Industries plc, (Various positions in UK, Africa, South America) 1965-87; Cadbury Schweppes plc, Group Finance Director 1987-89. *Biog: b.* 24 May 1940. *Nationality:* British. *m.* 1987 (2nd marriage), Susan; 2 s; 1 d. *Educ:* Enfield Grammar School. *Other Activities:* Member, Science and Engineering Research Council (SERC); Member, 100 Group (Finance Directors). *Professional Organisations:* Fellow, Institute of Chartered Accountants in England & Wales (FCA); Fellow, Association of Corporate Treasurers (FCT). *Recreations:* Most Sports.

NASH, Ian Eric; Company Secretary, The London International Financial Futures Exchange (Admin & Management), since 1989. *Career:* The General Electric Company plc, Assistant Company Secretary 1978-87; The London International Financial Futures Exchange 1987-. *Biog: b.* 18 March 1953. *Nationality:* British. *m.* 1978, Hilary (née Crowther); 4 s; 1 d. *Educ:* Bexleyheath School; University College, Cardiff (BSc Econ Hons). *Other Activities:* Member, The Parochial Church Council, St Helen's Church, Bishopsgate; Liveryman, Worshipful Company of Bakers. *Professional Organisations:* FCIS. *Clubs:* The National Club, Cambridge Harriers. *Recreations:* Athletics, Skiing, Windsurfing.

NASH, Paul Frank Anthony; Director, R P Martin plc.

NATALI, D P; Partner, Herbert Smith.

NATORI, T; Director & General Manager, The Industrial Bank of Japan Limited, since 1989; Banking. *Career:* Industrial Bank of Japan Ltd 1960-; IBJ (London) 1972; Dep Gen Mgr 1975; IBJ Australia Bank Ltd, Chief Gen Mgr 1984; Intl Headquarters, Tokyo, Gen Mgr 1987; Investment Banking Dept, Tokyo, Dir & Gen Mgr 1988. *Biog: b.* 24 July 1937. *Nationality:* Japanese. *m.* Noriko; 1 s; 1 d. *Educ:* Hitotsubashi University (BA Econ). *Directorships:* IBJ Intl 1989 (non-exec); Intermediate Capital Group Ltd 1990 (non-exec); Electra Kingsway Managers Holdings Ltd 1990 (non-exec). *Clubs:* Woburn Golf Club, Richmond Golf Club, Carlton Tennis Club, Overseas Bankers Club. *Recreations:* Golf, Tennis.

NAUDI, Robert E; Managing Director, Alexander Howden Reinsurance Brokers Limited.

NAULLS, Barry; Financial Controller/Operations Manager, The Bank of East Asia Ltd.

NAVARRO, Manuel; Deputy European Representative, Nacional Financiera Snc, since 1989; Financial Affairs & Activities Relating to Industrial Promotions Europe. *Career:* Department of Industry, Budget Analyst 1974-77; Nacional Financiera Snc, Multilateral Financing Organisation, Economic Analyst 1980-85; International Projects, Manager's Assistant 1985-88; London Rep Office, Dep European Rep 1989-. *Biog: b.* 2 July 1951. *Nationality:* Mexican. *m.* 1979, Susana (née Montano); 2 d. *Educ:* Autonomous University of San Luis Potosi, Mexico; Technological & Superior Studies, Inst of Monterrey (MBA); Institut Internationale d'Administration Publique de Paris (Diploma Economic & Social Planning); Universite de Paris, Pantheon, Sorbonne (Diploma Systemes Financiers). *Professional Organisations:* Certified Public Accountant. *Publications:* Accounting Standards in Mexico, 1974.

NEAL, P; Secretary, Candover Investments plc.

NEALE, D R; Joint Managing Director & Secretary, PWS Holdings plc.

NEALE, Frank L G; Partner, Phildrew Ventures, since 1988. *Career:* Economist Intelligence Unit, Consultant 1973-77; PA Management Consultants, Senior Consultant 1977-81; PA Developments, Managing Director 1981-83; Citicorp Venture Capital, Director and Head of Venture Capital Division 1983-87. *Biog: b.* 25 August 1950. *Nationality:* British. *m.* 1976, Helen (née Carter); 3 s. *Educ:* St Johns College, Cambridge (MA Economics); Manchester Business School (MBA). *Directorships:* Verson International Group plc 1985 (non-exec); Admiral Homes Ltd 1989 (non-exec); Normand Motor Group Ltd 1990 (non-exec); Carpetrite of London Ltd 1990 (non-exec); British Venture Capital Association Formerly Vice Chairman. *Professional Organisations:* MIMC (Inst of Management Consultants).

Clubs: Watford Football Club Supporters Club. *Recreations:* Football, Ballet, Swimming, Books.

NEALE, Timothy Peter Graham; Partner, Kidsons Impey, since 1990. *Career:* Hope Agar Partner 1967-88; Kidsons, Partner 1988-90. *Biog: b.* 1939. *Nationality:* British. *m.* 1970, Elizabeth (née Harvey); 2 d. *Educ:* Radley College. *Directorships:* Micklefield School (Reigate) Ltd 1980 (non-exec). *Other Activities:* Chm, Reigate Redhill and District Railway Users Association. *Professional Organisations:* FCA. *Clubs:* MCC, RAC. *Recreations:* Watching Sport, Gardening.

NEARY, Ms M; Director, Parrish Stockbrokers.

NEATE, Francis Webb; Partner, Slaughter & May, since 1972; Company and Commercial Law/Litigation. *Career:* Davis Polk & Wardwell, Associate 1963; Slaughter & May, Articled Clerk 1964-66; Asst Solicitor 1966-71. *Biog: b.* 13 May 1940. *Nationality:* British. *m.* 1962, Patricia Ann (née Mulligan); 2 s; 2 d. *Educ:* St Paul's School; Brasenose College, Oxford (BA); University of Chicago, Law School (JD). *Professional Organisations:* The Law Society, IBA; Chm, Commercial Banking Law Ctee of the Section on Business Law. *Clubs:* MCC, Berkshire County Cricket Club (VP). *Recreations:* Family, Cricket, Refereeing Coarse Rugby.

NEATHERCOAT, Simon John; Director, Kleinwort Benson Securities Ltd, since 1988; Director, Kleinwort Benson Limited, since 1989; Corporate Finance. *Career:* Gane Jackson & Walton 1969-74; The Law Debenture Corporation plc, Trustee Mgr 1974-79; Hoare Govett Ltd, Director, Corp Finance 1979-88. *Biog: b.* 13 February 1949. *Nationality:* British. *m.* 1974, Jacqueline (née Taylor); 2 s. *Educ:* St Johns, Leatherhead. *Clubs:* MCC, Wildernesse Golf Club. *Recreations:* Golf, Tennis.

NEAVE, Julius A S; CBE, JP, DL; Non-Executive Director, Prudential Corporation plc. *Career:* Mercantile & General Reinsurance Co plc, London 1938; 13/18th Royal Hussars, Adjutant/Major 1939-46; Mercantile & General Reinsurance Co plc 1946-; General Manager 1966; Director 1977; Managing Director 1980-82. *Educ:* Sherborne School. *Directorships:* Mercantile & General 1980-82 MD, 1982 (non-exec) on retirement. *Other Activities:* Director and Member of Board of Governors, International Insurance Seminars (Founder's Award for Excellence Gold Medal, 1977); Worshipful Company of Insurers, Member of Court of Assistants, Master, 1984; Managing Trustee, Worshipful Company of Insurers' Charitable Trust; JP (Essex), 1975; First Chairman, Reinsurance Officers Association 1969-74; Hon-President 1974; Chairman of Reinsurance Panel, British Insurance Association to 1982; GB Representative, Organising Committee, Rendez-Vous de Septembre 1969-; Association Internationale pour l'Etude de l'Economic de l'Assurance, Geneva, President 1982-86, President d'Honneur 1986-; Deputy Lieutenant for

County of Essex, 1983; Court of Essex University; Governor, Brentwood School; Member of Council of Order of St John, Essex and Chairman of Trustees for Centenary Appeal; High Sheriff of Essex, 1987-88; President, Brentwood & Ongar Conservative Association, 1984-87; President, Essex Club, 1985; President, Insurance Golfing Society. *Professional Organisations:* Past President, Insurance Institute of London; Chartered Insurance Institute, Member of Council, 1975-81; Deputy President, 1982; President, 1983-84; Hon Fellow, Royal Society of Arts 1975. *Recreations:* Golf, Shooting, Fishing, Tennis, Needlework.

NEAVE, R P S; Company Secretary, The Baltic Futures Exchange Ltd, since 1987; Company Secretary and Futures Markets Manager. *Career:* Kleinwort Benson Ltd 1969-84; The Baltic International Freight Futures Exchange Ltd 1985-87. *Biog: b.* 12 November 1947. *Nationality:* British. *m.* 1980, Elizabeth (née Riddell); 2 s. *Educ:* Eton College. *Professional Organisations:* Associate, Chartered Institute of Secretaries & Administrators.

NEBEKER, Gordon; Director, N M Rothschild & Sons Limited, since 1987; Merchant Banking. *Career:* Crocker National Bank, Japan Country Manager & Branch Manager, Banking 1981-84; Crocker National Bank (Hong Kong), Branch Manager 1984-85; Security National Bank (Tokyo), Japan Country Manager & Branch Manager 1985-86. *Biog: b.* 9 November 1945. *Nationality:* American. *m.* Anne (née Alston); 1 s; 1 d. *Educ:* Harvard University (AB Honours); New York University (MBA). *Directorships:* N M Rothschild & Sons Limited 1987; N M Rothschild & Sons (Hong Kong) Limited 1987; N M Rothschild & Sons (Singapore) Limited 1987. *Other Activities:* Tokyo American Club in Japan; American Chamber of Commerce in Japan; British Chamber of Commerce in Japan; Foreign Correspondents' Club of Japan.

NEBIOGLU, Ilhan; Senior Vice President, Turkish Garanti Bankasi, since 1987; European Bank Relations & Finance. *Career:* Publisher 1971-80; Comment Intertrade (Dusseldorf) MD 1980-82; Interbank (Turkey) VP 1982-85; Yapi Kredi Bank Rep in London 1985-87. *Biog: b.* 5 January 1946. *Nationality:* Turkish. *m.* 1978, Ruya (née Mocan). *Educ:* American Robert College, Istanbul; University of Freiburg, Germany (MA). *Other Activities:* Executive Committee, Europa Nostra. *Publications:* Who's Who of the Arab World, 1978 (as Publisher). *Clubs:* Brooks's. *Recreations:* Conservation, Heritage, Private Enterprise, Tennis, Books.

NEEDIIAM, G A; Senior Assistant General Manager, Arab Banking Corporation.

NEEDHAM KNOX, Gerald François; The Earl of Ranfurly; Chairman, Brewin Dolphin & Co Ltd.

NEESON, David; Managing Director, Morgan Stanley International, since 1987; Equities. *Career:* Bisgood Bishop & Co, Partner 1967-76; Merrill Lynch International, Vice President 1976-82. *Biog: b.* 19 October 1946. *Nationality:* British. *m.* 1972, Christine (née Hunt); 1 s; 1 d. *Educ:* Beal Grammar School, Ilford. *Other Activities:* Member, International Stock Exchange. *Clubs:* Wentworth, Wildernesse, Wisley. *Recreations:* Golf, Tennis, Shooting, Walking, Fine Wines.

NEGRETTI, Antony Simon Timothy; Dealing Director, Prudential Bache Capital Funding Money Brokers, since 1985; Stock Exchange Money Broker. *Career:* Page & Gwyther Ltd Dir 1972-82; Greig Middleton & Co Consultant 1982-85. *Biog: b.* 2 December 1945. *m.* 1982, Lucinda (née Lawrence); 1 s; 1 d. *Educ:* Eton College. *Directorships:* Meyrick Payne & Partners 1982 (non-exec). *Professional Organisations:* Member, The International Stock Exchange; Member of Lloyd's. *Clubs:* Boodle's, Queen's, Berkshire Golf Club. *Recreations:* Golf, Tennis, Squash, Skiing.

NEIL, A P; Partner, Simmons & Simmons.

NEILD, Paul; Economics Correspondent, ITN.

NEILL, Alistair; General Manager, Scottish Widows' Fund & Life Assurance Society, since 1988; Corporate Affairs. *Biog: b.* 18 November 1932. *Nationality:* British; 1 s; 2 d. *Educ:* George Watson's College, Edinburgh; University of Edinburgh (MA Hons 1st); University of Wisconsin (MS). *Other Activities:* Chm of the Pensions Ctee, The Life Insurance Council of the Assoc of British Insurers; Member, Pensions Panel, CBI; VP, formerly Treasurer, Faculty of Actuaries; Member, Institute of CAs of Scotland Disciplinary Proceedures. *Professional Organisations:* FFA; FIA; FCII; FPMI. *Publications:* Life Contingencies, 1977. *Clubs:* Caledonian, Baberton Golf Club. *Recreations:* Golf, Squash, Curling.

NEILL, James Ruary Drummond; Managing Director, Schroder Securities Hong Kong Ltd, since 1990; Hong Kong and SE Asian Equities. *Career:* Standard Chartered Bank (Abu Dhabi), Manager, Domestic Banking 1981-83; Standard Chartered Bank (Hong Kong), Manager, Trade Finance 1983-85; Warburg Securities, Salesman 1985-88; Schroder Securities, Director, European Sales Desk SE Asian Equities 1988-90; Schroder Securities Hong Kong, Managing Director 1990. *Biog: b.* 9 January 1959. *Nationality:* British. *m.* 1987, Hilary Jane Vipen (née Bourne); 1 d. *Educ:* Gresham School, Holt, Norfolk; School of Oriental and African Studies, London University (BA Hons Economics & Politics Majoring in Chinese Economics. *Directorships:* Schroder Securities Ltd 1989 (exec). *Recreations:* Reading, History, Shooting, Farming.

NEILL, John; Group Secretary, Legal & General Group plc, since 1973. *Biog: b.* 23 December 1937. *Nationality:*

British. *Educ:* FCIS. *Directorships:* Banner Life Insurance Company Limited 1983; Bridge End Properties Limited 1978; General Housing Company Limited 1973; Glanfield Securities Limited 1978; Gulliver Holdings Limited 1973; Legal & General Services Limited 1987; Paramount Realty Holdings Limited 1973; The Cavendish Land Company Limited 1973; Bear Holdings Limited 1973-1990; General Housing (Nottingham) Limited 1973-1989; Legal & General Independant Intermediaries Limited 1986-1987; Settle Speakman & Company Limited 1973-1989; Swithin's Investment Company Limited 1973-1989.

NEILLY, Gordon Joseph; Finance Director, Ivory & Sime plc, since 1990; Finance/Administration. *Career:* Ivory & Sime Management Servs Div, Divisional Dir Investment Admin & Co Secretarial Function for Clients of the Group 1988-90; Ivory & Sime, Accountant 1984-88; Peat Marwick McLintock, Chartered Accountant 1981-84. *Biog: b.* 2 July 1960. *Nationality:* British. *m.* 1985, Elizabeth Ruth. *Educ:* Edinburgh University (B Comm). *Directorships:* Ivory & Sime plc 1990 (exec) Fin Dir; Charlotte Investments Ltd 1990 (exec); Ivory & Sime (Bermuda) Ltd 1990 (exec); Ivory & Sime (Dallas) Inc 1990 (exec); Ivory & Sime (Guernsey) Ltd 1990 (exec); Ivory & Sime (Oil & Gas) Inc 1990 (exec). *Professional Organisations:* Institute of Chartered Accountants of Scotland 1984. *Recreations:* Football, Rugby, Water Skiing, Driving.

NEILSON, H; Partner, Nabarro Nathanson.

NELLEMOSE, P M; Partner, MacIntyre Hudson.

NELSON, Dr Elizabeth Hawkins; Chairman, Addison Consultancy Group plc, since 1989; Strategic Research. *Career:* Mars Ltd Research Psychologist 1953-55; Benton & Bowles Dir & MD, Market Research 1955-64; Mass Observation Dir 1964-65; Taylor Nelson Group Dir & Chm 1965-; Addison Consultancy Group Dir. *Biog: b.* 27 January 1931. *Nationality:* British/American. *m.* 1975, CJ Esterson; 2 s; 1 d. *Educ:* Hanover High School, NH, USA; Middlebury College, Vt. USA (BA); University of London (PhD). *Directorships:* The Royal Bank of Scotland 1988 (non-exec). *Other Activities:* Member & Court Assistant, Worshipful Company of Marketors; Council and Chairman of Fellowship, Royal Society of Arts; Member, Visiting Ctee, Open University; Member, Forum (UK). *Professional Organisations:* Member, Market Research Society; President, World Assoc of Public Opinion Research. *Publications:* Marketing in 1992 & Beyond, Journal of RSA, 1989. *Recreations:* Bridge, Choral Singing, Opera.

NELSON, The Hon James Jonathan; Managing Director, Foreign & Colonial Ventures Ltd, since 1985; Venture & Development Capital, Management Buy-Outs. *Career:* Morgan Guaranty Trust Co of New York, Commercial Banking Officer 1969-73; Foreign & Colonial Management Ltd, Dir 1974-. *Biog: b.* 17 June 1947. *Nationality:* British. *m.* 1977, Lucy (née Brown); 3 d. *Educ:* Ampleforth College; McGill University, Montreal (BCom). *Directorships:* F&C Enterprise Trust plc 1981 (exec); Kingsgrange plc 1984 (non-exec); US Ventures SA 1984 (non-exec); First Mortgage Securities Ltd 1987 (non-exec); Intermediate Capital Group Ltd 1989 (non-exec); Leveraged Opportunity Trust plc 1989 (non-exec). *Other Activities:* Liveryman, Worshipful Company of Goldsmiths. *Clubs:* Queen's, Hurlingham, New Zealand. *Recreations:* Golf, Tennis, Skiing, Shooting, Fishing.

NELSON, John Frederick; Vice Chairman, Lazard Brothers & Co Ltd, since 1986; Corporate Finance. *Career:* Kleinwort Benson Ltd 1971-86; Dir 1980-86. *Biog: b.* 26 July 1947. *Nationality:* British. *m.* 1976, Caroline (née Hannam); 2 s; 1 d. *Educ:* Marlborough College. *Professional Organisations:* FCA.

NELSON, Mike W; Director, Hoare Govett International Securities.

NELSON, Paul; Partner, Linklaters & Paines, since 1987. *Biog: b.* 22 August 1956. *Nationality:* British. *m.* 1983, Dora Lawson. *Educ:* Latymer Upper School, London; Corpus Christi College, Cambridge (BA Law, MA). *Professional Organisations:* Solicitor.

NELSON, Paul James Atkinson; Executive Director, Daiwa Europe Limited, since 1988; Fixed Income Sales. *Career:* Manufacturers Hanover Ltd, Senior Manager 1970-77; Exxon Overseas Services (Bermuda), Foreign Exchange Analyst 1977-81; Salomon Bros (NY & London) 1982-86; County NatWest, Managing Director 1986-88. *Biog: b.* 13 January 1949. *Nationality:* British. *m.* Jayne; 1 s; 1 d. *Educ:* Portsmouth Polytechnic. *Directorships:* Daiwa 1988 (exec). *Recreations:* Bridge, Tennis.

NELSON, Reginald Mason; Non Executive Chairman, Arbuthnot Latham Bank Ltd. *Career:* New Zealand Insurance Co (NZ, Singapore, Malaya, India), Various 1943-56; J M Sassoon & Co Stock & Sharebrokers (Singapore), Snr Ptnr 1964-72; New Zealand Insurance Co, West End Rep, London 1977-82; New Zealand Insurance plc, Chm 1982-87; NZI Corporation Ltd, UK Corporate Rep 1985-88; Investment Research of Cambridge Ltd 1987-90. *Biog: b.* 21 November 1923. *Nationality:* New Zealander. *m.* 1974, Joanna Mary Rose (née Fearnley-Whittingstall); 1 s; 3 d. *Educ:* Kings College, Auckland, NZ. *Directorships:* KLKI Holdings Ltd 1980 (exec) Chm; Yula Catto & Co plc 1987 (non-exec); Arbuthnot Fund Managers Ltd 1989 (non-exec). *Clubs:* MCC, Oriental, Singapore Cricket Club.

NELSON-JONES, John Austen; Chairman Development Committee, Field Fisher Waterhouse, since 1980; Business Strategy and Marketing, Company and Commercial Law. *Career:* Gregory Rowcliffe & Co, Articled Clerk 1960-63; Nicholas & Co, Assistant Solicitor 1964-66; Howard Kennedy & Co, Partner 1966-68; Field Fisher Waterhouse, Partner (Company and Commercial Law) 1968-. *Biog: b.* 26 July 1934. *Nationality:* British. *m.* 1963, Helene (née Wood); 2 s. *Educ:* Repton; Trinity College, Oxford (MA Hons). *Directorships:* Stiefel Laboratory (UK) Ltd 1974 (non-exec); Job Ownership Ltd 1985 (non-exec); National Consumer Council 1987 (non-exec); City Technology College Trust Ltd 1987 (non-exec). *Other Activities:* Council Member, National Consumer Council; Chairman, Travel and Tourism Law Committee of International Bar Association. *Professional Organisations:* Solicitor, Member Law Society. *Publications:* Practical Tax Saving, 1969; Package Holiday Law and Contracts, 1985; Employee Ownership Law, 1987. *Clubs:* Hurlingham. *Recreations:* Tennis, Classical Music, Reading.

NELSON-JONES, Rodney Michael; Medical Litigation Partner, Field Fisher Waterhouse, since 1983; Personal Injury Law. *Career:* L Bingham & Co, Partner 1977-83; Prothero & Prothero, Articled Clerk then Assistant Solicitor 1973-77. *Biog: b.* 11 February 1947. *Nationality:* British. *m.* 1988, Kusum (née Dhorajiwala). *Educ:* Repton; Hertford College, Oxford (MA). *Other Activities:* Member, M1 Air Disaster Steering Committee. *Professional Organisations:* Member, Law Society, Herbert Ruse Prize 1974. *Publications:* Product Liability - the new law under the Consumer Protection Act 1987, 1987; Medical Negligence Case Law, 1990; Nelson-Jones and Nuttalls Tax and Interest Tables, 1988, 1989, 1990. *Clubs:* Campden Hill LTC, RAC. *Recreations:* Cinema, Reading, Tennis, Travel.

NELSON-SMITH, David Austin; Director, Cargill UK Ltd, since 1983; European Public Affairs. *Career:* Tradax England Ltd, MD 1977-83. *Biog: b.* 6 April 1936. *Nationality:* British. *m.* 1965, Joyce (née Naef); 1 s; 1 d. *Educ:* Brighton College; Corpus Christi College, Cambridge (MA). *Directorships:* Sun Valley Poultry Ltd 1987 Chm (non-exec). *Other Activities:* (Past Vice Chm), British Cereals Export Ctee. *Professional Organisations:* Immediate Past President, COCERAL (European Grain Trade Assoc). *Recreations:* Sport, Gardening, Reading.

NENG, Ergin; Assistant General Manager & Local Director, Turkish Bank, since 1985; UK. *Career:* Akbank (Turkey), Inspector/Mgr 1961-71; Turkish Foreign Trade Bank (Turkey), Deputy Gen Mgr 1971-81. *Biog: b.* 28 February 1936. *Nationality:* Turkish. *m.* 1966, Sidika (née Karesioglu); 1 s; 1 d. *Educ:* Galatasaray Lyceum, Turkey; Marmara University, Turkey (BA Accounting). *Professional Organisations:* Board of Governors Member, Turkish-British Chamber of Commerce and Industry (UK).

NESBITT, S J; Director/Group Deputy Chairman, E D & F Man Ltd.

NESS, Donald Henry Rothwell; Manager, Scottish Investment Trust, since 1986; Investment Management. *Career:* Scottish Investment Trust 1970-. *Biog: b.* 25 March 1942. *Nationality:* British. *m.* 1966, Sheila (née Jamieson); 2 s; 1 d. *Educ:* Oundle School. *Professional Organisations:* CA. *Recreations:* Golf, Skiing.

NETHERTON, Derek Nigel Donald; Director, J Henry Schroder Wagg & Co Ltd, since 1981; Corporate Finance. *Career:* Bacon & Woodrow, Actuarial Student 1966-69. *Biog: b.* 4 January 1945. *m.* 1976, Pamela Jane (née Corkill); 4 s. *Educ:* Charterhouse; King's College, Cambridge (MA). *Professional Organisations:* FIA.

NEVILLE, Roger Albert Gartside; VRD; Director, Group Chief Executive, Sun Alliance Group plc. *Nationality:* British. *Directorships:* Sun Alliance and London Insurance plc; Sun Alliance and London Assurance; Alliance Assurance Company Ltd; Sun Insurance Office Limited; The London Assurance; Pheonix Assurance plc and other Subsidiary Companies of Sun Alliance and London Insurance plc. *Other Activities:* Dep Chm, Association of British Insurers. *Professional Organisations:* FCA.

NEVILLE BOWEN, W; Chairman, Hill Samuel Investment Management Ltd.

NEVILLE PEEL, G H; Partner, Booth & Co.

NEVIN, E; Director, Merchant Navy Investment Management.

NEW, Professor Christopher Colin; Deputy Director, Cranfield School of Management, since 1989; Graduate Programmes & Manufacturing Management. *Career:* Rolls-Royce Aero Engines Ltd, Graduate Apprentice 1962-66; O R Scientist 1966-71; London Business School, Lecturer in Operations Management 1971-78; Cranfield School of Management, Professor of Operations Management 1978-89; Director, MBA Programme 1982-85; Professor of Manufacturing Strategy & Deputy Director of School 1989-. *Biog: b.* 25 December 1944. *Nationality:* British. *m.* 1968, Hilary (née Bates); 2 s. *Educ:* King Edward's, Five Ways, Birmingham; Peterhouse, Cambridge (BA,MA); LBS, London University (MSc Business Studies, Distinction); London University (PhD). *Directorships:* Case Clearing House of Great Britain and Ireland 1986 (non-exec) Chairman. *Professional Organisations:* Fellow, British Production & Inventory Control Society; British Academy of Management; Institute of Directors. *Publications:* Material Requirements Planning, 1973; Managing The Manufacture of Complex Products, 1975; Operations Management: Text and Cases, 1976; Managing Manufacturing Operations in The US, 1975-85, 1986. *Recreations:* Horse Riding.

NEWBEGIN, John; Partner, Cameron Markby Hewitt, since 1977; General Commercial Law, Financial Services, Regulatory, Insurance Matters Services,. *Career:* Withers, London, Solicitor 1972-74; Cameron Kemm Nordon, London (became Cameron Markby, then Cameron Markby Hewitt) 1975-. *Biog: b.* 20 February 1949. *Educ:* King's College, London (LLB). *Other Activities:* City of London Solicitors Company.

NEWBIGGING, D K; Non-Executive Deputy Chairman, Ivory & Sime plc.

NEWBURY, Warwick John; Associate Director, Coutts & Co, since 1987; Head of Private Banking Division. *Biog: b.* 13 February 1946. *Nationality:* British. *m.* 1970, Karen (née Hyde); 2 d. *Educ:* Canford School. *Directorships:* Coutts & Co (Suisse) SA 1987 (exec); Coutts & Co (Isle of Man) Ltd 1990 (exec) Chm; Coutts & Co (Nassau) Ltd 1990 (exec). *Professional Organisations:* Member, Lloyd's.

NEWCOMB, David Martin; Managing Director, Alexanders Discount plc; Bill Director. *Directorships:* East Grinstead Properties Ltd (non-exec) Chm; East Grinstead Electronic Components Ltd (non-exec) Chm.

NEWEY, Peter; Executive Director, Lazard Bros.

NEWHOUSE, Anthony John Raymond; Partner, Slaughter and May.

NEWLANDS, David Baxter; Finance Director, General Electric Company plc, since 1989. *Career:* Touche Ross & Co, Ptnr 1963-86; Saatchi & Saatchi, Finance Director 1986-89; GEC, Finance Director 1989. *Biog: b.* 13 September 1946. *m.* 1973, Susan Helena (née Milne); 2 s; 2 d. *Educ:* Edinburgh Academy. *Professional Organisations:* FCA. *Clubs:* Sutton & Epsom Rugby Club, Walton Heath GS. *Recreations:* Golf, Bridge.

NEWMAN, Anthony Henry; Secretary General, Society of Investment Analysts, since 1987; Chief Executive. *Career:* Holloway Bros (London) Ltd, Asst Secretary (Admin) 1960-62; Stone Marine Holdings Ltd, Asst Sec 1962-65; J Stone & Co (Deptford) Ltd, Secretary 1965-68; Society of Investment Analysts, Secretary 1969-86. *Biog: b.* 11 July 1929. *Nationality:* British. *m.* 1956, Mary (née Fuller); 2 d. *Educ:* St Nicholas, Southampton; Peter Symonds, Winchester. *Professional Organisations:* Fellow, Institute of Chartered Secretaries.

NEWMAN, Anthony Michael; Partner, Lane Clark & Peacock, since 1984. *Biog: b.* 19 July 1955. *Nationality:* British. *Educ:* St Dunstan's College; Queens' College, Cambridge (MA). *Professional Organisations:* Fellow, Institute of Actuaries; Member, Association of Consulting Actuaries.

NEWMAN, B D; Director, Henderson Crosthwaite Institutional Brokers.

NEWMAN, David John; Pensions Director, General Manager, Pensions Division, London and Manchester Group plc.

NEWMAN, Helen; Partner & Solicitor, Simmons & Simmons, since 1985; Intellectual Property. *Nationality:* British. *Educ:* King's College, London (LLB, AKC). *Professional Organisations:* Member, United States Trademark Assoc; Assoc Member, Institute of Trademark Agents.

NEWMAN, J A; Executive Director, Allied Dunbar Assurance plc, since 1989; Sales Management. *Career:* Sun Life Assurance Co of Canada, Sales Representative/ Unit Manager 1972-78; The London Evening Standard, Display Advertising Sales Representative 1971-72; The Metropolitan Police, Detective Constable (CID) 1966-71; Voluntary Service Overseas, Community Work in the Gilbert & Ellice Islands, W Pacific 1965-66. *Biog: b.* 14 December 1947. *Nationality:* British. *m.* 1970, Sogra (née Ali); 3 s. *Educ:* Ossett Grammar School, West Yorkshire. *Recreations:* Squash, Tennis, Gardening, Fine Art, Family.

NEWMAN, J C; Director, Morgan Grenfell & Co Limited.

NEWMAN, P J; Partner, Arthur Andersen & Co Chartered Accountants, since 1989; Audit, Energy Group. *Career:* Arthur Andersen & Co, Trainee Accountant 1976-80; Mobil Oil Corporation, Corporate Auditor 1980-82; Mobil North Sea Ltd, Internal Auditor/Projects 1982-84; Arthur Andersen & Co, Manager 1984-89. *Biog: b.* 19 February 1955. *Nationality:* British. *m.* 1976, Donnas; 1 s; 1 d. *Educ:* Hertford College, Oxford (BA Hons); Hertford College, Oxford (MA). *Other Activities:* Secretary, Disclosure and Revenue & Financing Sub-Committees of the Oil Industry Accounting Committee. *Professional Organisations:* FCA (ICAEW). *Clubs:* Foxhills Country Club; *Clubs:* United Oxford & Cambridge University Club.

NEWMAN, Dr Paul Andrew; Director, Tranwood & Company Limited, since 1988; Corporate Finance. *Biog: b.* 7 February 1961. *Nationality:* New Zealander. *m.* 1990, Joanna Reesby. *Educ:* Kings College, Auckland; University of Auckland (MSc); Oxford University (DPhil). *Directorships:* Blackwood Financial Communications plc 1987 (non-exec). *Clubs:* The Auckland Club. *Recreations:* Opera, Architecture.

NEWMAN, William L; Assistant General Manager, Marketing, Moscow Narodny Bank Limited, since 1990;

Trade Finance, Joint Ventures, Project Finance, Asset Trading, Countertrade & Trade Development, Public Relations. *Career:* Moscow Norodny Bank Ltd, Senior Manager, Research 1988-90; Manager, Economics Department 1972-88. *Biog: b.* 12 September 1937. *Nationality:* British. *m.* 1963, Susan Mary (née Lockwood); 1 s; 1 d. *Educ:* Hull University (BA, Post Graduate Certificate of Education). *Professional Organisations:* Member, Royal African Society; Member, Society of Business Economists. *Publications:* Miscellaneous Articles on East-West Relations and Economic Analysis. *Recreations:* Music, Literature.

NEWMARCH, Michael George (Mick); Group Chief Executive, Prudential Corporation plc, since 1990. *Career:* Prudential Assurance Company Ltd, Economic Intelligence Analyst/Fund Manager 1958-79; Deputy Investment Manager 1979-80; Investment Manager 1980-89; Prudential Portfolio Managers Ltd, Chief Executive 1982-90; Prudential Assurance Co Ltd, Chairman 1990; Prudential Corporation plc, Group Chief Executive 1990. *Biog: b.* 19 May 1938. *Nationality:* British. *m.* 1959, Audrey (née Clark); 1 s; 2 d. *Educ:* London University (BSc Econ). *Directorships:* Prudential Corporation 1985 (exec); Prudential Portfolio Managers Ltd 1990 (exec) Chm; The Mercantile & General Reinsurance Co plc 1981 (exec); Prudential Pensions Ltd 1988 (exec); Prudential Holborn Ltd 1987 (exec); Jackson National Life Insurance Co 1990 (exec). *Professional Organisations:* Society of Investment Analysts. *Clubs:* Flyfishers Club. *Recreations:* Salmon and Trout Fishing, Bridge, Concert and Theatre Going.

NEWSOME, J M; Company Secretary/Chief Accountant, Walker Crips Weddle Beck plc, since 1989. *Career:* Arthur Andersen & Co, Articled Clerk 1979-83; The Spastics Society, Senior Internal Auditor 1983-86; Union International plc, Senior Internal Auditor 1986-87. *Biog: b.* 11 September 1957. *Nationality:* British. *Educ:* Kings College School, Wimbledon; University of Hull (BSc Hons Econ). *Professional Organisations:* Institute of Chartered Accountants in England & Wales (ACA); Registered Representative of the Securities Association. *Clubs:* Woking Golf Club. *Recreations:* Golf, Travel, Photography.

NEWSON, T J; Director/Underwriter, MFK Underwriting Agencies Ltd.

NEWTON, H P; Director, Hill Samuel Bank Limited, since 1988; Commercial Banking/Structured Finance. *Career:* Hill Samuel Bank (London), Shipping/Swaps 1981-87; Hill Samuel Bank (Tokyo), Head of Swaps 1987-90. *Biog: b.* 23 August 1959. *Nationality:* British. *m.* 1987, Beverley Jane (née Martyn). *Educ:* Maidenhead Grammar School; St Johns College, Oxford (BA PPE).

NEWTON, J A; Clerk, Coopers' Company.

NEWTON, John; Executive Director, Lombard Communications Limited.

NEWTON, Robert Charles; City/Economics Editor, Press Association, since 1988; The Economy and City & Company Affairs. *Career:* Evening Gazette, Colchester, Reporter/Sub Editor 1970-73; Birmingham Evening Mail, Sub Editor 1973-74; Press Association, Sub Editor 1974-77; Lloyd's List, Sub Editor 1977-78; East Essex Gazette, Dep Editor 1978-80; Harwich Standard, Editor 1980-83; Chambers Cox & Co, Publications Mgr 1983-84; Press Association, Sub Editor 1984-88. *Biog: b.* 13 July 1949. *Nationality:* British. *m.* 1976, Susan (née Rees). *Educ:* Colchester Royal Grammar; Leeds University (BA Hons).

NEWTON, Stewart Worth; Chairman & Managing Director, Newton Investment Management, since 1977. *Career:* Touche Ross, Trainee Accountant 1959-63; W Greenwell, Analyst 1963-68; Ivory & Sime, Fund Manager, Partner, Director 1968-77. *Biog: b.* 31 October 1941. *Nationality:* British. *m.* 1970, Jan (née Maples); 3 d. *Educ:* William Hume Grammar; Wrekin College. *Professional Organisations:* FCA. *Recreations:* Hockey, Cricket, Family, Reading.

NEWTON PRICE, R J; Partner, Cameron Markby Hewitt.

NEYENS, Frank A C V M; Executive Director, Credit Suisse First Boston Limited, since 1978; France/Benelux - Corporate Finance. *Career:* The First Boston Corporation 1970-73; First Boston (Europe) Ltd 1973-78; Director 1977; Credit Suisse First Boston Limited, Executive Director 1978-80; LTCB International Limited, Deputy Managing Director 1980-82; Credit Suisse First Boston Ltd, Executive Director 1982-. *Biog: b.* 4 February 1945. *Nationality:* Dutch. *m.* 1971, Dorrit E M (née Beynes); 2 d. *Directorships:* Credit Suisse First Boston France SA 1990 (non-exec); Credit Suisse First Boston Nederland NV 1989 (non-exec). *Recreations:* Walking, Reading, Skiing, Sailing.

NGUYEN-QUANG, Hoan; Senior Associate Director, Head of Corporate Fin & Banking, Société Générale Merchant Bank plc.

NIAS, P M W; Partner, Simmons & Simmons, since 1982; Solicitor, Corporate Commercial Tax. *Career:* Simmons & Simmons, Articled Clerk 1976-. *Biog: b.* 24 November 1953. *Nationality:* British. *m.* 1986, Monica (née Wing); 2 s. *Educ:* Dragon School, Oxford; William Hulme's School, Manchester; Manchester University (LLB). *Other Activities:* Member, Taxation Committee, International Chamber of Commerce. *Professional Organisations:* Member, International Fiscal Association. *Clubs:* Barsarkar och Vikingar (Swedish Club). *Recreations:* Music, Reading, Family Life.

NICHOL, David Brett; Director, Ivory & Sime plc, since 1980; Managing Director, Ivory & Sime Asia Ltd; Asian Pacific Investments. *Career:* County Bank Corp Fin 1968-70; Martin Corporation (Australia) Corp Fin 1970-71; WI Carr (Hong Kong) Research Analyst 1971-72; Ivory & Sime 1972-. *Biog: b.* 20 April 1945. *Nationality:* British. *m.* 1977, Judith Mary (née Parker); 4 d. *Educ:* Sedbergh School. *Directorships:* Pacific Assets Trust 1985 (non-exec). *Professional Organisations:* FCA. *Clubs:* New Club (Edinburgh), Hon Company of Edinburgh Golfers, Royal & Ancient Golf Club, Shek-o (Hongkong). *Recreations:* Shooting, Skiing, Golf.

NICHOLLS, Harry Anthony; Managing Director, Birmingham Technology (Venture Capital) Ltd, 1988; Overall Responsibility for the Company. *Career:* Royal Army Educational Corps 1957-60; Edinburgh University, Lecturer in Business Studies 1963-71; Director of Studies 1965-71; Ashorne Hill College, Deputy Director of Studies 1971-74; Aston University, Director of Postgraduate Studies 1974-82; Dean of Faculty of Management & Policy Sciences 1982-84; Head of Management Centre 1982-84; Birmingham Technology Limited, Director 1982-84; Chief Executive 1984-; Managing Director 1985-. *Biog: b.* 9 May 1937. *Nationality:* British. *Educ:* King Edward VII School, Sheffield; Leicester University (BA Soc Sci 2:i). *Directorships:* Birmingham Technology Limited 1985 MD; Birmingham Technology (Services) Ltd 1985; Birmingham Technology (Venture Capital) Ltd 1988; Birmingham Technology (Property) Limited 1988; AD2 Limited 1986; Aston Technical, Management & Planning Services 1984; Women's Enterprise Development Agency 1986. *Other Activities:* Member, CBI Smaller Firms Council; Member, CNAA Committee for Business, Management & Information Studies; Member, BIM National Council. *Professional Organisations:* CBIM; Chairman, West Midlands Regional Board of British Institute of Management. *Publications:* Numerous Publications on Venture Capital, University/Industry Interrelationships, Technology Transfer & Regional Development.

NICHOLLS, John Michael; Managing Director, Sun Life Properties Ltd, since 1975; Property Investments Management. *Biog: b.* 8 October 1934. *Nationality:* British. *m.* 1959, Janet (née Lea); 2 d. *Educ:* College of Estate Management. *Professional Organisations:* FRICS.

NICHOLLS, Mark Patrick; Director, S G Warburg & Co Ltd, since 1985; Corporate Finance. *Career:* Linklaters & Paines, Articled Clerk 1972-74; Solicitor 1974-76. *Biog: b.* 5 May 1949. *Nationality:* British. *m.* 1978, Catherine Mary (née Betts); 2 s; 2 d. *Educ:* Oundle School; Williston Academy, USA; Christ's College, Cambridge (MA). *Directorships:* S G Warburg & Co Ltd 1985 (exec); Sound Advantage plc 1990 (non-exec). *Other Activities:* Hon Treasurer, Royal National Institute for the Deaf. *Recreations:* Golf, Gardening.

NICHOLLS, P C; Director, James Capel Corporate Finance Ltd.

NICHOLLS, T H; Director, Hambros Bank Limited.

NICHOLS, Andrew John Fulford; Partner, Linklaters & Paines, since 1981; Property Law. *Career:* Linklaters & Paines, Articled Clerk 1969-71; Assistant Solicitor 1971-81. *Biog: b.* 7 February 1947. *Nationality:* British. *m.* 1976, Susan Mary (née Stry); 2 s. *Educ:* Marlborough College; University of Southampton (LLB). *Other Activities:* Freeman, City of London Solicitors' Company. *Professional Organisations:* Law Society. *Clubs:* Naval & Military. *Recreations:* Reading, Theatre.

NICHOLS, The Rev Canon Barry Edward; Partner, Ernst & Young, since 1970; Audit. *Career:* Arthur Young, Employee 1957-70; Partner 1970-89; Managing Partner 1983-86; Ernst & Young, Partner 1989-. *Biog: b.* 23 January 1940. *Nationality:* British. *m.* 1970, Anne (née Hastings); 1 s; 2 d. *Educ:* Epsom College. *Other Activities:* Church of England Priest; Member of Finance Ctee, Advisory Council for the Church's Ministry; Southwark Diocesan Synod; Southwark Diocesan Board of Finance; Dean for Ministers in Secular Employment in Kingston Episcopal Area. *Professional Organisations:* FCA. *Recreations:* Reading, Gardening.

NICHOLSON, Andrew Broadfoot; Chairman, Bell Lawrie Ltd.

NICHOLSON, B T G; Chairman, Marlar International Limited.

NICHOLSON, Brinsley Richard Ingebreth; Partner, Linklaters & Paines, since 1977; Financial Services, Insolvency and White Collar Crime. *Career:* Qualified Solicitor 1971. *Biog: b.* 11 April 1947. *Nationality:* British. *Educ:* Winchester College. *Other Activities:* Law Society; City of London Solicitors Company. *Professional Organisations:* Solicitor; Licensed Insolvency Practitioner. *Publications:* Joint Editor, A Handbook of Bankruptcy Law and Practice (3rd Edition), 1978. *Clubs:* Royal Wimbledon Golf Club, The Hurlingham Club. *Recreations:* Golf, Squash, Tennis, Antique Collecting.

NICHOLSON, C D; Director, Morgan Grenfell & Co Limited.

NICHOLSON, Graham Beattie; Managing Partner, Freshfields, since 1990. *Career:* Freshfields, Partner 1980-; Managing Partner, Company Department 1986-89. *Biog: b.* 22 February 1949. *Nationality:* British. *m.* 1982, Pamela (née Tan); 1 d. *Educ:* Bloxham School; Trinity Hall, Cambridge (MA). *Professional Organisations:* Law Society. *Recreations:* Music, Sailing.

NICHOLSON, Graham John; Partner, S J Berwin & Co, since 1990; Corporate Law. *Career:* Hancock &

Willis, Trainee Solicitor 1983-85; S J Berwin & Co, Assistant Solicitor 1985-90. *Biog: b.* 26 May 1959. *Nationality:* British. *Educ:* Sturton-by-Stow School; London School of Economics (LLB). *Professional Organisations:* Solicitor. *Recreations:* Cinema, Skiing, Squash.

NICHOLSON, Malcolm G C; Partner, Slaughter and May, since 1982; EEC/Competition Law and Regulation. *Biog: b.* 4 March 1949. *m.* 1975, Diana (née Jones); 4 d. *Educ:* Haileybury; Cambridge University (BA, LLB); Brussels (LIC, Droit Euro).

NICHOLSON, Martin; Joint Managing Director, Nicholson Chamberlain Colls Limited.

NICKSON, Sir David; KBE, DL; Chairman, Scottish Development Agency, since 1989. *Career:* Coldstream Guards 1949-54; William Collins/Publishers, Management Trainee 1954-61; Dir 1961-67; Jt MD 1967-76; Vice Chm 1976-79; Vice Chm & Group MD 1979-82; Scottish & Newcastle Breweries plc, Dep Chm 1982-83; Chm 1983-89; CBI Scotland, Vice Chm 1977-79; Chm 1979-81; CBI UK, Dep Pres 1985-86; Pres 1986-88; Scottish Development Agency, Dir 1988; Chm 1989-. *Biog: b.* 27 November 1929. *Nationality:* British. *m.* 1952, Helen Louise (née Cockcraft); 3 d. *Educ:* Eton College; Royal Military Academy, Sandhurst; Stirling University (Hon Doctor); Napier Polytechnic (Hon Doctor of Business Administration). *Directorships:* General Accident Fire & Life Assurance Corporation plc 1971 (non-exec); Clydesdale Bank plc 1981-88 (non-exec); 1989 (non-exec); Edinburgh Investment Trust plc 1982 (non-exec); Hambros plc 1988 (non-exec); Scottish United Investors Ltd 1970-82 (non-exec); Radio Clyde plc 1982-85 (non-exec); G & J Nickson & Co, Liverpool Food Manufacturers 1959-72 (non-exec). *Other Activities:* Member, Queen's Body Guard for Scotland, The Royal Company of Archers; Companion, British Institute of Management; Fellow, Royal Society of Arts; Fellow, Royal Society of Edinburgh; Chairman, Atlantic Salmon Trust; Member, Council CBI for Scotland (1974-83); Member, CBI Council (1977-); Member, National Training Task Force (1989-); Member, Top Salaries Review Body (1988-); Chairman, Top Salaries Review Body (1989-); Chairman, Countryside Commission for Scotland (1983-86); Member, Scottish Economic Council (1980-); Member, National Economic Development Council (1985-88); Scottish Industrial Development Advisory Board (1975-80); Scottish Committee, Design Council (1978-81). *Clubs:* Boodles, Flyfishers, MCC, Western (Glasgow). *Recreations:* Fishing, Bird Watching, The Countryside.

NICKSON, J D; Director, C Czarnikow Ltd.

NICOL, Alexander David; Deputy Chief Executive and Director, The British Linen Bank Ltd.

NICOL, Fiona Margaret; Director, Kleinwort Grieveson Securities.

NICOL, M J; Partner, Wedlake Bell (Solicitors), since 1963. *Biog: b.* 8 May 1940. *Nationality:* British. 3 d. *Educ:* London University (LLB). *Professional Organisations:* Solicitor; Member, Law Society. *Clubs:* MCC, Savage, British Sportsmens.

NICOLAOU, Serge; Deputy General Manager, BNP plc, since 1989. *Career:* Banque Nationale de Paris, Inspecteur, then Chef de Mission, Inspection Générale 1973-79; (Marseille), Directeur Adjoint, Chargé de l'Administration 1979-81; (Lille), Directeur Adjoint, Clientèle Entreprises 1981-83; (Ile de la Réunion), Directeur du groupe d'agences 1984-87; (Paris), Direction de l'Organisation, Responsable des systèmes étrangers 1987-89; (London), Deputy General Manager & Secrétaire Général 1989-. *Biog: b.* 17 April 1945. *Nationality:* French. *m.* Michèle; 2 d. *Educ:* Conservatoire des Arts et Métiers, Paris; Centre d'Etudes Supérieures de Banque, Paris.

NICOLI, E L; Chief Executive European Operations, United Biscuits (Holdings) plc.

NICOLSON, Charles Lancaster; Director, Mentor Fund Management Ltd. *Biog: b.* 26 June 1947. *m.* 1977, Hilary (née Warren); 2 s; 1 d. *Educ:* Haileybury (MSc). *Directorships:* Adam & Co (Group) plc (non-exec); Wendover Underwriting Agency Ltd (non-exec). *Clubs:* Brook's, RTYC.

NICOLSON, Sir David; Director, LASMO plc.

NICOLSON, Roy MacDonald; Managing Director, Scottish Amicable Life Assurance Society, since 1990. *Career:* Scottish Amicable Life Assurance 1960 -. *Biog: b.* 12 June 1944. *Nationality:* British. *m.* 1972, Jennifer; 1 s; 1 d. *Educ:* Paisley Grammar. *Directorships:* Scottish Amicable Life Assurance Society (exec); Scottish Amicable Nominees Limited (exec); Scottish Amicable Pensions Investments Limited (exec); Scottish Amicable Trustees Limited (exec); Scottish Amicable PEP Managers Limited (exec); Scottish Amicable PEP Nominees Limited (exec). *Other Activities:* Member, Council of the Faculty of Actuaries. *Professional Organisations:* FFA; FPMI.

NIEBOER, Jeremy; Partner, Gouldens, since 1982; Company/Commercial. *Career:* Barrister (Inner Temple) 1965-68; Fitzhugh Gates (Brighton), Partner 1970-77; Speechly Bircham, Partner 1978-82. *Educ:* Harrow School; Oriel College, Oxford (MA). *Professional Organisations:* Law Society. *Clubs:* Reform Club. *Recreations:* Cricket, Fishing.

NIMMO, James Alexander; Partner, Ashurst Morris Crisp, since 1988; Tokyo Office. *Biog: b.* 26 April 1956.

m. 1983, Lynda Goetz; 1 s; 1 d. *Educ:* Charterhouse; Peterhouse, Cambridge (BA Hons). *Recreations:* Sailing, Fishing.

NINOMIYA, R; Managing Director (Investment Management), Sanyo International Ltd.

NISBET, David Maltman; Director, County NatWest Securities Ltd, since 1989; Insurance Research. *Career:* Scottish Widows Fund & Life Assurance Society, Actuarial Trainee 1977-80; Wood Mackenzie (Now Part of County NatWest) 1980-. *Biog: b.* 14 February 1956. *Nationality:* Scottish. *m.* 1978, Janice (née Hislop); 1 s; 1 d. *Educ:* Tillicoultry Primary; Dollar Academy; University of St Andrews (BSc Hons Statistics). *Directorships:* County NatWest Securities 1989 (exec). *Professional Organisations:* FFA. *Publications:* Various Actoural Papers. *Clubs:* Craigmillar Golf Club, Edinburgh Southern Orienteering Club, Horsemaster Club. *Recreations:* Orienteering, Fell Mining, Hill Walking, Golf, Bridge, Reading.

NISHIMURA, M; Sales Director Leasing Division, Okasan International (Europe) Ltd.

NISHIMURA, T; Chairman, Triland Metals Ltd.

NISSAN, David; Editor, The Money Programme, BBC.

NISSE, Ian Bertram; Partner, Ashurst Morris Crisp, since 1987; Commercial Property. *Biog: b.* 5 January 1956. *Nationality:* British. *m.* 1987, Mary (née Pierce); 1 d. *Educ:* Bradford Grammar School; Durham University (BA). *Recreations:* Flying.

NISSEN, George Maitland; CBE; Chairman, Investment Management Regulatory Organisation, since 1989. *Career:* Pember & Boyle (Stockbrokers), Partner 1956-86; Senior Partner 1982-86; Morgan Grenfell Group plc, Director 1984-87; Adviser 1987-; Stock Exchange Council 1973-; Deputy Chairman 1978-81; The Securities Association, Board 1986-89; Gilt Edged Market Makers Association, Chairman 1986-. *Biog: b.* 29 March 1930. *Nationality:* British. *m.* 1956, Jane (née Bird); 2 s; 2 d. *Educ:* Eton; Trinity College, Cambridge (MA). *Directorships:* New Frontiers Development Trust 1987 Chairman; Union Discount 1988 (non-exec); Trades Union Unit Trust Managers 1988 (non-exec). *Other Activities:* Chairman of Governors, Reeds School; Chairman of Governors, St Paul's Girls Prep School; Governor, Godolphin & Latymer School; Governor, Royal Academy of Music. *Professional Organisations:* Associate; Society of Investment Analysts. *Clubs:* Brooks'. *Recreations:* Music, Railways, Walking.

NIVEN, Keith Melville; Director, Schroder Investment Management Ltd, since 1985; UK Institutional Fund Management. *Biog: b.* 14 August 1948. *m.* 1974,

Lesley Anne (née Wilson); 1 s; 1 d. *Educ:* The High School of Glasgow; Glasgow University (BSc Hons). *Recreations:* Golf, Hill Walking.

NIVEN, W G; Director, Sun Alliance and London Insurance plc.

NIX, P D A; Director, M & G Investment Ltd.

NIXON, Sir Edwin (Ronald); CBE, DL; Deputy Chairman, National Westminster Bank plc. *Career:* Dexion Ltd, Mgmnt Acct 1950-55; IBM (UK) Ltd Salesman/Mgmnt 1955-65; MD 1965-79; Chm & Chief Exec 1979-86; Chm 1986-90. *Biog: b.* 21 June 1925. *Nationality:* British. *m.* 1952, Joan Lillian (née Hill); 1 s; 1 d. *Educ:* Alderman Newton's School, Leicester; Selwyn College, Cambridge (MA). *Directorships:* Royal Insurance; Amersham Int plc Chm; Business in the Community. *Other Activities:* Council Member, Open University; Patron, Institute of Economic Affairs; VP, Opportunities for the Disabled; Pres, Nat Assoc for Gifted Children; Chm, Monteverdi Choir & Orchestra; The Prince's Youth Business Trust; Chichester Cathedral Development Trust; The Civil Service College. *Professional Organisations:* Chartered Institute of Marketing (Hon Fellow). *Clubs:* Athenaeum. *Recreations:* Music, Tennis, Golf, Sailing.

NIXON, John; Company Executive, Smith New Court plc, since 1985; Director in Charge of European Market Making. *Career:* Sun Life Assurance, Junior Trainee 1965-67; Halifax Building Society, Junior Trainee 1967-69; White & Cheeseman, Stock Exchange Dealer 1969-71. *Biog: b.* 6 February 1949. *Nationality:* British. *m.* 1980, Vivien (née Goldstone); 1 s. *Educ:* Clarks College, Southend. *Clubs:* Boyce Hill Golf Club, Flights Squash Club. *Recreations:* Golf, Squash, Tennis.

NIXON, W; Company Secretary, The Securities Association Limited.

NOAKES, Michael; Director (Convertible Sales), Hoare Govett International Securities.

NOAKES, Mike; Finance Director, Newmarket Venture Capital plc.

NOAKES, Simon John; Senior Partner, Beavis Walker, since 1987. *Career:* Beavis Walker, Articled Clerk 1968-73; Partner 1974-. *Biog: b.* 8 February 1948. *Nationality:* British. *m.* 1977, Rosemary Joan (née Cockburn); 3 s. *Educ:* Wallington GS. *Directorships:* West Wales Properties plc 1990 (non-exec) Chm; Mutual Accountants Professional Indemnity Company Ltd 1987 (non-exec); Structural Engineers Professional Indemnity Association Ltd 1990 (non-exec); Inpact International Ltd 1989 (non-exec). *Other Activities:* Council Member, Roehampton Institute. *Professional*

Organisations: FCA. *Clubs:* Carlton Club, Royal Wimbledon Golf Club. *Recreations:* Golf, Shooting.

NOBLE, E N; Financial Director, MFK Underwriting Agencies Ltd.

NOBLE, Professor Iain William; WS; Partner, Dundas & Wilson CS, since 1953; Conveyancing. *Biog:* b. 6 December 1925. *Nationality:* British. *m.* 1960, Dr Mary (née Bird); 1 s; 2 d. *Educ:* Inverness Royal Academy; University of Edinburgh (MA, LLB). *Clubs:* New Club, Edinburgh.

NOBLE, J J; Director, Kleinwort Benson Limited, since 1990; Corporate Finance. *Career:* Price Waterhouse, Chartered Accountant 1980-83. *Biog:* b. 22 March 1959. *Nationality:* British. *Educ:* Winchester College; New College, Oxford (BA). *Professional Organisations:* ACA.

NOBLE, N R; Head of Tax Dept, Field Fisher Waterhouse.

NOBLE, Peter; Director, Barclays de Zoete Wedd Limited, since 1986; Banking. *Career:* Barclays Bank plc Various 1956-76; Barclays Merchant Bank Ltd Various 1977-85; Director 1985-86. *Biog:* b. 29 September 1939. *m.* 1962, Cynthia Rosemary (née Munt); 1 s; 1 d. *Educ:* Rutlish College, Merton. *Professional Organisations:* AIB. *Clubs:* Old Rutlishians. *Recreations:* Egyptology, Gardening.

NOBUHARA, K; Chief Representative, The Hiroshima Bank Ltd, since 1988; UK. *Biog:* b. 19 January 1947. *Nationality:* Japanese. *m.* 1973, Kiyomi; 2 s. *Educ:* Kyoto University.

NODA, Hideki; Deputy Managing Director, Mitsui Finance International.

NODA, Yuzo; Managing Director, Maruman Securities (Europe) Ltd, since 1987. *Career:* The Tokai Bank Ltd (New York), Dep Gen Mgr 1979-84; (Tokyo), Gen Mgr 1984-86; Maruman Securities Co Ltd, Gen Mgr, Intl Dept 1986; (London Representative Office), Chief Rep 1987. *Biog:* b. 31 August 1939. *Nationality:* Japanese. *m.* 1968, Yoko (née Nakajima); 3 d. *Educ:* Hitotsubashi University (BA Economics). *Recreations:* Music, Reading, Travel, Sports.

NODDER, Edward John; Partner, Bristows, Cooke & Carpmael Solicitors, since 1986; Intellectual Property and Company Commercial Law. *Career:* Bristows, Cooke & Carpmael, Articles 1978-80; Bristows, Cooke & Carpmael, Assistant Solicitor 1980-86. *Biog:* b. 29 June 1956. *Nationality:* British. *m.* 1982, Rosalind (née Mackinney); 1 s. *Educ:* Lewes Grammar School; Christ's College, Cambridge (MA Natural Sciences & Law).

Professional Organisations: Solicitor, Member of the Law Society. *Recreations:* Natural History, Opera.

NOEL-PATON, Hon Frederick Ranald; Group Managing Director, John Menzies plc, since 1986. *Career:* British United Airways/British Caledonian Airways 1965-75; British Caledonian Airways (West Africa), Gen Mgr 1975-79; (Far East) Gen Mgr, Caledonian Far East Airways, Director 1980-86. *Biog:* b. 7 November 1938. *Nationality:* British. *m.* 1973, Patricia (née Stirling); 4 d. *Educ:* Rugby School; McGill University, Montreal (BA). *Directorships:* Pacific Assets Trust plc 1986 (exec); General Accident plc 1987 (non-exec); Royal Bank of Scotland plc 1988 (non-exec); Macallan-Glenlivet plc 1990 (non-exec). *Clubs:* Sheko Country Club, Hong Kong Club, New Club (Edinburgh). *Recreations:* Golf, Music, Ornithology, Walking.

NORBURY, J D; Director, Charterhouse Tilney.

NORBURY, Robert L; Deputy Chairman, Head of Corporate Finance, Wood Mackenzie & Co Ltd.

NORDBERG, Donald; Financial Editor, Europe, Middle East, Africa, Reuters Ltd, since 1989; To Supervise Reporting of All Business & Economic Affairs in the Region. *Career:* Fairchild Publications of New York, Reporter, News Editor & London Correspondent 1974-79; Reuters Ltd Sub-Editor 1979-80; Frankfurt Correspondent and Bureau Chief 1980-84; (Switzerland) Chief Correspondent 1984-88; Deputy News Editor 1988-89. *Biog:* b. 11 November 1949. *Nationality:* American. *m.* 1979, Hilary (née Glassborow); 2 s. *Educ:* Reed College, Portland, Oregon; University of Illinois (BA, MA).

NORDEN, Geoffrey R; Partner, Neville Russell.

NORFOLK, Jeremy Paul; Managing Director, Adam & Company plc, since 1988. *Career:* Bell Lawrie Robertson & Co 1973-75; Citibank NA 1975-83. *Biog:* b. 7 March 1948. *Nationality:* British. *m.* 1972, Rosemary Frances (née Raffan); 1 s; 1 d. *Educ:* Kingswood School, Bath; The King's School, Canterbury; Aberdeen University (MA). *Recreations:* Golf, Tennis, Gardening.

NORINDER, Jan Bertil; Director, Representative, Banque Scandinave En Suisse, since 1986; Portfolio Management. *Career:* S E Banken (Stockholm), Bond Trader 1962-69; (New York) Rep 1969-73; (Malmo), Snr VP 1973-76; Scandinavian Bank, Exec Dir 1976-86. *Biog:* b. 16 December 1937. *Nationality:* Swedish; 1 s; 1 d. *Educ:* Swedish Education. *Directorships:* Swedish British Chamber of Commerce 1987 Chm. *Recreations:* Skiing, Shooting, Art, Antiques.

NORLAND, Christopher Charles; Director, Rea Brothers Limited, since 1990; Head of Corporate Finance. *Career:* Finnie & Co Chartered Accountants (& its predecessor firms) 1958-82; IFICO plc 1982-89. *Biog: b.* 26 May 1937. *Nationality:* British. *m.* 1962, Patricia Ann (née Noel Jones); 1 s; 2 d. *Educ:* Leighton Park, Reading. *Directorships:* Frank Usher Holdings plc 1986 (non-exec) Chairman; Silk Industries Limited 1989 (non-exec) Chairman; Castle Communications plc 1986 (non-exec); Exmoor Dual Investment Trust plc 1988 (non-exec); Reliance Security Group plc 1980 (non-exec); Zeon Limited 1990 (non-exec). *Other Activities:* Freeman of the City of London. *Professional Organisations:* FCA. *Clubs:* The Lansdowne Club. *Recreations:* Tennis, Skiing, Walking, Music.

NORMAN, David Mark; Chairman & Chief Executive, Charles Barker plc, since 1987. *Career:* Norprint Ltd Mktg Dir 1968-69; MD 1969-72; Norcros Printing & Packaging Div Chief Exec 1971-75; Norcros Ltd Dir of Operations 1975-77; Russell Reynolds Associates Inc Exec Dir 1977-78; MD 1978-82; Norman Resources Ltd Founder & Chm 1982-83; Norman Broadbent International Ltd Founder & Chm 1983-. *Biog: b.* 30 January 1941. *Nationality:* British. *m.* 1966, Diana Anne (née Sheffield); 1 s; 3 d. *Educ:* Eton College; McGill University, Canada (BA Hons); Harvard Business School, USA (MBA). *Other Activities:* Governor, Royal Ballet School; Dir, Royal Opera House Ballet Board; Chm, The Tennis & Rackets Assoc of Great Britain. *Professional Organisations:* Founding Member, Business Graduates Association. *Clubs:* Boodle's, Queen's, All England Tennis Club, RAC. *Recreations:* Competitive Sport, Classical Music, Opera, Ballet.

NORMANDALE, O C T R; Master, Worshipful Company of Glass Sellers.

NORMARK, D; Director, The London Metal Exchange Ltd.

NORRIE, G B; Director, Wellington Underwriting Agencies Limited.

NORRINGTON, Humphrey Thomas; Executive Director, Barclays Bank plc, since 1987; Overseas Operations. *Career:* Barclays Bank UK Ltd, Gen Mgr 1981-85; Barclays Bank plc, Sen Gen Mgr, Finance 1985-86; Dep Chief Gen Mgr 1986-87. *Biog: b.* 8 May 1936. *Nationality:* British. *m.* 1963, Frances Guenn (née Bateson); 2 s; 2 d. *Educ:* Winchester College; Worcester College, Oxford (MA). *Other Activities:* Fin Ctee, British Red Cross Society; Fin Ctee, Nat Assoc of Boys' Clubs. *Professional Organisations:* FCIB. *Clubs:* United Oxford & Cambridge University. *Recreations:* Music, Tennis.

NORRIS, P M R; Director, Baring Brothers & Co Limited, since 1987; Corporate Finance. *Career:* Baring Brothers & Co Limited, Assistant Director 1976-84; Goldman Sachs & Co, Vice President 1984-87. *Biog: b.* 2 March 1955. *Nationality:* British. *Educ:* Magdalen Col-

lege, Oxford (Modern History & Modern Languages). *Directorships:* Baring Brothers & Co Limited 1987; Baring Brothers Asia Limited 1987-88; Cotton Nominees Ltd 1987; Baring Securities (HK) Limited 1987; Baring Futures (Hong Kong) Limited 1987; Baring Brothers Burrow & Partners Limited 1989; Baring Brothers Burrow & Partners (Securities) Limited 1989; China & Eastern Investment Co Ltd 1987; Commerce International Merchant Bankers Berhad 1990 Alternate Director; Baring Brothers & Wu Limited 1990; P T Baring Securities Indonesia 1990; Dukedove Limited 1985; Duff & Trotter Limited 1990. *Other Activities:* Hong Kong Committee on Takeovers & Mergers; Advisory Committee, Securities & Futures Commission, Hong Kong.

NORRIS, William V W; Partner, Allen & Overy. *Other Activities:* Chairman, Law Society Revenue Law Committee.

NORTH, Robert Murray; Partner, Clifford Chance, since 1990; Tax. *Biog: b.* 25 November 1956. *Nationality:* British. *m.* 1987, Victoria-Louise (née Harper). *Educ:* Brasenose College, Oxford (MA). *Professional Organisations:* Solicitor of the Supreme Court, (Formerly Barrister-at-Law). *Recreations:* Music, Theatre.

NORTH, S J; General Manager, Clydesdale Bank plc, since 1988; IT. *Career:* Loughborough University, Programmer 1972; Bovis Ltd, Senior Programmer 1973; Self-Employed Analyst Programmer 1973-75; Altergo (Ireland) Ltd, Senior Programmer/Analyst to Director 1975-83; PA Consulting Group, Senior Consultant to Director Business Development, Implementation Services 1983-88. *Biog: b.* 8 August 1951. *Nationality:* British. *m.* 1987, Margaret; 1 d. *Educ:* Doncaster Grammar School; Manchester University (BSc Computer Science). *Directorships:* Altergo (Ireland) Ltd 1979-83 (exec); BACS Ltd 1988-89 (non-exec). *Professional Organisations:* Member, British Computer Society; Chartered Engineer.

NORTHAM, J B; Senior Partner, Jaques & Lewis.

NORTHAM, P C; Renter Warden, Worshipful Company of Glass Sellers.

NORTHEDGE, Richard; Deputy City Editor, Daily Telegraph, since 1986. *Career:* Investors Chronicle, Property Editor 1976-78; Evening Standard, Property Editor 1978-80; Daily Telegraph, City Column 1980-83; Personal Fin Editor 1983-86. *Biog: b.* 1950. *Nationality:* British. *m.* Rosemary. *Educ:* Beverley Grammar School; Nottingham University (BA Hons). *Publications:* Consumers' Guide to Personal Equity Plans, 1987.

NORTHROP, Antony Patrick Clinton; Managing Director, Capital Markets, Swiss Bank Corporation.

NORTHWAY, Mark; Executive Director, First Interstate Capital Markets Limited, since 1989; Head of Eurosecurities Trading & Sales. *Career:* Deloitte Haskins & Sells, London; Ristalurgica De Santa Ana, Madrid, Spain; Costain/Tailor Woodrow JV, Dubai, UAE. *Biog:* b. 4 January 1960. *Nationality:* British. *m.* 1983, Roberta; 2 s. *Educ:* Downside School; Exeter University (BA Hons). *Directorships:* First Interstate Capital Markets Limited 1989 (exec); First Interstate Securities Limited 1989 (exec). *Professional Organisations:* AIBD Diploma; TSA Registration.

NORTON, Anthony David Longueville; Director, GNI Ltd, since 1985; Financial & Energy Futures. *Career:* 13th/18th Royal Hussars (QMO) 1973-77; Sultan of Oman's Land Forces 1977-79; Butler Till Ltd 1980-83; GNI Ltd 1983-. *Biog:* b. 17 February 1953. *Nationality:* British. *Educ:* Downside School.

NORTON, Hugh Edward; Managing Director, The British Petroleum Company plc, since 1989; Exploration, Production, East Asian Region,Information Technology. *Career:* British Petroleum Co plc 1959-; British Petroleum Co plc, Regional Co-Ordinator, Middle East 1977-78; BP Singapore, Managing Director 1978-81; British Petroleum Co plc, Director, Planning 1981-84; British Petroleum Co plc, Director, Administration 1984-86; BP Exploration Co Ltd, Chief Executive 1986-89. *Biog:* b. 23 June 1936. *Nationality:* British. *m.* 1965, Janet M (née Johnson); 1 s. *Educ:* Winchester College; Trinity College, Oxford (BA Hons, Lit Hum). *Directorships:* The British Petroleum Co plc 1989; BP Exploration Co Ltd 1981; Britoil plc 1989 (non-exec); BP Petroleum Dev Co Ltd 1981; BP Far East Ltd 1989; BP Southern Africa (Pty) Ltd 1990; BP-Japan Oil Development Co Ltd 1989. *Other Activities:* Advisory Board of Impact. *Professional Organisations:* Companion of British Institute of Management. *Recreations:* Painting, Ornithology, Tennis, Travel.

NORTON, James Henry Llewelyn; Compliance Director, Morgan Grenfell & Co Ltd, since 1989. *Career:* Touche Ross & Co, Chartered Accountant 1966-71. *Biog:* b. 16 February 1948. *Nationality:* British. *m.* 1988, Gillian Irena. *Educ:* Eton College. *Directorships:* Morgan Grenfell Group plc; Morgan Grenfell (Ireland) Ltd Chairman; Morgan Grenfell (Cayman) Ltd Chairman; Morgan Grenfell & Co Ltd; Morgan Grenfell (C I) Ltd Chairman. *Professional Organisations:* FCA. *Clubs:* Turf, Annabel's. *Recreations:* Golf, Tennis.

NORTON, John Charles; Partner, Arthur Andersen & Co, since 1971; Head of European Oil & Gas Practice. *Career:* Arthur Andersen & Co 1961-. *Biog:* b. 22 April 1937. *Nationality:* British. *m.* 1962, Dianne (née Lloyd); 2 s; 1 d. *Educ:* Dulwich College; University College, Oxford (MA). *Other Activities:* Member, Oil Industry Accounting Ctee. *Professional Organisations:* FCA; Institute of Petroleum. *Clubs:* Brooks's, United Oxford &

Cambridge Universities, Vincent's (Oxford). *Recreations:* Travel, Opera, Rugby.

NORTON, John Lindsey; Chairman, BDO Binder Hamlyn, since 1987; International. *Career:* Qualified with Blackburn Robson Coates & Co 1959-63; BDO Binder Hamlyn 1963-; Partnership, Initially Specialising in Taxation, then Financial Advice, Mergers and Acquisitions and Audit 1966; National Managing Partner 1981; Chairman, BDO Binder (International Firm) 1987; Chairman, National Partnership Committee of BDO Binder Hamlyn 1987. *Biog:* b. 21 May 1935. *Nationality:* British. *m.* 1959, Judith Ann; 3 d. *Educ:* Winchester College; Cambridge University (MA Economics). *Other Activities:* Member, Central Executive Committee of the National Society for the Prevention of Cruelty to Children(NSPCC); Member, Disciplinary Appeals Committee of the Institute of Chartered Accountants in England and Wales. *Professional Organisations:* ACA; FCA.

NORTON, T R P S; Director, Wise Speke Ltd.

NOTT, Sir John; Director, Royal Insurance Holdings plc.

NOTTAGE, William Bruce; Partner, Nabarro Nathanson, since 1990; Corporate Finance/Pension Fund Investments/Plant Finance. *Career:* Slaughter & May, Assistant Solicitor and Articled Clerk 1976-79; British Coal Pension Funds, Assistant Solicitor 1979-87; Head Financial Law 1987-90. *Biog:* b. 9 May 1954. *Nationality:* British. *Educ:* Waterloo Grammar School, Lancashire; Warwick University (LLB 2:1); College of Law, Guildford (Law Society Part II). *Clubs:* International Training in Communication. *Recreations:* Five a Side Goalkeeper.

NOTTON, William James Duncan; Principal Associate, Grimley J R Eve, since 1989; National Head of Public Sector Consultancy. *Career:* Inland Revenue, Valuation Office 1975-89; Ekins Dilley & Handley 1972-75; Corby Development Corporation 1969-72; Cambridge City Council 1968-69; Oxford City Council 1966-68; Kivell & Sons 1962-64. *Biog:* b. 21 February 1942. *Nationality:* British. *Educ:* Perse School, Cambridge; Bideford Grammar School. *Professional Organisations:* FRICS. *Recreations:* Shooting, Motorcycling.

NOWELL, Peter; Chief Executive, Prudential Corporate Pensions, since 1988; Global Fixed Income, Pension Fund Investment. *Career:* The Prudential Assurance Co Ltd, Equity Fund Mgmnt 1971-82; Prudential Portfolio Managers Ltd, Director 1982-87. *Biog:* b. 13 October 1948. *Nationality:* British. *m.* 1976, Wendy (née Bonfield); 2 d. *Educ:* Reading School; London School of Economics (MSc). *Directorships:* London Indemnity & General Insurance Co Ltd (non-exec); Dartford River Crossing Ltd (non-exec); Prudential Pensions Ltd (exec).

Professional Organisations: FIA. *Recreations:* Squash, Skiing, Local Politics.

NOWELL-SMITH, J C; Partner, Freshfields.

NOWLAN, Howard Malcolm; Partner, Slaughter and May, since 1976; Corporate Tax. *Biog: b.* 12 March 1946. *m.* 1974, Frances (née Raffety); 1 s; 2 d. *Educ:* St Edward's School, Oxford; Brasenose College, Oxford (MA).

NSOULI, Ali; Associate Director, Maruman Securities (Europe) Limited, since 1989; Sales/Trading Equity and Equity Related Instruments. *Career:* Intra Investment Company (Beirut, Lebanon), Portfolio Manager 1981-83; BAII, Banque Arabe et Internationale d'Investissement, Paris, Fonde de Pouvoir Principal, Equity Related Instruments Trader 1983-86; BAII plc London, Associate Director, Japanese German and Swiss Markets Portfolio Manager 1986-89; Maruman Securities 1989-. *Biog: b.* 23 January 1960. *Nationality:* Lebanese/French. *m.* 1987, Catherine (née Lorain); 2 s. *Educ:* American University of Beirut (BBA). *Professional Organisations:* AIBD Diploma. *Clubs:* Riverside. *Recreations:* Tennis, Swimming, Ski, Basketball, Sailing.

NSOULI, El-Walid; Managing Director, Morgan Guaranty Trust Company of New York.

NUNN, Christopher Leslie; Partner, Arthur Andersen & Co, since 1976; Accounting and Audit Partner, Specialising in Manufacturing Industries and Stock Exchange and Technical Practice. *Biog: b.* 14 March 1943. *Nationality:* British. *m.* 1969, Lynne (née Hughes); 2 s. *Educ:* Highgate School; London School of Economics (BSc). *Other Activities:* Member, NEDO Ctee on Manufacturing Systems; Chm, Accounting Standards Ctee on Stocks and Long-Term Contracts. *Professional Organisations:* FCA. *Publications:* ICAEW Accountants Digest £Valuation of Stocks and Work in Progress£.

NUNN, R; Director, Hill Samuel & Co Ltd Treasury.

NUNNELEY, Charles Kenneth Roylance; Deputy Chairman, Robert Fleming Holdings Ltd, since 1986; Investment Management. *Career:* Brown Fleming Murray, Articled Clerk 1956-61; Scottish Chartered Accountants, Qualified 1961; Flemings, Analyst 1962; Manager, Research Department 1965; Fund Manager, Portfolio Management Department 1967; Main Board Director 1968; Head of Department 1970; Robert Fleming Asset Management & Robert Fleming (France) SA, Chairman 1988; Robert Fleming Holdings, Deputy Chairman. *Biog: b.* 3 April 1936. *Nationality:* British. *m.* 1961, Catherine Elizabeth (née Buckley); 1 s; 3 d. *Educ:* Eton College. *Directorships:* Clerical Medical & General Life Assurance Society 1974 Dep Chm; Investment Management Regulatory Organisation Ltd (IMRO) 1986; Macmillan Ltd 1982; Monks Investment Trust plc

1977; Save and Prosper Group Limited 1989 Chm. *Other Activities:* Chairman, Institutional Fund Managers' Association & BMBA Asset Management Committee; Member of Court, Grocers Company (Master 1982-83); Governor, Oundle School, (Chairman of Finance Committee); Member of Finance Commitee, National Trust. *Clubs:* Hurlingham. *Recreations:* Tennis, Shooting, Photography, Walking, Reading.

NUSSBAUM, D; Director, Charterhouse Bank Limited; International Corporate Finance & International Development Capital. *Career:* Economist Intelligence Unit, Project Manager; Charterhouse Japhet Limited, Director International; Greyhound International Financial Services, Managing Director; Charterhouse Bank Limited.

NUTTALL, G J; Partner, Field Fisher Waterhouse, since 1988; Taxation. *Career:* Field, Fisher & Martineau, Articled Clerk 1982-84; Field, Fisher & Martineau, Assistant Solicitor 1984-88. *Biog: b.* 29 December 1959. *Nationality:* British. *m.* 1985, Elizabeth Jane (née Mayes); 1 s. *Educ:* Prices School/College; Peterhouse, Cambridge (MA); College of Law, Guildford. *Professional Organisations:* Law Society; Associate Member of Institute of Taxation. *Publications:* Employee Ownership - Legal & Tax Aspects, 1987 (Co-Author); Nelson-Jones' & Nuttall's Tax and Interest Tables, 1988, 1989 & 1990; Sponsorship, Endorsement & Merchandising, 1990 (Co-Author).

NUTTALL, Peter Scott; Joint Chairman, Carr Kitcat & Aitken Limited, since 1990; Overall Management. *Career:* Various in the Computer Industry and Consultancy Systems Analyst & Consultant 1959-68; Kitcat & Aitken Computer Mgr 1968-72; Ptnr 1972-74; Admin Ptnr 1974-75; Fin Ptnr 1975-80; Managing Ptnr 1980-82; Snr Ptnr 1982-86; MD 1986-88; RBC Dominion Securities International Ltd Vice Chairman 1988-90. *Biog: b.* 25 June 1934. *Nationality:* British. *Educ:* Oakham School; Worcester College, Oxford (MA). *Professional Organisations:* The Stock Exchange (Member); FBCS. *Recreations:* Walking, Cricket.

O

O'BRIEN, B J O; Partner, Freshfields, since 1986; Corporate Finance. *Career:* Slaughter and May, Articled Clerk and Solicitor 1976-83; Freshfields 1983-. *Biog: b.* 27 October 1952. *Nationality:* British. *m.* 1984, Susan Margaret; 1 s; 1 d. *Educ:* St Illtyd's College, Cardiff; University College, London (LLB). *Other Activities:* City of London Solicitors Company. *Professional Organisations:* Law Society. *Clubs:* Academicals. *Recreations:* Sport.

O'BRIEN, M R T; Clerk, Fishmongers' Company.

O'BRIEN, Michael J; Managing Director, Goldman Sachs International Finance Limited.

O'BRIEN, P; Company Secretary, James R Knowles Limited.

O'BRIEN, R F; Council Member, FIMBRA.

O'BRIEN, Timothy William; Chief Executive Officer UK, The Hong Kong and Shanghai Banking Corporation Ltd, since 1990. *Career:* Hong Kong and Shanghai Bkg Corp, Singapore, Manager Credit 1985-87; Hong Kong, Assistant General Manager Finance 1987-88; Hong Kong Assistant General Manager Corporate Banking 1988-89. *Biog: b.* 6 July 1947. *Nationality:* British. *m.* 1973, Cordelia (née Wykes-Sneyd); 2 d. *Educ:* Ampleford College, Yorks; University of Bristol (BA). *Directorships:* HongkongBank London Ltd 1989 (exec); HBL Nominees Ltd 1989 (exec); James Capel & Co Ltd 1989 (non-exec); Wardley Investment Services Intl Ltd 1990 (non-exec); Gatechurch Property Management Ltd 1990 (exec); HongkongBank Nominees UK Ltd 1990 (exec); Honggroup Nominees Ltd 1990 (exec); HSBC Holdings UK Ltd 1990 (exec); HBL Property Finance Ltd 1990 (exec); HongkongBank London Holdings Ltd 1990 (exec); Gatestock Ltd 1990 (exec); Marine Midland Bank (Nominees) Ltd 1990 (exec); Reachlift Ltd 1990 (exec). *Other Activities:* British and Overseas Commonwealth Banks' Association - Vice Chairman.

O'CATHAIN, Miss Detta; OBE; Managing Director, Barbican Centre for Arts and Conferences, since 1990; Arts Administration, Conference & Exhibition Administration. *Career:* Aer Lingus Economist 1961-66; Tarmac plc Group Economist 1966-69; Rootes Motors/Chrysler UK Economic Adviser 1969-72; Carrington Viyella Snr Economist 1972-73; British Leyland Dir, Market Planning 1973-76; Unigate plc Head of Corp Planning 1976-81; Milk Marketing Board Head, Strategic Planning 1981-84; Milk Marketing Board, Managing Direc-

tor Milk Marketing 1984-88. *Biog: b.* 3 February 1938. *Nationality:* British. *m.* 1968, William Bishop. *Educ:* Laurel Hill School, Limerick; University College, Dublin (BA). *Directorships:* Midland Bank plc 1984 (non-exec); Tesco plc 1985 (non-exec); Sears plc 1987 (non-exec). *Other Activities:* Fellow, Royal Society of Arts; Fellow, Chartered Institute of Marketing; Council Member, Industrial Society. *Recreations:* Reading, Music, Walking.

O'CONNOR, Ms Gillian; Editor, Investors Chronicle.

O'DOCHARTAIGH, Dr Aodh; Director, STC plc, since 1986; External Affairs and Communication. *Educ:* University College, Galway (BSc,BA); Cranfield Institute of Technology (PhD).

O'DONNELL, E; Director, R A McLean & Co Ltd.

O'DONNELL, J J; Director, County NatWest Limited.

O'DONNELL, James; Corporate First Vice President, Drexel Burnham Lambert Securities Ltd.

O'DONOGHUE, Dermot; Head of Treasury-Britain, Allied Irish Banks plc.

O'DONOGHUE, Martin John; Partner, Titmuss Sainer & Webb, since 1989; Commercial Property Development. *Career:* Witham Weld & Co, Articled Clerk 1978-79; City of London Corporation, Assistant Solicitor 1980-82; Nabarro Nathanson, Assistant Solicitor 1982-84; Turner Kenneth Brown, Assistant Solicitor 1984-87; Titmuss Sainer & Webb, Assistant Solicitor 1987-89. *Biog: b.* 1 November 1954. *Nationality:* British. *m.* 1979, Edaena (née Moloney); 1 s. *Educ:* Kings College, London (LLM). *Other Activities:* Liveryman, City of London Solicitors Company; Freeman of the City of London. *Professional Organisations:* Member, The Law Society. *Recreations:* Golf.

O'DONOVAN, F; General Manager, AIB Finance Ltd.

O'DONOVAN, II; Banking & Finance Partner, Richards Butler.

O'DONOVAN, Jerome Finbarr; General Manager-Business Banking, AIB Bank, since 1983; Business

Banking. *Career:* Allied Irish Banks plc Various 1961-75; Personnel Admin Mgr 1975-81; Head of Personnel 1981-83. *Biog: b.* 11 December 1941. *Nationality:* Irish. *m.* 1970, Moyra (née Murphy); 2 s; 3 d. *Educ:* Presentation Brothers' College, Cork; University College, Cork (BCom); University College, Dublin (MBA). *Other Activities:* Ctee Member, Co-operation Ireland. *Professional Organisations:* Institute of Personnel Management, Insitute of Directors; Fellow, Chartered Institute of Bankers in Ireland. *Clubs:* RAC, London Irish RFC, Middlesex CCC. *Recreations:* Sport, Art, Reading.

O'DRISCOLL, John Patrick; General Manager, Mellon Bank, since 1989. *Career:* Mellon Securities Limited Exec Dir (Syndications & Sales) 1987-88; Managing Director 1988-89. *Biog: b.* 24 June 1950. *Nationality:* Irish. *m.* 1977, Catherine E (née Fortier); 2 s; 1 d. *Educ:* Clongowes Wood College; Trinity College, Dublin (BA (Hons); Wharton School of Finance (MBA). *Directorships:* Mellon Securities Ltd 1988 (exec).

O'GORMAN, Robert Anthony Mary; Director, Banking Division, Barclays de Zoete Wedd Limited, since 1989; Acquisition and Mezzanine Financing. *Career:* Barclays Bank plc 1965-; Barclays de Zoete Wedd Limited (formerly Barclays Merchant Bank Limited). *Biog: b.* 19 April 1946. *Nationality:* Irish. *m.* 1973, Sheila (née Smith); 1 s; 2 d. *Educ:* Gunnersbury R C Grammar School. *Professional Organisations:* ACIB; Registered Representative, The Securities Association Ltd. *Clubs:* The Cornhill Club, Cannons. *Recreations:* Reading, Golf, Fishing, Gardening.

O'HANRAHAN, S; Executive Director, Daiwa Europe Limited.

O'HARA, Mark; Executive, Livingstone Fisher plc, since 1990; Mergers, Acquisitions, Disposals, Corporate Finance. *Career:* Neville Russell, Chartered Accountants 1982-85; Coopers & Lybrand, Chartered Accountants 1985-86; NESCO Investments plc, Financial Controller and Company Secretary 1986-88; Parallel Media Group plc, Group Finance Director 1988-90. *Biog: b.* 14 February 1961. *Nationality:* British. *m.* 1988, Angela (née O'Sullivan). *Educ:* King George V School, Hong Kong; University of Manchester (BA Econ Hons). *Professional Organisations:* Chartered Accountant. *Recreations:* Golf, Squash, Music, Drama.

O'HARA, Pat; General Manager, Bank of Ireland.

O'LEARY, Andrew George; Actuary & Secretary, Clerical Medical & General Life Assurance Society, since 1982; Corporate Finance. *Biog: b.* 4 July 1929. *Nationality:* British. *m.* 1964, Helen Elizabeth Worthington (née Evans); 1 s; 1 d. *Educ:* Mount St Mary's College; Trinity College, Cambridge (BA). *Directorships:* Clerical Medical (and Subsidiaries) 1975 (exec). *Other Activities:*

Dep Chm, BIIC; Guild of Guardians; Member, The Executive Ctee, Avon & Bristol Federation of Boys' Clubs. *Professional Organisations:* FIA, Society of Investment Analysts. *Clubs:* United Oxford & Cambridge, Clifton. *Recreations:* Walking, Singing.

O'LEARY, J C; Clerk, Apothecaries' Society.

O'MAHONEY, G J; Assistant General Manager, Administration and Operations, The Toronto-Dominion Bank, since 1989; In Charge of all Bank's Computer and Communications Systems, Foreign Exchange & Money Market Back Office, Loans Administration & Agency/ Syndications Function. *Career:* Bank of Ireland (Dublin) 1972-81; Computer Sciences Canada (Toronto), Marketing Representative 1981; The Bank of Montreal (Toronto), Senior Auditor, Corporate and Operations 1981-82; The Toronto-Dominion Bank (Toronto), Analyst, Office Automation 1982-; Manager, International Business Systems/Manager, Project Analysis 1985; Toronto Dominion Australia Limited (Melbourne), Director Administration 1985-88; The Toronto-Dominion Bank (London), Assistant General Manager Administration and Operations 1988-. *Biog: b.* 18 May 1954. *Nationality:* Irish/Canadian. *m.* Joan (née Mulvihill); 1 s; 1 d. *Educ:* University College Dublin (BCom). *Directorships:* Toronto Dominion Australia Limited. *Other Activities:* Member, General Committee of The British Overseas and Commonwealth Banks' Association. *Clubs:* Foxhills Golf and Country Club.

O'MAHONY, Jeremiah F; FCA; Financial Director, Ladbroke Group plc.

O'MALLEY, Christopher; Director, Samuel Montagu & Co Limited.

O'NEIL, Daniel; Investment Director, FS Investment Services.

O'NEILL, Derham; Partner, Clifford Chance.

O'NEILL, Nigel A; Partner, Moores Rowland, since 1980; Fraud & Corporate Investigations Human Resource Consultancy. *Career:* Articles with Edward Moore & Sons 1968-72; Mgr in Charge of Management Consultancy Division of South African Associated Firm in Johannesburg 1974-76; Mgr in Charge, Special Investigations Unit 1977-80; Partner in Charge, Hong Kong Office 1980-84; Involved with Operational Activities of Kingston upon Thames, Luxembourg and Monte Carlo Offices 1984-88. *Biog: b.* 16 March 1949. *Nationality:* British. *m.* Carolyn (née Galpin); 2 d. *Educ:* The Oratory, Berkshire. *Professional Organisations:* FCA. *Clubs:* RAC, London Welsh RFC, FCC (Hong Kong), Hong Kong Cricket Club. *Recreations:* Antiques, Rugby, Cricket.

O'NEILL, Dr Peter Terence (Terry); Partner, Clifford Chance, since 1980; Litigation in Shipping, Insurance, Banking, Commodities. *Career:* University College, London Lecturer in Law 1965-68; Brunel University, Lecturer in Law 1972-75; Barrister 1973-78; University College, London 1975-77. *Biog: b.* 18 September 1944. *Nationality:* British. *m.* 1976, Vivien (née Middleton); 1 s; 1 d. *Educ:* Ratcliffe College, Leicester; University College, London (LLB,PhD). *Professional Organisations:* The Law Society; London Maritime Arbitrators' Association; Association of Average Adjusters. *Recreations:* Trying to raise Children.

O'REILLY, Desmond; Director, Financial Services, Bank of Ireland.

O'REILLY, P J; Director, Panmure Gordon & Co Limited.

O'RILEY, H F; Partner, Jaques & Lewis.

O'SHEA, Daniel; Director, M&G Investment Management.

O'SHEA, E K; Group Chief Administrative Officer, Ultramar plc.

O'SHEA, S; Director, Hill Samuel Bank Limited, since 1988; Banking. *Career:* Wm C Ribbeck & Co, Accountants 1951-58; Albatros Fertilizer Co Ltd, Secretary/Accountant 1958-60; Irish Sea Fisheries Board (BIM), Accountant 1960-61; Industrial Credit Company Ltd, Loans Executive, Manager, Hire Purchase & Leasing Division; Branch Manager, Senior Executive Manager, Securities Division 1961-73; Hill Samuel Bank (Ireland) Ltd, General Manager 1973-; Director 1975-87; Managing Director 1987-. *Directorships:* Hill Samuel Bank Ltd 1988 (exec); Hill Samuel Bank (Ireland) Ltd 1975 (exec); Irish Pensions Trust Ltd 1987 (non-exec); Consolidated Land Corporation (Ireland) Ltd Subsidiaries 1988 (non-ex ec). *Professional Organisations:* FCA; FIB; FInstD; Council Member, Irish Bankers Federation.

O'SULLIVAN, (James) Roderic (Mary); Partner, Holman Fenwick & Willan, since 1973; Company/Commercial/Shipping Law. *Biog: b.* 30 May 1944. *Nationality:* British. *m.* 1975, Susan Lesley (née Hedderwick); 3 s; 1 d. *Educ:* Downside School. *Other Activities:* Freeman, Worshipful Company of Shipwrights. *Professional Organisations:* Solicitor. *Clubs:* RAC, Hurlingham. *Recreations:* Tennis, Sailing.

O'TOOLE, Shaun Anthony; Vice President, First Interstate Bank of California.

OAKES, Gillian; Executive Director, Samuel Montagu & Co Ltd, since 1987; Corporate Finance. *Career:* Coopers & Lybrand, Chartered Accountant 1976-80; Arbuthnot Latham & Co Ltd, Mgr 1980-84. *Biog: b.* 6

July 1953. *Nationality:* British; 1 s; 1 d. *Educ:* King's Head School for Girls, Warwick; St Hilda's College, Oxford (MA). *Professional Organisations:* ACA; InstAM.

OAKES, John Alfred Victor; Founder and Director, Morgan Harford Limited, since 1990; Industry Development House/Consultancy. *Career:* Ashurst, Morris, Crisp & Co, Articled Clerk/Assistant Solicitor 1976-79; Wood Gundy Limited, Head of Eurobond Syndications 1979-82; Chase Investment Bank Limited (formerly Chase Manhattan Limited), Director 1982-87; Wallace, Smith Trust Co Limited, Director, Corporate Finance 1987-90. *Biog: b.* 11 May 1951. *Nationality:* British. *m.* 1979, Sarah Jane (née Maxfield); 2 s. *Educ:* St Bees School, St Bees, Cumberland; Brasenose College, University of Oxford (BA). *Directorships:* Morgan Harford Limited 1990 (exec) Founder; Rickett & Co Limited 1989 (non-exec); Colmore Incentives Limited 1989 (non-exec); Sweetwater Properties Limited 1988 (exec). *Professional Organisations:* Solicitor; Law Society of England & Wales; Institute of Directors. *Clubs:* Royal Liverpool Golf Club. *Recreations:* Golf, Sailing, Skiing, Travel.

OAKES, Robin Geoffrey; Partner, Neville Russell, since 1985; Insurance Market Audit & Advice - Lloyd's, Syndicates; Brokers, Agents, General Company Audit & Technical. *Career:* Coopers & Lybrand (Birmingham), Audit Clerk to Gp Snr Mgr 1968-81; Neville Russell (London), Audit & Accounts Tech Mgr 1981-83; Snr Audit Mgr 1983-84. *Biog: b.* 18 February 1946. *Nationality:* British. *m.* 1969, Lorna (née O'Neill); 3 d. *Educ:* City of Norwich School; Birmingham University (BCom). *Other Activities:* Working Party of Auditing Practices Ctee (ICAEW). *Professional Organisations:* FCA. *Publications:* Business Briefing: Insurance Brokers, 1985, Revised & Reissued, 1990; Industry Audit and Accounting Guide: Insurance Brokers, 1990. *Clubs:* Lloyd's Club. *Recreations:* Church Leadership, Walking, Family.

OAKES, Mrs Sandra E; Partner, Touche Ross & Co.

OAKLEY, Andrew; National Partner - Marketing, Ernst & Young, since 1988; Accounting & Auditing, Computers, Marketing. *Career:* Ernst & Young, Various Staff Positions 1961-70; Ptnr 1971-. *Biog: b.* 4 March 1940. *m.* 1978, Patricia. *Educ:* King Edward VI Five Ways School, Birmingham; Birmingham University (BCom). *Professional Organisations:* FCA; FBCS. *Recreations:* Travel, Gastronomy, Coarse Golf.

OAKLEY, Christopher Hugh Alban; Partner, Clifford Chance, since 1990; Banking & International Finance, Securitisation, Secured Lending Housing Association Finance. *Career:* Coward Chance/Clifford Chance, Articled Clerk/Assistant Solicitor 1981-90. *Biog: b.* 18 December 1956. *Nationality:* British. *Educ:* Redborne School Ampthill, Beds; Worcester College,

Oxford (BA Jurisprudence). *Recreations:* Theatre, Opera, Travel, Photography, Windsurfing.

OAKLEY, G M; Director, National Investment Group plc.

OATEN, Michael John; Partner-Head of Corporate Finance, Arthur Andersen & Co.

OBAYASHI, K; Editor, Nihon Keisai Shimbun.

ODDIE, Alan James; Managing Director, M&G Assurance Group Limited, since 1988. *Biog: b.* 24 June 1950. *Nationality:* British. *m.* 1976, Elaine Anne. *Educ:* Hammonds Grammar School; Downing College, Cambridge (MA). *Directorships:* M&G Group plc 1988 (exec); M&G Assurance Group Limited 1988 (exec) MD; M&G Life Assurance Co Ltd 1988 (exec) Chm; M&G Pensions & Annuity Co Ltd 1988 (exec) Chm. *Professional Organisations:* Fellow, Institute of Actuaries. *Recreations:* Bridge, Chess, Golf, Hiking, DIY, Gardening.

ODDIE, Mrs Elaine Anne; Partner, Morison Stoneham, Chartered Accountants, since 1989; Head of Business Services Department. *Career:* Mason Charlesworth & Co, Chartered Accountants, Partner 1982-89; Yardley International Ltd, Financial Accountant 1979-82; Brebner, Allen & Trapp, Trainee Accountant 1976-79. *Biog: b.* 11 February 1955. *Nationality:* British. *m.* 1976, Alan. *Educ:* Kings College, Cambridge (MA Mathematics). *Other Activities:* President, South Essex Society of Chartered Accountants. *Professional Organisations:* FCA. *Recreations:* Squash.

ODENHEIMER, Michael; Area Manager, Central Europe, First Interstate Bank of California, since 1989; Corespondent Banking, Germany, Italy, Austria. *Career:* First Interstate, Mgr, Intl Portfolio Services (Credit) 1987-89; Corporate Product Development 1987; Mgr, Canada/UK, US Business 1985-87; Central Europe, Desk Officer 1982-85; Trainee, Corp Banking 1981-82; Los Angeles County Transportation Commission, Local Govt Liaison 1980-81; City of LA, Council Aides 1978-80; California, State University, Instructor 1972-78. *Biog: b.* 12 June 1945. *Nationality:* American. *m.* 1981, Leslie; 1 s; 1 d. *Educ:* North Western University (PhD); University of California (BA).

ODESCALCHI, Charles Mark; Head of Eastern European Department, James Capel, since 1990. *Career:* Bank of London & South America, Euro-Bond Analyst 1967-70; Williams de Broe Hill Chaplin Gilt-Edged, Exec 1974-79; Carr-Sebag, Gilt Edged, Exec 1979-82; James Capel Gilts, Director 1986-90. *Biog: b.* 30 October 1948. *Nationality:* British. *m.* 1971, Rosario (née Reixa Vizoso); 1 s; 1 d. *Educ:* Oratory School; London School of Economics (BSc). *Directorships:* James Capel Gilts 1986 (exec). *Professional Organisations:* Member, the International Stock Exchange; Registered Rep, National

Assoc of Securities Dealers (USA). *Recreations:* Tennis, Skiing.

ODGERS, G D W; Director, Dalgety plc.

ODLING-SMEE, J C; Deputy Chief Economic Adviser, HM Treasury.

OFFER, R A S; Director, S G Warburg Akroyd Rowe & Pitman Mullens Securities Ltd.

OGDEN, Alan; Managing Director (Corporate Division), Hill and Knowlton UK, since 1988. *Career:* Grenadier Guards, Captain 1969-78; Financial Times, Sales Mgr 1978-82; St James Corporate Communications Development Dir 1982-83; Charles Barker, City Dir, Public Relations 1983-88. *Biog: b.* 5 July 1948. *Nationality:* British. *m.* 1980, Josephine (née Hunter); 1 s. *Educ:* Eton College. *Professional Organisations:* MIPR; FBIM. *Recreations:* Travelling.

OGDEN, Jeremy Joseph; Partner, Wilde Sapte, since 1988; Insolvency and Litigation. *Career:* Boodle Hatfield, Articled Clerk 1981-83; Solicitor 1983-84; Wilde Sapte, Solicitor 1984-88; Partner 1988-. *Biog: b.* 16 May 1958. *Nationality:* English. *m.* 1987, Anne. *Educ:* Repton School; Sheffield University (LLB Hons). *Professional Organisations:* The Law Society. *Recreations:* Hockey, Children.

OGILVIE, Robert Bruce Challinor; Director, County NatWest Limited, since 1987; Corporate Advisory. *Career:* Lazard Brothers & Co Limited Mgr 1976-84. *Biog: b.* 27 May 1954. *Nationality:* British. *m.* 1985, Caroline Mary (née Noble-Jones). *Educ:* Rugby; Magdalene College, Cambridge (BSc). *Directorships:* County NatWest Subsidiaries. *Recreations:* Shooting, Gardening.

OGILVY, David; Chairman, W P P Group plc.

OGILVY, David George Coke Patrick; The Rt Hon The Earl of Airlie; Kt, GCVO, PC; Chairman, General Accident Fire & Life Assurance Corp.

OGILVY, The Hon James Donald Diarmid; Chief Executive, Foreign & Colonial Management Ltd, since 1988. *Career:* Rowe & Pitman, Ptnr 1959-84; Mercury Asset Management, Vice Chm 1985-88; Mercury Rowan Mullens, Chm 1985-88. *Biog: b.* 28 June 1934. *Nationality:* British. *m.* 1980, Lady Caroline (née Child-Villiers); 2 s; 2 d. *Educ:* Eton College. *Directorships:* Foreign & Colonial Management Ltd 1988 Chief (exec); Foreign & Colonial Unit Management Ltd 1988; Foreign & Colonial Investment Trust plc 1989 (exec); Mercury Asset Management 1985 (exec) Vice Chm; A Number of Investment Companies (non-exec). *Clubs:* White's. *Recreations:* Shooting, Golf.

OGLEY, Julian A; Partner, McKenna & Co, since 1982; Corporate Finance. *Career:* Herbert Smith, Articled Clerk 1970-72; Slaughter & May, Assistant Solicitor 1972-81; McKenna & Co, Partner 1982-. *Biog: b.* 29 September 1947. *Nationality:* British. *Educ:* Hertford College, Oxford; Kings College, Canterbury (BA History). *Professional Organisations:* Law Society. *Clubs:* RAC Club. *Recreations:* Music, Films, Theatre.

OHASHI, Yuji; Deputy Managing Director, Mitsubishi Trust International Limited.

OHI, Taizo; Joint General Manager, The Sumitomo Bank Limited.

OKABE, Yoji; Senior Managing Director, Member of the Executive Board, The Sumitomo Bank Ltd, since 1987; Supervising European, Middle Eastern & African Operations. *Career:* Sumitomo Bank Ltd (Japan) 1957-61; Head Office 1961-73; Sumitomo Bank Ltd (California) Intl Dept 1973-76; Sumitomo Finance International, MD 1976-80; Sumitomo Bank Ltd (Japan) Gen Mgr, Merchant Banking Dept 1980-82; Dir 1982-84; (London) Gen Mgr 1984-85; MD 1985-87; Senior Managing Director, stationed in London 1988-90. *Biog: b.* 16 August 1934. *Nationality:* Japanese. *m.* 1959, Takako (née Nakamura); 2 s; 1 d. *Educ:* Kyoto University (BA). *Directorships:* Sumitomo Bank 1982 (exec); Banca del Gottard 1984 (exec). *Recreations:* Philately, Golf.

OKAHASHI, Osamu; Joint General Manager, The Sumitomo Bank Limited.

OKAZAKI, Eisuke; Director, Schroder Securities Limited.

OKAZAKI, M; Director, Dowa Insurance Company (UK) Limited.

OKELL, P C; Director, Charterhouse Tilney.

OLDALE, J K; Partner, Rowe & Maw.

OLDFIELD, M H; Deputy Chairman, Schlesinger & Company Limited.

OLDHAM, M D; Head of Branch, Department of Trade and Industry.

OLDING, Goup Captain R C; CBE; Clerk, Shipwrights' Company.

OLDINGER, A; Director, PK English Trust Company Limited.

OLDMAN, Paul Anthony; Partner, Lovell White Durrant, since 1987; Banking Corporate Finance. *Biog: b.* 22 December 1952. *Nationality:* British. *Educ:* Gt Yarmouth Grammar School; Manchester University (LLB Hons). *Other Activities:* City of London Solicitors' Company. *Professional Organisations:* The Law Society. *Recreations:* Theatre, Cinema, Music.

OLDWORTH, Richard Anthony; Chief Executive, Buchanan Communications Ltd, since 1984. *Career:* Peat Marwick Mitchell 1976-80; County Bank Ltd, Corporate Finance Executive 1980-83; Bisgood Bishop, Corporate Finance Executive 1984; Buchanan Communications (Formerly Binns Cornwall), Chief Executive 1984-. *Biog: b.* 5 June 1957. *m.* 1989, Sarah. *Educ:* Radley; City of London Polytechnic. *Professional Organisations:* ACA. *Clubs:* City of London Club, Royal Solent Yacht Club. *Recreations:* Flying, Motorsport.

OLIVER, J A; Clerk, Ironmongers' Company.

OLIVER, Jasper William Dacres; Director, Hambros Bank Ltd, since 1981; Investment Management. *Career:* Hambros Bank Ltd Investment Mgr 1962-66; Allied Hambros Unit Trust Managers Ltd Dir 1966-76; Hambro Pacific Fund Management Ltd MD 1976-79; Hambro Investment Management Intl Ltd MD 1979-81; Hambros Bank Unit Trust Managers Ltd MD 1982-. *Biog: b.* 5 September 1938. *Nationality:* British. *m.* 1973, Virginia (née Whitaker); 2 d. *Educ:* Eton College. *Directorships:* Hambros Investment Management Services Ltd 1980; Hambros Investment Managers Intl Ltd 1980; Hambros Bank Ltd 1981; Hambros Bank Unit Trust Managers Ltd 1982; Hambros Bank 1983; Hambro American Special Si 1983-88; Hambro Fund Managers (CI) Ltd 1983; Hambro Pacific Fund Management Ltd 1983; Capital Reserve Fund 1983-84; Hambro Generali Fund Managers Ltd 1985; Hambros Australia Investment Management Ltd 1985; Hambros Investment Nominees Ltd 1986; Hambros Toshi Komon Kaisha 1987; Hambro Pacific Ltd 1988; Hambros Bank (Jersey) Ltd 1983; BBV-Hambros Asset Management (Guernsey) 1989; Hambro Eurobond and Money Market Fund Ltd 1990; Hambro Currency Fund Ltd 1990; Hambro Japanese OTC Fund Ltd 1990; Hambros Equity Selection Fund Ltd 1989. *Other Activities:* Ironmongers Company. *Clubs:* Boodle's MCC. *Recreations:* Farming, Shooting, Fishing, Gardening.

OLIVER, Group Captain K M; Clerk, Saddlers' Company.

OLIVER, Michael John; Senior Manager, Commerzbank AG, since 1986; Corporate Banking, Corporate Finance. *Career:* The National Bank Ltd 1965-67; The First National Bank of Boston (UK) 1967-73; (Luxembourg) 1973-75; (West Germany) 1975-79; (Australia) 1979-82; (USA) 1982-85. *Biog: b.* 9 July 1948. *m.* 1977, Sheridan Elizabeth (née Ray); 1 s; 1 d. *Recreations:* Family, House, Garden, Squash.

OLIVER, Peter James; Partner, Touche Ross & Co.

OLIVER, R N; Managing Director, Homes, George Wimpey plc.

OLIVER, Steven Wiles; Lazard Freres KK (Tokyo, Japan), since 1990; Mergers & Acquisitions. *Career:* Citibank NA VP 1972-80; Lazard Asia Ltd, Hong Kong Managing Director 1980-87; Lazard Freres & Co Ltd (London), Managing Director 1988-90. *Biog: b.* 27 May 1947. *Nationality:* American. *m.* 1971, Susan Elizabeth (née Peace); 1 s; 2 d. *Educ:* Claremont Men's College (AB); Vanderbilt University School of Law (JD). *Directorships:* Lazard Asia Asset Management 1986 (non-exec); Lazard Freres & Co Ltd 1988 (exec); Lazard Brothers & Co Ltd 1989 (non-exec). *Other Activities:* General Ptnr, Lazard Freres & Co, New York. *Clubs:* Tokyo American Club (Penang), Hong Kong Country Club (Leland). *Recreations:* Tennis, Jogging.

OLIVEY, Alan Keith; Partner, Business Services, Ernst & Young, since 1980; Taxation, Employee Share Schemes & Profit Related Pay. *Career:* Sydenham, Snowden, Nicholson & Co, Articled Clerk 1965-70; Qualified CA 1970-71; Turquands, Barton Mayhew & Co, Tax Senior 1971-75; Turquands (later Ernst & Whinney), Tax Manager 1975-80. *Biog: b.* 14 October 1947. *Nationality:* British. *m.* 1971, Janet Mary (née Hutton); 1 s; 1 d. *Educ:* Heath Clark Grammar School. *Professional Organisations:* FCA; ATII. *Recreations:* Badminton, Photography.

OLLEY, Mrs Jacqueline Rose (née Harvey); Marketing Manager, James Capel Unit Trust Management Limited, since 1988; Marketing. *Career:* John Govett & Co Limited, Production & Advertising Co-ordinator/Marketing 1983-87; Self Employed, Provision of Office Services 1981-83. *Biog: b.* 24 March 1951. *Nationality:* British. *m.* 1972, Stephen Thomas; 1 s. *Educ:* McEntee Technical High School. *Directorships:* James Capel Unit Trust Management Limited 1990 Associate Dir. *Professional Organisations:* Member, Chartered Institute of Marketing; Diploma of Marketing; Registered Representative, The Securities Association. *Clubs:* Valentines Tennis & Social Club, Aldborough Hall Equestrian Centre. *Recreations:* Tennis, Horse Riding.

OLLEY, Martin Burgess; Chief Estates Manager, Norwich Union Real Estate Managers Ltd, since 1983; Property Development Investment & Management. *Career:* Norwich Union 1950. *Biog: b.* 11 August 1932. *Nationality:* British. *m.* 1979, Moira (née Kelly); 2 s; 1 d. *Educ:* Gresham's School. *Directorships:* Norwich Properties (Scotland) Ltd 1983 (exec); Brownleigh Properties Ltd 1983 (exec); Norwich Properties (Belgium) S A 1983 (exec); Norwich Union Real Estate Managers Ltd 1990 (exec); British Council for Offices 1990 (non-exec); British Property Federation 1988 (non-exec). *Other Activities:* Woolman Livery, Freeman City of London. *Professional Organisations:* FRICS. *Clubs:* RAC.

Recreations: Golf, Boating, Tennis, Badminton, Cricket, Walking.

OLLIFF, B M; Managing Director, Olliff & Partners plc, since 1987; Business Development, Corporate Finance. *Career:* Rowe Swann 1962-63; Denny Brothers 1964-78; Laing & Cruickshank, Director Institutional Sales 1979-86; Olliff & Partners plc, Managing Director 1987-. *Biog: b.* 31 December 1944. *Nationality:* British. *m.* 1967, Margaret Ann; 1 s; 1 d. *Directorships:* Laing & Cruickshank 1983 (exec). *Recreations:* Cricket, Skiing, Travel.

OLNEY, P M; Partner, Slaughter and May, since 1990; Company/Commercial. *Career:* Slaughter and May, Assistant Solicitor 1983-90. *Biog: b.* 15 March 1957. *Nationality:* British. *m.* 1982, Judith Olney (née Geddes); 1 s; 2 d. *Educ:* Kingston Grammar School; Haywards Heath Grammar School; London School of Economics (BSc Econ - First Class, Hobhouse Memorial Prize). *Professional Organisations:* Law Society.

OLSEN, Lawrence Nigel Guy; *Career:* Investors in Industry 1961-88. *Biog: b.* 22 February 1934. *Nationality:* British. *m.* 1959, Rosemary (née Kies); 1 s; 1 d. *Educ:* Chaterhouse. *Directorships:* Compass Group Ltd 1987 (non-exec); The Frizzell Group Ltd 1985 (non-exec); Moore Group Ltd 1988 Chm; Cornwell Parker plc 1970 (non-exec); Smith New Court plc 1989 (non-exec). *Professional Organisations:* FCA. *Recreations:* Sailing.

OLSEN, R J; Director, Finance, Cable & Wireless plc.

OMATA, Shoji; President and Managing Director, Tokyo Securities Co (Europe) Limited, since 1990; Trading, Corporate Finance. *Career:* The Nikko Securities Co Ltd, Tokyo International Dept 1963-67; The Nikko Securities Co International Inc, San Francisco, Representative 1967-71; The Nikko Securities Co Ltd, Tokyo, 1971-73; Nikko Research Centre, Ltd, Tokyo, Manager 1973-83; Tokyo Securities Co Ltd, Tokyo, General Manager of International Investment & Research Dept 1983-90. *Biog: b.* 25 May 1935. *Nationality:* Japanese. *m.* 1971; 1 s; 1 d. *Educ:* Sophia University, Japan (Bachelor of Economics). *Recreations:* Golf.

ONIANS, Richard Anderson; Chief Executive, Baring Brothers Hambrecht & Quist Ltd, since 1984; Unquoted Investment Management & Corporate Finance. *Career:* Monsanto Chemicals Co (London) Marketing Mgr 1959-64; Monsanto Europe-SA (Brussels) Business Dir 1965-74; Monsanto Co (USA) Dir Human Resources 1975-77; Dir Pharmaceuticals 1977-78; Dir Corporate Strategy 1979-81; Dir Intl Development 1981-83; VP Electronics/Venture Capital 1983-4. *Biog: b.* 21 April 1940. *Nationality:* British. *m.* 1961, Marianne Dorothy (née Laidlaw); 1 s; 1 d. *Educ:* Thetford Grammar School. *Directorships:* Baring Brothers & Co Ltd 1985 (exec); Kratos Group plc 1984 (non-exec); Baring

Brothers Hambrecht & Quist Ltd 1984 (exec); Design Marketing Ltd 1986 (non-exec); Baring Capital Investors Ltd 1986 (non-exec); York Ltd 1989 (non-exec). *Other Activities:* FRSA, Club 54, House of Commons. *Professional Organisations:* EVCA. *Recreations:* Travel, Reading.

ONO, Kozo; Managing Director, Yamaichi International (Europe) Ltd, since 1988; Bond Sales. *Career:* Yamaichi Securities (Tokyo), Account Executive 1964-74; Yamaichi Investment Trust Fund Manager 1975-79; Yamaichi Securities (Tokyo), Manager of Foreign Stock Dept 1979-81; Yamaichi Switzerland, Deputy General Manager 1981-84; Yamaichi Securities (Tokyo), Gen Mgr of Intl Bond Marketing Dept 1984-88. *Biog: b.* 13 October 1940. *Nationality:* Japanese. *m.* 1967, Junko (née Ogawa); 1 s; 1 d. *Educ:* Kansei Gakuin University (BA). *Recreations:* Tennis, Skiing, Calligraphy, Golf.

OOI, D; Director, Kim Eng Securities (London) Limited.

OPATRNY, Donald Charles; Managing Director, Goldman Sachs International Limited, since 1987; Corporate Finance. *Career:* Morgan Guaranty Trust Co, Asst Treasurer 1976-78; Goldman, Sachs & Co, Ptnr 1978-87. *Biog: b.* 29 September 1952. *Nationality:* American. *m.* 1977, Judith (née Tindal); 1 s; 1 d. *Educ:* Cornell University (AB); University of Chicago (MBA). *Other Activities:* British Merchant Banking and Securities Houses Association, Corporate Finance Committee. *Recreations:* Golf, Sailing, Tennis.

OPPENHEIM-BARNES, Sally; The Rt Hon the Baroness Oppenheim-Barnes of Gloucester; Non-Executive Director, The Boots Co plc, since 1982; Non-Executive Director, The Fleming High Income Investment Trust plc, since 1989; Non-Executive Director, HFC Bank plc, since 1990. *Career:* Industrial and Investment Services Ltd, Executive Director 1964-69; MP (Con) for Gloucester (longest serving Member for this constituency and 1983 largest ever majority) 1970-87; Member of the General Advisory Council of the BBC 1972-74; National Union of Townswomens Guild, National Vice Chairman 1973-79; Royal Society for the Prevention of Accidents, National Vice Chairman 1973-79; Chairman of Conservative back bench Committee, Prices and Consumer Protection 1973; Appointed by Mr Heath Opposition Front Bench spokesman, Prices and Consumer Protection 1974; Appointed by Mrs Thatcher to the Shadow Cabinet (same portfolio) 1974-79; Privy Council 1979; Minister of State for Consumer Affairs, Department of Trade 1979-82; Chairman, Department of Environment Public Enquiry into Pedestrian Safety at Level Crossings Oppenheim Report 1986; Appointed Secretary of State for Trade and Industry 1987-89; Chairman, National Consumer Council; Chairman, National Waterways

Museum Trust 1988; Honorary Vice President, Free Trade League 1990. *Biog: b.* July 1930. *m.* 1984.

ORAM, William J; Chief Financial Officer, Alexander Howden Limited.

ORCHARD, Rupert Henry; Partner, Nabarro Nathanson, since 1990; Corporate Law. *Career:* Nabarro Nathanson, Articled Clerk 1980-87; Assistant Solicitor 1988-90; Robinson Cox, Perth, Western Australia, Senior Solicitor (Seconded) 1987-88. *Biog: b.* 30 May 1957. *Nationality:* British. *m.* 1985, Cecilia Mary (née Page); 1 d. *Educ:* Downside School; Magdalene College, Cambridge (MA). *Other Activities:* Liveryman, Drapers' Company. *Professional Organisations:* The Law Society. *Recreations:* Cricket, Travel.

ORCHARD-LISLE, P D; CBE, TD, DL; Senior Partner, Healey & Baker. *Career:* Healey & Baker 1961-. *Biog: b.* 3 August 1938. *Educ:* Marlborough College; Trinity Hall, Cambridge (MA). *Directorships:* Healey & Baker since 1969 Senior Partner; Slough Estates since 1983 (non-exec); Aula Securities since 1986 (exec). *Other Activities:* Chairman, Greater London TAVRA; Past President, Royal Institute of Chartered Surveyors; Member of Council, Reading University; Governor, Harrow School & Wat Buckland School. *Professional Organisations:* FRICS. *Clubs:* Athenaeum Club. *Recreations:* Golf.

ORCHART, P T; Director, S G Warburg & Co Ltd.

ORDERS, R W D; Director, Baring Brothers & Co Limited.

ORME, Jeremy; Group Director, Securities and Investments Board.

ORME, S; Managing Director, Morgan Stanley International.

ORMEROD, David A; Property Managing Director, Legal & General Group plc.

ORMEROD, John; Partner, Arthur Andersen & Co.

ORMROD, A D; Director, Economics & Strategy, Postel Investment Management Ltd.

ORMROD, Paul William; Director, British & Commonwealth Merchant Bank plc, since 1988. *Career:* Price Waterhouse, Mgmnt Consultant 1980-85; Lloyds Merchant Bank, Dir, Gilts & Stockbroking 1986-87. *Biog: b.* 31 January 1954. *Nationality:* British. *m.* 1972, Gaynor (née Hughes); 2 s. *Professional Organisations:* FCCA; Member, International Stock Exchange.

ORPWOOD PRICE, Gareth William; Partner, Lane Clark Peacock, since 1970. *Career:* LCP man and boy. *Biog: b.* 8 June 1937. *Nationality:* British. *m.* 1967, Sheila Ann; 3 s; 1 d. *Educ:* Reading School; Jesus College, Oxford (MA). *Professional Organisations:* FIA. *Recreations:* Gardening, Golf, Reading.

ORR, M L; Director, J O Hambro Magan & Co Ltd, since 1990; Corporate Finance. *Career:* Peat Marwick 1980-83; Hill Samuel & Co Ltd 1983-87; Barclays de Zoete Wedd Ltd 1987-89; J O Hambro Magan & Co Ltd 1989-. *Biog: b.* 29 August 1958. *Nationality:* Irish. *m.* 1984, Elizabeth; 1 d. *Educ:* Rugby School; Bristol University (BSc Economics & Accounting). *Directorships:* J O Hambro Magan & Co 1990 (exec). *Professional Organisations:* ACA.

ORR, Matthew; Partner, Killik & Co, since 1989; Marketing. *Career:* Penney Easton, Broker 1981-82; Quilter Goodison, Divisional Director Responsible for New Business Development and Shareshops 1982-87; Debenhams Investment Services plc, Founding Director Responsible for Establishing Business 1987-89. *Biog: b.* 14 October 1962. *Nationality:* British. *Educ:* Bedford School. *Other Activities:* Regular Lecturer on Dealing with Wider Shareownership. *Professional Organisations:* Member, Stock Exchange. *Recreations:* Rowing, Skiing, Tennis.

ORR, Michael William Major; Partner, Lawrence Graham, since 1989; Insurance & Commercial Litigation. *Career:* Lake, Ward Orr & Co, Partner 1979-89; Vizards, Partner 1976-79; Lawrence Graham, Partner 1971-74; Assistant Solicitor 1968-71; Articled Clerk 1963-68. *Biog: b.* 29 April 1944. *Nationality:* British. *m.* 1984, Candace Hope (née Clark). *Educ:* Shrewsbury; College of Law, Lancaster Gate. *Professional Organisations:* Deputy District Judge, High Court/County Court; Member, The Law Society. *Clubs:* National Liberal Club.

ORR, Roderick; Head of European Sales, Hoare Govett, since 1990; US and European Sales. *Career:* Vivian Gray & Co, Partner, UK Equity Sales 1981-87; Morgan Grenfell Securities, Head New York Office, UK/European Equity Sales 1987-89; Hoare Govett, Director, Overseas Sales 1989-. *Biog: b.* 17 December 1957. *Nationality:* British. *m.* Julia Margaret (née Brimacombe); 1 s. *Educ:* Bedford School; Salford University (Chemistry/Business Studies 2:1). *Professional Organisations:* Member, The Stock Exchange.

ORRELL, Jeremy Peter; Partner, Slater Heelis, since 1988. *Career:* Slater Heelis, Trainee Solicitor 1981-82; Asst Solicitor 1983-88. *Biog: b.* 14 June 1957. *Nationality:* British. *m.* 1983, Janette Elizabeth (née Lee); 1 s. *Educ:* Ampleforth College; Peterhouse, Cambridge (Entrance Scholarship & Exhibition MA). *Professional Organisations:* Member, The Law Society; Member, Manchester Law Society; Member, Manchester Young Solicitors. *Clubs:* Brooklands Cricket, Lawn Tennis &

Hockey Club. *Recreations:* Walking, Playing Tennis, Cricket, Squash.

ORSBORN, C M; Director, Charterhouse Tilney.

ORTON, Giles Anthony Christopher; Partner, Evershed Wells & Hind, since 1989; Litigation. *Career:* Broomheads, Sheffield (now Dibb Lupton Broomhead & Prior), Articled Clerk 1981-83; Assistant Solicitor 1983-85; Associate 1985-87; Wells & Hind, Associate 1987-89. *Biog: b.* 18 August 1959. *Nationality:* English. *m.* 1987, Jane (née Robinson); 1 s. *Educ:* King Edward VII School, Sheffield; The Queen's College, Oxford (MA Oxon Jurisprudence). *Other Activities:* Councillor, Derby City Council. *Professional Organisations:* Solicitor. *Recreations:* Field Sports.

OSAWA, Yoshio; Managing Director & Chief Executive Officer, IBJ International Ltd, since 1988. *Career:* IBJ International Ltd (UK), Dir, Corp Finance 1979-83; The Industrial Bank of Japan Ltd, Jt Gen Mgr, Int Finance Dept 1983-86; Gen Mgr, Intl Headquarters 1986-88; IBJ International Ltd, Managing Director & Chief Executive Officer 1988-. *Biog: b.* 23 February 1941. *Nationality:* Japanese. *m.* 1965, Yukiko (née Kojima); 1 s; 1 d. *Educ:* Gakushuin University (Faculty of Political Science & Economics). *Directorships:* Securities Association (TSA) 1988 Board; IPMA 1988 Board; Euro Clear Clearance System Societe Cooperative 1988 Board.

OSBALDESTON, Geoffrey; General Manager, Abbey National plc, since 1988; Estate Agency (Cornerstone). *Career:* College of Law, Lecturer 1963-67; Private Practice, Solicitor 1967-74; Abbey National, Asst Chief Solicitor 1974-78; Chief Solicitor 1978-80; Asst Gen Mgr 1980-88. *Biog: b.* 15 July 1940. *Nationality:* British. *m.* 1966; 2 d. *Educ:* King Williams College, Isle of Man; Law Society (Solicitor). *Directorships:* Abbey National Estate Agency Ltd 1989 (exec).

OSBORN-SMITH, Brent R; Investments Manager, Hodgson Martin Ltd, since 1989; Venture Capital/Global Securities. *Career:* Coldstream Guards, Officer 1984-88; L Messel & Co, Trainee Stockbroker 1984. *Biog: b.* 22 September 1961. *Nationality:* British. *Educ:* Eton; London University, Charing Cross Medical School; Edinburgh University (MBA). *Directorships:* Excalibur Investments Ltd 1985 (exec); Southern Securities Ltd 1985 (exec); Lombard Group plc 1990 (non-exec). *Clubs:* Cavalry & Guards. *Recreations:* Shooting, Flying, Skiing.

OSBORNE, David Francis; Executive Director, Electra Investment Trust plc, since 1987. *Career:* Unilever Ltd 1960-66; PA International Management Consultants Ltd 1966-82; Hill Samuel & Co Ltd 1982-87. *Biog: b.* 1937. *Nationality:* British. 1 s; 2 d. *Educ:* Dulwich College; Jesus College, Oxford (MA Litterae Humaniores). *Directorships:* UK Paper plc 1988 (non-exec); Sphere Drake 1988 (non-exec); Electra Kingsway Ltd 1989 (exec); Electra Investment Trust 1987 (exec); Electra Innvotec Ltd 1988 (non-exec); Italian Private Equity Fund 1990 (non-exec). *Professional Organisations:* Institute of Transport; Institute of Management Consultants; Institute of Cost & Management Accountants. *Clubs:* MCC. *Recreations:* Golf, Cricket, Bridge, Theatre.

OSBORNE, John; Partner, Clifford Chance.

OSBORNE, Trevor; Chairman and Managing Director, Speyhawk plc, since 1981. *Career:* Middlesex County Council, South Area Estate Manager 1960-65; APC (now PMI), Partner 1966-67; Private Property Interests, Principal 1967-73; Speyhawk Ltd, Chairman 1973-81; Speyhawk plc, Chairman and Managing Director 1981-. *Biog: b.* 7 July 1943. *Nationality:* British. *m.* 1969, Pamela (née Stephenson); 1 s; 1 d. *Educ:* Sunbury Grammar School. *Directorships:* Speyhawk plc 1981 (exec); Redland plc 1989 (non-exec). *Other Activities:* Liveryman, Worshipful Company of Chartered Surveyors; Member, Royal Opera House Development Board; Vice-President, British Property Federation; Council of Association of City Property Owners; Fellow, Royal Society of Arts; President, Windsor Arts Centre; Trustee, Wokingham Conservative Association. *Professional Organisations:* FRICS. *Publications:* Several Technical Papers on Planning and Property. *Clubs:* Carlton Club, Arts Club. *Recreations:* Art, Opera, Theatre, Travel.

OSLER, John Murray; Partner, S J Berwin & Co, since 1988; Corporate Law. *Career:* Frere Cholmley Asst Solicitor 1963-67; Stephenson Harwood Asst Solicitor 1967-71; Herbert Oppenheimer Nathan & Vandyk Partner 1972-88. *Biog: b.* 1 March 1937. *Nationality:* British. *m.* 1963, Pamela (née Scott); 3 s; 1 d. *Educ:* Charterhouse; Cambridge University (MA). *Other Activities:* City of London Solicitors' Company. *Professional Organisations:* The Law Society.

OSMAN, Christopher; Partner, Clifford Chance, since 1981; Litigation. *Career:* Coward Chance (now merged with Clifford Turner to form Clifford Chance) Articled Clerk 1974-76; Coward Chance Assistant Solicitor 1976-80; Coward Chance, Partner 1981-. *Biog: b.* 7 April 1951. *Nationality:* British. *m.* 1973, Maureen, (née Brigden); 1 d. *Educ:* Ramsden School; Southampton University (LLB). *Other Activities:* Liveryman, City of London Solicitors Company. *Professional Organisations:* The Law Society. *Recreations:* Badminton, Shooting.

OSTER, R M; Group Managing Director & Divisional Chief Executive, Cookson Group plc; Cookson America Division.

OSTLUND, H; Director, Chartered WestLB Limited.

OSUMI, Hidenobu; Managing Director, Daiwa Europe Limited, since 1988; Corporate Planning, Administration & Personnel. *Career:* Daiwa Securities Company Limited (Tokyo), Deputy General Manager 1982-87; Executive Director 1987-88. *Biog: b.* 13 July 1941. *Nationality:* Japanese. *Educ:* Kansai University. *Directorships:* Daiwa Europe Limited London 1988 Managing Director.

OSWALD, Eduard; Managing Director, Girozentrale Gilbert Eliott.

OTANI, Y; General Manager, Mitsui Trust & Banking Company Ltd.

OTT, C D; Director, Leslie & Godwin Limited.

OTTERBURN, S J; Director, Tullett & Tokyo Forex International Ltd.

OTTLEY, Robert Jeremy Mark Linn; Executive Director, Greenwell Montagu Stockbrokers.

OTTOLENGHI, Pierleone; Chairman & Managing Director, S G Warburg Italia SRL, since 1989; General Management/Corporate Finance. *Career:* Independent Financial Adviser 1981-89; S G Warburg Group plc, Adviser 1985-89; Caboto SPA (Milan), Deputy Chairman 1973-81; Comif Mobiliare SPA (Milan), Partner 1971-73; Pietro Gennaro & Associati SPA (Milan), Partner 1957-71. *Biog: b.* 28 June 1932. *Nationality:* Italian. 3 d. *Educ:* Harvard University Graduate School of Business (MBA); Georgetown University School of Foreign Service. *Directorships:* Johnson Wax SPA (Italy) 1974 (non-exec) Chm; 3i Investors in Industry SPA 1989 (non-exec); S G Warburg & Co Ltd (London) 1989 (exec). *Other Activities:* European Advisory Committee, Dana Corp, Toledo, Ohio. *Publications:* Revolution in the Printing Industry, 1954.

OUGHAM, D J; Director, Lowndes Lambert Group Holdings Limited.

OULD, Bernard John; Managing Director, Prudential-Bache Capital Funding (Money Brokers) Ltd, since 1985. *Career:* Albery Lund & Co Settlement Mgr 1959-62; Akroyd & Smithers plc Settlement Mgr 1962-69; Data Processing Mgr 1969-77; Tech Services Mgr 1977-80; Dep Mgr 1980-85. *Biog: b.* 5 December 1942. *m.* 1963, Brenda (née Wallis); 1 s; 1 d. *Educ:* Bermondsey Central School. *Professional Organisations:* The International Stock Exchange (Member, Managers' Ctee); MBCS. *Recreations:* All Sport.

OUTHWAITE, R H M; Director and Underwriter, R H M Outhwaite (Underwriting Agencies) Limited.

OUVRY, Jonathan G; Clerk, Weavers' Company.

OVER, D G; Director, Gerald Limited.

OWEN, (Arthur) Leslie; General Manager (Life & Pensions), Sun Life Assurance Society plc, since 1989; Pensions & Life Assurance: Administration, Product Development, Actuarial. *Career:* Sun Life Assurance Society plc, Mgr Group Servicing 1977-80; Mgr Pensions Mgmnt 1980-83; Asst Pensions Actuary 1983-86. *Biog: b.* 6 February 1949. *Nationality:* British. *m.* 1972, Valerie (née Emmott); 3 d. *Educ:* Holt High School, Liverpool; Manchester University (BSc Hons). *Directorships:* Company Pensions Information Centre 1986 (non-exec). *Other Activities:* Life Insurance Council (Pensions Administration Panel). *Professional Organisations:* FIA, FPMI. *Recreations:* Cricket, Soccer, Golf, Bridge, Reading.

OWEN, Glyn Aneurin; Chairman, Morgan Grenfell International Funds Management Ltd.

OWEN, J M; Director, Natwest Gilts Limited.

OWEN, John Leslie; Managing Director, Merrill Lynch, Pierce, Fenner & Smith Ltd, since 1971; North American Equities. *Biog: b.* 8 October 1934. *Nationality:* British. *m.* 1962, Susan Pamela (née Miller); 1 s; 1 d. *Educ:* Sedbergh School, Yorkshire; Oxford University (MA); London School of Economics (DBA). *Professional Organisations:* Society of Investment Analysts. *Recreations:* Fishing.

OWEN, Philip Anthony; Partner, Allen & Overy, since 1982; Company Law. *Career:* Allen & Overy, Asst Solicitor 1973-81. *Biog: b.* 25 August 1944. *Nationality:* British. *m.* 1984, Deborah Anne (née Lewin); 1 s; 1 d. *Educ:* Pitman's College, Hull; Queens' College, Cambridge (Cert of Advanced Study in English Law). *Other Activities:* City of London Solicitors Company. *Professional Organisations:* The Law Society; City of London Law Society; International Bar Association. *Clubs:* Royal Ocean Racing Club, Royal Yorkshire Yacht Club, Royal Wimbledon Golf Club. *Recreations:* Yachting, Golf, Tennis, Skiing.

OWEN, Precel James; Group Managing Director, RMC Group plc, since 1986; Manufacture and Distribution of Construction Materials. *Career:* RMC Group plc, Various 1954-. *Biog: b.* 21 February 1930. *Educ:* Fishguard County Grammar School. *Recreations:* Horse Racing.

OWEN, R; Partner, Bacon & Woodrow.

OWEN, Richard Wilfred; European Director Management Consultancy & Board of Partners, National Director, Personnel, Touche Ross & Co, since 1987, Management Consultancy. *Career:* Thomson McLintock, Audit Snr 1958-62; Crompton Parkinson, Asst Chief Accountant 1962-64. *Biog: b.* 26 October

1932. *Nationality:* British. *m.* 1966, Sheila (née Kerrigan); 3 s; 2 d. *Educ:* Gunnersbury Catholic Grammar School. *Professional Organisations:* FCA; Management Consultancies Assoc (Chm 1987).

OWENS, Bernard Charles; Member (Commissioner), Monopolies & Mergers Commission, since 1981. *Career:* Hobbs Savill & Bradford (Pensions) Ltd, Dir 1957-62; Stanley Bros Ltd, MD 1961-67; Unochrome International Ltd, Chm & MD 1964-79; Trinidad Sugar Estates Ltd, Alternate Dir 1965-67; Coronet Industrial Securities Ltd, MD 1965-67; T H & J Daniels Ltd, Chm 1968-74; Scottish Machine Tool Corporation Ltd, Chm 1969-74; Unochrome Australia Ltd, Chm 1970-73; Silverthorne Group Ltd, Chm 1970-79; Imperial Securities Intl Ltd (Singapore), Chm 1972-73. *Biog: b.* 20 March 1928. *Nationality:* British. *m.* 1954, Barbara Madeline (née Murphy); 2 s; 4 d. *Educ:* Solihull School; LSE. *Directorships:* Cornish Brewery Co Ltd 1987 (non-exec); British Jewellery & Giftware Federation Ltd 1987 (exec) VP; Land & Leisure - Tir A Hamdden Ltd 1990 (non-exec). *Other Activities:* Member, Lloyd's; Fellow, Zoological Society of London; Member, Order of Malta; Governor, RNLI; Member, HAC; Liveryman, Worshipful Company of Gardeners; Fellow, Royal Geographical Society; Fellow, Linnean Society; Fellow, Royal Society of Arts. *Clubs:* Carlton, City Livery, MCC, Wig & Pen, City Livery Yacht Club, Stroud RFC.

OWENS, C M; Director, CIN Venture Managers.

OWENS, John Robin; Director, Brown Shipley & Co Limited, since 1989; Personnel & Administration. *Career:* Armed Forces, Royal Engineers, Retd Captain 1958-68; Price Waterhouse 1968-73; Midland Montagu Leasing, Director 1973-80; Forward Trust Group, Director 1980-84; GATX Lease Finance, Director 1984-85; Park Place Finance, Managing Director 1985-86; Medens Trust, Managing Director 1986-89. *Biog: b.* 26 May 1939. *Nationality:* British. *m.* 1963, Margaret Ann (née Overton); 1 s; 1 d. *Educ:* Wellington College; Welbeck College; RMA Sandhurst; Cambridge University (MA). *Directorships:* Airlease International 1979 (exec) Chm. *Professional Organisations:* FCA. *Clubs:* CUOUC, Royal Temple Yacht Club. *Recreations:* Sailing, Tennis.

OXLADE, Michael Frank Leslie; Chairman & Managing Director (MD since 1984), Leslie & Godwin Special Risks Ltd.

OYLER, Edmund John Wilfrid; Partner, Ernst & Young, since 1967; Tax & Compliance. *Biog: b.* 8 February 1934. *Nationality:* British. *m.* 1961, Elizabeth Kathleen (née Larkins); 2 s; 1 d. *Educ:* Westminster School; Trinity College, Cambridge (MA); University College, London (LLM). *Professional Organisations:* FCA.

Clubs: Athenaeum, Gresham. *Recreations:* Music, Ski-touring.

OZAKI, K; Chief Representative, Japan Associated Finance Co Ltd, since 1990; Venture and Development Capital Investment.

P

PACKER, William Rees; National Tax Technical Director, Touche Ross, since 1984; Tax. *Career:* Royal Navy, Instructor Lieutenant 1953-55; Farrow Bursey Gain Vincent, Articled Clerk 1956-59; Down Kilner & Co, Ptnr 1960-70; Touche Ross, Tax Mgr 1970-72; Tax Ptnr 1972-. *Biog: b.* 7 October 1930. *m.* 1959, Annabel Monica (née Owen); 3 s. *Educ:* Truro Cathedral School; Gonville & Caius College, Cambridge (MA). *Other Activities:* Member, Chartered Accountants' Company. *Professional Organisations:* ACA (1959); FCA (1966). *Publications:* 101 Ways of Saving Tax, 1980; Tax Guide to Pay & Perks, 1982; Tax Guide for the Self-Employed, 1985; Tax Guide for the Family, 1986; Guide to Pension Planning & Retirement, 1989; VAT - A Business by Business Guide, 1988; Charter Guides to the Finance Act, 1988, 1989; Tax Practice Manual, 1982. *Recreations:* Gardening from a Deckchair.

PACKMAN, Martin John; Director, Baring Brothers & Co Ltd; Banking & Capital Markets - UK. *Biog: b.* 29 April 1949. *m.* 1978, Lyn (née Green); 1 s; 1 d. *Educ:* Simon Langton Grammar School, Canterbury; Lancaster University (MA). *Professional Organisations:* FCA. *Publications:* Co-Author, UK Companies Operating Overseas - Tax & Financial Strategics. *Recreations:* Riding, Tennis.

PACKSHAW, Charles Max; Executive Director, Lazard Brothers & Co Ltd, since 1987; Corporate Strategy, Mergers & Acquisitions. *Career:* Costain Group plc 1973-78; Cresap McCormick Snr Consultant 1980-84. *Biog: b.* 30 January 1952. *Nationality:* British. *m.* 1983, Helena (née Youngman); 2 s; 1 d. *Educ:* Westminster School; Bristol University (BSc Hons); London Business School (MSc). *Professional Organisations:* Institution of Civil Engineers (Member). *Recreations:* Squash.

PADBURY, Keith; Deputy Managing Director, Prelude Technology Investments Ltd, since 1987; Early Stage Venture Capital. *Career:* Coopers & Lybrand, Snr Mgr 1970-78; Hobsons Ltd, Dir of Finance 1979-85. *Biog: b.* 31 July 1946. *Nationality:* British. *m.* 1970, Christina (née Peel-Yates); 2 s. *Educ:* King Edwards School, Witley. *Professional Organisations:* FCCA. *Recreations:* Sailing, Motor Racing.

PADGETT, Robert Alan; Director of Finance, Postel Investment Management Ltd, since 1977. *Career:* NM Rothschild & Sons Ltd, Corp Fin Exec 1970-73; Cripps Warburg Ltd, Dir 1973-75; Brown Harriman International Banks Ltd, Mgr 1975-77. *Biog: b.* 27 May 1943; 1 s. *Educ:* Haileybury School; Wadham College, Ox-

ford (MA); Wharton School, University of Pennsylvania (MBA). *Directorships:* Gateway Building Society 1985-88 (non-exec); Beckenham Group plc 1987 (non-exec). *Professional Organisations:* FCA. *Publications:* Financial Reporting, 1987-88.

PADOVAN, John Mario Faskally; Deputy Chairman, BZW Limited, since 1989; Overall Head of Corporate Finance. *Career:* Price Waterhouse 1960-65; County Bank Limited 1970; Dir 1971; Dep Chief Exec 1974; Chief Exec 1976; Dep Chm 1982; Chm 1984; Hambros Bank Limited, Dep Chm 1984-86. *Biog: b.* 7 May 1938. *Nationality:* British. *m.* 1963, Sally Kay (née Anderson); 3 s. *Educ:* St George's College, Weybridge; King's College, University of London; Keble College, Oxford (LLB,BCL). *Directorships:* Barclays de Zoete Wedd Holdings Ltd 1986 (exec); Barclays de Zoete Wedd Limited 1986 (exec) Dep Chm; Barclays de Zoete Wedd Securities Ltd 1986 (exec); de Zoete & Bevan Limited 1986 (exec); MS Instruments plc 1985 (non-exec); Tesco plc 1982 (non-exec); Mabey Holdings Limited 1989 (non-exec). *Other Activities:* Liveryman, The Drapers' Company. *Professional Organisations:* FCA. *Clubs:* Oxford & Cambridge University Club, Royal St Georges Golf Club, West Surrey Golf Club. *Recreations:* Golf, Squash, Walking, Theatre, Contemporary Art.

PAGE, Christopher Roger; Director, Robert Fleming & Co Ltd.

PAGE, David A; Director, Bradstock Blunt & Thompson Ltd.

PAGE, David William; Partner, Clyde & Co, since 1986; Company/Commercial, Banking. *Career:* Elborne Mitchell, Solicitor 1982-85; Partner 1985-86. *Biog: b.* 8 August 1957. *Nationality:* British. *m.* 1985, Fiona (née Cameron); 1 s. *Educ:* Denbigh School; Leicester University (LLB Hons). *Recreations:* Share Investment, Walking.

PAGE, Henry C; Partner, Withers.

PAGE, Nicholas Hurst; Director, Hambro European Ventures Limited, since 1987; Management Buyouts, Development Capital. *Career:* Deloitte & Co, Audit Assistant 1974-77; Deloitte Haskins & Sells, Consultant 1977-82; Henderson & Co Ltd, Financial Controller 1982-83. *Biog: b.* 7 October 1952. *Nationality:* British. *m.* 1982, Rosalind (née Clifford); 2 d. *Educ:* Tonbridge School, Kent; Worcester College, Oxford (MA). *Direc-*

torships: Hambros Bank Ltd 1987 (exec); Hambros European Ventures Ltd 1988 (exec); Hambro Group Investments Ltd 1986 (exec); Consolidated Timber Holdings Ltd 1990 (non-exec); Rorzo Investments plc 1986 (non-exec). *Professional Organisations:* FCA. *Clubs:* RAC Club, Pall Mall. *Recreations:* Skiing, Sailing, Squash.

PAGE, Oliver; Head of Developing World Division, Bank of England. *Directorships:* European Investment Bank 1989 (non-exec).

PAGE, R M; Vice Chairman, Sedgwick Group plc.

PAGE, W A; Manager, Banque Belgo-Zaïroise SA.

PAGET, H; Director of Personnel, Barclays de Zoete Wedd, since 1988. *Career:* Barclays plc 1962-. *Biog: b.* 7 January 1945. *Nationality:* Welsh. *m.* 1969, Ann (née Morgan); 2 d. *Professional Organisations:* ACIB (Associate Chartered Institute of Bankers).

PAGNI, Patrick Robert Marie; Deputy Chief Executive, Societe Generale Strauss Turnbull Securities Limited, since 1989. *Career:* Societe Generale (New York Branch), Vice President International Banking 1978-80; (Los Angeles) Regional Manager for the Western USA 1981-84; (Hong Kong) General Manager 1984-88; Societe Generale Strauss Turnbull Securities Ltd, Executive Director 1988-89; Deputy Chief Executive 1989-. *Biog: b.* 15 July 1949. *Nationality:* French. *m.* 1978, Viviane (née Guyot). *Educ:* Ecole Saint Louis de Gonzagne, Paris; Université Paris IX Dauphine (Maîtrise); Harvard Business School (MBA). *Directorships:* Societe Generale Strauss Turnbull Securities Ltd 1988 (exec); Societe Generale Asia Limited 1984 (non-exec). *Clubs:* Royal Hong Kong Jockey Club. *Recreations:* Photography.

PAICE, Roger; Vice President, Transaction Finance, ScotiaMcleod.

PAIN, Mrs Josiane (née Lieberherr); Executive Director, Schroder Investment Management Limited, since 1985; European Fund Management. *Career:* European Fund Management. *Directorships:* Schroder Investment Management Limited; Schroder Investment Management (Denmark) A/S 1988 (exec); The Greece Fund 1989 (exec); The Mediterranean Fund 1989 (exec); Schroder Investment Management (Europe) Ltd 1990 (exec).

PAIN, Richard; Partner, Beachcroft Stanleys, since 1969; Commercial Property Lawyer. *Career:* Hyman Isaacs Lewis & Mills; Beachcroft Hyman Isaacs; Beachcrofts; Beachcroft Stanleys, Partner 1969-. *Biog: b.* 23 September 1942. *Nationality:* British. *m.* 1973, Adrienne Joyce; 1 s; 1 d. *Educ:* Westminster School. *Other Activities:* City of London Law Society. *Professional Organisations:* Law Society. *Clubs:* MCC. *Recreations:* Cricket.

PAINE, C Michael; Director, Jardine Insurance Brokers Limited.

PAINE, Graham Ernest Harley; Partner, Wilde Sapte, since 1984; Banking Insolvency Company and Commercial Law. *Career:* Wilde Sapte, Articled Clerk 1978-80; Asst Solicitor 1980-84. *Biog: b.* 2 September 1954. *Nationality:* British. *Educ:* Dulwich College; Bristol University (LLB Hons). *Other Activities:* London Young Solicitors' Group. *Professional Organisations:* Law Society. *Recreations:* Golf, Tennis, Skiing, Theatre.

PAINTER, Nicholas John; Partner, Simpson Curtis, since 1988; Company/Commercial Law, Company Acquisitions, Management Buy-outs, Stock Exchange Flotations. *Career:* Howes Percival, Company Dept Associate 1983-85; Simpson Curtis, Associate 1986-87. *Biog: b.* 3 February 1959. *Nationality:* British. *m.* 1981, Jayne (née Quinn); 1 d. *Educ:* Haverfordwest Grammar School; Keble College, Oxford (MA Hons). *Professional Organisations:* Member, The Law Society; Member, The Leeds Law Society. *Recreations:* Squash, Cricket, Theatre.

PAINTON, P Henry; Partner, Macnair Mason, since 1980. *Career:* Macnair Mason Evans, Articled Clerk 1969-73; Deloitte & Co Cape Town, Audit Senior 1974-76; Macnair Mason, Audit Senior 1976-. *Biog: b.* 20 July 1943. *Nationality:* British. *m.* Diana (née Shurlock); 1 s; 1 d. *Educ:* Abingdon School; Coventry Polytechnic (BSc Econ). *Professional Organisations:* Fellow, Institute of Chartered Accountants. *Clubs:* Saunton Golf Club. *Recreations:* Golf, Cricket.

PAIRMAN, L Annette; WS; Partner, W & J Burness WS, since 1985; Corporate/Commercial Law.

PAKENHAM, Kevin J T; Chief Executive, John Govett & Company Limited, since 1988. *Career:* Foreign & Colonial Management Ltd, MD 1983-88; American Express Bank, MD, Asset Management 1983; American Express Bank, Head of Securities Division 1979-83; American Express Bank, Group Economist 1977-79; Amex Bank Review, Editor 1975-79; Ivory & Sime Limited, Non-exec Director 1978-81; Rothschild International Bank, Chief Economist 1972-75; St Anthony's College, Oxford University, Junior Fellow 1969-72. *Biog: b.* 1 November 1947. *Nationality:* British. *m.* Clare. 3 s (& 1 steps) 2 d. *Educ:* Oxford University, (M Phil Economics); Oxford University (M A with Hons); Oxford University, Scholar, New College. *Clubs:* City of London Club, Hurlingham Club, Marylebone Cricket Club, Rye Harbour Sailing Club.

PALFREMAN, A; Director, Aitken Campbell & Co Ltd.

PALLETT, Julian Charles; Partner, Wragge & Co, since 1990; Banking and Insolvency. *Career:* Wragge & Co, Articled Clerk/Solicitor 1981-90. *Biog: b.* 22 September 1958. *Nationality:* British. *m.* 1982, Ann Munro (née Park). *Educ:* Waverley Grammar School, Birmingham; Wadham College, Oxford (MA). *Professional Organisations:* The Law Society; The Birmingham Law Society. *Recreations:* Music, Architectural History.

PALLEY, E M; Partner, Berwin Leighton, since 1985; Banking. *Career:* Allen & Overy, London, Articled Clerk 1976-78; Solicitor 1978-79; Allen & Overy, Dubai, Solicitor 1979-82; Allen & Overy, London, Solicitor 1982-85. *Biog: b.* 2 May 1954. *Nationality:* British. *m.* 1979, Sabina (née Fursdon); 3 s. *Educ:* Clifton College; St John's College, Oxford (BA Jurisprudence). *Professional Organisations:* Law Society.

PALLEY, Simon; Associate Director, Baring Capital Investors Limited, since 1990, Venture Capital and Buy-outs. *Career:* Chase Manhattan Bank, Assistant Manager, Corporate Banking 1978-81; Bain and Company, Manager, Strategy Consultant 1983-87; Bankers Trust Company, Vice President, Buy-outs 1987-90. *Biog: b.* 25 November 1957. *Nationality:* British. *m.* 1984, Midge (née Goldsmith); 2 s. *Educ:* Eton College; Christs College, Cambridge (BA,MA); Wharton (MBA).

PALLISER, Sir Michael; Deputy Chairman, British Invisibles & Midland Bank plc.

PALLISTER, Timothy John Barry; Partner, Slaughter and May, since 1972; International and Commercial Law/Arbitration. *Career:* Mills & Reeve, Articled Clerk 1958-62; Slaughter and May, Asst Solicitor 1963-71; (Paris), Ptnr 1973-80. *Biog: b.* 2 July 1940. *Nationality:* British. *m.* 1970, Christine (née Manners); 2 s; 1 d. *Educ:* Bloxham School. *Professional Organisations:* Member, The Law Society; IBA. *Clubs:* Royal Automobile, Norfolk, Sheringham Golf. *Recreations:* Motoring, Tennis, Skiing, Golf, Country Pursuits.

PALMER, A A H; Marketing Director, Berry Palmer & Lyle Ltd.

PALMER, Andrew William; Finance Director, Legal & General Investment Management Limited, since 1989; Back Office Operation: Finance, Portfolio Administration, Compliance, Personnel, Systems, Services. *Career:* Brewer & Company, Chartered Accountants 1971-76; Deloitte Haskins & Sells, Audit Senior/Manager 1976-81; Sabco Ram, Muscat, Vice President (Finance) 1981-82; Providence Capitol Life Assurance, Financial Controller/Company Sec 1982-86; Commercial Union/Commercial Union Trust Managers, Corporate Finance Manager/Financial Controller 1986-88; Legal & General Investment Management Limited, Deputy Finance Director 1988-89. *Biog: b.* 14 October 1953. *Nationality:* British. *m.* 1975, Jane; 2 s. *Educ:*

Dulwich College. *Directorships:* Legal & General Investment Management Limited 1989 (exec); Legal & General Pacific Limited 1989 (exec); Legal & General Ventures Limited 1989 (exec); Legal & General Assurance (Pensions Management) Limited 1989 (exec); Daytonian Limited 1988 (exec); James Capel (Pacific) Limited 1989 (exec); Alperton Inc 1989 (exec); Chalfont Corporation 1989 (exec); Glenworth Inc 1989 (exec); Highgate Inc 1989 (exec); Perivale Inc 1989 (exec); Rowney Inc 1989 (exec); Southfields Inc 1989 (exec). *Other Activities:* Clearing House Formation Committee; IFMA Standing Sub-Commitee on Practice; ISE Settlement Services Board. *Professional Organisations:* FCA.

PALMER, Anthony Eric Fletcher; Executive Director, Banking, Rea Brothers Limited, since 1989; Head of Banking Division. *Career:* Neville Russell & Co, Chartered Accountants 1965-69; Deloitte, Haskins & Sells 1969-71; Hambros Bank Ltd 1971-77; Grindlay Brandts Ltd, Assistant Director 1977-81; Anthony Gibbs & Sons Ltd, Executive Director 1981-88. *Biog: b.* 4 November 1945. *Nationality:* British. *m.* 1970, Nicola Mary (née Maude); 1 s; 2 d. *Educ:* Eton College. *Directorships:* Rea Brothers Limited 1989 (exec). *Professional Organisations:* Fellow of Institute of Chartered Accountants in England & Wales (FCA).

PALMER, Brian; Managing Director (Investment Management), Legal & General Group plc.

PALMER, C A; Partner, Grimley J R Eve.

PALMER, Christopher David; Partner, Cazenove & Co, since 1972. *Biog: m.* 1 s; 1 d. *Educ:* Eton College; Keble College, Oxford. *Directorships:* Electric & General Investment Trust 1983.

PALMER, Clifford Frederick; Active Underwriter of Lloyd's Syndicate, Ashley Palmer Holdings Limited, since 1980; Non-marine Insurance & Reinsurance. *Career:* National Farmers Union Mutual Insurance Society Limited, Clerk 1965-69; SA Meacock & Co, Lloyd's, Underwriting Assistant 1969-79. *Biog: b.* 7 September 1948. *Nationality:* British. *m.* 1984, Jill mary (née Steward); 4 d. *Educ:* Henley-in-Arden High School. *Directorships:* Ashley Palmer Holdings Ltd 1984 (exec); Clifford Palmer Underwriting Agencies Ltd 1979 (exec); Martin Ashley Underwriting Agencies Ltd 1984 (exec); Ashley, Palmer & Hathaway Ltd 1987 (exec). *Professional Organisations:* Fellow, Chartered Insurance Institute. *Clubs:* City of London.

PALMER, Group Captain D G F; OBE; Clerk, Glovers' Company.

PALMER, David Erroll Prior; Chief Executive, Financial Times Group, since 1990. *Career:* Trainee Journalist 1964-67; New York Correspondent 1967-70; Management Page Editor 1970-72; News Editor 1973-

77; Editorial Member of Frankfurt Project Team 1977-79; Foreign Editor 1979-81; Deputy Editor 1981-83; General Manager 1983-89; Deputy Chief Executive 1989-90. *Biog: b.* 20 February 1941. *Nationality:* British. *m.* 1974, Elizabeth; 2 s; 1 d. *Educ:* Christ Church, Oxford (MA Hons). *Directorships:* Financial Times Group Ltd 1984; The Financial Times Ltd 1983; The Financial Times (Europe) Ltd 1978; The Financial Times (France) Ltd 1990; The Financial Times (Japan) Ltd 1990; FT Business Information Ltd 1990. *Publications:* Atlantic Challenge, 1977. *Clubs:* Itchenor Sailing Club.

PALMER, H A; Chief Executive & Joint Managing Director, Taylor Woodrow plc.

PALMER, Dr Keith; Director, Corporate Finance, N M Rothschild & Sons Ltd, since 1984; Head, Natural Resources Division. *Career:* Finance Ministry, Papua New Guinea, First Secretary 1974-78; International Monetary Fund 1978-79; World Bank, Washington DC 1979-84. *Biog: b.* 26 July 1947. *Nationality:* British. *m.* 1974, Penny; 4 d. *Educ:* University of Birmingham (BSc Hons, PhD); University of Cambridge (DDE). *Professional Organisations:* Fellow, Geological Society of London; Institute of Directors.

PALMER, L W; Director, CCF Foster Braithwaite Ltd.

PALMER, Nigel S; Partner, S J Berwin & Co.

PALMER, Roger James Hume Dorney; Director/Chief Investment Strategist, Kleinwort Benson Securities, since 1987; Global Investment Strategy. *Career:* Grieveson Grant & Co 1965-86; Ptnr 1985-88; Kleinwort Benson Securities, Dir 1986-; Kleinwort Grieveson Securities Ltd, Dir 1986-. *Biog: b.* 21 March 1947. *Nationality:* British. *m.* 1979, Tsa (née Whitworth); 1 s; 2 d. *Educ:* Eton College; Gonville & Caius College, Cambridge (BA Hons 1st). *Clubs:* Groucho. *Recreations:* Wolves.

PALMER, Sue; Director of Marketing, Grant Thornton.

PALMER, Thomas Joseph; Director & Group Chief Executive, Legal & General Group Plc.

PALMER BROWN, Jonathan; Director, Nicholson Chamberlain Colls Limited.

PAMMENT, W R A; Deputy General Manager - Financial Control, Nomura Bank International plc.

PANGALOS, Phil; City Reporter, The Times.

PANK, Edward Charles; Company Secretary, Exco International plc, since 1987; Legal and Administrative.

Career: Stephenson Hanwood & Tatham, Articled Clerk 1967-69; Herbert Smith, Assistant Solicitor 1969-70; Slater Walker Ltd 1970-76; Director 1974-76; St Thomas's Hospital, Medical Student 1977-82; National Health Service, Medical Practitioner 1982-86. *Biog: b.* 5 June 1945. *Nationality:* British. *m.* 1983, Judith Clare (née Sommerville). *Educ:* Framlingham College, Suffolk; Trinity Hall, Cambridge (MA); St Thomas's Hospital (MRCS, LRCP, MB, BS). *Other Activities:* Liveryman, The Society of Apothecaries. *Professional Organisations:* Member, Law Society, Solicitor; Member, Royal College of Surgeons; Licentiate, Royal College of Physicians. *Publications:* Chapter on Moneybroking in Clay & Whebles Modern Merchant Banking, 1990. *Clubs:* Norfolk Print Club. *Recreations:* Riding, Beagling, Sailing, Gardening, Skiing.

PANTLING, Nigel Anthony; Director, J Henry Schroder Wagg & Co Ltd, since 1989; Corporate Finance. *Career:* Royal Artillery (Captain) 1968-76; Home Office (various appointments including Private Secretary to the Home Secretary) 1976-85; Schroders 1985-. *Educ:* Durham University (BSc).

PAPADOPOULOS, G S; Director, Bank of Cyprus (London) Ltd.

PAPASAVVAS, Demosthenis Kyriacou; Partner, Bacon & Woodrow, since 1990; Life Assurance (International) Consultant. *Career:* Mercantile and General Reinsurance Co, Trainee Actuary/Actuary 1977-89. *Biog: b.* 12 January 1956. *Nationality:* Cypriot/British. *Educ:* The English School, Nicosia; London School of Economics (BSc Econ). *Professional Organisations:* FSS; FIA. *Recreations:* Squash, Bridge, Skiing.

PARADISE, N; Partner, Nabarro Nathanson.

PARIS, Ronald John William; Director, J K Buckenham Ltd, since 1990; Accounts Dept.

PARISH, David William; Managing Director, Charterhouse plc, since 1990; Operations and Planning. *Career:* Coopers & Lybrand, Audit Manager 1967-70; RMC Group, PA To Finance Director 1970-73; Keyser Ullmann, Corporate Finance 1973-80; Charterhouse Bank, Corporate Finance Director 1980-86; Charterhouse plc, Finance Director 1987-90. *Biog: b.* 10 July 1945. *Nationality:* British. *m.* 1970, Aileen Clare (née Holder); 2 d. *Directorships:* Charterhouse plc 1987 (exec); Charterhouse Bank 1980 (exec); Charterhouse Development Capital Holdings 1988 (non-exec); Charterhouse Tilney 1986 (non-exec). *Professional Organisations:* FCA.

PARK, Charles Alan; Fund Manager, Framlington Investment Management Ltd, since 1986; High Yield UK Equities. *Career:* HM Forces (Army), Officer (Retired with rank of Major) 1956-69; Laurence Keen &

Gardner, Stockbrokers Clerk 1969-73; Laurence Prust & Co, Ptnr 1973-86. *Biog: b.* 7 March 1936. *m.* 1963, Gay (née Carling); 2 s. *Educ:* Winchester College; Cambridge University (MA). *Other Activities:* Member, Salters Company. *Recreations:* Skiing, Gardening, Music.

PARK, Chin Suk; Chief Representative, Bank of Korea.

PARK, Ian; Non-Executive Director, Reuters Holdings plc.

PARK, Margaret; Business Correspondent, Sunday Times Business News.

PARK, William Dennis; Partner, Linklaters & Paines, since 1971; Litigation. *Career:* Hart Jackson & Sons, Articled Clerk 1950-55; National Service (RASC) 1956-57; L G Powell, Asst Solicitor 1958-60; Morrison & Masters, Ptnr 1961-66; Linklaters & Paines, Asst Solicitor 1961-71. *Biog: b.* 28 May 1934. *Nationality:* British. *m.* 1959, Valerie (née Bayne); 1 s; 1 d. *Educ:* St Bees School. *Other Activities:* London Solicitors' Litigation Assoc (Past Pres); London Intl Arb Trust (Council Member); London Marine Arbs' Assoc (Supp Member); Member, Arb Commission, Intl Chamber of Commerce; City of London Solicitors' Co; Law Society, Representative Member of Board of Directors, London Court of International Arbitration; Brit Inst of Intl & Comparative (Council of Mgmnt); ILA. *Professional Organisations:* The Law Society; AC1Arb. *Publications:* Hire Purchase and Credit Sales, 1958; Collection of Debts, 1960; Discovery; Consulting Editor, Documentary Evidence, 1985, 1987. *Recreations:* Living and attempting to farm in W Cumbria, Fell Hunting.

PARKER, Alan; Managing Director, Brunswick Group, since 1987; Financial Public Relations. *Career:* Broadstreet Associates Public Relations Ltd, Dep MD 1981-87. *Biog: b.* 3 May 1956. *Nationality:* British. *m.* 1976, Caroline Louise (née Yates); 1 s; 2 d.

PARKER, Anthony John; Director, Hill Samuel Bank Ltd.

PARKER, C E; Executive Director, Eagle Star Insurance Co Ltd, since 1989; Investment & Property. *Career:* Eagle Star, Various Investment Positions 1958-. *Biog: b.* 4 October 1935. *Nationality:* British. *Educ:* Cambridge University (MA). *Directorships:* Eagle Pension Funds Ltd 1987; Eagle Star Asset Management Ltd 1987 Chm; Eagle Star Insurance Co Ltd 1989; Eagle Star Investment Managers Ltd 1987 Chm; Eagle Star Mortgages Ltd 1989; Eagle Star Properties Ltd 1989; Eagle Star Unit Managers Ltd 1987; Time Mission Ltd 1989. *Other Activities:* Past Chairman, Investment Committee of Association of British Insurers. *Professional Organisations:* FCIS; AMSIA.

PARKER, C H; Non-Executive Director, Johnson Matthey.

PARKER, C H J; Director of Finance & Administration, Waltons & Morse.

PARKER, Christopher John; General Manager, Saudi International Bank, since 1987. *Biog: b.* 5 September 1943. *m.* 1967, Jane; 2 s. *Educ:* St Peter's School, York. *Professional Organisations:* ACA.

PARKER, Colin; Director, Gresham Trust plc.

PARKER, E H; Resident Senior Partner, Bingham Dana & Gould, since 1990; Business Law. *Career:* US Army 1955-57; Bingham Dana & Gould 1957-; Associate 1957-63; Partner 1964-; Managing Partner 1984-89.

PARKER, Eric W; Deputy Chairman & Chief Executive, Trafalgar House plc, since 1988; Group Chief Executive. *Career:* Articled Clerk with Wheeler, Whittingham and Kent, Shrewsbury 1950-55; National Service Pay Corps 1956-58; Taylor Woodrow Group 1958-64; Trafalgar House plc 1965-; Trafalgar House plc, Finance/Administrative Director 1969-73; Deputy Managing Director 1973-77; Group Managing Director 1977-83; Group Chief Executive 1983-; Deputy Chairman 1988-. *Biog: b.* 8 June 1933. *Nationality:* British. *m.* 1955, Marlene Teresa; 2 s; 2 d. *Educ:* The Priory Grammar School for Boys, Shrewsbury. *Directorships:* Cunard Group Pensions Trustees Limited (non-exec); Hardy Oil & Gas plc (non-exec); MB Group plc (non-exec); RAC Motoring Services Limited (non-exec); SEPS Trustees Limited (non-exec); Trafalgar House Trustees Limited (non-exec); The Royal Automobile Club Limited (non-exec); Cunard Crusader World Travel Limited; Cunard Line Limited; Cunard Resorts Limited; Eider Enterprises Limited; John Brown plc; La Toc Holdings plc; Paradise Beach Limited; Scott Lithgow Limited; Scott Lithgow Holdings Limited; The Cementation Company (St Lucia) Limited; The Cunard Steam-Ship Company plc; The Reef (St Lucia) Limited; Trafalgar House Construction Holdings Limited; Trafalgar House Construction Limited; Trafalgar House Corporate Development Limited; Trafalgar House Group Services Limited; Trafalgar House Holdings Limited; Trafalgar House Investment Management Limited; Trafalgar House Property Limited; Trafalgar House Public Limited Company; CMB Packaging (UK) Limited (1) -1989; Eastern International Investment Trust plc (4) -1989; Touche Remnant Holdings Limited (1) -1989; Geoprosco International Limited (4) -1988; Poole Power Company Limited (4) -1988; Trafalgar House Finance NV (4) -1988; Trafalgar House Group Finance plc (4) -1988; Cementation International (Jersey) Limited (4) -1987; TR Holdings (1974) Limited (1) -1987; Associated Container Transportation (Australia) Limited (2) -1986; Cunard Cruise Ships Limited (4) -1986; Cunard Hotels Limited (4) -1986; Finance International Limited (4) -1986; The Ritz Hotel (London) Limited (4) -1986; Stafford Hotel Limited (4) -1986; European Assets Trust NV (1) -1985; Evening Standard Company Limited (2) -1985; RGC Offshore plc (4) - 1985. *Other Activities:* Committee for Industry and the City for the Royal Marsden Appeal; Development Board for the University of Kent; Fellow, Royal Society of Arts; Member, Lloyds; Member, Royal College of Surgeons (Appeal Committee). *Professional Organisations:* Companion, British Institute of Management; Fellow, Institute of Chartered Accountants (FCA). *Recreations:* Sports (Including Golf & Horse Racing), Wines.

PARKER, I J; Director, A P Leslie Underwriting Agencies Limited.

PARKER, L J; Business Development Manager, Arab Bank plc.

PARKER, Mrs M A; Partner, Touche Ross & Co.

PARKER, Michael D; Partner, Clyde & Co, since 1984; Commercial Litigation, particularly International Trade-Related and EEC. *Career:* Lovell White & King, Articled Clerk and Assistant Solicitor 1977-81; Clyde & Co, Assistant Solicitor 1981-84. *Biog: b.* 25 March 1955. *m.* 1979, Julie (née Youngs); 1 s; 2 d. *Educ:* Cardinal Vaughan GS; Magdalene College; Cambridge University (MA). *Recreations:* Rugby Union, Rowing.

PARKER, Norman; Senior General Manager, Lloyds Bank plc.

PARKER, Robert John; Executive Director, CSFB Investment Management Ltd, since 1985; Foreign Exchange, Fixed Income Investment. *Career:* Lloyds Bank International, Mgr 1973-76; N M Rothschild & Sons Ltd, Asst Dir 1976-82; Credit Suisse First Boston, Dir 1982-. *Biog: b.* 22 February 1952. *Nationality:* British. *m.* 1982, Claudia Jane (née Akerman); 1 s. *Educ:* Whitgift School; St John's College, Cambridge (MA). *Other Activities:* Livery Company of Farriers.

PARKER, S C Y; Director, Kleinwort Benson Ltd.

PARKER, William Northrop; Partner, Freshfields, since 1972. *Career:* Freshfields, Asst Solicitor 1967-72. *Biog: b.* 23 July 1941. *m.* 1977, Vanessa (née Brett); 1 s; 1 d. *Educ:* Herbert Strutt School, Belper; Sheffield University (LLB). *Professional Organisations:* The Law Society; The City of London Law Society. *Recreations:* Gardening, Opera.

PARKES, Anthony G; Director, Venture Link Investors Ltd, since 1987; Financial Director, Portfolio Administration. *Career:* Temple Gothard & Co, Articled Clerk 1967-72; Arthur Young & Co, to Principal Manager 1972-84; Mercia Venture Capital Ltd, Financial Director/Portfolio Administration 1984-87. *Biog: b.*

10 February 1949. *Nationality:* British. 1989, Elizabeth (née Grierson); 2 s; 1 d (by first marriage). *Educ:* Ardingly College. *Directorships:* Venture Link Investors Ltd 1987 (exec); Regisbrook Group Ltd 1989 (non-exec). *Professional Organisations:* Fellow, Inst of Chartered Accountants. *Clubs:* National Liberal Club. *Recreations:* Golf, Football, Racing.

PARKES, B W; Secretary, Ford Motor Credit Company.

PARKES, Christopher; Editor, Business.

PARKIN, M Adam; Director, John Govett & Co Limited.

PARKIN, R S; Partner, Pensions (Epsom), Bacon & Woodrow.

PARKINSON, Christopher; Partner, Gouldens.

PARKINSON, J C; Chairman, Anderson, Squires Ltd.

PARKINSON, John Whalley; Managing Director, Bell Houldsworth Fairmount Ltd, since 1988. *Career:* Bell White Hardy/Bell Houldsworth, Fin Ptnr 1974-86; Bell Houldsworth Fairmount Ltd, MD 1988-. *Biog: b.* 21 August 1946. *Nationality:* British. *m.* 1972, Barbara Helen (née Brierley); 2 s. *Educ:* Wrekin College. *Directorships:* Fairmount Trust Ltd 1986 (exec); Bell Houldsworth Fairmount Ltd 1986 (exec); Fairmount Wild Ltd 1986 (exec); Individual Pensions Fund Ltd 1988 (non-exec); Spinning Wheel (Management) Ltd 1984 (non-exec). *Professional Organisations:* FCA; Mem, The International Stock Exchange.

PARKINSON, Stuart; Associate, James Gentles & Son.

PARKS, Robert Ralph; Managing Director, Goldman Sachs International Ltd, since 1988; Investment Banking Services & Dept Capital Markets. *Career:* Merrill Lynch, MD 1970-81; Goldman Sachs & Co, VP 1981-86; Ptnr 1986-. *Biog: b.* 24 February 1944. *Nationality:* American. *m.* 1972, Gwendoline; 2 s; 1 d. *Educ:* Rice University, USA (BA); Columbia University (MBA). *Clubs:* RAC. *Recreations:* Shooting, Fishing, Tennis.

PARMEE, D S; Partner, Life & General (Epsom), Bacon & Woodrow.

PARNELL, C E; Director, Sturge Holdings plc.

PARNELL, Philip Edward; Director & Secretary, MFK Underwriting Agencies Ltd, since 1989; Legal, Administration, Personnel, Secretarial. *Career:* National Westminster Bank Ltd, Cashier/Clerk 1959-65; Yeoman Investment Trust Ltd, Asst Company Secretary 1965-72; J A Ewing & Co (London) Ltd, Asst Company

Secretary 1972-78; Harrisons & Crosfield plc, Asst Group Secretary 1978-81; MFK Underwriting Agencies Ltd, Company Secretary 1981-. *Biog: b.* 13 March 1942. *Nationality:* British. *m.* 1967, Irene F A (née Sumner); 2 s. *Educ:* Tom Hood Technical (Commercial) Secondary School. *Directorships:* MFK Underwriting Agencies Ltd 1989 (exec). *Professional Organisations:* Fellow, Chartered Institute of Secretaries & Administrators; Associate, Chartered Institute of Bankers. *Recreations:* Photography, Walking, Reading.

PARR, Oliver; Director, Samuel Montagu & Co Limited, since 1988. *Career:* Morgan Guaranty Trust Co of New York 1973-86. *Biog: b.* 11 June 1952. *Nationality:* British. *m.* 1978, Miranda (née Otten); 2 s; 1 d. *Educ:* Eton College; Worcester College, Oxford (BA PPE).

PARRIS, George Richard; Director, Hill Samuel Bank Limited.

PARRIS, R J W; Director and Company Secretary, J K Buckenham Limited.

PARRISH, Brian James; Executive, Parrish plc.

PARRITT, Clive; National Managing Partner, Baker Tilly; Management of Business - Also Expertise in Entertainment Industry & Corporate Finance. *Career:* Mann Judd/Fuller Jenks Beecroft, Gen Ptnr 1973-79; Touche Ross & Co, Gen Ptnr 1979-82; Howard Tilly & Co, Gen Ptnr 1982-85; Marketing Ptnr 1985-87; Managing Ptnr 1987-88. *Biog: b.* 11 April 1943. *Nationality:* British. 1985, Deborah (née Jones); 2 s; m1 2 s. *Educ:* Duff Miller School. *Directorships:* Hunters Estates Ltd 1986 (non-exec); Tony Long Opticals Ltd 1984 (non-exec); Baker Tilly Management Consultants Ltd 1986 (non-exec). *Other Activities:* Member of Council, ICAEW; Member, Committee CA's; Formerly Hon Treasurer British Theatre Association. *Professional Organisations:* FCA. *Publications:* Various Articles, Lectures & Papers. *Recreations:* Theatre, Gardening, Restaurants.

PARROTT, Graham J; Company Secretary, Granada Group.

PARROTT, John Leslie; Head of Research, Commercial Union Asset Management, since 1989. *Career:* British Petroleum, Commercial Apprentice 1967-71; Supply Economist 1971-73; Prudential Portfolio Managers, Research Analyst 1973-86; Head of UK Research 1986-89. *Biog: b.* 21 December 1948. *Nationality:* British. *m.* 1972, Virginia (née Parkinson); 1 s; 1 d. *Educ:* Hele's School, Exeter, Devon; Portsmouth Polytechnic (BA). *Professional Organisations:* AMSIA; Council Member, Society of Investment Analysts, 1984- (Chm 1987-).

PARRY, Dr Anthony; Director, International Corporate Finance, Charterhouse Bank Ltd, since 1990. *Career:* Hambros Bank Ltd, Director, European Mergers & Acquisitions/Director, Compliance 1987-90; HM Diplomatic Service, Legal Adviser 1985-87; European Commission (Brussels), Office of Vice President Christopher Tugendhat 1982-85; HM Diplomatic Service, Legal Adviser 1971-82. *Biog: b.* 18 January 1949. *Nationality:* British. *m.* 1979, Alison (née Sturdy-Morton); 1 s; 1 d. *Educ:* Rugby School; Queens' College, Cambridge (MA, PhD); European Studies Institute, Brussels University (Degree in European Law). *Directorships:* Charterhouse Bank Ltd 1990 (exec). *Professional Organisations:* Barrister. *Publications:* Co-Author, EEC Law, 1973, (2nd Ed 1981); Jt Editor, Encyclopedic Dictionary of International Law, 1986. *Clubs:* Royal Overseas League. *Recreations:* Europe.

PARRY, D; Partner, Nabarro Nathanson.

PARRY, David Ronald; Managing Director, Royal International Insurance Holdings Ltd, since 1989; Group's Direct Non-Life Business Throughout the World other than N America & UK. *Career:* Ipswich, Trainee 1959-61; Liverpool, Tutor at Training Centre 1961-62; Luton, Inspector 1963-66; City of London, Inspector then Asst Branch Manager 1966-70; Leicester, Area Life Branch Manager 1970-76; Royal Life, Liverpool, Life Sales Manager; Marketing Manager; Deputy General Manager; Assistant Managing Director 1976-89; Royal International London MD 1989-. *Biog: b.* 1 January 1937. *Nationality:* British. *m.* 1961, Averil Mary (née Leighton); 3 s. *Educ:* Northgate Grammar School. *Directorships:* Royal Life 1984 (exec). *Professional Organisations:* FCII, MBIM. *Clubs:* Hesnall Golf Club. *Recreations:* Golf, Gardening.

PARRY, Derek Joseph; Chairman & Managing Director, Derek Parry Ltd, since 1973; Investment Management. *Career:* Royal Air Force Officer in Gen Duties (Pilot) Branch (Fighter Test Pilot) 1955-72. *Biog: b.* 28 December 1934. *Nationality:* British. *m.* 1958, Gillian (née Fisher); 1 s; 2 d. *Educ:* Manchester Grammar School; University of Bristol. *Directorships:* FIMBRA 1980 (exec); Fortfield Nominees Ltd 1979 (exec); Derek Parry (Life & Pensions) Ltd 1984 (exec); Derek Parry (Holdings) Ltd 1987 (exec); Parry Management Ltd 1987 (exec). *Professional Organisations:* Institute of Directors (Fellow); Registered Insurance Broker. *Clubs:* RAF, Royal Western Yacht Club of England (Sidmouth). *Recreations:* Offshore Sailing, Travel, Wine, Snooker.

PARRY, G Mervyn; Partner, Allen & Overy, since 1985; Tax, Employee Benefits, Pension Schemes. *Career:* Allen & Overy, Assistant Solicitor 1975-85. *Biog: b.* 16 March 1951. *Nationality:* British. *m.* 1987, Jill (née Odiam); 1 d. *Educ:* Kings College School, Wimbledon; Downing College, Cambridge (BA); Solicitor (Law

Society Exams Hons). *Professional Organisations:* Law Society. *Recreations:* Walking, Travel, Wine, Photography, Sport.

PARRY, Judith; Associate Director, College Hill Associates Limited.

PARRY, Kenneth Ewart; Junior Warden, The Worshipful Company of Carmen. *Career:* CWS Ltd, Manchester, Accountancy 1947-53; Senior Assistant Elected Auditors 1953-58; CIS Limited, Manchester, Investment Manager, Home & Overseas (Equities) 1958-64; Airways Joint Pension Fund (BOAC & BEA), Investment Manager (Fixed Interest Equities and Direct Property) 1964-68; Iraq Petroleum Co Ltd, Pensions & Investment Manager 1968-85; Consultancy Appointments, City of London (Self Employed) 1985-. *Biog: b.* 2 March 1925. *Nationality:* British. *m.* 1955, Marian; 2 s; 1 d. *Educ:* Ardwick Central School, Manchester; Manchester High School of Commerce. *Directorships:* MIMs Asia & Australasia Exempt Trust Chairman. *Other Activities:* Immediate Past Master, Worshipful Company of Chartered Secretaries and Administrators; Life Member, Guild of Freemen, City of London; Member of the Court & Ex Hon Treasurer, Worshipful Company of Carmen; Trustee & Member of the Investment Committee of the Benevolent Fund, Worshipful Company of Chartered Secretaries and Administrators; Underwriting Member, Lloyd's of London; Trustee, International Wool Secretariat, Pension Fund; Member, Investment & Finance Committee of a large private charitable trust; Member, Investment & Finance Committees, Leukaemia Research Fund; Member of the Investment Committee, The Order of St John; Past Chairman of the Investment Protection Committee, NAPF; Previously served on the City Panel for Takeovers & Mergers, 1970-1980 under the Chairmanship of Lord Shawcross. *Professional Organisations:* Fellow, Chartered Institute of Secretaries & Administrators; Fellow, Pensions Management Institute; Associate Member, Society of Investment Analysts; Fellow, Royal Society of Arts. *Clubs:* Marylebone Cricket Club, The Oriental Club. *Recreations:* Cricket, Golf, Philately.

PARRY-HUSBANDS, Kenneth; Divisional Director, Citymax Integrated Information Systems Ltd; Corporate and Product Strategy. *Career:* Baric Computing Services, System Design/Development 1964; FM Support 1972; J Hoskyns & Sons Ltd, Senior Consultant, Project Manager in Finance 1973; Rank Xerox International, IS Project Manager of International Project 1979; Aanan Impey Morrish, Business Consultant 1982; MGE Systems, Financial Systems Consultant 1983; Total Systems Ltd, Financial Systems Consultant 1984. *Biog: b.* 13 November 1942. *Nationality:* British. *m.* 1966, Janet (née Green); 2 s. *Educ:* Enfield Grammar; Queen Mary College, London University (BSc Physics & Chemistry). *Directorships:* Citymax Integrated Information Systms

1986 (non-exec). *Recreations:* Fishing, Walking, Gardening.

PARSONAGE, Linda Susan; Partner, Bacon & Woodrow, since 1981; Consulting Actuary. *Biog: b.* 16 October 1951. *Nationality:* British. *Educ:* Cranborne Chase School; St Anne's College, Oxford (MA, MSc). *Other Activities:* President, Blackheath Lawn Tennis Club; Director, Blackheath Cricket, Football and Lawn Tennis Company Ltd. *Professional Organisations:* FIA, Association of Consulting Actuaries, International Association of Consulting Actuaries. *Recreations:* Tennis, Cooking and Eating.

PARSONS, C J; Director, Taylor Woodrow plc.

PARSONS, (Charles) Adrian (Haythorne); Unit Trust Ombudsman, The Insurance Ombudsman Bureau, since 1989; Consultant on Charity Matters to Wilde Sapte. *Career:* Coutts & Co Bankers 1952-64; Called to the Bar, Gray's Inn 1964; Charity Commission 1964-89; Deputy Commissioner 1972; Charity Commissioner in Charge of Northern Office of the Commission 1974; Charity Commissioner in Charge of the Legal Staff of the Commission 1981. *Biog: b.* 15 June 1929. *Nationality:* British. *m.* 1951, Hilary Caroline (née Sharpe); 1 d. *Educ:* Bembridge School; Wadham College, Oxford (MA). *Professional Organisations:* Barrister-at-Law. *Clubs:* United Oxford & Cambridge University Club.

PARSONS, Peter John; Director, Daiwa Europe Limited, since 1987; Corporate Finance/Capital Markets. *Career:* Shell International Petroleum Co Ltd 1964-72; Kleinwort Benson Limited, Director, Corporate Finance/Capital Markets 1973-87. *Biog: b.* 2 April 1940. *Nationality:* British. *m.* 1965, Jane; 2 s. *Educ:* Haileybury & ISC; Merton College, Oxford (MA Jurisprudence).

PARSONS, R E; Partner, Cameron Markby Hewitt.

PARSONS, Robert F J; OBE; Partner, Beachcroft Stanleys (Solicitors), since 1965; Property. *Career:* Cambridge University Conservative Association, Chairman 1956; Cambridge Union Society, Senior Committee Member 1956; Federation of University Conservative & Unionist Associations, Chairman 1957-58; Woking Constituency Young Conservatives, Chairman 1959-60; Surrey Young Conservatives, Chairman 1961-62; South East Area Young Conservatives, Chairman 1961-62; Conservative Candidate for Holborn & St Pancras South in General Elections of February and October 1974; North West Surrey Constituency Conservatives, Chairman 1979-82; North West Surrey Constituency Conservatives, President 1990-; Surrey Euro-Constituency Council, Chairman 1981-83; Surrey West Euro-Constituency Council, Chairman 1983-84; Surrey West Euro-Constituency Council, President 1984-87. *Biog: b.* 19 August 1935. *Nationality:* British. *Educ:* Kingswood School, Bath; Downing College, Cambridge (MA).

Directorships: Property Owners Building Society 1984-86. *Other Activities:* Member, Frimley & Camberley Urban District Council 1962-71 and 1972-74 (Leader 1965-67, 1969-71 and 1972-74, Chairman 1967-69); Member, Surrey County Council 1970-77; Governor, Frimley & Camberley Grammar School 1964-71; Governor, Collingwood School Camberley (incorporating F&CGS) since 1971 (Chairman 1979-89); Member, Standing Conference on London & South East Regional Planning 1974-77; Member (appointed by Secretary of State for the Environment) South East Regional Economic Planning Council 1975-78; Member (appointed by Secretary of State for Social Services), Surrey Family Practitioner Committee 1986-90; Member, Surrey Family Health Services Authority 1990-; Member, Committee of Harts Leap Cheshire Home Sandhurst 1971-72; Member, Committee (also Hon Solicitor) League of Helping Hand 1980-89, President since 1989; Chairman, Royal Stuart Society since 1965; President, Surrey Heath (formerly Camberley) Scout Council since 1969; President, Camberley & District Horticultural Society since 1985; Vice-President of various local sporting amenity and cultural societies. *Professional Organisations:* Law Society; Freeman, City of London Solicitors Company. *Publications:* The Role of Jacobitism in Modern Society, 1986. *Clubs:* Athenaeum, Travellers, St Stephens Constitutional. *Recreations:* Music, Travel, Reading.

PARSONS, Roger Michael Stanley; Managing Director, Robson Cotterell Ltd, since 1988. *Career:* Equity & Law Life Assurance, Investment Clerk 1954-55; Airways Pension Fund, Dep Investment Mgr 1955-59; Vickers Ltd, Sec's Office 1959-64; Unilever Pension Fund, Dep Investment Controller 1964-76; Panmure Gordon, Economist Ptnr 1976-88. *Biog:* b. 27 October 1935. *Nationality:* British. *m.* 1963, Sheila (née Reynolds); 2 d. *Educ:* Sherborne School. *Other Activities:* Stock Exchange Provincial Unit Committee. *Professional Organisations:* ASIA. *Recreations:* Sport, Charity Work, Politics, Philately.

PARSONS, Roger Wentworth; Joint Managing Director, Rea Brothers Group plc, since 1988. *Career:* Citibank NA 1963-73; European Banking Co Ltd Asst Dir 1974-77; Grindlay Brandts Dir 1977-80; Grindlays Bank plc MD 1981-85; Wentworth Parsons Ltd MD 1985-88. *Biog:* b. 16 February 1942. *Nationality:* British. *m.* 1969, Julie (née Deli); 2 d. *Educ:* Marlborough; St John's College, Cambridge (MA). *Directorships:* Rea Brothers (Guernsey) Ltd 1988 (non-exec); Rea Brothers (Investment Management) Ltd 1988 (non-exec); Mount Olympus Investments Ltd 1987 (non-exec); Mount Olympus Developments Ltd 1987 (non-exec). *Clubs:* Brooks's.

PARSONSON, Alan Geoffrey; Managing Director, Providence Capitol Fund Managers Ltd, since 1989. *Career:* Providence Capitol Life Assurance Company

Limited, Marketing Actuary 1987-88; National Mutual Life Assurance Society, Marketing Manager -1987. *Biog:* b. 10 July 1952. *Nationality:* British. *m.* 1978, Jane (née Turner); 1 s; 2 d. *Educ:* Lincoln College, Oxford (MA). *Directorships:* Providence Capitol Fund Managers Limited 1989 (exec). *Professional Organisations:* Fellow of Institute of Actuaries (FIA).

PARTINGTON, G; Group Finance Director, The Frizzell Group Limited.

PARTON, Nicholas; Partner and Head of Department, Taylor Joynson Garrett.

PARTRIDGE, Harry C; Non-Executive Director, Venture Link Investors Ltd.

PARVIN, Gilmour W; Chief Investment Manager, Life Association of Scotland, since 1990; Asset Management of the Funds of the Life Association of Scotland & its Subsidiaries. *Career:* LAS 1984-; Penney Easton & Co Stockbrokers (Glasgow), Head of Research 1975-84; Stirling Hendry & Co Stockbrokers (Glasgow), Investment Analyst 1974-75; Bell Lawrie & Co Stockbrokers (Edinburgh), Investment Analyst 1972-74. *Biog:* b. 3 September 1949. *Nationality:* British. *Educ:* Glasgow University (MA Hons Political Economy & Politics). *Professional Organisations:* Associate Member, Society of Investment Analysts.

PASCOE, B E A; Partner, Cazenove & Co.

PASCOE, R R; Company Secretary/UK Group General Counsel, Philips Electronic & Associated Industries Ltd, since 1987. *Career:* Hadfields Ltd, Salesman 1961-67; James Booth Aluminium, Assistant Secretary 1967-70; Alcan Booth Ltd, Assistant Secretary 1970-72; Ada Halifax Ltd, Legal Adviser 1972-75; Mullard Ltd, Company Secretary 1975-80; Philips TDS Division, Legal Adviser 1980-87. *Biog:* b. 12 January 1935. *Nationality:* British. *m.* 1972, Patricia Lilian (née Ellis); 2 s. *Educ:* Falmouth Grammar; Fitzwilliam College, Cambridge (History Pt 1 & Law Pt 2, MA). *Directorships:* Philips Pension Trustees Ltd 1987. *Other Activities:* Member, CBI Committees. *Recreations:* Singing, Walking, Reading.

PASRICHA, Nick; Partner, Ernst & Young, since 1980; Accounting, Tax & Financial Advisory Services. *Biog:* b. August 21 1950. *Nationality:* British. *m.* 1978, Lesley Ann (née Sampson); 1 s; 1 d. *Educ:* Sherwood College, India. *Professional Organisations:* FCA. *Recreations:* Badminton, Walking.

PASSEY, J D; Chairman & Managing Director, City Wall Securities Limited.

PATE, A M; Finance Director, Calor Group plc.

PATEK, C R; Managing Director, Allstate Reinsurance Co Limited.

PATEL, B K; Director, MIM Limited.

PATEL, Nimisha; Partner, Jaques & Lewis.

PATEL, V; Director, Macey Williams Insurance Services Ltd.

PATERSON, C H; Executive Director, Chartered WestLB Limited.

PATERSON, Christopher; Managing Director, Macmillan Publishers Ltd, since 1986; Macmillan Academic and Professional Ltd. *Career:* Macmillan Publishers Ltd, Export Manager 1972-74; Marketing Director, Trade Publications 1975-79; Publishing Director, Magazines 1980-81; The College Press (Pvt) Ltd Zimbabwe, Managing Director 1983-85; The Macmillan Press, Academic and Professional Division (Publishers Intl Stock Exchange Official Year Book), Managing Director 1986-90; Macmillan Publishers Ltd, Director 1990. *Biog:* b. 9 January 1947. *Nationality:* British/Zimbabwe. *m.* 1973, Gillian Diana; 1 s; 1 d. *Educ:* Peterhouse, Marondera, Zimbabwe; University of Exeter (BA Hons Economics). *Directorships:* Macmillan Boleswa (Pty) Ltd, Southern Africa 1986 Chm; The College Press (Pvt) Ltd, Zimbabwe 1987 Chm. *Other Activities:* Southern Africa Association, London. *Clubs:* Newbury & Henley RUFC, Harare Club. *Recreations:* Gardening, Running, Tennis, Watching Rugby Football.

PATERSON, Duncan; Finance Director, County NatWest Investment Management Ltd, since 1988. *Career:* Security Pacific Hoare Govett Ltd, Executive Director to CFO 1986-88; Touche Ross & Co, Senior Manager 1983-86; London School of Economics, Lecturer 1976-83; Coopers & Lybrand, Manager 1969-76. *Biog:* b. 11 January 1951. *Nationality:* British. *m.* 1972, Gillian; 1 s; 1 d. *Educ:* Glasgow Academy; Tonbridge School; London School of Economics (MSc Economics). *Directorships:* County NatWest Investment Management Limited 1988 (exec); County NatWest Investment Management Channel Isles 1988 (exec); County NatWest Investment Management Japan 1990 (exec). *Other Activities:* Member, 1949 Group. *Professional Organisations:* Fellow, Institute of Chartered Accountants in England & Wales. *Clubs:* Itchenor Sailing Club.

PATERSON, Mrs Jennie R (née Wilson); Marketing Director, Hill Samuel Investment Management Ltd, since 1989; Fund Management Marketing. *Career:* Lloyds Abbey Life Group plc, Marketing Operations Manager 1975-87; Hill Samuel Investment Management Ltd, Associate Director 1987-89. *Biog:* b. 31 July 1953. *Nationality:* British. *m.* 1977, John. *Educ:* George Abbot Girls' School, Guildford; University of Kent (BA Hons); Institute of Marketing (Diploma). *Professional Organisa-*

tions: Fellow, Chartered Institute of Marketing. *Clubs:* Royal Overseas League. *Recreations:* Fringe Arts, Current Affairs.

PATERSON, Maurice Dinsmore; Deputy Managing Director, Scottish Amicable Life Assurance Society, since 1990; Sales & Service. *Career:* Scottish Amicable 1959-; Director 1985-. *Biog:* b. 28 August 1941. *Nationality:* British. *m.* 1967, Avril (née Barclay); 2 s. *Educ:* Glasgow High School. *Directorships:* Origo Services Ltd 1989 (non-exec) Chairman. *Professional Organisations:* Fellow, Faculty of Actuaries. *Clubs:* Caledonian, Western Gailes GC, Pollok GC; Scottish Actuaries.

PATERSON, R N; Director, Barclays de Zoete Wedd Limited.

PATERSON, Ronald McNeill; Director of Accounting, Ernst & Young, since 1986; Financial Reporting. *Career:* Arthur Young 1970-89; Ernst & Young 1989-. *Biog:* b. 1 August 1950. *Nationality:* British. *m.* 1988, Frances (née Potter). *Educ:* Hillhead High School, Glasgow; Aberdeen University (LLB). *Other Activities:* Member, The Accounting Standards Ctee 1987-1990; Member, The Business Legislation Unit and the Accounting Standards Committee of The ICA Scotland; Member, The Financial Reporting Ctee of The ICAEW. *Professional Organisations:* CA. *Publications:* UK GAAP: Generally Accepted Accounting Practice in the UK (Jnt Author and Editor) Accounting for Pension Costs : the Implementation of SSAP24; Various Articles. *Clubs:* Deeside Scullers. *Recreations:* Tennis, Rowing, Travel.

PATIENT, Matthew Le May; Partner, Coopers & Lybrand Deloitte, since 1966; Senior Technical Partner, Accounting & Company Law. *Biog:* b. 16 March 1939. *Nationality:* British. *m.* 1967, Sue (née Soar); 1 s; 2 d. *Educ:* Brighton College (FCA). *Directorships:* Council of Lloyds 1989 Nominated Member; Retail Trades (Non-Food) Wages Council 1982 Independent Member; Brighton College Vice President. *Other Activities:* International Auditing Practices Committee (UK Representative); Committee of Governing Bodies Association; Company Affairs Committee of Institute of Directors. *Professional Organisations:* FCA (Council Member 1984-88). *Publications:* Accounting Provisions of the Companies Act (1985); Manual of Accounting (1990). *Clubs:* Gresham, RAC. *Recreations:* Home & Family.

PATON, Hamish Kinloch; Managing Director - Banking Services, TSB Bank plc, since 1990; Banking Services Operation. *Career:* Various Chartered Accountants, Articles & PQE 1962-70; Walter Alexander Industries, Management Accountant 1970-72; Heron Motor Group Ltd, Regional Dir & Financial Dir 1972-78; Transfleet Services Ltd, Managing Director 1979-84; United Dominions Trust Ltd, General Manager 1984-

88; TSB Bank plc, MD - Banking Services 1989-. *Biog:* *b.* 24 April 1945. *Nationality:* British. *m.* 1968, Marian (née Crew); 1 s; 1 d. *Educ:* George Watsons College; Glasgow University (CA). *Directorships:* United Dominions Trust Ltd. *Professional Organisations:* CA. *Recreations:* Golf, Tennis.

PATRICK, Bruce Robertson; Partner, Maclay Murray & Spens, since 1976; Company/Commercial Law. *Biog: b.* 26 November 1945. *m.* 1980, Hilary Jane (née Sutton); 1 s; 2 d. *Educ:* Glasgow Academy; Edinburgh Academy; Exeter College, Oxford (BA Hons); Edinburgh University (LLB). *Other Activities:* The Law Society's Company Law Ctee; Castle Rock Housing Assoc Mgmnt Ctee; Environmental Resource Centre Trust. *Professional Organisations:* The Law Society of Scotland; Royal Faculty of Procurators in Glasgow; Society of Writers to the Signet. *Clubs:* New, Prestwick, Luffness Golf Club. *Recreations:* Golf, Hill-Walking, Gardening.

PATRICK, E E; Non-Executive Director, Gravett & Tilling (Underwriting Agencies) Ltd.

PATRICK, Frederick Douglas; Chief Executive, Scottish Mutual Assurance Society, since 1990. *Biog: Nationality:* British. *Directorships:* Scottish Mutual Investment Managers Ltd; Scottish Mutual Pension Funds Investment Ltd. *Professional Organisations:* FFA.

PATRICK, Peter Laurence; Company Secretary, Hambros PLC, since 1986; Secretary of Hambros, Hambros Bank Ltd & Certain Subsidiaries. *Career:* Price Waterhouse & Co (Newcastle, London & Paris) Articled Clerk, Audit; Snr & Computer Audit Specialist 1967-76; Howard Tilly & Co Computer Audit Mgr 1976-78; Hambros Bank Ltd Head of Inspection 1978-86. *Biog: b.* 11 July 1946. *Nationality:* British. *m.* 1972, Teresa (née Mills); 1 s; 1 d. *Educ:* Alleyne's Grammar School, Herts; University College, Durham (BA Hons Chinese Studies). *Directorships:* Various Hambro Group Subsidiaries 1986; Towplan Securities Ltd 1986. *Other Activities:* District Councillor (Con), Basildon District Council, representing Billericay East; Chairman, Billericay & District Conservative Association. *Professional Organisations:* FCA; Assoc Member, British Computer Society; Member, Institute of Bankers. *Clubs:* Billericay Constitutional. *Recreations:* Politics, Church Choir, Gardening, Architecture, Music.

PATRICK, Roy; General Manager and Secretary, Scottish Equitable Life Assurance Society; Group Legal & Secretarial Affairs. *Career:* Boyds Solicitors, Partner 1975-84; Scottish Equitable Life Assurance Society, Jt Law Secretary 1984-85; Law Secretary 1986-88; AGM, Secretary 1988-89. *Biog: b.* 15 March 1950. *Nationality:* British. *m.* 1974, Linda Fairley (née Joyce); 1 s; 2 d. *Educ:* Lenzie Academy, Dunbartonshire; Glasgow University (LLB). *Professional Organisations:* Member, The

Law Society of Scotland; Notary Public. *Recreations:* Golf.

PATSALIDES, A C; Director, Bank of Cyprus (London) Ltd.

PATTERSON, John Allan; Director of Savings, Department for National Savings.

PATTERSON, Tony; Partner (Property), Frere Cholmeley.

PATTESON, Anthony I; Partner, Touche Ross & Co.

PATTISON, Tony Robert; Director, Capel Cure Myers Capital Management Ltd, since 1988; Head of Fund Management. *Career:* Capel Cure Carden 1968; Capel Cure Myers, Ptnr 1983; Capel Cure Myers & Co Ltd, Dir 1985. *Biog: b.* 18 January 1951. *Nationality:* British. *m.* 1984, Catherine (née Totman). *Directorships:* Capital Gearing Trust plc 1985 (exec). *Professional Organisations:* Member, The International Stock Exchange. *Clubs:* Naval and Military Club.

PATTON, Edwin; Partner, Clifford Chance.

PATTULLO, David Bruce; CBE; Group Chief Executive & Deputy Governor, Bank of Scotland, since 1988; General Management. *Career:* Bank of Scotland, Mgr (Investment Services Dept) 1967-71; Bank of Scotland Finance Co Ltd, Dep Mgr 1971-73; Gen Mgr 1973-77; The British Linen Bank Ltd, Dir & Chief Exec 1977-78; Bank of Scotland, Dep Treasurer 1978-79; Treasurer & General Manager 1979-88. *Biog: b.* 2 January 1938. *Nationality:* British. *m.* 1962, Fiona Jane (née Nicholson); 3 s; 1 d. *Educ:* Rugby School; Hertford College, Oxford (BA). *Directorships:* Melville Street Investments plc 1973 (non-exec); The British Linen Bank Ltd 1977 (non-exec); The Standard Life Assurance Company Ltd 1985 (non-exec); Bank of Wales plc 1986 (non-exec); NWS Bank plc 1986 (non-exec); Countrywide Banking Corporation Ltd 1987 (non-exec). *Other Activities:* Committee of Scottish Clearing Bankers; Royal Society of Edinburgh (FRSE). *Professional Organisations:* President, Institute of Bankers in Scotland, FIB (Scot). *Clubs:* New (Edinburgh), Caledonian. *Recreations:* Tennis, Hill Walking.

PAUK, M; Director, County NatWest Securities, since 1988. *Career:* BZW 1978-86. *Biog: b.* 23 July 1960. *Nationality:* British. *m.* 1990, Linda Irene (née Newell). *Other Activities:* Member, Stock Exchange. *Recreations:* Squash, Water Skiing, Soccer.

PAUL, Alan Dennis; Partner, Allen & Overy, since 1985; Corporate Law. *Career:* The Panel on Take-Overs and Merger (Secondment) Secretary 1985-87. *Biog: b.* 19 July 1954. *m.* 1978, Sarah (née Baxter); 1 s; 1 d. *Educ:* St Paul's School; University College, Oxford (MA).

PAUL, B; Assistant General Manager (Info Systems), National Provident Institution.

PAUL, Colin R H; Partner, S J Berwin & Co.

PAUL, Dr David M; Coroner for the City of London, Corporation of London.

PAUL, George William; Chief Executive, Harrisons & Crosfield plc, since 1986. *Career:* Pauls and Whites, Marketing Director 1968-85; Pauls and Whites, Managing Director 1972-85; Harrisons & Crosfield plc, Director 1985-; Pauls plc, Chairman 1985-; Harrisons & Crosfield plc, Joint CE 1986-87; Harrisons & Crosfield plc, CE 1987-. *Biog: b.* 25 February 1940. *Nationality:* British. *m.* 1963, Mary Annette (d. 1989) (née Mitchell); 2 s; 1 d. *Educ:* Harrow School; Wye College, University of London (BSc Hons Agriculture). *Directorships:* Harrisons & Crosfield plc 1985 (exec); Pauls plc 1972 (exec); Breckland Farms Ltd 1976 (exec); Norwich Union Life Insurance Society 1990 (non-exec). *Other Activities:* High Sheriff of Suffolk, 1990-91. *Clubs:* Boodle's, Farmers'. *Recreations:* Farming, Hunting, Shooting, Fishing.

PAUL, Julian Braithwaite; Managing Director, Guinness Mahon & Co Ltd, since 1989; Head of Banking and Corporate Finance Divisions. *Career:* Arthur Andersen & Co 1966-71; Citibank NA 1971-74; Banco Hispano Americano Ltd, Deputy MD 1974-87; Guinness Mahon & Co Ltd, Director 1987-. *Biog: b.* 18 May 1945. *Nationality:* British. *m.* 1973, Diana (née Davies); 1 s; 2 d. *Educ:* Wrekin College, Salop; St John's College, Oxford (MA PPE). *Directorships:* Guinness Mahon Asset Finance Ltd 1987 Chm; Guinness Yokohama Leasing Ltd 1989 Chm; Guinness Mahon Properties Ltd 1988 Chm. *Other Activities:* Member, Kent County Council (Representing Sevenoaks West) 1985-; Chm of Governors, Valence School, Westerham Kent. *Professional Organisations:* FCA. *Clubs:* Carlton, Coningsby, Bow Group.

PAUL, Nick; Partner, Competition, Cameron Markby Hewitt.

PAUL, Wesley I; Managing Director (Investment Management), Morgan (J P) Investment Management Inc.

PAULL, S J; Partner, Holman Fenwick & Willan.

PAVELY, R; Director, J H Minet & Co Ltd.

PAVIA, M J; Finance Director, LASMO plc, since 1988; Finance. *Career:* Allen Baldry Holman & Bert Chartered Accountants, Articled Clerk 1964-69; Price Waterhouse Chartered Accountants, Audit Senior 1970-73; Manager 1974-75; Senior Manager 1976-79; LASMO plc, Chief Accountant 1980-82; Controller 1983-85; Treasurer 1986-87; Finance Director 1988-. *Biog: b.* 7 October 1946. *Nationality:* British. *m.* 1976, Judith Elizabeth; 2 s; 2 d. *Educ:* King James I School, IOW. *Directorships:* LASMO plc 1988 (exec). *Other Activities:* Member, Oil Industry Accounting Committee. *Professional Organisations:* FCA. *Recreations:* Family, Music, Sport.

PAVITT, Roger John Provis; Lead IT Partner for Europe, Price Waterhouse, since 1988. *Career:* Ilford Ltd, Management Services (EDP and OR); Ilford Ltd, Marketing; Price Waterhouse (UK) 1970; Seconded Price Waterhouse Singapore 1974-76; Partner Responsible for Consulting Operations in Portugal 1984-87. *Biog: b.* 28 April 1944. *Nationality:* British. *m.* 1987, Helen; 2 s; 2 d. *Educ:* Manchester University (BA Econ & Soc Stud). *Professional Organisations:* Fellow, Institute of Management Consultants; Mem, British Computer Society.

PAWLOWICZ, Jerzy Andrzej; Partner-in-Charge, Information Systems Consulting, Ernst & Young Management Consultants, since 1986; Information Systems/Technology. *Career:* Innoxa Ltd, Management Trainee 1968-70; Foster Wheeler Ltd, Programmer Analyst 1970-72; Hill Samuel Group, Project Manager/Internal Consultant 1972-77; Lonsdale Systems Ltd, Project Manager/Consultant 1977-79; Percept System Consultancy, Consultant 1979-80. *Biog: b.* 24 May 1947. *Nationality:* British. *m.* 1968, Elizabeth (née Billington); 3 s. *Educ:* Cardinal Vaughan School, London; Aston University (BSc Chem). *Directorships:* ITUSA 1987 (exec). *Other Activities:* MCA (IT Ctee); ICC (IT Group). *Recreations:* Running, Squash.

PAWLYN, Doyran Allen David; Partner, Clark Whitehill, since 1973. *Biog: b.* 11 April 1949. *m.* 1976, Celia Elizabeth (née Sandeman); 3 d. *Educ:* Aldenham School, Elstree, Herts; Queen Elizabeth College, London (BSc Bioch, Chem). *Professional Organisations:* FCA.

PAWSON, Nicholas Charles Thoresby; Managing Director, FMI Limited, since 1983. *Career:* Price Waterhouse 1973-83. *Biog: b.* 7 March 1952. *Nationality:* British. *m.* 1985, Rosalind Jane (née Allhusen); 1 d. *Educ:* Woodcote House; Rugby School; Trinity Hall, Cambridge (MA Scholar). *Directorships:* FMI Limited 1983 (exec); London Fish & Game Co Ltd 1986 (non-exec). *Professional Organisations:* FIA; FCA. *Clubs:* Hawks. *Recreations:* Shooting, Fishing, Tennis, Southern Africa.

PAYNE, A; Partner, Bacon & Woodrow.

PAYNE, Professor A F T; Director, Centre for Services Management, Cranfield School of Management, since 1987; Professor of Services Marketing. *Career:* Steel Abrasive Co Pty Ltd, General Manager 1970-73; McPhersons Ltd, Corp Planner 1970-73;

Ronald J T Payne Pty Ltd, Director 1972-78; University of Melbourne, Senior Lecturer 1974-87. *Biog: b.* 3 May 1945. *Educ:* Melbourne Church of England Grammar School; Royal Melbourne Institute of Technology (FRMIT); University of Aston (MSc); University of Melbourne (PhD,MEd). *Directorships:* Executive Development Associates Pty Ltd 1981 (non-exec). *Professional Organisations:* Fellow, Chartered Institute of Marketing; Fellow, Institute of Directors. *Clubs:* Institute of Directors.

PAYNE, Colin; Director & Company Secretary, Ashley Palmer Holdings Limited, since 1984. *Biog: b.* 27 August 1955. *Nationality:* British. *m.* 1976, Christine (née Hayter); 2 d. *Educ:* Open University (BA Earth Sciences). *Directorships:* Ashley Palmer & Hathaway Ltd 1987 (exec); Clifford Palmer Underwriting Agencies Limited 1986 (exec); Martin Ashley Underwriting Agencies Limited 1986 (exec). *Professional Organisations:* FCIS.

PAYNE, James Michael; Chairman, E W Payne Companies Ltd, since 1978. *Nationality:* British. *Directorships:* Sedgwick Group plc Vice-Chm; Sullivan Payne Co (USA) Chm. *Other Activities:* Member of Lloyd's 1971-. *Professional Organisations:* ACII; Corporation of Insurance Brokers, Fellow 1971; Associate 1964-.

PAYNE, Jonathan William; Director, C Czarnikow Ltd, since 1989; Sugar Trading & Futures Markets. *Career:* C Czarnikow Ltd 1968-. *Biog: b.* 13 December 1949. *Nationality:* British. *m.* 1978, Claire Elizabeth (née Wall); 2 d. *Educ:* Worksop College. *Directorships:* London Fox 1988 (non-exec); Erlebach & Co 1984 (non-exec). *Other Activities:* Chairman, London Sugar Futures Market Committee. *Clubs:* Hendon Golf Club. *Recreations:* Golf.

PAYNE, Keith Howard; Deputy Chairman, Charles Barker City Ltd, since 1984; Financial Public & Investor Relations. *Career:* The Times 1958-68; Banking & Business Correspondent 1966-68; Charles Barker City Ltd, Dir 1970; Asst MD 1972; MD 1974; Charles Barker (Lyons), Vice-Chm & Dep Chief Exec 1976-83; Charles Barker, Group Dir 1984-. *Biog: b.* 16 July 1937. *Nationality:* British. *m.* 1984, Tania Jeannette; 1 d. *Educ:* Shooters Hill Grammer School. *Professional Organisations:* Institute of Public Relations. *Publications:* Contributor, How The City Works; Various Articles on Financial Affairs. *Recreations:* Swimming, Walking, Theatre.

PAYNE, M; Executive Director, Allied Dunbar Assurance plc.

PAYNE, M W; Deputy Chairman, Janson Green Limited.

PAYNE, R H; Director, Hoare Govett Corporate Finance Limited.

PAYNTER, John Gregor Hugh; Partner, Cazenove & Co, since 1986; Corporate Finance. *Career:* Barrister at Law (Grays Inn) 1977-79. *Biog: b.* 7 July 1954. *m.* 1983, Kym Elizabeth (née Sheldon); 1 s; 1 d. *Educ:* Merchant Taylors' School; University College, Oxford (MA Hons). *Professional Organisations:* The International Stock Exchange (Member).

PAYNTER, P J; Partner, Stoy Hayward.

PAYTON, Michael; Senior Partner, Clyde & Co.

PEACHEY, D J; Director, Janson Green Limited.

PEACOCK, Andrew J; Managing Director, Morgan Guaranty Trust Company of New York.

PEACOCK, David Walter; Senior Partner, Lane Clark & Peacock, since 1983. *Biog: b.* 16 July 1932. *Nationality:* British. *m.* 1973, Joan; 2 s; 1 d. *Educ:* Wolverhampton Grammar School; Trinity Hall, Cambridge (MA). *Directorships:* Alden Printing Group Ltd (non-exec) Chairman; IGIS Ltd (non-exec) Chairman. *Other Activities:* Chairman, Association of Consulting Actuaries, 1987-89; Member, Worshipful Company of Actuaries. *Professional Organisations:* Fellow, Institute of Actuaries.

PEACOCK, I R; Director, Kleinwort Benson Limited, since 1985; Joint Head of Banking, since 1990. *Career:* Unilever Ltd (Economics Department) 1968-72; Cripps Warburg Ltd 1972-75. *Biog: b.* 5 July 1947. *Nationality:* British. *m.* 1973, Alyanee; 1 s. *Educ:* Trinity College, Cambridge, 2:1. *Directorships:* Kleinwort Benson Group plc 1990 (exec); Kleinwort Benson Development Capital Ltd 1988 (non-exec); British Financial Union Ltd 1988 (non-exec); BFU (Contractors) Ltd 1990 (non-exec); Parc International Ltd 1988 (non-exec); British Fuels Group Ltd 1988 (non-exec).

PEACOCK, J Roderick B; Managing Director, Morgan Guaranty Trust Company of New York.

PEAK, D J; Director, County NatWest Limited.

PEAK, Stephen Victor; Director, Touche Remnant Investment Management Ltd, since 1988; Continental Europe-Fund Management. *Career:* Norwich Union Insurance Group, Investment Analyst 1975-83; ADIG Investment (Frankfurt), Fund Mgr 1983-84; Cornhill Insurance Group, Overseas Fund Mgr 1984-86; Touche Remnant Investment Management Ltd 1986-. *Biog: b.* 9 February 1957. *Nationality:* British. *Educ:* Denes High, Lowestoft. *Directorships:* Touche Remnant Unit Trust Management Limited 1988 (exec). *Recreations:* Bridge, Cinema, Theatre.

PEAKE, A C; Director, Hambros Bank Limited.

PEAKE, David Alphy Edward Raymon; Chairman, Benson Group plc, since 1989. *Career:* Banque Lambert (Brussels), Trainee 1958-59; J Henry Schroder Wagg & Co Ltd, Exec 1959-63; Kleinwort Benson Ltd 1963-. *Biog: b.* 27 September 1934. *Nationality:* British. *m.* 1962, Susanna (née Kleinwort); 1 s; 1 d. *Educ:* Ampleforth College; Christ Church, Oxford (MA Hons). *Directorships:* Banque Kleinwort Benson SA (Geneva) 1985-90; Banque Nationale de Paris plc 1974; The Hargreaves Group 1964-86 Chm; M & G Group plc 1979-87. *Other Activities:* Worshipful Company of Goldsmiths (Liveryman 1960). *Professional Organisations:* Institute of Directors; Institute of Bankers. *Clubs:* Brook's, Cavalry & Guards, Pratt's. *Recreations:* Country Sports, Reading.

PEAL, Charles Peter; Managing Director, Legal & General Ventures Limited, since 1988; Venture Capital. *Career:* 3i plc, Investment Director 1977-88; Prudential-Bache Capital Funding, MD European 1988. *Biog: b.* 11 December 1954. *Nationality:* British. *m.* 1983, Antonia (née Picton-Turbervill); 2 s; 1 d. *Educ:* Brighton College; St Catherine's College, Oxford (BA). *Directorships:* Cogent Limited 1988 (exec) Chm; Legal & General Investments Limited 1988 (exec). *Clubs:* Worthing Golf Club, Vincents.

PEARCE, Sir Austin; Non-Executive Director, Smiths Industries plc.

PEARCE, B W; Director, Robert Fleming Insurance Brokers Limited.

PEARCE, David Thomas Richard; Director, King & Shaxon Ltd.

PEARCE, G T; Clerk to the Company, The Worshipful Company of Carmen.

PEARCE, M J; Group Secretary, Lonrho plc.

PEARL, Howard George; Finance Co-ordinator, Ultramar plc.

PEARSE, Brian Gerald; Finance Director, Barclays Bank plc, since 1987; Finance, Planning, Risk Management. *Career:* Barclays Bank, Local Dir, Birmingham 1971-76; Reg Gen Mgr 1976-79; Gen Mgr 1979-82; CEO, N America 1982-87. *Biog: b.* 23 August 1933. *m.* 1959, Patricia (née Callaghan); 1 s; 2 d. *Educ:* St Edwards College, Liverpool. *Directorships:* 3i Group plc 1990 (non-exec). *Other Activities:* Chm, APACS. *Professional Organisations:* FCIB. *Clubs:* RAC. *Recreations:* Music, Opera, Travel.

PEARSON, Barrie; Managing Director, Livingstone Fisher plc, since 1976; Corporate Finance. *Career:* Dexion Comino International Ltd 1960-67; The Plessey Company plc 1967-73; The De La Rue Company plc 1973-76. *Biog: b.* 22 August 1939. *Nationality:* British. m1 1962 Georgina Ann (née Dix); 1 s; 1 d. m2 Catherine Campbell (née Walker). *Educ:* King's School, Pontefract; Nottingham University (BSc). *Directorships:* Information Transmission Ltd 1983-86 Chm (N). *Other Activities:* Visiting Fellow, Corporate Acquisitions and Disposals, City University Business School, 1987-. *Professional Organisations:* FCMA. *Publications:* Successful Acquisition of Unquoted Companies, 1989; Common Sense Business Strategy, 1987; Common Sense Time Management for Personal Success, 1988; Realising the Value of a Business, 1989; The Profit Driven Manager, 1990. *Recreations:* Theatre, Food Guide Inspector, Music.

PEARSON, C; Partner, Arthur Andersen & Co, since 1989; Business Services. *Career:* Arthur Andersen & Co 1978-. *Biog: b.* 18 July 1952. *Nationality:* British. *Educ:* St Johns College, Oxford (MA). *Professional Organisations:* Institute of Chartered Accountants (ACA). *Clubs:* Oxford & Cambridge. *Recreations:* Travel, Theatre, Cities, Walking.

PEARSON, Christopher Matthew Robertson; Solicitor & Group Company Secretary, CT Bowring & Co Ltd, since 1984; Legal and Property. *Career:* Coward Chance & Co, Articled Clerk 1970-72; The Bowring Group 1972-; CT Bowring & Co (Insurance) Ltd, Secretary 1974-81; CT Bowring Reinsurance Ltd, Secretary 1981-88. *Biog: b.* 21 June 1948. *Nationality:* British. *m.* 1973, Elizabeth Mary (née Britcher); 2 s; 1 d. *Educ:* Sevenoaks School; Kings College, London University (LLB Hons, AKC). *Directorships:* Tower Hill Property Company Ltd 1985 (exec) Chairman; Bowring Services Ltd 1983 (exec). *Professional Organisations:* The Law Society. *Recreations:* Gardening, Golf.

PEARSON, Hamish Alexander; Chairman, White Foster Sheldon Daly & Co Ltd.

PEARSON, John William; Director, J Henry Schroder Wagg & Co Limited, since 1989; Oil. *Career:* Bakelite Xylonite Limited, Business and Computer Analyst 1969-77; Tricentrol plc, Financial Analyst/Assistant Treasurer/Group Treasurer 1977-84. *Biog: b.* 27 November 1946. *Nationality:* German. *m.* 1971, Terry (née Muellek); 1 s; 1 d. *Educ:* Bristol Grammar School; UMIST (BSc Hons Chemistry). *Directorships:* J Henry Schroder Wagg 1989 (exec). *Recreations:* Renovating, Music.

PEARSON, Jonathan Michael Kuvey; Executive Director, Chartered WestLB Limited, since 1988; Capital Markets Trading. *Career:* Standard Chartered Merchant Bank Asia Ltd (Singapore), MD 1986-88. *Biog: b.* 4 November 1949. *Nationality:* British. *m.* 1974, Ruth Marilyn; 3 d. *Educ:* Winchester College; Gillingham School, Dorset. *Professional Organisations:* Associate, Institute of Bankers. *Clubs:* RAC. *Recreations:* Golf, Course Fishing, Chess.

PEARSON, Richard; Associate Director, College Hill Associates Limited.

PEARSON, Richard J C; Chairman UK Firm, Pannell Kerr Forster, since 1970; Audit. *Career:* Pannell Crewdson & Hardy, Articled Clerk 1962-65; Pannell Fitzpatrick/Pannell Kerr Forster, Partner 1970-. *Biog: b.* 4 May 1940. *Nationality:* British. *m.* 1968, Catriona (née Angus); 1 s; 1 d. *Educ:* St Edwards School, Oxford; St Andrews University (MA). *Other Activities:* The Barbers Company; General Commissioner of Taxes. *Professional Organisations:* FCA. *Clubs:* Reform. *Recreations:* Country Pursuits.

PEARSON, Robert W; Executive Director, Merrill Lynch International Bank Limited.

PEARSON LUND, Peter Graham; Director, Gartmore Investment Management Limited, since 1985; Promotion of Unitised Products. *Career:* Tilney & Co 1969-71; Cazenove & Co 1971-73; Anthony Gibbs 1973-75; Henderson Administration 1975-85. *Biog: b.* 9 September 1947. *Nationality:* British. *m.* Isabelle; 2 s. *Directorships:* Gartmore Inv. Management 1985; Gartmore Administration Limited; Gartmore Fund Managers (Isle of Man) 1986; Gartmore Luxembourg SA 1989; Various other Gartmore Boards; Henderson Unit Trust Management 1982-85 MD. *Other Activities:* Executive Committee, Unit Trust Association.

PEASE, Alexander Michael; Partner, Allen & Overy, since 1989; Aircraft Financing & General Banking Law. *Career:* Allen & Overy Asst Solicitor 1982-88; (Dubai) Asst Solicitor 1983-86. *Biog: b.* 14 March 1956. *Nationality:* British. *m.* 1989, Lucy (née Slater). *Educ:* Malvern College; Mansfield College, Oxford (MA). *Clubs:* The Royal Green Jackets London Club, Lambton Place Fitness Centre. *Recreations:* Spending Time with my Wife.

PEAT, Sir Gerrard; KVCO; *Career:* Peat Marwick McLintock & Co, Chartered Accountants, Partner 1956-87; Auditor to the Queen's Privy Purse 1980-88; Assistant Auditor 1969-80; Served War RAF and ATA, Pilot 1940-45; 600 City of London Auxiliary Sqdn, Pilot 1948-51. *Biog: b.* 14 June 1920. *m.* 1949, Margaret Josephine (née Collingwood); 1 s. *Educ:* Sedbergh School (FCA). *Directorships:* Johnson Wax Director; House of Fraser Trustees Director; Cleveland Trust Director. *Other Activities:* Underwriting Member, Lloyd's, 1973-; Member, Cttee, Association of Lloyd's Members, 1983-; Member, Council of Lloyd's, 1989-; Member, Corp of City of London, 1973-78; Worshipful Co of Turners, 1970-; Hon Treasurer, Assoc of Conservative Clubs, 1971-78. *Clubs:* Boodle's, City Livery. *Recreations:* Travel, Shooting, Fishing, Golf, Flying.

PEAT, R; Director, Hambros Bank Limited.

PECK, Andrew Michael; Partner, Linklaters & Paines, since 1983. *Career:* Linklaters & Paines 1971-76; N M Rothschild & Sons Limited 1976-81; Assistant Director 1979; Linklaters & Paines 1981-; Partner 1983. *Biog: b.* 1949. *Nationality:* British. *Educ:* Plymouth College; Gonvile & Caius College, Cambridge (MA, LLB). *Professional Organisations:* Law Society. *Publications:* Co-Author, Nelson's Tables of Company Procedure, Tenth Edition 1987. *Clubs:* United Oxford and Cambridge Universities Club.

PEDDIE, Peter Charles; CBE; Partner, Freshfields, since 1960. *Career:* Freshfields, Articled Clerk 1954-57; Assistant Solicitor 1957-60. *Biog: b.* 20 March 1932. *Nationality:* British. *m.* 1960, Charlotte Elizabeth (née Ryan); 2 s; 2 d. *Educ:* Canford School, Wimborne; St John's College, Cambridge (MA). *Other Activities:* Member, Law Society Standing Committee on Company Law; Special Trustee, Middlesex Hospital; Governor, Canford School, Wimborne, Dorset. *Professional Organisations:* Law Society; City of London Solicitors' Company. *Clubs:* City of London. *Recreations:* Gardening, Foreign Travel.

PEDELTY, Mervyn Kay; Finance Director, TSB Bank plc, Retail Banking Division, since 1989; Financial Management and Control, Purchasing and Administration, Credit Policy and Control. *Career:* TSB Group plc, Asst Director, Finance (Financial Control Deputise for Group Finance Director) 1987-89; Abacus Electronics Holdings plc, Finance Director and Asst Managing Director (Financial Management and Control, General Management) 1984-87; Gould Inc, Managing Director, Gould Bryans Instruments Group (GeneralManagement) 1982-84; Plantaion Holdings Ltd/PHICOM plc, Finance Director/Managing Director of Various Divisions/Subsidiaries 1976-82; British Leyland Ltd, Several Positions in Controller's Dept 1973-76. *Biog: b.* 16 January 1949. *Nationality:* British. *Educ:* Felixstowe Grammar School. *Directorships:* TSB Group Pension Trust Ltd 1989 (non-exec); United Dominions Trust Ltd 1989 (non-exec); Endeavour Financial Services Ltd 1989 (non-exec); Mortgage Express Ltd since 1989 (non-exec); Express Mortgage Management Ltd 1989 (non-exec); TSB Property Services Ltd since 1989 (non-exec); TSB Private Bank International SA (Luxembourg) 1990 (non-exec) Chairman. *Professional Organisations:* Fellow, Institute of Chartered Accountants in England & Wales. *Clubs:* Royal Automobile Club. *Recreations:* Music, Sport.

PEEBLES, A Douglas; Finance Director, The British Linen Bank Limited.

PEEBLES, David William; General Manager, London, State Bank of Victoria, since 1990; Chief Executive of London Branch. *Career:* State Bank of Victoria,

Assistant General Manager, London Branch 1989; Bank of America - Australia, Associate Director Investment Banking 1987-88; National Australia Bank - Chicago and Head Office Melbourne 1983-86. *Biog: b.* 1 September 1951. *Nationality:* Australian. *m.* 1973, Melinda Louise (née Mulholland); 2 s; 1 d. *Educ:* The Friends School, Hobart. *Professional Organisations:* British Bankers Association; Association of International Savings Banks in London; Australian Institute of Export; British and Commonwealth Banks Association. *Clubs:* Foxhills Country Club, Yarra Yarra Golf Club. *Recreations:* Field Hockey, Golf.

PEEK, Roger William; Treasurer, British Steel plc, since 1987; Treasury, Insurance, Property. *Career:* Esso Petroleum Ltd, Operations Research Analyst 1967-70; P A Management Consultants, Consultant 1970-71; United Dominions Trust Ltd Manager, Money Market Operations 1971-76. *Biog: b.* 11 May 1945. *Nationality:* British. *m.* 1968, Janice (née Arnold); 2 d. *Educ:* Palmers School; Exeter University (BSc, MSc). *Directorships:* Crucible Insurance Co Ltd 1988 (non-exec); Crownfields Ltd 1989 (non-exec). *Professional Organisations:* ACMA, MCT. *Publications:* British Steel - Treasury Organisation The Treasurer, 1989. *Recreations:* Golf, Squash, Dogwalking, Reading, Yachting.

PEEL, C E W; Chairman, Peel Hunt & Company Ltd.

PEEL, R M; Clerk, Feltmakers' Company.

PEELEN, J; Director, Unilever plc.

PEERS, Alan; General Manager, The Royal Bank of Scotland plc, since 1986; UK Banking. *Career:* Williams Deacon's Bank (then Williams & Glyn's) Various to Chief Inspector 1952-81; Asst Gen Mgr (Personnel) 1981-84; Asst Gen Mgr, UK Banking 1984-86. *Biog: Nationality:* British. *Professional Organisations:* FCIB. *Recreations:* Gardening, Golf, Walking, Swimming, Sport (general).

PEERS, James Roger; Director, Baring Brothers & Co Ltd, since 1987; Central Management. *Career:* Baring Brothers & Co Ltd, Various 1967-87. *Biog: b.* 13 November 1938. *Nationality:* British. *m.* 1977, Rosamond (née Hill); 2 d. *Educ:* Highgate School; King's College, Cambridge. *Other Activities:* Chm, WII Children's Opera Trust; Treasurer, National Listening Library; Dir, Ambache Orchestra. *Professional Organisations:* Solicitor. *Recreations:* Music, Gardening.

PEFFER, David W; Director of Internal Services & Company Secretary, The Financial Intermediaries, Managers & Brokers Regulatory Association, since 1986; Secretariat, Finance, Personnel, Administration. *Career:* Tozer Kemsley, Millbourn (Holdings) plc, Group Secretariat, Personnel, Admin 1959-86. *Biog: b.* 5 August 1943. *Nationality:* British. *m.* 1965, Brenda Ann (née

Krueger); 2 s; 1 d. *Educ:* City of London Grammar School. *Recreations:* Squash, Windsurfing, Photography.

PEGRUM, John; Director, UK Equities, BZW.

PEIRSON, Richard; Director, Kleinwort Benson Investment Management Ltd, since 1986; Investment Policy, Fund Management. *Career:* Arthur Andersen & Co, Computer Consultant 1970-72; Colegrave & Co, Account Exec 1972-73; J & A Scrimgeour, Account Exec 1973-75; W I Carr Sons & Co, Account Exec 1975-79; Carr Sebag & Co, Ptnr 1979-82; Grieveson Grant & Co, Ptnr 1982-86. *Biog: b.* 5 March 1949. *Nationality:* British. *m.* 1975, Jennifer Margaret (née Fernie) (div 1990); 1 s; 1 d. *Educ:* Purley County Grammar School; Liverpool University (BSc). *Professional Organisations:* Member, International Stock Exchange. *Recreations:* Watching Most Sports, Tennis, Bridge, Collecting Watercolours, Squash.

PELHAM BURN, Angus Maitland; JP, DL, OStJ; Self-employed. *Career:* Hudson's Bay Company Mgr 1951-58. *Biog: b.* 13 December 1931. *Nationality:* British. *m.* 1959, Anne Rosdew (née Forbes-Leith); 4 d. *Educ:* Harrow School; North of Scotland College of Agriculture (Diploma). *Directorships:* Scottish Provident Institution 1975 (non-exec); Pellet Administration Ltd 1973 Chm (non-exec); Aberdeen Fund Managers (now Aberdeen Trust Holdings plc) 1985 (non-exec); Bank of Scotland 1977 (non-exec); Status Timber Systems Ltd 1987 (non-exec); North of Scotland Finance Co Ltd (now AbTrust Scotland Investment Company plc) 1987 (non-exec). *Other Activities:* Dep Chm, Accounts Commn; Chm, Aberdeen AAPCA; Chm, Aberdeen Airport Consult Ctee; Mem, Grampian Reg Council; Royal Co of Archers; Member of Order Committee, St John's Hospital, Aberdeen; Justice of the Peace; Vice Lord Lieutenant of Kincardineshire; Council Member, Winston Churchill Memorial Trust. *Professional Organisations:* Fellow, Institute of Marketing; President, Aberdeen Branch. *Clubs:* New (Edinburgh), Royal Northern & University (Aberdeen). *Recreations:* Roe-Deer Stalking, Fishing, Vegetable Gardening.

PELL, Marian Priscilla; Partner, Herbert Smith, since 1984; Company & Commercial, Corporate Finance, The International Stock Exchange, Takeovers & Mergers, Insurance Companies. *Career:* Herbert Smith Asst Solicitor 1976-84. *Biog: b.* 5 July 1952. *Nationality:* British. *m.* 1973, Gordon F Pell; 2 s; 1 d. *Educ:* Watford Grammar School For Girls; Southampton University (LLB Hons). *Professional Organisations:* The Law Society. *Recreations:* Music, Walking.

PELL-ILDERTON, Richard John; Partner, Wilde Sapte, since 1989; Head of Japanese Unit. *Career:* Lawrence Graham, Articled Clerk 1983-85; Wilde Sapte, Assistant Solicitor 1985-87; Nishi, Tanaka & Takahashi, Tokyo, Seconded 1987-89. *Biog: b.* 24 October 1958. *Nationality:* British. *Educ:* Cheadle Hulme School; Kent University. *Professional Organisations:* The Law Society.

PELLETT, David; Divisional Director, Royal Trust Bank.

PELLY, Derek Roland (Derk); Director, The Private Bank and Trust Company Limited, since 1989. *Career:* Barclays Bank 1952-88; Vice Chairman 1977-86; Barclays International, Chairman 1986-87; Barclays Bank plc, Deputy Chairman 1986-88. *Biog: b.* 12 June 1929. *Nationality:* British. *m.* 1953, Susan (née Roberts); 1 s; 2 d. *Educ:* Marlborough; Trinity Hall, Cambridge (MA). *Directorships:* Chelmsford Diocesan Board of Finance. *Other Activities:* Governor, London House for Overseas Graduates; Ctee Member, The Family Assurance Society. *Professional Organisations:* FCIB. *Recreations:* Painting.

PELLY, John Henry Patrick Fuller; Director, Kleinwort Benson, since 1989; Institutional Equity Sales. *Career:* Kenneth Wilson, Grain Trader 1977-78; Blood Holman & Co, Grain Broker 1978-83. *Biog: b.* 27 September 1953. *Nationality:* British. *m.* 1980, Susan Elizabeth (née Briggs); 1 s; 2 d. *Educ:* Marlborough College; RAC Cirencester (Dip Agriculture). *Recreations:* Tennis, Cricket, Shooting, Skiing, Horse Racing.

PEMBERTON, G F; Director, Henry Cooke Lumsden plc.

PEMBERTON, J B; Director, Henry Cooke Lumsden plc.

PEMBERTON, P A; Director, Amalgamated Metal Trading Limited.

PEMBROKE, Jeremy William; Head International Equity Dealer, Hambros Bank, since 1972; Dealing Desk.

PENAHERRERA, Ramiro L; Managing Director (Investment Management), Merrill Lynch Pierce Fenner & Smith Limited.

PENN, G A; Partner, Cameron Markby Hewitt.

PENN, Ronald E; Treasurer, Esso UK plc, since 1988; Cash Management, Pension Fund Management, Corp Finance, Property. *Biog: b.* 5 June 1946. *Nationality:* British. *m.* 1984, Gillian (née Baird); 2 s. *Educ:* Imperial College, London (BSc). *Professional Organisations:* Fellow, Association of Corporate Treasurers (FCT).

PENNANT-REA, Rupert Lascelles; Editor, The Economist, since 1986. *Career:* Confederation of Irish Industry, Economist 1970-71; General & Municipal Workers Union, Economist 1972-73; Bank of England,

Economist 1973-77; The Economist, Economics Correspondent 1977-81; Economics Editor 1981-86. *Biog: b.* 23 January 1948. *Nationality:* British. *m.* 1986, Helen; 2 s; 1 d; 2 stepd. *Educ:* Peterhouse, Zimbabwe; Trinity College, Dublin (BA); Manchester University (MA). *Directorships:* The Economist Newspaper Ltd 1986 (exec). *Publications:* Gold Foil, 1978; Who Runs The Economy? (Jointly), 1979; The Pocket Economist (Jointly), 1981; The Economist Economics (Jointly), 1986. *Clubs:* MCC, Reform. *Recreations:* Music, Tennis, Fishing, Family.

PENNELLS, R F; Director, Hill Samuel Investment Management Ltd.

PENNEY, Charles David StJohn; Partner, Lovell White Durrant, since 1990; Corporate Finance. *Career:* Lovell White & King, Articled Clerk 1982-84; Secondment to 3i plc 1983-84; Lovell, White & King (became Lovell White Durrant 1988), Assistant Solicitor 1984-90; New York Office 1986-88. *Biog: b.* 12 April 1960. *Nationality:* British. *Educ:* Malvern College; Queen's College, Cambridge (MA). *Professional Organisations:* Law Society.

PENNEYCARD, Peter Kenneth; Group Taxation Controller, Sedgwick Group plc, since 1989; Corporate Taxation, Worldwide. *Career:* Arthur Andersen & Co, Articled Clerk & Audit Senior 1972-76; Price Waterhouse, Asst Tax Manager 1976-78; International Tax Services, Clients, Worldwide & Publications 1976-78; Tax Manager, Clients, Major UK Multinationals 1978-80; Senior Tax Manager, Clients, Major UK Multinationals 1980-84; Merck & Co Inc, European Tax Counsel, responsible for all European Taxation Matters 1985-89. *Biog: b.* 16 September 1950. *Nationality:* British. *Educ:* University of Sheffield(BA Hons). *Other Activities:* Ad hoc Charitable Treasurerships etc. *Professional Organisations:* FCA. *Recreations:* Sailing, Walking, Theatre, Music & Literature.

PENNIMAN, Michael H; Executive Director, Merrill Lynch International Bank Limited.

PENNINGTON, Anthony; Director of Finance, Hill Taylor Dickinson Solicitors, since 1988; Finance and Administration. *Career:* Sears plc, Asst Secretary/Senior Executive, Finance and Administration 1974-87; William Baird Finance & Services Ltd, Secretary & Chief Accountant 1973-74; Lindustries Ltd, Asst Group Accountant 1968-72; Barton Mayhew & Co, Chartered Accountants, Articled Clerk/Audit Senior 1963-68. *Biog: b.* 29 November 1943. *Nationality:* British. *m.* 1977, Helena Tara (née Harris); 1 s; 1 d. *Educ:* Ilford County High. *Directorships:* Sears Financial Services Ltd 1980-87 (exec); Sears Finance Ltd 1978-87 (exec). *Professional Organisations:* FCA. *Recreations:* Golf, Genealogy.

PENNY, Adrian; VP Director, International Equities, ScotiaMcLeod Incorporated.

PENROSE, D; Director, James Capel Corporate Finance Ltd.

PENRUDDOCKE, Charles Beresford; Director, Greig Fester Group Ltd.

PENSON, Alun John Alawfryn; Partner, Lovell White Durrant.

PENTLAND, Michael David; Investment Manager & Secretary, City of Glasgow Friendly Society.

PENTON, D M; Group Secretary & Director, George Wimpey plc.

PERCEPIED, Christian; Representative, International Bankers Incorporated SA, since 1988. *Career:* Banque Francaise du Commerce Exterieur, London Branch, Assistant General Manager 1980-85; IB Finance (UK) plc London, Manager 1985-88. *Biog: b.* 18 October 1948. *Nationality:* French. *m.* 1976, Anne; 1 s; 1 d. *Educ:* Faculté des Sciences Economiques de Paris (Licencié); Fondation Nationale des Sciences Politiques (Diplômé). *Directorships:* IB Finance (UK) plc, London 1988 Managing Director; Marine Cargo SA, Paris 1990 Chairman. *Other Activities:* Secretary, Société Française de Bienfaisance; Treasurer, Association Britannique des Anciens Sciences Po. *Clubs:* Golf de Saint Germain (France), Polo de Paris, Guards Polo Club (Londo), RAC (London).

PERCIVAL, N J; Director, Panmure Gordon & Co Limited.

PERCY, C M; Partner, Lawrence Graham.

PERCY, Humphrey Richard; Director, Barclays De Zoete Wedd Ltd, since 1986; Swaps and Derivative Products. *Career:* J Henry Schroder Wagg & Co Ltd 1974-80; Barclays Merchant Bank Ltd Dir 1980-86. *Biog: b.* 2 October 1956. *m.* 1985, Suzanne Patricia Spencer (née Holford-Walker); 2 s; 2 d. *Educ:* Winchester College. *Directorships:* Barclays De Zoete Wedd Capital Markets Ltd 1986 (exec). *Professional Organisations:* AIB, Forex Association, Futures & Options Society. *Clubs:* Cannons. *Recreations:* Literature, Travel.

PERCY, Keith Edward; Chief Executive, Morgan Grenfell Asset Management Ltd, since 1990. *Career:* Phillips & Drew, Head of Research 1978-83; Phillips & Drew Fund Management Ltd, Chairman 1983-90; UBS Asset Management (UK) Ltd, Chief Executive 1989-90. *Biog: b.* 22 January 1945. *Nationality:* British. *m.* 1970, Pamela (née Drake); 1 s; 1 d. *Educ:* Wanstead County High School; University of Manchester (BA Hons). *Directorships:* IMRO 1987 (non-exec); SIMS (non-exec).

Professional Organisations: Member, Society of Investment Analysts. *Clubs:* City. *Recreations:* Tennis, Badminton, Walking.

PERCY, Michael Hugh; Director, Hill Samuel Bank Ltd.

PERCY, S W; Chief Executive and Group Treasurer: BP Finance, The British Petroleum Company plc.

PERKIN, Roger Kitson; Partner, Ernst & Young, since 1979; Audit, Specialising in Banks & Law Firms. *Biog: b.* 30 April 1948. *m.* 1973, Lindsey (née Baird); 1 s; 1 d. *Educ:* Manchester Grammar School; Pembroke College, Cambridge (MA). *Professional Organisations:* FCA. *Recreations:* Golf, Gardening, Tennis.

PERKINS, Clifford; Group Treasury and Taxation Manager, Rank Organisation plc, since 1990; Group Treasury and Taxation Matters on a Worldwide Basis. *Career:* Procter & Gamble Ltd, Group Taxation Manager 1978-84; Imperial Group plc, Divisional Tax Manager 1984-85; Marks & Spencer plc, Group Taxation Manager 1985-88; J P Morgan Inc, Vice President 1989-90. *Biog: b.* 9 March 1953. *Nationality:* British. *m.* 1978, Janice (née Morgan); 3 s; 1 d. *Educ:* University College School. *Other Activities:* Editor, The British Tax Encyclopedia. *Professional Organisations:* Fellow, Institute of Taxation. *Publications:* Sweet & Maxwells Tax Computations & Tables, 1984, 1985.

PERKINS, David Charles Langrigge; Partner, Clifford Chance, since 1975; Intellectual Property. *Career:* Theodore Goddard & Co Articled Clerk/Asst Solicitor 1966-72. *Biog: b.* 31 May 1943. *m.* 1971, Sandra (née Buck); 3 s; 1 d. *Educ:* Uppingham School; Newcastle University (LLB Hons). *Professional Organisations:* Patent Solicitors Association; Associate Member,Chartered Institute of Patent Agents; Associate Member, Institute of Trade Mark Agents; European Communities Trade Mark Practitioners' Association; Union of European Practitioners in Industrial Property; AIPPI (Association Internationale pour la Protection de la Propriete Industrielle) The Law Society; Common Law Institute of Intellectual Property (Council Member); IBA; City of London Solicitor' Company; ABA; United States Trade Mark Assoc (Foreign Member); American Intellectual Property Law. *Publications:* Intellectual Property Protection for Biotechnology, 1983; Overview of the Protection available for Computer Hardware & Software in the UK under the Patents Act 1977 (Co-author), 1979. *Clubs:* Hurlingham, Northumberland Golf Club. *Recreations:* Golf, Tennis.

PERKINS, Ian Richard Brice; Director, James Capel & Co Ltd; Fixed Interest Dept. *Career:* WI Carr Private Clients 1969-72; Greenshields Inc Institutional Sales 1972-79; James Capel & Co Intl Bonds 1979. *Biog: b.* 15

November 1949. *Nationality:* British. *m.* 1975, Melissa (née Milne); 1 s; 2 d. *Educ:* Charterhouse. *Directorships:* James Capel Inc 1986 (exec); James Capel International 1988 (exec); James Capel Gilts 1988 (exec). *Other Activities:* Membership & Rules Ctee, LIFFE; The Skinners Company. *Clubs:* Boodles, Royal St Georges, Swinley Forest, The Berkshire, The Honourable Co of Edinburgh Golfers (Muirfield). *Recreations:* Golf, Tennis, Shooting, Skiing.

PERKINS, John; Managing Editor, Independent Radio News.

PERKS, David Rowland; Partner, Ashurst Morris Crisp, since 1980; Commercial Property. *Biog: b.* 16 May 1948. *Nationality:* British. *m.* 1975, Susan Lesley Riddiough; 2 d. *Educ:* The Leys School, Cambridge; University of Bristol (LLB Honours). *Professional Organisations:* Solicitor admitted 1973. *Recreations:* Shooting.

PERLIN, Howard; Executive Director, Sears plc, since 1984. *Directorships:* Asprey plc 1990 (non-exec). *Professional Organisations:* FCA.

PERRIN, Charles John; Deputy Chairman, Hambros Bank Ltd, since 1986. *Career:* Hambros Bank Ltd 1963-. *Biog: b.* 1 May 1940. *Nationality:* British. *m.* 1966, Gillian Margaret (née Hughes-Thomas); 2 d. *Educ:* Winchester College; New College, Oxford (MA Hons). *Directorships:* Hambros plc; Hambro Pacific Ltd (Hong Kong) Chm; Harland & Wolff plc (Belfast) 1984-89 (non-exec); Bishopsgate Trading & Export Co Ltd; Hambros Bank Executor & Trustee Co Ltd. *Other Activities:* Vice Chm, UK Ctee for UNICEF; Governor, Queen Anne's School, Caversham. *Professional Organisations:* Barrister-at-Law (Inner Temple, 1965). *Clubs:* Athenaeum.

PERRIN, Roger William Nasmith; Director, Hill Samuel Bank Limited, since 1987; Corporate Finance. *Career:* Coopers & Lybrand 1975-80; HM Treasury 1980-81; Coopers & Lybrand 1982-83; Hill Samuel Bank Limited 1983-. *Biog: b.* 19 May 1954. *Nationality:* British. *m.* 1975, Heather (née Grobecker); 2 s; 1 d. *Educ:* Marlborough College; Trinity College, Oxford (MA). *Professional Organisations:* ACA.

PERRY, The Hon Alan Malcolm; Partner, D J Freeman & Co, since 1988; Commercial Law. *Career:* Chancery Barrister 1974-78; The Rio-Tinto Zinc Corp Ltd, Assistant Legal Advisor 1979-81; Linklaters & Paines (Paris), Assistant Solicitor 1984-87. *Biog: b.* 6 February 1950. *Nationality:* British. *m.* 1976, Naomi Melanie (née Freedman); 3 s. *Educ:* George Heriot's, Edinburgh; Edinburgh University; Trinity College, Oxford (BA Hons). *Recreations:* Painting, Music.

PERRY, D A; Partner, Waltons & Morse.

PERRY, Gordon Climson; Executive Director, Aitken Campbell Co Ltd, since 1988; Dealing Director. *Career:* Aitken Campbell Co Ltd, Asst Office Mgr 1983-86; Head Dealer in Financials 1986-88. *Biog: b.* 11 April 1955. *Nationality:* British. *m.* 1978, Rosina. *Educ:* Uddingston High. *Recreations:* Golf.

PERRY, J D; Managing Partner, London Office, Simpson Curtis, since 1989; Partner-in-Charge (London Office), Principal Corporate Partner (London Office). *Career:* John D Perry & Co, Solicitors, Principal 1987-89; Knapp-Fishers, Partner and Head of Corporate Department 1975-87; McKenna & Co, Partner 1971-75; McKenna & Co, Articled Clerk and Assistant Solicitor 1966-71. *Biog: b.* 10 September 1941. *Nationality:* British. *m.* 1981, Kristian Avery (née Swengley). *Educ:* King Edward VII School, Sheffield; The Queen's College, Oxford (MA Jurisprudence, BCL). *Directorships:* Marriott UK Holdings Ltd 1983; Marriott Hotels & Catering (Holdings) Ltd 1979; Arbiter Group plc 1987; Ecuador Travel Ltd 1975; Brandtjen & Kluge (UK) Ltd 1986; Caterair UK Ltd since 1989. *Other Activities:* Liveryman, City of London Solicitors Company. *Professional Organisations:* The Law Society; International Bar Association. *Recreations:* Cricket, Tennis, Music, Gardening.

PERRY, Jonathan; Chairman, Ogilvy Adams & Rinehart.

PERRY, Michael Sydney; Director, Unilever, since 1985; Personal Products Coordinator. *Career:* Unilever (Various) 1957-; Chairman, Lever Brothers (Thailand) Ltd 1973-77; Chairman, Lever Asociados (Argentina) 1977-81; Chairman, Nippon Lever (Japan) 1981-83; Chairman, UAC International Ltd 1985-87; Personal Products Coordinator 1987-. *Biog: b.* 26 February 1934. *Nationality:* British. *m.* 1958, Joan Mary (née Stallard); 1 s; 2 d. *Educ:* King William's College, Isle of Man; St Johns College, Oxford (MA). *Directorships:* Unilever 1985 (exec); International Shakespeare Globe Centre Ltd (exec). *Other Activities:* British Overseas Trade Board; Japan Trade Advisory Group (Chm); Netherlands British Chamber of Commerce (Chm). *Clubs:* Oriental. *Recreations:* Music, Golf.

PERRY, Robert John; Director, NM Rothschild & Sons Limited, since 1987; Coporate Finance. *Career:* Arthur Andersen & Co 1969-76. *Educ:* University of Warwick (BSc). *Directorships:* NM Rothschild & Sons (Singapore) Limited 1987 (non-exec); NM Rothschild & Sons (Hong Kong) Limited 1987 (non-exec); Bumiputra Merchant Bankers, Berhad 1988 (non-exec). *Professional Organisations:* Fellow, Institute of Chartered Accountants. *Clubs:* Hurlingham.

PERSKE, G A; Joint Managing Director, Gerald Limited.

PERY, Patrick Edmund; The Earl of Limerick; KBE; *Career:* Peat Marwick Mitchell & Co 1953-58; Kleinwort Benson Limited 1958-72; Director 1967; Parliamentary Under Secretary of State for Trade 1972-74; Kleinwort Benson Limited 1974-90; Vice Chm 1983; Dep Chm 1985; Kleinwort Benson Group plc, Director 1982-90. *Biog: b.* 12 April 1930. *Nationality:* British. *m.* 1961, Sylvia Rosalind (née Lush); 2 s; 1 d. *Educ:* Eton; New College, Oxford (MA, PPE). *Directorships:* Kleinwort Benson Australian Income Fund Inc 1986; The De La Rue Company plc 1983; T R Pacific Investment Trust plc 1987; Polymeters Response International Limited 1988 (Chm); Pirelli UK plc 1989 (Chm); Pirelli Limited 1989; Pirelli General plc 1989. *Other Activities:* President, Institute of Export; Trustee, City Parochial Foundation; Board Member, British Overseas Trade Board; Trustee, Education 2000; President, Anglo-Swiss Society; Vice President, Alpine Club; City of London Polytechnic (Chm of the Court of Governors 1984, Vice Chm 1983,; British Invisible Exports Council (Chm 1984, Council Mem 1983); Festival of Switzerland in Britain Charitable Trust (1990). *Professional Organisations:* Member, Institute of Chartered Accountants in Scotland. *Recreations:* Skiing, Mountaineering, Gardening.

PESCOD, Michael; Partner, Slaughter and May, since 1977; Company and Commercial Department. *Biog: b.* 4 January 1946. *m.* 1988, Bettina; 1 d. *Educ:* Royal Grammar School, Newcastle Upon Tyne; University College, Oxford (BA). *Professional Organisations:* The Law Society. *Clubs:* Euston. *Recreations:* Sport, Music.

PETERSON, Michael Narramore; Director, Barclays De Zoete Wedd Ltd, since 1973; Banking. *Career:* J B Hughes & Lloyd, Articled Clerk 1954-69; Price Waterhouse & Co, Consultant 1960-64; Urwick Orr Co, Consultant 1965-69; S G Warburg & Co Ltd, Mgr 1970-71; Barclays Merchant Bank Ltd, Asst Dir 1972-73. *Biog: b.* 24 April 1938. *Nationality:* British. *m.* 1965, Lesley (née Mansie); 1 s. *Educ:* Birkenhead Institute. *Directorships:* Barclays Development Capital Ltd 1987 (non-exec). *Other Activities:* Worshipful Company of Chartered Accountants. *Professional Organisations:* FCA, Institute of Mgmnt Consultants (Member). *Recreations:* History, Gardening, Skiing, Water Skiing.

PETIT, B; Director, CCF Foster Braithwaite Ltd.

PETRI, Joseph M; Executive Director, Merrill Lynch International Bank Limited.

PETRIE, Sir Peter; Bt, CMG; Adviser to the Governor, Bank of England, since 1989; European Affairs. *Career:* HM Diplomatic Service 1956-89; UK Delegation to NATO in Paris 1958-61; UK High Commission, New Delhi 1961-64; Chargé d'Affaires, Kathmandu 1963; Cabinet Office 1965-67; FCO Economic Relations Department 1967-69; UK Mission to the United Nations, New York 1969-73; Counsellor and Head of Chancery, Bonn 1973-76; Head of European Integration Department, FCO 1976-79; Minister, Paris 1979-85; HM Ambassador to Belgium 1985-89. *Biog: b.* 7 March 1932. *Nationality:* British. *m.* 1958, Lydwine (née Countess v Oberndorff); 2 s; 1 d. *Educ:* Westminster School; Christ Church, Oxford (MA Litt Hum). *Clubs:* Brooks's, Jockey (Paris).

PETTIT, Graham Martin; General Manager, European Division, The Gulf Bank KSC.

PETTIT, Peter Charles Fenton; TD; Partner, Linklaters & Paines, since 1970; Commercial Property. *Biog: b.* 12 November 1935. *Nationality:* British. *Educ:* Sherborne School; Trinity Hall, Cambridge (MA).

PETTITT, Raymond Walter; Chairman, Minet Holdings plc.

PETTS, L; Director, Société Générale Strauss Turnbull.

PETTY, John; Correspondent, The Daily Telegraph, since 1970; Transport, Shipping, Commercial. *Career:* The Times Business News, News Editor.

PETTY, Ralph; Managing Director, Sun Alliance Group plc, since 1989. *Career:* Head of Spanish, St Olaves & St Saviours Grammar School, London 1958-6; Phoenix Assurance Co Ltd, (Overseas Dept) 1961-67; Cia de Seguros La Fenix Peruana (Lima, Peru), General Manager 1967-73; Phoenix Assurance plc, Various up to General Manager 1973-84; Sun Alliance Insurance Group, Assistant General Manager, General Manager and Managing Director 1984-90. *Biog: b.* 17 September 1935. *Nationality:* British. *m.* 1959, Janet (née Lawrence); 2 s. *Educ:* University of Nottingham (BA, Spanish and French). *Directorships:* A/S Forsikringsselskabet Codan; Alliance Assurance Company Limited; Century Insurance Company (Bermuda) Ltd; Fjerde Soforsikringsselskab A/S; Fortress Insurance Company of America; Guildhall Insurance Company Limited; London Guarantee & Accident Company of New York; London Guarantee & Reinsurance Company Limited; Phoenix Assurance Company of New York; Phoenix Assurance of South Africa Limited; Phoenix Assurance Overseas Holdings Limited; Phoenix Assurance plc; Protea Assurance Company Limited; Securitas Bremer Allgemeine Versicherungs AG; Sun Alliance and London Assurance Company; Sun Alliance and London Insurance plc; Sun Alliance Australia Limited; Sun Alliance Group plc; Sun Alliance Holdings Limited; Sun Alliance Insurance Company; Sun Alliance Insurance Limited; Sun Alliance Insurance Overseas Limited; Sun Alliance Life Assurance Limited; Sun Alliance Life Limited; Sun Alliance SA; Sun Alliance USA Inc; Sun Alliance Verzekering NV; Sun Insurance Company (Bermuda) Limited; Sun Insurance Company of New York; Sun Insurance Office Limited; The Century

Insurance Company Limited; The London Assurance; The Sea Insurance Company Limited; Verzekering Maatschappij Minerva NV; Wm H McGee & Co Inc. *Other Activities:* Worshipful Company of Insurers. *Professional Organisations:* ACII. *Recreations:* Music, Sailing.

PETZOLD, M W; Director, Wellington Underwriting Agencies Limited.

PEXTON, J M; Director, Fenchurch Insurance Group Limited.

PEZIER, Dr Jacques Pierre Paul; Director, Mitsubishi Finance International Ltd, since 1988; Arbitrage. *Career:* Dartmouth College Lecturer 1969-71; Centre d'Enseignement Supérieur des Affaires Asst Prof 1971-73; Stanford Research Institute Snr Decision Analyst 1973-76; SRI-International Mgr, Decision Analysis Gp, Europe 1976-81; Investment Intelligence Systems Corp Dir, European Consulting Services 1981-86; Barclays de Zoete Wedd (UK Equities Div) Dir, Risk Mgmnt 1986-88. *Biog: b.* 11 August 1943. *Nationality:* French. *m.* 1967, Florence T (née Lecouteux); 2 s; 2 d. *Educ:* Lycee P Corneille, Rouen, France; Ecole Centrale, Paris; Institut H Poincare, Paris (DEA); Dartmouth College, Hanover, NH, USA (MS, PhD). *Directorships:* London Maritime Investment 1984-85 (exec). *Recreations:* Tennis, Skiing.

PFEIFFER, Daniel D; Litigation Manager, Memery Crystal, since 1990; Property/Landlord & Tenant Litigation. *Career:* Isadore Goldman & Son 1964-65; EBV Christian & Co 1965-78; Druces & Atlee 1978-80; Memery Crystal 1980-. *Biog: b.* 11 February 1948. *Nationality:* British. *m.* 1970, Pauline Ann (née Woodlock); 2 d. *Educ:* Elliott Comprehensive School, Putney. *Publications:* Many in Angling Publications. *Clubs:* Guildford Angling Society, Godalming Angling Society, Dennis Angling Club. *Recreations:* Angling, All Sport, Music, Pubs.

PHAIR, Michael K; Executive Director, N M Rothschild & Sons Limited, since 1988; Corporate Finance Canada & Eastern Europe. *Career:* Toronto-Dominion Bank, Toronto, Canada, Management Trainee 1974; Assistant Branch Manager, Credit 1974-75; Representative Mexico City 1975-77; Senior Representative 1977-79; Banque Anval SA, Panama, President 1979-84; New York, Director and Consultant 1984-; Boston Capital Management Inc, Panama, Vice-President 1984; International Finance Corporation, Washington, Senior Investment Officer, Capital Markets Dept 1984-. *Biog: b.* 24 June 1950. *Nationality:* Canadian. *m.* Margaret N; 1 s; 1 d. *Educ:* University of Western Ontario (MBA) International Business Finance. *Clubs:* Hurlington Club. *Recreations:* Tennis, Golf, Sailing, Skiing.

PHAN, R; Director, International Commodities Clearing House.

PHAURE, Angus David; Director, County NatWest, since 1970; Investment Analyst, Building Sector. *Career:* Prudential Assurance Co; Royal London Mutual; Kemp-Gee. *Biog: b.* 20 December 1940. *m.* 1965, Susan Mary (née Zedgitt). *Recreations:* Dogs.

PHEASEY, Michael; Sales & Marketing Director, Bradford & Bingley Building Society, since 1989; Sales & Marketing, Development, Estate Management. *Career:* Bradford & Bingley Building Society Various 1969-76; Asst Gen Mgr 1976-80; Sec 1980-83; Gen Mgr 1983-88; Director & Deputy Chief Executive 1988-89. *Biog: b.* 12 May 1944. *Nationality:* British. *m.* 1965, Raynor Anne (née Mather); 2 s; 1 d. *Educ:* Buxton Grammar School. *Professional Organisations:* FCIS.

PHELAN, Robert; Director, International City Holdings.

PHELPS, Devereaux; Director, PaineWebber International (UK) Ltd.

PHELPS, John Christopher; Partner, Beachcroft Stanleys, since 1986; Commercial Conveyancing. *Biog: b.* 25 May 1954. *Nationality:* British. *m.* 1985, Isabelle; 1 s. *Educ:* Whitgift School; Liverpool University (LLB). *Professional Organisations:* Solicitor (Admitted October 1978), Law Society. *Publications:* Solicitors and VAT (Jointly with Julian Gizzi), 1986. *Clubs:* MCC, Crystal Palace Lifeline.

PHILBRICK, Ms Sarah; Director, Samuel Montagu & Co Ltd.

PHILLIPPS, P R; Partner, Lovell White Durrant.

PHILLIPS, Adrian Gerald; Director, Kleinwort Benson Securities, since 1981; European Equities. *Career:* Williams de Broe Hill Chaplin, Analyst 1979-81. *Biog: b.* 6 September 1956. *Educ:* King Edward VI School, Birmingham; Trinity College, Camp Hill, Cambridge (MA). *Clubs:* United Oxford & Cambridge University.

PHILLIPS, Alan Harry; Partner, Bacon & Woodrow, since 1985; Pensions. *Career:* Bacon & Woodrow 1979-85. *Biog: b.* 20 September 1957. *Nationality:* British. *m.* 1980, Jacqui (née Glam); 2 d. *Educ:* Haberdashers' Aske's School, Elstree; St Edmund Hall, Oxford (MA). *Professional Organisations:* FIA. *Recreations:* Golf.

PHILLIPS, Colin V; Director, Kleinwort Benson Securities Limited.

PHILLIPS, F P S; Director, Barclays de Zoete Wedd Securities Ltd.

PHILLIPS, G H; Deputy Secretary, HM Treasury.

PHILLIPS, J K; Director of Corporate Financial Services, Cable & Wireless plc.

PHILLIPS, M J W; Auditor, Bank of England.

PHILLIPS, P E; Director, Kleinwort Benson Securities Limited.

PHILLIPS, Robert John; Partner, McKenna & Co, since 1979; Major Projects. *Career:* McKenna & Co, Asst Solicitor; Partner 1979-83; Senior Resident Partner Hong Kong 1983-88; Partner London & Co-ordinator of Major Projects Unit, 1988; Head of Construction Dept 1990. *Biog: b.* 15 May 1947. *Nationality:* British. *m.* 1973, Eleanor Jean (née Jack); 1 s; 2 d. *Educ:* St Mary's College, Southampton (Solicitor). *Professional Organisations:* Law Society; Associate Member, Institute of Arbitrators. *Clubs:* Overseas Member Hong Kong Club. *Recreations:* Aquatic Sports.

PHILLIPS, S A S; Director, Wise Speke Ltd.

PHILLIPS, Simon; Director, PaineWebber International (UK) Ltd.

PHILLIPS, Simon Francis; Partner, Ernst & Young, since 1962. *Career:* Peat Marwick Mitchell, Articled Clerk to Asst Mgr 1950-60; Arthur Young, Mgr 1961-62; Principal 1962; Ptnr 1962-. *Biog: b.* 21 August 1934. *Nationality:* British. *m.* 1979, Sheila (née Wong Chong). *Educ:* Cranleigh School. *Professional Organisations:* FCA. *Publications:* Property Company Accounts. *Clubs:* British Racing Drivers Club, MCC, RAC. *Recreations:* Real Tennis, Skiing.

PHILLIPS, Thomas Bernard Hudson; Partner, Herbert Smith, since 1977; Corporate Finance. *Biog: b.* 12 August 1938. *Nationality:* British. *m.* 1979, Rosemary (née Sinclair); 1 s; 1 d. *Educ:* Kings School, Canterbury. *Other Activities:* Freeman, City of London Solicitors' Company. *Professional Organisations:* Solicitor; Member, The Law Society. *Recreations:* Sailing, Skiing, Golf.

PHILLIPSON, G R; Executive Director, Redland plc.

PHILO, Paul G; Director, Sphere Drake Insurance plc.

PHIPPS, P A C H; Non-Executive Chairman, LPH Group plc.

PHIPSON, John Norman; TD; Partner, Linklaters & Paines, since 1970. *Career:* Linklaters & Paines, Articled Clerk 1959-64; Assistant Solicitor 1964-70. *Biog: b.* 29 November 1940. *Nationality:* British. *m.* 1974, Harriet (née McCleery); 2 s; 2 d. *Educ:* Rugby School. *Other Activities:* Member, Honourable Artillery Company 1959-; Court of Assistants, Honourable Artillery Com-

pany 1972-; Treasurer, Honourable Artillery Company 1984-87; Vice President, Honourable Artillery Company 1988-90. *Professional Organisations:* The Law Society; City of London Solicitors' Company. *Clubs:* The Players' Theatre. *Recreations:* Family.

PHYTHIAN-ADAMS, Mark Vevers; Deputy Managing Director and Head of Corporate Finance, British and Commonwealth Merchant Bank plc, since 1989; Corporate Finance. *Career:* Drayton Corporation Ltd, Manager 1969-74; Samuel Montagu & Co Ltd, Assistant Director 1974-79; Director 1979-87; Henry Ansbacher & Co Ltd, Managing Director, Corporate Finance 1987-89. *Biog: b.* 24 February 1944. *Nationality:* British. *m.* 1978, Anne (née Colchester); 3 s. *Educ:* Rossall School; Queens' College, Cambridge. *Directorships:* Aviva Petroleum Inc 1989 (non-exec). *Other Activities:* Treasurer, Royal Archaeological Institute. *Professional Organisations:* Solicitor; Member, Law Society. *Recreations:* Fine Arts, Fell Walking.

PIA, Paul D; WS; Partner, W & J Burness WS, since 1974; Business Law. *Career:* W & J Burness, Qualified Lawyer 1970. *Biog: b.* 29 March 1947. *Nationality:* British. *m.* 1977, Anne C; 3 d. *Educ:* Holy Cross Academy, Edinburgh (University Entrance); University of Edinburgh (LLB Hons Economics and Law); University of Perugia (Diploma). *Directorships:* Caledonian Paper plc 1987 (non-exec); Shin-Etsu Hordobi Europe Limited 1984 (non-exec); Scottish International Childrens Festival 1989 (non-exec); Workwise 1990 (non-exec); Sweets Service Limited 1970 (non-exec); W & J Burness Pension Trustees 1974 (exec); W & J Burness WS Ltd 1974 Partner (exec). *Other Activities:* Council Member, Japan Society of Scotland. *Professional Organisations:* Law Society of Scotland; Member, Society of Writers to Her Majesty's Signet; Notary Public. *Publications:* Care Diligence and Skill; a Handbook for Arts Organisations - Written with T Mason - Published in 1986 and now in its third edition. *Clubs:* Institute of Directors, Dalmahoy Golf & Country Club. *Recreations:* Golf, Running, Foreign Languages.

PIANCA, Andrew; Partner, Clark Whitehill.

PICKARD, John Michael; Chief Executive, Sears plc, since 1986. *Career:* British Printing Corporation, Finance Director 1965-68; Trusthouses Ltd, Managing Director 1968-70; Trusthouse Forte Limited, Managing Director 1970-71; Happy Eater Limited, Founder Chairman 1972-86; Grattan plc, Chairman 1978-84; Courage Limited and Imperial Brewing & Leisure Limited, Chairman 1981-86. *Biog: b.* 29 July 1932. *Nationality:* British. *m.* 1959, Penelope Jane (née Catterall); 3 s; 1 d. *Educ:* Oundle School. *Directorships:* Sears plc Chief Exec; Asprey plc Alternate; British Shoe Corporation Holdings plc; British Shoe Corporation Ltd; Broadstoner Holdings plc; Brown Shipley Holdings plc (non-exec); Electra Investment Trust plc (non-exec); Electra

Kingsway General Partner Limited (non-exec); Electra Kingsway General Partner 'B' Limited (non-exec); Electra Kingsway Managers Holdings Limited (non-exec); Freemans plc; Galliford Sears Estates Ltd; Michael Pickard Limited; Miss Selfridge Ltd; Pickard Hotels Ltd; Sears Financial Services Ltd; Sears Investment Trust Limited; Sears Mens & Childrenswear plc; Sears Securities plc; Sears Sports & Leisurewear plc; Sears Trustees Limited; Selfridges Ltd; S H Services Ltd; Wallis Fashion Group Ltd; Warehouse Group plc. *Other Activities:* Member, The Court of Assistants of the Worshipful Company of Grocers; Chairman, Council Roedean School; Governor, Oundle School. *Professional Organisations:* Fellow, The Institute of Chartered Accountants; Companion, British Institute of Management. *Clubs:* MCC, Walton Heath Golf Club, Pilgrims. *Recreations:* Education, Sport.

PICKARD, Michael John; Chairman, Royal London Mutual Insurance Society Ltd.

PICKARD, Nigel Barry; Head of Corporate Tax, London, Ernst & Young, since 1989; Member of London Office Management Group. *Career:* Arthur Young, Ptnr Head of Tax, London 1975-89. *Biog:* b. 21 July 1941. *Nationality:* British. *m.* 1972, Diane Norah (née Dodsworth); 2 s; 1 d. *Educ:* Liskeard Grammar School. *Professional Organisations:* FCA, Institute of Taxation (Associate). *Recreations:* Golf.

PICKEN, G E; Managing Director, Forward Trust Group.

PICKERING, Christopher; Director, Merrill Lynch International Limited.

PICKERING, Professor J; Member, Monopolies and Mergers Commission.

PICKERING, R W; Director, Calor Group plc.

PICKERING, Robert F; Finance and Administration Partner, Broadbridge.

PICKIN, Andrew Jonathan; Partner, Evershed Wells & Hind, since 1988; Corporate Services Department. *Biog:* b. 13 April 1958. *Nationality:* British. *m.* 1981, Joy Elizabeth (née Highwood); 1 s; 2 d. *Educ:* King Edward VI Grammar School, Stafford; Balliol College, Oxford (BA). *Professional Organisations:* Licensed Insolvency Practitioner.

PICKLES, William; Controller, Yorkshire Bank plc, since 1988; Corporate Finance. *Career:* Yorkshire Bank plc, Assistant Chief Accountant 1971-83; Chief Accountant 1983-88. *Biog:* b. 6 January 1934. *Nationality:* British. *m.* 1958, Kathleen (née Seaton); 2 s; 1 d. *Directorships:* Yorkshire Bank Finance Ltd 1988; Yorkshire Bank Lease Management Ltd 1988; Yorkshire

Bank Commercial Leasing Ltd 1988; Yorkshire Bank Equipment Leasing Ltd 1988; Yorlease Ltd since 1988; Yorkshire Bank Home Loans Ltd 1988. *Professional Organisations:* Associate, Chartered Institute of Bankers.

PICKUP, Miss Alison Margaret; Director, Laurence Keen Ltd; Private Client Fund Management/Broking. *Career:* Laurence Prust, Private Client Exec 1977-85; Municipal Mutual Insurance, Fund Mgr 1985-86; Laurence Keen, Private Client Exec 1986-87. *Biog:* b. 12 April 1956. *Nationality:* British. *m.* 1983, Edward Bowman. *Educ:* Putney High School for Girls; Liverpool University (BSc Hons). *Directorships:* Laurence Keen Holdings Ltd 1990 (exec). *Professional Organisations:* Member, The International Stock Exchange. *Recreations:* Opera, Knitting, Crosswords.

PICKUP, Bryan J; Partner, S J Berwin & Co.

PIERCE, Julian; Partner, Holman Fenwick & Willan, since 1990; Maritime Law and Litigation. *Career:* Barrister 1977; Holman Fenwick & Willan, Articled Clerk 1977-81; Admitted Solicitor 1980; Oceanic Financial Services Ltd, Vice President 1981-85; Galbraith Montagu Ltd, Director 1985-87; Holman Fenwick & Willan, Solicitor 1988-89; Partner 1990-. *Biog:* b. 27 April 1955. *Nationality:* British. *m.* 1989, Cathy (née Day). *Educ:* Harvey Grammar School, Folkestone, Kent; Government High School, Nassau, Bahamas; Trinity Hall, Cambridge (MA); Lincoln's Inn (Barrister at Law); (Solicitor). *Other Activities:* Member, Law Society; Supporting Member, London Maritime Arbitrators Association. *Professional Organisations:* Solicitor. *Recreations:* Sailing, Skiing, Shooting, Hunting.

PIERS, Martin James; Litigation Partner, Gouldens, since 1983; Litigation/Insurance/Insolvency. *Biog:* b. 12 September 1954. *Nationality:* British. *m.* Nicola Susan (née Walker). *Educ:* Hertford Grammar School; University of Southampton (LLB Upper Second). *Professional Organisations:* Membership of Solicitors, 1979; Insolvency Practitioner, 1990. *Publications:* Directors & Officers Liability, 1989; Various Business Law Articles in the Financial Times, 1988, 1989, 1990. *Clubs:* The City Forum, The Wig & Pen Club, The Roof Gardens.

PIGOTT, Hugh Sefton; Partner, Clifford Chance, since 1960; International Banking. *Career:* Coward Chance (later Clifford Chance), Articled Clerk 1952-55; Assistant Solicitor 1955-60; Partner 1960. *Biog:* b. 21 December 1929. *Nationality:* British. m1 1957, Venetia Caroline Mary (née Stopford-Adams) (Diss 1984); 4s. m2 1986, Fiona (née Miller). *Educ:* Oundle School; King's College, Cambridge (BA Classics; MA). *Other Activities:* Liveryman, City of London Solicitors' Company; Member, Top Salaries Review Body. *Professional Organisations:* Member, International Bar Association. *Recreations:* Poetry & Literature, The Visual Arts, Piano Playing, Cooking.

PIGRAM, I; Secretary, Leslie & Godwin Limited.

PIKE, D M; Partner, Bacon & Woodrow, since 1989; Life Insurance. *Career:* The Scottish Mutual Assurance Society 1973-78; Cubie, Wood & Co 1978-81; General Accident Linked Life Assurance 1981-87. *Biog: b.* 22 February 1952. *Nationality:* British. *m.* 1986, Krystyna Barbara (née Zaremba); 1 s. *Educ:* The High School of Glasgow; University of Glasgow (BSc Hons). *Other Activities:* Treasurer, Insurance Orchestral Society. *Professional Organisations:* Fellow, Faculty of Actuaries. *Recreations:* Music.

PIKE, David Brian Elwis; Director, Brewin Dolphin & Co Ltd, since 1987; Portfolio Manager. *Career:* Brewin Dolphin & Co 1961-; Partner 1968. *Biog: b.* 16 March 1936. *Nationality:* British. *Educ:* Wellington College. *Clubs:* Guards & Cavalry.

PIKE, Francis Bruce; Director, MIM Ltd, since 1987; Japan & Far East, Investment Management. *Career:* MIM Tokyo KK MD 1986-88. *Biog: b.* 13 February 1954. *Educ:* Uppingham School; Selwyn College, Cambridge (MA Hons). *Directorships:* OUB Investment Management Ltd 1986 (non-exec); MIM Britania Okasan Investment Management Ltd 1986 (non-exec); MIM Tokyo KK 1988 (non-exec); Wetmore Financial Programs KK 1987 (non-exec); Nippon Warrant Fund (LUX) 1987 (non-exec); Asia Super Growth Fund (LUX) 1987 Chm (non-exec); Asia Tiger Fund (LUX) 1990 Chm (exec); European Warrant Fund (LUX) 1990 (non-exec); Drayton Asia Trust plc 1989 (exec); Drayton Far Eastern Trust plc 1988 (exec); Central European Asset Management Ltd 1990 Chm (exec). *Clubs:* Oriental Club. *Recreations:* Reading.

PILCHER, Robert; Partner, Clyde & Co.

PILKINGTON, Sir Alastair; Non-Executive Director, Wellcome plc.

PILKINGTON, George William; Director, S G Warburg Akroyd Rowe & Pitman Mullens.

PILKINGTON, I A D; Partner, Cazenove & Co.

PILKINGTON, J A B; Partner, Touche Ross & Co.

PILKINGTON, Nigel Douglas; Managing Director, Credit Suisse First Boston. *Career:* Rowe & Pitman 1972-83; Credit Suisse First Boston UK Ltd 1983-; Executive Director 1983.

PILKINGTON, Norman; Chief Executive, Globe Morley Ltd, since 1988. *Career:* Phillips & Drew, Analyst 1962-65; Pilkington Brothers Ltd, Assistant Investment Manager 1965-67; Shell International Petroleum Co Ltd, Assistant Investment Manager 1967-70; Investment Manager 1970-73; Baker Weeks & Co Inc,

Vice President, Head of European Research 1973-77; Geoffrey Morley & Partners Ltd, Director 1977-79; Deputy Chairman 1979-84; Chairman 1984-88; Globe Morley Ltd, Chief Executive 1988-. *Biog: b.* 25 April 1936. *Nationality:* British. *m.* 1960, Margaret Gordon (née Neville); 1 s; 1 d. *Educ:* Accrington Grammar School; Balliol College, Oxford (BA Hons OU Certificate in Statistics). *Professional Organisations:* Fellow, Society of Investment Analysts; Past Chairman (1975-1978) Society Investment Analysts. *Clubs:* United Oxford and Cambridge University Club.

PILLEY, J C D; Chairman, Russell Wood Ltd. *Career:* Henderson Administration Ltd, Director 1986-88. *Biog: b.* 25 January 1935. *Nationality:* British. *m.* 1985, Caroline (née Gilbert). *Educ:* Charterhouse; Christ Church, Oxford. *Directorships:* Falcon Capital Management 1989 Chairman. *Clubs:* Boodles.

PIMLOTT, Graham Fenwick; Chief Executive, Barclays De Zoete Wedd Limited, since 1989; Corporate Finance Division. *Career:* Lovell White & King (Now Lovell White Durrant) Solicitors 1974-86; Partner 1981-86; Secretary to Panel on Take-Overs and Mergers 1981-83; Kleinwort Benson Limited, Director Corporate Finance Division 1986-89. *Biog: b.* 22 October 1949. *Nationality:* British. *m.* 1974, Alison. *Educ:* St Edward's School, Oxford; Jesus College, Oxford University. *Professional Organisations:* Solicitor.

PINCHIN, Jeremy; Group Secretary, Sedgwick Group plc, since 1989; Legal & Secretariat Department. *Career:* Alexander Howden Group plc, Articled Clerk 1977-81; Reynolds Johnson & Green, Assistant Solicitor 1981-85; Alexander & Alexander Europe plc, Assistant Group Legal Advisor 1985-87; Reynolds Porter Chamberlain, Solicitor 1987-88. *Biog: b.* 20 July 1954. *Nationality:* British. *Educ:* Rossall School, Fleetwood, Lancashire. *Directorships:* Various Sedgwick Group Companies. *Professional Organisations:* Solicitor of Supreme Court; Member, Law Society. *Clubs:* Lloyds Yacht Club. *Recreations:* Sailing.

PINCKNEY, David Charles; Group Finance Director, Thornton and Co Ltd, since 1987; General & Financial Management. *Career:* Peat Marwick Mitchell & Co (Lyons), Ptnr in Charge 1975-77; (France), Snr Audit Ptnr 1977-83; Wrightson Wood Financial Services Ltd, MD 1983-86. *Biog: b.* 13 September 1940. *Nationality:* British. *m.* 1974, Susan Audrey (née Richards); 1 s; 2 d. *Educ:* Winchester College; New College, Oxford (MA Hons). *Other Activities:* Former Governor, British School in Paris. *Professional Organisations:* FCA, Ordre des Experts Comptables, Compagnie des Commissaires aux Comptes. *Clubs:* Brooks's, Hurlingham, Vincent's (Oxford). *Recreations:* Skiing, Tennis, Travel, Opera.

PINCUS, Barry Martin; Director, Dawnay, Day & Co Ltd, since 1985; Corporate Finance. *Career:* Keyser Ullmann Ltd, Asst Dir 1972-80; Charterhouse Japhet Ltd, Asst Dir 1980-81; Dawnay, Day & Co Ltd, Company Sec 1981-85. *Biog: b.* 9 December 1943. *Nationality:* British. 1989, Marion (née Weston); 2 s; 1d; 2 steps; 1 stepd. *Educ:* William Ellis School, London. *Directorships:* Union Group plc 1987 (non-exec). *Professional Organisations:* FCA.

PINFOLD, Mrs C E; Partner, Field Fisher Waterhouse, since 1989; Medico-Legal. *Career:* Field Fisher Waterhouse, Assistant Solicitor 1984-89. *Biog: Nationality:* British. *Educ:* King's College, University of London (BA).

PINKER, Keith Rodney; Senior Partner, Schaverien & Co.

PINLESS, David; Executive Director, Yamaichi International (Europe) Limited, since 1987; Financial Controller. *Career:* BNP Capital Markets Limited, Chief Accountant 1987; Libra Bank plc, Senior Manager Financial Services 1984-87; Manufacturers Hanover Trust Co, Accounting Officer 1979-83; Peat Marwick Mitchell & Co, Audit Senior 1976-79. *Biog: b.* 19 September 1953. *Nationality:* British. *Educ:* Imperial College, London University (BSc Hons). *Professional Organisations:* FCA; ARCS.

PINNER, Stephen John; Director, Citymax Integrated Information Systems Ltd, since 1990; Sales and Marketing. *Career:* Centre-File, Stockbroker Services Manager 1970-83; Extel Statistical Services, Marketing Director 1983-85; Extel Financial & Business Services, Director 1983-85; Financial Clearing & Services (UK) Ltd, Marketing Director 1985-87; Hoare Govett, Assistant Director 1985-87; Security Settlements plc, Chairman & Managing Director 1987-89; Security Settlements Options Ltd, Director 1988-90; Societe Generale Security Settlements Ltd, Managing Director 1989-90. *Biog: b.* 23 August 1951. *Nationality:* British. (div); 1 s 1 d. *Educ:* Enfield Grammar School; City of London College. *Directorships:* Citymax Integrated Information Systems Ltd 1990 (exec); Security Settlements Options Ltd 1988 (exec); Hoare Govett 1985 (exec). *Other Activities:* Committee Member, Stock Exchange Management Association. *Professional Organisations:* FA Referee. *Recreations:* Football, Theatre, Cycling, Music.

PINSENT, Antony Andrew MacPherson; Chairman & Managing Director, Leslie and Godwin Ltd, since 1989. *Career:* Willis Faber & Dumas 1966-75; CT Bowring, Dir 1975-80; Leslie & Godwin Aviation, Chm 1980-; Leslie & Godwin Limited, Managing Director 1985. *Biog: b.* 26 February 1946. *m.* 1969, Clare (née Reynolds); 1 s; 1 d. *Educ:* Radley College. *Directorships:* Various Subsidiary Companies within Leslie & Godwin Group. *Professional Organisations:* Member of Lloyd's.

Clubs: Hurlingham, Flyfishers. *Recreations:* Fishing, Shooting, Opera.

PIPER, Allan; Financial Journalist, The Mail On Sunday.

PIPER, C; Executive Director, Allied Dunbar Assurance plc.

PIPER, D J; Director, Minories Holdings Ltd.

PIRIE, Alistair; Staff Director, Securities and Investments Board.

PIRINTJI, Steven Michael; Legal Advisor & Company Secretary, Bank of Cyprus (London) Ltd, since 1985; Legal & Property Advice. *Career:* Howard Thomas & Petrou, Assistant Solicitor 1984-85. *Biog: b.* 24 December 1955. *Nationality:* British. *Educ:* University of Durham (BA Hons Sociology). *Professional Organisations:* Solicitors Qualification, Law Society. *Clubs:* Solicitors Anglo-Cypriot Association.

PIRRIE, David Blair; Director, UK Retail Banking, Lloyds Bank plc, since 1989. *Career:* Lloyds Bank, Gen Mgr (Brazil) 1975-81; Lloyds Bank Intl, Dir 1981-83; Gen Mgr 1983-85; Snr Gen Mgr, Intl, Dir Banking Div 1985-87; Snr Gen Mgr, UK Retail Banking 1987-89. *Biog: b.* 15 December 1938. *Nationality:* British. *m.* 1966, Angela (née Sellos); 3 s; 1 d. *Educ:* Strathallan School. *Directorships:* Alex Lawrie Factors Ltd 1987 (non-exec); Alex Lawrie Receivables Financing Ltd 1987 (non-exec); International Factors Ltd 1987 (non-exec); Lloyd's Bank Factors Ltd 1989 (non-exec); Confidential Invoice Discounting Ltd 1989 (non-exec); Independent Factors Ltd 1989 (non-exec). *Professional Organisations:* FCIB. *Clubs:* Wimbledon Park Golf Club. *Recreations:* Golf, Music.

PITCHER, Derek Ronald; Partner, Cyril Sweett and Partners.

PITCHER, George Martell; Industrial Editor, The Observer, since 1988. *Career:* Costain/Pitcher & Scott, Diver Linesman 1977-78; Bath Theatre Royal, Lighting Crew 1978; Western Clipper, Deckhand Barman 1978; Endeavour Training, Field Officer 1978-80; Haymarket Publishing, Journalist Marketing 1980-83; Braham-Hill Publications, MD 1983-85; Financial Marketing News, Editor 1983-85; Fund Management International, Editor 1983-85; Freelance, The Observer/Sunday Times/ Mirror 1983-85; The Observer, Associate Editor, Money Observer and City Reporter 1985-88; Marketing Week, Business Columnist 1988-; The Observer, Industrial Editor 1988-. *Biog: b.* 30 May 1955. *Nationality:* British. *m.* 1985, Lynda (née Mobbsetti); 2 s; 1 d. *Educ:* Blundells, Tiverton, Devon; Birmingham University (BA Hons Drama & Theatre Arts). *Other Activities:* Member, Room 74 Club Committee. *Professional Organi-*

sations: Member, Economic Research Council. *Publications:* The Public Faced (with Charles Stewart-Smith), 1989. *Clubs:* Room 74, London Press Club, Rags. *Recreations:* Journalism, Racing, PR.

PITCHER, K J; Director, S G Warburg Akroyd Rowe & Pitman Mullens Securities Ltd.

PITMAN, Brian Ivor; Director & Chief Executive, Lloyds Bank plc, since 1983. *Career:* Lloyds Bank 1952-; Joint Gen Mgr 1975; Lloyds Bank International, Exec Dir 1976-78; Dep Chief Exec 1978-81; Lloyds Bank plc, Dep Chief Exec 1982-83. *Biog: b.* 13 December 1931. *Nationality:* British. *m.* 1954, Barbara (née Darby); 2 s; 1 d. *Educ:* Cheltenham Grammar School. *Directorships:* National Bank of New Zealand Ltd 1982- (non-exec); Lloyds Bank (California) 1982-86 (non-exec); NBNZ Holdings Limited 1990- (non-exec). *Professional Organisations:* FCIB. *Publications:* Organising for the Future, 1985; Banking Through the Looking Glass, 1987; Banking in Ferment, 1989. *Clubs:* MCC, Gloucester County Cricket Club, St George's Hill Golf Club. *Recreations:* Golf, Music, Cricket.

PITROFF, Miss Vivienne E; Solicitor, Holman, Fenwick & Willan; Commercial Law. *Educ:* (LLM Law, Solicitor of the Supreme Court).

PITT, A A; Director, A J Archer Holdings plc.

PITT, R C; Director, Providence Capitol Life Assurance Ltd.

PITTIE, Bernard; Chief Financial & Administrative Officer, Paribas Limited, since 1986; Accounting, Budget, Technology, Operations, Facilities, Personnel. *Career:* Banque Paribas Paris, Internal Auditor 1970-81; Banque Paribas NY Branch, Head of Finance & Administration 1981-85; Paribas Limited, Head of Finance & Administration 1986-. *Biog: b.* 17 July 1990. *Nationality:* French. *m.* 1978, Françoise. *Educ:* Faculté de Droit et Sciences Economiques, Paris (Licence Sciences Economiques). *Recreations:* Golf.

PIX, Michael; Senior Executive Director, J H Minet & Co Ltd; Insurance of Jewellery and Fine Arts. *Career:* Hartley, Cooper & Co Ltd, Broker 1958-62; European Representative 1962-69; Cabinet Diot (Paris), Manager, International Department 1969-84; J H Minet & Co Ltd, Managing Director of Fine Arts and Jewellery Division 1984-87; Main Board Director 1984-; Senior Executive Director 1986-. *Biog: b.* 30 January 1940. *Nationality:* British. *m.* 1964, Jeanne (née Holzhauer). *Educ:* Streete Court School; Uppingham School. *Directorships:* J H Minet & Co Ltd 1984 (exec); Minet Europe Holdings Ltd 1989 (exec); Savoy Insurance Brokers Ltd 1982 (exec); Diot Minet (France) SA, Paris 1985 (exec); J H Minet Monaco SAM, Monte Carlo 1985 (exec); Minet Italia SRL, Florence 1987 (exec); Allen Insurance

Associates, Los Angeles 1990 (exec). *Other Activities:* Member, UK Insurance Brokers' International Committee. *Professional Organisations:* Chartered Insurance Practitioner; Associate, Chartered Insurance Institute; Registered Insurance Broker; Associate, Institute of Arbitrators. *Publications:* Insurance, 1962. *Recreations:* Arts, Gardening.

PLAISTOWE, William Ian David; Partner, Arthur Andersen & Co, since 1976; Accounting & Audit, Practice Director for UK. *Career:* Arthur Andersen & Co 1964-. *Biog: b.* 18 November 1942. *m.* 1968, Carolyn (née Wilson); 2 s; 1 d. *Educ:* Marlborough College; Queens' College, Cambridge (MA). *Professional Organisations:* FCA (Member of Council); Vice President, Institute of Chartered Accountants in England and Wales. *Clubs:* Carlton. *Recreations:* Golf, Tennis, Squash, Skiing, Gardening.

PLANT, Charles; Partner, Herbert Smith; Head of Litigation Department.

PLANT, Paul Gordon; Joint Managing Director, The Burton Group plc, since 1980. *Biog: b.* 1 March 1945. *Nationality:* British. *Directorships:* Burton Property Trust Limited 1984; Debenhams plc 1985; FPI Development Co Limited 1986; Freebody Properties Limited 1986; Pengap Estates Limited 1987.

PLATER, Alan G; Director, CSFB (Gilts) Limited.

PLATT, Adrian; Director, Sedgwick Group plc, since 1981; Various Overseas Group Companies and Worldwide Business. *Career:* Price Forbes & Co Ltd 1957-60; Sedgwick Collins & Co Ltd, Director 1960-74; Sedgwick Forbes Ltd 1974-79; Sedgwick Forbes Marine Ltd, Chairman 1977-79; Sedgwick Group plc 1979; Sedgwick Forbes Bland Payne Marine Ltd, Chairman 1979-81. *Biog: b.* 28 November 1935. *Nationality:* British. *m.* 1960, Valerie (née Bois); 2 d. *Educ:* Marlborough College; Grenobles University. *Directorships:* Various Sedgwick Group Directorships; Lloyds Insurance Brokers Marine Committee 1979 Chm; Lloyds Insurance Brokers Committee 1981 Dep Chm. *Other Activities:* Liveryman, Vintners Company; Liveryman, Shipwrights Company; Member, Honourable Artillery Co; Member, Institute of Directors; Trustee, Mary Rose Trust. *Publications:* Handling Risks of Privatisation, by Adam Smith Institute, 1990. *Clubs:* Effingham Golf Club, St Erudue Golf Club. *Recreations:* Golf, Tennis, Skiing, Shooting.

PLATT, John; Director, 3i plc.

PLATT, Robin; Partner, Morison Stoneham Chartered Accountants.

PLATT, William Peter; Deputy General Manager, Bank Handlowy w Warszawie SA. *Career:* Bank of England 1948-74; Wells Fargo Ltd 1976-79. *Biog: b.* 12

September 1926. *Nationality:* British. *m.* 1967, Felicity Anne (née Routledge); 2 s. *Educ:* Merchant Taylors' School; School of Oriental and African Studies, London. *Other Activities:* Mem, Honourable Artillery Company; Mem, Lombard Assoc. *Clubs:* Overseas Bankers', Royal Commonwealth Society. *Recreations:* Gardening, Reading, Fishing, Bird Watching, Country Pursuits.

PLATTS, D A; Director, Brewin Dolphin & Co Ltd.

PLAXTON, John K; Director, Merrill Lynch International Limited, since 1989; UK Corporate Finance. *Career:* Arthur Andersen & Co, Audit 1976-80; Merrill Lynch, New York 1982-84; Merrill Lynch, London 1984-. *Biog: b.* 2 July 1955. *Nationality:* British. *m.* 1984, Tian (née Tan); 2 s; 1 d. *Educ:* Scarborough High School for Boys; London School of Economics (BSc Economics); University of Chicago (MBA Honours). *Professional Organisations:* ACA. *Recreations:* Piano, Shooting, Jogging, Cinema.

PLENDERLEITH, Ian; Associate Director, Bank of England, since 1990; Official Market Operations and Monetary Policy; Government Broker, since 1989. *Career:* Bank of England, Various 1965-; IMF (Washington DC), Seconded-Tech Asst to UK Exec Dir 1972-74; Bank of England, Private Sec to Governor 1976-79; Head of Gilt-Edged Division 1982-90. *Biog: b.* 27 September 1943. *Nationality:* British. *m.* 1967, Kristina Mary (née Bentley); 1 s; 2 d. *Educ:* King Edward's School, Birmingham; Christ Church, Oxford (MA); Columbia Business School, New York (MBA). *Directorships:* European Investment Bank 1980-86 (non-exec); International Stock Exchange 1989 Stock Broker. *Other Activities:* Innholders' Company; Advisory Board, Institute of Archaeology Development Trust, University College, London; Member, The Council of The International Stock Exchange; Beta Gamma Sigma Award, Columbia University, 1971. *Professional Organisations:* Fellow, Association of Corporate Treasurers. *Clubs:* Tillington Cricket Club. *Recreations:* Archaeology, Theatre, Cricket.

PLOWDEN, Charles Edmund Philip; Partner, Baillie Gifford & Co, since 1988; UK Equity Manager. *Biog: b.* 1960. *Nationality:* British. *Educ:* Ampleforth College, York; Magdalen College, Oxford (BA Modern History).

PLOWRIGHT, David; Director, Granada Group.

PLUCINSKY, David Joseph; Chairman & Chief Executive Officer, Hoare Govett Securities Ltd, since 1990. *Career:* The Sequor Group, MD 1982-88; Security Pacific Hoare Govett (Group) Ltd, MD 1988-90. *Educ:* Rutger University; Montclair State College. *Directorships:* The Sequor Group 1986 (non-exec). *Recreations:* Golf, Tennis.

PLUMB, Charles Henry; Lord Plumb; Director, United Biscuits (Holdings) plc.

PLUMB, R H; Partner, Life & General (Epsom), Bacon & Woodrow.

PLUMMER, A C; Director, Hambros Bank Limited.

PLUMMER, J A; Director, Fenchurch Insurance Group Limited.

PLUMMER, Richard Martin; Director, MIM Ltd, since 1979; UK & International Property Investment, Marketing to Public Sector Pension Funds, Development Capital. *Career:* Knight Frank & Rutley, Mgr, Investment Dept 1972-79. *Biog: b.* 16 February 1950. *Nationality:* British. *m.* 1990, Hortense; 1 s. *Educ:* Warwick School; Oxford Polytechnic (Dip Est Man). *Directorships:* MIM Ltd 1982 (exec); MIM Trustee Corporation 1982 (exec); MIM Development Capital 1986 (exec); MIM Property Services 1985 MD. *Other Activities:* Member, Mgmnt Ctee, Paneuropean Property Unit Trust; Member, Mgmnt Ctee, Hanover Property Unit Trust. *Professional Organisations:* FRICS. *Clubs:* RAC. *Recreations:* Golf, Travel, Gardening.

PLUNKETT, Oliver D; Chairman, Bradstock Group plc.

POCKNEY, Penrhyn Charles Benjamin; Director, SG Warburg Akroyd Rowe & Pitman Mullens Securities, since 1986; UK Equity Division. *Career:* Saffery Sons & Co Chartered Accountants, Articled Clerk; J & A Scrimgeour Ltd, Dir 1963-80; Mullens & Co, Ptnr 1980-86. *Biog: b.* 22 May 1940. *m.* 1965, Patricia Jane (née des Voeux); 2 s. *Educ:* Winchester College. *Directorships:* Potter Warburg Ltd (Australia) 1989 (non-exec). *Other Activities:* Liveryman, Skinners' Company. *Professional Organisations:* FCA. *Clubs:* Boodle's, Lansdowne. *Recreations:* Fishing, Gardening, Painting.

POCOCK, Andrew Lovell Irwin; Director, Multilateral/Central Bank Relations for Midland Bank Group, since 1989, Samuel Montagu & Co Ltd; Coordiantion & Marketing of Group services to suprnational & central banking organisations. *Career:* Bank of London & South America Ltd, Management Trainee 1968-71; J Henry Schroder Wagg & Co Ltd, Assistant Manager 1971-74; Scandinavian Bank Ltd, Manager, Asst Gen Mgr 1975-82; Hong Kong, Credit & Marketing 1975-77; Singapore, Regional Representative 1978; Bahrain, General Manager 1978-80; Samuel Montagu & Co Ltd, Executive Director 1982-. *Biog: b.* 23 July 1946. *Nationality:* British. *m.* 1970, Penelope (née Heppell); 2 s; 1 d. *Educ:* Canford School; Fitzwilliam College, Cambridge (MA HONS). *Directorships:* Samuel Montagu & Co Ltd 1982 (exec); Midland Montagu Limited 1989 (non-exec). *Other Activities:*

Freeman, City of London. *Clubs:* Overseas Bankers Club, MCC. *Recreations:* Sailing, Squash, Tennis, Opera.

POGUE, R W; Director, Redland plc.

POIGNANT, B; Managing Director, BNP Capital Markets.

POLAND, Simon; Partner, Clyde & Co.

POLL, David John; Lloyd's Underwriter, Holdsure Motor Policies at Lloyd's, since 1972; Underwriter & Management of Composite Motor Insurer. *Career:* Bray Gibb, Motor Broker 1955-67; Swan Motor Policies, Deputy Motor Underwriter 1967-72. *Biog: b.* 14 September 1939; 3 s. *Educ:* Roan Grammar School, Blackheath. *Directorships:* David Holman & Co Ltd 1972 (exec); Holdsure Serv Co Ltd 1986 (exec); Erin Serv Co Ltd 1989 (exec).

POLLARD, David Nigel; Partner, Freshfields, since 1990. *Career:* Lewis Lewis & Co, Articled Clerk & Asst Solicitor 1978-80; Freshfields, Asst Solicitor 1980-90; Seconded to Singapore Office 1984-1987. *Biog: b.* 30 August 1956. *Nationality:* British. *Educ:* Cranbrook School; St John's College, Cambridge (MA). *Clubs:* Singapore Cricket Club. *Recreations:* Travel, Reading.

POLLARD, Garth; Partner, Clifford Chance, since 1975; Tax. *Career:* Ingledew, Brown, Bennison & Garrett Articled Clerk 1967-69; Clifford-Turner Asst Solicitor 1969-75; Partner 1975-87; Clifford Chance, Partner 1987-. *Biog: b.* 25 April 1945. *Nationality:* British. *m.* 1973, Lucy Petica (née Robertson); 3 s. *Educ:* Queen's College, Taunton; King's College, London (LLB). *Other Activities:* Member, City of London Solicitors' Company. *Professional Organisations:* Solicitor; The Law Society. *Publications:* Doing Business in The United Kingdom (Co-Editor), 1985. *Recreations:* Music, Walking.

POLLOCK, David Robert; Director, James Capel & Co Ltd, since 1990; International Equity Issues. *Career:* Samuel Montagu & Co Limited 1978-81; Morgan Grenfell & Co Limited 1981-88; James Capel & Co Limited 1989-. *Biog: b.* 1956. *Nationality:* British. *Educ:* City of London School; Worcester College, Oxford (BA).

POLLOCK, David T C; Partner, Touche Ross & Co, since 1987; Audit/Investigations/Student Recruitment. *Career:* Touche Ross & Co (Formerly Spicer & Oppenheim) 1979-; Student Chartered Accountant 1979-82; Audit Senior 1982-84; Manager 1984-87. *Biog: b.* 4 January 1958. *Nationality:* British. *m.* 1987, Nicole (née McAllister). *Educ:* Merchant Taylors' School; Southampton University (BSc). *Professional Organisations:* Institute of Chartered Accountants (ACA); Institute of

Taxation (ATII). *Clubs:* East India, Durrants. *Recreations:* Sport, Photography, Flying.

POLLOCK, Richard; Vice President & Personnel, Bank of America.

POLLOCK, The Hon Richard Charles Standish; TD; Partner, Simmons & Simmons, since 1982; Property. *Career:* Simmons & Simmons, Assistant Solicitor 1980-82; Macfarlanes, Assistant Solicitor 1976-80; Articled Clerk 1974-76. *Biog: b.* 6 February 1952. *Nationality:* British. *m.* 1982, Louise (née Lockhart); 2 s. *Educ:* Wellington College; Trinity College, Cambridge (MA). *Other Activities:* Grocers Company. *Recreations:* TAVR.

POLNIK, M J; Director, Charterhouse Tilney.

POLONIECKI, Piotr Bernard Hammersley; Managing Director, Midland Montagu Asset Management, since 1986; Investment Management. *Career:* Morgan Grenfell & Co Ltd, Director 1972-86. *Biog: b.* 15 July 1948. *Nationality:* British. *m.* (div); 3 s. *Educ:* Ampleforth College; Oriel College, Oxford (BSc). *Directorships:* Midland Bank Unit Trust Managers Ltd 1987 (exec); MMAM Holdings 1987 (exec); Midland Bank Trust Corporation (Jersey) Ltd 1989 (exec). *Other Activities:* Member of Council, Institute of Education, University of London. *Professional Organisations:* Society of Investment Analysts. *Recreations:* Tennis, Skiing.

POLONSKY, Mrs A E (née Glickman); Partner, Holman Fenwick & Willan, since 1990; Insurance/Reinsurance Litigation. *Career:* Clyde & Co, Assistant Solicitor, Reinsurance Litigation 1985-88; Reynolds Porter Chamberlaine, Assistant Solicitor, Professional Indemnity Litigation 1981-85; Bindman and Partners, Articled Clerk then Newly Qualified Assistant Solicitor, Litigation 1978-81. *Biog: b.* 28 August 1940. *Nationality:* Canadian. *m.* 1964, Prof Antony Polonsky; 1 s; 1 d. *Educ:* Humberside Collegiate Institute, Toronto; University of Toronto (BA Hons English Language and Literature); Somerville College, Oxford (BA, MA English, Course I); Queen Mary College, London University (LLB). *Professional Organisations:* Member, Law Society. *Recreations:* Reading, Music, Theatre, Films, Travel, Cooking.

POMEROY, Brian Walter; Partner In Charge, Management Consultancy, Touche Ross & Co Management Consultants, since 1987; Economics, Finance and General Management. *Career:* Touche Ross & Co, Ptnr 1976-. *Biog: b.* 26 June 1944. *Nationality:* British. *m.* 1974, Hilary (née Price); 2 d. *Educ:* The King's School, Canterbury; Magdalene College, Cambridge (MA). *Directorships:* The Rover Group plc 1985-88 (non-exec). *Other Activities:* Council Member, Lloyd's; Treasurer, Centrepoint Soho. *Professional Organisations:* FCA. *Recreations:* Tennis, Running, Photography.

POMEROY, Thomas; Executive Director, Yasuda Trust Europe Limited, since 1987.

POMERY, Michael Alan; Partner, Bacon & Woodrow, since 1973; Consulting Actuary. *Career:* Bacon & Woodrow Actuarial Trainee 1966-70; Voluntary Services Overseas Teacher 1970-72; Bacon & Woodrow Actuary 1972-73. *Biog: b.* 18 August 1944. *Nationality:* British. *m.* 1967, Mary (née Smallwood; 1 s; 1 d. *Educ:* Simon Langton GS, Canterbury; Keble College, Oxford (MA). *Other Activities:* Member, Council of National Association of Pension Funds, 1988-. *Professional Organisations:* FIA, FPMI, Member, Association of Consulting Actuaries.

POMFRET, David John; Partner, Pannell Kerr Forster, since 1987; Audit. *Career:* Pannell Kerr Forster, Articled Clerk to Audit Manager 1975-84; Corporate Advisory Manager 1984-86. *Biog: b.* 10 July 1954. *Nationality:* British. *m.* 1987, Janice Dora (née Rawstron); 2 s. *Educ:* Richmond School, Yorkshire; Warwick University (BSc Mathematics). *Professional Organisations:* FCA. *Recreations:* Music, Hiking, Reading.

PONSONBY, Rupert Charles; TD; Director, Samuel Montagu & Co Limited, since 1990; Corporate Finance. *Career:* Touche Ross & Co 1976-83; Samuel Montagu & Co Limited London, Corporate Finance 1983-85; Samuel Montagu & Co Limited Hong Kong, Corporate Finance 1985-88; Samuel Montagu & Co Limited London, Corporate Finance 1988-. *Biog: b.* 30 June 1957. *Nationality:* British. *Educ:* Eton. *Other Activities:* Major, Royal Wessex Yeomanry (TA). *Professional Organisations:* Associate of the Institute of Chartered Accountants in England and Wales, 1980. *Clubs:* Cavalry, Royal Hong Kong Jockey Club.

PONTIN, A J; Partner, Pannell Kerr Forster, since 1980; General Practice/Audit. *Biog: b.* 15 July 1948. *Nationality:* British. *Educ:* Marshalswick, St Albans. *Other Activities:* Gold & Silver Wyre Drawers; Past Chairman, Lunchtime Comment Club; City Livery Club. *Professional Organisations:* FCA. *Recreations:* Travel, Gardening, Flying.

PONTIN, J G; Non-Executive Director, Dartington & Co Group plc.

POOLE, The Hon David C; Chairman, James Capel Corporate Finance Ltd.

POOLE, James Nicholas; Chief Commodities and Futures Correspondent, Reuters Ltd, since 1989; Physical Commodities, Shipping and Futures Markets. *Biog: b.* 4 April 1953. *Nationality:* British. *Educ:* Trinity College, Cambridge (MA Hons). *Recreations:* Cricket, Squash.

POOLE, Kevin John; Partner, Wragge & Co, since 1990; Corporate Finance. *Career:* Rowe & Maw, Trainee

Solicitor then Solicitor 1981-85. *Biog: b.* 4 May 1959. *Nationality:* British. *m.* 1982, Geraldine (née Kettell); 2 s. *Educ:* Reigate Grammar School; Jesus College, Cambridge (MA). *Professional Organisations:* Member, Law Society; Solicitor.

POOLEY, Peter John; Managing Director, Secombe Marshall & Campion plc, since 1981. *Biog: b.* 16 August 1939. *m.* 1962, Jennifer Anne (née Grady); 1 s; 1 d. *Educ:* Ewell Castle School.

POPE, A Hugh; Chairman, Aerospace & Defence Systems Group, Smiths Industries plc.

POPE, Henry Martin John; Director, Hoare Govett Securities Limited, since 1987; Running Water & Electricity Market Making. *Career:* Henry Cooke Lumsden & Co, Dealer 1976-85. *Biog: b.* 20 July 1954. *Nationality:* British. *Educ:* Radley College. *Recreations:* Cricket, Horse Racing.

POPE, Ian W H; Partner, Hymans Robertson & Co, Consulting Actuaries, since 1987; UK Occupational Pension Schemes & Overseas Life Insurance Companies. *Career:* Hymans Robertson & Co, Trainee Actuary 1978-85; Qualified Actuary (FFA) 1985-87; Partner 1987-. *Biog: b.* 1 July 1961. *Nationality:* British. *m.* 1983, Jan Elisabeth (née Miller); 1 d. *Educ:* St Pauls School, London; Heriot Watt University, Edinburgh (Honours Degree in Actuarial Mathemaics & Statistics). *Directorships:* Robertson Trustees Limited 1990 (non-exec). *Professional Organisations:* Fellow, Faculty of Actuaries (FFA).

POPLE, J N; Partner, Chairman of the Management Committee, Hill Taylor Dickinson, ince 1979; Litigation. *Biog: b.* 17 August 1950. *Nationality:* British. *Educ:* University of Exeter (LLB). *Professional Organisations:* Solicitor. *Recreations:* Acting and Directing.

PORTER, Anthony Richard; Director, Wood Gundy Inc, since 1984; Stock Trading. *Biog: b.* 12 October 1939. *m.* 1969, Eileen (née Shiel); 1 s; 1 d. *Educ:* Selhurst Grammar School. *Clubs:* Croham Hurst Golf Club. *Recreations:* Golf, Skiing.

PORTER, D E; Director, LPH Group plc.

PORTER, David Robert; Director, de Zoete & Bevan Ltd; Barclays de Zoete Wedd Securities Ltd, since 1986; Managing Director Corporate Stockbroking. *Career:* de Zoete & Bevan, Partner.

PORTER, E R; Director, London International Financial Futures Exchange Ltd.

PORTER, Geoffrey; Vice President, Chemical Bank.

PORTER, Hamish S; Partner, Theodore Goddard, since 1984; Intellectual Property Litigation. *Career:* Theodore Goddard 1975-78; Deacons (Hong Kong) 1978-79; Mills & Reeve (Norwich) 1980-82; Theodore Goddard 1982-. *Biog: b.* 14 July 1952. *Nationality:* British. *m.* 1987, Patricia (née Holden); 1 s. *Educ:* The Leys School, Cambridge; Southampton University (LLB). *Clubs:* MCC. *Recreations:* Music, Theatre, Sport, Hill Walking.

PORTER, Ms Janet; Bureau Chief, The Journal of Commerce.

PORTER, Ms Leila (née Assassa); Partner, Gouldens, since 1990; Company/Commercial. *Career:* Lee & Pembertons, Articled Clerk 1981-83; Herbert Smith, Assistant Solicitor 1983-86; Gouldens, Assistant Solicitor 1986-90. *Biog: b.* 8 December 1958. *Nationality:* British. *m.* 1985, Alistair Campbell Porter; 2 d. *Educ:* Cheadle Hulme School; Leeds University (LLB Hons); Lancaster Gate College of Law. *Professional Organisations:* Member, Law Society (Qualified as Solicitor). *Recreations:* Reading, Sailing, Travel.

PORTER, M W; Partner, Allen & Overy, since 1978; Pensions Law. *Career:* College of Law 1972-74. *Educ:* King's College, Taunton; St John's College, Cambridge (Law). *Other Activities:* City of London Solicitors Company. *Professional Organisations:* Solicitor; Member, Law Society.

PORTER, Philip Ian; Executive Director, County NatWest Limited, since 1986. *Career:* Manufacturers Hanover Asia Ltd, Dir 1977-84; Manufacturers Hanover Ltd, Dir 1980-84; Merrill Lynch Capital Markets, MD 1984-86; Merrill Lynch Europe Ltd, Exec Dir 1984-86. *Biog: b.* 20 April 1948. *Nationality:* British. *Educ:* Eton College; Geneva University. *Recreations:* Sailing, Skiing, Golf, Photography, Tennis.

PORTER, Robert Howard; Partner, McKenna & Co, since 1990; Commercial Property. *Career:* Stones Porter & Co, Articled Clerk 1980-84; McKenna & Co, Asst Solicitor 1984-90. *Biog: b.* 22 April 1961. *Nationality:* British. *m.* 1983, Jane; 2 s. *Educ:* College of Law, Guildford. *Recreations:* Shooting, Riding.

PORTER, Robin Anthony; Partner, Wilde Sapte, since 1975; Partner in Commercial Property Department/Commercial Property Law and Property Finance. *Career:* Titmuss Sainer & Webb, Articled Clerk (Trainee Lawyer) 1968-70; Clifford-Turner & Co, Assistant Solicitor, Commercial Property Department 1971-72; McKenna & Co, Assistant Solicitor, Company and Commercial Department 1972-73; Penningtons, Assistant Solicitor, Company and Commercial Department 1974; Wilde Sapte, Assistant Solicitor, Commercial Property Department 1974-75; Partner, Commercial Property Department 1975-84; Partner in

Charge, New York Office 1984-87; Partner, Commercial Property Department 1987-. *Biog: b.* 15 September 1945. *Nationality:* British. *m.* 1974, Monica Jolán (née Halász); 2 s. *Educ:* Highgate School; The University of Leeds (LLB). *Other Activities:* Freeman, City of London; Liveryman, Worshipful Company of Musicians. *Professional Organisations:* Solicitor, 1971; The Law Society; International Bar Association (Section on Business Law); British-Hungarian Law Association. *Clubs:* English Speaking Union, Cumberland Lawn Tennis Club. *Recreations:* Music, Theatre, Tennis, Skiing, Cycling.

PORTER, Roger; Director, C S Investments Ltd, since 1987; Investment Manager, Private Clients. *Career:* Joseph Sebag & Co, Investment Analyst 1963-72; Slater Walker Investments, Dir 1972-78; Tower Fund Managers, Dir 1978-81; Dunbar Group plc, Dir 1981-84; C S Investments Ltd, Dir 1984-. *Biog: b.* 14 August 1942. *Nationality:* British. *m.* 1970, Diane (née Hailwood); 2 s. *Educ:* Ipswich School. *Professional Organisations:* Member, Lloyd's; AMSIA. *Clubs:* RAC, Sotogrande Golf Club. *Recreations:* Theatre, Gardening, Jogging, Family Interests.

PORTER, T E; UK Director, M W Marshall & Company Limited.

PORTINGTON, Michael; Senior Director, Risk Management, Continental Bank NA.

POSFORD, Stephen James Douglas; Managing Director, Greenwell Montagu Gilt Edged.

POST, Herschel; Chief Operating Officer & Director, Lehman Brothers International Inc, since 1990. *Career:* Daurs Polk & Wardwell (Attorneys), Attorney 1966-69; The Parks Council of New York City, Exec Dir 1969-72; City of New York (USA), Dep Admin, Parks, Recreation 1973; Morgan Guaranty Trust Co, Mgr, Euroclear Clearance System 1973-78; VP, Dep Head, Intl Inv Dept 1978-83; Shearson Lehman Global Asset Management, Pres & Dir 1984-. *Biog: b.* 9 October 1939. *Nationality:* American. *m.* 1963, Peggy (née Mayne); 1 s; 3 d. *Educ:* The Thacher School; Yale University (AB); Oxford University (BA, MA); Harvard Law School (LLB). *Directorships:* Shearson Global Asset Management SA 1984 (exec); Posthorn Global Asset Management (UK) Ltd 1984 (exec); International Stock Exchange, Intl Equity Mkt Ctee 1988 (non-exec) Chm; London Review of Books Ltd 1978 (non-exec); Earthwatch Europe 1988 Trustee; Lehman Brothers International Inc 1990 (exec); Lehman Brothers Securities Ltd 1990 (exec). *Professional Organisations:* Lawyer, Admitted to The Bar of the State of New York, USA. *Recreations:* Mountain Climbing, Skiing, Walking, Art Collecting.

POTASHNICK, Mark Peter; Director, Kleinwort Benson Securities Limited.

POTSIDES, C E; Area Financial Controller, The Hongkong and Shanghai Banking Corp.

POTTER, David Roger William; Chief Executive, Guinness Mahon & Co Limited, since 1990. *Career:* National Discount (now Gerrard & National) 1965-69; Credit Suisse First Boston, MD 1969-80; Midland Montagu/Samuel Montagu, MD 1980-89; David Potter Consultants 1989-90. *Biog: b.* 27 July 1944. *Nationality:* British. 2 d. *Educ:* Bryanston School, Dorset; University College, Oxford (PPE). *Directorships:* Tyndall Holdings 1990 (non-exec) Vice Chairman; Thomas Cook 1989 (non-exec). *Other Activities:* Ashmolean Museum, Oxford (Member of Development Committee); Bryanston School (Member of Council of Governors); Bruges Group (Supporter); UMDS, Guys & St Thomas's Hospital (Lay Governor, Chairman of Finance Committee). *Clubs:* United Oxford & Cambridge University Club. *Recreations:* Golf, Shooting, Theatre, Wine.

POTTER, Kenneth Harold; Group Partner, Touche Ross & Co.

POTTERTON, Ralph; Partner, Hepworth & Chadwick.

POTTINGER, Piers; Chairman, Lowe Bell Financial; Financial PR. *Biog: b.* 3 March 1954. *Nationality:* British. 1 s; 2 d. *Directorships:* Perkakuppe Coffee Filtration Systems SA (Sweden). *Clubs:* Famous Five. *Recreations:* Swirling.

POTTLE, Michael Adrian; Managing Director, Alexanders Discount plc, since 1984; Head of Sterling Money Market Operations. *Career:* Norman & Bennet Ltd, Mgr 1963-74; Jessel Toynbee & Co Ltd, Mgr 1974-83; Jessel Toynbee & Gillett, Asst to Dirs 1983-84. *Biog: b.* 18 December 1946. *Nationality:* British. *m.* 1965, Elizabeth Ann (née Lawry); 1 s; 1 d. *Educ:* Cheshunt Grammar School. *Directorships:* Alexanders Discount Futures Ltd 1989 (exec). *Recreations:* Shooting.

POTTS, D K; Director, United Dominions Trust Limited.

POTTS, J D; Chief Dealer, Treasury/Foreign Exchange, Société Générale Merchant Bank plc.

POUGATCH, Michael Seymour; Director, Singer & Friedlander Holdings, since 1973. *Biog: b.* 9 August 1933. *Nationality:* British. *m.* 1962, Pauline Sonia (née Clifton); 1 s; 2 d. *Educ:* Malvern College; Corpus Christi College, Cambridge (MA). *Directorships:* Singer & Friedlander Investment Management 1987. *Other Activities:* Worshipful Company of Broderers. *Clubs:* MCC, Guards & Cavalry. *Recreations:* Cricket, Horse Racing, Tennis, Walking.

POULET, Alain; General Manager, CIC-Union Européenne, International et Cie, since 1990. *Career:* Banque De L'Union Européenne (CIC Group), Senior Vice President, Corporate Banking, Domestic, Intl, Eurobond Dept 1971-85; CIC-Union Européenne, International et Cie (CIC Group), London Branch 1985-. *Biog: b.* 22 March 1944. *Nationality:* French. *m.* 1982, Dominique (née Orcel); 2 s; 1 d. *Educ:* Hautes Etudes Commerciales; University of Law, Paris; Harvard Business School (PMD). *Directorships:* CIC UK Ltd. *Recreations:* Golf.

POUND, John Alan; Director, since 1984; Secretary, since 1981, Cater Allen Holdings plc; Company Secretary/Administration. *Career:* Standard Bank of South Africa Clerk 1952-56; Allen Harvey & Ross (now Cater Allen Ltd) Secretary 1956-89. *Biog: b.* 23 February 1936. *Nationality:* British. *m.* 1960, Valerie Joy (née Bateman); 1 s; 1 d. *Educ:* Dulwich College. *Directorships:* Cater Allen Nominees Ltd 1968 (exec); Proudworth Ltd 1977 (exec); Cater Allen Investment Management Ltd 1978 (exec); Cater Allen Securities Ltd 1986 (exec). *Other Activities:* Walbrook Ward Club. *Professional Organisations:* FCIB; FCIS. *Clubs:* Shirley Wanderers RFC, Parkhouse FC, Beckenham Q Club, West Kent Golf Club. *Recreations:* Rugby, Golf, Snooker, Real Ale.

POUNTAIN, Sir Eric; Director, Midland Bank plc.

POUX-GUILLAUME, B; Chairman, Pechiney World Trade (Holdings) Ltd.

POVEY, George John; Secretary, National Westminster Bank plc, since 1986. *Career:* National Westminster Bank plc 1951-; Planning & Projects Executive 1984; Deputy Secretary 1985. *Biog: b.* 17 July 1931. *Nationality:* British. *m.* 1960, Jean Bernadette (née Mallon); 1 d. *Educ:* Glyn Grammar School, Epsom. *Directorships:* National Provincial Bank Ltd 1986 (non-exec); Westminster Bank Ltd 1986 (non-exec). *Professional Organisations:* ACIB. *Clubs:* Kent County Lawn Tennis Association, National Westminster Bank LTC. *Recreations:* Being Idle.

POWDRILL, Roger A; Partner, Touche Ross & Co; Corporate Recovery. *Career:* Beal Young & Booth 1965-69; Holman Williams & Co, Partner 1969-80; Spicer & Pegler, Partner 1980-90; Touche Ross, Partner 1990. *Biog: b.* 24 February 1946. *Nationality:* British. *m.* 1989, Rita; 4 d. *Educ:* Cheltenham College. *Professional Organisations:* FCA, Licensed Insolvency Practitioner, MIPA. *Clubs:* Naval Club. *Recreations:* Surrey CCC.

POWELL, Alan; Assistant General Manager, Banque Nationale de Paris plc, since 1989; Head of Banking Division (Corporate Banking). *Career:* The Skinners' School, Tunbridge Wells, History Master 1969-72; Montagu, Loebl, Stanley & Co, Oil Analyst 1972-75;

Westdeutsche Landesbank, Manager 1975-83; Banque Nationale de Paris plc 1984-; Manager, Banking Division 1984-89; Deputy Head of Banking Division 1989; Head of Banking Division 1990. *Biog: b.* 6 October 1946. *Nationality:* British. *m.* 1971, Claude Jacqueline Marie (née Garnier); 2 d. *Educ:* Drayton Manor School; New College, Oxford (BA Hons); Kings College, London (Post Graduate Certificate in Education). *Recreations:* Theatre, Cricket, Tennis.

POWELL, David; Chairman & CEO, A B Dick Company, since 1983. *Career:* The General Electric Company plc, Asst General Manager, Power Engineering Division, Witton, Asst Managing Director, Telecommunications Group, Director of Planning, GEC plc, Headquarters 1963; The Diesel Companies, Group Managing Director 1971; GEC Plc, Main Board Director 1978; A B Dick Company,Chicago, Illinois USA, Chairman & CEO 1983; Additional Responsibilities for Other GEC Companies in the USA 1987. *Biog: b.* 14 August 1928. *Nationality:* British. *m.* 1951, Kathleen (née Hill); 3 s; 1 d. *Educ:* De La Salle College, Salford, England; Metropolitan College, St Albans. *Directorships:* The General Electric Company plc 1978; Certain other Subsidiary Companies of GEC plc 1987. *Professional Organisations:* Fellow, Institute of Chartered Accountants in England & Wales. *Clubs:* RAC Club (Pall Mall, London), Michigan Shores Club (Wilmette, IllinoisUSA). *Recreations:* Golf, Swimming, Running.

POWELL, David Beynon; Group Legal Director, Midland Bank plc, since 1984. *Career:* BL Ltd (British Leyland) Dir of Legal Services 1973-84. *Nationality:* British. *Educ:* Gowerton Grammar School; Christ's College, Cambridge (MA, LLB); Yale Law School, LLM; Harvard Business School (SMP). *Directorships:* Midland California Holdings Ltd; Midland/Montagu Investment Co. *Recreations:* Reading, Music, Gardening.

POWELL, G B; Chief Operations Manager, Bank Hapoalim BM, since 1989; Banking Operations and Administration. *Career:* The National Bank of New Zealand Ltd, Bank Officer 1950-71; Bank Hapoalim BM, Chief Accountant, Accounting and Administration 197 1-89. *Biog: b.* 18 April 1930. *Nationality:* British. *m.* 1952, Lilian (née Dyer); 2 s; 2 d. *Educ:* Port Talbot Secondary School. *Directorships:* Ampal Leasing (UK) Ltd 1989 (exec). *Professional Organisations:* Ordinary Member, Chartered Institute of Bankers.

POWELL, Geoffrey Mark; Chief Executive, Laurence Keen Limited, since 1989. *Career:* L Powell Dawes & Co 1968-72; Powell Popham Dawes & Co, Partner 1972-77; Laing & Cruickshank, Director 1977-87; CL Alexanders Laing & Cruickshank Holdings Ltd, Director 1986-89; Chief Executive 1987-89. *Biog: b.* 14 January 1946. *Nationality:* British. *m.* 1971, Veronica Joan (née Rowland); 2 d. *Educ:* Tonbridge School; St Chad's College, University of Durham (BA). *Director-*

ships: Cavendish Wates Assured plc 1989 (non-exec). *Other Activities:* Member of Court of Assistants, Worshipful Company of Haberdashers. *Professional Organisations:* Member of International Stock Exchange; FRSA. *Clubs:* MCC, City of London.

POWELL, I N F; Deputy General Manager Administration, The Bank of East Asia Ltd.

POWELL, J; General Manager, Prudential Corporation.

POWELL, Paul Douglas; Senior Shipping Partner, Moore Stephens, Chartered Accountants, since 1983; Shipping Industry. *Career:* Frank J Smith & Co, Qualification 1957-64; Wine Importer & Wholesaler, Financial Accountant 1964-66; Industrial Manufacturers, Financial Accountant 1966-68; Moore Stephens 1968-; Partner 1974-. *Biog: b.* 6 May 1939. *Nationality:* British. 2 s. *Educ:* St Benedict's School, Ealing. *Other Activities:* Member, Society for Nautical Research. *Professional Organisations:* Fellow, Institute of Chartered Accountants in England and Wales; Associate, Institute of Taxation; Member, Baltic Exchange; Member, British Academy of Experts; Rep Member, International Maritime Industries Forum. *Recreations:* Maritime History, Humour.

POWELL, Richard Andrew; Partner, D J Freeman & Company, since 1983; Company/Commercial Law and Corporate Finance. *Career:* Anstey & Thompson, Articled Clerk 1970-75; Allen & Overy, Asst 1975-81; D J Freeman & Company, Asst 1981-83. *Biog: b.* 6 November 1948. *m.* 1975, Sarah (née John); 1 s; 1 d. *Educ:* Blundell's School; Birmingham University. *Other Activities:* City of London Solicitors' Company. *Professional Organisations:* The Law Society; IBA. *Recreations:* Motor Sport, Industrial Archaeology.

POWELL, Ms S R; Director, The Barnes Partnership.

POWELL, Tim; Board Director, Ogilvy Adams & Rinehart.

POWELL-SMITH, Christopher Brian; Partner, McKenna & Co, since 1964; Corporate Finance. *Career:* Henry B Sissmore & Co, Articles 1954-59; McKenna & Co, Asst Solicitor 1959; Fourth Regiment Royal Horse Artillery 1959-61; McKenna & Co, Asst Solicitor 1961-64; Ptnr 1964; Managing Ptnr 1982-86; Head of Corporate Department 1986-. *Biog: b.* 3 October 1936. *Nationality:* British. *m.* 1964, Jennifer (née Goslett); 2 s; 2 d. *Educ:* City of London School. *Other Activities:* Asst to the Court, The Honourable Artillery Company; Member, The London Concert Choir. *Professional Organisations:* The Law Society; Member, IBA. *Clubs:* City of London, Royal Mid-Surrey Golf Club, Thurleston Golf Club. *Recreations:* Golf, Music.

POWER, Christopher; Chairman, Spencer Stuart & Associates Ltd, since 1981. *Biog: b.* 5 May 1934.

POWER, Gordon; Managing Director, Guinness Mahon Development Capital Ltd, since 1988; Unquoted Investment. *Career:* H Graham King & Co, Audit Manager 1969-73; Thomas Borthwick & Sons (UK), International Audit Manager 1973-76; Spillers Ltd, Divisional Controller 1976-77; Guinness Peat Group plc (then Guinness Mahon Holdings plc), Group Financial Controller, Strategic Planning Acquisitions & Disposals 1977-88. *Biog: b.* 24 June 1953. *Nationality:* British. *m.* 1977, Brigid (née Collins); 1 s; 1 d. *Educ:* Romford Technical High School. *Directorships:* Guinness Mahon Development Capital Ltd 1988 (exec); Britt Allcroft Group Ltd 1989 (non-exec); Prospect Group Ltd 1990 (non-exec); Radiant Systems Technology Ltd 1990 (non-exec); Comtrad International Ltd 1987 (non-exec); Guinness Mahon Group Services Ltd 1988 (exec); Guinness Mahon Insurance Services Ltd 1988 (non-exec); Mobilia Ltd 1989 (non-exec). *Professional Organisations:* ACEA; MBIM. *Recreations:* Squash, Tennis, Golf.

POWER, M R P; Partner, Cazenove & Co.

POWLETT-SMITH, W; Partner, Ernst & Young.

POYNTER, John; Director, Schroder Securities Limited.

PRATI, M; Director, IMI Capital Markets (UK).

PRATT, Anthony Stewart; Head of Corporate Affairs, Allied-Lyons plc, since 1987; Media & Investor Relations, Public & Communisty Affairs.. *Biog: b.* 30 March 1945. *Nationality:* British. *m.* 1980, Sue.

PRATT, Wing Commander B C; Clerk, Painter-Stainers' Company.

PRATT, J R; Director, Touche Remnant Investment Management Ltd.

PRATT, P C; Director, Argosy Asset Management plc.

PRECIOUS, J R; Group Finance Director, Wellcome plc.

PREECE, Andrew Douglas; Partner, Herbert Smith, since 1977; Head of International Finance and Banking Section; Project & Aircraft Financing, Commercial Energy. *Career:* Hall Collins Solicitors, Articled Clerk/Assistant Solicitor 1968-71; Herbert Smith, Assistant Solicitor 1971-74; Associate Partner 1974-77. *Biog: b.* 28 September 1944. *Nationality:* British. *m.* 1968, Caroline Jane (née Bland); 1 s; 2 d. *Educ:* King Edward VI Grammar School, Stafford; Selwyn College, Cambridge (MA). *Other Activities:* The City of London Solicitors Company. *Professional Organisations:* Law Society; Inter-

national Bar Association; UK Oil Lawyers Group. *Clubs:* Royal Air Force Yacht Club, Moor Park Golf Club, The RNVR Yacht Club. *Recreations:* Sailing, Golf.

PRENTICE, Graham Noel; Partner, Freshfields, since 1986. *Career:* Wragge & Co (Birmingham) Articled Clerk 1978-80; Solicitor 1980-81; Freshfields Solicitor 1981-86. *Biog: b.* 7 March 1955. *Nationality:* British. *m.* 1975, Beverley Annette (née Meffen); 2 d. *Educ:* Peter Symonds, Winchester; Churchill College, Cambridge (BA Hons 1st). *Publications:* Irregular Resolution of Unincorporated Association May Not Be A Nullity; Protected Shorthold Tenancies - Traps for the Unwary; The Enforcement of Outsider Rights; Remedies of Building Sub-Contractors Against Employers. *Recreations:* Photography, Reading, Computing.

PRENTICE, J O; Chairman, A P Leslie Underwriting Agencies Limited & Wellington Underwriting Agencies Limited.

PRENTICE, Thomas; MC; Life President, Harrisons & Crosfield plc, since 1988. *Career:* Harrisons & Crosfield plc 1949-; Director 1969-; Chairman 1979-. *Biog: b.* 14 October 1919. *Nationality:* British. *m.* 1948, Peggy Ann (née Lloyd); 2 s; 2 d. *Clubs:* East India Club.

PRENTIS, Henry Barrell; Deputy Chairman, Leslie & Godwin Ltd, since 1983; Corporate Finance. *Career:* Ernst & Whinney, Audit Mgr 1968-71; Leslie & Godwin Ltd 1971-. *Biog: b.* 16 October 1944. *Nationality:* British. *m.* 1967, Lilia (née Nelson); 1 s; 1 d. *Educ:* St Olaves & St Saviour's Grammar School. *Directorships:* Leslie & Godwin Ltd and all subsidiary companies; Frank B Hall (UK) Ltd; Frank B Hall (Holdings) plc; Macey Williams Ltd; IEPA Bruno Sforni Spa (Italy); Reins India Ltd (India); MacDonagh & Boland Group Ltd; Godwins Ltd. *Other Activities:* Worshipful Company of Insurers; The City Livery Club. *Professional Organisations:* FCA. *Clubs:* City Livery, RAC. *Recreations:* Numismatist, Bibliophile, Fishing.

PRESCOTT, Jeremy Malcolm; Director, Samuel Montagu & Co Ltd, since 1987; Corporate Finance. *Career:* Peat Marwick Mitchell & Co, Assistant Manager 1970-76; Samuel Montagu 1977; 3i Controller 1979-82; Samuel Montagu 1982-. *Biog: b.* 26 March 1949. *Nationality:* British. *m.* 1982, Jackie (née Kirk); 1 s; 1 d. *Educ:* Ampleforth College; Fitzwilliam College, Cambridge (MA). *Professional Organisations:* FCA.

PRESLAND, Frank; Partner (Litigation), Frere Cholmeley.

PRESLAND, Peter Eric; Group Managing Director, CE Heath plc, since 1989; All duties relating to Managing Director of an International Insurance Broker with an overall responsibility forUnderwriting, Computer Services, Corporate Development and Litigation issues. *Career:* Arthur Andersen Audit Asst, Audit Snr 1974-76; BBDO Holdings Ltd, Group Finance Controller 1976-78; Arthur Andersen, Audit Snr, Audi 1978-80; CE Heath plc, Group Finance Controller 1980-81; Group Treasurer 1981-85; Group Finance Director 1985-89; Group Managing Director 1989. *Biog:* b. 5 April 1950. *Nationality:* British. *m.* 1973; 2 d. *Educ:* Sir Joseph Williamson's Mathem; King's College, London (LLB). *Directorships:* C E Heath (Agencies) Limited 1985; C E Heath (Broking Services) Limited 1989; Clausegate Limited 1981; Datasure Holdings Limited 1985; Erycinus Limited 1985; Financial Insurance & Reinsurance Management Limited 1986 Chm; C E Heath (Finance) Limited 1981 Chm; Heath Enterprises Limited 1990; Heath Financial Services Limited 1981 Chm; Heath Commodities & Securities Limited 1983 Chm; C E Heath Public Limited Company 1989 Group MD; C E Heath (Insurance Broking) Limited 1986; Indemnity International Limited 1990; Heath Nominees Limited 1984 Chm; C E Heath Overseas Broking 1987; Peterborough Software Limited 1986; Pinnacle Representatives Limited 1989 Chm; Repglow Limited 1981; Risk Management Holdings 1988 Chm; Rookhill Limited 1981; Heath Shipping Services Limited 1981 Chm; Streets Communications Limited 1990 (non-exec) Chm; C E Heath Underwriting (Holdings) 1982; Heath Fielding Australia Pty Limited 1988 Chm; C E Heath Underwriting and Insurance (Australia) Pty Limited 1988; C E Heath International Holdings Limited 1988; Prospect Insurance Limited 1988; Pinnacle Reinsurance Company Limited 1985; Lloyd's New York Insurance Group Inc 1989; HHL (Holdings) Limited 1988; C E Heath Management (Hong Kong) Limited 1987; Summit-Pasanisi-C E Heath 1981; C E Heath Holdings (Canada) Inc 1988; Valli Heath Fielding Spa 1990; C E Heath (Broking Services) Limited 1986; Chetlodge Limited 1984-89; Easthaven 1982; C E Heath (Financial Advisory Services) Limited 1981-86; The Heath Group Limited 1985; John Sherfield Art Department Limited 1978-82; John Sherfield Studio Limited 1979-81; John Wootton & Partners Limited 1977-83; Knoxville Investments Limited 1982; Motolease Finance Limited 1982; Motolease Limited 1982; Reliance Investments Limited 1982. *Professional Organisations:* Institute of Directors; Member, Lloyd's of London. *Clubs:* City of London, St James's. *Recreations:* Cricket, Horse Riding, Bowls.

PRESTON, Colin T; Director, Bradstock Financial Services Ltd.

PRESTON, Jeffrey William; CB; Deputy Director General, Office of Fair Trading, since 1990. *Career:* Ministry of Aviation, Assistant Principal 1963-66; Board of Trade, Private Secretary to Permanent Secretary 1966-67; Principal 1967-70; HM Treasury, Principal 1970-73; Dept of Trade and Industry, Principal 1973-75; Assistant Secretary 1975-1982; Under Secretary, Regional Director, Yorkshire and Humberside 1982-85;

(Welsh Office), Deputy Secretary, Economic and Industrial Affairs 1985-90. *Biog:* b. 28 January 1940. *Nationality:* British. *Educ:* Liverpool Collegiate School; Hertford College, Oxford (MA). *Other Activities:* Chairman, The Hertford Society. *Clubs:* United Oxford and Cambridge University. *Recreations:* Opera, Swimming, Motoring.

PRESTON, Michael; Executive Director, Broad Street Group plc.

PRESTON, N G; Partner, R Watson & Sons, since 1985; Pensions Advice. *Career:* Cubie Wood & Co Ltd, Principal Actuary 1976-84. *Biog:* b. 8 April 1946. *Nationality:* British. *m.* 1968, Helen (née Walmsley); 2 s. *Educ:* Sevenoaks School; Reading University (BSc Hons Mathematics). *Professional Organisations:* Fellow, Institute of Actuaries; Associate, Pensions Management Institute.

PRESTON, Robin M; Partner, Theodore Goddard.

PRESTON, Thomas Davis; Director, Harrisons & Crosfield plc, since 1981; Group Activities in the Pacific Region. *Career:* Colonial Service, Kenya, District Officer and District Commissioner 1954-63; Phillips, Harrisons & Crosfield Ltd, Kenya, Various to Chairman and Managing Director 1963-81; Sabah Timber Co Ltd, Director 1979; British Chrome & Chemicals Ltd, Director 1979; Durham Chemicals Ltd (subsidiaries of Harrisons & Crosfield plc, London), Director 1979; Harrisons & Crosfield plc, London, Regional Director 1980; Director Responsible for the Pacific 1981-; Harrisons & Crosfield (Australia) Ltd, Chairman and Chief Executive 1983-. *Biog:* b. 1 December 1932. *Nationality:* British. *m.* 1963, Jennifer Katharine (née Anderson); 2 d. *Educ:* Gillingham. *Directorships:* Harrisons & Crosfield (Aust) Ltd 1982 (exec) Chairman; Harcros Chemicals Pty Ltd, Australia 1982 (non-exec) Chairman; Harrisons & Crosfield (NZ) Ltd 1982 (non-exec) Chairman; Harrisons & Crosfield (PNG) Ltd 1982 (non-exec) Chairman; New Britain Palm Oil Development Ltd 1982 (non-exec) Chairman; Linatex Australia Pty Limited 1982 (non-exec) Chairman; Harcros Timber Australia Pty Ltd 1983 (non-exec) Chairman; Kapiura Plantations Pty Ltd 1985 (non-exec) Chairman; Harcros Chemicals (NZ) Ltd 1987 (non-exec) Chairman; Quaker Chemical (Australasia) Pty Limited 1989 (non-exec). *Other Activities:* Vice-President, Australia, Papua New Guinea Business Council. *Clubs:* Carlton (London), Elanora (Sydney), Karen (Nairobi), Wildernesse (Sevenoaks). *Recreations:* Golf, Opera.

PRESTRIDGE, Jeff; Personal Finance Editor, The Sunday Times, since 1990. *Career:* Money Management, Dep Editor. *Other Activities:* Unit Trust Association Journalist of the Year Award, 1989; BIIBA Journalist Award for 1989 Specialist Publications, 1990.

PREVETT, G J; Partner, Jaques & Lewis.

PREVETT, John Henry; Partner, Bacon & Woodrow, since 1962; Actuarial Advice on Pensions, Assessment of Damages, Interests in Settle. *Career:* North British & Mercantile Insurance Co Ltd, Actuarial Trainee 1950-55; Actuary (Life & Pensions) 1955-58. *Biog: b.* 6 April 1933. *Nationality:* British. *m.* 1959, Joy Maureen (née Goodchild); 2 s. *Educ:* Oxted County Grammar School; John Ruskin Grammar School. *Other Activities:* Member, Worshipful Company of Actuaries; Lab Member, Reigate & Banstead Borough Council; Chm, British Defence and Aid Fund for Southern Africa. *Professional Organisations:* FIA; FSS; FPMI; Member, Association of Consulting Actuaries (Chm 1983-85). *Publications:* Various Articles and Papers, particularly on Actuarial Assessment of Damages. *Clubs:* Lunchtime Comment. *Recreations:* Politics, Wining & Dining.

PRICE, Anthony John; General Manager, Berliner Bank, since 1980. *Career:* Bankers Trust Co FX Dealer 1955-65; Irving Trust Co Treasury Mgr 1965-70; Banca Commerciale Italiana Treasury Mgr 1970-75; Deutsche Bank Asst Gen Mgr 1975-80. *Biog: b.* 11 July 1935. *m.* 1959, Jeanette Frances (née O'Brien); 1 s; 1 d. *Educ:* Cranbrook College. *Recreations:* Golf, Bridge.

PRICE, Charles; Director, N M Rothschild & Sons Limited, since 1985; Banking Division. *Career:* National Westminster Bank 1967-70; County Bank 1970-71; N M Rothschild & Sons Limited 1972-76; N M Rothschild & Sons (Singapore) Limited, Managing Director 1976-79; N M Rothschild & Sons Limited, Assistant Director 1979-84; Director 1985-90. *Biog: b.* 7 November 1945. *Nationality:* British. *m.* 1971, Patricia Ann; 1 s; 1 d. *Educ:* King's College, Taunton; Queen Mary College, London (BA Hons History). *Professional Organisations:* Associate, Institute of Bankers. *Clubs:* Lombard Association. *Recreations:* Rugby.

PRICE, D; Executive Director, James R Knowles Limited.

PRICE, David William James; Joint Chairman, Mercury Asset Management plc, since 1985; Chief Executive. *Career:* S G Warburg & Co Ltd, Dir 1982-85. *Biog: b.* 11 June 1947. *Nationality:* British. *m.* 1971, Shervie Ann Lander (née Whitaker); 1 s; 1 d. *Educ:* Ampleforth College; Corpus Christi College, Oxford (MA). *Directorships:* Mercury Asset Mgmnt Group plc 1987 Dep Chm; Great Lakes Reinsurance (UK) 1989; Munich London Investment Management 1988 Jt Chm; Potter Warburg Asset Management 1986. *Clubs:* Brooks's.

PRICE, J R S; Partner, Field Fisher Waterhouse.

PRICE, John Aidan Joseph; Director, Kleinwort Benson Securities Ltd, since 1989; Head of Traded Option Sales. *Career:* Chase Manhattan Securities (Head of Options) 1988-89; County Securities Incorporating Fielding Newson-Smith 1985-88; Ranks Hovis McDougal plc, Various including Regional Manager 1977-84; Welsh Guards, Commissioned in 1973 (1973-77). *Biog: b.* 2 February 1953. *Nationality:* British. *m.* 1989, Deborah (née Thwaites Lastra). *Educ:* Glenalmond; Sandhurst. *Other Activities:* Merchant Taylor's Company. *Clubs:* Cavalry and Guards. *Recreations:* Shooting, Foxhunting, Sailing, Skiing.

PRICE, John J; Non-Executive Director, Quayle Munro Limited.

PRICE, Lionel D D; Head of Economics Division, Bank of England, since 1990; Europe. *Career:* Bank of England Various 1967-79; International Monetary Fund (Washington DC) Alternate Exec Dir for UK 1979-81; Bank of England Head of Information Div 1981-83; Head of International Div 1985-90. *Biog: b.* 2 February 1946. *Nationality:* British. *m.* 1968, Sara (née Holt); 2 s. *Educ:* Bolton School; Corpus Christi College, Cambridge (MA). *Clubs:* Overseas Bankers'. *Recreations:* Theatre, Family, Golf.

PRICE, R L; Managing Director, Group Operations, Midland Bank plc.

PRICE, Richard; Deputy Director-General, Confederation of British Industry, since 1990. *Career:* Queen's College Taunton, Head of Economics 1968-70; CBI, Junior Economist 1970-73; CBI, Head Economic Trends 1973-79; CBI, Deputy Director, Regions 1979-81; CBI, Director of Regions 1981-83; CBI, Director of Employment Affairs 1983-87; CBI, Executive Director, Government Relations 1987-90. *Biog: b.* 13 July 1944. *Nationality:* British. *m.* 1969, Sally Josephine (née McCowen); 3 s. *Educ:* Monmouth School; University College, London (BSc); Cambridge University (Cert Ed). *Directorships:* ACAS 1984 Council Member. *Other Activities:* UNICE (Union of EEC Industrial Federations); Chairman, Economic Trends Committee, 1976-80. *Professional Organisations:* Society of Business Economists. *Publications:* Various articles on aspects of Economic Forecasting. *Clubs:* United Oxford & Cambridge University. *Recreations:* Cricket, Golf, Skiing, Bridge, Gardening, Sleeping.

PRICE, Richard Charles; Partner, Taylor Joynson Garrett, since 1990; Intellectual Property/Head of Intellectual Property Dept. *Career:* Joynson-Hicks & Co, Articled Clerk 1968-70; Assistant Solicitor 1970-73; Partner 1973-75; Courts & Co, Partner 1975-77; Woodham Smith, Partner 1977-90. *Biog: b.* 7 January 1946. *Nationality:* British. *m.* 1982, Helen (née Fisher); 3 s. *Educ:* Kingston Grammar School; Bristol University (LLB); College of Law, Guildford. *Other Activities:* Secretary, Patent Solicitors Association; Member, Community Trade Mark Office, Executive Committee. *Professional Organisations:* Law Society; Solicitors' European

Group. *Clubs:* Royal Automobile Club, Riverside Racquets Club. *Recreations:* Natural History, Tennis, Sailing.

PRICE, Richard Stephen; Partner, McKenna & Co, since 1985; Mergers & Acquisitions. *Career:* McKenna & Co, Articled Clerk 1976-77; Assistant Solicitor, Bahrain Office 1977-79; Assistant Solicitor, London Office 1979-84; Overseas Manager, Bahrain 1984-85; Senior Resident Partner Bahrain 1985-88; Partner, London 1988-. *Biog: b.* 27 May 1953. *Nationality:* British. *m.* 1980, Nicola Mary (née Griffin); 1 s; 1 d. *Educ:* Cowbridge Grammar School; Leeds University (LLB). *Other Activities:* Member, Freedom of the City of London Solicitors Company. *Professional Organisations:* Member, The Law Society; City of London Solicitors Company. *Recreations:* Golf.

PRICE, Stephen David; Partner, Ernst & Young, since 1985; Financial Services & Eastern Europe. *Biog: b.* 30 May 1952. *Nationality:* British. *m.* 1985, Margaret Elizabeth (née Mills). *Educ:* Stationers Company School; Leeds University (BSc). *Professional Organisations:* FCA.

PRICE, W; Chief Manager, Northern Bank Ltd, since 1990; Financial Services. *Career:* Northern Bank Limited, Assistant General Manager, Corporate Finance Department 1981-84; Assistant General Manager, Business Development & Marketing 1984-87; Director, Financial Services 1987-90. *Biog: b.* 2 April 1933. *Nationality:* British. *m.* 1960, Elsie (née McKinty); 1 s; 2 d. *Directorships:* Northern Bank Insurance Services Limited 1987 (exec); Northern Bank Executor & Trustee Co Limited 1988 (non-exec). *Other Activities:* Northern Ireland Chamber of Commerce & Industry. *Professional Organisations:* Diploma in Executor & Trustee Work; Diploma of the Institute of Bankers in Ireland. *Clubs:* Royal Portrush Golf Club, Knock Golf Club.

PRICHARD, David; Director, Merrill Lynch International Limited.

PRICHARD, R D C; Director, Kleinwort Benson Investment Management.

PRIDAY, Blair Josephine; Executive Director, Merrill Lynch Europe Ltd, since 1985; Capital Markets. *Career:* James Capel & Co, Exec, Private Clients 1977-79; Credit Suisse First Boston Ltd, Mgr, Money Markets 1979-84; Merrill Lynch, Exec Dir 1984-87. *Biog: b.* 13 March 1954. *m.* 1988, Mark Winstanley; 1 s. *Educ:* Oxford High School; York University (BA Hons). *Clubs:* Hurlingham, Aldeburgh Golf Club. *Recreations:* Tennis, Golf, Squash, Bridge, Music.

PRIDEAUX, Sir John; Director, Arbuthnot Latham Bank Limited.

PRIESTLEY, Richard James; Director, BZW Equities Ltd.

PRINCE, J A P; Director, Morgan Grenfell & Co Limited.

PRINDL, Dr Andreas Robert; Chairman, Nomura Bank International plc, since 1990. *Career:* Morgan Guaranty Trust Co (NY), Mgmnt Trainee 1964-65; (Europe), Asst Treasurer (1966) 1965-67; (Frankfurt), Ass Vice Pres 1967-70; (London), Vice Pres (1972) 1970-76; (Tokyo), Gen Mgr 1976-80; Saudi International Bank, Exec Dir 1980-82; Morgan Guaranty 1982-84; Nomura International plc, MD 1984-86; Nomura Bank International plc, MD 1986-90. *Biog: b.* 25 November 1939. *Nationality:* American. *m.* 1963, Veronica Maria (née Koerber); 1 s; 1 d. *Educ:* Princeton University (BA); Bonn University; Kentucky University (MA,PhD); LSE. *Directorships:* Nomura Intl plc 1984 (non-exec); Nomura Bank Nederland NV, Amsterdam 1984 (non-exec); Nomura Bank Belgium SA, Brussels 1986 (non-exec); Nomura Bank (Luxembourg) SA, Luxembourg 1990 (non-exec). *Other Activities:* Central Council, CIOB; Steering Ctee, LSE Financial Markets Group; Editorial Board of Banking World; CBI City Advisory Group; Fellow, Assoc of Corporate Treasurers, Editorial Ctee; Advisory Panel, City University Business School; Board of Advisers, Patterson School of Diplomacy, University of Kentucky; CBI Task Force on Wider Share Ownership; Chairman, East Europe Ctee, Chartered Institute of Bankers. *Professional Organisations:* FCT; FCIB. *Publications:* Intl Money Management, 1972; Foreign Exchange Risk, 1976; Japanese Finance, 1981; Money in the Far East, 1986. *Clubs:* Reform. *Recreations:* Classical Music, Running.

PRINGLE, R D T; Director (UK Capitals), Hoare Govett Investment Research Limited.

PRIOR, James Michael Leathes; The Rt Hon Lord Prior; PC; Chairman, The General Electric Company plc. *Directorships:* United Biscuits (Holdings) plc.

PRIOR, The Lady Jane Primrose Gifford (née Lywood); Non-Executive Director, TSB Group plc, Tate & Lyle plc & Headbourne Worthy Medical plc, since 1985, 1984 & 1988 respectively. *Career:* Aston Boats Ltd Chm 1970-76; National Association of Youth Clubs Chm 1981-83. *Biog: b.* 5 October 1930. *Nationality:* British. *m.* 1954, James; 3 s; 1 d. *Educ:* St Agnes' School, Virginia, USA; St Felix School, Southwold. *Other Activities:* Chairman & Governor, St Felix School, Southwold, Suffolk; Governor, Atlantic College, Governor, Bradfield College; Trustee, CAF. *Recreations:* Farming, Politics, Gardening.

PRIOR, Tom; Director, Svenska Handelsbanken, since 1989; Treasury. *Career:* Saudi International 1978-88. *Biog: b.* 31 March 1949. *Nationality:* British. *m.* 1983, Gillian. *Educ:* Greshams School, Holt, Norfolk. *Clubs:* MCC, RORC.

PRIOR-PALMER, Simon Erroll; Executive Director, Credit Suisse First Boston Ltd, since 1986; UK Corporate Finance. *Biog: b.* 5 February 1951. *m.* 1984, Julia (née Lloyd George); 1 s. *Educ:* Christ Church, Oxford (MA Hons).

PRITCHARD, David Peter; Senior Vice President, The Royal Bank of Canada, since 1989; General Manager, Europe. *Career:* Hawker Siddeley Aviation, Contracts Mgr 1966-71; Wm Bradt's Sons & Co, Aircraft Finance Mgr 1971-72; Edward Bates & Sons, Leasing Dir 1972-78; Citicorp Investment Bank, MD 1978-86. *Biog: b.* 20 July 1944. *Nationality:* British. *m.* 1969, Angela C (née Pearce); 1 s; 1 d. *Educ:* Read Grammar School; Southampton University (BSc Eng). *Directorships:* Royal Bank of Canada (Europe) Ltd 1986 (exec) Vice Chm; RBC Dominion Securities International 1988 (non-exec). *Other Activities:* FRSA. *Recreations:* Bicycle Racing, Nordic Skiing, Photography.

PRITCHARD, Kathleen (née Pearce); Director, Queen Anne's Gate Asset Management Ltd, since 1989. *Career:* National Provident Inst Investment Analyst 1969-83; Water Authorities Supperannuation Fund, Investment Manager 1983-1989. *Biog: b.* 28 October 1950. *Nationality:* British. *m.* 1974, Raymond Henry Pritchard. *Educ:* Nonsuch High School for Girls. *Directorships:* Queen Anne's Gate Asset Management Ltd 1989 (exec). *Professional Organisations:* ACIS, Member of Society of Technical Analysts.

PRITCHARD, Michael John Oulton; Director, Bank of Tokyo International Ltd, since 1987; Finance, Compliance & Operations. *Career:* Deloitte Haskins & Sells, Articled Clerk & Audit Snr 1966-72; Kleinwort Benson Ltd, Gp Financial Accountant, Group Accounts & Tax 1972-84; Chief Accountant, Accounting 1977-84; Gota (UK) Ltd (now Gotabanken), Snr Mgr, Operations & Compliance 1984-86; Bank of Tokyo International Ltd, Dep Gen Mgr 1986-87; Company Sec 1986-; Dir 1987-; The Bank of Tokyo Ltd, Dep Gen Mgr 1990-. *Biog: b.* 13 October 1945. *Nationality:* British. *m.* 1971, Jennifer Mary (née Broadway); 2 d. *Educ:* Ipswich School. *Directorships:* Tokyo & Detroit Eurodeal (Continental) AG 1988 (exec). *Professional Organisations:* FCA. *Clubs:* Newbury Golf Club, Newbury Squash & Tennis Club. *Recreations:* Golf, Skiing, Squash, Tennis, Theatre.

PRIVETT, Robin Jarrard Campbell; Partner, Herbert Smith, since 1973. *Career:* Jacobs & Greenwood, Articles 1963-66; Norton Rose, Assistant Solicitor 1966-69; Herbert Smith 1969. *Biog: b.* 22 December 1940. *Nationality:* British. *m.* 1964, Penelope Lisbeth (née Bate); 2 s; 1 d. *Educ:* St Edward's School, Oxford; St Peter's College, Oxford (BA). *Professional Organisations:* Law Society. *Clubs:* Leander, City of London. *Recreations:* Shooting, Fishing, Theatre, Music.

PROCTER, D J; Director, S G Warburg & Co Ltd.

PROCTER, Susie E; Director, Midland Montagu Asset Management, since 1990; International Fixed Income Investment Management. *Career:* Citibank NA, Account Officer to Assistant Manager 1982-85; Citicorp Investment Bank Ltd, Eurobond Sales Manager 1985-86; LBS (Securities) Ltd 1986-88; Midland Montagu Asset Management 1988-; Director 1990-. *Biog: b.* 14 January 1961. *Nationality:* English. *Educ:* The Mount School, York; Bristol University (BSc Honours). *Directorships:* MMAM 1990.

PROCTER, Sidney; CBE; Commissioner, Buildings Societies Commission, since 1986. *Career:* Williams & Glyn's Bank Dep Dir 1970-75; Div Dir 1975-76; Asst Chief Exec 1976-78; Chief Exec 1978-82; The Royal Bank of Scotland Group Chief Exec 1982-85; Bank of England Adviser to the Governor 1985-87. *Biog: b.* 10 March 1925. *Nationality:* British. *m.* 1952, Isabel (née Simmons); 1 d. *Educ:* Ormskirk Grammar School. *Directorships:* Provincial Group plc 1985 (non-exec); Exeter Trust Ltd 1987 Chm. *Professional Organisations:* FCIB.

PROSSER, David; Group Director, Legal & General Group plc, since 1988; Investments. *Career:* Sun Alliance & London Assurance Co 1965-69; Hoare Govett & Co 1969-73; National Coal Board, Superannuation Investments Dept 1973-81; CIN Industrial Investments, Managing Director 1981-85; Chief Executive 1985-88. *Nationality:* British. *m.* 1971; 2 d. *Educ:* University College of Wales, Aberystwyth (BSc). *Directorships:* Legal & General Ventures Ltd 1988 Chm; Legal & General Group plc 1988; Legal & General Investment Management Ltd 1988 Chm; Legal & General Investment (Holdings) Ltd 1988; Legal & General Investment Trust Ltd 1988 Chm; Legal & General (Money Managers) Ltd 1988 Chm; Legal & General Assurance (Pensions Management) Ltd 1988; Legal & General Portfolio Managers Ltd 1988 Chm; Legal & General Property Fund Managers Ltd 1988 Chm; Legal & General (Unit Trust Managers) Ltd 1988; South Wales Electricity 1989 (non-exec). *Professional Organisations:* FIA.

PROSSER, Ian Maurice Gray; Chairman & Chief Executive, Bass plc.

PROSSER, Brigadier W K L; CBE, MC; Clerk, Tallow Chandlers' Company.

PROUDLOCK, Michael John Oliver; Director and Head of Development Capital, Granville & Co Ltd.

PROVAN, James L C; Executive Director, Scottish Financial Enterprise, since 1990; Heading Drive to Promote Awareness in the UK & Overseas of Scottish Expertise in Financial Management. *Career:* Farmer 1958-; Manager of Magazine Group with Outrams 1966-68; Baxters (Milnathort) Ltd (Engineering & Supply Co), Chairman 1969-74; Tayside Regional Council, Member, Chairman, Property Committee, Vice Chairman, Finance Committee 1974-82; Tay River Purification Board, Member 1978-82; The European Parliament, Conservative Member for North East Scotland Constituency 1979-89; Served on: Environment & Consumer Affairs Committee 1979-89; Agricultural & Fisheries Committee 1979-89; McIntosh Donald Ltd (Meat Producers), European Consultant, Chairman 1987-. *Biog: b.* 19 December 1936. *Nationality:* British. *m.* 1960, Roweena (née Lewis); 2 s; 1 d. *Educ:* Ardveck, Crieff; Oundle School, Northamptonshire; Royal Agricultural College, Cirencester (MRAC). *Directorships:* Scottish Financial Enterprise 1990 (exec); World Business Forum Ltd 1990 (non-exec); McIntosh Donald Ltd 1990 (non-exec); McIntosh of Dyce Ltd 1990 (non-exec). *Other Activities:* Farmer Member, Agricultural & Food Research Council. *Publications:* The European Community: An Ever Closer Union?, 1989. *Clubs:* Farmer's Club, East India, Royal Perth Golfing Society. *Recreations:* Country Pursuits, Sailing, Flying, Music, Travel.

PRYNN, Jonathan; City Reporter, The Times.

PSYLLIDES, Milton Nicholas; Partner, Evershed Wells & Hind, since 1984. *Career:* Evershed & Tomkinson, Articled Clerk 1976-78; Assistant Solicitor 1978-81; Associate 1981-84; Partner 1984-; Evershed & Tomkinson Merges with Wells & Hind to Create Evershed Wells & Hind 1989. *Biog: b.* 30 October 1953. *Nationality:* British. *m.* 1976, Lynne Josephine (née Rutherford); 1 s; 1 d. *Educ:* Brockley County Grammar School; Liverpool University (LLB Hons). *Directorships:* First Roman Property Trust plc 1988 (non-exec) Chairman; Roman Rentals 001 plc - 055 plc 1989 (non-exec) Chairman; Shire plc 1989 (non-exec); Burgmann (UK) Limited 1989 (non-exec); Drayton Hotels plc 1990 (non-exec) Chairman. *Other Activities:* Company and Commercial Law Committee, Birmingham Law Society. *Professional Organisations:* Member, The Law Society; Solicitor of The Supreme Court of Judicature. *Recreations:* Keep Fit, Family Life.

PUCHER, Andrew; Executive Vice President, Republic National Bank of New York, since 1986.

PUDDLE, David George Gordon; Executive Director, Midland Montagu Asset Management, since 1987; Investment Management - Marketing. *Career:* Brewer & Co, Articled Clerk 1972-77; Harris & Dixon Group Ltd Accountant 1977-78; Morgan Grenfell & Co Ltd, Asst Dir 1978-86; Morgan Grenfell Investment Management Ltd, Asst Dir 1986-87. *Biog: b.* 8 July 1953. *Nationality:* British. *m.* 1982, Jane (née Willock); 2 s; 1 d. *Educ:* Clifton College. *Professional Organisations:* FCA; IMRO. *Clubs:* Harlequin FC. *Recreations:* Rugby, Cricket, Squash, Gardening, Travel.

PUGET, M; Director, Barclays de Zoete Wedd Securities Ltd.

PUGH, Keith William; Partner, Nabarro Nathanson, since 1990; Employment Law/Litigation. *Career:* Articles with British Coal Corporation Western Area (Warrington) 1977-79; Assistant Solicitor 1980-83; British Coal Yorkshire Region (Doncaster), Assistant Solicitor 1983-88; British Coal HQ Legal Dept (Doncaster), Deputy Head of Employment Group 1988-90. *Biog: b.* 25 January 1955. *m.* Caroline (née Parker); 1 s; 1 d. *Educ:* Newcastle High School; Cannock Grammar School; Manchester Polytechnic (BA Hons Law); College of Law, Chester. *Professional Organisations:* Solicitor. *Recreations:* Music, Swimming, Walking, Gardening.

PUGH, R P; General Manager, Information Systems, Friends' Provident Life Office.

PULESTON JONES, Haydn; Partner, Linklaters & Paines, since 1979; International Finance and Banking. *Biog: b.* 16 September 1948. *Nationality:* British. *m.* 1973, Susan Elizabeth (née Karn); 2 s. *Educ:* Kings College, London (LLB Hons 1st AK). *Professional Organisations:* The Law Society; The City of London Law Society (Member of Banking Law Sub-Ctee). *Recreations:* Gardening, Classical Music, Genealogy.

PULLEN, Simon; Partner, Frere Cholmeley, since 1986; Company Commercial, Banking. *Biog: b.* 30 May 1954. *Nationality:* British. *m.* 1986, Gillian Mary (née Woolford); 1 s. *Educ:* Merchant Taylors School, Northwood; Magdalen College, Oxford (BA Hons).

PULLEY, J E; Director, W H Ireland Stephens & Co Ltd.

PULLMAN, Bruce John; Director, County NatWest Investment Management Ltd, since 1987; Business Development. *Career:* N M Rothschild & Sons Ltd Corporate Fin Analyst 1979-81; County Bank Fixed Income Fund Mgr 1981-82; County Investment Mgmnt Quantitative Fund Mgr 1983-86. *Biog: b.* 4 April 1957. *Nationality:* British. *m.* 1979, Joanna Alexis Hamilton (née Davies); 1 s; 2 d. *Educ:* Canford School, Wimbourne Dorset; Merton College, Oxford (BA Hons 1st) Chemistry. *Publications:* Portfolio Insurance, 1988. *Recreations:* Walking, Classical Music, Church.

PUMPHREY, Christopher Jonathan; TD; Chairman, Wise Speke Ltd, since 1987. *Career:* Wise Speke & Co, Partner 1961-87. *Educ:* Winchester; Magdalene College, Cambridge (MA). *Directorships:* Sturge Holdings plc 1987 (exec).

PURCELL, H; Non-Executive Director, Church, Charity and Local Authority Fund Managers Limited.

PURCELL, Roger; Staff Director, Securities and Investments Board.

PURCHON, Peter H; President, Chartered Insurance Institute, since 1990. *Career:* Royal Insurance Company Limited, Leeds 1949; Manchester, Inspector 1960; Matthews Wrightson Limited, Manchester 1963; London, Managing Director, Regional Organisation 1972; Stewart Wrightson UK Group Limited, Chairman 1977-86; Stewart Wrightson Mgmnt Services Limited, Chairman 1986-87; Willis Wrightson Limited, Deputy Chairman 1987-. *Biog: b.* 25 November 1932. *Nationality:* British. *m.* 1957, Sylvia (née Sadler); 1 s; 1 d. *Educ:* Dulwich College. *Directorships:* R Blackett & Son Ltd 1990 (non-exec) Chm. *Other Activities:* Worshipful Company of Insurers; British Institute of Management. *Professional Organisations:* Associate, Chartered Insurance Institute; Fellow, British Institute of Management; Fellow, Institute of Risk Management. *Clubs:* Royal Southern Yacht Club. *Recreations:* Music, The Arts, Sailing, Tennis, The Countryside.

PURDY, John Douglas; Director, Lombard North Central plc, since 1985; Financial Control. *Career:* Leslie A Ward, Articled Clerk 1953-59; Turquand Youngs & Co, Audit Manager 1959-71; National Westminster Bank, Controller, Group Accounts 1971-80; Lombard North Central, Mgr, Fin Control 1980-82; Dep Dir 1982-85; Dir 1985-. *Biog: b.* 22 June 1937. *Nationality:* British. *m.* 1963, Maureen (née Adkins); 2 d. *Educ:* Harrow Weald County Grammar. *Directorships:* Lombard North Central plc 1985 (exec); Farming & Agricultural Finance 1986 (non-exec); Harvey Plant Ltd 1985 (non-exec); Lex Vehicle Leasing Ltd 1982 (non-exec); Lombard Business Equipment Leasing 1986 (non-exec) Chm; Transfleet Services Ltd 1987 (non-exec). *Other Activities:* Finance Houses Association, Monetary & Economic Ctee. *Professional Organisations:* FCA. *Clubs:* Rotary. *Recreations:* Church & Parish Affairs, Rotary, Gardening.

PURSER, Christopher Robert; Group Treasurer, Glynwed International plc, since 1980; Treasury Management, Investor Relations. *Career:* Procter & Gamble Ltd, Industrial Engineering Production Management 1962-64; Mars Ltd, Sales Planner 1965-67; Allied Ironfounders Ltd, Sales Management 1968-69; Glynwed International plc, Marketing Services, Admin & Sec; AccountingTreasury, Investor Relations 1969-. *Biog: b.* 9 August 1939. *Nationality:* British. *m.* 1977, Barbara Ann (née MacDonald). *Educ:* Tiffin School; King's College, London (BA Hons); Warwick University (MBA). *Other Activities:* Deputy Chairman of Membership Ctee, ACT. *Professional Organisations:* FCIS; FCMA; MCIM; FCT. *Recreations:* Music, Opera, Canals, Travel.

PURSER, George Robert Gavin; Senior Partner, Lawrence Graham Solicitors, since 1987. *Biog: b.* 31 May 1936. *Nationality:* British. *m.* 1966, Mary Ruth (née Lowe); 2 d. *Clubs:* Athenaeum. *Recreations:* Gardening, Shooting, Tennis.

PURUSHOTHAMAN, A V; Company Secretary, The New India Assurance Company Limited.

PURVIS, Christopher Thomas Bremner; Director & Branch Manager, Tokyo Branch, S G Warburg Securities, since 1986; Japanese Equity Brokerage. *Career:* S G Warburg & Co Ltd Various 1974-83; Exec Dir 1983-86; Based in Japan 1982-87 & 1989-. *Biog: b.* 15 April 1951. *Nationality:* British. *m.* 1986, Phillida (née Seaward); 2 d. *Educ:* Bradfield College; Keble College, Oxford (MA).

PUSEY, K D; Director, United Dominions Trust Limited.

PUSINELLI, David Charles; Corporate Finance Director, Close Brothers Ltd; Corporate Finance, Compliance. *Career:* Coopers & Lybrand (London), Articles 1977-81; (South Africa), Gp Snr Mgr 1981-84; (London), Snr Mgr, Corp Finance 1984-86. *Biog: b.* 4 September 1956. *Nationality:* British. *Educ:* Bradfield College; Brasenose College, Oxford (MA). *Professional Organisations:* ACA. *Recreations:* Squash, Wine, Wild Life Photography, Skiing.

PUTNAM, Dr B H; Chief Economist and Director, Kleinwort Benson Limited, since 1989; Head of Economic Research. *Career:* Federal Reserve Bank of New York, Economist 1976-77; Chase Manhattan Bank New York, Vice President 1978-82; Stern Stewart & Co New York, Partner & Chief Economist 1982-84; Morgan Stanley & Co New York, Principal and Senior Economist 1984-88. *Biog: b.* 29 December 1950. *Nationality:* American. *Educ:* Eckerd College, St Petersburg Florida (BA); Tulane University, New Orleans (PhD). *Directorships:* Eckerd College, St Petersburg Florida 1988 (non-exec). *Publications:* The Blackwell Guide to Wall Street, 1986; The Monetary Approach to International Adjustment, 1978.

PUTNAM, Stephen Philip; Director, CIN Management Ltd; Marketable Securities Division. *Biog: m.* Janet Ann (née Jeffery); 2 d.

PUTTERGILL, Graham Fraser; Chairman, Gibbs Hartley Cooper Ltd, since 1985. *Career:* Antony Gibbs Pension Services Ltd 1972-77; MD 1977-82; Chm 1982-84. *Biog: b.* 20 February 1949. *Nationality:* South African. *m.* 1976, Susan (née Wilkinson); 2 s; 2 d. *Educ:* St Patrick's School, Port Elizabeth. *Directorships:* Antony Gibbs Pension Services Ltd 1976 (non-exec); Wardley Investment Services International Ltd 1982 (non-exec); HSBC Holdings (UK) Ltd 1986 (exec). *Professional Organisations:* FPMI, ACII.

PUYOL TOLEDO, Juan Jose; General Manager, Banco Exterior UK, since 1986; Overall Responsibility for the Management of the Bank. *Career:* Misr Exterior Bank (Banco Exterior - Egypt) in Cairo, Managing

Director & General Manager 1982-86; Banco Exterior de España in Moscow, Manager, Representative Office 1979-82; Banco Atlantico (Cadiz, Spain), Regional Manager 1977-79; Banco Atlantico, Sta Cruz de Tenerife, Canary Islands, Spain, Manager 1975-77; Banco Atlantico, Marbella, Spain 1973-75; Urgal, Paris, Manager 1970-73; Fabrica Conservera Catic, Casablanca, Manager 1968-70. *Biog: b.* 9 November 1943. *Nationality:* Spanish. *m.* 1975, Maria Isabel; 1 s; 1 d. *Educ:* French Lycée; Moscow University (Dr of Engineering and Master of Agricultural Sciences Hons). *Directorships:* Banco Exterior-UK 1986 (exec); Banco Exterior-France 1989 (non-exec); Banco Exterior-Belgium 1989 (non-exec); Banco Exterior-Deutschland 1989 (non-exec).

PYBUS, William Michael; Chairman, A A H Holdings plc, since 1986. *Career:* King's Dragoon Guards, Final Rank of Major 1944-46; Stephenson Harwood & Tatham, Articled Clerk 1948-50; Herbert Oppenheim, Nathan & Vandyk 1951-88; Partner 1953; Board of Amalgamated Anthracite Holdings Ltd (now AAH Holdings plc) 1967-; Chairman of Board 1968-; British Fuel Company, Chairman 1968-87; Siebe plc 1972-; Chairman of Board 1980-; Inter-Continental Fuels Ltd, Chairman 1975-88; Coal Industry Society, President 1976-81; Vice-President 1981; British Rail (Midlands & North-Western), Board 1977-89; Cornhill Insurance plc, Director 1977-; National Westminster Bank plc, Director (Outer London Regional Board) 1977-88; Homeowners Friendly Society, Director 1980-; R Mansell Limited, Deputy Chairman 1980-85; Leigh Interests plc, Chairman 1982-89; Bradford & Bingley Building Society 1982-; Director, South East Regional Board 1982-83; Director, Main Board 1983-; Denton, Hall, Burgin & Warrens, Consultant 1988-. *Biog: b.* 7 May 1923. *Nationality:* British. *m.* 1959, Elizabeth Janet (née Whitley); 2 s; 2 d. *Educ:* Bedford School; New College, Oxford (First Class Honours, Judisprudence). *Directorships:* Herbert Oppenheim, Nathan & Vandyk 1951-88; A A H Holdings plc 1967- (exec) Chairman; Siebe plc 1972- (exec) Chairman; Cornhill Insurance plc 1977- (exec); Homeowners Friendly Society 1980- (exec); Bradford & Bingley Building Society 1983- (exec). *Other Activities:* Master, The Worshipful Company of Pattenmarkers, 1972-73; Member of Court, The Worshipful Company of Fuellers, 1989-. *Professional Organisations:* CBIM; FRSA; Fellow, Chartered Institute of Marketing (FCIM). *Clubs:* Cavalry & Guards, MCC, Yorkshire CC. *Recreations:* Fishing.

PYM, Francis Jonathan; Partner, Travers Smith Braithwaite, since 1984; Company Department. *Biog: b.* 21 September 1952. *Nationality:* British. *m.* 1981, Laura Elizabeth Camille (née Wellesley); 2 s; 1 d. *Educ:* Eton College; Magdelene College, Cambridge (BA Hons History). *Professional Organisations:* Law Society, City of London Law Society. *Clubs:* Garrick. *Recreations:* Reading.

PYM, Hugh; Business Correspondent, ITN.

PYNE, T A; Finance Director, London and Manchester Group. *Biog: b.* 24 January 1947. *Nationality:* British. *Directorships:* London and Manchester Group plc since 1986; George Irlam and Dugdale Limited since 1988; London and Manchester (Agency Services) Limited 1987; London and Manchester (Commercial Agencies) Limited 1988; London and Manchester (Commercial Mortgages) (No 2) Limited 1989; London and Manchester (Managed Funds)Limited 1983; London and Manchester (Mortgages) (No 1) Limited 1986; London and Manchester (Mortgages) (No 2) Limited 1988; London and Manchester (Mortgages) (No 3) Limited 1989; London and Manchester (Mortgages) (No 4) Limited 1989; London and Manchester (Mortgages) Limited 1987; London and Manchester (Nominees) Limited 1986; London and Manchester (Pensions) Limited 1983; London and Manchester Assurance Company Limited 1983; Portnall Warren (Wentworth House) Limited 1990; Portnall Warren plc 1990. *Professional Organisations:* FIA.

PYSDEN, Edward Scott; Partner, Alexander Tatham, since 1974; Corporate Finance and Venture Capital. *Biog: b.* 6 May 1948. *Nationality:* British. *m.* 1971, Anna-Maria (née Peck); 3 d. *Educ:* Dulwich College; King's School, Macclesfield; Manchester University (LLB). *Directorships:* Umist Ventures Limited 1989 (non-exec). *Professional Organisations:* Law Society, Honours 2nd Class; Peacock Prize. *Clubs:* St James's Club. *Recreations:* Squash, Gardening, Music, Postcard Collecting.

Q

QUAILE, J A; Director, Barclays de Zoete Wedd Securities Ltd.

QUARRELL, John; Partner, Nabarro Nathanson, since 1978; Pensions Work. *Biog: b.* 27 October 1948. *Nationality:* British. *m.* 1970, Teresa; 2 d. *Educ:* London University (LLB). *Directorships:* Spicers Pensioneer Trustees Ltd (non-exec); Eagle Place Trustees Ltd (non-exec); Eagle Place Services Ltd (non-exec); Saunders Pension Trustees Ltd (non-exec); Pensions Management Institute (non-exec); Martin Cadman Trustees Ltd (non-exec). *Other Activities:* Member, Main Ctee, Assoc of Pensions Lawyers; Education Ctee Member, National Assoc of Pension Funds; Editor, Trust Law & Practice; Consultant Editor, NAPF/Butterworth Pension Handbook; Council Member, Pensions Management Institute. *Professional Organisations:* FPMI. *Publications:* The Law of Pension Fund Investment, 1990.

QUARTANO, Ralph Nicholas; CBE; Chairman, Postel Investment Management Limited, since 1987. *Career:* Bataafsche Petroleum MIJ, Process Engineer 1952-58; The Lummus Corporation, Snr Process Engineer 1959-60; Engineering Chemical & Marine Press, MD 1960-70; The Post Office Snr Dir & Member, Mgmnt Board 1971-74; Post Office Staff Superannuation Fund, Chief Exec 1974-83; Postel Investment Management Ltd, Chief Exec 1983-87. *Biog: b.* 3 August 1927. *Nationality:* British/Greek. *m.* 1954, Cornelia Johanna (née De Gunst); 2 d. *Educ:* Sherborne School; Pembroke College, Cambridge (MA); London Business School. *Directorships:* SIB 1986 (non-exec) Dep Chm; Britoil 1982-88 (non-exec); 3i's 1987 (non-exec); BUPA 1987 (non-exec)Governor; Clerical Medical & General Life Insurance 1987 (non-exec); John Lewis Partnership Pension Fund 1986-89 (non-exec); London American Energy 1981-88 (non-exec); Booker 1988 (non-exec); British Maritime Technology 1988 (non-exec). *Other Activities:* City Capital Mkts Ctee (Mem 1985); CBI City Advisory Group (Mem 1984); Invest Ctee of The PGGM Pension Fund (Holland) (Mem 1986); Monteverdi Trust (Trustee 1986); Financial Reporting Council (Mem 1990). *Professional Organisations:* MIChemE.

QUATTROPANI, Pier-Luigi; Director, AIBD (Systems & Information) Limited.

QUEISSER, H J; Managing Director International, Burns Fry Limited, since 1990. *Biog: b.* 22 January 1948. *Nationality:* German. *Educ:* HEC, Lausanne University (License És). *Directorships:* Burns Fry Limited, Toronto, CDA 1984 (exec).

QUEK, L C; Executive Chairman UK and International Racing, Benchmark Bank plc.

QUELCH, Professor John A; Professor of Business Administration, Harvard University Graduate School of Business Administration, since 1988; Strategic Marketing Management. *Career:* University of Western Ontario, School of Business Administration, Assistant Professor 1977-79; Harvard University, Graduate School of Business Administration 1979-. *Biog: b.* 8 August 1951. *Nationality:* British. *m.* 1978, Joyce (née Huntley). *Educ:* Exeter College, Oxford (BA); University of Pennsylvania (MBA); Harvard University (MS, DBA). *Directorships:* WPP Group plc 1987 (non-exec); Reebok International Ltd 1985 (non-exec). *Publications:* The Marketing Challenge of Europe 1992, 1990; How to Market to Consumers, 1989; Sales Promotion Management, 1989; Marketing Management, 1987; Multinational Marketing Management, 1987. *Clubs:* Harvard Club of Boston. *Recreations:* Squash, Tennis.

QUERN, Art; Director, Nicholson Chamberlain Colls Limited.

QUESTA, G; Chief Executive, IMI Capital Markets (UK).

QUICK, Dr Norman; DL; Non-Executive Chairman, Quicks Group plc, since 1985. *Career:* H & J Quick Ltd Trainee Mgr 1946-47; Dir 1947-54; Joint MD 1954; Sole MD 1957; Chm & MD 1965. *Biog: b.* 19 November 1922. *m.* 1949, Maureen Cynthia (née Chancellor); 4 d. *Educ:* Arnold School, Blackpool. *Directorships:* Victoria University of Manchester 1980-83 Chm of Council; 1983- Member, Court & Council; Motor Agents Association 1977-78; National Pres. *Other Activities:* Stretford Conservative Assoc (Chm 1957-72, Pres 1974-); Surface Transport Action Group (Chm 1974-); Wilmslow Prep School Trust (Chm 1987); Hon MA, Hon LLD, Manchester University. *Professional Organisations:* FIMI. *Clubs:* RAC, St James's (Manchester). *Recreations:* Golf.

QUICK, S; Director, J H Minet & Co Ltd.

QUIGLEY, Desmond; Director, Dewe Rogerson.

QUIGLEY, M; Director, Aitken Campbell & Co Ltd.

QUIGLEY, Dr (William) George (Henry); CB; Chairman, Ulster Bank Limited, since 1989; Ulster Bank Group. *Career:* Northern Ireland Civil Service 1955-88; Dept of Manpower Services, Permanent Sec 1974-76; Dept of Commerce, Permanent Sec 1976-79; Dept of Finance, Permanent Sec 1979-82; Dept of Finance & Personnel, Permanent Sec 1982-88; Northern Ireland Civil Service Commission, Chm 1983-88; Ulster Bank Ltd, Dep Chm 1988; Industrial Relations Review Body for Northern Ireland, Chm 1971-74; Review of Economics & Industrial Strategy for N Ireland, Chm 1976. *Biog: b.* 26 November 1929. *Nationality:* British. *m.* 1971, Moyra Alice (née Munn). *Educ:* Ballymena Academy; Queen's University, Belfast (BA Hons 1st, PhD). *Directorships:* National Westminster Bank plc 1990 (non-exec); Short Brothers plc 1989 (non-exec). *Other Activities:* Member, Management Ctee, Northern Ireland Economic Research Centre (1984-); Professorial Fellow, Queen's University, Belfast, 1988-. *Professional Organisations:* CBIM; Institute of Directors (Chairman, Northern Ireland Division); Fellow, Institute of Bankers in Ireland. *Publications:* Registrum Johannis Mey, 1972. *Recreations:* Historical Research, Reading, Music, Gardening.

QUILL, Roderick Michael; Chairman/Chief Executive, C T Bowring & Co Ltd, since 1984. *Career:* C T Bowring & Co Ltd, Various 1964-; A E Wilson Co, Toronto, Canada, Underwriter 1958-60; Progress Insurance Co, Asst Underwriter 1955-58; United Reinsurers Ltd, Asst Underwriter 1952-55; RAF National Service 1950-52; National Provincial Bank Limited, Clerk 1948-50. *Biog: b.* 16 June 1932. *Nationality:* British. *m.* 1957, Ruby (née Butterworth); 1 s; 1 d. *Educ:* Salesian College. *Directorships:* C T Bowring & Co Ltd 1983; C T Bowring & Co (Insurance) Ltd 1972-84 Chairman & Chief Executive; Bowring Aviation Ltd 1983; Bowring Marine & Energy Ltd 1983; Bowring Non Marine Insurance Brokers Ltd, now Bowring North America Ltd 1983-88; 1988; Bowring Financial & Professional Insurance Brokers Ltd 1988; Bowring Worldwide Services Ltd 1988; Bowring International Insurance Brokers Ltd 1988; Ruby Ltd 1987; Apsley Property Services Ltd 1990; Tudor Homes Ltd 1990 (non-exec). *Other Activities:* Company of Tallow Chandlers; FRSA; Lloyds Insurance Brokers Committee. *Professional Organisations:* Insurance Brokers Registration Council; Institute of Directors; Lloyds Insurance Brokers Committee. *Recreations:* Art, Literature, Golf, Travel, Photography, Music.

QUINN, Andrew; Director, Granada Group.

QUINN, Brian; Executive Director, Bank of England, since 1988; Banking Supervision & Banking Operations. *Career:* IMF Representative, Sierra Leone 1966-68; International Monetary Fund (Economic, Africa Dept) 1964-70; Bank of England, Economics Division 1970-74; Chief Cashier's Department 1974-77; Head of Information Division 1977-82; Assistant Director, Banking Supervision Division 1982-84; Assistant Director and Head of Banking Supervision Div 1984; Assistant Director and Head of Banking Supervision 1986; Executive Director 1988. *Biog: b.* 18 November 1936. *Nationality:* British. *m.* 1961, Mary (née Bradley); 2 s; 1 d. *Educ:* University of Glasgow (MA Hons); University of Manchester (MA Economics); Cornell University (PhD). *Directorships:* Bank of England 1988 (exec). *Clubs:* Overseas Bankers. *Recreations:* Fishing, Golf, Listening to Music.

QUINN, Patrick Joseph; Director, Chartered WestLB Ltd, since 1989; Banking. *Career:* National Westminster Bank, Various 1960-73; Rothschild Intercontinental Bank Various 1973-75; Amex Bank Ltd, Director 1975-83; Standard Chartered Asia Ltd (Hong Kong) Director 1983-88. *Biog: b.* 19 February 1944. *Nationality:* British. *m.* 1983, Elisabeth (née MacLean); 2 s; 2 d. *Educ:* High Wycombe Royal Grammar School; High Wycombe College of Technology and Art (Postgrad Dip in Mgmnt Studies, PhD). *Directorships:* CWB Nominees Ltd 1989 (exec); Charterd WestLB Nominees Ltd 1989 (exec); CWB Leasing Ltd 1990 (exec); CWB Scamba Leasing Ltd 1990 (exec); CWB Broadgate Leasing Ltd 1990 (exec); CWB Priorhouse Ltd 1990 (exec); Charterd WestLB Leasing Ltd 1990 (exec); Charterd WestLB Finance Ltd 1990 (exec); Pacific Bulk Carriers (1978) Ltd 1990 (exec); Turriff Developments (Telford) Ltd 1990 (exec). *Other Activities:* Ctee Member, London Chamber of Commerce Hong Kong Ctee.

QUINN, Thomas; Director, Barclays de Zoete Wedd Ltd, since 1987; Sterling Primary Markets. *Career:* Philips & Drew Fixed Interest 1955-65; James Capel & Co Fixed Interest 1965-67; W Greenwell & Co, Ptnr 1968; Greenwell, Exec 1973; Head, Equity Sales 1976-80; Corp Fin - Head, Fixed Interest 1980-87. *Biog: b.* 16 February 1939. *Nationality:* British. *m.* 1985, Susan (née Jackson); 1 s; 2 d. *Educ:* Watford Grammar School. *Directorships:* BZW Gilts Ltd 1987 (exec); BZW Capital Markets Ltd 1987 (exec); BZW Securities Ltd 1987 (exec); Ebbgate Holdings Ltd 1987 (exec). *Other Activities:* Bond Club of London. *Professional Organisations:* ASIA. *Clubs:* Woburn Golf and Country Club.

QUINNEN, Paul Nigel; Director, Lazard Investors Limited, since 1986; Investment Management. *Career:* Coopers & Lybrand, Tax Snr 1976-80; J Henry Schroder Wagg Fund, Mgr 1980-85. *Biog: b.* 10 October 1953. *Nationality:* British. *m.* 1977, Dinah (née Hetherington); 1 s; 1 d. *Educ:* St Benedict's School, Ealing; Wadham College, Oxford (BA). *Professional Organisations:* ACA. *Clubs:* Richmond Football Club, Royal Mid-Surrey Golf Club. *Recreations:* Rugby, Cricket, Golf, Public Houses.

QUINTON, Bryan P; Group Investment Director, MIM Ltd; Unit Trust and Pension Fund Management. *Biog: b.* 29 January 1934. *Professional Organisations:* FCA.

QUINTON, Sir John (Grand); Chairman, Barclays Bank plc, since 1987. *Career:* Barclays Bank Limited, General Manager 1975-82; Barclays Bank UK Management Limited, Director 1975; Barclays Bank Limited, Director and Senior General Manager 1982-84; Barclays Bank plc, Vice Chairman 1985; Barclays Bank plc, Deputy Chairman 1985-87. *Biog: b.* 21 December 1929. *Nationality:* British. *m.* 1954, Jean Margaret (née Chastney); 1 s; 1 d. *Educ:* Norwich School; St John's College, Cambridge (MA). *Directorships:* Bankers Clearing House 1987 (non-exec). *Other Activities:* Honorary Treasurer, Business in the Community; Governor, The Ditchley Foundation; Member, Court of Henley Management College; Chairman, Office of the Banking Ombudsman; Chairman, Advisory Council of the London Enterprise Agency; Governor, Motability; Fellow, Royal Society of Arts; Trustee, Royal Academy Trust; Council Member, Royal Shakespeare Theatre. *Professional Organisations:* FCIB. *Clubs:* Reform. *Recreations:* Golf, Gardening, Music.

QUIRICI, Daniel; Director, Credit Commercial de France (UK) Limited, since 1990; Corporate Finance. *Career:* Arthur D Little 1976-82; Credit Commercial de France Snr VP 1983-86. *Biog: b.* 8 June 1948. *Nationality:* French. *m.* 1972, Margaret (née Mann); 2 s; 1 d. *Educ:* Ecole des Hautes Etudes Commerciales (MBA); Stanford University, USA (PhD). *Directorships:* Compagnie Suisse et Française 1990 (exec); Credit Commercial de France Holdings Ltd 1988 (non-exec). *Other Activities:* Member, Knightsbridge Association Traffic Committee. *Clubs:* RAC.

QUIRKE, Maurice Gerard; Group Finance Director, CCF Holdings Limited, since 1989; Finance and Administration. *Career:* Ernst & Whinney, London 1981-86; County NatWest 1986-89. *Biog: b.* 1 February 1960. *Nationality:* British. *m.* 1986, Elsa (née Goldberg). *Educ:* London School of Economics (BSc Hons Econ). *Directorships:* Credit Commercial de France (UK) Limited 1989 (exec). *Professional Organisations:* ACA. *Recreations:* Travel, Skiing, Golf.

R

RABAGLIATI, Duncan Charles Pringle; Partner, McKenna & Co, since 1973; Overseas Purchasers of UK Property. *Career:* Booth & Co (Leeds) 1964-69; McKenna & Co, Asst Solicitor 1969-73. *Biog: b.* 3 January 1945. *Nationality:* British. *m.* 1971, Mair (née Williams); 2 s; 1 d. *Educ:* Seabergh School. *Professional Organisations:* Law Society; Westminster Law Society. *Publications:* History of Grand Prix & Voiturre Motor Racing Vols 1-7, 1985-; Formula One Record Book, 1977. *Recreations:* Historic Motor Racing, Motoring History, Genealogy.

RABBEN, Eivind; Director, Hambros Bank Ltd, since 1990; Norwegian Dept. *Career:* Norwegian Royal Navy, Lieutenant 1975-78; Bolnes Shipyard 1981; Unigas International 1982; Hambros Bank Ltd, Executive 1984-85; Manager 1985-86; Asst Director 1986-90; Director 1990-. *Biog: b.* 18 July 1956. *Nationality:* Norwegian. *m.* 1989, Clare Evelyn (née Hambro). *Educ:* Oslo Handels Gymnasium; Norwegian Royal Navy Officer School; University of Newcastle-upon-Tyne (BSc Marine Engineering); University of Durham (MSc Management Studies). *Directorships:* Hambros Bank Ltd 1990 (exec). *Clubs:* Den Norske Klubb, ShippingKlubben. *Recreations:* Skiing, Shooting.

RACE, R T; Director, Charlton Seal, A Division of Wise Speke Limited, since 1987; Corporate Finance. *Biog: b.* 13 June 1962. *Nationality:* English. *Educ:* Manchester Grammar School; The City University Business School (BSc Hons). *Professional Organisations:* Member, International Stock Exchange; Associate Member, Society of Investment Analysts.

RACE, Russell John; Corporate Finance Director, Hoare Govett Limited, since 1984; Corporate Finance. *Career:* British Steel Corporation, Economic Asst 1967-68; Sea Fish Authority, Asst Economist 1968-70. *Biog: b.* 28 May 1946. *Educ:* Liverpool University (BA Hons). *Professional Organisations:* Society of Business Economists; Society of Investment Analysts. *Recreations:* Hockey, Cricket, Music.

RADCLIFFE, Anthony J; Director, S G Warburg Securities.

RADCLIFFE, J G Y; TD; Director, Hogg Group plc, since 1984; Research & Development. *Career:* Hogg Group plc 1970-; Control Risks, Founding Director 1974-78; Investment Insurance International, Chairman 1972-. *Biog: b.* 29 August 1948. *Nationality:* British. *m.* 1981, Frances; 2 s; 1 d. *Educ:* Eton College; New College, Oxford (MA). *Directorships:* International Art and Antique Loss Register 1990 Chairman. *Other Activities:* Court, Weavers Livery Company; Chairman, Bolingbroke Primary School; Major, TA. *Clubs:* Cavalry & Guards, Carlton Club, City of London Club. *Recreations:* Farming, Military Studies.

RADFORD, K J; Executive Director, Henderson Crosthwaite Limited.

RADFORD, M F; Director, Bain Clarkson Limited.

RADLEY, Nigel Howard; Director, Baring Securities Ltd, since 1989; Japanese Equity Warrant Trading. *Career:* James Capel Ltd, Authorised Dealer 1970-77; Robert Fleming Securities Ltd, Mgr, Eurobonds 1977-85; Baring Securities Ltd, Dir, Warrant Trading 1985-. *Biog: b.* 15 March 1954. *Nationality:* British. *m.* 1977, Linda Barbara (née Biggs); 1 d. *Educ:* South East Essex Technical. *Recreations:* Golf, Snooker.

RAE, A A S; CBE; Non-Executive Director, Riggs A P Bank Ltd.

RAE, John McFadyen; Treasurer & Director, Arbuthnot Latham Bank Ltd, since 1988; Treasury and Capital Markets. *Career:* NZI Securities Ltd, Money Market Dealer 1982-83; NZ, Money Market Co-ordinator 1983-84; Funding Mgr 1984-85; Snr Treasury Mgr 1985-86; Snr Mgr, Domestic Operations 1986-87; Exec Projects Mgr, Capital Markets 1987-88. *Biog: b.* 31 July 1958. *Nationality:* New Zealand. *Educ:* Kings College, Auckland, NZ; Auckland University (LLB,BComm). *Directorships:* NZI Securities Europe Ltd 1988 (exec); Arbuthnot Latham Bank Ltd 1988 (exec); NZI Financial Corporation Europe Ltd 1990 (exec). *Professional Organisations:* Member, NZ Law Society. *Clubs:* Broadgate Club.

RAEBURN, Denis G; Managing Director (Investment Management), Global Asset Management (UK) Limited.

RAFF, David; Partner, Forsyte Kerman Solicitors, since 1987; Corporate Finance. *Career:* Clintons, Articled Clerk/Solicitor 1981-84. *Biog: b.* 8 January 1959. *Nationality:* British. *m.* 1982, Clare (née Clayton); 1 s. *Educ:* Manchester Grammar School; University College, London (LLB). *Professional Organisations:* Member, Law Society. *Recreations:* Tennis, Soccer.

RAFFERTY, John Campbell; Partner, W & J Burness WS, since 1977; Corporate and Financial Services Law. *Career:* W & J Burness, Asst Solicitor 1973-77. *Biog: b.* 30 June 1951. *Nationality:* British. *Educ:* The Edinburgh Academy; Edinburgh University (LLB Hons). *Directorships:* St Andrew Trust plc 1986 (non-exec). *Professional Organisations:* The Law Society of Scotland; Society of Writers to Her Majesty's Signet. *Recreations:* Swimming, Skiing, Hill Walking, Gardening.

RAHBEK, Jens; General Manager, Jyske Bank, since 1989. *Career:* Jyske Bank 1979-; Project Fin Mgr, Denmark 1981-85; Branch Mgr, Denmark 1985-86; Dep regional Mgr, Denmark 1986-89; Gen Mgr, London 1989-.

RAILTON, Timothy John; Partner, Hill Dickinson & Company.

RAINGOLD, Gerald Barry; Deputy Managing Director, Banque Paribas, since 1985; General Management. *Career:* Cole Dickens & Hill, Articles 1963-68; Coopers & Lybrand, Mgr 1968-72; Wallace Brothers Bank Ltd, Mgr 1972-76; Midland Montagu Group, Snr Mgr 1976-78. *Biog: b.* 25 March 1943. *m.* 1978, Aviva (née Petrie); 1 s; 2 d. *Educ:* St Paul's School; London Graduate Sch of Business Studies (MBA Sloan Fell). *Directorships:* Skandia Financial Services Ltd 1980 (non-exec); British Francophone Business Group 1986 (non-exec); Paribas Development Services Ltd 1985 (exec); Paribas Export Finance Ltd 1984 (exec); Paribas Finance Ltd 1982 (exec); Paribas Mortgage Services Ltd 1985 (exec). *Other Activities:* Freeman, City of London. *Professional Organisations:* FCA; Institute of Directors; Business Graduates' Association. *Recreations:* Theatre, Sports, Travel.

RAISMAN, J P; Partner, Jaques & Lewis.

RAISMAN, John Michael; CBE; Deputy Chairman, British Telecom, since 1987. *Career:* Shell UK Ltd 1953; Chm & Chief Exec 1978-85. *Biog: b.* 12 February 1929. *Nationality:* British. *m.* 1953, Evelyn Anne (née Muirhead); 1 s; 3 d. *Educ:* Rugby School; Queens College, Oxford (MA). *Directorships:* Vickers plc 1981 (non-exec); Glaxo Holdings plc 1982 (non-exec); Lloyds Bank plc 1985 (non-exec); Electra-Candover Partners 1985 Chm, Invest Brd. *Other Activities:* CBI (Member Council); Royal Academy Trust (Chm); Aston University (Pro-Chancellor); Governor, NIESR; Member of Council for Charitable Support; Hon LLD, Aberdeen; Chairman, Languages Lead Body. *Professional Organisations:* CBIM. *Clubs:* Brooks's, Sunningdale Golf Club, Royal Mid-Surrey. *Recreations:* Golf, Skiing, Travel, Music.

RAJANI, S H; Partner, Cameron Markby Hewitt.

RALSTON, Mrs Nicola T (née Thomas); Director, Schroder Investment Management Ltd, since 1987; UK Pension Fund Management. *Career:* Kitcat & Aitken, Retail Analyst 1977-79; Schroder Investment Management, Analyst 1979-84; Head of Research 1984-87. *Biog: b.* 29 November 1955. *Nationality:* British. *Educ:* King Edward VI High School for Girls, Birmingham; Somerville College, Oxford (BA). *Professional Organisations:* Council Member, AMSIA.

RAMANOËL, C M S; Director, Crédit Lyonnais Euro-Securities Ltd.

RAMEL, Axel K S M; Director, Merrill Lynch International Limited, since 1985; Corporate Finance; Scandinavia.

RAMFORS, Bo C E; Managing Director and Group Chief Executive, Skandinaviska Enskilda Banken. *Career:* Swedish Chamber of Commerce in Paris 1964-65; Hambros Bank Ltd 1966-76; Director and Member of The Board 1972-76; Statsforetag 1976-80; Finance Director 1976-78; Executive Vice President 1978-80; Skandinaviska Enskilda Banken Malmö, Deputy Managing Director 1980-83; Skandinaviska Enskilda Banken Gothenburg, Deputy Managing Director 1983-84; Managing Director 1985-89; Managing Director and Group Chief Executive 1989-. *Biog: b.* 2 June 1936. *Nationality:* Swedish. *m.* 1962, Gudrun (née Lindquist). *Educ:* Higher School Examination; Officer in The Reserve of the Royal Marine; University of Lund, Faculty of Law. *Directorships:* Nolato AB; Regnbagen AB; Scandinavium AB; Swedish Trade Fair, Gothenburg; Ruben Rausings Foundation; Bilspedition. *Recreations:* Shooting, Fishing, Music.

RAMIREZ-ESCUDERO, A; General Manager, Banco Bilbao Vizcaya.

RAMSAY, D W; Vice President, The Bank of Nova Scotia.

RAMSAY, G M; Director, Enterprise Oil.

RAMSAY, Ian Ross McGregor; Director, Robert Fleming & Co Limited, since 1984; Corporate Finance. *Career:* Price Waterhouse Articled Clerk to Mgr 1974-80; Robert Fleming Corp Fin 1980-. *Biog: b.* 3 September 1952. *m.* 1978, Tish (née Lawrence); 1 s; 1 d. *Educ:* Glenalmond College; Edinburgh University (BSc Hons). *Professional Organisations:* FCA. *Recreations:* Travel, Music, Woodwork.

RAMSAY, J P; Assistant Director, J K Buckenham Limited.

RAMSAY, R C; Director, Lehman Brothers Gilts Money Brokers Limited, since 1989. *Career:* Morgan Grenfell Securities Ltd, Assistant Director 1987-89;

Pinchin Denny & Co, Departmental Manager 1964-87. *Biog: b.* 15 September 1944. *Nationality:* British. *m.* 1977, Carol Anne (née Martin). *Educ:* Heathcote, Chingford, London. *Directorships:* Lehman Brothers Equity Money Brokers Limited 1989 (non-exec).

RAMSAY, Richard Alexander McGregor; Director & Managing Director, Corporate Finance Division, Barclays de Zoete Wedd Ltd, since 1988; Corporate Finance. *Career:* Grindlay Brandts Ltd, Exec Mgr 1975-78; Hill Samuel & Co Ltd, Exec Mgr, Asst Dir, Dir 1979-84; On Secondment to Dept of Trade & Industry, Dir Ind Dev Unit 1984-86; Hill Samuel & Co Ltd, Dir 1986-87. *Biog: b.* 27 December 1949. *m.* 1975, Elizabeth C M (née Blackwood); 1 s; 1 d. *Educ:* Trinity College, Glenalmond; Aberdeen University (MA Hons). *Professional Organisations:* FCA. *Recreations:* Skiing, Hill Walking, Classic Cars, Gardening.

RAMSAY, Roger Bryan Pointer; Assistant General Manager, Professional Services, Norwich Union Life Insurance Society Ltd, since 1989; Accountants, Actuaries, Solicitors and Valuation Team. *Career:* Norwich Union Life Insurance Society Ltd Actuary for NZ 1964-71; Overseas Actuary 1972-74; Ordinary Business Mgr 1974-78; Pensions Manager 1978-83; Assistant General Manager (Overseas Life) 1984-89. *Biog: b.* 17 September 1937. *Nationality:* British. *m.* 1961, Jill (née Hampshire); 1 s; 3 d. *Educ:* City of Norwich School. *Directorships:* London Indemnity & General Insurance Co 1976 Alternate Dir; 1980 Dir; Norwich Union Financial Holdings Ltd (Australia) 1987; Norwich Union Life Australia Ltd 1987. *Professional Organisations:* FIA; APMI; Member, Chartered Insurance Institute. *Recreations:* Bridge, Golf.

RAMSDEN, The Rt Hon James; Non-Executive Director, Prudential Corporation plc.

RAMSEY, Malcolm E; Associate Director, Coutts & Co.

RANCE, C C; Associate, Grimley J R Eve.

RANDALL, Graham James; Partner, Pannell Kerr Forster, since 1979; Audit Partner. *Career:* Woolger Hennell (merged with P D Leake & Co), Trainee Accountant 1969-74; P D Leake & Co (New York), Manager 1974-78; P D Leake & Co (UK), Senior Manager 1978-79; P D Leake & Co (merged with Ball Baker), Partner 1979-87; Ball Baker Leake (merged with Pannell Kerr Forster), Partner 1987-89; Pannell Kerr Forster, Partner 1989-. *Biog: b.* 1 March 1951. *Nationality:* British. *m.* 1982, Margaret Ann (née Madams); 1 s; 1 d. *Educ:* Brentwood School. *Professional Organisations:* Fellow, Institute of Chartered Accountants in England & Wales. *Clubs:* RAC. *Recreations:* Snooker, Gardening, Sport, Photography.

RANDALL, Jeff; City Editor, The Sunday Times, since 1989. *Career:* The Sunday Times, Deputy City Editor 1988-89; The Sunday Telegraph, City Correspondent 1986-88; Financial Weekly, Assistant Editor 1985-86. *Biog: b.* 3 October 1954. *Nationality:* British. *m.* 1986, Susan (née Fidler); 1 d. *Educ:* Nottingham University (BA Hons Economics). *Clubs:* Warley Park Golf Club. *Recreations:* Golf, Horseracing.

RANDALL, Peter Alan; Partner, Bacon & Woodrow, since 1985; Actuarial Research/International Employee Benefits. *Career:* Lane, Clark & Peacock, Actuary 1975-83; T G Arthur Hargrave (later Bacon & Woodrow), Actuary 1983-85; Partner 1985-. *Biog: b.* 15 June 1952. *Nationality:* British. *m.* 1984, Sarah Ann (née Middlemiss); 1 s; 2 d. *Educ:* Framlingham College; Selwyn College, Cambridge (MA). *Professional Organisations:* FIA; ASA (USA); Associate, Pension Management Institute (APMI). *Publications:* Actuaries, Pension Funds and Investment (with T G Arthur), IIA 1989. *Recreations:* Family, Skiing, Theatre, Squash.

RANDALL, R G L; Head of Group Corporate Relations, Royal Insurance Holdings plc.

RANDALL, Simon James Crawford; Partner, Lawrence Graham, since 1970; Local Government Law. *Biog: b.* 5 June 1944. *Nationality:* British. *m.* 1976, Glyneth (née Watson); 2 s. *Educ:* Westminster School; College of Law. *Directorships:* Housing Organisations Mobility and Exchange Services Ltd 1990 (non-exec); Social Housing Agency Ltd 1990; Social Care Management Ltd 1990; Churchill Theatre Trust Ltd 1978; Bethlem Royal & Maudsley SHA 1970 (non-exec). *Other Activities:* Member, London Borough of Bromley, 1968-; Member, Greater London Council, 1981-86; Chairman, London Committee for Accessible Transport; Chairman, London Boroughs Association, Housing & Social Services Committee. *Professional Organisations:* Society of Conservative Lawyers; Law Society. *Clubs:* Carlton. *Recreations:* Antiquarian Books, Mason's Ironstone Pottery.

RANDELL, Charles David; Partner, Slaughter and May, since 1989; Company and Commercial Department. *Career:* Slaughter and May, Asst Solicitor 1982-89. *Biog: b.* 6 June 1958. *Nationality:* British. *m.* 1983, Celia (née Van Oss); 1 s. *Educ:* Bradfield College; Trinity College, Oxford (BA). *Other Activities:* Member, Editorial Committee, 'Practical Law for Companies'. *Professional Organisations:* Mem, The Law Society; Mem, The City of London Solicitors' Company; Mem, UK Oil Lawyers' Group. *Recreations:* Sailing.

RANDLE, D S; Director, Macey Williams Insurance Services Ltd.

RANDS, D Harvey; Partner, Memery Crystal.

RANGER, F M; Director, County NatWest Limited.

RANKIN, Alick Michael; CBE; Chairman and Group Chief Executive, Scottish & Newcastle Breweries plc, since 1989. *Career:* National Service, Scots Guards 1953-55; Wood Gundy & Co, Investment Dealer, Toronto 1956-59; Scottish & Newcastle Breweries plc 1960-; Director 1974; Marketing Director 1977; Scottish Brewers Limited, Chairman 1982; Scottish & Newcastle Breweries plc, Chief Executive Officer 1983; Deputy Chm 1987. *Biog: b.* 23 January 1935. *Nationality:* British. *m.* 1976, Suzetta (née Nelson); 1 s; 3 d. *Educ:* Eton College; Christ Church, Oxford. *Directorships:* Bank of Scotland 1987 (non-exec); Christian Salvesen plc 1986 (non-exec); High Gosforth Park plc 1988; The Brewers' Society Limited 1990 Chm. *Other Activities:* Council, Scottish Confederation of British Industry; Trustee, Holyrood Brewery Foundation; Member, The Brewers' Court; Director, Edinburgh's Capital Limited. *Clubs:* Royal & Ancient (St Andrews), Hon Company of Edinburgh Golfers (Muirfield), New Club (Edinburgh), Vanderbilt Tennis (London), I Zingari Cricket. *Recreations:* Shooting, Fishing, Golf, Tennis, Ornithology, Oenology.

RANKIN, Brian; Investment Director (Edinburgh), Northern Venture Managers Limited.

RANKINE, Ian Gordon; Managing Director, Anglo Pierson Options Limited, since 1989; Technical Analyst, Traded Options Analyst. *Career:* Anglo American Options Ltd, Technical Analyst/Consultant, Associate Member 1988-89; NatWest/County Group, Divisional Director-Traded Options 1988-88; Walker, Crips, Weddle, Beck & Co, Associate Member 1975-88; Spence, Veitch & Co, Associate Member 1970-75; B Hansford & Co, Floor Trader 1962-70; Bradford & Paine (StockJobbers), Blue Button 1959-62. *Biog: b.* 2 March 1941. *m.* 1966, Heather Margaret Orr (née Claydon). *Educ:* Dulwich College. *Professional Organisations:* Member, International Stock Exchange. *Recreations:* Reading, Golf, Film-Making.

RANSOM, Robert S; Senior Partner, MacNair Mason.

RANSON, Roy Henry; Deputy General Manager, Joint Actuary, Equitable Life Assurance Society. *Biog: Nationality:* British. *Educ:* Christ College, Cambridge (MA). *Directorships:* Equitable Life Assurance Society; Equitable Investment Managers Ltd; Equitable Unit Trust Managers Ltd; University Life Assurance Society. *Other Activities:* Chairman, Life Supervision Committee, ABI. *Professional Organisations:* FIA; FPMI.

RAPHAEL, M; Director, Allied Trust Bank Limited.

RASHBROOK, Christopher Leonard; Senior Manager, Coutts & Co, since 1990; Responsible for the Day to Day Running of Robarts and Lloyd's Offices. *Career:* Coutts & Co, City Office, Manager 1978-79; Winchester Office, Manager 1979-83; Adelaide Branch, Manager 1983-88; Campbell's Office (Private Banking), Senior Manager 1988-90. *Biog: b.* 14 August 1938. *Nationality:* British. *m.* 1960, Shirley Ann (née Smith); 1 s; 1 d. *Educ:* King's College School, Wimbledon. *Other Activities:* Treasurer, Hampshire & The Islands Historic Churches Trust; Treasurer, Contact; Treasurer, Zahra Siddiqui Foundation; Freeman, City of London; Member, Royal Society of Arts. *Professional Organisations:* Institute of Bankers.

RASHLEIGH, Jonathan Michael Vernon; Financial Controller, 3i Group plc, since 1987; Finance, Planning, Information Sytems. *Career:* 3i Group, Chief Accountant 1985-87; Planning and Operations Manager 1979-84; Manager-Group Accounts Unit 1976-78; Ernst & Young, Audit Senior progressing to Assistant Manager 1974-76; Trainee 1969-73. *Biog: b.* 29 September 1950. *Nationality:* British. *m.* 1975, Sarah; 3 s; 1 d. *Educ:* Bryanston School. *Directorships:* 3i plc 1986 (exec). *Other Activities:* Member, Research Board, Institute of Chartered Accountants; Member, Business Support Group, ICA; Liveryman, Worshipful Company of Tobacco Blenders and Tobacco Pipe Makers; Freeman, City of London. *Professional Organisations:* FCA (Qualified 1974).

RATCLIFF, Michael; Partner, Wilde Sapte, since 1989; Corporate Tax. *Career:* Masons, Articled Clerk 1980-82; Lovell White & King, Assistant Solicitor 1982-88; Wilde Sapte, Assistant Solicitor 1988-89. *Biog: b.* 27 February 1957. *Nationality:* British. *m.* 1988, Catherine (née Pannell). *Educ:* Plympton Grammar School; Hertford College, Oxford (MA, BCL). *Professional Organisations:* Secretary, Exeter West Group (Railway Preservation Society); Member, Law Society. *Recreations:* Railway Enthusiast, Badminton, Walking.

RATCLIFFE, David E; Finance Director, Billiton Enthoven Metals Limited, since 1989; Finance & Administration. *Biog: b.* 6 January 1944. *m.* 1968; 1 s; 2 d. *Educ:* Repton School; Bristol University (BA). *Directorships:* Billiton Enthoven Metals Limited 1989 (exec). *Professional Organisations:* Fellow, Institute of Chartered Accountants. *Recreations:* Hockey, Tennis, Theatre.

RATH, James Winston; Secretary, The Association of Investment Trust Companies, since 1988; Overall Conduct of the Association's day to day Activities and Advising on Policy Matters. *Career:* Coopers & Lybrand, Articled Clerk 1969-72; Qualified Acct 1972-73; The Association of Investment Trust Companies Asst Sec 1973-87. *Biog: b.* 12 May 1944. *Nationality:* British. *Educ:* St Marylebone Grammar School; St Andrews University (MA). *Professional Organisations:* FCA.

RATNER, John G; Director, Svenska Handelsbanken plc.

RATTRAY, James Stephen; Group Overseas Manager, Commercial Union Assurance Company plc, since 1987; General Management of Overseas Insurance Operations. *Career:* F Rowland & Co (CA), Articled Clerk/Qualified Accountant 1958-64; Commonwealth Development Corporation (London/W Africa), Exec Asst 1964-70; Commercial Union Group 1970-; Various Fin Positions, Group Fin Controller 1982-84; Chief Fin Officer (US Subsidiary) 1984-86. *Biog:* b. 11 August 1940. *Nationality:* British. *m.* 1964, Muriel (née Annand); 2 s; 1 d. *Educ:* John Fisher School, Purley. *Directorships:* Commercial Union Group, Numerous Directorships of Overseas Subsidiaries & Associated Companies. *Professional Organisations:* FCA; FCT. *Recreations:* Tennis, Music, Travel.

RATZKE, B; Partner, Rowe & Maw, since 1989; Corporate Finance Mergers & Acquisitions. *Career:* Herbert Smith 1980 (Articles) 1987; Rowe & Maw 1988-. *Biog:* b. 27 July 1956. *Nationality:* West German. *m.* 1988, Karen Jane (née Bates). *Educ:* Sevenoaks School, Kent; University of Durham (BA Hons). *Professional Organisations:* Law Society. *Recreations:* Music, Opera, Gardening, Skiing.

RAVEN, F Barry; Partner (Nottingham), Evershed Wells & Hind.

RAVEN, P L; Group Chief Financial Officer, Ultramar plc.

RAVEN, Stephen Ernest John; Chairman and Managing Director, Charles Fulton Securities.

RAWLES, B J; Honorary Clerk, Worshipful Company of Glass Sellers.

RAWLINGS, John Barrington; Deputy Chairman, Morgan Grenfell & Co Ltd, since 1989; Banking. *Career:* H M Diplomatic Service 1968-73; Morgan Grenfell 1973. *Biog:* b. 10 February 1947. *m.* 1973, Sylvia. *Educ:* Whitgift School, Croydon; Trinity College, Cambridge (MA). *Professional Organisations:* FCIB, MCT.

RAWLINGS, Keith John; Chairman, Burlington Insurance Services Ltd, since 1969. *Career:* Royal Insurance 1959-69. *Biog:* b. 24 April 1940. *Nationality:* British. *m.* 1963, Susan Mary (née Johnson); 1 s; 1 d. *Educ:* Kent College, Canterbury. *Directorships:* Rutland Trust plc 1987 (exec); Rutland Ins Broking & Invest Group 1988; London & Edinburgh Trust plc 1985-86. *Professional Organisations:* Fellow, Chartered Ins Inst; Fellow, British Ins & Invest Brokers Assoc; Chartered Ins Practitioner. *Clubs:* St James's. *Recreations:* Tennis, Golf, Sailing, Travel, Shooting.

RAWLINS, D G; Head of Company/Commercial Dept, Field Fisher Waterhouse.

RAWLINS, Peter Jonathan; Chief Executive, The International Stock Exchange, since 1989. *Career:* Arthur Andersen & Co 1972-85; Audit Manager 1977-83; Partner 1983-84; UK Practice Development Partner 1984; Lloyd's of London, Seconded as PA to Deputy Chairman & Chief Executive 1983-84; Sturge Holdings plc, Director 1985-89; R W Sturge & Co, Managing Director 1985-89; Sturge Lloyd's Agencies Ltd, Director 1986-89; Wise Speke Holdings Ltd, Director 1987-89. *Biog:* b. 30 April 1951. *Nationality:* British. *m.* 1973, Louise (née Langton); 1 s; 1 d. *Educ:* Arnold House School; St Edward's School, Oxford; Keble College, Oxford (Honours Degree in English Language & Literature). *Directorships:* The Stock Exchange (Holdings) Ltd 1989 (exec); The Stock Exchange (Properties) Ltd 1989 (exec); The Birmingham Stock Exchange Buildings Ltd 1989 (exec); TOPIC Services Inc 1989 (exec); ISE Mutual Reference Ltd 1989 (exec); Securities Settlement & Clearing House Ltd 1989 (exec); London Option Clearing House Ltd 1989 (exec); London Equity Options Ltd 1989 (exec); London Traded Options Market Ltd 1989 (exec); SEPON Ltd 1989 (exec); SEPON (South Africa) Property Ltd 1989 (exec); SEPON (Australia) Property Ltd 1989 (exec); Talisman (Australia) Property Ltd 1989 (exec); The Stock Exchange (Nominees) Ltd 1989 (exec); LOCH (Nominees) Ltd 1989 (exec); S E (Global Custody) Ltd 1989 (exec); The International Stock Exchange (London) Inc 1989 (exec); Lloyd-Roberts & Gilkes Ltd 1989 (non-exec); Association for Business Sponsorship of the Arts 1982; London City Ballet Trust Ltd 1986. *Other Activities:* Fellow, The Royal Society for the Encouragement of Arts, Manufactures & Commerce. *Professional Organisations:* FCA; FRSA. *Clubs:* MCC, City of London. *Recreations:* Family, The Performing Arts, Tennis, Squash, Shooting Clays, Travelling.

RAWLINSON, Mark Stobart; Partner, Freshfields, since 1990; Corporate Finance. *Career:* Freshfields, Articled Clerk 1982-84; Assistant Solicitor 1984-90. *Biog:* b. 3 May 1957. *Nationality:* British. *m.* 1984, Julia Katrina Chiene (née Shepherd); 1 s. *Educ:* Manchester Grammar School; Haberdashers' Aske's School, Elstree; Sidney Sussex College, Cambridge (MA Hons). *Other Activities:* The City of London Solicitors' Company. *Professional Organisations:* The Law Society. *Publications:* Contributor, Practitioner's Guide to Corporate Finance and The Financial Services Act 1986, 1990. *Clubs:* Cambridge University Hawks Club. *Recreations:* Family, Skiing, Sailing, Windsurfing, Watching Rugby & Cricket.

RAWLINSON, Peter Anthony Grayson; The Rt Hon Lord Rawlinson of Ewell; PC, QC; *Career:* Barrister 1946; Practised until 1985; QC 1959; MP Epsom 1955-78; Solicitor General 1962-64; Defender, Salisbury 1960-62; Kingston-upon-Thames 1975-; Priory Councellor 1964; Attorney General 1970-74; Chairman of the Bar 1975; President of Senate of Inns of Court; Treasurer, Inns Temple 1984. *Biog:* b. 26 June

1918. *Nationality:* British. *m.* 1954, Elaine; 2 s; 4 d. *Educ:* Downside School; Christs College, Cambridge (Exhibitioner, Hon Fellow). *Directorships:* Pioneer Concrete Holdings (non-exec)Chm; Pioneer Investments, Sydney (non-exec); Daily Telegraph plc (non-exec); STC (non-exec); Anglo Group plc (non-exec). *Publications:* A Price Too High, 1988; The Jesuit Factor, 1989. *Clubs:* Whites, MCC, Pratts. *Recreations:* Painting.

RAWSON, Peter Robert; Group Secretary, Prudential Corporation plc, since 1989. *Career:* Prudential Corporation plc, Manager, Company Secretary's Office 1985; Assistant Secretary 1987; Group Secretary 1989. *Biog: b.* 13 May 1943. *Nationality:* British. *Directorships:* Prudential Registrars Limited 1988 (exec); Prudential Trustee Company Limited 1986 (exec); Plantagenet Limited 1986 (exec) Alternate. *Professional Organisations:* FCCA.

RAY, Colonel J B; Clerk, Curriers' Company.

RAY, P F; Secretary, Lowndes Lambert Group Holdings Limited.

RAYMOND, Hugh William; General Manager and Secretary, Scottish Widows' Fund and Life Assurance Society, since 1988; Company Secretary and Corporate Services. *Biog: b.* 2 June 1935. *Nationality:* British. *m.* 1958, Joan (née Cameron); 1 s. *Educ:* Royal High School, Edinburgh; Edinburgh University (MA Hons). *Professional Organisations:* FFA. *Clubs:* Caledonian. *Recreations:* Hill Walking, Curling, Philately.

RAYNER, D; Managing Director, Operations & Engineering, British Railways Board.

RAYNER, J A; Director, Morgan Grenfell & Co Limited.

RAZZALL, Tim; Chief Executive, since 1990, & Partner, since 1973, Frere Cholmeley, Company & Commercial, Corporate Finance, Mergers & Acquisitions. *Career:* Frere Cholmeley, Assistant Solicitor 1969-73. *Biog: b.* 12 June 1943. *Nationality:* British. *m.* 1982, Deirdre (née Taylor-Smith); 1 s; 1 d. *Educ:* St Paul's School; Worcester College, Oxford (BA). *Directorships:* CALA plc 1973 (non-exec); WEA Records Ltd 1984; Collins & Brown Ltd 1989; ISS (Holdings) Ltd 1989 (non-exec). *Other Activities:* Treasurer, Social & Liberal Democrat Party; Deputy Leader & Chairman of Policy & Resources Committee, London Borough of Richmond upon Thames. *Clubs:* National Liberal Club, MCC.

READ, Brigadier G; CBE; Clerk, Vintners' Company.

READ, Martin; Partner, Slaughter and May, since 1971; Company and Commercial Law. *Career:* Ham-

mond Suddards (Bradford), Articled Clerk 1960-62; Slaughter and May, Asst Solicitor 1963-70. *Biog: b.* 24 July 1938. *Nationality:* British. *m.* 1963, Laurette Gloria (née Goldsmith); 2 d. *Educ:* Queen Elizabeth's Grammar School, Alford, Lincs; Wadham College, Oxford (MA). *Professional Organisations:* Vice-Chm, The Law Society's Standing Ctee on Company Law; Past Chm, City of London Law Society, Company Law Sub-Ctee. *Clubs:* MCC, Royal St George's. *Recreations:* Golf, Lawn Tennis, Reading, Theatre.

READ, Martin James; Director, Sphere Drake Underwriting Management Limited, since 1982; Services Director. *Career:* Excess Insurance Group Ltd, Computer & Business Systems Manager 1974-78; Organisation & Methods Manager 1978-80; Underwriting Services Manager 1980-82. *Biog: b.* 23 May 1942. *Nationality:* British. *m.* 1962, Rosemary Anne; 1 s; 2 d. *Directorships:* Sphere Drake Underwriting Management Ltd 1982; Sphere Drake Insurance plc 1984; Sphere Drake Insurance Group plc 1986; Groves, John & Westrup (Underwriting) Limited 1986.

READER, C V; Chief Executive, Corporate Finance Division, Chancery plc, since 1990; Corporate Finance and BES. *Career:* Augustus Barnett & Son Limited, Financial Controller 1981-83; Laidlaw (Essex) Ltd & Laidlaw (Kent) Ltd, Financial Controller 1983-85; Entertainment Production Services plc Financial Controller 1985-86; Chancery plc, Corporate Finance Division, Executive 1986-88; Director 1988-90; Chief Executive 1990-. *Biog: b.* 7 January 1956. *Nationality:* British. *m.* 1982, Janet Caroline; 1 s; 1 d. *Educ:* Haberdashers Aske's School, Elstree, Hertfordshire; University of Kent at Canterbury (BA Hons Accounting). *Directorships:* Constellation Homes Companies 1989 (non-exec); Inca Gemstones plc 1989 (non-exec); Film Asset Developments plc 1988 (non-exec); London Town Assured Properties plc 1989 (non-exec); Worthing Premier Properties (Holdings) plc 1989 (non-exec); London Studio Properties (Holdings) plc 1989 (non-exec); Lomond Assured Properties (Holdings) plc 1989 (non-exec); Kent Assured Properties (Holdings) plc 1989 (non-exec); Broad Oak Pharmacy Companies 1990 (non-exec); Littlewood Nursery Schools (No 10) plc 1990 (non-exec). *Professional Organisations:* ACA. *Clubs:* Enfield Lawn Tennis Club.

REASON, David; Managing Director, Chemical Bank.

RECODER, E; Director, Barclays de Zoete Wedd Securities Ltd.

REDFERN, D A; Partner, Freshfields.

REDMAN, C T; Managing Director, County NatWest Limited, since 1988; Asset Finance Division. *Career:* National Westminster Bank plc, Career Banker.

Biog: b. 24 September 1933. *Nationality:* British. *m.* 1974, Josephine. *Directorships:* NatWest Property Ltd 1988 (exec) Chairman. *Other Activities:* Court Member, Worshipful Company of Farmers; Council Member, Shaftesbury Homes & Arethusa; Governor, West Surrey College of Art & Design. *Clubs:* Institute of Directors, Leander Club.

REDMAYNE, Mark John Studdert; Director, Sheppards, since 1988; Finance & Administration. *Career:* Ernst Whinney (Bahrain), Mgr 1976-78; BAII (Middle East), EC Mgr 1978-83; BAII plc, Dir 1983-88; BAII Holding Ltd, Company Sec 1986-88. *Biog: b.* 3 November 1948. *Nationality:* British. *m.* 1977, Irene (née Savage); 1 s; 3 d. *Educ:* Eton College. *Professional Organisations:* FCA. *Clubs:* Carlton. *Recreations:* Cricket, Football.

REDMAYNE, The Hon Sir Nicholas; Bt; Managing Director, Kleinwort Benson Limited, since 1989; Kleinwort Benson Securities Worldwide. *Career:* Grieveson Grant & Co 1965. *Biog: b.* 1 February 1938. *Nationality:* British. *m.* 1978, Christine Hewitt; 1 s; 1 d. *Educ:* Radley; RMA, Sandhurst. *Directorships:* Kleinwort Benson Ltd; Kleinwort Benson Group plc. *Recreations:* Skiing, Shooting.

REDMAYNE, Richard Charles Tunstall; Executive Director, County NatWest Wood Mackenzie & Co Ltd, since 1986; Corporate Stockbroking. *Career:* Brown Fleming & Murray Chartered Accountant Mgr 1956-62; Chaddesley Investments Ltd Dir 1962-66; Fielding Newson Smith & Co Ptnr 1966-86. *Biog: b.* 5 July 1938. *Nationality:* British. *m.* 1978, Patricia (née Burke); 4 s; 1 d. *Educ:* Eton College. *Directorships:* TVam plc 1989 (non-exec). *Other Activities:* Armourers and Brasiers. *Professional Organisations:* CA. *Clubs:* Braishfield Sports and Social, MCC. *Recreations:* Cricket, Shooting.

REDSHAW, Keith; Director, Land Securities plc, since 1990; Development, Portfolio, Management Activities. *Educ:* (BSc). *Professional Organisations:* FRICS.

REED, Adrian John Harbottle; Director, Hill Samuel Bank Ltd, since 1990; Corporate Finance. *Career:* Department of Environment 1975-76; J Henry Schroder Wagg & Co Ltd 1976-88. *Biog: b.* 8 May 1952. *Nationality:* British. *m.* 1984, Josie (née Henderson). *Educ:* Canford School; Brasenose College, Oxford (MA, BPhil). *Directorships:* Hill Samuel Securities Ltd 1988-1990 (exec); Moorgate Nominees Ltd since 1988 (exec). *Professional Organisations:* AIB.

REED, David Michael; Deputy Underwriter, Clifford Palmer Underwriting Agencies Ltd, since 1982; Insurance. *Career:* Carter Wilkes & Fane Ltd, Reinsurance Broker 1977-80; Syndicate 694 T J Hayday & Ors, Lloyds, Underwriting Assistant 1980-82; Syndicate 314 C F Palmer & Ors, Lloyds, Deputy Underwriter 1982-.

Biog: b. 26 August 1958. *Nationality:* British. *m.* 1983, Megan; 1 s; 1 d. *Educ:* Davenant Foundation Grammar School. *Directorships:* Clifford Palmer Underwriting Agencies Ltd 1984 (exec); Martin Ashley Underwriting Agencies Ltd (exec); Ashley Palmer & Hathaway Ltd (exec). *Professional Organisations:* Fellow, Chartered Insurance Institute. *Recreations:* Squash, Sailing, Hill Walking.

REED, J N; Partner, Pannell Kerr Forster.

REED, Paul Charles Rowe; Director, Argosy Asset Management plc, since 1986. *Career:* Friends' Provident Life Office, Asst Investment Sec 1958-82. *Biog: b.* 24 February 1942. *m.* 1974, Catherine (née O'Connell); 2 s. *Educ:* Reigate Grammar School. *Directorships:* Transcapital BV 1987 (exec); Clydesdale Investment Trust 1987 Alternate; Wemyss Coal Co 1988 (exec); Dublin City Properties 1988 (exec); Berland 1989 (exec). *Professional Organisations:* AIA. *Clubs:* Old Reigatians Rugby Club, Reigate Pilgrims Cricket Club, Racehorse Owners Assoc. *Recreations:* Horse-Racing & Breeding, Cricket, Rugby, Soccer, Wine & Food.

REES, Andrew Merfyn; Partner, Evershed Wells & Hind, Solicitors, since 1985; Head of Corporate Services Dept. *Career:* Evershed & Tomkinson 1980-85. *Biog: b.* 20 July 1954. *Nationality:* British. *m.* 1981, Monica; 4 s. *Educ:* Culford School; Fitzwilliam College, Cambridge (BA, MA). *Directorships:* Webb Lloyd Limited 1989 (non-exec); HROC Limited 1989 (non-exec). *Recreations:* Running, Shooting.

REES, Deborah Ann; Director, Kleinwort Benson Securities, since 1989; European Equities. *Career:* Grieveson Grant European Equities 1982-86. *Biog: b.* 26 August 1960. *Nationality:* British. *m.* 1988, Cooper. *Educ:* North London Collegiate School; St Edmund Hall, Oxford (BA Hons). *Recreations:* Committed Christian.

REES, J M; Partner, Waltons & Morse.

REES, Jeremy John; Director, IBJ International Ltd, since 1986; Data Processing & Accounting. *Career:* Peat Marwick Mitchell & Co, Supervising Audit Snr 1976-81; IBJ International Ltd 1981-. *Biog: b.* 13 February 1955. *Nationality:* British. *m.* 1980, Fiona Michelle (née Hudelist); 2 s. *Educ:* Felsted School; University of Southampton (LLB). *Professional Organisations:* ACA. *Recreations:* Cricket, Hockey, Squash.

REES, L S; Director, Larpent Newton & Co Ltd.

REES, Peter Wynford Innes; The Rt Hon Lord Rees of Goytre; QC, PC; Chairman, LASMO plc, since 1988; Director, since 1985. *Career:* Called to the Bar 1953; QC 1969; MP for Dover and Deal 1970-87; PPS to Solicitor General 1972; HM Treasury, Minister of State 1979-81; Minister for Trade 1981-83; Chief Secretary to HM Treasury 1983-85; Privy Councillor 1983; Created Baron 1987. *Biog: b.* 9 December 1926. *Nationality:* British. *m.* 1969, Anthea (née Hyslop). *Educ:* Stowe; Christ Church, Oxford. *Directorships:* LASMO plc 1988 (non-exec) Chm; EFG plc 1989 (non-exec) Chm; Leopold Joseph Holdings plc 1985 (non-exec) Dep Chm; James Finlay plc 1986 (non-exec); Fleming Mercantile Investment Trust 1987 (non-exec); Duty Free Confederation 1987 (non-exec) Chm; General Cable Limited 1990 (non-exec) Dir/Chm Desig; Westminster Industrial Brief 1990 (non-exec) Chm. *Other Activities:* Worshipful Company of Clockmakers; Member, Court and Council of The Museum of Wales; Member, Museum and Galleries Commission. *Clubs:* Boodles, Whites, Beefsteak.

REES-MOGG, William; Lord Rees-Mogg; Chairman & Proprietor, Pickering & Chatto Ltd, since 1981. *Career:* Financial Times 1952-60; Chief Leader Writer 1955-60; Asst Editor 1957-60; Sunday Times, City Editor 1960-61; Political and Economic Editor 1961-63; Deputy Editor 1964-67; The Times, Editor 1967-81; Times Newspapers Ltd, Mem Exec Board 1968-81; The Times Ltd, Director 1968-81; Times Newspapers Ltd, Director 1968-81; BBC Vice-Chairman, Board of Governors 1981-86; Arts Council of Great Britain, Chairman 1982-89; Sidgwick & Jackson, Chairman 1985-89; Broadcasting Standards Council, Chairman 1988-. *Biog: b.* 14 July 1928. *Nationality:* British. *m.* 1962, Gillian Shakespeare (née Morris); 2 s; 3 d. *Educ:* Charterhouse; Balliol College, Oxford (Brackenbury Scholar). *Directorships:* J Rothschild Holdings plc 1987 (non-exec); J Rothschild Investment Management 1987 (non-exec); London-Washington Publications 1984 (non-exec); M & G Group plc 1987 (non-exec); M & G Limited 1987 (non-exec); Pickering & Chatto Ltd 1981 (non-exec); Pickering & Chatto (Publishers) Ltd 1983 (non-exec); The General Electric Co plc 1981 (non-exec); Sinclair-Stevenson Ltd 1989 (non-exec); St James's Place Capital plc 1990 (non-exec). *Publications:* The Reigning Error: The Crisis of World Inflation (1974); An Humbler Heaven (1977); How to Buy Rare Books (1985); Blood in the Streets (with James Dale Davidson) (1988). *Clubs:* Garrick, Carlton. *Recreations:* Collecting.

REES-PULLEY, R; Partner, Ernst & Young.

REES SMITH, Peter; Partner, Holman Fenwick and Willan, since 1979; Crisis Management for and Advisor to third Party Liability Underwriter's in the Maritime Field; Handling Commercial Disputes for Shipowners with particular reference to Charterparty & Bill of Lading Claims; Maritime Pollution. *Career:* Herbert Smith & Co, Articled Clerk 1972-74; Holman Fenwick & Willan, Assistant Solicitor 1975-79; Partner 1979-. *Biog: b.* 17 February 1950. *Nationality:* British. *Educ:* Altrincham County Grammar School; University of Bristol (LLB 2:i). *Directorships:* RSR Ltd 1982 (non-

exec). *Clubs:* Wig & Pen. *Recreations:* Distance Running, Cycling, Sailing, Snow Skiing.

REESE, A S; Director, Charterhouse Bank Limited.

REEVE, John; Managing Director, Sun Life Corporation plc, since 1990. *Career:* Selbey Smith & Earle 1961-67; Peat Marwick McLintock 1967-68; Roneo Vickers Ltd Commercial Dir, Furniture & Systems Div 1968-; Mgr, Grp Financial Evaluation & Planning -1976; Wilkinson Match Ltd Dir, Accounting Services 1976-77; Amalgamated Metal Corporation Ltd Corp Controller 1977-80; The British Aluminium Company plc Grp Dir, Finance 1980-83; Mercantile House Holdings plc Grp Dir, Finance 1983-88; Sun Life Assurance Society plc Dep MD 1988. *Biog: b.* 13 July 1944. *Nationality:* British. *m.* Sally (née Welton); 1 d. *Educ:* Westcliff High School, Westcliff-on-Sea. *Directorships:* Sun Life Assurance Society plc 1989 MD; Sun Life Asset Management Ltd Chm; Sun Life Corporation plc; Sun Life Europe Ltd; HMC Group plc. *Other Activities:* Member, The Hundred Group of Chartered Accountants; Director, The English Concert; Council Member, Business in the Community. *Recreations:* Yachting, Music, Theatre.

REEVES, Christopher Reginald; Vice Chairman, Merrill Lynch International Ltd. *Career:* National Service, Rifle Brigade, Kenya & Malaya 1955-58; Bank of England 1958-63; Hill Samuel & Company Limited 1963-67; Morgan Grenfell & Co Limited 1968; Director 1970; Head of Banking Division 1972; Deputy Chairman and Deputy Chief Executive 1975; Joint Chairman 1985-87; Morgan Grenfell Holdings Ltd (now Morgan Grenfell Group plc), Deputy Chairman and Group Chief Executive 1985; Merrill Lynch Capital Markets, Senior Adviser to President 1988. *Biog: b.* 1936. *m.* 1965, Stella (née Whinney); 3 s. *Educ:* Malvern College. *Directorships:* Alliance International Insurance Co Limited; BICC plc; Oman International Bank, SARL; Andrew Weir & Company Limited; International Freehold Properties (Supervisory Board). *Other Activities:* Governor, Dulwich College Preparatory School; Companion, British Institute of Management; Member, City University Business Council. *Clubs:* Boodle's, Royal Southern Yacht Club, Itchenor Sailing Club. *Recreations:* Sailing, Shooting, Skiing.

REEVES, Ms Suzanne; Partner, Wedlake Bell, since 1986; Litigation/Construction. *Biog: b.* 13 August 1955. *Nationality:* British. *m.* 1983, W N Guppy; 1 s; 1 d. *Educ:* St Joseph's Convent, Reading; Exeter University (LLB Hons). *Professional Organisations:* Law Society. *Clubs:* Cannons. *Recreations:* Riding, Swimming.

REGAN, Edwin Thomas; General Manager, The Royal Bank of Scotland plc, since 1985; Administration/ Property. *Career:* The National Bank Ltd, Co Sec 1966-69; Williams & Glyn's Bank Ltd, Co Sec 1974-79; Asst Gen Mgr 1979-85. *Biog: b.* 16 January 1933. *Nationality:*

British. *m.* 1956, Marian (née Primarolo); 3 d. *Educ:* Plaistow County Grammar School. *Directorships:* The Cheque & Credit Clearing Co Ltd 1987 (non-exec) Chm. *Professional Organisations:* FCIB. *Clubs:* Forty. *Recreations:* Sport, Reading.

REGAN, Kevin; Managing Director, Money Markets, Sales & Trading, Merrill Lynch Europe Limited.

REID, A C; Director, Hill Samuel & Co Ltd.

REID, Alan; Director, Barclays de Zoete Wedd Ltd.

REID, Alexander J; Senior General Manager, The Royal Bank of Scotland plc.

REID, Alexander S; Group Director, MIM Ltd; Investment Trusts. *Directorships:* Drayton English & International Chairman; Drayton Consolidated (non-exec); City & Commercial Investment Trust Chairman; Cape & General Finance Ltd Chairman; City Merchants Bank Ltd (non-exec); MIM Development Capital Ltd Chairman; Delapena plc (non-exec).

REID, D; Partner, Allen & Overy.

REID, D H L; Director, Fleming Private Asset Management Limited.

REID, David Ernest; Tax Partner, Clifford Chance, since 1981; Corporate Commercial Taxation. *Biog: b.* 24 March 1952. *Nationality:* British. *Educ:* Stowe School; St John's College, Cambridge (MA Hons). *Other Activities:* New Bridge Street Consultants (Director); Wider Share Ownership Council (Trustee); ESOP Centre (Director). *Professional Organisations:* Institute of Taxation. *Publications:* Employee Share Ownership Plans in the UK - A Practitioner's Manual, 1990. *Clubs:* United Oxford & Cambridge University, Hurlingham. *Recreations:* Fly Fishing, Tennis, Squash.

REID, David R; WS; Partner, W & J Burness WS.

REID, George Malcolm; General Manager (Administration), Sun Life Assurance Society plc.

REID, Henry Anthony Caradoc; Director, Baring Securities Ltd, since 1988; Continental Europe. *Career:* Hill Samuel/Wood Mackenzie, Director (Europe) 1986-88; Warburg Investment Management, Manager 1981-86. *Biog: b.* 11 July 1958. *Nationality:* British. *Educ:* Lyceum Acpinum, Zuoz, Switzerland; London School of Economics (BSc Econ). *Other Activities:* Research Adviser to Greek Progress Fund SA.

REID, Malcolm; Chief Executive, Charlwood Leigh Ltd, since 1990; Investment Management. *Career:* Royal Navy 1959-64; Midland Bank plc 1964-66; RH Collier & Co Ltd, Sales Mgr 1966-69; Towry Law & Co Ltd,

Snr Fin Consultant 1969-75; Fairbridge Reid and Partners, Principal 1975-88; SKC Financial Services Ltd 1988-89. *Biog: b.* 13 January 1940. *Nationality:* British. *m.* 1971, Sheila Mary (née Welch); 1 s. *Educ:* King Edward's School, Fiveways, Birmingham. *Directorships:* FIMBRA 1986 (non-exec); Charlwood Leigh Ltd 1990 (exec); Charlwood Leigh Investment Management Ltd 1990 (exec); Charlwood Leigh Nominees Ltd 1990 (exec). *Other Activities:* FIMBRA; Rules & Legislation Ctee; Chairman, Financial Supervisory Rules Ctee. *Professional Organisations:* Member, Society of Technical Analysts. *Clubs:* Vintage Sports Car. *Recreations:* Vintage Cars, Fly Fishing, Conservation, Travel.

REID, Nigel; Partner, Linklaters & Paines.

REID, Sir Robert; CBE; Chairman, West Lambeth District Health Authority, since 1990. *Career:* Royal Tank Regiment 1941-46; London & North Eastern Railway, Traffic Apprentice 1947; Various including Goods Agent, Asst District Goods Mgr, District Passenger Mgr & Commercial Officer; Scottish Region of British Railways, Planning Mgr 1967; Doncaster Eastern Region, Div Mgr 1968; Southern Region, Dep Gen Mgr 1972; Southern Region, Gen Mgr 1974; British Railways Board, Full-time Member 1977; Chief Exec (Railways), responsible for Management of BR System 1989. *Nationality:* British. *m.* 1951, (widower since 1976); 1 s; 1 d. *Educ:* Malvern College; Brasenose Collge, Oxford (MA). *Directorships:* British Railways Board 1983 Vice Chm; 1983-87 & 1987-90 Chm. *Other Activities:* Master, Worshipful Company of Carmen, 1990; BR Boards Representative for Managing Board, Union of Intl Railways; Chm, Community of European Railways, 1988-89; Chm, Nationalised Industries Chairmen's Group, 1987. *Professional Organisations:* President, Chartered Institute of Transport, 1982-83; Companion, British Institute of Management; Fellow, Institute of Marketing; Honorary Fellow, Brasenose College, Oxford; Commander (Brother) of the Order of St John, 1986; Vice-President, Institute of Materials Handling, 1987; Doctor of Business Administration honoris causa, International Management Centre, Buckingham, 1988; President, Institute of Administrative Management, 1989; Honorary Colonel, 275 Railways Squadron, RCT(V), 1989; Doctor of Engineering honoris causa, Bristol University, 1990; Freeman, City of London; Immediate Past-Master, Company of Information Technologists. *Clubs:* Naval & Military. *Recreations:* Sailing, Shooting, Fishing & Mountaineering.

REID, Sir Robert Paul (Bob); Chairman, British Railways Board, since 1990. *Career:* Shell (Sarawak Oilfields & Brunei) 1956-59; Shell (Nigeria), Head of Personnel 1959-67; Africa & S Asia Regional Organisation (London) 1967-68; Shell & BP Services (Kenya), PA & Planning Adviser to Chm 1968-70; Shell (Nigeria), MD 1970-74; Shell UK Ltd, Chairman 1985-90. *Biog: b.* 1 May 1934. *m.* 1958, Joan Mary; 3 s. *Educ:* Bell

Baxter; St Andrews University (BA, LLD). *Directorships:* Thailand 1974-78 (exec); International Aviation & Products Trading 1978 (exec); Shell Co of Australia 1980 (exec); Supply & Marketing 1983 (exec); The Bank of Scotland 1987 (exec). *Other Activities:* Council Member, CBI; Board of Trustees, Civic Trust; Governing Council, Business in the Community & Scottish Business in Community; Foundation to Management Education; Fellow, Chartered Institute of Transport; Liveryman, Worshipful Company of Carmen. *Clubs:* MCC, Royal & Ancient GDF, Royal Melbourne, Frilford Heath Golf Club. *Recreations:* Golf, Sailing.

REID SCOTT, Malise; Director, Laurence Keen Ltd, since 1986; Investment Manager. *Career:* 11th Hussars (PAO) Subaltern 1967-70; Watney Mann & Co Ltd, Mgmnt Trainee 1970-72; Laurence Prust & Co Institutional Sales & Research, Investment Mgmnt 1972-86; Partner 1982-86. *Biog: b.* 28 September 1948. *Nationality:* British. *m.* 1978, Verity Fleur (née Comonte); 1 s; 1 d. *Educ:* Eton College. *Professional Organisations:* The International Stock Exchange. *Clubs:* Hurlingham. *Recreations:* Country Pursuits, Painting.

REIHL, Keith E; Vice President & Secretary-Treasurer, Euro Brokers Inc, since 1983. *Career:* Price Waterhouse (Pennsylvania), Senior Accountant 1974-80; (New York), Senior Audit Manager 1980-83; Euro Brokers Inc (New York), Vice President & Secretary-Treasurer 1983-. *Biog: b.* 20 April 1952. *Nationality:* American. *Educ:* Elizabeth Town College, Pennsylvania (BSc Accounting). *Professional Organisations:* Certified Public Accountant since 1976; Member, American Institute of Certified Public Accountants; Member, Pennsylvania Institute of Certified Public Accountants.

REILLY, Christopher L; Director, S G Warburg Securities, since 1982; International Corporate Finance. *Career:* McKinsey & Co Inc, Consultant 1974-77. *Biog: b.* 25 January 1948. *Nationality:* British. *m.* 1976, Chantal (née Davaux); 1 s; 2 d. *Educ:* Oundle School; Cambridge University (MA); INSEAD (MBA); Harvard Business School (MBA). *Other Activities:* International Stock Exchange Europe 1992 Ctee. *Clubs:* Roehampton. *Recreations:* Sport.

REILLY, J T; Partner, Cazenove & Co.

REINERT, Richard Arnim; Managing Director, Refco Overseas Ltd, since 1988; Futuresand Options Brokerage to Corporations & Financial Institutions.

REIS, J P; Executive Vice President and Manging Director Investment Banking, Kleinwort Benson North America Inc, since 1988; Investment Banking Activities with North American Companies, Cross Border Mergers & Acquisitions. *Career:* Darden School, University of Virginia, Morris Professor of Business Administration 1987-88; Morgan Stanley & Co Inc 1966-88; Managing

Director 1975-88; Principal 1975; Vice President 1973-74. *Biog: b.* 31 July 1942. *Nationality:* US Citizen. *m.* 1972, Kathryn (née Fortuin); 5 s. *Educ:* Washington & Lee University (BA Cum Laude); Harvard Business School (MBA with Distinction). *Directorships:* Philobolus Dance Company 1989 (non-exec). *Other Activities:* Fund Raising for various Schools and Political Campaigns. *Professional Organisations:* Bond Club of New York; Visiting Professor University of Virginia. *Publications:* The Fine Art of Valuation - The Mergers & Acquisitions Handbook, published by McGraw Hill (1987); Determining the Value of Restructuring Alternatives - Corporate Resructuring (1990). *Clubs:* The Links, NYC; The University Club, NYC; Bridgehampton Club, Bridgehampton, NY.

REISCH, Walter Anton; Executive Director, Group IT Services, International Commodities Clearing House.

REISS, R W; Partner, Cameron Markby Hewitt.

REIZENSTEIN, Anthony Jonathan; Director, SG Warburg & Co Ltd, since 1988; Corporate Finance. *Career:* Overseas Development Institute, Seconded to Nat Industrial Development Corp of Swaziland 1977-79; SG Warburg & Co Ltd, Various Posts in Banking & Corp Fin 1979-. *Biog: b.* 24 June 1956. *Nationality:* British. *m.* 1978, Susan Berenice (née Abrams); 2 s. *Educ:* St Paul's School; Clare College, Cambridge (Economics).

RELF, Diane; Partner, Clifford Chance.

REMNANT, The Hon Philip John; Director, Barclays de Zoete Wedd Limited, since 1990; Corporate Finance. *Career:* Peat Marwick Mitchell & Co, Latterly Manager 1976-82; Kleinwort Benson Limited 1982-90; Director 1988-90. *Biog: b.* 20 December 1954. *Nationality:* British. *m.* 1977, Caroline Elizabeth (née Cavendish); 1 s; 2 d. *Educ:* Eton College; New College, Oxford (MA). *Directorships:* Barclays de Zoete Wedd Limited 1990 (exec). *Other Activities:* Member of Council, The Marie Curie Memorial Foundation. *Professional Organisations:* ACA. *Recreations:* Cricket, Shooting.

REMNANT, James Wogan; The Rt Hon Lord Remnant; CVO; Chairman, National Provident Institution. *Career:* Touche Ross & Co, Ptnr 1958-70; Touche Remnant Holdings Ltd, MD 1970-81; Chm 1981-89. *Biog: b.* 23 October 1930. *Nationality:* British. *m.* 1953, Serena Jane (née Loehnis); 3 s; 1 d. *Educ:* Eton College. *Directorships:* Bank of Scotland (also Chm London Board) 1989; TR Pacific Investment Trust plc 1987 Chm; TR Technology Investment Trust plc 1959; Ultramar plc 1970 Dep Chm; Union Discount Company of London plc 1968; Westpool Investment Trust plc 1964. *Other Activities:* Australia & New Zealand Banking Group; (Mem, Intl Board of Advice); Royal Jubilee

Trusts (Trustee); National Council of YMCAs (Pres). *Professional Organisations:* FCA. *Clubs:* White's.

RENDELL, Edward G; Director, Bradstock Blunt & Crawley Ltd.

RENDELL, P F J; Director, Barclays de Zoete Wedd Securities Ltd.

RENDLE, M R; Non-Executive Director, Willis Corroon plc.

RENFREW, Glen; Managing Director, Reuters Holdings plc.

RENGER, M; Partner, Nabarro Nathanson, Solicitors; Environmental Law. *Career:* British Coal Legal Department, Environmental Solicitor 1980-90. *Biog: b.* 7 July 1955. *Nationality:* British. *m.* Caroline; 1 d. *Educ:* Emmanuel College, Cambridge (MA Law). *Professional Organisations:* Solicitor; Legal Associate of Royal Town Planning Institute.

RENNIE, G G; Director, Abbey Life Investment Services, since 1989; North American Equities. *Career:* Pannel Kerr Foster, Assistant Audit Manager 1971-78; Arthur Young McClelland Moore, Assistant Audit Manager 1978-79; Thomas C Gray, Financial Director 1979-82; Ivory & Sime plc, Divisional Director 1982-89; Abbey Life Investment Services, Director 1989-. *Biog: b.* 2 April 1953. *Nationality:* British. *m.* 1979, Lynda (née Fairgrieve); 1 s; 2 d. *Educ:* Institute of Scottish Chartered Accountants (CA). *Directorships:* Abbey Life Investment Services 1989 (exec). *Professional Organisations:* The Institute of Chartered Accountants of Scotland. *Recreations:* Squash, Tennis, Golf, Family.

RENNOLDSON, Gordon Harry; Vice President, Manufacturers Hanover Trust Company, since 1986; UK Corporate Banking. *Career:* Bankers Trust Company, Birmingham, Assistant Vice President, Relationship Manager 1979-84. *Biog: b.* 17 May 1948. *Nationality:* British. *m.* 1972, Heather; 2 s; 1 d. *Educ:* Watford Boys Grammar School; University of Salford (BSc Hons Business Operation and Control). *Clubs:* Cornhill.

RENSHAW, Peter Bernard Appleton; Partner, Slater Heelis, since 1982; Company Law. *Career:* Slater Heelis 1977-. *Biog: b.* 23 July 1954. *Nationality:* British. *m.* 1982, Patricia (née Caffrey); 1 s. *Educ:* Charterhouse; Selwyn College, Cambridge (Hons 1st). *Professional Organisations:* The Law Society. *Recreations:* Gardening, Walking, DIY.

RENTON, Simon Anthony; Partner, McKenna & Co, since 1986; Company Law and Insurance Law. *Career:* Slaughter and May, Articled Clerk 1973-75; Scottish Opera, Asst to Gen Administrator 1975-77; Bird & Bird, Solicitor & Ptnr 1977-83; British Gas,

Legal Adviser 1984; McKenna & Co, Solicitor 1985; Eurotunnel (Secondment), Legal Adviser 1986. *Biog: b.* 11 December 1948. *m.* 1977, Amanda (née Schrire); 2 d. *Educ:* Marlborough College; Trinity College, Oxford (BA). *Recreations:* Piano, Music.

RENWICK, George Frederick; Partner, Slaughter and May, since 1970; Commercial Taxation. *Career:* Northwestern University (Chicago), School of Law Teaching Associate 1962-63. *Biog: b.* 27 July 1938. *m.* 1974, Elizabeth Zoe (née Gordon); 1 d. *Educ:* Charterhouse; New College, Oxford (MA). *Other Activities:* Member, The Addington Society. *Professional Organisations:* The Law Society. *Clubs:* Athenaeum, MCC.

RENYI, John; Director, Singer & Friedlander Holdings Ltd, since 1980. *Career:* Singer & Friedlander Ltd, Trainee Exec 1948-49; Exec 1949-58; Investment Mgr 1958-61; Dir 1961-80. *Biog: b.* 23 July 1925. *Nationality:* British. *m.* 1963, Pierrette (née Lamuniere); 1 s. *Educ:* Chillon College, Glion, Switzerland; Geneva University (Lic Sc Econ). *Directorships:* Tokyo Trust SA 1969 Chm; Govett Oriental Investment Trust plc 1984; Singer & Friedlander Investment Management Ltd 1986. *Clubs:* RAC.

RESNICK, M J; Director, Allstate Reinsurance Co Limited.

RESTALL, R L W; Non-Executive Director, Aetna International (UK) Ltd.

REVELL, A; Director, Rowntree Limited.

REVELL, S M; Partner, Freshfields.

REW, Chris; Partner, Robson Rhodes.

REX, Paul James Laurence; Assistant General Manager, Head of Corporate Banking & Finance, Caisse Nationale de Credit Agricole, since 1989. *Career:* Chemical Bank, London Branch 1974-78; Various Positions, latterly Vice President - Ship Finance and Commodity Finance Europe/Scandanavia. *Biog: b.* 11 September 1952. *Nationality:* British. *m.* 1978, Josephine; 3 d. *Educ:* Kings School, Worcester; Queens College, Oxford (BA Honours German & French). *Clubs:* Royal Automobile, Overseas Bankers. *Recreations:* Theatre, Skiing, Squash.

REYNOLDS, David John Womersley; Partner, Clyde & Co, since 1985; Aviation, Offshore Oil & Gas. *Career:* Speechly Bircham, Articled Clerk/Solicitor 1976-81. *Biog: b.* 23 June 1953. *Nationality:* British. *m.* 1980, Anne Margaret (née Albone); 1 s; 1 d. *Educ:* Repton; Birmingham University (BSc). *Clubs:* RHKYC, CA, OGA. *Recreations:* Sailing, Cricket, Tennis, Squash.

REYNOLDS, Derek; Partner, Titmuss Sainer & Webb.

REYNOLDS, John Roderick; Director, J Henry Schroder Wagg & Co Limited, since 1984; Corporate Finance. *Career:* Price Waterhouse, Assistant Manager 1970-76; Schroder Wagg 1976-. *Biog: b.* 11 October 1948. *Nationality:* British. *m.* 1974, Jane (née Berridge); 2 s; 1 d. *Educ:* Oundle School; Imperial College, London University (BSc). *Professional Organisations:* ACA. *Clubs:* RAC, Hurlingham.

REYNOLDS, Michael J; Resident Partner in Brussels, Allen & Overy, since 1979; All Aspects of EEC Law; Head of EEC Unit, since 1988; Head of Eastern European Group, since 1989. *Career:* Allen & Overy, Asst Solicitor, Litigation Dept 1976-78; EC Commission 1978. *Biog: b.* 8 October 1950. *Nationality:* British. *Educ:* Felsted School, Essex; University of Keele (IIi Degree in Law & Politics). *Other Activities:* Member, British Invisible Exports Council 1992 Committee; Vice-Chairman, International Bar Association's Competition & Trade Committee. *Professional Organisations:* Solicitor of Supreme Court. *Publications:* Merger Control in EEC (EEC Chapter), 1988; Numerous Articles on EC Law, including Exclusive Purchasing Contracts, The International Contract, 1980; Merger Control in the EEC, Journal of World Trade Law, 1983; Extraterritorial Aspects of Mergers and Joint Ventures, International Business Lawyer, 1985; The New Form A/B: Notifying Agreements under Article 85, Fordham Corporate Law Institute, Yearbook 1985; Trade Associations and the EEC Competition Rules, Swiss Review of International Competition Law, 1985; The EEC Merger Control Regulation - an update, International Financial Law Review, 1987; 1992 and Lawyers, Solicitors' European Newsletter, 1988; The Recognition of Diplomas Directive, International Financial Law Review, 1988; EEC Merger Control at the Cross-roads, Acquisitions Monthly, 1988; Deadlock in Brussels, Mergers and Acquisitions International, 1988; The Regulation of the Securities Industry and 1992 ABA Institute Journal, 1989. *Clubs:* Cercle Royal Gaulois (Brussels), Club St Anne (Brussels).

REYNOLDS, Sir Peter; Director, Guardian Royal Exchange Assurance.

REYNOLDS, R F; Director, Hill Samuel & Co Ltd.

RHEAD, Colin K; Partner, Moores Rowland.

RHODES, Anthony John David; Executive Director, Bank of America International Limited.

RHODES, Philip John; Assistant General Manager, General Accident Fire & Life Assurance Corporation plc, since 1987; London Market. *Career:* General Accident plc Administration Controller 1978-85; City Mgr 1985-87. *Biog: b.* 23 August 1937. *Nationality:* British. *m.* 1965, Madeleine (née Blaza); 2 d. *Educ:* Lincoln City School. *Directorships:* MBL (Market Building Limited) 1989 (exec). *Other Activities:* Worshipful Company of Insurers. *Professional Organisations:* ACII. *Clubs:* Royal Commonwealth Society. *Recreations:* Golf, Tennis, Music.

RHODES, Richard John; Director, Warburg Securities, since 1986; Fixed Income Sales. *Career:* Legal & General Assurance 1967-70; Rowe & Pitman, Ptnr 1970-86. *Biog: b.* 12 February 1946. *m.* 1973, Barbara Mary (née Prichard); 2 s. *Educ:* Queen Elizabeth Grammar School; Durham University (BSc Hons). *Professional Organisations:* FIA; Member, The International Stock Exchange. *Recreations:* Tennis.

RICE, James; Partner, Linklaters & Paines, since 1989; Finance and Banking. *Career:* Linklaters & Paines since Articles. *Biog: b.* 10 March 1957. *Nationality:* British. *m.* 1987, Tessa; 2 d. *Educ:* Gravesend School for Boys; Christ Church, Oxford (1st Jurisprudence). *Professional Organisations:* Law Society.

RICE, Ladislas Oskar; Director, The Burton Group plc, since 1969. *Biog: b.* 20 January 1926. *Nationality:* British. *Directorships:* The Burton Group Pension Trustee Limited 1980; Stanley Gibbons Holdings plc; Data Recall Limited; Drayton Commercial Investment Company Limited; Drayton Consolidated Investment plc; Drayton Japan Trust plc; The Foundation for Management Education; Heredities Limited; Huntingdon Research Centre plc; National Trust (Enterprises) Limited; Polymark International plc; Scudden New Europe Fund Inc; Sovereign High Yield Investments Company NV.

RICE, M D; Director, Nicholson Chamberlain Colls Limited.

RICE, Michael; Treasurer, Citibank NA.

RICH, Charles; Partner, Bacon & Woodrow; Pension Funds, Takeovers/Mergers, FSA Compliance Officer. *Career:* Unilever, Trainee 1950-52; National Service RAF 1952-54; Prudential Assurance, Actuarial Trainee 1954-61; Bacon & Woodrow, Actuary 1961-65. *Biog: b.* 10 December 1934. *Nationality:* British. *Educ:* Watford Central School; Bushey Grammar School. *Other Activities:* Worshipful Company of Actuaries; Freeman, The City of London. *Professional Organisations:* FIA; ASA; FPMI; ATII. *Clubs:* RAC, Phiatus. *Recreations:* Chess, Bridge, Tennis.

RICH, Michael William; Partner, McKenna & Co, since 1977; Corporate Law. *Career:* McKenna & Co, Articled Clerk 1969-71; Asst Solicitor 1971-77. *Biog: b.* 23 July 1947. *m.* 1970, Eilis (née Clancy); 4 d. *Educ:* St Benedict's School, Ealing; St John's College, Cambridge (MA). *Directorships:* AC Nielsen Company Ltd 1983 (non-exec). *Professional Organisations:* The Law Society; Institute of Directors.

RICHARDS, Andrew Philip; Partner, Freshfields, since 1987. *Career:* Freshfields, Articled Clerk 1978-80; Asst Solicitor 1980-87. *Biog: b.* 28 January 1956. *Nationality:* British. *m.* 1983, Sarah Hope (née Edwards). *Educ:* Yardley Court School, Tonbridge, Kent; Sutton Valence School, Kent; Lincoln College, Oxford (MA). *Other Activities:* City of London Solicitors Company. *Professional Organisations:* Law Society. *Recreations:* Golf, Skiing, Fishing.

RICHARDS, G F; Director, Maxwell Pergamon Publishing Corporation plc.

RICHARDS, Gary Alan; Group Controller, Rea Brothers Limited.

RICHARDS, H; Partner, Nabarro Nathanson.

RICHARDS, Jane; Partner (Litigation), Frere Cholmeley.

RICHARDS, Jean E; Partner, Beachcroft Stanleys.

RICHARDS, Martin Edgar; Partner, Clifford Chance, since 1973; Corporate. *Career:* Clifford-Turner 1967-. *Biog: b.* 27 February 1943. *Nationality:* British. *m.* 1969, Caroline (née Billing Lewis); 1 s; 1 d. *Educ:* Harrow School. *Recreations:* Skiing, Fishing.

RICHARDS, Paul; Executive Director, Samuel Montagu & Co Limited, since 1980.

RICHARDS, Paul Howard; Managing Director, Shire Trust Ltd, since 1988; Corporate Finance & Banking. *Biog: b.* 17 July 1949. *Nationality:* British. *m.* 1983, Jeanette Marie (née Cardozo); 1 s; 1 d. *Educ:* Selwyn College, Cambridge (MA); London Business School (MSc). *Directorships:* Beaverco plc 1988 (non-exec). *Other Activities:* Member of Council, Society of Investment Analysts. *Professional Organisations:* ACIB; AMSIA. *Publications:* UK & European Share Price Behaviour: The Evidence, 1979.

RICHARDS, R L; Director, Foreign & Colonial Management Ltd.

RICHARDS, W S C; Non-executive Director, Steel Burrill Jones Group plc.

RICHARDS RODDEY, John Gardiner; LOM, DFC; Executive Vice President, NCNB National Bank, since 1990; Group Executive. *Career:* USAF, Captain 1959-65; USAF Reserve, Colonel 1965-89; NCNB (Charlotte, NC) VP, International Banking 1965-73; NCNB (London), General Manager 1974-76; NCNB (Charlotte), Corporate Finance Executive 1977-84; NCNB Investment Banking Company (Charlotte, NC), MD 1985-90. *Biog: b.* 12 February 1937. *Nationality:* American. *m.* 1961, Gail (née Baker); 2 s; 2 d. *Educ:* United States Naval Academy (BS Engineering). *Directorships:* NCNB Investment Banking Company 1985 MD; NCNB Equity Corporation 1984 Pres; NCNB Venture Corporation 1984 Pres; NCNB Lease Investments 1983 Chm; Panmure Gordon Bankers Ltd 1990 (exec); Panmure Gordon & Co 1990 (exec). *Clubs:* Overseas Bankers. *Recreations:* Soccer (Referee), Shooting, Fishing, Flying.

RICHARDSON, Baden Colin; Director, Granville & Co, since 1988; Managing Director, Private Client Stockbroking. *Career:* Vickers da Costa, Director 1968-85; Scrimgeour Vickers, Partner 1985-86. *Biog: b.* 11 August 1941. *Nationality:* British. *m.* 1963, Shirley (née Lucas); 3 s. *Educ:* Chigwell School. *Directorships:* Granville Davies & Co 1988 (exec); Granville Investment Management 1989 (exec); Torevell Mahon Granville Ltd 1989 (exec). *Professional Organisations:* Member, Securities Association. *Clubs:* Royal Ocean Racing Club. *Recreations:* Sailing, Skiing, Gardening.

RICHARDSON, Charles; Director, 3i plc, since 1989; Regional Director for Scotland and North of England. *Career:* 3i plc, Local Director, Cardiff 1985-88; 3i plc, Director, Manchester 1988-90. *Biog: b.* 26 October 1953. *Nationality:* British. *m.* 1982, Claire; 2 s. *Educ:* Abbeydale Boys Grammar Schhol, Sheffield; University of Bristol (BSc Econ); Manchester Business School (MBA). *Directorships:* 3i plc 1989 (exec). *Other Activities:* Member of Council, Manchester Business School. *Clubs:* St James's Club, Manchester. *Recreations:* Sailing.

RICHARDSON, H F; Director, S G Warburg & Co Ltd.

RICHARDSON, Ian; Partner, Hepworth & Chadwick.

RICHARDSON, Karen; Partner, Travers Smith Braithwaite.

RICHARDSON, Lindsey Anne; Director, County NatWest Investment Management Ltd, since 1987. *Career:* S G Warburg & Co Ltd, Mgr 1979-83; Citicorp Int Banking Ltd, Mgr 1983-84. *Biog: b.* 31 July 1955. *Nationality:* British. *m.* 1983, (div); 1 d. *Educ:* Cheadle Hulme School; Somerville College, Oxford (MA, MLitt). *Recreations:* Swimming, Tennis.

RICHARDSON, Mark Rushcliffe; Director, Lazard Brothers & Co Ltd, since 1985; Head of Institutional Fund Investment. *Career:* Lazard Brothers, Fund Mgr to Dir 1969-. *Biog: b.* 17 September 1947. *m.* 1973, Cherry Victoria (née Smart); 1 s; 2 d. *Educ:* Wellington

College; Christ Church, Oxford (BA Hons). *Clubs:* Boodle's. *Recreations:* Skiing, Country Pursuits.

RICHARDSON, Sir Michael; KB; Chairman, Smith New Court plc, since 1990. *Career:* Drayton Group 1949-52; Panmure Gordon, Partner 1952-71; Cazenove & Co, Partner 1971-81; N M Rothschild & Sons Limited, Managing Director 1981-90. *Biog: b.* 9 April 1925. *Nationality:* British. *m.* 1949, Octavia (née Mayhew); 1 s; 2 d. *Educ:* Harrow School; Kent School, USA. *Directorships:* Anglo-Scottish Amalgamated Corporate Limited 1972; Derby Trust Limited 1981 Chairman; Drayton Far Eastern Trust (Finance) Limited 1964; Drayton Far Eastern Trust plc 1961; English & International Trust plc 1961; Hyde Park Finance (Holdings) Ltd 1981; Hyde Park Finance Limited 1981; Mithras Investment Trust plc 1990; New Court Nominees Limited 1987; N M Rothschild & Sons Limited 1990 Vice Chairman; N M Rothschild & Sons (Wales) Ltd 1988 Chairman; Smith New Court plc 1990 Chairman; The Rank Foundation 1983; The Savoy Hotel plc 1979; Rothschild Continuation Limited 1989; Sedgwick Group plc 1984; NMR International NV 1983; Rothschild North America Inc 1983. *Other Activities:* Worshipful Company of Gunmakers. *Clubs:* Island Sailing Club. *Recreations:* Sailing.

RICHARDSON, Michael John; Director, Chartered WestLB Ltd, since 1986; Corporate Finance. *Career:* Price Waterhouse Audit/Investigation 1960-63; ICFC Investment Dept, ICFC Corp Fin Ltd (now 3i Corp Fin Ltd), MD 1963-8; Shandwick Communications Ltd Fin Dir 1980-81; Standard Chartered Merchant Bank Ltd Asst Dir 1980-83; Merchant Banking Div (India), Chief Exec 1983-86; Director, Corporate Finance 1986-. *Biog: b.* 28 March 1935. *Nationality:* British. *m.* 1959, Helen Patricia (née Bray); 1 s; 1 d. *Educ:* Epsom College. *Directorships:* CWB Nominees Ltd; Chartered WestLB Nominees Ltd. *Other Activities:* Liveryman, Worshipful Company of Chartered Accountants in England & Wales. *Professional Organisations:* FCA. *Publications:* Going Public, 1973. *Recreations:* Gardening, Swimming.

RICHARDSON, Michael Norman; Partner, Lawrence Graham, since 1985; Corporate Finance and Corporate Taxation. *Career:* Coward Chance & Co Solicitor 1960-62; Jaques & Co Ptnr 1963-73; Henry Ansbacher & Co Ltd Dep Chm 1970-77; Richardson & Oakley Ptnr 1977-85; Sarasota Technology plc Non-Exec Dir 1985-87. *Biog: b.* 23 February 1935. *m.* 1976, Rosemarie (née Moers); 4 d. *Educ:* Dulwich College; College of Law. *Directorships:* Several including A H Al-Zamil & Sons (UK) Ltd; Amp of Great Britain Ltd; GTE Products (UK) Ltd. *Professional Organisations:* The Law Society; Institute of Directors. *Clubs:* Oriental, MCC. *Recreations:* All Sports, Gardening.

RICHARDSON, P; Partner, Nabarro Nathanson.

RICHARDSON, P E; Credit & Loan Manager, Banca Popolare di Milano.

RICHARDSON, T G; Marketing Director, Pharmaceuticals Division, The Boots Co plc.

RICHARDSON-BUNBURY, Ms A M; Director, County NatWest Investment Management Ltd.

RICHES, D I; Director, Smith New Court plc.

RICHES, David Kenneth; Group Company Secretary, NM Rothschild & Sons Limited, since 1977. *Biog: b.* 19 July 1938. *Nationality:* British. *Professional Organisations:* FCIS, FCIB.

RICHMOND, C; Partner, Field Fisher Waterhouse.

RICHMOND-WATSON, Anthony Euan; Director, Morgan Grenfell & Co Ltd.

RICKARD, J; Partner, Nabarro Nathanson.

RICKARD, Miss Josanne; Partner, Freshfields.

RICKARDS, Adrian Charles; Executive Director, Midland Montagu Asset Management, since 1986; Investment Management - Administration. *Career:* Chapman Rowe 1953-55; RAPC (National Service) 1955-57; Quilter & Co 1957-65; Samuel Montagu & Co Ltd (inc MIM Ltd formerly Drayton Montagu Portfolio Mgmnt) Asst Dir, Securities Dept 1965-86. *Biog: b.* 4 May 1937. *Nationality:* British. *m.* 1960, Sheila Eleanor Margaret (née Townsend); 1 s. *Educ:* Aristotle School, London. *Directorships:* MMAM (Holdings) 1986 (exec); Accepting Houses Committee, Standing Ctee of Securities Mgrs 1986-87 Chm. *Recreations:* Squash, Tennis.

RICKETT, Peter David; Chairman & Managing Director, Rickett & Co Limited. *Career:* R Nivison & Co, Partner 1961-87; Corporate Finance & Administrative Director 1987-88; Rickett & Co, Chairman & Managing Director 1988-. *Biog: b.* 16 January 1937. *Nationality:* British. *m.* 1967, Sarah Jessica (née Norman); 2 d. *Educ:* St Andrews School, Eastbourne; Eton College; Trinity College, Cambridge. *Professional Organisations:* Member, Stock Exchange. *Clubs:* Waites, Pratts, Royal Yacht Squadron, St Moritz Tobogganing Club. *Recreations:* Dog Walking.

RICKSON, Derrick Gordon; Manager, Euro Brokers Ltd, since 1987; Administration. *Career:* National Provincial Bank Clerk 1957-61; Bank of America NTSA Dealer 1961-64; Leopold Joseph & Sons Ltd Dealer 1964-67; Banque Paribas Dealer/Chief Dealer 1967-69; Harlow Ueda Savage Broker FX Dir 1969-86. *Biog: b.* 21 January 1941. *m.* 1963, Pat (née Daniell); 4 d. *Educ:* Chislehurst & Sidcup Grammar School. *Other Activities:* Secretary/Treasurer, Foreign Exchange & Currency Deposit Brokers Assoc; RNLI Bromley Ctee. *Professional Organisations:* Forex Association. *Recreations:* Squash, Classical Music.

RIDDELL, Sir John Charles Buchanan; CVO; Deputy Chairman, Credit Suisse First Boston Ltd, since 1990. *Career:* IBRD, Loan Officer 1969-71; First Boston (Europe) Ltd, Director 1972-78; Credit Suisse First Boston Ltd, Executive Director 1978-85; TRH The Prince & Princess of Wales, Private Secretary & Treasurer 1985-90. *Biog: b.* 3 January 1934. *Nationality:* British. *m.* 1969, Sarah (née Richardson); 3 s. *Educ:* Eton; Christ Church, Oxford (MA). *Directorships:* Northern Rock Building Society 1990 (non-exec). *Professional Organisations:* CA. *Clubs:* Garrick, Northern Counties.

RIDDELL-CARRE, Ralph John; Partner, Ernst & Young, since 1974. *Biog: b.* 8 October 1941. *Nationality:* British. *m.* 1972, Valerie (née Tickler); 3 s. *Educ:* Harrow School. *Professional Organisations:* CA.

RIDDELL-CARRE, Walter Gervase; Director, Edinburgh Fund Managers plc, since 1988; Europe. *Career:* Kleinwort Benson Ltd, Mgr, Pension Funds 1968-72; Edinburgh Fund Managers 1972-. *Biog: b.* 10 January 1944. *Nationality:* British. *m.* 1975, Carolyn (née Ricketts); 2 s. *Educ:* Harrow. *Other Activities:* Member, Queen's Body Guard Scotland (Royal Company Archers). *Professional Organisations:* Institute of Chartered Accountants of Scotland. *Clubs:* New (Edinburgh), Honourable Company of Edinburgh Golfers, North Berwick Golf Club. *Recreations:* Golf.

RIDEHALGH, Kenneth; Partner, Beachcroft Stanleys.

RIDER, A T B; Partner, Field Fisher Waterhouse.

RIDER, F A G; Clerk, Tylers' & Bricklayers' Company.

RIDGE, J A; Under Warden, The Worshipful Company of Framework Knitters.

RIDGE, Peter; Partner, Neville Russell.

RIDGEON, David Howard; Director, Finance, Control and Compliance, Svenska International plc, since 1989; Finance, Accounts. *Career:* Quilter Goodison Company Limited, Director, Finance & Administration 1985-89; Coopers & Lybrand, Senior Consultant, MCS 1984-85; Bank of England, Adviser, Banking Supervision Division (Secondment) 1982-84; Audit, to Audit Manager 1975-82. *Biog: b.* 5 December 1952. *Nationality:* British. *m.* 1981, Cherryll (née Downer); 1 s; 1 d. *Educ:* New College, Oxford (MA Modern Languages); Haberdashers' Aske's School. *Directorships:* Svenska International plc 1989 (exec); Quilter Goodison Company Limited 1988-89 (exec). *Other Activities:* Member,

TSA Client Money Working Party. *Professional Organisations:* Associate, Institute of Chartered Accountants in England and Wales. *Recreations:* Rowing, Golf, Music, Fine Wines, Literature.

RIDGWELL, C J; Director, Allstate Reinsurance Co Limited.

RIDGWELL, Robert William; Chairman, The MDA Group plc, since 1988. *Career:* F J Meekins and Partners Quantity Surveyors, Quantity Surveyor 1953-60; Monk Dunstone Associates Quantity Surveyors, Senior Surveyor 1960-68; Associate 1968-70; Partner 1970-85; Director 1985-88. *Biog: b.* 24 June 1928. *Nationality:* British. *m.* 1959, Enid Mary; 1 s; 1 d. *Educ:* Highgate School; Regent Street Polytechnic; College of Estate Management, London University. *Directorships:* MDA Group plc 1985 (exec); MDA Group plc 1988 (exec) Chm; Monk Dunstone Associates 1970-85 (exec) Partner. *Professional Organisations:* ARICS; FRICS. *Clubs:* MCC, Hadley Wood Golf Club. *Recreations:* Golf, Football, Cricket, Tennis, Squash.

RIDING, Frederick Michael Peter; General Manager, Money Transmission & Bank Relations, UK Retail Banking Div, Lloyds Bank plc, since 1990; Correspondent Banking/UK Domestic & International Operations/Money Transmission. *Career:* Procter & Gamble Ltd, Marketing 1965-67; British Aluminium Co Ltd, Marketing 1967-69; Goode Durrant & Murray Ltd, Credit Mgr 1969-73; Chemical Bank, Account Exec 1973-75; (New York), Account Exec 1975-77; P T Multicor (Indonesia), Pres 1977-78; Chemical Bank (South East Asia), VP 1978-81; (Asia), Snr VP 1981-83; Lloyds Bank International Ltd Principal Mgr, Far East Div 1983-85; Lloyds Bank plc (Asia), Gen Mgr 1985-87; Lloyds Bank plc, General Manager, Trade Finance 1987-89; Lloyds Bank plc, General Manager, Commercial Banking 1989-90. *Biog: b.* 11 September 1943. *Nationality:* British. *m.* 1967, Vivian (née Dodds); 2 s; 1 d. *Educ:* Barnard Castle, Co Durham; Leeds University (BA Hons). *Other Activities:* Mem, Ship Mortgage Finance Company Advisory Committee. *Clubs:* Royal Lytham & St Annes Golf Club, Wildernesse Golf Club. *Recreations:* Theatre, Opera, Golf.

RIDLEY, Matthew White; Viscount Ridley; Chairman, Northern Rock Building Society.

RIDLEY, Sir Adam; Director, Hambros Bank Ltd, since 1985. *Career:* Accepted by Foreign Office but Seconded to Home Civil Service 1965; Department of Foreign Affairs, Economist 1965-70; Harkness Fellow, University of California, Berkeley, USA, on study leave 1968-69; HM Treasury, Economist 1970-71; Central Policy Review Staff ('Think Tank') No 10 Downing Street, Economist, responsible for studies on Nationalised Industries, Regional Policy, Energy Policy, Public Spending, Computer Industry 1971-74; Economic Adviser to Leader of Conservative Party & Shadow Cabinet 1974-79; Assistant Director and Director, Conservative Research Dept, Research into and preparation of the future Government's economic & industrial politics 1979; HM Treasury, Special Adviser to Chancellor of the Exchequer, Sir Geoffrey Howe 1979-83; Special Adviser to Chancellor of the Exchequer, Nigel Lawson 1983-84; Special Adviser to Lord Gowrie, Chancellor of the Duchy of Lancaster, Minister for the Arts & Civil Service 1985; Hambros Bank & Hambros plc, Executive Director 1985. *Biog: b.* 14 May 1942. *Nationality:* British. *m.* 1981, Margaret Anne (née Passmore); 3 s. *Educ:* Eton College; Oxford University (1st Class Hons Politics, Philosophy & Economics). *Directorships:* Clovelly Estate Co Ltd; Hambro Scotland Ltd 1988; Hambros Bank Ltd 1985; Hambros plc 1985; Soc Gen Strauss Turnbull & Co Ltd 1986 (non-exec); 1988 Dep Chm; The Sunday Correspondent Ltd 1988 (non-exec); The Sunday Newspaper Publishing plc 1988; ALM Ltd 1990. *Clubs:* Garrick.

RIDLEY, D; Director, Williams de Broë; Mining Compliance. *Career:* Williams de Broë 1966-. *Biog: b.* 25 May 1941. *Nationality:* British. *m.* 1968, Caroline (née Seton-Karr); 3 s. *Educ:* Stowe; Trinity College, Dublin (BComm, BA). *Directorships:* Williams de Broë 1970 (exec). *Clubs:* City University Club.

RIDLEY, D N; Partner, Waltons & Morse.

RIDLEY, Giles Mark; Partner, Slaughter and May, since 1978; Company & Commercial Law. *Career:* Slaughter and May 1969-. *Biog: b.* 17 August 1946. *Nationality:* British. *m.* 1970, Jane (née Daish); 2 s; 1 d. *Educ:* Winchester College; Magdalene College, Cambridge (MA, LLB). *Other Activities:* Mem, The Livery of the Weavers' Company. *Professional Organisations:* The Law Society; Associate of The Royal College of Organists. *Recreations:* Music, Sailing.

RIDLEY, N A; Partner, Hill Taylor Dickinson.

RIDLEY, P R; Partner, Arthur Andersen & Co Chartered Accts.

RIGG, John Eric Sagar; Director, Kleinwort Grieveson Investment Management Ltd, since 1978; Marketing/Business Development. *Career:* DQ Henriques & Co Investment Analyst 1964-70; Kleinwort Benson Group Investment Mgmnt, Snr Mgr 1971-78. *Biog: b.* 8 August 1942. *Nationality:* British. *m.* 1965, Inger (née Helsgaun); 1 s; 1 d. *Educ:* Charterhouse; University of Newcastle upon Tyne (BA). *Directorships:* Kleinwort Benson Investment Management KK (Japan) 1987 (non-exec). *Recreations:* Gardening, Reading.

RIIKONEN, (Yrja Pekka) Juhani; Deputy Managing Director, Skopbank, since 1989. *Career:* Skopbank, Hel-

sinki, Analyst 1970-74; Head of Accounting 1974-76; Second VP 1976-77; VP 1977-82; Snr VP 1982-83; Dep Mem of the Board 1983-84; Gen Mgr, Mem of the Board 1984-89; Dep MD, Mem of the Board 1989-. *Biog: b.* 1 September 1948. *Nationality:* Finnish. *m.* Soili; 1 s; 1 d. *Educ:* (BSc Econ). *Directorships:* Finnish Real Estate Bank Ltd 1985 Mem of Supervisory Bd; Interpolator Ltd 1988 Chm of the Bd; Tampella Ltd 1987 Mem of the Bd; Skopbank International SA 1989 Mem of the Bd.

RIJNVIS, A J; Director, Calor Group plc.

RILEY, Barry John; Investment Editor, Financial Times, since 1987; Investment, Personal Finance, Fund Management. *Career:* Investors Chronicle, Editorial Assistant 1964-66; Morning Telegraph, Sheffield, Deputy City Editor in the London Office 1966-67; Financial Times 1967-; Various including Editor, Lex Column 1977-82; Financial Editor 1982-86; Investment Editor and Columnist 1987-. *Biog: b.* 13 July 1942. *Nationality:* British. *m.* 1969, Anne (née Barry); 2 s; 1 d. *Educ:* Jesus College, Cambridge (BA). *Other Activities:* Member of the Domestic Promotions Committee, British Invisible Exports Council; Member, CBI Wider Share Ownership Task Force 1990.

RILEY, Ms Helen; Partner, Robson Rhodes, since 1986; Corporate & Business Taxation. *Career:* Robson Rhodes, Audit Trainee 1976-79; Tax Senior Manager 1979-83; Tax Consultant, International and Corporate Tax 1983-86. *Biog: b.* 26 November 1954. *Nationality:* British. *Educ:* Notre Dame High School; University College, London (LLB Hons). *Other Activities:* Treasurer & Council Member, Statute Law Society. *Professional Organisations:* Fellow, Institute of Chartered Accountants in England & Wales; Associate, Institute of Taxation. *Recreations:* Opera, Travel, Theatre.

RILEY, John Derek; Executive Director Sales, Allied Dunbar.

RILEY, Miss Kathryn M; Executive Director, County NatWest Limited, since 1988; Personnel. *Career:* Morgan Guaranty Trust Company of New York 1973-78; Head of Personnel Administration & Recruitment 1978-81; The Royal Bank of Canada Mgr, Personnel UK, Ireland, Nordic 1982-84; Mgr Compensation Europe, Middle East, Africa, 1984-85. *Biog: b.* 30 March 1951. *Nationality:* British. *Educ:* St Pauls, Sheffield; Polytechnic of North London (HND in Business Studies). *Professional Organisations:* Chm, Women in Banking 1983-85; Freedom of the City of London 1985; FIPM. *Clubs:* Women in Banking. *Recreations:* Chinese Health Arts, Shiatsu.

RILEY, Saxon; Director, Sedgwick Group plc.

RILEY, Stephen Martin; Partner, Clay & Partners, since 1985; Advice to Corporate Clients on Pensions & Associated Matters. *Career:* Commercial Union, Actuarial Trainee 1972-78; Actuary (Pensions Department) 1978-84; Clay & Partners, Actuary 1984-85. *Biog: b.* 22 April 1951. *Nationality:* British. *m.* 1984, Susan (née Baxter); 2 s. *Educ:* Brighton, Hove & Sussex Grammar School; University College London (BSc Hons Statistics). *Other Activities:* Liaison Officer, University College London. *Professional Organisations:* FIA; Member, Association of Consulting Actuaries; Member, International Actuarial Association. *Clubs:* RAC, Sussex County Cricket Club. *Recreations:* Cricket, Gardening, Golf, Rugby Football, Skiing, Travel.

RIMMER, Kenneth; Vice President & Manager, Bank of California (Mitsubishi Bank), since 1980; Correspondent Banking. *Career:* Australia & New Zealand Bank, Officer 1956-69; Bank Julius Baer, Officer 1969-73; The Bank of California 1973-. *Biog: b.* 30 January 1940. *Nationality:* British. *m.* 1966, Janice Lynne (née Pigrome); 1 s; 1 d. *Educ:* Buckhurst Hill County High School. *Professional Organisations:* ACIB. *Recreations:* Piano, Bowls, Reading.

RINEHART, Jonathan; Non-Executive Director, Ogilvy Adams & Rinehart.

RING, C J; Director, Wise Speke Ltd; Director in Charge - London Office Corporate Employee Services. *Career:* Coopers & Lybrand Chartered Accountants, Articles 1974-78; GKN Export Services, Financial Accountant 1978-80; Scrimgeour Kemp-Gee & Co/ Citicorp Scrimgeour Vickers/Scrimgeour Vickers Asset Management Ltd,1980-88 Partner from April 1983, Diretor from April 1985 (Private Client Department); Wise Speke 1988-. *Biog: b.* 30 April 1954. *Nationality:* British. *m.* 1980, Sally Ann Ring (née Johnson); 1 s; 1 d. *Educ:* Brighton, Hove & Sussex Grammar School. *Directorships:* Wise Speke 1988 (exec); Wise Speke Financial Services Ltd 1988 (exec). *Other Activities:* Treasurer, Kent Lawn Tennis Association. *Professional Organisations:* Chartered Accountant (ACA). *Clubs:* Bromley Cricket Club. *Recreations:* Tennis, Squash.

RING, Malcolm Spencer Humbert; TD; Managing Partner, Taylor Joynson Garrett, since 1989; Commercial Property/Banking. *Career:* Taylor & Humbert, Articled Clerk 1963-68; Asst Solicitor 1969-73; Partner 1973-80; Taylor Garrett, Partner 1980-89; Taylor Joynson Garrett, Partner 1989. *Biog: b.* 25 February 1944. *Nationality:* British. *m.* 1978, Elizabeth Anne (née Henman); 3 s; 1 d. *Educ:* Haileybury; ISC. *Other Activities:* Regimental Colonel of Honourable Artillery Company. *Professional Organisations:* The Law Society. *Clubs:* Oriental Club. *Recreations:* Fishing, Gardening.

RINGROSE, Colin Alan; Director, Technical Services, Gibbs Hartley Cooper.

RINK, J S; Partner, Allen & Overy, since 1977; Litigation. *Biog: b.* 25 October 1946. *Nationality:* British. *m.* 1971, Elizabeth; 1 s; 1 d. *Educ:* Sedbergh School; London University External (LLB). *Other Activities:* Governor, King College School, Wimbledon. *Clubs:* Royal Wimbledon GC, Royal West Norfolk GC. *Recreations:* Golf, Walking, Skiing, Music, Theatre.

RIORDAN, Joseph; Vice President, First Interstate Bank of California.

RISING, Hugh Wyman; Vice President, Corporate Finance, Toronto Dominion Bank.

RISK, Michael J R; WS; Partner, W & J Burness WS.

RISK, Sir Thomas (Neilson); Governor, Bank of Scotland, since 1981. *Career:* RAFVR, Flight Lt 1941-53; Maclay Murray & Spens, Ptnr 1950-81. *Biog: b.* 13 September 1922. *Nationality:* British. *m.* 1949, Suzanne (née Eiloart); 4 s. *Educ:* Kelvinside Academy, Glasgow; Glasgow University (BL,LLD). *Directorships:* Standard Life Ass Co 1965-88 (non-exec), 1969-77 Chm; The British Linen Bank Ltd 1968 (non-exec); Howden Group 1971-87 (non-exec); Merchants Trust 1973 (non-exec); MSA (Britain) Ltd 1958 (non-exec); Shell UK Ltd 1982 (non-exec); Barclays Bank 1983-85 (non-exec); Bank of Wales 1986 (non-exec); Scottish Financial Enterprise 1986-89 Chm. *Professional Organisations:* Member, Scottish Economic Council; Member, National Economic Development Council. *Clubs:* New (Edinburgh), RAF, Royal & Ancient, Prestwick Golf Club, Honourable Company of Edinburgh Golfers, Muirfield. *Recreations:* Art, Opera, Golf.

RITBLAT, John Henry; Chairman/Managing Director, The British Land Company plc, since 1971. *Career:* Articles with West End firm of Surveyors & Valuers 1952-58; Conrad Ritblat & Co, Consultant Surveyors and Valuers, Founder and Senior Partner 1958-; Union Property Holdings (London) Ltd, Managing Director 1969-71. *Biog: b.* 3 October 1935. *Nationality:* British. m1 1960, Isabel Paja (decd 1979). m2 1986, Jill Zilkha (née Slotover); 2 s; 1 d. *Educ:* Dulwich College; University of London; College of Estate Management (FSVA). *Directorships:* United Kingdon Property Company plc 1980 (exec); Regis Property Holdings plc 1970 (exec); Euston Centre Properties plc 1984 (exec); Rosehaugh Greycoat Estates plc 1988 (exec). *Other Activities:* Crown Estate Paving Commissioner, 1969-; Trustee, Zoological Society of London Dev Trust, 1986-; Member, Governing Body of The London Business School, 1990-; Member, Finance & Special Appeals Committee of The London Federation of Boys Clubs, 1990-; Hon Surveyor, King George's Fund for Sailors, 1979-; Member, Governing Council, Business in the Community; Prince of Wales Royal Parks Tree Appeal Committee; Executive Committee, The Weizmann Institute, 1970; Governor, The Hall School, Hampstead, 1977; Sole Sponsor,

The British Nat Ski Championships, 1978-. *Professional Organisations:* Fellow, Incorporated Society of Valuers & Auctioneers, 1965-. *Clubs:* RAC, MCC, Bath & Racquets Club, The Director's Club, The Cresta Club, St Moritz, Ham Manor & Littlehampton Golf Clubs. *Recreations:* Antiquarian Books & Libraries, Old Buildings, Squash, Golf, Skiing.

RITCHIE, David Cowan; Deputy Managing Director, Scottish Widows Fund & Life Assurance Society, since 1990; Investment Management & Corporate Strategy. *Career:* Scottish Widows Fund 1966-. *Directorships:* The Fleming Japanese Investment Trust plc (non-exec); Baillie Gifford Shin Nippon plc (non-exec). *Professional Organisations:* FFA.

RITCHIE, Hamish Martin Johnston; Chairman & Chief Executive, Bowring UK Ltd, since 1988; Direct Insurance. *Career:* Hogg Robinson UK Ltd, Dir 1974-80; MD 1980-81; Bowring London, Chief Exec 1981-85; Bowring UK Ltd, Chief Exec 1985-88. *Biog: b.* 22 February 1942. *Nationality:* British. *m.* 1967, Judith Carol (née Young); 1 s; 1 d. *Educ:* Loretto School, Musselburgh; Christ Church, Oxford (MA). *Directorships:* RAC Insurance Brokers 1985 (non-exec); BIIBA, Dep Chm 1987; RAC 1990. *Other Activities:* Chm of Governors, Caldicott School; Governor, Loretto School. *Professional Organisations:* CBIM; Institute of Directors. *Clubs:* MCC, Royal & Ancient, Denham Golf Club, Sunningdale Golf Club, RAC. *Recreations:* Golf, Music.

RITCHLEY, Martin Howard; Director & Chief Executive, Coventry Building Society since 1990; General Management. *Career:* Barton Mayhew & Co Audit Snr 1964-70; Coventry Building Society Chief Acct 1970-76; Sec 1976-89; Dir 1985-; Dep Chief Exec 1989-90; Chief Exec 1990-. *Biog: b.* 1 July 1946. *Nationality:* British. *m.* 1970, Elizabeth (née Burns); 1 s; 2 d. *Educ:* City of London School. *Professional Organisations:* FCA. *Clubs:* Coventry Golf Club. *Recreations:* Golf.

RIVANO, A; Director, IMI Capital Markets (UK).

RIVETT-CARNAC, Miles James; Deputy Chairman, Barings plc and Chairman, Baring Asset Management Ltd, since 1989. *Career:* Royal Navy to Commander (Commanded HMS Dainty & HMS Woolaston) 1950-70; Baring Brothers & Co Limited 1970; Outwich Limited (Merchant Banking Subsidiary of Barings) Johannesburg, Director 1976; Managing Director; Baring Brothers Inc, New York, President, 1978; Barings London, Member of Executive Committee responsible for International Operations 1980; Barings plc, Member of Board 1985; Baring Investment Management Holdings Ltd, Managing Director 1986. *Biog: b.* 7 February 1933. *Nationality:* British. *m.* 1958, April (née Villar); 2 s; 1 d. *Educ:* Royal Naval College, Dartmouth. *Directorships:* Baring Brothers Hambrecht & Quist Limited 1984; Baring Brothers Private Asset Management Limited 1989; Baring Capital Investors Limited 1986; The Baring Foundation 1989; Baring Group Holdings Limited 1986; BHB Management Limited 1984; BHC Management Limited 1985; BHE Management Limited 1985; BHI Management Limited 1985; Baring Institutional Realty Advisors Inc; Barings Nominees Limited 1976; Baring Quantitative Management Limited 1986; BVC Nominees Limited 1983; Iterate Securities Limited 1982; Stratton Investment Trust plc 1989; Tribune Investment Trust plc 1982; Tribune Finance Limited 1986; Baring America Asset Management Company Inc to 1989; Baring Investment Management Holdings Inc to 1986; Baring Brothers & Co Limited 1976-86; Baring Brothers International Limited 1981-86; Baring Fund Managers Limited 1986-89 Chairman; Baring International Investment Limited 1985-89; Baring International Investment Management Limited 1986-89; Baring Investment Management Limited 1986-89; Baring Investment Services Limited 1988-89; Baring Sterling Bonds 1985-86; Baring Securities (Japan) Limited to 1986; Baring Unit Trust Management Service Limited 1987-89; Iterate Investments Limited 1976-88; Landauer Associates Inc to 1986; Southampton Cable Limited; Willhire to Limited 1985. *Clubs:* White's, Naval & Military, Links (New York). *Recreations:* Tennis, Golf, Racing, Stamps.

RIX, P H W; Managing Director, Charterhouse Bank Limited.

ROACH, N; Director, Allied Dunbar Unit Trusts plc.

ROAD, Christopher John; Partner, Macfarlanes, since 1983; Corporate Finance. *Career:* British Council, Administrative Officer 1971-78. *Biog: b.* 7 May 1948. *Nationality:* British. *m.* 1971, Zofia Alicja (née Pialucha); 1 s; 1 d. *Educ:* St Paul's School; Trinity Hall, Cambridge (MA). *Other Activities:* The City of London Solicitors' Company. *Professional Organisations:* The Law Society.

ROAKE, S; Company Secretary, Panmure Gordon Bankers Limited.

ROBARTS, Anthony Julian; Managing Director, Coutts & Co, since 1986. *Career:* Coutts & Co, Trainee 1958-63; Dir 1963-; Head of Investment Operations 1970-71; Head of Operational Services 1971-75; Head of Business Development 1975-76; Dep MD 1976-86. *Biog: b.* 6 May 1937. *m.* 1961, Edwina B (née Hobson); 2 s; 1 d. *Educ:* Eton College. *Directorships:* Coutts Finance Co 1967 (non-exec); The International Fund for Institutions Inc (USA) 1983 (non-exec); National Westminster Bank plc (City & West End Region) 1971 Regional Dir. *Other Activities:* Hon Treasurer, Union Jack Club. *Professional Organisations:* Institute of Directors. *Clubs:* MCC. *Recreations:* Shooting, Gardening, Opera.

ROBB, George Alan; Director, Aberdeen Trust Holdings Ltd.

ROBB, J W; Chief Executive, Wellcome plc.

ROBBINS, Brian J; Director, Bradstock Blunt & Crawley Ltd.

ROBBINS, J V H; Chief Financial Officer, Willis Corroon plc.

ROBBSHAW, D; Director, Rudolf Wolff & Co Ltd.

ROBERTS, Commmander A J; OBE, RN; Clerk, Plumbers' Company.

ROBERTS, B M; Assistant Director, Macey Williams Insurance Services Ltd.

ROBERTS, C C; Director, Panmure Gordon & Co Limited.

ROBERTS, C W; Deputy Secretary, Department of Trade & Industry.

ROBERTS, Christopher Keepfer; Partner, Allen & Overy, since 1985; Corporate Finance, Banking, Regulatory Matters. *Career:* Allen & Overy Asst 1978-85. *Biog:* b. 26 March 1956. *Nationality:* British. *Educ:* Denbigh High School; Jesus College, Cambridge (MA). *Other Activities:* City of London Solicitors Company. *Professional Organisations:* The Law Society. *Recreations:* Sailing, Squash, Tennis.

ROBERTS, Clive; Director (Market-Making), Hoare Govett International Securities.

ROBERTS, Dr D H; CBE; Non-Executive Director, The General Electric Company plc.

ROBERTS, D J M; Director W H Smith Retail, W H Smith Group plc.

ROBERTS, David Edward Glyn; Managing Director, Quilter Goodison Company Limited, since 1988. *Career:* Royal Insurance, Actuarial Trainee 1949-55; Pensions Department 1957-61; Tilney & Co, Stockbrokers 1961-74; Roberts & Huish, Stockbrokers 1974-84; Ashton Tod McLaren, Stockbrokers 1984-90. *Biog:* b. 29 February 1932. *Other Activities:* Livery Company of Actuaries. *Professional Organisations:* FIA; FCII.

ROBERTS, David N; Treasurer, J Sainsbury plc.

ROBERTS, Derek Franklyn; Chief Executive, Yorkshire Building Society, since 1987; General Management. *Career:* Royal Insurance Group Systems Analyst 1961-72. *Biog:* b. 16 October 1942. *m.* 1969, Jacqueline (née Velho); 2 s; 1 d. *Educ:* Park High Grammar School, Birkenhead; Liverpool College of Commerce; Harvard Business School (AMP). *Directorships:* Yorkshire Building Society 1987 (exec); BWD Securities plc; Yorkshire Building Society Estate Agents Ltd 1988 Chm; Bradford Breakthrough Ltd 1990; Yorkshire Guernsey Ltd 1990. *Professional Organisations:* FCII, FCBSI. *Clubs:* Huddersfield Golf Club, Huddersfield Rugby Union Football Club.

ROBERTS, G; Executive Director, James R Knowles Limited.

ROBERTS, Ian M; Partner, Wilde Sapte.

ROBERTS, Ian Paul Hartin; Partner, Neville Russell, since 1987; Lloyd's Names Tax, Corporation Tax and Syndicate Tax. *Career:* Arthur Young Taxation Mgr 1979-83; Partridge, Muir & Warren Consultant 1983-85; Neville Russell Taxation Snr Mgr 1985-86. *Biog:* b. 3 July 1951. *Nationality:* British. *m.* 1982, Mary (née Bowen); 2 d. *Educ:* St Edmunds, Canterbury. *Other Activities:* Member, LSCA Taxation Working Party; Lecturer for ICAEW and CAET. *Professional Organisations:* FCA. *Recreations:* Christian Work, Gardening, Photography, Tennis.

ROBERTS, Julian Victor Frow; Group Finance Director, Nicholson Chamberlain Colls Limited, since 1988; Finance, Treasury & Systems. *Career:* Stuart Wrightson Holdings plc, Group Financial Controller 1987; C E Heath plc, Overseas Broking Financial Controller 1984-87; Price Waterhouse, Assistant Manager 1980-84. *Biog:* b. 7 June 1957. *Nationality:* British. *m.* 1981, Marion (née Macdonald); 2 s. *Educ:* Tonbridge School; Stirling University (BA Hons Accountancy & Business Law). *Directorships:* None other than Nicholson Chamberlain Colls Group of Companies. *Professional Organisations:* Chartered Accountant. *Recreations:* Rugby, Golf.

ROBERTS, K S; Director Structured Finance Group, County NatWest Ltd, since 1988. *Career:* Standard Chartered Bank 1980-83; County NatWest Limited 1983-. *Biog:* b. 21 January 1957. *Nationality:* British. *m.* 1981, Gill; 1 d. *Educ:* Chatham House Grammar School, Kent; Lincoln College, Oxford (BA Hons Chemistry). *Professional Organisations:* ACIB. *Clubs:* MCC. *Recreations:* Golf, Cricket, Family.

ROBERTS, Malcolm John Binyon; Director, Fleming Montagu Stanley Ltd, since 1986; Private Client Investment Management. *Career:* Montagu Loebl Stanley & Co Ptnr 1979-86. *Biog:* b. 3 July 1951. *Nationality:* British. *m.* 1984, Caroline Mary (née Scrutton); 1 s; 1 d. *Educ:* St Edmund's School, Canterbury. *Other Activities:* Freeman, Barbers Company. *Professional Organisations:* The International Stock Exchange. *Clubs:* City. *Recreations:* Tennis, Gardening.

ROBERTS, Martin John Dickin; Partner, Slaughter and May, since 1975; Company and Commercial Law. *Biog: b.* 20 March 1944. *m.* 1970, Ruth (née Packard); 3 d. *Educ:* Shrewsbury School; Trinity Hall, Cambridge (MA). *Professional Organisations:* The Law Society; City of London Law Society; IBA. *Publications:* Energy Finance, 1983; Article in Oil & Gas Law and Taxation Review, 1983. *Clubs:* RAC.

ROBERTS, Michael John; Director, Lazard Bros & Co Ltd, since 1981; Corporate Finance & International. *Career:* Lazard Brothers & Co Ltd 1966-. *Biog: b.* 24 June 1944. *m.* 1980, Rosemary (née Eccles); 1 s; 1 d. *Educ:* Rugby School; Queen's College, Oxford (BA). *Other Activities:* Worshipful Company of Shipwrights.

ROBERTS, Peter; Director, Royal Trust Bank.

ROBERTS, Peter David Thatcher; Director, Hays plc, since 1983. *Career:* Merchant Navy 1951-59; Leinster Maritime Agencies Ltd 1960-; Director 1963-; Managing Director 1965-69; Hays plc, Director of Various Subsidary Companies 1969-; Chairman, Marine Division 1981; Parent Board 1983. *Biog: b.* 1 March 1934. *Nationality:* British. *m.* 1959, Elizabeth (née Dodds); 1 s; 2 d. *Educ:* Alleyns School, Dulwich; King Edward VII Nautical College. *Directorships:* British Marine Mutual Insurance Assoc Ltd 1981-84 (non-exec); Shipowners Protection & Indemnity Assoc Ltd 1983- (non-exec); Shipowners Mutual P&I Association Luxembourg 1983- (non-exec); Spandilux SA 1990- (non-exec); Minories Holdings Ltd 1989- (non-exec). *Other Activities:* Junior Warden, Company of Waterman & Lightermen of the River Thames; Liveryman, Shipwrights Company; General Committee, Lloyds Register of Shipping. *Professional Organisations:* Member, Institute of Chartered Shipbrokers; Fellow, British Institute of Management. *Clubs:* Royal Ocean Racing, Royal Automobile, Wildernesse Golf. *Recreations:* Sailing, Golf.

ROBERTS, R A; Director (Personal Financial Planning), Granville & Co Limited.

ROBERTS, T J E; Corporate Director, Next plc, since 1985; Corporate Affairs, Property, Personnel. *Career:* Cuff Roberts North Kirk Solicitors, Liverpool, Partner 1970-85. *Biog: b.* 12 February 1943. *Nationality:* British. 1988, Anne Clarke (née Cunningham); 2 s (by first marriage). *Educ:* Rugby School; Liverpool University (LLB Hons). *Directorships:* Next plc 1985 (exec). *Other Activities:* Member, Council of British Retailers Association; Council Member, Leicestershire Training and Enterprise Council. *Professional Organisations:* Solicitor. *Clubs:* Royal & Ancient, Formby Golf Club, Royal County Down Golf Club. *Recreations:* Golf, Sport, Antiques, Period Property.

ROBERTS, Thomas; Director, General Accident Fire and Life Assurance Corp plc.

ROBERTS, Thomas Ian; Partner, Booth & Co, since 1988; Company/Commercial Department. *Career:* Simpson Curtis, Articled Clerk 1980-82; Booth & Co, Asst Solicitor 1982-86; Associate Solicitor 1986-88; Partner 1988-; Departmental Managing Partner 1990-. *Biog: b.* 8 November 1956. *Nationality:* British. *Educ:* Giggleswick; Queen's College, Oxford (BA Hons 1st, MA). *Directorships:* Kaye & Co (Huddersfield) Limited 1989 (non-exec). *Other Activities:* Yorkshire Archaeological Society; Secretary, Yorkshire Glass Manufacturers' Assoc, 1983-88; Rugby Fives Assoc. *Professional Organisations:* The Law Society; Leeds Law Society; Yorkshire Young Solicitors' Group (Treasurer 1987-88, Ctee 1985-88). *Publications:* A Walk Round Stackhouse, 1979. *Recreations:* Genealogy, Local History, Long Case Clocks, Fives.

ROBERTSHAW, John Desmond; Director, York Trust Ltd, since 1977; Corporate Finance. *Career:* Edward Bates & Sons Ltd & Associated Companies, Dir 1964-77. *Biog: b.* 19 December 1928. *m.* 1961, Lesley (née Carter); 1 s; 2 d. *Educ:* Bembridge School; St Peter's College, Oxford (MA). *Directorships:* Northern Ground Rents Trust Ltd 1965; Rights and Issues Investment Trust plc 1962; United Scientific Holdings plc 1965; Hubbacastle Investments Ltd 1965; Kode International plc 1979; Shorco Group Holdings Ltd 1980; Safe Computing Ltd 1982; Associated Farmers plc 1984; Phosyn Group Ltd 1985; Specialeyes plc 1985. *Other Activities:* Dep Chm, FIMBRA; Alternate Member, The Panel on Takeovers & Mergers. *Professional Organisations:* FCA. *Clubs:* MCC. *Recreations:* Golf.

ROBERTSON, D R C; Partner, Stephenson Harwood.

ROBERTSON, David Ritchie; General Manager Retail Banking, Clydesdale Bank plc, since 1988; Retail Banking. *Career:* Clydesdale Bank plc 1953-; Superintendent of Branches 1975-77; Gen Mgrs' Asst 1977-79; Asst Gen Mgr 1980-82; London Mgr 1982-84; Gen Mgr 1984-87. *Biog: b.* 21 July 1937. *m.* 1962, Christine A L (née White); 2 s; 1 d. *Educ:* Eastwood High School. *Directorships:* The Scottish Agricultural Securities Corporation 1987 (non-exec); Clydesdale Bank Finance Corporation 1985 (non-exec); Clyde General Leasing Ltd 1989 (non-exec). *Other Activities:* Council of Institute of Bankers in Scotland (Member); CBI Scotland Employment Ctee (Member 1987). *Professional Organisations:* FIB (Scot). *Clubs:* Western, Whitecraigs Golf Club, Royal Aberdeen Golf Club. *Recreations:* Golf.

ROBERTSON, Dennis Vernon; Partner, Stoy Hayward, since 1959; General Practice. *Biog: b.* 1 March 1932. *Nationality:* British. *m.* 1957, Barbara (née Anderson); 3 s. *Directorships:* Ambrose Investment Trust plc 1975 Chairman (exec). *Professional Organisations:* FCA.

ROBERTSON, Duncan Neil (Peter); Investment Director, M & G Investment Management Ltd, since 1971; Japan/Far East Investment Management. *Career:* R C Greig Clerk 1959-62; Philip Hill Higginson (now Hill Samuel) Fund Mgr 1962-65. *Biog: b.* 23 May 1940. *Nationality:* British. *m.* 1962, Diana Helen (née Barbor); 1 s; 1 d. *Educ:* Harrow School. *Directorships:* Drayton Far East Investment Trust 1982 (non-exec); External Investment Trust 1979 (exec). *Clubs:* Turf. *Recreations:* Golf, Shooting, Tennis, Rugby.

ROBERTSON, Eric Stuart; General Manager, Scottish Widows Fund & Life Assurance Society, since 1988; Servicing Division. *Career:* Scottish Widows Fund & Life Assurance Society, Various 1951-. *Biog: b.* 27 August 1932. *Nationality:* British. *m.* 1953, Jean (née Muir); 1 s; 2 d. *Educ:* George Heriot's School, Edinburgh. *Other Activities:* Vice President, Faculty of Actuaries. *Professional Organisations:* FFA. *Clubs:* Caledonian, Scottish Actuaries, Actuaries, Cyclists Touring Club. *Recreations:* Cycling, Photography, Computing.

ROBERTSON, Iain Samuel; Group Finance Director, County NatWest Ltd, since 1990. *Career:* Scottish Development Agency, Chief Executive 1985-89; Scottish Office 1978-84; Department of Energy 1975-77; Department of Trade & Industry 1973-75; Babcox & Wil, Nuclear Area Accountant 1971-72; Impetus Building Components, Company Accountant 1970; Peat Marwick Mitchell, Audit Senior 1969-70. *Biog: b.* 27 December 1945. *m.* 1972, Morag (née Johnston); 2 s; 2 d. *Educ:* Jordanhill College; Glasgow University (LLB). *Directorships:* County NatWest 1990 (exec); Selective Assets Trust 1988 (non-exec); Institute of Chartered Accountants. *Recreations:* Golf, Reading.

ROBERTSON, Ian; Financial Director, Alexander & Alexander Europe plc, since 1989; Finance & Admin throughout UK, Europe, Asia and Australasia. *Directorships:* Alexander Stenhouse & Partners Ltd 1979 Financial Dir; Alexander Stenhouse Ltd 1979 Financial Dir. *Professional Organisations:* Institute of Chartered Accountants of Scotland; Member of the Association of Corporate Treasurers. *Clubs:* Brookmans Park Golf Club, Hilton Park Golf Club. *Recreations:* Golf.

ROBERTSON, Margaret; Partner, Withers.

ROBERTSON, R; Director, County NatWest Securities Limited.

ROBERTSON, S G A; Divisional Director, City Merchants Bank Ltd; Private Banking. *Biog: b.* 13 June 1931. *Nationality:* British. *m.* 1972, Catherine Ann (née Shiel); 2 d. *Educ:* London School of Economics (BSc Econ). *Other Activities:* Trustee, City Merchant Bank (1978) Retirement Fund. *Clubs:* Three Rivers Golf & Country Club.

ROBERTSON, Simon Manwaring; Director, Kleinwort Benson Lonsdale plc.

ROBERTSON, William Nelson; Director, General Accident Fire & Life Assurance Corp plc.

ROBINSON, A H; Associate Director, Grandfield Rork Collins Financial Ltd.

ROBINSON, A L; Director, Barclays Bank plc.

ROBINSON, Anthony Leake; Managing Director, Centreway Development Capital Ltd, since 1988; Venture Capital. *Career:* London International Dir 1975; Chloride Group MD (O/S Div) 1979-87; Centreway Development Capital MD 1987-. *Biog: b.* 4 January 1945. *Nationality:* British. *m.* 1969, Judith (née Earnshaw); 1 s; 1 d. *Educ:* Fettes College, Edinburgh; Newcastle University (BA Econ). *Directorships:* Centreway Trust plc 1988 (exec); Westerly plc 1987 (non-exec); Plastiseal (upvc) plc 1987 (non-exec); ANS plc 1988 (non-exec). *Professional Organisations:* FCA. *Recreations:* Golf, Antiques, Historical Buildings.

ROBINSON, Brian Graham; Partner, Holman Fenwick & Willan, since 1969; Shipbuilding, Contracts, Shipping, Finance. *Career:* Peacock Fisher & Finch, Articled Clerk, Asst Solicitor 1960-64; Victoria University, (Wellington, New Zealand), Lecturer 1964-66. *Biog: b.* 27 March 1940. *m.* 1964, Jennifer Elizabeth (née Jones); 1 s; 1 d. *Educ:* Burnley Grammar School; London School of Economics (LLM). *Other Activities:* Liveryman, Worshipful Company of Shipwrights. *Professional Organisations:* Law Society. *Publications:* Various articles in New Zealand Universities Law Review, New Zealand Law. *Recreations:* Theatre, Travel, Golf.

ROBINSON, Christopher Ian; Partner, Pinsent & Co, since 1990; Corporate Law/Pensions. *Career:* Pinsent & Co, Trainee, Assistant Solicitor, Associate 1981-90. *Biog: b.* 30 July 1959. *Nationality:* British. *m.* 1988, Janet (née Cowen). *Educ:* British School of Brussels; University of Hull (LLB); College of Law, Guildford. *Professional Organisations:* Solicitor; Member, The Law Society; Associate Member, Association of Pension Lawyers.

ROBINSON, Christopher John Nield; Director, Leslie & Godwin Limited, since 1986; Business Development. *Career:* Reed Stenhouse (New York) Snr VP 1966-84. *Biog: b.* October 1934. *m.* 1976, Penny L (née Morley); 1 s. *Other Activities:* British American Chamber of Commerce (Exec Chm, UK Ctee, 1986-). *Clubs:* New York Yacht Club, Royal Canadian Yacht Club, Larchmont Yacht Club, Royal Thames Yacht Club. *Recreations:* Sailing.

ROBINSON, D F; Partner, Touche Ross & Co.

ROBINSON, David; Executive Director (Services), Royal Bank of Scotland plc.

ROBINSON, E C; Executive Director, Booker plc.

ROBINSON, F A L; Executive Director, UK Operations, Barclays Bank plc, since 1990. *Career:* Mercantile Credit Company 1959; General Manager 1971; Appointed to the Board 1978; Seconded to Barclays Bank International, Chairman of Executive Committee, Barclays American Corporation, Later Chief Executive Officer & President 1981; Barclays Bank International, Regional General Manager with Responsibility for Asia 1984; General Manager (Personnel) 1987; Executive Director (UK Operations) 1990-. *Biog: b.* 19 September 1937. *Nationality:* British. *m.* 1961, Lavinia; 2 d. *Educ:* Eton College. *Directorships:* Barclays plc; Barclays Bank plc; Barclays Financial Services Limited Chm. *Recreations:* Theatre, Opera, Ballet, Gardening, Golf, Tennis.

ROBINSON, Fred D P; Partner, Killik & Co, since 1989; PEPS. *Career:* Quilter Goodison, Various 1985-89. *Biog: b.* 20 June 1961. *Nationality:* British. *m.* 1988, Michelle; 1 d. *Educ:* Radley; Downing College, Cambridge (MA Cantab). *Professional Organisations:* Member, International Stock Exchange.

ROBINSON, I J R; Director, MIM Limited.

ROBINSON, Keith O'Dwyer; Director, Member Assessment, IMRO. *Career:* Lloyd's, Secretary to Council 1983-86; Accounting Standards Committee, Secretary 1980-83; Coopers & Lybrand, Senior Manager, Technical Department. *Biog: b.* 8 April 1949. *Nationality:* British. *Educ:* Bishop Vesey's Grammar School, Sutton Coldfield; Lancaster University (MA). *Other Activities:* Secretary, Hampton Deanery Synod. *Professional Organisations:* Fellow, Institute of Chartered Accountants. *Recreations:* Cricket, Football, Church Activities.

ROBINSON, M D; Head of Shipping Dept, Berwin Leighton, since 1980. *Career:* Merchant Navy - Navigation Officer 1961-69; Berwin Leighton 1973-. *Biog: b.* 1 February 1945. *Nationality:* British. *m.* 1972, Susan Mair (née Neeson). 3 s; (inc 1 set of twins). *Educ:* Hull Navigation College, Chief Officer, Certificate of Competency; University of Wales, Cardiff, BSc (Hons) Maritime Commerce; MSc Maritime Law; College of Law, London, Law Society Examination. *Other Activities:* Member of the Baltic Exchange. *Professional Organisations:* Member of the Royal Institute of Navigation. *Publications:* The Seafarer and the Law, 1973. *Recreations:* South Benfleet Social Club.

ROBINSON, Michael A; Director, J Trevor, Montleman & Poland Ltd.

ROBINSON, Michael John; Partner, Simpson Curtis, since 1990; Corporate Law. *Career:* Linklaters & Paines,

Articled Clerk 1983-85; Assistant Solicitor 1985-87; Simpson Curtis, Assistant Solicitor 1987-88; Associate 1988-90; Partner 1990-. *Biog: b.* 6 June 1961. *Nationality:* British. *m.* 1987, Ann Marie. *Educ:* Northallerton Grammar School; St Edmund Hall, Oxford (BA Jurisprudence 1st Class); Chester Law School. *Professional Organisations:* Solicitor. *Recreations:* Reading, Music.

ROBINSON, P C; Director, J Henry Schroder Wagg & Co Limited.

ROBINSON, Peter James; Director and Deputy Chief Executive, Woolwich Building Society; Business Operations. *Biog: b.* 28 April 1941. *Nationality:* British. *Educ:* Erith County Grammar School; City of London (HND). *Other Activities:* Freeman, The City of London; Livery, Chartered Secretaries. *Professional Organisations:* FCIS; FBIM; FCBSI. *Clubs:* City Livery, MCC. *Recreations:* Golf, Cricket, Gardening.

ROBINSON, Richard; Director, N M Rothschild Asset Management, since 1990; US Equities. *Career:* L Messel & Co 1982-85; John Govett & Company 1985-88; N M Rothschild Asset Management 1988-. *Educ:* Winchester College; Worcester College, Oxford (MA Hons). *Clubs:* Flyfishers'.

ROBINSON, Sheila M; TD; Clerk, The Company of Builders Merchants & Solicitors' Company.

ROBINSON, Stephen Howard; Partner, Grimley J R Eve Surveyors, since 1974; Managing Partner, National Planning Department. *Career:* J R Eve & Son, Partner 1969-88. *Biog: b.* 22 February 1947. *Nationality:* British. *m.* 1970; 1 s; 1 d. *Educ:* Kimbolton School; Sidney Sussex College, Cambridge (MA). *Directorships:* RTZ Estates Ltd 1984 (non-exec); Western Properties Ltd. *Professional Organisations:* Fellow, Royal Institution of Chartered Surveyors; Member, Royal Town Planning Institute. *Clubs:* United Oxford & Cambridge. *Recreations:* Tennis, History.

ROBINSON, T J; Director, Lonrho plc.

ROBINSON, William Simon Melland; Partner, Slaughter and May, since 1989; Company/Commercial Law. *Career:* Freshfields (London), Articled Clerk/Asst Solicitor 1978-84; (Singapore), Asst Solicitor 1984-86. *Biog: b.* 19 July 1955. *Nationality:* British. *m.* 1981, Nicola Jane (née de Selincourt); 1 s. *Educ:* Charterhouse; Clare College, Cambridge (BA). *Professional Organisations:* Member, The Law Society. *Clubs:* Oxford and Cambridge, Hollandse (Singapore).

ROBSON, Professor A; Professor of Management Accounting, Cranfield School of Management.

ROBSON, Clayton Hugo Wynne; Director, Kleinwort Grieveson Securities Ltd, since 1986; Institutional Equities. *Career:* Grieveson Grant & Co Ptnr 1963-86. *Biog: b.* 16 February 1932. *Educ:* Charterhouse; Magdalene College, Cambridge (BA Agriculture). *Professional Organisations:* Member, The International Stock Exchange. *Clubs:* Boodle's, Queen's, MCC, I Zingari, Free Forresters, City University, Royal Ashdown. *Recreations:* Golf, Royal Tennis, Fishing, Shooting, Bridge.

ROBSON, Clive Joseph Vermelles; Partner, Slaughter and May.

ROBSON, G W; Finance Director, Wise Speke Limited, since 1990; Finance. *Career:* Price Waterhouse 1980-87; Wise Speke Limited 1987-. *Biog: b.* 24 June 1958. *Nationality:* British. *Educ:* Trinity College, Glenalmond; Aberdeen University (MA). *Directorships:* Wise Speke Limited 1990 (exec); Pilgrim Unit Trust Management Ltd 1990 (exec). *Professional Organisations:* ACA. *Clubs:* Northern Counties Club, The Alnmouth Golf Club Limited. *Recreations:* Golf, Tennis, Bridge.

ROBSON, N; Group Treasurer, The Burton Group plc.

ROBSON, Nigel John; Chairman, Ottoman Bank, since 1987. *Career:* Arbuthnot Latham & Co Ltd Dir 1953-75; Chm 1969-75; Grindlays Bank plc Dir 1969-83; Dep Chm 1975-76; Chm 1977-83; Royal Trust Bank Chm 1984-89. *Biog: b.* 25 December 1926. *Nationality:* British. *m.* 1957, Anne (née Gladstone); 3 s. *Educ:* Eton College. *Directorships:* TSB Group plc 1985 (non-exec); Bank of Tokyo Ltd 1984 London Adviser; Bank of Tokyo International Ltd 1987 (non-exec); The National Bank of New Zealand Ltd 1973-77 (non-exec); British Sugar plc 1982-86 (non-exec); Royal Trustco Ltd 1985-89 (non-exec); TSB England & Wales plc 1986-90. *Other Activities:* Automobile Association (Vice-Chairman); British Heart Foundation (Member of Council); University of Surrey (Treasurer); King Edwards School, Witley (Governor). *Professional Organisations:* FCIB. *Clubs:* Brooks's, MCC, City of London, Overseas Bankers'. *Recreations:* Walking, Classical Music.

ROBSON, P J; Partner, Slaughter and May.

ROCHE, David; Managing Director (Investment Management), Morgan Stanley International.

ROCHE, Nicholas Alan; Partner, Richards Butler, since 1985; Corporate Finance. *Biog: b.* 3 June 1953. *m.* 1983, Elizabeth Louise (née Elton); 1 d. *Educ:* Cheltenham College; St Catherine's College, Cambridge (MA). *Professional Organisations:* The Law Society. *Clubs:* RAC, Hurlingham. *Recreations:* Tennis, Racing.

ROCHER, Richard Philip; Partner in Charge of the New York Office, Wilde Sapte, since 1988; International Litigation, Insurance. *Career:* Kenneth Brown Baker,

Trainee Solicitor 1979-81; Wilde Sapte, Assistant Solicitor 1981-85; Wilde Sapte (London) Partner 1985-88; Wilde Sapte (New York) Partner 1988-. *Biog: b.* 5 February 1956. *Nationality:* British. *m.* 1985, Lesley (née Dennis-Jones); 1 s; 1 d. *Educ:* Ashville College, Harrogate; Birmingham University (LLB 2:i). *Other Activities:* City of London Solicitors Company; American Bar Association; Law Society of England & Wales. *Professional Organisations:* Solicitor.

ROCHMAN, J H; Non-Executive Director, MFK Underwriting Agencies Ltd.

ROCK, John William; Director, J Henry Schroder Wagg & Co Ltd, since 1977; Banking. *Biog: b.* 28 January 1943. *Nationality:* British. *m.* 1970, Gaynor (née England); 1 s; 1 d. *Educ:* South West Essex Technical School. *Directorships:* Schroder Leasing Ltd 1986 Chm. *Professional Organisations:* ACIB.

ROCKEFELLER, R C; Non-Executive Director, Booker plc.

ROCKLEY, James Hugh; Lord Rockley; Vice Chairman, Kleinwort Benson Group plc, since 1986. *Career:* Wood Grundy & Company 1957-62; Kleinwort Benson Ltd 1962-. *Biog: b.* 5 April 1934. *Nationality:* British. *m.* 1958, Lady Rockley (née Cadogan); 1 s; 2 d. *Educ:* Eton; New College, Oxford (PPE). *Directorships:* Kleinwort Benson Group plc 1986 (exec); Kleinwort Benson Ltd 1970 (exec); Equity & Law plc 1987 (non-exec); Christies International plc 1989 (non-exec); FR Group plc 1990 (non-exec); Dartford River Crossing Ltd 1986 (non-exec),Chm; Abbey National plc 1990 (non-exec); Kleinwort Development Fund 1990 (non-exec). *Other Activities:* Member, Design Council; Salter's Company; Financial Reporting Council. *Clubs:* Pratt's, White's, MCC.

RODDAN, J; Director, County NatWest Securities Limited.

RODDICK, B M; Director, Holman Managers Ltd.

RODEN, D H; Director, Barclays de Zoete Wedd Securities Limited, since 1986. *Career:* City of London School, Mathematics Teacher 1971-76; St Albans School, Hertfordshire, Head of Mathematics 1976-80; de Zoete & Bevan 1981-86; Member of Stock Exchange 1984; de Zoete & Bevan, Partner 1985; Barclays de Zoete Wedd, Director 1986-; Barclays de Zoete Wedd Futures, Director. *Biog: b.* 9 December 1946. *Nationality:* British. *m.* 1968, Cynthia; 1 s; 1 d. *Educ:* Stockton-on-Tees Grammar School; Wadham College, Oxford; Kings College, London. *Directorships:* Barclays de Zoete Wedd Securities Limited 1989; Barclays de Zoete Wedd Futures Limited 1987. *Other Activities:* Member, Quality of Markets Committee; Member, LTOM Divisional

Board; Deputy Chairman, LTOM Clearing Committee; Member, FTSE Steering Committee.

RODGERS, J M; Non-Executive Director, Willis Corroon plc.

RODGERS, M B; Partner, Milne Ross.

RODGERS, P N; Associate Director Corporate Finance, Beeson Gregory Limited, since 1990; Corporate Finance. *Career:* Ernst & Young (Leeds), (Formerly Ernst & Whinney), Trainee Accountant, Audit Department 1981-84; Ernst & Young (London), Supervisor, Audit Department 1985-86; Manager, Corporate Advisory Department 1986-88; Seconded to; The Stock Exchange, Executive Quotations Department 1988-89; Ernst & Young (London), Senior Manager, Corporate Advisory Department 1989-89; Beeson Gregory Ltd 1989-. *Biog: b.* 14 January 1959. *Nationality:* British. *m.* 1984, Thea Elizabeth (née Comley); 1 s. *Educ:* Penistone Grammar School; Bootham School, York; Leeds University, Degree in Economics & History. *Professional Organisations:* Institute of Chartered Accountants in England & Wales (ACA). *Recreations:* Football, Cycling, Gardening.

RODITI, Spencer Nicholas; Director, J Rothschild Holdings plc, since 1986; Investments & Investment Management. *Career:* J Henry Schroder Wagg & Co Ltd Various 1970-82; Schroder Securities MD 1982-85. *Biog: b.* 30 August 1945. *Nationality:* British. *m.* 1983, Pamela Amanda (née Klaber); 1 s. *Educ:* Peterhouse, Zimbabwe; University of Cape Town (BComm, LLB); City of London University (MSc). *Directorships:* J Rothschild Investment Management Ltd 1986; Bishopsgate Progressive Unit Trust Management Co Ltd 1986; J Rothschild Fund Managers Ltd 1986; J Rothschild Investment Management Ltd 1986; J Rothschild Securities Ltd 1986.

RODWELL, Paul; Senior Equity Investment Manager, Crown Financial Management Limited.

ROE, James Kenneth; Director, N M Rothschild & Sons Ltd, since 1970. *Biog: b.* 28 February 1935. *Nationality:* British. *m.* 1958, Marion Audrey (née Keyte); 1 s; 2 d. *Educ:* King's School, Bruton. *Directorships:* Equity Consort Investment Trust Ltd 1967 (exec) Chairman; TCH Investments NV 1969; Tokyo Pacific Holdings NV 1969; Rothschild Trust Company Ltd 1970 (exec); N M Rothschild & Sons (CI) Ltd 1981 Chairman; Kleeneze Holdings plc 1985 (non-exec); Jupiter European Investment Trust plc 1990 (non-exec). *Professional Organisations:* ASIA; FRSA. *Clubs:* Carlton, MCC.

ROE, Mrs Sally Jean (née Petts); Partner, Freshfields, since 1990. *Career:* Dawson & Co, Lincoln's Inn, Articled Clerk 1979-81; Assistant Solicitor 1981-85;

Partner 1985-88; Freshfields, Assistant Solicitor 1988-90. *Biog: b.* 4 September 1956. *Nationality:* British. *Educ:* Wakefield Girls' High School; St Hilda's College, Oxford (BA). *Professional Organisations:* Law Society. *Recreations:* Walking, Skiing, Sailing, Theatre.

ROGEN, D; Director, Aitken Campbell & Co Ltd.

ROGER, Peter Charles Marshall; Partner, Speirs & Jeffrey Ltd, since 1974; Finance and Administration, Client Advisory Work. *Career:* Thomson McLintock & Co, Mgr 1966-71; Speirs & Jeffrey Ltd 1971-. *Biog: b.* 11 April 1942. *Nationality:* British. *m.* 1972, Fiona (née Murray); 2 s; 1 d. *Educ:* Glasgow High School. *Other Activities:* Chm, Scottish Unit, The International Stock Exchange. *Professional Organisations:* CA. *Clubs:* Caledonian, Royal Scottish Automobile. *Recreations:* Golf.

ROGERS, D F; General Manager, Operations & Administration, Yamaichi Bank (UK) plc.

ROGERS, David Allen; Director, Kleinwort Benson Securities.

ROGERS, Miss Dorcas Kay; Partner, Waltons & Morse, since 1989; Corporate Services: Shipping Finance, Competition Law. *Career:* Trowers & Hamlins, Articled Clerk/Assistant Solicitor 1982-87; Waltons & Morse 1987-. *Biog: b.* 17 January 1960. *Nationality:* British. *Educ:* Brighton & Hove High School; University College, London (LLB).

ROGERS, Ms Mary; Joint Chief Executive, Greater London Enterprise, since 1986. *Career:* Architectural Practice 1977-83; Greater London Council Industry & Employment Branch 1983-85; Greater London Enterprise Board, Property Director 1985-86. *Biog: b.* 20 September 1943. *Nationality:* British; 1 s; 1 d. *Educ:* St Margarets, Folkestone; Kingston College (BA); Royal College of Art (MA). *Directorships:* Greater London Enterprise 1986 (exec); GLE Subsidiaries 1986-90 (exec); GLE - Rosehaugh Developments 1989 (non-exec); Lewisham Phoenix 1989 (non-exec).

ROGERS, William Scofield; Head of Corporate Department, Theodore Goddard.

ROGERSON, Michael; Partner, Grant Thornton, since 1976; Business Advisory Services & Corporate Finance. *Career:* Spicer & Pegler, Trainee 1960-65; Spicer & Pegler (Australia), Manager 1965-67; Ernst & Young, Group Manager Investigations 1967-73; Grant Thornton 1974-. *Biog: b.* 19 February 1941. *Nationality:* British. *m.* 1969, Jane (née Blake); 1 s; 1 d. *Educ:* Harrow School. *Directorships:* Tech PR Ltd 1987 Chairman(non-exec); CMAC Ltd 1985 Chairman(non-exec). *Other Activities:* Vice Chairman, London Regional Council of CBI; Council Member, CBI; Liveryman, Skinner's Company; Chairman, Catholic Marriage Advisory Counsellor; Marriage Guidance Counsellor; Executive Member, Sherriff & Recorders Fund; Catholic Prisoners Social Service, Advisory Committee. *Professional Organisations:* FCA (Fellow, Institute of Chartered Accountants of England & Wales); FBIM (Fellow, British Institute of Management). *Publications:* Various Technical Accounting Articles. *Clubs:* Boodles, Worplesdon Golf Club, Trevose Golf Club. *Recreations:* Golf, Bridge, Gardening, Racing.

ROGERSON, Philip Graham; Group Treasurer, Imperial Chemical Industries plc.

ROGG, Howard Elliot; Partner, Nabarro Nathanson, since 1990; Property. *Career:* Malcolm Slowe & Co, Partner 1968-70; Rogg, Scott & Co, Partner 1970-72; Sole Practitioner 1972-75; Abroad 1975-79; Nabarro Nathanson 1979-. *Biog: b.* 2 May 1945. *Nationality:* Zimbabwean. *m.* 1979, Desiree (née Passov); 3 s; 1 d. *Educ:* Dulwich College. *Other Activities:* Member for Bourne End-Cum-Hedsor on Wycombe District Council; Member for Wooburn Town on Wooburn Parish Council. *Professional Organisations:* Law Society. *Clubs:* RAC. *Recreations:* Politics, Family, Sport (Not Necessarily in that Order!).

ROGLES, Brian David; General Manager (Finance), Woolwich Building Society, since 1988; Finance, Treasury, Internal Audit. *Career:* IBM Ltd, Acct 1961-62; BICC Ltd, Acct 1962-64; AEC/ACV Ltd, Fin Acct 1964-66; Dimplex Ltd, Sec & Chief Acct 1966-72; Temperance Permanent Building Society, Chief Acct 1972-77; Gateway Building Society AGM (Finance) 1977-81; Gen Mgr (Finance & Personnel) 1981-88. *Biog: b.* 14 August 1937. *Nationality:* British. *m.* 1959, Marina (née Wales); 3 d. *Educ:* Kingswood School, Bath. *Professional Organisations:* FCA.

ROHRBASSER, M; Managing Director Intl Corporate Finance, UBS Phillips & Drew Securities Limited.

ROLL, Eric; Lord Roll of Ipsden; President, S G Warburg Group plc.

ROME, D P; Director, Grandfield Rork Collins, since 1988; Corporate Public Relations/Investor Relations. *Career:* The Royal Hussars, PWO 1971-78; Financial Times 1978-83; GRC 1984-. *Biog: b.* 15 November 1949. *Nationality:* British. *m.* 1973, Penelope; 1 s; 2 d. *Educ:* Worth Abbey. *Professional Organisations:* Member, Investor Relations Institute. *Clubs:* Cavalry Club. *Recreations:* Country Pursuits.

ROMNEY, Charles D A; Partner (Property Department), Cameron Markby Hewitt, since 1975; General Commercial Proerty, Property Development, Property Funding, Property Investment, Property Insolvency. *Biog: b.* 29 December 1948. *Nationality:* British. *m.* 1968, Fiona (née Hood); 1 s; 1 d. *Educ:* Tonbridge School;

Leeds University (LLB). *Professional Organisations:* Member, British Council of Shopping Centres; Member, Law Society; Member, City of London Solicitor's Company. *Recreations:* Music, Reading, Skiing, Cycling, Walking, Gardening, Classic Cars, Scale Modelling.

ROOK, John Anthony James; Director, C Czarnikow Ltd. *Biog: b.* 6 December 1943. *Nationality:* British. *m.* 1966, Sarah Crundall (née Thicknesse); 3 s. *Directorships:* C Czarnikow Limited (non-exec); Czarnikow Holdings Limited (non-exec); Lion Mark Holdings Limited (non-exec). *Professional Organisations:* MBIM.

ROOK, Peter Francis Grosvenor; Director, C Czarnikow Ltd, since 1986; Non-Executive, alternate to brother, John Rook. *Career:* Barrister 1973-. *Biog: b.* 19 September 1949. *m.* 1978, Susanna (née Tewson); 1 s; 2 d. *Educ:* Charterhouse; Trinity College, Cambridge (MA); Bristol University (Dip SocSc). *Clubs:* Coolhurst Lawn Tennis & Squash Club, MCC (Assoc Member). *Recreations:* Tennis, Squash, Ornithology, Cricket.

ROOKE, Peter Leslie; Partner, Clifford Chance, since 1971; Corporate and International - Middle East and Eastern Erope. *Career:* Dawson & Burgess, Doncaster, Articled Clerk 1958-63; Longman & Co, Kitwe, Zambia, Assistant Solicitor 1963-65; Clifford Chance, London, Assistant Solicitor 1965-70. *Biog: b.* 19 March 1941. *Nationality:* British. *m.* 1981, Barbara (née Leach); 1 s; 2 d. *Educ:* Canford School; Leeds University (LLB). *Other Activities:* Chairman, International Bar Association, Arab Region; Chairman, Wingfield Arts & Music; Council Member and Honorary Solicitor, Japan Society. *Professional Organisations:* Solicitor. *Clubs:* Royal Ocean Racing. *Recreations:* Sailing.

ROOKER, Malcolm Francis; Executive Director, Henderson Crosthwaite Ltd, since 1987. *Biog: b.* 18 February 1944. *Nationality:* British. *m.* 1969, Susan Margaret (née Mackenzie); 1 s; 1 d. *Educ:* Shrewsbury School; Oxford University (BA). *Directorships:* Henderson Crosthwaite Ltd 1987 (exec); Footwear Developments Ltd 1976 (non-exec). *Professional Organisations:* FCA. *Clubs:* Leander Club, Royal Ocean Racing Club, Berkshire Golf Club.

ROOM, David James; Partner, Grimley J R Eve, since 1982; Head of National Rating Department; London Office Finance Partner. *Career:* Inland Revenue, Valuation Office, Valuer City of London 1975-82. *Biog: b.* 1953. *Nationality:* British. *m.* 1984, Jane Louisa Mary (née Titcombe); 2 d. *Educ:* St Olave's & St Saviour's Grammar School, London; London University (External) (BA Hons). *Other Activities:* Member, CBI Minerals Rating Committee; Chairman, NFCI Rating Committee. *Professional Organisations:* Fellow, Royal Institution of Chartered Surveyors; Member, Rating Surveyors' Association. *Clubs:* Royal Overseas League.

ROOTH, Anthony; Partner, Clyde & Co.

ROPER, J B; Partner, Jaques & Lewis, since 1981; Company, Banking, Insolvency. *Career:* Jaques & Lewis 1974-. *Biog: b.* 3 February 1951. *Nationality:* British. *m.* 1974, Gillian; 2 s; 2 d. *Educ:* King's College School, Wimbledon; Emmanuel College, Cambridge University. *Professional Organisations:* Law Society, Holborn Law Society. *Recreations:* Golf, Sailing, Skiing, Family (not in order !!).

ROPNER, G L J; Managing Director, Technical, Ropner Insurance Services Limited.

ROPNER, William Guy David; Director, Ropner plc, since 1953. *Career:* Lights Advisory Committee 1978-88; General Council of British Shipping, President 1979-80; Merchant Navy Welfare Board 1980-. *Biog: b.* 3 April 1924. *Nationality:* British. m2 1985, Charlotte Mary (née Piercy); 4 s; 1 d. *Educ:* Harrow School. *Directorships:* Ropner Holdings Ltd (now Ropner plc) 1973-84 Chm; Ropner plc 1953 (non-exec); Ropner Shipping Co Ltd 1972; Guidehouse Expansion Management Ltd 1984; Mainsforth Investments Ltd 1952; Cleveland Leasing 1982. *Other Activities:* General Committee, Lloyds Register of Shipping (1961-). *Recreations:* Gardening.

ROQUES, David John Seymour; Partner-in-Charge, Touche Ross & Co, since 1990. *Career:* Touche Ross & Co 1957-; Touche Ross, Partner 1967; Partner-in-Charge, Midlands Region 1973; Partner-in-Charge, Scottish Region 1978; Partner-in-Charge, London Office 1984; Managing Partner 1990; DRT International, Member, Executive Committee 1990. *Biog: b.* 14 October 1938. *Nationality:* British. *m.* 1963, Elizabeth Anne (née Mallender); 2 s; 1 d. *Educ:* St Alban's School. *Other Activities:* Fellow, Royal Society of Arts. *Professional Organisations:* Member, Institute of Chartered Accountants of Scotland (1962). *Clubs:* Edgbaston Golf Club, Wasps Football Club. *Recreations:* Rugby Football, Racing, Opera, Gardening.

ROSE, Barry Michael; General Manager (Investment), Scottish Provident, since 1988; Group Investment and Property Activities. *Career:* Cooperative Insurance Society, Asst Investment Mgr 1966-76; Scottish Life, Investment Mgr 1976-88. *Biog: b.* 10 March 1945. *Nationality:* British. *m.* March 1945. *Educ:* Manchester University (BSc Hons). *Directorships:* City Site Estates plc 1988 (non-exec); SPI Berkley Dev Cap Ltd 1988 (non-exec). *Professional Organisations:* FIA.

ROSE, Harvey Alexander; Senior Manager, National Australia Bank Limited, since 1987; London Branch Operations. *Career:* Charterhouse Bank Limited, Dir 1958-87; Charterhouse Tilney, Dir 1986-87. *Biog: b.* 22 February 1942. *Nationality:* British. *m.* 1964, Marion

(née Jacobs); 2 d. *Educ:* Grocers' Company, London. *Other Activities:* BBA; Sterling Market Committee.

ROSE, John I; Managing Director, Bankers' Trust Company, since 1986; Corporate Finance. *Career:* Citibank, NA Snr VP 1962-86. *Biog: b.* 22 September 1940. *m.* 1970, Margaret (née Landsiedel); 1 s; 1 d. *Educ:* Davidson College (AB); University of North Carolina (MBA).

ROSE, Michael; Partner, S J Berwin & Co, since 1988; EEC Law (Particularly Environment) and Eastern Europe. *Career:* Bartletts De Reya, Solicitors, Partner 1961-88. *Biog: b.* 29 June 1935. *Nationality:* British. *m.* 1959, Dr Susan Rose; 3 s; 1 d. *Educ:* Queen Elizabeths, Barnet; Exeter College, Oxford (BA Hons). *Other Activities:* Member, Law Society's Working Party on Eastern Europe. *Publications:* Contributor to Company Law and Competition (CBI), 1989; Passing Off, Unfair Competition and Community Law, European Intellectual Property Review, 1990. *Recreations:* Sailing.

ROSE, Michael Enderwick; Sole Practitioner, Rose & Associates, since 1970; Personal Financial Planning. *Career:* Unilever Subsidiaries (UK & Overseas), Various in Engineering Mgmnt 1951-66; International Life Ass, Direct Sales 1967-69. *Biog: b.* 10 March 1929. *Nationality:* British. *m.* 1951, Betty (née Westwell); 2 s; 1 d. *Educ:* Sherwood College, Hallett War School, India; Denstone College, UK; Salford Technical College (HNC, ONC). *Directorships:* FIMBRA 1988 (non-exec). *Professional Organisations:* CEng, MIMechE. *Recreations:* Complete conversion of stone barn to a home and fighting a losing battle.

ROSE, N C; Group Treasurer, Ford Motor Company Ltd.

ROSE, N P; Partner, Field Fisher Waterhouse.

ROSEMAN, R; Managing Director (Investment Management), Providence Capitol Life Assurance Ltd.

ROSENBERG, M S; Deputy Chairman/Director Corporate Finance, Raphael Zorn Hemsley Ltd, since 1989; Corporate Finance. *Career:* Samuel Montagu & Co Ltd Merchant Bankers 1957-74; Director Corporate Finance 1972-74; Allied Investments Ltd, Director 1974-79; United Medical Enterprises Ltd, Deputy Chairman 1979-87; Owner/Director of several businesses 1987-89. *Biog: b.* 27 June 1939. *Nationality:* British. *m.* 1965, Jacqueline; 1 s; 1 d. *Educ:* Aldenham School. *Directorships:* David Paradine Ltd 1974 (exec); Office Angels Ltd 1988 (non-exec); Raphael Zorn Hemsley Ltd 1989 Deputy Chairman; B Rosenberg Ltd 1980 Chairman; Nationwide Lawns Ltd 1988 (non-exec); Eastkings Ltd 1978 Chairman; Talsarn Investments Ltd 1987. *Other Activities:* Chairman, Hong Kong Trade Advisory Group; BOTB; Treasurer, Association of British Health Care Industries Ltd. *Professional Organisations:* AIB; ACIS. *Recreations:* Reading, Squash, Tennis, Chess.

ROSENSTEEL, J W; Director, Aetna International (UK) Ltd.

ROSIER, Frederick David Stewart; Chairman, Mercury Asset Management Private Investors, since 1988; Investment Management for Private Clients. *Career:* 1st The Queen's Dragoon Guards, Capt 1973-78; SG Warburg & Co Ltd 1978-86; Dir 1984. *Biog: b.* 10 April 1951. *Nationality:* British. *m.* 1975, Julia Elizabeth (née Gomme). *Educ:* Winchester College; Keble College, Oxford (MA). *Directorships:* Mercury Asset Management Group plc 1987 (exec); Mercury Asset Management plc 1986 Vice-Chairman; Warburg Asset Management Jersey Ltd 1985 (exec); Mercury Fund Managers Ltd 1990 (exec); Bank SG Warburg AG 1990 (non-exec). *Other Activities:* The Worshipful Company of Coachmakers & Coach Harness Makers. *Clubs:* Cavalry & Guards, Hurlingham, Fautasians. *Recreations:* Squash, Golf.

ROSKILL, Eustace Wentworth; The Right Hon The Lord Roskill; PC, DL.; Chairman, Appeal Committee of the Panel on Takeovers & Mergers. *Career:* Barrister, Middle Temple 1933; QC 1953; Chairman, Hampshire Quarter Sessions 1960-71; Judge of the High Court, Queen's Bench Division 1962-71; Chairman, Parole Board 1967-69; Chairman, Third London Airport Commission 1968-70; Lord Justice of Appeal 1971-80; President, Senate of the Four Inns of Court and the Bar 1972-74; Lord of Appeal in Ordinary 1980-86; Treasurer, Middle Temple 1980; Fellow, Winchester College 1981-86; Chairman, Fraud Trials Committee 1983-85. *Biog: b.* 6 February 1911. *Nationality:* British. *m.* 1947, Elisabeth Wallace (née Jackson); 1 s; 2 d. *Educ:* Winchester College; Exeter College, Oxford (BA 1st Class Honours Modern History, MA). *Other Activities:* Honorary Fellow, Exeter College, Oxford, 1963; Honorary Bencher, Inner Temple, 1980. *Professional Organisations:* Chairman, London Arbitration Trust, 1981. *Clubs:* Reform. *Recreations:* Swimming, Gardening, Music.

ROSS, Alan Waclaw Padmint; Marketing Director, Fund Management Division, Credit Suisse Buckmaster & Moore Ltd, since 1987. *Career:* Hill Samuel Life Agency Mgr, Dir 1972-81; Julian Gibbs Associates, Marketing Dir 1981-82; Tyndall Group Ltd, Dir, Project Dev 1983-84; Framlington Group plc, Various 1984-87. *Biog: b.* 23 December 1933. *Nationality:* British. *m.* 1961, Catherine (née Slade); 2 s; 1 d. *Educ:* Bradfield College, Berkshire; Balliol College, Oxford (Eng Hons 1st). *Clubs:* Royal Air Force. *Recreations:* Tennis, Squash, Politics, Collecting 18th-Century Glass.

ROSS, Colin Hamish; Managing Director, Edinburgh Fund Managers plc.

ROSS, Denis John; Consultant, S J Berwin & Co, since 1988; Corporate Finance. *Career:* Military Service (Captain, Royal Artillery) 1942-47; Articled to Hyman Isaacs Lewis & Mills (now Beechcroft Stanleys) 1948-52; Bartlett & Gluckstein (which became Bartletts de Reya), Assistant Solicitor 1952-55; Bartletts de Reya, Partner 1955-88; Senior Partner 1985-88. *Biog: b.* 10 July 1923. *Nationality:* British. *m.* 1956, Shifra (née Miller); 1 s; 3 d. *Educ:* Haberdashers' Aske's Hampstead School; University College, London (LLB Hons); College of Law (Solicitor Hons). *Other Activities:* President, City of Westminster Law Society, 1986-87; Member, Council of Family Holiday Association; Trustee, Victoria Community Centre. *Professional Organisations:* Law Society; Holborn Law Society. *Publications:* Commercial Editor of, and Author of Articles and Reviews in the Law Society's Gazette. *Clubs:* MCC, Royal Automobile Club. *Recreations:* Tennis, Cricket, Rugby, Reading, Music.

ROSS, Howard David; Partner, Clifford Chance, since 1981; Corporate Taxation. *Career:* Slaughter & May, Articled Clerk (as Qualified Solicitor in Tax Dept) 1968-72; Bank Leui, Israel, Legal Dept 1973-75; Slaughter & May, Tax Dept 1975-78; Clifford Turner/Clifford Chance 1978-. *Biog: b.* 12 August 1945. *Nationality:* British. *m.* 1972, Jennifer; 3 d. *Educ:* Owens Grammar School; LSE (LLB First Class Hons). *Other Activities:* Petroleum Revenue Committee of Law Society. *Professional Organisations:* Law Society. *Publications:* Doing Business in the UK (International Tax Chapters), 1986; Structuring Buyouts and other Investment Funds, 1989. *Clubs:* Reform. *Recreations:* Jogging, Cycling, Gardening.

ROSS, Hubert J; Partner, W & J Burness WS, since 1983; Tax Planning. *Career:* W & J Burness WS, Apprentice Solicitor 1972-76; Lord Advocates Department, Parliamentary Draftsman 1976-77; Leopold Joseph & Sons Limited, Director/Merchant Banker 1977-83. *Biog: b.* 26 November 1948. *Nationality:* British. *m.* 1975, Brenda; 2 s. *Educ:* Edinburgh University (MA Hons, LLB). *Directorships:* W & J Burness (Trustees) Limited; W & J Burness (Properties) Limited; W & J Burness (PEP Nominees) Limited. *Professional Organisations:* Law Society of Scotland.

ROSS, Ian; Partner, Clyde & Co.

ROSS, J D; Director, MIM Limited.

ROSS, John Dacre Hastings; Director, Barclays de Zoete Wedd Securities Ltd, since 1986; Investment Trust Corporate Finance. *Career:* Hobson Bates (Advertising), Time Buyer 1958-60; Ogilvy-Mather, Media Group Head 1960-69; Myers & Co, Investment Trust Sales 1969-70; Hoare Govett Ltd, Snr Ltd Shareholder, Invest Trust Sales 1970-79; de Zoete & Bevan, Consultant 1979-86. *Biog: b.* 28 May 1937. *Nationality:* British.

m. 1967, Gillian (née Thurnham); 2 s. *Educ:* Bradfield College. *Directorships:* Barclays de Zoete Wedd UK Equities Ltd 1986; Ebbgate Holdings Ltd 1987. *Clubs:* Naval, Cannons. *Recreations:* Tennis, Shooting, Golf.

ROSS, Kenneth A; Partner, W & J Burness WS. *Educ:* (LLB).

ROSS, M D; Deputy Managing Director, Scottish Widows' Fund & Life Assurance Society; Actuarial & Accounting Division.

ROSS, Murray John; Partner, Withers, since 1989; Head of Property Department. *Career:* Warmingtons & Hasties, Articled Clerk 1966-71; Wild Collins & Crosse, Asst Solicitor, Partner 1971-72; 3M United Kingdom plc, Company Secretary & General Manager Legal Affairs 1972-89. *Biog: b.* 31 March 1947. *m.* 1975, Myra Goldsman (née Brown); 2 s. *Educ:* Dulwich College. *Other Activities:* Member, Law Society's Land Law & Conveyancing Committee. *Publications:* Author, Drafting & Negotiating Commercial Leases, 3rd Edn 1989; Editor & Contributor, Vol 22 Encyclopaedia of Forms & Precidents, 5th Edn 1986; Co-Author, Drafting & Negotiating Commercial Leases in Scotland, 1985. *Clubs:* MCC, National Trust for Scotland.

ROSS, P F; Chairman, Henderson Crosthwaite Institutional Brokers.

ROSS, Thomas MacKenzie; Partner, Clay & Partners, since 1976; Pensions, Benefit Communications. *Career:* Scottish Life Assurance Co (Edinburgh), Trainee Actuary then Qualified Actuary 1966-71; Charles A Kench & Associates (Vancouver), Consulting Actuary 1971-76. *Biog: b.* 4 May 1944. *Nationality:* Scottish. *m.* 1967, Margaret (née Dewar); 1 s; 1 d. *Educ:* Dingwall Academy; Edinburgh University (BSc Hons). *Directorships:* Clay Communications Ltd 1987 (non-exec). *Other Activities:* CBI Pensions Panel, Assoc of Consulting Actuaries; Council of National Association of Pension Funds; Pensions Joint Committee of the Institute and Faculty of Actuaries. *Professional Organisations:* FFA; ASA; Fellow, The Canadian Institute of Actuaries; FPMI. *Recreations:* Golf, Horse-Racing, Gardening, Theatre.

ROSS-MCNAIRN, Edward; Partner, Clark Whitehill.

ROSS RUSSELL, G; Member of the Council, The International Stock Exchange.

ROSS RUSSELL, Graham; Chairman, Laurence Prust Holdings Ltd.

ROSS STEWART, David Andrew; OBE; Chairman, The Scottish Provident Institution, since 1989. *Career:* Alex Cowan & Sons Ltd, Mgmnt Trainee 1952-55;

Market Development 1955-59; Alex Cowan & Sons (NZ) Ltd (Wellington), Asst to Gen Mgr 1959-62; Alex Cowan & Sons (Stationery) Ltd, Gen Mgr 1962-66; Spicers (Stationery) Ltd, Gen Mgr 1966-68; John Bartholomew & Son Ltd 1968-89. *Biog: b.* 30 November 1930. *Nationality:* British. *m.* 1959, Susan Olive (née Routh); 2 s. *Educ:* Rugby School; Clare College, Cambridge (BA Hons). *Directorships:* St Andrew Trust plc Chm; East of Scotland Industrial Investments Ltd; Abbey National plc (Scottish Advisory Brd); West Lothian Enterprise Ltd Chm. *Other Activities:* Member, Trade Dev Ctee Scottish Council, Dev & Industry; Convener, University of Edinburgh Advisory Ctee on Business Studies. *Clubs:* New (Edinburgh), Honourable Company of Edinburgh Golfers, Muirfield. *Recreations:* Fishing, Gardening, Golf.

ROSSDALE, E G; Director, Byas Mosley & Co Ltd.

ROSSHANDLER, J; Partner, Nabarro Nathanson.

ROSSI, Francesco M; Managing Director Investment Banking, Brown Shipley & Co Ltd, since 1988; International Corporate Finance & Mergers & Acquisitions, Investment Banking Activities Worldwide. *Career:* Morgan Guaranty Bank (New York), Asst Treasurer 1980-84; Becker Paribas (New York) VP, Intl Corporate Finance 1984; Merrill Lynch (New York) VP, Mergers & Acquisitions; (London) VP, European Emerging Growth Companies 1984-88. *Biog: b.* 20 July 1957. *Nationality:* Italian. *m.* 1981, Alessandra (née Bertacchi); 2 s. *Educ:* Universita Bocconi.

ROTHERY, S; Director, Yorkshire Building Society.

ROTHSCHILD, (Nathaniel Charles) Jacob; Lord Rothschild; Chairman, St James's Place Capital plc. *Career:* N M Rothschild & Sons Ltd, Ptnr 1963; Dir 1968-80; RIT and Northern, Chm 1971; Co-Chm with Viscount Weir 1982; Charterhouse J Rothschild plc, Chm 1983-84. *Biog: b.* 29 April 1936. *Nationality:* British. *m.* 1961, Serena Mary (née Dunn); 1 s; 3 d. *Educ:* Eton College; Christ Church, Oxford (MA Hons 1st). *Directorships:* La Compagnie Financiere-Holding SA (France) 1975; Five Arrows Ltd 1980 Chm; Clifton Nurseries (Holdings) Ltd 1981; Colefax & Fowler Group Ltd 1986 (exec); J Rothschild Investment Mgmnt Ltd 1975. *Other Activities:* Chm of Board of Trustees, National Gallery, London; Member of Council, Royal College of Art; Commander of the Order of Henry the Navigator, 1985 (awarded by Portuguese Government). *Professional Organisations:* FRAS. *Clubs:* White's.

ROTHSCHILD, Simon Andrew Julian; Associate Director, College Hill Associates, since 1990; Financial Public Relations. *Career:* Dewe Rogerson, Account Executive 1983-87; Shandwick Consultants, Consultant 1987-89; College Hill Associates, Associate Director 1989-. *Biog: b.* 3 April 1959. *Nationality:* British. *Educ:*

Eton College; St Andrews University (MA Honours Modern History). *Directorships:* College Hill 1990 (exec).

ROTHWELL, John Dominic; Senior Partner, Waltons & Morse, since 1989; Commercial Property. *Career:* 2nd Lieutenant (National Service) 10th Royal Hussars 1956-57; Neish Howell & Haldane (became Macfarlanes), Articled Clerk 1960-63; Macfarlanes, Assistant Solicitor 1963-66; Allen & Overy, Assistant Solicitor 1966-68; Waltons Bright & Co, Assistant Solicitor 1968-69; Waltons Bright & Co, (renamed Waltons & Co and then Waltons & Morse on amalgamation with Sidney Morse & Co), Partner 1969-. *Biog: b.* 11 April 1937. *Nationality:* British. *m.* 1966, Anne Vivien (née Read); 2 d. *Educ:* Ampleforth; Brasenose College, Oxford (MA Jurisprudence). *Professional Organisations:* Law Society. *Clubs:* Cavalry & Guards, City University.

ROUECHE, Mossman; Director, Samuel Montagu & Co Limited, since 1986; Capital Markets: New Issues. *Career:* Standard Chartered Bank plc, Trainee 1973-75; Samuel Montagu & Co Ltd 1975-. *Biog: b.* 14 December 1947. *Nationality:* American. *m.* 1972, Charlotte (née Wrinch); 1 s; 1 d. *Educ:* Kenyon College, Ohio, USA (BA); State University of New York (MA). *Publications:* Various Articles on Byzantine Philosophy. *Recreations:* Archaeology.

ROUGET, Bernard John; Executive Director, County NatWest Limited, since 1988; Operational Audit & Compliance. *Career:* National Provincial Bank Clerk, Various Branches 1954-66; Acct 1966-71; National Westminster Bank, Asst Manager, Various Branches & HQ 1971-81; Snr Inspector 1981-85; Mgr 1985-87. *Biog: b.* 15 September 1937. *Nationality:* British. *m.* 1957, Brenda (née Manvell); 1 s; 1 d. *Educ:* Collyers School, Horsham. *Directorships:* County NatWest Ltd (exec). *Professional Organisations:* ACIB. *Clubs:* Royal Overseas League. *Recreations:* Church Work, Gardening.

ROUNDELL, Henry J; Managing Director, Morgan Guaranty Trust Company of New York.

ROUNDELL, P; Director, Leslie & Godwin Ltd.

ROUNDING, Albert; Regional Controller, Yorkshire Bank plc.

ROUNTHWAITE, Francis Anthony; Partner-In-Charge, West Midlands, Robson Rhodes.

ROUSE, Dr Lynda Margaret (née Cox); Director, Public Sector Unit, Barclays de Zoete Wedd Ltd.

ROUSE, R M; Partner, Ernst & Young.

ROUT, A E; Director, Wellington Underwriting Agencies Limited.

ROUTLEDGE, A G; Director, Bain Clarkson Limited.

ROWAN, Thomas Stanley; Executive Director, Singer & Friedlander Holdings Ltd. *Biog: b.* 11 April 1935. *Nationality:* British. *m.* 1964, Anne Strafford(née Sanderson); 1 s; 1 d. *Educ:* University of Natal (BA); Gonville & Caius College, Cambridge (LLB); Wellington School, Somerset. *Directorships:* Singer & Friedlander Investment Management Ltd; Singer & Friedlander (Jersey) Ltd. *Other Activities:* Member, Sub Committee of Taxation of the British Merchant Banking & Securities Association. *Professional Organisations:* FCA. *Clubs:* Leeds.

ROWBOTHAM, Graham William Henry; Partner, Simmons & Simmons, since 1981; Head of Banking and Capital Markets Group. *Career:* Arthur Andersen & Co 1969; Slaughter and May 1970-79; Simmons & Simmons 1980-. *Biog: b.* 25 June 1948. *Nationality:* British. *m.* 1977, Sue; 3 d. *Educ:* The King's School, Canterbury; St John's College, Oxford (MA). *Other Activities:* Member, Editorial Advisory Boards, International Financial Law Review and Computer Law and Practice; Member, Worshipful Company of Solicitors. *Professional Organisations:* Law Society; International Bar Association. *Clubs:* Roehampton, Royal Tennis Court. *Recreations:* Lawn Tennis, Golf, Walking, Reading.

ROWE, B V; Director, Parrish Stockbrokers.

ROWE, Heather; Partner, Lovell White Durrant, since 1988; Retail Banking, Electronic Banking, Debt Rescheduling, Secured Lending, Computer & Telecommunications Law. *Career:* Wilde Sapte Solicitor 1981-83; S J Berwin & Co Solicitor 1983-85; Durrant Piesse Solicitor 1985-88. *Biog: b.* 16 October 1957. *Nationality:* British. *Educ:* Stanborough School, Welwyn Garden City; Manchester University (LLB Hons). *Other Activities:* City of London Law Society; Freeman, Worshipful Company of Solicitors; Member, International Bar Association & Editor, Newsletter for the International Bar Association, Committe R. *Professional Organisations:* ACIArb. *Recreations:* Birdwatching, Fishing, Shooting, Tennis, Reading.

ROWE, John David Beaumont; Partner, Slaughter and May, since 1978; Competition Law. *Biog: b.* 2 October 1928. *Nationality:* British. *m.* 1957, Dorothy Mary (née Adam); 2 s. *Educ:* Wath-on-Dearne Grammar School; University College, Oxford (MA). *Professional Organisations:* The Law Society. *Publications:* Selling Industrial Products, 1968. *Clubs:* Saville, Huntercombe Golf Club. *Recreations:* Golf, History of Architecture.

ROWE, Michael F; Head of Systems Development, Leeds Permanent Building Society, since 1989; Computer Systems Development. *Biog: b.* 20 May 1953. *Nationality:* British. *m.* 1974, Sheila; 1 s; 1 d. *Educ:* St Michaels College, Leeds. *Recreations:* Football, Golf, Reading.

ROWE, Nigel; Partner, Cazenove & Co, since 1988; UK Equities. *Career:* Cazenove & Co 1979-. *Biog: b.* 7 October 1958. *Nationality:* British. *m.* 1986, Jane Elizabeth (née Peregrine); 1 d. *Educ:* Shrewsbury; Queens' College, Cambridge (MA Hons). *Directorships:* Cazenove Securities 1986.

ROWE-HAM, Sir David Kenneth; GBE; Consultant, Touche Ross & Co, since 1984. *Career:* Commissioned 3rd The King's Own Hussars; Smith Keen Cutler, Partner/Senior Partner 1964-82; Birmingham Municipal Bank, Chairman 1970-72; Smith Keen Cutler, Consultant 1982-84; London & Midland Industrials plc, Non-Executive Director 1978-79; Wiljay plc, Non-Executive Director 1980-84; 1928 Investment Trust plc, Director 1984-86; W Canning plc, Non-Executive Director 1981-86; Asset Trust plc, Chairman 1982-89; Jersey General Investment Trust Ltd, Chairman 1988-89. *Biog: b.* 19 December 1935. *Nationality:* British. *m.* 1980, Sandra Celia (née Nicholls); 3 s. *Educ:* Dragon School, Oxford; Charterhouse. *Directorships:* Touche Ross & Co 1984 Consultant; Lloyds Bank plc 1985 Regional Dir, London; Guinness Mahon Unit Trust Managers Ltd 1985 Chairman, Advisory Panel; Savoy Theatre Ltd 1986; Olayan Europe Ltd 1989 (non-exec) Chm; St Davids Investment Trust plc 1989. *Other Activities:* Lord Mayor of London, 1986-87; Sheriff of the City of London, 1984-85; Alderman of the City of London for the Ward of Bridge and Bridge Without 1976-; Governor, Christ's Hospital 1976- (Vice-President 1986-87); Court Member, City University 1981-86 (Chancellor 1986-87); Court Member, Worshipful Company of Chartered Accountants in England and Wales (Master 1985-86); Court Member, Worshipful Company of Wheelwrights; Honorary Liveryman, Worshipful Company of Launderers; Court Member, Honourable Artillery Company; Member, Guild of Freemen; Justice of the Peace, 1976-; Chief Magistrate of the City of London 1986-87; Governor, Royal Shakespeare Company; Trustee, Friends of D'Oyly Carte; Member, Lords Taverners; President, Black Country Museum Development Trust; Member, Stock Exchange 1964-84; Member, Birmingham City Council, 1965-72; Chairman, Junior Carlton Club Political Council 1977; Deputy Chairman, Carlton Club Political Committee 1977-79; Knight Grand Cross of the Most Excellent Order of the British Empire 1986; Knight of Justice of the Most Venerable Order of St John 1986; Commandeur de l'Ordre du Merite (France) 1984; Commander of the Order of the Lion of Malawi 1985; National Order of the Aztec Eagle (Class II) 1985; Order of King Abdul Aziz (Class 1) 1987; Grand Officier du Wissam Alouite 1987; Holder of the Pedro Ernesto Medal, Rio de Janeiro 1987; Order of Diego Losada of Caracas 1987; Her Majesty's Commission of Lieutenancy for the City of London 1987. *Professional Organisations:* Fellow, Institute of Chartered Accountants in England & Wales; Member, Society of Investment Analysts; Fellow, Institute of Chartered Secretaries and Administrators. *Clubs:* Carlton, Guildhall and City Livery.

ROWLAND, (John) David; Chairman, Sedgwick Group plc, since 1989. *Career:* Matthews Wrighton & Co 1956; Dir 1965; Matthews Wrighton Holdings, Dir 1972; Stewart Wrighton Holdings plc, Dep Chm 1978-81; Chm 1981-87; Westminster Insurance Agencies, Chm 1981-88; Royal London Mutual Insurance Society 1985-86; Willis Faber plc Dep Chm 1987-88; Project Fullemploy, Dir 1973-88; Sedgwick Group plc, Group Chief Executive 1988-89. *Biog: b.* 10 August 1933. *m.* 1957, Giulia (née Powell); 1 s; 1 d. *Educ:* St Paul's School; Trinity College, Cambridge (MA Natural Sciences). *Directorships:* Sedgwick Lloyd's Underwriting Agencies Ltd 1988 (exec); Fullemploy Group 1989. *Other Activities:* Member of Council, Lloyd's, 1987; Member, City of London Section, 1983-86; Vice-President, British Insurance & Investment Brokers, Association, 1980; Member, President's Ctee, Business in the Community, 1986; Member of Council, Industrial Society, 1983-88; Chm, Templeton College (Oxford Centre for Management Studies), 1985; Council Member, 1980; Contemporary Applied Arts (formerly British Crafts Centre),1985; Governor, College of Insurance, 1983-85. *Clubs:* MCC, Royal & Ancient Golf Club (St Andrews), Royal St George's (Sandwich), Royal Worlington & Newmarket Golf Club, Sunningdale Golf Club. *Recreations:* Golf, Running Slowly.

ROWLAND, Norman Leslie; Director, Smith Keen Cutler Ltd.

ROWLAND, Peter William Stuart; Group Secretary, TSB Group plc, since 1981; Company Secretarial, Legal, External Relations, Insurance. *Career:* Harveys of Bristol Ltd Secretarial Asst 1964-66; Showerings, Vine Products & Whiteways Ltd Secretarial Asst 1966-67; Smith Industries Ltd Asst Sec 1968-71; United Dominions Trust Ltd Asst Sec 1971-72; Sec 1973-81. *Biog: b.* 28 July 1941. *Nationality:* British. *m.* 1969, Monica Jane (née Brown); 1 s; 2 d. *Educ:* Repton School; Queens' College, Cambridge (MA). *Clubs:* MCC. *Recreations:* Golf, Tennis, Cricket.

ROWLAND, R W; Managing Director & Chief Executive, Lonrho plc.

ROWLAND, Richard Arthur Philip; Partner, Allen & Overy, since 1974; Company/Commercial Law. *Career:* Allen & Overy Asst Solicitor 1969-74. *Biog: b.* 18 July 1944. *m.* 1971, Cherry Ann (née Adcock); 2 s; 1 d.

Educ: St Paul's School; Selwyn College, Cambridge (BA, LLB). *Professional Organisations:* The Law Society; City of London Law Society (Company Law Sub-Ctee). *Recreations:* Print Making, Music, Vintage Car Restoration, Travel, Livestock Farming, Tennis.

ROWLAND, William Robin; Director & Group General Manager, Royal Insurance Holdings plc, since 1989; International Operations Mergers & Acquisitions, Strategic Planning. *Career:* Royal Insurance plc, Various Acturial 1958-63; Accounting Taxation 1964-71; Mgmnt Research Unit 1972-73; Group Chief Acct 1975-80; Dep Group Comptroller 1981; Group Comptroller 1982-85; Royal Life Holdings Ltd, Asst MD 1985-86; Royal International Insurance Holdings Ltd, MD 1987-89. *Biog: b.* 24 May 1940. *Nationality:* British. *m.* 1964, Valerie Leigh (née Rylance); 2 d. *Educ:* Shrewsbury School. *Directorships:* Subsidiary Cos of Royal Insurance Holdings plc. *Other Activities:* Trustee, Royal Insurance Benevolent Fund; Sponsor for Year 1550, Amersham Museum; BIEC; Japan Committee. *Professional Organisations:* FIA; FCCA; MCT. *Publications:* Several Accounting and Actuarial Papers. *Clubs:* Royal Horticultural Society. *Recreations:* Gardening, Music, Golf, Reading, Oil Painting, Family, Work.

ROWLANDS, J; Deputy Managing Director, Carnegie International, since 1988. *Career:* Touche Remnant, Analyst/Fund Manager 1981-83; Wood Gundy, European Sales 1983-85; Carnegie International 1985-. *Biog: b.* 16 November 1958. *Nationality:* British. *m.* 1985, Sally Louise (née Needham). *Educ:* Hertford College, Oxford (MA Hons Jurisprudence). *Directorships:* Carnegie International 1987 (non-exec); Carnegie Espania 1989 (exec); Carnegie Property Management 1989 (non-exec). *Recreations:* Rugby, Tennis.

ROWLAY, J T; Non-Executive Director, Next plc.

ROWLES, Michael J; Commercial Conveyancing Partner, Bristows Cooke & Carpmael.

ROWLEY, Geoffrey William; CBE; Town Clerk, Corporation of London.

ROWLEY, James Edward; Partner, Evershed Wells & Hind, since 1965; Housing Development. *Career:* Evershed & Tomkinson, Articled Clerk 1958-61; Assistant 1961-65; Partner 1965-. *Biog: b.* 25 March 1935. *Nationality:* British. *m.* 1965, Janet Mary (née Pinsent); 2 d. *Educ:* Kings School, Worcester; Cambridge (MA). *Professional Organisations:* Law Society. *Recreations:* Early Music.

ROWLEY, M E; Director, Tullett & Tokyo Forex International Ltd.

ROWLEY, Robert; Alternate Director, Reuters Holdings plc.

ROWLINSON, M; Senior Vice President and Branch Manager, Union Bank of Switzerland.

ROWSON, John Anthony; Senior Partner, Herbert Smith, since 1988; Company Law. *Career:* Herbert Smith 1960-. *Biog: b.* 6 May 1930. *Nationality:* British. 1989, Molly (née Lee-Warner); 2 s; 1 d (by previous marriage). *Educ:* Beckenham Grammar School. *Other Activities:* The Clockmakers' Company (Liveryman); City of London Solicitors' Company (Junior Warden). *Professional Organisations:* The Law Society; City of London Law Society. *Clubs:* Athenaeum, Royal Thames Yacht Club, City of London, Hurlingham. *Recreations:* Tennis, Skiing, Music.

ROY, D A; Director, County NatWest Securities Limited.

ROY, Paul David; Director, Smith New Court plc.

ROYDS, Richard George; Managing Director, John Govett Unit Management Ltd, since 1988; Controlling Company Activities, Product Design, Sales and Marketing. *Career:* London Weekend TV, Sales Executive 1976-79; Capital Radio, Sales Executive 1979-82; The Media Shop, Director 1982-86; Wardley Unit Trust Managers Ltd, Mktg Dir 1986-88; Managing Director 1988. *Biog: b.* 15 November 1957. *Nationality:* British. *m.* 1986, Lucinda (née McClean); 1 s. *Educ:* Charterhouse; City of London Polytechnic. *Directorships:* John Govett & Co Ltd 1988 (exec). *Other Activities:* Information Ctee Member, Unit Trust Association. *Clubs:* DWC, Sunningdale, Royal St Georges, Cricketers. *Recreations:* Golf, Fishing, Art.

ROYLE, Timothy Lancelot Fanshawe; Chairman, Control Risks Group, since 1974. *Career:* Commissioned 15th/19th King's Royal Hussars 1949; TA, Inns of Court Regt 1951-63; Hogg Robinson Group 1951; MD 1980-81; Wellmarine Reinsurance Brokers, Dep Chm 1976. *Biog: b.* 24 April 1931. *Nationality:* British. *m.* 1958, Jill (née Stedeford); 2 s; 1 d. *Educ:* Harrow; Mons Military Academy. *Directorships:* Hogg Robinson Group 1968 (exec); Control Risks Group 1974 (exec); Wellmarine Reinsurance Ltd 1978 (non-exec); Berry Palmer & Lyle 1984 (non-exec); Christian Weekly Newspaper 1978 (non-exec); Endley Educational Trust 1970 (non-exec); Central Board of Finance 1985 (non-exec). *Other Activities:* Member, Church Assembly of Church of England, 1960-70; Member, Gen Synod of the Church of England, 1985; Church Commissioner, 1966-83; Freeman, City of London; Marketors; Insurers. *Professional Organisations:* FCIM; FBBA. *Clubs:* Cavalry & Guards, St Moritz Tobogganning Club, MCC.

RUBEN, P; Associate, Grimley J R Eve.

RUBINS, B L; Director, Chancery plc, since 1987; Property Finance.

RUBINS, Jack; Chairman & Chief Executive Officer, McCann Erickson Group UK, since 1990. *Career:* DFS Dorland Advertising, Chairman & Chief Executive 1976-87; Saatchi Group, Consultant 1987-90. *Biog: b.* 4 August 1931. *Nationality:* British. *m.* Ruth; 3 s. *Educ:* Northern Polytechnic Architecture (FIPA). *Other Activities:* Chairman, National Advertising Benevolent Society, 1988. *Recreations:* Philately, Golf.

RUBNER, N; Director, S G Warburg Akroyd Rowe & Pitman Mullens Securities Ltd.

RUCK, Peter Thomas; Director, Leadenhall Associates Limited, since 1989. *Career:* Hertford Public Relations, Senior Account Executive 1968-71; Warwick Public Relations, Group Account Executive 1971-73; Industrial Communications, Director 1973-84; John Fowler & Partners, Head of London Office 1984-86; Shandwick Communications, Executive Director 1986-89. *Biog: b.* 25 May 1939. *Nationality:* British. *m.* 1963, Norah (née Lemmon); 1 d. *Educ:* Wotton School. *Clubs:* Bloggs, Scribes. *Recreations:* Shooting, Fishing, Forestry.

RUCK KEENE, David Kenneth Lancelot; Director, SG Warburg Akroyd Rowe & Pitman Mullens Ltd, since 1986; Institutional Client Liaison. *Career:* Binder Hamlyn, Articled Clerk 1967-73; W I Carr & Sons, Trainee 1973-74; Binder Hamlyn, Asst Mgr 1974-77; Rowe & Pitman, Institutional Salesman 1977-82; Ptnr 1982-86. *Biog: b.* 22 September 1948. *Nationality:* British. *m.* 1976, Tania Caroline (née Wild); 3 d. *Educ:* Eton College; Grenoble University. *Directorships:* S G Warburg Securities 1986 (exec). *Professional Organisations:* FCA; Member, The International Stock Exchange. *Clubs:* MCC, White's. *Recreations:* Rackets, Tennis, Golf, Fishing, Shooting, Music, Wildlife.

RUCKER, (Patrick) Antony S; Executive Director, Director of Compliance, London Fox, the Futures & Options Exchange, since 1986. *Career:* British Army, Sherwood Foresters 1951; Rucker & Bencraft 1960-62; Rubber Dept, Ptnr 1962-65; Commodity Market Services Ltd, Cocoa & Sugar Secretariat 1965-71; Cocoa & Sugar Secretariat, Sec 1971-73; The London Commodity Exchange Co Ltd, Exec Dir 1973-86. *Biog: b.* 23 October 1934. *Nationality:* British. *m.* 1988, Jane; 3 d. *Educ:* Eastbourne College; RMA Sandhurst. *Directorships:* Federation of Commodity Associations. *Other Activities:* Guild of World Traders.

RUDD, A J; Director, Hill Samuel Bank Limited.

RUDDELL, M F; Managing Director, Property Division, The Boots Co plc.

RUDGE, Anthony John de Nouaille; Regional Director, Barclays Bank plc.

RUDGE, Stanley Bickerton; Partner in Charge, Executive Office, Touche Ross & Co, since 1981; Audit, Corporate Finance, Financial Institutions, Board of Partnrs. *Career:* Touche Ross & Co 1967-. *Biog: b.* 28 September 1935. *Nationality:* British. *m.* 1962, Beryl; 2 s; 1 d. *Professional Organisations:* FCA.

RUDLOFF, Hans-Jorg; Chairman & Chief Executive, Credit Suisse First Boston Ltd.

RUDOLPH, Jochen; Correspondent, Frankfurter Allgemeine Zeitung, since 1967; Economy/Business/Finance. *Career:* Deutsche Zeitung & Wirtschafts Zeitung, Frankfurt, Stuttgart, Cologne, Hamburg, Taxation, Companies, Features, Correspondent 1952-64. *Biog: b.* 13 September 1926. *Nationality:* German. *m.* 1955, Brigitte. *Educ:* University, Erlangen-Nuremberg (Diplom-Kaufman). *Professional Organisations:* Foreign Press Association, London. *Publications:* Handbuch der englischen Wintschaftssprache, 1974/86/90.

RUFIAN-GARCIA, Miguel; Commercial Banking Manager, Banco Bilbao-Vizcaya.

RULE, C S; Secretary, W H Smith Group plc.

RUMSEY, Stephen John Raymond; Managing Director, Fixed Income Division, Barclays De Zoete Wedd, since 1986; Bonds. *Career:* Postel Investment Management 1977-85; Zoete & Bevan, Ptnr 1985-86. *Biog: b.* 6 November 1950. *m.* 1978, Anne (née Williamson); 2 s. *Educ:* Windsor Grammar School; London School of Economics (BSc). *Other Activities:* Council Member, RSPB, BTO; Chairman, Wetland Trust. *Publications:* Various Papers. *Recreations:* Agriculture, Ornithology.

RUNCIMAN, Walter Garrison; Lord Runciman; Deputy Chairman, Securities and Investments Board.

RUNDLE, Brian R; Executive Director, Bank of America International Limited.

RUSHBROOK, Ian Frank; Deputy Chairman, Ivory & Sime plc.

RUSHMORE, Patrick Joseph George; Partner, Macintyre Hudson, since 1985; International Partner, Practice Development Partner, Auditor, Advisor to Family Companies, Institutions and Trusts. *Career:* Ernst & Whinney, Accountant 1980-84. *Biog: b.* 13 January 1959. *Nationality:* British. *Educ:* Ratcliffe College, Leicestershire; Newcastle Upon Tyne University (BA Hons Economics/Accountancy). *Directorships:* Macintyre Sträter International Ltd 1990 (exec); Macintyre Investments Ltd 1988 (exec); Grangehouse Investments Ltd 1988 (exec); Eshwaite Estates Ltd 1987 (exec); Fairloch Investments Ltd 1988 (exec); Rydenford Ltd 1989 (exec); Bondneal Ltd 1987 (exec); Avonmore Stud Ltd

1988 (exec). *Other Activities:* Member, Various ICAEW Committee's (European, Independence of Audit; Small Audits Committee); Chairman, Young Chartered Accountants Group. *Professional Organisations:* Fellow of the Institute of Chartered Accountants in England & Wales. *Publications:* Various Articles and Interviews in Local and Trade Press. *Clubs:* City of London Club. *Recreations:* Shooting, Fishing, Riding, Sailing.

RUSHTON, D J F; Director, Hill Samuel Bank Limited.

RUSHTON, Ian Lawton; Group Chief Executive, Royal Insurance Holdings plc, since 1989. *Career:* Royal Insurance Co Ltd 1956-; Dep Gen Mgr for the UK 1972-81; Royal Group Inc (New York), Executive Vice President 1981-83; Royal Insurance (UK) Ltd, MD 1983-86; Royal Insurance plc, Dir & Gen Mgr 1986-88; Royal Insurance Holdings plc, Dep Group Chief Executive 1988-89; Group Chief Executive 1989-. *Biog: b.* 8 September 1931. *Nationality:* British. *m.* Anita. *Educ:* Rock Ferry High School, Birkenhead; Kings College, London (BSc). *Directorships:* ROINS Holding Ltd (Canada); Royal Group Inc (USA); Royal International Insurance Holdings Ltd; Royal Insurance (UK) Ltd; Royal Life Insurance Ltd; Royal Reinsurance Co Ltd; Aachener und Münchener Beteiligungs AG (W Germany); Royal Insurance Asset Management Ltd. *Other Activities:* Worshipful Company of Actuaries; Worshipful Company of Insurers. *Professional Organisations:* FIA; FSS; FCII; MAAA (USA).

RUSHWORTH, Jonathan Edwin Fletcher; Partner, Slaughter and May.

RUSSELL, Arthur Christie; Head of Insurance Division, Department of Trade & Industry, since 1987. *Career:* Department of Trade & Industry Head, Shipbuilding Policy Division 1978-83; Head, Finance & Resource Mgmnt Div 1983-87. *Biog: b.* 8 December 1934. *Nationality:* British. *m.* 1961, Gillian Mary (née Venables); 1 s; 1 d. *Educ:* Rugby; Jesus College, Oxford (BA).

RUSSELL, B J; Partner, Milne Ross.

RUSSELL, D W; Finance Director, T H March & Company Limited.

RUSSELL, Fiona Elizabeth; Partner, Gouldens, since 1989; Intellectual Property. *Career:* Coward Chance, Articled Clerk 1982-84; Gouldens, Solicitor 1984-. *Biog: b.* 5 March 1959. *Nationality:* British. *m.* 1985, Howard Barrie; 1 s. *Educ:* Godalming Grammar; Exeter University (LLB Hons); London University, Queen Mary College (Diploma in Intellectual Property). *Professional Organisations:* The Law Society; Associate Member, Chartered Institute of Patent Agents; Associate Member,

Institute of Trade Mark Agents. *Recreations:* Piano, Walking.

RUSSELL, Gary A M; Partner, Theodore Goddard, since 1980; Property Law. *Career:* Hart Forteane & Co, Articled Clerk 1975-77; Hart Forteane & Co, Partner 1977-80; Russel Blain, Partner 1980-85; Brooke Blain Russel, Partner 1985-90. *Biog: b.* 17 January 1952. *Educ:* Merchant Taylors School for Boys; (BA Law & German).

RUSSELL, Geoffrey Nicholas; Partner, Linklaters & Paines, since 1990; Property Law. *Career:* Linklaters & Paines, Articled Clerk 1981-83; Assistant Solicitor 1983-90. *Biog: b.* 11 May 1959. *Nationality:* British. *m.* 1988, Rhona Alison (née Inglis). *Educ:* Kings College School, Wimbledon; Downing College, Cambridge (BA, MA). *Professional Organisations:* Law Society.

RUSSELL, Gerald William; Partner, Ernst & Whinney.

RUSSELL, John Bayley; Partner, Bain & Company (Securities), since 1972; In Charge of London Branch. *Career:* Corser Henderson & Hale (Brisbane) Mgr, Research Dept 1964-67; Bain & Company (Sydney) Authorised Clerk 1968-70; Bain & Company Admin 1971-74; Private Client Sales 1974-76; Institutional Sales 1976-80; Ptnr in Charge, London 1980-84; Bain & Company (New York) Ptnr in Charge 1984-86; Ptnr in Charge, London 1986-. *Biog: b.* 22 January 1942. *Nationality:* Australian. *m.* 1968, Virginia; 1 s. *Educ:* Church of England Grammar School, Brisbane; University of Queensland (BComm). *Directorships:* Bain & Company (Securities) Ltd 1986 MD. *Other Activities:* The Australian British Chamber of Commerce. *Professional Organisations:* The Australian Stock Exchange Ltd; Institute of Directors. *Recreations:* Tennis, Swimming, Reading.

RUSSELL, The Hon John Hugo Trenchard; Director, Baring Brothers & Co Ltd.

RUSSELL, Keith B; Director, Investment Banking, Merrill Lynch International Limited, since 1989; Nordic Region. *Career:* Swiss Bank Corporation (London), Director, Nordic Investment Banking 1988-89; Salomon Brothers International Limited (London), Vice President, Corporate Finance 1982-88; Smith Barney, Harris Upham & Co (New York), Financial Analyst, Corporate Finance 1980-82. *Biog: b.* 23 April 1958. *Nationality:* British. *m.* 1982, Virginia B; 2 s. *Educ:* Harvard University (AB). *Directorships:* Merrill Lynch International Limited 1989 (exec). *Clubs:* Hurlingham, Harvard. *Recreations:* Tennis, Skiing, Sailing, Riding.

RUSSELL, R G; Director, Barclays de Zoete Wedd Securities Ltd.

RUSSELL, Richard Andrew; Managing Partner, Titmuss Sainer & Webb, since 1987. *Career:* Titmuss Sainer & Webb, Articled Clerk 1965-67; Solicitor in Corporate Dept 1967-69; Partner in Corporate Dept 1969-85; Head of Corporate Dept 1985-87. *Biog:* b. 16 October 1942; 1 s; 1 d. *Educ:* Nottingham High School; University College, Oxford (Honours Degree in Jurisprudence). *Other Activities:* City of London Solicitors Company; Howard League for Penal Reform. *Recreations:* Cooking, Bird-Watching, Opera, Cricket.

RUSSELL, Dr Thomas; Non-Executive Director, Saatchi & Saatchi Company plc.

RUTHERFORD, Brian William John; Director, Charterhouse Bank Limited, since 1989; Corporate Banking. *Career:* Bonar Mackenzie WS Solicitors, Edinburgh 1977-84; Partner 1980-1984, Continental Bank Chicago & London, Vice President 1984-89. *Biog:* b. 13 February 1956. *Nationality:* British. *m.* 1987, Louise (née O'Farrell); 1 d. *Educ:* George Watson's College; University of Dundee (LLB). *Professional Organisations:* Law Society of Scotland.

RUTHERFORD, D R; Director, Barclays de Zoete Wedd Securities Ltd.

RUTMAN, Laurence David; Senior Property Partner, Ashurst Morris Crisp, since 1974. *Career:* Paisner & Co, Partner 1966-74. *Biog:* b. 8 October 1937. *Nationality:* British. *m.* Sandra (née Colvin); 2 s; 1 d. *Educ:* Hendon County School; University College, London (LLB); Yale Law School (LLM). *Recreations:* Opera, Farming, Books.

RUTTEMAN, Paul Johannes; CBE; Partner, Ernst & Young, since 1970; Banking & Financial Services. *Career:* Joined Predecessor Firm from University 1960; Arthur Young, Partner 1970-. *Biog:* b. 9 November 1938. *Nationality:* British. *m.* 1981, Dorothy (née Storie); 3 s; 1 d. *Educ:* Merchant Taylors School, Northwood; London School of Economics (BSc Econ). *Other Activities:* Member of Council of Institute of Chartered Accountants; Chairman, Financial Reporting Committee, ICAEW. *Professional Organisations:* FCA. *Publications:* Various Articles and Chapters for Books. *Recreations:* Sailing, Walking, Photography.

RYAN, Charles N; Senior Representative, Banco Itau.

RYAN, K M T; Partner, Allen & Overy.

RYAN, Miss M A; Corporate Finance Director, County NatWest Limited, since 1989; Corporate Finance Advising Companis on Takeovers, Rights Issues, Acquisitions, Disposals etc. *Career:* Coopers & Lybrand, Chartered Accountants, Articled Clerk to Manager 1976-82; Fleet Holdings plc, Group Financial Controller 1983-85; County NatWest Limited, Corporate Finance De-partment 1985-. *Biog:* b. 30 November 1954. *Nationality:* British. *Educ:* St Michaels Convent, London; Reading University (BA Hons English); London Business School (MBA). *Directorships:* County NatWest Ltd 1989 (exec). *Professional Organisations:* ACA. *Recreations:* Theatre, Opera, Sailing, Windsurfing, Running.

RYAN, N J R; Director, UBS Phillips & Drew Futures Limited.

RYAN, Dr T A; Chairman and Group Chief Executive, GPA Group plc, since 1975. *Career:* Aer Lingus Teo 1956-75; GPA Group plc 1975-. *Biog:* b. 2 February 1936. *Nationality:* Irish. *m.* 3 s. *Educ:* CBS Thurles, Co Tipperary, Ireland; North Western University, Chicago. *Directorships:* Bank of Ireland 1988 (non-exec); Trafalgar 1989 (non-exec). *Other Activities:* Member, European Round Table; Counsel for Republic of Mexico to Ireland; Honorary Member, University of Limerick, 1986; Doctor of Laws, University College, Dublin, National University of Ireland 1987; Doctor of Laws, University of Dublin 1987; Member, Board of Governors, National Gallery of Ireland. *Recreations:* Farming, The Arts.

RYCROFT, J P; Vice Chairman , Skipton Building Society. *Directorships:* Gisburn Fabrics Ltd.

RYDER, Dudley Danvers Granville Coutts; The Rt Hon Earl of Harrowby; Deputy Chairman, Coutts & Co, since 1970. *Career:* National Provincial Bank, Dir 1964-69; Orion Bank Ltd, Chm 1979-81; Nat West Unit Trust Managers Ltd, Chm 1979-83; Powell Duffryn Group, Director 1976-86 & 1983-86; Chm 1981-86; The Bentley Engineering Co Ltd, Chm, Saudi International Bank Dir 1980-82; 1985-87; National Westminster Bank, Director 1968; Dep Chm 1971-87; Intl Nat West Bank plc, Chm 1977-87; Nat West Investment Bank, Chm 1986-87. *Biog:* b. 20 December 1922. *Nationality:* British. *m.* 1949, Jeannette Rosalthé (née Johnston-Sant); 1 s; 1 d. *Educ:* Eton College. *Directorships:* Dowty Group plc 1986 Chm; The Private Bank & Trust Company Ltd 1989 (non-exec) Chm. *Other Activities:* Mem, Trilateral Commission; Trustee, Psychiatry Research Trust; Mem, Royal Inst of Intl Affairs.

RYDER, N H D; Director, Cater Allen Limited.

RYLANCE, Paul; Director Professional Development, S J Berwin & Co, since 1990; PR Marketing of Firm, Training of Professional Staff. *Career:* Called to The Bar 1980; Practice at The Bar 1981-87; Inns of Court School of Law, Lecturer 1982-87; Surrey University, Lecturer 1984-85; Slaughter and May, Head of Education & Training 1987-90; S J Berwin & Co, Director, Professional Development 1990-; Queen Mary and Westfield College, London University, Visiting Fellow 1989-; Brunel University, Visiting Fellow

1989-. *Biog: b.* 10 December 1957. *Nationality:* British. *Educ:* St Andrews High School, Worthing; Kingston Polytechnic; Queen Mary College, London (BA Hons Law); Inns of Court School of Law (Barrister). *Directorships:* Westminster Management Consultants 1990 (non-exec). *Other Activities:* Founder/Chairman, Legal Education and Training Group (1988-90); Member, Law Society's Academic Consultative Ctee (1989-); Member, Council for the Accreditation of Teacher Education (Advises Minister of State for Education) (1990-). *Professional Organisations:* Middle Temple, Barrister. *Publications:* Contributor and Editor (UK Section), Business Law Europe. *Recreations:* Jazz, Ancient History, Oriental Cookery.

RYLAND, Charles; Executive Director, Lombard Communications Limited.

RYLAND, David Stuart; Partner, S J Berwin & Co, since 1988; Development Finance. *Career:* Clifford Chance (formerly Coward Chance) 1981-88. *Biog: b.* 27 October 1953. *Nationality:* British. *m.* 1986, Anne Helen. *Educ:* Dulwich College, (Mods Class 1); Exeter College, Oxford University (Greats Class 1). *Other Activities:* Freeman, City of London; Member, Law Society. *Publications:* Comment: Development Loan Considerations, 1988; Journal of International Bank Law: Single Property Vehicles, 1988; Institutional Investor: PINCS, 1989; Solicitors Journal: Guarantee of Development Obligations, 1990; Solicitors Journal: Special Purpose Vehicle Acquisitions, 1990; Journal of International Banking Law: Strategies on Enforcement, 1990; Journal of International Banking Law: APUTS (forthcoming); Estates Gazette: Joint Ventures.

RYLANDS, P D; Partner, Cazenove & Co.

S

SAATCHI, Charles; Director, Saatchi & Saatchi Company plc.

SAATCHI, Maurice; Chairman, Saatchi & Saatchi Company plc, since 1984. *Career:* Saatchi & Saatchi Company, Co-Founder 1970-. *Biog: b.* 21 June 1946. *m.* 1984, Josephine (née Hart); 2 s. *Educ:* LSE (BSc Hons 1st). *Recreations:* Gardens, Plays.

SAAVEDRA, Jose; General Manager, Banco Santander.

SABIN, N G D; Director, PK English Trust Company Limited.

SACH, Derek Stephen; Managing Director, 3i Group plc, since 1990; UK Investment. *Directorships:* London Chamber of Commerce & Industry 1990 (non-exec).

SACHS, Jon; Chief Executive, Bank of Ireland Corporate Finance Limited, since 1989; Corporate Finance. *Career:* Rowe, Swann & Co, Partner (1972) 1963-75; Sheppards and Chase, Partner 1975-85; James Capel & Co, Director, James Capel Corporate Finance Limited 1985-89. *Biog: b.* 27 December 1937. *Nationality:* British. *m.* 1966, Ann Elizabeth (née Holland); 1 s; 1 d. *Educ:* King Edward VI Grammar School, Chelmsford; University College, London (LLB); Law School, University of Michigan, USA. *Directorships:* Investment Bank of Ireland Corporate Finance Limited 1989 (exec); Bank of Ireland Corporate Finance Limited 1989 (exec). *Professional Organisations:* Associate, Chartered Institute of Secretaries and Administrators. *Clubs:* Slim Jim's. *Recreations:* Music, Gardening, Skiing, Walking, Travel.

SACHS, Kurt; General Manager, Bayerische Hypotheken-und-Wechsel Bank.

SACHS, Ned; Managing Director (Investment Management), Morgan Stanley International.

SADAKATA, S; Deputy General Manager, The Mitsubishi Bank Limited, since 1988; Corporate Finance, Special Finance. *Career:* Mitsubishi Bank, Manager of Corporate Banking 1980-83; Manager of International Finance 1983-85; Seconded for Training at Morgan Stanley, New York 1985-86; Assistant General Manager 1986-88; Deputy General Manager 1988-. *Biog: b.* 20 August 1951. *Nationality:* Japanese. *m.* 1978, Midori; 2 s. *Educ:* Hitotsubashi University (BA); Wharton Graduate (MBA).

SADLEIR, (Franc) Richard; Director, J Henry Schroder Wagg & Co Ltd, since 1984; Compliance. *Career:* Bank of London & South America Ltd Trainee 1967-70; Schroders 1970-. *Biog: b.* 27 December 1944. *m.* 1970, Frances Judith (née Wilson); 1 s; 1 d. *Educ:* Marlborough College; New College, Oxford (MA). *Directorships:* The Securities Association Ltd 1986-88 (non-exec). *Recreations:* Walking, Sailing, Reading.

SADLEIR, William Hugh Granby; Director, Samuel Montagu & Co Limited, since 1982; Chief Executive's Office. *Career:* Deloitte, Plender, Griffiths & Co, Articled Clerk 1966-70; Samuel Montagu & Co Limited, Executive/Manager 1970-75; Cedar Holdings Limited, Non-executive Director 1976-78; Samuel Montagu & Co Limited, Assistant Director/Director (Corporate Finance) 1978-88. *Biog: b.* 16 September 1945. *Nationality:* British. *m.* 1986, Yennor Christina (née Morris); 1 s; 1 d. *Educ:* Eton College; London School of Economics (BSc Econ). *Directorships:* Letinvest Plc 1987 (non-exec). *Professional Organisations:* FCA. *Clubs:* Naval. *Recreations:* Reading, Walking, Music.

SADLER, A; Operations Manager, Arab Bank plc, since 1989; All Operating Departments including Settlements, Payments, L/C, Comms, Building Management, Branch Offices. *Career:* Morgan Guaranty Trust Co, London 1973-75; Chemical Bank London, Manager Settlements Dept 1975-79; New York, Manager of International Funds Transfer Dept 1979-85; London, London Operations Manager 1985-89; Arab Bank, London Operations Manager 1989-. *Biog: b.* 26 January 1955. *Nationality:* British. *m.* 1986, Elaine Patricia (née Mattin); 1 s; 1 d. *Educ:* St Peter's, Merrow, Guildford.

SADLER, A Edward; Partner, Clifford Chance, since 1977; Corporate Taxation. *Career:* Farrer & Co, Articles 1971-73; Clifford-Turner, Assistant Solicitor 1973-77. *Biog: b.* 27 October 1947. *Nationality:* British. *m.* 1980, Patricia; 1 s. *Educ:* William Adams Grammar School, Newport, Shropshire; University College, Oxford (MA). *Other Activities:* Member, International Bar Association (Tax Committee); Member, Law Society Revenue Committee (Corporation Tax Sub-Committee); Member, City of London Solicitors Company (Revenue Committee). *Professional Organisations:* Solicitor. *Publications:* Equipment Leasing: An Analysis of UK Tax Considerations (with B C Reisbach and M R Thomas) (2nd edition), 1985. *Recreations:* Gardening, Opera, Fell-Walking.

SADLER, A G; Director, Barclays de Zoete Wedd Securities Ltd.

SADLER, John S; CBE; Director, Investment Management Regulatory Organisation Limited, since 1989. *Career:* John Lewis Partnership plc, Finance Director 1971-87; John Lewis Partnership plc, Deputy Chairman 1984-89. *Biog: b.* 6 May 1930. *Nationality:* British. *m.* 1952, Ella; 3 s. *Educ:* Reading School; Corpus Christi College, Oxford (MA). *Directorships:* Postel Properties Limited; Debenham Tewson & Chinnocks Holdings plc; British Telecommunications Pension Schemes Trustee; UK Board Australian Mutual Provident Society Dep Chairman; WRC plc - Environmental Research & Development Consultancy, Chairman. *Other Activities:* Member of Council of Royal London Society for the Blind; Member, Monopolies & Mergers Commission, 1975-85. *Clubs:* Oriental. *Recreations:* Reading, Golf.

SAFRAN, Henry W; Director, RBC Kitcat & Safran Ltd.

ST GEORGE, Peter Bligh; Managing Director, County NatWest Ltd, since 1990; Corporate Finance. *Career:* Hill Samuel Mgr 1974-83; Dir 1983-86; County NatWest, Director 1986-90. *Biog: b.* 23 July 1946. *m.* 1974, Elizabeth (née Williams); 1 s; 2 d. *Educ:* St Aidans College, South Africa; Natal University; Cape Town University (MBA). *Professional Organisations:* CA (South Africa).

ST GILES, Mark (Valentine); Chairman, Framlington Group plc. *Career:* Laurence Keen & Gardner, Inv Analyst 1964-69; Jessel Securities, Director 1969-75; Jessel Britania Group, Managing Director 1970-74; Hambros Bank Ltd, Director 1976-83; Allied Hambro Group, Managing Director 1975-83; GT Management plc, Director 1983-88. *Biog: m.* 1965, Susan Janet (née Turner); 1 s; 2 d. *Educ:* Winchester College; Clare College, Cambridge. *Directorships:* Cadogan Management Ltd 1988 (exec) Chm; Unit Trust Exchange Ltd 1988 (exec) Chm; Professional & Business Information plc 1989 (non-exec).

ST JOHN SMITH, Chris; Partner, Equipment Leasing, Cameron Markby Hewitt.

ST-LEGER HARRIS, S A; Partner (Bristol), Bacon & Woodrow.

SAITO, Hideo; Director, Kleinwort Benson Securities Limited.

SAKAL, Peter; Partner, Linklaters & Paines.

SAKAMOTO, Ichiro; Executive Director of UK & European Equities Division, Yamaichi International (Europe) Limited, since 1989; UK/European Equities Sales to Japanese Institutional Investors. *Career:* Nissan Motor Co, Planning Dept 1976-84; Yamaichi Securities Co Ltd (Tokyo) 1984-85; Yamaichi Intl (Europe) Ltd, Corporate Finance & M&A 1985-89; UK & European Equities Dept 1989-90. *Biog: b.* 24 October 1953. *Nationality:* Japanese. *m.* 1984, Akiko; 1 s. *Educ:* Osaka University (BA Japanese Commercial Law). *Recreations:* Skiing, Golf.

SAKAMOTO, T; Director, Sanyo International Ltd.

SAKURABA, Isao; Managing Director and Chief Executive Officer, The Nikko Securities Co (Europe) Ltd, since 1990; Overall Responsibility. *Career:* The Nikko Securities Co Ltd, Sendai, Japan 1967-70; The Nikko Securities Co Ltd, International Division, Japan 1970-71; The Nikko Securities Co (Europe) Ltd, London 1971-72; The Nikko Securities Co (Deutschland) GmbH, Frankfurt 1972-78; The Nikko Securities Co Ltd, Japan 1978-81; The Nikko (Switzerland) Finance Co Ltd, Zurich 1981-85; The Nikko Securities Co (Deutschland) GmbH, Frankfurt, Managing Director 1985-89; The Nikko Securities Co Ltd, Financial Institutions Division, Japan, General Manager 1989-90. *Biog: b.* 16 February 1944. *Nationality:* Japanese. *m.* 1968, Suwako; 2 s. *Educ:* Keio University (BA in Economics).

SALES, Christopher Hedley; Partner, Clark Whitehill, since 1980; Tax. *Career:* Ogden Hibberd Bull & Langton (subsequently Ogden Parsons & Co), Articled Clerk/Audit Senior 1961-69; British Steel Corporation, Taxation Accountant 1969-73; Clark Battams (subsequently Clark Whitehill), Tax Manager 1973-80. *Biog: b.* 24 October 1943. *Nationality:* British. *m.* 1970, Lynne; 1 s; 1 d. *Educ:* City of London School. *Other Activities:* Member, London Tax Study Group; FCA; ATII. *Publications:* A Number of Tax Articles Published in Accountancy & Other Professional Journals. *Clubs:* MCC. *Recreations:* Playing Tennis, Watching Cricket, Football.

SALES, Dr Martin; Partner, W & J Burness WS.

SALINA AMORINI, Marchese G L; Director, S G Warburg & Co Ltd.

SALLABANK, Mrs Charlotte Laura (née Iles); Partner, Wilde Sapte, since 1990; Corporate Tax. *Career:* National Westminster Bank plc, International Division, Corporate Finance 1978-81. *Biog: b.* 16 July 1957. *Nationality:* British. *m.* 1984, Nigel Edwin. *Educ:* St Denis School, Edinburgh; King's College, London (BSc, AKC). *Professional Organisations:* Law Society; ATII. *Recreations:* Rowing, Swimming, Music.

SALMON, J A; Director, Holman Managers Ltd.

SALMON, John H; Partner, Price Waterhouse, since 1988; London Audit and Business Advisory Services. *Career:* Price Waterhouse 1963-; Partner 1976. *Biog: b.*

10 January 1945. *Nationality:* British. *m.* 1970, Trisha (née Maunder Taylor); 2 s; 1 d. *Educ:* Eastbourne College. *Professional Organisations:* Fellow, Institute of Chartered Accountants in England and Wales. *Clubs:* Hadley Wood Golf Club.

SALMON, Roger; Executive Director, N M Rothschild & Sons Limited.

SALMON, T P; Director, Metheuen (Lloyds Underwriting Agents) Limited.

SALT, Julia Ann (née Richardson); Partner, Allen & Overy, since 1985; Banking and Company Law. *Career:* Allen & Overy, Asst Solicitor 1980-85. *Biog: b.* 4 May 1955. *Nationality:* British. *m.* 1980, David; 1 s; 1 d. *Educ:* St Mary's Senior High School, Hull; St Hilda's College, Oxford (BA). *Professional Organisations:* Law Society, City of London Law Society, City Women's Network. *Clubs:* Oxford & Cambridge. *Recreations:* Sailing, Bird-Watching, Literature, Opera, Languages.

SALTER, Christopher P; Director, Kleinwort Benson Securities Limited.

SALTER, Ian George; Director, Strauss Turnbull Co Ltd.

SALTER, Peter; Partner, Clark Whitehill.

SALTER, R D; Partner, Wedlake Bell.

SALTMARSH, P David; Company Secretary, Reckitt & Colman plc, since 1989. *Educ:* Shrewsbury School; St John's College, Cambridge (BA). *Professional Organisations:* FCA; MCT.

SALZ, Anthony Michael Vaughan; Partner, Freshfields, since 1980; Corporate Finance. *Career:* Turner Kenneth Brown, Articled Clerk/Asst Solicitor 1972-75; Freshfields, Asst Solicitor 1975-77; Davis Polk & Wardwell (New York) 1977-78; Freshfields 1978-. *Biog: b.* 30 June 1950. *Nationality:* British. *m.* 1975, Sally Ruth (née Hagger); 1 s; 2 d. *Educ:* Summerfields and Radley College; Exeter University (LLB Hons). *Professional Organisations:* The Law Society, IBA, City of London Law Society. *Publications:* Various Contributions to Legal Books. *Recreations:* Family, Golf, Fishing, Tennis.

SAMBROOK, Geoffrey Stephen; Director, Charles Davis (Metal Brokers) Ltd, since 1990. *Biog: b.* 14 October 1951. *Nationality:* British. *m.* Jennifer; 2 d. *Educ:* St Edmund Hall, Oxford (BA).

SAMMONS, D J; Director, Charlton Seal Schaverien Limited.

SAMMONS, Geoffrey Tait; Commissioner, The Building Societies Commission, since 1986. *Career:* Allen & Overy, Ptnr 1953-81; Snr Ptnr 1981-86. *Biog: Nationality:* British. *m.* 1949, Stephanie Anne (née Clark); 1 s; 1 d. *Educ:* Trinity College, Glenalmond; University College, Oxford (MA). *Directorships:* Spirax Sarco Engineering plc 1978 (non-exec). *Other Activities:* Governor, Lister Institute of Preventive Medicine. *Professional Organisations:* The Law Society. *Clubs:* Army and Navy. *Recreations:* Golf.

SAMMONS, K L; Director, J H Minet & Co Ltd.

SAMPSON, Gordon C; Director, W P P Group plc.

SAMPSON, Ian Godfrey; Managing Director, NM Schroder Unit Trust Managers Ltd.

SAMPSON, Michael; Director, John Govett & Co Limited, since 1986; Investment Management (Pension). *Career:* Simon & Coates, Investment Analyst 1964-77; Lloyds Investment Management, Investment Mgr 1977-85. *Biog: b.* 27 September 1942. *Nationality:* British. *m.* 1969, Elizabeth Victoria (née Hilliar); 2 d. *Educ:* Collyers School, Horsham; Southampton University (BSc Econ). *Professional Organisations:* Society of Investment Analysts. *Recreations:* Tennis.

SAMSON, J; Partner, Nabarro Nathanson.

SAMUEL, William Meredith; Director, J Henry Schroder Wagg & Co Ltd, since 1986; Corporate Finance. *Career:* Coopers & Lybrand 1973-77. *Biog: b.* 20 February 1952. *Nationality:* British. *m.* 1982, Dr Jane (née Evans); 1 d. *Educ:* Edinburgh Academy; Rugby School; Durham University (BSc Hons 1st). *Professional Organisations:* FCA. *Recreations:* Hockey, Tennis, Real Tennis.

SANBAR, S; Investment Manager, Sharjah Investment Co (UK) Ltd.

SANDARS, George Russell; Partner, Wilde Sapte, since 1986; Company & Commercial Law. *Career:* Slaughter and May, Articled Clerk 1976-78; Asst Solicitor 1978-79; Linklaters & Paines, Asst Solicitor 1979-83; Wilde Sapte, Asst Solicitor 1983-85. *Biog: b.* 14 February 1954. *Nationality:* British. *m.* 1984, Rosemary (née Yolland); 1 s; 2 d. *Educ:* Wellington College; Cambridge University (MA). *Professional Organisations:* Member, The Law Society. *Clubs:* City University Club. *Recreations:* Classical Music, Sailing, Walking.

SANDBERG, Alexander; Chairman & Chief Executive, College Group Limited, since 1987. *Career:* Tribe Clarke Painter & Darton; David Puttnam Associates; Visual Programme Systems Limited; Nathan Sandberg Ltd. *Biog: b.* 15 July 1949. *Nationality:* British. *m.* 1979, Clare (née Colman); 2 s; 2 d. *Educ:* Hawtreys; Milton

Abbey. *Directorships:* College Group Chm & Chief exec; College Hill Associates Ltd Chm; College Research Ltd Chm; College Design Ltd Chm; College Advertising Ltd Chm; CSC Limited Chm; Ultra Securities Limited (non-exec). *Clubs:* Queens. *Recreations:* Tennis, Fishing, Gardening, Shooting.

SANDELL, Kenneth Edwin; Director, Well Marine Reinsurance Brokers Limited, since 1985; Technical & Administration. *Career:* Samson, Menzies Limited, Clerk/Broker 1944-70; Fenchurch Marine Brokers Ltd, Broker/Director 1971-85. *Biog: b.* 28 April 1929. *Nationality:* British. *m.* 1960, Lillian Rose (née Buckingham); 1 s; 1 d. *Educ:* Tollington. *Directorships:* Well Marine Reinsurance Brokers Limited 1985 (exec); Samson, Menzies Limited 1972-85; Fenchurch Marine Brokers Limited 1971-85; Fenchurch Group International Ltd 1979-81. *Other Activities:* Member of Lloyds, 1976. *Recreations:* History, Reading, Theology, Youth Work.

SANDER, E E; Director, Benchmark Group plc.

SANDERS, John R; Chairman, Kitcat & Aitken (Division of RBC Dominion).

SANDERS, S J; Director, London International Financial Futures Exchange.

SANDERS, Terence John Robert; Joint Managing Director, Tullett & Tokyo Forex International Ltd, since 1987; Internationally Responsible for Currency Deposits, Eurocurrencies & Forwards. *Career:* Midland Bank plc 1956-65; Hill Samuel & Co Ltd 1965-72. *Biog: b.* 26 October 1941. *Nationality:* British. *m.* 1963, Christine Mary (née Slade); 4 s. *Educ:* Acton Central School. *Directorships:* Tullett & Tokyo (Eurocurrencies & Forwards) Ltd (exec); Tullett & Tokyo (Currency Deposits) Ltd (exec); Tullett & Tokyo (Money Markets) Ltd (exec); Tullett & Tokyo (Treasury Services) (exec). *Professional Organisations:* Member, Institute of Directors. *Clubs:* Ealing Golf Club, RAC. *Recreations:* Golf, Tennis, Swimming, Snooker.

SANDERSON, B K; Chief Executive, BP Chemicals, The British Petroleum Company plc.

SANDERSON, Brian; Chief Inspector, Yorkshire Bank plc.

SANDERSON, Eric Fenton; Director & Chief Executive, The British Linen Bank Ltd, since 1989. *Career:* Touche Ross & Co, Trainee CA 1973-76; British Linen Bank Ltd, Various 1976-. *Biog: b.* 14 October 1951. *Nationality:* British. *m.* 1975, Patricia Ann (née Shaw); 3 d. *Educ:* Morgan Academy, Dundee; Dundee University (LLB); Harvard Business School. *Directorships:* Cablevision (Scotland) plc 1984 (non-exec); Airtours plc 1987 (non-exec); English & Overseas Properties plc

1988 (non-exec). *Professional Organisations:* CA. *Clubs:* New Club, Edinburgh. *Recreations:* Photography, Gardening, Tennis.

SANDERSON, F L; Executive Director, J H Minet & Co Ltd.

SANDERSON, Robert Geoffrey; Director, Chartered West LB Limited, since 1988; Compliance and Administration. *Career:* Peat Marwick Mitchell & Co 1959-75; Partner 1965; Spain Brothers & Co, Snr Ptnr & Consultant 1976-87. *Biog: b.* 1931. *Nationality:* British. *m.* 1972, Anne (née Ryan); 1 s; 1 d. *Educ:* Queen's College, Oxford (MA). *Professional Organisations:* FCA; Associate, IMC.

SANDISON, Francis Gunn; Partner, Freshfields, since 1980; Corporate Tax. *Career:* Freshfields, Assistant Solicitor, Tax Department 1974-80. *Biog: b.* 25 May 1949. *Nationality:* American. *m.* 1981, Milva Lou (née McCaw); 1 s. *Educ:* Glasgow Academy; Charterhouse; Magdalen College, Oxford (BCL, MA). *Other Activities:* City of London Law Society; Revenue Law Sub-Committee. *Professional Organisations:* Law Society, 1974-; City of London Law Society, 1980-. *Publications:* Profit Sharing and other Share Acquisition Schemes, 1979; Co-Author, Whiteman on Income Tax, 3rd Edition 1988. *Recreations:* Fishing, Reading, Wine, Photography.

SANDLAND, Eric Michael; Chief Investment Manager, Norwich Union Insurance Group, since 1986; Fund Management. *Career:* Norwich Union Life Insurance Society Actuarial Student 1961-64; Actuarial Asst 1964-66; Asst Sec/Sec for France 1966-69; Group Statistician 1969-72; Investment Mgr 1972-86. *Biog: b.* 29 April 1938. *Nationality:* British. *m.* 1969, Jacqueline Marie-Ther (née Gauthier) (decd January 1990); 3 s. *Educ:* Edinburgh Academy; Trinity Hall, Cambridge (MA). *Directorships:* Various NU Group Directorships. *Other Activities:* Investment Committee, Association of British Insurers; Deputy Chairman, Institutional Shareholders' Committee. *Professional Organisations:* FIA, AMSIA. *Recreations:* Golf, Bridge, Music, DIY.

SANGHRAJKA, Jayant; Tax Partner, Morison Stoneham Chartered Accountants, since 1989; Taxation. *Career:* Coopers & Lybrand Deloitte, Manager 1976-85; Robson Rhodes, International Tax Senior Manager 1985-88. *Biog: b.* 20 March 1955. *Nationality:* British. *m.* 1981, Heena (née Rupani); 2 s. *Educ:* London School of Economics (BSc Econ Hons). *Directorships:* Plancity Properties Ltd 1990 (exec). *Other Activities:* Treasurer, Institute of Taxation (Harrow Branch). *Professional Organisations:* Fellow, Institute of Chartered Accountants in England & Wales; Associate, Institute of Taxation. *Recreations:* Walking, Sports.

SANKEY, Brian W; Managing Director, Chase Investment Bank Limited, since 1989; Group Executive Europe for Leveraged Acquisitions. *Career:* The Chase Manhattan Bank NA (London), Manager, Corporate Banking 1985-87; (London), Credit Supervising Officer UK 1987-89. *Biog: b.* 24 June 1952. *Nationality:* British. *m.* 1974, Linda (née Tysoe); 1 s. *Directorships:* Strand-VCI plc 1989 (non-exec).

SANKEY-BARKER, P; Partner, Waltons & Morse.

SANSOM, Dr Keith Geoffrey; Operations & Strategic Services Director, Laporte plc, since 1990. *Career:* Laporte, R & D 1968-72; Marketing 1972-79; Interox Australia, General Manager 1980-83; Laporte Australia, Chief Executive 1982-90. *Biog: b.* 9 November 1943. *Nationality:* Australian. *m.* 1966, Jennifer Jane (née Blakemore); 2 d. *Educ:* High Wycombe Royal Grammar School; University of Leeds (BSc, PhD). *Directorships:* Laporte plc 1990; Abel Lemon & Co Pty Limited 1984; Bitumen Products Pty Limited 1988; Great Lakes Biochemicals (New Zealand) Limited 1984; H Bleakley Pty Limited; H J Christoffel Chemicals Pty Limited 1988; Kaysanne Pty Limited 1988; Laporte Australia Pty Limited 1984; Laporte Group Australia Limited 1984; Laporte Industries (New Zealand) Limited; Laporte Industries Australia Pty Limited 1989; Laporte Investments Pty Limited 1983; Laporte Organisation Pty Limited 1989; Laporte Services Pty Limited 1982; Neuchatel Contracting Co (NSW) Pty Limited 1988; Neuchatel Contracting Co (QLD) Pty Limited 1988; Neuchatel Contracting Co Pty Limited; Ormonoid Limited 1988; Sovereign Chemicals (New Zealand) Limited 1985; Surface Treatment (SA) Pty Limited 1988; Surface Treatment Pty Limited 1988; Trinidad Lake Asphalt (Australia) Pty Limited 1988; Vermiculite Industries Pty Limited 1988; Laporte (New Zealand) Holdings Limited 1985; Interox Chemicals (New Zealand) Limited; Interox Chemicals Pty Limited 1986. *Other Activities:* Councillor, Milton Keynes Borough Council, 1975-76; Chairman, New South Wales Government Task Force on Chemical Industry in the State, 1988-90. *Publications:* Various research papers, 1967-70. *Clubs:* Oriental Club. *Recreations:* Sailing, Rotary.

SANSOM, Robert Anthony; UK Treasurer, Hill Samuel Bank Ltd, since 1988; Treasury Money Markets. *Career:* TSB England & Wales Treasurer, Treasury's Money Markets 1985-88. *Biog: b.* 25 January 1946. *Nationality:* British. *m.* 1988, Sandra (née Otley); 2 s; 1 d. *Educ:* Hove Grammar School. *Directorships:* Hill Samuel Bank Ltd 1988 (exec). *Other Activities:* Cornhill Club. *Professional Organisations:* ACIB. *Clubs:* Brighton & Hove Cricket Club. *Recreations:* Cricket.

SANSOME, N J; Director, Panmure Gordon & Company Limited.

SANTOS, Rui Mascarenhas; UK Representative, Banco Nacional Ultramario, since 1990; Representative Office of the Bank in London. *Career:* Banco Português Do Atlântico (Lisbon), Officer 1973-81; Banco Português Do Atlântico (London), Assistant General Manager 1981-83; Banco Português Do Atlântico (Paris), Deputy General Manager 1983-85; Banco Português Do Atlântico (London), Deputy General Manager 1985-88; Banif-Banco Internacional Do Funchal (Lisbon), Senior Manager, Head of International Division 1988-89. *Biog: b.* 16 February 1954. *Nationality:* Portuguese. *m.* 1976, Ana Matilde (née Sousa); 1 s. *Educ:* Technical University of Lisbon (Business Management). *Recreations:* Golf.

SANTS, H W H; Vice-Chairman Head of Equities, UBS Phillips & Drew Securities Limited.

SARGEANT, Peter Francis; Director, Standard Chartered Merchant Bank Ltd.

SARGENT, Michael Carlisle; Director, S G Warburg Group plc.

SARGINSON, John H; Partner (Nottingham), Evershed Wells & Hind.

SATCHELL, Keith; General Manager, Friends Provident Life Office, since 1987; Product and International Development. *Career:* Duncan C Fraser 1972-75; UK Provident, Various Actuarial Posts 1975-84; Mktg Mgr 1984-86; Friends Provident 1986-. *Biog: b.* 3 June 1951. *Nationality:* British. *m.* 1972, Hazel (née Burston); 2 s; 1 d. *Educ:* Hemel Hempstead Grammar; Aston University (BSc). *Directorships:* Friends Provident Linked Life Assurance Ltd 1986 (exec); FP Managed Pension Funds Ltd 1986 (exec); FP Unit Trust Managers Ltd 1986 (exec); FP Services Ltd 1987 (exec); Abbey National Personal Pensions Trustee Ltd 1988 (non-exec). *Professional Organisations:* FIA. *Recreations:* Football.

SATO, Haruo; Managing Director & Chief Executive, Yamaichi International (Europe) Ltd.

SATOH, Kenichi; Director, Kleinwort Benson Securities Limited.

SAUL, Andrew John; Partner, Penningtons, since 1988; Corporate Finance. *Biog: b.* 17 February 1962. *Educ:* Slough Grammar School; Oxford University (BA Hons). *Professional Organisations:* Law Society. *Clubs:* Stoke Poges Golf Club, Old Cranleighans RFC. *Recreations:* Golf, Rugby.

SAUL, Christopher Francis Irvin; Partner, Slaughter and May, since 1986; Company & Commercial Law, Corporate Finance, General Company Law & Capital Markets. *Career:* Slaughter and May, Asst Solicitor 1979-86. *Biog: b.* 29 June 1955. *m.* 1985, Anne (née Cartier);

1 s; 1 d. *Educ:* Tiffin School, Kingston-upon-Thames; St Catherine's College, Oxford (BA). *Other Activities:* City of London Solicitors' Company. *Professional Organisations:* The Law Society. *Recreations:* Cinema, Motor Cars, Collecting Clocks and Antique Maps.

SAUNDERS, Alan George; Investment Director, Lazard Investors, since 1986; Global Investment Strategy. *Career:* Simon & Coates 1970-78; Ptnr 1977-78; Royal Dutch Shell Chief Economist 1979-84; Head, Oil Pricing 1984-86. *Biog: b.* 13 April 1949. *Nationality:* British. *m.* 1978, (Pamela) Ann (née Robinson); 1 d. *Educ:* Taunton's School, Southampton; St Catharine's College, Cambridge (MA). *Recreations:* Sailing, Tennis, Reading, Walking, Cricket.

SAUNDERS, Christopher John; Partner, Slaughter and May.

SAUNDERS, David Norman; Deputy Managing Director, Mase Westpac Limited, since 1989. *Career:* N M Rothschild & Sons; Sharps Pixley Ltd, Director; Mocatta & Goldsmid Ltd, Director; Credit Suisse, London, Senior Vice President.

SAUNDERS, Emma Elizabeth; Chairman, The Analysis Corporation plc, 1988. *Career:* Lazard Bros & Co Ltd 1977-80; Bank of America International Mgr 1980-81; Bear Stearns International VP 1981-85; Tranwood Earl & Co, Director 1985-. *Biog: b.* 14 May 1955. *Nationality:* British. *m.* 1980, Peter R S Earl; 1 s; 1 d. *Educ:* Godolphin & Latymer School; Oxford University (MA Hons). *Directorships:* Sloane Corporation 1985 (exec); Sloane Wine Company 1987 (exec); Tranwood Earl & Co 1985 (exec). *Professional Organisations:* FIMBRA. *Clubs:* RAC.

SAUNDERS, H M; Finance Director, P & O Steam Navigation Company, since 1989. *Career:* Price Waterhouse 1968-75; Town & City Properties plc 1976-; Sterling Guarantee Trust plc 1976-; P & O Group 1976-. *Professional Organisations:* Fellow, Institute of Chartered Accountants.

SAUNDERS, Iain Ogilvy Swain; Chairman, Fleming Investment Management Ltd, since 1990. *Career:* Robert Fleming 1971-. *Biog: b.* 7 November 1947. *Nationality:* British. *m.* 1976, Robann; 1 d. *Educ:* Radley College; Bristol University (BSc Econ).

SAUNDERS, K F P; Director, Barclays de Zoete Wedd Securities Ltd.

SAUNDERS, Mark Bradley; Partner, Company Department, Nabarro Nathanson, since 1990; Company and Commercial Law. *Career:* Nabarro Nathanson, Articled Clerk 1983-85; Assistant Solicitor Company Department 1985-90; Occidental Petroleum Co Inc, Inhouse Lawyer 1985. *Biog: b.* 27 December 1959.

Nationality: British. *Educ:* The Coopers' Company and Coborn School; Leicester University (LLB). *Other Activities:* Law Society. *Recreations:* Music, Reading.

SAUNDERS, T J; Partner, Milne Ross Chartered Accountants, since 1988; Technical. *Nationality:* British. *Educ:* (BA Econ Hons). *Professional Organisations:* Member, Institute of Chartered Accountants in England & Wales. *Publications:* Contributor; The Accountants Manual, 1990.

SAUNDERS, (William) Howard; Partner, Keith Bayley, Rogers & Co, since 1970; Admin Finance/ Foreign Markets/Charities. *Career:* Keith Bayley & Rigg Members of the Stock Exchange (now Keith Bayley Rogers & Co) 1955-; Royal Army Pay Corps, Computer Conversion Team 1960-62. *Biog: b.* 29 June 1939. *Nationality:* British. *m.* 1960, Rita D (née Hardanay); 2 s. *Educ:* Alleyns, London. *Directorships:* Ebbark Nominees Ltd 1970 (exec) MD. *Professional Organisations:* International Stock Exchange. *Recreations:* Skiing, Travel, Reading.

SAUVARY, Paul; Director, Capital Markets Business, J Henry Schroder Wagg & Co Limited, since 1986; Overall Responsibility for Origination of Capital Markets Business. *Career:* Orion Royal Bank -1980; Schroders 1980-; Senior Representative in Japan 1983-86; Director & Head of Primary Markets 1986-90; Director & Head Capital Markets 1990-. *Educ:* Christ Church, Oxford (Greats, MLitt Mathematical Logic). *Clubs:* Reform Club.

SAVAGE, Paul; Vice President, First Interstate Bank of California.

SAVAGE, Peter James; Director, Chemicals & Industrial, Harrisons & Crosfields plc.

SAVAGE, Richard; Group Treasurer, British Telecommunications plc.

SAVAGE, Yvonne; Senior Executive, Hodgson Martin Limited.

SAVORY, James Howard; Partner, Slaughter and May, since 1985; Commercial Taxation. *Biog: b.* 5 May 1953. *m.* 1978, Diana Mary (née Wackerbarth); 2 s; 1 d. *Educ:* Winchester College; Queens' College, Cambridge (MA). *Professional Organisations:* The Law Society; ATII.

SAWADA, Takashi; General Manager, The Hokkaido Takushoku Bank Ltd, London Branch, since 1990. *Career:* Takugin Finance International Ltd (owned by Hokkaido Takushoku Bank Ltd), Managing Director & General Manager 1987-90. *Biog: b.* 14 December 1943. *Nationality:* Japanese. *m.* Kazuko; 2 d. *Educ:* Keio University, Tokyo, Japan (BA). *Directorships:* Takugin Finance International Ltd 1990 (non-exec).

SAWDY, Peter Bryan; Chairman, Peter Sawdy Associates, since 1985; General Responsibility. *Career:* Brooke Bond Group plc, Dep Chm & Chief Exec 1978-85. *Biog: b.* 17 September 1931. *Nationality:* British. *m.* 1989, Judith; 2 d. *Educ:* Ampleforth College; London School of Economics. *Directorships:* Hogg Group plc 1986 (non-exec) Dep Chm; Griffin International 1987 (exec); Costain Group plc 1978 (non-exec) Chm; Taylor Chess Ltd 1990 (non-exec) Chm; Opalbrown Ltd 1990 (non-exec) Chm. *Clubs:* Naval & Military, Royal Ashdown Golf Club, Annabel's. *Recreations:* Golf, Opera, Collecting 1st Editions.

SAWKINS, John William; Main Board Director, Bain Clarkson Limited, since 1987; Chairman, North American Division, North American Property/ Casualty/ Financial. *Career:* J H Minet & Co Ltd 1958-84; Main Board Dir 1981-84. *Biog: b.* 10 August 1941. *m.* 1962, Angela (née O'Donoghue); 1 s. *Educ:* Haberdashers' Aske's School. *Professional Organisations:* Member, Lloyd's Insurance Brokers Committee. *Recreations:* Golf.

SAWYER, D; Chief Dealer, Bayerische Vereinsbank.

SAXBY-SOFFE, Richard Nigel; Director, J Henry Schroder Wagg & Co Limited, since 1985; Investment Banking. *Career:* Peat Marwick Mitchell & Co, Assistant Manager 1972-78.

SAY, Stephen W; Partner, Stoy Hayward.

SAYEED, Sadeq; Executive Director, Crédit Suisse First Boston Limited.

SAYER, Stephen Thomas; Partner, Richards Butler, since 1974; Commercial & Competition Law. *Career:* Iliffe Sweet & Co Articled Clerk 1965-67. *Biog: b.* 8 July 1945. *Nationality:* British. 1 s; 1 d. *Educ:* Framlingham College. *Other Activities:* Liveryman, City of London Solicitors' Company; Lawyers Club; Freeman, City of London. *Professional Organisations:* Law Society; United Kingdon Assoc for European Law. *Publications:* Agency & Distribution Agreements (Contributor); Practical Commercial Precedents. *Clubs:* City of London, Reform, Queen's. *Recreations:* Real Tennis, Theatre, Reading, Racquets.

SCALES, J A; Partner, Stephenson Harwood.

SCAMMELL, S G A; Vice President, The Royal Bank of Canada.

SCANLAN, Charles Denis; Partner, Simmons & Simmons, since 1973; Tax, Life and Pensions Products & Financial Services. *Career:* Simmons & Simmons, Articled Clerk 1967-70; Asst Solicitor 1970-73. *Biog: b.*

23 December 1944. *Nationality:* British. *m.* 1971, Dorothy (née Quick); 2 s. *Educ:* St Benedicts School, Ealing; Balliol College, Oxford (BA Hons). *Other Activities:* Freeman, City of London Solicitors Co. *Professional Organisations:* Law Society.

SCANLAN, William; Managing Director, Royal Life Holdings, Royal Insurance Holdings plc.

SCANLON, James; Director, Bradstock Financial Services Ltd.

SCANNELL, D A; Group Treasurer & Director of Financial Planning, Jaguar Cars Ltd.

SCARGILL, Michael Philip; Partner, Allen & Overy; Corporate. *Career:* Slaughter and May, Articled Clerk 1978-80; Assistant Solicitor 1980-89; Allen & Overy, Assistant Solicitor 1989-90. *Biog: b.* 11 December 1955. *Nationality:* British. *m.* 1986, Claire Frances (née Nicholson); 2 s. *Educ:* Carlton Grammar School, Bradford; New College, Oxford (MA). *Professional Organisations:* The Law Society; The City of London Solicitors' Company. *Recreations:* Literature, Music, Travel.

SCARLETT, G; Head of Computer Services, Leeds Permanent Building Society, since 1990; Total Accountability for Service Delivery, including the Voice Network. *Career:* Leeds Permanent, Head of Systems, Planning and Support 1989-90; Leeds Permanent, Systems Development Manager 1988-89; Woolworths, Systems Development Mananger 1985-88; Business Consultant since 1985; Systems Manager since 1984; Project Manager 1982-83; Project Leader 1980-81; Applications Implementation Manager since 1979; Lloyds of London 1977-85; Project Leader 1977-78; Mouncey and Partners; Designed and Implemented New Systems Development 1975-78; Hotel Manager 1974-75; Lloyd's of London 1972-74; Mouncey and Partners 1967-72; Urwick Diebold 1966-67; NCR 1964-66;. *Biog: b.* 14 April 1942. *Nationality:* British. *m.* 1981, Susan (née Barker); 1 s. *Educ:* BA Hons, Business Studies. *Professional Organisations:* Member of the British Computer Society.

SCHADT, J P; Managing Director, Beverages Stream, Cadbury Schweppes plc.

SCHAEFER, Professor Stephen Martin; Director, Institute of Finance & Accounting; Chairman, Finance Area, London Business School, since 1985. *Career:* London Business School, Research Officer/Lecturer 1970-79; Stanford University, Asst Professor 1979-81. *Biog: b.* 18 November 1946. *Nationality:* British. *m.* 1969, Teresa Evelyn (née Ford); 2 s. *Educ:* Manchester Grammar School; Cambridge University (MA); London University (PhD). *Directorships:* The Securities Association 1989 Independent Board Member; Lawtex plc 1974 (non-exec). *Professional Organisations:* American Finance Association; European Finance Association. *Publications:* Several Papers in Academic Journals.

SCHAPIRA, J J; Partner, Pannell Kerr Forster, since 1987; Insolvency. *Career:* Leonard Finn & Co 1975-80; Stoy Hayward, Insolvency Administrator 1980-82; Pannell Kerr Forster 1985. *Biog: b.* 13 December 1954. *m.* 1983, Jacqueline (née Tempelhof); 2 s; 2 d. *Educ:* Hasmonean Grammar School. *Professional Organisations:* ACA (ICAEW).

SCHECK, Miss Gina Ruth; Director, J Henry Schroder Wagg & Co Limited, since 1989; Corporate Finance. *Biog: b.* 18 March 1954. *Nationality:* British. *Educ:* Lycee Français de Londres; Newnham College, Cambridge (MA).

SCHEPS, Adrian; Partner, Walker Martineau Stringer Saul.

SCHILD, P D; Senior Manager, Commerzbank AG.

SCHIRANO, Louis G; Non-Executive Director, First Interstate Capital Markets Limited.

SCHLOSS, Zvi; Chairman, Precious Metals Trust plc, since 1981. *Career:* J Rothschild Investment Management Ltd, Director 1979-; Bank Leumi (UK) plc, General Manager & Director 1962-79. *Biog: b.* 14 February 1925. *Nationality:* British/Israeli. *m.* 1952, Eva (née Geiringer); 3 d. *Educ:* Mainly Self-Educated; London (BComm Hons 1st). *Directorships:* J Rothschild Investment Management Ltd 1979; PMT Finance Ltd 1981; PMT Leasing Ltd 1981; Precious Metals Trust plc 1981. *Publications:* Variable Exchange Rates and the Quality of Credit in The AMEX Bank Review 1989. *Clubs:* LSE Club. *Recreations:* Reading, Walking, Gardening, Music, Charities.

SCHMITZ, Dr Ronaldo H; Executive Vice President, Deutsche Bank AG, since 1990; Member of the Board of Directors, 1991. *Career:* BASF AG, Member of the Treasury Department 1967-74; BASF Systems Inc, Chief Executive Officer 1974-75; BASF Espanola SA, Chief Executive Officer 1975-77; BASF Farben und Fasern AG, Chairman of the Board of Managing Directors 1977-80; BASF AG, Member of the Board of Managing Directors 1980-90. *Biog: b.* 30 October 1938. *Educ:* University of Cologne, West Germany (Diploma-Kaufman, Dr rer pol); INSEAD, Fontainebleau, France (MBA). *Directorships:* Villeroy & Boch, Mettlach; Linde AG, Wiesbaden; Deutsche Bank Capital Markets Ltd. (London) Chairman; Deutsche Bank Capital Corporation (New York) Vice Chairman; Deutsche Bank (Canada) Chairman; Morgan Grenfell Group plc; Banco Commercial Transatlantico, Barcelona.

SCHMÖLZ, Reinhard J; Chief Executive Officer, WPZ Bank (UK) Ltd, since 1987. *Career:* Swiss Volksbank, Zurich, Stock Exchange Dept 1963-65; G Eberstadt & Co Ltd, London, Eurobond Dealer 1965-66; Credit Commercial de France, Paris, Syndicate Department 1966-67; Smith Barney & Co Inc, New York, Vice President, Capital Market 1968-73; Mercur Bank SA, Luxembourg, Managing Director 1974-76; Credit Suisse, Luxembourg, Managing Director, Board Member 1976-83; Credit Suisse, London, Branch Manager 1983-85; CSFB, Frankfurt, Board Member, Securities Dealings 1985-87. *Biog: b.* 9 March 1942. *Nationality:* German. *m.* Marie-Paule (née Olinger); 2 d. *Educ:* Elementary and Commercial Schools in Munich. *Directorships:* Pedro Domecq International 1976-90 (non-exec); Pedro Domecq Financial 1976-90 (non-exec). *Clubs:* St George's Hill Golf Club. *Recreations:* Golf, Skiing.

SCHNEIDER-LENNÉ, Miss E R; Director, Morgan Grenfell Group plc.

SCHOCH, T; Partner, Cazenove & Co.

SCHOFIELD, B A; Partner, Cameron Markby Hewitt.

SCHOFIELD, G A; General Manager, The Royal Bank of Scotland plc.

SCHOLAR, Michael Charles; Deputy Secretary, H M Treasury, since 1987; Public Finance. *Career:* Harvard University, Loeb Fellow 1967; St John's College, Cambridge, Fellow 1969; H M Treasury 1969; Private Sec to Chief Secretary 1974-76; Barclays Bank International 1979-81; Private Sec to Prime Minister 1981-83; H M Treasury, Under Sec 1983-87. *Biog: b.* 3 January 1942. *Nationality:* British. *m.* 1964, Angela Mary; 3 s; 1 d d (decd). *Educ:* St Olave's Grammar School; St John's College, Cambridge (PhD); University of California at Berkeley (MA). *Professional Organisations:* ARCO. *Publications:* Contributions to Philosophical Journals. *Recreations:* Music, Walking.

SCHOLES, Jeremy Paul; Partner, Evershed Wells & Hind, since 1988; Corporate/Commercial. *Career:* Freshfields, Articled Clerk/Assistant Solicitor 1979-81; Waltons & Morse, Assistant Solicitor 1981-85; Wells & Hind/Evershed Wells & Hind, Assistant Solicitor/ Partner 1985-. *Biog: b.* 16 November 1956. *Educ:* Bacup & Rawtenstall Grammar School, Rossendale Lancashire; Churchill College, Cambridge (BA, MA); Collège d'Europe, Brugge, Belgium (Cert HEE). *Recreations:* Skiing, Cycling.

SCHOLES, Richard Thomas; TD; Director, Kleinwort Benson Securities Ltd, since 1986; Corporate Finnce. *Career:* Porter Matthews & Marsden 1965-69; Arthur Andersen 1969-70; Joseph Sebag & Co

Employee/Ptnr 1970-79; Carr Sebag & Co Ptnr 1979-82; Grieveson Grant & Co Ptnr 1982-86. *Biog: b.* 12 May 1945. *Nationality:* British. *m.* 1974, Carol (née Frith); 1 s; 2 d. *Educ:* Stowe School. *Directorships:* UKF Ltd 1986 (non-exec). *Other Activities:* Territorial Army. *Professional Organisations:* FCA.

SCHOLEY, Sir David; CBE; Chairman, S G Warburg Group plc, since 1984. *Career:* Thompson Graham & Co Ltd (Lloyd's Brokers) 1956-58; Dale & Co Ltd (Insurance Brokers), Canada 1958-59; Guinness Mahon & Co Ltd 1959-64; S G Warburg & Co Ltd 1965-. *Biog: b.* 28 June 1935. *Nationality:* British. *Educ:* Wellington College; Christ Church, Oxford. *Directorships:* Bank of England 1981 (non-exec); British Telecommunications plc 1986 (non-exec).

SCHOLTES, Cornelis A P; Director, S G Warburg and Co Ltd, since 1986; In Charge of Currency Advisory Group. *Career:* Chemical Bank In Charge, FX Advisory, Europe Dept 1977-82; Chief of Staff, European & Middle East Treasury Division 1982-84. *Biog: b.* 5 December 1948. *Nationality:* Dutch. *m.* 1974, Dominique (née Passau); 4 s; 1 d. *Educ:* Collège ND de la Paix; Faculté des Sciences Economiques, Namur, Belgium (MSc).

SCHRAGER VON ALTISHOFEN, Baroness N J; Secretary, Kleinwort Benson Securities Limited.

SCHRODER, Bruno Lionel; Director, J Henry Schroder Wagg & Company Ltd, since 1966. *Biog: b.* 17 January 1933. *Nationality:* British. *m.* 1969, Patricia (née Holt); 1 d. *Educ:* Eton College; University College, Oxford (MA); Harvard Business School (MBA). *Directorships:* Schroders plc 1963; Schroders Inc 1984; Schroder Charity Trust 1960. *Other Activities:* Liveryman, Goldsmith's Company (Court of Assistants, 1987); Member, Air Squadron Exec Ctee. *Clubs:* Brooks's. *Recreations:* Flying, Shooting, Continental Silver.

SCHUENEMAN, Diane L; Director, Merrill Lynch International Limited.

SCHUKKEN, F; Director, Calor Group plc.

SCHULZ, P F; Partner, Allen & Overy, since 1989; Banking, International Finance. *Career:* Allen & Overy 1981-. *Biog: b.* 5 October 1957. *Nationality:* British. *Educ:* Haberdashers' Aske's School; Downing College, Cambridge (MA Law). *Other Activities:* Member, City of London Solicitors' Company. *Recreations:* Flying (PPL Lapsed), Theatre, Music.

SCHWARZ, Jonathan Simon; Partner, Stephenson Harwood, since 1988; International Tax. *Career:* Fenerts, Robertson Fraser & Hatch, Associate 1978-81; Burnet, Duckworth & Palmer, In Charge of London Office 1981-88. *Biog: b.* 20 June 1953. *Nationality:* Canadian.

m. 1986, Denise (née Sheer); 2 s. *Educ:* Hyde Park High School; University of Witwatersrand (BA, LLB); University of California, Berkeley (LLM). *Other Activities:* Executive Committee, Association Internationale des Jeunes Avocats; Chairman, Legal Committee, Canada-UK Chamber of Commerce; Editor, Financial Times World Tax Report; UK Correspondent, Bulletin for International Fiscal Documentation; UK Correspondent, Juta's Foreign Tax Review. *Professional Organisations:* Solicitor, England & Wales; Barrister & Solicitor, Alberta, Canada; Advocate, South Africa; IBA; International Fiscal Association; Canadian Bar Association; Canadian Tax Foundation.

SCICLUNA, M A; Partner, Touche Ross & Co.

SCLATER, John Richard; Vice Chairman, Hill Samuel Bank Limited, since 1990; Corporate Finance. *Career:* Glyn, Mills & Co 1964-70; Williams, Glyn & Co, Director 1970-76; Nordic Bank, Managing Director 1976-85; Chairman 1985; Guinness Mahon & Co Ltd, Director 1985-87; Chairman 1987. *Biog: b.* 14 July 1940. *Nationality:* British. *m.* 1985, Grizel Elizabeth Catherine (née Dawson); 1 s; 1 d. *Educ:* Charterhouse; Cambridge University (MA); Harvard University (MBA); Yale University (MA). *Directorships:* Hill Samuel Bank Limited 1990 Vice Chairman; Berisford International plc 1990 Chm; Foreign and Colonial Investment Trust plc 1985 Chm; F & C Enterprise Trust plc 1986 Chm; Foreign & Colonial Ventures Advisors Limited 1988 Chm; Foreign & Colonial Ventures Limited 1990 Chm; Sclater Farming Limited 1979 Chm; County Catering & Leisure Limited 1990 Chm; The Union Discount Company of London plc 1986 Dep Chm; Yamaichi International (Europe) Limited 1987 Dep Chm; Berner Nicol & Co Limited 1968; James Cropper plc 1972; Economic Insurance Company Limited 1989; The Equitable Life Assurance Society 1985; Fuel-Tech Europe Limited 1990; Grosvenor Estate Holdings 1989; Hafnia Holdings (UK) Limited 1989; Holker Estates Company Limited 1974; Hypo Foreign & Colonial Management (Holdings) Ltd 1989; Prolific Group plc 1990; The Union Discount Superannuation Fund Trust Limited 1984; Wilrig AS 1989. *Other Activities:* Trustee, The Grosvenor Estate, 1973; Member, Council of the Duchy of Lancaster, 1987; Member, Confederation of British Industry City Advisory Group, 1988; Director & Governor, Brambletye School Trust Limited, 1976; International Students Trust Limited, 1976. *Clubs:* Brooks's, Pratts, University Pitt (Cambridge). *Recreations:* Country Pursuits.

SCOPES, Richard Henry; Partner, Wilde Sapte, since 1980; Company, Corporate Insolvency & Banking. *Biog: b.* 6 June 1944. *Nationality:* British. *m.* 1969, Jacqueline (née Monk); 1 d. *Educ:* University College School; Magdalene College, Cambridge (LLB). *Other Activities:* City of London Solicitors' Company;

Queenhithe Ward Club. *Professional Organisations:* The Law Society.

SCOTT, Charles; Finance Director, Saatchi & Saatchi Company plc.

SCOTT, Christopher; WS, NP; Partner, W & J Burness WS, since 1989; Company Law. *Career:* W & J Burness WS, Solicitor 1985-87; Travers Smith Braithwaite Solicitor 1987-88; W & J Burness WS, Solicitor 1988-89. *Biog: b.* 29 April 1960. *Nationality:* British. *Educ:* University of Edinburgh (LLB 1st Class Honours, Diploma in Legal Practice). *Directorships:* Non other than W & J Burness Related. *Professional Organisations:* Notary Public, Writer to HM Signet. *Recreations:* Fly Fishing, Motorcycling, Hillwalking.

SCOTT, Claude Hugo Cameron; Senior Partner, Gouldens. *Biog: b.* 20 September 1936. *m.* 1969, Elisabeth Juliet (née Brodie); 1 s; 2 d. *Educ:* St Edward's School, Oxford; Cambridge University (MA,LLM).

SCOTT, D R; Director, Hambros Bank Limited.

SCOTT, David; Managing Director, Weybourne Financial Services Limited, since 1987. *Career:* Legal & General 1959-68; Hill Samuel Life, Regional Manager 1968-73; Target Group, Marketing Director 1973-87. *Biog: b.* 23 April 1942. *Nationality:* British. *m.* 1965, Gwyneth; 2 d. *Directorships:* Target Group 1976-87 (exec); Weybourne Financial Services Ltd 1987 (exec); FIMBRA 1990 (exec). *Other Activities:* FIMBRA, Advertising Committee. *Recreations:* Golf, Health & Fitness, Chess.

SCOTT, G K; Director/Underwriter, MFK Underwriting Agencies Ltd.

SCOTT, G W; Chairman, Scott Underwriting Agencies Limited.

SCOTT, Hugo; Senior Partner, Gouldens.

SCOTT, I R H; Partner, Lane Clark & Peacock, since 1988. *Biog: b.* 18 June 1957. *Nationality:* Australian. *m.* 1985, Margaret (née Ayoung Chee); 1 d. *Educ:* University of Melbourne (BSc Hons). *Professional Organisations:* Fellow, Institute of Actuaries; Fellow, Institute of Actuaries of Australia. *Clubs:* Lansdowne Club. *Recreations:* Cricket, Squash.

SCOTT, Iain William St Clair; General Manager, Management Services, Bank of Scotland, since 1990; Information Technology. *Career:* Bank of Scotland, Cost Accountant 1970; Assistant Management Accountant 1972; Management Accountant 1973; Assistant Chief Accountant 1981; Manager, Corporate Planning 1983; Assistant General Manager, Corporate Planning 1985; Divisional General Manager, Accounting & Finance

1986; General Manager, Accounting & Finance 1989; General Manager, MSD 1990. *Biog: b.* 14 May 1946. *Nationality:* British. *m.* 1971, 'Jill' Noelle Margaret Gilmour (née Young); 1 s; 1 d. *Educ:* George Watsons College, Edinburgh; Edinburgh University. *Directorships:* Scottish Consultative Committee on the Curriculum 1987 (non-exec); NWS Bank plc 1988 (non-exec). *Professional Organisations:* CA; AIB (Scot). *Clubs:* Honourable Coy of Edinburgh Golfers, Bruntsfield Links GS. *Recreations:* Golf, Curling, Squash.

SCOTT, Ian; Sales Director, Henderson Unit Trust Management Ltd.

SCOTT, Ian A; Commercial Litigation Partner, Bristows Cooke & Carpmael.

SCOTT, Ian Jonathan; Director, Barclays de Zoete Wedd Ltd.

SCOTT, Ian Russell; Partner, Ashurst Morris Crisp, since 1972; Corporate Finance. *Career:* Sharpe Pritchard & Co, Asst Solicitor 1967-68; Ashurst Morris Crisp, Asst Solicitor 1968-72. *Biog: b.* 12 September 1942. *m.* 1969, Mary Peverell (née Wright); 1 s; 2 d. *Educ:* Sherborne School; London University (LLB Hons). *Clubs:* City of London, Roehampton. *Recreations:* Tennis, Golf, Hockey, Sailing, Theatre.

SCOTT, J D; Managing Director, Scott Underwriting Agencies Limited.

SCOTT, J M; Director, Wise Speke Ltd, since 1990; Private Clients. *Career:* Charlton Stott Dimmock & Co, Research Analyst 1970-80; Charlton Seal Dimmock & Co, Partner 1980-87; Charlton Seal Ltd, Director 1987-89; Charlton Seal Schaverien Ltd, Director 1987-90; Wise Speke Ltd, Director 1990-. *Educ:* Urmston Grammar School; University of London (BSc Econ). *Professional Organisations:* ASIA.

SCOTT, James; Director, BDO Consulting.

SCOTT, James A; CB, LVO; Chief Executive, Scottish Development Agency, since 1990. *Career:* Commonwealth Relations Officer 1956; UK High Commission, New Delhi, First Secretary 1958-62; UK Mission to UN, New York 1962-65; Transferred to Scottish Office 1965; Private Secretary to Secretary of State for Scotland 1969-71; Scottish Development Department, Assistant Secretary 1971-76; Industry Department for Scotland, Under-Secretary 1976-84; Scottish Education Department, Secretary 1984-87; Industry Department for Scotland, Secretary 1987-90. *Biog: b.* 5 March 1932. *Nationality:* British. *m.* 1957, Elizabeth (née Buchan-Hepburn); 3 s; 1 d. *Educ:* Dollar Academy; St Andrews University (MA Hons); Queen's University of Ontario. *Clubs:* Travellers'. *Recreations:* Music, Golf.

SCOTT, John Philip Henry S; Director, Lazard Brothers & Co, Limited, since 1988; Corporate Finance. *Career:* Jardine, Matheson & Co, Limited (Hong Kong) 1974-80; Lazard Brothers 1981-. *Biog: b.* 20 June 1952. *Nationality:* British. *m.* 1977, Jacqueline (née Rae); 2 s. *Educ:* Magdalene College, Cambridge (MA Economics); INSEAD, Fontainebleau (MBA). *Other Activities:* Freeman, Worshipful Company of Grocers(1981). *Professional Organisations:* Fellow, Chartered Insurance Institute (1980).

SCOTT, John Stearn; Director and Secretary, First National Bank plc, since 1989; Finance Director. *Career:* Evan Peirson & Co, Articled Clerk 1961-66; Touche Ross & Co, Supervisor 1967-70; First National Bank plc 1970-. *Biog: b.* 3 December 1944. *Nationality:* British. *m.* 1970, Jennifer (née Ockenden); 1 s; 2 d. *Educ:* Downer County Grammar. *Directorships:* First National Bank plc 1989 (exec); First National Leasing Ltd 1989 (exec); First National Credit Ltd 1989 (exec). *Other Activities:* Finance Houses Association, 2 Committees. *Professional Organisations:* FCA. *Clubs:* Chorleywood Golf Club. *Recreations:* Gardening, Squash.

SCOTT, Jonathan Pestwich; Director, S G Warburg & Co Ltd, since 1987; Specialist Finance. *Career:* Metal Box Asst Head, EEC Project 1971-73; Citicorp Leasing International Mgr, Leasing 1973-76; Citicorp International Bank Ltd VP, Specialist Finance 1976-80; Lloyds Bank International Dir, Merchant Banking Div 1980-85; Lloyds Merchant Bank Dir, Specialist Finance 1985-87. *Biog: b.* 24 April 1948. *Nationality:* British. *m.* 1979, Josephine (née Taylor); 1 s; 1 d. *Educ:* Sedbergh School; Durham University (BSc). *Other Activities:* Trustee of Scott Trust. *Publications:* Securitisation. *Recreations:* Golf, Walking.

SCOTT, Mrs Patricia Mary (née Rouse); Director of Taxation & Treasury, Thorn EMI plc, since 1989; Taxation & Treasury Worldwide. *Career:* Thorn EMI plc, Group Tax Manager 1986-89; Manager, International Tax & VAT 1985-86; Burmah Oil plc, Thistle Operations Accountant 1985-. *Biog: b.* 28 November 1954. *Nationality:* British. *m.* 1975, Anthony Vincent. *Educ:* Hredd Burna School, Swindon; Portsmouth Polytechnic (1 year only). *Directorships:* Many Thorn EMI Subsidiaries, None Public. *Other Activities:* Treasurer, St Augustines Church, Swindon. *Professional Organisations:* FCCA; MCT. *Recreations:* Gardening, Poultry Keeping.

SCOTT, Peter John; Chief Executive & Chairman, Aegis Group plc. *Career:* Ogilvy & Mather 1969; Invited to start a Scottish Office for the Company 1972; Ogilvy & Mather, Belgium Operation, Dep MD 1975; Funded, along with 3 partners, the advertising group WCRS listing on the British Stock Market 1983. *Biog: b.* 28 March 1947. *Nationality:* British. *m.* 1980, Jan Marie-Therese; 2 d. *Directorships:* Aegis Group plc 1979; Alan Pascoe Associates Ltd 1987; Groupe Belio-WCRS; Car-

at Holding SA; Church Green Engineering Ltd; Della Femina, McNamee WCRS, Inc; Euccom WCRS Della Femina Ball Ltd 1989; Fairstead Ltd; Gatebar Ltd; WCRS Investment Ltd 1988. *Clubs:* Harry's Bar. *Recreations:* Keen Polo Player.

SCOTT, Philip Gordon; Senior Investment Manager, Norwich Union Fund Managers Limited, since 1988; Head of Fund Management. *Career:* Norwich Union Actuarial Student 1973-79; Actuary 1979; Gilt Fund Mgr, Investment Dept 1979-81; Asst Actuary for New Zealand 1981-84; Asst Investment Mgr 1986-87; Investment Mgr 1987-88. *Biog: b.* 6 January 1954. *Nationality:* British. *m.* 1974, Helen Rebecca Evelyn (née Fearnley); 1 s; 1 d. *Educ:* Richard Hale School & Great Yarmouth Grammar; King's College, London. *Directorships:* Norwich Union Fund Managers Limited 1988 (exec); Norwich Union Venture Capital Limited 1988 (exec); Norwich General Trust Limited 1988 (exec); Norwich Union Real Estate Managers Limited 1990 (exec). *Professional Organisations:* FIA. *Recreations:* Sailing.

SCOTT, R D; Group Finance Director, Asda Group plc, since 1988. *Career:* Price Waterhouse & Company, Chartered Accountants 1972-76; Tilcon Ltd, Divisional Accountant/Divisional Financial Controller 1976-81; Wolstenholme Rink plc, Company Secretary/Chief Financial Officer 1981-85; Asda Stores Limited, Divisional Director/Finance Director 1985; Asda Group plc, Finance Director 1988-. *Biog: b.* 28 February 1949. *Nationality:* British. *m.* 1972, Sarah; 1 s; 2 d. *Educ:* Clitheroe Royal Grammar School; Merton College, Oxford (MA Oxon). *Directorships:* Burwood House Group (non-exec); MFI Furniture Group Limited (non-exec). *Professional Organisations:* FCA. *Recreations:* Outdoor Recreation, Sport.

SCOTT, Robert Avisson; Deputy General Manager (UK), General Accident Fire and Life Assurance Corporation plc, since 1990; UK. *Career:* The South British Insurance Co Ltd, Chief Manager 1979-81; The New Zealand Ins Co Ltd (N Zealand), Asst General Manager 1981-83; The New Zealand Ins Co Ltd (Australia), Asst General Manager 1983-85; General Manager 1985-87; NZI Insurance Australia Ltd & NZI Life Ltd, Chief General Manager 1987-90. *Biog: b.* 6 January 1942. *Nationality:* Australian. *Professional Organisations:* Associate, Insurance Institute of Australia & New Zealand.

SCOTT, Thomas Anthony; Partner, Linklaters & Paines, since 1989; Corporate Tax. *Career:* Lecturer in Law, Lincoln College, Oxford 1979-80; Overseas Lawyer, Hunton & Williams (Law Firm), Richmond, Virginia & Washington DC, USA 1980. *Biog: b.* 10 July 1958. *Nationality:* British. *m.* 1990, Patricia. *Other Activities:* City of London Solicitors' Company. *Publications:* Tolleys' Tax Planning (Chapter on Share Options and Share Incentive Schemes), Published Annually; Tolleys' Practical Guide To Company Acquisitions,

(Chapter on Planning the Tax Aspects), 1989. *Recreations:* Music, Reading.

SCOTT, William Andrew Black; General Manager & Deputy Chief Executive, Scottish Provident, since 1988; Customer Service. *Career:* Scottish Provident, Asst Actuary 1965-69; Dep Actuary 1969-72; Joint Sec 1972-75; Sec 1975-80; Assistant Gen Mgr & Sec 1980-88. *Biog: b.* 4 February 1938. *Nationality:* British. *m.* 1966, Marion (née Gow); 1 s; 1 d. *Educ:* Preston Lodge; Edinburgh University (MA). *Directorships:* Scottish Provident Institution 1990 (exec). *Professional Organisations:* FFA. *Recreations:* Golf.

SCOTT-BARRETT, A J; Partner, Cazenove & Co.

SCOTT-BARRETT, N H; Director, Hambros Bank Limited.

SCOTT BROWN, Ronald; Executive Chairman, Aberdeen Trust Holdings plc, since 1989; Investment Management. *Career:* Brander & Cruickshank, Advocates, Investment Management, Assistant 1961-66; Partner 1966-83; Aberdeen Fund Managers Ltd, Investment Management, Director 1986-. *Biog: b.* 14 February 1937. *Nationality:* British. *m.* 1966, Jean Leslie (née Booth); 3 s. *Educ:* Aberdeen Grammar School; Aberdeen University (MA,LLB). *Directorships:* Temple Bar Investment Trust plc 1978 (non-exec); Abtrust New Dawn Investment Trust plc 1989 (non-exec) Chm; Aberdeen Fund Managers Ltd 1983 (exec); Abtrust Management Ltd 1987 (exec). *Other Activities:* Governor, Northern College of Education; Member, University Court of University of Aberdeen. *Clubs:* Royal Northern & University Club, Aberdeen. *Recreations:* Skiing, Hill Walking.

SCOTT KNIGHT, A J; Director, Granville & Co Limited; Stockbroking.

SCOTT-MALDEN, John Nyren; Director, Barclays de Zoete Wedd Ltd, since 1990; Tobacco/Retail Analyst. *Career:* de Zoete & Bevan, Trainee/Research Analyst 1972-77; Tobacco Industry, Analyst 1977-86; Ptnr 1985; Barclays de Zoete Wedd, Tobacco Industry Analyst 1986-; Director, Head of European Research 1987-89. *Biog: b.* 10 September 1950. *Nationality:* British. *m.* 1973, Anne Marjorie (née Arthur); 2 s. *Educ:* Winchester College; King's College, Cambridge (MA Hons). *Professional Organisations:* ASIA. *Recreations:* Golf, Reading, Music.

SCOTT PLUMMER, J P; Director, Candover Investments plc.

SCOTT PLUMMER, Patrick Joseph; Director, Martin Currie Limited.

SCOTTER, Ray; General Manager, Woolwich Building Society, since 1988; Information Services. *Career:* Gateway Building Society, Assistant General Manager (Data Processing) 1980-88; Central Regional Council, Technical Manager 1978-80. *Biog: b.* 8 August 1948. *Nationality:* British. *m.* 1970, Deborah (née Bright); 2 d. *Educ:* Southampton University (BSc Hons Mathematics).

SCOURSE, Neil Richard; Director of Research, Barclays de Zoete Wedd, since 1986; Drinks Sector Research. *Career:* Fielding, Newson-Smith & Co, Various to Ptnr 1968-85. *Biog: b.* 4 July 1938. *Nationality:* British. *m.* 1969, Victoria (née Meyer). *Educ:* Bristol Grammar School; St John's College, Oxford (MA). *Directorships:* BZW Research Ltd 1986; BZW Securities Ltd 1986. *Professional Organisations:* ASIA; ISE. *Recreations:* Reading, Travel.

SCRASE, G E; Director, Crédit Lyonnais Rouse Limited.

SCRASE, P B; Partner, Holman Fenwick & Willan, since 1979; Commercial Litigation. *Career:* Howard Humphries Civil Engineering Consultants, Junior Engineer 1965-66; Solicitors' Articled Clerk 1966-69; Miscellaneous Jobs as a Solicitor 1969-72; Holman Fenwick & Willan 1972-. *Biog: b.* 7 March 1943. *Nationality:* British. *m.* 1965, Amanda; 1 s; 2 d. *Educ:* Cheltenham College; Emmanuel College, Cambridge (MA Engineering). *Recreations:* Walking, Riding, Skiing, Gardening, Workshop.

SCRIMGEOUR, Angus Muir Edington; Deputy Chairman, Henry Cooke Group plc, since 1990; Full Range of Financial Services, Including Banking; Corporate Finance & Stockbroking. *Career:* Citibank NA, VP 1974-84; Edington plc, Chief Exec 1985-; Chairman 1990. *Biog: b.* 19 February 1945. *Nationality:* British. *m.* 1968, Clare (née Murray); 1 s. *Educ:* Westminster School; New College, Oxford (MA); University College, London (MSc). *Directorships:* Henry Cooke Lumsden plc 1986 (non-exec).

SCRIVEN, J A; Partner, Allen & Overy.

SCRYMGEOUR-WEDDERBURN, James I; Director, MIM Limited.

SCURFIELD, Hugh Hedley; General Manager & Actuary, Norwich Union Insurance Group.

SCUTT, G H M; Chairman, Well Marine Reinsurance Brokers Limited.

SCUTT, S P; Director, Well Marine Reinsurance Brokers Limited.

SEABROOK, F; Executive Director, Daiwa Europe Limited.

SEABROOK, Michael Richard; Partner, Evershed Wells & Hind, since 1986; Corporate Finance. *Career:* Lovell White & King, Articled Clerk 1974-76; Clifford-Turner, Assistant Solicitor 1976-79; Needham & James, Assistant Solicitor 1980-81; Partner 1981-86; Evershed & Tomkinson (now Evershed Wells & Hind), Partner 1986-. *Biog: b.* 24 March 1952. *Nationality:* British. *m.* 1979, Hilary Margaret (née Pettitt); 2 s. *Educ:* King Edwards School, Birmingham; Exeter University (LLB). *Directorships:* LCL Limited 1988 (non-exec); Leicester Circuits Ltd 1988 (non-exec); Fourth Roman Property Trust plc 1989 (non-exec); Roman Rentals 056 plc to 109 plc 1989 (non-exec). *Professional Organisations:* Law Society. *Clubs:* Warwickshire Pilgrims Cricket Club, Warwickshire Imps Cricket Club, Knowle & Dorridge Cricket Club, Copt Heath Golf Club, Bacchanalians Golfing Society.

SEABY, M D; Director, Kellett (Holdings) Limited.

SEAL, K R; Chief Executive, BP Oil, British Petroleum Company plc.

SEAL, Michael Jefferson; Director, Charlton Seal (a division of Wise Speke Limited), since 1990. *Career:* The Carborundum Co Ltd 1957-59; Jefferson Seal & Co, Ptnr 1961-68; Seal Arnold & Co, Ptnr 1968-72; Henriques Seal & Co, Ptnr 1972-74; Charlton Seal Dimmock & Co, Ptnr 1974-87; Charlton Seal Ltd, Dir 1987-88; Charlton Seal Schaverien Limited, Chairman 1988-90. *Biog: b.* 17 October 1936. *Nationality:* British. *m.* 1962, Julia Mary (née Gaskill); 1 s; 2 d. *Educ:* Marlborough College. *Directorships:* Benchmark Group plc 1987 (exec); Jefferson Seal Ltd (Jersey) (non-exec). *Other Activities:* The Family Welfare Assoc of Manchester; The Humane Society of the Hundred of Salford; The Greater Manchester Educational Trust; Manchester Financial and Professional Forum. *Professional Organisations:* Member, International Stock Exchange (Northern Unit Ctee). *Clubs:* St James's (Manchester). *Recreations:* Country Activities.

SEAL, Russell; Managing Director & Chief Executive, British Petroleum Company plc, since 1988. *Career:* BP 1964-; Research, then Supply & Trading; (New York) 1970; (Rotterdam) set up Anro Oil, BP Group subsidiary; (London) New Ventures 1978; (Singapore) Chm, Marketing and Refining Business in Singapore, Malaysia & Hong Kong; Senior Representative for Southeast Asia 1980; (London) General Manager, Trade & Supply Dept, Intl Trading; Head of Refining Interest for Manufacturing & Supply Business Development Unit and International Marine Operations 1984. *Biog: b.* April 1942; 3 s. *Educ:* Keele University (Chemistry & Econ). *Directorships:* BP Oil.

SEALE, Jeremy; Executive Management, S J Berwin & Co.

SEALEY, Barry Edward; CBE; Non-Executive Director, Scottish Equitable Life Assurance Society, since 1984. *Career:* Christian Salvesen plc 1958-90; Trainee 1958; Director 1969; MD 1981; Dep Chm 1987. *Biog: b.* 3 February 1936. *Nationality:* British. *m.* 1960, Helen; 1 s; 1 d. *Educ:* Dursley Grammar School; St John's College, Cambridge (BA Hons); Harvard Business School (PMD). *Directorships:* Scottish American Investment Co Ltd 1983 (non-exec); Scottish Transport Group 1986 (non-exec); Morago Limited 1989 (non-exec); Albacom plc 1990 (non-exec); David A Hall Limited 1990 (non-exec); Warburton's Limited 1990 (non-exec); Logitek plc 1990 (non-exec); The Caledonian Brewing Company Ltd 1990 Dep Chm; National Westminster Bank, Northern Advisory Board 1989 (non-exec). *Other Activities:* Member, The High Constabulary of the Port of Leith; Chairman, Executive Ctee of the Industrial Society; Dep Chm, Governing Body of Napier Polytechnic of Edinburgh. *Professional Organisations:* CBIM; FINstD. *Clubs:* New Club. *Recreations:* Music, Walking.

SEAMAN, Thomas W; Managing Director, Merrill Lynch International Limited.

SEARJEANT, Graham; Financial Editor, The Times.

SEATON, Stuart Neil; Partner, Gouldens, since 1985; Company, Commercial and Corporate Finance Work. *Career:* Crossman, Block & Keith, Solicitor's Articled Clerk 1978-80; Gouldens, Assistant Solicitor 1980-85; Partner 1985-. *Biog: b.* 9 March 1956. *Nationality:* British. *Educ:* Blundell's School; Selwyn College, Cambridge (MA). *Directorships:* Portman Square Holdings plc 1986 (non-exec). *Other Activities:* The Girdlers' Company. *Professional Organisations:* Member, Law Society. *Recreations:* Tennis, Skiing, Cricket, Swimming, Bridge.

SEBAG-MONTEFIORE, Charles Adam Laurie; Director, Kleinwort Benson Securities Ltd, since 1986; Corporate Finance. *Career:* Touche Ross & Co Articled Clerk 1971-76; Joseph Sebag & Co 1976-79; Carr Sebag & Co Ptnr 1979-82; Grieveson Grant & Co Ptnr 1982-86. *Biog: b.* 25 October 1949. *Nationality:* British. *m.* 1979, Pamela Mary Diana (née Tennant); 1 s; 2 d. *Educ:* Eton College; University of St Andrews (MA). *Directorships:* Kleinwort Benson Securities Ltd 1986 (executive). *Other Activities:* National Art-Collections Fund (Chm of Projects Ctee 1978-88); Trustee, London Historic House Museums Trust; Liveryman,Spectacle Makers' Company; Treasurer, Friends of the National Libraries (1990); Treasurer, Friends of Lambeth Palace Library (1990). *Professional Organisations:* FCA. *Clubs:* Brook's. *Recreations:* Visiting Museums & Fine Libraries, Collecting Books.

SEBBA, M J; Director, Charterhouse Bank Limited.

SEDDON, Edward Jeremy; Managing Director, Barclays de Zoete Wedd Ltd, since 1987; Privatisation & Public Sector Advice. *Career:* Assoc Electrical Industries Ltd, Graduate Trainee to Corp Planning Mgr 1958-68; Dalgety Ltd, Corporate Planning Mgr 1968-73; Barclays Merchant Bank, Mgr to Asst Dir 1974-79; Barclays Development Capital, Dir 1979-87. *Biog: b.* 14 April 1941. *Nationality:* British. *m.* 1975, Prudence Mary (née Clarke); 1 s; 2 d. *Educ:* King's School, Bruton; Southampton University (BSc). *Directorships:* Victualic plc 1983 (non-exec); National Freight Consortium plc 1984-86 (non-exec). *Clubs:* Special Forces, Royal Thames Yacht Club. *Recreations:* Sailing, Gardening, Music.

SEDGWICK, Ian Peter; Group Managing Director, Schroders plc, since 1987; Investment Management. *Career:* National Westminster Bank 1952-59; Ottoman Bank 1959-69. *Biog: b.* 13 October 1935. *m.* 1956, Verna Mary (née Churchward); 1 s; 1 d. *Directorships:* Triplevest 1986 (non-exec); Schroder Global Trust plc 1986 (non-exec) Chm; Schroder Capital Management 1983 (exec) Chm; Schroder Investment Management 1984 Chief Exec; Schroder Unit Trusts Ltd 1987 (exec) Chm; City and Commercial Investment Trust Limited (non-exec); Fundinvest plc (non-exec); Greece Fund Limited (exec) Chm; Schroder Nominees Limited; Triplevest plc (non-exec).

SEDGWICK, Ivan Harry; Director, Schroder Securities Ltd, since 1989; Head of Japanese Equities, London. *Career:* New Japan Securities, London, Manager 1981-85; Morgan Stanley International, London, Associate 1985-89. *Biog: b.* 13 January 1959. *Nationality:* British. *m.* 1988, Elizabeth (née Heathcote); 1 s. *Educ:* Farnborough 6th Form College; Cambridge University (BA, MA); City University (MBA). *Directorships:* Schroder Securities Limited 1989 (exec); Spencer Estates (Assured Tenancies) Ltd (non-exec). *Recreations:* Opera, Shooting.

SEDGWICK ROUGH, William Roger Peter; Director, Murray Lawrence Members Agency Ltd, since 1985. *Career:* C T Bowing, Broker (Aviation) 1971-76; Assistant Director, International Non-Marine 1976-78; C T Bowring (Reinsurance) Ltd, Director 1978-85; Bowring Members Agency Ltd, Director 1985-88; Murray Lawrence Members Agency Ltd, Director 1988-. *Biog: b.* 29 June 1951. *Nationality:* British. *Educ:* Wellington College. *Directorships:* Murray Lawrence Members Agency Ltd 1988 (exec). *Clubs:* White's, MCC. *Recreations:* Skiing, Golf, Shooting.

SEE, John Gordon; Assistant General Manager, The Toronto-Dominion Bank, since 1988; Corporate Finance, Leveraged/Acquisition Finance, Loan Syndications/Sales. *Career:* The Toronto-Dominion Bank International Officer, Toronto 1981-82; Area Officer, Houston, Texas 1982-83; Snr Mgr Corp Ac-

counts, Houston 1984-87; Dir, Corp Fin, New York 1987-88. *Biog: b.* 1 April 1957. *Nationality:* Canadian. *m.* 1981, Kathryn Ann (née McColm); 1 s; 1 d. *Educ:* Woodruff High School; Queen's University (BSc); Queen's University (MBA). *Recreations:* Golf, Squash, Skiing.

SEEKINGS, Roger; Partner in Charge, London Tax Office, Price Waterhouse, since 1988; Taxation. *Career:* Inland Revenue, HM Inspector of Taxes 1970-78; Price Waterhouse 1978-; Partner 1981-. *Biog: b.* 17 January 1947. *Nationality:* British. *m.* 1968, Carole Elizabeth (née Jones); 2 d. *Educ:* Queen Elizabeth's Hospital; Victoria University of Manchester (BSc Hons Chemistry).

SEELY, Hilton Nigel; Director, Kleinwort Benson Securities Limited, since 1988; Equity Income.

SEET, Joe Lip Poh; Vice President Finance, Scotia McLeod Incorporated, since 1988; All Business Support Groups. *Career:* National Bank of Kuwaitsak, Kuwait City, Kuwait Deputy Controller, Finance, Accounting, Payroll, Treasury, Risk Management 1985-88; Chemical Bank (London Branch) Chief Accountant, Finance, Accounting, Treasury, Risk Management 1977-85; Hetherington & Company, Chartered Accountants Audit & Taxation Senior 1973-77; Mattesons Meats Limited; Trainee Cost Accountant 1972-73. *Biog: b.* 8 September 1952. *Nationality:* British. *m.* 1977, May (née Lee); 1 s; 1 d. *Other Activities:* Registered Manager, The Securities Association, United Kingdom; Officer, Director, Investment Dealers Association of Canada. *Professional Organisations:* Fellow, Institute of Chartered Accountants in England and Wales.

SEFTON, Ms O M; Partner, Holman Fenwick & Willan, since 1988; Commercial Litigation. *Career:* Holman Fenwick & Willan, Solicitor 1981-87. *Biog: b.* 3 August 1953. *Nationality:* British. *m.* 1980, Timothy Wormington; 1 s. *Educ:* Wycombe Abbey School; Somerville College, Oxford (BA Jurisprudence). *Professional Organisations:* Law Society.

SEGAL, Nicholas Alfred; Partner, Allen & Overy, since 1989; Law of Domestic & International Banking, Insolvency & Corporate Reconstruction. *Career:* Cameron Markby, Articled Clerk, Asst Solicitor, Prtnr 1980-88. *Biog: b.* 20 October 1956. *Nationality:* British. *m.* 1982, Genevieve (née Muinzer). *Educ:* Poole Grammar School; St Peter's College, Oxford (MA). *Other Activities:* Snr Visiting Fellow, Centre for Commercial Law Studies, Queen Mary College, University of London. *Publications:* Contributor, Gore-Browne on Companies, 1987-89; Contributor, Boyle & Bird's Company Law, 1988; Contributor, Totty & Jordan on Insolvency, 1987-89. *Recreations:* Golf, Reading, Writing.

SEGAL, Victor Maurice; Director, Singer & Friedlander Ltd.

SEGALL, Anne; Economics Correspondent, The Daily Telegraph. *Career:* Investors Chronicle; The Economist; Daily Telegraph, Banking Correspondent. *Other Activities:* Junior Wincott Award for Financial Journalism, 1981.

SEIBEL, Michael P; Senior Vice President & Financial Institutions, Bank of America.

SEIDL, Dr H; Operations Director, Laporte plc.

SEILERN-ASPANG, Count F C; Director, Hambros Bank Limited.

SEKI, N; Managing Director & General Manager, Credit, Yamaichi Bank (UK) plc.

SEKIYA, H; Chief Representative, Japan Development Bank, since 1989; Activities Regarding Issuing JDB Bonds, Promotion of Investment in Japan, etc. *Career:* The Japan Development Bank, Tokyo, Officer, Economic & Research Dept 1967; Officer, Loan Dept Bureau for Regional Development, 1968; JDB, Officer, Hiroshima Branch 1969; Officer, Credit Analysis Dept 1972; Research Institute of Capital Formation, Economist, Office of Management Research 1974; Deputy Manager, Loan Dept III 1978; JDB, Manager; Planning & Research Division, Osaka Branch 1981; Seconded to the Okinawa Development Finance Corporation 1984; Manager, Credit Analysis Dept 1986; Deputy Director & Adviser Project Planning Dept 1988; Chief Office of Information Management, Project Planning Dept 1988. *Biog: b.* 17 August 1943. *Nationality:* Japanese. *m.* 1973, Noriko; 2 d. *Educ:* Keio University (BA Economics). *Other Activities:* Advisory Member, Centre for Japanese and East Asian Studies. *Recreations:* Music, especially Classics, Tennis.

SELBY, George W; Senior Vice President & Senior Credit Officer, Bank of America.

SELIGMAN, D G; Director, S G Warburg & Co Ltd.

SELIGMAN, George Edward Spencer; Partner, Slaughter and May, since 1984; Company and Commercial Law. *Biog: b.* 29 November 1951. *Nationality:* British. *m.* 1978, Veronique Sybille (née Piat); 2 s. *Educ:* Charterhouse; Bristol University (BSc). *Professional Organisations:* The Law Society. *Clubs:* Hurlingham.

SELIGMAN, Mark Donald; Director, SG Warburg & Co Ltd, since 1989; Corporate Finance. *Career:* Price Waterhouse & Co 1977-81; Chloride Group plc 1981-83; SG Warburg & Co Ltd 1983-. *Biog: b.* 24 January 1956. *Nationality:* British. *m.* 1982, Louise Angela Mary (née De Zulueta); 1 s; 1 d. *Educ:* Eton College; Lincoln College, Oxford (MA PPE); Université De Grenoble (Diploma); Universität Wien (Diploma). *Directorships:* Lansdown Villa Hotel Ltd 1986 (non-exec). *Professional Organisations:* ACA. *Clubs:* Roehampton. *Recreations:* Piano, Stalking, Elderly Motor Cars.

SELIN, S H; Representative, Swedbank/Sparbankernas Bank.

SELL, John G; Partner (Resident in Paris), Theodore Goddard.

SELLIER, J M; Director, Philipp & Lion Ltd.

SELLIER, Robert Hugh; Group Managing Director, George Wimpey plc, since 1986; In Charge of Group Service Companies, Engineering, Offshore & Technology Divisions, North America & Canada. *Career:* Ideal Homes, MD 1972-75; Cementation International, Chm 1975-78; Cementation Construction, Chm 1978-84; Cementation Group, Chm 1984-85. *Biog: b.* 15 November 1933. *Nationality:* British. m1 1963, Cynthia Ann (decd 1985). m2 1987, Gillian (née Clark) 1 d. *Educ:* St Joseph's College, Oxford; Kings College, Durham University (BSc Civil Engineering). *Directorships:* Brown & Root-Wimpey Highlands Fabricators Ltd; George Wimpey Canada Investments Ltd; George Wimpey Inc; Grove Consultants Ltd; Monteith Travel Services Ltd; Wimpey Environmental Ltd; Wimpey Geotech Ltd; Wimpey Group Services Ltd; Wimpey Major Projects Ltd; Wimpol Ltd. *Professional Organisations:* FICE; FIHT. *Recreations:* Shooting, Skiing.

SEMMENS, Victor William; Chairman, Eversheds, since 1990. *Career:* Solictor 1964; Wells & Hind, Nottingham, Partner; Evershed Wells & Hind, Deputy Senior Partner. *Biog: b.* 10 October 1941. *Nationality:* British. *m.* 1964, Valerie; 2 s. *Educ:* Blundell's. *Directorships:* Sheriff Holdings plc 1988 (non-exec); John Howitt Group Limited 1985 (non-exec); Shamban Europa (UK) Limited 1985 (non-exec); Shamban Europa Bearings Co Limited 1985 (non-exec); F E Wood Holdings Limited 1986 (non-exec); Burall & Floraprint Limited 1987 (non-exec); College of Law 1983 (non-exec). *Professional Organisations:* Solicitor.

SEMPLE, Robert; Director, County NatWest Securities, since 1988; Market Strategy. *Career:* Economic Models (taken over by Data Resources), Snr Economist 1978-82; Wood Mackenzie, Snr Economist 1982-88. *Biog: b.* 17 December 1952. *Nationality:* British. *m.* 1974, Anne (née Johnston); 1 s; 1 d. *Educ:* Grove Academy, Dundee; Dundee University (MA); Southampton University (MSc). *Directorships:* County NatWest 1988 (non-exec); Hill Samuel 1988 (non-exec). *Professional Organisations:* The International Stock Exchange. *Recreations:* Songwriting, Playing Guitar and Piano, Squash, Tennis.

SENDROVE, Derek; Partner, Nabarro Nathanson; Commercial Property. *Career:* Qualified as a Solicitor 1972; Nabarro Nathanson, Partner 1974-77; Solicitor with own Practice 1977-87; Nabarro Nathanson, Partner 1987-. *Biog: b.* 3 August 1947. *Nationality:* British. 3 s; 1 d. *Educ:* Jesus College, Oxford (MA Hons). *Other Activities:* Member of Board, Institute of Polish-Jewish Affairs. *Professional Organisations:* Solicitor (Honours). *Clubs:* Lansdowne. *Recreations:* Marathon Running, Skiing, Tennis, Baroque Music.

SENIOR, C; Executive Director, County NatWest Limited.

SENIOR, D C; Director, Lowndes Lambert Group Limited.

SENIOR, R D; Partner, Pensions, Bacon & Woodrow.

SEPEL, Ralph; Managing Director, Albany Life Assurance Company Ltd.

SERGEANT, Sir Patrick (John Rushton); Chairman, Euromoney Publications plc, since 1985. *Career:* News Chronicle Asst City Editor 1948; Daily Mail Dep City Editor 1953; City Editor 1960-84; Euromoney Publications Founder & MD 1969-85. *Biog: b.* 17 March 1924. *Nationality:* British. *m.* 1952, Gillian (née Wilks); 2 d. *Educ:* Beaumont College. *Directorships:* Associated Newspapers Group 1971-84 (non-exec); Daily Mail & General Trust 1983 (non-exec). *Other Activities:* Fellow, The Royal Society for the encouragement of Arts, Manufactures & Commerce; Domus Fellow, St Catherine's College, Oxford (1988). *Professional Organisations:* Freeman of The City of London; Domus Fellow, St Catherine's College, Oxford. *Publications:* Another Road to Samarkand, 1955; Money Matters, 1967; Inflation Fighters Handbook, 1976. *Clubs:* RAC, Annabel's, Cumberland Lawn Tennis, The All England Lawn Tennis & Croquet Club. *Recreations:* Tennis, Skiing, Swimming, Talking.

SESSIONS, G; Manager (Corporate Banking), Banco Santander.

SETON, A; Director, Morgan Grenfell & Co Limited.

SETON, Bruce A; Director, Gartmore Investment Management Limited, since 1980; Far East. *Career:* Gartmore (Hong Kong) Ltd Dir 1973-. *Biog: b.* 5 August 1944. *Nationality:* British. *m.* 1973, Felicity Lee (née Aspin); 1 s; 2 d. *Educ:* London University (BSc Econ). *Directorships:* International Investment Trust Co Ltd.

SEWARD, Ian Graham; Executive Director, Management Services, Allied Dunbar Assurance plc.

SEWARD, W T; Managing Director Head of Research, UBS Phillips & Drew Securities Limited.

SEWELL, Richard George; Administration, Finance & Compliance Director, Laurence Keen Ltd, since 1990. *Career:* Grants of Ireland Ltd, MD 1963-71; Laurence Prust & Co, Controller 1972-75; Admin & Fin Ptnr 1975-86; Laurence Keen & Co, Admin & Finance Partner 1986-90. *Biog: b.* 6 August 1934. *Nationality:* British. *m.* 1958, Vivian (née Baker); 2 s; 1 d. *Educ:* Eton College. *Clubs:* Royal Ocean Racing Club, Irish Cruising Club. *Recreations:* Sailing.

SEWILL, Brendon; CBE, OBE; Clerk to the Council, Office of the Banking Ombudsman, since 1985. *Career:* Conservative Research Department, Director 1965-70; Special Assistant to The Chancellor of the Exchequer 1970-74; The Committee of London and Scottish Bankers, Adviser on Public Affairs 1975-90; National Consumer Council, Member 1977-82. *Biog: b.* 13 May 1929. *Nationality:* British. *m.* 1959, Hilary Margaret (née Boyd); 2 s; 2 d. *Educ:* Bryanston School; Clare College, Cambridge (MA). *Other Activities:* Vice President, British Trust for Conservation Volunteers; Governor, Centre for Policy on Ageing; Chairman, One World Trust. *Clubs:* Carlton, Emsworth Sailing.

SEYMOUR, Adam Peacock; Director, Charterhouse Bank Ltd, since 1989; Corporate Banking Services. *Career:* Citibank NA, Asset Based Finance Division 1978-84; Vice President, Leveraged Capital Group 1985-89. *Biog: b.* 14 October 1956. *Nationality:* British. *m.* 1986, Jo-Anne (née Gordon); 2 d. *Educ:* Blundell's School, Tiverton, Devon; Emmanuel College, Cambridge (MA).

SEYMOUR, H L; Director, Martin Currie Investment Management Ltd.

SEYMOUR-NEWTON, C T; Director, Wendover Underwriting Agency Limited.

SHAAR, Susan; Director, Moorgate Public Relations.

SHACKELTON, Richard; Financial Writer, The Scotsman.

SHACKLOCK, Timothy Anthony; Director, Kleinwort Benson Limited, since 1989; Corporate Finance. *Career:* Spicer & Pegler 1975-80; Pannell Kerr Forster 1980-88; Partner 1985-88; Kleinwort Benson Limited 1988-. *Biog: b.* 12 July 1956. *Nationality:* English. *m.* 1985, Barbara (née Stephenson); 2 d. *Educ:* Nottingham High School. *Directorships:* Kleinwort Benson Limited 1989 (exec). *Professional Organisations:* Associate, Institute of Chartered Accountants. *Recreations:* Old Cars, Skiing.

SHADBOLT, Richard Andrew; Partner, McKenna & Co, since 1971; International Construction & Major Projects, Contracts, Litigation and Arbitration. *Career:* Commercial Bank of Australia, Graduate Trainee 1964;

E T Ray & Co (Leighton Buzzard), Articled Clerk 1965-67; McKenna & Co, Asst Solicitor 1967-71; Ptnr 1971. *Biog: b.* 18 December 1942. *Nationality:* British. *m.* 1970, Diane (née Taylor); 1 s; 2 d. *Educ:* Kings College, London (LLB Honours). *Other Activities:* IBA; Associate Member, American Bar Association; Chairman, European Lawyers Discussion Group; Council Member, British Polish Legal Association; Major Projects Association (Oxford); Participant, International Chamber of Commerce; CBI London Chamber of Commerce; Occasional Lecturer, University of Kent; Institute of Advanced Legal Studies, London; Steering Committee, Government Legal Advisers Course. *Professional Organisations:* Solicitor, Hong Kong; Member, Law Society England and Wales. *Publications:* Co-Author, Construction Industry Forms Book, USA 1988; Co-Author, Proving and Pricing Construction Claims, USA 1990; Contributor to Construction Periodicals (UK and Elsewhere) on Construction Law and European Business Topics, Particularly Eastern Europe. *Recreations:* Family Life.

SHAH, A M P; Chairman, Meghraj Bank Ltd.

SHAH, V M P; Director, Meghraj Bank Ltd.

SHAHABI, K; Non-Executive Director, Sheppards.

SHAKERLEY, Charles F E; Chairman, Provincial Group PLC.

SHAKESHAFT, Richard Kenneth; Executive Director Sales, Allied Dunbar Assurance plc, since 1985; Sales Management. *Career:* Barclays Bank 1959-65; Equity & Law Life Assurance 1965-70; Abbey Life 1970; Hambro Life/Allied Dunbar 1971-. *Biog: b.* 21 March 1942. *Nationality:* British. *m.* 1978, Rosemary (née Saunders). *Educ:* Stockport Grammar School. *Clubs:* Isle of Purbeck Golf Club. *Recreations:* Golf, Sailing, Travelling.

SHAMA, F; Non-Executive Chairman, C S Investments Limited.

SHANAHAN, Francis P; Non-Executive Director, First Interstate Capital Markets Limited.

SHAND, Kenneth D; Partner, Maclay Murray & Spens, since 1989; Corporate Law. *Career:* Maclay Murray & Spens Trainee Solicitor 1982-84; Assistant Solicitor 1984-88; McKenna & Co, Assistant Solicitor 1988-89. *Biog: b.* 29 April 1960. *Nationality:* British. *m.* 1985, Valerie Anne (née Callaghan); 1 s. *Educ:* Glasgow Academy; University of Glasgow (LLB Honours & Diploma in Legal Practice). *Professional Organisations:* Law Society of Scotland. *Recreations:* Golf, Tennis, Football.

SHAND, Peter R; Director, Brown, Shipley & Co Limited.

SHAPLAND, Nicholas; Director, 3i plc, since 1984; Treasury. *Career:* Investors in Industry, Controller 1973-76; Leasing Controller 1976-78; (Ireland), MD 1978-84. *Biog: b.* 9 August 1949. *m.* 1980, Barbara-Anne; 2 s; 1 d. *Educ:* Royal Grammar School, Guildford; North Wales University (BSc). *Directorships:* Societe Generale Merchant Bank 1987 (non-exec); Investors in Industry International BV 1987 MD. *Professional Organisations:* MCT. *Recreations:* Sailing, Skiing, Riding.

SHARDLOW, W D; Group Personnel Director, Grand Metropolitan plc, since 1989; Personnel. *Career:* Mobil Oil Company, Graduate Trainee to Employee Relations Manager 1963-83; Watney Mann & Truman Brewers Ltd (Grandmet), Personnel & Administration Director 1983-86; Brewing & Retailing Div (Grandmet), Personnel & Administration Director 1986-87; International Distillers & Vintners Ltd, Personnel Director 1987-89; Grand Metropolitan plc, Group Personnel Director 1989-. *Biog: b.* 28 July 1940. *Nationality:* British. *m.* 1965, Phyllis; 1 s; 2 d. *Educ:* Ludlow Grammar School; Oxford University (MA PPE). *Professional Organisations:* Member, Institute Personnel Management (MIPM).

SHARMAN, D S; Director, R H M Outhwaite (Underwriting Agencies) Limited.

SHARMAN, Frederick Joseph; Director, County NatWest Securities Ltd, since 1988; Market Making - Smaller Companies. *Career:* Wedd Durlacher Mordaunt & Co, Senior Dealer 1954-86. *Biog: b.* 20 November 1931. *Nationality:* British. *m.* 1955, Mary Julia Sarah (née West); 2 s. *Educ:* Leyton County High School. *Professional Organisations:* Member, the International Stock Exchange. *Recreations:* Golf.

SHARP, B H; Director, Forward Trust Group.

SHARP, C; Associate, Grimley J R Eve.

SHARP, E E; Director, BTR plc.

SHARP, Ernest H; Board Member, Unigate plc.

SHARP, G K; Institutional Director, Albert E Sharp Holdings plc.

SHARP, J C B; Director, Hill Samuel Bank Limited.

SHARP, James Christopher; Managing Director, Northern Rock Building Society, since 1985; Chief Executive Officer. *Career:* Shropshire CC, Articled Clerk/Asst Solicitor 1963-68; GH Morgan & Co, Asst Solicitor 1968-70; Northern Rock Building Society 1970-. *Biog: b.* 24 December 1939. *Nationality:* British. *m.* 1963, Mary (née Bromfield); 1 s; 2 d. *Educ:* Stockport Grammar School; Pembroke College, Oxford (MA). *Directorships:* Northern Rock Housing Trust Ltd

1985 (non-exec); Northern Rock Property Services Ltd 1987 (non-exec); NHBC Building Control Services Ltd 1985 (non-exec); National House-Building Council 1984 (non-exec); North Housing Association Ltd 1980 (non-exec); North Housing Ltd 1980 (non-exec); North Housing Trust Ltd 1986 (non-exec); Building Societies Ombudsman Co Ltd 1987 (non-exec) Chm; The Newcastle Initiative 1988 (non-exec); Tyneside Training & Enterprise Council 1989 (non-exec); Rock Asset Management Ltd 1988 (non-exec); Northern Rock Financial Services Ltd 1989 (non-exec). *Other Activities:* Board of Governors, Newcastle Polytechnic, 1988; Board of Governors, Durham University Business School, 1987. *Professional Organisations:* The Law Society; Deputy Chairman, Building Societies Assoc; FCBSI; CBIM. *Clubs:* Oxford & Cambridge, Northern Counties. *Recreations:* Home.

SHARP, Nicholas John Gordon; Deputy Chairman, Duncan Lawrie Limited.

SHARP, Peter John; Partner, Wilde Sapte, since 1984; Commercial Litigation. *Career:* A J Harry & Co, Articled Clerk then Assistant Solicitor 1978-81; Wilde Sapte, Assistant Solicitor 1981-84. *Biog: b.* 16 April 1956. *Nationality:* British. *m.* 1984, Philippa (née Body); 1 s; 1 d. *Educ:* Berkhamstead School; Oxford University (BA Hons). *Professional Organisations:* Solicitor; Member, Law Society. *Recreations:* Cycling, Motor Racing.

SHARP, R B; Partner, Ernst & Young.

SHARP, Ralph Julian; Partner, Touche Ross & Co.

SHARP, Simon Dumville; Chairman, Albert E Sharp Holdings plc.

SHARPLES, The Hon Christopher John; Director, GNI Ltd. *Career:* C Czarnikow Ltd (sugar brokers) 1968-72; Inter Commodities Ltd (brokers in futures, options and foreign exchange), Co-Founder and Director 1972-; International Petroleum Exchange, Director 1981-86; Vice Chairman 1986-87; Served on Committees of London Commodity Exchange (Public Relations); London International Financial Futures Exchange (Clearing); British Federation of Commodity Associations (Taxation); London Commodity Exchange Regulatory Advisory Group; International Petroleum Exchange (Public Relations); Advisory Panel to the Securities and Investments Board 1986-; Association of Futures Brokers and Dealers (Rules Committee) 1987-; Membership Committee 1987-; Finance and General Purposes Committee 1987-; ICV Ltd, Chairman 1981-; Intercom Data Systems Ltd, Director 1982; Chairman 1982-89; Association of Futures Brokers and Dealers (AFBD), Chairman 1987-; BT Vision, Member Advisory Panel 1988-. *Biog: b.* 24 May 1947. *m.* 1975, Sharon (née Sweeney); 1 s; 2 d. *Educ:* Eton College; Business

School of Neuchatel, Switzerland. *Directorships:* Inter Commodities Ltd 1972; Inter Commodities Trading Ltd 1976; ICV Ltd 1981 Chairman; GNI Ltd 1982; Intercom Data Systems 1982 (non-exec)Chm; GNI Holdings Ltd 1984; GNI (Jersey) Ltd 1985; GNI Bullion (Jersey) Ltd 1985; GNI Fund Management Ltd 1985; GNI Holdings (Jersey) Ltd 1985; GNI Wallace Ltd 1986; Association of Futures Brokers and Dealers 1987 Chairman. *Clubs:* White's, Royal Yacht Squadron. *Recreations:* Sailing, Shooting, Tennis.

SHARPLEY, M A; Director, Amalgamated Metal Trading Limited.

SHATTOCK, Nicholas Simon Keith; Partner, S J Berwin & Co, since 1990; Development Property/ Hotels/France. *Career:* Brown Cooper, Assistant Solicitor 1984-86. *Biog: b.* 28 October 1959. *Nationality:* British. *m.* 1985, Cora Ann (née Roberts); 2 d. *Educ:* Lancing College, Sussex (BA Hons Law). *Professional Organisations:* Law Society. *Clubs:* MCC. *Recreations:* Cricket.

SHAW, Alec; Director, Hogg Group plc, since 1987; Insurance Broking Management. *Career:* North British & Mercantile Ins Co, Insurance Official 1950-56; Stenhouse Organisation, Dir/MD/Chief Exec (UK Div) 1957-85; Hogg Robinson Ltd, MD 1985-. *Biog: b.* 5 April 1934. *Nationality:* British. *m.* 1958, Iris (née Webster); 1 s; 1 d. *Educ:* Burnage Grammar School, Manchester. *Directorships:* Hogg Insurance Brokers Limited Dep Chm; Gardner Mountain Financial Services Chm; Hogg Insurance Brokers UK Division Chm & MD; Gardner Mountain Financial Services Ltd Chm; Hogg Insurance Management Ltd, Guernsey Chm. *Other Activities:* Worshipful Company of Insurers. *Professional Organisations:* ACII; Reg Member, BIBA; Member, Lloyd's. *Clubs:* Copt Heath Golf Club. *Recreations:* Golf, Reading.

SHAW, Andrew Martin; Director, J Henry Schroder Wagg & Co Limited, since 1988; Corporate Finance. *Career:* Peat, Marwick, Mitchell & Co 1977-80; Audit Continental SA (Paris) 1980-82. *Biog: b.* 21 December 1953. *Nationality:* British. *Educ:* Berkhamsted School; Corpus Christi College, Oxford (MA). *Professional Organisations:* ACA.

SHAW, Sir Brian; Director, Enterprise Oil.

SHAW, David Robert; Managing Director, County NatWest Ventures Limited, since 1989; Venture Capital. *Career:* Hardie Caldwell, Aberdeen, Articled Clerk 1971-74; 3i Aberdeen, General Manager 1974-81; 3i USA, President 1981-86; 3i London, Director 1986-89; County NatWest Ventures, Managing Director 1989-. *Biog: b.* 29 May 1948. *Nationality:* British. *m.* 1971, Judith; 2 s; 1 d. *Educ:* Heriot Watt University, Edinburgh. *Directorships:* County NatWest Ventures 1989 (exec); County NatWest 1989 (exec); Aqualisa Products Ltd 1989 (non-exec). *Professional Organisations:* CA of Scotland (1974). *Clubs:* Caledonian Club. *Recreations:* Golf, Music.

SHAW, Brian R; Managing Director, Britannia Building Society.

SHAW, Gary Alexander; Vice President & Director, Wood Gundy Inc.

SHAW, J R E; Partner, Cameron Markby Hewitt.

SHAW, J S; Director, Brandeis Limited.

SHAW, Professor John Calman; Director, Bank of Scotland, since 1990. *Career:* Deloitte Haskins & Sells (Edinburgh), Ptnr 1960-86; Local Snr Ptnr 1980-86. *Biog: b.* 10 July 1932. *Nationality:* British. *m.* 1960, Shirley (née Botterill); 3 d. *Educ:* Strathallan School; Edinburgh University (BL). *Directorships:* Scottish Mortgage and Trust plc 1982 (non-exec); Scottish American Investment Company plc 1986 (non-exec); Scottish Industrial Development Advisory Board 1987; TR European Growth Trust plc 1990; Financial Reporting Council 1990; Scottish Enterprise 1990. *Other Activities:* Dir, Scottish Chamber Orchestra; Part-time Professor of Accountancy, Johnstone-Smith, 1972-82; Visiting Professor, Glasgow University. *Professional Organisations:* CA (Pres 1983-84); FCMA. *Publications:* Bogie-Group Accounts, 3rd Ed, 1973; The Audit Report, 1980. *Clubs:* New (Edinburgh), Western (Glasgow), Caledonian. *Recreations:* Walking, Opera, Foreign Travel.

SHAW, Martin; Partner, Simpson Curtis, since 1971; Corporate Finance. *Career:* Simpson Curtis, Articled Clerk 1966-69; Solicitor 1969-71. *Biog: b.* 31 October 1944. *Nationality:* British. *m.* 1967, Christine (née Whitwam); 2 s; 1 d. *Educ:* Leeds Grammar School; University College, London (LLB Hons). *Directorships:* Legal Resources Limited 1988 (non-exec)Chm; Leeds Business Venture 1982 (non-exec); Richmond House & Far Headingley School Assoc Ltd 1979 (non-exec); Gateways Educational Trust Ltd 1986 (non-exec); Minstergate plc 1985-89 Chm (non-exec); Minster Corporation plc 1988-89 Chm (non-exec). *Other Activities:* Headingley Rotary Club; Chm of Govs, Richmond House Sch; Gov, Gateways Sch; Mem, Economic & Trade Ctee, Leeds Chamber of Commerce & Ind; Board Mem, Leeds Business Group; Solicitors European Group; American Bar Association; International Bar. *Clubs:* Leeds, Alwoodley Golf Club, Chapel Allerton Lawn Tennis & Squash Club. *Recreations:* Running, Golf, Tennis, Squash.

SHAW, Neil M; Non-Executive Director, Smiths Industries plc.

SHAW, R M; Director, Baring Asset Management Ltd.

SHAW, R M; Director, Greenwell Montagu Gilt-Edged.

SHAW, Richard John Gildroy; Chief Executive/ Chairman, Lowndes Lambert Group Ltd, since 1979; Insurance Broker. *Career:* J H Minet & Co Ltd, Insurance Broker 1957-66; H J Symons & Co, Asst Dir 1967-70; C E Heath & Co (Insurance Broking Ltd), Dep Chm 1970-79; C E Heath (International), Chm & MD 1970-79; C E Heath (Latin America), Chm 1970-79. *Biog: b.* 7 June 1936. *m.* 1973, Yvonne Kathleen (née Maskell); 1 s. *Educ:* Dragon School, Oxford; Eton College. *Directorships:* Hill Samuel Group Ltd 1979 (exec); Hill House Hammond 1983 (exec); Christies Fine Art Security Services 1984 (exec). *Other Activities:* Member of Lloyd's, Lords Taverners, British Boxing Board of Control (Appeal Steward). *Clubs:* Sunningdale Golf Club, Portland, Clermont, St James's, Royal Thames, Yacht Club, Lloyd's Golf Club, Lloyd's Yacht Club. *Recreations:* Golf, Yachting, Reading, Cricket.

SHAW, Roland Clark; CBE (Hon); Chairman and Chief Executive, Premier Consolidated Oilfields plc, since 1979. *Biog: b.* 22 October 1921. *Nationality:* American. *m.* 1952, Felicitas (née von Frankenberg und Proschlitz); 2 d. *Educ:* Kimball Union Academy, US (Grad); Princeton University US (BA); London School of Economics (Post-Grad). *Directorships:* Premier Consolidated Oilfields plc 1971 (exec); Burmah Castrol plc 1986 (non-exec). *Publications:* AIME; IP; SPE. *Clubs:* Travellers (Paris), Special Forces, Princeton (NY), Bucks.

SHAW, S S; Partner, Pannell Kerr Forster.

SHAW STEWART, D H; Director, Stewart Ivory & Company Limited.

SHAWYER, Peter Michael; Group Tax Partner, Touche Ross & Co, since 1982; International Taxation Especially United States. *Biog: b.* 11 September 1950. *Nationality:* British. *m.* 1979, Margot (née Bishop); 1 s; 1 d. *Educ:* Enfield Grammar School; Sheffield University (BA Hons). *Professional Organisations:* FCA. *Publications:* Numerous articles on taxation. *Clubs:* Enfield Golf Club, Broxbourne SRC. *Recreations:* Sport generally.

SHEA, Christopher William; Director, Gill and Duffus Ltd, since 1987; Finance. *Career:* Thomson McLintock & Co, Articled Clerk 1976-81; BP Oil, Intl Accountant 1981-83. *Biog: b.* 25 June 1954. *Nationality:* British. *m.* 1981, Susan (née Shepherd); 3 s. *Educ:* St Thomas Aquinas Grammar School; Christ's College, Cambridge (MA). *Directorships:* London Fox 1987 (non-exec). *Professional Organisations:* ACA. *Recreations:* Sailing, Theatre.

SHEAD, A D; Chairman, Wendover Underwriting Agency Limited.

SHEARD, Edward Martin; Partner, Grimley J R Eve, since 1978; Valuation, Compulsory Purchase, Property Taxation, Expert Evidence. *Career:* Smith-Woolley & Co, Assistant Land Agent, Rural Estate Management 1967-71; Strutt & Parker, Assistant Land Agent, Rural Estate Management 1971-72; J R Eve & Son/J R Eve/ Grimley J R Eve, Senior Assistant 1972-. *Educ:* Sedbergh School; Sidney Sussex College, Cambridge (Exhibition, MA). *Other Activities:* Member, RICS Mineral Public Affairs Committee; Former Chartered Land Agents' Society Hugh Cooke Prize in Practical Exam. *Professional Organisations:* Fellow, Royal Institution of Chartered Surveyors. *Publications:* Contributor of Chapter on Land Transactions to Strategic Tax Planning Encyclopedia, 1987; Chapter on Surveyor in Court to Chartered Surveyors Fact Book, 1990; Chapter on Institutional Properties to Rating Service. *Clubs:* United Oxford & Cambridge University Club. *Recreations:* Fly Fishing.

SHEARER, Anthony Patrick; Financial Director, M & G Group plc, since 1988; Finance. *Career:* Deloitte Haskins & Sells, Various 1967-80; Partner 1980-88. *Biog:* b. 24 October 1948. *Nationality:* British. *m.* 1972, Jenny (née Dixon); 2 d. *Educ:* Rugby School. *Directorships:* Littlegarth School (Dedham) Ltd 1987 (non-exec); M & G Ltd 1988 (exec); Transatlantic & General Securities Company Ltd 1988 (exec); M & G Financial Services Ltd 1988 (exec); M & G Securities Ltd 1988 (exec). *Professional Organisations:* FCA. *Clubs:* Brooks's. *Recreations:* Tennis, Garden, Family, Rock'n'Roll.

SHEARMUR, Robert Laurence; KSG; Joint Managing Director, Kleinwort Benson Unit Trusts, since 1983; Unit Trust & Mutual Fund Administration/ Finance. *Career:* John Shelbourne & Co Ltd Chief Acct 1963-72; Colegrave & Co Chief Acct 1972-75; Grieveson Grant & Co Unit Trust Admin 1975-86; Kleinwort Benson Investment Mgmnt Ltd Unit Trust Admin 1986-. *Biog:* b. 26 October 1939. *Nationality:* British. *m.* 1962, Valerie (née Mickleburgh); 1 s; 1 d. *Educ:* Forest School. *Directorships:* Kleinwort Benson Unit Trusts Ltd 1983 (exec); Kleinwort Benson Investment Management Ltd 1989 (exec). *Other Activities:* Honorary Treasurer, Society of Friends of Westminster Cathedral. *Clubs:* Buck's. *Recreations:* Music, Theatre, Sailing.

SHEDDEN, Alfred Charles (Fred); Managing Partner, McGrigor Donald Solicitors, since 1985; Management of Whole Practice. *Career:* McGrigor Donald, Apprentice 1967-69; Assistant Solicitor 1969-71; Partner, (Specialising in Corporate Law until 1985) 1971-. *Biog:* b. 30 June 1944. *Nationality:* British. *m.* 1979, Irene; 1 s; 1 d. *Educ:* Arbroath High School; Aberdeen University (MA, LLB). *Directorships:* Scottish Financial Enterprise 1989 (non-exec). *Professional Organisations:* Law Society of Scotland. *Clubs:* Glasgow Art Club, Glasgow Golf Club. *Recreations:* Golf, Music, Cricket.

SHEEHAN, Richard A P; Chairman, GHC Financial Institution Insurance Services Ltd, since 1985; Broking Crime & Liability Insurance for Financial Institutions Worldwide. *Career:* Bowring Non-Marine Ins Brokers Ltd, Dir 1982-85; CT Bowring (Ins) Ltd, Dir 1984-85. *Biog:* b. 20 July 1945. *m.* 1976, Mary Lucy (née Elcomb); 1 s. *Educ:* Beaumont College; City of London Polytechnic (MA). *Directorships:* Gibbs Hartley Cooper Ltd 1986 (exec); Gibbs Hartnett & Richardson Intl Ltd 1987 (exec). *Professional Organisations:* Underwriting Member of Lloyd's; Barrister-at-Law; ACII; ACIArb. *Publications:* Articles on Insurance, Computer Crime & Products Liability. *Clubs:* Lloyd's Saddle (Hon Sec). *Recreations:* Family, Hunting, Gardening, Jogging, Serpentine Swimming, English Pubs.

SHEFFIELD, John Julian Lionel George; Director, Guardian Royal Exchange Assurance plc.

SHEINBERG, Eric P; Managing Director - Equities Trading, Goldman Sachs International Limited.

SHELBOURNE, Sir Philip; Chairman, Henry Ansbacher Holdings plc, since 1988. *Career:* Barrister-at-Law 1950-62; N M Rothschild & Sons, Ptnr 1962-71; Drayton Group Ltd, Chm 1971-74; Samuel Montagu & Co Ltd, Chm 1974-80; The British National Oil Corp, Chm 1980-82; Britoil plc, Chm 1982-88. *Biog:* b. 15 June 1924. *Nationality:* British. *Educ:* Radley College; Corpus Christi College, Oxford (MA Hons). *Directorships:* Allied Lyons plc 1976 (non-exec); Rolls Royce Ltd 1986 (non-exec); IBM World Trade Europe/Middle East/Africa Corp 1983 (non-exec). *Other Activities:* Panel on Takeovers & Mergers (Dep Chm 1987). *Clubs:* Brook's. *Recreations:* Music.

SHELDON, Jeremy Nigel; Partner, Ashurst Morris Crisp, since 1987; Company/Commercial Law. *Career:* Brighton Museum, Exhibition Officer 1974-75; Ranks Hovis McDougall, Marketing Exec 1975-76; Ashurst Morris Crisp 1978-. *Biog:* b. 10 October 1952. *Nationality:* British. *m.* 1983, Maryline (née Marti); 1 s; 1 d. *Educ:* Haileybury College; Leeds University (BA Hons 1st). *Recreations:* Music, Reading, Walking.

SHELDON, Mark Hebberton; Senior Partner, Linklaters & Paines, since 1988. *Career:* Linklaters & Paines Articled Clerk 1953-57; Asst Solicitor 1957-59; Partner 1959; (New York) Ptnr in Charge 1972-74. *Biog:* b. 6 February 1931. *Nationality:* British. *m.* 1971, Catherine Eve (née Ashworth); 1 s; 1 d. *Educ:* Wycliffe College; Corpus Christi College, Oxford (MA). *Other Activities:* The City of London Solicitors Co, Master,1987-88. *Professional Organisations:* The Law Society (Member of Council 1978; Treasurer 1981-86; Deputy Vice-President 1990-; Financial Reporting Council (Member, 1990); The City of London Law Society (Pres 1988),Nominated Member of the Council of Corp of Lloyds (1989-). *Clubs:* City of London,

Travellers. *Recreations:* Music, English, Watercolours, Swimming.

SHELDON, T J; Partner, Life & General, Bacon & Woodrow.

SHELDON, Timothy James Ralph; Group Finance Director, GNI Ltd, since 1987. *Career:* Armitage & Norton Chartered Accountant 1978-82; Robert Fleming & Co Ltd Corporate Finance Manager 1982-87. *Biog: b.* 9 July 1956. *Nationality:* British. *m.* 1984, Susan Jean (née Best); 2 s; 1 d. *Educ:* Eton; Exeter University (BA). *Directorships:* Harry Ferguson Ltd 1983 (non-exec); GNI Ltd 1987 (exec); GNI Wallace Ltd (exec); GNI Freight Futures Ltd; GH Asset Management Ltd; AGVEN Asset Management Ltd; Trifutures. *Professional Organisations:* ACA. *Clubs:* Royal Yacht Squadron, Queens. *Recreations:* Sailing, Swimming, Farming, Tennis, Shooting, Piano.

SHELDRICK, J N; Executive Director, Finance, Johnson Matthey.

SHELFORD, Peter Bengt McNeill; Partner, Clyde & Co, since 1979; Commercial Litigation. *Career:* Clyde & Co, Articled Clerk 1973-75; Clyde & Co, Assistant Solicitor 1975-79. *Biog: b.* 20 February 1951. *Nationality:* British. *m.* 1977, Patricia Evelyn (née Pullen); 1 s; 2 d. *Educ:* St John's School, Leatherhead; Southampton University (LLB). *Professional Organisations:* The Law Society, Member. *Clubs:* Hurst Green Tennis Club (Secretary). *Recreations:* Tennis, Badminton, Bridge.

SHELFORD, William T C; Senior Partner, Cameron Markby Hewitt, since 1990; Senior Partner and Partner in Property Department (Funding, Acquisition and Disposal of Commercial Real Estate). *Career:* Cameron Markby Hewitt Partner 1970-. *Biog: b.* 27 January 1943. *Nationality:* British. *m.* 1972, Annette (née Heap-Holt); 2 s; 1 d. *Educ:* Eton College; Christ Church, Oxford (MA Jurisprudence). *Other Activities:* Member, Worshipful Company of Upholders. *Professional Organisations:* Member, Law Society. *Publications:* City of London and Brook's. *Recreations:* Gardening, Small Holding, Tennis, Skiing.

SHELLARD, Jeanette A; Partner, Theodore Goddard.

SHELLEY, M John; Director, MIM Limited.

SHELTON, S W; Vice President & General Manager, State Street Bank & Trust Co.

SHENAI, G A; Chief Ecexutive, Canara Bank.

SHENKMAN, G A; Director, Kleinwort Benson Limited.

SHENTON, T; Director, Kellett (Holdings) Limited.

SHEPHERD, Miss Elizabeth Margaret; Partner, Alexander Tatham, since 1984; Company/Commercial. *Career:* Alexander Tatham, Articles 1982-84. *Biog: b.* 3 March 1959. *Nationality:* British. *Educ:* Penwortham Girls' Grammar School; Churchill College, Cambridge (MA First); Chester College of Law, Solicitors Finals. *Other Activities:* Manchester Board Member, Prince of Wales Youth Business Trust. *Professional Organisations:* Member, Law Society. *Recreations:* Theatre, Opera, Ballet, Walking.

SHEPHERD, Michael Lloyd; Partner, Hammond Suddards, since 1974; Corporate Law. *Career:* Town Clerks Office, Manchester Articled Clerk 1966-69; Assistant Solicitor 1969-72; AV Hammond, Assistant Solicitor 1972-74. *Biog: b.* 26 September 1944. *Nationality:* British. *m.* 1969, Carole Catherine (née Hill); 2 s; 1 d. *Educ:* Bradford Grammar School; Queen's College, Oxford (MA). *Professional Organisations:* Solicitor (admitted 1969); Member, Law Society. *Recreations:* Football, Cricket.

SHEPHERD, Nick; Partner, Drivers Jonas.

SHEPHERD, R; Director, Gerrard & National Securities Limited.

SHEPHERD, Robert Priestley; JP, DL; Deputy Chairman, Pentland Group plc, since 1987. *Career:* Priestley Footwear Limited (now wholly owned subsidiary of Pentland Group plc), Chairman. *Biog: b.* 1 December 1931. *Nationality:* British. *m.* 1954, Anne (née Heyworth); 2 s; 1 d. *Educ:* Rossall School, Fleetwood; Leicester College of Technology (ACFI). *Directorships:* Pentland Group plc; Priestley Footwear Limited Chm; HH Refrigeration Limited; SATRA. *Other Activities:* Renter Warden, Worshipful Company of Pattenmakers. *Professional Organisations:* FRSA; FIOD. *Recreations:* Royal Windermere Yacht Club.

SHEPLEY, J E; Partner, Clay & Partners, since 1981; Actuary to Company Pension Schemes. *Career:* London & Manchester Assurance Co Ltd, Actuarial Trainee 1971-75; Hymans Robertson Consulting Actuaries, Actuarial Trainee 1975-78. *Biog: b.* 10 May 1950. *Nationality:* British. *m.* 1984, Joanne (née Hume); 2 s. *Educ:* Sussex University (BSc Physics). *Professional Organisations:* FIA. *Publications:* Contributor, Management Buyouts (Author Krieger), 1989. *Recreations:* Cycling, Walking, Music.

SHEPPARD, Sir Allen John George; Chairman & Group Chief Executive, Grand Metropolitan plc, since 1987. *Career:* Ford 1958-68; Chrysler 1968-71; British Leyland 1971-75; Grand Metropolitan 1975-. *Biog: b.* 25 December 1932. *Nationality:* British. *m.* 1980, Mary (née Stewart). *Educ:* Ilford County High School; London School of Economics (BSc Econ). *Directorships:* Meyer International 1989 Director (non-exec); Business in the

Community 1988 Deputy Chairman; London School Economics 1988 Governor; Brewers Society 1987 Vice President; British Rail 1985-1990 Part Time Member; Mallinson-Denny 1985-1987 (non-exec) Chairman; UBM Group 1983-1985 (non-exec). *Other Activities:* Chairman, Prince's Youth Business Trust; Member, National Training Task Force; Member, National Economic Development Council; Member, Advisory Board, British-American Chamber of Commerce. *Professional Organisations:* Institute of Cost Management Accountants; Institute of Chartered Secretaries & Administrators. *Publications:* Your Business Matters 1958. Various Articles in Professional Journals. *Recreations:* Gardens, Reading, Red Setter Dogs.

SHEPPARD, David; MBE; Chairman, David Sheppard & Partners Ltd, since 1967. *Career:* Royal Navy, Retired as Lieutenant Commander, Specialised in Communications 1936-55; Tube Investments, Assistant Director of Personnel 1955-62; Rank Xerox Management Ltd, Director of Manpower 1962-67; David Sheppard & Partners, Chairman & Managing Director 1967-. *Biog: b.* 1 May 1921. *Nationality:* British. *m.* 1947, Mary Seton (née Burnell); 1 s; 1 d. *Educ:* Royal Naval College, Dartmouth. *Professional Organisations:* MIPM. *Clubs:* Brooks's, Fox, Army & Navy.

SHEPPARD, J C; Partner, Holman Fenwick & Willan, since 1963; All Areas of Maritime Law, excluding Collision, Salvage & Ship Finance. *Career:* Holman Fenwick & Willan, Articled Clerk 1955; Solicitor 1959; Partner 1963-: has laboured in the ups and downs of the Shipping Market since the beginning of his career, and still enjoys it, particularly advising P&I Clubs, Owners & Charterers. *Biog: b.* 15 November 1932. *Nationality:* British. *m.* 1983, Alexandra Mandaracas; 2 s; 2 d. *Educ:* Oundle (HSC History/English); Exeter College, Oxford (Stapleton Exhibition in History MA Jurisprudence, Oxon); Law Society (Solicitors Finals, Honours). *Professional Organisations:* Law Society. *Clubs:* Portmadoc Gwynedd Golf Club. *Recreations:* Trying with Varying Degrees of Success to Keep up with 3 Year Old Son.

SHEPPERD, Sir Alfred; Director, Mercury Asset Management Group plc.

SHEPPERD, John William; Sterling Bond Economist, Warburg (SG) Akroyd Rowe & Pitman Mullens Securities Ltd, since 1982; Gilt-Edged Market. *Career:* University of Calgary, Alberta, Canada, Lecturer 1973-78; Economic Models Ltd, Economist (Manager, Macroeconomic Forecasting) 1978-80; Laing & Cruickshank, Gilt Edged Economist 1980-82; Mullens and Co (Part of Warburg Securities since 1986), Economist 1982-. *Biog: b.* 26 February 1951. *Nationality:* British. *m.* 1975, Margot (née Hickey); 1 d. *Educ:* Tottenham Grammar School; University College of Wales, Aberystwyth (BSc Hons); University of Manchester (MA Econ). *Directorships:* Warburg Securities 1990 (exec). *Professional Organisations:* Member, International Stock Exchange; Member, Royal Economic Society.

SHEPTYCKI, W J; Managing Director, Ultramar Exploration Limited, since 1980; UK & Northwest Europe Exploration and Production. *Career:* Texaco Exploration, Calgary, Geologist 1952-58; Texaco Exploration, District Geologist 1958-65; Senior Staff Geologist 1965-68; Ultramar Exploration, Calgary, Chief Geologist 1968-69; Vice President & General Manager 1970-74; Ultramar Iran, Tehran, Iran, Managing Director 1975-77; Ultramar Indonesia, Jakarta, Indonesia, Vice President & Resident Manager 1977-80; Ultramar Exploration, London, Managing Director 1980-; Ultramar plc, London, Director 1984-. *Biog: b.* 24 August 1929. *Nationality:* Canadian. *m.* 1958, Roseanne (née Donaghy); 1 s; 1 d. *Educ:* University of Alberta, Canada (BSc Geology). *Directorships:* Blackfriars Oil & Gas Ltd 1988 (exec); Ultramar Exploration Ltd 1980 (exec); Ultramar Holdings Ltd 1984 (exec); Ultramar plc 1984 (exec); Ultramar Exploration (Netherlands) BV 1982 (exec). *Professional Organisations:* Canadian Society of Petroleum Geologists; Association of Professional Engineers, Geologists and Geophysicists of Alberta. *Clubs:* Highgate Golf Club, London.

SHER, Victor Herman; Group Managing Director, Amalgamated Metal Corporation plc, since 1988. *Career:* Fuller-Jenks Beachcroft, Chartered Accountant 1972-73; Amalgamated Metal Corporation plc, Taxation Manager 1973; Finance Manager 1977; Director of Corporate Finance 1978; Director of Corporate Treasury 1981; Finance Director 1983; Finance & Trading Director 1986. *Biog: b.* 13 January 1947. *Nationality:* British. *m.* 1979, Molly (née Soloman); 1 s; 3 d. *Educ:* King Edward VII School, Johannesburg; University of the Witwatersrand, Johannesburg (BComm, CA, SA). *Directorships:* Various within the Subsidiaries of Amalgamated Metal Corporation. *Other Activities:* Chairman of Trustees, AMC Pension Scheme. *Professional Organisations:* South African Institute of Chartered Accountants. *Recreations:* Tennis & Snow Skiing.

SHERGOLD, H E C; Director, Allstate Reinsurance Co Limited.

SHERIDAN, Christopher Julian; Deputy Chairman and Chief Executive, Samuel Montagu & Co Ltd, since 1984. *Career:* Samuel Montagu & Co Ltd Joined 1962; Asst Mgr 1968; Mgr 1972; Asst Dir 1973; Dir 1974; MD 1981. *Biog: b.* 18 February 1943. *Nationality:* British. *m.* 1972, Diane (née Wadey); 1 d. *Educ:* Berkhamsted School. *Directorships:* Guyerzeller Bank AG; Montagu Holdings SA; Midland Montagu (Holdings) Ltd; Montagu Int Investment BV. *Clubs:* Buck's. *Recreations:* Skiing, Theatre.

SHERIDAN, Philip Ogilvie; General Manager (International), Norwich Union Insurance Group, since

1989; Group Non-European Overseas Life & Non-Life Business. *Career:* Norwich Union Insurance Group Various in Branch & Head Office 1952-73; Assistant Production Manager 1973-74; Planning Manager 1974-78; Home Fire Manager 1978-83; Assistant General Manager (Staff) 1983-86; Asst Gen Manager (Staff & Admin) 1986-89. *Biog: b.* 1 August 1934. *Nationality:* British. *m.* 1959, Lorna (née Martin); 3 s. *Educ:* Morgan Academy, Dundee. *Directorships:* Norwich Union (Services) Ltd 1986 (exec); Norwich Winterthur Holdings Ltd 1988 (exec); Norwich Winterthur Reinsurance Group Ltd 1988 (exec); Norwich Winterthur Overseas Ltd 1988 (exec); Stronghold Insurance Co Ltd 1988 (exec); Various Other Group Subsidiaries and Associated Companies. *Other Activities:* Chairman of Governors, Norwich City College; Member of Council, Norwich & Norfolk Chamber of Commerce; Member of Anglia Regional Council, British Institute of Management. *Professional Organisations:* FCII; FBIM. *Clubs:* Eaton Golf Club. *Recreations:* Fishing, Shooting, Golf.

SHERIDAN, William Henry; Director, Sedgwick Group plc.

SHERLEY-DALE, Michael B; Director, County NatWest Wood Mackenzie, since 1990; Bank & Insurance Shares (UK), Specialist Sales. *Career:* Grenfell & Colgrave 1980-82; Philips & Drew 1982-87; County NatWest, Director 1987-; City North Properties plc, Managing Director 1988-. *Biog: b.* 3 January 1954. *Nationality:* British. *m.* 1985, Dawn Elizabeth; 2 d. *Educ:* Ampleforth College; York University (2i). *Directorships:* County NatWest 1990 (exec); City North Properties plc 1988 (exec) MD; Clocktower Properties Ltd 1983; Clocktower Design & Construction 1989. *Other Activities:* Management Committee, Enfield Christian Action Housing Association. *Professional Organisations:* Stock Exchange Exams (4). *Recreations:* Fishing, Painting.

SHERLING, Clive Richard; Director, Alan Patricof Associates Limited, since 1987; Director of Venture Capital Investment. *Career:* Arthur Andersen & Co 1970-87; Partner, Insolvency Practice 1982-87. *Biog: b.* 20 October 1949. *Nationality:* British; 2 s. *Educ:* London School of Economics (BSc Econ). *Directorships:* Alan Patricof Associates Ltd 1987 (exec); Lowndes Lambert Group Holdings Ltd 1988 (non-exec); Seasons Garden Centres plc 1990 (non-exec); Rotaprint Industries Ltd 1988 (non-exec); Sports Aid Foundation Ltd 1985 (non-exec). *Other Activities:* Chairman of Trustees, Sports Aid Foundation Charitable Trust. *Professional Organisations:* Fellow, Institute of Chartered Accountants in England & Wales.

SHERLOCK, (Edward) Barry (Orton); General Manager & Actuary Director, The Equitable Life Assurance Society, since 1972. *Career:* The Equitable Life Assurance Society 1956-. *Biog: b.* 10 February 1932. *Nationality:* British. *m.* 1955, Lucy (née Willey); 2 d.

Educ: Merchant Taylors' School; Pembroke College, Cambridge (MA Hons 1st). *Directorships:* Equitable Investment Managers Ltd 1987 (exec) Chm; Equitable Reversionary Interest Society Ltd 1970 (exec); The Equitable Life Assurance Society 1972 (exec); Lautro Ltd 1987 (non-exec) Chm; Percy Street Investments Ltd 1977 (exec); Reversionary Interest Society Ltd 1970 (exec); Universities Superannuation Scheme Ltd 1978 (non-exec); University Life Assurance Society 1972 (non-exec); Equitable Unit Trust Managers Ltd 1972 (exec) Chm. *Other Activities:* Liveryman, Worshipful Co of Actuaries. *Professional Organisations:* Institute of Actuaries (VP 1981-84); ABI (Dep Chm 1985-86). *Clubs:* Actuaries', Gallio. *Recreations:* Classical Music, Gardening.

SHERLOCK, Nigel; Director, Wise Speke Limited, since 1987; Corporate Fund Management. *Career:* Sherlock & Edmenson Ptnr 1963-68; Wise Speke & Co Ptnr 1969-87. *Biog: b.* 12 January 1940. *Nationality:* British. *m.* 1966, Helen Diane Frances (née Sigmund); 2 s; 1 d. *Educ:* Barnard Castle School; Nottingham University (BA). *Other Activities:* High Sheriff of Tyne & Wear, 1990-91; Chairman of Northern Sinfonia Orchestra; Chairman, Northumberland Scout Association; Council Member of University of Newcastle; Council Member of St John's College, University of Durham; Freeman of the city of Newcastle upon Tyne; Bishops Council, Diocese of Newcastle. *Professional Organisations:* FBIM, AMSIA. *Clubs:* Northern Counties Club (Newcastle upon Tyne), New Club (Edinburgh). *Recreations:* The Countryside.

SHERLOCK, Peter; Editorial Director, Equity International.

SHERMAN, Henry Charles; Partner, McKenna & Co, since 1987; Construction Litigation. *Career:* Frere Cholmeley, Articled Clerk 1975-77; Asst Solicitor 1977-83; McKenna & Co, Asst Solicitor 1983-85; Partner in Hong Kong 1985-87; Partner in London 1987-. *Biog: b.* 16 February 1952. *Nationality:* British. *m.* 1982, Caroline; 3 s. *Educ:* Oxford University (BA).

SHERVINGTON, Richard; Director of Recruitment, Price Waterhouse.

SHERWIN, David Michael Weldon; Partner, Ernst & Young, since 1985; Fraud Investigations and Financial Services. *Career:* Arthur Young (Predessor Firm of Ernst & Young) 1977-; Arthur Young, Chartered Accountant 1980; Arthur Young (Now Ernst & Young), Partner 1985-; Partner in Charge of E & Y Fraud Group & Audit Partner Specialising in Financial Services Clients and Investigations. *Biog: b.* 24 March 1954. *Nationality:* British. *m.* 1981, Rachel; 1 s; 1 d. *Educ:* Peterhouse, Rhodesia; University of Natal, Durban, South Africa (B Com). *Other Activities:* Freeman, City of London. *Professional Organisations:* ACA (Qualified 1980). *Publications:*

Fraud '89 - The Extent of Fraud Against Large Companies and Executive Views on What Should Be Done About It. *Clubs:* Wimbledon Club. *Recreations:* Golf, Stamp Collecting, Hockey, Gardening.

SHERWOOD, Dr Martin Anthony; Head of Public Relations, Wellcome plc, since 1983; Investor Relations/Corporate Communications. *Biog: b.* 10 January 1942. *Nationality:* British. *Educ:* University of Montreal (BSc); University of Exeter (PhD). *Directorships:* L-Tech Ltd 1989 (non-exec). *Recreations:* Cookery, Gardening.

SHIBANO, K; Deputy Managing Director, LTCB International Limited.

SHIBUYA, F; Coordinator, Triland Metals Ltd.

SHIELDS, Frank Cox; Director and General Manager, Maruman Securities (Europe) Ltd, since 1987. *Career:* London School of Economics, Research Staff 1969-71; Cazenove & Co, Stockbroker 1971-73; Grieveson, Grant & Co, Stockbroker 1973-78; European Banking Co Ltd, Exec Dir 1978-85; EBC Amro Bank Ltd, Exec Dir 1985-86; Maruman Securities Co Ltd, Snr Rep 1987. *Biog: b.* 10 September 1944. *Nationality:* American. *m.* 1971, Elizabeth (née Kinross); 2 s; 1 d. *Educ:* Harvard College (AB Hons); Wharton School of Finance (MBA). *Clubs:* Buck's. *Recreations:* Architecture, Reading, Travel.

SHIER, Philip; Partner, Bacon & Woodrow, Pensions.

SHIHATA, George; Manager, Credit and Private Banking, Jordan International Bank plc, since 1984; Credit Control and Investments. *Career:* Allied Arab Bank (now Allied Trust Bank plc), Senior Foreign Exchange Officer 1979-84; Associated Biscuits plc (Peak Freens), Cost and Management Accountant 1976-79. *Biog: b.* 15 September 1990. *Nationality:* Sudanese. *m.* Maha K Shihata; 2 s. *Educ:* Strathclyde University, Glasgow (Postgraduate Diploma in Finance & Economics); Cairo University (BCom); Oxford University. *Other Activities:* Member, Arab Bankers Association, London; Member, Christian Coptic Orthodox Community in London.

SHILLINGFORD, James Hugh; Managing Director, M & G Investment Management, since 1987; Investment Management. *Career:* Coopers & Lybrand, Audit Supervisor 1975-79. *Biog: b.* 18 August 1953. *Educ:* Westminster School; Christ Church, Oxford (MA); London Business School (MSc). *Directorships:* M & G Group plc; M & G Second Dual Trust. *Professional Organisations:* ICA.

SHIM, O S; General Manager, Bank of Seoul.

SHIMA, Hiroaki; Group Legal Advisor and Company Secretary, Yamaichi International (Europe) Limited.

SHIMIZU, Haruhisa; Chief Representative, Norinchukin Bank, London Representative office, since 1987. *Career:* The Norinchukin Bank, Mgr 1981-87. *Biog: b.* 12 October 1945. *m.* 1970, Michiko; 3 d. *Educ:* Tokyo University.

SHINNICK, Mathis; Vice President, Manufacturers Hanover Trust Co.

SHIPP, Arnold; OBE; Executive Director, Samuel Montagu and Co Limited, since 1975; Project Advisory/Privatisation. *Career:* UK Diplomatic Service with Postings in Brussels (European Communities) and Lima 1962-68; Executive in the Industrial Reorganisation Corporation, an Agency of the UK Government with Responsibility for Strengthening UK Industry through Mergers, Acquisitions & Restructuring 1968-70; Samuel Montagu and Co Limited, Director, Project Advisory Unit, Responsible for Advising Governments, Central Banks & other Public Sector Institutions on Financial Matters 1970-. *Biog: b.* 25 January 1938. *Nationality:* British. *m.* 1975, Gilda Ann. *Educ:* Balliol College, Oxford (BA 1st Class Honours in Philosophy, Politics and Economics); University of Pennsylvania (MA in International Relations). *Directorships:* Samuel Montagu and Co Limited 1975 (exec). *Other Activities:* Chairman, Caribbean Trade Advisory Group; Member of the Governing Body, School of Oriental and African Studies.

SHIPTON, J K; Senior Partner, J K Shipton and Company.

SHIPTON, Tim; Partner, Linklaters & Paines.

SHIPWRIGHT, Adrian John; Partner, S J Berwin & Co, since 1987. *Career:* Denton Hall Burgin and Warren, Partner 1982-87; Christ Church, Oxford, Official Student and Tutor in Law, Oxford University, Lecturer in Law 1977-82; Linklaters & Paines, Assistant Solicitor and Articled Clerk 1973-77. *Biog: b.* 2 July 1950. *Nationality:* British. *m.* 1974, Diana (née Treseder); 1 s; 1 d. *Educ:* King Edward VI School, Southampton; Christ Church, Oxford (BCL, MA). *Other Activities:* Visiting Professor, Kings College, London; Governor, King Edward VI School, Southampton. *Professional Organisations:* Solicitor Law Society. *Publications:* Strategic Tax Planning (2nd Ed), 1988; Tax Planning and UK Land Development (2nd Ed), 1990; Co-Author, Capital Gains Tax Strategies - The New Regime, 1989; Vol 5 CCH British Tax Reporter (Capital Gains), 1985; Co-Author, UK Taxation and Intellectual Property, 1989; VAT, Property and The New Rules (Forthcoming).

SHIRAO, Ryoichi; Director, Tokyo Securities Co (Europe) Ltd; Management of Sales of Japanese Equities. *Biog: b.* 7 April 1947. *Nationality:* Japanese. *m.* 1972,

Toshiko (née Kawada); 1 s; 1 d. *Educ:* Kajiki Senior High School; Kagoshima University.

SHODA, Toshio; Managing Director, The Nikko Securities Co (Europe) Ltd, since 1987; Corporate Finance. *Career:* The Nikko Securities Co Ltd (Singapore), Chief Rep 1979-84; The Nikko Securities Co Ltd Joint Gen Mgr, Intl Fin Div 1984-85; Joint Gen Mgr, Intl Underwriting Div 1985-87. *Biog: b.* 12 March 1938. *Nationality:* Japanese. *m.* 1964, Keiko (née Abe); 1 s; 1 d. *Educ:* Meiji University (BEcon). *Recreations:* Music, Skiing.

SHOEMAKER, A V; Director, Royal Insurance Holdings plc. *Career:* The First Boston Corporation, Chairman of the Board 1983-89. *Nationality:* American. *Directorships:* Royal USA Chairman; Paramount Petroleum Co Inc 1990 Chairman; United Gas Pipe Line Co 1990 Chairman. *Other Activities:* Chairman, Board of Trustees, University of Pennsylvania.

SHONE, Steven; Partner, Nabarro Nathanson, since 1988; Commercial Property. *Career:* Hunt Dickens (Nottingham), Trainee Solicitor 1980-82; Vintners (Cambridge), Assistant Solicitor 1982-84; Shoosmiths & Harrison (Milton Keynes), Assistant Solicitor 1984-86; Nabarro Nathanson, Assistant Solicitor 1986-88. *Biog: b.* 18 March 1957. *Nationality:* Welsh. *m.* 1980, Janet (née Dodd); 2 d. *Educ:* Elfed High School, Buckley, Clwyd; University of Birmingham (LLB Hons). *Professional Organisations:* Solicitor; Member of the Law Society. *Recreations:* Computers, Photography.

SHOOLBRED, C F; Secretary, Mercantile Credit Company Limited.

SHORE, Sydney Frederick; General Manager Corporate Banking, Lloyds Bank plc, since 1987. *Career:* Asst Gen Mgr 1959-87. *Biog: b.* 13 March 1933. *Nationality:* British. *m.* 1955, Joyce M L (née Englist); 1 s; 1 d. *Educ:* Wanstead County High School. *Directorships:* Lloyds Leasing Ltd & Associated Companies. *Other Activities:* FRSA. *Professional Organisations:* FCIB. *Recreations:* Music, Theatre, Sport.

SHORT, B A; Treasury Manager, Arab Bank plc.

SHORT, B D; General Manager, Scottish Widows' Fund and Life Assurance Society, since 1988; Information Technology. *Career:* Bank of Scotland Computer Services, Analyst/Project Leader 1967-71; Systems Consultants Ltd, Computer Consultant 1971-76; Peat Marwick Mitchell, Management Consultant 1977-79; Scottish Widows, Data Processing Manager 1979-88. *Biog: b.* 25 April 1944. *Nationality:* British. *m.* Kate McLauchlan (née Murray); 2 s; 1 d. *Educ:* George Heriots School; Edinburgh University (BSc Hons). *Clubs:* Caledonian Club London, Royal Burgess Golfing

Society. *Recreations:* Bridge, Golf, Curling, Shooting, Music.

SHORT, Mrs J E; Director, Charterhouse Bank Limited.

SHORT, J M; Director, Morgan Grenfell & Co Limited.

SHORTT, Michael Brian; Director, Kleinwort Benson Securities Ltd.

SHOURBAJI, Mohamed; Director, Merrill Lynch Pierce Fenner & Smith Limited.

SHRAGER, Andrew Henry; Executive Director, Lazard Brothers & Co Limited, since 1990; Corporate Finance. *Career:* Lazard Brothers 1986-; British Petroleum Co plc, Manager, Various Departments 1979-86; The Confederation of British Industry, PA to Director General 1974-79. *Biog: b.* 2 January 1945. *Nationality:* British. *m.* 1968, Susan Mary (née Hayes); 1 s; 1 d. *Educ:* Stowe School, Buckingham; University of Reading (BA Economics); The City University (MSc Business Administration).

SHREEVE, G; Editor, The Banker.

SHRIMPTON, David E; General Practice Partner, Stoy Hayward, since 1990; Medium Sized Public Companies, Member of Management Committee. *Career:* Deloitte Haskins & Sells, Investigation Mgr 1973-75; Industrial Development Unit, DOI, Principal 1975-77; Midland Bank, Corp Fin Exec 1977-79; Stoy Hayward, Snr Ptnr Corp Fin & Investigations Dept 1979-90. *Biog: b.* 19 May 1943. *Nationality:* British. *m.* 1969, Rosemary (née Fone); 3 s. *Educ:* Dulwich College. *Other Activities:* Freeman of City of London; Chairman, St Dunstan's College Society. *Professional Organisations:* FCA. *Publications:* Obtaining a Stock Exchange Quotation, 1983 (Revision 1989). *Clubs:* British Sportsmans. *Recreations:* Children, Fulham FC.

SHURMAN, Laurence Paul Lyons; Banking Ombudsman, The Office of The Banking Ombudsman, since 1989. *Career:* John H Sinton & Co (Newcastle) Articled Clerk 1954-57; Haswell Croft (Newcastle) Asst Solicitor 1955-58; Hall Brydon (London) Asst Solicitor 1958-60; Kaufman & Seigal (London) Asst Solicitor 1960-61; Shurman Bindman (London) Ptnr 1961-64; Shurman & Co (London) Ptnr 1964-67; Kingsley Napley (London) Ptnr 1967-75; Kingsley Napley (London) Ptnr 1975-89. *Biog: b.* 25 November 1930. *Nationality:* British. *m.* 1963, Mary Seamans (née McMullan); 1 d. *Educ:* Newcastle upon Tyne Royal Grammar; Magdalen College, Oxford (MA). *Other Activities:* Legal Member Mental Health Review Tribunal (1976-); President, City Westminster Law Society (1980-81); Member, Council of Justice (1973-); Gov (Vice Chm),

Channing School (1985-). *Professional Organisations:* The Law Society. *Publications:* The Practical Skills of The Solicitor, 1981, 1985-. *Clubs:* Leander. *Recreations:* Law Reform, Literature, Walking, Swimming, Jogging.

SHUTTLEWORTH, Richard James Christopher; Partner, Freshfields, since 1969. *Career:* Freshfields, Articled Clerk 1961-64; Assistant Solicitor 1964-69. *Biog: b.* 22 June 1938. *Nationality:* English. *m.* 1965, Sheila (née Attenborough). *Educ:* Christ's Hospital; St John's College, Oxford (BA). *Directorships:* Dragon School Trust Limited. *Professional Organisations:* The Law Society; City of London Solicitor's Company.

SIBLEY, Edward; Solicitor, Attorney at Law, Partner, Berwin Leighton, since 1970; Litigation Dept. *Career:* Berwin & Co, Partner 1965-70. *Biog: b.* 21 July 1935. *Nationality:* British. *m.* 1957, Sonia (née Beynon); 2 s; 1 d. *Educ:* Rhymney Grammar School, Gwent; University College of Wales (LLB Hons). *Other Activities:* Member, National Committee, Union Internationale des Avocats; Member, City of London Law Society Litigation Sub-Committee; Liveryman, City of London Solicitors Company. *Professional Organisations:* Member, New York State Bar; Member, Law Society; Member, International Bar Association; Member, American Bar Association. *Clubs:* Reform. *Recreations:* Theatre, Opera, Literature, Rugby, Running.

SIBLEY, Nicholas Theobald; TD; Director, Barclays de Zoete Wedd Holdings Ltd.

SICH, P F G W; Director, Parrish Stockbrokers.

SIDAWAY, Mrs Janet F (née Cochrane); Engineering Analyst, Kleinwort Benson Securities Limited, since 1988; Mechanical Engineering, Metals, Electricals. *Career:* TI Group, Systems Manager, Industrial Engineer, Production Controller 1970-77; National Economic Development Office, Organiser of Process Plant and Foundries Sector Working Party 1977-83; Laing and Cruickshank, Engineering Analyst 1983-85; Citicorp Scrimgeour Vickers, Engineering Analyst 1985-88. *Biog: b.* 11 December 1948. *Nationality:* British. *Educ:* Midhurst Grammar School; York University (BA English Literature); Strathclyde University (MBA). *Professional Organisations:* London Business School Graduates Association; British Institute of Management. *Recreations:* Wagner, Medieval Art.

SIDDALL, Sir Norman; Non-Executive Director, CIN Management Limited.

SIDDICK, Allan Said Ali; Partner, Bacon & Woodrow, since 1987; Employee Benefits. *Career:* Northern Assurance Company Limited, Clerk, Actuarial Student 1962-66; Abbey Life Assurance Company Limited, Assistant Manager, Actuarial Department 1966-68; Bacon & Woodrow London, Member of Professional Staff 1968-69; Bacon Woodrow & De Souza Trinidad, General Manager and Later Partner 1969-73; Bacon & Woodrow, Partner 1973-. *Biog: b.* 9 August 1944. *Nationality:* British; 1 s; 1 d. *Directorships:* Director, Chairman & Member of various companies within Bacon & Woodrow Group. *Professional Organisations:* Fellow, Institute of Actuaries; Associate, Society of Actuaries; Fellow, Pensions Management Institute. *Clubs:* Cottons, Lambs, Coolhurst. *Recreations:* Reading, Music, Swimming, Squash, Walking.

SIDDIQI, K A; Executive Vice President, Habib Bank AG Zurich, since 1988; Head of Computer Division. *Career:* State Bank of Pakistan, Karachi, Trainee Officer, Trainee 1964-65; National Bank of Pakistan, Karachi, Sub-Accountant, Officer 1965-67; National Bank of Pakistan (DP Dept) Sub/Asst Acct, Programmer 1967-71; Standard Bank Ltd (Computer Dept) Officer GR II Systems Analyst 1971-73; Habib Bank Ltd (Computer DN HO); Officer GR II Systems Analyst, 1973-75; Office GR I, Systems Manager, 1976-78; Asst Vice President, Project Manager 1979-80; Habib Bank (London), Asst Vice President, Project Manager 1980-81; Vice President, DP Manager 1982-84; Senior Vice President, DP Manager (UK & Europe) 1985-88; Habib Bank AG Zurich, London; Senior Vice President, Head, Computer Division 1988-89; Executive Vice President, Head, Computer Division 1990. *Biog: b.* 16 February 1943. *Nationality:* British. *m.* 1972, Rehana Anjum; 2 s; 1 d. *Educ:* Karachi University, Pakistan (MA Economics); Institute of Bankers in Pakistan (DAIBP); British Computer Society (MBCS). *Professional Organisations:* Diplomaed Associate, Institute of Bankers in Pakistan; Member, British Computer Society.

SIDDONS, Benjamin Charles Reid; Director, Kleinwort Benson Investment Management, since 1984; Head of Research. *Career:* Hubbard, Durose & Pain Acct 1963-68. *Biog: b.* 15 May 1945. *Nationality:* British. *m.* 1971, Elaine (née Naylor); 1 s; 1 d. *Educ:* Oundle School. *Directorships:* Kleinwort Smaller Companies Investment Trust 1986 (exec); Kleinwort Benson Investment Management 1984 (exec); Kleinwort Benson Ventures Management Ltd; First Debenture Finance plc; The Brunner Investment Trust plc (alt); The Merchants Trust plc (alt); Langbourne Financial Services Ltd; KB Berkeley Management Co Ltd; Jos Holdings plc (alt). *Professional Organisations:* FCA. *Clubs:* St George's Hill Golf Club, SWS Club GS. *Recreations:* Golf, Trout Fishing, Painting.

SIDEBOTTOM, Peter Charles Chappe; Director, Hill Samuel Bank Ltd, since 1988; Corporate Finance. *Career:* Herring Son & Daw Partner 1972; Director 1976-85; Robert Fraser Estates Director 1985-86. *Biog: b.* 1 October 1943. *Nationality:* British. *m.* 1972, Susan (née Anderson); 1 s; 1 d. *Educ:* Eton College; Trinity Hall, Cambridge (MA). *Other Activities:* Worshipful Company of Grocers. *Professional Organisations:* FRICS.

Clubs: Boodles, Whites. *Recreations:* Hunting, Polo, Skiing, Reading.

SIDWELL, Graham Robert; Partner, Robson Rhodes, since 1985; Corporate Financial Services. *Career:* Robson Rhodes 1975-. *Biog: b.* 25 October 1953. *Nationality:* British. *m.* 1975, Susan; 1 s; 1 d. *Educ:* University of Hull (BSc Econ). *Professional Organisations:* FCA. *Recreations:* Squash.

SIDWELL, John; Director, Chartfield & Co Limited.

SIGLER, P; Partner, Nabarro Nathanson.

SILCOCK, John; Non-Executive Director, NM Rothschild & Sons Limited, since 1989; Natural Resources Group. *Career:* Shell Petroleum Co Ltd, Various Positions ending up as Assistant Treasurer 1955-63; Shell Do Brazil SA, Finance Director 1963-65; N M Rothschild & Sons, Associate Partner 1968; Director 1970-. *Biog: b.* 1929. *Nationality:* British. *m.* 1958, Jennifer Joy (née Rust); 5 s. *Educ:* Bradfield College; Worcester College, Oxford (MA). *Directorships:* Silcock Associates Ltd 1989 (exec); Francarep SA 1986 (non-exec); HMC Technology 1989 (non-exec). *Other Activities:* British National Executive Committee, World Energy Council.

SILK, Mrs Anne Christine (née Arnold); Private Practice; Contact Lenses & Ocular Health. *Biog: b.* 19 December 1931. *Nationality:* British. *m.* 1957, Frederick Silk. *Educ:* Christ Hospital; University of Oxford (External Diploma of Archaelogy). *Directorships:* Dollond & Aitchison 1975-80 (non-exec); Hamblin & Wingate 1975-79 (exec). *Other Activities:* Master, Worshipful Company of Spectacle Makers; Past President, Association of Dispensing Opticians 1974-76; Member: General Optical Council, Contact Lens Committee, ABDO Contact Lens Committee, SMC Liaison Committee; Contact Lens Problem Panel, Optician 1985; LW various contributions to the Optical Press on matters of general dispensing and contact lens interest, especially prosthetic and special lenses, and non-ionising radiation; Occasional radio broadcasts on Contact Lens matters; Royal Society of Medicine. *Professional Organisations:* Hon Fellow, Association of Dispensing Opticians; Fellow, Faculty of Dispensing Opticians; Fellow, Royal Society of Arts. *Publications:* Various Scientific Papers. *Recreations:* Archaeology, Geophysics.

SILLITOE, N; Director, Framlington Unit Management Ltd, since 1990; Marketing to Institutions. *Career:* Brown Shipley Unit Trust Managers Ltd, Sales Manager 1986-87; Arbuthnot Unit Trust Managers Ltd, Sales Consultant 1983-86; Bishop Cavanagh, Consultant 1979-83; J H Minet, Reinsurance Broker 1977-79. *Biog: b.* 13 March 1961. *Nationality:* British. *Educ:* Aldenham School, Elstree. *Other Activities:* Merchant Taylors Livery Company. *Professional Organisations:* Stock Exchange

Registered Representative. *Recreations:* Clay Pidgeon Shooting, Travel.

SILVER, Henry; Secretary, Sun Alliance and London Insurance plc.

SILVERMAN, Martin Barry; Senior Partner, Morison Stoneham, since 1988; Development of International Relations, Strategic Planning. *Career:* Stoy Hayward & Co (London), Qualified as Chartered Accountant 1961-67; Backer Winter, Partner 1967-70; Acquired Mercers, Chartered Accountants, London (Merged in 1974 to Become Mercers Bryant) 1971-79; Hartley Baird plc and its Subsidiary H J Baldwin plc, Non-Executive Director, Subsequently Chairman of Baldwin 1975-79; The Marpro Group, Director of Corporate Affairs, Responsible for Finance, Group Structure and Organisation of offices in US, Latin America, Europe, Asia 1979-83; Morison Stoneham, Consultant, Specialising in Corporate Finance and Strategy 1983-; Partner 1984; Management Ctee 1985; Senior Partner 1988-; Dwyer plc Executive Finance Director 1986-. *Biog: b.* 30 May 1945. *Nationality:* British. *m.* Angela (née Silverman); 2 s; 1 d. *Educ:* Harrow County Grammar School. *Directorships:* Angelis Estates Ltd; Annstar Properties Ltd; M S Management Consultants Ltd; M S Corporate Finance Ltd; Dwyer Property Ltd; Dwyer (UK) Holdings Ltd; Dwyer plc (Ireland); Dwyer Investments Ltd; Hulburds (Sittingbourne) Ltd; Acelease Ltd; Mainscene Ltd. *Professional Organisations:* FCA. *Clubs:* RAC, Gresham. *Recreations:* Tennis, Golf, Theatre, Music.

SILVESTER, Peter; Director & General Manager, Investments, Friends' Provident Life Office.

SILVIRI, J J; Director, British & Commonwealth Merchant Bank plc.

SIMISON, Sheila; Partner, Clyde & Co.

SIMMONDS, Michael; Group Finance Director, Greig Fester Group Ltd, since 1985; Finance and Administration. *Career:* de Paula Turner Turner Lake & Co, Articled Clerk/Chartered Acct 1960-64; Price Waterhouse & Co, Chartered Acct 1964-65; British West Africa Corporation, Chief Acct 1965-68; Fergusson Wild & Co Ltd, Acct/Sec 1968-72; Greig Fester Ltd, Acct/Sec/Fin Dir 1972-. *Biog: b.* 15 May 1932. *m.* 1963, Jennifer Jill (née Williamson); 3 d. *Educ:* Shrewsbury School. *Directorships:* Toa Re-Oatley Underwriting Management Ltd 1978 (non-exec); Greig Fester (Agencies) 1979 (non-exec); Subsidiary Companies of Greig Fester Group. *Other Activities:* Liveryman, Worshipful Company of Turners of London (Member of Court). *Professional Organisations:* FCA; ATII; FBIM. *Clubs:* City of London, Naval and Military, Walton Heath Golf Club, St Enodoc Golf Club, The Berkshire Golf Club. *Recreations:* Golf.

SIMMONDS, N J; Director, Walker Crips Weddle Beck plc, since 1990; In Charge of Direct Share Dealing Service. *Career:* Walker Crips, Various. *Biog: b.* 1 August 1962. *Nationality:* British. *m.* 1986, Louise Margaret. *Educ:* The Deans Comprehensive. *Recreations:* Badminton, Squash, Tennis.

SIMMONDS, Peter Graham William; Group Managing Director, Pauls plc, since 1986; MD of Pauls plc, the Food & Agriculture Division of Harrisons & Crosfield plc. *Career:* R & W Paul Limited, Management Trainee 1962-65; Roy Benton Poultry, Commercial Manager 1965-67; R & W Paul (Maltsters) Limited, Export Sales Manager 1967-76; Pauls & Sandars Limited, Sales Director 1976-82; Managing Director 1982-86. *Biog: b.* 9 May 1940. *Nationality:* British. *m.* 1969, Jennifer Jane (née Cook); 1 d. *Educ:* Harrow; Wye College, University of London (BSc Agric). *Directorships:* Harrisons & Crosfield plc 1987 (exec); The Grain Terminal (Ipswich) Limited 1983 (exec); The St Elizabeth Hospice Limited 1989 (non-exec). *Other Activities:* Institute of Brewing Council & Executive Committees; Chairman of Appeal Committee, St Elizabeth Hospice Appeal, Ipswich. *Professional Organisations:* Fellow, Institute of Brewing. *Recreations:* Shooting, Fishing.

SIMMONDS, R A G; Director, County NatWest Securities Limited.

SIMMONS, Mrs Petrea Alyson (née Lacey); Partner, Lane Clark & Peacock, since 1990; Pensions. *Career:* Clerical Medical & General Life Assurance Society, Rating & Valuing Life Business 1976-79 (During University Vacations); Actuarial Assistant, Valuations & Design of Pension Schemes 1979-84; Bacon & Woodrow, Partner, Advising Corporate Clients on Pensions Matters 1984-90; Lane Clark & Peacock, Partner 1990-. *Biog: b.* 16 November 1957. *Nationality:* British. *m.* 1976, Peter Frank Simmons; 1 s. *Educ:* Beaverwood Girls School; Rochester Grammar School; City University (BSc Actuarial Science). *Professional Organisations:* Fellow, Institute of Actuaries. *Recreations:* Swimming, Walking, Music.

SIMMONS, Richard John; Partner, Arthur Andersen & Co, since 1979; Head of Industrial and Commercial Group. *Biog: b.* 2 June 1947. *Nationality:* British. *m.* 1983, Veronica (née Sinkins); 1 s; 1 d. *Educ:* Moseley Grammar School, Birmingham; LSE (BSc Econ); University of California, Berkeley. *Directorships:* Cranfield Information Technology Institute Ltd 1985-90 (non-exec). *Other Activities:* Royal Academy of Arts Advisory Board; Carlton Club Political Ctee; Chm of Bow Group, 1980-81. *Professional Organisations:* FCA. *Clubs:* Carlton. *Recreations:* Tennis, Horse Racing, Gardening.

SIMON, D A G; Deputy Chairman & Chief Operating Officer, British Petroleum Company plc.

SIMON, Gary I; Partner, Touche Ross & Co.

SIMON, J J; Partner, Pensions (Epsom), Bacon & Woodrow.

SIMON, Peter Walter; *Career:* Legal & General Group plc 1955-87; Legal & General Group plc, Director and General Manager Investment 1973-87. *Biog: b.* 25 November 1929. *Nationality:* British. *m.* 1960, Sheila (née Brimacombe); 1 s; 1 d. *Educ:* Thames Valley Grammar; London School of Economics (BSc Econ, PhD Econ). *Directorships:* British Land 1987 (non-exec); Conrad Rifflet Residential Properties 1989 (non-exec) Chm. *Professional Organisations:* ACII. *Clubs:* East India, Teddington Hockey & Cricket, MCC.

SIMON, Richard F J; Partner, Lawrence Graham, since 1974; Corporate & Commercial. *Biog: b.* October 1947. *Educ:* Gresham's School; Trinity Hall, Cambridge (MA Hons). *Professional Organisations:* Law Society; City of London Solicitors Company. *Recreations:* Choral Singing.

SIMON-BARBOUX, Bernard; Executive Vice-President, Banque Indosuez, since 1984. *Career:* Groupe Drouot (French Insurance Group) 1963; Financial Director 1973; General Manager of the Commercial, Financial and Foreign Departments 1977; General Manager for all the Departments 1979; Immofice, Chairman 1973-83. *Biog: b.* 15 July 1938. *Nationality:* Française. *m.* 1961, Marie-Thérèse (née Renard); 2 s; 2 d. *Educ:* Ingénieur EcoleCentrale De Paris. *Directorships:* Cheuvreux, De Virieu (Paris) Member of the Board; Cie D'Investissement Astorg (Paris) Member of the Board; Etablissement Poron (Troyes) Member of the Board; Financiere Strafor (Strasbourg) Member of the Board; Union Financiere De France (Paris) Member of the Board; Indosuez Gartmore Gestion Member of the Board; Banque De Suez Nederland NV (Amsterdam) Member of the Board; Indosuez Asia Ltd (Hong Kong) Member of the Board; Indosuez Italia Holding SpA Milan Member of the Board; Gartmore Investment Management Ltd London Member of the Board; France Growth Fund Member of the Board; Indosuez Investment Management Services (California) Member of the Board; Carr Indosuez Securities (Paris) Chm; Finanziaria Indosuez SpA (Milan) Chm; Gartmore Indosuez Asset Management Chm; Indosuez Asia Investment Services (Hong Kong) Chm; APAC Holdings Chm.

SIMONDS, Gavin Napier; Director, Kleinwort Benson, since 1989; Corporate Finance. *Career:* Peat Marwick 1975-81; Rowe & Pitman Exec, Corp Finance 1982-85; UBS/Phillips & Drew Dir, Corp Finance 1985-88. *Biog: b.* 1 January 1955. *Nationality:* British. *m.* 1980, Venetia (née Steele); 1 s; 3 d. *Educ:* Eton College. *Professional Organisations:* ACA; ATII. *Recreations:* Family, Tennis, Sailing.

SIMONELLI, Dr Leonardo; Managing Director, Etrufin Reserco Ltd, since 1985; UK Representative and Consultant to 9 Italian Savings Banks. *Career:* Instituto Mobiliare Italiano 1969-85; UK Rep 1977-79; Chm of London Subsidiary 1979-82; Head of Foreign Fin Dept 1983-84; Head of Foreign Div 1984-85. *Biog: b.* 12 June 1939. *Nationality:* Italian. *m.* 1968, Joan Carole (née Wehrlin); 1 s; 2 d. *Educ:* Florence University (Hons 1st); Illinois University (MSc Physics). *Directorships:* Intl Fin Products Sales Co Ltd (Cayman Islands) 1980-82; Interfund (Luxembourg) 1980-85; Industrial Multinational Investments Ltd (Jersey) 1981-84; FONDITALIA Mgmnt Co 1983-85; Italian Chamber of Commerce Dep Chm; Palazzuolo SpA; Belladonna Srl. *Other Activities:* Assoc of Intl Savings Banks, London (Chm 1988-); Italian Chamber of Commerce, London (Dep Chm). *Professional Organisations:* Italian Assoc of Chemists; Foreign Banks Assoc; AISBL, FIMBRA. *Publications:* Various Articles on Solid State Physics; Surface Chemistry; Economic Aspects of Industrial Research; Various Articles on International Banking; Various Financial Articles for Il Corricre Della Sera. *Clubs:* Rotary, Overseas Bankers', Hurlingham, Queen's, Club di Londra. *Recreations:* Tennis, Shooting, Fishing.

SIMPER, S V; Administrative Director, Walker Crips Weddle Beck plc.

SIMPSON, C C; Partner, Simmons & Simmons.

SIMPSON, Geoffrey J; Partner, Moores Rowland.

SIMPSON, James Robert; Finance Director, Sedgwick Lloyd's Underwriting Agents Ltd, since 1988; Finance & Systems. *Career:* Price Waterhouse 1977-83; Chandos Insurance (Bass plc subsidiary) 1983-86; Sedgwick Lloyd's Underwriting Agents Ltd 1986-. *Biog: b.* 6 July 1955. *Nationality:* British. *m.* 1980, Julia (née Hornor); 1 s; 1 d. *Educ:* Radley College; Mansfield College, Oxford (BA). *Professional Organisations:* ACA.

SIMPSON, John; Partner, Linklaters & Paines.

SIMPSON, Keith C F; Assistant General Manager, Yorkshire Bank plc; Retail Banking. *Professional Organisations:* Fellow, Chartered Institute of Bankers.

SIMPSON, Neil; Financial Journalist, Daily Mirror.

SIMPSON, Peter F; Partner, S J Berwin & Co Ltd, since 1983; Corporate Finance. *Career:* Stephenson Harwood Articles 1971-73; Asst Solicitor 1973-77; Ptnr 1977-83. *Biog: b.* 23 June 1948. *Nationality:* British. *m.* 1978, Helen (née Anisfeld); 1 s. *Educ:* Royal Grammar School, High Wycombe; Oriel College, Oxford (MA). *Other Activities:* Various Israeli Charities Ctees. *Professional Organisations:* The Law Society. *Recreations:* Opera, Music, Theatre.

SIMPSON, R N; Partner, Kidsons Impey.

SIMPSON, Rachel; City Reporter, Daily Express, since 1989. *Career:* Marketing Magazine 1985-88; Freelance 1988-89; Daily Express, City Reporter 1989-.

SIMPSON, Roger T; Vice President, Chemical Bank.

SIMPSON, T C F; Director, Bunzl Plc.

SIMS, Christopher; Deputy City Editor, The Glasgow Herald (London Office).

SIMS, M H; Director, Stewart Ivory & Company Limited.

SIMSON, Peregrine Anthony Litton; Partner, Clifford Chance, since 1972; Litigation. *Career:* Limmer & Trinidad Asphalt Co Ltd, Assistant Sec 1966-67; Clifford Turner, Articled Clerk/Assistant Solicitor 1967-72; Partner 1972-87; Clifford Chance, Partner 1987-. *Biog: b.* 10 April 1944. *Nationality:* British. *m.* 1967 (divorced 1979) Caroline Basina (née Hosier); 1 s; 1 d. *Educ:* Charterhouse School; Worcester College, Oxford (BA Hons Jurisprudence). *Professional Organisations:* Law Society; Honorable Solicitor's Company; Former Member, Inner Temple, Inns of Court; Admitted as Solicitor, 1970. *Clubs:* Hurlingham. *Recreations:* Shooting, Tennis, Cricket.

SINCLAIR, Charles J F; Director, Schroders plc.

SINCLAIR, David Bruce; Director, National Investment Group plc, since 1988; London Trading, Southern Administration. *Career:* Grieveson Grant & Co County Bank, Assistant Director 1967-86; NatWest Stockbrokers, Director 1986-87; Smith New Court 1987-88; National Investment Group, Director 1988-. *Biog: b.* 20 May 1946. *Nationality:* British. *m.* 1973, Gail (nee Fitzherbert); 1 s; 2 d. *Educ:* Gordonstoun. *Professional Organisations:* Member, ISE. *Clubs:* RYS, RLYC. *Recreations:* Sailing, Tennis, Skiing, Family.

SINCLAIR, Ian G; Managing Director (Underwriting), Continental Reinsurance London.

SINCLAIR, Jeremy; Deputy Chairman & Director, Saatchi & Saatchi Company. *Biog: b.* 4 November 1946. *m.* 1976, Jacqueline (née Metcalfe); 2 s; 1 d.

SINCLAIR, John Ian; General Manager, Royal Bank of Scotland.

SINCLAIR, Kenneth Brian; Chairman, Barclays de Zoete Wedd Fixed Income, since 1986; Government Securities. *Career:* Eagle Star Insurance, Clerical Officer, Gilt Edged Portfolio 1947-54; National Coal Board, Clerical Officer Inv Dept 1954; David A Bevan Simpson, Clerk 1954-60; Ptnr 1960-70; de Zoete &

Bevan, Ptnr 1970-86; Exec Ptnr 1974-86. *Biog: b.* 14 March 1931. *Nationality:* British. *m.* 1957, Yvonne Joan (née Tucker); 1 s. *Educ:* Heath Clark School, Croydon. *Directorships:* BZW Securities Ltd 1986 (exec) Dep Chm; BZW Gilts Ltd 1986 Chm; BZW Ltd 1986 (exec) Dep Chm; BZW Holdings Ltd 1986 (exec); BZW Capital Markets 1986 (exec); BZW Futures Trading 1986 (exec); Latonia Investment Co Ltd 1986; BZW Money Market Services Ltd 1986; The International Stock Exchange 1988; Barclays Bank 1988. *Professional Organisations:* The International Stock Exchange. *Clubs:* City of London, Gresham. *Recreations:* Bridge, Chess, Historical Biographies, Football.

SINCLAIR, M J; Partner, Raphael Zorn Hemsley Ltd.

SINCLAIR, Neil; Partner, Berwin Leighton, since 1971; Corporate Finance, Taxation, Property Unitisation. *Career:* Nabbaro Nathanson, Asst Solicitor and Ptnr 1963-66; Berwin & Co, Asst Solicitor and Ptnr 1966-70. *Biog: b.* 17 September 1937. *m.* 1964, Susan (née Frazer); 3 s. *Educ:* King George V, Southport; Caius College, Cambridge (BA Hons 1st). *Professional Organisations:* The Law Society. *Publications:* Warranties and Indemnities on Share Sales, 1984; Practical Commercial Precedents (Editorial Board and Contributor), 1986. *Recreations:* Mathematics, Cycling.

SINCLAIR, Roderick John; Chairman, Thamesway Investment Services Ltd, since 1987; Soft Commission. *Career:* Scots Guards, 2 Lt 1963-66; L Messel Inst Salesman 1969-77; de Zoete & Bevan, Ptnr 1977-86; Barclays de Zoete Wedd Securities Ltd, Director 1986-; Consultant 1989. *Biog: b.* 10 July 1944. *Nationality:* British. *m.* 1977, Sarah Margaret (née Dolphin); 1 s; 1 d. *Educ:* Gordonstoun School. *Directorships:* Broker Services BZW Securities Ltd 1986-88 Chairman; Thamesway Investment Services 1987 (exec) Chm; BZW Securities 1984. *Professional Organisations:* International Stock Exchange. *Clubs:* Boodle's, British Ski Club. *Recreations:* Tennis, Sailing, Skiing.

SINCLAIR, T J; Director, Barclays de Zoete Wedd Securities Ltd.

SINCLAIR, Walter Isaac; Partner, Kidsons Impey, since 1976; Taxation. *Career:* Bernard Phillips & Co, Articled Clerk 1953-59; Fuller Jenks Beecroft, Qualified Senior 1960-66; Blick Rothenberg, Tax Specialist 1967-76; Kidsons Impey, Tax Partner 1976-90. *Biog: b.* 29 May 1934. *Nationality:* British. *m.* 1964, Margaret (née Halle); 1 s; 2 d. *Educ:* Hendon County Grammar School. *Professional Organisations:* FCA. *Publications:* Author, The Allied Dunbar Law Guide (originally the Hambro Law Guide)(19th Ed), 1972-; Co-Author, The Allied Dunbar Capital Laws and Estate Planning Guide (5th Ed), -1990; Co-Author, The Allied Dunbar Business Law and Law Guide (2nd Ed), -1989. *Recreations:* Tennis, Bridge, Classical Music, Theatre.

SINDZINGRE, M J; Executive Vice-President, Imetal, since 1987; International Holding. *Career:* School of Mines of Paris, Professor 1966-72; Societe Le-Nickel, Research Director 1972-75; Minemet Recherche, Chairman 1977-87; Imetal, Research & Industrial Manager 1975-87; Executive Vice-President 1987-. *Biog: b.* 6 May 1937. *Nationality:* French. *m.* 1960, Claudette (née Robert); 3 s. *Educ:* Grammar School Carnot Dijon, ENSM Paris; Polytechnique School, Paris (Mining Engineer). *Directorships:* Mircal 1985 Chairman (exec); Damrec 1985 Chairman (exec); Cookson Group 1982 Director (non-exec); Copperweld Steel Co 1987 Director (non-exec); Francarep 1979 Director (non-exec). *Recreations:* Skiing, Theatre, Music.

SINGER, A E; Director, Henry Ansbacher Holdings plc.

SINGER, J B; Director (Corporate Finance), Granville & Co Limited.

SINGER, Keith; Head of Projects, Citymax Integrated Information Systems Ltd, since 1990. *Career:* Software Sciences Ltd, Analyst, Programmer 1980-82; Buckmaster & Moore, Consultant 1982-86; Citymax Integrated Information Systems Ltd, Director 1984 -. *Biog: b.* 25 August 1958. *Nationality:* British. *m.* 1986, Susan (née Lewis). *Educ:* Dulwich College; Merton College, Oxford (MA Hons, Physics). *Directorships:* Citymax 1984 (exec). *Recreations:* Theatre, Walking, Travelling.

SINGER, R N; Chairman, Jardine Insurance Brokers Ltd, since 1989; General Management. *Career:* Tozer Kemsley & Millbourne (South Africa), Trainee 1956-61; Credit Guarantee Insurance Corporation of South Africa, Branch Manager 1961-64; Willis Faber Dumas & Roward (South Africa), Director 1964-71; The Hedbank Group (South Africa), Corporate Planner, Chairman Insurance Br 1971-77; Leslie & Godwin Holdings Ltd, Chairman 1977-83; ARRCS Investments, Joint Chairman 1983-87; Jardine Insurance Brokers Ltd 1987-. *Biog: b.* 12 August 1934. *Nationality:* British. *m.* 1987, Juliet (née Whitehead); 1 s; 2 d. *Educ:* Glasgow Academy; Uppingham; University of Cape Town (PhD). *Directorships:* Crusader Life Assurance (South Africa) 1986 Director (non-exec); Pegasus Life (Bristol) 1990 Director (non-exec); Cellcom Ltd 1987-89 (exec); Frank B Hall Inc (New York) 1978-84 (exec). *Other Activities:* Member, Insurers Livery Co. *Professional Organisations:* FCIS. *Clubs:* Royal & Ancient Golf Club of St Andrews, RAC, Sunningdale, Hurlingham. *Recreations:* Golf.

SINGER, Ms Wendy M; Partner, Gibson Dunn & Crutcher, since 1987. *Career:* Cleary Gottlieb Steen & Hamilton, Associate 1974-83; Gibson Dunn & Crutcher, Associate 1984-86. *Biog: b.* 5 February 1950. *Nationality:* American. *m.* 1980, J P Legrand; 1 s; 1 d.

Educ: Harvard (BA, JD). *Professional Organisations:* Member, NY Bar; Conseil Juridique, France. *Clubs:* Reform.

SINGLETON-GREEN, Brian; Editor, Accountancy, since 1990. *Career:* Harmood Banner/Deloitte & Co, Trainee Chartered Accountant 1973-76; H M Treasury, Accountant 1977-78; Binder Hamlyn, Audit Supervisor 1979-80; Institute of Chartered Accountants in England and Wales, Various Positions in the Technical Directorate 1980-89; Secretary, Accounting Standards Ctee 1984. *Biog: b.* 26 April 1951. *Nationality:* British. 1986, Barbara Ann (née Dyer) 1 d stepd. *Educ:* Eltham College; Clare College, Cambridge (MA). *Professional Organisations:* FCA.

SIRS, Bill; Council Member, Office of the Banking Ombudsman. *Career:* Hartlepool and Knutsford, Justice of the Peace 1963; Iron & Steel Trades Confederation, General Secretary 1975-85; Trades Union Congress, General Council 1975-85; European Coal & Steel Consultative Committee, Member 1975-85; Employment Appeal Tribunal, Member 1976-90; Winston Churchill Memorial Trust, Council Member 1985-90; Northern Home Counties Productivity Association, President 1985-; International Metalworkers Fed, Iron & Steel Non-Ferrous Metals Section, President 1975-85; Hertfordshire Groundwork Trust, Director 1985-; School Governor 1988-; Hertfordshire Colleges, Governor 1990. *Biog: b.* 6 January 1920. *Nationality:* British. *m.* 1941, Joan (née Clark); 1 s; 1 d. *Educ:* Middleton St Johns School. *Other Activities:* Freeman, City of London. *Professional Organisations:* City & Guilds Steelmaking. *Publications:* Hard Labour, 1985. *Recreations:* Golf, Squash, Running, Weight Training.

SISSON, J D; Senior Manager-Resources, Allied Trust Bank Limited.

SISSON, P C; Director, County NatWest Securities Limited.

SISSONS, Michael John; Assistant General Manager, Guardian Royal Exchange plc, since 1985; Personnel. *Career:* Atlas Assurance Co Ltd (Nairobi) Asst 1960-64; Royal Exchange Assurance Group (Manchester) Inspector 1965-67; (Bristol) Branch Mgr 1967-69; Guardian Royal Exchange (Exeter) Branch Mgr 1969-72; (Bristol) Branch Mgr 1972-76; (Glasgow) Branch Mgr 1976-80; (Nottingham) Area Mgr 1980-84; Snr Personnel Mgr 1984-85. *Biog: b.* 6 June 1933. *Nationality:* British. *m.* 1962, Patricia Ann (née Portch); 2 s; 2 d. *Educ:* Taunton School. *Professional Organisations:* Chartered Insurance Institute; Institute of Personnel Management. *Recreations:* Keeping Track of my Family.

SISSONS, T B; Director, Panmure Gordon & Co Limited.

SISTO, Vittorio; General Manager, Banco di Roma, since 1987; Great Britain & Scandinavian Countries. *Career:* Banco di Roma, Italy 1965-74; Sub Mgr (London) 1974-76; Dep Gen Mgr (London) 1976-79; Gen Mgr (Hong Kong) 1979-83; Pres & Chief Officer (Chicago) 1984-86; Foreign Banks & Securities Houses Assoc, Vice Chairman; Italian Chamber of Commerce for Great Britian, Vice Chairman. *Biog: b.* 7 August 1939. *m.* 1963, Laura (née Papa); 1 s; 1 d. *Educ:* Naples University. *Other Activities:* Decorations: Commendatore of the Italian Republic (Merit of Honour conferred by the President of the Republic of Italy); Counsellor, Italian Chamber of Commerce for GB. *Clubs:* Club di Londra.

SITARAM, A K; Financial Adviser, The New India Assurance Company Limited.

SITTAMPALAM, A; Managing Director (Investment Management), Sanwa International Ltd.

SIVA-JOTHY, Mrs C S T; Agency Director, Gravett & Tilling (Underwriting Agencies) Ltd.

SIVELL, George; City News Editor, The Times.

SIVYER, Jeremy Duncan; Partner, Simmons & Simmons, since 1984; International & Commercial Law. *Career:* Simmons & Simmons, Articled Clerk 1977-79; Assistant Solicitor 1979-83; Partner 1984-. *Biog: b.* 13 May 1955. *Nationality:* British. *m.* 1983, Lisa (née Matthews); 1 s. *Educ:* The Royal Liberty School, Romford; University of Sheffield (LLB). *Professional Organisations:* Law Society. *Recreations:* Cricket, Gardening.

SJÖWALL, Björn Mikael Axel; Director, Kleinwort Benson Securities Ltd, since 1983; Scandinavian Equities. *Educ:* Stockholm School of Economics (Civilekonom); New York University Graduate Business School (APC).

SKAE, John Michael; Director and General Manager (Group Resources), Legal & General Group plc.

SKAE, John Robin; Group Company Secretary, Midland Bank plc, since 1985; Secretary's Office and Head Office Administration. *Career:* Bamfords Ltd, Dir & Sec 1963-75; Dowty Group plc, Group Sec 1975-85. *Biog: b.* 11 July 1936. *Nationality:* British. *m.* 1961, Cynthia (née Forrest); 1 s; 2 d. *Educ:* Oundle School. *Other Activities:* Justice of the Peace. *Professional Organisations:* FCA. *Clubs:* RAC Pall Mall London. *Recreations:* Sport, Gardening, Outdoor Pursuits.

SKAILES, J A D; Director, Gerrard Vivian Gray Limited.

SKELTON, John Martin; Partner, Macfarlanes, since 1987; Banking/Corporate. *Career:* Withers Ptnr 1980-87. *Biog: b.* 22 May 1952. *m.* 1982, Clare Louise (née Le Gassick); 1 s; 1 d. *Educ:* Westminster School; Brasenose College, Oxford (BA). *Professional Organisations:* The Law Society.

SKEY, C H A; Director, Sturge Holdings plc.

SKINGLEY, G M L; Director, United Dominions Trust Limited.

SKINNER, Andrew Urquhart; Executive Director, James Capel Corporate Finance Limited; UK Corporate Finance. *Career:* Antony Gibbs & Sons Limited Asst Dir 1977-83; Wardley London Limited Dir 1983-85; Hongkong Bank Limited Head of Corporate Finance 1985-86. *Biog: b.* 18 June 1952. *Nationality:* British. *m.* 1984, Jane Elizabeth (née Wood). *Educ:* Woodbridge School; Fitzwilliam College, Cambridge (MA LLM). *Other Activities:* Hon Treasurer, St Mark's Research Foundation. *Professional Organisations:* Barrister (Lincolns Inn).

SKINNER, David Lennox; Managing Director, Martin Currie Ltd.

SKINNER, G; General Manager, Bayerische Vereinsbank AG, since 1988; Treasury, Operation, Administration. *Career:* Midland Bank Group, Manager, Treasury 1964-74; EBC Amro Bank, Executive Director, Treasury 1974-87. *Biog: b.* 9 November 1947. *Nationality:* British. *m.* 1972, Jennifer (née Pettitt); 2 d. *Educ:* Preston Manor County Grammar. *Professional Organisations:* Institute of Bankers; Association of International Bond Dealers. *Recreations:* Family, DIY, Sailing.

SKINNER, I R; Partner, R Watson & Sons Consulting Actuaries.

SKINNER, Jeremy John Banks; Partner, Linklaters & Paines, since 1967; Corporate Law & Taxation. *Biog: b.* 15 November 1936. *Nationality:* British. *m.* 1963, Judith (née Austin); 1 s; 2 d. *Educ:* Rugby School; Clare College, Cambridge (BA). *Directorships:* Institute for Fiscal Studies 1969 (non-exec). *Other Activities:* Senior Warden, Worshipful Co of Cordwainers; Governor, Rugby School. *Professional Organisations:* Law Society. *Clubs:* Brooks's. *Recreations:* Hunting.

SKINNER, Kevin John; Partner, Bacon & Woodrow, since 1988; Pensions Consultancy. *Career:* Bacon & Woodrow 1980-. *Biog: b.* 29 December 1957. *Nationality:* British. *Educ:* Dr Challoner's Grammar School, Amersham, Bucks; St Catherine's College, Oxford (MA). *Professional Organisations:* FIA.

SKIPPER, B J; Executive Director, Booker plc.

SKOYLES, Dr Kathryn J; Partner, Titmuss Sainer & Webb, since 1990; Investigations. *Career:* Monash University, Tutor in Law 1984-85; Titmuss Sainer & Webb, Articled Clerk 1986-88; Solicitor 1988-90; Partner 1990-. *Biog: b.* 16 July 1958. *Nationality:* British. *Educ:* The King's School, Ely; London School of Economics (LLB Hons); University of London (LLM); Monash University, Victoria, Australia (PhD). *Professional Organisations:* Member, Society of Genealogists; Member, Norfolk & Norwich Genealogical Society; Member, The Law Society; Member, International Bar Association; Member, Society of English and American Lawyers; Member, Society for Computers and Law. *Publications:* The Fiduciary Basis of Insider Trading Liability-Dirks Down Under?, 1984; The Right of Target Companies' Directors to Use Corporate Funds in Defence of Take-Over, (with Y Danziger), 1984; The Pitfalls of Being a Director, 1990. *Recreations:* Genealogy, Reading Detective Novels, Travel.

SKRABB, H; Director, FennoScandia Bank Limited.

SLACK, M R; Partner, Lane Clark & Peacock, since 1976. *Biog: b.* 29 June 1949. *Educ:* The Leys School, Cambridge; Churchill College, Cambridge. *Other Activities:* Liveryman, Company of Actuaries. *Professional Organisations:* FIA.

SLADE, L; Deputy Ombudsman, Insurance Ombudsman Bureau, since 1988; Share with Ombudsman Responsibility for Decisions in Reference to Bureau. *Career:* Chartered Institute of Arbitrators, Legal Adviser 1982-88. *Biog: b.* 12 February 1944. *Nationality:* Kenyan. *Educ:* Magdalen College, Oxford (MA); Lincoln's Inn (Barrister). *Professional Organisations:* Associate, Chartered Institute of Arbitrators. *Recreations:* Painting, Theatre.

SLADEN, A M; Managing Director, Wendover Underwriting Agency Limited.

SLAGEL, Paul; Corporate Finance Manager, National Westminster Bank, since 1989; Corporate Finance. *Career:* Peat Marwick Mitchell, Audit Supervising Senior 1977-83; Robson Rhodes, Special Services Section, Manager Venture Capital, Assistance to Clients 1983-85; Kibun Co (UK) Ltd, Financial Controller, Financial Strategy, Financial Reporting, Monitoring and Control 1985-89; National Westminster Bank, Corp Finance Manager, Corp Investigations, Venture Capital Appraisal & Deal Completions 1989-. *Biog: b.* 1 June 1956. *Nationality:* British. *Educ:* Merchant Taylors School; Liverpool University (BCom 2:i). *Professional Organisations:* ACA; Associate, Institute of Linguists. *Recreations:* Reading, The Arts, Tennis, Squash, Meteorology, Travel.

SLATER, Anton Geoffrey; Partner, Clifford Chance, since 1967; Shipping and International Trade. *Biog: b.* 31 January 1936. *m.* 1964, Ann (née Morgan); 4 s. *Educ:*

Chesterfield Grammar School; Balliol College, Oxford (BA, BCL). *Professional Organisations:* The Law Society.

SLATER, Gerald Antony; Director, The Burton Group plc, since 1980. *Biog: b.* 19 May 1934. *Nationality:* British. *Directorships:* The British Life Office Limited 1990; Lingfords Limited; The Reliance Fire & Accident Insurance Corporation Limited 1990; Reliance Mutual Insurance Society Limited 1990; Reliance Pension Scheme Trustees Limited 1990; Reliance Unit Managers Limited 1990; Trireme Enterprises Limited.

SLATER, Graham Robert; Senior Dealer, Rudolf Wolff & Co Ltd, since 1983; London Metal Exchange Dealings, Options, Foreign Exchange. *Biog: b.* 19 October 1946. *Nationality:* British. *m.* 1969, Carol Ann (née Woodage); 2 d. *Recreations:* National Film Theatre, Organic Vegetable Growing.

SLATER, Richard; Partner, Slaughter and May, since 1979; Company & Commercial Law. *Career:* Slaughter and May 1970-; (Hong Kong) 1981-86. *Biog: b.* 18 August 1948. *m.* 1975, Julie (née Ward); 2 s; 1 d. *Educ:* University College School; Pembroke College, Cambridge (MA). *Professional Organisations:* The Law Society.

SLATER, Richard Ewart Hollis; Partner, Simmons & Simmons, since 1980; Corporate Finance and Financial Services. *Career:* Simmons & Simmons, Articled Clerk 1975-77; Asst Solicitor 1977-80. *Biog: b.* 9 November 1950. *Nationality:* British. *m.* 1985, Jane (née Liversedge); 2 s; 1 d. *Educ:* Cheltenham College; City University, London (BSc); Cambridge University (BA). *Directorships:* Huntingdon International (Holdings) plc 1983 (non-exec). *Recreations:* Family, Opera.

SLATTER, C B; Director, Leslie & Godwin Limited.

SLAUGHTER, Tony; Chief Executive & Director, St James Public Relations.

SLAVIN, J R; Partner, Milne Ross.

SLEE, William Robert; Group Managing Director, Credit & Capital Market Division, Schroders plc, since 1984; Banking, Capital Markets, Project Finance. *Career:* Citibank, VP & European Petroleum Co-ordinator 1963-73; European Banking Co Ltd, MD & Chief Operating Officer 1973-84. *Biog: b.* 13 January 1941. *m.* 1981, Heidi (née Burklin); 2 s. *Educ:* Holy Cross College, Massachusetts (BSc). *Directorships:* J Henry Schroder Wagg & Co Ltd 1984 (exec). *Clubs:* Royal Ocean Racing Club, Royal Lymington Yacht Club. *Recreations:* Sailing, Tennis.

SLEEMAN, John Keith; Executive Director, Samuel Montagu & Co Limited, since 1989; Project Advisory. *Career:* Touche Ross & Co, Articled Clerk/ Assistant Manager 1970-75. *Biog: b.* 24 July 1949. *Nationality:*

British. *m.* 1975, Gail Erica (née Blair); 2 s; 1 d. *Educ:* University of Durham (BSc Hons in Physics). *Directorships:* Samuel Montagu & Co Limited 1989 (exec). *Other Activities:* Liveryman, Worshipful Company of Wax Chandlers. *Professional Organisations:* Fellow, Institute of Chartered Accountants in England and Wales; Associate, Chartered Institute of Bankers. *Recreations:* Piano, Reading.

SLEIGH, Charles Frederick; Partner, Grant Thornton, since 1955; General Practice. *Biog: b.* 21 October 1929. *m.* 1957, Gillian Anne Clark (née Cormack); 1 s; 2 d. *Educ:* The Edinburgh Academy. *Directorships:* Investors Capital Trust plc 1964 (non-exec); Scottish Equitable Life Assurance Soc 1970 (non-exec); Baillie Gifford Technology plc 1984 (non-exec). *Other Activities:* Chm, ASC Working Party which Produced SORPI on 'Pension Scheme Accounts'; Mem, ASC Working Party which Produced ED39 'Accounting for Pension Costs'. *Professional Organisations:* CA. *Clubs:* New Club (Edinburgh). *Recreations:* Fishing, Shooting.

SLIWERSKI, Trevor Zygmunt; Director, Baring Securities Ltd, since 1985; Japanese Equity Warrants/ Convertible Bonds. *Career:* Savory Milln Dealer 1968-71; R Layton Dealer 1971-74; Nomura Dealer 1978-80; Robert Fleming Dir 1980-85. *Biog: b.* 30 December 1950. *Nationality:* British. *m.* 1981, Lynn (née Francis); 1 s; 1 d. *Educ:* John Fisher School, Purley. *Clubs:* Stock Exchange Athletics Club, Surrey Walking Club.

SLOAN, Derek Scott; Partner, Allen & Overy, since 1977; Head of Pensions Department. *Biog: b.* 25 June 1948. *Nationality:* British. *m.* 1980, Sarah Elizabeth (née Rash); 2 s. *Educ:* Cranleigh School; New College, Oxford (BA). *Other Activities:* City of London Solicitors' Company. *Professional Organisations:* Solicitor. *Recreations:* Horse Racing, Cards.

SLOAN, Robert B; Regional Sales Director, Private Client (Central Europe), Merrill Lynch Europe, since 1986; Executive Director, Private Banking Group (Central Europe), Merrill Lynch International Bank, since 1986; Marketing, Sales, Banking. *Career:* Continental Bank, Banking Officer, Wholesale Corporate Banking-International Banking 1979-82; Security Pacific Bank, Assistant Vice President, Wholesale Corporate Banking-Energy 1982-84; Canadian Imperial Bank of Commerce, Team Leader, Vice Pres, Wholesale Corporate Banking, Fortune 500/Energy 1984-86; Merrill Lynch International Bank, Regional Business Head Private Banking Group (Central Europe) 1986-; Merrill Lynch Europe, Regional Sales Director, Private Client (Central Europe) 1990-. *Biog: b.* 1948. *Nationality:* American. *m.* 1990, Rebecca. *Educ:* Southern Illinois University (BSc Econ, MBA Hons Accounting/Finance). *Directorships:* Merrill Lynch International Bank 1989 (non-exec); 1990 (exec). *Professional Organisations:* Series 7 Registered. *Clubs:* Mosimann's. *Recreations:* Tennis, Skiing, Golf.

SLOANE, J; Partner in Charge of Management Consultancy, Robson Rhodes, since 1990; Management Consultancy, Information Technology. *Career:* Arthur Andersen, Consultant 1977-82; Chicago Bridge & Iron, Financial Systems Manager 1982-85; Robson Rhodes, Consultant 1985-87; Partner 1987-. *Biog: b.* 25 May 1954. *Nationality:* British. *Educ:* Bedford School; University of Manchester, Institute of Science & Technology (BSc Management Science). *Recreations:* Walking, Skiing.

SLOPER, Ted; Partner, Clark Whitehill.

SLY, C; Partner, Jaques & Lewis.

SMAILL, P M; Director, County NatWest Ventures Ltd, since 1989; Venture Capital. *Career:* 3i plc, Investment Controller 1978-84; County Bank, Manager 1984-86; Gresham Trust plc, Senior Investment Executive 1986-87; County NatWest Ventures, Director 1987-. *Biog: b.* 21 August 1954. *Nationality:* British. *m.* 1988, Anna (née Whitworth); 1 d. *Educ:* High School of Stirling; Univerisity of Edinburgh (LLB Hons, DBA). *Directorships:* Wren Investments Limited 1987 (exec); Crestacre Holdings plc 1987 (non-exec). *Professional Organisations:* Certified Diploma in Accounting & Finance. *Publications:* Various Articles in Accountancy Age, Taxation, Investors Chronicle. *Clubs:* Reform.

SMALE, T A; Partner, Waltons & Morse.

SMALL, David Nigel Geoffrey; Managing Director, Woolwich (Europe) Ltd, since 1990; Development of Markets within the EEC. *Career:* London Borough of Bromley Articled Clerk 1965-69; Private Practice Asst Solicitor 1969-71; Woolwich Building Society Asst Solicitor 1971-74; Joint Solicitor 1974-81; Asst Gen Mgr, Planning 1981-83; Gen Mgr, Planning 1983-86; Gen Mgr, Housing 1986-87; Gen Mgr, Housing & Legal Services 1987-89; Gen Mgr, Lending 1989-90. *Biog: b.* 13 May 1943. *Nationality:* British. *m.* 1968, Diana (née Narbeth); 1 s; 1 d. *Educ:* St Dunstan's College, Catford; Leeds University (LLB Hons). *Directorships:* Woolwich Homes Ltd 1983; Electronic Funds Transfer Ltd 1985 (non-exec); Hyde Housing Association 1986 (non-exec); Woolwich Homes (1987) Ltd 1987; Building Societies Ombudsman Co Ltd 1987 (non-exec); Hyde Charitable Trust 1986 (non-exec); Hyde Community Services 1986 (non-exec); Hyde Housing Developments Ltd 1986 (non-exec); Leegate Housing Society Ltd 1986 (non-exec); North West Kent Housing Association Ltd 1986 (non-exec); Woolwich Assured Homes Ltd 1989; The Federation of Community Urban Specialists 1989 (non-exec); Lewisham Phoenix Development Corporation Ltd 1989 (non-exec); Woolwich (Europe) Ltd 1990. *Other Activities:*

Commerce and Industry Group of The Law Society; Member, Hyde Housing Association Management Committee. *Professional Organisations:* The Law Society. *Clubs:* Wildernesse. *Recreations:* Golf, Bridge, Skiing, Tennis.

SMALL, Michael John; Director, Fenchurch Insurance Holdings.

SMALLWOOD, Matthew; Associate Director, College Hill Associates Limited.

SMART, Adrian Michael Harwood; Partner, Slaughter and May, since 1969; Company and Commercial Law. *Biog: b.* 20 November 1935. *Nationality:* British. *m.* 1963, Sara (née Morrish); 1 s; 1 d. *Educ:* Eastbourne College. *Professional Organisations:* The Law Society; IBA. *Clubs:* Oriental, Hong Kong Club. *Recreations:* Gardening.

SMART, F J; Partner, Field Fisher Waterhouse.

SMART, Peter Charles; Partner, Walker Morris Scott Turnbull.

SMEDLEY, Charles William Oliver; Director, James Capel & Co, since 1988; Continental Europe. *Career:* Kleinwort Benson Ltd Dealer 1970; Royal Trust Co of Canada Investment Mgr 1974; Galloway and Pearson Analyst/Salesman 1975; James Capel & Co Salesman 1979; Partner 1981; James Capel Inc (New York) Pres 1984-86; James Capel International Dir 1986. *Biog: b.* 18 April 1951. *Nationality:* British. *m.* 1978, Victoria Jane (née Angell); 2 s. *Educ:* Monkton Combe, Bath. *Directorships:* Brown Baldwin Nisker James Capel Inc (Toronto) 1988 (non-exec); DLP James Capel (Paris) 1988 (exec); Van Meer James Capel (Amsterdam) 1988 (exec). *Professional Organisations:* AIB. *Recreations:* Fine Art, Theatre, Music, Shooting.

SMELLIE, K G; Compliance Director, Albert E Sharp & Co.

SMERTNIK, G; Director, Crédit Commercial de France (UK) Limited.

SMETHURST, M S; Director, Hambros Bank Limited.

SMETHURST, Richard Good; Director, Investment Management Regulatory Organisation, 1987. *Career:* St Edmund Hall, Oxford Research Fellow 1964-65; Fellow & Tutor in Economics 1965-66; Worcester College, Oxford Fellow & Tutor in Economics 1967-76; Professorial Fellow 1976-86; University of Oxford, Dept for External Studies Dir 1976-86; Monopolies and Mergers Commission, Commissioner, 1978-86; Deputy Chairman 1986-89; University of Oxford, General Board of Faculties, Chairman 1989-91. *Biog: b.* 17 January 1941.

m. 1964, Dorothy Joan (née Mitchenall); 2 s; 2 d. *Educ:* Liverpool College; Worcester College, Oxford (BA); Nuffield College, Oxford (MA). *Directorships:* Investment Management Regulatory Organisation Ltd 1987; Templeton College (Oxford Centre for Mgmnt Studies Ltd) 1974. *Other Activities:* Open University (Member, Academic Consultative Ctee); Trustee, European Community Baroque Orchestra; Music at Oxford (Advisory Board); Life Governor, Liverpool College. *Publications:* Impact of Food Aid (Co-author), 1965; New Thinking About Welfare, 1969; Economic System in the UK (Co-Author), 1977, 1979; Continuing Education in Universities & Polytechnics (Co-Author), 1982; Contributions to Journal of Development Economics, Oxford Review of Education. *Recreations:* Good Food.

SMIDDY, Francis Paul; Director, Kleinwort Benson Securities Ltd, since 1988. *Career:* Price Waterhouse, Mgr 1975-82; J Sainsbury plc, Fin Analyst 1982-84; Capel-Cure Myers, Research Analyst 1984-85; County NatWest Woodmac, Associate Dir 1985-88. *Biog: b.* 13 November 1953. *Nationality:* British. *m.* 1978, Katy (née Watson); 2 s. *Educ:* Winchester College; Manchester University (BA Econ Hons). *Professional Organisations:* FCA. *Publications:* Several Articles on Accounting & Retail Matters in the Professional Press. *Recreations:* Flying, Motor Sport, Squash, Theatre, Running.

SMIDS, A; Chairman, English Trust Company Limited.

SMILLIE, W H; Director, Head of Settlement Services and Financial Futures Clearing, Hill Samuel Bank Ltd, since 1989; Settlement Services and Financial Futures. *Career:* Thomson McLintock & Co (London), Chartered Accountants, Manager 1963-72; Aiken & Carter, Chartered Accountants, Manager 1972-79; Hill Samuel (South Africa) Ltd, Divisional Head/Director 1979-89; Hill Samuel Bank Ltd, London, Director/Head of Settlement Services and Financial Futures Clearing 1989-. *Biog: b.* 19 February 1938. *Nationality:* British. *m.* 1968, Geraldine (née Arnott); 2 s; 2 d. *Educ:* Buckhaven High School, Fife. *Directorships:* Hill Samuel (South Africa) Ltd 1985 (exec); Hill Samuel Bank Ltd 1989 (exec). *Professional Organisations:* Institute of Chartered Accountants of Scotland (CA); The South African Institute of Chartered Accountants (CA (SA)). *Clubs:* Johannesburg Country Club. *Recreations:* Tennis, Golf, Squash.

SMIT, W J; Director, J H Rayner (Mincing Lane).

SMITH, Colonel A C; Chief Executive, Unit Trust Association, since 1980. *Career:* British Army, Logistics Planning Appointments in the Ministry of Defence and NATO 1946-78; Campaign Against Building Industry Nationalisation (CABIN), Director 1978-79; UTA, Chief Executive 1980. *Biog: b.* 3 January 1928. *Nationality:* British. *m.* 1981, Shirley; 2 s; 2 d. *Educ:* Scunthorpe Grammar School; Army Staff College Camberley (Graduate); United States Army Staff College (Graduate). *Directorships:* UTA (Services) Ltd 1988 (exec). *Other Activities:* Member, Institute of Directors. *Recreations:* Travel, Gardening, Photography.

SMITH, A G; Managing Director, Finance & Admin, Ropner Insurance Services Limited.

SMITH, A J C; Director, C T Bowring & Co Limited.

SMITH, A J C; Vice President, The Faculty of Actuaries.

SMITH, A L; Director, CCF Foster Braithwaite Ltd.

SMITH, Alan; Secretary, Smiths Industries plc, since 1986; Secretary's Office, Legal & Patents Departments. *Career:* Procter & Gamble Ltd, Brand Assistant 1961-62; Penningtons (Solicitors), Articled Clerk 1963-66; Smiths Industries plc, Assistant Solicitor 1966-69; Solicitor & Head of Legal Department 1969-77; Solicitor & Deputy Secretary 1977-86; Secretary & Solicitor 1986-. *Biog: b.* 15 May 1938. *Nationality:* British. *Educ:* Pembroke College, Oxford (MA). *Professional Organisations:* Law Society.

SMITH, Alan Frederick; Compliance Director, Brown Shipley Stockbroking Ltd; Compliance, Finance, Administration. *Career:* Heseltine Powell & Co, Succeeded by Brown Shipley Stockbroking Ltd 1952-. *Biog: b.* 9 October 1936. *Nationality:* British. *m.* 1968, Pauline Wendy (née Spragg); 1 s; 4 d. *Educ:* Upton House. *Directorships:* Brown Shipley Stockbroking Holdings Ltd 1987-89 (non-exec); Brown Shipley Stockbroking (CI) Ltd 1988 (exec); International Stock Exchange of UK & Eire 1988 (non-exec); The Securities Association 1988 (non-exec); Wilshere Baldwin & Co 1986-89 (non-exec); Brown Shipley PEP Managers Ltd 1987 (exec); Brown Shipley Stockbroking Ltd 1986 (exec). *Other Activities:* Member, The Guild of the Freeman of the City of London; Member, City Livery Club; Board Member of TSA. *Professional Organisations:* Member, The International Stock Exchange. *Clubs:* Berkshire & Attenian Club, RSPB, RNLI, Wildfowl Trust, National Trust. *Recreations:* Theatre, Music, Nature, Bird Watching, Steam Railway's, Sport.

SMITH, Anthony Simon; Managing Director, White Foster Sheldon Daly & Co Ltd.

SMITH, B; Executive Director, Banque Paribas London.

SMITH, Brian Philip; Manager, A Bell & Son (Paddington) Ltd, since 1984; Control of Decorating Division. *Career:* W J Brooker Ltd, Estimator Surveyor 1958-61; J Cole (Painting) Ltd, Estimator Surveyor 1961-62; Ernie Bayliss, Estimator Surveyor/Director

1962-83. *Biog: b.* 21 September 1937. *Nationality:* British. *m.* 1960, Jeanette Margaret (née Lampard); 1 s; 2 d. *Educ:* Hassenbrook School. *Other Activities:* Worshipful Company of Joiners & Ceilers (Upper Warden). *Clubs:* City Livery Club. *Recreations:* Golf, Fishing.

SMITH, C; Director, The Frizzell Group Limited.

SMITH, C S; Manager, Corporate Affairs, Ultramar plc.

SMITH, Dr (Charles Edward) Gordon; CB; Deputy Chairman, Wellcome Trust, since 1983. *Career:* HM Colonial Service Malaysia, Virologist 1948-57; London School of Hygiene & Tropical Medicine, Senior Lecturer, Reader 1957-64; Microbiological Research Establishment MOD, Director 1964-70; London School of Hygiene & Tropical Medicine, Dean 1970-89; Public Health Laboratory Service Board Chairman 1972-89. *Biog: b.* 12 May 1924. *Nationality:* British. *m.* 1948, Elsie (née McClellan); 1 s; 2 d. *Educ:* Forfar Academy; St Andrews University (Mh, ChB, MD, DSc Honorary). *Other Activities:* Liveryman, The Goldsmith's Company 1974-; Assistant 1981; Warden 1988; Prime Warden 1991-92. *Professional Organisations:* FRCP; FRCPath. *Publications:* Some 200 Scientific Papers. *Clubs:* Savile, Bramshaw Golf, New Zealand Golf. *Recreations:* Golf, Gardening.

SMITH, Christopher Gordon; Director, Noble Grossart Limited, since 1989; Treasury. *Career:* C R McRitchie & Co Ltd, Dir 1977-84; Nobel Grossart Ltd 1985-; Asst Dir 1988-89. *Biog: b.* 3 September 1952. *Nationality:* British. *m.* 1980, Jean Helen (née Inglis); 1 s; 1 d. *Educ:* The Abbey School, Fort Augustus. *Directorships:* Norloch Ltd 1977-84 (non-exec). *Clubs:* Edinburgh Sports Club. *Recreations:* Squash, Running.

SMITH, Christopher Michael Peter; Associate Director, Beeson Gregory Ltd, since 1989; Institutional Sales. *Career:* Capel-Cure Myers 1985-89. *Biog: b.* 11 March 1962. *Nationality:* British. *m.* Nicole (née Livingstone-Smith). *Educ:* Rugby School; Leeds University.

SMITH, Christopher Raphael; Partner, Slaughter and May, since 1987; Company/Commercial. *Career:* Slaughter and May, Articled Clerk 1978-80; Asst Solicitor 1980-87. *Biog: b.* 29 May 1956. *m.* 1985, Carolyn Mary (née Povey); 1 s. *Educ:* Finchley High School; Bristol University (LLB Hons). *Other Activities:* City of London Solicitors' Company. *Professional Organisations:* The Law Society. *Recreations:* Theatre, Reading, Rugby Union.

SMITH, Colin Ferguson; Director, Smith Keen Cutler, since 1986; Investment Management (Private Clients). *Career:* Tangyes Ltd, Production Controller 1960-62; Chief Buyer 1962-64; Company Secretary & Ac-

counts Manager 1964-67; Central Wagon Co Ltd, Assistant Company Secretary 1967-69; Smith Keen Barnett, Research Partner 1971-86. *Biog: b.* 12 October 1932. *Nationality:* British. *Educ:* Leighton Park School; Gonville & Caius College, Cambridge (MA, LLB). *Directorships:* Smith Keen Cutler 1986 (exec). *Professional Organisations:* FCIS. *Clubs:* Carlton.

SMITH, David Alexander; Partner, Shepherd & Wedderburn, since 1974; Commercial Property. *Biog: b.* 17 November 1947. *Nationality:* British. *m.* 1979, Anne (née Hamilton-Douglas); 1 s; 1 d. *Educ:* Fettes College; Edinburgh University (LLB). *Other Activities:* Member, Society of Writers to Her Majesty's Signet. *Professional Organisations:* The Law Society of Scotland. *Clubs:* The Honourable Company of Edinburgh Golfers (Muirfield), The Bruntsfield Links Golfing Society. *Recreations:* Hockey, Golf, Walking.

SMITH, David D; Chief Executive, The Gateway Corporation Ltd.

SMITH, David Henry; Economics Editor, Sunday Times Business News, since 1989; Economics, Statistics, Energy. *Career:* Lloyds Bank, Economic Report Writer 1976-77; Henley Centre for Forecasting, Economist 1977-79; Now! Magazine, Journalist 1979-81; Financial Weekly, Economics & Assistant Editor 1981-84; The Times, Economics Correspondent 1984-89; The Sunday Times, Economics Editor 1989-. *Biog: b.* 3 April 1954. *Nationality:* Welsh. *m.* 1980, Jane (née Howells); 2 s; 1 d. *Educ:* University College, Cardiff (BSc Econ); Birkbeck College, University of London (MSc Econ). *Publications:* The Rise and Fall of Monetarism, 1987; Mrs Thatcher's Economics, 1988; North and South, 1989. *Clubs:* St James. *Recreations:* Squash, Tennis.

SMITH, David M; Director, Robert Fleming & Co Ltd, since 1987; Foreign Exchange & Money Markets. *Biog: b.* 20 March 1950. *Nationality:* British. *m.* Lynn; 2 d. *Recreations:* Golf.

SMITH, David Michael Walker; Partner, Richards Butler, since 1989; Asset Financing/Banking. *Career:* Richards Butler, Articled Clerk 1982-84; Solicitor 1984-89. *Biog: b.* 13 May 1960. *Nationality:* British. *m.* 1987, Catherine (née Wright). *Educ:* Queen Elizabeth Grammar School, Wakefield; Brasenose College, Oxford (BA Hons 2nd Class, MA); College of Law, Chester (Law Society Final Examinations, 2nd Class Hons). *Professional Organisations:* Law Society; Baltic Exchange. *Recreations:* Walking, Reading, Driving.

SMITH, Edward Richard; Director, Hill Samuel Bank Ltd, since 1974; Senior Credit Director. *Career:* Martins Bank Ltd 1954-68. *Biog: b.* 19 March 1936. *Nationality:* British. *m.* 1960, Pamela Margaret (née Mundy); 2 s. *Educ:* Highgate School. *Directorships:* Control Securities plc (non-exec); European Equity Corporation Ltd (non-exec); Gross Hill Properties Ltd (non-exec); Sydney and London Properties Ltd (non-exec). *Other Activities:* Member, Worshipful Company of Pattenmakers. *Professional Organisations:* FCIB. *Clubs:* Royal Automobile, MCC, East India. *Recreations:* Gardening, Antiquarian, Second-Hand Books.

SMITH, Ms Eleanor; Finance Director, Williams de Broe plc, since 1990; Finance, Operations, IT. *Career:* Peat Marwick McLintock, Articled Clerk, Latterly Audit Senior 1973-78; Hill Samuel & Co Ltd, Internal Auditor 1978-79; Lazard Brothers & Co Ltd, Leasing Executive 1979-81; Lloyds Bank plc, Manager, International Leasing, Merchant Banking Division 1982-84; Manager, Financial Control and Planning, International Banking Division 1984-89. *Biog: b.* 16 May 1951. *Nationality:* British. *Educ:* Queen Elizabeth School, Crediton; St Anne's College, Oxford (MA Hons, Mathematics); University of Heidelburg, West Germany (German Language Course). *Professional Organisations:* FCA. *Clubs:* Oxford & Cambridge, Little Ship. *Recreations:* Shooting, Fishing, Tennis, Travel.

SMITH, Geoffrey; Deputy Chairman, Bradstock Financial Services Ltd.

SMITH, George Ronald; MBE; Director Operations and Deputy Chief Executive, IMRO, since 1990; (Director, Compliance, IMRO, 1987-90); Regulation of Investment Business. *Career:* Wallace & Sommerville (Edinburgh), CA Apprenticeship 1956-65; Ptnr 1965-69; Whinney Murray & Co (Edinburgh), Ptnr 1969-71; Ernst & Whinney Continental Firm (Hamburg), Ptnr 1971-74; Ptnr in Charge 1974-76; (The Netherlands), Managing Ptnr 1976-84; Dep Chm & Snr Ptnr 1984-85; Chm & Snr Ptnr 1985-86. *Biog: b.* 14 July 1939. *m.* 1966, Frances Margaret; 1 s; 1 d. *Educ:* George Watson's College, Edinburgh; University of Edinburgh (MA,LLB). *Professional Organisations:* CA; ICA. *Publications:* De Vierde Richtlijn (Contributor), 1978. *Recreations:* Gardening, Angling, Occasional Golf, Reading.

SMITH, Mrs Gillian Sara (née Oppenheim); Partner, S J Berwin & Co, since 1985; Banking. *Career:* Linklaters & Paines, Articles 1977-79; Assistant 1979-81; Nordic Bank plc 1981-83; S J Berwin & Co 1983-. *Biog: b.* 1953. *Nationality:* British. *m.* 1987, Lindsay M; 1 s. *Educ:* St George's School for Girls, Edinburgh; Newnham College, Cambridge (MA Hons). *Professional Organisations:* Law Society; Solicitor. *Recreations:* Being with my Family.

SMITH, Graham Frederick; Partner, Ernst & Young, since 1975. *Career:* Barton Mayhew & Co/Turquands Barton Mayhew & Co/Ernst & Whinney, Qualified 1964; Mgr 1969-75. *Biog: b.* 17 February 1943. *Nationality:* British. *m.* 1966, Wendy Elizabeth (née Maltby); 1 s; 2 d. *Educ:* Royal Grammar School, High Wy-

combe. *Professional Organisations:* FCA. *Clubs:* Oriental. *Recreations:* Golf, Garden, Music.

SMITH, Graham Paul; Partner, Clifford Chance, since 1987; Commercial Law. *Career:* Clifford-Turner, Ptnr 1981-87. *Biog: b.* 25 December 1949. *Nationality:* British. *Educ:* Royal Grammar School, High Wycombe; University of Durham (BA); Osgoode Hall Law School, Toronto (LLM). *Other Activities:* Member, Editorial Board, Computer Law Strategist. *Professional Organisations:* The Law Society; Computer Law Association; City of London Solicitors Company. *Publications:* Contributor to Doing Business in the United Kingdom; Contributor to Encyclopaedia of Information Technology Law; Contributor to Computer Law (ed by C Reed). *Clubs:* MCC. *Recreations:* Opera, Cricket.

SMITH, Graham Richard Elliott; Partner, Wilde Sapte, since 1987; Solicitor Company & Commercial. *Career:* Wilde Sapte Articled Clerk 1980-82; Solicitor 1982-. *Biog: b.* 24 February 1958. *Nationality:* British. *m.* 1987, Sharon (née Mulroney); 1 d. *Educ:* Royal Grammar School Guildford; Nottingham University (BA Hons). *Other Activities:* Freeman of the Worshipful Company of Solicitors of The City of London. *Professional Organisations:* The Law Society; IBA. *Recreations:* Theatre, Travel, Skiing.

SMITH, Ian; Director, Livingstone Fisher plc, since 1989; Corporate Finance. *Career:* Grant Thornton 1979-82; International Thomson Organisation (Head office), Group Accountant 1982-4; Thomson Publishing, Assistant to Finance Director 1984-85; Thomson Consumer Magazines, Finance Director 1985-88; Livingstone Fisher plc, Executive 1988-89. *Biog: b.* 10 March 1959. *Nationality:* British. *m.* 1987, Shona Ann (née Nicoll). *Educ:* Allen Glen's School, Glasgow; University of Strathclyde (BA). *Professional Organisations:* Institute of Chartered Accountants of Scotland. *Recreations:* Athletics, Badminton, Tennis.

SMITH, J A; Director, Barclays de Zoete Wedd Securities Ltd.

SMITH, J C; Director, Morgan, Grenfell & Co Ltd.

SMITH, J D M; Executive Director, BTR plc, since 1988; Europe. *Career:* Distillers Co Ltd, Various Marketing Positions 1960-68; BTR Silvertown Ltd, Business Manager 1969-72; Managing Director 1972-76; BTR Industries Ltd, Various Chief Executive Appointments 1976-87. *Biog: b.* 24 September 1939. *Nationality:* British. *m.* Sherry (née Burges); 2 s. *Educ:* Midsomer Norton Grammar School; University College, London (BSc Hons Chemistry). *Directorships:* BTR plc 1988 (exec); British Rubber Manufacturers' Association 1989 (non-exec).

SMITH, J T; Director, Laurence Keen Limited.

SMITH, Jill A K; Investment Director, Henderson Administration Group plc.

SMITH, Sir John L E; CBE; Director, Coutts & Co.

SMITH, John Patrick; Managing Director, Equity & Law Investment Managers Limited, since 1989; Investment Management. *Career:* Equity & Law 1956-; Dir 1983-. *Biog: b.* 25 August 1932. *m.* 1961, Ann Felicity (née Hawker); 2 s; 1 d. *Educ:* St Edward's School, Oxford; Brasenose College, Oxford (MA). *Directorships:* Equity & Law Life Assurance Society plc 1984; Equity & Law (Estate Management) Ltd 1978; Equity & Law (Managed Funds) Ltd 1976; Equity & Law Home Loans Ltd 1988; Equity & Law Home Loans (No 2) Ltd 1989; Equity & Law Home Loans (No 3) Ltd 1989; Equity & Law Unit Trust Managers Ltd 1972; Equity & Law Commercial Loans Ltd 1990; Grandvista Properties Ltd 1984; Watling Street Properties Ltd 1985 (non-exec); Newmarket Venture Capital plc 1972 (non-exec); Kings (Estate Agents) Limited 1988 (non-exec); Tern plc 1989 (non-exec); The Golf Fund plc 1989 (non-exec); Equity & Law Investment Managers Limited 1989; Venture Lighting International Inc 1988 (non-exec). *Professional Organisations:* FIA. *Clubs:* Dale Hill Golf Club. *Recreations:* Golf, Gardening.

SMITH, K S; Managing Director, Mocatta & Goldsmid Ltd.

SMITH, Keith Ramsay; TD; Group Managing Director, Parrish plc, since 1990. *Career:* Boyes & Gaskarth, Ptnr Private Clients 1968-71; Earnshaw Haes & Sons, Ptnr, Private Clients/Corp Finance 1971-74; Sternberg Thomas Clarke & Co, Ptnr, Private Clients/Corp Finance 1974-86; Finance Ptnr 1980-86; Snr Ptnr 1986; Dir, Private Clients/Corp Finance 1986-87; Parrish Stockbrokers, Chief Executive 1987. *Biog: b.* 1938. *Nationality:* British. *m.* 1987, Rosalind Judith. *Educ:* St Paul's School. *Directorships:* Parrish Stockbrokers 1987 (exec); Tamaris plc 1988 (non-exec); Lifecare International plc 1988 (non-exec) Chm; Aims International Medical Services Ltd 1982 (non-exec)Chm; Charterhouse Mercantile Securities Ltd 1985 (non-exec); Parrish plc 1988 (exec); Viencode Ltd 1990 (non-exec). *Professional Organisations:* Fellow, BIM; AMSIA. *Clubs:* City of London.

SMITH, Leslie J; Dealing Director, Brewin Dolphin & Co Ltd. *Career:* Birch & Co Stockbrokers, Office Boy 1943-45; Sidney Cooper & Son Stockbrokers, Clerk 1945-48; National Service, RHA 1948-50; Francis Havalowndes Stockbrokers (now part of Brewin Dolphin & Co Ltd), Clerk to Director 1950-. *Biog: b.* 19 October 1929. *Nationality:* British. *m.* 1958, June Margaret (née Dupouy); 2 d. *Educ:* Erkenwald. *Directorships:* Brewin Dolphin & Co Ltd 1980 (exec). *Recreations:* Golf, Swimming, Badminton.

SMITH, M; Associate, Grimley J R Eve.

SMITH, M J; Director, Philipp & Lion Ltd.

SMITH, Mark; Director, Lowe Bell Financial Ltd.

SMITH, Mark Aynsley; Executive Director, S G Warburg & Co Ltd, since 1971; Corporate Finance. *Career:* Peat Marwick Mitchell & Co CA 1958-66; S G Warburg & Co Ltd, Corp Finance Exec 1966-71. *Biog: b.* 24 May 1939. *Nationality:* British. *m.* 1964, Carol Ann (née Jones); 1 s; 1 d. *Educ:* Kings College School, Wimbledon. *Professional Organisations:* FCA. *Recreations:* Collecting, Exercise.

SMITH, Michael D C; Managing Director, Citicorp Venture Capital Ltd.

SMITH, Michael Gordon; Senior Partner Head of Lloyd's Office, Titmuss Sainer & Webb, since 1990; Lloyd's and Non-Lloyd's Insurance and Reinsurance. *Career:* Titmuss Sainer & Webb 1963-. *Biog: b.* 30 May 1945. *Nationality:* British. *m.* 1969, Wendy (née Major); 1 s; 1 d. *Educ:* Cheltenham College; Sorbonne University, Paris. *Directorships:* Lloyd-Roberts & Gilkes Ltd (Lloyds Underwriting Agency). *Other Activities:* The Law Society. *Recreations:* Music, Opera, Skiing.

SMITH, Michael Thomas Ramsay; Head of Industrial Finance Division, Bank of England, since 1987; Relations between Industry and Finance. *Career:* Bank of England Various 1963-. *Biog: b.* 1 May 1940. *Nationality:* British. *m.* 1968, Susan (née Cruikshank); 2 s. *Educ:* George Watson's College, Edinburgh; Hamilton College, Clinton, New York State; Edinburgh University (MA Hons). *Professional Organisations:* Chartered Institute of Bankers. *Recreations:* Music, Sport (Tennis & Golf), Walking.

SMITH, Nicholas Andrew; Head of Personnel, Norwich Union Insurance Group, since 1989; To Ensure Staff Worldwide are Appropriate in Quality and Number and we are well motivated and Properly Utilized. *Career:* Commission on Industrial Relations 1973-74; Esso Petroleum, Employment and Public Relations Manager 1977-86; Prudential Corporation, Group Personnel Operations Manager 1986-89; Norwich Union Insurance Group, Head of Personnel 1989-. *Biog: b.* 5 October 1950. *Nationality:* British. *m.* 1979, Julie Mary; 2 s. *Educ:* Hall Mead Secondary Modern School; East Berks College of Further Education; University of East Anglia (BA Hons). *Professional Organisations:* Devonshire House Personnel Executives.

SMITH, P; Director, Allied Dunbar Assurance plc.

SMITH, P E; Director, Morgan Grenfell & Co Limited.

SMITH, The Hon P R; Director, W H Smith Group plc.

SMITH, Paul Edward Hill; Partner, Stoy Hayward, since 1984; Corporate Finance. *Biog: b.* 7 August 1951. *Nationality:* British. *m.* 1975, Lynn; 1 s; 1 d. *Educ:* Hampton School; University College of Wales, Aberystwyth (BSc Econ Hons). *Professional Organisations:* FCA. *Recreations:* Playing Rugby, Cricket, Golf, Watching Sport, Reading.

SMITH, Peter Nicholas; Partner, McKenna & Co, since 1987; Corporate Finance and Financial Services. *Career:* Bischoff & Co, Solicitor 1978-84; McKenna & Co, Asst Solicitor 1984-87. *Biog: b.* 10 November 1954. *m.* 1986, Isabelle (née Martin). *Educ:* King Alfred's School, Wantage; Bristol University (LLB). *Professional Organisations:* The Law Society; City of London Solicitors Company.

SMITH, Peter Webster; Partner, Wragge & Co, since 1983; Corporate Law and Tax. *Nationality:* British. *Educ:* West Bromwich Grammar School; Jesus College, Oxford (MA). *Professional Organisations:* Law Society.

SMITH, Philip Henry; Group Treasurer, ASDA Group plc, since 1986; Funding & Investment Management. *Career:* Leicestershire County Council, Accountancy/Audit Asst 1964-69; Lusaka City Council (Zambia), Snr Acct 1969-72; Dairy Produce Board (Zambia), Area Acct 1972-74; Dorada Holdings plc, Div Fin Dir 1974-81; Brooke Tool Holdings plc, Div Fin Dir 1981-83; ASDA Group plc Controller, Grp Fin Services 1983-86. *Biog: b.* 24 November 1946. *Nationality:* British. *m.* 1968, Sonia Idena (née Moody); 2 s; 1 d. *Educ:* Loughborough College Grammar School; Leicester Regional College of Technology; Nottingham Polytechnic. *Directorships:* ASDA Finance Ltd 1989 (exec); McLagan Investments (Jersey) 1989 (exec); ASDA International Finance BV 1989 (exec). *Other Activities:* Member, Programme Committee, Association of Corporate Treasurers. *Professional Organisations:* MBIM; CIPFA (Associate Member); CIMA (Fellow Member); ACT (Member). *Recreations:* Sport, Wine, Gardening.

SMITH, R B; Partner, Cazenove & Co, since 1977. *Educ:* St Edward's School, Oxford; St Peter's College, Oxford (BA). *Directorships:* Lowland Investment Co plc (non-exec).

SMITH, R B; Managing Director, LMX, Denis M Clayton & Co Limited.

SMITH, R F; Director, Lazard Investors Ltd.

SMITH, R G; Chairman, Taylor Woodrow Construction Ltd, since 1989. *Career:* Taylor Woodrow, Various Positions 1953-. *Biog: b.* 4 June 1929. *Nationality:* British. *m.* 1958, Molly; 1 s; 1 d. *Educ:* Birmingham College of Technology. *Directorships:* Taylor Woodrow plc 1985 (Director); Taylor Woodrow Construction Ltd 1989 (Chairman); Taylor Woodrow Construction Northern Ltd 1986 (Chairman). *Other Activities:* Council Member, Building Employers Confederation (London Region); Council Member, Confederation of British Industry (London Region); Liveryman, Worshipful Company of Joiners and Ceilers. *Professional Organisations:* Chartered Institute of Building (FCIOB). *Recreations:* Offshore sailing.

SMITH, R G F; Secretary, Redland plc.

SMITH, Ramon Allan; Senior Manager, Commerzbank.

SMITH, Robert Haldane; Director, Morgan Grenfell & Co Limited; Chief Executive, Morgan Grenfell Development Capital Limited. *Career:* Charterhouse Development Capital Limited, Director; Charterhouse Bank Limited, Executive Director 1985-89; Royal Bank of Scotland plc, General Manager, Corporate Finance Division; National Commercial & Glyns Limited, Managing Director 1983-85; ICFC (now 3i) 1968-82; Area Manager, Brighton 1973; Business Development Manager 1978; Asst General Manager 1981; Robb Ferguson & Co, Glasgow, Articles 1963-68. *Biog: b.* 8 August 1944. *Nationality:* m.; 2 d. *Educ:* Allan Glen's School, Glasgow; Glasgow University. *Directorships:* include TIP Europe plc; MFI Furniture Group Ltd. *Other Activities:* Member, Board of Trustees, National Museums of Scotland; Commissioner, Museums and Galleries Commission. *Publications:* Managing your Company's Finances (Co-author). *Recreations:* Amateur Dramatics, Public Speaking, Spectator Sports, Historic and Listed Buildings, Music.

SMITH, Robert John; Partner, Lawrence Graham, since 1980; Pensions Law. *Biog: b.* 17 January 1953. *Nationality:* British. *m.* 1978, Michele; 1 s. *Educ:* Bablake School, Coventry; Oriel College, Oxford (BA). *Professional Organisations:* Law Society; APMI. *Publications:* Contributor to: Organization and Management of a Solicitor's Practice, 1980.

SMITH, Robert William; Vice President and International Controller, The Riggs National Bank of Washington, DC, since 1989; Accounting, Taxation, Systems, Management; Acquisitions and Strategic Planning in Europe. *Career:* Riggs Bank 1980-; VP Finance (Washington) 1986-89; Branch Accountant 1980-86; Arthur Andersen (formerly Tansley Witt) 1987-80; Wheawill & Sudworth CA 1974-77. *Biog: b.* 27 September 1951. *Nationality:* British. *m.* 1978, Geraldine (née Taylor); 2 s. *Educ:* Chislehurst & Sidcup GS; Pembroke College, Oxford (MA). *Professional Organisations:* FCA. *Recreations:* Philately, Music, Cricket.

SMITH, Professor Roland; Chairman, British Aerospace plc.

SMITH, Ronald; Deputy Chief Executive, Investment Management Regulatory Organisation Ltd.

SMITH, Stephen; Chief Executive, Addison Consultancy Group plc.

SMITH, Thomas Alfred Guy; Vice President & General Manager, NBD Bank NA (formerly National Bank of Detroit), since 1984; General Management. *Career:* Toy, Campbell & Co, Articled Clerk, Qualified Asst 1950-57; Pannell Crewdson & Hardy, Qualified Asst 1957-60; Davies Investments Ltd, Chief Acct 1960-67; E R Nicholson FCA, Qualified Asst 1967-68; National Bank of Detroit, Chief Acct, Overseas Office 1968-76; The Gulf Bank KSC (Kuwait), Fin Controller 1976-82; National Bank of Detroit, Dep Gen Mgr 1982-84. *Biog: b.* 5 November 1933. Nationality: British. *m.* 1959, Stella (née Kedge). *Educ:* Christ's Hospital. *Other Activities:* The Woolnoth Society Charitable Trust (Treasurer). *Professional Organisations:* FCA. *Clubs:* Overseas Bankers'. *Recreations:* Gardening, Cricket, Music.

SMITH, Thomas Anthony; General Manager Finance, Yorkshire Building Society, since 1984; All Aspects of Finance. *Career:* Walker Fullerton Hartley & Co, Articled Clerk 1956-60; Price Waterhouse, Snr Audit Clerk 1961-64; Allied Breweries, Various, Chief Acct Britvic Ltd 1965-72; United Drapery Stores Alexanders Tailors Ltd 1972-74; Bradford Permanent Building Soc, Chief Acct 1974-75; Huddersfield & Bradford Building Soc,Chief Acct 1975-80; Yorkshire Building Soc, Asst Gen Mgr, Fin 1980-83. *Biog: b.* 19 October 1938. *Nationality:* British. *m.* 1964, Christine Mary (née Whitaker); 1 s; 1 d. *Educ:* Aireborough Grammar School. *Directorships:* Funds Transfer Sharing Ltd 1986 (non-exec); Yorkshire Building Society 1988 (exec); Yorkshire Building Society Estate Agents Limited 1988 (non-exec); Link Interchange Network Ltd 1989 (non-exec); Y B S Properties Ltd 1990 (non-exec). *Professional Organisations:* FCA. *Clubs:* Horsforth Golf Club, Woodhall Hills Golf Club. *Recreations:* Golf.

SMITH, W J; Director, Brandeis Limited.

SMITH, William Blades Berwick; Managing Director, Leslie & Godwin Aviation Holdings Ltd, since 1989; Aviation, Aerospace and Satellite Insurance. *Career:* Sedgwick Aviation Ltd, Director 1973-86. *Biog: b.* 10 November 1956. *Nationality:* British. *m.* 1983, Katherine Ann (née Wright); 1 d. *Educ:* Whitgift School. *Directorships:* Leslie & Godwin Ltd 1990 (exec); Leslie & Godwin AXL Ltd 1990 (exec). *Other Activities:* Member of LIBC Aviation Sub-Committee; Member of Lloyds.

SMITH, William James; Chief Equity Strategist, BZW, since 1990; Asset Allocation. *Career:* Standard Life, Pension Fund Manager 1977-84; Prudential-Bache, Director of European Research/European Strategist 1984-90. *Biog: b.* 2 December 1954. *Nationality:* British. *m.* 1978, Marion Anne (née Slevin); 1 s; 2 d. *Educ:* St Aloysius College, Glasgow; Heriot Watt University (BSc Hons). *Directorships:* BZW Securities 1990 (exec). *Other Activities:* Financial Times Actuarial Indices Committee; Institute of Actuaries Financial Risk Committee; Worshipful Company of Actuaries. *Professional Organisations:* Associate, Society of Investment Analysts; Graduate Member, Institute of Mathematics; Fellow, Faculty of Actuaries. *Recreations:* Running.

SMITH, William Nicolson; Director, Robert Fleming & Co Limited, since 1990; Administration, Corporate Finance Department. *Career:* Robert Fleming Investment Management Ltd, Director Responsible for Administration 1974-86; Director Responsible for Compliance 1986-90. *Directorships:* Robert Fleming & Co Limited 1990 (exec); Robert Fleming Management Services Limited 1986 (exec). *Other Activities:* Responsible for Flemings Collection of Scottish Art. *Professional Organisations:* FCIS; FBIM.

SMITHSON, Antony John; Deputy Managing Director, Murray Lawrence Members Agency Ltd, since 1988 (Managing Director 1991). *Career:* Willis Faber & Dumas, Insurance Broker 1964-78; Michael Payne & Others, Assistant Underwriter Members Agency Manager 1978-86; Murray Lawrence & Partners, Members Agency Manager 1986-88. *Biog: b.* 26 November 1945. *Nationality:* British. *m.* 1969, Margaret (née Fogell); 2 s; 1 d. *Educ:* Merchant Taylors' School, Northwood. *Directorships:* Murray Lawrence Members Agency Limited 1988 (exec).

SMITHSON, Simon F; Director, Kleinwort Benson Securities Limited.

SMOUHA, Brian Andrew; Partner, Touche Ross & Co, since 1970; Audit Services to Financial Institutions. *Career:* Secondment to Dept of Industry Under-Sec 1979-80. *Biog: b.* 3 September 1938. *Nationality:* British. *m.* 1961, Hana (née Btesh); 2 s. *Educ:* Harrow School; Magdalene College, Cambridge (MA). *Professional Organisations:* FCA. *Publications:* Regulation of Banks in UK, 1990.

SMURFIT, D F; Director, Macey Williams Ltd.

SMYTH, G R T; Partner, Cameron Markby Hewitt.

SMYTH, John Rodney; Partner, Lovell White Durrant, since 1985; Company Law, Compliance. *Career:* Barrister 1975-79; Holman, Fenwick & Willan, Asst Solicitor 1980-82; Durrant Piesse (now Lovell White Durrant), Asst Solicitor 1982-85. *Biog: b.* 23

August 1953. *Nationality:* British. *Educ:* Shrewsbury School; Magdalene College, Cambridge (MA). *Professional Organisations:* Member, The Law Society. *Recreations:* Birdwatching, Paintings.

SMYTH, Joyce A; Partner, Theodore Goddard.

SMYTH, M J; Clerk, Makers of Playing Cards' Company.

SMYTH, Michael Anthony; Partner, Lawrence Graham, since 1987; Corporate Finance. *Career:* Knapp Fishers, Ptnr 1982-87. *Biog: b.* 17 April 1954. *Educ:* Dr Challoner's Grammar School, Amersham; Pembroke College, Cambridge (MA Hons 1st). *Directorships:* Friends of the Earth Ltd 1983-86 (non-exec); Friends of the Earth Trust Ltd 1983 (non-exec); Media Natwa Trust Ltd 1987 (non-exec). *Professional Organisations:* Law Society. *Recreations:* Bridge, Fell Walking, Cycling.

SMYTH, Michael Thomas; Partner, Clifford Chance, since 1990; Commercial Litigation. *Career:* Lovell White Durrant (then Lovell White & King), Articled Clerk and Assistant Solicitor 1980-84; Clifford Chance (then Clifford-Turner), Assistant Solicitor and Partner 1985-. *Biog: b.* 3 March 1957. *Nationality:* British. *m.* 1983, Joyce Anne (née Young). *Educ:* Royal Belfast Academical Institution; Clare College, Cambridge (MA). *Professional Organisations:* Law Society; City of London Solicitors Company; Admitted as Solicitor in Hong Kong.

SNEDDEN, David; Non-Executive Director, Reuters Holdings plc.

SNEDDON, A C B; Director, R A McLean & Co Ltd.

SNEDDON, Alan Drysdale; Chief General Manager, Co-operative Insurance Society Ltd.

SNELL, Thomas Markley; Managing Director, J P Morgan, since 1989; European Advisory/Analysis. *Biog: b.* 2 June 1955. *Nationality:* American. *m.* 1978, Virginia (née Joy); 1 s; 1 d. *Educ:* University of Chicago (MBA); University of North Carolina (BA).

SNELSON, Robin Edward; Partner, Clay & Partners, since 1988; Insurance Division, Actuarial Advice on Major Issues Affecting Insurance Companies. *Career:* Legal & General plc 1955-88; Actuary for Australia 1969-74; Pensions Actuary (UK) 1974-79; Actuary (UK) 1979-84; Head of Group Actuarial Services 1984-88. *Biog: b.* 11 April 1938. *Nationality:* British. *m.* 1961, Mary Christine (née Johnson); 4 s. *Educ:* Melton Mowbray Grammar School. *Directorships:* Financial Insurance Group 1988 (non-exec). *Other Activities:* Council Member, Institute of Actuaries. *Professional Organisations:* Fellow, Institute of Actuaries; Fellow, Institute of Actuaries of Australia; Fellow, Pensions Management Insti-

tute. *Publications:* Modern Methods of Costing Insured Pension Schemes (Journal of the Institute of Actuaries Students' Society), 1970; Pensions and Company Finance, 1970; Joint Author with G T Humphrey, F R Langham & J D Sparks.

SNOW, Antony E; Chairman, Hill & Knowlton (UK) Ltd, since 1991. *Career:* Balding & Mansell Limited, Sales Trainee 1956; W S Crawford Limited, Graduate Trainee 1958; W S Crawford Limited, Account Executive 1959; Charles Barker & Sons Limited, Account Executive 1961; Charles Barker Birmingham, Chief Executive Officer 1971; Charles Barker Recruitment, Chief Executive Officer 1973; Charles Barker Hill & Knowlton UK, Chairman 1975; Charles Barker Group, Deputy Chairman 1975; Charles Barker Watney & Powell, Chairman; Charles Barker Lyons, Chairman; Charles Barker City, Chairman; Steuben Glass, USA, Vice President, Market Planning; Corning Museum of Glass, USA, Deputy Director 1976; Rockwell Museum, USA, Director 1978; Arnot Art Museum, USA, Trustee; Chemung Valley Arts Council, Trustee 1979; Corning Chamber of Commerce, Chairman; Corning Glass Works, Corporate Management Group 1980; Steuben Glass, Vice President, Corporate Planning 1982; Charles Barker plc, Chairman and Chief Executive 1983; BNB Resources plc, Non-Executive Director; The Heritage Group, Consultant; Hogg Group plc, Non-Executive Director 1988; The PFISTER Co, Chairman 1990; Hill & Knowlton (UK) Ltd, Chairman 1991. *Biog: b.* 5 December 1932. *m.* 1961, Caroline (née Wilson); 1 s; 2 d. *Educ:* American School, Bogota, Columbia; Sherborne School; National Service Commissioned in 10th Royal Hussars, Skiing and Athletics for 2nd Division, BOAR; New College, Oxford (Prelims and Finals in Law); London School of Printing (Diploma); IPA Intermediate and Finals, Advertising and Marketing. *Other Activities:* Member, Ancient Monuments Advisory Committee, English Heritage, 1989; Member, Appeals Committee, Ashmolean Museum, Oxford; Member, Executive Committee, Courtauld Institute of Art, 1986; Member, Executive Committee, National Art Collections Fund, 1986; Member, The Design Council, 1989; Trustee, Monteverdi Choir, 1988; Trustee, Corning Museum of Glass, New York, 1983. *Professional Organisations:* Fellow, Institute of Practitioners in Advertising; Member, Public Relations Society of America; Companion, British Institute of Management; Member, Institute of Public Relations; Member, Public Relations Consultants Association; Member, American Association of Museums; Member, Royal Society of Arts. *Clubs:* Cavalry & Guards Club, City of London Club, Pilgrims.

SNYDER, Maurice W; Director, J Henry Schroder Wagg & Co Limited.

SOAMES, The Hon Jeremy; Executive Director, N M Rothschild & Sons Limited.

SOAMES, W A; Director, Panmure Gordon & Co Limited.

SOAR, Adrian Richard; Managing Director, Macmillan Press Ltd, since 1989. *Career:* Book Development Council, Head of Research 1967-69; Macmillan Group 1969-; Export Manager 1969-71; Macmillan India, Managing Director 1972-73; Academic & Magazines, Marketing Director 1973-78; Macmillan Reference, Publishing Director 1973-78; Managing Director, Academic Division 1979-84; Managing Director, Educational, Professional & Reference Group 1984-89. *Biog:* b. 5 March 1941. *Nationality:* British. *m.* 1973, Micaela (née Coltofeanu); 1 s; 1 d. *Educ:* Tonbridge School; Jesus College, Oxford (BA, MA Classics). *Directorships:* Macmillan India Ltd 1972 (non-exec); Macmillan Shuppan KK, Tokyo 1974 (non-exec); Macmillan de Mexico 1980 (non-exec); Macmillan Boleswa 1985 (non-exec); Macmillan Language House Tokyo 1987 (non-exec); Stockton Press Inc 1985 (non-exec); Macmillan Education Ltd 1987 (exec) Chm; Macmillan Academic & Professional 1987 (exec) Chm; Macmillan LT 1987 (exec) Chm; Modern English Publications Ltd 1987 (exec) Chm; Macmillan Publishers Ltd 1980 (non-exec); Macmillan Ltd 1983 (non-exec). *Recreations:* Work, Reading, Cooking, Gardening.

SOBCZAK, A W; Director, Barclays de Zoete Wedd Securities Ltd.

SODEN, I; Director, J H Minet & Co Ltd.

SODEN, Robert; Vice President, Operations, Scotia McLeod Inc, since 1987. *Career:* Wardley (London) Limited, Assistant Director 1985-87; The United Bank of Kuwait Ltd 1973-85.

SOFER, Zamir; General Manager, UK Branches and UK Rep, Bank Hapoalim, since 1989; Foreign Exchange, Loans & Deposits, Commercial Customer Service Unit. *Career:* Agrexco Ltd, Fin Dir 1979-81; Bank Hapoalim, Mgr, Subsidiaries Dept 1981-86. *Biog:* b. 25 February 1946. *m.* 1972, Dorit; 1 s; 1 d. *Professional Organisations:* CPA (Israel). *Clubs:* Overseas Bankers'.

SOLANDT, Jean Bernard; Vice-Chairman, J Henry Schroder Wagg & Co Ltd, since 1984; Treasury & Trading. *Career:* Société Générale; Strasbourg/Paris/London FX Dealer 1954-68; Société Générale (London) Dep Chief Dealer 1965-; J Henry Schroder Wagg & Co Ltd 1968-. *Biog:* b. 23 December 1936. *m.* 1965, Sheila (née Hammill); 1 s; 1 d. *Educ:* Collège Moderne de Strasbourg; Collège Technique Commercial, Strasbourg. *Directorships:* Schroders plc 1985 MD; Schroder Securities Ltd 1986 Chm; Schroder Securities Int Ltd 1986 Chm. *Other Activities:* Member, Executive Committee British Bankers' Association 1990. *Recreations:* Music, Skiing, Reading, Walking.

SOLDEN, Lester David; Director, Dealing, Mase Westpac Ltd.

SOLITANDER, J E; Director, Hambros Bank Limited.

SOLLY, D S; Director, Kleinwort Benson Limited.

SOLOMON, A; Non-Executive Director, S G Warburg Group plc.

SOLOMON, Gerald Oliver; Senior General Manager, Lloyds Bank plc, since 1989; UK Retail Banking. *Career:* Lloyds Bank plc, Asst Treasurer 1976-78; Dep Chief Acct 1978-80; Reg Dir, South Wales 1980-82; Asst Gen Mgr 1982-84; General Manager, London 1984-89. *Biog:* b. 18 June 1935. *Educ:* University College, London (LLB). *Directorships:* Travellers Cheque Associates Ltd 1986 Chm. *Professional Organisations:* FCIB; MBIM. *Clubs:* Royal Overseas League, United Club (Jersey), MCC. *Recreations:* Golf, Fell Walking.

SOLOMON, Michael James; Partner, Cyril Sweett and Partners.

SOLOMON, Stephen; Vice President, Manufacturers Hanover Trust Co.

SOLOMONS, A N; Chairman, Singer & Friedlander Group plc, since 1976. *Career:* Qualified Chartered Accountant 1952; Wilkins Kennedy & Co 1954-55; Lobitos Oilfields Ltd 1955-58; Singer & Friedlander Ltd 1958-; Director 1964; Chief Executive 1973; Chairman & Chief Executive 1976-89; Singer & Friedlander Group plc, Chairman 1987-. *Biog:* b. 26 January 1930. *Nationality:* British. *m.* 1957, Jean (née Golding); 2 d. *Educ:* Oundle. *Directorships:* Bullough plc (non-exec); Invesco MIM plc (non-exec); ACT plc (non-exec); Milton Keynes Development Corporation (non-exec). *Other Activities:* Member, Property Advisory Group to Department of Environment; Member, Educational Assets Board. *Professional Organisations:* FCA; FBIM. *Clubs:* Carlton.

SOLOMONS, Bernard; Chairman & Chief Executive, Allied Provincial plc, since 1986; Stockbroking. *Career:* Scottish Mutual Assurance 1967; Parsons & Co, Stockbrokers 1968; Partner in Charge of Institutional Sales/Research 1976; Responsible for the Formation of Allied Provincial Securities plc, Group Chairman & Chief Executive 1986. *Biog:* b. 4 May 1944. *Nationality:* British. *m.* 1968, Maureen; 1 s; 1 d. *Educ:* Hutchesons Boys Grammar School; University of Glasgow (MA Hons Economics & Statistics). *Directorships:* Scottish Financial Enterprise 1988. *Other Activities:* Member, Stock Exchange Council, 1984-85; Chairman, Society of Investment Analysts (Scottish Branch), 1976-82. *Clubs:* Bonnyton Golf Club. *Recreations:* Golf, Gardening.

SOLON, Paul C M; Partner, Beachcroft Stanleys.

SOLVAY, J E; Non-Executive Director, Laporte plc.

SOLWAY, G R; Director, North American Pharmaceuticals Division, The Boots Co plc.

SOMMERVILLE, A J C; Director, Parrish plc.

SOPER, Derek Ronald; Director, Kleinwort Benson Ltd, since 1986; Leasing, Asset Based Finance. *Career:* Barclays Mercantile Industrial Fin Ltd, Dir. *Biog: b.* 16 August 1937. *Nationality:* British. *m.* 1963, Janet (née Booth); 3 d. *Educ:* Scarborough College. *Directorships:* Kleinwort Benson Subsidiary Companies. *Professional Organisations:* Member of Management Committee, Equipment Leasing Assoc. *Clubs:* Wig & Pen. *Recreations:* Walking, Skiing.

SORKIN, Alexander Michael; Vice Chairman, Hambros Bank Limited.

SORRELL, J; Director, Touche, Remnant & Co.

SORRELL, Martin Stuart; Group Chief Executive, WPP Group plc.

SOUBRIER, Jean-Marie; Director, Gartmore Investment Management Limited.

SOUL, Michael J; Partner, Withers.

SOUNDY, Andrew John; Partner, Ashurst Morris Crisp, since 1969; Acquisitions, Corp Finance, Competition, Venture Capital. *Biog: b.* 29 March 1940. *Nationality:* British. *m.* 1963, Jill Marion (née Steiner); 1 s; 2 d. *Educ:* Shrewsbury School; Trinity College, Cambridge (MA). *Professional Organisations:* Solicitor. *Clubs:* Cavalry and Guards. *Recreations:* Pedigree Cattle Breeding, Tennis, Opera, Good Living.

SOUNESS, J M; Managing Director, LAS Unit Trust Managers.

SOUTH, Dr Robert; Director of Strategic Planning, British Gas plc.

SOUTH, W L; CBE; Technical Director, Philips Electronics, since 1982. *Career:* Mullard Ltd, Technical Director 1980-82; Pye of Cambridge Ltd, Technical Director 1977-80; Mullard Mitcham, Pland Director 1974-77. *Biog: b.* 3 May 1933. *Nationality:* British. *m.* 1960, Lesley (née Donaldson); 1 s; 2 d. *Educ:* Purley County Grammar School. *Directorships:* Philips Electronics 1982 (exec); OTIB Holdings Ltd 1990 (non-exec). *Other Activities:* Member, ITAB; Chairman, Devices Committee (DTI/SERC); Member, Supervisory Board of The National Physical Laboratory. *Clubs:* Chichester Yacht Club.

SOUTHCOTT, Barry John; Managing Director, Marketable Securities Division, CIN Management Ltd, since 1983; Quoted Equity & Bond Portfolios British Coal, Pension Funds. *Career:* Phillips & Drew, Investment Analyst 1971-75; British Coal Superannuation Investments Department 1975-85; Deputy Managing Director 1980; Managing Director, Marketable Securities Division 1983-; CIN Management Ltd, set up as a subsidiary of British Coal to do work previously carried out by Superannuation Investments Department, Employment Transferred from British Coal 1985-. *Biog: b.* 27 March 1950. *Nationality:* British. *m.* 1978, Lesley Anne (née Parkinson); 1 s. *Educ:* Latymer Upper School; Bradford University (BSc Hons Econ); Four Stock Exchange Exams. *Directorships:* Black Diamonds Pensions Ltd; The British Investment Trust plc; CIN Investments plc; CIN Industrial Finance Holdings Ltd; CIN Contractors Management Ltd; Citystone Assets plc; Drayton Premier Investment Trust plc; BZW Convertible Investment Trust plc; Globe Investment Trust, Edinburgh Fund Managers plc; TR Industrial & General Trust plc. *Professional Organisations:* AMSIA, 1973. *Recreations:* Tennis, Football, Music, Gardening.

SOUTHERN, Guy Hugo; Partner, Frere Cholmeley, since 1959; Private Clients. *Career:* Crossman Block & Co, London, Assistant Solicitor 1955-57; Alfred Blundell, London, Partner 1957-58. *Biog: b.* 12 October 1929. *Nationality:* British. *m.* 1958, R Antonia (née McAndrew); 1 s; 2 d. *Educ:* Harrow School, Middx. *Professional Organisations:* Law Society. *Clubs:* Beefsteak.

SOUTHEY, Verner George; Partner, Clyde & Co, since 1986; Head of Company/Commercial Department. *Career:* In Legal Practice in S Rhodesia 1962-75; Wedlake Bell Asst 1975-78; Wedlake Bell Ptnr 1978-79; Elborne Mitchell Ptnr 1979-86. *Biog: b.* 1 October 1942. *m.* 1965, Marilyn (née MacKendrick); 1 s; 1 d. *Educ:* St Aidan's College, Grahamstown, South Africa; University of Cape Town (BA); University of London (LLB).

SOUTHGATE, C G; Chairman and Chief Executive, Thorn EMI plc.

SOUTHGATE, Colin; Non-Executive Director, Prudential Corporation plc.

SOUTHGATE, Crispin John; Director, Charterhouse Bank Ltd, since 1987; Capital Markets. *Career:* Price Waterhouse, Asst Mgr 1977-82; Charterhouse Bank 1982-. *Biog: b.* 16 February 1955. *Nationality:* British. *m.* 1979, Joanna Mary (née Donaldson); 2 s; 1 d. *Educ:* Christ's Hospital; Merton College, Oxford (MA). *Directorships:* Charterhouse Bank Ltd 1987 (exec). *Other Activities:* Treasurer, The Rainer Foundation. *Professional Organisations:* ACA. *Recreations:* Music, Family.

SOUTHWOOD, Kevin Charles; Director & General Manager, Northern Rock Building Society, since 1990; Marketing, Insurance, Research & Planning, Information Technology, Retail Banking, Estate Agency. *Career:* Barclays Bank, Branch Banking 1969-71; Olivetti I T Marketing 1971-72; Hill Samuel Group, Insurance Broking 1972-75; Northern Rock Building Society, Various Mktng, Planning & Mgmnt Positions 1975-. *Biog: b.* 9 September 1950. *Nationality:* British. *m.* 1972, Christine Mary (née Edwards); 2 s. *Educ:* St Cuthberts Grammar School; Hatfield Polytechnic (DMS); Newcastle University (MBA). *Directorships:* Northern Rock Property Services 1987 Chm; Northern Rock Financial Services 1990 Dep Chm; Link Interchange Network Ltd 1989 (non-exec); Funds Transfer Sharing Ltd 1989 (non-exec). *Other Activities:* Visiting Lecturer in Marketing, Newcastle University; Examiner, Chartered Building Societies Institute. *Professional Organisations:* FCBSI; MCIM; MBIM. *Recreations:* Playing Rugby, Cricket & Tennis.

SOUVIRON, P; Director, Crédit Lyonnais Capital Markets plc.

SOWERBUTTS, Kevin; Head of International Finance and Legal, Paribas Limited.

SPACEY, Roger; Director (Market-Making), Hoare Govett International Securities.

SPACKMAN, Michael Kenneth Maurice; Director, Singer & Friedlander Investment Management Ltd, since 1987; Specialising in Spain since 1963. *Career:* Hong Kong and Shanghai Banking Corp, Foreign Staff 1948-57. *Biog: b.* 5 February 1926. *Nationality:* British. *m.* 1960, Ann Veronica (née Cook); 2 d. *Educ:* Marlborough College. *Directorships:* First Spanish Investment Trust 1987 (non-exec); Vallehermoso SA 1989 (non-exec). *Recreations:* Horse Trials.

SPAREY, Jonathan Nigel Edward; Executive Director, Samuel Montagu & Co Limited, since 1987; Specialised Financing. *Career:* Samuel Montagu & Co Limited, Assistant Manager 1981-; Manager 1983-; Assistant Director 1985-. *Biog: b.* 7 August 1957. *Nationality:* British. *m.* 1981, Hazel (née Presdee). *Educ:* Monkton Combe, Somerset; University of St Andrews (Double First Class Honours, MA Modern and Medieval History); City University Business School (MBA). *Directorships:* Northern Mortgage Corporation Ltd 1985/89 (non-exec). *Clubs:* Sea View Yacht Club, Isle of Wight. *Recreations:* Tennis, Sailing, Hill-Walking.

SPARKES, Michael James; Overseas Equities Manager, British Airways Pension Fund, since 1986; Head of Overseas Equities Portfolio Management Team. *Career:* British Airways plc, Management Trainee 1980-81; British Airways Pension Fund 1981-; Investment Analyst 1981-84; US Equities Manager 1984-86. *Biog: b.* 29 January 1957. *Nationality:* British. *m.* 1984, Caroline Anne (née Macqueen). *Educ:* Cranbrook School; Emmanuel College, Cambridge (MA). *Other Activities:* Company Secretary, Oliver Northcote Ltd; Management Committee, Hounslow Hockey Club. *Clubs:* Oriental, Hounslow Hockey. *Recreations:* Theatre, Sport, Travel, Gardening.

SPARKES, Russell Kevin; Senior Investment Manager, Refuge Group plc.

SPARKS, David; Partner, Lovell White Durrant.

SPARKS, John Drummond; Partner, Bacon & Woodrow, since 1971; Pensions. *Career:* Northern Assurance Co Ltd 1959-65. *Biog: b.* 23 April 1938. *m.* 1965, Jennifer; 2 s; 2 d. *Educ:* Brentwood School; Bristol University (BA). *Directorships:* Triskel Communications 1978 (non-exec); Hothorpe Hall Ltd (Christian Conference Centre) 1984 (non-exec). *Professional Organisations:* Association of Consulting Actuaries; Fellow, Pensions Management Institute. *Recreations:* Anglican, Music, Badminton.

SPARKS, V J; Director, Knight & Day Ltd.

SPARROW, E C A; Partner, Ashurst Morris Crisp.

SPEARING, David Nicholas; Partner, Freshfields, since 1984. *Career:* Gordon Dadds & Co 1976-78; Freshfields 1978-. *Biog: b.* 4 May 1954. *Nationality:* British. *m.* 1980, Annemarie (née Gatford); 1 s; 2 d. *Educ:* Caterham School; Hertford College, Oxford (MA Hons). *Other Activities:* Chm, Law Society Solicitors' European Group; Mem, Joint Bar Law Society Working Party on Competition Law; City of London Solicitors' Co. *Publications:* Contributor, Butterworths Encyclopaedia of Forms and Precedents; Articles in Professional Journals. *Recreations:* Theatre, Tennis, Reading.

SPEDDING, (Stephen) Paul; Director, Kleinwort Benson Securities.

SPEKE, Ian Benjamin; Director, Wise Speke Ltd, since 1980; Private Clients. *Career:* Army 9/12 Royal Lancers Short Service Commission 1968-72; Pinchin Denny Blue Button/Dealer 1974-77; Hoare Govett Institutional, Sales 1977-80. *Biog: b.* 12 March 1950. *m.* 1983, Ailsa Elizabeth (née Fenwick); 1 s; 2 d. *Educ:* Eton College. *Clubs:* Pratt's, Cavalry & Guards, Northern Counties. *Recreations:* Field Sports, Horse Racing, Real/Lawn Tennis, Cricket, Golf.

SPELLER, Stuart M; Managing Director, GP Eliot & Company Ltd.

SPELMAN, R; General Manager, Halifax Building Society, since 1989; Marketing. *Career:* Halifax Building Society 1964; Assistant District Manager 1969; Assistant

Advertising Manager 1974; Advertising Manager 1979; Marketing Controller 1982; Assistant General Manager, Marketing Services 1985; General Manager, Marketing 1989. *Biog: b.* 6 July 1946. *Nationality:* British. *m.* Marian; 2 d. *Directorships:* Halifax Homes Limited 1989; Halifax Urban Renewal Limited 1989; Halifax Loans Limited 1989; The Partnership Renewal of The Built Environment Ltd (Probe Ltd) 1990. *Other Activities:* Member of Council, Advertising Standards Board of Finance; Chairman, Building Societies Association Advertising Panel; HM Treasury, Adviser to Government on Advertising, 1990. *Clubs:* Reform. *Recreations:* Golf.

SPENCE, C D; Managing Director, Sedgwick Lloyd's Underwriting Agents Limited.

SPENCE, C J; Deputy Chairman & Chief Executive, English Trust Company Limited.

SPENCE, Christopher; Chairman, Tyndall Holdings plc.

SPENCE, David Lane; Partner, Grant Thornton, since 1970; Investigations, Corporate Finance & Recovery. *Career:* C F Middleton & Co 1962-67; Grant Thornton, Chairman, Investigation Panel 1974-84; European Practice Partner 1974-79; Executive Partner 1984-89. *Biog: b.* 5 October 1943. *Nationality:* Scottish. *m.* 1966, Beverley Esther (née Cardale); 1 s; 2 d. *Educ:* Fettes College, (CA). *Other Activities:* Worshipful Company of Glaziers; DTI Inspector 1989, County NatWest Ltd; Member, ICAS (Business Legislation Unit). *Professional Organisations:* ICAS, 1967. *Clubs:* Caledonian, Sunningdale. *Recreations:* Golf, Skiing, Music, Family.

SPENCER, Christopher Robert; Director, Kleinwort Benson Investment Management.

SPENCER, Paul; Associate Director-Treasurer, Hanson plc, since 1986; Corporate Financing, Risk Management, Cash Management, Insurance. *Career:* Keyser Ullman Investment Asst 1969-72; ICI Pension Fund Investment Mgr 1972-76; British Leyland Ltd Treasury Mgr 1976-80; Rolls Royce plc Group Treasurer 1980-86. *Biog: b.* 3 January 1950. *m.* 1975, Lorna (née Nykerk); 2 s; 1 d. *Educ:* Ampleforth College; CNAA Thames Polytechnic (BA Hons). *Other Activities:* Chm of Editorial Board, 'The Treasurer'. *Professional Organisations:* ACMA, Council Member, FCT. *Recreations:* Cricket, Rugby, Tennis, Opera.

SPENCER, R D; Director, LMX, Denis M Clayton & Co Limited.

SPENCER MARTINS, L; Deputy General Manager (London Branch), Banco Espirito Santo e Comercial de Lisboa, since 1989; Credit/Treasury. *Career:* Banco Totts & Acores (London Branch), Manager (Credit) 1985-87; Banco Espirito Santo e Comercial de Lisboa (Lisbon),

Senior Manager (Credit) 1988-89. *Biog: b.* 4 March 1950. *Nationality:* Portuguese. *m.* 1975, Hilary; 2 d. *Educ:* (BSc Economics, MBA).

SPENDLOVE, Justin T; Partner, Wilde Sapte.

SPENS, John Alexander; Director, Scottish Amicable Life Assurance Society, since 1963. *Career:* Maclay Murray & Spens, Ptnr 1960; Consultant 1990; Carrick Pursuivant 1974-85; Standard Property Investment plc, Director 1977-87; Scottish Amicable Life Assurance Society, Chairman 1978-81; Albany Herald 1985. *Directorships:* The Planning Exchange Limited. *Other Activities:* Member, Scottish Episcopal Church Finance Committee; Chairman, Diocese of Glasgow and Galloway Administration Board.

SPENSLEY, P M; Director, Treasury-Money Market Division, SG Warburg & Co Ltd, since 1990; Sterling Treasury. *Career:* Phillips & Drew, Manager 1972-82; TSB England & Wales, Assistant Treasurer 1982-87; S G Warburg & Co Assistant Director 1987-90. *Biog: b.* 3 June 1950. *Nationality:* British. *m.* 1979, Wendy; 2 s. *Educ:* Chislehurst & Sidcup Grammar School For Boys. *Professional Organisations:* Member, Stock Exchange.

SPERRING, Michael W; Analyst, Smith New Court Research.

SPICER, John Vincent; Director, Kleinwort Benson Securities, since 1986; Brewery Analyst. *Career:* Kodak Business Planner 1975-77; Whitbread & Co plc, Strategic Planner 1978-82; Grenfell & Colegrave, Brewery Analyst 1982-84. *Biog: b.* 2 March 1951. *Nationality:* British. *m.* 1973, Patricia Ann Spicer (née Bracher). *Educ:* Sheffield University (BA Hons 1st). *Professional Organisations:* Member, The International Stock Exchange. *Recreations:* Golf, Squash.

SPICER, P G B; Director, Lonrho plc.

SPICER, Q; Partner, Wedlake Bell.

SPIEGEL, S; Director, Lehman Brothers Equity Money Brokers Ltd.

SPIEGELBERG, Richard George; Director of Corporate Communications, Merrill Lynch Europe Limited, since 1987. *Career:* The Economist Intelligence Unit 1965-67; The Times, Business Journalist & Mgmnt Editor 1967-74; Department of Industry, Principal 1974-75; National Economic Development Office 1975-76; J Walter Thompson & Co, Associate Director 1976-80; Coopers & Lybrand, Associate Director 1980-84; Streets, Financial Dir and Joint MD 1984-87. *Biog: b.* 21 January 1944. *Nationality:* British. *m.* 1980, Suzanne Louise (née Dodd); 3 s; 1 d. *Educ:* Marlborough College and Hotchkiss School (USA); New College, Oxford (MA Hons). *Publications:* The City, 1973. *Clubs:* Brooks's. *Recreations:* Walking, Golf, Opera.

SPIERENBURG, M; Director, S G Warburg Akroyd Rowe & Pitman Mullens Securities Ltd.

SPILLER, Richard John; Partner, D J Freeman & Company, since 1985; Insurance/Commercial & Competition Law. *Career:* Derby Cook Quinby & Tweedt (San Francisco), Legal Clerk 1977-78; Hedleys, Asst Solicitor 1978-81; Norton Rose Botterell & Roche, Asst Solicitor 1982-83; D J Freeman & Co, Asst Solicitor 1983-85. *Biog: b.* 31 December 1953. *Nationality:* British. *m.* 1982, Hilary (née Wright); 1 s; 1 d. *Educ:* Royal Belfast Academical Institution; Exeter University (LLB); City of London Polytechnic (MA). *Other Activities:* City of London Solicitors' Company (Commercial Law Sub-Committee). *Professional Organisations:* The Law Society. *Recreations:* Sport, Gardening, Cinema, Dining Out.

SPILSBURY, Steven Graham; General Manager, Bradford & Bingley Building Society, since 1985; Marketing, Business Development, Investment Management, New Business Research. *Biog: b.* 20 December 1944. *Nationality:* British. *m.* 1967, Diane Mary (née Legard); 2 s. *Educ:* Bradford Grammar School. *Directorships:* Bradford & Bingley (IOM) Limited 1985 (exec); Bradford & Bingley (PEPS) Limited 1987 (exec); Bradford & Bingley Pensions Ltd 1988 (exec). *Professional Organisations:* Chartered Building Societies Institute. *Clubs:* Shipley Golf Club. *Recreations:* Golf.

SPINELLI, F; Joint Managing Director (Operations), Refco Overseas Ltd.

SPINK, J D; Non-Executive Director, British Land. *Biog: b.* 23 December 1924. *Nationality:* British. *Professional Organisations:* FRICS (Chartered Surveyor).

SPINK, John L; Senior Manager, Commerzbank AG.

SPIRA, Peter John Ralph; Deputy Chairman, County NatWest Limited, since 1988; Group Business Development. *Career:* S G Warburg & Co Vice-Chm 1957-74; Sotheby Parke Bennet Group Fin Dir 1974-82; Goldman Sachs Intl Corp Vice-Chm 1983-87. *Biog: b.* 2 March 1930. *Nationality:* British. *m.* 1969, Anne (née Landon); 4 s; 2 d. *Educ:* Eton College; King's College, Cambridge (MA). *Directorships:* NatWest Investment Bank Ltd 1989 (exec); Societe Generale de Surveillance Holdings SA (exec). *Other Activities:* Council of Birthright. *Clubs:* Buck's. *Recreations:* Music, Reading, Photography.

SPOONER, Graham; Director, 3i plc. *Other Activities:* London Business School Centre for Enterprise; London Chamber of Commerce Regional Affairs.

SPOONER, Sir James; Director, John Swire & Sons Ltd, since 1970. *Career:* Dixon Wilson & Co Chartered Accts, Ptnr 1963-72; Coats Viyella plc, Chm 1969-89; NAAFI, Chm 1973-86; National Mutual Life Assurance Society, Dep Chm 1972-82; Hogg Robinson Group plc, Dep Chm 1971-85; Bentalls plc, Chm 1978-82. *Biog: b.* 11 July 1932. *Nationality:* British. *m.* 1958, Alyson (née Glover); 2 s; 1 d. *Educ:* Eton College; Christ Church, Oxford (MA). *Directorships:* Abingworth plc 1973 (non-exec); The Morgan Crucible Co plc 1978 Chm; J Sainsbury plc 1981 (non-exec); Barclays Bank plc 1983 (non-exec). *Other Activities:* King's College, London (Chairman & Fellow); Royal Opera House (Director); Eton College (Fellow). *Professional Organisations:* FCA. *Clubs:* Beefsteak, White's. *Recreations:* History, Music, Shooting, Travel, Walking.

SPORBORG, Christopher Henry; Deputy Chairman, Hambros Bank Ltd, since 1983; Chief Executive of Non-Banking Activities. *Career:* Hambros Bank Ltd 1962-; Dir 1970; Exec Dir, Corp Fin 1975; Hambros plc, Dir 1983; Vice-Chm 1986. *Biog: b.* 17 April 1939. *m.* 1961, Lucinda Jane (née Hanbury); 2 s; 2 d. *Educ:* Rugby School; Emmanuel College, Cambridge (BA Hons). *Directorships:* Subsidiary & Associated Companies of Hambros; Atlas Copco UK Holdings Ltd 1984 Chm; Huntingdon Steeplechases Ltd 1984; TNT (UK) Ltd 1981; Jockey Club Estates Ltd 1985; Lambourn Holdings Ltd 1984; Thinkmajor Ltd 1986. *Other Activities:* Hon Treasurer, British Field Sports Society; Trustee, Sir Jules Thorn Charitable Trust; Member, Horse Race Betting Levy Board; Joint Master, Puckeridge & Thurlow Foxhounds; Member, Jockey Club. *Professional Organisations:* CBIM. *Clubs:* Boodle's. *Recreations:* Racing, Hunting, Ballet.

SPRAGGS, Peter David; Director, Gerrard & National Securities Ltd.

SPRAGUE, Christopher William; Partner, Ince & Co, since 1975; Insurance and Maritime Law. *Career:* Messrs Simmons & Simmons, Articled Clerk 1966-69; Messrs Ince & Co, Assistant Solicitor 1970-74; Partner 1975-. *Biog: b.* 19 August 1943. *Nationality:* British. *m.* 1971, Clare (née Bradshaw); 4 d. *Educ:* St Edwards School, Oxford; Christ Church, Oxford (MA). *Other Activities:* Liveryman, Barbers' Company. *Professional Organisations:* Law Society; Supporting Member, London Maritime Arbitrators' Association; Subscribing member, Association of Average Adjusters. *Clubs:* United Oxford and Cambridge University, London Rowing, Leander. *Recreations:* Reading, History, Rowing, Bellringing.

SPRATT, Sir Greville Douglas; GBE, KStJ, TD, JP, DL; Regional Director, NatWest, since 1989; City & West End. *Career:* Coldstream Guards 1945-46; Arab Legion 1946-48; Lloyd's Underwriting (Hogg Robinson) 1948-61; J & N Wade Group, Electrical Distribution, Director 1969-76; MD 1971-76; Honourable

Artillery Company, Active Member 1950-70; LT Col 1962-65; Regtl Col 1966-70; Chairman of City of London TAVRA 1977-82; Alderman, City of London 1978-; Chancellor, City University 1987-88; ADC to HM The Queen 1973-78; Magistrate of the City of London 1978-; Sheriff of the City of London 1984-85; Lord Mayor of London 1987-88; Lieutenant of the City of London 1972-; Deputy Lieutenant of Greater London 1986-; Hon Col City of London & NE Sector ACF 1983-; Hon Col Queens Fusiliers 1988-. *Biog: b.* 1 May 1927. *Nationality:* British. *m.* 1954, Sheila (née Wade); 3 s. *Educ:* Leighton Park; Charterhouse; RMA Sandhurst. *Directorships:* Williams Lea Group 1989. *Other Activities:* Chairman, Governing Body, Charterhouse; Chairman, Action Research; Chairman, Greater London TAVRA; Chairman, Anglo Jordanian Society; Vice President, King Edwards School, Witley; Governor, St Paul's Cathedral Choir School; Governor, Christs Hospital; Council Member, City University; Court Member, Ironmongers Co; Corporation Police Planning Music; Special Trustee, St Barts. Hospital. *Professional Organisations:* FRSA. *Clubs:* Cowdray, City Livery, Guildhall. *Recreations:* Tennis, Music, Military History.

SPRATT, Timothy; Managing Director (Investment Management), Broad Street Associates PR Ltd.

SPRING, Michael; Associate Director, GCI Sterling, since 1989; European Communications/Public Affairs. *Career:* PA Marketing Communications, Director 1984-89. *Biog: b.* 22 July 1952. *Nationality:* British. *m.* 1984, Vanessa; 1 s; 1 d. *Educ:* Queen's University, Belfast (BA American Studies/English). *Clubs:* Arsenal Football, RITL Snooker. *Recreations:* Admiring Sportsmen, Learning.

SPRINGBETT, D J; Deputy Chairman, PWS Holdings plc. *Career:* C T Bowring 1956-64; PWS, Founder Member 1964-. *Biog: b.* 2 May 1938. *Nationality:* British/Australian; 2 s; 4 d. *Educ:* Dulwich College. *Other Activities:* Council Member, Royal Philatelic Society. *Clubs:* Waterskiing, Snooker, Philately, Travel.

SPROULE, I T B; Financial Accountant, Hill Samuel Bank Limited, since 1990; Finance. *Career:* S B Quin Knox (Chartered Accountants) 1963-69; Coopers & Lybrand 1969-72; Hill Samuel Bank Limited 1972-. *Biog: b.* 22 September 1944. *Nationality:* British. *m.* 1974, Elizabeth (née McVicker); 1 s. *Educ:* Rossall School, Fleetwood, Lancs. *Professional Organisations:* FCA. *Recreations:* Theatre, Sports.

SPURRIER, J A; Director of Administration, Hill Samuel Bank Limited, since 1990; Administration. *Career:* City of London Corporation. *Biog: b.* 21 June 1936. *m.* 1965, Barbara Eileen; 1 s; 1 d. *Educ:* Friern Barnet County. *Recreations:* Cricket, Computers, Theatre.

SQUIRE, Wing Commander H C F; Clerk, Fuellers' Company.

SQUIRES, K R; Director, Barclays de Zoete Wedd Securities Ltd.

SRINIVASAN, R; Director, The New India Assurance Company Limited.

SRODES, James; American Business Correspondent, The Sunday Telegraph; Weekly View from Wall St Column.

STACEY, Dennis James; Director, Finance & Legal Services, Abbey Life Assurance Co Ltd, since 1989; Finance. *Career:* Beecham Products, Economist 1972-77; Rank Xerox Ltd, Business Analyst 1977-78; Rank Xerox (UK) Ltd, Various Finance Roles 1978-88; Fin Controller 1987-88; X/Open Company Ltd, VP, Business Planning & Finance 1988. *Biog: b.* 25 January 1950. *Nationality:* British. *m.* 1972, Jean (née Clayton). *Educ:* Frederick Gough Grammar, Scunthorpe; Pembroke College, Cambridge (MA). *Directorships:* Abbey Life Assurance Company Ltd 1990 (exec); Abbey Life Trustee Services Ltd 1989 (exec). *Professional Organisations:* FCMA. *Recreations:* Travel, Reading.

STACEY, Maré N; Partner, Theodore Goddard.

STACEY, P H; Partner, Slaughter and May.

STACY, Graham; Director of Professional Services, Price Waterhouse.

STAEHLI, Roland E; General Manager, Swiss Cantobank (International), since 1989. *Career:* Swiss Volksbank, Zurich, St Moritz 1967-70; Swiss Volksbank, Zurich, Head of Section, Securities Dept 1970-71; Union Bank of Switzerland, Lausanne, FX Dealer 1971-73; Swiss Volksbank, Zurich, FX & MMKT Dealer 1974-76; Banque Populaire Suisse SA, Luxembourg, Head of FX & MMKT 1976-78; Swiss Volksbank, London, UK Representative, VP 1979-82; Swiss Volksbank, Berne, Int Division, VP 1982-84; BSI-Bancasvizzera Italiana, London, UK Representative, SVP 1985-87; BSI-Bancasvizzera Italiana, London, Dep Branch Mgr, Branch Mgr, SVP 1987-89; Swiss Cantobank (Int), London, Gen Mgr 1989-. *Biog: b.* 20 September 1950. *Nationality:* Swiss. *m.* 1976, Elisabeth (née Huber); 1 s; 1 d. *Educ:* Mercantile College, Zurich (Federal Diploma); Graduate School of Business Administration, Zurich (MBA). *Directorships:* Swiss Cantobank Securities Ltd 1989 (exec). *Clubs:* RAC. *Recreations:* Classic Cars, Golf.

STAFFORD, P M; Managing Partner, Touche Ross & Co.

659

STAFFORD, W J; Chief Manager (Retail), Northern Bank Limited, since 1990; Branch Network. *Career:* NBG, Assistant General Manager, Corporate Finance 1984-86; Manager, Waring Street Branch 1986-88; Regional Manager, Belfast Region 1988-90; Chief Manager (Retail), Head Office 1990-. *Biog: b.* 13 July 1938. *Nationality:* British. *m.* 1963, Norma; 1 s; 1 d. *Educ:* Wallace High School. *Directorships:* Causeway Credit Limited 1990 (non-exec); Northern Bank Commercial Leasing Limited 1990 (non-exec); Northern Bank Equipment Leasing Limited 1990 (non-exec); Northern Bank Factors Limited 1990 (non-exec); Northern Bank Industrial Leasing Limited 1990 (non-exec); Northern Bank Leasing Limited 1990 (non-exec); Strangford Brick Co Limited 1988 (non-exec); Tyrone Brick Limited 1983 (non-exec). *Professional Organisations:* Institute of Bankers Certificate in Banking; Institute of Bankers Trustee Diploma. *Clubs:* Ulster Reform Club. *Recreations:* Gardening, Reading, Music.

STAFFORD-DEITSCH, Andrew; Executive Director, St James's Place Capital plc, since 1985; Corporate Finance. *Career:* N M Rothschild & Sons Ltd, Corp Fin Exec 1979-83; J Rothschild Holdings plc 1983-; Appointed to the Board 1985. *Educ:* Eton College; Oriel College, Oxford (BA). *Directorships:* RIT Capital Partners plc (non-exec); Amerpharm Investments NV; J Rothschild Capital Management Ltd; Anglo Group plc. *Other Activities:* Trustee, Chemical Dependency Centre.

STAKHOVITCH, A; Director, IBJ International Limited.

STALEY, B; General Manager & Director, Triland Metals Ltd.

STALHAM, Derek; Administration Director, Framlington Unit Management Ltd, since 1985; Unit Trust, Investment Management Administration. *Career:* Save & Prosper Group, Chief Cashier 1963-69; M&G Group Comptroller 1969-78. *Biog: b.* 23 November 1944. *m.* 1971, Barbara Ann (née Willy); 1 s; 1 d. *Educ:* William Morris Technical School. *Directorships:* Framlington Administration Services Ltd 1983 (exec); Framlington Nominees Ltd 1988 (exec).

STALLARD, Christopher David; Director, Panmure Gordon & Co Ltd, since 1987; Dealing. *Biog: b.* 24 August 1949. *Nationality:* British. *m.* 1973, Gillian; 1 s; 1 d. *Educ:* Chase Cross Boys School.

STALLWOOD, J; Renter Warden, The Worshipful Company of Spectacle Makers.

STAMMERS, L J; Director, BTR plc.

STANCLIFFE, John C G; Director, Warburg Securities.

STANDEN, John Francis; Managing Director, Barclays de Zoete Wedd, since 1985; Corporate Finance. *Career:* Barclays 1970-; Barclays National Merchant Bank (South Africa) 1977-80; Barclays Merchant Bank 1980-86. *Biog: b.* 14 October 1948. *m.* 1975, Kathleen Mary (née Quilty); 2 s; 1 d. *Educ:* St James' School, Burnt Oak; Durham University (BA). *Directorships:* Property Equity Fund 1987 (non-exec). *Professional Organisations:* AIB. *Recreations:* Relaxing, Walking, Family Fun, Theatre, Opera.

STANDISH, P J; Partner, Ernst & Young.

STANFORD, Adrian Timothy James; Director, Samuel Montagu & Co Limited, since 1972; Specialised Financing. *Career:* Samuel Montagu & Co Limited 1958-; Samuel Montagu & Co Limited, Company Secretary 1965-77; Samuel Montagu & Co Limited, UK Banking, Specialised Financing 1977-. *Biog: b.* 19 July 1935. *Nationality:* British. *Educ:* Rugby School; Merton College, Oxford (MA Jurisprudence); The Sherwood Foresters, 2nd Lieutenant. *Directorships:* Samuel Montagu & Co Limited and various subsidiaries 1972 (exec). *Other Activities:* Lay Member, Investigation Committee of Institute of Chartered Accountants. *Professional Organisations:* FCIS. *Clubs:* Boodle's, Brooks's. *Recreations:* Architecture, Gardening.

STANGENBERG-HAVERCAMP, Dr F; Director, Baring Brothers & Co Limited.

STANGER, Keith Burroughs; General Manager, Lloyds Bank plc, since 1990; Finance. *Career:* Bank of London and Montreal, Chief Acct 1972-76; Lloyds Bank Int (New York), Asst Mgr 1976-78; (Chicago), Mgr 1978-80; Bank of London & South America (Uruguay), Principal Mgr 1980-82; Lloyds Bank plc (Brazil), Asst Gen Mgr 1982-86; (London), General Manager Strategic Planning 1987-88; General Manager Corporate Banking & Treasury 1988-90. *Biog: b.* 17 September 1939. *Nationality:* British. *m.* 1967, Susan Margaret; 2 s. *Educ:* Leeds Grammar School; St Andrews University (MA Hons); Harvard Business School (PMD). *Directorships:* Lyfet SA 1982 (non-exec). *Professional Organisations:* Institute of Bankers. *Clubs:* Montevideo Cricket Club, Sao Paulo Country Club. *Recreations:* Fell Walking, Tennis, Orchids, Bassets.

STANIFORTH, Ms Alison; Partner, Hepworth & Chadwick, since 1990; Building/Construction Litigation. *Career:* Herbert Smith, Articled Clerk 1983-85; Assistant Solicitor 1984-85; Hepworth & Chadwick, Assistant Solicitor 1985-90. *Biog: b.* 13 December 1957. *Nationality:* British. *Educ:* University of Leeds (LLB); University of Cambridge (MLit). *Professional Organisations:* Member, Law Society. *Recreations:* Hockey, Squash, Rowing.

STANLEY, Ian George; Partner, Allen & Overy, since 1990; Corporate Finance. *Educ:* Selwyn College, University of Cambridge (MA).

STANLEY, Juanita Linda Fortuné; Investment Director, Glasgow Investment Managers Limited, since 1987. *Career:* British Gas Corp Various 1972-80; Snr Fin Analyst 1980; Murray Johnstone Ltd Various 1980-83; Fund Mgr 1983-87; Pension Mgmnt Dir 1985; Investment Dir 1987. *Biog: b.* 18 July 1951. *m.* 1982, N D Stanley; 1 s. *Educ:* Frimley & Camberley Grammar School; Exeter University (BA Hons). *Directorships:* Glasgow Investment Managers Ltd; Drummond Fund Management Ltd. *Clubs:* Western Lawn Tennis & Squash Club. *Recreations:* Piano, Squash, Tennis.

STANLEY, M; Assistant Director, J K Buckenham Limited.

STANLEY, Peter Henry Arthur; Chairman & Chief Executive Officer, Williams de Broe plc, since 1984. *Career:* Grenadier Guards, 2nd Lt 1951-53; Dixon Wilson & Co, Articled Clerk 1953-58; Qualified Acct 1958-60; Peat Marwick Mitchell (New York), Acct 1959-60; Williams de Broe Hill Chaplin & Co, Dir 1960-. *Biog: b.* 17 March 1933. *Nationality:* British. *m.* 1990, Lucy; 1 s; 1 d. *Educ:* Eton College. *Directorships:* Capital Plus Luxembourg. *Professional Organisations:* Ex Officio Member, The Intl Stock Exchange Council (Chm Accounts Cte, Dep Chm Quotations Ctee); Board Member, The Securities Assoc (Chm, Capital Adequacy Ctee). *Clubs:* White's, City of London, Queen's, Swinley Forest Golf Club. *Recreations:* Travel, Gardening, Shooting, Tennis.

STANLEY, The Hon Richard Morgan Oliver; Director, Draw Lane Transport Group plc, since 1988; Investment Management. *Career:* Metal Box plc, Dir 1958-85; UKPI, Dep Chm 1985-86. *Biog: b.* 30 April 1931. *Nationality:* British. *m.* 1956, Phyllida Mary Katherine (née Austin); 2 s; 2 d. *Educ:* Winchester College; Oxford University (MA). *Directorships:* Friends Provident 1986 (non-exec); GA Securities Ltd 1989 (non-exec); Draw Lane Transport Group plc 1989 (exec); Blackwell GT 1987 (non-exec); Midland Fox Ltd 1989 Chm; North British Bus Co 1990 Chm; Beeline Bus Co 1989 Chm. *Other Activities:* Warden, Bradfield College; Chm, Carr Gomm Society; Trustee, Disabled Living Foundation; Member of Lloyd's; Governor, Thomas Coram Foundation. *Clubs:* Boodle's.

STANNARD, Ms Jan; , Director, GCI Sterling, since 1987; Public Relations, European Communications Programmes & Information Technology. *Career:* Can Byoir & Associates Ltd, Account Manager 1979-84.

STANNERS, K C; Director, Robert Fleming Insurance Brokers Limited.

STANSBURY, Robert Irvin; Director, Hill Samuel Bank Limited.

STANTON, M J; Director, Corporate Finance, Hill Samuel Bank, since 1988; International & Corporate Taxation. *Career:* Arthur Andersen, Taxation Specialist 1975-82. *Biog: b.* 15 November 1953. *Nationality:* British. *m.* 1984, Sarah Louisa (née Fulford); 1 s. *Educ:* Lancing College; Oriel College, Oxford (MA). *Professional Organisations:* ACA. *Clubs:* Turf. *Recreations:* Skiing, Sailing, Marathon Running for Charity.

STANTON-REID, Richard Ian; Partner, Forsyte Kerman, since 1989; Corporate and Commercial Law. *Career:* Forsyte Kerman, Articled Clerk 1983-85; Assistant Solicitor 1985-88. *Biog: b.* 15 October 1957. *Nationality:* British. *m.* 1982, Alyce Louise (née Rae); 1 s; 1 d. *Educ:* Parktown Boys High School, Johannesburg, South Africa; Queen Mary College, London University (LLB Hons). *Professional Organisations:* Law Society; Institute of Taxation. *Recreations:* Golf.

STAPLE, George; Partner, Clifford Chance. *Other Activities:* Treasurer, The Law Society, 1989-.

STAPLE, William; Director, N M Rothschild & Sons Limited, since 1986; Corporate Finance. *Career:* Cazenove & Co, Executive, Corporate Finance 1973-81; N M Rothschild & Sons Limited 1982-. *Biog: b.* 28 September 1947. *Nationality:* British. 1977,Jennifer (née Walker) (diss) 1986; 1 s; 1 d. *Educ:* Haileybury. *Directorships:* Grampian Holdings plc 1984 (non-exec). *Professional Organisations:* Barrister. *Clubs:* Whites. *Recreations:* Theatre, Fishing.

STAPLES, Francis A; Director, Bradstock Blunt & Thompson Ltd.

STAPLETON, Andrew John; Controller (Advances), Yorkshire Bank plc, since 1990; Commercial Lending in East Region. *Biog: b.* 26 February 1938. *m.* 1962, Patricia Georgina (née Hill); 1 d. *Educ:* King Edward VI Grammar School, Retford. *Professional Organisations:* ACIB.

STAPLETON, N J; Finance Director, Reed International plc, since 1986. *Career:* Unilever United States Inc, Vice President of Finance 1983-86; Commercial Advisor to Unilever's Regional Director for North America 1980-83; BOCM-Silcock (UK Subsidiary of Unilever), Development Director 1978-80; Corporate Planning Manager 1975-78; Unilever, Various Roles Worldwide 1968-75. *Biog: b.* 1 November 1946. *Nationality:* British. *m.* 1982, Johanna (née Molhoek); 1 s; 1 d. *Educ:* City of London School; Fitzwilliam College, Cambridge (MA Economics First Class Honours). *Directorships:* Reed International plc 1986 (exec). *Other Activities:* Member, NEDO Committee on Industry & Finance; Member, Hundred Group (of UK Finance Directors); Chairman, Hundred Group Technical

Committee; Member, Hundred Group Main Committee. *Professional Organisations:* FCMA. *Clubs:* United Oxford & Cambridge Club (London), Navy & Military Club (London). *Recreations:* Classical Music, Opera, Gardening, Tennis.

STAPYLTON SMITH, Duncan; Partner (Conseil Juridique & Solicitor), Theodore Goddard, since 1990; Commercial Property, Tax (French Law). *Career:* Lovell, White & King (London), Articles 1981-83; Clifford Turner/Clifford Chance (Paris), Assistant Solicitor & Conseil Juridique 1983-89. *Biog: b.* 1 May 1958. *Nationality:* British/French. *Educ:* Tonbridge School; University of Leicester (LLB Hons). *Other Activities:* Chairman of the Junior Section of the Franco-British Chamber of Commerce, Paris (1989-). *Professional Organisations:* Member, The Law Society.

STARKER, Alexandre; Executive Director, Banque Paribas, since 1988; Head of Private Banking. *Career:* Office Suisse d'Expansion Commercial (Lausanne), Assistant 1972-73; Mannesmann-UHDE-JV Delegate Office (Cairo), Mgr 1973-81; Banque Paribas (Saudi Arabia) Mgr, MD Industrial Joint Ventures 1981-84; (Bahrain) Dep Gen Mgr 1985-88. *Biog: b.* 18 February 1946. *Nationality:* Swiss. *m.* 1978, Patricia. *Educ:* Jesuit School, Cairo; University of Lausanne (Doctorat). *Publications:* Des Concessions aux Concentrations Petrolieres dans les Pays du Moyen Orient. *Recreations:* Sailing, Skiing.

STARLING, David Henry; Joint Chairman, Carr Kitcat & Aitken Limited, since 1984. *Career:* Galloway & Pearson 1959-84; Ptnr 1966-84; Snr Ptnr 1982-84. *Biog: b.* 11 August 1935. *Nationality:* British. *m.* 1967, Judith Penelope (née Lindo); 1 s; 1 d. *Educ:* Eton College. *Directorships:* Le Masurier; James & Chinn Ltd 1987 (non-exec). *Professional Organisations:* Council Member, The Int Stock Exchange, 1975-79. *Clubs:* Boodle's, Royal Naval Sailing Association. *Recreations:* Sailing.

STARLING, Robert; Director, Hill Samuel Bank Ltd, since 1988; Treasury. *Career:* Essex Trustee Savings Bank, Various 1964-73; Central Trustee Savings Bank Ltd, Treasury 1973-84; Asst Treasurer 1984-85; TSB England & Wales plc, Asst Treasurer 1985-88. *Biog: b.* 26 December 1947. *Nationality:* British. *m.* 1969, Maureen (née Douglas); 1 s; 1 d. *Educ:* Erkenwald School, Barking. *Professional Organisations:* ACIB. *Clubs:* Essex County Cricket Club. *Recreations:* Sport, Music, Photography.

STARNES, Kenneth; Group Treasurer, Harrisons & Crosfield plc, since 1985; Treasury. *Career:* National Westminster Bank Ltd Clerical 1962-66; ANZ Banking Group Ltd Snr Accounts Clerk 1966-75; American Express Company Foreign Exchange Mgr 1975-84; F Int Ltd Treasury Consultant 1984-85. *Biog: b.* 20

December 1944. *m.* 1967, Helen Linda (née Ward); 1 s; 1 d. *Educ:* Varndean Grammar School, Brighton. *Other Activities:* Leader of Church Youth Club. *Professional Organisations:* ACIB, FCT. *Recreations:* Cricket, Theatre, Reading, An active family life.

STARR, Richard Knowles; Managing Director, Laurence Prust Broking Ltd.

STARR, Robert; Resident Member, Cole Corette & Abrutyn, since 1986; Legal Aspects of International Trade, Finance and Investment; including East-Westmatters. *Career:* US Government Service 1965-72; Private Law Practice 1973-. *Biog: b.* 19 November 1937. *Nationality:* American. *Educ:* Northwestern University, (Graduate Institute of Intl Studies, Geneva (Certif); University of Chicago Law School (BA, JD); University of Aix-Marseilles (Docteur en Droit). *Professional Organisations:* Mem, District of Columbia and Illinois Bars; Admitted to Practice before The US Supreme Court; ABA; IBA. *Publications:* Numerous Books and Articles on International Trade, Investment and Finance. *Clubs:* Savile.

STAVELEY, B W; Partner, Freshfields.

STAVELEY, P G; Director, County NatWest Ltd, since 1989; SE Asia - Head of Institutional Equity Sales. *Career:* Jardine Matheson & Co 1980-84; Vickers SA Costa Ltd 1985-88; County NatWest Ltd 1988-. *Biog: b.* 1957. *Nationality:* British. *m.* 1983, Judith Mary (née Allan); 1 s; 1 d. *Educ:* Durham School; St Andrew's University (MA Hons). *Directorships:* County NatWest Ltd 1989 (exec). *Recreations:* Sport, Family.

STAVELEY-TAYLOR, Miss Victoria A; Partner, Theodore Goddard, since 1987; Commercial Property.

STEAD, Jacqueline A; Partner, J K Shipton and Company.

STEADMAN, Howard Ian; Portfolio Manager, BP Pensions Services Ltd, since 1982; Investment Management, UK & Europe. *Career:* McAnally Montgomery & Co, Various to Ptnr 1966-74; BP Pensions Services Ltd 1974-. *Biog: b.* 17 December 1939. *Nationality:* British. *m.* 1969, Joy Elaine (née Fisher); 1 s; 2 d. *Educ:* Kilburn Grammar School; Jesus College, Oxford (MA). *Professional Organisations:* MSIA. *Recreations:* Bridge, Badminton, Tennis.

STEANE, C J; Director, Baring Brothers & Co Limited.

STEBBINGS, Simon Brent; Partner, Freshfields, since 1990; Litigation (Construction/Engineering Disputes). *Career:* Freshfields, Articled Clerk 1981-83; Assistant Solicitor (London) 1983-85; Assistant Solicitor (Singapore) 1986-87; Assistant Solicitor (London) 1988-

90. *Biog: b.* 31 March 1958. *Nationality:* British. *Educ:* St Albans School; Worcester College, Oxford (BA Hons); College of Law, Lancaster Gate (Final Examination of the Law Society). *Professional Organisations:* Solicitor, Supreme Court of England and Wales, 1983; Solicitor, Supreme Court of Hong Kong, 1986; Member, Singapore Institute of Arbitrators. *Clubs:* Singapore Cricket Club.

STEDMAN, D G; Managing Partner, Penningtons.

STEEDS, David William Howitt; Director, Granville & Co Ltd.

STEEL, Sir David; Director, Kleinwort Benson Group plc.

STEEL, R M; Director, Ropner Insurance Services Limited.

STEEL, Robert King; Managing Director, Goldman Sachs International Corporation, since 1976; Equity Capital Markets. *Nationality:* American. *Educ:* Duke University (BA); University of Chicago (MBA).

STEEL, Rodney; Director, SG Warburg Akroyd Rowe & Pitman Mullens Securities Ltd. *Career:* Chase Manhattan Bank NA, Vice President, Assistant General Manager, Operations & Systems 1976-88; Arthur Andersen & Co, Manager, Consulting Division 1970-76. *Biog: b.* 12 January 1946. *Nationality:* British. *m.* 1967, Sylvia Kathleen (née Lyon); 1 s. *Educ:* Magdelene College, Cambridge (MA). *Professional Organisations:* Member, British Computer Society, Chartered Engineer.

STEER, Ian; Executive Director, Samuel Montagu & Co Limited, since 1988; Specialised Finance. *Career:* Barclays Bank, Management Development Programme 1975-77; County Bank, Executive 1977-81; Samuel Montagu, Manager, Assistant Divisional Director 1981-88. *Biog: b.* 24 July 1954. *Nationality:* British. *m.* 1987, Maria (née Keane); 1 s. *Educ:* Maidstone Grammar School; Christchurch, Oxford (Chemistry). *Directorships:* Anglo Soviet Development Corporation 1989 (non-exec); Assetname 1988 (non-exec); Law 190 1989 (non-exec); Total Flag 1990 (non-exec); Samuel Montagu & Co Ltd 1988 (non-exec). *Professional Organisations:* AIB; Cert Dip A/C Fin. *Recreations:* Squash, Music, Reading, Travel.

STEERS, I S; Director, Kleinwort Benson Group plc.

STEFFENS, G; Director, Thornton Management Limited.

STEFFENS, Guenter Z; General Manager, Dresdner Bank AG.

STEGGLE, R K; Director, S G Warburg Akroyd Rowe & Pitman Mullens Securities Ltd.

STEIN, Cyril; Chairman & Managing Director, Ladbroke Group plc, since 1966.

STEIN, Keith Peter Sydney; Senior Partner in Management Consultancy Practice, Ernst & Young, since 1987; Strategic Management/Planning, Management Consultancy, Financial Management. *Career:* International Wool Secretariat Snr Operational Researcher 1968-70; Unigate Mgmnt Services Division & Food Division Snr Consultant/Ops Mgr/Div Planning/ Strategic Planning Manager 1971-76. *Biog: b.* 27 July 1945. *Nationality:* British. *m.* 1970, Linda (née Collins); 1 s; 1 d. *Educ:* Preston Manor Grammar School; Leeds University (BA); London School of Economics (MSc). *Directorships:* Renown Sportwear (Wemblex) Ltd; Wemblex Manufacturing Co Ltd; Arthur Young (Information Engineering Services) Ltd. *Professional Organisations:* FCMA, MIMC. *Clubs:* Moor Park Golf Club. *Recreations:* Sports - County, Schools & University Cricket, Soccer, Table Tennis, Golf, Skiing, Bridge.

STEINBICHLER, Alois; Deputy General Manager/ Deputy Chief Executive, Creditanstalt-Bankverein, since 1990. *Career:* Continental Bank, Vice President (Vienna, London, Zuerich) 1978-84; State Street Bank, Director (Zuerich, Switzerland) 1984-87; Creditanstalt-Bankverein, Vienna, Assistant General Manager/ International Division 1987-90. *Biog: b.* 1953. *Nationality:* Austrian. *m.* 1981, Dr Michaela. *Educ:* University for Economic & Trade Sciences, Vienna (Mag Rer Soc Oec); Kraumert Graduate School of Management, Purdue University, USA (Master of Science in Management). *Publications:* Financial Futures - An Instrument to Hedge against Interest Rate Volatility, 1982.

STEINER, Clive; Partner, Morison Stoneham, Chartered Accountants, since 1988; Corporate Fnance. *Career:* Courtaulds plc 1967-69; British Leyland Group 1969-75; Pullmaflex International Ltd 1975-78; Clive Steiner & Associates 1978-88; Profund Management 1985-88. *Biog: b.* 12 May 1943. *Nationality:* British. *m.* 1967, Rowena; 2 d. *Educ:* Highgate Public School. *Directorships:* Morison Stoneham Corporate Finance Ltd 1988 (exec); Morison Stoneham Management Consultants 1985 (exec); Financial Selection Services 1985 (non-exec). *Other Activities:* Past President, Knightsbridge Speakers Club; Honorary Treasurer, JBG Housing Society. *Professional Organisations:* Fellow, Institute of Chartered Accountants in England & Wales; Fellow, British Institute of Management; Fellow, Institute of Financial Accountants. *Recreations:* Tennis, Swimming, The Arts, Reading, Languages.

STEINFIELD, Michael Robert; Partner, Titmuss Sainer & Webb, since 1972; Head of Corporate Department, Corporate Finance. *Career:* Titmuss Sainer &

Webb, Trainee Solicitor 1968-70; Assistant Solicitor 1970-72. *Biog: b.* 3 December 1943. *Nationality:* British. *m.* 1980, Elizabeth Ann (née Watson); 2 d. *Educ:* William Ellis School; Pembroke College, Oxford (BA); College of Law (Solicitor). *Professional Organisations:* The Law Society. *Recreations:* Football, Skiing, Walking, France, Cinema, Food.

STEMP, P; Senior Executive Director, Allied Dunbar Assurance plc.

STENHAM, Anthony William Paul (Cob); Non-Executive Chairman for Europe, Bankers Trust Company, since 1986; Managing Director, Bankers Trust Company, New York, since 1986. *Career:* Price Waterhouse 1956-62; Phillip Hill Higginson Erlanger 1962-64; William Baird & Co, Dir/MD 1964-69; Unilever NV & plc, Fin Dir 1970-86; Corp Development Dir 1970-86; Unilever United States, Chm 1978-79. *Biog: b.* 28 January 1932. *Nationality:* British. m2 1983, Anne (née O'Rawe) 1 d. *Educ:* Eton College; Trinity College, Cambridge (MA). *Directorships:* Capital Radio plc 1982 (non-exec); Colonial Mutual 1987 (non-exec); Rank Organisation plc 1987 (non-exec); Rothmans International plc 1988 (non-exec); VSEL Consortium plc 1986 (non-exec); Unigate plc 1989 (non-exec); STC plc 1990 (non-exec). *Other Activities:* Board of Governors, Museum of London; Member of Court, Royal College of Art; Advisory Board, Institute of Contemporary Arts; FRCA; FRSA. *Professional Organisations:* CA. *Clubs:* Turf, White's. *Recreations:* Cinema, Modern Art, Theatre.

STENHOUSE, David Harvey; Personnel Director, Charterhouse Group, since 1987. *Career:* Hoover Ltd, Management Trainee 1968-72; National Institute of Industrial Psychology, Lecturer 1972-73; STC/ITT, Various Personnel Roles 1973-87; STC Submarine Systems Ltd, Director, Personnel & Business Planning 1980-87. *Biog: b.* 12 December 1945. *Nationality:* British. *Educ:* Dumfermline High School; Ealing College (BA Hons). *Directorships:* Charterhouse Bank Ltd 1987 (exec); Charterhouse Pensions Ltd 1987 (exec); Charterhouse Pensions Ltd 1988 (exec) Chm. *Professional Organisations:* Member, IPM National Committee on Compensation & Employment Benefits; Fellow, Institute of Personnel Management.

STENLAKE, R; Partner, Pensions (Epsom), Bacon & Woodrow.

STENNING, Michael; Director, Samuel Montagu & Co Limited.

STENSON, Roger; Management Services, Norwich Union Insurance Group, since 1987; Computer Services, Communications, Office Systems. *Career:* Westland Aircraft 1965-77; Urwick Orr & Ptnr 1970-73; Leyland Truck & Bus 1977-79; BSG Computer Services Ltd MD

1979-83; The Boots Company plc Dir, Mgmnt Services 1983-87. *Biog: b.* 6 February 1936. *Nationality:* British. *m.* 1960, Janet Elisabeth (née McCall); 2 s; 1 d. *Educ:* Mundella Grammar School, Nottingham; Keble College, Oxford (MA). *Professional Organisations:* FBCS. *Recreations:* Orienteering, Bridge, Classical Music.

STEPHEN, Alexander Moncrieff Mitchell; Director, Scottish Widows Fund & Life Assurance Society.

STEPHEN, Jeremy D; Director, Bradstock Blunt & Thompson Ltd.

STEPHENS, David V J; Director and Company Secretary, G P Eliot & Company Ltd.

STEPHENS, Mrs Fiona Jane Fitzgerald; Managing Director, Stephens Associates, since 1976; International Executive Search. *Career:* Haymarket Publishing Ltd, Manager 1970-76. *Biog: b.* 1 October 1950. *Nationality:* British; 1 s; 2 d. *Educ:* Convent of the Sacred Heart, Perthshire. *Directorships:* Stephens Consultancies Ltd Founder & Chairman; Vicky Mann & Associates; Kennedy Stephens Ltd; A & M Stephens Ltd; Wilson Stephens Ltd; Cripps Sears & Partners Ltd; G Z Stephens Inc; De Lisle Stephens Ltd. *Professional Organisations:* FECI. *Recreations:* Children.

STEPHENS, J; Director, W H Ireland Stephens & Co Ltd.

STEPHENS, Jeremy James Trevelyan; Partner, Lovell White Durrant, since 1968; Business Law. *Educ:* Downside School; Cambridge University (BA). *Professional Organisations:* Law Society; City of London Solicitors' Company. *Clubs:* Cavalry & Guards. *Recreations:* Offshore Sailing.

STEPHENS, Malcolm George; Chief Executive, Export Credits Guarantee Department, since 1987. *Career:* Commonwealth Relations Office 1953-65; Civil Service, College Dir (Economic & Social Admin) 1971-72; ECGD, Various to Principal Fin Officer 1965-82; Barclays Bank Intl, Intl Fin Dir 1982; Barclays Bank, Export Fin Dir 1983-87. *Biog: b.* 14 July 1937. *Nationality:* British. *m.* 1975, Lynette Marie (née Caffery). *Educ:* Shooters Hill Grammar School; St John's College, Oxford (BA Hons 1st). *Other Activities:* Member, Overseas Projects Board, 1985-87; British Overseas Trade Board, 1987. *Professional Organisations:* FIB; Fellow, Institute of Export. *Clubs:* Travellers'. *Recreations:* Gardening, Reading.

STEPHENS, Michael J G; Managing Director, Alexander Howden Reinsurance Brokers Limited.

STEPHENS, Philip Francis; Political Editor, Financial Times, since 1988; Politics. *Career:* Financial

Times, Economics Correspondent; Reuters, Brussels Correspondent.

STEPHENS, R G R; Partner, Jaques & Lewis.

STEPHENS, Robert D; Director, Beazer plc, since 1986; Deputy Chairman, Beazer Europe & Overseas. *Career:* G Wimpey & Co Dept 9 Luton, Senior Land Negotiator 1968-73; Taylor Woodrow Homes Ltd, Senior Land Negotiator 1973-75; Divisional Director 1975-78; Director 1978-82; Land Acquisition, UK, USA (California); Land Development Research, Far East & Australia. *Biog: b.* 10 March 1947. *Nationality:* British. *m.* 1971, Eileen (née Roberts); 2 s. *Educ:* Scarborough High School, Yorkshire; Hertfordshire College of Building. *Directorships:* Beazer plc 1986; Beazer Europe & Overseas 1989; Beazer Homes Ltd 1984; Beazer Property Ltd 1987; Beazer Properties Inc (USA) 1987; Beazer Construction 1989; Beazer National Construction 1989; Beazer Projects 1989; Beazer Property France SA 1989; Immobliaria Beazer Espania SA 1989.

STEPHENSON, Timothy Congreve; Managing Director, Stephenson Cobbold Limited, since 1987. *Career:* Welsh Guards 1959-65; Gallaher Limited 1965-79; Grafton Limited, Managing Director 1980-86. *Biog: b.* 7 March 1940. *Nationality:* British. *m.* 1980, Diana-Margaret (née Soltmann); 5 s; 2 d. *Educ:* Harrow School. *Directorships:* Stephenson Cobbold Limited 1987 (exec) MD; IED Associates Limited 1985 (non-exec); Grafton Limited 1980-86 (exec) MD; Grafton Office Products (Inc) 1982-86 (exec) Chm. *Other Activities:* Member, Industrial Tribunals (NI), 1974-79; Member, Board of Labour Relations (NI), 1976-79. *Professional Organisations:* IOD; RSA. *Clubs:* Brooks's, Beefsteak, Pratts, City of London, MCC.

STERLING, Sir Jeffrey Maurice; CBE; Chairman, The Peninsular and Oriental Steam Navigation Company, since 1983. *Career:* Paul Schweder & Co, (Stock Exchange) 1955-57; G Eberstadt & Co 1957-62; General Guarantee Corporation, Financial Director 1962-64; Gula Investments Ltd, Managing Director 1964-69; Sterling Guarantee Trust plc, Chairman 1969-85; British Airways Board, Member 1979-82; Secretary of State for Industry, Special Adviser to 1982-83; World Ort Union, Member Executive 1966-; Chairman Organisation Committee 1969-73; Ort Technical Services 1974-; British Ort, Vice President 1978-; London Celebrations Committee, Queen's Silver Jubilee, Deputy Chairman & Honorary Treasurer 1975-83; Young Vic Co, Chairman 1975-83. *Biog: b.* 27 December 1934. *Nationality:* British. *m.* 1985, Dorothy Ann (née Smith); 1 d. *Educ:* Reigate Grammar School; Preston Manor County School; Guildhall School of Music. *Directorships:* Royal Ballet School 1983 Chairman of Governors; Royal Ballet 1986 Governor; Motability 1977 Vice Chairman & Chairman of Exec; General Council of British Shipping 1990-91 President; Pall Mall Properties 1990.

Clubs: Garrick, Carlton, Hurlingham. *Recreations:* Music, Swimming, Tennis.

STERN, Charles Roger; Group Finance Director, Aegis Group plc, since 1986. *Career:* Delta Group, Australia, Managing Director 1984-86; Delta Group Industrial Services Division, Financial Director 1979-84; Delta RA Ltd, Financial Director 1976-79; Delta Group Overseas Ltd, Planning Assistant 1973-76. *Biog: b.* 16 April 1950. *Nationality:* British. *m.* Nicky; 3 s. *Educ:* Marlborough College (Scholar); Cambridge University (MA Mathematics & Operations Research Upper Second); London Business School (MSc Econ). *Directorships:* TMD Advertising Holdings plc 1989 (non-exec). *Professional Organisations:* ACMA. *Recreations:* Opera.

STERN, Dr P G; Non-Executive Director, STC plc.

STERNBERG, Nigel P; Partner (Nottingham), Evershed Wells & Hind.

STERRY, R L; Director, Field Operations, United Dominions Trust Limited, since 1990; All Retail Motor, Caravan & Home Improvement Finance Activities in Great Britain & Northern Ireland. *Career:* UDT, Manager, Administration 1983-86; Manager, Management Services, Organisation & Methods/Systems Development 1986-87; Director, Central Operations, Credit, Collection, Legal & Administration 1987-90. *Biog: b.* 7 November 1945. *Nationality:* British. *m.* 1976, Christine; 1 s. *Directorships:* United Dominions Trust Ltd 1990 (exec); Shogun Finance Ltd 1990 (exec); International Motors Finance Ltd 1990 (exec); MCL Finance Ltd 1990 (exec). *Professional Organisations:* Associate, Institute of Bankers.

STEVENS, Alan Michael; Partner, Linklaters & Paines, since 1987; International Finance. *Biog: b.* 8 April 1955. *Nationality:* British. *m.* 1987, Lynn (née Hoffinger); 1 s; 1 d. *Educ:* Malvern College; Selwyn College, Cambridge (MA Law). *Other Activities:* City of London Solicitors Company. *Professional Organisations:* Law Society. *Recreations:* Tennis, Skiing, Sailing, Water-Skiing, Reading, Music, Films, Travel.

STEVENS, Andrew Mark; City/Economics Correspondent, Press Association, since 1990; The Economy, City and Company Affairs. *Career:* Burnie Advocate, Reporter/Sub-Editor 1980-83; Northern Leader, Chief Reporter 1983; Australian Financial Review, Correspondent 1984-85. *Biog: b.* 1 March 1961. *Nationality:* Australian. *Educ:* Don College, Tasmania, Australia.

STEVENS, David Robert; The Lord Stevens of Ludgate; *Career:* Elliott Automation, Management Trainee 1959; Hill Samuel Securities 1959-68; Drayton Group 1968-74; Alexander Proudfoot Holdings (formerly City & Foreign) 1976-; Drayton Far East 1976-; English & International 1976-; Consolidated Venture (formerly Montagu Boston) 1979-; Drayton Consolidated 1980-88; Drayton, Japan 1980-; United Newspapers plc, Director 1974, Chairman 1981; Express Newspapers 1985-; MIM Britannia Ltd (formerly Montagu Investment Management Ltd), Chief Executive 1980-87; Chairman, MIM (formerly Britannia Arrow Holdings) 1989-. *Biog: b.* 26 May 1936. m1 Patricia Rose (div 1971). m2 1977, Melissa; 1 s; 1 d; m3 1990, Meriza Giori. *Educ:* Stowe School; Sidney Sussex College, Cambridge (MA Hons Econ). *Other Activities:* Chm, EDC for Civil Engineering, 1984-86. *Clubs:* White's, Sunningdale Golf. *Recreations:* Golf.

STEVENS, M T; Partner, Holman Fenwick & Willan, since 1981; Admiralty. *Career:* H F & W, Assistant Solicitor, Clerk 1973-81; Sail Training Association, Chief Officer Schooner 'Sir Winston Churchill' 1970-72; Blue Star Line, Howard Smith Ind (Sydney NSW), Deck Officer 1960-70. *Biog: b.* 30 March 1943. *Nationality:* British. *m.* 1972, Suzanne (née Page); 1 s. *Educ:* Wolverton Grammar School; School of Navigation, Warsash (Masters Foreign-going Cert). *Other Activities:* Member, Hon Company of Master Mariners; Member, Nautical Institute; Member, Warsash Association (Committee). *Professional Organisations:* Master Mariner. *Recreations:* Sailing, Walking.

STEVENS, Mrs Marie Adelaide Grizella (née Powell); Group Solicitor, Ladbroke Group plc, since 1990; Head of Group Legal Services. *Career:* Slaughter & May 1972-77; Colgate Palmolive Limited 1980-87; Ladbroke Group plc 1987-. *Biog: b.* 5 July 1950. *Nationality:* British. *m.* 1988, David Cooper; 1 s; 3 d. *Educ:* Wadhurst College; London School of Economics (LLB Hons). *Other Activities:* Member, Medico-Legal Society. *Professional Organisations:* Solicitor. *Clubs:* Belgravia Breakfast Club. *Recreations:* Opera.

STEVENS, Peter Rupert; Chief Executive, G T Management plc, since 1989. *Career:* Grieveson Grant & Co 1960-68; Laurie Milbank & Co Ptnr 1968-81; Snr Ptnr 1981-86; Chase Manhattan Gilts Ltd 1986-89. *Biog: b.* 14 May 1938. *Nationality:* British. *m.* 1963, Sarah Venetia Mary (née Hogan); 1 s; 2 d. *Educ:* Winchester College; Taft School, USA. *Directorships:* The International Stock Exchange 1988; The Securities Association Ltd 1986; GT Management plc 1989; GT Management (UK) Ltd 1989; GT Unit Managers Ltd 1989; GT Pensions Management Ltd 1989; Bank in Liechtenstein (UK) Ltd 1989; GT Chile Growth Fund 1989. *Other Activities:* The Securities Assoc Ltd (Board Member 1987-). *Professional Organisations:* The International Stock Exchange (Member of Council, 1974-87; 1988-). *Recreations:* Cricket, Tennis, Gardening, Country Pursuits.

STEVENS, Philip Martin Colin Jude; Director, Lazard Investors Limited, since 1986; Private Clients, Unit Trusts. *Career:* Military Service - The King's

Shropshire Light Infantry 1963-69; Norwich Union Life Insurance Society, Life Assurance Inspector 1969-73; Chandler Hargreaves Whittall & Co Ltd (Manager, Life Assurance & Estate Planning) 1973-76; Henderson Administration Ltd (Assistant Director then Director Henderson Financial Management Ltd) 1976-84; Hambros Bank Ltd (Director, Investment Management Services) 1984-85; Lazard Brothers & Co Ltd (Director, Lazard Investors; Director, Lazard Unit Trust Managers; Private Portfolio Manager and Director, Unit Trusts) 1986-. *Biog: b.* 1 August 1945. *Nationality:* English. *m.* 1971, Veronica Mary (née Allen); 3 s; 1 d. *Educ:* Beaumont; RMA Sandhurst. *Directorships:* Lazard Investors 1986 (exec); Lazard Unit Trust Managers 1987 (exec). *Recreations:* Sailing, Reading, Holidays for Handicapped Children.

STEVENS, Robin; Partner Corporate Finance, Moores Rowland, since 1989; Corporate Finance and Business Advisory Services. *Career:* MacIntyre Hudson, Trainee Chartered Accountant 1977-80; Longcrofts, Audit/Investigations Manager 1980-85. *Biog: b.* 27 September 1953. *Nationality:* British. *m.* Diana (née Pendleton); 3 s; 1 d. *Educ:* Chancellors School; Hatfield Polytechnic (BA Hons). *Directorships:* Moores Rowland Corporate Finance plc 1989 (non-exec); Edmorson Trustee Company Limited 1990 (non-exec). *Professional Organisations:* Associate of the Institute of Chartered Accountants (ACA). *Recreations:* Cricket, Golf, History, Music.

STEVENS, S C G; Director, MIM Limited.

STEVENSON, David D; Director, Hodgson Martin Limited.

STEVENSON, Dennis; Non-Executive Director, Pearson plc.

STEVENSON, Hugh Alexander; Group Director for Administration Information Technology, SG Warburg Group plc; Deputy Chairman & Managing Director of SG Warburg Group Ltd. *Career:* Linklaters & Paines 1964-70. *Biog: b.* 7 September 1942. *Nationality:* British. *m.* 1965, Catherine (née Peacock); 2 s; 2 d. *Educ:* Harrow; University College, Oxford (BA). *Directorships:* SG Warburg Group plc 1986 (exec); Mercury Asset Management Group plc 1987 (non-exec).

STEVENSON, J A; Chief Executive, Johnson Matthey.

STEVENSON, James Roger; Director, Building Investment Analyst, Kleinwort Benson Securities.

STEVENSON, Jane; Associate Director, GCI Sterling.

STEVENSON, Nicholas John; Managing Director, Close Brothers Ltd, since 1990; Lending, Property Development. *Career:* William & Glyns Bank Ltd, Asst Legal Adviser 1978-81; Societe Generale, Legal Adviser 1981-84. *Biog: b.* 8 January 1955. *Nationality:* British. *m.* 1979, Joanna (née Tatchell); 1 s; 1 d. *Educ:* Culford School; Trinity Hall, Cambridge (MA). *Directorships:* Close Properties Ltd 1988 (exec); Clearbrook Trust Ltd 1988 (exec). *Professional Organisations:* Barrister-at-Law (Gray's Inn). *Recreations:* Ornithology.

STEVENSON, Paul Edwin; General Manager, Union Bank of Norway, since 1987; Head of London Branch. *Career:* Chemical Bank VP 1980-84; Den Norske Creditbank plc Dir 1984-87. *Biog: b.* 1 February 1952. *Nationality:* British. *m.* 1978, Joan (née England); 2 s. *Educ:* Trent Polytechnic (BA).

STEVENSON, Paul Trevor; Finance Director, Alexanders Discount plc, since 1990; Finance, Administration, Compliance. *Career:* Williams Deacons Bank Ltd, Management Trainee 1965-68; Cater Ryder & Co Ltd, Management Trainee 1968-70; Alexanders Discount plc, Head of Securities/Settlements 1970-80; Assistant Accountant 1980-84; Chief Accountant 1984-89; Managing Director (Finance) 1990-. *Biog: b.* 28 August 1947. *Nationality:* English. *m.* 1967, Linda (née Coombs); 1 s; 2 d. *Educ:* Beal Grammar School, Ilford. *Directorships:* JTG Leasing Ltd 1988 (exec). *Professional Organisations:* Associate, Chartered Institute of Bankers. *Recreations:* Football, Tennis.

STEVENSON, R; Executive Director, Daiwa Europe Limited.

STEVENSON, Samuel; Managing Director, CS Investments Ltd, since 1983; Investment Management. *Career:* Arthur Young & Co, Ptnr 1962-69; Gartmore Investment Mgmnt Ltd, MD 1969-83. *Biog: b.* 14 March 1933. *Nationality:* British. *m.* 1986, Christine (née Galkin). *Educ:* Charterhouse School. *Directorships:* Arlington Securities Ltd 1983-89 (non-exec); Group Development Capital Trust plc 1986 (exec); The Henry Venture Fund Ltd 1983-90 (non-exec); Sapphire Petroleum plc 1981-86 (non-exec); Lloyd's Life Assurance Ltd 1973-85 (exec); Altifund plc 1978-86 (exec); English & Scottish Investors plc 1981-83 (exec). *Professional Organisations:* CA. *Clubs:* City of London, Brooks's, MCC. *Recreations:* Golf.

STEWARD, G L; Director, Hambros Bank Limited.

STEWART, Alan James; Partner, McGrigor Donald, since 1985; Corporate Finance/General Corporate. *Career:* McGrigor Donald, Asst Solicitor 1979-82; Herbert Smith, Asst Solicitor 1982-84; McGrigor Donald, Asst Solicitor 1984-85. *Biog: b.* 21 February 1957. *Nationality:* British. *m.* 1982, Fiona Janet (née Harrison); 2 s. *Educ:* Glasgow Academy; Glasgow University (LLB). *Professional Organisations:* The Law Society of Scotland.

STEWART, Alexander Donald; Partner, McGrigor Donald, since 1965; Company Law. *Career:* MacAndrew Wright & Murray, Apprentice/Asst Solicitor 1955-59; Brodie Cuthbertson & Watson, Asst Solicitor 1960-61; MacLay Murray & Spain, Asst Solicitor 1961-63; Moncrieff Warren Paterson & Co (Now McGrigor Donald), Asst Solicitor 1964; Partner, Corporate Law 1965-. *Biog: b.* 18 June 1933. *Nationality:* British. *m.* 1970, Virginia Mary (née Washington); 1 s; 5 d. *Educ:* Wellington College; Trinity College, Oxford (BA); Edinburgh University (LLB). *Directorships:* Clyde Cablevision 1983 (non-exec); Scottish Amicable Life Assurance Society 1985 (non-exec). *Other Activities:* Dep Lieutenant for County of Perth; Honorary Consul for Thailand in Scotland. *Professional Organisations:* The Law Society of Scotland, Society of Writers to the Signet. *Clubs:* Puffin's. *Recreations:* Field Sports, Winter Sports, Music.

STEWART, Andrew; Consultant (Capital Markets), BBM Associates.

STEWART, Callum John Tyndale; Director, C E Heath plc, since 1986. *Career:* Bland Welch & Co Ltd London, Executive Director 1963-72; C E Heath plc London, Director 1972-75; Fielding Group of Companies London, Director 1975-86; C E Heath plc London, Executive Director 1986-. *Biog: b.* 2 February 1945. *Nationality:* British. *m.* 1991, Anna (née Balmer). *Educ:* Wellington College. *Directorships:* C E Heath plc 1986 (exec); C E Heath (North America) Holdings 1989 Chairman; C E Heath (North America) Ltd 1989 (exec); Heath North American 1987 (exec); Reinsurance Broking Limited; C E Heath (Insurance Broking) 1989 (exec); C E Heath (Aviation Reinsurance Broking) Limited; C E Heath (Aviation) Limited 1986 (exec); Hughes Aubrey & Partners Ltd 1988 (exec); Lloyd's New York Insurance Group 1989 (exec); Cornwall & Stevens 1989 (exec); Alexander J Wayne & Associates 1990 (exec). *Recreations:* Tennis, Jogging, Antiques.

STEWART, Charles Gordon; Senior Manager, Retail Banking Division, Allied Trust Bank, since 1987; Head of Retail Banking Division, Specialising in 'Distance' Banking/Deposit Raising. *Career:* Standard Chartered Bank (Salisbury, Rhodesia), Branch Accountant, Senior Advances Officer 1965-78. *Biog: b.* 17 April 1947. *Nationality:* British. *m.* 1971, Margaret. *Educ:* Prince Edward School, Salisbury, Rhodesia; City University Business School, London (MBA). *Professional Organisations:* Associate, Institute of Bankers (SA). *Clubs:* Old Hararians. *Recreations:* Golf, Photography, Reading.

STEWART, D R J; Group Company Secretary/Director, United Biscuits(Holdings) plc, since 1972/1987; Statutory, Pensions, Legal, Employee Share

Schemes. *Career:* Scottish American Mortgage Co, Secretary 1962-65; W J Burness WS, Accountant 1965-72. *Biog: b.* 17 January 1935. *Nationality:* British. *Educ:* Edinburgh Academy; Edinburgh University (MA, LLB). *Professional Organisations:* CA (Scottish).

STEWART, David Howat; General Manager & Chief Executive, Creditanstalt-Bankverein London Branch, since 1987. *Career:* National Westminster Bank 1963-70; County NatWest Ltd, Executive Director 1970-87. *Biog: b.* 27 October 1945. *Nationality:* British. *m.* 1985, Susan Andrea (née Laing); 1 s; 2 d. *Educ:* Grangefield Grammar School, Stockton-on-Tees. *Directorships:* Industriebeteiligung BV, Amsterdam 1988 (non-exec); Austrian Schilling Bond SA, Luxembourg 1988; Semperit Industrial Products Ltd 1987; CA Industrial Finance Ltd 1987; CA Export Finance Ltd 1988; CA (London) Ltd 1988; CA Leasing Ltd 1987; Creditanstalt Investment Management Ltd 1988. *Other Activities:* Chairman, European Committee, Foreign Banks and Securities Association. *Professional Organisations:* ACIB. *Recreations:* Music, Tennis.

STEWART, Duncan A; Regional Director, Banco Real SA.

STEWART, Gordon; Partner, Simmons & Simmons, since 1985; Banking & Capital Markets. *Career:* Slaughter and May, Articled Clerk 1976-78; Asst Solicitor 1978-83; Simmons & Simmons, Asst Solicitor 1983-85. *Biog: b.* 18 April 1953. *Nationality:* British. *m.* 1982, Teresa Violet (née Henry); 2 s. *Educ:* Luton Grammar School; Van Mildert College, Durham (BA Hons). *Professional Organisations:* The Law Society.

STEWART, Gordon Colin; Partner, Allen & Overy, since 1989; Partner in the Company Commercial Dept, Specialising in Insolvency and Banking. *Career:* Cameron Markby, Articled Clerk-Ptnr 1978-88. *Biog: b.* 16 May 1956. *Nationality:* British. *m.* 1987, Fiona (née Gatchfield); 1 d. *Educ:* Hutchinsons' Boys Grammar School, Glasgow; University College, Oxford (MA). *Professional Organisations:* The Law Society; Assoc Mem, AEPPC; Insolvency Lawyers' Association. *Publications:* Administrative Receivers and Administrators, 1987. *Clubs:* Barbican Health & Fitness Centre, Royal Scottish Automobile Club. *Recreations:* Running, Golf, Chess, Bridge, Literature, Humour.

STEWART, The Rt Hon Ian; RD, MP; Chairman, The Throgmorton Trust plc, since 1990. *Career:* Seccombe Marshall and Campion Ltd 1959-60; Brown, Shipley & Co Ltd 1960-83; Director 1971-83; Victory Insurance Co Ltd (non-executive) 1976-83; MP for North Hertfordshire (formerly Hitchin) 1974-; PPS to Chancellor of the Exchequer (Sir G Howe) 1979-83; Parliamentary Under-Secretary of State for Defence Procurement 1983; Economic Secretary to the Treasury 1983-87; Ministers of State for the Armed Forces 1987-

88; Minister of State, Northern Ireland 1988-89. *Biog: b.* 10 August 1935. *m.* 1966, Deborah; 1 s; 2 d. *Educ:* Haileybury; Jesus College, Cambridge (MA, DLITT). *Directorships:* Standard Chartered plc 1990 (non-exec); Diploma plc 1990 (non-exec); Framlington Group plc 1990 (non-exec); Seccombe Marshall & Campion Holdings Ltd 1989 (non-exec); The New Throgmorton Trust (1983) plc 1990 (non-exec); The Throgmorton Dual Trust plc 1990 (non-exec); The Throgmorton Trust plc 1990 (non-exec). *Other Activities:* Trustee, Sir Halley Stewart Trust, 1978-. *Professional Organisations:* FBA; FRSE. *Publications:* The Scottish Coinage, 1955, 1967; Coinage in Tenth-Century England, 1989, with C E Blunt and C S S Lyon. *Clubs:* MCC, Hawks, Pitt (Cambridge). *Recreations:* Archaeology, Tennis.

STEWART, Ian R; Partner, Dennis Murphy, Campbell & Co.

STEWART, J M; Director, S G Warburg Akroyd Rowe & Pitman Mullens Securities Ltd.

STEWART, Malcolm de M A; Partner, MacNair Mason, since 1966; Personal Taxation, Including Underwriters Tax. *Career:* Hill Vellacott & Co, Chartered Accountants, London 1951-59; KPMG Peat Marwick, Chartered Accountants, London 1959-61; KPMG Peat Marwick, Chartered Accountants, Wellington, New Zealand 1961-63; MacNair Mason, Chartered Accountants, London 1963-. *Biog: b.* 7 November 1932. *Nationality:* British. *m.* 1962, Barbara (née Taylor); 4 d. *Educ:* Stone School. *Directorships:* PRA Plastics (and Developments) Ltd since 1977 (non-exec); PRA Aids for the Handicapped Ltd since 1977 (non-exec). *Other Activities:* Worshipful Company of Chartered Accountants in England and Wales. *Professional Organisations:* FCA - Institute of Chartered Accountants in England & Wales. *Clubs:* City of London.

STEWART, Mark; Partner, Clifford Chance.

STEWART, Mark Antony; Director, County NatWest Ltd, since 1988; Property Finance. *Career:* Chase Manhattan Bank Second VP, Property Finance 1979-86; County Natwest Dir, Property Finance 1986-87. *Biog: b.* 24 July 1956. *Nationality:* British. *m.* 1989, Fiona (nee Schemeil). *Educ:* Ratcliffe College, Leicester; London School of Economics (BSc Econ); Imperial College, London (MSc). *Directorships:* County Natwest Property Ltd since 1986 (non-exec); Stanhope County Ltd since 1990 (exec); Stanhope County St George Ltd since 1990 (exec); County NatWest Investments Ltd since 1990 (exec).

STEWART, Peter James Robert; Partner, Field Fisher Waterhouse, since 1985. *Career:* Field Fisher Waterhouse (Then Field Fisher & Martineau), Articled Clerk 1980; Solicitor 1982. *Biog: b.* 3 February 1956. *Nationality:* British. *m.* 1985, Amanda Louise (née Walker). *Educ:* Campbell College; Pembroke College, Cambridge. *Other Activities:* Member, Institute of Travel & Tourism; Member, International Forum of Travel & Tourism Advocates; Member, International Bar Association. *Professional Organisations:* Law Society. *Publications:* A Practical Guide to Package Holiday Law and Contracts, (1st Edition) 1985, (2nd Edition) 1989; Product Liability - The New Law Under The Consumer Protection Act 1987, (1st Edition) 1987, (2nd Edition) 1988. *Recreations:* Golf, Tennis.

STEWART Jr, S A; Director, Sedgwick Group plc.

STEWART-BROWN, Brian; Director & Chairman, Nicholson Stewart-Brown Ltd; Aviation Reinsurance Business. *Career:* C T Bowring & Co, Director, Aviation Division 1980-; Nicholson Stewart Wrighton, (now Nicholson Stewart-Brown Ltd, Part of Nicholson Chamberlain Colls Group), Chairman 1980-. *Biog: b.* 24 September 1946. *Nationality:* British. *m.* 1972, Veronica (née Round); 2 d. *Educ:* St Edmund's College, Old Hall Green. *Recreations:* Sailing, Reading, History, Music.

STEWART-ROBERTS, Andrew K; Vice Chairman, S G Warburg & Co Ltd.

STILLING, Peter John; Senior Professional Partner, Touche Ross & Co, since 1987; Accounting and Auditing Policy Gp of Touche Ross Intl. *Career:* Touche Ross & Co Consultant 1957-63; Audit Ptnr 1964-73; Nat Dir (Accounting & Audit) 1974-87. *Biog: b.* 8 November 1931. *Nationality:* British. *m.* 1957, Elyane. *Educ:* Bromley County Grammer School, Matriculation Exemption. *Directorships:* T.R.I. Holdings Limited 1988 (non-exec chm); T.R.I. Indemnity Limited 1985 (non-exec chm); Professional Asset Indemnity Limited 1986 (non-exec vice chm); Padua Limited 1988 (non-exec vice chm). *Other Activities:* United Kingdom Board; Member, International Accounting Standards Committee. *Professional Organisations:* FCA, ACMA. *Clubs:* City of London Club. *Recreations:* Music, Literature, Walking.

STIMPSON, K; Partner, Nabarro Nathanson.

STIRLING, James; Director, Scottish Widows Fund & Life Assurance Society.

STIRRUP, Peter; Chief Executive Officer, Universities Superannuation Scheme Ltd, since 1974. *Career:* Royal Insurance Pensions Deputy Actuary 1956-74. *Biog: b.* 8 March 1933. *Nationality:* British. *m.* 1957, Kathleen; 2 s; 1 d. *Educ:* Wade Deacon Grammar School, Widnes; Sidney Sussex College, Cambridge (MA). *Other Activities:* Chm, National Association of Pension Funds, 1989. *Professional Organisations:* FIA; FBCS; FPMI. *Clubs:* United Oxford and Cambridge University.

STOBART, Eric St Clair; Director, Hill Samuel Bank Ltd, since 1987; Corporate Finance. *Career:* Foreman Frank & Co (Lewes, Sussex) Articled Clerk 1966-70; Coopers & Lybrand (London) Audit Supervisor 1970-75; London Business School MBA Student 1975-77; Hill Samuel & Co Ltd Mgr, Intl Dept 1977-80; Hill Samuel Australia Ltd Asst Dir, Corp Finance 1980-83; Hill Samuel & Co Ltd Asst Dir, Corp Finance 1983-87. *Biog: b.* 12 September 1948. *Nationality:* British. *m.* 1979, Virginia Charlotte (née Howkins); 1 d. *Educ:* Lewes Grammar School; London Business School (MSc). *Professional Organisations:* FCA. *Clubs:* Roehampton Club. *Recreations:* Walking, Squash, Rugby.

STOBART, F J; Member of Board of Management, SG Warburg Soditic SA, since 1989; Investment Banking. *Career:* S G Warburg Group plc 1981-. *Biog: b.* 1 April 1957. *Nationality:* British/French. *Educ:* Worth Abbey; Ceram, France (Diploma in Business Administration). *Directorships:* S G Warburg & Co Ltd 1987; Bacot-Allain-Farra SA 1989 Member, Supervisory Board; SG Warburg, France SA 1988-89 Directeur Général.

STOBART, Mrs Kate Lucinda (née Fraser); Associate Director, GCI Sterling, since 1990; Financial and Corporate Public Relations Consultancy. *Career:* Freelance Consultancy, New York and London 1987-90; Lowe Bell Financial, Director (Previously Good Relations City) 1985-87; Sterling Financial, Account Director 1983-85; Charles Barker Lyons, Account Executive, (Including One Year on Secondment at Guildhall as Assistant Press Officer for the Corporation of the City of London) 1980-83. *Biog: b.* 30 December 1960. *Nationality:* British. *m.* 1987, Paul Stobart. *Educ:* St Paul's Girls School; St Michaels, Burton Park, Petworth. *Recreations:* Tennis, Golf, Skiing, Riding, Driving.

STOCKDALE, R A; Director, Skipton Building Society. *Directorships:* Yorkshire Salmon Ltd.

STOCKEN, Oliver Henry James; Chief Operations Officer & Chief Executive, Merchant Banking Division, Barclays de Zoete Wedd. *Career:* Arthur Andersen & Co 1964-68; N M Rothschild & Sons Ltd 1968-77; Dir 1972-77; Esperanza Ltd Dir 1977-79; Barclays Merchant Bank Dir 1979-81; Barclays Australia Ltd MD 1982-84; Barclays Merchant Bank MD 1984-86. *Biog: b.* 22 December 1941. *Nationality:* British. *m.* 1967, Sally (née Dishon); 2 s; 1 d. *Educ:* Felsted School; University College, Oxford (BA). *Professional Organisations:* ICA.

STOCKS, F W R; Finance Director, TSB Unit Trusts Ltd, since 1988; Finance & Investments. *Career:* TSB Trust Co Ltd, Divisional Manager, Finance 1980-88; Save & Prosper Group Ltd, Group Finance Manager 1968-80; Wm Brandt's Sons & Co, Asst Chief Accountant 1965-68; Peat Marwick Mitchell, FCA 1959-65. *Biog: b.* 28 March 1940. *Nationality:* English. *m.* 1988,

Paula (née St John Smith); 1 s; 2 d. *Educ:* Tonbridge School. *Directorships:* TSB Unit Trusts 1988 (exec). *Other Activities:* Unit Trust Association Tax Committee. *Professional Organisations:* FCA. *Clubs:* St George's Hill Golf Club, Littlestone Golf Club, St George's Hill Lawn Tennis Club, The Royal Tennis Court.

STOCKWELL, Anthony Howard; Partner, Stephenson Harwood, since 1978; Banking and Finance Law. *Career:* Stephenson Harwood, Articled Clerk 1972-74; Assistant Solicitor 1974-78; Partner 1978-. *Biog:* m. Karen (née Richardson). *Educ:* The Grammar School, Enfield; Clare College, Cambridge (BA). *Other Activities:* Liveryman, City of London Solicitors' Company; Member, City of London Law Society, Banking Law Sub-Committee; Member, City of London Law Society, Insolvency Law Sub-Committee. *Professional Organisations:* Member, Law Society; Solicitor, England and Wales; Solicitor, Hong Kong.

STOCKWELL, Tony F R; Master, Worshipful Company of Joiners and Ceilers.

STODDART, Michael Craig; Chairman, Electra Investment Trust plc, since 1986, Electra Kingsway Group 1988. *Career:* Singer & Friedlander Limited, Joint Chief Executive 1955-73; Electra Investment Trust plc, Deputy Chairman & Chief Executive 1974-86; Chairman (Executive) 1986-; Electra Kingsway Limited, Chairman (Executive) 1988-; Electra Kingsway Managers Holdings Limited, Chairman (Executive) 1988-. *Biog:* b. 27 March 1932. *Nationality:* British. *m.* 1961, (Susan) Brigid (née O'Halloran); 2 s; 2 d. *Educ:* Marlborough College. *Directorships:* Advent Capital Limited 1982 (non-exec); Advent Eurofund Limited 1982 (non-exec); BPOC Limited 1989 (non-exec) Chm; Bullough plc 1968 (non-exec); Electra Corporate Ventures Limited 1988 (non-exec) Chm; Electra Investment Trust plc 1986 (exec) Chm; Electra Kingsway Limited 1988 (exec) Chm; Electra Kingsway Managers Limited 1988 (exec) Chm; Electra Kingsway Managers Holdings Limited 1988 (exec) Chm; Electra Leisure Group 1990 (non-exec) Chm; Electra Risk Capital plc 1981 (exec) Chm; Oppenheimer & Co Inc 1975 (non-exec); Next plc 1974 (non-exec); Sphere Drake Holding plc 1987 (non-exec); The Summit Group plc 1990 (non-exec); Candover Investments plc; Charterhouse Group International Inc; Goldcrest Films International Limited; Mercantile House Holdings plc; Hepworths Limited; CT Bowring & Co Limited; Singer & Friedlander Limited. *Other Activities:* Member, Council of Business in the Community; Member, Council of Aims of Industry; Trustee, All Hallows Church; Member, Archbishop's Council for the Church Urban Fund; Member, Worshipful Company of Chartered Accountants in England and Wales. *Professional Organisations:* FCA. *Clubs:* Boodle's. *Recreations:* Country Pursuits, Shooting, Tennis, Golf, Theatre.

STODDART, Peter Laurence Bowring; Chairman, Robert Fleming Insurance Brokers Ltd, since 1983. *Career:* C T Bowring & Co Ltd; C T Bowring & Co (Insurance) Ltd; C T Bowring (Insurance) Holdings Ltd; English & American Insurance Co Ltd; Singer & Friedlander Ltd; C T Bowring (Underwriting Agencies) Ltd; C T Bowring Underwriting Holdings Ltd; Crusader Insurance Co Ltd to 1980. *Biog:* b. 24 June 1934. *Nationality:* British. *m.* 1957, Joanna (née Adams); 1 s; 2 d. *Educ:* Eton College; Trinity College, Oxford. *Directorships:* Robert Fleming Insurance Brokers Ltd 1980 (exec); Robert Fleming Marine Ltd 1982 (exec); Robert Fleming Non Marine Management Ltd 1985 (exec); Robert Fleming Insurance Brokers (UK) Ltd 1987 (exec); Fox Craig & Co Ltd 1990 (exec); Robert Fleming Fox Craig & Co Ltd 1990 (exec); Greenfriar Investment Company plc 1972 (non-exec); Fleming Mercantile Investment Trust plc 1977 (non-exec); Hunt Servants Benefit Society (non-exec). *Other Activities:* Master of Salters Company, 1986. *Clubs:* Cavalry & Guards Club, White's, MCC.

STOFFBERG, L D; Director, Gibbs Hartley Cooper Ltd.

STOKELD, J T; Director, Charterhouse Tilney.

STOKELY, Guy Robert; General Manager, Saudi International Bank, since 1987. *Career:* Manufacturers Life Insurance Co of Canada, Financial VP 1966-78; Saudi International Bank, Head of Investment 1978-81; Asst Gen Mgr 1981-87. *Biog:* b. 30 October 1943. *m.* 1968, Wendy (née Carter); 3 s; 1 d. *Educ:* Forest School; Oxford University (BA Hons). *Clubs:* RAC. *Recreations:* Golf, Windsurfing.

STONE, Chris L T; City Editor, Glasgow Herald (London Office), since 1990; General Financial Coverage. *Career:* Financial Times 1959-67; Thomson Newspapers 1967-69; United Newspapers (Dep City Editor) 1969-73; Glasgow Herald (Dep City Editor) 1973-. *Biog:* b. 7 October 1938. *Nationality:* English. *m.* 1965; 1 s; 2 d. *Educ:* Christ's Hospital.

STONE, Gilbert Seymour; Chairman, Manganese Bronze Holdings plc, since 1987. *Career:* RAF (Air Crew) to Sqn Ldr 1939-45; ICFC to Asst Gen Mgr 1945-59; Gresham Trust plc, Executive Director 1959-61; Director of Public Companies 1961-72; 1974-; DTI, Industrial Development Unit, Dir 1972-74; Manganese Bronze Holdings plc, Dir 1979-. *Biog:* b. 4 February 1915. *m.* 1941, Josephine (née Tolhurst); 1 s. *Educ:* Clifton College, Bristol. *Directorships:* Smith New Court plc 1984 (non-exec); HMC Group plc 1986 (non-exec); Babcock International Group plc 1987 (non-exec). *Professional Organisations:* FCA. *Clubs:* Garrick, Sunningdale Golf Club.

STONE, John; Deputy Chairman, Target Group plc.

STONE, Jonathan M L; Consultant, S J Berwin & Co.

STONE, Michael John Christopher; Group Chairman, ED & F Man Limited, since 1983; General Overall Responsibility for the Commodity Division. *Career:* ED & F Man Ltd, Sugar Trader 1957-62; Ptnr 1962-; Dir 1965-77; ED & F Man (Sugar) Limited, Chm 1977-83. *Biog: b.* 10 May 1936. *Nationality:* British. *m.* 1966, Louisa (née Dyson); 2 s; 1 d. *Educ:* Bradfield College, Berkshire. *Directorships:* London Sugar Futures Market 1981-84 Chm; Holco Trading Co 1984; Farr Man Inc (NY); London Fox 1986. *Other Activities:* Business in the Community; The Game Conservancy Trust (Council Member); Worshipful Co of Shipwrights (Freeman); Hon Artillery Co. *Clubs:* Brook's. *Recreations:* Shooting, Fishing, Farming, Skiing, Gardening.

STONE, Peter John; Banking Director, Close Brothers Ltd.

STONE, Richard Anthony; Head of Corporate Finance Services, Coopers & Lybrand Deloitte, since 1986; Mergers, Acquisitions, Disposals, Turnaround Recovery & Reconstruction. *Career:* Cork Gully Articled Clerk 1965-68; Outwich SA (part of Barings) Snr Mgr 1969-72; Regional Properties Ltd Fin Dir 1972-75; Coopers & Lybrand Ptnr 1982-. *Biog: b.* 3 March 1943. *Nationality:* British. *m.* 1975, Susan Joan; 2 d. *Educ:* Shrewsbury School; Emmanuel College, Cambridge (BA). *Other Activities:* Worshipful Company of Chartered Accountants; Worshipful Company of Glaziers (Member of Court of Assts). *Professional Organisations:* FCA, Insolvency Practitioners' Assoc; Institute of Directors. *Clubs:* Carlton, Ascot Race Course. *Recreations:* Golf, Opera, Ballet, Tennis.

STONE, Terence John; Partner, Ernst & Young, since 1979; Banking & Finance/Middle East Liaison. *Career:* Ham Jackson & Brown Articled Clerk 1953-59; National Service Commissioned 1959-61; Barton Mayhew Employee 1961-69; Ptnr 1969-71; Turquands Barton Mayhew Ptnr 1972-79; Ernst & Whinney/Ernst & Young 1979-89. *Biog: b.* 28 July 1937. *m.* 1960, Hazel (née Glisson); 1 s; 2 d. *Educ:* City of Bath Boys' Grammar School. *Other Activities:* Middle East Assoc (Member); Saudi British Friendly Soc (Member). *Professional Organisations:* FCA. *Clubs:* City of London, Oriental. *Recreations:* Music, Theatre, Travel.

STONEHAM, Michael Peter; Partner, Dundas & Wilson, CS, since 1987; Banking/Reconstructions and Corporate Finance. *Career:* Allen & Overy Articles 1978-80; Asst Solicitor Intl Banking and Fin 1980-84. *Biog: b.* 12 January 1955. *Nationality:* British. *m.* 1984, Helen Frances (née How); 2 s. *Educ:* Chatham House, Ramsgate; Downing College, Cambridge (Exhibitioner, BA Hons). *Other Activities:* Hon Legal Adviser to Project North East; Newcastle Youth Enterprise Centre; PNE Projects and Edinburgh Cancer Help Centre. *Professional*

Organisations: The Law Society; The Law Society of Scotland (Member of Company Law Ctee). *Publications:* North Sea Oil Financing; Taking Security, 1985 (IFLR). *Clubs:* United Oxford & Cambridge University. *Recreations:* Tennis, Hockey, Art, Autogenics, Shooting.

STONES, R J L; Partner, Lovell White Durrant, since 1987; Corporate and Securities Law. *Career:* Exeter College, Oxford, Research Lecturer in Ancient History 1972-76; Lovell White Durrant, Articled Clerk 1977-80; Assistant Solicitor 1980-87. *Biog: b.* 16 April 1948. *Nationality:* British. *m.* 1980, Elizabeth (née Madeley); 2 d. *Educ:* Glasgow Academy; Balliol College, Oxford (MA). *Other Activities:* Member, City of London Solicitors Company. *Recreations:* Cycling, Swimming, Model Railways.

STONOR, Ralph Thomas Campion George Sherman; Lord Camoys; Deputy Chairman, Barclays de Zoete Wedd Holdings Limited, since 1988. *Career:* NM Rothschild & Sons Ltd 1962; Joint Manager (set up National Provincial and Rothschild London Limited, became Rothschild Inter-Continental Bank) 1967; Rothschild Inter-Continental Bank, Managing Director, (bought by American Express in 1975 changed to Amex Bank Limited) 1969-75; Amex Bank, Chairman 1977-78; Barclays Merchant Bank Ltd, Managing Director 1978-84; Executive Vice-Chairman 1984-86; Barclays de Zoete Wedd Limited, Chief Executive 1987-88; Barclays de Zoete Wedd Holdings Limited, Deputy Chairman 1988-. *Biog: b.* 16 April 1940. *Nationality:* British. *m.* 1966, Elisabeth Mary (née Hyde Parker); 1 s; 3 d. *Educ:* Eton; Balliol College, Oxford (MA). *Directorships:* The Administrative Staff College 1989 (exec) Dir & Governor; Barclays Bank plc 1979 (exec); Barclays plc 1984 (exec); Barclays Development Capital Limited 1979 (exec) Chairman; National Provident Institution 1982 (exec). *Other Activities:* Court of Assistants, Fishmongers' Company; Member, Royal Commission on Historical Manuscripts. *Clubs:* Boodle's, Pratt's, Leander, Henley-on-Thames. *Recreations:* The Arts, Shooting.

STOR, T; Managing Director (Investment Management), MGA (UK) Ltd.

STORER, Jane; Partner (Birmingham), Evershed Wells & Hind.

STOREY, Sir Richard; Bt; Non-Executive Director, Reuters Holdings plc.

STORK, John J; UK Managing Partner, Korn/Ferry International Ltd, since 1989; UK, Middle East, Africa; Advising Clients on Top Executive Appointments. *Career:* S Simpson Ltd, Cloth Buyer 1958-60; Attwood Statistics Ltd, Client Service Executive 1960-62; D'Arcy Masius Benton & Bowles, Research Director, Subsequently International Board Director with Worldwide Client Responsibilities 1962-74; John Stork International Group, Chairman of Leading UK-Based Executive Search Gp (Merged with Korn/Ferry Intl 1988) 1974-88. *Biog: b.* 25 December 1935. *Nationality:* British. *m.* 1963, Delphine M (née Bowie); 2 s. *Educ:* Charterhouse; Leeds University (BCom Hons Textile Technology & Economics). *Directorships:* Association of Executive Search Consultants (USA) 1988-89 (non-exec) Chairman of Intl Ctee; Dryflow Ltd 1982 (non-exec); C G Bevan Associates Ltd 1978 (non-exec); EEL Pie Marine Ltd 1983 (non-exec) Chairman; Pintab Associates Ltd 1984 (non-exec) Chairman. *Clubs:* Royal Thames YC, Royal Southern YC. *Recreations:* Sailing.

STORMONTH DARLING, Sir James; Director, Scottish Widow's Fund and Life Assurance Society.

STORMONTH DARLING, Peter; Chairman, Mercury Asset Management Group plc, since 1979. *Biog: b.* 1932. 3 d. *Educ:* Winchester College; Oxford University (MA). *Directorships:* Mercury Asset Management Group plc 1969; The Orion Insurance Company plc 1987; S G Warburg Group plc 1985; Mercury International Investment Trust Ltd 1990; Mercury Selected Trust 1985; The First Hungary Fund Ltd 1989.

STOUGHTON, N M; Director, M W Marshall & Company Ltd.

STOUTZKER, Ian Isaac; Chairman, Dawnay Day International Ltd, since 1985; Corporate Finance. *Career:* Samuel Montagu & Co Ltd, Investment Research 1951-55; A Keyser & Co, Dir 1956-76. *Biog: b.* 21 January 1929. *Nationality:* British. *m.* 1958, Mercedes (née Cohen); 1 s; 1 d. *Educ:* Berkhamsted School; London School of Economics (BSc Econ); Royal College of Music (ARCM, FRCM). *Directorships:* Dawnay Day & Co 1985 (exec). *Other Activities:* Live Music Now (Chm 1980-); Musicians' Benevolent Fund (Exec Ctee 1980-); Royal College of Music (Exec Ctee 1968-). *Clubs:* Carlton. *Recreations:* Music, Cross-Country Walking.

STOW, G H; Director, Asda Group plc.

STOYE, Mrs Anne Christine (née Merillees); Partner, Clay & Partners, since 1983; Company Pension Schemes. *Biog: b.* 19 July 1953. *Nationality:* British. *m.* 1977, Simon Craig. *Educ:* Merchant Taylors' School for Girls; Newnham College, Cambridge (MA). *Other Activities:* Liveryman, Worshipful Company of Actuaries; Member, Association of Consulting Actuaries Pensions Legislation Committee; Secretary, Occupational Pension Schemes Joint Working Group, 1990-91; Member, Institute of Actuaries' Board of Examiners. *Professional Organisations:* FIA; Member, Association of Consulting Actuaries. *Recreations:* Reading, Cooking, Sewing, Skiing.

STOYE, Simon; Partner, Clay & Partners, since 1980; Actuarial Computing. *Educ:* Magdalen College School,

Oxford; Trinity College, Cambridge (MA). *Professional Organisations:* FIA. *Clubs:* Savile, Royal Ocean Racing Club.

STRACHAN, David; Partner, Hepworth & Chadwick.

STRACHAN, J R; Director, James Finlay Bank Limited.

STRACHAN, Robert Blackwood; Vice President, Leeds Permanent Building Society, since 1989. *Career:* Hargreaves Group plc, MD 1979-87. *Biog: b.* 21 February 1926. *Nationality:* British. *m.* 1952, Iris Anne (née Logan); 2 s; 2 d. *Educ:* Dumbarton Academy; Glasgow University (MA, LLB). *Directorships:* Leeds Permanent Building Society 1986 (non-exec); Property Leeds Ltd 1989 (non-exec); Ward Group plc 1988 (non-exec). *Other Activities:* UEFA. *Professional Organisations:* Solicitor & Notary Public, The Law Society of Scotland; FCIS; CBIM.

STRADLING, Graham Ivor; Director, Kleinwort Grieveson Securities, since 1987; Institutional Sales. *Career:* Grieveson Grant & Co, Ptnr 1982-86; WI Carr/Carr Sebag, Clerk 1976-82; Laurie Milbank, Clerk 1973-76. *Biog: b.* 3 April 1947. *m.* 1979, Barbara Ann (née Spooner); 2 s. *Educ:* Merchant Taylors School, Northwood. *Clubs:* Rye Golf, Royal & Ancient. *Recreations:* Golf.

STRADLING, Stuart Rhys; Head of Corporate Finance, SG Warburg Akroyd, Rowe & Pitman, Mullens, since 1976. *Career:* Smallfield, Fitzhugh, Tillett & Co, Articled Clerk 1962-67; Thornton Baker & Co, Audit Mgr 1967-68; Turquand Young & Co, Audit Mgr 1968-69. *Biog: b.* 9 August 1944. *Nationality:* British. *m.* 1969, Susan (née Whatmore); 3 s; 1 d. *Educ:* Merchant Taylors School, Northwood. *Professional Organisations:* FCA. *Recreations:* Theatre, Golf, Rugby.

STRANG, Andrew David; Managing Director, Schroder Properties Ltd, since 1988; Property Investment Management & Development. *Career:* Richard Ellis, Surveyor 1975-78; Hillier Parker May & Rowden, Snr Surveyor 1978-82; Hill Samuel Property Services Ltd, Dir, Responsible for HS Property Unit Trust 1982-88. *Biog: b.* 25 January 1953. *Nationality:* British. *m.* 1980, Miranda Caroline (née Francis); 3 s. *Educ:* Radley College; Durham University (BSc Hons). *Directorships:* Schroder Investment Management Ltd 1988 (exec). *Professional Organisations:* FRICS. *Recreations:* Sailing.

STRANG, David Ivor; Partner, Travers Smith Braithwaite, since 1988; Commercial Law, Intellectual Property Law and UK & EEC Competition Law. *Career:* Slaughter and May, Asst Solicitor 1982-86. *Biog: b.* 3 May 1956. *Nationality:* British. *m.* 1983, Anna (née Turnbull-Walker); 2 s; 1 d. *Educ:* King George V

Grammar School, Southport; New College, Oxford (BA Hons); Université d'Aix/Marseille III (DES); Institut d'Etudes Européennes, Brussels (Lic Special en Droit Européen). *Professional Organisations:* Member, The Law Society; Member, Institute of Linguists. *Recreations:* Cycling, Family Life.

STRANG, Richard William; Director, Morgan Grenfell & Co Ltd, since 1986; Corporate Finance. *Career:* Peat Marwick Mitchell 1971-77. *Biog: b.* 19 June 1950. *Nationality:* British. *m.* 1990, Victoria (née Gibson). *Educ:* Radley College; Corpus Christi College, Oxford (MA). *Directorships:* Morgan Grenfell Australia Holdings Ltd 1987 (non-exec). *Professional Organisations:* FCA. *Recreations:* Sailing, Skiing, Tennis, Bridge, Opera.

STRANG STEEL, Malcolm G; WS; Partner, W & J Burness WS, since 1973; Agricultural & Tax Law. *Career:* Davidson & Syme WS, Apprentice 1970-72; W & J Burness WS, Assistant 1972-73. *Biog: b.* 24 November 1946. *Nationality:* British. *m.* 1972, Margaret Philippa (née Scott); 1 s; 1 d. *Educ:* Eton College; Trinity College, Cambridge (BA); Edinburgh University (LLB). *Directorships:* Aysgarth School Trust Ltd 1986 (non-exec); Taymount Timeshare Nominees Ltd 1988 (non-exec). *Other Activities:* Member of Council, Law Society of Scotland, 1984-90; Member of Taxation & Law & Parliamentary Committees, Scottish Landowners Federation; Trustee, Scottish Dyslexia Trust. *Professional Organisations:* WS Society. *Clubs:* New (Edinburgh), MCC. *Recreations:* Fishing, Shooting, Skiing, Tennis, Reading.

STRANGE, John Cope; Senior Partner, Hill Osborne & Co.

STRANGER-JONES, Anthony John; Director, Barclays de Zoete Wedd Ltd, since 1986; International Investment Banking. *Career:* Rib Finance Ltd (HK), MD 1974-76; Amex Bank Ltd, Dir 1976-79; Korea Merchant Banking Corp, Dir 1979-82; Barclays Merchant Bank Ltd, Dir 1979-86. *Biog: b.* 30 December 1944. *Nationality:* British. *m.* 1976, Kazumi (née Matsuo); 1 s; 2 d. *Educ:* Westminster School; Christ Church, Oxford (MA). *Professional Organisations:* AIB. *Clubs:* MCC, Hong Kong Club.

STRATHDEE, I C; Executive Director, James R Knowles Limited.

STRATTAN, Richard Charles Weir; Partner, Clay & Partners, since 1979; Pensions & Employee Benefits. *Career:* Legal & General Assurance Pensions Actuarial Dept 1971-76. *Biog: b.* 13 March 1950. *Nationality:* British. *m.* 1973, Jane; 2 d. *Educ:* Worcester Royal Grammar School; Birmingham University (BSc Maths). *Professional Organisations:* Fellow, Institute of Actuaries. *Clubs:* Kingswood Golf Club, RAC Club, St Mellion Golf & Country Club. *Recreations:* Golf, Squash, Piano.

STRATTEN, Malcolm D; Director, Bradstock Blunt & Crawley Ltd.

STRATTON, David M; Director, Bradstock Blunt & Crawley Ltd.

STRAUSS, Derek Ronald; Chairman, Strauss, Turnbull & Co Ltd.

STREATFIELD, Peter Stopford; Partner, Freshfields.

STREDDER, P J; Director, Privatisation Advisory Unit, Barclays de Zoete Wedd Ltd, since 1989. *Career:* Department of Trade and Industry, Grade 7 1976-83; HM Treasury, Grade 7 1983-86; Policy Unit, Prime Minister's Office 1986-88; Barclays de Zoete Wedd Ltd, Assistant Director 1988-89. *Biog: b.* 5 May 1949. *Nationality:* British. *m.* 1981, Theresa Mary (née O'Donnell); 1 d. *Educ:* Kent College, Canterbury; King's College, Cambridge (BA MA); University of Warwick (PhD). *Directorships:* Barclays de Zoete Wedd Ltd 1989 (exec). *Other Activities:* Member of Committee of Management, London & Quadrant Housing Trust. *Recreations:* Family, Travel.

STREETER, K R; Director, Capability Trust Managers Limited.

STRICK, Robert C G; Clerk, Drapers' Company.

STRICKLAND, Benjamin Vincent Michael; Group Managing Director, Operations, Schroders plc, since 1983; Strategy, Finance, Information Technology. *Career:* National Service Officer (BAOR), Lt 17/21st Lancers 1959-60; Price Waterhouse, Junior Manager 1963-68; J Henry Schroder Wagg & Co Ltd, Director Corporate Finance 1974; Schroders (Australia), Chief Executive 1978-82. *Biog: b.* 20 September 1939. *Nationality:* British. *m.* 1965, Tessa Mary Edwina (née Grant); 1 s; 1 d. *Educ:* Mayfield College; University College, Oxford (MA, PPE); Harvard Business School (AMP Diploma). *Directorships:* J Henry Schroder Wagg & Co 1974 (exec); Schroders plc 1983 (exec). *Other Activities:* FRSA. *Professional Organisations:* FCA. *Publications:* Bow Group Pamphlet on Resources of the Sea with Laurance Reed, 1965; Chapter on Globalisation of Financial Services in the Financial Services Handbook, 1986. *Clubs:* Boodle's, Hurlingham. *Recreations:* Travel, Military & General History, Shooting, Theatre, Reading.

STRINGFELLOW, Richard B; Partner (Nottingham), Evershed Wells & Hind.

STRONG, Barry N; Director, Jardine Insurance Brokers Ltd, since 1981. *Professional Organisations:* ACII; FBIBA.

STRONG, Donald Malcolm David; Partner, Ince & Co, since 1970; Ship Finance and Related Corporate Matters. *Career:* F T Jones & Sons Office Junior 1960; Ince & Co Articled Clerk 1965-67; Solicitor 1967-69. *Biog: b.* 28 May 1941. *Nationality:* British. *m.* 1969, Hilary (née Wheeler); 1 d. *Educ:* Highgate School; Sidney Sussex College, Cambridge (MA/LLM). *Other Activities:* Member, City of London Law Society Shipping and Aerospace Law Sub-Ctee. *Professional Organisations:* The Law Society. *Recreations:* Music, Gardening, Cricket.

STROUD, A W; Partner, Milne Ross, since 1966; Taxation Specialist. *Career:* McNair, Mason, Evans, Articled Clerk 1948-54; Army 1954-56; West Wake Price, Accountant 1956-61; Deloitte Plender Griffiths, Tax Specialist 1961-66; Jones Ross Howell (later Milne Ross), Partner/Tax Specialist 1966-. *Biog: b.* 17 January 1931. *Nationality:* British. *Educ:* Gravesend Grammar School (Matric). *Directorships:* Milne Ross Associates 1980 (exec); Lycap Financial Consultants Limited (Jersey) 1989 (exec). *Professional Organisations:* FCA; ATII; MOI. *Publications:* The Accountant's Manual, 1990. *Clubs:* Les Ambassadeurs. *Recreations:* Running.

STROUTHOS, Andreas Nicholas; Chief Representative Officer, Bank of Crete, since 1986. *Career:* National Bank of Greece (Nicosia, Cyprus), Chief Acct 1959-66; Asst Mgr 1966-67; Mgr 1967-78; (London) Mgr 1978-85. *Biog: b.* 14 September 1929. *Nationality:* Cypriot. *m.* 1954, Helen (née Nicolaidou); 3 s. *Educ:* Pancyprian Gymnasium, Nicosia; College of Higher Education, Nicosia. *Other Activities:* Ctee Member, AGII Anargyri Church. *Clubs:* ENAD Athletic Club (Nicosia), Cyprus Philatelic Society.

STROWGER, C; Member of the Council, The International Stock Exchange.

STRUZ, Jan; Managing Director, Zivnostenska Banka, since 1990. *Career:* Zivnostenska Bank, Head Office, Prague, Manager of the International Dept 1973; Head of the International Dept; Deputy General Manager of Head Office 1979; Deputy Managing Director, London Office 1986; Managing Director 1990. *Biog: b.* 5 May 1949. *Nationality:* Czechoslovakian. *m.* 1974, Vera; 1 s; 2 d. *Educ:* Prague School of Economics, Faculty of Foreign Trade. *Professional Organisations:* Member, European Committee of Foreign Banks & Securities Houses Association.

STUBBINGS, Barry; Director, James Capel Corporate Finance Ltd, since 1987; UK Corporate Finance. *Career:* James Capel & Co, Gaining Experience in Stockbroking 1960-67; Began Specialising in Corp Fin 1967-; Snr Exec 1986-. *Biog: b.* 14 March 1943. *Nationality:* British. *Educ:* Catford Central School for Boys. *Directorships:* James Capel Corporate Finance Ltd

1987 (exec). *Professional Organisations:* Member, International Stock Exchange. *Recreations:* Travel, Walking.

STUBBINGS, J Simon; Partner, Theodore Goddard, since 1977; Taxation. *Career:* Theodore Goddard, Articled Clerk 1969-72; Solicitor 1972-77. *Biog: b.* 16 January 1945. *Nationality:* British. *m.* 1976, Joan (née Darby); 1 s; 1 d. *Educ:* Michael House, South Africa; Trinity College, University of Dublin (BA Mod). *Directorships:* Dandia Charitable Trust 1986 (non-exec). *Other Activities:* City of London Law Society, Revenue Law Committee. *Professional Organisations:* Law Society. *Recreations:* Squash, Cycling, Walking.

STUBBLEFIELD, Rodney George; Senior Partner, Gamlens, Penningtons Incorporating Gamlens, since 1989; General and Commercial Property. *Career:* Qualified as Solicitor 1961; Gamlens, Partner 1962-89; Senior Partner 1989-90; Penningtons Incorporating Gamlens, Partner 1990-. *Biog: b.* 10 October 1937. *Nationality:* British. *m.* 1967, Jenny (née Instone); 1 s; 1 d. *Educ:* Durston House, Ealing; Sutton Valence School, Kent; University College, London (LLB). *Other Activities:* President, Holborn Law Society, 1990-91; Governor, Sutton Vallence School, Kent; Conveyancing Standing Committee, Holborn Law Society (Past Chairman). *Clubs:* RAC, Wentworth. *Recreations:* Bridge, Squash, Tennis.

STUBBS, John; Director, BDO Consulting.

STUCHFIELD, N J; Director, Securities, Barclays de Zoete Wedd, since 1989; Equity Trading, IT. *Career:* Wedd Durlacher Mordaunt & Co 1981-86; Head of Arbitrage 1983-85; Partner 1985-86; Barclays de Zoete Wedd 1986-; Director, UK Equities 1986-; UK Equity Risk Manager 1986-88; Small Order Execution 1987-; Head of Equities IT 1988-. *Biog: b.* 13 January 1960. *Nationality:* British. *m.* 1986, Jill (née Pendleton). *Educ:* Forest School, London; Magdalen College, Oxford (MA). *Directorships:* British American Arts Association 1989 (non-exec); The Options & Futures Society 1985-1988 (exec) Chairman. *Other Activities:* Member, FT-SE 100 Index Future Committee (1985); Chairman, Options & Futures Examination Committee (1987-88). *Clubs:* Oxford & Cambridge. *Recreations:* Opera, Theatre.

STUDZINSKI, J; Executive Director, Morgan Stanley International.

STULZ, Viviane H; Partner, Theodore Goddard, since 1990; Commercial Company and Labour Law. *Career:* Theodore Goddard 1983-. *Biog: b.* 11 October 1950. *Nationality:* French. *Educ:* Paris University (Licence English, Maîtrise Notarial Law, Diplôme d'Etudes Appliquées Labour Law).

STUNT, C W; Partner, Allen & Overy.

STURMER, Raymond Creuzé; Director of Group Finance & Administration, W I Carr Group.

STURMEY, Martin George; Partner, Bacon & Woodrow, since 1988; Actuarial Consulting & Software Development for Life Assurance Companies. *Career:* Pearl Assurance, Mgr 1975-81; Liberty Life, Deputy Actuary 1981-84; Crown Financial Management, Asst Actuary 1984-86; Bacon & Woodrow 1986-. *Biog: b.* 30 April 1954. *Nationality:* British. *Educ:* Hitchin Boys Grammar School; Manchester University (BSc Hons 1st). *Professional Organisations:* FIA.

STURROCK, Ms Fiona; Director, Phillips & Drew Fund Management Limited.

STUTTARD, John Boothman; Director of Corporate Planning & Marketing, Coopers & Lybrand Deloitte, since 1990; Senior Corporate Finance, Support Services & Audit Partnership, since 1975; Head of Scandinavian Market Groups since 1987; UK Representative on EUROMAS, (European Mergers & Acquisitions Services Group), since 1987. *Career:* Cooper Brothers & Co Trainee Acct 1967-70; Qualified Acct 1970-75; Coopers & Lybrand Deloitte, Partner 1975-; UK Government Central Policy Review Staff,Cabinet Office Adviser 1981-83. *Biog: b.* 6 February 1945. *Nationality:* British. *m.* 1970, Lesley (née Daish); 2 s. *Educ:* Shrewsbury School; Churchill College, Cambridge (MA Hons). *Directorships:* Totteridge Manor Association. *Other Activities:* Cambridge University Appointments Board (1977-81). *Professional Organisations:* FCA. *Clubs:* Naval & Military. *Recreations:* Travel, Theatre, Squash, Old Cars, Tennis.

STYANT, Alan James; Managing Director, Tullett & Tokyo Forex Int Ltd.

STYLE, Christopher John David; Partner, Linklaters & Painnes, since 1985; Commercial Litigation. *Career:* Linklaters & Paines, Articled Clerk 1977-79; Solicitor 1979-85. *Biog: b.* 13 April 1955. *Nationality:* British. *m.* 1990, Victoria Jane Style (née Miles). *Educ:* St Bees School; Trinity Hall, Cambridge (MA Law). *Other Activities:* City of London Solicitors Company; International Bar Association; The Law Society. *Publications:* Documentary Evidence (3rd Edition), 1990. *Recreations:* Fell Walking, Climbing.

STYLES, Commander M T H; Clerk, Fruiterers' Company.

SUCHOPAR, Ladislav Vaclav; Director, Allied Dunbar Assurance plc, since 1987; Admin of Life and Pension Business, Unit Trusts & Mortgages. *Career:* Allied Dunbar, Mgmnt Services, Chief Systems Designer 1971-75; Head of Pensions Div 1975-77; Exec Dir, Data Processing Div 1978-83; Exec Dir, Developments 1983-87; Dunbar Bank MD 1983-87. *Biog: b.* 20 September 1943. *Nationality:* British. *m.* 1972, Susan Ann (née Ward); 1 s; 1 d. *Educ:* The Czech Technical University in Prague (MSc Hons 1st). *Professional Organisations:* Member, British Computer Society; Institute of Chartered Engineers; Institute of Directors. *Recreations:* Arts, Travels, Photography, Food & Wine.

SUCHY, Anthony Rudolf Sascha; Partner, Ince & Co, since 1980; Shipping Finance & Related Corporate Work. *Career:* Goodman Derrick, Articled Clerk 1968-71; R I Lewis, Asst Solicitor 1971-73; Bennett & Seigal, Asst Solicitor 1973-74; Norton Rose, Asst Solicitor 1974-77; Ince & Co, Asst Solicitor 1977-80. *Biog: b.* 16 February 1945. *Nationality:* British. *m.* 1981, Dr Gabrijela (née Kocjan). *Educ:* St Marylebone Grammar School; Leeds University (LLB). *Professional Organisations:* The Law Society. *Clubs:* Cumberland. *Recreations:* Walking, Squash, Tennis, Opera.

SUDDARDS, Roger Whitley; CBE, DL; Chairman, Yorkshire Building Society, since 1988. *Career:* Admitted as Solicitor 1952; Royal Army Service Corps, Army Legal Aid 1952-54; Last Suddards, Partner 1952-88; Hammond Suddards 1988-. *Biog: b.* 5 June 1930. *Nationality:* British. *m.* 1963, Elizabeth Anne (née Rayner); 2 d. *Educ:* Bradford Grammar School. *Directorships:* Hammond Suddards Research Ltd; Bradford Breakthrough Ltd 1988; Yorkshire Building Society 1988 Chm; Yorkshire Television Telethon Trust Ltd 1990 Chm; The Independent Broadcasting Telethon Trust Ltd 1990 Chm. *Other Activities:* Visiting Lecturer, Leeds School of Town Planning 1964-74; Planning Law Consultant to UN 1974-77; Government of Mauritius 1981-82 and 1989; Government of Nevis 1990; Former Chairman, Examinations Board ISVA; Advisory Committee for Land Commission for Yorkshire and Humberside; Former part-time Chairman of Industrial Tribunals; Secretary, Hand Knitting Association 1958-75; Working Party on Future of Bradford Churches, Chairman 1978-79; Member of Board 1969-86, Vice Chairman and Chairman, Bradford Grammar School (to 1986); Member Law Society Bye-Laws Revision Committee 1984-87; Law Society Planning Law Committee 1964-81; Chairman, Bradford Disaster Appeal Trust 1985-89; President, Bradford Law Society 1969; Legal Member, The Royal Town Planning Institute; Pro-Chancellor and Chairman of Council, Bradford University 1987-; Member of West Yorkshire Residuary Body 1986-89; Member of Committee, The National Museum of Photography Film and Television 1984-; Member, National Property Advisory Group for the National Health Service 1988-; Member, English Heritage Historic Areas Advisory Committee; Trustee, Civic Trust 1988-; Trustee, National Historical Building Crafts Institute 1989-; Trustee, The Sam Chippindale Foundation; The Butterfield Charitable Foundation; The David Hockney Charitable Foundation; The Wm Morrison Enterprise Trust. *Professional Organisations:* Law Society; The Royal Town Planning Institute; Hon

Fellow, Incorporated Society of Valuers and Auctioneers. *Publications:* Town Planning Law of West Indies, 1974; History of Bradford Law Society, 1975; Listed Buildings,1982, 2nd edition, 1988; A Lawyer's Peregrination, 1984, 2nd edition, 1987; Bradford Disaster Appeal, 1986; Articles in Journal of Planning and Environmental Law (Member of Editorial Board), and Law Society Gazette. *Clubs:* Arts, Bradford (Bradford). *Recreations:* Theatre, Music, Reading, Travel.

SUÈR, Egbertus Gerardus M; Deputy General Manager, AmRo Bank NV.

SUESS, Nigel Marcus; Director, The British Linen Bank Ltd, since 1979; Investment Banking. *Career:* N M Rothschild & Sons Ltd Asst Dir 1967-77; The British Linen Bank Ltd 1978-. *Biog: b.* 13 December 1945. *Nationality:* British. *m.* 1978, Maureen (née Ferguson); 1 d. *Educ:* Chigwell School; Gonville & Caius College, Cambridge (MA). *Directorships:* British Linen Securities Ltd 1986 (exec); Lothian Homes Ltd 1986 (non-exec); The Murrayfield plc 1982 (non-exec); Stonedale Ltd 1982 (non-exec); Hibberds Holdings Limited 1988 (non-exec). *Professional Organisations:* FCIB; FCCA. *Clubs:* Junior Mountaineering Club of Scotland. *Recreations:* Mountaineering, Chess, Ornithology.

SUGAR, Steven Charles; Partner, Frere Cholmeley, since 1981; Company Law. *Career:* Bristol University, Lecturer 1972-73; Liberal Party, Research Officer 1973-74. *Biog: b.* 2 November 1949. *Nationality:* British. *m.* 1981, Jane Ann (née Skerrett); 1 s. *Educ:* St Peter's, York; Peterhouse, Cambridge (BA); LSE (MSc Econ). *Professional Organisations:* The Law Society. *Recreations:* Resting.

SUGGETT, Gavin Robert; Executive Director, The Alliance Trust plc, since 1987; Finance Treasury Banking and Savings Subsidiaries. *Career:* Deloittes, Articled Clerk 1962-66; Weir Group, Financial Controller 1971-73; The Alliance Trust plc, Company Secretary 1973-87. *Biog: b.* 11 May 1944. *Nationality:* British. *m.* 1971, Louise (née Thomson); 1 s; 2 d. *Educ:* Felsted School; Christ's College, Cambridge (MA); London Business School (MSc). *Directorships:* The Alliance Trust plc 1987 (exec); The Second Alliance Trust plc 1987 (exec); Alliance Trust Finance Ltd 1979 MD; Alliance Trust Savings 1986 MD. *Other Activities:* Dundee University, P/T Lecturer in Finance & Computing. *Professional Organisations:* FCA (ICAE W). *Clubs:* New Club Edinburgh, Royal Perth Golf. *Recreations:* Gardening, Skiing.

SULLIVAN, Aline; Finance Reporter, Lloyd's List.

SULLIVAN, David Dimitri; Managing Director, NM Rothschild & Sons Limited, since 1988; Personnel/Administration/Finance. *Career:* Herbert Hill & Co 1959-65; Clark Battams & Co 1965-67; NM Rothschild

& Sons Limited 1967-. *Biog: b.* 19 March 1943. *Nationality:* British. *m.* 1967, Lesley June (née Berks); 1 s; 1 d. *Educ:* Mayfield College, Sussex. *Professional Organisations:* FCA, ATII. *Recreations:* Golf, Skiing.

SULLIVAN, J L; Director, Manufacturers Hanover Ltd.

SULLIVAN, Robert Sean; Senior Manager, Corporate Banking, Commerzbank AG, since 1987; Corporate Banking/Corporate Finance. *Career:* Bank of England; Grindlay Brandts; Irving Trust Co; Royal Trust Bank. *Biog: b.* 12 February 1951. *Nationality:* British. *m.* 1975, Mary (née Garvan); 3 d. *Educ:* Wallasey Grammar School; Emmanuel College, Cambridge (BA, MA). *Recreations:* Family, Walking, Gardening, Rugby.

SULTOON, Jeffrey Alan; Partner, Ashurst Morris Crisp, since 1986; Company/Securities Law. *Career:* Freshfields, Asst Solicitor 1978-81. *Biog: b.* 8 October 1953. *Nationality:* British. *m.* 1985, Vivien Caryl (née Woodbridge). *Educ:* Haberdashers' Aske's School; St Edmund Hall, Oxford (MA). *Publications:* Tolley's Company Law, 1990 (Dividends, Universal Checklist for any Transaction).

SUMMER, Julian Philip; Managing Director, Merrill Lynch International Ltd, since 1987; Head of Equity New Issues. *Career:* Ashurst Morris Crisp & Co, Solicitor 1974-77; County Bank Ltd, Asst Dir 1978-82; Swiss Bank Corporation International Ltd, Exec Dir (Canadian New Business and Privatisation Issues) 1982-87. *Biog: b.* 24 May 1952. *Nationality:* British. *m.* 1981, Julia (née Collins); 1 s; 2 d. *Educ:* Eton College; St Catherine's College, Cambridge (MA Law). *Directorships:* Merrill Lynch International Ltd 1977 (exec); Indonesia Capital Fund 1989 (non-exec); Bankok Investments Ltd 1990 (non-exec). *Other Activities:* Worshipful Company of Glovers. *Clubs:* Bucks. *Recreations:* Hunting, Skiing, Sleeping.

SUMMERFIELD, Peter William; Partner, Nabarro Nathanson, since 1988; International Litigation and International Commercial Law. *Career:* National Service (Egypt and Malta) 1952-54; Oppenheimers, Articled Clerk and Assistant Solicitor 1957-65; Oppenheimers, Partner 1965-88; Austrian Government and Embassy, Honorary UK Solicitor 1984-; Swiss Government and Embassy, Honorary UK Solicitor 1988-. *Biog: b.* 3 June 1933. *Nationality:* British. *m.* 1973, Marianne (née Granby); 2 s; 1 d. *Educ:* The Hall School, Hampstead; William Ellis School; Pembroke College, Oxford (MA Hons Jurisprudence). *Directorships:* Eagle Place Services Ltd 1990 (exec). *Other Activities:* Member, Law Society of England & Wales; Member, European Group of The Law Society; Member, International Bar Association; Member, American Bar Association; Member, British-German Jurists' Association; Member, Society of English and American Lawyers; Member, American Chamber of

Commerce (UK); Member, German Chamber of Industry & Commerce in the UK; Member, Japan Association; Member, Anglo-Austrian Society; Member, Anglo-German Society; Member, Anglo-Swiss Society; Member, Anglo-Finnish Society; Member, British-Swiss Chamber of Commerce; Member, British Chamber of Commerce in Germany; Member, Franco-British Chamber of Commerce & Industry; Member, British Chamber of Commerce in Spain; Member, Finnish-British Trade Guild; Member, Norwegian Chamber of Commerce in the UK; Member, Swedish Chamber of Commerce in the UK. *Professional Organisations:* Visiting Professor & Chairman of International Board of Advisers,; McGeorge School of Law,; University of the Pacific, California, USA; Arbitrator, International Chamber of Commerce, Paris. *Publications:* Co-Editor of Effective Dispute Resolution for the International Commercial Lawyer, 1988. *Clubs:* The Institute of Directors. *Recreations:* Tennis, Reading.

SUMMERS, Andrew; Vice President, Morgan Stanley Asset Management.

SUMMERS, David James; Director, Kleinwort Benson Securities Ltd.

SUMMERS, Dr Richard; Director, 3i plc.

SUMMERS, S B; Investment Manager, West Midlands Metropolitan Authorities Superannuation Fund. *Professional Organisations:* IFPA.

SUMMERSCALE, John Nelson; Director, Barclays de Zoete Wedd Securities, since 1986; Head of UK Research. *Career:* Coopers & Lybrand, Articled Clerk/Snr 1965-68; Market Investigations Ltd, Acct 1969-70; De Zoete & Bevan, Investment Analyst/Ptnr 1970-86. *Biog: b.* 27 July 1944. *m.* 1981, Lynda Susan (née Stewart); 2 s. *Educ:* Bryanston School; Pembroke College, Cambridge (BA). *Directorships:* Barclays de Zoete Wedd Research Ltd 1986. *Other Activities:* Treasurer of FULPAC (Fulham Parents and Children). *Professional Organisations:* FCA; ASIA. *Recreations:* Bridge, Tennis, Reading.

SUMNERS, David; Managing Director, Morgan Stanley International, since 1989; European Foreign Exchange Activities. *Career:* National Westminster Bank plc 1968-69; Australia & New Zealand Bank 1969-73; First National Bank of Chicago, Vice-President, Chief Foreign Exchange Dealer 1973-83; Morgan Stanley International 1983-. *Biog: b.* 6 March 1950. *Nationality:* British. *m.* 1990, Francine; 2 s; 1 d. *Educ:* Bexley Grammar School.

SUMSION, John W; Senior Director, Continental Bank NA, since 1988; Management Buy-Outs, Leveraged Finance & Debt Restructuring. *Career:* Chase Manhattan Bank NA (NY, London) Manager, Commer-

cial Accounts 196376. *Biog: b.* 30 October 1941. *m.* 1985, Margo (née Yearwood). *Educ:* Brigham Young University, USA (BA). *Recreations:* Hunting, Conservation.

SUNDERLAND, Frank Graham; Director, Yorkshire Bank plc, since 1988; General Manager, since 1978; Group Chief Executive. *Career:* Yorkshire Bank. *Biog: b.* 13 June 1932. *m.* 1957, Sheila (née Normanton); 2 d. *Educ:* Elland Grammar School. *Directorships:* Eden Vehicle Rentals Ltd 1987 Chm (non-exec); Yorkshire Bank Finance Ltd 1975 (non-exec); & Other Yorkshire Bank Trading Subsidiaries. *Other Activities:* Harrogate Intl Festival (Chm). *Professional Organisations:* FCIB.

SUNDERLAND, M J; Finance Director, Walker Crips Weddle Beck plc.

SUNLEY, Keith Austin; Regional Controller, Yorkshire Bank plc.

SUPRAN, Jonathan Michael; Finance Director, Argosy Asset Management plc, since 1986; Finance/Compliance. *Career:* National Research Development Corporation 1969-73; Commonwealth Development Finance Co Ltd 1973-85. *Biog: b.* 16 November 1943. *Nationality:* British. *m.* 1973, Liora (née Buksdorf); 2 d. *Educ:* Christ's College, Finchley. *Professional Organisations:* Fellow, Institute of Chartered Accountants. *Recreations:* Table Tennis, Swimming, Walking, Reading, Cinema, Music.

SURATGAR, David; Group Director, Morgan Grenfell & Co Ltd, since 1975; Government Advisory & Project Finance Services. *Career:* Sullivan & Cromwell (New York) Foreign Law Adviser 1962-64; World Bank Snr Attorney 1964-73; Surrey & Morse European Counsel 1976-85; Jones, Day, Reavis & Pogue Consultant 1987-; Georgetown University, Adjunct Professor of International Financial Law 1967-73. *Biog: b.* 23 October 1938. *Nationality:* British. *m.* 1962, Barbara Lita (née Low); 1 s; 1 d. *Educ:* Silcoates School; New College, Oxford (MA); Columbia University (MIA); Hague Academy of International Law (Cert). *Directorships:* Sifida SA (Switzerland) 1985 (non-exec); Major Projects Assoc 1987 (exec). *Other Activities:* Chm, The West India Ctee (Royal Charter Company); Trustee, Caribbean Central American Action Organisation (USA); Centre for World Development Education (Member of Council); Federal Trust for Education and Research (Member of Council); Oxford Playhouse Theatre Trust (Member of Board). *Publications:* Articles in Journals; International Financial Law (Co-Author), 2nd Ed 1984; Default and Rescheduling-Sovereign and Corporate Borrowers in Difficulty (Editor and Co-Author), 1984; Build, Own and Operate as an Approach to Third World Project Financing (Co-Author). *Clubs:* Travellers', Chelsea Arts. *Recreations:* Book Collecting, Shooting, Theatre.

SURFACE, Richard C; General Manager (Corporate Development), Sun Life Corporation plc, since 1989; Group Diversification, Corporate Strategy and Business Development. *Career:* National Life & Accident Insurance Company, Nashville Tennessee, Actuarial Assistant 1970-72; Mobil Oil Corporation, New York, Corporate Treasury Analyst 1974-77; Northwest Industries Inc, Chicago Illinois, Director Corporate Planning 1977-81; American Express Company, London/Frankfurt, Regional Vice-President (Card Strategic Planning); Division Vice-President (Business Development); Division Vice-President (Card Marketing); Division Vice-President & General Manager (Personal Financial Services) 1981-89. *Biog: b.* 16 June 1948. *Nationality:* American. *m.* 1977, Stephanie M (née Hentschel von Gilgenheimb); 2 s; 1 d. *Educ:* University of Minnesota; University of Kansas (Bachelors Degree in Mathematics); Harvard Business School (Master in Business Administration). *Recreations:* Antiquarian Books, Skiing, Opera, Theatre.

SURSOCK, R K; Chairman, Sheppards.

SUSSMAN, Steven Anthony; Director, Granville & Co Ltd, since 1988; Head of Finance & Administration Department. *Career:* Binder Hamlyn, Audit Snr 1977-81; London Brick plc, Internal Audit 1982-83; Hong Kong International Trade Finance Ltd, Gp Accountant 1983-85; Granville & Co Ltd 1985-. *Biog: b.* 16 October 1953. *Nationality:* British. *m.* 1979, Jennifer Anne (née Young); 1 s; 1 d. *Educ:* Buckhurst Hill County High; Hatfield Polytechnic (BA Hons). *Professional Organisations:* ACA. *Recreations:* Reading, Squash, Walking.

SUTCH, Andrew Lang; Partner, Stephenson Harwood, since 1984; Company/Commercial. *Biog: b.* 10 July 1952. *Nationality:* British. *m.* 1982, Shirley Anne (née Teichmann); 2 s. *Educ:* Haileybury School; Oriel College, Oxford (Literae Humaniores). *Other Activities:* City of London Solicitors' Co. *Professional Organisations:* The Law Society. *Recreations:* Territorial Army.

SUTCLIFFE, Allan; Managing Director, Group Finance, British Gas plc, since 1986. *Career:* British Rail, Graduate Trainee 1957-60; British Rail (W, E & S Regions & HQ), Various Positions in Finance 1960-70; Wales Gas Board, Chief Accountant 1970; Director of Finance 1972; British Gas West Midlands, Deputy Chairman 1980; British Gas North Thames, Deputy Chairman 1983; British Gas plc, Director 1986. *Biog: b.* 30 January 1936. *Nationality:* British. *m.* 1983, Pauline. *Educ:* Neath Grammar School; University College, London (LLB). *Professional Organisations:* FCMA, CIGasE. *Clubs:* RAC. *Recreations:* Music, Books.

SUTHERLAND, D M; Assistant General Manager, Nedperm Bank Limited.

SUTHERLAND, Donald Gilmour; Member of UK Executive, Ernst & Young, since 1988; Regional Managing Partner (South), since 1990; Financial Services. *Career:* Wm Home Cook & Coy Apprentice 1958-63; Whinney Murray Snr Acct 1963-66; (Glasgow) Snr Acct 1966-68; Partner 1968-73; Ernst & Whinney (Edinburgh) Partner 1973-; Managing Partner 1985-88; Regional Managing Partner (North) 1988-90; Regional Managing Partner (South) 1990-. *Biog: b.* 15 April 1940. *Nationality:* British. *m.* 1970, Linda (née Malone); 2 s; 1 d. *Educ:* George Watson's College, Edinburgh. *Directorships:* Murray Johnstone Ltd 1986-89 (non-exec); Murray Int Trust plc 1986-89 (non-exec); Murray Income Trust plc 1986-89 (non-exec); Murray Smaller Markets plc 1986-89 (non-exec); Standard Life Assurance Company 1990. *Other Activities:* National Trust for Scotland (Member, Exec Ctee & Council); George Watson's College (Vice-Chairman, Governing Council). *Professional Organisations:* CA. *Clubs:* New Club (Edinburgh). *Recreations:* Golf, Antique Clocks, Conservation.

SUTHERLAND, Ian M; General Manager, The Royal Bank of Scotland plc.

SUTTIE, F I; Head of Commercial Unit, Simpson Curtis, Solicitors, since 1988; Commercial Law, Intellectual Property and Joint Ventures. *Career:* Falkirk College of Technology, Senior Lecturer in Law 1976-82; Walker Morris & Coles (Leeds), Trainee Solicitor 1983-85; Simpson Curtis (Leeds), Solicitor 1985-. *Biog: b.* 8 March 1954. *Nationality:* British. *m.* 1977, Anne (née MacCallum); 2 d. *Educ:* Kirkaldy High School; University of Stirling (BA Accountancy and Business Law); University of London (LLB). *Professional Organisations:* Member, The Law Society; Member, The Society for Computers and the Law. *Publications:* Statutory Sick Pay - An Employer's Guide, 1982. *Recreations:* Swimming, Tennis.

SUTTON, D StJ; Partner, Allen & Overy.

SUTTON, Michael Philip; Director, Singer & Friedlander Ltd.

SUTTON, Paul Reginald; Executive Director & Credit Controller, FennoScandia Bank Limited, since 1987; Credit Control, Compliance, Loan Administration. *Career:* Barclays Bank Ltd, various 1960-65; The Royal Bank of Scotland, various 1965-73; Canadian Assignment 1973-75; Assistant Manager, Loans; Assistant Manager, Administration 1976-80; Assistant Manager, Loans 1980-81; Manager, Corporate Banking (Metropolitan London) 1981-84; Manager Lending (UK, Ireland & Nordic Countries) 1984. *Biog: b.* 2 April 1944. *Nationality:* British. *m.* 3 s. *Educ:* Erith Technical School; Numerous RBC and other courses and seminars. *Other Activities:* Institute of Bankers Examinations. *Rec-*

reations: Sports, especially Squash, Photography, Breeding Foreign Finches, Canaries & Budgerigars.

SUTTON, R M; Director, Brewin Dolphin & Co Ltd.

SUTTON, Robert Hiles; Partner, Macfarlanes, since 1983; Corporate and Securities Law. *Biog: b.* 19 January 1954. *Nationality:* British. *m.* 1981, Carola Jane (née Dewey); 1 s; 1 d. *Educ:* Winchester College; Magdalen College, Oxford (BA Hons 1st). *Professional Organisations:* The Law Society; IBA. *Clubs:* City of London. *Recreations:* Rackets, Poker.

SUZUKI, Shigehiro; Managing Director, Sanwa International.

SWAIN, P; Director, Bain Clarkson Limited.

SWAINSON, Eric; CBE; Director, Lloyds Bank plc.

SWAMINATHAN, D; Director, The New India Assurance Company Limited.

SWAN, F J; Chief Executive Officer, Cadbury Schweppes Australia Limited, since 1988. *Career:* Schweppes New Zealand Pty Ltd, Auckland, Chief Chemist 1964-73; Cadbury Schweppes Australia Limited, Production Manager 1973-76; Technical Services Manager 1977; Regional Manager, Drinks Division 1977-79; Appointed Director of Cadbury Schweppes Pty Ltd 1977; Marketing and Sales Director, Drinks Division 1979; Managing Director, Drinks Division 1979-88. *Biog: b.* 26 September 1940. *Nationality:* Australian. *m.* 1967, Helen Margaret; 3 s; 1 d. *Educ:* De La Salle College, Marrickville; University of New South Wales (Bachelor Degree in Science). *Directorships:* Cadbury Schweppes plc 1988-. *Other Activities:* Member, Business Council of Australia. *Professional Organisations:* Fellow, Australian Institute of Company Directors. *Recreations:* Tennis, Reading.

SWANN, Andrew Blyth; Director, Baring Brothers & Co Ltd, since 1989; Banking and Capital Markets. *Biog: b.* 27 October 1952. *Nationality:* British. *m.* 1980, Wendy (née Benning); 1 s; 2 d. *Educ:* George Heriots School/Dr Challoner's School; Pembroke College, Cambridge (MA). *Recreations:* Swimming, Hill Walking.

SWANN, William Frederick Cecil; Partnership Secretary, Cyril Sweett & Partners, since 1980; Finance/Secretarial. *Biog: b.* 13 June 1939. *Nationality:* British. *Educ:* Midhurst G S; Trinity College, Oxford (MA). *Professional Organisations:* FCA.

SWANNELL, Robert William Ashburnham; Director, J Henry Schroder Wagg & Co Ltd, since 1985; Corporate Finance. *Career:* Peat Marwick Mitchell 1969-73; Bar Exams/Pupilage 1975-77; J Henry Schroder Wagg & Co Asst Dir 1977-83; United Gulf Ltd Dir 1983-84; J Henry Schroder Wagg & Co Dir 1985-. *Biog: b.* 18 November 1950. *m.* 1982, Patricia Ann (née Ward); 1 s; 1 d. *Educ:* Rugby School. *Directorships:* Property Intelligence Ltd 1984 (non-exec). *Professional Organisations:* FCA; Barrister at Law (Lincolns Inn).

SWANSON, Magnus Paton; Partner, Maclay Murray & Spens, since 1987; Corporate and International Law. *Career:* Maclay Murray & Spens, Asst 1982-85; Paul Weiss Rifkind Wharton & Garrison (New York), Foreign Attorney 1986-87. *Biog: b.* 25 April 1958. *m.* 1984, Alayne Elizabeth (née Lawrie); 1 s. *Educ:* Thurso High School; The Edinburgh Academy; Edinburgh University (LLB Hons). *Professional Organisations:* The Law Society of Scotland. *Publications:* Aircraft Finance - Registration, Security & Enforcement (Scottish Chapter), 1989. *Clubs:* Royal Scottish Automobile Club. *Recreations:* Golf, Skiing.

SWASH, Peter Charles; Partner, Pannell Kerr Forster, since 1988; Technical: Corporate Tax Planning, Tax Planning for International groups, Insurance Tax, Industries Insurance, Building Materials, Hotels. *Career:* Hugill & Co, Articled Clerk 1972-77; Deloitte Haskins & Sells, Tax Senior 1977-80. *Biog: b.* 26 November 1953. *Nationality:* British. *m.* 1978, Paulene; 2 s; 1 d. *Educ:* Parmiters, London. *Professional Organisations:* ICAEW; FCA; ATII.

SWATMAN, Philip Hilary; Director, N M Rothschild & Sons Limited, since 1988; Corporate Finance. *Career:* KPMG Peat Marwick McClintock 1971-77; National Enterprise Board 1977-79; N M Rothschild & Sons Limited 1979-87; Chase Property Holdings plc 1987-88. *Biog: b.* 1 December 1949. *Nationality:* British. *m.* 1972, Rosemary Anne (née Cox); 1 s; 2 d. *Educ:* St Edwards School, Oxford; Christ Church, Oxford (PPE Hons). *Professional Organisations:* Fellow, Institute of Chartered Accountants. *Recreations:* Sailing, Squash, Opera, Theatre.

SWAYNE, Thompson M; Area Executive, Chase Manhattan Bank NA, since 1990; Global Bank Operations in Europe, Africa & Middle East. *Career:* Chase (New York), Credit Training 1976-77; Financial Analysis 1977-78; Relationship Manager, Consumer Good Division 1978-81; Capital Goods Team, Divisional Executive 1981-86; Diversified Industries, Component Executive 1986-87; Structured Finance Component, Senior Vice President 1987-88; Chase Investment Bank Ltd (London), Senior Vice President & Corporate Finance Product Executive, Europe 1988-90; EAME, Area Executive 1990-. *Biog: b.* 28 January 1951. *Nationality:* American. *m.* Susie (née Sumner); 2 s; 1 d. *Educ:* Ripon College, USA (BA Economics). *Directorships:* Chase Investment Bank Limited 1988 Snr MD. *Clubs:* Overseas Bankers'. *Recreations:* Golf.

SWEENEY, K; Partner, McGrigor Donald.

SWEETING, Malcolm John; Partner, Clifford Chance, since 1990; Banking and International Finance. *Other Activities:* City of London Solicitor's Company. *Professional Organisations:* Law Society.

SWEETLAND, Brian William; General Manager (Professional Services), Friends' Provident Life Office, since 1989; Secretariat, Legal, Human Resources, Personnel, Compliance, Internal Audit, Office Services. *Career:* South Eastern Gas Board Trainee Solicitor 1967-72; Lawrance Messer & Co Solicitors, Asst Solicitor 1972-74; Friends' Provident Life Office 1974-; Asst Solicitor 1974-77; Asst Mgr, Legal Dept 1977-78; Mgr, Legal Dept 1978-80; Office Solicitor 1980-83; Solicitor & Secretary 1983-87; AGM (Legal & Secretarial) 1987-89; General Manager (Professional Services) 1989-. *Biog:* b. 18 April 1945. *Nationality:* British. *m.* 1972, Jenifer Ann (née Sendall); 1 s; 1 d. *Educ:* Cathays High School; Cardiff & Glyn Grammar School, Epsom; London School of Economics (LLB Hons). *Professional Organisations:* The Law Society. *Recreations:* Theatre, Sport.

SWIFT, Robert; Partner, Linklaters & Paines, since 1975; Head of Intellectual Property Department. *Career:* EMI Ltd Solicitor, Patent Dept 1967-71; Linklaters & Paines Solicitor 1971-74; White & Case (New York) Seconded 1974. *Biog:* b. 13 August 1941. *Nationality:* British/American. *m.* 1963, Hilary (née Casson); 2 s; 1 d. *Educ:* John Marshall High School, (LA LSE LLB). *Other Activities:* Vice Chm, City of London Law Society Intellectual Property Sub-Ctee; Mem, Jt Bar-Law Society Working Party on Intellectual Property. *Professional Organisations:* Member, Law Society; Member, City of London Solicitors' Company; Member, Patent Solicitors' Association. *Publications:* Occasional articles. *Recreations:* Books, Music, Walking, A Bit of Gentle Squash.

SWINBURNE-JOHNSON, A R; General Manager, London and Manchester Group plc.

SWINGLEHURST, John James Hutton; Director, Sedgwick Group plc, since 1979; Group Development. *Career:* Price Forbes 1949-53; C T Bowring 1953-57; Sedgwick Group 1957-. *Biog:* b. 27 December 1931. *Nationality:* British. *m.* 1964, Patrice (née Philippe-Bowen); 1 s. *Educ:* St Bees School. *Directorships:* Sedgwick Ltd 1986 (exec); Sedgwick Overseas Investments Ltd 1975; Sedgwick Group (Africa) Ltd 1982. *Other Activities:* Lloyd's of London. *Recreations:* Tennis, Swimming, Skiing, Music.

SWINGLER, Peter John; Director, Barclays de Zoete Wedd Ltd, since 1986; Treasury. *Career:* Midland Bank Principal Sterling Dealer 1959-79; Barclays Merchant Bank Asst Dir 1979-86; Barclays de Zoete Wedd Ltd Dir 1986. *Biog:* b. 6 January 1936. *m.* 1960, Anthea Elizabeth (née Rossiter); 1 s; 1 d. *Educ:* Trinity Grammar School, Wood Green. *Directorships:* Barclays de Zoete Wedd Futures Ltd 1986 (non-exec).

SWINSON, Christopher; Partner, BDO Binder Hamlyn, since 1981; National Managing Partner. *Career:* Price Waterhouse Mgr 1970-78; Binder Hamlyn Snr Mgr 1979-81. *Biog:* b. 27 January 1948. *m.* 1972, Christine (née Hallam); 1 s. *Educ:* Wadham College, Oxford (MA). *Other Activities:* Navy Records Society (Hon Treasurer). *Professional Organisations:* FCA (Member of Council); Member, Management Committee; Chairman, Financial Reporting and Auditing Group. *Publications:* Companies Act 1989, published 1990. *Clubs:* Athenaeum. *Recreations:* Collecting Books on Naval history.

SWIRE, Rhoderick Martin; Managing Director, G T Venture Management Holdings Ltd. *Directorships:* Baronsmead Venture Capital plc 1985; Elite Wines Ltd 1990; GT Land Colorado Inc (Formerly GT Land Inc) 1982; GT Venture Investment Company plc 1987; GT Venture Management Holdings Ltd 1988; GT Venture Management Inc 1988; GT Venture Management Ltd (Formerly GT Special Developments Ltd) 1988; Vicarage Holdings Limited 1989; Allen House Finance Limited -1988; Aurora Products Corporation (Liquidated) 1981; Blackwell GT plc -1988; Blackwell GT Property Enterprises plc 1986; Drive Glare Ltd -1987; GT Land Ltd 1987-89; GT Management (UK) Limited 1982-86; GT Management plc 1987-88; Santa Elena Ltda -1987; The London Docklands Finance Co Ltd -1989.

SYKES, A; Non-Executive Director, Willis Corroon plc.

SYKES, Andrew Francis; Director, J Henry Schroder Wagg & Co Ltd, since 1987; Treasury, FX and Swaps. *Career:* J Henry Schroder Wagg & Co Ltd, Banking Div 1978-83; Treasury 1983-90. *Biog:* b. 24 July 1957. *Nationality:* British. *m.* 1987, Laura Jane (née Stephenson); 1 d. *Educ:* Winchester College; Christ Church College, Oxford (MA).

SYKES, David; Senior Partner, Hepworth & Chadwick.

SYKES, Gerard; Partner, Grant Thornton.

SYKES, Mrs Patricia Anne (née Soames); Partner, Field Fisher Waterhouse, since 1979; Private Client Department. *Career:* Field Fisher & Martineau, Articled, Assistant Solicitor 1972-79. *Biog:* b. 27 August 1952. *Nationality:* British. *m.* 1974, Timothy R; 1 s. *Educ:* St Mary's School, Calne, Wiltshire. *Other Activities:* Freeman, City of London Solicitors Company. *Professional Organisations:* Solicitor. *Recreations:* Fishing, Gardening.

SYKES, Richard Hugh; Partner, Allen & Overy.

SYMECKO, Daniel E; Senior Vice President, Morgan Guaranty Trust Company of New York, since 1985; Financial Director. *Career:* Marine Midland Bank, VP

1969-77; Morgan Guaranty Trust Company, VP 1977-85. *Biog: b.* 31 July 1946. *Nationality:* American. *m.* 1969, Barbara (née Eaton); 2 d. *Educ:* Fordham University (BS).

SYMES, J; Administration Director, Wardley Investment Services International Limited.

SYMES, Tom; Partner, Nabarro Nathanson, since 1986; Commercial Property & Environmental Law. *Biog: b.* 15 May 1956. *Nationality:* British. *m.* 1984, Elizabeth (née Noakes); 1 d. *Educ:* Ampleforth College, York; Reading University (LLB). *Other Activities:* Committee Member, Land Aid Charitable Trust Limited. *Professional Organisations:* Law Society. *Recreations:* Skiing, Mountaineering.

SYMINGTON, C H; Director, S G Warburg Akroyd Rowe & Pitman Mullens Securities Ltd.

SYMONDS, P G; Investment Manager, Candover Investments plc, since 1983. *Career:* KPMG Peat, Marwick Mclintock, Articled Clerk 1973-76; Qualified Accountant/Audit Senior 1976-79; Supervising Senior 1979-81; Assistant Manager 1981-83. *Biog: b.* 11 September 1951. *Nationality:* British. *m.* 1975, Gillian Ann (née Spooner). *Educ:* Dartford Grammar School; Bristol University (1st Class Hons, Mathematics/Physics). *Directorships:* Builders Mate Ltd 1984 (non-exec); Swan Hunter Ltd 1986 (non-exec). *Professional Organisations:* Fellow, Institute of Chartered Accountants in England & Wales. *Recreations:* Gardening, Listening to Music, Swimming.

SZPIRO, George; Chairman, Wintrust Securities Ltd, since 1970. *Biog: b.* 1906. *m.* 1940, Halina (née Milstein); 1 s. *Educ:* Russian School, Danzig; Liège University, Belgium (MCom). *Recreations:* Study of Languages, Art, Literature.

SZPIRO, Richard David; Managing Director, Wintrust plc.

T

TABAKSBLAT, M; Director, Unilever plc.

TABERNER, Neil; Partner In Charge of National Human Resources, Coopers & Lybrand Deloitte, since 1988; General Practice Partner in charge of all personnel and training matters in the firm; Senior Partner for a number of listed companies including Maxwell Communication Corporation and Rothmans International. *Career:* Coopers & Lybrand 1966; Coopers & Lybrand, Partner 1977-. *Biog: b.* 5 April 1944. *Nationality:* British. *m.* 1969, Angela Jane (née Barren); 3 s. *Professional Organisations:* FCA; ATII. *Clubs:* MCC, Hawks, Roehampton, Richmond Rugby. *Recreations:* Golf, Rugger, Cricket.

TADIELLO, Derek C; Partner, Wilde Sapte.

TAFFINDER, Dr Paul; Executive Director, BDO Consulting, since 1990; Organization Development and Human Resources. *Career:* Anglo-American Corporation, South Africa, Personnel Officer, Responsible for Personnel Policies and Procedures 1983; National Institute for Personnel Research, Johannesburg, South Africa, Psychologist, Responsible for Research into Organizational Functioning and Consulting Work to Companies, Regarding Human Resources Issues, Particularly Organizational Change 1983-87; PA Consulting Group (Human Resources) London, Manager and Consultant Responsible for Consultancy Assignments in Business Psychology, Assessment and Selection and Management Development 1987-90; BDO Consulting, London, Director 1990-. *Biog: b.* 24 November 1960. *Nationality:* British. *m.* 1988, Mandy. *Educ:* St Davids College (Marist Brothers); University of the Witwatersrand (BA Hons, MA Psychology, PhD Psychology). *Directorships:* BDO Consulting 1990 (exec). *Professional Organisations:* Member, The British Psychological Society; Chartered Psychologist. *Publications:* The Nominal Group Technique in Management Training (with C Viedge), 1987, in Industrial and Commercial Training (Vol 19)'. *Recreations:* Writing.

TAGAYA, Tadayuki; General Manager, The Chuo Trust & Banking Co Ltd, since 1989; General Banking Business. *Career:* The Chuo Trust & Banking Co Ltd, Deputy General Manager, New York Branch 1981-82; Deputy General Manager, International Dept 1983-88; Chuo Trust International, Managing Director 1988-89; The Chuo Trust & Banking Co Ltd, General Manager, London Branch 1989-. *Biog: b.* 8 March 1942. *National-*

ity: Japanese. *m.* 1969, Fumiko (née Obata). *Educ:* Keio Gijuku University (BA).

TAGG, D E; Chief Executive Retailing & Property, Grand Metropolitan plc.

TAHANY, J; EEC Development Executive, Macey Williams Insurance Services Ltd.

TAIT, Brian Clayton; Director, Dunedin Fund Managers Limited, since 1985; Investment Management, UK. *Career:* Robertson & Maxton Graham CA Apprentice 1960-66; Uniroyal Internal Auditor 1966-67; Christian Salvesen Investment Mgr 1967-71; First Scottish American Trust Investment Mgr 1971-85. *Biog: b.* 1942. *Nationality:* British. *m.* 1966, Kathleen (née Christie); 1 s; 2 d. *Educ:* Sedbergh School. *Professional Organisations:* CA.

TAJIMA, H; Managing Director & Company Secretary, Yamaichi International (Europe) Limited. *Nationality:* Japanese.

TAKAGI, Michio; Managing Director, Norinchukin International Ltd, since 1988. *Career:* Norinchukin Bank, Gen Mgr Intl Capital Markets 1987-88. *Biog: b.* 5 July 1940. *Nationality:* Japanese. *m.* 1966, Reiko; 1 s; 1 d. *Educ:* Kyoto University.

TAKAGISHI, S; Executive Director, Daiwa Europe Limited.

TAKAHASHI, T; Deputy Managing Director, Nippon Credit International Limited.

TAKAYAMA, Teruji; Managing Director, Marusan Europe Ltd, since 1986; General. *Career:* Marusan Securities Co Ltd, Sales Dept Mgr, Various Divs and Branches incl Private & Corp Div 1960-85; (London Representative Office) Chief Rep 1985-86. *Biog: b.* 11 June 1935. *Nationality:* Japanese. *m.* 1961, Tomiko (née Sanehisa). *Educ:* Shudo High School, Horishima, Japan; Chuo University, Japan (BA). *Professional Organisations:* Mem, AIBD; TSA. *Recreations:* Golf, Music.

TAKEMOTO, Yoshiyuki; President & Chief Operating Officer, Daiwa Europe Limited, since 1989. *Career:* Daiwa Securities Co Ltd, Nagoya, Salesman 1968-72; Daiwa Securities, Tokyo International Sales 1972; Daiwa Europe NV, Amsterdam, Assistant Mgr 1972-75; Daiwa Securities (HK) Ltd, Manager 1975-80; Daiwa

Europe Limited, London Associate Dir 1980-85; Daiwa Securities Co Ltd, Tokyo, Dep Gen Mgr 1985-87; Daiwa Securities (HK) Ltd, Managing Dir 1987-89; Daiwa Europe Ltd, London, President & Chief Operating Officer 1989-. *Biog: b.* 3 July 1945. *Nationality:* Japanese. *m.* 1972, Kazumi (née Sekiguchi); 2 d. *Educ:* Waseda University (BA Law). *Clubs:* Camberley Heath Golf Club. *Recreations:* Golf.

TAKEMURA, Wataru; Managing Director, Okasan International (Europe) Ltd, since 1989. *Career:* Okasan (Switzerland) Finance Ltd, Managing Director 1986-89. *Biog: b.* 10 May 1948. *Nationality:* Japanese. *m.* 1973, Kumiko; 1 s; 1 d. *Educ:* Rikkyo University (BA). *Directorships:* Okasan International (Europe) Ltd 1989 (non-exec). *Other Activities:* Member of Palmerston, Kai; Ichimoku-kai Member/Nigetsu-kai Member; Member, Japanese Chamber of Commerce & Industry. *Recreations:* Golf, Skiing.

TAKENAKA, Shigeo; Company Secretary, Tokyo Securities Co (Europe) Ltd, since 1987; General Affairs. *Career:* Tokyo Securities Co Ltd (Nagoya), Sales Dept 1983-84; (Tokyo), Admin Dept 1984-85; (Tokyo), Intl Dept 1985-86; Tokyo Securities Co (Europe) Ltd 1986-. *Biog: b.* 13 August 1960. *Nationality:* Japanese. *Educ:* Meiji University (Bachelor of Law).

TAKETANI, Junichirou; Executive Director, Yamaichi International (Europe) Limited, since 1988; Capital Markets, Derivatives, New Products. *Career:* Sanyo Electric Co Ltd (Overseas Div), Legal Dept, in charge of a US anti-trust litigation 1977-83; Yamaichi Securities Co Ltd, International Finance Dept/Syndicate Dept 1983-86; Yamaichi International (Europe) Ltd 1986-. *Biog: b.* 27 November 1950. *Nationality:* Japanese. *Educ:* University of Tokyo (LLB). *Recreations:* Music.

TAKEUCHI, Isao; General Manager, The Sumitomo Trust & Banking Co Ltd, since 1989. *Career:* Sumitomo Trust & Banking Co Ltd Dep Gen Mgr 1985-87; Sumitomo Trust International Ltd, Managing Director 1987-89. *Biog: b.* 30 March 1945. *m.* 1973, Junko; 1 s; 1 d. *Educ:* Keio High School; Keio University. *Clubs:* Finchley Manor Tennis Club, Woburn Golf and Country Club. *Recreations:* Tennis, Skiing.

TAKEUCHI, Yoshiyuki; Executive Director, Svenska International plc.

TALBOT, John Andrew; Partner, Head of UK Corporate Recovery Practice, Arthur Andersen & Co, since 1983. *Biog: b.* 2 August 1949. *m.* Jennifer; 1 s; 3 d. *Professional Organisations:* FCA.

TALBOT, Paul Darius; Managing Director, Brown Shipley Unit Trust Managers Ltd.

TALEV, George V; Vice President, Manufacturers Hanover Trust Co.

TAME, Leonie; Research/Financial Journalist, The Mail On Sunday.

TAMPIN, M P; Director (UK Capitals), Hoare Govett Investment Research Limited.

TANAKA, Hideaki; Resident Partner, Hamada & Matsumoto.

TANAKA, Kunihiko; Managing Director, Administration and Company Secretary, The Nikko Securities Co (Europe) Ltd, since 1988; Administration (Personnel, Corporate Communications, Data Processing, Compliance, Company Secretarial, Finance/Accounting. *Career:* The Nikko Securities Co Ltd (Tokyo), Personnel Officer 1971-85; General Manager (Personnel) 1985-88; Managing Director (Aministration), Company Secretary, Member of the Board 1988-. *Biog: b.* 6 January 1947. *Nationality:* Japanese. *m.* 1971, Noriko (née Ozeki); 1 d. *Educ:* Waseda University, Tokyo, Japan (Bachelor of Laws). *Directorships:* The Nikko Securities Co (Europe) Ltd 1988 (exec). *Recreations:* Classical Music, Golf.

TANAKA, Tsukasa; Deputy Managing Director, Nomura Bank International plc.

TANAMURA, Harutoshi; Executive Director, Nikko Securities Co (Europe) Ltd.

TANDY, David; Partner, Titmuss Sainer & Webb, since 1976; Head of Private Client Department. *Career:* Inland Revenue, Estate Duty Office 1967-73; Titmuss Sainer & Webb, Articles 1973-75; Admitted 1975; Assistant Solicitor 1975-76; Partner 1976. *Biog: b.* 25 June 1944. *Nationality:* British. *m.* 1967, Catherine (née Jaggs); 2 d. *Educ:* Bexley Grammar; University of London (External LLB); City of London College (Diploma in Civil Law). *Other Activities:* City of London Solicitors' Company. *Recreations:* Shooting.

TANG, Stephen; Treasury Manager, The Bank of East Asia Ltd.

TANNER, Stephen Lesley; Director, Kleinwort Benson Investment Management Ltd, since 1986; Head, Institutional Fund Management, 1986-88, Compliance Director, 1988-. *Career:* Grieveson Grant & Co, Ptnr 1968-86. *Biog: b.* 11 March 1936. *Nationality:* British. *m.* 1959, Caroline (née Leggatt); 1 s; 2 d. *Educ:* Marlborough College; Trinity College, Oxford. *Directorships:* Transatlantic Ventures NV 1988 (non-exec). *Other Activities:* Mem, Regulation & Taxation Ctee, IFMA. *Professional Organisations:* The International Stock Exchange. *Clubs:* MCC. *Recreations:* Golf, Theatre, Opera, Biography.

TAPNER, John Walter; Deputy Senior Partner, Slaughter and May.

TAPNER, N R; Director, S G Warburg Securities, since 1990; Corporate Finance. *Career:* Rowe & Pitman (Merged with S G Warburg Group plc) 1983-. *Biog: b.* 30 September 1959. *Nationality:* British. *m.* 1988, Alexandra (née Boldero). *Educ:* Radley College; King's College, London (LLB); Lancaster Gate Law School. *Directorships:* S G Warburg, Akroyd, Rowe & Pitman, Mullens Securities Ltd 1990; Rowe & Pitman Ltd 1987; Pan Nominees 1989. *Clubs:* Roehampton Club. *Recreations:* Golf, Photography, Collecting Watercolours.

TAPPER, D J; Director, Hambros Bank Limited.

TAPPER, R Q; Director, Barclays de Zoete Wedd Securities Limited, since 1990; Equity Derivatives/Worldwide Risk Management. *Career:* Wedd Durlacher Mordaunt 1971; Back Office 1971-72; Trainee Dealer 1972-75; Dealer (Foods & Wines) 1975-77; Options 1977-84; Head of Options Trading 1984; Wedd Durlacher Mordaunt, Partner & Member of Equity Management Committee 1985; Set Up Option Trading for BZW in Australia 1988; Set Up Options Trading (DTB) 1990; Barclays de Zoete Wedd Securities Ltd, Director (Wedd Durlacher Mordaunt was taken over by BZW in 1986) 1990. *Biog: b.* 7 March 1950. *Nationality:* British. *m.* 1972, Anne (née Barlow). *Educ:* Alleyns School, Dulwich; Royal Holloway College, London. *Directorships:* Barclays de Zoete Wedd Securities Limited 1990.

TAPSFIELD, Richard Harold; Partner, Linklaters & Paines, since 1982; Commercial Litigation, Particularly Insurance & Construction. *Career:* Linklaters & Paines, Articles, Assistant Solicitor 1974-78; Assistant Solicitor 1978-82. *Biog: b.* 21 May 1951. *Nationality:* British. *m.* 1974, Penelope; 2 s. *Educ:* The Manchester Grammar School for Boys; Selwyn College, Cambridge (MA). *Other Activities:* The Insurance Institute of London; Society of Construction Law.

TARANTELLI, Dr Panfilo; Director, J Henry Schroder Wagg & Co Limited, since 1989; Merger & Acquisition in Southern Europe. *Career:* Banca Commerciale Italiana, Executive, UK Marketing 1979-83; S G Warburg & Co Ltd, Manager, Southern Europe 1983-86. *Biog: b.* 14 June 1955. *Nationality:* Italian. *Educ:* University of Rome (Hons Degree Econ). *Directorships:* J Henry Schroder Wagg & Co Ltd 1989 (exec).

TARLING, Nikolas Daniel; Partner, Freshfields, since 1974; Company Law. *Career:* Herbert Oppenheimer, Articled Clerk 1964-66; Freshfields, Assistant Solicitor 1968-73; Freshfields, Resident Partner, Paris 1974-75. *Biog: b.* 1 May 1941. *Nationality:* British. *m.* 1969, Elizabeth (née Lawson); 3 d. *Educ:* Repton School; Jesus College, Oxford (MA). *Directorships:* The

Yarlet Trust 1970 (non-exec). *Other Activities:* City of London Law Society. *Clubs:* City of London, Hurlingham. *Recreations:* Fishing, Skiing, Music, Old Master Drawings.

TARRANT, Stuart; Group Finance Director, Sedgwick Group plc, since 1988. *Biog: b.* 14 October 1940. *Nationality:* British. *m.* Jennie; 1 s; 1 d. *Professional Organisations:* FCA; FCT.

TARREL, B L J; Director, Barclays de Zoete Wedd Securities Ltd.

TARSH, P M; Director, Lonrho plc.

TASCO, F J; Director, C T Bowring & Co Limited.

TATCH, Brian; Partner, Clay & Partners, since 1975; Occupational Pension Schemes, Interests in Settled Property. *Career:* Guardian Assurance Co Ltd, Actuarial Trainee 1964-68; Sentinel Insurance Co Ltd, Actuarial Trainee 1968-69; Clay & Partners, Actuarial Trainee 1969-75. *Biog: b.* 24 April 1943. *Nationality:* British. *m.* 1965, Denise Ann (née Puckett); 2 s; 1 d. *Educ:* Central Foundation; University College, London (BSc). *Directorships:* Clay & Partners Pension Trustees Ltd 1984 (exec); Clay Clark Whitehill Ltd 1985-87 (non-exec) Chm; The Bridford Group Limited 1987-89 (non-exec)Chm; Leopold Joseph Pensioneer Trustee Co Ltd 1987 (non-exec). *Other Activities:* Founder Member, Past Treasurer, Chairman (1981-85), Assoc of Pensioneer Trustees; Member of Various Pensions and Actuarial Assocs, National and International. *Professional Organisations:* FIA; FPMI. *Publications:* Sundry Articles in Various Periodicals. *Recreations:* Mainly Sedentary, some Fell Walking in Lake District.

TATE, David Alfred; Clerk, Worshipful Company of Joiners & Ceilers, since 1984; Administration of Livery Company. *Career:* Caldwell & Braham, Partner 1963-81; Ellis & Tate, Partner 1981-. *Biog: b.* 23 October 1934. *Nationality:* British. *m.* 1958, Doreen Hilda (née Wilson); 2 s; 1 d. *Educ:* Latymer Upper School, Hammersmith. *Other Activities:* Liveryman, Worshipful Company of Joiners & Ceilers. *Clubs:* East India, Public.

TATE, David Henry; Partner, Clifford Chance, since 1987; Energy and Corporate Law. *Career:* Clifford-Turner, Ptnr 1962-87. *Biog: b.* 18 May 1929. *Nationality:* British. *m.* 1955, Norah (née Graham); 3 d. *Educ:* St Peter's School, York; King's College, Durham (LLB). *Other Activities:* Trustee, Royal Philharmonic Orchestra Trust. *Professional Organisations:* The Law Society; IBA (General Business, Energy & Natural Resources Law Sections); UK Oil Lawyers' Group; Canadian Petroleum Law Foundation; Asia-Paci. *Recreations:* The Arts, Gardening, Kitchen Bridge, Fishing.

TATE, Mike; Deputy City Editor, The Times.

TATE, Saxon; Chairman, London Fox, since 1985. *Career:* Redpath Industries Ltd, President and Chief Executive Officer 1965-73; Tate and Lyle plc, Managing Director 1973-80; Vice Chairman 1980-82; Industrial Development Board for Northern Ireland, Chief Executive 1982-85. *Biog: b.* 28 November 1931. *Nationality:* British. *m.* 1975, Virginia Joan (née Sturm); 4 s. *Educ:* Eton; Christ Church, Oxford. *Directorships:* London Fox; Tate & Lyle plc; The Robertson Group plc; CMS Ltd; CMS (Japan); Tate Appointements. *Other Activities:* Chairman, Joint Exchanges Committee, London Exchanges; Council Member, BIEC.

TATGENHORST, R Barry; Joint General Manager, The Sumitomo Bank Limited.

TAUBE, Nils; Director, J Rothschild Holdings plc.

TAUNTON, Terence Grosvenor; Managing Director, Fenchurch Insurance Brokers Ltd, since 1984; All Activities within UK. *Career:* Sedgwick International, Director 1975-82; Sedgwick Construction Services, Director 1973-82; Fenchurch Construction Services, MD 1982-84. *Biog: b.* 16 August 1938. *Nationality:* British. *m.* 1964, Kay (née Rochester); 2 s. *Educ:* Faversham Grammar School. *Directorships:* Fenchurch Ins Group Ltd 1989; Fenchurch Ins Brokers Ltd 1984 MD; Fen London 1984 MD; Fen Northern 1984; Fen North Western 1984; Fen Midlands 1986; Fen Financial Services 1989. *Professional Organisations:* ACII. *Recreations:* Sailing, Golfing, Gardening, Walking.

TAWIL, Morris; Executive Vice President, Republic National Bank of New York, since 1986; Head of Trading Management. *Career:* Trade Development Bank Trading Mgr 1965-83; American Express Bank Trading Mgr 1983-84. *Biog: b.* 22 September 1938. *m.* 1968, Nancy (née Dwek); 3 s; 1 d. *Educ:* Alliance Universelle, Beirut; Ecole du Commerce, Beirut. *Professional Organisations:* Member, Association Cambiste Internationale. *Recreations:* Tennis, Swimming, Bridge.

TAYANGANON, Thira; Senior Vice President & General Manager, Bangkok Bank Ltd.

TAYLOR, (Charity); Lady Taylor; Director, Taylor Woodrow plc.

TAYLOR, A; Director, Wellington Underwriting Agencies Limited.

TAYLOR, Bernard John; Executive Director, Baring Brothers & Co Ltd, since 1987; Corporate Finance. *Career:* Smiths Industries plc, Business Planning & Acquisitions 1979-82; Dir, Medical Div 1982-85; Baring Bros & Co Ltd, Corporate Fin Dept Mgr, Asst Dir 1985-. *Biog: b.* 2 November 1956. *Nationality:* British. *m.* 1984, Sarah Jane (née Taylor). *Educ:* Cheltenham College; St John's College (Open Scholar), Oxford

(MA). *Professional Organisations:* Royal Society of Chemistry; Royal Photographic Society. *Publications:* Photosensitive Film Formation on Copper (I), 1974; Photosensitive Film Formation on Copper (II), 1976; Oxidation of Alcohols to Carbonyl Compounds, Synthesis, 1979. *Clubs:* United Oxford & Cambridge University. *Recreations:* Gardening, Photography, History.

TAYLOR, Cavan; Deputy Senior Partner, Lovell White Durrant, since 1966; Commercial Law. *Biog: b.* 23 February 1935. *Nationality:* British. *m.* 1962, Helen (née Tinling); 1 s; 2 d. *Educ:* King's College School, Wimbledon; Emmanuel College, Cambridge (MA, LLM). *Directorships:* Cooper Estates Ltd 1982-88 Chm; Tissunique Ltd 1967 (non-exec); Various Energy Related Companies (non-exec); Hampton Gold Mining Areas plc. *Other Activities:* City of London Solicitors' Co; Governor, King's College School, Wimbledon (Chm of Governing Body, 1973-90). *Professional Organisations:* The Law Society; IBA; UK Oil Lawyers' Group. *Publications:* Occasional Articles in Legal Journals. *Recreations:* Reading, Sailing, Gardening.

TAYLOR, Christopher S; Financial Director, Smiths Industries plc, since 1989. *Career:* William Collins plc, Financial Director 1988-89; Babcock International plc, Financial Director 1986-87; Tarmac plc, Group Treasurer & Asst Financial Director 1976-86. *Biog: b.* 28 May 1941. *Nationality:* British. *m.* 1971, Alexandra (née Howard); 1 s; 2 d. *Educ:* Stanford University, USA (Business MBA); Clare College, Cambridge University (Physics MA); Clifton College. *Directorships:* Smiths Industries plc 1989 (exec). *Professional Organisations:* FCT. *Clubs:* RAC, Royal Western. *Recreations:* Sailing, Tennis, Opera.

TAYLOR, Christopher Thomas; Chief Adviser, European Division, Bank of England, since 1990; European Economy Isues, ERM, EMU etc. *Career:* Canadian Pacific Railway Research Officer 1961-65; Cambridge University (Applied Economics Dept) Research Officer & Dep Dir 1966-74; Bank of England Asst Adviser 1974-81; Intl Monetary Fund (Secondment) Alternate Dir for UK 1981-83; Bank of England, Head of Economics Division 1983-90; Chief Advisor, European Division 1990-. *Biog: b.* 15 October 1938. *Nationality:* British. *m.* 1964, Rosemary Elsie (née Peel); 1 s; 1 d. *Educ:* High Storrs Grammar School, Sheffield; King's College, Cambridge (BA, MA); McGill University, Montreal (MA). *Publications:* Various. *Recreations:* Gardening, Reading, Listening to Music.

TAYLOR, Colin Edward; Director, Smith New Court plc, since 1983. *Career:* Sambourne & Co Ptnr 1960-74. *Biog: b.* 2 September 1938. *m.* (née 1962). *Educ:* Christ's College, Finchley; London School of Economics (BSc Econ). *Professional Organisations:* The Intl Stock Exchange (Member).

TAYLOR, Derek Roger; Executive Director, Halifax Building Society; Estate Agency Network. *Career:* West Pennine Water Board, Chief Acct 1968-74; North West Water Authority, Div Fin Officer 1974-80; Halifax Building Society, Acct 1980-82; Asst Gen Mgr, Finance 1982-83; Gen Mgr, Finance 1983-86; Halifax Estate Agencies Ltd, Managing Director 1986-. *Biog:* b. 25 August 1940. *Nationality:* British. *m.* 1986, Vivienne (née Holroyd); 1 s. *Educ:* Sir Joseph Williamsons Mathematical School for Boys; Chadderton Grammar School, Oldham. *Directorships:* Halifax Estate Agencies Ltd & 23 Subsidiary Companies MD; Oldham Athletic Football Club; Halifax Building Society. *Professional Organisations:* IPFA; MBIM. *Recreations:* Various Sporting Activities.

TAYLOR, Ms Elizabeth Rose; Group Risk Manager, Insurance, Harrisons & Crosfield plc.

TAYLOR, Gordon Lindsay; Finance Director, IMI plc, since 1987. *Career:* Thomson McLintock, Audit Manager 1960-61; ICI, Financial Accountant 1961-68; IMI, Chief Accountant 1972-87. *Biog:* b. 10 April 1932. *m.* 1961, Sybil Heather; 1 s; 1 d. *Educ:* Hutchesons Boys School; Glasgow University (MA). *Professional Organisations:* CA, FCT.

TAYLOR, I; Partner, Freshfields.

TAYLOR, I D; Director, Legal & General Ventures Ltd, since 1989; Venture Capital.

TAYLOR, J R; Director, Larpent Newton & Co Ltd.

TAYLOR, John; Managing Director, AIBD (Systems & Information) Ltd.

TAYLOR, John A F; Sheriff, Corporation of London.

TAYLOR, John H; Partner, Theodore Goddard.

TAYLOR, Jonathan Jeremy Kirwan; Group Marketing Director, Baring Asset Management Ltd, since 1989; Marketing of Investment Services for all Baring Asset Management Worldwide Subsidiaries. *Career:* Baring Brothers & Co Limited 1969-73; Baring Sanwa Multinational Ltd Hong Kong, Assistant Director 1973-76; Henderson Baring Management Hong Kong, Marketing Director 1976-77; Henderson Baring Management London, Marketing Director & Representative 1978-84; Subsequently Managing Director London Branch and UK Subsidiaries; Baring International Investment Management Limited, Marketing Director 1985-89; Baring Fund Managers Ltd, Managing Director 1990. *Biog:* b. 12 October 1943. *Nationality:* British. *m.* 1966, Victoria Mary Caroline (née McLaren); 4 d. *Educ:* Eton; Edmund Hall, Oxford (MA). *Directorships:* Baring Fund Managers Ltd (Authorised Unit Trusts) (exec) Chairman & Managing Director; Baring International Fund Managers

Limited (Offshore Funds) (non-exec) Chairman; Baring International Investment Management Australia Ltd Chairman; Baring International Investment (Canada) Chairman. *Professional Organisations:* Barrister at Law, Middle Temple 1968. *Clubs:* Turf, Royal Thames, Hong Kong, City.

TAYLOR, Mrs L A; Partner, Pannell Kerr Forster.

TAYLOR, Les; Partner, Clark Whitehill.

TAYLOR, M R; Partner, Hill Taylor Dickinson.

TAYLOR, Martin Gibbeson; Vice Chairman, Hanson plc, since 1988. *Career:* Mann Judd & Co, Articles 1958-61; Dow Chemical (UK), Co Sec 1963-69. *Biog:* b. 30 January 1935. *Nationality:* British. *m.* 1960, Gunilla (née Bryner); 2 s. *Educ:* Haileybury School; St Catharine's College, Cambridge (MA). *Directorships:* Vickers plc 1986 (non-exec); The Securities Assoc 1987-90; National Westminster Bank plc 1990. *Other Activities:* Council Member, CBI and Member, the Panel on Takeovers & Mergers (Representing CBI). *Professional Organisations:* FCA. *Clubs:* MCC. *Recreations:* Books, Pictures, Sport, Theatre.

TAYLOR, Nigel; Partner, Clay & Partners, since 1988; Investment, Benefits Consultancy. *Biog:* b. 26 January 1963. *Nationality:* British. *Educ:* London School of Economics (BSc). *Professional Organisations:* FIA. *Recreations:* Music, Travel, Skiing.

TAYLOR, Peter; Partner, Clifford Chance.

TAYLOR, Dr R; Director, Equity Syndication, BZW Ltd, since 1989; Primary Issues, International Equities and Derivatives. *Career:* Savory Milln, Corporate Finance Director 1982-86; Morgan Stanley, Equity Syndicate, Vice President 1986-89. *Biog:* b. 5 April 1954. *Nationality:* British. *m.* Wiesia. *Educ:* St Catherine's, Cambridge (MA Engineering); Imperial College, London (PhD Industrial Sociology). *Professional Organisations:* Member, Stock Exchange.

TAYLOR, R I; Executive Director, Chartered WestLB Ltd; Treasury. *Biog:* b. 13 July 1945. *m.* Yvonne; 2 s; 1 d. *Professional Organisations:* AIB.

TAYLOR, R M; Partner, Hill Taylor Dickinson.

TAYLOR, R W; Chief Operating Officer, County NatWest Securities Ltd, since 1990; Settlements, Finance, Control, Information Technology globally. *Career:* British Petroleum, Positions including: Director, Finance Control Systems, BP Exploration America; Member, BP America, Gas Management Committee; General Manager, Planning and Systems, responsible for Corporate Planning, New Ventures, Services, Purchasing, Information Technology, fifth largest overseas associate; Manager, Corporate Informations Systems, Worldwide Control Systems and GHO IT; Manager, Systems Support, BP Trading; Prior to that ten years industrial experience including: Major Clearing Bank, Project Manager covering MIS and Internal Consultancy; Major Computer Bureau, Manager Internal Services, Computer Manufacturer, Area Systems Executive. *Biog: b.* 15 April 1944. *m.* Valerie Mary. *Educ:* (BSc Industrial Economics, Diploma in Business Administration). *Directorships:* County NatWest Securities Ltd 1990 (exec); County NatWest Investment Bank Ltd 1990 (non-exec). *Other Activities:* Member, Guild of Freemen.

TAYLOR, Richard John Johnson; Partner, McKenna & Co, since 1974; European Community and UK Competition Law. *Career:* McKenna & Co, Articled Clerk 1967-69; Assistant Solicitor 1969-74; Partner & Head of EC & UK Competition Practice 1974-; Head of Commercial & Litigation Department 1988-. *Biog: b.* 6 February 1945. *Nationality:* British. *m.* Jean; 1 d. *Educ:* Oxford University (MA).

TAYLOR, Robert Mortimer John; Director, Morgan Grenfell & Co Ltd, since 1983; Management Services. *Career:* Accountancy Profession 1967-72; Morgan Grenfell 1972-. *Biog: b.* 12 February 1946. *Nationality:* British. *Educ:* Rossall School; Emmanuel College, Cambridge (MA). *Directorships:* Pendle & Rivett Ltd 1973. *Professional Organisations:* FCA.

TAYLOR, Roger John; Director, Sun Alliance & London Insurance plc.

TAYLOR, Ms Sue; Partner, Frere Cholmeley, since 1986. *Career:* Frere Cholmeley, Articles, Assistant Solicitor 1976-86. *Educ:* Beverley High School; Exeter University (LLB); St Anne's College, Oxford (BCL). *Professional Organisations:* Member, Law Society.

TAYLOR, T H; General Manager, Banco Totta & Açores.

TAYLOR, Tim; Partner, S J Berwin & Co.

TAYLOR, Timothy J; Partner, Withers.

TAYLOR, Timothy William Simpson; Partner, Hill Taylor Dickinson, since 1989. *Career:* Hill Dickinson & Co, Articled Clerk 1976-78; Assistant Solicitor 1978-82; Partner 1982-89. *Biog: b.* 22 June 1954. *Nationality:* British. *m.* 1986, Alison Elizabeth (née Wells); 1 d. *Educ:* Clifton College. *Professional Organisations:* Law Society. *Clubs:* Walton Heath Golf Club. *Recreations:* Golf, Fishing.

TAYLOR, W N; Head of Planning, Berwin Leighton.

TAYLOR, Francis; The Rt Hon Lord Taylor of Hadfield; Life President, Taylor Woodrow plc.

TEAGUE, David W H; Managing Director, Svenska Iberica SA; Corporate Finance, Spain. *Career:* J P Morgan, Vice President 1974-86; Bankers Trust Company, Vice President 1986-89. *Biog: b.* 13 January 1941. *Nationality:* British. (div); 1 s 3 d. *Educ:* Harvard Business School (MBA). *Professional Organisations:* American Institute of Certified Public Accountants. *Clubs:* Hurlingham. *Recreations:* Tennis.

TEBBUTT, G F; Director, Robert Fleming Insurance Brokers Limited.

TEDDER, Gerald Leon; Deputy Chairman, BAII plc.

TEEUW, A E; Director, Barclays de Zoete Wedd Securities Ltd.

TEGNER, Ian Nicol; Senior Vice President, Institute of Chartered Accountants of Scotland, since 1990. *Career:* Jenks Percival Pidgeon & Co Chartered Accountants, London, Apprentice 1952-57; Qualified as Scottish Chartered Accountant 1957; Clarkson Gordon & Co, Toronto 1958; Barton Mayhew & Co, Chartered Accountants (now Ernst & Young) London, Audit Manager 1959; Partner 1965-71; Bowater Corporation Ltd (later Bowater Industries plc), Finance Dir 1971-86; Midland Bank plc, Director, Group Finance 1987-89. *Biog: b.* 11 July 1933. *Nationality:* British. *m.* 1961, Meriel Helen (née Lush); 1 s; 1 d. *Educ:* Perthshire Rugby School; Harvard Business School (AMP). *Directorships:* Barton Mayhew & Co 1965-71 Ptnr; Bowater Industries plc 1971-86 Fin Dir; Midland Bank plc 1987-89 Dir Group Fin; Wiggins Teape Appleton plc 1990 Indep Dir; Control Risks Group Ltd 1990 Indep Dir; The Hundred Group of Finance Directors 1988 Chairman. *Other Activities:* Council Member, Institute of Chartered Accountants of Scotland, 1978-86; Vice-President, 1986-87; Member, Accounting Standards Committee CCAB; Lindley Educational Trust. *Professional Organisations:* Chartered Accountant (Scotland). *Publications:* Contributions to various professional publications. *Clubs:* Caledonian Club. *Recreations:* Antiquarian Books, Choral Singing, Hill Walking, Travel.

TEITLER, E; Manager, Senior Vice President, American Express Bank.

TEJASAKULSIN, P; Branch Manager, Bangkok Bank Ltd, since 1989; Overall Branch Operations. *Career:* Bangkok Bank Ltd, HO, Operation Officer, Documentary Bills 1971-72; Saigon BR, Sub-Accountant, Documentary Bills 1973-75; Hong Kong BR, Admin Officer, Documentary Bills 1975-79; Tokyo BR, Asst Manager, Overall Branch Operations 1979-82; Kuala Lumpur BR, Asst Manager, Overall Branch Operations 1982-87; London BR, Deputy Manager, Overall Branch Operations 1987-89. *Biog: b.* 1 November 1946. *Nationality:* Thai. *m.* 1975, Areerat; 1 s; 2 d. *Educ:* South-West London College (AIB). *Professional Organisations:* Associate, Institute of Bankers.

TELFER, Barry; Vice President, Chemical Bank.

TELFORD, Sir Robert; Chairman, Prelude Technology Investments Limited.

TELLIER, Christian; UK Representative, Caisse Centrale des Banques Populaires, since 1986; Representative. *Biog: b.* 4 November 1946. *Nationality:* French; 2 s. *Educ:* University of Nantes, France (Hons Law); Institut D'Administration des Entreprises. *Professional Organisations:* Conseiller du Commerce Exterieur de la France.

TEMPLE, (John) Nicholas; Group Legal Director & Company Secretary, Lloyds Abbey Life plc. *Career:* C & A Modes Exec Trainee 1972-74; Group Lotus Car Companies plc PA to Dep Chm 1974-76; RHP Group plc Mgr, Legal & Property Dept 1976-82; Westland plc Group Legal Adviser 1982-84; Robinson & Sons plc Group Sec & Legal Adviser 1984-86; Stormgard plc Exec Dir 1986-88. *Biog: b.* 11 March 1951. *Nationality:* British. *m.* 1979, Patricia Janet (née Dickinson); 1 s; 2 d. *Educ:* Durham School; Manchester University (LLB Hons). *Directorships:* Abbey Life Assurance Co Ltd 1988 (exec); Ambassador Life Assurance Co Ltd 1988 (exec); 22 Abbey Life Subsidiary Companies 1988 (exec). *Professional Organisations:* Barrister. *Recreations:* Walking, Classic Cars.

TEMPLE, Michael Nicholas Fraser; Partner, Arthur Andersen & Co, since 1982; Audit & Investigative Work (Marketing, Services, Property). *Career:* Arthur Andersen & Co, Articled Clerk 1971-74; Audit Senior 1974-76; Manager 1976-82; Partner 1982; Assistant Division Head, Accounting and Audit Division 1984-86; Partner in Charge of Financial Consulting Practice, Queensland, Australia 1986-89. *Biog: b.* 30 December 1949. *Nationality:* British. *m.* 1973, Yvonne (née Forsyth); 1 s; 2 d. *Educ:* Radley College; University of Bristol (BSc). *Professional Organisations:* Fellow, Institute of Chartered Accountants in England and Wales; Fellow, Institute of Chartered Accountants in Australia.

TEMPLE, P W; Director, Hill Samuel Bank Limited.

TEMPLETON, Richard; Director, Robert Fleming & Co Ltd; Corporate Finance. *Career:* J Henry Schroder Wagg, Clerical 1965-66; Phillips & Drew, Junior Analyst 1969-70; Robert Fleming, Analyst 1971-75; Save and Prosper, Fund Mgr 1975-78. *Biog: b.* 11 April 1945. *m.* 1986, Belinda (née Timlin). *Educ:* Clifton College; Reading University (BA Hons); Bradford University (MSc). *Directorships:* West of England Trust Ltd 1986 (non-exec); Fleming Fledgeling Investment Trust

plc 1989 (non-exec). *Professional Organisations:* ASIA. *Clubs:* Turf, MCC. *Recreations:* Beagling, Reading.

TENBY, William Lloyd-George; Viscount Tenby; Non-Executive Chairman, St James Public Relations Ltd, since 1990; Financial Public Relations. *Career:* United Dominions Trust Group, PR/Advertising Manager 1955-70; Old Broad St Securities, PR/Advertising Manager 1970-74; Kleinwort Benson, PR Advisor to Chairman 1974-88. *Biog: b.* 7 November 1927. *m.* 1955, Ursula (née Medlicott); 1 s; 2 d. *Educ:* St Catharines College, Cambridge (Late Exhibitioner) (BA History). *Directorships:* Williams Lea & Co (non-exec). *Other Activities:* Chairman, Odiham Bench; Member, Magistrates' Court Committee, Hampshire; Member, Police Authority, Hampshire; Involvement with a Number of Charities at National and Local Level.

TENNANT, James Robert; Director, Lazard Investors Ltd, since 1987; Pension Funds. *Career:* Lloyds Bank Trust Division, Trust Officer 1973-78; IMI plc, Investment Analyst 1978-83. *Biog: b.* 16 June 1953. *Nationality:* British. *m.* 1978, Maria Pilar (née Maldonado Somoza); 2 s; 2 d. *Educ:* Loughborough Grammar School. *Clubs:* Royal Anglesey Yacht Club. *Recreations:* Sailing, Shooting.

TENNANT, Mark E; Director, Hill Samuel Investment Services Group Ltd, since 1986; Chairman, Bell Lawrie White & Co Ltd (Stockbrokers); Chairman, Hill Samuel Unit Trust Managers Ltd. *Career:* Scots Guards, Army Officer, Left at Rank of Captain 1966-73; Hambros Bank Ltd, Trainee 1974-75; Manager, Banking Control Dept 1975-76; Manager, International Fixed Interest Management 1976-81; Hambro Pacific Ltd (Hong Kong), Managing Director 1981-83; Hambro Investment Management Services Ltd, Marketing Director 1983-; Fidelity International, Director in Charge of UK Pension Funds; Marketing Director International Erisa Funds 1983-86; Hill Samuel Investment Services Group Ltd, Director 1986-. *Biog: b.* 9 April 1947. *Nationality:* Scottish. *m.* 1971, Hermione (née Howe); 1 s; 2 d. *Educ:* Eton College. *Directorships:* Hambro Pacific Ltd 1989 (exec); Fidelity International Investment Advisors Ltd 1983 (exec); Hill Samuel Investment Services Group Ltd 1986 (exec); Hill Samuel Private Client Management Ltd 1986 (exec); Wood McKenzie Private Client Services Ltd 1986 (exec); Robert White & Co Ltd 1988 (exec); Bell Lawrie White & Co Ltd 1989 (exec); Hill Samuel Unit Trust Management Ltd 1988 (exec). *Other Activities:* Member, Unit Trust Association Executive Committee, 1988-90; Member, Executive Committee, Scottish Tory Reform Group, 1989-. *Professional Organisations:* Member of Institute of Bankers. *Clubs:* Boodles. *Recreations:* Shooting, Deerstalking, Golf, Bridge, Playing the Bagpipes.

TERAO, Yasushi; Assistant General Manager, The Sumitomo Bank Limited.

TERASKIEWICZ, Eddie; Director, International City Holdings.

TERAZAWA, Ms Kumiko; Director, Baring Securities Ltd, since 1988; Warrant Sales. *Career:* Morgan Stanley Inc, Associate 1984-88. *Nationality:* Japanese. *Educ:* Harvard University Graduate School of Business (MBA); Harvard College (BA).

TERENGHI, Mario; Managing Director, Credito Italiano International Ltd, since 1984; Merchant Banking. *Career:* Credito Italiano SpA 1946-75; Orion Banking Group, Exec Dir 1975-80; Credito Italiano SpA, Snr Mgr 1981-84. *Biog: b.* 28 May 1927. *Nationality:* Italian. *m.* 1983, Airdrie (née Armstrong). *Educ:* High School of Commerce, Monza; Catholic University of Milan. *Directorships:* Orion Multinational Services Ltd 1975-80 Chm; Orion Pacific Ltd (Hong Kong) 1975-80; Orion Leasing Holdings Ltd 1975-80; Libra Bank Ltd 1975-84. *Professional Organisations:* Fellow, Institute of Directors; Foreign Banks Association. *Clubs:* Hurlingham, Overseas Bankers', Lombard Association. *Recreations:* Music, Photography.

TERNENT, K L; Partner (Leeds), Bacon & Woodrow.

TERRY, I K; Partner, Freshfields.

TERRY Jr, Luther L; Executive Director, Crédit Suisse First Boston Limited.

TESTER, S K; Partner, Cameron Markby Hewitt.

THAINE, C E A; Banking & Finance Partner, Richards Butler.

THATCHER, M; Clerk, Cooks' Company.

THELWALL JONES, G M; Director, Charterhouse Tilney. *Biog:* 1 s.

THEODOLI-BRASCHI, Giovanni Angelo; Director, Southern Europe, County NatWest Ltd; Investment Banking, Business Development in Italy, Spain, Portugal & Greece. *Career:* Texaco Spa (Italy), Sales Representative 1967-70; The First Boston Corp, NY, Assoc in Underwriting Dept 1972-73; First Boston (Europe) Ltd, London Mgr, Syndication Dept 1974-75; Citicorp Investment Bank Ltd, London VP, Syndication Dept 1975-82; Citibank Espana, Madrid General Mgr, Investment Banking 1983-86; County NatWest Ltd, Dir 1987-89; Executive Dir 1989-. *Biog: b.* 1 May 1942. *Nationality:* Italian. *m.* 1977, Maria (née Milstein); 1 s; 1 d. *Educ:* Liceo Luigi Galvani, Bologna; University of Bologna (JD); Cornell University (MBA). *Professional Organisations:* Member, New York Stock Exchange; Member, NASD, New York. *Clubs:* Circolo Della Caccia, Puerta de Hierro, Hurlingham. *Recreations:* Tennis, Scuba Diving, Horseback Riding.

THIELE, Patrick A; Director, Minet Holdings plc.

THOLSTRUP, Jens Jorgen; Director, Warburg Securities.

THOM, Graeme C A; Managing Director, Shaw & Co Limited.

THOM, James Demmink; Treasurer, BTR plc.

THOM, P R; Chief Accountant, Henry Ansbacher Holdings plc.

THOMAS, Adrian Anthony Michael; Partner, Clark Whitehill, since 1988; International Tax. *Career:* Clark Whitehill 1978-. *Biog: b.* 12 January 1954. *Nationality:* British. *m.* 1990, Ann. *Educ:* Trinity College, Cambridge (BA). *Professional Organisations:* ATII, ACA. *Recreations:* Bridge, Golf.

THOMAS, Anthony David; Director, Kleinwort Benson Securities, since 1989; Economic Research. *Career:* Bank of England, Economist 1979-85. *Biog: b.* 13 July 1989. *Nationality:* British. *Educ:* Pembroke College, Oxford; LSE.

THOMAS, Brian Michael; Executive Director, Allied Dunbar Assurance plc, since 1987; Actuarial Finance/ Product Development. *Career:* Commercial Union Assurance plc Asst Actuary 1973-80. *Biog: b.* 14 November 1952. *m.* 1974, Jane Elizabeth (née Humphreys); 1 s; 1 d. *Educ:* Tiverton Grammar School; Oxford University (MA Hons). *Professional Organisations:* FIA. *Recreations:* Photography, Food & Wine, Theatre.

THOMAS, D K; Director, C & G Guardian.

THOMAS, David George; Director, The Equitable Life Assurance Society, since 1989; Investment Management. *Career:* Sun Life Assurance Society plc, Various 1965-84; The Equitable Life Assurance Society, Asst Gen Mgr 1984-88. *Biog: b.* 25 July 1944. *Nationality:* British. *m.* 1967, Janet Natalie; 1 s; 1 d. *Educ:* Exeter University (BSc Hons). *Directorships:* The Baptist Insurance Co plc 1979 (non-exec); Percy Street Investments Ltd 1984 (exec); Equitable Unit Trust Managers Ltd 1984 (exec); University Life Assurance Soc Ltd 1985 (exec); Equitable Investment Mgrs Ltd 1986 (exec). *Professional Organisations:* FIA.

THOMAS, David Hugh; Director, Morgan Grenfell & Co Ltd, since 1988; Risk Management, Financial Compliance & Planning. *Career:* Morgan Grenfell & Co Ltd, Eurocurrency Dept Specialising in Italian Exports 1978-83; Asst Dir, Eurobond Div 1983-84; Head, Swaps Dept 1984-87. *Biog: b.* 6 December 1951. *Nationality:* British. *m.* 1978, Frances Mary (née Brown); 1 s; 1 d. *Educ:* Hertford Grammar School; Corpus Christi College, Oxford (BA Hons 1st); St John's College, Oxford

(MA,DPhil). *Clubs:* Oxford Union Society - Secretary Trinity 1973, Librarian Michaelmas, 1973. *Recreations:* Playing the Piano (very badly).

THOMAS, E S; Partner, Bacon & Woodrow.

THOMAS, Geraint Edward Bowen; Finance Director, Kleinwort Benson Investment Management.

THOMAS, Glyn Collen; Group Treasurer, Kingfisher plc, since 1986; Financial Operations. *Career:* Peat Marwick Mitchell, Audit Senior, Tax & Audit 1972-76; Rothmans International, Group Financial Controller, Group Accounts, Group MIS, Group Treasury 1976-86. *Biog:* b. 30 July 1951. *Nationality:* British. *m.* 1984, Heather; 1 s; 1 d. *Educ:* Bec Grammar; Cardiff High; University of Wales, Cardiff (BSc Econ Hons). *Directorships:* Time Retail Finance Limited 1988 Chairman; Triptych Insurance NV 1988 (non-exec). *Professional Organisations:* Institute of Chartered Accountants; Society of Business Economists; Association of Corporate Treasurers.

THOMAS, Gordon Henry Evan; Deputy General Manager, Banco Di Roma, since 1986; Business Development, International Department. *Career:* Standard Bank of S Africa/Standard Chartered Bank Various 1957-70; Bankers' Trust Co VP, Intl Banking 1970-86. *Biog:* b. 7 October 1936. *m.* (Div); 1 s; 1 d. *Educ:* St Dunstan's College. *Professional Organisations:* FCIB; ATTI. *Clubs:* Overseas Bankers'. *Recreations:* Cricket, Squash, Sailing.

THOMAS, H; Partner, Hays Allan.

THOMAS, Jeremy David; Partner, Allen & Overy, since 1990; Corporate Finance. *Career:* Allen & Overy, Articled Clerk 1980-82; Assistant Solicitor 1982-89; Partner 1990-. *Biog:* b. 2 December 1957. *Nationality:* British. *Educ:* Dynevor School, Swansea; Christ's College, Cambridge (BA, MA Law). *Other Activities:* Freeman, City of London Solicitors' Company. *Professional Organisations:* Member, Law Society. *Recreations:* Golf, Theatre, Reading.

THOMAS, M W; Director, Martin Currie Investment Management Ltd.

THOMAS, Nicholas Andrew; Partner, Macfarlanes, since 1981; Corporate and Commercial. *Biog:* b. 14 April 1953. *Nationality:* British. *Educ:* Kelly College, Tavistock; Exeter College, Oxford (BA). *Other Activities:* City of London Solicitors' Co. *Professional Organisations:* The Law Society. *Recreations:* Golf, Walking, Classical Music, Opera.

THOMAS, P M; Director, Private Clients, NCL Investments Limited. *Career:* L Nessel & Co 1971-87; Shearson Lehman Securities 1987-88.

THOMAS, Patricia E; Partner, S J Berwin & Co.

THOMAS, Peter; Executive Director, Corporate Affairs, P & O Steam Navigation Company, since 1986; Public Affairs, Personnel, Administration, Pay & Pension. *Career:* Journalist, (Australia & England) 1959; P & O 1961-67; Overseas Containers Australia Pty Ltd (Sydney) 1967; P & O, Director of Information; Smith's Industries plc 1973-; P & O, Director of Information 1980. *Biog:* b. 1933. *Nationality:* Australian.

THOMAS, R A; Director, Hambros Bank Limited.

THOMAS, R H L; Director, Robert Fleming Holdings Limited.

THOMAS, R Lance; Chief Executive & Managing Director, Jonathan Wren & Co Ltd, since 1990; Financial Recruitment. *Career:* Gibraltar Savings and Loan, California, Senior Vice President 1970-80; Encino Savings and Loan, California, President & Chief Exec Officer 1980-82; Bel-Air Savings and Loan, California, President & Chief Exec Officer 1982-89; Executive Bank, California, President & Chief Exec Officer 1989-90. *Biog:* b. 26 December 1946. *Nationality:* American. *m.* 1985, Susan; 1 s; 2 d. *Educ:* Bristol Old Vic School; San Diego State College; University of Southern California. *Directorships:* Jonathan Wren & Co (London) 1990 MD; Arth Corporation (Los Angeles) 1989 Chm of the Board. *Other Activities:* Young Presidents Organization.

THOMAS, R W; Executive Director, James R Knowles Limited.

THOMAS, Robert Lorne; Director International Research and Chief International Economist, Greenwell Montagu Gilt-Edged & Midland Montagu, since 1986; Currency Forecasts & Forecasting Impact of International Events on Currencies & Bond Markets. *Career:* W Greenwell & Co, Economist 1966-76; W Greenwell & Co, Partner 1976-86. *Biog:* b. 11 June 1945. *Nationality:* British. *m.* 1970, Joanna; 2 s. *Educ:* Malvern College; Jesus College, Cambridge (MA 2:1 Economics). *Directorships:* Greenwell Montagu Gilt-Edged 1986 (exec). *Other Activities:* Liveryman, Glass Sellers Company; Liveryman, Actuaries Company; Trustee, Charles S French Charitable Trust. *Professional Organisations:* Fellow, Institute of Actuaries. *Clubs:* City Livery. *Recreations:* Beekeeping, Travel, Tennis.

THOMAS, Robin Noel; Director, Clive Discount Co Ltd.

THOMAS, T J; Managing Director, Co-operative Bank, since 1988. *Career:* Joint Credit Card Co, Research Manager 1971-72; Joint Credit Card Co, National Sales Manager 1972. *Biog:* b. 19 October 1937. *Nationality:* British. *m.* Lynda; 3 s. *Educ:* Queen Elizabeth Grammar School; Bath University, School of Management (Post Graduate Diploma, Business Administration). *Directorships:* Co-operative Bank plc MD; Unity Trust Bank plc Chm; Co-operative Pension Funds Unit Trust Managers Ltd; Co-operative Bank Financial Advisers; International Co-operative Alliance Banking Commitee Pres; Co-operative Development Agency; CAPRA Limited (Advertising Agency); Employee Share Ownership Plan Limited; Manchester Ringway Developments Alternate Dir; Venture Technic (Cheshire) Limited Chm; Office of the Banking Ombudsman; EFT/POS Limited; Llanelli Radiators Holdings Limited; Holyoake Insurance Brokers Limited; First Co-operative Finance Limited (later known as Credit Services); Cleveland Finance Limited; Cleveland Guaranty Limited; F C Finance Limited; Co-operative Commercial Limited; First Roodhill Leasing Co Limited; Second Roodhill Leasing Co Limited; Third Roodhill Leasing Co Limited; Fourth Roodhill Leasing Co Limited; Worldtech Ventures Limited; Unity Balloting Services Limited; Unity Communications; Unity Financial Services Limited; Unity Investment Management Limited; Unity Pension Services; Unity Trust Unit Trust Management Limited; Manchester Phoenix Initiative -1990. *Other Activities:* Visiting Professor, University of Stirling (MBA Banking Course); Member of the General Council of the Chartered Institute of Bankers; Board of Trustees of CAMPUS (Campaign to Promote the University of Salford). *Professional Organisations:* Fellow, Chartered Institute of Bankers; Fellow, Chartered Institute of Marketing. *Publications:* Worker Cooperatives, Past, Present and Future. *Recreations:* Grandson, Jogging, Rugby.

THOMLINSON, B N; Director, Granville Davies Limited.

THOMPKINS, P D G; Partner, Lane Clark & Peacock.

THOMPSETT, Maurice Edward; Partner, Touche Ross & Co; Taxation. *Career:* Touche Ross & Co Ptnr 1969-. *Biog: b.* 15 April 1932. *Nationality:* British. *m.* 1956, Joyce (née Cook); 2 d. *Educ:* Dartford Grammar School. *Professional Organisations:* FCA; ATII. *Clubs:* MCC. *Recreations:* Cricket, Horse Racing.

THOMPSON, C Simon; Group Treasurer, Trafalgar House Public Limited Company.

THOMPSON, D A R; Group Finance Director, The Boots Company plc, since 1990. *Career:* Thomas Bourne & Co, Chartered Accountants, Articles 1964; The Boots Company plc 1966-; Group Management Accountant 1973-77; Vice President Finance, Boots Drug Stores, Canada 1977-80; Finance Director, Retail Division 1980-89; Group Financial Controller 1989-90; Group Finance Director 1990-. *Biog: b.* 4 September 1942. *m.* 1966, Stella Eunice (née Durrow); 2 s. *Educ:* Burton

Grammar School. *Directorships:* The Boots Company plc 1990 (exec); Do It All Ltd 1990 (exec). *Other Activities:* The Hundred Group of Finance Directors; The Midlands Industry Group of Finance Directors. *Professional Organisations:* Fellow, Institute Chartered Accountants in England & Wales. *Recreations:* Swimming.

THOMPSON, D C; Director, Brewin Dolphin & Co Ltd.

THOMPSON, Dennis; Head of Property Services, Leeds Permanent Building Society, since 1988; Management of the Society's Property Portfolio. *Career:* Leeds Permanent Building Society 1952-69; Asst Chief Surveyor 1969-83; Asst General Mgr 1983-88. *Biog: b.* 9 November 1931. *Nationality:* British. *m.* 1955, Jean (née Willis); 1 s; 1 d. *Educ:* Morley Grammar School. *Professional Organisations:* FRICS. *Recreations:* Golf, Gardening.

THOMPSON, Gerald Vincent Bodenham; Director, Hambros Bank Limited, since 1990; Corporate Finance, Specialisation in Continental Europe. *Career:* Morgan Grenfell & Co Limited, Corporate Finance 1978-90; Director 1989; Peat Marwick Mitchell 1974-78. *Biog: b.* 7 January 1951. *Nationality:* British. *Educ:* Ampleforth College; Jesus College, Cambridge (MA). *Directorships:* Hambros Bank Limited 1990 (exec); Morgan Grenfell & Co Limited 1989. *Other Activities:* Grocers Company. *Professional Organisations:* FCA. *Clubs:* Oxford & Cambridge. *Recreations:* Music, Skiing, Tennis.

THOMPSON, Hugh Edward; Partner, Beharrell Thompson & Co, since 1990; Banking. *Career:* Thompson Quarrell, Partner 1971-75; National Westminster Bank, Head Office Legal Dept 1975-77; Standard Chartered Merchant Bank, Senior Assistant Director International Project Finance 1981-88; Lawrence Graham, Partner 1988-90. *Biog: b.* 29 September 1944. *Nationality:* British. *m.* 1972, Anne Elizabeth (née Bygott); 3 d. *Educ:* Bradfield College; Christ Church, Oxford (MA Hons). *Directorships:* Metasa Limited 1978 (non-exec). *Other Activities:* Freeman, Grocers Company. *Professional Organisations:* Member, The Law Society. *Publications:* Articles on Banking Law. *Recreations:* Travel, Literature, Gardening.

THOMPSON, James Francis Cherry; Investment Manager & Director,, James Finlay Investment Management Ltd, since 1981; Private Clients. *Career:* Singer and Friedlander, Local Director 1975-81; The Glasgow Herald, Business Editor. *Biog: b.* 11 March 1939. *Nationality:* British. *m.* 1967, Alison Margaret (née Cowan); 3 d. *Educ:* Loretto School. *Professional Organisations:* AMSIA. *Clubs:* West of Scotland FC, London Scottish FC, Buchanan Castle Golf Club.

THOMPSON, Jeremy Sinclair; Managing Director, Tranwood & Co Ltd, since 1986; Corporate Finance.

Career: Peat Marwick Mitchell & Co Articled Clerk/ Audit Snr 1976-80; Air Florida Europe Ltd Dir of Accounting Services 1980-82; Coopers & Lybrand Assoc Consultant 1982-84; Sinclair Thompson Assoc Mgmnt Consultant 1985-86. *Biog: b.* 6 April 1954. *Nationality:* British. *m.* 1982, Lucy Jane (née Wagner); 2 d. *Educ:* Durham School; Keble College, Oxford (MA). *Directorships:* Lester Brothers Ltd 1986 (non-exec); Tranwood plc 1987 (exec); Tranwood & Co Ltd 1986 (exec); Filofax Group plc 1990 (non-exec). *Professional Organisations:* ACA. *Clubs:* Leander, Vincents, Royal Ocean Racing Club. *Recreations:* Sailing, Rowing, Marathon Running, Sheep Farming.

THOMPSON, John C; Corporate Treasurer, Reed International plc. *Biog: b.* 1 April 1941. *Nationality:* British. *Professional Organisations:* FCCA; MBA; FCT.

THOMPSON, K D; Director/Company Secretary, Scott Underwriting Agencies Limited.

THOMPSON, M N B; Director, S G Warburg Securities, since 1989; Equity Syndication. *Career:* S G Warburg 1981-. *Biog: b.* 22 April 1958. *Nationality:* British. *m.* 1983, Vivien (née Whitley); 1 s; 2 d. *Educ:* Sherborne School; Brasenose College, Oxford (MA Modern History and Modern Languages Class I). *Clubs:* Travellers Club.

THOMPSON, M W; Director, Alliance & Leicester Building Society.

THOMPSON, Michael; Partner, Freshfields, since 1985; Corporate Taxation. *Career:* Freshfields, Articled Clerk 1977-79; Manager 1979-85. *Biog: b.* 18 June 1954. *Nationality:* British. *Educ:* Bradford Grammar School; Trinity College, Cambridge (MA Classics and Law). *Other Activities:* PCC Member and Deanery Synod Representative for St Helen's, Bishopsgate; Member, Law Society Petroleum Revenue Tax Committee. *Professional Organisations:* Law Society; City of London Solicitors Company. *Recreations:* Walking, Munro Bagging.

THOMPSON, Michael Herbert; Director, Parrish Stockbrokers, since 1987; Private Clients, Fund Management. *Career:* Thomas Clarke & Co, Partner 1960-74; Senior Partner 1969-74; Sternberg Thomas Clarke & Co, Partner 1974-87. *Biog: b.* 9 June 1934. *Nationality:* British. *m.* 1957, Veronica (née Myddelton); 1 s; 3 d. *Educ:* Dulwich College; Trinity College, Cambridge (MA). *Directorships:* Lethos Holdings Ltd 1967; Parrish Stockbrokers 1987. *Other Activities:* Committee Member, City Liaison Group. *Clubs:* Reform. *Recreations:* Reading, Music, Woodcutting.

THOMPSON, Norman Victor; Head of Corporate Communications, Leeds Permanent Building Society, since 1988; Corporate Affairs, Internal & External Communications, Public Relations. *Career:* Anglian Water Authority, Chief Information Officer 1974-80; Access Joint Credit Card Co Manager, Corporate Communications 1980-88. *Biog: b.* 9 September 1934. *Nationality:* British. *m.* 1956, Stella Anne (née Bailey); 2 s; 2 d. *Educ:* Kibworth Beauchamp Grammar. *Professional Organisations:* MIPR; Member, British Association of Industrial Editors. *Recreations:* Art, Theatre.

THOMPSON, P J; Director, S G Warburg & Co Ltd.

THOMPSON, Peter John Stuart; Managing Partner, Hepworth & Chadwick, since 1989. *Career:* Articled in London 1969-71; Hepworth & Chadwick 1971-; Partner 1974. *Biog: b.* 28 September 1946. *Nationality:* British. *m.* 1970, Morven Mary Thompson (née Hanscome). 1s (decd); 1 d. *Educ:* Rossall; Leeds University (LLB). *Directorships:* Eversheds Legal Services Ltd 1990. *Other Activities:* Chartered Inst Arbitrators (Chairman of Branch 1987-88). *Professional Organisations:* Law Society. *Clubs:* RAC, Leeds.

THOMPSON, Richard; Chairman, G T Venture Management Holdings Ltd.

THOMSON, A J R; Vice-President, The Institute of Bankers in Scotland.

THOMSON, Sir Adam; CBE; Chairman, Gold Stag Ltd.

THOMSON, Charles Grant; General Manager (Finance) and Actuary, The Scottish Mutual Assurance Society, since 1990. *Career:* The Scottish Mutual Assurance Society 1969-; Asst Actuary 1974-79; Snr Asst Actuary 1979-80; Dep Jt Actuary 1980-82; Actuarial Mgr 1982-84; Assistant General Manager 1984-90. *Biog: b.* 23 September 1948. *Nationality:* British. *m.* 1970, Pamela; 1 s; 1 d. *Educ:* Jordanhill College School; Glasgow University (BSc Hons 1st). *Directorships:* Scottish Mutual Pension Funds Investment Ltd 1990 (exec); Scottish Mutual Investment Managers Ltd 1990 (exec); Scottish Mutual Portfolio Managers Ltd 1990 (exec); Scottish Mutual Nominees Ltd 1990 (exec). *Other Activities:* Member, Faculty Council 1983-86, 1989-; Chm, Faculty Examinations Board 1989-. *Professional Organisations:* FFA. *Clubs:* Windyhill Golf Club (Handicap 8), Western Club, Glasgow Golf Club. *Recreations:* Golf, Photography, Wine, Foreign Travel.

THOMSON, Chilton; Director, Gartmore Investment Limited, since 1989; International Investment. *Career:* Posthorn Global Asset Management (London); Director International Equity Portfoio Management 1984-89; Morgan Guaranty (London), Vice President & Portfolio Manager 1977-84; US Army, Sergent 1963-66. *Biog: b.* 20 October 1942. *Nationality:* British. *m.* 1971, Alyson (née Vero); 1 s; 2 d. *Educ:* Deerfield Academy (US High School Diploma); Yale University (BA); Keble College, Oxford (MA); Stanford University (MBA).

Directorships: Gartmore 1989 (exec); Nippon Credit Bank/ Gartmore (Joint Venture) 1990 (exec). *Professional Organisations:* Chartered Financial Analyst; New York Society of Security Analysts; UK Society of Investment Analysts. *Clubs:* Hurlingham Club. *Recreations:* Skiing, Gardening.

THOMSON, David Graham; Director, Panmure Gordon & Co, since 1989; Corporate Finance. *Career:* Clarke Pickering & Co, Articled Clerk 1956-61; Peat Marwick Mitchell & Co, Chartered Accountant 1961-63; S G Warburg & Co Ltd, Executive 1963-69; W Greenwell & Co, Partner 1969-87. *Biog: b.* 15 April 1939. *Nationality:* British. *m.* 1962, Brenda Evelyn (née Rogers); 2 s. *Educ:* Raynes Park Grammar. *Professional Organisations:* FCA.

THOMSON, David P; Director General, British Invisibles.

THOMSON, David Paget; RD; Member, Monopolies and Mergers Commission, since 1984. *Career:* National Service in Navy, Sub-Lt RNVR/Lt-Cmdr RNR 1953-55; Lazard Brothers, Exec 1956-65; Exec Dir 1965-84; British Embassy (Bonn), Counsellor 1971-73; Lazard Brothers, Non-Exec Dir 1984-86. *Biog: b.* 19 March 1931. *Nationality:* British. *m.* 1959, Patience Mary (née Bragg); 2 s; 2 d. *Educ:* Rugby School; Grenoble University; Trinity College, Cambridge (BA, MA). *Directorships:* Monopolies and Mergers Commission 1984 (non-exec); Jufcrest Ltd 1984-89 (non-exec) Chm; Henley Distance Learning Ltd 1985 (non-exec); FC Germany Investment Trust plc 1990 (non-exec) Chm; Medical Sickness Society 1990 (non-exec). *Other Activities:* Past Master, The Worshipful Co of Plumbers; Trustee, Lucy Cavendish College, Cambridge; Trustee, Portsmouth Naval Base Property Trust; Chairman, Fitzwilliam Museum Trust, Cambridge. *Professional Organisations:* The Royal Institution (Chm of Council 1985-87); Henley Mgmnt College (Court of Governors, Chm Finance Ctee). *Clubs:* Athenaeum. *Recreations:* Hill-Walking, Gardening.

THOMSON, Duncan W; WS; Partner, W & J Burness WS, since 1984; Trusts, Landed Estates, Farms. *Biog: b.* 23 October 1954. *Nationality:* British. *m.* 1985, Alyson; 1 d. *Educ:* George Watsons College, Edinburgh; University of Aberdeen (LLB). *Clubs:* New Club (Edinburgh), Guernsey Yacht Club. *Recreations:* Sailing, Skiing, Fishing.

THOMSON, F Sinclair; Chief Executive, Hepworth plc, since 1986; Overall Corporate Strategy and Achievement of Financial Targets for Group. *Career:* De La Rue Group, Marketing Trainee 1964-69; Midland Aluminium Co Ltd (Worked for subsidiary, Glow-Worm), Marketing Director/Managing Director/Main Board Member 1970-77; TI Group plc, Managing Director, Domestic Appliance Div 1977-86. *Biog: b.* 20

January 1943. *Nationality:* British. *m.* 1967, Elizabeth Annie; 2 s. *Educ:* Manchester University (BA Econ). *Directorships:* Hepworth plc 1986 (exec); Hepworth Building Products Ltd (exec) Chm; Hepworth Home Products Ltd (exec) Chm; Hepworth Minerals & Chemicals Ltd (exec) Chm; Hepworth Refractories Ltd (exec) Chm; Hepworth Industrial Products Ltd (exec) Chm; Societe Financiere Saunier Duval SA 1990 Chm; Hepworth Properties Ltd 1989 (exec) Chm. *Other Activities:* Joint Chairman, Sheffield Percent Club. *Professional Organisations:* Companion, British Institute of Management; Institute of Directors. *Recreations:* Gardening, Decorating.

THOMSON, Ian; Partner, Dennis Murphy, Campbell & Co.

THOMSON, James Alexander; Director, Hambros Bank Ltd, since 1986; Commercial Banking. *Career:* Charterhouse Japhet 1970-73; Hill Samuel & Co Ltd 1973-78; Deutsche Bank AG 1978-85. *Biog: b.* 10 April 1948. *m.* 1970, Sylvia (née McNulty); 2 s. *Educ:* The King's School, Canterbury; Oriel College, Oxford (MA). *Directorships:* Hambros Bank (Jersey) Ltd 1986; Hambros Bank (Gibraltar) Ltd 1986.

THOMSON, John Murray; Chairman, London & Manchester Group plc, since 1985; Life Assurance & Financial Services. *Career:* Lazard Brothers & Co Ltd 1950-59; Manufacturers Hanover, Asst Vice-President 1959-66; Brooke Bond Group plc, Group Finance Dir, Managing Director, Dep Chief Exec 1966-84; London & Manchester Group plc, Dep Chm, Chm 1985-. *Biog: b.* 30 January 1928. *Nationality:* British. *m.* 1959, Ingrid (née Haugas); 1 s; 1 d. *Educ:* High School of Falkirk; Edinburgh University (MA). *Directorships:* Scottish & Newcastle Breweries plc 1979 (non-exec); J Bibby & Sons plc 1981 (non-exec) Vice-Chm; Thames Water Authority 1984 (non-exec); Czarnikow (Holdings) Ltd 1985 (non-exec); London & Manchester 1985 (non-exec) Chm; Borthwicks plc 1987 (non-exec) Chm. *Other Activities:* Carr-Gomm Society. *Recreations:* Skiing, Walking, Theatre.

THOMSON, Keith; Partner, Linklaters & Paines, since 1986; Capital Markets & Banking. *Biog: b.* 22 September 1953. *Nationality:* British. *m.* 1979, Janet; 3 d. *Educ:* University of Durham (BA); University of Cambridge (LLB). *Other Activities:* City of London Solicitors Company. *Professional Organisations:* Law Society. *Recreations:* Squash, Tennis.

THOMSON, R E; Director, Metheuen (Lloyds Underwriting Agents) Limited.

THOMSON, R S; Partner, Clay & Partners, since 1986; Advice to Corporate Clients on Pensions & Associated Matters. *Career:* Clay & Partners, Actuarial Trainee 1979-84; Actuary 1984-86. *Biog: b.* 18 February

1955. *Nationality:* British. *m.* 1982, Alison Mary (née Bonnett); 1 s. *Educ:* Royal Liberty Grammar, Romford; Leeds University, (BSc Hons First Class Mathematics); Cambridge University (Diploma in Statistics). *Professional Organisations:* Fellow, Institute of Actuaries; Member, Association of Consulting Actuaries; Member, International Actuarial Association. *Clubs:* Biddenden Squash, Biddenden Tennis. *Recreations:* Tennis, Squash, Golf, Reading, Gardening.

THOMSON, R T A; Partner, Pannell Kerr Forster.

THOMSON, S; CBE; Staff Operations Director, Ford Motor Credit Company.

THOMSON, George Morgan; The Rt Hon Lord Thomson of Monifieth; Kt, PC; Non-Executive Chairman, Value & Income Trust, since 1986. *Career:* Journalism 1937-40; RAF 1941-46; Political Journalism, Editor Forward 1946-56; East Dundee MP (Lab) 1952-72; Foreign & Commonwealth Affairs, Cabinet Minister 1964-70; Regional Development, EEC Commissioner 1973-77; Advertising Standards Authority, Chairman 1977-80; First Crown Estate Commissioner; Independent Broadcasting Authority, Chairman 1980-88; House of Lords, Liberal Democrats Broadcasting Spokesman, 1989-. *Biog: b.* 16 January 1921. *Nationality:* British. *m.* 1948, Grace (née Jenkins); 2 d. *Educ:* Grove Academy, Dundee. *Directorships:* Value & Income Trust plc 1986 Chairman (non-exec); Grant Leisure Ltd 1988 Chairman (non-exec); Woolwich Building Society 1979 Deputy Chairman (non-exec); Royal Bank of Scotland 1977-90 (non-exec); ICI plc 1977-89 (non-exec). *Other Activities:* Trustee, Pilgrim Trust; Trustee, Leeds Castle Foundation; Chairman, Suzy Lamplugh Trust. *Professional Organisations:* Fellow, Royal Television Society; Royal Society (Edinburgh). *Clubs:* Brooks's. *Recreations:* Swimming, Cycling.

THORBURN, Ian Gordon; Executive Director, Johnson Matthey, since 1983; Administration. *Career:* Johnson Matthey, Financial Controller 1982-83; Executive Director, Finance 1983-87; Administration 1987-. *Biog: b.* 23 August 1940. *Nationality:* British. *m.* 1968, Susan Patricia (née Walton); 1 s; 1 d. *Educ:* Glenalmond College; Trinity College, Oxford (MA). *Professional Organisations:* FCA. *Clubs:* Various Golf Clubs. *Recreations:* Music & Sport.

THORN, David; Chairman, Target Group plc.

THORN, David Bruce; Deputy Managing Director, TSB Group plc.

THORN, John Leonard; Independent Board Member, The Securities Association, since 1987; Conduct of Business Rules Committee, Membership & Disciplinary Appeals Tribunal. *Career:* Clifton College, Bristol, Asst Master 1949-61; Repton School, Derby, Headmaster 1961-68; Winchester College, Headmaster 1968-85; Headmasters' Conference, Chm 1981. *Biog: b.* 28 April 1925. *Nationality:* British. *m.* 1955, Veronica Laura (née Maconochie); 1 s; 1 d. *Educ:* St Paul's School; Corpus Christi College, Cambridge (BA, MA). *Other Activities:* Stowe School (Governor); Oakham School (Trustee); Cancer Research Campaign (Exec Ctee); Hampshire Buildings Preservation Trust; Southampton University Dept of Education (Visiting Fellow). *Professional Organisations:* Headmasters' Conference (Hon Associate Member). *Publications:* A History of England, 1961; The Road to Winchester, 1989; Many Articles. *Clubs:* Garrick. *Recreations:* Writing, Reading, Gardening, The Arts.

THORNBOROUGH, R M; Director, NCL Investments Limited.

THORNE, Anthony Charles; Managing Director, Smith Barney & Co.

THORNE, Barry; Partner, Titmuss Sainer & Webb.

THORNE, Matthew W J; Investment Director, Beazer plc, since 1985; Corporate Finance/Acquisitions. *Career:* Price Waterhouse, London 1975-78; County NatWest, London 1978-83. *Biog: b.* 27 June 1952. *Nationality:* British. *m.* 1978, Sheila Leigh (née Phillimore); 3 s; 1 d. *Educ:* Dragon School, Oxford; Kings School, Canterbury; Trinity College, Oxford (MA). *Professional Organisations:* FCA.

THORNE, R N; Director, Barclays de Zoete Wedd Securities Ltd.

THORNE, Ms R P; Group Financial Controller, Grand Metropolitan plc, since 1990. *Career:* BOC Ltd, Accountant 1974-77; Mothercare plc, Chief Accountant 1977-82; Habitat Mothercare plc, Group Financial Controller 1982-85; Storehouse plc, Group Financial Controller 1986-86; House of Fraser-Harrods Ltd, Financial Director & Company Secretary 1986-90; Grand Metropolitan plc, Group Financial Controller 1990-. *Biog: b.* 12 February 1952. *Nationality:* British. *m.* 1976 (divorced 1984), Peter Humphrey. *Educ:* Warwick University (BSc Hons - Mathematics & Economics). *Directorships:* Bioproductors Ltd 1990; Biosensors Ltd 1990; Caxton Pension Trust Ltd 1990; Flexigage Instruments Ltd 1990; Flexigage Ltd 1990; Flexigage Manufacturing Ltd 1990; Grand Metropolitan Biotechnology Ltd 1990; Grand Metropolitan Finance plc 1990; Grand Metropolitan Innovation Ltd 1990; Grand Metropolitan Nominee Company (No 2) Ltd 1990; Grand Metropolitan Research No 2 Ltd 1990; Grand Metropolitan Research No 3 Ltd 1990; Grand Metropolitan Second Investments Ltd 1990; Grand Metropolitan Third Investments Ltd 1990; Grandmet Hotels & Catering Ltd 1990; Leisure International Ltd 1990; Precis (175) Ltd 1990; Watney Mann & Truman Holdings plc 1990; Habitat Mothercare Employee Share Trustees Ltd -1986;

Harrodian Trustees Ltd -1990; Harrods (Continental) Ltd -1990; Harrods (Management) Ltd -1990; Harrods Bank Ltd -1990; Harrods Estates Offices Ltd -1990; Harrods Heinemann Ltd -1990; Harrods Ltd -1990; Micromono Ltd -1986; Mothercare Finance Ltd -1986; Precis (689) Ltd -1990; TCR Properties Ltd -1986; Wylie & Company Ltd -1990; Conran Mothercare US Inc -1986. *Other Activities:* Council Member, CIMA. *Professional Organisations:* FCMA, MCT.

THORNEYCROFT, Maxwell Bennett; Managing Partner, Gouldens, since 1987; Corporate Finance. *Career:* Macfarlanes, Articled Clerk 1973-75; Norton Rose Botterell & Roche, Solicitor 1975-81; Gouldens, Solicitor 1981-83; Ptnr 1983-. *Biog: b.* 2 September 1949. *Nationality:* British. *m.* 1978, Jennifer C P (née Archbold); 1 s; 1 d. *Educ:* The King's School, Macclesfield; Lincoln College, Oxford (BA Hons). *Professional Organisations:* The Law Society. *Recreations:* Opera, Hill Walking, Tennis.

THORNHAM, David Alan; Managing Director, Midland Montagu Corporate Banking, Midland Bank plc, since 1990. *Career:* Midland Bank, Group Reg Dir 1978-80; Asst Gen Mgr 1980-82; Forward Trust Group MD 1982-84; Credit & Risk Director, Domestic 1984-86; Global Banking 1986-88; Group Risk Management & Audit Director 1988-90. *Biog: b.* 21 November 1937. *Nationality:* British. *m.* 1962, Gwendoline (née Clayton); 1 s; 1 d. *Educ:* Hymers College, Hull. *Professional Organisations:* FCIB; BBA. *Recreations:* Golf.

THORNHILL, Richard John; Partner, Slaughter and May, since 1986; Corporate Finance. *Biog: b.* 13 November 1954. *m.* 1980, Nicola (née Dyke); 1 s. *Educ:* Malvern College; St John's College, Oxford (MA). *Professional Organisations:* The Law Society. *Clubs:* RAC, Royal Hong Kong Jockey Club.

THORNTON, B; Partner, Moores Rowland.

THORNTON, D R; Financial Director & Secretary, Denis M Clayton & Co Limited.

THORNTON, John L; Managing Director, Goldman Sachs International Limited.

THORNTON, Jonathan; Managing Director, Close Investment Management Limited, since 1984; Venture & Development Capital. *Career:* Arthur Andersen & Co, Accountant 1968-71; 3i Group plc, Investment Controller 1972-77; Aregon Group Limited, Finance Director 1977-81; CIN Venture Managers Limited, Director, then Deputy MD 1981-85. *Biog: b.* 5 March 1947. *Nationality:* British. *m.* 1973, Caroline Mary (née Dewar); 2 s. *Educ:* Marlborough College; Lincoln College, Oxford (MA Hons PPE); Cranfield School of Management. *Directorships:* Close Brothers Group plc 1985 (exec); Close Investment Management Limited

1984 MD; Crown Industrial Group 1987 (non-exec); Euroventures Management UK Ltd 1990 Chm. *Other Activities:* Churchwarden, St James's Church, Muswell Hill, London. *Professional Organisations:* Fellow, Institute of Chartered Accountants in England and Wales. *Recreations:* Swimming, Tennis.

THORNTON, Nicholas; Executive Director, Bank of Wales plc.

THORNTON, Paul Noel; Partner, R Watson & Sons, since 1977; Advice on Pension Arrangements, Marketing of the Firms Services. *Career:* Friends Provident Life Office, Actuarial Trainee 1972-74; R Watson & Sons, Various to Partner 1974-77. *Educ:* City of London School; Worcester College, Oxford (MA). *Directorships:* Watsons Services Ltd 1990 (exec). *Other Activities:* Hon Sec, Inst of Actuaries. *Professional Organisations:* FIA; Member, Intl Actuarial Assoc; Member, Intl Assoc of Consulting Actuaries.

THORNTON, Richard Chicheley; Chairman, Thornton Management Ltd.

THORNTON, Robert; Partner, Forsyte Kerman.

THORNTON, Timothy Kenneth; Director, Kleinwort Grieveson Securities Ltd, since 1986; UK Equity Institutional Sales. *Career:* Joseph Sebag Ptnr 1963-79; Carr Sebag Ptnr 1979-82; Grieveson Grant Ptnr 1982-86; Kleinwort Grieveson Dir 1986-. *Biog: b.* 7 March 1935. *Nationality:* British. *m.* 1966, Jacqueline Green (née Hillman); 1 s; 1 d. *Educ:* Eton College. *Professional Organisations:* Member, The Intl Stock Exchange. *Clubs:* White's, Pratt's. *Recreations:* Gardening, Skiing.

THORP, Clive Robert; Partner, Clyde & Co, since 1981; Shipping Law. *Career:* Holman Fenwick and Willan, Assistant Solicitor 1976-78; Clyde & Co, Assistant Solicitor 1978-81. *Biog: b.* 28 August 1950. *Nationality:* British. *m.* 1976, Jean Rosemary (née Barclay); 2 s. *Educ:* Malvern College, University of Hull (BSc Econ); College of Law. *Professional Organisations:* Law Society. *Clubs:* Landsdowne.

THORP, David; Director, 3i plc, since 1985; UK Investment Support. *Career:* Alcan Production Eng 1967-69; 3i plc 1971-. *Biog: b.* 22 July 1945. *Nationality:* British. *m.* 1969, Christine Janice (née Kenyon); 3 s. *Educ:* Portsmouth Grammar School; Queens' College, Cambridge (MA); London Business School (MSc). *Directorships:* 3i plc 1985. *Professional Organisations:* Institute of Directors (Corporate Affairs Ctee). *Recreations:* Cricket, Tennis.

THORPE, Christopher R; Director, Panmure Gordon Bankers Ltd.

THORPE, David Hedley; Director, Kleinwort Benson Securities Limited.

THORPE, Phillip; Chief Executive & Director, The Association of Futures Brokers and Dealers Limited.

THORPE, W P; Finance Director, City Merchants Bank Ltd.

THRALL, Andrew; Staff Director, Securities and Investments Board.

THREADGOLD, Dr Andrew Richard; Chief Executive & Director of Securities Investment, Postel Investment Management Ltd, since 1987. *Career:* The International Wool Secretariat Mgr, Economics Information 1971-74; Bank of England Adviser Economics Div 1974-84; Postel Investment Mgmnt Ltd On Secondment-Chief Economist 1984-86; Bank of England Adviser and Subsequently Head of Fin Supervision Gen Div 1986-87. *Biog: b.* 8 February 1944. *Nationality:* British. *m.* (Sep). *Educ:* Brentwood School; Nottingham University (BA); Melbourne University (PhD). *Directorships:* Allied Provincial Securities Ltd 1987 (non-exec); IBM UK Pensions Trust Ltd 1990.

THRING, Peter Streatfeild; TD; Partner, Ernst & Young, since 1989; Banking and Financial Services Industry - Audit. *Career:* Barton, Mayhew & Co Articled Clerk 1957-60; Acct 1960-67; Ptnr 1967-71; Turquands, Barton, Mayhew & Co Ptnr 1972-79; Ernst & Whinney Ptnr 1979-89; Ernst & Young, Ptnr 1989-. *Biog: b.* 31 December 1933. *Nationality:* British. *m.* 1962, Joanna Elizabeth (née Duff); 1 s; 1 d. *Educ:* Winchester College; Corpus Christi College, Oxford (MA). *Professional Organisations:* FCA. *Clubs:* United Oxford & Cambridge University. *Recreations:* Local Church, Gardening, Bee-Keeping.

THRUSH, P; Senior Vice President and Branch Manager, Union Bank of Switzerland.

THUM, Maximilien John Alexandre; Senior Litigation Partner, Ashurst Morris Crisp, since 1967; Arbitration & General Commercial Litigation, Defamation Trade Libel, Judicial Review Intellectual Property, Product Liability, Professional Negligence. *Career:* RAF, Pilot Officer 1955-57; Rodyk & Davidson, Singapore, Advocate & Solicitor 1957-60; Law Society, Assistant Solicitor, Professional Purposes 1961; Sharpe Pritchard & Co, Assistant Solicitor & Partner 1961-66; Ashurst Morris Crisp, Senior Litigation Partner 1966. *Biog: b.* 15 February 1933. *Nationality:* British. *m.* 1982, Valerie (née Kay); 2 s; 1 d. *Educ:* Ecole Internationale de Genéve; Chigwell School, Essex; Law Society College of Law (Solicitors Final Examination). *Professional Organisations:* International Bar Association; American Bar Association. *Clubs:* RAC. *Recreations:* Photography, Opera, Swimming, Tennis, Cars.

THURNHAM, Anthony; Partner, Linklaters & Paines.

THURSTANS, Kenneth John; Managing Director, Chambers & Remington Ltd. *Directorships:* Lloyds Bank Stockbrokers Ltd (non-exec). *Professional Organisations:* FCA; AMSIA; Member, The International Stock Exchange.

THURSTON, Julian Paul; Partner, McKenna & Co, since 1986; Technology, Marketing (Intellectual Property). *Career:* McKenna & Co, Articled Clerk 1977-79; Asst Solicitor 1979-86. *Biog: b.* 11 May 1955. *Nationality:* British. *m.* Julia; 1 s; 1 d. *Educ:* Oxford (MA). *Publications:* Various Articles, 1987-89.

TICKEL, Ra; Company News Editor, The Daily Telegraph, since 1987. *Career:* The Daily Telegraph 1963.

TICKELL, Tom; Deputy Personal Finance Editor & Diary Editor, The Sunday Telegraph.

TICKNER, Richard; Director, Samuel Montagu & Co Ltd, since 1983; Head of Capital Markets. *Career:* Lloyds Bank, Trainee 1971-73; Samuel Montagu, Various 1973-. *Biog: b.* 19 March 1951. *m.* 1977, Jane Frances (née Boulton); 3 s. *Educ:* Beckenham Grammar School; Lancaster University.

TIDBURY, Sir Charles; Director, Mercantile Credit Company Limited.

TIDMAN, J; Executive Director, Daiwa Europe Limited.

TIERNAN, Gary L; Director, County NatWest, since 1990; Traded Options. *Career:* Credit Suisse (Zurich), Head Dealer in Soffex 1989; Morgan Grenfell Securities (London), Senior Dealer Traded Options & Euro-Sterling Convertibles 1985-88. *Biog: b.* 28 March 1963. *Nationality:* British. *m.* 1989, Noelle (née Nusslé). *Educ:* Sheffield University (BA Economics, Accounting & Financial Management). *Recreations:* Bridge, Skiing, Golf, Tennis.

TIGUE, Jeremy John; Director, Foreign & Colonial Management Limited, since 1990; UK Investment Management. *Career:* Foreign & Colonial Management 1981. *Biog: b.* 21 August 1959. *Nationality:* British. *Educ:* Oxford University (MA). *Directorships:* F&C Smaller Companies plc 1989 (exec). *Professional Organisations:* AMSIA.

TILBROOK, John Jeremy; Finance Director, Beeson Gregory Limited, since 1989. *Career:* JF Nash Securities Limited, Finance Director 1968-81; Allebone & Sons plc, Chief Executive 1982-88. *Biog: b.* 7 August 1942. *Nationality:* British. *m.* 1986, Dianne (née Kirk); 2 s;

1 d. *Directorships:* The Video Store Group plc 1990 (non-exec). *Professional Organisations:* Fellow, Institute of Chartered Accountants in England & Wales.

TILBY, Alan; Deputy Chairman, W C R S Mathews Marcantonio.

TILEY, J S; Partner, Touche Ross & Co.

TILLER, L; Director, Hambros Bank Limited.

TILLEY, Charles Basil; Group Finance Director, Hambros plc, since 1989. *Career:* Peat Marwick McLintock, Partner 1974-88. *Biog: b.* 22 December 1950. *m.* 1984, Sarah (née Morgan); 1 s; 1 d. *Educ:* Seaford College. *Clubs:* Seaview Yacht Club, Brading Haven Yacht Club. *Recreations:* Sailing, Squash, Running, Skiing.

TILLING, J P; Underwriting Director, Gravett & Tilling (Underwriting Agencies) Ltd.

TIMBRELL, Martin Clive; Head of Economics Department, University of Exeter, since 1990; Lecturer in Economics, since 1976. *Career:* Shell International Computer Programmer 1967; Ministry of Technology, Assitant Statistician 1970; University of Manchester, Research Assistant, Dept of Economics 1971-74; University of Southampton, Lecturer in Economics 1974-76; University of Exeter, Lecturer in Economics 1976-; Academic Secretary 1986-89. *Biog: b.* 14 July 1949. *Educ:* Latymer Upper School; Churchill College, Cambridge (MA Econ IIi); University of Warwick (MA Econ). *Other Activities:* Vice Chairman of Governors, Cullompton St Andrew's Junior School; Former Chairman, PTA; Treasurer, East Devon Federation of PTAs; Examiner, London External Degree, (BSc Econ) 1978-80; Examiner, Civil Service Commission, Civil Service Entrance Examinations 1981-84; Examiner, Institute of Statisticians Graduate Diploma in Statistics 1981-; External Examiner, Nottingham Polytechnic, BSc Econ, BA in Social Studies, 1988-; Pennsylvania State University Program, Lecturer; Individual Lectures and Courses for a variety of outside bodies including the Workers Education Association, Extramural Studies, Schoolteachers conferences and Sixth Form conferences; University of Exeter, Devon District Manpower Committee 1980-84; Treasurer, Readers and Lecturers Association 1981-86; Board of the Faculty of Social Studies 1981-82 & 1987-; SSDPU Committee 1983-90; Senate 1983-86, 1990-; Computer Committee 1983-86; Library Committee 1983-86 & 1990-; Faculty Planning Committee 1986-89; Standing Committee 1990-. *Publications:* Mathematics for Economists, 1985; International Stock Exchange Official Yearbook, editor, 1990; Journal of Interdisciplinary Economics (with K J Penney) editor; Numerous other books, articles and papers. *Recreations:* Sport.

TIMMS, Jonathan Richard; Director of Research, Charterhouse Tilney, since 1987; Head of Building Industry Research Team. *Career:* Friends Provident, Trainee 1967-68; Simon & Coates, Building Analyst 1968; Research Mgr 1973; Tilney & Co, Building Analyst 1975; Partner 1977; Charterhouse Tilney, Director 1986; Director of Research 1988. *Biog: b.* April 1945. *m.* 1969, Judith (née Blay); 2 s; 1 d. *Educ:* St John's College, Leatherhead; Oriel College, Oxford (MA). *Professional Organisations:* ASIA.

TIMMS, Robert Lionel; Human Resources Executive, The Chase Manhattan Bank.

TINDALE, Lawrence Victor Dolman; CBE; Deputy Chairman, 3i Group plc, since 1974. *Career:* McClelland Ker, Articled Clerk 1938-39; Manager 1946-50; Partner 1951-59; ICFC 1959; DTI, Dir of Industrial Devt 1972-74. *Biog: b.* 29 April 1921. *m.* 1946, Beatrice Mabel (née Barton); 1 s; 1 d. *Educ:* Upper Latymer School. *Directorships:* National Research Dev Corp 1974 (non-exec); Northern Engineering Industries plc 1974 (non-exec); National British Canadian Investment Co plc 1979 (non-exec); National Enterprise Board 1980 (non-exec); British Technology Group 1981 (non-exec); C & J Clark Ltd 1986 Chairman; Polly Peck Intl plc 1985 (non-exec); Shandwick plc 1985 (non-exec); Subsidiaries of 3i Group plc (exec). *Other Activities:* Treasurer, Society for the Protection of Ancient Buildings. *Professional Organisations:* BIM (Member of Council); IIM, Institute of Directors. *Clubs:* Reform, St James's (Manchester), Australia Club (Melbourne). *Recreations:* Opera.

TINDALL, Daniel Purser; Partner, Holman Fenwick & Willan, since 1987; Company Commercial including Shipping Finance. *Career:* Heald & Nickinson, Solicitor 1980-82; Holman Fenwick & Willan, Solicitor 1982-86. *Biog: b.* 6 October 1955. *Nationality:* British. *m.* 1990. *Educ:* London School of Economics (LLB). *Clubs:* Chelsea Arts.

TINDALL, Terence William; Director, Banking Division, Barclays de Zoete Wedd Limited, since 1988; Specialist Property Finance and Limited and Non-Recourse Finance. *Career:* Barclays Bank plc Various to Jnr Mgmnt 1967-78; Barclays Merchant Bank/BZW Asst Mgr to Asst Dir 1978-87. *Biog: b.* 3 June 1949. *m.* 1974, Jean Doreen (née Gentry); 1 s; 1 d. *Educ:* Slough Grammar School; Open University (BA). *Directorships:* Ebbgate Holdings Ltd 1988 (exec). *Professional Organisations:* ACIB. *Recreations:* Golf.

TIPLADY, Charles Edward; Director, Touche, Remnant & Co, since 1987; Administration and Information Technology. *Career:* L Messel & Co, Computer Services Manager & Information Technology Manager 1970-86; The Stock Exchange, Systems Analyst 1968-70. *Biog: b.* 23 August 1945. *Nationality:* British. *m.* 1972, Anne;

3 d. *Educ:* University of Newcastle upon Tyne (BA). *Directorships:* Touche Remnant & Co 1987 (exec). *Recreations:* Shooting, Training Gundogs, Early English Furniture.

TISBURY, M H; Associate, Grimley J R Eve.

TISCH, P P; Director, Société Générale Strauss Turnbull.

TITCOMB, Malcolm; Partner (Birmingham), Evershed Wells & Hind.

TITCOMB, Simon James; Non-Executive Director, Barclays de Zoete Wedd Holdings Ltd, since 1986. *Career:* Singleton Fabian & Co Articled Clerk 1949-55; Royal Army Pay Corps 2nd Lt 1955-57; de Zoete & Bevan Partner 1962-66; Managing Partner 1966-76; Snr Partner 1976-86. *Biog: b.* 10 July 1931. *Nationality:* British. *m.* 1957, Ann Constance (née Vokins); 2 s; 1 d. *Educ:* Brighton College. *Directorships:* T R City of London Investment plc 1982 Chm; E C C plc 1986 (non-exec); Ling Dynamic Systems Ltd 1982 Chm; Astrac Ltd 1988 Chm; Taylor Clark plc 1989 Dep Chm. *Professional Organisations:* FCA; CBIM. *Clubs:* Brooks's, City of London. *Recreations:* Golf, Bridge, Conservation.

TOALSTER, John Raymond; Director, Hoare Govett, since 1987; Investment Research. *Career:* University of Sierra Leone University Teacher 1964-68; Mobil Oil Corp Planner 1969-70; Hedderwick, Borthwick Snr Oil Analyst 1970-77; Kuwait International Investment Co Banking Mgr 1977-81. *Biog: b.* 12 March 1941. *Nationality:* British. *m.* 1963, Christine Anne (née Paget); 1 s; 2 d. *Educ:* Kingston High School, Hull; LSE (BSc Hons). *Professional Organisations:* London Oil Analysts Group, Institute of Petroleum. *Publications:* BP Oil Discovery Costs, Limited Circulation. *Clubs:* Economics Society, LSE. *Recreations:* Sailing, Tennis, Swimming, Travel.

TOBIN, T T; Director, Leslie & Godwin Limited.

TOD, M N; Head of Private Client Dept, Field Fisher Waterhouse.

TODD, James; Director, Lazard Brothers & Co Ltd, since 1977; Group Compliance Director. *Career:* United Dominions Trust Clerical 1953-56; Martins Bank Ltd Clerical 1956-59; Lazard Brothers & Co Ltd 1959-. *Biog: b.* 19 February 1932. *Nationality:* British. *m.* 1953, Isabella S J (née Green); 1 s; 3 d. *Educ:* John Street Senior Secondary School, Glasgow; Harvard Business School. *Directorships:* Lazard Brothers & Co (Jersey) Ltd 1987 (non-exec); (Guernsey) 1987 (non-exec). *Professional Organisations:* ACIB. *Clubs:* RAC. *Recreations:* Golf, Travel.

TOFTE JENSEN, K; Executive Director, Unibank plc.

TOGAWA, Masahide; Executive Director, Yamaichi International (Europe) Limited.

TOGNINO, John N; Managing Director, Merrill Lynch International Limited, since 1988; Equities Internationally. *Career:* Merrill Lynch 1957-70; A G Becker 1970-72; Merrill Lynch 1972-. *Biog: b.* 20 September 1938. *Nationality:* American. *m.* 1959, Norma (née Borelli); 2 s; 1 d. *Educ:* Fordham University, New York (BA Economics Summa Cum Laude). *Directorships:* Merrill Lynch 1988 (exec) MD; Merrill Lynch, Pierce, Fenner & Smith Inc 1977 VP. *Other Activities:* Past Chairman, National Security Traders Association and now Chairman of its Advisory Board; Member, Trading Committee, SOES User Committee; Member, International Committee of the National Association of Securities Dealers (USA); Former Member, OTC Trading Committee of the Securities Industry Association (USA); Member, International Equity Dealers Association; Member of the Investment Assoc (New York); Mem & Past Pres, Securities Assoc (New York); Member, Executive Committee of Merrill Lynch Europe & the Middle East; Trader of the Year, Traders Monthly Magazine 1983; OTC Man of the Year, OTC Digest Magazine 1986. *Clubs:* Scarsdale Golf Club. *Recreations:* Tennis, Golf, Opera, Theatre.

TOKER, Sencar; Managing Director, Midland Montagu Ltd, since 1988; Midland Group's Network of European Branches, Subsidiaries, Associated Companies and Representative offices; Trust Corporations in Channel Islands, Isle of Man & Cayman Islands. *Career:* BCI Ltd, Exec Dir 1975-80; Midland Bank SA (France), Exec Dir 1980-82; Handelsfinanz Midl (Switzerland), Chief Exec Officer 1982-84; Credit Risk Intl, Midland Credit Mgr 1984-86. *Biog: b.* 3 March 1940. *Nationality:* Italian. *m.* 1964, Paola (née Pirogalli); 2 s. *Educ:* W London College of Business Administration (HND). *Directorships:* Handelsfinanz Midl 1985 (non-exec); EURAB Ltd 1985 (non-exec); Thomas Cook Group 1986 (non-exec); UBAF Ltd 1986 (non-exec).

TOKLEY, Ms Jacqueline Margaret; Managing Director, Citioptions Ltd, since 1990; Derivatives. *Career:* Edward Moore & Sons, Graduate Chartered Accountant 1980-81; International Commodities Clearing House Ltd, International Clearing Manager, International Clearing Derivatives Mkts 1981-87; Chicago Board of Trade, Assistant Director, European Office, Marketing & Education Derivatives 1987; Citioptions, Citicorp Managing Director 1987-. *Biog: b.* 22 July 1956. *Nationality:* British. *Educ:* Birmingham University (Economics/Political Science Soc Sci Jt Hons 2:i). *Directorships:* Citioptions Ltd 1990 (exec). *Professional Organisations:* Individual Member, Intl Stock Exchange; Securities Industry Association Diploma.

TOKUHIRO, K; Chairman, Dowa Insurance Company (UK) Limited.

TOLAND, G K; Partner, Lovell White Durrant.

TOLKIEN, Richard Ian; Director, Morgan Grenfell & Co Ltd, since 1989; Corporate Finance. *Career:* H M Treasury Principal 1977-82; Morgan Grenfell & Co Various 1982-89. *Biog: b.* 9 January 1955. *Nationality:* British. *m.* 1985, Sally (née Rowley); 1 d. *Educ:* King Edward VI School, Totnes; Exeter College, Oxford (BA Hons 1st). *Directorships:* MG & Co Ltd 1989 (exec). *Other Activities:* Trustee, David Tolkien Trust for Stoke Mandeville. *Clubs:* RORC, RWYC. *Recreations:* Sailing, Family.

TOLLER, Mark Geoffrey Charles; Director, British & Commonwealth Merchant Bank plc, since 1987; Private Banking. *Career:* Dixon Wilson & Co, Articled Clerk 1969-74; Helicopter Marketing Ltd, Acct 1974-75; Guinness Mahon & Co Ltd, Asst Dir 1976-87. *Biog: b.* 23 October 1950. *m.* 1981, Anna (née McGregor); 1 s; 2 d. *Educ:* Harrow School. *Professional Organisations:* ACA. *Recreations:* Horse Racing, Shooting, Golf.

TOLLETT, Michael J; Partner (Birmingham), Evershed Wells & Hind.

TOLMIE, M; Director, Allied Provincial plc.

TOMBS, Francis Leonard; The Rt Hon The Lord Tombs of Brailes; *Career:* General Electric Company Ltd, Witton, Birmingham 1939-45; Birmingham Corporation Electricity Supply Dept 1946-47; British Electricity Authority 1948-57; General Electric Co Ltd Gen Mgr 1958-67; James Howden & Co Dir Gen Mgr 1967-68; South of Scotland Electricity Board, Director of Engineering 1969-73; Deputy Chm 1973-74; Chm 1969-77; Electricity Council for England & Wales Chm 1977-80; The Weir Grp plc Chm 1981-83; T & N plc Chm 1982-89. *Biog: b.* 17 May 1924. *Nationality:* British. *m.* 1949, Marjorie (née Evans); 3 d. *Educ:* University of London (BSc Hons). *Directorships:* N M Rothschild & Sons Ltd 1981; Rolls Royce Ltd 1982; Shell - UK Ltd 1983; Rolls Royce plc 1985 Chm. *Other Activities:* Visiting Professor, Hon LLD, Strathclyde University, 1979; Hon DSc Aston University, 1979; Lodz University Poland, 1980; Cranfield Institute of Technology, 1985; The City University London, 1986; The University of Bradford 1986; Queen's University, Belfast; Surrey University, 1988; Nottingham University, 1989; Warwick University, 1990; Cambridge University, 1990; Hon DTech Loughborough University, 1979; Hon D Ed Council for National Academic Awards, 1989; Hon Fellow, Institute of Civil Engineers; Institute of Mechanical Engineers; Institute of Chemical Engineers; Institute of Production Engineers; Hon Member, British Nuclear Energy Society; Freeman, City of London; Liveryman and Assistant Warden, Goldsmiths' Company; Pro-Chancellor and Chairman, The Council of Cranfield Institute of Technology, 1985; Vice-President, Engineers for Disaster Relief, 1985; Chairman, Molecule Theatre Limited (science for schoolchildren), 1985. *Professional Organisations:* Fellow and past Vice President, Fellowship of Engineering; Fellow and past President, Institution of Electrical Engineering.

TOMKINS, Matthew Lionel Lance; Partner, Field Fisher Waterhouse, since 1988; Property. *Career:* Wild Sapte, Articled Clerk 1981-83; Assistant Solicitor 1984-. *Biog: b.* 27 June 1957. *Nationality:* New Zealander; 1 s. *Educ:* Wanganui College; Winchester College; Jesus College, Cambridge (BA Cantab).

TOMPKINS, Peter David Gordon; Partner, Lane Clark & Peacock, since 1989; Research and Development. *Career:* National Mutual Life Assurance Society, Actuarial Trainee 1982-84. *Biog: b.* 22 December 1959. *Nationality:* British. *Educ:* Birkenhead School; Trinity College, Cambridge (MA Diploma in Mathematical Statistics). *Other Activities:* Vice-Chairman, Society of Young Freemen of the City of London; Editor, The Actuary. *Professional Organisations:* Fellow, Institute of Actuaries. *Publications:* The Tompkins Table, Annually; Flexibility and Fairness, 1989. *Recreations:* Bee Keeping, Cycling, Guide-Lecturing, Property Restoration.

TONER, Charles Gerard; General Manager, Abbey National Building Society.

TONNER, James E; Managing Director & Chief Investment Officer, Chemical Investment Group (London) Ltd.

TOOMEY, Dr Robert; Director, 3i plc. *Professional Organisations:* ACMA.

TOOTAL, Christopher Peter; Partner, Herbert Smith, since 1968; Head of Intellectual Property Group. *Career:* Trainee Patent Agent 1958-62; Chartered Patent Agent 1962-64; Herbert Smith, Articled Clerk 1964-67. *Biog: b.* 10 March 1936. *Nationality:* British. *m.* 1968, Alison Jane (née Forbes); 1 s; 1 d. *Educ:* Repton School; The Queen's College, Oxford (BA, BSc). *Other Activities:* Liveryman, Tallow Chandlers Company; Chairman, Patent Solicitors Association; President, British Group of International Association for the Protection of Industrial Property; Chairman, Joint Working Party of Bar and Law Society on Industrial Property; Member, Standing Advisory Committee on Industrial Property. *Professional Organisations:* Law Society; Chartered Institute of Patent Agents. *Publications:* The Law of Industrial Design - Registered Designs, Copyright and Design Right, 1990. *Clubs:* Royal Harwich Yacht Club. *Recreations:* Sailing, Music, Photography.

TOPLEY, R E; Partner, Cameron Markby Hewitt.

TOPPING, J; Deputy Chairman, Taylor Woodrow plc.

TORA, Brian Roberto; Head of Retail Marketing, James Capel & Co; Private Clients, Financial Services, Unit Trusts. *Career:* Grieveson Grant & Co Various 1963-74; Singer & Friedlander Ltd Investment Mgr 1974-79; van Cutsen & Associates Ltd Investment Dir 1979-82; Touche Remnant Financial Management Ltd Investment Dir 1982-85. *Biog: b.* 21 September 1945. *Nationality:* British. m1 1975, Jennifer (née Blanckensee) (diss 1988). m2 1989, Elizabeth (née Edgecombe); 2 s. *Educ:* Bancrofts. *Directorships:* James Capel Unit Trust Management Ltd 1985 (exec); James Capel Financial Services Ltd 1986 (exec). *Other Activities:* Trustee, The Mobility Trust. *Professional Organisations:* Member, The International Stock Exchange. *Recreations:* Travel, Gardening (through necessity), Reading.

TOREVELL, Alan; Managing Director, Torevell Mahon Granville Ltd, since 1973; Personal Financial Planning. *Career:* Leeds Grammar School Head of Economics Dept 1962-68; Sheffield Education Authority Asst Education Officer 1968-70. *Biog: b.* 16 January 1937. *Nationality:* British. *m.* 1961, Barbara (née Hartley); 1 s. *Educ:* Bacup & Rawtenstall Grammar; LSE (BSc); Leeds University. *Directorships:* Granville & Co Ltd 1986 (non-exec); Granville Trust 1987 (non-exec). *Recreations:* Golf, Walking, Cutting Logs.

TORII, Y; Managing Director, National Securities of Japan (Europe) Ltd.

TORREIRA, Manuel Santos; Representative, Caja de Ahorros de Galicia.

TORRENS, Samuel Henry; Director & Chief Executive, Northern Bank Ltd, since 1988. *Career:* Northern Bank Ltd, Various 1951-78; Reg Dir 1978-82; Gen Mgr 1982-85; Dep Chief Exec 1985-87; Midland Bank plc, Reg Dir 1986-87. *Biog: b.* 24 August 1934. *Nationality:* British. *m.* 1967, Marjorie (née Gillespie); 3 s; 1 d. *Educ:* Coleraine Academical Institution. *Directorships:* Northern Bank Development Corp Ltd 1985 Chm; Northern Bank Executor & Trustee Co Ltd 1985 (non-exec); Northern Bank Financial Services Ltd 1985 Chm; Northern Bank Nominees Ltd 1985 Chm; Belfast Bank Executor & Trustee Co Ltd 1985 Chm; Belfast Banking Co Ltd 1985 Chm; Northern Bank Factors Ltd 1987 Chm; Northern Bank Insurance Services Ltd 1987 Chm; National Australia Finance (UK) Ltd 1987 (non-exec). *Other Activities:* President, Institute of Bankers in Ireland, 1990-91; Member of Council, Royal Ulster Agricultural Society, 1990-; Member of Board of Governors, Coleraine Academical Instution, 1987-. *Professional Organisations:* FIB (Ireland). *Clubs:* Ulster Reform Club. *Recreations:* Gardening.

TORRIE, John; Senior Partner, Torrie & Co, since 1975. *Biog: b.* 5 May 1941. *Nationality:* British. *m.* 1964, Elizabeth Patricia (née Dennison); 1 s; 1 d. *Educ:* Dunfermline High School; Edinburgh University (MA, BCom). *Other Activities:* The Intl Stock Exchange Scottish Unit Ctee, Stock Exchange Regional Ctee. *Professional Organisations:* Member, The International Stock Exchange. *Clubs:* New Club (Edinburgh). *Recreations:* Golf.

TORRINGTON, P G; Director, Berry Palmer & Lyle Ltd.

TOSCANO, José Manuel; General Manager, Banco Portugues do Atlantico, since 1988; Banking. *Career:* Companhia Uniao Fabril Textile Div, Dept of Research & Development of New Products 1969-71; Banco de Fomento Nacional Economic Research Dept 1971-78; Banco de Portugal Credit Dept 1978-88; Instituto Emissor de Macau Chairman 1982-87; Banco Português do Atlântico Manager 1988-. *Biog: b.* 10 August 1945. *Nationality:* Portuguese. *m.* 1969, Liseta (née Vinagre); 2 s; 1 d. *Educ:* Instituto Superior de Economia (MBA). *Publications:* Industria Metalomecanica Pesada, 1976; Avaliação Economica de Projectos, 1978.

TOTTY, P G; Partner, Allen & Overy.

TOUCHE, Sir Anthony George; Bt; Deputy Chairman, Friend's Provident Life Office, since 1969. *Professional Organisations:* FCA.

TOVELL, M; Partner, Waltons & Morse.

TOWERS, William Lennox; Managing Partner, Booth & Co, since 1990. *Career:* Booth & Co, Articled Clerk 1969-71; Asst Solicitor 1971-74; Commercial Law/Taxation, Partner 1974-90. *Biog: b.* 24 September 1946. *Nationality:* British. *m.* 1972, Jan (née Morrill); 2 s; 1 d. *Educ:* Hutchesons' Boys' Grammar School, Glasgow; Leeds Grammar School; Exeter University (LLB). *Directorships:* H Foster & Co (Stearines) Ltd 1983 (non-exec)Chm; Aire Place Property Co Ltd 1983 (non-exec)Chm. *Professional Organisations:* The Law Society.

TOWNEND, A J P; Director, CCF Foster Braithwaite Ltd.

TOWNER, Richard Edward; Partner, Richards Butler.

TOWNSEND, G P; Director, Fenchurch Insurance Group Limited.

TOWNSEND, John Anthony Victor; Chairman, Rea Brothers Ltd, since 1988; Non-Executive. *Career:* Brown Shipley & Co Ltd Asst Mgr 1969-74; Rea Brothers Ltd Dir 1975-79; John Townsend & Co (Holdings) Ltd Dir 1979-87. *Biog: b.* 24 January 1948.

Nationality: British. *m.* 1971, Carolyn Ann (née Salomon); 1 s; 1 d. *Educ:* Harrow School; Selwyn College, Cambridge (MA). *Directorships:* Finsbury Asset Management Ltd 1987 (exec); Immuno AG (Switzerland) 1989. *Other Activities:* Member, Lloyd's; Member of the Court, The Worshipful Company of Pattenmakers; Governor, Cranleigh School. *Clubs:* Gresham, RAC, Broadgate.

TOWNSON, Howard; Partner, Clyde & Co.

TOYOTA, T; Chief Representative, The Hyogo Bank Limited.

TOZIER, William Harley; Director, Senior Vice President, Smith Barney Harris Upham Europe Ltd, since 1989; Sales. *Career:* Kuhn Loeb & Co 1975-78. *Biog: b.* 4 November 1936. *Nationality:* American. *m.* 1961, Lesley Preston (née Liversidge); 2 d. *Educ:* Brown University (BA).

TRACEY, Eric Frank; Partner, Touche Ross & Co, since 1980; Public Sector Audits, Privatisation. *Career:* Inland Revenue (NZ), Clerk 1965-67; M L Chatfield, CA (NZ), Clerk/Office Mgr 1967-68; Accountancy Dept, Auckland University, Snr Tutor/Junior Lecturer 1970-2; Touche Ross & Co, Various 1973-80. *Biog: b.* 3 July 1948. *m.* 1970, Patricia (née Gamble). *Educ:* Mount Albert Grammar; Auckland University (MCom). *Other Activities:* Trustee, The Waltargi Foundation; Chairman, London Branch, NZ Society Accountants. *Professional Organisations:* FCA; ACIS. *Recreations:* Rugby, Cricket, Cooking, Walking.

TRACY, Charles Peter Gervais; Managing Director, N M Rothschild & Sons (C I) Limited, since 1981; Merchant Banking. *Career:* Hambros Bank Ltd 1967-72; Samuel Montagu & Co Ltd, Manager 1972-75; N M Rothschild & Sons Ltd, Manager 1975-78; (Hong Kong) Director 1978-. *Biog: b.* 23 October 1945. *Nationality:* British. *m.* 1986, Vera (née Morrison); 1 s; 2 d. *Educ:* Rugby School (Scholar); Trinity College, Cambridge (II.1 Economics II.2 Nat Sciences). *Other Activities:* Member, Council of Friends of St James Association; Chairman, Association of Guernsey Banks. *Recreations:* Singing, Skiing, Gardening.

TRACY, P R; Operations Director, USA, Wellcome plc.

TRAILL, Sir Alan; Former Lord Mayor (elected 1984), Corporation of London.

TRAILL, N D; Partner, Waltons & Morse.

TRAINER, Miss (Margaret) Lorraine; Head of Human Resources, London Stock Exchange, since 1990. *Career:* Citibank NA 1975-90; Senior Human Resources Head, Europe, Middle East and Africa 1989-90; Divi-

sional Human Resources Head, UK and Northern Europe 1988-89; Chief of Staff to the Head of the London Treasury 1986-88. *Biog: b.* 13 March 1952. *Nationality:* British. *Educ:* L'Université de la Sorbonne, Paris (Diplôme Supérieure de Langue et Civilisation Française); University of Stirling, University of St Andrews (MA Hons, French IIi). *Other Activities:* Windsor Fellowship; St Andrew's University Career Advisory Board. *Publications:* Moving to London, 1978. *Clubs:* Hurlingham. *Recreations:* Skiing, Opera, France.

TRAMPE, Ulrik Christian Greve; Sales Manager, Kleinwort Benson North America Inc, since 1988; Equities. *Career:* Boston Consulting Group, Consultant 1981-82; Merrill Lynch & Co, Associate; Institutional Salesperson 1982-88; Sales Manager 1982-88. *Biog: b.* 2 December 1957. *Nationality:* Danish. *m.* 1982, Kathryn Anne (née McVey). *Educ:* University of Copenhagen (Cand Polit); Harvard Business School (MBA). *Directorships:* Kleinwort Benson North America Inc 1989 (exec); Kleinwort Benson Securities Ltd 1990 (exec). *Other Activities:* Member, Konsistorium, Koebenhavns Universitat 1978-80.

TRAN-BA-HUY, Christian; General Manager, Banque Française du Commerce Extérieur, since 1986. *Career:* BFCE (Head Office) Account Mgr 1971-76; (New York) VP 1976-81; (Singapore) Gen Mgr 1981-84; (Head Office) Sous Directeur 1985-86. *Biog: b.* 12 November 1946. *Nationality:* French. *m.* 1976, Catherine (née Grosscurth); 1 s; 2 d. *Educ:* Lycée Louis le Grand, Paris; Université de Droit (Dip); Institut d'Etudes Politiques de Paris (Dip).

TRASK, Michael A; Partner, S J Berwin & Co.

TRAVERS, I; Partner, Nabarro Nathanson.

TREGONING, Christopher; Deputy Managing Director, Den Norske Bank plc, since 1986; Finance and Administration. *Career:* Thomson McLintock & Co Chartered Accountants 1970-74; Barclays Bank plc 1974-79; Den Norske Bank plc (Formerly Nordic Bank plc) 1979-. *Biog: b.* 15 June 1948. *Nationality:* British. *m.* 1973, Antonia (née Critcley-Salmonson); 3 s. *Educ:* Harrow School; Fitzwilliam College, Cambridge (Law IIi). *Professional Organisations:* FCA.

TREMLETT, Thomas Fabian; Director, Gerrard & National Securities Ltd, since 1987. *Biog: b.* 10 May 1946. *Nationality:* British. *Educ:* Stowe School. *Professional Organisations:* The Intl Stock Exchange. *Clubs:* Turf, MCC, Royal St George's, Sunningdale Golf Club. *Recreations:* Golf.

TRENCHARD, Hugh; The Viscount Trenchard; Director, Kleinwort Benson Limited; International Corporate Finance, Japan. *Biog: b.* 12 March 1951. *Nationality:* British. *m.* 1975, Fiona Elizabeth; 2 s; 2 d. *Educ:*

Eton College; Trinity College, Cambridge (BA Hons). *Directorships:* Kleinwort Benson Ltd 1986 (exec); Kleinwort Benson International Inc 1988 President; KB Berkeley Japan Development Capital Ltd 1987; Dover Japan Inc 1985-87 (non-exec). *Other Activities:* Member, General Affairs Committee, Japan Security Dealers' Association, 1987-88; Member, Japan Association of Corporate Executives, 1987-; Member, Japan Committee, British Invisible Exports Council.

TREVES, Vanni Emanuele; Senior Partner, Macfarlanes, since 1987; Corporate Law. *Career:* Macfarlanes Solicitor 1965-68; White & Case (New York) Visiting Attorney 1968-69; Macfarlanes Ptnr 1970-87. *Biog: b.* 3 November 1940. *Nationality:* British. *m.* 1971, Angela (née Fyffe); 2 s; 1 d. *Educ:* St Paul's School; University College, Oxford (MA); University of Illinois (LLM). *Directorships:* BBA Group plc 1986 (non-exec) Dep Chm; Oceonics plc 1984 (non-exec). *Other Activities:* City of London Solicitors' Co. *Professional Organisations:* The Law Society. *Clubs:* Boodles, Buck's City of London. *Recreations:* Eating, Walking, Collecting Watercolours.

TREVOR, John C; Non-Executive Director, J Trevor, Montleman & Poland Ltd.

TRIANTARFYLLIDES, S A; Director, Bank of Cyprus (London) Ltd.

TRICKS, Stephen; Partner, Clyde & Co.

TRIPP, M H; Assistant General Manager, Guardian Royal Exchange Assurance.

TRISTEM, N J; Partner, Milne Ross.

TRITTON, Alan George; Director, Barclays Bank Ltd.

TRITTON, Group Captain J W; Clerk, Guild of Air Pilots and Air Navigators.

TROLLIP, Ms Arabella; Director, S G Warburg & Co Ltd, since 1990; Overseas Advisory. *Career:* S G Warburg & Co Ltd 1981-. *Biog: b.* 14 February 1959. *Nationality:* British.

TROLLOPE, D E; Partner, Grimley J R Eve.

TROLLOPE, Patrick Haward; Master, Worshipful Company of Glaziers, since 1990. *Career:* Trollope & Colls, Building Contractors 1947-87; Trollope & Colls (City) Ltd, Director 1971-87. *Biog: b.* 8 September 1920. *Nationality:* British. *m.* 1942, Diana Mary (née Newbold); 1 s; 1 d. *Educ:* St Edmunds School, Hindhead; Harrow School. *Other Activities:* Master, Worshipful Company of Glaziers. *Professional Organisa-*

tions: Fellow, Chartered Institute of Building. *Recreations:* Gardening, Shooting.

TROMANS, G E; Investment Director, Chambers & Remington Ltd.

TROUGHTON, A A J L; Director, Steel Burrill Jones Group plc.

TROUGHTON, S R V; Partner, Cazenove & Co.

TROUP, John Edward Astley; Partner, Simmons & Simmons, since 1984; Corporate Tax. *Career:* Simmons & Simmons, Assistant Solicitor 1981-84. *Biog: b.* 26 January 1955. *Nationality:* British. *m.* 1978, Siriol Jane (née Martin); 1 s; 1 d. *Educ:* Oundle; Oxford University (MA, MSc). *Other Activities:* Institute of Fiscal Studies Working Party on Capital Taxation; Law Society, Revenue Law (Corporation Tax) Committee; Freeman of the Grocers' Company. *Professional Organisations:* ATII. *Publications:* Numerous Articles in Professional Journals. *Recreations:* Cinema, Wagner, Reading Moby Dick, Sleep.

TROWBRIDGE, Martin E O'K; CBE, HM; Chairman & Chief Executive Officer, Martin Trowbridge Limited, since 1972; General Management. *Career:* ICI plc, Technical Officer 1947-49; Fluor-Head Wrightson, Commercial Manager 1949-52; Sharples Corporation, Managing Director 1952-62; Pennwalt Corporation, International Managing Director 1962-72; Pegler Hattersley Group, Group Managing Director 1972-73; Chemical Industries Association, Director General 1973-87; Confederation Européen des Federations des Industries Chimique, President du Conseil d'Administration 1982-87. *Biog: b.* 9 May 1925. *Nationality:* European. *m.* 1946, Valerie; 1 s. *Educ:* Imperial College, London; Royal College of Science, London University (BSc, ACGI); City and Guilds College, London University (BSc Eng, Chem Eng); AMI College, New York, (Diploma in Business Studies). *Directorships:* National Radiological Protection Board (NRPB) 1987 (non-exec); Investment Management Regulatory Organisation Ltd (IMRO) 1987 (non-exec). *Other Activities:* European Business Institute, Halton National Chemical Musuem (Trustee). *Professional Organisations:* Fellow, Institute of Chemical Engineers; Fellow, City and Guilds Institute; Member, SCI; FRSA; C Eng. *Publications:* Heat Sinks, 1953; Purification of Oils for Marine Service, 1960; Scaling Up Centrifugal Separation, 1962; Collected Poems, 1963; Centrifugation, 1966; Exhibiting for Profit, 1969; Market Research & Forecasting, 1969; Financial Performance of Process Plant Companies, 1970; More Poems, 1983; Mineral Collecting in Norway 1978. *Clubs:* Old Siberions, Boffles (New York), Frensham Gun. *Recreations:* Shooting, Painting, Mineralogy, Sailing.

TROWELL, Timothy Martin; Director, Brown Shipley & Co Limited, since 1980; Compliance/Editor, Investment Review. *Career:* Laurence, Keen & Gardner, Investment Analyst 1964-70. *Biog: b.* 22 September 1938. *Nationality:* British. *m.* 1987, Alison Theodora (née Rundle Clark); 3 d; 3 steps. *Educ:* Monkton Combe; St John's College, Cambridge (MA). *Clubs:* City University. *Recreations:* Poetry, Vegetable Gardening.

TRUEGER, Arthur I; Executive Chairman, John Govett & Co Ltd, since 1986. *Career:* Berkeley International Capital Corporation, Executive Chairman 1977-; Berkeley Govett & Company Ltd and related Companies, Executive Chairman 1985-. *Biog: b.* 15 November 1948. *Nationality:* American. *m.* 1986, Cordelia J (née Fraser); 3 s. *Educ:* University of California, Berkeley USA (BA, MA); Hastings College of Law, San Francisco (JD). *Directorships:* Integral Systems Inc 1983 (non-exec); James Hardie Industries Ltd 1987 (non-exec). *Recreations:* Skiing, Sailing.

TRUELL, Edmund; Director, Hambro European Ventures Limited, since 1987; Management Buyouts. *Career:* Hambro Linsandro Limited, Director, Tax-Efficient Asset Finance 1986-; Bankers Trust Co, Associate, LBO Group 1984-86. *Biog: b.* 13 October 1962. *Nationality:* British. *m.* 1985, Lynne (née Murphy). *Educ:* Collingwood College, Durham University (BA Hons Economics); Wellington College, Berkshire. *Directorships:* Hambro European Ventures Ltd 1987 (exec); Hambro Linsandro Ltd 1987 (non-exec, previously exec); Flexible Securities Ltd 1986 (exec). *Professional Organisations:* Associate Member, Society of Investment Analysts. *Clubs:* Riverside. *Recreations:* Tennis, Hockey, Skiing.

TRUEMAN, John Francis; Director, S G Warburg & Co Ltd, since 1983.

TRUMP, E F; Director, Robert Bruce Fitzmaurice Ltd.

TRUP, Michael; Sales Director, Continental Europe, Dean Witter Capital Markets International Ltd, since 1989; Institutional Sales. *Career:* Price Waterhouse Management Consultants, Consultant Economist 1982-83; Merrill Lynch Pierce Fenner & Smith Inc, Stockbroker 1983-85; Dean Witter Reynolds Inc, Institutional Equity Sales (US Equities and Derivatives) 1985-. *Biog: b.* 22 July 1955. *Nationality:* British. *m.* 1979, Sophie (née Rybeczko); 2 s; 1 d. *Educ:* Highgate School, London; Queen Mary College, University of London (BSc Economics 1st Class Hons); University of Exeter, University of Belgrade (Research Student). *Directorships:* Dean Witter Reynolds International SA 1990 (exec); Dean Witter Capital Markets 1989 (exec). *Professional Organisations:* National Association of Securities Dealers (US Series 7, Series 3); Commodity Futures Trading Commission. *Clubs:* National Liberal Club. *Recreations:* Karate, Travel, Philosophy, Politics.

TRUSLER, Colin Harold; Chairman & Chief Executive, Shandwick Consultants Ltd, since 1987. *Career:* Public Relations Partners Ltd, Trainee 1963-66; Brook-Hart Ruder Finn Ltd, Account Dir 1966-69; Lloyds Bank plc, Public Relations Adviser 1969-72; Head of Marketing 1972-86; Shandwick Consultants Ltd, Dir 1986-. *Biog: b.* 1942. *m.* 1982, Fiona (née Parsons); 3 s; 1 d. *Educ:* Loughborough Grammar School; Wadham College, Oxford (MA). *Directorships:* Shandwick Public Affairs Ltd 1987; Fairfax Design Ltd 1989. *Professional Organisations:* MInstM.

TRUST, Howard Bailey; Group Legal Director, Barclays de Zoete Wedd Holdings Limited, since 1989; Legal Services. *Career:* Lovell White & King, Solicitor 1980-85; Morgan Grenfell & Co Limited, Solicitor 1985-87; Morgan Grenfell Group plc, Company Secretary 1987-89. *Biog: b.* 6 October 1954. *Nationality:* British. *m.* 1982, Jennifer (née Marshall). *Educ:* Quarry Bank High School, Liverpool; Gonville & Caius College, Cambridge (MA Cantab). *Directorships:* Barclays de Zoete Wedd Securities Limited 1989 (exec). *Other Activities:* Law Society; International Bar Association; City of London Solicitors Company. *Professional Organisations:* Solicitor.

TRUSTRAM EVE, C; Associate, Grimley J R Eve.

TRUSTRAM EVE, J R; Joint Senior Partner, Grimley J R Eve, since 1990; Chartered Surveyors. *Career:* Strutt & Parker, Surveyor 1956-59; J R Eve & Sons, Partner 1960-78; J R Eve, Senior Partner 1978-88; Grimley J R Eve, Joint Managing Partner 1988-90; Joint Senior Partner 1990-. *Biog: b.* 30 April 1936. *Nationality:* British. *m.* 1961, Pipyn (née Beale); 2 s; 1 d. *Educ:* Winchester College; University College, London (MSc Econ). *Other Activities:* Immediate Past-Master, Worshipful Company of Chartered Surveyors; Past-President, RICS Planning & Development Committee; Member, CBI Council and London Regional Council. *Professional Organisations:* Fellow, Royal Institution of Chartered Surveyors. *Clubs:* Royal Mid Surrey Golf Club, Royal Albert Yacht Club.

TSUCHIYA, N; Director, S G Warburg Securities (Japan Inc), since 1990; Head of International Fixed Income Sales. *Career:* Yamaichi Securities Co 1974-85. *Biog: b.* 10 July 1951. *Nationality:* Japanese. *m.* 1990, Yumiko Tsuchiya; 2 s; 1 d. *Educ:* Sophia University (BA Economics).

TSUGAWA, Kiyoshi; Chairman & President, S G Warburg Securities (Japan) Inc, since 1987; Mainly Japan. *Career:* The Bank of Tokyo Ltd, Director in Charge of International Finance & Member of the Board 1956-87. *Biog: b.* 20 October 1933. *Nationality:* Japanese. *m.* 1958, Keiko (née Okuno). *Educ:* University of Tokyo (Degree of Law). *Directorships:* S G Warburg, Akroyd, Rowe & Pitman, Mullens Securities Ltd 1987; S G

Warburg Securities (Japan) Inc 1987 Chairman & President; Warburg Soditic SA 1988. *Clubs:* Tokyo Golf Club. *Recreations:* Golf, Journey, Painting.

TUCK, Brian; Finance Director, PaineWebber International Bank Ltd.

TUCK, Peter John; Partner, Grant Thornton, since 1984. *Career:* Robson Rhodes 1974-81. *Biog: b.* 8 December 1952. *Nationality:* British. *m.* 1977, Ann Victoria (née Mortlock); 2 s. *Educ:* Isleworth Grammar School; University of Kent (BA). *Professional Organisations:* Fellow, Institute of Chartered Accountants in England and Wales.

TUCKER, John Channon; Partner, Linklaters & Paines, since 1990; International Finance & Banking. *Career:* Finlaysons, South Australia, Articled Clerk/ Assistant Solicitor 1979-84; Finlaysons, Partner 1984-89. *Biog: b.* 31 July 1958. *Nationality:* Australian. *m.* 1983, Madeleine Jane Penn (née Boucaut); 3 s. *Educ:* St Peter's College, South Australia; University of Adelaide (LLB Hons); South Australian Institute of Technology (BA Accountancy). *Professional Organisations:* Australian Society of Accountants; Law Society. *Clubs:* The Adelaide Club, Royal South Australian Yacht Squadron. *Recreations:* Reading, Running, Family.

TUCKER, Paul Thomas; Director of Information Technology, Morgan Grenfell & Co Ltd, since 1990; Information Technology. *Career:* Pinchin Denny & Co, Data Processing Manager 1971-78; Office Manager & Data Processing Manager 1979-81; Partner Technology & Administration 1982-86; Morgan Grenfell Securities Ltd, Director Technology, Business Planning & Management Information 1987-89; Morgan Grenfell & Co Ltd, Director of Information Technology 1990-. *Biog: b.* 15 June 1944. *Nationality:* British. *m.* 1967, Dorothy (née Jakes); 3 s. *Educ:* Ealing Technical College. *Directorships:* Morgan Grenfell & Co Ltd 1990 (exec); Morgan Grenfell Securities Ltd 1987 (exec); Pinchin Denny & Co 1982 (exec). *Other Activities:* Chairman, Sub Group of International Markets Committee of the Stock Exchange (1988); Member, Talisman Review Panel of the London Stock Exchange (1977-80). *Professional Organisations:* Member, International Stock Exchange; MBCS; MIDPM; MENSA. *Clubs:* City of London Club, Crondall Park Golf Club. *Recreations:* Golf, Chess, Music.

TUCKEY, Andrew Marmaduke Lane; Chairman, Baring Brothers & Co Ltd, since 1989; Corporate Finance, Banking and Capital Markets. *Career:* Dixon Wilson & Co 1962-66; British-American Tobacco Corporate Planning 1966-68; Baring Brothers & Co Ltd 1968-; (Hong Kong) 1972-74. *Biog: b.* 28 August 1943. *Nationality:* British. *m.* 1967, Louise (née Barnes); 1 s; 2 d. *Educ:* Plumtree School, Zimbabwe. *Directorships:* Barings plc 1985 Jt Dep Chm; Commerce Intl Merchant Bankers Berhad 1977; Baring Securities Ltd 1984. *Other Activities:* Treasurer of The Friends of Covent Garden; Trustee, Esmee Fairbairn Charitable Trust. *Professional Organisations:* FCA. *Clubs:* City of London, Roehampton. *Recreations:* Music, Tennis, Windsurfing.

TUCKWELL, Paul Hamilton; Director, N M Rothschild & Sons Limited, since 1989; Loan Syndications & Corporate Treasury Desk. *Career:* N M Rothschild & Sons Ltd, Assistant Manager (Bahrain Division) 1984; Lloyds Bank International Ltd, 2 years Training in Uruguay and Paraguay; Account Executive (Bahrain); Credit Officer (London) 1978-84. *Biog: b.* 1956. *Nationality:* British/Brazilian. *m.* 1980, Maria del Rosario; 1 d. *Educ:* St Julian's School, Portugal; Eastbourne College; Loughborough University (BSc Hons Banking & Finance). *Directorships:* N M Rothschild & Sons Limited 1989 (exec). *Recreations:* Walking, Theatre, Music.

TUDBALL, Peter C; Vice-Chairman/Group Business Development, The Baltic Exchange Limited.

TUDOR JOHN, William; Partner, Allen & Overy, since 1972; International Finance, Financial Services. *Career:* Allen & Overy, Articled Clerk 1967-69; Assoc Lawyer 1969-70; Orion Bank Ltd, Banker 1970-72. *Biog: b.* 26 April 1944. *Nationality:* British. *m.* 1967, Jane (née Clark); 3 d. *Educ:* Cowbridge School; Downing College, Cambridge (MA). *Directorships:* Suttons Seeds (Holdings) Ltd 1978 (non-exec) Chm; Horticultural & Botanical Holdings Ltd 1985 (non-exec) Chm; Carters Tested Seeds Ltd 1985 (non-exec); R & G Cuthbert Ltd 1985 (non-exec); Samuel Dobie & Son Ltd 1985 (non-exec); W Weibull (UK) Ltd 1978 (non-exec). *Other Activities:* Associate Fellow, Downing College, Cambridge; Steward of Appeal, British Boxing Board of Control; City of London Solicitors' Co. *Professional Organisations:* The Law Society; IBA. *Publications:* Chapters on Law Relating to Sovereign Immunity in Euromoney's Internatio. *Clubs:* The Justinians. *Recreations:* Shooting, Rugby Football, Music, Books.

TUDOR WILLIAMS, D; Joint Managing Director, A J Archer Holdings plc.

TUDWAY, R H; Managing Partner, Waltons & Morse, since 1987; Company Law & Banking. *Career:* Waltons & Morse, Partner 1977-; Sydney Mobe & Co, Assistant Solicitor 1973-75; Stanley Wasborough & Co, Articled Clerk 1970-73. *Biog: b.* 28 April 1947. *Nationality:* British. *Educ:* Clifton College, Bristol; Peterhouse, Cambridge (BA History). *Other Activities:* The City of London Solicitors' Company; Council Member, Statute Law Society. *Professional Organisations:* Solicitor. *Clubs:* Little Ship Club. *Recreations:* Sailing.

TUFFLEY, David John; Managing Director, Tullett & Tokyo (Foreign Exchange) Co Ltd, since 1987;

Global Responsibility for Spot Foreign Exchange. *Career:* National Westminster Bank, General Clerk 1966-67; Standard Chartered Bank, Foreign Exchange Clerk 1967-69; Emigrated to Australia 1969-72; Dalton Barton Bankers, Foreign Exchange Clerk 1972-74; Tullett & Tokyo, International Broker 1974-. *Biog: b.* 13 May 1948. *Nationality:* British. *m.* 1978, Jeanette (née Parker); 2 s; 2 d. *Educ:* Hurstmere Secondary School, Sidcup. *Directorships:* Tullett & Tokyo (London) Ltd 1987; Tullett & Tokyo (International) Ltd 1988. *Clubs:* Chislehurst Golf Club. *Recreations:* Golf.

TUFFNELL, Kevin Douglas; Partner, Macfarlanes, since 1989; Corporate Finance. *Career:* MacFarlanes, Articled Clerk/Assistant Solicitor 1982-89. *Biog: b.* 6 October 1959. *Nationality:* British. *m.* 1982, Ruchanee; 1 s; 1 d. *Educ:* St Albans School; Sidney Sussex College, Cambridge (BA, MA). *Recreations:* Sailing, Reading.

TUGENDHAT, Sir Christopher Samuel; Chairman, Civil Aviation Authority, since 1986. *Career:* Financial Times, Leader/Feature Writer 1960-70; MP (Conservative) 1970-76; European Commission, Commissioner 1977-81; VP 1981-85. *Biog: b.* 23 February 1937. *Nationality:* British. *m.* 1967, Julia (née Dobson); 2 s. *Educ:* Ampleforth College; Cambridge University (MA). *Directorships:* The BOC Group 1985 (non-exec); National Westminster Bank 1986 Dep Chm 1990 (non-exec); Commercial Union plc 1988 (non-exec). *Other Activities:* Chm, Royal Institute of International Affairs (Chatham House); VP, British Lung Foundation. *Publications:* Oil: The Biggest Business, 1968; The Multinationals, 1971; Making Sense of Europe, 1986; Options for British Foreign Policy in the 1990's, (with William Wallace), 1988. *Clubs:* Carlton, Anglo-Belgian, Bucks. *Recreations:* Reading, Family.

TUGWELL, John; Director and Chief Executive, International Businesses, National Westminster Bank, since 1989. *Career:* National Westminster Bank plc Advances Mgr, Group Advances 1974-78; Dep Mgr, Lothbury 1978-80; Mgr, Leeds City Office 1980-84; Regional Gen Mgr, N America 1984-87; Gen Mgr, Business Development Div 1987-89. *Biog: b.* 1 October 1940. *Nationality:* British. *m.* 1962, Janice Elizabeth (née Santer); 1 s; 1 d. *Educ:* Hove Grammar School. *Professional Organisations:* ACIB; Mem Mgmnt Board, The Prince's Trust; Mem, CBI Europe Ctee; Mem, America/European Community Assoc. *Recreations:* Cricket, Gardening.

TUKE, Sir Anthony; Deputy Chairman, Royal Insurance Holdings plc.

TUKE, John Fintan; Director, Treasury and Capital Markets Dept, Hambros Bank Limited, since 1990; Off Balance Sheet Trading. *Career:* Hambros Bank Limited 1972-90; Hambros Australia Limited, Seconded as Foreign Exchange Manager 1984-86. *Biog: b.* 20 July 1954.

Nationality: British. *m.* 1978, Judith Mary (née Rayner); 1 s; 3 d. *Educ:* Wimbledon College Jesuit Grammar School. *Recreations:* Cricket, Golf.

TUKE, Michael Edward; Finance Director, Woolwich Building Society, since 1987; Finance, Treasury, Data Processing, Personnel. *Career:* Standard Telephones & Cables, Progress Chaser 1959-62; Woolwich Building Society, Various Clerical 1962-72; Asst Acct 1972-75; Mgr Accounts Dept 1975-76; Sec 1976-83; Gen Mgr 1983-87. *Biog: b.* 29 May 1938. *Nationality:* British. *m.* 1965, Doreen Margaret (née Bailey); 1 s; 1 d. *Educ:* St Joseph's Academy, Blackheath. *Directorships:* Keat Thames-Side Groundwork Trust 1990 (non-exec). *Other Activities:* School Governor; Ctee Member, Church Housing Assoc. *Professional Organisations:* FCCA. *Recreations:* Music particularly Jazz, Supporting Son's Motor Racing Activities.

TULLETT, Derek; Chairman, Tullett & Tokyo Forex International Ltd.

TULLOCH, Alastair; Partner, Frere Cholmeley, since 1988; Company and Commerce. *Career:* Lovell White & King, Articled Clerk 1977-80; Asst Solicitor 1980-82; McNeill & Co, Dubai, Asst Solicitor 1982-84; Clifford Turner, Asst Solicitor 1984-86; Frere Cholmeley, Asst Solicitor 1987-88. *Biog: b.* 1 October 1955. *Nationality:* British. *m.* 1987, Hilary; 1 d. *Educ:* Magdalen College, Oxford (MA Oxon). *Professional Organisations:* Law Society. *Recreations:* DIY.

TULLOCH, Edward Archibald William; Director, Stewart, Ivory & Company Ltd.

TULLOCH, N S; Director, James Capel Fund Managers Ltd.

TULLY, David John; Managing Partner, Addleshaw Sons & Latham Solicitors, since 1989; Property and Private Taxation. *Career:* Addleshaw Sons & Latham, Articled 1959-64; Solicitor 1965; Partner 1969. *Biog: b.* 13 March 1942. *Nationality:* British. *m.* 1965, Susan P (née Arnott); 1 s; 2 d. *Educ:* Twyford Preparatory School; Sherborne; Rylands Fletcher (Scholarship Prize). *Directorships:* Cobden Commercial Properties Ltd 1975 (non-exec); Norton Rose MS Ltd 1989 (non-exec); Manchester Young Solicitors Past Chairman; National Young Solicitors Past Chairman; Manchester Law Society Past President; Governors of Crawley School for Girls Past Chairman; Manchester Grammar Governor; The St James's Club Manchester Past Chairman. *Professional Organisations:* Law Society; Manchester Law Society. *Clubs:* St James's Club Manchester. *Recreations:* Fishing, Shooting, Golf.

TULOUP, Y; Director, Société Générale Strauss Turnbull Securities Ltd.

TURCAN, William James; Finance Director, Harrisons & Crosfield plc, since 1988. *Career:* Binder Hamlyn 1965-70; Pauls Malt Ltd 1970-86; Pauls plc, Finance Director 1986-88. *Biog: b.* 4 January 1943. *Nationality:* British. *Educ:* Rugby School; Trinity College, Oxford (MA). *Professional Organisations:* ACA.

TURKINGTON, John; Group Treasurer UK, Racal Group Services Ltd, since 1986; All aspects of Treasury Management. *Career:* T Brittain & Co, Articled Clerk 1963-67; Price Waterhouse & Co, Audit Snr 1967-74; Charterhouse Group plc, Subsid Fin Controller 1970-74; Aladdin Industries Ltd, Group Chief Accountant 1974-77; Chubb & Son plc, Group Treasurer 1977-85. *Biog: b.* 16 October 1944. *Nationality:* British. *m.* 1972; 2 *s. Professional Organisations:* FCA; FCT.

TURNBULL, Andrew D C; Partner, Walker Morris Scott Turnbull.

TURNBULL, Sir George Henry; Kt; Chairman & Chief Executive, Inchcape plc, since 1986. *Career:* Standard Motors Ltd, PA/Liaison Officer/Exec 1950-55; Petters Ltd, Works Mgr 1955-56; Standard Motors, Div Mgr, Gen Mgr 1956-62; Standard-Triumph Intl, Dir & Gen Mgr/Dep Chm 1962-69; British Leyland Motor Corp, Dir/Dep MD/MD 1967-73; Hyundai Motors (Seoul), VP & Dir 1974-77; Iran National Motor Co (Tehran), Consultant Adviser to Chm/Dep MD 1978-79; Talbot UK, Chm 1979-84; Inchcape plc, Group MD/Group Chief Exec 1984-86. *Biog: b.* 17 October 1926. *m.* 1950, Marion (née Wing); 1 s; 2 d. *Educ:* King Henry VIII School, Coventry; Birmingham University (BSc Hons). *Directorships:* Hong Kong and Shanghai Banking Corporation 1985 Member, London Advisory; The Industrial Society 1987 Chm of Council; Korea-Europe Fund Ltd 1987 (non-exec) Chm; Euro-Asia Centre 1987 (exec); Bank in Liechtenstein (UK) Ltd 1988 (non-exec); Kleinwort Benson Group plc 1988 (non-exec). *Other Activities:* SMMT (Pres 1982-83, Dep Pres 1984-). *Professional Organisations:* FIMechE; FIProdE; FIMI; Fellow, Institute of Directors. *Publications:* Report on the Future of the Korean Car Industry, 1976. *Recreations:* Skiing, Court Tennis, Golf, Fishing.

TURNBULL, John; Partner, Linklaters & Paines, since 1989; Litigation. *Career:* College of Law 1979-80; Philip Ross & Co, Articled 1980-82; Linklaters, Assistant Solicitor 1982-89. *Biog: b.* 15 April 1958. *Nationality:* British. *m.* 1983, Janet. *Educ:* Leicester University (LLB). *Professional Organisations:* Solicitor, Supreme Court.

TURNBULL, Nigel; Finance Director, The Rank Organisation plc.

TURNBULL, Steven; Partner, Linklaters & Paines, since 1985; Corporate/Corporate Finance. *Biog: b.* 24 October 1952. *Nationality:* British. *m.* 1984, Mary Ann;

1 s; 1 d. *Educ:* Monkton Combe School; University College, Oxford (BA Modern History & Modern Languages). *Other Activities:* City of London Solicitors Company, Company Law Sub-Committee. *Clubs:* Royal Wimbledon Golf Club, Oxford & Cambridge Golfing Society. *Recreations:* Golf, Tennis, Music, Family.

TURNER, A C; Director, Byas Mosley & Co Ltd.

TURNER, Andrew; Private Banking Director, Royal Trust Bank. *Career:* N M Rothschild & Sons Ltd; Price Waterhouse. *Professional Organisations:* FCA.

TURNER, D; Director, C & G Guardian.

TURNER, D J; Executive Director, Booker plc.

TURNER, John Kenelm; Partner, Gouldens Solicitors, since 1968; Pensions. *Career:* National Service, Middlesex Regiment 1952-54; Bower, Cotton & Bower, Articled Clerk 1957-60; Linklaters & Paines, Asst Solicitor 1960-65; Gouldens, Asst Solicitor 1965-68. *Biog: b.* 6 May 1934. *Nationality:* British. *m.* 1965, Anne (née Barescti); 3 s. *Educ:* Whitgift School; Kings College, London (LLB). *Directorships:* Solicitor to the Hearing Aid Council 1987. *Professional Organisations:* Solicitor (Honours); Law Society. *Recreations:* Bird Watching, Art History, Travel, Foreign Languages.

TURNER, John Lawrence; Director, Bain Clarkson Limited, since 1987; Chairman, European Division. *Career:* Royal Insurance Various 1957-63; WG Holmes & Co Ltd, Various 1963-64; Bain Dawes plc, Various 1965-. *Biog: b.* 28 June 1933. *Nationality:* British. *m.* 1958, Ursula (née Laycock); 2 s; 1 d. *Educ:* Bradford Grammar School; Magdalene College, Cambridge (MA). *Directorships:* Inchape Insurance Holdings plc 1989 (exec); RICS Insurance services Ltd 1989 (non-exec). *Professional Organisations:* FCII; FBIBA; FBIM. *Recreations:* Bridge, Sailing.

TURNER, Michael John; Audit Group Partner, Touche Ross & Co, since 1990; Partner in charge of Japanese Business. *Career:* Hamilton & Rowland Chartered Accountants, Student 1968-72; Touche Ross & Co 1972-; Partner 1979. *Biog: b.* 8 February 1950. *Nationality:* British. *m.* 1975, Kazine; 2 d. *Educ:* King Edward VI Grammar School, Southampton. *Professional Organisations:* FCA. *Clubs:* Teddington Hockey Club (Vice President). *Recreations:* Golf, Tennis.

TURNER, Norman; Head of Housing Services, Leeds Permanent Building Society, since 1988; Mortgage Products, Lending, Insurance Products, Services & Sales. *Career:* Legal & General Assurance Society Ltd, Marketing of Personal Lines Insurance 1970-81; Leeds Permanent Building Society Insurance Services Mgr 1981-88. *Biog: b.* 10 March 1947. *Nationality:* British. *m.* 1969, Patricia (née Haydock); 2 s. *Directorships:* Leeds Permanent Financial Planning Ltd 1989 (exec). *Professional Organisations:* FCII; MCIM; Registered Insurance Broker; Chartered Insurance Practitioner.

TURNER, P G C; Representative, First National Bank of Southern Africa Limited.

TURNER, The Hon (Philip Noel) Nigel; Executive Director, Lazard Bros & Co Ltd, since 1985; Corporate Finance, UK/USA/Canada/Mexico. *Career:* The Northern Trust Co, Dep Gen Mgr 1970-83; Barclays Merchant Bank, Exec Dir 1983-85. *Biog: b.* 8 May 1949. *Nationality:* British. *m.* 1988, Jennifer Anne(née Armstrong); 2 s; 3 d. *Educ:* Rugby School; Worcester College, Oxford (MA). *Clubs:* MCC, I Zingari, Royal St George's Golf Club. *Recreations:* Cricket, Golf, Shooting, Tennis, Music, Gardening.

TURNER, R T; OBE; Group Marketing Director, STC plc, since 1988. *Career:* Rolls Royce plc, Last Position Commercial Director, Civil Engine Group 1965-88. *Biog: b.* 17 August 1942. *Nationality:* British. *m.* 1982, Margaret (née Corbett); 2 d. *Educ:* Shrewsbury School; University of Manchester (BA Hons Politics and Modern History). *Directorships:* STC plc 1989 (exec). *Professional Organisations:* Associate of RACS. *Clubs:* IOD. *Recreations:* Music, Opera, Rugby Football, Farming.

TURNER, Raymond T; Partner, Neville Russell.

TURNER, Roy G; Executive Vice President & Chief Financial Officer, Beazer USA, Inc, Beazer plc.

TURNER-SAMUELS, Michael Bryan; Group Treasurer, Unigate plc, since 1990. *Career:* Abbey National Building Society, Articled Clerk 1975-77; United Glass Ltd, Assistant Solicitor 1977-79; Hassey-Ferguson Holdings Ltd, European Legal Counsel 1979-82; European Treasury Manager 1982-85; Varity Corporation, General Treasury Manager 1985-88; Assistant Treasurer 1988-90. *Biog: b.* 17 August 1946. *Nationality:* British/Canadian. *m.* 1973, Hilary S (née Martin); 1 s; 1 d. *Educ:* King's College, Wimbledon; Southampton University (LLB). *Directorships:* Polygon Reinsurance Company Ltd 1989-90 (exec). *Professional Organisations:* Member, Association of Corporate Treasurers; Member, Law Society.

TURNOR, R W C; Partner, Allen & Overy, since 1985; Private Clients. *Career:* Allen & Overy, Articled Clerk and Assistant Solicitor 1978-85. *Biog: b.* 15 March 1956. *Nationality:* British. *m.* 1985, Louisa (née Forbes); 1 s; 1 d. *Educ:* Eton College; Keble College, Oxford, College of Law (BA). *Other Activities:* City of London Solicitors International Bar Association. *Professional Organisations:* Law Society, Solicitor. *Publications:* A Few Articles. *Clubs:* Bucks, Millenium. *Recreations:* Field Sports, Forestry, Skiing.

TURTLE, T W; Partner, Herbert Smith.

TUTEN, Henderson; Non-Executive Director, N M Rothschild & Sons Limited.

TWACHTMANN, P; Director, S G Warburg & Co Ltd.

TWEEN, Richard Leo; Managing Director, Lowndes Lambert Australia Limited, since 1976; Total Responsibility for the Australian Operations. *Career:* MLC Fire & General Insurance, Inspector Marketing 1960-68; Sedgwick Collins, Director Service/Marketing 1968-73; Lowndes Lambert, Managing Director 1974-. *Biog: b.* 21 August 1940. *Nationality:* Australian. *m.* 1964, Cynthia (née Greathead); 3 s. *Educ:* University of NSW (BCom). *Directorships:* Lowndes Lambert Australia Limited 1974 (exec); Lowndes Lambert Group Holdings Limited 1988 (exec). *Clubs:* Safari Club International. *Recreations:* Big Game Hunting.

TWINING, Dennis Russell; Executive Director, Lazard Brothers, since 1989; Head of Real Estate Finance. *Career:* International Nickel Co, Application Engineer 1964-70; Amax, Asst Gen Mgr 1970-73; Freeport McMoran,Various, Responsible for all Metals Divisions Commercial Activities 1973-86; Salomon Brothers, Vice Pres, Real Estate Finance 1986-89. *Educ:* University of Michigan (BSe Metallurgical Engineering); New York University (MBS Finance and Marketing). *Other Activities:* American Society. *Clubs:* Racquet, Tennis (NYC USA), St Georges Hill Tennis (Weybridge).

TWIST, George Patrick; Partner, Pinsent & Co, since 1988; Banking and Corporate Finance. *Career:* Bank of Scotland, Head of Legal Services (London) 1982-87. *Biog: b.* 1952. *m.* 1981; 1 s; 1 d. *Educ:* Downside School; Keele University. *Clubs:* Bohemian. *Recreations:* Cricket, Forestry.

TWISTON DAVIES, Audley William; Director, Foreign & Colonial Management Ltd.

TYERMAN, Robert; Assistant City Editor, The Sunday Telegraph, since 1977; City Topics, Mining, Australia, Lloyd's, Hong Kong, Fraud, City Diary. *Career:* Investors' Chronicle, Specialising on USA, Italy & France; Sunday Telegraph, Albany Column 1975-77.

TYLER, Colin Douglas; Partner, Wragge & Co, since 1963; Commercial & Trade Matters. *Career:* Frank A Plate & Beaizley (Walsall), Articled Clerk 1955-58; Hopkin & Sons (Mansfield), Asst Solicitor 1958-60; Wragge & Co, Asst Solicitor 1960-62. *Biog: b.* 13 July 1932. *Nationality:* British. *m.* 1958, Margaret Marie (née Hughes); 2 s. *Educ:* Queen Mary's Grammar School, Walsall; Emmanuel College, Cambridge (MA). *Directorships:* Ingleby Nominees Ltd (non exec); Ingleby Services (non-exec); Ingleby Holdings Ltd (non-exec); W J

Wild Nominees Ltd (non-exec). *Other Activities:* Chm (part-time), Birmingham Medical Appeal Tribunal; Mem, Advisory Board of Institute of European Law, University of Birmingham. *Professional Organisations:* The Law Society. *Clubs:* Birmingham; Moseley Golf Club. *Recreations:* Golf, Classical Music, Theatre, Fine Art, French, Walking.

TYLER, P S; Director, County NatWest Securities Limited.

TYLER, R G; Director & Company Secretary, Edwards & Payne (Underwriting Agencies) Limited.

TYLOR, John; Director, Samuel Montagu & Co Ltd, since 1981; Corporate Finance. *Career:* Herbert Smith Solicitors 1966-73; Samuel Montagu 1973-. *Biog: b.* 1 July 1942. *Nationality:* British. *m.* 1975, Heather (née Budgett); 2 s. *Educ:* Eton; Dublin University (MA). *Directorships:* Samuel Montagu & Co Ltd. *Professional Organisations:* Solicitor.

TYRRELL, James Michael; General Manager & Finance Director, Abbey National Building Society, since 1982 & 1989; Finance, Treasury, Banking. *Career:* Coopers & Lybrand, Articles 1962-66; Associated British Picture Corp, PA to Group Fin Dir 1967-69; Associated British Cinemas Ltd, Fin Dir 1970-73; EMI Leisure Enterprises Ltd, Dir of New Ventures 1974-75; EMI Records Ltd, Dir of Fin & Admin 1975-78; HMV Shops Ltd (Retail), MD 1979-82. *Biog: b.* 6 March 1941. *Nationality:* British. *m.* 1970, Jill Elizabeth (née Scott); 1 s; 2 d. *Educ:* Bradfield College; Lincoln College, Oxford (MA Hons). *Other Activities:* Bradfield College (Governor); Downe House (Governor). *Professional Organisations:* FCA; The 100 Group. *Clubs:* Huntercombe Golf Club.

TYSON, Professor Shaun; Professor of Human Resource Management, Cranfield School of Management, since 1979; Chairman of Human Resource Department. *Career:* Thorn Group (TV), Personnel Manager 1964-69; Bestobell Group, Personnel Manager 1969-75; Civil Service College, Lecturer in Management 1975-79. *Biog: b.* 22 July 1940. *Nationality:* British. *Educ:* London University, Goldsmith's College (BA); London School of Economics (PhD). *Directorships:* Cranfield School of Management Human Resource Research Centre 1985 (exec). *Other Activities:* Member, Post Graduate Courses Board, CNAA; Member, Editorial Boards of: Journal of Human Resource Management, MBA Review, Management Monitor. *Professional Organisations:* Fellow, Institute of Personnel Management; Member, British Psychological Society; Member, British Academy of Management. *Publications:* Personnel Management Made Simple, 1982 (Revised 1988); Evaluating the Personnel Function, 1986; Cases in Human Resource Management (Ed), 1987; Appraising and Exploring Organisations (Ed), 1988; International Comparisons in Human Resource Management (Ed), 1991. *Clubs:* National Liberal Club.

U

UCHIMURA, T; Managing Director, Sumitomo Finance International, since 1988. *Career:* The Sumitomo Bank Ltd, served in a domestic branch 1968-71; Univeristy of Exeter (UK) 1971-73; The Sumitomo Bank Ltd (Tokyo), Foreign Business Dept 1973-74; International Planning Dept 1974-80; (Sydney) Representative Office 1980-84; (Tokyo) Deputy General Manager 1984-85; (New York) Joint General Manager 1985-88; Sumitomo Finance International (London), Managing Director 1988-. *Educ:* Kyusha University (BA).

UDELL, Roger Barry; Administration Director/Compliance Officer, Gibbs Hartley Cooper, since 1985. *Career:* Pearl Assurance Co, Clerk 1949-54; Gibson & Co, Mgr 1954-59; Glanville Enthoven & Co, Acct Exec 1959-69; Gibbs Hartley Cooper & Co, Dir 1969-. *Biog: b.* 10 December 1932. *Nationality:* British. *m.* 1964, Anne (née Cooper); 1 s. *Educ:* St Alban's County Grammar School. *Other Activities:* Member, The Worshipful Company of Insurers; Freeman of the City of London; Underwriting Member of Lloyd's. *Professional Organisations:* ACII, Registered Insurance Broker. *Recreations:* Golf.

UETADANI, T; General Manager, Yasuda Trust & Banking Co Ltd.

UFLAND, Richard Mark; Partner, Stephenson Harwood, since 1986; Corporate Finance. *Career:* Stephenson Harwood, Articled Clerk 1979-81; Asst Solicitor 1981-86. *Biog: b.* 4 May 1957. *m.* 1985, Jane Camilla (née Rapaport); 2 s. *Educ:* St Paul's School; Downing College, Cambridge (MA). *Other Activities:* City of London Solicitors' Company. *Professional Organisations:* The Law Society. *Recreations:* Opera, Theatre, Bridge.

UHRYNUK, Mark R; Associate, Mayer Brown & Platt, since 1986; Corporate and Commercial. *Biog: b.* 20 December 1958. *Nationality:* Canadian. *Educ:* University of Western Ontario (MBA, LLB with distinction); Dartmouth College (AB). *Professional Organisations:* American Bar Association; Canadian Bar Association.

UJIHARA, Kosaku; Director, Chief Representative, Baring Brothers & Co Limited, 1983-89; Corporate Finance, Capital Markets. *Career:* Sheffield University, Lecturer of the Centre of Japanese Studies 1971-76; British Embassy in Japan, Head of British Embassy Kamakura School 1976-83. *Biog: b.* 1 January 1947.

Nationality: Japanese. *m.* 1971, Reiko; 1 s; 2 d. *Educ:* Waseda University (BA). *Directorships:* ORIX Capital Corporation 1986; Baring Brothers & Co Limited 1989; Suntory-Allied Lyons Ltd 1989 Auditor. *Recreations:* Reading, Music.

UKON, Tokuo; Managing Director & Chief Executive, Yamaichi International (Europe) Ltd, since 1990. *Career:* Yamaichi Securities Co, Japan 1969; Stock Sales, Marubiru Branch 1969; International Finance Department 1974; Yamaichi International (Europe) Ltd, Japanese Equities Institutional Sales 1982; Yamaichi Bank (Switzerland), President 1986; Yamaichi Securities Co, General Manager, Convertive Bonds and Warrants Department 1989; Yamaichi International (Europe) Ltd, Managing Director & Chief Executive 1990. *Biog: b.* 24 March 1990. *Nationality:* Japanese; 1 s; 1 d. *Educ:* Wased University, Tokyo Japan (Politics & Economics). *Directorships:* Yamaichi International (Europe) Ltd 1990 Managing Director & Chief Executive. *Recreations:* Walking, Skiing.

UMEZAKI, Yasunori; Managing Director, Yamaichi International (Europe) Ltd; UK & European Equities. *Career:* Bond Trading Department, Deputy Managing Director 1989. *Biog: b.* 6 January 1944. *Nationality:* Japanese. *m.* 1972, Mieko Umezaki (née Muramatsu); 2 d. *Educ:* Hosei University (Bachelor). *Recreations:* Swimming, Reading.

UNDERHILL, C W Y; Partner, Slaughter and May, since 1990. *Biog: b.* 30 June 1959. *m.* Virginia; 1 s; 1 d. *Educ:* London School of Economics (LLB).

UNDERHILL, Peter John; Managing Director, Capital Ventures Limited, since 1981. *Career:* Coopers & Lybrand, London, Articled Clerk then Senior Manager 1969-77; Peerless Group Limited, Chief Accountant/Commercial Mgr of BSK Aluminum Ltd (subsidiary company) 1977-78; Star Aluminum Co (a division of Alusuisse (UK) Ltd, Fin Controller 1978-81; Capital Ventures Ltd & TriVenture Ltd, Director then Managing Director 1981-. *Biog: b.* 14 February 1948. *Nationality:* British. *m.* Susan; 1 s; 1 d. *Educ:* Bridgenorth Grammar School; University of London; London School of Economics (BSc Econ Hons). *Directorships:* Capital Ventures Ltd 1981 (exec); Alan Paul plc (non-exec); Bristol Commercial Developments Limited (previously Datepress Limited) (non-exec); Beeches Homes Limited (non-exec); Bristol Commercial Developments plc (non-exec); Capital Inns Limited (non-exec); Capital Inns (3) (non-exec); Capital Inns (5) Limited (non-exec); Capital Securities Limited (non-exec); Capital Ventures Limited (non-exec); Cave Nominees Limited (non-exec); Chevin Lodge Limited (non-exec); Combustion Developments Limited (non-exec); Crusoe Music Limited (non-exec); CV Leasing Limited (non-exec); EP Packaging Limited (previously Foray 236 Limited) (non-exec); Executive Action Link (non-exec); Fenland Sheepskin Limited (non-exec); First Roman Property Trust plc (non-exec); The Fourth Roman Property Trust plc (non-exec); Hawthorn Homes Limited (previously Dollarmoor Limited) (non-exec); Jamasque Limited (non-exec); Jingles International Limited (non-exec); Lobbyglen Limited (non-exec); Markwide Limited (non-exec); Powerplant Music & Recording Limited (non-exec); Roman Homes plc (non-exec); Scarlett Recordings Limited (non-exec); TriVenture Limited (non-exec); UBA (Developments) plc (non-exec); United British Artists Limited (non-exec); Whitmore Holdings plc 1990 (non-exec); Arthur Woolacott Holdings Limited (non-exec); Admiral Inns Limited (non-exec); Aegis Insurance Services (Holdings) Limited (non-exec); Ken Read & Son (Wholesale Meat) Limited (exec); Park Rose Limited (non-exec); Jayvision Limited (non-exec); Gostin of Liverpool Limited (non-exec); Chase Property Holdings (Northern) Limited (non-exec); Harcourt Holdings plc (previously Thorpac Group plc) (non-exec); Coppice Foil Containers Limited (non-exec); Alupack Foil Containers Limited (non-exec); ATP Management Limited (non-exec); Avon Tin Printers Limited (non-exec); Orbital Data Systems Limited (non-exec); Skanfish Limited (non-exec); Trice Frozen Foods Limited (non-exec); The Harrogate International Hotel plc (non-exec). *Professional Organisations:* FCA.

UNDERWOOD, S G B; Clerk, Broderers' Company.

UNDERWOOD, William Greaves; Director, Majedie Investments plc, since 1988; Executive. *Career:* Deloitte & Co, Asst Mgr 1961-66; Antony Gibbs Holdings, Dir 1966-82; Riggs AP Bank, Dir 1982-88. *Biog: b.* 16 June 1936. *Nationality:* British. *m.* 1960, Susan Elizabeth, (née Cogswell); 1 s; 2 d. *Educ:* Uppingham. *Directorships:* Majedie Investments plc 1988 (exec); Haymills Holdings Ltd 1986 (non-exec). *Other Activities:* Chm, Thomley & Bernwood Association; Member of Council, London Chamber of Commerce, 1982-89. *Professional Organisations:* FCA; FRSA. *Clubs:* City of London Club. *Recreations:* Preservation of the Countryside, Skiing, Music.

UNSWORTH, Edwin; Correspondent, The Journal of Commerce.

UNWIN, C A; Member, Monopolies & Mergers Commission.

UNWINS, John; Partner, McKenna & Co.

UPSALL, Terence John; Chairman, Beazer Europe & Overseas Ltd; Europe & Overseas. *Career:* Local Government Planning Department 1955-72; Beazer plc 1972-. *Biog: b.* 22 March 1937. *Nationality:* British. *m.* 1961, Sheila Ann; 1 s; 1 d. *Educ:* Kings School, Bruton. *Other Activities:* Senior Vice President, HBF. *Professional Organisations:* FRICS; FSVA.

URE, D; Managing Director, Reuters Ltd, since 1989; Europe, Middle East & Africa. *Biog: b.* 8 September 1947. *Nationality:* British. *m.* Elizabeth (née Millar); 1 d. *Educ:* Merton College, Oxford (BA Hons Modern History). *Directorships:* Reuters Holdings plc 1989 (exec). *Clubs:* RAC Club.

URQUHART, L M; Chairman and Chief Executive, Burmah Castrol plc, since 1990. *Career:* Price Waterhouse 1957-62; Shell International Petroleum 1962-64; PA Management Consultants 1964-68; Charterhouse Group Ltd, Snr Group Executive 1968-74; Tozer, Kemsley & Millbourn, Group Finance Dir 1974-77; Burmah Oil Co Ltd, Group Finance Dir 1977-82; Castrol Limited, Chief Executive 1982-85; Burmah Oil plc, Group Managing Dir 1985-90. *Biog: b.* 24 September 1935. *Nationality:* British. *m.* 1961, Elizabeth Catherine (née Burns); 3 s; 1 d. *Educ:* Strathallan School, Perthshire; Kings College, London University (LLB CA). *Directorships:* Premier Consolidated Oilfields 1986 (non-exec); South Western Regional Health Authority 1990 (non-exec). *Other Activities:* Liveryman, Worshipful Company of Coach and Coach Harness Makers; British Institute of Management (CBIM) F Inst Pet. *Professional Organisations:* Institute of Chartered Accountants CA, Scotland. *Clubs:* Lilley Brook, Frilford Heath Golf Club, Southerness Golf Club. *Recreations:* Golf, Music.

URSELL, Bruce Anthony; Chairman, British & Commonwealth Merchant Bank plc, since 1990. *Career:* Standard Bank Ltd, Mgr 1961-68; Western American Bank, Gen Mgr 1968-74; Guinness Mahon & Co, Snr Banking Dir 1974-84; MD 1984-87. *Biog: b.* 28 August 1942. *m.* 1966, Anne Carole (née Pitt); 1 s; 2 d. *Educ:* William Ellis School, Highgate. *Directorships:* Lockton Dev 1985 (non-exec) Chm; Survey Broadcasting (USA) 1986 (non-exec) Chm. *Recreations:* Theatre, Music, Tennis, Cinema.

URWIN, Mrs Ailsa; Partner, Freshfields.

URWIN, Jeffrey; Executive Director, Developing Countries Group, Samuel Montagu & Co Ltd, since 1987. *Career:* Lloyds Bank International 1979-83. *Biog: b.* 18 January 1956. *Nationality:* British. *m.* Ailsa; 1 s; 1 d. *Directorships:* Banco Roberts SA 1988 (non-exec); Argentine Private Development Trust 1990 (non-exec); Samuel Montagu & Co Ltd 1987 (exec).

USAGAWA, Naoto; Joint General Manager, The Sumitomo Bank Limited.

USHER, Andrew Michael; Partner, Baillie Gifford & Co, since 1986; Administration. *Career:* Park Nelson Dennes Redfern & Co, Assistant Solicitor 1964-67; Partner 1967-69; The British Investment Trust plc, Investment Assistant 1969-77; Portfolio Manager 1977-79; Secretary 1979-86; Baillie Gifford & Co, Partner 1986-. *Biog: b.* 15 October 1938. *Nationality:* British. *m.* 1964, Anne (née Whittington); 3 s; 1 d. *Educ:* Cheltenham College; The College of Law. *Directorships:* The Fleming Fledgeling Investment Trust plc 1978 (non-exec). *Professional Organisations:* Solicitor. *Clubs:* The New (Edinburgh), The Hon Co of Edinburgh Golfers Muirfield. *Recreations:* Music, Golf, Genealogy.

USHER, Catherine F; Partner, Turner Kenneth Brown; Commercial Property.

UTTING, Harry William; General Manager & Secretary, Norwich Union Insurance Group, since 1990; Central, Corporate Services & Company Secretary. *Career:* Norwich Union Insurance Clerk 1955-56; RAF National Service 1956-58; Norwich Union Motor Insurance Clerk 1958-65; Computer Programmer/Systems Analyst 1965-71; Asst Head, Motor Research 1972-73; Head, Motor Research 1973-77; Asst Mgr, City Office 1977-78; Home Motor Supt 1978-80; Asst Home Motor Mgr 1980-81; Home Accident Mgr 1981-84; Asst General Mgr (Branches) 1984-89; Asst General Mgr (Personal Insurances) 1989-90. *Biog: b.* 25 July 1937. *Nationality:* British. *m.* 1959, Jean Edna (née Loome); 1 d. *Educ:* City of Norwich School. *Directorships:* Norfolk & Waveney Training & Enterprise Council 1990 (non-exec). *Other Activities:* Committee Member, Community Action Trust. *Professional Organisations:* FCII, Chartered Insurer. *Clubs:* Royal Norwich Golf Club, Norfolk Bowling Club. *Recreations:* Golf, Watching Soccer, DIY, Popular Music.

UWINS, John Trevor; Partner, McKenna & Co, since 1987; Construction, Major Projects & Dispute Resolutions. *Career:* McKenna & Co, Articled Clerk 1979-81; Assistant Solicitor 1981-85; Overseas Partner, Singapore 1985-87; Partner & Senior Resident Partner in Singapore 1987-90; Partner, London 1991-. *Biog: b.* 28 July 1956. *Nationality:* British. *m.* 1984, Adele (née Meyer). *Educ:* Fitzwilliam College, Cambridge (MA). *Other Activities:* American Business Council, Singapore; British Business Association, Singapore. *Professional Organisations:* Law Society England & Wales; Singapore Institute of Arbitration. *Recreations:* Golf, Rugby, Tennis, Squash.

UZIELLI, William John; Director, Hogg Group plc, since 1987; Marine Insurance Broking. *Biog: b.* 2 March 1937. *Nationality:* British. *m.* 1968, Angela Mary (née Carrick); 1 s; 1 d. *Educ:* Marlborough College; Trinity College, Oxford (MA). *Directorships:* GIL Carvajal & Partners (non-exec); Gardner Mountain Capel-Cure (Agencies) (non-exec). *Clubs:* City of London, Royal & Ancient Golf Club, Berkshire Golf Club, Trevose Golf Club. *Recreations:* Golf, Gardening.

V

VAILE, Ian; European Director of Tax Services, Price Waterhouse.

VALDINGER, Jan Robin; Director, UK Corporate Finance, Chartered WestLB Limited, since 1986; Corporate & Project Finance. *Career:* Clifford Turner & Co Solicitor 1970-74; Morgan Grenfell & Co Ltd Exec 1974-79; Standard Chartered Merchant Bank (India) Head 1979-83; (Hong Kong) Head 1983-87. *Biog: b.* 28 September 1945. *m.* 1974, Rosemary Jane (née O'Conor Donelan); 1 s; 2 d. *Educ:* Cranbrook School; Newcastle University (LLB Hons). *Professional Organisations:* The Law Society. *Clubs:* Hong Kong Club, Royal Hong Kong Jockey Club, Burhill Golf Club. *Recreations:* Golf, Tennis.

VALENTINE, G R P N; Chairman, Janson Green Limited.

VALENTINE, Michael Robert; Director, S G Warburg Group plc, since 1967. *Career:* Cooper Brothers & Co, Snr Mgr 1951-60; S G Warburg & Co Ltd, Vice Chm/Head of Corporate Finance 1960-88. *Biog: b.* 16 January 1928. *Nationality:* British. *m.* 1957, Shirley Josephine (née Hall); 1 s; 2 d. *Educ:* Shrewsbury; Corpus Christi College, Cambridge (MA). *Directorships:* Croda International plc 1982 Chairman; Reckitt & Colman plc 1986 (non-exec). *Professional Organisations:* FCA. *Recreations:* Opera, Vintage Cars.

VALNER, Nicholas; Partner, Frere Cholmeley, since 1985; Commercial Litigation. *Career:* Frere Cholmeley, Articled Clerk 1977; Solicitor 1979; Partner 1985. *Biog: b.* 14 September 1953. *Nationality:* British. *m.* 1979, Jane; 3 s. *Educ:* Stonyhurst College; Mansfield College, Oxford (BA Jurisprudence). *Other Activities:* Chairman, Arbitration Users Programme (CAUP), sub-committee of The Chartered Institute of Arbitrators; Mansfield College Fund Raising Committee. *Professional Organisations:* Associate Member, Chartered Institute of Arbitrators; Member, International Bar Association. *Recreations:* Fishing, Gardening, Shooting.

VAN AREM, H W; Managing Director (Investment Management), KAS Clearing Agent Ltd.

VAN DER SPEK, C N; Executive Vice President & General Manager - UK, Amro Bank, since 1986; UK, Ireland, Africa. *Career:* Amsterdam-Rotterdam Bank NV 1977-. *Biog: b.* 17 September 1948. *Nationality:* Dutch. *m.* 1978, Mariette (née Heyning); 2 d. *Educ:* Willem de Zwijeer-Lyceum (Gymnasium B); University of Leyden (MA Law); Balliol College, Oxford. *Directorships:* Amro Bank Mortgage Finance 1990 (exec); Amro (Nominees) Ltd 1986 (exec); Amro Holdings Ltd 1986 (exec); Amro Leasing (UK) Ltd 1986 (exec); Amro Fiducia (UK) Ltd 1986 (exec); Netherlands-British Chamber of Commerce 1986 (exec). *Clubs:* Overseas Bankers. *Recreations:* Skiing, Sailing, Reading, Music.

VAN DER WYCK, Herman Constantyn; Vice Chairman, S G Warburg Group plc; International Investment Banking Sovereign Advisory Services. *Career:* Royal Dutch/Shell Group of Companies, Marketing, Supply & Planning 1959-69. *Biog: b.* 17 March 1934. *Nationality:* Dutch. (div); 3 s 1 d. *Educ:* Graduate Institute of Political Science, Geneva University (MA); The Rotterdam University/University of Michigan Program (MBA). *Directorships:* Energy International NV; Automobiles Peugeot SA; Peugeot Talbot Motor Company Ltd; S G Warburg & Co Ltd Jt Chm. *Publications:* Various Articles on International Financing. *Recreations:* Snow/Water Skiing, Swimming, Tennis.

VAN DER WYCK, Otto; Chief Executive, Baring Capital Investors Limited.

VAN PELT, Guy; Managing Director, Morgan Guaranty Trust Company of New York.

VAN ZWEEDEN, Frederick; Partner, Clark Whitehill.

VARDEY, Giles Edwin; Managing Director, Equities, Swiss Bank Corporation, since 1990. *Career:* Salomon Bros, VP, Fixed Income Sales 1982-86; County NatWest, MD, Head of European Equities & Derivatives 1986-89; Salomon Bros, VP, Head of European Equities 1989-90.

VARDEY, Richard J; Secretary, The Union Discount Company of London plc.

VARDIGANS, P J; Director, York Trust Group plc.

VARLEY, A J; Retail Director, Next plc.

VARLEY, John Silvester; Director, Barclays de Zoete Wedd Securities Ltd.

VARTAN, J B R; Director, Charterhouse Tilney, since 1989; Marketing. *Career:* Hill Osborne, Partner

1964-79; Barratt Vartan & Co, Partner 1979-81; Buckmaster & Moore, Partner 1981-86; Credit Suisse Buckmaster & Moore, Director 1986-89; Charterhouse Tilney, Director 1989-. *Biog: b.* 13 September 1937. *Nationality:* British. *m.* 1963, Frances (née Bowser); 1 s; 1 d. *Educ:* Bilton Grange; Uppingham; Caius College, Cambridge. *Other Activities:* Court Member, The Worshipful Company of Glaziers; Trustee, Peterborough Cathedral; Member, The Council of The Stock Exchange, 1974-81; Chairman, The Provincial Unit of The Stock Exchange, 1979-81. *Professional Organisations:* Member, The International Stock Exchange. *Clubs:* The Hawks Club, The Royal & Ancient Golf Club of St Andrews, The Naval Club. *Recreations:* Golf, Tennis, Shooting, Fishing, Walking.

VARZI, Mehdi; Director, Oil Research, Kleinwort Benson Securities, since 1986; World Oil Market, with Special Reference to OPEC. *Career:* National Iranian Oil Co, Snr Analyst, Intl Oil Mkt 1968-72; Iranian Foreign Ministry, Various Positions in Economic and Political Sections 1972-81; Grieveson Grant & Co, Oil Consultant (OPEC & World Oil Mkt) 1982-86; Kleinwort Benson Securities, Dir, Oil Research 1986-. *Biog: b.* 23 July 1945. *Nationality:* Iranian. *m.* 1974, Soraya (née Ehsani); 2 s; 1 d. *Educ:* Oundle School; LSE (BSc); School of Oriental & African Studies (MA). *Professional Organisations:* London Oil Analysts Group. *Recreations:* Piano, Photography, Squash, Swimming, Table Tennis.

VASTA, U; General Manager, Banca Popolare di Milano.

VAUGHAN, Dr Caroline Lesley; Chief Executive, Newmarket Venture Capital plc, since 1990; Venture Capital. *Career:* W R Grace, Financial Analyst 1969-72; Marketing Manager 1972-74; Tube Investments, Commercial Planner - Group 1974-76; Divisional Planner - Domestic Appliance Division 1976-78; National Enterprise Board, Divisional Executive 1978-80; Celltech, Director of Market Development 1980-82; Director of Business Development 1982-84; Newmarket Venture Capital, Director 1984-89; Chief Executive 1990-. *Biog: b.* 5 February 1941. *Nationality:* British. *Educ:* Croydon High School; Manchester University (BSc Biochemistry); London University (PhD Pharmaceutical Chemistry). *Directorships:* Newmarket Venture Capital plc 1987 (exec); Synoptics 1986 (non-exec); Cell Systems 1986 (non-exec); Archaeus 1987 (non-exec); Limbic 1986 (non-exec); Gelosia 1990 (non-exec); UMI 1990 (non-exec).

VAUGHAN, R; Director, CCF Foster Braithwaite Ltd.

VAUGHAN, R B; Director, Dalgety plc.

VAUGHAN-FOWLER, M; Director, J H Minet & Co Ltd.

VAUGHAN-NEIL, J; Partner, Nabarro Nathanson.

VAUGHN, James Hurd; Chairman, Hogg Robinson & Gardner Mountain plc, since 1987. *Career:* Vaughn & Blake Pres & Chief Exec Officer 1954-71; Fred S James Snr VP 1971-75; Chm 1975-81; Hogg Robinson Group plc Non-Exec Dir 1983-87; Hogg Robinson North America Chm 1984-87; BNB Resources plc Non-Exec Dir 1983-90; Jenner Fenton & Slade Ltd Non-Exec Dir 1988-. *Biog: b.* 7 April 1927. *Nationality:* American. *m.* 1954, Charlotte W (née Blaine); 1 s; 2 d. *Educ:* Cranbrook School, Michigan; Cornell University (BA). *Directorships:* J S Johnson 1985 (non-exec); The Children's Aid Society 1984 Trustee; Portals Group Ltd NA 1984 (non-exec); Kleinwort Benson NA 1983 (non-exec); Markel Corporation 1983 (non-exec). *Other Activities:* Underwriting Member of Lloyd's. *Clubs:* Queen's, City of London, Brook's, Brook River (New York). *Recreations:* Tennis, Skiing, Golf, Gardening.

VAUSE, Alan Charles; Senior Partner, Milne Ross, since 1985; Corporate Finance. *Career:* Middletons, Articled Clerk 1948-54; Royal Army Pay Corps, 2 Lt 1954-56; Jones Ross Howell (Subsequently Merged to form Milne Ross), Partner 1956-. *Biog: b.* 10 August 1931. *Nationality:* British. *m.* 1955, Diane; 2 s; 1 d. *Educ:* Surbiton Grammar School. *Other Activities:* Court of Worshipful Company of Environmental Cleaners. *Professional Organisations:* Fellow, Institute of Chartered Accountants. *Clubs:* MCC, RAC, Saunton Golf Club. *Recreations:* Golf, Skiing.

VAZ DE MASCARENHAS, A; UK Representative, Banco Pinto & Sotto Mayor; London Representative Office.

VEIT, David; President, Pearson Inc, since 1985. *Biog: b.* 21 October 1938. *Nationality:* British. *m.* 1969, Marsha Frances Veit (née Robbins); 2 s; 2 d. *Educ:* Brasenose College, Oxford (MA); Stanford University (MBA). *Directorships:* Camco International Inc 1976 Chairman; Cedar Fair Management Company 1986 (non-exec). *Other Activities:* Senior Livery, Clothworkers Company. *Clubs:* University Club (New York).

VEITCH, George; Partner, Baillie Gifford & Co, since 1982; Japan & Far East Investment Management. *Career:* Edinburgh Investment Trust Investment Analyst 1961-69; Baillie Gifford & Co Investment Analyst 1969-82. *Biog: b.* 2 May 1943. *m.* 1966, Muriel J F (née Fraser); 2 s; 1 d. *Educ:* George Heriot's School, Edinburgh. *Directorships:* Baillie Gifford Shin Nippon plc 1985 (exec); Baillie Gifford Japan Trust plc 1989 (exec). *Professional Organisations:* ACIS. *Recreations:* Squash, Badminton, Golf.

VENABLES, Peter; Assistant General Manager (Lending), Banque Internationale à Luxembourg.

VENN, K E; Partner, Lawrence Graham.

VENNING, John; Partner, Robson Rhodes.

VENTOSO, Alfonso L; Executive Director, Merrill Lynch International Bank Limited.

VERBINNEN, Paul; Non-Executive Director, Ogilvy Adams & Rinehart.

VEREY, David John; Chief Executive, Lazard Brothers & Co Ltd, since 1990. *Biog: b.* 8 December 1950. *m.* 1990, Emma (née Laidlaw); 2 s; 1 d. *Educ:* Eton College; Trinity College, Cambridge (MA). *Directorships:* British Bond & Mortgage Corporation Ltd 1985; Lazard Investments Ltd 1985; Lazard Overseas Holdings Ltd 1985; LB Ltd 1985; Silicon (Organic) Developments Ltd 1985; Sunberg Ltd 1985; Lazard Overseas Investments Ltd 1985; Eurafrance SA 1985; Minden Securities 1985; Actionace Ltd 1986; Cushion Trust Ltd 1986; Lazard Brothers Money Broking 1986; Maison Lazard 1986. *Recreations:* Shooting, Stalking, Tennis, Bridge.

VEREY, Henry Nicholas; Director, S G Warburg Group plc.

VERILGHEN, Etienne; Director, Brown, Shipley & Co Limited.

VERNEY, His Honour Judge Lawrence; High Steward of Southwark & Recorder, Corporation of London.

VERNON, M D L; Financial Director, Gravett & Tilling (Underwriting Agencies) Ltd.

VERO, Geoffrey Osborne; Director, Causeway Capital Limited, since 1987; Investment Management, Unquoted Investments. *Career:* Ernest Young, Articled Clerk 1965-70; Savills, Chief Accountant 1970-75; The Diners Club Ltd, Group Finance Director 1976-84; Lazard Development Capital Ltd, Investment Director 1985-86. *Biog: b.* 9 January 1947. *Nationality:* British. *m.* 1975, Ann Frances (née Walton); 2 s; 1 d. *Educ:* Mill Hill School, London. *Directorships:* Causeway Capital Ltd 1987 (exec); Causeway Group Ltd 1989 (exec); Westcane Ltd 1987 (non-exec); Beaumont Industrial Holdings Ltd 1987 (non-exec); Shogun Jewellery Ltd 1988 (non-exec). *Other Activities:* Chairman, Chobham Conservative Association; Member, Public Schools Golfing Society Committee; Liveryman, W C of Feltmakers. *Professional Organisations:* FCA. *Clubs:* Carlton, Sunningdale GC, Rye GC, Salcombe Yacht Club. *Recreations:* Golf, Tennis, Cricket.

VERRILL, John Rothwell; Partner, Lawrence Graham, since 1986; Company and Commercial Law (Oil and Gas, Insolvency). *Career:* Ward Bowie, Asst Solicitor 1981-82; Lawrence Graham, Asst Solicitor 1982-86. *Biog: b.* 25 March 1954. *Nationality:* British. *m.* 1980, Katharine (née Spensley); 2 s. *Educ:* University College School; University College, London (LLB Hons). *Professional Organisations:* The Law Society; Westminster Law Society; City of London Solicitors Company; Insolvency Lawyers Association; Licensed Insolvency Practitioner. *Clubs:* Leander, Aldeburgh Yacht Club. *Recreations:* Rowing, Sailing.

VERSEN, R F; Director, Granville Davies Ltd.

VERSTRAETEN, Anne Marie; Executive Director, Banque Belge Limited.

VERULAM, John Duncan; The Earl of Verulam; Director, Baring Brothers & Co Ltd, since 1987; Corporate Finance. *Career:* Delta Metal Ltd Graduate Tnee 1973-75; Grimston Trust Ltd Chief Exec 1975-82; Baring Brothers & Co Ltd Exec 1982; Mgr 1984; Asst Dir 1986. *Biog: b.* 21 April 1951. *Nationality:* British. *m.* 1976, Dione (née Smith); 3 s; 1 d. *Educ:* Eton College; Oxford University (MA). *Directorships:* Grimston Trust Ltd 1982 Chm (non-exec). *Clubs:* White's, Beefsteak, Turf. *Recreations:* Country Pursuits.

VESTERI, Topi Heikki; General Manager, Postipankki Ltd, London Branch, since 1990. *Career:* Postipankki Ltd, Tokyo Representative Office, Chief Representative 1988-90; Postipankki Ltd, International Capital Markets, Senior Manager 1986-88. *Biog: b.* 7 January 1956. *Nationality:* Finnish. *m.* 1980, Anna-Stina Vesteri (née Sirén); 1 s; 1 d. *Educ:* University of Helsinki (LLM). *Directorships:* PSP (UK) Limited 1990 (exec) MD. *Clubs:* Jurecon r y.

VICE, Henry Anthony; Director, N M Rothschild & Sons Ltd, since 1972. *Career:* Financial Times 1953-58; Daily Telegraph 1958-64; Sunday Times 1964-67; The Times Founder/Ed Business News 1967-71. *Biog: b.* 24 December 1930. *Nationality:* British. *m.* 1954, Elizabeth J S (née Wright); 1 s; 2 d. *Educ:* Hymers College, Hull; Queen's College, Oxford (Scholar, Hons 1st). *Directorships:* I J Dewhirst Holdings plc Chm; Bowthorpe Holdings plc 1978 (non-exec); Drummond Group plc 1986 (non-exec); Cavaghan and Gray Ltd 1988; Evident Dental Co Ltd 1989 (non-exec); Chaucer Estates Ltd 1990 (non-exec). *Publications:* Bid for Power (with G Bull), 1959; Strategy of Takeovers, 1971; Financier at Sea, 1986.

VICINELLI, Gaetano; Managing Director, Morgan Guaranty Trust Company of New York.

VICKERS, Adrian; Director, Abbott Mead Vickers plc.

VIGRASS, C; Litigation Partner, Ashurst Morris Crisp; Commercial Litigation. *Career:* Linklaters &

Paines, Articled Clerk 1978-80; Assistant Solicitor, Litigation Department 1980-86; Ashurst Morris Crisp, Assistant Solicitor, Litigation Department 1986-87; Associate 1987-88. *Biog: b.* 8 August 1955. *Nationality:* British. *m.* 1978, Gael (née Bowman); 1 s; 2 d. *Educ:* Bradford Grammar School; Gonville & Caius, Cambridge (MA). *Professional Organisations:* Member, Society of Construction Law; British Insurance Law Association. *Recreations:* Squash, Fell Walking.

VILE, Martin; Group Director, Securities and Investments Board, since 1991.

VILLENEUVE, André; Executive Director, Reuters Holdings plc.

VILLIERS, Charles Nigel; Managing Director, Abbey National plc, since 1988; Corporate Development. *Career:* Arthur Andersen 1963-67; Industrial Commercial Finance Corporation 1967-72; County Bank 1972-; Deputy Chief Executive 1977-83; Chairman and Chief Executive 1984-86; County NatWest, Chairman 1986-88. *Biog: b.* 25 January 1941. *Nationality:* British. *m.* 1970, Sally Priscilla (née Magnay); 1 s; 1 d. *Educ:* Winchester College; Oxford University (MA). *Directorships:* Conder Group plc 1989 (non-exec). *Professional Organisations:* FCA. *Clubs:* Hurlingham. *Recreations:* Opera, Squash, Skiing, Tennis.

VINCENT, Leslie; Director, Svenska International plc.

VINCENT, Sir William P M; Head of International Development, Société Générale Touche Remnant, since 1990; USA, Asia, M East. *Career:* Touche Remnant, Investment Director 1986-90; US Investment Director 1985-86; Save & Prosper, US Investment Director 1977-85; Robert Fleming, US Fund Manager 1976-77; E F Hutton 1974-76; James Capel 1967-74. *Biog: b.* 1 February 1949. *Nationality:* British. *m.* 1976, Christine (née Walton); 3 s. *Educ:* Eton. *Directorships:* Société Générale Touche Remnant Asset Management 1990; Société Générale Touche Remnant Corp USA 1990 Chairman; Touche Remnant & Co 1985. *Clubs:* Household Division Yacht Club.

VINE, A R C; Director, Holman Macleod Limited.

VINE-LOTT, A K; Managing Director, Barclays Broker Services Ltd, since 1988; Stockbroking. *Career:* Honeywell Computers UK Ltd, Education Manager, Network Services Division 1978-81; Wang UK Ltd, National Mktg & Technical Support Manager 1981-86; Cleaver Co, Managing Director 1986-88. *Biog: b.* 24 October 1947. *Nationality:* British. *m.* 1982, Dr Ailsa (née Webb). *Educ:* King Edward VII, Macclesfield; Sheffield Polytechnic (HND Building Construction). *Directorships:* Thermal Structures Ltd (non-exec); Cleaver UK Ltd 1986 (exec); JPC Holdings 1987 (exec);

Grace & Templar Ltd 1989 (non--exec); Grace & Templar West Ltd 1989 (non-exec); Barclays Broker Services Ltd (exec). *Other Activities:* Member, The International Stock Exchange Glasgow Unit Committee. *Professional Organisations:* Royal Institute of Marketing. *Clubs:* Naval Club, Royal Yachting Assoc. *Recreations:* Sailing.

VINKEN, Pierre; Chairman and CEO, Elsevier, since 1979. *Career:* Univ of Amsterdam NL, Neurosurgeon & Senior Scientific Officer, Boeshaave Clinic Amsterdam, Consultant Neurosurgeon 1960-70; Elsevier Scientific Publishing Co, Managing Director 1971-73; Elsevier Amsterdam, Exec Dir 1972-79; Chairman and CEO 1979-. *Biog: b.* 25 November 1927. *Nationality:* Dutch. *Educ:* University of Utrecht NL (MD); University of Amsterdam NL (Neurosurgeon). *Directorships:* Wereldhave Real Estate Inv Co, The Hague 1979 (non-exec); INTERCOIN, Amsterdam 1981 (non-exec); Bank Pierson, Helding & Pierson, Amsterdam 1981 (non-exec); Logica, Rotterdam 1985 (non-exec) Chm; Halder Investment Co, The Hague 1988 (non-exec) Chm; Pearson, London 1988 (non-exec) Chm; The Economist Newspaper, London 1989; Logica, London 1990. *Other Activities:* Extra-Ord Professor, Medical Database Technology, Univ of Leyden (NL); Adv Ctee, Univ of Leyden; Chairman Balis Fdn, Hospital Information Systems, Leyden. *Professional Organisations:* Doctor Honoris Causa, University of Paris; Hon Mem, Société Française Neurologie; Hon Mem, Neurol Soc India; Hon Mem, Peru Soc Psychiatry, Neurol and Neurosurgery; Hon Mem, Neurol Soc Amsterdam; Knight Order Netherlands Lion; Commander Order of Hipolito Unanne, Peru. *Publications:* Handbook of Clinical Neurology (57 Vols), 1968-.

VINTCENT, John; Managing Director, CCF Foster Braithwaite Ltd, since 1988. *Career:* Laurence Keen & Gardner, Partner 1966-70; Warburg Investment Management Ltd 1970-79; Director, Vice Chairman 1979-; Non-Executive Director Private Client Investment Management 1985-; Hanford Farms Ltd, Managing Director 1979-87. *Biog: b.* 13 November 1937. *m.* 1959, Elizabeth Susan; 2 s; 1 d. *Educ:* Winchester College. *Directorships:* CCF Holdings Ltd 1989 (exec). *Other Activities:* General Commissioner for Income Tax, 1984-. *Clubs:* Brooks', Grasshoppers.

VINTER, Graham David; Partner, Allen & Overy, since 1988; Corporate Finance. *Career:* Allen & Overy. *Biog: b.* 4 March 1956. *Nationality:* British. *m.* 1990, Anne Elizabeth (née Baldock). *Educ:* Chichester High School for Boys; Brasenose College, Oxford (BA). *Recreations:* Squash, Chess.

VINTON, Alfred Merton; Chief Operating Officer, N M Rothschild & Sons Limited, since 1988. *Career:* J P Morgan, Various 1962-87; Morgan Guaranty Trust Company, General Manager London Office; J P Morgan

Securities Ltd, Vice-Chairman. *Biog: b.* 11 May 1938. *Nationality:* American. *m.* 1983, Anna Maria (née Dugan-Chapman); 1 s; 1 d. *Educ:* Choate School, Connecticut; Harvard (AB). *Directorships:* N M Rothschild & Sons Ltd 1988 (exec); Rothschilds Continuation Ltd 1989 (exec); Rothschild Ventures Limited 1988 (exec); Shield Trust Limited 1988 (exec); Rothschild Gold Limited 1990 (exec); Rothschild North America Inc 1988 (exec). *Recreations:* Riding, Tennis, Country Life, Classical Music.

VISUTTIPORN, Pipat; Assistant Vice President & Branch Manager, Thai Farmers Bank London Branch, since 1990; General Management. *Career:* Thai Farmers Bank, Assistant Manager, Head Office 1982-85; Division Manager 1985-88; Silom Major Branch, Assistant Marketing Manager 1988-89. *Biog: b.* 20 March 1955. *Nationality:* Thai. *Educ:* Chulalongkorn University, Bangkok (B Eng Chemical Engineering); New York University, New York USA (MBA).

VIVIAN, Jonathan Mark; Partner, McKenna & Co, since 1989; Commercial Property with a particular Emphasis on Development Work. *Career:* Frere Cholmeley, Articled Clerk 1978-80; Asst Solicitor 1980-81; Bells, Asst Solicitor 1981-82; Ptnr 1982-89. *Biog: b.* 28 August 1954. *Nationality:* British. *m.* Tessa; 1 s. *Educ:* St John's College, Cambridge (LLB, MA). *Professional Organisations:* Law Society.

VLASTO, Anthony Alexander; Partner, Clifford Chance, since 1981; Shipping/International Trade. *Career:* Coward Chance, Articled Clerk/Asst Solicitor 1973-81. *Biog: b.* 10 January 1951. *m.* 1975, Catherine Isolde (née Badenoch); 1 s. *Educ:* Charterhouse School; Southampton University (LLB Hons 1st). *Other Activities:* City of London Solicitors' Company. *Professional Organisations:* Average Adjuster's Assoc; London Maritime Arbitrators' Assoc; Baltic Exchange. *Clubs:* Hurlingham. *Recreations:* Squash, Fishing, Sailing, Theatre.

VOADEN, A H C; Joint Senior Partner, Grimley J R Eve.

VOADEN, W J; Associate, Grimley J R Eve.

VOGEL, David Norman; Partner, Titmuss Sainer & Webb, since 1974; Corporate Finance. *Career:* Titmuss Sainer & Webb, Articled Clerk 1970-72; Assistant Solicitor 1972-74. *Biog: b.* 2 August 1948. *Nationality:* British. *m.* 1975, Michele (née Beaumont); 3 d. *Educ:* Haberdasher Aske's School; University College, London (LLM). *Professional Organisations:* Law Society.

VOGT, Paul Johan; Chairman & Managing Director, Vogt & Maguire Ltd, since 1970; Shipbroking. *Biog: b.* 6 December 1938. *Nationality:* British. *m.* 1962, Ruth (née Tyrrell); 2 d. *Educ:* Rugby School. *Directorships:* The

Baltic Exchange Ltd 1989-91 Chairman; Windle Shipping Company Ltd; R J Johnson & Co (Liverpool) Ltd; The Transmarine Mutual Strike Association Ltd; The Transmarine Mutual Loss of Hire Assurance Association; The Sunderland Steamship Protecting & Indemnity Association; The Charterers Mutual Assurance Association Ltd; Charles Johnson & Co (London) Ltd; The United Kingdom Freight Demurrage & Defence Association Ltd; Vogt Futures Ltd. *Professional Organisations:* FICS. *Recreations:* Bridge.

VOISEY, D J; Director, Ropner Insurance Services Limited.

VOLDSTAD, Conrad; Managing Director, Debt Markets, Merrill Lynch Europe Limited.

VON BRENTANO, Michael; Managing Director, Deutsche Bank Capital Markets Limited, since 1985; Secondary Markets and Corporate Finance. *Career:* Berliner Handels-Gesellschaft, SVP/EVP 1964-74; Deutsche Bank AG, SVP 1974-85; Deutsche Bank Capital Markets Limited, Managing Director 1985-. *Biog: b.* 6 August 1933. *Nationality:* German. *m.* 1966, Elke (née Hassel); 1 d. *Educ:* In Switzerland and Germany. *Directorships:* Deutsche Bank Capital Corporation; International Primary Markets Association Chairman. *Clubs:* Frankfurter Gesellschaft fur Handel, Industrie und Wissenschaft, Royal Mid-Surrey Golf Club.

VON CLEMM, Michael; Director, Merrill Lynch Europe Limited.

VON DER GROEBEN, Hans-Eric; Executive Director, Svenska International plc.

VON DONNERSMARCK, Count W Henckel; Director, Hambros Bank Limited.

VON EISENHART-ROTHE, Ruediger; Managing Director, Chase Investment Bank Limited, since 1982; Structured Finance, Loan Syndication, Asset Sales, Tax Effective Finance, Project Finance, Leasing Private Placements. *Career:* Chase Bank AG, Frankfurt, Head of Credit Department 1971; Chase Düsseldorf & Hamburg, Lending Officer and Deputy Branch Manager 1972-73; CMB New York, Orion Bank, Liaison Officer, Policy Support and Marketing 1973-75; Chase Manhattan Limited, London, Executive Director 1975-76; Chase London, Division Mgr & Assistant General Mgr, Credit and Marketing, UK Corp Banking 1976-81; Chase Merchant Banking Unit, New York, Division Mgr, In Charge Latin America & Certain Corporate Ind Grps In The USA 1981-82; Chase Investment Bank Limited, London, Managing Director 1982-. *Biog: b.* 22 October 1939. *Nationality:* German. *m.* Britta; 2 s; 2 d. *Educ:* University of Heidelberg and Frankfurt (DR in Law). *Clubs:* City of London Club. *Recreations:* Tennis.

VON HALLE, Timothy W L; Director, Merrill Lynch International Limited.

VON SIMSON, Piers; Director, S G Warburg Group plc, since 1979; International Mergers & Acquisitions. *Career:* S G Warburg & Co Ltd 1973-; Director 1979; S G Warburg Group plc, Director 1989. *Biog: b.* 23 September 1946. *Nationality:* British. *m.* 1977, Lindsay (née Corner); 1 s; 2 d. *Educ:* Lancing College, Sussex; New College, Oxford (BA Hons Jurisprudence); University of California, Berkeley (LLM). *Directorships:* S G Warburg USA Inc (exec); S G Warburg France SA (exec); S G Warburg Espana SA (exec); Ladbroke Square Montessori School Ltd (exec) Chm. *Professional Organisations:* Barrister-at-Law (Middle Temple). *Clubs:* Turf. *Recreations:* Music, Gardening, Winter Sports.

VON UNGERN STERNBERG, Alexander; Managing Director, Deutsche Bank Capital Markets Ltd, since 1989; Syndicate, Swaps, UK Corporate Finance. *Career:* Price Waterhouse, UK and Germany 1971-79; Security Pacific International Leasing Inc, Germany and UK, Senior Vice President 1979-84; Deutsche Bank AG, Senior Vice President Head of International Leasing 1985-87; Head of Global Swaps 1987-90. *Biog: b.* 21 October 1950. *Nationality:* German. *m.* 1971, Lindy (née Skilbeck); 2 s; 2 d. *Educ:* St Paul's School, London; St John's College, Oxford (MA Oxon). *Professional Organisations:* Institute of Chartered Accountants in England and Wales. *Clubs:* Übersee Club (Hamburg).

VON WALLWITZ, Dr B; Graf von Wallwitz; General Manager, Bayerische Vereinsbank.

VONK, E; Non-Executive Director, C S Investments Limited.

VORPERIAN, Dikran; Director, Moutafian Commodities Ltd, since 1987; Management, Administration, Trading, Documentation. *Career:* Artistic Stationers Ltd (Addis Ababa), Company Secretary 1968-79; Artistic Printers Ltd (Addis Ababa), Company Secretary 1968-79. *Biog: b.* 20 August 1940. *Nationality:* British. *m.* 1960, Shenorig (née Khatchadourian); 1 s; 2 d. *Educ:* Melkonian Educational Institute, Cyprus (Diploma in Commerce); State Conservatoire of Yerevan Named After Komitas, Armenia, USSR (Masters Degree in Music). *Directorships:* Gagarin Mercantile Ltd (London) 1984 Company Secretary. *Other Activities:* Honourary Secretary, Armenian General Benevolent Union London Branch; Conductor, Ararat Choir, London. *Clubs:* AGBU, Tekeyan Cultural Association. *Recreations:* Music (Opera, Violin, Choir), Tennis.

VORYS, A I; Non-Executive Director, Willis Corroon plc.

VOULTERS, Marc; Partner, Neville Russell, since 1988; Head of General Practice Division. *Career:* Berke Fine, Partner 1983-88; KMG Thomson McLintock 1977-83. *Biog: b.* 14 February 1956. *Nationality:* British. *m.* 1981, Lynn Rochelle (née Pollack); 2 s. *Educ:* Dulwich College; Hull University (BSc Econ). *Directorships:* Aston Chase Limited 1985 (non-exec). *Professional Organisations:* ACA. *Recreations:* Keeping Fit, Tennis, Skiing, Food & Drink.

W

WACKER, Thomas J; Chairman, Royal Trust International Limited, since 1990; Chairman of all Royal Trust International companies with Responsibility for Important International Client Relationships/Marketing Assistance to International Units. *Career:* CitiBank NA, Junior Positions up to Vice President covering all aspects including Corporate Financing/Multinational Clients/ Petroleum, Chemical and Mining Industries 1969-82; Crocker National Bank, Senior Vice-President, Corporate Finance 1982-83; Bank of Montreal, Senior Vice-President, Corporate Finance 1983-87. *Biog: b.* 11 August 1943. *Nationality:* American. *m.* 1964, Penny (née Hunter); 2 s; 2 d. *Educ:* Indiana University (AB History and Geography MBA Intl Business & Finance). *Directorships:* Royal Trust Bank, UK 1987 (non-exec); Royal Trust Merchant Bank, Singapore 1987 (non-exec); Royal Trust International Ltd UK 1987 (exec); RTC Holdings Company, UK 1987 (non-exec); Royal Trust Bank (Jersey) Ltd UK 1987 (non-exec); Royal Trust Asia Limited, Hong Kong 1987 (non-exec); The Royal Trust Company of Canada (CI) Ltd 1987 (non-exec); Royal Trust Bank (Switzerland) 1987 (non-exec); Royal Trust Bank (Austria) AG 1988 (non-exec); Property Investments Ltd 1987 (non-exec); Maple Oak plc 1989 (non-exec). *Clubs:* London Irish Rugby Football Club, Wentworth, Royal Automobile Club, Royal Hong Kong Golf Club, Hong Kong Club; *Clubs:* Royal Hong Kong Yacht Club, Cannons Sports Club. *Recreations:* Reading, Golf, Fishing, Hunting, Rugby.

WADA, Kenji; Senior Managing Director (European Headquarters), The Nikko Securities Co (Europe) Ltd, since 1990; Responsible for Co-ordinating Nikko's European Activities. *Career:* The Nikko Securities Co Ltd (Tokyo), Analyst in Research Dept 1960-74; Nikko Securities (Beirut Office), Gen Mgr 1974-75; The Nikko Securities Co Ltd (Tokyo), Mgr/Intl Investment & Research Dept 1975-80; The Nikko Securities Co (Europe) Ltd, Dep MD 1980-82; The Nikko Securities Co Intl Inc (New York), Exec Vice Pres 1982-86; The Nikko Securities Co Ltd (Tokyo), Gen Mgr/Intl Investment & Research Dept 1986-88; Snr Gen Mgr, Asia & Oceania Headquarters 1988-90; The Nikko Securities Co (Europe) Ltd, Snr MD (European Headquarters) 1990. *Biog: b.* 8 January 1938. *Nationality:* Japanese. *m.* 1963, Tsuneko (née Arai); 3 d. *Educ:* Tokyo University (Bachelor of Economics). *Professional Organisations:* General Registered Representative (Japan); Registered Representative (USA); Registered Principal (USA); Member, The Securities Association. *Recreations:* Golf, Reading.

WADDELL, Alan Alexander Wallace; Director, Speirs & Jeffrey, since 1962; General. *Career:* Lazard Brothers, Clerk/Analyst 1959-61. *Biog: b.* 17 February 1933. *Nationality:* British. *m.* 1959, Marjorie Ann (née Hay Smith); 2 s; 2 d. *Educ:* Fettes; Cambridge University (BA); Harvard (MBA). *Directorships:* Ferguson & Menzies 1967 (non-exec). *Clubs:* Glasgow Golf Club, Honourable Company of Edinburgh Golfers. *Recreations:* Golf, Squash, Swimming.

WADDELL, Robert Steele; Chairman, Speirs & Jeffrey Ltd, since 1978. *Career:* Speirs & Jeffrey 1960-. *Biog: b.* 3 August 1931. *Nationality:* British. *m.* 1960, Eileen (née Sturrock); 4 d. *Educ:* Fettes College; Pembroke College, Cambridge (BA). *Directorships:* SSK Ltd 1984 (non-exec) Chm; John Hamilton 1985 (non-exec) Chm. *Professional Organisations:* CA. *Recreations:* Golf.

WADDINGTON, J P; Partner, Touche Ross & Co.

WADDINGTON, Robert; Director, Hambros Bank Ltd, since 1984; Corporate Finance. *Career:* Hambros Bank Ltd 1971-. *Biog: b.* 20 January 1942. *Nationality:* British. *m.* 1976, Jennifer Ann (née Jenkinson); 2 s. *Educ:* Uppingham School. *Professional Organisations:* FCA. *Recreations:* Shooting, Sailing, Gardening.

WADE, I D; Private Client Director, Albert E Sharp & Co.

WADE, Michael John; Chairman, Holman Wade Ltd and Holman Wade Insurance Brokers Ltd, since 1980 & 1989; Financial Insurances for Members of Lloyds. *Career:* C E Heath (Underwriting) Box Staff 1975-76; Hartley Cooper & Co Reinsurance Broker 1976-80. *Biog: b.* 22 May 1954. *Nationality:* British. *Educ:* Royal Russell School; North Staffordshire College. *Directorships:* Holman Wade Group 1984 (exec); Horace Clarkson plc 1986 (exec). *Other Activities:* Member, Council of Lloyd's (1987-1991); Trustee, Lloyd's Music Foundation. *Professional Organisations:* CII; Underwriting Member of Lloyd's; Member, Baltic Exchange. *Clubs:* Turf. *Recreations:* Music, Politics, Flying, Shooting.

WADE-GERY, Sir Robert; KCMG, KCVO; Executive Director, Barclays de Zoete Wedd Ltd, since 1987; International Development & Governmental Relations. *Career:* HM Diplomatic Service 1951-87; High Commissioner (UK Ambassador) in India 1982-87; Deputy Secretary of the Cabinet, London 1979-82; HM Minister in Moscow 1977-79; HM Minister in Madrid 1973-77; Central Policy Review Staff, Cabinet Office, Under Secretary 1970-73; Head of Financial Policy Dept, FCO 1970; Seconded to Bank of England 1969; Service in London (Foreign Office), Bonn, Nicosia, Tel Aviv & Saigon 1951-68. *Biog: b.* 22 April 1929. *Nationality:* British. *m.* 1962, Sarah (née Marris); 1 s; 1 d. *Educ:* Winchester College; New College, Oxford (BA,MA). *Directorships:* Barclays Bank (Spain) SAE 1989 (exec). *Other Activities:* Chairman, Governing Body, London School of Oriental & African Studies; Fellow, All Souls College, Oxford; Trustee, Help the Aged; Chairman, Finance Committee, International Institute for Strategic Studies. *Professional Organisations:* Royal Institute of International Affairs. *Clubs:* Athenaeum. *Recreations:* Walking, Sailing, Travel, History.

WADIA, G R J; Director, J Henry Schroder Wagg & Co Limited.

WADIA, Jim; Head of London Tax Practice, Arthur Andersen & Co, since 1982; Responsible for London Tax Practice, Specialization International Tax. *Career:* Chalmers Impey & Co Articled Clerk-Tax Mgr 1970-77. *Biog: b.* 12 April 1948. *Nationality:* British. *m.* 1972, Joelle (née Garnier); 1 s; 1 d. *Educ:* Le Rosey Rolle, Vaud, Switzerland; Inner Temple (Barrister). *Professional Organisations:* FCA; Barrister. *Recreations:* Tennis, Theatre.

WADSWORTH, Arthur John; Company Secretary & Executive Director, Samuel Montagu & Co Ltd, since 1987. *Career:* Midland Bank plc, Various Branches/Head Office Depts in London 1958-67; Various Appointments in Leicester, Nottingham & London 1967-82; Assistant General Manager 1982-86; Samuel Montagu & Co Ltd, Executive Director & Company Secretary 1987-. *Biog: b.* 13 June 1939. *Nationality:* British. *m.* 1966, Sheila (née Blythe); 1 s; 2 d. *Educ:* King's College School, Wimbledon. *Directorships:* Sundry Companies within Midland Bank plc; Epsom Sports Club Ltd 1988 (non-exec); London International Financial Futures Exchange Ltd 1982-85. *Professional Organisations:* Associate, Chartered Institute of Bankers; Member, British Institute of Management. *Clubs:* Epsom Hockey Club. *Recreations:* Hockey, Gardening.

WADSWORTH, David Jeffrey; Partner, Kidsons.

WADSWORTH, Michael; Partner, Insurance & Reinsurance & Insurance Litigation, Cameron Markby Hewitt.

WADWELL, David Martin; Director, Barclays de Zoete Wedd (Securities) Ltd, since 1986; Corporate Finance. *Career:* De Zoete & Bevan, Ptnr 1973-86. *Biog: b.* 12 March 1946. *Educ:* Ipswich School; Southampton University (BSc); LSE (MSc). *Professional Organisations:* FCA. *Recreations:* Sailing.

WAGENMANN, Dr Bernard A; Director, IBJ International Limited, since 1990; Fund Management and Asset Allocation. *Career:* Senior Research Associate at Latin American Institute at University of St Gall, Switzerland 1972-75; JP Morgan Investment Management Inc Vice President (Responsible for Multi-Currency Fixed Income Accounts and Strategist) 1978-90. *Biog: b.* 29 May 1946. *Nationality:* German. *Educ:* University of Lausanne; University of St Gall (Switzerland) (lic oec MBA equivalent); University of St Gall (Dr oec PhD economics). *Directorships:* Minerva Capital Corporation 1990 (non-exec). *Publications:* Latinamerika (co-author JM Baumer), 1977; Developing Countries and the International Exchange of Goods, Capital and Ideas, 1980 (in German). *Clubs:* RAC. *Recreations:* Game Shooting, Riding, Tennis.

WAGHORN, B P; Director, Leslie & Godwin Limited.

WAGNER-KNUDSEN, Jorgen; Managing Director, Morgan Guaranty Trust Company of New York.

WAILEN, Margaret J L; Partner, Cameron Markby Hewitt.

WAINMAN, Simon; Executive Director, Walter Judd Limited.

WAINWRIGHT, Sam; CBE; *Career:* Glasgow Herald, Financial Journalist and Dep City Editor 1950-55; Grieveson Grant & Co Head of Research 1955-58; W Greenwell & Co Head of Research 1958-60; Rea Brothers Ltd MD 1960-77; National Girobank MD 1977-85; The Post Office Board Member 1977-85; Dep Chm 1981-85; Stothert & Pitt plc Dir 1970-77; Chm 1975-77; Furness Withy & Co Ltd Non-exec Dir 1971-77; Aeronautical & General Instruments Ltd, Non-exec Dir 1968-77. *Biog: b.* 2 October 1924. *Nationality:* British. *m.* 1952, Ruth (née Strom); 3 s; 1 d. *Educ:* Regent Street Polytechnic; LSE (BSc Econ, Banking MSc Econ, Banking). *Directorships:* Monopolies & Mergers Commission 1985 Member; BICC plc 1985-90 (non-exec); Amdahl (UK) Ltd 1985 (non-exec); Manders (Holdings) plc 1972-87 (non-exec); 1985-86 Dep Chm; 1986-87 Chm; Various Investment Trusts 1963-77 (non-exec); Postel Investment Management 1981-85 (non-exec); Aeronautical & General Instruments Ltd 1968-77 (non-exec). *Other Activities:* Member, Post Office Audit Committee, 1985-; Trustee, Post Office Pension Fund, 1981-85; Chairman, BICC Audit Committee, 1985-90; Chairman, BICC Pension Fund, 1985-90. *Professional Organisations:* Hon FSIA (Council Member, 1961-75); Founder and First Editor, The Investment Analyst (1961-74). *Publications:* Articles in various Bank Reviews. *Clubs:* Reform. *Recreations:* Reading, Bridge.

WAITE, Ian A; Deputy Chairman, Alexander Howden Limited.

WAITES, Christopher; Managing Partner, Bacon & Woodrow, since 1987. *Career:* Bacon & Woodrow, Actuarial Student 1966-68; Unilever plc, Various Pensions/Actuarial 1968-76; Financial Group 1976-78; UAC International, Various latterly Dir Consumer Products Div 1978-84; Commercial Member Chemical Co-ordination 1984-85; Commercial Director PPF International 1985-87. *Biog: b.* 30 October 1944. *Nationality:* British. *Educ:* Brentwood School; Emmanuel College, Cambridge (MA). *Professional Organisations:* FIA.

WAKABAYASHI, Kazuhiko; Deputy General Manager, The Bank of Tokyo Limited.

WAKABAYASHI, Tokuji; Managing Director, Taiheiyo Europe Ltd.

WAKE-WALKER, David Christopher; Director, Kleinwort Benson Limited, since 1981; Corporate Banking. *Career:* Kleinwort Benson Ltd Various to Dir 1969-83; Kleinwort Benson (Hong Kong) Ltd MD 1983-86. *Biog: b.* 11 March 1947. *Nationality:* British. *m.* 1979, Jennifer Rosemary (née Vaulkhard); 2 s. *Educ:* Winchester College; St Andrew's University (MA). *Directorships:* Kleinwort Benson Group plc 1990 (exec); Town & Country Building Society 1990 (non-exec); Kleinwort Benson (Guernsey) Ltd 1979 (non-exec); Kleinwort Benson (Jersey) Ltd 1979 (non-exec); Kleinwort Benson (Hong Kong) Ltd 1983 (non-exec); British Financial Union Ltd 1988 (non-exec); BFU Contractors Ltd (non-exec). *Professional Organisations:* ACIB. *Clubs:* Wanderers, Hurlingham, Shek O Country Club, Hong Kong Club, Aldeburgh Yacht. *Recreations:* Music.

WAKEFIELD, Gerald Hugo Cropper; Director, C T Bowring & Co Limited, since 1983; Insurance Broking. *Career:* Joseph W Hobbs & Co, Clerk 1961-63; Anderson Finch-Villiers (Insurance) Ltd 1963-67; C T Bowring & Co 1968-. *Biog: b.* 15 September 1938. *Nationality:* British. *m.* 1971, Victoria Rose (née Feilden); 1 s. *Educ:* Eton College; Trinity College, Cambridge (MA). *Directorships:* CT Bowring Reinsurance Ltd 1988 Chm; Guy Carpenter & Co Inc (USA) 1990 Dep Chm. *Clubs:* White's. *Recreations:* Shooting, Fishing, Skiing.

WAKEFIELD, Sir Norman; Non-Executive Director, Lloyds Abbey Life plc.

WAKEFIELD, Peter; Director, G T Management plc.

WAKEFIELD, R; Partner, Nabarro Nathanson.

WAKEFIELD, G H C, ; Chairman, C T Bowring Reinsurance Ltd, since 1988. *Career:* Joseph & Hobbs

Ltd, Clerk 1961-63; Anderson Finchvilliers (Insurance) Ltd, Broker 1963-67; C T Bowring & Co Ltd, Various 1968-. *Biog: b.* 15 September 1938. *Nationality:* British. *m.* 1971, Victoria; 1 s. *Educ:* Eton College; Trinity College, Cambridge (MA). *Directorships:* C T Bowring & Co Ltd 1983 (exec); C T Bowring & Co Reinsurance Ltd 1988 Chm; Guy Carpenter & Co Inc Dep Chm. *Clubs:* Whites. *Recreations:* Shooting, Fishing, Skiing.

WAKEFORD, C; Partner, Nabarro Nathanson.

WAKEFORD, G M M; Clerk, Mercers' Company.

WAKEHAM, John; Lecturer, South West London College; Business Studies. *Career:* Councillor LB Camden 1982-; Board Member Greater London Enterprise 1986-; Chair ALA Planning & Transport Committee 1986-89. *Biog: b.* 4 January 1942. *Nationality:* British. *Educ:* Bristol University (BA). *Directorships:* None Outside GLE Group.

WAKELEY, Martin J; Managing Director, Jardine Insurance Brokers Ltd.

WAKELEY, Timothy Grey; Managing Director, Investments, Greenwell Montagu Stockbrokers; Fund Management and Asset Allocation for Private Investors; Trust and Charities. *Career:* W Greenwell & Co Training 1961-64; Portfolio Mgr 1964-71; Ptnr 1972-85. *Biog: b.* 13 December 1943. *Nationality:* British. *m.* 1967, Anne (née Bush); 2 s; 2 d. *Educ:* Carshalton College. *Directorships:* Greenwell Montagu & Co 1986; Smith Keen Cutler 1987 (non-exec); Greenwell Montagu Financial Services 1987. *Professional Organisations:* Society of Investment Analysts. *Clubs:* City of London. *Recreations:* Tennis, Skiing, Vintage Cars.

WAKELIN, A C; Chief Executive, Allied Arab Bank.

WAKELING, Richard Keith Arthur; Chief Executive, Johnson Matthey plc, since 1991. *Career:* The BOC Group, Group Treasurer 1973-83; John Brown plc, Finance Director 1983-86; Charter Consolidated plc, Acting Chief Executive 1986-89; Johnson Matthey plc, Deputy Chief Executive 1990-. *Biog: b.* 19 November 1946. *Nationality:* British. *m.* Carmen; 3 s. *Educ:* Churchill College, Cambridge (MA Cantab). *Directorships:* Johnson Matthey plc 1990 (exec); Charter Consolidated plc 1990 (non-exec). *Professional Organisations:* Barrister at Law; FCT. *Recreations:* Mediaeval History & Architecture, Soccer, American Football, Golf, Music, Gardening.

WALDEN, Herbert Richard Charles; CBE; Building Societies Commissioner, Building Societies Commission, since 1986. *Career:* War Service Royal Warwickshire Regt & Royal Leicestershire Regt (UK & Gold Coast), Captain 1944-47; Warwick Building Society, Various -1955; Assistant Secretary 1955-1957; Joint

Secretary 1957-62; Director & General Manager 1962-67; Rugby & Warwick Building Society, Director & Joint General Manager 1967-72; Director & General Manager 1972-74; Heart of England Building Society; Director & Joint General Manager 1974-76; Director & General Manager 1976-86. *Biog: b.* 6 October 1926. *Nationality:* British. *m.* 1940, Margaret (née Walker); 2 d. *Educ:* Westgate School, Warwick. *Directorships:* Midland Association of Building Societies 1969-71 Hon Sec; 1971 Dep Chm; 1972-73 Chm; Building Societies Association 1974-86 Mem of Council; 1981-83 Dep Chm; 1983-85 Chm; Chartered Building Societies Institute 1977-82 Mem of Council; 1988 Vice-Pres; Housing Corporation 1986-89 Board Member. *Other Activities:* Member, Warwick Borough Council, 1955-63; Member, South Warwickshire Hospital Management Committee, 1963-74 (Chairman 1964-72); Governor, Warwick Schools Foundation (Warwick School, King's High School for Girls and Warwick Preparatory School), 1962-90 (Chairman, 1986-90); Trustee and Former Chairman, Thomas Okens Charity, Warwick; Trustee and Former Chairman, King Henry VIII Charity, Warwick; Chairman, Austin Edwards Charity, Warwick; Vice President, Warwickshire Scout Council (Former Hon Treasurer); Founder President, Rotary Club of Warwick, 1965; Chairman of Finance Committee, Northgate Methodist Church, Warwick; Commissioner of Taxes. *Professional Organisations:* FCIS; FCBSI. *Clubs:* Naval & Military. *Recreations:* Watching Cricket & Soccer.

WALFORD, Christopher Rupert; Partner, Allen & Overy, since 1970. *Career:* Allen & Overy, Asst Solicitor 1962-70. *Biog: b.* 15 October 1935. *Nationality:* British. *m.* 1967, Anne Elizabeth (née Viggars); 2 s. *Educ:* Charterhouse; Oriel College, Oxford (MA). *Other Activities:* Alderman of the Ward of Farringdon Within, Worshipful Co of Makers of Playing Cards (Past Master); Institute of Directors (Policy & Exec Ctee); King Edward's School, Witley, Governor; Sheriff, The City of London (1990-91). *Professional Organisations:* The Law Society; The City of London Law Society. *Clubs:* MCC, City Livery, Farringdon Ward. *Recreations:* Music, Sport (Watching), Bridge.

WALFORD, Ms Janet; Editor, Money Management Magazine, since 1986; Pensions, Life Assurance, Personal Finance. *Career:* Life Insurance Companies 1971-78; Money Management Magazine Staff Writer 1978; Asst Editor 1979; Dep Editor 1982; Pensions Management Magazine Founding Editor 1985-86. *Nationality:* British. *m.* 1975, John Harrison. *Educ:* Wembley High School; Harrow College of Technology & Art. *Other Activities:* Insurance Journalist of the Year (1984 & 1987); Pensions Journalist of the Year (1985 & 1986). *Publications:* FT Personal Pensions Handbook, 1991. *Recreations:* Glider Pilot (Solo Licence).

WALFORD, M K; Partner, Wedlake Bell.

WALFORD, Dr Thomas Leonard Howard; Director, John Govett & Co Ltd, since 1988; Strategic Investment and Small Companies. *Career:* RHP Project Engineer 1977-81; Welwyn Electronics Ltd Gen Mgr 1981-84; Robert Fleming & Co Ltd Mgr, Unquoted Investments 1984-87. *Biog: b.* 18 May 1955. *Nationality:* British. *m.* 1986, Catherine (née O'Flaherty); 1 s. *Educ:* Cheltenham College; Bristol University (BSc; PhD). *Professional Organisations:* MIMechE; MIEE. *Recreations:* Sailing, Walking, Horology.

WALKDEN, Gerald Livesey; London Representative, Banco Economico, SA, since 1984; European Representation. *Career:* Midland Bank plc, Various 1941-83; (Latin America), Snr Exec/Regional Dir 1973-83. *Biog: b.* 18 April 1925. *Nationality:* British. *m.* 1950, Dorothy (née Stott); 1 s; 1 d. *Educ:* Manchester Grammar School. *Directorships:* Banque Europeenne Pour L'Amerique; Latine (Brussels) 1974-81 (non-exec). *Professional Organisations:* Chartered Inst of Bankers. *Clubs:* Overseas Bankers'. *Recreations:* Music, Natural History.

WALKER, A R; Director, CIN Properties.

WALKER, Alan James; Director, 3i plc, since 1990; Planning, Investor Relations & Special Projects. *Career:* Royal Military Academy, Sandhurst, Lecturer 1969-70; Burmah-Castrol Co, Operational Research Analyst 1970-71; National Westminster Bank, Manager 1971-82; 3i plc, Various Positions to Director 1982-. *Biog: b.* 16 January 1947. *Nationality:* British. *m.* 1976, Marsali; 2 s; 1 d. *Educ:* Trinity School, Croydon; Southampton University (BSc First Class Hons Mathematics, MSc Applied Mathematics). *Directorships:* Ship Mortgage Finance Company plc 1990 (non-exec). *Other Activities:* Chairman of Governors, Reigate St Mary's Preparatory School. *Professional Organisations:* ACIB; AIA. *Recreations:* Music, Golf, Walking, Squash.

WALKER, Andrew William; Partner, Simpson Curtis, since 1974; Stock Exchange Issues, Corporate Finance, Banking, Company Takeovers, Mergers International Law. *Career:* Linklaters & Paines Articled Clerk/Asst Solicitor 1966-72; Bury & Walkers Asst Solicitor 1972-74. *Biog: b.* 9 January 1944. *Nationality:* British. *m.* 1972, Jennifer Massey (née Harrison); 1 s; 1 d. *Educ:* Leeds Grammar School; Magdalene College, Cambridge (MA). *Other Activities:* Elmet Conservative Association. *Professional Organisations:* The Law Society, Leeds Law Soc, Licensing Execs' Soc, Solicitors' European Group, American Bar Assoc, IBA. *Clubs:* The Leeds. *Recreations:* Tennis, Golf, Riding, Skiing, Gardening, Theatre.

WALKER, Archibald George Orr; Deputy Chairman, Singer & Friedlander Ltd, since 1983; General. *Career:* Coldstream Guards 2nd Lt 1955-57; McClelland Moores (Glasgow) Apprentice 1957-62; John Beresford & Co (Development) Ltd 1962-67; Singer & Friedlander

Limited 1968-. *Biog: b.* 14 February 1937. *Nationality:* British. *m.* 1967, Fiona Mary Elizabeth (née Barr); 1 s; 1 d. *Educ:* Eton College. *Directorships:* Singer & Friedlander Group plc 1987 (exec); Clyde Petroleum plc 1973-88 (non-exec); Scottish National Trust plc 1984 (non-exec); John Beresford & Co (Development) Ltd 1965 Chm; Pionsheads Ltd 1968 Chm; Irvine Development Corp 1987. *Other Activities:* Member of the Queen's Bodyguard for Scotland, Royal Company of Archers. *Professional Organisations:* CA. *Clubs:* Royal and Ancient Golf Club, Western (Glasgow), Prestwick Golf Club, Hon Co of Edinburgh Golfers, Machrihanish Golf Club. *Recreations:* Golf, Shooting, Stalking, Skiing, Tennis.

WALKER, Barry Matthew; Partner, Ashurst Morris Crisp, since 1974; Company & Commercial Law. *Career:* Gouldens, Articled Clerk & Assistant Solicitor 1957-63; Paisner & Co, Asst Solicitor 1963-67; Ptnr 1967-74. *Biog: b.* 30 August 1939. *Nationality:* British. *m.* 1961, Hazel (née Jenkins); 2 s; 2 d. *Educ:* Cranleigh School. *Directorships:* Diploma plc 1982 (non-exec). *Other Activities:* Membership of Committees. *Professional Organisations:* The Law Society; The City of London Law Society, Company Law Sub-Committee.

WALKER, David; Managing Editor, Financial Times.

WALKER, Sir David Alan; Chairman, Securities & Investments Board, since 1988. *Career:* HM Treasury 1961-77; Private Sec to Joint Permanent Sec 1964-66; IMF Washington (Secondment) Staff 1970-73; HM Treasury Asst Sec 1973-77; Bank of England Chief Adviser/Chief of Economic Intelligence Dept 1977-80; Asst Dir 1980-; Executive Dir, Finance & Industry 1982-88. *Biog: b.* 31 December 1939. *Nationality:* British. *m.* 1963, Isobel (née Cooper); 1 s; 2 d. *Educ:* Chesterfield School; Queens' College, Cambridge (MA). *Directorships:* Bank of England 1988 (non-exec); Council of Lloyd's of London 1988 Nom Mem; National Power Company plc 1988 (non-exec); Securities and Investments Board 1988 Chm; Financial Markets Group, LSE 1987 Chm. *Other Activities:* Honorary Fellow, Queens' College Cambridge. *Professional Organisations:* FBIM. *Clubs:* Reform. *Recreations:* Mountain Walking, Running, Opera, Reading.

WALKER, David R; Chairman, Jardine (Lloyds Underwriting Agents) Ltd, Jardine Insurance Brokers Group.

WALKER, David Secker; Director, Causeway Capital Ltd.

WALKER, Derek James; Lloyd's Underwriter, Gooda Walker Ltd.

WALKER, Donald; Director, MIM Ltd.

WALKER, Graham Arthur James; Partner, Arthur Andersen & Co; Financial and General Business Consultancy Services. *Career:* British Steel Corporation Engineering Scholar 1967-71; Arthur Andersen & Co 1971-; The Prince's and Royal Jubilee Trusts Honorary Treasurer 1989-. *Biog: b.* 24 April 1949. *Nationality:* British. *m.* 1972, Susanna (née Coryndon); 2 s; 1 d. *Educ:* Westminster School; Trinity Hall, Cambridge (MA). *Professional Organisations:* ICA. *Clubs:* RAC. *Recreations:* Fell Walking, Cycling, Squash, Golf.

WALKER, Graham Roderick; Deputy Managing Director, Scimitar Asset Management Limited, since 1989; Management. *Career:* Thomson McLintock & Co, Audit Senior 1967-72; Queen Street Trust Limited, Director 1972-74; Wardley Limited, Director 1974-86; Thomson Mckinnon Securities Inc, Director 1986-89; Scimitar Asset Management Limited, Director 1989-. *Biog: b.* 14 January 1947. *Nationality:* British. *m.* 1989, Susan Jane Walker (née Field); 6 s. *Educ:* Merchant Taylors School, Northwood. *Directorships:* Scimitar Asset Management Limited 1989 (exec). *Other Activities:* Freeman of City of London; Freeman of Merchant Taylors Company. *Professional Organisations:* Institute of Chartered Accountants of Scotland. *Clubs:* Beaconsfield Golf Club, Royal Hong Kong Golf Club, Hong Kong Club. *Recreations:* Golf, Philately.

WALKER, J D; European Insurance Analyst, Baring Securities Limited, since 1990. *Career:* Greenwell Montagu Securities, European Insurance Analyst 1985-87; Kleinwort Benson Securities, European Insurance Analyst to 1990; Baring Securities, European Insurance Analyst 1990-. *Biog: b.* 13 July 1964. *Nationality:* British. *Educ:* University College School, London; Manchester University (BA Econ). *Other Activities:* Fellow, Royal Geographical Society. *Professional Organisations:* Member, International Stock Exchange. *Publications:* European Insurance Review, 1988. *Recreations:* Skiing, Swimming, Wind Surfing.

WALKER, Michael; Managing Director, Clive Discount Company Ltd, since 1990; Money Market Trading. *Career:* Westpac Banking Corporation 1965-71; Clive Discount Co Ltd 1972-. *Biog: b.* 1 November 1948. *Nationality:* British. *m.* 1970, Jacqueline Margaret (née Bowen); 1 s; 2 d. *Educ:* Thomas Lethaby School. *Directorships:* Clive Discount Holdings International Limited; Clivwell Securities Limited. *Professional Organisations:* Fellow, Chartered Institute of Bankers (Member, City of London Centre Ctee, VP & Past Chm of Financial Studies Group). *Recreations:* Various Sports, Photography.

WALKER, Michael; Director, Gresham Trust plc.

WALKER, Michael John; Partner, Maclay Murray & Spens, since 1981; Head of Corporate Department. *Career:* Dundas & Wilson, Articled Clerk 1974-76;

Maclay Murray & Spens Legal Asst, Company Dept 1976-79; Lovell White & King Legal Asst, Company Dept 1979-81. *Biog: b.* 23 October 1952. *m.* 1978, Elspeth Raeburn Lyle (née Reid); 1 s; 1 d. *Educ:* Trinity College, Glenalmond; Dundee University (LLB). *Other Activities:* Notary Public. *Professional Organisations:* The Law Society of Scotland; International Bar Association. *Clubs:* New (Edinburgh), Honourable Company of Edinburgh Golfers, Puffins', Royal Scottish Automobile, Prestwick Golf Club, The Addington Golf Club. *Recreations:* Golf, Travel, Reading.

WALKER, Nicholas Gordon; Secretary, IMRO (Investment Management Regulatory Organisation Limited), since 1990. *Career:* Public Prosecutions Dept, Director 1975-87; Lawyer, Fraud Investigation Group 1983-87; IMRO 1987-. *Biog: b.* 13 December 1949. *Nationality:* British. *m.* 1985, Jane (née Shaw); 1 s; 2 d. *Educ:* Harrow School. *Other Activities:* Council of Legal Education. *Professional Organisations:* Barrister, Member of Middle Temple. *Recreations:* Music, Reading, Walking.

WALKER, Nicola S; Partner, S J Berwin & Co.

WALKER, Patrick Nicholas Charles; Director, Morgan Grenfell Asset Management Ltd, since 1987; Investment Management. *Career:* Imperial Chemical Industries Ltd Commercial Asst 1975-77; Morgan Grenfell 1977-80; (New York) 1980-84; (London) 1984-87; (Tokyo) 1987-89; (London) 1989-. *Biog: b.* 13 December 1951. *m.* 1986, Sara Rose (née Hepburn). *Educ:* Winchester College; University of St Andrews (MA Hons). *Directorships:* Morgan Grenfell Investment Services Ltd 1986 (non-exec); Morgan Grenfell International Fund Management Ltd 1989. *Recreations:* Tennis, Squash, Music.

WALKER, Paul Christopher; Partner, Lawrence Graham, since 1986; Solicitor Specialising in Corporate Finance. *Career:* Home Office, Admin Trainee 1972-74; Allen & Overy, Articled Clerk/Asst Solicitor 1974-79; Hill Samuel & Co Ltd, Exec Mgr Corp Fin Dept 1979-84; J Henry Schroder Wagg & Co Ltd, Asst Dir Corp Fin Dept 1985-86. *Biog: b.* 27 August 1950. *Nationality:* British. *m.* 1979, Sandra (née Hunt); 2 d. *Educ:* Charterhouse; St John's College, Oxford (MA Hons). *Professional Organisations:* Law Society; City of London Solicitors' Company. *Publications:* The City Institutions - A Guide to their Financial Services, 1984.

WALKER, Paul L; Partner, Walker Morris Scott Turnbull.

WALKER, The Rt Hon Peter Edward; MBE, MP; Non-Executive Director, Smith New Court plc, since 1990; Strategic Planning. *Career:* Lloyds Brokers Rose Thomson Young & Company, Chm 1954-70; Walker Young & Company, International Brokers, Chm 1954-

70; Secretary of State for the Environment 1970-72; Secretary of State for Trade and Industry 1972-74; Wigham Poland & Company Limited, Dir 1974-79; Adwest Engineering Group, Dir 1974-79; Minister of Agriculture 1979-83; Secretary of State for Energy 1983-87; Secretary of State for Wales 1987-90. *Biog: b.* 25 March 1932. *Nationality:* British. *m.* 1969, Tessa Joan (née Pout); 3 s; 2 d. *Educ:* Latymer Upper School. *Directorships:* Smith New Court plc 1990 (non-exec); Worcester Group plc 1990 (non-exec); British Gas plc 1990 (non-exec); N M Rothschild & Sons (Wales) Ltd 1990 (non-exec); Dalgety plc 1990 (non-exec); Tate & Lyle plc 1990 (non-exec); DC Gardner Group plc 1990 (non-exec); Thornton & Company Limited 1990 (non-exec); CBC UK Limited 1990 (non-exec). *Publications:* The Ascent of Britain, 1976; Trust the People, 1987. *Clubs:* Buck's Club, Union & County (Worcester). *Recreations:* Tennis, Reading, Music.

WALKER, Ron L; Director, Jardine Insurance Brokers Ltd.

WALKER, Sandy; Director, 3i plc.

WALKER-ARNOTT, E I; Partner, Herbert Smith.

WALKER-HAWORTH, J L; Director, S G Warburg & Co Ltd.

WALKLEY, Geoffrey; Partner, Nabarro Nathanson, since 1988; Head of Intellectual Property Section. *Career:* Bartletts de Reya, Articled Clerk 1966-68; Assistant 1968-71; Ptnr 1971-88. *Biog: b.* 25 July 1944. *Nationality:* British. *m.* 1969, Barbara (née Dunstan); 1 s; 1 d. *Educ:* East Ham Grammar School for Boys; Kings, Durham (LLB). *Other Activities:* Secretary, Maylandsea Bay Yacht Club. *Professional Organisations:* The Law Society. *Clubs:* Maylandsea Bay Yacht Club. *Recreations:* Sailing, Skiing, Reading, Woodwork.

WALKLING, Anthony Kim; Partner, S J Berwin & Co, since 1988; Banking/Asset Finance. *Career:* Slaughter & May, Articled Clerk 1980-82; Farley & Williams, Assistant Solicitor 1982-87. *Biog: b.* 27 September 1957. *Nationality:* British. *m.* 1986, Margaret Caroline Deirdre (née Moore). *Educ:* Sutton High School, Plymouth; University of London (LLB Hons). *Professional Organisations:* Holborn Law Society; Europe Air Law Association; Law Society. *Recreations:* Music, Photography.

WALL, John Anthony; Partner, Litigation Department, Lawrence Graham, since 1977; General Litigation/All Litigation other than Insurance Work. *Career:* Middleton Lewis, Partner 1974-77; National Local Government Officers Assoc, Legal Officer 1956-74. *Biog: b.* 4 June 1930. *Nationality:* British. *m.* 1956, Joan Doreen; 4 s. *Educ:* Worcester College for the Blind; Baliol College, Oxford (BA Jurisprudence, MA). *Other Activities:* Chairman, Royal National Institute for the Blind. *Professional Organisations:* Solicitor. *Publications:* A Retailer's Guide to Trading Law, 1956; A Businessman's Guide to the Restrictive Trade Practices, 1956, 1957; Articles in Periodicals. *Clubs:* Reform Club. *Recreations:* Chess, Music, Swimming.

WALLACE, Graham M; Group Finance Director, Granada Group plc, since 1989. *Career:* Turner & Newall Ltd, Graduate Management Trainee 1969-71; Cost Accountant 1971-72; Brandhurst Co Ltd, Assistant Company Accountant 1972-73; Company Accountant 1973-74; Rank Xerox Ltd, Business Analyst 1974-76; Manager, Currency Planning & Control 1976-78; Controller, Balance Sheet Planning & Control 1978-80; Rank Xerox Corp USA (on assignment), Manufacturing Operations Analysis Manager 1980-82; Rank Xerox Ltd, Performance Assurance Manager 1982; Imperial Group Ltd, Senior Financial Planning Manager 1983-84; Finance Director, Imperial Inns & Taverns 1984-85; Finance Director, Imperial Leisure & Retailing 1985-86; Granada Group plc, Head of Finance & Planning 1986-87; Director of Corporate Finance 1988-89; Finance Director 1989-. *Biog: b.* 26 May 1948. *Nationality:* British. *m.* 1974, Denise (née Dyer); 1 s; 1 d. *Educ:* Slough Grammar School; Imperial College, London University (BSc Civil Engineering). *Professional Organisations:* Fellow, Chartered Institute of Management Accountants.

WALLACE, J B; Executive Director, Willis Corroon plc.

WALLACE, J R; General Manager, Information Technology, National Westminster Bank plc.

WALLACE, J W M; Non-Executive Director, Redland plc.

WALLACE, R J; Director, Janson Green Limited.

WALLACE, T J; Director, Leslie & Godwin Ltd.

WALLAS, Brian Stanley; Non-Executive Director, Greig Fester Group Ltd, since 1984; General. *Career:* Fester Fothergill & Hartung Partner 1954-74; Greig Fester Ltd Dep Chm 1974-84. *Biog: b.* 11 September 1924. *Nationality:* British. *m.* 1952, Shirley Carol (née Dunbar); 2 s; 2 d. *Educ:* Lancing College; Magdalen College, Oxford (MA). *Professional Organisations:* CII; ACII; FCIB. *Clubs:* Union Club, Seaford. *Recreations:* Golf, Bridge, Philately.

WALLER, Margaret M; Director, County NatWest Investment Management Ltd.

WALLER, Martin; City Reporter, The Times.

WALLER, Paul; Director, 3i plc, since 1987; Continental Europe. *Career:* Botswana Development Corpora-

tion, Investment Officer 1975-77; 3i London, Investment Controller 1978-82; 3i Brighton, Local Dir 1983-86; 3i London, Local Dir 1986-88; 3i, Regional Director 1988-90. *Biog: b.* 6 June 1954. *Nationality:* British. *m.* 1980, Jennifer Margaret (née Rout); 1 s; 1 d. *Educ:* Haberdashers' Aske's School; UMIST (BSc Hons). *Other Activities:* Past Fellow, The Overseas Development Institute. *Recreations:* Squash, Tennis, Skiing, Travel.

WALLEY, K H; Deputy Chairman, Johnson Matthey.

WALLINGER, John David Arnold; Director, SG Warburg Securities.

WALLIS, Andrew James; Partner, Jaques & Lewis, since 1974; Litigation, especially Banking, Insolvency & Related Commercial & Financial Aspects. *Career:* LB Southwark, Articles 1968-70; Suburban firms 1970-72; Jaques & Co (later Jacques & Lewis), Partner 1974-. *Biog: b.* 5 December 1945. *Nationality:* British. *Educ:* Emanuel School; King's College, London University (LLB). *Professional Organisations:* The Law Society. *Recreations:* Politics, Theatre, Art, History, Music, Sailing.

WALLIS, Clifford E; Director, SG Warburg Akroyd Rowe & Pitman.

WALLIS, Captain D A; RN; Clerk, Merchant Taylors' Company.

WALLIS, D R; Executive Director & Underwriter, Gresham Underwriting Agencies Limited.

WALLIS, J K; Direct Response Director, Next plc.

WALLIS, R H; Partner, Hill Taylor Dickinson.

WALLS, Alan Patrick Randal; Partner, Holman Fenwick & Willan, since 1985; Personal Injury Litigation. *Career:* Lee & Pembertons, Assistant Solicitor 1973-75; Holman Fenwick & Willan, Assistant Solicitor 1975-85. *Biog: b.* 24 January 1944. *Nationality:* British. *m.* 1977, Celia Elizabeth (née Moss); 2 s. *Educ:* Charterhouse School; Gonville & Caius College, Cambridge(MA). *Clubs:* Lloyds Club. *Recreations:* Music.

WALLS, (John) Russell (Fotheringham); Group Finance Director, Coats Viyella plc, since 1990. *Career:* Coats Patons, Management Trainee 1966-69; Donbros Ltd (Scotland), Accountant 1969-71; Coats Patons (Peru), Finance Director 1971-76; (Benelux) Finance Director 1976-78; (Italy) Finance Director 1978-82; (Brazil) Finance Director 1982-87; Coats Viyella plc, Executive Assistant 1987-89; Group Finance Director 1990-. *Biog: b.* 22 February 1944. *Nationality:* British. *m.* 1968, Sheila May (née Goodwin); 1 s; 1 d. *Educ:* Dollar Academy; University of Glasgow (BSc). *Professional Organisations:* ACCA; FCCA. *Recreations:* Classic Cars.

WALLS, William Alan; Partner, Linklaters & Paines, since 1987; Commercial Litigation, Insolvency, Employment. *Career:* Linklaters & Paines, Articled Clerk 1979-81; Articled Solicitor 1981-87. *Biog: b.* 18 September 1956. *Nationality:* British. *m.* 1977, Julie (née Brown); 1 s; 1 d. *Educ:* Trinity Hall, Cambridge (MA Law Cantab). *Other Activities:* City of London Solicitors Company; Association Européenne des Praticiens des Procédures Collectives; International Bar Association. *Professional Organisations:* Member, Law Society; Licensed Insolvency Practitioner. *Recreations:* Sailing, Walking, Theatre, Opera.

WALMISLEY, Mrs P; Clerk, The Company of Information Technologists.

WALMSLEY, J A; Managing Director, Finance & Business Development, Enterprise Oil plc, since 1988; Board Responsibility for all Aspects of the Group's Finance. *Career:* Spicer & Pegler, Chartered Accountant - 1973; Arthur Andersen, Chartered Accountant 1973-80; Partner, Tax Division 1980-84; Enterprise Oil plc, Finance Director 1984-88; MD, Finance & Business Development 1988-. *Biog: b.* 5 December 1946. *Nationality:* British. *m.* Louise (née Harrison); 1 s; 1 d. *Educ:* University of Leicester (BA Hons English). *Directorships:* AMI Healthcare Group plc 1988 (non-exec); Seeboard plc 1990 (non-exec). *Professional Organisations:* FCA.

WALSH, A S; CBE; Chairman, and Chief Executive, STC plc.

WALSH, Andrew Geoffrey; Partner, McKenna & Co, since 1986; Company & Commercial Law/Acquisitions & Mergers. *Career:* Payne Hicks Beach, Articled Clerk 1977-79; Norton Rose Botterell & Roche, Asst Solicitor 1979-83. *Biog: b.* 26 July 1954. *Nationality:* British. *m.* 1989, Emma (née Belmonte). *Educ:* Queen Elizabeth's Grammar School, Blackburn; Magdalen College, Oxford (MA); Trinity Hall, Cambridge (LLB). *Other Activities:* City of London Solicitors' Company. *Publications:* Companies Bill, 1989; Global M & A, Chapter on Legal Aspects, 1989. *Clubs:* Cannons. *Recreations:* Soccer, Squash, Cycling, Theatre, Visiting Historic Buildings.

WALSH, Andrew Selby Lister; Director, Panmure Gordon Bankers Ltd, since 1985; Banking and Development Capital. *Career:* Chemical Bank; Rowe Swann; Price Waterhouse. *Biog: b.* 15 June 1947. *Nationality:* British. *m.* 1973, Jennifer (née Bamford); 2 s. *Educ:* Wellington College. *Professional Organisations:* FCA. *Clubs:* RAC, RMYC, Roehampton.

WALSH, B; Managing Director (Investment Management), Bankers Trust Company.

WALSH, D; Assistant General Manager (Information Systems), C & G Guardian.

WALSH, Fiona; Assistant City Editor, Sunday Times Business News.

WALSH, Geoffrey Brian Whittington; Non-Executive Director, Duncan Lawrie Limited.

WALSH, Graham Robert; Managing Director, Bankers Trust Company, since 1988; Corporate Finance, Mergers & Acquisitions, Strategic Planning. *Career:* Hill Samuel & Co Ltd Dir, Corp Finance 1964-73; Morgan Grenfell Group plc Dir, Head of Corp Finance 1973-87; Panel on Takeovers & Mergers, Dir Gen 1979-81; Issuing Houses Association, Chm 1985-87. *Biog: b.* 30 July 1939. *Nationality:* British. *m.* 1968, Margaret Ann (née Alexander); 1 s; 1 d. *Educ:* Hurstpierpoint College, Sussex. *Directorships:* Moss Bros Group plc 1988 (non-exec); Haslemere Estates plc 1989 (non-exec). *Professional Organisations:* FCA. *Recreations:* Gardening, Walking, Theatre, Music.

WALSH, Ms Jane; Director, Merrill Lynch Pierce Fenner & Smith (Brokers & Dealers) Ltd; Futures/Commodity Sales & Trading.

WALSH, Jeremy H; Executive Director, First Interstate Capital Markets Limited, since 1989; Legal Services, Compliance. *Career:* Randall Rose & Co, Partner 1975-86; First Interstate Capital Markets Ltd 1986-. *Biog: b.* 4 March 1949. *Nationality:* British. *m.* 1974, Mary (née Hardwick); 3 s; 1 d. *Educ:* University College, London (LLB Hons). *Directorships:* First Interstate Capital Markets Limited 1989 (exec); First Interstate Securities Limited 1989 (exec). *Professional Organisations:* Solicitor, 1973.

WALSH, Jonathan; Partner & Head of Private Client Dept, Taylor Joynson Garrett, since 1989; Family Law & Divorce. *Career:* Holloway Blunt & Duke, Articles 1963-68; Bircham & Co, Assistant Solicitor 1968-70; Joynson-Hicks, Assistant Solicitor 1970; Partner 1973. *Biog: b.* 21 April 1944. *Nationality:* British. *m.* 1968, Angela (née Miers); 4 s. *Educ:* Eton College; Sorbonne. *Other Activities:* Liveryman, Worshipful Company of Tin Plate Workers. *Professional Organisations:* Law Society. *Clubs:* Boodles, Queens. *Recreations:* Sport, Gardening.

WALSH, Patrick Keiran; Company Secretary, Sphere Drake Underwriting Management Ltd, since 1982. *Career:* Haines Watts, Accountants, Berkshire, Trainee Company Secretary 1977; Sphere Drake Underwriting Management Ltd, Asst to Secretary 1978-81. *Biog: b.* 16 August 1953. *Nationality:* British. *Educ:* University of Leeds (LLB Hons); College of Law, Chester. *Professional Organisations:* Fellow, Institute of Chartered Secretaries and Administrators.

WALSH, Paul Anthony; Partner, Bristows Cooke & Carpmael, since 1988; Intellectual Property Litigation and Licensing. *Career:* Linklaters & Paines, Articles 1980-82; Bristows Cooke & Carpmael, Assistant Solicitor 1983-87; Partner 1988-. *Biog: b.* 21 December 1956. *Nationality:* British. *m.* 1988, Caroline. *Educ:* Salvatorian College, Harrow; Oxford University (BA Jurisprudence). *Professional Organisations:* Solicitor. *Publications:* The Licensing of Biotechnology, 1989. *Recreations:* Literature, Theatre, Film, Sport.

WALSOM, Roger Benham; Partner, Ashurst Morris Crisp, since 1988; Company, Commercial and Financial Law. *Career:* Slaughter and May, Articled Clerk 1978-80; Asst Solicitor 1980-83; Ashurst Morris Crisp, Asst Solicitor 1983-86; Associate 1986-88. *Biog: b.* 2 March 1953. *Nationality:* British. *m.* 1984, Susan Christina (née Pitcairn); 1 s. *Educ:* Brighton Hove & Sussex Grammar; Southampton University (LLB). *Professional Organisations:* Law Society. *Recreations:* Photography, Reading, Travel.

WALTER, Jeremy Canning; Partner, Simmons & Simmons, since 1976; Corporate Law, Financial Services and Insurance Law, Head of East European Group. *Career:* Ellis Peters Young Jackson, Articled Clerk 1971-73; Simmons & Simmons, Assistant Solicitor 1973-76. *Biog: b.* 22 August 1948. *Nationality:* British. *m.* 1973, Judith Jane (née Rowlands) (div); 2 d. *Educ:* Kings School, Canterbury; Sidney Sussex College, Cambridge (MA Double First Class Honours, LLB First Class Honours). *Other Activities:* Member of Council, British-Polish Legal Association; Member, British-Hungarian Legal Association. *Professional Organisations:* Law Society; International Bar Association (Business Law Section, Energy and Natural Resources Section); American Bar Association. *Publications:* Various Articles on Eastern Europe. *Clubs:* MCC. *Recreations:* Cricket, Golf, Reading, Theatre.

WALTERS, Geoffrey; Partner, Titmuss Sainer & Webb.

WALTERS, M E B; Director, Charlton Seal Schaverien Limited.

WALTERS, Michael; Deputy City Editor, Daily Mail.

WALTON, David; CStJ, JP; Chairman, Stirling Hendry & Co and Scottish Metropolitan Property plc, since 1987; Finance. *Educ:* (LLB Hons). *Professional Organisations:* Hon FRCPS (Glasgow).

WALTON, David A; Partner, Moores Rowland.

WALTON, Leonard Joseph; Deputy Chairman, Riggs AP Bank Ltd, since 1976. *Career:* Martins Bank, Dep Chief Gen Mgr 1963-69; Barclays Bank plc, Gen Mgr 1969-71; Barclays Merchant Bank, Dep Chm & Chief Exec 1969-76. *Biog: b.* 30 May 1911. *Nationality:* British. *m.* 1937, Vera Freda; 1 d. *Educ:* Wallasey

Grammar School. *Directorships:* Regalian Properties plc 1983-90 Chm; Institute of Bankers 1966-80 Hon Treasurer. *Professional Organisations:* FCIB. *Clubs:* Royal Liverpool Golf Club, Wyresdale Anglers. *Recreations:* Fishing, Golf.

WALTON, Miles Henry; Partner, Wilde Sapte, since 1984; Corporate Tax. *Career:* Slaughter and May, Asst Solicitor 1980-83. *Biog: b.* 15 July 1955. *Nationality:* British. *m.* 1985, Lorraine (née Nunn); 1 s. *Educ:* Ratcliffe College; Brasenose College, Oxford (MA). *Professional Organisations:* The Law Society; Institute of Taxation (ATII). *Publications:* Business Tax Anti-Avoidance (Chapter in ICAEW Taxation Service), 1987; Co-Author, Taxation & Banking, 1990. *Recreations:* Saxophone, Wine Tasting, Sailing, Scuba Diving.

WALTON, Paul A; Managing Director, Chemical Bank.

WALTON, Philip; Group Property Director, Midland Bank plc.

WALZAK, M; Assistant General Manager, Credit, The Toronto-Dominion Bank.

WAMBOLD, Ali Edward; Chief Executive Officer, Lazard Freres & Co Limited, since 1990; Mergers & Acquisitions Advisory, Investments. *Career:* Corporate Partners, Managing Director, Co-Head 1988-90; Lazard Frères & Co, General Partner, Mergers & Acquisitions Advice and Corporate Finance 1985-90; Lehman Brothers, Vice President, Mergers & Acquisitions Advice 1981-85. *Biog: b.* 10 April 1954. *Nationality:* American. *m.* 1981, Monica Gerard-Sharp; 2 d. *Educ:* Pembroke-Hill School; Harvard University (BA); Columbia University (MBA). *Directorships:* Corporate Partners 1988 (non-exec); The Albert Fisher Group plc 1990 (non-exec); Zapata Gulf Marine Corporation 1990 (non-exec); Lazard Frères & Co 1987 General Partner. *Professional Organisations:* Chartered Financial Analyst.

WANLESS, Derek; Chief Executive, National Westminster Bank plc, since 1990; UK Financial Services. *Career:* National Westminster Bank plc, Snr Project Mgr, Domestic Banking Div 1979-80; Marketing Mgr, Domestic Banking Div 1980-82; Attached to Domestic Banking Div 1982; Area Dir, North East England 1982-85; Area Dir, West Yorkshire 1985-86; Dir of Personal Banking Services 1986-88; General Manager, UK Branch Business 1989-90. *Biog: b.* 29 September 1947. *Nationality:* British. *m.* 1971, Vera (née West); 1 s; 4 d. *Educ:* Royal Grammar School, Newcastle; Kings College, Cambridge (MA). *Directorships:* National Westminster Home Loans Ltd 1986 (exec); National Westminster Personal Financial Management Ltd 1987 (exec); National Westminster Insurance Services Ltd 1989 (exec); NatWest Stockbrokers Ltd 1989 (exec); Joint Credit Card Co Ltd 1987-89 (non-exec);

MasterCard International Inc 1989 (non-exec); Eurocard International SA 1989 (non-exec) Vice Chm; MasterCard and Eurocard Members (UK and Republic of Ireland) 1989 (non-exec) Chm. *Professional Organisations:* ACIB; Member, Institute of Statisticians. *Recreations:* Watching All Sports, Gardening, Walking, Music.

WANSBROUGH, David; Director, Prelude Technology Investments Limited.

WARBURTON, M A; Partner, Waltons & Morse.

WARBURTON, M C; Partner, Slater Heelis.

WARD, Miss A; Secretary, LAS Unit Trust Managers.

WARD, A D; Director, C S Investments Limited.

WARD, B M; Director, Parrish Stockbrokers.

WARD, David J; Partner, Touche Ross & Co.

WARD, Graham Norman Charles; Director of Electricity Services, Price Waterhouse, since 1990. *Career:* Price Waterhouse, Student/Snr Manager 1974-86; Accounting Standards Committee (Secondment), Personal Assistant to Chairman 1978-79; HM Treasury (Secondment), Accounting Consultant 1985; Price Waterhouse, Partner 1986-. *Biog: b.* 9 May 1952. *Nationality:* British. *m.* 1975, Imogen (née Baden-Powell) (div 1981); 2 s. *Educ:* Dulwich College; Jesus College, Oxford (MA). *Other Activities:* Chairman, London Society of Chartered Accountants; Vice-President, Chartered Accountant Students' Society of London; President, Jesus College Association. *Professional Organisations:* Fellow, The Institute of Chartered Accountants in England and Wales. *Publications:* The Work of a Pension Scheme Actuary, 1987; Pensions: Your Way Through the Maze, 1988. *Clubs:* Carlton, Vincent's (Oxford), Oxford University Amateur Boxing Club (VP). *Recreations:* Boxing, Rugby, Jazz.

WARD, Lady Helen Madeleine (née Gilbert); Partner, Penningtons, since 1978; Family Law, Head of Family Law Department. *Career:* Ward Bowie Solicitors (now Penningtons), Qualified as Solicitor, Partner 1978. *Biog: b.* 28 May 1951. *Nationality:* British. *m.* 1983, Sir Alan Ward; 2 d twins. *Educ:* King Alfred's School, Hampstead; Birmingham University, (LLB Hons). *Other Activities:* Treasurer, Solicitors Family Law Association; Fellow, International Academy of Matrimonial Lawyers.

WARD, J M; Director, Crédit Lyonnais Rouse Limited.

WARD, M; Partner, Baillie Gifford & Co, since 1975; UK Equities. *Career:* Baillie Gifford & Co, Investment Trainee 1971-75. *Biog: b.* 22 August 1949. *Nationality:* British. *m.* 1982, Sarah (née Marsham); 2 s; 1 d. *Educ:* Harrow; St Catharine's, Cambridge (MA). *Directorships:*

Scottish Equitable Life Assurance Society 1988 (non-exec). *Clubs:* New Club. *Recreations:* Tennis, Squash, Bridge, County Pursuits.

WARD, M J; Partner, Bacon & Woodrow.

WARD, Maxwell Colin Bernard; Partner, Baillie Gifford & Co, since 1975; UK Equities. *Career:* Baillie Gifford & Co, Trainee 1971-75. *Biog: b.* 22 August 1949. *Nationality:* British. *m.* 1982, Sarah (née Marsham); 2 s; 1 d. *Educ:* Harrow; St Catharine's, Cambridge (MA). *Directorships:* Scottish Equitable Life Assurance Society 1988 (non-exec). *Clubs:* New Club. *Recreations:* Tennis, Squash, Bridge, Country Pastimes.

WARD, Peter Geoffrey; General Manager, Commercial Union Assurance, since 1988; General Management - Composite Insurance. *Career:* Commercial Union (Australia), Asst Actuary 1968-72; (South Africa), Actuary 1972-77; Dep Gen Mgr 1977-78; (UK) Planning Mgr 1978-81; Life Mgr 1981-83; Divisional Dir 1983-87; Dep Gen Mgr 1987-88. *Biog: b.* 5 May 1942. *Nationality:* British. *m.* 1961, D Annette (née Hedley); 2 s. *Educ:* Chesterfield Grammar School; King's College, London (BSc). *Directorships:* CU Life Assurance Co Ltd 1986 (exec); CU Risk Management Ltd 1985 (non-exec); Northern Assurance Co Ltd 1986 (exec); Midland Life Ltd 1988 (non-exec); CU Financial Services Ltd 1985 (exec); British & European Re Co Ltd 1988 (exec); Hiberian Group plc 1989 (non-exec); CU Unit Trust Managers Ltd 1987 (exec); Travellers Insurance Association 1988 (exec). *Other Activities:* Vice President, CII; Member, Worshipful Company of Insurers. *Professional Organisations:* FIA; FCII. *Recreations:* Golf, Gardening.

WARD, R G; Director, S G Warburg Group plc.

WARD, Robert Dennis; Finance Director, Laing & Cruickshank, since 1988; Accounting and Administration. *Career:* Binder Hamlyn (formerly Marsh Wood Drew), Audit Supervisor 1968-73; Henry Ansbacher Holdings plc, Group Financial Accountant 1973-85; Mercantile House Holdings plc, Group Financial Controller 1985-87. *Biog: b.* 25 October 1948. *Nationality:* British. *m.* 1979, Hilary Else (née Hutchinson); 1 d. *Educ:* St William of York; North Western Polytechnic; City of London College. *Professional Organisations:* FCA; Member, The International Stock Exchange. *Recreations:* Skiing, Tennis, Soccer.

WARD, Roger; Vice President, Chemical Bank.

WARD, Simon Charles Vivian; Director, Fleming Private Asset Management Ltd, since 1986; Discretionary Private Client Fund Management. *Career:* Govett Sons & Co, Trainee Stockbroker 1963-65; Hedderwick Hunt & Co, Ptnr's Asst 1965-67; Hedderwick Borthwick & Co, Ptnr's Asst 1967-70; Montagu Loebl Stanley & Co 1970-86; Ptnr 1972-86. *Biog: b.* 23 March

1942. *Nationality:* British. *m.* 1965, Jillian (née East); 3 d. *Educ:* Shrewsbury School; Trinity College, Cambridge (MA Hons). *Professional Organisations:* Member, The International Stock Exchange; Member, The Securities Association. *Recreations:* Skiing, Tennis, Gardening, Opera, Ballet.

WARD, Simon Roderick; Partner, Slaughter and May.

WARD, Steven; Managing Director (Investment Management), Morgan Stanley International.

WARD, Ms Victoria Ann; Director Product Development, LIFFE, since 1990; Developing New Derivative Products and Maintaining and Reviewing Existing Products. *Career:* Fiamass Ltd, Graduate Trainee/Research Analyst in Financial Futures & Options 1981-82; Messel Futures Limited (Subsequently Part of Shearsan), Trainee Broker to Director of Futures Company 1982-85; Michael Page City, Recruitment Consultant 1985-87; LIFFE, Index Products Specialist/Director UK Business Development/Director Product Development 1987-. *Biog: b.* 25 November 1959. *Nationality:* British. *m.* 1990, Neil J D Nokes; 1 d. *Educ:* Nottinghill & Ealing High School for Girls; Selwyn College, Cambridge (Hons Modern Languages 2i). *Directorships:* Nokes & Co 1990 Company Secretary. *Recreations:* Tennis, Gardening, Nokes & Daughter, 20th Century Art.

WARD, W P; Director, Yorkshire Building Society.

WARDLE, John Wilkinson; Director, Wise Speke Ltd.

WARDLE, Philip John; Financial Editor UK & Ireland, Reuters Ltd, since 1988; UK Financial, Economic, Commodity NES. *Career:* Reuters 1967; Economic Editor, France 1969-72; Economic Editor, Asia, in Hong Kong 1972-76; Economic News Editor in London 1976-80; Asian Editor in Hong Kong 1980-82; Commodities Editor, US & Canada, in Chicago 1982-85; Commodities Editor, Europe 1985-88; Financial Editor, UK 1988-. *Biog: b.* 30 September 1944. *Nationality:* British. *Educ:* Manchester Grammar School; St Cuthbert's Society, University of Durham (BA Hons). *Professional Organisations:* NUJ. *Clubs:* Hong Kong Foreign Correspondents Club.

WARE, T; Secretary, Cookson Group.

WAREHAM, O A; Partner, Slaughter and May, since 1990. *Career:* Slaughter and May, Articled Clerk 1981-83; Assistant Solicitor 1983-90. *Biog: b.* 3 April 1958. *Nationality:* British/Swiss. *m.* 1986, Joanna (née Rowley); 1 s. *Educ:* Westminster School; Magdalen College, Oxford (BA Hons,PPE). *Professional Organisations:* The Law Society.

WARING, R B C; Master, The Worshipful Company of Furniture Makers.

WARMAN, G W B; Director, Charterhouse Tilney.

WARMINGTON, Anthony Marshall; Director, Burson-Marsteller, since 1989; Head of Investor Relations. *Career:* Queen's Dragoon Guards, Lieutenant 1965-68; Stockjobber Kitcat and Aitken, Investment Manager 1968-70; Bisgood Bishop & Co, Stockjobber 1970-75; Ionian Bank Ltd, Investment Manager 1975-77; Streets Financial Ltd, Financial PR 1977-88; Director 1981; Manning Selvage & Leg, Head of Financial PR 1988-89; Burson-Marsteller, Head of Investor Relations 1989. *Biog: b.* 1 July 1946. *Nationality:* British; 1 s; 1 d. *Educ:* Charterhouse; Grenoble University. *Directorships:* Burson-Marsteller 1989 (exec); Burson-Marsteller Financial 1989 (exec); Streets Financial 1981-87 (exec). *Other Activities:* Member, Mensa; Member, Investor Relations Society. *Clubs:* MCC, Cavalry and Guards. *Recreations:* Golf, Tennis, Theatre.

WARNER, Michael Leslie; Managing Director, Hartley Cooper & Warner Ltd, since 1981; Lloyd's Guaranteeing Broker. *Career:* Wigham-Poland (Motor) Ltd Dir 1979-81; Wigham-Poland (Agency Services) Ltd Dir 1980-81. *Biog: b.* 22 April 1947. *m.* 1983, Jane (née Twomey). *Educ:* Southchurch High School, Southend-on-Sea. *Directorships:* Gibbs Hartey Cooper Ltd 1986 (exec). *Other Activities:* Motor Executive Ctee, Lloyd's Insurance Brokers. *Professional Organisations:* Registered Insurance Broker. *Recreations:* Walking.

WARNER, P L; Director, P & O Steam Navigation Company.

WARNER-ALLEN, C; Associate Director, Beeson Gregory Limited.

WARNFORD-DAVIS, Miss Karelyn Mandy; Partner, Rowe & Maw, since 1985; General Company Law and Corporate Finance. *Career:* Titmuss Sainer & Webb, Solicitor 1979-82; Rowe & Maw, Solicitor 1982-. *Biog: b.* 19 June 1954. *Nationality:* British. *Educ:* Heathfield School, Ascot; St Hugh's College, Oxford (BA Hons). *Professional Organisations:* The Law Society.

WARREN, A B; Director, Knight & Day Ltd.

WARREN, B J; Chairman & Chief Executive, Crawley Warren Group plc.

WARREN, George John; General Manager, Ottoman Bank.

WARREN, Jack; Associate Director, Candover Investments plc, since 1990; Management Buyouts. *Career:* Coopers & Lybrand Deloitte, Student Accountant, Audit Senior 1974-77; Continental Illinois Limited, Management Accountant 1978; Allied Irish Investment Bank Limited, Lending Officer 1979-80; 3i plc (Formerly ICFC Limited), Local Director/Assistant Manager/ Investment Controller/Director 1980-89; Candover Investments plc, Associate Director & Senior Investment Manager 1990-. *Biog: b.* 6 September 1951. *Nationality:* British. *m.* 1984, Geraldine Margaret (née Lloyd). *Educ:* Watford Boys Grammar School; Corpus Christi College, Cambridge (MA Hons). *Directorships:* 3i plc 1988-89 (exec). *Professional Organisations:* FCA. *Clubs:* MCC. *Recreations:* Sport, Theatre, Opera, Travel.

WARREN, M E; Chief Executive & Director, Dalgety plc.

WARREN, Michael; Chairman, International City Holdings.

WARREN, Peter; Non-Executive Director, Ogilvy Adams & Rinehart.

WARWICK, Leonard; Director, Securities and Investments Board.

WASDELL, Donald Charles; Director, Smith Keen Cutler Ltd, since 1985; Financial Adviser. *Career:* Smith Keen Barnett/Smith Keen Cutler Ptnr 1962-85. *Biog: b.* 15 August 1934. *Nationality:* British. *m.* 1968, Susan Margaret (née Joseph); 2 s. *Educ:* Bromsgrove School. *Directorships:* Samuel Royston Developments Ltd 1986 (non-exec); Wasdell Packaging Ltd 1976 (non-exec); Birmingham Stock Exchange Buildings Ltd 1981 (non-exec). *Other Activities:* Midlands & Western Stock Exchange Unit (Ctee Member); General Commissioner of Income Tax; British Merchant Banking and Securities Houses Association, Securities Sub-Committee. *Professional Organisations:* FCA; Mem, Sub-Ctee, British Merchant Banking & Securities Houses Assoc. *Clubs:* Oriental, Phyllis Court. *Recreations:* Gardening, Reading.

WASHIZAWA, Shigeru; Executive Director, Yamaichi International (Europe) Ltd.

WASILEWSKI, M; Director, CIN Marketable Securities.

WASS, Sir Douglas; GCB; Co-Chairman, Nomura International Ltd.

WATANABE, Hiroshi; Managing Director, Bank of Tokyo International Limited.

WATANABE, Yoshihiro; Deputy General Manager, The Bank of Tokyo Ltd.

WATERER, Robin Alistair; Partner, Macfarlanes, since 1988; General Corporate Law and Employee Share Schemes. *Career:* Macfarlanes, Articled Clerk/Asst Solicitor 1980-. *Biog: b.* 7 August 1956. *Nationality:* British. *m.* 1981, Florence (née Dherse); 2 s; 1 d. *Educ:* Radley College; Sidney Sussex College, Cambridge (MA). *Clubs:* Hawks.

WATERHOUSE, Dame Rachel; DBE, CBE; Chairman, Centre for Consumer Research, since 1989. *Career:* Health and Safety Commission, Member 1990-; Office of the Banking Ombudsman, Council Member 1986-; National Economic Development Council, Member 1981-. *Biog: b.* 2 January 1923. *Nationality:* British. *m.* 1947, John A H; 2 s; 2 d. *Educ:* King Edward VI High School for Girls, Birmingham; St Hugh's College, Oxford (MA); University of Birmingham (PhD); Loughborough (Hon Ditt); Birmingham (Hon D Soc Sci). *Directorships:* Association for Consumer Research 1967 (non-exec) Chairman 1982-90; Securities and Investment Board 1985 (non-exec). *Clubs:* Royal Commonwealth Institute.

WATERLOW, Lady (née Skyrme); JP; Director, the Securities Association, since 1988.

WATERMAN, Howard John; Partner, Departmental Manager, Banking Department, Cameron Markby Hewitt, since 1984; Banking Law (International Banking & Trade Finance). *Career:* Admitted as a Solicitor 1977. *Biog: b.* 23 May 1953. *Nationality:* British. *m.* 1981, Sharon; 1 d. *Educ:* Southampton University 1971-74 (LLB Hons). *Professional Organisations:* Member, City of London Solicitors' Company; The Law Society. *Recreations:* Chess, Bridge, Sports.

WATERS, Brian Wallace; Director, European Affairs.

WATERS, G R; Partner, Wedlake Bell.

WATERS, William F; Non-Executive Director, Merrill Lynch International Bank Limited.

WATES, Sir Christopher; Chairman, Wates Building Group Limited.

WATKIN, Geoffrey; London Joint General Manager, Banco Bilbao Vizcaya.

WATKINS, D J; Member of the Council, The International Stock Exchange.

WATKINS, David J; Deputy Chief Executive, Industrial Development Board, since 1989; Corporate Services Group. *Career:* European Commission, Competition Directorate 1978-79; Dept of Economic Development (NI), Responsible for Government Sponsorship of Short Bros plc and Harland & Wolff plc 1979-88; IDB 1989-. *Biog: b.* 3 August 1948. *Nationality:* British. *m.* 1974, Valerie; 1 s; 1 d. *Educ:* Royal Belfast Academical

Institution; Trinity College, Dublin (BA Hons Modern Languages).

WATKINS, G; Partner, Nabarro Nathanson.

WATKINS, James Arthur; Partner, Linklaters & Paines, since 1975; Senior Partner of the Hong Kong Office. *Career:* Linklaters & Paines, Articled Clerk 1967-69; Solicitor 1969-75. *Biog: b.* 26 September 1945. *Nationality:* British. *m.* 1967, Ursula Barbara (née Richards) (div 1984); 2 d. *Educ:* Archbishop Holgate's School, York; Leeds University (LLB). *Directorships:* Bankers Trustee Company Limited 1984 (non-exec). *Other Activities:* Member, City of London Solicitors' Company. *Professional Organisations:* Member, Law Society. *Clubs:* Hurlingham, Annabel's, Hanbury Manor, Shek-O (Hong Kong), Hong Kong Club. *Recreations:* Tennis, Golf, Reading, Theatre, Music.

WATKINS, Mark Christopher; Chairman, MFK Underwriting Agencies Ltd, since 1989; Underwriter, Syndicate 457. *Career:* Sphere Drake Insurance, Deputy Underwriter 1970-77; MFK Underwriting Agencies Ltd, Deputy Underwriter Syndicate 457 1977-89; Director 1983-; Underwriter Syndicate 904 1983-90; Underwriter Syndicate 457 1989-; Chairman 1989-. *Biog: b.* 28 May 1951. *Nationality:* British. *m.* 1972, Elizabeth Georgina Mary (née Abbott); 2 s; 1 d. *Educ:* St Edward's School, Oxford. *Directorships:* Watkins Newson McCord Holdings Ltd 1989 (exec); WNM Dream Software Ltd 1989 (exec); MFK Underwriting Agencies Ltd 1983 (exec). *Professional Organisations:* Fellow, Chartered Insurance Institute. *Recreations:* Skiing, Travel, Reading, Films, Eating.

WATKINS, Nigel G; Partner (London), Evershed Wells & Hind.

WATKINS, Richard Valentine; Chief Executive, Schroder Securities Limited; UK, South East Asia, Japan, Korea, European Securities Sales and Trading. *Career:* Phillips & Drew Inc 1972-77; Kleinwort Benson Mgr & Overseas Rep 1977-83; Phillips & Drew Inc (New York) MD 1983-86; Hoare Govett Inc (New York) Pres 1986-88; Burns Fry Hoare Govett Inc (New York) Chm 1988. *Biog: b.* 23 September 1950. *Nationality:* British. *m.* 1976, Charlotte (née de Laszlo); 2 s; 1 d. *Educ:* Wellington; Loughborough University (BSc). *Directorships:* J Henry Schroder Wagg & Co Ltd 1988 (exec); Schroder Securities (Hong Kong) Ltd 1988 (exec); Schroder Securities (Japan) Ltd 1988 (exec). *Clubs:* Turf, Racquet Club (New York). *Recreations:* Skiing.

WATKINS, William George; Partner, Lovell White Durrant, since 1970. *Career:* Slaughter and May, Asst Solicitor 1960-69. *Biog: b.* 29 August 1933. *Nationality:* British. *m.* 1965, Anne (née Roper); 3 s; 1 d. *Educ:* King's School, Canterbury; University College, Oxford (MA). *Other Activities:* The City of London Solicitors'

Company. *Professional Organisations:* The Law Society. *Recreations:* Walking, Industrial Archaeology.

WATSHAM, Robert; Director, Marlar International Limited.

WATSON, A; Director, Charlton Seal Schaverien Limited.

WATSON, B; Managing Director, McCann-Erickson Advertising Ltd.

WATSON, B P; Director, Providence Capitol Life Assurance Ltd.

WATSON, D E; Director, LMX, Denis M Clayton & Co Limited.

WATSON, Garry Sanderson; Director, Hill Samuel Bank Ltd, since 1976; Development Capital. *Career:* Hill Samuel Bank Ltd 1965-. *Biog: b.* 31 July 1940. *Nationality:* British. *m.* 1967, Elizabeth Ann; 4 d. *Educ:* Glasgow Academy (CA). *Other Activities:* Honorary Treasurer, National Assoc of Citizens Advice Bureaux. *Professional Organisations:* Institute of Chartered Accountants of Scotland. *Recreations:* Skiing, Swimming, Walking, Theatre.

WATSON, Graham Forgie; Director, Noble Gossart Ltd, since 1987; Corporate Finance. *Career:* KPMG Peat Marwick McLintock, Trainee 1979-82; KPMG Peat Marwick McLintock International Career Development Programme, Audit Senior 1982-83; Noble Gossart Ltd, Executive 1984-86; Assistant Director 1986-87; Director 1987-. *Biog: b.* 14 January 1958. *Nationality:* British. *m.* 1983, Elspeth Margaret (née Brewster); 1 d. *Educ:* George Heriot's School, Edinburgh; University of Edinburgh (LLB). *Directorships:* Noble Gossart Ltd 1987 (exec); Waverley Cameron plc 1988 (non-exec); Balmoral International Ltd 1989 (non-exec); Barnfather Associates Ltd 1989 (non-exec); The Pan Drop Co Ltd 1989 (non-exec); Creos International Ltd 1989 (non-exec); John Fleming & Company (Holdings) plc 1989 (non-exec); Edinburgh Crystal Ltd 1990 (non-exec). *Professional Organisations:* The Institute of Chartered Accountants of Scotland (CA). *Clubs:* New Club, Edinburgh; *Clubs:* The Bruntsfield Links Golfing Society, Edinburgh; *Clubs:* The Golf House Club, Elie. *Recreations:* Golf, Curling, Skiing, Squash.

WATSON, I P; Director, Macey Williams Ltd.

WATSON, Ian Roland; Tax Partner, Touche Ross, since 1986; Banking and Securities Industry. *Career:* Thos Bowden & Glenton, Student 1958-63; Spicer & Pegler, Audit Supervisor 1963-65; Coopers and Lybrand, Tax Mgr 1965-73; Thornton Baker, Snr Tax Mgr 1973-74; Price Waterhouse, Snr Tax Mgr 1974-77; Bankers Trust Company VP, Eur Tax Adviser 1977-86;

Spicer & Oppenheim (now Touche Ross) 1986-. *Biog: b.* 21 August 1941. *Nationality:* British. *m.* 1968, Sheila Margaret (née Roebuck); 2 d. *Educ:* Blaydon Grammar School. *Other Activities:* American Banks Association Tax Committee, 1984-86; Committee of Invisible Exports (Bank of England), 1984-86; British Bankers Association (Member of Fiscal Ctee). *Professional Organisations:* FCA; ATII. *Publications:* Taxation and Accounting for Financial Instruments, 1987. *Recreations:* Showjumping/ Eventing, Reading, Music, Art.

WATSON, J G; Partner, Ashurst Morris Crisp, since 1989; Tax. *Career:* Qualified as Barrister 1975-84; Solicitor 1984; Neville Russell, Chartered Accountants 1978-83; Ashurst Morris, Solicitors 1983-. *Biog: b.* 23 April 1951. *Nationality:* British. *m.* 1988, Janis June (née Higgie); 1 d. *Educ:* Christs College, Cambridge (MA Maths Tripos). *Professional Organisations:* Solicitor. *Clubs:* Naval & Military. *Recreations:* Fishing.

WATSON, John Tinto; Director, Robert Fleming & Co Limited, since 1989; Corporate Finance. *Career:* Arthur Young 1973-76; Coopers & Lybrand (Tehran) 1977-79; Coopers & Lybrand (London) 1979-86; Department of Industry Secondment 1981-82; Robert Fleming & Co Limited 1986-. *Biog: b.* 19 October 1951. *Nationality:* British. *m.* 1978, Tricia (née Nolde); 1 s; 1 d. *Educ:* Winchester College; City of London Polytechnic (BA Hons). *Professional Organisations:* FCA.

WATSON, M; Executive Director, Daiwa Europe Limited.

WATSON, Michael John Bannatyne; Director, Hambros Bank Limited, since 1989; Corporate Finance. *Career:* Linklaters & Paines, Articles 1979-81; Assistant Solicitor 1981-85; Hambros Bank Limited, Corp Fin Dept, Senior Executive 1985-86; Manager 1986-87; Assistant Director 1987-89; Director 1989-. *Biog: b.* 9 May 1956. *Nationality:* British. *m.* 1985, Susan Elizabeth Ann (née Grundy); 1 s; 1 d. *Educ:* Eton College; Trinity College, Cambridge (BA). *Directorships:* Hambros Bank Limited 1989 (exec). *Professional Organisations:* Solicitor. *Recreations:* Shooting, Golf, Tennis.

WATSON, P; Senior Underwriter, Allstate Reinsurance Co Limited.

WATSON, P M; Partner, Allen & Overy.

WATSON, R M C; Director, Barclays de Zoete Wedd Limited.

WATSON, Richard Timothy; Director, Foreign and Colonial Management Ltd; Managing Dir of Foreign & Colonial Pensions Management Ltd. *Career:* Kemp-Gee & Co, Partner's Assistant 1969-73; SG Warburg & Co, Pension Fund Manager 1974-80; Tyndall & Co, Investment Manager 1980-82; Universities Superannuation

Scheme, Investment Manager, UK Equities 1982-88. *Biog: b.* 7 November 1947. *Nationality:* British. *m.* 1970, Jennifer Ann (née Maclean); 2 s; 1 d. *Educ:* St Joseph's Academy, SE3. *Directorships:* Foreign & Colonial Pensions Management Ltd 1988 (exec). *Professional Organisations:* ACIB. *Recreations:* Tennis, Reading.

WATSON, Ronald Henry; Non-Executive Director, Barclays Development Capital Ltd, since 1979. *Career:* Barclays Bank Ltd, Local Director; Barclays Merchant Bank Ltd, Deputy Managing Director. *Biog: b.* 23 September 1924. *Nationality:* British. *m.* 1948, Joan Renee; 1 s; 2 d. *Educ:* Ilford County High School. *Directorships:* CI de Rougemont Holdings Ltd (non-exec); NFC plc (non-exec); Amalgamated Manufacturing Ltd (non-exec); Robert Leonard Holdings Ltd (non-exec); IG Investments Ltd (non-exec); European Investments & Development (UK) Ltd plc (non-exec); Ron Watson Consultancies Ltd Chairman; Mercury Communications Ltd -1984. *Professional Organisations:* ACIB. *Clubs:* Romford Golf Club.

WATSON, Ross; Director, Gartmore Scotland Ltd.

WATSON, Sean Michael; Partner, McKenna & Co, since 1979; Corporate Finance and Banking Law. *Career:* Slaughter and May Solicitor 1970-78. *Biog: b.* 5 April 1948. *m.* 1973, Sarah Margaret (née Coombes); 3 d. *Educ:* St Mary's, Melrose, Scotland; Manchester University (LLB Hons). *Professional Organisations:* The Law Society; Solicitor of Supreme Court (Hong Kong). *Clubs:* St George's Hill Lawn Tennis Club, The Hong Kong Club. *Recreations:* Tennis, Skiing, Gardening.

WATT, Iain Alasdair; Director, Edinburgh Fund Managers.

WATT, J F; Production Director, Enterprise Oil.

WATT, J P; Partner, Dundas & Wilson CS.

WATT, Michael John; Director, Touche Remnant Investment Management Limited, since 1988; Investment Management (Far East). *Career:* Scottish Widows Fund, Investment Mgr 1969-73; Gilbert Eliott & Co, Investment Analyst 1973-76; Panmure Gordon & Co, Investment Analyst 1976-79; Touche Remnant & Co, Investment Mgr 1979-. *Biog: b.* 2 February 1947. *Nationality:* British. *m.* 1969, Irene (née Fyfe); 2 s. *Educ:* Quarry Bank High School, Liverpool; St Andrews University (MA Hons). *Directorships:* TR Pacific Basin Investment Trust (in Liquidation) 1987 (exec); TR Pacific Investment Trust 1987 (exec). *Professional Organisations:* Society of Investment Analysts. *Recreations:* Skiing, Japanese Art and Literature.

WATTERS, B D; General Manager, Treasury, Nomura Bank International plc.

WATTERS, James Andrew Donaldson; Partner, Stephenson Harwood, since 1985; Company Commercial Work. *Career:* Stephenson Harwood, Articled Clerk/Solicitor 1970-75; Norton Rose, Solicitor 1976-79; Investors in Industry plc, Snr Legal Adviser 1980-81; Goodwille & Co, Ptnr 1982-85. *Biog: b.* 16 March 1948. *m.* 1972, Lesley Jane Aves (née Churchman); 2 s; 1 d. *Educ:* King's College School, Wimbledon; Pembroke College, Oxford (BA). *Other Activities:* City of London Solicitors' Company. *Professional Organisations:* The Law Society. *Recreations:* Cooking, Eating.

WATTS, David Walter; Managing Director, Gartmore Pension Fund Managers Ltd.

WATTS, F R; Executive Director, Sheppards.

WATTS, Gareth Lougher; Director, John Govett & Co Ltd, since 1988; Senior Fund Manager, North American Equities. *Career:* Legal & General Assurance Soc Ltd, Actuarial Trainee/Fund Manager 1978-83; Morgan Grenfell (Asset Management) Ltd, Fund Manager 1983-86; Scrimgeour Vickers (Asset Management), Fund Manager 1986-88. *Biog: b.* 16 February 1956. *Nationality:* British. *m.* 1982, Diane; 2 s.

WATTS, Graham J; Head of Operations, Continental Bank NA.

WATTS, Kevan Vincent; Managing Director, Investment Banking, Merrill Lynch International Ltd, since 1987; Corporate Finance in UK, France and Italy. *Career:* HM Treasury 1974-81; Merrill Lynch (New York) Associate 1981-83; Merrill Lynch (London) Vice-Pres 1983; Associate Dir 1984; Exec Dir 1985. *Biog: b.* 27 December 1950. *m.* 1972, Prudence Mary Lloyd (née Vine); 1 s; 2 d. *Educ:* Kent College, Canterbury; University College, Oxford (BPhil, MA Hons). *Other Activities:* Member, London Regional Council of Confederation of British Industry; Member, Corporate Finance Committee of British Merchant Banking and Securities Houses Association. *Professional Organisations:* Certified Diploma of Accounting and Finance. *Recreations:* Music, Gardening, Tennis, Golf and Family Life.

WATTS, Ms Lesley Mary Samuel; Director, Kleinwort Benson Ltd, since 1986; Corporate Finance. *Career:* Slaughter and May Solicitor 1976-79; Shearman & Sterling (New York) Attorney 1979-80; Kleinwort Benson Ltd 1980-. *Biog: b.* 19 September 1953. *Nationality:* British. *m.* divorced. *Educ:* Cheltenham Ladies' College; Churchill College, Cambridge (MA Hons). *Professional Organisations:* Solicitor, The Supreme Court. *Recreations:* Fly Fishing, Contemporary Art, Piano, Peace and Quiet.

WATTS, Michael John Colin; Director, Brown, Shipley & Co Limited.

WATTS, Nicholas Michael; Chief Investment Officer, John Govett & Co Limited, since 1988; Head of Overall Investment Management Activity. *Career:* Alexanders Discount Co Grad Trainee/Dealer 1974-75; Teacher of Business English (London & Madrid) 1975-76; W Greenwell & Co Inv Analyst (Electronics) 1977-79; N M Rothschild & Sons Ltd Asst Dir/Snr Pension Fund Mgr 1979-86; Citicorp Investment Management Co Head, Intl Equity Mgmnt Unit 1986-88. *Biog: b.* 10 October 1952. *Nationality:* British. *m.* 1981, Rolande. *Educ:* Ampleforth College, York; Oxford Polytechnic (BSc Hons). *Directorships:* John Govett & Co Ltd 1988 (exec). *Clubs:* MCC. *Recreations:* Golf, Racing, Cricket.

WATTS, R; Chairman, Lowndes Lambert Group Holdings Limited.

WATTS, Timothy Eatough; Partner, Richards Butler, since 1986; Company Law, Corporate Finance. *Career:* Cameron Kemm Nordon, Articled Clerk 1976-78; Richards Butler, Asst Solicitor 1978-86. *Biog: b.* 21 February 1953. *Educ:* Rugby School. *Professional Organisations:* The Law Society; Institute of Directors. *Publications:* Chapter in Tolley's Company Law, 1990; Chapter in A Practitioner's Guide to Corporate Finance & the Financial Services Act 1986, 1990. *Clubs:* Travellers', MCC, Sandy Lodge Golf Club.

WAUCHOPE, Michael Owen Charles; Director, Panmure Gordon & Co Ltd, since 1987; Private Client Management, both Advisory and Discretionary, Unit Trust Management for In-House Trust. *Career:* Grieveson Grant & Co, Private Client Exec 1960-63; Panmure Gordon & Co, Private Client Exec 1964-75; Ptnr 1975-. *Biog: b.* 8 November 1937. *Nationality:* British. *m.* 1972, Susan Margaret (née Hodgson). *Educ:* Winchester College. *Directorships:* Panmure Gordon Bankers Ltd 1987 (exec). *Other Activities:* Ctee Member, Turf Club. *Professional Organisations:* Member, The International Stock Exchange. *Clubs:* MCC, Turf, New Zealand Golf Club, Royal Dornoch Golf Club. *Recreations:* Golf, Snooker, Poetry, Shooting, Fishing, Racing.

WAUGH, A; Director, A P Leslie Underwriting Agencies Limited.

WAUGH, Ian L; Branch Partner, Broadbridge.

WAY, Bertie; Director, Lowe Bell Financial Ltd.

WAY, Patrick Edward; Corporate Tax Partner, Gouldens, since 1987; Corporate Tax. *Career:* Lawrence Graham, Articled Clerk and Assistant Solicitor 1977-82; Nabarro Nathanson, Assistant Solicitor and Tax Partner 1982-87; Gouldens, Corporate Tax Partner 1987. *Biog: b.* 6 February 1954. *Nationality:* British. *m.* 1978, Judith (née Williams); 3 s. *Educ:* Solihull School; Leeds University (BA). *Directorships:* Banner Residential Properties plc 1989 (non-exec); Housebuilding Portfolio I plc 1990 (non-exec); Housebuilding Portfolio II plc 1990 (non-exec); The BES Association 1990 (non-exec). *Other Activities:* Tax Committee of the BES Association. *Professional Organisations:* Law Society. *Publications:* Death and Taxes, 1986; Maximising Opportunities Under The BES, 1987; BES and Assured Tenancies: The New Rules, 1989; Share Sales and Earnouts, 1991; Contributor to Tolley's Tax Planning, 1991. *Recreations:* Gardening, Tennis.

WAY, Robert Michael; Director-Banking (& Compliance Officer), Duncan Lawrie Limited.

WEATHERILL, B N A; Senior Partner, Wedlake Bell.

WEBB, Anthony Clifford; Managing Director, Chartered Trust PLC.

WEBB, John Howard; Director, Group Actuary, Commercial Union Assurance Co plc.

WEBB, Nigel Kenneth Lamboll; Group Managing Director, Byas Mosley & Co Ltd, since 1984; Corporate Development. *Career:* Byas Mosley & Co Ltd 1978-. *Biog: b.* 13 November 1954. *Nationality:* British. *m.* 1976, Tessa; 2 s; 1 d. *Educ:* Harrow. *Directorships:* Byas Mosley Group Ltd 1989 (exec); Byas Mosley & Co Ltd (Lloyd's Broker) 1981 (exec). *Professional Organisations:* Insurance Brokers Regristration Council (IBRC). *Clubs:* City of London Club, HAC, St Moritz Toboganning Club. *Recreations:* Shooting, Fishing.

WEBB, P J R; Company Secretary, James Capel & Co Ltd, since 1987. *Career:* Ernst & Young, Articled Clerk 1965-69; Peat Marwick McLintock, Manager 1969-81; Touche Remnant & Co, Company Secretary 1981-85; James Capel & Co Ltd, Company Secretary 1986-. *Biog: b.* 31 March 1944. *Nationality:* British. *m.* 1969, Joanna (née Burton); 2 s; 1 d. *Educ:* St Edward's School; Trinity Hall, Cambridge. *Directorships:* James Capel Unit Trust Management Ltd 1989 (exec). *Other Activities:* Chairman, Brailey School Governors; Treasurer, Betchworth Conservative Association. *Professional Organisations:* Chartered Accountant (FCA). *Recreations:* Golf, Music, Tennis.

WEBB, R A; UK Director, M W Marshall & Company Limited.

WEBB, Richard Murton Lumley; Chairman, Morgan Grenfell & Co Ltd, since 1989; Corporate Finance/Banking/Credit Control. *Career:* Brown Fleming & Murray/Whinney Murray & Co, Articled Clerk/Qualified Acct/Asst Mgr 1961-67. *Biog: b.* 7 March 1939. *m.* 1966, Juliet (née Devenish); 1 s; 1 d. *Educ:* Winchester College; New College, Oxford (BA). *Directorships:* Morgan Grenfell Group plc 1988. *Other Activities:* NEDO; Member, Committee on Industry &

Finance. *Professional Organisations:* CA. *Clubs:* Hurlingham.

WEBB, S W; Director, Baring Securities, since 1989; Eurobonds (Equity Related). *Career:* Grieveson Grant & Co 1972-84. *Biog: b.* 7 June 1955. *Nationality:* British. *m.* 1977, Lorraine; 2 s. *Recreations:* Golf, Racquet Sports.

WEBB, Stuart Campbell; Managing Director, Lazard Brothers & Co Ltd, since 1985; Chief Executive, Lazard Investors. *Career:* Robert Fleming & Co Ltd, Dir 1971-77; Saudi International Bank, Mgr 1977-82; Chase Manhattan Bank, Dir 1982-85. *Biog: b.* 16 May 1940. *Nationality:* British. *m.* 1964, Jacqueline (née Lindsley); 1 s; 1 d. *Educ:* Michael House, South Africa; Cornell University (BSc); Cornell Graduate Business School (MBA). *Directorships:* Raeburn Investment Trust plc 1988; Romney Trust plc 1988. *Professional Organisations:* Institute of Chartered Financial Analysts; New York Society of Security Analysts. *Recreations:* Mountaineering, Cycling, Music.

WEBB, Vernon; Clerk, The Worshipful Company of Insurers.

WEBB, W F; Deputy General Manager (Non-Life), Co-operative Society Ltd.

WEBBER, M; Director, IBJ International Limited.

WEBBER, Nigel John; Director, Pine Street Investments Limited, since 1987; Investment in Unquoted Companies in the Financial Services Sector. *Career:* Peat Marwick Mitchell & Co 1974-79; Citibank NA, Vice Pres Mergers Acquisitions & Corp Fin 1979-84; Mercantile House Holdings plc, Group Dev Mgr 1984-87. *Biog: b.* 18 February 1953. *Nationality:* British. *m.* 1980, Heather (née McCallum); 1 s; 1 d. *Educ:* King's School, Canterbury; University of Manchester Institute of Science (BSc Hons). *Directorships:* Genesis Investment Management Ltd; Pine Street Corporate Finance Ltd; The Seventy Three Group Limited; Crosby Holdings Limited. *Professional Organisations:* ACA. *Clubs:* Roehampton. *Recreations:* Skiing, Golf, Cornwall.

WEBER, C A L; Partner, Wedlake Bell.

WEBER, David Henry; Partner, Linklaters & Paines, since 1984; Project Finance, Particularly in Energy and Infrastructure and Related Areas. *Career:* Linklaters & Paines, Articles 1976-78; Assistant Solicitor 1978; On Secondment to Fulbright & Jaworski, Houston, Texas 1980-81. *Biog: b.* 11 August 1953. *Educ:* Haberdashers' Aske's School, Elstree, Hertfordshire; Clare College, Cambridge (MA Cantab). *Other Activities:* City of London Solicitors' Company. *Professional Organisations:* Law Society; International Bar Association; UK Oil Lawyers Group. *Recreations:* Music, Theatre, Travel.

WEBER, Menahem; General Manager, United Mizrahi Bank.

WEBSTER, D E; Partner, Waltons & Morse.

WEBSTER, Dean Leslie; Partner, Cyril Sweett and Partners.

WEBSTER, Francis Michael; Director, Barclays de Zoete Wedd Limited, since 1988; Corporate Finance.

WEBSTER, Frank John; Chief Investment Manager, Refuge Assurance plc, since 1988. *Career:* L Messel and Co Gilt Analyst 1968-71; Grieveson Grant & Co Gilt Analyst 1971-72; Refuge Assurance Various Positions in Investment Area 1972-88. *Biog: b.* 17 January 1947. *Nationality:* British. *m.* 1971, Juliet (née Guthrie); 2 d. *Educ:* Manchester Grammar School; St Edmund Hall, Oxford (BA Hons). *Directorships:* Refuge Unit Trust Managers Ltd 1986; Refuge Assurance plc 1988. *Professional Organisations:* FCIS; FCII; AMSIA.

WEBSTER, John Dudley; Managing Director, Sun Life Asset Management Ltd, since 1989. *Career:* Sun Life Assurance Society plc 1961-; Investment Mgr & Asst Exec 1974-76; Investment Mgr & Exec 1976-78; Asst Gen Mgr (Investment) & Dir 1978-80; Gen Mgr (Investment) 1980-84; Gen Mgr (Investment) & Sec 1984-89; Sun Life Asset Management Ltd, Managing Director 1989-. *Biog: b.* 13 November 1939. *Nationality:* British. *m.* 1967, Barbara Joan (née Cheese); 1 d. *Educ:* Merchant Taylors' School; University College, London (BSc). *Directorships:* Subsidiary Companies of Sun Life; The Securities Assoc 1986; Save & Prosper Return of Assets Investment Trust plc 1984. *Other Activities:* The International Stock Exchange (Lay Member of the Council 1985-86; 1988-); Trustee, The Charities' Office Investment Fund, 1988-. *Professional Organisations:* FIA, AMSIA. *Clubs:* Surrey County Cricket Club. *Recreations:* Gardening, Reading, Watching Cricket.

WEBSTER, M J B; Partner, Rowe & Maw, since 1973; Corporate Finance & Computer Law. *Career:* Herbert Smith, Articled Clerk/Assistant Solicitor 1963-67; McKenna & Co, Assistant Solicitor 1967-70; Travers, Smith Braithwaite, Assistant Solicitor 1970-73; Rowe & Maw, Partner 1973-; Senior Partner, Commercial Dept. *Biog: b.* 10 February 1942. *Nationality:* British. *m.* 1968, Penny (née Brown); 1 s; 1 d. *Educ:* Berkhamsted School; Bristol University (LLB Hons). *Other Activities:* International Bar Association (Computer & Technology Law - Committee R); The Computer Law Group. *Professional Organisations:* The Law Society. *Clubs:* The Honourable Artillery Company, Ashridge Golf Club. *Recreations:* Walking in Remote Places with Binoculars, Golf, Tennis, Theatre, Bridge.

WEBSTER, P M; Partner, Pensions (Epsom), Bacon & Woodrow.

WEBSTER, Trevor; City Editor, Daily Express, since 1989. *Career:* Financial World, Reporter 1960-62; Investors Review, Editor 1962-63; Stock Exchange Gazette Company New Editor 1963-65; Scotsman, Deputy City Editor 1965-66; Daily Express, City Reporter 1966; Scotsman, Dep City Editor 1966-70; City Editor 1970-86; Daily News, Dep City Editor 1987; Daily Telegraph, Questor 1987-88; Daily Express, Dep City Editor 1988-89. *Biog: b.* 1 November 1937. *Nationality:* British. *Educ:* Leeds Grammar School; Leeds University (LLB). *Publications:* Where to go in Greece, 1985; Athens Mainland & North Aegean Isles, 1986; Corfu and Ionian Isles, 1986; Rhodes and the Dodecannese, 1987; Crete and the Cyclades, 1988; Greek Island Delights, 1989. *Clubs:* National Liberal, City Golf, Globe Lawn Tennis. *Recreations:* Tennis, Skiing, Travel.

WEDGWOOD, John Arthur Thomas; Director and Secretary, Guinness Mahon Holdings plc, since 1988; Secretarial, Legal & Administration. *Career:* Westminster Bank Ltd 1960-66; Wiggins Teape Ltd Asst Co Sec 1966-72; Slater Walker Securities Ltd Asst Co Sec 1970-76; Ozalid Group Holdings Ltd Co Sec 1976-78; GPG plc 1978-88. *Biog: b.* 14 September 1940. *Nationality:* British. *m.* 1966, Elizabeth (née Handscomb); 1 s; 1 d. *Educ:* Merchant Taylors' School, Moor Park. *Directorships:* Guinness Mahon Group Ltd; Guinness Mahon Insurance Services Ltd; Guinness Mahon Pension Fund Trustees Ltd; Guinness Mahon Group Services Ltd. *Professional Organisations:* FCIS. *Recreations:* Rugby, Tennis, Squash.

WEDLAKE, G A O; Partner, Travers Smith Braithwaite.

WEDLAKE, William John; Finance Director, J Henry Schroder Wagg & Co Limited, since 1990. *Career:* Arthur Andersen & Co 1978-82; Price Waterhouse (Hartford, USA), Senior Manager 1982-84; (London) 1984-86; Continental Bank, Vice President 1986-87. *Other Activities:* Chairman, British Merchant Banks and Securities Houses Association Committee of Accountants. *Professional Organisations:* Chartered Accountant.

WEEKS, Clive A; Partner, Moores Rowland, since 1975; National Staff, Training and Administration. *Career:* Rowland & Co Chartered Accountants, Manager 1969-75; Rowland & Co, Partner 1975-76; Rowland Nevill, Partner 1975-85; Moores Rowland, Partner 1985-. *Biog: b.* 5 September 1947. *Nationality:* British. *m.* 1970, Teresa (née Forrester); 1 s; 2 d. *Educ:* Wimbledon College. *Other Activities:* Governor, Ursuline Convent High School, Wimbledon. *Professional Organisations:* FCA. *Recreations:* Music, Cricket.

WEEVER, Patrick; City Reporter, The Sunday Telegraph.

WEGELIUS, (Harald) Christopher; Chief General Manager, Skopbank, since 1989. *Career:* Oy Credit Ab, Assistant Lawyer 1966-67; Skopbank, Presenter of Credit Applications 1970-71; Skopbank, Credit Manager's Assistant 1971-77; Finnish Real Estate Bank Ltd, Bank Manager 1973-77; Skopbank, Board Member 1977-84; Skopbank, Managing Director 1985-89. *Biog: b.* 13 September 1944. *Nationality:* Finnish. *m.* 2 s. *Educ:* Helsinki University (LLB, trained on the Bench 1972). *Directorships:* Finnish Real Estate Bank Ltd 1990 Member of the Supervisory Board; Skop Finance Ltd 1990 Member of the Supervisory Board; Tampella Ltd 1987 Chairman of the Board; Metsä-Serla Oy 1990 Member of the Board. *Other Activities:* Chairman, The Equestrian Federation of Finland. *Recreations:* Show Jumping.

WEGUELIN, John Richard McLean; Executive Director, Bank of America International Limited.

WEIL, Charles-Henri; Financial Consultant, Dawnay Day & Co Ltd, since 1982; Corporate Finance. *Career:* Banque OBC (Paris), Mgr 1962-71; Compagnie Financiere (Paris), Mgr 1972-77; Havas SA (Paris), Chief Fin Officer 1978-82. *Biog: b.* 9 February 1937. *m.* 1967, Claire (née Hauser); 1 s; 2 d. *Educ:* Hautes Etudes Commerciales, France. *Directorships:* Dawnay Day & Co 1982 (non-exec); Nord Est France 1984 (non-exec); Minnesota Rubber (France) 1986 (non-exec); Equity Ventures 1985 (non-exec); Duc Lamothe (France); Creeldean Ltd (England); Harringtel Ltd (England); Intergestion SA (France); Société Parisienne des Sciures; Definance SA (Belgium). *Recreations:* Tennis.

WEINBERG, C L; Director, Parrish Stockbrokers.

WEINBERG, Sir Mark Aubrey; Chairman, Allied Dunbar Assurance plc, since 1978. *Career:* Barrister (South Africa) 1955-61; Abbey Life Assurance Company, Managing Director 1962-70; Hambro Life Assurance (now Allied Dunbar Assurance), Managing Director 1971-78. *Biog: b.* 9 August 1931. *Nationality:* British. *m.* 1980, Anouska; 1 s; 3 d. *Educ:* King Edward VII, Johannesburg; University of Witwatersrand (BCom, LLB); University of London LSE (LLM). *Directorships:* J Rothschild Holdings 1984-89 (non-exec); BAT Industries 1985-89 (non-exec); Securities & Investments Board 1985-90 Deputy Chairman. *Other Activities:* Trustee, Tate Gallery; Joint Chairman, The Per Cent Club; Deputy Chairman, Business in The Community. *Publications:* Take-Overs & Mergers (5th Edition), 1989. *Clubs:* Portland.

WEINSTOCK, Arnold; Lord Weinstock; Managing Director (Investment Management), The General Electric Company plc.

WEINSTOCK, Hon Simon; Director, The General Electric Company plc.

WEIR, William Kenneth James; The Viscount Weir; Vice Chairman, J Rothschild Holdings plc.

WEISS, John Roger; Head of Chief Executive's Division, Export Credits Guarantee Department, since 1987; Secretariat, ECGD Management Board & Export Guarantees Advisory Council, Business Planning, International Relations Press & Publicity, Legislation. *Career:* HM Inland Revenue Tax Officer 1961-64; Export Credits Guarantee Department Exec Officer 1964-70; Higher Exec Officer 1970-76; Snr Exec Officer 1976-78; Principal 1978-82; Head of Division 1982-. *Biog: b.* 27 December 1944. *Nationality:* British. *m.* 1967, Hazel Kay (née Lang). *Educ:* St Helen's College, Surrey. *Recreations:* Music, Archaeology, Walking.

WELBURN, Peter Robert; Senior Partner, Holman Fenwick & Willan, since 1987; Commercial Property. *Career:* Boodle, Hatfield & Co Solicitors, Articled Clerk 1979-83; Herbert Oppenheimer Nathan & Vandyk, Solicitor 1983-86; Thornton Lynne & Lawson, Solicitor 1986-87; Holman Fenwick & Willan, Solicitor/Partner 1987-. *Biog: b.* 6 May 1956. *Nationality:* British. *m.* 1988, Eliana; 1 d. *Educ:* University College, Durham (BA Hons Politics). *Other Activities:* Anglo-Hungarian Law Association. *Professional Organisations:* Law Society. *Clubs:* Wig & Pen.

WELCH, David Michael; Partner (Company Department), Nabarro Nathanson, since 1975; General Commercial/Company. *Career:* Goodman Derrick & Co, Articles; Partner. *Educ:* Norwich School; University College London (LLM). *Professional Organisations:* Law Society.

WELCH, Sir John (Reader); Bt, CStJ; Partner, Wedlake Bell, since 1972; Commercial Property. *Career:* Freshfields, Articled Clerk 1957-60; Bell Brodrick & Gray, Partner 1961-71. *Biog: b.* 26 July 1933. *Nationality:* British. *m.* 1962, (Margaret) Kerry; 1 s; 2 d. *Educ:* Marlborough College; Hertford College, Oxford (MA). *Directorships:* John Fairfax (UK) Limited 1977 (non-exec). *Other Activities:* Liveryman, Haberdashers Company (1st Warden 1988-90); Freeman, Parish Clerks Company (Master 1967-68); Registrar, Archdeaconry of London. *Professional Organisations:* The Law Society; Ecclesiastical Law Association; Ecclesiastical Law Society. *Clubs:* City Livery Club (Pres 1986-1987), MCC, Surrey County Cricket Club, Hulingham Club.

WELDON, George Francis Daryl; Management Consultancy Group Partner, Touche Ross & Co, since 1987; Strategic Planning, Organisation Structure and Related Management Information Systems. *Career:* C & J Clark, Various 1968-75; Touche Ross Management Consultants, Consultant 1975-78; Ptnr 1978-85; Touche Ross & Co, National Dir of Marketing 1985-87. *Biog: b.* 9 December 1946. *Nationality:* British. *m.* 1981, Jane Margaret (née Knapman); 2 d. *Educ:* Wellington

College; Keble College, Oxford (MA); Carnegie-Mellon University, Pittsburgh, USA (MBA). *Professional Organisations:* CBI (London Regional Council). *Clubs:* United Oxford & Cambridge University.

WELFARE, Jonathan W; Managing Director, Venture Link Investors Ltd, since 1990. *Career:* Drivers Jonas & Co, Consultant 1966-68; Sir Colin Buchanan and Partners, Consultant 1968-70; Milton Keynes Development Corporation, Corporate Planning Manager 1970-74; South Yorkshire Metropolitan County Council, Chief Economist, Deputy Chief Executive 1974-84. *Biog:* b. 21 October 1944. *Nationality:* British. *m.* 1969, Deborah Louise (née Nesbitt); 1 s; 3 d. *Educ:* Bradfield College, Berkshire; Emmanuel College, Cambridge (MA). *Directorships:* Landmark Trust 1984-86; Oxford Ventures Group 1986-89; Granite Television and Film Productions Ltd 1988 (non-exec); Systematica Ltd 1990 (non-exec); Oxford Innovation Centres Ltd 1989. *Other Activities:* Chairman, Northmoor Trust (General Charitable); Chairman, Oxford Trust (Charitable Trust for Promotion of Science and Technology). *Publications:* Sources of EEE Funding for Local Authorities, 1976. *Clubs:* Hawks. *Recreations:* Tennis, Sailing.

WELFORD, Anthony; Deputy General Manager Administration, Postipankki Ltd.

WELHAM, George; Chairman, Burson-Marsteller Financial Ltd, since 1989; Financial and Investor Relations. *Career:* Journalist 1961-69; Welham McAdam Public Relations, Co-Founder & Chairman 1969-76; Extel PR & Advertising, Director 1976-79; Hill & Knowlton, Director 1979-80; Dep Managing Director 1980-84; Gavin Anderson Ltd, Managing Director 1984-88; Burson-Marsteller Ltd, Director 1988-; Burson-Marsteller Financial, Chief Exec, then Chairman 1988-. *Biog:* b. 9 July 1938. *Nationality:* British. *m.* 1975, Penny (née Connell); 3 s; 2 d. *Educ:* Dulwich College. *Recreations:* Opera, Theatre, Books, Singing, Gardening, Sport.

WELLEMEYER, John Charles; Co-Head, Morgan Stanley International, since 1986; International Research, London. *Career:* Morgan Stanley Group (New York), Energy Analyst 1973-86; Faulkner Dowkins & Sullivan, Energy Analyst 1966-73; Exxon Corporation, Financial Analyst 1964-66; Cities Service, Chemical Engineer 1959-62. *Biog:* b. 2 October 1937. *Nationality:* American. *Educ:* University of Chicago Graduate School of Business (MBA); Yale University (BE Chemical Engineering). *Professional Organisations:* Chartered Financial Analyst; Member, New York Society of Security Analysts; Member, American Institute of Chemical Engineers; Member, Oil Analyst Group of New York.

WELLER, Christopher Stewart; Deputy Managing Director, Svenska International plc, since 1983; Financial Control and Operations. *Career:* Dunn Wylie & Co,

Audit Staff 1962-67; Guinness Mahon & Co Ltd, Asst Acct 1968-72; Merrill Lynch International Bank Ltd, VP 1972-82; Svenska Handelsbanken, VP 1982-. *Biog:* b. 11 October 1944. *Nationality:* British. *m.* 1967, Dorothy (née Hurlow); 1 s; 1 d. *Educ:* Monkton Combe School. *Directorships:* Svenska and Company Limited 1987 (exec); Svenska Development Capital plc. *Other Activities:* Fiscal Ctee of Foreign Banks Association. *Professional Organisations:* FCA. *Recreations:* Church Finances, Gardening.

WELLESLEY WESLEY, D; Director, The Growth Fund Limited.

WELLESLEY WESLEY, J D; Director, Granville & Co Ltd, since 1988; UK Public Company Corporate Finance. *Career:* Morgan Guaranty Trust Company of New York, Assistant Treasurer (Banking) 1979-83. *Biog:* b. 9 July 1957. *Nationality:* British. *m.* 1982, Elizabeth (née Romones); 3 d. *Educ:* Eton College; Cambridge University (MA). *Directorships:* Unistrut Europe plc 1988 (non-exec).

WELLESLEY-WOOD, Mark Michael; Director, Kleinwort Benson Securities.

WELLING, Mark Ronald; Partner, Allen & Overy; International Capital Markets. *Career:* Allen & Overy Solicitor 1981-. *Biog:* b. 22 March 1956. *Nationality:* British. *m.* 1987, Vanessa (née Barker). *Educ:* Derby School; Emmanuel College, Cambridge (MA). *Other Activities:* Royal Borough of Kingston upon Thames Council (Councillor 1986-90). *Professional Organisations:* The Law Society; City of London Solicitors' Company.

WELLINGS, David Gordon; Managing Director, Group Confectionery, Cadbury Schweppes plc, since 1989; Chocolate & Sugar Confectionery Worldwide (except Australasia). *Career:* Cadbury Brothers Ltd, Sales & Marketing Training, Management 1962-68; Associated Fisheries & Foods Ltd, Marketing Manager, Director 1968-73; Northway Farm Products, (ITT), Managing Director 1973-78; Imperial Group; Ross Foods, Director Fish Operations 1978-80; Golden Wonder, Managing Director 1980-83; Golden Wonder & HP, Chairman & Chief Executive 1983-85; Director of Business Development 1985-86; Cadbury Schweppes plc; Cadbury Ltd Managing Director 1986-89; Managing Director, Group Confectionery 1989-. *Biog:* b. 13 December 1940. *Nationality:* British. *m.* 1962, Jennifer (née Simpson); 1 s; 1 d. *Educ:* Manchester Grammar School; Oriel College, Oxford (BA Hons Modern Languages). *Directorships:* Cadbury Schweppes plc 1989 (exec); Cadbury Ltd 1986 (non-exec); Trebor Bassett Ltd 1990 (non-exec).

WELLINGTON, P; Director, County NatWest Securities Limited.

WELLS, Andrew; Partner, Clyde & Co.

WELLS, Boyan Stewart; Partner, Allen & Overy, since 1987; Capital Markets, Swaps, Corporate Finance. *Biog: b.* 3 June 1956. *Nationality:* British. *m.* 1984, Alison Jayne (née Good); 2 d. *Educ:* Colston's School, Bristol; Wadham College, Oxford (MA). *Other Activities:* City of London Solicitors' Company. *Professional Organisations:* The Law Society. *Clubs:* Richmond Hockey Club, Friends of Dulwich Society. *Recreations:* Hockey, Squash.

WELLS, David Patrick Casey; Partner, Titmuss Sainer & Webb, since 1988; Commercial Property and Banking. *Career:* Reynolds Porter Chamberlain, Partner, Commercial Property 1980-88; Herbert Smith, Assistant Solicitor, Commercial Property 1976-80. *Biog: b.* 24 November 1950. *Nationality:* British. *Educ:* St Joseph's College, Blackpool; Queen Mary College, Mile End, London (LLB Hons). *Other Activities:* City of London Solicitors Company. *Professional Organisations:* Law Society. *Clubs:* Blackheath Rugby Club. *Recreations:* Squash.

WELLS, Gary G; Partner, Hymans Robertson & Co.

WELLS, John Richard Lancaster; Partner, Laurence Keen & Co, since 1988; Private Clients. *Career:* Laurie Milbank & Co, Ptnr 1966-1986; Head of Private Client Dept 1971-1986. *Biog: b.* 23 August 1932. *Nationality:* British. *m.* 1963, Rosemary (née Dickson); 1 s; 2 d. *Educ:* Marlborough College; Oriel College, Oxford (MA). *Recreations:* Tennis, Golf, Bridge.

WELLS, Nicholas C; Marketing Director Pharmaceuticals Division, Sun Life Trust Management Limited.

WELLS, R F; Director, J H Minet & Co Ltd.

WELLS, Stuart H; Associate Director, Coutts & Co. *m.* 2 s; 1 d.

WELLS, W A A; Company Secretary, Minories Holdings Ltd & Clerk, The Company of Watermen & Lightermen of the River Thames.

WELMAN, J M P; Managing Director, Rea Brothers Investment Management Limited, since 1989; Investment Management. *Career:* Baring Brothers & Co Ltd Baring Investment Management Ltd 1979-89; Director 1989. *Biog: b.* 2 January 1958. *Nationality:* British. *m.* 1988, Alex (née Burell); 1 s. *Educ:* Radley College, Oxford; Exeter University (BSc Econ Hons). *Directorships:* Rea Brothers Investment Management 1989 (exec); Rea Brothers Limited 1989 (exec). *Clubs:* MCC, Liphook Golf Club. *Recreations:* Shooting, Fishing, Golf.

WELSBY, J K; CBE; Chief Executive, Railways, British Railways Board, since 1990. *Career:* British Railways Board, Executive Board Member, with special responsibility for Channel Tunnel Matters and Private Sector Involvement 1987-89; Managing Director, Procurement 1985-87; Director, Manufacturing & Maintenance Policy 1984-85; Director, Provincial Services 1982-84; Director, Strategic Studies 1979-82; Senior Economic Adviser, Dept of Transport 1972-79; Transport & Road Research Laboratory, Economic Adviser, Advanced Systems Division 1971-72; University of British Columbia, Vancouver, Canada, Asst Professor, Business School 1969-71; Ministry of Transport, Economic Adviser, Economic Planning Directorate 1966-69; The Electricity Council, London, Economist 1965-66. *Biog: b.* 26 May 1938. *Nationality:* British. *m.* Jill; 1 s; 1 d. *Educ:* University of Exeter (BA Hons Economics); University of London (MSc). *Professional Organisations:* Fellow, Chartered Institute of Transport. *Publications:* Several Articles of Economics of Transport. *Recreations:* Walking, Music.

WELSFORD, Robert Arthur Mills; Partner, Slaughter and May, since 1980; Company & Commercial Law. *Career:* Slaughter and May, Asst Solicitor 1973-80. *Biog: b.* 17 June 1948. *Nationality:* British. *m.* 1975, Susan (née Catling); 1 s; 2 d. *Educ:* Winchester College; New College, Oxford (MA). *Professional Organisations:* The Law Society; City of London Law Society. *Recreations:* Music, Theatre.

WEMYSS, Rear Admiral M La T; CB; Clerk, Brewers' Company.

WENHAM, I J; Director, Barclays de Zoete Wedd Securities Ltd.

WENT, David; Chief Executive, Ulster Bank Ltd, since 1988. *Career:* Citibank NA (Ireland), Gen Mgr 1970-75; (Jeddah) Gen Mgr 1975-76; Ulster Investment Bank, Dir, Banking 1976-87; Chief Exec 1982-87; Ulster Bank Ltd, Dep Chief Exec 1987. *Biog: b.* 25 March 1947. *Nationality:* Irish. *m.* 1972, Mary (née Milligan); 1 s; 1 d. *Educ:* High School, Dublin; Trinity College (BA, LLB). *Directorships:* Ulster Investment Bank 1976 (non-exec); Lombard & Ulster Ltd 1987 (non-exec); Lombard & Ulster Banking Ltd 1987 (non-exec); Ulster International Finance 1989 (non-exec). *Professional Organisations:* Barrister at Law, King's Inn, Dublin; FIB. *Clubs:* University, Reform, Royal Belfast Golf Club, Royal North of Ireland Yacht Club. *Recreations:* Tennis, Squash, Reading, Sport.

WENTWORTH-STANLEY, D M; Partner, Cazenove & Co.

WEPPE, Bernard Jacky Pierre; Director, C Czarnikow Ltd, since 1987; Soft Commodities. *Career:* Euro-Africaine De Transactions (Paris), Trader 1974-76; Foreign Trading Agency, Trader 1976-81; C Czarnikow Ltd, Snr Trader & Dir 1981-. *Biog: b.* 27 December 1949. *Nationality:* French. *m.* 1973, Pamela (née Blackburn); 2 s. *Educ:* College of Chateauneuf,

Loiret, France; Conservatoire National Des Arts et Metiers, Paris. *Directorships:* C Czarnikow SA 1984 (exec).

WESBROOM, K R; Partner (Bristol), Bacon & Woodrow.

WEST, J D; Head of Business Development, Enterprise Oil.

WEST, J J; Director, Dalgety plc.

WEST, James Glynn; Managing Director, Globe Investment Trust plc.

WEST, Martin; Director (Market-Making), Hoare Govett International Securities.

WEST, Richard; UK Equity Manager, Crown Financial Management Limited.

WEST, Stephen; Head of Fixed Income, New Issues, Paribas Limited, since 1988. *Career:* Orion Royal Bank Ltd, Canadian Entities, New Issues & Swaps 1983-87; Paribas Limited 1987-. *Biog:* b. 13 November 1959. *Nationality:* British. *Educ:* University College London (LLB Hons). *Other Activities:* IPMA Market Practices Committee, 1988-. *Professional Organisations:* Member of Grays Inn, Barrister.

WEST, T W R; Chairman, Potts, West, Trumbull (UK) Limited.

WESTACOTT, S J; Head of Administration, Grimley J R Eve.

WESTAWAY, Mark; Partner, Memery Crystal.

WESTBROOK, Bruce; Partner, Cameron Markby Hewitt, since 1981; Corporate Finance. *Career:* Cameron Markby Hewitt (& Predecessor Firms) 1976-; Articled Clerk 1976-78; Assistant Solicitor 1979-81; Partner 1981-. *Educ:* Kings School, Macclesfield; University College, London (LLB). *Professional Organisations:* Law Society.

WESTBROOK, S; Managing Director, Mynshul Bank plc.

WESTBY, David John; Group Treasurer, Prudential Corporation plc, since 1989; Foreign Exchange Exposure Management, Banking and Financial Relationships, Financing the Corporation, Developing Financial Strategies. *Career:* Standard Chartered Bank 1967-71; Monsanto plc, Banking Mgr 1971-74; Commercial Union, Head of Treasury 1974-79; Fisons plc, Gp Treasurer 1979-82; Metal Box plc (now MB Group), Gp Treasurer 1982-87; Dir, Gp Purchasing 1987-88. *Biog:* b. 16 November 1942. *Nationality:* British. *m.* 1966,

Josephine; 2 s. *Educ:* Cranleigh School. *Other Activities:* Former Council Member of ACT; Chm, Electoral Ctee of Treasurer 1983-87. *Professional Organisations:* AIB; FCT; MInstPS. *Clubs:* Royal Photographic Society. *Recreations:* Photography, Skiing, Running.

WESTCOTT, David; National Director-Personnel, BDO Binder Hamlyn.

WESTCOTT, Richard H; Managing Director, Merrill Lynch International Limited.

WESTERBURGEN, J W B; Secretary, Unilever plc.

WESTLEY, Peter; Partner, Gouldens.

WESTMACOTT, Philip G; Intellectual Property Partner, Bristows Cooke & Carpmael.

WESTMACOTT, Simon Field; Executive Director, Chartered WestLB Limited, since 1989; Corporate Finance. *Career:* Standard Chartered ASIA Ltd (Tokyo), Chief Representative 1985-88; Standard Chartered Merchant Bank Ltd, Corporate Finance 1982-85; Antony Gibbs & Sons Ltd, Corporate Finance 1978-82; Barclays Merchant Bank Ltd, Corporate Finance 1976-77; Deloitte Haskins & Sells, Investigation Dept 1972-75; Black Geoghegan & Till, Articled Clerk 1969-72; Ranks Hovis McDougall plc, Management Trainee 1967-69. *Biog:* b. 31 October 1944. *Nationality:* British. *m.* 1972, Patricia (née Airey); 1 s; 2 d. *Educ:* Taunton School; Wye College, University of London (BSc Agriculture Hons). *Directorships:* Chartered WestLB Ltd 1989 (exec); Scamba Nominees Ltd 1989 (non-exec). *Professional Organisations:* FCA. *Recreations:* sailing, Skiing, Fishing, Garden.

WESTON, Christopher J; Chairman, Phillips.

WESTON SMITH, John Harry; Finance Director and Group Secretary, The British Land Company plc, since 1973. *Career:* Abbey National Building Society, Secretary, Assistant Secretary, then Joint General Manager. *Biog:* b. 3 February 1932. *Nationality:* British. *m.* 1955, Margaret Fraser Milne; 1 s; 2 d. *Educ:* Cambridge University (Master of Arts). *Professional Organisations:* FCIS; ACII; ACBSI.

WESTROPP, George Victor; Partner, Touche Ross & Co.

WETHERED, (James) Adam (Lawrence); Member of the London Management Committee, Senior VP, Director, Morgan Guaranty Trust Company of New York, since 1990; Finance, Personnel, Operations, Technology, Legal & Compliance, Audit & Administration, Europe 1992. *Career:* J P Morgan; Strategic Planning & Management Reporting (New York) 1988-89; Head, Specialised Finance 1986-88; Specialised Industries 1984-86; Corporate Finance, Petroleum & Project Finance 1983-84; Bank Lending Officer, Scandinavia & Shipping 1976-83. *Biog: b.* 2 April 1953. *Nationality:* British. *m.* 1984; 1 s; 1 d. *Educ:* Eton; Christ's College (MA, LLB Law); Inner Temple (Barrister). *Directorships:* J P Morgan Securities Ltd (exec). *Other Activities:* Inner Temple; Merchant Taylors.

WETHERED, Simon Richard; Partner, Alsop Wilkinson, since 1978; Insolvency. *Career:* Simmons & Simmons, Partner 1970-78. *Biog: b.* 1 March 1945. *Nationality:* British. *m.* 1978, Victoria (née Le Fanu); 2 s; 1 d. *Educ:* Clifton College; Worcester College, Oxford (BA). *Directorships:* Academy Concerts Society 1984 (non-exec); FIMBRA 1987 (non-exec). *Other Activities:* City of London Solicitors' Company. *Professional Organisations:* Law Society; AEPPC. *Recreations:* Wine, Music, Walking.

WETHERED, Thomas Owen Gilbert; Partner, Linklaters & Paines, since 1986; Corporate Law. *Biog: b.* 25 September 1953. *Nationality:* British. *m.* 1979, Colleen Mary (née Ruane); 3 s; 1 d. *Educ:* Charterhouse; Christ Church, Oxford (MA English Language and Literature); Trinity, Cambridge (BA Law).

WETHERELL, J M H P; Director, Janson Green Limited.

WEYER, Martin Laurence Vander; Director, Barclays de Zoete Wedd Limited, since 1987; Chief Operations Officer, Corporate Finance Division. *Career:* J Henry Schroder Wagg & Co Ltd, London 1976-81; Brussels 1979-81; Barclays Merchant Bank Limited (subsequently Barclays de Zoete Wedd Group) 1981-; Malaysia 1984-85; Deputy Representative, Tokyo 1985-87; Managing Director, Asia (Based in Hong Kong) 1987-89; Chief Operations Officer, Corporate Finance Division, London 1990-. *Biog: b.* 24 January 1955. *Nationality:* British. *Educ:* Glenalmond School; Worcester College, Oxford (BA PPE). *Clubs:* Bucks, Tokyo Club.

WHAITE, Robin; Partner, Linklaters & Paines.

WHALLEY, G A; Partner, Freshfields.

WHARFE, Major W H; RM; Clerk, Coachmakers' & Coach Harness Makers' Company.

WHATMUFF, P W; Partner, Wedlake Bell.

WHEAL, Anthony Nevill; Financial Director, Fenchurch Insurance Group Ltd, since 1979. *Career:* Bland Payne Ltd, Fin Dir 1972-79; Price Waterhouse & Co; Peat Marwick Mitchell & Co. *Biog: b.* 16 August 1939. *Nationality:* British. *m.* 1978, Margaret (née Bruce); 1 s; 2 d. *Educ:* St John's College, Johannesburg; University of South Africa (CA, SA). *Directorships:*

Temple Wheal & Co Ltd 1979 (exec). *Other Activities:* Chairman, Suffolk Coastal Consultative Council. *Clubs:* Rand, Inanda, Country. *Recreations:* Shooting, Children.

WHEAL, G T; Partner, Wedlake Bell.

WHEATCROFT, C J; Partner, Touche Ross & Co.

WHEATCROFT, G S; Partner, Ashurst Morris Crisp.

WHEATLEY, Alan Edward; Senior Partner, London Office, Price Waterhouse, since 1985. *Career:* Norton Slade, Student 1954-60; Qualified 1960; Price Waterhouse 1960-; Partner 1970-; Member, UK Policy Committee 1981-; Senior Partner, London Office 1985-; Member, European Policy Board 1988-; Member, World Board 1988-. *Biog: b.* 25 May 1938. *Nationality:* British. *m.* 1962, Marion; 2 s; 1 d. *Educ:* Ilford Grammar School. *Directorships:* British Steel plc 1984 (non-exec); Industrial Development Advisory Board 1985 Board Member; Cable & Wireless plc 1981-84 (non-exec) Govt Dir; 1984-85 (non-exec) Dep Chm; EBS Investments Ltd (wholly owned subsidiary of Bank of England) 1977-90. *Professional Organisations:* Member, Institute of Chartered Accountants in England & Wales. *Clubs:* Wildernesse Golf Club. *Recreations:* Golf, Tennis, Badminton, Bridge.

WHEATLEY, Alan Michael; Director, Morgan Grenfell Investment Services Ltd, since 1985; International Fund Management. *Career:* Morgan Grenfell & Co Ltd, Fund Mgr 1974-85; Morgan Grenfell Investment Services, Fund Mgr 1985; Morgan Grenfell Asset Management, Dir 1986-. *Biog: b.* 4 June 1951. *m.* 1974, Elizabeth (née Pinkerton); 1 s; 2 d. *Educ:* King's College School, Wimbledon; Emmanuel College, Cambridge (BA Hons 1st, MA). *Professional Organisations:* ASIA. *Recreations:* History, Choral Singing.

WHEATON, James Bernard; Partner, Clifford Chance, since 1978. *Biog: b.* 13 November 1948. *Nationality:* British. *m.* 1973, Rosemary (née Thompson); 3 s. *Educ:* Godalming County Grammar; University of Birmingham (LLB). *Professional Organisations:* Law Society; City of London Solicitors Company. *Clubs:* Foxhills. *Recreations:* Tennis, Squash.

WHEELER, Adrian; Managing Director (Investment Management), GCI Sterling.

WHEELER, Mrs C M K; Partner, Ernst & Young.

WHEELER, David Perrin; Managing Director, J P Morgan, since 1990; Head of European Media and Communications Group. *Career:* J P Morgan 1976-. *Biog: b.* 4 October 1952. *Nationality:* American. *m.* 1981, Lee (née Montross); 1 s; 1 d. *Educ:* Bowdoin College (BA History Summa Cum Laude); Wharton Business

School (MBA Finance). *Clubs:* RAC, Hurlingham. *Recreations:* Squash, Shooting, Tennis.

WHEELER, Kenneth; Group Finance Director/ Company Secretary, Broad Street Group plc, since 1988. *Career:* Ardingly College, Haywards Heath School Master 1974-75; Arthur Andersen & Co (London), Audit Manager 1975-83; Chase Manhattan Bank NA, Audit Manager 1983-85; Burgess Daring Advertising, Finance Director 1985-88. *Biog: b.* 10 February 1952. *Nationality:* British. *m.* 1986, Sally (née Lineham); 1 *s. Educ:* Danum Grammar School; Fitzwilliam College, Cambridge (MA Hons Natural Sciences, Theoretical Physics); Worcester College of Education, University of Birmingham (Postgraduate Certificate of Education, Mathematics and Physics). *Directorships:* Broad Street Group plc 1989 (exec). *Professional Organisations:* FCA. *Recreations:* Theatre, Cinema, Sports.

WHEELER, Raymond; Director, C S Project Consultants.

WHEELER, Timothy Carpenter; Partner, Clifford Chance, since 1987; Commercial Property. *Career:* Lewis & Lewis and Gisborne, Articled Clerk 1951-56; Clifford-Turner, Asst Solicitor 1958-64; Ptnr 1964-87. *Biog: b.* 20 September 1933. *Nationality:* British. *m.* 1967, Diana Katherine (née Hillson); 1 *d. Other Activities:* Member, International Bar Association; City of London Solicitors' Company; British Property Federation. *Professional Organisations:* The Law Society; City of London Law Society(Chm of Land Law Sub-Ctee). *Clubs:* Effingham Golf Club, Esher Cricket Club. *Recreations:* Walking, Gardening.

WHEELEY, Edward George; Assistant General Manager, Banque Nationale de Paris plc, since 1989; Administration/Operations. *Career:* Ford Motor Company Ltd, Various Roles in Personnel Management 1966-75; Banque Nationale de Paris plc, Staff Manager 1975-81; Manager, then Senior Manager, Commercial Banking Department 1981-88; Senior Manager, Administration 1989. *Biog: b.* 14 October 1944. *Nationality:* British. *m.* 1967, Eleanor Randall (née Telfer); 2 s; 1 *d. Educ:* Brentwood School, Brentwood, Essex; Caius College, Cambridge (MA History). *Other Activities:* Vice Chairman, Mid-Essex Relate. *Professional Organisations:* Member, The Chartered Institute of Bankers; Member, Institute of Personnel Management; Member, British Institute of Management. *Recreations:* Mountain Walking, Tennis.

WHEEN, Richard Francis; Partner, Linklaters & Paines, since 1973; Corporate Finance. *Career:* Nicholas Williams & Co, Articles & Assistant Solicitor 1964-68; Linklaters & Paines, Assistant Solicitor 1968-73. *Biog: b.* 27 May 1941. *Nationality:* British. *m.* 1983, Anne (née Keegan); 5 *s. Educ:* Harrow School; Peterhouse, Cambridge (MA). *Other Activities:* Member, City of London

Solicitors Company. *Professional Organisations:* Solicitor of The Supreme Court; Member, Law Society. *Publications:* Editor, Joint Ventures, 1990; Bridge Player, Series of Computer Programs, 1984. *Clubs:* Army & Navy, Worplesdon Golf Club, Players Theatre Club. *Recreations:* Golf, Shooting, Bridge, Computer Programming.

WHELDON, Timothy J; Partner, Booth & Co (Solicitors), since 1990; Company Law. *Career:* Gosschalks (Solicitors) 1981-90; Partner 1985-90. *Biog: b.* 29 January 1959. *Nationality:* British. *m.* 1980, Sharon Ann (née Wallhead); 2 s; 1 *d. Educ:* Hymers College, Hull; Manchester Polytechnic (BA Hons Law with French). *Professional Organisations:* Solicitor. *Recreations:* Sailing, Skiing, Horse Riding.

WHERITY, William Gerard; Director, Abbey Life Investment Services Ltd; Fixed Interest Markets. *Career:* London Borough of Hillingdon, Mathematics Teacher 1975-78; Eagle Star Group, Snr Fund Mgr 1978-87; Fuji International Finance, Assoc Dir 1986-87. *Biog: b.* 12 December 1953. *Nationality:* British. *m.* 1979; 2 s; 2 *d. Educ:* Bristol University (BSc). *Directorships:* Abbey Life Investment Services Ltd. *Professional Organisations:* FIA.

WHETNALL, Norman; Stock Market Correspondent, The Daily Telegraph, since 1960. *Career:* The Financial Times. *Publications:* How The Stock Exchange Works.

WHETSTONE, M J; Partner, Grimley J R Eve.

WHIDDETT, J D; Director, Hill Samuel Investment Management Ltd.

WHITAKER, John Christopher; Director, County NatWest Investment Management Ltd, since 1986; Investment Management. *Career:* Imperial Life of Canada Investment Mgr 1967-71; British Steel Corp Asst Pensions Investment Mgr 1971-76; Badix Properties Dir 1976-78; Fielding Newson-Smith & Co 1978-82; Ptnr 1982-86. *Biog: b.* 4 October 1943. *Nationality:* British. *m.* 1981, Susan Mary (née Donaldson); 2 *s. Educ:* Bryanston School; Trinity College, Dublin (MA Hons). *Professional Organisations:* Society of Investment Analysts; Member, The International Stock Exchange. *Clubs:* Sunningdale Golf Club. *Recreations:* Golf, Tennis, Shooting.

WHITAKER, Paul Simpson; Director, Hill Samuel Bank Ltd, since 1988; Treasury. *Career:* National Mutual Life Assurance Society, Actuarial Student 1975-78; Provident Mutual Life Assurance Association, Snr Investment Analyst 1978-82; Central Trustee Savings Bank Ltd, Fund Mgr, Gilts 1982-85; TSB England & Wales plc, Treasury Co-ordinator 1985-88. *Biog: b.* 29 October 1953. *Nationality:* British. *m.* 1987, Erika Nicole (née Berentemfel). *Educ:* Warwick School;

Sidney Sussex College, Cambridge (MA). *Professional Organisations:* FIA.

WHITAKER, R A; Company Secretary, General Accident Fire Life Assurance Corp.

WHITAKER, Robert Anthony Mattievich; Director, Hoare Govett Securities Limited, since 1987; UK Equity Sales. *Biog: b.* 13 November 1943. *Nationality:* British. *Clubs:* City of London, Groucho, Canning.

WHITBOURN, G A; Director, Wise Speke Ltd.

WHITBREAD, B D; Deputy Secretary, The Securities Association Limited.

WHITBREAD, S C; Director, Sun Alliance and London Insurance plc.

WHITE, Adrian Harold Michael; Director, Midland Montagu Asset Management, since 1987; Finance and Planning. *Career:* Peat Marwick Mitchell & Co, Articled Clerk/Audit Senior 1964-70; Brown Shipley & Co Ltd, Exec 1970-72; Old Broad Street Securities Ltd, Exec 1972-75; Hill Samuel & Co Ltd, Internal Audit Mgr 1975-78; Morgan Grenfell & Co Ltd, Snr Asst Dir 1978-87. *Biog: b.* 20 November 1945. *Nationality:* British. *m.* 1970, Helen (née Cox); 1 s. *Educ:* Ampleforth College. *Professional Organisations:* FCA. *Clubs:* MCC, North London Rifle Club. *Recreations:* Rifle Shooting.

WHITE, Andrew John; Director, Kleinwort Benson Ltd.

WHITE, Clarence; Director, White Foster Sheldon Daly & Co Ltd.

WHITE, D M; Director, County NatWest Ltd.

WHITE, David Julian; Deputy Chairman, Cater Allen Holdings plc, since 1984. *Career:* Union Discount Co of London Ltd Mgr 1965-79; Cater Ryder Ltd Dir 1979-84. *Biog: b.* 17 July 1942. *m.* 1967, Claire (née Emett); 3 d. *Educ:* Marlborough College.

WHITE, Graham; Consultant, Sabin Bacon White.

WHITE, Graham Peter; Partner, Slaughter and May, since 1987; Property. *Biog: b.* 28 May 1955. *Nationality:* British. *Educ:* Haberdashers' Aske's School, Elstree; St Catherine's College, Oxford (MA Jurisprudence).

WHITE, Ian Shaw; Director, Kleinwort Benson Securities Limited, since 1988; Pharmaceutical Research. *Career:* Simon & Coates, Investment Analyst 1973-77; Hedderwick Stirling Grumbar & Co, Investment Analyst 1977-81; W Greenwell & Co, Investment Analyst 1981-84; Research Ptnr, Pharmaceuticals 1984-86; Greenwell Montagu, Dir, Pharmaceutical Research

1986-87; Dir, Head of Research 1987-88. *Biog: b.* 30 July 1952. *Nationality:* British. *m.* 1980, Susan Elizabeth (née Bacon) (dec 1989); 2 s. *Educ:* Bromsgrove School; Churchill College, Cambridge (MA). *Directorships:* Kleinwort Benson Securities Ltd 1988 (exec). *Professional Organisations:* ASIA. *Recreations:* Thinking, Travel, Board Games, Reading.

WHITE, John; Senior Partner, London & South East, Peat Marwick McLintock.

WHITE, John J; Partner, Banking UK, Cameron Markby Hewitt.

WHITE, Keith Geoffrey; Regional Director (Birmingham), County NatWest Ltd, since 1986; Investmen Banking, Corporate Advice. *Career:* Grant Thornton, Snr Ptnr, Corporate Fin 1974-84; Causeway Capital Dir 1984-86. *Biog: b.* 16 June 1941. *Nationality:* British. *m.* 1969, Susan Patricia (née Kitchen); 1 s; 1 d. *Educ:* Cheltenham Grammar School. *Directorships:* County NatWest Ltd 1988; County NatWest Ventures Ltd 1988; Bank Street Investments Ltd 1988. *Other Activities:* The Worshipful, Company of Chartered Accountants in England & Wales. *Professional Organisations:* FCA. *Clubs:* Birmingham Club. *Recreations:* Golf, Theatre, Opera.

WHITE, Keith William; Executive Director, Societe Generale Strauss Turnbull, since 1988; Europroducts. *Career:* Strauss Turnbull & Co, Dir 1963-80; Societe Generale Strauss Turnbull, Sec 1980-88. *Biog: b.* 18 July 1948. *m.* 1970, Una (née Campbell); 2 s; 1 d. *Educ:* St Martin's County Secondary School. *Clubs:* Bond Club of London. *Recreations:* Golf, Tennis.

WHITE, Peter Richard; Managing Director & Deputy Group Chief Executive, Alliance & Leicester, since 1989; Marketing, Branch & Agency Operations, Estate Agency; strategic Planning, Liquidity Management & Wholesale Funding. *Career:* Price Waterhouse Auditing & Investigations 1965-69; Abbey National Building Society, Mgmnt Acct, Chief Internal Auditor, Fin Controller 1970-82; Alliance Building Society, Gen Mgr, Fin & Mgmnt Services 1982-85; Alliance & Leicester Building Society, Gen Mgr, Admin & Treasury 1985-87; Gen Mgr, Development 1987-89. *Biog: b.* 11 February 1942. *Nationality:* British. *m.* 1968, Mary Angela (née Bowyer); 1 s; 1 d. *Educ:* St Paul's School. *Directorships:* Alliance & Leicester Property Services Ltd Chm; EFTPOS (UK) Ltd (non-exec); EFT (Clearings) Ltd (non-exec); Girobank plc (non-exec); Alliance & Leicester (Isle of Man) Ltd (non-exec). *Professional Organisations:* FCA; Institute of Directors; Assoc of Corporate Treasurers. *Recreations:* Golf, Opera.

WHITE, Philip Martin; Assistant Company Secretary, Asda Group Plc, since 1989; Company Secretary, Asda Stores Limited, since 1989. *Career:* Asda 1977-. *Biog: b.* 9

December 1959. *Nationality:* British. *m.* 1983, Melanie; 1 s. *Educ:* Batley Grammar School; Dewsbury Technical College (OND Business Studies); Huddersfield Technical College (P/T). *Directorships:* Various companies within the Asda Group. *Professional Organisations:* Member, Association of Accounting Technicians (MAAT); Student, Institute of Chartered Secretaries and Administrators. *Recreations:* Football, Photography.

WHITE, Rupert Haydon; Director, David Sheppard & Partners Ltd, since 1980. *Career:* Kleinwort Benson Ltd 1968-72; Daniel Greenaway & Sons 1972-80. *Biog: b.* 17 September 1948. *Nationality:* British. *m.* 1975, Charlotte (née Ovens); 1 s; 2 d. *Educ:* Eton. *Clubs:* Boodles.

WHITE, S C; Director, British & Commonwealth Merchant Bank plc.

WHITE, Stephen Frank; Director, Foreign & Colonial Management Ltd, since 1986; Management of Continental European Equity Portfolios. *Career:* Price Waterhouse Audit Snr 1977-81; Phillips & Drew Analyst 1981-83; Hill Samuel Investment Management Investment Mgr 1983-85. *Biog: b.* 29 September 1955. *Educ:* Eton College; Bristol University (BA Hons). *Directorships:* F & C Eurotrust plc 1987 (exec); F & C Germany Investment Trust 1990 (exec). *Other Activities:* Freeman of the Worshipful Company of Merchant Taylors. *Professional Organisations:* ACA. *Recreations:* Opera, Walking, Gardening.

WHITE-COOPER, W R P; Director, Sedgwick Group plc.

WHITEHAND, Robert; Managing Director (Investment Management), Morgan Stanley International.

WHITEHEAD, A J; Director, Bain & Company (Securities) Ltd.

WHITEHEAD, Darryl; Executive Partner, Grant Thornton, Chartered Accountants, since 1989; Client Services. *Career:* Grant Thornton, General Practice/Business Adviser 1970-; Partner 1981-; Grant Thornton International, Regional Director 1986-89. *Biog: b.* 11 July 1948. *Nationality:* British. *m.* 1975, Naomi (née Freund); 2 d. *Educ:* London University (BSc Econ). *Directorships:* Grant Thornton Management Consultants Ltd 1989 (non-exec). *Other Activities:* Hon Auditor, Guild of Freemen of City of London. *Professional Organisations:* Institute of Chartered Accountants in England and Wales; London Society of Chartered Accountants; Institute of Directors. *Recreations:* Family, Tennis, Travel, Historic Studies, Languages.

WHITEHEAD, G; Director, Greenwell Montagu Gilt-Edged.

WHITEHOUSE, Brian Paul; Director, Hambros Bank Ltd, since 1970; Direct Investments. *Biog: b.* 24 May 1919. *Nationality:* British. *m.* 1959, Jane Margaret (née Roberts-West); 2 s; 2 d. *Educ:* Oxford (MA). *Directorships:* Berkeley Hambro Property Co Ltd 1985; Cunningham Hart Holdings Ltd 1985; Hambro Group Investments Ltd 1974 Deputy Chairman; Network Security Holdings Ltd 1987 (non-exec) Chairman; DSL Holdings Ltd 1990. *Recreations:* Racing, Opera, Croquet, Bridge.

WHITEHOUSE, Christopher Michael; Partner, Wragge & Co, since 1987; Acquisitions & Mergers, Flotations & Prospectus, Commercial. *Career:* Slaughter and May, Solicitor 1977-81. *Biog: b.* 21 October 1952. *m.* 1982, Helen (née Marshall). *Educ:* Malvern College; University of Liverpool (LLB). *Other Activities:* Chm, Birmingham Railway Museum Trust. *Clubs:* Grand Junction. *Recreations:* Railways, Photography, Travel.

WHITEHOUSE, M G; General Manager, Halifax Building Society.

WHITEHOUSE, Richard Timothy; Partner, Lovell White Durrant, since 1986; Corporate Law. *Career:* Lovell White & King 1977-88. *Biog: b.* 13 December 1952. *Nationality:* British. *m.* 1981, Alison (née Chappell). *Educ:* Dulwich College; Trinity College, Cambridge (MA). *Other Activities:* Member, City of London Solicitors' Company. *Professional Organisations:* Law Society. *Recreations:* Amateur Musical Stage.

WHITELAM, Richard John; Partner, Bacon & Woodrow, since 1985; Pensions. *Career:* Bacon & Woodrow 1979. *Biog: b.* 8 February 1958. *Nationality:* British. *m.* 1985, Clare Elizabeth (née Olive). *Educ:* Westcliff High School for Boys; Jesus College, Oxford (MA Mathematics). *Professional Organisations:* Fellow, Institute of Actuaries. *Recreations:* Walking, Cycling.

WHITELY, Miss C A; Executive Director, Chartered WestLB Limited.

WHITER, John Lindsay Pearce; Managing Partner, Neville Russell, since 1988; Audit. *Career:* Honey Barrett & Co (Eastbourne) Articled Clerk/Audit Snr 1968-72; Butt Cozens (Colchester); Brebner, Allen & Trapp Mgr 1973-74; Neville Russell Ptnr 1976-. *Biog: b.* 10 May 1950. *Nationality:* British. *m.* 1975, Janet Dulcie Sarah (née Vickery); 2 s; 1 d. *Educ:* Eastbourne Grammar School. *Other Activities:* Freeman, City of London. *Professional Organisations:* FCA. *Clubs:* The National, City of London, Bishopsgate Ward Club. *Recreations:* Golf, Squash, Tennis, Reading.

WHITEWOOD, David R H; Director, Bradstock Blunt & Crawley Ltd.

WHITFIELD, R J; Compliance Director, Charterhouse Tilney, since 1989.

WHITHAM, P B; Director, Hill Samuel & Co Ltd.

WHITHEAR, Edward Roy; Finance Director, Greenwell Montagu Stockbrokers, since 1987; Financial Control and Commercial Management. *Career:* British Airways Apprentice/Auditor/Systems Analyst 1958-65; The Observer Dep Chief Acct 1965-67; IBM (UK) Ltd Financial & Support Mgmnt 1967-77; Kingston RBC Dir of Finance & Admin 1977-78; Computer Technology Financial Dir & Co Sec 1978-80; Gestetner Manufacturing Finance Dir to Gen Mgr 1980-85; Midland Bank Group Financial/Systems Mgmnt, (International Sector) Snr Systems Mgr, Financial Controller 1985-87. *Biog: b.* 10 July 1940. *Nationality:* British. *m.* 1962, Ann (née Mager); 2 s; 1 d. *Educ:* Isleworth Grammar School. *Directorships:* Greenwell Nominees Ltd 1987 (exec); Greensward Nominees Ltd Brokers 1987 (exec); Mergelike Ltd 1987 (exec); Montagu Securities Ltd 1987 (exec); Shenfield Nominees Ltd 1987 (exec). *Professional Organisations:* FCCA; FBIM; MBCS. *Clubs:* Stocks. *Recreations:* Family, Watford FC Supporter.

WHITING, D A; Chairman, International Petroleum Exchange.

WHITLEY, Edward Thomas; Partner, Cazenove & Co, since 1988; South East Asia, Australasia. *Career:* Price Waterhouse 1976-81; Cazenove & Co 1981-. *Biog: b.* 6 May 1954. *Nationality:* British. *m.* 1984, The Hon Tara (née Chichester-Clark). *Educ:* Harrow; University of Bristol (BSc). *Directorships:* Strata Investments plc 1990 (non-exec). *Professional Organisations:* ACA.

WHITLEY, Ms Sarah Jane MacKay; Partner, Baillie Gifford & Co, since 1986; Far East Department. *Career:* Baillie Gifford, Investment Trainee 1980-. *Biog: b.* 6 August 1958. *Nationality:* British. *m.* 1987, W Graham Whyte. *Educ:* Edinburgh Academy; Somerville College, Oxford (BA Experimental Psychology). *Clubs:* Scottish Arts Club. *Recreations:* Sailing, Rowing.

WHITLING, D A; Director, London Fox.

WHITMEY, Nicholas; Partner, Theodore Goddard.

WHITNEY, John Norton Braithwaite; Chairman, Really Useful Group plc, since 1990. *Career:* Ross Radio Productions Founder 1951; Autocue, Founder/Chm 1955; Saggita Productions, Founder Dir 1968-82; Capital Radio, MD 1973-82; Consolidated Productions, Dir 1980-82; Independent Broadcasting Authority, Dir Gen 1982-89. *Biog: b.* 20 December 1930. *Nationality:* British. *m.* 1956, Roma Elizabeth (née Hodgson); 1 s; 1 d. *Educ:* Leighton Park Friends' School. *Directorships:* Friends Provident Life Office 1982 (non-exec); Really Useful Group 1989 (non-exec). *Other Activities:* Board Member, National Theatre, 1982-; Hon FRCM; FRSA; Pres, London Marriage Guidance Council, 1983-89; Board Member, Open College, 1987-89; Fellow & VP, Royal Television Society; Soundaround (National Sound Magazine for the Blind, 1981-); Artsline, 1983-; VP, RNID; Chairman, Theatre Investment Fund, 1990-; Board Member, English National Ballet, 1990-. *Clubs:* Garrick, Whitefriars, Pilgrims, Thirty. *Recreations:* Photography, Chess, Sculpting, Music.

WHITNEY, Dr Paul Michael; Chief Executive, CIN Management Ltd, since 1985; Chief Executive with overall responsibility to Trustees for investment management. *Career:* Industrial & Commercial Fin Corp Investment Controller 1980-83; CIN Industrial Investments Ltd Dir 1984-85; MD 1985-87; Industrial Investment Branch Managing Director, responsible for venture capital activities of both schemes 1985-87; CIN Management Ltd, Subsidiary company of NCB 1985-; Chief Executive 1988-. *Biog: b.* 4 May 1948. *Nationality:* British. *Educ:* Aston University (BSc Hons, PhD); Cranfield College (MBA). *Directorships:* CIN Management Ltd; Acorn Pictures Ltd; The British Investment Trust plc; Black Diamonds Pensions Ltd; CIN Agricultural Services Ltd; CIN Industrial Finance Holdings Ltd; CIN Investments plc; CIN Properties Ltd; CIN Venture Managers Ltd; CIN Venture Nominees Ltd; United Shoe Machinery Group 1987; MFI Furniture Group Ltd; Citystone Assets plc; East Anglian Real Property Co Ltd 1988; Marlvern UK Index Trust plc; MFI Furniture Group Ltd; United Shoe Machinery Group Ltd.

WHITTAKER, Geraldine; General Manager, Banque Belge Limited.

WHITTAKER, John Daniel; Partner, Clyde & Co, since 1986; Shipping, Insurance & International Trade. *Career:* Simmons & Simmons, Articled Clerk 1980-82; Clyde & Co, Solicitor 1982-86; Clyde & Co, Partner 1986-. *Biog: b.* 29 April 1956. *Nationality:* British. *m.* 1986, Nicola (née Lusty); 1 s; 1 d. *Educ:* Rossall School; Newcastle University (LLB); Max Plank Institute for Patent, Trademark & Copyright Law Munich. *Recreations:* Walking, Climbing & Family.

WHITTAKER, Miss (Rosemary) Jane; Partner, Macfarlanes, since 1989; EEC and UK Competition Law. *Career:* Macfarlanes, Solicitor. *Biog: b.* 27 February 1955. *Nationality:* British. *m.* 1988, Colin M Brown. *Educ:* Queen Mary School, Lytham St Annes; Manchester University (LLM Hons). *Professional Organisations:* International Bar Association; Law Society; Legal Committee, Chambers of Commerce. *Publications:* Articles in European Finance Director and 1992 Publications. *Clubs:* Riverside. *Recreations:* Tennis, Collecting Antiques.

WHITTEN, R E; Finance Director, Lonrho plc.

WHITTINGHAM, Leigh Nattrass; Chief Financial Officer, Jardine Insurance Brokers Ltd, since 1988; Finance. *Career:* Price Waterhouse (London) Asst Mgr - Audit 1972-79; Garnar Booth plc Group Co Sec 1979-86; Jardine Insurance Services Ltd Group Financial Controller 1986-88. *Biog: b.* 13 June 1951. *Nationality:* British. *m.* 1977, Penny (née Bush); 1 s; 2 d. *Educ:* Shrewsbury School; Newcastle-upon-Tyne University (BA). *Directorships:* Jardine Insurance Brokers Limited & Subsidiaries 1988 (exec). *Professional Organisations:* FCA. *Recreations:* Sport, Music.

WHITTINGTON, C M J; Chairman, Morgan Grenfell & Co.

WHITTINGTON, Professor Geoffrey; Price Waterhouse Professor of Financial Accounting, University of Cambridge, since 1988. *Career:* Chartered Accountants, Articled Clerk 1959-62; University of Cambridge, Research Officer 1962-72; University of Edinburgh, Professor & Head of Dept of Accounting 1972-75; University of Bristol, Professor, Head of Dept of Economics, Dean of Faculty of Social Sciences 1975-88. *Biog: b.* 21 September 1938. *Nationality:* British. *m.* 1963, Joyce E (née Smith); 2 s. *Educ:* Dudley Grammar School; LSE (BSc); Fitzwilliam College, Cambridge (MA, PhD). *Directorships:* Cambridge Econometrics 1990 (non-exec). *Other Activities:* Part-Time Member, Monopolies & Mergers Commission; Academic Adviser, Accounting Standards Board. *Professional Organisations:* FCA. *Publications:* Five Books and Over Fifty Other Publications. *Recreations:* Music, Squash, Badminton, Walking.

WHITWORTH, Francis John; Non-Executive Chairman, Merchant Navy Officers Pension Fund Trustees Ltd, since 1987. *Career:* The Cunard Steam-Ship Co Ltd, Mgmnt Trainee to Personnel Dir 1950-68; Cunard Line, MD 1968; Gp Administration, Dir 1969; British Shipping Federation General Council of British Shipping, Various to Dep Dir Gen 1972-87; International Shipping Federation, Exec Dir 1980-87. *Biog: b.* 1 May 1925. *Nationality:* British. *m.* 1956, Auriol Myfanwy Medwyn (née Hughes); 1 s; 1 d. *Educ:* Charterhouse School; Pembroke College, Oxford (MA). *Directorships:* Argosy Asset Management plc 1987 (non-exec); Merchant Navy Pensions Administration Ltd 1987 (non-exec) Chm; Pensions Ltd 1988 (non-exec) Chm; The General Council of British Shipping Contributory Pension Fund Trustees Ltd 1985 (non-exec); Conway Merchant Navy Trust 1980 (non-exec). *Other Activities:* Member, Economic and Social Ctee of the European Communities, 1986; Member, Industrial Tribunals for England and Wales, 1978. *Professional Organisations:* Barrister, Middle Temple, 1950. *Clubs:* United Oxford and Cambridge University. *Recreations:* Racing, Opera, Music, Cricket.

WHYBROW, Stephen Kennedy; Managing Partner, McKenna & Co, since 1986; Commercial. *Career:* McKenna & Co, Articled Clerk 1969; Assistant Solicitor 1971; Partner 1977; Managing Partner 1986. *Biog: b.* 13 March 1946. *Nationality:* British. *m.* 1980, Joan Annette (née Griffiths); 1 s; 1 d. *Educ:* Bishop's Stortford College; St John's College, Cambridge (MA,LLB). *Professional Organisations:* Institute of Directors; Law Society. *Publications:* Joint Author of Employment Section, Longmans Practical Commercial Precedents, 1987.

WHYSALL, William F; Partner (Nottingham), Evershed Wells & Hind.

WICHELOW, Phillip Arthur; Director, Robert Fleming & Co Ltd.

WICKHAM, Robert Joseph Johnstone; General Manager, Bank of Scotland, since 1989; UK Banking, England. *Career:* Chief Manager, Bank of Scotland, London Chief Office 1977-85; Divisional General Manager, Bank of Scotland 1985-89; General Manager, Bank of Scotland 1989-. *Biog: b.* 25 March 1934. *Nationality:* British. *m.* 1959, Isabella Margaret (née Walls); 2 d. *Educ:* Dornoch Academy. *Directorships:* Bank of Wales 1988 (non-exec). *Other Activities:* Member of the Lombard Association. *Professional Organisations:* Fellow of the Institute of Bankers in Scotland; Advanced Management Program Harvard Business School 1975. *Clubs:* Caledonian Club, Overseas Bankers Club. *Recreations:* Sailing.

WICKS, N L; Second Permanent Secretary, HM Treasury.

WIDDOWSON, D G; Partner, Hill Taylor Dickinson.

WIEGMAN, Albert Edward Bernard; Managing Director, Security Pacific Hoare Govett Equity Ventures Ltd, since 1987; Origination and Financing of Large Management Buy-Outs. *Career:* County Bank, Asst Dir, Venture Capital Subsidiary 1978-87. *Biog: b.* 4 March 1952. *Nationality:* British. *m.* m1 1973, (div), m2 1990, Gail (née Fleming); 1 s; 1 d. *Educ:* Carshalton College of Further Education; Manchester University. *Directorships:* VF International Ltd 1988 (non-exec). *Professional Organisations:* ACIB. *Clubs:* RAC. *Recreations:* Sailing, Golf.

WIELECHOWSKI, J S; Director, Phillips & Drew Fund Management Limited.

WIESNER, Miss Helena; Self-Employed (Sole Proprietor); Consumer Affairs Consultant. *Career:* Consumers' Association, Publishers of Which? Magazine 1971-89; Verifier; Various Research and Editorial Jobs; Head of Economic and Social Group, (Money, Food & Health and Public Affairs); Responsible for Research Output and for Various Outputs (Magazine, Campaigning, Books, TV etc); Personally involved in lobbying on Financial Services Act and other related topics; Self-Employed, Consumer Affairs Consultant 1989. *Biog: b.* 31 July 1945. *Nationality:* British. *Educ:* Lady Margaret Hall, Oxford University (BA Hons Physics); St Bartholomew's Medical College, London University (PhD Radiation Biology). *Directorships:* Lautro Ltd 1990 (non-exec); Investors Compensation Scheme 1990 (non-exec). *Other Activities:* Board Member, Occupational Pensions Board; Council Member, Insurance Brokers Registration Council; Consumers' Association Representative: Unit Trust Forum (set up by SIB), Quality of Information Consultative Group (set up by SIB). *Publications:* PhD Thesis: The Relative Biological Effectiveness of 15 MEV Electrons as a Function of Depth of Tissue Traversed, 1970; The Which? Book of Saving and Investing, Editor, 1982; The Which? Book of Money, 1980 and The Which? Book of Tax, 1984, Joint Editor; Numerous Articles in Which? Magazine. *Clubs:* Groucho. *Recreations:* Gardening, Reading.

WIGGINS, N C; Managing Director, Langbourn Property Investment Services Ltd. *Career:* Kleinwort Benson Investment Management Ltd, Director Responsible for Property Asset Management 1980-89. *Biog: b.* 26 November 1949. *Nationality:* British. *m.* 1970, Annie-France; 1 s. *Educ:* Christ's Hospital, Horsham; London University (BSc Econ Hons). *Directorships:* Big Yellow Self Storage Company Limited; Broad Street Mall Limited; Hallsworth (Horkesley) Limited; Hallsworth (Farmland Trust) Limited; Hallsworth Farming (Cambridgeshire) Limited; Langbourn Property Investment Services Limited; Langbourn Financial Services Limited; Langbourn Properties plc; Pentstone plc; South Street Management Limited; Kleinwort Benson Investment Management Limited -1989; Danstock Limited -1988. *Other Activities:* Member of Committee, Association of Property Unit Trusts. *Professional Organisations:* FRICS. *Recreations:* Running Slowly.

WIGGLESWORTH, Jack; Head of International Fixed Interest Investment, Henderson Administration Ltd, since 1989; Bond & Related Instruments Investment. *Career:* Phillips & Drew, Bond Economist & Salesman 1963-71; Member, Stock Exchange 1968; W Greenwell & Co, Gilt Salesman 1971-86; Partner 1973-86; Lloyds Merchant Bank, Head of Gilt Sales 1986-87; The Securities Association, Membership Committee 1987; LIFFE, Chairman, Membership Committee 1988. *Biog: b.* 9 October 1941. *Nationality:* British. *m.* 1970, Carlota Josephine (née Paz); 1 s; 1 d. *Educ:* Jesus College, Oxford (MA Hons). *Directorships:* LIFFE 1982 (non-exec); Henderson Investment Services 1989 (exec); Lloyds Bank Financial Futures 1986-87 (non-exec). *Other Activities:* TSA, Membership Committee; TSA, Individuals Registration Panel; LIFFE, Chairman, Membership & Clubs Committee. *Professional Organisations:* Society of Business Economists; Society of Investment

Analyst; Institute of Directors. *Recreations:* Reading, Gardening, Swimming, Travel, Films.

WIGHTMAN, David Richard; Senior Partner, Turner Kenneth Brown, since 1987; Corporate. *Biog: b.* 3 April 1940. *Nationality:* British. *Educ:* King's College School, Wimbledon. *Directorships:* Hydril (UK) Ltd 1982 (non-exec); Disley Paper Company Ltd 1989 (non-exec). *Other Activities:* International Construction Law Review (Editor-in-Chief); National Farmers Union; Business in the Community (Governing Council); City of London Solicitors' Company; Fellow, Royal Society of Arts. *Professional Organisations:* The Law Society; Institute of Directors; IBA; Society of Construction Law. *Clubs:* Travellers'.

WIGHTMAN, John Martin; Director, Barclays de Zoete Wedd Securities Ltd, since 1986; Corporate Finance. *Career:* David A Bevan Simpson Analyst 1968-70; de Zoete & Bevan 1970-86, Ptnr 1977. *Biog: b.* 27 January 1944. *Nationality:* British. *m.* 1970, Anne Leigh (née Paynter); 2 s; 5 d. *Educ:* The Oratory School. *Directorships:* de Zoete & Bevan 1977-86 (exec); de Zoete & Bevan Ltd 1986 (exec). *Other Activities:* General Committee, Gresham Club. *Professional Organisations:* Society of Investment Analysts. *Clubs:* Gresham. *Recreations:* Sports.

WIGHTMAN, Nigel; Managing Director, N M Rothschild Asset Management Limited, since 1988; International Investment Activities. *Career:* Samuel Montagu & Co 1976-80; Chemical Bank 1980-84; N M Rothschild Asset Management Ltd 1984-. *Biog: b.* 1953. *m.* 1987; 2 s. *Educ:* Oxford University (MA, MPhil).

WIGLEY, Carole E; Partner (Nottingham), Evershed Wells & Hind.

WIGLEY, John Robert; Partner, R Watson & Sons, since 1973; Pensions and Investment Consultancy. *Career:* Guardian Assurance Co, Actuarial Trainee 1967-69. *Biog: b.* 22 December 1945. *m.* 1973, Sam (née Major); 2 s. *Educ:* Latymer Upper School; Jesus College, Cambridge (MA). *Directorships:* CAPS Ltd 1984 (exec). *Professional Organisations:* FIA; FPMI; AMSIA; FSS.

WIKSTROM, Svante; Executive Director, Svenska International plc.

WILCOCK, Miss Susan M; Partner, Lane Clark & Peacock, since 1969; Occupational & Personal Pensions. *Career:* Lane Clark & Peacock, Actuarial Student, Qualified 1969. *Educ:* Roedean. *Other Activities:* Member of Council, Wycombe Abbey School (Chairman, Finance Ctee); Governor, Commonwealth Trust. *Professional Organisations:* Fellow, Institute of Actuaries. *Clubs:* Commonwealth Trust. *Recreations:* Walking.

WILD, David W; Partner (Derby), Evershed Wells & Hind.

WILD, Gordon; Chief Accountant, Cooperative Insurance Society Ltd, since 1984; Finance Accounting & Taxation. *Career:* J Wild & Co Chartered Accountants, Articled Clerk 1954-59; Taxation Snr 1959-63; Ernest Francis & Son, Audit Snr 1963-67; Cooperative Insurance Society Ltd, Asst Accountant 1967-84. *Biog: b.* 3 March 1938. *Nationality:* British. *m.* 1961, Joan (née Fell); 1 s; 2 d. *Educ:* Bury Grammar School. *Professional Organisations:* FCA.

WILD, Kenneth (Ken); Accounting Research Partner, Touche Ross & Co, since 1984; Financial Reporting & Company Law. *Career:* Peat Marwick Mitchell & Co, Trainee/Snr 1974-78; ICAEW Under Sec to Accounting Standards Ctee 1978-80; Touche Ross & Co, Manager 1980-84. *Biog: b.* 25 July 1949. *m.* 1974, Johanna (née Wolf); 1 s; 1 d. *Educ:* Chadderton Grammar School; University of York (BA Hons). *Other Activities:* ICAEW; Business Law Committee; Financial Reporting Commitee & Research Board. *Professional Organisations:* FCA. *Publications:* Company Accounting Requirements - A Practical Guide (Joint Author), 1985; Accounting for Associated Companies, 1982; Manual of Financial Reporting and Accounting (Joint Author). *Recreations:* Reading, Gardening.

WILD, R; Group Director, Export Credits Guarantee Department.

WILDBLOOD, P; Chief Executive, International Petroleum Exchange.

WILDE, Malcolm James; Managing Director, British & Commonwealth Merchant Bank plc, since 1987. *Career:* Western American Bank (Europe) Ltd, Mgr 1969-75; Crocker National Bank, VP 1975-77; Guinness Mahon & Co Ltd, Dir & Head of Banking 1977-87; Guinness Mahon Holdings Ltd, Dir 1986-87. *Biog: b.* 9 October 1950. *m.* 1973, Helen Elaine (née Bartley); 1 s; 2 d. *Directorships:* BCMB Group Ltd 1987 MD; British & Commonwealth Merchant Bank (Guernsey) Ltd 1988 Chm; Provincial Bank plc (non-exec); R J Shrubb & Co Ltd 1988 (non-exec). *Clubs:* Piltdown Golf Club, Overseas Bankers' Club. *Recreations:* Golf, Tennis, Antiques, Music.

WILDER, Gay E; Partner, Beachcroft Stanleys.

WILDIG, M J; Partner, Financial Markets Group, Arthur Anderson & Co, since 1984; Financial Services.

WILDISH, Nigel Denis; Partner, Turner Kenneth Brown, since 1983; Company/Commercial and Intellectual Property. *Career:* EF Turner & Sons, Articled Clerk 1970-72; Asst Solicitor 1972-74; Ptnr 1974; Turner Peacock, Ptnr 1974-83. *Biog: b.* 6 April 1948.

Nationality: British. *m.* 1978, Ruth (née Tammer); 1 s; 1 d. *Educ:* Haileybury & ISC; Clare College, Cambridge (BA). *Directorships:* Schott & Co Ltd 1987 (non-exec). *Other Activities:* Federation Against Software Theft; City of London Solicitors' Company; PCC, St James, Friern Barnet. *Professional Organisations:* International Bar Association; British Computer Society. *Clubs:* MCC, Cumberland Lawn Tennis Club. *Recreations:* Family, Church, Squash, Running, Theatre, Concerts.

WILDRIDGE, M J; Director, Lowndes Lambert Group Limited.

WILES, Rupert; Director, 3i plc, since 1989; Investment in the Larger Company. *Career:* Touche Ross & Co, Senior Manager 1977-81; 3i plc, Investment Executive 1981-89; Director 1989. *Biog: b.* 27 July 1947. *Nationality:* British. *m.* 1972, Marjorie (née Hayward); 2 s. *Educ:* Uppingham School. *Directorships:* 3i plc 1989 (exec); Allders Limited 1989 (non-exec); Gomme Limited 1988-89 (non-exec). *Professional Organisations:* FCA. *Recreations:* Tennis, Fishing, Cycling, Rambling.

WILKES, Christopher J; Partner, Beachcroft Stanleys.

WILKES, Richard Geoffrey; CBE, TD, DL; Chartered Accountant. *Career:* Bolton Bullivant & Co Chartered Accountants (Leicester), Partner 1953-69; Price Waterhouse (Leicester), Partner-in-Charge 1969-80; (London), Director, International Relations 1981-89. *Biog: b.* 12 June 1928. *Nationality:* British. *m.* 1953, Wendy (née Ward); 1 s; 3 d. *Educ:* Repton (Exhibitioner). *Directorships:* Cassidy Davis Holdings Ltd 1989 (non-exec); Chartered Accountants Compensation Scheme 1990 (non-exec) Chm; Adviser to Lloyds of London on Self-Regulation 1983-85. *Other Activities:* President, Leicestershire & Northamptonshire Society of Chartered Accountants, 1967-68; Institute of Chartered Accountants in England & Wales, Member of Council 1969-90, President 1980-81; International Federation of Accountants, Member of Council 1983-90, President 1987-90; Territorial Army, Royal Leicestershire Regt 1948-71, Commanding Officer, 4/5 Bn Royal Leicesters 1965-68, Territorial Colonel, East Midlands District 1968-71, Aide De Camp To HM Queen (TA) 1972-77; Commandant, Leicestershire Special Constabulary 1972-78; Worshipful Company of Chartered Accountants in England & Wales, Court 1977-, Junior Warden 1989-90, Senior Warden 1990-91; Governor, Care for Mentally Handicapped People 1971-; Deputy Lieutenant, Leicestershire 1967-. *Professional Organisations:* FCA. *Clubs:* Army & Navy.

WILKINS, H D F N; Director, Nicholson Chamberlain Colls Limited.

WILKINS, Nick; Director, Nicholson Chamberlain Colls Limited.

WILKINSON, Christopher; Partner, Simmons & Simmons, since 1985; Company/Corporate Finance. *Career:* Heald & Nickinson, Articled Clerk 1976-78; Assistant Solicitor 1978-80; Simmons & Simmons, Assistant Solicitor 1980-85. *Biog:* b. 11 May 1954. *Nationality:* British. *m.* 1980, Caroline Susan (née Munslow); 2 s. *Educ:* Wintringham Grammar School, Grimsby; University College, London (LLB Hons). *Professional Organisations:* Law Society. *Recreations:* Reading.

WILKINSON, Christopher John; Corporate Finance Director, Panmure Gordon & Co Ltd, since 1988. *Career:* Ernst & Whinney Snr Accountant 1979-84; Tillotson Financial Options Ltd Options Broker 1984; Panmure Gordon & Co Ltd Corp Finance Exec 1984-. *Biog:* b. 28 February 1958. *Nationality:* British. *m.* 1986, Henrietta (née Rankin); 1 s. *Educ:* Epsom College; Exeter University (BA). *Directorships:* Panmure Gordon & Co Ltd 1988 (exec). *Professional Organisations:* ACA. *Clubs:* Walton Heath Golf Club. *Recreations:* Golf, Cricket, Squash.

WILKINSON, David; Director, 3i plc, since 1989; Yorkshire & Humberside. *Career:* Spicer & Oppenheim, Chartered Accountants, Qualified 1978; Joined 3i, 1978. *Biog:* b. 30 August 1950. *Nationality:* British. *m.* Alison; 1 d. *Educ:* Liverpool University (BCom). *Directorships:* 3i plc 1989. *Professional Organisations:* Chartered Accountant.

WILKINSON, David S; Partner, Theodore Goddard.

WILKINSON, Norman; Partner, James Gentles & Son.

WILKINSON, P R; Director, County NatWest Securities Limited.

WILKS, Colin Neville Joseph; Chief Financial Officer, Lloyds Bank plc, since 1988; Exec Committee Member; Broad Range of General Management & Financial Skills. *Career:* Lloyds Bank plc 1957-; (Humberside) Regional Gen Mgr 1980-82; Gen Mgr, Planning & Mktg Div & Corp Communications Div 1982-86; (N American HQ, New York) Snr Exec VP & Gen Mgr 1986-88. *Biog:* b. 28 May 1936. *Nationality:* British. *m.* 1964, Patricia (née Waters); 2 s; 2 d. *Educ:* Secondary. *Professional Organisations:* FRSA; FIB. *Recreations:* Wood Carving.

WILL, James Robert; Partner, Shepherd & Wedderburn WS, since 1981; Corporate Law. *Career:* Tods Murray WS, Solicitor 1978-79; Clifford-Turner, Corporate Lawyer 1979-81. *Biog:* b. 30 April 1955. *Nationality:* British. *m.* 1983, Jane Anne Denham; 1 s; 1 d. *Educ:* Merchiston Castle School, Edinburgh; Aberdeen University (LLB). *Professional Organisations:* Law Society of Scotland; Writer to Her Majesty's Signet. *Clubs:* New Club. *Recreations:* Skiing, Shooting, Fishing.

WILLIAMS, A A; Director, Kellett (Holdings) Limited.

WILLIAMS, A J; Director, Macey Williams Ltd.

WILLIAMS, Alan E; Deputy Chairman, Alexander Howden Reinsurance Brokers Limited.

WILLIAMS, Andrew Christopher; Director, J Henry Schroder Wagg & Co Limited.

WILLIAMS, Charles Robert Grant; Partner, Wilde Sapte, since 1989; Shipping & International Trade. *Career:* Thomas Cooper & Stibbard, Articled Clerk 1977-79; Lovell White & King, Solicitor 1979-82; Richards Butler, Solicitor 1982-88; Wilde Sapte, Solicitor 1988-89; Partner 1989-90. *Biog:* b. 17 December 1953. *Nationality:* British. *m.* 1983, Lesley (née Dowler); 2 s. *Educ:* Shrewsbury School; University of Birmingham (LLB Hons). *Other Activities:* Member, City of London Solicitors Company; Member, The Law Society.

WILLIAMS, Clive F; Managing Director, Sun Life Europe Ltd, since 1986; Europe. *Career:* Keith Shipton & Co Ltd MD 1966-72; Abbey Life Dir Broker Div & Joint Mktg Dir 1973-74; Sedgwick Forbes UK Ltd Midland Reg Dir 1974-77; Leslie & Godwin (Holdings) Ltd Dir 1977-81; Independant Consultant 1981-83; Alexander & Alexander Ltd Dep Chm & Chief Operations Officer 1983-86. *Biog:* b. 2 April 1936. *m.* Lorna; 2 s; 1 d. *Educ:* Friars School, Bangor. *Directorships:* Sun Life Trust Management Ltd; Sun Life Global Portfolio. *Other Activities:* Governor, St Martin's School, Northwood. *Professional Organisations:* ACII. *Clubs:* RAC, Moor Park Golf Club, Duquesa Golf & Country Club. *Recreations:* Golf, Swimming.

WILLIAMS, D; Director, Jarden Morgan (UK).

WILLIAMS, D R; Managing Director, Coca-Cola & Schweppes Beverages Limited, Cadbury Schweppes plc.

WILLIAMS, David Brynle; Director & General Manager, Bank of Wales plc.

WILLIAMS, David Howard; Managing Director, Glasgow Investment Managers Ltd, since 1986; Investment Management. *Career:* Shell Intl Petroleum Co Ltd Fin Exec 1965-74; Murray Johnstone Ltd Investment Mgr 1974-78; Dir 1978-83; Dep MD 1983-85. *Biog:* b. 7 August 1944. *Nationality:* British. *m.* 1970, Phyllis Jane (née Brodie); 1 s; 1 d. *Educ:* High School of Glasgow; Glasgow University (MA Hons). *Directorships:* Murray Johnstone Ltd 1978-85 (exec); Society of Investment Analysts 1982-85 (non-exec); EFT Group plc 1987 (exec); City of Edinburgh Life Assurance Co Ltd 1987-89 (non-exec). *Professional Organisations:* Society of Investment Analysts. *Clubs:* Glasgow High School Club, Milngavie Golf Club, Royal Scottish Automobile Club,

West of Scotland Football Club, Caledonian Club. *Recreations:* Athletics, Golf, Music.

WILLIAMS, Donald James; Partner, Robson Rhodes.

WILLIAMS, Donald Lynedoch; Partner, Linklaters & Paines.

WILLIAMS, Edward F; Commercial Conveyancing Partner, Bristows Cooke & Carpmael.

WILLIAMS, G D; Director, Metheuen (Lloyds Underwriting Agents) Limited.

WILLIAMS, Geoffrey Guy; Deputy Chairman, J Henry Schroder Wagg & Co Limited.

WILLIAMS, Glyn Mark; Partner, Neville Russell, since 1990; Business Services. *Career:* Trainee Chartered Accountant, Neville Russell 1982-85; Senior Auditor, Foreign & Commonwealth Office 1985-87; Business Services Manager, Neville Russell 1987-89. *Biog: b.* 31 December 1960. *Nationality:* British. *Educ:* Eltham College; Southampton university (BSc). *Professional Organisations:* Associate of Institute of Chartered Accountants in England and Wales. *Recreations:* Most Sports.

WILLIAMS, Graham E H; Partner, MacNair Mason.

WILLIAMS, H Stephen; Partner (Birmingham), Evershed Wells & Hind.

WILLIAMS, H V; Member of Board/ Partner in charge of Insurance Dept, Jaques & Lewis, since 1988; Insurance. *Career:* Russell Jones & Walker, Partner 1980-88; Alexander Rubens, Partner 1976-80. *Biog: b.* 24 October 1950. *Nationality:* British. *m.* 1980, Gillian; 1 s; 2 d. *Educ:* Christs College, Cambridge (MA). *Other Activities:* Chairman, The Tideway Scullers School. *Professional Organisations:* Solicitor. *Publications:* Various articles in insurance publications regarding legal issues.

WILLIAMS, Howard Glyn; Chairman, Clark Whitehill, since 1990. *Career:* Partner in Charge of Investigations Group dealing with Flotations, Acquisitions, Mergers, Fund Raising & Financial Investigations. *Biog: b.* 3 September 1941. *Nationality:* British. *m.* 1970, Angela Margaret (née Fitzgerald); 1 s; 1 d. *Educ:* Kings College School, Wimbledon. *Professional Organisations:* FCA. *Recreations:* Family, Theatre, Tennis, Skiing.

WILLIAMS, Hugh Rodney; Chief Operating Officer UK, The Hongkong & Shanghai Banking Corporation, since 1988; Corporate & General Banking Services in the UK. *Career:* The Hongkong & Shanghai Banking Corporation, Posts in HK, Singapore, India 1964-85; The British Bank of the Middle East (Oman), Manager Main Office 1981-83; Area Manager 1985-87. *Biog: b.* 20 September 1941. *Nationality:* British. *m.* 1969, Sylvia

(née den Broeder); 1 s; 1 d. *Educ:* Dover College. *Directorships:* Anthony Gibbs & Sons Ltd 1988; Anthony Gibbs Benefit Consultants Ltd 1988; Anthony Gibbs (Middle East) Ltd 1988; Anthony Gibbs Securities Ltd 1988; Hongkong & Shanghai Bank (Pension Trustee) Ltd 1988; HongkongBank International Trade Finance (Holdings) Ltd 1988; HongkongBank Mortgage Fin Ltd (formerly A Gibbs & Sons Ltd) 1988; HBL Nominees Ltd 1988; James Capel Bankers Ltd 1988; James Capel Mortgage Finance Ltd 1988. *Professional Organisations:* ACIB. *Clubs:* Worplesdon Golf Club. *Recreations:* Tennis, Golf.

WILLIAMS, J D; Director, Steel Burrill Jones Group plc.

WILLIAMS, J P; Director, Baring Asset Management Ltd.

WILLIAMS, J Paul; Director, Clerical Medical Unit Trust Managers.

WILLIAMS, J R; Clerk, Gold & Silver Wyre Drawers' Company & Loriners' Company.

WILLIAMS, J T M; Director, Pechiney World Trade (Holdings) Ltd.

WILLIAMS, John F G; Partner, S J Berwin & Co.

WILLIAMS, John Kenrick; Chief UK Financial Officer, American Express Bank, since 1985; Financial Control & Taxation. *Career:* Price Waterhouse & Co Audit Snr 1968-73; Deltec International Ltd Fin Controller & Treasurer 1973-80; Trade Development Bank Fin Controller 1980-83; Samuel Montagu Fin Controller 1983-84. *Biog: b.* 27 November 1946. *Educ:* King's School, Chester. *Professional Organisations:* FCA. *Recreations:* Golf, Swimming, Reading.

WILLIAMS, K T; Director, Hambros Bank Limited.

WILLIAMS, M D; Deputy General Manager, Credit, Nomura Bank International plc.

WILLIAMS, M F; Director, Kleinwort Benson Limited.

WILLIAMS, M J R; Director, Brewin Dolphin & Co Ltd.

WILLIAMS, Martin Gwynne; Director, Credit Commercial De France (UK) Limited, since 1990; Corporate Finance. *Career:* Coopers & Lybrand 1969-81; Laurence Prust & Co/CCF Laurence Prust Ltd 1981-90; Laurence Prust & Co, Partner 1985-86. *Biog: b.* 13 March 1948. *Nationality:* British. *Educ:* Westminster School; Trinity Hall, Cambridge. *Other Activities:* Hon Treasurer, Trinity Hall Association; Governor, Arnold House School.

Professional Organisations: FCA; Member, Stock Exchange. *Clubs:* City of London, United Oxford & Cambridge University.

WILLIAMS, Sir Max; Kt; Senior Partner, Clifford Chance.

WILLIAMS, P; Director, Investors in Industry.

WILLIAMS, P J; Director, UBS Phillips & Drew Futures Limited.

WILLIAMS, Paul Joseph; Group Partner, Touche Ross & Co, since 1984; Tax. *Career:* Allan Charlesworth & Co (Liverpool), Articled Clerk 1970-74; Touche Ross & Co, Tax Snr/Mgr 1974-80; Tax Ptnr 1980-; Group Staff Ptnr 1981-84; Tax Dept, Personnel Ptnr 1982-90; Group Ptnr 1984-. *Biog: b.* 2 July 1951. *Nationality:* British. *m.* 1977, Susan Venetia (née Berendt); 4 s; 3 d. *Educ:* Ampleforth College. *Other Activities:* Member, British Property Federation Tax Ctee. *Professional Organisations:* FCA; ATII. *Clubs:* Wig & Pen. *Recreations:* Travelling with the Family, Answering the Phone.

WILLIAMS, Peter; Editor, Accountancy Age.

WILLIAMS, Philip Kendrick; Director, Hill Samuel Bank Ltd, since 1987; Investment Finance. *Biog: b.* 20 March 1941. *Nationality:* British. *m.* 1977, Susan J C (née Wellspring); 3 s. *Educ:* Epsom College; London University (BSc); Birmingham University (MSc). *Directorships:* Western National (Holdings) Ltd 1987 (non-exec).

WILLIAMS, Robert James; Partner, Linklaters & Paines.

WILLIAMS, Robin John Arthur; Partner, McKenna & Co, since 1979; Head of Commercial Litigation, Insurance and Reinsurance. *Career:* McKenna & Co, Articled Clerk 1971-73; Asst Solicitor 1973-79. *Biog: b.* 6 February 1949. *Nationality:* English; 1 s; 1 d. *Educ:* University College, Oxford (MA). *Professional Organisations:* Law Society; British Insurance Law Association; American Bar Association; Associate Member, Lloyd's. *Publications:* Comment in The Changing Insurance Market, 1989; Reoccuring Questions - Reactions, 1989; Towards a Greener Spain - Reactions, 1989; Environmental Impairment Liability Policies - Envirorisk, 1990; Environmental Risks: Who Pays the Bill? - Global Reinsurance, 1990; Current International Issues in Environmental Claims Journal, 1990. *Recreations:* Soccer, Golf, Theatre, Cooking, Gardening.

WILLIAMS, Roger; Partner, Nabarro Nathanson, since 1990; Litigation and Employment. *Career:* British Coal Corporation 1971-90; Asst Solicitor 1971-75; Deputy Regional Solicitor and Head of Litigation, East Midlands Region 1975-84; Solicitor (South Wales) 1984-88; Head of Employment Group, HQ Legal Dept 1988-90; Nabarro Nathanson, Partner 1990. *Biog: b.* 5 August 1947. *Nationality:* British. *m.* 1974, Sheila Mary (née Hyland); 2 s; 2 d. *Educ:* Lewis School, Pengam; University College of Wales, Aberystwyth (LLB Hons). *Professional Organisations:* Law Society. *Recreations:* Walking, Swimming, Reading.

WILLIAMS, Stanley Killa; Company Secretary & Solicitor, BTR plc, since 1989; Legal & Administration. *Career:* Devon County Council, Solicitor 1969-74; Oxon County Council, Assistant County Secretary 1974-80; Rowntree plc, Deputy Company Secretary 1980-89. *Biog: b.* 2 July 1945. *Nationality:* British. *m.* 1972, Dheidre Rhona (née Westerman); 1 s; 1 d. *Educ:* Bromsgrove School; Merton College, Oxford (BA, MA). *Directorships:* BTR Industrial Holdings Ltd 1989 (exec); Dunlop Ltd 1989 (exec); Thomas Tilling International Ltd 1989 (exec). *Professional Organisations:* Solicitor; Law Society. *Recreations:* Sport, Travel.

WILLIAMS, Stephen; Partner, Frere Cholmeley, since 1989; Company & Commercial. *Career:* Slaughter & May, Articled Clerk 1979-81; Assistant Solicitor 1981-85; Saunders Sobell Leigh & Dobin, Assistant Solicitor 1985-87; Frere Cholmeley, Assistant Solicitor 1987-89; Partner 1989-. *Biog: b.* 27 October 1954. *Nationality:* British. *m.* 1981, Sabina (née Salvati); 2 d. *Educ:* Magdalen College, Oxford (Italian and French). *Professional Organisations:* Member, Law Society; British-Italian Law Association. *Publications:* Contributor to Frere Cholmeley Guide to the Companies Act, 1989-90. *Recreations:* Photography, Sailing, Badminton.

WILLIAMS, Stephen Geoffrey; Joint Secretary, Unilever plc, since 1986. *Career:* Slaughter & May, Solicitor 1972-75; Imperial Chemicals Industries plc, Legal Adviser 1975-84; Assistant Company Secretary 1984-86; Unilever plc, Joint Secretary 1986-. *Biog: b.* 31 January 1948. *Nationality:* British. *m.* 1972, Susan (née Cottam); 1 s. *Educ:* Brentwood School, Essex; King's College London (LLB Hons). *Directorships:* Associated Enterprises Limited 1986 (exec); Margarine Union (1930) 1986 (exec); Unilever Employee Benefit Trustees Limited 1990 (exec). *Other Activities:* Companies Committee, Confederation of British Industry; Law Society's Company Law Committee; Company Secretaries Group. *Professional Organisations:* Law Society. *Clubs:* RAC, Euston, 2 Brydges Place. *Recreations:* Contemporary Art, Professional Football, 20th Century Fiction, Cinema, Swimming.

WILLIAMS, T; General Manager, Anderson, Squires Ltd.

WILLIAMS, T G; Director, County NatWest Securities Limited.

WILLIAMSON, Andrew J; Partner, Walker Morris Scott Turnbull.

WILLIAMSON, David Simon; Director, Granville & Co Ltd, since 1988; Corporate Finance. *Career:* Lovell White & King, Solicitor 1980-83; Granville & Co Ltd 1983-. *Biog: b.* 9 October 1957. *Nationality:* British. *m.* 1987, Lisa (née Solcati); 1 s. *Educ:* Millfield School; Christ Church, Oxford (MA). *Directorships:* RFS Industries Ltd 1987 (non-exec); Priday Metford & Co Ltd 1988 (non-exec); Norman Magnetics Ltd 1988 (non-exec); Onix Group Ltd 1990 (non-exec). *Professional Organisations:* Solicitor.

WILLIAMSON, David Thomas; Group Taxation Manager, Harrisons & Crosfield plc, since 1978; Taxation Worldwide. *Career:* Inland Revenue, Tax Officer (Higher Grade), Section Leader 1962-65; Thomson McLintock & Co, Senior Tax Assistant, Mixed Client Base 1965-71; Trafalgar House Investments Ltd, Tax Assistant, UK Corporation Tax 1971-76; Inco Europe Ltd, Senior Tax Assistant, UK and European Tax 1976-78. *Biog: b.* 16 April 1942. *Nationality:* British. *m.* 1976, Jacqueline Patricia (née Heaton). *Educ:* The Grammar School, Hampton, Middx. *Professional Organisations:* Associate, The Institute of Taxation. *Recreations:* Squash, DIY.

WILLIAMSON, G A; Partner, Cameron Markby Hewitt.

WILLIAMSON, J M M; Director, County NatWest Securities Limited.

WILLIAMSON, M J; Finance Director, Gresham Underwriting Agencies Limited.

WILLIAMSON, Michael Richard; Director, S G Warburg Akroyd Rowe & Pitman Mullens Securities, since 1987; Financing Division. *Career:* Continental Illinois National Bank & Trust Company of Chicago, 2nd VP, Multinational Banking Div 1977-80; Continental Illinois Ltd, Mgr, Syndicate 1980-82; Samuel Montagu & Co Ltd, Asst Dir, Intl Capital Mkts 1982-85. *Biog: b.* 2 December 1954. *Nationality:* British. *m.* 1982, Anne (née Campbell); 2 s. *Educ:* Glenaemond; St Andrews University (MA); LSE (MSc).

WILLIAMSON, Neil Morton; Managing Director, 3i Corporate Finance Limited, since 1979; Corporate Finance. *Career:* Henry Ansbacher & Co Limited 1965-78; Director 1972-78; 3i Corporate Finance Limited 1978-. *Biog: b.* 14 May 1943. *Nationality:* British. *Educ:* Tonbridge School; Worcester College, Oxford (MA Jurisprudence). *Directorships:* 3i Corporate Finance Limited; Ashdown House School Trust Limited; Pellipar Investments Limited; Tonbridge School Clubs Limited; Tonbridge Services Limited; Skinners' Investment Company Limited; Skinners' (Cheapside) Limited; Waterloo Ven-

tures Inc. *Other Activities:* Court of Skinners' Company. *Clubs:* East India Club. *Recreations:* Golf.

WILLIAMSON, Robert Brian; CBE; Chairman, Gerrard & National Holdings plc, since 1989. *Biog: b.* 16 February 1945. *Nationality:* British. *m.* 1986, Diane (née de Jacquier de Rosee). *Educ:* Trinity College, Dublin. *Directorships:* LIFFE 1985 Board Dir; GNI Ltd 1985-89 Chm; Securities & Investment Board 1986; Bank of Ireland Britain Holdings Board 1986; Court of the Bank of Ireland 1990; The Fleming International High Income Investment Trust plc 1990. *Other Activities:* Council Member, The British Invisible Exports Council, 1985-88 (European Ctee Member, 1985-).

WILLIAMSON, Rodney Turner; Senior Vice President, Frank B Hall & Co Overseas Inc.

WILLINS, John; Partner, James Gentles & Son.

WILLIS, Antony Martin Derek; Head of Litigation, Clifford Chance, since 1989; *Career:* Justice Department and Practices in Wellington before qualification in 1965; Perry Wylie Pope & Page, Barristers & Solicitors, Wellington; Coward Chance, London 1970-; London, Partner Litigation Department 1973; Managing Partner 1987; Clifford Chance, Joint Managing Partner 1987. *Biog: b.* 29 November 1941. *Nationality:* New Zealand. *m.* 1975, Tilly; 1 s; 5 d (including 3 from previous marriage). *Educ:* Wanganui Collegiate School, Wanganui; Victoria University of Wellington (LLB). *Other Activities:* Wellington District Law Society; Law Society of England and Wales; City of London Solicitors Company; International Bar Association; Lawasia; Associate, Institute of Arbitrators; American Arbitration Association. *Professional Organisations:* Barrister and Solicitor, High Court of New Zealand; Solicitor, Supreme Court of England and Wales; Solicitor, Supreme Court of Hong Kong. *Clubs:* Reform, Hurlingham.

WILLIS, David; Head of Private Clients Department, Frere Cholmeley, since 1989; Taxation/Trusts/Family Law.

WILLISON, William David; Senior Vice President & Head Intl Systems Infrastructure, Morgan Guaranty Trust Company of New York, since 1989; Technology Infrastructure. *Career:* IBM UK Ltd, Various Positions in Systems Engineering and Product Management 1963-74; Logica, Principal Consultant 1974-77. *Biog: b.* 6 July 1941. *Nationality:* British. *m.* Jillian; 1 s; 2 d. *Educ:* Marlborough College; King's College, London University (BSc). *Recreations:* Theatre, Reading, Gardening, Sailing.

WILLOTT, Dr (William) Brian; Under Secretary, Financial Services Division, Department of Trade & Industry, since 1987; Regulation of Financial Services. *Career:* University of Maryland Research Associate 1965-

67; Board of Trade Various 1967-73; Treasury Principal 1973-75; Department of Industry Asst Sec 1975-80; National Enterprise Board, British Technology Group Sec, then Chief Exec 1980-84; Dept of Trade and Industry Under-Sec 1980-. *Biog: b.* 14 May 1940. *Nationality:* British. *m.* 1970, Alison (née Pyke-Lees); 2 s; 2 d. *Educ:* Queen Elizabeth Grammar School, Wakefield; Trinity College, Cambridge (MA, PhD). *Recreations:* Music, Walking, Ancient History, Gardening.

WILLOUGHBY, Professor Peter Geoffrey; Partner, Turner Kenneth Brown, since 1986; Vat, Hong Kong Taxation, Training & Recruitment. *Career:* Solicitor 1962; College of Law, Lecturer 1962; Nigerian Law School, Snr Lecturer 1962-66; College of Law, Lecturer 1966-69; Snr Lecturer 1969-72; Principal Lecturer 1972-73; University of Hong Kong, Dir, Professional Legal Education 1973-75; Peter C Wong & Co, Consultant 1973-85; University of Hong Kong, Professor of Law 1975-86. *Biog: b.* 17 February 1937. *Nationality:* British. *m.* 1962, Ruth M (née Brunwin); 1 s; 1 d. *Educ:* Merchant Taylors' School; London School of Economics (LLB, LLM, Solicitor Hons). *Other Activities:* City of London Solicitors' Company; The Law Society's VAT Sub-Ctee; The Law Society's Revenue Law Committee; JP (Hong Kong); Chm, HK Joint Taxation Liaison Ctee; Member, HK Standing Ctee on Company Law Reform; HK Air Traffic Licensing Authority; HK Inland Revenue Board of Review. *Professional Organisations:* The Law Society; Nigerian Bar Assoc; Law Society of Hong Kong. *Publications:* Hong Kong Revenue Law, Vols 1, 2 & 3, 1981; Articles in Journals. *Clubs:* Royal Ocean Racing Club, Royal Fowey Yacht Club, Royal Hong Kong Yacht Club, Law Society Yacht Club, Middlesex County Cricket Club. *Recreations:* Sailing, Cricket, Rugby, Gardening, Siamese Cats, Model Ships, Railways, Wine.

WILLOUGHBY, Phillip John; Partner, Clark Whitehill, since 1968; Audit - Financial Sector, Offshore , Far East & Nigeria, Fraud Investigations. *Career:* Predecessor Firms 1957. *Biog: b.* 6 October 1939. *Nationality:* British. *m.* 1964, Susan Elizabeth (née Humphriss); 1 s; 1 d. *Educ:* Merchant Taylors' School. *Directorships:* Pottery & Glass Trades Benevolent Institution 1974 Hon Treasurer; 1980-81 Chm. *Other Activities:* JP (City of London Bench); Governor, City of London Freemens School; Worshipful Company of Glass Sellers (Master 1986-87, Hon Clerk 1976-89); Hon. Treasurer, Bishopsgate Ward Club; Council Member, City Livery Club; Governor, Northwood College for Girls (1987). *Professional Organisations:* FCA. *Clubs:* MCC, City Livery Club, Moor Park Golf Club, Castletown Golf Club. *Recreations:* Music, Wine, Cricket, Golf, Sea Fishing.

WILLOUGHBY, R W; Finance Director, Mobil Oil Company.

WILLOUGHBY, Thomas Jeremy; Director, Co Sec, Solicitor, Compliance Dir, Gartmore Investment Management Ltd, since 1989. *Career:* Lloyds and Bolsa International Ltd, Research Officer 1971-73; Open University, Part-Time Tutor 1972-73; Addleshaw Sons & Latham, Articled Clerk 1973-76; Philip Con & Co, Assistant Solicitor 1977-78; Messrs Allen & Overy, Assistant Solicitor 1978-81; Gartmore Investment Management Ltd 1981-88; Solicitor/Asst Dir & Asst Co Sec to Gartmore Group of Companies; Director and Secretary of a number of subsidiaries 1981-88; Company Secretary, Solicitor, and Compliance Officer with direct responsibility to the Chairman/Chief Executive 1989-. *Biog: b.* 3 June 1948. *Nationality:* British. *Educ:* University College of Wales, Aberystwyth (IIi Political Science); London School of Economics and Political Science (MA Latin American Studies). *Directorships:* Gartmore Investment Management Ltd 1989 (exec); Gartmore Investment Ltd 1989 (exec); Gartmore Investment Trust Management Ltd 1983 (exec); Gartmore Money Management Ltd 1989 (exec); Gartmore Overseas Ltd 1989 (exec); Gartmore Pension Fund Trustees Ltd 1988 (exec). *Professional Organisations:* Qualified as a Solicitor in 1977. *Clubs:* Groucho's, City of London Club, MCC. *Recreations:* Opera, Theatre, Art, Squash, Collecting Prime Miniterial memorabilia.

WILLS, David John; Managing Director, Brown Shipley Development Capital Ltd, since 1987; Development Capital. *Career:* Charterhouse Development Capital Ltd Dir 1980-86. *Biog: b.* 22 September 1946. *Educ:* Uppingham School; London University (BSc); London Business School (MSc). *Directorships:* Brown Shipley Development Capital; Brown Shipley Venture Managers. *Professional Organisations:* Business Graduates' Assoc. *Clubs:* Brooks's.

WILLS, Derek; Marine Underwriter at Lloyd's & Partner, Barder Marsh.

WILLS, Sir John; Bt, TD, JP; Chairman, Bristol & West Building Society. *Career:* Served Coldstream Guards 1946-49; North Somerset Yeomanry 1954-67; Brevet Colonel 1967; Honorary Captain, Royal Navy Reserve 1988; Honorary Colonel, 37th (Wessex and Welsh) Signal Regiment 1975-87; Formerly Alderman of Somerset County Council and a Deputy Lieutenant for Somerset; High Sheriff of Somerset 1968. *Biog: b.* 3 July 1928. *m.* 1953; 4 s. *Educ:* Eton; Royal Agricultural College, Cirencester. *Directorships:* Bristol Waterworks Company Chm; Bristol Evening Post Dep Chm; Bristol United Press Dep Chm. *Other Activities:* Member, National Water Council; Chairman, Wessex Water Authority, 1973-82; Lord-Lieutenant and Keeper of the Rolls of the County of Avon since 1974-; Knight of the Order of St John of Jerusalem, 1978; Pro Chancellor of the University of Bath, 1979-; Patron: Avon Wildlife Trust; Bristol Branch, The Royal Commonwealth Society; Somerset and South Avon Branch, Royal British

Legion; President: Abbeyfield Weston-Super-Mare Society; Avon Community Council; Avon Scout Association; Avon/Somerset Branch, Country Landowners Association; Avon Talking Magazine Association for the Blind; Avon Youth Association; Bristol Contributory Welfare Association; Council of the Order of St John for Avon; Council of the St Monica Home of Rest; Royal Bath and West and Southern Counties Society, 1979-80 (Dep Pres 1985-86); Somerset and South Avon Magistrates' Association; Territorial Auxiliary and Volunteer Reserve Association for Western Wessex, 1979-81 and 1989-. *Professional Organisations:* FRICS; Hon LLD, University of Bristol; Member, Society of Merchant Venturers (Master 1985-86).

WILLS, M D; Executive Director, James R Knowles Limited.

WILLS, R M; Partner, Field Fisher Waterhouse.

WILLSMORE, R W; Secretary, Shell Contributory Pension Fund.

WILLSON, Ronald; General Manager, Business Development, Republic National Bank of New York.

WILLSON, Stephen Phillip; Partner, S J Berwin & Co, since 1982; Head of Property Department. *Career:* Burton & Ramsden (Solicitors), Articled Clerk 1966-71; Assistant Solicitor 1971-73; Partner 1973-82. *Biog: b.* 27 July 1948. *Nationality:* British. *m.* 1975, Susan Mary (née Hunter); 1 s; 2 d. *Educ:* Battisborough School, Plymouth; College of Law (Solicitor). *Directorships:* Private Companies Only. *Professional Organisations:* Solicitor; Member, Law Society. *Clubs:* RAC. *Recreations:* Squash, Tennis, Country Persuits.

WILMOT SITWELL, Peter Sacheverell; Chairman, Warburg Securities, since 1986; Vice Chairman, S G Warburg Group plc. *Career:* Hambros Bank Trainee 1958; Rowe & Pitman Trainee 1959; Ptnr 1960; Snr Ptnr 1982-86. *Biog: b.* 28 March 1935. *m.* 1960, Clare Veronica (née Cobbold); 2 s; 1 d. *Educ:* Eton College; Worcester College, Oxford (BA Hons). *Directorships:* W H Smith plc 1987 (non-exec); S G Warburg Group plc 1987 Vice-Chm. *Clubs:* White's, Pratt's. *Recreations:* Shooting, Golf, Tennis.

WILSON, Alan John; Partner, Clay & Partners.

WILSON, Anthony Charles; Director, Barclays de Zoete Wedd Securities Ltd.

WILSON, Anthony P J; Executive Director, Daiwa Europe Ltd, since 1989; Short & Medium Term Securities (Euro Communities Paper & Euro Medium Term Notes). *Career:* Bank of Nova Scotia, Commercial Banking Division 1971-80; Wood Gundy, Fixed Income Dept, Sales & Trading 1980-85; Citicorp, Commercial

Paper, Trading 1985-86; Lloyds Merchant Bank, Commercial Paper, Dept Head 1986-87; Daiwa Europe Ltd, Commercial Paper, Dept Head 1987-. *Biog: b.* 12 June 1948. *Nationality:* British. *m.* 1972, Sarah B (née James); 1 s; 1 d. *Educ:* Harrow School. *Other Activities:* Chairman, Euro Commercial Paper Association. *Professional Organisations:* Fellow, Institute of Canadian Bankers (FICB). *Clubs:* Hurlingham & Queen's Clubs. *Recreations:* Real Tennis, Racquets, Bridge, Travel.

WILSON, Brian John; Partner in Charge of Specialist Industries, Ernst & Young, since 1988. *Career:* Charles Comins & Co, Articled Clerk 1960-66; Ernst & Whinney 1966-; Ptnr 1973-. *Biog: b.* 17 May 1944. *Nationality:* British. *m.* 1966, Pamela (née Wansell); 2 d. *Educ:* Enfield Grammar School. *Professional Organisations:* FCA. *Recreations:* Sailing.

WILSON, Brian Kenneth; Partner, Bacon & Woodrow, since 1983; Pensions Research. *Career:* Dulwich College, Assistant Master 1971-74; The King's School, Canterbury, Assistant Master 1974-76; Bacon & Woodrow, Actuarial Staff 1976-83. *Biog: b.* 8 October 1947. *Nationality:* British. *m.* 1972, Susan Lynda (née Elbourne); 1 s; 1 d. *Educ:* Lewes County Grammar School; Oriel College, Oxford (MA). *Professional Organisations:* Fellow, The Institute of Actuaries.

WILSON, C E; Director, Hambros Bank Limited.

WILSON, D R; Finance Director, Slough Estates plc, since 1986; Finance and Treasury. *Career:* Wilkinson Match Ltd, Financial Controller 1978-82; Cadbury Schweppes plc, Director of Finance 1982-86. *Biog: b.* 10 October 1944. *Nationality:* British; *m.* 1 s; 1 d. *Educ:* Bristol University (BA). *Professional Organisations:* FCA.

WILSON, Sir David; Bt; Senior Tax Partner, Simmons & Simmons.

WILSON, David Philip; Manager, Banca Nazionale del Lavoro, since 1973; General. *Career:* Martins Bank Ltd (West End Branches) 1949-57; Foreign Exchange Dealer 1957-60; Seconded to BNCI (Paris) Stagiaire; (Liverpool) Asst Mgr, Overseas Branch 1961-64; (Manchester) Mgr, Overseas Branch 1965-66; (London) Dep Mgr, Chief Overseas Branch 1967-68; Martins Bank acquired by Barclays Bank Mgr, West End Foreign Branch 1968-69; (Chicago) Rep, responsible for the Opening of the Barclays Group of Banks 1969-70; Mgr, Chief Foreign Branch 1971-72; Barclays Bank International Intl Mgr 1972-73; Banca Nazionale del Lavoro Established London Branch 1973-; (Singapore) Gen Mgr 1984-85. *Biog: b.* 6 February 1928. *Nationality:* British. *m.* 1952, Mary Leslie (née Armstrong); 1 s; 1 d. *Educ:* Alleyn's School, Dulwich; International Banking Summer School, Moscow; Administrative Staff College, Henley-on-Thames. *Professional Organisations:* MIB.

Clubs: Overseas Bankers, MCC, Bath & County. *Recreations:* Golf, Cricket, Choral Music.

WILSON, David Thomas; Head of Marketing and of Business Services, Ernst & Young, since 1990. *Career:* Ernst & Young 1970-; Qualified Chartered Accountant 1973; Seconded Singapore 1977-80; Partner 1982; Head of Computer Audit 1982-89; Head of Business Services 1985-; Head of Marketing 1990-. *Biog: b.* 24 November 1947. *Nationality:* British. *m.* 1985, Judith (née Hindshaw); 1 s; 1 d. *Educ:* Battersea Grammar School; Southampton University (BSc 2i Economics). *Professional Organisations:* Institute of Chartered Accountants, England & Wales, 1973. *Recreations:* Soccer, Squash, Hill-Walking, Cooking, Travel.

WILSON III, Don M; European Regional Manager & General Manager London Branch, Chemical Bank.

WILSON, Duncan M; Director, Charterhouse Bank Ltd, since 1988; Capital Markets. *Career:* Chemical Bank, Treasury 1980-82; Manager, Treasury 1982-83; Assistant Vice President, Treasury 1983-85; Charterhouse Bank, Manager 1985-87; Assistant Director 1987-88. *Biog: b.* 14 May 1957. *Nationality:* British. *Educ:* Winchester College; Bristol University (LLB). *Professional Organisations:* Barrister at Law; Member, Inner Temple. *Recreations:* Tennis, Skiing.

WILSON, The Hon Geoffrey Hazlitt; Chairman, Delta plc, since 1982. *Directorships:* Johnson Matthey (non-exec).

WILSON, Graham; Finance Director, United Newspapers plc, since 1982; Finance Director, Chairman Information Services Division. *Career:* Trident Television, Company Secretary 1979-82; Crosse & Crosse Solicitors, Partner 1972-79; Regular Army, Officer 1963-71. *Biog: b.* 23 January 1943. *Nationality:* British. *m.* 1969, Mary; 2 s; 1 d. *Educ:* Sevenoaks School; Wadham College, Oxford (MA). *Directorships:* United Newspapers plc. *Clubs:* Travellers.

WILSON, Guy Edward Nairne Sandilands; Partner, Ernst & Whinney, since 1979; Corporate Finance. *Career:* Ernst & Whinney 1967-; Currently on Secondment to HM Treasury. *Biog: b.* 10 April 1948. *Nationality:* British. *m.* 1979, Sue (née D'Arcy Clark); 2 s. *Educ:* Eton College; Aix-en-Provence University. *Professional Organisations:* FCA. *Clubs:* Brooks's, MCC, Royal St George's Golf Club, IZ, Berkshire Golf Club. *Recreations:* Golf, Cricket, Football, Tennis, Squash.

WILSON, Guy Neave; Partner, Allen & Overy, since 1972; Corporate Finance. *Career:* Allen & Overy, Articled Clerk 1964-66; Asst Solicitor 1966-72. *Biog: b.* 4 June 1942. *m.* 1978, Annabel Alexandra (née Crone); 1 s; 2 d. *Educ:* Westminster School; Trinity College, Cambridge (BA). *Other Activities:* City of London Solici-

tors' Company. *Professional Organisations:* The Law Society. *Recreations:* Family, Walking, Skiing, Sailing.

WILSON, I M; Partner, Milne Ross.

WILSON, I R; Chief Executive & Director, Charlton Seal Schaverien Limited.

WILSON, J A; Partner, Field Fisher Waterhouse.

WILSON, J H; Partner, Pensions (Epsom), Bacon & Woodrow.

WILSON, John Frederick Reynell; Director, Kleinwort Benson Securities.

WILSON, Keith John; Director, Henry Cooke Lumsden plc; Investment Dept. *Biog: b.* 15 May 1944. *Nationality:* British; 2 s. *Directorships:* Arkwright Management Ltd.

WILSON, Kevin Michael Hamilton; Director, Lazard Brothers & Co; Manager, Lazard Money Broking Ltd.

WILSON, Lyn S; Director, Friends' Provident Life Office.

WILSON, M H; Director, Morgan Grenfell & Co Limited.

WILSON, Margaret Faye (née Perry); Managing Director & SVP, Security Pacific Hoare Govett.

WILSON, Michael Gerald; Partner, Berwin Leighton (Solicitors), since 1979; Commercial Litigation. *Biog: b.* 6 December 1942. *Nationality:* British. *m.* 1965, Maureen Brenda (née Hiron); 1 s; 1 d. *Directorships:* Spreckley Villers Hunt & Co Ltd 1987 (non-exec). *Other Activities:* Freeman, City of London; Member, The City of London Solicitors' Company. *Professional Organisations:* Law Society; IBA; South Western Legal Foundation; Asian Pacific Lawyers Association; Associate Member, Lloyd's of London. *Recreations:* Tennis, Squash, Swimming, Travel, Reading, Music.

WILSON, Michael Sumner; Group Chief Executive, Allied Dunbar Assurance plc, since 1988. *Career:* Equity & Law 1963-68; Abbey Life, Broker Manager 1968-70; Hambro Life/Allied Dunbar 1971-; Executive Director 1973; Main Board Director 1976; Deputy Managing Director 1982; Managing Director 1984; Group Chief Executive 1988. *Biog: b.* 5 December 1943. *Nationality:* British. *m.* 1975, Mary (née Drysdale); 1 d. *Educ:* St Edwards School, Oxford. *Other Activities:* Member of Lloyd's; Trustee, Mental Health Foundation. *Professional Organisations:* Honorary Life Member, Life Insurance Association. *Recreations:* Tennis, Racing.

WILSON, Nicholas Samuel; Member, Executive Committee, National Westminster Bank plc, since 1990. *Career:* National Service, Royal Artillery 2nd Lt 1954-56; Keeble Hawson, Steele Carr & Co, Articled Clerk 1956-61; Harvard University (Law School), Post-Graduate Student 1961-62; University of California (Berkeley), Post-Graduate Student 1962-63; Slaughter and May, Asst Solicitor 1963-67; Partner 1968-90. *Biog: b.* 27 September 1935. *Nationality:* British. *m.* 1982, Penelope Mary Elizabeth (née Hewetson-Brown); 2 s; 1 d. *Educ:* Repton School; Sheffield University (LLB); Harvard University (LLM); University of California at Berkeley, Law School (Post Graduate Research). *Other Activities:* Chairman, City Capital Markets Ctee; City of London Solicitors' Company. *Professional Organisations:* The Law Society. *Recreations:* Music, Gardening.

WILSON, Nigel Richard; Director, C S Investments Ltd, since 1988; Charities and Private Client Dept. *Career:* McAnally Montgomery & Co, Ptnr 1970-82; Private Client, Ptnr 1980-82; Mgmnt Ctee 1982-83; Laing & Cruickshank, Dir 1982-88; Private Client, Mgmnt Ctee 1982-88; Responsible for Front Office Computer Systems 1983-88; Unit Trusts & Client Deposits 1984-88; Man Dir, Investment Mgmnt Div 1987-88; CL-Alexanders Laing & Cruickshank Main Board, Dir 1987-88. *Biog: b.* 18 February 1946. *Nationality:* British. *m.* 1 s; 1 d. *Educ:* Radley College. *Directorships:* C S Investment Management Ltd 1988 (exec); CSIM Nominees Ltd 1988. *Other Activities:* Chm, Ski Club of Great Britain, 1979-82; Director, National SK: Federation, 1979-82; Multiple Sclerosis Finance Ctee, 1983-. *Professional Organisations:* Member, International Stock Exchange, 1970-. *Publications:* Editor, Silk Cut Ski Guide, 1974. *Clubs:* Ski Club of Great Britain. *Recreations:* Skiing, Tennis, Cricket, Fishing, Shooting.

WILSON, P F; DFC; Clerk, Bakers' Company.

WILSON, Patrick Nicholas Gerald; Director, County NatWest Ltd, since 1988; Corporate Finance. *Career:* Grieveson Grant & Co, Investment Analyst 1977-79; Capel-Cure Myers, Investment Analyst & Corp Fin Exec 1979-83; County Bank Corp Fin Dept 1983-. *Biog: b.* 23 February 1956. *Nationality:* British. *m.* 1984, Nicola Suzanne (née Newton); 2 d. *Educ:* Buckhurst Hill County High; Jesus College, Cambridge (BA Hons). *Clubs:* London Rowing Club, Leander Club. *Recreations:* Rowing, Skiing, Gardening, Horse Racing.

WILSON, Philip Derek; Senior Manager, Development Capital, AIB Capital Markets plc, since 1986; Venture/Development Capital. *Career:* Arthur Andersen & Co Staff Snr, Audit Div 1978-82; Staff Snr, Mgmnt Consultancy Div 1982-83; Investors In Industry plc Investment Controller 1983-86. *Biog: b.* 18 July 1957. *Nationality:* British. *m.* 1988, Susan (née Lennon); 1 s. *Educ:* Peter Symonds College, Winchester; Gonville & Caius College, Cambridge (BA). *Directorships:* Alumet

Systems Ltd 1989 (non-exec); AIB Venture Capital Ltd 1989 (non-exec). *Professional Organisations:* ACA. *Recreations:* Flying.

WILSON, R G; Partner, Holman Fenwick & Willan.

WILSON, R J; Deputy Secretary, HM Treasury.

WILSON, R M A; Director, Hoare Govett Corporate Finance Limited.

WILSON, Richard; Assistant General Manager, Saudi International Bank.

WILSON, Robert Henry; Director, International Marketing, James Capel Fund Managers Ltd, since 1985; Global Marketing of Fund Management Services. *Career:* Estabrook & Co, European Equity Analyst 1964-67; James Capel & Co Ptnr, Head of European Dept 1967-76; Ptnr, Head of Intl Bonds 1976-81; Ptnr & Fund Mgr 1981-85. *Biog: b.* 22 February 1939. *Nationality:* British. *m.* 1965, Anne Christine (née Pypendop); 1 s; 1 d. *Educ:* Whitby Grammar School, N Yorks. *Clubs:* City of London Club. *Recreations:* Jogging, Sailing, Travel.

WILSON, Stewart Roger Devine; Director, Lowndes Lambert Group Ltd.

WILSON, Tom; Partner in Charge of Corporate Finance, Price Waterhouse.

WILSON, W D; Partner, Pannell Kerr Forster.

WILSON, William Moore; Chairman and Chief Executive, Alexander & Alexander Europe plc, since 1989. *Career:* Stenhouse Holdings Ltd (Glasgow), Group Accountant 1961-64; Secretary 1964-66; Finance Director 1966-73; Reed Stenhouse Companies Limited (Toronto), Vice-President Finance & Chief Financial Officer 1973-79; President & Chief Executive Officer 1979-88; Alexander & Alexander International Inc (New York), Chairman & Chief Executive Officer 1985-88; Director 1985-; Executive Vice President 1987-89. *Biog: b.* 21 May 1937. *Nationality:* British. *m.* 1966, Margaret (née Spalding); 1 s; 2 d. *Educ:* Merchiston Castle School, Edinburgh; Deloittes, Glasgow (CA Apprenticeship); Post-Qualifying, Peat Marwick, Mitchell, Glasgow 1960-61. *Directorships:* Alexander & Alexander Services Inc (New York) Dep Chm; Reed Stenhouse Companies Limited (Toronto); Noble Grossart Ltd, Edinburgh (Merchant Bankers). *Professional Organisations:* Member, Institute of Chartered Accountants of Scotland. *Clubs:* Royal Canadian Yacht Toronto, Royal Scottish Automobile Glasgow, Caledonian London; Toronto Toronto. *Recreations:* Yachting, Skiing, Cycling.

WILTSHIRE, H P; Chairman & Managing Director, J H Rayner (Mincing Lane).

WINCKLER, Andrew; Deputy Chairman, European Capital Company Limited, since 1990; Corporate Finance. *Career:* H M Treasury 1970-78; British Embassy, Washington DC USA, First Secretary (Financial) 1978-81; H M Treasury 1981-82; Lloyds Bank International 1982-85; Lloyds Merchant Bank, Director 1985-87; Security Pacific Hoare Govett Limited, Executive Director; Corporate Finance Limited, Divisional Director 1987-90; European Capital, Deputy Chairman 1990-. *Biog: b.* 8 January 1949. *Nationality:* British. *m.* 1971, Marie; 3 s. *Educ:* Bedford Modern School; Christ's College, Cambridge (MA, Dip Econ). *Directorships:* The Securities Association Deputy Chairman. *Clubs:* United Oxford and Cambridge University Club. *Recreations:* Gardening, White Water Rafting.

WINDMILL, Robert John; Partner, McKenna & Co, since 1976; Head of Mergers & Acquisitions Dept, Partnerships, Corporate Litigation & Japan. *Career:* Freshfields, Assistant Solicitor 1964-69; Clifford Chance, Assistant Solicitor 1971-73; McKenna & Co, Assistant Solicitor 1973-76. *Biog: b.* 30 October 1941. *Nationality:* British. *m.* 1990, Lesley; 3 d. *Educ:* Blundell School, Tiverton. *Directorships:* National Heritage Ltd; Debat Ethical & Cosmetic Preparations; Scottish Trust Managers Ltd; Gresham Street Nominees Ltd; Harvey Hubbell Ltd; Grelco Ltd; Grelco Realisations Ltd; Crofthill Investments Ltd; Oberman (Watford) Ltd; LaBour Pump Company Ltd; Linhay Meats Ltd; Fairlawn Ltd; Dickensons Quality Meats Ltd; Colquoun Lowson & Co Ltd; Chattem (UK) Ltd; Inveresk Secretaries Ltd; Kumagai Glengate Ltd; Katun (UK) Ltd; Carlton Cards Ltd; Leaning Tower Restaurant Ltd; Casa Porrelli (Kensington) Ltd; Kumagai Glengate (Properties) Ltd; Kumagai Gumi UK Ltd. *Other Activities:* City of London Solicitors Company. *Professional Organisations:* The Law Society; City of London Law Society. *Clubs:* Little Ship Club, Royal Motor Yacht Club. *Recreations:* Fishing, Shooting, Power Boat Racing.

WINKWORTH, M J B; Director of Finance, Berwin Leighton, since 1982. *Career:* Price Waterhouse & Co, Chartered Accountants 1969-77; Coopers & Lybrand (Canada), Chartered Accountants 1977-78; General Guarantee Corporation Ltd, Company Secretary 1978-80; Forward Trust Group, Financial Planning Manager 1980-82. *Biog: b.* 21 March 1947. *Nationality:* British. *m.* 1972, Janis; 1 s; 1 d. *Educ:* Royal Naval School, Malta GC; University of Exeter (BSc Engineering Science). *Professional Organisations:* Fellow, Institute of Chartered Accountants of England & Wales. *Clubs:* Little Ship Club. *Recreations:* Sailing, Rugby, Soccer.

WINKWORTH, Peter Leslie; Director, Close Brothers Group plc, since 1984; Corporate Finance. *Career:* JH Champness, Corderoy, Beesley & Co Articled Clerk 1966-70; Peat Marwick Mitchell & Co Accountant 1970-73; Baring Brothers & Co Ltd Exec 1973-76. *Biog: b.* 9 August 1948. *Nationality:* British. *m.* 1973, Tessa

Anne (née Page); 1 s; 2 d. *Educ:* Tonbridge School. *Directorships:* Close Brothers Holdings Ltd 1979 (exec); Close Brothers Ltd 1977 (exec); Safeguard Investments Ltd 1984 (exec); Clifford Brown Group plc 1987 (non-exec); Jackson-Stops & Stoff Ltd 1990 (non-exec). *Professional Organisations:* FCA; ATII. *Clubs:* St George's Hill Lawn Tennis Club. *Recreations:* Tennis, Horse Riding, National Hunt Racing and Breeding.

WINN, Martin; City Reporter, Today.

WINNINGTON, Anthony Edward; Director, Sales, Hoare Govett Securities, since 1969; UK Equities. *Biog: b.* 13 May 1948. *Nationality:* British. *m.* 1978, Karyn; 1 s; 2 d. *Educ:* Eton College; Grenoble University. *Professional Organisations:* International Stock Exchange. *Clubs:* Boodles.

WINTER, Charles Milne; Group Chief Executive, The Royal Bank of Scotland Group plc.

WINTER, Paul; Partner, Hepworth & Chadwick, Solicitors, since 1989; Planning and Commercial Property. *Career:* Leeds City Council, Articled Clerk/Group Co-ordinator 1972-76; Gordons and H M Dawson & Co, Solicitor/Partner 1976-89; Hepworth & Chadwick, Solicitor/Partner 1989-. *Biog: b.* 24 April 1949. *Nationality:* British. *Educ:* Leeds University (LLB). *Professional Organisations:* Solicitor. *Recreations:* Music, Reading, Walking.

WINTER, Richard Thomas; Partner, Eversheds, since 1981; Commercial. *Career:* Evershed & Tomkinson, Articled Clerk 1971-73; Litigation Solicitor 1973-75; Fisons plc, Litigation & Commercial Solicitor 1975-78; Evershed & Tomkinson, Litigation & Commercial Solicitor 1978-81; Commercial Partner 1981-89; Evershed Wells & Hind, Commercial Partner 1989-90; Eversheds, Commercial Partner 1990-. *Biog: b.* 6 March 1949. *Nationality:* British. *m.* 1989, Dorothy Sally (née Filer); 1 d. *Educ:* Warwick School; Birmingham University (LLB). *Directorships:* Tarmac-Burford (Southern) Limited 1988 (non-exec); Ninadock Limited 1985 (non-exec); Biocheck Limited 1986 (non-exec); Monsport Limited 1989 (non-exec); Devon Invest SA 1989 (non-exec). *Professional Organisations:* The Law Society. *Clubs:* Roehampton Club. *Recreations:* Sailing.

WINTERFLOOD, Brian; Managing Director, Winterflood Securities Limited, since 1988. *Career:* Greener Dreyfus, Stockbroker 1953-58; National Service 1958-60; Bisgood Bishop & Co, Stockjobber 1960-86; Bisgood Bishop & Co, Partner 1967-71; Bisgood Bishop & Co, Director 1971-80; Bisgood Bishop & Co, Joint Managing Director 1981-86; County NatWest Ltd, Executive Director 1987-88; Winterflood Securities Ltd, Managing Director 1988-. *Biog: b.* 31 January 1937. *Nationality:* British. *m.* 1966, Doreen Stella (née McCartney); 2 s; 1 d. *Educ:* Frays College. *Directorships:*

Winterflood Securities Ltd 1988 Managing Director; Union Discount Co of London plc (exec). *Other Activities:* Vice President, REMEDI; Joint Chairman, USM Initiative for the Prince's Youth Business Trust. *Professional Organisations:* Institute of Directors. *Recreations:* Travel.

WINTERTON, Michael Anthony Campbell; TD; Legal Director, FIMBRA, since 1987; Legal Department. *Career:* The Law Debenture Corporation plc, Assistant Trust Mgr 1971-74; The Renwick Group plc, Gp Co Sec & Head of Legal Services 1974-83; The Law Society, Dep Dir, Solicitors Complaints Bur 1984-87. *Biog: b.* 10 June 1937. *Nationality:* British. *m.* 1965, Carolyn (née Webber); 1 s; 1 d. *Educ:* Charterhouse; Pembroke College, Cambridge (MA). *Other Activities:* Upper Bailiff, The Worshipful Company of Weavers (1988-89); Officer Commanding, NGLO Section RA(V). *Professional Organisations:* Member, The Law Society. *Recreations:* Sailing, Hill-Walking, Territorial Army.

WINTOUR, R D; Partner, Cazenove & Co.

WINUP, F W; Managing Director, Mercantile Credit Co.

WIPPELL, M A; Partner, Ashurst Morris Crisp, since 1990; Company and Commercial Law. *Career:* Withers, Articled Clerk 1981-83; Assistant Solicitor 1983-86; Carter, Ledyard & Milburn, New York, Associate 1986-87 (Admitted New York State Bar 1987); Ashurst Morris Crisp, Assistant Solicitor 1987-88; Associate 1988-90. *Biog: b.* 12 June 1958. *Nationality:* British. *m.* 1984, Michèle Joan (née Nicholson). *Educ:* Sherborne School; Oxford University (MA); Tulane University (LLM). *Professional Organisations:* Law Society; American Bar Association; Union Internationale des Avocats.

WISCARSON, Christopher Michael; Group Director, Europe, Lloyds Abbey Life plc, since 1990; European Operations. *Career:* Equitable Life Principal 1972-79; Liberty Life of South Africa Mgr, Actuarial Administration 1979-80; Southern Life Assoc of South Africa, Gen Mgr 1980-86; Save and Prosper Insurances, Chief Executive 1986-90. *Biog: b.* 25 March 1951. *Nationality:* British. *m.* 1972, Gillian (née Deeks); 2 d. *Educ:* Welbeck College, Worksop, Notts; Kings College, London (BSc Hons); Harvard Business School (Program for Management Development). *Directorships:* Save & Prosper Group 1988-90 (exec); Lloyds Abbey Life 1990 (exec). *Other Activities:* Guest Speaker to the Henley Management College. *Professional Organisations:* FIA (1976); Program for Management Development-Graduate of Harvard Business School (1985). *Publications:* Assistance to Actuarial Students, 1983; Marketing and Product Development, 1987. *Clubs:* Phyllis Court, Henley on Thames. *Recreations:* Public Speaking, Art Appreciation, Opera.

WISE, Andrew John; Partner, R Watson & Sons, since 1976; Consulting Actuary to Pension Fund Clients. *Career:* Scicon Analyst/Mathematician 1970-71. *Biog: b.* 12 June 1948. *Nationality:* British. *m.* 1974, Zoe Patricia (née Marlowe); 1 s; 1 d. *Educ:* St Dunstan's College; Trinity College, Cambridge (MA Hons 1st). *Directorships:* Country Home Holidays Ltd 1984 (non-exec). *Other Activities:* Member, Council & Pensions Ctee, Institute of Actuaries. *Professional Organisations:* FIA; FSS; FPMI; Assoc of Consulting Actuaries; Intl Assoc of Consulting Actuaries; Intl Actuarial Association. *Publications:* Research Papers in Journal of Institute of Actuaries 1984, 1986, 1987, 1989. *Recreations:* Golf.

WISE, D J; Chairman, Co-operative Insurance Society.

WISENFIELD, G M; Deputy General Manager & Company Secretary, Bank Leumi (UK) plc.

WISHER, P S; Director, Charterhouse Bank Limited.

WITHALL, Maurice; Partner, Grant Thornton.

WITHERS, A R; Director, S G Warburg & Co Ltd, since 1989; UK, Ireland. *Career:* Citibank NA, Manager 1975-80; Bank of Montreal, Manager 1982-85; S G Warburg & Co Ltd, Director 1985-. *Biog: b.* 31 March 1954. *Nationality:* British. *m.* 1983, Carla Maria (née Raffo); 2 s. *Educ:* Christ's College, Cambridge (MA Econ). *Directorships:* S G Warburg & Co Ltd 1989 (exec). *Professional Organisations:* MBA Imede 1981. *Clubs:* RAC.

WITHERS GREEN, Philip Richard; Vice-Chairman, Barclays de Zoete Wedd Investment Management, since 1990; Local Government Superannuation Schemes. *Career:* de Zoete & Bevan 1961; Partner 1970; Barclays de Zoete Wedd Investment Management Ltd, Director, Head of Investment Operation 1986. *Biog: b.* 1 August 1942. *Nationality:* British. *m.* 1966, Diana Mary; 1 s; 2 d. *Educ:* St Paul's School, London. *Directorships:* BZW Convertible Investment Trust Ltd 1990 (exec); Barclays de Zoete Wedd Asset Management Ltd (exec); Barclays de Zoete Wedd Property Investment Management Ltd (exec). *Other Activities:* Trustee, Old Pauline Club; Chairman of Governors, St David's School for Girls, Ashford, Middx; Member of the Livery, Mercer's Company. *Professional Organisations:* Member, Stock Exchange. *Clubs:* City of London Club, Old Pauline Club, Harlequin FC, Old Pauline Football Club, Royal Wimbledon GC. *Recreations:* Rugby, Golf.

WITHERSBY, Anthony B; Director, Continental Reinsurance London.

WITHNELL, Aloysius Luke Hamilton Lowndes; Director, County NatWest Limited, since 1989; Corporate Finance. *Career:* Coopers & Lybrand, Articled Clerk to Senior Manager 1977-84. *Biog: b.* 21 November 1955.

Nationality: British. *m.* 1989, Marilyn. *Educ:* Stonyhurst College; London School of Economics (BSc). *Professional Organisations:* Associate, Institute of Chartered Accountants. *Recreations:* Running, Squash, Skiing, Fishing.

WITTS, Richard A; Director, Schroder Securities Limited.

WOHANKA, Richard; Head of Bond Fund Management, Paribas Limited.

WOHRER, M; Director, Crédit Commercial de France (UK) Limited.

WOLF, Colin Piers; Partner, Evershed Wells & Hind, since 1973; Company Law. *Career:* March Pearson & Skelton, Articled Clerk 1961-66; Freshfields, Assistant Solicitor 1966-72. *Biog: b.* 26 January 1943. *Nationality:* English. *m.* 1972, Jennifer (née Fox); 1 s; 1 d. *Educ:* Bedford School. *Directorships:* Arden International Business Services Limited 1990 (non-exec). *Other Activities:* The Law Society's Company Law Committee. *Professional Organisations:* The Law Society.

WOLF, P G D; Director, Touche Remnant Investment Management Ltd.

WOLF, R; General Manager, Bayerische Hypotheken-und-Wechsel Bank.

WOLFF, John Philip Anthony; Director, Rudolf Wolff & Co Limited, since 1974. *Biog: b.* 26 April 1940. *Nationality:* British. *m.* 1964, Anne-Louise (née Ortoli); 3 s; 4 d. *Educ:* Beaumont College. *Directorships:* London Metal Exchange Ltd Chairman; John Wolff (Commodities) Ltd (exec); Everest Trading & Investments Co Ltd (exec); Amari World Steel Ltd (non-exec); Wolff Steel Ltd (non-exec); London Bullion Market Association (exec).

WOLFF, R J; Director, County NatWest Securities Ltd, since 1989; Derivatives. *Career:* Pinchin Denney/ Morgan Grenfell Securities Ltd 1982-89. *Biog: b.* 31 October 1961. *Nationality:* British. *Educ:* Merchant Taylors School, Northwood; Manchester University (BA Econ). *Recreations:* Sport, Arts.

WOLFSON, Sir Donald; Chairman, Next plc.

WOLLNER, M; Director, Bain Clarkson Limited.

WOLMAN, Clive; City Editor, The Mail On Sunday.

WOLSTENHOLME, Peter Houghton; Partner, Touche Ross, since 1975; Taxation. *Career:* Inland Revenue Inspector of Taxes 1961-70. *Biog: b.* 4 August 1939. *Nationality:* British. *m.* 1962, Susan (née Sharp); 3 d. *Educ:* Accrington Grammar School; Christ Church, Oxford (MA). *Professional Organisations:* FCA. *Publica-*

tions: Taxation of Lloyd's Underwriters, 1980, 1985 & 1988; Purchase & Redemption by a Company of its Own Shares, 1982; Share Options and Incentives for Directors and Employees, 1986. *Clubs:* City of London. *Recreations:* Tennis, Golf, Skiing.

WONG, George; Non-Executive Director, N M Rothschild & Sons Limited.

WOOD, A R; Director, Barclays de Zoete Wedd Limited.

WOOD, Brian David; Director, Schroder Investment Management Limited, since 1987; Investment Management/Marketing. *Career:* Barclays Bank Ltd, Economist 1962-66; Standard Bank, Economist 1966-67; Centre for Interfirm Comparisons, Business Consultant 1967-69; Morgan Grenfell & Co Ltd, Investment Mgmnt 1969-87. *Biog: b.* 25 April 1940. *Nationality:* British. *m.* 1963, Valerie Pearl (née Footitt); 1 s; 1 d. *Educ:* Chigwell School; Exeter University (BA Hons). *Directorships:* Morgan Grenfell Investment Management Ltd 1985-87 (exec); Bicester Real Estate Ltd 1978-87 (exec). *Other Activities:* Branch Treasurer, Muscular Dystrophy Group; Member, General Council, Society of Pension Consultants. *Professional Organisations:* Institute of Directors. *Clubs:* Woodford Wells Sports Club. *Recreations:* Squash, Tennis, Music, Walking.

WOOD, Bryan; Managing Director, Alta Berkeley Associates.

WOOD, Charles Edward Peter Neil; The Rt Hon Earl of Halifax; JP, DL; Director, Hambros Bank Ltd, since 1978. *Biog: b.* 14 March 1944. *m.* Camilla (née Younger); 1 s; 2 d. *Educ:* Eton College; Christ Church, Oxford (BA Hons). *Directorships:* Boral (UK) Ltd 1983; Yorkshire Post Newspapers Ltd. *Clubs:* White's, Pratt's.

WOOD, Ian Clark; CBE; Chairman & Managing Director, John Wood Group plc, since 1967. *Biog: b.* 21 July 1942. *Nationality:* British. *m.* 1970, Helen (née Macrae); 3 s. *Educ:* Robert Gordon's College; Aberdeen University (BSc Hons 1st). *Directorships:* J W Holdings Ltd 1967 (exec); Aberdeen Harbour Ltd 1972 Board Member; Scottish Development Agency 1984-90 (non-exec); Royal Bank of Scotland 1988 (non-exec). *Other Activities:* Dir, Aberdeen Beyond 2000; Mem, Offshore Industry Advisory Board; Mem, Scottish Economic Council; Mem, Scottish Sub-Ctee of University Grants Ctee; Mem, Carnegie Trust; Chm, Grampian Enterprise Ltd. *Professional Organisations:* FRSA; CBIM. *Recreations:* Squash, Tennis, Family, Art.

WOOD, J D B; Director, Dunedin Fund Managers Ltd, since 1981. *Educ:* LLB.

WOOD, J R L; Executive Director, James R Knowles Limited.

WOOD, Jerry; Director, Lowe Bell Financial Ltd.

WOOD, John Michael Alderton; Senior Director, Commercial Bank NA. *Nationality:* British; *m.* 1 d. *Educ:* St John's College, Cambridge (MA); Wharton School; University of Pennsylvania (MBA).

WOOD, Jonathan Paul; Director, Kleinwort Benson Securities, since 1987; Head of Derivatives and Risk Arbitrage. *Career:* Wedd Durlacher Options Market Maker 1983-86. *Biog: b.* 27 August 1961. *Nationality:* British. *m.* 1987, Cheryl Anne May (née Phillips). *Educ:* St Edmunds, Canterbury; Loughborough University (BSc Hons). *Professional Organisations:* Member, International Stock Exchange. *Clubs:* Wentworth Golf Club, Queen's Club. *Recreations:* Golf, Tennis.

WOOD, K H; Director (US), Ivory & Sime plc.

WOOD, Keith George; Head of Personnel, S J Berwin & Co, since 1990. *Career:* Drexel Burnham Lambert, Head of Human Resources, Europe 1988-90; EBC Amro Bank, Executive Director, Head of Human Resources 1984-88; Orion Royal Bank, Associate Director, Head of Personnel 1975-84; Lloyd Executive Selection, Management and Recruitment Consultant 1973-75; Bank of England, Management Trainee Development Programme 1966-73. *Biog: b.* 14 October 1947. *Nationality:* British. *m.* 1988, Ruth (née Stanage). *Educ:* Northampton Grammar School. *Recreations:* Sport.

WOOD, Malcolm James; WS; Partner, W & J Burness WS, since 1985; Corporate Law. *Career:* Brodies WS, Law Apprentice 1979-81; Herbert Smith, Assistant Solicitor 1981-82; Brodies WS, Assistant Solicitor 1982-83; W & J Burness WS, Assistant Solicitor 1983-85. *Biog: b.* 12 September 1955. *Nationality:* British. *m.* 1980, Nicola (née Ross); 2 d. *Educ:* Robert Gordons College; Edinburgh University (LLB); University of California, Berkeley (Visiting Scholar). *Other Activities:* Member, Scottish Committee of Marie Curie Memorial Foundation; Trustee, Church Hymnary Trust. *Professional Organisations:* Member, Law Society of Scotland; Member, Society of Writers to HM Signet. *Clubs:* Scottish Arts. *Recreations:* Singing, Real Tennis.

WOOD, Mark; Editor-in-Chief, Reuters, since 1989; News Operations. *Career:* Reuters, Correspondent, Vienna 1977-78; Correspondent, East Berlin 1978-81; Correspondent, Moscow 1981-85; Chief Correspondent, West Germany 1985-87; European Editor 1987-89; Editor-in-Chief 1989-. *Biog: b.* 28 March 1952. *Nationality:* British. *m.* 1986, Helen (née Lanzer); 1 d. *Educ:* University of Leeds; University of Warwick; St Edmund Hall, Oxford (BA Hons, MA). *Directorships:* Reuters Holdings plc 1989 (exec); Visnews Ltd 1989 (non-exec).

WOOD, Neil; JP,DL; Director, Hambros Bank Ltd, since 1978. *Biog: b.* 14 March 1944. *m.* Camilla (née Younger); 1 s; 2 d. *Educ:* Eton College; Christ Church, Oxford (BA Hons). *Directorships:* Boral (UK) Ltd 1983; Yorkshire Post Newspapers Ltd. *Clubs:* White's, Pratt's.

WOOD, Peter Anthony; Director Treasury, Barclays Bank plc, since 1987. *Career:* Barclays Bank International, Treasurer 1983-85; Barclays Bank plc, Treasurer 1985-87. *Biog: b.* 1943. *Nationality:* British. *m.* 1965, Janet Catherine (née Brown); 1 s; 1 d. *Educ:* Oldershaw Grammar School, Wallasey; Manchester University (BSc Hons); London University (MSc). *Directorships:* ICCH 1987 (non-exec). *Professional Organisations:* ACIB; ACT; Royal Statistical Society. *Recreations:* Golf, Bird Watching.

WOOD, Philip Richard; Partner, Allen & Overy, since 1973; Banking & Capital Markets, Corp Fin, Shipping, Insolvency. *Career:* Allen & Overy Asst Solicitor 1970-73. *Biog: b.* 20 August 1942. *Nationality:* British. *m.* 1980, Marie-Elisabeth (née Marciniak); 2 s; 1 d. *Educ:* St John's College, Johannesburg; University of Cape Town (BA); University of Oxford (BA). *Other Activities:* Visiting Professor, Queen Mary and Westfield College, University of London; Faculty of Laws, King's College, London (Visiting Fellow); Editorial Boards of Journal of Intl Banking Law, Intl Fin Law Review, Intl Banking & Fin Law Bulletin; Butterworth's Journal of International Banking and Financial Law plc. *Professional Organisations:* The Law Society, City of London Law Society (Banking Sub-Ctee), IBA. *Publications:* Law & Practice of International Finance, 1980; Encyclopaedia of Banking; English and International Set-Off, 1989; The Law of Subordinated Debt, 1990. *Recreations:* Motor Touring, Landscaping, Walking, Piano-Playing.

WOOD, Roger Bryan Savage; Corporate Finance Director, Smith Keen Cutler (a division of Greenwell Montagu Stockbrokers), since 1986. *Career:* Harrison West Ledsam Articled Clerk 1957-63; Birmingham Industrial Trust Dir's Asst 1963-67; Neville Industrial Securities Investment Mgr 1967-70; Smith Keen Cutler 1970-. *Biog: b.* 11 April 1939. *m.* 1970, Dinah (née Cookson); 1 s; 1 d. *Educ:* Bromsgrove School. *Professional Organisations:* FCA. *Clubs:* Birmingham Club, Harborne Hockey Club, Edgbaston Priory, Edgbaston Golf Club, Aberdovey Golf Club. *Recreations:* Squash, Golf, Hockey, Skiing, Sailing, Water Skiing.

WOOD, Simon Richard Browne; Director, Cater Allen Holdings plc.

WOOD, Stephen Fitzmaurice; Chief Investment Manager, Co-operative Insurance Society Ltd, since 1983. *Career:* CIS Various 1959-. *Biog: b.* 20 December 1938. *m.* 1979, Helen (née Keelan); 1 s; 1 d. *Educ:* St Bede's College, Manchester. *Directorships:* Housing Finance Corp 1987 (non-exec). *Other Activities:* Investment Adviser, GMS Pension Fund. *Professional Organisations:* FIA. *Recreations:* Running.

WOOD, Tom; Clerk, Wax Chandlers' Company.

WOOD, William Michael; Deputy Managing & Finance Director, The Burton Group plc, since 1980. *Biog: b.* 11 October 1939. *Nationality:* British. *Directorships:* Burton Retail Limited 1990; Champion Sport Retail Limited 1990; Debenhams plc 1985; Dorothy Perkins Retail Limited 1987; Evans Limited 1987; Harvey Nichols and Company Limited 1989; Principles for Men Limited 1990; Principles for Women Limited 1990; Peter Robinson Limited 1987; Top Man Retail Limited 1990.

WOODALL, Timothy Robert William; Partner, Clifford Chance, since 1980; Litigation. *Career:* Clifford Turner, Assistant Solicitor 1974-80. *Biog: b.* 24 July 1949. *Nationality:* British. *m.* 1974, Jennifer Margaret (née Woolf); 2 s. *Educ:* Allhallows School; Solicitors Exams. *Professional Organisations:* Law Society. *Recreations:* Squash, Tennis.

WOODBRIDGE, R J; Managing Director, Riggs A P Bank Limited, since 1989. *Biog: b.* 2 December 1945. *Nationality:* British. *m.* Gillian Margaret; 1 s; 1 d. *Educ:* Liverpool University (BA Hons). *Directorships:* Riggs Valmet SA, Geneva 1989 (non-exec); Riggs Valmet Holdings Ltd, Gibraltar 1989 (non-exec); Riggs Keep Limited 1990 (non-exec); Riggs Asset Finance Limited 1989 (non-exec). *Professional Organisations:* FCA. *Clubs:* Royal Automobile Club, Gresham Club, Vanderbilt Racquet Club. *Recreations:* Golf, Skiing, Tennis.

WOODBURN, Tom; Partner, Clifford Chance.

WOODFORD, R; Head of Corporation Services, Lloyd's of London.

WOODGATE, C N; Chief Executive Officer, IMI Securities Ltd.

WOODHEAD, Robin George; Chairman/Chief Executive, National Investment Group plc, since 1986; Management of Broking Business/Financial Services. *Career:* Standard & Chartered Bank (Zimbabwe), Trust Officer 1972-74; Stoneham Langton & Passmore, Articled Clerk 1974-76; Freshfields 1976-77; Solicitors' Law Stationery Assoc plc, PA to Chm 1977-79; Premier Consolidated Oilfields plc Co 1979-80; Intl Petroleum Exchange of London Ltd, Chm & Dir 1981-86; Premier Man Ltd, MD 1981-86. *Biog: b.* 28 April 1951. *Nationality:* Irish. *m.* 1980, Mary (née Allen). *Educ:* Mt Pleasant College, Salisbury; University College of Rhodesia & Nyasaland, Rhodesia (LLB Hons, Lond). *Directorships:* National Investment Group plc 1986 (exec); National Investment Holdings plc 1986 (exec); Godfray Derby & Co 1986 (exec); Hanson & Co (Stockbrokers) Ltd 1986 (exec); Hillman Catford Board Ltd 1986 (exec); Lyddon Ltd 1986 (exec); Margetts & Addenbrooke Ltd 1986 (exec); Milton Mortimer & Co Ltd 1986 (exec);

Richarson Chubb Love Rogers Ltd 1986 (exec); Societe Generale Settlement Holdings Ltd 1989 (exec); National Investment Group High Technology Ltd 1989 (exec); NIG PEP Nominees Ltd 1989 (exec); Holland House Nominees Ltd 1987 (exec); McLellan Ballard & Co Ltd 1987 (exec); Finsbury Circus Nominees Ltd 1988 (exec); Northern Stockbrokers Ltd 1989 (exec); Contemporary Art Society Projects Ltd 1988 (non-exec); Mercury Theatre Trust Ltd 1990 (non-exec); Ballet Rambert Ltd 1990 (non-exec). *Other Activities:* The Contemporary Art Society; Whitechapel Art Gallery Foundation Ltd; Rambert Dance Company. *Professional Organisations:* The Law Society. *Clubs:* City of London Club. *Recreations:* Contemporary Art, Skiing, Tennis, Riding.

WOODHOUSE, Colin Frank; Director, Brandeis Limited, since 1990; Eastern Europe. *Career:* Brandeis Limited 1979-; Rhodesian Banking Corp (Harare), Assistant Accountant and Various 1969-79. *Biog: b.* 4 April 1950. *Nationality:* British. *m.* 1972, Bridget (née Barclay Thomas); 1 s; 1 d. *Educ:* Fort Victoria High School, Rhodesia.

WOODHOUSE, J G; Director, Lombard North Central plc.

WOODHOUSE, John Patrick; Partner, Clay & Partners, since 1982; Pensions. *Career:* Sun Life Assurance, Actuarial Trainee 1971-73. *Biog: b.* 16 June 1950. *Nationality:* British. *m.* (decd); 2 s. *Educ:* King Edward VII School, Sheffield; University College, London (BSc Hons). *Directorships:* Masterwood Ltd 1985 (exec). *Professional Organisations:* FIA. *Recreations:* Wine, Horse Racing, Cricket, Golf.

WOODIFIELD, N R; Director, Williams de Broë plc.

WOODIFIELD, P; Business Editor, The Scotsman.

WOODING, Dr Norman Samuel; CBE; Non-Executive Chairman, Agricultural Genetics Company Ltd, since 1988. *Career:* Courtaulds plc Dep Chm 1976-87; Early's of Witney Chm 1978-83. *Biog: b.* 20 April 1927. *Nationality:* British. *m.* 1949, Dorothy (née Smith); 1 s; 2 d. *Educ:* Lawrence Sheriff, Rugby; London University; Leeds University; Manchester University (BSc, PhD). *Directorships:* Royal London Mutual Insurance Society Ltd 1987 (non-exec) Dep Chm; British Nuclear Fuels plc 1987 (non-exec); British Textile Technology Group 1988 (non-exec). *Other Activities:* Pres, British-Soviet Chamber of Commerce; Chm, East European Trade Council; Member of Governing Body, Great Britain/East Europe Centre and of Great Britain/USSR Association; *Professional Organisations:* CBIM. *Publications:* Articles in Physical Chemistry, Fibre Structure, Eastern Europe. *Clubs:* Reform. *Recreations:* Hill Walking, Photography, Fast Cars.

WOODMAN, M H J; Partner, Field Fisher Waterhouse.

WOODMAN, Robert Charles; Director, The Burton Group plc, since 1980. *Biog: b.* 24 October 1936. *Nationality:* British. *Directorships:* LCA Computer Services Limited 1980; Debenhams plc 1985-86.

WOODROFFE, S R; Director, Hambros Bank Limited.

WOODS, Alan Thomas; Chairman & Managing Director, Woods River Services Ltd, since 1973. *Career:* Apprenticed Waterman and Lighterman 1953; Freeman of the River Thames 1960. *Biog: b.* 31 October 1937. *Nationality:* British. *m.* 1971, Jane Lesley (née Cleverly); 2 s; 1 d. *Educ:* Bermondsey Central School. *Directorships:* Woods River Services Ltd (exec); W R S Marine Ltd (exec); Riverwoods Caterers Ltd (exec); Tower Pier Launches Ltd (exec); Minories Holdings Ltd (exec). *Other Activities:* Chairman, Thames Passenger Services Federation; Junior Warden, Company of Waterman and Lighterman of the River Thames; Freeman of the River Thames; Freeman of the City of London.

WOODS, David Ernest; Managing Director, Scottish Provident Institution, since 1988; Life Assurance & Investment. *Career:* Equity & Law Life Assurance Snr Asst Secretary 1969-79; Equity & Law Levensverzekeringen (Holland) Adjunkt Directeur 1979-83; Equity & Law Life Pensions Actuary 1983-86; Royal Life Holdings Planning & Development Mgr 1986-88. *Biog: b.* 27 December 1947. *Nationality:* British. *m.* 1970, Barbara Elizabeth (née Boothroyd); 2 s; 1 d. *Educ:* Huddersfield New College; Churchill, Cambridge (MA); Sheffield University (MSc). *Directorships:* Scottish Provident Managed Funds 1988 (exec); Scottish Provident Asset Management 1988 (exec); Scottish Provident Investment Management 1988 (exec); Scottish Provident Trustees 1988 (exec); LAUTRO 1988 (non-exec); Scoplife SA (Greek Life Assurance Co) 1989 (non-exec) Chm; British Life SA (Spanish Life Assurance Co) 1990 (non-exec) Chm. *Professional Organisations:* FIA; FSS. *Clubs:* Nieuwe Societeit de Witte (The Hague), New Club (Edinburgh). *Recreations:* Reading, Travel.

WOODS, N J; Director, T H March & Company Limited.

WOODS, Roger; Deputy Managing Director, GCI Sterling.

WOODWARD, Christopher; Marketing Director, 3i plc.

WOODWARD, David C; Chairman & Chief Executive, Citicorp Insurance Brokers Ltd.

WOODWARD, John Charles; Chief Executive, British Airways Pensions, 1984; Investment Management & Benefits Management of BA Pension Schemes. *Career:* Refuge Assurance Actuarial Trainee 1958-61; Co-operative Insurance Investment Management 1961-66; Cotterell & Co Executive - Stockbroking 1966-68; Colegrave & Co Ptnr - Institutional Stockbroking 1968-75; Reed International, Investment Mgr of Group Pension Schemes 1975-83. *Biog: b.* 31 October 1935. *Nationality:* British. *m.* 1962, Kathleen (née Ashton); 1 s; 2 d. *Educ:* Herbert Strutt G S, Derbyshire; Manchester University (BSc Hons). *Directorships:* NFC Trustees Ltd 1987 (non-exec). *Other Activities:* Chm, National Association of Pension Funds; Investment Committee 1982-84; Representative on Takeover Panel, Stock Exchange Liaison Committee; Institutional Shareholders Committee, Chm 1982-83; National Association of Pension Funds Council, Chm 1987-89, Vice President 1989-. *Professional Organisations:* FIA. *Recreations:* Photography, Travel, Philately, Growing Dahlias.

WOODWARD, Dr Michael Trevor; Investment Director, Ivory and Sime plc, since 1990; Overall Investment Management Function. *Career:* Ivory and Sime plc, Trainee 1983-85; Junior Fund Manager (Europe) 1985-88; Senior Fund Manager, Divisional Director (Europe) 1988-90; Investment Director 1990-. *Biog: b.* 25 November 1957. *Nationality:* British. *m.* 1989, Anne McWalter (née Russell). *Educ:* Dartmouth Comprehensive, Sandwell; University of Aberdeen (MA Hons, PhD). *Directorships:* Ivory and Sime plc 1990 (exec). *Clubs:* Edinburgh Sports. *Recreations:* Squash, Golf.

WOODWARK, R G; Clerk, Turners' Company.

WOOLDRIDGE, Felicity; Partner, Jaques & Lewis.

WOOLF, Mrs Fiona; Partner, McKenna & Co, since 1981; Energy & Natural Resources, Regulation of Public Utilities. *Career:* Coward Chance, Assistant Solicitor 1973-78; McKenna & Co, Assistant Solicitor 1978-81. *Biog: b.* 11 May 1948. *Nationality:* British. *m.* 1990, Nicholas. *Educ:* Strasbourg University (Comparative Law); Keele University (BA). *Other Activities:* Bank of England City EEC Committee. *Professional Organisations:* Council of Law Society England & Wales; International Committee, Law Society England & Wales; Law Society Company Law Committee.

WOOLF, John Nicholas; Partner, Arthur Andersen & Co, since 1979; Taxation. *Career:* Arthur Andersen 1968-. *Biog: b.* 7 September 1946. *Nationality:* British. *m.* m2 1990, Catherine Fiona (née Swain); 1 s; 1 d. *Educ:* Hampton School; University of London (BSc). *Professional Organisations:* FCA; FTII; Institute of Petroleum. *Clubs:* RAC. *Recreations:* Golf, Squash, Tennis.

WOOLFENDEN, J B; Member of the Council, The International Stock Exchange.

WOOLFENDEN, J G; Director, Private Banking, Guinness Mahon & Co Ltd.

WOOLFSON, Philip; Partner, Theodore Goddard, since 1987; Corporate, Commercial & Property Law in France, EEC Law. *Career:* Articled Clerk, Admitted as Solicitor 1979-81; Certificate of Advanced European Studies, Bruges, Belgium 1981-82; Traineeship, Legal Service, Council of the European Communities (Brussels) 1982-83; Theodore Goddard, (Paris) 1983; Conseil Juridique & Partner 1987; Theodore Goddard (Paris & Brussels) 1987-. *Biog: b.* 23 December 1955. *Nationality:* British. *m.* 1986, Suzanne Logstrup; 1 s; 1 d. *Educ:* High School of Glasgow; University of Glasgow (MA, LLB Hons); College of Europe, Bruges, Belgium (Certificate of Advanced European Studies). *Other Activities:* Association Nationale Des Conseils Juridiques; Franco-British Chamber of Commerce and Industry. *Recreations:* Skiing, Music, Reading, Golf.

WOOLHOUSE, J T; Partner, R Watson & Sons Consulting Actuaries, since 1987; Insurance. *Career:* Lloyds Life Assurance, Managing Director and Actuary 1974-85; Royal Life Assurance (result of takeover), Director 1985-87.

WOOLLGAR, K R; Secretary, Well Marine Reinsurance Brokers Limited.

WOOLTERTON, Peter William; Assistant General Manager, Norwich Union Fire Insurance Society Ltd, since 1990; Personal Insurances. *Career:* Norwich Union, Agency Department 1953; RAF, Junior Technician, Instrument Fitter 1954-55; Motor Department 1956; Two Fire Courses, Burglary Dept, Third Party Dept & all other Accident Depts 1956-59; Stoke Branch 1958; Glasgow Branch 1959; Motor Department 1959; Section Leader 1964; Senior Section Leader, Head of Motor Department 2 1965; Setting up Motor Research Unit prior to non-Tarriff 1968; Home Motor Superintendent 1973; Australia and New Zealand, Analysing and Reporting their Motor Problems 1974-76; Assistant Manager, London City 1978-79; Assistant Motor Insurance Manager 1980; Home Motor Manager 1982; Motor Insurance Manager 1985; Senior Motor Insurances Manager 1987; Senior Personal Insurances Manager 1989. *Biog: b.* 13 August 1935. *Nationality:* British. *m.* 1957, Brenda Angela (née Thacker); 3 s. *Educ:* City of Norwich School. *Directorships:* Haven Insurance Policies Ltd 1986 Gen Mgr; St Stephens Policies Ltd 1987 (exec); Policy Master Ltd 1990 (non-exec); Norwich Union Healthcare Ltd 1990 (exec); The Motor Insurance Repair Research Centre, Thatcham (non-exec). *Other Activities:* ABI; Intermediaries Co-ordinating Committee; Chairman, Motor Risk Statistics Panel;

General Intermediaries Committee. *Professional Organisations:* Fellow, Chartered Insurance Institute (FCII).

WOOTTON, Brian John; Managing Director, Hill Samuel Property Services Limited, since 1985; Institutional Property Investment. *Career:* Manufacturer Life Insurance Company, Property Manager 1963-80; Hill Samuel Property Services Ltd, Senior Surveyor 1980-85. *Biog: b.* 5 October 1931. *Nationality:* British. *m.* (div); 2 d. *Educ:* Spalding Grammar School; Plymouth College; College of Estate Management. *Directorships:* Hill Samuel Investment Management Limited 1986. *Other Activities:* Part Chairman of Association of Property Unit Trusts and a Current Member of the Management Committee. *Professional Organisations:* FRICS. *Recreations:* Music, Singing.

WOOTTON, D H; Partner, Allen & Overy, since 1979; Corporate Finance. *Career:* Allen & Overy, Articled Clerk 1973-75; Assistant Solicitor 1975-79. *Biog: b.* 21 July 1950. *Nationality:* British. *m.* 1977, E R (née Knox); 2 s; 2 d. *Educ:* Bradford Grammar School; Jesus College, Cambridge (MA). *Other Activities:* City of London Solicitors Company. *Professional Organisations:* Solicitor; Member, Law Society. *Clubs:* Leander.

WOOTTON, J P; Partner, Allen & Overy.

WORBY, John G; Group Finance Director, Unigate plc, since 1987; Group Finance, Investor Relations. *Career:* Coopers & Lybrand, Various to Audit Manager 1972-78; Wincanton Group, Financial Controller 1978-81; Unigate plc, Group Treasurer 1981-83; Unigate Dairy Holdings, Finance Director 1983-84; Wincanton Group, Finance Director 1984-87. *Biog: b.* 27 November 1950. *Nationality:* British; 2 d. *Educ:* Trinity School of John Whitgift; Bristol University (BSc Mathematics First Class Honours). *Directorships:* Unigate plc 1987 (exec). *Professional Organisations:* FCA; MCT. *Publications:* Contributor, Mergers & Acquisitions; Contributor, Corporate Finance Treasury Management.

WORKMAN, R S; Director, UK Consumers, Hoare Govett Investment Research Ltd, since 1986; Food Manufacturing, Tobacco, Overseas Traders. *Career:* Fielding, Newson-Smith & Co 1977-80; Lawrence Prust & Co 1980-82; Wood Mackenzie 1982-86; Hoare Govett 1986-. *Nationality:* British.

WORMS, D; Director, Metallgesellschaft Ltd.

WORRALL, Anthony David; Managing Director, C S Project Consultants.

WORSLEY, Francis Edward (Jock); Chairman, The Financial Training Co Ltd, since 1972. *Career:* Anderson Thomas Frankel, Partner 1966-71; The Financial Training Co Ltd, Chairman & Managing Director 1972-85; Chairman 1985-; Institute of Chartered Accountants in

England & Wales, President 1988-89. *Biog: b.* 15 February 1941. *Nationality:* British. *m.* 1963, Caroline (née Hatherell); 2 s; 2 d. *Educ:* Stonyhurst College; Sorbonne. *Directorships:* Lautro 1990 (non-exec) Public Interest Dir; Court Holdings Ltd 1989 (non-exec). *Other Activities:* Junior Warden, The Worshipful Company of Chartered Accountants in England & Wales; Chairman Finance Committee, Cancer Research Campaign; Governor, Ludgrove School. *Professional Organisations:* FCA. *Clubs:* Carlton. *Recreations:* Tennis, Wine, Cooking, Reading.

WORTHINGTON, Philip; Partner, Bacon & Woodrow, since 1988; Pensions. *Career:* Duncan C Fraser (now William M Mercer Fraser Ltd), Various to Partner 1976-86; Consultant 1986-87; TG Arthur Hargrave (merged with Bacon & Woodrow 1989) 1988-. *Biog: b.* 19 December 1955. *Nationality:* British. *m.* 1978, Elizabeth Anne (née Dawson); 2 s; 2 d. *Educ:* Priory Grammar School, Shrewsbury; Birmingham University (BSc). *Professional Organisations:* FIA. *Recreations:* Sailing.

WORTHINGTON, Richard Philip; Director, Exco International plc, since 1972; Money Broking. *Career:* Alexanders Discount Co 1963-70. *Biog: b.* 9 February 1941. *Nationality:* British. *m.* 1967, Sara Mary (née Callender); 1 s; 2 d. *Educ:* Eton College; Trinity College, Cambridge (BA). *Clubs:* Turf, New Zealand Golf Club, Swinley Rivers Golf Club. *Recreations:* Golf, Shooting.

WRANGHAM, James Russell; Group Treasurer, Courtaulds plc, since 1978. *Biog: b.* 8 June 1938. *Nationality:* British. *Educ:* Eton College; King's College, Cambridge (BA). *Professional Organisations:* FCT.

WRANGHAM, Peter John; Executive Director Europe, The Hongkong and Shanghai Banking Corporation Limited, since 1988. *Career:* The Hongkong and Shanghai Banking Corporation Limited (HongkongBank), Asia Pacific Area 1955; General Manager with Responsibility for Retail and Commercial Banking Operations in Hong Kong 1982. *Biog: b.* 30 April 1934. *Nationality:* British. *m.* 1963, Bridget Ann; 1 d. *Directorships:* The Hong Kong and Shanghai Banking Corporation Limited 1987; The British Bank of the Middle East (UK) 1988; HSBC Holdings UK Limited (UK) 1988; Hong Kong Bank Nominees (UK) Limited (UK) 1988; HSBC Holdings BV 1989; International Commercial Bank plc (UK) 1988 (non-exec) Chm; James Capel & Co Limited (UK) 1989-90 (non-exec) Chm; James Capel Holdings Limited (UK) 1989; Midland Bank plc (UK) 1988; Gibbs Insurance Holdings Limited 1989 (non-exec) Chm; 99 Bishopsgate Limited 1989; Hong Kong Bank Trustee Holdings Limited (Alternate) 1989; Hang Seng Bank 1987-; Cathay Pacific Airways 1987-; Mass Transit Railway Corporation 1987-. *Other Activities:* Past Member, Consultative

Committee for the Basic Law of the Hong Kong Special Administrative Region of The People's Republic of China and Hong Kong Banking Advisory Committees; Member, Council, Trade Development Council, 1982-88. *Professional Organisations:* Fellow, Chartered Institute of Bankers.

WRAY, J C; General Manager, Allied Arab Bank.

WREFORD, Peter Graham; Kabbans Securities Ltd. *Career:* Coutts & Co 1937-40; RAF Flying Officer 1940-46; Industrial & Commercial Finance Corp Ltd Various 1946-58; Gresham Investment Trust Ltd Chm 1958-82; Gresham Trust Ltd Chm 1958-82. *Biog: b.* 12 February 1918. *Nationality:* British. *m.* 1949, Rosemary Billie; 1 s; 3 d. *Educ:* University College School, Hampstead; London School of Economics (BSc Econ). *Directorships:* London Atlantic Inv Trust plc (non-exec); Candover Investments plc (non-exec); Wates Ltd (non-exec); Alwen Hough Johnson & Co Ltd (non-exec); Capital Trust Ltd (non-exec); Investment Trust of Guernsey plc (non-exec). *Other Activities:* Esher Cricket Club (Pres); Royal College of Surgeons (Lay Adviser). *Professional Organisations:* AIB; ACIS. *Clubs:* Marylebone Cricket Club. *Recreations:* Cricket, Horticulture.

WREN, Alan Christopher; Chief Executive, Prudential Holborn Ltd, since 1987. *Career:* Hoare & Co 1968-74; Gartmore Fund Managers, Director 1974-83; Touche Remnant, Managing Director, UT Subsidiary, Director, Parent Co 1983-85; Prudential Corporation, Managing Director, Prudential Unit Trust Managers Limited 1985. *Biog: b.* 24 November 1948. *Nationality:* British. *m.* 1987, Belinda (née Irons); 1 s; 2 d. *Educ:* Harvey Grammar School, Folkestone, Kent. *Directorships:* Prudential Holborn Unit Trusts Ltd 1985 (exec); Prudential Holborn Personal Equity Plans Ltd 1986 (exec); Prudential Holborn Life Ltd 1987 (exec); Prudential Holborn Pensions Ltd 1987 (exec). *Other Activities:* Member, UTA Executive Committee. *Professional Organisations:* Fellow, Institute of Directors. *Clubs:* Lansdowne Club. *Recreations:* Horses, Golf, Water Skiing, Walking, Squash.

WREY, Benjamin Harold Bourchier; Deputy Chairman, Henderson Administration Group plc, since 1983; Investment Management. *Career:* Legal & General Assurance Society, Pension Fund, Technical Dept 1963-66; Hambros Bank, Investment Analyst 1966-69; Henderson Admin Group plc 1969-; Dir 1971-. *Biog: b.* 6 May 1940. *Nationality:* British. *m.* 1970. *Educ:* Blundell's School; Clare College, Cambridge (BA Hons,MA). *Directorships:* Electric & General Investment Co plc 1977 (exec). *Clubs:* City of London Club, Boodle's. *Recreations:* Shooting, Fishing, Photography, Skiing.

WRIGHT, A; Partner, Nabarro Nathanson.

WRIGHT, A W F; Director, Williams de Broë plc.

WRIGHT, Adrian C; Partner, Moores Rowland.

WRIGHT, Brian Alfred; Group Executive Director, Sun Alliance Insurance plc, since 1989. *Career:* Norwich Union 1950-61; Sun Alliance 1961-81; Gen Mgr 1981-84; Executive Dir 1984-89; Group Executive Dir 1989-. *Biog: b.* 6 February 1930. *Nationality:* British. *m.* 1952, Sheila Marion (née Wood); 2 d. *Educ:* Haberdasher's Aske's, Hatcham. *Directorships:* Subsidiary Companies of Sun Alliance; Alliance Assurance Company Limited; Bradford Insurance Company Limited; Foxstern Limited; Hogg Robinson Property Services Limited; Phoenix Assurance plc; Property Growth Assurance Company Limited; Property Growth Pensions and Annuities Limited; Sal Pension Fund Limited; SAW Mortgage Company Limited; Sun Alliance and London Assurance Company Limited; Sun Alliance and London Insurance plc; Sun Alliance Fund Management Limited; Sun Alliance Group plc; Sun Alliance Insurance International Limited; Sun Alliance Insurance Overseas Limited; Sun Alliance Insurance UK Limited; Sun Alliance Life Limited; Sun Alliance Linked Life Insurance Limited; Sun Alliance Management Services Limited; Sun Alliance Pensions Limited; Sun Alliance Unit Trust Management Limited; Sun Insurance Office Limited; Swinton (Holdings) Limited; The London Assurance; The Pennine Insurance Company Limited. *Professional Organisations:* FIA. *Recreations:* Golf, Gardening, Music.

WRIGHT, C; Director, Kleinwort Benson Limited.

WRIGHT, D W R; Company Secretary, Johnson Matthey.

WRIGHT, David Ernest; Chief Executive, Citigate Communications Group Ltd, since 1988; Corporate Policy, Financial Controls, Senior Appointments, Acquisitions throughout the Group. *Career:* Financial Times, Financial Journalist 1960-78; Universal McCann, Director of PR 1979-83; Financial Strategy, Director 1983-84; Streets Financial Strategy, Managing Director 1984-87. *Biog: b.* 11 June 1944. *Nationality:* British. *m.* 1968, Marsha; 1 s; 1 d. *Directorships:* Citigate Design Ltd 1988 Chm; Citigate Publishing Ltd 1988 Chm; Citigate Marketing Ltd 1989 Chm; Citigate Advertising Ltd 1989 Chm; Nexus Graphics Ltd 1990 Chm.

WRIGHT, David J; Partner, Turner Kenneth Brown. *Biog: b.* 17 December 1946. *m.* 1973, Patricia; 1 s; 1 d. *Educ:* Bishop Vesey's Grammar School; Bristol University (LLB IIi). *Directorships:* Direct Wines (Windsor) Limited 1973 (non-exec). *Recreations:* Golf, Gardening.

WRIGHT, E; Director, GNI Ltd.

WRIGHT, Ian Kenneth; Director, Foreign & Colonial Management Ltd, since 1984; Head of Far East Department. *Career:* Clerical, Medical & General Life Assurance Investment Analyst 1974-78; Buckmaster & Moore Investment Mgr 1978-81. *Biog: b.* 7 March 1953. *Nationality:* British. *Educ:* Latymer School, Edmonton; Southampton University (BSc). *Directorships:* F & C Pacific Investment Trust plc 1987 (exec). *Professional Organisations:* AIA. *Recreations:* Golf, Bridge, Squash.

WRIGHT, J C W; Director, Steel Burrill Jones Group plc.

WRIGHT, J H; Director, Granville Davies Limited.

WRIGHT, J M; Director, Parrish plc.

WRIGHT, John Gordon Laurence; Director, Stewart Ivory & Co Ltd, since 1972; Far East Investment. *Career:* Hambros Bank Ltd Investment Analyst 1967-71. *Biog: b.* 6 June 1944. *Nationality:* British. *m.* 1974, Faith Alison (née Guy); 2 s. *Educ:* Glenalmond College; Brasenose College, Oxford (MA Hons). *Clubs:* New (Edinburgh). *Recreations:* Skiing, Photography, Shooting.

WRIGHT, Dr Kenneth Campbell; CMG, OBE; Director, British Invisible Exports Council, since 1989; Europe/Public Affairs. *Career:* Royal Air Force, Flight Lieutenant 1957-60; Educational Development Aid & University Lecturing, Congo (Zaire) & Ghana 1960-65; H M Diplomatic Service 1965-89; Overseas Postings to Bonn (First Secretary Economic); UK Permanent Representation to the EC, Brussels (Counsellor), Paris (Counsellor Political); Assistant Under-Secretary of State 1985-89. *Biog: b.* 31 May 1932. *Nationality:* British. *m.* 1958, Diana (née Binnie); 1 s; 2 d. *Educ:* George Heriot's School; University of Edinburgh (MA, PhD); University of Paris (L és L). *Directorships:* City Communications Centre (until merged into BIEC) 1989 (exec). *Other Activities:* The Royal Institution. *Publications:* Articles on the City and Invisible Exports. *Clubs:* Athenaeum. *Recreations:* People, Places, Books, Hill Walking.

WRIGHT, M J; Partner, Field Fisher Waterhouse.

WRIGHT, M J P; Director, Laurence Keen Limited.

WRIGHT, Martin Clive; Partner, S J Berwin & Co, since 1990; Commercial Property/Development. *Career:* Herbert Smith & Co 1979-87. *Biog: b.* 28 February 1954. *Nationality:* British. *m.* 1976, Charlotte Anne (née Jay). *Professional Organisations:* Law Society.

WRIGHTSON, Sir (Charles) Mark (Garmondsway); Director, Hill Samuel Bank Ltd, since 1984; Corporate Finance. *Biog: b.* 18 February 1951. *m.* 1975, Stella Virginia (née Dean); 3 s. *Educ:* Eton College; Queens' College, Cambridge (BA Hons).

Other Activities: Worshipful Company of Haberdashers. *Professional Organisations:* Barrister-at-Law.

WRIGLEY, T J B; Managing Director, First National Securities Ltd.

WRISTON, Walter; Non-Executive Director, Reuters Holdings plc.

WROUGHTON, Philip Lavallin; Chairman & Chief Executive, C T Bowring & Co Limited, since 1988. *Career:* King's Royal Rifle Corps, Lieutenant 1951-53; Price Forbes & Co 1954-61. *Biog: b.* 19 April 1933. *Nationality:* British. *m.* 1957, Catriona H I (née MacLeod); 2 d. *Educ:* Eton College. *Directorships:* C T Bowring Reinsurance Ltd; C T Bowring & Co (Insurance) Ltd 1986; Bowring UK Limited 1986; Winchester Bowring Ltd 1977; Marsh & McLennan Companies Inc 1988; Marsh & McLennan Incorporated 1990 Dep Chm. *Other Activities:* High Sheriff of Berkshire, 1977-78; Governor, St Mary's School, Wantage, 1986-; Member of Lloyd's. *Professional Organisations:* BIIBA. *Clubs:* White's, RAC. *Recreations:* Racing, Shooting.

WU, Kung Chao; Adviser, Bank of China, since 1989. *Biog: b.* 20 November 1922. *Nationality:* Chinese. *m.* 1951, Daisy (née Chan); 1 s; 1 d. *Educ:* Anglo-Chinese College, Amoy, China; London School of Economics. *Other Activities:* Member of the National Committee of the Chinese People's Political Consultative Conference, Beijing, China. *Professional Organisations:* FCIB. *Clubs:* Overseas Bankers'. *Recreations:* Tennis, Reading, Travel.

WUNDERLICH, Herbert; Managing Director, dresdnerbank investment management (dbi), since 1988. *Career:* Dresdner Bank, Trainee in all Major Depts 1969; dresdnerbank investment management (dbi), Portfolio Manager 1970; Director, Head of Portfolio Management Dept 1976; General Manager, Portfolio Management, Organisation 1984; Deputy Managing Director 1987; Managing Director 1988. *Biog: b.* 14 July 1941. *Nationality:* German. *m.* 1989, Ursula. *Educ:* Johann-Wolfgang-Goethe-Universität (Diplom-Kaufmann, Graduate Degree Business Economics). *Directorships:* Thornton Management Ltd, London 1988; Thornton Unit Managers Ltd, London 1988; Thornton Investment Management, London 1988; Thornton Management (ASIA) Ltd, Hong Kong 1988; Thornton Management (Australia) Ltd, Sydney 1988; Dresdner Global Asset Management, Frankfurt 1988 Managing Director; Thornton Asian Emerging Markets Investment Trust plc 1989; Thornton Pacific Investment Fund SA 1988. *Other Activities:* Member of Group Executive Committee, Thornton & Co Limited; Member of Board of Directors, Thornton & Co limited; Member of Board of Directors, dresdnerbank asset management (dam) SA Luxembourg. *Professional Organisations:* Member of the Committee for International Affairs of BVI,

Bundesverband, Deutscher Investment Gesellschaften eV, Frankfurt.

WYAND, Anthony Blake; General Manager, Commercial Union Assurance Co plc.

WYATT, R L; Vice Chairman & Chief Executive, Forward Trust Group.

WYATT, Richard Edward John; Director, County NatWest Securities Ltd, since 1987; UK Equities Sales. *Career:* James Capel & Co Fund Management 1980-84; Henderson Administration 1989-90; County NatWest Securities 1990-. *Biog: b.* 4 April 1959. *Nationality:* British. *Educ:* University College, London (LLB); Queens' College, Cambridge. *Directorships:* County Natwest Securities Ltd 1987 (exec). *Professional Organisations:* Member, International Stock Exchange. *Clubs:* RAC. *Recreations:* Tennis, Opera, Hang Gliding, Conservation.

WYATT, Thomas James; Director, Hill Samuel Bank, since 1989; Corporate Finance. *Career:* Grieveson Grant & Co 1971-86; Ptnr 1981-86; Kleinwort Grieveson Securities, Dir 1986-89. *Biog: b.* 17 May 1949. *Nationality:* British. *m.* 1976, Kay (née Roberts); 1 s. *Educ:* Bristol Grammar School; St John's College, Oxford (MA). *Professional Organisations:* Society of Investment Analysts; Member of the Stock Exchange, 1979-. *Recreations:* Wine.

WYCKS, Charles John; Head of Visa & Unsecured Lending, Leeds Permanent Building Society, since 1988; Visa Credit Cards, Personal Loans. *Career:* Leeds Permanent Building Society, Advertising Mgr 1984-86; Branch Mgr 1986-87; Regional Mgr 1987-88. *Biog: b.* 31 October 1950. *Nationality:* British. *m.* 1977, Helen (née Goodwin); 2 s; 1 d. *Educ:* Bramcote Hills, Nottingham; Kingston on Thames Polytechnic. *Directorships:* Leeds Permanent Financial Services Ltd 1988 (exec). *Professional Organisations:* FCBSI; MBIM.

WYER, John Daryl; Partner, Touche Ross & Co.

WYLIE, I R; Director, David Holman & Co Ltd.

WYMAN, M J; Partner, Simmons & Simmons.

WYMAN, T H; Director, United Biscuits (Holdings) plc.

WYMAN, T H; Non-Executive Director, S G Warburg Group plc.

WYNESS, James; Managing Partner, Linklaters & Paines.

WYNN, H J; Director, Steel Burrill Jones Group plc.

WYNNE-GRIFFITH, Huw Rees; Senior Partner, Barnett Waddingham & Company, since 1990; Consulting Actuary. *Career:* Duncan C Fraser & Co (Consulting Actuaries), Partner 1973-86; William M Mercer Fraser Ltd (Consultants & Actuaries), Head of City Office 1986-89; Barnett Waddingham & Co (Consulting Actuaries), Founding Partner 1989; Senior Partner 1990. *Biog: b.* 5 March 1944. *Nationality:* Welsh. *m.* 1972, Helen (née Sandover); 1 s; 1 d. *Educ:* University of Wales, Aberystwyth (BSc, MSc). *Directorships:* Barnett Waddingham Trustees Ltd 1989 (exec); Whitehall Computing Ltd 1989 (exec). *Other Activities:* Worshipful Company of Actuaries; Association of Consulting Actuaries (Committee). *Professional Organisations:* Fellow, Institute of Actuaries; Fellow, Royal Statistical Society; Associate, Society of Actuaries. *Publications:* Various papers & monographs. *Clubs:* Reform. *Recreations:* Skiing, Music, Painting (poorly), Drawing (better).

WYNNE-MORGAN, David; Chairman & Chief Executive, Hill and Knowlton.

WYNTER BEE, John Roy; Consultant, Walker Martineau Stringer Saul. *Career:* RAF, Flight Lt 1942-47; Walker Martineau, Articled Clerk 1947-50; Asst Solicitor 1950-53; Ptnr 1953-87; Senior Partner 1987-. *Biog: b.* 30 December 1924. *m.* 1950, Margaret Goward (née Hargreaves); 1 s; 2 d. *Educ:* Sherborne School; Durham University. *Other Activities:* Member, Coachmakers & Coach Harness Makers Company. *Professional Organisations:* Holborn Law Society. *Clubs:* RAF.

Y

YABLON, Gordon Anthony; Partner, Jaques & Lewis, since 1966; Company/Commercial Department. *Biog: b.* 16 April 1940. *Nationality:* British. *m.* 1964, Rosemary; 1 s; 1 d. *Educ:* Rugby School; Pembroke College, Oxford (MA). *Directorships:* Bytem Properties Limited 1977 (non-exec); Eccentrics Limited 1986 (non-exec); Educational Audio Visual Limited 1968 (non-exec); Excellet Investments Limited 1981 (non-exec); Ian Hodgkins & Co Limited 1972 (non-exec); Kerr Herrman & Stagg Limited 1983 (non-exec); Limitbrook Limited 1986 (non-exec); Matred Investments Limited 1967 (non-exec); Quickness Limited 1981 (non-exec); Phaseproud Limited 1990 (non-exec); Strand Pharmaceutical Co Limited 1977 (non-exec); The Yablon Family Charity Co Limited 1983 (non-exec); Zephyr Properties Limited 1988 (non-exec); Allied Innkeepers (UK) Limited -1990 (non-exec); Agricultural Development Co Limited -1986 (non-exec); Business & Finance Publishers (Scotland) Ltd -1989 (non-exec); Dial Holdings Limited -1986 (non-exec); Envoyred Limited -1987 (non-exec); Grenadier Knitwear Co Limited -1986 (non-exec); Penntotime Limited -1985 (non-exec); Woodstock Accessories Limited -1985 (non-exec); Commonwealth Holiday Inns of Canada (UK) Ltd -1989 (non-exec); Commonwealth Holiday Inns of UK Limited -1989 (non-exec); Envoyisle Limited -1990 (non-exec); Holborn Court Services -1986 (non-exec). *Professional Organisations:* Member, Law Society; Member, New York Bar. *Clubs:* Oxford & Cambridge. *Recreations:* Squash.

YALLOP, John Mark; Director, Morgan Grenfell & Co Limited, since 1990; Treasury & Trading. *Career:* Baring Brothers & Co Limited 1982-85; Morgan Grenfell & Co Limited 1985-. *Biog: b.* 16 March 1960. *Nationality:* British. *m.* 1988, R J Yallop (née Moore). *Educ:* Allhallows School; University College, Oxford (BA Natural Science).

YAMADA, Masamichi; Managing Director and Chief Executive, Mitsubishi Finance International Ltd.

YAMADA, S; Director, S G Warburg & Co Ltd.

YAMADA, Taro; Chairman, Yamaichi International (Europe) Ltd, since 1988; Senior Managing Director Yamaichi Securities Co Ltd, in charge of Europe and Middle East. *Career:* Yamaichi Securities Co Ltd Various 1957-75; Dep Gen Mgr of Foreign Capital Dept 1975-79; Yamaichi International (America) Inc, Pres 1979-83; Yamaichi Securities Co Ltd, Gen Mgr, Foreign Capital

Dept 1983-85; Dir & Gen Mgr, Intl Fin Dept 1985-87; MD 1987-88; Snr MD 1990. *Biog: b.* 19 November 1934. *Nationality:* Japanese. *m.* 1961, Nobuko; 2 s. *Educ:* Keio University (Economics). *Directorships:* Yamaichi Bank (UK) plc. *Other Activities:* Board Member, AIBD.

YAMAMOTO, Y; Deputy Chairman, Dowa Insurance Company (UK) Limited.

YAMAMURO, Y; Deputy General Manager Administration, Sumitomo Trust & Banking Corp.

YAMATAKA, Hiroaki; Director, Kleinwort Benson Securities Ltd, since 1987; Japanese Equity Sales to the Institutional Investors. *Career:* The Nikko Securities Co Ltd (Osaka), Equity Sales Exec 1968-72; Company Scholarship to the University of Wisconsin 1972-74; Nikko Asia (Hong Kong), Asst Mgr 1974-78; Wako Securities Co Ltd (Tokyo), Sales Mgr 1978-79; Wako Securities (Europe) Ltd 1979-84. *Biog: b.* 13 October 1944. *Nationality:* Japanese. *m.* 1970, Harue (née Maruyama); 2 d. *Educ:* High School attached to Kumamoto University; Tokyo College of Economics (BA); The University of Wisconsin, USA. *Directorships:* Grieveson Grant Pacific Ltd 1984 (exec); The London Symphony Orchestra 1987 (non-exec) Intl VP; Wako International Europe Ltd 1979 (exec). *Clubs:* Japan Society, Naval & Military Club. *Recreations:* Attending Classical Music Concerts, Opera, Reading Books, Painting in Oils.

YAMEY, Professor B S; CBE, FBA; Economic Consultant. *Career:* London School of Economics, Professor of Economics 1960-84; Emeritus Professor 1984-. *Biog: b.* 4 May 1919. *Nationality:* British. *m.* 1948, Helen (née Bloch); deceased 1980; 1 s; 1 d. *Educ:* Tulbagh High School; University of Cape Town (BCom). *Directorships:* Private Bank and Trust Co Ltd 1989- (non-exec). *Other Activities:* Managing Trustee, Institute of Economic Affairs. *Publications:* Books and Articles on Applied Economics and History of Accounting; Art & Accounting, 1989.

YANAGISAWA, Tadashi; Deputy General Manager, The Bank of Tokyo Limited.

YARDLEY, G J; Director, BTR plc.

YARDLEY, Michael John; Executive Director, The Royal London Mutual Insurance Society Limited, since 1989; Investment Management. *Career:* Pearl Assurance

Co Ltd 1975-78; The Royal London Mutual Insurance Society Limited, Fund Manager 1978-87; Investment Manager 1987-. *Biog: b.* 26 November 1956. *Nationality:* British. *m.* 1976, Heather (née Nicholls); 2 s. *Educ:* Maldon Grammar School. *Directorships:* Lion Insurance Company Ltd 1987 (exec); Royal London Asset Management Ltd 1988 (exec); Triton Fund Managers Ltd 1987 (exec). *Professional Organisations:* Fellow, Institute of Actuaries. *Recreations:* Local History.

YARDLEY, Noel Peter; Finance Director, City & Commercial Communications plc, since 1989; Company Finance. *Career:* Coopers & Lybrand Deloitte, Auditor 1978-83; Security Centres plc, Financial Controller 1984-85; City & Commercial Communications plc, Financial Controller 1985-90. *Biog: b.* 8 January 1957. *Nationality:* British. *m.* 1989, Carmen. *Educ:* University College, London (BSc Hons Econ). *Professional Organisations:* ACA (Institute of Chartered Accountants). *Clubs:* Foxhills Golf & Country Club. *Recreations:* Golf, Squash.

YARROW, Alan Colin Drake; Director, Kleinwort Benson Securities Ltd, since 1986; Equity Sales. *Career:* Grieveson Grant Ptnr 1981-86. *Biog: b.* 27 June 1951. *m.* 1975, Gillian F J A (née Clarke); 2 s. *Educ:* Harrow School. *Directorships:* Kleinwort Benson Ltd 1990. *Clubs:* Hurlingham. *Recreations:* Tennis, Bridge, Art.

YARROW, Sir Eric; MBE, DL; Chairman (Non-Executive), Clydesdale Bank plc, since 1985. *Career:* G & J Weir Ltd, Engineering Apprentice 1938-39; Royal Engineers, left at rank of Major 1939-45; English Electric Co Ltd, Engineering Apprentice 1945-46; Yarrow plc (formerly Yarrow & Co Ltd), Director 1948-; Managing Director 1958-67; Chairman 1962-85; President 1985-87. *Directorships:* Clydesdale Bank plc 1962- (Joint Dep Chm); The Standard Life Assurance Co; National Australia Bank Ltd. *Other Activities:* Member, Scottish Committee of Lloyd's Register of Shipping (1956-87); Council Member, Royal Institution of Naval Architects (Appointed Vice President 1965, Hon Vice President 1972) (1957-); President, Scottish Convalescent Home for Children (1958-70); Member, General Committee of Lloyd's Register of Shipping (1960-89); Deacon, Incorporation of Hammermen of Glasgow (1961-62); Chairman, Yarrow (Shipbuilders) Ltd and Member of Committees in Connection with Shipbuilding Industry (1962-79); Officer (Brother), Order of St John (1965); Director, Scottish International Trust Ltd (1965-72); Vice Chairman, Watertube Boilermakers' Association (1965-76); Council Member, Institution of Shipbuilders & Engineers in Scotland (1966-67); Director, Croftinloan (Holdings) Ltd (1967-81); Deputy Lieutenant, County of Renfrewshire (1970-); Prime Warden, Worshipful Company of Shipwrights (1970-71); Fellow, Royal Society of Edinburgh(1974-); Chairman, Executive Committee of Princess Louise Scottish Hospital, Erskine (Appointed Hon President 1986) (1980-86); President, Smeatonian Society of Civil

Engineers (1983-84); Chairman, The 'Saints and Sinners' Club of Scotland(1983-84); Council Member, Institute of Directors (1983-90); President, The Marlburian Club (1984-85); Committee Member, Institute of Directors Scottish Division (1984-87); Member, Glasgow Action (1985-); President, British Naval Equipment Association (1987-90); President, Scottish Area, Burma Star Association (1990-); Vice President, Royal Highland and Agricultural Society for Scotland (1990-).

YASSUKOVICH, Stanislas Michael; Non Executive Director, Henderson Administration Group plc, since 1990; International. *Career:* US Marine Corps 1957-61; Banque Galland SA (Lausanne), Trainee; Samuel Montagu and Co Ltd (London), Trainee; White Weld & Co (Zurich) 1961; International Dept, Head Office (New York); London Office 1962; Branch Manager 1967; General Partner (New York) 1969; Managing Director (London) 1969; European Banking Company Ltd, MD; Merrill Lynch Europe & Middle East, Chm 1985-89; Merrill Lynch & Co, Senior Adviser, International Advisory Council 1990-. *Biog: b.* 5 February 1935. *Nationality:* American. *m.* 1961, Diana (née Townsend); 2 s; 1 d. *Directorships:* Flextech plc Chm. *Other Activities:* Chm, Association of International Bond Dealers (1975-79); Chm, The Securities Association; Mem, City Panel on Takeovers and Mergers; Member, City Advisory Group, CBI; Member, Development Council of Royal National Theatre and National Art Collection Fund, Council for Charitable Support. *Professional Organisations:* FRSA. *Clubs:* Buck's, Travellers' (Paris), Brook (NY), Union (NY). *Recreations:* Hunting, Shooting, Polo.

YASUDA, Kazuma; Managing Director, Cosmo Securities (Europe) Limited.

YASUNAGA, N; General Manager/Director, The Mitsubishi Bank Ltd.

YATES, James; Director, N M Rothschild & Sons Ltd, since 1987; Group Finance. *Career:* Turquand Youngs, Articled Clerk/Manager 1966-73. *Biog: b.* 9 September 1944. *Nationality:* British. *m.* 1976, Margaret Josephine (née McCourt); 2 s; 2 d. *Educ:* Beaumont College; Durham University (BA Econ); Newcastle University (BA Hons). *Directorships:* N M Rothschild & Sons Ltd 1987 (exec); N M Rothschild & Sons (CI) Ltd 1986 (non-exec). *Professional Organisations:* Institute of Chartered Accountants (FCA). *Recreations:* Gardening, Music.

YATES, Paul Tennant; Director, Phillips & Drew Fund Management, since 1988; Pension Fund Management & Marketing. *Career:* MIM Ltd (previously Subsidiary of Samuel Montagu & Co) Asst Dir 1980-85. *Biog: b.* 21 June 1957. *Nationality:* British. *m.* 1986, Madeleine (née Haddon); 1 s; 1 d. *Educ:* Rugby; Edinburgh University (BCom). *Directorships:* Phillips &

Drew Fund Management 1989 (exec); Phildrew Ventures 1990 (exec). *Recreations:* Home & Family.

YEATMAN, Ivan; Deputy Managing Director, CIN Properties Ltd, since 1981; Property - UK (Acquisition, Developments, Refurbishments) - America. *Career:* Adkin Belcher & Bowen, Trainee; W H Smith & Son, Mgmnt; Hall & Ham River, Mgmnt; Ready Mixed Concrete, Mgmnt; W H Smith & Son, Estate Mgmnt. *Biog: b.* 25 October 1937. *m.* 1967, Catherine (née Kavanagh); 1 s; 2 d. *Educ:* King Alfred's School, Wantage; College of Estate Management; London Business School. *Directorships:* CIN Subsidiary Companies. *Professional Organisations:* FRICS. *Clubs:* RAC. *Recreations:* Bridge, Golf, Gardening.

YEEND, V; Partner, Nabarro Nathanson.

YELDHAM, C W; Director, Fenchurch Insurance Group Ltd, since 1987; Managing Director, Fenchurch Underwriting Agencies Ltd; Underwriting Activities. *Career:* Chandler Hargreaves Whittall & Co Ltd 1960-77; Director, North American Responsibilty 1971-77; Devitt Group, Director 1977-87; Devitt (North America) Ltd, Director 1977-87; Crockford Devitt (Underwriting Agencies) Ltd, Director 1981-90.

YEO, Stephen Francis; Partner, Clay & Partners, since 1987; Occupational Pension Schemes. *Career:* Hill Samuel Life, Actuarial Trainee 1975-77; Clay & Partners, Actuarial Trainee 1977-85; Actuary 1985-87. *Biog: b.* 24 June 1957. *Nationality:* British. *m.* 1987, Alison (née Brown). *Educ:* Whitgift School, Croydon. *Other Activities:* Member, Staple Inn Actuarial Society Committee. *Professional Organisations:* Fellow, Institute of Actuaries. *Clubs:* RAC. *Recreations:* Sailing, Cycling, Chess.

YEOMANS, Brian; Tax Partner, Arthur Andersen & Co, since 1989; Corporate & International Tax. *Biog: b.* 7 October 1954. *Nationality:* British. *Educ:* Cambridge University (MA). *Other Activities:* Tax Publications Committee, ICAEW. *Professional Organisations:* FCA.

YEOMANS, R David; Managing Director, Wincanton Group Limited, since 1982; Managing Director, 6 National Operating Companies, comprising 36 Garages, Distribution Services, Car Contract Hire, Car, Commercial Vehicle & Plant Auctions Group; Commercial Vehicle Contract Hire. *Career:* Milk Marketing Board, Sampler Tester to Regional Transport Officer 1965-71; Wincanton Transport, Area Manager 1971-72; Transport Manager (Milk) 1972-75; General Manager (Milk) 1975-78; Wincanton Transport (Group), Managing Director 1978-82; Wincanton Group, Managing Director 1982-; Unigate plc, Main Board Member 1982-. *Biog: b.* 15 February 1943. *Nationality:* British. *m.* 1968, Doreen Ann (née Herring); 1 s; 1 d. *Educ:* Hartley Wintney County Secondary Modern School;

Hampshire College of Agriculture (Credit Pass Certificate in Agriculture); Shuttleworth Agricultural College (Nat Diploma in Agriculture). *Directorships:* Groundwork Foundation 1988 (non-exec); Unigate plc 1982 (exec). *Other Activities:* Trustee, the National Motor Museum, Beaulieu; Member, CBI Economic Situation Committee; Chairman, CBI Transport Policy Committee; Liveryman, Worshipful Company of Carmen; Chairman, Bristol Avon Groundwork Trust. *Professional Organisations:* Fellow, British Institute of Management; Fellow, Chartered Institute of Transport. *Clubs:* RAC. *Recreations:* Shooting, Opera, Gardening, Photography, Good Wine.

YEOWART, Geoffrey Bernard Brian; Partner, Lovell White Durrant, since 1985; Banking & Corporate Law. *Career:* Durrant Piesse, Partner 1985-88. *Biog: b.* 28 March 1949. *Nationality:* British. *m.* 1979, Patricia Eileen (née Anthony); 2 s; 1 d. *Educ:* Ardingly College; Southampton University (LLB); King's College, London (LLM). *Professional Organisations:* The Law Society; Admitted as Solicitor in England & Wales and Hong Kong. *Recreations:* Sailing, Skiing.

YESCOMBE, Edward Raymond; Director, Bank of Tokyo International Ltd, since 1987; Special Finance. *Biog: b.* 21 April 1948. *Nationality:* British. *m.* 1973, Frances (née Mathews); 2 s; 1 d. *Educ:* Oriel College, Oxford (MA Jurisprudence).

YETMAN, John Andrew; Director, 3i Corporate Finance Ltd, since 1980; Corporate Finance. *Career:* Tube Investments Ltd, Budget Accountant 1966-68; 3i, Investment Executive 1968-70; 3i Corporate Finance Ltd 1970. *Biog: b.* 1 August 1943. *Nationality:* British. *m.* 1972, Marion Hunter (née Hardie); 2 s; 1 d. *Educ:* Dynevor Grammar School, Swansea. *Professional Organisations:* FCA.

YOLLAND, J; Partner, Ashurst Morris Crisp.

YOSHIDA, S; Director, Sanyo International Ltd.

YOSHIOKA, Takaaki; Deputy General Manager, The Mitsubishi Bank Ltd.

YOSHITAKE, Takao; Executive Director, Yamaichi International (Europe) Ltd.

YOUDE, J; Director, CIN Marketable Securities.

YOUELL, J R L; Active Underwriter, since 1986. *Biog: b.* 23 September 1942. *Nationality:* British. *m.* 1979, Tessa Claridge (née Tulk-Hart); 1 s; 1 d. *Educ:* Keble College, Oxford (MA Jurisprudence). *Directorships:* Janson Green Properties Ltd; Janson Green Holdings Ltd.

YOUENS, Sir Peter William; CMG, OBE; Director, Lonrho plc. *Career:* Colonial Administrative Service, Naval Service 1938-40; Sub Lt Cadet SL 1939; Asst Dist Commissioner 1942; Dist Commissioner 1948; Sierra Leone Legislative Council, Colony Commissioner and Member 1950; Asst Sec Nyasaland 1951; Dep Chief Sec 1953-63; Secretary to the Prime Minister and to the Cabinet Malawi (Nyasaland, 1963-64) 1964-66; Nyasaland Legislative Council, Member 1954-61; Retired 1966; Lonrho Ltd, Executive Director 1966-69; John Tyzack & Partners Ltd, Partner 1969-81; Lonrho Ltd, Non-Executive Director 1980-81; Lonrho plc, Executive Director 1981-. *Biog: b.* 29 April 1916. *Educ:* King Edward VII's School, Sheffield; Wadham College, Oxford (MA). *Clubs:* East India, Devonshire, Sports & Public Schools, Vincent's (Oxford).

YOUNES, M S; Director, Baring Brothers & Co Limited.

YOUNG, A R; Director, Allied Dunbar Assurance plc.

YOUNG, D E; Finance Director, John Lewis Partnership plc.

YOUNG, David Tyrrell; Deputy Chairman, Touche Ross & Co, since 1990. *Career:* Gerard Van De Linde & Son, Audit Senior 1955-61; James Edwards Dangefield, Audit Manager 1961-65; Spicer and Pegler (later Oppenheim; merged with Touche Rouche & Co 1990), Audit Manager 1965-68; Ptnr 1968-82; Managing Ptnr 1982-88; Senior Ptnr 1988-90. *Biog: b.* 6 January 1938. *Nationality:* British. *m.* 1965, Madeline (née Philips); 3 d. *Educ:* Charterhouse. *Other Activities:* Court of Assistants, Fishmongers' Company. *Professional Organisations:* FCA. *Clubs:* City of London, HAC, Royal St George Golf, Royal Worlington Golf. *Recreations:* Golf, Tennis, Skiing.

YOUNG, Derek Alfred; Director, James Capel Corporate Finance; Corporate Finance. *Career:* Southend BC, Brighton BC, Slough BC, City of Coventry BC 1958-70; M W Marshall & Co Ltd, Dir M W Marshall (Sterling) Ltd 1972-80; Saturn Management Ltd, Dir 1980-83. *Biog: b.* 21 July 1941. *Nationality:* British. *m.* 1963, Daphne (née Thurman); 3 s; 1 d. *Professional Organisations:* Member, CIPFA.

YOUNG, G J; Director, Ropner Insurance Services Limited.

YOUNG, Hugh Kenneth; General Manager & Secretary, Member of Management Board, Bank of Scotlnd, since 1984; Secretary's Department, Legal Services and Compliance Departments, Personal Financial Services Div. *Career:* ICFC 1962-67; J Henry Schroder Wagg & Co Ltd, Mgr 1968-73; Edward Bates & Sons Ltd, Local Dir 1973-75; The British Linen Bank Ltd, Dir & Dep Chief Exec 1975-84. *Biog: b.* 6 May 1936. *Nationality:*

British. *m.* 1962, Marjory Bruce (née Wilson); 2 s; 1 d. *Educ:* The Edinburgh Academy. *Directorships:* Pentland Oil Exploration Ltd 1980-87 (non-exec); Edinburgh Sports Club Ltd 1983-87 Chm; Uberior Investments plc 1986 (non-exec); Bank of Wales (Jersey) Ltd 1986 (non-exec); Bank of Scotland (Jersey) Ltd 1986 Chm; Bank of Scotland Insurance Services Ltd 1986 (non-exec); Scottish Agricultural Securities Corporation plc 1988 (non-exec); Scotland International Finance BV 1988 (non-exec); Bank of Scotland Independent Financial Advisers Ltd 1989 Chm. *Professional Organisations:* CA; FIB (Scot). *Clubs:* New Club (Edinburgh), Edinburgh Sports Club. *Recreations:* Squash, Tennis, Hill-Walking.

YOUNG, J A; Director, Chartered WestLB Limited, since 1990; Export & Project Finance. *Career:* Johnson Matthey, Research Chemist 1961-63; Export Credits Guarantee Department, Executive Officer then Principal 1963-84; Chartered WestLB Limited, Director, Export & Project Finance Division 1984-. *Biog: b.* 28 April 1943. *Nationality:* British. *m.* 1972, Linda Williams (née Stewart); 1 s; 1 d. *Educ:* Finchley County Grammar School. *Directorships:* Chartered WestLB Limited 1990 (exec); CWB Export Finance Limited 1990 (exec). *Recreations:* Golf, Football, Cricket.

YOUNG, J A E; Partner, Cameron Markby Hewitt.

YOUNG, Janet Mary (née Baker); The Rt Hon The Baroness Young of Farnworth; PC, DL; Non Executive Director, National Westminster Bank plc; Non Executive Director, Marks & Spencer plc. *Career:* Baroness in Waiting (Govt Whip) 1972-73; Parliamentary Under-Secretary of State, DoE 1973-74; Minister of State, DES 1979-81; Chancellor, Duchy of Lancaster 1981-82; Leader of House of Lords 1981-83; Lord Privy Seal 1982-83; Minister of State, FCO 1983-87; Conservative Party Organisation, A Vice Chairman 1975-83; Deputy Chairman 1977-79; Women's National Commn, Co-Chairman 1979-83; Oxford City Council, Councillor 1957; Alderman 1967-72; Leader of Conservative Group 1967-72. *Biog: b.* 23 October 1926. *m.* 1950, Geoffrey Tyndale; 3 d. *Directorships:* UK Provident Institution 1975-79; National Westminster Bank 1987-; Marks and Spencer plc 1987-. *Other Activities:* Chairman, Independent Schools Joint Council, 1989; Deputy Lieutenant, Oxfordshire, 1989; Member, BR Advisory Board, Western Region 1977-79; A Vice-President, W India Ctee 1987-. *Recreations:* Music.

YOUNG, John Andrew Gordon; Director, Smith New Court plc, since 1987; Managing Director of Smith New Court International Market Making. *Career:* Baring Brothers & Co Exec 1970-73; N M Rothschild & Sons Ltd, Exec Dir 1973-87; Non-Exec Dir 1987-89; Smith New Court plc Exec Dir 1987-. *Biog: b.* 18 March 1945. *Nationality:* British. *m.* 1989, Sylvie (née Burton); 1 s; 1 d. *Educ:* King's College School. *Directorships:* Cabra Estates plc 1989 (non-exec). *Professional Organisa-*

tions: CA. *Clubs:* Oriental, West Sussex Golf Club, Hong Kong Jockey Club, Hurlingham. *Recreations:* Golf, Travelling.

YOUNG, John Cedric Keith; Group Treasurer, RMC Group plc, since 1977; Corporate Accounting, Finance. *Career:* Macnair & Mason Articled Clerk 1959-65, Peat Marwick Mitchell Co Audit Snr 1965-66; Cooper Scott & Co Ptnr 1966-69; RMC Group plc Various Fin Appointments 1969-. *Biog: b.* 22 May 1941. *m.* 1966, Barbara (née Young); 2 s; 1 d. *Educ:* Emanuel School. *Professional Organisations:* FCA; Fellow, Institute of Corporate Treasurers. *Clubs:* Rosslyn Park FC. *Recreations:* Sports: Tennis, Squash, Rowing.

YOUNG, John D C; Partner (Nottingham), Evershed Wells & Hind.

YOUNG, John E; Partner, Cravath, Swaine & Moore, since 1968; Corporate Securities & Finance (Resident in London since 1990). *Career:* Cravath, Swaine & Moore (New York), Associate 1961-67; Partner 1968-; Resident Partner in Paris 1971-73; Resident Partner in London 1990-. *Biog: b.* 11 July 1935. *Nationality:* American. *m.* 1966, Mary (née Nason); 2 d. *Educ:* California Institute of Technology (BS Honors); Harvard Law School (LLB Magna cum laude). *Directorships:* Trustee, Brearley School, New York 1980-1986. *Other Activities:* Harvard Law Review (Editor), 1958-59; Sheldon Traveling Fellow (Harvard), 1959-60. *Professional Organisations:* American, New York State, New York City and New York County Bar Associations. *Clubs:* Century, Down Town, Harvard.

YOUNG, John Robert Chester; Chief Executive, The Securities Association, since 1987. *Career:* Simon & Coates, Members of the Stock Exchange 1961-82; Partner 1965-82; Deputy Senior Partner 1976-82; The Stock Exchange, Director of Policy & Planning 1982-86; The International Stock Exchange, Vice Chairman of the Executive Board 1986-89; The Securities Association (TSA), Chief Executive 1987-. *Biog: b.* 6 September 1937. *Nationality:* British. *m.* 1963, Pauline (née Yates); 1 s; 1 d. *Educ:* Bishop Vesey's GS; St Edmund Hall, Oxford University (Hons Sch Jurisprudence Class II); Gray's Inn, London (Bar Finals). *Other Activities:* Member of Council, Stock Exchange, 1978-82; Member of Selection Committee, The Rugby Football Union, 1979-82. *Clubs:* Harlequins FC (Trustee), Surrey RFC (Vice President), Dorking RFC (Vice President), Vincents. *Recreations:* Rugby Football, Cooking.

YOUNG, John Todd; Partner, Lovell White Durrant, since 1987; Practice, Corporate & Insurance Law. *Career:* Lovell, White & King 1979-. *Biog: b.* 14 January 1957. *Nationality:* British. *m.* 1981, Elizabeth Jane (née Grattidge). *Educ:* The Manchester Grammar School; Sidney Sussex College, Cambridge (MA). *Other Activities:* City of London Solicitors' Company. *Professional*

Organisations: The Law Society. *Clubs:* Cannons Sports Club. *Recreations:* Mountaineering, Windsurfing.

YOUNG, Lionel H; Corporate Finance Partner, Touche Ross & Co, since 1987; Corporate Finance. *Career:* Spicer and Pegler, (Merged with Touche Ross & Co 1990) 1977; Qualified 1980. *Biog: b.* 9 June 1955. *Nationality:* British. *Educ:* Greshams School, Holt, Norfolk; Durham University (BSc Joint Honours, Applied Physics/Chemistry); Harvard Business School (Programme for Management Development). *Other Activities:* Liveryman, Worshipful Company of Fishmongers and Worshipful Company of Turners. *Professional Organisations:* ACA. *Recreations:* Tennis, Golf, Croquet, Skiing, Theatre, Cinema, Good Food & Wine.

YOUNG, M D; Vice Chairman, Ford Motor Credit Company.

YOUNG, Philip James; Director, County NatWest Ltd, since 1987; Head of International Consultancy. *Career:* Peat Marwick Mitchell Supervisor 1977-81; Deloitte Haskins & Sells Management Consultancy Snr Mgr 1981-87. *Biog: b.* 30 January 1956. *Nationality:* British. *Educ:* Glyn Grammar School; Bristol University (BSc). *Directorships:* County NatWest 1987 (exec). *Professional Organisations:* Member, ICAEW. *Recreations:* Bridge, Walking, Squash.

YOUNG, R J; Director, Lombard North Central plc.

YOUNG, Richard John Neville; Partner, Lane, Clark & Peacock, since 1970; Consulting Actuary and Pensions Consultant. *Career:* Equity & Law, Actuarial Trainee 1962-66. *Biog: b.* 15 December 1940. *m.* 1971, Hilary Mary (née Sawdon); 3 s. *Educ:* Marlborough College; Oxford University (MA). *Professional Organisations:* FIA. *Recreations:* Sailing, Skiing, Squash, Tennis, Filmgoing.

YOUNG, Dr Richard Michael; Director, Merill Lynch Pierce Fenner & Smith Ltd. *Career:* ANZ McCaughan Securities, Director, Portfolio Strategy & Economic Research 1987-89; Chase Econometrics, Senior Vice President, Director of International Operations 1982-87; Trinity University, Chairman & Associate Professor, Dept of Economics 1980-81; Wharton Econometrics, Managing Director 1975-80; University of Birmingham, Lecturer 1973-5; Federal Reserve Bank of Philadelphia, Economist 1971-73. *Biog: b.* 24 February 1941. *Nationality:* American. *m.* 1989, Deborah (née Grady); 1 s. *Educ:* University of Delaware (BA High Honours Economics); University of Pennsylvania (PhD Economics). *Directorships:* Merrill Lynch 1990 (non-exec). *Professional Organisations:* Society of Investment Analysts. *Publications:* An Introduction to Econometric Forecasting Models (with L R Klein), 1980; Academic Articles in Books, Pamphlets & Journals including

American Economic Review & Econometrica. *Clubs:* Vanderbilt Club. *Recreations:* Skiing, Tennis.

YOUNG, Robin; Non-Executive Director, Scottish Equitable Life Assurance Society. *Career:* Scottish American Mortgage Co Ltd, Sec 1956-62; Mgr 1963-66; Martin Currie & Co, Ptnr 1966-85; Martin Currie Investment Management Ltd 1985-89. *Biog: b.* 7 January 1927. *Nationality:* British. *m.* 1959, Fiona M (née Ritchie); 3 s; 1 d. *Educ:* Brentwood College, British Columbia; Merchiston Castle School. *Directorships:* Edinburgh Investment Trust Ltd 1968 (non-exec); Scottish Equitable Life Assurance Society Ltd 1976 (non-exec); Securities Trust of Scotland plc 1986 (non-exec); James Donaldson & Sons Ltd 1985 (non-exec). *Other Activities:* High Constable and Guard of Honour of Holyrood House. *Professional Organisations:* CA. *Clubs:* New (Edinburgh), Honourable Company of Edinburgh Golfers. *Recreations:* Golf, Gardening.

YOUNG, William Victor; Executive Vice President, Bank of America, since 1986; Europe, Middle East & Africa. *Career:* 2 Years in the U S Army; Bank of America, Trainee 1966; Nigeria 1968-71; Amsterdam 1971-73; Rotterdam, Manager 1973-76; Central America, Regional Manager 1976-81; Latin America/Caribbean Division 1981-86; International Division, Exec Vice President 1986-88; EMEA Division, Exec Vice President 1988-. *Biog: b.* 25 April 1937. *Nationality:* American. *m.* 1962, Jenny (decd); 2 s; 1 d. *Educ:* San Jose University; University of Oregon (MA); London Business School; Harvard University (Advanced Mgt Programme). *Directorships:* Bank of America Intl (exec). *Clubs:* Overseas Bankers Club, Mosimann's. *Recreations:* Jogging, Travel, Wine Appreciation.

YOUNG HERRIES, W M; Director, Hambros Bank Limited.

YOUNGER, George Kenneth Hotson; TD, PC, DL, MP; Chairman, Royal Bank of Scotland, since 1990. *Career:* Argyll and Sutherland Highlanders Command 1950; Served in Baor and Korea 1951; 7th Battalion Argyll and Sutherland Highlanders TA 1951-65; Hon Col 154 (Lowland) Transport Regiment RCT T&AVR 1977-85; George Younger & Sons Ltd, Alloa, Director 1958-68; G Thomson & Co Ltd 1962-66; MacLachlans Ltd 1968-70. *Biog: b.* 22 September 1931. *m.* Diana Rhona (née Tuck); 3 s; 1 d. *Educ:* Cargilfield School, Edinburgh; Winchester College and New College, Oxford (MA Hons Modern History). *Directorships:* Royal Bank of Scotland Group plc 1989 (non-exec); 1990 Dep Chm; Scottish Equitable Life Assurance Society 1990; Murray Investment Trusts 1989 (non-exec); Tennent Caledonian Breweries Ltd 1977-79. *Other Activities:* Conservative Member of Parliament for Ayr, 1964-; Contested North Lanarkshire, 1959 (unsuccessful); Unionist Candidate for Kinross and West Pertshire, 1963 (stood in favour of Sir Alec Douglas-home); Scottish

Conservative Whip, 1965-67; Parliamentary Under-Secretary of State for Development, Scottish Office 1970-74; Minister of State for Defence, 1974; Secretary of State for Scotland 1979-86; Chairman, Conservative Party in Scotland, 1974-75; Deputy Chairman 1967-1970; Secretary of State for Defence, 1986-89; President, National Union of Conservative and Unionist Associations 1987-88; Brigadier, Queen's Body Guard for Scotland (Royal Company of Archers); DL Stirlingshire 1968. *Recreations:* Music, Tennis, Sailing, Golf.

YOUNGMAN, D W; Director, Wise Speke Ltd, since 1990; Institutional Sales/Research. *Career:* Computer Programmer 1971-72; Trainee Investment Analyst 1973-74; Investment Research Analyst 1975-80; Stockbroker 1980; Charlton Seal Dimmock & Co, Partner, Investment Research 1980-87; Charlton Seal Ltd, Finance Director 1987-88; Chief Operating Officer 1988-88; Benchmark Group plc, Exec Director 1987-90; Charlton Seal Schaverien Ltd, Deputy Managing Director 1988-90. *Biog: b.* 26 June 1950. *Nationality:* British. *m.* 1981, Lesley Carole; 2 s. *Educ:* Felixstowe Grammar; University of Hull (BSc Hons); University of Birmingham (MSc). *Professional Organisations:* ASIA. *Recreations:* Tennis, Golf.

YOXALL, George Thomas; Managing Director, Abbey Life Investment Services Ltd, since 1989. *Directorships:* Abbey Unit Trust Managers 1989; Abbey Global Investment Fund (Luxembourg) 1989; First Philippines Investment Trust 1989.

YU Jr, Raymundo A; Executive Director, Merrill Lynch International Bank Limited.

Z

ZACCOUR, Makram M; Regional Director, Merrill Lynch, Pierce, Fenner & Smith Ltd, since 1983; Europe & Middle East. *Career:* Industries Textiles Ultratex Sales 1957-64; Gen Mgr 1964-66; Merrill Lynch (Middle East SAL) Financial Consultant 1967-73; (Middle East) Mgr Beirut Office 1973; (Paris) Mgr Beirut & Paris 1976; (London) Mgr 1977-83. *Biog: b.* 19 August 1935. *Nationality:* Columbian/Lebanese. *Educ:* International College of American University of Beirut; California University, Berkeley (BSc). *Clubs:* Annabel's, Harry's Bar, Mark's, Les Ambssadeurs.

ZANDANO, Professor G; Director, Hambros plc.

ZANGER, Claus Dietrich; Director, Branch Manager Düsseldorf, Chartered West LB Limited, since 1990; Structured Financing. *Career:* Westdeutsche Landesbank Girozentrale, Director in Charge of Special Financing Group 1987-90; Chase Manhattan Bank, London and Düsseldorf, Relationship Manager 1984-87. *Biog: b.* 13 September 1958. *Nationality:* German. *m.* 1987, Barbara. *Educ:* University of Cologne (Diplom-Kaufmann). *Other Activities:* Member of the Board, International Bankers Forum.

ZAPHIRIOU-ZARIFI, A C; FCA; Non-Executive Director, Beeson Gregory Limited.

ZEALLEY, C B; Non-Executive Chairman, Dartington & Co Group plc.

ZEFFMAN, David Charles; Partner, Company & Commercial Dept, Frere Cholmeley, since 1989. *Career:* Frere Cholmeley, Articled Clerk/Solicitor 1981-89.

ZEIKEL, Arthur; Managing Director, Merrill Lynch Global Asset Management Limited.

ZELKHA, Morris Sion; Tax Partner, Arthur Andersen & Co, since 1981; Corporate Finance. *Career:* Deloitte & Co, Qualifying Accountant to Tax Mgr 1966-77; Tansley Witt & Co, Snr Tax Mgr 1977-79; Arthur Andersen &Co, Snr Tax Mgr to Tax Ptnr 1979-81. *Biog: b.* 22 June 1948. *Nationality:* British. *Educ:* St Paul's School. *Professional Organisations:* FCA; ATII. *Recreations:* Bridge, Tennis, Reading.

ZELL, David J; Director, Merrill Lynch International Ltd, since 1990; Head European Insurance Industry, Corporate Finance. *Career:* J Henry Schroder Wagg (London) US/German Commercial Banking Groups

1969-72; Manufacturers Hanover Trust Company Export Finance Manager, Frankfurt 1974-78; Representative, Munich, Germany 1978-81; Branch Manager, Rome, Italy 1981-83; Chase Manhattan Bank (London) VP, Marketing Manager, Europe 1984-87. *Biog: b.* 30 December 1947. *Nationality:* British. *m.* 1978, Noemi (née Barlev); 1 s; 1 d. *Educ:* Nicolaus Cusanus Gymnasium, Bonn; Nottingham University (BA Hons). *Recreations:* Photography, Community Affairs.

ZELTNER, Robert V; Managing Director, Treasury and Fixed Income Securities, Swiss Bank Corporation, since 1989; Head of Treasury Division. *Career:* Swiss Bank Corporation, General Management (Zurich) Snr VP, Global Treasury 1989. *Biog: b.* 13 October 1946. *Nationality:* Swiss. *m.* 1975, Sumiko; 2 s.

ZERETZKE, U C; Director, WBB Commodities.

ZIEGLER, D; Finance Editor, The Economist.

ZIEGLER, Kurt; Senior Vice President, Republic National Bank of New York, since 1987; Head of International Lending. *Career:* Wells Fargo Bank Area Mgr 1969-85. *Biog: b.* 15 February 1942. *Nationality:* Austrian. *m.* 1967, Joan Marie (née Wilson); 2 s. *Educ:* University of Vienna (Law). *Directorships:* Republic (UK) Ltd 1987 (non-exec). *Clubs:* Overseas Bankers'. *Recreations:* Skiing.

ZIERKE, U; Deputy Chief Executive, Chartered West LB Ltd, since 1990; Capital Markets, LDC-Asset Trading, Structured Finance, Treasury & Swaps. *Career:* Westdeutsche Landesbank (Spain), Director General 1989-90; (Japan), General Manager 1982-89; (New York), Vice President, Latin American Office 1980-82; (Dusseldorf), Assistant Vice President, International Division 1979-80; Libra Bank (London & Mexico), Assistant General Manager 1974-78; Westdeutsche Landesbank (Dusseldorf), Assistant Manager Int Division 1972-73. *Biog: b.* 24 June 1944. *Nationality:* German. *m.* 1975, Kornelia (née Saur). *Educ:* Lessing Gymnasium, Frankfurt (Abitur); Johann-Wolfgang von Goethe University, Frankfurt, Dipl-Kaufmann (MA).

ZIMAN, Lawrence D; Partner, Nabarro Nathanson, since 1977; Company/Commercial. *Career:* Herbert Oppenheimer Nathan & Vandyck, Partner 1965-66; Berwin & Co, Partner 1966-70; Industrial Reorganisation Corporation, Executive 1969-70; Ziman & Co, Partner 1970-77. *Biog: b.* 10 August 1938. *Nationality:*

British. *m.* Joyce; 2 s. *Educ:* City of London School; Trinity Hall, Cambridge (BA 1st Class Hons, MA). *Other Activities:* Consulting Editor, Butterworths Company Law Service.

ZIMMERMAN, J S; Partner, Bingham, Dana & Gould, since 1986; US Law. *Biog: b.* 15 March 1954. *Nationality:* American. *m.* 1979, Laura; 2 d. *Educ:* Harvard College (BA); Harvard Law School (JD). *Professional Organisations:* American Bar Association; International Bar Association; Boston Bar Association. *Clubs:* Harvard Club.

ZIMMERMAN, Stephen Anthony; Joint Chairman, Mercury Asset Management Ltd.

ZUBAIDA, Sabah D; Director, IBJ International Ltd, since 1989; In Charge of Eurobond Trading and Sales. *Career:* Wood Gundy Inc, London, Vice President & Director in Charge of Eurobond Trading & Sales 1976-89. *Biog: b.* 10 July 1949. *Nationality:* British. *m.* 1978, Brighty (née Shashou); 2 s. *Educ:* Queen Mary College, University of London (BSc Econ Hons).

ZUBAIRI, Salim Ahmad; Chief Executive Vice-President & General Manager, Habib Bank AG Zurich, since 1976. *Career:* Habib Bank Ltd, Pakistan Probationary Officer to Senior Exec 1953-76. *Biog: b.* 20 September 1932. *Nationality:* Pakistani/British. *m.* 1967, Zakia (née Hafeezullah); 1 s; 2 d. *Educ:* Karachi University (BA Econ). *Professional Organisations:* Pakistan Institute of Bankers. *Clubs:* Swiss Club (London), Karachi Gymkhana.

ZUCKERMAN, P S; Director, S G Warburg & Co Ltd, since 1985; Overseas Advisory. *Career:* Ford Foundation 1968-71; World Bank 1973-80; S G Warburg 1980-. *Biog: b.* 22 June 1945. *Nationality:* British. *Educ:* Rugby School; Trinity College, Cambridge (MA); Reading University (PhD). *Clubs:* Brooks's.

ZURIDIS, Emmanuel Pericles; Director, Samuel Montagu & Co Ltd, since 1986; Southern Europe. *Career:* Richard Thomas & Baldwins Ltd Technical Sales 1959-64; Chaseside Engineering Ltd MD (German Subsidiary) 1964-66; PA Management Consultants Snr Consultant 1966-71; Balfour Williamson & Co Ltd Mgr 1971-73; Italian International Bank plc Gen Mgr 1973-86. *Biog: b.* 11 March 1937. *Nationality:* British. *m.* 1972, Rosalind (née Orlando); 1 s; 1 d. *Educ:* Victoria College; Alexandria, Egypt; Prior Park College, Bath; Battersea College of Advanced Technology (Mechanical Engineer). *Directorships:* Alpha Finance AE, Athens 1989 (non-exec) Dep Chm; Euromobiliare Investmenti Spa, Milan 1990 (non-exec); James Capel-Midland ADV, Madrid 1990 (non-exec); Midland Montagu Fininter SGPS, Lisbon 1990 (non-exec) Chm. *Clubs:* Hurlingham, RAC. *Recreations:* Skiing, Sailing, Tennis.

ZUTTER, John Daniel; Executive Vice President & Country Manager, Manufacturers Hanover Trust Company; UK Operations. *Career:* Manufacturers Hanover, Various Mainly in Intl Div 1971-; SVP & Regional Mgr, Middle East, Africa and Eastern Europe/USSR 1981-88; (New York), Exec VP, Global Financial Institutions 1988. *Nationality:* American. *Educ:* St Michael's College, Vermont; Fordham University Graduate School of Business (MBA); Harvard Business School (Advanced Management Program). *Directorships:* Adelphi Management Company Limited; Epsom Leasing Limited; Hanover Nominees Limited; Manufacturers Hanover Export Finance Limited; Manufacturers Hanover Finance Limited; Manufacturers Hanover Industrial Finance Limited; Manufacturers Hanover Leasing (UK) Limited; Manufacturers Hanover Limited; Manufacturers Hanover Property Services Limited; Manufacturers Hanover UK Holdings Limited; MH Dealerplan Limited; MH London Limited.

INDEX
OF COMPANIES

Index of Companies

3i Corporate Finance Ltd
91 Waterloo Road
London SE1 8XP
Tel: 071 928 3131
Telex: 917844
Fax: 071 928 1875

Managing Director: Neil Williamson
Director:
David Chassels
David Hughes
Philip Marsden
John Yetman

3i Group plc
91 Waterloo Road
London SE1 8XP
Tel: 071 928 3131
Telex: 917844
Fax: 071 928 0058

Chairman: Sir John Cuckney
Deputy Chairman:
Lawrence Tindale
Jon Foulds
Chief Executive: David Marlow
Director:
Dr David Atterton
Sir Donald Barron
William Govett
Ralph Quartano
Sir Max Williams
Secretary: Peter Brown

3i plc
91 Waterloo Road
London SE1 8XP
Tel: 071 928 3131
Telex: 917844
Fax: 071 928 0058

Chairman: Sir John Cuckney
Deputy Chairman:
Jon Foulds
Lawrence Tindale
Chief Executive: David Marlow
Director:
Eric Barton
D Cheesman
Donald Clarke
Dr Neil Cross
Stephen Denford

Director:
Rodney Drew
Christopher Edge
Marc Gillespie
Malcolm Gloak
David Hunter
John Kirkpatrick
Brian Larcombe
Roger Lawson
Alan Lewis
Joe McGrane
Robin McIntosh
Ewen Macpherson
Keith Mair
Jim Martin
John Platt
Hugh Richards
Charles Richardson
Derek Sach
Graham Spooner
Dr Richard Summers
David Thorp
Dr Robert Toomey
Alan Walker
Sandy Walker
Paul Waller
Rupert Wiles
David Wilkinson
Peter Williams
David Wilson
Head of Personnel: Peter Ewins
Chief Legal Adviser: Colin Garrett
Chief Industrial Adviser: Nigel Lewis
Financial Controller:
Jonathan Rashleigh
Corporate Treasurer: Nick Shapland
Marketing Director:
Christopher Woodward
Secretary: Peter Brown

3i Portfolio Management Ltd
91 Waterloo Road
London SE1 8XP
Tel: 071 928 3131
Telex: 917844
Fax: 071 928 0058

Managing Director: John Davies

A A H Holdings plc
5 Chancery Lane
Clifford's Inn
London EC4A 1BU
Tel: 071 242 1212
Telex: 263567 BURGIN G
Fax: 071 831 2085

Chairman: William M Pybus

Abbey Life Assurance Company Limited
Abbey Life House
PO Box 33
80 Holdenhurst Road
Bournemouth BH8 8AL
Tel: 0202 292373
Telex: 41310
Fax: 0202 296816

Chairman: M L Hepher
Managing Director: A J Frost
Director:
C D Evans
D J Stacey
J N Temple
G T Yoxall

Abbey Life Investment Services Limited
Abbey Life House
PO Box 33
80 Holdenhurst Road
Bournemouth BH8 8AL
Tel: 0202 292373
Telex: 41310
Fax: 0202 296816

Chairman: M L Hepher
Managing Director: G T Yoxall
Deputy Managing Director:
P A K Laband
Director:
P D Chesterfield
T M Forbes
A J Frost
R E Milton
G G Rennie
W G Wherity

Abbey National plc
Abbey House
Baker Street
London NW1 6XL
Tel: 071 486 5555
Telex: 266103
Fax: 071 486 5555

Chairman: Sir Campbell Adamson
Deputy Chairman: P A Davis
Group Chief Executive:
    Peter G Birch
Managing Director, Retail Operations:
    J Bayliss
*Managing Director, New Business
    Operations:* Richard J Baglin
*Managing Director, Corporate
    Development:* C N Villiers
General Manager/Director:
    John M Fry
General Manager:
    R F Knighton
    G Osbaldeston
    Charles G Toner
Finance Director/General Manager:
    James M Tyrrell
General Manager & Secretary: B
    John Ellis
Non-Executive Director:
    Sir John Garlick KCB
    M A Heap
    J E Hugh-Rees
    Sir Myles Humphreys
    •Dame Jennifer Jenkins DBE
    M E Llowarch
    • Sara Morrison
    Lord Rockley

Aberdeen Trust Holdings plc
10 Queen's Terrace
Aberdeen AB9 1QJ
Tel: 0224 631999
Telex: 73683
Fax: 0224 647010

Chairman: Ronald Scott Brown
Director:
    Martin J Gilbert
    Andrew A Laing
    George A Robb

Abtrust Management Limited
99 Charterhouse Street
London EC1M 6AB
Tel: 071 490 4466
Telex: 945065
Fax: 071 490 4436

Chairman: Martin J Gilbert
Deputy Chairman: Richard Luders
Managing Director: Bev Hendry

Adam & Company Group plc
22 Charlotte Square
Edinburgh EH2 4DF
Tel: 031 225 8484
Telex: 72182
Fax: 031 225 5136

Chairman: Sir Charles Fraser
*Deputy Chairman and Managing
    Director:* J T Laurenson
Deputy Managing Director:
    I M Dalziel
Executive Director:
    R M Entwistle
    J P Norfolk

ADT Finance plc
6th Floor, Lansdowne House
Berkeley Square
London W1X 5DH
Tel: 071 629 6252
Telex: 266557
Fax: 071 491 3626

Group Treasurer: R J Phillips

Aegis Group plc
6 Eaton Gate
London SW1W 9BL
Tel: 071 730 1001
Fax: 071 823 6750

Chief Executive: Peter Scott
Group Finance Director:
    Charles Stern

Aetna International (UK) Ltd
2/12 Pentonville Road
London N1 9XB
Tel: 071 837 6494
Telex: 27797
Fax: 071 837 3967

Chairman & Chief Executive:
    James R Bailey
Executive Director, Finance:
    Peter Brady
Director:
    G G Benanav
    T Heron
    P W Kenny
    J W Rosensteel
Non-Executive Director:
    D P Charters

Non-Executive Director:
    A B Henderson
    C S S Lyon
    R L W Restall

Afghan National Credit & Finance Ltd
New Roman House
10 East Road
London N1 6AD
Tel: 071 251 4100
Telex: 883243
Fax: 071 253 3058

Managing Director: A W Khurami
Director: Mrs R Latif

AIB Finance Ltd
Bank Centre Britain
Belmont Road
Uxbridge UB8 1SA
Tel: 0895 72222
Telex: 925659
Fax: 0895 39774

General Manager: F O'Donovan
*Divisional Director, Business
    Mortgages:* R Bradley

AIB Venture Capital
12 Old Jewry
London EC2 8DP
Tel: 071 606 5800
Fax: 071 606 5818

Group General Manager:
    T P Mulcahy
Manager: P D Wilson

Aitken Campbell & Co Ltd
Stock Exchange House
7 Nelson Mandela Place
Glasgow G2 1BY
Tel: 041 248 6966
Fax: 041 221 5797

Chairman: W B Carmichael
Director: D J Bowes-Lyon
Director (Secretary): J Cornyn
Director:
    G E Gilchrist
    A C McSporran
    A Palfreman
    G C Perry
    M Quigley
    D Rogen

Aitken Campbell (Gilts) Ltd
Stock Exchange House
7 Nelson Mandela Place
Glasgow G2 1BY
Tel: 041 248 6966
Fax: 041 221 5797

Chairman: W B Carmichael
Director: D J Bowes-Lyon
Director (Secretary): J Cornyn
Director:
  G E Gilchrist
  M Quigley
  D Rogen

Aitken Hume International plc
30 City Road
London EC1Y 2AY
Tel: 071 638 6011
Telex: 8811791
Fax: 071 628 4008

Chairman & Chief Executive:
  Z H Idilby
Financial Controller: C J Charlwood
Company Secretary: J J F Hills

Alan Patricof Associates Ltd
24 Upper Brook Street
London W1Y 1PD
Tel: 071 872 6300
Fax: 071 629 9035

Chairman: Ronald M Cohen
Director: Adrian Beechcroft

Albert E Sharp & Co
Edmund House
12-22 Newhall Street
Birmingham B3 3ER
Tel: 021 200 2244
Telex: 336550
Fax: 021 200 2245

Chairman: Simon D Sharp
Institutional Director: G K Sharp
Dealing Director: T Morris-Jones
Private Client Director: I D Wade
Compliance Director: K G Smellie

Alexander & Alexander Europe plc
8 Devonshire Square
London EC2M 4PL
Tel: 071 623 5500
Telex: 882171 Howden G
Fax: 071 621 1511

Chairman and Chief Executive Officer:
  William M Wilson

Chief Financial Officer:
  Ian Robertson
Chief Executive Officer, Alexander Stenhouse Europe Ltd:
  Michael J Barrett
Chief Executive Officer, Alexander Stenhouse Ltd: Kenneth J Davis
Chief Executive Officer, The Alexander Consulting Group:
  R Allan Durward
Chairman, Alexander Howden Reinsurance Brokers Limited:
  Ronald A Iles
Chairman, Alexander Howden Limited: Dennis L Mahoney

Alexander Howden Limited
8 Devonshire Square
London EC2M 4PL
Tel: 071 283 3456
Telex: 882171 HOWDEN G
Fax: 071 621 1511

Chairman: Dennis L Mahoney
Deputy Chairman and Chief Operating Officer: F Paul Chilton
Deputy Chairman: Ian A Waite
Director:
  Brian C Ainsworth
  T Michael R Gauge
  Reginald W Larkin
  Ross L McKenzie
Chief Financial Officer:
  William J Oram
Director:
  John W Hanna
  Dan E Kestenbaum
  Michael R McDermott

Alexander Howden Reinsurance Brokers Limited
8 Devonshire Square
London EC2M 4PL
Tel: 071 623 5500
Telex: 882171 HOWDEN G
Fax: 071 621 1511

Chairman: Ronald A Iles
Deputy Chairman: Alan E Williams
Managing Director:
  Simon S Barnes
  Bryan Burnside
  Charles P T Cantlay
  Alan J Cranfield
  Robert S Curzey
  David I Evans
  Alan F Griffin
  Reginald W Larkin
  Alistair W MacDonald

Managing Director:
  Barry G Mackay
  Robert E Naudi
  Michael J G Stephens
Chief Financial Officer:
  Francis N Marjoribanks

Alexander Stenhouse Limited
10 Devonshire Square
London EC2 4LE
Tel: 071 621 9990
Telex: 920368
Fax: 071 621 9950

Chairman: J B Devine
Chief Executive: K J Davis
Finance Director: I Robertson
Director: R A Durward
Company Secretary: I Falconer

Alexanders Discount plc
Broadwalk House
5 Appold Street
London EC2A 2DA
Tel: 071 626 5467
Telex: 883126
Fax: 071 623 1116

Chairman: I F Hay Davison
Chief Executive: R A S Moser
Director:
  G L Blacktop
  P L Fava
  D M Newcomb
  M A Pottle
  P T Stevenson

Alliance & Leicester Building Society
49 Park Lane
London W1Y 4EQ
Tel: 071 629 6661
Telex: 265027
Fax: 071 408 1399

Chairman: C J Baker
Deputy Chairman:
  F W Crawley
  S Everard
Group Chief Executive: A S Durward
Deputy Group Chief Executive:
  P R White
Group Management Services Director:
  P Clifton
Group Finance Director:
  W I Hamilton
Director:
  E J Baden
  Lord Campbell of Croy

Director:
G N Corah
R E M Elborne
M W Thompson

The Alliance Trust plc
Meadow House
64 Reform Street
Dundee DD1 1TJ
Tel: 0382 201700
Telex: 76195
Fax: 0382 25133

Chairman: Sir Robert Smith
Managing Director: Lyndon Bolton
Director:
Professor Christopher Blake
Sir Douglas Hardie
Gavin Suggett
Andrew Thomson

Allied Dunbar Assurance plc
Allied Dunbar Centre
Station Road
Swindon SN1 1EL
Tel: 0793 514514
Telex: 449129
Fax: 0793 29343

Chairman: Sir Mark Weinberg
Deputy Chairman: J G Joffe
Group Chief Executive: M S Wilson
Joint Managing Director:
K A Carby
A P Leitch
Director:
D P Allvey
L Churchill
K W B Inglis
P Smith
L V Suchopar
A R Young
Senior Executive Director:
J W Grayburn
P Stemp
Executive Director:
D M Anderson
K Baldwin
M R S Bateman
D J Beynon
D J Boulton
J G M Burt
N F Burton
M Cooper-Smith
P J Da Costa
K J Davies
Ms R Day
P A Emms
G Fletcher
C Johnson

Executive Director:
N R Leslie
I Lovett
A McColville
R McGonigle
B Metters
D Miller
S F Myers
J A N Newman
M Payne
C Piper
J D Riley
I G Seward
R K Shakeshaft
S Smith
B M Thomas
Secretary: P B Hamilton

Allied Dunbar Unit Trusts plc
9 Sackville Street
Piccadilly
London W1X 1DE
Tel: 071 434 3211
Telex: 291755
Fax: 071 494 3066

Chairman: M S Wilson
Director:
J P Gurney
K W B Inglis
J G Joffe
N Roach
L V Suchopar
Sir Mark Weinberg
Secretary: P C Howe

Allied Irish Banks plc
Bankcentre-Britain
Belmont Road
Uxbridge UB8 1SA
Tel: 0895 72222
Telex: 9413570
Fax: 0895 39774

Group General Manager - Britain:
P R Douglas
General Manager - Business Banking:
J F O'Donovan
General Manager - Corporate Development: T P A Carey
General Manager - Group Treasury:
Dermot O'Donoghue
General Manager - Personal Banking:
T Morris

Allied-Lyons plc
24 Portland Place
London W1N 4BB

Tel: 071 323 9000
Telex: 267605
Fax: 071 323 1742

Chairman: Sir Derrick Holden-Brown
Vice-Chairman & Chief Executive:
R G Martin
Vice-Chairman: M C J Jackman
Director:
D Beatty
D Brown
J A Giffen
S T Graham
Sir John Grenside
M J Griffiths
A J Hales
M R Lampard
D Marshall
W E Mason
R Moss
Sir Philip Shelbourne
Finance Director: H C Hatch Jr
Secretary: D S Mitchell
Head of Corporate Affairs: A S Pratt
Group Treasurer: T M H Dalton

Allied Provincial plc
Town Centre House
The Merrion Centre
Leeds LS2 8NA
Tel: 0532 420169
Fax: 0532 421527

Chairman: B Solomons
Deputy Chairman: B H Foster
Director:
J M A Hanbury-Williams
H A Kitching
D J F Lawrence
C R T Laws
I Mackay
R C Mather
R J Mills
M Tolmie

Allied Provincial Securities Ltd
Shackleton House
4 Battlebridge Lane
London SE1 2HY
Tel: 071 378 0015
Fax: 071 378 0286

Chairman: B Solomons
Chief Executive: J M A Hanbury-Williams
Administration Director: M Tolmie
Finance Director: I Mackay

Allied Trust Bank Limited
Granite House
97-101 Cannon Street
London EC4N 5AD
Tel: 071 283 9111
Telex: 8813401
Fax: 071 626 1213

Chairman: Dr A M Hegazy
Deputy Chairman: A R P Carden
Chief Executive: A C Wakelin
Director:
　J A Champion
　S Jawhary
　C Moharram
　M Raphael
General Manager: J C Wray
*General Manager-Commercial
　Banking:* A M James
Group Financial Controller:
　J D R Margarson
Senior Manager-Resources: J D Sisson
Senior Manager-Retail Banking:
　C G Stewart
Chief Dealer: R A Goodgame
Company Secretary:
　J D R Margarson

Allstate Reinsurance Co Limited
Fountain House
130 Fenchurh Street
London EC3M 5AU
Tel: 071 626 5273
Telex: 889311
Fax: 071 929 4734

Chairman: R T S MacPherson
Managing Director: C R Patek
Finance Director: P W Donovan
Director:
　K Angst
　J D Callahan
　W E Hedien
　M J Resnick
　C J Ridgwell
　H E C Shergold
London Branch Manager:
　S Humphries
Senior Underwriter: P Watson

Amalgamated Metal Trading Limited
Ground Floor
Adelaide House
London Bridge
London EC4R 9DP
Tel: 071 626 4521
Telex: 888704
Fax: 071 623 3982

Chairman: T G Lock
Managing Director: K H Gaunt
Finance Director: J W Land
Director:
　M J Beale
　K D Latcham
　P A Pemberton
　M A Sharpley
　V H Sher

American Express Bank
60 Buckingham Palace Rd
London SW1W 0RU
Tel: 071 583 6666
Telex: 8956274
Fax: 071 730 3602

*General Manager & Executive Vice
　President:* J Flaherty
Manager, Senior Vice President:
　S Duncan
　E Teitler
Manager, First Vice President:
　Mrs C Jap
　A Marrs
　J Williams

AmRo Bank NV
101 Moorgate
London EC2M 6SB
Tel: 071 638 2700
Telex: 887139
Fax: 071 588 4794

General Manager: C N van der Spek
Deputy General Manager:
　E G M Suer
Senior Manager:
　D Bonnerman
　Robert W Lyons

S P Angel & Co
Biiba House
14 Bevis Marks
London EC3A 7NT
Tel: 071 623 3427
Telex: 8955762
Fax: 071 623 1097

Senior Partner: P C Angel

Anglo Pierson Options Ltd
99 Gresham Street
London EC2V 7PH
Tel: 071 600 1711
Fax: 071 600 1988

Managing Director: I Rankine

Anglo-Romanian Bank
42 Moorgate
London EC2R 6EL
Tel: 071 588 4150
Telex: 886700

Managing Director/General Manager:
　F Lungoci
Deputy General Manager:
　G Anderson

ANZ Merchant Bank Limited
Palace House
3 Cathedral Street
London SE1 9AN
Tel: 071 378 2300
Telex: 881741/2/3/4
Fax: 071 403 8782

Chairman: W M Clarke
Managing Director: J F Curry
Director: Lord Bancroft

Arab Bank plc
PO Box 138
15 Moorgate
London EC2R 6LP
Tel: 071 315 8500
Telex: 887110 ARABBK G
Fax: 071 600 7620

Regional Manager: Elie El-Hadj
Senior Manager: J C Carney
Business Development Manager:
　L J Parker
Treasury Manager: B A Short
Operations Manager: A Sadler

Arab Banking Corporation
Arab Banking Corporation House
1-5 Moorgate
London EC2R 6AB
Tel: 071 726 4599
Telex: 893748
Fax: 071 606 9987

SVP & General Manager: M C Hay
Senior Assistant General Manager:
　G A Needham
Assistant General Manager: S Hinds

Arbuthnot Latham Bank Limited
131 Finsbury Pavement
Moorgate
London EC2A 1AY
Tel: 071 628 9876
Telex: 885970
Fax: 071 638 1545

Chairman: R M Nelson
Chief Executive: L Ivory
Director:
P Ashley Miller
P Ashton
A Bradshaw
A E Field
L F Heasman
J R Kaye
I J McBride
R J Morbin
Sir John Prideaux
J M Rae
Director General Accident:
B Holder
I C Menzies
Director New Zealand: J B Macaulay

A J Archer Holdings plc

Holland House
1/4 Bury Street
London EC3A 5JA
Tel: 071 283 8020
Fax: 071 623 3419

Chairman: R J Maylam
Joint Deputy Chairman: G S Blacker
Joint Managing Director:
C M Burton
D Tudor Williams
Director:
I R Binney
M J Harris
A A Pitt

Argosy Asset Management plc

30 Finsbury Circus
London EC2M 7QQ
Tel: 071 588 6000
Telex: 888607
Fax: 071 588 1224

Chairman: Eric Nevin
Managing Director: G C Musson
Director:
A J Ashmore
A A Charlwood
Ms J A Cogswell
P G V Dingemans
C M Gilchrist
P W A Henderson
G R Henry
P G McEwen
P C Pratt
P C R Reed
J M Supran
F J Whitworth

Asda Group plc

Asda House
Southbank
Great Wilson Street
Leeds LS11 5AD
Tel: 0532 435435
Telex: 556623
Fax: 0532 418666

Chairman & Chief Executive:
J N Hardman
Finance Director: R D Scott
Director:
L A Campbell
G S Carr
G H Stow
Non Executive Director:
K J Morton
Sir Godfrey Messervy
Group Company Secretary:
J A L Miller
Assistant Company Secretary:
P M White
Group Treasurer: P H Smith
Group Solicitor: F B Atkinson

Ashley, Palmer & Hathaway Limited

9/13 Fenchurch Buildings
London EC3M 5HR
Tel: 071 488 0103
Fax: 071 481 4995

Chairman: M Ashley
Managing Director: R F Hathaway
Director:
J I Gordon
C F Palmer
D M Reed
Director & Secretary: C Payne

Ashley Palmer Holdings Limited

9/13 Fenchurch Buildings
London EC3M 5HR
Tel: 071 488 0103
Fax: 071 481 4995

Chairman: M Ashley
Managing Director: R F Hathaway
Director: C F Palmer
Director & Secretary: C Payne

ASLK-CGER Bank London Branch

22 Eastcheap
London EC3M 1EU

Tel: 071 975 1000
Telex: 920322
Fax: 071 895 1098

General Manager: J Gilman

The Association of Futures Brokers and Dealers Limited

B Section, 5th Floor
Plantation House
5-8 Mincing Lane
London EC3M 3DX
Tel: 071 626 9763
Fax: 071 626 9760

Chairman: The
Hon Christopher Sharples
Chief Executive: Phillip Thorpe

BAA plc

Corporate Office
130 Wilton Road
London SW1V 1LQ
Tel: 071 834 9449
Telex: 919268 BAAPLC G
Fax: 071 932 6734

Group Finance Director: N G Ellis

Bacon & Woodrow

(Offices also in Epsom, St Albans,
Guernsey, Bristol, Leeds &
Birmingham)
St Olaf House
London Bridge City
London SE1 2PE
Tel: 071 357 7171
Telex: 8953206 BWLON G
Fax: 071 378 8428/8470

Senior Partner (London): C D Lever
Managing Partner (London):
C Waites
Partner, Insurance (London):
S Benjamin
A S Brown
M S Burrows
D H Craighead
D G R Ferguson
M H Field
A E M Fine
H W Frogatt
F E Guaschi
J A Kamienicki
D M Pike
M G Sturmey
Partner, Investment (London):
T G Arthur
M A Evans
N D Fitzpatrick
D P Hager

Partner, Investment (London):
M H D Kemp
Partner, Pensions (London):
N S Buckland
D R Halliday
P D Hancock
P R Hardcastle
M D Harris
M A Jones
P J Morgan
R Owen
L S Parsonage
M A Pomery
J H Prevett
C R Rich
P S Shier
E S Thomas
M J Ward
Partner, International Pensions (London):
R L M Arnold
P A Randall
Partner, Pensions (Epsom):
A S Cairns
I Edwards
S A Fox
M G J Gannon
H M Gregson
A R Hewitt
M Jones
P R C Jowett
K D Lelliott
M J Lowes
R S Parkin
R D Senior
J J Simon
J D Sparks
R Stenlake
P M Webster
B K Wilson
J H Wilson
Partner, Pension Fund Administration (Epsom): A K M Lion
Partner, Pensions Research (Epsom):
V M Miller
R K Mulcahy
Partner, Life & General (Epsom):
M J Brockman
D R Campbell
H E Clarke
L M Eagles
I El-Deweiny
A B English
C Hazzard
D Papasavvas
D S Parmee
R H Plumb
T J Sheldon

Partner, Pensions (St Albans):
K Barton
R J Chapman
J E M Curtis
G R Farren
A Hale
R J Jagelman
A H Phillips
A S A Siddick
K J Skinner
R J Whitelam
Partner (Guernsey):
S J Ainsworth
R M Benjamin
S M Jones
P E Merriman
Partner (Leeds):
I F Banks
K L Ternent
Partner (Bristol):
T P Kimpton
R D Moore
A Payne
S A St-Leger Harris
K R Wesbroom
Partner (Birmingham):
C M Atkin
D G Hargrave
A S McKinnon
P Worthington

Bahrain Middle East Bank
1 College Hill
London EC4R 2RA
Tel: 071 236 0413
Telex: 933045
Fax: 071 236 0409

Senior Vice President/Snr Rep:
David L Dale

Baillie Gifford & Co
10 Glenfinlas Street
Edinburgh EH3 6YY
Tel: 031 225 2581
Telex: 72310
Fax: 031 225 2358

Joint Senior Partner:
Gavin Gemmell
Douglas McDougall
Partner:
James Anderson
Richard Burns
Alex Callander
William Carnegie
John Carson
Stewart Clark
Ross Lidstone
Brian Malcolm

Partner:
Robin Menzies
Charles Plowden
Michael Usher
George Veitch
Max Ward
Ms Sarah Whitley

Bain & Company (Securities) Ltd
115 Houndsditch
London EC3A 7BU
Tel: 071 283 9133
Telex: 887862
Fax: 071 626 7090

Managing Director: J B Russell
Director:
J Brennan
A J Whitehead

Bain Clarkson Limited
15 Minories
London EC3N 1NJ
Tel: 071 481 3232
Telex: 8813411
Fax: 071 480 6137

Chairman & Chief Executive:
S R Arnold
Deputy Chairman: D M Berliand
Director:
P R Askew
D N Botsford
C L Burgess
K A Chaplin
T R Goulder
K Hodgson
J L Kavanaugh
P K King
I Marshall
D C Millwater
J B Morley Cooper
M F Radford
T Roberts
A G Routledge
J W Sawkins
P Swain
J L Turner
M Wollner

The Baltic Exchange Limited
14-20 St Mary Axe
London EC3A 8BU
Tel: 071 623 5501

Chairman: Paul J Vogt

Vice-Chairman: Peter C Tudball
Secretary & Chief Executive:
    Derek J Walker

The Baltic Futures Exchange Limited
24/28 St Mary Ave
London EC3A 8EP
Tel: 071 626 7985
Telex: 916434
Fax: 071 623 2917

Chairman: P Elmer
Vice-Chairman: P M W Fletcher
Secretary General: S M Carter
Director of Futures Markets:
    W J Englebright
Secretary: R P S Neave

Banca Commerciale Italiana
42 Gresham Street
London EC2V 7LA
Tel: 071 600 8651
Telex: 885927
Fax: 071 606 1071

Chief Manager: F Marcotti
Deputy Chief Manager: G Mandelli
Senior Manager: R Barkley

Banca del Gottardo
Salisbury House
Finsbury Circus
London EC2M 5QQ
Tel: 071 382 9873
Telex: 925361

Representative: J S Platts

Banca d'Italia and UIC
39 King Street
London EC2V 8JJ
Tel: 071 606 4201
Telex: 886965
Fax: 071 606 4065

Chief Representative:
    Dr Luigi Marini

Banca Nazionale del Lavoro
33-35 Cornhill
London EC3V 3QD
Tel: 071 623 4222
Telex: 888094
Fax: 071 929 7982/83

Chief Manager: W Golinelli
Manager: David P Wilson
Deputy Manager: F Lanza

Banca Nazionale dell'Agricoltura
85 Gracechurch Street
London EC3V 0AR
Tel: 071 623 2773
Telex: 884651
Fax: 071 623 8435

General Manager: P Di Giorgio

Banca Novara (UK) Limited
6th Floor, Bucklersbury House
Walbrook
London EC4N 8EL
Tel: 071 489 0404
Telex: 8811511
Fax: 071 236 2033

Managing Director: S Gattinara

Banca Popolare di Milano
London Branch
London EC2R 6AE
Tel: 071 6284210
Telex: 885998
Fax: 071 6284491

General Manager: U Vasta
Controller & Compliance Manager:
    L Battaglia
Operations & Finance Manager:
    F Codo
Chief Dealer: G H Green
Credit & Loan Manager:
    P E Richardson

Banca Serfin SNC
Stratton House
Stratton Street
London W1X 6AY
Tel: 071 408 2151
Telex: 886873
Fax: 071 408 2134

London General Manager:
    George M Gunson

Banco Bilbao Vizcaya
100 Cannon Street
London EC4N 6EH
Tel: 071 623 3060
Telex: 8811693
Fax: 071 929 4718

London General Manager:
    Alberto Ramirez-Escudero
London Joint General Manager:
    Alfonso Camano
    Geoffrey Watkin
Manager, Corporate Banking:
    Juan Madinaveitia

Manager, Commercial Banking:
    Miguel Rufian-Garcia
Manager, Treasury: Sidney Buckland

Banco Central
Triton Court
Finsbury Square
London EC2A 1AB
Tel: 071 588 0181
Telex: 8812997
Fax: 071 256 7850

London General Manager: F Alonso

Banco de la Naciòn Argentina
Longbow House
14-20 Chiswell Street
London EC1Y 4TD
Tel: 071 588 2738
Telex: 883950
Fax: 071 588 4034

General Manager: Jorge Mozzino

Banco de Sabadell
Sabadell House
120 Pall Mall
London SW1Y 5EA
Tel: 071 321 0020
Telex: 8814314
Fax: 071 321 0075

General Manager: J M Grumé

Banco di Roma
87 Gresham Street
London EC2V 7NQ
Tel: 071 726 4106
Telex: 888074
Fax: 071 895 1800

General Manager: Dr Vittorio Sisto
Senior Deputy General Manager:
    Dr Corrado Amari
Deputy General Manager:
    Gordon H E Thomas

Banco di Sicilia
99 Bishopsgate
London EC2P 2LA
Tel: 071 638 0201
Telex: 888078
Fax: 071 638 4796

General Manager: M Cali

Banco Economico SA
London Representative Office
1 Gracechurch Street
London EC3R 0DD

Tel: 071 283 8141
Telex: 888647
Fax: 44 71 626 9467

London Representative:
Gerald L Walkden

Banco Español de Crédito SA

33 King Street
London EC2V 8EH
Tel: 071 606 4883
Telex: 8811360
Fax: 071 606 3921

Representative: Andres
Cuenca Toribio

Banco Espirito Santo e Comercial de Lisboa

4 Fenchurch Street
London EC3M 3AT
Tel: 071 283 5381
Telex: 883064
Fax: 071 626 8369

Deputy General Manager: I G Brodie
General Manager: L Spencer Martins

Banco Exterior - UK

9 King Street
London EC2V 8HB
Tel: 071 796 4100
Telex: 886820
Fax: 071 796 3898

General Manager: Juan J
Puyol Toledo

Banco Itau

66 Gresham Street
London EC2V 7LB
Tel: 071 606 4906
Telex: 8955752
Fax: 071 726 8869

Senior Representative:
Charles N Ryan

Banco Nacional Ultramarino

Walbrook House
7th Floor
23 Walbrook
London EC4N 8LD
Tel: 071 283 5535
Telex: 887477
Fax: 071 283 6762

UK Representative: Rui
Mascarenhas Santos

Banco Pinto & Sotto Mayor

London Representative Office
5th Floor
10 Philpott Lane
London EC3M 8AA
Tel: 071 626 5021
Telex: 8951212
Fax: 071 623 3379

UK Representative: A Vaz de
Mascarenhas

Banco Portugues do Atlantico

77 Gracechurch Street
London EC3V 0BQ
Tel: 071 626 1711
Telex: 8956297
Fax: 071 626 4441

General Manager: J M Toscano

Banco Real SA

3rd Floor
20 St Dunstan's Hill
London EC3R 8HY
Tel: 071 638 6474
Telex: 8952875
Fax: 071 638 4997

Regional Director: Duncan A Stewart

Banco Santander

10 Moorgate
London EC2R 6LB
Tel: 071 606 7766
Telex: 8812851
Fax: 071 606 0352

General Manager: J Saavedra
Deputy General Manager: J Eulate
Assistant General Manager (Treasury):
T Bush
Manager (Corporate Banking):
M Greenwood
G Sessions

Banco Totta & Açores

68 Cannon Street
London EC4N 6AQ
Tel: 071 236 1515
Telex: 887609
Fax: 071 236 7717

General Manager: T H Taylor

Bangkok Bank

61 St Mary Axe
London EC3A 8BY

Tel: 071 929 4422
Telex: 8812448
Fax: 071 283 5547

Senior Vice President & General
Manager: T Tayanganon
Vice President & Branch Manager:
P Tejasakulsin

Bank für Gemeinwirtschaft

33 Lombard Street
London EC3V 9BS
Tel: 071 283 1090
Telex: 887628
Fax: 071 929 1473

General Manager:
W Dressel
U Mauersberg

Bank Handlowy w Warszawie

London Branch
4 Coleman Street
London EC2R 5AS
Tel: 071 606 7181
Telex: 8811681
Fax: 071 726 4902

General Manager and Managing
Director: T Barlowski
Deputy General Manager: W P Platt

Bank Hapoalim BM

8-12 Brook Street
London W1Y 1AA
Tel: 071 872 9912
Telex: 886805
Fax: 071 872 9924

General Manager: Z Sofer
Chief Operations Manager:
G B Powell

Bank in Liechtenstein (UK) Limited

1 Devonshire Square
London EC2M 4UJ
Tel: 071 377 0404
Telex: 8811714
Fax: 071 247 1171

Chief Executive Officer:
Reinhard J Schmölz

Bank Julius Baer & Co Ltd

Bevis Marks House
Bevis Marks
London EC3A 7NE

Tel: 071 623 4211
Telex: 887272
Fax: 071 283 6146

*Senior Vice President and Branch
    Manager:* P N Amphlett
Senior Vice President:
    J W Baker
    R J Davis
    J C Minter
    C F Smith

Bank Leumi (UK) plc

4/7 Woodstock Street
London W1A 2AF
Tel: 071 629 1205
Telex: 888738
Fax: 071 493 1426

General Manager & Executive Director:
    D Efrima
*Deputy General Manager & Company
    Secretary:* G M Wisenfield
Deputy General Manager:
    G Doubtfire

Bank Negara Indonesia 1946

London Branch
3 Finsbury Square
London EC2A 1DL
Tel: 071 638 4070
Telex: 887758
Fax: 071 256 9945

General Manager: I W Tantra

Bank of America

25 Cannon Street
London EC4P 4HN
Tel: 071 634 4000
Telex: 888412
Fax: 071 634 4549

Executive Vice President:
    William V Young
*Executive Vice President, Relationship
    Management:* Riad Ghali
Senior Vice President, Capital Markets:
    P Gerald Doherty
*Senior Vice President, Senior Credit
    Officer:* George W Selby
*Senior Vice President, Global Payments
    Services:* Bruce W Mitchell
*Senior Vice President, Financial
    Institutions:* Michael P Seibel
*Senior Vice President, Corporate
    Finance:* Robert Morrow
Vice President, Personnel:
    Richard Pollock

Vice President, FX Trading and Sales:
    Paul Chappell
*Vice President, Financial Engineering
    and Risk Mgt:* David Blatchford

Bank of America
International Limited

1 Watling Street
PO Box 262
London EC4P 4BX
Tel: 071 634 4000
Telex: 884552
Fax: 071 236 0154

Managing Director: P
    Gerald Doherty
Deputy Managing Director:
    William B Morrow
Executive Director:
    A Richard Abraham
    Ralph Brandt
    Peter J Hodgson
    Anthony J D Rhodes
    Brian R Rundle
    John R M Weguelin

The Bank of California
(Mitsubishi Bank)

18 Finsbury Circus
London EC2M 7BP
Tel: 071 628 1883
Telex: 8814323
Fax: 071 628 1864

Vice President & Manager:
    K Rimmer

Bank of China

8/10 Mansion House Place
London EC4N 8BL
Tel: 071 626 8301
Telex: 886935
Fax: 071 626 3892

Director & General Manager:
    J S Chen
Senior Deputy General Manager:
    K C Wu

Bank of Crete

8 Moorgate
London EC2R 6DD
Tel: 071 606 7971
Telex: 945852
Fax: 071 796 4347

Chief Representative Officer:
    A N Strouthos

Bank of Cyprus (London)
Ltd

27-31 Charlotte Street
London W1P 2HJ
Tel: 071 637 3961
Telex: 22114
Fax: 071 637 1677

Chairman: G C Christofides
Director & General Manager:
    C C Ioannides
Director:
    T N Clarke
    J A Legon
    G S Papadopoulos
    A C Patsalides
    S A Triantarfyllides
Financial Controller: S H Evangelou
Company Secretary: S M Pirintji

The Bank of East Asia Ltd

75 Shaftesbury Avenue
London W1V 8BB
Tel: 071-734 3434
Telex: 262006 BEALDN
Fax: 071-734 0523

General Manager: Joseph Chow
Deputy General Manager:
    I N F Powell
*Financial Controller/Operations
    Manager:* Barry Naulls
Lending Manager: Michael Hood
Treasury Manager: Stephen Tang

Bank of England

Threadneedle Street
London EC2R 8AH
Tel: 071 601 4878

Governor: The Rt
    Hon Robert Leigh-Pemberton
Deputy Governor: E A J George
Director:
    Dr David V Atterton CBE
    The Hon Sir John F H Baring
        CVO
    Sir Adrian Cadbury
    Frederick B Corby
    Sir Colin R Corness
    Sir Robert Haslam
    Sir Martin W Jacomb
    Professor Mervyn King
    Sir Hector Laing
    Gavin H Laird CBE
    Sir David G Scholey CBE
    David A Walker
Executive Director:
    A L Coleby
    Andrew D Crockett

Executive Director:
Brian Quinn
Associate Director:
H C E Harris
P H Kent
Ian Plenderleith
Chief Monetary Adviser to the
Governor: A L Coleby
Adviser to the Governors:
J P Charkham
Sir Peter Petrie Bt
Head of Foreign Exchange Division:
W A Allen
Assistant Director & Head of Banking
Supervision: R A Barnes
Auditor: M J W Phillips
Head of Financial Statistics Divisions:
P A Bull
Head of Financial Markets:
T A Clark
Chief Registrar & Chief Accountant:
D A Bridger
Head of Foreign Exchange Division:
W A Allen
Chief of Banking Department & Chief
Cashier: G M Gill
Head of Finance & Industry Area:
M E Hewitt
General Manager - Printing Works:
A W Jarvis
Head of Industrial Finance Division:
M T R Smith
Head of Economics Division:
L D D Price
Head of Wholesale Markets Supevision:
J S Beverly
Head of Information Division:
J R E Footman
Head of Developing World Division:
Oliver Page
Head of European Division:
M D K W Foot
Head of International Finance,
Economy and Debt Division:
A R Latter
Head of North America and Japan
Division: D W Green
Special Adviser on European Monetary
Questions: C T Taylor

Bank of Ireland
36 Queen Street
London EC4R 1BN
Tel: 071 329 4500
Telex: 8812635
Fax: 071 489 1886

Chief Executive: Richard Keatinge

General Manager:
Pat O'Hara
Des O'Reilly

Bank of Ireland Corporate Finance Limited
36 Queen Street
London EC4R 1BN
Tel: 071 329 4500
Telex: 892616
Fax: 071 236 7170

Chief Executive: Jon Sachs

Bank of Japan
27-32 Old Jewry
London EC2R 8EY
Tel: 071 606 2454
Telex: 884517
Fax: 071 726 4819

Chief Representative: K Matsuda

Bank of Korea
London Representative Office
Plantation House
31-35 Fenchurch Street
London EC3
Tel: 071 626 8321
Telex: 883285
Fax: 071 626 7201

Chief Representative: Chin Suk Park

The Bank of Kyoto Ltd
7th Floor
62 Cornhill
London EC3V 3NH
Tel: 071 626 6897
Telex: 933044
Fax: 071 626 1079

Chief Representative: T Hayashi

Bank of Montreal
11 Walbrook, 2nd Floor
London EC4N 8ED
Tel: 071 236 1010
Telex: 889068
Fax: 071 236 2821

Senior Vice President & Manager:
Soren K Christensen

Bank of New England
Dexter House
2 Royal Mint Court
London EC3N 4QN

Tel: 071 481 8181
Telex: 887866
Fax: 071 481 4111

Senior Vice President & General
Manager: J D Dorman

Bank of New York
46 Berkeley Street
London W1X 6AA
Tel: 071 499 1234
Telex: 883265/883266
Fax: 071 322 6030

Senior Vice President/Resident
Manager: G W Bennet

Bank of New Zealand
91 Gresham Street
PO Box 402
London EC2V 7BL
Tel: 071 726 4060
Telex: 888451
Fax: 071 606 7751

Chief Manager: Earl W Hartstonge

The Bank of Nova Scotia
Scotia House
33 Finsbury Square
London EC2A 1BB
Tel: 071 638 5644
Telex: 885188/9
Fax: 071 638 8488

Executive Vice President: L L Fox
Senior Vice President:
P J Hefferman
B R F Luter
Vice President:
R N L Brandman
P Kluge
G E Marlatte
I J McCannah
D W Ramsay
Assistant General Manager: K C Bird

Bank of Oman
Coventry House
3 South Place
London EC2P 2NH
Tel: 071 638 2271
Telex: 883429
Fax: 071 638 2110

Chief Manager: F H Naboulsi

Bank of Scotland
PO Box No 5
The Mound
Edinburgh EH1 1YZ

Tel: 031 442 7777
Telex: 72275
Fax: 031 243 5437

Governor: Sir Thomas N Risk
Deputy Governor: The Rt Hon
Lord Balfour of Burleigh
Deputy Governor & Group Chief
Executive: D Bruce Pattullo
Director:
A Scott Bell
J E Boyd
Thomas O Hutchison
Professor Robert B Jack
Norman Lessels
Duncan J MacLeod
John M Menzies
Angus M Pelham Burn
A M Rankin
Sir Bob Reid
The Rt Hon Lord Remnant
Professor Jack C Shaw
Sir Robert Smith
Treasurer & Chief General Manager:
Peter A Burt
General Manager:
Thomas Bennie
J R Browning
Archie T Gibson
Gavin G Masterton
Iain W St C Scott
Robert J J Wickham
General Manager & Secretary:
Hugh K Young

Bank of Seoul

3 Finsbury Square
London EC2A 1AD
Tel: 071 588 6162
Telex: 8951507
Fax: 071 588 9655

General Manager: O S Shim

The Bank of Tokyo Capital Markets Ltd

20-24 Moorgate
London EC2R 6DH
Tel: 071 628 3000
Telex: 88254

Managing Director: T Moriguchi
Deputy Managing Director:
K Nakazato
Head of Operations: J P Harris

Bank of Tokyo International Limited

20/24 Moorgate
London EC2R 6DH

Tel: 071 628 3000
Telex: 883254
Fax: 071 628 8464

Chairman: T Naruse
Managing Director: T Kawamoto
Director:
T Moriguchi
I Nakagawa
M J O Pritchard
Y Watanabe
E R Yescombe
Director (Non-Executive):
N J Robson

The Bank of Tokyo Limited

Northgate House
20/24 Moorgate
London EC2R 6DH
Tel: 071 638 1271
Telex: 884819
Fax: 071 628 8241

Managing Director:
Tomonori Naruse
General Manager:
Yoshihiko Nagaya
Deputy General Manager:
Toshihiro Kashizawa
Kazuhiko Wakabayashi
Yoshihiro Watanabe
Tadashi Yanagisawa

Bank of Wales plc

Kingsway
Cardiff CF1 4YB
Tel: 0222 229922
Telex: 497288
Fax: 0222 397193

Executive Director:
T Eric H Crawford
Nicholas Thornton
David B Williams

Bank of Yokohama Ltd

40 Basinghall Street
London EC2V 5DE
Tel: 071 628 9973
Telex: 887995
Fax: 071 638 1886

General Manager: S Asai

Bankers Trust Company

1 Appold Street
Broadgate
London EC2A 2HE
Tel: 071 982 2500
Telex: 883341
Fax: 071 982 3366

Managing Director:
A W Capitman
B Classon
J Clayton
M Clerin
C R Cochin de Billy
B R Cook
O M Cordes
B L M F de Saint Remy
N Doyle
D Dwyer
D Evans
J B Giannotti
D W Godfrey
L Hoagland
C Keer
J Leitner
R McLauchlan
M D Moore
B A Nachamkin
J I Rose
A W P Stenham
B Walsh
G R Walsh
J Zarfaty
General Counsel, Europe: S Ball

Banque Belge Limited

3 St James's Square
London SW1Y 4JU
Tel: 071 930 7000
Telex: 886604/886788
Fax: 071 930 4360

Managing Director: John N Cotton
Executive Director: Anne
Marie Verstraeten
General Manager:
Geraldine Whittaker

Banque Belgo-Zaïroise SA

48-54 Moorgate
London EC2R 6EL
Tel: 071 588 9801
Telex: 888528
Fax: 071 628 1722

Manager: W A Page

Banque Française de l'Orient

31 Berkeley Square
London W1X 5HA
Tel: 071 493 8942
Telex: 23875 BFO WG
Fax: 071 493 7193

General Manager: R C Sturmer
Deputy General Manager:
M Darkazally

Banque Française du Commerce Extérieur
4-6 Throgmorton Avenue
London EC2N 2PP
Tel: 071 638 0088
Telex: 894191

General Manager: C Tran-Ba-Huy

Banque Internationale à Luxembourg
Priory House
1 Mitre Square
London EC3A 5BS
Tel: 071 623 3110
Telex: 884032
Fax: 071 623 5833

Chief Executive: Edward Charlton
General Manager: Brian Wood
Assistant General Manager (Treasury):
  Robert Bird
  Peter Venables
Head of Syndications:
  Robert Halcrow

Banque Nationale de Paris plc
8-13 King William Street
London EC4P 4HS
Tel: 071 895 7070
Telex: 883412
Fax: 071 929 0310

Chairman: The Lord Hunt of
  Tanworth GCB
Managing Director: R Amzallag
General Manager: A P J Kinnison
Deputy General Manager: S Nicolaou
Assistant General Manager:
  C Hallam
  A Powell
  E G Wheeley

Banque Paribas London
68 Lombard Street
London EC3V 9EH
Tel: 071 929 4545
Telex: 945881
Fax: 071 726 6761

Senior Managing Director: F de
  Rancourt
Managing Director: D Bazin
Deputy Managing Director:
  G Raingold
Executive Director:
  C Balfour
  P Cater
  P Cohen
  J de Naurois

Executive Director:
  D Farmer
  D Griffith
  B Smith
  A Starker

Banque Scandinave en Suisse
10 Hill Street
London W1X 7FU
Tel: 071 629 3634
Telex: 886642
Fax: 071 493 4847

Representative: J B Norinder

Barclays Bank plc
Johnson Smirke Building
4 Royal Mint Court
London EC3N 4HJ
Tel: 071 626 1567
Telex: 884970

Chairman: Sir John Quinton
Deputy Chairman:
  Sir Martin Jacomb
  Peter E Leslie
Vice Chairman:
  Andrew R F Buxton
Director:
  Dr David V Atterton CBE
  Mrs Mary Baker
  David Band
  Sir Timothy Bevan
  A E Brown
  John D Birkin
  Ian G Butler
  Lord Camoys
  A R P Carden
  M C Deverell
  The Hon S H Fortescue
  Sir Michael Franklin KCB CMG
  W J Gordon
  Sir Denys Henderson
  Henry U A Lambert
  The Rt Hon Nigel Lawson MP
  G R Miller
  Sir Nigel Mobbs DL
  Humphrey T Norrington
  Brian G Pearse
  A L Robinson
  F A L Robinson
  Anthony J de N Rudge
  K B Sinclair
  Sir James Spooner
  Sir Charles Tidbury DL
  Sir Alan G Tritton
  J H C Whicker
  P A Wood
Secretary: J M D Atterbury
Chief Accountant: N J Brittain

Barclays Broker Services Limited
Pickfords Wharf
Clink Street
London SE1 9DG
Tel: 071 403 4833

Chairman: J Broadhurst
Deputy Chairman: R F Durlacher
Managing Director: A K Vinc-Lott

Barclays de Zoete Wedd Asset Management
Seal House
1 Swan Lane
London EC4R 3UD
Tel: 071 623 7777
Telex: 9413073
Fax: 071 621 9411

Chairman: D A Acland
Vice Chairman: P R Withers Green
Managing Director: D H Brydon

Barclays de Zoete Wedd Holdings Limited
Ebbgate House
2 Swan Lane
London EC4R 3TS
Tel: 071 623 2323
Telex: 8812124
Fax: 071 623 6075

Chairman: Sir Martin Jacomb
Deputy Chairman: Lord Camoys
Vice Chairman: K B Sinclair
Chief Executive: D Band
Director:
  H B Coates
  T B L Coghlan
  J R Davie
  S M de Zoete
  K D Green
  P R Kerridge
  J M F Padovan
  N T Sibley
  O H J Stocken
Non-Executive Director:
  A R P Carden
  Sir Nigel Mobbs DL
  H T Norrington
  Sir James Spooner
  S J Titcomb
  P A Wood
Secretary: T J P Hart

Barclays de Zoete Wedd Limited

Ebbgate House
2 Swan Lane
London EC4R 3TS
Tel: 071 623 2323
Telex: 8812124
Fax: 071 623 6075

Chairman: Sir Martin Jacomb
Deputy Chairman:
    J M F Padovan
    K B Sinclair
Chief Executive: D Band
Director:
    C J F Arnander
    P W Bingham
    Lord Camoys
    P J R Carter
    A H Christie
    R O Cloke
    C E Condren
    R W Crick
    A S Cullen
    M R Cumming
    N B Denison
    N J Durlacher
    M H Forster
    D C Franklin
    L D Goodman
    K D Green
    N Harland
    C P Haviland
    N P J Hawke
    N F Keegan
    P R Kerridge
    D L Knight
    M J Lemay
    C J Mallett
    B J Martin
    T C Martin
    M C McCarthy
    E D Morris
    M C Mowat
    P Noble
    R A M O'Gorman
    R N Paterson
    H R Percy
    M N Peterson
    G F Pimlott
    T Quinn
    R A M Ramsay
    Dr L M Rouse
    I J Scott
    E J Seddon
    J F Standen
    O H J Stocken
    A J Stranger-Jones
    P J Stredder

Director:
    P J Swingler
    R Taylor
    T W Tindall
    Sir Robert Wade-Gery
    R M C Watson
    F M Webster-Smith
    M L V Weyer
    A R Wood

Barclays de Zoete Wedd Securities Ltd

Ebbgate House
2 Swan Lane
London EC4R 3TS
Tel: 071 623 2323
Telex: 8812124
Fax: 071 623 6075

Chairman: Sir Martin Jacomb
Deputy Chairman: K B Sinclair
Chief Executive: D Band
Director:
    G R Austin
    Miss C J C Barnes
    S M W Bishop
    N O Brigstocke
    A E Brown
    D P Brown
    Lord Camoys
    A W F Clapperton
    H B Coates
    T B L Coghlan
    P G Couche
    J S Cousins
    T R Crammond
    S Crane
    A S Cullen
    T A Daniels
    J D David-Jones
    J R Davie
    P De Bray
    S M de Zoete
    R F Durlacher
    N G A Everingham
    B C France
    Miss C E Gale
    N George
    M Gibson
    D J Gillespie
    K D Green
    B F Gregory
    T Grimes
    G N Guinness
    N P H Hadow
    S Hak
    R L Harding
    S J Harker
    E J G Harkness

Director:
    C P Haviland
    P B Hilliar
    D J Hills
    J P Hudson
    M Hughes
    K M Hui
    C A Jessua
    H A Joules
    G R Kelly
    R J Kyle
    W K E Lamond
    I H Macdonald
    J F X Mahe
    Y J F Mahe
    K McGivern
    J E Mernagh
    R E B Mews
    S I Millman
    E D Morris
    J M F Padovan
    H Paget
    J Pegrum
    F P S Phillips
    D R Porter
    R J Priestley
    M Puget
    J A Quaile
    T Quinn
    E Recoder
    A Reid
    P F J Rendell
    D H Roden
    J D H Ross
    S J R Rumsey
    R G Russell
    D R Rutherford
    A G Sadler
    K F P Saunders
    J N Scott-Malden
    N R Scourse
    N T Sibley
    R J Sinclair
    T J Sinclair
    J A Smith
    W J Smith
    A W Sobczak
    K R Squires
    N J Stuchfield
    J N Summerscale
    R Q Tapper
    B L J Tarrel
    A E Teeuw
    R N Thorne
    H B Trust
    J S Varley
    D M Wadwell

Director:
I J Wenham
J M Wightman
A C Wilson

Barclays Development Capital Limited

Pickfords Wharf
Clink Street
London SE1 9DG
Tel: 071 407 2389
Telex: 914912
Fax: 071 407 3362

Chairman: Lord Camoys
Managing Director: M R Cumming
Deputy Managing Director:
C H McLintock
Director:
L S Allan
E S O Bishop
F J Harding
Non-Executive Director:
E B Atling
J W G Cotton
J M F Padovan
M N Peterson
O H J Stocken
R H Watson

Baring Asset Management Ltd

155 Bishopsgate
London EC2M 3XY
Tel: 071 628 6000
Telex: 885888
Fax: 071 638 7928

Chairman: M J Rivett-Carnac
Chief Executive: J D Bolsover
Director:
W Backhouse
M W Banton
G S Cass
M T Chamberlayne
G S Giles
L I Greenlees
P S Hartley
J E Heskett
J A Morrell
R M Shaw
J J K Taylor
J P Williams

Baring Brothers & Co Limited

8 Bishopsgate
London EC2N 4AE

Tel: 071 280 1000
Telex: 883622
Fax: 071 283 2633

Chairman: A M L Tuckey
Managing Director: R D Broadley
Director:
A M G Baring
G G F Barnett
S P F Best
S A Borrows
N D Brown
P E Bugge
M L Burch
K G Cox
J A Dare
J M de Bunsen
J R F Fairbrother
N R Gold
A J D Hawes
C J Heath
P Heininger
I W Hopkins
C L A Irby
J R C Lupton
G A MacLean
A C O McGrath
N E Melville
J M A Menendez
J P Moon
P M R Norris
R A Onians
R W D Orders
M J Packman
J R Peers
The Hon J H T Russell
Dr F Stangenberg-Havercamp
C J Steane
A B Swann
B Taylor
K Ujihara
O W Van Der Wyck
Lord Verulam
M S Younes
Non-Executive Director: W A Black

Baring Brothers Hambrecht & Quist Ltd

140 Park Lane
London W1Y 3AA
Tel: 071 408 0555
Telex: 295082
Fax: 071 493 5153

Chief Executive: Richard A Onians

Baring Capital Investors Limited

140 Park Lane
London W1Y 3AA
Tel: 071 408 1282
Fax: 071 493 1368

Chief Executive: Otto van der Wyck
Executive Director:
John Burgess
Paul Griffiths
Associate: Simon Palley

Baring Securities Limited

Lloyds Chambers
1 Portsoken Street
London E1 8DF
Tel: 071 621 1500
Telex: 887714
Fax: 071 623 1873

Chairman: J A Dare
Managing Director:
Christopher J Heath
Director:
S A Aldridge
A M G Baring
A R L Baylis
J R E Campbell-Lamerton
B Y Cho
Dr C J Derricott
The Hon A A M Fraser
Ms V Gibson
J A Guy
M C Hatcher
R D T Johnson
R Katz
R D A Kelly
I J Martin
A T Murray
W T Murray
N H Radley
H A C Reid
T Z Sliwerski
Ms K Terazawa
A M L Tuckey
S W Webb

Barings plc

8 Bishopsgate
London EC2N 4AE
Tel: 071 280 1000
Telex: 883622
Fax: 071 283 2633

Chairman: P Baring
Deputy Chairman:
M J Rivett-Carnac
A M L Tuckey
Director: R D Broadley

Non-Executive Director:
The Hon Sir John Baring
KCVO
N H Baring
R Malpas CBE
H M P Miles OBE

Barnett Waddingham & Company
11 Tufton Street
London SW1P 3QB
Tel: 071 222 1961
Fax: 071 222 6783

Senior Partner: H R Wynne-Griffith

Baronsmead plc
Clerkenwell House
67 Clerkenwell Road
London EC1R 5BH
Tel: 071 242 4900
Fax: 071 242 2048

Chairman: Paul Borrett
Managing Director: R Hargreaves

Bass plc
66 Chiltern Street
London W1M 1PR
Tel: 071 486 4440

Chairman: I M G Prosser
Financial Director: D G Inns

Bayerische Hypotheken-und-Wechsel Bank
41 Moorgate
London EC2R 6AE
Tel: 071 638 2728
Telex: 894624
Fax: 071 638 1712

General Manager:
Kurt Sachs
R Wolf
General Manager Property Finance:
Georg Funke

Bayerische Landesbank Girozentrale
Bavaria House
13/14 Appold Street
London EC2A 2AA
Tel: 071 247 0056
Telex: 886437

General Manager and Chief Executive:
G Mann
General Manager:
C Butcher
M King

Bayerische Vereinsbank
1 Royal Exchange Buildings
London EC3V 3LD
Tel: 071 626 1301
Telex: 889196

General Manager:
Dr B Graf von Wallwitz
G Skinner
Manager Corporate Banking:
M Korwin
Chief Dealer: D Sawyer

Beazer plc
Beazer House
Lower Bristol Road
Bath BA2 3EY
Tel: 0225 428401
Telex: 449497
Fax: 0225 339279

Chairman & Chief Executive:
Brian C Beazer
Deputy Chairman & Deputy Chief Executive: John W Matthews
Finance Director, Beazer Europe & Overseas Ltd: John H Bennett
Group Finance Director:
Alan Chapple
Chairman & Chief Executive, Beazer USA, Inc: Thomas B Howard Jr
Deputy Chairman, Beazer Europe & Overseas Ltd: Robert D Stephens
Investment Director:
Matthew W J Thorne
Executive Vice President & Chief Financial Officer, Beazer USA, Inc: Roy G Turner
Chairman, Beazer Europe & Overseas Ltd: Terry J Upsall
Group Legal Advisor and Company Secretary: D J Heathcote
Group Finance Controller:
J M Miners
Group Tax Manager: C W Davey
Group Treasurer: Peter Coates

Beeson Gregory Limited
The Registry
Royal Mint Court
London EC3N 4EY
Tel: 071 488 4040
Fax: 071 481 3762

Non-Executive Chairman:
R N D Langdon
Chief Executive: A N W Beeson
Director:
J H Flower
J E Gordon

Director:
J F Gregory
R A M Lederman
J W J Moxon
Finance Director: J J Tilbrook
Non-Executive Director:
N F Baldock
A C Zaphiriou-Zarifi
Associate Director:
D F Langmead
P N Rodgers
C M P Smith
C Warner-Allen

Bell Houldsworth Fairmount Limited
PO Box No 329
Fountain Court
68 Fountain Street
Manchester M60 2QL
Tel: 061 228 2228

Managing Director: J W Parkinson

Bell Lawrie White & Co Ltd
17 Tokenhouse Yard
London EC2R 7LB
Tel: 071 588 5699
Telex: 886202
Fax: 071 726 4455

Chairman: Mark E Tennant
Deputy Chairman:
Michael P Goodman
Managing Director:
Christopher Jeal
D J H McIntosh

Benchmark Bank plc
Benchmark House
86 Newman Street
London W1P 3LD
Tel: 071 631 3313
Fax: 071 323 9321

Executive Chairman: L C Quek
Deputy Chairman: L A W Evans
Managing Director: R Williams
Deputy Managing Director:
P A Bendall
Financial Director: B R B Carrick
Lending Director: G J Horton
Associate Director/Financial Controller: W R Dobbie
Associate Director/Recoveries:
V A Millgate
Director, Leasing Division:
G D H Main
Sales Director, Leasing Division:
R W Lilwall

Benchmark Group plc

Benchmark House
86 Newman Street
London W1P 3LD
Tel: 071 631 3313
Fax: 071 323 9320

Executive Chairman: L C Quek
Group Managing Director:
L A W Evans
Director:
L H Kwek
J H B Muenter
K R Pinker
E E Sander
M J Seal
R Williams
D W Youngman

Benitz and Partners Limited

24-25 New Bond Street
London W1Y 9HD
Tel: 071 495 1859
Fax: 071 409 3134

Chairman: Bryan Benitz

Beogradska Banka DD

Representative Office
108 Fenchurch Street
London EC3M 5JJ
Tel: 071 488 3766
Telex: 887689
Fax: 071 481 1902

Director: M Marinkovic

Berliner Bank AG

Berliner House
81-82 Gracechurch Street
London EC3V 0DS
Tel: 071 929 4060
Fax: 884131

General Manager:
W F Bruehl
A J Price

Berry Palmer & Lyle Ltd

24/26 Minories
London EC3N 1BY
Tel: 071 265 1921
Telex: 928459
Fax: 071 480 7036

Chairman: T L F Royle
Managing Director: J C H Berry
Marketing Director: A A H Palmer
Director:
B de Haldevang
G E J A Doughty

Director:
R A W Lyle
A J Miller
P G Torrington
Secretary: S L Liu

BICC

Devonshire House
Mayfair Place
London W1X 5FH
Tel: 071 629 6622
Telex: 23463
Fax: 071 409 0365

Treasurer: D H Goodman

Bikuben

London Representative Office
65-66 Queen Street
London EC4R 1EH
Tel: 071 248 0863
Telex: 926577
Fax: 071 236 4839

Senior Representative:
Finn Bergmann

Billiton-Enthoven Metals Limited

84 Fenchurch Street
London EC3M 4BY
Tel: 071 480 7290
Telex: 8953341
Fax: 071 488 1986

Chairman: D C Heath
Managing Director: F W R Beck
Director:
T J Bartlett
M J G Linington
D E Ratcliffe
Secretary: Mrs J M Lloyd

Birmingham Midshires Building Society

PO Box 81
35-49 Lichfield Street
Wolverhampton WV1 1EL
Tel: 0902 710710
Fax: 0902 713412

Chairman: C J James
Chief Executive: D A McDonald
Finance Director: Stephen Bright

Birmingham Technology (Venture Capital) Limited

Aston Science Park, Love Lane
Aston Triangle
Birmingham B7 4BJ

Tel: 021 359 0981
Telex: 334535
Fax: 021 359 0433

Managing Director: H A Nicholls

Blue Circle Industries plc

84 Eccleston Square
London SW1V 1PX
Tel: 071 828 3456
Telex: 927757
Fax: 071 245 8169

Group Treasurer: Colin Hunter

BNP Capital Markets Limited

8-13 King William Street
London EC4N 7DN
Tel: 071 548 9548
Telex: 935850
Fax: 071 548 9513

Managing Director: B Poignant

BOC Group plc

Chertsey Road
Windlesham GU20 6HJ
Tel: 0276 77222
Telex: 859363
Fax: 0276 71333

Group Treasurer: S A Bowles

Booker plc

Portland House
Stag Place
London SW1E 5AY
Tel: 071 828 9850
Telex: 888169
Fax: 071 630 8029

Non-Executive Chairman:
Sir Michael Caine
Chief Executive: Jonathan Taylor
Executive Director:
L Hoskins
R A McKenzie
E C Robinson
B J Skipper
D J Turner FCA
Non-Executive Director:
M H Fisher
J A Haynes
Sir Michael Palliser GCMG PC
R N Quartano
R C Rockefeller

The Boots Co plc

Nottingham NG2 3AA

Tel: 0602 506111
Telex: 378431
Fax: 0602 592727

Chairman: Sir Christopher Benson
Vice Chairman: A B Marshall
Managing Director, Retail Division:
    K Ackroyd
Managing Director, Pharmaceuticals
    Division: E E Cliffe
Finance Director: D A R Thompson
Personnel Director:
    A H Hawksworth TD
Managing Director, Boots The
    Chemists: G M Hourston
Marketing Director, Pharmaceuticals
    Division: T G Richardson
Managing Director, Property Division:
    M F Ruddell
Director, North American
    Pharmaceuticals Division:
    G R Solway
Director:
    I M G Prosser
    Sir Peter Reynolds CBE
    The Rt Hon Sally the Baroness
        Oppenheim-Barnes of
        Gloucester
Secretary: I A Hawtin
Group Treasurer: M G Bunting

C T Bowring & Co Limited

The Bowring Building
Tower Place
London EC3P 3BE
Tel: 071 357 1000
Telex: 882191
Fax: 071 929 2705

Chairman & Chief Executive:
    P L Wroughton
Director:
    A H Bolton
    C J S Cullum
    B R E Hibbert
    R M Quill
    H M J Ritchie
    A J C Smith
    F J Tasco
    G H C Wakefield
Company Secretary: C M R Pearson
Group Personnel Executive:
    E J B Leach

BP Pensions Services Ltd

Britannic House
Moor Lane
London EC2Y 9BU

Tel: 071 920 4287
Telex: 888811
Fax: 071 920 3736

General Manager: J W Martin
Property Manager: W J Cox
Compliance Officer: G R Cridlan
Portfolio Manager:
    S M Butler
    T J Dillon
    S C Harris
    H I Steadman

BPB Industries

Langley Park House
Uxbridge Road
Slough SL3 6DU
Tel: 0753 73273
Telex: 847694
Fax: 0753 823397

Finance Director: B J Hogben

Bradford & Bingley Building Society

PO Box 2
Main Street
Bingley BD16 2LW
Tel: 0274 568111
Telex: 51210
Fax: 0274 569116

Chairman: P T Duxbury
Chief Executive: G R Lister

Operations Director: D Hanson
Sales & Marketing Director:
    M Pheasey
General Manager & Secretary:
    F M Hallam
General Manager:
    J G Lodge
    S G Spilsbury

Bradstock Blunt & Crawley Ltd

58/59 Fenchurch Street
London EC3M 4AB
Tel: 071 436 7878
Telex: 884234
Fax: 071 488 4834

Chairman: Oliver D Plunkett
Managing Director:
    Robert E G Gibson
    David C Huntington
Director:
    Peter H Bentley
    Vincent J Byrne
    Susan Christiansen
    John C Cliff

Director:
    George W Cocks
    Nigel E N Collins
    Peter W J Cresswell
    Giles C Gleadell
    David W Haspineall
    John G Laver
    Michael H Morland
    Edward G Rendell
    Brian J Robbins
    Malcolm D Stratten
    David M Stratton
    David R H Whitewood

Bradstock Blunt & Thompson Ltd

52/53 Russell Square
London WC1B 4HP
Tel: 071 436 7878
Telex: 8812183
Fax: 071 436 9770

Chairman and Managing Director:
    Edmund B McGrath
Deputy Managing Director:
    Stephen W Calcroft
Director:
    Robin E Bradford
    Philip M Branch
    Nicholas M Bryce-Smith
    Kevin L Davies
    David W Hill
    Peter R Horsman
    Victor I Knope
    Peter F J Monnickendam
    David A Page
    Francis A Staples
    Jeremy D Stephen

Bradstock Financial Services Ltd

52/53 Russell Square
London WC1B 4HP
Tel: 071 436 7878
Telex: 8812183
Fax: 071 323 4635

Chairman: Edmund B McGrath
Deputy Chairman: Geoffrey Smith
Managing Director:
    Terence C Monk
Director:
    William E Bennington
    John N Cosslett
    Timothy P Culverhouse
    Robert E G Gibson
    Colin T Preston
    James Scanlon

Bradstock Group plc

18 London Street
London EC3R 7JP
Tel: 071 436 7878
Telex: 884234
Fax: 071 481 8896

Chairman: Oliver D Plunkett
Managing Director and Chief
   Executive: Robert E G Gibson
Director:
   David M Backhouse
   Peter W J Cresswell
   Edmund B McGrath

Brandeis (Brokers) Limited

4 Fore Street
London EC2P 4NU
Tel: 071 638 5877
Telex: 884401
Fax: 071 638 3031

Chairman: B Poux-Guillaume
Managing Director: V J Davies
Director:
   A G Fergusson
   D T Griffin
   G Hauser
   W J Smith
Finance Director & Company
   Secretary: S E Fishburn

Brandeis Limited

4 Fore Street
London EC2P 2NU
Tel: 071 638 5877
Telex: 884401
Fax: 071 638 3031

Chairman: B Poux-Guillaume
Managing Director: D P Hargrave
Director:
   P E Brau
   V J Davies
   B J Edmondson
   D T Griffin
   G Hauser
   I Markson
   J S Shaw
   W J Smith
   C Woodhouse
Finance Director and Company
   Secretary: S E Fishburn

Branston & Gothard Ltd

52-58 Tabernacle Street
London EC2A 4PL
Tel: 071 250 1180
Telex: 9419098
Fax: 071 490 1301

Director:
   G M Branston
   K A Brown
   R I Cummings
   P M Marks

Brewin Dolphin & Co Ltd

5 Giltspur Street
London EC1A 9DE
Tel: 071 248 4400
Telex: 21423
Fax: 071 236 2034

Chairman: The Earl of Ranfurly
Managing Director: J P Hall
Director:
   I R D Andrew
   R A Andrew
Compliance Director: D J Gates
Director:
   J S Gordon
   S R H Hosford
   C D Legge
   M R I Lilwall
   W H Main
   J R Maunsell-Thomas
   D B E Pike
   D A Platts
   L J Smith
   M St. Giles
   R M Sutton
   D C Thompson
   M J R Williams
Associate Director:
   R P H Corden
   R J Hardwicke
   R J F Lynn

Bristol & West Building Society

PO Box 27
Broad Quay
Bristol BS99 7AX
Tel: 0272 294271
Telex: 44741
Fax: 0272 211632

Chairman: Sir John Wills
President: A Breach
Managing Director & Chief Executive:
   P A Fitzsimons
Finance Director: P J F Breach
General Manager:
   J J Burke
   R M Coverdale
   A J Draper
   I D Kennedy
Secretary: D W Abecassis

Britannia Building Society

PO Box 20
Newton House
Leek
Staffs ST13 5RG
Tel: 0538 399399
Fax: 0538 399149

Managing Director: F Michael Shaw
Treasurer/General Manager:
   Philip Davis

British Aerospace plc

11 Strand
London WC2N 5JT
Tel: 071 930 1020
Telex: 919221
Fax: 071 839 4774

Treasurer: J D Hanson

British Airways Pensions

Alton House
177 High Holborn
London WC1V 7AA
Tel: 071 836 3511
Telex: 268635
Fax: 071 240 7468

Chief Executive: J C Woodward
Investment Manager: Peter Moon
UK Equities Manager: Chris Wright
Overseas Equities Manager:
   Mike Sparkes
Fixed Interest Manager:
   Andrew Lang
Property Manager: Chris Keable

British Airways plc

PO Box 10
London Heathrow Airport
Hounslow TW6 2JA
Tel: 081 759 5511
Telex: 8813983
Fax: 081 839 2311

Treasurer: R Galbraith

British Bank of The Middle East

Falcon House
18c Curzon Street
London W1Y 8AA
Tel: 071 493 8331
Telex: 27544
Fax: 071 409 1140

Director: Ian Gill

British & Commonwealth Merchant Bank plc
66 Cannon Street
London EC4N 6AE
Tel: 071 248 0900
Telex: 884040
Fax: 071 248 0906

Chairman: John H Gunn
Deputy Chairman & Chief Executive:
   Bruce A Ursell
Managing Director:
   Malcolm J Wilde
Director, Treasury: Geoffrey J Clay
*Director (Research and Fund
   Management):*
   R Philip R Darwall-Smith
   Christopher C Edge
Director, Media Finance:
   Jorge Gallegos
Director, Treasury & Capital Markets:
   Peter A Haring
Director (Banking):
   Robin C Holliday
Director, Compliance:
   Ian C McAndrew
Director (Syndications):
   David A Milne
   Peter Morley
Director, Private Banking:
   Mark G C Toller
Director (Human Resources):
   J F Rayman
Director:
   R E Basher
   Sir P T Miles
   Paul W Ormrod
   M V Phythian-Adams
   J J Silviri
   S C White

British Coal Corporation
Hobart House
Grosvenor Place
London SW1X 7AE
Tel: 071 235 2020

Group Treasurer: M Garrett

British Gas plc
Rivermill House
152 Grosvenor Road
London SW1V 3JL
Tel: 071 821 1444
Telex: 938529
Fax: 071 821 8522

Managing Director, Group Finance:
   Allan Sutcliffe
Group Treasurer: Arthur W Burgess

Director of Strategic Planning:
   Dr Robert South
Head of Investor Relations:
   Allan H Curran

British Invisibles
6th Floor Windsor House
39 King Street
London EC2V 8DQ
Tel: 071 600 1198
Telex: 9413342
Fax: 071 606 4248

Chairman: The Earl
   of Limerick KBE
Deputy Chairman:
   Sir Michael Palliser GCMG
Director General: David P Thomson
Executive Director: Richard G Mason
Director:
   Ms M Gaye Murdoch MBE
   Kenneth C Wright CMG OBE
Secretary: M C Nicolle

British Land
No 10 Cornwall Terrace
Regent's Park
London NW1 4QP
Tel: 071 486 4466
Telex: 28411
Fax: 071 935 5552

Chairman and Managing Director:
   J H Ritblat
Finance Director and Secretary:
   J H Weston Smith
Director:
   D C Berry
   S L Kalman
   C Metliss
Non-Executive Director:
   P W Simon
   J D Spink

The British Linen Bank Limited
PO Box No 49
4 Melville Street
Edinburgh EH3 7NZ
Tel: 031 453 1919
Telex: 727221
Fax: 031 243 8393

Governor: J Edward Boyd
Chief Executive: Eric F Sanderson
Depty Chief Executive:
   Alexander D Nicol
Finance Director: A Douglas Peebles
Director:
   John S Hunter

Director:
   W Donald Marr
   M Douglas McPhail
   Alan A Murray
   Nigel M Suess

The British Petroleum Company plc
Britannic House
1 Finsbury Circus
London EC2M 7BA
Tel: 071 920 8000
Telex: 888811
Fax: 071 920 8263

Chairman and Chief Executive Officer:
   R B Horton
*Deputy Chairman and Chief Operating
   Officer:* D A G Simon
Managing Director:
   B R R Butler OBE
   P J Gillam
   R R Knowland
   H E Norton
Chief Executive, BP Oil: K R Seal
Chief Executive, BP Exploration:
   E J P Browne
Chief Executive, BP Chemicals:
   B K Sanderson
Chief Executive, BP Nutrition:
   R Gourlay
*Chief Executive and Group Treasurer,
   BP Finance:* S W Percy
Company Secretary: R C Grayson

British Railways Board
Euston House
PO Box 100
24 Eversholt Street
London NW1 1DZ
Tel: 071 928 5151
Telex: 299431
Fax: 071 922 6994

Chairman: Sir R P Reid
Deputy Chairman: D Fowler
Chief Executive, Railways:
   J K Welsby
*Managing Director, Operations &
   Engineering:* D Rayner
Managing Director, Group Services:
   J C P Edmonds
Non-Executive Member:
   Ms A Biss
   J B Cameron
   Sir Oscar De Ville
   Sir Derek Hamby
   Miss K T Kantor
   A J G Sheppard

British Steel plc
9 Albert Embankment
London SE1 7SN
Tel: 071 735 7654

Group Treasurer: R W Peek

British Technology Group
101 Newington Causeway
London SE1 6BU
Tel: 071 403 6666
Telex: 894397
Fax: 071 403 7586

Chairman: C Barker
Chief Executive: I A Harvey

British Telecommunications plc
81 Newgate Street
London EC1A 7AJ
Tel: 071 356 5000

Group Treasurer: Richard Savage
*Director Financial Control, Personal
   Communications Division:*
   B J Cameron Smail

British Venture Capital Association
3 Catherine Place
London SW1E 6DX
Tel: 071 233 5212
Fax: 071 931 0563

Chairman: Michael Denny

Broadbridge
Wellington Plaza
31 Wellington Street
Leeds LS1 4DL
Tel: 0532 443721
Fax: 0532 420134

Joint Senior Partner:
   Christopher J Corlett
   Stephen Hastings
Branch Partner: Ian L Waugh
Finance and Administration Partner:
   Robert F Pickering
Compliance Partner: M A Elviss
Partner: D J Hall

Brown, Shipley & Co Limited
Founders Court
Lothbury
London EC2R 7HE
Tel: 071 606 9833
Telex: 886704
Fax: 071 600 1517

Chairman: The Rt Hon
   Lord Farnham
Deputy Chairman: John P de Blocq
   van Kuffeler
*Managing Director, Corporate
   Banking:* Charles P Barrington
Managing Director: G Geoffrey Bell
Managing Director, Offshore Banking:
   David J Berkeley
*Managing Director, Management
   Services:* Robert C Carefull
Managing Director, Corporate Finance:
   Derek J Connolly
*Managing Director, International
   Investment Banking:*
   Francesco M Rossi
Director:
   David K Anslow
   Timothy R Bacon
   Stewart J C Dick
   Charles S Fairhurst
   John A B Kelly
   C Richard F Kemp
   Jeremy P Knight
   Alastair J Lawson
   Dominic E D McCarthy
   J Robin Owens
   Peter R Shand
   Timothy M Trowell
   Etienne Verilghen
   Michael J C Watts
   David J Wills
Secretary: Michael J Halsey

Brown Shipley Development Capital Ltd
Founders Court
Lothbury
London EC2R 7HE
Tel: 071 606 9833
Telex: 886704
Fax: 071 600 2279

Managing Director: David Wills

Brown Shipley Stockbroking Ltd
Founders Court
Lothbury
London EC2R 7HE
Tel: 071 726 4059
Telex: 918795

Managing Director: M A Ingram

BSI-Banca della Svizzera Italiana
London Branch
Windsor House
39 King Street
London EC2V 8DQ
Tel: 071 600 0033
Telex: 884821
Fax: 071 606 3484

Senior Vice President: N R L Hudson

BTR plc
Silvertown House
Vincent Square
London SW1P 2PL
Tel: 071 834 3848
Telex: 22524
Fax: 071 834 3879

Chairman: Sir Owen Green
Chief Executive: A Jackson
Group Finance Director: C R H Bull
Company Secretary: S K Williams
Director:
   R F Faircloth
   N C Ireland
   A R Jackson
   H W Laughland
   E E Sharp
   J D M Smith
   L J Stammers
   G J Yardley
Group Treasurer: J D Thom

J K Buckenham Limited
Chesterfield House
26/28 Fenchurch Street
London EC3M 3DQ
Tel: 071 929 1754
Telex: 883920 BUCKEN G
Fax: 071 283 8365

Chairman: J K Buckenham
Director:
   M J Attenborough
   J A Buckenham
   P J Horner
   M J Hughes
Director and Company Secretary:
   R J W Parris
Assistant Director:
   D W Monk
   J P Ramsay
   M Stanley

Buckmaster Management Company Limited
Beaufort House
15 St Botolph Street
London EC3A 7JJ
Tel: 071 247 7474
Telex: 883229 BANDM G
Fax: 071 247 4539

Chairman & Chief Executive:
　Harry J France
Head of Marketing: A W P Ross
Finance Director: Mervyn N Jones
Head of Fund Management Division:
　F J Ewers

The Building Societies Commission
15 Great Marlborough Street
London W1V 2AX
Tel: 071 437 9992
Fax: 071 437 1612

First Commissioner (Chairman):
　Mrs R E J Gilmore
Commissioner:
　D C Hobson
　T F Mathews
　S Procter CBE
　G T Sammons
　H W Walden CBE

Bunzl plc
Stoke House
Stoke Green
Stoke Poges
Slough SL2 4JN
Tel: 0753 693693
Telex: 847503
Fax: 0753 694694

Chairman and Chief Executive:
　J White
Director:
　K R Anderson
　B P Ford
　D C Latimer
　P G Lorenzini
　T C F Simpson
Non-Executive Director:
　G C Hoyer Millar
　D W Kendall
　B McGillivray
Group Treasurer: Philip Godbold

The Burmah Oil plc
Burmah House
Pipers Way
Swindon SN3 1RE

Tel: 0793 511521
Telex: 449221
Fax: 0793 612524

Chairman/Chief Executive:
　L M Urquhart
Chief Executive, Shipping, Energy Investments: M J Cooper
Chief Executive, Speciality Chemicals:
　J H Ellicock
Chief Executive, Lubricants and Fuels:
　J M Fry
Director, Finance: B Hardy
Secretary: J B Jones
Non-Executive Director:
　G C Butcher
　I G Dobbie
　H S Mellor
　R C Shaw CBE

Burns Fry
4 Broadgate
London EC2M 7LE
Tel: 071 895 0650
Telex: 884645

Managing Director: H J Queisser

The Burton Group plc
214 Oxford Street
London W1N 9DF
Tel: 071 636 8040
Telex: 21484
Fax: 071 927 0580

Chairman: Sir John Hoskyns
Chief Executive: Laurence Cooklin
Managing Director: Paul G Plant
Director:
　Gerald A Slater
　Richard T Harris
　Mark Littman
　Ladislas O Rice
　William M Wood
　Robert C Woodman
Group Treasurer: N Robson
Group Secretary: J O Davies

Byas Mosley & Co Ltd
William Byas House
14/18 St Clare Street
London EC3N 1JX
Tel: 071 481 0101
Telex: 894266
Fax: 071 480 5305

Non-Executive Chairman:
　A J Hamilton
Managing Director: N K L Webb
Finance Director: A Mirza

Director:
　N Chapman
　A J Duggan
　J Elliott
　A J Ellison
　S F D Knight
　E G Rossdale
　A C Turner

Byblos Bank Sal
7 Berkeley Square
London W1X 5HF
Tel: 071 493 3537

Chairman & General Manager:
　Dr F Bassil
Manager: Gaby G Fadel

C & G Guardian
(Central Lending Division of Cheltenham & Gloucester Building Society)
120 High Holborn
London WC1V 6RH
Tel: 071 242 3142
Fax: 071 242 6364

Chairman: V A Dawson
Managing Director: P L Coster
Director:
　D Barnes
　G M McKenzie
　D K Thomas
　D Turner
General Manager & Secretary:
　T E Howes
Assistant General Manager (Finance):
　C Imison
　F Jones
　D Walsh

C S Investments Limited
125 High Holborn
London WC1V 6PY
Tel: 071 242 1148
Telex: 291986
Fax: 071 831 7187

Non-Executive Chairman: F Shama
Managing Director: S Stevenson
Director:
　R C Buist
　D H Davenport
　M C C Davies
　A B Fisher
　R Porter
　A D Ward
　N R Wilson
Non-Executive Director:
　M Cannon Brooks

Non-Executive Director:
The Hon C Lyttleton
G van Riemsdijk
E Vonk

Cable & Wireless plc
26 Red Lion Square
London WC1R 4UQ
Tel: 071 315 4000
Telex: 920000
Fax: 071 315 5000

Director, Finance: R J Olsen
Director of Corporate Financial
Services: J K Phillips

Cadbury Schweppes plc
1-4 Connaught Place
London W2 2EX
Tel: 071 262 1212
Telex: 334413 CSPLC G
Fax: 071 262 1212 extn 2121

Non-Executive Chairman:
Sir Graham Day
Chief Executive: N D Cadbury
Finance Director and Deputy Chief
Executive: N C Bain
Managing Director, Beverages Stream:
J P Schadt
Chief Executive, Cadbury Schweppes
Australia Ltd: F J Swan
Managing Director, Confectionery
Stream: D G Wellings
Managing Director, Coca-Cola &
Schweppes Beverages Limited:
D R Williams
Secretary: M A C Clark
Director of Treasury: J Grout
Director, Corporate Communications:
R C Milburn

Caisse Centrale des Banques Populaires
4 London Wall Buildings
Blomfield Street
London EC2M 5NT
Tel: 071 588 3281
Telex: 8812428
Fax: 071 374 6787

UK Representative: C Tellier

Caisse Nationale de Credit Agricole
Condor House
14 St Paul's Churchyard
London EC4M 8BD

Tel: 071 248 1400
Telex: 8811521
Fax: 071 248 0788

General Manager, CAFCO: A de
Truchis
Deputy General Manager: D Barrows
Managing Director: D Kingsmill
Assistant General Manager, Corporate
Banking & Finance Division:
Paul Rex

Caja de Ahorros de Galicia
125 Kensington High Street
London W8 5SF
Tel: 071 938 1805
Telex: 919284
Fax: 071 376 1194

Representative: Manuel
Santos Torreira

Calor Group plc
Appleton Park
Datchet
Slough SL3 9JG
Tel: 0753 40000
Telex: 848384
Fax: 0753 48121

Company Secretary: Jonathan Dance
Chairman: A M Davies
Chief Executive: D J Mitchell
Director:
R W Pickering
A J Rijnvis
F Schukken
Finance Director: A M Pate

Cambridge Capital Limited
13 Station Road
Cambridge CB1 2JB
Tel: 0223 312856
Fax: 0223 65704

Chairman: Mark Hoffman
Managing Director:
Francis Madden TD

Cambridge Capital Management Limited
13 Station Road
Cambridge CB1 2JB
Tel: 0223 312856
Fax: 0223 65704

Chairman: Richard King
Managing Director:
Stephen Bloomfield

Campbell Lutyens Hudson Co Ltd
4 Clifford Street
London W1X 1RB
Tel: 071 439 7191
Telex: 21888
Fax: 071 437 0153

Chairman: B N Kelly
Director:
A J W Campbell
W J A Dacombe
D W Hudson
J M Loizaga
R D Lutyens
P Muuls

Canara Bank
Longbow House
14/20 Chiswell Street
London EC1Y 4SR
Tel: 071 628 2187
Telex: 8956961
Fax: 071 374 2468

Chief Executive: G A Shenai

Candover Investments plc
8/9 East Harding Street
London EC4A 3AS
Tel: 071 583 5090
Telex: 928035
Fax: 071 583 0717

Chairman: C R E Brooke
Deputy Chairman: A P Hichens
Chief Executive: S W Curran
Deputy Chief Executive:
G D Fairservice
Director:
G A Elliot
R A P King
J P Scott Plummer
J G West
Secretary: P Neal
Associate Director: J Warran
Investment Manager:
C J Bultin
M S Gumienny
P G Symonds
Financial Controller: M E Murphy

Capability Trust Managers Limited
65 Holborn Viaduct
London EC1A 2UE
Tel: 071 236 3053
Telex: 886653
Fax: 071 248 0296

Chairman: J C Henderson

Director:
C C Ball
The Earl of Euston
J S Hillyer OBE
A L Klahr
K G S Levy
J Loudon
K R Streeter

Capel-Cure Myers Capital Management Ltd
The Registry
Royal Mint Court
London EC3N 4EY
Tel: 071 488 4000
Telex: 9419251 PROCURG
Fax: 071 481 3798

Chairman: I H Leslie Melville
Chief Executive: J C Henderson
Finance Director: The Earl
    of Euston
Director:
C C Ball
R O W Derby
R F Down
P M T Jones
K G S Levy
T R Pattison

Capital Ventures Ltd
Rutherford Way
Cheltenham GL51 9TR
Tel: 0242 584380
Fax: 0242 226671

Chairman: D Fredjohn
Managing Director: P J Underhill

Cargill UK Ltd
3 Shortlands
London W6 8RT
Tel: 081 741 9090
Telex: 298965
Fax: 081 846 0950

Chairman: R Murray
Director:
A Blankestijn
The Earl of Carrick
D L Holy
D A Nelson-Smith
Company Secretary: John Reynolds

Carnegie International Ltd
Carthusian Court
12 Carthusian Street
London EC1M 6EB
Tel: 071 606 0055
Fax: 071 796 2617

Managing Director: C Bouckley
Deputy Managing Director:
    J Rowlands

Carr Kitcat and Aitken Limited
No 1 London Bridge
London SE1 9TJ
Tel: 071 378 7050
Telex: 8956121
Fax: 071 403 0755

Co Chairman:
P Nuttall
D H Starling

Carswell Ltd
Stock Exchange House
7 Nelson Mandela Place
Glasgow G2 1BU
Tel: 041 221 3402
Fax: 041 221 2979

Chairman: D McGuinness
Director:
Thomas S Carswell
George H Montgomery

Cassa di Risparmio di Genova e Imperia
Wax Chandlers Hall
Gresham Street
London EC2V 7AD
Tel: 071 606 8225
Telex: 886529
Fax: 071 726 2694

UK Representative: L Castello

Cater Allen Limited
20 Birchin Lane
London EC3V 9DJ
Tel: 071 623 2070
Telex: 888553
Fax: 071 929 1641

Chairman & Managing Director:
James C Barclay
Managing Director:
C J W Frost
J E Illsley
D J White
S R B Wood
Director:
P G Cairns
E R R Jewson
M D Lee
I T Liss
N H D Ryder

Cater Allen Securities Limited
20 Birchin Lane
London EC3V 9DJ
Tel: 071 623 2070
Telex: 888553

Chairman: J C Barclay
Managing Director: J E Illsley
Director:
A W Bumstead
D J Coe
J L Derx
M D Lee
J A Pound

Causeway Capital Limited
7 Hanover Square
London W1R 9HE
Tel: 071 495 2525
Fax: 071 491 2050

Director:
Lionel Anthony
Ian Cameron
Andrew Joy
Geoffrey Vero
David Secker Walker
Secretary: Christopher Jenkins

Cazenove & Co
12 Tokenhouse Yard
London EC2R 7AN
Tel: 071 588 2828
Telex: 886758
Fax: 071 606 9205

Senior Partner:
A D A W Forbes
J Kemp-Welch
Partner:
The Lord Faringdon
M P Archer
U D Barnett
R A R Bradfield
D R Brazier
P J Brown
M Calvert
G S P Carden
C J Cazalet
P C J Dalby
S J Daniels
B M de L Cazenove
H de L Cazenove
S J Dettmer
P K F Donlea
A P A Drysdale
J W Findlay
D C Godwin
N A Gold

Partner:
R de C Grubb
Hon J E R Harbord-Hamond
H M Henderson
L D E Hollingworth
J C Hubbard
D R Hunter
C P Kindersley
R M U Lambert
The Hon V M G A Lampson
M A Loveday
R L H Lyster
D L Mayhew
P B Mitford-Slade
S P Morant
A H J Muir
C D Palmer-Tomkinson
B E A Pascoe
J G H Paynter
I A D Pilkington
M R P Power
J T Reilly
N Rowe
P D Rylands
T Schoch
A J Scott-Barrett
C Smith
R B Smith
S R V Troughton
D M Wentworth-Stanley
E T Whitley
R D Wintour

CCF Foster Braithwaite Ltd

27 Finsbury Square
London EC2A 1BD
Tel: 071 588 6111
Telex: 8954140
Fax: 071 256 5505

Chairman: A B Greayer
Deputy Chairman: M Haski
Managing Director: J Vintcent
Director:
J N Braithwaite
D C Gascoigne
T M Halton
H L Holloway
D R Larcombe
L W Palmer
B Petit
G Ross Russell
A L Smith
R K Starr
A J P Townend
R Vaughan
Secretary: J R Arthur OBE

Central Bank of the Republic of Turkey Representative Office

391 Centric House
Strand
London WC2R 0LT
Tel: 071 379 0548

Deputy Representative:
Mustafa H Gurtin

Chambers & Remington Ltd

Canterbury House
85 Newhall Street
Birmingham B3 1LS
Tel: 021 236 2577
Fax: 021 200 2343

Managing Director: K J Thurstans
Dealing Director: C D H Blackshaw
Investment Director: G E Tromans
Director:
R A D Froy
P D Minchin

Chancery plc

100 Avenue Road
London NW3 3HF
Tel: 071 722 0099
Fax: 071 722 5226

Chairman & Chief Executive:
H Cohen
Deputy Chief Executive: G D Berger
Finance Director: R T Graham
Director:
M D Hill
B L Rubins
Chief Executive, Corporate Finance Div: C V Reader
Chief Executive, Stockbroking Div:
G M Branston

Charles Davis (Metal Brokers) Ltd

9/13 Fenchurch Buildings
London EC3M 5HR
Tel: 071 702 9735
Telex: 883928
Fax: 071 702 9333

Managing Director: C P Danin
Financial Director: S W F Ford
Director: G Sambrook

Charles Stanley & Co Ltd

25 Luke Street
London EC2A 4AR
Tel: 071 739 8200
Telex: 8952218
Fax: 071 739 7798

Chairman: Sir Edward Howard Bt
GBE
Director:
E M Clark
D H S Howard
P A Hurst

Charles Stanley Corporate Finance Ltd

25 Luke Street
London EC2 4AR
Tel: 071 739 8200
Fax: 071 739 7798

Director: P A Hurst

Charlton Seal Schaverien Limited

18½ Sekforde Street
London EC1R 0HN
Tel: 071 782 0044
Telex: 262120 SCHVRING
Fax: 071 251 3983

Chairman: M J Seal
Chief Executive: I R Wilson
Managing Director: K R Pinker
Deputy Managing Director:
D W Youngman
Director:
P F Barlow
W L Beevers
L A W Evans
P R Goodbody
N R Harding
R E Holmes
N R Lawrence
M P W Lloyd
J J W R Main
I G Mavroleon
R T Race
D J Sammons
J M Scott
M E B Walters
A Watson
C J Weston
R Williams

Chartered Trust plc

24-26 Newport Road
Cardiff CF2 1SR
Tel: 0222 473000
Telex: 498268
Fax: 0222 485517

Chairman: J Hoddell
Deputy Chairman: W J Franklin
Managing Director: A C Webb
Director:
P A Barry

Director:
  B P P Blake
  M C Hart
  J Mackenzie

Chartered WestLB Limited
33-36 Gracechurch Street
London EC3V 0AX
Tel: 071 623 8711
Telex: 884689
Fax: 071 626 1610

Chairman & Chief Executive:
  P L Macdougall
Deputy Chief Executive:
  A D Gemmill
  U H H Zierke
Executive Director:
  W B Blyth
  O G Dereham
  N E Doughty
  H A P Farmar
  D W H Farmer
  A J A Grey
  W D Hayes
  R Hoffmann
  I E Lapping
  J McNeill
  N D Melvill
  C H Paterson
  J M K Pearson
  P J Quinn
  M J Richardson
  R G Sanderson
  R I Taylor
  J R Valdinger
  S F Westmacott
  Miss C A Whitely
  J A Young
  D Zanger
Managing Director:
  P R Godwin
  R Mathrani
  M P Milbourn
  P F Sargeant
Director:
  D Berry
  M Brook
  J L Dazin
  H Ostlund

Charterhouse Bank Limited
1 Paternoster Row
St Paul's
London EC4M 7DH
Tel: 071 248 4000
Telex: 884276
Fax: 071 248 6522

Chairman and Chief Executive:
  M V Blank
Vice Chairman:
  M R B Gatenby
  R P Kilsby
Managing Director:
  I M Beith
  A W Muirhead
  P H W Rix
Director:
  P M Baines
  P M A Bryans
  P C Button
  Mrs J Cohen
  E G Cox
  S P de Albuquerque
  R W Dix
  P F Doye
  I Edward
  W H W Edwardes
  R D Fuller
  E H Gilmour
  E D Glover
  R W Grant
  P D Green
  N J Hamway
  M J Higgins
  J H High
  C A Horan
  I A Houston
  T A Lebus
  M H Legge
  J S Liddle
  P N J May
  D Nussbaum
  D W Parish
  A Parry
  A S Reese
  B W J Rutherford
  M J Sebba
  A P Seymour
  Mrs J E Short
  C J Southgate
  D H Stenhouse
  D M Wilson
  P S Wisher

Charterhouse plc
1 Paternoster Row
St Paul's
London EC4M 7DH
Tel: 071 248 4000
Telex: 884276
Fax: 071 248 6522

Chairman: P E G Balfour
Chief Executive: M V Blank
Director:
  E G Cox

Director:
  H E Farley
  M R B Gatenby
  M H Mason
  D W Parish
  C M Winter
Secretary: M G Hotchin

Charterhouse Tilney
Royal Liver Building
Pierhead
Liverpool L3 1NY
Tel: 051 236 6000
Telex: 627367
Fax: 051 236 6000 ext 274

Chairman: M H Mason
Managing Director:
  J P D Hancox
  J D Mitchell
Director:
  S Adams
  A C Binks
  R A Burgess
  C C Cannon
  G L Collins
  H Dawson
  A M M Dodd
  P C English
  A Fowler
  P R Green
  R P Hall
  C L W Jackson
  R W Jackson
  A K R Jacomb
  I M Kirk
  J Marr
  J S McAllester
  D J McEntyre
  J H J McQueen
  J D Norbury
  P C Okell
  C M Orsborn
  D W Parish
  M J Polnik
  J T Stokeld
  G H Thelwall Jones
  J R Timms
  J B R Vartan
  G W B Warman
  R J Whitfield

Chartfield & Co Limited
24/26 Baltic Street
London EC1Y 0TB
Tel: 071 608 1451
Fax: 071 608 3158

Chairman: Nicholas Branch

Director:
Richard Beamiss
Alex Hunter
Sir John Lucas-Tooth
John Sidwell

Chase Investment Bank Limited
PO Box 16
Woolgate House
Coleman Street
London EC2P 2HD
Tel: 071 726 5000
Telex: 892101

Senior Managing Director & Europe
Corporate Finance Executive:
Thompson Swayne
Senior Managing Director & Europe
Risk Management Executive:
Paul Brandow
Managing Director (Structured
Finance):
Oliver Greene
Ruediger Eisenhart Rothe
Director/Company Secretary & UK
Compliance Officer: Brian Harte
Managing Director & Mergers and
Acquisitions Executive:
Robert Hinaman
Financial Controller: Laurence Jopp
Managing Director & Global Risk
Management Executive:
Warren McLeland
Managing Director & Europe Equity
Investment Group Executive:
Brian Sankey

Cheltenham & Gloucester Building Society
Barnett Way
Gloucester GL4 7RL
Tel: 0452 372372
Telex: 43513
Fax: 0452 373970

Managing Director: A H Longhurst
Finance Director: D Barnes
Assistant General Manager (Finance):
A M Kidd
Treasurer: D J Bennett

Chemical Bank
Chemical Bank House
180 Strand
London WC2R 1EX
Tel: 071 379 7474
Telex: 264766

European Regional Manager &
Managing Director:
Don M Wilson III
Managing Director:
Michael Cornford
Mark S Garvin
David Reason
Paul A Walton
Vice President:
Alan C Brann
Jonathan Butterfield
Albemarle J Cator
William J Clark
Timothy R Elliott
Ms Jane Mecz
Michael J Mulley
Geoffrey Porter
Roger T Simpson
Barry Telfer
Roger Ward

Chemical Investment Group (London) Ltd
Chemical Bank House
180 Strand
London WC2R 1EX
Tel: 071 379 7474
Telex: 264766

Managing Director & Chief Investment
Officer: James E Tonner

J F Chown & Company Limited
51 Lafone Street
London SE1 2LX
Tel: 071 403 0787
Telex: 883571
Fax: 071 403 6693

Chairman & Managing Director:
John Chown

The Chuo Trust & Banking Co Ltd
10th Floor
Woolgate House
Coleman Street
London EC2R 5AT
Tel: 071 726 6050
Telex: 8812700 CTRUST

General Manager: T Tagaya

Church, Charity and Local Authority Fund Managers Limited
(CCLA Fund Managers Ltd)
St Alphage House
2 Fore Street
London EC2Y 5AQ
Tel: 071 588 1815
Telex: 8954509
Fax: 071 588 6291

Non-Executive Chairman: T G Abell
Non-Executive Director:
W T Griffin
H Purcell
I P Sedgwick
Chief Executive:
Viscount Churchill
Financial Director: D Fitton
Investment Director: A G Gibbs
Chief Surveyor: J McAuslan

CIC-Union Européenne Internationale et Cie
74 London Wall
London EC2M 5NE
Tel: 071 638 5700
Telex: 886725
Fax: 071 588 6038

General Manager: A Poulet
Treasury Manager: T Curtis

CIN Management Limited
PO Box 10, Hobart House
Grosvenor Place
London SW1X 7AD
Tel: 071 245 6911
Telex: 885770
Fax: 071 235 2822

Non-Executive Chairman: C Barker
Chief Executive: Dr P M Whitney
Non-Executive Director:
Dr D V Atterton
M H Butler
J R Cowan
J F G Emms
W J R Govett
Sir Norman Siddall

CIN Marketable Securities
PO Box 10, Hobart House
Grosvenor Place
London SW1X 7AD
Tel: 071 245 6911
Telex: 885770
Fax: 071 235 2822

Managing Director: B J Southcott
Deputy Managing Director: H P Hill

Director:
  J Abel
  G Bennett
  W Beresford
  S Putnam
  M Wasilewski
  J Youde

CIN Properties
PO Box 10, Hobart House
Grosvenor Place
London SW1X 7AD
Tel: 071 245 6911
Telex: 885770
Fax: 071 235 2822

Managing Director: R K Juddery
Deputy Managing Director:
  I Yeatman
Director:
  B Ellinthorpe
  B R Fossett
  P Mason
  A R Walker

CIN Venture Managers
PO Box 10, Hobart House
Grosvenor Place
London SW1X 7AD
Tel: 071 245 6911
Telex: 885770
Fax: 071 235 2822

Managing Director: R A Hall
Deputy Managing Director:
  J F Brown
Director:
  M G W Burgess
  G B Davison
  M W Jelbart
  B A Linden
  A W Marchant
  P J Maskell
  C M Owens

Citicorp Insurance Brokers Ltd
St Clare House
30-33 Minories
London EC3N 1DD
Tel: 071 488 1388
Telex: 883485
Fax: 071 480 5111

Chairman & Chief Executive:
  David C Woodward
Chief Operating Officer:
  Edward W Hahn

Citicorp Venture Capital Ltd
Cottons Centre
Hays Lane
London SE1 2QT
Tel: 071 234 2779
Telex: 299831
Fax: 071 234 2784

Managing Director:
  Michael D C Smith

Citioptions Limited
Regis House
43-45 King William Street
London EC4R 9AR
Tel: 071 234 2340
Fax: 071 929 4762

Managing Director: Jackie Tokley

City Merchants Bank Ltd
PO Box 408
13 Austin Friars
London EC2N 2AJ
Tel: 071 638 3511
Telex: 886532
Fax: 071 638 2187

Chairman: P M Bunce
Managing Director: J Denton-Clark
Deputy Managing Director:
  S Hamilton
Divisional Director:
  D C Eley
  S G A Robertson
Finance Director: W P Thorpe
Non-Executive Director:
  C A Barnes
  N E Foster
  A S Reid

City Wall Securities Limited
65 London Wall
London EC2M 5TU
Tel: 071 638 7422
Fax: 071 638 7789

Chairman & Managing Director:
  J D Passey

Citymax Integrated Information Systems Ltd
Citymax House
6 Laurence Pountney Hill
London EC4R 0BL
Tel: 071 929 5005
Telex: 914682
Fax: 071 621 1531

Chairman: Harry J France
Deputy Chairman: Dr Hans Geiger

Managing Director: Ahmad Abu El-Ata
Director:
  Hassan Bakr
  Margaret Borland
  Amr El-Kashef
  David Haynes
  R M Major
  Ken Parry Husbands
  Stephen J Pinner
  Keith Singer
Non Executive Director:
  Bruno Aschwanden
  Roland Eggli
  Mervyn Jones
  D Marti

Clay & Partners Consulting Actuaries
61 Brook Street
London W1Y 2HN
Tel: 071 071 408 1600
Telex: 27167
Fax: 071 499 0711

Partner:
  I S Aitken
  N R Bankhead
  R Bannister
  G Booth
  J R P Checkley
  P J Cross
  Miss Jacqueline Daldorph
  C F B Dallard
  Mrs Lynne Davis
  M S Demwell
  M Dyson
  J D Fisher
  A S Fishman
  S L Gooch
  Mrs Helen James
  J A Jenkins
  P R Lockyer
  G Mitchell
  S M Riley
  T M Ross
  J E Shepley
  R F Snelson
  Mrs Anne Stoye
  S C Stoye
  R C W Strattan
  B Tatch
  N Taylor
  R S Thomson
  A J Wilson
  J P Woodhouse
  S F Yeo

Clerical Medical Unit Trust Managers
Narrow Plain
Bristol BS2 0JH
Tel: 0272 290566
Fax: 0272 269031

Non-Executive Chairman:
  William P Gunn
Chief Executive: A G Harrison
Director:
  D M Claisse
  Roger D Corley
  Andrew G O'Leary
  J Paul Williams
Finance Director & Company
  Secretary: Nigel R Gardner

Clifford Palmer Underwriting Agencies Limited
9/13 Fenchurch Buildings
London EC3M 5HR
Tel: 071 488 0103
Fax: 071 481 4995

Chairman: K C Combe TD
Director:
  M Ashley
  J I Gordon
  C F Palmer
  D M Reed
Director & Secretary: C Payne

Clive Discount Company Ltd
9 Devonshire Square
London EC2M 4HP
Tel: 071 548 4000
Telex: 8958901
Fax: 071 220 7238

Chairman: Nicholas H Chamberlen
Managing Director:
  S J St F Dare
  M A Jameson-Till
  R N Thomas
  M Walker
Secretary: W N H Jones

Close Brothers Limited
36 Great St Helen's
London EC3A 6AP
Tel: 071 283 2241
Telex: 8814274
Fax: 071 623 9699

Chairman and Managing Director:
  R D Kent
Director:
  L M Bland

Director:
  V L Cannock
  T D Cansick
  D G Hardisty
  S R Hodges
  C D Keogh
  H A Lloyd
  D C Pusinelli
  N J Stevenson
  P J Stone
  J G T Thornton
  P L Winkworth

Close Investment Management Limited
36 Great St Helen's
London EC3A 6AP
Tel: 071 283 2241
Telex: 8814274
Fax: 071 638 5624

Managing Director:
  Jonathan Thornton

Clydesdale Bank plc
30 St Vincent Place
Glasgow G1 2HL
Tel: 041 248 7070
Telex: 77135
Fax: 041 204 0828

Chairman: Sir Eric Yarrow
Deputy Chairman:
  Sir William Coats
Chief Executive:
  A Richard Cole-Hamilton
General Manager, Corporate &
  International: J Cook
General Manager, Credit Bureau:
  D E Eccleshall
General Manager, Financial Services:
  K C Green
General Manager, Personnel:
  G M D Heron
General Manager, Finance:
  J K McNeillage
General Manager, Information
  Technology: S J North
General Manager, Retail:
  D R Robertson
Director:
  W R Alexander CBE
  The Viscount of Arbuthnott
    CBE DSC JP
  D R Argus
  T N Biggart CBE WS
  D Birrell WS
  Sir William Coats
  A R Cole-Hamilton
  A W Diplock

Director:
  Ian D Grant CBE
  Sir Douglas Hardie
  A Ledingham
  Sir Norman Macfarlane
  Sir David McNee
  Sir David Nickson KBE DL

Coats Viyella plc
28 Savile Row
London W1X 2DD
Tel: 071 734 5321

Finance Director: J R F Walls

Commercial Bank of Kuwait
3rd Floor
Fitzherbert House
49 Park Lane
London W1Y 4EQ
Tel: 071 495 2096
Telex: 22138 TIJARI G
Fax: 071 495 2094

European Representative: W Major

Commercial Union plc
PO Box 420
St Helen's
1 Undershaft
London EC3P 3DQ
Tel: 071 283 7500
Telex: 887626

Chairman: N H Baring
Deputy Chairman:
  Sir Martin Jacomb
Chief Executive: A L Brend
Executive Director:
  J G T Carter
  A B Wyand
Director:
  R A Brooks
  M H Fisher
  R C Hampel
  Sir Christopher Tugendhat
Group Actuary: J H Webb
General Manager Investments:
  M A Evans
Group European Manager: M D Ford
Group Overseas Manager: J S Rattray
General Manager UK Division:
  P G Ward
Secretary: K N Grant

Commerzbank AG
10/11 Austin Friars
London EC2N 2HE
Tel: 071 638 5895
Telex: 8954308

General Manager:
    Gottfried O Bruder
    Juergen Lemmer
Assistant General Manager:
    Gordon S Anderson
    Anthony V Eland
Senior Manager:
    Juergen Jahn
    Michael J Oliver
    Patrick D Schild
    Colin Smith
    Ramon A Smith
    John L Spink
    Robert S Sullivan

Confederaciòn Española de Cajas de Ahorros (CECA)
16 Waterloo Place
London SW1
Tel: 071 925 2560
Telex: 296984

General Manager: J Bonet

Consolidado UK Ltd
Vestry House
Laurence Pountney Hill
London EC4R 0EH
Tel: 071 283 0801
Telex: 291109 CONSUK G
Fax: 071 283 0875

Managing Director: D Kantorowicz-
    Toro

Consolidated Credits Investment Capital
West World
West Gate
London W5 1DT
Tel: 081 991 2551
Telex: 8812983
Fax: 081 991 5263

Director:
    C Lewis
    J Lewis

Continental Bank NA
Continental Bank House
162 Queen Victoria Street
London EC4V 7444
Tel: 071 236 7444
Telex: 883620
Fax: 071 248 1244

Executive Vice President:
    William M Goodyear
Managing Director, Europe:
    J R Degenhardt

*Managing Director, London
    Origination:* Charles Law
Senior Director, Corporate Funding:
    Anthony C Barber
Chief Credit Officer:
    Philip A Carraro
Senior Director, Risk Management:
    Michael Portington
*Senior Director, European Structured
    Finance:* Terry Hughes
Managing Director, Foreign Exchange:
    Simon J Morris
Managing Director, Global:
    Igor Hurcik
Senior Director, London Origination:
    Howard Chinner
    John Dragic
    John W Sumsion
    John Wood
Head of Operations: Graham J Watts
*Managing Director, International
    Leasing:* David A Kliefoth
Managing Director, Corporate Finance:
    Tony Moody
Managing Director, Capital Markets:
    David Gates
*Managing Director, LDC Asset
    Trading:* Alex McLeod
Senior Director: Jeffrey R Macklin
Tax Advisory: Richard Briffett

Continental Reinsurance London
(Comprising Continental
Reinsurance Corporation (UK)
Limited, Unionamerica Insurance
Company Limited)
77 Gracechurch Street
London EC3V 0PA
Tel: 071 548 5900
Telex: 886851/883148
Fax: 071 929 3160

Chairman/Chief Executive:
    Philip M Marcell
Managing Director (Underwriting):
    Ian G Sinclair
Chief Financial Officer and Director:
    Peter J Cooper
Director:
    Gary French
    Martin D Haber
    Edward J Harvey
    Michael A J Hayden
    Hugh B G G Jago
    John H Loynes
    Andrew E Marks
    Ralph F Morrison
    Anthony B Withersby

Cookson Group
130 Wood Street
London EC2V 6EQ
Tel: 071 606 4400
Telex: 884141
Fax: 071 606 2851

Chairman & Chief Executive:
    M J G Henderson
Group Managing Director: Dr R Iley
*Group Managing Director & Director,
    Group Development:* R M Oster
Group Financial Controller: I S Barr
Director, Finance & Planning:
    F F C Munro
Director of Human Resources:
    J L Bickers
Non-Executive Director:
    I G Butler
    Sir Peter Matthews AO
    Sir Nigel Mobbs DL
    M J Sindzingre
Secretary: T Ware
*Divisional Chief Executive, Metals &
    Chemical Division & Member of
    Group Executive Committee:*
    B B Carey
*Divisional Chief Executive, Ceramics
    & Plastics Division & Member of
    Group Executive Committee:*
    M Batey
*Chief Executive, Vesuvius Group &
    Member of Group Executive
    Committee:* D L Carcieri
*Chief Executive Cookson America &
    Member of Group Executive
    Committee:* D L Carcieri

Co-operative Bank plc
1 Balloon Street
Manchester M60 4EP
Tel: 061 832 3456
Telex: 667274
Fax: 061 829 4475

Chairman: T Agar
Managing Director: T J Thomas
Director:
    R V Gorvin
    B Jones
    J Marper
Secretary: G J Melmoth

Co-operative Insurance Society Ltd (CIS)
Miller Street
Manchester M60 0AL
Tel: 061 832 8686
Telex: 668621
Fax: 061 837 4048

Chairman: D J Wise
Chief General Manager:
 A D Sneddon
Deputy Chief General Manager &
 Secretary: P D Johnson
Chief Investment Manager: S F Wood
Deputy General Manager & Actuary
 (Life): D S Hollas
Deputy General Manager (Non-Life):
 W F Webb
Chief Accountant: G Wild
Deputy General Manager (Admin):
 P Kirkham

Corporation of London

PO Box 270
Guildhall
London EC2P 2EJ
Tel: 071 606 3030
Fax: 071 260 1119

Lord Mayor: Sir Alexander
 Michael Graham GBE
Former Lord Mayor (elected 1989):
 Sir Hugh Bidwell
Former Lord Mayor (elected 1988):
 Sir Christopher Collett
Former Lord Mayor (elected 1985):
 Sir William Davis
Former Lord Mayor (elected 1983):
 Dame Mary Donaldson
Former Lord Mayor (elected 1979):
 Sir Peter Gadsden
Former Lord Mayor (elected 1976):
 Sir Robin Gillett
Former Lord Mayor (elected 1981):
 Sir Christopher Leaver
Former Lord Mayor (elected 1986):
 Sir David Rowe-Ham
Former Lord Mayor (elected 1987):
 Sir Greville Spratt
Former Lord Mayor (elected 1984):
 Sir Alan Traill
Sheriff:
 John Arthur Taylor TD
 Alderman Christopher Rupert
 Walford
Recorder: His Honour
 Judge Lawrence Verney
Chamberlain: Bernard Peter Harty
Town Clerk: Geoffrey
 William Rowley CBE
Common Serjeant:
 Judge Robert Lymbry
Commissioner of the City Police:
 Owen Kelly QPM
Comptroller and City Solicitor:
 Andrew James Colvin

Remembrancer: Adrian Francis
 Patrick Barnes
Secretary and Under-Sheriff and High
 Bailiff of Southwark:
 Gp Capt John Hurn Constable
Medical Officer for the Port & City of
 London: Dr Herbert Hugh John
Coroner for the City of London:
 Dr David Manuel Paul
High Steward of Southwark: His
 Honour
 Judge Lawrence Verney

Cosmo Securities (Europe) Limited

Garden House
18 Finsbury Circus
London EC2M 7BP
Tel: 071 588 6733
Telex: 8811382
Fax: 071 628 6703

Managing Director: K Yasuda
Director: T Akatsuka
Company Secretary: W Arimoto

County NatWest Investment Management Ltd

Fenchurch Exchange
43-44 Crutched Friars
London EC3N 2ES
Tel: 071 374 3000
Telex: 882121
Fax: 071 374 3277

Chairman: Sir Richard Butler
Chief Executive: Nigel M Lester
Deputy Chief Executive: D J Gamble
Director:
 A M Clapperton
 J Clark Hallmann
 R Layard-Liesching
 Simon Le Fevre
 B Melton
 D Patterson
 B J Pullman
 Ms L A Richardson
 Ms A M Richardson-Bunbury
 Ms M M Waller
 J C Whitaker

County NatWest Limited

135 Bishopsgate
London EC2M 3UR
Tel: 071 375 5000
Telex: 882121
Fax: 071 375 5050

Chairman & Chief Executive:
 J H Macdonald

Deputy Chairman: P J R Spira
Managing Director:
 I C Ferguson
 D C Macpherson
 C T Redman
 I S Robertson
 D R Shaw
 P B St George
Executive Director:
 D M Cardale
 A J Cole
 S J Dobbie
 J L Fender
 C M S Kaye
 D G Liddle
 A P Marsden
 C C McCann
 S R Metcalf
 S R Moore
 R L Norbury
 P I Porter
 Miss K M Riley
 B J Rouget
 C Senior
 G A Theodoli-Braschi
Director:
 J B Aitken
 K H Anderson
 P J Augar
 A T Baker
 R C J Baker
 D M Barclay
 N Barton
 M Blackman
 I Carlton
 J G Colman
 S R C Davies
 R J Demeza
 G Dewhirst
 P Donald
 S M Donald
 C E H Drury
 A J S Ewen
 J Furlong
 S B Gibb
 J R Glancy
 R J Grantham
 B S Gray
 D Head
 A T Hopkinson
 Miss S J Kellett
 I R Longworth
 J L K McBride
 D M McMullan
 C J J McQueen
 S P Meredith Hardy
 C R Mills
 R S Mully
 J J O'Donnell

COUNTY NATWEST SECURITIES LIMITED

Director:
R B C Ogilvie
D J Peak
A D Phaure
F M Ranger
R C T Redmayne
K S Roberts
M Rowe
M A Ryan
P G Staveley
M A Stewart
R W Taylor
L Tzidon
D M White
P N G Wilson
A L Withnel
P J Young
Director (France): P Esteva
Director (Leeds): J M B Frank
Director (Birmingham): K G White

County NatWest Securities Limited
135 Bishopsgate
London EC2M 3UR
Tel: 071 375 5000
Telex: 916041
Fax: 071 375 5050

Chief Executive: I C Ferguson
Deputy Chairman & Managing Director: R L Norbury
Vice Chairman: S Dobbie
Executive Director:
P J Augar
A J Cole
S R C Davies
A J S Ewen
J Furlong
J R Glancy
D R J Head
C J J McQueen
S P Meredith Hardy
C R Mills
J J O'Donnell
F M Ranger
R W Taylor
Director:
J B Aitken
D Allchorne
G Allum
R J Angus
P Aynsley
D M Baker
A M Barker
D I G Barlow
P Y Bartlett
J Beatson-Hird
R C Boxall

Director:
A C W Boyle
W W Brodie
H N Buchan
W Calder
P S Chantrey
A E Davey
H De Lusignan
P J Deighton
P J Donald
N Downer
C E H Drury
J E Fineberg
A B Fitzgerald
T P Friend
M E C Gilbard
R J Grantham
P D Gregory
D Heilbron
A J Hibbert
M R W Hildrey
A T Hopkinson
R M Hulett
I Johnston
R M S U Kaufmann
P Kersey
J Lafferty
D Leaf
J M Lyon
D M McMullan
A J MacNeary
I G McNeil
J J McNeill
T F E Marchant
E G Meek
R Miller-Bakewell
David D B Morrison
D Nisbet
M Pauk
A D Phaure
R C T Redmayne
J Richards
R Robertson
J Roddan
M Rowe
D A Roy
R Semple
F J Sharman
M B Sherley-Dale
R A G Simmonds
P C Sisson
J A Spens
R K Starr
P S Streatfield
G L Tiernan
P S Tyler
P Wellington
D M White
P R Wilkinson

Director:
T G Williams
J M M Williamson
R J Wolff
R E J Wyatt

County NatWest Ventures Limited
135 Bishopsgate
London EC2M 3UR
Tel: 071 375 5000
Telex: 882121
Fax: 071 375 6262

Chairman: J H Macdonald
Managing Director: D R Shaw
Director:
G Dewhirst
S M Donald
A R Gibbons
C C McCann
J Moran
P M Smaill
K G White

Courtaulds plc
18 Hanover Square
London W1A 2BB
Tel: 071 629 9080
Telex: 28788
Fax: 071 629 2586

Group Treasurer: J Wrangham

Coutts & Co
440 Strand
London WC2R 0QS
Tel: 071 753 1000
Telex: 268612

Chairman: David B Money-Coutts
Managing Director: A Julian Robarts
Director:
The Hon Nicholas Assheton
E William Barron
The Hon M Albemarle Bowes Lyon
Denis M Child CBE
G Anthony Davies
Roger Flemington
David C Macdonald
Stuart W Marshall
Carel M Mosselmans TD
Sir John L E Smith CBE
Secretary & Senior Associate Director:
Christopher M Horne
Associate Director:
Anthony H Corin
Clifford E Franklin
Kevin Garvey

Associate Director:
Henry G Hopper
Warwick J Newbury
Malcolm E Ramsey
Stuart H Wells
Senior Manager, City Office:
Christopher Rashbrook

Coventry Building Society
Economic House
PO Box 9
High Street
Coventry CV1 5QN
Tel: 0203 555255
Fax: 0203 222820

Chairman: B Gillitt
Chief Executive: M H Ritchley
Secretary: M R Edwards

Crawley Warren Group plc
8 Lloyds Avenue
London EC3N 3HD
Tel: 071 488 1414
Telex: 8956151/2
Fax: 071 265 1453

Chairman & Chief Executive:
B J Warren
Deputy Chairman: J H Howes
Financial Director: R Hargrave
Company Secretary: B J Fitzpatrick
Director:
R A Eckersley
M Forbes-Wilson
D F Howard

Crédit Commercial de France (UK) Limited
Corporate Member
27 Finsbury Square
London EC2A 1LP
Tel: 071 628 1111
Telex: 924081
Fax: 071 638 7661

Chairman: A B Greayer
Director:
N Aylwin
M A Borrelli
P Cazalaa
V de Maredsous
T Descamps
P Diers
K W Hamer
M-O Laurent
J Laurent-Bellue
D Quirici
M G Quirke

Director:
G Smertnik
M G Williams
M Wohrer

Crédit du Nord
66 Mark Lane
London EC3R 7HS
Tel: 071 488 0872

General Manager:
Philippe R M Jouan

Crédit Lyonnais
UK Head Office
PO Box 81
84-94 Queen Victoria Street
London EC4P 4LX
Tel: 071 634 8000
Telex: 885479
Fax: 071 489 1559

General Manager UK: Jean-
Claude Goubet
Deputy General Manager UK:
M Bonnet
Credit Manager: Michel Barthelemy
*Assistant General Manager,
Administration:* Jacques Jambon
*Assistant General Manager, Market
Group:* Steven McGuire
*Assistant General Manager, General
Banking:* Denis Long
*Assistant General Manager, Corporate
Banking:* Ian Menage

Crédit Lyonnais Bank Nederland NV
41-43 Maddox Street
London W1R 0BS
Tel: 071 499 6343
Telex: 8953651
Fax: 071 499 0588

Joint UK General Manager:
D J Herod
P M Kellner

Crédit Lyonnais Capital Markets plc
Broadwalk House
5 Appold Street
London EC2A 2DA
Tel: 071 638 6076
Fax: 071 588 0299/0301

Chairman: Ian F Hay Davison
Chief Executive: C P Ménard
Group Legal & Compliance Director:
M J Harty
Head of Finance: B F Armstrong

Head of Futures: W B Bradwell
Head of Equities:
R M Leiman
G C Mordaunt
Head of Corporate Finance:
M S Evans
B Hautefort
Head of Investment Management:
M N C Kerr-Dineen
Head of Discount House:
R A S Moser
Head of Euro-Securities: G Gibson
Director:
M Andrews
Sir K Couzens
G de Kerangal
J S Fforde
J-Y Haberer
Mme C Lanchon
P Souviron

Crédit Lyonnais Euro-Securities Ltd
Broadwalk House
5 Appold Street
London EC2A 2DA
Tel: 071 638 6201
Telex: 264037
Fax: 071 588 0107

Chairman: M A L Camoin
Chief Executive: G M Gibson
Director:
M S Anastassiades
J Bellut
A J Bouckaert
C P Edwards
B Hautefort
I F Hay Davison
M J Lawrence
R K Mannes
C P M J Ménard
C M S Ramanoël
Finance Director: T J Griffiths
Director and Company Secretary:
M J Harty

Crédit Lyonnais Rouse Limited
Broadwalk House
5 Appold Street
London EC2A 2DA
Tel: 071 374 6100
Telex: 8950831/0 CLR G
Fax: 071 638 0327

Chairman: I F H Davison
Deputy Chairman: C P Ménard
Vice Chairman: R S Leighton
Managing Director: W Bradwell

Finance Director: P J Bramble
Director:
  N A Bents
  P A Bonner
  A J Cooper
  G Croft-Smith
  E P Dablin
  D A P Elkin
  J V Hannam
  G E Scrase
  J M Ward

Crédit Suisse First Boston Limited
2a Great Titchfield Street
London W1P 7AA
Tel: 071 322 4000
Telex: 892131
Fax: 071 580 2541

Chairman & Chief Executive: Hans-Joerg Rudloff
Deputy Chairman:
  Oswald J Gruebel
  Sir John C B Riddell
Executive Director:
  Lugman Arnold
  P Joan Beck
  David L Benson
  Brian S Berry
  Richard H Briance
  I Christopher Carter
  Jean-Christian Cheysson
  Phillip M Colebatch
  Adrian R T Cooper
  Michel R de Carvalho
  P Anthony de Liedekerke
  Marcus A L Everard
  Christopher A Goekjian
  Stephen A M Hester
  Pedro-Pablo Kuczynski
  Karl J Kuehne
  Claus G Labes
  Robert D Loverd
  Arturo C-F Mathieu
  Daniel J Meade
  R Ian Molson
  Frank A Neyens
  Simon E Prior-Palmer
  Sadeq Sayeed
  Luther L Terry Jr
Director:
  Manfred J Adami
  N D Pilkington

Creditanstalt-Bankverein
29 Gresham Street
London EC2V 7AH

Tel: 071 822 2600
Telex: 894612
Fax: 071 822 2663/2644

General Manager and Chief Executive:
  David Stewart
Deputy General Manager and Deputy Chief Executive:
  Alois Steinbichler

Credito Italiano
17 Moorgate
London EC2R 6HX
Tel: 071 606 9011
Telex: 883456
Fax: 071 606 3920

Chief Manager: L W Durden

Credito Italiano International Ltd
95 Gresham Street
London EC2V 7NB
Tel: 071 600 3616
Telex: 8814392
Fax: 071 726 8927

Managing Director: M Terenghi

Crown Financial Management Limited
Crown House
Crown Square
Woking GU21 1XW
Tel: 0483 715033
Telex: 859618
Fax: 0483 720718

Group Investment Manager:
  John Arnold
Senior Equity Investment Manager:
  Paul Rodwell
UK Equity Manager: Richard West
International Equity Manager:
  Gregory Allen
Fixed Interest Manager: John Gray

CSFB (Gilts) Limited
2a Great Titchfield Street
London W1P 7AA
Tel: 071 322 4000
Telex: 892131

Chairman: Richard H Briance
Managing Director: David L Benson
Executive Director: Luther L Terry Jr
Director:
  Brian S Berry
  Oswald J Gruebel
  Alan G Plater

CSFB Investment Management Limited
2a Great Titchfield Street
London W1P 7AA
Tel: 071 322 4000
Telex: 892131
Fax: 071 322 4434/3042

Chairman: Hans-Joerg Rudloff
Managing Director:
  Dr Manfred J Adami
Executive Director: Robert J Parker

C Czarnikow Ltd
66 Mark Lane
London EC3P 3EA
Tel: 071 480 9300
Telex: 885011
Fax: 071 480 9500

Chairman: M D Chataway
Vice-Chairman: Michael R Liddiard
Director:
  J H Barneby
  C Bellew
  J S Collecott
  J A de Havilland
  J J Garry
  N E H Mason
  R D P Mullion
  J D Nickson
  J W Payne
  J A J Rook
  P F G Rook
  J M Thomson
  B J P Weppe
Secretary: C Godfrey

Daewoo Securities Co Ltd
London Representative Office
3rd floor
1 London Wall Buildings
London EC2M 5PP
Tel: 071 638 7207
Telex: 9413098
Fax: 071 638 7144

Chief Representative: J S Koo

The Dai-Ichi Kangyo Bank Ltd
DKB House
24 King William Street
London EC4R 9DB
Tel: 071 283 0929
Telex: 884042
Fax: 071 626 2800

Joint General Manager:
  W Akihama

Joint General Manager:
  M Iwamoto
  H Matsudaira
  T Takayama

Daiwa Bank (Capital Management)
Commercial Union Building
PO Box 432
St Helens, 1 Undershaft
London EC3A 8LQ
Tel: 071 623 1494
Telex: 8956907
Fax: 071 623 2717

Managing Director: T Morishige

The Daiwa Bank Limited
Commercial Union Building
St Helen's, 1 Undershaft
London EC3A 8JJ
Tel: 071 623 8200
Telex: 886569
Fax: 071 623 2718

Director & General Manager:
  Y Kiyoyanagi

Daiwa Europe Limited
5 King William Street
London EC4N 7AX
Tel: 071 548 8080
Telex: 884121
Fax: 071 548 8303

Chairman & Chief Executive:
  M Mori
President & Chief Operating Officer:
  Y Takemoto
Vice Chairman: N P Clegg
Managing Director:
  J M Bunting
  S Kashiwa
  N Miyata
  H Osumi
Executive Director:
  J Band
  K Egashira
  F Glock
  S Hakuta
  Y Hashimoto
  Y Hirai
  C Jorge
  S Kawamura
  A Monnas
  P Nelson
  S O'Hanrahan
  P Parsons
  F Seabrook
  R Stevenson

Executive Director:
  S Takagishi
  J Tidman
  M Watson
  A Wilson

Dalgety plc
19 Hanover Square
London W1R 9DA
Tel: 071 499 7712
Telex: 21148
Fax: 071 493 0892

Chairman: Sir Peter Carey
Chief Executive: M E Warren
Director:
  B Fawcett
  P A J Gardiner
  R N Harris
  E C Humphreys
  Sir Christopher Laidlaw
  J R Martyn
  G D W Odgers
  R B Vaughan
  J J West

Dartington & Co Group plc
70 Prince Street
Bristol BS1 4QD
Tel: 0272 213206
Fax: 0272 230379

Non-Executive Chairman:
  C B Zealley
Chief Executive: C Dunlearley
Director:
  C E Breed
  D W R Johnstone
Non-Executive Director:
  D Astor
  J Burrow
  J G Hemingway
  D O May
  J G Pontin

Dartington & Co Limited
10 The Crescent
Plymouth PL1 3AB
Tel: 0752 673873
Telex: 0752 672106

Chairman: D W R Johnstone
Managing Director: C E Breed

Dawnay Day and Co Limited
15 Grosvenor Gardens
London SW1W 0BD
Tel: 071 834 8060
Telex: 8955547
Fax: 071 828 1992

Chairman: G A Naggar
Director:
  D E Cicurel
  Sir David L Nicolson
  B M Pincus
  I I Stoutzker
  C H Weil

DCC Corporate Finance Limited
103 Mount Street
London W1Y 5HE
Tel: 071 491 0767
Fax: 071 499 1952

Chairman & Chief Executive:
  Jim Flavin
Managing Director:
  Peter Featherman

DCC Ventures Limited
103 Mount Street
London W1Y 5HE
Tel: 071 491 0767
Fax: 071 499 1952

Chief Executive: Jim Flavin

Dean Witter Capital Markets International Ltd
1 Appold Street
6th Floor, Broadgate 5
London EC2A 2AA
Tel: 071 480 8500
Telex: 925380
Fax: 071 956 1244

Managing Director:
  Richard M Furber
Director:
  Thomas Indaco
  Michael P Lee
  Michael Trup

Den Danske Bank
10 Broadgate
London EC2M 2QS
Tel: 071 628 3090
Telex: 896229
Fax: 071 588 7400

General Manager: B Jagd
Deputy Manager: A J MacLennan

Den Norske Bank plc
20 St Dunstan's Hill
London EC3R 8HY
Tel: 071 621 1111
Telex: 887654-5
Fax: 071 626 7400

Chairman: Tom Grøndahl
Managing Director: Brian Hudson
*Deputy Managing Director, Shipping
& Asset Finance:* Bruce Lambie
*Deputy Managing Director, Finance
and Administration:*
  Christopher Tregoning

Denis M Clayton & Co Limited

Landmark House
69 Leadenhall Street
London EC3A 2AD
Tel: 071 480 6410
Telex: 884600 CLAYTN G
Fax: 071 488 9022

Chairman: J S Goldsmith
Managing Director, LMX: R B Smith
Managing Director, USA:
  R C Howard
*Managing Director, Management
Services:* A B Abbiss
Financial Director & Secretary:
  D R Thornton
Director, LMX:
  G A Marsh
  R D Spencer
  D E Watson
Director, USA:
  P J Allen
  C R Green

Dennis Murphy, Campbell & Co

2 Russia Row
London EC2V 8BP
Tel: 071 726 8631

Senior Partner:
  Anthony Dawson Paul
Partner:
  Jonathan J Ewbank
  A Paul A Inness
  Ian R Stewart
  Ian Thomson

Department for National Savings

Charles House
375 Kensington High Street
London W14 8SD
Tel: 071 605 9437
Fax: 071 605 9432

Director of Savings: John Patterson
Deputy Director of Savings:
  David Butler
Controller Marketing & Information:
  Mrs Sarah Cullum

Department of Trade and Industry

1 Victoria Street
London SW1H 0ET
Tel: 071 215 5000

Permanent Secretary:
  Sir Peter Gregson KCB
Deputy Secretary:
  Dr R Coleman
  David M Dell CB
  G A Hosker CB
  W M Knighton CB
  R Mountfield CB
  C W Roberts CB
  R Williams CB
Under Secretary:
  Mrs Sarah E Brown
  J A Cooke
  A C Hutton
  A C Russell
  W Brian Willott
Head of Branch:
  David W Hellings
  V F Lane
  M D Oldham

Deutsche Bank AG

6 Bishopsgate
London EC2P 2AT
Tel: 071 971 7000
Telex: 889287
Fax: 071 626 1377

General Manager:
  Dr Klaus L Albrecht
  Charles Low

Deutsche Bank Capital Markets Limited

150 Leadenhall Street
London EC3V 4RJ
Tel: 071 283 0933
Telex: 8958261
Fax: 071 626 5010

Joint Managing Director:
  Michael von Brentano
  Alexander von Ungern-
    Sternberg

Development Capital Group Ltd

44 Baker Street
London W1M 1DH
Tel: 071 935 2731
Fax: 071 935 9831

Chairman: M C Bingham
Chief Executive: T C Glucklich

DG Bank

Deutsche Genossenschaftsbank
PO Box 596
10 Aldersgate Street
London EC1A 4XX
Tel: 071 726 6791
Telex: 886647
Fax: 071 606 2738

General Manager: F G Leitner

Discount Corporation of New York (London) Limited

16 St Helen's Place
London EC3A 6DE
Tel: 071 588 8486
Telex: 887610
Fax: 071 638 2469

Managing Director: Guy A Fulbrook

DKB International Limited

DKB House
24 King William Street
London EC4R 9DB
Tel: 071 929 7777
Telex: 932931

Managing Director: H Nagamatsu
Deputy Managing Director:
  T Matsuoka
  F Miyako
Company Secretary: M J Conway

Donaldson, Lufkin & Jenrette International

Jupiter House
Triton Court
14 Finsbury Square
London EC2A 1BR
Tel: 071 638 5822
Telex: 8811356
Fax: 071 588 0120

Managing Director: C M Hale

Dowa Insurance Company (UK) Limited

14 Trinity Square
London EC3N 4ET
Tel: 071 481 0733
Telex: 8811587
Fax: 071 481 0920

Chairman: K Tokuhiro
Deputy Chairman : Y Yamamoto
Managing Director: A F Catt
Director:
  P Ellacott

Director:
E Nagano
S Nagata
M Okazaki

Dresdner Bank AG
Dresdner Bank House
125 Wood Street
London EC2V 7AQ
Tel: 071 606 7030
Telex: 885540
Fax: 071 600 6310

General Manager:
Robert E Beale
Stefan M Duderstadt
Guenter Z Steffens

Duncan Lawrie Limited
1 Hobart Place
London SW1W 0HU
Tel: 071 245 1234
Telex: 917046
Fax: 071 245 6276

Chairman & Managing Director:
Nicholas Airth Grant
Deputy Chairman: Nicholas John
Gordon Sharp
Non-Executive Director:
John Newton Butterwick
Geoffrey Brian Whittington
Walsh
Director - Finance: William
Mark Dawson
Director - Investment: Barrie
Jonathan Martin
*Director - Banking (& Compliance
Officer):* Peter John Field
Director - Banking: Robert
Michael Way

Dunedin Fund Managers Limited
Dunedin House
25 Ravelston Terrace
Edinburgh EH4 3EX
Tel: 031 315 2500
Telex: 72229
Fax: 031 315 2222

Chairman & Chief Executive:
W D Marr
Deputy Chief Executive: A S Kemp
Director:
G Anderson
J D Anderson
G M A Crawford
D M Fortune
J F X Hettich

Director:
R G H McGeorge
B C Tait
J D B Wood

E S Securities Limited
Pembroke House
40 City Road
London EC1Y 2BL
Tel: 071 253 1163
Telex: 915697
Fax: 071 251 6484

Managing Director: Brian A Myerson
Director: David J Cooley
Finance Director: James A Croxton

Eagle Star Insurance Company Limited
60 St Mary Ave
London EC3A 8JQ
Tel: 071 929 1111
Telex: 914926
Fax: 071 626 1266

Chairman & Chief Executive:
M A Butt
Executive Director & Chief Actuary:
R E Brimblecombe
*Executive Director (Management
Services):* I Dunbar
*Executive Director (Information
Technology):* J C Bradley
Executive Director (Finance):
C F Coates
Executive Director (Marketing):
A M Heath
Executive Director (Life):
A S Melcher
Executive Director:
L A Agius
G H Lockwood
Director: D P Allvey

Earnshaw Haes & Sons Ltd
17 Tokenhouse Yard
London EC2R 7LB
Tel: 071 588 5699
Telex: 886202
Fax: 071 726 4455

Managing Director:
Michael P Goodman

EC1 Ventures
Brettenham House
Lancaster Place
London WC2E 7EN
Tel: 071 606 1000
Fax: 071 240 5050

Managing Partner:
David Wansbrough

Edinburgh Fund Managers plc
4 Melville Crescent
Edinburgh EH3 7JB
Tel: 031 226 4931
Telex: 72453
Fax: 031 226 2359

Chairman: A M M Grossart
Chief Executive: C H Ross
Director:
C Barker
A A Bissett
J W Blair
M J Bullick
A J Gowars
W S Johnstone
Sir Norman Macfarlane
W G Riddell-Carre
B J Southcott
I A Watt
Dr P M Whitney

Edwards & Payne (Underwriting Agencies) Limited
18 London Street
London EC3R 7JP
Tel: 071 623 3556
Fax: 071 481 4924

Chairman: C H A Skey
Director:
B Blamey
P A Davis
D M W Farley
R G M Finn
A J Mitchell-Harris
Director & Company Secretary:
R G Tyler

Electra Investment Trust plc
65 Kingsway
London WC2B 6QT
Tel: 071 831 6464
Telex: 265525
Fax: 071 404 5388

Chairman: Michael C Stoddart
Joint Deputy Chairman:
Michael J Bentley

Executive Director:
Clive T Clague
R Glyn Morris
Hugh A L H Mumford
David F Osborne

Electricity Supply Pension Scheme
PO Box 648
30 Millbank
London SW1P 4RD
Tel: 071 834 2333
Telex: 23385
Fax: 071 828 8922

Chairman: David Jefferies
Chief Executive: M B Cannan
Property Investment Director: T Bell
Securities Investment Director:
R J M Gibson
Finance Director: W B Matthews

G P Eliot & Company Ltd
Lloyds
Lime Street
London EC3M 7HA
Tel: 071 283 3412
Fax: 071 283 8552

Chairman and Underwriter:
Robin F Eliot
Managing Director: Stuart M Speller
Director and Deputy Underwriter:
Roger L Bradley
Director and Assistant Underwriter:
Ian M Crane
Director and Company Secretary:
David V J Stephens

Enterprise Oil
5 The Strand
London WC2N 5HU
Tel: 071 930 1212
Telex: 8950611
Fax: 071 930 0321

Chairman: W E Bell CBE
Chief Executive: G J Hearne
Managing Director, Finance:
J A Walmsley
Managing Director, Technical:
P E Kingston
Exploration Director:
J M Bowen OBE
International Operations Director:
E J Harris
Production Director: J F Watt
Director:
S E Churchfield OBE
J A Gardiner

Director:
G M Ramsay
P G Rogerson
Sir Brian Shaw
Secretary: G B Jennings
Financial Controller: G Mather
Head of Business Development:
J D West
Head of Legal Affairs:
Vivien M Gaymer
Director, Corporate Affairs:
R M Dafter

The Equitable Life Assurance Society
Walton Street
Aylesbury HP21 7QW
Tel: 0296 393100
Fax: 0296 384100

President: Professor Roland Smith
Vice President:
T G Abell
A G Tritton
Director:
R Q Bowley
W T J Griffin
S M Kinnis
Peter Martin
R H Ranson
J R Sclater
E B O Sherlock
David G Thomas
Sir Christopher Wates
Assistant General Manager: A Nash

Equity & Law Life Assurance Society plc
Amersham Road
High Wycombe HP13 5AL
Tel: 0494 463463
Telex: 83385
Fax: 0494 461989

Chairman & General Manager:
C J Brocksom
Director & Assistant General Manager:
W M Brown
J S Hawken
Director:
L Brossier
A Brunet
J C Damerval
Director & Chief Actuary: D A Kerr

Esso UK plc
Esso House
Victoria Street
London SW1E 5JW
Tel: 071 834 6677

Group Treasurer: R E Penn

Etrufin Reserco Ltd
3 St Helen's Place
London EC3A 6AU
Tel: 071 638 4231
Telex: 269821
Fax: 071 588 5809

Managing Director: Dr L Simonelli

Euro Brokers Holdings Limited
Adelaide House
London Bridge
London EC4R 9EQ
Tel: 071 626 2691
Telex: 883033
Fax: 071 626 3820

Director:
C J Buggins
U N Cohen
D R A Marshall
K B Mason
M C Morrison
K E Reihl
Non-Executive Director:
N R L Hudson

Eurobids
Suite G10
Butlers Wharf Business Centre
45 Curlew Street
London SE1 2ND
Tel: 071 403 8785
Fax: 071 403 8707

Editor: Peter Shearlock

N T Evennett and Partners Ltd
Suite 785
Lloyds
Lime Street
London EC3M 7DQ
Tel: 071 626 3064

Chairman: Norman T Evennett
Managing Director: David Evennett
Director:
John Collings
Hugh Robert Hart
Paul Jenks

Director:
Bryan Missenden
Secretary and Compliance Officer:
Jonathan Bracken

Exco International plc
80 Cannon Street
London EC4N 6LJ
Tel: 071 623 4040
Fax: 071 283 8450

Chairman: Richard Clifford Lacy
Finance Director: Geoffrey Dunn
Director:
Paul W Burnand
Peter J Edge
Richard P Worthington
Company Secretary: Edward Pank

Export Credits Guarantee Department
PO Box 272
Export House
50 Ludgate Hill
London EC4M 7AY
Tel: 071 382 7000
Telex: 883601
Fax: 071 382 7649

Chief Executive: M G Stephens
Group Director:
G E Breach
C Foxall
M V Hawtin
R Wild
Secretary: J R Weiss

Export-Import Bank of Japan
Warnford Court
Throgmorton Street
London EC2N 2AT
Tel: 071 638 0175
Telex: 8952604

Chief Representative: M Agata

F S Investment Managers Ltd
190 West George Street
Glasgow G2 2PA
Tel: 041 332 3132
Telex: 779921
Fax: 041 332 3343

Executive Director:
Peter Burdon
Danny O'Neil

Fenchurch Insurance Group Limited
136/138 Minories
London EC3N 1QN
Tel: 071 488 2388
Telex: 884442
Fax: 071 481 9467

Executive Chairman: G E Knight
Managing Director: R L Earl
Non-Executive Director:
T H Bartlam
Director:
P W Bedford
B J Blacker
S B Cassey
C A G Keeling
J M Pexton
J A Plummer
M J Small
T G Taunton
G P Townsend
C W Yeldham
Financial Director: A N Wheal
Director/Company Secretary:
D H Griffiths

FennoScandia Bank Limited
The Old Deanery
Dean's Court
London EC4V 5AA
Tel: 071 236 4060
Telex: 892458
Fax: 071 248 4712

Chairman: C H Wegelius
Managing Director:
J G T S Ankarcrona
Executive Director, UK & International: D H Adamson
Executive Director, Treasury: J J Hall
Executive Director (Company Secretary):
A C Rogers
P R Sutton
Director:
Y P J Riikonen
H Skrabb
Senior Manager, Corporate Finance:
J A M Greig

FIMBRA
Herstmere House
Hertsmere Road
London E14 4AB
Tel: 071 538 8860

Chairman: Sir Gordon Downey
Deputy Chairman: J D Robertshaw

Council Member:
G G Appelboam
D O Brown
B S Burnell
Sir Kenneth Clucas
B P Cochrane
N C Conyers
W G Curran
R E Gee
A S Gordon
J A Hendry
Ms M Jennings
G B Kangley
Ms C Leach
Sir Denis Marshall
M H B Musgrave
D J Parry
M Reid
M E Rose
D Scott
S R Wethered
Chief Executive: R F O'Brien
Deputy Chief Executive: P J Dickison
Director:
R R Cockroft
J J Gaskin
M Gore
C Lanch
Ms F Monro
M A C Winterton
Director & Secretary: D W Peffer

J M Finn & Co
Salisbury House
London Wall
London EC2M 5TA
Tel: 071 628 9688
Telex: 887281
Fax: 071 628 7314

Senior Partner: C A Feather
Finance Partner: C T H Beck

First Austrian International Limited
Eldon House
2 Eldon Street
London EC2M 7BX
Tel: 071 247 7626
Telex: 9419084
Fax: 071 377 2600

Managing Director: G P Cooper

First Bank of Nigeria Limited
29-30 King Street
London EC2V 8EH

Tel: 071 606 6411
Telex: 893013
Fax: 071 606 3134

Branch Manager: F S Abiela-Cudjoe

First City, Texas - Houston NA
13 George Street
London W1
Tel: 071 224 4400
Telex: 884815/6
Fax: 071 224 6020

Executive Vice President:
Dr Odeh Aburdene
Senior Vice President and General Manager: Wolfgang E Jaschob

First Interstate Bank of California
First Interstate House
6 Agar Street
London WC2H 4HN
Tel: 071 836 3560
Telex: 883307
Fax: 071 872 0781

Senior Vice President & General Manager: John Duncan Harris
Senior Vice President: Jurgen Heinrich Lindemann
Vice President:
Robert D Farquharson
Shaun Anthony O'Toole
Michael Odenheimer
Joseph Riordan
Paul Savage

First Interstate Capital Markets Limited
First Interstate House
6 Agar Street
London WC2H 4HN
Tel: 071 379 5915
Telex: 947161
Fax: 071 836 2040

Managing Director: David G Lord
Executive Director:
John D Harris
Jurgen H Lindemann
John T McGurran
Mark Northway
Jeremy H Walsh
Non-Executive Director:
William J Bogaard
Theodore F Craver
William J Doomey

Non-Executive Director:
Harold J Meyerman
Louis G Schirano
Francis P Shanahan

First National Bank of Boston
39 Victoria Street
London SW1H 0ED
Tel: 071 799 3333
Telex: 885125
Fax: 071 222 5649

Vice-President:
T Bubier
C Chesney
N Flux
Vice-President & General Manager:
I Levack

The First National Bank of Maryland
London Representative Office
12 Old Jewry
London EC2R 8DP
Tel: 071 726 4082
Fax: 071 600 1106

Vice President and Representative:
Rosemary A Farmer

First National Bank of Southern Africa Limited
4th Floor
10 Foster Lane
London EC2V 6HH
Tel: 071 606 7050
Telex: 933038

Representative: P G C Turner

First National Bank plc
First National House
College Road
Harrow HA1 1FB
Tel: 081 861 1313
Telex: 923119
Fax: 081 861 0597

Group Chief Executive:
T J B Wrigley
Group Director:
D F Cowham
J I Kamiel
Director:
K L Dalwood
K W Horlock
M T J Horton
D A P Jeffryes
M A Mew
Director and Secretary: J S Scott

Fleet National Bank
40-41 St Andrew's Hill
London EC4V 5DE
Tel: 071 248 9531
Telex: 887791
Fax: 071 236 1473

General Manager: G P Clayson III
Deputy General Manager:
M R Cowdery

Fleming Private Asset Management Limited
31 Sun Street
London EC2M 2QP
Tel: 071 377 9242
Telex: 885941
Fax: 071 247 3594

Chairman: P J Manser
Managing Director: G W Ball
Director:
A K Barrowman
A R Fleming
D L P Lutyens
D H L Reid
M J B Roberts
S C V Ward
Marketing Manager: C K Macfarlane

Fleming Ventures Ltd
World Trade Centre
International House
1 St Katharine's Way
London E1 9UN
Tel: 071 480 6211
Fax: 071 481 1156

Partner:
Peter English
Bernard Fairman

Ford Motor Company Ltd
Eagle Way
Brentwood CM13 3BW
Tel: 0277 253000
Telex: 995311
Fax: 0277 211445

Group Treasurer: N C Rose

Ford Motor Credit Company
Jubilee House
The Drive
Brentwood CM13 3AR
Tel: 0277 692200
Telex: 995184
Fax: 0277 233722

Chairman: D D Barron
Vice Chairman: M D Young

Managing Director: A B Murray
Finance Director: M P Lang
Field Operations Director:
  W D Butler
Staff Operations Director:
  P L S Green
  R F Humm
  S Thomson CBE
  R D Warner
Secretary: B W Parkes

Foreign & Colonial Management Ltd

1 Laurence Pountney Hill
London EC4R 0BA
Tel: 071 623 4680
Telex: 886197 or 8811745
  FORCOL G
Fax: 071 626 4947

Chairman: O N Dawson
Managing Director: The
  Hon James D D Ogilvy
Director:
  A C Barker
  M J Boxford
  R G Donkin
  E C Elstob
  C J B Faherty
  J A Findlay
  M J Hart
  C P Helmore
  S E V James
  J R Mathias
  J J Nelson
  R L Richards
  J J Tigue
  A W Twiston Davies
  R T Watson
  S F White
  I K Wright

Foreign & Colonial Ventures Ltd

6 Laurence Pountney Hill
London EC4R 0BL
Tel: 071 782 9829
Telex: 881697/8811745
Fax: 071 782 9834

Chairman: John Sclater
Managing Director: The
  Hon James Nelson

Forward Trust Group

145 City Road
London EC1V 1JY
Tel: 071 251 9090
Telex: 8952620
Fax: 071 251 0064

Chairman: H E Lockhart
Vice Chairman & Chief Executive:
  R L Wyatt
Managing Director: G E Picken
Director:
  D W Gilman
  B H Sharp

Fox-Pitt Kelton Limited

Eldon House
2 Eldon Street
London EC2P 2AY
Tel: 071 377 8929
Telex: 884163
Fax: 071 247 5013

Chairman: R C Kelton

Framlington Unit Management Limited

155 Bishopsgate
London EC2M 3FT
Tel: 071 374 4100
Fax: 071 628 3731

Director:
  J Gaisford-St Lawrence
  J B Holford
  P E Jordan
  P J Loach
  Anne McMeehan
  A B Milford
  C A Park
  N Sillitoe
  D Stalham
Director & Secretary:
  W M McDonald

Frank Fehr & Co Ltd

Prince Rupert House
64 Queen Street
London EC4R 1ER
Tel: 071 248 5066
Telex: 888960
Fax: 071 248 4225

Chairman: B H F Fehr CBE
Secretary: R E J Barker

French Bank of Southern Africa Limited

64 Bishopsgate
London EC2N 4AR
Tel: 071 638 8712
Telex: 888688
Fax: 071 588 5856

General Manager: R Kopke

Friends' Provident Life Office

Pixham End
Dorking RH4 1QA
Tel: 0306 740123
Telex: 859262
Fax: 0306 740150

Chairman: The Rt Hon the
  Lord Jenkin of Roding
Deputy Chairman:
  Sir Anthony Touche Bt
Managing Director:
  Frederick G Cotton CBE
Deputy Managing Director:
  Michael F Doerr
Director:
  Sir Arthur Bryan
  John de Havilland
  Michael P Fox
  Ian T Johnstone
  Michael E L Melluish
  The Hon Richard M O Stanley
  John N B Whitney
  Lyn S Wilson
Director, General Manager & Actuary:
  G K Aslet
Director & General Manager,
  Investments: P Silvester
General Manager, Marketing & Sales:
  A J Griffiths
General Manager, Customer Services:
  R C Hallett
General Manager, Information Systems:
  R P Pugh
General Manager, Professional Services
  & Secretary: B W Sweetland
General Manager, Product &
  International Development:
  K Satchell

The Frizzell Group Limited

Frizzell House
14/22 Elder Street
London E1 6DF
Tel: 071 247 6595
Telex: 8811077
Fax: 071 377 9114

Chairman: C F Frizzell
Deputy Chairman: A M Graham
Group Chief Executive:
  I H N Mackay
Group Finance Director:
  G Partington
Director:
  J G K Borrett
  R P Brett
  K M Davidson

Director:
   C Smith
Non-Executive Director:
   L N G Olsen

Fuji International Finance Limited
7-11 Finsbury Circus
London EC2M 7NT
Tel: 071 256 8888
Telex: 884275
Fax: 071 588 2033

Managing Director: M Iwasaki

Fyshe Horton Finney Ltd
Charles House
148-149 Great Charles Street
Birmingham B3 3HT
Tel: 021 236 3111/7
Fax: 021 236 4875

Managing Director: F Keeling

G T Management plc
8 Devonshire Square
London EC2M 4YJ
Tel: 071 283 2575
Telex: 886100
Fax: 071 626 6176

Chairman: David FitzWilliam-Lay
Chief Executive: P R Stevens
Director:
   Michael Beard
   Sir Marc Cochrane
   Antony Dick
   Philip Douglas
   Alex Dundas
   Peter Glossop
   John Griffin
   Michael Hill
   Nigel Ledeboer
   Peter Wakefield
Finance Director:
   Anthony Littlejohn

G T Venture Management Holdings Ltd
Stafford House
5 Stafford Street
London W1X 3PD
Tel: 071 493 5685
Fax: 071 629 0844

Chairman: Richard Thompson
Managing Director: Rhoderick Swire

J S Gadd & Co Ltd
45 Bloomsbury Square
London WC1A 2RA

Tel: 071 242 5544
Telex: 23260
Fax: 071 405 0977

Chairman: J S Gadd
Managing Director: C A Good
Director:
   M S Carnwath
   P Engstrom
   S L Goschalk
   N J Mardon Taylor

Gartmore Investment Management Limited
Gartmore House
16-18 Monument Street
London EC3R 8QQ
Tel: 071 623 1212
Telex: 896873
Fax: 071 283 6070

Chairman & Chief Executive:
   Paul Myners
Director:
   Vivian Paul Bazalgette
   Michael John Bishop
   Andrew Jonathan Brown
   Pierre Henri Daviron
   Jean-Francois Lepetit
   Peter Graham Pearson Lund
   Lewis John McNaught
   Bruce Alexander Seton
   Bernard Simon-Barboux
   Jean-Marie Soubrier
   Chilton Thomson
   David Walter Watts
   Thomas Jeremy Willoughby

Gartmore Scotland Limited
Charles Oakley House
125 West Regent Street
Glasgow G2 2SG
Tel: 041 248 3972
Telex: 778875
Fax: 041 226 4390

Managing Director:
   Peter N B Kennedy TD
Director: Ross Watson

The Gateway Corporation Ltd
Stockley House
130 Wilton Road
London SW1V 1LU
Tel: 071 233 5353
Fax: 071 233 5254

Chief Executive: David D Smith

General Accident Fire & Life Assurance Corp
Pitheavlis
Perth PH2 0NH
Tel: 0738 21202
Telex: 76237
Fax: 0738 21843

Chairman: The Rt Hon The Earl
   of Airlie
Deputy Chairman: R W Adam
Director (General Manager):
   J C Corcoran
   J C Frangoulis
   B Holder
Director:
   L Bolton
   Anthony B Cleaver
   Sir Nicholas Goodison
   H J Kember
   Sir Duncan McDonald
   Sir Norman Macfarlane
   The Rt Hon The Earl of
      Mansfield
   I C Menzies
   The Rt Hon Lord Moore of
      Wolvercote
   Sir David W Nickson
   The Hon F R Noel-Paton
   T Roberts
   W N Robertson
General Manager (Estate Agents):
   J H Boxall
Deputy General Manager (UK):
   W H Jack
   R A Scott
Deputy General Manager (Overseas):
   C R Barker Bennett
Assistant General Manager (UK):
   N G Lister
   P J Rhodes
Company Secretary: R A Whitaker

The General Electric Company plc
1 Stanhope Gate
London W1A 1EH
Tel: 071 493 8484
Telex: 22451
Fax: 071 493 1974

Chairman: The Rt Hon
   Lord Prior PC
Vice Chairman:
   Sir Kenneth Bond
   Sir Ronald Grierson
Managing Director: Lord Weinstock
Deputy Managing Director:
   M R Bates
Legal Director: M Lester

Finance Director: D B Newlands
Director:
    Sir Robert Davidson
    J D Gadd
    Dr I G MacBean CBE
    Hon Mrs Sara Morrison
    D Powell
    Hon Simon Weinstock
    R J Williams
Non-Executive Director:
    Lord Catto
    S Z de Ferranti
    Professor E T Hall CBE
    Lord Rees-Mogg
    Dr D H Roberts CBE
Treasurer: R K Anderson
Secretary: J H Caplin

Gerald Limited

Europe House
World Trade Centre
St Katharine by the Tower
London E1 9AA
Tel: 071 867 9400
Telex: 884377
Fax: 071 867 9499

Chairman: G L Lennard
Joint Managing Director:
    R Kestenbaum
    G A Perske
Director:
    D J Hands
    D G Over

Gerrard & National Holdings plc

33 Lombard Street
London EC3V 9BQ
Tel: 071 623 9981
Telex: 883589
Fax: 071 623 6173

Chairman: R B Williamson
Deputy Chairman:
    The Earl of Eglinton & Winton
    T W Fellowes
Director:
    H J Askew
    D A Brayshaw
    D H Clarke
    R J Elkington
    A S R Jones
Non-Executive Director:
    M E T Davies
    R G Gibbs
    C A E Goodhart
    D B Money-Coutts

Gerrard & National Securities Limited

33 Lombard Street
London EC3V 9BQ
Tel: 071 623 9981
Telex: 883589
Fax: 071 623 6173

Chairman: R B Williamson CBE
Director:
    H J Askew
    D A Brayshaw
    R J Elkington
    A S R Jones
    R Shepherd
    P D Spraggs
    T F Tremlett

Gerrard Vivian Gray Limited

Burne House
88 High Holborn
London WC1V 6LS
Tel: 071 831 8883
Telex: 887080
Fax: 071 831 9938

Chairman: The Earl of Eglington & Winton
Chief Executive: S P Cooke
Director:
    R J Elkington
    J A D Skailes

Ghana Commercial Bank

69 Cheapside
London EC2P 2BB
Tel: 071 248 2384
Telex: 888597
Fax: 071 489 9058

Deputy Chief Manager:
    P S M Koranteng

Gibbs Hartley Cooper Ltd

Bishops Court
27-33 Artillery Lane
London E1 7LP
Tel: 071 247 5433
Telex: 8950791
Fax: 071 377 2139

Chairman: G F Puttergill
Director:
    L P R Ahlas
    J F Barnett
    R W Cook
    J S Evans
    H M Hall
    S R Harrap
    B D Hough

Director:
    M J Hunt
    T Kemp
    P M Maynard
    C A Ringrose
    R A P Sheehan
    L D Stoffberg
    R B Udell
    M L Warner
Secretary: C E R Ledsam

Girobank plc

10 Milk Street
London EC2V 8JH
Tel: 071 600 6020
Telex: 885700
Fax: 071 606 1020

Chairman: A S Durward
Deputy Chairman: F W Crawley
Managing Director & Chief Executive:
    E J Baden
Deputy Managing Director:
    T I Hardie
Director:
    C J Baker
    P Clifton
    N Crowley
    W I Hamilton
    D N Legg
    B V Moult
    P R White

Girozentrale Gilbert Eliott

Salisbury House
London Wall
London EC2M 5SB
Tel: 071 628 6782
Telex: 888886
Fax: 071 628 3500

Managing Director:
    G P Mills
    E Oswald

GKN plc

PO Box 55
psley House
psley Church Lane
Redditch BG8 0TL
Tel: 0527 517715
Fax: 0527 517715

Group Treasurer: W G McLuskie

Glasgow Investment Managers Ltd

29 St Vincent Place
Glasgow G1 2DR

Tel: 041 226 4585
Telex: 779503
Fax: 041 226 3632

Chief Executive: David H Williams
Finance Director: W G Gardiner
Investment Director:
    Mrs Juanita L F Stanley

Glaxo Holdings plc
Clarges House
6-12 Clarges Street
London W1Y 8DH
Tel: 071 493 4060
Telex: 25456
Fax: 071 493 4809

Group Treasurer: R P Gent

Global Asset Management (UK) Limited
GAM House
12 St James's Place
London SW1A 1NX
Tel: 071 493 9990
Telex: 296099
Fax: 071 493 0715

Chairman: Gilbert de Botton
Deputy Chairman: Nils O Taube
Managing Director:
    Denis G Raeburn
Director:
    Jeffrey Ginsberg
    David J Miller

Globe Investment Trust plc
Globe House
4 Temple Place
London WC2R 3HP
Tel: 071 836 7766
Telex: 24101
Fax: 071 240 0841

Chairman: David W Hardy
Deputy Chairman: Colin H Black
Managing Director: James G West
Director - Pension Funds:
    Norman Pilkington
Financial Controller:
    T M Gillingham

Glynwed International plc
Headland House
54 New Coventry Road
Sheldon
Birmingham B26 3AZ
Tel: 021 742 2366
Telex: 336608
Fax: 021 742 0403

Chairman & Chief Executive:
    Gareth Davies
Group Finance Director:
    David L Milne
Group Treasurer:
    Christopher R Purser

GNI Limited
Colechurch House
1 London Bridge Walk
London SE1 2SX
Tel: 071 378 7171
Telex: 884962
Fax: 071 407 3848

Chairman: D A Brayshaw
Director:
    J G Burridge
    M E T Davies
    P M W Fletcher
    K F Harbour
    S W Harragan
    C G Hellyer
    A S R Jones
    P C S Mehta
    A D L Norton
    The Hon C J Sharples
    T J R Sheldon
    E Wright

Goldman Sachs Futures Limited
133 Fleet Street
London EC4A 2BB
Tel: 071 248 6464
Fax: 071 489 2607

Director: Andrew Coulton

Goldman Sachs International Finance Limited
133 Fleet Street
London EC4A 2BB
Tel: 071 248 6464
Fax: 071 489 2236

Managing Director:
    Michael J O'Brien

Goldman Sachs International Limited
133 Fleet Street
London EC4A 2BB
Tel: 071 489 2000

Managing Director & Chairman:
    Eugene V Fife
Managing Director - Economics:
    Gavyn Davies
    David Morrison

Managing Director - Fixed Income:
    John R Farmer
    Fredric B Garonzik
Managing Director - Investment Banking: James N Lane
Managing Director - Foreign Exchange:
    Michael J O'Brien
Managing Director - Investment Banking:
    Donald C Opatrny, Jr
    R Ralph Parks, Jr
Managing Director - Equities Trading:
    Eric P Sheinberg
Managing Director - Equities:
    Robert K Steel
Managing Director - Investment:
    John L Thornton

Goldman Sachs Limited
133 Fleet Street
London EC4A 2BB
Tel: 071 248 6464
Fax: 071 489 5723

Chairman: Eugene V Fife
Managing Director: Frank E DuBose

Granada Group
36 Golden Square
London W1R 4AH
Tel: 071 734 8080
Telex: 27937

Chairman: Alex Bernstein
Chief Executive: Derek C Lewis
Finance Director:
    Graham M Wallace
Director:
    E W E Andrewes
    David Plowright
    Andrew Quinn
Company Secretary:
    Graham J Parrott
Group Treasurer: Peter Coleridge

Grand Metropolitan plc
11-12 Hanover Square
London W1A 1DP
Tel: 071 629 7488
Telex: 299606
Fax: 071 408 1246

Chairman and Group Chief Executive:
    A J G Sheppard
Deputy Chairman: Sir John Harvey-Jones
Chief Executive, Drinks: G J Bull
Chief Executive, Food: I A Martin
Chief Executive, Retailing & Property:
    D E Tagg

Group Finance Director: D P Nash
Non-Executive Director:
  R V Giordano
  Sir Colin Marshall
  D A G Simon
Group Treasurer: M D McCann
Group Financial Controller:
  Ms R P Thorne
Group Legal Director:
  R H Myddelton
Group Personnel Director:
  W D Shardlow
Group Strategy Development Director:
  P E B Cawdron
Group Public Affairs Director:
  W T Halford
Director of Investor Relations:
  R C Mitchell

Granville & Co Limited
Mint House
77 Mansell Street
London E1 8AF
Tel: 071 488 1212
Telex: 8814884
Fax: 071 481 3911

Chairman: M E R Allsopp
Managing Director: R G Hodgson
Deputy Managing Director:
  C H N Moy
Director (Corporate Finance):
  J M Blanc
Director (Stockbroking): W E Drake
Director (Development Capital):
  H G Eastman
Director (Corporate Finance):
  N C Harvey
Director (Discretionary Fund Mgmnt):
  A W K Merriam
Director (Development Capital):
  M J O Proudlock
Director (Stockbroking):
  B C Richardson
*Director (Personal Financial
  Planning):* R A Roberts
Director (Stockbroking): A J Scott
  Knight
Director (Corporate Finance):
  J B Singer
Director (Development Capital):
  D W H Steeds
Director (Finance & Administration):
  S A Sussman
*Director (Personal Financial
  Planning):* A Torevell
Director (Corporate Finance):
  J D Wellesley Wesley DS
  D S Williamson JD

Granville Davies Limited
Mint House
77 Mansell Street
London E1 8AF
Tel: 071 488 1212
Telex: 8814884
Fax: 071 481 3911

Director:
  W E Drake
  R Hodgson
  D C King
  C H N Moy
  M F Nally
  B C Richardson
  R J D Schiff
  A J Scott Knight
  B N Thomlinson
  R F Versen
  J H Wright
Company Secretary: S A Sussman

Gravett & Tilling (Underwriting Agencies) Ltd
(Underwriting Agents at Lloyds)
Baltic Exchange Chambers
24 St Mary Axe
London EC3A 8DE
Tel: 071 623 3002
Fax: 071 623 5718

Chairman: C A Cheesman
Underwriting Director:
  R O Garratt
  M A Gravett
  J P Tilling
Financial Director: M D L Vernon
Agency Director:
  P J Burton
  Mrs C S T Siva-Jothy
Non-Executive Director: E E Patrick

Greater London Enterprise
63-67 Newington Causeway
London SE1 6BD
Tel: 071 403 0300
Telex: 896616
Fax: 071 403 1742

Chairman: John Wakeham
Joint Chief Executive:
  Richard Minns
  Ms Mary Rogers

Greenwell Montagu Gilt-Edged
10 Lower Thames Street
London EC3R 6AE

Tel: 071 260 9900
Telex: 27783
Fax: 071 220 7113

Managing Director: J B Lake
Financial Director: A M de Steiger
Director:
  G R Addison
  J C Beaven
  R P Bootle
  R J Brewer
  A L Bucknell
  R M Shaw
  R L Thomas
  G Whitehead

Greenwell Montagu Stockbrokers
(Inc Smith Keen Cutler)
114 Old Broad Street
London EC2P 2HY
Tel: 071 588 8817
Telex: 925363
Fax: 071 588 1673

Chairman: R H Lawson
Chief Executive: E J Fenton
Executive Group:
  D Baker
  J D Loudon
  C W Melly
  R L Ottley
  C F Smith
  T G Wakeley
  E R Whithear

Greig Fester Group Ltd
43/46 King William Street
London EC4R 9AD
Tel: 071 623 3177
Telex: 883206
Fax: 071 623 8735

Chairman: J S Greig
Chief Executive: D R Losse
Director:
  T G Abell
  R J Carless
  P G S Keats
  C B Penruddocke
  B S Wallas
Financial Director: M Simmonds
Company Secretary: F H Hitchman

Greig, Middleton & Co Ltd
66 Wilson Street
London EC2A 2BL
Tel: 071 247 0007
Telex: 887296

Chairman: M N Kemp-Gee
Deputy Chairman: S H J A Knott
Managing Director: N F Andrews

Gresham Trust plc

Barrington House
Gresham Street
London EC2V 7HE
Tel: 071 606 6474
Fax: 071 606 3370

Chairman: Norman F Baldock
Deputy Chairman: Michael Carr
Managing Director: Trevor Jones
Director:
    David Ascott
    Clive F Coates
    Leslie J Davies
    Antony R Diment
    Colin Parker
    Michael Walker

Gresham Underwriting Agencies Limited

Asia House
31/33 Lime Street
London EC3M 7HR
Tel: 071 621 9362
Fax: 071 929 0903

Chairman and Underwriter:
    T G Green
Managing Director: J H Goodger
Finance Director: M J Williamson
Compliance Officer: T H Bayman
Executive Director and Underwriter:
    J S Darling
    D R Wallis
*Executive Director and Deputy
    Underwriter:* M F Ellis
Non-Executive Director:
    R H M Outhwaite
    D S Sharman

Grosvenor Venture Managers Limited

Commerce House
2-6 Bath Road
Slough SL1 3RZ
Tel: 0753 32623
Telex: 848314
Fax: 0753 34879

Chairman: David Beattie
Managing Director:
    Robert Drummond

The Growth Fund Limited

4th Floor
24-26 Baltic Street
London EC1Y 0TB
Tel: 071 251 9111
Telex: 94011991
Fax: 071 251 2609

Director:
    P Silvester
    D Wellesley Wesley

Gruppo Arca Nordest

3 St Helen's Place
Bishopsgate
London EC3A 6AU
Tel: 071 628 0365
Telex: 8952649
Fax: 071 374 0640

UK Representative: Cesare Combi

Guardian Royal Exchange Assurance

Royal Exchange
London EC3V 3LS
Tel: 071 283 7101
Telex: 883232
Fax: 071 623 3587

Chairman: Charles E A Hambro
Deputy Chairman: J
    Julian L G Sheffield
Managing Director: S A Hopkins
Director & Senior General Manager:
    S M F Harris
Director & General Manager:
    Miss C M Burton
    J Morley
Secretary: J M R Evans
Director:
    The Hon G E Adeane
    P R Dugdale
    Donald Gordon
    Alastair McCorquodale
    John M Menzies
    Sir Peter Reynolds
General Manager: D F Cooper
Assistant General Manager:
    M K Bewes
    N L Feldman
    M F W Jenkin
    B R King
    J W King
    J T McDonough
    M J Sissons
    M H Tripp

The Guidehouse Group plc

Durrant House
8-13 Chiswell Street
London EC1Y 4UP
Tel: 071 628 5858
Fax: 071 606 7002

Chairman: David Michaels
Chief Executive: J R A East
Director:
    Harold Bach
    Jonathan L Davis
    M E W Jackson

Guidehouse Securities Limited

Durrant House
8-13 Chiswell Street
London EC1Y 4UP
Tel: 071 628 5858
Fax: 071 628 4473

Chairman: David Michaels
Managing Director: John East
Director:
    Stefan Adams
    Keith Bellingham
    William Marle
    Nicholas H J Miller

Guinness Flight Global Asset Management Ltd

Lighterman's Court
5 Gainsford Street
Tower Bridge
London SE1 2NE
Tel: 071 522 2100
Telex: 8811299 GFGAM G
Fax: 071 522 2102/2104

Joint Managing Director:
    H E Flight
    T W N Guinness

Guinness Mahon & Co Ltd

32 St Mary at Hill
London EC3P 3AJ
Tel: 071 623 9333
Telex: 884035
Fax: 071 283 4811

Vice Chairman: P Moorsom
Managing Director, Treasurey:
    A W Broughton
*Managing Director, Banking and
    Corporate Finance:* J B Paul
Director, Private Banking:
    J G Woolfenden

Guinness Mahon Development Capital Ltd
32 St Mary at Hill
London EC3P 3AJ
Tel: 071 623 9333
Telex: 884035
Fax: 071 623 4313

Managing Director: Gordon Power
Senior Executive: Malcolm Moss

Guinness Mahon Holdings plc
32 St Mary at Hill
London EC3P 3AJ
Tel: 071 623 6222
Telex: 83065
Fax: 071 626 7007

Chairman: G L Bell
Director:
    D I R Bruce
    J A T Wedgwood

Guinness plc
39 Portman Square
London W1H 9HB
Tel: 071 486 0288
Telex: 23368
Fax: 071 486 4968

Director of Treasury: Ian Scott

The Gulf Bank KSC
European Representative Office
1 College Hill
London EC4R 2RA
Tel: 071 248 2843
Telex: 887688
Fax: 071 489 0407

General Manager (European Division):
    G M Pettit

Gulf International Bank BSC
2-6 Cannon Street
London EC4M 6XP
Tel: 071 248 6411
Telex: 8812889
Fax: 071 236 3082

Senior Vice President & UK Branch Manager: D Drumm

Gyllenhammar & Partners International Limited (GPI)
Little Tufton House
3 Dean Trench Street
London SW1P 3HB

Tel: 071 222 8151
Telex: 914024
Fax: 071 222 0893

Director: Dr Lars Åhrell

Habib Bank AG Zurich
92 Moorgate
London EC2P 2EX
Tel: 071 638 1391
Telex: 888056
Fax: 071 638 8318

Chief Executive Vice President:
    S A Zubairi
Executive Vice President:
    I M Kadwani
    K A Siddiqi
Senior Vice President:
    M Y Chowdhury
Assistant Vice President: P Dayal

Halifax Building Society
Trinity Road
Halifax HX1 2RG
Tel: 0422 333333
Telex: 517441
Fax: 0422 333000

Chairman: H Jon Foulds
Director and Chief Executive:
    J D Birrell
Finance Director: G J Folwell
Group Personnel & Services Director:
    D C Laughlan
Managing Director, Halifax Estate Agencies Limited: D R Taylor
Operations Director (Building Society):
    M G Whitehouse
Managing Director, Halifax Financial Services (Holdings) Limited:
    M Fearnsides
General Manager:
    R Barrow
    D Gilchrist
    G K Jackson
    R Spelman
Secretary: C S Cockroft

Hall Graham Bradford
5 London Wall Buildings
Finsbury Circus
London EC2M 5NT
Tel: 071 628 7961

Senior Partner: M D Bradford

Hambro European Ventures Limited
41 Tower Hill
London EC3N 4HA

Tel: 071 480 5000/702 3593
Telex: 883851
Fax: 071 702 9827

Managing Director: Gilbert Chalk
Director:
    Anthony Mallin
    Nicholas Page
    Edmund Truell

J O Hambro Magan & Co Ltd
No 32 Queen Anne's Gate
London SW1H 9AB
Tel: 071 233 1400
Telex: 934267
Fax: 071 222 4978

Chairman: Rupert Hambro
Joint Managing Director:
    James Hambro
    Alton Irby
    George Magan
Executive Director:
    O L Griffith
    D B MacFarlane
    M L Orr

Hambros Bank Limited
41 Tower Hill
London EC3N 4HA
Tel: 071 480 5000
Telex: 883851
Fax: 071 702 4424

Chairman and Chief Executive:
    J C L Keswick
Deputy Chairman:
    C J Perrin
    C H Sporborg
Vice Chairman:
    J N Heywood
    P D Hill-Wood
    A M Sorkin
Director:
    The Hon Edward Adeane
    P M Allen
    Count P Antonelli
    C R D Arbuthnot
    D M Arr
    M H L X Aubrey
    D D Bailey
    C R Balfour
    A R Beevor
    A J Bell
    P L Binder
    J D Blumsom
    T A J Boyce
    A F Brignall
    K F Buckle
    Sir Michael Butler

Director:
T F Candy
G J Chalk
C Colao
J F Cook
T A Cooper
Mrs J C Cowell
C R B Cox
N R Craig Harvey
D C Cross
A G Curtin
H N Darling
W G Davis
G J T G de Nadaillac
J C de Tuba
J F Dryer
J F Dymock
P M Evans Lombe
D O Ewart-James
D H FitzHerbert
D P Gibbs
P J Goodey
R A Goodwin
The Earl of Halifax
C E Hambro
Sir David Hancock
R W G Harvey
J D Hicks
N J Holden
C R Hollick
A Howard
T E Humphreys
Dr A Jozzo
J D Klein
G P Knight
J T P Lawes
D G Lewis
A G Mallin
Dr A W Mallmann
M T N Mansfield
A E Martin Smith
J M May
Miss S R Mitchell
N McG Moore
R P Mountford
A W W Munro
T H Nicholls
J W D Olivier
N H Page
A C Peake
R Peat
J W Pembroke
A C Plummer
D R Scott
N H Scott-Barrett
Count F C Seilern-Aspang
M S Smethurst
J E Solitander
G L Steward

Director:
D J Tapper
R A Thomas
G V B Thompson
J A Thomson
L Tiller
C B Tilley
J F Tuke
Count W Henckel von
    Donnersmarck
R Waddington
M J B Watson
B P Whitehouse
K T Williams
C E Wilson
S R Woodroffe
W M Young Herries

Hambros plc
41 Tower Hill
London EC3N 4HA
Tel: 071 480 5000
Telex: 883851
Fax: 071 638 0480

Chairman: C E A Hambro
Deputy Chairman: J M Clay
Vice Chairman:
    J C L Keswick
    C H Sporborg
Director:
    The Hon Hugh W Astor
    A R Beevor
    Sir Michael Butler
    Sir David Hancock
    J N Heywood
    M R Lampard
    Sir E Mas Montanes
    Sir Ian Morrow
    Sir David Nickson
    C J Perrin
    Sir Adam Ridley
    A M Sorkin
    C B Tilley
    Professor G Zandano
Secretary: P L Patrick

Hammerson Property Investment and Development Corporation plc
100 Park Lane
London W1Y 4AR
Tel: 071 629 9494
Fax: 071 629 0498

Director and Company Secretary:
    R S Johnson

Hanson plc
1 Grosvenor Place
London SW1X 7JH
Tel: 071 245 1245
Telex: 917698
Fax: 071 235 3455

Associate Director-Treasurer:
    Paul Spencer

Harrisons & Crosfield plc
20 St Dustan's Hill
London EC3R 8LQ
Tel: 071 626 4333
Telex: 885636
Fax: 071 782 0112

Life President: Thomas Prentice MC
Chairman: David Hugh
    Laing Hopkinson CBE RD DL
Chief Executive: George
    William Paul
Finance Director: William
    Janes Turcan
Director, Chemicals & Industrial:
    Michael James Hadley
    Peter James Savage
Director, Timber & Building Supplies:
    James Miller
Director, Food & Agriculture: Peter
    Graham William Simmonds
Director, Plantations: Geoffrey
    Edward Martyn Brown
Director, Pacific: Thomas
    Davis Preston
Non-Executive Director:
    Sir Richard Lloyd Bt
    John Newcombe Maltby CBE
Secretary: Christopher Gill
Group Accountant: Danial Delaney
Group Pensions Manager:
    Mrs Andrea Bannister
Group Risk Manager, Insurance:
    Ms Elizabeth Rose Taylor
Group Taxation Manager: David
    Thomas Williamson
Group Treasurer: K Starnes

Havana International Bank Ltd
20 Ironmonger Lane
London EC2V 8EY
Tel: 071 606 0781
Telex: 886577
Fax: 071 726 4278

Managing Director: J Lebredo

Hawker Siddeley Group plc

18 St James's Square
London SW1Y 4LJ
Tel: 071 930 6177
Telex: 919011
Fax: 071 627 7767

Treasurer: Jeffery Hume

C E Heath plc

Cuthbert Heath House
150 Minories
London EC3N 1NR
Tel: 071 488 2488
Telex: 8813001
Fax: 071 488 4001

Chairman: R W Fielding
Director:
　J M Clay
　P W J Duffield
　P J Hughes
　M H Kier
　J G Mackenzie Green
　A J Money
　Sir Ian Morrow
　P E Presland
　C J T Stewart
Secretary: M J Burton

Henderson Administration Group plc

3 Finsbury Avenue
London EC2M 2PA
Tel: 071 638 5757
Telex: 884616
Fax: 071 377 5742

Chairman: B H B Wrey
Director:
　J E Brown
　T F Conlon
　Jeremy J C Edwards
　D H Gibson
　R G Holland-Martin

Henderson Crosthwaite Institutional Brokers

32 St Mary at Hill
London EC3P 3AJ
Tel: 071 623 9992
Telex: 884035
Fax: 071 528 0884

Chairman: P F Ross
Director:
　P K O Crosthwaite
　D P Lang
　B D Newman

Henderson Crosthwaite Limited

32 St Mary at Hill
London EC3P 3AJ
Tel: 071 283 8577
Telex: 884035
Fax: 071 283 1997

Chairman: K M H Millar
Managing Director: P T Crosthwaite
Executive Director:
　B W M Cowper
　K J Radford
　M F Rooker

Henry Ansbacher Holdings plc

One Mitre Square
London EC3A 5AN
Tel: 071 283 2500
Telex: 8812459
Fax: 071 626 0866

Chairman: Sir Philip Shelbourne
Chief Executive: R D Fenhalls
Director:
　W L S Guinness
　A E Singer
Secretary & Chief Accountant:
　P R Thom

Henry Cooke Lumsden plc

PO Box 369
1 King Street
Manchester M60 3AH
Tel: 061 834 2332
Telex: 667783
Fax: 061 832 6024

Chairman: D I Hunter
Chief Executive: D H Adams
Director:
　K R Ashworth-Lord
　E B Bibby
　M J Brown
　J Davenport
　P R Green
　J R Grice
　N Hyman
　C S Jones
　T Kerrigan
　David M Lumsden
　G F Pemberton
　J B Pemberton
　A M E Scrimgeour
　K J Wilson

Henry G Nicholson (Underwriting) Ltd

12/14 Folgate Street
London E1 6BX
Tel: 071 377 1800
Telex: 883516
Fax: 071 377 9430

Chairman: B J Harvey
Director and Agency Manager:
　Mrs J Hook
Director:
　N Hart
　R J d'O Hope
Director and Company Secretary:
　R A Everest

Hill Osborne & Co

Royal Insurance Building
Silver Street
Lincoln LN2 1DU
Tel: 0522 513838
Fax: 0522 513965

Senior Partner: John C Strange

Hill Samuel Bank Limited

100 Wood Street
London EC2P 2AJ
Tel: 071 628 8011
Telex: 888822
Fax: 071 726 4671

Chairman: Sir Richard Lloyd
Deputy Chairman: D Bucks
Chief Executive: H Donaldson
Director:
　M H F Anderson
　P W Bonney
　J O P Bourke
　P W Brading
　T F Brockbank
　M R Brown
　C W E R Buchan
　P Bucks
　S J Campkin
　A Camu
　A W Clark
　Sir Robert Clark DSC
　Sir Hugh Cortazzi GCMG
　R S Davenport
　R W Devlin
　J C Doerr
　E A Emerson
　J A Fordham
　C R Forster
　T C Frankland
　R C G Gardner
　A C Gidman
　H R Gillespie

Director:
R D Gollings
G P Gonszor
P J Gooding
M C Gray
M J B Green
R S Grindy
P Guy
R W Heley
B Hesketh
L J Hirsch
W S James
J Jawanmardi
A W Jukes
J P Knights
J S Ledbury
D J E Longridge
R J Mackay
M S Mander
G M McEnery
B G McNamara
R H Meddings
J C S Mills
R R C Moore
D C Mootham
J A Naish
H P Newton
R Nunn
S O'Shea
C Oakley
A J Parker
G R Parris
M H Percy
R W N Perrin
A J H Reed
A C Reid
R F Reynolds
A J Rudd
D J F Rushton
R A Sansom
J C B Sharp
P C C Sidebottom
G M L Skingley
W H Smillie
E R Smith
I T B Sproule
J A Spurrier
R I Stansbury
M J Stanton
R Starling
E StC Stobart
P W Temple
G S Watson
P S Whitaker
P B Whitham
J K S Wilkinson
P K Williams
C M G Wrightson
T J Wyatt

Hill Samuel Development Capital
100 Wood Street
London EC2P 2AJ
Tel: 071 628 8011
Telex: 888822
Fax: 071 588 5281

Director:
Garry S Watson
Philip K Williams

Hill Samuel Investment Management Ltd
45 Beech Street
London EC2P 2LX
Tel: 071 638 1774
Telex: 887363
Fax: 071 588 4738

Chairman: W Neville Bowen
Director:
P E Beaven
R A Cawdron
J Daniels
H Fane
A A Gaitskell
E H Gold
A S Greenhorn
J C Grieve
D Ives
L Johnson
W MacDougall
H J Maguire
D S Manning
J R T Miller
J R Paterson
R F Pennells
J D Whiddett
B J Wootton

The Hiroshima Bank Ltd
18 King William Street
London EC4N 7BR
Tel: 071 623 2442
Telex: 8814908
Fax: 071 283 9209

Chief Representative: K Nobuhara

HM Treasury
Parliament Street
London SW1P 3AG
Tel: 071 270 3000
Telex: 9413704
Fax: 071 270 5653

Permanent Secretary:
Sir Peter Middleton
Chief Economic Adviser To The Treasury: Sir Terence Burns

Second Permanent Secretary:
A J C Edwards
N J Monck
N L Wicks
Chief Accountancy Adviser:
A J Hardcastle
Deputy Chief Economic Adviser:
J C Odling-Smee
Deputy Secretary:
H P Evans
G H Phillips
M C Scholar
R J Wilson

C Hoare & Co
37 Fleet Street
London EC4P 4DQ
Tel: 071 353 4522
Telex: 24622
Fax: 071 353 4521

Chairman and Managing Partner:
H C Hoare
Deputy Chairman and Managing Partner: D J Hoare
Managing Partner:
A M V Hoare
Alexander S Hoare
M R Hoare
Q V Hoare OBE
R Q Hoare
General Manager, Administration:
K E Mason

Hoare Govett Corporate Finance Limited
4 Broadgate
London EC2M 7LE
Tel: 071 601 0101
Telex: 297801
Fax: 071 374 1587

Chairman: Peter Meinertzhagen
Deputy Chairman: L H P Conner
Managing Director: F William Hulton
Director:
A Ayres
R H Bunn
C I Collins
W N David
Miss V E G Harper
C G James
R H Laird
P W Lord
N G Mills
Miss E Milner
C H Munday
R H Payne
R J Race

Director:
Mrs M F Wilson
R M A Wilson
A Winckler

Hoare Govett International Securities

4 Broadgate
London EC2M 7LE
Tel: 071 601 0101
Telex: 297801
Fax: 071 256 8500

Chairman: Tony C Lowrie
Managing Director:
Tim G E Kilpatrick
Director:
Peter M Berry
Peter G Bristowe
Steve A Crockford
Steve G Denby
Jill Hawkins
Finance Director: Neil A Linwood
Directors:
Barry L Murrell
Mike W Nelson

Hoare Govett Investment Research Limited

4 Broadgate
London EC2M 7LE
Tel: 071 601 0101
Telex: 297801
Fax: 071 256 8500

Managing Director, International Research: Jill Hawkins
Managing Director, UK Research: S Clegg
Managing Director, Economists: R S Jeffrey
Director (UK Consumers):
A J Culverwell
W Currie
G W Douglas
C D Hitchings
W J Houlihan
N G Hugh-Smith
Miss C Munro
R D T Pringle
M P Tampin
J R Toalster
R S Workman

Hoare Govett Securities Limited

4 Broadgate
London EC2M 7LE

Tel: 071 601 0101
Telex: 297801
Fax: 071 256 8500

Managing Director & Chief Executive Officer: D Plucinsky
Director, Head of Market-Making: N B Hughes
Director, Head of Sales: G A Houston
Director (Sales):
Shaun Allison
Graham Ayres
James Calvocoressi
Director (Market-Making):
Robert Chambers
Giles Fitzpatrick
Director (Sales): Douglas Gordon
Director (Market-Making):
Peter Greenwood
Director (Sales):
Marcus Hall
Keith Hiscock
Director (Market-Making):
Ian Jamieson
Director (Sales):
John Knox
John MacGowan
Director (Market-Making):
David Marshall
Ray Minsky
John Monnery
Director (Sales): Lee Morton
Director (Convertible Sales):
Michael Noakes
Director (Sales): Roderick Orr
Director (Market-Making):
H Martin Pope
Clive Roberts
Roger Spacey
Director (Sales): Jeremy Thompson
Director (Market-Making):
Michael Walker
Martin West
Director (Sales):
Robert Whitaker
Anthony Winnington

Hodgson Martin Limited

36 George Street
Edinburgh EH2 2LE
Tel: 031 226 7644
Telex: 727039
Fax: 031 226 7647

Managing Director: Allan F Hodgson
Director:
George D Gwilt
Dr Thomas L Johnston
G Arnold Kingsnorth
David D Stevenson

Assistant Director:
Lindsay J Boyd
Sheila C D Mackie
Senior Executive:
Brent R Osborn-Smith
Yvonne Savage

Hoenig & Co Ltd

5 London Wall Buildings
Finsbury Circus
London EC2M 5NT
Tel: 071 588 6622
Telex: 9312110378 HS
Fax: 071 588 6497

Chief Executive: N Johnson-Hill

Hogg Group plc

Lloyds Chambers
1 Portsoken Street
London E1 8DF
Tel: 071 480 4000
Telex: 884633
Fax: 071 480 4007

Chairman: J H Vaughn
Deputy Chairman & Managing Director: A G C Howland Jackson
Deputy Chairman: P B Sawdy
Finance Director: P A T Davidson
Director:
N B Bovingdon
H C Davies
Sir John Greenborough
C E Keller
D A McClure Fisher
S J C Minoprio
J C Y Radcliffe
A Shaw
A E Snow
W J Uzielli

The Hokkaido Takushoku Bank Ltd

Garrard House
31-45 Gresham Street
London EC2V 7BD
Tel: 071 606 8961
Telex: 884353
Fax: 071 606 7872

General Manager: T Sawada

Holman Franklin Ltd

Minster House
Arthur Street
London EC4R 9AB

Tel: 071 929 4037
Telex: 8954000
Fax: 071 621 0205

Chairman: David M Holman
Director:
    M D Beales
    J M Dennes
    J L Franklin
    B W C Graham
    P A Minter
    I R Wylie

Holman Macleod Limited
Minster House
Arthur Street
London EC4R 9AB
Tel: 071 929 4037
Telex: 8954000
Fax: 071 621 0205

Chairman: David M Holman
Director:
    J M Dennes
    B W C Graham
    R S T Gunter
    A M Macleod
    A R C Vine
    I R Wylie

Holman Managers Ltd
Minster House
Arthur Street
London EC4R 9AB
Tel: 071 929 4037
Telex: 8954000
Fax: 071 621 0205

Chairman: David M Holman
Director:
    J M Dennes
    B W C Graham
    B M Roddick
    J A Salmon
    I R Wylie

The Hongkong and Shanghai Banking Corp
PO Box 199
99 Bishopsgate
London EC2P 2LA
Tel: 071 638 2366
Telex: 885945
Fax: 071 588 3318

Executive Director Europe:
    P J Wrangham
Chief Operating Officer UK:
    H R Williams
Senior Manager Corporate Banking:
    J R Morley

Chief Treasury Manager Europe & M
    East: G Heald
Senior Manager General Banking:
    J R Fletcher
Area Financial Controller:
    C E Potsides
Legal Adviser Europe: P M Maynard

Hymans Robertson & Co
190 Fleet Street
London EC4A 2AH
Tel: 071 831 9561
Telex: 8813716
Fax: 071 831 6800

Senior Partner: Norman D Freethy
Partner:
    Michael Arnold
    Stuart H Bell
    Francis W Bowden
    Ronald S Bowie
    Ian W H Pope
    Gary G Wells

The Hyogo Bank Ltd
2nd Floor
Phoenix House
18 King William Street
London EC4N 7BR
Tel: 071 623 7602
Telex: 265474
Fax: 071 623 3288

Chief Representative: T Toyota

IBJ International Limited
Bucklersbury House
3 Queen Victoria Street
London EC4N 8HR
Tel: 071 236 1090
Telex: 925621
Fax: 071 236 0484

Managing Director & Chief Executive:
    Y Osawa
Managing Director: S Kubo
Deputy Managing Director:
    O Kurihara
    M Nakagawa
Director:
    K Ametani
    J H Dalhuisen
    M Hama
    T G Jensen
    S Kashiwagi
    Y Kudo
    T Natori
    J J Rees
    A Stakhovitch

Director:
    B Wagenmann
    M Webber
    S Zubaida

ICI Pension Fund
ICI Investment Management
Limited
1 Adam Street
London WC2N 6AW
Tel: 071 930 1262
Telex: 22497
Fax: 071 839 7479

Chairman: B C Hines
Managing Director: T Heyes
Investment Director: G K Allen
Finance & Operations Director:
    C A Amos

ICI plc
ICI Group Headquarters
9 Millbank
London SW1P 3JF
Tel: 071 834 4444
Telex: 21324
Fax: 071 834 2042

General Manager - Finance:
    P G Rogerson

IMI Capital Markets (UK)
Walbrook House
23-29 Walbrook
London EC4N 8BB
Tel: 071 283 6264
Telex: 941 9091 IMI CAP
Fax: 071 283 2279

Chairman: M J Balfour
Chief Executive: G Questa
Director:
    L Brunozzi
    E Celin
    L Cohen
    L F MacRae
    G F O Mattei
    M Prati
    A Rivano

IMI plc
PO Box 216
Witton
Birmingham B6 7BA
Tel: 021 356 4848
Telex: 336771
Fax: 021 356 3526

Chief Executive: G J Allen
Finance Director: G L Taylor
Company Secretary: J Metcalf

IMI Securities Ltd
Walbrook House
23-29 Walbrook
London EC4N 8BB
Tel: Trading 071 929 5202
Tel: Switchboard 071 283 6264
Telex: 941 9091 IMI CAP
Fax: Trading 071 283 9382
Fax: Research 071 623 9340

Chairman: M J Balfour
Chief Executive Officer:
  C N Woodgate
Director:
  M Amato
  L Cohen
  E Coliva
  L F MacRae
  T Meine
Head Dealer: R N Cunningham
Head of Research: A Peaker

Imperial Investments Limited
Bull Wharf
Redcliff Street
Bristol BS1 6QR
Tel: 0272 298444
Telex: 44791
Fax: 0272 290779

Joint Managing Director:
  P W Dunscombe
  W G Mather

Inchcape plc
St James's House
23 King Street
London SW1Y 6QY
Tel: 071 321 0110
Telex: 885395
Fax: 071 321 0604

Group Treasurer: J M Long

Industrial Development Board for Northern Ireland
IDB House
Chichester Street
Belfast BT1 4JX
Tel: 0232 233233
Telex: 747025
Fax: 0232 231328

Chief Executive:
  Anthony S Hopkins
Deputy Chief Executive:
  Frank Hewitt
  Bruce Robinson
  David Watkins

Instinet UK Ltd
Kildare House
Dorset Rise
London EC4P 4AJ
Tel: 071 353 2182
Fax: 071 353 0943

Managing Director: B J Cavill

Interallianz Bank Zurich AG
Representative Office
Cleary Court
21-23 St Swithin's Lane
London EC4N 8AD
Tel: 071 283 6211
Telex: 918677
Fax: 071 626 2012

Chief Executive: P M N Jennings

International Bankers Incorporated SA
Representative Office
11 Golden Square
London W1R 3AF
Tel: 071 437 4337
Telex: 936058 IBIF G
Fax: 071 287 9050

Representative: Christian Percepied

International City Holdings
34-40 Ludgate Hill
London EC4M 7JT
Tel: 071 248 3242
Telex: 893413
Fax: 071 248 1042

Chairman: Michael Warren
Director:
  William Duffy
  Richard Hottinger
  Robert Phelan
  Eddie Teraskiewicz
  Mrs Angela Howarth

International Clearing Services Limited
99 Gresham Street
London EC2V 7PH
Tel: 071 696 0500
Telex: 265704
Fax: 071 600 1732

Managing Director: G Möller

International Commodities Clearing House
Roman Wall House
1-2 Crutched Friars
London EC3N 2AN
Tel: 071 488 3200

Chairman: D M Child
Director:
  K B Alberti
  E W Barron
  A W Burr
  M A Cruttenden
  J M Eades
  P W Fowler
  D M Hardy
  J M Mather
  J A W Maxwell
  R Phan
  W A Reisch
  P A Wood

International Mexican Bank
29 Gresham Street
London EC2V 7ES
Tel: 071 600 0880
Telex: 8811017
Fax: 071 600 9891

Managing Director: G Legrain

International Petroleum Exchange
International House
1 St Katharine's Way
London E1 9UN
Tel: 071 481 0643
Telex: 927479
Fax: 071 481 8485

Chairman: D A Whiting
Chief Executive: P Wildblood

The International Stock Exchange
London EC2N 1HP
Tel: 071 588 2355
Telex: 886557

Chairman: A C Hugh Smith
Deputy Chairman:
  H Post
  I G Salter
Chief Executive: P J Rawlins
Secretary to the Council: M E Fidler
Managing Director, Primary Markets
  Division: S C H Douglas-Mann
Managing Director, Trading Markets
  Division: G A Hayter
Managing Director, Settlement Services
  Division: R J Margree

Head of Human Resources:
Ms L Trainer
Member of the Council:
K Beaton
G H Chamberlain
S P Cooke
N R Elwes
P-J K Etzel
J H Hale
M R Heath
M Inagaki
D L Jones
G N Kennedy
W N H Legge-Bourke
J McFarlane
C S McVeigh III
P D Minchin
P B Mitford-Slade
Nobuo Nakazawa
A B Nicholson
G M Nissen
S E J Raven
G Ross Russell
K B Sinclair
P R Stevens
C Strowger
D J Watkins
J D Webster
Sir Max Williams
J B Woolfenden
The Government Broker:
I Plenderleith

Investment Management Regulatory Organisation Ltd
Broadwalk House
5 Appold Street
London EC2A 2LL
Tel: 071 628 6022
Telex: 918768 IMRO G
Fax: 071 920 9285

Chairman: George M Nissen
Chief Executive: John A Morgan
Director:
S J David Corsan
David S Enock
Clive A K Fenn-Smith
H Robin Hutton
Melvyn L Jones
Douglas C P McDougall
John J McLachlan
Charles K R Nunneley
Keith E Percy
John S Sadler
Richard G Smethurst
Martin E O'K Trowbridge
Deputy Chief Executive:
Ronald Smith

Legal Director: David Brewster
Policy Director: Philip A R Brown
Finance & Support Services Director:
Tom Cotton
Member Assessment Director:
Keith Robinson
Company Secretary: Nick Walker

W H Ireland Stephens & Co Ltd
8 St John Street
Manchester M3 4DU
Tel: 061 832 6644
Fax: 061 833 0935

Director:
C T Ellis
H Fitzsimmons
J M Hamlyn
J E Pulley
J Stephens

Istituto Bancario San Paolo di Torino
9 St Paul's Churchyard
London EC4M 8AB
Tel: 071 822 7800
Telex: 8811148/9, 887268
Fax: 071 236 2698

Chief Manager: M Cotto
Deputy Chief Manager: B Mazzola

Ivory & Sime plc
One Charlotte Square
Edinburgh EH2 4DZ
Tel: 031 225 1357
Telex: 727242
Fax: 031 225 2375

Non-Executive Chairman:
R A Hammond-Chambers
Non-Executive Deputy Chairman:
G C Musson
D K Newbigging
Finance Director: G J Neilly
Investment Director: M T Woodward
Marketing Director: R I E Carswell
Director:
P de Salaberry
A Munro
D B Nichol
Director (US): K H Wood
Non-Executive Director:
M J K Belmont
I F Rushbrook

Iyo Bank
Level 6, City Tower
40 Basinghall Street
London EC2V 5DE
Tel: 071 588 2791
Telex: 949011
Fax: 071 588 2715

Chief Representative: M Akagashi

Jaguar Cars Ltd
Browns Lane
Coventry CV5 9DR
Tel: 0203 402121
Telex: 31622
Fax: 0203 405451

*Group Treasurer & Director of
   Financial Planning:* D A Scannell

James Capel & Co Ltd
James Capel House
PO Box 551
6 Bevis Marks
London EC3A 7JQ
Tel: 071 621 0011
Telex: 888866
Fax: 071 621 0496

Non-Executive Chairman:
P J Wrangham
Joint Chief Executive:
D J Dugdale
F J Fergusson
Executive Director:
R J Atkins
R J Benton
N A Fraser
M W Geering
J L Green
D L N Heron
G N Kennedy
P A Letley
S Lofthouse
I R B Perkins
C M Q Rampton
C W O Smedley
Non-Executive Director:
B H Asher
J M Gray
T W O'Brien

James Capel Corporate Finance Ltd
James Capel House
6 Bevis Marks
London EC3A 7JQ
Tel: 071 621 0011
Telex: 888866
Fax: 071 621 0496

Chairman: The Hon David C Poole
Director:
  T R Attwood
  J H Cripps
  D J Dugdale
  R W F Green
  R E Greenwood
  R J Harrison
  D M J Hickey
  F A Lilley
  Sir Raymond Lygo
  N C McCarthy
  P C Nicholls
  D Penrose
  D R Pollock
  A U Skinner
  B Stubbings
  D A Young

James Capel Fund Managers Ltd
7 Devonshire Square
London EC2M 4HU
Tel: 071 626 0566
Telex: 9413578
Fax: 071 621 0426

Executive Chairman: S Lofthouse
Director:
  W J Babtie
  A J Dunsford
  N A Fraser
  N S Tulloch
  R H Wilson
Company Secretary: R D W Haas

James Capel Gilts Ltd
James Capel House
6 Bevis Marks
London EC3A 7JQ
Tel: 071 621 0011
Telex: 888866
Fax: 071 621 0496

Chairman: I R B Perkins
Director:
  I C Collier
  E W Felstead
  A S Herbert
  T J Issaias
  J E Morrell
  C M Odescalchi

James Capel Moneybroking Ltd
James Capel House
6 Bevis Marks
London EC3A 7JQ

Tel: 071 621 0011
Telex: 888866
Fax: 071 621 0496

Director:
  R I Capel
  D J Dugdale
  G N Kennedy
  J M Latham

James Capel Unit Trust Management Ltd
James Capel House
6 Bevis Marks
London EC3A 7JQ
Tel: 071 626 0566
Fax: 071 626 4129

Chairman: N A Fraser
Managing Director: J J Custance
  Baker
Director:
  R J Bisson
  R S Brooks
  S M Corbett
  D J Dugdale
  N R Legge
  S Lofthouse
  B R Tora
  P J R Webb
Associate Director:
  W E S Carey
  Mrs J R Olley

James Finlay Bank Limited
Finlay House
10/14 West Nile Street
Glasgow G1 2PP
Tel: 041 204 1321
Telex: 777844
Fax: 041 204 4254

Chairman: R J K Muir
Deputy Chairman: R G Capper
Managing Director: J M Ingleby
Director:
  J A L Cumming
  P N Homer
  J R Strachan
  J F C Thompson
General Manager: C D Bustard

Janson Green Limited
6/7 Crescent
London EC3N 2LX
Tel: 071 480 6440
Telex: 893432
Fax: 071 481 9702

Chairman: G R P N Valentine

Deputy Chairman:
  W W Maitland
  M W Payne
Finance Director: S P Burns
Director:
  W F Goodier
  D J Peachey
  R J Wallace
  J M H P Wetherell
  J R L Youell

Japan Associated Finance Co Ltd
Nomura House
24 Monument Street
London EC3R 8AJ
Tel: 071 929 0926
Fax: 071 929 1692

Chief Representative: K Ozaki

Japan Development Bank
Level 4, City Tower
40 Basinghall Street
London EC2V 5DE
Tel: 071 638 6210
Telex: 888907
Fax: 071 638 6467

Chief Representative: H Sekiya

Jardine Insurance Brokers Group
Jardine House
6 Crutched Friars
London EC3N 2HT
Tel: 071 528 4444
Telex: 941 3847 JIS LDN
Fax: 071 528 4185

Group Chairman: Rodney Leach
Group Chief Executive: John Barton
*Group Director; Chairman & Chief
  Executive Jardine Reinsurance
  Holdings (UK) Ltd:*
  David E Corben
*Group Director; Chief Executive
  Jardine Insurance Brokers
  International Ltd:*
  Michael C Gribbin
*Group Director; Chief Exective Jardine
  Insurance Brokers Ltd & Group
  Director responsible for Asia:*
  Martin J Wakeley
*Chairman, Jardine (Lloyds
  Underwriting Agents) Ltd:*
  David R Walker

Jardine Insurance Brokers Limited

Jardine House
6 Crutched Friars
London EC3N 2HT
Tel: 071 528 4444
Telex: 924093
Fax: 071 528 4437

Chairman: Robin N Singer
Chief Executive: Martin J Wakeley
Director:
David J Cowley
Paul A Dawson
John Hastings-Bass
Barry A Kirby
Nicholas J Lee
C Michael Paine
Barry N Strong
Ron L Walker
Leigh N Whittingham

John Govett & Co Limited

Shackleton House
4 Battle Bridge Lane
London SE1 2HR
Tel: 071 378 7979
Telex: 884266
Fax: 071 638 3468

Chairman: Arthur I Trueger
Chief Executive:
Kevin J T Pakenham
Director:
M James Barstow
Peter L G Cotgrove
Charles A Fowler
Brian R Jervis
A Bruce McIntosh
M Adam Parkin
Richard G Royds
Michael Sampson
Thomas L H Walford
Gareth L Watts
Nicholas M Watts

John Lewis Partnership plc

171 Victoria Street
London SW1E 5NN
Tel: 071 828 1000
Telex: 941991/2
Fax: 071 828 6609

Finance Director: D E Young

John Siddall & Son Ltd

The Stock Exchange
4 Norfolk Street
Manchester M60 1DY
Tel: 061 832 7471
Fax: 061 835 3130

Managing Director: S H Alexander

Johnson Fry plc

20 Regent Street
London SW1Y 4PZ
Tel: 071 321 0220
Fax: 071 437 4844

Chairman: C A Fry
Chief Executive: C N A Castleman
Director:
K L Barker
M G Fletcher
P S Gildersleeves
C M J Whittington

Johnson Matthey

New Garden House
78 Hatton Garden
London EC1N 8JP
Tel: 071 269 8000
Telex: 267711
Fax: 071 269 8133

Chairman: D J Davies
Deputy Chairman: K H Walley
Chief Executive: J A Stevenson
Deputy Chief Executive:
R K A Wakeling
Executive Director, Administration:
I G Thorburn
Executive Director, Catalytic Systems:
C R N Clark
Executive Director, Finance:
J N Sheldrick
*Executive Director, Materials
Technology & Research:*
B S Cooper
Non-Executive Director:
H E Fitzgibbons
H M P Miles
C H Parker
The Hon G H Wilson
Company Secretary: D W R Wright

Jordan International Bank plc

103 Mount Street
London W1Y 6AP
Tel: 071 493 7528
Telex: 8814135
Fax: 071 355 4359

Acting General Manager:
Timothy Barnes
Treasury Manager: Bassel Kekhia
Private Banking Manager:
George Shihata
*Business Development and
Correspondent Banking Manager:*
Anis Naamani

Jugobanka DD

UK Representative Office
Salisbury House
London Wall
London EC2M 5RT
Tel: 071 628 9081
Telex: 883031

Chief Representative: M Ilic

Jyske Bank

119-120 Chancery Lane
London WC2A 1HU
Tel: 071 831 2778
Telex: 266093

General Manager: Jens Rahbek
Deputy General Manager:
Guy Loosmore

KAS Clearing Agent Ltd

Suite 560, Salisbury House
London Wall
London EC2M 5SH
Tel: 071 588 6400
Fax: 071 528 8829

Managing Director: H W van Arem

KDB International (London) Limited

Plantation House
31-35 Fenchurch Street
London EC3M 3DX
Tel: 071 623 2960
Telex: 886903
Fax: 071 283 4593

Chief Representative: D S Kim

Keith Bayley Rogers & Co

Ebbark House
93-95 Borough High Street
London SE1 1NL
Tel: 071 378 0657
Telex: 888437
Fax: 071 378 1795

Senior Partner: David H Covell
Managing/Finance Partner: W
Howard Saunders

Corporate Finance Partner:
A H Drummon
Senior Analyst: John Goodchild

Kellett (Holdings) Limited
Greenly House
40 Dukes Place
London EC3A 7LP
Tel: 071 623 9104
Fax: 071 626 5981

Chairman: B P D Kellett
Director:
B F G Cockhill
W Deem
M D Seaby
T Shenton
A A Williams

Killik & Co
24/25 Manchester Square
London W1M 5AP
Tel: 071 224 2050
Fax: 071 486 3562

Senior Partner: Paul Killik
Partner:
Matthew Orr
F D P Robinson
Non-Executive Partner:
P M Barclay CBE
P R Hartley

Kim Eng Securities (London) Limited
37 Park Street
London W1Y 3HG
Tel: 071 355 2320
Telex: 261687
Fax: 071 409 2191

Chairman and Managing Director:
A W Hobbs
Director:
M C Franklin
A Gunn Forbes
D Ooi

King & Shaxson Limited
52 Cornhill
London EC3V 3PD
Tel: 071 623 5433
Telex: 888869
Fax: 071 929 0075

Chairman: W E C D'Abbans
Director:
D R Jarrett
D T R Pearce
Secretary: D E Mason

King & Shaxson Money Brokers Limited
52 Cornhill
London EC3V 3PD
Tel: 071 626 7406
Telex: 888869
Fax: 071 929 0075

Chairman: W E C D'Abbans
Non-Exec Director: D T R Pearce
Director: J A Beard

Kingfisher plc
North West House
119 Marylebone Road
London NW1 5PX
Tel: 071 724 7749
Telex: 267007
Fax: 071 724 1160

Treasurer: Glyn Thomas

Kleinwort Benson Gilts Limited
20 Fenchurch Street
London EC3P 3DB
Tel: 071 623 8000
Telex: 922241
Fax: 071 623 4572

Chairman: J N Abanto
Deputy Chairman: P M Clarke
Director:
J M Duchin
J Duckett
Dr R J A Golding
R Helyar
R C H Jeens
B W J Manning

Kleinwort Benson Group plc
20 Fenchurch Street
London EC3P 3DB
Tel: 071 623 8000
Telex: 888531
Fax: 071 626 4069

Chairman: D A E R Peake
Group Chief Executive:
J G W Agnew
Vice-Chairman/Group Business Development:
The Lord Rockley
D H Benson
R T Fox
Director:
J N Abanto
T G Barker
C H Black
R A Brooks
D C Clementi

Director:
Sir Philip Haddon-Cave KBE CMG
C J Hue Williams
Sir Kenneth Kleinwort Bt
N S MacEwan
C C Maltby
B W J Manning
K J Morton
I R Peacock
The Hon Sir Nicholas Redmayne Bt
Sir David Steel
I S Steers
Sir George Turnbull
D C Wake-Walker

Kleinwort Benson Investment Management
10 Fenchurch Street
London EC3M 3LB
Tel: 071 956 6600
Fax: 071 956 7125

Chairman: C H Black
Chief Executive: C C Maltby
Deputy Chairman: P J Ellis
Director:
F P L Adams
P G Ainsworth
P J Allen
M E Beaumont
P J Bebb
A C Begg
R J Boden
D V Clasper
J F Dale
B M Dean
J Garbutt
D G Glasgow
A R Gregory
N F Haynes
Ms M A Kerr
K King
D A C Lawrence
D Loffstadt
M E Luboff
A R Marlow
R Peirson
R D C Prichard
J E S Rigg
R L Shearmur
B C R Siddons
C R Spencer
S L Tanner
G E B Thomas
N C Wiggins

Kleinwort Benson Limited

20 Fenchurch Street
London EC3P 3DB
Tel: 071 623 8000
Telex: 888531
Fax: 071 623 4069

Chairman: J G W Agnew
Vice Chairman: T G Barker
Director:
N C à Brassard
J N Abanto
G F O Alford
M D Allen
M G Baker
M J N Barnett
B Bennett
D H Benson
S H A Bobasch
R J Boden
P C Boothman
A L J Bowen
R A Brooks
A D G Brown
A B Buckwell
P L Button
D R O'C Cameron
J A N Cameron
Lord Chandos
P M Clarke
D C Clementi
A N Coppell
A L Craft
M J L Cramsie
P A d'Anyers Willis
P H P de Pelet
B M Dean
M Defriend
J L E G Delvaulx
A C Dolbey
G B Duncan
C A A P Eugster
C J Farrow
R T Fox
R J Garvey
D M F A Gautier-Sauvagnac
H G Geier
R D Gillingwater
R J A Golding
B P R Guerin
J I M Hamilton
R D N Harley
R W Harvey
J R P Healing
Miss R Hedley-Miller
D Hinshaw
B M Hiorns
T H Holland-Bosworth
C J Hue Williams

Director:
G H F Irwin
R C H Jeens
N Jefcoat
R A Jenkins
Ms M Kerr
C P Kirwan-Taylor
M G Lethbridge
R C Lough
D W A Loyd
N S MacEwan
B W J Manning
M Martin
P J Martin
K S McCormick
W H Mellen
K J Morton
R A Murley
S J Neathercoat
J J Noble
R J H D Palmer
S C Y Parker
I R Peacock
D A E R Peake
B H Putnam
Sir Nicholas Redmayne
J P Reis
The Hon P J Remnant
S M Robertson
C H W Robson
The Lord Rockley
T A Shacklock
G A Shenkman
G N Simonds
D S Solly
D R Soper
Viscount Trenchard
D C Wake-Walker
Mrs L M S Watts
A J White
M F Williams
C Wright
A C D Yarrow

Kleinwort Benson Securities Limited

20 Fenchurch Street
London EC3P 3DB
Tel: 071 623 8000
Telex: 922241
Fax: 071 623 4572

Chairman: J G W Agnew
Vice-Chairman: D C Clementi
Joint Managing Director:
C J Hue Williams
Sir Nicholas Redmayne
Deputy Managing Director:
B M Hiorns

Finance Director: S P Ball
Secretary: Baroness N J Schrager
Von Altishofen
Director:
Nicholas Allan
Ian S Andrews
Kiyoshi Arai
Miss Barbara J Arzymanow
Michael Geoffrey Bedford
Andrew Richard Bell
Barrie Bennett
Jeremy D Chantry
Nicholas A Christie
Michael James Costello
Robert Gwynne Cottam
James I Crammond
Graeme Frank Cull
Geoffrey de Sibert
Vernon Nicholas John Dempsey
James Edmund Dodd
Simon Douglas-Home
Gary Robert Dudman
John L Duffy
Laurence John Faulkner
Colin Rodney Fell
Colin Digby Thomas Fitch
Bruce Douglas Hayden Froud
Victor Gordon David Halle
Jeremy Ian MacAulay Hamilton
Robert Dryburgh Nisbet Harley
David G Harper
Roger Martin Harvey
Julian Robert Peter Healing
Christopher John Honnor
Verity Susan Stowell Hunt
David A Jervis
David Philip Joyner
David Brian Knox
Philip S Lambert
Vincent W Leader
William Nigel Henry Legge-
Bourke
Chung Lew
Martin Neil Lupton
Simon P Maclean
Miss Bromwen M Maddox
Robin James McDonagh
William Henry Mellen
Philip Meredith
Piers M Mizen
Simon John Nethercoat
Miss Fiona Margaret Nicol
Roger James Hune Dorney
Palmer
John Henry Patrick Fuller Pelly
Adrian Gerald Phillips
Colin V Phillips
Peter Edward Phillips
Mark Peter Potashnick

Director:
John Aidan Joseph Price
Ms Deborah Ann Rees
Clayton Hugo Wynne Robson
David Allen Rogers
Hideo Saito
Christopher P Salter
Kenichi Satoh
Richard Thomas Scholes
Charles Adam Laurie Sebag-
    Montefiore
Hilton Nigel Seely
Michael Brian Shortt
Janet F Sidaway
B Mikaela Sjowall
Francis Paul Smiddy
Simon F Smithson
Stephen Paul Spedding
John Vincent Spicer
James Robertson Stevenson
Graham Ivor Stradling
David James Summers
Anthony David Thomas
Timothy Kenneth Thornton
David Hedley Thorpe
Ulrik T Trampe
Mehdi Varzi
Mark Michael Wellesley-Wood
Ian Shaw White
John Frederick Reynell Wilson
Jonathan Paul Wood
Hiroaki Yamataka
Alan Colin Drake Yarrow

Kleinwort Benson Unit Trusts Limited

10 Fenchurch Street
London EC3M 3LB
Tel: 071 956 6600
Telex: 9413545
Fax: 071 956 5810

Chairman: C R T Edwards
Deputy Chairman:
    D G Glasgow
    C C Maltby
Joint Managing Director:
    A R Gregory
    R L Shearmur
Director:
    M E Beaumont
    R J Boden
    G R Davies
    P J Ellis
    D A C Lawrence
    G E B Thomas

Knight & Day Ltd (Birmingham Division)

3/8 Vyse Street
Birmingham B18 6LT
Tel: 021 236 9045
Telex: 339084
Fax: 021 236 7670
Fax: 021 212 1175

Chief Executive: R D P Knight
Group Managing Director:
    P A Knight
Deputy Managing Director:
    R G Eastwood
Director:
    R T Benwell
    M L Hughes
    V J Sparks
    A B Warren

Knight & Day Ltd (London Division)

City Central Two
Seward Street
London EC1V 3PA
Tel: 071 250 1188
Telex: 264891
Fax: 071 490 2104

Chief Executive: R D P Knight
Managing Director: P A Knight
Director:
    C R Green
    T V Melvill

Korea Development Bank

Plantation House
31-35 Fenchurch Street
London EC3M 3DX
Tel: 071 623 2960
Telex: 886903
Fax: 071 283 4593

Chief Representative: D S Kim

Korea Exchange Bank

1 Old Jewry
London EC2R 8DU
Tel: 071 606 0191
Telex: 886398
Fax: 071 606 9968

Regional Senior Vice President: Yung-
    Woo Lee

Korea First Bank

80 Cannon Street
London EC4N 6HH

Tel: 071 626 9264
Telex: 8956724
Fax: 071 626 2840

General Manager: K W Chong

Kredietbank NV

Level 7, City Tower
40 Basinghall Street
London EC2V 5DE
Tel: 071 638 5812
Telex: 8951024/6
Fax: 071 588 0882

General Manager: Marc Bernaert
Senior Manager Treasury:
    Keith Benson
Senior Manager Operations:
    Paul Knapen
*Senior Manager Corp Banking &
    Finance:* David Monahan

Kredietbank SA Luxembourgeoise

London Representative Office
Founders Court, Lothbury
London EC2R 7HE
Tel: 071 600 0332
Telex: 888709
Fax: 071 726 6417

London Representative:
    Ms M J Horbaczewska

Kuwait Investment Office

St Vedast House
150 Cheapside
London EC2V 6ET
Tel: 071 606 8080
Telex: 886301
Fax: 071 606 1605

Chairman: Sheikh Fahd M Al Sabah
Deputy Chairman & Chief Executive:
    K N Al Sabah

Kyowa Bank

93-95 Gresham Street
London EC2V 7NA
Tel: 071 606 9231
Telex: 883317
Fax: 071 606 0565

General Manager: K Ando

Ladbroke Group plc

Chancel House
Neasden Lane
London NW10 2XE

Tel: 081 459 8031
Telex: 22274
Fax: 081 459 8618

Treasurer: B Barker
Group Solicitor: Mrs Marie Stevens
Chairman and Managing Director:
Cyril Stein
Director and Secretary:
Christopher H Andrews
*Corporate Planning Director and
Executive Chairman, Texas
Homecare:* Keith G Edelman
*Executive Chairman, UK and
International Racing:*
Peter M George
*Executive Chairman, UK and
International Hotels:*
Michael B Hirst
Financial Director:
Jeremiah F O'Mahony
Vice Chairman:
Sir Kenneth Cork GBE
Non-Executive Director:
The Rt Hon The Earl of
Gowrie
John B H Jackson BA LLB
The Hon Greville Janner QC
MP

Laing & Cruickshank
Broadwalk House
5 Appold Street
London EC2A 2DA
Tel: 071 588 4000
Telex: 888397/8
Fax: 071 588 0290

Chairman: I F H Davison
Chief Executive: C P Ménard
Director:
B Armstrong
M S Evans
M J Harty
B Hautefort
R M Leiman
A R K Mackintosh
G C Mordaunt
R D Ward

Land Securities plc
21 New Fetter Lane
London EC4P 4PY
Tel: 071 353 4222
Telex: 934019
Fax: 071 353 7871

Chairman and Managing Director:
P J Hunt
Deputy Chairman: John Hull

Director:
R A W Caine
H I Connick
M R Griffiths
I J Henderson
D H MacKeith
W Mathieson
J M Moar
K Redshaw

Lane Clark & Peacock
30 Old Burlington Street
London W1X 1LB
Tel: 071 439 2266
Fax: 071 439 0183

Senior Partner: D W Peacock
Partner:
C R C Hawkes
R J N Young
Susan M Wilcock
G W Orpwood Price
M R Slack
A Bradley
R R Heard
A M Newman
F J Morrison
A D Mason
I R H Scott
A P Cunningham
P D G Thompkins
Petrea A Simmons
N Curry
Consultant: B J Clark
Chief Executive: David Ellis

Laporte plc
Laporte House
Kingsway
Luton LU4 8EW
Tel: 0582 21212
Telex: 82221
Fax: 0582 31818

Non-Executive Chairman:
R Bexon CBE
*Chief Executive and Managing
Director:* K J Minton
Finance Director: R E Dickinson
Operations Director:
M A Fearfield
Dr H Seidl
Personnel and Administration Director:
B A Hall
Strategic Planning Operations Director:
Dr K G Sansom
Non-Executive Director:
G Duncan
M J Evans

Non-Executive Director:
C Loutrel
J E Solvay
Group Treasurer: Jim Cudmore

Larpent Newton & Co Ltd
4th Floor
24-26 Baltic Street
London EC1Y 0TB
Tel: 071 251 9111
Fax: 071 251 2609

Managing Director: C J Breese
Director:
L S Rees
J R Taylor

LAS Unit Trust Managers
10 George Street
Edinburgh EH2 2YH
Tel: 031 225 8494
Telex: 727128
Fax: 031 225 3618

Managing Director: J M Souness
Chief Executive: M A Forrest
Director:
S D Brookhouse
K R L Luckhoo
N P Magee
K McLean
G W Parvin
Secretary: Miss A Ward

LASMO plc
100 Liverpool Street
London EC2M 2BB
Tel: 071 945 4545
Telex: 8812970
Fax: 071 606 2893

Chairman: The Rt Hon
Lord Rees QC
Deputy Chairman:
J Cordingley OBE
Chief Executive: W W C Greentree
Director Corporate, Development:
C N Davidson Kelly
Director, Finance: M J Pavia
Director, Production: T G King
Director:
Professor Sir James Ball
M J K Belmont
Sir David Nicolson
Group Treasurer: J G George

Laurence Keen Limited
49/51 Bow Lane
London EC4M 9LX

Tel: 071 489 9493
Telex: 916966
Fax: 071 489 8638

Chairman: W H Keatley
Chief Executive: G M Powell
Director:
  T F M Bebb
  A C O Bell
  D H W Bell
  D M Davis
  I W Gammell
  Miss C M Gore Langton
  Miss A M Pickup
  M Reid Scott
  R G Sewell
  J T Smith
  J R L Wells
  M J P Wright

Lautro Ltd
Centre Point
103 New Oxford Street
London WC1A 1QH
Tel: 071 379 0444
Fax: 071 379 4121

Chairman: E B O Sherlock
Deputy Chairman:
  J A Freeman
  Sir Michael Kerry KCB QC
  I G Sampson
Chief Executive: C F Jebens
Director:
  R W S Baker
  P Bateman
  J Bridel
  R Calver
  J Elbourne
  Mrs P Lambert
  D R Loughborough
  C S S Lyon
  T P F Miller
  R Sepel
  M St Giles
  Ms Helena Wiesner
  D Woods
  F E Worsley

Lazard Brothers & Co Limited
21 Moorfields
London EC2P 2HT
Tel: 071 588 2721
Telex: 886438
Fax: 071 628 2485

Chairman: M A David-Weill
Chief Executive: D J Verey

Vice Chairman:
  M A P Agius
  J F Nelson
Executive Director:
  D J L F Anderson
  M C Baughan
  A L Blakesley
  M C Bottenheim
  A G Catto
  R D Clegg
  G M Craig-McFeely
  T Cross Brown
  R J G Davies
  E W Dawnay
  J S Dear
  C C Fisher
  M C Francis
  W W Gridley
  Mrs Frances A Heaton
  F J C G Hervey-Bathurst
  P G Hock
  A D Johnston
  N M H Jones
  J A Kitchen
  N T Lukes
  N D M Mackay
  C B Melluish
  P Newey
  A P C Northrop
  C M Packshaw
  M R Richardson
  M J Roberts
  J P H S Scott
  A H Shrager
  J Todd
  The Hon P N N Turner
  D R Twining
  S C Webb
  K M H Wilson
Director:
  R F Agostinelli
  R Bexon
  Viscount Blakenham
  M W Burrell
  D H Bushell
  Sir John Cuckney
  Sir Ian Fraser
  T C Glucklich
  J C Haas
  D E C Hudson
  J A B Joll
  Lord Kindersley
  Hon T H Manners
  S W Oliver
Secretary: A J Eady

Lazard Frères & Co Limited
21 Moorfields
London EC2P 2HT
Tel: 071 528 9966
Fax: 071 374 6614

Chief Executive Officer:
  Ali E Wambold
Managing Director: J Gotbaum

Lazard Investors Limited
21 Moorfields
London EC2P 2HT
Tel: 071 588 2721
Telex: 886438
Fax: 071 628 2485

Chairman: M C Baughan
Chief Executive: S C Webb
Director:
  Mrs Patricia R Book
  P Chrimes
  D R Graham
  P M Hope-Falkner
  K Jones
  Miss P J Maxwell-Arnot
  C B Melluish
  P N Quinnen
  M R Richardson
  A G Saunders
  Miss J A K Smith
  R F Smith
  P M C J Stevens
  J R Tennant
  D J Verey

Leeds Permanent Building Society
Permanent House
The Headrow
Leeds LS1 1NS
Tel: 0532 438181
Fax: 0532 352569

President: J M Barr
Vice-President: R B Strachan
Director & Chief Executive:
  J M Blackburn
Commercial Director:
  C N P Chadwick
Finance Director: R F Boyes
Information Systems Director:
  P G Lumb
General Manager Field Operations:
  R G Humphreys
General Manager Finance & Estates:
  R F Bennett
Head of Computer Services: G Scarlett
Head of Corporate Communications:
  N V Thompson

Head of Direct Marketing: R Ivey
Head of Housing Services: N Turner
Head of Human Resource Management:
  D Jarratt
Head of Property Services:
  D Thompson
Head of Savings & Investment:
  D Andrew
Head of Systems Development:
  M F Rowe
Head of Treasury: P J Green
Head of Visa & Unsecured Lending:
  C J Wycks
Secretary: H J Briggs
Group Planning Control &
  Compliance Officer: P Martin

Legal & General Group plc

Temple Court
11 Queen Victoria Street
London EC4N 4TP
Tel: 071 528 6200
Telex: 892971
Fax: 071 528 6222

Chairman: Professor Sir James Ball
Vice Chairman: K H M Dixon
Group Chief Executive: T J Palmer
Managing Director:
  Colin C Harris
  Brian Palmer
Group Director:
  John K Elbourne
  Anthony Hobson
  David Prosser
  John M Skae
Director:
  R H Clutton
  Sir Frederick Crawford
  Sir John Egan
  W J R Govett
  Lady Howe
  J F C Hull
  J S Kerridge
  Sir Richard E B Lloyd
  The Hon T J Manners
Group Secretary: John Neill
Property Managing Director:
  David A Ormerod

Legal & General Ventures Ltd

Temple Court
11 Queen Victoria Street
London EC4N 4TP
Tel: 071 248 9678
Telex: 892971
Fax: 071 248 9678 ext 3379

Chairman: D J Prosser

Managing Director: C P Peal
Director:
  E L Cooper
  A R B Johnson
  P Laszlo
  A W Palmer
  I D Taylor

Lehman Brothers Equity Money Brokers Ltd

1 Broadgate
London EC2M 7HA
Tel: 071 260 2025
Telex: 888881
Fax: 071 260 3152

Chief Executive: J DiRocco
Director:
  D McHugh
  M F K Moursy
  H Post
  S Spiegel

Lehman Brothers Gilt Money Brokers Ltd

One Broadgate
London EC2M 7HA
Tel: 071 601 0011
Telex: 888881
Fax: 071 260 2999

Director:
  J DiRocco
  D McHugh
  M F K Moursy
  R Ramsay
  S Spiegel

Leslie & Godwin Limited

PO Box 219
6 Braham Street
London E1 8ED
Tel: 071 480 7200
Telex: 8950221
Fax: 071 480 7450

Chairman & Managing Director:
  A A M Pinsent
Deputy Chairman: H B Prentis
Director:
  J H Barder
  D J Brodrick
  N R G Christian
  R R Davies
  M W Eve
  R A D Fyshe
  R A Gladdis
  B G Hayden
  M C Hughesdon
  I M E Jeffery

Director:
  Sir Francis Kennedy
  D J Martin
  D J C Mekie
  J S R Monk
  C D Ott
  M F L Oxlade
  C J N Robinson
  P Roundell
  C B Slatter
  W B B Smith
  T T Tobin
  B P Waghorn
  T J Wallace
  R T Williamson
Secretary: I Pigram

A P Leslie Underwriting Agencies Limited

120 Fenchurch Street
London EC3M 5BA
Tel: 071 929 2811
Fax: 071 220 7234

Chairman: J O Prentice
Director:
  H R Dumas
  W G Ibett
  A P Leslie
  I J Parker
  A Taylor
  A Waugh
Secretary: T G S Busher

Lewis & Peat Holdings Ltd

PO Box 50
32 St Mary-at-Hill
London EC3R 8LT
Tel: 071 623 3111
Telex: 887973
Fax: 071 623 3351

Chairman: Hon R D Kissin
Life President: Lord Kissin of
  Camden
Executive Director: D L Cowley

Livingstone Fisher plc

Acre House
11-15 William Road
London NW1 3ER
Tel: 071 388 7000
Fax: 071 380 4900

Managing Director: Barrie Pearson
Director:
  Tim Lyle
  Ian Smith
Executive: Mark O'Hara

Ljubljanska Banka Representative Office
7 Birchin Lane
London EC3V 9BY
Tel: 071 626 8848
Telex: 888394
Fax: 071 626 0710

Senior Vice President: G Koprivec

Lloyds Abbey Life plc
80 Holdenhurst Road
Bournemouth BH8 8AL
Tel: 0932 850888
Fax: 0932 846597

Chairman and Managing Director:
Michael L Hepher
Deputy Managing Director and Group Finance Director: Stephen Maran
Group Marketing Director: M Gary Jones
Group Director, Europe:
C M Wiscarson
Executive Director:
P S Constable
A J Frost
Group Legal Director and Company Secretary: J N Temple
Non-Executive Director:
Sir Lindsay Alexander
Dr C John Constable
N W Jones CBE TD
C R Smith CBE
Sir Norman Wakefield

Lloyds Bank plc
71 Lombard Street
London EC3P 3BS
Tel: 071 626 1500
Telex: 888301
Fax: 071 623 1863

Chairman:
Sir Jeremy Morse KCMG
Deputy Chairman:
Sir John Hedley Greenborough KBE
Sir Robin Ibbs KBE
Vice Chairman:
A J Davis RD
N W Jones CBE TD
Chief Executive: B I Pitman
Deputy Chief Executive:
M H R Thompson
Director of Corporate Banking & Treasury: A E Moore CBE
Director of International Banking:
J T Davies

Director of Private Banking & Financial Services: P G Brown
Director of UK Retail Banking:
D B Pirrie
Director:
Sir Lindsay Alexander
Sir William Harding KCMG CVO
M L Hepher
Sir Simon Hornby
G C Kent
Sir Peter Matthews AO
Lord Plumb DL
I M G Prosser
J M Raisman CBE
C R Smith CBE
Eric Swainson CBE
Senior General Manager:
F E Jones
N Parker
G O Solomon
General Manager:
P J Bareau
C Bruce-Jones
A B Buchanan
I D Cheyne
M A Cruttenden
J A Davies
C M Fisher
D H A Harrison
P J Leech
B J Milne
N J Minchinson
F M P Riding
S F Shore
K B Stanger
Chief Financial Officer: C N J Wilks
Secretary: A J Michie
Chief Economic Adviser: C L McI Johnson
Chief Legal Adviser: P B Lawson

Lloyd's Bank Stockbrokers Ltd
48 Chiswell Street
London EC1Y 4XX
Tel: 071 522 5000
Telex: 888301
Fax: 071 522 5563

Managing Director: Robert A D Froy

Lloyds Development Capital Limited
40-66 Queen Victoria Street
London EC4P 4EL
Tel: 071 236 4940
Fax: 071 329 4900

Managing Director: R Hollidge

Lloyds Merchant Bank Limited
48 Chiswell Street
London EC1Y 4XX
Tel: 071 522 5000
Telex: 888301
Fax: 071 522 5163

Chairman and Chief Executive:
D O Horne
Deputy Chairman: P D Minchin
Managing Director (Corporate Finance): R C G Fortin
Managing Director (Lloyds Development Capital Limited):
R Hollidge
Managing Director (Lloyds Bank Stockbrokers Limited):
R A D Froy
Managing Director (Support Services):
G Morgan
Managing Director (Lloyds Investment Managers): Peter C Axten

Lloyd's of London
1 Lime Street
London EC3M 7DQ
Tel: 071 623 7100
Telex: 987321
Fax: 071 626 2389

Chairman: David Coleridge
Deputy Chairman:
Alan Francis Jackson
John Greig
Deputy Chairman & Chief Executive:
Alan Lord CB
Member of the Council:
Dr Mary Archer
Sir Nicholas Bonsor Bt
Michael Henry Cockell
David Ean Coleridge
Sir Alcon Copisarow
Henry Roy Dobinson
Norman Gordon Edward Dunlop
Patrick Egan
Arthur Mark Farrer
John Scott Greig
Anthony Gordon Hines
Sir Maurice Hodgson
Bryan Philip David Kellett
The Rt Hon Lord Kimball
Stephen Roy Merrett
Sir Jeremy Morse
Matthew Le May Patient
Nicholas Charles Thoresby Pawson
Sir Gerrard Peat KVCO
Brian Walter Pomeroy

Member of the Council:
  J David Rowland
  Mark Hebberton Sheldon
  Michael John Wade
  David Alan Walker
Solicitor to the Corporation:
  W C Beckett
Head of Regulatory Services:
  R A C Hewes
Head of Finance: J H F Gaynor
Head of Systems & Communications:
  J D Lee
Head of Corporation Services:
  R Woodford
Head of Market Services: A A Duguid
Secretary to the Council: A P Barber

Lombard North Central plc

Lombard House
3 Princess Way
Redhill
Surrey RH1 1NP
Tel: 0737 774111
Telex: 268742
Fax: 0737 760031

Chairman: Sir Hugh Cubitt
Chief Executive: B A Carte
Director:
  E W Barron
  R G Crotty
  C W Finnerty
  R Flemington
  Sir Brian Kellett
  M A Maberly
  A A Mitchener
  J M Morgan
  J D Purdy
  J G Woodhouse
  R J Young

London and Manchester Group plc

Eldon House
Eldon Street
London EC2M 7LB
Tel: 071 247 2000
Fax: 071 247 2859

Chairman: J M Thomson
Chief Executive: D A L Jubb
Investment Director: Simon McClean
Pensions Director: D J Newman
Finance Director: T A Pyne
General Manager:
  W H Lea
  A R Swinburne-Johnson

London Fox

1 Commodity Quay
St Katharine Docks
London E1 9AX
Tel: 071 481 2080
Telex: 884370
Fax: 071 702 9924

Chairman and Chief Executive:
  M A B Saxon Tate
Director:
  M D Chataway
  J Kerr-Muir
  A D McClumpha
  J A Patterson
  J Payne
  C W Shea
  M J C Stone
  D A Whitling
Compliance Director: P A S Rucker

London International Financial Futures Exchange

Royal Exchange
London EC3V 3PJ
Tel: 071 623 0444
Telex: 893893
Fax: 071 588 3624

Chairman: A D Burton
Deputy Chairman: N J Durlacher
Chief Executive: M N H Jenkins
Director:
  N G Ackerman
  M R Bailey
  R R St J Barkshire
  P C Barnett
  R M Eynon
  Mrs C H F Furse
  Mrs S S Hanbury-Brown
  C Henry
  D J Keegan
  D M Kyte
  A P La Roche
  B J Lind
  E R Porter
  S J Sanders
  J Wigglesworth
  R B Williamson
Company Secretary: I E Nash

The London Metal Exchange Ltd

Plantation House
Fenchurch Street
London EC3M 3AP
Tel: 071 626 3311
Telex: 8951367
Fax: 071 626 1703

President: J K Lion
Vice Chairman: J P A Wolff
Chief Executive: D E King
Company Secretary: N D Banks
Director:
  R K Bagri
  P C F Crowson
  E P Dablin
  C P Danin
  K C Davies
  C J Farrow
  R Kestenbaum
  S C Lowe
  C I C Mackinnon
  D Normark
  K S Smith

Long Term Credit Bank of Japan

18 King William Street
London EC4N 7BR
Tel: 071 623 9511
Telex: 885305
Fax: 071 929 1672

Director & General Manager: Y Fujtt

Lonrho plc

Cheapside House
138 Cheapside
London EC2V 6BL
Tel: 071 606 9898
Telex: 885908
Fax: 071 606 2285

Chairman: The Rt Hon
  Sir Edward du Cann
Managing Director & Chief Executive:
  R W Rowland
Director:
  R G Badger
  R F Dunlop
  N Kruger
  M J J R Leclézio
  T J Robinson
  P G B Spicer
  P M Tarsh
  R E Whitten
  Sir Peter W Youens
Associate Director: J S Kato
Group Secretary: M J Pearce
Group Chief Accountant:
  C Matthews

Lowndes Lambert Group Holdings Limited

53 Eastcheap
London EC3P 3HL
Tel: 071 283 2000
Fax: 071 283 1970

Chairman: R Watts
Chief Executive: R J G Shaw
Director:
   M A Barnfield
   J Bartington
   B P Blackshields
   C R E Brooke
   M J Caley
   P W Kininmonth
   D B Margrett
   C Mineraud
   D J Ougham
   C R Sherling
   R L Tween
   S R D Wilson
Secretary: P F Ray

Lowndes Lambert Group Ltd
53 Eastcheap
London EC3P 3HL
Tel: 071 283 2000
Telex: 8814631
Fax: 071 283 1970

Chairman & Chief Executive:
   R J G Shaw
Managing Director:
   P W Kininmonth
Director:
   M A Barnfield
   J Bartington
   B P Blackshields
   M J Caley
   J A Champness
   J R Crisford
   M J Fitchen
   J D Forder
   A G Hazell
   A A Ledamun
   D B Margrett
   D C Senior
   M J Wildridge
   S R D Wilson
Financial Director: D J Ougham
Secretary: P F Ray

LPH Group plc
St Michael's Rectory
St Michael's Alley
Off Cornhill
London EC3V 9DS
Tel: 071 283 9831
Telex: 8952051 LEGPOR
Fax: 071 283 9859

Non-Executive Chairman:
   P A C H Phipps
Joint Managing Director:
   D A Howard
   J J R Leggett

Director:
   R M Dresner
   Sir M Harrison
   Jan Kratke
   Mark Letheren
   D E Porter

LTCB International Limited
18 King William Street
London EC4N 7BR
Tel: 071 623 3765
Telex: 892579
Fax: 071 626 1100

Managing Director: T Aizawa
Deputy Managing Director:
   B F Gadow
   M Imamura
   S Matsunaga
   K Shibano

Lucas Automotive Ltd
International Headquarters
Stratford Road
Shirley
Solihull B90 4LA
Tel: 021 627 3939
Telex: 338682
Fax: 021 627 4000

Managing Director: R A Dale

M & G Group plc
Three Quays
Tower Hill
London EC3R 6BQ
Tel: 071 626 4588
Telex: 887196
Fax: 071 623 8615

Deputy Chairman & Managing
   Director: D B Money-Coutts
Director:
   R A Brooks
   A G Down
   J S Fairbairn
   H J Haden
   C A McLintock
   T P F Miller
   A J Oddie
   Lord Rees-Mogg
   A P Shearer
   J H Shillingford
Secretary: A J Ashplant

M & G Investment Management Limited
Three Quays
Tower Hill
London EC3R 6BQ

Tel: 071 626 4588
Telex: 887196
Fax: 071 623 8615

Chairman: L E Linaker
Managing Director: J H Shillingford
Director:
   J P Allard
   J W Boeckmann
   J A T Caulfield
   G P Craig
   R S Hughes
   D L Morgan
   N D Morrison
   P D A Nix
   D O'Shea
   D N Robertson

Macey Williams Insurance Services Ltd
10 New Street
London EC2M 4TP
Tel: 071 623 4344
Telex: 896618MACWIL
Fax: 071 929 0414

Director:
   M O B Menzies
   V Patel
   D S Randle
EEC Development Executive:
   J Tahany
Assistant Director:
   M W Hamilton
   B M Roberts

Macey Williams Ltd
10 New Street
London EC2M 4TP
Tel: 071 623 4344
Telex: 896618 MACWIL
Fax: 071 929 0414

Chairman: E A MacRedmond
Managing Director: R D M Macey
Director:
   C F Lynch
   H B Prentis
   D F Smurfit
   I P Watson
   A J Williams

R A McLean & Co Ltd
44 West George Street
Glasgow G2 1DW
Tel: 041 332 5311
Fax: 041 221 3884

Director:
   D A R Lawrie

Director:
R A McLean
E O'Donnell
A C B Sneddon

Madoff Securities International Limited
43 London Wall
London EC2M 5TB
Tel: 071 374 0891
Telex: 947369
Fax: 071 374 0923

Chairman: Bernard L Madoff

MAI plc
8 Montague Close
London Bridge
London SE1 9RD
Tel: 071 407 7624
Fax: 071 407 0002

Chairman: Sir Ian Morrow
Deputy Chairman: Sir Graham Day
Managing Director: Clive Hollick
Deputy Managing Director:
Charles Gregson
Finance Director: Nicholas Cosh

Malayan Banking Berhad
74 Coleman Street
London EC2R 5BN
Tel: 071 638 0561
Telex: 888586

General Manager: R W C Chang

E D & F Man Ltd
Sugar Quay
Lower Thames Street
London EC3R 6DU
Tel: 071 626 8788
Telex: 885431
Fax: 071 621 0149

Chairman: M J C Stone
Managing Director:
Harvey A McGrath
Director:
D Federman
S Fink
B C Green
G Harris
J M Kinder
F J Lavooij
H A McGrath
M Metcalfe
S J Nesbitt

Manning Beard Ltd
3/5 Crutched Friars
London EC3N 2HT
Tel: 071 488 9881
Telex: 885475 MANBEA G
Fax: 071 480 7213

Chairman: M J Manning
Director:
T W Hughes
G A Latham
W J N Ling
D M Menzies

Manufacturers Hanover Limited
The Adelphi
1-11 John Adam Street
London WC2N 6HT
Tel: 071 932 4000
Telex: 884901
Fax: 071 932 4100

Managing Director: John L Sullivan

Manufacturers Hanover Trust Company
The Adelphi
1-11 John Adam Street
London WC2N 6HT
Tel: 071 932 3000
Telex: 898371
Fax: 071 839 8380

Executive Vice President:
John D Zutter Jr
Senior Vice President:
Morten Arntzen
Thomas F Hyland Jr
Managing Director:
Peter Bickerton
James H Hohorst
Richard Smith
Vice President:
Bruce Bettencourt
Andrew Brett
Edward Charles
Derek A Clapton
Joseph A Coneeny
Clifford J Fairley
Rainer Gebhardt
Nicholas G Handras
David G Hodgson
A John Hollis
William E Lawes
Peter R Lighte
Roger P Lockwood
Ian R H Mason
Gordon H Rennoldson

Vice President:
Mathis Shinnick
Stephen Solomon
George V Talev

Manulife International Investment Management Limited
Broad Street House
55 Old Broad Street
London EC2M 1TL
Tel: 071 638 6611
Telex: 885650
Fax: 071 638 2059

Head of Investment Office:
Richard Bowles

T H March & Company Limited
St Dunstan's House
Carey Lane
London EC2V 8AD
Tel: 071 606 1282
Fax: 071 606 6759

Chairman (Non-Executive):
R F Ferraro
Managing Director & Chief Executive:
R C H Mumford
Finance Director: D W Russell
Director:
J Barber
M J Ferraro
N J Woods

March Investment Fund Limited
35-39 Waterfront Quay
Salford Quays
Manchester M5 2XW
Tel: 061 872 3676
Fax: 061 872 3324

Director:
William J Hopkins
Richard S Marshall
Investment Analyst: Mark Judkowski

Marks & Spencer plc
Michael House
47-67 Baker Street
London W1A 1DN
Tel: 071 935 4422
Telex: 267141
Fax: 071 487 2679

Corporate Treasurer: J I Denton

Marsden W Hargreave Hale & Co

8-10 Springfield Road
Blackpool FY1 1QN
Tel: 0253 21575
Fax: 0253 293511

Senior Partner: C O Hargreave

M W Marshall & Company Limited

Lloyds Chambers
1 Portsoken Street
London E1 8DF
Tel: 071 481 1511
Telex: 888286
Fax: 071 702 3951

Chairman: C J K Kelson
Joint Managing Director: S Muller
Finance Director: P J Bentley
UK Director:
  T E Porter
  N M Stoughton
  R A Webb

Martin Ashley Underwriting Agencies Limited

9/13 Fenchurch Buildings
London EC3M 5HR
Tel: 071 488 0103
Fax: 071 481 4995

Chairman: K C Combe TD
Director:
  M Ashley
  J I Gordon
  C F Palmer
  D M Reed
Director & Secretary: C Payne

Martin Currie Investment Management Ltd

29 Charlotte Square
Edinburgh EH2 4HA
Tel: 031 225 3811
Telex: 72505
Fax: 031 225 2322

Chairman: D L Skinner
Joint Managing Director:
  W M C Kennedy
  P J Scott Plummer
Director:
  J M A Fairweather
  J K R Falconer
  M J Gibson
  T J D Hall
  Marianne L Hay
  A G D Johnston

Director:
  E D McAuslan
  H L Seymour
  M W Thomas

Martin Currie Unit Trust

48 Melville Street
Edinburgh EH3 7HF
Tel: 031 226 4372
Fax: 031 225 5618

Chairman: Sir Gerald Elliot
Managing Director:
  Alan T Maidment
Director:
  T Hall
  I Macpherson
  David L Skinner

Maruman Securities (Europe) Limited

1 Liverpool Street
London EC2M 7NH
Tel: 071 374 4000
Telex: 929347
Fax: 071 382 9143

Managing Director: Yuzo Noda
Director & General Manager:
  F C Shields
Chief Financial Officer:
  Mark F Deacon
Associate Director:
  Derek G Gibson
  Ali Nsouli

Marusan Europe Limited

35 Moorgate
London EC2R 6AR
Tel: 071 588 2698
Telex: 934392
Fax: 071 256 5374

Director: T Takayama

Mase Westpac Limited

Westpac House
75 King William Street
London EC4N 7HA
Tel: 071 621 7800
Telex: 884491
Fax: 071 283 4659

Chairman: R J Dent
Managing Director: D Gazmararian
Deputy Managing Director:
  D N Saunders
Director & Company Secretary:
  A T F Hunter

Director:
  F M B Kershaw
  L D Solden

Maxwell Pergamon Publishing Corporation plc

PO Box 283
33 Holborn Circus
London EC1N 2NE
Tel: 071 822 2345
Telex: 888804
Fax: 071 583 4261

Director:
  R H Bunn
  D L Frueling
  B D Gilbert
  M Heller
  B M Martell
  K F H Maxwell
  B T Moss
  G F Richards

MB Group plc

Apex Plaza
Forbury Road
Reading
Berkshire RG1 1AX
Tel: 0734 581177
Fax: 0734 587078

Chairman: Antony Hichens
Chief Executive: Peter Jansen

Meghraj Bank Ltd

Meghraj Court
18 Jockey's Fields
London WC1R 4BW
Tel: 071 831 6881
Telex: 261838
Fax: 071 430 1328

Chairman: A M P Shah
Managing Director: D C Lewis
Director:
  Sir Jay Gohel
  D N Karanjia
  H S Mellor
  V M P Shah
Legal Adviser & Company Secretary:
  A M Chapman

Mellon Bank NA

6 Devonshire Square
London EC2M 4LB
Tel: 071 626 9828
Telex: 885962
Fax: 071 283 9323

General Manager: J P O'Driscoll
Treasury Manager: Keith R Baker

Risk Assessment Manager:
Parkson Cheong
Finance Director: Michael Lyons
Marketing Manager: Robert D Miller
Operations Manager:
Raymond C Luckhurst

Mellon Securities Limited
6 Devonshire Square
London EC2M 4LB
Tel: 071 220 7073
Telex: 885962
Fax: 071 623 5023

Executive Director:
John P O'Driscoll

Mercantile Credit Company Limited
Churchill Plaza
Churchill Way
Basingstoke RG21 1GP
Tel: 0256 817777
Telex: 859202
Fax: 0256 791950

Chairman: S W Buckley
Managing Director: F W Winup
Director:
T M Clark
The Hon S H Fortescue
R S Simblet
Sir Charles Tidbury
A G Tritton
Secretary: C F Shoolbred

Mercury Asset Management Group plc
33 King William Street
London EC4R 9AS
Tel: 071 280 2800
Telex: 8953927
Fax: 071 280 2820

Chairman: P Stormonth Darling
Deputy Chairman: D W J Price
Vice-Chairman:
L S Licht
S A Zimmerman
Director:
R O Bernays
A S Dalton
C J P Dawnay
H J Foulds
Miss C Galley
C N Hurst-Brown
L Levy
R P B Michaelson

Director:
F D S Rosier
Sir Alfred Shepperd
H A Stevenson

Merrill Lynch Asset Management UK Limited
Ropemaker Place
25 Ropemaker Street
London EC2Y 9LY
Tel: 071 867 2000
Telex: 8811047
Fax: 071 867 2867

Managing Director:
Alan J Albert
Terry K Glenn
Managing Director: Arthur Zeikel

Merrill Lynch Europe Limited
Ropemaker Place
25 Ropemaker Street
London EC2Y 9LY
Tel: 071 867 2000
Telex: 8811047
Fax: 071 867 2867

Managing Director:
J Michael Giles
John T McGowan
Costas P Michaelides
Director:
John A Angus
Atilla S Ilkson
David L Jalving
Paul S J Kerrigan
Charles R Kirkman
Richard W Lyon
Richard G Spiegelberg
Michael von Clemm

Merrill Lynch Global Asset Management Limited
Ropemaker Place
25 Ropemaker Street
London EC2Y 9LY
Tel: 071 867 2000
Telex: 8811047
Fax: 071 867 2867

Managing Director: Jeffrey Lawrence
Director:
Bernard J Durnin
John J Frawley Jr
Arthur Zeikel

Merrill Lynch International Bank Limited
Ropemaker Place
25 Ropemaker Street
London EC2Y 9LY
Tel: 071 867 2000
Telex: 8811047
Fax: 071 867 2867

Chairman and Managing Director: J
Michael Giles
Managing Director:
Michele Di Stefano
Benjamin H Lorenz
Executive Director:
Robert G Harada
Joakim J Helenius
Leslie F Hill
David L Jalving
Philip R Ker
Robert W Pearson
Michael H Penniman
Joseph M Petri
Robert B Sloan
Alfonso L Ventoso
Raymundo A Yu Jr
Non-Executive Director:
Alfred B Berger
Mario C Brupbacher
John G Heimann
John T McGowan
Costas P Michaelides
William F Waters

Merrill Lynch International Limited
Ropemaker Place
25 Ropemaker Street
London EC2Y 9LY
Tel: 071 867 2000
Telex: 8811047
Fax: 071 867 2867

Managing Director:
Jeffrey A Bennett
C Anders Bergendahl
Jerome J Corcoran
Paul Dennison
Thomas J Doyle
Anthony J Freeman
Geoffrey A Hodson
Thiam J Lim
Martin E Loat
John F Lyness
John T McGowan
John McNiven
Kevin Regan
Thomas W Seaman
Julian P Summer
John Tognino

Managing Director:
 Kevan V Watts
 Richard H Westcott
Director:
 Clive H Austin
 Flavio C Bartman
 Steven A Blakey
 Rodney P Colwell
 Patrick R Currie
 Louis d'Alancon
 Clifford Dent
 Adriano Dispenza
 Ahmass Fakahany
 Mehrdad Farimani
 Karl H Hauptmann
 Simon Howell
 Terence X Hurley
 Atilla S Ilkson
 Clive Jackson
 Charles E Lillis
 Stephen C Marquardt
 Costas P Michaelides
 A Rawle Michelson
 William S Miller
 Christopher Pickering
 John K Plaxton
 David Prichard
 Blair J Priday
 Axel J S Ramel
 Keith B Russell
 Diane L Schueneman
 Timothy W L von Halle
 David J Zell

Merrill Lynch Limited

Ropemaker Place
25 Ropemaker Street
London EC2Y 9LY
Tel: 071 867 2000
Telex: 8811047
Fax: 071 867 2867

Managing Director: John N Tognino
Director:
 Ahmass Fakahany
 Stephen H Groom
 Terence X Hurley
 John T McGowan
 Costas P Michaelides

Merrill Lynch Pierce Fenner & Smith (Brokers & Dealers) Limited

Ropemaker Place
25 Ropemaker Street
London EC2Y 9LY
Tel: 071 867 2000
Telex: 8811047
Fax: 071 867 2867

Managing Director:
 Ramiro L Penaherrera
Director:
 Stephen M Bellotti
 Andrew J Dowse
 Stuart S Gordon
 David L Jalving
 Paul Lewis
 John T McGowan
 Mark T Mills
 Mohamed Shourbaji
 Jane Walsh

Merrill Lynch Pierce Fenner & Smith Limited

Ropemaker Place
25 Ropemaker Street
London EC2Y 9LY
Tel: 071 867 2000
Telex: 8811047
Fax: 071 867 2867

Managing Director:
 Alfred G Lutz
 George K Martin
 John L Owen
 Ramiro L Penaherrera
 Conrad Voldstad
 M Makram Zaccour
Director:
 Indira Anand
 Charles J S Beazley
 Walter S Elliott
 Ahmass Fakahany
 Ruth Hennefeld
 Terence X Hurley
 John T McGowan
 Costas P Michaelides
 Mohamed Shourbaji
 R Michael Young

Metallgesellschaft Ltd

4th Floor
Three Quays, Tower Hill
London EC3R 6DS
Tel: 071 626 4221
Telex: 888971
Fax: 071 621 0213

Chairman: G Maunes
Joint Managing Director:
 M J Hutchinson
 J H Murmann
Director:
 N Fussell
 R H Y Mills
 D Worms
Controller: P M Harris

Methuen (Lloyds Underwriting Agents) Limited

5th Floor
Bankside House
107/112 Leadenhall Street
London EC3A 4AP
Tel: 071 621 1755
Telex: 918958 G
Fax: 071 283 1954

Chairman: P R Chandler
Director:
 J F Acheson
 S J Cox
 G R Deveson
 J M Gordon
 B A Hardy
 J P Landais
 J D Lloyd
 T P Salmon
 R E Thomson
 G D Williams

MFK Underwriting Agencies Ltd

6th Floor
117 Fenchurch Street
London EC3M 5AL
Tel: 071 480 6971
Fax: 071 488 1737

Chairman: M C Watkins
Director/Underwriter:
 R J Blunt
 M P P McCord
 T J Newson
 G K Scott
Director/Agency Manager:
 O A W Biggs
Financial Director: E N Noble
Director/Secretary: P E Parnell
Non-Executive Director:
 J H Rochman

MGA (UK) Ltd

Suite 555, Salisbury House
London Wall
London EC2M 5SH
Tel: 071 638 0857
Fax: 071 256 5934

Managing Director: T Stor

Middle East Bank

1 Lombard Street
London EC3V 9AA

Tel: 071 283 2201
Telex: 8956506
Fax: 071 626 6721

General Manager: D Dasgupta

Midland Bank plc
Poultry
London EC2P 2BX
Tel: 071 260 8000
Telex: 8811822
Fax: 071 260 7065

Chairman: Sir Peter Walters
Group Chief Executive: Brian Pearse
Deputy Group Chief Executive:
  B L Goldthorpe
Deputy Chairman:
  Sir Alex Jarratt
  Sir Patrick Meaney
  Sir Michael Palliser
Chief Executive - UK Banking &
  Group Operations: H E Lockhart
Chief Executive - Intl/Inv Banking:
  G Loudon
Managing Director - UK Banking:
  R Baker-Bates
Managing Director - Corporate
  Finance: I A N McIntosh
Managing Director - Group
  Operations: R L Price
Managing Director - Intl Banking:
  Sencar Toker
Managing Director - Midland Montagu
  Corporate Banking: David
  Alan Thornham
Director:
  Sir Kenneth Corfield
  A W Forster
  G Maitland Smith
  Miss D O'Cathain
  Sir Eric Pountain
Director - Risk Management:
  S D Gager
Director - Fixed Income: B J Lind
Director - Treasury Sales:
  T R A Lockett
Director - UK Corporate Banking:
  A I Mullen
Director - Global Corporate Banking:
  D R W Potter
Director - Group Finance:
  R Delbridge
Group Legal Director: D B Powell
Group Property Director: P Walton
Head of Capital Markets: R Tickner
Head of Correspondent Banking:
  R A Hubbard

Head of Group Compliance:
  A R Morris
Group Personnel Director: G P White
Secretary: J R Skae

Midland Montagu Asset Management
10 Lower Thames Street
London EC3R 6AE
Tel: 071 260 9922
Telex: 8956886
Fax: 071 260 9140

Managing Director:
  P B H Poloniecki
Deputy Managing Director:
  C N Lindsell
Director:
  G R Cervenka
  Dr A L M Davies
  G A Hall
  I W Hunter
  Miss Dinah McKenzie
  A D Moore
  D G G Puddle
  A C Rickards
  A H M White
Head of International Fixed Income:
  Miss Suzie Procter

Midlantic National Bank
Prince Rupert House
64 Queen Street
London EC4R 1AD
Tel: 071 236 7232
Telex: 885607
Fax: 071 489 8748

European Representative: J P Beebe

MIM Limited
11 Devonshire Square
London EC2M 4YR
Tel: 071 626 3434
Telex: 886108
Fax: 071 623 3339

Chairman: Lord Stevens
Chief Executive:
  Nicholas A D Johnson
Director:
  Jeffrey C Attfield
  Streten Bakovljev
  Stephen D Barber
  Mrs S C Bates
  Geoffrey J Bowling
  Mrs A Cabot-Alletzhauser
  Alistair C Calder
  M D Callaghan
  Richard Connell

Director:
  W L Davidson
  P S Dawson
  R A Di Mascio
  P R Ehrmann
  Ratan Engineer
  David C Gillan
  K E Hewett
  M N B Higlett
  David C Hypher
  Bryan R Keene
  B K Patel
  Francis B Pike
  Richard M Plummer
  Mrs A Powell
  Bryan P Quinton
  Alexander S Reid
  I J R Robinson
  J D Ross
  James I Scrymgeour-
    Wedderburn
  M John Shelley
  S C G Stevens
  Donald Walker

J H Minet & Co Ltd
Minet House
100 Leman Street
London E1 8HG
Tel: 071 481 0707
Telex: 8813901
Fax: 071 488 9786

Chairman: J T Gore
Deputy Chairman: P H Foster
Senior Executive Director:
  B Beamish
  P Cotterill
  J M Dewen
  C R Dixey
  I Genders
  M Pix
Executive Director:
  M T Hagerty
  F L Sanderson
Finance Director & Company
  Secretary: R J Allam
Director:
  T Brundage
  R Cooney
  M T Ellis
  J Hollinrake
  K Khartabil
  D A Klima
  R Pavely
  S Quick
  K L Sammons

Director:
  I Soden
  M Vaughan-Fowler
  R F Wells

Minet Holdings plc
Minet House
100 Leman Street
London E1 8HG
Tel: 071 481 0707
Telex: 8813901
Fax: 071 488 9786

Chairman: Raymond W Pettitt
Deputy Chairman:
  Brian B Chapple
  Christopher W Keey
Director:
  Michael A Brown
  Peter S Christie
  Paul Cotterill
  Charles R Dixey
  Peter H Foster
  John T Gore
  Robert W Hatton
  Bryan J Hayes
  Alan B Middleton
  Richard Murray
  Patrick A Thiele

Minories Holdings Ltd
16 St Mary-at-Hill
London EC3R 8EE
Tel: 071 283 2373
Fax: 071 283 0477

Chairman: C P Braithwaite
Director:
  J G Adams
  J G P Crowden
  H G Mack
  D J Piper
  P D T Roberts
  A T Woods
Company Secretary: W A A Wells

Minster Trust Limited
Minster House
Arthur Street
London EC4R 9BH
Tel: 071 623 1050
Telex: 883823
Fax: 071 626 1471

Chairman: A R G McGibbon
Managing Director: T C H Lyons
Director:
  A F Elmer
  H J H C Hildreth
  G T A W Horton

Mito Europe Limited
1st Floor
Crescent House
14-15 Grosvenor Crescent
London SW1X 7EE
Tel: 071 259 6521
Telex: 9413561
Fax: 071 235 3116

Managing Director: T Matsui

The Mitsubishi Bank Ltd
6 Broadgate
London EC2M 2SX
Tel: 071 638 2222
Telex: 8958931 BISHBK G
Fax: 071 334 0140/0150

General Manager/Director:
  N Yasunaga
Senior Deputy General Manager:
  M Aoki
Deputy General Manager:
  J R Bunn
  T Kakumoto
  K Kamiya
  Y Mogi
  S Sadakata
  T Yoshioka

Mitsubishi Finance International Limited
6 Broadgate
London EC2M 2AA
Tel: 071 628 5555
Telex: 8954381 BISHFI G
Fax: 071 782 9144

Managing Director & Chief Executive:
  Masamichi Yamada
Deputy Managing Director:
  Paul Gold
  Yoichi Kambara
  Fumiaki Maeda
Director, Head of Corporate Finance:
  Yoshitaka Akamatsu
Director, Syndicate: Peter Crane
Director, Risk Mgmnt/Technical
  Products: Ken Cunningham
Director, Head of Trading:
  Naoshi Fujihara
Director, Deputy Head of Trading:
  Robert Dowman
Director, Head of Investment &
  Arbitrage: Desmond Fitzgerald
Director, Arbitrage Group:
  Jacques Pezier
Director, Research Department:
  Dr Brendan Brown

Mitsubishi Trust International Limited
24 Lombard Street
London EC3V 9AJ
Tel: 071 929 2866
Telex: 945759
Fax: 071 929 3471

Managing Director & Chief Executive:
  M Fujii
Deputy Managing Director:
  Yuji Ohashi

The Mitsui Taiyo Kobe Bank Ltd
Ground & First Floors
6 Broadgate
London EC2M 2RQ
Tel: 071 638 3131
Telex: 888902
Fax: 071 638 1260

General Manager: T Abiru
Senior Deputy General Manager:
  K Miyagi

Mitsui Taiyo Kobe International Limited
6 Broadgate
London EC2M 2RQ
Tel: 071 638 7595
Telex: 886107 MTKINT G
Fax: 071 638 1285

Managing Director and Chief
  Executive: Hirokazu Ishikawa
Deputy Managing Director Trading
  and Sales: Hideki Noda
Deputy Managing Director Corporate
  Finance: Takeshi Naito
Deputy Managing Director General
  Affairs: Akira Hara
Deputy Managing Director Fund
  Management: Atsushi Hiraguchi
Deputy Managing Director Sales:
  Peter Larkin

Mitsui Trust & Banking Company Ltd
5th Floor
6 Broadgate
London EC2M 2TB
Tel: 071 638 0841
Telex: 920280
Fax: 071 588 6910

General Manager:
  J Hisasue
  Y Otani
Deputy General Manager: N Ikeda

Mitsui Trust International Ltd

Towergate
41 Tower Hill
London EC3N 4DU
Tel: 071 702 1477
Telex: 945831
Fax: 071 702 9857

Managing Director & Chief Executive:
  T Hasegawa

MMG Patricof & Co

24 Upper Brook Street
London W1Y 1PD
Tel: 071 872 6300
Fax: 071 629 9035

Chairman: Ronald M Cohen
Managing Director: Keith R Harris

MMG Patricof Buy-Ins Limited

24 Upper Brook Street
London W1Y 1PD
Tel: 071 872 6300
Fax: 071 629 9035

Chairman: Ronald M Cohen
Director: Ian Fisher

The MMG Patricof Group plc

24 Upper Brook Street
London W1Y 1PD
Tel: 071 872 6300
Fax: 071 629 9035

Chairman: Ronald M Cohen

MNC International Bank

Mercury House
195 Knightsbridge
London SW7 1RE
Tel: 071 581 9990
Telex: 887432
Fax: 071 581 9795

Managing Director:
  R G Edwards
  D Feld

Mobil Oil Company

54-60 Victoria Street
London SW1E 6QB
Tel: 071 828 9777

Finance Director: R W Willoughby

Monopolies and Mergers Commission

New Court
48 Carey Street
London WC2A 2JT
Tel: 071 324 1467
Fax: 071 324 1400

Chairman: M S Lipworth
Deputy Chairman:
  P H Dean
  H H Hunt CBE
  H Liesner CB
Member:
  A Armstrong
  C C Baillieu
  I Barter
  Professor M E Beesley CBE
  Mrs C Blight
  F E Bonner CBE
  P Brenan
  J S Bridgeman
  L Britz
  K S Carmichael CBE
  R Davies
  Professor S Eilon
  J Evans
  A Ferry MBE
  D G Goyder
  M R Hoffman
  J D Keir QC
  L Kingshott
  Miss Patricia K R Mann
  G Mather
  L Mills
  Professor P Minford
  J Montgomery
  B C Owens
  Professor J Pickering
  D P Thomson
  C A Unwin MBE
  S Wainwright CBE
  Professor G Whittington
  R Young
Secretary: S N Burbridge

Morgan Grenfell & Co Limited

23 Great Winchester Street
London EC2P 2AX
Tel: 071 588 4545
Telex: 8953511
Fax: 071 826 6155

Chairman: R M L Webb
Joint Deputy Chairman:
  G N Dawson
  J B Rawlings
Group Compliance Director:
  J H L Norton

Group Personnel Director:
  D C F Hoysted
Group Treasury Director: G T Munn
Director:
  R D Abbott
  J P Asquith
  S T Badger
  A P J Ball
  C B B Beauman
  S R Bell
  C M Berry
  N M Berwin
  M N Biggs
  R F Binyon
  E A Bradman
  N J D Bull
  P H G Cadbury
  B J Cook
  J A Craven
  J P S Crawford
  C de Joncaire Narten
  M W R Dobson
  D A C Douglas-Home
  L J Dowley
  R J Dowsett
  J F T Dundas
  S G P Eccles-Williams
  P I Espenhahn
  P A Flannery
  J H Forsyth
  J A Franklin
  R J Freeman
  R J Halcrow
  F Z Haller
  P M Harvey
  R W Heyman
  M E Hildesley
  Hsieh Fu Hua
  G S Hutton
  C J Knight
  G A F Lickley
  J C B Lucas
  J G McCurrie
  J A McLaren
  R P Macnamara
  W G M Michie
  N L Murray
  J C Newman
  C D Nicholson
  J A P Prince
  J A Rayner
  A E Richmond-Watson
  A Seton
  J M Short
  J C Smith
  P E Smith
  R H Smith
  R W Strang
  D Suratgar

Director:
  R M J Taylor
  D H Thomas
  R I Tolkien
  P T Tucker
  M H Wilson
  J M Yallop
Secretary: R P Elliston
Non-Executive Director: G L Law

Morgan Grenfell Asset Management Limited

20 Finsbury Circus
London EC2M 1NB
Tel: 071 256 7500
Telex: 896009
Fax: 071 256 6960

Chairman: M W R Dobson
Managing Director: Michael Bullock
Finance Director: H C Benson
Director:
  N R Dunford
  W P Dwerryhouse
  G A E Fraher
  A W Mallinson
  I C Marris
  M J Meyrick
  R P Morris
  Glyn A Owen
  P N C Walker
  A M Wheatley
Secretary: P A Hogwood

Morgan Grenfell Group plc

23 Great Winchester Street
London EC2P 2AX
Tel: 071 588 4545
Telex: 8953511
Fax: 071 826 6155

Chairman: John A Craven
Joint Deputy Chairman:
  H Kopper
  A E Richmond-Watson
Chief Executive: M W R Dobson
Director:
  Dr Rolf-Ernst Breuer
  J H L Norton
  Dr R H Schmitz
  Miss E R Schneider-Lenné
  R M L Webb
Secretary: R P Elliston

Morgan Guaranty Trust Company of New York

1 Angel Court
London EC2R 7AE

Tel: 071 600 2300
Telex: 896631
Fax: 071 325 8212

Managing Director and Chairman of London Management Committee:
  Walter A Gubert
Senior Vice President:
  Gerard G Cameron
  Kenneth J Garrod
  Derek G Hall
  Colin B Jelley
  Terry R Mills
  Daniel E Symecko
  J Adam L Wethered
  William D Willison
Managing Director:
  R Andrew Bruce
  Thomas H Donaldson
  Terence C Eccles
  Peter Hancock
  Maureen A Hendricks
  Richard F Johnson
  Thomas L Kalaris
  R Vincent Lynch
  El-Walid Nsouli
  Andrew J Peacock
  J Roderick B Peacock
  Henry J Roundell
  Thomas Snell
  Guy Van Pelt
  Gaetano Vicinelli
  Jorgen Wagner-Knudsen
  David P Wheeley

J P Morgan Futures Inc

1 Angel Court
London EC2R 7AE
Tel: 071 325 5304
Telex: 8955711
Fax: 071 325 8228

Vice President: Ms S Hanbury-Brown

J P Morgan Investment Management Inc

83 Pall Mall
London SW1Y 5ES
Tel: 071 930 9444
Telex: 8954543
Fax: 071 839 3115

Managing Director:
  Kenneth W Anderson
  Anthony G Bird
  Roger Dubois
  Rudolph Leuthold

Managing Director:
  Thomas P Madsen
  Wesley I Paul
Director: Martin E Harrison

Morgan Stanley Asset Management

15th Floor, Commercial Union Building
Leadenhall Street
London EC3P 3HB
Tel: 071 709 3000
Telex: 917141
Fax: 071 283 4455

Principal:
  P Dominic Caldecott
  Michael J J Cowan
Vice President:
  Jonathan Allum
  Michael J W Daley
  James Lyle
  Andrew Summers
Managing Director: Stephen C Butt

Morgan Stanley International

Kingsley House
1a Wimpole Street
London W1M 7AA
Tel: 071 709 3000
Telex: 8812564
Fax: 071 709 3937

Managing Director:
  Martin Angle
  Keith Brown
  Stephen Butt
  Miguel Capaross
  Robert Diamond
  Amir Eilon
  Spencer Fleischer
  Mario Francescotti
  Alan Goodhill
  David Haythe
  John Hepburn
  John Holmes
  Peter Kellner
  William Kneisel
  Deborah McLean
  David Neeson
  Simon Orme
  David Roche
  Ned Sachs
  David Smith
  John Studzinski
  David Sumners
  Steven Ward
  John Wellemeyer

Managing Director:
Robert Whitehand
Managing Director (Head of London Office): Timothy A Hultquist

Moscow Narodny Bank Limited
81 King William Street
London EC4P 4JS
Tel: 071 623 2066
Telex: 885401
Fax: 071 283 4840

Chairman: A S Maslov
Deputy Chairman and General Manager: E M Grevtsev
Deputy General Manager:
Raymond A King
Assistant General Manager:
William L Newman

Moutafian Commodities Ltd
2/4 Eastcheap
London EC3M 1AL
Tel: 071 623 3311
Telex: 884412
Fax: 071 623 1484

Chairman & Managing Director:
A N Moutafian
Finance Director: M E Markarian
Director:
Mrs H Moutafian MBE
D Vorperian

MSB Corporate Finance Limited
8 & 9 Giltspur Street
London EC1A 9DE
Tel: 071 248 2894
Fax: 071 489 1672

Director: Simon Morris
Associate: Azhiz Basirov

MTI Managers Limited
70 St Albans Road
Watford WD1 1RP
Tel: 0923 50244
Fax: 0923 247783

Chief Executive: Dr Paul Castle
Deputy Chief Executive:
Richard Ford

Murray Lawrence Members' Agency Limited
32 Threadneedle Street
London EC2R 8AY
Tel: 071 588 7447
Fax: 071 374 2640

Chairman: W N M Lawrence
Managing Director: A C Mitchell
Director:
The Earl of Annandale and Hartfell
P N Archard
J C Langman
Sir Bayley Laurie BART
W R P Sedgwick Rough
A J Smithson
Director & Company Secretary:
Mrs H R Hayden

Mynshul Bank plc
John Dalton House
121 Deansgate
Manchester M3 2AB
Tel: 061 839 9000
Fax: 061 839 1691

Managing Director: S Westbrook

Nacional Financiera
17th Floor, 99 Bishopsgate
London EC2M 3XD
Tel: 071 628 0016
Telex: 888863
Fax: 071 374 0716

Deputy European Representative:
N Manuel

NASDAQ International
43 London Wall
London EC2M 5TB
Tel: 071 374 6969
Fax: 071 374 4488

Managing Director: J Lynton Jones
Assistant Director - Marketing:
Ms Isobel Carter
Assistant Director - Markets Policy:
Nicholas Barker

National Australia Bank Limited
6-8 Tokenhouse Yard
London EC2R 7AJ
Tel: 071 606 8070
Telex: 888912
Fax: 071 588 8356

Chief General Manager: A W Diplock
Senior Manager:
K Hodgson
H A Rose

The National Commercial Bank
Bevis Marks House
24 Bevis Marks
London EC3A 7JB
Tel: 071 283 4233
Telex: 8952594
Fax: 071 929 4373

General Manager: Dennis Ford
European Representative and Manager, Correspondent Banking:
Jinx Grafftey-Smith

National Investment Group plc
Holland House
1-4 Bury Street
London EC3A 5AT
Tel: 071 283 8050
Telex: 886594
Fax: 071 283 5045

Chairman & Chief Executive:
A C Bull
J C R Downing
J W Eardley
A R Elder
A M Hedley
A R Holt
D C Jarrett
P J Leatherdale
W J Long
G M Oakley
D B Sinclair
R G Woodhead

National Provident Institution
National Provident House
Tunbridge Wells TN1 2UE
Tel: 0892 515151
Telex: 957316
Fax: 0892 705611

Chairman:
Richard F Barclay
Lord Remnant
Director:
G V Bayley
Lord Camoys
A D Garrett
M C Harris
P W L Morgan
Director and General Manager:
K H McBrien
Director and Assistant General Manager (Assets):
B J Brindley
C J Holmes

Assistant General Manager (Customer Services): B G Blake
Assistant General Manager (Sales): J H Cook
Assistant General Manager (Marketing): L M Edmans
Assistant General Manager (Personnel): T Mullins
Assistant General Manager (Info Systems): B Paul

National Securities of Japan (Europe) Ltd
10 Finsbury Square
London EC2A 1AD
Tel: 071 588 3517
Telex: 929078

Managing Director: Y Torii

National Westminster Bank plc
41 Lothbury
London EC2P 2BP
Tel: 071 726 1000
Telex: 888388
Fax: 071 726 1035

Chairman: Lord Alexander of Weedon QC
Deputy Chairman:
    Sir Edwin Nixon
    Sir Christopher Tugendhat
Director:
    J A Burns
    The Hon Sir Richard C Butler
    Denis M Child
    Roger Flemington
    Graeme A Elliot
    Thomas P Frost
    Martin R Harris
    Robin A E Herbert
    Sir Brian Hill
    Sir Brian Kellett
    J H Macdonald
    Sir Ian MacLaurin
    J W Melbourn
    A Morris
    Sir Antony Pilkington
    Dr W G H Quigley
    J Tugwell
    The Rt Hon the Baroness Young PC
Group Chief Executive: T P Frost
Chief Executive, UK Financial Services: Derek Wanless
General Manager, Subsidiary & Assoc Business: E W Barron
General Manager, Group Personnel: D Duffield

General Manager, Corporate Banking: R W Byatt
General Manager, Strategy & Comms: B P Horn
General Manager, Corporate & Institutional Finance: M A Jones
General Manager, Information Technology: J R Wallace
General Manager, Property Development: David Edmonds
Group Treasurer: Dr J M Owen
Chief Economic Adviser: Dr David Lomax
Chief Economist & Head of Market Intelligence: David Kern
Secretary of the Bank: G J Povey

National Westminster Growth Options Ltd
King's Cross House
200 Pentonville Road
London N1 9LH
Tel: 071 239 8563
Fax: 071 239 8900

Director: R C King
Manager:
    Ian Andrews
    Chris Cook
    Alan Hinton
    Simon Lee
    Paul Slagel

Nationwide Anglia Building Society
Chesterfield House
15/19 Bloomsbury Way
London WC1V 6PW
Tel: 071 242 8822
Telex: 264549
Fax: 071 242 8822 ext 2024

Chief Executive:
    Timothy D Melville-Ross
Deputy Chief Executive and Finance Director: Daniel H Hodson
Resources Director: Dr Brian E Davis
Retail Director: John Hutchinson
Group Secretary: Frank C Kraus

NBD Bank NA
28 Finsbury Circus
London EC2M 7AU
Tel: 071 920 0921
Telex: 886998/883501
Fax: 071 638 0093

Vice President & General Manager: T A G Smith

NCL Investments Limited
Bartlett House
9-12 Basinghall Street
London EC2V 5NS
Tel: 071 600 2801
Telex: 885893
Fax: 071 726 6201/2

Director & Chief Executive: The Hon C C Lyttelton
Director:
    M Cannon Brookes
    Lord Chetwode
    R T Eddleston
    P M Thomas
    R M Thornborough
Secretary: Mrs J R Z Boyce

NCNB National Bank of North Carolina
14 Moorfields Highwalk
London EC2Y 9DS
Tel: 071 588 9133
Telex: 883938
Fax: 071 588 1904

Regional Executive: Dr P C James
Executive Vice President: J G Richards Roddey
Senior Vice President & General Manager: R C Hollmeyer
Senior Vice President:
    J R A Mark
    Dr C R Thorpe
    A S L Walsh
Senior Vice President and Treasury Manager: R Mullings
Senior Vice President and Deputy General Manager: P C Keller

Nedperm Bank Limited
20 Abchurch Lane
London EC4N 7AD
Tel: 071 623 1077
Telex: 886208
Fax: 071 621 9304

General Manager: M F Byrne
Assistant General Manager:
    D M Sutherland

The New India Assurance Company Limited
Lloyd's Avenue House
6 Lloyd's Avenue
London EC3N 3AP
Tel: 071 480 6626
Telex: 944026 NEWIN
Fax: 071 702 2736

Chairman/Managing Director:
　S V Mony
Director:
　D N Desai
　J S Gore
　S Kannan
　R Srinivasan
　D Swaminathan
General Manager:
　A E Dalvie
　D N Desai
　J S Gore
　K C Mittal
Company Secretary:
　A V Purushothaman
Financial Adviser: A K Sitaram

Newmarket Venture Capital plc

14-20 Chiswell Street
London EC1Y 4TY
Tel: 071 638 2521
Fax: 071 638 8409

Chairman: Alan Duncan
Executive Director:
　Alan B Henderson
　Dr Caroline Vaughan
Finance Director: Mike Noakes

Newton Investment Group

No 2 London Bridge
London SE1 9RA
Tel: 071 407 4404
Telex: 291931
Fax: 071 407 4371

Chairman & Managing Director:
　Stewart W Newton
Director:
　David A Baxter
　Arthur T Boanas
　Stephen H Burgess
　L Barrie Green
　Colin R Harris
　Paul Harwood
　Raymond A Henley
　Richard M A Horlick
　Nicholas J Kirk

Next plc

Desford Road
Enderby
Leicester LE9 5AT
Tel: 0533 866411
Telex: 34415
Fax: 0533 848998

Chairman: Sir Donald Wolfson
Chief Executive: D C Jones

Finance Director: P E Lomas
Corporate Director: T J B Roberts
Retail Director: A J Varley
Home Shopping Director:
　M J Bottomley
Direct Response Director: J K Wallis
Non-Executive Director:
　B S Marker
　A C Mitchell-Innes
　J T Rowlay
　M C Stoddart
Group Treasurer: David W Keens
Secretary: P Bailey

Nichiboshin (UK) Ltd

6th Floor
56-60 Gresham Street
London EC2V 7BB
Tel: 071 606 3633
Telex: 918452
Fax: 071 600 9885

Managing Director: K Wada
Director & Company Secretary:
　N Kanazome

Nicholson Chamberlain Colls Limited

PO Box 615
Beaufort House
15 St Botolph Street
London EC3A 7QQ
Tel: 071 247 4466
Telex: 929464
Fax: 071 377 1157

Chairman: Alan Colls
Joint Managing Director:
　Nigel Chamberlain
　Martin Nicholson
Director:
　Graham Addiscott
　Colin Bryan
　Peter Butler
　Tony Fell
　Richard Holt
　Andrew Johnson
　Paul Milton
　Jonathan Palmer Brown
　Art Quern
　Mike Rice
　Brian Stewart-Brown
　Nick Wilkins
Finance Director: Julian Roberts
Secretary: John Jennings

Nikko Bank (UK) plc

17 Godliman Street
London EC4V 5BD

Tel: 071 528 7070
Telex: 928703
Fax: 071 528 7077

Chairman: John R Cunningham
Co-Chairman & Executive Director:
　Y Imaizumi
Managing Director & Chief Executive:
　T Kato
Managing Director:
　Sir John Hall
　D Hughes
Director:
　G Fujimoto
　M Inagaki
　Y Kanzaki

The Nikko Securities Company (Europe) Ltd

55 Victoria Street
London SW1H 0EU
Tel: 071 799 2222
Telex: 884717

Chairman: Masao Inagaki
Senior Managing Director:
　Kenji Wada
Managing Director & Chief Executive:
　Isao Sakuraba
Director: Miss Haruko Fukuda
Managing Director - Fixed Income:
　Kiyoshi Fukunaga
Managing Director - Investment:
　Tetsuya Murakami
Managing Director - Stock Trading:
　Hiroshi Watanabe
Managing Director - Corporate Finance: Toshio Shoda
Managing Director - Administration & Company Secretary:
　Kunihiko Tanaka
Managing Director - Operations:
　Harutoshi Tanamura

Nippon Credit International Limited

City Tower
40 Basinghall Street
London EC2V 5DE
Tel: 071 638 6911
Telex: 947861
Fax: 071 638 3460

Managing Director: M Kusano
Deputy Managing Director:
　K Hoshino
　T Takahashi

Noble Grossart Ltd
48 Queen Street
Edinburgh EH2 3NR
Tel: 031 226 7011
Fax: 031 226 6032

Managing Director: Angus Grossart
Director:
Ewan Brown
Brian Dick
David Mathewson
Chrisopher Smith
Graham Watson

Nomura Asset Management (Int) Ltd
Nomura House
One St Martin le Grand
London EC1A 4NP
Tel: 071 929 2366
Telex: 9413063
Fax: 071 626 0851

President & Managing Director:
M Iijima
Managing Director: Y Watanabe

Nomura Bank International plc
Nomura House
One St Martin le Grand
London EC1A 4NP
Tel: 071 929 2366
Telex: 9413063/4/5/6
Fax: 071 626 0851

Chairman: Dr A R Prindl
Managing Director: T Tanaka
General Manager Administration and Company Secretary: K Mii
General Manager - General Banking: R V Emerson
General Manager - Treasury: B D Watters
Deputy General Manager - Forex: T Maule
Deputy General Manager - Asset Management: O Morita
Deputy General Manager - Credit: M D Williams
Deputy General Manager - Marketing: J G S Macdonald
Deputy General Manager - Operations: K G Moodey
Deputy General Manager - Financial Control: W R A Pamment

Nomura Capital Management (UK) Limited
36 Monument Street
London EC3R 8LJ
Tel: 071 621 1466
Telex: 934015/6
Fax: 071 623 3894

Managing Director: I Komatsu

Nomura International Limited
Nomura House
One St Martin le Grand
London EC1A 4NP
Tel: 071 283 8811
Telex: 883119
Fax: 071 621 1286

President: T Kondo
Deputy President: John Howland Jackson
Chairman: N Nakazawa
Co-Chairman: Sir Douglas Wass

Norddeutsche Landesbank
20 Ironmonger Lane
London EC2V 8EY
Tel: 071 600 1721
Telex: 884882
Fax: 071 726 8417

General Manager: Hans W Meyers

Norinchukin Bank
131 Finsbury Pavement
London EC2A 1AY
Tel: 071 588 6589
Telex: 892698
Fax: 071 588 6585

Chief Representative: H Shimizu

Norinchukin International Ltd
131 Finsbury Pavement
London EC2A 1AY
Tel: 071 588 6593
Telex: 936122
Fax: 071 588 6586

Chairman: A Kodama
Managing Director: M Takagi
Senior Adviser: A Lund
Deputy Managing Director: T Yoshioka
Director:
T Minematsu
H Sato
H Shimizu

Northern Bank Limited
PO Box 183
Donegall Square West
Belfast BT1 6JS
Tel: 0232 245277
Telex: 747674
Fax: 0232 893214

Chairman: Sir Desmond Lorimer
Chief Executive: S H Torrens
General Manager (Banking):
W J H McPherson
G H Moore
Chief Manager (Corporate):
M M Brown
W Price
W J Stafford

Northern Foods
Beverley House
St Stephens Square
Hull HU1 3XG
Tel: 0482 25432
Telex: 597149
Fax: 0482 226136

Treasurer: J Jepson

Northern Rock Building Society
Northern Rock House
Regent Centre
Gosforth
Newcastle Upon Tyne NE3 4PL
Tel: 091 285 7191
Fax: 091 2848470

Chairman: Viscount Ridley
Managing Director: J C Sharp
Deputy Managing Director: Leo P Finn
Director and General Manager: Kevin C Southwood

The Northern Trust Company
155 Bishopsgate
London EC2M 3XS
Tel: 071 628 2233
Telex: 884641
Fax: 071 982 5200

Senior Vice President and General Manager: W R Dodds Jr
Vice President - Operations: M S Casady
Vice President - Foreign Exchange: I G Clark

Second Vice President - Commercial Banking: Julia E Cormier
Second Vice President - Master Trust: S L Fradkin

Northern Venture Managers Limited

Northumberland House
Princess Square
Newcastle upon Tyne NE1 8ER
Tel: 091 232 7068
Fax: 091 232 4070

Chairman: Michael Denny
Managing Director: Alastair Conn
Investment Director: Tim Levett
Investment Director (Edinburgh): Brian Rankin
Company Secretary: Chris Mellor

Norwich Union Fund Managers Ltd

PO Box 4
Surrey Street
Norwich NR1 3NG
Tel: 0603 622200
Telex: 97388
Fax: 0603 683659

Senior Investment Manager:
    Adrian Gunson
    Philip G Scott

Norwich Union Insurance Group

Surrey Street
Norwich NR1 3NG
Tel: 0603 622200
Telex: 97388
Fax: 0603 683659

Chairman: M G Falcon
Vice-Chairman:
    F Cator
    Sir James Cleminson
Group Chief Executive:
    A Bridgewater
General Manager & Actuary:
    H H Scurfield
General Manager & Secretary:
    H W Utting
General Manager:
    R J Burke
    R Calver
    A G Mills
    P O Sheridan
Assistant General Manager:
    B H Bannock
    R Bellinger
    E J Brister

Assistant General Manager:
    T A Kelly
    G Loades
    R B P Ramsay
    N A Smith
    R Stenson
    P W Woolterton
Chief Estates Manager: M B Olley
Chief Investment Manager:
    E M Sandland

NWS Bank plc

NWS House
City Road
Chester CH99 3AN
Tel: 0244 690000
Telex: 61211
Fax: 0244 312067

Chairman: The Rt Hon
    Lord Balfour of Burleigh
Managing Director: C H Bush

Office of Fair Trading

Field House
15-25 Bream's Buildings
London EC4A 1PR
Tel: 071 242 2858
Telex: 269009
Fax: 071 831 2195

Director General:
    Sir Gordon Borrie QC
Deputy Director General:
    J W Preston CB
Director: Dr M Howe

Okasan International (Europe) Ltd

5 Devonshire Square
London EC2M 4YD
Tel: 071 626 1682
Telex: 8811131
Fax: 071 626 1342

Chairman: S Kato
Managing Director: W Takemura
Financial, Operations and Personnel Director: S Matsuda
Sales Director: M Nishimura
Secretary: S Machida

Olliff & Partners plc

Saddlers House
Gutter Lane
Cheapside
London EC2V 6BR
Tel: 071 374 0191
Telex: 919325
Fax: 071 374 2063

Managing Director: B M Olliff
Finance Director: W C Cole
Director: J E Howson

Ottoman Bank

Representative Office
King William House
2a Eastcheap
London EC3M 1AA
Tel: 071 626 5932
Fax: 071 626 2337

General Manager: G J Warren

R H M Outhwaite (Underwriting Agencies) Limited

85 Gracechurch Street
London EC3V OAA
Tel: 071 623 1481
Fax: 071 283 4912

Non-Executive Chairman: The Rt
    Hon The Lord Havers
Deputy Chairman: M W Hussey
Chief Executive: W E Bloxham
Director and Underwriter:
    R H M Outhwaite
Director:
    R N Alwen
    D S Sharman
Non-Executive Director:
    R M H Gilkes
    S M Mitchell
Company Secretary: N A Bradfield

P & O Steam Navigation Company

79 Pall Mall
London SW1Y 5EJ
Tel: 071 930 4343
Telex: 885551
Fax: 071 839 9338

Chairman: Sir Jeffrey Sterling CBE
Managing Director: B D MacPhail
Director:
    B W Baillie
    A K Black
    P J Ford
    T J R Harding
    T C Harris
    A G Hatchett CBE
    Sir Frank Lampl
    H M Saunders
    P Thomas
    P L Warner
Non-Executive Director:
    Sir Peter Cazalet

Non-Executive Director:
  C E A Hambro
  O Marriott
Secretary: J M Crossman

PaineWebber International Bank Ltd

47 Berkeley Square
London W1X 5DB
Tel: 071 629 5474
Telex: 295088
Fax: 071 491 0796

Chairman: Robin Baillie
Chief Executive: Geoffrey Bignell
Finance Director: Brian Tuck

PaineWebber International (UK) Ltd

1 Finsbury Avenue
London EC2M 2PA
Tel: 071 377 0055
Telex: 297361
Fax: 071 247 4058

Director:
  John Bult
  Brian Havill
  P Michael Malcolmson
  Charles Milligan
  Ian Myers
  Devereaux Phelps
  Simon Phillips

Panel on Takeovers & Mergers

PO Box 226
Stock Exchange Building
London EC2P 2JX
Tel: 071 382 9026
Fax: 071 638 1554

Chairman: D C Calcutt QC
Deputy Chairman:
  J F Goble
  J F C Hull
  Sir Philip Shelbourne
Member:
  R D Broadley
  Sir Adrian Cadbury
  P E Couse
  Sir Gordon Downey
  J S Fairbairn
  C M Gilchrist
  M J Hart
  A C Hugh Smith
  I A N McIntosh
  G M Nissen
  T J Palmer
  Sir Austin Pearce

Member:
  Sir John Quinton
  M G Taylor
  S M Yassukovich
Chairman of the Appeal Committee of the Panel: Lord Roskill
Deputy Chairman of the Appeal Committee of the Panel:
  Sir Michael Kerr

Panmure Gordon & Co Limited

9 Moorfields Highwalk
London EC2Y 9DS
Tel: 071 638 4010
Telex: 883832/3
Fax: 071 920 9305

Group Chief Executive: Dr P James
Chairman: J G Lithiby
Managing Director: The Lord McGowan
Finance Director and Company Secretary: A T Jamieson
Director:
  P J Baker
  D D R Banks
  J C Banner
  D S Black
  J G Bos
  B C Bruce
  I D Cameron
  D S S Chichester
  T Clarke
  C G Climie
  M M Cooke
  M J Cunnane
  Miss D Darlington
  M Davies
  D R J Foster
  R M Fry
  M M Guterres
  R J L Hall
  P J F Hart
  D M Hawkins
  M A Henderson
  R C Hollmeyer
  A T Jamieson
  C Jobling
  J M Kerner
  A Learoyd
  G C Lees
  G Liberman
  N S Little
  J R A Mark
  P J G C Martin
  S C Melsom
  P J O'Reilly
  N J Percival

Director:
  C C Roberts
  N J Sansome
  T B Sissons
  W A Soames
  C D Stallard
  D G Thomson
  M O C Wauchope
  C J Wilkinson

Panmure Gordon Bankers Limited

14 Moorfields Highwalk
London EC2Y 9DS
Tel: 071 628 4821
Telex: 8953587
Fax: 071 588 1904

Group Chief Executive:
  J G R Roddey
Chief Executive: Dr P C James
Director:
  P J Baker
  D S S Chichester
  M J Cunnane
  D L Henderson
  M A Henderson
  H Hodgson
  R C Hollmeyer
  M J Howells
  A T Jamieson
  J G Lithiby
  J R A Mark
  P J G C Martin
  The Lord McGowan
  J Meakin
  A C Moir
  P J O'Reilly
  W A Soames
  C R Thorpe
  A S L Walsh
Company Secretary: S Roake

Paribas Limited

33 Wigmore Street
London W1H 0BN
Tel: 071 355 3000
Telex: 296723
Fax: 071 895 2555

Managing Director: Alec de Lezardière
Deputy Managing Director:
  John Davies
Head of Bond Fund Management:
  Richard Wohanka
Head of Bond Trading and Sales:
  Claes Hesselgren
Head of Bond Syndicate:
  Stephen West

Head of Fixed Income Trading and
  Sales: Darryl Green
Head of Fixed Income Research:
  James Durrant
Head of Swaps and Fixed Income
  Marketing: David Brunner
Head of Swaps European Currencies:
  Filippo Friedenberg
Head of Swaps Other Currencies:
  Jacques D'Estais
Head of Financing Desk:
  Guillaume d'Angerville
Head of Equity Syndicate:
  Anthony Bourne
Head of Equity Derivative:
  Sanjay Dighe
Head of Equity Sales and Trading:
  Christopher Cartwright
Head of Equity Trading:
  Philip Leung
Head of Equity Sales: Seno Bril
Head of Corporate Finance:
  Philip Evans
Head of Structured Finance:
  David Hudd
Head of International Finance and
  Legal: Kevin Sowerbutts
Head of Finance and Administration:
  Bernard Pittié

Parrish plc
1 London Wall Buildings
London EC2M 5PP
Tel: 071 638 1282
Telex: 883787
Fax: 071 628 1973

Director:
  D J Clark
  P M N Jennings
  B J Parrish
  K Smith
  A J C Sommerville
  J M Wright

Parrish Stockbrokers
4 London Wall Buildings
London EC2M 5NX
Tel: 071 638 1282
Fax: 071 588 2449

Director:
  J R Anderton
  Mrs E Bayer
  G L W Burlton
  Mrs M A Cave
  D J Clark
  A W Dewar
  G H J Edwards
  J Harris St John

Director:
  J C Heath
  P J P Johnson
  G A Living
  Mrs D A Lock
  D S Maker
  Ms M Neary
  B V Rowe
  P F G W Sich
  K R Smith
  A J C Sommerville
  M H Thompson
  B M Ward
  C L Weinberg

Paul E Schweder Miller & Co
46-50 Tabernacle Street
London EC2A 2LB
Tel: 071 588 5600
Telex: 886793
Fax: 071 250 0802

Senior Partner: Sydney Davis

E W Payne Companies Limited
Aldgate House
33 Aldgate High Street
London EC3N 1AJ
Tel: 071 623 8080
Telex: 8952031
Fax: 071 375 0361

Chairman: J M Payne
Deputy Chairman: R D Espe
Director:
  A J Campbell-Hart
  J C Garner
  C J Grey
  M C Howard
  W H Sheridan

Pearl Assurance plc
Pearl Assurance House
Thorp Wood
Peterborough PE3 6SA
Tel: 0733 63212
Telex: 296 350 PEARL G
Fax: 0733 312743

Chairman: G E Bowles
Director:
  R W Bevitt
  D W Davies
  D C Furness
  D M Gordon
  N C Haygarth
  I C Worner

Pearson plc
Millbank Tower
Millbank
London SW1P 4QZ
Tel: 071 828 9020
Telex: 8953869
Fax: 071 828 3342

Chairman and Chief Executive:
  Viscount Blakenham
Managing Director and Chief
  Operating Officer: Frank Barlow
Finance Director: James Joll
Executive Director:
  Mark Burrell
  David Veit
Non-Executive Director:
  Michel David-Weill
  Pehr Gyllenhammar
  Jean-Claude Haas
  John Hale
  Sir Simon Hornby
  Reuben Mark
  Dennis Stevenson
  Pierre Vinken

Pechiney World Trade (Holdings) Ltd
4 Fore Street
London EC2P 2NV
Tel: 071 638 5877
Telex: 884401
Fax: 071 638 3031

Chairman: B Poux-Guillaume
Director:
  V J Davies
  D T Griffin
  G Hauser
  J T M Williams
Secretary: S E Fishburn

Peel Hunt & Company Ltd
37 Lombard Street
London EC3V 9BQ
Tel: 071 283 9666
Fax: 071 283 0219

Chairman: C E W Peel
Managing Director: C Holdsworth
  Hunt

Phibro Salomon
Victoria Plaza
111 Buckingham Palace Road
London SW1W 0SL
Tel: 071 721 2000
Telex: 886441
Fax: 071 222 7062

Finance Director: J R Bradurne

Philadelphia National Bank

3 Gracechurch Street
London EC3V 0AD
Tel: 071 623 8144
Telex: 926911
Fax: 071 623 5346

*Senior Vice-President & General
    Manager, Chief Executive Officer &
    Managing Director:* A J C Geddes

Phildrew Ventures

Triton Court
14 Finsbury Square
London EC2A 1PD
Tel: 071 628 6366
Fax: 071 638 2817

Partner:
    Charles Gonszor
    Tim Hart
    Ian Hawkins
    Ron Hobbs
    Robert Jenkins
    Frank Neale

Philipp & Lion Ltd

Chapel Court
Chapel Place
Rivington Street
London EC2A 3DQ
Tel: 071 628 3060
Telex: 888555
Fax: 071 628 4392

Chairman & Chief Executive Officer:
    M C E Lion
Director:
    J H Anderson
    M J Curwen
    D N Lion
    J M Sellier
    M J Smith
Finance Director: R L Monaghan

Philipp Brothers Ltd

Victoria Plaza
111 Buckingham Palace Road
London SW1W 0SL
Tel: 071 721 4000
Telex: 883801
Fax: 071 222 4299

Director:
    P H Brent
    D G Chambers
Finance Director: M Lambert
Group Secretary & Director:
    G C Howsden

Philips Electronic & Associated Industries Ltd

Philips House
188 Tottenham Court Road
London W1P 9LE
Tel: 071 436 4044
Telex: 267518
Fax: 071 436 9449

Chairman & Managing Director:
    C A M Busch
Financial Director: M A Inwards
Director: W L South
Company Secretary: R R Pascoe
Director of Finance: J T Harwood

Phillips & Drew Fund Management Limited

Mercury House
Triton Court
14 Finsbury Square
London EC2A 1PD
Tel: 071 901 5050
Telex: 916976
Fax: 071 929 0487/9

Executive Chairman:
    Paul M C Meredith
Deputy Chief Executive: Tony Dye
Managing Director: J B Marsh
Director:
    M F Brooks
    T W Buckland
    C H V Collins
    D J Gold
    R F Green
    J C Hayes
    J Hemingway
    D H S Hobbs
    W J Horwood
    Mrs L C How
    J P McCaughan
    M A Murray
    Ms Fiona Sturrock
    J S Wielechowski
    P T Yates
Non-Executive Director:
    J M Marriott

Pierson, Heldring & Pierson

99 Gresham Street
London EC2V 7PH
Tel: 071 696 0500
Telex: 885119
Fax: 071 600 1732

Managing Director: G A Möller

Pilkington plc

Prescot Road
St Helens
Merseyside WA10 3TT
Tel: 0744 28882
Telex: 627441
Fax: 0744 23042

Treasurer: I L Bradley

Pine Street Investments Limited

Bowater House West
68 Knightsbridge
London SW1X 7LT
Tel: 071 225 3911
Fax: 071 581 0131

Director:
    N J Case
    N J Webber

PK English Trust Company Limited

Carthusian Court
12 Cartusian Street
London EC1M 6EB
Tel: 071 796 1200
Telex: 8814900
Fax: 071 796 1510

Chairman: A Smids
Deputy Chairman & Chief Executive:
    C J Spence
Director:
    G P L Addison
    A F Arscott
    R F Baum
    J R Gilmour
    J F Molyneux
    A Oldinger
    N G D Sabin
Secretary: D O Kimberley

Postel Investment Management Ltd

Standon House
21 Mansell Street
London E1 8AA
Tel: 071 702 0888
Telex: 888947
Fax: 071 702 9452

Chairman: Ralph Quartano
Chief Executive: A R Threadgold
Director, Economics & Strategy:
    A D Ormrod
Director of Finance: R A Padgett
Director of Property Investment:
    Richard A Harrold

Postipankki Ltd
10-12 Little Trinity Lane
London EC4V 2AA
Tel: 071 489 0303
Telex: 894818
Fax: 071 489 1142

General Manager: Topi Vesteri
Deputy General Manager:
Geoffrey Fitton
Anthony Welford

Potts, West, Trumbull (UK) Limited
3 Cleary Court
21-23 St Swithins Lane
London EC4N 8DE
Tel: 071 283 5024
Telex: 887049
Fax: 071 626 5543

Chairman: T W R West

Prelude Technology Investments Limited
No 280, Cambridge Science Park
Milton Road
Cambridge CB4 4WE
Tel: 0223 423132
Fax: 0223 420869

Managing Director: Robert Hook
Deputy Managing Director:
Keith Padbury
Executive Director: Stephen Jones
Director:
George Anson
Paul Auton
Mark Burgess
Richard Jones
David Wansbrough
Chairman: Sir Robert Telford

Price Waterhouse
Southwark Towers
32 London Bridge Street
London SE1 9SY
Tel: 071 939 3000
Telex: 884609
Fax: 071 378 0647

Senior Partner: Jeffrey Bowman
Managing Partner: Howard Hughes
Director of Regional Offices:
Christopher Ames
Partner in Charge, Financial Services Consulting (Europe):
Mark Austen
Director of Independent Business Services & EC Co-ordinator re 1992 Initiatives: Barry Baldwin

Partner in Charge of London Corporate Reconstruction & Insolvency Department: Colin Bird
Partner in Charge of Computerised Information Systems & Audit Business Services: David Bridger
Director of Technical Services:
Ian Brindle
Director of Privatisation Services:
Anthony Browne
Director of Finance (Europe):
Colin Brown
Partner in Charge of Banking & Financial Services:
Nigel Buchanan
Director of Inward Investment (Europe): Chris Bull
Senior Partner, Management Consultancy (Europe):
Neville Cheadle
Chairman, PW World Regulatory Advisory Practice: Peter Cooke
Mergers and Acquisitions Partner:
Martin Foley
National Director of Corporate Reconstruction & Insolvency Services: Mark Homan
National Director of Audit & Business Advisory Services: Tim Hoult
Partner in Charge, Corporate Finance (Europe): Howard Hyman
Joint Partner in Charge of London Audit & Business Advisory Services:
Geoffrey Johnson
Partner in Charge of London Management Consultancy Services:
Pat Kiernan
Partner, European Human Resources Consultancy: Alan Little
Partner in Charge, International Tax and Trade Consultancy Services:
Mike Maskall
Lead Information Technology Partner, Management Consultancy Services:
Roger Pavitt
Joint Partner in Charge of London Audit and Business Advisory Services: John Salmon
Senior London Tax Partner:
Roger Seekings
Director of Recruitment:
Richard Shervington
Director of Professional Services:
Graham Stacy
European Director of Tax Services:
Ian Vaile
Director of Electricity Services:
Graham Ward

Senior Partner (London):
Alan Wheatley
Partner in Charge of Corporate Finance: Tom Wilson

The Private Bank and Trust Company Limited
Lansdowne House
Berkeley Square
London W1X 5DG
Tel: 071 491 9111
Telex: 262175 PBTCLN G
Fax: 071 872 3706

Chairman: The Earl
of Harrowby TD
Chief Executive: C J W Ball
Director:
P J Borrett
G K Elliott
Dr S J Latsis
D R Pelly
Professor B S Yamey CBE
Executive Director, Banking:
A L Kingshott
Director, Fund Management:
G L A Galitzine
Director, Information Systems:
M S K Harrison
Director, Finance & Control:
A J Marshall
Director, Treasury: R W Fetzer
Director, Banking: W F Hanna

Providence Capitol Fund Managers Ltd
Providence House
30 Uxbridge Road
London W12 8PG
Tel: 081 749 9111
Telex: 934227
Fax: 081 749 9777

Chairman: M J Levett
Managing Director: A G Parsonson
Director:
J S G Baker
K C Carter
T J R Gordon
B A Marquard
R Roseman

Providence Capitol Life Assurance Ltd
Providence House
30 Uxbridge Road
London W12 8PG
Tel: 081 749 9111
Telex: 934227
Fax: 081 749 9777

Chairman: M J Levett
Managing Director: R Roseman
Director:
M J J Arney
J S G Baker
T J R Gordon
D Hepburn
B A Marquard
G M Mattin
R C Pitt
B P Watson

Pru-Bache Capital Funding (Moneybrokers) Ltd
3 Gracechurch Street
London EC3V 0AT
Tel: 071 626 1443
Telex: 933096/7
Fax: 071 929 0634

Chairman: B J Ould
Non-Executive Director:
W L Custard
S J St F Dare
Financial Director: A S T Negretti
Administration Director: J C Jones

Prudential-Bache Capital Funding (Equities) Ltd
9 Devonshire Square
London EC2M 4HP
Tel: 071 548 4000
Telex: 8958901
Fax: 071 623 4546

Chairman: W L Custard
Joint Managing Director:
J D Best
G C Bunting
Director:
N Atkinson
N H Chamberlen
D E Duffy
G G Lloyd
Secretary: W N H Jones

Prudential-Bache Securities (UK)
5 Burlington Gardens
London W1X 1LE
Tel: 071 439 4191
Telex: 263779
Fax: 071 437 9110

Executive Vice President - Manager:
Stephen Massey
Vice President: H G Garioch
Vice President - Investments:
Peter F Dickinson

Prudential Corporation plc
142 Holborn Bars
London EC1N 2NH
Tel: 071 405 9222
Telex: 266431
Fax: 071 548 3363

Chairman: Sir Brian Corby
Deputy Chairman:
Sir Trevor Holdsworth
Sir Alex Jarratt CB
Group Chief Executive:
Michael Newmarch
Non-Executive Director:
Michael Abrahams MBE
Ronald Artus
Mrs Mary Baker
The Rt Hon Lord Butterfield OBE
Sir Ronald Dearing CB
The Hon Sir Victor Garland KBE
The Rt Hon Lord Hunt of Tanworth GCB
Peter Moody CBE
Julius Neave CBE JP DL
The Rt Hon James Ramsden
Colin Southgate
Chief Executive - Prudential Portfolio Managers: Hugh Jenkins
Group Finance Director:
Michael Lawrence
Managing Director - Mercantile & General Reinsurance: John Lock
Managing Director - International Division: Brian Medhurst
Managing Director - UK Individual Division: Anthony Freeman
Group Taxation Manager:
Michael Cole
Group Financial Controller:
John Hughes
Group Treasurer: David Westby
Group Chief Actuary: Hugh Jarvis
Group Legal Adviser:
Mrs Shelley Grey
Group Property Legal Adviser:
Alan Brakefield
General Manager - Group Strategic Planning: Donald Sirkett
General Manager - Personnel & Business Manager:
Geoffrey Keeys
Group Personnel Policy Manager:
Andrew Jones
Director - Prudential Business Services:
Nicholas Alliston
Group General Manager - Management Services: Ernest Morris

Group Secretary: Peter Rawson
Home Service Division Director and General Manager, Field Operations and Marketing:
Keith Bedell-Pearce
Managing Director - Commercial and Broker General Insurance Division:
John Powell
Chief Executive - Prudential Holborn:
Alan Wren
Finance Director - Prudential Property Services: Michael Dudley
Chief Executive - Prudential Corporate Pensions: Peter Nowell

PWS Holdings plc
52/56 Minories
London EC3N 1JJ
Tel: 071 480 6622
Telex: 887265
Fax: 071 283 5594/480 7470

Chairman: The Lord Pearson of Rannoch
Deputy Chairman:
J J S Farmer
D J Springbett
Joint Managing Director: P J English
Joint Managing Director & Secretary:
D R Neale

Quadrex Securities
80-82 Regent Street
London W1R 6QX
Tel: 071 439 2131
Telex: 297401
Fax: 071 437 3637

Chairman: A G Klesch
Managing Director: K Marthaler

Quanta Group (Holdings) Limited
Empire House
8-14 St Martin's-le-Grand
London EC1A 4AD
Tel: 071 606 7491
Telex: 886318
Fax: 071 606 9827

Managing Director: Tarek J Kassem

Quayle Munro Limited
42 Charlotte Street
Edinburgh EH2 4HQ
Tel: 031 226 4421
Telex: 72244
Fax: 031 225 3391

Chairman: Sir Alan Smith
Chief Executive: Ian Q Jones

Executive Director:
Jo C Elliot
Robert W L Legget
D Michael Munro
Non-Executive Director:
John J Price
David L Skinner
Robin Young

Queen Anne's Gate Asset Management Limited
1 Queen Anne's Gate
London SW1H 9BT
Tel: 071 222 0106
Fax: 071 222 3843

Managing Director:
Charles Crowther
Director:
P Adderson
Mrs Kathleen Pritchard

Quill Underwriting Agency Limited
12/13 Lime Street
London EC3M 7AA
Tel: 071 626 3004
Fax: 071 623 1626

Chairman: H J M Blakeney
Underwriter: S A Holmes
Finance Director: R J Ingham Clark
Director: A P Leslie

Quilter Goodison Company Ltd
St Helen's
1 Undershaft
London EC3A 8BB
Tel: 071 600 4177
Telex: 883719
Fax: 071 726 8826

Managing Director: D E G Roberts

Racal Electronics plc
Western Road
Bracknell RG12 1RG
Tel: 0344 481222

Group Treasurer: J Turkington

The Rank Organisation plc
No 6 Connaught Place
London W2 2EZ
Tel: 071 706 1111
Telex: 263549
Fax: 071 262 9886

Finance Director: Nigel Turnbull
Group Tax & Treasurey Manager:
Clifford Perkins

Ranks Hovis McDougall plc
R H M Centre
PO Box 178, Alma Road
Windsor SL4 3ST
Tel: 0753 857123
Telex: 847314
Fax: 0753 846537

Group Financial Controller &
Treasurer: R J Endacott

Raphael Zorn Hemsley Ltd
10 Throgmorton Avenue
London EC2N 2DP
Tel: 071 628 4000

Chairman: G T Laing
Partner:
D Betts
O A Hemsley
T J Leader
C H Moore
M S Rosenberg
M J Sinclair

J H Rayner (Mincing Lane)
1 Prescot Street
London E1 8AY
Tel: 071 481 9144
Telex: 883461
Fax: 071 481 8859

Chairman & Managing Director:
H P Wiltshire
Director:
D J Allen
R T Burgess
W J Smit
Head of Coffee: D J Barry
Head of Sugar: N Blum
Head of Metals: L B Grossmann
Head of Cocoa: N Labram

RBC Dominion Securities International Ltd
71 Queen Victoria Street
London EC4V 4DE
Tel: 071 489 1133
Telex: 888011
Fax: 071 248 3940

Chairman: J R Sanders
Managing Director: F S H Ma

RBC Kitcat & Safran Ltd
71 Queen Victoria Street
London EC4V 4DE

Tel: 071 489 1966
Telex: 888297
Fax: 071 329 6149

Director: Henry W Safran

Rea Brothers Limited
Alderman's House
Alderman's Walk
London EC2M 3XR
Tel: 071 623 1155
Telex: 886503
Fax: 071 626 0130

Chairman: J A V Townsend
Managing Director: R W Parsons
Director:
M J E G Bower
P Franklin
A A Hall
J D Knox
C C Norland
A E F Palmer
G A Richards
J M P Welman
Director & Company Secretary:
G M Muir

Reckitt & Colman plc
One Burlington Lane
London W4 2RW
Tel: 081 994 6464
Telex: 21268
Fax: 081 994 8920

Secretary: P D Saltmarsh

Redland plc
Redland House
Reigate
Surrey RH2 0SJ
Tel: 0737 242488
Telex: 28626
Fax: 0737 221938

Chairman: Sir Colin Corness
Managing Director: R S Napier
Financial Director: G M N Corbett
Executive Director:
K A Abbott
P M Johnson
G R Phillipson
Non-Executive Director:
Sir Christopher Laidlaw
T Osbourne
R W Pogue
J W M Wallace
J White
Secretary: R G F Smith
Group Controller: R D Andrews
Treasurer: S East

Reed International plc

Reed House
6 Chesterfield Gardens
London W1A 1EJ
Tel: 071 499 4020
Telex: 25771
Fax: 071 491 8212

Chairman & Chief Executive:
  P J Davis
Finance Director: N J Stapleton
Corporate Treasurer: J Thompson

Refco Overseas Ltd

5th Floor, Europe House
World Trade Centre
London E1 9AA
Tel: 071 488 3232
Telex: 887438
Fax: 071 480 7069

Joint Managing Director (Sales):
  R Reinert
  F Spinelli

Refuge Assurance plc

Investment Office
66 Gresham Street
London EC2V 7PQ
Tel: 071 600 0339
Telex: 295958
Fax: 071 606 3842

Chief Investment Manager:
  Frank J Webster
Senior Investment Manager:
  Adrian J Brown
  Russell K Sparkes

Republic National Bank of New York

30 Monument Street
London EC3R 8NB
Tel: 071 860 3000
Telex: 889217
Fax: 071 623 2866

Executive Vice President & General
  Manager: Andrew Pucher
Executive Vice President:
  Adrian Fletcher
  Morris Tawil
  Ronald Willson
Senior Vice-President: Kurt Ziegler

Reuters Holdings plc

85 Fleet Street
London EC4P 4AT
Tel: 071 250 1122
Telex: 23222
Fax: 071 353 0156

Chairman: Sir Christopher Hogg
Executive Director:
  Peter Job
  Nigel Judah
  Glen Renfrew
  David Ure
  André Villeneuve
Non-Executive Director:
  James Evans
  Pehr Gyllenhammar
  Andrew Knight
  Rupert Murdoch AC
  Ian Park
  David Snedden
  Sir Richard Storey Bt
  Walter Wriston
Alternate Director:
  Robert Rowley
  Mark Wood

Rickett & Co Limited

3/5 St John Street
London EC1M 4AE
Tel: 071 253 7174
Fax: 071 251 2359

Chairman: Peter David Rickett
Director: Joseph Kelley Fritz
Non-Executive Director: John Victor
  Alfred Oakes

Riggs A P Bank Ltd

21 Great Winchester Street
London EC2N 2HH
Tel: 071 588 7575
Telex: 888218
Fax: 071 920 9457

Chairman: Sir James Cleminson MC
  DL
Joint Deputy Chairman:
  J L Allbritton
  L J Walton
Managing Director: R Woodbridge
Corporate Finance Director:
  A P Brown
Banking Director:
  P A Bishop
  R Bryant
Finance Director:
  A W P Comber
  P J Haycock
Non-Executive Director:
  Sir Hugh Bidwell GBE
  T C Coughlin
  J W Dyson
  L I Hebert
  A G Keel Jr
  A A S Rae CBE

The Riggs National Bank of Washington DC

21 Great Winchester Street
London EC2N 2HH
Tel: 071 588 7772
Telex: 892807
Fax: 071 256 7369

Vice President & General Manager:
  John W T Hunt
Vice President & Deputy General
  Manager: Edmund S Muskie Jr
Vice President & International
  Comptroller: Robert W Smith

River & Mercantile Investment Management

7 Lincoln's Inn Fields
London WC2A 3BP
Tel: 071 405 7722

Chairman: A E Foucar
Managing Director: P M Godfrey
Executive Director: Ms V Gould
Non-Executive Director:
  P S S Macpherson

RMC Group plc

RMC House
Coldharbour Lane
Thorpe
Egham
Surrey TW20 8TD
Tel: 0932 568833
Telex: 918150
Fax: 0932 568933

Chairman: J Camden
Managing Director: P J Owen
Finance Director: D W Jenkins
Secretary: P H F Bullard
Group Treasurer: J C K Young

Robert Bruce Fitzmaurice Ltd

Byward House
16 Byward Street
London EC3R 5BA
Tel: 071 480 5158
Telex: 8955710
Fax: 071 488 0166

Chairman: H M F McCall
Director:
  P T Adler
  J V C Butcher
  S W G Hedley
  R M Mansell Jones
  E F Trump
Director and Company Secretary:
  P E Chapman

Robert Fleming & Co Limited

25 Copthall Avenue
London EC2R 7DR
Tel: 071 638 5858
Telex: 297451
Fax: 071 588 7219

Chairman: P J Manser
Deputy Chairman: W L Banks
Director:
A C Armstrong
P H G Bradley
J H M Bruce
A C Chambers
R H Cooper
J D Crosland
J D Drysdale
O B Ellingham
I K C Ellison
A I Findlay
V P Fleming
A M Golding
Ms E J Holt
L V Ingrams
P L A Jamieson
M J C Ladenburg
I W Lindsey
D J Lowes
C M Moore
C R Page
I R M Ramsay
D M Smith
W N Smith
M Takagi
R Templeton
J T Watson
P A Wichelow

Robert Fleming Holdings Limited

25 Copthall Avenue
London EC2R 7DR
Tel: 071 638 5858
Telex: 297451
Fax: 071 588 7219

Chairman: Robin Fleming
Deputy Chairman:
Charles K R Nunneley
Group Chief Executive: P J Manser
Director:
Lawrence Banks
P T Bateman
R H Cooper
John Drysdale
John Emly
Lord Mark Fitzalan Howard
Adam Fleming
Val Fleming

Director:
John Galvanoni
William Garrett
Patrick Gifford
Leonard Ingrams
Peter Jamieson
Chris Moore
C I C Munro
Iain Saunders
R H L Thomas
Phillip Wichelow

Robert Fleming Insurance Brokers Limited

Staple Hall
Stone House Court
London EC3A 7AX
Tel: 071 621 1263
Telex: 883735
Fax: 071 623 6175

Chairman: P L B Stoddart
Chief Executive: C J Bowring
Director:
H C Bowring
R P de L Cazenove
J D Drysdale
A F C Fox
S H de B Galwey
B C F Granville
R W Holmes
P S Little
C McGarrigle
B W Pearce
K C Stanners
G F Tebbutt

Robson Cotterell Ltd

Bourne Chambers
St Peters Road
Bournemouth BH1 2JX
Tel: 0202 557581
Fax: 0202 556131

Managing Director: R M S Parsons

Rolls-Royce plc

65 Buckingham Gate
London SW1E 6AT
Tel: 071 222 9020

Director (Finance):
Peter F Macfarlane

Ropner Insurance Services Limited

Boundary House
7/17 Jewry Street
London EC3N 2HP

Tel: 071 488 4533
Telex: 897074
Fax: 071 481 0830

Chairman: M G Gladwyn
Managing Director, Finance & Admin:
A G Smith
Managing Director, Technical:
G L J Ropner
Director:
C W P Chase
A G Costin
A H S de Pree
D J Elcox
D L Ewer
M A Fountaine
B V Gaitley
B R Morris
W G D Ropner
R M Steel
D J Voisey
G J Young
Secretary: E G Hull

J Rothschild Capital Management Limited

15 St James's Place
London SW1A 1NW
Tel: 071 493 8111
Telex: 883625/896568
Fax: 071 493 5765

Chairman: The Lord Rothschild
Director:
Duncan Budge
John Cracknell
The Hon Clive Gibson
John Johnston
Andrew Stafford-Deitsch

J Rothschild Holdings plc

15 St James's Place
London SW1A 1NW
Tel: 071 493 8111
Telex: 883625/896568
Fax: 071 493 5765

Chairman: The Lord Rothschild
Vice Chairman: The Viscount Weir
Director:
Nathaniel de Rothschild
The Hon Clive Gibson
A Jiskoor
The Lord Rees-Mogg
S Nicholas Roditi
Andrew Stafford-Deitsch
Nils Taube

J Rothschild Investment Management Ltd
15 St James's Place
London SW1A 1NW
Tel: 071 493 8111
Telex: 883625/896568
Fax: 071 493 5765

Chairman: Nils Taube
Director:
John Cracknell
John Hodson
The Lord Rees-Mogg
S Nicholas Roditi
The Lord Rothschild
Zvi Schloss

N M Rothschild & Sons Limited
PO Box No 185
New Court
St Swithin's Lane
London EC4P 4DU
Tel: 071 280 5000
Telex: 888031
Fax: 071 929 1643

Chairman: Sir Evelyn de Rothschild
Vice-Chairman: Michael Richardson
Chief Operating Officer:
Alfred Vinton
Managing Director:
Anthony Alt
Russell Edey
Bernard Myers
David Sullivan
Executive Director:
Malcolm Aish
Charles Alexander
Richard Bailey
Caroline Banszky
John Bishop
David Blackett
Peter Byrom
Graham Curds
Penny Curtis
Richard Davey
Leopold de Rothschild
Paul ffolkes Davis
Nicholas Field-Johnson
Anthony Fry
Alan Graham
Robert Guy
Timothy Hancock
David Harris
Peter Johns
Martyn Konig
Simon Linnett
Charles Mercey
Gordon Nebeker

Executive Director:
Keith Palmer
Robert Perry
Michael Phair
Charles Price
Roger Salmon
The Hon Jeremy Soames
William Staple
Philip Swatman
Paul Tuckwell
James Yates
Non-Executive Director:
Lord Armstrong of Ilminster
Michael Cominos
Sir Frank Cooper
John Craig
David de Rothschild
Edmund de Rothschild
Eric de Rothschild
Kenneth Dick
Hubert Faure
Christopher French
Ruben Goldberg
Gerald Goldsmith
John Green-Armytage
Dr Alfred Hartmann
Graham Hearne
Georges Karlweis
Richard Katz
Grant Manheim
Robert Pirie
James Roe
John Silcock
Lord Tombs
Charles Tracy
Henderson Tuten
Anthony Vice
George Wong
Secretary: David Riches

N M Rothschild International Asset Management Limited
Five Arrows House
St Swithin's Lane
London EC4N 8NR
Tel: 071 280 5000
Telex: 888031
Fax: 071 929 1643

Chairman: Carel M Mosselmans
Managing Director:
Nigel Wightman
Executive Director:
Rosalind Altmann
Mark Connolly
William Currey
Gareth Evans

Executive Director:
Patrick Foster
Richard Lamb
Richard Robinson

Rowntree Limited
York YO1 1XY
Tel: 0904 653071
Telex: 57846
Fax: 0904 622467

Chairman: P H Blackburn
Director:
T Gardiner
G Millar
A Revell

Roy James & Co
Stock Exchange Buildings
33 Great Charles Street
Birmingham B3 3JS
Tel: 021 200 2200

Managing Director: R D James

The Royal Bank of Canada
RBC Centre
71/71a Queen Victoria Street
London EC4V 4DE
Tel: 071 489 1188
Telex: 929111
Fax: 071 329 6144

Senior Vice President:
R A Masleck
D P Pritchard
Vice President:
R J Goom
K N Kikano
M G Klingsick
S G A Scammell

Royal Bank of Canada Europe Limited
71 Queen Victoria Street
London EC4V 4DE
Tel: 071 489 1177
Telex: 929111
Fax: 071 329 6144

Chairman & Managing Director:
R A Masleck
Vice Chairman: D P Pritchard
Director:
N C Achen
C J H Fisher
R J Goom
K N Kikano
J R Sanders
S G A Scammell

The Royal Bank of Scotland plc

42 St Andrew Square
Edinburgh EH2 2YE
Tel: 031 556 8555
Telex: 72230
Fax: 031 557 6565

Chairman: The Rt
  Hon George K H Younger
Vice Chairman:
  Peter E G Balfour
  Sir Austin Pearce
Managing Director:
  Robert M Maiden
Executive Director:
  John A Barclay
  Sir Michael Herries
  Lewis S McGill
  David Robinson
Director:
  Professor Derek F Channon
  David B Clark
  Sir Robin Duthie
  Henry E Farley
  Ian F H Grant
  Henry L C Greig
  Angus McF McL Grossart
  Alexander M Hamilton
  Dr George R Mathewson
  Dr Elizabeth Hawkins Nelson
  The Hon F Ranald Noel-Paton
  Norman Quick
  Charles F E Shakerley
  Sir Adam Thomson
  Charles M Winter
  Ian C Wood
Senior General Manager:
  Kenneth J Duncombe
  Alexander J Reid
General Manager:
  Wilfred Allen
  Donald A Cameron
  Stanley J Comber
  James Grier
  Norman M Irvine
  Joseph M Macdonald
  Robert M McInnes
  John M Mather
  Alfred W Moon
  Dr M Mosson
  Alan Peers
  Edwin T Regan
  G A Schofield
  John I Sinclair
  Ian M Sutherland
Secretary: James S Lindsay

Royal Insurance Holdings plc

1 Cornhill
London EC3V 3QR
Tel: 071 283 4300
Telex: 8956701
Fax: 071 623 5282

Chairman: Sir John Cuckney
Deputy Chairman:
  Sir Anthony Tuke
Director:
  Sir Derek Alun-Jones
  R D Broadley
Group Finance Director: R A Gamble
Director:
  Sir John Milne
  Sir Edwin Nixon
  Sir John Nott
  A V Shoemaker
  Sir Max Williams
Director & Group General Manager:
  W R Rowland
Director & Group Chief Executive:
  I L Rushton
Director & Managing Director (Royal UK): P F Duerden
Director & Managing Director (Royal Life): W Scanlan
Group General Manager: R A Elms
Deputy Group General Manager:
  D Malcolm
Managing Director (Royal International): D R Parry
General Manager (Royal Reinsurance):
  K J Dare
Secretary: D Morgan
Assistant Group General Manager (Personnel): C J Evans
Head of Group Corporate Relations:
  R G L Randall

Royal London Mutual Insurance Society Limited

Royal London House
27 Middleborough
Colchester CO1 1RA
Tel: 0206 761761
Telex: 987723
Fax: 0206 578449

Chairman: M J Pickard
Deputy Chairman:
  Dr N S Wooding
Managing Director, Operations:
  J B Knights
Chief Investment Manager: C Brill
General Manager & Actuary:
  B R Jones
Investment Manager: M J Yardley

Royal Trust Bank

Royal Trust House
48-50 Cannon Street
London EC4N 6LD
Tel: 071 236 6044
Telex: 8952879
Fax: 071 248 0828

Chairman: Thomas J Wacker
Managing Director: Jan-Arne Farstad
Director:
  Brian Barr
  Philip Holbeche
  Doug Keller Hobson
  Peter Roberts
Senior Associate Director:
  Michael Brierley
  Michael Burns
  Neil Millward
Divisional Director:
  Steven Barlow
  Charles Baxter
  Paul Brunning
  Stephen Denham
  Barry Jenkinson
  David Jones
  Arthur Jordan
  David Lockwood
  David Pellett
  Andrew Turner

Rudolf Wolff & Co Ltd

Second Floor, D Section
Plantation House
31-35 Fenchurch Street
London EC3M 3DX
Tel: 071 626 8765
Telex: 885034
Fax: 071 626 3939

Chairman & Managing Director:
  Francis Holford
Director:
  Mohammed Ahmadzadeh
  Ian Anderson
  Gary German
  John Hampton
  Derek Robbshaw
  Graham Slater
  John Wolff

The Rural & Industries Bank of Western Australia

Park House
16 Finsbury Circus
London EC2M 7DJ

Tel: 071 256 5600
Telex: 298971
Fax: 071 256 7979

Chief Manager: Andrew P Cornish

Russell Wood Ltd
4th Floor
30 Great Guildford Street
London SE1 0HS
Tel: 071 928 0505
Telex: 927665
Fax: 071 928 8931

Chairman: J C D Pilley

Rutland Trust plc
Rutland House
Rutland Gardens
London SW7 1BX
Tel: 071 225 3391
Fax: 071 225 1364

Chairman: J L Beckwith
Chief Executive: M R F Langdon
Director:
  B S Briggs
  C B Dowling
  R D Headlam
  G A Loughney
  K J Rawlings
Non-Executive Director:
  A Cassels
  B J M Dally
  C Giacomotto
  P S McDonald
Company Secretary: M R Douglas

J Sainsbury plc
Stamford House
Stamford Street
London SE1 9LL
Tel: 071 921 6000
Telex: 264241
Fax: 071 921 6413

Treasurer: David N Roberts

The Saitama Bank Ltd
30 Cannon Street
London EC4M 6XH
Tel: 071 248 9421
Telex: 886400
Fax: 071 248 3862

General Manager: K Ito
Senior Deputy General Manager:
  M Aosaki
  J Kosuge

Salomon Brothers International Limited
Victoria Plaza
111 Buckingham Palace Road
London SW1W 0SB
Tel: 071 721 2000
Telex: 886441
Fax: 071 222 7062

Chairman: Charles S McVeigh III
Chief Executive: James L Massey
Managing Director:
  Nicholas C Bedford
  Bruce Brittain
  Peter R Clarke
  Ronald M Freeman
  J Nicholas Garrow
  David T Goldmuntz
  Jean Grall
  David Jarvis
  David S Karat
  Denis J Keegan
  Peter McSloy
  Christopher M Mitchinson
  Stephen J D Posford

Samba Capital Management International Ltd
65 Curzon Street
London W1Y 7PE
Tel: 071 355 4411
Telex: 885124
Fax: 071 355 4416

Executive: Richard P Keigher

Sampo Insurance Company (UK) Limited
117 Fenchurch Street
London EC3M 5EJ
Tel: 071 488 2972
Fax: 071 702 2535

Managing Director: W H Morris
Director: D H Meadows
Company Secretary: N J Hudson

Samuel Montagu & Co Limited
10 Lower Thames Street
London EC3R 6AE
Tel: 071 260 9000
Telex: 887213
Fax: 071 488 1630

Chairman: The Rt Hon
  Sir Michael Palliser GCMG
Deputy Chairman: George Loudon
Deputy Chairman & Chief Executive:
  Christopher Sheridan

Deputy Chief Executive:
  Ian McIntosh
Managing Director: Ernest Cole
Director:
  Anthony Arfwedson
  Robert Barry
  Anthony Blaiklock
  Gervase Boote
  Trevor Botham
  Douglas Bull
  David Burnett
  Clive Chalk
  Christopher Clarke
  Simon Clayton
  John Cutts
  James Dominguez
  Ms Irene Dorner
  Ian Dunn
  Derek Eastment
  John Evangelides
  Rupert Faure Walker
  Andrew Galloway
  Richard Gillingham
  Marcus Gregson
  John Griffiths
  Charles Hanbury-Williams
  Anthony Hass
  David Hinde
  Ms Patricia Hudson
  Stanley Hurn
  Peter Jones
  Philip Kendall
  John Kerr
  Timothy Lynn
  Sir Laurence Magnus Bt
  Christopher O'Malley
  Ms Gillian Oakes
  Oliver Parr
  Ms Sarah Philbrick
  Andrew Pocock
  Rupert Ponsonby
  Jeremy Prescott
  Paul Richards
  Mossman Roueche
  William Sadleir
  Arnold Shipp OBE
  John Sleeman
  Jonathan Sparey
  Adrian Stanford
  Ian Steer
  Michael Stenning
  Richard Tickner
  John Tylor
  Jeffrey Urwin
  Emmanuel Zuridis
Director (Secretary):
  Arthur Wadsworth

Sanwa International Ltd

PO Box 245
Commercial Union Building
1 Undershaft
London EC3A 8BR
Tel: 071 623 7991
Telex: 887132
Fax: 071 623 3208

Chief Executive: S Arai
Managing Director:
  S Akita
  J Goldstein
  A Sittampalam
  S Suzuki

Sanyo International Ltd

Roman House
Wood Street
London EC2Y 5BP
Tel: 071 628 2931
Telex: 8812979
Fax: 071 628 4179

Chairman: L A B Dodge
Managing Director: R Ninomiya
Director:
  P H Hill
  K Katsuoka
  G Murakawa
  T Sakamoto
  S Yoshida

Saudi American Bank

65 Curzon Street
London W1Y 7PE
Tel: 071 355 4411
Telex: 885124
Fax: 071 355 4416

Branch Manager: George E Kanaan

Saudi International Bank

99 Bishopsgate
London EC2M 3TB
Tel: 071 638 2323
Telex: 8812261/2
Fax: 071 628 8633

*Executive Director and Chief Executive
  Officer:* Peter J de Roos
General Manager:
  Christopher J Parker
  Guy R Stokely
Assistant General Manager:
  Ford M Fraker
  Clive Hanover
  Robin McIlvenny
  Richard Wilson

Scandinavian Bank Group plc

Scandinavian House
2/6 Cannon Street
London EC4M 6XX
Tel: 071 236 6090
Telex: 889093
Fax: 071 248 6612

Chairman: Bo C E Ramfors
Chief Executive: Gerard De Geer
Director, Finance and Administration:
  C Niel Daubeny
Director and Company Secretary:
  Malcolm K Crow
Banking Division: Per O F Ahlqvist
Treasury Division: Sven I Bjorkman
Debt Capital Markets Division: M
  Roger Gifford

Schlesinger & Company Limited

International House
1 St Katharine's Way
London E1 9UN
Tel: 071 488 4888
Fax: 071 488 3480

Chairman: N R Tribble
Deputy Chairman:
  D Gradel
  M H Oldfield
Chief Executive: B R MacIlwaine
Director: G H Brown
Associate Director:
  S R Barnes
  N L Davies
  K E Lillie

Schroder Investment Management Ltd

36 Old Jewry
London EC2R 8BS
Tel: 071 382 6000
Telex: 885029
Fax: 071 382 3950

Chief Executive: I Peter Sedgwick
Deputy Chief Executive: C
  John Govett
Executive Director:
  R F Cheetham
  W R Eyres
  J A Hill
  B C Hillard
  Roger E Hills
  J A Kingzett
  J R Lambert
  P A Leonard
  P A R Meyer

Executive Director:
  David J Mumford
  Keith M Niven
  Mrs J L Pain
  Mrs Nicola T Ralston
  A D Strang
  B D Wood

Schroder Securities Limited

120 Cheapside
London EC2V 6DS
Tel: 071 382 6000
Telex: 885029
Fax: 071 382 3977

Chief Executive: Richard V Watkins
Director:
  Roger J Brocklebank
  Rupert M Caldecott
  John G Conor Killeen
  Edward S Cumming-Bruce
  Michael G Eddy
  Nicholas I Hamilton
  William J Harkett
  Richard C Harwood
  Young Tae Kim
  Michael B H Law
  Iain A G Menzies
  Pierre Morgue d'Algue
  Takeshi Murakami
  James R D Neill
  Eisuke Okazaki
  John Poynter
  Paul N Sauvary
  Ivan H Sedgewick
  Andrew C Williams
  Richard A Witts

Schroder Ventures

20 Southampton Street
London WC2E 7QG
Tel: 071 632 1000
Fax: 071 240 5072

Managing Partner: Jon Moulton

J Henry Schroder Wagg & Co Limited

120 Cheapside
London EC2V 6DS
Tel: 071 382 6000
Telex: 885029
Fax: 071 382 2950

Chairman: W F W Bischoff
Vice Chairman: J B Solandt
Director:
  John Aston
  Raymond Badrock
  Bernard F Barham

Director:
Robin Blunden
H W Bolland
R D Bown
J Desmond Boyle
A H C Broadbent
Richard Broadbent
John Burnham
C J Cairns
Rupert Caldecott
D A Cameron DL
Alison J Carnwath
David Challen
Robin Corner
Susan M Cox
Bernard Dewe Mathews TD
Patrick Drayton
Michael J Dunne
Giles Elliott
Nicholas Ferguson
A E Forsyth
Dr Erik B Gasser
I R L Gordon
Gerald Grimstone
P M Hargreaves-Allen
G C Harington
E J Henbrey
Jeremy Hill
Clive Jobson
Richard Lazarus
R Lis
The Hon N R MacAndrew
Christopher A A E Mackenzie
George W Mallinckrodt
B E Marenbach
David J H Morris
D N D Netherton
Nigel Pantling
John Pearson
John Reynolds
P C Robinson
J W Rock
F R Sadleir
William M Samuel
Paul Sauvary
Nigel Saxby-Soffe
Gina Scheck
Bruno L Schroder
Andrew M Shaw
William R Slee
M W Snyder
B V Strickland
R W A Swannell
Andrew F Sykes
Panfilo Tarantelli
G R J Wadia
Richard Watkins
Andrew C Williams

Finance Director:
William J Wedlake
Secretary: A M Gaulter

Schroders plc
120 Cheapside
London EC2V 6DS
Tel: 071 382 6000
Telex: 885029
Fax: 071 382 3950

Executive Chairman:
George W Mallinckrodt
Group Chief Executive:
W F W Bischoff
Director:
A H C Broadbent
Baron Daniel Janssen
Sir Ralph H Robins
Bruno L Schroder
I Peter Sedgwick
Charles J F Sinclair
William R Slee
J B Solandt
B V Strickland
Geoffrey G Williams
Secretary: Raymond Badrock

Scimitar Asset Management Ltd
22 Billiter Street
London EC3A 2BE
Tel: 071 588 6868
Telex: 918738
Fax: 071 702 2737

Managing Director: The
Hon Michael D Benson
Deputy Managing Director:
Graham Walker

Scimitar Development Capital Limited
Osprey House
78 Wigmore Street
London W1H 9DQ
Tel: 071 487 5914
Fax: 071 487 5048

Executive Director:
Richard Arthur
Peter Dale
Dennis Hallahane
Assistant Director: John Dixon

ScotiaMcLeod Incorporated
3 Finsbury Square
London EC2A 1AD

Tel: 071 256 5656
Telex: 889283
Fax: 071 256 8476/7/8

Managing Director:
Christopher J Church
Senior VP Director, Bonds: Ian Berry
VP Director, Bond Trading:
Simon Last
VP Bond Sales: Heather Mackay
VP Director, Transaction Finance:
Roger Paice
VP Director, International Equities:
Stuart Hensman
Adrian Penny
VP Director, Equities:
Geoffrey Garsten
VP Finance: Joe Seet
VP Operations: Bob Soden
VP Compliance: Roy Keirstead

Scott Underwriting Agencies Limited
3rd Floor
Ibex House
42/47 Minories
London EC3N 1PR
Tel: 071 481 1943
Fax: 071 480 7607

Chairman: G W Scott
Managing Director: J D Scott
Director:
R J Butler
J M Ferguson
F G Howard
R C Kingsley
Director/Company Secretary:
K D Thompson

Scottish & Newcastle Breweries Ltd
111 Holyrood Road
Edinburgh EH8 8YS
Tel: 031 556 2591
Telex: 72356
Fax: 031 556 4665

Group Treasurer: John Laurie

Scottish Amicable Life Assurance Society
150 St Vincent Street
Glasgow G2 5NQ
Tel: 041 248 2323
Telex: 77171
Fax: 041 221 3893

Chairman: W Brown
President: The Rt Hon The Earl
of Elgin and Kincardine

Deputy Chairman: A D Stewart
Director:
R Anderson
T M Bisset
T Johnston
J R Johnstone
W G Knox
R A B Miller
J A Spens
Managing Director: R M Nicolson
Deputy Managing Director (Sales & Service): M D Paterson

Scottish Development Agency
120 Bothwell Street
Glasgow G2 7JP
Tel: 041 248 2700
Telex: 777600
Fax: 041 221 3217

Chairman: Sir David Nickson KBE DL
Deputy Chairman:
Sir Douglas Hardie CBE
Chief Executive: James A Scott CB LVO
Agency Secretary: David A Lyle

Scottish Equitable Life Assurance Society
28 St Andrew Square
Edinburgh EH2 1YF
Tel: 031 556 9101
Telex: 72610
Fax: 031 556 7801

Chairman: C F Sleigh
Director:
E I Cuthbertson
R Gordon
H M Inglis
B E Sealey
M B A Ward
R Young
Rt Hon G Younger MP
Chief Executive: D A Berridge
Deputy Chief Executive: P H Grace
General Manager (Sales):
J G Elliott
D A Henderson
D J Kirkpatrick
R Patrick

Scottish Financial Enterprise
91 George Street
Edinburgh EH2 3ES
Tel: 031 225 6990
Fax: 031 220 1353

Chairman (Non-Executive): J Raymond Johnstone CBE
Executive Director:
James C L Provan
Director:
A Scott Bell
Angus M M Grossart CBE
Dr George Mathewson CBE
A C (Fred) Shedden
Bernard Solomons
Assistant Director: Mike B Foulis

The Scottish Investment Trust plc
6 Albyn Place
Edinburgh EH2 4NL
Tel: 031 225 7781
Telex: 727888
Fax: 031 226 3663

Chairman: Angus Grossart CBE
Managing Director: J R Glen
Manager:
I C McLeish
D H R Ness
Director:
Lord Balfour of Burleigh
D H Davidson
J G Gulliver
G R Mathewson CBE
Secretary: I M Harding

The Scottish Mutual Assurance Society
109 St Vincent Street
Glasgow G2 5HN
Tel: 041 248 6321
Telex: 777145
Fax: 041 221 1230

Chairman: J H Forbes Macpherson
Chief Executive: F D Patrick
General Manager:
A G Blakeley
J W D Campbell
R S Clarkson
L J Gray
W M Henderson
C G Thomson
Secretary: C G Kirkwood

The Scottish Provident Institution
6 St Andrew Square
Edinburgh EH2 2YA
Tel: 031 556 9181
Telex: 72631
Fax: 031 558 2486

Chairman: D A Ross Stewart

Deputy Chairman:
Charles R Connell
Managing Director: D E Woods
Director:
J D S Bennett
J C R Inglis
Duncan J MacLeod
A M Pelham Burn
M D Pentland
General Manager (Customer Service) & Deputy Chief Executive:
W A B Scott
General Manager (Corporate Development): N M Bryson
General Manager (Sales & Marketing):
P G FitzGerald
General Manager (Finance) & Actuary: H W Gillon
General Manager (Investment):
B M Rose

Scottish Widow's Fund and Life Assurance Society
PO Box 902
15 Dalkeith Road
Edinburgh EH16 5BU
Tel: 031 655 6000
Telex: 72654
Fax: 031 662 4053

Chairman: Colin H Black
Deputy Chairman: J E Boyd
Managing Director: J Elder
Deputy Managing Director:
D C Ritchie
M D Ross
Director:
The Viscount of Arbuthnott
Robert C Buist
Sir Charles Fraser
Gavin J N Gemmell
G R G Graham
Sir Michael Herries
Alistair J Low
A M M Stephen
James Stirling
Sir James Stormonth Darling
General Manager:
F E G Attrill
A Neill
E S Robertson
B D Short
General Manager & Secretary:
H W Raymond

Sears plc
40 Duke Street
London W1A 2HP
Tel: 071 408 1180

Chairman: Geoffrey Maitland
  Smith
Chief Executive: J Michael Pickard
Executive Director: Howard S Perlin
Finance Director: John D Lovering
Group Treasurer: Michael Bryant

Seccombe Marshall & Campion plc

7 Birchin Lane
London EC3V 9DE
Tel: 071 283 5031
Telex: 269759
Fax: 071 621 0973

Chairman: The Earl of Clarendon
Managing Director:
  Christopher A Chapman
  Peter J Pooley
Director:
  Henri Cukierman
  Philippe Delienne
  Olivier Mirat

Securities and Investments Board

Gavrelle House
2-14 Bunhill Row
London EC1Y 8RA
Tel: 071 283 2474
Telex: 291829
Fax: 071 929 0433

Chairman: Sir David Walker
Deputy Chairman:
  Ralph Quartano
  Lord Runciman
Executive Director & Chief Operating
  Officer: Roy Croft
Executive Director: Derek Fellows
Secretary: T E Allen
Director:
  Denis Child
  John Craven
  John Gardiner
  Norman Lessels
  John Manser
  Graham Ross Russell
  Leonard Warwick
  Dame Rachel Waterhouse
  Brian Williamson
Group Director:
  Michael Blair
  Colette Bowe
  Jeremy Orme
  Martin Vile
Staff Director:
  Richard Britton
  Barry Gittins
  Alistair Pirie

Staff Director:
  Roger Purcell
  Brian Smith
  Andrew Thrall

The Securities Association Limited

The Stock Exchange Building
London EC2N 1EQ
Tel: 071 256 9000
Fax: 071 334 8945

Chairman: S M Yassukovich
Deputy Chairman:
  R H Lawson
  A S Winckler
Board Member and Chief Executive:
  J R C Young
Board Member:
  A J Blair Agnew
  J R S Boas
  R A Brooks
  J A de Gier
  N J Durlacher
  A C Hugh Smith
  C W Jonas
  D J E Longridge
  I J Martin
  J McFarlane
  P D Minchin
  N Nakazawa
  Y Osawa
  A F Smith
  P H A Stanley
  P R Stevens
Independent Member:
  Lord Bridges
  Viscount Colville of Culross
  Professor R B Jack
  Professor S M Schaefer
  M G Taylor
  J L Thorn
  Lady Waterlow
  J D Webster
Company Secretary: W Nixon
Deputy Secretary: B D Whitbread

Security Pacific Hoare Govett Equity Ventures Limited

4 Broadgate
London EC2M 7LE
Tel: 071 374 1798
Telex: 887887
Fax: 071 374 4399

Managing Director: A E B Wiegman

Security Pacific Venture Capital

130 Jermyn Street
London SW1Y 4UJ
Tel: 071 925 2395
Fax: 071 930 2348

Managing Director: Dmitry Bosky

Sedgwick Group plc

Sedgwick House
Sedgwick Centre
London E1 8DX
Tel: 071 377 3456
Telex: 882131
Fax: 071 377 3199

Chairman: J D Rowland
Vice Chairman:
  R M Page
  J M Payne
  S Riley
Director (Non-Executive):
  H R Collum
  Lord Fanshawe
Director: J S Gilbert
Director (Non-Executive):
  R N Hambro
  J R Harvey
  F C Herringer
  F J Lutolf
  P L Moussa
Director: A Platt
Director (Non-Executive):
  Sir Michael Richardson
Director:
  S A Stewart
  J J H Swinglehurst
  S S Tarrant
  W R P White-Cooper
Director Corporate Communications:
  J C Fish
Group Secretary: J Pinchin
Group Financial Controller:
  H M J McGarel-Groves
Group Treasurer: J A V Montague
Group Personnel Director:
  M C Harrison
Group Taxation Controller:
  P K Penneycard

Sedgwick Lloyd's Underwriting Agents Limited

(Lloyd's Members Agent)
Aldgate House
33 Aldgate High Street
London EC3N 1AJ

Tel: 071 247 3224
Telex: 927014
Fax: 071 247 5331

Chairman: M J Crispin
Managing Director: C D Spence
Director:
R J A Brett
A G Godson
J D Rowland
Finance Director: J R Simpson
Non-Executive Director:
H M P Miles
Director and Company Secretary:
C H Murphy

Seventy-Seven Bank
7th Floor, Northgate House
20-24 Moorgate
London EC2R 6DH
Tel: 071 628 5506
Telex: 933055
Fax: 071 628 0561

Chief Representative: Y Nagayama

Sharjah Investment Co (UK) Ltd
Suite 1-2
14 Old Park Lane
London W1Y 3LH
Tel: 071 493 6000
Telex: 298861
Fax: 071 493 0217

Managing Director: S Khanachet
Director: I Mohamed
Investment Manager: S Sanbar

Sharps Pixley Limited
10 Rood Lane
London EC3M 8BB
Tel: 071 623 8000
Telex: 892817
Fax: 071 626 9509

Managing Director: T L Edgar
Deputy Managing Director:
A F Baker
Director:
J M Ball
P J H Govier

Shaw & Co Limited
4 London Wall Buildings
Blomfield Street
London EC2M 5NT
Tel: 071 638 3644
Telex: 888949/8956236
Fax: 071 374 2010

Deputy Chairman: J S Murdoch
Managing Director:
Graeme C A Thom

Shell Contributory Pension Fund
Shell Centre
London SE1 7NA
Tel: 071 934 1234
Fax: 071 934 6699

Investment Manager: R N Gaskell
Secretary: R W Willsmore

Shell Transport and Trading Company plc
Shell Centre
London SE1 7NA
Tel: 071 934 1234
Telex: 919651
Fax: 071 934 8060

Group Treasurer: M Harvey

Sheppards
No 1 London Bridge
London SE1 9QU
Tel: 071 378 7000
Telex: 886268
Fax: 071 378 7585

Chairman: R K Sursock
Executive Director:
I C Buckley
I Maxwell Scott
Dr T May
M J S Redmayne
F R Watts
Non-Executive Director:
R Gardiner
J Ginsbury
K Shahabi
G L Tedder

Sheppards Moneybrokers Ltd
20 Gresham Street
London EC2V 7HT
Tel: 071 606 6064
Telex: 269770
Fax: 071 606 0327

Non-Executive Chairman:
J C Barclay
Chief Executive: T S Hibbitt

J K Shipton and Company
Ridgway House
41/42 King William Street
London EC4R 9EN
Tel: 071 327 3399
Fax: 071 283 8003

Senior Partner: J K Shipton
Partner:
N H H Adams
R E Dudley
Jacqueline A Stead

Singer & Friedlander Investment Management Ltd
21 New Street
Bishopsgate
London EC2M 4HR
Tel: 071 623 3000
Telex: 886977
Fax: 071 623 2122

Chairman: A N Solomons
Deputy Chairman:
J Hodson
M E L Melluish
Director:
B H Buckley
R R Clough
A Hanbury
T R Howe
M S Pougatch
J Renyi
T S Rowan
M K M Spackman
A G O Walker

Singer & Friedlander Limited
21 New Street
Bishopsgate
London EC2M 4HR
Tel: 071 623 3000
Telex: 886977
Fax: 071 623 2122

Chairman: A N Solomons
Deputy Chairman:
B H Buckley
A G O Walker
Chief Executive: J Hodson
Director:
E P Bruegger
P W Burditt
L A Coppel
R P Corbett
P G Cordrey
D C Courtman
A R J Dyas
N C England
B N Gorst
B D F Mansfield
P Moores
V M Segal
M P Sutton

Skipton Building Society

59 High Street
Skipton BD23 1DN
Tel: 0756 700500
Fax: 0756 798793

Chairman: H G Fell
Chief Executive & Director: T Adams
Director:
B Braithwaite-Oxley
H T Fattorini
J B Haggas
J P Rycroft
R A Stockdale
General Manager & Secretary:
J A Jeanes
General Manager:
J G Goodfellow
I R Hepworth

Slough Estates plc

234 Bath Road
Slough SL1 4EE
Tel: 0753 37171
Telex: 847604
Fax: 0753 820585

Chairman and Chief Executive:
Sir Nigel Mobbs
Executive Vice Chairman: G A Elliot
Executive Director:
R W Carey
J C Harding JP
D R Wilson
Non-Executive Director:
C R E Brooke
D Kramer
W J Mackenzie OBE
Sir Donald Maitland GCMG
OBE
P D Orchard-Lisle
Group Treasurer: Ms J A Bentley

Smith Barney Harris Upham Europe Ltd

Brewers' Hall
Aldermanbury Square
London EC2V 7HR
Tel: 071 600 5633
Telex: 886595
Fax: 071 726 8217

Managing Director:
R L Hall
R L Hamburger
A C Thorne
Director:
H H Luetzow
W H Tozier

W H Smith Group plc

Strand House
7 Holbein Place
London SW1W 8NR
Tel: 071 730 1200

Chairman: Sir Simon Hornby
Managing Director: M D Field
Deputy Managing Director:
R N Thomas
Finance Director: J A Napier
Director, W H Smith Retail:
D J M Roberts
Director:
E E Elson
C J M Hardie
S H Honeyman
Dr J P Morgan
The Hon P R Smith
P S Wilmot-Sitwell
Lord Windlesham
Secretary: C S Rule
Treasurer: S K Leadill

Smith Keen Cutler

(A Division of Greenwell Montagu
Stockbrokers)
Exchange Buildings
Birmingham B2 4NN
Tel: 021 643 9977
Telex: 336730
Fax: 021 643 0345

Chairman: R H Lawson
Chief Executive: E J Fenton
Managing Director: C W Melly
Director:
S V Glazzard
N A Harrison
D M Horton
J D Loudon
N L Rowland
C F Smith
D C Wasdell
R B S Wood

Smith New Court plc

PO Box 293, Chetwynd House
24-30 St Swithin's Lane
London EC4N 8AE
Tel: 071 626 1544
Telex: 884410
Fax: 071 623 3947

Non-Executive Chairman:
Sir Michael Richardson
Chief Executive: M J P Marks
Director:
A S Abrahams
Baron N L Banszky von Ambroz

Director:
G F Casey
R M P Davis
M A Dritz
G D Freedman
J H Gunn
M R Heath
N J Holt
P B Kay
G A Lewis
D M Marks
E S Marks
B I Myers
J Nixon
L N G Olsen
D I Riches
P D Roy
M W Sperring
G S Stone
C E Taylor
R L Timms
P E Walker
J A G Young
Company Secretary: J R Garwood

Smiths Industries plc

765 Finchley Road
London NW11 8DS
Tel: 081 458 3232
Telex: 928761
Fax: 081 458 4380

Chairman: Sir Alex Jarratt
*Chief Executive and Managing
Director:* F Roger Horn
Financial Director:
Christopher S Taylor
*Chairman, Smiths Industries Medical
Systems Group:*
George M Kennedy
*Chairman, Aerospace & Defence
Systems Group:* A Hugh Pope
Chairman, Industrial Group:
Ron Williams
Non-Executive Director:
Sir James Hamilton
Sir Austin Pearce
Neil M Shaw
Sir Peter Thompson
Secretary: Alan Smith

Société Générale

60 Gracechurch Street
London EC3V 0HD
Tel: 071 626 5400
Telex: 886611
Fax: 071 929 1332

UK General Manager: Jean Huet
Deputy General Manager:
    Patrick Froger

Société Générale Merchant Bank plc
60 Gracechurch Street
London EC3V 0ET
Tel: 071 626 5622
Telex: 8812527
Fax: 071 626 4190

Managing Director: P H Collas
Deputy General Manager,
    Administration: C R Atkins
Senior Associate Director: H Nguyen-
    Quang
Compliance Director: G Luchini
Adviser: F Legros
Chief Dealer, Treasury/Foreign
    Exchange: J D Potts

Société Générale Strauss Turnbull Securities Ltd
Exchange House
Primrose Street
London EC2A 2DD

Chairman: P Duverger
Deputy Chairman:
    Sir Adam Ridley
    D R Strauss
Chief Executive: P L Hogarth
Deputy Chief Executive: P Pagni
Director:
    D Attard
    W J Dunn
    The Hon K I M Fraser
    L Petts
    P P Tisch
    Y Tuloup
    K W White

Sogemin Metals Ltd
4th Floor
98 Cannon Street
London EC4N 6EN
Tel: 071 621 0330
Telex: 885244
Fax: 071 283 6788

Chairman and Managing Director:
    D C Blundell
Deputy Managing Director:
    R W Kelly
Trading Director: D Jackman
Finance Director: D C Hogan
Director: D N Manners

Company Secretary: P J Miall
Compliance Officer: B M Harrison
Operations Manager: L A Doman

Speirs & Jeffrey Ltd
36 Renfield Street
Glasgow G2 1NA
Tel: 041 248 4311
Telex: 777902

Chairman: R S Waddell
Director:
    J R Gibb
    J R McCulloch
    P C M Roger
    A A W Waddell

Sphere Drake Insurance plc
52-54 Leadenhall Street
London EC3A 2BJ
Tel: 071 480 7340
Telex: 935015
Fax: 071 481 3828

Chairman, General Manager & Chief
    Executive: Ian H Dean
Director:
    Peter H Chilton
    Richard W Gray
    John C Head
    John R Llambias
    Paul G Philo
    Martin J Read
Secretary: P K Walsh
Marine Underwriter: J N Bloxham
Non-Marine Underwriter:
    D C Long
    R C Marks
Actuary: F Duncan
Personnel Controller: Mrs S R Gilbert

State Bank of India
1 Milk Street
London EC2P 2JP
Tel: 071 600 6444
Telex: 884589
Fax: 071 726 2739/2740

General Manager (UK):
    K R Maheshwari
Chief Manager (UK Branches):
    P S Mehrotra
Development Manager: K K Narula

State Bank of New South Wales
110-112 Fenchurch Street
London EC3M 5DR

Tel: 071 481 8000
Telex: 8952331
Fax: 071 265 0740

Treasurer: J E Masters

State Bank of Victoria
30 Old Jewry
London EC2R 8EY
Tel: 071 726 0081
Telex: 262052
Fax: 071 600 9925

General Manager: D W Peebles

State Street Bank & Trust Co
12 Nicholas Lane
London EC4N 7BN
Tel: 071 283 0091
Telex: 8955361
Fax: 071 283 7238

Vice President & General Manager:
    S W Shelton

STC plc
1B Portland Place
London W1N 3AA
Tel: 071 323 1000
Telex: 22385

Chairman and Chief Executive:
    A S Walsh CBE
Deputy Chief Executive, and
    Chairman and Managing Director,
    ICL: P L Bonfield CBE
Managing Director, Communications
    Systems: R A Gardner
Finance Director: L G Cullen
Director of Mergers and Acquisitions:
    W K Gardener
Group Marketing Director, and
    Chairman, Submarine Systems:
    R T Turner OBE
Non-Executive Director:
    E O M Eilledge
    E B Fitzgerald
    D W Kendall
    HRH Prince Michael of Kent
    Dame Anne Mueller DBE
    The Rt Hon Lord Rawlinson of
        Ewell PC QC
    A W P Stenham
    Dr P G Stern
    F S Thomson
Alternate Director:
    Sir David Nicolson
Secretary: J G Bates
Personnel Director: D F Beattie
Director, Commercial and Legal
    Affairs: R Christou

Director, External Affairs and
    Communication:
    Dr A C O'Dochartaigh

Steel Burrill Jones Group plc
One Hundred Whitechapel
London E1 1JG
Tel: 071 247 8888
Telex: 886129
Fax: 071 377 0022

Chairman: D Beresford Jones
Deputy Chairman:
    G Boden
    J M Horwell
Finance Director: A J Keys
Director:
    W M Barratt
    B J Bell
    J Davies
    D J Forcey
    G K Moore
    A A J L Troughton
    J D Williams
    J C W Wright
    H J Wynn
Non-executive Director:
    W S C Richards
Company Secretary: C R S Birrell

Stewart Ivory & Company Limited
45 Charlotte Square
Edinburgh EH2 4HW
Tel: 031 226 3271
Telex: 72500
Fax: 031 226 5120

Chairman: J G D Ferguson
Director:
    P A Campbell Fraser
    D W R Ferguson
    A Finlay
    D J Hume
    I E Ivory
    J Ivory
    B McCorkell
    Miss J G K Matterson
    J H Murray
    D H Shaw Stewart
    M H Sims
    A Tulloch
    E A W Tulloch
    J G L Wright

Stirling Hendry & Co
Royal Exchange House
100 Queen Street
Glasgow G1 3DL
Tel: 041 248 6033
Fax: 041 204 2155

Chairman: D Walton
Administration Director: I R Lydall
Finance Director: F Kinloch

Stopanska Banka AD Skopje
Representative Office
Kingsway House, 103 Kingsway
London WC2B 6QX
Tel: 071 405 6053
Telex: 268314
Fax: 071 831 1577

Director: J Angelkoski

Storehouse plc
The Heal's Building
196 Tottenham Court Road
London W1P 9LD
Tel: 071 631 0101
Telex: 296475
Fax: 071 631 3091

Treasurer: Lance S Moir

Sturge Holdings plc
9 Devonshire Square
London EC2M 4YL
Tel: 071 623 8022
Telex: 894156
Fax: 071 623 3386

Chairman: D E Coleridge
Finance Director: P A Davis
Director:
    M B H Maughan
    C E Parnell
    C J Pumphrey
    C H A Skey
Non-Executive Director:
    Lord N Gordon-Lennox
    D W Hardy
    E I Walker-Arnott
Company Secretary: A J Brown

Sumit Equity Ventures Limited
Edmund House
12 Newhall Street
Birmingham B3 3ER
Tel: 021 200 2244
Fax: 021 233 4628

Managing Director: John Kerr

The Sumitomo Bank Limited
Temple Court
11 Queen Victoria Street
London EC4N 4TA
Tel: 071 971 1000
Telex: 887667
Fax: 071 236 0049

Senior Managing Director:
    Yoji Okabe
*Managing Director & General
    Manager:* Yoichi Abe
Joint General Manager:
    Yasuyuki Kimoto
    Tanekiyo Kunitake
    Kiyotaka Kurokawa
    C Philip Martyn
    Osamu Okahashi
    R Barry Tatgenhorst
    Yasushi Terao
    Naoto Usagawa
Deputy General Manager:
    Takeo Hida
    Masao Iwase
*Joint General Manager - Treasury
    Dept:* Taizo Ohi
*Joint General Manager - Intl Credit
    Dept:* Yasufumi Kitamoto

Sumitomo Finance International
107 Cheapside
London EC2V 6DT
Tel: 071 606 3001
Telex: 8811043
Fax: 071 606 4615

Chairman: T Shimizu
President: T Nakamitsu
Managing Director:
    K Nagasaki
    T Uchimura

Sumitomo Trust & Banking Corp
Bishopsgate Exchange
155 Bishopsgate
London EC2M 3XU
Tel: 071 945 7000
Telex: 888924

Deputy General Manager:
    Y Yamamuro
Joint General Manager:
    T Kimura
    I Takeuchi

Sun Alliance and London Insurance plc

1 Bartholomew Lane
London EC2N 2AB
Tel: 071 588 2345
Telex: 888310
Fax: 071 638 3728

Chairman: H U A Lambert
Deputy Chairman:
  Sir Derrick Holden-Brown
Vice Chairman:
  The Earl of Crawford and
    Balcarres
  J N C James
Group Chief Executive:
  R A G Neville
Group Executive Director:
  R J Taylor
  B A Wright
Director:
  A R C Arbuthnot
  Sir Christopher Benson
  R K Bishop
  G Bowler
  G E Browne
  L D de Rothschild
  M L Dew
  H N L Keswick
  The Lord Kindersley
  D B Money-Coutts
  W G Niven
  R Petty
  S C Whitbread
Secretary: H Silver

Sun Life Assurance Society plc

107 Cheapside
London EC2V 6DU
Tel: 071 606 7788
Telex: 881871
Fax: 071 378 1865

Chairman: Peter J Grant
Deputy Chairman: Lord Bancroft
Managing Director: John Reeve
*Director, Group Secretary & Managing
  Director, SLAM:*
  John D Webster
*General Manager (Corporate
  Development):* R C Surface
General Manager, SLAS (UK):
  Michael J Turner
General Manager (Marketing & Sales):
  Geoffrey Harrison-Dees
General Manager (Life & Pensions): A
  Leslie Owen

General Manager (Administration):
  George M Reid
Chief Surveyor: John M Nicholls

Sun Life Corporation plc

107 Cheapside
London EC2V 6DU
Tel: 071 606 7788
Telex: 881871
Fax: 071 378 1865

Chairman: Peter J Grant
Deputy Chairman: Lord Bancroft
Managing Director: John Reeve
*Director, Group Secretary & Managing
  Director, SLAM:*
  John D Webster
*General Manager (Corporate
  Development):* R C Surface

Sun Life Europe Ltd

107 Cheapside
London EC2V 6DU
Tel: 071 606 7788
Telex: 881871
Fax: 071 378 1865

Managing Director, SLE:
  Clive F Williams

Sun Life Trust Management Limited

Granite House
101 Cannon Street
London EC4N 5AD
Tel: 071 606 4044 (General)
Telex: 9419073
Fax: 071 283 0715

Managing Director: Ian G Sampson
Finance Director:
  Stuart D Mathieson
Marketing Director:
  Nicholas C Wells

Svenska International plc

Svenska House
3-5 Newgate Street
London EC1A 7DA
Tel: 071 329 4467
Telex: 894716
Fax: 071 329 0036/7

Managing Director: Lars P Evander
Deputy Managing Director:
  Leif I Hedberg
Executive Director:
  John Berntsson
  Terry Hubble
  John G Ratner
  Yoshiyuki Takeuchi

Executive Director:
  David W H Teague
  Michael J Turner
  Hans-Eric von der Groeben
  Christopher S Weller
  Svante Wikstrom
Director:
  George Anastasi
  Claes G M Carlon
  David Clark
  Peter G Colmer
  Birgitta C Dahllof
  Andre P de Havilland
  Martin Hankey
  Noel Meredith
  Nicholas Miller
  Philip Moss
  Tom Prior
  David Ridgeon
  Leslie Vincent

Swedbank/Sparbankernas Bank

The Old Deanery
Dean's Court
London EC4V 5AA
Tel: 071 236 4060
Telex: 892458
Fax: 071 248 4712

Representative: S H Selin

Swiss American Securities

24 Bishopsgate
London EC2N 4BQ
Tel: 071 283 2284
Telex: 928291
Fax: 071 220 7558

Branch Manager: Peter R May

Swiss Bank Corporation

Swiss Bank House
1 High Timber Street
London EC4V 3SB
Tel: 071 329 0329
Telex: 887434 SBCO G
Fax: 071 329 8700

President: J A de Gier
Chief Executive: R Bogni
Chairman - Equities: R F Erith
Executive Director - Equities:
  A P Anderson
Executive Director - Human Resources:
  P T Cole
*Managing Director - Merchant
  Banking:* C L Badcock
*Managing Director - Commercial
  Banking:* W M Gabitass

Managing Director - Equities:
G E Vardey
Managing Director - Operations:
C W Abbott
Managing Director - Private Banking:
U Eberhardt
Managing Director - Treasury:
R V Zeltner
Director - Financial Control: S Myers
Consultant: The Rt
Hon David Howell MP

Swiss Cantobank (International)
5th Floor
Moor House, London Wall
London EC2Y 5ET
Tel: 071 920 9696
Telex: 8813560
Fax: 071 588 1313

General Manager: R E Staehli

Swiss Volksbank
48-54 Moorgate
London EC2R 6EL
Tel: 071 628 7777
Telex: 917777
Fax: 071 628 2786

Branch Manager: Alfred Huber
Deputy Branch Manager:
Lawrie Arduino

Syndicate Bank
2a Eastcheap
London EC3M 1AA
Tel: 071 626 9681
Telex: 894649
Fax: 071 283 3830

Deputy General Manager: U M Kini

T C Ziraat Bankasi
48 Bishopsgate
London EC2N 4AJ
Tel: 071 374 4554
Telex: 887582
Fax: 071 638 8332

General Manager: Resat M Duran

Taiheiyo Europe Ltd
74/78 Finsbury Pavement
London EC2A 1AT
Tel: 071 588 0603
Telex: 917139
Fax: 071 588 3469

Managing Director: T Wakabayashi
Director: J Arai

Target Group plc
Alton House
174-177 High Holborn
London WC1V 7AA
Tel: 071 836 8040
Telex: 269879
Fax: 071 836 4012

Chairman: David Thorn
Managing Director: Paul Taylor
Deputy Chairman: John Stone
Executive Director Finance:
John Rathbone
Executive Director Operations:
Paul Roberts
Director:
David Gordon
The Hon Robert Loder

Taylor Woodrow plc
10 Park Street
London W1Y 4DD
Tel: 071 499 8871
Telex: 22513
Fax: 071 629 5393

Life President: The Rt Hon
Lord Taylor of Hadfield
Chairman: P R L Drew OBE
*Chief Executive & Joint Managing
Director:* H A Palmer
Deputy Chairman: J Topping
*Deputy Chairman & Joint Managing
Director:* P Hedges
Joint Managing Director: W Hogbin
Director:
G B Borwell
J Millar
C J Parsons
R G Smith
Lady Taylor
Finance Director: D A Green
Non-Executive Director:
The Rt Hon Lord Bellwin JP
C E A Hambro

Templeton Unit Trust Managers Limited
13 Atholl Crescent
Edinburgh EH3 8HA
Tel: 031 228 3932
Fax: 031 228 4506

Director:
Douglas W Adams
Dickson B Anderson
Martin L Flanagan
Kenneth J Greig
Thomas L Hansberger

Tesco plc
Tesco House
Delamare Road
Cheshunt EN8 9SL
Tel: 0992 32222
Telex: 24138
Fax: 0992 30794

Chairman: Sir Ian Maclaren
Finance Director: D E Reid
Company Secretary: R S Ager
Treasurer: R Howell

Texaco Ltd
1 Knightsbridge Green
London SW1X 7QJ
Tel: 071 584 5000

Financial Director: J Gatens

The Thai Farmers Bank Ltd
80 Cannon Street
London EC4N 6HH
Tel: 071 623 4975
Telex: 8811173
Fax: 071 283 7437

Manager: Pipat Visuttiporn

The Thomson Corporation
180 Wardour Street
London W1A 4YG
Tel: 071 437 9787

Group Treasurer: M Jones
Financial Planning Adviser:
S J H Coles
Company Secretary: M D Knight

Thorn EMI plc
4 Tenterden Street
Hanover Square
London W1A 2AY
Tel: 071 355 4848
Telex: 935825

Chairman and Chief Executive:
C G Southgate
Finance Director: M E Metcalf
Director of Taxation & Treasury:
Mrs P M Scott
Group Financial Controller:
W R Murray

Thornton Management Limited
33 Cavendish Square
London W1M 0DH
Tel: 071 493 7262
Telex: 923061
Fax: 071 409 0590

Chairman: Richard C Thornton
Finance Director: D C Pinckney
Managing Director: P Dew
Director:
L Aitkenhead
A C B Chancellor
S Neritt
G Steffens
H Wunderlich

Tokai International Limited
Mercury House
Triton Court, 14 Finsbury Square
London EC2A 1DR
Tel: 071 638 6030
Telex: 8812649 TOKINT G
Fax: 071 588 5875

Managing Director: A Murakami

Tokyo Securities Co (Europe) Ltd
1 London Wall Buildings
London Wall
London EC2M 5PP
Tel: 071 248 0433
Telex: 8811484
Fax: 071 248 0106

Managing Director: S Omata
Director: R Shirao
Company Secretary: S Takenaka

Top Technology Limited
20/21 Tooks Court
Cursitor Street
London EC4A 1LB
Tel: 071 242 9900
Fax: 071 405 2863

Chairman: Peter Hill-Wood
Marketing Manager:
Kimberley Johnson

The Toronto-Dominion Bank
Triton Court
14/18 Finsbury Square
London EC2A 1DB
Tel: 071 920 0272
Telex: 886142
Fax: 071 638 1042

Vice President & Regional Treasurer:
R E Burgess
Vice President, Corporate Finance:
H W Rising
Assistant General Manager, Corporate Finance: J G See
Assistant General Manager, Credit:
M Walzak

Assistant General Manager, Foreign Exchange/Money Market:
R H Guest
Assistant General Manager, Operations: G J O'Mahoney
Senior Manager, Capital Markets:
P Roberts

Torrie & Co
37 Frederick Street
Edinburgh EH2 1EP
Tel: 031 225 1766
Fax: 031 220 2363

Senior Partner: J Torrie

Touche Remnant & Co
Mermaid House
2 Puddle Dock
London EC4V 3AT
Tel: 071 236 6565
Telex: 885703
Fax: 071 248 9756

Chairman and Chief Executive:
P V S Manduca
Senior Managing Director:
H J Gittings
Sir William Vincent
Director:
L W Baker
P J Bushnell
M I Henderson
L R Maclean
J R Pratt
J Sorrell
C E Tiplady

Touche Remnant Investment Management Ltd
Mermaid House
2 Puddle Dock
London EC4V 3AT
Tel: 071 236 6565
Telex: 885703
Fax: 071 248 9756

Chairman and Chief Executive:
P V S Manduca
Chief Investment Officer:
Sir William P M Vincent
Director:
J R Alexander
B J D Ashford-Russell
F P L Bedwell
P J Bushnell
J S Curtis
G S de Nemeskeri-Kiss
P J Duffy
J R S Escott

Director:
H J Gittings
M W Hammond
N B Holliday
S L Hunter-Jones
C J Kirman
M B Moule
S V Peak
J R Pratt
M J Watt
P G D Wolf

Town & Country Building Society
215 Strand
London WC2R 1AY
Tel: 071 353 2438
Fax: 071 583 2933

Chairman: Terence S Mallinson
Managing Director: I Bell
Deputy Chief Executive: B J Grinyer
General Manager: D B Hind
Secretary: G Maydon

The Toyo Trust & Banking Company Ltd
5th Floor, Bucklersbury House
83 Cannon Street
London EC4N 8AJ
Tel: 071 236 4020
Telex: 885619
Fax: 071 236 5319

General Manager: C Hikokubo

Toyo Trust International Limited
36 Queen Street
London EC4R 1BN
Tel: 071 236 5272
Telex: 8811456
Fax: 071 236 5316

Managing Director: Shoji Wakita

Trafalgar House Public Limited Company
1 Berkeley Street
London W1A 1BY
Tel: 071 499 9020
Telex: 921341
Fax: 071 493 5484

Chairman: Sir Nigel Broackes
Deputy Chairman and Chief Executive: Eric W Parker
Finance Director: John R W Ansdell
Director:
D M Calverley
John W S Fletcher

Director:
Allan G Gormly
Vincent A Grundy
Dermot St J McDermott
Non-Executive Director:
Geoffrey H B Carter
Alan W Clements
Geoffrey E Knight
Dr T A Ryan
The Marquess of Tavistock
Director and Secretary: Ian Fowler
Group Treasurer:
C Simon Thompson

Tranwood Earl & Company Limited
123 Sloane Street
London SW1X 9BW
Tel: 071 824 8181
Telex: 932016
Fax: 071 730 5770

Executive Chairman: Peter R S Earl
Managing Director:
Jeremy S Thompson
Director:
John W A Gilmore
Desmond G Mitchell
Paul A Newman
Ms Emma E Saunders

J Trevor, Montleman & Poland Ltd
Wigham House
16-30 Wakering Road
Barking
Essex IG11 8PB
Tel: 081 594 7222
Telex: 263695
Fax: 081 594 4907

Chairman: Michael G Livingstone
Managing Director: G W
Roy Beckley
Director:
Brian J Hinchcliffe
Brian G Montleman
Michael A Robinson
Non-Executive Director & Company Secretary: Michael S Clarke
Non-Executive Director:
John C Trevor

Triland Metals Ltd
Bow Bells House
Bread Street
London EC4M 9BQ
Tel: 071 236 5551
Telex: 888677

Chairman: T Nishimura
General Manager & Director: B Staley
Director: F Shibuya

Trust Bank of Africa
90 Long Acre
London WC2E 9SE
Tel: 071 236 7424
Telex: 886258
Fax: 071 236 1945

General Manager: O D Grobler

Trusthouse Forte plc
166 High Holborn
London WC1V 6TT
Tel: 071 836 7744
Telex: 264678
Fax: 071 240 9611

Group Treasurer: M Grossfeld

TSB Bank Scotland plc
PO Box 177
Henry Duncan House
120 George Street
Edinburgh EH2 4TS
Tel: 031 225 4555
Telex: 727512
Fax: 031 220 0240

Chairman: J H
Forbes Macpherson CBE
Chief Executive: C M Love
Executive Director:
A C Dempster
R McGregor
Finance Director: J McConville

TSB Group plc
25 Milk Street
London EC2V 8LU
Tel: 071 606 7070
Telex: 8812487
Fax: 071 606 0510

Chairman: Sir Nicholas Goodison
Deputy Chairman:
P Charlton
Sir Robert Clark
Sir Ian Fraser
Chief Executive: D C McCrickard
Executive Director:
H Donaldson
P B Ellwood
D C Mootham
D B Thorn
Director:
D M Backhouse
L Bolton
W M Carson

Director:
M H Field
R R Jeune
Sir Richard Lloyd
J H F Macpherson
Lady Jane P G Prior
N J Robson
Secretary: P W S Rowland

TSB Unit Trusts Limited
Charlton Place
Andover SP10 1RE
Tel: 0264 56789
Telex: 477018
Fax: 0264 50091

Managing Manager: G G Gray
Director:
P A Brooks
B M J Brown
F W R Stocks

Tullett & Tokyo Forex International Ltd
Cable House
54-62 New Broad Street
London EC2M 1JJ
Tel: 071 895 9595
Telex: 884997
Fax: 071 895 0819

Chairman: D Tullett
Deputy Chairman: M J L Everett
Managing Director:
T J R Sanders
A J Styant
Director:
S J Otterburn
M E Rowley
D J Tuffley
Company Secretary: D L Lowe

Turkish Bank Ltd
84-86 Borough High Street
London SE1 1LN
Tel: 071 403 5656
Telex: 8955666 TURBOR-G
Fax: 071 407 7406

Assistant General Manager & Local Director: E Neng

Turkiye Garanti Bankasi AS
141 Fenchurch Street
London EC3M 6BL
Tel: 071 626 3803
Telex: 8813102
Fax: 071 929 5582

Representative: I Nebioglu

Tyndall Holdings plc
25 Bucklersbury
London EC4N 8TH
Tel: 071 248 3399
Telex: 914684
Fax: 071 236 4547

Chairman: Christopher Spence
Managing Director: Garnet Harrison
Director:
   N Jonathan Bradley
   Peter Glossop
   Kevin A Kenny
   Ian Meier
   James Mellon
Director (Finance): Richard Horton

UBAF Bank Limited
30 Gresham Street
London EC2V 7LP
Tel: 071 606 7777
Telex: 22961
Fax: 071 600 3318

Director:
   I Cotterill
   J de Mandat-Grancey
   G A Freestone
   S Toker
Chief Executive: P J W Taplin
*Deputy Chief Executive & General
   Manager:* Mohamed Fezzani
Assistant General Manager:
   A D Holloway
   Ahmed Khalil

UBS Phillips & Drew Futures Limited
100 Liverpool Street
London EC2M 2RH
Tel: 071 901 3333
Telex: 923333
Fax: 071 901 2345

Chairman & Director: R G Mueller
Vice-Chairman & Director:
   C J Lewis
   H W H Sants
Director:
   M H Burns
   N J R Ryan
   P J Williams
Executive Director & Head of Sales:
   Ms C Furse

UBS Phillips & Drew Gilts Limited
100 Liverpool Street
London EC2M 2RH

Tel: 071 901 3333
Telex: 923333
Fax: 071 901 2345

Chairman & Director: R G Mueller
Vice-Chairman & Director:
   C J Lewis
Director:
   M H Burns
   R L Lawrence

UBS Phillips & Drew Intl Investment Ltd
Triton Court
14 Finsbury Square
London EC2A 1PD
Tel: 071 588 7114
Telex: 926454
Fax: 071 628 9417

Executive Chairman:
   Paul M Meredith
Managing Director:
   Jim P McCaughan

UBS Phillips & Drew Securities Limited
100 Liverpool Street
London EC2M 2RH
Tel: 071 901 3333
Telex: 923333
Fax: 071 901 2345

Chairman: R G Mueller
*Vice-Chairman Head of Corporate
   Finance:* S J M Brisby
Vice-Chairman Head of Debt:
   C J Lewis
Vice-Chairman Head of Equities:
   H W H Sants
*Managing Director Finance &
   Accounting:* P R Bennett
Managing Director UK Trading:
   J S Dalby
*Managing Director Intl Corporate
   Finance:* M Rohrbasser
*Managing Director UK Corporate
   Finance:* M L B Emley
Managing Director Head of Research:
   W T Seward

Uco Bank
Finsbury House
23 Finsbury Circus
London EC2M 7UY
Tel: 071 256 7435
Telex: 916456
Fax: 071 374 2230

Deputy General Manager:
   H N Maskara

Ulster Bank Limited
PO Box 232
47 Donegall Place
Belfast BT1 5AU
Tel: 0232 320222
Telex: 747334
Fax: 0232 328243/322097

Chairman: Dr G Quigley
Deputy Chairman: Victor Chambers
Executive Director & Chief Executive:
   David Went
Executive Director:
   Ronald D Kells
   Brian W McConnell
   John J McNally

Ulster Development Capital Limited
1 Arthur Street
Belfast BT1 4GA
Tel: 0232 246765
Fax: 0232 232982

Chairman: Victor Chambers
Chief Executive:
   Edmund W Johnston
Director:
   Derek Cheatley
   Leo Conway
   Denis Desmond
   Frank Ledwidge

Ultramar plc
141 Moorgate
London EC2M 6TX
Tel: 071 256 6080
Telex: 885444
Fax: 071 256 8556

Chairman: J O R Darby
Group Chief Executive Officer:
   J Gaulin
Director: L Bensen
*Executive Chief Exploration and
   Production Officer:* R W Bland
Executive Director of Ultramar plc:
   D O Elton
Group Chief Administrative Officer:
   E K O'Shea
Group Chief Financial Officer:
   P L Raven
*Managing Director, North Sea &
   European Exploration and
   Production:* W J Sheptycki
Secretary & Legal Co-ordinator:
   T J Hunt
Special Projects Co-ordinator:
   R J Martin

Finance Co-ordinator: H G Pearl
Manager, Corporate Affairs:
    C S Smith

Unibanco-Uniao de Bancos Brasileiros
22 Lovat Lane
London EC3R 8EB
Tel: 071 621 0965
Telex: 886740
Fax: 071 621 9504

Representative: N R Infante

Unibank plc
3rd Floor
107 Cheapside
London EC2V 6DA
Tel: 071 726 6000
Telex: 924123
Fax: 071 726 4638

Chief Executive: Carsten Esphavn
    Jensen
Director:
    J J Bennett
    W E Davis
    P Dodds
Secretary: R W Kempen
Executive Director:
    P Green Lauridsen
    M Lister
    J Mellor
    K Tofte Jensen

Unigate plc
Unigate House
58 Wood Lane
London W12 7RP
Tel: 081 749 8888
Telex: 927592
Fax: 081 749 7166

Chairman & Chief Executive:
    John Clement
Board Member:
    Andrew R Dare
    Sir Brian Kellett
    John S Kerridge
    Ernest H Sharp
    A W P (Cob) Stenham
    John G Worby
    R David Yeomans
Secretary: Nicholas G U Morris
Group Treasurer: Michael Turner-
    Samuels

Unilever plc
Unilever House
PO Box 68
Blackfriars
London EC4P 4BQ
Tel: 071 822 5252
Telex: 28395
Fax: 071 822 5951

Chairman: Sir Michael Angus
Vice Chairman: F A Maljers
Director:
    J I W Anderson
    R W Archer
    M Dowdall
    P V M Egan
    H Eggerstedt
    N W A Fitzgerald
    A S Ganguly
    W K Grubman
    M G Heron
    C M Jemmett
    A Kemner
    C Miller Smith
    O O H Mueller
    J Peelen
    M S Perry
    M Tabaksblat
Secretary:
    J W B Westerburgen
    S G Williams
Controller: B F Atsma
Group Treasurer: P E Martin

Union Bank of Finland Ltd
46 Cannon Street
London EC4N 6JJ
Tel: 071 248 3333
Telex: 886144
Fax: 071 236 0450

General Manager: Carl-
    Johan Granvik
Assistant General Manager - Treasury:
    David Britton
Assistant General Manager - FX:
    Peter Holloway
*Assistant General Manager -
    Commercial Banking:*
    Theo Mezger
*Assistant General Manager - Finance &
    Operations:* Peter Mobsby

Union Bank of Norway
20 St Swithins Lane
London EC4N 8AD
Tel: 071 929 2391
Telex: 8951828

General Manager: P E Stevenson

Union Bank of Switzerland
122 Leadenhall Street
London EC3V 4QL
Tel: 071 901 6111
Telex: 887341/2
Fax: 071 929 4111

*First Vice President and Branch
    Manager:* P Braunwalder
Senior Vice President:
    M Rowlinson
    P Thrush
Executive Vice President:
    R G Mueller

The Union Discount Company of London plc
39 Cornhill
London EC3V 3NU
Tel: 071 623 1020
Telex: 886434
Fax: 071 626 9069

Chairman: Robin A E Herbert
Deputy Chairman: John R Sclater
*Deputy Chairman (Managing
    Director):* Graeme E Gilchrist
Director:
    William B Carmichael
    Brian S P Gent
    Derek J Lyons
    Robert M Munro
    George M Nissen
    The Rt Hon Lord Remnant
    Brian M Winterflood
Finance Director: George Lynn
Secretary: Richard J Vardy

Union International plc
13-16 West Smithfield
London EC1A 9JN
Tel: 071 248 1212

Finance Director: Michael Brand

United Biscuits (Holdings) plc
Grant House
PO Box 40
Syon Lane
Isleworth TW7 5NN
Tel: 081 560 3131
Telex: 8954657
Fax: 081 847 5302

Chairman & Chief Executive:
    R C Clarke
Deputy Group Chief Executive:
    F W Knight
Finance Director: J Blyth

Chief Executive European Operations:
  E L Nicoli
Director & Group Company Secretary:
  D R J Stewart
Vice Chairman: Sir Charles Fraser
Director:
  T M Garvin
  W P Gunn
  M A Heller
  Lady Howe
  Lord Plumb
  The Rt Hon Lord Prior PC
  N M Shaw
  T H Wyman
UK Treasurer: P Butler

United Dominions Trust Limited
116 Cockfosters Road
Barnet EN4 0DY
Tel: 081 449 5533
Fax: 081 449 2899

Chairman: H K Paton
Managing Director: J L Davies
Director:
  G R Bird
  M L Ingham
  M K Pedelty
  D K Potts
  K D Pusey
  G M L Skingley
  R L Sterry
Secretary: B J Marsh

United Mizrahi Bank Limited
Finsbury House
23 Finsbury Circus
London EC2M 7UB
Tel: 071 628 7040
Telex: 896654
Fax: 071 588 3361

General Manager: M Weber
Senior Manager: J Doherty

United Newspapers
Ludgate House
245 Blackfriars Road
London SE1 9UY
Tel: 071 921 5000
Telex: 892389
Fax: 071 928 2728

Financial Director: Graham Wilson

United Overseas Bank (Banque Unie Pour Les Pays d'Outre-Mer) Geneva
London Branch
103 Mount Street
London W1Y 5HE
Tel: 071 491 1530
Telex: 25119
Fax: 071 493 7925

General Manager: Michael F Deller
Manager of Trade Finance Department:
  Helene Cassaigne
*Manager of Private Banking
  Department:* Vincent Mahon
Operations Manager: Bruce Clarke

Vale & Weetman Ltd
111 Spencer Street
Birmingham B18 6DA
Tel: 021 554 1656
Telex: 333791
Fax: 021 554 2786

Director: T H Fletcher

Vauxhall Motors
Kimpton Road
Luton LU2 0SY
Tel: 0582 21122 Ext 6441

Treasurer: F Lara

Venture Link Investors Ltd
Tectonic Place
Holyport Road
Maidenhead
Berks SL6 2YG
Tel: 0628 771050
Fax: 0628 770392

Managing Director:
  John V Hatch
  Derek C Laval
  Anthony G Parkes
  Jonathan W Welfare
Non-Executive Director:
  Anthony J V Cheetham
  Harry C Partridge

Vojvodjanska Banka DD
308 Regent Street
London W1R 5AL
Tel: 071 734 8333/071 323 1707
Fax: 071 323 1669

Director: Mrs M Milicic

W B B Commodities Ltd
39 Hatton Garden
London EC1N 8BX

Tel: 071 242 5491
Telex: 262547
Fax: 071 831 7894

Managing Director: U C Zeretzke

W P P Group plc
27 Farm Street
London W1X 6RD
Tel: 071 408 2204
Fax: 071 493 6819

Chairman: David Ogilvy
Deputy Chairman: John R Symonds
Chief Executive Officer:
  Martin S Sorrell
Finance Director: Robert E Lerwill
Director:
  Jeremy J D Bullmore
  Stephen H M King
  John A Quelch
  Gordon C Sampson

Wako International (Europe) Ltd
Park House
16 Finsbury Circus
London EC2M 7DJ
Tel: 071 374 6055
Telex: 884029
Fax: 071 374 8611

Managing Director:
  Shuzo Nakamura
Deputy Managing Director:
  Kazuo Kinkozan
Compliance Officer: J T Moriyama

Walker Crips Weddle Beck plc
1st Floor, Sophia House
76/80 City Road
London EC1Y 2BJ
Tel: 071 253 7502
Telex: 291509
Fax: 071 253 7500

Chairman: L G Byford
Finance Director: M J Sunderland
Compliance Director: R Field
Administrative Director: S V Simper
Investorlink Director: N J Simmonds
Company Secretary: J M Newsome

S G Warburg Akroyd Rowe & Pitman Mullens Securities Ltd
1 Finsbury Avenue
London EC2M 2PA

Tel: 071 606 1066
Telex: 8952485/937011
Fax: 071 382 4800

Chairman: P S Wilmot-Sitwell
Director:
B J A Allain
F D Bacot
W E A Bain
O A G Baring
P Bass
J D Battye
K F Baugh
P Berwein
G P Blunden
H W Bolsterli
S J J Boswell
A L Brooke
C A M Buchan
D J S Burnett
T J Bush
J L Callahan
E Cameron-Watt
S P Carr
E J Chandler
D T H Clarke
W J Conn
M Cook
W S Cornish
G W Cossey
L G Cox
H de la Morinière
C V Dinwiddy
A P W Durrant
C N J Edwards
C R J Eglington
M J Ekers
S T Ellen
C C Ellerton
P F Ellick
N R Elwes
R M Eynon
K M Feeny
R F Fitzpatrick
D C G Framhein
D A Freud
M G D Giedroyc
J D Goodwin
M L Gordon
J R Hall
J K Hamilton
P R Hamilton
N J Hanbury-Williams
P B Hardy
T R N Harrison-Topham
I Harwood
D J Haysey
M J Hesketh
R C Huff

Director:
A W V Ireland
Y Kamina
J H Leigh-Pemberton
L N Leuzzi
O M Lewisohn
U Lichtenberg
J N Littlewood
M J S Loveland
D C W Macdonald
V D Mackney
G Magnus
R C R Mallows
P J Mars
T J W Maxwell
J H McDowell
D W J McGirr
H N Millward
G P D Milne
J W Morosani
R A S Offer
G W Pilkington
K J Pitcher
P C B Pockney
C T B Purvis
A J Radcliffe
C L Reilly
R J Rhodes
N Rubner
D K L Ruck Keene
M C Sargent
J W Sheppard
M Spierenburg
J C G Stancliffe
R Steel
R K Steggle
J M Stewart
S R Stradling
C H Symington
N R Tapner
J J Tholstrup
M N B Thompson
P Thompson
N Tsuchiya
K Tsugawa
H C van der Wyck
H N Verey
J D A Wallinger
C E Wallis
R G Ward
M R Williamson
J C Woodman

S G Warburg & Co Ltd

2 Finsbury Avenue
London EC2M 2PA
Tel: 071 860 1090
Telex: 22941
Fax: 071 382 4800

Joint Chairman:
The Rt Hon The Earl Cairns
H C van der Wyck
Deputy Chairman: O M Lewisohn
Vice Chairman:
A D Loehnis CMG
A K Stewart-Roberts
Director:
M E S Adda
D V Allatt
L Arber
J W Bailey
S W S Barnes
O H Bayoumi
D M M Beever
R P Binks
J D Birney
J R S Boas
R F Budenberg
A D Burton
E Cazaly
J W J Coleman
T C Colville
K J Costa
N J Coulson
A N C Defriez
J F Difford
M Dwek
M B Edelshain
A C R Elliott
K D Elliott
D S Fielden
M H Fisher
N R L Fry
R A J Gillespie
H M Glyn Davies
P A Gómez-Baeza
M B G Gore
R W J Hardie
M R Hardwick
D A Higgs
D C D Hobley
M E A Innes
A B S Jackson
H Kahnamouyipour
P C Keevil
A Kidel
S Latner
S W Leathes
J W Ledóchowski
E R Macdonald
K R P Marshall
J C Mayo
J W Mayo
Sir Ronald McIntosh KCB
M P Nicholls
P T Orchart
P Ottolenghi
D J Procter

Director:
A J Reizenstein
H F Richardson
Marchese G L Salina Amorini
C A P Scholtes
J P Scott
D G Seligman
M D Seligman
M A Smith
P M Spensley
F J Stobart
P J Thompson
A E L Trollip
J F Trueman
P Twachtmann
P von Simson
N J Wakefield
J L Walker-Haworth
A R Withers
S Yamada
P S Zuckerman

S G Warburg Group plc
1 Finsbury Avenue
London EC2M 2PA
Tel: 071 606 1066
Telex: 937011/8952485
Fax: 071 382 4800

President:
H Grunfeld
Lord Roll of Ipsden
Chairman: Sir David Scholey
Vice Chairman:
Earl Cairns
H C van der Wyck
P S Wilmot-Sitwell
Director:
M B G Gore
P B Hardy
D A Higgs
O M Lewisohn
J N Littlewood
A D Loehnis
J W Mayo
M C Sargent
J C G Stancliffe
H A Stevenson
A K Stewart-Roberts
P Stormonth Darling
M R Valentine
H N Verey
P von Simson
R G Ward
Non-Executive Director:
T Cedraschi
Sir Colin Corness
F R Hurn
Dr Horst K Jannott

Non-Executive Director:
Baron Kraijenhoff
A Solomon
T H Wyman

Wardley Investment Services International Limited
3 Harbour Exchange Square
London E14 9GJ
Tel: 071 955 5050
Telex: 920451 WISLON G
Fax: 071 955 5052

Managing Director: The Rt Hon The
Earl of Buckinghamshire
Investment Director:
C J Galleymore
I R Henderson
Administration Director: J Symes
*Company Secretary/Compliance
Officer:* D W Evans
Group Financial Controller:
J K Jeyakumar

Wardley Unit Trust Managers Limited
3 Harbour Exchange Square
London E14 9GJ
Tel: 071 955 5051
Telex: 920451 WISLON G
Fax: 071 955 5052

Chairman: The Rt Hon The Earl
of Buckinghamshire
Executive Director:
P D M Bridgman
I R Henderson
J K Jeyakumar
S McLaughlin
J Symes
*Company Secretary/Compliance
Officer:* D W Evans

Wasserstein Perella & Co International Ltd
10-11 Park Place
London SW1A 1LP
Tel: 071 499 4664
Fax: 071 495 2772

Managing Director: Jim Downing

Waters Lunniss & Co Ltd
Member of The Norwich &
Peterborough Group
5 Queen Street
Norwich NR2 4SG
Tel: 0603 622265
Fax: 0603 630127

Managing Director: R J Larner

R Watson & Sons Consulting Actuaries
Watson House
47-49 London Road
Reigate RH2 9PQ
Tel: 0737 241144
Telex: 946070
Fax: 0737 241496

Senior Partner: L J Martin
Partner:
G R Alexander
R G Ashurst
G McD Bell
M J de H Bell
J M Bibby
V J Chambers
P A Cockbain
J A Geddes
H Gracey
J M Hill
R P Jessett
J A Jolliffe
P A Kelly
P Lofthouse
R D Masding
M D May
N G Preston
I R Skinner
P N Thornton
J R Wigley
A J Wise
J T Woolhouse

Well Marine Reinsurance Brokers Limited
14 Trinity Square
London EC3N 4AA
Tel: 071 481 2935
Fax: 071 702 3007

Chairman: G H M Scutt
Director:
A S Dalton
N W Found
M A Hawkins
T L F Royle
K E Sandell
S P Scutt
Secretary: K R Woollgar

Wellcome plc
Unicorn House
160 Euston Road
London NW1 2BP
Tel: 071 387 4477
Telex: 8951486
Fax: 071 388 3530

Chairman: Sir Alistair Frame

Chief Executive: J W Robb
Vice President Research, Development and Medical, Burroughs WellcomeCo, USA:
Dr D W Barry
Research, Development and Medical, UK Director: Dr T M Jones
Director: D Godfrey
Operations Director:
J M T Cochrane
R C Devereux
K J Merrifield
Operations Director, USA: P R Tracy
Group Corporate Planning Director:
H Copestick
Group Finance Director: J R Precious
Group Personnel Director:
P T G Hobbs
Non-Executive Director:
Sir Michael Butler
A W Clausen
Dr A T James
J F Lever
Sir Alastair Pilkington
Secretary: H Mitchell
Finance Controller: D F Beeton
Head of Public Relations:
Dr M A Sherwood

Wellington Underwriting Agencies Limited

120 Fenchurch Street
London EC3M 5BA
Tel: 071 929 2811
Fax: 071 220 7234

Chairman: J O Prentice
Managing Director: A G Cooper
Director:
Sir Lindsay Alexander
T G S Busher
B Coleman
H R Dumas
A M England
R E George
C R Howel
W G Ibbett
J W Mayo
R J Morse
P D Morsman
G B Norrie
M W Petzold
A E Rout
A Taylor
Secretary: T G S Busher
Alternate Director:
P J Freeman
D M Golding

Alternate Director:
N E M Goulder
H C V Keeling
A A Waugh

Wendover Underwriting Agency Limited

3 St Helen's Place
London EC3 6AU
Tel: 071 628 1317
Fax: 071 628 1713

Chairman: A D Shead
Managing Director: A M Sladen
Finance Director: J A Loveless
Director:
J R Bovington
J W E Butcher
J R Cackett
A S Feasey
R J Ikin acii
J P Johnson
C L Nicolson
C T Seymour-Newton
Company Secretary: R A Godfrey

West Midlands Metropolitan Authorities Superannuation Fund

Finance Department
Civic Centre
St Peters Square
Wolverhampton WV1 1RL
Tel: 0902 312089
Telex: 335060
Fax: 0902 314655

Director of Finance: B Bailey
Investment Manager: S B Summers

West Yorkshire Superannuation Fund

Britannia House
Hall Ings
Bradford BD1 1HX
Tel: 0274 752317
Telex: 51677
Fax: 0274 308016

Investment Manager: Stuart Imeson

Westdeutsche Landesbank Girozentrale

51 Moorgate
London EC2R 6AE
Tel: 071 638 6141
Telex: 887984
Fax: 071 374 8546

General Manager:
John Gilbert

General Manager:
Reinhold Mestwerdt
Managing Director, WestLB UK Ltd:
Thomas Gaffney
Hans Leukers

Westlake & Co

(A division of Allied Provincial
Securities Ltd)
St Catherine's House
Notte Street
Plymouth PL1 2TW
Tel: 0752 220971
Telex: 45438
Fax: 0752 225846

Senior Director: B H Foster

Westpac Banking Corp

Westpac House
75 King William Street
London EC4N 7HA
Tel: 071 867 7000
Telex: 888641
Fax: 071 623 9428

General Manager - European Division:
Tony Aveling

White Foster Sheldon Daly & Co Ltd

96 Sandmere Road
London SW4 3JT
Tel: 071 710 6780
Telex: 49287

Managing Director: A S Smith
Director:
H A Pearson
C White

Williams de Broë plc

PO Box 515
6 Broadgate
London EC2M 2RP
Tel: 071 588 7511
Telex: 893277 G
Fax: 071 588 1702

Chairman and Chief Executive:
P H A Stanley
Non-Executive Director:
T P Lambrecht
Director:
D E Ackroyd
D A B Curling
Y A Gachoud
C E Lusty
J P Millar
D Ridley
Ms E Smith

Director:
N R Woodifield
A W F Wright
Company Secretary: D J Heigham

Williams Holdings plc
Pentagon House
Sir Frank Whittle Road
Derby DE2 4XA
Tel: 0332 364257
Telex: 37685
Fax: 0332 295339

Group Treasurer:
Brian Cunningham

Willis Corroon plc
Ten Trinity Square
London EC3P 3AX
Tel: 071 488 8111
Telex: 882141
Fax: 071 488 8223

Executive Chairman: R J Elliott
Chief Executive: R M Miller
Chief Financial Officer:
J V H Robbins
Executive Director:
A A Gregory
R B Keville
D R King
J R Lamberson
J B Wallace
Non-Executive Director:
R F Corroon
A T Gregory
M R Rendle
J M Rodgers
A Sykes
A I Vorys
Secretary:
J V Ambrose
M P Chitty

Wilson Smithett & Cope Limited
PO Box 50
32 St Mary at Hill
London EC3R 8LT
Tel: 071 623 3111
Telex: 883983
Fax: 071 623 3351

Director:
C A J Bloggs
D L Cowley
R D Kissin

George Wimpey plc
26/28 Hammersmith Grove
London W6 7EN
Tel: 081 748 2000
Telex: 25666
Fax: 081 748 0076

Chairman: Sir Clifford Chetwood
Chief Executive: J A Dwyer
Managing Director, Homes:
R N Oliver
Managing Director, Engineering/
Technology/Canada/USA/Group
Services: R H Sellier
Finance Director: M J Dowdy
Director: G M Davies
Non Executive Director:
J D Birkin
P A M Curry
W P C Grassick
Dr D J T Graves
Group Secretary: D M Penton
Group Treasurer: M J Lavers

Winterflood Securities Ltd
Knollys House
47 Mark Lane
London EC3R 7QH
Tel: 071 621 0004
Fax: 071 623 9482

Chairman: Graeme Gilchrist
Managing Director:
Brian Winterflood
Finance Director: David Codd

Wintrust Securities
21 College Hill
London EC4R 2RP
Tel: 071 236 2360
Telex: 885493
Fax: 071 236 3842

Chairman: George Szpiro
Managing Director:
Richard D Szpiro

Wise Speke Ltd
Commercial Union House
39 Pilgrim Street
Newcastle upon Tyne NE1 6RQ
Tel: 091 261 1266
Telex: 537681
Fax: 091 261 1616

Chairman: C J Pumphrey
Director:
Sir David Chapman Bt
P Cooper
N T Garbutt
B J Gillespie

Director:
P B R Houghton
P T Howells
M Lyons
A Martell
T R P S Norton
S A S Phillips
C J Ring
N Sherlock
J A Speight
I B Speke
J W Wardle
G A Whitbourn
J J Wright
D W Youngman
Secretary: A J Brown
Financial Controller: G W Robson

Wood Gundy Inc
Cottons Centre
Cottons Lane
London SE1 2QA
Tel: 071 234 7100
Telex: 886752
Fax: 071 407 6453

Vice Chairman: John N Abell
Director:
R J Edge
N C Hobson
M J Keenan
D G Leith
A R Porter
G A Shaw

Woolwich Building Society
Corporate Headquarters
Watling Street
Bexley Heath
Kent DA6 7RR
Tel: 081 298 5000
Fax: 0322 555733

Chairman: C A McLintock
Deputy Chairman: The Rt Hon
Lord Thomson of Monifieth
Executive Vice Chairman:
Alan Cumming
Michael J Gibbs
Chief Executive: Donald H Kirkham
Executive Director:
Peter J Robinson
Michael E Tuke
General Manager:
Richard J Groom
Gordon M Law
Neil MacMahon
Brian D Rogles
Ray Scotter
David N G Small

Yamaichi Bank (UK) plc

Guildhall House
81-87 Gresham Street
London EC2V 7NQ
Tel: 071 600 1188
Telex: 919549
Fax: 071 600 1169

Managing Director & Chief Executive:
P W Bulfield
*Managing Director & General
Manager, Credit:* N Seki
General Manager, Treasury:
C R Grumball
*General Manager, Operations &
Administration:* D F Rogers
Deputy General Manager, Credit:
P Fickling
Manager, Banking:
M Clark
S Trevelyan

Yamaichi International (Europe) Limited

111-117 Finsbury Pavement
London EC2A 1EQ
Tel: 071 638 5599
Telex: 887414
Fax: 071 588 4602

Chairman: Taro Yamada
Deputy Chairman: John Sclater
Managing Director & Chief Executive:
Tokuo Ukon
*Managing Director & Company
Secretary:* Hiroshi Tajima
*Managing Director, Japanese Corporate
Investment Services:* Shigeichi Ito
Managing Director, Bond Sales:
Kozo Ono
*Managing Director, UK & European
Equities:* Yasunori Umezaki
Managing Director, Corporate Finance:
Michael Hutchinson
Keiichi Mitake
*Deputy Managing Director, Corporate
Finance:* Giles Bethenod
Deputy Managing Director, Syndicate:
David Butcher
*Deputy Managing Director, Corporate
Planning:* Isami Hata
*Deputy Managing Director, Bond
Trading:* Shinichi Kobuse
Deputy Managing Director, Syndicate:
Yasuo Konishi
*Deputy Managing Director, Japanese
Equity Sales:*
Shigeru Washizawa
*Executive Director, Japanese Stock
Trading:* Masao Asakawa

Executive Director, Money Markets:
Phillip Bloodworth
*Executive Director, UK & European
Equities:* David Butler
Executive Director, Corporate Finance:
Masaaki Fujimoto
*Executive Director, Japanese Equity
Sales:* Tony Furlong
Executive Director, Compliance:
Lyn Hall
Executive Director, Bond Trading:
Takeshi Inosaki
*Executive Director, Japanese Equity
Sales:* Masakazu Ishida
*Executive Director, Japanese Corporate
Investment Services:*
Motoji Ishikawa
Executive Director, Bond Sales:
Toshio Jinjugi
Executive Director, Bond Trading:
David Johnson-Biggs
*Executive Director, Japanese Stock
Trading:* Kazue Kido
Executive Director, Corporate Finance:
James Kyle
Executive Director, Personnel:
Kath Lawrence
*Executive Director, Investment
Strategy:* Neil MacKinnon
Executive Director, Bond Sales:
Brian Moriarty
*Executive Director, Japanese Equity
Sales:* Noriyasu Nakajo
Executive Director, Operations:
Shoji Nishihara
*Executive Director, Corporate
Planning:* John O'Donnell
Executive Director, Financial Control:
David Pinless
*Executive Director, UK & European
Equities:* Ichiro Sakamoto
Executive Director, Corporate Finance:
Hiroaki Shima
*Executive Director, UK & European
Equities:* Michael Simmonds
Executive Director, Corporate Finance:
Junichirou Taketani
Masahide Togawa
*Executive Director, Japanese Equity
Sales:* Takao Yoshitake

Yasuda Trust & Banking Co Ltd

1 Liverpool Street
London EC2M 7NH

Tel: 071 628 5721
Telex: 922040 YSDTBL G
Fax: 071 374 4941/4894

General Manager: T Uetadani

Yasuda Trust Europe Ltd

No 1 Liverpool Street
London EC2M 7NH
Tel: 071 256 6188
Telex: 915192
Fax: 071 374 0831/2

Managing Director:
Yoshio Mikoshiba
Deputy Managing Director:
Tsutomu Kameda
Executive Director:
Thomas Pomeroy

York Trust Group plc

3 Finsbury Square
London EC2A 1AD
Tel: 071 588 6272
Telex: 889341
Fax: 071 588 9210

Chairman: N R Balfour
Deputy Chairman: A M Hughes
Director:
J V Babcock
P G Barker
P J Vardigans
Finance Director: K M Mellors

Yorkshire Bank plc

20 Merrion Way
Leeds LS2 8NZ
Tel: 0532 441244
Telex: 556292
Fax: 0532 420733

Chairman: Lord Clitheroe
General Manager:
F Graham Sunderland
*Assistant General Manager (Retail
Banking):* Keith C F Simpson
*Assistant General Manager (Strategic
Planning):* David Knight
Controller:
Michael Allsopp
James S Fox
John C Howley
B Jones
David Mortimer
William Pickles
Andrew J Stapleton
Chief Inspector: Brian Sanderson
Regional Controller:
Albert Rounding
Keith A Sunley

Yorkshire Building Society

Yorkshire House
Westgate
Bradford BD1 2AU
Tel: 0274 734822
Fax: 0274 306031

Chairman: Roger W Suddards CBE
  DL
Chief Executive: D F Roberts
Chairman Elect: D K MacNaught
Director:
  H S Ambler JP
  J Atkinson
  F R Bentley
  Sir James F Hill
  S Rothery
  W P Ward
General Manager & Director:
  T A Smith
*General Manager (Marketing
  Premises):*

General Manager (Marketing
  D Anderson
  B W Davies
  P A Ireland
  R B Jackson

Yorkshire Enterprise Limited

Elizabeth House
Queen Street
Leeds LS1 2TW
Tel: 0532 420505
Fax: 0532 420266

Chairman: John Gunnell
Managing Director: Donald Law
Assistant Managing Director:
  Peter Claydon
Finance Director: Phillip Day
Company Secretary & Solicitor:
  James Gervasio

The Zenshinren Bank

London Representative Office
103 Cannon Street
London EC4N 5AD
Tel: 071 621 1763
Telex: 927776
Fax: 071 621 0782

Chief Representative: T Miura

Zivnostenska Banka NC

104-106 Leadenhall Street
London EC3A 4AA
Tel: 071 623 3201
Telex: 885451
Fax: 071 283 5372

Branch Manager: Jan Struž

INDEX OF
SERVICE COMPANIES &
ORGANISATIONS

PLEASE HELP MAKE OLD AGE DIFFERENT

Our Trust is engaged in Research Projects, Training Programmes, Award Schemes and the organisation of International Symposia, all with the shared objective of improving knowledge and standards of care for infirm elderly people.

Long life, good health, sustained dignity and happiness are what we wish each other. But wishes are not enough. In every family in the land members one day have to face up to frailty, physical disability, anxiety, often loneliness. Courage may be abundant, but it feeds on hope. Hope that, in the family 'Carer' in our own homes, in those who run residential homes, in those who treat our debilities and nurse us when there's need, there will be understanding, knowledge and loving help.

This is why we care greatly about Homes and standards, our own as much as others. Why we reward others for excellence in design and amenities. Why we provide rehabilitation, respite and long term care, and place great emphasis on sustaining ability and quality of life. Why we seek knowledge internationally and amongst our peers, and share it.

With our sister charity, the Royal Surgical Aid Society, we have just opened a brand new home which, from its inception to completion, demonstrates standards befitting the 21st Century. It, and our other homes, match our philosophy of 'Complete Care' — safe havens of excellent standard.

We depend on gifts for our building, research and training funds also for the sponsorship of care for poorer infirm people.

Please help. For information or a gift write to

DEVELOPMENT TRUST
FOR THE FRAIL OR PHYSICALLY DISABLED ELDERLY

Index of Service Companies & Organisations

Barristers

1 Brick Court
Temple
London EC4Y 9BY
Tel: 071 583 0777
Telex: 892687 1BRICK G
Fax: 071 583 9401

Head of Chambers:
    Christopher Clarke QC
Richard Aikens QC
Nicholas Chambers QC
Mark Cran QC
Nicholas Forwood QC
John Griffiths CMG, QC
Miss Hilary Heilbron QC
Jonathan Hirst QC
Sydney Kentridge QC
Sir Nicholas Lyell QC, MP
Philip L W Owen QC
Jonathan Sumption QC
David Vaughan QC
David Anderson
Gerald Barling
Peter Brunner
Timothy Charlton
David Garland
Nicholas Green
Mark Hapgood
Charles Hollander
Mark Howard
Peter Irvin
Cyril Kinsky
George Leggatt
David Lloyd Jones
Richard Lord
Julian Malins
Harry Matovu
Miss Catharine Otton-Goulder
Andrew Popplewell
Stephen Ruttle
The Hon Peregrine Simon
Richard Slade
Paul Walker
Martin White
William Wood

3 New Square
Lincoln's Inn
London WC2A 3RS
Tel: 071 405 5577
Fax: 071 404 5032

Head of Chambers:
    Sir William Goodhart QC
David Rowell

12 New Square
Lincoln's Inn
London WC2A 3SW
Tel: 071 405 3808
Fax: 071 831 7376

Head of Chambers:
    John Mowbray QC
Stuart Barber
Ross Crail
Sara Hill
Nicholas Le Poidevin
John Macdonald QC
Margaret McCabe
William Poulton
Charles Purle QC
Christopher Russell QC
Leigh Sagar
Stephen Smith
Claire Staddon
Lynton Tucker

13 Old Square
Lincoln's Inn
London WC2A 3UA
Tel: 071 404 4800
Telex: 22487
Fax: 071 405 4267

David Oliver QC

24 Old Buildings
Lincoln's Inn
London WC2A 3UJ
Tel: 071 404 0946
Telex: 94014909
Fax: 071 405 1360

Head of Chambers: C A Brodie QC

Lawrence Cohen
John Davies
Adrian Francis
Michael Gadd
Mrs Helen Galley
Daniel Gerrans
Roger Kaye QC
Michael King
Dennis Levy QC
Martin Mann QC
Stephen Moverley Smith
Richard Ritchie
Alan Steinfield QC
Paul Teverson
Miss Julienne Walker
Miss Elizabeth Weaver

4 Stone Buildings
Lincoln's Inn
London WC2A 3XT
Tel: 071 242 5524
Telex: 892300
Fax: 071 831 7907

Head of Chambers: Peter Currie QC
John Bertin
A G Bompas
John Brisby
Jonathan Crow
Malcolm Davis White
Edward Evans-Lombe QC
Peter Griffiths
Sarah J Harman
Philip Heslop QC
Robert Hildyard
Robert Miles
Rosalind Nicholson

7 Stone Buildings
Lincoln's Inn
London WC2A 3SZ
Tel: 071 405 3886/7
Telex: 071 242 3546
Fax: 071 242 8502

Patrick Howell QC
John Lindsay QC
David Unwin

4/5 Gray's Inn Square
Gray's Inn
London WC1R 5AY
Tel: 071 404 5252
Telex: 8953743
Fax: 071 242 7803/831 0202

Head of Chambers:
    Miss Elizabeth Appleby QC
Michael Beloff QC
Sam Aaron
Miss Genevra Caws
Stuart Isaacs
Julian Chichester
Mark Temleman
Jonathan R McManus
Hodge Malek
Peter Havey
Miss Jane Wilson
Kishore Sharma
Neil Calver
Senior Clerk: Leslie Page

1 Essex Court
Temple
London EC4Y 9AR
Tel: 071 583 2000
Telex: 889109 ESSEX G
Fax: 071 583 0118/071 353 8958

S J Burnton QC
C Carr QC
I B Glick QC
A S Grabiner QC
P L O Leaver QC
S A Stamler QC
N A Strauss QC
R U Thomas QC
A A R Thompson QC
S R Auld
M R P Barnes
R V M E Behar
Miss S J Benster
Miss J M Bernard
M G Bloch
W R Davies
Miss S P Fitzgerald
I D Grainger
C Graham
A P Griffiths
R M Hayward
G W Hobbs
T P G Ivory
V H Joffe
M E Jones
A Lenon
J McCaughran
A R Macgregor

K W Maclean
M J Malone
Miss M A F Morgan
J Onions
L Rabinowitz
T A E Sharpe
Miss F Stockton

3 Essex Court
Temple
London EC4Y 9AL
Tel: 071 583 9294
Telex: 893468
Fax: 071 583 1341

Head of Chambers:
    Anthony B R Hallgarten QC
Philip J Allott
Andrew Baker
Richard Bentham
Ms Elizabeth B Birch
Derek W Bowett QC
Edmund J Broadbent
Geraldine Clark
John G Collier
Julian H S Cooke
Clifford Gill
Nicholas A Hamblen
Christopher Hancock
A Mark D Havelock-Allan
David B Johnson QC
Elihu Lauterpacht QC
P Nicholas Legh-Jones QC
Stephen M Males
Duncan Matthews
Iain A Milligan
Martin J Moore-Bick QC
David Owen
Ms Patricia J Phelan
Murray A Pickering
Richard O Plender QC
Bernard A Rix QC
Kenneth S Rokison QC
Christopher C Russell
Sir Francis Vallat QC
Richard G Wood
Timothy N Young QC

Four Essex Court
Temple
London EC4Y 9AJ
Tel: 071 583 9191
Telex: 888465
Fax: 071 583 2422

Head of Chambers:
    Anthony Colman QC
Miss Geraldine Andrews

Steven Berry
Stewart Boyd QC
Simon Bryan
Michael Collins QC
Roderick Cordara
Simon Crookenden
Graham Dunning
Bernard Eder QC
David Foxton
Steven Gee
Jonathan Gilman QC
Angus Glennie
Jeffrey Gruder
Mrs Rosalyn Higgins QC
Ian Hunter QC
Richard Jacobs
David Joseph
John Lockey
Victor Lyon
David Mildon
Gordon Pollock QC
Malcolm Shaw
Richard Silberry
Mark Smith
Joe Smouha
John Thomas QC
Mrs Karen Troy-Davies
V V Veeder QC

7 King's Bench Walk
Temple
London EC4Y 7DS
Tel: 071 583 0404
Telex: 887491
Fax: 071 583 0950

Head of Chambers:
    Adrian Hamilton QC
Jeremy Cooke QC
Michael Dean QC
John Franklin Willmer QC
Andrew Longmore QC
Jonathan Mance QC
Stephen Tomlinson QC
David Bailey
Robert Bright
Christopher Butcher
Julia Dias
David Edwards
Adam Fenton
Julian Flaux
Jonathan Gaisman
Gavin Geary
Stephen Hofmeyr
Chirag Karia
Gavin Kealey
Dominic Kendrick
Stephen Kenny

Charles Priday
Timothy Saloman
Alistair Schaff
Richard Southern
Alastair Stewart-Richardson

·

Hamilton House
1 Temple Avenue
Victoria Embankment
London EC4Y 0HA
Tel: 071 353 0491
Fax: 071 353 4358

Head of Chambers:
   Mrs Clare Tritton QC

Abbott Mead Vickers plc
191 Old Marylebone Road
London NW1 5DW
Tel: 071 402 4100
Telex: 888876
Fax: 071 935 1642

Chairman: David Abbott
Chief Executive: Peter Mead
Finance Director: James McDanell
Director:
   Michael Baulk
   Adrian Vickers
Secretary: Peter Gill

Accountancy
40 Bernard Street
London WC1N 1LD
Tel: 071 833 3291
Telex: 884443
Fax: 071 833 2085

Editor: Brian Singleton-Green

Accountancy Age
VNU House
32-34 Broadwick Street
London W1A 2HG
Tel: 071 439 4242
Telex: 23918
Fax: 071 437 7001

Editor: Peter Williams
Associate Editor: Robert Bruce

Actuaries' Company
25 Thomas a Becket Close
Wembley
Middlesex
Tel: 081 904 9971

Clerk: P D Esslemont

Addleshaw, Sons & Latham
Dennis House
Marsden Street
Manchester M2 1JD
Tel: 061 832 5994
Telex: 668886
Fax: 061 832 2250

Senior Partner: R G M Dykstra
Managing Partner: D J Tully

The Age (Melbourne)
Suite 626, International Press
   Centre
76 Shoe Lane
London EC4A 3JB
Tel: 071 353 5193/9321

Financial Correspondent:
   Gideon Haigh

Agence France-Presse
Chronicle House
72/78 Fleet Street
London EC4Y 1HY
Tel: 071 353 7461
Telex: 28703
Fax: 071 353 8359

Bureau Chief: F Grangie

AIBD (Systems & Information) Limited
Seven Limeharbour
Docklands
London E14 9NQ
Tel: 071 538 5656
Telex: 8813069
Fax: 071 538 4902

Director:
   Patrick Brown
   Paul Dart
   Dr Osama El-Ansari
   Roy Lambert
   John Langton
   Pier Luigi Quattropani
   John Taylor
Company Secretary:
   Barry McCormack

Alexander Tatham
30 St Ann Street
Manchester M2 3DB
Tel: 061 236 4444
Telex: 666666
Fax: 061 832 5337

Senior Partner: Lionel Freedman
Head of Corporate Dept:
   John Boardman

Partner:
   Geoffrey Blower
   Peter Cole
   Ronald Graham
   Janet Knowles
   Edward Pysden
   Elizabeth Shepherd
   John Walsh

Allen & Overy
9 Cheapside
London EC2V 6AD
Tel: 071 248 9898
Telex: 8812801
Fax: 071 236 2192

Senior Partner: J M Kennedy
Managing Partner: A J Herbert
Finance Director: I M Dinwiddie
Administration Director: R J E Barker
Partner:
   A H Asher
   Anne E Baldock
   Alison M Beardsley
   P H D Bedford
   G G Beringer
   N M H Bird
   P E M Borrowdale
   J L F Brayne
   A T Brodie
   R M Brown
   Katherine A Buckley
   S P Chater
   P Chedgy
   A J C Clark
   R W L Cranfield
   P Crook
   R G Davies
   S R N Denyer
   M G Duncan
   J V O D Dunstan
   I F Elder
   M W Friend
   K G Godfrey
   J M Goodwin
   J Gould
   B W Harrison
   G Henderson
   A D Hewat
   P B Hockless
   P R J Holland
   J Horsfall Turner
   R Horsfall Turner
   G D Hudson
   D C Hughes
   A R Humphrey
   N D Johnson
   R J L Jones
   E W Jowett

Partner:
- A C Keal
- G J Kendall
- D E Lewis
- D L Mackie
- Clare M Maurice
- D M McGown
- C McKenna
- P M Mears
- P H T Mimpriss
- P N Monk
- C P Morgan
- D H Morley
- J A Morton
- W V W Norris
- P A Owen
- G M Parry
- A D Paul
- A M Pease
- M W Porter
- D Reid
- M J Reynolds
- J S Rink
- C K Roberts
- R A P Rowland
- K M T Ryan
- Julia A Salt
- M P Scargill
- P F Schulz
- J A Scriven
- N A Segal
- D S Sloan
- I G Stanley
- G C Stewart
- C W Stunt
- D StJ Sutton
- R H Sykes
- J D Thomas
- P G Totty
- H J Trembath
- W Tudor John
- R W C Turnor
- G D Vinter
- C R Walford
- P M Watson
- M R Welling
- B S Wells
- D L Williams
- G N Wilson
- P R Wood
- J P Wootton
- D H Wotton

Anderson, Squires Ltd
127 Cheapside
London EC2V 6BU
Tel: 071 606 1706
Fax: 071 726 4031

Chairman: J C Parkinson
General Manager: T Williams

Apothecaries' Society
Apothecaries' Hall
Blackfriars Lane
London EC4V 6EJ
Tel: 071 236 1180

Clerk: J C O'Leary

Arbitrators' Company
19 Tavistock Court
Tavistock Square
London WC1H 9NE
Tel: 071 387 4232

Clerk: J Minshull-Fogg TD

Armourers' & Brasiers' Company
Armourers' Hall
81 Coleman Street
London EC2R 5BJ
Tel: 071 606 1199

Clerk: Lt Col R F Cowe

Arthur Andersen & Co Chartered Accts
1 Surrey Street
London WC2R 2PS
Tel: 071 438 3000
Telex: 8812711
Fax: 071 831 1133

Managing Partner: R J Chapman
Partner:
- D J Ashton
- R W Burton
- D P G Cade
- D R Chester
- R M Cooke
- B M Currie
- D S Darbyshire
- R S Elfick
- M A Fishman
- S R Hailey
- P R Hinton
- D C Hughes
- A Hunking
- S M Kingsley
- D F Kirk
- I S Krieger
- V R Levy

Partner:
- R G Linger
- I D Luder
- R A Matthews
- W Meisenkothen
- T Minowa
- D J Murby
- P J Newman
- J C Norton
- C L Nunn
- M J Oaten
- J Ormerod
- C Pearson
- W I D Plaistowe
- P A Randall
- P R Ridley
- R J Simmons
- J A Talbot
- N F Temple
- J Wadia
- G A J Walker
- M J Wildig
- J N Woolf
- B Yeomans
- M S Zelkha

Ashurst Morris Crisp
Broadwalk House
5 Appold Street
London EC2A 2HA
Tel: 071 638 1111
Telex: 887067
Fax: 071 972 7990

Senior Partner: M G H Bell
Partner:
- D E P Albert
- C J Amos
- C J Ashworth
- L A Bailey
- A S Clark
- C D Crosthwaite
- C M Crosthwaite
- M D Cunliffe
- A A Dear
- J J Ellison
- J C Evans
- R J Finbow
- G S Green
- R S Gubbins
- W Innes
- R B James
- M C Johns
- D R Kershaw
- A W N Kitchin
- C J Leach
- D J MacFarlane
- S J Machin
- M A F MacPherson

Partner:
J N May
J A Nimmo
I B Nisse
D R Perks
L D Rutman
I R Scott
J N Sheldon
A J Soundy
E C A Sparrow
J A Sultoon
M J A Thum
C Vigrass
B M Walker
R B Walsom
J G Watson
G S Wheatcroft
M A Wippell
J Yolland

Association of British Consortium Banks
c/o UBAF Bank Ltd
30 Gresham Street
London EC2V 7LP
Tel: 071 606 7777
Telex: 22961
Fax: 01 600 3318

Chairman: G Legrain
Secretary: John W Mills

Association of British Insurers
Aldermary House
10/15 Queen Street
London EC4N 1TT
Tel: 071 248 4477
Telex: 937035
Fax: 071 489 1120

Chairman: T J Palmer CBE
Deputy Chairman:
R A G Neville
M J Pickard
Chief Executive: M A Jones

Association of Investment Trust Companies
6th Floor
Park House
16 Finsbury Circus
London EC2M 7JJ
Tel: 071 588 5347
Fax: 071 638 1803

Chairman: Michael J Hart
Deputy Chairman:
William T Carnegie
Mark R Cornwall-Jones

Deputy Chairman:
Paul V S Manduca
Secretary: James W Rath
Adviser: E Philip Chappell

Australian Financial Review
12 Norwich Street
London EC4
Tel: 071 353 9321
Telex: 262836
Fax: 071 583 0348

London Correspondent:
Joseph J Dowling

Baker Tilly
2 Bloomsbury Street
London WC1B 3ST
Tel: 071 413 5100
Telex: 8952387
Fax: 071 413 5101

Chairman: Richard J B Blake
Deputy Chairman: Roger Clark
Managing Partner: Clive Parritt
London Managing Partner:
David Knapman

Bakers' Company
Bakers' Hall
Harp Lane
Lower Thames Street
London EC3R 6DP
Tel: 071 623 2223

Clerk: P F Wilson DFC

The Banker
102-108 Clerkenwell Road
London EC1M 5SA
Tel: 071 251 9321/7
Telex: 23700
Fax: 071 251 4686

Editor: G Shreeve

Barbers' Company
Barber-Surgeons' Hall
Monkwell Square
London EC2Y 5BL
Tel: 071 606 0741

Clerk: Col A B Harfield CBE

The Barnes Partnership
Saddlers House
Gutter Lane
London EC2V 6DA
Tel: 071 606 1188
Fax: 071 796 4234

Chairman: J H Barnes

Managing Director: J M F Dixon
Director:
Ms L de Zulueta
H G Delves
Ms S R Powell

Basketmakers' Company
5 The Spinney
Warren Road
Purley
Surrey
Tel: 081 668 0757

Clerk: Denis J Farrier

BBC Television
Lime Grove Studios
Lime Grove
London W12 7RJ
Tel: 081 743 8000
Fax: 081 740 8549

Editor, The Money Programme:
David Nissan

BBC TV (Economics & Business Unit)
Television Centre, Room 7090
Spur
Wood Lane
London W12 7RJ
Tel: 081 576 7485
Fax: 081 746 0787

Economics Correspondent:
Graham Ingham
Steve Levinson
Business Correspondent:
Iain Carson
Peter Morgan
Industrial Correspondent: John Fryer

BBM Associates
76 Watling Street
London EC4M 9BJ
Tel: 071 248 3653
Fax: 071 248 2814

Partner:
Kevin Byrne
Ms Susan A L Mummé
Consultant (Capital Markets):
Andrew Stewart
Consultant (Equities & Fund Management): Nick Bennett
Consultant (Corporate Finance):
Jane Hayes
Niall MacNaughton

BDO Binder Hamlyn

20 Old Bailey
London EC4M 7BH
Tel: 071 489 9000
Telex: 8812282
Fax: 071 489 6060

Senior Partner: The Lord Lane
   of Horsell
Chairman, BDO Policy Board:
   John Norton
National Managing Partner:
   Chris Swinson
London Managing Partner:
   Adrian Burn
National Director, Marketing:
   James Broomfield
National Director, Finance:
   John Deane
National Director, Professional
   Services: Martin Gairdner
National Director, Training:
   Peter Smith
National Director, Personnel:
   David Westcott
Director, Private Client Services:
   Frank Akers-Douglas
Director, Corporate Services:
   Richard Hall
Director, Company Tax Services:
   Paul Morris
Managing Director, Binder Hamlyn
   Investment Management:
   Paul Cattermull

BDO Consulting

20 Old Bailey
London EC4A 4DA
Tel: 071 489 9000
Telex: 8812282
Fax: 071 489 6060

Chairman: Chris Swinson
Managing Director: William Casey
Director:
   John Bishop
   Simon Bryan
   Adrian Burn
   Alistair Durie
   Ronald A Fisher
   Rodney Graves
   Paul James
   Anthony Leon
   Michael Mainelli
   James Scott
   John Stubbs
   Paul Taffinder

Beachcroft Stanleys

20 Furnival Street
London EC4A 1BN
Tel: 071 242 1011
Telex: 264607 BEALAW G
Fax: 071 831 6630

Chief Executive: James A Kennedy
Senior Partner: Andrew D Kennedy
Partner:
   Elizabeth J Adams
   Malcolm P Alistwick
   Trevor Blythe
   Peter A Brazel
   Ian E Cairns
   Tony Cherry
   Richard C Evans
   Barry H Francis
   George P Francis
   Julian A Gizzi
   C Nicholas Hall
   Simon J Hodson
   David J F Hunt
   John R Hurdley
   Peter J L Illion
   Julian S Korn
   Peter A Kraus
   Ivan M H Kremer
   Philip A Lawrence
   Lawrence P Markham
   Steven M E Mitchell
   David R P Morgan
   Philip Murphy
   Richard Pain
   Robert F J Parsons
   John C Phelps
   Jean E Richards
   Kenneth Ridehalgh
   Paul C M Solon
   Gay E Wilder
   Christopher J Wilkes

Beavis Walker

14 Southampton Place
London WC1A 2AJ
Tel: 071 430 1111
Fax: 071 831 0439

Senior Partner: Simon Noakes
Partner:
   Peter Bennetts
   Peter Drown
   Simon Hammerton
   John Handley
   Peter Hoskin

Beharrell, Thompson & Co

(Solicitors in association with
Coudert Brothers International
Attorneys)
4 Dean's Court
London EC4V 5AA
Tel: 071 895 9668
Telex: 887071
Fax: 071 236 4349

Resident Partner:
   Steven R Beharrell
   Hugh E Thompson

S J Berwin & Co

236 Grays Inn Road
London WC1X 8HB
Tel: 071 278 0444
Telex: 8814928
Fax: 071 833 2860

Senior Partner: Christopher F Haan
Partner:
   Charles Abrams
   Alan Aisbett
   Peter W Anderson
   Rhonda Baker
   Jonathan E Blake
   Martin J Bowen
   Robert P Burrow
   Peter J Davis
   Brian Eagles
   John Eldridge
   Bruce Gardner
   Josyane R Gold
   Philip Goldenberg
   David T D Harrel
   Nicholas A C Higham
   Ian A E Insley
   Stephen D Kon
   Graeme D Levy
   Julian D M Lew
   Peter McInerney
   Jonathan A Metliss
   Russell Mishcon
   Neil Morrison
   Graham J Nicholson
   John M Osler
   Nigel S Palmer
   Colin R H Paul
   Bryan J Pickup
   Michael Rose
   David S Ryland
   Nicholas Shattock
   Adrian Shipwright
   Peter F Simpson
   Gillian S Smith
   Jeffrey S Smith
   Tim Taylor
   Patricia E Thomas

Partner:
Michael A Trask
Nicola S Walker
Kim Walkling
John F G Williams
Stephen P Willson
Martin Wright
Consultant:
Lord Clinton-Davis
Denis J Ross
Jonathan M L Stone
Executive Management:
Michael Crawford
Paul Rylance
Jeremy Seale
Keith Wood

Berwin Leighton
Adelaide House
London Bridge
London EC4R 9HA
Tel: 071 623 3144
Telex: 886420
Fax: 071 623 4416

Chairman of Board: M H Brummer
Principal Executive: O M Harpur
Head of Corporate Finance Dept:
B J Bartlett
Head of Property Department:
R M Buck
Head of Litigation Dept: M G Wilson
Head of Tax Dept: R E Downhill
Head of Shipping: M D Robinson
Head of Planning: W N Taylor
Head of Banking: E M Palley
Head of Construction: M R Gibson
Head of Commercial & European Law:
L H Evans
Marketing Partner: L H Evans
Staff Partner: L H A Homan
Senior Partner:
V W Benjamin
G M Chinn
J R Fenner
L Heller
E Sibley
N Sinclair
Finance Director: M J B Winkworth

Bingham Dana & Gould
39 Victoria Street
London SW1H 0EE
Tel: 071 799 2646
Telex: 888179
Fax: 071 799 2654

Resident Partner:
E H Parker
J S Zimmerman

Birmingham Post
Clan House
19-21 Tudor Street
London EC4Y 0LA
Tel: 071 353 0811
Telex: 337552
Fax: 071 353 1762

City Editor: Nevill Boyd Maunsell

Blacksmith's Company
27 Cheyne Walk
Grange Park
London N21 1DB
Tel: 081 364 1522

Clerk: R C Jorden

BMP Business
54 Baker Street
London W1M 1DJ
Tel: 071 486 5566
Fax: 071 486 0763

Managing Director: S Anson
Director of New Business Development:
J Hoare
Creative Director: A Melsom
Executive Director:
J Horsfall
J Hudson
M Innes

Booth & Co
P O Box 8
Sovereign House
South Parade
Leeds LS1 1HQ
Tel: 0532 832000
Telex: 557439
Fax: 0532 832060

Senior Partner: George H Cox
Partner (Head of Department):
Maurice C Cowen
Partner:
William F Charnley
Mark A Chidley
Ian W McIntosh
John B Morgan
G H Neville Peel
T Ian Roberts
W Lennox Towers
Timothy J Wheldon

Bowyer's Company
2 Serjeants' Inn
London EC4Y 1LL
Tel: 071 353 5385

Clerk: A Black CBE, DL

Bracewell & Patterson
43 Brook Street
London W1Y 2BL
Tel: 071 355 3330
Telex: 261414
Fax: 071 629 2621

Partner: Kevin J Alexander

Brewers' Company
Brewers' Hall
Aldermanbury Square
London EC2V 7HR
Tel: 071 606 1301

Clerk: R/Admiral M
La T Wemyss CB

Bristows Cooke & Carpmael
10 Lincoln's Inn Fields
London WC2A 3BP
Tel: 071 242 0462
Telex: 27487
Fax: 071 242 1232/071 831 3537

Commercial Conveyancing Partner:
Michael J Rowles
Edward F Williams
Commercial Litigation Partner:
Kevin E Appleton
Nigel R Cornwell
Richard de Ste Croix
James J S Hudson
Ian A Scott
Company Commercial Partner:
Q G Paul Cooke
Dan W Graham
John D Lace
Edward J Nodder
Intellectual Property Partner:
John P M Allcock
David J C Brown
Laurence J Cohen
Simon H Cooke
Sally A Field
Alan Johnson
Ian M Judge
Paul A Walsh
Philip G Westmacott

British Bankers Association
10 Lombard Street
London EC3V 9EL
Tel: 071 623 4001
Telex: 888364
Fax: 071 283 7037

President: Sir Jeremy Morse
Senior Vice-President:
Sir John Quinton
Vice-President: Sir Martin Jacomb

Chairman: H T Norrington
Deputy Chairman: R T Fox
Secretary General: Lord Inchyra
Senior Deputy Secretary:
  M N Karmel
Press & Information Officer:
  Mrs Pauline Hedges

The British Insurance and Investment Brokers' Association

BIIBA House
14 Bevis Marks
London EC3A 7NT
Tel: 071 623 9043

Chairman: H R L Lumley
Deputy Chairman:
  G J Hayman
  B R Marsh
  J L McKirdy
  H M J Ritchie

British Merchant Banking and Securities Houses Association

6 Frederick's Place
London EC2R 8BT
Tel: 071 796 3606
Fax: 071 796 4345

Chairman: Sir Martin Jacomb
Director General: H Robin Hutton
Chairman's Committee:
  J G W Agnew
  Hon Sir John Baring
  R A Brooks
  Sir Evelyn de Rothschild
  J G Heimann
  I A N McIntosh
  C K R Nunneley
  M A Smith
  P S Wilmot-Sitwell

Broad Street Associates PR Ltd

30 Furnival Street
London EC4A 1JE
Tel: 071 831 3113
Fax: 071 831 7961

Chairman and Chief Executive:
  Brian Basham
Managing Director: Timothy Spratt
Finance Director/Secretary:
  Kenneth Wheeler

Broad Street Group plc

30 Furnival Street
London EC4A 1JE
Tel: 071 831 3113
Fax: 071 831 6469

Deputy Chairman: Brian Basham
Managing Director: Andrew Elliott
Executive Director:
  Paul Howie
  Anthony Knox
  Michael Preston
  Kenneth Wheeler

Broderers' Company

Westminster Bank Chambers
11A Bridge Road
East Molesey
Surrey
Tel: 081 979 2153

Clerk: S G B Underwood

Brunswick PR Ltd

17 Lincoln's Inn Fields
London WC2A 3ED
Tel: 071 404 5959
Fax: 071 831 2823

Managing Director: Alan Parker
Director:
  Christopher Ashton-Jones
  Louise Charlton
  Andrew Fenwick
  Alison Hogan
  Tom Kyte

Buchanan Communications Ltd

36 St Andrew's Hill
London EC4V 5DE
Tel: 071 489 1441

Chief Executive: R A Oldworth
Managing Director: T J Anderson

The Building Societies Association

3 Savile Row
London W1X 1AF
Tel: 071 437 0655
Telex: 24538
Fax: 071 734 6416

Director-General: Mark J Boleat
Head of Legal Services:
  Ron Armstrong
Head of External Relations:
  Adrian Coles
Head of Financial Policy:
  Christopher French

W & J Burness WS

16 Hope Street
Charlotte Square
Edinburgh EH2 4DD
Tel: 031 226 2561
Telex: 72405
Fax: 031 225 2964

Senior Partner:
  Sir Charles Fraser KCVO
Partner:
  Donald B Caskie WS
  Caroline S Drummond WS
  David B Gibson
  David A Gifford WS
  Adam R Gillingham WS
  Alastair J Gordon WS
  Alasdair F Hardman WS
  W Bruce Logan WS
  Simon A Mackintosh WS
  James A McLean WS
  George M Menzies WS
  Gordon L K Murray WS
  Marsali C Murray
  L Annette Pairman WS
  Paul D Pia WS
  John C Rafferty WS
  David R Reid WS
  Michael J R Risk WS
  Hubert J Ross
  Kenneth A Ross
  Dr Martin Sales
  Christopher Scott WS
  Malcolm G Strang Steel WS
  Duncan W Thomson WS
  Malcolm J Wood WS

Burson-Marsteller Financial Limited

24-28 Bloomsbury Way
London WC1A 2PX
Tel: 071 831 2969

Chairman: George Welham
Chief Executive: John Mattison
Director:
  Robin Baillie
  Brian Coleman-Smith
  Tony Warmington

Business

234 King's Road
London SW3 5UA
Tel: 071 351 7351
Telex: 914549
Fax: 071 351 2794

Editor: Christopher Parkes

Business Television Limited

The Trocadero
Third Floor
19 Rupert Street
London W1V 8AA
Tel: 071 287 4444
Fax: 071 494 3837

Chairman (and Executive Producer, C4 Business Daily):
Michael D Braham
Managing Director (and Associate Producer, C4 Business Daily):
Ciaran J Fenton
Director (and Editor, C4 Business Daily): Andrew Clayton

Business Week International

34 Dover Street
London W1X 4BR
Tel: 071 491 8985
Telex: 892191
Fax: 071 493 9896

London Bureau Chief:
Richard Melcher
London Correspondent:
Mark Maremont

N T Butterfield & Son (Bermuda) Ltd

10 Old Jewry
London EC2R 8EA
Tel: 071 248 4871
Fax: 071 606 2405

Managing Director: C Grant Hall

C S Project Consultants

(Project Consultants for the Construction Industry)
35 John Street
London WC1N 2AT
Tel: 071 405 6136
Fax: 071 831 8843

Chairman: Ronald William Clarke
Managing Director:
Michael David Gibbons
Anthony David Worrall
Director:
David John Baker-Falkner
Francis Robert Ives
Dean Leslie Webster
Raymond Wheeler
Company Secretary: William Frederick Cecil Swann

Cameron Markby Hewitt

Sceptre Court
40 Tower Hill
London EC3 4BB
Tel: 071 702 2345
Telex: 925779
Fax: 071 702 2303

Senior Partner: Bill Shelford
Partner:
N S D Agar
Jimmy Aitchison
P D Aldred
J S Armstrong
M Aspery
M F Baker
G S Barrett
D G Bellhouse
O A Bolton
Simon Boome
William Brafman
Clive Brown
Andrew Bryce
Penelope A Bruce
M J Burke
James Burnett-Hitchcock
Brian Cain
Amanda J Chumas
Andrew Crawford
Frank Dufficy
M E M Elborne
Anthony Fincham
M J J Freeman
M R Galaud
R A Goodman
R Griggs
Keith Gregory
J E Hall
S H Hallam
P L Hewes
A J Hobkinson
N R James
Nigel Johnson
Arfon Jones
D J Kidd
R D Lambourne
C Larlham
Anthony Lewis
Sara Lovick
A McKnight
P Maguire
R G Martin
Raymond Mayes
K H Miller
Anne P Morris
Simon Morris
Tony Morris
John Newbegin
R J Newton Price

Partner:
R E Parsons
Nick Paul
G A Penn
S H Rajani
R W Reiss
Charles Romney
B A Schofield
J R E Shaw
Chris St John Smith
G R T Smyth
S K Tester
R E Topley
Michael Wadsworth
Margaret J L Wailen
Howard Waterman
Bruce Westbrook
John White
G A Williamson
J A E Young
Consultants:
D Allibone
J E Cama
R E Denoon Duncan

Carpenters' Company

Carpenters' Hall
Throgmorton Avenue
London EC2N 2JJ
Tel: 071 588 7001

Clerk: Capt K G Hamon RN

Charles Barker City Ltd

30 Farringdon Street
London EC4A 4EA
Tel: 071 634 1000

Chairman: Ms Angela Heylin
Deputy Chairman: Keith Payne
Chief Executive: Christopher Joll

Chartered Architects' Company

39 Park Lane
Broxbourne
Herts
Tel: 0992 463890

Clerk: L Groome OBE

The Chartered Institute of Bankers

10 Lombard Street
London EC3V 9AS
Tel: 071 623 3531
Telex: 265871
Fax: 071 283 1510

President & Chairman of the Council:
P Charlton OBE

Deputy Chairman of the Council:
R Flemington
Secretary General: Eric Glover
Treasurer: D G Cracknell

The Chartered Insurance Institute

20 Aldermanbury
London EC2V 7HY
Tel: 071 606 3835
Telex: 957092
Fax: 071 726 0131

President: Peter Purchon
Deputy President: C P Harris
Director General: David Bland

Chartered Secretaries' and Administrators' Company

The Irish Chamber
Guildhall Yard
London EC2V 5AE
Tel: 071 726 2955

Clerk: G H Challis

Chartered Surveyors' Company

16 St Mary at Hill
London EC3
Tel: 071 623 2761

Clerk: Mrs A L Jackson

Christopher Bosanquet Ltd

56/60 St John Street
London EC1M 4DT
Tel: 071 490 4611
Fax: 071 490 4405

Managing Director:
Christopher Bosanquet

Citigate Communications Group Ltd

7 Birchin Lane
London EC3V 9BY
Tel: 071 623 2737
Fax: 071 623 9050

Chairman: A Campbell-Harris
Deputy Chairman: Leo Cavendish
Chief Executive: D Wright

City & Commercial Communications plc

Bell Court House
11 Blomfield Street
London EC2M 7AY
Tel: 071 588 6050

Chairman: Norman Chalmers

Chief Executive: Jeremy Carey
Director:
Timothy C Brown
Alan M Bulmer
Kim Harris
Bobby Leach
Noel Yardley

City of London PR Group plc

Triton Court
Finsbury Square
London EC2A 1BR
Tel: 071 628 5518
Telex: 262128
Fax: 071 628 8555

Chairman & Managing Director:
John Greenhalgh
Director:
Peter Doye
Ian Forsyth
Stewart McAlpine

CJA (Management Recruitment Consultants) Ltd

3 London Wall Buildings
London Wall
London EC2M 5PJ
Tel: 071 588 3588
Telex: 887374
Fax: 071 256 8501

Chairman: G Campbell-Johnston

Clark Whitehill

25 New Street Square
London EC4A 3LN
Tel: 071 353 1577
Telex: 887422
Fax: 071 583 1720

Chief Executive: Hugh Butterworth
Partner:
John Adams
Laurence Baehr
David Betton
Donald Broad
George Cranston
David Davis
David Devon
Zahir Fazal
William Field
Michael Fletcher
Philip Forwood
David Furst
Mike Garland
James Gemmell
Julian Glicher

Partner:
Robin Gorringe
Christopher Greene
Anne Gregory-Jones
Andrea Grimshaw
Derek Haynes
Brian Ing
Damian Keeling
Ian Kelly
Mark Ladd
Peter Lobbenberg
Clive Malcolm
Tony Meadows
Shirley Mitchard
Allen Pawlyn
Andrew Pianca
Edward Ross-McNairn
Chris Sales
Peter Salter
Ted Sloper
Les Taylor
Adrian Thomas
Frederick Van Zweeden
Richard White
Howard Williams
Philip Willoughby

Cleary, Gottlieb, Steen & Hamilton

99 Bishopsgate
London EC2M 3XD
Tel: 071 638 5291
Telex: 887659
Fax: 071 600 1698/588 5163

Resident Partner:
Manley O Hudson Jr
Christof von Dryander

Clifford Chance

Royex House
Aldermanbury Square
London EC2V 7LD
Tel: 071 600 0808
Telex: 8959991
Fax: 071 726 8561

Senior Partner: Nigel Fox Bassett
Managing Partner:
Geoffrey M T Howe
Partner:
James Barlow
Ms Rosalind Bax
Roger Best
Teddy Bourne
David Bows
David Bowyer
Edward Bradley
Michael Bray
Tony Briam

Partner:
Peter Brooks
Michael Brown
Ronald Brown
Jeremy Brownlow
Tom Budgett
Robin Burleigh
Jeremy Carver
Armel Cates
David Childs
Keith Clark
Katherine Coates
Richard Coleman
Rodney Davis
Paul Downing
Mark Dyer
John East
John Edwards
Michael Edwards
Peter J Elliott
David Griffiths
Ben Hawkes
Martin Herbert
John Hanby Holmes
Stephen Hood
Michael J Howell
Martin Hughes
Ian Jackson
Paul Jacobs
Alan Jones
Barry Lock
Simon MacLachlan
Richard Marre
Michael Mathews
David Maunder
David McCarthy
Christopher McGonigal
Richard McIlwee
Michael Mockridge
Murray North
Derham O'Neill
Terry O'Neill
Chris Oakley
John Osborne
Christopher Osman
Edwin Patton
David Perkins
Hugh Pigott
Garth Pollard
David E Reid
Diane Relf
Martin E Richards
Peter Rooke
Howard Ross
Edward Sadler
P Simson
Anton G Slater
Graham P Smith
Michael Smyth

Partner:
George Staple
Mark Stewart
Malcolm Sweeting
David H Tate
Peter Taylor
Anthony A Vlasto
Jim Wheaton
Timothy Wheeler
Geoffrey White
Antony Willis
Tim Woodall
Tom Woodburn

Clockmakers' Company
St Dunstan's House
Carey Lane
London EC2V 8AA
Tel: 071 606 2366

Clerk: A/Cmdr B G Frow

Clothworkers' Company
Clothworkers' Hall
Dunster Court
Mincing Lane
London EC3R 7AH
Tel: 071 623 7041

Clerk: Christopher M Mowll

Clyde & Co
51 Eastcheap
London EC3M 1JP
Tel: 071 623 1244
Telex: 884886
Fax: 071 623 5427

Senior Partner: Michael Payton
Partner:
Jane Andrewartha
David Best
John Blacker
Nigel Brook
Benjamin Browne
Paul Bugden
Nigel Chapman
Robert Chapman
Corinna Cresswell
John Dunt
Gordon Elliot
Ralph Evers
Peter Farthing
Simon Fletcher
Colin Franke
Richard Glencross
Christopher Gooding
Nicholas Greensmith
David Hall
Michael Harrison

Partner:
Robert Heanley
Aidan Heathcote
Patrick Heffernan
Derek Hodgson
Margaret Kelly
Stirling Leech
Stuart Macdonald
Francis Mackie
Paul Manser
Jane Martineau
Peter Morgan
David Page
Michael Parker
Robert Pilcher
Simon Poland
David Reynolds
Anthony Rooth
Ian Ross
Peter Shelford
Sheila Simison
Roderick Smith
Verner Southey
Anthony Thomas
Clive Thorp
Howard Townson
Stephen Tricks
Andrew Wells
John Whittaker

Coachmakers' & Coach Harness Makers' Company
149 Banstead Road
Ewell, Epsom
Surrey
Tel: 081 393 5394

Clerk: Major W H Wharfe RM

Wm F Coates & Co
North Bank House
8-9 Donegall Square North
Belfast BT1 5LX
Tel: 0232 323456

Senior Partner: H T Morrison

Cole Corette & Abrutyn
21 Upper Brook Street
London W1Y 1PD
Tel: 071 491 3735
Telex: 264598
Fax: 071 408 0843

Senior Partner: Robert Starr

College Hill Associates Limited
4 College Hill
London EC4R 2RA
Tel: 071 236 2020
Telex: 071 248 3259

Chairman & Chief Executive:
  Alex Sandberg
Director: Peter Belchamber
Associate Director:
  Mark Garraway
  Judith Parry
  Richard Pearson
  Simon Rothschild
  Matthew Smallwood

The Company of Builders Merchants
128 Queen Victoria Street
London EC4P 4JX

Clerk: Sheila M Robinson TD

The Company of Constructors
Graves End House
Woodbury Salterton
Exeter
Devon
Tel: 0395 33202

Clerk: Anthony W J Appleton

The Company of Information Technologists
13 Mansfield Street
London W1M 0BP
Tel: 071 637 0471

Clerk: Mrs P Walmisley

The Company of Watermen & Lightermen of the River Thames
Watermen's Hall
18 St Mary at Hill
London EC3R 8EE
Tel: 071 283 2373

Clerk: W A A Wells TD

Confederation of British Industry
Centre Point
103 New Oxford Street
London WC1A 1DU
Tel: 071 379 7400
Telex: 21332
Fax: 071 240 1578

President: Sir Brian Corby

Director General: John Banham
Executive Director:
  Maurice Hunt
  Richard Price
Chief Economic Adviser:
  Professor Douglas McWilliams

Cooks' Company
49 Queen Victoria Street
London EC4N 4SE
Tel: 071 248 3024

Clerk: M Thatcher

Coopers & Lybrand Deloitte
Plumtree Court
London EC4A 4HT
Tel: 071 583 5000
Telex: 887470
Fax: 071 822 4652/4663

Chairman & Joint Senior Partner:
  Brandon Gough
Deputy Chairman, Joint Senior Partner & Chairman of Coopers & Lybrand Europe: John Bullock
Deputy Chairman and Chairman of Management Consultancy Services:
  Peter W Allen
Managing Partner: Alan McFetrich
Executive Partner in charge of Regions:
  Barrie Cottingham
Executive Partner in charge of London City Office: Peter Smith
Executive Partner in charge of Central London Office: David Stewart
Executive Partner in charge of Management Consultancy Services:
  Malcolm Coster
Head of Audit: Brian Jenkins
Deputy Head of Audit:
  Bryan Blackborn
Head of Corporate Finance:
  Richard Stone
Head of Business Services:
  Roderick Boswell
Deputy Head of Business Services:
  John Belton
Head of Tax: John M Andrews
Chairman of Cork Gully (Insolvency):
  Michael Jordan
Deputy Chairman of Cork Gully (Insolvency): Ian Bond
Head of Cork Gully (Insolvency):
  Chris Hughes
Head of Litigation Support:
  Tim Lawrence
Head of Public Sector Audit:
  John Tedder

Director of Corporate Planning and Marketing: John B Studdard
Director of Human Resources:
  Neil Taberner

Coopers' Company
Coopers' Hall
13 Devonshire Square
London EC2M 4TH
Tel: 071 247 9577

Clerk: J A Newton

Cordwainers' Company
Eldon Chambers
30 Fleet Street
London EC4
Tel: 071 353 4309

Clerk: Capt C T Codrington CBE, RN

Coudert Brothers
(International Attorneys associated in London with Beharrell, Thompson & Co.)
4 Dean's Court
London E4V 5AA
Tel: 071 236 5591
Telex: 887071
Fax: 071 248 3153

Resident Partner: Barry Metzger

Council of Mortgage Lenders
3 Savile Row
London W1X 1AF
Tel: 071 437 0655
Telex: 24538
Fax: 071 734 6416

Secretary: Christopher French

Cranfield School of Management
Cranfield MK43 0AL
Tel: 0234 751122

Director of School:
  Professor L G Murray
Deputy Director, Professor of Marketing and Logistics Systems:
  Professor M G Christopher
Deputy Director, Professor of Manufacturing Strategy:
  Professor C C New
Director of Research, Professor of Strategic Management:
  Professor G Johnson

Professor of Finance and Accounting:
Professor D R Myddelton
Professor of Management Accounting:
Professor A Robson
Professor of International Financial Management:
Professor A Buckley
Association of Corporate Treasurers Professor of Treasury Management:
Professor J Broyles
National Westminster Bank Professor in the Development of Small Business: Professor P J Burns
Professor of Enterprise Development:
Professor M H Harper
Professor of Management Development:
Professor A Kakabadse
Professor of Marketing Planning:
Professor M H B McDonald
Professor of Services Marketing:
Professor A F T Payne
Professor of Human Resource Management: Professor S Tyson

Cravath, Swaine & Moore
33 King William Street
London EC4R 9DU
Tel: 071 606 1421
Telex: 8814901
Fax: 071 860 1150

John E Young

Curriers' Company
Hornbeam House
Middle Winterslow
Salisbury
Wilts

Clerk: Col J B Ray

Cutlers' Company
Cutlers' Hall
Warwick Lane
London EC4M 7BR
Tel: 071 248 1866

Clerk: K S G Hinde TD

Cyril Sweett and Partners
(Quantity Surveyors for the Construction Industry)
37/41 Bedford Row
London WC1R 4LE
Tel: 071 242 9777
Fax: 071 430 0603

Senior Partner:
Ronald William Clarke
Partner:
Paul John Braithwaite

Partner:
Michael David Gibbons
Ernest Paul Gulley
Julian John Lennox Heard
Andrew Robert Hemsley
James David Ian Hossack
Francis Robert Ives
Derek Ronald Pitcher
Michael James Solomon
Dean Leslie Webster
Partnership Manager: Christopher John Cooper
Company Secretary: William Frederick Cecil Swann

Daily Express
245 Blackfriars Road
London SE1 9UX
Tel: 071 928 8000
Fax: 071 620 1645

City Editor: Trevor Webster
Deputy City Editor: Stephen Kahn
Money Editor: Julia Finch
City Reporter:
Nick Fletcher
Rachel Simpson
Personal Finance Writer & City Reporter: Niki Chesworth

Daily Mail
Temple House
Temple Avenue
London EC4Y OJF
Tel: 071 938 6000
Fax: 071 937 3214

City Editor: Andrew Alexander
Deputy City Editor: Michael Walters
Assistant City Editor: Chris Falton
Market Reporter: Geoff Foster
Financial Reporter:
Ken Allen
Michel Bows
Tim Freeborn
Mark Hotopf

Daily Mirror
Holborn Circus
London EC1P 1DQ
Tel: 071 353 0246
Fax: 071 822 3402

City Editor: John Husband
Deputy City Editor: Stephen Ellis
Financial Journalist:
William Keenan
Ian Miller
Neil Simpson

The Daily Telegraph
City Office
2nd Floor
Salters Hall
4 Fore Street
London EC2Y 5DT
Tel: 071 538 5000
Telex: 22874
Fax: 071 628 0343

City Editor: Neil Collins
Deputy City Editor:
Richard Northedge
City Diary Editor: Sally White
Personal Finance Editor: Ian Cowie
Banking Correspondent:
Antonia Feuchtwanger
Commercial Property Correspondent:
Bruce Kinloch
City Reporter: Paul Murphy
Reporter:
Charlotte Beugge
Duncan Hughes
Annabel Lagden
Charles McVeigh
Sonia Purnell
Kate Rankine
David Wighton

David Holman & Co Ltd
Minster House
Arthur Street
London EC4R 9AB
Tel: 071 929 4037
Telex: 8954000
Fax: 071 621 0205

Chairman: David M Holman
Director:
B W C Graham
R S T Gunter
C B Holman
C A Lilley
D J Poll
I R W Wylie

David Sheppard & Partners Ltd
21 Cleveland Place
St James's
London SW1Y 6RL
Tel: 071 930 8786
Fax: 071 839 3649

Chairman: David Sheppard MBE
City Director:
Benedict Fenwick
Rupert White

De Lisle Stephens
20 Cousin Lane
London EC4R 3TE
Tel: 071 236 7307
Fax: 071 489 1130

Managing Director: Freddie de Lisle

Dewe Rogerson
3½ London Wall Buildings
London Wall
London EC2M 5SY
Tel: 071 638 9571
Telex: 883610
Fax: 071 628 3444

Director: Desmond Quigley

Dickson Minto
22/25 Finsbury Square
London EC2A 1DS
Tel: 071 628 4455
Telex: 9413550
Fax: 071 628 0027

Senior Partner: Alastair Dickson
Partner:
   Michael Barron
   James Birrell
   Roderick Bruce
   Gordon Davidson
   A Graham Martin
   Kevan McDonald
   Bruce Minto
   David Mitchell

Distillers' Company
60 Montford Place
Kennington Lane
London SE11 5DF
Tel: 071 793 0183

Clerk: Bruce Dehn

Drapers' Company
Drapers' Hall
Throgmorton Street
London EC2N 2DQ
Tel: 071 588 5002

Clerk: Robert C G Strick

Drivers Jonas
30 Watling Street
London EC4M 9JN
Tel: 071 248 9731
Telex: 917080
Fax: 071 329 4923

Partner-in-Charge: George Gillon
Senior Partner: Christopher Jonas

Partner:
   Ian Menzies
   Nick Shepherd

Dundas & Wilson CS
25 Charlotte Square
Edinburgh EH2 4EZ
Tel: 031 225 1234
Telex: 72404
Fax: 031 225 5594

Senior Partner: J N Fergusson
Executive Partner: R O Blair
Partner:
   R D D Bertram
   C R J Campbell
   Miss Maureen S Coutts
   D I Cumming
   D Hardie
   C R M Hook
   P Mackay
   Professor I W Noble
   M P Stoneham
   J P Watt

Dyers' Company
Dyers' Hall
Dowgate Hill
London EC4R 2ST
Tel: 071 236 7197

Clerk: J R Chambers

The Economist
25 St James's Street
London SW1A 1HG
Tel: 071 839 7000
Telex: 24344
Fax: 071 839 2968

Editor: R Pennant-Rea
Economics Editor: C Crook
Business Affairs Editor: W Emmott
Finance Editor: D Ziegler
World Business Editor: D Manasian

Engineers' Company
19 Old Broad Street
London EC2
Tel: 071 839 3097

Clerk: Cmdr B D Gibson

Environmental Cleaners' Company
Whitehorns
Rannoch Road
Crowborough
East Sussex
Tel: 0892 655780

Clerk: S J Holt

Equity International
Suite G10
Butlers Wharf Business Centre
45 Curlew Street
London SE1 2ND
Tel: 071 403 8785
Fax: 071 403 8707

Editorial Director: Peter Sherlock
Editor: Ray Heath

Ernst & Young
Becket House
1 Lambeth Palace Road
London SE1 7EU
Tel: 071 928 2000
Telex: 885234
Fax: 071 928 1345

Chairman: G A Anderson
Firm's Managing Partner:
   P R Edwards
Managing Partner, London:
   R J Butler
Senior Partner: E O M Eilledge
Partner:
   S J L Adamson
   J P Allday
   L J Allen
   E E Anstee
   M J Arnold
   C R Attwood
   C D Bishop
   A D Black
   N R Bowman
   M N M Boyd
   A V B Broke
   G D A Brown
   H R Brown
   B F Burns
   A T Cabourn-Smith
   F Carbutt
   N F R Carratu
   A D Chessells
   L J Chrisfield
   C Collett
   H Cottam
   T J A Curry
   J W Dixon
   N H Dobson

Partner:
Ms A Mairi Eastwood
D A D Essex
J D Fairley
R N Findlater
C J Frankland
M I M Gardiner
P L Gillett
S H Hall
N J Hamilton
B D Harmon
R Harris
R D J Heath
B J Herring
R W Holman
G J Howe
J R Howells
R C Hughes
P S Jenkins
A B Jones
J F D Knust
N C E Land
N Le Neve Foster
I A Leeson
D C Lindsell
M D Lynch-Bell
N C L Macdonald
A E Macfarlane
K P McNamara
R B Mead
A T Meller
N S J Moore
J R Morgan
C J Munro
B E Nichols
A Oakley
A K Olivey
E J W Oyler
N Pasricha
R M Paterson
J A Pawlowicz
R K Perkin
S F Phillips
N B Pickard
W Powlett-Smith
S D Price
R Rees-Pulley
R J Riddell-Carre
R M Rouse
R W Russell
P J Rutteman
R B Sharp
D M W Sherwin
G F Smith
P J Standish
K P S Stein
T J Stone
Donald G Sutherland
P S Thring

Partner:
B W Waters
Mrs C M K Wheeler
B J Wilson
D T Wilson
G E N S Wilson

Euromoney Publications plc
Nestor House
Playhouse Yard
London EC4V 5EX
Tel: 071 236 3288
Telex: 8814985/6
Fax: 071 329 4349

Chairman: Sir Patrick Sergeant
Chief Executive: Padraic Fallon

The Evening Standard
Temple House
Temple Avenue
London EC4
Tel: 071 938 6000
Fax: 071 936 2061

City Editor: Michael Smith
Deputy City Editor: Michael Foster
Assistant City Editor:
Andrew Cornelius
Patricia Knox
Financial Reporter:
Tim Blackstone
Andrew Garfield
Sarah Griffin
Kirstie Hamilton
Amanda McCrystal
Michael Neill
Peter Oborne
Patricia Tehan

Evershed Wells & Hind
(Offices also in London,
Nottingham & Derby)
10 Newhall Street
Birmingham B3 3LX
Tel: 021 233 2001
Telex: 336688
Fax: 021 236 1583

Partner (Birmingham):
Michael R Arnold
Peter G Battye
Partner (Nottingham):
C Rupert Bear
Partner (Birmingham):
Adrian D Bland
David Blyth
Peter R Bromage
Partner (Nottingham):
Hilary P Campion

Partner (Nottingham):
Andrew R S Cooper
Richard G L Davis
Partner (Birmingham):
Stephen L Duffield
Harry O Forrester
David S Haggett
Partner (Nottingham): Peter Hands
Partner (Birmingham):
Meg E M Heppel
Partner (Derby): Paul J Hilsdon
Partner (Birmingham):
Martin W Hopkins
Partner (Nottingham):
Lionel M Howard
Partner (Birmingham):
David J Hubball
Andrew G D Inglis
John M Jennings
W Ian Jollie
Partner (London):
William J Keating
Partner (Birmingham):
Susan Lewis
Peter J McHugh
Alex J R Mackay
Martin N McKenna
Partner (London): Peter Manford
Partner (Nottingham): R Keith Muir
Partner (Derby): Giles A C Orton
Partner (Nottingham):
Andrew J Pickin
Partner (Birmingham):
Milton N Psyllides
Partner (Nottingham):
F Barry Raven
Partner (Birmingham):
Andrew M Rees
Jim E Rowley
Partner (Nottingham):
John H Sarginson
Jeremy P Scholes
Partner (Birmingham):
Michael R Seabrook
Partner (Nottingham):
Victor W Semmens
Partner (Birmingham):
Brian R Shaw
Partner (Nottingham):
Nigel P Sternberg
Partner (Birmingham): Jane Storer
Partner (Nottingham):
Richard B Stringfellow
Partner (Birmingham):
Malcolm Titcomb
Michael J Tollett
Partner (London): Nigel G Watkins
Partner (Nottingham):
William F Whysall

Partner (Nottingham):
Carole E Wigley
Partner (Derby): David W Wild
Partner (Birmingham): H
Stephen Williams
Partner (London):
Richard T Winter
Partner (Birmingham): C Piers Wolf
Partner (Nottingham):
John D C Young

The Faculty of Actuaries
23 St Andrew Square
Edinburgh EH2 1AQ
Tel: 031 557 1575
Fax: 031 557 6702

President: J M Souness
Vice President:
A U Lyburn
E S Robertson
A J C Smith
Past President:
J M Macharg
W M Morrison
Honorary Secretary:
G M Murray
F D Patrick
Honorary Treasurer: H W Gillon

Farmers' Company
Pel House
35 Station Square
Petts Wood
Kent
Tel: 0689 891238

Clerk: J P Jackson

Farriers' Company
37 The Uplands
Loughton
Essex
Tel: 081 508 6242

Clerk: H W H Ellis

FCB Advertising Ltd
82 Baker Street
London W1M 2AE
Tel: 071 935 4426
Telex: 263526
Fax: 071 486 7571

Chairman & Chief Executive:
R A Dalton
Deputy Chairman: R Ballin

Feltmakers' Company
10 Carteret Street
Queen Anne's Gate
London SW1H 9DR
Tel: 071 222 8844

Clerk: R M Peel

Field Fisher Waterhouse
41 Vine Street
London EC3N 2AA
Tel: 071 481 4841
Telex: 262613 ADIDEM
Fax: 071 488 0084

Senior Partner: U W Bankes
Chairman, Management Committee:
W R I Crewdson
Chairman, Development Committee:
J A Nelson-Jones
Head of Company/Commercial Dept:
D G Rawlins
Head of Commercial Litigation Dept:
D M Lowe
Head of Commercial Property Dept:
D K Birley
Head of Private Client Dept:
M N Tod
Head of Licensing Dept:
P G Glazebrook
Head of Tax Dept: N R Noble
Partner:
P M Abell
R S Bagehot
I S Barnard
C A Baylis
E D Berton
C M Bond
R E Buxton
N B Carr
F H Coffell
T J Davies
J R Facer
J K Fife
A M Fisher
S G Gibbs
P B Hayes
A P P Honigmann
J A Lemkin CBE
M C Mackenzie
C McArthur
R M Nelson-Jones
G J Nuttall
C E Pinfold
J R S Price
C Richmond
A T B Rider
N P Rose
F J Smart
P J Stewart

Partner:
P A Sykes
M L L Tomkins
R M Wills
J A Wilson
M H J Woodman
M J Wright

Financial Dynamics Limited
Sentinel House
2 Eyre Street Hill
London EC1R 5AE
Tel: 071 278 7441
Fax: 071 278 0004

Chairman: Anthony Knox
Chief Executive: Justin Downes
Director/Secretary:
Julian Hanson-Smith
Director:
Robin Christopher Butler
Stephen Jacobs
Sally-Anne Moss

Financial Times
Number One
Southwark Bridge
London SE1 9HL
Tel: 071 873 3000
Telex: 922186
Fax: 071 407 5700

Chief Executive: David Palmer
Managing Editor: David Walker
Editor: Richard Lambert
Deputy Editor: Ian Hargreaves
Principal Economic Commentator:
Samuel Brittan
Personal Finance Editor:
John Edwards
Finance Editor: Peter Martin
Political Editor: Philip Stephens
Investment Editor: Barry Riley
News Editor: Alain Cass
Commentator: John Plender
Financial Services Correspondent:
David Lascelles
Accountancy Correspondent:
David Waller
Insurance Correspondent:
Patrick Cockburn
Personal Finance Writer:
Terry Dodsworth
Sara Webb
Pensions, Unit Trusts: Eric Short

Financial Weekly
14 Greville Street
Hatton Garden
London EC1N 8SB
Tel: 071 405 2622/3
Fax: 071 831 2625

Editor-in-Chief: Tom Lloyd
Editor: Maurice Anslow

Fishmongers' Company
Fishmongers' Hall
London Bridge
London EC4R 9EL
Tel: 071 626 3531

Clerk: M R T O'Brien

Fleet Communications
100 Fleet Street
London EC4Y 1DE
Tel: 071 353 1174
Fax: 071 353 4194

Managing Director: Ian James

Fletcher Jones Limited
9 South Charlotte Street
Edinbrugh EH2 4AS
Tel: 031 226 5709
Telex: 031 220 1940

Managing Director:
Richard A Fletcher

Fletchers' Company
Farmers & Fletchers Hall
3 Cloth Street
London EC1A 7LD
Tel: 071 628 4361

Clerk: J R Garnett

Foreign Banks and Securities Houses Association
68 Lombard Street
London EC3V 9LJ
Tel: 071 955 5495

Chairman: F H Brittain
Vice-Chairman: V Sisto

Foreign Exchange & Currency Deposit Brokers Association
Adelaide House
London Bridge
London EC4R 9EQ
Tel: 071 626 2691
Telex: 883033
Fax: 071 623 1137

Chairman: P F A Nash
Secretary & Treasurer:
Derrick Rickson

Forsyte Kerman
79 New Cavendish Street
London W1M 8AQ
Tel: 071 637 8566
Telex: 22122
Fax: 071 436 6088

Partner:
Michael Bronstein
Peter Carter
Rabinder Chaggar
Ivor Collins
Paul di Biase
Catherine Diggle
Wendy Fillery
Norman Fisher
Vivienne Furneaux
Beverley Jones
Polly Joseph
Alan Kaufman
Anthony Kerman
Isidore Kerman
Keith Laws
Michael Lewis
Nigel Middlemass
David Raff
Richard Stanton-Reid
Robert Thornton

Founders' Company
Founders' Hall
Number One Cloth Fair
London EC1A 7HT
Tel: 071 606 3171

Clerk: A J Gillett

Frankfurter Allgemeine Zeitung
c/o Financial Times
1 Southwark Bridge
London SE1 9HL
Tel: 071 407 5624/071 873 4138
Fax: 071 873 3070

Economic & Financial Correspondent:
Jochen Rudolph

D J Freeman & Co
43 Fetter Lane
London EC4A 1NA
Tel: 071 583 4055
Telex: 894579 DX 103
Fax: 071 353 7377

Partner:
J C Christopher Comyn

Partner:
Charles A Crick
David J Freeman
Antony Gostyn
Toby J Greenbury
Catherine D Hope
Coling S Joseph
Stephen D Koehne
N Anthony Leifer
Jonathan M Lewis
Stuart R Lippiatt
Alan M Magnus
Alan Perry
Richard A Powell
Richard J Spiller

Frere Cholmeley
28 Lincoln's Inn Fields
London WC2A 3HH
Tel: 071 405 7878
Telex: 27623
Fax: 071 405 9056

Chairman: Bruce Brodie
Partner:
Nicholas Baker
Rosemary Bott
Michael Carl
Howard Cooke
Craig Eadie
Sheila Fyfe
Ian Gibson
Ben Gough
Bruce Gripton
Max Hudson
Peter Martin
Simon Pullen
Steven Sugar
Ms Sue Taylor
Alastair Tulloch
Stephen Williams
David Zeffman
Partner (Property):
Hew Billson
Norman Chapman
Charmian Glyn Davies
Christopher Digby-Bell
John Drewitt
Ian Gascoigne
William Gibbs
Sophie Hamilton
Peter Harding
Patrick Isherwood
Alan Jenkins
Tony Patterson
Frank Presland
Jane Richards
Paul Roberts
David Robinson

Partner (Property):
Hugo Southern
Roger Steel
Nicholas Valner
David Willis
Director of Finance and
Administration: Danny Gesna
Chief Executive: Tim Razzall

Freshfields
Whitefriars
65 Fleet Street
London EC4Y 1HS
Tel: 071 936 4000
Telex: 889292
Fax: 071 832 7001

Senior Partner: J K Grieves
Partner:
D C ap Simon
R M Ballard
P J R Bloxham
D C Bonsall
P Bowden
Miss Rachel Brandenburger
J N Byrne
A L Chapman
M L H Clode
G L B Darlington
J P L Davis
K N Dierden
R J Dyer
E T H Evans
I M Falconer
I M Fisher
J C T Foster
J E Francis
Miss Penelope Freer
P S Gaynor
J P A Goddard
S A D Hall
R W Harris
T W R Head
I L Hewitt
S L Hoyle
J M H Hunter
P J Jeffcote
T W Jones
C L A July
Miss Vanessa Knapp
J A H Lawden
G le Pard
P M Leonard
T A Ling
A Littlejohns
M M MacCabe
P R Macklin
L G D Marr
J K McCall

Partner:
J L McKeand
A S McWhirter
T A Moore
G W Morton
G B Nicholson
J C Nowell-Smith
B J O'Brien
W N Parker
P C Peddie
D N Pollard
G N Prentice
M S Rawlinson
D A Redfern
S M Revell
A P Richards
Miss Josanne Rickard
Mrs Sally Roe
A M Salz
F G Sandison
R J C Shuttleworth
D N Spearing
B W Staveley
S B Stebbings
P S Streatfield
N D Tarling
I Taylor
I K Terry
M Thompson
Mrs Ailsa Urwin
G A Whalley

Froriep Renggli & Partners
(Swiss Lawyers)
1 Knightrider Court
London EC4V 5JP
Tel: 071 236 6000
Fax: 071 248 0209

Resident Partner: Bruno W Boesch

Fruiterers' Company
Denmead Cottage
Chawton, Alton
Hants
Tel: 0420 88627

Clerk: Cmdr M T H Styles

Fuellers' Company
4 Maycross Avenue
Morden
Surrey
Tel: 081 543 9446

Clerk: W/Cmdr H C F Squire

Gardeners' Company
14 & 15 Craven Street
London WC2N 5AD
Tel: 071 625 0303

Clerk: A L McGeachy WS

Gardiner Morgan International
27 Throgmorton Street
London EC2N 2AN
Tel: 071 638 1891
Fax: 071 588 8442

Senior Partner: Don Gardiner

GCI Sterling
1 Chelsea Manor Gardens
London SW3 5PN
Tel: 071 351 2400
Telex: 9413121
Fax: 071 352 6244

Chairman: John Brill
Managing Director: Adrian Wheeler
Deputy Managing Director:
Roger Woods
Financial Director: Derek Dalby
Director:
Colin Ainger
Susanna Beard
Philip Dewhurst
Roger Edwards
Harriet Mouchty-Weiss
Jan Stannard
Associate:
Sue Harris
Carolyn Martin
Michael Spring
Jane Stevenson
Kate Lucinda Stobart

Gibson Dunn & Crutcher
30/35 Pall Mall
London SW1Y 5LP
Tel: 071 925 0440
Telex: 27731
Fax: 071 925 2465

Anthony Bonanno
Bruce L Gitelson
John J A Hossenlopp
Ms Wendy M Singer

Girdlers' Company
Girdlers' Hall
Basinghall Avenue
London EC2V 5DD
Tel: 071 638 0488

Clerk: E B Fleming

The Glasgow Herald

195 Albion Street
Glasgow G1 1QP
Tel: 041 552 6255
Fax: 041 552 2288

Business Editor: Ronald Dundas
Associate Business Editor: Eric Baird

The Glasgow Herald (London Office)

1 Jerome Street
London E1 6NJ
Tel: 071 377 0890
Fax: 071 375 2001

City Editor: Chris Stone
Deputy City Editor:
    Christopher Sims

Glovers' Company

Glovers
Tismans Common
Rudgwick
West Sussex
Tel: 0403 722536

Clerk: Gp Capt D G F Palmer OBE

Goddard Kay Rogers & Associates Ltd

Old London House
32 St James's Square
London SW1Y 4JR
Tel: 071 930 5100
Telex: 263218
Fax: 071 321 0605/930 7470

Chairman: David Kay
Managing Director: Paul Buchanan-
    Barrow

Gold & Silver Wyre Drawers' Company

50 Cheyne Avenue
London E18 2DR
Tel: 081 989 0652

Clerk: J R Williams

Good Relations Ltd

59 Russell Square
.London WC1B 4HJ
Tel: 071 631 3434
Telex: 265903
Fax: 071 631 1399

Chairman and Managing Director:
    Jeffrey Lyes

Gouldens

22 Tudor Street
London EC4Y 0JJ
Tel: 071 583 7777
Telex: 21520
Fax: 071 583 3051

Senior Partner: Hugo Scott
Partner:
    Patrick Burgess
    James Campbell
    Ms Claire Edeleanu
    Adam Greaves
    Jeremy Nieboer
    Christopher Parkinson
    Ms Leila Porter
    Neil Seaton
    Ms Diana Spoudeas
    Max Thorneycroft
    John Turner
    Patrick Way
    Christopher Cruttwell
    Tom Auber
    David East
    David Cooper
    Charters MacDonald-Brown
    Philip Jones
    Julian Doyle
    Ms Clare Deanesly
    Martin Piers
    Ms Jennet Davies
    Christopher Berry
    Ms Angela Turner
    Ms Carrie Faller
    Ms Fiona Russell
    Ms Kay Balaam
    Ian Lupson
    Peter Westley

Grandfield Rork Collins Financial Ltd

Prestige House
14-18 Holborn
London EC1N 2LE
Tel: 071 242 2002

Chairman: A J Cardew
Vice Chairman: J R Archer
Deputy Chairman: R G Fallowfield
Managing Director: J P Grove
Director:
    Ms J J N Basset
    R J Carroll
    C N Cook
    R G Dalrymple
    D P Rome
Associate Director:
    Mrs T J Atkin
    S N Leasor
    A H Robinson

Grant Thornton

Grant Thornton House
Melton Street
Euston Square
London NW1 2EP
Tel: 071 383 5100
Telex: 28984
Fax: 071 383 4715

National Managing Partner:
    David McDonnell
Executive Partner:
    Ann Baldwin
    Darryl Whitehead
Director of Marketing: Sue Palmer
London Managing Partner:
    Michael Cleary
Partner:
    Jason Cross
    Philip Kabraji
    Simon Morris
    Michael Rogerson
    David Spence
    Gerard Sykes
    John Tuck
    Maurice Withall

Grimley J R Eve

10 Stratton Street
London W1X 5FD
Tel: 071 895 1515
Telex: 269155
Fax: 071 499 4723

Joint Senior Partner:
    J R Trustram Eve
    A H C Voaden
Partner:
    B G Abbey
    N B Asbury
    R J Bould
    J W Clark-Lowes
    P Craig
    N J de Lotbiniere
    M de Vick
    G T G Eccles
    A M Hall
    D W Henson
    R A Hepher
    M M Mark
    J P Meredith
    R S Morgan
    C A Palmer
    S H Robinson
    D J Room
    E M Sheard
    D E Trollope
    M J Whetstone
Associate:
    P B Dixon

Associate:
G P Gatland
S R Gubbins
R C L Gunn
M Hardy
M Haycocks
T J Jackson
H S Kilner
D F G Locke
S Morley
W Notton
C C Rance
P Ruben
C Sharp
M Smith
M H Tisbury
C Trustram Eve
W J Voaden
Partner (City Office): G Davies
Head of Administration:
S J Westacott

Grocers' Company
Grocers' Hall
Princes Street
London EC2R 8AQ
Tel: 071 606 3113

Clerk: C G Mattingley CBE

The Guardian
119 Farringdon Road
London EC1R 3ER
Tel: 071 278 2332
Telex: 8811746
Fax: 071 837 2114

Managing Editor(City):
Nicholas Bannister
Financial Editor: Alex Brummer
Deputy Financial Editor:
Ben Laurence
Economics Editor: Will Hutton

Guild of Air Pilots and Air Navigators
Cobham House
291 Gray's Inn Road
London WC1X 8QF
Tel: 071 837 3323

Clerk: Gp Capt J W Tritton

Gunmakers' Company
The Proof House
48/50 Commercial Road
London E1 1LP
Tel: 071 481 2695

Clerk: F B Brandt

Haberdashers' Company
Haberdashers' Hall
Staining Lane
Gresham Street
London EC2V 7DD
Tel: 071 606 0967

Clerk: Capt M E Barrow DSO, RN

Hamada & Matsumoto
Bow Bells House
Bread Street
London EC4M 9BQ
Tel: 071 329 4438
Fax: 071 329 4463

Resident Partner: Hideaki Tanaka

Hammond Suddards
Empire House
10 Piccadilly
Bradford BD1 3LR
Tel: 0274 734700
Telex: 517201
Fax: 0274 737547

Joint Senior Partner:
A I Bottomley
D T Lewis
Partner:
D W K Armitage
R Burns
W N Downs
G N I Greenfield
C N Hutton
S R Inman
A R Jordan
R J Marshall Smith
J P Mitchell
M L Shepherd

Hays Allan
Southampton House
317 High Holborn
London WC1V 7NL
Tel: 071 831 6233
Telex: 887929
Fax: 071 831 2416

Senior Partner: J W Gordon
Partner:
D C Dietz
A J MacDonald
H Thomas

Haythe & Curley
23 Albemarle Street
London W1X 3HA
Tel: 071 499 3112
Fax: 071 495 4712

Roger H Lloyd

Hepworth & Chadwick
Cloth Hall Court
Infirmary Street
Leeds LS1 2JB
Tel: 0532 430391
Telex: 557917
Fax: 0532 456188

Senior Partner: David Sykes
Partner:
Raymond Ainscoe
Ian Bramley
Neil Brown
Howard Bryan
Peter Chadwick
Robert Chapman
Richard Davis
John Finnigan
John Foster
David Gray
Jonathan Guest
John Heaps
Julian Horrocks
Andrew Latchmore
Peter Margerison
Ralph Potterton
Ian Richardson
Paul Smith
Alison Staniforth
David Strachan
Peter Thompson
Paul Winter

Herbert Smith
Exchange House
Primrose Street
London EC2A 2HS
Tel: 071 374 8000
Telex: 886633
Fax: 071 496 0043

Senior Partner: J A Rowson
Partner:
S G Barnard
S J Barton
P T Bellis
D M Bolton
R D Bond
D M B Clarke
A C Congreve
R D A Fraser
Ms Caroline M H Goodall

Partner:
S C Hancock
C H Harrison
G R R Hart
R A Jowett
P T C King
M I Kingston
G F Kinmonth
Ms Dorothy K Livingston
A D Macaulay
D Martin
Ms Margaret Mountford
D P Natali
Ms Marian P Pell
T B H Phillips
C W Plant
A D Preece
R J C Privett
C P Tootal
T W Turtle
E I Walker-Arnott

Hill & Knowlton (UK) Ltd
5/11 Theobald's Road
London WC1X 8SH
Tel: 071 413 3000
Telex: 264100
Fax: 071 413 3111

Chairman & Chief Executive:
D Wynne-Morgan
Managing Director, Financial &
Corporate: A Ogden
Finance Director: M R Glynn

Hill Taylor Dickinson
Irongate House
Duke's Place
London EC3A 7LP
Tel: 071 283 9033
Telex: 888470
Fax: 071 283 1144

Partner:
P S Albertini
P F Barfield
N R Clift
S Cropper
Malcolm G Entwistle
J C Evans
C S Goldsmith
J E Isaacs
A Johnson
S S Kakkad
M F Mallin
P N Moore
J N Pople
T J Railton
N A Ridley
M R Taylor

Partner:
R M Taylor
T W S Taylor
R H Wallis
D G Widdowson
Director of Finance: A Pennington

Holman Fenwick & Willan
Marlow House
Lloyds Avenue
London EC3N 3AL
Tel: 071 488 2300
Telex: 8812247
Fax: 071 481 0316

Senior Partner: W A Bishop
Partner:
L A Bell
S K Blows
H M Brown
T P Butler
The Lord Byron
D E Charity
R W Crump
D V G de Pass
S P Drury
J P J Duff
J M Fine
J G Gosling
C A Hales
G E T Hogg
H J Livingstone
C R Lowe
T R Marshall
I M McLachlan
K Michel
G S Moore
J R M O'Sullivan
S J Paull
J C Pierce
V E Pitroff
A E Polonsky
P Rees Smith
B G Robinson
P B Scrase
O M Sefton
J C Sheppard
M T Stevens
D P Tindall
A P R Walls
P Welburn
R G Wilson

Horners' Company
11 Hobart Place
London SW1W 0HL
Tel: 081 946 9767
Telex: 915719
Fax: 071 823 1379

Master: N K Grant
Warden:
D S du Parc Braham
H Kleeman
Clerk: Dr E M Hunt

Ince & Co
Knollys House
11 Byward Street
London EC3R 5EN
Tel: 081 623 2011
Telex: 8955043
Fax: 081 623 3225

Partner:
C W Sprague
D M D Strong
A Suchy

The Independent
40 City Road
London EC1Y 2DB
Tel: 071 253 1222
Telex: 9419611
Fax: 071 608 1205

Editor, Business & City:
Hamish McRae

Independent Radio News
Crown House
72 Hammersmith Road
London W14 8YE
Tel: 071 603 2400
Fax: 071 371 2199

Managing Editor: John Perkins
Financial Editor: Douglas Moffitt
Deputy Financial Editor:
Robin Amlôt

The Institute of Bankers in Scotland
19 Rutland Square
Edinburgh EH1 2DE
Tel: 031 229 9869
Fax: 031 229 1852

President: D B Pattullo
Vice-President:
A C Dempster
R M Maiden
D R Robertson
A J R Thomson
Secretary: Dr C W Munn

Institute of Chartered Accountants in England and Wales

PO Box 433
Chartered Accountants' Hall
Moorgate Place
London EC2P 2BJ
Tel: 071 628 7060
Fax: 071 920 0547

President: Michael G Lickiss
Deputy President: Ian R McNeil
Vice President: W Ian D Plaistowe
Secretary: Andrew Colquhoun

The Institute of Chartered Accountants of Scotland

27 Queen Street
Edinburgh EH2 1LA
Tel: 031 225 5673/9
Telex: 727530
Fax: 031 225 3813

President: J P Percy
Vice President:
    J A Denholm
    I N Tegner

The Institute of Economic Affairs

2 Lord North Street
Westminister
London SW1P 3LB
Tel: 071 799 3745

Publishing Director: Walter Allen

The Insurance Ombudsman Bureau

31 Southampton Row
London WC1B 5HJ
Tel: 071 242 8613
Fax: 071 242 7516

Chairman of Council: Mrs K M Foss
Insurance Ombudsman:
    Dr Julian Farrand
Deputy Insurance Ombudsman:
    L Slade
Unit Trust Ombudsman:
    C A H Parsons
Bureau Manager: C J Hamer

International Financing Review

IFR Publishing Ltd
South Quay Plaza II
183 Marsh Wall
London E14 9FU

Tel: 071 538 5384
Telex: 889365
Fax: 071 377 0978

Editor-in-Chief: Peter Krijgsman

International Herald Tribune

63 Long Acre
London WC2E 9JH
Tel: 071 836 4802
Telex: 262009
Fax: 071 240 2254

City Editor: Leigh H Bruce

International Management

7-11 St John's Hill
London SW11 1TE
Tel: 071 978 4955
Telex: 892084
Fax: 071 978 4862

Editor: Michael Johnson

Investment Trusts

4 Malvern Drive
Woodford Green
Essex IG8 0JR
Tel: 081 504 6862

Editor: John Davis

Investors Chronicle

Financial Times Magazines
Greystoke Place, Fetter Lane
London EC4A 1ND
Tel: 071 405 6969
Telex: 883694
Fax: 071 405 5276

Editor: Ms Gillian O'Connor

Ironmongers' Company

Ironmongers' Hall
Barbican
London EC2Y 8AA
Tel: 071 606 2726

Clerk: J A Oliver

ITN

200 Grays Inn Road
London WC1X 8XZ
Tel: 071 833 3000

Business Correspondent: Hugh Pym
Economics Correspondent: Paul Neild

James Gentles & Son

(Chartered Quantity Surveyors)
Gogar Park
167 Glasgow Road
Edinburgh EH12 9DJ
Tel: 031 317 7474
Telex: 72256
Fax: 031 317 7575

Senior Partner: Wallace Begg
Partner:
    George Henderson
    George Houston
    John McMillan
    Norman Wilkinson
    John Willins
Associate:
    Stewart Anderson
    John Fletcher
    Gordon Hood
    John Martin
    Stuart Parkinson

James R Knowles Limited

Wardle House
King Street
Knutsford
Cheshire WA16 6PD
Tel: 0565 55512
Fax: 0565 54990

Chairman and Managing Director:
    James R Knowles
Deputy Managing Director: P Jensen
Executive Director:
    C S Archibald
    G R Brewer
    L Burkitt
    A Dunn
    R M Entwhistle
    M S Hall
    W A Knowles
    P J Lineen
    P A MacGillivray
    M K Milne
    D Price
    G Roberts
    I C Strathdee
    R W Thomas
    M D Wills
    J R L Wood
Company Secretary: P O'Brien
Group Administrator:
    B C Hill-Samuel

Jaques & Lewis

2 South Square
Gray's Inn
London WC1R 5HR

Tel: 071 242 9755
Telex: 27938
Fax: 071 405 4464

Senior Partner: J B Northam
Partner:
Elaine Aarons
R R Ainsworth
C R Bailey
Judith Barnes
I P Bell
A H Biggs
D R Brown
G R F Butler
J H Butler
R Button
R W Bynoe
Elizabeth Cairns
Ann Churchill
T M Daltry
J D Denman
Shelia Dobson
Janet Evans
D I Fowell
Elizabeth Gant
J Glasson
J A Godby
Aleen Gulvanessian
Brenda Harris
Linda Harrison
C S Heaps
B Hollingsworth
Rosalind Kellaway
C T Lambrick
Linda J Lawrence
H Lewis
R K Lewis
T J Maloney
N D Morris
H F O'Riley
Nimisha Patel
G J Prevett
J P Raisman
J B Roper
P J Scott
C Sly
R G R Stephens
A J Wallis
H V Williams
Felicity Wooldridge
G A Yablon

John Bretton Financial Public Relations
Warnford Court
Throgmorton Street
London EC2N 2JN
Tel: 071 638 0877

Managing Director: John Bretton

Jonathan Wren and Co Ltd
No 1 New Street
Off Bishopsgate
London EC2M 4TP
Tel: 071 623 1266
Telex: 8954673
Fax: 071 626 5258

Chief Executive & Managing Director:
R L Thomas

The Journal of Commerce
18-20 Laystall Street
London EC1R 4PA
Tel: 071 278 2727

Bureau Chief: Ms Janet Porter
Correspondent: Edwin Unsworth

Kidsons Impey
Russell Square House
10/12 Russell Square
London WC1B 5AE
Tel: 071 436 3636
Telex: 263901
Fax: 071 436 6603

Partner:
E Battarbee
D Botterill
M M Bowler
S L Bright
J F Buckle
P E Haynes
W G Herriott
J R Hetherington
R W Knox
R P G Lewis
I Macfarlane
T P G Neale
R N Simpson
W I Sinclair
D J Wadsworth

Kogan Page Limited
120 Pentonville Road
London N1 9JN
Tel: 071 278 0433
Telex: 263088
Fax: 071 837 6348

Managing Director: Philip Kogan
Director: Ben Kogan
Sales And Marketing Director:
Tom Davy
Production Director: Peter Chadwick
Publishing Director:
Ms Pauline Goodwin
*Finance Director and Company
Secretary:* Praba Kan

Korn/Ferry International Ltd
Pepys House
12 Buckingham Street
London WC2N 6DF
Tel: 071 930 4334
Telex: 914860
Fax: 071 930 8085

Managing Partner: John Stork
*Managing Director (Financial
Services):* Edward W Kelley

Lafferty Publications Ltd
Axe & Bottle Court
70 Newcomen Street
London SE1 1YT
Tel: 071 357 7200

Chief Executive Officer:
Michael J Lafferty

Launderers' Company
Launderers' Hall
9 Montague Close
London Bridge
London SE1 9DD
Tel: 0372 274309

Clerk: W E Kingsland

Lawrence Graham
190 Strand
London WC2R 1JN
Tel: 071 379 0000
Telex: 22673
Fax: 071 379 6854

Senior Partner: Gavin R G Purser
Partner:
D M S Barnes
R N H Benson
P A Burroughs
J Clift
R A Cooper
D K Davies
A C Dobson
M J Duffy
M D Edwards
A W Elliott
R D Field
Martyn Gowar
M J Graham
H R B Hamilton
D P Hayward
C E Ince
P Kilsella
Michael Lax
J D M Mackintosh
B R J Manford
P L R Mitchell

Partner:
  M W M Orr
  C M Percy
  S J C Randall
  M N Richardson
  R F J Simon
  R J Smith
  M A Smyth
  K E Venn
  J R Verrill
  P Walker
  J A Wall

Leadenhall Associates Ltd
Lindsey House
40-42 Charterhouse Street
London EC1M 6JH
Tel: 071 253 5523
Fax: 071 253 5523 ext 34

Chairman: A Watson
Managing Director: J Bray
Director:
  Ms Vivienne Carlton
  Peter Ruck

Leathersellers' Company
Leathersellers' Hall
St Helen's Place
London EC3A 6DQ
Tel: 071 588 4615

Clerk: Capt Neil MacEacham

Lightmongers' Company
53 Leithcote Gardens
Streatham
London SW16 2UX
Tel: 081 675 6635

Clerk: S H Birch

Linklaters & Paines
Barrington House
59-67 Gresham Street
London EC2V 7JA
Tel: 071 606 7080
Telex: 884349
Fax: 071 606 5113

Senior Partner: Mark Sheldon
Managing Partner: James Wyness
Partner:
  Beverly Adam
  Ralph Aldwinkle
  Bill Allan
  Charles Allen-Jones
  Anthony Angel
  Jeffrey Bailey
  Richard Bailey
  Alan Barker

Partner:
  David Barnard
  David Barnes
  Keith Benham
  Elizabeth Bennett
  Len Berkowitz
  Eryl Besse
  Alan Black
  Ralph Bonnett
  Margaret Bonsall
  Stephen Boughton
  Andrew Brackfield
  Guy Brannan
  Graeme Brister
  Jeremy Brown
  Adrian Burn
  Malcolm Campbell
  Michael Canby
  Anthony Cann
  Andrew Carmichael
  David Cheyne
  Charles Clark
  Simon Clark
  Tim Clarke
  Christopher Cooke
  Christopher Coombe
  Peter Cornell
  Stephen Cromie
  James Croock
  Martin Day
  Robyn Durie
  Nick Eastwell
  Stephen Edlmann
  John Edwards
  David Egerton-Smith
  John Ellard
  Martin Elliott
  Peter Farren
  Maeve Feeny
  Robert Finch
  Caird Forbes-Cockell
  Malcolm Gammie
  Ron Gibbs
  Richard Godden
  Diana Good
  Christopher Gorman
  William Grant
  Peter Gray
  David Greenhalgh
  Shane Griffin
  Alan Ground
  Tony Grundy
  David Hall
  Paul Harris
  Tony Hickinbotham
  Richard Holden
  Robin Human
  Raymond Jackson
  Christopher James

Partner:
  Raymond Jeffers
  Christopher Johnson-Gilbert
  John Kilner
  Peter King
  Terence Kyle
  Andrew Legg
  Marshall Levine
  David Lloyd
  Hilary Lord
  Chris McFadzean
  Derek McMenamin
  Alexandra Marks
  Jeremy Marriage
  Julia Maynard
  Nikhil Mehta
  Matthew Middleditch
  Adrian Montague
  Anthony Morris
  David Mullarkey
  Jane Murphy
  Iain Murray
  Paul Nelson
  Andrew Nichols
  Brinsley Nicholson
  Bill Park
  Andrew Peck
  Charles Pettit
  John Phipson
  Haydn Puleston-Jones
  Nigel Reid
  James Rice
  Geoffrey Russell
  Peter Sakal
  Tom Scott
  Tim Shipton
  John Simpson
  Jeremy Skinner
  Alan Stephens
  Christopher Style
  Robert Swift
  Richard Tapsfield
  Keith Thomson
  Anthony Thurnham
  John Tucker
  John Turnbull
  Steven Turnbull
  Alan Walls
  James Watkins
  David Weber
  Tom Wethered
  Robin Whaite
  Richard Wheen
  Donald Williams
  Robert Williams
  Stephen Williams

Lloyd's List

Lloyd's of London Press
1 Singer Street
London EC2A 4LQ
Tel: 071 250 1500
Fax: 071 250 0660

Editor/Chief Executive:
    David Gilbertson
Business Editor:
    Christopher Brown-Humes
Business Correspondent: Paul Berrill
Finance Reporter: Aline Sullivan
Deputy Editor/News Editor:
    Tony Gray

Lombard Communications Limited

12 Groveland Court
Bow Lane
London EC4M 9EH
Tel: 071 236 5858
Fax: 071 236 6128

Chairman: Philip Birch
Executive Director:
    David Bick
    John Newton
    Charles Ryland

London Business School

Sussex Place
Regent's Park
London NW1 4SA
Tel: 071 262 5050
    Professor Sir James Ball
    Professor Richard Brealey
    Professor David Currie
    Professor Elroy Dimson
    Professor Julian Franks
    Professor John Kay
    Professor Andrew Lickierman
    Professor Paul Marsh
    Professor P G Moore
    Professor Steve Schaefer

London School of Economics

Houghton Street
London WC2A 2AE
Tel: 071 405 7686

    Professor Michael Bromwich
    Professor Charles A E Goodhart
    Professor Anthony Hopwood
    Professor Mervyn King

Lord Day & Lord, Barrett Smith

35 Old Jewry
London EC2R 8DD
Tel: 071 726 4451
Telex: 291629
Fax: 071 726 6559/4387

    Franklin G Hunt

Loriners' Company

50 Cheyne Avenue
London E18 2DR
Tel: 081 989 0652

Clerk: J R Williams

Lovell White Durrant

65 Holborn Viaduct
London EC1A 2DY
Tel: 071 236 0066
Telex: 887122
Fax: 071 248 4212

Senior Partner: P N Gerrard
Deputy Senior Partner: C Taylor
Partner:
    Miss C M Allinson
    J Cooper
    T A R Curran
    A C R Davis
    P J Fisher
    A Gamble
    P D Gershuny
    A S Gordon
    D F Gray
    D Harris
    D C Kelly
    J R H Kitching
    A D Lickorish
    A J Lutley
    D C Mace
    C I Major
    M B Maunsell
    R H R McKean
    G J McQuater
    A G Murray-Jones
    P A Oldman
    C D StJ Penney
    A J A Penson
    P R Phillipps
    Ms H Rowe
    J R Smyth
    D Sparks
    J J T Stephens
    R J L Stones
    G K Toland
    W G Watkins
    A J White

Partner:
    R T Whitehouse
    G B B Yeowart
    J T Young

Lowe Bell Financial Ltd

1 Red Lion Court
London EC4A 3EB
Tel: 071 353 9203
Fax: 071 353 7392/7980

Chairman: Piers Pottinger
Deputy Chairman: Jem Miller
Director:
    Nick Miles
    Mark Smith
    Bertie Way
    Jerry Wood

McCann-Erickson Advertising Ltd

36 Howland Street
London W1A 1AT
Tel: 071 580 6690
Telex: 28570
Fax: 071 323 2883

Chairman: I Rubins
Managing Director: B Watson

Macfarlanes

10 Norwich Street
London EC4A 1BD
Tel: 071 831 9222
Telex: 296381
Fax: 071 831 9607

Senior Partner: V E Treves
Managing Partner: R M Formby
Partner:
    B C Barker
    G J M Buckley
    N J L Doran
    A D Evans
    D Hayes
    W L King
    J S Macfarlane
    C D Z Martin
    C J Road
    J M Skelton
    R H Sutton
    N A Thomas
    K D Tuffnell
    P H Turnbull
    R A Waterer
    R J Whittaker

McGrigor Donald

Solicitors in Scotland
Finsbury Chambers
74-78 Finsbury Pavement
London EC2A 1AT
Tel: 071 638 6388
Fax: 071 638 6232/638 6233

Senior Partner: Professor R B Jack
Partner:
  I P Bankier
  Dean Carswell
  R M Glennie
  I Gordon
  M Maclean
  A D Stewart
  A J Stewart
  K Sweeney

MacIntyre Hudson

28 Ely Place
London EC1N 6RL
Tel: 071 242 0242
Telex: 25177
Fax: 071 405 4786

Senior Partner: E G Barratt
Partner:
  R J E Bamford
  G A Crowther
  C J Gee
  G T Gower
  N M Hanlon
  B M Jones
  R H MacIntyre
  P M Nellemose
  P J G Rushmore

McKenna & Co

Mitre House
160 Aldersgate Street
London EC1A 4DD
Tel: 071 606 9000
Telex: 27251
Fax: 071 606 9100

Partner:
  Neil Cameron Aitken
  Jonathan Paul Beckitt
  Guy Billington
  George Anthony John Bowles
  Nicholas Arthur Brown
  Richard Hamilton Burnett-Hall
  Timothy James Burton
  Brian Anthony Ross Concanon
  John Malcolm Cunliffe
  Robert Stephen Derry-Evans
  Ian Charles Dodds-Smith
  John Bentley Driffield
  Alan Meredith Edwards

Partner:
  Paul Robert Ellington
  John Corti Emmerson
  Robert Charles Campbell Gait
  Francis Stephen Garford
  Ian Cheyne Gatenby
  Nicholas Martin Hadley
  Timothy Paul Frank Hardy
  Gary Robert Hickinbottom
  Christopher John Stratford
    Hodges
  Julian Pendrill Warner
    Holloway
  Andrew Selwyn Ivison
  Simon Baden Jeffreys
  Elizabeth Kate Kelleher
  Antony Bernard Kitson
  Robert Charles Lane
  Michael Charles Langdon
  Peter Halford Lawson
  Gordon Ionwy David Llewelyn
  Peter James Long
  Anthony Francis Loring
  Richard Harold Malthouse
  Anthony Louis Marks
  Martin Charles Mendelssohn
  Elizabeth Ann Minogue
  Robert Wallace Muir
  Julian Anthony Ogley
  Robert John Phillips
  Robert Howard Porter
  Christopher Brian Powell-Smith
  Richard Stephen Price
  Duncan Charles Pringle
    Rabagliati
  Simon Anthony Renton
  Michael William Rich
  Richard Andrew Shadbolt
  Henry Charles Sherman
  Peter Nicholas Smith
  Richard John Johnson Taylor
  Julian Paul Thurston
  John Trevor Uwins
  Jonathan Mark Vivian
  Andrew Geoffrey Walsh
  Sean Michael Watson
  Stephen Kennedy Whybrow
  Robin John Arthur Williams
  Robert John Windmill
  Fiona Woolf

Maclay Murray & Spens

151 St Vincent Street
Glasgow G2 5NJ
Tel: 041 248 5011
Telex: 77474
Fax: 041 248 5819/221 2968

Managing Partner: J
  Anthony S Murray
Partner:
  Andrew S Fleming
  Robert J Laing
  Thomas M Lawrie
  Ian G Lumsden
  Bruce R Patrick
  Kenneth D Shand
  Magnus P Swanson
  Michael J Walker

Macmillan Publishers Ltd

4 Little Essex Street
London WC2R 3LF
Tel: 071 836 6633
Telex: 262024
Fax: 071 379 4204

President: Lord Stockton
*Chairman and Group Managing
  Director:* Nicholas Byam Shaw
*Managing Director, Macmillan Press
  Ltd:* Adrian Soar
Director, Macmillan Press Ltd:
  Christopher J Paterson
Publishing Director, Reference Books:
  Julian Ashby
Senior Financial Editor:
  Andrea Hartill

MacNair Mason

St Clare House
30/33 Minories
London EC3N 1DU
Tel: 071 481 3022
Telex: 886189
Fax: 071 488 4458

Senior Partner: Robert S Ransom
Partner:
  Geoffrey A Boardman
  Graham N Hall
  G Anton Luck
  Stuart J Markley
  Richard J S Mason
  Gwilym R Morgan
  P Henry Painton
  Malcolm de M A Stewart
  Graham E H Williams

The Mail On Sunday

Temple House
Temple Avenue
London EC4Y OJA
Tel: 071 938 6000

City Editor: Clive Wolman
Financial Editor: Lawrence Lever
Deputy City Editor: Richard Milner

Research/Financial Journalist:
Leonie Tame
Financial Journalist: Allan Piper
Personal Finance Editor:
Anne Ashworth
Business Editor: Timon Day

Makers of Playing Cards' Company
6 The Priory
Godstone
Surrey
Tel: 0883 842300

Clerk: M J Smyth

Marketors' Company
42 Tottenham Lane
Hornsey
London N8
Tel: 081 348 7890

Clerk: Benson F Catt JP

Marlar International Limited
12 Well Court
London EC4M 9DN
Tel: 071 235 9614
Telex: 261260
Fax: 071 489 8316

Chairman: B T G Nicholson
Director:
Gordon Chatterton
Robert Watsham

Martineau Johnson
St Philip's House
St Philip's Place
Birmingham B3 2PP
Tel: 021 200 3300
Telex: 339793
Fax: 021 200 3330

Senior Partner: C J James
Partner: J J Martineau

Masons' Company
106-114 Borough High Street
London SE1 1LB
Tel: 071 407 7604

Clerk: T F Ackland

Master Mariners' Company
HQS Wellington
Temple Stairs
Victoria Embankment
London WC2
Tel: 071 836 8179

Clerk: D W Field

Mayer Brown & Platt
162 Queen Victoria Street
London EC4V 4BS
Tel: 071 248 1465
Telex: 8811095

Partner:
Richard A Cole
Ian R Coles
Associate:
David Carpenter
Jeffrey I Gordon
Rob F Hugi
Nabil L Khodadad
Mark R Uhrynuk

The MDA Group plc
Amy Johnson House
15 Cherry Orchard Road
Croydon
Surrey CR9 6BJ
Tel: 081 686 5566
Telex: 946655
Fax: 081 688 1280

Chairman: Robert W Ridgwell
Chief Executive: G Robert Boot
Director:
Michael J Dwelly
Daniel P J Flynn
J Neil Kenworthy
Raymond J Liechti
Group Marketing Director:
Stephen J O Godfrey
Group Company Secretary:
Miss Charlotte Blake
Group Financial Controller:
Alastair J Mitchell

Memery Crystal
31 Southampton Row
London WC1B 5HT
Tel: 071 242 5905
Telex: 298957 MEMLAW
Fax: 071 242 2058

Partner:
David A Connick
Peter M Crystal
Jonathan P Davies
Lesley A Gregory
D Harvey Rands
Mark Westaway
Litigation Manager:
Daniel D Pfeiffer
Consultant: W V John Memery

Mercers' Company
Mercers' Hall
Ironmonger Lane
London EC2V 8HE
Tel: 071 726 4991

Clerk: G M M Wakeford

Merchant Taylors' Company
30 Threadneedle Street
London EC2R 8AY
Tel: 071 588 7606

Clerk: Capt D A Wallis RN

Milne Ross
Chapel House
24 Nutford Place
London W1H 6AE
Tel: 071 262 7788
Telex: 299272 MILNE G
Fax: 071 724 6953

Senior Partner: A C Vause
Managing Partner: R B Fear
Partner:
R J B Alexander
S H Berger
R C Bloomer
J N Burns
R C Casling
N Dennis
B Dunton
D Glassman
W S Gregg
R J G Holman
K B Humphrey
N G Keen
D A Locke
D K McSweeney
H Mercer
P R Miller
M B Rodgers
B J Russell
T J Saunders
J R Slavin
A W Stroud
N J Tristem
I M Wilson
Consultant:
T J Dean
C D Masters
Partnership Secretary: J R Curtis

Le Monde
29 Old Church Street
London SW3
Tel: 071 351 0505
Fax: 071 351 5605

Economic Correspondent: Dominique-
Andre Dhombres

Money Management & Unitholder
Financial Times Magazines
Greystoke Place
Fetter Lane
London EC4A 1ND
Tel: 071 405 6969
Telex: 883694
Fax: 071 831 2181

Editor: Ms Janet Walford

Money Observer
Chelsea Bridge House
Queenstown Road
London SW8 4NN
Tel: 071 627 0700
Telex: 888963
Fax: 071 627 5572

Editor: John Davis
Specialist Writer:
Sue Baker
Peter Bugler
Michael Dineen
Wendy Elkinson
William Kay
Sylvia Morris
Iain Murray
Helen Pridhan
Joanna Slaughter
Peter Watson

Moore Stephens
St Pauls House
8-12 Warwick Lane
London EC4P 4BN
Tel: 071 248 4499
Telex: 884610
Fax: 071 248 3408

Senior Partner: Richard Moore
Partner:
Robert Bates
John Coleman
Alan Cox
Andrew Cunningham
Arthur Davey
Norman Epstein
Norman Farrant
Peter Griffiths
Nicholas Hilton

Partner:
Stephen Hogg
Gervase Hulbert
Robert Kenworthy
David La Niece
Paul Powell

Moores Rowland
Clifford's Inn
Fetter Lane
London EC4A 1AS
Tel: 071 831 2345
Telex: 886504
Fax: 071 831 6123

Senior Partner: Cyril F Dashwood
Managing Partner:
Victor H J Clements
Partner:
T Baldwin
Charles S Bunker
C Chadburn
John L Clarke
Graham S Coopey
Michael K Down
Simon Footerman
Brian F Gilligan
E J Max Goodall
Bryan M Graham
Christopher L Howard
G Nicholas V Jenkins
Leslie J P Livens
Edward P Magrin
H Charles E Maynard
Joseph M Michaelson
Peter G G Miller
Nigel A O'Neill
Colin K Rhead
Geoffrey J Simpson
Robin Stevens
B Thornton
David A Walton
Clive A Weeks
Adrian C Wright

Moorgate Public Relations
Moorgate House
56 Artillery Lane
London E1 7LS
Tel: 071 377 2400
Fax: 071 377 5820

Chairman: John Allison
Director: Susan Shaar

Morison Stoneham Chartered Accountants
6th Floor
805 Salisbury House
31 Finsbury Circus
London EC2M 5SQ
Tel: 071 628 2040
Fax: 071 628 7531

Senior Partner:
Stephen Chang
Martin Silverman
Partner:
Michael Bailey
Chris Chapman
Richard Green
Bernard Harrington
Richard Harvey
Peter Hill
Nick Jones
Richard Kennett
Perry Lewis
David Mannooch
Elaine Oddie
Robin Platt
Jay Sanghrajka
Clive Steiner
Human Resources Director:
Michael Leaney
Marketing Director: Gillian Angel
Financial Director: Barrie Davies

Morrison & Foerster
23 Albemarle Street
London W1X 3HA
Tel: 071 408 1943
Fax: 071 629 3035

James R Beery
Bradford S Gentry

Musicians' Company
1 The Sanctuary
Westminster
London SW1P 3JT
Tel: 071 222 5381

Clerk: M J G Fletcher

Nabarro Nathanson
50 Stratton Street
London W1X 5FL
Tel: 071 493 9933
Telex: 8813144 NABARO G
Fax: 071 629 7900

Senior Partner:
Geoffrey Greenwood
Managing Partner: John Heller
Partner:
D Abram

Partner:
A Ali
A Barsh
M Bennett
G Benwell
J Blackwell
R Boddington
D Bramson
M Bridgewater
J Byrne
S Carroll
N Cheffings
B Clark
R Collingham
C Cox
A Cree
C Davey
J Dawson
C Daykin
F Denley
H Dunne
C Edwards
L Elks
R Evans
P Fitzmaurice
G Freer
R Gershuny
P Gorty
R Gulliver
D Hawkins
T Herbert-Smith
E Hide
R Holt
C Hopkins
I Howe
N Hughes
K Hutcheson
S Johnston
G Jones
M Joscelyne
M Kemp
P Kempster
P Kendall
L Kovacs
B Land
G Lander
C Lister
S Loble
N Logan
C Luck
G Lust
A MacAdie
I MacPherson
W Martin
L McCaw
G McGowan
S McKenna
M Mendelblat
P Moon

Partner:
J Murray
H Neilson
W Nottage
R Orchard
N Paradise
D Parry
A Pennington
K Pugh
J Quarrell
M Renger
H Richards
P Richardson
J Rickard
H Rogg
J Rosshandler
J Samson
M Saunders
D Sendrove
S Shone
P Sigler
K Stimpson
P Summerfield
T Symes
I Travers
J Vaughan-Neil
R Wakefield
C Wakeford
G Walkley
G Watkins
D Welch
R Williams
A Wright
V Yeend
L Ziman

National Association of Pension Funds

12-18 Grosvenor Gardens
London SW1W 0DH
Tel: 071 730 0585
Fax: 071 730 2595

Chairman: P Stirrup
Vice Chairman:
    C M Gilchrist
    B S MacMahon
Hon Treasurer: R J Amy
Vice President:
    D H Brydon
    J C Woodward
Director General: M A Elton

Needlemakers' Company

17 Southampton Place
London WC1A 2EH
Tel: 071 242 6017

Clerk: M G Cook

Neville Russell

246 Bishopsgate
London EC2M 4PB
Tel: 071 377 1000
Telex: 883410
Fax: 071 377 8931

Senior Partner: Alan W Dyer
Managing Partner: John L P Whiter
Partner:
    David M Berke
    Anthony M Blake
    B John Dore
    John V Drury
    Ms Barbara A Furley
    Mark J Grice
    Andrew J Hubbard
    John S Hughesdon
    Peter R Hyatt
    David R B Ingmire
    Andrew B Jacob
    Glyn F MacAulay
    John S Mellows
    Gerry I Moscrop
    Geoffrey R Norden
    Robin G Oakes
    Peter Ridge
    Ian P H Roberts
    Derek Smith
    Raymond T Turner
    Marc Voulters
    Glyn M Williams

Nicholas Angell Limited

11 Waterloo Place
London SW1Y 4AU
Tel: 071 930 7971
Fax: 071 925 2369

Managing Director: Nicholas Angell

Nihon Keisai Shimbun

Bush House
North West Wing
Aldwych
London WC2B 4PJ
Tel: 071 379 4949
Telex: 884356
Fax: 071 379 5400

Editor: K Obayashi

Noel Alexander Associates

91 Gresham Street
London EC2V 9BL
Tel: 071 796 4322
Fax: 071 796 3309

Managing Director: Noel A de Berry

Norman Broadbent International
65 Curzon Street
London W1Y 7PE
Tel: 071 629 9626
Fax: 071 629 9900

Chairman: David Norman
Chief Executive: Miles Broadbent

The Observer
Chelsea Bridge House
Queenstown Road
London SW8 4NN
Tel: 071 627 0700
Telex: 888963
Fax: 071 627 5570

Editor, Observer Business & City
Editor: Melvyn Markus
Deputy Editor, Observer Business:
Nick Goodway
Economics Editor: William Keegan
Financial Editor: Ms Christine Moir
Industrial Editor: George Pitcher
Investment Editor: John Davis

The Office of the Banking Ombudsman
Citadel House
5/11 Fetter Lane
London EC4A 1BR
Tel: 071 583 1395

Banking Ombudsman:
Laurence Shurman
Chairman of Council:
Dame Mary Donaldson CBE
Clerk to the Council:
Brendon Sewill GBE
Council Member:
Eddie Atkinson
Sir Alastair Burnet
Professor Roy Goode OBE
Bert Morris
Alastair Reid
Bill Sirs
Dame Rachel Waterhouse CBE

The Office of the Building Societies Ombudsman
Grosvenor Gardens House
35-37 Grosvenor Gardens
London SW1X 7AW
Tel: 071 931 0044
Fax: 071 931 8485

Building Society Ombudsman:
Stephen Edell

Ogilvy Adams & Rinehart
Chancery House
Chancery Lane
London WC2A 1QU
Tel: 071 405 8733
Fax: 071 831 0339

Chairman: Jonathan Perry
Vice Chairman Joint Managing
Director: Alex Hurst
Managing Director: David Duffy
Board Director:
Martin Druce
Patrick Heaton-Ward
Tim Powell
Non-Executive Director:
Tom Cook
Jonathan Rinehart
Paul Verbinnen
Peter Warren

Overton Shirley & Barry Partnership
Prince Rupert House
64 Queen Street
London EC4R 1AD
Tel: 071 248 0355
Fax: 071 489 1102

Managing Partner: Colin Barry
Partner:
John Denny
Keith Fisher
Consultant: Caroline Magnus

Painter-Stainers' Company
Painters' Hall
9 Little Trinity Lane
London EC4V 2AD
Tel: 071 236 6258

Clerk: W/Cmdr B C Pratt

Pannell Kerr Forster
New Garden House
78 Hatton Garden
London EC1N 8JA
Tel: 071 831 7393
Telex: 071 405 6736
Fax: 295928

Chairman: C R Brown
Managing Partner: J S Baird
Partner:
S R Armstrong
R S Bint
A M Bolton
D W Boud
S C Bourne
M J Boyle
M Bridge

Partner:
S M Bruck
R A G Bryson
R J Claxton
J G Collard
C Cox
K Crofton-Martin
K S Davies
S J Davies
A D Foreman
R H French
N Gilbert
J C Giles
M R Goodchild
J F Goodson
B C Head
J W M Hills
A K T Hopper
G Littlewood
J F McHale
A F J Mead
R G Mendelssohn
E B Middleton
W J D Moberly
D H Nash
B I Pearl
R J C Pearson
D J Pomfret
A J Pontin
G J Randall
J N Reed
J J Schapira
S S Shaw
P C Swash
Mrs L A Taylor
R T A Thomson
W D Wilson

Parish Clerks' Company
General Synod Office
Church House
Great Smith Street
London SW1
Tel: 071 222 9011

Clerk: J D Hebblethwaite

Paviors' Company
Cutlers' Hall
Warwick Lane
London EC4M 7BR
Tel: 071 236 1710

Clerk: R F Coe

Penningtons
37 Sun Street
London EC2M 2PY

Tel: 071 377 2855
Telex: 859640
Fax: 071 430 2210

Managing Partner: D G Stedman
Partner:
  P J Alexander
  R J Allsopp
  C R Benzecry
  D M Davidson
  P E Eaton
  M B Fellingham
  L C Fynn
  P Hadow
  P R Hay
  D H Kemp OBE
  B I Lewis
  Lesley Joan Lintott
  R A Loveland
  J R E M Mathé
  A J Saul
  R G Stubblefield
  Lady Helen Ward

Philip Allan Publishers Limited
Market Place
Deddington
Oxford OX5 4SE
Tel: 0869 38652
Fax: 0869 38803

Managing Director: Philip Allan
Editorial Director: Philip Cross
Marketing Director: David Cross

Pinsent & Co
26 Colmore Circus
Birmingham B4 6BH
Tel: 021 200 1050
Telex: 335101
Fax: 021 200 1040

Senior Partner: David C Cooke
Partner:
  David J Cooke
  Andrew K Eastgate
  Michael J Embleton
  Patrick J Green
  David J Hughes
  Christopher I Robinson
  Patrick Twist

Plaisterers' Company
Plaisterers' Hall
1 London Wall
London EC2Y 5JU
Tel: 071 606 1361

Clerk: Henry Mott

Plumbers' Company
21 Fleet Street
London EC4Y 1AA
Tel: 071 353 9658

Clerk: Cmdr A J Roberts OBE, RN

Poulters' Company
c/o Armourers' Hall
81 Coleman Street
London EC2R 5BJ
Tel: 071 606 1199

Clerk: Lt Col R R F Cowe

The Press Association
85 Fleet Street
London EC4P 4BE
Tel: 071 353 7440
Telex: 922330
Fax: 071 936 2363

City & Economics Editor:
  Bob Newton
City & Economics Correspondent:
  Andrew Stevens

Reuters
85 Fleet Street
London EC4P 4AJ
Tel: 071 955 0011
Telex: 265339
Fax: 071 583 3769

Financial Editor Europe, M East
  Africa: Donald Nordberg
Financial Editor UK and Ireland:
  Philip Wardle
Chief Commodities/Futures
  Correspondent: James Poole

Richards Butler
Beaufort House
15 St Botolph Street
London EC3A 7EE
Tel: 071 247 6555
Telex: 949494 RBLAW G
Fax: 071 247 5091

Senior Partner: S N Beare
Executive Partner: J M Aylwin
Company Partner:
  D J Boutcher
  F J Donagh
  H L Goldingham
  D J F Innes
  J A Keliher
  D L Marchese
  P G Michelmore
  D L Morgan
  N A Roche

Company Partner:
  S T Sayer
  R E Towner
  T E Watts
Banking & Finance Partner:
  C Bamford
  I M Fletcher
  H O'Donovan
  D M W Smith
  C E A Thaine

Robson Rhodes
186 City Road
London EC1V 2NU
Tel: 071 251 1644
Telex: 885734
Fax: 071 250 0801

Managing Partner: H G Aldous
Partner:
  F A Attwood
  S Bayfield
  M J Biles
  J P Carty
  C Connor
  R Denton
  Geoff Field
  Robert Hale
  M K Hardy
  David Medland
  Chris Rew
  Helen Riley
  Francis A Rounthwaite
  Graham Sidwell
  J Sloane
  John Venning
  D J Williams

Rogers & Wells
58 Coleman Street
London EC2R 5BE
Tel: 071 628 0101
Telex: 884964
Fax: 071 638 2008

Senior Resident Partner:
  Eric C Bettelheim

Rowe & Maw
20 Black Friars Lane
London EC4V 6HD
Tel: 071 248 4282
Telex: 262787 MAWLAW G
Fax: 071 248 2009

Senior Partner: N N Graham Maw
Partner:
  C P Ashcroft
  S J Bottomley
  S C James

Partner:
R D Linsell
J K Oldale
B Ratzke
Ms K M Warnford-Davis
M J B Webster

Saatchi & Saatchi Company plc
Berkeley Square
London W1X 5DH
Tel: 071 495 5000
Telex: 8950391
Fax: 071 495 3575

Chairman: Maurice Saatchi
Chief Executive Officer:
Robert Louis-Dreyfus
Finance Director: Charles Scott
Deputy Chairman and Director:
Jeremy Sinclair
Director:
Simon Mellor
Charles Saatchi
Non-Executive Director:
Professor Theodore Levitt
Dr Thomas Russell
Group Treasurer:
Christopher Bunton
Secretary: David Binding

Saddlers' Company
Saddlers' Hall
Gutter Lane
London EC2V 6BT
Tel: 071 726 8661

Clerk: Gp Capt K M Oliver

St James Public Relations
63 St Martin's Lane
London WC2 4JS
Tel: 071 379 5646
Fax: 071 379 5951

Chairman: Viscount Tenby
Chief Executive: Tony Slaughter

Salters' Company
Salters' Hall
Fore Street
London EC2Y 5DE
Tel: 071 588 5216

Clerk: J M Montgomery

Scientific Instrument Makers' Company
Scientific Instrument Makers' Hall
9 Montague CLose
London SE1 9DD
Tel: 071 407 4832

Clerk: F G Everard

The Scotsman
20 North Bridge
Edinburgh EH1 1YT
Tel: 031 225 2468
Telex: 72255
Fax: 031 226 7420

Associate Editor (Business):
Frank Frazer
Business Editor: P Woodifield
Financial Editor: David Appleton
City Editor: Clifford German
Glasgow Business Correspondent:
Neil Fitzgerald
Business Reporter: Gordon Milne
Financial Writer:
Angus McCrone
Richard Shackleton
Ian Harper

Scriveners' Company
Griffin House
135 High Street
Crawley
West Sussex

Clerk: H J W Harman

Shandwick Consultants Ltd
Dauntsey House
Frederick's Place, Old Jewry
London EC2R 8AB
Tel: 071 726 4291

Chairman & Chief Executive:
C Trusler
Deputy Chairman: D Millham

Shearman & Sterling
St Helen's
1 Undershaft
London EC3A 8HX
Tel: 071 283 9100
Telex: 884274
Fax: 071 626 1211

Thomas Joyce Jr
John A Marzulli Jr
James M Bartos

Shepherd & Wedderburn WS
16 Charlotte Square
Edinburgh EH2 4YS
Tel: 031 225 8585
Telex: 727251
Fax: 031 225 1110/6543

Senior Partner:
W Denys C Andrews
Ian S Boyd
James W Brydie
Thomas H Drysdale
Ivor R Guild
Paul W Hally
Ian B Inglis
D Ian K MacLeod
Iain M C Meiklejohn
David A Smith
James R Will

Shipwrights' Company
Ironmongers' Hall
Barbican
London EC2Y 8AA
Tel: 071 606 2376

Clerk: Gp Capt R C Olding CBE, DSC

Simmons & Simmons
14 Dominion Street
London EC2M 2RJ
Tel: 071 628 2020/528 9292
Telex: 888562
Fax: 071 588 4129/588 9418

Senior Partner: S L James
Partner:
D B Barker
A F Bird
J M Bradshaw
P J Bretherton
B N Buckley
A J Butler
John Calvert
A M Campbell
A M Carr
H P Chalmers
W I Cullen
P D Daniels
D D de Carle
P A de Chazal
A C Dove
G A A Durell
M A Ellis
S R Elvidge
S J Evans
P J Freeman
C A Garner
Mrs Janet Gaymer

Partner:
W E M Godfrey
C P Goodall
N F B Heald
Miss Janet Hollway
G R Kennedy
P D Kennerley
O J R Kinsey
W J L Knight
C E Leaver
H S G Mather
K M Mooney
A P Neil
Mrs Helen Newman
P M W Nias
W F P Noad
R C S Pollock
G W H Rowbotham
C D Scanlan
C C Simpson
J D Sivyer
R E H Slater
G Stewart
J E A Troup
J C Walter
C Wilkinson
Sir David Wilson Bt
M J Wyman

Simpson Curtis
41 Park Square
Leeds LS1 2NS
Tel: 0532 433433
Telex: 55376
Fax: 0532 445598

Senior Partner: Anthony Blackmore
Partner:
D W J Crone
A W Gosnay
N J Painter
J D Perry
M J Robinson
M Shaw
F I Suttie
A W Walker

Simpson Thacher & Bartlett
99 Bishopsgate
London EC2M 3XD
Tel: 071 638 3851
Telex: 886077
Fax: 071 628 0977

Resident Partner: D Rhett Brandon

Skinners' Company
Skinners' Hall
8 Dowgate Hill
London EC4R 2SP
Tel: 071 236 5629

Clerk: M H Glover

Slater Heelis
71 Princess Street
Manchester M2 4HL
Tel: 061 228 3781
Telex: 669568
Fax: 061 236 5282

Partner:
E R Brooks
C F Dunn
J P Orrell
P B A Renshaw
M C Warburton
Consultant: J P Barker

Slaughter and May
35 Basinghall Street
London EC2V 5DB
Tel: 071 600 1200
Telex: 883486
Fax: 071 726 0038

Senior Partner: G B Inglis
Partner:
G J Airs
N J Archer
A G Balfour
G P Balfour
Mrs E A Barrett
D J Beales
R R S Beaumont
P F J Bennett
The Hon N P Boardman
T G M Buckley
M S E Carpenter
R V Carson
P P Chappatte
G D Child
T N Clark
E A Codrington
R D B Cooper
R J N Cripps
Miss J S Edge
S M Edge
S L Edwards
J M Featherby
G P J Finn
C F FitzGerald
St J Flaherty
Miss R M Fox
D T Frank
T G Freshwater

Partner:
I W Goldie
R M G Goulding
R N S Grandison
P A S Grindrod
A R F Hall
C Hall
R C Harvey
J S Haw
G I Henderson
C J Hickson
J Hine
C M Horton
M Hughes
L St J T Jackson
H R Jacobs
G W James
P T Jennings
P Jolliffe
P J L Kett
T A Kinnersley
P J Langley
J H Macaskill
F M Mitchell
R R Montague-Johnstone
Miss F Murphy
F W Neate
A J R Newhouse
M G C Nicholson
H M Nowlan
P M Olney
T J B Pallister
M Pescod
C D Randell
M Read
G F Renwick
G M Ridley
M J D Roberts
W S M Robinson
C J V Robson
P J Robson
J D B Rowe
J E F Rushworth
C F I Saul
C J Saunders
J H Savory
G E S Seligman
R Slater
A M H Smart
C R Smith
P H Stacey
J W Tapner
R J Thornhill
C W Y Underhill
S R Ward
O A Wareham
R A M Welsford
G P White
N S Wilson

The Society of Investment Analysts
211-213 High Street
Bromley BR1 1NY
Tel: 081 464 0811
Fax: 081 313 0587

Chairman: J L Parrott
Member of the Council:
S R Boshell
T F Brown
C J Clark
C C Davis
G J J Dennis
P F Diggle
G M Fuller
P J Greenslade
L F Heasman
D P Johnson
R D Matthews
J A Miller
Mrs N T Ralston
P H Richards
Secretary General: A H Newman

Solicitors' Company
14 Charterhouse Square
London EC1
Tel: 071 251 0531

Clerk: Sheila M Robinson TD

The Spectator
56 Doughty Street
London WC1N 2LL
Tel: 071 405 1706
Fax: 071 242 0603

City Correspondent:
Christopher Fildes
Financial Journalist: Tim Congden

Spencer Stuart & Associates Ltd
16 Connaught Place
London W2 2ED
Tel: 071 493 1238
Fax: 071 973 0893

Chairman: C D Power
Managing Director: D H S Kimbell

Stationers' & Newspaper Makers' Company
Stationers' Hall
Ludgate Hill
London EC4M 7DD
Tel: 071 248 2934

Clerk: Capt P Hames RN

Stephens Associates
20 Cousin Lane
London EC4R 3TE
Tel: 071 236 7307
Fax: 071 489 1130

Managing Director:
Ms Fiona Stephens

Stephenson Cobbold Limited
84 Palace Court
London W2 4JE
Tel: 071 727 5335/243 1383
Fax: 071 221 3698

Chairman: Nicholas S Cobbold
Managing Director: T C Stephenson

Stephenson Harwood
One St Paul's Churchyard
London EC4M 8SH
Tel: 071 329 4422
Telex: 886789 SHSPC G
Fax: 071 606 0822

Senior Partner: A H Isaacs
Partner:
R H Aydon
J T Bach
P J Diss
P J M Fidler
J G Fleming
C A W Gibbons
J R C Howison
A S R Mair
P D Maloney
D M D McCann
D R C Robertson
J A Scales
J S Schwarz
A H Stockwell
A L Sutch
R M Ufland
J A D Watters

Stoy Hayward
8 Baker Street
London W1M 1DA
Tel: 071 486 5888
Telex: 267716
Fax: 071 487 3686

Senior Partner: Paul Hipps
Managing Partner: Stephen Greene
Partner:
George A Auger
S B Benaim
Peter R Copp
Stephen Davis
Michael Grunberg
Michael R Haan

Partner:
David K Harris
Ian Harvey
Phillip R Jacobson
Gervase MacGregor
Adrian H Martin
Dermot C A Mathias
P J Paynter
Dennis V Robertson
Stephen W Say
David E Shrimpton
Paul E H Smith

Sunday Express
Ludgate House
245 Blackfriars Road
London SE1 9UX
Tel: 071 928 8000
Telex: 21841/21842
Fax: 071 633 0244

City Editor: Chris Blackhurst
Deputy City Editor: Paul Dickins
Personal Finance Editor:
Lynne Bateson

The Sunday Telegraph
2nd Floor
Salters Hall
4 Fore Street
London EC2Y 5DT
Tel: 071 538 5000

City Editor: John Jay
Deputy City Editor: Bill Jamieson
Assistant City Editor:
Robert Tyerman
Economics Editor: Sarah Hogg
Personal Finance Editor:
Jeff Prestridge
Deputy Personal Finance Editor &
Diary Editor: Tom Tickell
City Reporter: Patrick Weever
American Business Correspondent:
James Srodes
City Journalist:
Judy Bevan
Jonathan Gregson
Frank Kane
Raymond Mgadzah

Sunday Times Business News
1 Pennington Street
London E1 9XW
Tel: 071 782 5000
Telex: 262139
Fax: 071 782 5658

Editor: Roger Eglin
City Editor: Jeff Randall

Economics Editor: D Smith
Business Editor: Andrew Lorenz
Deputy City Editor: Gareth David
Assistant City Editor: Fiona Walsh
Business Correspondent:
    David Brierley
    Margaret Park
European Correspondent: Iain Jenkins

Tallow Chandlers' Company
Tallow Chandlers' Hall
4 Dowgate Hill
London EC4R 2SH
Tel: 071 248 4726

Clerk: Brig W K L Prosser CBE,
    MC

Taylor Joynson Garrett
180 Fleet Street
London EC4A 2NT
Tel: 071 430 1122
Telex: 25516
Fax: 071 528 7145

Senior Partner:
    Anthony Lewis
    Michael Morrison
Managing Partner: Malcolm Ring
Partner and Head of Department:
    Christopher Bell
    Colin Fraser
    Gordon Jackson
    Richard Marsh
    Nicholas Parton
    Richard Price
    Jonathan Walsh

Thames Television
306-316 Euston Road
London NW1 3BB
Tel: 071 387 9494
Telex: 22816
Fax: 071 387 6297

Editor, The City Programme:
    Terry Kelleher

Theodore Goddard
150 Aldersgate Street
London EC1A 4EJ
Tel: 071 606 8855
Telex: 884678
Fax: 071 606 4390

Senior Partner: W H Stuart May
Partner:
    Michael G T Allen
    Charles E G Ashton
    David R Barrett
    Philip M Bulley

Partner:
    F John Calderan
    Martin G Chester
    Christopher D S Clogg
    Peter S Cooke
    Michael A Croft Baker
    J Nicholas de Beristain
        Humphrey
    Douglas F Evans
    Mark Gilbert
    Simon N Goodworth
    Paddy Grafton Green
    Rosemary Guilding
    Diana Guy
    Geoff N Haley
    James H K Harman
    M John Harris
    Alan Hart
    Michael E Hatchard
    Antony Heald
    David M Hodson
    Leslie I Jackson
    David E M Janney
    Peter R M Kavanagh
    John R Kelleher
    David W Kilshaw
    Martin C Kramer
    Peter S Laskey
    Guy I F Leigh
    Christine Lerry
    Derek W Lewis
    John H Lomas
    Bruce W C McGregor
    C Julian J Maples
    Ken C Mildwaters
    John T Murphy
    Hamish S Porter
    Robin M Preston
    William S Rogers
    Gary A M Russell
    Jeanette A Shellard
    Joyce A Smyth
    Maré N Stacey
    Victoria A Stavely-Taylor
    J Simon Stubbings
    John H Taylor
    Nicholas Whitmey
    David S Wilkinson
Partner (Resident in Brussels):
    Peter G Jackson
    Christopher E Lloyd
    Christopher H Lovell
    Dominic McClusky
    Angus M M Murray
    John G Sell
    Duncan B Stapleton-Smith
    Viviane H Stulz
    Philip Woolfson

J Walter Thompson Co Ltd
40 Berkeley Square
London W1X 6AD
Tel: 071 499 4040
Telex: 22871
Fax: 071 493 8432/8418

Chairman: A Thomas
Managing Director: C Jones

Time-Life News Service
Time & Life Building
153 New Bond Street
London W1Y 0AA
Tel: 071 499 4080

Bureau Chief: William Mader

The Times
1 Pennington Street
London E1 9XN
Tel: 071 782 5000
Telex: 262141
Fax: 071 782 5112

Executive Editor - Finance & Industry:
    David Brewerton
City Editor: John Bell
News Editor: Rob Ballantyne
Economics Editor: Kaletsky Anatole
Financial Editor: Graham Searjeant
Family Money Editor:
    Ms Lindsay Cook
Small Business Editor: Derek Harris
Deputy City Editor: Mike Tate
City News Editor: George Sivell
Industrial Editor: Philip Bassett
Banking Correspondent:
    Neil Bennett
Economics Corrrespondent:
    Colin Narbrough
European Biz Correspondent:
    Wolfgang Munchau
Stock Market Correspondent:
    Micheal Clark
City Diary: Carol Leonard
Finance Reporter: Angela Mackay
City Reporter:
    Martin Barrow
    Matthew Bond
    Gillian Bowditch
    Phil Pangalos
    Jonathan Prynn
    Martin Waller

Tin Plate Workers Alias Wireworkers' Company
14 Talbot House
98 St Martin's Lane
London WC2N 4AX
Tel: 071 379 0788

Clerk: Mrs A M Irving

Titmuss Sainer & Webb
2 Sarjeants Inn
London EC4Y 1LT
Tel: 071 583 5353
Telex: 23823
Fax: 071 353 3683

Senior Partner: Michael Smith
Partner:
    Simon Arscott
    Paul Berry
    Jeremy Butler
    David Byrne
    Ciaran Carvalho
    Frank Collier
    Keith Conway
    Charles Corman
    Peter Crockford
    Geoffrey Davies
    Tamsin Eastwood
    Christopher Edwards
    David Fairfield
    Steven Fogel
    William Fryzer
    Michael Garland
    Gillian Gelding
    Patrick Gloyens
    Peter Gold
    John Goldstein
    Jeremy Grose
    Michael Hallowell
    Paul Harding
    Jack Harper
    Sharon Hazell
    Andrew Hearn
    Carol Holmes
    John Hume
    Andrew Hutchinson
    Georgina Keane
    Alan Kerfoot
    Michael Lacey
    Simon Leonard
    Julian Lewis
    Ian Marsh
    Michael Max
    Reg Morton
    Martin O'Donoghue
    Derek Reynolds
    Dick Russel
    Kathryn Skoyles
    Michael Steinfeld

Partner:
    David Tandy
    Barry Thorne
    David Vogel
    Geoffrey Walters
    David Wells

Tobacco Pipe Makers' & Tobacco Blenders' Company
4th Floor
Bouverie House
154 Fleet Street
London EC4A 2HX
Tel: 071 353 3290

Clerk: I J Kimmins

Today
Allen House
70 Vauxhall Bridge Road
Pimlico
London SW1V 2RP
Tel: 071 630 1300
Telex: 919925
Fax: 071 630 6839

City Editor: Ms Cathy Gunn
Deputy City Editor:
    George Campbell
Personal Finance Editor:
    John Coppock
Financial Reporter: Diane Boliver
City Reporter:
    Peter Davies
    Liz Dolan
    Edward Evans
    Martin Winn

Touche Ross & Co
Hill House
1 Little New Street
London EC4A 3TR
Tel: 071 936 3000
Telex: 884739
Fax: 071 583 8517

Chairman: M J Blackburn
Senior Partner: D T Young
Managing Partner: P M Stafford
Partner-in-Charge: D J S Roques
Partner:
    R K Baldwin
    William D Barnes
    Robert I Beard
    John H Bentley
    R J Blackburn
    John R Bloxsome
    Gerald W Boon
    M Braithwaite
    Diana H Bromley

Partner:
    T M Browne
    Jeremy Casson
    D J Chapman
    Roger G Cheesley
    D Clark
    M C Clarke
    W A Comyn
    J P Connolly
    The Hon R Constantine
    J E Cornish
    Peter H Cowell
    Nigel T Davey
    Colin P David
    Colin G Davis
    Miss Celia Denton
    F A Falk
    R S Field
    P M Gregson
    Clifford S H Hampton
    Nicholas Handley-Jones
    Simon C Hardy
    J Harrison
    Simon M Haslam
    A G Herron
    Michael Holland
    William R H Inglis
    S Ives
    D S Jenkins
    Gareth D Jones
    Thomas J Kendall
    Miss A D M Kennedy
    Julia Le Blan
    A D Llewellyn
    Nicholas R Lyle
    J Magill
    B Marsh
    John M Massey
    David L Morgan
    Peter J Morgan
    C Morris
    C Musgrave
    Mrs Sandra E Oakes
    Peter J Oliver
    R W Owen
    W R Packer
    Mrs M A Parker
    Anthony I Patteson
    J A B Pilkington
    David T C Pollock
    B W Pomeroy
    K H Potter
    Roger A Powdrill
    D F Robinson
    S B Rudge
    M A Scicluna
    Ralph J Sharp
    P M Shawyer
    Gary I Simon

Partner:
B A Smouha
P J Stilling
M E Thompsett
J S Tiley
E F Tracey
M J Turner
John P Waddington
David J Ward
Ian R Watson
G F D Weldon
G V Westropp
C J Wheatcroft
K Wild
P J Williams
P H Wolstenholme
J D Wyer
Lionel H Young

Travers Smith Braithwaite
10 Snow Hill
London EC1A 2AL
Tel: 071 248 9133
Telex: 887117
Fax: 071 236 3728

Senior Partner: A C Humphries
Partner:
David Adams
Oliver Barnes
Christopher Bell
Nigel Campion-Smith
Christopher Carroll
Michael Combes
Roger Dixon
Alasdair Douglas
P W J Duffield
Christopher Hale
Alan Keat
John Longdon
Jonathan Pym
Ms Karen Richardson
D I Strang
G A O Wedlake

Trevor Bass Associates Ltd
70-74 City Road
London EC1Y 2BJ
Tel: 071 253 5858
Fax: 071 253 5255

Managing Director: Trevor Bass

Turner Kenneth Brown
100 Fetter Lane
London EC4A 1DD
Tel: 071 242 6006
Telex: 297696
Fax: 071 242 3003

Senior Partner: David R Wightman
Partner:
Peter R Allen
Stephen J Arthur
Stuart H Benson
Timothy C Cornick
Thomas H R Crawley
Giles Dixon
John Duckworth
Adrian C Hall
Andrew P Inkester
Rhidian H B Jones
Ms Rosemary Martin-Jones
Barry J Moughton
Catherine F Usher
Nigel D Wildish
Professor Peter G Willoughby
David J Wright

Turners' Company
33a Hill Avenue
Amersham
Bucks
Tel: 0494 725903

Clerk: R G Woodwark DSC

Tylers' & Bricklayers' Company
Union House
6 Martin Lane
Cannon Street
London EC4R 0DP
Tel: 071 283 1531

Clerk: F A G Rider

Unit Trust Association
65 Kingsway
London WC2B 6TD
Tel: 071 831 0898
Fax: 071 831 9975

Chairman: J S Fairbairn
Chief Executive: A C Smith
Committee Member (Legal & General):
Mrs M Barber
Committee Member (Fidelity):
B R Bateman
Committee Member (Henderson):
R K Berrill
Committee Member (Target Trust Managers): A Booth
Committee Member (Baring Fund Managers): S Burr
Committee Member (Perpetual):
R Cornick
Committee Member (James Capel):
J Custance Baker

Committee Member (Barclays Unicorn): P Dennis
Committee Member (GT Unit Managers): R Eates
Committee Member (Morgan Grenfell):
A Fraher
Committee Member (Touche Remnant): J Gittings
Committee Member (Abbey Unit Trust Managers): R Haynes
Committee Member (Midland):
R G Heape
Committee Member (Framlington):
Ms A McMeehan
Committee Member (Martin Currie Unit Trusts): A T Maidment
Committee Member (Gartmore Fund Managers): P Pearson Lund
Committee Member (Brown Shipley):
P D Talbot
Committee Member (Prudential Holborn): A C Wren

University College of North Wales
Bangor LL57 2DG
Tel: 0248 351151 ext 2277

Director, Institute of European Finance:
Professor E P M Gardener
Consultant Director, Institute of European Finance:
Professor J R S Revel

University of Cambridge
Economics Department
Sidgwick Avenue
Cambridge CB3 9DD
Tel: 0223 337733
Professor Geoffrey Whittington

University of Exeter
Economics Department
Amory Building
Rennes Drive
Exeter EX4 4RJ
Tel: 0392 263263

Head of Economics:
Martin C Timbrell
Lecturer and Director of the MA in Finance and Investment:
John Matatko
Senior Reader in Economics:
Dr Desmond Corner

Upholders' Company
c/o Kern Ltd
B3 Woolborough Lane
Crawley
Sussex
Tel: 0293 512023

Clerk: W A Garnett

US News and World Report
72 New Bond Street
London W1Y 0RD
Tel: 071 493 4643

Senior European Editor:
Robin Knight

Vintners' Company
Vintners' Hall
Upper Thames Street
London EC4V 3BE
Tel: 071 236 1863

Clerk: Brig G Read CBE

Volkskas Bank Ltd
52-54 Gracechurch Street
London EC3V 0EH
Tel: 071 528 8296
Telex: 920226
Fax: 071 528 8298

General Manager: A G Lewis

W C R S Mathews Marcantonio
41-44 Great Queen Street
London WC2B 5AR
Tel: 071 242 2800
Telex: 25574
Fax: 071 831 3080

Chairman: Robin Wight
Deputy Chairman: Alan Tilby
Chief Executive: Roger Mathews
Director of Finance: Gary Bickerton

Walker Martineau Stringer Saul
64 Queen Street
London EC4
Tel: 071 236 4232
Telex: 28843
Fax: 071 236 2525

Managing Partner: Peter Hawley
Partner:
Peter Aldis
Diana Benjamin
Terence Cole
Roger Duncan
Richard Ham

Partner:
Josselyn Hill
Medwyn Jones
Adrian Scheps
John Wynter-Bee

Walker Morris Scott Turnbull
Kings Court
12 King Street
Leeds LS1 2HL
Tel: 0532 832500
Telex: 557455
Fax: 0532 459412

Senior Partner: Leslie Morris
Partner:
Alan B Baker
Christopher S Caisley
Brian Crawford
David J Duckworth
Derek J Duffy
Robert S Eatwell
Ian M Gilbert
Andrew L T Hurst
Richard H R Innes
John R Kelsall
Michael Kempley
Roger S G Limbert
Richard B Manning
Neil M McLean
Philip J Mudd
Peter C Smart
Andrew D C Turnbull
Paul L Walker
Andrew J Williamson

Wall Street Journal
International Press Centre
76 Shoe Lane
London EC4A
Tel: 071 334 0006
Telex: 22504
Fax: 071 353 4893

London Bureau Chief: Glynn Mapes
Economics Correspondent:
Tim Carrington
City Reporter: Craig Forman

Walter Judd Limited
1A Bow Lane
London EC4M 9EJ
Tel: 071 236 4541
Fax: 071 248 8139

Chairman: James Judd
Executive Director:
William Fergusson
Julian Judd

Executive Director:
Simon Wainman
Head of Public Relations:
Peter Bicknell

Waltons & Morse
Plantation House
31-35 Fenchurch Street
London EC3M 3NN
Tel: 071 623 4255
Telex: 884209
Fax: 071 626 4153

Senior Partner: J D Rothwell
Managing Partner: R H Tudway
Partner:
H H Bohling
J F Brooks
M T Brown
M A Buckley
I Charles-Jones
R K Ginsberg
D P Lewis
D A Perry
J M Rees
D N Ridley
D K Rogers
P Sankey-Barker
T A Smale
M Tovell
N D Traill
M A Warburton
D E Webster
Consultant: R I Hattrick
Director of Finance & Administration:
C H J Parker

Washington Post
25 Upper Brook Street
London W11Y 2AB
Tel: 071 629 8958
Telex: 263555
Fax: 071 629 0050

Bureau Chief: Glenn Frankel

Wax Chandlers' Company
Wax Chandlers' Hall
Gresham Street
London EC2V 7AD
Tel: 071 606 3591

Clerk: Tom Wood

Weavers' Company
1 The Sanctuary
London SW1P 3JT
Tel: 071 222 1983

Clerk: Jonathan G Ouvry

Wedlake Bell
16 Bedford Street
Covent Garden
London WC2E 9HF
Tel: 071 379 7266
Telex: 25256
Fax: 071 836 6117

Senior Partner: B N A Weatherill
Partner:
  G R Andersen
  A P Baker
  M J Burton
  M J Butcher
  T Cheshire
  J P Cornthwaite
  J P Cowlishaw
  R A Dolman
  R J L Eatwell
  J R Fluker
  N E Goodeve-Docker
  A P Gubbins
  R J Hewitt
  C A Hicks
  P Matthews
  J M McKean
  M J Nicol
  Suzanne Reeves
  R D Salter
  Q Spicer
  M K Walford
  G R Waters
  C A L Weber
  Sir John Welch
  P W Whatmuff
  G T Wheal

Wheelwrights' Company
Greenup
Milton Avenue
Gerrards Cross
Bucks
Tel: 0753 888290

Clerk: M R Francis

Wilde Sapte
Queensbridge House
60 Upper Thames Street
London EC4V 3BD
Tel: 071 236 3050
Telex: 887793
Fax: 071 236 9624

Senior Partner: Charles G J Leeming
Deputy Senior Partner:
  Malcolm Glover
Managing Partner: Philip N Brown
Partner:
  Mark B Andrews

Partner:
  Andrew M S Beer
  Graham R Bennett
  Richard J S Bethell-Jones
  Stephan Bird
  James S Blakeley
  Mary P Bonar
  Stephen J Brower
  Richard F Caird
  John A Campbell
  Christopher A Cardona
  Helen M Cleaveland
  Andrew D Collins
  James A Curtis
  Robert K Dibble
  David F C Evans
  John A Fell
  Guy N Fifield
  Mark S Gill
  Geoffrey W Harding
  John K Hull
  Alan L Jarvis
  Charles J Jennings
  Gregory R Kahn
  Robert S McCaw
  Andrew M MacLaren
  Stuart K McLeish
  David W M Menhennet
  Adrian S Miles
  Aynia M Mulligan
  Joseph J Ogden
  Graham E H Paine
  Richard J Pell-Ilderton
  Robin A Porter
  Michael Ratcliff
  Ian M Roberts
  Richard P Rocher
  Charlotte L Sallabank
  George R Sandars
  Richard H Scopes
  Peter J Sharp
  Graham R E Smith
  Justin T Spendlove
  Derek C Tadiello
  Miles H Walton
  Charles R G Williams

Winthrop Stimson Putnam & Roberts
2 Throgmorton Avenue
London EC2N 2AP
Tel: 071 628 4931
Fax: 071 638 0443

  Peter S Brown

Withers
20 Essex Street
London WC2R 3AL

Tel: 071 836 8400
Telex: 24213 WITHER G
Fax: 071 240 2278

Partner:
  David M Dixon
  Philip W Durrance
  Jonathan J Eastwood
  Theresa J Grant Peterkin
  Ian Johnson
  Alexis P Maitland Hudson
  Henry C Page
  Margaret Robertson
  Murray J Ross
  Michael J Soul
  Timothy J Taylor

Woolmens' Company
Kingsmead House
250 King's Road
Chelsea
London SW3 5UE
Tel: 071 352 8638

Clerk: D R L Humble RD

The Worshipful Company of Butchers
Butchers' Hall
Bartholemew Close
London EC1A 7EB
Tel: 071 606 4106
Fax: 071 600 2777

Clerk to the Company: Alan H Emus

The Worshipful Company of Carmen
Britannic House
Moor Lane
London EC2Y 9BU
Tel: 071 920 8509

Master: Sir Robert Reid
Senior Warden: E R Britt
Junior Warden: K E Parry
Clerk to the Company: G T Pearce

The Worshipful Company of Chartered Accountants in England & Wales
The Grove
Hinton Parva
Swindon
Wiltshire SN4 0DH
Tel: 0793 790471
Fax: 0793 790234

Master: Alderman Brian Jenkins

Senior Warden:
Richard G Wilkes CBE TD DL
Junior Warden: F E Worsley

The Worshipful Company of Fan Makers

2 Bolts Hill
Castle Camps
Cambridgeshire CB1 6TL
Tel: 079 984 840

Clerk: I R P Green

The Worshipful Company of Framework Knitters

Apothecaries' Hall
Black Friars Lane
London EC4V 6EL
Tel: 071 489 8469

Master: G N Corah DL
Upper Warden: A M Chapman
Under Warden: J A Ridge
The Clerk: C J Eldridge

The Worshipful Company of Furniture Makers

30 Harcourt Street
London W1H 2AA
Tel: 071 724 5160

Master: R B C Waring
Clerk: Wg Cdr G Acklam

Worshipful Company of Glass Sellers

43 Aragon Avenue
Thames Ditton
Surrey KT7 OPY
Tel: 081 398 4712
Fax: 081 398 5481

Master: O C T R Normandale
Prime Warden: V E Emms
Renter Warden: P C Northam
Honorary Clerk: B J Rawles

The Worshipful Company of Glaziers

Glaziers Hall
9 Montague Close
London Bridge
London SE1 9DD
Tel: 071 403 3300
Fax: 071 407 6036

Master: P H Trollope
Upper Warden: D S Cobbett
Renter Warden: A R Fisher
Clerk: P R Batchelor

The Worshipful Company of Goldsmiths

Goldsmith's Hall
Foster Lane
London EC2V 6BN
Tel: 071 606 7010
Fax: 071 606 1511

Prime Warden: Dr C E Gordon
Smith
Clerk: R D Buchanan-Dunlop

The Worshipful Company of Insurers

The Hall
20 Aldermanbury
London EC2V 7HY
Tel: 071 606 3835
Telex: 957017
Fax: 071 726 0131

Master: R K Bishop
Senior Warden: R C W Bardell
Junior Warden: J S Greig
Clerk: Vernon Webb

Worshipful Company of Joiners and Ceilers

Parkville House
Bridge Street
Pinner
Middlesex HA5 1SJ
Tel: 081 429 0605
Fax: 081 866 8856

Master: Tony F R Stockwell
Upper Warden: Brian P Smith
Renter Warden: John W Farrar
Clerk: David A Tate

Worshipful Company of Pattenmakers

25 Wellesley Road
Chiswick
London W4 4BU
Tel: 081 995 1252
Fax: 081 995 0717

Master: J P H M S Cunynghame
Renter Warden: R P Shepherd JP DL
Clerk: Paul Merritt

Worshipful Company of Pewterers

Pewterers Hall
Oat Lane
London EC2V 7DE
Tel: 071 606 9363

Master: B J Fazan
Upper Warden: C G Grant
Renter Warden: C J M Hull
Clerk: Major General J St J Grey
Beadle: M R Smith

The Worshipful Company of Spectacle Makers

Apothecaries' Hall
Black Friars Lane
London EC4 6EL
Tel: 071 236 2932

Master: Mrs A C A Silk
Upper Warden: J L Kennerley
Bankes
Renter Warden: J Stallwood
The Clerk: C J Eldridge

Wragge & Co

Bank House
8 Cherry Street
Birmingham B2 5JY
Tel: 021 632 4131
Telex: 338728
Fax: 021 643 2417

Senior Partner: Sir Patrick Lawrence
Partner:
S J Braithwaite
J R A Crabtree
Maurice J Dwyer
R M Gilbert
John H Hall
David W Hamlett
C W Hughes
David J Marsh

Julian C Pallett
Kevin J Poole
Peter W Smith
Colin D Tyler
C M Whitehouse

Yorkshire Post Newspaper Ltd
23 Tudor Street
London EC4Y 0HR
Tel: 071 353 3424
Fax: 071 353 7796

City Editor: John Heffernan

SECTOR INDEX

Sector Order

Academic Institutions
Accountants
Actuaries
Advertising Consultants
Analysts
Barristers
British Merchant Banks
Building Societies
Bullion Dealers
Chartered Surveyors
Commodity Brokers
Corporate Finance Advisers
Discount Houses
Exchanges and Societies
Finance Houses
Fund Management Companies
Gilt-Edged Market Makers
Industrial and Commercial Companies
Insurance Brokers
Insurance Companies
Livery Companies
Media
Moneybrokers
Ombudsmen
Other British Banks
Overseas Banks
Overseas Lawyers
Pension Funds
PR Companies
Professional Bodies and Associations
Public Sector
Publishers
Recruitment Consultants
Retail Bank Groups
Securities/Stock Market Firms, Investment Banks
    and Other Financial Groups
Solicitors
Stock Exchange Moneybrokers
The Securities and Investments Board, and Self-regulatory Organisations
Underwriters
Underwriting Agents
Venture Capital Companies

*   see Index of Companies
†   see Index of Service Companies & Organisations

Academic Institutions†

Cranfield School of Management
London Business School
London School of Economics
University College of North Wales
University of Cambridge
University of Exeter

Accountants†

Arthur Andersen & Co Chartered
  Accts
Baker Tilly
BDO Binder Hamlyn
Beavis Walker
Clark Whitehill
Coopers & Lybrand Deloitte
Ernst & Young
Grant Thornton
Hays Allan
Kidsons Impey
MacIntyre Hudson
MacNair Mason
Milne Ross
Moore Stephens
Moores Rowland
Morison Stoneham Chartered
  Accountants
Neville Russell
Pannell Kerr Forster
Robson Rhodes
Stoy Hayward
Touche Ross & Co

Actuaries*

Bacon & Woodrow
Barnett Waddingham & Company
Clay & Partners Consulting
  Actuaries
Hymans Robertson & Co
Lane Clark & Peacock
R Watson & Sons Consulting
  Actuaries

---

* see Index of Companies
† see Index of Service Companies & Organisations

Advertising Consultants†

Abbott Mead Vickers plc
BMP Business
FCB Advertising Ltd
McCann-Erickson Advertising Ltd
Saatchi & Saatchi Company plc
J Walter Thompson Co Ltd
W C R S Mathews Marcantonio

Analysts†

Albert E Sharp & Co
  Del Barrett (Motors)
  Paddy Barrett (Motors)
  Tim Bennett (Engineering)
  Sue Cox (Smaller Companies,
    Aerospace)
  Jonathan Getz (Engineering)
  Robert Griffiths (Other Industrial
    Materials, Building Materials,
    Smaller Companies)
  John Paterson (Electricals &
    Electronics)
  Colin Porter (Other Industrial
    Materials, Building Materials)
  Andrew Rogers (Aerospace)
  Mitchel Teager (Smaller
    Companies)
  Ben Thefaut (Smaller
    Companies)

Baring Securities Limited
  J D Walker (European Insurance)

Carr Kitcat & Aitken Limited
  Stephen Benzikie (Leisure)
  Robin Bhar (Metals)
  Wiktar Bielski (Mining)
  Alan Butler Henderson
    (Investment Strategy)
  Derek Chambers (Banks)
  John Chataway (Stores)
  Robin Christie (Property)
  Tony Cooper (Food Retailing/
    Stores)
  Charles Graham (Food
    Manufacturing)
  Mark Hake (Building &
    Construction)
  Martin Hawkins (Breweries)
  Chris Hibbert (Mining)

Analysts – *continued*

  Charles Kernot (Mining)
  Mark Laurence (Shipping &
    Transport)
  John Marshall (Food
    Manufacturing)
  Keith Morris (Oils)
  Christopher Rathbone
    (Insurance)
  Graham Roberts (Head of
    Mining)
  Martin Smith (Engineering)
  Khaleeq Taimuri (Textiles)
  Alan Thomas (Oils, Head of
    Research)
  Chris Tucker (Electronics &
    Telephone Networks)

County NatWest Securities
  Philip Augar (Head of Research)

Goldman Sachs International Corp
  Rod Barrett (Banks)
  Anders Bartanivts (Scandinavia)
  John Beaumont (Breweries)
  Paola Bergamaschi (Italy)
  Gabriel Besson (France)
  Charles Brown (Chemicals)
  Christopher Buckley (Oils)
  Jose Cerezo (Spain)
  Liz Christie (Electric)
  Gavyn Davies (Currency
    Forecasting, UK Economics)
  Paul Deacon (Stores)
  Stephen Dias (Insurance)
  Philip Dorgan (Food Retailing)
  Mark Edmiston (Germany)
  Andrea Kirkby (Conglomerates)
  Paul Morris (Stores)
  David Morrison (Currency
    Forecasting, International
    Economics)
  Christopher Page (Leisure)
  Susan Sternglass (European
    Banks)
  Philip Van Den Berg
    (Netherlands)
  Graham Warren (Insurance)
  Jeffrey Weingarten (Head of
    Equity Research, Strategist)
  Keith Wills (Stores)

Greenwell Montagu
  Peter Coombs (Research
    Director)
  David Gillott (UK Equities)
  Peter Jones (Head of Research)
  Ian Williams (UK Equities)

Analysts – *continued*

Henderson Crosthwaite
Institutional Brokers Limited
Anthony M Alves (Special
Situations)
Louise M Barton (Paper &
Packaging)
Douglas B Bird (Oils)
Valerie A Connor (Paper &
Packaging)
Richard J Dyett (Electricals)
Julian K Easthope (Leisure)
Paul F Heath (Leisure)
Patrick M Hickey (Electricals)
Michael R Landymore (Food
Manufacturing)
David P Lang (Food
Manufacturing)
William J Myers (Food Retailing)
Brian D Newman (Electricals)
Peter Spring (Oils)

Hoare Govett
Donald Anderson (Building
Materials, Textiles)
Nick Antill (Oil & Gas)
Nigel Barnes (Health &
Household)
Krystyna Brzeskwinski
(Contracting & Construction)
Andrew Buchanan (Brewers &
Distillers)
Emma Burdett (Food Retailing,
Stores)
Melissa Carrington (Economics)
Richard Churchman
(Contracting & Construction)
Simon Clegg (Head of Research)
Angela Coad (Insurance Life)
Nick Collier (Banks, Merchant
Banks, Financial Services)
Sara Collinson-Jones (Food
Manufacturing)
Philippa Cross (Smaller
Companies/USM)
James Culverwell (Health &
Household)
Bill Currie (Food Retailing,
Stores)
William de Winton (Food
Manufacturing)
Hamish Dickson (Brewers &
Distillers, Leisure & Agencies)
John Dorée (Chemicals)
Mark Finnie (Textiles)
David Grimbley (Leisure &
Agencies)
Linda Harte (Food Retailing,
Stores)

Analysts – *continued*

Nigel Hawkins (Electricity/
Water)
Richard Hickinbotham (Smaller
Companies/USM)
Chris Hitchings (Insurance
Brokers/Composite)
John Houlihan (Smaller
Companies/USM)
Nigel Hugh-Smith (Economics)
Andrew Hunter (Leisure &
Agencies)
David Ireland (Conglomerates,
Other Industrial Materials)
Richard Jeffrey (Deputy Head of
Research, Economics)
Andrew Lansdown (Publications
Manager)
Roger Leboff (Property)
Peter Lincoln (Banks, Merchant
Banks, Financial Services,
Insurance Brokers/Composite/
Life)
Bruce McInroy (Electricals &
Electronics)
Monty Mills (Convertibles)
Chris Munro (Packaging and
Paper, Printing and Publishing)
Sandra Murphy (Research
Accountant)
Peter Nolan (Smaller
Companies/USM)
Bob Pringle (Deputy Head of
Research, Electricals &
Electronics, Telephone
Networks)
Richard Rae (Conglomerates,
Other Industrial Materials)
Emma Roe (Administration
Assistant)
Andrew Stone (Electricity/
Water)
Mike Tampin (Aerospace,
Engineering, Metals & Metal
Forming)
Colin Tennant (Packaging and
Paper, Printing and Publishing)
Brendan Wilders (Oil & Gas)
Richard Workman (Food
Manufacturing, Overseas
Traders)
Mark Wright (Metals & Metal
Forming)

James Capel & Co
Rosemary Banyard (Textiles)
Bob Barber (Engineering/Metals
& Metal Forming/Motors)

Analysts – *continued*

Paul Beaufrere (Industrial
Materials/Conglomerates/
Tobaccos/Overseas Traders)
Neil Blackley (Publishing &
Printing/Agencies)
Michael Blogg (Engineering)
Malcolm Brown (Building
Materials/Contracting &
Construction)
Charles Burrows (Electricals/
Electronics)
Andrew Causer (Property)
Julie Crampton (Brewers &
Distillers)
Richard Coleman (Banks/
Merchant Banks/Other
Financial)
Frank Davidson (Food Retailng)
Max Dolding (Leisure)
John Elston (Food
Manufacturing)
Ewan Fraser (Engineering/Metals
& Metal Forming/Motors)
David Gibbons (Electronics)
Robin Gilbert (Health &
Household)
David Gray (Oil & Gas)
Robin Griffiths (Technical
Analysis)
Brian Harding (Engineering/
Metals & Metal Forming)
Roger Hardman (Waste;
Employment)
Yasmin Harrison (Transport)
Lucy Henley (Health &
Household)
Lucas Herrmann (Chemicals)
David Ingles (Chemicals)
James Joseph (Oil & Gas)
Roy Maconochie (Stores)
David Mathers (Building
Materials/Contracting &
Construction)
Chris Murphy (Water)
Jenny Nibbs (Stores)
Allan Nichols (Insurance)
Stephen Owen (Telephone
Networks)
Tony Pennie (Packaging &
Paper/Publishing & Printing)
Fiona Perrott-Humphrey
(Industrial Materials/
Conglomerates)
Quintin Price (Publishing &
Printing/Agencies)
Alan Richards (Insurance)
Nan Roger (Property)

935

Analysts – *continued*

Chris Mitchinson (Equity Strategy, Japan)
Robin Mitra (Insurance)
Ken Monaghan (Corporate Bonds)
Martin Murch (Construction)
Ron Napier (Macro-Economic and Policy Analysis, Japan)
Les Pugh (Food Manufacturing)
Francesco Ricciulli (Italy)
James Ritchie (Conglomerates)
Richard Ryder (Telecommunications)
Michael Sayers (Utilities)
Christopher Walls (Property)
Philip Wylie (Motors)

Smith New Court Europe Ltd
Lorenzo Colucci (Spain, Italy & General Sales)
Dr Alexander Dehmel (Managing Director & Germany)
James Duckworth (Holland)
John Ferrario (Italy)
Pascal Hautcoeur (France)
Bernd Janssen (Germany)
Arjen Los (Holland)
Ian McCormick (France)
Martin Newson (Switzerland)
Nichola Pease (Managing Director, Holland & General Sales)
Elaine Redler (Germany & Switzerland)
Christophe Reynier (France)
Philip Richards (France, Belgium & General Sales)

Smith New Court Far East
Geoffrey Barker (Pacific Economies - Japan Specialist)
Augustus Cheah (Pacific Economies - Singapore and Malaysia Specialist)
Tony Conway (Hong Kong Strategist)
Martin Wedgwood (South East Asia Strategist)

Smith New Court plc
John Aldersley (Health & Household Products - Specialist Sales)
Chris Avery (Engineering)
Steven Bird (Composite Insurance Companies & Insurance Brokers)
Alistair Buchanan (Electricity)

Analysts – *continued*

Bob Bucknell (Engineering)
Kevin Cammack (Building Materials & Construction)
Jacquelyne Cantle (Health & Household Products)
Sara Carter (Food Retailing & Stores)
Roman Cizdyn (Life Insurance & Insurance Brokers)
Nick Clayton (Oils)
Terry Connor (Media, Printing, Publishing)
Arthur Copple (Investment Trust)
Bruce Davidson (Industrial Holdings Companies, Tobacco)
Alison Deuchars (Banks & Merchant Banks)
Chris Dickman (Food Retailing & Stores)
Stephen Doe (Water)
Mary Fleming (Smaller Companies)
Martin Green (Banks, Merchant Banks & Other Financials)
Alastair Irvine (Smaller Companies)
Bruce Jones (Leisure & Office Equipment)
Peter Joseph (Leisure & Office Equipment)
Julian Lakin (Food Manufacturing)
Charles Lambert (Chemicals, Smaller Companies)
Michael Lever (Banks)
Ian Lowe (Engineering)
Peter Lyon (Portfolio Stategist)
Mike McCarthy (Breweries & Distillers)
Chris McFadden (Electricals, Electronics & Telephone Networks)
Philip Middleton (Investment Trust)
Emil Morfett (International Mining)
Andrew Mitchell (Industrial Holdings Companies)
Philip Morrish (Chemicals)
Adam Murza (Property)
Steve Oldfield (Food Retailing & Stores)
Roy Owens (Leisure & Office Equipment)
Catherine Pickers (Food Manufacturing - Specialist Sales)

Analysts – *continued*

Tim Potter (Food Manufacturing)
Tim Read (International Mining)
Derek Reed (Building Materials & Construction)
Alex Robinson (Banks & Other Financials)
Martin Ruscoe (Engineering, Specialist Sales)
Alan Sinclair (Oils)
Maureen Sinclair (Building Materials & Construction - Specialist Sales)
Owen Smyth (Smaller Companies - Specialist Sales)
Mike Sperring (Electricals, Electronics & Telephone Networks)
Mike Styles (Electricals, Electronics & Telephone Networks)
Keith Sykes (Electricals, Electronics & Telephone Networks)
David Tunstall (Property)
Paul Turnbull (Economist)
Steve Turner (Oils)
John Walters (Breweries & Distillers)
Nick Ward (Media, Printing, Publishing)
Graham Webster (Engineering - Specialist Sales & Industrial Holdings Companies)
Paul Woodhouse (Health & Household Products)

Swiss Bank Corporation
Robert Balan (Technical Analysis, Foreign Exchange, Bonds Futures)
Peter Bradshaw (Sweden, Finland Scandinavian Paper, Pulp & Forestry)
David Brown (UK Economics, International Bonds)
Anthony Duckworth (Germany)
Tessa Gilks (Spain)
Marie-Christine Keith AD (Italy)
Vanessa Kennerley-Rossi (Director of Research - Economics & Strategy)
Theo Kitz (Germany)
Gordon Maclean (Sweden, Norway, Scandinavian Shipping)
Gabriella Muzio AD (Italy)

Analysts – *continued*

Jim O'Neill (Director of Research - Foreign Exchange, International Bonds)

Nicola Stevens (France)

Roland Sturm (Switzerland, Seconded from Basle)

Luc van Lent (The Netherlands)

UBS Phillips & Drew

Thomas Albrecht (Banks)

Latkis P Athansiou (Water)

John W Atkins (Senior Analyst, Property)

Peter Beck (Head of European Company Research)

Roger D Beedell (Economist, UK)

Ian Blackford (Specialist Sales, Netherlands)

Roddy M Bridge (Country Strategist, Scandinavia)

Malcolm Brown (Specialist Sales, Oils, Water, Electricity)

Mark F Brown (Chief Strategist, UK)

Chris D Burbridge (Senior Analyst, Chemicals/Textiles)

C Paul Compton (Engineering)

Hilary Cook (Specialist Sales, Breweries & Distillers)

Nuala Corry (East European/ German Companies)

Erich Daehler (Country Strategist, Switzerland)

Kevin J Darlington (Economist, UK)

Mark Dixson (Oil Companies - UK)

Michael Drozd (Oil Companies - Europe)

Peter J Dupont (Engineering/ Metals)

Andrew Forshaw (Specialist Sales, Consumer)

Dorian Foyil (Electronics)

Eric Frankis (Breweries & Distillers)

Gideon Franklin (Electricals)

Scott Fulton (Conglomerates/ OIM/Misc)

Ian R G Furnivall (Country Strategist, France)

Andrew W Goodwin (Senior Analyst, Insurance Composites)

Carl A Gough (Property)

John Graham (Food)

Martin Hall (Health & Household)

Analysts – *continued*

Richard Hannah (Senior Analyst, Shipping/Transport)

Jeffrey Harwood (Leisure)

Jill Johnson (Food - Retailing)

Alun P Jones (Head of Sector Strategy & Quant)

Jack A Jones (Senior Analyst, Conglomerates/OIM/Misc)

Tony Lancelott (Motors)

P Filippo Lardera (Country Strategist, Italy)

Robert Lind (Economist, UK)

Malcolm MacLachlan (Retailing)

William Martin (Head of UK Economics and Chief Economist)

Charles Mills (Food - Manufacturing)

Ian D Moore (Health & Household)

Nick J Measham (Telecomms/ Electricals)

Kalid Nazir (Building & Construction)

Charles Nichols (Senior Analyst, Stores/Food Retailing)

Alasdair Nisbet (Chemicals)

Warren W Oliver (Economist, France, Germany, Netherlands)

Liz Padley (Specialist Sales, Consumer)

David Poutney (Merchant Banks/ Financials)

Geoff Pyne (Oil Products)

Adam D L Quinton (Electronics/ Electricals)

Dr Richard D G Reid (Head of European Economics)

Steve M Reitman (Motors)

Guy Rigden (Head of Strategy & Markets and Chief Strategist, Europe/Germany)

Janet E Robson (Leisure)

Joe D Roseman (European Economist)

Paul Sawyer (Engineering)

Alan E Scowcroft (Quantitative Analyst)

Amanda Sells (Technical Analysis)

William T Seward (Head of Equity Research)

Howard D Seymour (Building & Construction)

Jonathan Shantry (Smaller Companies)

Juliet M Shaughnessy (Insurance)

Analysts – *continued*

Mark Shepperd (Senior Analyst, Agencies)

Mark A Simpson (Shipping/ Transport)

Andrew Smith (Precious Metals)

John D G Smith (Senior Analyst, Stores/Food Retailing)

Peter M Smith (Pharmaceuticals)

Terry C Smith (Head of UK Company Research)

Lawson Steele (Country Strategist, Spain)

Peter Tennyson (Country Analyst, Spain/Italy)

Derek N Terrington (Senior Analyst, Publishing & Printing)

Rupert Thompson (Economist, G/Economics)

Steven Thorn (Banks)

Christianne Thorne (Retailing)

Peter Toeman (Banks)

William Vincent (Banks)

Urs Waldvogel (Building & Construction)

Stephen Weller (Paper & Packaging)

Darren Williams (Economist, Italy, Scandinavia, Spain)

John M R Wilson (Electricity)

Geraldine Wright (Leisure)

John Wriglesworth (Building Societies)

Andrew Yeo (Smaller Companies)

Youssef Ziai (Insurance - Life)

Barristers†

see the beginning of Index of Service Companies & Organisations

British Merchant Banks*

Arab Bank plc

Arbuthnot Latham Bank Limited

Bank of Ireland

Bank of Tokyo International Limited

Banque Internationale à Luxembourg

Baring Brothers & Co Limited

British Merchant Banks

– continued

Barings plc
British & Commonwealth
  Merchant Bank plc
Brown, Shipley & Co Limited
Chartered WestLB Limited
Charterhouse Bank Limited
Charterhouse plc
City Merchants Bank Ltd
Close Brothers Limited
Consolidated Credits Investment
  Capital
Dartington & Co Group plc
Dartington & Co Limited
First Interstate Capital Markets
  Limited
Gresham Trust plc
Guinness Mahon & Co Ltd
Guinness Mahon Holdings plc
Hambros Bank Limited
Hambros plc
Havana International Bank Ltd
Henry Ansbacher Holdings plc
Hill Samuel Bank Limited
International Mexican Bank
James Finlay Bank Limited
Kleinwort Benson Limited
Lazard Brothers & Co Limited
Lloyds Merchant Bank Limited
Merrill Lynch International Bank
  Limited
Morgan Grenfell & Co Limited
Morgan Grenfell Group plc
Noble Grossart Ltd
PK English Trust Company
  Limited
Rea Brothers Limited
Riggs A P Bank Ltd
Robert Fleming & Co Limited
Robert Fleming Holdings Limited
N M Rothschild & Sons Limited
Samuel Montagu & Co Limited
Saudi International Bank
Schroders plc
J Henry Schroder Wagg & Co
  Limited
Singer & Friedlander Limited
Société Générale Merchant Bank
  plc
S G Warburg & Co Ltd
Wintrust Securities

Building Societies*

Alliance & Leicester Building
  Society
Birmingham Midshires Building
  Society
Bradford & Bingley Building
  Society
Bristol & West Building Society
Britannia Building Society
C & G Guardian
Cheltenham & Gloucester Building
  Society
Coventry Building Society
Halifax Building Society
Leeds Permanent Building Society
Nationwide Anglia Building
  Society
Northern Rock Building Society
Skipton Building Society
Town & Country Building Society
Woolwich Building Society
Yorkshire Building Society

Bullion Dealers*

Knight & Day Ltd
Mase Westpac Limited
Sharps Pixley Limited
Vale & Weetman Ltd

Chartered Surveyors†

C S Project Consultants
Cyril Sweett and Partners
Drivers Jonas
Grimley J R Eve
James Gentles & Son
James R Knowles Limited
The MDA Group plc

Commodity Brokers*

Amalgamated Metal Trading
  Limited
Billiton-Enthoven Metals Limited
Brandeis (Brokers) Limited
Brandeis Limited

Commodity Brokers *– continued*

C Czarnikow Ltd
Cargill UK Ltd
Charles Davis (Metal Brokers) Ltd
Crédit Lyonnais Rouse Limited
E D & F Man Ltd
Frank Fehr & Co Ltd
Gerald Limited
GNI Limited
Goldman Sachs Futures Limited
Lewis & Peat Holdings Ltd
Merrill Lynch Pierce Fenner &
  Smith (Brokers & Dealers)
  Limited
Metallgesellschaft Ltd
Moutafian Commodities Ltd
Pechiney World Trade (Holdings)
  Ltd
Philipp & Lion Ltd
Philipp Brothers Ltd
JH Rayner (Mincing Lane)
Refco Overseas Ltd
Rudolf Wolff & Co Ltd
Sogemin Metals Ltd
Triland Metals Ltd
W B B Commodities Ltd
Wilson Smithett & Cope Limited

Corporate Finance Advisers*

3i Corporate Finance Ltd
Bank of Ireland Corporate Finance
  Limited
Campbell Lutyens Hudson Co Ltd
Crédit Commercial de France (UK)
  Limited
Hoare Govett Corporate Finance
  Limited
J F Chown & Company Limited
J O Hambro Magan & Co Ltd
J S Gadd & Co Ltd
James Capel Corporate Finance Ltd
Lazard Frères & Co Limited
Livingstone Fisher plc
MSB Corporate Finance Limited
Quayle Munro Limited
Tranwood Earl & Company
  Limited
Wasserstein Perella & Co
  International Ltd
White Foster Sheldon Daly & Co
  Ltd

Discount Houses*

Alexanders Discount plc
Cater Allen Limited
Clive Discount Company Ltd
Gerrard & National Holdings plc
King & Shaxson Limited
Seccombe Marshall & Campion plc
The Union Discount Company of
London plc

Exchanges and Societies*

The Baltic Exchange Limited
The Baltic Futures Exchange
Limited
Eurobids
International Commodities
Clearing House
International Petroleum Exchange
The International Stock Exchange
Lloyd's of London
London Fox
London International Financial
Futures Exchange
The London Metal Exchange Ltd
NASDAQ International
Scottish Financial Enterprise

Finance Houses*

AIB Finance Ltd
Chartered Trust plc
Commercial Bank of Kuwait
Ford Motor Credit Company
Forward Trust Group
Lloyds Abbey Life plc
Lombard North Central plc
Mercantile Credit Company
Limited
Nichiboshin (UK) Ltd
Nomura International Limited
NWS Bank plc
Rutland Trust plc
Toyo Trust International Limited
United Dominions Trust Limited

Fund Management Companies*

3i Portfolio Management Ltd
Abbey Life Investment Services
Limited
Aberdeen Trust Holdings plc
Abtrust Management Limited
Aetna International (UK) Ltd
Allied Dunbar Unit Trusts plc
Argosy Asset Management plc
Baillie Gifford & Co
Baring Asset Management Ltd
C S Investments Limited
Capability Trust Managers Limited
Chemical Investment Group
(London) Ltd
Church, Charity and Local
Authority Fund Managers
Limited
CIN Management Limited
Clerical Medical Unit Trust
Managers
County NatWest Investment
Management Ltd
CSFB Investment Management
Limited
Dunedin Fund Managers Limited
Edinburgh Fund Managers plc
Electra Investment Trust plc
F S Investment Managers Ltd
Foreign & Colonial Management
Ltd
Framlington Unit Management
Limited
G T Management plc
Gartmore Investment Management
Limited
Gartmore Scotland Limited
Glasgow Investment Managers Ltd
Global Asset Management (UK)
Limited
Guinness Flight Global Asset
Management Ltd
Henderson Administration Group
plc
Hill Samuel Investment
Management Ltd
Hodgson Martin Limited
Ivory & Sime plc
James Capel Fund Managers Ltd
James Capel Unit Trust
Management Ltd
John Govett & Co Limited
Kleinwort Benson Investment
Management

Fund Management Companies
– *continued*
Larpent Newton & Co Ltd
LAS Unit Trust Managers
Lazard Investors Limited
M & G Group plc
M & G Investment Management
Limited
Martin Currie Investment
Management Ltd
Martin Currie Unit Trust
Mercury Asset Management Group
plc
Merrill Lynch Asset Management
UK Limited
Merrill Lynch Global Asset
Management Limited
Midland Montagu Asset
Management
MIM Limited
Morgan Grenfell Asset
Management Limited
Morgan Stanley Asset Management
Newton Investment Group
Nomura Asset Management (Int)
Ltd
Nomura Capital Management (UK)
Limited
Norwich Union Fund Managers
Ltd
Phillips & Drew Fund Management
Limited
Postel Investment Management Ltd
Providence Capitol Fund Managers
Ltd
Queen Anne's Gate Asset
Management Limited
River & Mercantile Investment
Management
J Rothschild Capital Management
Limited
J Rothschild Holdings plc
J Rothschild Investment
Management Ltd
N M Rothschild International Asset
Management Limited
Rutland Trust plc
Samba Capital Management
International Ltd
Schroder Investment Management
Ltd
Scimitar Asset Management Ltd
The Scottish Investment Trust plc
Singer & Friedlander Investment
Management Ltd
Stewart Ivory & Company Limited
Templeton Unit Trust Managers
Limited
Touche Remnant & Co

Fund Management Companies
– *continued*

Touche Remnant Investment
  Management Ltd
UBS Phillips & Drew Intl
  Investment Ltd
Wardley Investment Services
  International Limited
Wardley Unit Trust Managers
  Limited

Gilt-Edged Market Makers*

Aitken Campbell (Gilts) Ltd
Cater Allen Securities Limited
CSFB (Gilts) Limited
Gerrard & National Securities
  Limited
Greenwell Montagu Gilt-Edged
Kleinwort Benson Gilts Limited
UBS Phillips & Drew Gilts Limited

Industrial and Commercial Companies*

A A H Holdings plc
ADT Finance plc
Aegis Group plc
Allied-Lyons plc
Asda Group plc
BAA plc
Bass plc
Beazer plc
BICC
Blue Circle Industries plc
BOC Group plc
Booker plc
The Boots Co plc
BPB Industries
British Aerospace plc
British Airways plc
British Coal Corporation
British Gas plc
British Land
The British Petroleum Company
  plc
British Steel plc
British Telecommunications plc
BTR plc

Industrial and Commercial Companies – *continued*

Bunzl plc
The Burmah Oil plc
The Burton Group plc
Cable & Wireless plc
Cadbury Schweppes plc
Calor Group plc
CIN Properties
Coats Viyella plc
Cookson Group
Courtaulds plc
Dalgety plc
Enterprise Oil
Esso UK plc
Ford Motor Company Ltd
The Gateway Corporation Ltd
The General Electric Company plc
GKN plc
Glaxo Holdings plc
Glynwed International plc
Granada Group
Grand Metropolitan plc
Guinness plc
Hammerson Property Investment
  and Development Corporation
  plc
Hanson plc
Harrisons & Crosfields plc
Hawker Siddeley Group plc
ICI plc
IMI plc
Inchcape plc
Jaguar Cars Ltd
John Lewis Partnership plc
Johnson Matthey
Kingfisher plc
Ladbroke Group plc
Land Securities plc
Laporte plc
LASMO plc
Lonrho plc
Lucas Automotive Ltd
Marks & Spencer plc
Maxwell Pergamon Publishing
  Corporation plc
MB Group plc
Mobil Oil Company
Next plc
Northern Foods
P & O Steam Navigation Company
Pearson plc
Phibro Salomon
Philips Electronic & Associated
  Industries Ltd
Pilkington plc
Racal Electronics plc
The Rank Organisation plc
Rank Hovis McDougall plc

Industrial and Commercial Companies – *continued*

Reckitt & Colman plc
Redland plc
Reed International plc
Reuters Holdings plc
RMC Group plc
Rolls-Royce plc
Rowntree Limited
J Sainsbury plc
Scottish & Newcastle Breweries Ltd
Sears plc
Shell Transport and Trading
  Company plc
W H Smith Group plc
Slough Estates plc
Smiths Industries plc
STC plc
Storehouse plc
Taylor Woodrow plc
Tesco plc
Texaco Ltd
Thorn EMI plc
Trafalgar House Public Limited
  Company
Trusthouse Forte plc
Ultramar plc
Unigate plc
Unilever plc
Union International plc
United Biscuits (Holdings) plc
United Newspapers
Vauxhall Motors
W P P Group plc
Wellcome plc
Williams Holdings plc
George Wimpey plc

Insurance Brokers*

Alexander & Alexander Europe plc
Alexander Howden Limited
Alexander Howden Reinsurance
  Brokers Limited
Alexander Stenhouse Limited
A J Archer Holdings plc
Bain Clarkson Limited
Banque Française de l'Orient
Berry Palmer & Lyle Ltd
C T Bowring & Co Limited
Bradstock Blunt & Crawley Ltd
Bradstock Blunt & Thompson Ltd
Bradstock Financial Services Ltd
Bradstock Group plc
J K Buckenham Limited
Byas Mosley & Co Ltd

Insurance Brokers – *continued*
Citicorp Insurance Brokers Ltd
Crawley Warren Group plc
Denis M Clayton & Co Limited
Fenchurch Insurance Group Limited
The Frizzell Group Limited
Gibbs Hartley Cooper Ltd
Greig Fester Group Ltd
C E Heath plc
Hogg Group plc
Jardine Insurance Brokers Group
Jardine Insurance Brokers Limited
Leslie & Godwin Limited
Lowndes Lambert Group Holdings Limited
Lowndes Lambert Group Limited
LPH Group plc
Macey Williams Insurance Services Ltd
Macey Williams Ltd
Manning Beard Ltd
T H March & Company Limited
J H Minet & Co Ltd
Minet Holdings plc
Nicholson Chamberlain Colls Limited
E W Payne Companies Limited
Price Waterhouse
PWS Holdings plc
Robert Bruce Fitzmaurice Ltd
Robert Fleming Insurance Brokers Limited
Ropner Insurance Services Limited
Sedgwick Group plc
Steel Burrill Jones Group plc
Sturge Holdings plc
J Trevor, Montleman & Poland Ltd
Well Marine Reinsurance Brokers Limited
Willis Corroon plc

Insurance Companies*

Abbey Life Assurance Company Limited
Allied Dunbar Assurance plc
Allstate Reinsurance Co Limited
Commercial Union plc
Continental Reinsurance London
Co-operative Insurance Society Ltd (CIS)
Dowa Insurance Company (UK) Limited
Eagle Star Insurance Company Limited

Insurance Companies – *continued*
The Equitable Life Assurance Society
Equity & Law Life Assurance Society plc
Friends' Provident Life Office
General Accident Fire Life Assurance Corp
Guardian Royal Exchange Assurance
Legal & General Group plc
London and Manchester Group plc
Lowndes Lambert Group Ltd
Manulife International Investment Management Limited
National Provident Institution
The New India Assurance Company Limited
Norwich Union Insurance Group
Pearl Assurance plc
Providence Capitol Life Assurance Ltd
Prudential Corporation plc
Refuge Assurance plc
Royal Insurance Holdings plc
Royal London Mutual Insurance Society Limited
Sampo Insurance Company (UK) Limited
Scottish Amicable Life Assurance Society
Scottish Equitable Life Assurance Society
The Scottish Mutual Assurance Society
The Scottish Provident Institution
Scottish Widow's Fund and Life Assurance Society
Sphere Drake Insurance plc
Sun Alliance and London Insurance plc
Sun Life Assurance Society plc
Sun Life Corporation plc
Sun Life Europe Ltd
Target Group plc
TSB Unit Trusts Limited

Livery Companies†

Actuaries' Company
Apothecaries' Society
Arbitrators' Company
Armourers' & Brasiers' Company
Bakers' Company
Barbers' Company
Basketmakers' Company

Livery Companies – *continued*
Blacksmith's Company
Bowyer's Company
Brewers' Company
Broderers' Company
Carpenters' Company
Chartered Architects' Company
Chartered Secretaries' and Administrators' Company
Chartered Surveyors' Company
Clockmakers' Company
Clothworkers' Company
Coachmakers' & Coach Harness Makers' Company
The Company of Builders Merchants
The Company of Constructors
The Company of Information Technologists
The Company of Watermen & Lightermen of the River Thames
Cooks' Company
Coopers' Company
Cordwainers' Company
Curriers' Company
Cutlers' Company
Distillers' Company
Drapers' Company
Dyers' Company
Engineers' Company
Environmental Cleaners' Company
Farmers' Company
Farriers' Company
Feltmakers' Company
Fishmongers' Company
Fletchers' Company
Founders' Company
Fruiterers' Company
Fuellers' Company
Gardeners' Company
Girdlers' Company
Glovers' Company
Gold & Silver Wyre Drawers' Company
Grocers' Company
Guild of Air Pilots and Air Navigators
Gunmakers' Company
Haberdashers' Company
Horners' Company
Ironmongers' Company
Launderers' Company
Leathersellers' Company
Lightmongers' Company
Loriners' Company
Makers of Playing Cards' Company
Marketors' Company
Masons' Company
Master Mariners' Company

Livery Companies – *continued*

Mercers' Company
Merchant Taylors' Company
Musicians' Company
Needlemakers' Company
Painter-Stainers' Company
Parish Clerks' Company
Paviors' Company
Plaisterers' Company
Plumbers' Company
Poulters' Company
Saddlers' Company
Salters' Company
Scientific Instrument Makers' Company
Scriveners' Company
Shipwrights' Company
Skinners' Company
Solicitors' Company
Stationers' & Newspaper Makers' Company
Tallow Chandlers' Company
Tin Plate Workers Alias Wireworkers' Company
Tobacco Pipe Makers' & Tobacco Blenders' Company
Turners' Company
Tylers' & Bricklayers' Company
Upholders' Company
Vintners' Company
Wax Chandlers' Company
Weavers' Company
Wheelwrights' Company
Woolmens' Company
The Worshipful Company of Butchers
The Worshipful Company of Carmen
The Worshipful Company of Chartered Accountants in England & Wales
The Worshipful Company of Fan Makers
The Worshipful Company of Framework Knitters
The Worshipful Company of Furniture Makers
Worshipful Company of Glass Sellers
The Worshipful Company of Glaziers
The Worshipful Company of Goldsmiths
The Worshipful Company of Insurers
Worshipful Company of Joiners and Ceilers
Worshipful Company of Pattenmakers

Livery Companies – *continued*

Worshipful Company of Pewterers
The Worshipful Company of Spectacle Makers

Media†

Accountancy
Accountancy Age
The Age (Melbourne)
Agence France-Presse
Australian Financial Review
The Banker
BBC Television
BBC TV (Economics & Business Unit)
Birmingham Post
Business
Business Television Limited
Business Week International
Daily Express
Daily Mail
Daily Mirror
The Daily Telegraph
The Economist
Equity International
The Evening Standard
Financial Times
Financial Weekly
Frankfurter Allgemeine Zeitung
The Glasgow Herald
The Glasgow Herald (London Office)
The Guardian
The Independent
Independent Radio News
International Financing Review
International Herald Tribune
International Management
Investment Trusts
Investors Chronicle
ITN
The Journal of Commerce
Lloyd's List
The Mail On Sunday
Le Monde
Money Management & Unitholder
Money Observer
Nihon Keisai Shimbun
The Observer
The Press Association
Reuters
The Scotsman
The Spectator
Sunday Express
The Sunday Telegraph

Media – *continued*

Sunday Times Business News
Thames Television
Time-Life News Service
The Times
Today
US News and World Report
Wall Street Journal
Washington Post
Yorkshire Post Newspaper Ltd

Moneybrokers*

Crown Financial Management Limited
Euro Brokers Holdings Limited
Exco International plc
International City Holdings
King & Shaxson Money Brokers Limited
Lehman Brothers Equity Money Brokers Ltd
Lehman Brothers Gilt Money Brokers Ltd
M W Marshall & Company Limited
Sheppards Moneybrokers Ltd
Tullett & Tokyo Forex International Ltd

Ombudsmen†

The Insurance Ombudsman Bureau
The Office of the Banking Ombudsman
The Office of the Building Societies Ombudsman

Other British Banks*

Adam & Company Group plc
Allied Trust Bank Limited
Bank Leumi (UK) plc
Bank of Wales plc
Barclays de Zoete Wedd Holdings Limited
Barclays de Zoete Wedd Limited
Benchmark Bank plc
Benchmark Group plc
British Bank of The Middle East

Other British Banks – *continued*
The British Linen Bank Limited
Chancery plc
Clydesdale Bank plc
Dawnay Day and Co Limited
Duncan Lawrie Limited
First National Bank plc
Granville & Co Limited
Jordan International Bank plc
Minster Trust Limited
Moscow Narodny Bank Limited
Nikko Bank (UK) plc
Northern Bank Limited
PaineWebber International Bank
  Ltd
The Private Bank and Trust
  Company Limited
Rothschild (J) Capital Management
  Limited
Royal Trust Bank
Schlesinger & Company Limited
State Bank of New South Wales
Unibank plc

Overseas Banks*

Afghan National Credit & Finance
  Ltd
AIB Venture Capital
AmRo Bank NV
Anglo-Romanian Bank
ANZ Merchant Bank Limited
Arab Banking Corporation
ASLK-CGER Bank
Bahrain Middle East Bank
Banca Commerciale Italiana
Banca del Gottardo
Banca d'Italia and UIC
Banca Nazionale del Lavoro
Banca Nazionale dell'Agricoltura
Banca Novara (UK) Limited
Banca Popolare di Milano
Banca Serfin SNC
Banco Bilbao Vizcaya
Banco Central
Banco de la Naciòn Argentina
Banco de Sabadell
Banco di Roma
Banco di Sicilia
Banco Economico SA
Banco Español de Crédito SA
Banco Espirito Santo e Comercial
  de Lisboa
Banco Exterior - UK
Banco Itau
Banco Nacional Ultramarino

Overseas Banks – *continued*
Banco Pinto & Sotto Mayor
Banco Portugues do Atlantico
Banco Real SA
Banco Santander
Banco Totta & Açores
Bangkok Bank
Bank für Gemeinwirtschaft
Bank Handlowy w Warszawie
Bank Hapoalim BM
Bank Julius Baer & Co Ltd
Bank Negara Indonesia 1946
Bank of America
The Bank of California (Mitsubishi
  Bank)
Bank of China
Bank of Crete
Bank of Cyprus (London) Ltd
The Bank of East Asia Ltd
Bank of Japan
Bank of Korea
The Bank of Kyoto Ltd
Bank of Montreal
Bank of New England
Bank of New York
Bank of New Zealand
The Bank of Nova Scotia
Bank of Oman
Bank of Seoul
The Bank of Tokyo Limited
Bank of Yokohama Ltd
Bankers Trust Company
Banque Belge Limited
Banque Belgo-Zaïroise SA
Banque Française du Commerce
  Extérieur
Banque Nationale de Paris plc
Banque Paribas London
Banque Scandinave en Suisse
Bayerische
  Hypotheken-und-Wechsel Bank
Bayerische Vereinsbank
Beogradska Banka DD
Berliner Bank AG
Bikuben
BSI-Banca della Svizzera Italiana
N T Butterfield & Son (Bermuda)
  Ltd
Byblos Bank Sal
Caisse Centrale des Banques
  Populaires
Caisse Nationale de Credit Agricole
Caja de Ahorros de Galicia
Canara Bank
Cassa di Risparmio di Genova e
  Imperia
Central Bank of the Republic of
  Turkey Representative Office
Chase Investment Bank Limited

Overseas Banks – *continued*
Chemical Bank
The Chuo Trust & Banking Co Ltd
CIC-Union Européenne
  Internationale et Cie
Commerzbank AG
Confederaciòn Espãnola de Cajas de
  Ahorros (CECA)
Consolidado UK Ltd
Continental Bank NA
Crédit du Nord
Crédit Lyonnais
Crédit Lyonnais Bank Nederland
  NV
Crédit Suisse First Boston Limited
Creditanstalt-Bankverein
Credito Italiano
Credito Italiano International Ltd
The Dai-Ichi Kangyo Bank Ltd
Den Danske Bank
Den Norske Bank plc
Deutsche Bank AG
DG Bank
Dresdner Bank AG
Etrufin Reserco Ltd
Export-Import Bank of Japan
FennoScandia Bank Limited
First Bank of Nigeria Limited
First City, Texas - Houston NA
First Interstate Bank of California
First National Bank of Boston
The First National Bank of
  Maryland
First National Bank of Southern
  Africa Limited
Fleet National Bank
French Bank of Southern Africa
  Limited
Ghana Commercial Bank
Goldman Sachs International
  Finance Limited
Goldman Sachs Limited
Gruppo Arca Nordest
The Gulf Bank KSC
Gulf International Bank BSC
Habib Bank AG Zurich
The Hiroshima Bank Ltd
The Hokkaido Takushoku Bank
  Ltd
The Hongkong and Shanghai
  Banking Corp
The Hyogo Bank Ltd
IBJ International Limited
Interallianz Bank Zurich AG
International Bankers Incorporated
  SA
Istituto Bancario San Paolo di
  Torino
Iyo Bank

Overseas Banks – *continued*
Japan Development Bank
Jugobanka DD
Jyske Bank
Korea Development Bank
Korea Exchange Bank
Korea First Bank
Kredietbank NV
Kredietbank SA Luxembourgeoise
Kyowa Bank
Ljubljanska Banka
Long Term Credit Bank of Japan
Malayan Banking Berhad
Manufacturers Hanover Limited
Manufacturers Hanover Trust
  Company
Mellon Bank NA
Middle East Bank
Midlantic National Bank
The Mitsubishi Bank Ltd
The Mitsui Taiyo Kobe Bank Ltd
Mitsui Trust & Banking Company
  Ltd
MNC International Bank
Morgan Guaranty Trust Company
  of New York
Nacional Financiera
National Australia Bank Limited
The National Commercial Bank
NBD Bank NA
NCNB National Bank of North
  Carolina
Nedperm Bank Limited
Nomura Bank International plc
Norddeutsche Landesbank
Norinchukin Bank
The Northern Trust Company
Ottoman Bank
Panmure Gordon Bankers Limited
Philadelphia National Bank
Pierson, Heldring & Pierson
Postipankki Ltd
Republic National Bank of New
  York
The Riggs National Bank of
  Washington DC
The Royal Bank of Canada
Royal Bank of Canada Europe
  Limited
The Rural & Industries Bank of
  Western Australia
The Saitama Bank Ltd
Saudi American Bank
Scandinavian Bank Group plc
Seventy-Seven Bank
Société Générale
State Bank of India
State Bank of Victoria
State Street Bank & Trust Co

Overseas Banks – *continued*
Stopanska Banka AD Skopje
The Sumitomo Bank Limited
Sumitomo Trust & Banking Corp
Svenska International plc
Swedbank/Sparbankernas Bank
Swiss Bank Corporation
Swiss Cantobank (International)
Swiss Volksbank
Syndicate Bank
T C Ziraat Bankasi
The Thai Farmers Bank Ltd
The Toronto-Dominion Bank
The Toyo Trust & Banking
  Company Ltd
Trust Bank of Africa
Turkish Bank Ltd
Turkiye Garanti Bankasi AS
UBAF Bank Limited
Uco Bank
Unibanco-Uniao de Bancos
  Brasileiros
Union Bank of Finland Ltd
Union Bank of Norway
Union Bank of Switzerland
United Mizrahi Bank Limited
United Overseas Bank (Banque
  Unie Pour Les Pays d'Outre-Mer)
  Geneva
Vojvodjanska Banka DD
Volkskas Bank Ltd
Westdeutsche Landesbank
  Girozentrale
Westpac Banking Corp
Yamaichi Bank (UK) plc
Yasuda Trust & Banking Co Ltd
The Zenshinren Bank
Zivnostenska Banka NC

Overseas Lawyers†

Bingham Dana & Gould
Bracewell & Patterson
Cleary, Gottlieb, Steen & Hamilton
Cole Corette & Abrutyn
Coudert Brothers
Cravath, Swaine & Moore
Froriep Renggli & Partners
Gibson Dunn & Crutcher
Hamada & Matsumoto
Haythe & Curley
Lord Day & Lord, Barrett Smith
Mayer Brown & Platt
Morrison & Foerster
Rogers & Wells
Shearman & Sterling

Overseas Lawyers – *continued*
Simpson Thacher & Bartlett

Pension Funds*

Beeson Gregory Limited
BP Pensions Services Ltd
British Airways Pensions
Electricity Supply Pension Scheme
ICI Pension Fund
Imperial Investments Limited
Shell Contributory Pension Fund
West Midlands Metropolitan
  Authorities Superannuation Fund
West Yorkshire Superannuation
  Fund

PR Companies†

Broad Street Associates PR Ltd
Broad Street Group plc
Brunswick PR Ltd
Buchanan Communications Ltd
Burson-Marsteller Financial
  Limited
Charles Barker City Ltd
Christopher Bosanquet Ltd
Citigate Communications Group
  Ltd
City & Commercial
  Communications plc
City of London PR Group plc
College Hill Associates Limited
Dewe Rogerson
Financial Dynamics Limited
Fleet Communications
GCI Sterling
Good Relations Ltd
Grandfield Rork Collins Financial
  Ltd
Hill & Knowlton (UK) Ltd
John Bretton Financial Public
  Relations
Leadenhall Associates Ltd
Lombard Communications Limited
Lowe Bell Financial Ltd
Moorgate Public Relations
Ogilvy Adams & Rinehart
St James Public Relations
Shandwick Consultants Ltd
Trevor Bass Associates Ltd
Walter Judd Limited

Professional Bodies and Associations†

AIBD (Systems & Information)
  Limited
Association of British Consortium
  Banks
Association of British Insurers
Association of Investment Trust
  Companies
British Bankers Association
The British Insurance and
  Investment Brokers' Association
British Merchant Banking and
  Securities Houses Association
The Building Societies Association
The Chartered Institute of Bankers
The Chartered Insurance Institute
Confederation of British Industry
Council of Mortgage Lenders
The Faculty of Actuaries
Foreign Banks and Securities
  Houses Association
Foreign Exchange & Currency
  Deposit Brokers Association
The Institute of Bankers in Scotland
Institute of Chartered Accountants
  in England and Wales
The Institute of Chartered
  Accountants of Scotland
National Association of Pension
  Funds
The Society of Investment Analysts
Unit Trust Association

Public Sector*

Bank of England
British Invisibles
British Railways Board
The Building Societies Commission
Corporation of London
Department for National Savings
Department of Trade and Industry
Export Credits Guarantee
  Department
HM Treasury
Industrial Development Board for
  Northern Ireland
Minories Holdings Ltd
Monopolies and Mergers
  Commission
Office of Fair Trading

Public Sector – *continued*
Scottish Development Agency

Publishers†

Euromoney Publications plc
The Institute of Economic Affairs
Kogan Page Limited
Lafferty Publications Ltd
Macmillan Publishers Ltd
Philip Allan Publishers Limited

Recruitment Consultants†

Anderson, Squires Ltd
The Barnes Partnership
BBM Associates
BDO Consulting
CJA (Management Recruitment
  Consultants) Ltd
David Sheppard & Partners Ltd
De Lisle Stephens
Fletcher Jones Limited
Gardiner Morgan International
Goddard Kay Rogers & Associates
  Ltd
Jonathan Wren and Co Ltd
Korn/Ferry International Ltd
Marlar International Limited
Nicholas Angell Limited
Noel Alexander Associates
Norman Broadbent International
Overton Shirley & Barry
  Partnership
Spencer Stuart & Associates Ltd
Stephens Associates
Stephenson Cobbold Limited

Retail Bank Groups*

Abbey National plc
Allied Irish Banks plc
Bank of Scotland
Barclays Bank plc
Co-operative Bank plc
Coutts & Co
Girobank plc
C Hoare & Co

Retail Bank Groups – *continued*
Lloyds Bank plc
Meghraj Bank Ltd
Midland Bank plc
National Westminster Bank plc
The Royal Bank of Scotland plc
TSB Bank Scotland plc
TSB Group plc
Ulster Bank Limited
Yorkshire Bank plc

Securities/Stock Market Firms, Investment Banks, and other Financial Groups*

Aitken Hume International plc
Albert E Sharp & Co
The Alliance Trust plc
Allied Provincial plc
Allied Provincial Securities Ltd
American Express Bank
S P Angel & Co
Anglo Pierson Options Ltd
Bain & Company (Securities) Ltd
Bank in Liechtenstein (UK)
  Limited
Bank of America International
  Limited
The Bank of Tokyo Capital
  Markets Ltd
Barclays Broker Services Limited
Barclays de Zoete Wedd Asset
  Management
Barclays de Zoete Wedd Securities
  Ltd
Baring Securities Limited
Bayerische Landesbank
  Girozentrale
Bell Houldsworth Fairmount
  Limited
Bell Lawrie White & Co Ltd
Benitz and Partners Limited
BNP Capital Markets Limited
Branston & Gothard Ltd
Brewin Dolphin & Co Ltd
Broadbridge
Brown Shipley Stockbroking Ltd
Buckmaster Management Company
  Limited
Burns Fry
Cambridge Capital Limited
Capel-Cure Myers Capital
  Management Ltd

Securities/Stock Market Firms, Investment Banks, and other Financial Groups – *continued*

Carnegie International Ltd
Carr Kitcat and Aitken Limited
Cazenove & Co
CCF Foster Braithwaite Ltd
Chambers & Remington Ltd
Charles Stanley & Co Ltd
Charles Stanley Corporate Finance Ltd
Charlton Seal Schaverien Limited
Charterhouse Tilney
CIN Marketable Securities
Citioptions Limited
City Wall Securities Limited
Citymax Integrated Information Systems Ltd
Cosmo Securities (Europe) Limited
County NatWest Securities Limited
Crédit Lyonnais Capital Markets plc
Crédit Lyonnais Euro-Securities Ltd
Daewoo Securities Co Ltd
Daiwa Bank (Capital Management)
The Daiwa Bank Limited
Daiwa Europe Limited
Dean Witter Capital Markets International Ltd
Dennis Murphy, Campbell & Co
Deutsche Bank Capital Markets Limited
Discount Corporation of New York (London) Limited
DKB International Limited
Donaldson, Lufkin & Jenrette International
E S Securities Limited
Earnshaw Haes & Sons Ltd
J M Finn & Co
First Austrian International Limited
Fleming Private Asset Management Limited
Fox-Pitt Kelton Limited
Fuji International Finance Limited
Fyshe Horton Finney Ltd
Gerrard Vivian Gray Limited
Girozentrale Gilbert Eliott
Globe Investment Trust plc
Goldman Sachs International Limited
Granville Davies Limited
Greenwell Montagu Stockbrokers
The Guidehouse Group plc
Guidehouse Securities Limited
Hall Graham Bradford
Henderson Crosthwaite Institutional Brokers
Henderson Crosthwaite Limited

Securities/Stock Market Firms, Investment Banks, and other Financial Groups – *continued*

Henry Cooke Lumsden plc
Hill Osborne & Co
Hoare Govett International Securities
Hoare Govett Investment Research Limited
Hoare Govett Securities Limited
Hoenig & Co Ltd
IMI Capital Markets (UK)
IMI Securities Ltd
Instinet UK Ltd
International Clearing Services Limited
W H Ireland Stephens & Co Ltd
James Capel & Co Ltd
James Capel Gilts Ltd
Johnson Fry plc
KAS Clearing Agent Ltd
KDB International (London) Limited
Keith Bayley Rogers & Co
Killik & Co
Kim Eng Securities (London) Limited
Kleinwort Benson Group plc
Kleinwort Benson Securities Limited
Kleinwort Benson Unit Trusts Limited
Kuwait Investment Office
Laing & Cruickshank
Laurence Keen Limited
Lloyd's Bank Stockbrokers Ltd
LTCB International Limited
R A McLean & Co Ltd
Madoff Securities International Limited
MAI plc
Maruman Securities (Europe) Limited
Marusan Europe Limited
Mellon Securities Limited
Merrill Lynch Europe Limited
Merrill Lynch International Limited
Merrill Lynch Limited
Merrill Lynch Pierce Fenner & Smith Limited
MGA (UK) Ltd
Mito Europe Limited
Mitsubishi Finance International Limited
Mitsubishi Trust International Limited
Mitsui Taiyo Kobe International Limited
Mitsui Trust International Ltd

Securities/Stock Market Firms, Investment Banks, and other Financial Groups – *continued*

J P Morgan Investment Management Inc
Morgan Stanley International
National Investment Group plc
National Securities of Japan (Europe) Ltd
NCL Investments Limited
The Nikko Securities Company (Europe) Ltd
Nippon Credit International Limited
Norinchukin International Ltd
Okasan International (Europe) Ltd
Olliff & Partners plc
PaineWebber International (UK) Ltd
Panmure Gordon & Co Limited
Paribas Limited
Parrish plc
Parrish Stockbrokers
Paul E Schweder Miller & Co
Peel Hunt & Company Ltd
Potts, West, Trumbull (UK) Limited
Prudential-Bache Capital Funding (Equities) Ltd
Prudential-Bache Securities (UK)
Quadrex Securities
Quanta Group (Holdings) Limited
Quilter Goodison Company Ltd
Raphael Zorn Hemsley Ltd
RBC Dominion Securities International Ltd
RBC Kitcat & Safran Ltd
Rickett & Co Limited
Robson Cotterell Ltd
Roy James & Co
Russell Wood Ltd
Salomon Brothers International Limited
Sanwa International Ltd
Sanyo International Ltd
Schroder Securities Limited
ScotiaMcLeod Incorporated
Security Pacific Hoare Govett Equity Ventures Limited
Sharjah Investment Co (UK) Ltd
Shaw & Co Limited
Sheppards
Smith Barney Harris Upham Europe Ltd
Smith Keen Cutler
Smith New Court plc
Société Générale Strauss Turnbull Securities Ltd
Speirs & Jeffrey Ltd

Securities/Stock Market Firms, Investment Banks, and other Financial Groups – *continued*

Speirs & Jeffrey Ltd
Stirling Hendry & Co
Sumitomo Finance International
Sun Life Trust Management
   Limited
Swiss American Securities
Taiheiyo Europe Ltd
Thornton Management Limited
Tokai International Limited
Tokyo Securities Co (Europe) Ltd
Torrie & Co
Tyndall Holdings plc
UBS Phillips & Drew Futures
   Limited
UBS Phillips & Drew Securities
   Limited
Wako International (Europe) Ltd
Walker Crips Weddle Beck plc
S G Warburg Akroyd Rowe &
   Pitman Mullens Securities Ltd
S G Warburg Group plc
Waters Lunniss & Co Ltd
Westlake & Co
Williams de Broë plc
Winterflood Securities Ltd
Wise Speke Ltd
Wood Gundy Inc
Yamaichi International (Europe)
   Limited
Yasuda Trust Europe Ltd
York Trust Group plc

Solicitors†

Addleshaw, Sons & Latham
Alexander Tatham
Allen & Overy
Ashurst Morris Crisp
Beachcroft Stanleys
Beharrell, Thompson & Co
Berwin Leighton
S J Berwin & Co
Booth & Co
Bristows Cooke & Carpmael
W & J Burness WS
Cameron Markby Hewitt
Clifford Chance
Clyde & Co
Dickson Minto
Dundas & Wilson CS
Evershed Wells & Hind
Field Fisher Waterhouse
Forsyte Kerman

Solicitors – *continued*

D J Freeman & Co
Frere Cholmeley
Freshfields
Gouldens
Hammond Suddards
Hepworth & Chadwick
Herbert Smith
Hill Taylor Dickinson
Holman Fenwick & Willan
Ince & Co
Jaques & Lewis
Lawrence Graham
Linklaters & Paines
Lovell White Durrant
Macfarlanes
McGrigor Donald
McKenna & Co
Maclay Murray & Spens
Martineau Johnson
Memery Crystal
Nabarro Nathanson
Penningtons
Pinsent & Co
Richards Butler
Rowe & Maw
Shepherd & Wedderburn WS
Simmons & Simmons
Simpson Curtis
Slater Heelis
Slaughter and May
Stephenson Harwood
Taylor Joynson Garrett
Theodore Goddard
Titmuss Sainer & Webb
Travers Smith Braithwaite
Turner Kenneth Brown
Walker Martineau Stringer Saul
Walker Morris Scott Turnbull
Waltons & Morse
Wedlake Bell
Wilde Sapte
Winthrop Stimson Putnam &
   Roberts
Withers
Wragge & Co

Stock Exchange Moneybrokers*

Carswell Ltd
Greig, Middleton & Co Ltd
James Capel Moneybroking Ltd
John Siddall & Son Ltd
Marsden W Hargreave Hale & Co

Stock Exchange Moneybrokers – *continued*

Pru-Bache Capital Funding
   (Moneybrokers) Ltd

The Securities and Investments Board, and Self-Regulatory Organisations*

Aitken Campbell & Co Ltd
The Association of Futures Brokers
   and Dealers Limited
FIMBRA
Investment Management
   Regulatory Organisation Ltd
Lautro Ltd
Panel on Takeovers & Mergers
Securities and Investments Board
The Securities Association Limited

Underwriters*

G P Eliot & Company Ltd
N T Evennett and Partners Ltd
Kellett (Holdings) Limited

Underwriting Agents*

Ashley, Palmer & Hathaway
   Limited
Ashley Palmer Holdings Limited
David Holman & Co Ltd
Edwards & Payne (Underwriting
   Agencies) Limited
Gravett & Tilling (Underwriting
   Agencies) Ltd
Gresham Underwriting Agencies
   Limited
Henry G Nicholson (Underwriting)
   Ltd
Holman Franklin Ltd
Holman Macleod Limited
Holman Managers Ltd
Janson Green Limited
A P Leslie Underwriting Agencies
   Limited

Underwriting Agents – *continued*

Martin Ashley Underwriting
   Agencies Limited
Methuen (Lloyds Underwriting
   Agents) Limited
MFK Underwriting Agencies Ltd
Murray Lawrence Members'
   Agency Limited
Clifford Palmer Underwriting
   Agencies Limited
Quill Underwriting Agency
   Limited
R H M Outhwaite (Underwriting
   Agencies) Limited
Scott Underwriting Agencies
   Limited
Sedgwick Lloyd's Underwriting
   Agents Limited
J K Shipton and Company
The Thomson Corporation
Wellington Underwriting Agencies
   Limited
Wendover Underwriting Agency
   Limited

Venture Capital Companies*

3i Group plc
3i plc
Alan Patricof Associates Ltd
Barclays Development Capital
   Limited
Baring Brothers Hambrecht &
   Quist Ltd
Baring Capital Investors Limited
Baronsmead plc
Birmingham Technology (Venture
   Capital) Limited
British Technology Group
British Venture Capital Association
Brown Shipley Development
   Capital Ltd
Cambridge Capital Management
   Limited
Candover Investments plc
Capital Ventures Ltd
Causeway Capital Limited
Chartfield & Co Limited
CIN Venture Managers
Citicorp Venture Capital Ltd
Close Investment Management
   Limited
County NatWest Ventures Limited
DCC Corporate Finance Limited

Venture Capital Companies
 – *continued*

DCC Ventures Limited
Development Capital Group Ltd
EC1 Ventures
Fleming Ventures Ltd
Foreign & Colonial Ventures Ltd
G T Venture Management
   Holdings Ltd
Greater London Enterprise
Grosvenor Venture Managers
   Limited
The Growth Fund Limited
Guinness Mahon Development
   Capital Ltd
Gyllenhammar & Partners
   International Limited (GPI)
Hambro European Ventures
   Limited
Hill Samuel Development Capital
Japan Associated Finance Co Ltd
Legal & General Ventures Ltd
Lloyds Development Capital
   Limited
March Investment Fund Limited
MMG Patricof & Co
MMG Patricof Buy-Ins Limited
The MMG Patricof Group plc
J P Morgan Futures Inc
MTI Managers Limited
Mynshul Bank plc
National Westminster Growth
   Options Ltd
Newmarket Venture Capital plc
Northern Venture Managers
   Limited
Phildrew Ventures
Pine Street Investments Limited
Prelude Technology Investments
   Limited
Schroder Ventures
Scimitar Development Capital
   Limited
Security Pacific Venture Capital
Sumit Equity Ventures Limited
Top Technology Limited
Ulster Development Capital
   Limited
Venture Link Investors Ltd
Yorkshire Enterprise Limited

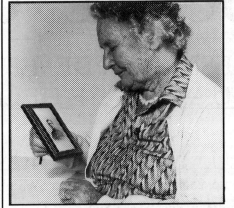

WHO FIGHTS FOR THE SOLDIER WHEN THE SOLDIER CAN'T FIGHT?

When a man has given his youth and strength to help us, it's our privilege and duty to help him and his loved ones when in need – even if he's still in the Service.

And when a Serviceman leaves the Army, Navy or Air Force, he and his family may have to face problems never encountered before. In fact, he may, in the defence of his country, have become disabled or have left behind a widow and children who desperately need advice and help.

A legacy in your will ensures that we can continue doing something in return. Please remember us. And please help.

SSAFA, 19 Queen Elizabeth Street, London SE1 2LP
Tel: 071 403 8783 or 071 962 9696

SOLDIERS', SAILORS' AND AIRMEN'S FAMILIES ASSOCIATION

949

YOUR LIFE DEPENDS ON YOUR LUNGS

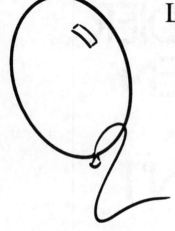

LUNG RESEARCH DEPENDS ON <u>YOU</u> — PLEASE HELP.

BRITISH LUNG FOUNDATION

Kingsmead House, 250 Kings Road, London SW3 5UE
Telephone: 071 376 5735. Registered charity no 326730
Patron: HRH The Princess of Wales

Breathing life into lung research

The British Lung Foundation is one of the UK's fastest growing charities. With the Princess of Wales as its committed Patron, its lively balloon logo and professional approach, the British Lung Foundtion has already raised over £XX million since it was set up in 1985.

One person in ten has a lung problem in this country and lung disease results in over 50 million working days being lost each year. Five million people — from premature babies and young children through to the elderly — have to cope with often disabling diseases such as asthma, bronchitis, pneumonia and emphysema, and one if five of these will die from them.

Despite these facts, the British Lung Foundation is the only charity in the UK funding research into the prevention, diagnosis and treatment of all kinds of lung diseases.

The British Lung is offering unparalled opportunities for business partners to benefit from its success as it grows. Whether it is corporate hospitality, public relations or sales promotions, the British Lung Foundation can offer joint sponsorships and promotions which are good for your business as well as your staff, suppliers, clients and shareholders.

The British Lung Foundation's Business Partners
Beazer, British Airways
BOC Group, Grand Metropolitan
Midlands Electricity, National Power
and Trusthouse Forte
are all business partners of the British Lung Foundation.

Ring Sarah Woolf at the British Lung Founation and find out how your company could work with the British Lung Foundation as it breathes new life into lung research.

BRITISH LUNG FOUNDATION

250 KING'S ROAD · LONDON SW3 5UE
TEL 071-376 5735 · CHARITY NUMBER 326730

The Brave and Living Dead

As a nation we honour those brave men and women from all the services who gave their lives for the safety of our Country.

But what of the many who faced the same horrors and survived . . . but with their minds shattered?

Men and women such as these come from all the Services, some young, some now elderly, with varying degrees of mental illness from total twilight to mild infirmity.

Thanks to the Ex-Services Mental Welfare Society not one need be abandoned as human wreckage. We have our own Convalescent Homes and, for the old, there is our Veterans' Home where they can see out their days with dignity and comfort.

To put it bluntly; for this work the Society needs money badly. Please help us to help those who have given their most precious possession after life itself. A donation, legacy, covenant or a gift inter vivos – all are urgently required.

"They've given more than they could. Please give as much as you can."

COMBAT STRESS

EX-SERVICES MENTAL WELFARE SOCIETY

Broadway House, The Broadway, Wimbledon SW19 1RL.
Telephone: 081-543 6333

OVER 70 YEARS OF CARING
COMBAT STRESS
EX-SERVICES MENTAL WELFARE SOCIETY

Ex-Services Mental Welfare Society

BROADWAY HOUSE,
THE BROADWAY,
WIMBLEDON SW19 1RL.
Telephone: 081-543 6333

The Ex-Services Mental Welfare Society is the only organisation specialising in the mental problems of ex-Service men and women of H.M. Forces and the Merchant Navy. In undertaking this work it fills a void. Men and women breaking down through service to their country, have two alternatives; either to go into a mental hospital, or to have treatment in their own homes. Although mental hospitals here are as good as any in the world, they are overcrowded and have a vast civilian problem. As far as patients remaining in their own homes are concerned, no one with a close knowledge of mental breakdown would expect the family of this sufferer to carry this burden throughout their entire lives. In the words of the late Admiral of the Fleet, Sir Arthur Power, "You can give a man an artificial limb, but you cannot give him an artificial mind. Somewhere, somehow, he has to be looked after under specialist care."

The Society visits ex-Service men and women in mental hospitals, runs its own convalescent homes, provides cottages, a hostel, a veterans' home and a pensions appeal department. But this work costs more and more every year. Support is vital and the Society asks everybody to "remember those who can't forget." Some of its patients are only nineteen, some are ninety, and all need the Society's help because there's no one else.

Assured of Care
for the rest of their lives

For 90 years Princess Christian Homes, Knaphill, Surrey have been home to men who might otherwise spend their declining years in loneliness and difficulty.

Now, among the ex-service community as in the rest of the population, the number of frail elderly is increasing, and the care which the Homes can at present give is not enough.

THE FORCES HELP SOCIETY therefore plans to add a fully staffed, well equipped care unit with all its own facilities, to accommodate both men and women. For this your help is needed by donations, covenants and legacies.

In their old age help us to care for those who served us so well

The Forces Help Society
& Lord Roberts Workshops

122 Brompton Road, London SW3 1JE   Tel: 01-589 3243

Registered Charity No. 209753

Many of those now becoming unable to fend for themselves are the men and women who served well and loyally in World War II and came back, more or less unscathed, to live useful lives in the civilian world. Others came back with disabilities they could cope with while young, but which cause increasing difficulty as they grow older. Yet others, still relatively young in years, need day to day care through crippling injuries sustained in troubled regions from Korea to Northern Ireland.

As well as helping individuals in need, the FORCES HELP SOCIETY has carried out a number of building projects for the benefit of ex-service men and women with disabilities, whether resulting from their service or from injury, illness or ageing after their return to civilian life. Over the past decade it has built and now maintains 33 bungalows designed for the disabled. In 1987 a new wing was built at the Society's Retirement Home at Knaphill, Surrey, with facilities to enable the wheelchair-bound to live there. Purpose-built holiday apartments for the disabled and those who care for them opened in April 1990 on the Isle of Wight.

None of these projects would have been possible without the generous support of Trusts, Companies and individuals. The Society earnestly hopes that even more will wish to be associated with its newest project to being security and comfort in their old age to some of those who served.

In the life of a Great Ormond Street patient – these people are.

For some children, Great Ormond Street Children's Hospital is their world. The most important people in this world are not only their parents, but also the staff who support their courageous efforts to stay alive.

Founded in 1852, to look after only 10 children, Great Ormond Street Children's Hospital now admits 12,000 in-patients and sees some 50,000 out-patients a year.

The Hospital has always touched the hearts of the Nation. It moved people like Charles Dickens to read some of his own work to raise funds. It motivated Sir James Barrie to bequeath the copyright of Peter Pan to the Hospital. And it has compelled

people like you and I, through our whole-hearted support, to make the present Hospital possible.

To make a donation, or for information on the Hospital's history, its present and its future, please phone me on 071-831 1199 or write to me at the address below. I'm Ann Gillespie, and I look forward to hearing from you.

Great Ormond Street Children's Hospital Fund
The Hospitals for Sick Children,
Great Ormond Street,
LONDON WC1N 3JH

The Haemophilia Society

123 Westminster Bridge Road
London SE1 7HR
Telephone: 071-928 2020

Patron: HRH The Duchess of Kent
Established 1950
Regd. Charity No. 288260

Haemophilia is a disorder of the blood clotting mechanism which can lead to progressive crippling unless properly treated.

The Haemophilia Society exists to:

☐ **Provide our members with factual information on their condition.**

☐ **Provide advice on all aspects of treatment and care.**

☐ **Provide practical help with any matter arising from haemophilia.**

☐ **Provide financial help where necessary.**

THE SOCIETY URGENTLY NEEDS FUNDS TO CONTINUE AND EXPAND IT MUCH NEEDED WORK.

For further details of the Society's work please write to us at the above address.

Donations should be sent to: *The Treasurer, 123 Westminster Bridge Road, London SE1 7HR.*

HAEMOPHILIA SOCIETY

123 Westminster Bridge Road, London SE1 7HR.
(Tel: 071–928 2020). Registered Charity No: 288260.

Haemophilia is an inherited blood disorder which can lead to progressive crippling unless properly treated by the infusion of blood concentrates, the use of which represents an important medical advance.

Haemophilia means life long anxiety for those affected and acute worry for the parents of young children. The Society provides help and advice and issues publications which can bridge the gap between hope and despair.

The Society is a small charity with a staff of only six. The strain upon its slender resources from all these demands is enormous.

We need covenants, donations and legacies. Thank you.

The Institute of Cancer Research, Royal Cancer Hospital, 17A Onslow Gardens, London, SW7 3AL (Tel: 071-352 8133). Founded in 1911, the objects of the Institute are to carry out research into the nature, causes and prevention of cancer and allied diseases and in collaboration with the medical staff of The Royal Marsden Hospital — formerly, the Royal Cancer Hospital — to improve methods of diagnosis, treatment and the alleviation of suffering. Research is organised on a multi-disciplinary basis and covers the full spectrum of fundamental and clinical work. During 1989-1990, the Institute spent some £16 million on research of which an amount in excess of £2 million was received in the form of legacies and donations. A large proportion of the Institute's revenue comes from its principal sponsor, the Cancer Research Campaign, together with the Medical Research Council and others, but the Institute does depend on considerable public support to ensure the continuity of its research from year to year. The present research facilities are located at two main sites, the Chester Beatty Laboratories in Chelsea, London, and the Institute's laboratories at Sutton, Surrey. The Institute is part of the University of London and devotes considerable effort to attracting the best scientific graduates and training them in the specific disciplines necessary. For more information please contact the Legacy Officer at the Institute.

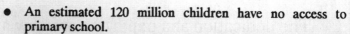
958

The formation of the PDSA in 1917 was the inspiration of social worker Maria Dickin, who was moved by the plight of animals whose owners found themselves unable to afford veterinary fees. From a point of commencement in London's East End the Society's enterprise spread nation-wide and ultimately internationally, with its continuance ever dependent upon public subscription of funds.

During the second world war and subsequently, overseas services have been progressively withdrawn and a commitment now remains only in Cairo, although the Society's name is also associated with a charitable veterinary service in Cape Town.

Society activity is now substantially concentrated upon its service to eligible clients within the United Kingdom, and its precise objectives and limitations are defined by two relevant Acts of Parliament. Currently it undertakes responsibility for the cost of almost 1.4 million treatments annually. Today the eligibility of clients for Society services is judged in the first instance upon their receipt of a range of state benefits:

State Retirement Pension
Sickness/Invalidity Benefit or Pension
Unemployment Benefit or Training Allowance
Income Support
Family Credit
Widows Benefits
Housing Benefit

Other owners of a low income category and experiencing difficulty in meeting the cost of an unusually expensive veterinary treatment may be referred for Society help, usually through the intervention of a private veterinary surgeon. In addition to these categories, the Society, in common with private veterinary practices, provides necessary emergency treatment for any animal in a situation of genuine need, regardless of its owners status.

The bulk of society expenditure is upon services provided within its 55 veterinary centres which employ a total of 190 full time veterinary staff, 230 veterinary nurses and additional supporting staff. These are located in major conurbations and areas of high population density, but in a further 70 smaller communities a PDSA Pet-Aid service is offered through participating private sector practices. In these situations eligible clients living within specified postal-code districts have access to full veterinary services from their local veterinary practice at the Society's expense.

In all circumstances the pets of clients are offered veterinary services at standards comparable with those available in private practices, but there is a limited range of elective procedures excluded from offer. All forms of cosmetic surgery and such elective procedures as neutering of female or male animals (other than tom cats) are excluded, as is routine vaccination of dogs and cats, since these are all items for which pre-planning and budgeting may be reasonably anticipated.

Nonetheless, expenditure on necessary services now exceeds £10.5 million annually and costs continue to escalate as increasingly sophisticated veterinary treatments become mainstream.

As a charity dependent upon income from continuous public subscription, the Society faces the additional problem that in times of particular recession, as such income inevitably declines, the demand upon its services increases noticeably and sometimes dramatically. Professional fund raising is therefore a necessary adjunct to the provision of veterinary services and the Society operates a team of 'Appeals' Staff, as well as approximately 70 retail outlets in which the services of volunteers are utilised under the supervision of salaried staff.

Assistance from well wishers is appreciated, but inevitably has to be confined to fund raising activities since the work of veterinary staff is highly specialised and not allowing of non-professional participation. However, the objectives of all are that the valuable inter-relationship of pets and people be afforded maximum support in situations in which the stress of accident or illness is exacerbated by lack of financial solvency. In this way the Society remains entirely loyal to the objectives of its founder.

The PDSA, as Britain's major veterinary charity, undertakes financial responsibility for approximately 1.4 million veterinary treatments annually.

The continuance and expansion of this service to eligible pet owners nation wide remains dependent upon donations from a general public approving of its effort.

The Society has remained true to its objective for more than 70 years and continues in this practical way to facilitate the beneficial bond between pet and person.

Head Office: PDSA
Whitechapel Way,
Priorslee,
Telford,
Shropshire TF2 9PQ.
Tel: (0952) 290999
Fax: (0952) 291035

"NOW IT'S GRANDPA'S HOUR OF NEED, IT'S THE RAF BENEVOLENT FUND THAT DESERVES A MEDAL"

"Grandpa was admired for many brave acts, but he won his DFM for his part in the Battle of Britain. Now he's been in the wars himself, he says it's the RAF Benevolent Fund that really deserves a medal."

Over 70,000 RAF men and women died for our country during the last War. Many thousands more were left disabled. Since 1945, too, the RAF has incurred casualties in its training, peace-preserving missions and operations.

From 1919, the Fund has been helping past and present RAF members of all ranks, their widows and children. In 1989, over 13,000 people benefited from grants of over £7.4 million. Inflation and old age increases that figure annually.

Where does the money go? To helping families maintain a semblance of the life they had before, by providing housing and funds to overcome financial difficulties, by looking after the infirm in our rest homes and many other ways in which the Fund contributes to the well being of those who have an hour of need.

We urgently need your clients' support to repay the debt we owe those who have suffered on our behalf. All donations will be gratefully received. We'll also be happy to advise on legacies, covenants and payroll giving.

THE ROYAL AIR FORCE BENEVOLENT FUND

Dept. WIC90, 67 Portland Place,
London W1N 4AR.
Telephone: 071-580 8343. Ext. 257

Charity Reg. No 207327

Royal Air Force Benevolent Fund

67 PORTLAND PLACE, LONDON W1N 4AR.
Also at:
20 QUEEN STREET, EDINBURGH EH2 1JX.
Registered Charity No. 207327

The Royal Air Force Benevolent Fund was founded in 1919 for the relief of distress or need amongst past and present members of all ranks of the Royal Air Force, including the Women's Services, the Royal Auxiliary Air Force, the Royal Air Force Reserves, and their widows, children and other dependants.

There are no hard and fast rules about how those eligible may be helped or how much help may be given. Each person's needs are considered in the light of his or her particular circumstances, the object being to provide relief in the many cases where assistance from the State is either not forthcoming or is inadequate. Where dependants are concerned, the Fund endeavours to help them maintain some semblance of the life to which they are accustomed and to enable children to follow careers that their fathers might reasonably have expected them to follow.

The Duke of Kent School at Woolpit, Surrey is an independent preparatory boarding school supported and administered by the Fund for sons and daughters of Royal Air Force personnel of all ranks. Preference for admission is given to children (Foundationers) whose fathers died or were seriously disabled whilst serving. Children of retired Royal Air Force personnel are also accepted, particularly if the father died through illness or disablement attributable to his service. The Fund also assists with boarding and education fees to the completion of "A" level examinations. Where there is a need, help may also be given for higher education at university or polytechnic.

Princess Marina House at Rustington in Sussex provides convalescent and residential accommodation for partially disabled and elderly past or present members of all ranks of the Royal Air Force and their adult dependants. Residential accommodation for 31 residents only is available at Alastrean House, Tarland, Grampian.

An increasing number of beneficiaries are now reaching advanced age and it is essential for the Fund to raise its income to ensure that it will always be able to meet the demands of the coming years; it must never fail, through lack of money, to help someone in need.

A legacy or bequest to the Fund is an acknowledgement of the debt we owe and can form a permanent memorial to someone who gave a life or performed gallant service with the RAF. Full advice on legacies, bequests and covenants will gladly be supplied by Secretary (Appeals). Telephone 071-580 8343 or in Scotland 031-225 6421.

The Sue Ryder Foundation
In aid of the sick and disabled

Founder — Lady Ryder of Warsaw, CMG, OBE

The Sue Ryder Foundation was established by Sue Ryder during the post-war years after she had been doing social relief work on the Continent. Its purpose was, and is, the relief of suffering on a wide scale by means of personal service, helping the sick and disabled everywhere, irrespective of race, religion or age, and thus serving as a **Living Memorial** to all those who suffered or died in the two World Wars and to those who undergo persecution or die in defence of human values today.

At present there are Homes in Britain in **Berkshire, Bedfordshire, Cambridgeshire, Cumbria, Gloucestershire, Hampshire, Hertfordshire, Lancashire, Leicestershire, Norfolk, Suffolk, Yorkshire, Berwickshire and West Lothian,** but many more are needed. They care for the **physically handicapped, cancer** patients both terminal and convalescent, the **mentally ill, Huntington's Chorea** patients, and the **elderly**. Domiciliary care is also undertaken. These and all our patients desperately need your help — with a legacy, deed of convenant or donation in finance or kind. Also, the Foundation will be pleased to advise companies whose employees wish to contribute via the *Give As You Earn Scheme.*

New Homes are planned in Birmingham, Cambridgeshire, Kent, London, Nottinghamshire, Shropshire and North East England.

Please write for any further information to:

The Sue Ryder Foundation
Cavendish, Sudbury, Suffolk CO10 8AY

962

It costs us over £15,000 a day to support our dependents. That's an awful lot of coins (or one or two legacies).

It's easy to see why legacies are vital to us. Just one can equal hundreds, even thousands, of smaller donations.

So if they stop, so does our work.

That would mean the end of much-needed support for many deserving people who are unable to make ends meet after their retirement.

Not just dedicated ex-professionals (and others from a similar background) who have spent their lives serving the community, but also those who have shown unstinting devotion to their family, even to the detriment of their own careers. RUKBA care for such people in a number of ways.

Primarily by the granting of life-long annuities or, if necessary, by offering a place in one of our residential homes.

Either way our costs are rising daily.

As are the number of people who deserve our support.

To help us, tell your clients about our work because legacies are our lifeblood. And the more we receive the more help we can give.

RUKBA

6, Avonmore Road, London W14 8RL. Tel: 071-602 6274

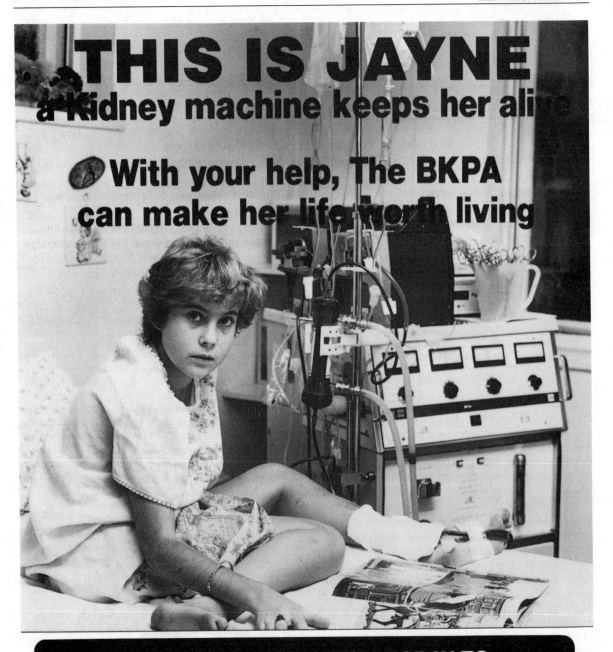

WOOD GREEN ANIMAL SHELTERS
FOUNDED 1924

The Progressive Charity

The aims of Wood Green Animal Shelters are:
*To shelter any animal. *To nurse them back to health. *To endeavour to find them new homes.
*To encourage responsible attitudes towards animals.
The need for Wood Green Animal Shelters will not diminish. However, to achieve these aims, Wood Green Animal Shelters must meet its objectives.
*Maintain long-term financial support. *Increase fundraising activities. *Extend existing facilities.
A business link with the Wood Green Animal Shelters creates a mutually beneficial publicity campaign and offers important sales and marketing opportunities:
*To work in partnership with companies and businesses. Our highly motivated marketing team will undertake presentations to client's briefs and provide full in-house production from concept to completion.
*To adapt specific projects to meet your corporate needs.
*To enhance one's corporate image. *To increase one's target market.
*To improve community relations. *To motivate staff.

For full details about the work of the Shelters, please contact:-
Wood Green Animal Shelters, Dept M155, Chishill Road, Heydon, Nr. Royston, Herts, SG8 8PN.
Telephone (0763) 838329   Fax: 0763 838318
Registered Charity 298348

Each of Wood Green Animal Shelters' branches has the most up-to-date facilities and technology to care for all types of animals in need. Animals placed in the Charity's care receive dedicated devotion from caring professional staff. The Shelters employ their own veterinary surgeons and veterinary nurses and are an approved training and examination centre for veterinary nurses.

At any given time the Shelters are able to accommodate over 2,000 animals at their premises and continue to care for the well-being of all animals that have been re-homed. In many cases pre-visits are carried out before adoption to ascertain that the facilities being offered are suitable for the animals chosen. Follow-up visits are made for the remainder of the animals' lives. Strict vaccination and worming programmes are carried out and neutering policies are adhered to, to prevent an even greater number of unwanted litters being born for which homes would have to be found.

The construction of a multi-purpose complex at the Cambridgeshire Shelter consists of an international sized indoor arena, conference and education centre, restuarant and gift shop. The arena was built primarily for the Shelters' Riding and Driving for the Disabled Scheme which gives physically and mentally disabled people the opportunity to enjoy the benefits of riding, and play an active role within the community. The hire of the arena for dog and cat shows, equestrian events and trade shows generates additional income which is used for the benefit of the Charity. These bring thousands of visitors to the centre every week. The conference and education centre provides excellent facilities for companies and businesses to hold meetings and seminars. Full backing is provided with audio/visual equipment. The restaurant offers Self Service and a la Carte menus which can be specially prepared to suit your needs.

Wood Green Animal Shelters' constructive approach towards educating people in the field of animal welfare is playing a key role in the promotion of responsible pet ownership. Wood Green Animal Shelters has implemented a valuable syllabus of educational programmes dealing with a wide variety of animal related subjects.

Wood Green Animal Shelters has founded the College of Animal Welfare which offers a wide range of courses and seminars which are beneficial to staff, members of the public and those wishing to pursue a career in animal welfare. The Shelters' nationally recognised Animal Welfare Officer Training Course is providing highly trained officers to work within local communities on a contractual basis or full-time employment. In addition to Veterinary Nurse training the College operates courses for Kennel & Cattery Management, YTS Kennel Craft and many others for people of all ages. The Shelters launched the National Schools Challenge which is a nationwide animal related quiz. Schools throughout the U.K participate which attracts considerable publicity and media coverage.

We will never forget you

Please Remember

A donation, a covenant, a legacy or through the Payroll Giving Scheme to The Army Benevolent Fund will help soldiers, ex-soldiers and their families in distress.

THE ARMY BENEVOLENT FUND

DEPT. WIC90, 41 QUEEN'S GATE, LONDON SW7 5HR

Army Benevolent Fund

41 QUEENS GATE,
SOUTH KENSINGTON,
LONDON SW7 5HR.

The Army Benevolent Fund is the Army's Central Charity. Its aim is to give help where State assistance is either inapplicable, inadequate or unable to meet the immediate need at the time it is required. Any man or woman who is serving, or has served, in the British Army and their families are eligible. Help is given either directly to individuals through Corps and Regimental Associations, or by very substantial financial support for those national charities which provide specialised forms of help for soldiers, ex-soldiers and their dependants. More than seventy such charities are helped annually, examples being the British Limbless Ex-Servicemen's Association, the Ex-Services Mental Welfare Society and SSAFA.

Included in those helped are the widows of those who fought in South Africa; the many ex-soldiers of the two World Wars and their dependants; those who participated in subsequent campaigns world-wide; and now the casualties from Northern Ireland, where to date over 4800 soldiers have been killed or wounded in the present troubles, and from the recent operations in the Falklands.

Army Benevolence disbursed over £5.4 million last year in such work. Those now serving in the Army contribute over £2.3 million annually; the fund is dependent on the public for the remainder – and still more is needed. Their continued generosity is essential if Army Benevolence is to be able to continue its vital work. Every case is fully investigated and help is only given where it is really required.

Index of Advertisers